November 3–7, 2014
Orlando, Florida, USA

Association for
Computing Machinery

Advancing Computing as a Science & Profession

MM'14

Proceedings of the 2014 ACM Conference on Multimedia

Sponsored by:

ACM SIGMM

Supported by:

FX PAL, NFS, Symantec, UCM, Google, IBM Research, Microsoft Research, NASA, Yahoo! Labs, and Yandex

Association for
Computing Machinery

Advancing Computing as a Science & Profession

The Association for Computing Machinery
2 Penn Plaza, Suite 701
New York, New York 10121-0701

ISBN: 978-1-4503-3063-3 (Digital)

ISBN: 978-1-4503-3425-9 (Print)

Additional copies may be ordered prepaid from:

ACM Order Department
PO Box 30777
New York, NY 10087-0777, USA

Phone: 1-800-342-6626 (USA and Canada)
+1-212-626-0500 (Global)
Fax: +1-212-944-1318
E-mail: acmhelp@acm.org
Hours of Operation: 8:30 am – 4:30 pm ET

Printed in the USA

Message from the General Chairs

Welcome to ACM Multimedia 2014 in Orlando! As in the past, this year's conference is being organized as a full week of events from November 3rd to November 7th, 2014. The 3-day main conference is preceded by eight tutorials and followed by 12 workshops on current topics in multimedia computing, communications, and applications.

Orlando, nicknamed "The City Beautiful," is one of the busiest American cities for conferences and conventions. The city's famous attractions and vibrant downtown make Orlando the most visited American city, with approximately 50 million tourists a year. The greater Orlando metropolitan area has a population of over two million residents, with a rapidly growing technology industry of more than 2,600 companies. It serves as the divisional headquarters for many major companies such as Siemens, Mitsubishi, Lockheed Martin, L-3 Communications, SAIC, and Electronic Arts. The city is home to the University of Central Florida, currently the 2nd largest university in the United States. The Central Florida Research Park, located adjacent to the university, is the 7th largest research park in the country. Metro Orlando is also home to the simulation procurement commands for the U.S. Army, Navy, Air Force, Marines, and Coast Guard. Forbes magazine lists Metro Orlando among the "Best Places for Business and Careers." Entrepreneur Magazine rates Orlando as the "Number One City for Entrepreneurs." BusinessWeek featured Metro Orlando among its picks of "global hot spots" in its issue titled "What makes a Winner: The Competition Issue." Orlando is one of the three communities in the world to be featured.

Since the founding of ACM SIGMM in 1993, ACM Multimedia has been the worldwide premier conference and a key world event to present scientific achievements and innovative industrial products in the field of multimedia. At ACM Multimedia 2014, we celebrate its twenty-second iteration with an extensive program consisting of technical sessions covering all aspects of the multimedia field in the forms of oral and poster presentations, tutorials, panels, exhibits, demonstrations, and workshops, bringing into focus the principal subjects of investigation, competitions of research teams on challenging problems, and also an interactive art program stimulating artists and computer scientists to come together to take contemporary art to a new level with multimedia interaction.

We are happy that we were able to maintain registration fees at about the same levels as in 2011, the last time the conference was held in the U.S. This is possible with the generous financial support from our many sponsors of the conference. In particular, we are indebted to our host, the University of Central Florida, who provided substantial financial contributions in the early stage to give us a solid basis for organizing a successful conference. It is also our privilege to acknowledge the generous support of Symantec, our Platinum sponsor; FXPAL and Google, our Gold sponsors; and IBM, Microsoft Research, NASA Florida Space Grant Consortium, Yahoo Lab, and Yandex, our Silver sponsors.

ACM Multimedia has a long tradition of financially supporting student participation. We are thankful for a grant from US National Science Foundation, which with additional fund from SIGMM has allowed us to continue this tradition by providing substantial number of student travel grants. We have also organized a lunch for the Doctoral Symposium to give the students the opportunity to meet and interact with leaders of the research community. ACM SIGMM also provided special funds for us to organize the 'Women's Research Meeting' lunch, an annual SIGMM event started by Klara Nahrstedt in 2010 to strengthen the social networking among junior and senior female researchers and to work on increasing the participation of women in the SIGMM community.

Organizing a conference with the magnitude of ACM Multimedia requires a large number of enthusiastic volunteers. We have truly enjoyed working with an outstanding group of colleagues in the organization committee, who have generously contributed their time and effort for over two years. This conference would not have been possible without their dedication and hard work.

We thank all those who contributed to the organization of the outstanding technical programs through a highly selective review process: Technical Program Committee Chairs Alan Hanjalic, Apostol Natsev, and Wenwu Zhu; Workshop Chairs Andreas Mauthe, Max Muhlhauser, and Hari Sundaram; Technical Demo Chairs Shu-Ching Chen, Stefan Gobel, and Carsten Griwodz; Interactive Art Exhibit Chairs Andrea Cavallaro and Cheryl Cabrera; Tutorial Chairs Hermann Hellwagner and Wei Tsang Ooi; Industry Exhibit Chairs Minoru Etoh and Dulce Ponceleon; "High-Risk High-Reward Papers" Chairs abdulmotaleb El Saddik, Rainer Lienhart, and Balakrishnan Prabhakaran, "Multimedia Grand Challenge Papers" Chairs Changsheng Xu and Cha Zhang, Open Source Competition Chairs Andreas Girgensohn and Lynn Wilcox; Research Panel Chairs Wolfgang Klas and Chang Wen Chen; Industrial Panel Chairs, Borko Furth and Ivica Rimac; and Author's Advocate Chair Pablo Cesar.

We also thank all those who worked tirelessly behind the scenes to make sure everything running smoothly: Web Chair Alex Aved; Local Arrangement Chairs Mainak Chatterjee and Cliff Zou; Finance and Registration Chairs Tai Do, Ning Jiang, and Ming Li; Proceedings Chairs Wallapak Tavanapong and Ying Cai; Publicity and Social Media Chair Grace Ngai; Travel Grant Chairs Danzhou Liu and Junghwan Oh; Sponsorship Chairs Hassan Foroosh and Mark Liao; and History Preservation Chairs Duc Tran and Roy Villafane.

We want to thank former ACM SIGMM Chair Klara Nahrstedt, former SIGMM Director of Conference Mohan Kankanhalli, current SIGMM Chair, Shih-Fu Chang, and current SIGMM Director of Conference Nicu Sebe for their advice and help in all stages of the organization of the conference. Last, but not least, we gratefully acknowledge Sheridan Printing Company for their help with the preparation of the conference proceedings.

It was our great honor to accept the responsibility of Conference General Chairs. We hope that you will find ACM Multimedia 2014 to be a stimulating, informative, and enriching experience. We are sure that you will also find time to enjoy the beautiful city of Orlando with the many entertainment options.

Kien A. Hua Yong Rui Ralf Steinmetz
ACM Multimedia 2014 General Chairs

Report from the Technical Program Chairs

It is our pleasure to introduce to you the Technical Program of the *ACM International Conference on Multimedia 2014*. While we built this year's program upon the best practices from previous editions of the conference, we also introduced several adjustments with the goal to define the set of submission areas to reflect the current and emerging research directions in the multimedia field and to improve the quality of the review process and the feedback provided to the authors.

Papers were submitted to 14 areas: *Big and Broad Multimedia, Deep Learning for Multimedia, Emotional and Social Signals in Multimedia, Media Transport and Delivery, Multimedia and Society, Multimedia and the Crowd, Multimedia Art, Entertainment and Culture, Multimedia HCI and QoE, Multimedia Search and Recommendation, Multimedia Security, Privacy and Forensics, Multimedia Systems and Middleware, Multimodal Analysis and Description, Music, Speech and Audio Processing in Multimedia*, and *Social Media and Collective Online Presence*. This set of areas resulted from revising and expanding the areas from previous years, and based on the discussion within the Technical Program Committee (TPC) that aimed at highlighting new and emerging research directions (e.g., big and broad multimedia, multimedia and society, QoE), promising new technical approaches not traditionally covered at ACM Multimedia (e.g., deep learning), and reaching out to related communities with complementary expertise (e.g., emotional and social signals). At the same time, some areas were discontinued, either due to the sub-standard number of submissions over the past several years (e.g. multimedia authoring and collaboration) or due to the fact that some technologies and platforms have become mainstream and need no special emphasis any more (e.g. mobile and multi-device).

For each area, a team of Area Chairs (ACs) was appointed to handle the paper review process. In total, 38 ACs were appointed. The sizes of the teams were defined based on the anticipated number of submissions per area. Consequently, the teams ranged from two to seven ACs. The TPC consisted of both experienced and junior ACs. Also, some ACs were new to the ACM Multimedia venue, with the intention to broaden the ACM Multimedia community and open it up to related communities. ACs were given autonomy to define the Call for Papers (CfP) for their areas, select reviewers, assign papers to them (either manually or through a bidding process), assess papers based on their reviews, and provide initial acceptance recommendation as input for the TPC meeting.

The activities of the ACs were steered at the meta level by the following guidelines defined by the TPC Chairs to maximize the program quality:

- The conference must preserve its unique multimedia character in order to stand out among related scientific venues and attract highest-quality submissions.
- The papers were handled in a double-blind fashion and for each paper a minimum of three reviews were required.
- The CfPs for different areas were defined so as to minimize overlap among areas, optimally highlight the focus of individual areas, and maximize the overall topic coverage of the conference program. For this purpose, ACs were requested to share their CfPs with other ACs, and to collaboratively resolve any overlap or ambiguity issues. This resulted in several area-CfP adjustments.
- ACs were also requested to share their lists of reviewers so as to maximize the level of expertise per area and to make the lists non-overlapping in order to control the review load per reviewer (a reviewer was allowed to participate in multiple areas only with the explicit agreement of the reviewer and the corresponding ACs).

- ACs were instructed to administratively reject improperly formatted papers and to move papers to other tracks if they believed there was a better fit for the paper. This required the agreement of ACs from both the outgoing and the receiving area.
- Conflict of Interest (CoI) handling: ACs were allowed to submit at most one full paper and one short paper to their own area. Since the submission system (EasyChair) only allowed the ACs to have access to papers and reviews in their own track, any submission by ACs were moved to a separate meta track, which included only papers with conflicts of interest. All of these papers were handled by another qualified AC, either from the same area or from another area. If the papers co-authored by ACs passed the threshold for discussion during the TPC meeting, the discussion was led by the handling AC and the author-AC was asked to leave the room.

An elaborate ***EasyChair Paper Management Guidelines*** document was written containing instructions for the ACs on how to implement the TPC Chair's guidelines and how to navigate the submission management system (EasyChair). This Guidelines document will be made available to the SIGMM Director of Conferences to share with future TPCs of the ACM Multimedia conference. As an aside, we would strongly suggest to future TPCs to explore alternative conference management systems as EasyChair presented a number of challenges over the course of this process.

Regarding the paper submission and review process,

- There was no pre-submission of abstracts. This led to a simplification of the submission process, and given the large number of submissions, we feel it did not negatively influence the paper submission process.
- Submission of full and short papers were separated from each other, with short papers being submitted only after the full paper submission had been closed. This improved the ease of managing different types of submissions, and allowed authors to more easily plan for both full and short papers, if desired. This may be a possible explanation for the noticeable increase in the number of submissions this year.
- For full papers, we organized a two-stage review process, and authors were invited to submit a rebuttal based on the first stage reviews. The reviewers were then instructed to consider the rebuttal, to revise their reviews accordingly, and to enter discussion with each other aiming to improve review consensus on each paper. The results of the second round reviews and discussion were then summarized by the ACs into meta reviews, which included tentative ACCEPT/REJECT/BORDERLINE recommendations, to be discussed and finalized during the TPC meeting.
- Compared to 2013, the full paper submission deadline was moved back to the end of March, while keeping the two-stage review process. Despite the significantly shortened review period, all full papers received at least three reviews on time (some as many as six!). We really appreciate the effort by our ACs and reviewers and thank them for the great job they did!
- Following the successful experience from 2013, an Author's Advocate (AA) role was created to provide authors with an independent channel to express concerns about the quality of the reviews for their papers, and to engage into a discussion with ACs on how to handle these concerns. The AA received requests for mediation for a total of 22 of the full papers (8%). The AA reviewed all the cases and successfully handled them in a collaborative effort with the ACs in charge of the corresponding papers. As a result of the mediation, 4 new reviews were generated and 14 other reviews were revised. The mediation from the AA happened

before the TPC meeting, so the material serving as input for the discussions during the meeting did not include any low-quality review.

- We received 300 full and 397 short papers by the corresponding submission deadlines, or in total 697 papers. After removing improperly anonymized or otherwise invalid papers, 286 full and 393 short papers remained and entered the regular review process. The latter numbers served as the reference for computing the acceptance rate.
- Based on the first review results for full papers (after notification), 14 papers were withdrawn by the authors and removed from the system, leaving 665 papers in the review processing pipeline: 272 full papers and 393 short papers. This is the number that served as input for TPC meeting. The table below gives a distribution of these papers across areas.

Area	Full papers	Short papers
Big and Broad Multimedia	10	8
Deep Learning for Multimedia	23	21
Emotional and Social Signals in Multimedia	16	29
Media Transport and Delivery	18	15
Multimedia and Society	11	13
Multimedia and the Crowd	7	8
Multimedia Art, Entertainment and Culture	19	19
Multimedia HCI and QoE	20	38
Multimedia Search and Recommendation	56	80
Multimedia Security, Privacy and Forensics	10	23
Multimedia Systems and Middleware	17	25
Multimodal Analysis and Description	43	75
Music, Speech and Audio Processing in Multimedia	8	18
Social Media and Collective Online Presence	14	21

Decisions on full and short papers were made at the two-day TPC meeting held at Google Inc. in Mountain View, CA, USA on 18-19 June 2014. Two TPC Chairs and 28 ACs attended the meeting. While not all ACs were requested to be present, it was required that all areas are represented in the meeting. AC-teams per area were requested to agree on their recommendations on all papers in the area before the meeting so the representing AC(s) can lead the discussion for the entire area. On the first day, full papers were handled, and on the second day the short papers together with the discussion on awards nominees. We accepted 55 full and 117 short papers, leading to acceptance rates of 19.2% and 29.8% for full and short papers, respectively.

The discussion on both full and short papers was conducted per area, leaving the ACs the opportunity to nominate the papers from their area into the pool of accepted papers. The discussion was at all times plenary, enabling ACs from any area to comment on any paper being discussed from the point of view of their individual expertise, experience, or rating criteria. The discussion went over all areas, and covered all papers flagged for discussion from each area by the ACs, as well as all papers scoring above a certain threshold in terms of their average review score. This way, we made sure to discuss both high-scoring and borderline papers as well as any controversial papers (with large review score discrepancy or with discrepancy between the scores and recommendations from the ACs). The discussion on the papers was intensive, taking into account all the information collected per paper, including reviews, the scores, the authors' rebuttals, the initial recommendations by the ACs (in the form of a meta review) and the reviews performed by other ACs during the meeting.

After the meeting the TPC Chairs finalized the program by grouping the accepted papers into sessions, and the ACs finalized the meta reviews to include extra information based on the TPC meeting discussion. The sessions were formed based on research topics and do not necessarily reflect the submission areas. After notification, all accepted full papers were shepherded to make sure that the revised papers adequately addressed reviewers' concerns and the authors implemented any changes promised in their rebuttals.

The TPC has done everything in their power to ensure that the technical program of the conference is of the highest possible quality. This would not have been possible without the commitment of the Area Chairs and the reviewers. We would like to thank them for their rigor and engagement, and we look forward to having a strong and engaging technical program in Orlando, FL!

We hope you enjoy the program!

Alan Hanjalic
Delft University of Technology
The Netherlands

Apostol (Paul) Natsev
Google Inc.
USA

Wenwu Zhu
Tsinghua University
PR China

Table of Contents

Session: Multimedia Grand Challenge

Session Chair: Cha Zhang *(Microsoft Research)*

Session: Multimedia HCI and QoE

Session Chair: Judith Redi *(Delft University of Technology)*

Session: Multimedia Analysis and Mining

Session Chair: Benoit Huet *(Eurecom)*

Session: Multimedia Systems

Session Chair: Carsten Griwodz *(University of Oslo)*

Session: Emotional and Social Signals in Multimedia

Session Chair: Hayley Hung *(Delft University of Technology)*

Doctoral Symposium 1
Session Chair: Oge Marques *(Florida Atlantic University)*

Doctoral Symposium 2
Session Chair: Christian Breiteneder *(Vienna University of Technology)*

Open Source Software Competition 1
Session Chair: Andreas Girgensohn *(FXPAL)*

Open Source Software Competition 2
Session Chair: Lynn Wilcox *(FXPAL)*

Art Exhibit
Session Chair: Cheryl Cabrera *(University of Central Florida)*

Demos 1: Searching and Finding

Session Chair: Shu-Ching Chen *(Florida International University)*

Demos 2: Senses and Sensors

Session Chair: Stefan Göbel *(Technische Universität Darmstadt)*

Demos 3: Systems

Session Chair: Carsten Griwodz *(Simula Research Laboratory)*

Posters Session 1

Session Chair: Duc Tran *(University of Massachusetts at Boston)*

Posters Session 2

Session Chair: Roy Villafane *(Andrews University)*

Posters Session 3

Session Chair: Roy Villafane *(Andrews University)*

Tutorials

Workshop Summaries

MM 2014 Conference Organization

General Chairs:	Kien A. Hua *(University of Central Florida, USA)* Yong Rui *(Microsoft Research, China)* Ralf Steinmetz *(Technische Universität Darmstadt, Germany)*
Technical Program Committee Chairs:	Alan Hanjalic *(Delft University of Technology, Netherlands)* Apostol (Paul) Natsev *(Google, USA)* Wenwu Zhu *(Tsinghua University, China)*
Author's Advocate:	Pablo Cesar *(CWI, Netherlands)*
High-Risk High-Reward Papers Chairs:	Abdulmotaleb El Saddik *(University of Ottawa, Canada)* Rainer Lienhart *(Augsburg University, Germany)* Balakrishnan Prabhakaran *(University of Texas at Dallas, USA)*
Multimedia Grand Challenge Chairs:	Changsheng Xu (*Chinese Academy of Sciences, China)* Cha Zhang *(Microsoft Research, USA)*
Technical Demo Chairs:	Shu-Ching Chen (*Florida International University, USA*) Stefan Göbel *(Technische Universität Darmstadt, Germany)* Carsten Griwodz *(Simula Research Laboratory, Norway)*
Industrial Exhibit Chairs:	Minoru Etoh (Mick) *(NTT DoCoMo, Japan)* Dulce Ponceleón *(IBM Research, USA)*
Interactive Art Exhibit Chairs:	Andrea Cavallaro *(Queen Mary University of London, UK)* Cheryl Cabrera *(University of Central Florida, USA)*
Panel Chairs:	Wolfgang Klas *(University of Vienna, Austria)* Chang Wen Chen *(State University of New York at Buffalo, USA)*
Industrial Panel Chairs:	Borko Furth (*Florida Atlantic University, USA)* Ivica Rimac *(Bell Labs / Alcatel-Lucent, USA)*
Open Source Competition Chairs:	Andreas Girgensohn (*FX Palo Alto Laboratory, Inc., USA)* Lynn Wilcox *(FX Palo Alto Laboratory, Inc., USA)*
Doctoral Symposium Chairs:	Laszlo Böszörmenyi *(University of Klagenfurt, Austria)* Christian Breiteneder *(Technical University of Vienna, Austria)* Oge Marques *(Florida Atlantic University, USA)*
Tutorial Chairs:	Hermann Hellwagner *(University of Klagenfurt, Austria)* Wei Tsang Ooi *(National University of Singapore, Singapore)*

Workshops Chairs: Andreas Mauthe *(University of Lancaster, UK)*
Max Mühlhäuser *(Technische Universität, Germany)*
Hari Sundaram (*University of Illinois at Urbana Champaign, USA)*

Web Chair: Alex Aved *(U.S. Air Force Research Lab, USA)*

Local Arrangements Chairs: Mainak Chatterjee *(University of Central Florida, USA)*
Cliff Zou *(University of Central Florida, USA)*

Finance and Registration Chairs: Tai Do *(Microsoft, USA)*
Ning Jiang *(Institute for Systems Biology, USA)*
Ming Li *(California State University, USA)*

Sponsorship Chairs: Hassan Foroosh *(University of Central Florida, USA)*
Mark Liao *(Academia Sincia, Taipei, Taiwan)*

Travel Grant Chairs: Danzhou Liu *(NetApp, USA)*
JungHwan Oh *(University of North Texas, USA)*

Proceedings Chairs: Ying Cai *(Iowa State University, USA)*
Wallapak Tavanapong *(Iowa State University, USA)*

History Preservation Chairs: Duc Tran *(University of Massachusetts in Boston, USA)*
Roy Villafane *(Andrews University, USA)*

Publicity and Social Media Chair: Grace Ngai *(Hong Kong Polytechnic University, S.A.R. China)*

MM 2014 Area Chairs

Big and Broad Multimedia: Nuria Oliver *(Telefonica, Spain)*
Vivek Singh *(MIT, USA)*
Alan Smeaton *(Dublin City University, Ireland)*

Deep Learning for Multimedia: Marc'Aurelio Ranzato *(Facebook, USA)*
Kai Yu *(Baidu, China)*
George Toderici *(Google, USA)*

Emotional and Social Signals in Multimedia: Hatice Gunes *(Queen Mary University of London, United Kingdom)*
Hayley Hung *(Delft University of Technology, Netherlands)*
Bjorn Schuller *(TU Munich, Germany)*

Media Transport and Delivery: Carsten Griwodz *(University of Oslo, Norway)*
Baochun Li *(University of Toronto, Canada)*

Multimedia and Society: Jenny Benois-Pineau *(University of Bordeaux, France)*
Wallapak Tavanapong *(Iowa State University, USA)*

Multimedia and the Crowd: Kuan-Ta Chen *(Academia Sinica, Taiwan)*
Martha Larson *(Delft University of Technology, Netherlands)*

Multimedia Art, Entertainment and Culture: Teresa Chambel *(University of Lisbon, Portugal)*
Frank Nack *(University of Amsterdam, Netherlands)*

Multimedia HCI & QoE: Marc Cavazza *(Teesside University, United Kingdom)*
Touradj Ebrahimi *(EPFL, Switzerland)*

Multimedia Search and Recommendation: Xian-Sheng Hua *(Microsoft Research, USA)*
Qi Tian *(University of Texas San Antonio, USA)*
Shuicheng Yan *(National University of Singapore, Singapore)*
Hector Yee *(Google, USA)*

Multimedia Security, Privacy and Forensics: Gerald Friedland *(ICSI Berkeley, USA)*
Mohan Kankanhalli *(National University of Singapore, Singapore)*

Multimedia Systems and Middleware: Jiangchuan Liu *(Simon Fraser University, Canada)*
Roger Zimmermann *(National University of Singapore, Singapore)*

Multi-modal Analysis and Description:

Alex Hauptmann *(Carnegie-Mellon University, USA)*
Benoit Huet *(Eurecom, France)*
Xuelong Li *(Chinese Academy of Sciences, China)*
Ansgar Scherp *(Kiel University and Leibniz Information Center for Economics, Germany)*
Mubarak Shah *(University of Central Florida, USA)*
Cees Snoek *(University of Amsterdam, Netherlands)*
Rong Yan *(Square, USA)*

Music, Speech and Audio Processing in Multimedia:

Xavier Anguera *(Telefonica, Spain)*
Cynthia Liem *(Delft University of Technology, Netherlands)*

Social Media and Collective Online Presence:

Peng Cui *(Tsinghua University, China)*
Lexing Xie *(Australian National University, Australia)*

MM 2014 Program Committee

Alberto Abad
Sheikh Ahamed
Lffat Ahmed
Luca Maria Aiello
Ceyhun Akgül
Albert Ali Salah
Francesc Alias
Tim Althoff
Noam Amir
Mostafa Ammar
Kristina Andersen
Oya Aran
Shervin Ardeshir
Pradeep Atrey
Yannis Avrithis
Sileye Ba
Lamberto Ballan
Sabina Barakovic
Vittorio Baroncini
Alessio Bazzica
Emmanuelle Beauxis-Aussalet
Georgios Bebis
Ali C. Begen
Nathalia Beloff
Nadia Berthouze
Marco Bertini
Subhabrata Bhattacharya
Giulia Boato
Victor Boer
Olga Bondarenko
Lubomir Bordev
Damian Borth
Nicolas Boulanger-Lewandowski
Jeffrey Boyd
Alessandro Bozzon
Francois Bremond
Alexia Briasouli
Kjell Brunnstrom
Yaroslav Bulatov
Felix Burkhardt
Ian Burnett
Carlos Busso
Daragh Byrne
Deng Cai
Antonio Camurri
K. Selcuk Candan
Yu Cao
Mark Cartwright
Pablo Cesar
Gary Chan
Surendar Chandra
Guillaume Chanel
Carl Chang
Shih-Fu Chang
Fred Charles
Vincent Charvillat
Gal Chechik
Trista Chen
Tao Chen
Minghua Chen
Kuan-Ta Chen
Songqing Chen
Berlin Chen
Wen-Huang Cheng
Elaine Chew
Ed Chi
Sumit Chopra
Wei-Ta Chu
Ching-Hua Chuan
Chloé Clavel
Kathy Clawson
Mark Claypool
Matthew Cooper
Nuno Correia
Eduardo Coutinho
Marco Cristani
Peng Cui
Kevin Curran
Kerstin Dautenhahn
Larry Davis
Piet de Groen
Fernando de La Torre
Giorgio De Michelis
Giovanni De Poli
Afshin Dehghan
Alberto Del Bimbo
Cheng Deng
Giusy Di Lorenzo
Klaus Diepold
Jana Dittmann
Christian Dittmar
Sidney Dmello
Michael Dorr
Zhiyao Duan
Alan Dunning
Pinar Duygulu Sahin
Serge Egelman
Sebastian Egger
David Eigen
Hazım Kemal Ekenel
Dan Ellis
Sabu Emmanuel
Herman Engelbrecht
Gorka Epelde Unanue
Julien Epps
Dumitru Erhan
Slim Essid
Georg Essl
Sebastian Ewert
Tiago Falk
Giulia Fanti
Benoit Favre
Wu-Chi Feng
Karel Fliegel
Soren Forchhamer
Piero Fraternali
Jason Freeman
Jonathan Freeman
Enrique Frias-Martinez
Andrea Frome
Raymond Fu
Takuya Fujishima
Luciano Gamberini
Xinbo Gao
Kevin Gao
Chenqiang Gao
Yue Gao
Zan Gao
Jason Gauci
David Geerts
Bo Geng
Bogdan Ghita
Andreas Girgensohn
Stefan Goebel
Emilia Gomez
Andrew Gordon

Masataka Goto
Luke Gottlieb
José Goutierez
Guillaume Gravier
Carsten Griwodz
Peter Grosche
Lei Guo
Michael Gurevich
Pal Halvorsen
Raffay Hamid
Yahong Han
Mei Han
Jungong Han
Allan Hanbury
Philippe Hanhart
Lynda Hardman
Jonathon Hare
Xiaofei He
Junfeng He
Mohamed Hefeeda
Dirk Heylen
Andrew Hines
Jason Hockman
Steven C.H. Hoi
Richang Hong
Tobias Hossfeld
Cheng-Hsin Hsu
Winston Hsu
Yao Hu
Yuheng Hu
Ke Hu
Gang Hua
Zixia Huang
Jiwu Huang
Zi Huang
Qingming Huang
Thomas Mensink

Chung-Lin Huang
Benoit Huet
Mark Hughes
Inseok Hwang
Haroon Idrees
David Imseng
Omer Inan
Bogdan Ionescu
Panos Ipeirotis
Ignasi Iriondo
Yuri Ivanov
Christian Jacquemin
Giulio Jacucci
Alejandro Jaimes
Lucjan Janowski
Mostafa Javed
Omar Javed
Dinesh Babu Jayagopi
Rongrong Ji
Jia Jia
Shen Jialie
Yu-Gang Jiang
Wei Jiang
Lu Jiang
Ajita John
Maritza Johnson
Gareth Jones
Dhiraj Joshi
Lina Karam
Stefan Katzenbeisser
Koray Kavukcuoglu
Gabriella Kazai
Aisling Kelliher
Lyndon Kennedy
Salman Khokhar
Ben Knapp
Wei Pan

Peter Knees
Hiroki Kobayashi
Yiannis Kompatsiaris
Pavel Korshunov
Dejan Kostic
Alex Krizhevsky
Eleni Kroupi
Antonio Kruger
Dragan Kukolj
Shiro Kumano
C.-C. Jay Kuo
Gregorij Kurillo
Vivek Kwatra
Zhenzhong Lan
Nicholas D. Lane
Jakob Larsen
Rasmus Larsen
Martha Larson
Neal Lathia
Patrick Le Callet
Jeongkyu Lee
Sune Lehmann
Riccardo Leonardi
Bruno Lepri
Alexander Lerch
Thomas Leung
Mark Levy
Miachel Lew
Baoxin Li
Xi Li
Zhifeng Li
Ming Li
Xirong Li
Huan Li
Haibo Li
Hongzhi Li
Mukesh Saini

Mark Liao
Cynthia Liem
Yu-Ru Lin
Suzanne Little
Feng Liu
Jingen Liu
Yong-Jin Liu
Fangming Liu
Jiangchuan Liu
Si Liu
Xueliang Liu
Zheng Liu
Xueliang Liu
Zicheng Liu
Dong Liu
Luoqi Liu
Xiaoqiang Lu
Huchuan Lu
Lie Lu
Jiebo Luo
Jordi Luque
Mathias Lux
Zhigang Ma
Kevin Ma
Mathew Magimai Doss
Stephane Marchand-Maillet
Jose Martinez
Andreas Mauthe
Ketan Mayer-Patel
Stephen Mckenna
Gary McKeown
Andre McPherson
Remi Megret
Tao Mei
Nasir Memon
Deyu Meng
Mohammad Soleymani

Bernard Merialdo
Michele Merler
Florian Metze
Rada Mihalcea
Yue Ming
Prasenjit Mitra
Vicki Moulder
Emily Mower-Provost
Yadong Mu
Sudhir Mudur
Henning Mueller
Meinard Mueller
Vittorio Murino
Klara Nahrstedt
Alok Nandi
Paolo Nesi
Edith Ngai
Chong-Wah Ngo
Bingbing Ni
Feiping Nie
Oliver Nina
Jasminko Novak
Junghwan Oh
Igor Olaizola
Eckehard Olbrich
Sean O'Malley
Eng-Jon Ong
Wei Tsang Ooi
Omar Oreifej
Vincent Oria
Nicola Orio
Jörg Ott
Daniel Overholt
Katsunori Oyama
Manohar Paluri
Sudheendra Vijayanarasimhan
Tuomas Virtanen

Yanwei Pang
Bryan Pardo
Alexandre Passos
Geoffroy Peeters
Catherine Pelachaud
Yuxin Peng
Fernando Pereira
Fernando Perez-Gonzalez
Andrew Perkis
Stavros Petridis
Dinh Phung
Fabio Pianesi
Massimo Piccardi
Claudio Pinhanez
Antonio Pinheiro
Hamed Pirsivash
Ronald Poppe
Reid Porter
Kishore Prahallad
Michael Pucher
Guojun Qi
Daniele Quercia
Alexander Raake
Zafar Rafii
Nitendra Rajput
Sanjay Rao
Judith Redi
Ulrich Reiter
Martin Rerabek
Elisa Ricci
Gaël Richard
Michael Riegler
Andreas Riener
Stevan Rudinac
Bahjat Safadi
Yan Wang
Xinxi Wang

Albert Ali Salah
Imran Saleemi
Dasarathi Sampath
Jose San Pedro
Jitao Sang
Emre Sargin
Shin'Ichi Satoh
Markus Schedl
Peter Schelkens
Nicu Sebe
Doree Seligmann
Subhabrata Sen
Pierre Sermanet
Joan Serrà
Mubarak Shah
Cyrus Shahabi
David A. Shamma
Shiguang Shan
Sgshan Shan
Xiaowei Shao
Ling Shao
Jialie Shen
Jacky Shen
Jianbing Shen
Yi Shen
Prashant Shenoy
Fuming Shih
Shervin Shirmohammadi
Jon Shlens
Erez Shmueli
Börkur Sigurbjörnsson
Gwendal Simon
Athanassios Skodras
Lea Skorin-Kapov
Paris Smaragdis
Yi Yang
Linjun Yang

Mingli Song
Khurram Soomro
Nitish Srivastava
Jacopo Staiano
Eckehard Steinbach
Arkadiusz Stopczynski
Ramanathan Subramanian
Av Subramanyam
Sainbayar Sukhbaatar
Aixin Sun
Lingfen Sun
Yaniv Taigman
Jinhui Tang
Dacheng Tao
Wallapak Tavanapong
Tony Thomas
Bruce Thomas
Christian Timmerer
Steve Tjoa
George Toderici
Giorgos Tolias
Wei Tong
Naoko Tosa
Khiet Truong
Michael Carl Tschantz
Alexey Tsymbal
Mika Tuomola
George Tzanetakis
Andreas Uhl
Jasper Uijlings
Marian Ursu
Gonzalo Vaca-Castano
Michel Valstar
Jan van Gemert
Martin Varela
Wojciech Zaremba
Eric Zavesky

Gualtiero Volpe
Stefanos Vrochidis
Yi Wang
Meng Wang
Qi Wang
Hanzi Wang
Xiaogang Wang
Zhi Wang
Fei Wang
Xiaoyu Wang
Jingdong Wang
Meng Wang
Ye Wang
Ju-Chiang Wang
Jingbin Wang
Xiangjun Wang
Zhiyong Wang
Jing Wang
Leon Watts
Robert Wechsler
Lynn Wilcox
Johnny Wong
Chuck Wooters
Marcel Worring
Chuan Wu
Wanmin Wu
Min Wu
Fei Wu
Zhong Wu
Lingxi Xie
Changsheng Xu
W. Yan
Tom Yan
Weiqi Yan
Ming Yang
Fei Yang
Weilong Yang
Yi-Hsuan Yang
Kuiyuan Yang
Guangnan Ye
Yangli Hector Yee
Woon Seung Yeo
Jude Yew
Junyong You
Ehsan Younessian
Shoou-I Yu
Meng Yu
Yuan Yuan
Xiaotong Yuan
Titus Zakharia
Massimo Zancanaro
Zhengjun Zha
Zheng-Jun Zha
Lijun Zhang
Longfei Zhang
Shiliang Zhang
Yongdong Zhang
Lei Zhang
Liang Zheng
Huiyu Zhou
Will Zhou
Hanning Zhou
Wengang Zhou
Jinfeng Zhuang
Michael Zink

MM 2014 Grand Challenge Program Committee

Chairs: Changsheng Xu *(Chinese Academy of Sciences)*
Cha Zhang *(Microsoft Research)*

Program Committee: ***New York City 360o Challenge:***
Yuan-Chi Chang *(IBM Research)*
John R. Smith *(IBM Research)*
Liangliang Cao *(IBM Research)*

MSR-Bing Image Retrieval Challenge
Xian-Sheng Hua *(Microsoft Research)*
Ming Ye *(Microsoft Bing)*

VideoLectures.NET Challenge
Gaber Cerle *(VideoLectures.NET)*
Vasileios Mezaris *(CERTH)*

Emotional Response to Multimedia Content Grand Challenge
Christel Chamaret *(Technicolor)*
Philippe Guillotel *(Technicolor)*
Patrick Pérez *(Technicolor)*
Christophe Diot *(Technicolor)*

Machine Learning for Computational Photography
Qing Zhang *(Huawei)*

MM 2014 Doctoral Symposium Committee

Chairs: Laszlo Böszörmenyi *(Klagenfurt University, Austria)*
Christian Breiteneder *(Vienna University of Technology, Austria)*
Oge Marques *(Florida Atlantic University, USA)*

Program Committee: Vincent Charvillat *(University of Toulouse, France)*
Marco Cristani *(Università degli Studi di Verona, Italy)*
Dubravko Culibrk *(University of Novi Sad, Serbia)*
Xavier Giró-i-Nieto *(UPC, Barcelona, Catalunya, Spain)*
Pål Halvorsen *(University of Oslo and Simula Research, Norway)*
Hayley Hung *(Technical University of Delft, The Netherlands)*
Hari Kalva *(Florida Atlantic University, USA)*
Mohan S. Kankanhalli *(National University of Singapore, Singapore)*
Ralf Klamma *(RWTH Aachen University, Germany)*
Harald Kosch *(Passau University, Germany)*
Stephane Marchand-Maillet *(University of Geneva, Switzerland)*
Liam Mayron *(Florida Institute of Technology, USA)*
Pier Luca Montessoro *(University of Udine, Italy)*
Klara Nahrstedt *(University of Illinois, USA)*
Arnold Smeulders *(University of Amsterdam, The Netherlands)*
Ooi-Wie Tsang *(National University of Singapore, Singapore)*
Andreas Uhl *(Salzburg University, Austria)*
Svetha Venkatesh *(Deakin University, Australia)*

Panelists: **Session 1**
Laszlo Böszörmenyi *(Klagenfurt University, Austria)*
Christian Breiteneder *(Vienna University of Technology, Austria)*
Xavier Giró-i-Nieto *(UPC, Barcelona, Catalunya, Spain)*
Session 2
Vincent Charvillat *(University of Toulouse, France)*
Hayley Hung *(Technical University of Delft, The Netherlands)*
Oge Marques *(Florida Atlantic University, USA)*
Arnold Smeulders *(University of Amsterdam, The Netherlands)*
Wallapak Tavanapong *(Iowa State University, USA)*

MM 2014 Technical Demos Program Committee

Chairs:
Shu-Ching Chen *(Florida International University, U.S.A.)*
Stefan Göbel *(Technische Universität Darmstadt, Germany)*
Carsten Griwodz *(Simula Research Laboratory, Norway)*

Program Committee:
Ramazan Aygun *(University of Alabama in Huntsville, USA)*
Fernando Boronat *(Polytechnic University of Valencia - IGIC Institute, Spain)*
Yu Cao *(University of Massachusetts Lowell, USA)*
Richard Chbeir *(University of Bourgogne in Dijon, France)*
Kuan-Ta Chen *(Academia Sinica, Taiwan)*
Chao Chen *(Capital One Bank, USA)*
Min Chen *(University of Washington Bothell, USA)*
Songqing Chen *(George Mason University, USA)*
Ching-Hua Chuan *(University of North Florida, USA)*
Mario Montagud Climent *(Universitat Politècnica de València (UPV), Spain)*
Simon Clippingdale *(NHK Science & Technical Research Laboratories, Japan)*
Cyril Concolato *(Telecom ParisTech, France)*
Tim Dutz *(TU Darmstadt, Germany)*
Wolfgang Effelsberg *(University of Mannheim, Germany)*
Jianping Fan *(University of North Carolina at Charlotte, USA)*
William Grosky *(University of Michigan-Dearborn, USA)*
Yang Guo *(Bell Labs, USA)*
Michael Gutjahr *(Tu Darmstadt, Germany)*
Zifang Huang *(Western Union Digital, USA)*
Wolfgang Huerst *(Utrecht University, Germany)*
Mohan Kankanhalli *(National University of Singapore, Singapore)*
Ashfaq Khokhar *(Illinois Institute of Technology, USA)*
Seon Ho Kim *(University of Southern California, USA)*
Johannes Konert *(Technische Universität Darmstadt, Germany)*
Ying Li *(IBM T.J. Watson Research Center, USA)*
Lin Lin *(American National Standards Institute, USA)*
Zhu Liu *(AT&T Research Labs, USA)*
Dianting Liu *(University of Miami, USA)*
Hongli Luo *(Indiana University - Purdue University Fort Wayne, USA)*
Robin Mellecker *(The University of Hong Kong, Institute of Human Performance, China)*
Tao Meng *(University of Miami, USA)*
André Miede *(Hochschule für Technik und Wirtschaft des Saarlandes, Germany)*
Nilesh Patel *(Oakland University, USA)*
Nicholas Race *(Lancaster University, United Kingdom)*
Nabil Sarhan *(Wayne State University, USA)*
Ishwar Sethi *(Oakland University, USA)*
Mei-Ling Shyu *(University of Miami, USA)*
Leonel Sousa *(Universidade de Lisboa, Portugal)*
Yonghong Tian *(Peking University, China)*
Gareth Tyson *(Queen Mary, University of London, United Kingdom)*
Zhen Wen *(IBM T.J. Watson Research Center, USA)*

Technical Demo Program Committee (continued):

Viktor Wendel *(TU Darmstadt, Germany)*
Chuan Wu *(The University of Hong Kong, China)*
Jianhua Yan *(Amazon, USA)*
Chengcui Zhang *(The University of Alabama at Birmingham, USA)*
Tong Zhang *(HP Labs, USA)*
Qiusha Zhu *(SENZARI, USA)*

MM 2014 Open Source Software Competition Organization Committee

Chairs: Andreas Girgensohn *(FX Palo Alto Laboratory)*
Lynn Wilcox *(FX Palo Alto Laboratory)*

Program Committee: Jerome Berclaz *(Microsoft, USA)*
Surendar Chandra *(Datrium, USA)*
Huizhong Chen *(Stanford University, USA)*
Michael Cutter *(University of California at Santa Cruz, USA)*
Laurent Denoue *(FXPAL, USA)*
Luis Francisco-Revilla *(The University of Texas at Austin, USA)*
Gang Hua *(Stevens Institute of Technology, USA)*
Lyndon Kennedy *(Yahoo Labs, USA)*
Thommen Korah *(Microsoft, USA)*
Qiong Liu *(FXPAL, USA)*
Les Nelson *(Palo Alto Research Center, Inc., USA)*
Wei Tsang Ooi *(National University of Singapore)*
Timo Pylvanainen *(Microsoft, USA)*

MM 2014 HRHR Program Committee

Abdulmotaleb El Saddik *(University of Ottawa, Canada)*
Rainer Lienhart *(University of Augsburg, Germany)*
Balakrishnan Prabhakaran *(University of Texas at Dallas, USA)*

MM 2014 Sponsor & Supporters

Sponsor:

SIGMM

Platinum Supporters:

FX PAL

NSF

Symantec.

UCF College of Engineering & Computer Science

Gold Supporter:

Google

Silver Supporters:

IBM Research

Microsoft Research

NASA Florida Space Grant Consortium

Yahoo! Labs

Yandex

Bing, the Fastest Growing Image Search Engine

Harry Shum
EVP, Technology and Research
Microsoft
hshum@microsoft.com

ABSTRACT

Since the launch of Bing (www.bing.com) in June 2009, we have seen Bing web search market share in the US more than doubled and Bing image search query share quadrupled. In this talk, I will share our experience building Bing image search as the fastest growing image search engine, and discuss the challenges and opportunities in image search. Specifically, I will talk about how we have significantly improved image search quality, and built differentiated image search user experience using NLP, entity, big data, machine learning and computer vision technologies. By leveraging big data from billions of search queries, billions of images on the web and from the social networks, and billions of user clicks, we have designed massive machine learning systems to continuously improve image search quality. With the focus on natural language and entity understanding, for instance, we have improved Bing's ability to understand the user intent beyond queries and keywords. I will demonstrate with many examples how Bing has delivered a superior image search user experience, quantitatively, qualitatively and aesthetically, by utilizing computer vision techniques.

Author Keywords

Search engines; image search

ACM Classification Keywords

Web searching and information discovery; Web mining; information retrieval query processing; multimedia and multimodal retrieval

BIO

Former managing director of Microsoft Research Asia, Dr. Harry Shum, after leading Bing product development for several years as a Corporate Vice President, has taken the new role of Microsoft Executive Vice President, Technology and Research.

Dr. Shum is an Institute of Electrical and Electronics Engineers (IEEE) Fellow and an Association for Computing Machinery (ACM) Fellow. He served on the editorial board of the International Journal of Computer Vision, and was a Program Chair of the International Conference of Computer Vision (ICCV) 2007. Dr. Shum has published more than 100 papers in computer vision, computer graphics, pattern recognition, statistical learning, and robotics. He holds more than 50 U.S. patents.

Dr. Shum joined Microsoft Research in 1996 where he worked in Redmond, WA as a researcher on computer vision and computer graphics. In 1999, Shum moved to Beijing to help start Microsoft Research China (later renamed Microsoft Research Asia). His tenure there began as a research manager and subsequently moved up to Assistant Managing Director, Managing Director of Microsoft Research Asia, Distinguished Engineer, and Corporate Vice President. In 2007, Shum became Microsoft Corporate Vice President responsible for Bing product development. In 2013, he took on the responsibilities of Microsoft Executive Vice President including oversight of Microsoft Research.

Dr. Shum received a doctorate in robotics from the School of Computer Science at Carnegie Mellon University. In his spare time, he enjoys playing basketball, rooting for the Pittsburgh Steelers, and spending quality time with his family.

MM'14, November 3–7, 2014, Orlando, Florida, USA.
ACM 978-1-4503-3063-3/14/11.
http://dx.doi.org/10.1145/2647868.2647958

Affective Media and Wearables: Surprising Findings

Rosalind W. Picard
Professor of Media Arts and Sciences, MIT Media Lab
Cambridge, MA USA
Twitter: @rosalindpicard

ABSTRACT

Over a decade ago, I suggested that computers will need the skills of emotional intelligence in order to interact with regular people in ways that they perceive as intelligent. Our lab embarked on this journey of "affective computing" with a focus on first enabling computers to better understand and communicate human emotion. Our main tools have been wearable sensors (several which we created), video, and audio, coupled with signal processing, machine learning and pattern analysis of multimodal human data. Along the way we encountered several surprises. This talk will highlight some of the challenges we have faced, some accomplishments, and the most surprising and rewarding findings. Our findings reveal the power of the human emotion system not only in intelligence, in social interaction, and in everyday media consumption, but also in autism, epilepsy, and sleep memory formation.

Author Keywords

Affective computing, wearable sensors, emotion, autonomic nervous system, measuring engagement, stress and frustration

ACM Classification Keywords

A.0 General: Biographies, I.5 Pattern Recognition, J.3 Life and Medical Sciences, Health

BIO

Professor Rosalind W. Picard, Sc.D., FIEEE, is founder and director of the Affective Computing Research Group at the Massachusetts Institute of Technology (MIT) Media Lab where she also leads the Media Lab's Technology for Health initiative. Picard has co-founded two businesses, Empatica, Inc. creating wearable sensors and analytics to improve health, and Affectiva, Inc. delivering technology to help measure and communicate emotion using video.

Picard holds a bachelor's degree in electrical engineering with highest honors from the Georgia Institute of Technology, and masters and doctorate degrees, both in electrical engineering and computer science, from MIT. She started her career as a member of the technical staff at AT&T Bell Laboratories, where she designed VLSI chips for digital signal processing and developed algorithms for image compression. In 1991 she joined the MIT Media Lab Faculty where she rose to the level of full professor. Picard became known internationally for her work designing novel analytical models for content-based retrieval of images and for work pioneering methods of automated search and annotation in digital video, including the Photobook system. In 1996 she wrote and published the book Affective Computing, which envisioned a new area of research and today is credited as starting a new field by that name. Today that field has its own journal, international conference, and professional society. Picard also served as a founding member of the IEEE Technical Committee on Wearable Information Systems in 1998, helping launch the field of wearable computing.

Picard has authored or co-authored over two hundred scientific articles and chapters spanning computer vision, pattern recognition, machine learning, human-computer interaction, wearable sensors and affective computing. She is a recipient of several best paper prizes, including work on machine learning with multiple models (with Minka, 1998), a best theory paper prize for affect in human learning (with Kort and Reilly, 2001) a best paper prize for work with facial expressions (with McDuff, Kaliouby and Demirdjian, 2013) and a best UBICOMP 2013 paper for an automated conversation coach (with Hoque et al, 2013). Her paper (with Healey, 2005) on how to measure driver stress won best paper of the decade 2000-2009 for IEEE Intelligent Transportation Systems.

Picard is an active inventor with patents including wearable and non-contact sensors, algorithms, and systems for sensing, recognizing, and responding respectfully to human affective information. Her inventions have been applied in autism, epilepsy, sleep, stress, autonomic nervous system disorders, human and machine learning, health behavior change, market research, customer service, and human-computer interaction. In 2005 she was named a Fellow of the IEEE for contributions to image and video analysis and affective computing. Picard has been honored with dozens of distinguished and named lectureships and other international awards, and has given over 100 keynote talks.

MM'14, November 3–7, 2014, Orlando, Florida, USA.
ACM 978-1-4503-3063-3/14/11.
http://dx.doi.org/10.1145/2647868.2647959

Prof. Picard has served on international and national science and engineering program committees, editorial boards, and review panels, including the Advisory Committee for the National Science Foundation's (NSF's) division of Computers in Science and Engineering (CISE), the Advisory Board for the Georgia Tech College of Computing, and the Editorial Board of User Modeling and User-Adapted Interaction: The Journal of Personalization Research. Picard has also served on non-profit boards, including a school for children with special needs, and a pro-life organization that helps educate and support women with crisis pregnancies.

Picard interacts regularly with industry and has consulted for many companies including Apple, AT&T, BT, HP, i.Robot, Merck, Motorola, and Samsung. Her group's achievements have been featured in forums for the general public such as The New York Times, The London Independent, National Public Radio, Scientific American Frontiers with Alan Alda, ABC's Nightline and World News Tonight, Time, Vogue, Wired, Voice of America Radio, New Scientist, and BBC programs such as "Hard Talk" and BBC Horizon with Michael Mosley. Picard lives in Newton, Massachusetts with her amazing husband and three energetic sons.

REFERENCES

[1] R.W. Picard (2009), "Future Affective Technology for Autism and Emotion Communication," *Philosophical Transactions of the Royal Society B: Biological Sciences*, doi: 10.1098/rstb.2009.0143 Phil. Trans. R. Soc. B 12 December 2009 vol. 364 no. 1535 3575-3584.

[2] M.Z. Poh, N.C. Swenson, R.W. Picard (2010), "A Wearable Sensor for Unobtrusive, Long-term Assessment of Electrodermal Activity," *IEEE Transactions on Biomedical Engineering*, Volume 57, Number 5, pp. 1243-1252. May 2010. doi: 10.1109/TBME.2009.2038487.

[3] Picard, R.W. (2010), "Emotion research by the people, for the people," *Emotion Review,* Volume 2, Issue 3, July 2010.

[4] Poh, M.Z., Loddenkemper, T., Reinsberger, C., Swenson, N.C., Goyal, S., Madsen, J.R., Picard, R.W. (2012) "Autonomic Changes with Seizures Correlate with Postictal EEG Suppression," *Neurology*, Volume 78, Number 23, 1868-1876, June 5, 2012.

[5] Hoque, M.E., McDuff, D.J., Picard, R.W. (2012), "Exploring Temporal Patterns in Classifying Frustrated and Delighted Smiles," *IEEE Transactions on Affective Computing*, Volume 3, Issue 3, September 2012.

[6] Dinakar, K., Jones, B., Havasi, C., Lieberman, H., Picard, R.W. (2012) "Common Sense Reasoning for Detection, Prevention, and Mitigation of Cyber bullying." *ACM Transactions on Interactive Intelligent Systems,* archive, Volume 2 Issue 3, September 2012, Article No. 18,. doi>10.1145/2362394.2362400.

[7] Sano A., Picard R.W., "Recognition of Sleep Dependent Memory Consolidation with Multi-modal Sensor Data", *The 10th Annual Body Sensor Networks Conference 2013*, Cambridge, MA, May 2013.

[8] McDuff D., Kaliouby R., Senechal T., Amr M., Cohn J., Picard R.W., "AMFED Facial Expression Dataset: Naturalistic and Spontaneous Facial Expressions Collected In-the-Wild", *The 2013 IEEE Computer Society Conference on Computer Vision and Pattern Recognition Workshops (CVPRW'10),* Portland, OR, USA, June 2013.

[9] Hoque, M. E., Courgeon, M., Martin, J.-C., Mutlu, B., Picard, R. W., "MACH: My Automated Conversation coacH", 15th International Conference on Ubiquitous Computing (Ubicomp), September 8-12, 2013.

[10] Ahn, H.I. and Picard R.W., "Measuring Affective-Cognitive Experience and Predicting Market Success," *IEEE Transactions on Affective Computing*, (To Appear) 2014.

[11] McDuff, D., Gontarek, S. & Picard, R. W., "Improvements in Remote Cardio-Pulmonary Measurement Using a Five Band Digital Camera." *Transactions on Biomedical Engineering*, (To Appear) 2014.

[12] Picard, R. W., Fedor, S., & Ayzenberg Y., "Multiple Arousal Theory and Daily-Life Electrodermal Activity Asymmetry" *Emotion Review*, (To Appear) 2014.

Back and to the Future: Quality Provisioning for Multimedia Content Delivery

Klara Nahrstedt
Professor of Computer Science
University of Illinois at Urbana-Champaign
klara@illinois.edu

ABSTRACT

Quality Provisioning concept has been with us for at least 25 years and it started with the claim to be one of the necessary building blocks for multimedia content distribution and delivery. A lot of research has been done on Quality of Service and Quality of Experience by the ACM Special Interest Group on Multimedia (SIGMM) community and other research communities. So where are we with respect to broader impact and deployment of Quality Provisioning in multimedia networks, systems and applications? Did it become a necessary building block for multimedia content delivery or not?

During the talk I will go back and to the future, discussing my journey regarding quality topics ranging from Quality of Service (QoS) in multimedia networks and end systems, to Experiential Quality (QoE) for current and future multimedia applications. I will reflect on successes and failures of Quality Provisioning mechanisms, policies, algorithms, protocols and management frameworks in multimedia networks, systems and applications as they evolved from up to the point of an almost ubiquitous presence of multimedia services to the on-going discussions about network neutrality and multimedia service provisioning. I will also argue that the future for Quality Provisioning is bright with numerous exciting research problems since users expect at this point nothing but high quality multimedia content delivery anytime, anywhere, any content, and on any device.

Author Keywords

Quality of Service, Quality of Experience, Multimedia Systems, Multimedia Communication, Computing and Applications

ACM Classification Keywords

C. Computer Systems Organization, C.2. Computer-Communication Networks, C.2.4 Distributed Systems, Subject: Distributed Applications, C.3. Special-Purpose and Application-Based Systems

BIO

Klara Nahrstedt is the Ralph and Catherine Fisher Full Professor at University of Illinois at Urbana-Champaign, Computer Science Department, and the Acting Director of Coordinated Science Laboratory. She is the co-author of the textbooks "*Multimedia Computing, Communications and Applications*", published by Prentice Hall 1995, "*Multimedia Systems*", published by Spring Verlag in 2004, and the author of the online book "*QoS in Wireless Networks over Unlicensed Spectrum*", published by Morgan & Claypool in 2012. She is the recipient of the Early NSF Career Award, the Junior Xerox Award, the IEEE Communication Society Leonard Abraham Award for Research Achievements, the University Scholar Award, the Humboldt Research Award, and IEEE Computer Society Technical Achievement Award. She was the editor-in-chief of the ACM/Springer Multimedia Systems Journal (2000-2007), associate editor of ACM Transactions on Multimedia Computing, Communications and Applications (2005-2011), associate editor of IEEE Transactions on Multimedia (2012-now), associate editor of IEEE Transactions on Information Forensics & Security, general co-chair of ACM Multimedia 2006, general chair of ACM NOSSDAV 2007, general chair of IEEE PerCom 2009, and Ralph and Catherine Fisher Professor (2002-2012). She was elected to serve as the chair of the ACM SIG Multimedia (2007-2013).

Klara Nahrstedt received her BA in mathematics from Humboldt University, Berlin, in 1984, and M.Sc. degree in numerical analysis from the same university in 1985. She was a research scientist in the Institute for Informatik in Berlin until 1990. In 1995 she received her PhD from the University of Pennsylvania in the Department of Computer and Information Science. She is the ACM Fellow, IEEE Fellow, and the Member of Leopoldina German National Academy of Sciences.

MM14, November 3–7, 2014, Orlando, Florida, USA.
ACM 978-1-4503-3063-3/14/11.
http://dx.doi.org/10.1145/2647868.2647959

Cross-modal Retrieval with Correspondence Autoencoder

Fangxiang Feng
Beijing University of Posts and Telecommunications
Beijing, China
f.fangxiang@gmail.com

Xiaojie Wang
Beijing University of Posts and Telecommunications
Beijing, China
xjwang@bupt.edu.cn

Ruifan Li
Beijing University of Posts and Telecommunications
Beijing, China
rfli@bupt.edu.cn

ABSTRACT

The problem of cross-modal retrieval, e.g., using a text query to search for images and vice-versa, is considered in this paper. A novel model involving correspondence autoencoder (Corr-AE) is proposed here for solving this problem. The model is constructed by correlating hidden representations of two uni-modal autoencoders. A novel optimal objective, which minimizes a linear combination of representation learning errors for each modality and correlation learning error between hidden representations of two modalities, is used to train the model as a whole. Minimization of correlation learning error forces the model to learn hidden representations with only common information in different modalities, while minimization of representation learning error makes hidden representations are good enough to reconstruct input of each modality. A parameter α is used to balance the representation learning error and the correlation learning error. Based on two different multi-modal autoencoders, Corr-AE is extended to other two correspondence models, here we called Corr-Cross-AE and Corr-Full-AE. The proposed models are evaluated on three publicly available data sets from real scenes. We demonstrate that the three correspondence autoencoders perform significantly better than three canonical correlation analysis based models and two popular multi-modal deep models on cross-modal retrieval tasks.

Categories and Subject Descriptors

H.3.3 [**Information Search and Retrieval**]: Retrieval Models; I.2.6 [**Artificial Intelligence**]: Learning

General Terms

Algorithms; Design

Keywords

Cross-modal; retrieval; image and text; deep learning; autoencoder

MM'14, November 03–07, 2014, Orlando, FL, USA.

http://dx.doi.org/10.1145/2647868.2654902.

1. INTRODUCTION

The inclusion of multi-modal data in webpages has become a widespread trend. For example, a webpage telling a story often contains some illustrations and other images accompanying the text. A travel photo shared on the web is usually tagged with words. The presence of massive multimodal data on the Internet brings huge cross-modal retrieval requirements, such as using an image query to search for texts and using a text query to search for images. Unlike traditional information retrieval tasks in a single modality, such as using a text query to search for text, cross-modal retrieval focuses on mining the correlations between data from different modalities.

1.1 Previous Work

Many approaches have been proposed to develop solutions to these challenging tasks. There are two main strategies for modeling cross-modal correlations among previous work.

One strategy involves modeling the correlation between different modalities with a shared layer.

A portion of them use topic models to achieve it. Correspondence LDA (Corr-LDA) [4] extended LDA [5] to find the topic-level relationships between images and text annotations, where topics' distributions act as middle layer for both images and texts. For images with loosely-coupled text, a mixture of directed and undirected probabilistic graphical model, called MDRF, was proposed in [14]. This model was built using a Markov random field over LDA. These LDA-based models essentially can be understood as a two-layer architecture with only one hidden layer.

Recently, there has been a trend of developing deep architecture for tackling complex AI problems [2], which is inspired by the architectural depth of the brain. Some representative models, such as deep autoencoders (DAE) [11], deep belief networks (DBN) [13], and deep Boltzmann Machine (DBM) [21], and their corresponding learning algorithms have been proposed. These models also have been extended to model multi-modal data. Ngiam et al. [17] used multimodal DAE to learn a shared representation for both speech and visual inputs. Srivastava and Salakhutdinov [25] used multimodal DBM and DBN to learn a unified representation for both images and texts. We also noticed several deep learning methods [29, 9, 23] for learning a joint embedding space of image and text very recently. Those models have shown significant advantages at image annotation, objective classification and zero-shot learning tasks. But, to our best knowledge, neither of them has been used for cross-modal retrieval up to now.

Figure 1: An image and its tags. "sky" and "blue" are common information in both image and text modalities. "nikon" and "nikkor" are text modality-specific information while "flowers" and "clouds" are image modality-specific information. Common information are the key to cross-modal retrieval tasks.

The other strategy involves a two-stage framework. It first learns or extracts features for each modality separately then uses canonical correlation analysis (CCA) [10] to build a lower-dimensional common representation space. This choice is more straightforward for cross-modal retrieval task. CCA is a method of data analysis used to discover a subspace of multiple data spaces. Given the training pairs p and q, CCA finds matrices U and V such that Up and Vq have maximum correlations. The first d canonical components of U and V could be used for projecting new input pairs into a d-dimension space where cross-modal retrieval could be conducted by calculating a simple similarity measurement, such as Euclidean or cosine distance. Rasiwasia et al. [19] proposed correlation matching mapping the features of images and texts extracted by LDA into same representation space using CCA. Ngiam et al. [17] used DAE to extract features and suggested using CCA to form a shared representation of audio and video data. As in Ngiam et al.'s work, Kim et al. [15] learned the shared semantic space of different language with DAE and CCA.

1.2 Motivation

In the first strategy, the shared layer was built by jointly learning from different modalities. We think the shared layer learnt in this way might no fit the need of cross-modal retrieval. Perceived data from different modalities for a same object normally comprise of common information in all modalities and modality-specific information. Figure 1 gives an example. There is a picture accompanying with several text tags in figure 1, where "sky" and "blue" are common information in both image and text modalities. "nikon" and "nikkor" are text modality-specific information which can hardly be acquired from the image. While "flowers" and "clouds" are only image modality-specific information which can not be captured in text tags. Intuitively, common information like "sky" and "blue" are key to cross-modal retrieval. Both text modality-specific and image modality-specific information are not necessary and even harmful to cross-modal retrieval. A shared representation learns both common and modality-specific information. Although it showed its strength on learning complementarity of data from different modalities, it is therefore not a exactly well-fitting representation for cross-modal retrieval. A representation which can learn only common information for different modalities is a better choice. This is the first motivation to build our model in this paper.

The second strategy separates correlation learning from representation learning. This strategy is too weak to exploit the complex correlations of representations from different modalities, especially when autoencoders are used to learn representations. Autoencoders can be used learn different level representation for inputs with different reconstruction errors, one problem for building correlations between data from two different modalities is that it is difficult to decide which level is best for building correlations. In other words, two different modalities may be correlated at different abstract levels of representation. Therefore, correlation learning need be considered with representation learning as a whole. This is the second motivation to build our model in this paper.

1.3 Contribution

In this paper, we propose correspondence autoencoder (Corr-AE) based on two basic uni-modal autoencoders. The difference between two-stage methods and our Corr-AE is illustrated in Figure 2. The two-stage methods ignore the correlation between different modalities when perform representation learning. Corr-AE incorporates representation learning and correlation learning into a single process. A novel loss function is here designed. It includes not only the loss of different autoencoders for all modalities, but also the loss of correlation between different modalities. This model is evaluated using three publicly available data sets. Compared against several multi-modal deep learning models, our Corr-AE demonstrate its effectiveness. Besides, based on two other multi-modal autoencoders, we extend Corr-AE to two correspondence models, Corr-Cross-AE and Corr-Full-AE. Experimental results show that based on different autoencoders, the combination of representation learning and correlation learning is more effective than the two-stage methods.

The remainder of this paper is organized as follows. In the next section, the details of the basic Corr-AE are described. The Corr-AE are then extended to Corr-Cross-AE and a combinational model. Section 3 describes the experimental results and compares the performance of different models. Conclusions are presented in Section 4.

2. LEARNING ARCHITECTURE

In this section, the details of the architecture of the basic Corr-AE are described. Then a loss function suitable for training Corr-AE for learning similar representations of different modalities is proposed. Next, two extensions of the Corr-AE are introduced. Lastly, the deep architecture with the training algorithms is described.

2.1 Correspondence Autoencoder

As illustrated in Figure 3, the Corr-AE architecture consists of two subnetworks, each a basic autoencoder. These two networks are connected by a predefined similarity measure on the code layer. Each subnetwork in the Corr-AE is

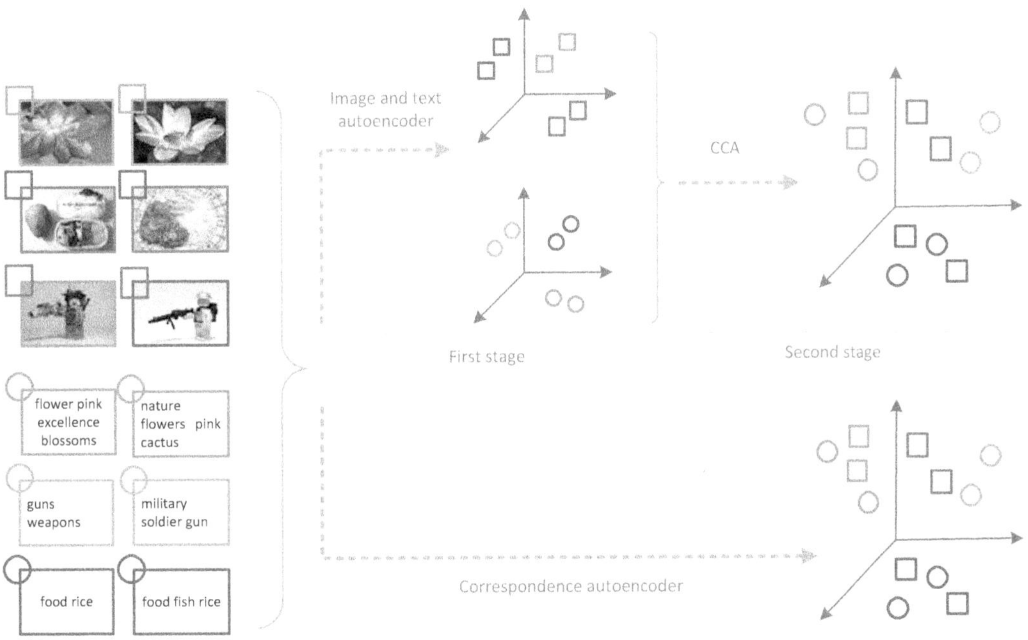

Figure 2: Difference between two-stage methods and our Corr-AE: Corr-AE incorporates representation learning and correlation learning into a single process while two-stage methods separate the two processes.

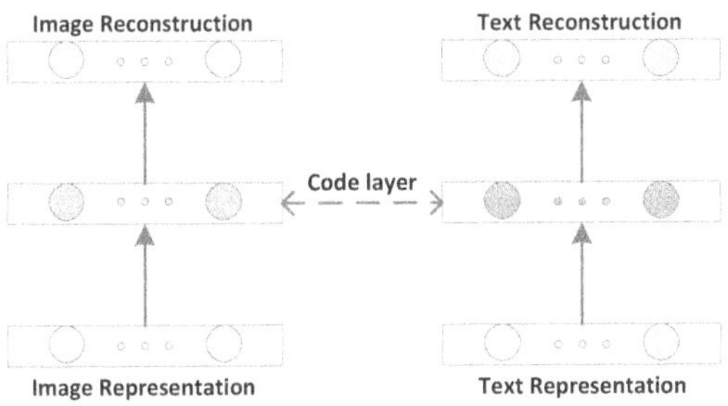

Figure 3: Correspondence autoencoder

responsible for each modality. In this way, the inputs to each subnetwork are features from one modality. During learning, the two subnetworks are coupled at their code layer using a similarity measure. After learning, the two subnetworks in the Corr-AE exhibit different parameters even if they have the same architecture. As a result, the code for new inputs can be obtained using the learned network parameters.

Formally, the mapping from the inputs of these two subnetworks to the code layers is denoted as $f(p; W_f)$ and $g(q; W_g)$, in which, f is image modality and g is text modality; W denotes the weight parameters in these two subnetworks. The subscripts denote the corresponding modalities. f and g are logistic activation function. The similarity measure between ith pair of image representation $p^{(i)}$ and the given text representation $q^{(i)}$ are here defined as follows:

$$C(p^{(i)}, q^{(i)}; W_f, W_g) = \left\| f(p^{(i)}; W_f) - g(q^{(i)}; W_g) \right\|_2^2 \quad (1)$$

where $\|\cdot\|_2$ is the $\mathcal{L}_2$ norm.

To learn the similar representations of these two modalities for one object, a loss function given input image representation $p^{(i)}$ and its text representation $q^{(i)}$ are established. To simplify the notation, the network parameters W_f, W_g are grouped as Θ. The loss function on any pair of inputs can then be defined as follows:

$$\begin{aligned} L(p^{(i)}, q^{(i)}; \Theta) =& (1-\alpha)\left(L_I(p^{(i)}; \Theta) + L_T(q^{(i)}; \Theta)\right) \\ &+ \alpha L_C(p^{(i)}, q^{(i)}; \Theta) \end{aligned} \quad (2)$$

where

$$L_I(p^{(i)}, q^{(i)}; \Theta) = \left\| p^{(i)} - \hat{p}_I^{(i)} \right\|_2^2 \quad (3a)$$

$$L_T(p^{(i)}, q^{(i)}; \Theta) = \left\| q^{(i)} - \hat{q}_T^{(i)} \right\|_2^2 \quad (3b)$$

$$L_C(p^{(i)}, q^{(i)}; \Theta) = C(p^{(i)}, q^{(i)}; \Theta) \quad (3c)$$

Here, $\|\cdot\|_2$ is the $\mathcal{L}_2$ norm. L_I and L_T are the losses caused by data reconstruction errors for the given inputs (an image and its text) of two subnetworks, specifically image and text modalities. $\hat{p}_I^{(i)}$ and $\hat{q}_I^{(i)}$ are the reconstruction data from $p^{(i)}$ and $q^{(i)}$ respectively; L_C is the correlation loss; $\alpha (0 < \alpha < 1)$ in the total loss function (2) is a parameter used to trade off between two groups of objectives: correlation losses and reconstruction losses. An appropriate value for α is crucial. If $\alpha = 0$, the loss function degenerates to the loss function of the autoencoders. It cannot then capture any correlations between inputs from different modalities. At the other extreme, considering only correlation loss, α is set to 1. This assumes that any pair of inputs has correlations, regardless of whether the image and text inputs match or not. An intuitive interpretation for this is that the cost function only focuses on the constraints of correlations and ignores the characteristics of the data completely.

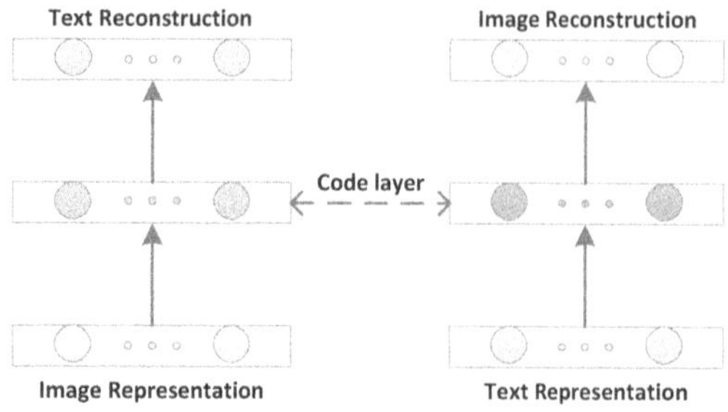

Figure 4: Correspondence cross-modal autoencoder

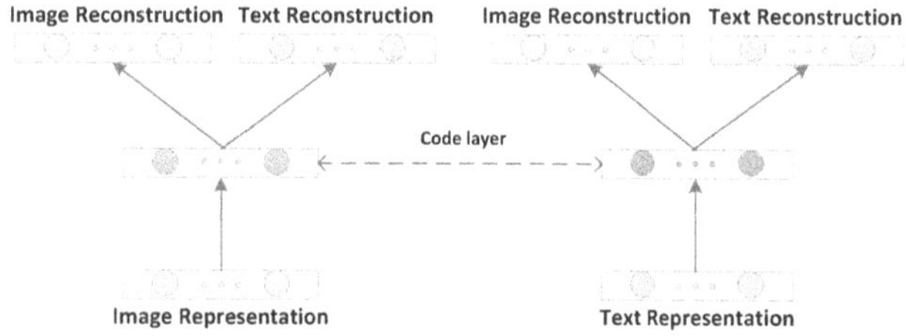

Figure 5: Correspondence full-modal autoencoder

In summary, minimizing the loss function defined in Eq. (2) enables our Corr-AE to learn similar representations from bimodal feature representations.

2.2 Correspondence Cross-modal Autoencoder

As illustrated in Figure 4, we propose the Corr-Cross-AE, which replace the basic autoencoders to cross-modal autoencoders. Unlike the basic autoencoders, which reconstruct the input itself, cross-modal autoencoders reconstruct input from different modalities. The loss function on any pair of inputs of the Corr-Cross-AE is defined as follows:

$$L(p^{(i)}, q^{(i)}; \Theta) = (1-\alpha)\Big(L_I(p^{(i)}, q^{(i)}; \Theta) + L_T(p^{(i)}, q^{(i)}; \Theta)\Big) + \alpha L_C(p^{(i)}, q^{(i)}; \Theta) \quad (4)$$

where

$$L_I(p^{(i)}, q^{(i)}; \Theta) = \left\|q^{(i)} - \hat{q}_I^{(i)}\right\|_2^2 \quad (5a)$$

$$L_T(p^{(i)}, q^{(i)}; \Theta) = \left\|p^{(i)} - \hat{p}_T^{(i)}\right\|_2^2 \quad (5b)$$

$$L_C(p^{(i)}, q^{(i)}; \Theta) = C(p^{(i)}, q^{(i)}; \Theta) \quad (5c)$$

Here, $\hat{q}_I^{(i)}$ and $\hat{p}_T^{(i)}$ are the reconstruction data from image and text subnet, respectively. The meanings of other symbols are the same as in Eq. (2).

The representation learning of image modality in cross-modal autoencoder considers the information from the text modality and vice-versa. This causes some correlations to be captured in the reconstruction loss.

2.3 Correspondence Full-modal Autoencoder

The full-modal autoencoder can be viewed as a combination of a basic autoencoder and cross-modal autoencoder. This autoencoder is proposed to model the audio and video data in [17]. The basic Corr-AE are also easy to extend to Corr-Full-AE based on full-modal autoencoder. As illustrated in Figure 5, the autoencoder reconstruct not only the input itself but also input from different modalities. This "full" representation space contains information from both modalities. The loss function of any pair of inputs of the Corr-Full-AE is defined as follows:

$$L(p^{(i)}, q^{(i)}; \Theta) = (1-\alpha)\Big(L_I(p^{(i)}, q^{(i)}; \Theta) + L_T(p^{(i)}, q^{(i)}; \Theta)\Big) + \alpha L_C(p^{(i)}, q^{(i)}; \Theta) \quad (6)$$

where

$$L_I(p^{(i)}, q^{(i)}; \Theta) = \left\|p^{(i)} - \hat{p}_I^{(i)}\right\|_2^2 + \left\|q^{(i)} - \hat{q}_I^{(i)}\right\|_2^2 \quad (7a)$$

$$L_T(p^{(i)}, q^{(i)}; \Theta) = \left\|p^{(i)} - \hat{p}_T^{(i)}\right\|_2^2 + \left\|q^{(i)} - \hat{q}_T^{(i)}\right\|_2^2 \quad (7b)$$

$$L_C(p^{(i)}, q^{(i)}; \Theta) = C(p^{(i)}, q^{(i)}; \Theta) \quad (7c)$$

Here, $\hat{p}_I^{(i)}$ and $\hat{q}_I^{(i)}$ are the reconstruction data from $p^{(i)}$ and $q^{(i)}$ in the image subnet; $\hat{p}_T^{(i)}$ and $\hat{q}_T^{(i)}$ are the reconstruction data from $p^{(i)}$ and $q^{(i)}$ in the text subnet. The meanings of other symbols are the same as in Eq. (2).

2.4 Deep Architecture

Data from different modalities may have very different statistical properties. This makes it difficult to capture correlations across modalities directly. To address this, a deep architecture is here proposed. This first involves using some stacked modality-friendly models to learn higher-level representations that remove such modality-specific properties. Then the Corr-AE are used to learn similar representations at a higher level.

As illustrated in Figure 6, the deep architecture has three stacked components. The first two components are all restricted Boltzmann machines (RBMs). There are two extended RBMs for the first component and two basic RBMs for the second component. To be brief, RBM[22] is an undirected graphical model with stochastic binary units in a vis-

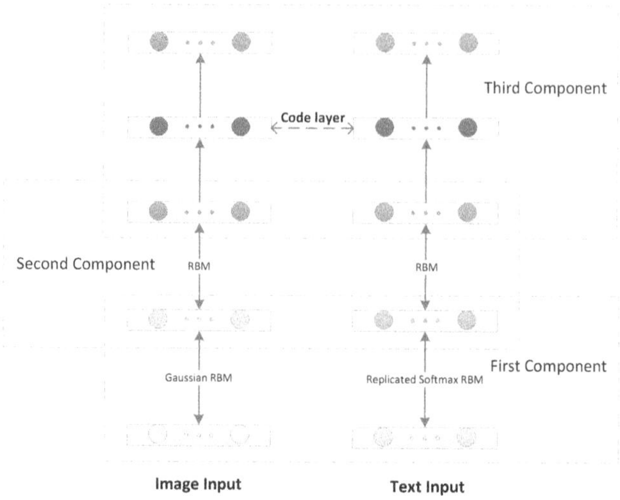

Figure 6: Deep architecture

ible layer and hidden layer but without connections between the units within these two layers. Given that each unit is distributed by Bernoulli distribution with logistic activation function, a joint probabilistic distribution of visible units and hidden units can be defined. The basic RBM can be extended to exponential family. All the models can be efficiently learned by using the contrastive divergence approximation (CD) [12]. For the first layer, Gaussian RBM [28] and replicated softmax RBM [20] can be used to model the real-valued feature vectors for image and the discrete sparse word count vectors for text, respectively. After learning the RBMs, the hidden layer can then be used as the input for the second component. The second component involves two basic RBMs, which are used to learn higher-level features for image and text. The third component can involve any one of the three correspondence autoencoders given above. The learning for Corr-AE can be performed using standard back-propagation algorithm.

Because different modalities are mapped into the same representation space by the deep architecture, it is straightforward to use the model for cross-modal retrieval tasks. For example, given a text query, we expect the relevant images could be returned[1]. After learning this deep architecture, all test images are mapped into the representation space from the three-layer image subnetwork. A new text query is mapped into the same space from the three-layer text subnetwork. The similarity between the text query and all the candidate images can be calculated by a simple distance metric in the representation space. In this way, in searching for image using text, image ranked list will return by increasing distance for any text query.

3. EXPERIMENTS

We evaluate our models on three public available real-world data sets. In this section, we first give a detailed description of these data sets. Then, the evaluation protocol used in the experiments is introduced. Next, the performance of several models is reported. Finally, an analysis of the impact of α on the models is given.

3.1 Data sets and Feature Extraction

Wikipedia. The data set [19] was collected from "Wikipedia featured articles". It contains 2,866 image/text pairs belonging to 10 semantic categories. The data set was split into three subsets: 2,173 cases as training set, 231 cases as validation set and 462 cases as testing set. For image representation, we extract the following three types of features:

- Pyramid Histogram of Words (PHOW) [6]. For PHOW features, dense SIFT descriptors is first extracted by VLfeat [27] from per training image and then a 1000-dimensional visual word codebook learned with K-means clustering.
- Gist [18]. The gist descriptor is extracted by the public available package[2] with default parameters. This results in a 512-dimensional feature vector.
- MPEG-7 descriptors [16]. We use the public available software [1] to extract four different visual descriptors (CSD, SCD, CLD, EHD) defined in MPEG-7 for image representations. The dimension of obtained MPEG-7 feature vector is 784.

[1]Text retrieval using an image query can be done in a similar way.

[2]`http://people.csail.mit.edu/torralba/code/spatialenvelope/`

Thus, each image is represented by a 2296-dimensional feature vector. For text representation, we use bag of words model. A dictionary of 3000 high-frequency words is built from all training texts. We use Python Natural Language Toolkit [3] to stem the text. This data set is available at `http://www.svcl.ucsd.edu/projects/crossmodal/`.

Pascal. The data set [8] contains 1,000 image/text pairs from 20 categories, 50 cases per categories. The images are randomly selected from 2008 PASCAL development kit. Each image is labeled with 5 sentences. We split the data into three subsets, 800 for training (40 cases per category), 100 for validation (5 cases per category) and 100 for testing (5 cases per category). The feature extraction for images and texts is the same as for the Wikipedia data set except that the dimension of text is 1,000. This data set is available at `http://vision.cs.uiuc.edu/pascal-sentences/`.

NUS-WIDE-10k. This data set is a subset of NUS-WIDE [7], which contains about 270k images with tag annotations from 81 categories. We only choose 10 categories with the largest quantity and 1,000 image/text pairs per category from NUS-WIDE. Each pair of our NUS-WIDE-10k only belongs to a single category. The 10 categories are animal, clouds, flowers, food, grass, person, sky, toy, water and window. We randomly split the data set into three subsets: 8,000 cases for training (800 cases per category), 1,000 for validation (100 cases per category) and 1,000 for testing (100 cases per category). Each image is represented by six descriptors, including 64-D color histogram, 144-D color correlogram, 73-D edge direction histogram, 128-D wavelet texture, 225-D block-wise color moments and 500-D bag of words based on SIFT descriptions. Each text is represented by 1000-dimensional bag of words. This data set with extracted features is available at `http://lms.comp.nus.edu.sg/research/NUS-WIDE.htm`.

As we can see, these data sets have very distinct properties. For example, the text modality of the three data sets Wikipedia, Pascal and NUS-WIDE-10k is quite different, which are article, sentences and tags, respectively. Besides, the sizes of these data sets range from 1k to 10k and the number of the categories range from 10 to 20.

3.2 Evaluation metric

We consider two cross-modal retrieval tasks: text retrieval from an image query, and image retrieval from a text query. Following [30], retrieval performance is evaluated using two metrics, mean average precision (mAP) and top 20% percentage. The first one represents the ability of learning discriminative cross-modal mapping functions while the later one reveals the ability of learning corresponding latent concepts.

mAP Given one query and first R top-ranked retrieved data, the average precision is defined as

$$\frac{1}{M}\sum_{r=1}^{R} p(r) \cdot rel(r) \qquad (8)$$

where M is the number of relevant data in the retrieved result, $p(r)$ is precision of at r, and $rel(r)$ presents the relevance of a given rank (one if relevant and zero otherwise). The retrieved data is considered as relevant if it has the same semantic label as the query. mAP is obtained by averaging AP of all the queries. We report $mAP@50$ ($R = 50$) in all experiments. Semantic labels are only used for evaluation. Training of our models does not need any semantic label.

Top 20% Jia et al. [14] proposed this evaluation metric for data sets without semantic label. Because there is only one ground-truth for each image-text pair in this case, the position of the ground-truth image/text in the ranked list is used to evaluate performance. Specifically, top 20% percentage is the relative number of images/texts correctly retrieved in the first 20% of the ranked list.

3.3 Baseline

For a fair comparison, the inputs to our models and baseline methods[3] are all features learned by first two components of deep architecture described in section 2.4. That means that the only difference is the third component of the deep architecture. Besides, cosine distance is used to measure the similarity in all experiments. We compare our models with three CCA based models and two multi-modal models:

- CCA-AE[15]. We first use two uni-modal autoencoders to learn higher level image feature and text feature respectively, and then use CCA[4] to learn a common representation space on the learned features.
- CCA-Cross-AE. Instead of using the uni-modal autoencoders with CCA, this method combines immediately cross-modal autoencoders and CCA.
- CCA-Full-AE. Literally, this method combines full-modal autoencoders and CCA.
- Bimodal AE[17]. We train a bimodal autoencoder to perform shared representation learning. Follow the training algorithm described in [17], we add training examples that have zero values for one of the input modalities (e.g., image) and original values for the other input modality (e.g., text), but still require the network to reconstruct both modalities (image and text). Thus, one-third of the training data has only image for input, while another one-third of the data has only text, and the last one-third of the data has both image and text. After learning the bimodal autoencoder, a single modality input(image or text) can be mapped into the shared representation space.
- Bimodal DBN[17, 24]. A bimodal DBN is obtained by connecting image and text features with a joint layer. The model does not give a direct matching function of image and text input. However, it can generate the unknown modality conditioned on a given modality. In other words, queries can be mapped into the feature space of the other modality and a suitable similarity measure can be used to retrieve results that are close to the query.

3.4 Model Architecture

We perform grid search for the number of hidden units of each layer with the setting 32, 64, 128, 256, 512, 1024. In all models, to reduce the search space, the number of units for all hidden layers in the deep architecture is restricted to the same. The validation sets are used to determine the best number of hidden units. The dimensionality of the CCA latent space and the iterations of Bimodal AEs and our three correspondence models are also determined by the validation sets. For our three correspondence models, we need to choose an appropriate value for the parameter α. The parameter α is not sensitive to data sets. So, in all data sets, the value of α for Corr-AE and Corr-Full-AE is set to 0.8. For Corr-Cross-AE, α is set to 0.2. A detailed analysis of α will be given at the end of this section.

For the models involving CCA, to achieve a better performance, CCA is applied to learn the correlation between the image and text hidden layers with different number of units. Three copies of all training data are used in Bimodal AE training. The first copy remains data from both modalities (original data). The second is only image data with text data setting to zeros. And the third is only text data with image data setting to all zeros. We do not weight the reconstruction errors from different modalities. So do our correspondence models. For the Bimodal DBN, variational mean field with ten steps is used to generate the unknown modality conditioned on a given modality. Gibbs sampling does not show improvement in our experiments. The code with parameter specifications of our three models and the baseline methods are available online[5].

3.5 Results

Table 1 summarizes the mAP scores and top 20% of the two cross-modal retrieval tasks for Wikipedia, Pascal and NUS-WIDE-10k data sets respectively. On all data sets, our three correspondence autoencoders significantly outperform other models on both tasks of text and image retrieval. Taking Corr-Full-AE as an example, we compare it with the best results on each task achieved by the five baseline models. It improves mAP scores 12.3% and 16.6% respectively on searching texts by images and searching images by texts on Wikipedia data set, improves 12.4% and 2.2% respectively on the two tasks on Pascal data set, improves 32.4% and 10.2% respectively on the two tasks on NUS-WIDE-10k data set.

Compared with CCA-AE, our Corr-AE improves average mAP value of two tasks 53.6%, 81.5%, 48.3% on Wikipedia, Pascal, NUS-WIDE-10k data sets respectively. Compared with CCA-Cross-AE, our Corr-Cross-AE improves 57.9%, 73.6%, 28.3% on the three data sets. Compared with CCA-Full-AE, our Corr-Full-AE improves 12.8%, 71.2%, 46.7% on the three data sets. Based on three different multi-modal autoencoders, our correspondence models significantly outperform the two-stage methods. The advantage of our correspondence models over two-stage models is that correspondence models combined representation learning and correlation learning into a whole. In other words, compared with our correspondence models, the two-stage methods are suboptimal. It is also noticeable that the difference within the three correspondence autoencoders are found to be smaller than the difference among the three CCA-AEs. This also demonstrates the effectiveness of the combination of representation learning and correlation learning processes.

Compared with Bimodal AE, our Corr-AE improves mAP scores 15.6% and 10.4% respectively on searching texts by

[3]The code for all baseline models are available online at `https://github.com/nitishsrivastava/deepnet`.

[4]Matlab code of the CCA can be downloaded at `http://www.davidroihardoon.com/Professional/Code.html`.

[5]https://github.com/fangxiangfeng/deepnet

Table 1: **Results of two retrieval protocols: mAP scores and top 20% on three data sets.**

(a) Wikipedia

Model	mAP			Top 20%		
	Image Query	Text Query	Average	Image Query	Text Query	Average
CCA-AE[15]	0.213	0.235	0.224	28.35	23.59	25.97
CCA-Cross-AE	0.197	0.230	0.214	25.54	28.14	26.84
CCA-Full-AE	0.293	0.331	0.312	51.08	49.57	50.33
Bimodal AE[17]	0.282	0.327	0.305	44.16	42.42	43.29
Bimodal DBN[17, 24]	0.189	0.222	0.206	26.19	31.6	28.90
Corr-AE	0.326	0.361	0.344	56.06	55.19	55.63
Corr-Cross-AE	**0.336**	0.341	0.338	55.41	**58.66**	57.04
Corr-Full-AE	0.335	**0.368**	**0.352**	**57.36**	57.79	**57.58**

(b) Pascal

Model	mAP			Top 20%		
	Image Query	Text Query	Average	Image Query	Text Query	Average
CCA-AE[15]	0.161	0.153	0.157	36	30	33
CCA-Cross-AE	0.137	0.182	0.159	18	16	17
CCA-Full-AE	0.148	0.177	0.163	32	35	33.5
Bimodal AE[17]	0.250	0.270	0.260	68	68	68
Bimodal DBN[17, 24]	0.219	0.219	0.219	55	61	58
Corr-AE	**0.290**	0.279	**0.285**	72	67	69.5
Corr-Cross-AE	0.271	**0.280**	0.276	**78**	**75**	**76.5**
Corr-Full-AE	0.281	0.276	0.279	74	73	73.5

(c) NUS-WIDE-10k

Model	mAP			Top 20%		
	Image Query	Text Query	Average	Image Query	Text Query	Average
CCA-AE[15]	0.199	0.268	0.234	37	33.8	35.4
CCA-Cross-AE	0.199	0.344	0.272	29	47.7	38.35
CCA-Full-AE	0.241	0.242	0.242	37.1	38.2	37.65
Bimodal AE[17]	0.250	0.297	0.274	30.2	35.4	32.8
Bimodal DBN[17, 24]	0.173	0.203	0.188	25.3	27	26.15
Corr-AE	0.319	0.375	0.347	47.1	53.5	50.3
Corr-Cross-AE	**0.349**	0.348	0.349	**53.1**	**59.7**	**56.4**
Corr-Full-AE	0.331	**0.379**	**0.355**	49.6	56.5	53.05

images and searching images by texts on Wikipedia data set, improves 16.0% and 3.3% respectively on the two tasks on Pascal data set, improves 27.6% and 26.3% respectively on the two tasks on NUS-WIDE-10k data set. Both Bimodal AE and Bimodal DBN model the multi-modal inputs with a shared hidden layer. Representation learned in shared hidden layer should cover difference between two modalities for achieving good performance in both autoencoders or RBMs. It therefore focuses more on learning complementarity instead of correlation across data from different modalities.

Figure 7 shows three examples of text-based cross-modal using our Corr-Full-AE and the best baseline method. In these examples, the top four retrieved images by Corr-Full-AE are all relevant to correspondence text query. Figure 8 shows several failure cases of Corr-Full-AE on the NUS-WIDE-10k test data set.

As for the top 20% percentage metric, our three correspondence autoencoders also significantly outperform the other baseline models. There is only one ground-truth for each image-text pair under this evaluation metric. Figure 9 shows several top-1-hit retrieval examples by our Corr-Full-AE. In these cases, the first returned results by the query are all ground truth on both image query text and text query image tasks.

3.6 Analysis of α

Here, mAP values of three correspondence autoencoders with different values of α in all data sets are given in Figure 10. Both too small values and too large values of α show poor performance in the three data sets. This is consistent with the impact of α in the present models. Too small values of α overemphasize the "individuality" of data and ignore the correlations. Too large values overemphasize the correlations and ignore the "individuality" of the data.

To validate the hypothesis of the effect of α to the "individuality" of data, we use tSNE [26] to visualize the image and text representation learned by our Corr-Full-AE. As shown in Figure 11, when $\alpha = 0.01$, image and text representation space are almost disjoint. In this case, image and text have strong "individuality" so that the learned representation of image and text have no correlations. To the other extreme of the α, when $\alpha = 0.99$, "individuality" of im-

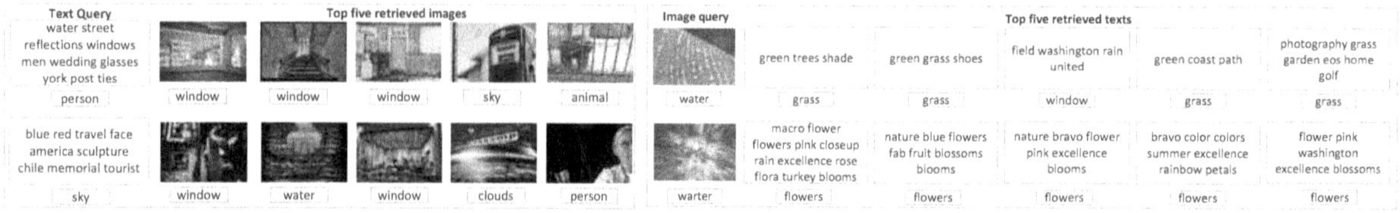

(a) Failure cases: text query image (b) Failure cases: image query text

Figure 8: Several failure cases of Corr-Full-AE on the NUS-WIDE-10k test data set. The words under the texts/images are the correspondence semantic labels. In the cases of text query images, the images are related to the subset of the text query. For example, in the first case, the first retrieved image is related to the "windows" and "glasses". In the cases of image query texts, the image queries are too difficult to be recognized. For example, in the second case, the image query is easy to be recognized as the flowers falsely.

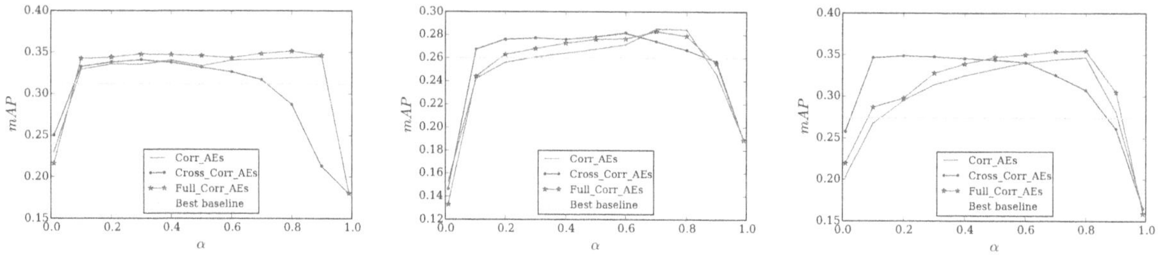

(a) Wikipedia (b) Pascal (c) NUS-WIDE-10k

Figure 10: mAP values of three correspondence autoencoders with different values of α in all data sets. The X-axis gives values for α. The Y-axis gives the mAP scores. The yellow line denotes the mAP score of the best baseline model, which does not change with α.

(a) $\alpha = 0.01$ (b) $\alpha = 0.8$ (c) $\alpha = 0.99$

Figure 11: Image and text representation visualization of different value for α on the NUS-WIDE-10k test data set. Different shapes denote different modalities: "square" for image, "plus" for text. Different colors denote different semantic categories.

age and text representation is missing due to the confusion representation space. In this case, any image-text pair has correlations, regardless of whether the image and text inputs match or not.When α is set to 0.8, the representation space is quite effective to the cross-modal retrieval task, since a large number of image-text pairs with same semantic labels are clustered.

As shown in Figure 10, the yellow line denotes the mAP scores of the best baseline model. On all data sets, our three correspondence autoencoders outperform the best baseline when α is in a quite large range.

4. CONCLUSION

In this work, a cross-modal learning model, Corr-AE, is presented. This model incorporates representation learning and correlation learning into a single process, so combining autoencoder cost with correlation cost. Corr-AE is here extended to Corr-Cross-AE by replacing the basic autoencoder with a cross-modal autoencoder. Finally, Corr-Full-AE is built by combining Corr-AE and Corr-Cross-AE. These three models are compared to CCA-based and multi-modal deep learning models and found to be effective in cross-modal retrieval of information from three publicly available data sets.

5. ACKNOWLEDGEMENTS

This work was partially supported by National Natural Science Foundation of China(No. 61273365), National High Technology Research and Development Program of China(No. 2012AA011103), discipline building plan in 111 base(No. B08004), the Fundamental Research Funds for the Central Universities (No. 2013RC0304) and Engineering Research Center of Information Networks, Ministry of Education.

6. REFERENCES

[1] M. Bastan, H. Cam, U. GÍźdÍźkbay, and z. Ulusoy. Bilvideo-7: an mpeg-7- compatible video indexing and retrieval system. *IEEE MultiMedia*, 17(3):62–73, 2010.

[2] Y. Bengio. Learning deep architectures for AI. *Foundations and Trends in Machine Learning*, 2(1):1–127, 2009.

[3] E. L. Bird, Steven and E. Klein. In *Natural Language Processing with Python*. O'Reilly Media Inc., 2009.

[4] D. M. Blei and M. I. Jordan. Modeling annotated data. *ACM SIGIR*, pages 127–134, 2003.

[5] D. M. Blei, A. Y. Ng, and M. I. Jordan. Latent dirichlet allocation. *JMLR*, 3:993–1022, 2003.

[6] A. Bosch, A. Zisserman, and X. Muñoz. Image classification using random forests and ferns. In *ICCV*, pages 1–8. IEEE, 2007.

[7] T.-S. Chua, J. Tang, R. Hong, H. Li, Z. Luo, and Y.-T. Zheng. Nus-wide: A real-world web image database from national university of singapore. In *CIVR*, Santorini, Greece., 2009.

[8] A. Farhadi, S. M. M. Hejrati, M. A. Sadeghi, P. Young, C. Rashtchian, J. Hockenmaier, and D. A. Forsyth. Every picture tells a story: Generating sentences from images. In K. Daniilidis, P. Maragos, and N. Paragios, editors, *ECCV (4)*, volume 6314 of *Lecture Notes in Computer Science*, pages 15–29. Springer, 2010.

[9] A. Frome, G. Corrado, J. Shlens, S. Bengio, J. Dean, M. Ranzato, and T. Mikolov. Devise: A deep visual-semantic embedding model. In *NIPS*, pages 2121–2129, 2013.

[10] D. R. Hardoon, S. Szedmĺčk, and J. Shawe-Taylor. Canonical correlation analysis; an overview with application to learning methods. *Neural Computation*, 16:2639–2664, 2004.

[11] G. Hinton and R. Salakhutdinov. Reducing the dimensionality of data with neural networks. *Science*, 313(5786):504–507, 2006.

[12] G. E. Hinton. Training products of experts by minimizing contrastive divergence. *Neural Computation*, 14(8):1771–1800, 2002.

[13] G. E. Hinton, S. Osindero, and Y. Teh. A fast learning algorithm for deep belief nets. *Neural Computation*, 18(7):1527–1554, 2006.

[14] Y. Jia, M. Salzmann, and T. Darrell. Learning cross-modality similarity for multinomial data. *ICCV*, pages 2407–2414, 2011.

[15] J. Kim, J. Nam, and I. Gurevych. Learning semantics with deep belief network for cross-language information retrieval. *COLING*, pages 579–588, 2012.

[16] B. S. Manjunath, J. R. Ohm, V. V. Vinod, , and A. Yamada. Color and texture descriptors. *IEEE Trans. Circuits and Systems for Video Technology, Special Issue on MPEG-7*, 11(6):703–715, June 2001.

[17] J. Ngiam, A. Khosla, M. Kim, J. Nam, H. Lee, and A. Y. Ng. Multimodal deep learning. *ICML*, pages 689–696, 2011.

[18] A. Oliva and A. Torralba. Modeling the shape of the scene: A holistic representation of the spatial envelope. *IJCV*, 42(3):145–175, 2001.

[19] N. Rasiwasia, J. C. Pereira, E. Coviello, G. Doyle, G. R. G. Lanckriet, R. Levy, and N. Vasconcelos. A new approach to cross-modal multimedia retrieval. *ACM MM*, pages 251–260, 2010.

[20] R. Salakhutdinov and G. Hinton. Replicated softmax: an undirected topic model. *NIPS*, pages 1607–1614, 2009.

[21] R. R. Salakhutdinov and G. G. Hinton. An efficient learning procedure for deep Boltzmann machines. *Neural computation*, 24(8):1967–2006, 2012.

[22] P. Smolensky. Parallel distributed processing: explorations in the microstructure of cognition, vol. 1. chapter Information processing in dynamical systems: foundations of harmony theory, pages 194–281. MIT Press, Cambridge, MA, USA, 1986.

[23] R. Socher, M. Ganjoo, C. D. Manning, and A. Ng. Zero-shot learning through cross-modal transfer. In *NIPS*, pages 935–943, 2013.

[24] N. Srivastava and R. Salakhutdinov. Learning representations for multimodal data with deep belief nets. *ICML Representation Learning Workshop*, 2012.

[25] N. Srivastava and R. Salakhutdinov. Multimodal learning with deep Boltzmann machines. *NIPS*, pages 2231–2239, 2012.

[26] L. van der Maaten and G. Hinton. Visualizing high-dimensional data using t-sne. *JMLR*, 2008.

[27] A. Vedaldi and B. Fulkerson. Vlfeat: an open and portable library of computer vision algorithms. In A. D. Bimbo, S.-F. Chang, and A. W. M. Smeulders, editors, *ACM MM*, pages 1469–1472, 2010.

[28] M. Welling, M. Rosen-Zvi, and G. Hinton. Exponential family harmoniums with an application to information retrieval. In *NIPS*, pages 501–508, Vancouver, 2004. Morgan Kaufmann.

[29] J. Weston, S. Bengio, and N. Usunier. Large scale image annotation: Learning to rank with joint word-image embeddings. In *ECML*, pages 21–35, 2010.

[30] Y. Zhuang, Y. F. Wang, F. Wu, Y. Zhang, and W. Lu. Supervised coupled dictionary learning with group structures for multi-modal retrieval. In *AAAI*, 2013.

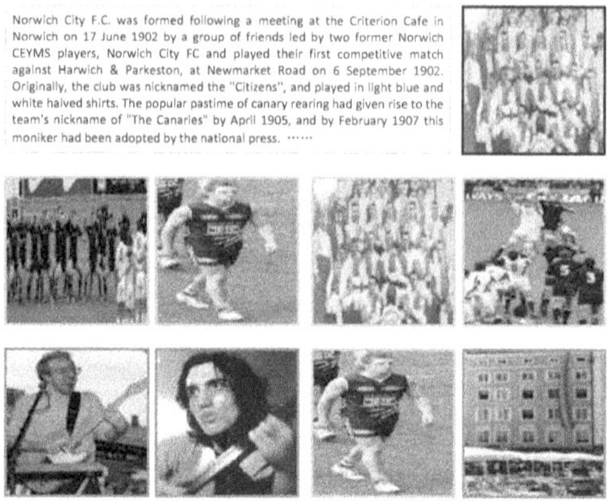

(a) Wikipedia

(b) Pascal

(c) NUS-WIDE-10k

Figure 7: Three examples of text-based cross-modal using our Corr-Full-AE and best baseline method. In each example, the query text and its correspondence image are shown on the top; retrieved images of our Corr-Full-AE are presented in the middle; retrieved images of the best baseline model are presented at the bottom. Relevant matches are shown with green bounding box. Irrelevant matches are shown with red bounding box. The text queries come from sport, aeroplane and grass category respectively.

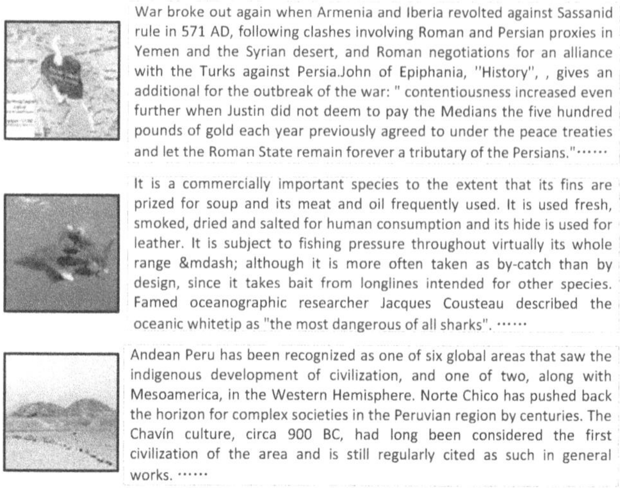

(a) Wikipedia

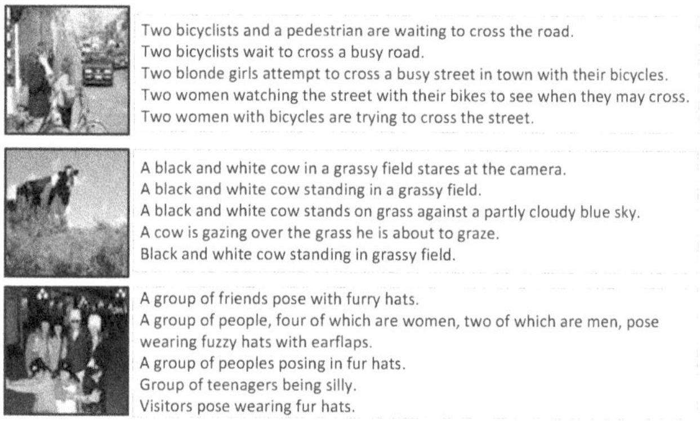

(b) Pascal

(c) NUS-WIDE-10k

Figure 9: Several image-text pairs of three data sets. In these pairs, the closest images(texts) to the text(image) queries are all ground truth. In figure (a), three image-text pairs come from warfare, biology, history category respectively. In figure (b), three pairs come from bicycle, cow, person category respectively. In figure (c), three pairs come from animal, flower, food category respectively. Various images(texts) can be retrieved effectively.

VideoStory: A New Multimedia Embedding for Few-Example Recognition and Translation of Events

Amirhossein Habibian, Thomas Mensink, Cees G. M. Snoek
ISLA, Informatics Institute, University of Amsterdam
Science Park 904, 1098 XH
Amsterdam, The Netherlands
{a.habibian, tmensink, cgmsnoek}@uva.nl

ABSTRACT

This paper proposes a new video representation for few-example event recognition and translation. Different from existing representations, which rely on either low-level features, or pre-specified attributes, we propose to learn an embedding from videos *and* their descriptions. In our embedding, which we call *VideoStory*, correlated term labels are combined if their combination improves the video classifier prediction. Our proposed algorithm prevents the combination of correlated terms which are visually dissimilar by optimizing a joint-objective balancing descriptiveness and predictability. The algorithm learns from textual descriptions of video content, which we obtain for free from the web by a simple spidering procedure. We use our VideoStory representation for few-example recognition of events on more than 65K challenging web videos from the NIST TRECVID event detection task and the Columbia Consumer Video collection. Our experiments establish that *i)* VideoStory outperforms an embedding without joint-objective and alternatives without any embedding, *ii)* The varying quality of input video descriptions from the web is compensated by harvesting more data, *iii)* VideoStory sets a new state-of-the-art for few-example event recognition, outperforming very recent attribute and low-level motion encodings. What is more, VideoStory translates a previously unseen video to its most likely description from visual content only.

Categories and Subject Descriptors

I.2.10 [**Artificial Intelligence**]: Vision and Scene Understanding—*Video analysis*

General Terms

Algorithms, Experimentation, Measurement

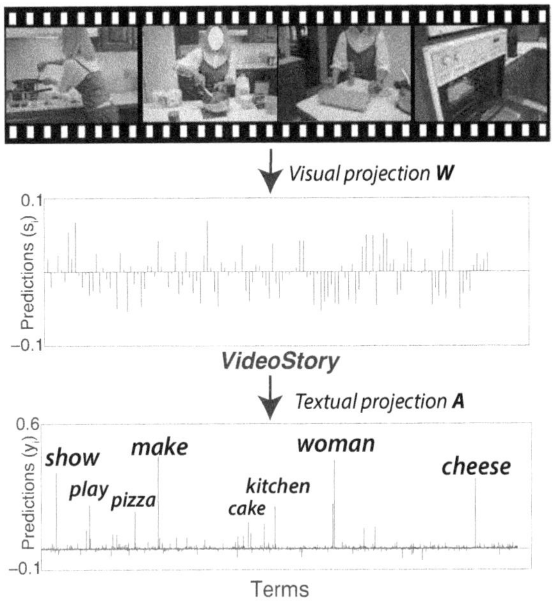

Figure 1: VideoStory at work. We propose an algorithm that learns from web data an optimal multimedia embedding optimizing both the visual projection for recognition and the textual projection for translation. For unseen videos it recognizes events from just ten examples and it predicts the most likely description from visual content only.

1. INTRODUCTION

The goal of this paper is to recognize *and* translate events in web video from ten examples only. For multimedia challenges where examples are scarce, a traditional solution is to rely on clever combinations and rerankings of as many extracted information sources as possible *e.g.,* [25,28]. In principle, such approaches would be well-suited for event recognition, despite the fact that none of them is able to provide a semantic interpretation of the obtained result. We adhere to a different solution. The main contribution of this paper is a new video representation for few-example event recognition and translation, which we learn from freely available web videos and their descriptions. We call our new video representation *VideoStory*, since it strives to encode the story of a video rather than a collection of single words (Figure 1). Before detailing our contributions we discuss related work on representations for event recognition, learning from the web, and multimedia embedding.

MM'14, November 3–7, 2014, Orlando, Florida, USA.
Copyright is held by the owner/author(s). Publication rights licensed to ACM.
ACM 978-1-4503-3063-3/14/11 ...$15.00.
http://dx.doi.org/10.1145/2647868.2654913.

Representations for Event Recognition The state-of-the-art in event recognition represents a video in terms of low-level audiovisual features [2,6,16,27,34,37]. These methods first extract from the video various descriptors *e.g.*, color SIFT [36], or motion boundary histograms [37]. Then, the descriptors are quantized and aggregated as bag-of-word histograms or Fisher vectors [32,37]. Despite good recognition performance, low-level representations suffer from two drawbacks. First, they are incapable of providing a semantic interpretation of an event. Second, because of their high-dimensionality, training effective event classifiers on the low-level representation often requires a sufficient number of training examples. When only a few event exemplars are available, the applicability of the low-level representation is limited [22,23].

Semantic video representations provide an alternative, they are achieved by representing a video by their attribute (or concept) scores. Yang *et al.* [41] obtain the attributes by compressing their low-level features in three consecutive unsupervised clustering steps. The obtained attributes are shown to outperform the low-level audiovisual features they started from. However, attributes obtained by unsupervised clustering of low-level features still have no semantic interpretation. In [22], Ma *et al.* learn the attribute classifiers and event classifiers jointly. In their work, the attribute classifiers are trained to optimize the event recognition, without explicitly optimizing the individual attribute classifier accuracies. As a consequence, the obtained representation does not necessarily have a semantic interpretation either. We aim for a representation that is both robust for recognition and interpretable by humans.

Semantic representations for event recognition that are both accurate and interpretable rely on the prediction scores made by a set of pre-trained attribute classifiers [11,13,21,22,24,26]. In [26], Merler *et al.* obtain the attribute classifiers by training 280 SVMs on a manually labeled collection of images, including objects, people, and scenes. Habibian *et al.* [11] study the properties of 1,346 attribute classifiers trained from ImageNet [8] and TRECVID [29] for representing and recognizing events in web video. In [24], Mazloom *et al.* learn a semantic representation per event by feature selection of a subset of attributes, from the same 1,346 used in [11], which maximizes the event recognition accuracy. While effective and promising, a considerable drawback of attribute representations is their dependence on individual attribute classifiers. They demand a considerable classifier training and video representation construction effort. However, the biggest limitation is the need to pre-specify and manually label the attributes in advance, often leading to a mismatch between the representation and the events of interest. Rather than specifying and labeling the attributes one by one to represent video, we propose an algorithm that *discovers* the semantic representation without the need for specification or annotation.

Representation Learning from the Web Many have used annotations from the web to learn individual attributes, *e.g.,* [17,35,39], without considering their utility as a representation. We are inspired by the work on image representations by Berg *et al.* [4], who start by collecting a set of web pages, relevant to the (visual) attributes of interest, by submitting attribute names to an Internet search engine. The retrieved web pages are mined to discover the most frequent terms and their associated images. Subsequently, a classifier is trained by using all the images corresponding to a certain term as positive annotations and randomly sampling images from other terms as negatives. They hold out a portion of the training data as a validation set, which they use to select the most reliable term classifiers for the final representation. While their work is proposed for images, it is easily extended to video. However, a drawback is that many terms rarely occur. For these infrequent terms only a limited number of positive examples are available, which leads to a biased estimation of their reliability. As a consequence, many of the discovered visual terms might be overfitted to their small training set and do not generalize well for new videos. We also discover our representation from the Internet, but rather than selecting individual, and often unreliable, classifiers per term, we prefer to combine terms automatically into more descriptive attributes. By combining terms, more training examples are available and a more robust representation is obtained, without losing descriptive ability.

Representation by Multimedia Embedding Current representations for video (and image) translation also combine terms, typically by multimedia embeddings of visual features and descriptions from labels [40], attributes [1] or documents [7,31] into a joint low dimensional space. Most multimedia embeddings are proposed for image classification [1,40] and cross-media retrieval [31], we are not aware of any multimedia embeddings for few-example event recognition and translation. Das *et al.* [7] focus on generating video translations. They model the relation between low-level video-features and textual terms by an embedding founded on multimodal latent dirichlet allocation; a probabilistic topic model which models the videos and their descriptions as mixed memberships over a set of latent topics. Despite their effectiveness for translating video to text, this method is not intended to recognize events in video. As an aside we note that by design multimodal topic models are only applicable for discrete features. Therefore, they cannot leverage recent state-of-the-art video encodings such as Fisher vectors [32] or deep learned representations [19], which would undermine the effectiveness of multimodal topic models for the purpose of event recognition. In addition to generating event video translations, we aim for state-of-the-art video event recognition using a multimedia embedding that leverages the benefits of modern encodings.

Contributions We make the following contributions:

- We propose a multimedia embedding for few-example event recognition and translation, which we learn from videos and their descriptions.
- We introduce an algorithm that combines correlated terms if their combination improves the video classifier prediction by optimizing a joint-objective trading of descriptiveness and predictability (Section 2).
- The algorithm learns from textual descriptions of video content, for which we introduce a new dataset obtained for free from the web by a simple spidering procedure (Section 3).

We use our VideoStory representation for few-example recognition and translation of events on more than 65K challenging web videos from the NIST TRECVID event detection task [33] and the Columbia Consumer Video collection [15] (Section 4). State-of-the-art results support our proposed contributions (Section 5). We conclude in Section 6.

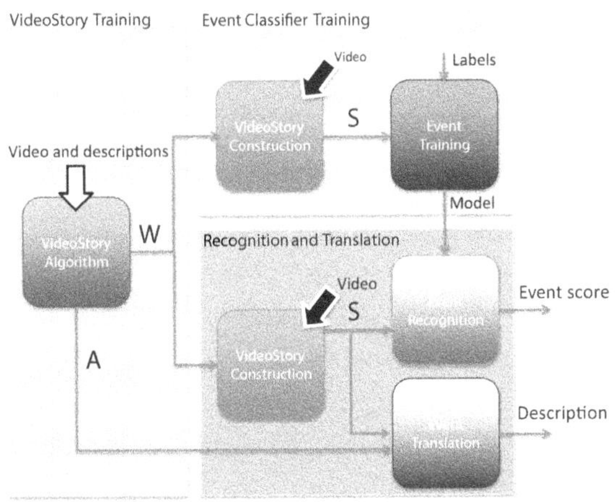

Figure 2: Dataflow for learning the VideoStory and using it for event recognition and translation.

2. VIDEOSTORY FRAMEWORK

Our VideoStory framework contains three major parts, schematically illustrated in Figure 2.

1. The VideoStory training, where we learn our multimedia embedding from a dataset consisting of videos with descriptions. This training outputs two projection matrices: a visual projection matrix $\boldsymbol{W}$, and a textual projection matrix $\boldsymbol{A}$. The VideoStory representation $\boldsymbol{S}$ is computed from the visual projection matrix $\boldsymbol{W}$ and low-level video features.
2. The event classifier training, where we use off-the-shelf SVMs to train classifiers on a dataset consisting of videos with a few event labels. The videos are encoded with our VideoStory representation.
3. The recognition and translation stage, where we evaluate the event classifiers, and use the semantics of our representation to describe videos.

In this section we introduce the VideoStory embedding, its design principles and how it is obtained by learning.

2.1 Objective Function

Using the notation summarized in Table 1, we will describe the objective function we minimize to obtain the VideoStory representation. To learn the embedding we use a dataset of videos, represented by low-level video features $\boldsymbol{X}$, and their descriptions, represented by binary term vectors $\boldsymbol{Y}$, indicating which terms are present in each video description. While we use and emphasize low-level visual features in this work, our approach is generic and can create a VideoStory from any multimedia feature.

The aim of the VideoStory representation is to balance two compelling forces:

1. *Descriptiveness*, to preserve the information encoded in the video descriptions $\boldsymbol{Y}$ as much as possible, and
2. *Predictability*, to ensure that the VideoStory could be effectively recognized from visual video content $\boldsymbol{X}$.

Notation	Description
N	Number of videos
M	Number of unique terms in descriptions
D	Dimensionality of visual feature
k	Dimensionality of VideoStory embedding
$\boldsymbol{X} \in \mathbb{R}^{D\times N}$	Matrix of low-level video features
$\boldsymbol{Y} \in \{0,1\}^{M\times N}$	Matrix of binary term vectors
$\boldsymbol{W} \in \mathbb{R}^{D\times k}$	VideoStory visual projection
$\boldsymbol{A} \in \mathbb{R}^{M\times k}$	VideoStory textual projection
$\boldsymbol{S} \in \mathbb{R}^{k\times N}$	VideoStory embedding
$\boldsymbol{x}_i, \boldsymbol{y}_i, \boldsymbol{s}_i$	The column representing the i-th video

Table 1: Summary of notation.

Therefore, we learn the VideoStory representation by both objectives in a joint optimization framework.

The VideoStory representation is learned by minimizing:

$$L_{\text{VS}}(\boldsymbol{A},\boldsymbol{W}) = \min_{\boldsymbol{S}} L_d(\boldsymbol{A},\boldsymbol{S}) + L_p(\boldsymbol{S},\boldsymbol{W}), \quad (1)$$

where $\boldsymbol{A}$ is the textual projection matrix, $\boldsymbol{W}$ is the visual projection matrix, and $\boldsymbol{S}$ is the VideoStory embedding. The loss function L_d corresponds to our first objective for learning a descriptive VideoStory, and the loss function L_p corresponds to our second objective for learning a predictable VideoStory. The VideoStory embedding $\boldsymbol{S}$ interconnects the two loss functions. To the best of our knowledge this joint embedding framework is novel.

Descriptiveness For the L_d function, we use a variant of regularized Latent Semantic Indexing [38]. This objective minimizes the quadratic error between the original video descriptions $\boldsymbol{Y}$, and the reconstructed translations obtained from $\boldsymbol{A}$ and $\boldsymbol{S}$:

$$L_d(\boldsymbol{A},\boldsymbol{S}) = \frac{1}{N}\sum_{i=1}^{N}\|\boldsymbol{y}_i - \boldsymbol{A}\boldsymbol{s}_i\|_2^2 + \lambda_a\Omega(\boldsymbol{A}) + \lambda_s\Psi(\boldsymbol{S}), \quad (2)$$

where $\Psi(\cdot)$ and $\Omega(\cdot)$ denote regularization functions, and $\lambda_a \geq 0$ and $\lambda_s \geq 0$ are regularizer coefficients. We use the squared Frobenius norm for regularization, which is the matrix variant of the ℓ_2 regularizer, *i.e.*, $\Omega(\boldsymbol{A}) = \|\boldsymbol{A}\|_{\text{F}}^2 = \sum_i\|\boldsymbol{a}_i\|_2^2 = \sum_{ij} a_{ij}^2$, the sum of the squared matrix elements. Similarly for the VideoStory matrix $\Psi(\boldsymbol{S}) = \|\boldsymbol{S}\|_{\text{F}}^2$.

The main difference with regularized Latent Semantic Indexing [38] is that they used an ℓ_1 regularizer, $\Omega(\boldsymbol{A}) = \sum_i\|\boldsymbol{a}_i\|_1$, which enforces sparsity in the textual projection $\boldsymbol{A}$. However, with our larger representation (typically we use k between 256 and 1,024 in our experiments compared to only $k = 20$ used in [38]) and fewer number of unique terms (around 10K, compared to 100K), enforcing sparsity is not necessary for good performance.

Note that many other textual embedding methods, such as Sparse Coding and probabilistic Latent Semantic Indexing [12] can be formulated similar to Eq. (2), when appropriate regularization functions $\Omega(\cdot)$ and $\Psi(\cdot)$ are used. Furthermore, when the textual projection matrix $\boldsymbol{A}$ is constrained such that each column has a single non-zero value, *i.e.*, selects a single term, our objective becomes very close to methods that select the best single term labels, such as [4].

Predictability The L_p function measures the occurred loss between the VideoStory $\boldsymbol{S}$ and the embedding of low-level videos features using $\boldsymbol{W}$. Since the VideoStory $\boldsymbol{S}$ is real valued, as opposed to a binary or multi-class encoding, we can not rely on standard classification losses such as the hinge-loss used in SVMs. Therefore, we define L_p as a regularized regression, similar to ridge regression:

$$L_p(\boldsymbol{S}, \boldsymbol{W}) = \frac{1}{N}\sum_{i=1}^{N} \|\boldsymbol{s}_i - \boldsymbol{W}^\top \boldsymbol{x}_i\|_2^2 + \lambda_w \Theta(\boldsymbol{W}), \quad (3)$$

where we use (again) the Frobenius norm for regularization of the visual projection matrix W, $\Theta(\boldsymbol{W}) = \|\boldsymbol{W}\|_F^2$, and λ_w is the regularization coefficient.

2.2 Learning Algorithm

To handle large scale datasets and state-of-the-art high-dimensional visual features, *e.g.*, Fisher vectors [32] on low-level video features [37] or deep learned representations [19], we employ SGD (Stochastic Gradient Descent) [5]. SGD is an efficient online procedure and converges fast to the (global) minimum of a model. At each step, training with SGD consists of (i) choosing a random sample from the dataset consisting of a video and a description, (ii) computing the sample estimate of the gradient of the parameters in the model, and (iii) updating the parameters in the direction of the gradient with step-size η. The number of passes over the datasets, often denoted as *epochs*, and the step-size η are hyper-parameters of SGD.

The VideoStory objective function, as given in Eq. (1), is convex with respect to matrix $\boldsymbol{A}$ and $\boldsymbol{W}$ when the embedding $\boldsymbol{S}$ is fixed. In that case, the joint optimization is decoupled into Eq. (2) and Eq. (3), which are both reduced to a standard ridge regression for a fixed $\boldsymbol{S}$. Moreover, when both $\boldsymbol{A}$ and $\boldsymbol{W}$ are fixed, the objective Eq. (1) is convex *w.r.t.* $\boldsymbol{S}$. Therefore we use standard SGD by computing the gradients of a sample *w.r.t.* the current value of the parameters, and we minimize $\boldsymbol{S}$ jointly with $\boldsymbol{A}$ and $\boldsymbol{W}$.

Lets denote a randomly sampled video and description pair at step t by $(\boldsymbol{x}_t, \boldsymbol{y}_t)$, and let $\boldsymbol{s}_t$ denote the current VideoStory embedding of sample t. The gradients of Eq. (1) for this sample *w.r.t.* $\boldsymbol{A}, \boldsymbol{W}$ and $\boldsymbol{s}_t$ are given by:

$$\nabla_{\boldsymbol{A}} L_{\mathrm{VS}} = -2\left(\boldsymbol{y}_t - \boldsymbol{A}\boldsymbol{s}_t\right)\boldsymbol{s}_t^\top + \lambda_a \boldsymbol{A}, \quad (4)$$

$$\nabla_{\boldsymbol{W}} L_{\mathrm{VS}} = -2\, \boldsymbol{x}_t \left(\boldsymbol{s}_t - \boldsymbol{W}^\top \boldsymbol{x}_t\right)^\top + \lambda_w \boldsymbol{W}, \text{ and} \quad (5)$$

$$\nabla_{\boldsymbol{s}_t} L_{\mathrm{VS}} = 2\left[\boldsymbol{s}_t - \boldsymbol{W}^\top \boldsymbol{x}_t - \boldsymbol{A}^\top\left(\boldsymbol{y}_t - \boldsymbol{A}\boldsymbol{s}_t\right)\right] + \lambda_s \boldsymbol{s}_t. \quad (6)$$

Our algorithm is summarized in Algorithm 1.

The effect of joint learning the descriptiveness and the predictability, becomes clear in Eq. (6), where both the textual projection matrix $\boldsymbol{A}$ and visual projection matrix $\boldsymbol{W}$ contribute to learning the VideoStory embedding $\boldsymbol{S}$. This embedding $\boldsymbol{S}$ is subsequently used to obtain the textual projection $\boldsymbol{A}$ matrix, in Eq. (4), and the visual projection $\boldsymbol{W}$ matrix, in Eq. (5). This leads to the VideoStory embedding, which is both descriptive, by preserving the textual information, and predictable, by minimizing the visual prediction loss.

2.3 Using the VideoStory Embedding

The result of training our VideoStory embedding is the visual projection matrix $\boldsymbol{W}$ and the textual projection matrix $\boldsymbol{A}$. These are used to encode a new video i into our VideoStory representation $\boldsymbol{s}_i$.

In the case that both a video $\boldsymbol{x}_i$ and description y_i are given, we could obtain the semantic embedding by returning $\boldsymbol{s}_i$ from Eq. (1), while keeping both $\boldsymbol{A}$ and $\boldsymbol{W}$ fixed.

```
input  : X, Y, k, η (step-size), m (max-epochs)
output: W and A
A, W, and S ← random (zero-mean, unit variance)
for e ← 1 to m do
    for i ← 1 to N do
        Pick a random video-description pair (x_t, y_t)
        Compute gradients w.r.t. A, W and s_t
        Update parameters:
            A   ← A − η_t ∇_A L_VS        see Eq. (4)
            W   ← W − η_t ∇_W L_VS        see Eq. (5)
            S   ← s_t − η_t ∇_{s_t} L_VS   see Eq. (6)
    end
end
return: W and A
```

Algorithm 1: Pseudocode for learning VideoStory

However, in practice most videos are not provided with a description. Therefore, we use:

$$\boldsymbol{s}_i = \boldsymbol{W}^\top \boldsymbol{x}_i, \quad (7)$$

to construct our VideoStory representation from the low-level video features $\boldsymbol{x}_i$. Given an embedded video $\boldsymbol{s}_i$, we can translate a video by:

$$\hat{\boldsymbol{y}}_i = \boldsymbol{A}\boldsymbol{s}_i, \quad (8)$$

where the terms with the highest values are most relevant for this video.

3. HARVESTING VIDEOS AND THEIR DESCRIPTIONS FROM THE WEB

Rather than describing the video content manually, we opt to harvest both videos and descriptions from the web. Video sharing web sites, such as YouTube and Vimeo, provide a rich and varied source of videos and user provided descriptions, such as their title captions and comments. Although video title captions do not necessarily correspond to the visual content of the videos, we will show that by harvesting a large number of these captioned videos and applying a set of quality filters we obtain reliable video descriptions.

We start from an initial pool of descriptions, as the collection seeds, and iteratively collect videos and their title captions from YouTube. For the collection seeds, we rely on 3,000 sentence descriptions from the training partition of the NIST TRECVID HAVIC corpus [33]. Then each description within the pool is queried to YouTube and the 25 most relevant videos are retrieved, based on YouTube's textual similarity search. Every retrieved video is passed through a set of quality filters. The videos which pass all the filters are added to the collection and their title captions are added to the description pool. We iteratively repeat this procedure until enough videos are collected. We will first detail our quality filters before providing the statistics of our harvested video and description dataset.

3.1 Quality Filters

Event Filter Events are generally described by their actors, actions, and possible involved objects [10]. Hence we assume that a description of an event video should contain actors, actions and objects. For this purpose, we parse the

Figure 3: Terms from the VideoStory46K dataset occurring in more than 500 title captions of the harvested YouTube videos.

grammatical structure of title captions using a probabilistic context free grammar parser [18]. Then we accept a video only if its caption includes verbs, subjects, and objects.

Visualness Filter There are many terms in title captions which do not refer to visually depictable attributes, such as `buy`, `God`, and `genius`. These attributes are not recognizable by present-day visual classifiers, so should not be included in the collection. For this filter we evaluate the visualness of caption terms. Rather than relying on visual features [4, 9, 20], which are expensive to extract and limit the scalability, we evaluate the visualness of each term in the title caption by measuring its similarities to the ImageNet synsets [8] in the WordNet hierarchy. We measure the similarity of each synset pair by following [3], which finds overlaps between the glosses of two synsets as well as their directly linked synsets. Finally, we define the visualness of a title caption by averaging the visualness of all its terms. The captions whose visualness exceeds a threshold of 0.5 are accepted by our harvesting procedure.

Reality Filter A considerable amount of YouTube videos are related to celebrities, TV series, and movie trailers. We observe these professional videos are typically semantically dissimilar to the event videos which we are interested in. Moreover, they often infringe intellectual property rights. Therefore, we prefer to filter out the corresponding videos. Our reality filter relies on a list of keywords from Wikipedia, which provides an extensive index of celebrity, TV series and movie names[1]. We exclude the videos whose description matches any of the keywords from the list.

Temporal Filter Our last filter rests on the assumption that short videos better match their title captions, compared to long videos. It is because long videos usually contain a broad set of attributes that are typically not specified completely by their captions. Hence, we only retrieve the YouTube videos which are shorter than 120 seconds.

3.2 VideoStory46K Dataset

Following the proposed procedure, including all quality filters, we harvest 45,826 videos from YouTube. The videos have an average length of 58.4 seconds and the whole collection contains 743 hours of videos. Every video comes with a short title caption provided by the user who has uploaded the video. Every caption is made of 7.7 individual terms on average, with a standard deviation of 1.8 terms. There are 19,159 unique terms in the captions, most of them occurring infrequently in the collection, *i.e.*, 50% of the terms occur only once in the collection, and only 0.4% of the terms occur more than 500 times. Some examples of these frequent terms are shown as a tag cloud in Figure 3. Our dataset of videos and their descriptions, which we call VideoStory46K, is available for download at `http://www.mediamill.nl`. Illustrative examples from the dataset are shown in Figure 4.

[1]`wikipedia.org/wiki/List_of_American_television_series`

4. EXPERIMENTAL SETUP

4.1 Evaluation Datasets

We perform our experiments on the challenging NIST TRECVID HAVIC corpus [33] and the Columbia Consumer Video collection [15], together containing more than 65K videos collected from the web. To the best of our knowledge these are the largest publicly available video corpora in the literature for event recognition containing user-generated video with a large variation in quality, length and content.

NIST TRECVID HAVIC [33] The 2013 public release of this dataset comes with five partitions of videos: Event Kit training, Background training, test set MED, test set Kindred, and a Research collection, including about 200, 5K, 27K, 14K, and 10K videos, respectively[2]. Apart from the Research partition (which we only use in experiment 2), all four other partitions come with ground truth annotation at video-level for 20 event categories. We follow the *10Ex evaluation procedure* outlined by the NIST TRECVID event recognition task [29] for all our experiments. It means that for each event the training data is composed of 10 positive videos from the Event Kit training data along with about 5K negative videos from the Background training data. We report event recognition results of each event classifier on both the test set MED and test set Kindred datasets.

Columbia Consumer Video [15] This dataset contains 9,317 user-generated videos from YouTube. It consists of over 210 hours of videos in total, where each video has an average length of 80 seconds. Moreover, the dataset contains ground truth annotations at video-level for 20 semantic categories, where 15 of them are events. The other 5 categories are objects and scenes, which are excluded from the dataset in our experiments: "bird", "cat", "dog", "beach" and "playground". We use the standard partitioning of the dataset, but we use only 10 positive examples per event in the training data. These 10 are selected based on alphabetical order of the respective video names, we ignore the remaining positive examples in the train set. We report event recognition results on the standard test partition.

4.2 Event Recognition Protocol

Our event recognition pipeline consists of the following consecutive steps:

1. Extracting low-level features. For all videos we compute MBH descriptors [37] along the motion trajectories. The extracted 288-dimensional descriptors are reduced to 128 dimensions using PCA and are then aggregated per video using a Fisher vector [32], with 128 Gaussians resulting in a 32K dimensional vector. Each Fisher vector is power

[2]There is also a PROGRESS set with 98K videos, but this partition is for blind testing by NIST only.

Figure 4: Example videos and title captions from our introduced VideoStory46K dataset.

normalized, with $\alpha = 0.2$, as in [14]. This representation is shown to be state-of-the-art for recognizing events using a single modality [37].

2. Learning the VideoStory. We learn the VideoStory on the MBH-encoded videos from the VideoStory46K dataset using the algorithm described in Algorithm 1, we use 75% of the dataset for training and 25% for validation to set the hyper-parameters of our model $(\lambda_w, \lambda_a, \lambda_s)$ and of SGD (number of epochs, η).

3. Applying the VideoStory. We apply the learned VideoStory on all the MBH-encoded training and test videos in the NIST TRECVID HAVIC and Columbia Consumer Video datasets.

4. Training event classifiers. On top of the VideoStory we train event classifiers using the 10-example *training sets* of the NIST TRECVID HAVIC and Columbia Consumer Video datasets. We train SVM classifiers with RBF kernels, which is shown to be effective for learning events from semantic representations [26]. We obtain the parameters for the SVM regularization cost and the RBF kernel by 2-fold cross-validation.

5. Testing event classifiers. We apply the event classifiers on the VideoStory embedding of the MED test, Kindred test and Columbia Consumer Video test sets, and rank the video classification results.

As an evaluation criteria for the ranked lists, we follow the standard convention in the literature [15,29] by relying on the average precision (AP) per event, and we report the mean average precision (mAP) for overall accuracy.

4.3 Experiments

4.3.1 Effect of Embedding

In our first experiment we quantify the merit of the VideoStory, by comparing it with three baselines: an embedding without joint optimization and two baselines without embedding inspired by the work on image representations by Berg *et al.* [4].

Baseline 1: ***Description embedding***. In this baseline we learn the embedding in two stages. First, the descriptions are embedded using regularized Latent Semantic Indexing [38], according to Eq. (2). Then the video embedding is learned separately, by minimizing the error of predicting the embedded descriptions from the videos using ridge regression, according to Eq. (3).

Baseline 2: ***Visual terms***. We learn this representation directly from the terms in the description following Berg *et al.* [4] (see Section 1). A linear SVM classifier is trained per term. The classifiers which have the highest prediction accuracy, based on a 2-fold cross-validation, are selected as visual terms in the video representation.

Baseline 3: ***Frequent terms***. This representation is similar to baseline 2, but rather than using cross-validation to select terms it simply selects the terms with the highest frequency in the descriptions. The occurrences of these terms in the description accompanying a video are considered as labels which are used for training the classifiers.

We evaluate all four video representations for recognizing events from few-examples using a varying dimensionality of the representation, from 32 up to 8,192.

4.3.2 Description Quality and Quantity

In our second experiment we assess the influence of the quality and quantity of the videos and descriptions that we use as input to learn our VideoStory. We compare the VideoStory learned from the VideoStory46K dataset with two baselines.

Baseline 4: ***ExpertSentences10K***, includes 10K videos from the Research partition of the NIST TRECVID HAVIC corpus [33]. Each video in this collection comes with an expert written description. The descriptions are made of a few sentences written by a team of 60 expert annotators with the purpose of summarizing the visual content of the videos. Consequently, there is always a strong correspondence between a description and its video in this collection.

Baseline 5: ***VideoStory10K***, includes 10K random videos and descriptions from the VideoStory46K dataset, which we collected as discussed in Section 3. This collection includes the same number of videos and captions as the ExpertSentences10K dataset, but the captions are generally of lower quality for event recognition because of the non-expert descriptions and the fact that video captions on YouTube do not necessarily correspond to the visual content.

Again we use a varying dimensionality of the representation, starting from 32 up to 2,048, and we compare their effectiveness for recognizing events from few examples.

4.3.3 VideoStory vs Others

In this experiment we compare the VideoStory with alternative representations for event recognition. We consider three state-of-the-art baselines.

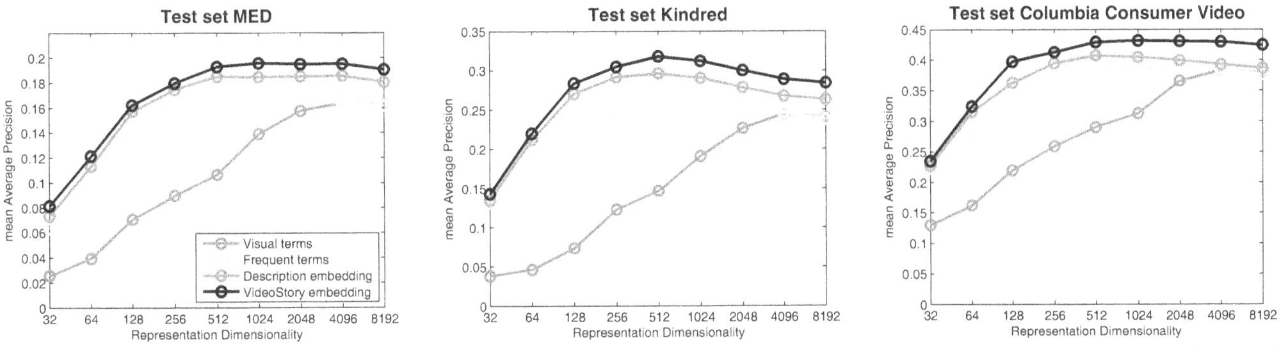

Figure 5: Effect of embedding. The VideoStory, which is learned by our proposed algorithm, outperforms all three alternatives on all three test sets. The Description embedding is the closest competitor, but it suffers from the embedding of correlated terms which are visually dissimilar. Representations without term label combinations, *i.e.*, the Visual terms and Frequent terms, inspired by Berg *et al.* [4], are always worse.

Baseline 6: ***Attributes*** [11]. This representation uses 1,346 pre-specified attribute classifiers to represent a video. Every image and key frame is represented as a Fisher vector encoding of densely sampled color SIFT descriptors [36] with spatial pyramids. Each individual attribute classifier is trained by a linear SVM on annotated images from TRECVID and ImageNet. The video representation is obtained by applying the trained classifiers on the video frames, extracted every two seconds, and then averaging over the entire video [11].

Baseline 7: ***Informative Attributes*** [24]. This baseline automatically selects informative attributes per event, and uses the selected subset as video representation. The informative attributes are selected from the same 1,346 attribute classifiers used for *baseline 6* by using mRMR feature selection [30] on the training data, with 2-fold cross validation. The reported results are based on the optimal number of selected attributes per event.

Baseline 8: ***Low-Level*** [37]. The last baseline is the state-of-the-art Fisher vector representation using MBH descriptors, explained in Section 4.2. In this case the event classifiers are trained directly on the low-level video representations, without extracting an embedding.

Different from the low-level baseline, the attributes and the informative attributes baselines rely only on static visual features, since they are trained, in part, on the ImageNet dataset. These baselines are included because of their translation ability, a capability the low-level features cannot achieve. For this experiment we use a fixed 1,024 dimensional VideoStory representation, since this resembles most closely with the dimensionality of the other semantic baselines (using at most 1,346 dimensions), although it is not necessarily the optimal VideoStory dimensionality.

5. RESULTS

5.1 Effect of Embedding

The results are shown in Figure 5. The VideoStory, which is learned by our proposed algorithm, outperforms all three alternatives on all three test sets.

The lowest performing representation is obtained with Visual terms, which relies on the estimated reliability of individual term classifiers. As expected, this representation suffers from two drawbacks. First, many of the visual terms refer to very specific terms, which are incapable of characterizing the events of interest *i.e.*, `necklace`, `suitcase`, `cellphone`, `elevator` and `earring`. Although these terms can be accurately predicted from videos, they are incapable of providing a characteristic representation of the events. Second, many of the terms rarely occur in video descriptions. For these infrequent terms there are only a limited number of positive examples available, which leads to a biased estimation of their reliability. As a consequence, many of the discovered visual terms might be overfitted to their small training set and do not generalize well for new videos.

The drawbacks of Visual terms are relaxed by Frequent terms, by simply relying on the most frequent terms. We observe the most frequent terms usually refer to characterizing attributes of events which are frequently used by humans when describing a video, *i.e.*, `car`, `girl`, `man`, `kid`, and `truck`. Moreover, because of their large number of positive examples, the trained visual classifiers are in general more reliable. Hence, Frequent terms consistently outperform Visual terms on the MED test, the Kindred test, and the Columbia Consumer Video datasets.

Both the Visual terms and Frequent terms use no embedding. However, a Description embedding, without joint optimization, is always better than using no embedding at all. We explain it by the fact that the Description embedding represents the terms in a reduced-dimensional space, where the correlated terms are usually combined together. Combining correlated terms per dimension leads to less correlation between dimensions. Moreover, as the positive examples for all correlated terms are combined, it provides more positive video examples to train visual classifiers, often leading to better accuracy. The results demonstrate that a more effective video representation is obtained by considering correlated terms together.

Finally, our proposed VideoStory outperforms the Description embedding, especially for higher dimensional representations. For example, by extracting a 1,024 dimensional Description embedding we obtain an event recognition mAP of 0.183, 0.287 and 0.405 on MED test, Kindred test, and Columbia Consumer Video test, respectively. However, by extracting a VideoStory of the same dimensionality we obtain an event recognition mAP of 0.196, 0.312, and 0.432, which is a relative improvement of 7%, 9%, and 7%. Given the difficulty of recognizing events from only ten positive examples [29], this is a considerable improvement. We explain the improvement by the fact that combining the terms based on textual correlation only does not necessarily imply that the corresponding video is visually correlated as well. For example, the terms `puppy` and `kid` have a high

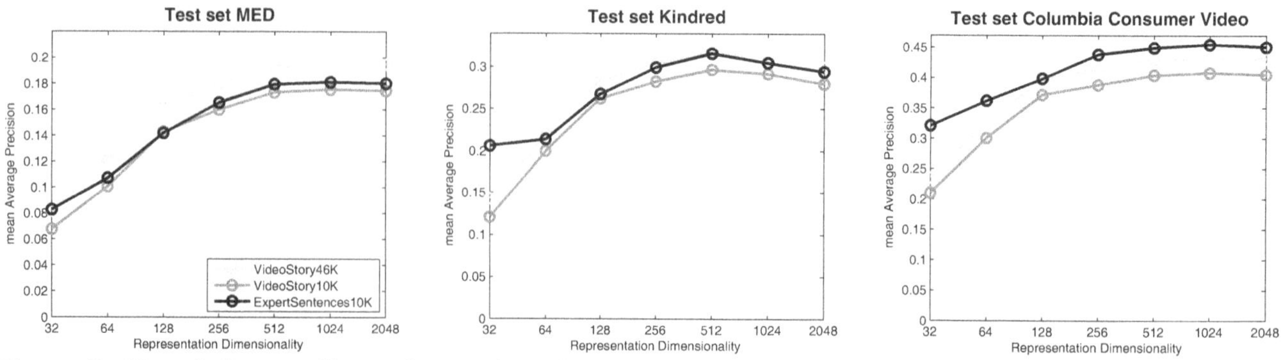

Figure 6: Description quality and quantity. As expected, the more reliable the correspondence between description and video content, the better the result. The event recognition accuracy obtained by ExpertSentences10K can be approached, and even improved, by simply harvesting more descriptions from the web.

correlation in the descriptions but are visually dissimilar. Combining these two terms together, as is done by Description embedding, undermines the accuracy of the classifiers predicting them from videos. In contrast, our VideoStory learns the embedding by taking both the term correlations and their visual similarity into account. In other words, in a VideoStory the correlated terms are combined only if their combination improves their classifier prediction. It prevents the combination of correlated terms which are visually dissimilar.

5.2 Description Quality and Quantity

The results of experiment 2 are presented in Figure 6. As expected, the more reliable the correspondence between the description and the video content it describes, the better the result. A VideoStory learned from ExpertSentences10K always performs better than an embedding learned from the same amount of descriptions from VideoStory10K. Yet it should be noted that the expert descriptions are generally unavailable or hard to obtain. Interestingly, the event recognition accuracy obtained by expert descriptions can be approached, and even improved (for both the test set MED and test set Kindred) by simply harvesting more descriptions from the web. When considering all results, the complete VideoStory46K dataset is the best choice overall. The embedding reduces the influence of noisy video descriptions, especially when the number of input videos and descriptions are large. It demonstrates the value of user generated videos and descriptions as an unlimited, free, yet precious resource for constructing an effective VideoStory.

5.3 VideoStory vs Others

Table 2 and Table 3 show that the VideoStory outperforms all three state-of-the-art video representations on all three test sets. By comparing the VideoStory and the low-level representation we observe a higher event recognition accuracy of 0.196 vs 0.174 for the MED test, 0.312 vs 0.263 for the Kindred test, and 0.432 vs 0.409 for the Columbia Consumer Video test set. It demonstrates that the VideoStory enriches the video representation by transferring and incorporating semantics from the descriptions.

The results further demonstrate that the VideoStory outperforms the attributes and the informative attributes with ease. We provide two reasons to explain this. First, both the attributes and the informative attributes rely on the TRECVID Semantic Indexing task and the ImageNet categories as attributes. However, many of these pre-specified attributes are not semantically relevant for the events. For example, a considerable number of ImageNet categories are devoted to specific animal species, which are not characteristic for representing events. Although the informative attributes address this problem by selecting only the most relevant subset of attributes per event, their performance is limited to the availability of relevant attributes. If the relevant attributes are unavailable in the initial pool, they can never be selected. In contrast to pre-specified attributes, the VideoStory embedding is automatically derived from the VideoStory46K dataset, which includes many descriptions relevant to events. Second, 1,000 out of 1,346 pre-specified attributes are derived from ImageNet images, for which we can only extract static visual features. As a consequence, all the pre-specified attribute representations, which rely on image data to train attribute predictors, can not benefit from the state-of-the-art motion features for event recognition. Hence, it limits their performance in comparison to our VideoStory which is trained from *video* data. The results demonstrate the importance of learning a representation from event descriptions and their corresponding video data, which are both achieved by using the VideoStory.

Apart from their better event recognition accuracy, the VideoStory is also extracted much more efficiently compared to the attribute based representation. The attribute based representation is trained on images and so can only be applied to video frames. Hence, extracting the attribute-based

Table 3: VideoStory vs Others. VideoStory outperforms state-of-the-art video representations on the Columbia Consumer Videos dataset.

	Test set Columbia Consumer Video			
Event	Attributes [11]	Informative [24]	Low-Level [37]	VideoStory
Basketball	0.293	0.317	0.485	**0.553**
Baseball	0.401	**0.463**	0.298	0.299
Soccer	0.336	0.302	0.469	**0.505**
Ice skating	0.632	0.649	0.646	**0.675**
Skiing	0.641	0.651	0.610	**0.671**
Swimming	0.520	0.489	0.691	**0.764**
Biking	0.324	0.307	0.420	**0.561**
Graduation	0.083	0.058	**0.135**	0.121
Birthday	0.149	0.216	0.187	**0.257**
Wedding reception	0.147	**0.201**	0.124	0.117
Wedding ceremony	0.216	0.248	**0.387**	0.324
Wedding dance	0.243	0.294	**0.550**	0.521
Music performance	**0.279**	0.247	0.225	0.201
Non-music performance	0.195	0.190	**0.334**	0.282
Parade	0.247	0.295	0.579	**0.634**
mean	0.314	0.328	0.409	**0.432**

Table 2: VideoStory vs Others. VideoStory outperforms the state-of-the-art on MED and Kindred test set.

	Test set MED				Test set Kindred			
Event	Attributes [11]	Informative [24]	Low-Level [37]	VideoStory	Attributes [11]	Informative [24]	Low-Level [37]	VideoStory
Birthday party	0.089	0.103	0.083	**0.118**	0.365	**0.379**	0.224	0.331
Changing vehicle tire	0.217	**0.239**	0.106	0.103	0.087	0.109	0.167	**0.180**
Flash mob gathering	0.432	0.434	**0.544**	0.535	0.078	0.080	0.248	**0.309**
Getting vehicle unstuck	0.307	0.309	0.137	**0.319**	0.354	0.371	0.301	**0.393**
Grooming animal	0.102	0.110	0.114	**0.151**	0.328	0.336	0.381	**0.501**
Making sandwich	0.055	0.054	0.073	**0.074**	0.297	0.296	**0.356**	0.278
Parade	0.195	0.198	0.352	**0.452**	0.056	0.059	0.106	**0.146**
Parkour	0.170	0.184	0.705	**0.721**	0.023	0.037	0.619	**0.792**
Repairing appliance	0.143	0.163	0.174	**0.184**	0.111	0.131	**0.540**	0.534
Working sewing project	0.081	0.106	0.085	**0.151**	0.022	0.047	0.327	**0.488**
Attempting bike trick	0.135	**0.144**	0.033	0.061	0.042	0.041	0.099	**0.198**
Cleaning appliance	0.007	0.033	0.072	**0.078**	0.008	0.034	0.110	**0.162**
Dog show	0.164	0.187	**0.409**	0.354	0.133	0.156	**0.479**	0.416
Giving directions location	0.007	0.018	**0.047**	0.004	0.003	**0.014**	0.004	0.003
Marriage proposal	0.002	**0.018**	0.007	0.004	0.003	**0.019**	0.008	0.008
Renovating home	0.047	0.047	**0.072**	0.051	0.141	**0.142**	0.112	0.131
Rock climbing	0.090	0.101	**0.118**	0.100	0.244	0.255	0.557	**0.618**
Town hall meeting	0.157	**0.176**	0.149	0.118	0.097	**0.116**	0.065	0.061
Winning race without vehicle	0.206	0.210	0.130	**0.217**	0.243	0.255	0.308	**0.413**
Working metal crafts project	0.090	0.101	0.068	**0.118**	0.083	0.104	0.241	**0.278**
mean	0.135	0.147	0.174	**0.196**	0.136	0.149	0.263	**0.312**

representation for video includes many predictions for each individual frame, before they are aggregated per video. In contrast, our proposed VideoStories are directly trained on videos and thus provide video-level predictions, which makes it significantly more efficient.

Finally, we evaluate the video descriptions generated by VideoStory and by the attribute baseline [11]. Following the protocol of [7], we use the ROUGE-1 metric on the automatically generated descriptions, with the expert-provided descriptions as ground truth. For the generated descriptions we predefine the length k, and use the highest scoring terms from Eq. (8) for VideoStory, see Figure 8 for some examples of videos and their predicted terms. As baseline, we use the highest scoring attributes names.

In Figure 7 we show the results on the MED test and Kindred test sets, where expert-provided descriptions are available for each video. Since ROUGE-1 is a recall based metric, it computes the recall of the ground truth terms in the provided description, we evaluate different values of k. From the results we observe that VideoStory generates more accurate video translations, and the performance gap increases for a higher value of k. This could be explained by the fact that the attribute baseline uses only terms of TRECVID and ImageNet categories, many being very specific and rarely used by humans to describe videos. In contrast, VideoStory relies on human-provided descriptions obtained from the web, which leads to a video description that is more in-line with the ground truth descriptions.

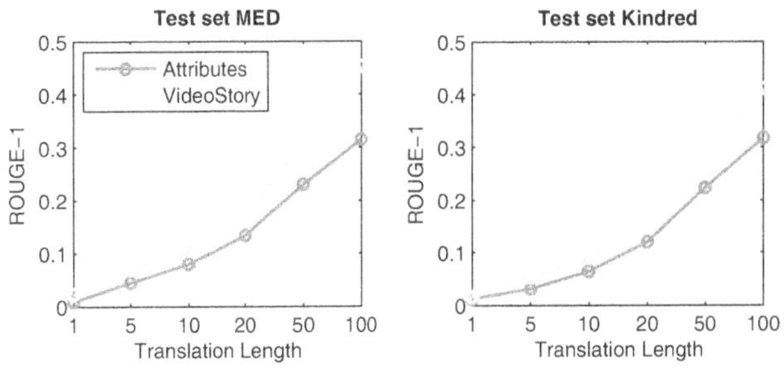

Figure 7: VideoStory vs Others. VideoStory generates more accurate descriptions.

6. CONCLUSION

In this paper we propose *VideoStory* a new multimedia embedding for few-example event recognition and translation. Our joint objective function aims to optimize the textual descriptiveness as well as the visual predictability of the embedding. In contrast to previous approaches, VideoStory allows both to train event classifiers using just a few examples in a low-dimensional, yet highly-discriminative, embedding space and to translate embedded videos to text. For training our VideoStory embedding, we rely on the weak supervision of easy to harvest descriptions from web videos. Therefore, we have introduced the VideoStory46K dataset, consisting of 46K YouTube videos with their title captions as descriptions. Results on three challenging test sets show that our event classification framework outperforms the current state-of-the-art. Moreover, we are able to generate human interpretable translations for previously unseen videos, opening up new connections with natural language processing and computational linguistics for describing and querying videos.

Acknowledgments This research is supported by the STW STORY project, the Dutch national program COMMIT, and by the Intelligence Advanced Research Projects Activity (IARPA) via Department of Interior National Business Center contract number D11PC20067. The U.S. Government is authorized to reproduce and distribute reprints for Governmental purposes notwithstanding any copyright annotation thereon. Disclaimer: The views and conclusions contained herein are those of the authors and should not be interpreted as necessarily representing the official policies or endorsements, either expressed or implied, of IARPA, DoI/NBC, or the U.S. Government.

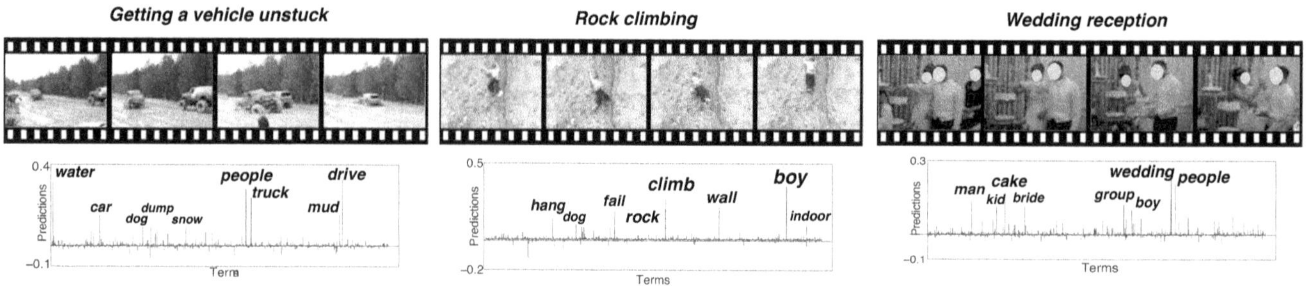

Figure 8: VideoStory event recognition and translation results on previously unseen videos.

7. REFERENCES

[1] Z. Akata, F. Perronnin, Z. Harchaoui, and C. Schmid. Label-embedding for attribute-based classification. In *CVPR*, 2013.

[2] R. Aly et al. The AXES submissions at trecvid 2013. In *TRECVID*, 2013.

[3] S. Banerjee and T. Pedersen. Extended gloss overlaps as a measure of semantic relatedness. In *IJCAI*, 2003.

[4] T. Berg, A. Berg, and J. Shih. Automatic attribute discovery and characterization from noisy web data. In *ECCV*, 2010.

[5] L. Bottou. Large-scale machine learning with stochastic gradient descent. In *ICCS*, 2010.

[6] Q. Chen et al. Spatio-temporal fisher vector coding for surveillance event detection. In *ACM MM*, 2013.

[7] P. Das, R. Srihari, and J. Corso. Translating related words to videos and back through latent topics. In *WSDM*, 2013.

[8] J. Deng, W. Dong, R. Socher, L.-J. Li, K. Li, and L. Fei-Fei. ImageNet: A large-scale hierarchical image database. In *CVPR*, 2009.

[9] J. Dodge et al. Detecting visual text. In *NAACL*, 2012.

[10] S. Guadarrama et al. Youtube2text: Recognizing and describing arbitrary activities using semantic hierarchies and zero-shot recognition. In *ICCV*, 2013.

[11] A. Habibian and C. Snoek. Recommendations for recognizing video events by concept vocabularies. *CVIU*, 124, 2014.

[12] T. Hofmann. Probabilistic latent semantic indexing. In *ACM SIGIR*, 1999.

[13] H. Izadinia and M. Shah. Recognizing complex events using large margin joint low-level event model. In *ECCV*, 2012.

[14] M. Jain, H. Jégou, and P. Bouthemy. Better exploiting motion for better action recognition. In *CVPR*, 2013.

[15] Y.-G. Jiang, G. Ye, S.-F. Chang, D. Ellis, and A. Loui. Consumer video understanding: A benchmark database and an evaluation of human and machine performance. In *ICMR*, 2011.

[16] Y.-G. Jiang, X. Zeng, G. Ye, S. Bhattacharya, D. Ellis, M. Shah, and S.-F. Chang. Columbia-ucf trecvid2010 multimedia event detection: Combining multiple modalities, contextual concepts, and temporal matching. In *TRECVID*, 2010.

[17] L. Kennedy, S.-F. Chang, and I. Kozintsev. To search or to label?: predicting the performance of search-based automatic image classifiers. In *ACM MIR*, 2006.

[18] D. Klein and C. Manning. Accurate unlexicalized parsing. In *ACL*, 2003.

[19] A. Krizhevsky, I. Sutskever, and G. Hinton. Imagenet classification with deep convolutional neural networks. In *NIPS*, 2012.

[20] P. Kuznetsova, V. Ordonez, A. Berg, T. Berg, and Y. Choi. Generalizing image captions for image-text parallel corpus. In *ACL*, 2013.

[21] J. Liu et al. Video event recognition using concept attributes. In *WACV*, 2013.

[22] Z. Ma, Y. Yang, Y. Cai, N. Sebe, and A. Hauptmann. Knowledge adaptation for ad hoc multimedia event detection with few exemplars. In *ACM MM*, 2012.

[23] Z. Ma, Y. Yang, Z. Xu, N. Sebe, and A. Hauptmann. We are not equally negative: fine-grained labeling for multimedia event detection. In *ACM MM*, 2013.

[24] M. Mazloom, E. Gavves, K. van de Sande, and C. Snoek. Searching informative concept banks for video event detection. In *ICMR*, 2013.

[25] T. Mei, Y. Rui, S. Li, and Q. Tian. Multimedia search reranking: A literature survey. *ACM CS*, 46(3), 2014.

[26] M. Merler, B. Huang, L. Xie, G. Hua, and A. Natsev. Semantic model vectors for complex video event recognition. *IEEE TMM*, 14(1), 2012.

[27] P. Natarajan et al. Multimodal feature fusion for robust event detection in web videos. In *CVPR*, 2012.

[28] A. Natsev, M. Naphade, and J. Tešić. Learning the semantics of multimedia queries and concepts from a small number of examples. In *ACM MM*, 2005.

[29] P. Over, J. Fiscus, G. Sanders, et al. TRECVID 2013-an overview of the goals, tasks, data, evaluation mechanisms and metrics. In *TRECVID*, 2013.

[30] H. Peng, F. Long, and C. Ding. Feature selection based on mutual information criteria of max-dependency, max-relevance, and min-redundancy. *IEEE TPAMI*, 27(8), 2005.

[31] N. Rasiwasia, J. Costa Pereira, E. Coviello, G. Doyle, G. Lanckriet, R. Levy, and N. Vasconcelos. A new approach to cross-modal multimedia retrieval. In *ACM MM*, 2010.

[32] J. Sánchez, F. Perronnin, T. Mensink, and J. Verbeek. Image classification with the fisher vector: Theory and practice. *IJCV*, 105(3), 2013.

[33] S. Strassel et al. Creating havic: Heterogeneous audio visual internet collection. In *LREC*, 2012.

[34] A. Tamrakar et al. Evaluation of low-level features and their combinations for complex event detection in open source videos. In *CVPR*, 2012.

[35] A. Ulges, C. Schulze, M. Koch, and T. Breuel. Learning automatic concept detectors from online video. *CVIU*, 114(4), 2010.

[36] K. van de Sande, T. Gevers, and C. Snoek. Evaluating color descriptors for object and scene recognition. *IEEE TPAMI*, 32(9), 2010.

[37] H. Wang and C. Schmid. Action recognition with improved trajectories. In *ICCV*, 2013.

[38] Q. Wang, J. Xu, H. Li, and N. Craswell. Regularized latent semantic indexing. In *ACM SIGIR*, 2011.

[39] X.-J. Wang, L. Zhang, X. Li, and W.-Y. Ma. Annotating images by mining image search results. *IEEE TPAMI*, 30(11), 2008.

[40] J. Weston, S. Bengio, and N. Usunier. Wsabie: Scaling up to large vocabulary image annotation. In *IJCAI*, 2011.

[41] Y. Yang and M. Shah. Complex events detection using data-driven concepts. In *ECCV*, 2012.

Say Cheese vs. Smile: Reducing Speech-Related Variability for Facial Emotion Recognition

Yelin Kim and Emily Mower Provost
Electrical Engineering and Computer Science
University of Michigan, Ann Arbor, Michigan, USA
{yelinkim, emilykmp}@umich.edu

ABSTRACT

Facial movement is modulated both by emotion and speech articulation. Facial emotion recognition systems aim to discriminate between emotions, while reducing the speech-related variability in facial cues. This aim is often achieved using two key features: (1) *phoneme segmentation*: facial cues are temporally divided into units with a single phoneme and (2) *phoneme-specific classification*: systems learn patterns associated with groups of visually similar phonemes (visemes), e.g. /P/, /B/, and /M/. In this work, we empirically compare the effects of different temporal segmentation and classification schemes for facial emotion recognition. We propose an unsupervised segmentation method that does not necessitate costly phonetic transcripts. We show that the proposed method bridges the accuracy gap between a traditional sliding window method and phoneme segmentation, achieving a statistically significant performance gain. We also demonstrate that the segments derived from the proposed unsupervised and phoneme segmentation strategies are similar to each other. This paper provides new insight into unsupervised facial motion segmentation and the impact of speech variability on emotion classification.

Categories and Subject Descriptors

I.5.4 [**Computing Methodologies**]: Pattern Recognition Applications

General Terms

Emotion

Keywords

emotion recognition; dynamics; dynamic time warping; phoneme; segmentation; viseme; facial expression; speech

MM'14, November 3–7, 2014, Orlando, Florida, USA.

http://dx.doi.org/10.1145/2647868.2654934.

1. INTRODUCTION

The expression of emotion is complex. It modulates facial behavior, vocal behavior, and body gestures. Emotion recognition systems must decode these modulations in order to gain insight into the underlying emotional message. However, this decoding process is challenging; behavior is often modulated by more than just emotion. Facial expressions are strongly affected by the articulation associated with speech production. Robust emotion recognition systems must differentiate speech-related articulation from emotion variation (e.g., differentiate someone saying "cheese" from smiling). In this paper we explore methods to model the temporal behavior of facial motion with the goal of mitigating speech variability, focusing on temporal segmentation and classification methods. The results suggest that proper segmentation is critical for emotion recognition.

One common method for constraining speech variation is by first segmenting the facial movement into temporal units with consistent patterns. Commonly, this segmentation is accomplished using known phoneme or viseme boundaries. We refer to this process as *phoneme segmentation* [1]. The resulting segments are then grouped into categories with similar lip movements (e.g., /P/, /B/, /M/, see Table 1). Emotion models are trained for each visually similar phoneme group, a process we refer to as *phoneme-specific classification*. These two schemes have been used effectively in prior work [2, 14, 19, 20]. However, it is not yet clear how facial emotion recognition systems benefit from each of these components. Moreover, these phoneme-based paradigms are costly due to their reliance on detailed phonetic transcripts. In this paper we explore two *unsupervised* segmentation methods that do not require phonetic transcripts. We demonstrate that phoneme segmentation is more effective than fixed-length sliding window segmentation. We describe a new unsupervised segmentation strategy that bridges the gap in accuracy between phoneme segmentation and fixed-length sliding window segmentation. We also demonstrate that phoneme-specific classification can still be used given unsupervised segmentation by coarsely approximating the phoneme content present in each of the resulting segments.

Studies on variable-length segmentation and the utility of phoneme-specific classification have recently received attention in the emotion recognition field. Mariooryad and Busso studied lexically constrained facial emotion recogni-

[1] We refer to the process as phoneme segmentation when the vocal signal, rather than the facial movement, is used to segment the data. These audio-derived segmentation boundaries are applied to the facial movement.

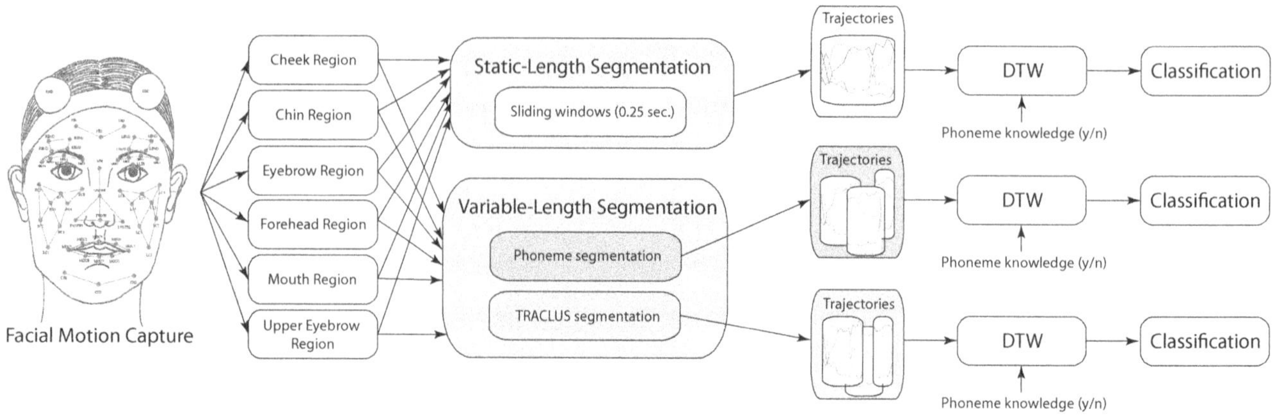

Figure 1: *Overview of the system. We separately segment the facial movement of the six facial region using (1) fixed-length and (2) variable-length methods. For variable-length segmentation, we investigate both phoneme-based segmentation and unsupervised, automatic segmentation using the TRACLUS algorithm [17]. We calculate the time-series similarity between each segment using Dynamic Time Warping (DTW). We use the time-series similarity between testing and training segments to infer the testing utterances' labels. We compare the performance of the systems both with and without knowledge of phoneme content.*

Table 1: *Phoneme to viseme mapping.*

Group	Phonemes	Group	Phonemes
1	P, B, M	8	AE, AW, EH, EY
2	F,V	9	AH,AX,AY
3	T,D,S,Z,TH,DH	10	AA
4	W,R	11	AXR,ER
5	CH,SH,ZH	12	AO,OY,OW
6	K,G,N,L,HH,NG,Y	13	UH,UW
7	IY,IH, IX	14	SIL

tion systems using phoneme segmentation and phoneme-specific classification. They introduced feature-level constraints, which normalized the facial cues based on the underlying phoneme, and model-level constraints, phoneme-specific classification [19]. Metallinou et al. [20] also proposed a method to integrate phoneme segmentation and phoneme-specific classification into facial emotion recognition systems. They first segmented the data into groups of visually similar phonemes (visemes) and found that the dynamics of these segments could be accurately captured using Hidden Markov Models. These methods demonstrate the benefits of phoneme segmentation and phoneme-specific classification. However, there remain open questions relating to how similar performance can be achieved absent a detailed phonetic transcript.

In this paper we empirically compare phoneme segmentation with two unsupervised segmentation methods. The first uses fixed-length sliding window segmentation and the second uses variable-length segmentation. In the fixed-length window approach, windows slide over an utterance, segmenting it at regular intervals. The challenge with this approach is that it may inappropriately disrupt important dynamics relating to emotion expression. We propose the second method, based on the TRACLUS algorithm [17], to address these challenges. TRACLUS is an unsupervised technique that segments an utterance into variable-length components based on the dynamics of the signal, mitigating the speech-related variability in facial movements by focusing on short-time patterns that operate at the time-scale of phoneme expression. Figure 1 describes our system: the system segments the facial motion capture data using one of three segmentation methods (phoneme, TRACLUS, fixed window), classifies the emotion content of these segments, and then aggregates the segment-level classification into an utterance-level estimate. We use Dynamic Time Warping (DTW) to compare the similarity between testing segments and held out training segments. We additionally compare the advantages associated with phoneme-specific classification. We perform phoneme-specific classification by comparing a testing segment only to training segments from the same phoneme class. We perform *general classification* by comparing the testing segment to all training segments. We create a segment-level Motion Similarity Profile (MSP), which is a four-dimensional measure that captures the distribution of the emotion class labels over the c closest training segments (class labels are from the set {angry, happy, neutral, sad}). We estimate the final emotion label by calculating an average MSP using the set of segment-level MSPs associated with a single utterance.

We present a novel system that explores the importance of variable-length segmentation, segmentation focused on the natural dynamics of the signal, and the benefit derived from phoneme-specific classification, an approach that restricts the impact of the modulations in the facial channel due to associated acoustic variability. Our results demonstrate that variable-length segmentation and phoneme-specific classification provide complementary improvements in classification. We show that variable-length segmentation and phoneme-specific classification can improve performance over fixed-length sliding window segmentation by 4.04%, compared to a system that uses a sliding window and general classification, results supported by prior research [19]. One of the advantages associated with our system is that it captures the dynamics of facial movement, rather than the behavior of static utterance-length features. This is critical for a detailed understanding of emotion expression behavior. The performance of our system suggests that our method can be used to provide insight into frame-level movement while providing accurate classification performance. Finally, our results demonstrate that the accuracy derived from a variable-length TRACLUS segmentation approach has higher accuracy than a fixed-length sliding window approach and comparable accuracy to a phoneme segmentation approach, suggesting that segmentation informed by the temporal properties of the signal is crucial for emotion classification systems.

This paper is organized as follows. In Section 2, we provide an overview of previous research. In Section 3, we describe the database. In Section 4, we detail the methodology underlying our approach. In Section 5, we describe experimental setup including the cross-validation scheme and performance measure. In Section 6, we present and analyze the results. We discuss our findings in Section 7. We conclude our work in Section 8.

2. RELATED WORK

Automatic emotion recognition is the process of predicting the high-level affective content of an utterance from the low-level signal cues produced by a speaker. Comprehensive surveys can be found in [9, 11, 30].

2.1 Segmentation

Temporal segmentation is commonly employed in speech emotion recognition. In the pioneering study of Lee et al., the authors designed and compared the standard emotion-specific Hidden Markov Models (HMM) and HMMs trained on individual phoneme groups for each emotion and found that vowel sounds were the most effective for emotion classification compared to the other four phoneme groups [16]. Batliner et al. treated words as the basic unit of emotion expression. They combined words either into syntactically and semantically meaningful chunks or into sequences of words that belonged to the same emotion class [1]. Jeon et al. investigated different sub-sentence segment units (words, phrases, time-based segments) using a two-level system that focused both on segment-level and utterance-level emotion prediction. They found that time-based segments achieved the best performance [13]. Schuller et al. also investigated different timing patterns for segmentation using absolute and relative time intervals. Utterances were either segmented at fixed time intervals (absolute) or at fixed relative positions such as halves or thirds (relative) [27]. They demonstrated that absolute time intervals of one second achieved the highest accuracy (also demonstrated in [21]). Additionally, they found that systems based on relative time intervals were more accurate than those that used absolute time intervals. Ringeval et al. proposed a speech feature extraction method based on a pseudo-phonetic speech segmentation technique combined with a vowel detector [24]. They compared MFCC acoustic features from these pseudo-phonetic segments (vowels, consonants) with segments created by identifying regions of voiced and unvoiced speech. They showed that the voiced segments could be modeled more accurately than the vowel or consonant segments for emotion recognition.

There have also been research efforts in temporal segmentation for facial emotion expression recognition. As seen in audio modeling, these methods include phoneme-based segmentation [7, 12] and the standard fixed-length and multiple fixed-length segmentation [21, 23, 26]. Cohen et al. proposed a multi-level HMM for the automatic segmentation and classification of facial expressions [7]. The proposed method automatically segments and classifies a video consisting of six sequences that display each of the six basic emotions (*anger, disgust, fear, happiness, sadness, and surprise*). The multi-level HMM makes an assumption that the transitions between emotions pass through the *neutral* state. They compare this with the standard emotion-specific HMM, where the input video is pre-segmented for each emotion. They found that the accuracy of their proposed system was similar to that of the standard emotion-specific HMM. Hoey used a manual segmentation of facial cues into segments presenting a subject's underlying emotion [12]. He proposed a multi-level weakly supervised dynamic Bayesian network that learns the high-level dynamics of facial expressions.

There has also been work focused on unsupervised segmentation of facial expression data. Zhou et al. presented an unsupervised segmentation and clustering method of facial events [31]. They used k-means clustering with a Dynamic Time Alignment Kernel [29] to segment and cluster posed and unposed facial events. They found moderate intersystem agreement with the Facial Action Coding System (FACS). However, most of the previous works used facial data not modulated by spoken content, rendering it challenging to understand the impact of speech-related variability (a notable exception includes [31]). Our work is differentiated from the previous studies, by its focus on how we can better estimate emotion class by reducing the variability of facial movements caused by speech, while using unsupervised techniques.

2.2 Phoneme-Specific Classification

Phoneme-specific classification systems have been used to decrease speech-related variability and capture emotion-specific variability. These systems segment facial cues into phoneme segments and build phoneme-specific emotion classifiers over each phoneme group [19, 20]. Mariooryad and Busso presented two different types of phoneme-specific classification: feature-level (each phoneme segment was normalized based on the underlying phoneme content) and model-level (phoneme-specific classification) [19]. They estimated utterance-level emotion content by aggregating the posterior probabilities of the phoneme-level estimates. They found that the model-level constrained system performed more accurately than the feature-level system and that both systems outperformed the phoneme-independent baseline. The model-level system used static features, statistics extracted within phoneme segments, in contrast to dynamic features, features that capture the dynamics of frame-level cues, as used in our paper. Metallinou et al. modeled the frame-level dynamics of facial motion-capture data using HMMs and estimated the phoneme-level emotion as a single hard label [20]. They estimated utterance-level emotion using a majority vote over the phoneme-level labels. The previous studies demonstrated the benefits of phoneme segmentation and phoneme-specific classification. However, an open question remains in how similar levels of accuracy can be achieved without knowledge of phoneme transcript.

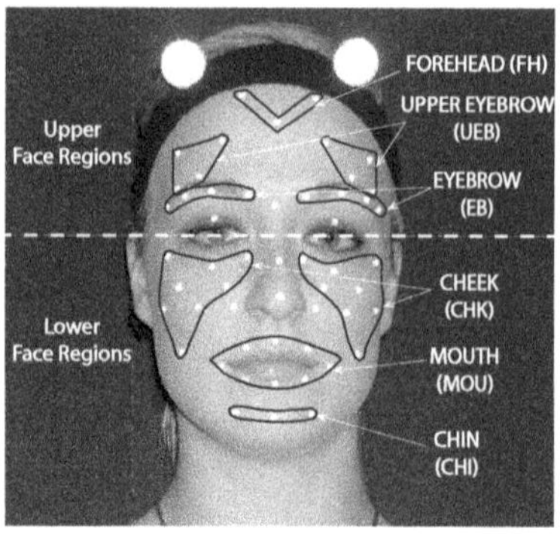

Figure 2: *Positions of face markers and six face regions: chin, forehead, cheek, upper eyebrow, eyebrow, and mouth. The upper face contains the forehead, upper eyebrow, and eyebrow regions, whereas the lower face contains the chin, cheek, and mouth regions.*

3. DATABASE

In this work we use the IEMOCAP audio-visual emotion database [3], also used in [19, 20]. The IEMOCAP database contains audio-visual and motion capture recordings of interactions between five male-female pairs of actors, performing from plays and improvised scenarios. The motion capture data includes the three-dimensional motion of fifty-three markers on the face with sample rate of 120 Hz (Figure 2). Rotation effects were reduced by transforming the facial coordinate space such that the nose tip is always at the origin. The dataset also includes a detailed phonemic transcript.

We assign an emotion class to each utterance, or speech turn, as the majority vote over the three human annotators. The human annotators assign labels from the set of anger, sadness, happiness, disgust, fear and surprise, frustration, excited neutral, and other. For purposes of consistency with the literature [19, 20], we use data annotated as *anger, happiness, sadness,* and *neutrality* and merge the classes of excitement and happiness. There are an average of 61.1 ± 27.53 angry utterances, 122.4 ± 24.86 happy utterances, 58.1 ± 21.61 neutral utterances, and 64.4 ± 25.18 sad utterances per speaker. The mean length of an utterance is 4.73 ± 3.34 seconds.

4. PROPOSED METHODS

We present a system operating at two-levels: segment-level and utterance-level. We test six classification schemes for segment-level classification that combine segmentation approaches (phoneme, TRACLUS, sliding window) and classification approaches (phoneme-specific or general). Phoneme-specific classification compares test segments only to training segments with the same phoneme content. General classification compares test segments to all training segments.

The classification schemes are as follows (Figure 3):

1. General phoneme ("Gen/Phon"): phoneme segmentation and general classification.
2. General TRACLUS ("Gen/TRA"): TRACLUS segmentation and general classification.
3. General window ("Gen/Win"): fixed-length sliding window segmentation and general classification.
4. Phoneme-specific phoneme ("PS/Phon"): phoneme segmentation and phoneme-specific classification.
5. Phoneme-specific TRACLUS ("PS/TRA"): TRACLUS segmentation and phoneme-specific classification. A phoneme label is assigned by identifying the phoneme with the longest duration within each TRACLUS segment.
6. Phoneme-specific window ("PS/Win"): fixed-length window segmentation and phoneme-specific classification. Again, a phoneme label is assigned by identifying the phoneme with the longest duration within each window segment.

We aggregate the segment-level estimates to form an utterance-level estimate of emotion content. In the following sections, we first introduce the preprocessing that we apply to the motion capture data that serve as our input for segmentation (Section 4.1). We then describe our segmentation approaches (Section 4.2). Finally, we provide a description for how we estimate segment-level emotion and aggregate these estimates into utterance-level emotion labels (Section 4.3).

4.1 Motion Capture Preprocessing

We group the motion capture data points into six facial regions: chin, forehead, cheek, upper eyebrow, eyebrows, and mouth. There are 3 markers in both the *Chin* and *Forehead regions*, 16 markers in the *Cheek region*, and 8 markers in the *Upper Eyebrow, Eyebrow*, and *Mouth regions* as shown in Figure 2. This results in 9 (x, y, z)-coordinates for the *Chin* and *Forehead regions*, 48 coordinates for the *Cheek region*, and 24 coordinates for the *Upper Eyebrow, Eyebrow*, and *Mouth regions*, for a total of 138 marker coordinates. We perform median-filter smoothing using a window size of three over each of the six regions.

Each segment is represented by six different trajectories, one for each facial region. Each trajectory can be described by a $N \times K$ motion-capture trajectory, where N is the number of motion-capture frames within the segment and K is the number of 3-D marker coordinates in the face region. We exclude the five nose markers because of their limited movement and the two eyelid markers because they are often occluded, as in [20]. We also exclude data with less than seven frames (threshold number of frames were chosen empirically) or 0.058 seconds, 43.5% of all phoneme segments, 0.67% of all TRACLUS segments, and 0.86% of all fixed-length segments (the last fixed-length segments within an utterance is less than 0.25 seconds). We drop segments with any missing values in the 46 markers we use. This results in different sets of utterances for each segmentation scheme. Hence, we use the set of intersecting utterances for all experiments; fixed-length, TRACLUS, phoneme segmentation schemes. In total, we test our system using 3,060 utterances.

4.2 Segmentation

In this section we present the three temporal segmentation schemes that we use to segment the facial motion capture data. The sliding window and TRACLUS segmentation strategies do not require transcripts, while the phoneme segmentation strategy does require transcripts.

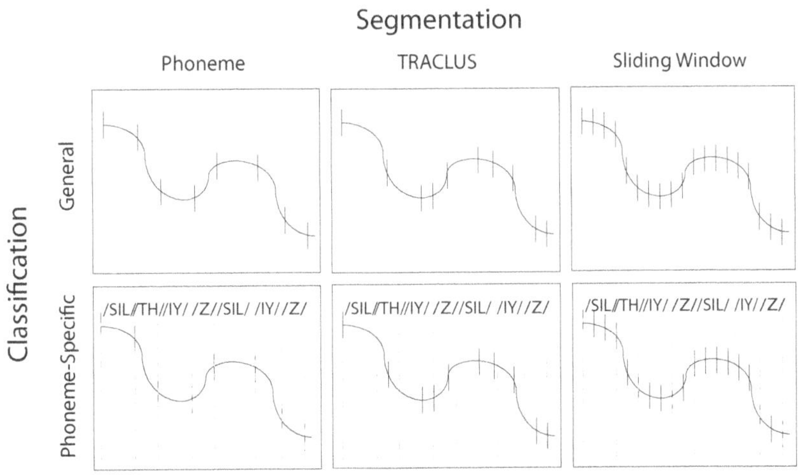

Figure 3: *The proposed six schemes using different temporal segmentation and classification methods. The two rows demonstrate general and phoneme-specific classification methods, and the three columns show phoneme, TRACLUS, and fixed-length segmentation methods. The dashed lines of the three phoneme-specific schemes (bottom row) show the phoneme boundaries. The hash marks of all schemes demonstrate different segment boundaries. Notice the potential mismatch between the hash markers and dashed lines in TRACLUS and fixed-length segmentation*

4.2.1 Sliding Window Segmentation ("Win")

We obtain fixed-length segments using a sliding window of length 0.25 seconds without overlapping. We also include the last remaining segment at the end of an utterance, even if that segment is less than 0.25 seconds. In our initial experiments, we tested windows of length {0.15, 0.25, 0.5, 1, 1.5, 2} seconds, window sizes demonstrated to be effective in previous work [15,21]. We found that the differences in performance between window lengths of 0.15 seconds and 1.5 seconds were not statistically significantly different. Performance using the 2-second windows was significantly lower.

4.2.2 Phoneme Segmentation ("Phon")

We obtain phoneme segments by force aligning the audio to the known transcript. We use the phoneme time boundaries to segment the motion-capture data into phoneme segments. We refer to the segments as phoneme segments, rather than viseme segments, to indicate that we are using the features of the audio to segment the data, rather than the features of the video. We group the phoneme segments into categories based on similar articulatory configurations (Table 1), as in [19,20].

4.2.3 TRACLUS Segmentation ("TRA")

We obtain unsupervised variable-length segments using a trajectory partitioning algorithm called TRACLUS (Trajectory Clustering) [17]. TRACLUS takes a trajectory as input, automatically recognizes regions of consistent dynamics, and identifies *characteristic points* as the end-points for these regions (Figure 4). We treat the characteristic points as segment boundaries. Although the TRACLUS algorithm both partitions and clusters time series data, we only use the partition portion of the algorithm.

The input to TRACLUS segmentation is the smoothed 24-dimensional mouth trajectory using a median filter with a window size of three. We use the resulting characteristic points to segment the data from all six regions. We segment based only on the mouth trajectory because our preliminary results demonstrated that the accuracy of the classifiers operating on the mouth-derived segmentation boundaries were more accurate than those operating on boundaries derived from the remaining five regions.

TRACLUS identifies characteristic points using Minimum Description Length (MDL) coding. MDL is a widely used information theoretic concept positing that the best hypothesis H for given data D is the one that derives the best compression of that data, mitigating both the complexity associated with the compressed representation and the loss between the compression and the original data. The encoding of the data is a line connecting the first and last points (the characteristic points) of the region. The implication is that the variations between the first and last points represent noise around a period of consistent dynamics. The TRACLUS segments are formed by segmenting the motion capture data at the characteristic points.

The cost of approximating D as H is calculated in two parts: $L(H)$ and $L(D|H)$. $L(H)$ is the length, in bits, of the description of the hypothesis, and $L(D|H)$ is the length, in bits, of the description of the data when encoded by the hypothesis. The goal is to find the best hypothesis H to explain D that minimizes $L(H)+L(D|H)$. Given an M-length trajectory $TR = p_1 p_2 \cdots p_j \cdots p_M$ and a set of n characteristic points $= \{c_1, c_2, \cdots, c_n\}$ (where $c_1 = 1, c_n = M$), let $len(p_{c_j} p_{c_{j+1}})$ be the length of a line segment $p_{c_j} p_{c_{j+1}}$, i.e. the Euclidean distance between p_{c_j} and $p_{c_{j+1}}$. The optimization method formula is described in equation 1. The values $d_\perp$ and d_θ are the perpendicular distance and angular distance, adapted from a similarity measure using line segments [5]. Since our trajectory is multi-dimensional, we use multi-dimensional Euclidean distance between each trajectory point. Please see [17] for more details.

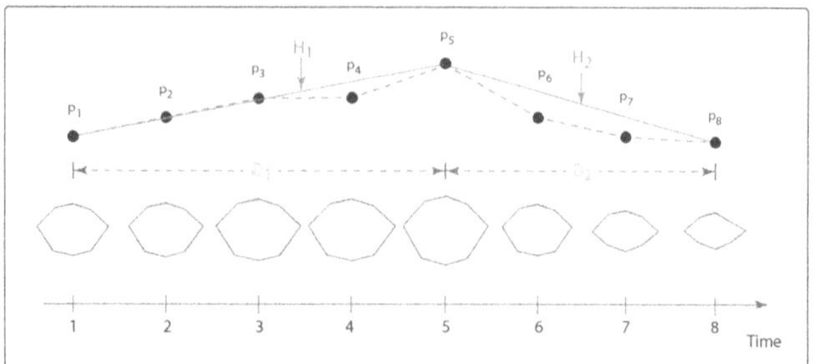

Figure 4: *TRACLUS segmentation example. Each point $\{p_1, p_2, ..., p_8\}$ represents frame-level mouth motion capture (illustrated as eight 2-D marker points for visualization purposes). In this example, TRACLUS identifies characteristic points $\{c_1 = 1, c_2 = 5, c_3 = 8\}$. H_1 and H_2 are the lines connecting p_1 and p_5 and p_5 and p_8, and D_1 and D_2 are the sets of original line segments $\{p_1p_2, p_2p_3, p_3p_4, p_4p_5\}$, and $\{p_5p_6, p_6p_7, p_7p_8\}$, respectively.*

$$\begin{aligned}
&\arg\min_{H} && L(H) + L(D|H) \\
&\text{where} && L(H) = \sum_{j=1}^{n-1} \log_2\left(len(p_{c_j}p_{c_{j+1}})\right), \\
& && L(D|H) = \sum_{j=1}^{n-1}\sum_{k=c_j}^{c_{j+1}-1} \log_2\left(d_\perp(p_{c_j}p_{c_{j+1}}, p_kp_{k+1})\right) \\
& && \quad + \log_2\left(d_\theta(p_{c_j}p_{c_{j+1}}, p_kp_{k+1})\right)
\end{aligned} \tag{1}$$

Due to the cost of finding the optimal partitioning, the algorithm seeks to identify an approximate solution that treats the set of local optima as the global optima [17]. The approximate solution computes the MDL costs both when a point p_j is a characteristic point and when it is not. It denotes $cost_{par}(p_i, p_j)$ as the MDL cost ($= L(H) + L(D|H)$) of a trajectory between p_i and p_j ($i < j$) when p_i and p_j are the only characteristic points. On the other hand, it denotes $cost_{nopar}(p_i, p_j)$ as the MDL cost without partitioning, i.e. $L(D|H) = 0$ and $L(H)$ is the sum of the lengths of all components of the trajectory (e.g., length between all consecutive pairs of points ($p_{i,j}, i = j - 1, 2 \leq j \leq 5$ in Figure 4). If the former ($cost_{par}$) is larger than the latter ($cost_{nopar}$), it chooses p_{j-1} as a characteristic point. This approach identifies the longest trajectory partition p_ip_j that satisfies $cost_{par}(p_i, p_k) \leq cost_{nopar}(p_i, p_k)$ for $\forall k, i < k \leq j$. Otherwise, it advances p_j by increasing j. In our work, we partition the trajectory when $cost_{par} \geq cost_{nopar} + 10$, since $cost_{par} \geq cost_{nopar}$ resulted in segmenting at all frames. Our preliminary results demonstrated that there is not a significant difference in terms of classification accuracy when we use $\{10, 20, 30, 40\}$.

For example, consider the trajectory in Figure 4. The figure displays the mouth motion capture data for an unsegmented region. TRACLUS has identified two segments, H_1 and H_2, based on identified characteristic points $c_1 = 1, c_2 = 5$, and $c_3 = 8$, which are the lines connecting p_1 and p_5 and p_5 and p_8, respectively. The components of the cost associated with this segmentation can be calculated as the length of H_1 and the cost of approximating D_1 as H_1 and the length of H_2 and the cost of approximating D_2 as H_2.

4.3 Emotion Classification

4.3.1 Emotion Similarity Calculation: DTW

The segment-level similarity between the motion capture data within each segment is calculated using DTW, a widely used time-series similarity measure [28]. Unlike HMM, DTW does not make any statistical assumptions about the temporal data, instead explicitly measuring temporal similarity, rather than probabilistic state transitions [15]. Multi-dimensional DTW measures the time-series similarity between two multi-dimensional trajectories with the same dimensionality (the lengths of the trajectories can be different). All of our calculations are multidimensional and we will refer to multi-dimensional DTW as DTW. DTW uses dynamic programming to calculate an optimal match between two time-series [25]. We compute a local cost matrix Q, that contains distances between the two trajectories at every instance in time. For instance, as we described in Section 4.1, let two K-dimensional face movement trajectories of length M_1 and M_2 be $T_1 \in \mathbb{R}^{M_1 \times K}$ and $T_2 \in \mathbb{R}^{M_2 \times K}$. The multi-dimensional DTW algorithm populates the M_1-by-M_2 local cost matrix Q according to the following equation:

$$Q(i, j) = \sum_{k=1}^{K} (T_1(i, k) - T_2(j, k))^2, \tag{2}$$

where i and j represent the frame-level point of T_1 ($1 \leq i \leq M_1$) and T_2 ($1 \leq j \leq M_2$), respectively. Each local cost element of Q is an aggregate of the individual multi-dimensional distances between points in the trajectory calculated using the 2-norm, the sum of the squared differences across all dimensions. DTW then finds the optimal warping path that minimizes the accumulated distances in Q [28]. The accumulated distance along the optimal path is the final DTW distance. We use Sakoe-Chiba normalization, which adds 2 weights to the diagonal path when calculating the local distance cost and divides the final distance by the sum of the lengths of two trajectories [25].

4.3.2 Use of Phoneme Knowledge

Phoneme-specific and general classification refer to whether or not knowledge of the phoneme content of a segment is used during the similarity calculation (Figure 3). In phoneme-specific classification, knowledge of phoneme content is used in the modeling process to constrain the number of training segments to which each testing segment is compared. Phoneme content is defined as the dominant phoneme in the segment. We group the phonemes into the fourteen groups outlined in Table 1, as used in previous work [18, 20]. For a given testing segment, we calculate the DTW distance from this testing segment to all other training segments within the phoneme group (Section 4.3.1). This allows us to reduce the lexical variability of the facial movement (Figure 5). In general classification, the testing segments are compared to all training segments, independent of phoneme group.

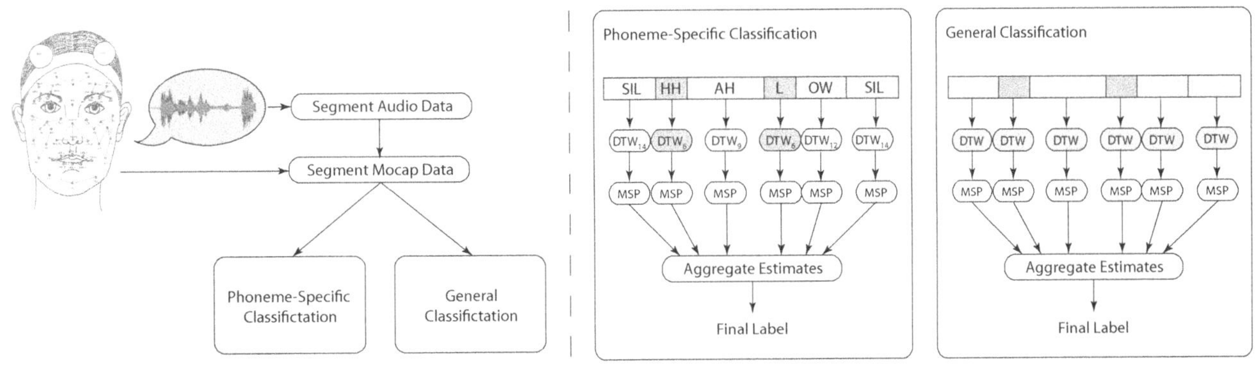

Figure 5: *The utterance-level MSP calculation. All the segments are grouped into 14 phoneme groups (differentiated by colors, Table 1). The group is directly assigned for phoneme segments. The dominant phoneme (in terms of duration) is assigned for the fixed-length and TRACLUS segments. In phoneme-specific classification we calculate the DTW similarity only between segments within the same phoneme group. In general classification we calculate the DTW similarity between the test segments and every training segment. The c closest neighbors are identified and the distribution of the c emotion labels are stored in the segment-level MSPs. The final utterance-level aggregated MSP is an average of the segment-level MSPs.*

4.3.3 Utterance-Level Classification

The DTW calculation allows us to identify a set of training segments to which the testing segments are most similar. We retain the c closest neighbors, using the MSP representation to describe the distribution of the emotion labels amongst the c neighbors. This allows us to estimate the emotion content of the testing segment. For instance, if c=10 and the segment-level labels of the c closest training segments include 3 angry, 6 happy, 1 neutral, and 0 sadness segments, then the MSP is $[0.3, 0.6, 0.1, 0]$. In our experiments, we set $c = 20$, based on preliminary analyses.

For each facial region, we calculate the segment-level MSPs (e.g., $MSP_{mouth,1} \ldots MSP_{mouth,L}$). We create an utterance-level MSP by averaging the segment-level MSPs (e.g., $MSP_{mouth} = mean(\{MSP_{mouth,1} \ldots MSP_{mouth,L}\})$. This results in a single four-dimensional emotion estimate for each facial region. We average the six facial region MSPs to obtain the final utterance-level MSP. We normalize each of the four dimensions using speaker-specific z-normalization. We assign an utterance-level label based on the maximum of the aggregated MSP. This is based on the assumption that the largest component in the MSP corresponds to the class to which the utterance is most similar.

5. EXPERIMENTAL SETUP

Speaker normalization: We use the speaker normalization method used in [20] to mitigate the intrinsic differences in the facial configuration of the speakers. For each speaker i, we calculate the mean of each marker coordinate j of a speaker ($m_{i,j}$). We then calculate M_j, the mean of each marker coordinate j across all speakers. We then calculate the normalization coefficient, $c_{i,j}$, where $c_{i,j} = M_j / m_{i,j}$. In the calculation of $c_{i,j}$, i represents each speaker from 1 to 10, and j represents each marker coordinate from 1 to 138. We multiply each i-th speaker's j-th marker coordinate by $c_{i,j}$ to make the mean of each speaker's facial marker positions equal.

Cross-validation: We use a subject-independent training paradigm, leave-one-speaker-out cross validation (one speaker is used for testing, the other nine for training).

Performance measure: We include three experiments to understand the contribution and utility of each of the six facial regions: (1) AV mouth: the single mouth region, (2) AV 4 faces: four facial regions of chin, cheek, upper eyebrow, and mouth, excluding forehead and eyebrow, and (3) AV 6 faces: all six facial regions. Note that AV represents "average."

In all cases, the reported accuracy is unweighted recall (UW). UW is an average of the per-emotion class recall. It is used to offset the class imbalance observed in the data. We calculate the UW for each speaker. We then average the UW over speakers and report the mean and standard deviation as the final UW.

6. RESULTS

The results demonstrate that phoneme-specific classification is more accurate than general classification for both the phoneme and TRACLUS segmentation strategies across all three experiments: AV mouth, AV 4, and AV 6. The AV mouth and AV 4 experiments have similar levels of accuracy. Both outperform the AV 6 experiment. General classification is more accurate for fixed-length sliding window segmentation in the AV 4 experiment.

Given phoneme-specific classification, variable-length segmentation (phoneme and TRACLUS) outperforms fixed-length sliding window segmentation for the AV mouth and AV 4 experiments, the performance is comparable for the AV 6 experiment. This trend was not seen in general classification. In fact, in general classification, fixed-length sliding window segmentation outperforms variable-length segmentation in the AV mouth and AV 4 experiments.

The overall UW comparison is summarized in Table 2. The results are presented as the average unweighted recall over the ten subjects. We test the significance of the difference between the classification schemes using paired t-tests over the 10 subjects, suggested in [8]. In the remainder of this section, we provide additional details regarding the effect of segmentation, phoneme-specific classification, and statistical significance. The results will be discussed in terms of the AV mouth and AV 4 experiments.

Table 2: *Unweighted classification accuracy (%) using six schemes of: (1) general phoneme segments, (2) general TRACLUS segments, (3) general window segments, (4) phoneme-specific phoneme segments, (5) phoneme-specific TRACLUS segments, and (6) phoneme-specific window segments. The experiments include: (1) AV mouth: the single mouth region, (2) AV 4 faces: four facial regions of chin, cheek, upper eyebrow, and mouth, excluding forehead and eyebrow, and (3) AV 6 faces: all six facial regions. The results are presented as mean and standard deviation over the 10 speakers.*

Classification	Segment Length	Segmentation	AV Mouth		AV 4		AV 6	
			Mean	Std	Mean	Std	Mean	Std
General	Variable	Phoneme	51.13	3.66	54.04	6.55	52.05	7.02
		TRACLUS	51.79	4.78	53.38	5.82	52.47	6.00
	Fixed	Window	52.04	5.15	55.04	5.12	52.49	6.06
Phoneme-Specific	Variable	Phoneme	56.07	3.05	56.14	4.53	55.60	6.36
		TRACLUS	56.08	4.97	56.18	4.12	54.99	6.16
	Fixed	Window	52.63	4.76	54.83	5.29	54.92	5.50

6.1 Variable-length Segmentation

In this section we compare the UW of the system using fixed-length segments and variable-length segments (phoneme and TRACLUS) to understand the contribution of the segmentation.

The UW for PS/Phon is 56.14%, for PS/TRA is 56.18%, and PS/Win is 54.83%, all in the AV 4 experiment. This trend suggests that phoneme-specific classification benefits from meaningful segmentation. In the AV mouth experiment, the UW for PS/Phon is 56.07%, for PS/TRA is 56.08%, and for PS/Win is 52.63%. In this experiment, both PS/Phon and PS/TRA performed statistically significantly more accurately than PS/Win at $p<0.05$, providing additional evidence that phoneme-specific classification benefits from segmentation tied to the dynamics of the signal. PS/Phon uses the dynamics of the speech signal during segmentation and and PS/TRA uses the dynamics of the mouth movement signal during segmentation. The unweighted recall associated with the PS/Phon and PS/TRA schemes are not statistically significantly different ($p<0.05$). The importance of variable-length segmentation was also demonstrated in previous work [22]. However, this is the first demonstration of the efficacy of unsupervised variable-length segmentation for raw facial movements.

The highest UW for Gen/Phon is 54.04%, for Gen/TRA is 53.38%, and Gen/Win is 55.04%, all within the AV 4 experiment. In the AV mouth experiment, the UW for Gen/Phon is 51.13%, for Gen/TRA is 51.79%, and for Gen/Win is 52.04%. The differences between experiments and within experiments are not statistically significantly different. The trend in the results demonstrates that when using general classification (i.e., the phoneme content is not known) it is advantageous to model the dynamics of more than just the mouth region. It further demonstrates that absent knowledge of phoneme content, it may be beneficial to model longer-term dynamics (captured by windows of 0.25 seconds, compared to 0.17 and 0.16 second windows for phoneme and TRACLUS segmentation, respectively, see Section 6.3).

6.2 Phoneme-specific Classification

In this section we compare the UW of the system using phoneme-specific and general classification. This analysis allows us to understand the importance of constraining variability by limiting the content to which we compare testing segments.

We present the results in terms of improvements in performance, moving from general classification to phoneme-specific classification for each of the three segmentation schemes. We analyze the improvement in performance in terms of AV mouth and AV 4, respectively. The improvement for phoneme segmentation was 4.94% and 2.10%, for TRACLUS segments was 4.28% and 2.80%, and for sliding window segments was 0.59% and -0.21%. The improvements for both variable-length segmentation schemes are statistically significant at $p<0.05$ (for both AV mouth and AV 4). The performance was not statistically significantly different for fixed-length sliding window segmentation.

These results demonstrate that the knowledge of phoneme content within a segment contributes less when segmentation is not tied to the dynamics of the signal (compare fixed-length segments to variable-length phoneme and TRACLUS segments). Consider the results of the AV mouth experiment, the experiment in which the phoneme segmentation and TRACLUS segmentation strategies saw the greatest increase in performance. The experiment is unique, because it operates only on the mouth, the region of the face most influenced by lexical content. Phoneme segmentation explicitly controls for the dynamics introduced by lexical variability by segmenting at phoneme boundaries. TRACLUS segmentation identifies points at which dynamics change, capturing an approximation of this variability. Therefore, the improvement observed for variable-length segmentation emphasizes the importance of proper segmentation when integrating higher-level knowledge (phoneme content) that could account for fluctuations in the signal. It further suggests that given effective segmentation, emotion can be estimated from a smaller set of facial motion capture data (AV mouth vs. AV 4/6).

The improvement in classification, going from general to phoneme-specific classification (observed in all cases excepting general classification with window segmentation, AV 4 experiment), demonstrates the importance of removing variation due to speech-related articulation when considering the dynamics of frame-level facial movement.

6.3 Details of Segments

Both the fixed-length window and TRACLUS segments contain more than one phoneme on average. The fixed-length segments contain 2.67 ± 1.49 phonemes. The TRACLUS segments contain 2.13 ± 1.01 phonemes. The phoneme

Table 3: *Unweighted recall (%) across facial regions*

Forehead	U. Eyebrow	Eyebrow	Cheek	Mouth	Chin
40.43	45.07	40.14	44.92	**56.07**	49.96

segments are 0.17 ± 0.01 seconds in length, the TRACLUS segments are 0.16 ± 0.01 seconds in length, and the fixed-length sliding windows are 0.25 seconds in length.

7. DISCUSSION

We find that phoneme-specific classification with variable-length segmentation (phoneme and TRACLUS segmentation) performs more accurately than phoneme-specific classification with fixed-length sliding window segmentation. This suggests that when modeling emotion expressions it is critical to focus both on the lexical content of the signal and the underlying dynamics of the signal. Phoneme-specific classification with variable-length segmentation significantly outperforms general classification with sliding window segmentation in the AV mouth experiment (improvement of 4.03% and 4.04% for phoneme segmentation and TRACLUS segmentation, respectively, $p < 0.05$).

We find that phoneme-specific classification using the lower face regions (mouth, cheek, chin) performs more accurately than systems using the upper face regions (forehead, eyebrow, upper eyebrow) (Table 3). This finding aligns with the previous findings [19]. Further, we are able to extract the emotion information from the mouth region more accurately than from any other single face region. We hypothesize that the relative accuracy of the mouth-region classification is due to the lexical constraint that is placed on the modeling, we explicitly control for the variability that effects the mouth region (i.e., speech). The segmentation and phoneme-specific classification mitigates a large degree of the variability associated with speech. Therefore, the majority of the differences observed in the trajectories of the mouth region are tied to emotion or speaker variability. The other regions are not temporally constrained in the same manner. Research has demonstrated that eyebrow movements are related to prosodic patterns [4, 19]. However, these patterns are not generally time-synchronous with the production of phonemes.

In this paper we explicitly model the dynamics of the raw facial movement. This reliance on raw facial movement will provide new insight into emotionally salient facial behaviors and facial dynamics. Our current method performs comparably to the best result of Metallinou et al. [20], the previous state-of-the-art in raw facial movement modeling (we demonstrate an increase in performance of 0.44%). The presented PS/TRA scheme (phoneme-specific classification with TRACLUS segmentation) achieves comparable accuracy to their PS/Phon scheme. This suggests that frame-level dynamics can be comparably measured with unsupervised segmentation and a coarse knowledge of phoneme content, which has the potential to decrease the cost of transcription.

8. CONCLUSIONS

In this work, we investigate the advantages of variable-length segmentation and phoneme-specific classification for facial emotion recognition. We found that both variable-length segmentation and phoneme-specific classification improve overall performance. This highlights the importance of carefully considering segmentation when preprocessing for emotion classification.

However, phoneme segmentation requires the use of a transcript, which can be costly to obtain. The results demonstrated that absent knowledge of phoneme timing we could still improve performance over a fixed-length window baseline using TRACLUS, an unsupervised, automatic variable-length segmentation method. In phoneme-specific classification, the variable-length segmentation significantly outperforms the fixed-length segmentation when modeling the mouth data. This is promising because in real world feature extraction the mouth region can be extracted and tracked reliably (for example, [6, 10]).

In the future, we will investigate the utility of multiple variable-length segmentation techniques. The relatively low accuracy of the upper face regions suggests that the upper face regions may require longer time frames to capture the emotion-specific modulations (e.g. a frown of disapproval may last longer than phoneme-level time frames). Finally, our focus on the movement of raw feature points precludes the effects of facial structure. Future work will address modeling strategies that incorporate structural modeling. The presented study will be a building block for our future investigations on feature interaction at the different levels, such as sub-utterance-level, utterance-level, and dialog-level. We will also explore the inclusion of audio data based on pitch, energy, or frequency variations. Finally, we will explore the performance of our system on additional facial motion capture databases.

9. ACKNOWLEDGMENTS

We thank Dr. Donald Winsor and Laura Fink for offering computing resources. We thank Chansoo Lee and Yuan (June) Shangguan for their many helpful comments on this paper. We also wish to thank our anonymous reviewers for their insightful feedback.

10. REFERENCES

[1] A. Batliner, D. Seppi, S. Steidl, and B. Schuller. Segmenting into adequate units for automatic recognition of emotion-related episodes: a speech-based approach. *Advances in Human Computer Interaction, Special Issue on Emotion-Aware Natural Interaction*, January 2010.

[2] E. Bevacqua and C. Pelachaud. Expressive audio-visual speech. *Computer Animation and Virtual Worlds*, 15(3-4):297–304, 2004.

[3] C. Busso, M. Bulut, C. Lee, A. Kazemzadeh, E. Mower, S. Kim, J. Chang, S. Lee, and S. Narayanan. Iemocap: Interactive emotional dyadic motion capture database. *Language Resources and Evaluation*, 42(4):335–359, 2008.

[4] C. Busso and S. Narayanan. Interrelation between speech and facial gestures in emotional utterances: a single subject study. *IEEE Transactions on Audio, Speech, and Language Processing*, 15(8):2331–2347, 2007.

[5] J. Chen, M. K. Leung, and Y. Gao. Noisy logo recognition using line segment hausdorff distance. *Pattern recognition*, 36(4):943–955, 2003.

[6] S. Cheng, A. Asthana, S. Zafeiriou, J. Shen, and M. Pantic. Real-time generic face tracking in the wild with cuda. In *ACM Multimedia Systems Conference*, pages 148–151, Singapore, Singapore, 2014.

[7] I. Cohen, A. Garg, and T. S. Huang. Emotion recognition from facial expressions using multilevel hmm. In *Neural Information Processing Systems (NIPS)*, Denver, CO, November 2000.

[8] T. G. Dietterich. Approximate statistical tests for comparing supervised classification learning algorithms. *Neural Computation*, 10(7):1895–1923, 1998.

[9] M. El Ayadi, M. Kamel, and F. Karray. Survey on speech emotion recognition: Features, classification schemes, and databases. *Pattern Recognition*, 44(3):572–587, 2011.

[10] G. Galatas, G. Potamianos, and F. Makedon. Audio-visual speech recognition incorporating facial depth information captured by the kinect. In *European Signal Processing Conference (EUSIPCO)*, pages 2714–2717, Bucharest, Romania, August 2012.

[11] H. Gunes, B. Schuller, M. Pantic, and R. Cowie. Emotion representation, analysis and synthesis in continuous space: A survey. In *IEEE International Conference on Automatic Face & Gesture Recognition and Workshops (FG)*, pages 827–834, Santa Barbara, CA, March 2011.

[12] J. Hoey. Hierarchical unsupervised learning of facial expression categories. In *IEEE Workshop on Detection and Recognition of Events in Video*, pages 99–106, Vancouver, BC, July 2001.

[13] J. H. Jeon, R. Xia, and Y. Liu. Sentence level emotion recognition based on decisions from subsentence segments. In *IEEE International Conference on Acoustics, Speech and Signal Processing (ICASSP)*, pages 4940–4943, Prague, Czech Republic, May 2011.

[14] G. Kalberer, P. Müller, and L. Van Gool. Speech animation using viseme space. In *Vision, Modeling, and Visualization (VMV)*, pages 463–470, Erlangen, Germany, November 2002.

[15] Y. Kim and E. M. Provost. Emotion classification via utterance-level dynamics: A pattern-based approach to characterizing affective expressions. In *IEEE International Conference on Acoustics, Speech and Signal Processing (ICASSP)*, pages 3677–3681, Vancouver, BC, May 2013.

[16] C. M. Lee, S. Yildirim, M. Bulut, A. Kazemzadeh, C. Busso, Z. Deng, S. Lee, and S. Narayanan. Emotion recognition based on phoneme classes. In *INTERSPEECH*, pages 205–211, 2004.

[17] J.-G. Lee, J. Han, and K.-Y. Whang. Trajectory clustering: a partition-and-group framework. In *ACM SIGMOD International Conference on Management of Data*, pages 593–604, Beijing, China, June 2007.

[18] P. Lucey, T. Martin, and S. Sridharan. Confusability of phonemes grouped according to their viseme classes in noisy environments. In *Australian International Conference on Speech Science & Tech*, pages 265–270, 2004.

[19] S. Mariooryad and C. Busso. Feature and model level compensation of lexical content for facial emotion recognition. In *IEEE International Conference on Automatic Face and Gesture Recognition (FG)*, Ljubljana, Slovenia, May 2013.

[20] A. Metallinou, C. Busso, S. Lee, and S. Narayanan. Visual emotion recognition using compact facial representations and viseme information. In *IEEE International Conference on Acoustics Speech and Signal Processing (ICASSP)*, pages 2474–2477, Dallas, TX, March 2010.

[21] E. Mower and S. Narayanan. A hierarchical static-dynamic framework for emotion classification. In *IEEE International Conference on Acoustics, Speech and Signal Processing (ICASSP)*, pages 2372–2375, Prague, Czech Republic, May 2011.

[22] E. Mower Provost. Identifying salient sub-utterance emotion dynamics using flexible units and estimates of affective flow. In *IEEE International Conference on Acoustics, Speech and Signal Processing (ICASSP)*, pages 3682–3686, Vancouver, BC, May 2013.

[23] J. Nicolle, V. Rapp, K. Bailly, L. Prevost, and M. Chetouani. Robust continuous prediction of human emotions using multiscale dynamic cues. In *ACM international conference on Multimodal interaction*, pages 501–508. ACM, 2012.

[24] F. Ringeval and M. Chetouani. Exploiting a vowel based approach for acted emotion recognition. In *Verbal and Nonverbal Features of Human-Human and Human-Machine Interaction*, pages 243–254. Springer, 2008.

[25] H. Sakoe and S. Chiba. Dynamic programming algorithm optimization for spoken word recognition. *IEEE Transactions on Acoustics, Speech and Signal Processing*, 26(1):43–49, 1978.

[26] G. Sandbach, S. Zafeiriou, M. Pantic, and D. Rueckert. A dynamic approach to the recognition of 3d facial expressions and their temporal models. In *IEEE International Conference on Automatic Face & Gesture Recognition and Workshops (FG)*, pages 406–413, Santa Barbara, CA, March 2011.

[27] B. Schuller and G. Rigoll. Timing levels in segment-based speech emotion recognition. In *INTERSPEECH*, pages 1818–1821, Pittsburgh, Pennsylvania, September 2006.

[28] P. Senin. Dynamic time warping algorithm review. *Information and Computer Science Department University of Hawaii at Manoa Honolulu, USA*, pages 1–23, 2008.

[29] H. Shimodaira, K.-i. Noma, M. Nakai, and S. Sagayama. Dynamic time-alignment kernel in support vector machine. In *Neural Information Processing Systems (NIPS)*, volume 14, pages 921–928, Vancouver, BC, December 2001.

[30] Z. Zeng, M. Pantic, G. Roisman, and T. Huang. A survey of affect recognition methods: Audio, visual, and spontaneous expressions. *IEEE Transactions on Pattern Analysis and Machine Intelligence*, 31(1):39–58, 2009.

[31] F. Zhou, F. De la Torre, and J. F. Cohn. Unsupervised discovery of facial events. In *IEEE Conference on Computer Vision and Pattern Recognition (CVPR)*, pages 2574–2581, San Francisco, CA, June 2010.

Analysis/Synthesis Approaches for Creatively Processing Video Signals

Javier Villegas
School of Information: Science, Technology, and Arts
University of Arizona
javier.villegasp@gmail.com

Angus Graeme Forbes
University of Illinois at Chicago
Department of Computer Science
aforbes@uic.edu

ABSTRACT

This paper explores methods for the creative manipulation of video signals and the generation of animations through a process of analysis and synthesis. Our approach involves four distinct steps, and different creative outputs based on video inputs can be obtained by choosing different alternatives at each of the steps. First, we decide which features to extract from an input video sequence. Next, we choose a matching strategy to associate the features between a pair of video frames. Then, we choose a way to interpolate between corresponding features within these frames. Finally, we decide how to render these elements when resynthesizing the signal. We illustrate our approach with a range of different examples, including video manipulation experiments, animations, and real-time multimedia installations.

Categories and Subject Descriptors

I.3.3 [**Computer Graphics**]: Picture/Image Generation; I.4.9 [**Image Processing and Computer Vision**]: Applications; J.5 [**Computer Applications**]: Art and Humanities—*fine arts, performing arts*

General Terms

Algorithms, Design, Experimentation

Keywords

Analysis/Synthesis; resynthesis techniques; video processing; animation; media arts; computer graphics

1. INTRODUCTION

Signal alteration is a well established means for artistic expression in the visual arts. Popular tools such as Photoshop, Instagram, and After Effects enable a user to explore creative effects by, for instance, applying filters to an input image or video. We introduce a powerful strategy for the manipulation of video signals that combines the processes of *analysis* and *synthesis*. After an *analysis* process a signal is represented by a series of elements or features. This representation can be more appropriate than the original for a wide range of applications, including, for example, the compression and transmission of video signals [27], or, as we describe in this paper, this representation can be used to generate new modified instances of the starting signal. In the audio domain, Analysis/Synthesis (hereafter, A/S) strategies have been used extensively in creative applications. The phase vocoder is perhaps the best known A/S audio processing algorithm [8]. With the phase vocoder it is possible to manipulate the duration of a signal and the pitch of a signal independently. Other popular effects include dispersion, robotization, whisperization and automatic tuning [44]. However, although A/S techniques are sometimes used for processing videos, in general there is less of an emphasis on using A/S for creative, real-time techniques on video signals.

In one sense, many effects applied on static images, including mosaicing, pointillism, and other non-photorealistic representations, can be thought of as A/S processes. In these processes, a particular set of features (e.g, regions, lines, or objects) are identified through an *analysis* of the input image. These features are then used to describe new elements, which are then *synthesized* into a modified version of the original image. Thus, despite even potentially extreme modifications, the newly-created, non-photorealistic image nonetheless retains many aspects of the identity of the original input. In extending this technique to video input, a common problem with the A/S techniques, and many other non-photorealistic rendering approaches, is that when frames are analyzed independently the detected features can vary abruptly between consecutive frames. This is due to the nature of the detection algorithm or its sensitivity to noise. These rapid variations create distracting artifacts when the independently synthesized frames are put together in an animation. According to Bénard et al., this issue of temporal coherence has prevented non-photorealistic techniques, or stylized animations, from being more widely adopted for video manipulation [1].

We present a novel approach to the implementation of A/S techniques applied to video signals. Our approach involves matching elements between image pairs, i.e., video frames, and involves constructing video processing techniques over one or more of four distinct stages, each one of which enables different creative decisions to be made. These matchings are not necessarily constrained to the image itself, but instead, as we show in Section 4, can take place in a different do-

MM'14, November 03 - 07 2014, Orlando, FL, USA.

ACM 978-1-4503-3063-3/14/11 $15.00.
http://dx.doi.org/10.1145/2647868.2654944.

main. Moreover, we utilize creative criteria for choosing the matching strategy across image pairs. These criteria may be sub-optimal in some senses, and we show that by selecting unconventional interpolation paths and exploring new rendering techniques we can achieve interesting results that are not based on emulating existing methods. The first step of our approach is the *analysis* of the input image. During this step a series of elements are extracted from the image, each described by a set of parameters. The second step is the *matching* of elements between frames. Again, different criteria can be used to do this matching. The problem of matching elements can be thought of as an assignment problem [5]; although efficient solutions exists for finding assignments that are in some sense optimal, these solutions may not be realizable in real-time, and thus not appropriate for interactive experiences. In this paper, we evaluate the possibilities and limitations of *sub-optimal* matching algorithms that can be implemented in real-time. Once the assignment between elements is defined, the next step is to decide on an *interpolation* trajectory in the parameter space; that is, how the elements from one image are going to become the elements of the other. The final step is the *rendering* of the output image. The output does not neeed to be a faithful representation of the input, but ideally aspects of its identity should be maintained. Many narrative possibilities can be explored in this last step.

The contributions of the paper are as follows:

- We introduce a method for thinking of video processing in a particular set of stages in order to enable a range of creative possibilities (Section 3).
- We adapt signal processing approaches common in the audio domain (such as the FFT vocoder, matching pursuits, and cross-synthesis) to the processing of video sequences (Section 2).
- We introduce techniques for creative video processing, including the use of instantaneous frequency manipulation for image transitions (Section 4.6) and the use of 2D Gaussian decomposition to create fluid morphing between video frames (Section 4.3).
- We show that in some cases, sub-optimal matching and other alternative interpolation strategies lead to creative approaches especially useful for real-time video processing (Section 3.2).
- We introduce example artworks that illustrate how to create computer animations that extend algorithmic art techniques by showing that multiple scales (global and local) can be used to explore simultaneous narratives (Section 4).

In addition to describing details of our four-step A/S approach in Section 3, we introduce a series of example projects that utilize this approach in Section 4. We show how radical modifications in the *synthesis* stage can produce engaging results.

The first two examples explore the use of simple feature vectors that describe points defined solely by their x and y position within the image. The third example presents a dictionary-based method that can be combined with a finite state machine to create animations with micro-narratives at local level. In the fourth example we describe an application

Figure 1: An art installation showing trees created in real-time from the output of a dithering algorithm using the sub-optimal matching strategy. Section 4.1 discusses this project. Image copyright ©Javier Villegas.

of a two-dimensional Gaussian decomposition. The fifth example, similar to the previous example, instead uses Fourier descriptors of the closed contours from a level set representation of a grayscale image. The interaction of video data with different media streams is illustrated in the example presented in section 4.5. Finally, in the last example we present interactive animations that can be created by manipulating the transition of the frequency components of a two-dimensional DFT. We discuss the audience reception of our work in Section 5, as well as possibilities for future work in Section 6.

2. RELATED WORK

Much of our present work is inspired by the impact that A/S audio tools have had in the music community, which have motivated the use of new artificial sonic textures in various music genres. In one of the examples we present here, we use a strategy similar to the audio phase vocoder [8]. We detect the phases of different frequency components in consecutive video frames and then use them to manipulate the instantaneous frequency during the synthesis. We have also created animations where the synthesis objects are detected using a template matching algorithm whose structure resembles dictionary-based methods, such as matching pursuits [18]. We also explore the concept of cross-synthesis [44] applied to moving images, that is, images that are synthesized with information from two different sources.

Different works of figurative computer art have used A/S strategies since the 1960s. Mosaic-like versions of photographs have been created by a variety of artists, including Kenneth Knowlton [19], Chuck Close [7], and Robert Silvers [32]. Golan Levin has used similar strategies to algorithmically modify photographs [20, 21]. Daniel Rozin's work has investigated algorithmic "mirrors," interactive systems that recreate input images from a camera in real-time [2].

A/S strategies are also widely used for the effective compression and coding of images [6], since frequency domain representations of real world images tend to concentrate the energy of the image in few coefficients. In Section 4.6 we explore the use of the frequency domain representation of an image to explore different paths for transitions and instant frequency modifications.

The implementation of A/S on moving sequences has also been used to create "rewriting" video applications. In these applications, the frames of a long video are rearranged to create a new video. Bergler et al. used the audio channel on speech videos to associate "visemes" with phonemes, and then automatically generated a video with a new audio signal via a concatenation of visemes at different temporal positions [4]. Schödl and Essa created a technique, "Video Sprites," that can rearrange and correct the perspective of long video sequences of animals moving freely [30]. Our approach to video resynthesis is somewhat different as we are not simply reorganizing the existing video frames, but rather recreating new ones through resynthesizing and concatenating particular components of the video.

Non-photorealistic rendering (NPR) techniques investigate the automatic recreation of different styles of hand painting. Hetzmann unified many of those techniques under the term "stroke-based rendering" [15]. In his survey, Hertszmann describes the general problem as designing an optimization algorithm that minimizes the placement error of different types of strokes. Similarly, Gooch et al. [13] illustrate a technique with two clear steps: first, finding the best position for strokes and, second, rendering those brush strokes on the virtual canvas. Other authors have used techniques where an A/S process is more evident. For instance, Li and Huang [22], Hausner [14], and Wen et al. [42] discuss the detection of regions to be used as a stroke container or as a render primitive, and Lin et al. [23] uses a combinatorial matching algorithm to track the propagation of strokes. In our work we also suggest the use of combinatorial optimization to find correspondences between the elements of pairs of frames, but we propose the use of different matching optimization criteria as an important part of the creative control. A recent review of different NPR techniques and applications can be found in [29].

Gooch et al. emphatically state that the NPR community has surpassed the stage of mimicking art styles from the past and should instead be looking forward to generating novel rendering styles that are only possible with computers [12]. We are also interested in creating visual experiences that promote interaction and that can be implemented on mobile devices. The computational power and hardware capabilities of today's mobile devices are an invitation to use them as the destination platform for real-time A/S based manipulations. Many contemporary artists have chosen to create artworks for mobile platforms [9, 16, 33, 41].

Our approach can also be used to create transitions between two dissimilar images. Many morphing techniques have been created to generate fluid transitions between pairs of images [43]. In most of these techniques, there is a tradeoff between the complexity of the definition of the correspondent points and the warping function. With our system, new smooth transitions between pairs of images can be generated even when it is not possible to define correspondent points by visual similarity.

We present a variety of rendering primitives that are *not* based on any form of painting or illustration (a common approach of NPR techniques [15]) and that can moreover be used with the combinatorial optimization matching algorithms we present here to create animations and video effects. Furthermore, we also present sub-optimal alternatives that can be used effectively in interactive applications, including on mobile devices.

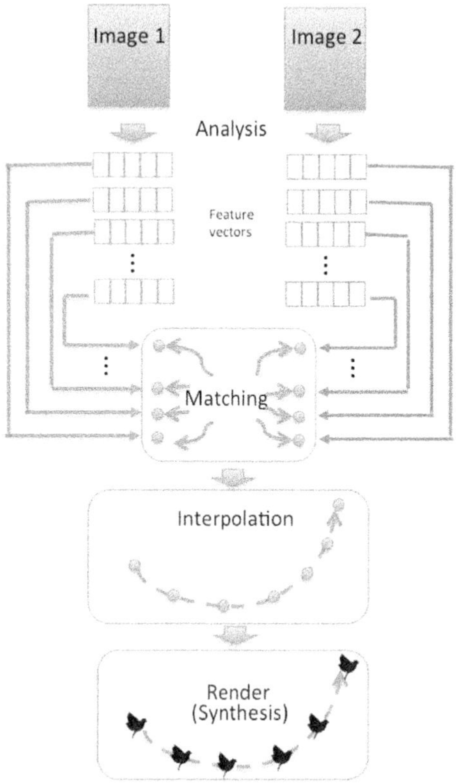

Figure 2: An overview diagram showing the four stages of the system. For step 1, we determine which feature to extract (and how to extract them) from the video sequence. For step 2, we choose a matching strategy to associate specific features between image pairs. For step 3, we decide how to interpolate between corresponding features. Finally, in step 4, we choose a rendering technique that resynthesizes the features and places them in an output video sequence. Creative choices can be made at each of these four stages.

3. GENERAL DESCRIPTION

An overview of our four-step approach to A/S is depicted in Figure 2. Pairs of images are analyzed to extract descriptive elements from them. These elements are then matched and the transitions between the correspondent pairs are calculated. In the final stage a new image is created by rendering the modified elements back to screen.

3.1 Analyzing the Input Image

The first step in the process is the *analysis* of the image. By definition, an analysis is the process of separating a whole into its component parts, but many different alternatives can be considered as "component parts." We interpret this stage

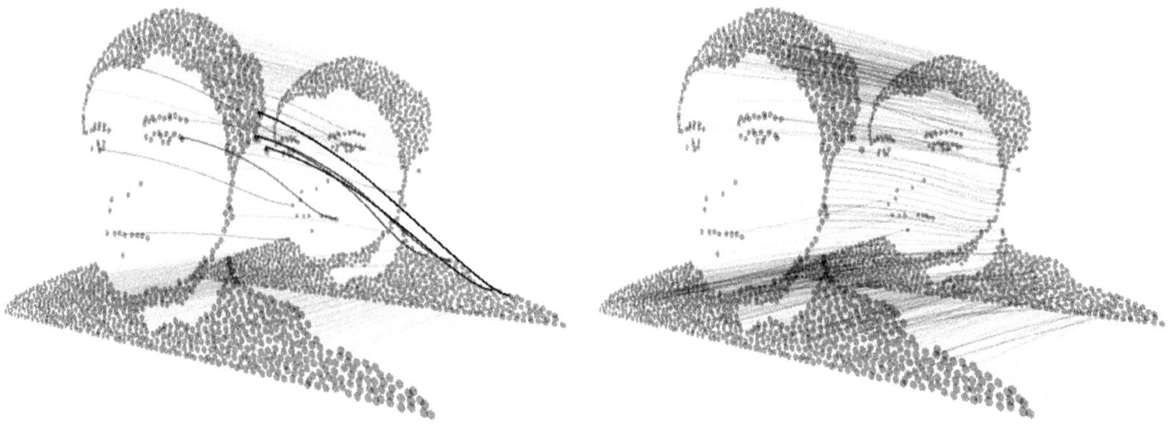

(a) (b)

Figure 3: These figure depict different matching criteria between frames. In (a), two consecutive frames and the lines joining the matched objects. The darkness of the lines is proportional to the distance. In (b), the same two frames as the previous example but with matchings defined using the minimum maximum criterion. Here, we see that it is less likely that any one match will jump a significant distance.

broadly, considering it as a process of identifying and extracting information that can then be used in later steps. We explore a range of possible outputs from this stage, including: the decomposition of the image into a transformed domain, such as the DFT [11]; or the list of features from a feature detection algorithm (e.g., black points in a dithered image, straight lines from the edge map, connected regions, or corners) [25]. After this process the input image is represented as a set of points in the transformed domain, that is, in the space formed by the parameters of the detected features.

3.2 Matching Elements between Frames

3.2.1 Optimal Matching

The features on each frame are matched with the features of the next frame. If the number of detected features is the same on all frames then the matching can be posted as an assignment problem as follows:

- Define the cost matrix $\mathbf{C}[n, n+1]$ of size $M \times M$ where M is the number of features on each frames, and each matrix element C_{ij} represents the Euclidean distance between the vector of parameters $\mathbf{z}$ of every feature i on frame n to every feature j on frame $n+1$. That is,

$$\mathbf{C}_{i,j} = d\left(\mathbf{z}_i[n], \mathbf{z}_j[n+1]\right). \tag{1}$$

- We then want to find the assignment matrix $\mathbf{X}[n]$ with elements X_{ij}, where $X_{ij} = 1$ if the feature i on frame n is matched to feature j on frame $n+1$ and $X_{ij} = 0$ otherwise.

- The assignment matrix is restricted so that each feature on frame n is assigned to one and only one feature on frame $n+1$ and reciprocally each feature on frame $n+1$ is matched to one and only one feature on frame n. That is,

$$\sum_{j=1}^{M} X_{ij} = 1 \qquad (i = 1.2...M)$$

and,

$$\sum_{i=1}^{M} X_{ij} = 1 \qquad (j = 1.2...M)$$

with,

$$X_{ij} \in \{0, 1\} \qquad (i, j = 1.2...M)$$

- If the assignment matrix that is chosen is the one that minimizes the sum of distances between features, that is, if the matrix $\mathbf{X}[n]$ is chosen such that

$$\sum_{i=1}^{M}\sum_{j=1}^{M} C_{ij} X_{ij} \tag{2}$$

is minimized, the optimization problem is known as the linear assignment problem, and many algorithms for solving this problem efficiently can be found in the literature [5]. But on the other hand, if the matching criterion is not to minimize the sum of distances but to make the maximum distance as small as possible, the assignment problem is transformed to the bottleneck assignment problem. The problem now is to minimize the maximum of $C_{ij}X_{ij}$ $\forall i, j = 1 \cdots M$ with the same constrains presented previously. This is a very well known variation of the original assignment problem for which, fortunately, efficient algorithms also exist [5].

Figure 3a shows two frames of an animation where, for simplicity of illustration, the synthesis objects are circles with fixed color and size. Every feature can be described by a vector of only two parameters (the x and y position) and the matching between the objects is done using the minimum sum criterion. Larger distances are plotted with a darker tone. Note that in order to minimize the total sum, most of the matchings are done between near objects. Figure 3b shows the result of the bottleneck assignment problem with the same two frames. Note that, though many matches have significant distances (darker lines), there are no big jumps.

3.2.2 Sub-optimal strategies

Although some of the limitations of the combinatorial optimization approaches, such as the restriction on having the same number of elements, can be easily overcome (for instance by repeating elements on the less populated images), they are nonetheless not feasible for real-time implementation. We explore a sub-optimal alternative to the matching of elements that consists of these following steps:

- A maximum number of elements N is defined so that the number of detected features in the analysis stage is never larger than this number;
- At the beginning, N random elements are created;
- Starting with an arbitrary element, each one of them is assigned to the closest (in the parameter space) unassigned feature in the currently analyzed frame;
- If all the target features are assigned, the closest one with less source elements associated to it is chosen.

Despite the simplicity of this alternative and its sensitivity to the starting element, we have obtained good results using this algorithm in real-time interactive experiences. Some of these results are described in section 4.1.

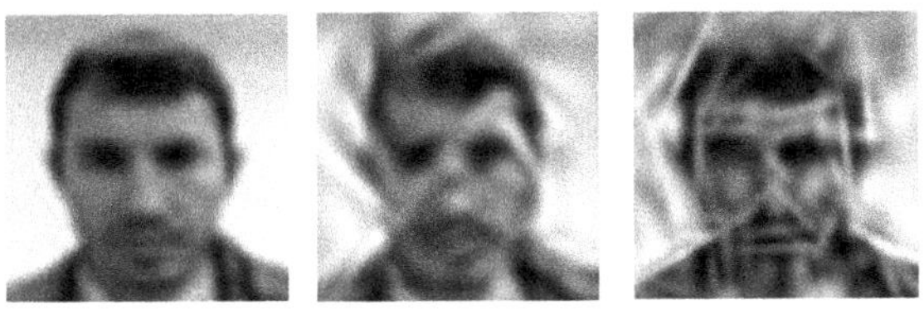

Figure 4: Using different paths to get to the same target image. The left image is the final reconstruction with a linear combination of two-dimensional Gaussian functions. In the middle image the last parameter to be updated was the angle. In the right image the last parameter was the variance.

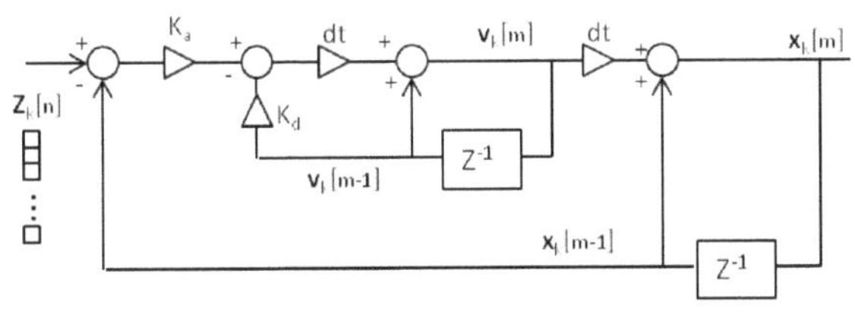

Figure 5: Block diagram of an Euler integrator used to generate a transition trajectory. $Z_k[n]$ is the current detected feature, $X_k[n]$ is the interpolated output.

3.3 Creating Intermediate Images by Interpolation

Once the matching between elements has been decided, the next aspect to be determined is the path in parameter space that each source element will follow to become its correspondent target element. One of the alternatives that we have used is illustrated in Figure 5. The vector of the difference between the current and desired position is used as a steering force, and then the velocity and position of the elements in parameter space is calculated by discrete time integration. The two parameters K_a and K_d control the degree of influence of the steering and drag forces and can be modified to generate different trajectories.

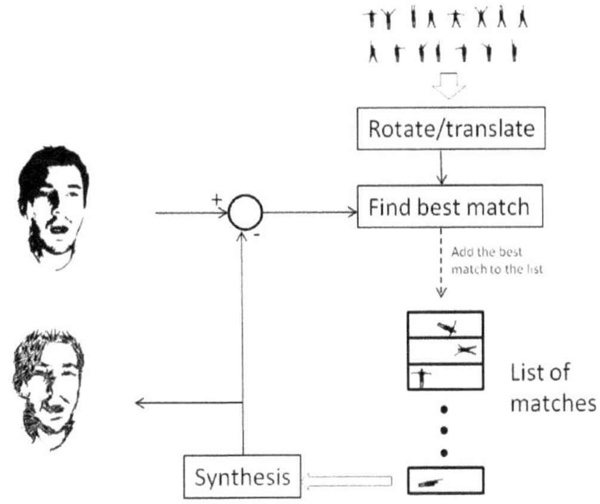

Figure 6: A dictionary-based strategy to detect different silhouettes in a black and white image.

Figure 7: The frame of an animation created with the dictionary-based scheme. Every small element is a human silhouette in a different pose. Image copyright ©Javier Villegas.

In many of the representations that are obtained after the analysis stage, the visual salience of the parameters that conform each element is not necessarily uniform (e.g., in the Fourier representation of images, phase is much more important than amplitude [11]). Therefore, perceptually different transitions can be obtained if the parameters of each element do not change in perfect synchronicity (See Figure 4).

Table 1: Summary of steps used in example projects

Project	Analysis	Features	Matching	Interpolation	Synthesis	Interactive?
Ant Theater (Section 4.1)	Corner detection	2D points	Sub-optimal	Euler integration	Ant textures	Yes
Herbaceous (Section 4.1)	Dithering	2D points	Sub-optimal	Euler integration	Tree structures	Yes
Background Singer (Section 4.2)	Dictionary of silhouette templates	2D oriented elements with state	Minimum maximum	Euler Integration; Viterbi	Human silhouettes	No
Untitled (Section 4.3)	Nonlinear least squares	2D Gaussian functions (6D vectors)	Minimum sum	Euler integration	2D Gaussian functions	No
Untitled (Section 4.4)	Connected regions; Contour detection	128D Fourier descriptors	Minimum sum	Euler integration	Filled regions	No
Slave of Your Words (Section 4.5)	Luminance value	Rectangular regions	Identity; One on one	Zero-order hold	Audio waveforms	Yes
The Fitting Dance (Section 4.5)	Ellipse Fitting	Ellipses	Sub-optimal	Euler integration	Ellipses w/audio-controlled contours	Yes
Untitled (Section 4.6)	2D FFT	256x256 coefficient matrix	Identity; One on one	Asymmetric frequency-dependent Euler integration	Frequency modulation of the IFFT	Yes

In section 4.6 we illustrate these possibilities with specific examples.

3.4 Resynthesizing the Output Image

The final step is to recreate a new image, that is, to render the elements that have been interpolated previously. It is in this step where narrative meanings can be injected into the animation, for example, by replacing corners detected in the original frame with new images related to a particular theme (Section 4.1), or by introducing visual motifs taken from other modalities (Section 4.5). This can allow the artist to emphasis an aspect of the original video or reveal a new story superimposed upon the original video. As we will illustrate in Section 4, the elements drawn on screen do not have to be exactly the same ones that were detected, nor do they need to be abstract entities. Rather they can have an identity of their own, based perhaps on the aesthetic goals of the artwork. They can also be used as a starting point or as input parameters for a more sophisticated final rendering process.

4. EXAMPLES

In this section we will present examples of animations and real-time installations that follow the approach presented above. Table 1 summarizes the characteristics of each of the examples, illustrating how our method enables a variety of creative techniques at various stages of our A/S approach, including feature extraction, matching, interpolation, and rendering. We also indicate which techniques are appropriate for interactive contexts; in general, techniques that use a sub-optimal matching strategy can occur at real-time rates.

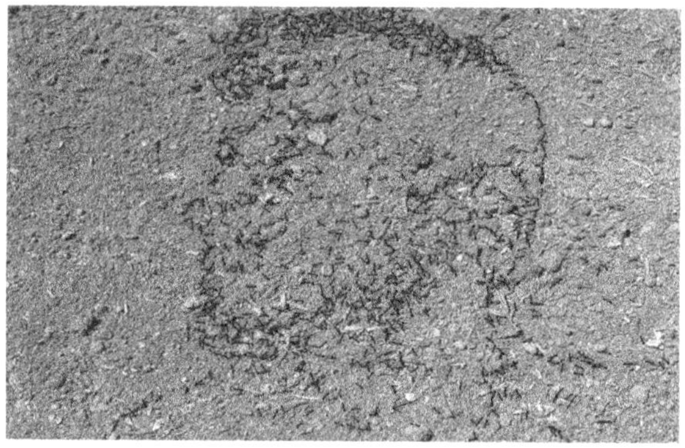

Figure 8: An "interactive mirror" using the sub-optimal algorithm and rendering points as ants.

4.1 Point-like Features

We developed a real-time installation, *Ant Theater* [37], where an input image is analyzed in real-time using a Shi-Tomasi corner detection algorithm [31] (see Figure 8). The assignment between frames is done using the sub-optimal algorithm described in Section 3.2.2. To handle the different number of elements detected on each frame, a maximum number of elements is predefined (it is a number that is always bigger than the maximum number of corners that the algorithm can return). Some elements are matched to to the same target point, so at render time some ants will be simply hiding behind others. Intermediate positions are calculated using the Euler integration scheme presented in section 3.3. The features are the points detected as corners but they are rendered as ants.

A similar approach was used for the real-time installation, *Herbaceous*, shown in Figure 1 [39]. Here the analysis stage instead uses a Floyd-Steinberg dithering algorithm [34] modified to return a restricted maximum number of points (the points that represent darker areas). The points are again two dimensional features that are matched using the sub-optimal approach and then rendered as the leaves of a tree. The body of the tree is constructed using the position of the leaves, as suggested by Rodkaew et al. [28].

4.2 Template Matching

Figure 7 shows a frame from an animation where the analysis stage involved the detection of human silhouettes in different positions and orientations. This scheme, depicted in Figure 6, resembles dictionary-based decompositions such as the matching pursuits algorithm [18]. Matching between frames is done using the minimum maximum optimization criterion. Elements in this representation have position, orientation and state. Position and orientation can be interpolated with the strategy depicted in Figure 5, but for the interpolation of states, a variation of the Viterbi algorithm was used to generate the intermediate states [24]. This technique was used for the creation of a short animation that explored the possibilities of narratives a two different levels [38].

4.3 Gaussians in a 6D Space

Figure 11 shows the morphing between two images using features that belong to a six dimensional space. The features are Gaussian functions. The target image was analyzed using non-linear least squares [26] to find the best fit of a linear combination of 2D Gaussian functions. That is, a grayscale image is approximated by:

$$I(x,y) \approx \sum_{n=1}^{N} g_n(x,y) \quad (3)$$

where

$$g_n(x,y) = A_n e^{-a_n(x-\mu_{xn})^2 + 2b_n(x-\mu_{xn})(y-\mu_{yn}) + c_n(y-\mu_{yn})^2}$$

with

$$a_n = \frac{\cos^2\theta_n}{2\sigma_{xn}^2} + \frac{\sin^2\theta_n}{2\sigma_{yn}^2}$$

$$b_n = -\frac{\sin 2\theta_n}{4\sigma_{xn}^2} + \frac{\sin 2\theta_n}{4\sigma_{yn}^2}$$

$$c_n = \frac{\sin^2\theta_n}{2\sigma_{xn}^2} + \frac{\cos^2\theta_n}{2\sigma_{yn}^2}$$

Thus, each Gaussian function can be represented as a point in a six-dimensional space using the six parameters: A_n, μ_{xn}, μ_{yn}, σ_{xn}, σ_{yn}, θ_n.

In the sequence depicted in Figure 11, 144 Gaussian functions are used to represent each one of the images. The Gaussian functions are then matched using the minimum sum criterion, and the parameters from the source image are slowly transformed to the destination image.

4.4 Fourier Descriptors in a 128D Space

A similar experiment in morphing two images can be repeated with a different set of features. This time we used the set of closed contours of a level set representation of a grayscale image (see Figure 9).

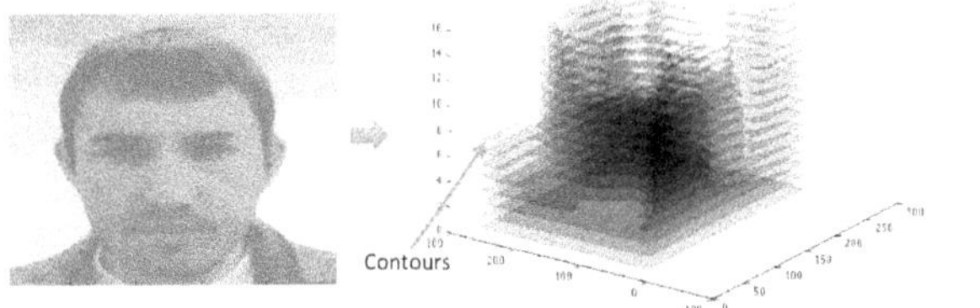

Figure 9: Generating a list of the level sets of a grayscale image.

Each contour is represented using a 128-length vector of its Fourier descriptors [17]. The list of contours of the original image is matched using the minimum sum criterion with the list of contours of the destination image. To calculate the cost matrix $\mathbf{C}[n, n+1]$ of equation 1, we used the Euclidean distance between the magnitude of all but the first element of each vector of Fourier descriptors. By doing that we consider differences in shape, scale and position and ignore differences in starting point and (unfortunately) orientation. Figure 13 shows a sequence of frames created in the morphing between the two representations.

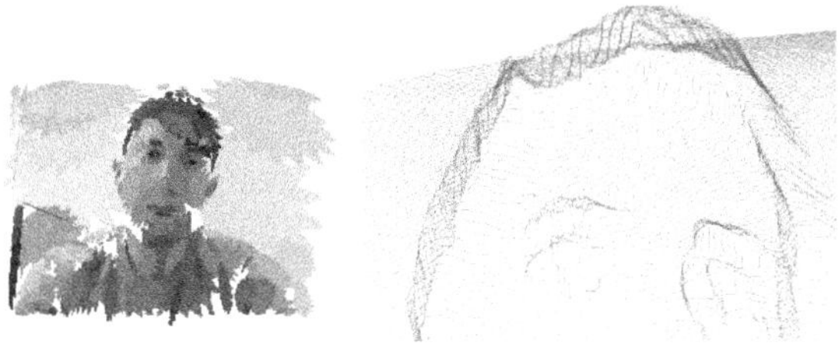

Figure 10: Two images showing the use of an audio signal before the resynthesis. On the left the RMS value of the audio signal is used to change the contours of the ellipses. In the picture on the right the waveform of the audio signal is used to draw the input image.

4.5 Intermodality

A/S approaches are powerful in part because strong manipulations can be performed before rebuilding the output. Figure 10 shows examples where an external signal (i.e. an audio stream) is used to transform the input image. The left image shows an image where the RMS value of a musical input is used to determine the amplitude of the sinusoidal signal added to the ellipse contours. This strategy was used for the creation of a short animation titled *The Fitting Dance* [35]. The right image shows a zoom in to a frame of the interactive installation *Slave of Your Words* [36]. In this installation the waveforms themselves are used as synthesis elements.

4.6 A/S in the Frequency Domain

The Fourier transform is a powerful analytical tool commonly used for signal transformations [3]. For this last example, we use the two-dimensional Fourier transform in the

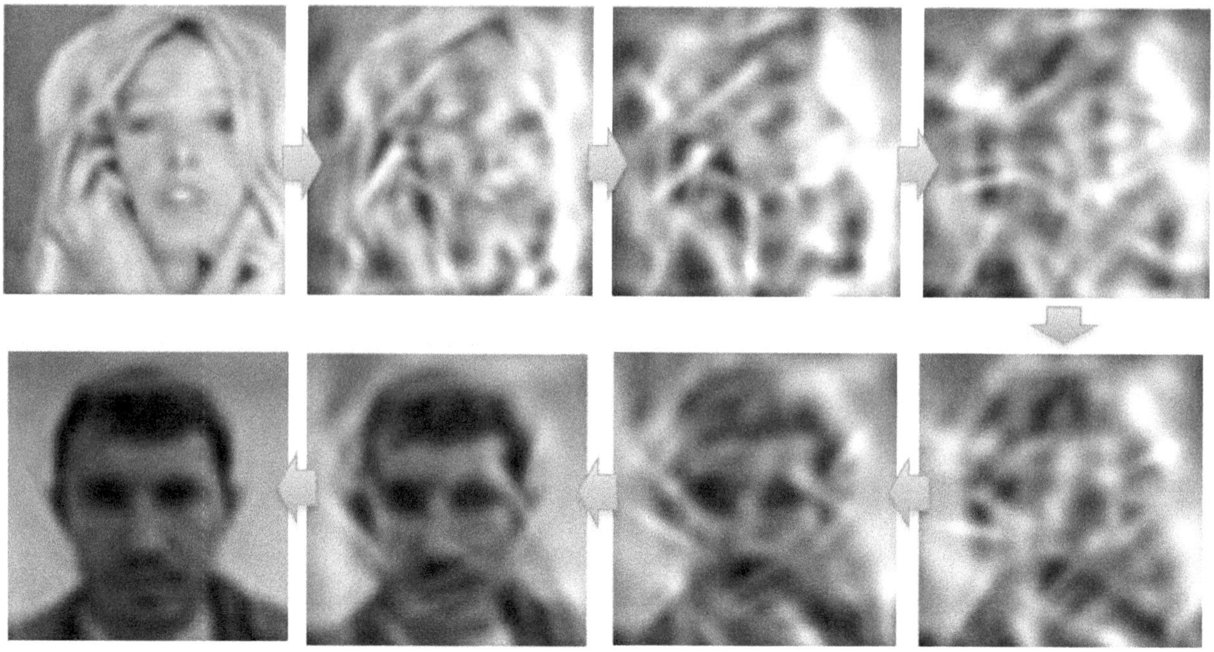

Figure 11: Morphing between two images using a six-dimensional representation for each of the detected feature (a 2D gaussian function), and matching them with a minimum sum criterion.

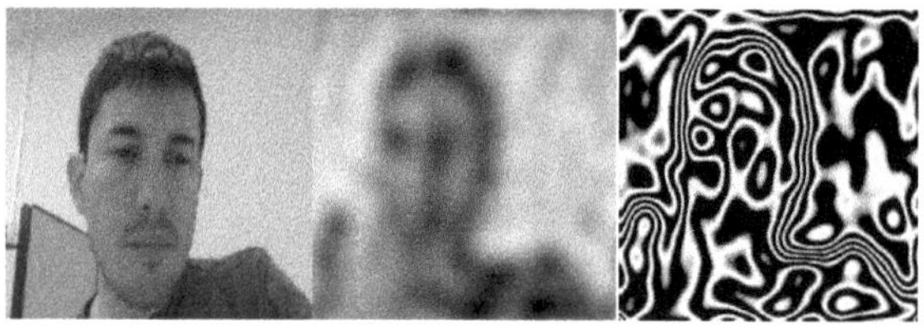

Figure 12: A frame of the FFT animation. The right side shows the resynthesized version created by frequency modulation of the IFFT of the phase interpolated version of the input. The middle image shows that low frequencies are updated first.

analysis stage. After this process, the image is represented as a linear combination of two-dimensional sinusoidal functions of different phases and amplitudes. We used a trivial identity assignment of the frequency components from frame to frame, but we used the interpolation scheme shown in Figure 5 for the phases of the low-frequency detected components. The high frequency components are updated only after the low frequency elements are close enough to their targets. The resulting animation is rendered as the frequency modulation of the inverse Fourier transform of the interpolated components. To interact with the piece, the phase of the low frequency components can be manipulated in real time with dragging gestures. This example is illustrated in Figure 12.

5. EVALUATION

In this paper, we presented a novel approach for thinking about how to generate moving sequences from video data. We have used this approach to create a wide range of animations and real-time installations that have been received positively by audiences and curators.

In many of the applications we have created, the rendered elements are constantly moving towards a target. Because of that, a faithful reconstruction of the input is accomplished only when the image stays still for a few frames. That constraint defines what type of sequences work best as subject matter. For instance, we have used slow moving faces in animations like *The Fitting Dance* [35] and *Background Singer* [38], both of them were presented in multiple international venues, including the 2009 Japan Media Arts Festival[1] (more than 10,000 attendees), the 2011 Byte Gallery International Exhibition[2], and the 2012 Portland Experimental Film Festival[3] (each with ~1,000 visitors). Audience reaction was enthusiastic as the artworks engaged the audience with a narrative in which the synthesis elements changed with time according to a backstory. There is always a mixture of joy and surprise when familiar objects (like human faces) are created slowly from the synthesis objects.

In real-time installations we have found that, rather than being a limitation, the non-immediate response of the system in fact adds suspense. It becomes a way to engage the viewer as a participant and to invite him or her to spend some time with the artwork. We have observed this behavior in some of the more popular installations, such as *Herbaceous* [39] and *Ant Theater* [37]. Both of these pieces have been presented in international exhibitions, including the 2014 Digital Latin America Festival[4] (still ongoing, ~5,000 attendees expected), Currents 2013: The Santa Fe International New Media Festival[5] (>5,000 attendees), and the 2012

[1] http://j-mediaarts.jp/about/index?locale=en

[2] http://www.transy.edu/music/BYTE_GALLERY

[3] http://effportland.com/

[4] http://issuu.com/516artsabq/docs/digital_latin_america_program_guide

[5] http://currentsnewmedia.org/

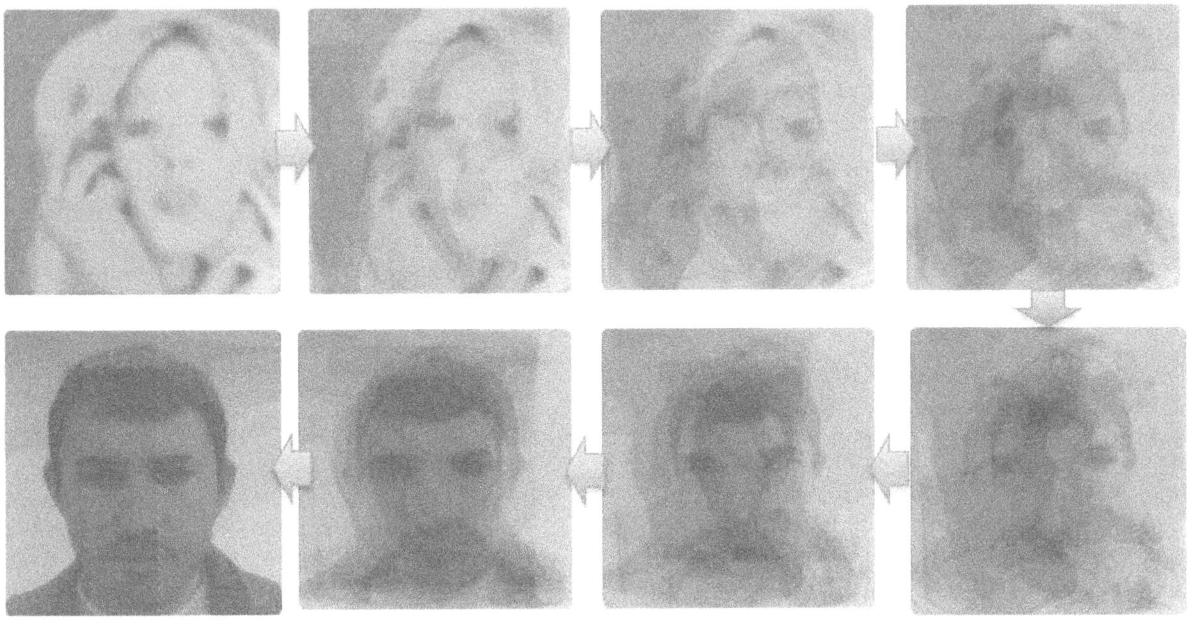

Figure 13: Features of dimension 128 matched between two images and the intermediate images that they generate.

Prospectives International Festival of Digital Art[6] (~1,000 attendees).

6. FUTURE WORK

We have shown that it is possible to use our approach to create A/S techniques for video sequences similar in many ways to A/S techniques in the audio domain. Despite the perceptual differences between aural and visual stimuli, the most successful audio tools can still be used as inspiration to explore the possibilities of A/S in animation. In particular, we showed how the two-dimensional Fourier transform can be used to create a continuous manipulation of frequency components at interactive rates, similar to the way the phase vocoder does for the manipulation of audio partials. Future work can include the use of an oscillator bank in the resynthesis stage instead of the IFFT. That implementation will allow more direct manipulation of frequency, orientation, phase, and amplitude before the resynthesis step.

We strongly believe that the use of A/S techniques on video sequences can support the creation of new visual narratives. For example, we showed in section 4.1 that the rendering step can be used to impose an additional "local" meaning to the elements to be rendered. This simultaneity of subject matters at multiple scales can be used to explore new parallel narratives [40].

We have shown that our approach is general enough to be adequate for the creation of non-photorealistic representations that are not intended to mimic art styles from the past, but instead seek to find novel creative renditions of moving images. Although some of the alternatives we presented here are currently not suitable for real-time implementation, we expect that in the near future that situation will be overcome.

We have created animations [38, 35], real-time installations [10, 37, 39, 36] and tablet applications [41] with our techniques, but an interesting direction to distribute and further evaluate the creative potential of our work will be to create public domain tools that allow other people to experiment with our techniques. Although not discussed here in this text, future work will explore the creation of plugins and interfaces that help artists to better make use of A/S techniques, such as those described above. Additionally, we plan to introduce authoring tools that enable multimedia programmers to more easily develop and test novel A/S techniques appropriate for their own projects.

7. REFERENCES

[1] P. Bénard, A. Bousseau, and J. Thollot. State-of-the-art report on temporal coherence for stylized animations. In *Computer Graphics Forum*, volume 30, pages 2367–2386. Wiley Online Library, 2011.

[2] J. D. Bolter and D. Gromala. *Windows and Mirrors: Interaction Design, Digital Art, and the Myth of Transparency*. The MIT Press, Oct. 2005.

[3] R. N. Bracewell. The Fourier transform and its applications. 1980.

[4] C. Bregler, M. Covell, and M. Slaney. Video rewrite: Driving visual speech with audio. In *Proceedings of the 24th annual conference on Computer graphics and interactive techniques*, pages 353–360. ACM Press/Addison-Wesley Publishing Co., 1997.

[5] R. Burkard, M. Dell'Amico, and S. Martello. *Assignment problems*. Society for Industrial Mathematics, 2009.

[6] R. J. Clarke. Transform coding of images. *Astrophysics*, 1, 1985.

[7] C. Finch. *Chuck Close: Work*. Prestel Publishing, Oct. 2007.

[6] `www.unr.edu/art/prospectives12.html`

[8] J. L. Flanagan and R. Golden. Phase vocoder. *Bell System Technical Journal*, 45(9):1493–1509, 1966.

[9] A. G. Forbes, T. Höllerer, and G. Legrady. Generative fluid profiles for interactive media arts projects. In *Proceedings of the International Symposium on Computational Aesthetics in Graphics, Visualization, and Imaging*, pages 37–43, 2013.

[10] A. G. Forbes and J. Villegas. Creative applications of microvideos. In *MMEDIA 2014, The Sixth International Conferences on Advances in Multimedia*, pages 108–111, 2014.

[11] R. C. Gonzalez and R. E. Woods. Digital image processing, 2nd. *SL: Prentice Hall*, 2002.

[12] A. A. Gooch, J. Long, L. Ji, A. Estey, and B. S. Gooch. Viewing progress in non-photorealistic rendering through heinlein's lens. In *Proceedings of the 8th International Symposium on Non-Photorealistic Animation and Rendering*, pages 165–171. ACM, 2010.

[13] B. Gooch, G. Coombe, and P. Shirley. Artistic vision: painterly rendering using computer vision techniques. In *Proceedings of the 2nd international symposium on Non-photorealistic animation and rendering*, pages 1–11. ACM, 2002.

[14] A. Hausner. Simulating decorative mosaics. In *Proceedings of the 28th annual conference on Computer graphics and interactive techniques*, pages 573–580. ACM, 2001.

[15] A. Hertzmann. A survey of stroke-based rendering. *IEEE Computer Graphics and Applications*, 23(4):70–81, 2003.

[16] L. Jevbratt. Zoomorph. `http://zoomorph.net`, 2011.

[17] B. JÃd'hne. *Digital Image Processing 6th Edition*. Springer, Berlin [u.a.], 2005.

[18] G. Kling and C. Roads. Audio analysis, visualization, and transformation with the matching pursuit algorithm. In *Proceedings of the 7th International Conference on Digital Audio Effects (DAFx-04)*, pages 33–37, 2004.

[19] Knowlton. Knowlton mosaics - portraits by computer assisted art pioneer Ken Knowlton. `http://www.knowltonmosaics.com`, Accessed July 2014.

[20] G. Levin. Floccular portraits - interactive art by Golan Levin and collaborators. `http://www.flong.com/projects/floccugraph`, Accessed July 2014.

[21] G. Levin. Segmentation and symptom - interactive art by Golan Levin and collaborators, Accessed July 2014.

[22] N. Li and Z. Huang. A feature-based pencil drawing method. In *Proceedings of the 1st international conference on Computer graphics and interactive techniques in Australasia and South East Asia*, pages 135–ff. ACM, 2003.

[23] L. Lin, K. Zeng, H. Lv, Y. Wang, Y. Xu, and S.-C. Zhu. Painterly animation using video semantics and feature correspondence. In *Proceedings of the 8th International Symposium on Non-Photorealistic Animation and Rendering*, pages 73–80. ACM, 2010.

[24] H. Lou. Implementing the viterbi algorithm. *Signal Processing Magazine, IEEE*, 12(5):42–52, 1995.

[25] M. S. Nixon and A. S. Aguado. *Feature Extraction & Image Processing for Computer Vision*. Academic Press, 2012.

[26] J. Nocedal and S. J. Wright. *Numerical Optimization*. Springer, New York, 2nd edition, 2006.

[27] C. Poynton. *Digital video and HD: Algorithms and Interfaces*. Elsevier, 2012.

[28] Y. Rodkaew, P. Chongstitvatana, S. Siripant, and C. Lursinsap. Particle systems for plant modeling. *Plant Growth Modeling and Applications*, pages 210–217, 2003.

[29] P. Rosin and J. Collomosse. *Image and Video-Based Artistic Stylisation*, volume 42. Springer, 2013.

[30] A. Schödl and I. A. Essa. Controlled animation of video sprites. In *Proceedings of the 2002 ACM SIGGRAPH/Eurographics symposium on Computer animation*, pages 121–127. ACM, 2002.

[31] J. Shi and C. Tomasi. Good features to track. In *Proceedings of IEEE Computer Society Conference on Computer Vision and Pattern Recognition*, pages 593–600, 1994.

[32] R. Silvers. Robert silvers. `http://www.photomosaic.com`, 2003.

[33] S. Snibbe. Studio apps. `http://www.snibbestudio.com/apps`, accessed July 2014.

[34] T. Strothotte and S. Schlechtweg. *Non-Photorealistic Computer Graphics: Modeling, Rendering and Animation*. Morgan Kaufmann, 1 edition, June 15 2002. ISBN: 1558607870, pages 472.

[35] J. Villegas. The fitting dance - animation, 2009. `https://vimeo.com/12137723`.

[36] J. Villegas. Slave of your words - interactive installation, 2011. `https://vimeo.com/31750240`.

[37] J. Villegas. Ant theater - interactive installation, 2012. `https://vimeo.com/74593738`.

[38] J. Villegas. Background singer - animation, 2012. `https://vimeo.com/43152993`.

[39] J. Villegas. Herbaceous - interactive installation, 2012. `https://vimeo.com/55131863`.

[40] J. Villegas and A. Forbes. Double-meaning: Interactive animations with simultaneous global and local narrative. In *Proceedings of the Re-new Digital Arts Festival*, pages 302–306, October 2013.

[41] J. Villegas and A. Forbes. Interactive non-photorealistic video synthesis for artistic user experience on mobile devices. In *Proceedings of the 8th International Workshop on Video Processing and Quality Metrics for Consumer Electronics (VPQM)*, Chandler, Arizona, February 2014.

[42] F. Wen, Q. Luan, L. Liang, Y.-Q. Xu, and H.-Y. Shum. Color sketch generation. In *Proceedings of the 4th international symposium on Non-photorealistic animation and rendering*, pages 47–54. ACM, 2006.

[43] G. Wolberg. Image morphing: A survey. *The visual computer*, 14(8):360–372, 1998.

[44] U. Zölzer. *DAFX: Digital Audio Effects*. Wiley, 2011.

Exploring Principles-of-Art Features For Image Emotion Recognition

Sicheng Zhao†, Yue Gao‡, Xiaolei Jiang†, Hongxun Yao†, Tat-Seng Chua‡, Xiaoshuai Sun†

†School of Computer Science and Technology, Harbin Institute of Technology, China.
‡School of Computing, National University of Singapore, Singapore.
{zsc, xljiang, h.yao, xiaoshuaisun}@hit.edu.cn; {dcsgaoy,dcscts}@nus.edu.sg

ABSTRACT

Emotions can be evoked in humans by images. Most previous works on image emotion analysis mainly used the elements-of-art-based low-level visual features. However, these features are vulnerable and not invariant to the different arrangements of elements. In this paper, we investigate the concept of principles-of-art and its influence on image emotions. Principles-of-art-based emotion features (PAEF) are extracted to classify and score image emotions for understanding the relationship between artistic principles and emotions. PAEF are the unified combination of representation features derived from different principles, including *balance*, *emphasis*, *harmony*, *variety*, *gradation*, and *movement*. Experiments on the International Affective Picture System (IAPS), a set of artistic photography and a set of peer rated abstract paintings, demonstrate the superiority of PAEF for affective image classification and regression (with about 5% improvement on classification accuracy and 0.2 decrease in mean squared error), as compared to the state-of-the-art approaches. We then utilize PAEF to analyze the emotions of master paintings, with promising results.

Categories and Subject Descriptors

H.3.1 [**Information storage and retrieval**]: Content Analysis and Indexing; I.4.7 [**Image processing and computer vision**]: Feature Measurement; J.5 [**Computer Applications**]: Arts and Humanities

General Terms

Algorithms, Human Factors, Experimentation, Performance

Keywords

Image Emotion; Affective Image Classification; Image Features; Art Theory; Principles of Art

1. INTRODUCTION

Humans are able to perceive and understand images only at high level semantics (including cognitive level and affective level [10]), rather than at low level visual features. Most previous works on image content analysis focus on understanding the cognitive aspects of images, such as object detection and recognition. Little research effort has been dedicated to the understanding of images at the affective level, due to the subjective evaluation on emotions and the "affective gap", which can be defined as "the lack of coincidence between the measurable signal properties, commonly referred to as features, and the expected affective state in which the user is brought by perceiving the signal" ([10], p. 91). However, with the increasing use of digital photography technology by the public and users' high requirement for image understanding, the analysis of image content at higher semantic levels, in particular the affective level, is becoming increasingly important.

For affective level analysis, how to extract emotion related features is the key problem. Most existing works target low level visual features based on the elements-of-art, such as *color*, *texture*, *shape*, *line*, *etc*. Obviously, these features are not invariant to their different arrangements and their link to emotions is weak, while different element arrangements share different meanings and evoke different emotions. Therefore, elements must be carefully arranged and orchestrated into meaningful regions and images to describe specific semantics and emotions. The rules, tools or guidelines of arranging and orchestrating the elements-of-art in an artwork are known as the principles-of-art, which consider various artistic aspects including *balance*, *emphasis*, *harmony*, *variety*, *gradation*, *movement*, *rhythm*, and *proportion* [6, 12]. Different combinations of these principles can evoke different emotions. For example, symmetric and harmonious images tend to express positive emotions, while images with strong color contrast may evoke negative emotions [31] (see Section 5.2). Further, the artistic principles are more interpretable by humans than elements [5].

Inspired by these observations, we propose to study, formulate, and implement the principles-of-art systematically, based on the related art theory and computer vision research. After quantizing each principle, we combine them together to construct image emotion features. Different from previous low level visual features, PAEF take the arrangements and orchestrations of different elements into account, and it can be used to classify and score image emotions evoked in humans. The framework of our proposed method is shown in Figure 1. We then apply the proposed PAEF to predict the emotions implied in famous artworks to capture the masters' emotional status.

The rest of this paper is organized as follows. Section 2 introduces related work on affective content analysis, aesthetics, composition and photo quality assessment. We summarize the elements-of-art-based low level emotion features (EAEF) and their limitations in emotion prediction as a preliminary in Section 3. The proposed PAEF are described in Section 4. Experimental evaluation, analysis and applications are presented in Section 5, followed by conclusion and future work in Section 6.

MM '14, November 03 - 07 2014, Orlando, FL, USA.

http://dx.doi.org/10.1145/2647868.2654930.

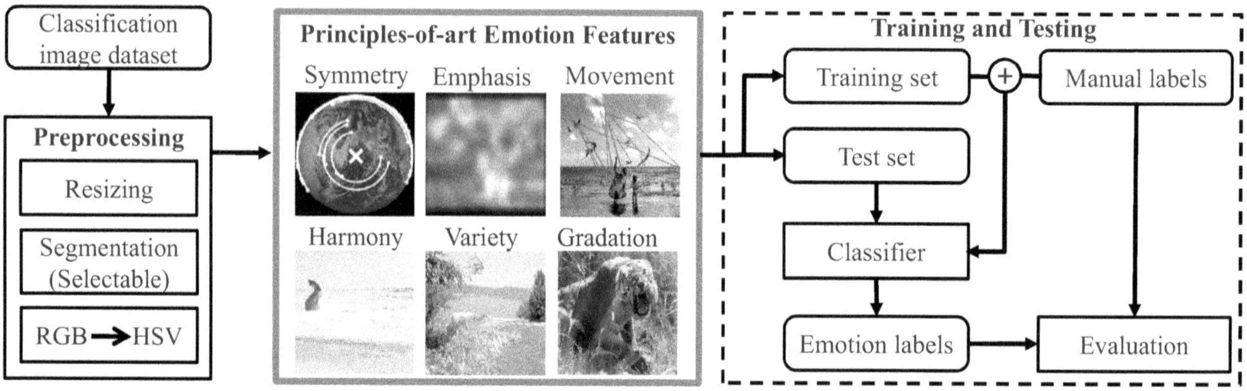

Figure 1: The framework of our proposed method. The main contributions, principles-of-art-based emotion features (PAEF), lie in the central feature extraction part in blue solid rectangle.

Table 1: Related works on affective content analysis

Category	Classification		Publications
Data type	Still images		[26, 38, 42, 24, 20, 15, 29, 33]
	Dynamic videos		[10, 17, 41, 43, 39, 3, 13]
Emotion model	Categorical		[26, 38, 42, 43, 24, 20, 15, 17, 39, 13]
	Dimensional		[10, 24, 29, 41, 3, 33]
Features	Generality	Generic	[42, 29, 4]
		Specific	[10, 26, 38, 43, 24, 20, 15, 17, 41, 39, 3, 13, 33]
	Level	Low	[10, 26, 38, 42, 24, 20, 15, 29, 17, 41, 39, 3]
		Mid	[26, 13, 33]
		High	[26, 4, 43]
	Art theory	Elements	[26, 38, 42, 24, 20, 15, 33]
		Principles	[26]

2. RELATED WORK

Affective content analysis. Some research efforts have been made recently to improve the accuracy of affective understanding in images and videos. Table 1 presents the related works, which can be divided into different types, according to the analyzed multimedia type, the adopted emotion model and the extracted features.

Generally, there are two typical models to represent emotions: categorical emotion states (CES), and dimensional emotion space (DES). CES methods [26, 38, 42, 24, 20, 15, 17, 39, 13] consider emotions to be one of a few basic categories, such as *fear*, *contentment*, *sadness*, *etc.* DES methods mostly employ the 3-D valence-arousal-control emotion space [32], 3-D natural-temporal-energetic connotative space [3], 3-D activity-weight-heat emotion factors [33], and 2-D valence-arousal emotion space [10, 24, 29, 41] for affective representation and modeling. CES in the classification task is easier for users to understand and label, while DES in the regression task is more flexible and richer in the descriptive power. Similar to [26, 42], we adopt CES to classify emotions into eight categories defined in a rigorous psychological study [27], including *anger*, *disgust*, *fear*, *sadness* as negative emotions, and *amusement*, *awe*, *contentment*, *excitement* as positive emotions. We also use valence-arousal DES to predict the scores of image emotions as in [24].

From a feature's view point, most methods extract low level visual and audio features. Lu *et al.* [24] investigated the computability of emotion through *shape* features. Machajdik and Hanbury [26] exploited theoretical and empirical concepts from psychology and art theory to extract image features that are specific to the domain of artworks. In their method, *color* and *texture* are used as low level features, *composition* are used as mid level features, while image *semantic content* including human faces and skin are used as high level features. Besides color features, Jia *et al.* [15] also extracted social correlation features for social network images. Solli and Lenz [33] classified emotions using emotion-histogram features and bag-of-emotion features derived for patches surrounding each interest point. Irie *et al.* [13] extracted mid level features based on affective audio-visual words and proposed a latent topic driving model for video classification task. Borth *et al.* proposed to infer emotions based on the understanding of visual concepts [4]. A large-scale visual sentiment ontology composed of adjective noun pairs (ANPs) is constructed and SentiBank is proposed to detect the presence of ANPs. Popular features in previous works on image emotion analysis are mainly based on elements-of-art, such as *color*, *texture*, *shape*, *etc.* Machajdik and Hanbury [26] extracted composition features, some of which can be considered as principles. However, there is still no systematic study on the use of principles-of-art for image emotion analysis.

Aesthetics, composition and photo quality assessment. Aesthetics, composition in images and the quality of photos are strongly related to humans' emotions. Joshi *et al.* [16] and Datta *et al.* [7] discussed key aspects of the problem of computational inference of aesthetics and emotions from natural images. Liu *et al.* [21] evaluated the composition aesthetics of a given image based on measuring composition guidelines and changed the relative position of salient regions using a compound operator of crop-and-retarget. Aesthetics and interestingness are predicted through high level describable attributes, including compositional, content and sky-illumination attributes [8]. Compositional features are also exploited for scene recognition [30] and category-level image classification [37]. Based on professional photography techniques, Luo and Tang [25] extracted the subject region from a photo and formulated a number of high-level semantic features based on this subject and background division. Sun *et al.* [35] presented a computational visual attention model to assess photos by using the rate of focused attention. In this work, we expand related research on computer vision and multimedia to measure the artistic principles for affective image classification and score prediction.

3. ELEMENTS OF ART: A PRELIMINARY

Low level features extracted for emotion recognition are mostly based on the elements-of-art (EAEF), including *color*, *value*, *line*, *texture*, *shape*, *form* and *space* [12], as shown in Figure 2. In this section, we briefly introduce EAEF and their limitations in image emotion prediction.

3.1 Elements-of-art-based Low Level Features

Color. An element of art which has three properties: hue, intensity, and value, representing the name, brightness and lightness or darkness of a color. Color is often used effectively by artists to induce emotional effects, such as *saturation*, *brightness*, *hue*, and *colorfulness* [26, 38, 20, 15].

Value. An element of art that describes the lightness or darkness of a color. Value is usually found to be an important element in works of art. This is true with drawings, prints, photographs, most sculpture, and architecture. The description of *lightness* or *darkness* is often used as value features [26, 38].

Line. An element of art which is a continuous mark made on some surface by a moving point. There are mainly two types of lines, emphasizing lines and de-emphasizing lines. Emphasizing lines, better known as contour lines, show and outline the edges or contours of an object. When artists stress contours or outlines in their work, the pieces are usually described as lines. Not all artists emphasize lines in their works. Some even try to hide the outline of objects in their works. De-emphasizing lines are used to describe works that do not stress the contours or outlines of objects.

Lines can be used to suggest movement in some direction. They are also used in certain ways to give people different feelings. For example, horizontal lines suggest calmness and usually make people feel relaxed, vertical lines suggest strength and stability, diagonal lines suggest tension, and curved lines suggest flowing movement [26]. Usually, the *amounts* and *lengths* of *static* and *dynamic* lines are calculated by Hough transform to describe lines [26].

Texture. An element of art which is used to describe the surface quality of one object. It refers to how things feel, or look as if they might feel if you were able to touch it. Some artists paint carefully to give their paintings a smooth appeal, while others use a lot of paint to produce a rough texture. The most frequently used texture features are *wavelet-based* features, *Tamura* features, *gray-level co-occurrence matrix* [26, 20] and *LBP* features.

Shape and *Form.* Shape is flat and has only 2 dimensions, height and width. The descriptions of *roundness*, *angularity*, *simplicity*, and *complexity* are used as shape features [24]. Form is 3 dimensional with height, width and depth, thus having mass and volume.

Space. An element of art which refers to the distance or area between, around, above, below or within things.

3.2 Limitations of EAEF

These elements-of-art based low level visual features are easy to extract based on current computer vision and multimedia research. However, there are several disadvantages using them to model image emotions:

(1) **Weak link to emotions** [1, 26]. EAEF suffer from the greatest "affective gap" and are vulnerable and not invariant to the different arrangements of elements, resulting in the poor performance on image emotion recognition. These low level features cannot represent high level emotions well.

(2) **Not interpretable by humans** [1]. As EAEF are extracted from low level view point. Humans cannot understand the meanings of these features and why such a set of features induce a particular emotion.

4. PROPOSED EMOTION FEATURES

In this section, we systematically study and formulize 6 artistic principles. For each principle, we first explain the concepts and meanings, under the art theory in [6, 12], and then translate

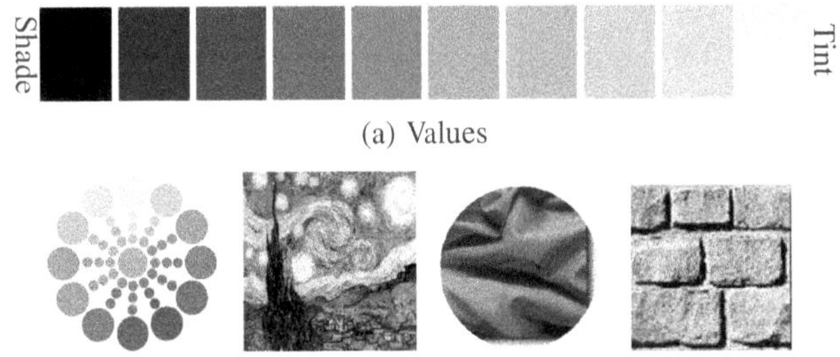

(a) Values

(b) Colors (c) Lines (d) (e)Textures and Shapes

Figure 2: Low-level representation features of emotions based on elements-of-art.

these concepts into mathematical formulae for quantization measurement. As rhythm and proportion are ambiguously defined, we do not take them into account here.

4.1 Balance

Balance (symmetry) refers to the feeling of equilibrium or stability of an art work. The artists arrange balance to set the dynamics of a composition. There are three types of balances: symmetrical, asymmetrical and radial. Symmetrical balance is the most visually stable, and characterized by an exact or nearly exact compositional design on both sides of the horizontal, vertical or any axis of the picture plane. If the two halves of an image are identical or very similar, it is symmetrical balance. Asymmetry uses compositional elements that are offset from each other, creating a visually unstable balance. Asymmetrical balance is the most dynamic because it creates a more complex design construction. Radial balance refers to balance within a circular shape or object, offering stability and a point of focus at the center of the composition [6, 12].

Since the asymmetrical balance is difficult to measure mathematically, in this paper we only consider symmetry, including bilateral symmetry, rotational symmetry [22] and radial symmetry [23, 28]. Symmetry can be seen as the reverse measurement of asymmetry.

To detect bilateral and rotational symmetry, we use the symmetry detection method in [22], which is based on matching symmetrical pairs of feature points. The method for determining feature points should be rotationally invariant, so SIFT is a good choice, although scale-invariance is not necessary. Each feature can be represented by a point vector describing its location in x, y coordinates, its orientation and (optionally) scale. Every pair of feature points is a potential candidate for a symmetrical pair. In the case of bilateral symmetry, each pair of matching points defines a potential axis of symmetry passing perpendicularly through the mid-point of the line joining these two points. Unlike bilateral symmetry detection, detecting rotational symmetry does not require the development of additional feature descriptors. It can be simply detected by matching the features against each other. Given a pair of non-parallel feature point vectors, there exists a point about which feature vector can be rotated to precisely align with another feature vector. The Hough transform [2] is used to find dominant symmetry axes or centers. Each potential symmetrical pair casts a vote in Hough space weighted by their symmetry magnitude. The rotational symmetry magnitude may be set to unity, while the bilateral symmetry magnitude may involve the discrepancy between the orientation of one feature point and the mirrored orientation of another feature point. Finally the symmetries exhibited by all individual pairs in a voting space are accumulated to determine the dominant symmetries present in the image. The result is blurred with a Gaussian and

Figure 3: Symmetrical gray scale images. The first row is images in bilateral symmetry with symmetry axis and symmetrical feature points. The second row is images in rotational symmetry with symmetry center and symmetrical feature points.

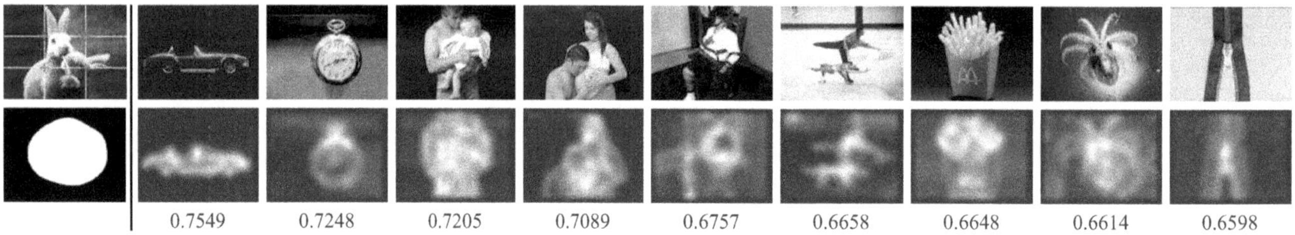

Figure 4: Images with *high* RFA based on statistic subject mask in [35]. The first column is "Rule of the third" composition and this mask. The three rows on the right of the black line are related images, saliency maps and RFA scores.

the maxima are identified as dominant axes of bilateral symmetry or centres of rotational symmetry. We compute symmetry number, radius, angle and strength of the maximum symmetry for bilateral symmetry, symmetry number, center and strength of the maximum symmetry for rotational symmetry, as shown in Figure 3.

Based on the symmetry detection method in [23], we compute the distribution of symmetry map after radial symmetry transformation for radial symmetry (see Section 4.4).

4.2 Emphasis

Emphasis, also known as contrast, is used to stress the difference of certain elements. It can be accomplished by using sudden and abrupt changes in elements. Emphasis is usually used to direct and focus viewers' attention to the most important area or centers of interests of a design, because it catches your attention [12]. We adopt Itten's color contrasts [14] and Sun's rate of focused attention (RFA) [35] to measure the principle of emphasis.

Itten defined and identified strategies for successful color combinations [14]. Seven methodologies were devised to coordinate colors using hue's contrasting properties. Itten contrasts include contrast of saturation, light and dark, extension, complements, hue, warm and cold and the simultaneous contrast. We calculate six color contrasts by the mathematical expressions in [26] and represent the contrast of extension as the standard deviation of the pixel amount of 11 basic colors as in Section 4.4.

RFA was proposed to measure the focus rate of an image when people watch it [35]. FRA is defined as the attention focus on some predefined aesthetic templates or some statistical distributions according to image's saliency map. Here we adopt Sun's response map method [34] to estimate saliency. Besides the statistic subject mask coincidence with "Rule of the third" composition method, defined in [35], we use another two diagonal aesthetic templates [21]. A 3 dimensional RFA vector is obtained by computing,

$$RFA(i) = \frac{\sum_{x=1}^{Wid}\sum_{y=1}^{Hei} Saliency(x,y)Mask_i(x,y)}{\sum_{x=1}^{Wid}\sum_{y=1}^{Hei} Saliency(x,y)}, \quad (1)$$

where Wid and Hei denote the width and height of image I, while $Saliency(x,y)$ and $Mask_i(x,y)$ are the saliency value and mask value at pixel (x,y), respectively. In Eq. (1), $i = 1,2,3$, representing different aesthetic templates. Illustrations of different masks are shown in Figure 4, 5, and 6, together with related images, saliency maps and RFA scores.

4.3 Harmony

Harmony, also known as unity, refers to a way of combining similar elements (such as *line*, *shape*, *color*, *texture*) in an artwork to accent their similarities. It can be accomplished by using repetition and gradual changes when the components of an image are perceived as harmonious. Pieces that are in harmony give the work a sense of completion and have an overall uniform appearance [12].

Inspired by Kass' idea of smoothed filters for local histogram [18], we compute the harmony intensity of each pixel on its hue and gradient direction in a neighborhood. We divide the circular hue or gradient direction equally into eight parts, which are separated into two adjacent groups $c = \{i_1, i_2, \ldots, i_k | 0 \le i_j \le 7, j = 1, 2, \ldots, k\}$ and $I \backslash c$ (see Figure 7(a)), where $i_{k+1} \equiv i_k + 1(mod 8)$, $I = \{0, 1, \ldots, 7\}$. The harmony intensity at pixel $p(x,y)$ is defined as

$$H(x,y) = \min_c e^{-|h^m(c)-h^m(I\backslash c)|}|i^m(c) - i^m(I \setminus c)|, \quad (2)$$

where

$$\begin{aligned} h^m(c) &= \max_{i\in c} h^i(c) \\ i^m(c) &= \arg\max_{i\in c} h^i(c), \end{aligned} \quad (3)$$

where $h_i(c)$ is the hue or gradient direction in groups c. The harmony intensity of the whole image is the sum of all pixels' harmony intensity, that is

$$H = \sum_{(x,y)} H(x,y). \quad (4)$$

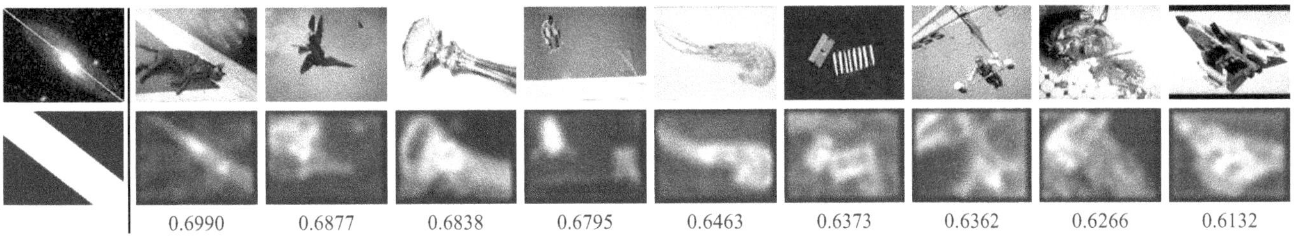

Figure 5: Images with *high* RFA based on diagonal mask [21], shown in the first column. The three rows on the right of the black line are related images, saliency maps and RFA scores.

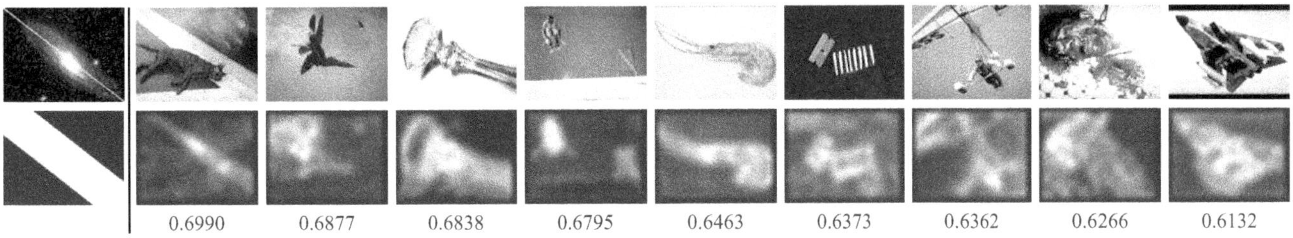

Figure 6: Images with *high* RFA based on back diagonal mask [21], shown in the first column. The three rows on the right of the black line are related images, saliency maps and RFA scores.

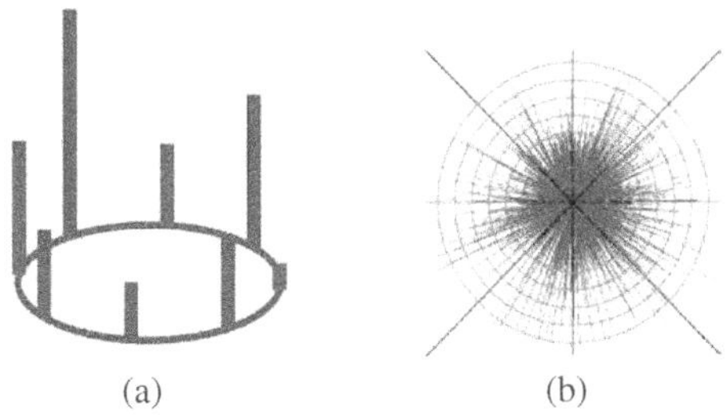

Figure 7: (a) Local histogram on eight equal parts. (b) The gradient distribution of '1300.jpg' in IAPS on red channel.

Figure 10: Images of different texture gradations, but with similar content meanings and emotions.

4.4 Variety

Variety is used to create complicated images by combining different elements. A picture made up of many different *hues*, *values*, *lines*, *textures*, or *shapes* would be described as a complex picture, which increases humans' visual interestingness [12].

However, harmony and variety are not opposites. A careful blend of the two principles is essential to the success of almost any work of art. Artists who focus only on harmony and ignore variety might find it easier to achieve balance and unity; but the visual interest in the piece could be lost. On the other hand, artists who focus only on variety and not harmony would make their works too complex; and consequently, the overall unity of the piece could be lost, which makes viewers confused [12].

Each color has a special meaning and is used in certain ways by artists. We count how many basic colors (black, blue, brown, green, gray, orange, pink, purple, red, white, and yellow) are present and the pixel amount of each color using the algorithm proposed by Weijer *et al.* [36]. Image examples of different color variety are shown in Figure 8.

Gradient depicts the changes of values and directions of pixels in an image. We calculate the distribution of gradient statistically (Figure 7(b)). For directions, we count the number of pixels in the eight regions equally divided of the circle. For lengths, we divide the relative maximum length (RML) into 8 parts equally, by computing RML as,

$$RML = \mu + 5\sigma, \tag{5}$$

where μ and σ are respectively the mean and standard deviation of the gradient matrix.

4.5 Gradation

Gradation refers to a way of combining elements by using a series of gradual changes. For example, gradation may be a gradual change of a dark value to a light value [12].

We adopt the concepts of pixel-wise *windowed total variation* and *windowed inherent variation* proposed by Xu *et al.* [40] and their combination to measure gradation for each pixel. The *windowed total variation* for pixel $p(x, y)$ in image I is defined as

$$D_x(p) = \sum_q g_{p,q}|(\partial_x I)_q|, \; D_y(p) = \sum_q g_{p,q}|(\partial_y I)_q|, \tag{6}$$

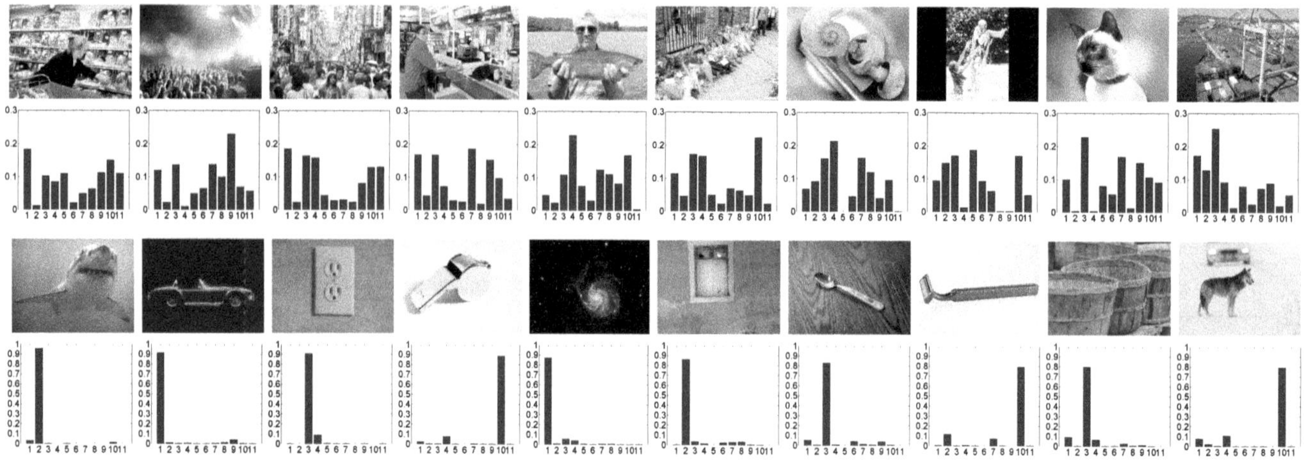

Figure 8: Images of different color variety. The first row shows images of *high* color variety with their color distributions in terms of 11 basic colors shown in row 2. The third and fourth rows respectively show images of *low* color variety and related distributions of the 11 basic colors.

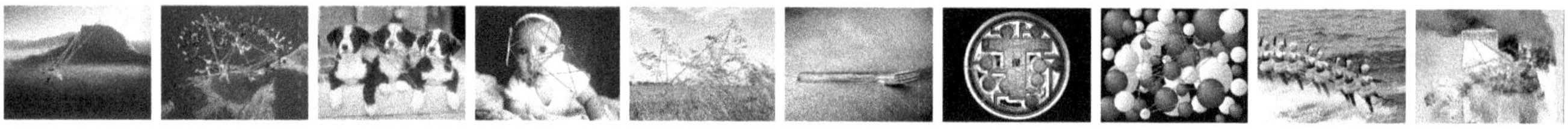

Figure 9: Eye scan path for measuring the principle of movement.

where $q \in R(p)$, $R(q)$ is a rectangular region centered at p, $D_x(p)$ and $D_y(p)$ are windowed total variations in the x and y directions for pixel p, which count the absolute spatial difference within the window $R(q)$. $g_{p,q}$ is a weighting function

$$g_{p,q} = exp\left(-\frac{(x_p - x_q)^2 + (y_p - y_q)^2}{2\sigma^2}\right), \qquad (7)$$

where σ controls the spatial scale of the window.

The *windowed inherent variation* for pixel $p(x, y)$ in image I is defined as

$$L_x(p) = |\sum_q g_{p,q}(\partial_x I)_q|, \; L_y(p) = |\sum_q g_{p,q}(\partial_y I)_q|. \qquad (8)$$

Different from $D_x(p)$ and $D_y(p)$, $L_x(p)$ and $L_y(p)$ capture the overall spatial variation, without incorporating modules.

It has been proven that in the *relative total variation* (RTV) defined in Equ. (9), opposite gradients in a window cancel out each other (Figure 10), regardless whether the pattern is isotropic or not. We adopt the sum of RTV, the sum of *windowed total variation* and the sum of *windowed inherent variation* to measure an image's relative gradation and absolute gradation, respectively.

$$RG = \sum_p RTV(p) = \sum_p \left(\frac{D_x(p)}{L_x(p) + \varepsilon} + \frac{D_y(p)}{L_y(p) + \varepsilon}\right), \qquad (9)$$

$$AGT_x = \sum_p D_x(p), AGT_y = \sum_p D_y(p), \qquad (10)$$

$$AGI_x = \sum_p L_x(p), AGI_y = \sum_p L_y(p). \qquad (11)$$

4.6 Movement

Movement is used to create the look and feel of action. It guides and moves the viewers' eye throughout the work of art. Movement is achieved through placement of elements so that the eye follows a certain path, like the curve of a line, the contours of shapes, or the repetition of certain colors, textures, or shapes [12].

Based on Super Gaussian Component analysis, Sun *et al.* [34] obtained a response map by filtering the original image and adopted the winner-takes-all (WTA) principle to select and locate the simulated fixation point and estimate a saliency map. We calculate the distribution of eye scan path obtained using Sun's method (see Figure 9).

4.7 Application to Emotion Classification and Score Prediction

From the above six subsections describing the measurements for each principle, we can see that: (1) PAEF are more interpretable and semantic than EAEF; and are easier for humans to understand. For example, humans can understand *symmetry* and *variety* better than *texture* and *line*. (2) PAEF take the arrangements and orchestrations of elements into consideration and are more relevant to image emotions and more robust in image emotion prediction, as demonstrated in Sections 5.2 and 5.3.

We then apply the proposed PAEF to image emotion classification and score prediction. Firstly, we combine the representation of the six principles into one feature vector consistently. The dimensions of these principles are 60, 18, 2, 60, 9 and 16 respectively. The measurements for each principle are summarized in Table 2. Secondly, we adopt Support Vector Machine (SVM) and Support Vector Regression (SVR) both with radial basis function (RBF) kernel to classify categorial emotions and predict dimensional emotion

Table 2: Summary of the measurements for principles of art. '#' indicates the dimension of each measurement.

Principles	Measurement	#	Short Description
Balance	*Bilateral symmetry*	12	Symmetry number, Maximum symmetry radius, angle and strength
	Rotational symmetry	12	Symmetry number, Maximum symmetry center (x and y), strength
	Radial symmetry	36	Distribution of symmetry map after radial symmetry transformation
Emphasis	*Itten color contrast*	15	Average contrast of saturation, contrast of light and dark, contrast of extension, contrast of complements, contrast of hue, contrast of warm and cold, simultaneous contrast
	RFA	3	Rate of focused attention based on saliency map and subject mask
Harmony	*Rangeability of hue and gradient direction*	2	The first and second maximums of local maximum hues and gradient directions in relative histograms of an image patch, and their differences; the combination of all patches of an image
Variety	*Color names*	12	Color types of black, blue, brown, gray, green, orange, pink, purple, red, white, yellow and each color's amount
	Distribution of gradient	48	The distribution of gradient on eight scales of direction and eight scales of length
Gradation	*Absolute and relative variation*	9	Pixel-wise windowed total variation, windowed inherent variation in x and y direction respectively, and relative total variation
Movement	*Gaze scan path*	16	The distribution of gaze vector

scores, respectively. We use the LIBSVM[1] to conduct the emotion classification and score prediction task.

5. EXPERIMENTS

To evaluate the effectiveness of the proposed PAEF, we carried out two experiments, affective image classification and emotion score prediction. PAEF were then applied to predict emotions of masterpieces.

5.1 Datasets

IAPS dataset. The International Affective Picture System (IAP-S) is a standard emotion evoking image set in psychology [19]. It consists of 1,182 documentary-style natural color images depicting complex scenes, such as portraits, babies, animals, landscapes, *etc.* Each image is associated with an empirically derived mean and s-tandard deviation of valance, arousal, and dominance ratings in a 9-point rating scale. In this rating setting, rating score 9 represents a high rating on each dimension (i.e. high pleasure, high arousal, high dominance), and 1 represents a low rating on each dimension (low pleasure, low arousal, low dominance). This dataset and related emotion ratings were used for DES modeling. Similar to [24], we only modelled on the valence and arousal dimension, without considering the dominance dimension for its relatively small contributing scope on emotions [11].

Subset A of the IAPS dataset (**IAPSa**). Mikels *et al.* [27] selected 395 pictures from **IAPS** and categorized them into eight discreet categories: *Anger, Disgust, Fear, Sadness, Amusement, Awe, Contentment*, and *Excitement.*

Artistic dataset (**ArtPhoto**). This dataset consists of 806 artistic photographs from a photo sharing site searched by emotion categories [26].

Abstract dataset (**Abstract**). This dataset includes 228 peer rated abstract paintings without contextual content [26].

The latter three datasets (IAPSa, ArtPhoto, Abstract for short) were used for CES modeling. The summary of these datasets is listed in Table 3.

5.2 Affective Image Classification

We compared our emotion classification method with Wang *et al.* [38], Machajdik *et al.* [26] and Yanulevskaya *et al.* [42]. We

[1]http://www.csie.ntu.edu.tw/~cjlin/libsvm/

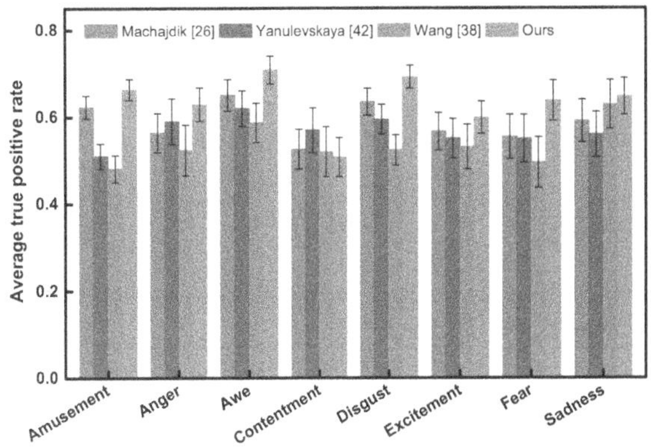

Figure 11: Classification performance on the IAPSa dataset compared to Machajdik *et al* [26], Yanulevskaya *et al* [42] and Wang *et al* [38].

adopted a "one category against all" strategy for experimental setup. The data was separated into a training set and a test set using K-fold Cross Validation (K=5) for 10 runs. Similar to [26], we optimized for the *true positive rate per class* averaged over the positive and negative classes, to overcome the limit of unbalanced data distribution of each category. We utilized PCA to perform dimensionality reduction on the feature vectors. Figures 11 to 13 illustrate the comparison of average classification performance and standard deviation between the proposed method and those of Machajdik *et al.* [26], Wang *et al.* [38] and Yanulevskaya *et al.* [42] on the IAPSa dataset, the Abstract dataset and the Artistic dataset, respectively.

From the results, it is clear that our method outperforms the state-of-the-art methods, achieving an improvement of about 5% on classification accuracy on average. This improvement arises because the state-of-the-art methods only consider the value of different low-level visual features, without considering the relationships of elements, while our proposed PAEF takes the elements' arrangements and orchestrations into account. The classification improvement demonstrates that principles-of-art are important in expressing image emotions. From the results of standard deviation, we can conclude that the proposed features are more robust for affective image classification than the use of low-level visual features.

Table 3: **Summary of the three datasets with discrete emotion categories for affective image classification.**

Dataset	Amusement	Anger	Awe	Contentment	Disgust	Excitement	Fear	Sadness	Sum
IAPSa	37	8	54	63	74	55	42	62	395
ArtPhoto	101	77	102	70	70	105	115	166	806
Abstract	25	3	15	63	18	36	36	32	228
Combined	163	88	171	196	162	196	193	260	1429

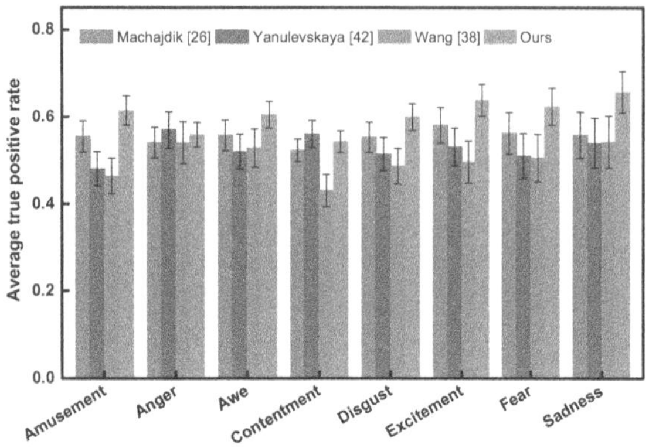

Figure 12: Classification performance on the Abstract dataset compared to Machajdik *et al* [26], Yanulevskaya *et al* [42] and Wang *et al* [38].

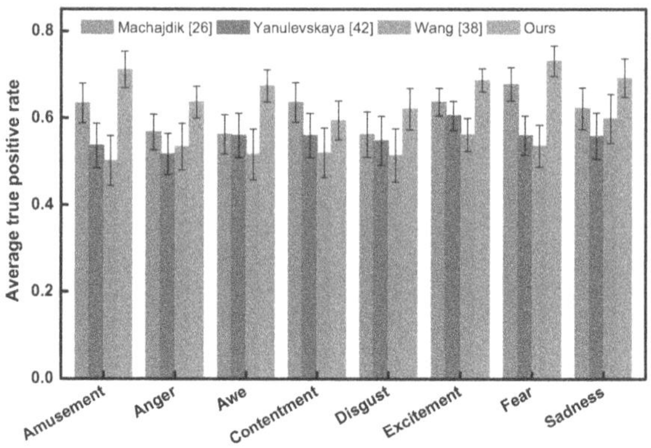

Figure 13: Classification performance on the ArtPhoto dataset compared to Machajdik *et al* [26], Yanulevskaya *et al* [42] and Wang *et al* [38].

Table 4: Measurements ranking list for the contribution to affective image classification.

	IAPSa	Abstract	ArtPhoto
Amusement	jbeghacdkifl	egdhkbfacjli	gedjkhfcaibl
Anger	bgkdfacjlehi	efgjklabcidh	befgjklacdih
Awe	bjefgldchkai	edkclbghafji	cbkhfldegaji
Contentment	bfhjegkdilac	ebfkhacljdig	fbcekhagdjli
Disgust	ecdajhfbkigl	eklghbcadfji	gelbadhcfkji
Excitement	fghdbcjkleia	gjcdhkafiebl	cbejdgkahifl
Fear	dcghkaejfbli	bgdhakcejfil	cgdkhejlabif
Sadness	fbecljhkagdi	efkbcdgahjli	fbhjdkglciea

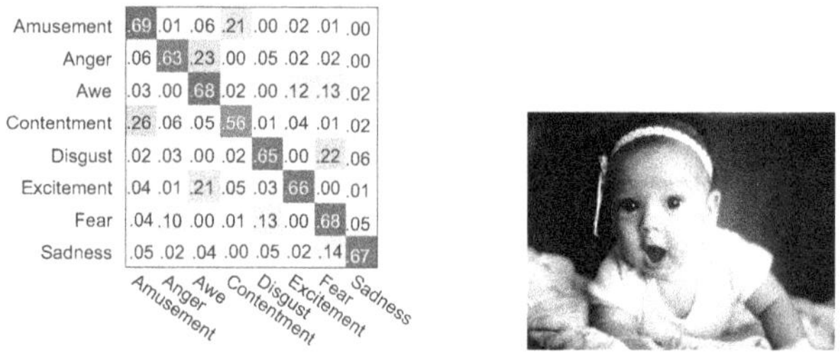

(a) (b)

Figure 14: (a) The average confusion matrix of classification results on the three dataset. (b) The image named '2070.jpg' in the IAPS dataset.

Comparing different datasets, we can also observe that the classification accuracy on the Abstract and ArtPhoto datasets is better than that on the IAPSa dataset. This is because in the IAPSa dataset, the emotions are usually evoked by certain objects in the images, while in the other two datasets, the images are taken by artists who understand and utilize the principles-of-art better.

The 8-class confusion matrix of our final results is shown in Fig. 14(a). Some pair-wise emotions are difficult to classify, such as *amusement* and *contentment*, *fear* and *disgust*. This is easy to understand, because one image can evoke different emotions. For example, for the image shown in Fig. 14(b), some people may feel *amusement* while others may feel *contentment*.

In order to evaluate the effectiveness of the measurements for each principle and its contribution for affective image classification, we built classifiers for each measurement. We sorted the measurements based on the classification accuracy in a descending order with the results in Table 4. The letters from 'a' to 'l' represent the measurements of *Bilateral symmetry*, *Rotational symmetry*, *Radial symmetry*, *Itten color contrast*, *RFA*, *Rangeability of hue and gradient direction*, *Color names*, *Distribution of gradient*, *Absolute variation*, *Relative variation*, *Relative total variation* and *Gaze scan path*, respectively. Readers can refer to Table 2 for the detailed meanings of each measurement.

From the results and the visulization results for different principles, we draw the following conclusions: (1) The best features for affective image classification are dependent on the emotion category, which means that different combinations of principles express different emotions. (2) The best features for affective image classification are dependent on the dataset, this is because the three datasets vary greatly from each other. Hence, based on the above two observations, we use all the principle features instead of selecting optimal feature combinations for different datasets and different emotions. (3) In terms of roles of different principles, symmetry (balance) and harmony tend to express positive emotions more often, while emphasis (contrast) and variety play an important role in classifying all the 8 categories of emotions. (4) Relative variation performs better than absolute variation, the eye scan path (movement) mainly focuses on the emphasis area, while RFA is extremely effective for emotion classification in the Abstract dataset.

Table 5: Comparison of MSE (standard deviation) for VA dimensions in the IAPS dataset.

	Machajdik [26]	PAEF	Combination
Valence	1.49(0.21)	1.31(0.15)	1.27(0.13)
Arousal	1.06(0.13)	0.85(0.10)	0.82(0.09)

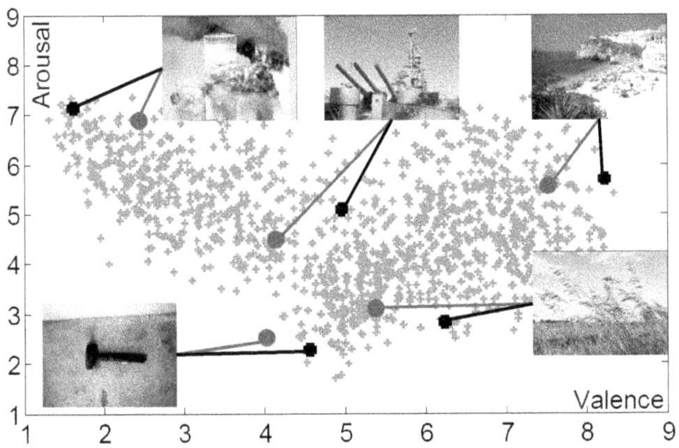

Figure 15: Emotion prediction results of our method. The black plus signs and blue circles represent the ground truth and our predicted values of image emotions, respectively.

5.3 Emotion Score Prediction

We used SVR with RBF kernel to model the VA dimensions on the IAPS dataset, and computed the mean squared error (MSE) of each dimension as the evaluation measurement. The lower the MSE is, the better the regression is. We compared our method with Machajdik's features [26] and the combination, using 5-cross validation for 10 runs. From Table 5, we can see that: (1) both valence and arousal are more accurately modeled by our principles-of-art features than Machajdik's features; (2) both our principles-of-art features and Machajdik features predict arousal better than valence; and (3) there is little improvement (3.05% and 3.53% decrease in MSE for valence and arousal) by combining them together, indicating that the principle features provide a strong enough ability in understanding image emotions. Some regression results are given in Fig. 15, which demonstrates the effectiveness of our image emotion prediction method.

We also conducted the VA emotion regression task using each of the six principles. From the MSE results in Table 6, we find that *variety*, *emphasis*, *gradation* and *balance* have higher correlations with valence, while *emphasis*, *variety*, *harmony* and *movement* are more correlated with arousal.

5.4 Inferring Masters' Moods

Masters have strong abilities to capture scenes or subjects into artworks which evoke strong emotional responses [42, 15]. Inferring the emotions implied in the masterpieces can immensely help in understanding the essential moods that the masters intended to express at that time.

Here we gathered 1,029 paintings and 158 watercolors of Vincent van Gogh, a famous Post-Impressionist painter, to infer his moods at different life periods, including early years (1881-1883), Nuenen (1883-1886), Antwerp (1883-1886), Paris (1886-1888), Arles (1888-1889), Saint-Remy (1889-1890) and Auvers (1890).

We used PAEF to predict the implied image emotions from van Gogh's artworks based on the training results of the three different datasets, IAPSa, Abstract and ArtPhoto, respectively. Some representational paintings and our predicted emotions are shown in Figure 16. We can observe that the training result in ArtPhoto dataset performs best. So we used this training result to predict all the artworks. The prediction result is shown in Table 7, from which we can see the distribution of the number of his paintings and watercolors. Note that one image can evoke different emotions. For each life period of van Gogh in Table 7, the first and second rows of each entry represent the numbers of paintings and watercolors, respectively. Take the painting "Wheat Field with Crows" (van Gogh's last painting) as example, the comments from *vangoghgallery* (www.vangoghgallery.com) are heavy, lonely, gloom, and melancholy, and our prediction emotion is *sadness*, clearly indicting the emotional status of his final days.

Table 6: MSE of each principle for VA dimensions in the IAPS dataset.

	Ban	Emp	Har	Var	Gra	Mov
Valence	1.85	1.72	2.16	1.67	1.78	2.37
Arousal	1.52	0.98	1.12	1.07	1.61	1.15

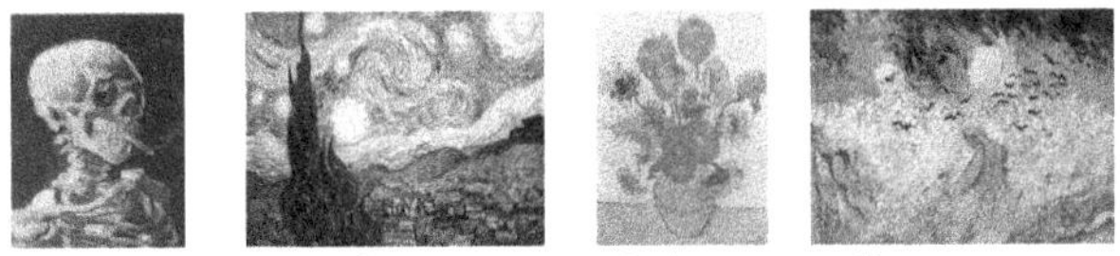

Figure 16: van Gogh's masterpieces, and our predicted emotions. The paintings are "Skull with burning cigarette", "Starry night", "Still life vase with fourteen sunflowers" and "Wheat field with crows" from left to right. The three rows of predicted emotions below the paintings are based on the training results in IAPSa, Abstract and ArtPhoto datasets, respectively.

Table 7: Emotion prediction result of van Gogh's artworks.

Period	Am	An	Aw	Co	Di	Ex	Fe	Sa	Ne	Sum
Early	0	0	0	1	4	3	9	22	8	35
	0	0	0	1	7	3	15	22	45	88
Nuenen	0	0	1	3	41	26	73	75	25	200
	0	0	0	0	3	1	3	10	9	24
Antwerp	0	0	0	0	3	0	5	2	1	7
	0	0	0	0	0	0	0	0	0	0
Paris	11	1	3	7	35	47	44	45	53	224
	0	0	0	0	1	0	3	2	4	10
Arles	11	5	1	19	45	69	52	49	87	304
	1	0	0	0	6	7	3	1	3	21
SaintRemy	8	12	3	11	36	36	22	11	57	177
	1	0	0	0	1	6	1	1	2	11
Auvers	6	0	5	3	7	22	6	8	29	82
	0	0	0	0	0	0	1	2	2	4

5.5 Discussion

From the classification results in Section 5.2 and the regression results in Section 5.3, we can conclude that PAEF can indeed help to improve the performance of image emotion recognition. The results demonstrate that the principles-of-art features can model image emotions better and are more robust in image emotion recognition than the elements-of-art features. PAEF are especially helpful and accurate to handle the abstract and artistic images, the emotions of which are mainly determined by the composition.

However, as our method does not consider the semantics of images, it does not work so well for the images whose emotions are dominated by some specific objects, concepts or scenes; and the emotion recognition performance is relatively low for these images. For example, in one image containing snakes, the emotion of *fear* may directly be evoked by the presence of snakes. In such cases, our method may fail. Combining the visual concept detection method, such as SentiBank [4], may help to tackle this problem and further improve the emotion recognition performance.

6. CONCLUSION AND FUTURE WORK

In this paper, we proposed to extract emotion features based on principles-of-art (PAEF) for image emotion classification and scoring task. Different from previous works that mainly extract low level visual features based on elements-of-art, we drew inspirations from the concept of principles-of-art for higher level understanding of images. Experimental results on affective image classification and regression have demonstrated that the performance of the proposed features is superior over the state-of-the-art approaches. The application of PAEF in emotion prediction of masterpieces is also interesting and has much potential for future research. PAEF can also be used to develop other emotion based applications, such as image musicalization [44] and affective image retrieval [45].

For further studies, we will continue our efforts to quantize the principles using more effective measurements and to improve the efficiency for real time implementation. Applying high level content detection and recognition methods may improve the performance of emotion recognition. In addition, we will consider using social network (e.g., Flickr) data, combining the descriptions and images to jointly learn the expected emotion of specified image based on visual-textual-social features [9] and analyzing the comments to distinguish expected emotion and actual emotion. How to analyze videos using visual features together with acoustic signals from an emotional perspective is also worth studying.

7. ACKNOWLEDGEMENTS

This work was supported by National Natural Science Foundation of China (No. 61071180) and Key Program (No. 61133003), and partially supported by the Singapore National Research Foundation under its International Research Centre @ Singapore Funding Initiative and administered by the IDM Programme Office.

Sicheng Zhao was also supported by the Ph.D. Short-Term Overseas Visiting Scholar Program of Harbin Institute of Technology.

8. REFERENCES

[1] R. Arnheim. *Art and visual perception: A psychology of the creative eye*. University of California Press, 1954.

[2] D. H. Ballard. Generalizing the hough transform to detect arbitrary shapes. *Pattern Recognition*, 13(2):111–122, 1981.

[3] S. Benini, L. Canini, and R. Leonardi. A connotative space for supporting movie affective recommendation. *IEEE Transactions on Multimedia*, 13(6):1356–1370, 2011.

[4] D. Borth, R. Ji, T. Chen, T. Breuel, and S.-F. Chang. Large-scale visual sentiment ontology and detectors using adjective noun pairs. In *ACM MM*, 2013.

[5] S. Calahan. Storytelling through lighting: a computer graphics perspective. *SIGGRAPH course notes*, 96, 1996.

[6] R. G. Collingwood. *The principles of art*, volume 62. Oxford University Press, USA, 1958.

[7] R. Datta, J. Li, and J. Z. Wang. Algorithmic inferencing of aesthetics and emotion in natural images: An exposition. In *ICIP*, 2008.

[8] S. Dhar, V. Ordonez, and T. Berg. High level describable attributes for predicting aesthetics and interestingness. In *CVPR*, 2011.

[9] Y. Gao, M. Wang, Z.-J. Zha, J. Shen, X. Li, and X. Wu. Visual-textual joint relevance learning for tag-based social image search. *IEEE Transactions on Image Processing*, 22(1):363–376, 2013.

[10] A. Hanjalic. Extracting moods from pictures and sounds: Towards truly personalized tv. *IEEE Signal Processing Magazine*, 23(2):90–100, 2006.

[11] A. Hanjalic and L.-Q. Xu. Affective video content representation and modeling. *IEEE Transactions on Multimedia*, 7(1):143–154, 2005.

[12] J. Hobbs, R. Salome, and K. Vieth. *The visual experience*. Davis Publications, 1995.

[13] G. Irie, T. Satou, A. Kojima, T. Yamasaki, and K. Aizawa. Affective audio-visual words and latent topic driving model for realizing movie affective scene classification. *IEEE Transactions on Multimedia*, 12(6):523–535, 2010.

[14] J. Itten. *The art of color: the subjective experience and objective rationale of color*. Wiley, 1974.

[15] J. Jia, S. Wu, X. Wang, P. Hu, L. Cai, and J. Tang. Can we understand van gogh's mood? learning to infer affects from images in social networks. In *ACM MM*, 2012.

[16] D. Joshi, R. Datta, E. Fedorovskaya, Q. Luong, J. Z. Wang, J. Li, and J. Luo. Aesthetics and emotions in images. *IEEE Signal Processing Magazine*, 28(5):94–115, 2011.

[17] H. Kang. Affective content detection using hmms. In *ACM MM*, 2003.

[18] M. Kass and J. Solomon. Smoothed local histogram filters. *ACM Transactions on Graphics*, 29(4):100, 2010.

[19] P. Lang, M. Bradley, B. Cuthbert, et al. *International affective picture system (IAPS): Affective ratings of pictures and instruction manual*. NIMH, Center for the Study of Emotion & Attention, 2005.

[20] B. Li, W. Xiong, W. Hu, and X. Ding. Context-aware affective images classification based on bilayer sparse representation. In *ACM MM*, 2012.

[21] L. Liu, R. Chen, L. Wolf, and D. Cohen-Or. Optimizing photo composition. In *Computer Graphics Forum*, 2010.

[22] G. Loy and J. Eklundh. Detecting symmetry and symmetric constellations of features. In *ICCV*, 2006.

[23] G. Loy and A. Zelinsky. Fast radial symmetry for detecting points of interest. *IEEE Transactions on Pattern Analysis and Machine Intelligence*, 25(8):959–973, 2003.

[24] X. Lu, P. Suryanarayan, R. B. Adams Jr, J. Li, M. G. Newman, and J. Z. Wang. On shape and the computability of emotions. In *ACM MM*, 2012.

[25] Y. Luo and X. Tang. Photo and video quality evaluation: Focusing on the subject. In *ECCV*, 2008.

[26] J. Machajdik and A. Hanbury. Affective image classification using features inspired by psychology and art theory. In *ACM MM*, 2010.

[27] J. Mikels, B. Fredrickson, G. Larkin, C. Lindberg, S. Maglio, and P. Reuter-Lorenz. Emotional category data on images from the international affective picture system. *Behavior research methods*, 37(4):626–630, 2005.

[28] J. Ni, M. Singh, and C. Bahlmann. Fast radial symmetry detection under affine transformations. In *CVPR*, 2012.

[29] M. A. Nicolaou, H. Gunes, and M. Pantic. A multi-layer hybrid framework for dimensional emotion classification. In *ACM MM*, 2011.

[30] M. Redi and B. Merialdo. Enhancing semantic features with compositional analysis for scene recognition. In *ECCV Workshop*, 2012.

[31] J. Ruskan. *Emotion and Art: Mastering the Challenges of the Artist's Path*. R. Wyler & Co., 2012.

[32] H. Schlosberg. Three dimensions of emotion. *Psychological review*, 61(2):81, 1954.

[33] M. Solli and R. Lenz. Color based bags-of-emotions. In *CAIP*, 2009.

[34] X. Sun, H. Yao, and R. Ji. What are we looking for: Towards statistical modeling of saccadic eye movements and visual saliency. In *CVPR*, 2012.

[35] X. Sun, H. Yao, R. Ji, and S. Liu. Photo assessment based on computational visual attention model. In *ACM MM*, 2009.

[36] J. Van De W., C. Schmid, and J. Verbeek. Learning color names from real-world images. In *CVPR*, 2007.

[37] J. C. van Gemert. Exploiting photographic style for category-level image classification by generalizing the spatial pyramid. In *ICMR*, 2011.

[38] W. Wang, Y. Yu, and S. Jiang. Image retrieval by emotional semantics: A study of emotional space and feature extraction. In *IEEE SMC*, 2006.

[39] X. Xiang and M. Kankanhalli. Affect-based adaptive presentation of home videos. In *ACM MM*, 2011.

[40] L. Xu, Q. Yan, Y. Xia, and J. Jia. Structure extraction from texture via relative total variation. *ACM Transactions on Graphics*, 31(6):139, 2012.

[41] M. Xu, J. S. Jin, S. Luo, and L. Duan. Hierarchical movie affective content analysis based on arousal and valence features. In *ACM MM*, 2008.

[42] V. Yanulevskaya, J. Van Gemert, K. Roth, A. Herbold, N. Sebe, and J. Geusebroek. Emotional valence categorization using holistic image features. In *ICIP*, 2008.

[43] S. Zhao, H. Yao, X. Sun, P. Xu, X. Liu, and R. Ji. Video indexing and recommendation based on affective analysis of viewers. In *ACM MM*, 2011.

[44] S. Zhao, H. Yao, F. Wang, X. Jiang, and W. Zhang. Emotion based image musicalization. In *ICMEW*, 2014.

[45] S. Zhao, H. Yao, Y. Yang, and Y. Zhang. Affective image retrieval via multi-graph learning. In *ACM MM*, 2014.

From Writing to Painting: A Kinect-Based Cross-Modal Chinese Painting Generation System

Jiajia Li[1], Grace Ngai[1], Stephen C.F. Chan[1], Kien A. Hua[2], Hong Va Leong[1] and Alvin Chan[1]

[1]Department of Computing
Hong Kong Polytechnic University
Kowloon, HONG KONG
{csjjli, csgngai, csschan, cshleong, cstschan}@comp.polyu.edu.hk

[2]School of Electrical Engineering and Computer Science
University of Central Florida
Orlando, FL32816-2362
kienhua@cs.ucf.edu

ABSTRACT

As computer and interaction technologies mature, a much broader range of media is now used for input and output, each of which has its own rich repertoire of techniques, instruments, and cultural heritage. The combination of multiple media can produce novel multimedia human-computer interaction approaches which are more efficient and interesting than traditional single media methods. This paper presents CalliPaint, a system for cross-modal art generation that links together Chinese ink brush calligraphy writing and Chinese landscape painting. We investigate the mapping between the two modalities based on concepts of metaphoric congruence, and implement our findings into a prototype system. A multi-step evaluation experiment with real users suggests that CalliPaint provides a realistic and intuitive experience that allows even novice users to create attractive landscape paintings from writing. Comparison with a general-purpose digital painting software suggests that CalliPaint provides users with a more enjoyable experience. Finally, exhibiting CalliPaint in an open-access location for use by casual users without any training shows that the system is easy to learn.

Categories and Subject Descriptors

H.5.2 [**Information Interfaces and Presentation**]: User Interfaces – *graphical user interfaces, interaction styles, input devices and strategies.*

General Terms

Design, Human Factors.

Keywords

Cross-modal interaction; writing; paintings; creativity

1. INTRODUCTION

Computer technology is very useful, fast growing and evolving. When it is integrated with other media such as music, photography and video, it can unleash astonishing creativity. This has resulted in a diversity of methods that use the computer to aid creative self-expression [14, 5, 19, 22, 25]. Many of these focus on the cross-modal mapping of one art form to another – for example, from body movement to music or lights, or from pen-based interaction to music generation [13, 14, 22, 25, 26].

Figure 1. Chinese Calligraphy (left) and Chinese ink-brush painting. The tools used in both art forms and the techniques (i.e. the way the pen is grasped) is the same.

There has also been a lot of interest in using computer technologies to re-interpret human cultural artifacts [23, 27, 30, 39, 40]. These invariably involve the computerization of one or more art forms and augmenting them with interaction or multimedia techniques. They widen the audience to these cultural heritages and also create new art forms or interactivities.

This paper focuses on the computerization of an ancient art form (in fact, two related art forms) with thousands of years of rich cultural heritage. Chinese ink brush calligraphy and landscape painting are believed to be interlinked or even homologous with each other. While this has not been the focus of much objective research, the two art forms do share many commonalities. They use the same tools for creation, and are produced on the same media (Figure 1). This is in contrast to Western calligraphy and painting, which uses different tools and work on different media. Upon closer inspection of the mechanics, it has been pointed out that Chinese calligraphy and Chinese ink painting share a number of commonalities that are used to produce the artwork. These include the way in which the brush is held and the manner in which the strokes are made.

CalliPaint is a novel cross-modal art generation system that is designed to allow novices that do not have a background in Chinese painting to compose Chinese ink painting artworks through the writing of Chinese ink brush calligraphy. It uses a painting model and a calligraphy model to correlate the two art forms at the semantic, mechanical and spatial levels. The motivation behind the conception of the system is the observation that many more people can write calligraphy than can draw, and this mode of combining the rich heritage of Chinese art with state-of-the-art computer interaction technologies can create a platform that has the potential to afford a large diversity of users an exploration into art forms that take years to master.

MM '14, November 3–7 2014, Orlando, FL, USA
Copyright 2014 ACM 978-1-4503-3063-3/14/11$15.00.
http://dx.doi.org/10.1145/2647868.2654911

We assessed CalliPaint on its functionality, usability, as well as its potential to facilitate creativity through two experiments: a multi-step guided evaluation with real users and a large-scale, 7-day, unguided experiment involving 72 users. The results show that CalliPaint is intuitive, easily learned and controlled, and successfully facilitates creative expression in a variety of users.

The contribution of this paper can therefore be summarized as follows: we have (1) devised a novel input device based on the writing mechanics of a Chinese calligraphic brush; (2) developed a multi-level mapping from writing dynamics to visualization of an object in a painted scene; and (3) demonstrated the feasibility and viability of the concept in a real system which has been evaluated by multiple users.

2. RELATED WORK

2.1 Cross-modal Art Generation

Previous work has introduced the concept of combining diverse modalities/media through cross-modal mappings to create new art forms. For instance, Wanderley and Depalle [32] presented a hands-free painting system based on speech and pointing gestures, and Schkolne [26] used motion recognition to create a semi-immersive 3D painting system. Drawings and music have also been linked through visual-audio/audio-visual relationships [12, 13, 17]. The Hé system [12] detects calligraphic symbols and converts them to a sound composed of pitch, pitch length and volume though MIDI and serial communication. Harmonic paper [13] uses a microcontroller and photocells to detect features from physical drawings on paper, and converts them into music with visual feedback. DrawSound [17] is a drawing instrument for sound performances that combines multi-touch input technology with the expressive character of drawing.

2.2 Pen-based Input

There has also been much interest in pen-based interactions. Previous work has explored potential usages of different pen manipulations, such as tilting [36], rolling [3] and even gripping [28]. Some support creative art generation or interactions based on the writing instruments. For instance, I/O brush [25] is a novel paintbrush that can pick up color, texture, and movement of everyday objects for creative art generation. DAB [2] is a haptic painting system that uses a haptic stylus to paint on a virtual canvas. Vignette [15] is an interactive system that facilitates texture creation in pen-and-ink illustrations with interactive refinement and editing capabilities to provide a high level of texture control. FluidPaint [31] uses vision-based techniques to allow painting with real wet brushes on a custom hardware installation that uses infrared total internal reflection to detect the brush bristles. Finally, vision-based bimanual pen and touch interaction has been explored recently [4, 18] based on a number of algorithms that are developed for object extraction [11, 32, 34].

2.3 Computerized Generation of Chinese Calligraphy and Paintings

Computerized generation of Chinese calligraphy and paintings has attracted much interest from the research community. Much previous work focus on modeling Chinese calligraphy in the digital domain; for example, modeling the appearance of the real brush strokes and simulating the behavior of a brush with wet paint on paper [6, 9, 29, 39]. Wong and Ip [35] present a parameterized model that captures the writing brush's 3D geometric parameters, simulates the physical process of brush stroke creation and synthesizes realistically Chinese calligraphic writings. Xu et al [38] present a solid model-based virtual hairy brush system for interactive digital painting and calligraphy. A virtual brush model based on droplet operation was developed by Mi et al., [21], which efficiently simulates Chinese calligraphy and traditional Chinese painting in real time. There has also been much work in real-time generation of new handwritten character fonts. For example, intelligent systems [37] have been deployed to automatically create novel, aesthetically appealing Chinese calligraphy from a few training examples of existing calligraphic styles writings. Dolinsky and Takagi [7] modeled characters using nonlinear techniques to generate handwriting of unique, personalized form.

There has been some previous work on the cross-modal modeling of Chinese art forms. Kang and Chien [12] and Huang et al. [10] associated Chinese calligraphy with music through a mapping between visual input and the Chinese pentatonic scale. However, to our knowledge, little work has been done to link Chinese calligraphy and Chinese ink painting based on a real-time mapping between the two modalities. The ZENetic computer [30], perhaps the most similar to our system, enables semi-automatic generation of Chinese-style paintings through dragging and dropping icons onto a pictorial canvas. Compared with ZENetic, CalliPaint uses a more sophisticated and flexible mapping from written character to image representation.

3. METHODOLOGY

Despite the recent interest in digitization of Chinese calligraphy, research on the mechanics of writing Chinese calligraphy or on capturing/using Chinese calligraphy as input is still at an early stage. Our presented system CalliPaint generates a pictorial scene in the classical Chinese landscape painting style, corresponding to written calligraphic characters from the user. It therefore involves the mapping between two different modalities that are connected through strokes of a soft brush: the strokes that make up the written character, and those that make up a pictorial image. Our system links these two modalities on multiple dimensions.

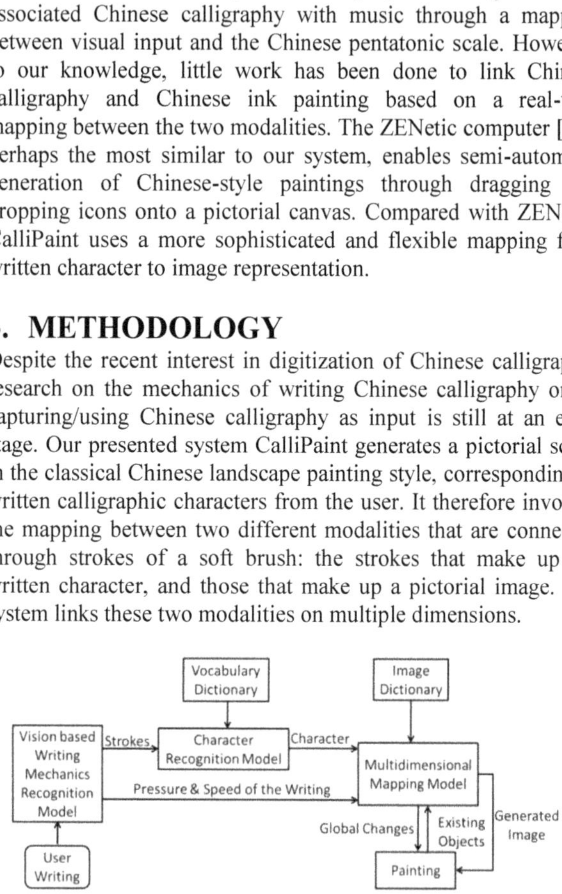

Figure 2. Framework of the CalliPaint System.

Figure 2 illustrates the framework of the system. Essentially, the system performs a multidimensional mapping from Chinese calligraphy to Chinese ink paintings. When the user writes a character on the writing interface, a vision-based writing mechanics recognition model captures the stroke sequence and mechanics (pressure and speed) of the writing through a Microsoft Kinect depth camera. The character recognition model then matches the stroke sequence to a written character inside the vocabulary dictionary. If the written character is in the dictionary, the multidimensional mapping model then executes the mapping between character and image on physical, semantic and spatial levels. Finally, an image of the written object in the image dictionary that accords with the mapping rules will be selected to be the generated image and displayed in the painting. For coherence, if the character is traditionally associated with any allegorical aspects, global changes of existing objects will also be introduced into the painting based on the semantic mapping rules.

The following subsections present the details of the mapping process. We first introduce the vocabulary dictionary, which determines the objects supported by the system. Next, we cover the tri-level mapping from written character to object image. We finally describe the image dictionary, which determines the appearance and variation of the objects in the scene.

3.1 A Vocabulary from Characters to Images

The main idea behind CalliPaint is the "translation", so to speak, of a written character on a virtual parchment or writing surface into a pictorial image of the object that it represents in a scene. Since the focus of our system is not to perform a deep semantic understanding of a written sentence or phrase, we use a simple 1-1 mapping of character to object, as defined by a pre-set dictionary.

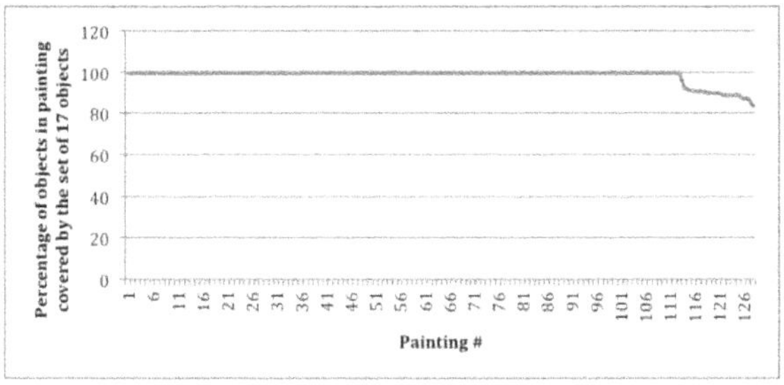

Figure 3. Coverage of objects in each painting by the set of 17 object types in the CalliPaint dictionary.

To populate our dictionary, we collected a set of 128 well-known Chinese landscape paintings to serve as a representative sample of their genre [1]. We then enumerated and analyzed the objects depicted in these paintings. We found that though the paintings exhibit much complexity, the number of object *types* that they contained was relatively constrained: indeed, a small set of 17 object "types" is sufficiently rich (with variations) to fully characterize all objects in 90% of those paintings. For the remaining 10%, this set covers over 80% of all objects (Figure 3). Some of these objects also carry significant meanings or popularly understood symbolisms.

Given these findings, we incorporated these 17 objects into a pre-set dictionary for our system. These 17 objects are: mountain, river, tree, human, house, bird, land, boat, sun, moon, cloud, plum, bridge, bamboo, chrysanthemum, pine and willow.

3.2 A Tri-Level Mapping from Written Character to Object Image

A character written on the CalliPaint writing surface is mapped into an object, and then the object's pictorial representation. This mapping of the character to an object is done on three levels: mechanical, semantic and spatial (Table 1). The principles behind the mapping on each level are governed by rules of metaphoric congruence, conventions and physical properties.

[1] These paintings are from the Song (960-1279) (21%), Yuan (1271-1368) (17%), Ming (1368-1644) (27%) and Qing (1644-1912) (35%) Dynasties, regarded as periods of high productivity in the development of Chinese landscape painting [1, 8]

Table 1. Writing-Image Mappings in CalliPaint.

Principles	Mapping	
Physics and Convention	Spatial (Section 3.2.3)	
Chinese characters and language	Semantic (Section 3.2.2)	Contextual
		Literal
Metaphoric congruence, Intuition and Experimentation	Physical (Section 3.2.1)	

3.2.1 Physical Mapping: from Writing to Graphical Appearance

Chinese calligraphy and Chinese ink painting share a number of commonalities, both in the instruments that are used for creation, as well as the mechanics involved in the generation. Our first level of cross-modal mapping therefore works at a physical level with a design based on intuition and experience to link the mechanics of the written character with the appearance of the pictorial image.

To arrive at an intuitive mapping between writing a character and drawing an image, we draw upon concepts in metaphorical congruence, which has been demonstrated by research in neuroscience to produce pleasing results in the processing of multi-modal sensory input in the brain [20, 24], and deployed in MelodicBrush, which links Chinese calligraphy with music generation [11]. Among the physical mechanics that are used to write a calligraphic character using a soft brush, two of the most easily controlled and understood are the "firmness" of the stroke, which is roughly indicated by the pressure exerted upon the brush, and the speed with which the stroke is made. On the pictorial aspect, the most obvious characteristics of a given image are its level of detail, as defined by the granularity and the number of the strokes that make up the image, and its sharpness.

Given these writing mechanics, we hypothesize that there exists some correlation between the pressure and speed of the writing and the level of detail and sharpness of the painted objects. To test this hypothesis, we invited 12 subjects aged 21–30 to participate in an experiment. All were university students fluent in written Chinese, and three had some training in Chinese calligraphy.

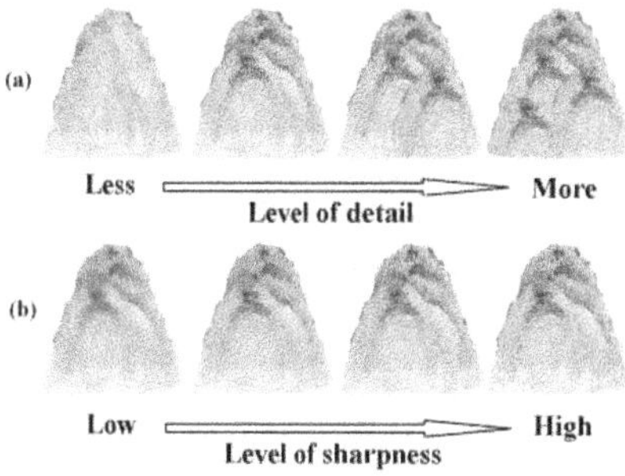

Figure 4. Images used in experiment investigating the correlation between writing mechanics and the appearance of the pictorial image. The shape and general form of the images are identical, but vary in levels of (a) detail, and (b) sharpness.

Our experiment assumes that there may be a 1-1 mapping between each writing dynamic and each object feature. We first investigate the correlation between the pressure of writing and the painting feature. The participants were asked to write the Chinese character for "mountain" (山) twice, once with a heavy hand (high pressure), and once with a lighter hand (low pressure). They were then presented with two pre-prepared sets of images of a mountain painted in the style of Chinese ink paintings (Figure 4). In the first set, Figure 4(a), the images had different levels of detail, but were otherwise identical. The second set, Figure 4(b) contained images of the same mountain with the same amount of detail, but varying levels of sharpness (b). The participants were asked to select one image from each set that they felt best corresponded to the character that they had just written.

Table 2. Perceived congruence between pressure of writing and image quality. Most subjects perceive strong congruence between a heavy hand and a highly detailed image, and weak congruence between writing pressure and sharpness of image.

Writing Pressure	Level of Detail of Associated Image				Sharpness of Associated Image			
	less	→		more	low	→		high
Light	7	4	0	1	4	2	0	6
Heavy	1	0	2	9	5	1	1	5

Table 2 shows the results of this experiment. 11 of the 12 participants picked a highly-detailed image to associate with a character written with a heavy hand, suggesting that a high pressure of writing is perceived as positively correlated to the level of detail in the image. In contrast, there is no clear correlation between the pressure of writing and the level of sharpness of the image, as the experiment subjects were as likely to correlate writing with a heavy hand with a blurred image as with a sharp one.

A similar experiment investigates the correlation between writing speed and painting features. The subjects were asked to write the character for "mountain" twice again, but this time with different speeds, once quickly, and once slowly. Likewise, the participants were then asked to select one image from each set that they felt most correlated with each written character.

Table 3. Perceived congruence between speed of writing and image quality. Most subjects perceive strong congruence between fast writing speed and low level of image sharpness, and weak congruence between speed and level of detail.

Writing Speed	Level of Detail of Associated Image				Sharpness of Associated Image			
	less	→		more	low	→		high
Slow	6	1	0	5	10	2	0	0
Fast	4	3	2	3	0	0	2	10

Table 3 shows the results of the second experiment. It can be seen that there is a clear correlation between the speed of writing and the sharpness of the image. In other words, most people associate writing quickly with a blurred image. In contrast, the correlation between speed of writing and image sharpness is quite ambiguous.

Our experiment therefore corroborates our hypothesis of the types of linkage between the writing mechanics of a written character and the appearance of the perceived associated image. Given these results, CalliPaint maps the pressure of writing to the level of detail of the image, and the speed of writing to the sharpness.

3.2.2 Semantic Mapping: Language, Context and Meaning

At the semantic level, the physical object is identified and inserted into the scene. The contextual level deploys the motifs and allegorical aspects of the objects in the painting, and allows certain objects to induce a change in the global picture. An obvious case is "sun" and "moon", which do not normally appear in the sky at the same time. Therefore, the writing of one will remove the other from the scene. Other examples are taken from common allegories in Chinese culture – such as certain plants (e.g., plum, orchid, chrysanthemum and pine), which symbolize different seasons, and hence are not allowed to appear together.

3.2.3 Spatial Mapping: Size and Position

The third level of our cross-modal mapping links the size and position of the written character with the spatial position and the image size of the object in the scene.

In our investigations of the representative set of 128 paintings, we observe that the composition of these paintings usually consists of three parts: the background, midground and foreground. The upper part of the scene usually contains objects that are distant and lofty, such as the sky, clouds and mountains. The midground usually contains mountains and lakes. The foreground is usually in the lower third of the canvas and depicts objects that are close to the viewer, such as trees and animate objects.

CalliPaint uses these principles of composition to map the size and the vertical coordinate of the written character to the spatial location of the image in the scene. Objects in the foreground occlude those in the background, as governed by the physical laws of optics, based on their vertical coordinate values. To allow for more diversity in the appearance of the objects, the physical size of the written character for inanimate objects (e.g. mountains and trees) is also mapped to the size of the image object.

The spatial mapping between written characters and the image representations of the objects allows users to construct their artwork without needing to be too concerned about the order in which the objects are placed into the picture, or with how newly placed objects should interact with the rest of the scene.

3.3 A Dictionary of Image Variations

The image dictionary of the objects supported in CalliPaint is based upon the results of the object identification step and the metaphorical congruence mapping of the writing mechanics.

At this stage, our primary focus is on facilitating and maximizing control and usability for the user. To that end, we built a core image library by selecting one reference image from a real painting in the public domain to represent each object in our dictionary. Each reference image is then further preprocessed with image editing software to achieve the desired effect corresponding to different levels of pressure and writing speed.

The granularity in pressure or writing speed that would be supported by the system was determined through experimentation.

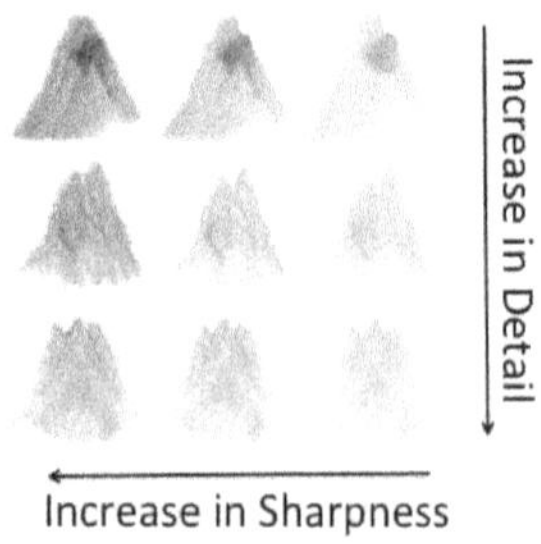

Figure 5. Mountain images that would be generated from varying different writing mechanics.

We ran another experiment with 11 subjects to test the system by using different levels of pressure and speed to "select" an image with a given level of sharpness and detail.

We found that beyond 3 discrete levels, many subjects spent a lot of time choosing between images because the difference between visual variants at adjacent levels was too small to discern. Subjects also had difficulty exercising precise control on the writing tool beyond three levels of either speed or pressure.

We therefore feel that for prototyping purposes, it is sufficient to use three levels of granularity both for writing pressure (light, normal and hard), and writing speed (slow, normal and fast). The original image is preprocessed for each combination of the desired effects – therefore, each object is expressed as a set of nine possible images. Figure 5 shows an example for the object "mountain". This approximation was done for the purposes of prototyping, but since the image effects can also be produced in real time, the number of levels can be increased or decreased as deemed appropriate.

The writing pressure and writing speed is similarly quantized into three discrete levels for prototyping purposes. We determine the level of writing pressure based on the average distance from the top of the brush to the writing surface, which roughly translates to the amount of deformation of the bristles. Specifically speaking, light pressure is applied when the bristles are practically perpendicular to the writing; while heavy pressure is applied when the bristles are almost completely lying horizontally against the surface. To calibrate the writing speed, we collected writing samples from one of the authors, who is also a skilled calligrapher. Analysis of the speed of the brush from the samples gives us three quantized levels of writing speed.

Figure 6. Appearance of the "Person" image corresponding to different speeds of writing: slow (sitting), normal (standing) and fast (walking).

An exception is made for the mapping of dynamic and animate objects that commonly appear in the foreground of paintings (i.e. they are often the subject of the painting). The only such object currently in the vocabulary of CalliPaint is "person" (人). We map the writing speed for this character to the most commonly-occurring human activities found in our reference set of Chinese landscape paintings: a person sitting, standing and walking (Figure 6). The writing pressure is ignored for such objects.

4. SYSTEM INTERFACE AND IMPLEMENTATION

The objective of CalliPaint's writing component is to enable the creation of a computer representation of the written calligraphy, and to capture the writing mechanics for painting generation. We wish to create a writing experience for the user that would be as normal and natural as possible, while, at the same time, to facilitate the user's control over the appearance of the painting and to give him/her a sense of working directly on the painting.

To achieve this objective, CalliPaint borrows from previous approaches [10] that use the Microsoft Kinect depth camera to capture the writing mechanics of a user writing with a normal calligraphic brush, and to repurpose an ordinary LCD display panel as a writing surface.

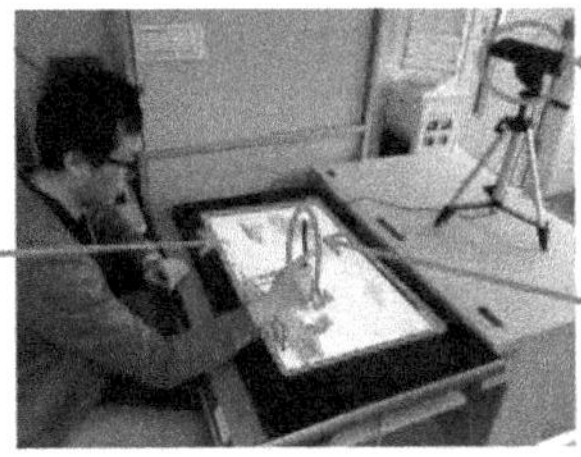

Figure 7. The System Interface for Callipaint. The writing mechanics are captured by the Kinect. The brush strokes are generated in real-time and converted to images.

Figure 7 shows the setup of our system. The Kinect depth camera captures the position and movement of a user and the position of the brush used. The brush positions are converted into *((x,y), time, pressure)* data points, where *(x,y)* are the coordinates of the brush position, *time* records when the brush was located at that coordinate, and *pressure* measures how hard the user is pressing down on the writing interface. The data point sequences are then smoothed by a 2D Gaussian filter and down-sampled for noise reduction. The visual appearances of the brush trajectories are then generated as real-time feedback and displayed on the LCD panel. Analysis of the geometry of the smoothed trajectory path gives us the type of calligraphic stroke. The *time* and *pressure* data provides us with writing mechanics like writing speed and pressure. The stroke sequence is then mapped to the written character using a stroke sequence-to-character mapping dictionary. If the stroke sequence is recognized as a character, the strokes fade out and are replaced by the corresponding image. Non-recognized stroke sequences also fade out; here, the lack of a replacement image serves as user feedback.

In addition to the recognition of characters as they are written, our system also provides three editing functions: delete, move and resize, which offers users more control over their painting.

5. EVALUATION

The usability and functionality of CalliPaint was evaluated through two experiments. The first assesses CalliPaint as a tool for self-expression and education. The second assesses CalliPaint as a tool for entertainment in an unconstrained, unguided scenario.

5.1 Experiment 1: CalliPaint in a Supervised / Guided Environment

Our first experiment targets users who are reasonably good at writing Chinese, and who may have some expertise in calligraphy, but may not be particularly gifted at drawing and painting.

The evaluation involved 10 subjects. They were aged between 20-35 and were all fluent in written Chinese. One was a primary school teacher while the others were university and graduate students. Four subjects have formal training in Chinese calligraphy and three of them consider themselves "comfortable" with drawing, though not at painting. Seven subjects have previously used digital graphics software (e.g. Adobe Illustrator or Microsoft Paint). None have expertise in Chinese painting.

The experiment consists of 4 stages. Both qualitative and quantitative evaluations were applied. The first stage evaluates the writing interface of the system. The second stage assesses the learnability, controllability and ease of use. A third stage

Table 4. Evaluation Feedback Results from Subjects in the Guided / Supervised Experiment.

Dimension of Evaluation	Lowest rating (1) stands for:	Highest rating (5) stands for:	Average
Overall Experience	Not enjoyable	Extremely enjoyable	3.9
Realism of interface	Artificial, contrived	Feels like the real thing	4.1
Realism of writing tool	Artificial, contrived	Feels like the real thing	4.3
Effectiveness in encouraging correct and standard practices of writing	Not helpful	Helpful	3.7
Ease of use (pressure control)	Difficult	Easy	3.9
Ease of use (speed control)	Difficult	Easy	3.7
Attractiveness of copy of real artwork	Ugly	Attractive	4.0
Attractiveness of self-generated artwork	Ugly	Attractive	3.7
Effectiveness in facilitating creativity	Not helpful	Helpful	4.4

investigates the ability of the system to create aesthetically-pleasing pictures. Conclusions drawn from these three stages are mainly from statistical analysis. For the sake of brevity, the details are not shown here. The fourth and final stage evaluates the degree to which the system supports and facilitates creativity. After that, the subjects were asked to complete an assessment form rating various aspects of the system on a scale from 1 to 5 (as in Table 4), and to participate in a post-experiment interview. Finally, two external experts in Chinese painting and design, respectively, evaluated the artwork created by the subjects.

All 10 subjects participated in all 4 stages in the prescribed order.

5.1.1 *Stage 1: Intuitiveness and Realism of Writing Interface*

The first stage of the experiment is designed to assess the writing interface for its intuitiveness and realism and the precision of character recognition, with a secondary purpose to familiarize the experiment subjects with the system.

The subjects were given 15 minutes to complete this stage. They were provided with the list of characters in the system dictionary, with annotations denoting the correct stroke order of writing for each character. They were then asked to copy the characters into the system via the writing interface.

The writing interface obtained high scores in the post-experiment assessment feedback. Table 4 shows that the subjects gave the writing interface a score of 4.1 and the writing tool (the brush) 4.3. This was corroborated in the post-experiment interviews, where most of the subjects said that the writing interface was intuitive and realistic.

The performance of the system can further be assessed by the number of characters successfully entered by the user. In our experiments, characters were successfully recognized by the system about 90% of the time. In the remaining 10%, the character was either rejected as being out of vocabulary, or misrecognized as another character. The main reason is nonstandard writing practices (e.g. wrong stroke sequence) on the part of the user. The recognition of the character is therefore an indirect reflection of the quality of the user's writing. Users with prior experience in calligraphy made fewer errors, but even users weaker in Chinese writing significantly reduced their errors with correction and practice. Users gave CalliPaint 3.7 on effectiveness in encouraging correct and standard writing practices.

In post-experiment interviews, some subjects suggested that they would have been able to perform better (i.e. have more characters successfully recognized by the system) if more time had been available for practice. Some subjects were surprised when the system did not recognize their writing because of a nonstandard order of strokes. The primary school teacher was very interested in the system as a potential tool for teaching younger children to write and to encourage them to practice writing correctly. Indeed, we noted that seeing images generated in real time based on the written character was exciting and enjoyable for the users.

5.1.2 *Stage 2: Learnability and Controllability of System*

The second stage of the experiment assess CalliPaint based on how easy it is to learn how to use the system, including selecting the desired effect (sharpness and level of detail) of an image and placing it at the desired location. To obtain an objective comparison with currently available software, we also include a comparison in which subjects repeat the same activity with Adobe Photoshop, a commonly-used digital graphics editing software.

We start with a short (5 minutes) introduction to provide some background. Using only the mountain (山) character, one of the authors demonstrated how one can vary the writing mechanics in CalliPaint to obtain dramatically different appearances (as in Figure 5.) This particular character is chosen because it is easy to write, and because mountains are commonly-occurring objects popularly associated with Chinese landscape painting. After the introduction, the subjects were given 10 minutes to experiment with the system on their own. To evaluate their ability to use the different controls, they were then shown a sample painting that had been developed on CalliPaint and asked to duplicate it as closely as possible, within a time limit of 30 minutes. Upon completion, the subjects were asked to repeat the same task within the same time limit on Adobe Photoshop. To ensure fairness, subjects that did not have prior experience with Photoshop were given 30 minutes' training and practice before starting the task.

During the pre-experiment practice session, we noticed that most of the subjects tried to recall the mapping rules by vocalizing the rules to themselves before they wrote. The majority were able to remember the rules correctly. In the first few attempts, the subjects usually failed to get the effects they wanted because they were not able to control the writing pressure and speed properly. These problems were usually easily solved by repeatedly adjusting the writing pressure or speed until they achieved the effect they desired. 70% of the subjects thought that pressure was easier to control than speed, but the average scores were similar – the pressure dimension got a score of 3.9, as compared to the speed

(a) Original Picture (CalliPaint expert) | Copies made with CalliPaint. Left (b): user with some art training; right (c): novice user. | Copies made with Photoshop. Left (d): expert user; right (e): novice user.

Figure 8. Artwork created in Stage 2 of Guided / Supervised Experiment - Evaluation of Learnability and Controllability.

dimension's 3.7. The main problem reported with speed is that it is relatively more difficult to maintain a consistent speed of writing across multiple strokes within the same character.

Figure 8 shows the artwork generated during this stage of the experiment. The sample artwork Figure 8(a) was deliberately made moderately complex, with nine mountains, four trees, two water elements, one moon, one stone and one piece of land in the scene. Despite this being their first attempt, the experiment subjects performed well on CalliPaint, with all of the subjects completing the task within the allotted time. The creator of Figure 8(b) had some prior art training, while the creator of Figure 8(c) was a novice both at calligraphy and drawing. It can be seen that the composition of the copies is basically the same as the sample except for a few deviations in the placement and size of certain objects. Both subjects tried to copy the template as much as they could except that the creator of Figure 8(b) explicitly changed the arrangement of the group of mountains in the upper part of the scene to make the painting look more "balanced".

To objectively evaluate the subjects' ability to control the system, we compare each object in the subject's artwork with its counterpart from the original. If the level of detail of the objects is the same, it means that the subject has successfully used writing pressure to control the graphical effect of the object. Similarly, the accuracy of speed control is calculated based on comparing the sharpness of the corresponding objects.

Our experiment subjects achieved an average pressure control accuracy of 77% and an average speed control accuracy of 72%. This is an impressive performance, considering that the subjects had only 30 minutes' practice before the task. We believe that the performance would have been better, had the subjects been allowed more time for practice.

Figure 8(d) and Figure 8(e) are created with Adobe Photoshop. Figure 8(d) was generated in 28 minutes by a subject who happened to be a Photoshop expert, and unsurprisingly, the composition closely matches the original. Users who had experience with Photoshop predictably felt that Photoshop was more efficient, but the others felt that CalliPaint was easier to use. Figure 8(e) was produced by one such novice user, who ran out of time and was not able to finish the task within the allotted time. Interestingly, in post experiment surveys, 40% of the subjects, including some of the Photoshop users, stated that they found it more enjoyable to use a brush to generate paintings, as compared to using a mouse and clicking on buttons. They also felt that working on Photoshop, as compared with CalliPaint, was more technical and mechanical. Finally, all subjects, including the Photoshop experts, reported that comparatively, using painting software requires more practice and dexterity, as compared to CalliPaint's low entry barrier.

5.1.3 Stage 3: Functionality and Potential for Art Creation

The third stage of the experiment evaluates CalliPaint on its functionality and its potential as a tool to create realistic, aesthetically pleasing artwork. In other words, we are interested in seeing whether CalliPaint is able to support the generation of a complex scene from a genuine Chinese landscape painting.

In this experiment, the subjects were presented with a real Chinese landscape painting produced using traditional ink-and-brush methods. The subjects were then asked to duplicate the painting as closely as they could within 35-40 minutes.

Figure 9. Artwork created in Stage 3 of Guided / Supervised Experiment -- Evaluation of Functionality. While the style and some of the details of the objects differ from the original[2], the composition and the arrangement are the same.

Figure 9 shows some representative examples of the experiment subjects' results[2]. It can be seen that though the style and some of the details of the objects in the scene differ from the original artwork, the composition and arrangement of the objects in the copied paintings are quite similar. Some of the subjects added their own refinements to the paintings. For example, one of the subjects added birds to the scene. Other subjects added boats, water, bamboo, etc.

Upon the completion of the task, they were asked to rate the attractiveness of their artwork. Most of the subjects were happy with their own work, giving it a rating of 4.0.

5.1.4 Stage 4: Support for Artistic Creation

Compared with the other tasks, creating an original Chinese landscape painting was perceived to be a big challenge, especially to the subjects with little art background. The objective of the last experiment is to observe the degree to which CalliPaint is able to support users' creativity. The experiment subjects were asked to create a painting of their own – no further instructions were provided – and were allowed to take as long as they wished to complete the task.

---

[2] The originals are not reproduced in this paper. Links to the original artworks at:
http://www.nipic.com/show/1759204.html
http://www.taopic.com/tuku/201101/22400.html

Figure 10. Artwork created in Stage 4 of Guided / Supervised Experiment – Support for Artistic Creation. All pieces were created after ~1.5 hrs of training. (a) "Mid-Autumn Night", (b) "An Idyllic Life", (c) "In the Sunset" and (d) "On the way to visit a friend".

Figure 10 shows a selection of the artwork, and Table 6 shows the objects they contained and the control functions that were deployed in their creation. It can be seen that there is significant complexity (multiple objects and control functions) and substantial diversity between the pieces. Even though the component objects are all drawn from the same image dictionary, the variation in size and the graphical effects that are supported by CalliPaint allows users to create scenes that are quite dissimilar.

A closer inspection reveals some interesting artistic concepts incorporated by the experiment subjects. The subjects had a sense of how the scene of the painting should be composed to highlight the embedded story. This is worth noting especially as the majority of the subjects did not have prior training in art and drawing, and none of them had experience specifically with Chinese landscape painting. For example, the scene *"Mid-autumn night"* includes a sitting person in the moon, depicting the Moon Goddess from Chinese mythology. *"An idyllic life"* includes a long, rugged path between two mountain ranges and a person travelling to a distant mountain, evoking a feeling of mystery – a mysterious hermit who in a mountain far removed from the crowd. *"On the way to visit a friend"* uses a bridge separating two houses to indicate a journey that must be undertaken in the process. *"In the sunset"* incorporates a composition of large mountains in the distance and a small human figure in the foreground to create a feeling of vast space and to evoke a sense of calm over the whole scene.

Table 5. Third-party expert assessments on artwork created in Stage 4 of Guided / Supervised Experiment.

	Average score (from 1: disagree to 5: agree)
The painting is in the Chinese style.	5
The composition is good.	3.3
The painting is interesting / creative.	3.9
The overall effect is pleasing.	3.7

Most of the experiment subjects consciously used the control functions to produce their preferred graphical effect for the objects in the scene. For example, when creating *"Mid-autumn night"*, the subject wanted a group of mountains that were highly detailed with sharp features. Her explanation was that she wanted the mountains to *"look close"* and to be imposing and grand, almost as if the mountain was right on top of the viewer. The corresponding character (山, mountain) was written slowly and deliberately with a very firm hand. Similarly, to generate the three identical trees in the right of the foreground, the user deliberately tried to be consistent with the pressure and speed of writing, repeating the process until the desired effect was achieved.

Table 6. Evaluation of Support for Creativity. Objects and control functions that were used in the creation of the artwork pieces shown in Figure 10.

Painting	Objects contained	Control functions
Mid-autumn night	Moon, cloud, human, mountain, tree, land, boat, bridge, bamboo, house, stone.	Pressure, speed
An idyllic life	Moon, mountain, land, bamboo, tree, house, boat, bridge, stone, human	Speed
In the sunset	Sun, land, tree, willow, human, house, bird	Pressure
On the way to a friend's house	Sun, cloud, mountain, land, bamboo, pine tree, human, tree, house, bridge	Pressure, speed

The subjects gave CalliPaint an average score of 4.4 on its effectiveness in facilitating creativity. They were also mostly satisfied with their artwork and gave it an average rating of 3.7.

Table 5 shows the evaluations of the expert judges, who were asked to evaluate the paintings from multiple dimensions. The judges fully agreed that the artwork resembles Chinese-style paintings, and they also felt that the paintings were interesting and creative, with good composition. One judge commented that the paintings clearly tell different stories and leaves room for the viewers to imagine the relationship between the objects. Another judge said that the composition is not bad, but the spatial relationship between the objects (in particular the sun and moon) could have been better presented. Overall, however, they were pleased with the aesthetics of the artwork.

5.1.5 Summary of Guided Experiment

The subjects' overall impression of CalliPaint was unanimously positive. All found the experience enjoyable. In the post-experiment feedback assessment, the subjects rated the overall experience an average of 3.9. The interface and the tool were found intuitive and the functions interesting and easy to use. Specifically, the effectiveness of the control functions was noted by the experiment subjects – most (70%) of them felt that the control functions was the most useful feature of CalliPaint, since it allowed them to achieve a fine-grained control over the graphical effects intuitively through controlling their writing style and mechanics. Many experiment subjects wanted to continue using the system after the experiment was over, and some bystanders asked if they could try to create their own artwork.

It is worth noting that even though all of our experiment subjects could write Chinese, none of them had previous expertise in Chinese landscape painting, a complex art form that takes years to master; and only a few of them had limited experience in Chinese calligraphy. The amount of practice that they were given prior to creating their own artwork in the final task of the experiment was also limited (the average time that each person spent on the previous stages was about 1-1.5 hours). However, all of our subjects were able to create an attractive artwork using the system. Indeed, during the creativity experiment, we observed that many of the subjects were particular about aspects such as composition of the scene and placement of the objects – in fact, they were behaving as if they were familiar with the primary techniques that are often deployed in visual art creation. The artwork that they created is also realistic and complex.

5.2 Experiment 2: CalliPaint in an Unguided / Unsupervised Environment

In contrast to the multistage experiment, which demonstrates that CalliPaint can be successfully used by novices with a minimum of training and guidance, the objective of the second experiment is to ascertain the potential of CalliPaint to be used by people without any training or guidance at all.

For this experiment, we exhibited the system in a high-traffic student activity room in a local university for one week, during which it was available to numerous undergraduates and graduate students. No training or help was given except for a short introductory video playing in a loop on an accompanying display, a printout of the characters contained in the dictionary with the correct stroke order for each character, and a note stating the purpose of this display, informing users that their activities would be recorded for research, and inviting the reader to try it out.

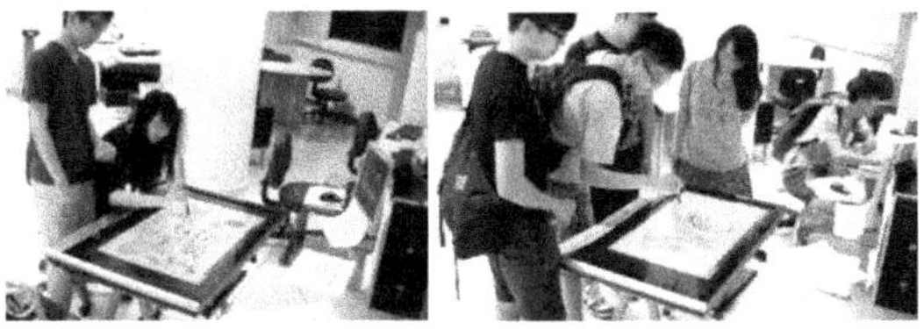

Figure 11. Scenes from the unguided experiment. Most users were able to learn the system controls on their own or through collaboration with other users.

Reviews of the video recordings (Figure 11) give us insight into the behavior of casual passers-by in interacting with CalliPaint. In total, 72 people tried the system. As expected, most (47) just gave it a try and did not seriously spend time learning it. However, a significant number (17) did give the system a serious attempt, spending up to 30 minutes figuring out the controls and comparing their work with others. In addition, 8 made serious effort to learning the system, spending upwards of an hour on creating and perfecting their artwork.

Figure 12. Artwork created with CalliPaint in the open experiment. Figure (a) was created by a student who spent around half an hour on the drawing. Figure (b) was created by a curious bypasser in less than 10 minutes.

This experiment shows that CalliPaint can be learned even without explicit training, by casual passers-by, and through experimentation and trial and error. Similarly to the guided experiments, we noted that in most of the cases where the user had difficulty with the system, the problems were usually caused by incorrect writing practices (e.g. wrong stroke sequence). In quite a few instances, students collaborated in figuring out the controls or "debugging" each other's mistakes.

Figure 12 shows two samples generated during the open experiment. The level of control – and hence the physical appearance of the individual objects – is definitely inferior to those generated during the evaluation experiment, but the composition of the scene is still attractive and interesting. This is especially significant given that the authors were simply casual passers-by who had little motivation except innate curiosity. It suggests that CalliPaint is learnable and usable, and is able to facilitate creative self-expression even in untrained individuals.

Table 7. Third-party expert assessments on artwork created during the Unguided / Unsupervised Experiment.

	Average score (from 1: disagree to 5: agree)
The painting is in the Chinese style.	4.0
The composition is good.	2.5
The painting is interesting / creative.	2.25
The overall effect is pleasing.	2.25

Table 7 presents the evaluations from our expert judges on the artwork created during the unguided experiment. As expected, the judges consider these paintings to be less attractive than the ones created in the guided experiment. On the other hand, it is encouraging that the judges still consider the composition of the paintings to be acceptable, and the style to be consistent with that of Chinese landscape paintings.

5.3 Overall Evaluation

Our experiments have demonstrated the effectiveness of the CalliPaint system as a creativity-facilitating tool for the generation of Chinese landscape-style artwork. It provides enough flexibility and functionality to facilitate the creation of diverse and attractive art pieces, enough control to allow subtle variations in the graphical effects, and is easy to use even by untrained novices.

We therefore believe that one of the biggest contributions of our system is to bring these complex art forms within reach of the novice or casual observer. Indeed, some of our experiment subjects opined that this was the most useful feature – the general applicability of CalliPaint, which enables people to create attractive Chinese landscape art without extensive training.

6. CONCLUSION AND FUTURE WORK

We have presented CalliPaint, a Kinect-based novel digital system that generates Chinese ink painting from Chinese calligraphy. Images corresponding to the written characters are generated through a cross-modal mapping between the two art forms on both semantic level and mechanical level. Experimental evaluation with real users proved the intuitiveness, controllability, usability and potential to support creativity of our system.

This work studies Chinese as an example of a logographic language, where a character/grapheme may represent an object (pictographic), an idea (ideographic), or a sound (phonetic). There are other examples, e.g., hieroglyphs. Here we focus on how one specific culture (Chinese) makes use of such symbols. In future work, we plan to investigate how our approach can be adapted to other logographic languages and/or related media, and how diverse cultures make use of them. We plan to also develop more sophisticated methods of generating images that capture the style of the characters. Finally, we also plan to further investigate how our approach can be applied to use of graphemes in other contexts such as child education, graphical design, etc.

7. ACKNOWLEDGMENTS
We thank all our evaluation subjects, the design artists and subject experts for their time and suggestions. We also thank the anonymous reviewers and our shepherd for their comments and suggestions. This work is supported in part by grants PolyU 5248/10E and PolyU 5222/13E from the Hong Kong Polytechnic University and the Hong Kong Research Grants Council, respectively.

8. REFERENCES
[1] Barnhart, R., Yang, X., Nie, C., Cahill, J., Lang, S. and Wu, H. 2002. Three Thousand Years of Chinese Painting. *New Haven*, CT: Yale University Press.

[2] Baxter B, Scheib V, Lin MC, Manocha D. 2001. DAB: interactive haptic painting with 3D virtual brushes. In *Proc. of SIGGRAPH'01*, pp 461-468.

[3] Bi X., Moscovich, T., Ramos, G., Balakrishnam, R. and Hinckley, K. 2008. An exploration of pen rolling for pen-based interaction. In *Proc. of UIST'08*, pp 191-200.

[4] Brandl P., Forlines, C., Wigdor, D., Haller, M. and Shen, C. 2008. Combining and measuring the benefits of bimanual pen and direct-touch interaction on horizontal interfaces. *AVI'08*, pp 154-161.

[5] Cao X, Lindley SE, Helmes J, Sellen A. 2010. Telling the whole story: anticipation, inspiration and reputation in a field deployment of TellTable. In *Proc. of CSCW'10*, pp 251-260.

[6] Chu, NS, Tai, CL. 2004. Real-Time Painting with an Expressive Virtual Chinese Brush. *IEEE Comput. Graph. Appl. Mag.*, 24(5): 76-85.

[7] Dolinsky J, Takagi H. 2007. Synthesizing Handwritten Characters Using Naturalness Learning. In *Proc. of ICCC'07*, pp.101-106.

[8] Ebrey, P.B. 2010. The Cambridge Illustrated History of China. *Cambridge*: University Press; 2nd edition.

[9] Guo Q, Kunii, TL. 2003. Nijimi rendering algorithm for creating quality black ink paintings. In *Proc. of CGI'03*, pp 152-159.

[10] Huang, M.X., Tang, W., Lo, K.W.K., Lau, C.K., Ngai, G. and Chan, S. 2012. MelodicBrush: A Novel System for Cross-Modal Digital Art Creation Linking Calligraphy and Music. *DIS'12*, pp 418-427.

[11] Kalal Z, Mikolajczyk K, and Matas J. 2010. Face-TLD: Tracking-Learning-Detection Applied to Faces. In *Proc. of ICIP'10*, pp 3789-3792.

[12] Kang L, Chien HY. 2010. Hé: Calligraphy as a Musical Interface. In *Proc. of NIME'12*, pp 352-355.

[13] Kang L, Gu T, Gay G. 2013. Harmonic paper. In *CHI EA'13*, pp 763-768.

[14] Kazi, R.H., Chua, K.C. 2011.SandCanvas: a multi-touch art medium inspired by sand animation. In *Proc. of CHI'11*, pp 1283-1292.

[15] Kazi, R.H., Igarashi, R., Zhao, S. and Davis, R. 2012. Vignette: interactive texture design and manipulation with freeform gestures for pen-and-ink illustration. In *Proc. of CHI'12*, pp 1727-1736.

[16] Knorig, A., Muller, B., Wettach, R. 2007. Articulated paint: musical expression for non-musicians. In *Proc. of NIME'07*, pp 384-385.

[17] Jo, K. 2008. DrawSound: a drawing instrument for sound performance. In *Proc. of TEI'08*, pp 59-62.

[18] Lopes P, Mendes D, Araújo B, Jorge JA. 2011. Combining bimanual manipulation and pen-based input for 3D modelling. In *Proc. of SBIM'11*, pp 15-22.

[19] Lu, F., Tian, F., Jiang, Y., Cao, X., Luo, W., Li, G., Zhang, X., Dai, G. and Wang, H. 2011. ShadowStory: creative and collaborative digital storytelling inspired by cultural heritage. In *Proc. of CHI'11*, pp 1919-1928.

[20] Maurer D, Pathman T, Mondloch CJ. 2006. The shape of boubas: Sound-shape correspondences in toddlers and adults. *Developmental Science*, 9(3): 316-322.

[21] Mi, XF, Tang M, Dong JX. 2004. Droplet: a virtual brush model to simulate Chinese calligraphy and painting. J. *Computing Science Technologies* 19(3): 393–404.

[22] Otsuki, M., Sugihara, K., Kimura, A., Shibata, F., and Tamura, H. 2010. MAI painting brush: an interactive device that realizes the feeling of real painting. In *Proc. of UIST'10*, pp 97-100.

[23] Raffle H, Vaucelle, C., Wang, R., Ishii, H. 2007. Jabberstamp: embedding sound and voice in traditional drawings. In *Proc. of IDC'07*, pp 137-144.

[24] Ramachandran VS, Hubbard EM. 2001. Synaesthesia: A window into perception, thought and language. *Journal of Consciousness Studies*, vol. 8, pp 3–34.

[25] Ryokai K, Marti S, Ishii H. 2004. I/O brush: drawing with everyday objects as ink. In *Proc. of CHI'04*, pp 303–310.

[26] Schkolne S. 2002. Drawing with the Hand in Free Space: Creating 3D Shapes with Gesture in a Semi-Immersive Environment. *Leonardo*, 35(4): 371-375.

[27] Shen IF, Ma KL, Stompel A. 2003. A new form of traditional art - visual simulation of Chinese Shadow play. In *SIGGRAPH'03 Sketches & Applications, pp 1-1.*

[28] Song, H., Benko, H., Guimbretière, F., Izadi, S., Cao, X. and Hinckley, K. 2011. Grips and gestures on a multi-touch pen. In *Proc. of CHI'11*, pp 1323-1332.

[29] Strassmann S. 1986. Hairy brush. In: *Proc. of SIGGRAPH'86*, pp 225-232.

[30] Tosa, N., Matsuoka, S., Ellis, B., Ueda, H., Nakatsu, R. 2005. Cultural Computing with Context Aware Application: ZENetic Computer. In *Proc. of ICEC'05*, pp 13-23.

[31] Vandoren, P., Claesen, L., Van Laerhoven, T., Taelman, J., Raymaekers, C., Flerackers, E., and Van Reeth, F. 2009. FluidPaint: an interactive digital painting system using real wet brushes. In *Proc. of ITS'09*, pp 53-56.

[32] Wanderley MM. and Depalle P. 2004. Gestural control of sound synthesis. In *Proc. IEEE 2004*, 92(4): 632- 644.

[33] Wang L, Zhang C, Yang R, Zhang C. 2010. Tofcut: towards robust real-time foreground extraction using a time-of-flight camera. In *P Proc. of DPVT'10.*

[34] Wilson AD. 2010. Using a depth camera as a touch sensor. In: *Proc. of ITS'10*, pp 69-72.

[35] Wong HTF and Ip HH. 2000. Virtual brush: a model-based synthesis of Chinese calligraphy. *Computers & Graphics*, 24(1): 99-113.

[36] Xin Y, Bi X and Ren X. 2011. Acquiring and pointing: an empirical study of pen-tilt-based interaction. *In Proc. of CHI'11*, pp 849-858.

[37] Xu, S., Jiang, H., Lau, F.C.M. and Pan, Y. 2007. An Intelligent system for Chinese Calligraphy. In *Proc. of AAAI'07*, pp 1578-1583.

[38] Xu S, Lau, FCM, Xu C, Pan Y. 2005. Virtual hairy brush for digital painting and calligraphy. *Science in China*, Series F: Information Science (Springer), 48(3): 285–303.

[39] Yu JH, Luo GM, Peng QS. 2003 Image-based synthesis of Chinese landscape painting, *Journal of Computer Science and Technology*, vol. 18, pp. 22-28.

[40] Zhu Y, Li C, Shen, IF. 2004. A new style of ancient culture: Animated Chinese Dunhuang murals. In *SIGGRAPH'04* pp 130.

Gibber: Abstractions for Creative Multimedia Programming

Charles Roberts, Matthew Wright, JoAnn Kuchera-Morin, Tobias Höllerer
Media Arts & Technology Program, University of California at Santa Barbara
charlie@charlie-roberts.com, {matt,jkm}@create.ucsb.edu, holl@cs.ucsb.edu

ABSTRACT

We describe design decisions informing the development of *Gibber*, an audiovisual programming environment for the browser. Our design comprises a consistent notation across modalities in addition to high-level abstractions affording intuitive declarations of multimodal mappings, unified timing constructs, and rapid, iterative reinvocations of constructors while preserving the state of audio and visual graphs.

We discuss the features of our environment and the abstractions that enable them. We close by describing use cases, including live audiovisual performances and computer science education.

Categories and Subject Descriptors

D.2.6 [**Programming Environments**]: Interactive Environments; J.5 [**Arts and Humanities**]: Performing Arts

General Terms

Design, Human Factors

Keywords

Multimodal Programming; Live coding; Audio; Graphics; Web; JavaScript; Creative Coding

1. INTRODUCTION

Creative coding environments have often favored one modality at the expense of others. Popular audio programming environments like ChucK [33] and SuperCollider [14] come with minimal or no graphics capabilities out of the box, while the example audio code for Processing [22], one of the most popular environments for teaching programming to visual artists, is buried in nested submenus. In some cases, the design of a domain-specific language (DSL) specific to one modality potentially affects its ability to be adapted to others. The syntax of the ChucK language, for example, contains abstractions affording terse graph formation, but in a way that is arguably specific to audio programming. Researchers have argued in favor of using DSLs for teaching creative coding [18, 33], as they enable abstractions affording creative expressivity to be encoded within language syntax. However, we argue that multimodal content creation often requires the use of general-purpose programming languages to accommodate the needs of differing representations. General-purpose languages for creative coding also provide an opportunity to use and teach syntax and other elements that, assuming a given language has wide adoption, transfer to other environments.

We seek to bring the expressivity often found in domain-specific languages for creative coding to a general-purpose programming language through the use of high-level abstractions. We address this challenge in the design of an audiovisual, creative coding environment for the browser, *Gibber* [25]. In this paper, we begin by discussing the motivation and philosophy behind Gibber and other creative coding environments that inform Gibber's design. We then provide an overview of Gibber's multimedia affordances and examine the notation used by Gibber end-users, as the notation is intricately tied to the abstractions that are a focus of our research. After discussing three abstractions for creative coding that we have found particularly rewarding, we conclude with a description of selected audiovisual performances that were realized with Gibber and discuss end-user feedback gathered about the environment.

MM'14, November 03 - 07 2014, Orlando, FL, USA.

ACM 978-1-4503-3063-3/14/11 $15.00.
http://dx.doi.org/10.1145/2647868.2654949.

2. MOTIVATION AND AUDIENCE

Gibber began its development as an environment for *live coding* performance, a practice discussed further in Section 3. As its development continued, the educational potential of a browser-based programming environment became appealing to us, and we began to target both performers and beginning programmers as our audience. In particular, Gibber is appropriate for people interested in learning JavaScript who also have interest in audiovisual programming. The youngest group of users we know of to program with Gibber started at age eleven; it has also been used to teach at the university level. With this audience in mind, there were four principles that motivated Gibber's development:

Capitalize on Browser Features and Ubiquity

Due to its ubiquity and recent additions to its feature set, the web browser provides an accessible vehicle for disseminating audiovisual works and the tools to create them. Gibber takes advantage of this ubiquity, providing a programming environment usable by anyone running a modern web browser.

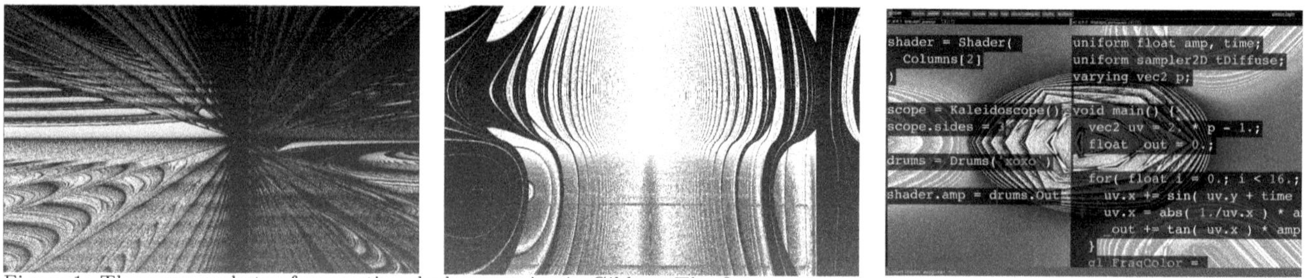

Figure 1: Three screenshots of generative shaders running in Gibber. The first two images show graphical output while the final image also depicts overlaid JavaScript and GLSL editors, which can be hidden and revealed via keystroke macros.

No installation of software is required, removing an immediate barrier to entry: anyone with the URL of Gibber's homepage can immediately begin using it. The browser offers a variety of affordances for creative practice, including 3D graphics, realtime audio synthesis, realtime audio and video input, networked communications, and support for touch, mouse, and keyboard interactions; Gibber takes advantage of all of these. Gibber also encourages social aspects of content production in the browser by providing a centralized database for publishing and browsing audiovisual projects and a variety of tools for realtime collaboration.

Use JavaScript, not a Domain-Specific Language
JavaScript was selected as the end-user programming language in Gibber due to its first-class status in the browser as well as its use as a scripting language in commercial, multimedia applications such as Max/MSP[1], Apple's Logic Pro[2], various Adobe applications including Photoshop, Illustrator, and Flash[3], and game engines such as Unity[4] and DX Studio[5]. JavaScript's dynamic language features and its ability to meld functional and object-oriented programming techniques make it particularly well suited to exploratory creative practice. It has also been identified as an excellent language for introducing computer science students to programming [23].

One important constraint when designing Gibber was to avoid requiring pre-processing of end-user code to make it valid for execution by the JavaScript runtime. That is, all code written by Gibber end-users must be valid JavaScript. By avoiding application-specific language extensions, we increase the likelihood that syntax and other lessons learned while programming in Gibber will transfer to other environments with a JavaScript API. In contrast, some of the knowledge gained while using domain-specific languages (at minimum, a knowledge of syntax) is inevitably lost when users attempt to transfer it to domains employing different languages. Our concern regarding knowledge transfer also drove our decision to use a textual programming language rather than a visual one, as visual programming languages are often application specific.

Support Audio, Visual and Interactive Programming
Gibber emphasizes equal treatment of audio, visual, and interactive modalities, and was designed so that users can easily connect inputs and outputs across modalities without requiring special code considerations. The API for each modality is designed with a low threshold for beginning programmers and a high ceiling for users with more experience. For example, the graphics subsystem affords placing a 3D geometry on the screen with a single function call (example: `Cube()`) but also enables advanced users to live code vertex and fragment shaders. Similarly, the audio subsystem affords the creation and playback of a drum loop in a single function call (example: `Drums('xoxo')`) but also enables advanced users to perform audio-rate modulation of sample-accurate scheduling.

Provide an Expressive Notation
Given the motivations and constraints listed above, one resulting challenge was to design a consistent, expressive notation that lends itself to creative practice; the result is discussed in Section 5 and Section 6.

3. RELATED WORK

We limit our discussion here to representative *creative coding environments* that, in contrast to visual programming environments, use text editing as the primary coding mechanism. We use the term *creative coding*, widely used colloquially, to discuss programming practice geared towards artistic content production; it has also been found effective in computer science education [9]. The software used for creative coding often includes an integrated development environment, libraries for generating audiovisual output, and, in many cases, a domain-specific language designed to ease creative exploration.

One of the first and most successful languages for creative coding was *Logo* [20]; at current count, over two-hundred and fifty Logo implementations have been authored [5]. Originally created as a Lisp dialect to control the movements of a drawing robot, Logo became famous in the 1980s after it was altered to create graphics on computer monitors and subsequently taught around the world. Research on Logo and creative coding flourished at MIT, where Seymour Papert, one of the original creators of Logo, was a professor. During the 1990s the creative coding environment *Design By Numbers* (DBN) [11] was developed by John Maeda and his Aesthetics and Computation Group at MIT. DBN moved away from the concept of the turtle to provide a new, domain-specific language for creating non-interactive visual artworks. Two of Maeda's students, Casey Reas and Ben Fry, drew inspiration from using DBN to teach and designed their own creative coding environment, *Processing*, which is now widely used and taught. Processing sketches are written in Java;

[1]http://cycling74.com/products/max/
[2]http://www.apple.com/logic-pro/
[3]https://www.adobe.com/creativecloud.html
[4]http://unity3d.com
[5]http://www.dxstudio.com/

as a result its output is fairly cross-platform and can be embedded in web pages as Java applets. Java applets do not, however, run in most mobile operating systems. Developer John Resig solved this problem by porting the main Processing classes to JavaScript in a version called *Processing.js* [24]. In a clever twist, he also wrote a pre-processor that takes Processing programs written in Java as input and compiles them to JavaScript. This enables many of the demos and examples available in the Processing ecosystem to be compiled and subsequently run in the browser without any modification to the original Java source code. However, many important library extensions for Processing have not been ported to Processing.js; as one example, the audio functionality provided by the *minim* [19] library is not available at the time of this writing. Work has begun on *p5.js*[6], a port of Processing that, unlike Processing.js, uses JavaScript as the end-user programming language.

The audio community has also been active in the development of creative coding environments; much of this activity stems from the performance practice known as *live coding*, where works of audiovisual art are programmed in front of audiences while the programmer-performer's code is projected for audience members to see and potentially follow [6, 13]. Live coding was one of the motivations for the first iteration of Gibber, and Gibber has since drawn inspiration from a number of environments and languages that enable such performances. *SuperCollider* [14] is one popular audio programming environment with a language based on ideas from Smalltalk and functional programming. The Supercollider language is coupled to a flexible sound synthesis server that serves as the basis for a number of live coding environments, most notably *ixi lang* [12] and *Overtone* [4]. The proxy system described in Section 6.3 was heavily inspired by techniques pioneered in SuperCollider. ChucK [33], another popular live coding system for audio, provides a domain-specific language catered towards audio graph construction, concurrency, and sample-accurate scheduling.

None of these live coding environments provide significant built-in graphics capabilities, though SuperCollider's basic 2D drawing API can be extended with OpenGL functionality via the SCGraph library [2] and Overtone is designed to interoperate with a number of graphics applications [3, 1]. LuaAV [32] and Extempore [30] are creative coding platforms that include both audio and visual affordances. LuaAV uses the Lua general-purpose language and Extempore a uses a combination of Scheme and the custom language *xtlang*. Although Gibber is similar in that it uses a general-purpose language (in this case JavaScript), we argue that our research enables end-users to create audiovisual works at a higher level of abstraction, easing the burdens of multimodal programming for beginning creative coders. The abstractions also afford a terseness to Gibber programming that makes it well-suited for live coding performances, where language verbosity is one factor that directly impacts the potential for virtuosity. Almost the entirety of the Gibber environment, from the end-user language to the server to the 2D and 3D graphics APIs, is programmed in JavaScript[7]; this means that users can modify and augment any part of the environment within the constraints of the browser.

[6]http://p5js.org/

[7]The one exception to this is fragment and vertex shaders, which are programmed in GLSL.

Alex McLean's *Tidal* language for live coding pattern represents a middle road between general-purpose and domain-specific languages [17]. Tidal is a DSL that is used within Haskell to define patterns controlling sound synthesis. When Tidal syntax is parsed each token becomes a Haskell function. Although it is possible to instead create similar patterns solely using Haskell, McLean believes the extra verbosity required would not lend itself to live coding performance practice [16]. Inspired by the sequencing capabilities of Tidal, we are currently exploring strategies using JavaScript to define and manipulate patterns[8].

Fluxus [10] is a live coding environment by David Griffiths that uses Scheme to define and manipulate 3D scenes made with OpenGL. It also comes with an extension named Fluxa that provides basic audio synthesis capabilities. In comparison with Gibber, Fluxus has impressively superior 3D graphics functionality, but does not include 2D graphics or shader programming capabilities.

Other live coding environments run in the browser, however, most use DSLs instead of JavaScript for their end-user programming language. One such example is *Livecodelab* [7], which primarily provides capabilities for controlling and sequencing 3D graphics and shaders. The authors of Livecodelab began with JavaScript as the end-user language, moving to CoffeeScript (an expressive language that compiles to JavaScript) and finally to developing their own custom DSL. Thus, instead of seeking greater expressivity through abstraction, Livecodelab's developers focused on designing a language customized to their needs. Like Gibber, *Lich.js* [15] provides both audio and graphics programming in the browser, and is notable for its flexibility in creating and customizing musical patterns. Similar to the authors of Livecodelab, the author of Lich.js designed a Haskell-inspired DSL as its end-user programming language, creating a compiler that converts the end-user code to JavaScript for execution.

4. AN OVERVIEW OF GIBBER

Gibber is a creative coding environment that runs in most modern web browsers, including Chrome, Safari, and Firefox. Gibber programs (aka *giblets*) are created and edited at runtime. Users enter code and dynamically evaluate code fragments with simple keystroke macros. Execution of selected code can optionally be delayed until the beginning of the next musical measure to ensure that musical sequences created at different moments in time are rhythmically synchronized with sample-accurate precision.

The graphics engine provides 2D and 3D APIs and also a variety of pre-built generative and post-processing shaders. The post-processing shaders work in both 2D and 3D giblets; we accomplish this in 2D by drawing to a canvas which is subsequently used to texture a full-screen OpenGL quad. The ease of combining 2D drawing with post-processing shaders is relatively unique among creative coding environments; these effects can add visual complexity and interest to simple 2D forms that beginning programmers may produce. Gibber also provides the capability to live-code fragment and vertex shaders. Its editing window can be divided into multiple columns; in a live shader editing session there is typically one column of JavaScript and one or two columns

[8]For a demo of JavaScript patterns in Gibber see: http://gibber.mat.ucsb.edu/?p=charlie/pattern_demo

of GLSL. Shaders can be edited and recompiled with the same keystroke macros used to execute JavaScript; Gibber notes the column that is currently focused when keystroke events are triggered and executes the macro appropriate to the language being edited. Abstractions are also provided to easily pass information from the JavaScript runtime to the GLSL environment as uniforms; a new uniform can be defined and mapped in a single line of JavaScript. Fig. 1 shows multi-column shader programming.

Gibber's audio capabilities include low-level elements such as oscillators and filters, as well as higher-level, aggregate instruments designed to immediately provide an interesting sonic palette for musical performance and composition. These instruments include an emulation of a classic analog drum machine, a two-operator FM synthesizer, a three-oscillator monosynth, a sampler, and many other options. A variety of audio effects are also included along with flexible mechanisms for routing and defining audio graphs.

Graphics and audio can be synchronized with relative ease in Gibber. Scheduling of events is sample-accurate and can be performed using various measures of time including audio samples, milliseconds, seconds, or musical beats. Gibber's support for live coding dance music includes a visual metronome in the upper hand corner that defaults to 4/4 time but can be set to other meters or turned off entirely.

Gibber provides interactive control of audiovisual objects by generating control signals from the cursor position in the browser window or from keystroke events. A companion GUI library, *Interface.js*, is included in Gibber to support the creation of more elaborate user interfaces [26, 27].

Maximizing the social potential of content creation in the browser is an important consideration in Gibber's design. Users can publish giblets to a centralized database and disseminate associated URLs to friends and colleagues who might want to view their work. When users publish giblets they can tag them with metadata and provide a description; a browser is provided that allows users to easily search the database and view each giblet's associated metadata. Gibber's built-in chat system enables users to easily ask questions of one another and is extended with a simple mechanism for entering into collaborative editing sessions. Clicking on another user's name in the chat window and selecting a code fragment to share is all that is required to begin a joint programming session, or, potentially, a joint networked performance.

5. NOTATION DESIGN

We designed Gibber's notation to provide a consistent end-user programming experience across modalities; it is an integral part of the abstractions described in this paper. It contains some debatable design decisions; each was considered carefully in the context of creative coding and we believe the results well serve the needs of creative coding community. Important aspects of the notation include:

- *Abuse of Global Namespace* - The majority of constructors in Gibber are typically invoked in the global namespace. This makes calls to constructors extremely terse and simple, and avoids any required initial discussion of namespaces with beginning programmers. Gibber includes a simple module system for publishing and using JavaScript extensions to its environment. As users advance in skill and want to customize their programming experience they can learn about and employ namespaces in the design of their own extensions.

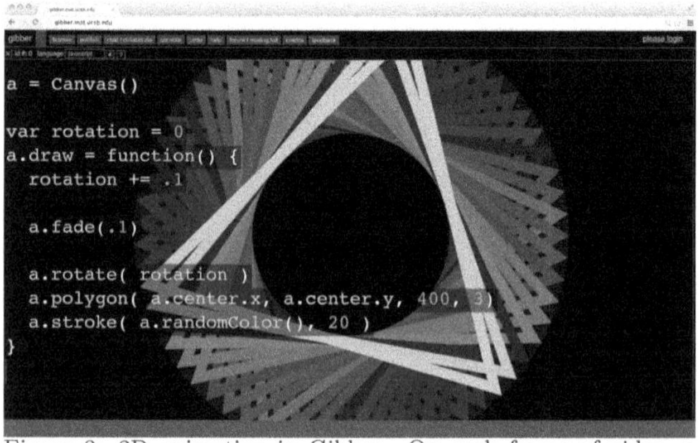

Figure 2: 2D animation in Gibber. On each frame of video, a polygon is drawn with a random color while previous output is faded by ten percent.

- *Constructor Syntax* - Gibber provides three different methods of passing arguments to object constructors. The first is an ordered list of comma-separated arguments, in a notation similar to C++ or Java. The second is an unordered dictionary of key/value pairs to assign to the generated object as properties. In contrast to a comma-separated list this shows exactly which properties are being set on the new object, which is useful for programmers, students, and potentially audience members. The third method is to pass a string naming a constructor *preset* that contains a set of predefined property values, along with an optional dictionary to selectively override aspects of the preset.

- *Capitalization* - The name of any function that returns an object, whether or not it would traditionally be referred to as a constructor, is capitalized. This allows for disambiguation of names that might return different values. For example, `rndf()` returns a single random number, whereas `Rndf()` (useful for sequencing) returns a function that in turn returns a random number. Capitalizing property names of Gibber objects triggers the mapping abstractions discussed in Sec 6.2 by implicitly creating an object that handles the complexities of multi-rate signal mapping.

- *Cascading method calls* - Many calls to object methods in Gibber return the object itself. This allows commands to easily be chained together. In practice, this is often used after calling constructors to customize the resulting object with effects or temporal sequencing.

A short example of the resulting notation, in which the rotation of 3D object is tied the output envelope of a distorted synth line, is given below:

```
mySynth = Synth({ attack:ms(1), decay:ms(200) })
  .note.seq( ['c4','g4'], 1/4 )
  .fx.add( Distortion() )

myCube = Cube()
myCube.rotation.x = mySynth.Out
```

6. ABSTRACTIONS FOR MULTIMEDIA PROGRAMMING

Gibber provides several programming abstractions that simplify exploratory programming practice and multimodal authoring.

6.1 Time, Scheduling, and Rhythm

6.1.1 Rhythmic Notation

Initially, all time values in Gibber were measured in audio samples. To indicate a rhythmic duration, variables preceded by underscores were used that stored the number of samples for particular metric subdivisions. For example, `_4` equaled the number of samples in a quarter note, `_16` equaled the number of samples in a sixteenth note etc. This was reasonably terse except in situations where long durations needed to be specified; for example, ten measures would be notated as the expression `_1 * 10` .

We were subsequently inspired by considering more traditional rhythmic notations, such as using `1/4` to represent a quarter note, `1/8` to represent an eighth note and `1` to represent a whole note. Using this notation the value `10` represents the duration of ten measures of music in 4/4 time. However, problems arise when subsequently considering how to represent temporal values that are not expressed in terms of rhythmic meter. As one example, suppose a user wants to indicate the attack of an amplitude envelope in samples? A very short attack might have a duration of fifty samples, but to define this duration Gibber requires a mechanism to differentiate between fifty samples and fifty measures. Accordingly, we declare a variable, `Gibber.maxMeasures`, that denotes the maximum number of measures that can be indicated as a duration. The default value for this variable is forty-four; this means that any higher duration value is considered to be measured in samples while any lower value is measured in terms of meter. Users can also notate time using the `ms()`, `seconds()` or `measures()` functions, which translate their arguments into samples.

6.1.2 Scheduling

Most scheduling is performed Gibber's audio callback with one exception that will be discussed momentarily. This affords audio-rate modulation of scheduling, a rare feature even in dedicated music authoring environments. It also enables experimental generative techniques where unit generators can be created and added to the audio graph (and subsequently removed if desired) within the bounds of a single execution of the audio callback; another feature that is rare in musical programming environments. The price for this flexibility is the potential for blocking, a problem that is exacerbated by the (predominantly) single-threaded nature of the JavaScript runtime. We have mitigated this problem via the creation of a highly-optimized JavaScript audio library, *Gibberish.js*, discussed in [26].

There are three main ways that events are scheduled in Gibber. The first is through calls to the `future` function, which accepts an arbitrary function and a time duration (measured in samples) to wait before executing it. It is similar to the standard `setTimeout` method included in most JavaScript runtimes, but the `future` method has better temporal accuracy through its reliance on the audio clock. Providing a functional approach to sample-accurate scheduling also affords a live coding idiom known as *temporal recursion* [31], where a function generating audiovisual output is repeatedly executed at various moments of time and iterated to gain complexity.

The second scheduling method is the use of `Seq` (sequencer) objects in Gibber. `Seq` objects are flexible vehicles for changing properties and calling methods on objects at defined temporal intervals; they can also be used to execute anonymous functions. The `Seq` object has a `durations` property that determines when it triggers actions and can either loop its actions indefinitely or perform them a pre-defined number of times. One unique abstraction in Gibber is a shorthand wherein every property and method of Gibber's standard library has its own `seq()` method, allowing properties to be sequenced in an extremely terse manner, as seen when sequencing the `frequency` and `amp` properties in the code example at the end of this section.

The final method is tied to Gibber's graphics engine as opposed to the audio clock. Any graphical object can be assigned an `onupdate()` event handler that is called for every frame of video presented. This enables a more traditional model of graphics scheduling as found in creative coding environments like Processing, while also ensuring that elements such as shader uniforms are only updated at visually salient moments in time.

The code example below illustrates the three methods of scheduling discussed in this section.

```
// use the sequencer included in each property to
// schedule changes in frequency and amplitude
a = Sine()
  .frequency.seq( [440,880], 1/4 )
  .amp.seq( [.5, .25, .1, 0], 1/8 )

// use future to schedule a function call
future( function() { a.fadeOut( 1 ) }, ms(2000) )

// use the onupdate method to increment a property
// in each frame of rendering
b = Cube()
b.onupdate = function() {
  b.rotation += .01
}
```

6.2 Multimodal Mappings

Creating mappings between modalities is complex enough to deter creative coders from regular experimentation. It involves the application of filters and envelope followers (or raw sample-rate conversion), as well as various affine transformations. The goal of Gibber's mapping abstractions is to enable people to think of audiovisual and interactive objects in Gibber the same way audio synthesists think of patching in a modular synthesis environment, where all signals are normalized to a standard control voltage; the result is that anything can freely be patched (mapped) from one object to any other.

Initially presented in the context of designing musical instruments [27], here we expand our discussion of Gibber's mapping abstractions to include mappings between audio and visual modalities. We have created a system and notation that enables, as one example, the rotation of a cube to be continuously controlled by the frequency envelope of a synthesizer using a single line of code:

```
cube.rotation = synth.Frequency
```

The capitalization of Frequency in `synth.Frequency` denotes that we should assign a mapping object providing a continuous translation of the synthesizer's frequency to the rotation of the cube. If **Frequency** were lowercase the instantaneous value of the synth's frequency property when the line of code was executed would be mapped to the rotation; the frequency would not be translated to a range of values appropriate to geometric rotations and would most likely yield non-interesting results. In contrast, when a capitalized property name is mapped to another property two actions occur:

- Gibber compares the timescales of the two properties; here the **synth** is an audio object (operating at 44.1 kHz) while the **cube** is a graphical object (ideally operating at 60 Hz). To accommodate these differing timescales, Gibber places an envelope follower on the frequency of the synth and modulates the cube's rotation with the envelope follower's output. If the mapping was reversed, Gibber would place a low-pass filter on the cube's rotation and assign the result to control the synth's frequency.
- Gibber recognizes that the two properties have different ranges of possible values, and attaches an affine transform to the envelope follower to ensure that it outputs values which make sense as rotations. In effect, it converts a value in the range of 50–3500 Hz to 0–2π radians.

Mapping objects can have different output curves associated with them so that properties such as amplitude can be mapped logarithmically (for perceptual accuracy) while rotation is mapped linearly.

In addition to meta-data on operational timescale and perceptual output curve, every object property in Gibber includes a default output range with the goal of providing intelligent default behaviors for cross-modal mappings. With certain properties we choose a narrower default range than what is capable of being perceived. For example, with oscillator frequency it does not make sense to always map between 20 Hz and the Nyquist limit, even though this is arguably the range of frequencies perceivable. Instead, we choose a narrower range of frequency values, 50Hz to 3500 Hz, which are more commonly used musically. These settings are freely customizable, as even mappings using a narrower frequency range will still generate little effect if the pitch of the unit generator consistently remains low, such as for a bass line. In such cases, users may override the default range specified by the mapping object as follows:

```
cube.rotation.y = synth.Frequency
synth.Frequency.min = 40
synth.Frequency.max = 400
```

Similarly, we can constrain the rotation of our cube to a narrower range than the default of $(0,2\pi)$:

```
cube.rotation.Y.min = 0
cube.rotation.Y.max = Math.PI * .5
```

The properties of mapping objects (such as `min` and `max`) also employ Gibber's mapping abstractions. This enables the creation of complex feedback networks where properties of one object affect another and the amount of the effect is continuously controlled by a property on yet another object.

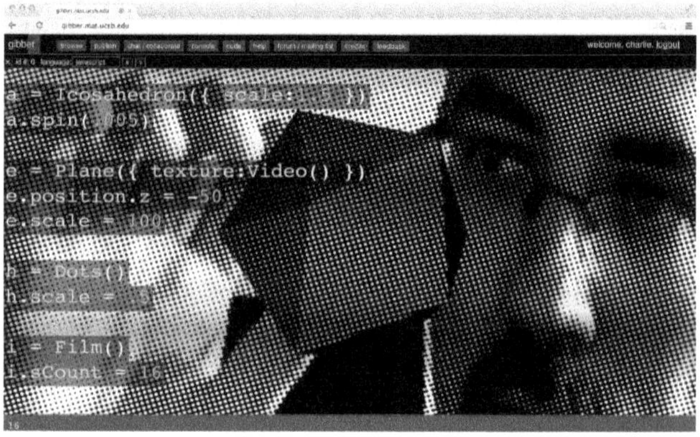

Figure 3: Two shaders post-process a scene consisting of a spinning icosahedron and a background quad textured with a live video feed, made in nine lines of JavaScript.

In the example below, the rotation of a geometry controls the pitch of a drum loop, while the output envelope of a bass line controls the effect of the geometry's rotation on the drum loop's pitch.

```
tetra = Tetrahedron().spin( .005 )
drums = Drums('xoxo')
drums.pitch = tetra.rotation.X
bass = FM('bass').note.seq( [0,7], 1/8 )
drums.Pitch.max = bass.Out
```

End-users can also sequence mapping properties using the sequencing abstraction discussed in Section 6.1.2. The example below randomly changes the `max` property of a mapping every 250ms and inverts it every two seconds.

```
sphere = Sphere({ scale:Mouse.X })
sphere.Scale.max.seq( Rndf(1,3), ms(250) )
sphere.Scale.invert.seq( null, ms(2000) )
```

The abstraction described in this section is similar to that found in UrMus [8], a multimedia programming toolkit for creating mobile applications. Although there are number of notable differences between the multi-rate mapping strategies adopted by Gibber and UrMus, we believe that the most important distinction is the notation itself. Gibber provides a mechanism for creating multimodal mappings that requires nothing more than the capitalization of a object property name, while UrMus (which provides greater flexibility in how multi-rate mappings are composed) requires multiple lines of code to achieve a similar effect. The goal of our abstraction was to remove the cognitive burdens associated with programming multimodal mappings and we believe our notation accomplishes this; all end users need to remember is to use a capital letter when they wish to make a continuous mapping between two properties.

As mentioned in Section 4, shader uniforms also utilize Gibber's mapping abstractions enabling users to easily incorporate audio signal analysis or geometric object properties into GPU programming.

6.3 Proxies and Maintenance of State

Consider the results of executing the following two lines of code, one after another:

```
a = Sine( 440, .5 )
a = Sine( 880, .5 )
```

An intuitive expectation is that the second sine oscillator, being assigned to the same variable a as the first one, would simply replace it in the audio graph; you would be left hearing a single sine oscillator at 880 Hz. This is, in fact, the result of executing these two lines in Gibber thanks to the implementation of *proxy* objects for nodes in the audio and visual graphs. In the above example, the variable a represents a proxy object. Whenever an object is assigned to it, the proxy looks at the node it currently holds and removes it from whatever graph it is attached to. The new object then replaces the old object's position in the graph.

In practice, this has a very important effect: the same line or block of code that calls a constructor can be called repeatedly with different argument variations without creating duplicate nodes in the audio or visual graphs. This is much more immediate than manipulating individual properties of objects after a constructor has been called; instead of subsequently typing names and targeted properties one can simply change the arguments to the original constructor call and re-execute it.

In a more complex relationship, sequencing objects that are not themselves stored in proxies are still bound to side effects of their behaviors. Whenever a sequencer is assigned to target a particular audiovisual object, that object retains a reference to the sequencer as well. When a proxy is assigned a new object, it checks to see if the object it contains holds any sequencer references. If it does, the proxy object re-routes the sequencers to target the new object stored in the proxy instead of the old one that is removed from the audio or visual graph. This allows users to easily experiment with different sound sources that will all be controlled by the same sequencer. The following block of code shows a sequencer targeting a synth and a variety of commented out potential replacements for the synth.

```
a = Sine( 440, .5 )
// a = Synth({ attack:1/4, decay: 1/4 })
// a = FM({ index:19, cmRatio: 3.011 })
// a = Mono( cutoff:.1, resonance:4 })

b = Seq({
  note:[ 440,660,880,1100 ].random(),
  durations:[ 1/4,1/8,1/2 ].random(),
  target:a
})
```

Thanks to proxies, executing any of the commented-out redefinitions of the variable a will change the timbre of the sequenced notes with no interruption in the sequence itself. Not having to create a new sequencer for each iteration or re-execute the constructor of the existing sequencer to pass a new reference makes the process of iteration more immediate and, in our opinion, conceptually simpler. The target of the sequencer is always whatever object is currently held in the global variable a, not just the object that was the value of a when the sequencer was instantiated.

Proxies are identified in Gibber through the use of variable names that are single, lower-case letters. This convention exists because JavaScript does not possess a language feature known as *catchalls*; that is, there is no way to metaprogram behaviors for any arbitrarily named variable added to an object. The alternative used here is to create a collection of properties on the global object and perform the meta-programming in question only when these properties are assigned to. This requires some initial discussion when introducing Gibber, as the following two lines have completely different effects if they are are executed repeatedly:

```
a = Sine( rndi(400, 800) )
aa = Sine( rndi(400, 800) )
```

In the first line of code the Sine constructor is generating an object assigned to a proxy; therefore any previous objects stored in the proxy will be removed from the audio graph. It can be executed repeatedly, always yielding a single sine oscillator generating sound at any given moment. In contrast, the second line of code does not assign to a proxy object. Every time this line is executed a new node will be placed in the audio graph and the old node that was formerly held in the variable will continue to generate audio but will no longer be referenced in the global namespace. Executing the second line of code ten times will result in ten different sine waves running simultaneously at randomized frequencies.

The mapping abstractions discussed in Section 6.2 are also subject to proxy behaviors. This means that if a proxy object A is replaced, any object B that contained mappings referring to object A will now use the new replacement object for mapping.

The idea of using proxies in audio graphs was initially explored in SuperCollider [28]; here we extend its use to graphics and interactive subsystems while also providing compatibility with Gibber's multi-rate mapping abstractions.

7. USE AND EVALUATION

Our evaluation begins with a brief comparison illustrating how the notation for the various abstractions in this paper compares with the notations of other environments. We then look at use of Gibber in live performance and in the classroom, and end with the results of a feedback survey completed by twenty-eight Gibber users.

7.1 Comparison of Notation

It is easy to cherry-pick comparisons where Gibber's terseness makes another environment look excessively verbose. In one comparison we performed it took seventeen lines of Processing code to mirror a two-line giblet which mapped cursor position to the frequency of a sine oscillator; the frequency of the oscillator then controlled the rotation of a cube. Such comparisons can easily be discredited: for example, although Processing might be substantially more verbose for the above task, it provides functionalities that are not available to Gibber. In order avoid such comparisons, we chose two code examples directly from the documentation of other creative coding environments and attempted to replicate their functionality in Gibber. For more information about differences between Fluxus, Tidal and Gibber, please refer to Section 3.

7.1.1 Audiovisual Mapping in Fluxus and Gibber

Though few environments enable easy mappings between audio and visual modalities, the very first code example in the Fluxus documentation renders a cube whose 3D scaling is modified by the frequency content of an input audio signal, as shown here:

```
(define (render)
  (scale (vector (gh 1) (gh 5) (gh 9) ))
  (draw-cube))
(every-frame (render))
```

In the above example, the gh function (short for getHarmonic) retrieves the magnitude of the given bin of a FFT analysis performed on the audio input. Three calls to this function are used to scale the rendering context, after which a cube is drawn to the screen. In Gibber, the same effect is achieved with the following code:

```
cube = Cube()
input = Input()
fft = FFT() // defaults to measuring master output
cube.scale = Vec3( fft.Bin1, fft.Bin5, fft.Bin9 )
```

Here we see an object-oriented approach, where instead of explicitly defining a render function we add an object to the visual graph (this occurs in the constructor), which handles rendering for us. We use identifiers such as bin1, bin2 etc. to identify FFT bin magnitudes; these are capitalized in the example above to use the continuous mapping abstraction discussed in Section 6.2. Although Gibber can mimic the introductory Fluxus example using a code fragment of similar length, it is important to note Fluxus does not generally have the flexibility in mapping that Gibber possesses. For example, there is no capability in Fluxus to tersely map the current frequency of an oscillator to the cube's scale or rotation. Instead, Fluxus users would have to manually track the appropriate variable and explicitly perform the required transformations. In Gibber, making the cube, the oscillator, and creating the continuous mapping can be done in two lines of code:

```
sine = Sine()
cube = Cube({ rotation:sine.Frequency })
```

7.1.2 *Sequencing in Tidal and in Gibber*

As sequencing and the creation of musical pattern is Tidal's primary motivation, we compare Gibber's sequencing abstraction to Tidal's. For simple cases the two notations closely mirror. For example, the following Tidal code (slightly modified from Tidal's documentation) sequences a simple drum pattern with changes to pan and speed:

```
d1 $ sound "bd sn sn"
    |+| speed ".25 .5 1"
    |+| pan "0 0.5 1"
```

In the example above all code in quotes above uses the Tidal DSL, while the rest is Haskell. The equivalent code in Gibber is the following:

```
Drums()
  .note.seq( [0,1,1], 1/3 )
  .pitch.seq( [.25,.5,1] )
  .pan.seq( [-1,0,1] )
```

As mentioned in Section 3, Tidal offers many sophisticated options for pattern creation and customization that Gibber currently lacks. But for simple cases like the one above, Gibber's notation is of comparable verbosity and, in our opinion, comparable clarity to that of Tidal without requiring the use of a DSL.

7.2 Performances

Networked live coding performances using Gibber have been given by the CREATE Ensemble, an electroacoustic group at UC Santa Barbara that places experimental interaction techniques at the center of its improvisatory practice. In the first such performance, Gibber's server enabled members of the ensemble to send code to a central computer for execution, while Gibber's built-in chatroom was used for ensemble members to communicate throughout the performance. The central computer was connected to a stereo audio feed as well as a video projector; the projected video showed both the code that members were sending to the central computer as well as the accompanying chat dialogue. An interesting side effect of the decision to send code to be executed on a central computer was that individual performers could audition the code on their laptops using personal headphones before they sent it over the network for public consumption.

The resulting piece, *G.meta* was performed on April 12th, 2012. The performance went smoothly but with some glitches in the audio due to high CPU usage. This problem with CPU inefficiency was an influential factor in deciding to begin work on a dedicated audio library for Gibber, Gibberish.js. An iteration of G.meta was also performed as part of the Santa Barbara New Music Series in August of 2012. In this version there were only three performers and the optimized audio library had been integrated into Gibber. Fewer performers and a better audio engine led to a performance free of audio stutters due to CPU performance.

In a subsequent networked live coding performance titled *Passages*, Gibber was augmented so that ensemble members could easily pass code fragments over a local area network. Building off the concept of the *Exquisite Corpse*, as code was passed around the ensemble each member receiving the fragment would modify it before it was passed to the next member and executed. The performance was conducted with ensemble members scattered throughout the audience using no amplification other than their built-in laptop speakers, a concept originally explored by the live coding group *powerbooks unplugged* [29].

Gibber has also been featured in many solo live coding performances in the United States, Europe, and Asia. One recent performance took place on July 3rd, 2014 at an Algorave[9] in London, where the majority of performers were live coders using a variety of environments and tools. The first author gave a twenty minute performance, creating both music and a generative, full-screen fragment shader from scratch using Gibber. Towards the end of the performance many of Gibber's pre-defined shaders were also employed, using the output of the live-coded fragment shader as their initial input. We look forward to future duo performances where each performer is responsible for the content of a single modality while using Gibber's abstractions to easily create mappings between them.

Audience feedback after a May 2013 solo performance by the first author was particularly interesting. During the performance, a critical error was made approximately three minutes into the performance that caused the audio processing in Gibber to begin a digital stutter, much in the fashion of a CD skipping. With no ability to resolve the problem, the performer simply copied all the code (minus the error which had been identified), refreshed the website, pasted in

[9] http://algorave.com

the copied code and executed it. This basically restarted the performance from the point immediately prior to the error. At a later point, another error again caused stuttering; however, this time the performer was able to resolve the problem after a brief moment of tension. After the performance, multiple audience members commented on how the errors lent the performance a sense of danger, and emphasized the improvisatory nature of the performance. Some went as far as to say the errors were their favorite part; we remain unclear what this says about the quality of the error-free segments of the performance.

7.3 CS Education

An interview was conducted with Carl Plant [21], a partner at *bitjam*, a company that (among other initiatives) has led a series of hacking workshops in England for teenagers. These workshops featured Arduino programming, working with Raspberry Pis, and programming music in Gibber. Each workshop hosted approximately ten students; after conducing six of them Plant estimated that he has taught Gibber to roughly sixty children between the ages of eleven and sixteen. In Plant's words the best aspect of Gibber was the "immediate gratification" it provided:

> "Kids are able to setup a beat straight away and modify it... add synth bass, wobble it."

Plant also mentioned that Gibber was preferred over other options as it is "not just long winded python coding, it can be exciting". His stated goal with the workshops was not explicitly to teach programming but rather to get kids excited about exploring it, and he believed Gibber was a much better fit for this goal than other musical (or non-musical) programming environments.

In addition to teaching teenagers, Gibber has been taught in a variety of university settings, including the University of Florida, Istanbul Technical University, Louisiana State University, Goldsmiths University of London, and the University of California at Santa Barbara.

7.4 Feedback Survey

Since December 4th, 2013, a survey link has been prominently displayed inside of Gibber. Twenty-eight users completed the survey as of July 24nd, 2014, providing qualitative and Likert scale feedback on which aspects of Gibber they enjoy and which they dislike. Of these twenty-eight users, 60% used Gibber for less than an hour before completing the survey. 62% of users had three or more years of programming experience and 85% had at least some experience programming JavaScript. 72% of users agreed or strongly agreed that they would consider using Gibber to teach or partially teach a class on programming.

88% of users either agreed or strongly agreed with the statement that they enjoyed programming in Gibber. User 20, the sole user who disagreed or strongly disagreed with the statement, expressed a dislike for web-based text editors, preferring to use vim or emacs for editing. In a similar vein, a number of users noted that they wished there was an offline version of the software:

> User 11: "I also dislike that it can't be used stand-alone without a back-end. I'd skip the social features and try to allow the app to stand-alone without the need for a remote web server."

> User 12: "(I don't like) the fact that i cant download it, and if you're offline, its a massive massive disappointment"

User 26 also expressed a desire to use Gibber within his/her bash shell. However, the same user also noted how easy it was to use since no installation is required:

> "It is very easy to setup. I already tried SuperCollider, Overtone and all this other stuff, it's nice that it's all browser based and there aren't any dependencies, build issues, etc."

In addition to allowing users with no internet connection to use Gibber, an offline version could also potentially offer improved end-user filesystem integration, easier communication with interactive devices, and more flexible options for defining the GUI used by the IDE. However, this would come with the expense of dealing with compatibility issues on different platforms.

When asked to name aspects of Gibber users found particularly enjoyable, many comments mentioned the audiovisual capabilities:

> User 13: "Simple and ultra lisible language. Audio and graphics programming in the same interface. Web based."

> User 8: "How simple and fun it is. Within a day I had visuals synced to music through my input on a projector for a new years party with 50+ people. I can spend hours playing with the software, I've never quite seen anything like it!"

> User 4: "Incredible sound and incredible graphics."

Although confident in our rationale for using a text-based environment, we were curious to learn if users thought this decision impacted Gibber's ease of use and asked users to respond to the statement "Gibber is easier to use than many visual programming environments." 50% of users agreed or strongly agreed with this statement. 17% of users had no experience with visual programming environments, and 25% of users were neutral on the subject. Only two users disagreed.

8. CONCLUSION

By integrating high-level abstractions for JavaScript into Gibber, we provide new possibilities for creative output and enable users to transfer knowledge acquired through programming in JavaScript to other domains. Three such abstractions we have integral to creative, multimodal coding are the use of proxies to manage removal/insertion of nodes in audiovisual graphs, multi-rate mapping strategies to afford mappings across modalities, and a unified system for scheduling and sequencing.

Our implementation of these abstractions provides an accessible, cross-platform, browser-based programming environment with audio, visual, and interactive affordances[10]. The system described here has been successfully used both in education and in live performance. A running instance of

[10]Gibber is open-source under the MIT license and available on GitHub at http://github.com/charlieroberts/Gibber

Gibber can be accessed on a central server hosted by the Media Arts and Technology program at UC Santa Barbara[11].

Moving forward, we will focus on the social aspects of Gibber and on improving its educational potential. For example, fine-grained sharing permissions would enable teachers and students to selectively share course-related giblets with members of their class. We plan to increase the ways giblets are consumed by enabling users to download giblets (along with the necessary supporting libraries) to embed in their own personal websites. Based on end-user feedback, we will explore creating a version of Gibber that runs without requiring internet access.

9. ACKNOWLEDGMENTS

The Robert W. Deutsch Foundation generously supported this research. This work was partially supported by ONR grant N00014-14-1-0133 and ARL/ARO MURI grant W911NF-09-1-0553.

10. REFERENCES

[1] Quil. https://github.com/quil/quil.

[2] SCGraph - a graphics server for SuperCollider. http://scgraph.github.io.

[3] ShaderTone. https://github.com/overtone/shadertone.

[4] S. Aaron and A. F. Blackwell. From sonic Pi to overtone: creative musical experiences with domain-specific and functional languages. In *Proceedings of the first ACM SIGPLAN workshop on Functional art, music, modeling & design*, pages 35–46. ACM, 2013.

[5] P. Boytchev. Logo tree project. http://elica.net/download/papers/LogoTreeProject.pdf, 2007.

[6] N. Collins, A. McLean, J. Rohrhuber, and A. Ward. Live coding in laptop performance. *Organised Sound*, 8(3), 2004.

[7] D. Della Casa and G. John. LiveCodeLab 2.0 and its language LiveCodeLang. In *Proceedings of the second ACM SIGPLAN workshop on Functional art, music, modeling & design*. ACM, 2014.

[8] G. Essl. *Playing with Time: Manipulation of Time and Rate in a Multi-rate Signal Processing Pipeline.* Ann Arbor, MI: MPublishing, University of Michigan Library, 2012.

[9] I. Greenberg, D. Kumar, and D. Xu. Creative coding and visual portfolios for CS1. In *Proceedings of the 43rd ACM technical symposium on Computer Science Education*, pages 247–252. ACM, 2012.

[10] D. Griffiths. Fluxus. In A. Blackwell, A. McLean, J. Noble, and J. Rohrhuber, editors, *Collaboration and learning through live coding*, Report from Dagstuhl Seminar 13382, pages 149–150. Dagstuhl, Germany, 2013.

[11] J. Maeda. *Design by numbers.* The MIT Press, 2001.

[12] T. Magnusson. ixi lang: a SuperCollider parasite for live coding. In *Proceedings of the International Computer Music Conference.* University of Huddersfield, 2011.

[13] T. Magnusson. Herding cats: Observing live coding in the wild. *Computer Music Journal*, 38(1):8–16, 2014.

[11] http://gibber.mat.ucsb.edu

[14] J. McCartney. Rethinking the computer music language: Supercollider. *Computer Music Journal*, 26(4):61–68, 2002.

[15] C. McKinney. Quick live coding collaboration in the web browser. In *Proceedings of the 2014 Conference on New Interfaces for Musical Expression*, pages 379–382, 2014.

[16] A. McLean. Tidal – mini language for live coding pattern. http://toplap.org/tidal/.

[17] A. McLean and G. Wiggins. Tidal–pattern language for the live coding of music. In *Proceedings of the 7th sound and music computing conference*, 2010.

[18] C. A. McLean et al. *Artist-Programmers and Programming Languages for the Arts.* PhD thesis, 2011.

[19] J. A. Mills III, D. Di Fede, and N. Brix. Music programming in minim. In *Proceedings of the 2010 Conference on New Interfaces for Musical Expression (NIME 2010). Sydney, Australia*, pages 37–42, 2010.

[20] S. Papert. *Mindstorms: Children, computers, and powerful ideas.* Basic Books, Inc., 1980.

[21] C. Plant. Interview, 12 2013. Technical Director: bitjam, ltd.

[22] C. Reas and B. Fry. Processing: programming for the media arts. *AI & SOCIETY*, 20(4):526–538, 2006.

[23] J. Resig. Javascript as a first language. http://ejohn.org/blog/javascript-as-a-first-language/, 20011.

[24] J. Resig. Processing.js. http://ejohn.org/blog/processingjs/, 2008.

[25] C. Roberts and J. Kuchera-Morin. Gibber: Live coding audio in the browser. *Proceedings of the International Computer Music Conference*, 2012.

[26] C. Roberts, G. Wakefield, and M. Wright. The web browser as synthesizer and interface. In *Proceedings of the 2013 Conference on New Interfaces for Musical Expression (NIME 2013)*, volume 2013, 2013.

[27] C. Roberts, M. Wright, J. Kuchera-Morin, and T. Höllerer. Rapid creation and publication of digital musical instruments. In *Proceedings of New Interfaces for Musical Expression*, volume 2014, 2014.

[28] J. Rohrhuber, A. de Campo, and R. Wieser. Algorithms today notes on language design for just in time programming. In *Proceedings of the International Computer Music Conference*, 2005.

[29] J. Rohrhuber, A. de Campo, R. Wieser, J.-K. van Kampen, E. Ho, and H. Hölzl. Purloined letters and distributed persons. In *Music in the Global Village Conference (Budapest)*, 2007.

[30] A. Sorensen. Extempore. http://extempore.moso.com.au.

[31] A. Sorensen. The Many Faces of a Temporal Recursion. http://extempore.moso.com.au/temporal_recursion.html, 2013.

[32] G. Wakefield, W. Smith, and C. Roberts. LuaAV: Extensibility and Heterogeneity for Audiovisual Computing. *Proceedings of Linux Audio Conference*, 2010.

[33] G. Wang and P. R. Cook. *The ChucK Audio Programming Language. a Strongly-timed and On-the-fly Environ/mentality.* PhD thesis, 2008.

Multiple Features But Few Labels? A Symbiotic Solution Exemplified for Video Analysis

Zhigang Ma
Carnegie Mellon University
kevinma@cs.cmu.edu

Yi Yang
The University of Queensland
yi.yang@uq.edu.au

Nicu Sebe
University of Trento
sebe@disi.unitn.it

Alexander G. Hauptmann
Carnegie Mellon University
alex@cs.cmu.edu

ABSTRACT

Video analysis has been attracting increasing research due to the proliferation of internet videos. In this paper, we investigate how to improve the performance on internet quality video analysis. Particularly, we work on the scenario of few labeled training videos being provided, which is less focused in multimedia. To being with, we consider how to more effectively harness the evidences from the low-level features. Researchers have developed several promising features to represent videos to capture the semantic information. However, as videos usually characterize rich semantic contents, the analysis performance by using one single feature is potentially limited. Simply combining multiple features through early fusion or late fusion to incorporate more informative cues is doable but not optimal due to the heterogeneity and different predicting capability of these features. For better exploitation of multiple features, we propose to mine the importance of different features and cast it into the learning of the classification model. Our method is based on multiple graphs from different features and uses the Riemannian metric to evaluate the feature importance. On the other hand, to be able to use limited labeled training videos for a respectable accuracy we formulate our method in a semi-supervised way. The main contribution of this paper is a novel scheme of evaluating the feature importance that is further casted into a unified framework of harnessing multiple weighted features with limited labeled training videos. We perform extensive experiments on video action recognition and multimedia event recognition and the comparison to other state-of-the-art multi-feature learning algorithms has validated the efficacy of our framework.

Categories and Subject Descriptors

H.3.1 [**Information Search and Retrieval**]: Content Analysis and Indexing; I.2.10 [**Vision and Scene Understanding**]: Video analysis

General Terms

Algorithms, Experimentation, Performance

MM'14, November 3–7, 2014, Orlando, Florida, USA.

http://dx.doi.org/10.1145/2647868.2654907.

Keywords

Video Analysis; Multi-feature; Weighted Features; Riemannian Distance; Semi-supervised Learning

1. INTRODUCTION

The sheer amount of videos and their expansion demand effective content analysis for indexing, retrieval and management. Video analysis is essentially a task to understand the semantics, for which it has to bridge the semantic gap between the low-level features and the high-level semantic content description [7].

Encouraging progress on video analysis has been made in recent years. At early times, video analysis was focused on controlled video analysis such as news videos. The attention has been gradually shifted to unconstrained video analysis such as videos recorded by amateurs. Current trend is to analyze internet quality videos due to the exponential growth of videos online. Typical internet quality video analysis includes action recognition and multimedia event analysis, which are studied in this paper. Video action recognition aims to understand the human motions contained in videos, *e.g.*, *running*. More dynamic information is included and it is usually beneficial to analyze several video sequences. Multimedia event analysis is much more complicated than action recognition as a multimedia event contains several concepts, actions within one or various scenes. For example, the event *making a cake* consists of a combination of several concepts such as *cake*, *people*, *kitchen* together with the action *making* within a longer video sequence. To attain reasonable accuracy, we usually need the entire video clip for extracting discriminative cues. In spite of various approaches for video analysis, extracting robust features and building classifiers based on them are the essential thrust. On one hand, a variety of features have been proposed in the literature for video analysis. For example, researchers have proposed capturing spatial-temporal volumes to address the local variations in both space and time. Since both spatial and temporal information are leveraged, this kind of feature has more reliable performance for video semantic analysis. Among others, STIP feature is mostly used [14]. Besides the STIP feature, another recent feature type, *i.e.*, MoSIFT shows promising performance in video semantic analysis [2]. Dense trajectory [33] is gaining increasing attention as it has been shown to be very robust for video analysis. Apart from visual features, some other modalities, which provide different yet complementary information, can also be used to represent videos. For example, auditory features based on Mel-frequency Cepstral Coefficients (MFCC) have also been frequently used to represent videos [13]. Focusing on different characteristics of the videos, these features intuitively should complement each other. That said, it is highly

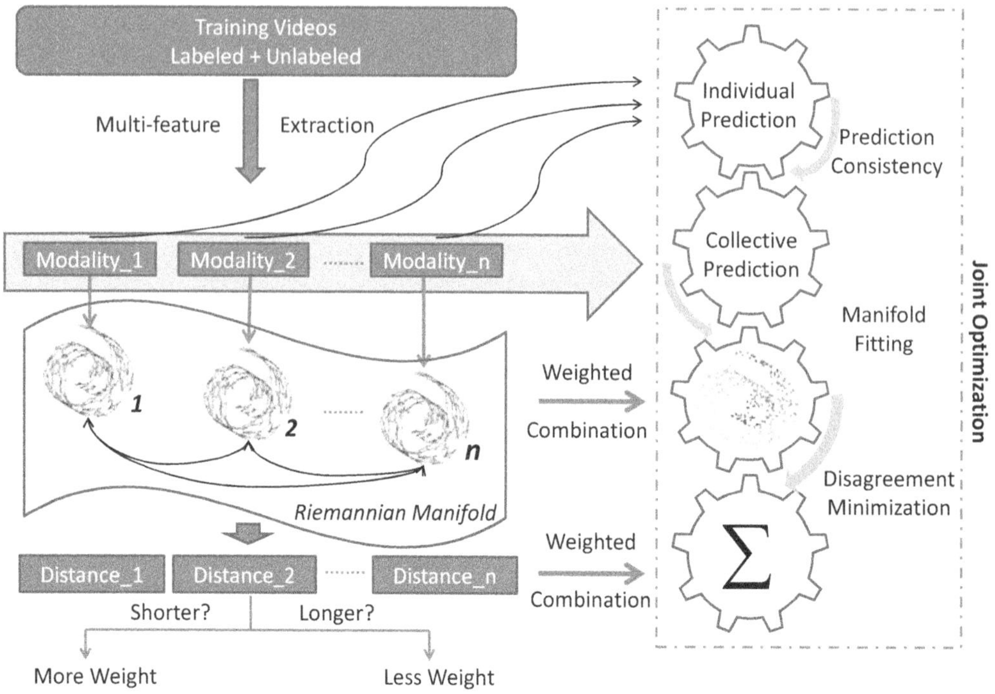

Figure 1: The illustration of our multi-feature learning framework.

possible to further boost the analysis accuracy by utilizing different features together. A simple way is to concatenate feature vectors of different types as the final representation. However, each feature has its own statistical property and simple concatenation is potentially limited in mining the informative cues from different features.

On the other hand, the performance of video analysis is also affected by the classifiers. Traditional classifiers such as Support Vector Machine (SVM) [33] usually require a large amount of accurately labeled training data. But in practice, we usually do not have a large number of precisely labeled videos as the training data and manual labeling is tedious and time-consuming. Using a small number of training data for classifier learning, however, is prone to over-fitting.

This paper aims to boost internet quality video analysis by simultaneously addressing the two aforementioned issues, *i.e.*, how to effectively integrate different features to better utilize the evidences from each feature, and how to guarantee a reasonable performance when only few labeled training data are provided. We propose a unified framework which deals with the two issues simultaneously, thus resulting in improved performance for video analysis.

Previous work has shown that multi-feature learning is a promising way to analyze different features simultaneously. Among others, Canonical Correlation Analysis [8][32], two-view support vector machines, namely SVM-2K and their variants [11][15] are the representative algorithms. Some other algorithms in the literature include [4][1][36][40], *etc.* Nonetheless, the aforementioned work mostly treats each feature equally while in fact for a specific data set usually one type of feature has higher recognition capability than other counterparts. Having been a common issue for other applications such as image annotation, differentiating feature capability in classification was investigated in multi-feature learning. Since we have a similar assumption that different features possibly have different contributions to the video analysis performance *w.r.t.* different datasets, we propose to mine the inconsistency of observations from different features and subsequently, their importance adaptively in our framework.

The second issue to be tackled in this paper is grounded on semi-supervised learning. Semi-supervised learning relieves the burden of manual labeling by properly using unlabeled data together with labeled data. A review of the progress on semi-supervised learning is [43] and constructing graphs from both labeled and unlabeled data to utilize manifold structure is the mainstream approach of semi-supervised learning. We opt to build a normalized Laplacian graph of each feature type to utilize the corresponding unlabeled data. Another usage of these graphs is for mining the inconsistency of different features raised by the first issue we mentioned before. In this paper, we assume that the inconsistency can be evaluated by distances between different graphs. If a graph constructed from one feature type is comparatively farther away from those constructed from other features, this feature is possibly inconsistent with other features from the classification perspective. Our learning scheme considers this inconsistency and balances between different features to attain a more robust classifier. As for the distance calculation, the Riemannian metric is exploited to measure that between different graphs. The underlying reason is that the normalized Laplacian graphs are Symmetric Positive Definite (SPD) matrices. Previous work has suggested that the Riemannian metric is a good measure of dissimilarity between two SPD matrices as SPD matrices exist on the Riemannian manifold [9].

Figure 1 illustrates how our method learns feature importance and the related classifiers jointly. After extracting multiple features (denoted as Modality 1 to Modality n), multiple graphs are constructed. We then calculate the Riemannian distance of each graph *w.r.t.* other graphs. It is reasonable that some features have better prediction capability but less noise than other features. Hence, these stronger features tend to better uncover the manifold structure of the data and it would be beneficial to give them more weights in the learning process. Based on the assumption about the quality of features, that they have roughly similar performance, with some noise on the results, we propose to learn such importance by distance measuring following some recent work [35]. Shorter distance indicates the related feature has more agreement with other features, thus also meaning the feature is more important. Larger distance indicates the related feature is an outlier *w.r.t.* other features, thus making it less important. The importance is reflected by the weights which are used to combine the graphs and the distances. In the following joint optimization module, there are three constraints to be satisfied. First, the predictions from each single modality should be consistent with the prediction from the combined modalities. Second, the prediction should fit the manifold structure uncovered by the combined graphs. Third, the weights should balance the Riemannian distances to minimize the disagreement from different modalities. For example, if the distance is larger (meaning the feature might have worse performance in prediction), the weight should be smaller. Through the joint optimization process, the weights and the classifiers for predictions are properly learned. In the following step, they can be applied to the testing videos to obtain decision values and weighted fusion.

In summary, the main contributions of this paper are as follows:

- A scheme is developed to evaluate the importance of each feature type by leveraging Riemannian distance atop multimedia manifold structure.
- The effective utilization of weighted features is embedded into a multi-feature semi-supervised learning framework.
- The proposed approach is desirable for internet quality video analysis when only limited labeled training data are available.
- The method is general and can be used in other applications when multiple features are provided with limited labeled training data.

We name our method **R**iemannian weighted **S**emi-**S**upervised **M**ulti-feature learning (RSSM).

2. RELATED WORK

In this section, we briefly review the related work. Some typical work on video analysis is first reviewed. Then we give some discussion on semi-supervised learning and multi-feature learning.

2.1 Video Analysis

Existing work on video analysis is focused on different levels. Video concept analysis aims to understand the abstract or general idea inferred from specific instances and has been widely studied in recent years [18][28][27][31]. Video action recognition, by contrast, makes more effort on analyzing the human motions contained in videos. Hence, how to capture the motion information has been the major focus. A representative work in earlier time is the Space-time Interest Points proposed by Laptev and Lindeberg [14]. By using differential descriptors to detect the local structures in the spatial-temporal domain, they generate features of the videos and show their efficacy for action recognition. Chen *et al.* introduce a novel descriptor, namely MoSIFT for action recognition [2]. MoSIFT is built atop the SIFT descriptor by integrating local motion information. Wang *et al.* show that describing videos by dense trajectories boosts the action recognition accuracy remarkably [33]. Positioned in a higher level with more difficulties, multimedia event analysis is gradually attracting more research interest. An event builds upon many concepts and is unlikely to be inferred with a single image or a few video frames. Some representative work includes [10][20][23][22]. Generally speaking, the research on multimedia event analysis is still based on robust low-level features. Visual features such as STIP and dense trajectories have proved to be effective. Meanwhile, other modalities such as audio features are also helpful in event analysis. This is different from video action recognition which is more dependent on visual features only.

Robust features are essential for video analysis. Nonetheless, each single feature has its advantage but is pragmatically insufficient to capture all the variations of different actions or events. Concerned with this limitation, some work has been proposed to fuse the evidences from multiple features for better multimedia analysis [29][16][37]. Yet they are supervised methods which require a good amount of labeled training data. By contrast, we aim to get reasonable performance with only few labeled training data.

2.2 Semi-supervised Learning

To handle the paucity of labeled training data, semi-supervised learning is a good way as it simultaneously exploits labeled and unlabeled training data [43]. Within the area of video analysis, semi-supervised learning has been widely used for concept analysis [38][42][6]. By contrast, limited work has investigated its usage on more complicated tasks such as action recognition and event analysis [19][34][41]. In [19], Ma *et al.* have proposed a semi-supervised feature analyzing framework integrating $l_{2,1}$-norm regularized feature selection and manifold learning and have applied it to 3D action recognition. Wang *et al.* cast shared structural subspace learning into a semi-supervised learning framework for action recognition and demonstrate its advantage over supervised classifiers [34]. In [41], Yu *et al.* have proposed a semi-supervised algorithm for tracking in the surveillance videos. Though showing the potential of semi-supervised learning, the aforementioned work does not take into account how to reasonably fuse evidences from different features in a statistical way. Hence, in this paper we focus on video action recognition and multimedia event analysis with a newly proposed semi-supervised model that integrates multi-feature learning.

2.3 Multi-feature Learning

Canonical Correlation Analysis (CCA) [8][32] is a classical multi-feature learning approach that maximizes the correlations between two features. Subsequent representative work includes two-view support vector machines (SVM-2K) [11] and multiple kernel learning (MKL) [24] that both build upon SVM. However, CCA and SVM-2K can only analyze two features simultaneously while MKL induces a heavy computational burden due to the computation of multiple kernels. Gehler *et al.* propose learning the correct weighting of different features based on LPBoost for object recognition [5]. Xu *et al.* propose a method to learn the weights, thresholding and smoothing parameters jointly and apply it to action recognition and multimedia event detection [37]. The algorithms mentioned above all work in a supervised fashion. Yang *et al.* have proposed a regression model which integrates semi-supervised learning and multi-feature learning [39]. The model optimizes the classifier inferred from each feature but does not consider the fact that different features have different prediction capability. Additionally, it is a linear algorithm but nonlinear algorithms are more robust for video analysis. Though we can apply some mapping method such as KPCA to preprocess the data to make their method comparable to a nonlinear approach, it is a two-step fashion and the two processes are not tightly coupled.

We develop a nonlinear algorithm that aims to progress beyond existing semi-supervised multi-feature learning algorithms by uncovering the feature importance and using such information for classifier learning. In a nutshell, we formulate our multi-feature learning based on uncovering feature disagreement motivated by [3] which argues that different features may have different capabilities for a classification task. By analyzing the feature disagreement we may exert more influence from the more powerful features on learning the classifier. Particularly, we couple it with the semi-supervised learning process. Normalized Laplacian graphs are constructed for semi-supervised learning and we analyze the distances of one graph from other graphs. These distances serve for the evaluation scheme of the feature disagreement and are fed into the framework. Here a thought should be given to how we choose the distance metric. Normalized Laplacian graphs are Symmetric Positive Definite (SPD) matrices lying on a Riemannian manifold. Though Eucliean distance can be also used to approximate the distance between two SPD matrices, previous work has suggested that the Riemannian metric is a more precise measurement [9]. Hence, we choose the Riemannian distance in measuring the distances between graphs to achieve the uncovering of the feature dissimilarity.

3. PROBLEM FORMULATION

Suppose we have n training data represented by m different features and denote them as $X_v|_{v=1}^m \in \mathbb{R}^{d_v \times n}$. d_v is the feature dimension. $X_v = [x_1^v, x_2^v, \ldots, x_n^v]$ among which l data are labeled. Let $Y \in \{0,1\}^{n \times c}$ be the label matrix. c stands for the class number and $y_i \in \mathbb{R}^c (1 \le i \le n)$ is the label vector with c classes. Let Y_{ij} denote the j-th datum of y_i then $Y_{ij} = 1$ if x_i^v is in the j-th class, while $Y_{ij} = 0$ otherwise. If x_i^v is not labeled, y_i is set to a vector with all zeros, namely, $\forall i > l$, $y_i|_{i=(l+1)}^n = 0^{c \times 1}$.

We begin formulating our algorithm with the classical regularized empirical error that results in a classifier f based on a set of training data $\{x_i, y_i\}_{i=1}^n$ where y_i indicates the label of x_i:

$$\min_f \sum_{i=1}^n loss(f(x_i), y_i) + \gamma\Omega(f). \tag{1}$$

$loss(\cdot,\cdot)$ is a loss function and $\Omega(f)$ is the regularization function on f with γ as its parameter.

Considering the ease of implementation, we use the following linear transformation:

$$f(x_i) = W^T x_i + b_i, \tag{2}$$

where W is the projection matrix used for classification and b_i is the bias. Using the matrix form and considering each feature type, Eq. (1) can be rewritten as:

$$\min_{W_v, b_v} \sum_{v=1}^m \left\| X_v^T W_v + 1_n b_v^T - F_v \right\|_F^2 + \gamma \sum_{v=1}^m \|W_v\|_F^2 \tag{3}$$

where $1_n \in \mathbb{R}^n$ denotes a column vector with all ones; the second item is added to avoid over-fitting. Note that we replace Y with a predicted label matrix F_v because: 1) many of the training data are unlabeled and F_v can reflect the possible labels of them; 2) it is useful in integrating the predictions from different features as will shown later.

The second step is to construct the normalized Laplacian graph L_i from each feature type. Following the traditional way, we formulate $\tilde{L}_i = D_i - G_i$ where D_i is a diagonal matrix with its diagonal elements as $\sum_{j=1}^n G_{ij}$ and G_i is a weight matrix whose element G_i^{pq} reflects the similarity between x_p and x_q. Next, $L_i = D_i^{-1/2} \tilde{L}_i D_i^{-1/2}$ which is an SPD matrix. Based on L_i, we calculate the Riemannian distance of each L_i to other graphs. For two graphs L_i and L_j, their distance is calculated as $\left\| \log(L_i^{-1/2} L_j L_i^{-1/2}) \right\|_F$. We therefore obtain the specific values for each graph *w.r.t.* to all the other graphs. We sum the values and denote it as R_i for each graph.

Next, we show how to associate the observations from each feature. Since we decide the feature importance by using the Riemannian distance based on the graphs, we assign a weight λ_i to R_i and L_i when performing multi-feature learning. Meanwhile, the feature vectors from all the features are concatenated to form a data matrix $X = [X_1; \cdots; X_v] \in \mathbb{R}^{d \times n}$ and we propose to similarly learn a predicted label matrix F from X. F is supposed to satisfy three conditions: 1) consistent with the known ground truth labels of the training data [44][43]; 2) smooth on the combined manifold of the weighted graphs [44][43]; 3) consistent with the predicted labels from each single feature. By incorporating these constraints, we get the following objective function:

$$\begin{aligned} \min_{F, F_v, W, W_v, \lambda_v, b, b_v} & \|X^T W + 1_n b^T - F\|_F^2 + \sum_{v=1}^m \|X_v^T W_v + 1_n b_v^T - F_v\|_F^2 \\ & + \sum_{v=1}^m \|F_v - F\|_F^2 + Tr\left(F^T (\sum_{v=1}^m \lambda_v L_v) F\right) + Tr\left((F-Y)^T U (F-Y)\right) \\ & + \alpha \sum_{v=1}^m \lambda_v R_v + \mu \sum_{v=1}^m \lambda_v \log \lambda_v + \gamma (\sum_{v=1}^m \|W_v\|_F^2 + \|W\|_F^2) \\ & s.t. \quad \sum_{v=1}^m \lambda_v = 1, \lambda_v \in [0,1]. \end{aligned} \tag{4}$$

In Eq. (4), the maximum entropy regularization $\sum_{v=1}^m \lambda_v \log \lambda_v$ is added to avoid the trivial solution that $\lambda_k' = 1$ and $\lambda_k = 0$, $\forall k \ne k'$; U is a diagonal matrix whose diagonal element $U_{ii} = \infty$ if x_i is labeled and $U_{ii} = 1$ otherwise. Note that Eq. (4) mixes several types of constraints involving different objects. All the constraints are based on comparable numerical values so they can be mixed in the same objective function.

As nonlinear classifiers have proved to be advantageous for video analysis, we further extend Eq. (4) by introducing a kernel function k defined by the nonlinear feature mapping, *i.e.*, $k(a,b) = \varphi(a)^T \varphi(b)$ for any two data a and b. Thus, we rewrite Eq. (4) as:

$$\begin{aligned} \min_{F, F_v, \varphi(W), \varphi(W_v), \lambda_v, b, b_v} & \|\varphi(X)^T \varphi(W) + 1_n b^T - F\|_F^2 \\ & + \sum_{v=1}^m \|\varphi(X_v)^T \varphi(W_v) + 1_n b_v^T - F_v\|_F^2 + \sum_{v=1}^m \|F_v - F\|_F^2 \\ & + Tr\left(F^T (\sum_{v=1}^m \lambda_v L_v) F\right) + Tr\left((F-Y)^T U (F-Y)\right) + \alpha \sum_{v=1}^m \lambda_v R_v \\ & + \mu \sum_{v=1}^m \lambda_v \log \lambda_v + \gamma \left(\sum_{v=1}^m \|\varphi(W_v)\|_F^2 + \|\varphi(W)\|_F^2 \right) \\ & s.t. \quad \sum_{v=1}^m \lambda_v = 1, \lambda_v \in [0,1]. \end{aligned} \tag{5}$$

4. SOLUTION

Our objective function is non-smooth so we propose an alternating algorithm to solve it.

(1) Fixing λ_v to optimize $\varphi(W_v)$, F_v, b_v, $\varphi(W)$, F and b:

By setting the derivative *w.r.t.* b_v to 0, we have:

$$b_v^T = \frac{1}{n} \left(1_n^T F_v - 1_n^T \varphi(X_v)^T \varphi(W_v) \right). \tag{6}$$

Denote a centering matrix as $H = I_n - \frac{1}{n} 1_n 1_n^T$ where $I_n \in \mathbb{R}^{n \times n}$ is an identity matrix. Substituting Eq. (6) into Eq. (5), the problem subsequently converts to the following one when optimizing $\varphi(W_v)$:

$$\min_{\varphi(W_v)} \sum_{v=1}^{m} Tr\left((H\varphi(X_v)^T\varphi(W_v) - HF_v)^T(H\varphi(X_v)^T\varphi(W_v) - HF_v)\right)$$
$$+\gamma\sum_{v=1}^{m} Tr\left(\varphi(W_v)^T\varphi(W_v)\right)$$
$$\Rightarrow \min_{\varphi(W_v)} \sum_{v=1}^{m} Tr\left(\varphi(W_v)^T\varphi(X_v)H\varphi(X_v)^T\varphi(W_v) - 2\varphi(W_v)^T\varphi(X_v)HF_v\right) \quad (7)$$
$$+\gamma\sum_{v=1}^{m} Tr\left(\varphi(W_v)^T\varphi(W_v)\right)$$
$$\Rightarrow \min_{\varphi(W_v)} \sum_{v=1}^{m} Tr\left(\varphi(W_v)^T[\varphi(X_v)H\varphi(X_v)^T + \gamma I_v]\varphi(W_v) - 2\varphi(W_v)^T\varphi(X_v)HF_v\right)$$

where $I_v \in \mathbb{R}^{d_v \times d_v}$ is an identity matrix. By setting the derivative *w.r.t* $\varphi(W_v)$ to 0, we have:

$$2\varphi(X_v)H\varphi(X_v)^T\varphi(W_v) - 2\varphi(X_v)HF_v + 2\gamma\varphi(W_v) = 0$$
$$\Rightarrow \varphi(W_v) = \left(\varphi(X_v)H\varphi(X_v)^T + \gamma I_v\right)^{-1}\varphi(X_v)HF_v \quad (8)$$

Let $A_v = \left(\varphi(X_v)H\varphi(X_v)^T + \gamma I_v\right)^{-1}$ and substitute $\varphi(W_v)$ and b_v into the objective function, the optimization of F_v equals to:

$$\min_{F_v} \sum_{v=1}^{m} \|H\phi(X_v)^T A_v\phi(X_v)HF_v - HF_v\|_F^2 + \sum_{v=1}^{m} \|F_v - F\|_F^2$$
$$+\gamma\sum_{v=1}^{m} \|A_v\phi(X_v)HF_v\|_F^2$$
$$\Rightarrow \min_{F_v} \sum_{v=1}^{m} Tr\left(F_v^T(H\phi(X_v)^T A_v\phi(X_v)H - I_n)^2F_v\right) + \sum_{v=1}^{m} Tr(F_v^T - F^T)(F_v - F) \quad (9)$$
$$+\gamma\sum_{v=1}^{m} Tr\left(F_v^T H\phi(X_v)^T A_v^2\phi(X_v)HF_v\right)$$
$$\Rightarrow \min_{F_v} \sum_{v=1}^{m} Tr\left(F_v^T[(H\varphi(X_v)^T A_v\varphi(X_v)H - I_n)^2 + I_n + \gamma H\varphi(X_v)^T A_v^2\varphi(X_v)H]F_v\right)$$
$$-2\sum_{v=1}^{m} Tr(F_v^T F)$$

By setting the derivative *w.r.t.* F_v to 0, we have:

$$\left((H\phi(X_v)^T A_v\phi(X_v)H - I_n)^2 + I_n + \gamma H\phi(X_v)^T A_v^2\phi(X_v)H\right)F_v = F$$
$$\Rightarrow F_v = J_vF \quad (10)$$

where $J_v = \left(I_n - H\varphi(X_v)^T A_v\varphi(X_v)H\right)^{-1}$. In the same manner, we can get:

$$b^T = \frac{1}{n}\left(1_n^T F - 1_n^T\varphi(X)^T\varphi(W)\right), \quad (11)$$

$$\varphi(W) = \left(\varphi(X)H\varphi(X)^T + \gamma I\right)^{-1}\varphi(X)HF \quad (12)$$

where $I \in \mathbb{R}^{d\times d}$ is an identity matrix. Let $M = \left(\varphi(X)H\varphi(X)^T + \gamma I\right)^{-1}$ and substitute $\varphi(W_v)$, b_v, F_v, $\varphi(W)$, b into the objective function, we then arrive at:

$$\min_F \|H\varphi(X)^T M\varphi(X)HF - HF\|_F^2$$
$$+\sum_{v=1}^{m} \|\left(H\varphi(X_v)^T A_v\varphi(X_v)HJ_v - HJ_v\right)F\|_F^2 + \sum_{v=1}^{m} \|(J_v - I_n)F\|_F^2$$
$$+Tr\left(F^T(\sum_{v=1}^{m}\lambda_vL_v)F\right) + Tr\left((F-Y)^TU(F-Y)\right) \quad (13)$$
$$+\gamma\left(\sum_{v=1}^{m}\|A_v\varphi(X_v)HJ_vF\|_F^2 + \|M\varphi(X)HF\|_F^2\right)$$

By setting its derivative *w.r.t.* F to 0, we obtain:

$$F = \begin{pmatrix} \sum_{v=1}^{m} J_v(H - \varphi(X_v)^T A_v\varphi(X_v)H)J_v \\ +H - H\varphi(X)^T M\varphi(X)H \\ +\sum_{v=1}^{m}\lambda_vL_v + \sum_{v=1}^{m}(J_v - I_n)^2 + U \end{pmatrix}^{-1} UY \quad (14)$$

(2) Fixing $\varphi(W_v)$, F_v, b_v, $\varphi(W)$, F and b to optimize λ_v:
The problem is equivalent to:

$$\min_{\lambda_v} Tr\left(F^T(\sum_{v=1}^{m}\lambda_vL_v)F\right) + \mu\sum_{v=1}^{m}\lambda_v\log\lambda_v + \alpha\sum_{v=1}^{m}\lambda_vR_v$$
$$s.t. \quad \sum_{v=1}^{m}\lambda_v = 1, \lambda_v \in [0,1] \quad (15)$$

By using a Lagrange multiplier ξ we convert the above problem to a Lagrange function as:

$$L(\lambda_v,\xi) = Tr(F^T\sum_{v=1}^{m}\lambda_vL_vF) + \mu\sum_{v=1}^{m}\lambda_v\log\lambda_v$$
$$+\alpha\sum_{v=1}^{m}\lambda_vR_v - \xi(\sum_{v=1}^{m}\lambda_v - 1) \quad (16)$$

By setting its derivative *w.r.t.* λ_v and ξ to 0 respectively, we have:

$$\begin{cases} Tr(F^TL_vF) + \mu\log\lambda_v + \mu + \alpha R_v - \xi = 0 \\ \sum_{v=1}^{m}\lambda_v - 1 = 0 \end{cases} \quad (17)$$

We thus obtain:

$$\lambda_v = \frac{\exp\left(\frac{-Tr(F^TL_vF)-\alpha R_v-\mu}{\mu}\right)}{\sum_{v=1}^{m}\exp\left(\frac{-Tr(F^TL_vF)-\alpha R_v-\mu}{\mu}\right)} \quad (18)$$

Note that for any matrix Q, $Q(Q^TQ+\mu I)^{-1} = (QQ^T+\mu I)Q$. Hence, we can rewrite $\varphi(W_v)$, J_v, $\varphi(W)$ and F as:

$$\varphi(W_v) = \varphi(X_v)H\left(H\varphi(X_v)^T\varphi(X_v)H + \gamma I_n\right)^{-1}F_v, \quad (19)$$

$$J_v = \left(I_n - H\varphi(X_v)^T\varphi(X_v)H[H\varphi(X_v)^T\varphi(X_v)H + \gamma I_n]^{-1}\right)^{-1}, \quad (20)$$

$$\varphi(W) = \varphi(X)H\left(H\varphi(X)^T\varphi(X)H + \gamma I_n\right)^{-1}F, \quad (21)$$

$$F = \left(\sum_{v=1}^{m}J_vHJ_v - \sum_{v=1}^{m}J_v\varphi(X_v)^T\varphi(X_v)H[H\varphi(X_v)^T\varphi(X_v)H + \gamma I_n]^{-1}J_v\right.$$
$$+H - H\varphi(X)^T\varphi(X)H\left(H\varphi(X)^T\varphi(X)H + \gamma I_n\right)^{-1} + \sum_{v=1}^{m}\lambda_vL_v \quad (22)$$
$$\left. + \sum_{v=1}^{m}(J_v - I_n)^2 + U\right)^{-1} UY$$

Let $K_{tr}^v \in \mathbb{R}^{n\times n}$ and $K_{tr} \in \mathbb{R}^{n\times n}$ denote the kernel matrices calculated from X_v and X. Let $K_{te}^v \in \mathbb{R}^{n_{te}\times n}$ and $K_{te} \in \mathbb{R}^{n_{te}\times n}$ denote the kernel matrices between the testing data and the training data based on the v-th feature and the concatenated feature respectively. n_{te} indicates the number of testing data. We can therefore arrive at Algorithm 1.

Discussion on the computational complexity:

Computing the graph Laplacian is $O(n^2)$ and computing the kernel matrix from the training data is $O(d_vn^2)$. During the training process, computing the inverse of a few matrices in training has the complexity of $O(n^3)$. During the testing process, computing the kernel matrix between the testing data and the training data is $O(d_v n n_{te})$.

Algorithm 1: Optimization procedure for RSSM.

Input:

K_{tr}^v, K_{tr}, K_{te}^v, K_{te}, L_v, U, R_v and Y;
Parameters α, μ and γ.

Output:

Optimized classification model.

1: Set $t = 0$ and initialize $\lambda_v = \frac{1}{m}$;

2: **repeat**

Update J_v as $J_v = \left(I_n - HK_{tr}^v H(HK_{tr}^v H + \gamma I_n)^{-1}\right)^{-1}$;

Update F as

$F = [\sum_{v=1}^{m} J_v H J_v - \sum_{v=1}^{m} J_v K_{tr}^v H(HK_{tr}^v H + \gamma I_n)^{-1} J_v + H - HK_{tr}H(HK_{tr}H + \gamma I_n)^{-1} + \sum_{v=1}^{m} \lambda_v L_v + \sum_{v=1}^{m} (J_v - I_n)^2 + U]^{-1} UY$;

Update F_v as $F_v = J_v F$;

Update λ_v according to Eq. (18);

Update the objective function value obj;

$t = t + 1$.

until *Convergence:* $|obj_{t+1} - obj_t| / obj_t \leq 10^{-3}$;

3: $Model = H(HK_{tr}^v H + \gamma I_n)^{-1} F_v$.

---

5. EXPERIMENTS

We evaluate our algorithm on two tasks of video analysis: video action recognition and multimedia event recognition. The comparison to several state-of-the-art algorithms is first presented with discussion. Additionally, we have some experimental study on the weights learned by our method, the contributions of different features and different BoW representations.

5.1 Datasets

We use four datasets in the experiments. For action recognition, Youtube action dataset [17], UCF50 action dataset [25] and HMDB dataset [12] are used. Youtube dataset has 1600 video sequences from 11 actions. UCF50 consists of 6681 video sequences from 50 actions. HMDB is made up of 6849 video clips from 51 actions. For multimedia event recognition, we use the TRECVID MED 2013 MEDTEST data. In this dataset, there are positive videos of 20 events and the remaining videos are null videos. As our experiment is to evaluate the performance for recognition, we only use all the positive videos, thus resulting in a subset of 3489 videos. We name this subset Multimedia Event Dataset (MED) for convenience.

Following [30], we extract three dynamic visual features, *i.e.*, STIP [14], MoSIFT [2] and dense trajectories (Trajectory) [33] for all the four datasets. We additionally extract MFCC feature from MED dataset as the audio information has been shown to be helpful for multimedia event analysis. Based on each feature type, we generate the 4096 dimensional bag-of-words representation for the videos.

5.2 Comparison Algorithms

The following is a brief introduction of the comparison algorithms in our experiments.

- RSSM: The proposed method in this paper. We apply the χ^2 kernel due to its robustness for bag-of-words features [33].
- SVM: We use SVM with χ^2 kernel as it has demonstrated to be advantageous for video analysis [33]. As both early fusion and late fusion are typical for using multiple features, we implement SVM with both approaches and denote them as SVM_{ef} and SVM_{lf}.
- SVM-2K [11]: A representative multi-feature learning algorithm.
- SimpleMKL [24]: An algorithm that utilizes multiple features through multiple kernel learning.
- LP-β [5]: A variant of LPBoost which is designed particularly for feature combination problem in multi-class classification.
- Feature Weighting via Optimal Thresholding (FWOT) [37]: A recent feature fusion method that learns the weights, thresholding and smoothing parameters jointly.
- Multi-feature Learning via Hierarchical Regression (MLHR) [39]: A regression model which integrates semi-supervised learning and multi-feature learning.

To transform SVM-2K and MLHR to nonlinear approaches so that they are comparable to other methods, we perform full rank principal component analysis [26] with the χ^2 kernel to map the low-level features into a Hilbert space $\mathcal{H}$. The representations in $\mathcal{H}$ are the input for these two methods.

5.3 Setup

Similarly to [34], we randomly split Youtube and UCF50 to multiple (5 in our experiments) training and testing sets in a half-and-half fashion. For HMDB, we use the three provided partitions to form the training and testing sets. All the results reported on these three datasets are the average results from these splits. For MED data, NIST already provided the standard development (training) set and evaluation (testing) set so we use the provided partition. Mean Average Precision (MAP) is used as the evaluation metric. For the training sets, 2%, 10%, 25%, 50% and 75% training data are labeled respectively and the supervised algorithms only use the labeled data for training.

The parameters involved are set as follows. The parameter for kernel calculation is fixed to the mean of the pairwise distances among the training samples, which is a widely adopted strategy in the literature; the regularization parameters are all tuned from $\{0.001, 0.1, 10, 1000\}$. For SVM-2K and SimpleMKL, we use the code shared by the authors and follow their parameter settings. We report the best results for each algorithm.

5.4 Recognition Results

The recognition results on different datasets are shown from Table 1 to Table 4. It can be seen that our method is consistently better than other comparison algorithms with different percentage of training data labeled on all the four datasets. Our method is significantly better judged by the t-test (with a significance level of 0.001). Specifically, we have the following observations and discussion: 1) Semi-supervised algorithms, *i.e.*, RSSM and MLHR, perform better than supervised algorithms probably due to the usage of unlabeled training data; 2) The advantage of RSSM and MLHR over other supervised algorithms is especially visible when only few training video are labeled, *e.g.*, 2%, 10% or 25% of the training videos. 3) RSSM outperforms MLHR, which indicates that properly mining feature importance can give us extra benefit; 4) When increasing the number of labeled training data, the recognition accuracy of all comparison algorithms improves, which is

Table 1: **Action recognition results on Youtube dataset (MAP±Standard Deviation). The best results are highlighted in bold.**

Comparison Algorithms	2%	10%	25%	50%	75%
RSSM	**0.275±0.021**	**0.498±0.014**	**0.689±0.021**	**0.798±0.016**	**0.864±0.016**
SVM_{ef}	0.115±0.010	0.265±0.032	0.532±0.014	0.657±0.015	0.731±0.014
SVM_{lf}	0.117±0.007	0.271±0.006	0.537±0.008	0.667±0.010	0.740±0.005
SimpleMKL	0.216±0.030	0.364±0.009	0.528±0.017	0.627±0.021	0.673±0.020
LP-β	0.120±0.014	0.285±0.030	0.564±0.038	0.660±0.033	0.732±0.018
FWOT	0.137±0.013	0.291±0.009	0.589±0.011	0.681±0.008	0.769±0.011
MLHR	0.260±0.011	0.483±0.012	0.663±0.010	0.772±0.015	0.824±0.016

Table 2: **Action recognition results on UCF50 dataset (MAP±Standard Deviation). The best results are highlighted in bold.**

Comparison Algorithms	2%	10%	25%	50%	75%
RSSM	**0.292±0.019**	**0.577±0.016**	**0.796±0.011**	**0.871±0.005**	**0.920±0.016**
SVM_{ef}	0.140±0.001	0.334±0.014	0.673±0.013	0.802±0.011	0.867±0.011
SVM_{lf}	0.141±0.001	0.377±0.014	0.703±0.007	0.826±0.008	0.885±0.006
SimpleMKL	0.177±0.021	0.387±0.017	0.544±0.010	0.650±0.004	0.703±0.005
LP-β	0.126±0.003	0.388±0.015	0.650±0.007	0.826±0.008	0.888±0.006
FWOT	0.162±0.001	0.394±0.014	0.713±0.010	0.841±0.010	0.894±0.009
MLHR	0.283±0.019	0.557±0.014	0.771±0.008	0.869±0.006	0.913±0.005

Table 3: **Action recognition results on HMDB dataset (MAP±Standard Deviation). The best results are highlighted in bold.**

Comparison Algorithms	2%	10%	25%	50%	75%
RSSM	**0.095±0.003**	**0.197±0.013**	**0.265±0.002**	**0.334±0.001**	**0.382±0.004**
SVM_{ef}	0.058±0.001	0.101±0.013	0.225±0.015	0.280±0.006	0.319±0.008
SVM_{lf}	0.058±0.001	0.115±0.012	0.232±0.013	0.285±0.008	0.324±0.011
SimpleMKL	0.053±0.005	0.104±0.013	0.145±0.002	0.190±0.008	0.212±0.008
LP-β	0.058±0.001	0.135±0.010	0.173±0.010	0.257±0.008	0.309±0.006
FWOT	0.063±0.001	0.133±0.010	0.239±0.016	0.299±0.007	0.338±0.010
MLHR	0.071±0.001	0.182±0.016	0.256±0.003	0.317±0.002	0.357±0.006

Table 4: **Multimedia event recognition results on MED dataset (MAP). The best results are highlighted in bold.**

Comparison Algorithms	2%	10%	25%	50%	75%
RSSM	**0.229**	**0.414**	**0.538**	**0.601**	**0.662**
SVM_{ef}	0.115	0.265	0.396	0.503	0.551
SVM_{lf}	0.117	0.271	0.401	0.510	0.554
SimpleMKL	0.186	0.271	0.345	0.397	0.438
LP-β	0.156	0.234	0.404	0.521	0.569
FWOT	0.137	0.291	0.410	0.533	0.577
MLHR	0.211	0.401	0.514	0.585	0.630

Table 5: **Riemmanian distances and the learned weights on Youtube dataset *w.r.t.* different percentage of training data labeled.**

Modality	Riemmanian Distance	2%	10%	25%	50%	75%
STIP	56.7962	0.3363	0.3423	0.3418	0.3430	0.3440
MoSIFT	57.1440	0.3356	0.3414	0.3412	0.3365	0.3334
Trajectory	57.4910	0.3282	0.3162	0.3170	0.3205	0.3227

consistent with our experience that more labeled training data always help; 5) The advantage of semi-supervised methods over supervised methods tends to plateau as more training data are labeled, which is especially visible on UCF50 dataset; 6) FWOT generally obtains more robust performance in comparison with other supervised multi-feature learning methods such as SimpleMKL and LP-β. The better performance of RSSM validates the effectiveness of our approach that simultaneously leverages unlabeled data and feature importance.

5.5 Riemmanian Distances v.s. Weights

Our method leverages the Riemmannian distances between multiple graphs constructed from multiple modalities for learning the weights of the corresponding modalities. In this subsection, we

Table 6: **Riemmanian distances and the learned weights on UCF50 dataset *w.r.t.* different percentage of training data labeled.**

Modality	Riemmanian Distance	2%	10%	25%	50%	75%
STIP	37.6956	0.3331	0.3333	0.3418	0.3334	0.3347
MoSIFT	38.2276	0.3309	0.3323	0.3412	0.3331	0.3302
Trajectory	35.1621	0.3360	0.3344	0.3170	0.3335	0.3351

Table 7: **Riemmanian distances and the learned weights on HMDB dataset *w.r.t.* different percentage of training data labeled.**

Modality	Riemmanian Distance	2%	10%	25%	50%	75%
STIP	36.7737	0.3334	0.3334	0.3335	0.3336	0.3336
MoSIFT	39.3522	0.3333	0.3333	0.3328	0.3327	0.3325
Trajectory	36.6340	0.3334	0.3334	0.3337	0.3337	0.3339

Table 8: **Riemmanian distances and the learned weights on MED dataset *w.r.t.* different percentage of training data labeled.**

Modality	Riemmanian Distance	2%	10%	25%	50%	75%
STIP	83.5899	0.2513	0.2500	0.2501	0.2526	0.2560
MoSIFT	83.7743	0.2506	0.2500	0.2501	0.2505	0.2487
Trajectory	83.5189	0.2518	0.2506	0.2502	0.2546	0.2580
MFCC	85.7730	0.2459	0.2463	0.2494	0.2422	0.2373

give the weights learned by our algorithm in pair of the distances from Table 5 to Table 8. It can be seen that different features have varying importance on a particular dataset. On Youtube dataset, the graph constructed from STIP feature is closer to those constructed from MoSIFT and Trajectory features. The resulting weights learned from our model reflect the distances with more weight given to STIP feature. On UCF50 dataset, the graph constructed from Trajectory feature is closer to those constructed from STIP and MoSIFT features. Though the difference between the weights learned from our model is not so obvious as on Youtube dataset, we can still see that more weights are given to Trajectory feature. On HMDB dataset, we similarly observe that the graph constructed from Trajectory feature is closer to other graphs and it obtains subtly more weight from our model. On MED dataset, Trajectory feature similarly gets more weights in comparison with other three features. MFCC feature is given least weight by our model, which is consistent with previous experience on TRECVID MED that visual features are still more discriminative than audio features. The slight difference of the learned weights on UCF50, HMDB and MED datasets may indicate that these three datasets are more difficult to analyze than Youtube dataset. Our model is still able to learn proper weights of different features, thus resulting in a reasonable way to fuse the heterogeneous evidences. On the other hand, in our algorithm the weights and the corresponding classifiers for different features are learned jointly. The integration of both contributes to the performance gain. In spite of the slight difference of the weights, the classifiers are still optimized under the influence of the learned weights.

We also observe that the relative importance of different feature does not change a lot over different datasets. This result may be because that for all the datasets we have the same feature extraction pipeline. Besides, the literature has also shown that STIP and Trajectory are better for video analysis, especially action recognition and event analysis. It is worth pointing out that all the other comparison algorithms have used the same features as our method but our method still outperforms other methods, which again indicates the efficacy of our method.

5.6 Performance *w.r.t.* Different Features

As a classical multi-feature learning algorithm, SVM-2K can only handle two features. To compare our method to this classical algorithm, we conduct experiments on Youtube dataset by leaving one feature out. We therefore have three combinations, *i.e.*, STIP+MoSIFT, STIP+Trajectory and MoSIFT+Trajectory. In this way, we can also study the predicting capability of different features. We would point out that using only two features actually restrains the performance of RSSM since the feature disagreement loses its power ($R_1 = R_2$). However, we can see from the comparison in Figure 2 that our method still consistently outperforms SVM-2K no matter which two features are used. The advantage is possibly attributed to the usage of unlabeled training data.

5.7 BoW v.s. Spatial BoW

The spatial BoW representation introduced in [21] has shown good performance for video analysis. In this subsection, we show the performance gain by using spatial BoW compared to standard BoW representation on Youtube dataset. We use 1x1, 2x2 and 3x1 spatial grids to generate the spatial BoW representation. For each grid, we use the standard BoW representation with 4,096 dimensions, thus resulting in 32,768 dimension spatial BoW feature for each feature type. Note that we did not use the spatial BoW representation in the above experiments due to the consideration of computational efficiency. The comparison is presented in Figure 3. We observe from the figure that using spatial BoW representation can further boost the accuracy in comparison with using standard BoW representation.

6. CONCLUSION

We have studied how to improve the performance of internet quality video analysis, particularly on action recognition and multimedia event recognition. Considering that: 1) Discriminative features are the basis of video analysis; 2) A variety of good features are available with different capability of capturing the information from videos; and 3) Traditional classifiers work with many labeled training data which are costly to obtain in practice, we tackled the

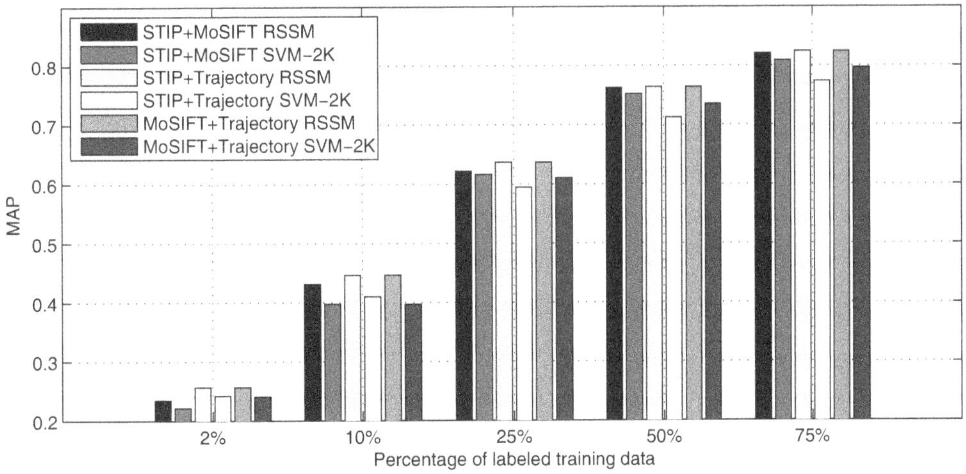

Figure 2: Action recognition results using different combinations of two features on Youtube dataset. Both the results of RSSM and SVM-2K are given in the figure. RSSM is consistently better than SVM-2K.

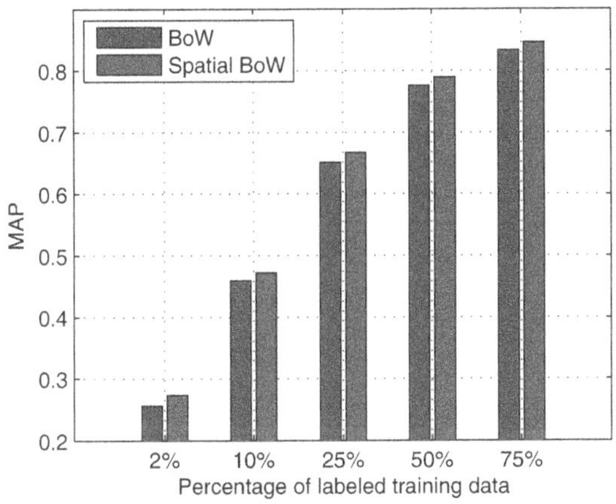

Figure 3: Performance comparison between using BoW representation and using spatial BoW representation on Youtube dataset. It can be seen that using spatial BoW representation results in better performance than using BoW representation.

problem by proposing a joint learning framework that integrates semi-supervised learning, multi-feature learning and the Riemannian metric. Specifically, the main merit of our method is its ability of effectively exploiting multiple features with the consideration of the different predicting capability of these features. On top of that, our method can attain reasonable performance when only few training videos are labeled, which makes our method desirable in real-world scenarios. We have tested our method on video action recognition and multimedia event recognition using four widely used datasets. Our method is advantageous compared to several other state-of-the-art algorithms. The experimental results suggest that unlabeled data, multiple features and feature importance as priors all contribute to the boosted recognition accuracy. Lastly, it is worth mentioning that our framework can be also used in other applications when we have multiple features but few labeled training data, which is another nice property.

7. ACKNOWLEDGMENTS

This paper was partially supported by the European Commission project xLiMe, the Open Project Program of the State Key Lab of CAD&CG (Grant No. A1402), Zhejiang University, the US Department of Defense the U. S. Army Research Office (W911NF-13-1-0277) and the Intelligence Advanced Research Projects Activity (IARPA) via Department of Interior National Business Center contract number D11PC20068. The U.S. Government is authorized to reproduce and distribute reprints for Governmental purposes notwithstanding any copyright annotation thereon. Disclaimer: The views and conclusions contained herein are those of the authors and should not be interpreted as necessarily representing the official policies or endorsements, either expressed or implied, of IARPA, DoI/NBC, ARO, or the U.S. Government.

8. REFERENCES

[1] R. K. Ando and T. Zhang. Two-view feature generation model for semi-supervised learning. In *ICML*, pages 25–32, 2007.

[2] M.-Y. Chen and A. G. Hauptmann. Mosift: Recognizing human actions in surveillance videos. In *Technical Report CMU-CS-09-161, Carnegie Mellon University*, 2009.

[3] C. M. Christoudias, R. Urtasun, and T. Darrell. Multi-view learning in the presence of view disagreement. In *UAI*, 2008.

[4] M. A. Davenport, C. Hegde, M. F. Duarte, and R. G. Baraniuk. Joint manifolds for data fusion. *IEEE Transactions on Image Processing*, 19(10):2580–2594, 2010.

[5] P. V. Gehler and S. Nowozin. On feature combination for multiclass object classification. In *ICCV*, pages 221–228, 2009.

[6] Y. Han, Y. Yang, Y. Yan, Z. Ma, N. Sebe, and X. Zhou. Semi-supervised feature selection via spline regression for video semantic recognition. *IEEE Transactions on Neural Networks and Learning Systems*, 2014.

[7] A. G. Hauptmann, R. Yan, W.-H. Lin, M. G. Christel, and H. D. Wactlar. Can high-level concepts fill the semantic gap in video retrieval? a case study with broadcast news. *IEEE Transactions on Multimedia*, 9(5):958–966, 2007.

[8] H. Hotelling. Relations between two sets of variates. *Biometrika*, 28(3).

[9] S. Jayasumana, R. Hartley, M. Salzmann, H. Li, and M. T. Harandi. Kernel methods on the riemannian manifold of symmetric positive definite matrices. In *CVPR*, pages 73–80, 2013.

[10] L. Jiang, A. G. Hauptmann, and G. Xiang. Leveraging high-level and low-level features for multimedia event detection. In *ACM Multimedia*, pages 449–458, 2012.

[11] T.-K. Kim, J. Kittler, and R. Cipolla. Discriminative learning and recognition of image set classes using canonical correlations. *IEEE Trans. Pattern Anal. Mach. Intell.*, 29(6):1005–1018, 2007.

[12] H. Kuehne, H. Jhuang, E. Garrote, T. Poggio, and T. Serre. Hmdb: A large video database for human motion recognition. In *ICCV*, pages 2556–2563, 2011.

[13] Z.-Z. Lan, L. Bao, S.-I. Yu, W. Liu, and A. G. Hauptmann. Multimedia classification and event detection using double fusion. *Journal of Multimedia Tools and Applications*, 2013.

[14] I. Laptev and T. Lindeberg. Space-time interest points. In *ICCV*, pages 432–439, 2003.

[15] G. Li, S. C. H. Hoi, and K. Chang. Two-view transductive support vector machines. In *SDM*, pages 235–244, 2010.

[16] Y. Li, B. Geng, D. Tao, Z.-J. Zha, L. Yang, and C. Xu. Difficulty guided image retrieval using linear multiple feature embedding. *IEEE Transactions on Multimedia*, 14(6):1618–1630, 2012.

[17] J. Liu, J. Luo, and M. Shah. Recognizing realistic actions from videos. In *CVPR*, pages 1996–2003, 2009.

[18] J. Luo, J. Yu, D. Joshi, and W. Hao. Event recognition: viewing the world with a third eye. In *ACM Multimedia*, pages 1071–1080, 2008.

[19] Z. Ma, F. Nie, Y. Yang, J. R. R. Uijlings, N. Sebe, and A. G. Hauptmann. Discriminating joint feature analysis for multimedia data understanding. *IEEE Transactions on Multimedia*, 14(6):1662–1672, 2012.

[20] Z. Ma, Y. Yang, Y. Cai, N. Sebe, and A. G. Hauptmann. Knowledge adaptation for ad hoc multimedia event detection with few exemplars. In *ACM Multimedia*, pages 469–478, 2012.

[21] M. Marszalek, C. Schmid, H. Harzallah, and J. van de Weijer. Learning object representations for visual object class recognition. In *Visual recognition challenge workshop*, 2007.

[22] M. Mazloom, E. Gavves, K. E. A. van de Sande, and C. Snoek. Searching informative concept banks for video event detection. In *ICMR*, pages 255–262, 2013.

[23] M. Merler, B. Huang, L. Xie, G. Hua, and A. Natsev. Semantic model vectors for complex video event recognition. *IEEE Transactions on Multimedia*, 14(1):88–101, 2012.

[24] A. Rakotomamonjy, F. Bach, S. Canu, and Y. Grandvalet. SimpleMKL. *Journal of Machine Learning Research*, 9:2491–2521, 2008.

[25] K. K. Reddy and M. Shah. Recognizing 50 human action categories of web videos. *Mach. Vis. Appl.*, 24(5):971–981, 2013.

[26] B. Schölkopf, A. J. Smola, and K.-R. Müller. Nonlinear component analysis as a kernel eigenvalue problem. *Neural Computation*, 10(5):1299–1319, 1998.

[27] M.-L. Shyu, Z. Xie, M. Chen, and S.-C. Chen. Video semantic event/concept detection using a subspace-based multimedia data mining framework. *IEEE Transactions on Multimedia*, 10(2):252–259, 2008.

[28] C. Snoek, M. Worring, J. van Gemert, J.-M. Geusebroek, and A. W. M. Smeulders. The challenge problem for automated detection of 101 semantic concepts in multimedia. In *ACM Multimedia*, pages 421–430, 2006.

[29] J. Song, Y. Yang, Z. Huang, H. T. Shen, and R. Hong. Multiple feature hashing for real-time large scale near-duplicate video retrieval. In *ACM Multimedia*, pages 423–432, 2011.

[30] A. Tamrakar, S. Ali, Q. Yu, J. Liu, O. Javed, A. Divakaran, H. Cheng, and H. S. Sawhney. Evaluation of low-level features and their combinations for complex event detection in open source videos. In *CVPR*, pages 3681–3688, 2012.

[31] V. S. Tseng, J.-H. Su, J.-H. Huang, and C.-J. Chen. Integrated mining of visual features, speech features, and frequent patterns for semantic video annotation. *IEEE Transactions on Multimedia*, 10(2):260–267, 2008.

[32] A. Vinokourov, J. Shawe-Taylor, and N. Cristianini. Inferring a semantic representation of text via cross-language correlation analysis. In *NIPS*, pages 1473–1480, 2002.

[33] H. Wang, A. Kläser, C. Schmid, and C.-L. Liu. Action recognition by dense trajectories. In *CVPR*, pages 3169–3176, 2011.

[34] S. Wang, Y. Yang, Z. Ma, X. Li, C. Pang, and A. G. Hauptmann. Action recognition by exploring data distribution and feature correlation. In *CVPR*, pages 1370–1377, 2012.

[35] X. Wang, W. Bian, and D. Tao. Grassmannian regularized structured multi-view embedding for image classification. *IEEE Transactions on Image Processing*, 22(7):2646–2660, 2013.

[36] D. P. Williams. Bayesian data fusion of multiview synthetic aperture sonar imagery for seabed classification. *IEEE Transactions on Image Processing*, 18(6):1239–1254, 2009.

[37] Z. Xu, Y. Yang, I. Tsang, N. Sebe, and A. G. Hauptmann. Feature weighting via optimal thresholding for video analysis. In *ICCV*, pages 3440–3447, 2013.

[38] Y. Yang, F. Nie, D. Xu, J. Luo, Y. Zhuang, and Y. Pan. A multimedia retrieval framework based on semi-supervised ranking and relevance feedback. *IEEE Trans. Pattern Anal. Mach. Intell.*, 34(4):723–742, 2012.

[39] Y. Yang, J. Song, Z. Huang, Z. Ma, N. Sebe, and A. G. Hauptmann. Multi-feature fusion via hierarchical regression for multimedia analysis. *IEEE Transactions on Multimedia*, 15(3):572–581, 2013.

[40] S. Yu, B. Krishnapuram, R. Rosales, H. Steck, and R. B. Rao. Bayesian co-training. In *NIPS*, 2007.

[41] S.-I. Yu, Y. Yang, and A. G. Hauptmann. Harry potter's marauder's map: Localizing and tracking multiple persons-of-interest by nonnegative discretization. In *CVPR*, pages 3714–3720, 2013.

[42] T. Zhang, C. Xu, G. Zhu, S. Liu, and H. Lu. A generic framework for video annotation via semi-supervised learning. *IEEE Transactions on Multimedia*, 14(4):1206–1219, 2012.

[43] X. Zhu. Semi-supervised learning literature survey. In *Technical Report 1530, University of Wisconsin, Madison*, 2007.

[44] X. Zhu, Z. Ghahramani, and J. D. Lafferty. Semi-supervised learning using gaussian fields and harmonic functions. In *ICML*, pages 912–919, 2003.

Latent Tensor Transfer Learning for RGB-D Action Recognition*

Chengcheng Jia[1], Yu Kong[1], Zhengming Ding[1], Yun Fu[1,2]
[1]Electrical and Computer Engineering, [2]Computer and Information Science, Northeastern University, USA
{cjia, allanding}@coe.neu.edu, {yukong, yunfu}@ece.neu.edu

ABSTRACT

This paper proposes a method to compensate RGB-D images from the original target RGB images by transferring the depth knowledge of source data. Conventional RGB databases (*e.g.*, UT-Interaction database) do not contain depth information since they are captured by the RGB cameras. Therefore, the methods designed for RGB databases cannot take advantage of depth information, which proves useful for simplifying intra-class variations and background subtraction. In this paper, we present a novel transfer learning method that can transfer the knowledge from depth information to the RGB database, and use the additional source information to recognize human actions in RGB videos. Our method takes full advantage of 3D geometric information contained within the learned depth data, thus, can further improve action recognition performance. We treat action data as a fourth-order tensor (row, column, frame and sample), and apply latent low-rank transfer learning to learn shared subspaces of the source and target databases. Moreover, we introduce a novel cross-modality regularizer that plays an important role in finding the correlation between RGB and depth modalities, and then more depth information from the source database can be transferred to that of the target. Our method is extensively evaluated on public by available databases. Results of two action datasets show that our method outperforms existing methods.

Categories and Subject Descriptors

I.5.4 [**Pattern Recognition**]: Applications; H.2.8 [**Database Applications**]: Data Mining

Keywords

RGB-D Action Recognition; Transfer Learning; Latent Tensor.

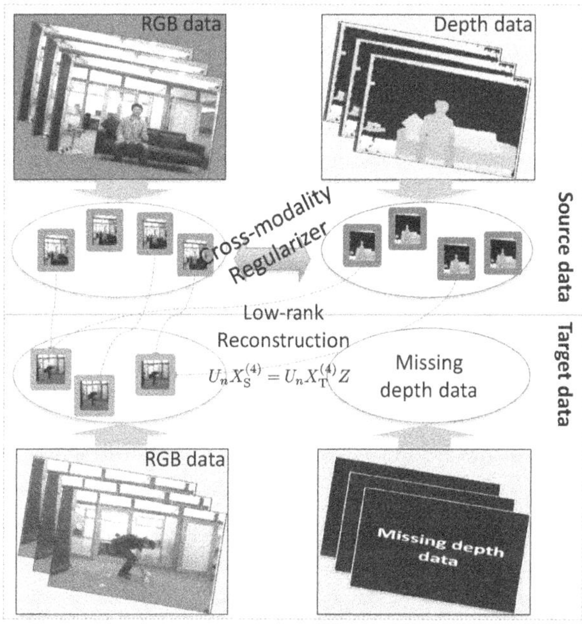

Figure 1: Our method is able to transfer knowledge from the RGB-D dataset to the RGB dataset, so missing depth information can be compensated for. Using a latent low-rank constraint $U_n X_S = U_n X_T Z + L U_n X_S + E$, the missing depth information in the target is uncoverable. A novel cross-modality regularizer is added to couple the RGB and depth modalities to properly align and transfer more depth information to that of the target.

1. INTRODUCTION

Due to the recent advent of the cost-effective Kinect sensors, action recognition from RGB-D cameras has received an increasing interest through out the computer vision community. Compared with conventional RGB cameras, Kinect sensors provide depth information, computing 3D-structural information of the entire scene. The 3D-structural information can facilitate the recognition task by simplifying intra-class motion variation and removing cluttered background noise. Recent work [48, 49, 8, 52] has shown that the performance of recognition systems can be improved by applying depth information to yield RGB-D databases (*e.g.*, MSR DailyAction3D database [51] and MSR PairAction3D database [30]).

*This research is supported in part by the NSF CNS award 1314484, ONR award N00014-12-1-1028, ONR Young Investigator Award N00014-14-1-0484, and U.S. Army Research Office Young Investigator Award W911NF-14-1-0218.

MM'14, November 3–7, 2014, Orlando, Florida, USA.
Copyright 2014 ACM 978-1-4503-3063-3/14/11 ...$15.00.
http://dx.doi.org/10.1145/2647868.2654928.

The useful depth information is not incorporated in most of the popular RGB action databases[1] (e.g., UT-Interaction [37], UCF Sports [35], UCF 101 [41], KTH [38], and Hollywood database [18]), as conventional RGB cameras were used to capture data. Therefore, methods [51, 20, 3, 34, 11] that were designed for these RGB action databases cannot utilize the rich 3D-structural information to reduce large intra-class variations. Thus, the performance is limited. Even with the state-of-the-art methods having achieved high performance on some action classes, they often fail to understand actions in more challenging scenarios (*e.g.*, occluded body parts) due to the lack of 3D structural information. On the other hand, several methods [21, 49, 52, 8] have been proposed to utilize 3D-structural information, but require real RGB-D databases, and cannot be directly applied to RGB databases.

In this paper, we propose a novel action recognition method for learning the "missing" depth information[2] that is not included in conventional RGB action databases (Figure 1) to further improve the recognition performance. We utilize a RGB-D database as the source data, and learn the knowledge about the correlations between the two modalities: RGB data and depth data of the source data. This knowledge is then transferred to the target data, which only has RGB information. Consequently, depth information can be compensated for in the target data. Moreover, a cross-modality regularizer is added to the two modalities of source data so that RGB and depth information can be well coupled, and more depth information can be transferred to the target database. Therefore, on the target database, our method can extract useful 3D-structural information, improving the performance over methods that only uses the real RGB data.

The significance of our method is that we incorporate the knowledge about the correlations between RGB and depth data into our model. The use of this rich knowledge allows us to use additional source of information for recognition. Even though this knowledge does not exist in the target training and testing data, we can still learn this knowledge from an additional RGB-D source data, and then transfer it to the RGB target data. Our experimental results demonstrate that the learned knowledge significantly improves the recognition performance when compares with the case that only RGB information is used. In addition, we bridge the gap between RGB database and RGB-D database. Previous methods treat them as different application subjects, *i.e.*, action recognition [51, 20, 3] and RGB-D action recognition [21, 49, 52, 8]. By comparison, in this work, we show that RGB-D database can be used as strong depth information for the RGB database. Consequently, conventional RGB action databases can be reused as "RGB-D" databases, and provide action recognition methods with rich depth information fused within. Furthermore, compared with attribute-based methods [27, 15, 16] for recovering missing training samples, the knowledge in our work is data-driven, and is automatically discovered from data rather than being manually specified by experts. This helps us mine useful knowledge and avoid subjective labeling in an automated fashion.

There are many previous studies that used tensor for high dimensional data representation [42], in order to distinguish their various factors (*e.g.*, identity, expression, illumination, color in face recognition [46, 32], object classification [44], and action video recognition [45, 22, 12]). Motivated by these methods, here we use a tensor to represent by an action sequence. Specifically, a RGB or depth action video is represented as a third-order tensor, while a RGB-D action video is composed of two third-order tensors. It can also be constructed as a fourth-order tensor, when there is a "missing" modality (e.g., RGB or depth), the fourth-order tensor can be truncated to a third-order tensor.

Suppose the data with "missing" depth modality is a third-order tensor, and the whole dataset is taken as a fourth-order tensor. We apply latent low-rank transfer learning on the fourth-mode of the tensor data. Using the latent low-rank constraint, the source database with complete modalities can transfer the knowledge of the depth information to the target database, and help compensate for the missing modality in the target database. Furthermore, we add a cross-modality regularizer on the two modalities of source database to properly align the two modalities. In this way, the knowledge about the RGB and depth channels can be balanced, and more depth information in source database can be transferred to the target one in order to better discover missing information in the target/test.

Our method can be generalized to satisfy many applications. First, our method can recognize RGB videos when only RGB videos in target database are used for training. We learn knowledge of the depth data from RGB-D source data. Second, our method can recognize RGB/depth videos when only depth/RGB target videos are used for training. Third, our method can recognize RGB-D videos when only RGB target videos are used for training. We treat RGB and depth information as two separate modalities. If one modality is missing in training/testing, our method can still recognize the video, and make use of both appearance and 3D-structural information.

Our method has fundamental differences from existing action recognition methods [48, 49, 8, 52] with RGB-D videos. RGB-D data was previously both available in the training set and the testing set, while we now only have RGB data in both target training set and testing set. The depth information in the source data is not directly used for recognition, but is transferred as the learned knowledge to the target data. Experiments show that our method can achieve competitive performance with using this transferred knowledge.

2. RELATED WORK

2.1 Action Recognition

Conventional action recognition methods mainly focus on RGB videos. These methods can roughly be divided into two categories: low-level feature-based methods and mid-level knowledge-based methods. Low-level feature-based methods [6, 38, 17, 13, 19] use spatio-temporal interest points, body shape feature [26], structure information [36], key poses [34], etc., to represent human actions. These methods rely on hand-crafted features, which the actions directly learn from. Recent work also shows that action features can be learned using deep learning techniques [11].

Even though these studies yielded promising results in action recognition, they show little promise with representing actions due to the large semantic gap between low-level features and high level understanding. In order to solve this problem, mid-level features, such as attributes [27], optical flow [50], semantic descriptions [15], context [4], and relations [43], are learned from low-level features, then used for the recognition task. The learned mid-level features can be considered as knowledge discovered from the same database used for training or having been specified by experts. Com-

[1]In this work, RGB action database means the one that is captured by a conventional RGB camera. Only RGB data are available in the RGB action database; depth data are not available. RGB-D action database is the one that is captured by a RGB-D camera. Both RGB data and depth data are available in the RGB-D action database.

[2]In this work, the missing depth data means that they are not included in the conventional RGB action databases, or we intentionally remove them from a RGB-D database to build a RGB database for evaluation.

pared with these methods, the knowledge in our work is homogeneous and is used in a cross-database fashion, while they use inhomogeneous knowledge in the same database. The knowledge used in our work is discovered in the RGB-D source database, and transferred to another RGB target database. Differently, they discover knowledge (or specify knowledge) in RGB database and use it throughout the same RGB database.

Recently, due to the advent of the cost-effective Kinect sensor, researchers have put lots of attentions to the recognizing actions from RGB-D data [48, 49, 8, 52, 28, 30]. Compared with conventional RGB data, the additional depth information allows us to capture 3D structural information, which is very useful in removing background information and simplifying intra-class motion variations. Depth information is on available in the target training and testing databases in this work. We use additional RGB-D data as the source database, and learn the correlations between RGB data and depth data. The learned correlation knowledge is then transferred to the target database where the depth information does not exist. With the learned depth information, the performance on the target RGB data improves from when only the RGB data in the target data are used.

2.2 Transfer Learning

Transfer learning techniques attract lots of attention those recent years, which aim to transfer existing, well-instituted knowledge to the new datasets or new problems. Generally, transfer learning techniques can be categorized by domains and tasks. Among them, inductive transfer learning is defined by the same data domain, but by different tasks. In addition, transductive transfer learning [39, 10] uses different data domains for the same task. In transfer learning problems, target data and source data should share common properties, as the information in the source domain is available for the target domain to reference. Additional detailed references are available in the survey of transfer learning [31].

More recently, a low-rank constraint was introduced to transfer learning [39, 10]. Low-rank representation (LRR) [24, 23] can discover the structure information of the data, especially the data come from various subspaces. LRR aims to find the lowest rank representation amongst all the data, which can be represented as the linear combinations of the basis. Such a low rank representation can uncover the dataset in its entire global structure, grouping the correlated candidates into one cluster. In addition, LRR handles more noise and gross corruption of data than other traditional methods that only consider the Gaussian noise. Moreover, Liu et al. proposed a latent low-rank representation (LatLRR) method to handle the limited observed data problem [25]. LatLRR discovers the latent information of the unobserved data from the observed, making the recovery more stable.

Even more recently, a low-rank constraint was used in transfer learning. LTSL [39] and LRDAP [10] are two typical transfer learning methods that include the low-rank constraint. LTSL aims to find a common subspace where the source data can well represent the target in the low-rank framework. LRDAP aims to find a rotation on source domain data to be represented by the target domain in the low-rank framework. LRDAP considers that the rotated source data can be used to test the target data when the rotated source data can be reconstructed in the target domain.

Different from the previous work, our method aims to solve missing modality problem by transferring depth from RGB-D source data to the RGB target data in tensor framework. By introducing a new cross-modality regularizer on the source data, our method can couple the two RGB and depth modalities to transfer more depth information into the target domain to compensate for the missing depth information in the target data.

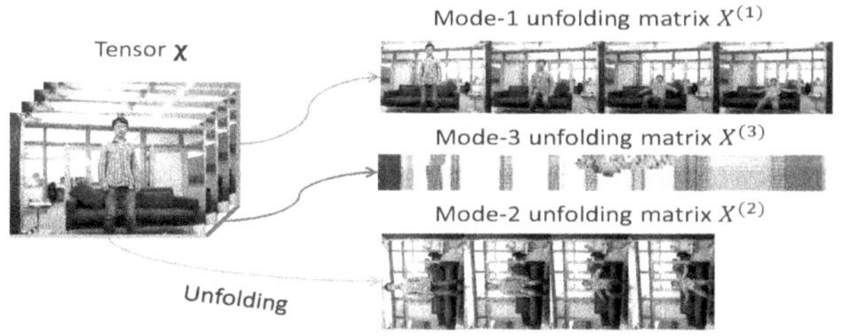

Figure 2: Illustration of tensor *mode-n* unfolding. An action sequence is represented as a 3D tensor $\mathcal{X}$, and we get *mode-n* unfolding matrix $X^{(n)}$ along its *x, y, z-axis*.

3. LATENT LOW-RANK TENSOR TRANSFER LEARNING

3.1 Preliminary

A multi-dimensional array $\mathcal{X} \in \mathbb{R}^{I_1 \times \ldots \times I_n \times \ldots \times I_N}$ is called an *Nth-order* tensor, where I_n is the size of n-th dimension. For example, a vector $x \in \mathbb{R}^{I_1}$ can be taken as a *first-order* tensor, a matrix $X \in \mathbb{R}^{I_1 \times I_2}$ is called a *second-order* tensor. Each element of $\mathcal{X}$ is represented as $\mathcal{X}_{i_1 \ldots i_n \ldots i_N}$, where i_n is the index of n-th dimension (or mode). The n-th mode of $\mathcal{X}$ is of size I_n, while each fiber $x \in \mathbb{R}^{I_n}$ of n-th mode is a *mode-n* vector [14].

Definition 1: Mode-n unfolding
An Nth-order tensor $\mathcal{X}$ can be stretched by fixing the mode-n vectors to be a matrix $X_{(n)} \in \mathbb{R}^{I_n \times (I_1 \cdot I_2 \ldots I_{n-1} \cdot I_{n+1} \ldots I_N)}$, where $\cdot$ is used for scalar product.

Definition 2: Tucker decomposition
Given a tensor $\mathcal{X} \in \mathbb{R}^{I_1 \times \ldots \times I_N}$, and projection matrices $U_n \in \mathbb{R}^{I_n \times J_n} (1 \leqslant n \leqslant \mathrm{N})$, the decomposition is performed by

$$\mathcal{S} = \mathcal{X} \times_1 U_1 \times_2 U_2 \ldots \times_n U_n \ldots \times_{\mathrm{N}} U_{\mathrm{N}}, \quad (1)$$

where $\mathcal{X} = \mathcal{S} \times_1 U_1^{\mathrm{T}} \times_2 U_2^{\mathrm{T}} \ldots \times_n U_n^{\mathrm{T}} \ldots \times_{\mathrm{N}} U_{\mathrm{N}}^{\mathrm{T}}$, $\times_n$ indicates mode-n product. $\mathcal{S} \in \mathbb{R}^{J_1 \times J_2 \times \ldots \times J_{\mathrm{N}}}$ is called the core tensor.

The illustration of the *mode-n* unfolding of $\mathcal{X}$ is shown in Figure 2. By unfolding along *x-axis* we get a matrix ordered by images side-by-side, and along *y-axis* all the images are ordered in a column, while along *z-axis* we put the cross section side-by-side.

3.2 Latent Problem Formulation

Given two action databases in fourth-order tensor representation, $\mathcal{X}_{\mathrm{S}} \in \mathbb{R}^{(I_1 \times I_2 \times I_3) \times I_{\mathrm{S}}}$ and $\mathcal{X}_{\mathrm{T}} \in \mathbb{R}^{(I_1 \times I_2 \times I_3) \times I_{\mathrm{T}}}$, where I_1 and I_2 mean the row and column dimensions of one frame, I_3 indicates the number of frames in one action sample, and I_{S}, I_{T} are the numbers of action samples in source and target databases, respectively. Each database has two modalities: RGB and depth, which are combined in the fourth-order of the data tensor, *i.e.*, $\mathcal{X}_{\mathrm{S}} = [\mathcal{X}_{\mathrm{S \cdot RGB}}, \mathcal{X}_{\mathrm{S \cdot D}}]$ and $\mathcal{X}_{\mathrm{T}} = [\mathcal{X}_{\mathrm{T \cdot RGB}}, \mathcal{X}_{\mathrm{T \cdot D}}]$. Traditional transfer learning methods would consider the transfer between modalities within one database, (e.g, $\mathcal{X}_{\mathrm{S \cdot RGB}} \rightarrow \mathcal{X}_{\mathrm{S \cdot D}}$ and $\mathcal{X}_{\mathrm{T \cdot RGB}} \rightarrow \mathcal{X}_{\mathrm{T \cdot D}}$), or the transfer between two databases in one modality, (e.g. $\mathcal{X}_{\mathrm{S \cdot RGB}} \rightarrow \mathcal{X}_{\mathrm{T \cdot RGB}}$ and $\mathcal{X}_{\mathrm{S \cdot D}} \rightarrow \mathcal{X}_{\mathrm{T \cdot D}}$). However, when one modality of the target is missing, both the kinds of traditional transfer learning would fail. How can we uncover the information of the lost modality? In this paper, we propose a latent low-rank tensor transfer learning by introducing a graph regularizer to couple RGB and depth information in the source database, then transfer to the target database. We consider the transfer $\mathcal{X}_{\mathrm{S}} \rightarrow \mathcal{X}_{\mathrm{T}}$, where the source has two modalities, while the target contains only one modality.

Since $\mathcal{X}_{\mathrm{S}}$ and $\mathcal{X}_{\mathrm{T}}$ are two different databases lying in different spaces, $\mathcal{X}_{\mathrm{S}} \subsetneq \mathcal{X}_{\mathrm{T}}$. Suppose the source data $\mathcal{X}_{\mathrm{S}}$ and target data $\mathcal{X}_{\mathrm{T}}$ in the same space, both projected with U_n $(n = 1, 2, 3)$ on the first three modes of databases, *i.e.*, $U_n \mathcal{X}_{\mathrm{S}} \subseteq U_n \mathcal{X}_{\mathrm{T}}$. First, we assume $\mathcal{X}_{\mathrm{T\cdot D}}$ is known and unfold both the tensors in the fourth-order to get $U_n X_{\mathrm{S}}^{(4)}, U_n X_{\mathrm{T}}^{(4)}$, see **Figure 2**. As many previous researches have shown, low-rank representation in transfer learning helps preserve the locality in reconstruction and find the block structure of the source data. We define the low-rank tensor transfer learning with unfolded tensor data as

$$\begin{aligned} &\min_{Z} \|Z\|_*, \\ &\text{s.t. } U_n X_{\mathrm{S}}^{(4)} = U_n X_{\mathrm{T}}^{(4)} Z, \\ &U_n^{\mathrm{T}} U_n = \mathrm{I}, \quad n = 1, 2, 3, \end{aligned} \tag{2}$$

where $\|\cdot\|_*$ is the nuclear norm and Z is called "low-rank representations" of source data $X_{\mathrm{S}}^{(4)}$ with respect to the target data $X_{\mathrm{T}}^{(4)}$. We focus on the unfolded tensor in the fourth-order, so we omit the superscript "$\cdot^{(4)}$" for simplicity, since the source and target data are well-aligned after projected by U_n $(n = 1, 2, 3)$.

We propose to find the relationship between X_{S} and X_{T} via SVD, *i.e.*, $U_n[X_{\mathrm{S}}, X_{\mathrm{T}}] = H\Sigma V^{\mathrm{T}}$, where $V = [V_{\mathrm{S}}; V_{\mathrm{T}}]$ by row partition. Therefore, $U_n[X_{\mathrm{S}}, X_{\mathrm{T}}] = H\Sigma[V_{\mathrm{S}}; V_{\mathrm{T}}]^{\mathrm{T}} = [H\Sigma V_{\mathrm{S}}^{\mathrm{T}}; H\Sigma V_{\mathrm{T}}^{\mathrm{T}}]$, and $U_n X_{\mathrm{S}} = H\Sigma V_{\mathrm{S}}^{\mathrm{T}}, U_n X_{\mathrm{T}} = H\Sigma V_{\mathrm{T}}^{\mathrm{T}}$ can be derived. The above constraint can be written as

$$H\Sigma V_{\mathrm{S}}^{\mathrm{T}} = H\Sigma V_{\mathrm{T}}^{\mathrm{T}} Z. \tag{3}$$

Therefore, Eq. (2) can be transformed into

$$\begin{aligned} &\min_{Z} \|Z\|_*, \\ &\text{s.t. } V_{\mathrm{S}}^{\mathrm{T}} = V_{\mathrm{T}}^{\mathrm{T}} Z. \end{aligned} \tag{4}$$

According to **Theorem 3.1** [25], the optimal low-rank representation Z_* can be found as follows:

$$\begin{aligned} Z_* &= V_{\mathrm{T}} V_{\mathrm{S}}^{\mathrm{T}} \\ &= [V_{\mathrm{T\cdot RGB}}; V_{\mathrm{T\cdot D}}] V_{\mathrm{S}}^{\mathrm{T}}, \end{aligned} \tag{5}$$

where V_{T} has been row partitioned into $V_{\mathrm{T\cdot RGB}}$ and $V_{\mathrm{T\cdot D}}$. Then the constrained part can be rewritten as

$$\begin{aligned} U_n X_{\mathrm{S}} &= U_n X_{\mathrm{T}} Z_* \\ &= U_n [X_{\mathrm{T\cdot RGB}}, X_{\mathrm{T\cdot D}}] Z_* \\ &= U_n [X_{\mathrm{T\cdot RGB}}, X_{\mathrm{T\cdot D}}][V_{\mathrm{T\cdot RGB}}; V_{\mathrm{T\cdot D}}] V_{\mathrm{S}}^{\mathrm{T}} \\ &= U_n X_{\mathrm{T\cdot RGB}} V_{\mathrm{T\cdot RGB}} V_{\mathrm{S}}^{\mathrm{T}} + U_n X_{\mathrm{T\cdot D}} V_{\mathrm{T\cdot D}} V_{\mathrm{S}}^{\mathrm{T}} \\ &= U_n X_{\mathrm{T\cdot RGB}} (V_{\mathrm{T\cdot RGB}} V_{\mathrm{S}}^{\mathrm{T}}) + U\Sigma V_{\mathrm{T\cdot D}}^{\mathrm{T}} V_{\mathrm{T\cdot D}} V_{\mathrm{S}}^{\mathrm{T}} \\ &= U_n X_{\mathrm{T\cdot RGB}} \tilde{Z} + (U\Sigma V_{\mathrm{T\cdot D}}^{\mathrm{T}} V_{\mathrm{T\cdot D}} \Sigma^{-1} U^{\mathrm{T}}) U_n X_{\mathrm{S}} \\ &= U_n X_{\mathrm{T\cdot RGB}} \tilde{Z} + \tilde{L} U_n X_{\mathrm{S}}, \end{aligned} \tag{6}$$

where $\tilde{Z}$ indicates the low-rank structure of source data on the target data only with RGB, and $\tilde{L} = U\Sigma V_{\mathrm{T\cdot D}}^{\mathrm{T}} V_{\mathrm{T\cdot D}} \Sigma^{-1} U^{\mathrm{T}}$ should also be low-rank, as $V_{\mathrm{T\cdot D}}^{\mathrm{T}} V_{\mathrm{T\cdot D}}$ aims to uncover the block structure of $U_n X_{\mathrm{T\cdot D}}$.

Therefore, when $X_{\mathrm{T\cdot D}}$ is unobserved (that is, $X_{\mathrm{T}} = X_{\mathrm{T\cdot RGB}}$), the objective function could be written as

$$\begin{aligned} &\min_{\tilde{Z}, \tilde{L}} \|\tilde{Z}\|_* + \|\tilde{L}\|_*, \\ &\text{s.t. } U_n X_{\mathrm{S}} = U_n X_{\mathrm{T}} \tilde{Z} + \tilde{L} U_n X_{\mathrm{S}}, \\ &U_n^{\mathrm{T}} U_n = \mathrm{I}, \ n = 1, 2, 3. \end{aligned} \tag{7}$$

With Eq. (7), we can handle the problem where part of the target data is missing by referencing the recovered data from the source domain. For simplicity, we remove the tildes from $\tilde{Z}$ and $\tilde{L}$.

In reality, the data is sometimes corrupted. So we need to add an error term as done previously in [24, 39, 23], then the general model in Eq. (7) is represented as

$$\begin{aligned} &\min_{Z, L, E} \|Z\|_* + \|L\|_* + \lambda \|E\|_{2,1} \\ &\text{s.t. } U_n X_{\mathrm{S}} = U_n X_{\mathrm{T}} Z + L U_n X_{\mathrm{S}} + E, \\ &U_n^{\mathrm{T}} U_n = \mathrm{I}, \ n = 1, 2, 3, \end{aligned} \tag{8}$$

where $\lambda > 0$ is the parameter to balance the error, and $\|E\|_{2,1} = \sum_{i=1}^{I_{\mathrm{S}}} \sqrt{\sum_{j=1}^{(I_1 \times I_2 \times I_3)} ([E]_{ij})^2}$ is $L_{2,1}$ norm, which can make E sample specific (column sparsity), resulting in the formula detecting some outliers.

As shown in [25], LatLRR provides a way to reconstruct the hidden data matrix from two directions: column and row of the observed data. Our algorithm also has such an advantage. The source data $U_n X_{\mathrm{S}}$ is reconstructed from both the fourth-order of $U_n X_{\mathrm{T}}$ and the first three orders of $U_n X_{\mathrm{S}}$. That is, when some data in the target domain is missing, $U_n X_{\mathrm{S}}$ will make sense in reconstruction, and uncover the latent information of the missing data. When solving the previous problem, the objective testing modality is the missing part of the target data. We can then uncover more latent information from the source data in transfer subspace learning.

3.3 Cross-Modality Regularizer

The latent low-rank tensor model can uncover the lost modality of the target using the source dataset. In this section, we introduce a cross-modality regularizer to capture the modality information in the source data, so that more depth information from the source dataset can be transferred to the target dataset. The learned Z can be treated as a new low-rank representation of the projected source data $U_n X_{\mathrm{S}}$, which is a combination of RGB data Z_{RGB} and depth data Z_{D}. Our goal is to couple the different RGB and depth modalities of the same class by the similar low-rank coefficients. We define z_i as the i-th column of Z, which correlates with the i-th sample x_i of X_{S}. According to this property, we introduce a novel regularization term.

$$\begin{aligned} &\min_{z_i, z_j} \sum_{i=1}^{I_{\mathrm{S}}} \sum_{j=1}^{I_{\mathrm{S}}} (z_i - z_j)^2 w_{ij}, \\ &\forall i, j, w_{ij} \in \mathcal{W}, \end{aligned} \tag{9}$$

where $w_{ij} = 1$, if x_i and x_j have the same label; $w_{ij} = 0$ otherwise. From this formulation, we saw that Eq. (9) enforces z_i and z_j to be similar if w_{ij} is 1. Mathematically, Eq. (9) can be rewritten as $\mathrm{tr}(Z^{\mathrm{T}} \mathcal{L} Z)$, where $\mathcal{L} = \mathcal{D} - \mathcal{W}$ and $\mathcal{D}$ is a diagonal matrix with the rows sum of $\mathcal{W}$ as the element. It can be seen that $\mathcal{L}$ is very similar to graph Laplacian, which has been extensively used in spectral clustering [47] and graph embedding [53]. However, different from them, the proposed term $\mathcal{W}$, as it carries discriminative label information between modalities for source data, where RGB and depth data with the same label are coupled. By adding the regularization term $\mathrm{tr}(Z^T \mathcal{L} Z)$ to Eq. (9), our final objective function results as follows:

$$\begin{aligned} &\min_{Z, L, E} \|Z\|_* + \|L\|_* + \lambda \|E\|_{2,1} + \tfrac{\beta}{2} \mathrm{tr}(Z^{\mathrm{T}} \mathcal{L} Z), \\ &\text{s.t. } U_n X_{\mathrm{S}} = U_n X_{\mathrm{T}} Z + L U_n X_{\mathrm{S}} + E, \\ &U_n^{\mathrm{T}} U_n = \mathrm{I}, \ n = 1, 2, 3, \end{aligned} \tag{10}$$

where $\beta \geq 0$ is the balanced parameter. When $\beta = 0$ there is no couples between the two modalities in the source data.

With the above formula, two modalities of the source dataset can be well coupled when reconstructed by the target data with a low-rank constraint. Therefore, the information of the lost modality in target dataset can be more uncovered using the complete modality source dataset in transfer learning. In the experiment, we show that the cross-modality regularizer can help with transferring the depth information of source data to uncover the missing depth modality of the target data.

3.4 Solving Objective Function

To solve Eq. (10), we rewrite the objective function by introducing some auxiliary matrices as

$$\min_{\substack{K,Z,W,\\L,E}} \|K\|_* + \|W\|_* + \frac{\beta}{2}\mathrm{tr}(Z^T\mathcal{L}Z) + \lambda\|E\|_{2,1},$$
$$\text{s.t. } U_nX_S = U_nX_TZ + LU_nX_S + E, \quad (11)$$
$$Z = K, \; L = W, \; U_n^TU_n = \mathrm{I}, \; n = 1,2,3.$$

Augmented Lagrangian Multiplier [33, 9] is applied to achieve better convergence of the Eq. (11), the augmented Lagrangian function is:

$$\begin{aligned}\min_{\substack{K,W,Z,L,\\U_n,E}} \quad & \|K\|_* + \|W\|_* + \lambda\|E\|_{2,1} \\ & +\mathrm{tr}[Y_1^T(U_nX_S - U_nX_TZ - LU_nX_S - E)] \\ & +\mathrm{tr}[Y_2^T(Z-K)] + \mathrm{tr}[Y_3^T(L-W)] \\ & +\frac{\beta}{2}\mathrm{tr}(Z^T\mathcal{L}Z) + \frac{\mu}{2}\left[\|Z-K\|_F^2 + \|L-W\|_F^2\right. \\ & \left.+\|U_nX_S - U_nX_TZ - LU_nX_S - E\|_F^2\right],\end{aligned} \quad (12)$$

where Y_1, Y_2, Y_3 are Lagrange multipliers and $\mu > 0$ is a penalty parameter. All the variables in the Eq. (12) are difficult to calculate jointly, however, we can optimize them one-by-one in an iterative manner. We use the Augmented Lagrangian Multiplier [33, 9] for the above problem, which converges well even when some of the data is not smooth. In details, we alternately update the variables Z, L, E, K, W and U_n in the $t+1$ iteration as follows:

For K:

$$K_{t+1} = \arg\min_K \frac{1}{\mu}\|K\|_* + \frac{1}{2}\|K - (Z_t + Y_2/\mu)\|_F^2. \quad (13)$$

For Z:

$$\beta\mathcal{L}Z_{t+1} + \mu Z_{t+1}(X_TX_T^T + \mathrm{I}) + \mu M_t = 0, \quad (14)$$

where $M_t = \frac{Y_2 - Y_1X_T^T}{\mu} - K_t - (X_S - L_tX_S - E_t)X_T^T$.

For W:

$$W_{t+1} = \arg\min_W \frac{1}{\mu}\|W\|_* + \frac{1}{2}\|W - (L_t + Y_3/\mu)\|_F^2. \quad (15)$$

For L:

$$\begin{aligned}L_{t+1} = [&(U_{n,t}X_S - U_{n,t}X_TZ_t - E_t)(X_S^TU_{n,t}^T) + W_t + \\ &\frac{Y_1X_S^TU_{n,t}^T - Y_3}{\mu}](U_{n,t}X_SX_S^TU_{n,t}^T + \mathrm{I})^{-1}.\end{aligned} \quad (16)$$

For $U_n, (n = 1,2,3)$:

$$U_{n,t+1} = (\frac{-Y_1}{\mu} + E_t)(X_S^{(n)} - X_T^{(n)}Z_t - L_tX_S^{(n)})^{-1}, \quad (17)$$

where $X_S^{(n)}$ and $X_T^{(n)}$ mean $\mathcal{X}_S$ and $\mathcal{X}_S$ unfolded in mode n, $n = 1,2,3$.

For E:

$$E_{t+1} = \arg\min_E \frac{\lambda}{\mu}\|E\|_{2,1} + \frac{1}{2}\|E - \widehat{E}_t\|_F^2, \quad (18)$$

where $\widehat{E}_t = U_{n,t}X_S - U_{n,t}X_TZ_t - L_tU_{n,t}X_S + Y_1/\mu$.

Amongst them, Eqs. (13)(15) can be solved by Singular Value Thresholding (SVT) [2], also it can be solved by fixed-rank representation [29] for faster speed and lower computational cost. Eq. (18) is solved by the shrinkage operator [54]. Eq. (14) is updated by a Lyap [1]. The details of the algorithm are outlined in **Algorithm 1**. The parameters μ_0, ρ, ϵ and $\max_\mu$ are set empirically, while other balance parameters are tuned for the experiment. Note, we will show the effluence of β across different values to indicate how this cross-modality regularizer helps.

Algorithm 1 LTTL (Solving Problem Eq. (12))

Input: $X_T, X_S, \lambda, \beta, \mathcal{L}$

Initialize: $Z = K = 0, W = L = 0, E = 0, Y_1 = 0, Y_2 = 0, Y_3 = 0, \mu_0 = 10^{-6}, \rho = 1.2, \max_\mu = 10^6, \epsilon = 10^{-6}$.

---

while not converged **do**

1. Fix the others and update K_{t+1} by Eq. (13).
2. Fix the others and update L_{t+1} by Eq. (16).
3. Fix the others and update Z_{t+1} by Eq. (14).
4. Fix the others and update W_{t+1} by Eq. (15).
5. Fix the others and update $U_{n,t+1}$ by Eq. (17) and $U_{n,t+1} \leftarrow$ **orthogonal**$(U_{n,t+1})$.
6. Update the multipliers Y_1, Y_2, Y_3 by
   $Y_1 = Y_1 + \mu(U_nX_S - U_nX_TZ - LU_nX_S - E)$;
   $Y_2 = Y_2 + \mu(Z - K)$;
   $Y_3 = Y_3 + \mu(L - W)$.
7. Update the parameter μ by $\mu = \min(\rho\mu, \max_\mu)$
8. Check the convergence conditions
   $\|U_{n,t+1}X_S - U_{n,t+1}X_TZ_{t+1} - L_{t+1}U_{n,t+1}X_S - E_{t+1}\|_\infty < \epsilon$,
   $\|W_{t+1} - L_{t+1}\|_\infty < \epsilon$,
   $\|Z_{t+1} - K_{t+1}\|_\infty < \epsilon$.

end while

---

output: Z, W, L, K, E, U_n.

3.5 Complexity Analysis

The main computational cost of our algorithm is the latent low-rank transfer part. For simplicity, assume both the unfolded data X_S and $X_T \in \mathbb{R}^{m\times n}$. Then the time-consuming components of **Algorithm 1** are

- Trace norm computation of an $n \times n$ matrix (Step 1 and 4).
- Matrix multiplication and inverse (Step 2 and 5).
- Lyap equation (Step 3).

Here, we discuss the computation complexity in detail. First, the trace norm solved by SVD computation in Step 1 and Step 4 take $O(n^3)$. When n is very large, this step would cost a lot. Second, the general multiplication costs $O(n^3)$, and the inverse takes $O(n^3)$. Step 2 and 5 cost $2O(n^3)$. Finally, Step 3 is Lyap function, which takes $O(m^3)$, and is related with the dimensionality of the data.

3.6 Discussion

By borrowing an auxiliary dataset, with both RGB and depth data, our method can transfer the complete modality information from the source domain to the target. We highlight some important properties of our method, and show the differences comparing with existing methods.

Uncover missing depth information in the target data. The latent low-rank constraint assumes that the transformed RGB-D source data can be represented by a transformed RGB target data plus latent information (missing depth information). This allows us to discover the missing depth information, and then use it as additional cue for recognition.

Coupling two modalities. We propose a cross-modality regularizer on the RGB and depth of source data to couple the two modalities. Therefore, they can be well aligned, and transfer more depth information to the target.

Capturing structure information. Our method captures both RGB and depth information. In addition, our tensor-based method elegantly captures spatial geometric information.

Compared with traditional transfer learning methods, such as LTSL and GFK, they do not consider the missing information in the target, as they only consider the transfering between modalities within one dataset, and transfer between two datasets in one modality. Compared with L^2TSL [5], which also considers the missing modality information, our method is tensor-based; therefore, our method can uncover more time spatial information from the action video. To the best of our knowledge, we are the first to consider transfer learning to uncover the depth information to help action recognition. Our novel cross-modality regularizer to compensate for the diversity of the two modalities in source data would help transfer more depth information to the target, so that our method can improve action recognition with only RGB data.

4. EXPERIMENTS

In the experimental part, we classify the test samples of various modalities via borrowing the missing information from the source database. Both the source and target databases are used for training, while the target database is used as reference for testing. In the source database, the RGB-D data is used throughout every experiment. Combinations of target database and testing database are listed in Section 4.4. We first introduce the experimental database and setting, then compare other transfer learning methods with our method.

4.1 Databases

In the experimental section, we use two action databases to evaluate the proposed method: MSR daily action 3D database and MSR pair action 3D database[3]. Both have two modalities, RGB images and depth images.

In the MSR daily action database, there are 16 categories of actions: *drinking, eating, reading book, calling cellphone, writing on a paper, using laptop, using vacuum cleaner, cheering up, sitting still, tossing paper, playing game, lying down on sofa, walking, playing guitar, standing up, sitting down.* All these actions are performed by 10 subjects, each performs every action twice. There are 320 RGB samples and 320 depth samples. Figure 3(a) and 4(a) show the RGB and depth sequence of one sitting action.

In the MSR pair action database, there are six pairs of actions: *picking up a box/putting down a box, lifting a box/placing a box, pushing a chair/pulling a chair, wearing a hat/taking off a hat, putting on a backpack/taking off a backpack, sticking/removing a poster.* There are a total of 360 RGB samples and 360 depth action samples. There are ten subjects performing three trails for each action, and the first five subjects for testing. Figure 3(b) shows the RGB sequence of pushing a chair action.

To unify the tensor size, we extracted 10 frames from each video sequence at specific intervals. We use the whole frame to extract feature instead of tracking, because (1) the background of the video are static, (2) we apply HOG descriptors to extract feature. Thus, the background will not contribute to the feature too much and human tracking is not necessary here.

In both databases, RGB and depth action samples were subsampled to be $80 \times 80 \times 10$, whose HOG feature [4] were exacted to represent the action samples. The HOG feature of source RGB data is shown in Figure 4(b).

[3]http://research.microsoft.com/en-us/um/people/zliu/ActionRecoRsrc/

[4]http://www.vlfeat.org/overview/hog.html

(a) Sitting sequence

(b) Pushing a chair sequence

Figure 3: RGB sequence of (a) MSR daily action 3D database and (b) MSR pair action 3D database.

4.2 Experimental Settings

4.2.1 MSR pair action recognition

In this experiment, we aim to recognize one modality of pair action by another modality. This is done by transferring the knowledge of the missing modality from other database.

Source database: MSR daily action 3D database, which contains 16 action categories by 10 subjects with 640 samples, composed of 320 RGB samples and 320 corresponding depth samples. **Target database:** MSR pair action 3D database, which includes 12 interaction categories by 10 subjects with 720 samples, containing 360 RGB samples and 360 depth samples.

We separate the target database into two parts for training and testing, respectively. Therefore, we can test each part reversely by alternating orders, which is listed in Case 1 and Case 2 situations.

Case 1: The actions of the first five subjects are used for training in the target database, while the last five subjects for testing.

Case 2: The actions by the last five subjects are employed for training, while the rest for testing.

By these two cases, we can see the recognition results for the whole pair action database.

4.2.2 MSR daily action recognition

In this experiment, we aim to classify the daily actions by transferring the knowledge from the pair action database. The setting is detailed as follows.

Source database: MSR pair action 3D database, which contains 720 samples of 12 categories by 10 subjects with 360 RGB and 360 depth samples, respectively. **Target database:** MSR daily action 3D database, which includes 640 actions of 16 categories and has 320 RGB and 320 depth samples, respectively.

We separate the target database into two parts for training and testing, respectively. Therefore, we can test each part reversely by alternating their orders, which is listed in Case 3 and Case 4 situations.

Case 3: The actions of the first five subjects are used for training in the target database, while the last five subjects for testing.

Case 4: The actions by the last five subjects are employed for training, while the rest for testing.

By this two cases, we can see the recognition result of the whole daily action database.

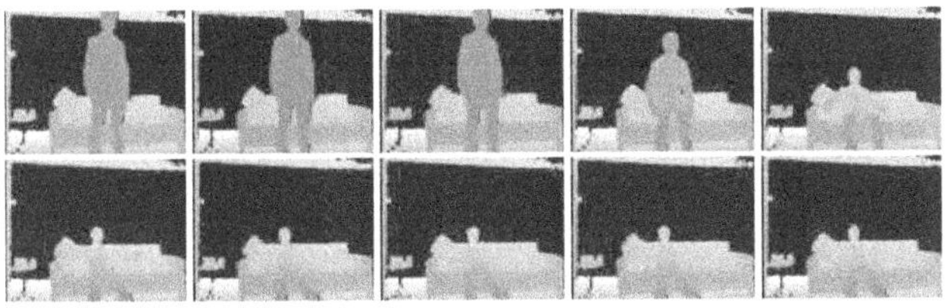

(a) MSR daily depth image sequence

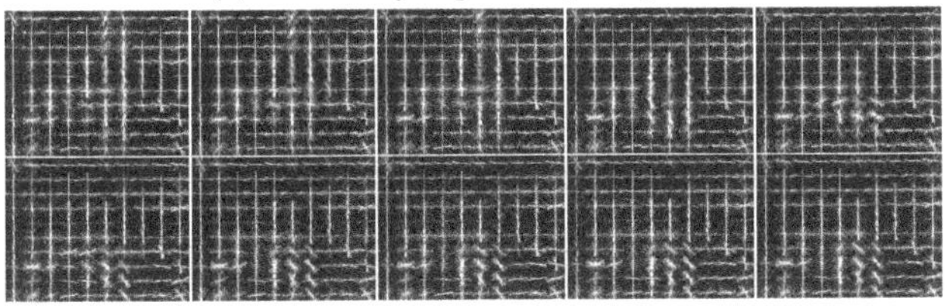

(b) MSR daily HOG feature of RGB sequence

Figure 4: MSR daily action 3D database, (a) is the depth sequence of sitting, (b) is the HOG feature of RGB sequence.

Table 1: Best accuracy (%) of Test 1 on two action databases

Test 1: RGB-RGB				
Methods	Case 1	Case 2	Case 3	Case 4
GFK [7]	64.46	61.67	20.63	20.63
LTSL [40]	57.85	46.67	6.88	5.63
HOG-KNN	76.03	64.17	19.38	18.13
Ours	**86.78**	**90.00**	**40.00**	**33.75**

4.3 Compared methods

In this section we mainly use three compared methods: LTSL [40], GFK [7], and HOG-KNN. LTSL learns a common subspace by transfer learning between two domains for objective and face recognition, which is performed through a low-rank constraint. GFK calculates a common subspace by finding the correlation of the two subspaces of source and target domains, which is an unsupervised method for objective classification. The HOG-KNN does not use transfer learning as a baseline, *i.e.*, the source database is not used in the training phase.

4.4 Comparison results

In this section, LTSL [40], GFK [7], and HOG-KNN are used for comparison in different test settings. We adopt five group testing in the target database:

4.4.1 Test 1

We set Training - Testing data: **RGB - RGB** tensor samples. In order to testify the performance of the depth information transferred from the source database X_S on the RGB samples classification, we use the source data and target RGB data for training.

In Case 1, we use 640 source data and 120 target RGB data for training, and 121 RGB data for testing. Table 1 shows the accuracy results of all the methods. It can be seen that our result is around 10% higher than the original space, which indicates that it works when transferring depth information for RGB action testing. While the LTSL and GFK is lower than the HOG-KNN, meaning the two methods have transferred negative knowledge about depth, and is not suitable for RGB-D action recognition. The result is reasonable because (1). In the object/face recognition, there is NO complex background in the data, so the environmental interference is very low compared to the human action data; (2). In the action recognition, there is much larger diversity between two categories, which is different from the object/face recognition containing the similar knowledge between two subjects.

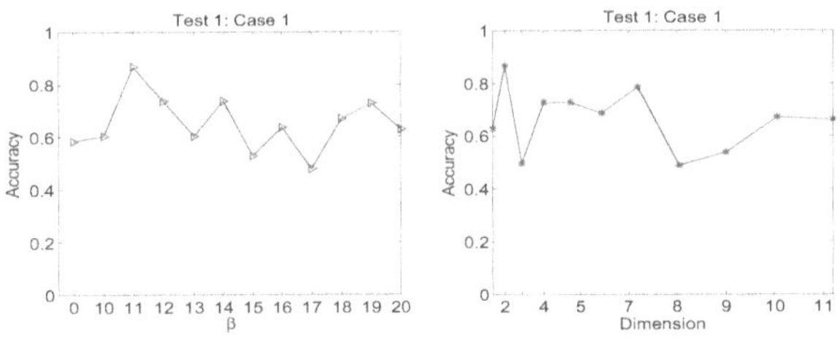

Figure 5: Accuracy under different dimensions β and Dimension on Test 1: Case 1.

The corresponding testing with different parameters has made for a better experimental setting. There are two important parameters, β and Dimension. First, we give a sequence of β values by fixing the Dimension to get the accuracy, which is shown in the left of Figure 5. It is seen that β is best around 11. When $\beta = 0$, the accuracy is lower than some other $\beta > 0$ cases. Therefore, it indicates that the Cross-modality regularizer, tr($Z\mathcal{L}Z^T$), has contributed to our model.

Second, we change the Dimension by fixing the best β learned during the last step, which is shown in the right of Figure 5. The digits [1,11] of the x-axis indicate the dimension $\{[20, 20, 5]$, $[30, 30, 5]$, $\cdots$, $[120, 120, 5]\}$, respectively. For selecting the dimension, it shows that the smaller dimension about [30,30,5] can achieve better performance than larger dimensions. This also indicates that the learned subspace can align the original and supplementary RGB samples efficiently. Notice that we obtain the best performance at certain parameters β and dimension, once tuned.

The learned projection matrix U_n ($n = 1, 2, 3$) is illustrated in Figure 6. The *mode-1,2* matrices are similar to each other, whose value scale is [-0.5,0.5], while *mode-3* matrix value is learned in larger scale [-1,1]. We show the performance of U_3 in Figure 7, from which we can see that the human information is immersed in the background. However, the eigenPush (by *mode-3* projection) kept the basic contour of the pairwise human and chair, which means U_3 can perform well by capturing the essential energy of the sequence.

4.4.2 Test 2

We set Training - Testing data: **Depth - Depth** tensor samples. Conversely, we also want to know if RGB knowledge is transferred from the source database, would it be helpful to improve the accuracy of the depth images recognition? So we use the depth samples as the target data for training, and other depth samples for testing.

Table 2 shows the results of depth testing, from which we can see the depth samples performs better than the RGB samples for recognition in Test 1. And compared with the Test 1, the transferred RGB information had minimal impact for improving the performance when compared with HOG-KNN.

4.4.3 Test 3

We set Training - Testing data: **RGB - Depth** tensor samples. As we know, the RGB and depth images are two different modalities, and the matching degree will be low between them. However, if we transfer the knowledge of one modality to another, it makes sense that the matching degree between different modalities will increase, as the sharing information is transferred from the other database. Table 3 shows the results of all the compared methods. We can see the accuracy is not as high as Test 1,2, because of the matching between the different modalities. However, it shows that the transferred depth knowledge helps to improve the performance by more than 10% compared with the original space.

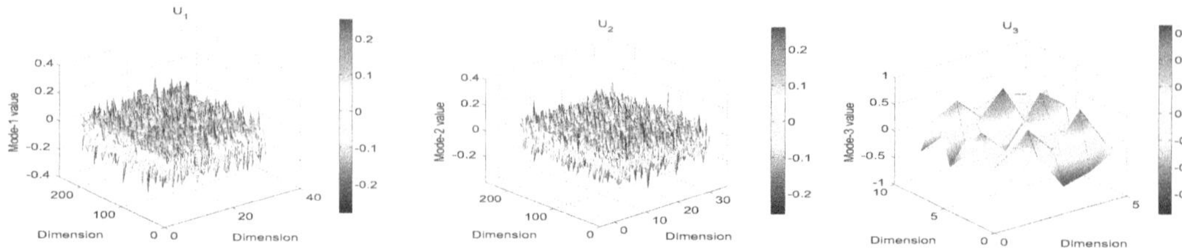

Figure 6: Illustration of *mode-n* projection matrices. U_1, U_2 perform on the *mode-1, 2* feature, while U_3 on the sequence dimension.

Table 2: Best accuracy (%) of Test 2 on two action databases

Test 2: Depth-Depth				
Methods	Case 1	Case 2	Case 3	Case 4
GFK [7]	71.59	74.58	36.25	39.38
LTSL [40]	60.80	69.49	5.63	5.63
HOG-KNN	90.91	89.27	34.38	38.75
Ours	**91.48**	**92.09**	**40.00**	**41.25**

Table 3: Best accuracy (%) of Test 3 on two action databases

Test 3: RGB-Depth				
Methods	Case 1	Case 2	Case 3	Case 4
GFK [7]	18.18	11.86	22.50	16.25
LTSL [40]	10.80	7.34	6.88	5.00
HOG-KNN	22.73	24.29	28.75	26.25
Ours	**35.23**	**31.07**	**29.38**	**34.38**

4.4.4 *Test 4*

We set Training - Testing data: **Depth - RGB** tensor samples. Considering Test 3, we transferred some RGB information from source database to compensate for the existing depth samples, and to see the performance on the RGB action testing. Table 4 shows the results of RGB classification by the depth images. We can see the transferred RGB information helped improve by more than 10%, but it shows that compensating depth knowledge in Test 3 works better than transferring RGB information, as done for this test.

4.4.5 *Test 5*

We set Training - Testing data: **RGB - RGB** & **Depth (RGB-D)** tensor samples. With RGB samples in the target database, can it be employed for new RGB-D samples classification? We suppose to generate the new samples containing both RGB and depth knowledge in the subspace, which align them with the testing RGB-D sample. All the compared results for the RGB-D action recognition are shown in Table 5. It shows that we can make use of the existing RGB images to classify the new RGB-D samples, and achieve better performance by transferring the depth knowledge from other known RGB-D database.

According to the five tests presented, all the tables show that our method performs better than the original space, which means the transfer learning between the two modalities does work for action recognition. And some other transfer methods, which work well on the RGB objective and face recognition, may transfer the negative knowledge of the RGB or depth action samples.

4.4.6 *Convergence and Cross-modality regularizer*

We use the [Test 1: Case 1] introduced in Section 4.2.1 to analyze the properties of the convergence and constraint term.

Table 4: Best accuracy (%) of Test 4 on two action databases

Test 4: Depth-RGB				
Methods	Case 1	Case 2	Case 3	Case 4
GFK [7]	7.44	19.17	15.63	14.38
LTSL [40]	7.44	12.50	5.63	5.00
HOG-KNN	12.40	22.50	17.50	16.88
Ours	**23.14**	**23.33**	**35.00**	**31.88**

Table 5: Best accuracy (%) of Test 5 on two action databases

Test 5: RGB-(RGB-D)				
Methods	Case 1	Case 2	Case 3	Case 4
GFK [7]	37.04	31.99	21.56	18.44
LTSL [40]	23.23	23.23	6.88	5.31
HOG-KNN	42.09	40.40	24.06	22.19
Ours	**51.85**	**51.52**	**34.38**	**33.44**

Convergence

The Figure 8 shows the error for a different number of iterations. The convergence condition is given in **Algorithm 1**. We can see the curves are stable within 50 iterations.

Cross-modality regularizer

In order to testify the importance of the Cross-modality regularizer, $\beta\text{tr}(Z\mathcal{L}Z^T)$, we set different β values to tune weight of the term. When $\beta = 0$, the accuracy is 58.33%, which is not competitive with the cases that $\beta > 0$. This indicates it will not improve without the constraint term.

We also illustrate the structure of Z to see whether the transfer learning works or not. There are 640 samples in the source database, in which the first 320 are RGB samples and second 320 are depth samples respectively. Z indicates the number of source and target databases in the x, y direction of the matrix.

In the source database, Z should be asymmetrical when initialized because of the two different modalities. In Figure 9, the left shows the structure after 1 iteration, from which we can see the left 320 is quite different for the right 320 part. After several iterations of learning, the structure of Z turns closely to be symmetrical as middle (3 times iterations) and right (5 times) show, which means the transfer learning exploits the connection of the two modalities, RGB and depth samples.

4.4.7 *Training Time*

We also compare our method with GFK [7] and LTSL [40] on the training time. We use MSR daily action 3D as source data and MSR pair action 3D as target data. All the tests are run on a PC (Intel Xeon E5 2650 CPU at 2.00 GHz and 128GB memory).

Results shown in Table 6 indicate that our method is significantly faster than the GFK method and the LTSL method. Our method spent 0.5 minutes training, which is 10 × faster than the GFK method and 20 × faster than the LTSL method.

Figure 7: Illustration of performance by U_3. Left: RGB samples; Medium: HOG feature; Right: eigenPush.

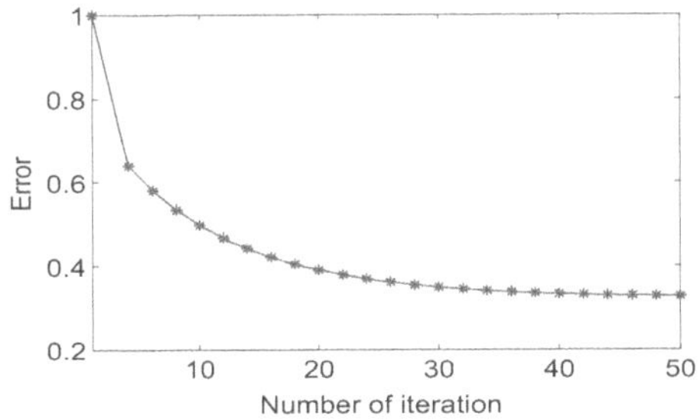

Figure 8: Mode-n (n=1,2,3) error with different number of iterations.

4.5 Discussion

For action recognition by transferring missing knowledge from an existing source database, we did some experiments on the common RGB-D databases. MSR daily action 3D and MSR pair action 3D got results compared with the state-of-the-art transfer methods; LTSL, GFK. The experiments of different setting testified our previous expectation, and we present a discussion to follow.

First, our method can outperform other compared algorithms. In this paper, we aim to improve the performance of recognition by transferring the depth information from the source domain to the target, using a latent low-rank framework. Test 1 and 2 were not traditional transfer learning cases, so that LTSL and GFK perform worse than the HOG-KNN method, as they would transfer more negative information from another database. Another reason, we consider, is that those traditional transfer learning methods does not consider the latent information and the cross-modality structure, so they would fail to transfer the depth information; on the contrary, they add more negative RGB information from the source data.

Second, our novel cross-modality regularizer plays an important role in coupling the two modalities. Obviously, it can be seen that from the structure of Z, whose left part is similar to the right part, those two parts are correlated with RGB and depth data in source, respectively. Also, we tune the parameter β to control the influence of the cross-modality regularizer. $\beta = 0$ means no cross-modality information is coupled, so the result is worse than the case when $\beta > 0$. Moreover, the learned U_n, $n = 1, 2, 3$ can be treated as a subspace projection, so we can tune their dimensions to achieve the best result. We have shown the results in different dimensions. Generally, reduced dimension combination would reach the highest recognition rate, which indicates subspace projections on three modes of the data could remove redundancies. Also, reducing dimensions can be much easier to align the source and target in the same space during the low-rank reconstruction.

Third, we use two databases made up of different action categories. Therefore, there is a large difference between two action categories. For example, pushing a chair and sitting on the sofa, which are very different from the object/face recognition. For instance, two faces from various people contain more similar information, as the location of eyes and mouth can match respectively easily. So it makes sense that the state-of-the-art transfer methods do not work well in the situation of limited common knowledge. Notice, the source database is related to the target database to some extent, they should have similar visual contents, *e.g.*, limbs moving. Besides, we can see results from different cases and find that our method performs well on the action recognition, regardless of the complex background, meaning it is more robust than the other transfer methods that mainly rely on simple experimental situation.

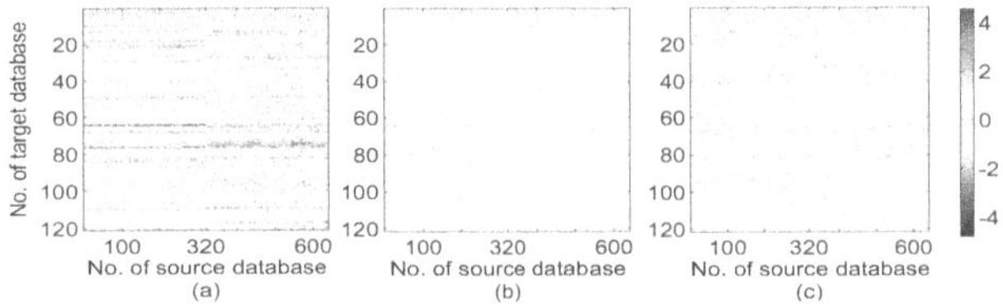

Figure 9: Illustration of low-rank matrix Z. From (a) to (c) is updated Z under 1, 3 and 5 times of iterations.

Table 6: Training time cost of methods.

Methods	GFK [7]	LTSL [40]	Ours
Training time	5 minutes	10 minutes	0.5 minutes

5. CONCLUSION

We addressed the problem transferring depth information to the target RGB action data (depth data is not available in the target data), and used both RGB data and the learned depth data for action recognition. A novel transfer learning method is proposed to use a RGB-D dataset as the source data, and to learn a shared subspace for RGB and depth data. The learned knowledge about the depth information is then effectively transferred to the target data to enrich action representations. Extensive experiments show that our method achieves superior performance over existing methods.

6. REFERENCES

[1] R. H. Bartels and G. Stewart. Solution of the matrix equation ax+ xb= c [f4]. *Communications of the ACM*, 15(9):820–826, 1972.

[2] J.-F. Cai, E. J. Candès, and Z. Shen. A singular value thresholding algorithm for matrix completion. *SIAM Journal on Optimization*, 20(4):1956–1982, 2010.

[3] Y. Cao, D. Barrett, A. Barbu, S. Narayanaswamy, H. Yu, A. Michaux, Y. Lin, S. Dickinson, J. M. Siskind, and S. Wang. Recognize human activities from partially observed videos. In *CVPR*, pages 2658–2665. IEEE, 2013.

[4] W. Choi, K. Shahid, and S. Savarese. Learning context for collective activity recognition. In *CVPR*, pages 3273–3280, 2011.

[5] Z. Ding, M. Shao, and Y. Fu. Latent low-rank transfer subspace learning for missing modality recognition. *AAAI*, 2014.

[6] P. Dollar, V. Rabaud, G. Cottrell, and S. Belongie. Behavior recognition via sparse spatio-temporal features. In *VS-PETS*, pages 65–72, 2005.

[7] B. Gong, Y. Shi, F. Sha, and K. Grauman. Geodesic flow kernel for unsupervised domain adaptation. In *CVPR*, pages 2066–2073, 2012.

[8] S. Hadfield and R. Bowden. Hollywood 3D: Recognizing Actions in 3D Natural Scenes. In *CVPR*, pages 3398–3405, 2013.

[9] M. R. Hestenes. Multiplier and gradient methods. *Journal of optimization theory and applications*, 4(5):303–320, 1969.

[10] I.-H. Jhuo, D. Liu, D. Lee, and S.-F. Chang. Robust visual domain adaptation with low-rank reconstruction. In *CVPR*, pages 2168–2175, 2012.

[11] S. Ji, W. Xu, M. Yang, and K. Yu. 3D Convolutional Neural Networks for Human Action Recognition. *IEEE TPAMI*, 35(1):221–231, 2013.
[12] C. Jia, G. Zhong, and Y. Fu. Low-rank tensor learning with discriminant analysis for action classification and image recovery. In *AAAI*, 2014.
[13] A. Klaser, M. Marszalek, and C. Schmid. A spatio-temporal descriptor based on 3d-gradients. In *BMVC*, pages 1–10, 2008.
[14] T. G. Kolda and B. W. Bader. Tensor decompositions and applications. *SIAM review*, 51(3):455–500, 2009.
[15] Y. Kong, Y. Jia, and Y. Fu. Interactive phrases: Semantic descriptions for human interaction recognition. In *IEEE TPAMI*, 2014.
[16] Y. Kong, D. Kit, and Y. Fu. A discriminative model with multiple temporal scales for action prediction. In *ECCV*, 2014.
[17] I. Laptev. On space-time interest points. *IJCV*, 64(2):107–123, 2005.
[18] I. Laptev, M. Marszałek, C. Schmid, and B. Rozenfeld. Learning realistic human actions from movies. In *CVPR*, pages 1–8, 2008.
[19] K. Li and Y. Fu. Prediction of human activity by discovering temporal sequence patterns. *TPAMI*, 36(8):1644–1657, 2014.
[20] W. Li and N. Vasconcelos. Recognizing activities by attribute dynamics. In *NIPS*, pages 1106–1114, 2012.
[21] W. Li, Z. Zhang, and Z. Liu. Action recognition based on a bag of 3d points. In *CVPR workshop*, pages 9–14, 2010.
[22] X. Li, S. Lin, S. Yan, and D. Xu. Discriminant locally linear embedding with high-order tensor data. *IEEE T SYST MAN CY B*, 38(2):342–352, 2008.
[23] G. Liu, Z. Lin, S. Yan, J. Sun, Y. Yu, and Y. Ma. Robust recovery of subspace structures by low-rank representation. *IEEE TPAMI*, 35(1):171–184, 2013.
[24] G. Liu, Z. Lin, and Y. Yu. Robust subspace segmentation by low-rank representation. In *ICML*, pages 663–670, 2010.
[25] G. Liu and S. Yan. Latent low-rank representation for subspace segmentation and feature extraction. In *ICCV*, pages 1615–1622, 2011.
[26] J. Liu, S. Ali, and M. Shah. Recognizing human actions using multiple features. In *CVPR*, pages 1–8, 2008.
[27] J. Liu, B. Kuipers, and S. Savarese. Recognizing human actions by attributes. In *CVPR*, pages 3337–3344, 2011.
[28] L. Liu and L. Shao. Learning discriminative representations from rgb-d video data. In *IJCAI*, pages 1493–1500, 2013.
[29] R. Liu, Z. Lin, F. De la Torre, and Z. Su. Fixed-rank representation for unsupervised visual learning. In *CVPR*, pages 598–605, 2012.
[30] O. Oreifej and Z. Liu. HON4D: Histogram of Oriented 4D Normals for Activity Recognition from Depth Sequences. In *CVPR*, pages 716–723, 2013.
[31] S. J. Pan and Q. Yang. A survey on transfer learning. *IEEE TKDE*, 22(10):1345–1359, 2010.
[32] Y. Pang, X. Li, and Y. Yuan. Robust tensor analysis with l1-norm. *IEEE Trans. Circuits Syst. Video Technol.*, 20(2):172–178, 2010.
[33] M. J. D. Powell. A method for nonlinear constraints in minimization problems. *Optimization*, 60(1):283–298, 1969.
[34] M. Raptis and L. Sigal. Poselet key-framing: A model for human activity recognition. In *CVPR*, pages 2650–2657. IEEE, 2013.
[35] M. D. Rodriguez, J. Ahmed, and M. Shah. Action mach: A spatio-temporal maximum average correlation height filter for action recognition. In *CVPR*, pages 1–8, 2008.
[36] M. Ryoo and J. Aggarwal. Spatio-temporal relationship match: Video structure comparison for recognition of complex human activities. In *ICCV*, pages 1593–1600, 2009.
[37] M. Ryoo and J. Aggarwal. UT-Interaction Dataset, ICPR contest on Semantic Description of Human Activities (SDHA), 2010.
[38] C. Schuldt, I. Laptev, and B. Caputo. Recognizing human actions: A local svm approach. In *ICPR*, pages 32–36, 2004.
[39] M. Shao, C. Castillo, Z. Gu, and Y. Fu. Low-rank transfer subspace learning. In *ICDM*, pages 1104–1109, 2012.
[40] M. Shao, D. Kit, and Y. Fu. Generalized transfer subspace learning through low-rank constraint. *IJCV*, pages 1–20, 2014.
[41] K. Soomro, A. R. Zamir, and M. Shah. Ucf101: A dataset of 101 human action classes from videos in the wild. In *CRCV-TR-12-01*, 2013.
[42] J. Sun, D. Tao, S. Papadimitriou, P. S. Yu, and C. Faloutsos. Incremental tensor analysis: Theory and applications. *TKDD*, 2(3):11, 2008.
[43] I. Sutskever, J. B. Tenenbaum, and R. Salakhutdinov. Modelling relational data using bayesian clustered tensor factorization. In *NIPS*, pages 1821–1828, 2009.
[44] D. Tao, X. Li, X. Wu, W. Hu, and S. J. Maybank. Supervised tensor learning. *KNOWL INF SYST*, 13(1):1–42, 2007.
[45] D. Tao, X. Li, X. Wu, and S. J. Maybank. General tensor discriminant analysis and gabor features for gait recognition. *TPAMI*, 29(10):1700–1715, 2007.
[46] D. Tao, M. Song, X. Li, J. Shen, J. Sun, X. Wu, C. Faloutsos, and S. J. Maybank. Bayesian tensor approach for 3-d face modeling. *IEEE Trans. Circuits Syst. Video Technol.*, 18(10):1397–1410, 2008.
[47] U. Von Luxburg. A tutorial on spectral clustering. *Statistics and computing*, 17(4):395–416, 2007.
[48] J. Wang, Z. Liu, J. Chorowski, Z. Chen, and Y. Wu. Robust 3D Action Recognition with Random Occupancy Patterns. In *ECCV*, pages 872–885, 2012.
[49] J. Wang, Z. Liu, Y. Wu, and J. Yuan. Mining actionlet ensemble for action recognition with depth cameras. In *CVPR*, pages 1290–1297, 2012.
[50] Y. Wang and G. Mori. Hidden part models for human action recognition: Probabilistic vs. max-margin. *IEEE TPAMI*, 33(7):1310–1323, 2011.
[51] Z. Wang, J. Wang, J. Xiao, K.-H. Lin, and T. S. Huang. Substructural and boundary modeling for continuous action recognition. In *CVPR*, pages 1330–1337, 2012.
[52] L. Xia and J. Aggarwal. Spatio-temporal depth cuboid similarity feature for activity recognition using depth camera. In *CVPR*, pages 2834–2841, 2013.
[53] S. Yan, D. Xu, B. Zhang, H.-J. Zhang, Q. Yang, and S. Lin. Graph embedding and extensions: a general framework for dimensionality reduction. *IEEE TPAMI*, 29(1):40–51, 2007.
[54] J. Yang, W. Yin, Y. Zhang, and Y. Wang. A fast algorithm for edge-preserving variational multichannel image restoration. *SIAM Journal on Imaging Sciences*, 2(2):569–592, 2009.

3D Human Activity Recognition with Reconfigurable Convolutional Neural Networks

Keze Wang[1], Xiaolong Wang[1], Liang Lin[1]*, Meng Wang[2], Wangmeng Zuo[3]
[1]Sun Yat-Sen University, Guangzhou 510006, China
[2]School of Computer Science and Information Engineering, Hefei University of Technology
[3]School of Computer Science and Technology, Harbin Institute of Technology
linliang@ieee.org; {kezewang,dragonwxl123,eric.mengwang,cswmzuo}@gmail.com

ABSTRACT

Human activity understanding with 3D/depth sensors has received increasing attention in multimedia processing and interactions. This work targets on developing a novel deep model for automatic activity recognition from RGB-D videos. We represent each human activity as an ensemble of cubic-like video segments, and learn to discover the temporal structures for a category of activities, i.e. how the activities to be decomposed in terms of classification. Our model can be regarded as a structured deep architecture, as it extends the convolutional neural networks (CNNs) by incorporating structure alternatives. Specifically, we build the network consisting of 3D convolutions and max-pooling operators over the video segments, and introduce the latent variables in each convolutional layer manipulating the activation of neurons. Our model thus advances existing approaches in two aspects: (i) it acts directly on the raw inputs (grayscale-depth data) to conduct recognition instead of relying on hand-crafted features, and (ii) the model structure can be dynamically adjusted accounting for the temporal variations of human activities, i.e. the network configuration is allowed to be partially activated during inference. For model training, we propose an EM-type optimization method that iteratively (i) discovers the latent structure by determining the decomposed actions for each training example, and (ii) learns the network parameters by using the back-propagation algorithm. Our approach is validated in challenging scenarios, and outperforms state-of-the-art methods. A large human activity database of RGB-D videos is presented in addition.

*Corresponding author is Liang Lin. This work was supported by the Hi-Tech Research and Development Program of China (no.2013AA013801), Guangdong Natural Science Foundation (no.S2013050014548), Program of Guangzhou Zhujiang Star of Science and Technology (no.2013J2200067), Special Project on Integration of Industry, Educationand Research of Guangdong (no.2012B091100148), and Fundamental Research Funds for the Central Universities (no.13lgjc26).

MM'14, November 3–7 2014, Orlando, FL, USA.

http://dx.doi.org/10.1145/2647868.2654912.

Categories and Subject Descriptors

I.4 [**Computing Methodologies**]: Image Processing and Computer Vision

General Terms

Algorithms; Experimentation; Performance

Keywords

Video Parsing; 3D Activity; Deep Learning; Structured Model

1. INTRODUCTION

In the research of multimedia, there is a particular interest in the last decades on developing intelligent systems of human activity understanding with different application backgrounds, e.g. intelligent surveillance, robotics and video content search. Recently developed 3D/depth sensors have opened up new opportunities with enormous commercial values, which provide more rich information compared with the traditional cameras (e.g., three-dimensional structure information of scenes and subjects/objects). Building upon these technologies, human poses can be easily access to, and modeling complicated human activities becomes facilitated.

This paper focuses on recognizing complex human activities from RGB-D videos that are captured by a Microsoft Kinect camera. There exist two main difficulties despite the additionally provided depth information:

- Representing complex human appearance and motion information. Due to diverse poses/views of individuals, it is usually hard to retrieve accurate body information with motions. The depth maps are often unavoidably contaminated [20], and may become unstable due to sensor noises or self-occlusions of bodies.
- Capturing large temporal variations of human activities. An activity can be considered as a sequence of actions occurred over time [3]. For instance, the activity of "microwaving food" can be decomposed into several actions such as picking up food , walking and operating microwave. The variance of a category of human activities can be hence very large, as it is uncertain how the activities to be decomposed in the temporal domain. Figure 1 shows two activities belonging to the same category, where the temporal lengths of decomposed actions are variant by different subjects.

Most of previous methods recognize 3D human activities by training discriminative or generative classifiers based on carefully designed features [36, 20, 35, 30]. These approaches

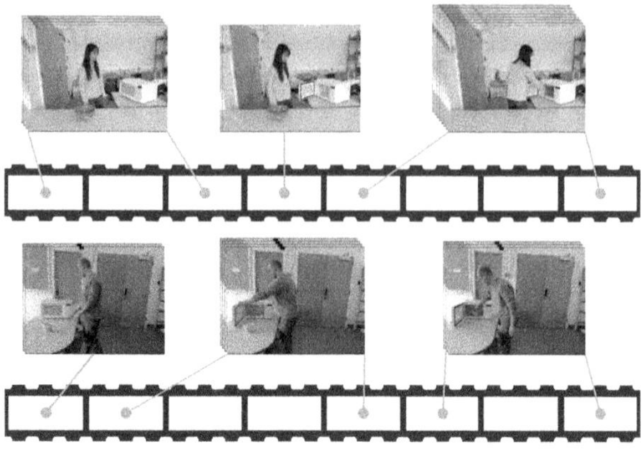

Figure 1: Two activities of the same category. We consider one activity as a sequence of actions occurred over time, and temporal compositions of actions are diverse by different subjects.

often require sufficient domain knowledge and heavy burden of feature engineering, which could limit their applications. Some compositional methods [33, 3] attempt to model activities by representing videos as sequences of fixed length temporal segments. However, they may have problems on handling complex activities composed by actions of diverse temporal durations, e.g., the example in Figure 1.

In this work, we develop an expressive configurable human activity model to address the above mentioned issues, absorbing the powers of two promising techniques of broad interests: deep learning [13, 7, 11, 8, 34, 18, 32] and reconfigurable part-based models [41, 1, 22, 16]. We represent one human activity as a sequence of separated actions, each of which is associated with a cubic-like video segment of unfixed length, as Figure 2 illustrates, and learn to discover the temporal structures for a category of human activities in terms of classification. In brief, our model is built upon the deep convolutional neural networks (CNNs) [13, 8], and we allow the network to be reconfigured to capture the varying temporal compositions of activities. We thus regard our model as a deep structured model, as it incorporates structure alternatives into a deep architecture. We consider following advantages of the deep structured model for 3D human activity recognition.

First, the deep architecture enables us to act directly on grayscale-depth data rather than relying on hand-crafted features. We build the layered network stacked up by convolutional layers, max-pooling operators and full connection layers, where the raw segmented videos are treated as inputs. We firstly apply the 3D convolutional kernel [8] over the bottom to extract features from both spatial and temporal domains, thereby encoding the motion information over adjacent frames. The 2D convolutions are then deployed upon to abstract the higher-level information. The convolutional layers for the segmented videos are computed independently to each other, in order to generate features for actions within the video segments. Afterwards, the convolution results coming from different segments are merged together into two full connection layers, giving rise to the activity classification.

Second, the structure of our model can be flexibly adjusted during inference, which is a key to improve the capability of modeling complex patterns [41, 22, 14]. Specifically, in each convolutional layer, we impose the latent variables to manipulate the activation of neurons, so that the network can be partially enabled to explicitly handle large temporal variations of activities. For example, some of the neurons can be turned-off to adapt the different temporal durations of separated actions. During the inference for activity recognition, we aggregate the responses in each layer of network while searching for the optimal network configuration. It is worth mentioning that we can conduct the inference in a parallel manner using GPU (Graphic Processing Unit) programming, in order to counterbalance the extra computational demand.

Training the structured deep model is another innovation of this work, as it is required to simultaneously optimize parameters and latent structure in the deep architecture. Thus we propose an EM-type optimization method, namely Latent Structural Back Propagation (LSBP), which iterates with two steps: (i) Fixing the current model parameters, it performs activity classification while discovering the temporal composition (i.e. determining the separated actions) for each training example. (ii) Fixing the decompositions of input videos, it learns the parameters in each layer of the network using the back-propagation algorithm.

Moreover, collecting RGB-D data is relatively expensive in practice, while the amount of training data plays a critical role in deep feature learning [11]. Thus we propose to pre-train the network on the common RGB video data, taking advantage of existing databases of human activities. The trained parameters are then transferred into our model as the initializations.

The key contribution of this work is a novel deep structured model. To the best of our knowledge, it is original in literature to make the deep architecture reconfigurable to adaptively account for data variations. We demonstrate superior performances over state-of-the-art approaches in several challenging scenarios. In addition, we construct a new database of RGB-D data, which includes 1180 human activities of 20 categories.

This paper is organized as follows. Section 2 presents a review of related work. Then we present our deep structured model in Section 3, followed by a description of model learning algorithm in Section 4. Section 5 discusses the inference procedure. The experimental results and comparisons are exhibited in Section 6. Section 7 concludes this paper.

2. RELATED WORK

A batch of works on human action/activity understanding mainly focused on developing robust and descriptive features [35, 6, 20, 19, 40, 37, 24]. Xia and Aggarwal [35] extracted spatio-temporal interest points from depth videos (DSTIP) and developed a depth cuboid similarity feature (DCSF) to model human activities. Oreifej and Liu [20] proposed to capture spatio-temporal changes of activities by using a histogram of oriented 4D surface normals (HON4D). Most of these methods, however, overlooked detailed spatio-temporal structure information, and limited in periodic activities.

Several compositional approaches were studied for complex scenarios and achieved substantial progresses[33, 29, 39, 21, 23, 30, 4, 15], and they decomposed an activity into deformable parts and enriched the models with contextual information. For instance, Wang et al. [33] recognized

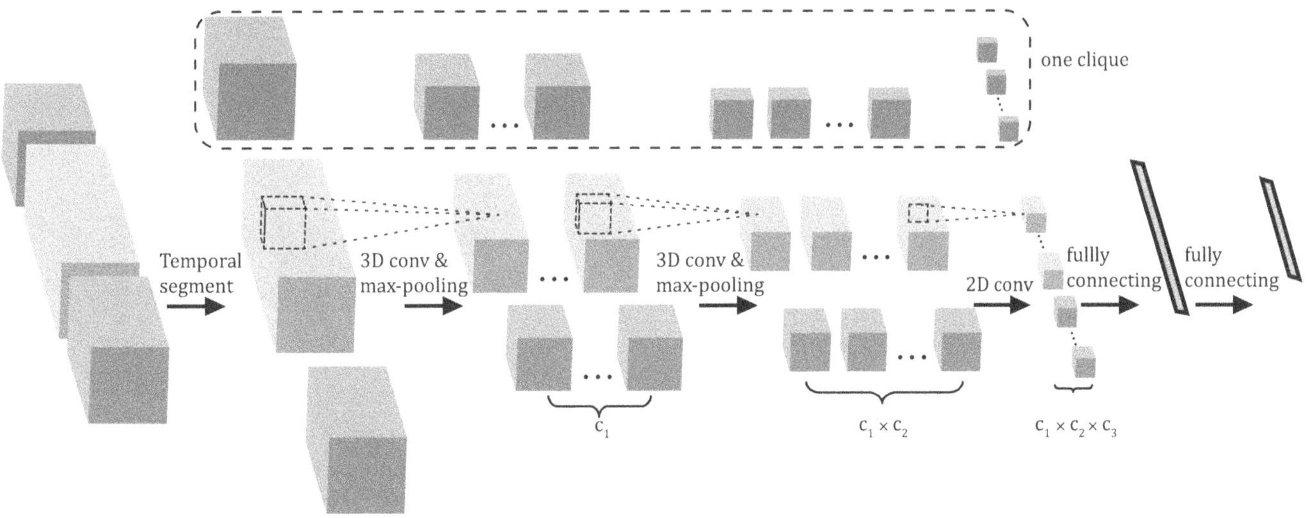

Figure 2: The architecture of our deep structured model. The network is stacked up by convolutional layers, max-pooling operators and full connection layers, where the raw segmented videos are treated as the input. A clique is defined as a subpart of the network stacked up for several layers, extracting features for one segmented video. Moreover, the architecture can be partially enabled to explicitly handle different temporal compositions of the activities.

human activities in common videos by training the hidden conditional random fields in a max-margin framework. For activity recognition in RGB-D data, Packer et al. [21] employed the latent structural SVM to train the model with part-based pose trajectories and object manipulations. An ensemble model of actionlets were studied in [30] to represent 3D human activities with a new feature called local occupancy pattern (LOP). To handle more complicated activities with large temporal variations, some powerful models [26, 31, 2] further discovered temporal structures of activities by localizing sequential actions. For example, Wang and Wu [31] proposed to solve the temporal alignment of actions by maximum margin temporal warping. Tang et al. [26] captured the latent temporal structures of 2D activities based on the variable-duration hidden Markov model. Koppula and Saxena [10] applied the Conditional Random Fields to model the sub-activities and affordances of the objects for 3D activity recognition.

Recently, the reconfigurable models were developed in the form of And-Or graphs [41, 22, 14, 28, 32], and yielded competitive performance in several challenging scenarios. The key idea of these approaches was to discover different ways of compositions by making the models reconfigured during learning and inference. Zhu and Mumford [41] first explored the And-Or graph models for image parsing. Pei et al. [22] then introduced the models for video event understanding, but their approach required elaborate annotations. Liang et al. [14] proposed to automatically train the reconfigurable action model by a non-convex formulation. However, the above mentioned models were built on hand-crafted features.

On the other hand, the past few years have seen a resurgence of research in the design of deep neural networks, and impressive progresses were made on learning image features from raw data [7, 27, 12, 11, 17, 5]. To address human action recognition from videos, Ji et al. [8] developed a novel deep architecture of convolutional networks, where they extracted features from both spatial and temporal dimensions. Amer and Todorovic [1] applied Sum Product Networks (SPNs) to model human activities based on variable primitive actions. Our deep structured model can be viewed as an extension of these existing architectures, in which we make the network reconfigurable during learning and inference.

3. STRUCTURED DEEP MODEL

In this section, we firstly introduce the structure of our deep structured model, and then explain how it can handle large intra-class variance with the latent structure.

3.1 Spatio-temporal CNNs

Our deep model is presented as a spatio-temporal convolutional neural network, as shown in Figure 2. To model the complex human activities, it comprises of M network cliques, which jointly conduct the final output. We define a clique as a subpart of the network stacked up for several layers. In particular, each clique extracts features from one decomposed video segment associated to one separated sub-action from the complete activity, and an illustration is highlighted in Figure 2. Specifically, for each clique, two 3D convolutional layers are first built upon the raw input (i.e. grayscale and depth data), which consists with at most m video frames, and then followed by one 2D convolutional layer. Note that a max-pooling operator is applied on each 3D convolutional layer making our model robust to local body deformations and surrounding noises. Afterwards, the convolution results generated by different cliques are merged and concatenated into a long feature vector, upon which we build two full connection layers to associate with the activity labels. In the following, we introduce the detailed definitions for these components of our model.

3D Convolutional Layer. The 3D convolutional kernels in one clique are computed independently to those from different cliques. For example, the kernels belonging to the first clique will only be applied to perform convolutions on

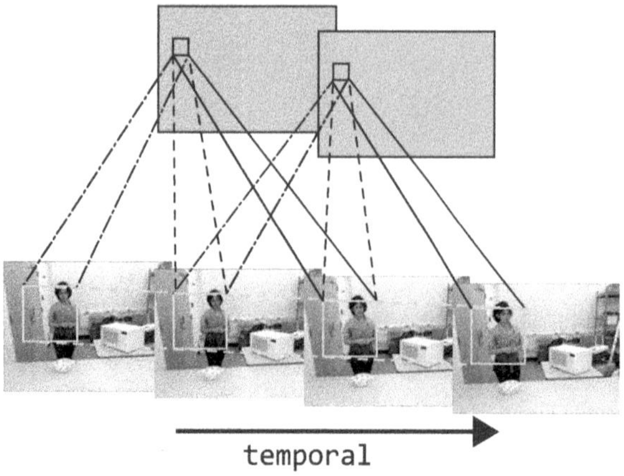

Figure 3: Illustration of the 3D convolution across both spatial and temporal domains. In this example, the temporal dimension of the 3D kernel is 3. That is to say, each feature map is obtained by performing 3D convolutions across 3 adjacent frames.

the first temporal segment of the activity. Motivated by [8], we perform the 3D convolutions spanning over both spatial and temporal dimensions of the input videos, and our model thereby captures both appearance and motion information for the observations. Suppose the width and the height of each frame are w and h, and the size of the 3D convolutional kernel is $w' \times h' \times m'$, where w', h', m' represents the width, height and temporal length, respectively. As Figure 3 illustrates, we can obtain a feature map via performing 3D convolutions across the sth to the $(s+m'-1)$th frames. The response for the position (x,y) in the feature map can be represented as,

$$v_{xys} = \tanh(b + \sum_{i=0}^{w'-1}\sum_{j=0}^{h'-1}\sum_{k=0}^{m'-1} \omega_{ijk} \cdot p_{(x+i)(y+j)(s+k)}), \quad (1)$$

where $p_{(x+i)(y+j)(s+k)}$ is the input pixel value at position $(x+i, y+j)$ in the $(s+k)$th frame, ω_{ijk} is the parameter for the convolutional kernel, and b is the bias for the feature map. Thus we can obtain $m-m'+1$ feature maps, each with size of $(w-w'+1, h-h'+1)$. Note that one convolutional kernel only extracts one kind of feature. Thus we employ several kernels to generate different kinds of feature in each convolutional layer. For each model clique, we define that the number of 3D convolutional kernels in the first and second layers as c_1 and c_2.

After the first 3D convolutions, we obtain c_1 sets of $m-m'+1$ feature maps. For each set of feature maps, we further perform 3D convolutions on it, and generate another set of feature maps on a deeper layer. Note that as we employ c_2 kernels on the c_1 sets of feature maps, we can obtain $c_1 \times c_2$ sets of new feature maps in the next layer.

Max-pooling Operator. In our model, we apply a max-pooling operator after each 3D convolution result. This is a procedure widely applied to obtain deformation and shift invariance [11, 38]. Given a set of feature maps, the max-pooling operator performs subsampling on them, which leads to the same number of feature maps with lower spatial resolution. More specifically, if a 2×2 max-pooling operator is performed on a $a_1 \times a_2$ feature map, we collect the max

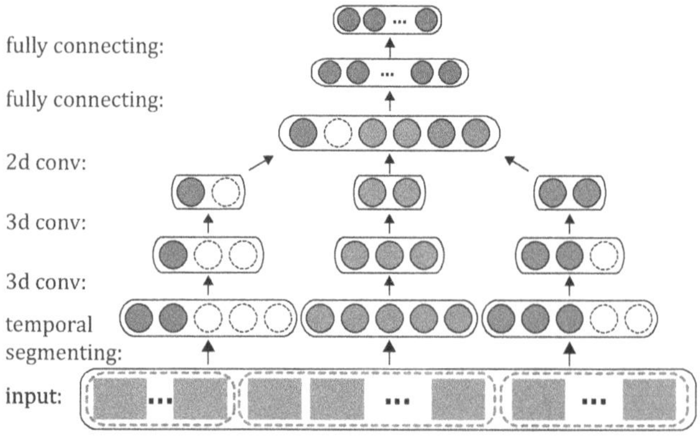

Figure 4: Illustration of our deep model incorporating the latent structure. Different model cliques are represented by different colors. As the temporal segmentation for an input video can be variant, different cliques might have different number of input frames. For the cliques whose input frame number less than m, part of the neurons in the network are inactivated, as represented by the dotted blank circles.

value in each 2×2 non-overlap regions to form a new feature map with size of $a_1/2 \times a_2/2$.

2D Convolutional Layer. After two layers of 3D convolution followed with max-pooling, each set of feature maps reduces to relatively a small temporal dimension. We then further apply 2D convolutional kernels to extract higher-level complex features from them. The 2D convolution can be viewed as a special case of 3D convolution by setting the temporal dimension of the 3D kernel to one, i.e. $m' = 1$. By performing 2D convolution on a set of feature maps, we can obtain the same number of feature maps in a new set. Suppose the number of 2D convolutional kernels is c_3, by performing 2D convolutions on $c1 \times c2$ sets of feature maps, we can obtain $c_1 \times c_2 \times c_3$ sets of new feature maps.

Full Connection Layer. There are two full connection layers in our model. We first concatenate different sets of feature maps from the M model cliques into a long feature vector. Then each unit of this vector are further connected with all neurons in the first full connection layer, which are further fully connected with output neurons. Note that the number of the output neurons is K, which is the same as the number of categories of activities K, and each of the neurons represents the probability of an activity hypothesis. To normalize the probabilities of the output labels, we apply the softmax function on them,

$$\sigma(z_i) = \frac{\exp(z_i)}{\sum_{k=1}^{K} \exp(z_k)}, \quad (2)$$

where z_i is the ith value computed by multiplying the neuron values in the second last layer with the weights connected to the ith output neuron, and $\sigma(z_i)$ is the output probability. Note that $\sum_{i=1}^{K} \sigma(z_i) = 1$.

Input Data Details. In our experiment, we obtain the gray and depth image from the raw data, which are taken from the gray channel and the depth channel of each video frame. To perform convolutions, we duplicate the channels for the 3D convolutional kernels in the first layer. The convolution results for these two channels are summed up together, thus the dimensions of the convolved feature maps remain the same. Note that our model can be generalized to apply on multi-channel video frames.

3.2 Reconfigurable Latent Structure

One key contribution of this paper is incorporating latent structure in deep model. Given different activity videos, the starting anchor frame and the number of input frames for each model clique can be variant. To illustrate it, we present a toy example in Figure 4, in which three model cliques represented by different colors are presented. Accordingly, the whole activity is decomposed into three action segments. The starting frame for each clique is flexible and the video is not evenly segmented. In this scheme, a clique is trained to handle the missing data by inactivating parts of the neurons. In other words, for the clique whose input anchor frame number is less than m, part of the neurons in the network are inactivated, as represented by the dotted blank circles in the first and third model cliques. Given input segments, classification on activities can be achieved with the deep model by performing forward propagation.

Formally, given a video sample, we define the index of starting anchor frames for M cliques as $(s_1, ..., s_M)$ and the corresponding number of input frames are $(t_1, ..., t_M)$ where $1 \leq t_i \leq m$. Thus, the latent variables for our model can be represented as $H = (s_1, ..., s_M, t_1, ..., t_M)$, which infers the video segments for each model clique. Given the input video X, latent variables H, and model parameters ω (including different layer parameters and biases), we represent the classification results obtained by our model as $F(X, \omega, H)$, which is a vector of the probabilities for each activity. For simplicity, we define the probability for the ith activity as $F_i(X, \omega, H)$.

Note that our model explicitly decomposes the input activity into sub-actions by incorporating the latent variables. But the sub-actions will be not directly co-related with semantic meaning. The different values of M (i.e. the number of sub-actions for one activity) will affect the final classification performance. When there is only one clique, the reconfigurability would be disregarded, and our model is simplified as the traditional CNN such as [8], which is compared in Sect. 6. We can empirically tune M, just like setting the number of parts for the deformable part-based model in object detection. The model with a small M could be less expressive to handle activity temporal variations, while a large M could lead to over-fitting for the high model complexity. In practice, we can roughly estimate M using traditional parameter tuning methods, e.g., the cross validation. We have shown the effectiveness of our method by setting $M = 4$ on the databases.

4. LEARNING

As our deep model incorporates latent structure, the standard back propagation algorithm [13] is not applicable to optimize the model parameters. Thus we propose an EM-type optimization algorithm, namely Latent Structural Back Propagation (LSBP), to learn our model. Due to the large number of our model parameters and the insufficience of RGB-D data in human activities, we introduce a pre-training scheme to borrow the data strength from 2D data to optimize our model.

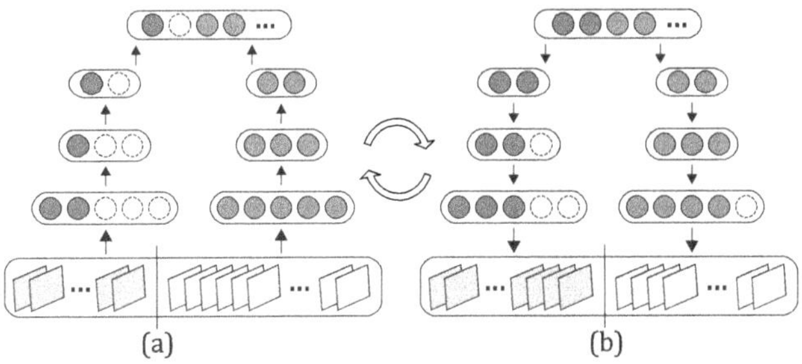

Figure 5: Illustration for the Latent Structural Back Propagation (LSBP). It is an iterative algorithm with two steps: (a) Given the current model parameters ω, estimate the latent variables H by adjusting the video segmentation; (b) Given the estimated latent variables H^* which infers a video segmentation proposal, perform back propagation to optimize model parameters ω. Note that the network neurons can be partially inactivated (as the dotted circles) according to the input segments.

4.1 Latent Structural Back Propagation

Given a video with different latent variables, the input segments for each model clique will be different. During learning, the model parameters ω and the latent variables H are required to be optimized at the same time. We propose an EM-type algorithm to iteratively optimize ω and H in two steps: (i) Given the model parameters ω we can compute the latent variables H (Figure 5.(a)); (ii) Given the input frames decided by H, we can perform back propagation to optimize the model parameters ω (Figure 5.(b)).

Suppose there are a set of N training samples (X_1, y_1), ... , (X_N, y_N), where X is the video, $y \in \{1, ..., K\}$ represents the activity classes and K is the number of activity classes. For simplicity, we also define the set of latent variables for all samples as $\mathbf{H} = \{H_1, ..., H_N\}$. We apply the logistic regression to define the cost function $J(\omega, \mathbf{H})$ in training, which is defined as,

$$\begin{aligned} J(\omega, \mathbf{H}) &= -\frac{1}{N}(\sum_{i=1}^{N}\sum_{k=1}^{K}\mathbf{1}(y_i = k)\log F_k(X_i, \omega, H_i) \\ &\quad +(1 - \mathbf{1}(y_i = k))\log(1 - F_k(X_i, \omega, H_i))) \\ &\quad +||\omega||^2, \end{aligned} \tag{3}$$

where $\mathbf{1}(\cdot) \in \{0, 1\}$ is the indicator function. The first two terms in Eq.(3) are the opposite of the log-likelihood and the last one is the regularization term. To minimize the cost $J(\omega, \mathbf{H})$, we optimize parameters ω and $\mathbf{H}$ in a 2-steps iteration as below.

(i) Given the model parameters ω obtained from the last iteration, we can minimize Eq.(3) by maximizing the probability $F_{y_i}(X_i, \omega, H_i)$ for each sample (X_i, y_i), which is achieved by finding the most appropriate latent variable H,

$$H_i^* = argmax_{H_i} F_{y_i}(X_i, \omega, H_i). \tag{4}$$

Recall that we apply softmax operator on the output results as Eq.(2), thus the maximization of $F_{y_i}(X_i, \omega, H_i)$ also depresses the probabilities of other labels $F_k(X_i, \omega, H_i), \forall k \neq y_i$. It leads to the increase of the log-likelihood and decrease the cost $J(\omega, \mathbf{H})$.

(ii) Given the latent variables $\mathbf{H} = \{H_1, ..., H_N\}$ for each sample, we can obtain the input sample segments for the deep structured model. After computing the cost $J(\omega, \mathbf{H})$ with the current inputs, we can obtain the gradients of $J(\omega, \mathbf{H})$ with respect to parameters ω. By performing the back propagation algorithm, we can further decrease the cost $J(\omega, \mathbf{H})$ and optimize the model parameters ω. Note that during back propagation, we apply stochastic gradient descent to update the parameters, and the update stops when it runs through all the training samples for one time.

The optimization algorithm iterates between these two steps until Eq.(3) converges.

4.2 Model Pre-training

To handle the insufficient RGB-D data for training and to boost the activity recognition results, we apply a pre-training scheme to initialize our model before optimizing the parameters with our LSBP algorithm on 3D data.

Given the large sum of 2D activity videos with labels, we train our deep model in a supervised manner. In this procedure, we first initialize the model parameters randomly, and each 2D video is evenly segmented to the number as the number of model cliques. To train on the 2D data, we directly apply back propagation instead of the proposed LSBP algorithm. It is mainly because of the following two reasons: (i) The initial model parameters are unstable, and it is not reliable to estimate latent variables H with them; (ii) The training efficiency can be improved without considering the latent variables.

After training on the 2D data, we apply the parameters of the convolutional layers to initialize our model. Note that we have gray and depth channels for each input frame in 3D data and only one gray channel for the 2D data. We thus duplicate the dimension of the 3D convolutional kernels in the first layer and initialize the parameters for the depth channel by the parameters for the gray channel. For the full connection layers, we set the parameters to random values. The reason is that we only need to borrow the feature learned in the 2D data, because the higher level information should be learned directly from the specific 3D activity dataset.

We summarize the whole learning procedure as Algorithm 1.

Algorithm 1 Learning Framework

Input:
The labelled 2D and 3D activity dataset.
Output:
Model parameters ω.
Initialization:
Pre-train the Spatial-Temporal CNN in the 2D dataset.

Learning on 3D dataset:
repeat
1. Estimate the latent variables $\mathbf{H}$ by fixing model parameters ω.
2. Optimize ω given the input sample segments indicated by $\mathbf{H}$.

until $J(\omega, \mathbf{H})$ in Eq.(3) converges.

5. INFERENCE

The inference task is to recognize the category of the activity given a video X. Formally, we perform the standard procedure of brute search for the activity label y and the latent variables H by maximizing the probability of $F_i(X, \omega, H)$,

$$(y^*, H^*) = argmax_{(y,H)} F_y(X, \omega, H). \quad (5)$$

To do this, we search across all the labels $y (1 \leq y \leq K)$ and calculate the maximum probability $F_y(X, \omega, H)$ by optimizing H. Given the domain space of $H = (s_1, ..., s_M, t_1, ..., t_M)$, we constrain the input frame number for each model clique as $\tau \leq t_i \leq m$, and different video segments should not have overlaps (i.e., $s_i + t_i \leq s_{i+1}$). In all our experiments, we set the constant $\tau = 5$ during training and inference. We enumerate all the possibilities of H under these constraints, and calculate the corresponding probabilities $F_y(X, \omega, H)$ via forward propagations. By selecting the highest probability, we obtain the optimal $F_y(X, \omega, H^*)$. Though this optimization is a procedure of brute search, we can take advantage of parallel computation with GPU for that the forward propagations decided by different H are independent of each other. In our experiment, parallel computation via GPU highly accelerates the inference speed.

6. EXPERIMENT

We validate our approach on the CAD-120 activity dataset [9] and a larger dataset newly created by us, namely Office Activity (OA) dataset. Comparisons with state-of-arts and empirical analysis are presented in the experiments as well.

The CAD-120 dataset contains 120 RGB-D activity sequences of 10 categories, which is widely used in 3D human activity recognition. These activities were performed by four different subjects, and each activity was repeated three times by the same actor. The challenges on this dataset lie in the large variance in object appearance, human pose, and viewpoint. The proposed OA dataset is more comprehensive, covering the regular daily activities taken place in an office, and it is the largest activity dataset of RGB-D videos, which includes 1180 sequences. Three RGB-D sensors (i.e. Microsoft Kinect cameras) are utilized to capture data in three different viewpoints, and more than 10 actors are involved. The activities are captured in two different offices to increase the variability, where each actor performs the same activity twice for each viewpoint. It is worth mentioning that this dataset also includes the activities performed by two subjects with interactions. In particular, it is divided into two sub-sets, each of which contains 10 categories of activities: OA1 (activities by a single subject) and OA2 (activities by two subjects). The categories in OA1 are: {*answering-phones, arranging-files, eating, moving-objects, going-to-work, finding-objects, mopping, sleeping, taking-water, wandering*}, and in OA2, we have {*asking-and-away, called-away, carrying, chatting, delivering, eating-and-chatting, having-guest, showing, seeking-help, shaking-hands*}. The OA database is publicly accessible[1].

Several sampled frames and depth maps from the databases are exhibited in Figure 6.

Following [9], we apply four-fold cross validation procedure for testing in the CAD-120 dataset. That is, the model is trained on the activities of three subjects and tested on a new subject each time. The final outputs are averaged on the results of all four validations. For the OA dataset, we apply five-fold cross validation in the similar way.

[1]http://vision.sysu.edu.cn/projects/3d-activity/

Figure 6: Activity examples from the testing databases. Several sampled frames and depth maps are presented. (a) CAD-120, (b) OA1, (c) OA2, respectively, show two activities of the same category selected from the three databases.

6.1 Implementation

Given the RGB-D videos, we first normalize them into the same temporal length as preprocessing. For each video, we extract 120 frames by removing the ones with similar appearances in gray-scale. Then we further obtain 30 anchor frames with a step size of 4 in the 120 frames. Suppose we index the 120 frames from 1 to 120, then the selected frames are indexed by $1, 5, 9, ..., 120$. We apply these 30 anchor frames as the inputs for our model.

We scale the input frame to $w = 80$ and $h = 60$ in our experiments. The number of decomposed video segments (i.e. actions) is $M = 4$, and the length of the maximum number of input frames of each segment is $m = 9$. Recall that the actual input frames can be less than m, as we introduce the latent variables manipulating the temporal decomposition. The networks in each clique are of the same structures (e.g. kernels). For each clique, the number of 3D convolutional kernels in the first layer is $c_1 = 7$, and the size of the kernel is $9 \times 7 \times 3$, where each number represents the width, height and temporal length. In the second layer, the number of 3D kernels is $c_2 = 5$, and the size is $7 \times 7 \times 3$. We apply 3×3 max-pooling operator over the 3D convolutions. In the 2D convolutional layer, we have $c_3 = 4$ kernels with size of 6×4. Hence we can obtain 700 feature maps with size 1×1 as the outputs for each network clique, and we merge the feature maps together into a vector of $700 \times 4 = 2800$ dimensions. Each unit in this vector is linked to 64 neurons in the next full connection layer. At last, the 64 neurons are fully connected to associate with the activity labels.

The experiments are executed on a desktop with an Intel i7 3.7GHz CPU, 8GB RAM and GTX TITAN GPU. For model learning, we set the learning rate as 0.002 for applying the stochastic gradient descent algorithm. The training times of one fold are 2 hours for CAD-120 (including 120 videos and occupying 0.2GB), 5 hours for OA1 (including 600 videos and occupying 1.0GB), and 5 hours for OA2 (including 580 videos and occupying 0.9GB) dataset, respectively. Each iteration of training costs similar time, and the convergence of our model over iterations is shown in Figure. 8 and 9. For inference, as we fully take advantage of parallel computation with GPU, it only takes around 0.4 seconds to complete recognition on a given video.

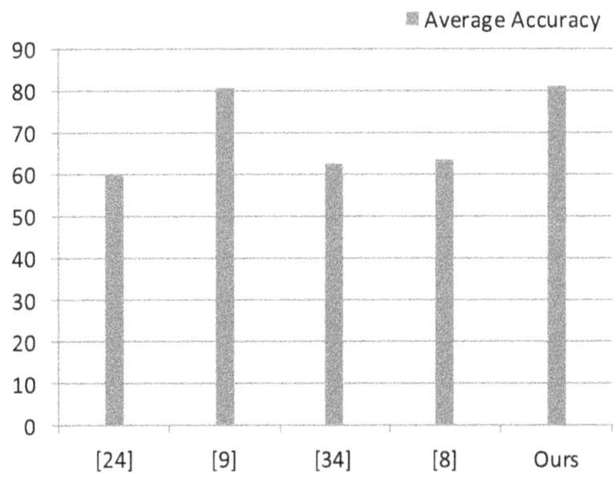

Figure 7: The average accuracy on the CAD-120 database.

	Xia et al [35].	Ji et al [8].	Ours
arranging-objects	75.0%	68.3%	**82.3%**
cleaning-objects	68.3%	60.0%	**79.7%**
having-meal	41.7%	60.0%	**71.0%**
making-cereal	76.7%	77.6%	**91.5%**
microwaving-food	36.7%	71.7%	**85.3%**
picking-objects	75.0%	58.3%	**97.2%**
stacking-objects	**75.0%**	48.3%	61.0%
taking-food	83.3%	73.3%	**93.5%**
taking-medicine	58.3%	76.7%	**96.8%**
unstacking-objects	33.3%	36.7%	**54.0%**
Average accuracy	62.3%	63.1%	**81.2%**

Table 1: Accuracy of all categories on the CAD120 dataset.

	Xia et al [35]	Ji et al[8]	Ours
answering-phones	12.5%	**40.0%**	35.0%
arranging-files	59.7%	53.3%	**84.4%**
eating	40.3%	41.7%	**65.5%**
moving-objects	48.6%	51.7%	**61.1%**
going-to-work	34.7%	41..7%	**92.2%**
finding-objects	**65.3%**	36.7%	53.9%
mopping	63.9%	66.7%	**72.2%**
sleeping	25.0%	**45%**	43.9%
taking-water	**58.3%**	40.0%	51.7%
wandering	**56.9%**	50.0%	40.6%
Accuracy	46.5%	46.7%	**60.1%**

Table 2: Quantitative results on the OA1 dataset. Accuracy per activity category and average accuracy of all categories are reported.

	Xia et al [35]	Ji et al[8]	Ours
asking-and-away	12.5%	**39.6%**	25.3%
called-away	45.8%	44.8%	**57.5%**
carrying	**66.7%**	56.8%	53.5%
chatting	37.5%	17.2%	**25.3%**
delivering	20.1%	**34.5%**	32.8%
eating-and-chatting	50.0%	35.8%	**69.5%**
having-guest	37.5%	34.1%	**43.7%**
seeking-help	16.7%	44.8%	**59.2%**
shaking-hands	41.7%	32..8%	**59.8%**
showing	**37.5%**	29.3%	23.0%
Accuracy	36.6%	37.0%	**45.0%**

Table 3: Quantitative results on the OA2 dataset. Accuracy per activity category and average accuracy of all categories are reported.

	grayscale	depth	grayscale + depth
OA1	44.9%	57.2%	60.1%
OA2	41.6%	43.6%	45.0%

Table 4: Channel analysis on the three dataset. Average accuracy of all categories are reported.

6.2 Results and Comparisons

CAD-120 dataset. On this dataset, we adopt four state-of-the-art methods for comparison. As shown in Figure 7, our approach obtains the average accuracy of 81.2%, distinctly superior than results generated by other four competing methods, such as 59.7% [25], 80.6% [9], 62.3% [35] and 63.1% [8]. In Table 1, we report the detailed accuracies on all the categories, compared with the method based on hand-crafted feature engineering [35], and the deep architecture of convolutional neural networks [8]. Note that for different methods we train the models using the same data annotation, which only includes the activity labels on videos.

OA dataset. In this experiment, we apply our approach on the two sub-sets, respectively. Our deep structured model outperforms the state-of-the-art methods on average. On the OA1 set, our approach outperforms on 5 out of 10 categories and obtains the highest average accuracy of 60.1%, as Table. 2 reports. On the OA2 set, the average accuracy of our method is 45.0% and we have 6 classes of activities achieve better results than the other two competing methods, as Table 3 reports. By reviewing the results, we find the failure cases probably caused by the lack of contextualized scene understanding. For example, understanding the activities of *taking-water* and *sleeping* actually requires to extra higher level information. We will consider it in future work. Moreover, the depth data is very useful. Since the testing is performed on the new subject, we observe that large appearance variances existed in grayscale data lead to worse performance. The depth data has much smaller variance, and does help to capture the motion information. Table 4 illustrates that depth data can boost the performance a lot, especially in OA1.

6.3 Empirical Analysis

For further evaluation, we conduct two following empirical analysis under different settings.

(I) To clarify significance of using the pre-training, we discard the parameters trained on 2D videos and learn the model directly on the RGB-D data. Then we compare the model with the original version by the test error rate, which is defined as one minus the classification accuracy. This testing is implemented on the OA1 dataset. In Figure 8, we visualize the test error rates with the increasing of iteration numbers during training. Each test error rate on a specific iteration number is calculated by applying the currently trained model. It is shown that the model using the pre-training converges after 25 iterations, while the other one without the pre-training requires 140 iterations. More importantly, the pre-training can effectively reduce the error rate in the testing, say 8% less than without the pre-training.

(II) We demonstrate the effectiveness of incorporating reconfigurable structure in the deep architecture. That is, we can fix the latent variables in our model and train it using the standard back propagation algorithm. In this model without latent structure, each network clique receives m input frames that are evenly segmented from the video. In Figure 9, we visualize the test error rates with different iterations of the two models: structured v.s. non-structured, from the same initialization. We observe that the error rates of the structured model decrease faster and reach to the lower result, compared with the non-structured model. This experiment is executed on the OA1 dataset.

7. CONCLUSIONS

This paper studies a novel deep structured model by incorporating model reconfigurability into layered convolutional neural networks. This model has been shown to handle well realistic challenges in 3D activity recognition, and it enables us to perform recognition from raw RGB-D data rather than relying on hand-crafted features. Moreover, we consider two aspects in future work. First, we can integrate high level semantic information into our model to deal with more complicated events with underlying intentions. Second, we plan to deploy our model into cloud computing platforms so that thin clients can expediently access the ability of 3D human activity understanding.

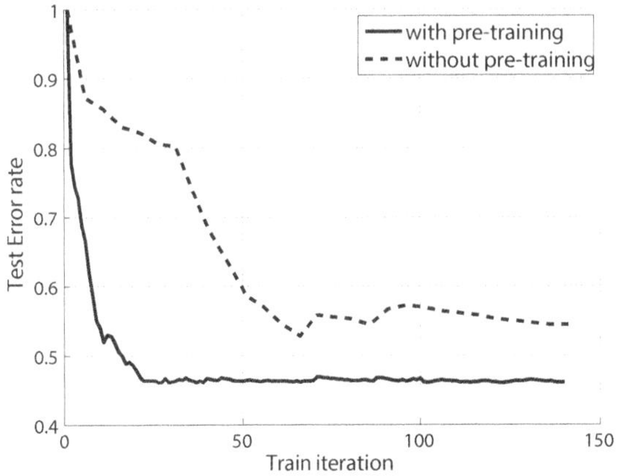

Figure 8: Test error rates with/without using the pre-training.

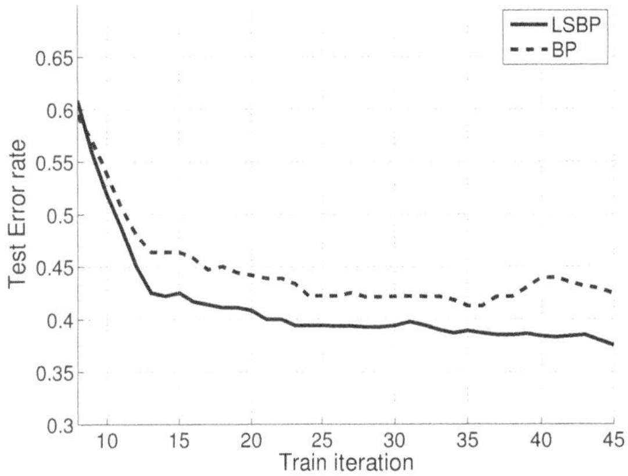

Figure 9: Test error rates with/without incorporating the latent structure in the deep model. The solid curve represents the structured deep model trained by the proposed LSBP optimization method, and the dashed curve represents the non-structured model using standard back propagation.

8. REFERENCES

[1] M. R. Amer and S. Todorovic. Sum-product networks for modeling activities with stochastic structure. In *CVPR*, pages 1314–1321, 2012.

[2] W. Brendel and S. Todorovic. Learning spatiotemporal graphs of human activities. In *ICCV*, pages 778–785, 2011.

[3] J. M. Chaquet, E. J. Carmona, and A. Fernandez-Caballero. A survey of video datasets for human action and activity recognition. *Computer Vision and Image Understanding*, 117(6):633–659, 2013.

[4] Z. Cheng, L. Qin, Q. Huang, S. Jiang, S. Yan, and Q. Tian. Human group activity analysis with fusion of motion and appearance information. In *ACM Multimedia*, pages 1401–1404, 2011.

[5] R. Girshick, J. Donahue, T. Darrell, and J. Malik. Rich feature hierarchies for accurate object detection and semantic segmentation. In *CVPR*, 2014.

[6] R. Gupta, A. Y. Chia, D. Rajan, E. S. Ng, and E. H. Lung. Human activities recognition using depth images. In *ACM Multimedia*, pages 283–292, 2013.

[7] G. E. Hinton and R. R. Salakhutdinov. Reducing the dimensionality of data with neural networks. *Science*, 313(5786):504–507, 2006.

[8] S. Ji, W. Xu, M. Yang, and K. Yu. 3d convolutional neural networks for human action recognition. *IEEE Trans. Pattern Anal. Mach. Intell.*, 35(1):221–231, 2013.

[9] H. S. Koppula, R. Gupta, and A. Saxena. Learning human activities and object affordances from rgb-d videos. *International Journal of Robotics Research (IJRR)*, 32(8):951–970, 2013.

[10] H. S. Koppula and A. Saxena. Learning spatio-temporal structure from rgb-d videos for human activity detection and anticipation. In *ICML*, pages 792–800, 2013.

[11] A. Krizhevsky, I. Sutskever, and G. E. Hinton. Imagenet classification with deep convolutional neural networks. In *Advances in neural information processing systems*, pages 1097–1105, 2012.

[12] Q. V. Le, W. Y. Zou, S. Y. Yeung, and A. Y. Ng. Learning hierarchical invariant spatio-temporal features for action recognition with independent subspace analysis. In *CVPR*, pages 3361–3368, 2011.

[13] Y. LeCun, B. Boser, J. Denker, D. Henderson, R. Howard, W. Hubbard, and e. a. L.D. Jackel. Handwritten digit recognition with a back-propagation network. In *Advances in neural information processing systems*, 1990.

[14] X. Liang, L. Lin, and L. Cao. Learning latent spatio-temporal compositional model for human action recognition. In *ACM Multimedia*, pages 263–272, 2013.

[15] L. Lin, H. Gong, L. Li, and L. Wang. Semantic event representation and recognition using syntactic attribute graph grammar. *Pattern Recognition Letters*, 30(2):180–186, 2009.

[16] L. Lin, T. Wu, J. Porway, and Z. Xu. A stochastic graph grammar for compositional object representation and recognition. *Pattern Recognition*, 42(7):1297–1307, 2009.

[17] P. Luo, X. Wang, and X. Tang. A deep sum-product architecture for robust facial attributes analysis. In

ICCV, pages 2864–2871, 2013.
[18] P. Luo, X. Wang, and X. Tang. Pedestrian parsing via deep decompositional neural network. In *ICCV*, pages 2648–2655, 2013.
[19] B. Ni, Z. L. Y. Pei, L. Lin, and P. Moulin. Integrating multi-stage depth-induced contextual information for human action recognition and localization. In *International Conference and Workshops on Automatic Face and Gesture Recognition*, pages 1–8, 2013.
[20] O. Oreifej and Z. Liu. Hon4d: Histogram of oriented 4d normals for activity recognition from depth sequences. In *CVPR*, pages 716–723, 2013.
[21] B. Packer, K. Saenko, and D. Koller. A combined pose, object, and feature model for action understanding. In *CVPR*, pages 1378–1385, 2012.
[22] M. Pei, Y. Jia, and S. Zhu. Parsing video events with goal inference and intent prediction. In *ICCV*, pages 487–494, 2011.
[23] S. Sadanand and J. J. Corso. Action bank: A high-level representation of activity in video. In *CVPR*, pages 1234–1241, 2012.
[24] P. Scovanner, S. Ali, and M. Shah. A 3-dimensional sift descriptor and its application to action recognition. In *ACM Multimedia*, pages 357–360, 2007.
[25] J. Sung, C. Ponce, B. Selman, and A. Saxena. Unstructured human activity detection from rgbd images. In *ICRA*, pages 842–849, 2012.
[26] K. Tang, L. Fei-Fei, and D. Koller. Learning latent temporal structure for complex event detection. In *CVPR*, pages 1250–1257, 2012.
[27] G. W. Taylor, R. Fergus, Y. LeCun, and C. Bregler. Convolutional learning of spatio-temporal features. In *ECCV*, pages 140–153, 2010.
[28] K. Tu, M. Meng, M. W. Lee, T. Choi, and S. Zhu. Joint video and text parsing for understanding events and answering queries. *IEEE Transactions on Multimedia*, 21(2):42–70, 2014.
[29] C. Wang, Y. Wang, and A. L. Yuille. An approach to pose-based action recognition. In *CVPR*, pages 915–922, 2013.
[30] J. Wang, Z. Liu, Y. Wu, and J. Yuan. Mining actionlet ensemble for action recognition with depth cameras. In *CVPR*, pages 1290–1297, 2012.
[31] J. Wang and Y. Wu. Learning maximum margin temporal warping for action recognition. In *ICCV*, pages 2688–2695, 2013.
[32] X. Wang, L. Lin, L. Huang, and S. Yan. Incorporating structural alternatives and sharing into hierarchy for multiclass object recognition and detection. In *CVPR*, pages 3334–3341, 2013.
[33] Y. Wang and G. Mori. Hidden part models for human action recognition: Probabilistic vs. max-margin. *IEEE Trans. Pattern Anal. Mach. Intell.*, 33(7):1310–1323, 2011.
[34] P. Wu, S. Hoi, H. Xia, P. Zhao, D. Wang, and C. Miao. Online multimodal deep similarity learning with application to image retrieval. In *ACM Mutilmedia*, pages 153–162, 2013.
[35] L. Xia and J. Aggarwal. Spatio-temporal depth cuboid similarity feature for activity recognition using depth camera. In *CVPR*, pages 2834–2841, 2013.
[36] L. Xia, C. Chen, and J. K. Aggarwal. View invariant human action recognition using histograms of 3d joints. In *CVPRW*, pages 20–27, 2012.
[37] X. Yang, C. Zhang, and Y. Tian. Recognizing actions using depth motion maps-based histograms of oriented gradients. In *ACM Multimedia*, pages 1057–1060, 2012.
[38] K. Yu, Y. Lin, and J. Lafferty. Learning image representations from the pixel level via hierarchical sparse coding. In *CVPR*, pages 1713–1720, 2011.
[39] X. Zhao, Y. Liu, and Y. Fu. Exploring discriminative pose sub-patterns for effective action classification. In *ACM Multimedia*, pages 273–282, 2013.
[40] X. Zhou, X. Zhuang, S. Yan, S. F. Chang, M. H. Johnson, and T. S. Huang. Sift-bag kernel for video event analysis. In *ACM Multimedia*, pages 229–238, 2009.
[41] S. Zhu and D. Mumford. A stochastic grammar of images. *Foundations and Trends in Computer Graphics and Vision*, 2(4):259–362, 2007.

Dynamic Background Learning through Deep Auto-encoder Networks

Pei Xu
School of CSE, University of Electronic Science and Technology of China, P.R. China
xupei268@gmail.com

Mao Ye *
School of CSE, University of Electronic Science and Technology of China, P.R. China
cvlab.uestc@gmail.com

Xue Li
School of ITEE, The University of Queensland, Australia
xueli@itee.uq.edu.au

Qihe Liu
School of CSE, University of Electronic Science and Technology of China, P.R. China
qiheliu@uestc.edu.cn

Yi Yang
School of ITEE, The University of Queensland, Australia
yi.yang@uq.edu.au

Jian Ding
Tencent Group
dingjianhl@126.com

ABSTRACT

Background learning is a pre-processing of motion detection which is a basis step of video analysis. For the static background, many previous works have already achieved good performance. However, the results on learning dynamic background are still much to be improved. To address this challenge, in this paper, a novel and practical method is proposed based on deep auto-encoder networks. Firstly, dynamic background images are extracted through a deep auto-encoder network (called Background Extraction Network) from video frames containing motion objects. Then, a dynamic background model is learned by another deep auto-encoder network (called Background Learning Network) using the extracted background images as the input. To be more flexible, our background model can be updated on-line to absorb more training samples. Our main contributions are 1) a cascade of two deep auto-encoder networks which can deal with the separation of dynamic background and foregrounds very efficiently; 2) a method of online learning is adopted to accelerate the training of Background Extraction Network. Compared with previous algorithms, our approach obtains the best performance over six benchmark data sets. Especially, the experiments show that our algorithm can handle large variation background very well.

*Mao Ye is the corresponding author and works for the School of Computer Science and Engineering, Center for Robotics, Key Laboratory for Neuro-Information of Ministry of Education, University of Electronic Science and Technology of China, Chengdu 611731, P.R. China

MM'14, November 03 - 07 2014, Orlando, FL, USA.

http://dx.doi.org/10.1145/2647868.2654914.

Categories and Subject Descriptors

I.4.8 [**Image Processing and Computer Vision**]: Scene Analysis

Keywords

Motion detection; Dynamic background; Deep auto-encoder network

1. INTRODUCTION

Extracting moving objects from a video is a fundamental and basis step in multimedia applications such as crowd detection, action recognition, etc [36, 42]. There have already existed lots of works on this problem. Roughly, they can be classified into two categories. The first category is to learn a foreground model to get the moving objects. The other category is to extract the moving objects by learning the background model.

In the first category, there are two approaches. The first approach is called motion segmentation[26, 5, 6, 18, 33, 40]. With the assumption of rigid or smooth motion, the method of segmentation or optical flow is used to model foreground motion. However, the moving objects are always complicated with nonrigid shapes, complicated texture and illumination changes caused by dynamic background. Recently, another approach is proposed based on deep models. Human motion, which can be viewed as foreground, is learned by a factored conditional Restricted Boltzman Machine [23, 24]. In real-world applications, these methods are not available because moving objects are infinite in variety and it would be a huge project to learn a neural network for each kind of motion.

Instead of extracting the moving object directly, another category of methods try to model the dynamic background. There exist two kinds of approaches in this category. The first one is probability model based, such as Mixture of Gaussian (MOG) [31, 22, 11] and Hidden Markov model (HMM) [19], which are used to model the background. The parameters of these models are learned to describe the background. In this approach, the background is assumed to fit a specific probability model, which is limited when the distribution of real background is unknown, because the real background could be very complex including dynamical texture variations and illumination changes.

The second approach is based on a deterministic model, such as Support Vector Machine (SVM), linear regression model, sparse dictionary, and low-rank strategy, etc. In [3, 4, 41, 16, 38, 9, 14, 2], the authors proposed to use a SVM classifier, linear regression model and sparse dictionary learning based methods to learn the background respectively. These methods need clean background images (without foregrounds), which cannot be achieved in real world applications. For example, in traffic monitoring of crossroad, there always exist moving cars in the video. The low-rank strategy assumes the background images are linear correlated with each other. This assumption has some tolerances of linear variations in the background [42]. In [35], a couple of auto-encoder networks is proposed to separate foregrounds from background images. This method can achieve good performance with static background. When the variation of background is nonlinear, such as water surface, all of these methods perform poorly.

As we stated, the above mentioned methods cannot simultaneously achieve: 1) learning the background with large variations and 2) separating foregrounds from background images. To address these challenges, in this paper, a novel and practical method is proposed based on deep auto-encoder networks by a technically designed cost function. Firstly, background images are extracted using a deep auto-encoder network (called Background Extraction Network, BEN). Then, a succeed deep auto-encoder network (called Background Learning Network, BLN) is used to model dynamic background with the background images from the BEN as input. Using the deep architecture, the large dynamic background changes can be learned. Furthermore, to be more flexible for the dynamic background changes, a method of searching and substituting the minimizing effect parameters in different hidden layers, is used to learn the background online.

Our main contributions are: 1) A learning method of dynamic background based on deep auto-encoder networks is proposed. A Background Extraction Network is designed to extract background images from video frames which may contain motion objects. The Background Learning Network is used to learn dynamic background based on the extracted background images. This strategy can handle large variations of background; 2) A method of searching and substituting the minimizing effect parameters in different hidden layers is adopted to accelerate the on-line training of the Background Extraction Network. Our experiments have demonstrated the superior performance than the state-of-the-art approaches.

In the rest of this paper, we first review the deep auto-encoder network in Section 2. Our approach is introduced in Section 3. And the experimental results and conclusions are given in Section 4 and Section 5, respectively.

2. PRELIMINARIES

In this paper, we use deep auto-encoder network in [1, 17] as a building block. In the encoding stage, the input data $\mathbf{x} \in [0,1]^N$ is encoded by a function $\mathbf{h}_1 = f(\mathbf{x})$ ($\mathbf{h}_1 \in [0,1]^{M_1}$), which is defined as follows

$$\mathbf{h}_1 = f(\mathbf{x}) = sigm(W_1\mathbf{x} + b_1) \quad (1)$$

where $W_1 \in R^{M_1 \times N}$ is a weight matrix, $b_1 \in R^{M_1}$ is a hidden bias vector, and $sigm(z) = \frac{1}{1+exp(-z)}$ is the sigmoid function. Then, $\mathbf{h}_1$ as the input is also encoded by another function $\mathbf{h}_2 = f(\mathbf{h}_1)(\mathbf{h}_2 \in [0,1]^{M_2})$, which is written as,

$$\mathbf{h}_2 = f(\mathbf{h}_1) = sigm(W_2\mathbf{h}_1 + b_2) \quad (2)$$

where $W_2 \in R^{M_2 \times M_1}$ is a weight matrix and $b_2 \in R^{M_2}$ is a bias vector.

In the decoding stage, $\mathbf{h}_2$ is the input of function

$$\mathbf{h}_1^{'} = g(\mathbf{h}_2) = sigm(W_2^T\mathbf{h}_2 + b_3) \quad (3)$$

where $b_3 \in R^{M_1}$. Then the reconstructed output $\hat{\mathbf{x}} \in [0,1]^N$ is computed by the decoding function,

$$\hat{\mathbf{x}} = g(\mathbf{h}_1^{'}) = sigm(W_1^T\mathbf{h}_1^{'} + b_4) \quad (4)$$

where $b_4 \in R^M$ is a bias vector. Here, $W_i(i = 1,2)$ and $b_j(j = 1,2,3,4)$ are model parameters which are learned by minimizing a cost function defined as,

$$\mathcal{E}(\mathbf{x}) = -\sum_{i=1}^{N}\left(\mathbf{x}_i \log \hat{\mathbf{x}}_i + (1-\mathbf{x}_i)\log(1-\hat{\mathbf{x}}_i)\right), \quad (5)$$

which is called a cross-entropy function [43, 27].

3. PROPOSED METHOD

3.1 Dynamic Background Modeling

Our cascade architecture of two deep auto-encoder networks is shown in Fig 1. Firstly, the video frames are reshaped into 1-dimensional vectors and the pixel values of each frame are mapped into the interval [0, 1]. In this paper, the RGB images are changed into gray ones. Thus, the video frames are denoted as $\mathbf{x} = \{\mathbf{x}^1, \cdots, \mathbf{x}^D\}(\mathbf{x}^j \in [0,1]^N)$ where D is the number of frames and N is the number of pixels of a frame. The video frame set $\mathbf{x}$ is the input of the Background Extraction Network (BEN). The vector $B^0 \in [0,1]^N$ represents the extracted background image. The output h_1 and h_2 are from the different encoder stages, respectively. The $h_1^{'}$ and $\hat{\mathbf{x}}$ are the decoding and reconstruction outputs, respectively. A separation function $\mathcal{S}(\hat{\mathbf{x}}_i^j, B_i^0)$ is used to formulate the input data $\boldsymbol{B}$ of the Background Learning Network (BLN) where $i = 1, 2, \cdots, N$. The outputs h_{B1} and h_{B2} are from the two encoding layers. The $h_1^{'}$ and $\hat{\mathbf{B}}$ are the outputs of the hide decoding and reconstruction layers, respectively. In this work, we assume the neurons in the same layer are independent of each other.

3.1.1 *Dynamic Background Extraction*

Detecting foregrounds from dynamic background is a challenge task because it is very difficult to find a set of clean background images and the background also dynamically changes. Some parts of video frames are clean background when the foreground vanishes or occurs in video sequences. So the pixel belongs to background at most of time. This is a basic observation of our work.

Inspired by previous denoising works using deep auto-encoder networks, we view dynamic background and foregrounds as 'clean' data and 'noise' data, respectively. We use a deep auto-encoder network (named Background Extraction Network, BEN) to get background images. The

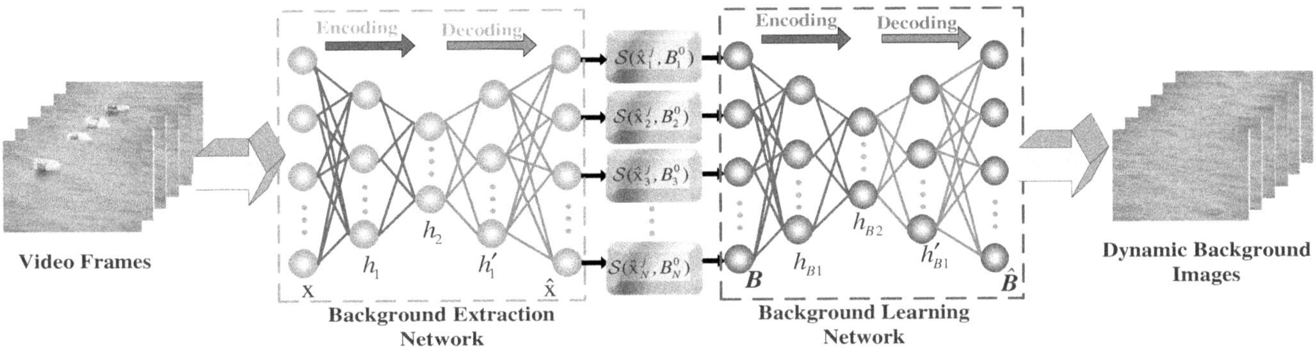

Figure 1: The cascade architecture of two deep auto-encoder networks.

cost function of the BEN is defined as

$$\min_{\theta_E, B^0, \sigma} \mathcal{L}(\mathrm{x}^j; \theta_E, B^0, \sigma) = \mathcal{E}(\mathbf{x}^j) + \sum_{i=1}^{N} \left| \frac{\hat{\mathbf{x}}_i^j - B_i^0}{\sigma_i} \right| + \lambda \sum_{i=1}^{N} |\sigma_i| \tag{6}$$

where $j = 1, 2, \cdots, D$ (D is the number of video frames), and N is the dimensionality. In formula (6), B^0 is a parameter vector representing a background image, and σ is the tolerance value vector of B^0.

The first item in the right hand side of formula (6) is the network reconstruction part of BEN which contains the standard deep auto-encoder network parameters $\theta_E = \{W_{Ei}(i = 1, 2), b_{Ej}(j = 1, \cdots, 4)\}$. The second item forces the reconstructed frames approach to a background image B^0. In the second and third items, the parameter vector σ represents the tolerance of dynamic background variances. At different pixels, the tolerances are different. To be resilient to large variance tolerances, in the second term, we divide the approximate error by the parameter σ_i at the ith pixel for $i = 1, \cdots, N$. However, the large variances should be controlled. Otherwise, the good background images cannot be obtained. The third term is a regularization item which controls the solution range of σ. For σ is trained from the BEN, the tolerance threshold of background variances is adaptive.

Next, we train the parameters of BEN by optimizing the cost function (6). The training of parameters θ_E, B^0 and σ will be executed respectively. The parameter θ_E represents the weight matrices and bias vectors in BEN respectively. The updating of θ_E is,

$$\theta_E = \theta_E - \eta \nabla \theta_E, \tag{7}$$

where η is the learning rate, and $\nabla \theta_E$ is defined as the following,

$$\nabla \theta_E = \frac{\partial \mathcal{L}(\mathrm{x}^j; \theta_E, B^0, \sigma)}{\partial \theta_E} = \frac{\partial \mathcal{E}(\mathbf{x}^j)}{\partial \theta_E} + \frac{\partial \left(\sum_{i=1}^{N} \left| \frac{\hat{\mathrm{x}}_i^j - B_i^0}{\sigma_i} \right| \right)}{\partial \theta_E}. \tag{8}$$

The second item in the right hand side of formula (6) is not differentiable. We adopt a *sign* function to roughly compute the derivative. So we can obtain

$$\nabla \theta_E = \frac{\partial \mathcal{E}(\mathbf{x}^j)}{\partial \theta_E} + \sum_{i=1}^{N} sign\left(\frac{\hat{\mathbf{x}}_i^j - B_i^0}{\sigma_i} \right) \frac{\partial \hat{\mathrm{x}}_i^j}{\partial \theta_E}, \tag{9}$$

where $sign(a) = 1 (a > 0)$, $sign(a) = 0 (a = 0)$ and $sign(a) = -1 (a < 0)$. Then, the parameter θ_E can be updated by the formulas (7) and (9).

Now, after fixing the parameter θ_E, we show the details about the training of B^0. In this paper, we view D frames as a batch data set. So the optimal problem about B^0, from the formula (6), can be represented equally as

$$\sum_{i=1}^{N} \left(\min_{B_i^0} \sum_{j=1}^{D} |\hat{\mathrm{x}}_i^j - B_i^0| \right). \tag{10}$$

It also can be written as

$$\min_{B_i^0} \sum_{j=1}^{D} |\hat{\mathrm{x}}_i^j - B_i^0|, \tag{11}$$

for $i = 1, \cdots, N$. According to previous works [28, 14] about l^1-norm optimization, the optimal B_i^0 is the median of $\{\hat{\mathrm{x}}_i^1, \hat{\mathrm{x}}_i^2, \cdots, \hat{\mathrm{x}}_i^D\}$ for $i = 1, \cdots, N$.

After B^0 and θ_E are fixed, the cost function for each σ_i can be rewritten as

$$L(\sigma_i) = \left| \frac{\hat{\mathbf{x}}_i^j - B_i^0}{\sigma_i} \right| + \lambda |\sigma_i|, \tag{12}$$

for $i = 1, \cdots, N, j = 1, \cdots, D$. Optimizing $L(\sigma_i)$ equals to minimize its logarithmic form, written as $\ln L(\sigma_i)$. Let the derivative of $\ln L(\sigma_i)$ be zero. It follows that

$$\frac{\partial \ln L(\sigma_i)}{\partial \sigma_i} = \frac{2\lambda\sigma_i}{\lambda\sigma_i^2 + |\hat{\mathrm{x}}_i^j - B_i^0|} - \frac{1}{\sigma_i} = 0, \tag{13}$$

for $j = 1, \cdots, D$. The optimal σ_i is

$$\sigma_i^* = \sqrt{\left| \frac{\hat{\mathrm{x}}_i^j - B_i^0}{\lambda} \right|} \tag{14}$$

for $j = 1, \cdots, D$, where λ is a tunable parameter and $0 < \lambda < 1$ in our work. For the batch data set of D frames, we compute the average value of σ_i^* for $j = 1, \cdots, D$. It follows that

$$\sigma_i^* = Average_{j=1,\cdots,D} \left(\sqrt{\left| \frac{\hat{\mathrm{x}}_i^j - B_i^0}{\lambda} \right|} \right). \tag{15}$$

When the error $\sum_{j=1}^{D} \|\hat{\mathbf{x}}^j - \mathbf{x}^j\|_2 < \delta_E$ (δ_E is a threshold closed to zero), the updating is terminated. The details can be found in **Algorithm 1** (line 2-12).

Different from previous works ([23, 24, 8, 38, 9, 14, 2]), we do not need clean background images. Our assumption is that each pixel belongs to the background at most of time which is reasonable in practical applications. When the number D of training frames is larger, the learned result is much better. Compared with the method in [35], the tolerance measure of dynamic background, σ, is learned adaptively by our proposed method. Thus, our deep auto-encoder network can handle large variations of dynamic background very efficiently.

After the training of BEN is finished, for the video frames $x^j, j = 1, \cdots, D$, we can get a clean and static background B^0, and the tolerance measure σ of background variations. However, the reconstructed output $\hat{x}^j$ is not exact the background image though the deep auto-encoder network BEN can move some foregrounds in some sense. So we adopt a separation function to clean the output furthermore, which is

$$B_i^j = \mathcal{S}(\hat{\mathbf{x}}_i^j, B_i^0) = \begin{cases} \hat{\mathbf{x}}_i & |\hat{\mathbf{x}}_i^j - B_i^0| \leq \sigma_i, \\ B_i^0 & |\hat{\mathbf{x}}_i^j - B_i^0| > \sigma_i \end{cases} \tag{16}$$

where $B^j (j = 1, \cdots, D)$ are the cleaned background images. If $|\hat{\mathbf{x}}_i^j - B_i^0| \leq \sigma_i$, then at the ith pixel of the jth background image B_i^j equals $\hat{\mathbf{x}}_i^j$. Otherwise, B_i^j equals B_i^0. For these D video frames, we obtain the clean background image set $\boldsymbol{B} = \{B^1, \cdots, B^D\} (B^j \in [0, 1]^N)$ in some sense.

Algorithm 1 Dynamic Background Modeling

1: **Input:** samples $\mathbf{x} = \{\mathbf{x}^1, \cdots, \mathbf{x}^D\}$; randomly initialized matrix $W_{Ei}(i = 1, 2), B^0$; zero vectors $b_{Ej}(j = 1, \cdots, 4)$; learning rate η_E; parameter λ.
2: **repeat**
3:   **for** each $j = 1, \cdots, D$ **do**
4:     Compute $h_1 \leftarrow sigm(W_{E1}\mathbf{x}^j + b_{E1})$
5:     Compute $h_2 \leftarrow sigm(W_{E2}h_1 + b_{E2})$
6:     Compute $h_1^{'} \leftarrow sigm(W_{E2}^{\mathrm{T}}h_2 + b_{E3})$
7:     Compute $\hat{\mathbf{x}}^j \leftarrow sigm(W_{E1}^{\mathrm{T}}h_1^{'} + b_{E4})$
8:     Update parameters $\theta_E \leftarrow \theta_E - \eta_E \nabla \theta_E$, θ_E can be substituted for $W_{Ei}(i = 1, 2), b_{Ej}(j = 1, \cdots, 4)$
9:     $B_i^0 \leftarrow median(\hat{\mathrm{x}}_i^1, \cdots, \hat{\mathrm{x}}_i^j)(i = 1, \cdots, N)$
10:   **end for**
11:   σ is updated according to formula (15)
12: **until** $\sum_{j=1}^{D} \|\hat{\mathbf{x}}^j - \mathbf{x}^j\|_2 < \delta_E$
13: Obtain the background images $\boldsymbol{B} = \{B^1, \cdots, B^D\}$ based on formula (16). Initialize the parameters of BLN as $W_{Li} \leftarrow W_{Ei}(i = 1, 2)$ and $b_{Lj} \leftarrow b_{Ej}(j = 1, \cdots, 4)$.
14: **repeat**
15:   **for** each $j = 1, \cdots, D$ **do**
16:     Compute $h_{B1} \leftarrow sigm(W_{L1}B^j + b_{L1})$
17:     Compute $h_{B2} \leftarrow sigm(W_{L2}h_{B1} + b_{L2})$
18:     Compute $h_{B1}^{'} \leftarrow sigm(W_{L2}^{\mathrm{T}}h_{B2} + b_{L3})$
19:     Compute $\hat{B}^j \leftarrow sigm(W_{L1}^{\mathrm{T}}h_{B1}^{'} + b_{L4})$
20:     Update parameters $\theta_L \leftarrow \theta_L - \eta_L \nabla \theta_L$, θ_E can be substituted for $W_{Li}(i = 1, 2), b_{Lj}(j = 1, \cdots, 4)$
21:   **end for**
22: **until** $\sum_{j=1}^{D} \|\hat{B}^j - B^j\|_2 < \delta_L$
23: **Output:** $\theta_E, \theta_L, B^0, \sigma$

3.1.2 Dynamic Background Learning

We use another deep auto-encoder network (called Background Learning Network, BLN) to further learn the dynamic background model from the extracted background images. $\boldsymbol{B}$ as the input data is used to train the parameters of the BLN. To decrease the training time, the parameters of this deep auto-encoder Network, written as $\theta_L = \{W_{Li}(i = 1, 2), b_{Lj}(j = 1, \cdots, 4)\}$, are initialized by $\theta_E = \{W_{Ei}(i = 1, 2), b_{Ej}(j = 1, \cdots, 4)\}$. The cost function of Background Network is

$$\mathcal{L}(B^j, \theta_L) = -\sum_{i=1}^{N} \left(B_i^j \log \hat{B}_i^j + (1 - B_i^j) \log(1 - \hat{B}_i^j) \right) \tag{17}$$

for $j = 1, 2, \cdots, D$, where $\hat{B}^j$ is the reconstruction result of BLN.

The gradient decent method is used to train θ_L, where $\nabla \theta_L$ is computed as

$$\nabla \theta_L = \frac{\partial \mathcal{L}(B^j, \theta_L)}{\partial \theta_L} \tag{18}$$

where θ_L can be substituted for $W_{Li}(i = 1, 2)$ and $b_{Lj}(j = 1, \cdots, 4)$. When $\sum_{j=1}^{D} \|\hat{B}^j - B^j\|_2 < \delta_L$ is satisfied, the iteration is finished. δ_B is a small threshold parameter. The training details also can be found in **Algorithm 1** (line 13-22).

The first auto-encoder performs like a denoising auto-encoder which learns the 'clean' background image and the tolerance of background variations for each pixel. The tolerance can help obtain the background images for each of the first D frames. Simply fitting B to the frames using L_1 optimization cannot achieve good results. The extracted background images contain the foregrounds. The deep architecture learns a more invariant representation of the background which enables us to better reconstruct the 'clean' background image and remove the foregrounds. It will make our algorithm more robust.

The reason we use two deep auto-encoder networks is that the background of different frames may have dramatic variations, so the learned background images from the first D frames may not fit the subsequent frames well. In the next section, we will introduce the online learning method which is essential for obtaining robust performance given dramatic inter-frame variations and adaptively learns the network parameters. Besides, the second network is used to model dynamic background, which can further reduce the noise of the background images by learning the variation distributions of the background implicitly. Although two auto-encoders are used, our algorithm is still real time.

3.2 Online Learning

In previous section, D video frames are used to train the dynamic background model. The number of samples is limited which may produce the overfitting problem. So we propose an online learning method to incorporate more data such that a more generalized model can be obtained.

The online learning executes on the BEN to update the trained parameters θ_E, B^0 and σ. To discriminate the symbols of these parameter, we denote the parameters as $\theta_E^o = \{W_{Ei}^o(i = 1, 2), b_{E,j}^o(j = 1, \cdots, 4)\}$, B^{o0} and σ^o. Firstly, the parameters, θ_E^o, B^{o0} and σ^o, are initialized by $\theta_{E,t-h}^o$, B_{t-h}^{o0} and σ_{t-h}^o where $t-h$ means the previous trained BEN. And in each turn, there are h frames to update the network. To speed up the online learning of the two layer weights $W_{Ei}^o(i = 1, 2)$, motivated by the method in [34] that is to search and eliminate the weights which lead to the minimal change effect of cost function, instead of eliminating these weights, we substitute these weights by the weights with large change effects. This strategy can help us use all connections between neurons more efficiently which also help the training stop earlier.

Firstly, the weight matrices $W^o_{Ei}(i=1,2)$ are rewritten as $W^o_{E1} = [W^o_{E1,1}, W^o_{E1,2}, \cdots, W^o_{E1,M_1}]$ and $W^o_{E2} = [W^o_{E2,1}, W^o_{E2,2}, \cdots, W^o_{E2,M_2}]$ where M_1 and M_2 are the neural number respect to the first two hidden layers respectively. $W^o_{E1,\cdot}$ is an N-dimensional vector and $W^o_{E2,\cdot}$ is an M_1-dimensional vector. Based on the method [34] on single hidden layer, our optimal problem on two hidden layers is to solve

$$\begin{aligned} \min_{\Delta W^o_{Ei}} \quad & \Delta\mathcal{L}(W^o_{E1}, W^o_{E2}) = \textstyle\sum_{i=1}^{2} tr(\frac{1}{2}\Delta W^{oT}_{Ei}\mathbf{H}_i\Delta W^o_{Ei}) \\ \text{s.t.} \quad & \Delta W^o_{E1}e_j = -W^o_{E1,j}, \Delta W^o_{E2}e'_k = -W^o_{E2,k} \end{aligned} \quad (19)$$

where e_j is the jth column of $N \times M_1$ identity matrix, e'_k is the kth column of $M_1 \times M_2$ identity matrix and $\mathbf{H}_i$ is the Hessian matrix respect to the ith layer weights. $\Delta\mathcal{L}$ denotes a disturbance from the weight changes. We assume the weight matrices W^o_{E1} and W^o_{E2} to be independent to each other which means $\Delta\mathcal{L}(W^o_{E1}, W^o_{E2}) = \Delta\mathcal{L}(W^o_{E1}) + \Delta\mathcal{L}(W^o_{E2})$ abbreviated as $\Delta\mathcal{L} = \Delta\mathcal{L}_1 + \Delta\mathcal{L}_2$.

Let

$$\begin{aligned} \Delta\mathcal{L}_{1j} &= {W^o_{E1,j}}^T W^o_{E1,j}/\mathbf{H}^{-1}_{1,jj}, \\ \Delta\mathcal{L}_{2k} &= {W^o_{E2,k}}^T W^o_{E2,k}/\mathbf{H}^{-1}_{2,kk} \end{aligned} \quad (20)$$

where $\mathbf{H}^{-1}_{i,jj}$ means the jth diagonal element of $\mathbf{H}^{-1}_i$. The computation of $\mathbf{H}^{-1}_i$ is achieved by several iterative operations. The solutions of minimizing the cost functions $\Delta\mathcal{L}_1$ and $\Delta\mathcal{L}_2$ are to find the vectors $W^o_{E1,j*}$ and $W^o_{E2,k*}$ such that the $\Delta\mathcal{L}_{1j}$ and $\Delta\mathcal{L}_{2k}$ are minimal for $j = 1, \cdots, M_1$ and $k = 1, \cdots, M_2$ respectively. More details are referred to [34]. Thus, we sort the results of $\Delta\mathcal{L}_{ij}(i=1,2)$ for $j = 1, \cdots, M_1$ and $j = 1, \cdots, M_2$ respectively. The vector $W^o_{Ei,j}$ with some j, which satisfies $\Delta\mathcal{L}_{ij} < \zeta$, is substituted by a randomly chosen vector $W^o_{Ei,r}$ satisfying $\Delta\mathcal{L}_{ir} > \zeta$, where ζ is an artificial parameter. Then, we retrain the BEN based on new samples. The details are shown in **Algorithm 2**.

There exist a few online learning methods ([43, 20, 39, 32]). These methods find a metric to merge similar weights. In fact, merging similar weights may affect the cost function enormously. Such operation may cause the network needs more iterative times to converge. Different from these works, our online strategy is to find the weights corresponding to the minimal effects of cost function in order to update and sufficiently use all connections. The saturation effects will be avoided by substituting these weight vectors by the weight vectors with large change effects of cost function.

3.3 Foreground Detection

In this section, we introduce the foreground detection flow based on the method proposed in previous sections. For an input image y, the outputs of the BEN and the BLN are $\hat{y}$ and $\hat{B}^y$ respectively. Combining $\hat{y}$ and $\hat{B}^y$, the foreground is computed as

$$F_i = \begin{cases} 0 & |\hat{y}_i - \hat{B}^y_i| \le \epsilon \\ 1 & |\hat{y}_i - \hat{B}^y_i| > \epsilon \end{cases} \quad (21)$$

for $i = 1, 2, \cdots, N$, where ϵ is a threshold representing the error of BEN input and BLN output.

Suppose there are D' frames in a video. Firstly, we use $D(D < D')$ frames to pre-train the BEN and BLN using **Algorithm 1**. Then, D foreground images $\mathbf{F} = \{F^1, \cdots, F^D\}$ are computed according to the formula (21). In each round of the online learning, h frames are used to train the BEN by **Algorithm 2**. The foreground images are saved in $\mathbf{F}$. These details are shown in **Algorithm 3**.

Algorithm 2 Online Learning of BEN

1: **Input:** samples $\mathbf{x} = \{\mathbf{x}^{t-h+1}, \cdots, \mathbf{x}^t\}$; initialized parameters as $W^o_{Ei} \leftarrow W_{Ei,t-h}, b^o_{Ej} \leftarrow b^o_{Ej,t-h}, B^{o0} \leftarrow B^{o0}_{t-h}, \sigma^o \leftarrow \sigma^o_{t-h}$
2: Use (20) to find the minimal effect vectors in $W^o_{Ei}(i = 1, 2)$.
3: Substitute these vectors by the randomly chosen vectors in $W^o_{Ei}(i = 1, 2)$ satisfying $\Delta\mathcal{L} > \zeta$.
4: **repeat**
5:   **for** each $j = t - h + 1, \cdots, t$ **do**
6:     Compute $h_1 \leftarrow sigm(W^o_{E1}\mathbf{x}^j + b^o_{E1})$
7:     Compute $h_2 \leftarrow sigm(W^o_{E2}h_{B1} + b^o_{E2})$
8:     Compute $h'_1 \leftarrow sigm(W^{oT}_{E2}h_2 + b^o_{E3})$
9:     Compute $\hat{\mathbf{x}}^j \leftarrow sigm(W^{oT}_{E1}h'_1 + b^o_{E4})$
10:     Update weight matrices $\theta^o_E \leftarrow \theta^o_E - \eta\nabla\theta^o_E$ using formula (9), where θ^o_E can be substituted for W^o_{Ei}, b^o_{Ej}
11:     $B^{o0}_i \leftarrow median(\hat{x}^1_i, \cdots, \hat{x}^j_i)(i = 1, \cdots, N)$
12:   **end for**
13:   σ^o is updated according to formula (15)
14: **until** $\sum_{j=t-h+1}^{t} \|\hat{\mathbf{x}} - \mathbf{x}\|_2 < \delta_o$
15: **Output:**$\theta^o, B^{o0}, \sigma^o$

Algorithm 3 Foreground Detection

1: **Input:** samples $\mathbf{x} = \{\mathbf{x}^1, \cdots, \mathbf{x}^{D'}\}$;
2: Use D samples to initialize the BEN and BLN by **Algorithm 1**.
3: Use the formula (21) to obtain D foreground images $\mathbf{F} = \{F^1, \cdots, F^D\}$.
4: $t \leftarrow D + 1$.
5: **repeat**
6:   Obtain samples $\{\mathbf{x}^{t-h+1}, \cdots, \mathbf{x}^t\}$ from $\mathbf{x}$
7:   Use these h samples to process online-learning by **Algorithm 2**.
8:   Re-train BLN using **Algorithm 2** line 13-22
9:   $\mathbf{F} \leftarrow \mathbf{F} \cup \{F^{t-h+1}, \cdots, F^t\}$
10:   $t \leftarrow t + h$
11: **until** $t \ge D'$
12: **Output:F**

4. EXPERIMENTAL RESULTS

In this section, we evaluate the performance of our methods to extract foregrounds from dynamic background. We firstly introduce the data sets and some experiment details in Section 4.1. Then we compare our experiment results to previous works in Section 4.2. Lastly, we discuss the online learning strategy in Section 4.3.

4.1 Experiment Setup

We use six publicly available video data sets in our experiments, including Jug [41], Railway [21], Lights [3], Trees [25], Water-Surface [12], and Fountain [21] to evaluate the performance of **Algorithm 3** which detailed the foreground detection from dynamic background.

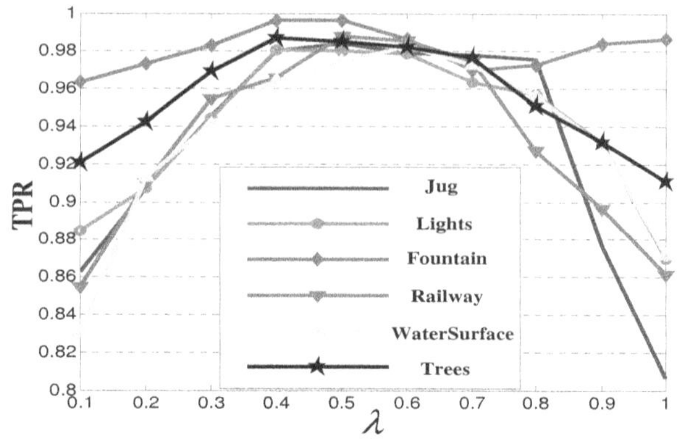

Figure 2: TPR vs λ on six data sets.

The Jug data set [41] contains 207 frames. In this data set, the dynamic background is moving river surface and foreground is a bottle floating on the surface. **The Railway data set [21]** contains 500 images. The dynamic background consists of moving trees and foreground is a walking person and a moving car. **The Lights data set [3]** contains 1546 images whose dynamic background is the room scene with illumination variations and foregrounds are pedestrians. **Trees [25]** contains 287 frames. There are a moving tree as a part of dynamic background and a walking man as the foreground. **Water-Surface [12]** contains 432 frames whose dynamic background consists of the moving water and the foreground is a walking man. **Fountain [21]** contains 1957 frames. There are several moving fountains in the background and walking men as foregrounds.

We measure the accuracy of detection to evaluate quantitatively. Actually, the foreground detection is a classification problem. If the pixel is classified as foreground, the output is positive. Otherwise it is negative. We evaluate detection results using TPR (True Positive Rate) and FPR (False Positive Rate), which are defined as

$$\mathrm{TPR} = \frac{\mathrm{TP}}{\mathrm{TP}+\mathrm{FP}}, \mathrm{FPR} = \frac{\mathrm{FN}}{\mathrm{TP}+\mathrm{FN}} \tag{22}$$

where TP, FP, TN and FN are the number of true positives, false positives, true negatives and false negatives at the pixel level for all test frames, respectively.

Some of previous works uses F-measure (or called F-score) to evaluate the performance. F-measure is defined as

$$\text{F-measure} = \frac{2 \cdot \mathrm{TPR} \cdot (1-\mathrm{FPR})}{\mathrm{TPR} + (1-\mathrm{FPR})}. \tag{23}$$

The higher F-measure means the better performance.

For each of data sets mentioned above, we trained our deep auto-encoder networks, respectively. The input dimensionality N on these six data set is 80×60(Jug), 180×120(Railway), 80×64(Lights), 80×60(Water-Surface), and 180×120(Fountain), respectively. The number of frames, D' in **Algorithm 3**, is 50 on all these data sets. According to our method, the larger D' obtains the better learning results. We find that, on these six data set, the experimental results are almost the same when D' is larger than 50. No more accuracy can be gained. And in **Algorithm 3**, each online learning contains $h = 35$ frames to re-train the network. In **Algorithm 1**, the parameters, δ_E, δ_L, are set to the 5% and 10% of the initial error between the input and the reconstruction output. This setting is adaptive for different data sets than that of previous work in [35] whose δ is a fixed value. Parameter ϵ in formula (21) is tunable. We will show our ROC curves in the next section depend on ϵ.

Parameter λ in **Algorithm 1** is tunable. The Different values of λ provide different tolerances of dynamic background. We compute the TPR on six data sets with different λ (see Figure 2). In our discussion below, we choose the value of λ which is corresponding to the highest TPR on each data set. Specifically, $\lambda = 0.5, 0.4, 0.4, 0.5, 0.6, 0.4$ correspond to the Jug, Lights, Fountain, Railway, Water-Surface, and Trees, respectively.

4.2 Comparisons to Previous Works

In this section, we compare some of benchmark methods on which the authors have provided the ROC curves in their papers. Firstly, we compare our method to previous works: 1-SVM [3], Bayesian method of [21], struct-SVM (S-SVM) method from [4], Mixture of Gaussian (MOG) in [11] and DCOLOR (Detecting Contiguous Outliers of Low-Rank) [42] on Jug, Lights, Railway, and Trees data sets. Sheikh *et al* use Bayesian model to learn background. But this work cannot obtain competitive results on dynamic background. 1-SVM and S-Svm are two previous methods which are proposed to use support vector machines to subtract background from dynamic scenes online. These two methods obtain some competitive results on dynamic scene. The Mixture of Gaussian based method is a popular method to background subtraction. The MOG has been proven to be very competitive compared to some sophisticated methods. But it is not good enough for dynamic scene. DCOLOR is an state-of-the-art method to dynamic background learning and get good results on many complex and dynamic background data sets. But this method is based on the assumption that the background images are linearly correlated with each other. This assumption limits the method to the case with large variations of background.

The comparisons of their ROC curves are shown in Fig. 3. From Fig. 3, it can be observed that these methods perform not very well comparing to our method on data sets Jug, Lights, Trees. On the Railway data set, only the results of S-SVM are competitive to ours. Our method uses deep auto-encoder network (BLN) to model the dynamic background. Unlike DCOLOR, there is no linear assumption about the background variations. BLN can learn large variations of dynamic background. So our method performs better.

We also compare our method to some works on data set WaterSurface and Fountain. For the WaterSurface data set, our method obtain the best performance among RPMF (Robust Probabilistic Matrix Factorization) [29], RP CA (Robust PCA) [13], GRASTA (Grassmannian Robust Adaptive Subspace Tracking) [7], and DCOLOR [42]. RPMF, RPCA, and GRASTA are three baseline methods on background substraction. There exist nonlinear moving and large variations of moving water in data set WaterSurface. RPCA and DCOLOR are not robust for this kind of dynamic change background. GRASTA [7] is also a method based on the Low-Rank model which imposes a sparsity penalty on its norm. But this method only works well for the static background. So on the dynamic background data set, such as WaterSurface, GRASTA cannot achieve good performance. RPMF [29] is based on the method of non-negative ma-

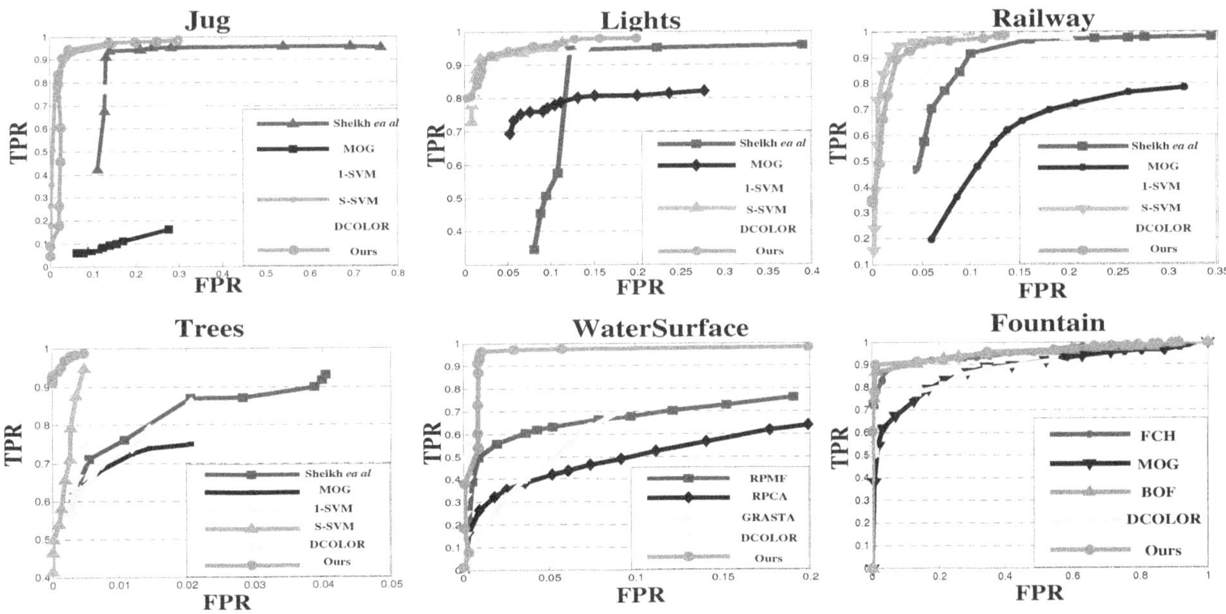

Figure 3: Comparisons of ROC Curves.

trix factorization which provides competitive performance on static background data set and is not good enough for dynamic background. The reason of our better performance is that BEN can subtract dynamic background images with considering the variations and BLN trains these dynamic background images using a deep auto-encoder network that can learn large variations of background.

For the Fountain data set, we compare our results to FCH (Fuzzy color Histogram) [10], BOF (Bag of Feature), MOG [11], and DCOLOR [42]. FCH learns color information of background. BOF is based on the learning of background texture. The feature selection is very important for the good results of FCH and BOF. Our deep learning strategy combines these two phases of feature selection and object detection. Deep neural networks can learn the object information from pixels and show powerful functionality of classification.

Some of previous works use F-measure (or called F-score) to evaluate the performance. To compare with these works directly, we also compute the F-measure of our method. The comparison results are shown in Table 1 and Table 2. In Table 1, we compare our work to MOG, FCH, BOF, ROFS, DCOLOR, RPCA, RPMF, and GRASTA on four data sets. On the Fountain and WaterSurface data sets, the F-measure values of MOG, FCH, BOF, and ROFS are copied from [37]. And the F-measure values of RPCA, RPMF, GRASTA are copied from [7]. On the Trees and Lights data sets, the F-measure values of FCH, BOF, and ROFS are from our implementation according to their algorithms. And the F-measure values of FCH, BOF, and ROFS are also from [7]. In Table 1, the F-measure values of DCOLOR are all from the open code provided by the authors. From Table 1, one can find that our method is consistently better than all of these baseline methods, though RPMF and DCOLOR can obtain rather good performances on these data sets, respectively. This demonstrates our method has more competitiveness for motion detection from dynamic background.

In Table 2, we compare our work to MOG, ORDL (Online Robust Dictionary Learning) [14], BRDL (Batch Robust Dictionary Learning) [38], Mairal *et al* [15], DECOLOR, and MDAEN (Motion Detection with Auto-encoder Network) [35] on the Jug and Railway data sets. The method of ORDL is based on the l^1 norm to learn the background dictionary. And BRDL is based on l^2 norm to learn the dictionary. Mairal *et al* proposed to learn the background by matrix factorization and sparse coding. These three methods always need clean background images to learn the dictionary. This limitation does not fit with real world applications. And these three methods can perform very well on static background when the learned dictionary expresses the static background good enough. The authors of MDAEN also proposed to use a couple of auto-encoder networks to learn the background. But this work is only based on a fixed vector to describe the tolerances of background variations while our strategy is to learn an adaptive tolerance vector. On the dynamic background set its performance is worse than that of ours. From Table 2, one can find that our method obtains the best performance.

In Fig. 4, we show some examples of foreground extraction for different methods on the six data sets. The first row in Fig. 4 shows a bottle floating on the moving surface of water. Our method subtracts the background accurately. MOG and DCOLOR output some false negatives. Sheikh *et al*'s work, 1-SVM, and S-SVM produce some false positives. The fourth row in Figure 4 is a walking person with dynamic background of a waving tree. The tree is waving faster than that of the walking man. MOG, Sheikh *et al*'s work, 1-SVM , and S-SVM show some false negatives. The method of DECOLOR shows both of false negatives and false positives. On these six data sets of dynamic background, our method shows the best foreground extraction results than all of previous benchmark methods.

Table 1: Comparisons of F-measure on Fountain, WaterSurface, Trees, and Lights

Video	MOG	FCH	BOF	ROFS	DCOLOR	RPCA	RPMF	GRASTA	Ours
Fountain	0.601	0.900	0.901	0.859	0.860	0.940	0.940	0.690	**0.962**
WaterSurface	0.534	0.721	0.819	0.926	0.910	0.730	0.840	0.870	**0.950**
Trees	0.553	0.732	0.795	0.8785	0.79	0.74	0.840	0.870	**0.970**
Lights	0.63	0.846	0.871	0.864	0.88	0.87	0.92	0.620	**0.943**

Table 2: Comparisons of F-measure on Jug and Railway

Video	MOG	ORDL	BRDL	Mairal *et al*	DECOLOR	MDAEN	Ours
Jug	0.613	0.712	0.711	0.623	0.76	0.853	**0.92**
Railway	0.736	0.886	0.833	0.794	0.932	0.914	**0.954**

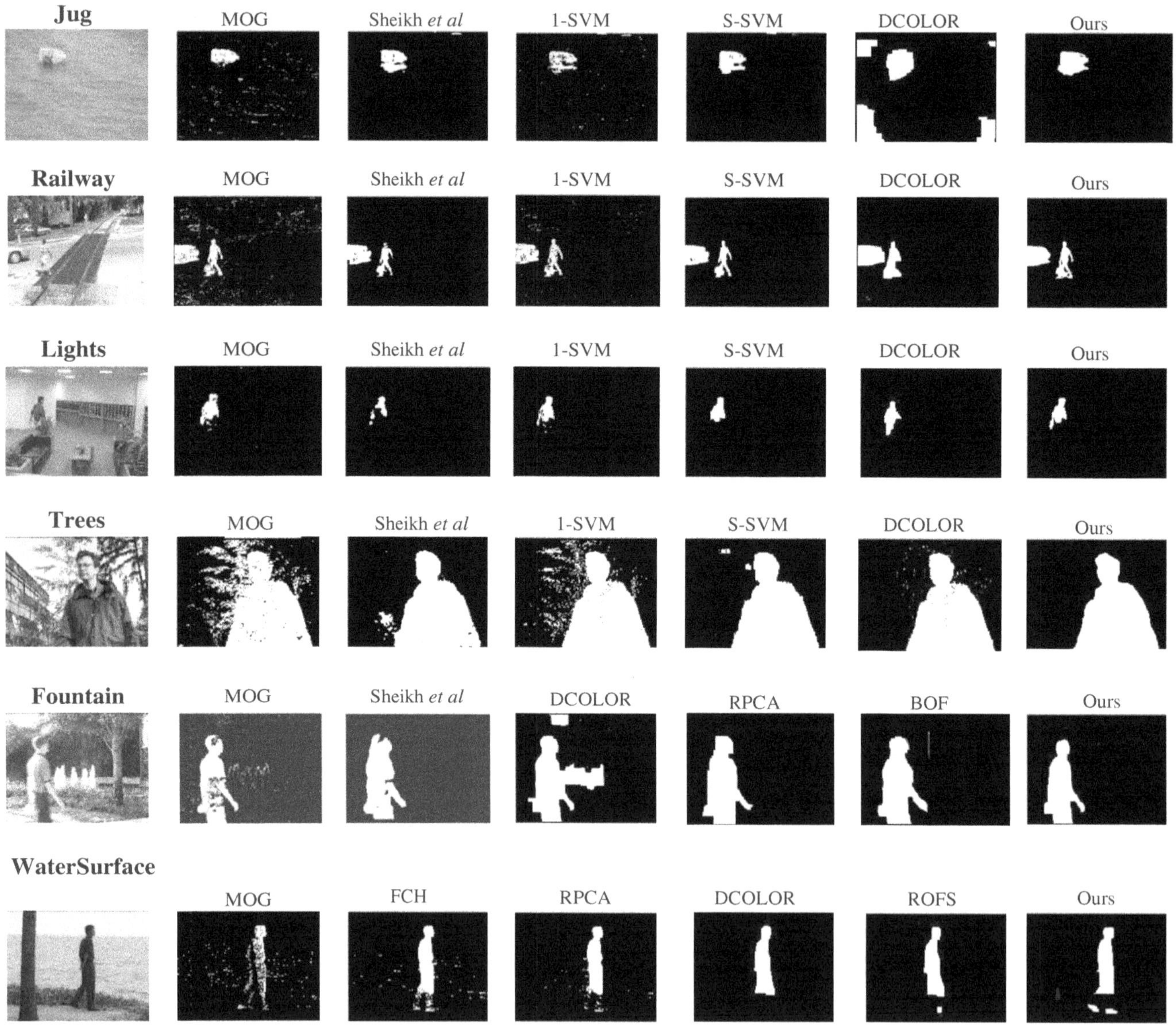

Figure 4: Comparisons of foreground extraction. The first column contains the original images. The second to the end columns are the extracted results of different methods.

4.3 Online Learning Strategy Comparison

In this section, we compare the online strategy to previous works. Our aim is to compare the iterative times in **Algorithm 2** with other strategies. ESCWL (Exact Soft Confidence-Weighted Learning) [30] is the newest online learning methods which assume the weight vector fits Gaussian distribution. Based on this assumption, this method constructs a loss function about the weight vector. And the weights are updated according to the mean and covariance of weight vectors. OI (Online Incremental) [43] is an online method to compute the similarity between two weight vectors. This method will combine the similar weight vectors. Besides, we also compare the online learning strategy which is directly updating weights (DUW) using

$$W = W - \eta \Delta W \tag{24}$$

without any preprocessing.

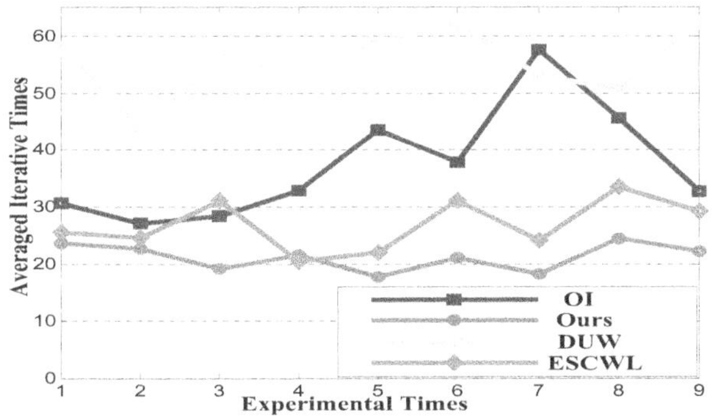

Figure 5: Comparisons of online learning strategies.

On all the six data sets, we evaluate **Algorithm 2** nine times. The h frames of each time is 35, 40, 27, 43, 50, 28, 32, 47, 23 on each data set. Every time we average the iterative times of six data sets. In **Algorithm 2**, the parameters ζ and δ are different for the data sets. So we average the iterative times on the six data sets.

The results are shown in Fig. 5. The OI strategy is almost better than that of DUW except the seventh test. This means that merging similar weights can not always obtain better results than the method of directly updating weights. The ESCWL method is better than or comparable with OI. ESCWL is based on the assumption that the weight vector is fit to a Gaussian distribution. Our strategy can obtain least iterative times which is better than that of ESCWL, OI and DUW. Because the minimal effect weights are substituted for large effect weights according to the cost function, this strategy can reduce the iterative times and make the training converges fast.

5. CONCLUSIONS

We propose a novel and practical method to deal with moving object detection from dynamic background based on deep auto-encoder networks. Firstly, dynamic background images are extracted using a deep auto-encoder network (called Background Extraction Network, BEN). Then, another deep auto-encoder network (called Background Learning Network, BLN) is used to model dynamic background using the dynamic background images as input. To be more resilient to the large dynamic background variances, a method of searching and substituting the minimizing effect parameters, in different hidden layers, is used for online-learning. In our framework, a specific method is used to learn the variance tolerance measure adaptively. Experiments on six benchmark data sets confirmed the superior performance of our method on dynamic background.

6. ACKNOWLEDGMENTS

This work was supported in part by the National Natural Science Foundation of China (61375038), 973 National Basic Research Program of China (2010CB732501) and Fundamental Research Funds for the Central University (ZYGX2012YB028). The work of Yi Yang is in part supported by the ARC DECRA project.

7. REFERENCES

[1] Y. Bengio, P. Lamblin, D. Popovici, and H. Larochelle. Greedy layer-wise training of deep networks. In *Advances in Neural Information Processing Systems (NIPS)*, pages 153-160, 2007.

[2] V. Cevher, A. Sankaranarayanan, M. Duarte, D. Reddy, R. Baraniuk, and R. Chellappa. Compressive sensing background subtraction. In *European Conference on Computer Vision (ECCV)*, pages 155-168, 2008.

[3] L. Cheng, S. V. N. Vishwanathan, and D. Schuurmans et al. Implicit online learning with kernels. In *Advances in Neural Information Processing Systems (NIPS)*, pages 249-256, 2006.

[4] L. Cheng, and M. Gong. Realtime Background Substraction from Dynamic Scenes. In *IEEE International Conference on Computer Vision (ICCV)*, pages 2066-2073, 2009.

[5] D. Cremers and S. Soatto. Motion competition: A variational approach to piecewise parametric motion segmentation, *International Journal of Computer Vision (IJCV)*, 62(3):249-265, 2005.

[6] C. Farabet, C. Couprie, L. Najman, and Y. Lecun. Learning Hierarchical Features for Scene Labeling. *IEEE Transactions on Pattern Analysis and Machine Intelligence (TPAMI)*, 35(8):1915 - 1929, 2013.

[7] J. He, L. Balzano, and A. Szlam. Incremental gradient on the grassmannian for online foreground and background separation in subsampled video. In *IEEE International Conference on Computer Vision and Pattern Recognition (CVPR)*, pages 1568-1575, 2012.

[8] N. Heess, N. L. Roux, and J.Winn. Weakly supervised learning of foreground-background segmentation using masked RBMs. In *International Conference on Artificial Neural Networks (ICANN)*, pages 9-16, 2011.

[9] J. Huang, X. Huang, and D. N. Metaxas. Learning with dynamic group sparsity. In *IEEE International Conference on Computer Vision (ICCV)*, pages 64-71, 2009.

[10] W. Kim, C. Kim. Background subtraction for dynamic texture scenes using fuzzy color histograms. *IEEE Signal Process Letter*, 19(3):127-130, 2012.

[11] D. Lee. Effective gaussian mixture learning for video background substraction. *IEEE Transactions on Pattern Analysis and Machine Intelligence (TPAMI)*, 27(5):827-832, 2005.

[12] L. Li, W. Huang, I. Gu, and Q. Tian. Statistical modeling of complex backgrounds for foreground object detectiong. *IEEE Transactions on Image Processing (TIP)*, 13(11):1459-1472,2004.

[13] Z. Lin, M. Chen, L. Wu, and Y. Ma. The augmented lagrange multiplier method for exact recovery of corrupted low-rank matrices. *UIUC Technical Report UILU-ENG-09-2215*, 1009.5055, 2009.

[14] Cewu Lu, Jianping Shi, and Jiaya Jia. Online Robust Dictionary Learning. In *IEEE International Conference on Computer Vision and Pattern Recognition (CVPR),* pages 415-422, 2013.

[15] J. Mairal, F. Bach, J. Ponce, and G. Sapiro. Online learning for matrix factorization and sparse coding. *The Journal of Machine Learning Research,* 11(3):19-60, 2010.

[16] A. Monnet, A. Mittal, N. Paragios, and V. Ramesh. Background modeling and subtraction of dynamic scenes. In *IEEE International Conference on Computer Vision (ICCV),* pages 1305-1312, 2005.

[17] Marc'Aurelio Ranzato, F. J. Huang, Y. L. Boureau, Y. LeCun. Unsupervised learning of invarient feature hierarchies with applications to object recognition. In *IEEE International Conference on Computer Vision and Pattern Recognition (CVPR),* papges 1-8, 2007.

[18] Z. Ren, L. Chia, D. Rajan, and S. Gao. Background subtraction via coherent trajectory decomposition. In *ACM international conference on Multimedia (MM),* pages 545-548, 2013.

[19] J. Rittscher, J. Kato, S. Joga, and A. Blake. A probabilistic background model for tracking. In *European Conference on Computer Vision (ECCV),* pages 336-350,2000.

[20] F. Rosenblatt. The perceptron: A probabilistic model for information storage and organization in the brain. *Psychological Review,* 65(6):386-408, 1958.

[21] Y. Sheikh and M. Shah. Bayesian object detection in dynamic scenes. In *IEEE International Conference on Computer Vision and Pattern Recognition (CVPR),* pages 74-79, 2005.

[22] C. Stauffer and W. Grimson. Adaptive Background Mixture Models for Real-Time Tracking. In *IEEE International Conference on Computer Vision and Pattern Recognition (CVPR),* pages 2246-2252, 1999.

[23] G. W. Taylor, and G. E. Hinton. Factored Conditional Restricted Boltzmann Machines for Modeling Motion Style. In *International Conference on Machine Learning (ICML),* pages 129-137, 2009.

[24] G. W. Taylor, G. E. Hinton, and S. Roweis. Modeling Human Motion Using Binary Latent Vairiables. In *Advances in Neural Information Processing Systems (NIPS),* pages 1345-1352, 2006.

[25] K. Toyama, J. Krumm, B. Brumitt, and B. Meyers. Wallflower: Principles and practice of background maintenance. In *IEEE International Conference on Computer Vision (ICCV),* pages 255-261, 1999.

[26] R. Vidal and Y. Ma. A unified algebraic approach to 2-d and 3-d motion segmentations. In *European Conference on Computer Vision (ECCV),* pages 1-15, 2004.

[27] P. Vincent, H. Larochelle, Y. Bengio, and P. Manzagol. Extracting and composing robust features with denoising auto-encoders. In *International Conference on Machine Learning (ICML),* Pages 1096-1103, 2008.

[28] A. Wagner, J. Wright, A. Ganesh, Z. Zhou, H. Mobahi, and Y. Ma. Towards a practical face recognition system: Robust alignment and illumination by sparse representation. *IEEE Transactions on Pattern Analysis and Machine Intelligence (TPAMI),* 34(2):372-386, 2012.

[29] N.Wang, T. Yao, J.Wang, and D.-Y. Yeung. A probabilistic approach to robust matrix factorization. In *European Conference on Computer Vision (ECCV),* pages 126-139, 2012.

[30] J. Wang, P. Zhao, and S. C. H. Hoi. Exact soft confidence-weighted learning. In *International Conference on Machine Learning (ICML),* pages 121-128, 2012.

[31] C. R. Wren, A. Azarbayejani, T. Darrell, and A. P. Pentland. Pfinder: Real-time tracking of the human body. *IEEE Transactions on Pattern Analysis and Machine Intelligence (TPAMI),* 19(2):780-785, 2002.

[32] P. Wu, S. C. H. Hoi, H. Xia *et al.* Online Multimodal Deep Similarity Learning with Application to Image Retrieval. In *ACM international conference on Multimedia (MM),* pages 153-162, 2013.

[33] Q. Wu, P. Boulanger, and W. F. Bischof. Bi-Layer Video Segmentation with Foreground and Background Infrared Illumination. In *ACM international conference on Multimedia (MM),* pages 1025-1026, 2012.

[34] Jinhua Xu, DanielW. C. Ho. A new training and pruning algorithm based on node dependence and Jacobian rank deficiency. *Neurocomputing,* 70(1):544-558, 2006.

[35] P. Xu, M. Ye, Q.H. Liu, *et al.* Motion detection via a couple of auto-encoder networks. In *IEEE International Conference on Multimedia and Expo (ICME),* 2014.

[36] A. Yilmaz, O. Javed, and M. Shah. Object tracking: A survey. *ACM computing survey,* 38(4):1-45, 2006.

[37] S. Yoo, and C. Kim. Background subtraction using hybrid feature coding in the bag-of-features framework. *Pattern Recognition Letters,* 34(16): 2086-2093, 2013.

[38] C. Zhao, X. Wang, and W.K. Cham. Background subtraction via robust dictionary learning. *EURASIP Journal on Image and Video Processing,* 2011(972961):1-12, 2011.

[39] P. Zhao, S. C. H. Hoi, and R. Jin. Double updating online learning. *Journal of Machine Learning Research,* 12(5):1587-1615, 2011.

[40] Y. Zheng, S. Gu, and C. Tomas. Detection motion synchrony by video tubes. In *ACM international conference on Multimedia (MM),* pages 1197-1200, 2011.

[41] J. Zhong and S. Sclaroff. Segmenting foreground objects from a dynamic textured background via a robust Kalman filter. In *IEEE International Conference on Computer Vision (ICCV),* pages 44-50, 2003.

[42] X. Zhou, C. Yang, and W. Yu. Moving object detection by detecting contiguous outliers in the low-rank representation. *IEEE Transactions on Pattern Analysis and Machine Intelligence (TPAMI),* 35(3):597-610, 2013.

[43] G. Zhou, K. Sohn, and H. Lee. Online Incremental Feature Learning with Denoising Auto-encoders, *Proceedings of the Fifteenth International Conference on Artificial Intelligence and Statistics (ICAIS)*, pages 1453-1461, 2012.

Music Emotion Recognition by Multi-label Multi-layer Multi-instance Multi-view Learning

Bin Wu[1], Erheng Zhong[1], Andrew Horner[1], Qiang Yang[1,2]
[1]Department of Computer Science and Engineering,
Hong Kong University of Science and Technology, Hong Kong
[2]Noah's Ark Lab, Huawei, Hong Kong
{bwuaa,ezhong,horner,qyang}@cse.ust.hk

ABSTRACT

Music emotion recognition, which aims to automatically recognize the affective content of a piece of music, has become one of the key components of music searching, exploring, and social networking applications. Although researchers have given more and more attention to music emotion recognition studies, the recognition performance has come to a bottleneck in recent years. One major reason is that experts' labels for music emotion are mostly song-level, while music emotion usually varies within a song. Traditional methods have considered each song as a single instance and have built models based on song-level features. However, they ignored the dynamics of music emotion and failed to capture accurate emotion-feature correlations. In this paper, we model music emotion recognition as a novel *multi-label multi-layer multi-instance multi-view learning* problem: music is formulated as a hierarchical multi-instance structure (e.g., song-segment-sentence) where multiple emotion labels correspond to at least one of the instances with multiple views of each layer. We propose a Hierarchical Music Emotion Recognition model (HMER) – a novel hierarchical Bayesian model using sentence-level music and lyrics features. It captures music emotion dynamics with a song-segment-sentence hierarchical structure. HMER also considers emotion correlations between both music segments and sentences. Experimental results show that HMER outperforms several state-of-the-art methods in terms of F_1 score and mean average precision.

Categories and Subject Descriptors

H.5.5 [**Sound and Music Computing**]: Methodologies and Techniques, Systems

Keywords

Music Emotion Recognition; Multi-label Multi-layer Multi-instance Multi-view Learning

MM'14, November 03–07, 2014, Orlando, FL, USA.

http://dx.doi.org/10.1145/2647868.2654904.

1. INTRODUCTION

The famous 19th century Russian novelist Leo Tolstoy once said, "Music is the shorthand of emotion". Music is the most direct artistic form of expressing and riding the roller-coaster of emotion[1]. Researchers have given increasing attention to this area because of many interesting and important applications of music emotion. For example, *Sensbeat*[2] is a social network where users connect with one another by sharing music and emotions, and *Stereomood*[3] is a music website which enables users to explore music based on emotion queries.

Music emotion recognition, which aims to automatically recognize the affective content of a piece of music, is the key component of the above-mentioned music emotion applications. Many previous studies have been devoted to improve the accuracy of music emotion recognition. However, the recognition accuracy is still far from satisfactory and has come to a bottleneck in recent years despite sufficient labeled data [28]. As reported in MIREX – an annual Audio Music Mood Classification Evaluation Exchange[4], the best classification accuracies have been around 68% on a five-emotion classification task since 2011, and no improvement was made in 2013.

One major reason for the performance bottleneck is that previous methods considered each song as a single instance and assumed that emotions are consistent over the entire songs [6]. However, music emotion is time-varying [19, 15]. For example, theme A of the song "I believe I can fly" by R. Kelly expresses a "reflective" emotion, while theme B conveys an "ambitious" emotion. More specifically, based on our observations from data, we propose a structure of music emotion dynamics as follows:

- Music emotion can vary greatly between music segments.
- Music emotion is mostly consistent within each segment.
- Music emotion is almost always consistent within each sentence.

Previous methods were not aware of such a structure. They extract song-level features by averaging features over the entire song, which may lead to inaccurate feature representation, and may therefore degrade recognition performance. Attempts have been made to capture the dynamics

[1]"Emotion" and "mood" are often used interchangeably. In this paper, we use "emotion".
[2]`https://itunes.apple.com/hk/app/sensbeat/id725472587?mt=8`
[3]`https://itunes.apple.com/hk/app/stereomood-tuning-my-emotions/id524634435?mt=8`
[4]http://www.music-ir.org/mirex/wiki

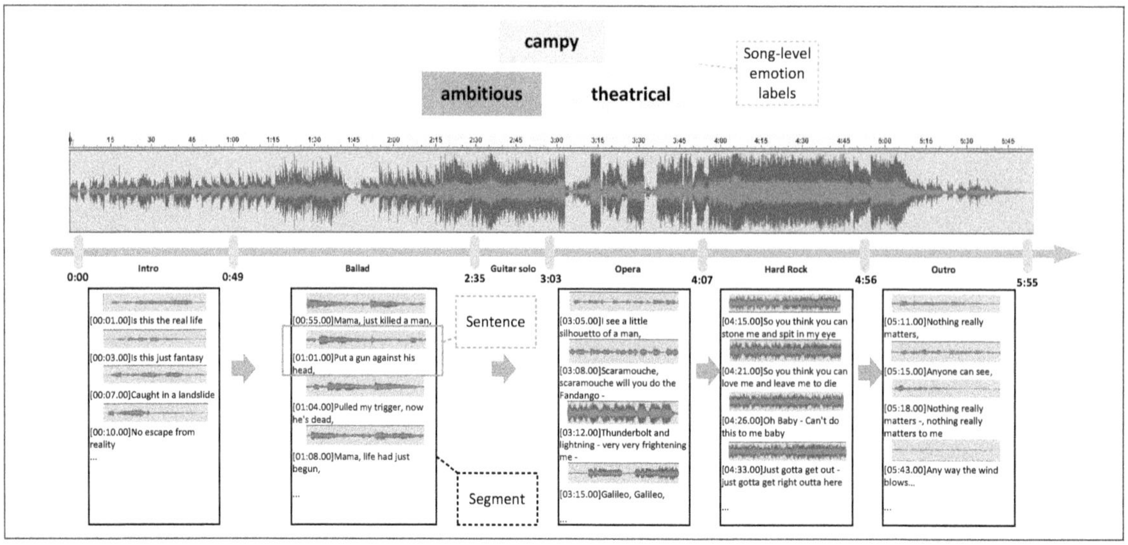

Figure 1: Music structure of the song "Bohemian Rhapsody" by Queen. This song has three song-level emotion labels. Emotion varies between segments, but is mostly consistent within each segment, and almost always consistent within each sentence.

of music emotion to some extent. For example, Schmidt *et al.* [20] and Lu *et al.* [15] exploited segment-level labeled data of music, assuming that emotions being conveyed within the same segment were usually consistent. Their approaches, however, is not scalable because labeling each segment requires a great deal of effort by music experts, which is difficult to come by in practice. Therefore, other label sources are desired.

Fortunately, the large number of song-level labels can be utilized without making strong assumptions like traditional single-instance methods. For example, multi-instance learning methods assume that each song is a bag of instances (e.g., segments, sentences, or music notes), where the song-level labels correspond to at least one of the instances [16]. This assumption allows different music emotions to correspond to different music segments.

Also, lyrics are another good source of labels in describing the dynamics of music emotion [9, 13]. Lyrics and music are always highly synchronized and carefully composed to match each other in terms of emotion. LRC formatted lyrics files, which are available for many songs on the Internet, provide sentence-level synchronized lyrics by indicating start and end playback timestamps for each sentence. Using this information may allow us to obtain more fine-grained and accurate music-lyrics correlations and improve feature representation.

Motivated by the structure of music emotion dynamics, as well as the two sources of labels, we propose a novel *multi-label multi-layer multi-instance multi-view learning* problem that formulates music emotion recognition as follows: "multi-label" means that a song usually has multiple emotions [21]; "multi-layer multi-instance" means that the multi-instance structure is multi-layer (e.g., song-segment-sentence), and the multiple labels correspond to at least one of the instances; "multi-view" means that multiple views (such as music and lyrics) co-exist in each instance layer (e.g., song, segment, and sentence).

To approach music emotion recognition as the novel *multi-label multi-layer multi-instance multi-view learning* problem, we propose a Hierarchical Music Emotion Recognition model (HMER) – a novel hierarchical Bayesian model which accurately captures the dynamic structure of music emotion. More specifically, HMER requires lyrics with timestamps, uses sentence-level music and lyrics features, and captures music emotion dynamics by a song-segment-sentence hierarchical structure. Also, HMER not only considers emotion correlations within a song by assuming its segments follow correlated emotion distributions, but also considers stricter emotion correlations within each segment by assuming its sentences follow the same emotion distributions. The experimental results show that HMER outperforms several state-of-the-art methods on both mean average precision and F_1 scores. Note that our model is aimed for offline processing so computational time is a secondary issue.

We summarize our main contributions as follows:

- We propose a novel hierarchical Bayesian model to approach music emotion recognition as a novel *multi-label multi-layer multi-instance multi-view learning* problem.
- We empirically prove the effectiveness of our proposed model on music emotion recognition using a real-world dataset.

2. PROBLEM DEFINITION

In this section, we first provide an example to illustrate the features and structure of music emotion dynamics. Then, we give the formal problem definition and formulation motivated by the observations from the example. We also provide a preliminary introduction to the concepts of *multi-label multi-layer multi-instance multi-view learning.*

2.1 An Illustrating Example

Figure 1 presents an example to illustrate the problem using the song "Bohemian Rhapsody" by Queen[5]. This song

[5]Music video of the song can be found at `http://www.youtube.com/watch?v=fJ9rUzIMcZQ`. LRC file can be down-

was labeled by AllMusic as "campy", "ambitious", and "theatrical" [1]. The full waveform is shown in the figure for illustration. The song has six segments: Intro, Ballad, Guitar solo, Opera, Hard rock, and Outro [2]. For each segment, we show part of the lyrics. Using the corresponding LRC file, we can locate the start timestamp for each sentence. We also extracted the waveform of each sentence for illustration.

Overall, we can observe from the complete waveform that the amplitude changes dramatically over the song (amplitude significantly correlates with strength of emotion [12]). More specifically, amplitude is weakest during the Intro and Outro, medium in the Ballad and Opera, and strongest in the Hard rock, indicating emotion varies greatly in different segments. For each segment, we can see that the amplitude of each sentence is of a similar level, implying that emotions are generally consistent within the same segment. Nevertheless, we can observe some special cases. For example, consider the sentence at 03:12 in Opera, the amplitude level is obviously larger than the others. This is because composers sometimes make use of contrasts to express emotion. Furthermore, amplitude level is almost always consistent within each sentence.

In summary, three assumptions can be made: 1) music emotion varies greatly between music segments; 2) music emotion is mostly consistent within each segment; 3) music emotion is almost always consistent within each sentence. Based on these assumptions, the three emotion labels "campy", "ambitious", and "theatrical", which are not similar with one another, are probably describing different segments. Intuitively, this is problematic for traditional single-instance methods which assume that multiple labels simultaneously describe song-level features.

2.2 Problem Formulation

Consider a set of songs X of size D. Each song X_d has a set of labels Y_d of size $|Y_d|$, and I_d segments. The ith segment X_{di} has $S_d^{(i)}$ sentences. The sth sentence X_{dis} has two perspectives/views: a music view and a lyrics view, where the corresponding music and lyrics tokens are denoted as m_{dis} and l_{dis}, respectively. Following [31], each music token is represented as a bag of prototypes $\mathcal{C} = \{c_1, \ldots, c_C\}$ for the music corpus of size C by clustering acoustic features. Each lyrics token is represented as a bag of words $\mathcal{W} = \{w_1, \ldots, w_W\}$ of size W by constructing a word corpus. The objective is to predict labels for testing songs X_{test} given a set of training songs and labels $\{X_{train}, Y_{train}\}$. Notations are listed in Table 1.

In this paper, we formulate music emotion recognition as a novel *multi-label multi-layer multi-instance multi-view learning* problem as follows: the multiple-labeled nature of music emotion makes it a multi-label classification problem; the fact that song-level labels correspond to at least one of the song segments and sentences fits this problem to a multi-layer multi-instance learning problem; finally, since music and lyrics are synchronized, we always have two views for each layer: from song-layer to music note layer. However, since LRC data only provides synchronization on the sentence-layer and emotions are usually consistent within a sentence as observed in Figure 1, we only consider song, segment, and sentence layers in this paper.

loaded at `http://music.baidu.com/data2/lrc/1831720/1831720.lrc`

Table 1: Notation.

Notation	Definition
D	Number of songs (bags).
K	Number of topics.
X_d	Song d, including music and lyrics content.
Y	Label set.
Y_d	Labels of song d.
$\|Y_d\|$	Number of labels.
y_{dn}	The n-th label in Y_d.
θ_d	Topic distritution of song X_d.
γ	Dirichlet prior of θ_d.
φ	Label distribution for topics.
β	Dirichlet prior of φ.
z_{dn}	Topic assignments of label y_{dn} in song X_d.
I_d	Number of segments (instances) in song d.
$\theta_d^{(i)'}$	Label distribution of the i-th segment.
$\alpha_d^{(i)}$	Dirichlet prior of θ'_{di}.
$\xi_d^{(i)}$	Parameter for song d and instance i which co-decides $\alpha_d^{(i)}$.
ξ	Fixed parameter for initializing $\xi_d^{(i)}$.
η	Fixed parameter which co-decides $\alpha_d^{(i)}$.
$S_d^{(i)}$	Number of sentences in the i-th segment of song X_d.
v'_{dis}	Label assignment of the song X_d, i-th segment, s-th sentence.
m_{dis}	Music token of song X_d, i-th segment, s-th sentence.
l_{dis}	Lyrics token of song X_d, i-th segment, s-th sentence.
$\varphi^{(m)}$	Music token distribution over label assignment.
$\varphi^{(l)}$	Lyrics token distribution over label assignment.
$\beta^{(m)}$	Dirichlet prior of $\varphi^{(m)}$.
$\beta^{(l)}$	Dirichlet prior of $\varphi^{(l)}$.
C	Number of music prototypes.
W	Number of lyrics words.

2.3 Preliminary

In this subsection, we give a preliminary introduction to *multi-label multi-layer multi-instance multi-view learning*: 1) Multi-label learning aims to classify an instance into multiple labels simultaneously; 2) Multi-view learning aims to learn from multiple perspectives/views/modals of instances to improve accuracy [27]; 3) Multi-instance learning assumes that labels are provided on bags of instances to cope with the fact that labels may correspond to different instances instead of the entire bag of instances [31].

Multi-instance learning is usually also a multi-label learning problem, i.e., multi-label multi-instance [31, 30, 17]. Multi-instance learning sometimes have multiple layers of instances, i.e., multi-layer multi-instance [8]. Nevertheless, to the best of our knowledge, multi-view learning has only been applied to bag-level (i.e., multi-view multi-instance learning) [17], but neither to instance-level nor to multi-layer instance-level in a multi-instance learning setting (i.e., (multi-layer) multi-instance multi-view learning). *Multi-label multi-layer multi-instance multi-view learning* is what we propose and focus on in this paper.

3. HIERARCHICAL MUSIC EMOTION RECOGNITION MODEL

We elaborate our proposed Hierarchical Music Emotion Recognition (HMER) Model in this section. We first introduce our proposed generative model of music emotion.

Then, following the generative process, parameters such as emotion distribution over music and lyrics can be trained given the emotion labels and sentence-level music-lyrics. Finally, we can predict emotions of songs given the trained parameters and observed music and lyrics content in the test set.

3.1 The Generative Model

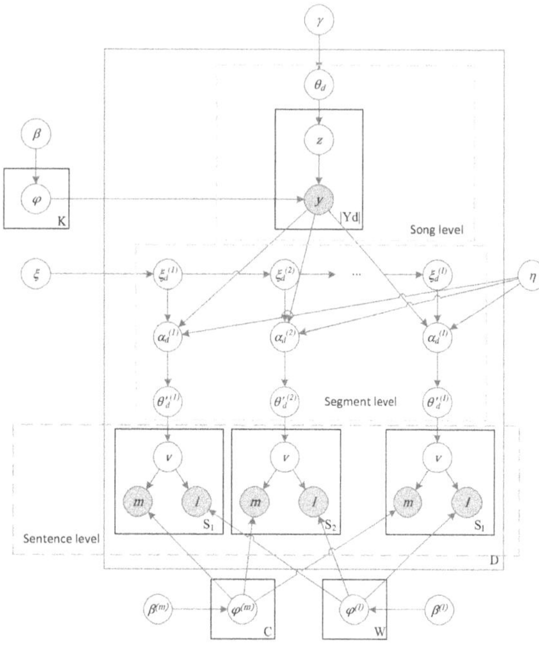

Figure 2: Graphical model of the proposed model.

We consider music and emotion as a top-down generative model as follows. First, composers are inspired by some musical ideas/topics perhaps based on non-musical associations. Then, when creating music and lyrics, composers design the segment structure (i.e., emotions expressed in each segment) to express the overall emotions. Next, within each segment, multiple sentences with music and lyrics content are generated by the underlying segment emotions[6]. Note that the above generative model is a probabilistic assumption for modeling purposes instead of what takes place in the real-life composition process.

More specifically, HMER represents emotions for each segment i as a probability distribution $\theta_d^{(i)}$ because emotion can vary greatly between segments as observed in Figure 1. Also, since the segment emotions are correlated within the same song, we require emotion distributions of the segments to be similar using a Markov chain $\boldsymbol{\xi_d}$ ($\boldsymbol{\xi_d}$ affects how similar the Dirichlet prior between segments are, thereby how similar the distributions are). Moreover, since emotions of sentences can sometimes vary but are mostly consistent within the same segment, we assume sentences in the same segment follow the same emotion distribution, which restricts sentences to be highly similar. Finally, each sentence is restricted to a single emotion because emotion is almost always consistent within each sentence.

[6]The generative process can continue until the music note level, but we ignore these in this paper to simplify the problem because emotion is usually consistent within a sentence and LRC files only provide sentence-level music-lyrics synchronization.

The generative process is described in Figure 2 as a graphical model and stated in Algorithm 1, where we refer to the topic-label generation process as the topic-label part, and the other processes as the label-token part (i.e., label-music and label-lyrics). Notations of variables in Algorithm 1 are listed in Table 1.

Algorithm 1: Generative process of the proposed model.

for *each song* X_d **do**
- –Sample a topic distribution of labels $\theta_d \in Dirichlet(\gamma)$; θ_d is a K-dimensional Dirichlet distribution parameterized by γ.
- **for** *each label* y_{dn} **do**
  - –Sample a topic assignment $z_{dn} \sim Multinominal(\theta_d)$.
  - –Sample a label from $p(y_{dn}|z_{dn}, \varphi_{z_{dn}}) = Multinominal(\varphi_{z_{dn}})$ from the topic z_{dn}.
- –Compute the label priors for X_d: $\boldsymbol{\alpha_d^{(i)}} = \{\eta \times N_1/|Y_d| + f(\xi_{d1}^{(i)}), \ldots, \eta \times N_{|Y_d|}/|Y_d| + f(\xi_{d|Y_d|}^{(i)})\}$, where N_n is the number of y_{dn} in Y_d; $\xi_{dn}^{(i)} \sim \mathcal{N}(\xi_{dn}^{(i-1)}, \sigma^2)$, and $\xi_d^{(0)} = \xi$.
- **for** *each segment* $\boldsymbol{x_{di}} \in X_d$ **do**
  - **for** *each sentence* $\boldsymbol{x_{dis}} \in \boldsymbol{x_{di}}$ **do**
    - –Sample a label assignment $v_{dis} \sim Multinomial(\theta_d^{(i)'})$.
    - –Sample a music sentence $\boldsymbol{m_{dis}}$ from $p(\boldsymbol{m}|v_{dis}, \varphi^{(m)}) = \prod_{c=1}^{C}(\varphi_{c,v_{dis}}^{m})^{\boldsymbol{m_c}}$; $\varphi_{\cdot,v_{dis}}^{(m)}$ is a C-dimensional Multinominal for the label v_{dis}.
    - –Sample a lyrics sentence $\boldsymbol{l_{dis}}$ from $p(\boldsymbol{l}|v_{dis}, \varphi^{(l)}) = \prod_{w=1}^{W}(\varphi_{w,v_{dis}}^{l})^{\boldsymbol{l_w}}$; $\varphi_{\cdot,v_{dis}}^{(l)}$ is a W-dimensional Multinominal for the label v_{dis}.

The innovations of HMER are three-folds:

1) Music and lyrics are generated simultaneously to express the same emotions on the sentence level (i.e., music and lyrics tokens m and l are generated by the sentence emotion v), while other models only assume music and lyrics convey the same emotions on the song-level [21, 18, 17];

2) The song-segment-sentence hierarchical structure captures the dynamics of music emotion, which cannot be handled by previous methods since they are one layer multi-instance models (i.e., either segments or sentences) [18, 17], while HMER has two layers (i.e., both segments and sentences).

3) Emotion correlations between music segments in the same song are captured by $\xi_d^{(i)}$ as a Markov process (i.e., emotions of music segment $\theta_d^{(i)}$ are generated for both song-level emotions Y_d and the preceding segment's emotions $\theta_d^{(i-1)}$), while music segments are considered exchangeable by other multi-instance learning methods [18, 17].

Following the generative process, HMER is first trained by iteratively assigning labels to each sentence and updating topic-song distribution θ_d, the label-segment distribution $\theta_d^{(i)}$ and its prior $\alpha_d^{(i)}$, the topic-label distribution φ, the music-label distribution $\varphi^{(m)}$, and the lyrics-label distribution $\varphi^{(l)}$ accordingly. Then, fixing the trained φ, $\varphi^{(m)}$, and $\varphi^{(l)}$, we can obtain label distributions of test songs by sampling label assignments through the generative process iteratively. Details of the training and testing processes are elaborated in the following subsections.

3.2 Training Process

Optimizing the segment label distribution's Dirichlet prior $\alpha_d^{(i)}$ and the other parameters jointly is computationally difficult. Therefore, we use an alternative optimization process, where φ, $\varphi^{(m)}$, and $\varphi^{(l)}$ are estimated using Gibbs sampling, and $\alpha_d^{(i)}$ is then optimized given the current model likelihood estimation.

Fixing $\boldsymbol{\alpha}$ *and maximizing the joint probability* $p(X, Y, v, z)$.

Given $\boldsymbol{\alpha}$, the topic-label part and the label-token part are decoupled. Therefore, the two parts can be estimated separately [18, 17]. The topic-label part is a standard Latent Dirichlet Allocation model [4], which can be solved by existing methods.

In the following, we estimate the label-token part using a collapsed Gibbs Sampling [7]. We denote N_{ydi} as the number of times label y is assigned to segment x_{di}, $N_{cy}^{(m)}$ as the number of times label y is assigned to music prototype c, and $N_{wy}^{(l)}$ as the number of times label y is assigned to word w. Then, we use the Gibbs sampling equation to update the label assignment of $\boldsymbol{x_{dis}}$ as follows:

$$\begin{aligned}
&P(v_{dis} = y | \boldsymbol{x_{dis}}, \boldsymbol{x_{di-s}}, \boldsymbol{v_{di-s}}, \boldsymbol{\alpha}_d^{(i)}, \beta^{(m)}, \beta^{(l)}) \\
&\propto \frac{N_{ydi,-s} + \alpha_{dy}^{(i)}}{N_{\cdot di,-s} + \Sigma_{y'} \alpha_{dy'}^{(i)}} \\
&\times \frac{\prod_{c=1}^{C} \prod_{p=1}^{m_{disc}} (N_{cy,-s} + m_{disc} - p + \beta^{(m)})}{\prod_{r=1}^{N_{dis}} (N_{\cdot y,-s}) + N_{dis} - r + C\beta^{(m)}} \\
&\times \frac{\prod_{w=1}^{W} \prod_{q=1}^{l_{disw}} (N_{wy,-s} + l_{disw} - q + \beta^{(l)})}{\prod_{r=1}^{N_{dis}} (N_{\cdot y,-s}) + N_{dis} - r + W\beta^{(l)}},
\end{aligned} \quad (1)$$

where

$$\alpha_{dy}^{(i)} = \eta \times N_{yd}/|Y_d| + f(\xi_{dy}^{(i)}), \quad (2)$$

and $f()$ is a problem-specific transformation function that can take many forms, such as $f(x) = x$, $f(x) = e^x$, and $f(x) = log[1 + e^x]$.

Optimizing $\boldsymbol{\xi}$.

The joint probability of $\boldsymbol{\xi}$ and the label assignment v for each sentence is:

$$\begin{aligned}
&P(\boldsymbol{v}, \boldsymbol{\xi}) = p(\boldsymbol{v}|\boldsymbol{\xi})p(\boldsymbol{\xi}) \\
&= \prod_{d=1}^{D} \prod_{i=1}^{I_d} \left\{ \frac{\Gamma(\Sigma_y \alpha_{dy}^{(i)})}{\Gamma(N_{\cdot di} + \Sigma_y \alpha_{dy}^{(i)})} \prod_{y=1}^{|Y_d|} \frac{\Gamma(\alpha_{dy}^{(i)} + N_{ydi})}{\Gamma(\alpha_{dy}^{(i)})} \right\} \\
&\times \prod_{d=1}^{D} \prod_{i=1}^{I_d} \prod_{y=1}^{|Y_d|} p(\xi_{dy}^{(i)} | \xi_{dy}^{(i-1)}),
\end{aligned} \quad (3)$$

where $\xi_{dy}^{(0)} = \xi_y$, $\xi_{dy}^{(i)} \sim \mathcal{N}(\xi_{dy}^{(i-1)}, \sigma^2)$, and ξ_y is a fixed parameter for each label y. Let $\mathcal{L} = log(P(\boldsymbol{v}, \boldsymbol{\xi}))$, for each segment $i > 0$ we have:

$$\begin{aligned}
\frac{\partial \mathcal{L}}{\partial \xi_{dy}^{(i)}} &= \Big[\Psi(\Sigma_{y'} \alpha_{dy'}^{(i)}) - \Psi(N_{\cdot di} + \Sigma_{y'} \alpha_{dy'}^{(i)}) \\
&+ \Psi(\alpha_{dy}^{(i)} + N_{ydi}) - \Psi(\alpha_{dy}^{(i)}) \Big] \times \frac{\partial f(\xi_{dy}^{(i)})}{\xi_{dy}^{(i)}} \\
&- \frac{\xi_{dy}^{(i)} - \xi_{dy}^{(i-1)}}{\sigma^2},
\end{aligned} \quad (4)$$

where Ψ is the digamma function. Then, $\xi_{dy}^{(i)}$ is updated as:

$$\xi_{dy}^{(i)} = \xi_{dy}^{(i)} - \lambda * \frac{\partial \mathcal{L}}{\partial \xi_{dy}^{(i)}}, \quad (5)$$

where λ is the learning rate. $f()$ is defined as $f(x) = x$ in this paper. Note that the choice of $f()$ depends on the problem and data. $f(x) = e^x$ and $f(x) = log[1 + e^x]$ can be adopted if updating $\xi_{dy}^{(i)}$ leads to negative $\alpha_{dy}^{(i)}$. After training, the posterior estimates of $\hat{\varphi}$, $\hat{\varphi}^{(m)}$, and $\hat{\varphi}^{(l)}$ are:

$$\hat{\varphi}_{yk} = \frac{N_{yk} + \beta}{N_{\cdot k} + |Y_d|\beta}, \quad (6)$$

$$\hat{\varphi}_{cy}^{(m)} = \frac{N_{cy}^{(m)} + \beta^{(m)}}{N_{\cdot y}^{(m)} + C\beta^{(m)}}, \quad (7)$$

$$\hat{\varphi}_{wy}^{(l)} = \frac{N_{wy}^{(l)} + \beta^{(l)}}{N_{\cdot y}^{(l)} + W\beta^{(l)}}, \quad (8)$$

where $\hat{\varphi}_{yk}$ is the estimated probability of label y given topic k, $\hat{\varphi}_{cy}^{(m)}$ is the estimated probability of music prototype c given label y, and $\hat{\varphi}_{wy}^{(l)}$ is the estimated probability of word w given label y. The training algorithm is shown in Algorithm 2.

Algorithm 2: Training algorithm.

Input: Song set $\boldsymbol{X}$; label set Y_d and segmentation for each song X_d; sentence-level aligned music and lyrics observation $\boldsymbol{x}_{dis} = \{\boldsymbol{m}_{dis}, \boldsymbol{l}_{dis}\}$ for the i-th segment and s-th sentence.
Output: Topic-label distribution φ; label-music token distribution $\varphi^{(m)}$; label-lyrics word distribution $\varphi^{(l)}$.
for *each song* X_d **do**
  –Sample $\boldsymbol{z}$ using a Gibbs sampler [7] and obtain φ.
  for *each segment* x_{di} **do**
    $\xi_{dy}^{(i)} \sim \mathcal{N}(\xi_{dy}^{(i-1)}, \sigma^2)$.
    $\alpha_{dy}^{(i)} = \eta \times N_{yd}/|Y_d| + f(\xi_{dy}^{(i)})$.
    repeat
      for *each observed sentence* $\{\boldsymbol{m}_{dis}, \boldsymbol{l}_{dis}\}$ **do**
        –Sample v_{dis} using Eq. 1 for several iterations.
      –Update $\xi_{dy}^{(i)}$ using Eq. 4 and 5 until convergence.
      –Compute $\boldsymbol{\alpha}$ using Eq. 2.
    until *several iterations*;

3.3 Testing Process

In the testing process, since the labels for each song are no longer available, the topic-label and label-token parts are estimated in a combined way. To make the procedure more efficient, we use the fast inference method [18], where in each iteration $\boldsymbol{\alpha}_d^{(i)}$ is directly computed as:

$$\boldsymbol{\alpha}_d^{(i)} = \eta(\hat{\boldsymbol{\theta}}_d \boldsymbol{\varphi}) + f(\boldsymbol{\xi}_d^{(i)}) \quad (9)$$

Other steps are similar to the training process. The testing algorithm is listed in Algorithm 3. The point estimate of song d's topic distribution $\hat{\theta}_d$ and segment i's label distribution $\hat{\theta}_d^{'(i)}$ are as follows:

$$\hat{\theta}_{dk} = \frac{N_{dk} + \gamma}{N_{d\cdot} + K\gamma} \quad (10)$$

$$\hat{\theta}'^{(i)}_{dy} = \frac{N_{ydi} + \alpha^{(i)}_{dy}}{N_{\cdot di} + |Y|\alpha^{(i)}_{dy}} \tag{11}$$

Then, the label distribution $\mathcal{L}_d$ of song d can be predicted by:

$$\mathcal{L}_d = \frac{\sum_{i=1}^{I_d} \hat{\boldsymbol{\theta}}'^{(i)}_{\boldsymbol{d}}}{I_d} \tag{12}$$

Algorithm 3: Testing algorithm.

Input: Song set $\boldsymbol{X}$; Segmentation for each song X_d; sentence-level aligned music and lyrics observation $\boldsymbol{x}_{dis} = \{\boldsymbol{m}_{dis}, \boldsymbol{l}_{dis}\}$ for the i-th segment and s-th sentence. Trained topic-label distribution φ; trained label-music token distribution $\varphi^{(m)}$; and trained label-lyrics word distribution $\varphi^{(l)}$.

Output: Topic distribution $\hat{\boldsymbol{\theta}}_d$; label distribution $\hat{\boldsymbol{\theta}}'^{(i)}_d$ over segments, and song d's label distribution $\mathcal{L}_d$.

for *each song* X_d **do**
- –Initialize $\boldsymbol{\theta}_d$.
- **repeat**
  - **for** *each segment* x_{di} **do**
    - $\boldsymbol{\xi}^{(i)}_d \sim \mathcal{N}(\boldsymbol{\xi}^{(i-1)}_d, \sigma^2\boldsymbol{I})$.
    - $\boldsymbol{\alpha}^{(i)}_d = \eta(\hat{\boldsymbol{\theta}}_d\boldsymbol{\varphi}) + f(\boldsymbol{\xi}^{(i)}_d)$.
    - **repeat**
      - **for** *each observed sentence* $\{\boldsymbol{m}_{dis}, \boldsymbol{l}_{dis}\}$ **do**
        - –Sample v_{dis} using Eq. 1 for several iterations.
      - –Update $\xi^{(i)}_{dy}$ using Eq. 4 and 5 until convergence.
    - **until** *several iterations*;
- **until** *a few iterations*;

3.4 Computational Complexity

Consider when $\boldsymbol{\alpha}^{(i)}_d$ is fixed, the computational complexity of the topic-label part model (i.e., LDA) is $\mathcal{O}(|Y_d|K)$ for song d per iteration. As for the label-token part, the complexity of updating segment i is bounded by $\mathcal{O}(|Y_d|(C+W))$. Therefore, the complexity of the label-token part is $\mathcal{O}(|Y_d|I_d(C+W))$, and the complete complexity given $\boldsymbol{\alpha}^{(i)}_d$ is $\mathcal{O}(\sum_{d=1}^{D}|Y_d|[K+I_d(C+W)])$. The complexity of updating $\boldsymbol{\alpha}^{(i)}_d$ is $\mathcal{O}(\sum_{d=1}^{D} I_d|Y_d|)$. In sum, the total complexity is $\mathcal{O}(\sum_{d=1}^{D}|Y_d|[K+I_d(C+W)]) + \mathcal{O}(\sum_{d=1}^{D} I_d|Y_d|) = \mathcal{O}(\sum_{d=1}^{D}|Y_d|[K+I_d(C+W)])$. In practice, the complexity can be much lower since the size of the music prototypes and lyrics words are usually much smaller than C and W in each song (e.g., a 15 second music segment usually contains 3 music prototypes and 10 lyrics words)

4. EXPERIMENTS

We empirically answer the following questions in this section: 1) Does the proposed *multi-label multi-layer multi-instance multi-view* formulation fit the music emotion recognition problem and improve the recognition performance? 2) How do parameters such as learning rate affect the performance? 3) How can the output be interpreted for real-world applications?

To answer these questions, we first illustrate the data we used. Then, multiple state-of-the-art multi-label music recognition models and multi-view multi-label multi-instance models are introduced as baselines along with the corresponding feature extraction details. Next, we compare the music emotion recognition performance of our method to the baseline methods. We also study the influence of parameters. Furthermore, we study the effectiveness of our method by interpreting its outputs for music emotion clustering and music keywords extraction.

4.1 Datasets

We construct our dataset based on the All Music Guide [1], which lists thousands of English Pop songs labeled by experts with emotion words. We used these songs and labels as the ground truth. There are a total of 183 emotion labels and 5106 label-song entries. We then link the songs with the Million Song Dataset [3] using song titles and artists for acoustic feature extraction. For LRC lyrics matching, we searched the song titles and artists in Baidu[7] and downloaded all matched LRC files. The start and end time-stamps for music segments and sentences were retrieved from the Million Song Dataset and LRC files respectively. All in all, there were a total of 1493 songs and 122 labels. The average number of labels per song was 1.85, and the median number of songs per label was 10. The data is summarized in Table 2.

Table 2: Data summary.

Statistics	Number
#Songs	1493
#Segments	6055
#Sentences	31388
#Labels	122
#Label-song pairs	2767
Average #labels per song	1.85
Median #songs per label	10
Standard Deviation of #songs per label	6.6

4.2 Baseline Methods

We introduce several baseline methods for comparing the experimental results, including random guessing by top labels (Random), previous methods on multi-label music emotion classification such as binary relevance (BR), label powerset (LP), random k-labelsets (RAKEL) [21], and a state-of-the-art multi-view multi-label multi-instance method M3LDA [17]. BR, LP, and RAKEL are single-instance models while M3LDA and our proposed model HMER are multi-instance models. For M3LDA, either a segment or sentence can be regarded as an instance, leading to the two baselines M3LDA-seg and M3LDA-sen.

4.3 Feature Extraction

To describe the acoustic features from a music emotion perspective, we consider features such as timbre, pitch, rhythm, and loudness, which have been found to be effective in describing music emotion [28]. We extracted Mel-Frequency Cepstral Coefficient (MFCC)-like features with 12 bands, including timbre and pitch from the Million Song

[7]http://music.baidu.com

Dataset. Also, we use the maximum loudness of each segment to outline the overall loudness of the music.

For single-instance models (BR, LP, and RAKEL), we represent lyrics using term frequency-inverse document frequency (TF*IDF) [25]. Since the size of the lyrics dictionary is too large (more than 10,000), we adopted the most frequent 1000 words. For acoustic features, we take the mean and Standard Deviation (STD) every five seconds (i.e., the texture window), and take the mean and STD again for the complete song [23]. For rhythm, we use the overall tempo (beats per minute) and take the STD of beat intervals to represent the tempo regularity [11]. Finally, aggregating all four features, we have a 102-dimension acoustic feature vector. Finally, there are 1102 dimensions for feature vectors in single-instance models.

For multi-instance models (M3LDA and HMER), we simply count the word frequency for lyrics features. The size of lyrics dictionary is 17851. For acoustic features, we first extract timbre, pitch, loudness, and rhythm features every five seconds. Then, to construct the music token dictionary, we conducted a 1000-prototypes k-means clustering across the whole dataset. Then, each instance (segment for M3LDA-seg and sentence for M3LDA-sen and HMER) is represented by a 1000-dimension vector, where each dimension is the number of times the prototypes appear in the instance. For the sake of fairness, we also test single-instance models with prototype feature representation to be consistent with multi-instance methods, which are coined BR-Pro, LP-Pro, and RAKEL-Pro, respectively.

Lyrics features were used differently in different models because using all lyrics would result in too many dimensions for single-instance models; while in multi-instance models, a sentence is much shorter than a song, so using only 1000 lyrics would reduce most sentences to zero words.

4.4 Experimental Setup

Experiments on BR, LP, and RAKEL were conducted on MEKA[8] and MULAN [22], using random tree as the base classifier with recommended parameters.

Both M3LDA and HMER are iterative methods. The number of training and testing iterations were set as 500; the number of topics K was set to 10 motivated by psychology studies such as Hevner's 8-cluster model [28]; η was 250 [17]; γ was set to 0.1; ξ_y was set to 0.1 for each label y; Dirichlet priors of topic-label β, label-music β_m, and label-lyrics β_l were all set to 0.01. For M3LDA, the weights of music and lyrics were both set to 0.5. For HMER, $\boldsymbol{\xi}$ was updated every 200 iterations; learning rate was set to 0.05; the threshold of convergence in updating $\boldsymbol{\xi}$ was 0.1.

We examine the performance of HMER both with and without updating $\boldsymbol{\xi}$, namely "HMER" and "HMER-ξ". For "HMER", we set $\xi_d^{(i)} = \xi_y$ and kept it stable during the whole training and testing process.

Note that all experiments were conducted using out-of-sample manner.

4.5 Music Emotion Recognition Results

We evaluated the performance using two standard metrics: F_1 score and mean average precision at ten (MAP@10). F_1 score is a binary based metric commonly used in evaluating a classifier, which is defined as follows:

[8]http://meka.sourceforge.net/

$$F_1 = \frac{2 * Precision * Recall}{Precision + Recall} \tag{13}$$

In this paper, we return ten predicted emotions to calculate F_1. Mean average precision at 10 (MAP@10) is a ranking metric commonly used in evaluating recommender systems, which is defined as:

$$MAP@10 = \frac{\sum_{d=1}^{D}\left[\frac{\sum_{k=1}^{10} P(k)}{10}\right]}{D} \tag{14}$$

where $P(k) = \frac{\#Correct}{k}$, and D is the number of songs. In music emotion recognition, F_1 score shows how accurate songs are classified into each emotion label, while MAP@10 shows how well the top ten relevant songs are ranked for each emotion label.

The ten-run-average results of F_1 score and MAP@10 are listed in Table 3 along with standard deviations. The best performances are highlighted in bold-font. Statistical tests (Friedman test followed by Nemenyi post-hoc test at 5 percent significance level) are also listed in Table 3 to show the significance of performance difference, where $\{a, b\} \succ \{c, d\}$ indicates that both methods a and b perform significantly differently with methods c and d.

Overall, single-instance methods such as BR, LP, and RAKEL did not perform well, with the best F_1 score at 0.11 by RAKEL and MAP@10 at 0.09 by LP. Multi-instance methods achieved significantly better performance, with at least 0.150 for F_1 score and 0.184 for MAP@10. The results show the benefits in assuming music emotions to be different for each instance, and the fitness of multi-instance models to music emotion recognition.

HMER-ξ achieved the best performance, by 49% F_1 score and 326% MAP@10 improvement compared to the best-existing multi-label music emotion recognition baseline RAKEL, and 7.9% F_1 score and 8.0% MAP@10 improvement over M3LDA. HMER-ξ also outperformed HMER by 5.1% on F_1 score and 3.6% on MAP@10, which shows that the optimization of ξ captures the emotion correlation between music segments. Moreover, isolating the benefits of updating ξ, HMER still outperformed M3LDA by 2.6% and 4.2% on F_1 score and MAP@10 respectively, which clearly indicates the advantages of the *multi-layer multi-instance multi-view* formulation.

Table 3: Performance comparison in terms of F1 Score and MAP@10 (higher is better).

Methods	F_1 Score	MAP@10
Random	0.002	0.006
BR-Pro	0.045±0.003	0.047±0.01
LP-Pro	0.03±0.003	0.054±0.006
RAKEL-Pro	0.035±0.004	0.05±0.001
BR	0.071±0.001	0.054±0.007
LP	0.094±0.001	0.09±0.001
RAKEL	0.110±0.008	0.087±0.002
M3LDA-sen	0.152±0.005	0.184±0.004
M3LDA-seg	0.150±0.002	0.213±0.004
HMER	0.156±0.004	0.222±0.001
HMER-ξ	**0.164±0.003**	**0.230±0.002**

$\boldsymbol{F_1}$: {HMER-ξ} $\succ$ All others; {HMER} $\succ$ All others except for {M3LDA-sen}. **MAP@10**: {HMER-ξ} $\succ$ All others; {HMER} $\succ$ All others except for {M3LDA-seg}.

Discussion.

BR performed the worst because it simply transforms multi-label classification tasks into multiple single-label tasks, without considering label correlations. LP assumes the label powerset as a set of single labels, which considers label correlations and therefore performed better than BR. RAKEL ensembles multiple LP weak learners and further improved the performance. However, since these single-instance methods built models on song-level features, they failed to capture the music emotion dynamics structure. As for features representation, prototype representation was too sparse for single-instance models and led to the worst performance.

Both M3LDAs (i.e., M3LDA-seg and M3LDA sen) and HMERs (i.e., HMER-ξ and HMER) can capture the multi-view multi-instance nature of music emotion dynamics. However, M3LDAs cannot deal with the *multi-layer multi-instance multi-view* property of music emotion and did not perform as well as HMERs due to two main reasons.

First, on one hand, M3LDAs are single-layer multi-instance models, which only consider either segments or sentences as instances (corresponding to M3LDA-seg and M3LDA-sen respectively). Also, M3LDAs only assume instances to follow the same emotion distribution, and emotion within each instance to be consistent; while HMERs assume segments to follow different yet correlated emotion distributions, sentences in the same segment to follow the same emotion distribution, and each sentence to have a consistent emotion. Apparently, compared to M3LDAs, HMERs highly match the observations that music emotions are usually different in different segments, mostly consistent within each segment, and almost always consistent within each sentence, which resulted in superior performance.

Second, since HMERs are multi-layer multi-view models, they can capture sentence-level music-lyrics correlations. Nevertheless, being bag-level multi-view models, M3LDAs can only capture song-level music-lyrics correlations, which are less accurate compared to HMERs. Such a difference also contributed to HMERs' better performance[9].

Computational Time.

The experiments were all conducted on a 64-bit computer with a 3.3GB CPU and a 4GB memory. Overall, single-instance methods such as BR, LP, and RAKEL finished in a very short time. For example, RAKEL spent 3 seconds for the whole training and testing process. Single-instance methods have lower computational complexity and smaller number of instances because they are song-level methods. The computational time of M3LDA-sen and HMERs are similar, with less than 1.5 hours for the whole process. M3LDA-seg spent half of the time compared to M3LDA-sen and HMERs because it is a segment-level method where the number of instances is much smaller. For prediction time, BR, LP, and RAKEL took 0.02, 4e-4, and 6e-4 seconds for testing a song, while M3LDA-sen and HMERs took 0.9 seconds, and M3LDA-seg took 0.5 seconds.

4.6 Parameter Study

In this section, we examine how parameters affect the performance of HMER. Three parameters (η which decides $\alpha_d^{(i)}$, number of topics K, and the learning rate λ) were studied for both F_1 score and mean average precision at ten (MAP@10). The results are shown in Figure 3.

[9]Note that the performance may further improve using more advanced and sophisticated feature representation and selection as well as multi-modal fusion strategies.

According to Figure 3(a) and 3(b), when η is between 200 to 300, both F_1 score and mean average precision achieve their best. When η is greater than 400, the performance starts to decrease. The larger η is, the larger $\alpha_d^{(i)}$ tends to be, and the more labels are assumed in each instance. Therefore, this result implies that the assumption of fewer emotions existing in a music segment is more reasonable.

Figure 3(c) and 3(d) show that when $K = 5$, both F_1 score and mean average precision achieve their best, which means that the best number of music emotion clusters is about five. For learning rate λ, the influence on both F_1 score and MAP@10 are smaller compared to η and K as shown in Figure 3(e) and 3(f), where F_1 score is in [0.165, 0.170] and the mean average precision is in [0.225, 0.235].

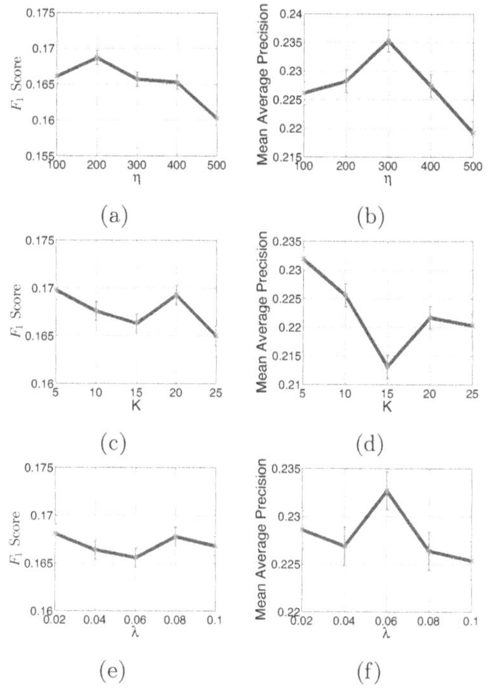

Figure 3: Parameter study for HMER.

4.7 φ: Music Emotion Clusters

Music emotion clustering is useful to enhance the user-experience in emotion-based music exploration because it avoids showing the large number of music emotions (e.g., there are 187 emotions defined by the All Music Guide). The topic-label distribution φ trained by HMER can be interpreted as music emotion clusters. The top five topics/clusters for music emotions are listed in Table 4. The weight of each emotion represents its relevance to the topic/cluster. The representative emotions of the five topics/clusters are: happy, acerbic, sentimental, aggressive, and sad. The five clusters cover most clusters in the valence-arousal emotion plane [29].

4.8 $\varphi^{(l)}$: Correlation Between Music Emotion and Lyrics

HMER can also provide emotion-lyrics correlation using the label-lyrics distribution $\varphi^{(l)}$. Five emotions (delicate, cheerful, restrained, rollicking, and sweet) are presented and the corresponding major words are listed in Table 5. Personal pronouns and articles were filtered out. Overall, there

Table 4: **Top five topics of music emotion.**

Topic	Major emotions(weight)
Topic 1	happy(0.137), carefree(0.137), fun(0.091), joyous(0.091), innocent(0.091), cheerful(0.082)
Topic 2	acerbic(0.308), sarcastic-cynical(0.264), fiery(0.089), snide(0.045), rollicking(0.045)
Topic 3	sentimental(0.170), poignant(0.170), reserved(0.114), soothing(0.114), rousing(0.058), wistful(0.058)
Topic 4	aggressive(0.184), menacing(0.153), rebellious(0.153), malevolent(0.123), angry(0.062)
Topic 5	sad(0.295), somber(0.253), nocturnal(0.169), nihilistic(0.085), enigmatic(0.002)

are no contradictory words for each emotion. Some words are frequently related to the reported emotions. For example, river and snow relate to delicate, dream and need relate to sweet. This result shows that our proposed model captures reasonable keywords describing emotions.

Table 5: Top three lyrics words of music emotion.

Emotion	Major words(weight)
Delicate	river(0.016), snow(0.013), night(0.012)
Cheerful	forever(0.019), remember(0.018), happy(0.016)
Restrained	little(0.016), ocean(0.015), love(0.012)
Rollicking	Saturday(0.023), night(0.021), baby(0.018)
Sweet	dream(0.022), need(0.021), call(0.017)

The label-lyrics distribution $\varphi^{(l)}$ can also be useful in music exploration. For example, keywords/tags recommendation can be made for each song by the element-wise product of $\varphi^{(l)}$ and the song-label distribution $\mathcal{L}_d$, which is useful in music previewing and indexing.

5. RELATED WORK

In this section, we give an overview of two aspects of related work: 1) music emotion recognition; 2) multi-view multi-label multi-instance models.

Music emotion recognition.

Music emotion recognition is usually formulated as either a *classification* problem or a *regression* problem. For *classification* formulation, music is classified into multiple predefined emotion adjectives or clusters [28, 6], where Support Vector Machines [14] and Gaussian Mixture Models [15] were commonly used to solve it as a multi-class classification problem. However, these methods usually work on a small number of music emotion categories (e.g., four to eight), while a much larger number is needed (e.g., more than 50) for emotion based music recommender systems to provide fine-grained retrieval. When the number of emotions gets large, multiple similar yet different emotion labels can be used to describe music simultaneously. Therefore, music emotion recognition becomes a typical multi-label classification problem, where traditional multi-class methods fail since they assume each song has only one label.

To this end, multi-label classification methods have been proposed [21]. However, these methods assume that music emotions are consistent over each song, which ignores the fact that multiple labels may apply to different segments, but not necessarily the entire song. Thus, models trained for song-level labels and features may not be accurate.

Music emotion recognition is also commonly formulated as a *regression* problem to improve indexing accuracy. Emotion adjectives are translated into two dimensional real values, representing positiveness and strength of emotions respectively [5]. Then, regression models such as label propagation [26], Gaussian Mixture Models [24], and Support Vector Machine [11] are usually adopted. Specifically, LRC data was considered by Hu *et al.* in this line of research on song-level [10]. Although regression approaches provide accurate indexing, multiple labels are usually averaged as one single label [26] or fitted to a Gaussian distribution for each song [24], which does not consider the dynamics of music emotion. Schmidt *et al.* proposed to utilize music emotion dynamics to improve regression accuracy [20]. However, their method requires segment-level music emotion labels, and is therefore not scalable in real-world application.

Multi-view multi-label multi-instance learning.

Multi-label multi-instance learning has been well studied in multi-label image classification [31, 30, 17]. In particular, M3LDA was proposed to address multi-view/modal multi-label image classification [17], where each image has two views: image and tags. Replacing image regions with music segments, and tags with lyrics, M3LDA can capture the dynamic nature of music emotion to some extent using the large number of song-level labels and lyrics. However, for music emotion recognition, lyrics and music are highly synchronized, which is different from the relation between image regions and tags. Also, the song-segment-sentence structure as well as music emotion correlation between both music segments and sentence cannot be handled by M3LDA due to single layer multi-instance structure and its exchangeability assumption for music segments.

6. DISCUSSION AND FUTURE WORK

Applicable scenarios.

Our proposed model shows promising fitness to music emotion recognition. However, since HMER is in the multi-instance learning framework, the number of actual instances is much larger than single-instance learning methods, which is one major factor that slows down training and testing. Thus, HMER is mainly useful for off-line music emotion recognition tasks such as emotion based music indexing and context-free music recommendation. More efficient yet effective methods are still needed for real-time context-aware and personalized music recommendation.

In the future, we may consider parallel implementation of HMER by observing that each segment can be sampled independently given the prior obtained from the last iteration. Also, we may consider only segment-level music-lyrics synchronization to speed up HMER.

Extension to more views.

Although we only consider music and lyrics views in this paper, HMER can be easily extended to more views given proper data. For example, in music videos, music, lyrics, and clips/images are highly synchronized and consistent in terms of expressed emotions. HMER can easily include clips/images to improve music emotion recognition by introducing a third view-variable on the sentence-layer.

7. CONCLUSION

In this paper, we investigated the dynamic nature of music emotion and modeled music emotion recognition as a novel *multi-label multi-layer multi-instance multi-view learning* problem. We propose a novel hierarchical Bayesian model which uses sentence-level music and lyrics features, captures music emotion dynamics by a song-segment-sentence hierarchical structure. Our model also considers emotion correlations within a song by assuming its music segments follow correlated emotion distributions, and considers stricter emotion correlations within music segment by assuming its sentences follow the same emotion distributions. Experimental results have shown that our method outperforms several state-of-the-art models in terms of both F_1 score and mean average precision (MAP).

8. ACKNOWLEDGMENT

This work has been supported by Hong Kong Research Grants Council grants HKUST613112.

9. REFERENCES

[1] AllMusic moods. Online: http://www.allmusic.com/moods (9 Dec 2011).

[2] Bohemian rhapsody. Online (22 March 2014): http://www.queensongs.info/the-book/songwriting-analyses/no-synth-era/a-night-at-the-opera/bohemian-rhapsody.html.

[3] T. Bertin-Mahieux, D. P. Ellis, B. Whitman, and P. Lamere. The million song dataset. In *Proceedings of the International Society for Music Information Retrieval Conference*, pages 591–596, 2011.

[4] D. M. Blei, A. Y. Ng, and M. I. Jordan. Latent dirichlet allocation. *the Journal of Machine Learning Research*, 3:993–1022, 2003.

[5] M. M. Bradley and P. J. Lang. Affective norms for English words (ANEW): Instruction manual and affective ratings. *Psychology*, (C-1):1–45, 1999.

[6] R. Cai, C. Zhang, C. Wang, L. Zhang, and W.-Y. Ma. Musicsense: contextual music recommendation using emotional allocation modeling. In *Proceedings of the 15th ACM International Conference on Multimedia*, pages 553–556, 2007.

[7] T. L. Griffiths and M. Steyvers. Finding scientific topics. *Proceedings of the National Academy of Sciences of the United States of America*, 101(Suppl 1):5228–5235, 2004.

[8] Z. Gu, T. Mei, X.-S. Hua, J. Tang, and X. Wu. Multi-layer multi-instance learning for video concept detection. *IEEE Transactions on Multimedia*, 10(8):1605–1616, 2008.

[9] X. Hu and J. S. Downie. Improving mood classification in music digital libraries by combining lyrics and audio. In *Proceedings of the 10th Annual Joint Conference on Digital Libraries*, pages 159–168. ACM, 2010.

[10] Y. Hu, X. Chen, and D. Yang. Lyric-based song emotion detection with affective lexicon and fuzzy clustering method. In *Proceedings of the International Society for Music Information Retrieval Conference*, pages 123–128, 2009.

[11] B. Jun Han, S. Rho, R. B. Dannenberg, and E. Hwang. Smers: Music emotion recognition using support vector regression. In *Proceedings of the International Society for Music Information Retrieval Conference*, pages 651–656, 2009.

[12] P. N. Juslin and J. A. Sloboda. *Music and emotion: Theory and research.* Oxford University Press, 2001.

[13] C. Laurier, J. Grivolla, and P. Herrera. Multimodal music mood classification using audio and lyrics. In *International Conference on Machine Learning and Applications*, pages 688–693. IEEE, 2008.

[14] T. Li and M. Ogihara. Content-based music similarity search and emotion detection. In *IEEE International Conference on Acoustics, Speech, and Signal Processing.*, volume 5, pages 705–708, 2004.

[15] L. Lu, D. Liu, and H. Zhang. Automatic mood detection and tracking of music audio signals. *IEEE Transactions on Audio, Speech, and Language Processing*, 14(1):5–18, 2006.

[16] M. I. Mandel and D. P. Ellis. Multiple-instance learning for music information retrieval. In *Proceedings of the International Society for Music Information Retrieval Conference*, pages 577–582, 2008.

[17] C.-T. Nguyen, D.-C. Zhan, and Z.-H. Zhou. Multi-modal image annotation with multi-instance multi-label lda. In *Proceedings of the Twenty-Third International Joint Conference on Artificial Intelligence*, pages 1558–1564, 2013.

[18] T. N. Rubin, A. Chambers, P. Smyth, and M. Steyvers. Statistical topic models for multi-label document classification. *Machine Learning*, 88(1-2):157–208, 2012.

[19] E. M. Schmidt and Y. E. Kim. Prediction of time-varying musical mood distributions using kalman filtering. In *IEEE International Conference on Machine Learning and Applications*, pages 655–660, 2010.

[20] E. M. Schmidt and Y. E. Kim. Modeling musical emotion dynamics with conditional random fields. In *Proceedings of the International Society for Music Information Retrieval Conference*, pages 777–782, 2011.

[21] K. Trohidis, G. Tsoumakas, G. Kalliris, and I. P. Vlahavas. Multi-label classification of music into emotions. In *Proceedings of the International Society for Music Information Retrieval Conference*, volume 8, pages 325–330, 2008.

[22] G. Tsoumakas, I. Katakis, and I. Vlahavas. Mining multi-label data. In *Data mining and knowledge discovery handbook*, pages 667–685. Springer, 2010.

[23] G. Tzanetakis and P. Cook. Musical genre classification of audio signals. *IEEE Transactions on Audio, Speech, and Language Processing*, 10(5):293–302, 2002.

[24] J.-C. Wang, Y.-H. Yang, H.-M. Wang, and S.-K. Jeng. The acoustic emotion gaussians model for emotion-based music annotation and retrieval. In *Proceedings of the 20th ACM International Conference on Multimedia*, pages 89–98, 2012.

[25] X. Wang, X. Chen, D. Yang, and Y. Wu. Music emotion classification of chinese songs based on lyrics using tf*idf and rhyme. In *Proceedings of the International Society for Music Information Retrieval Conference*, pages 765–770, 2011.

[26] B. Wu, E. Zhong, D. H. Hu, A. Horner, and Q. Yang. Smart: Semi-supervised music emotion recognition with social tagging. In *SIAM International Conference on Data Mining*, pages 279–287. SIAM, 2013.

[27] C. Xu, D. Tao, and C. Xu. A survey on multi-view learning. *arXiv preprint arXiv:1304.5634*, 2013.

[28] Y.-H. Yang and H. H. Chen. Machine recognition of music emotion: A review. *ACM Transactions on Intelligent Systems and Technology*, 3(3):40, 2012.

[29] Y.-H. Yang and J.-Y. Liu. Quantitative study of music listening behavior in a social and affective context. *IEEE Transactions on Multimedia*, 15(6):1304–1315, 2013.

[30] Z.-J. Zha, X.-S. Hua, T. Mei, J. Wang, G.-J. Qi, and Z. Wang. Joint multi-label multi-instance learning for image classification. In *IEEE Conference on Computer Vision and Pattern Recognition*, pages 1–8, 2008.

[31] Z.-H. Zhou and M.-L. Zhang. Multi-instance multi-label learning with application to scene classification. In *Advances in Neural Information Processing Systems*, pages 1609–1616, 2006.

Song Recommendation for Social Singing Community

Kuang Mao[1] Ju Fan[2] Lidan Shou[1] Gang Chen[1] Mohan Kankanhalli[2]
[1]College of Computer Science, Zhejiang University, Hangzhou, China
[2]School of Computing, National University of Singapore, Singapore
mbill@zju.edu.cn; fanj@comp.nus.edu.sg; {should,cg}@zju.edu.cn; mohan@comp.nus.edu.sg

ABSTRACT

Nowadays, an increasing number of singing enthusiasts upload their cover songs and share their performances in online social singing communities. They can also listen and rate other users' song renderings. An important feature of the social singing communities is to recommend appropriate singing-songs which users are able to perform excellently.

In this paper, we propose a singing-song recommendation framework to make song recommendation in social singing community. Instead of recommending songs that people like to listen, we recommend suitable songs that people can sing well. We propose to discover the song difficulty orderings from the song performance ratings of each user. We transform the difficulty orderings into a difficulty graph and propose an iterative inference algorithm to make singing-song recommendation on the difficulty graph. The experimental result shows the effectiveness of our proposed framework. To the best of our knowledge, our work is the first study of singing-song recommendation in social singing communities.

Categories and Subject Descriptors

H.3.3 [**Information Search and Retrieval**]: Information filtering; H.5.5 [**Sound and Music Computing**]: Systems

General Terms

Algorithms; Experimentation

Keywords

Singing-song recommendation; social singing community; recommender systems

1. INTRODUCTION

Singing and listening in Karaoke is an enjoyable form of entertainment for many people. With the popularity of high-speed wireless connectivity, the Web today is increasingly seeing a new form of online Karaoke known as the *Social Singing Community* (SSC). A singer in a SSC can record a

MM '14, November 3-7,2014, Orlando, USA
Copyright 2014 978-1-4503-3063-3/14/11...$15.00
http://dx.doi.org/10.1145/2647868.2654921.

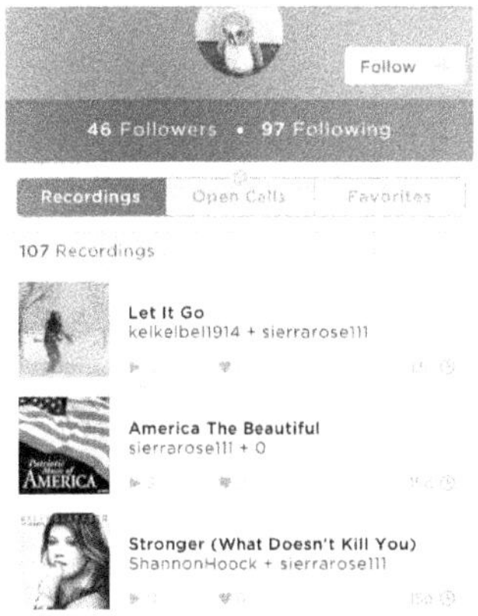

Figure 1: Screenshot of Sing! interface

performance (or album) via her/his device, and then publish to SSC, allowing for access to it at any place and any time. On the other hand, a listener, after enjoying the performances disseminated by the system, gives ratings, likes, or comments to the performances or singers. To date, a great number of SSCs have emerged on the Web. Some popular ones include *Smule*[1], *5sing*[2], and *Sing!*[3]. For example, 5sing has a population of 1.3 million active users and a repository of 7.5 million cover songs sung by its users by 2013. Figure 1 shows the interface of a well-known mobile SSC application called Sing!.

While SSC can serve as a conventional platform of listening to songs for the listeners, it provides an essential "virtual stage" for the amateur singers. Unlike conventional music communities in which listeners rate the songs and interact with other listeners, SSC focuses more on the *singers*, by encouraging interaction between the singers and the listeners via ratings on the performances.

One important service in SSC is to provide singing-song recommendation for singers. Despite the abundance of studies in song recommendation [7], the problem of singing-song recommendation in SSC has its unique characteristic which has not been addressed adequately in the literature. Specifically, the conventional song recommendation focuses on discovering songs that a user likes to listen. In contrast, singing-song recommendation aims to find the songs which are easier to lead to high *singing performances*. In particular, higher singing performance in SSC means the corre-

[1]http://www.smule.com/
[2]http://www.5sing.com/
[3]https://itunes.apple.com/app/sing!-karaoke-by-smule/id509993510?mt=8

sponding songs can help a singer obtain more appreciation and higher ratings from the listeners. Acquiring higher rating is very important to the singer, because it can not only bring acknowledgement and encouragement, but also help her promote the influence in the community and further attract more fans. In the rest of the paper, for ease of presentation, we use "song s_1 is easier than s_2" to represent that s_1 is easier to incur higher singing performance than s_2. Note that this may not necessarily reflect the difficulty in terms of acoustic features (melody, pitch range, etc.): some easy-to-sing songs may not bring impressive performances and high ratings due to their unattractive melodies.

Although a previous study published in [15] has considered singing-song recommendation, it cannot address our problem in SSC. The work in [15] proposed a solution called competence based song recommendation, which relies on complex modeling of singer's vocal competence and song profiles, and conducts a matching between singer competence and songs using a machine learning algorithm. Unfortunately, this approach is impractical for singing-song recommendation in SSC, due to the following reasons: First, the vocal competence modeling in [15] employs an expensive recording process which requires the user to sing every pitch in his/her pitch range from the softest to the loudest, under the supervision of music professionals. This requirement cannot be practically achieved in SSC. Second, the song profiles are acquired from music scores and manually annotated singing intensity data. Such process requires prohibitive manual works of cleaning, calibration, and annotation, which is impossible under the circumstance of large-scale SSC.

In this paper, we report our research on *SInging-song Recommendation* (SIR) for a social singing community. The main objective is to study how to recommend songs that users have large potentials to perform well and finally obtain high ratings from the listeners. Specifically, we develop a SIR framework which takes a user's singing history as input, and, from the singing history, predicts which songs the user can perform well. Our song recommendation is different from the traditional song retrieval which focuses only on matching users' listening interests. We pay particular attention to matching the users' singing performance needs. It also differs with Shou [15]'s work which focuses on matching songs with singer's singing model. We discover the songs' difficulty evidences in terms of performance from listener ratings and recommend songs that are most probable to incur better performance than the songs sung by a user in the history. To the best of our knowledge, this is the first work to deal with the SIR in a SSC.

Our singing-song recommendation faces two main technical challenges. The first one is how to determine whether a song is easier than another one, i.e., the difficulty relation in performance between two songs. As such knowledge of difficulty relation is not off-the-shelf, one approach is to ask a group of singers to judge the difficulty in performance between two songs. However, it is costly to employ people to compare the difficulty. Another approach is to indirectly discover the difficulty comparison results from SSC. The problem is we need to determine how reliable the obtained difficulty relations are.

The second challenge is how to make recommendation based on the aforementioned song difficulty relations. To make full use of these relations, we need to model these song difficulty relations so that we can infer new difficulty relations from existing ones. For song recommendation, it is challenging to estimate whether a user can perform a specific song well based on the inference from their singing history.

To solve the first challenge, we propose to discover the *song difficulty ordering* from the singing performance rating of the songs in users' singing history. We derive song difficulty orderings from the performance ratings given to the songs sung by the same user. This is not easy, however, as the diversity in singer's vocal competence and listener's preference may probably lead to inconsistent ratings. Such uncertainty poses the following questions to us: Is the discovered difficulty ordering valid for every singer? Are there "common" orders which are valid for most singers and ad-hoc ones which depend largely on individual singers. To answer these questions, we need to measure the *reliability* of song difficulty orderings as the result of derivation from human judgments.

To address the second challenge, we capture all the song difficulty orderings in a *difficulty graph*, where each vertex represents a song. We evaluate whether the user can sing a song well, using a quantity called *performance degree*. Given a song (vertex), this quantity can be estimated from its neighboring vertices in the graph, using a probabilistic inference technique. Since a user's singing history covers only a few vertices in the difficulty graph, we propose an *Iterative Probabilistic Inference (IPI)* algorithm in the graph which iteratively "spreads" the performance degrees from the user's singing history to other songs. Note that, the proposed recommendation framework can also be generalized to other competence-related recommendation problems such as books, games, where we only need to determine the difficulty relations between vertices in the difficulty graph.

The advantage of this approach in the current problem is that, the difficulty orderings discovered in one SSC can be reused and updated in another SSC system which is a way to ease the cold start problem in recommendation system. Given sufficient resources, it is also possible to employ music experts to build an ever-expanding song difficulty ordering database and then provide singing-song recommendation services for any social singing community. In this paper, we publish the very first difficulty ordering database of the songs used in our experiments[4].

Our contributions can be summarized as follows:

(1) We propose a singing song recommendation framework to solve the song recommendation problem for a social singing community.

(2) We propose a method for discovering the song difficulty orderings from the social singing community and measure the reliability of the discovered difficulty orderings.

(3) We present a difficulty graph to model song difficulty orderings and build up a probabilistic inference technique to estimate a song's performance degree.

(4) We introduce a ranking algorithm for singing song recommendation from a difficulty graph.

(5) Our experiment shows promising results for the proposed recommendation framework.

The rest of the paper is organized as follows: Section 2 introduces the related work. In Section 3, we define our research problem and provide an overview of the framework. Section 4 describes how to discover the song difficulty orderings from social singing community. Section 5 introduces

[4]http://db.zju.edu.cn/dataDownload/index.html

the inference technique in difficulty graph and describes the song recommendation algorithm. Section 6 describes the details of the experiments and the results. Finally, in Section 7 we conclude the paper.

2. RELATED WORK

In this paper, we study the problem of singing song recommendation for social singing community. This research is related to the traditional song recommendation, singing song recommendation and graph ranking algorithms. We will give a brief review of these works and explain the differences with our work.

2.1 Traditional Song Recommendation

Traditional song recommendation systems are designed for discovering songs that satisfy user's listening interests. The early methods for song recommendation such as [10] explore techniques in the domain of content based song recommendation. These techniques use low level features to represent user's preferences of the songs such as moods and rhythms and recommend songs that have a large similarity on low level features. However, it suffers from the semantic gap between low level features and user's preferences.

The classic way to recommend songs is via Collaborative Filtering (CF) [8], which can be divided into user-based CF [6] and item-based CF [14]. The user-based CF first predicts the human ratings for unrated items (songs) from a group of similar users and makes recommendation by ranking the predicted rating of each items. The intuition of CF (user-based) comes from the assumption that if users A and B have a strong similarity in the choice of listening songs, their songs can be recommended to each other. However, it is not always valid for recommending songs for singing. People will tend to sing some popular songs which are liked by many people, however they will also sing some unique songs. It is inappropriate to recommend such unique songs to others without considering the songs' difficulty in performance.

Another straightforward way is to use an ordinary graph to do song recommendation, it first builds a user-item bi-graph and performs random walk to get the song ranking where those songs that share many connected users with the query song will get higher ranks. It intuitively recommends popular songs to satisfy user's interest needs. It also ignores taking song's difficulty in performance into consideration. Wu [16] proposed a next-song recommendation strategy for online karaoke users using personalized markov embedding. They also focus on matching user's singing interests, while ignoring singer's demands for high performance in karaoke.

In our proposed approach, we will discover song's difficulty in performance. The recommendation is based on the song difficulty orderings which guarantees that recommended songs are easier than the user's past sung songs.

2.2 Singing Song Recommendation

Singing song recommendation is a relatively new research area which was first proposed by Mao *et al.* [13] in 2012. Then Shou *et al.* [15] presented a competence based song recommendation system which utilizes a singer's digitized voice recording to recommend a list of songs based on the analysis of singer's vocal competence. They require a professional recording process to acquire user's vocal competence, called singer profile, and model the song profile which is the singing notes distribution within each song. After that, they propose a learning to rank scheme for recommending songs using the singer profile. Their system has two major drawbacks for recommending songs for a social singing community. The first one is that it requires a complex user's vocal competence acquisition process which is not fit for the social singing community. Another drawback is that it needs each song's score to build the song model which is hard to acquire for large number of songs in the social singing community setting.

In our work, we avoid modeling user's vocal competence and do not need to know song's score for singing song recommendation. We only need the users' singing history to do the recommendation.

2.3 Ranking on the Graph

Graph ranking studies the ranking method for the graph vertices. Most methods [4, 5, 18] are based on regularization theory for graphs. Zhou *et al.* [19] propose a universal ranking algorithm, which can exploit the intrinsic manifold structure of the data. They first build a weighted graph, define and normalize the weight of the edge. During each iteration, each vertex spreads its rank to the neighbors via the weighted network until the ranks converge. Agarwal [1] develops an algorithmic framework for learning ranking functions on both directed and undirected graph data. They build the graph which acts as a regularizer to make sure closely connected document will get a similar value. Baluja [3] proposed a video co-view graph and developed a random walk algorithm to do video recommendation.

For our graph ranking method, the basic idea is similar to that of Zhou *et al.* [3, 19]. We use a probabilistic modeling technique to model our difficulty graph. We rank the songs by iteratively doing probabilistic inference in the graph.

3. SINGING-SONG RECOMMENDATION

In this section, we formalize the problem of song recommendation for social singing community in Section 3.1 and introduce our recommendation framework in Section 3.2.

3.1 Problem Statement

Social Singing Community. Our work studies a social singing community with a set of users $U = \{u_1, u_2, \ldots, u_m\}$ and a collection of songs $S = \{s_1, s_2, \ldots, s_n\}$. In the community, each user $u_k \in U$ has a singing history that consists of a subset of songs in S, denoted by $S_k \subseteq S$. The user u_k could post this history in the community to let other users listen to the songs in S_k. Then, the listeners may evaluate u_k's performance on these songs by providing ratings on a scale from 1 to 5. We compute the average rating of listeners on each song $s_i^k \in S_k$ performed by u_k and denote this rating as r_i^k. The input phase of Figure 2 provides an example of user's singing histories. In this example, the user u_1 has a history consisting of songs s_1, s_2, etc., where the songs are associated with the average rating by listeners, e.g., rating for s_1 is 4.3 for user u_1.

Singing-song Recommendation. In this work, we aim to recommend the songs that users have the potential to perform well. To better illustrate this recommendation objective, let us consider a user u_k and two songs s_i and s_j in the song set $S - S_k$. If the performance of u_k on s_i could attract more attention from the listeners and the listeners would give higher ratings to this song, then song s_i would be preferable than s_j in our recommendation.

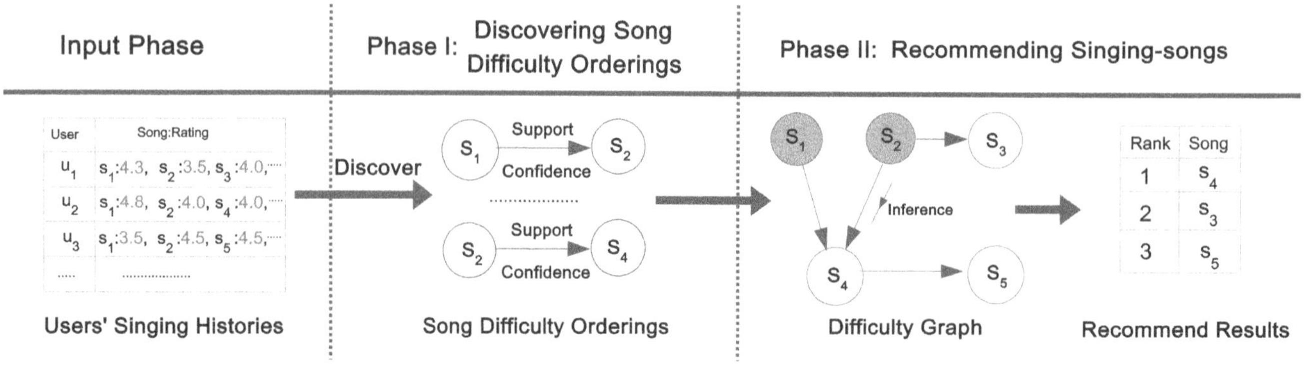

Figure 2: Overview of the singing-song recommendation framework

3.2 Recommendation Framework

Our framework for singing-song recommendation is illustrated in Figure 2. The framework takes as input the users' singing histories in the community and recommends songs to each individual user. As mentioned in the introduction, the basic idea is to infer whether a user can perform well on a song by considering song rendition difficulty. Intuitively, if a song is much more difficult than the singing history of a user, then the song is more likely to be inappropriate for the user, and it would not be recommended. Specifically, the framework recommends songs through two phases.

Phase I - Discovering song difficulty orderings. In this phase, we discover the ordering of any two songs in terms of *difficulty*, which captures whether song s_i is more difficult to perform well than s_j to the users, denoted by $s_i > s_j$. We discover the difficulty orderings from users' singing histories: if s_i has lower ratings than s_j in many singing histories, we conjecture that s_i is more difficult than s_j. Then, we evaluate the reliability of the conjecture by considering the following two factors.

1) The first factor is the *support* of the ordering, that is, how many singers support s_i is more difficult than s_j.

2) The second factor is the *confidence* of the ordering, that is, whether there are many other singing histories support the opposite conclusion, i.e., s_j is more difficult than s_i.

We will formally define song difficulty ordering and present our method of estimating support and confidence of difficulty ordering in Section 4.

Phase II - Recommending singing-songs. In this phase, we recommend songs that users have the potential to perform well. To this end, given a user u_k, we need to infer which songs are easier to get a good performance compared to the songs in u_k's singing history. We make the inference with the help of the difficulty orderings obtained in the first phase. More specifically, we first construct a difficulty graph based on difficulty orderings, where each vertex represents a song and a directed edge captures the difficulty ordering of two songs. Then, we develop an iterative probabilistic inference algorithm to obtain songs which are most likely to be "easier" to perform well for a user than those in her/his singing history. We will discuss the details of the algorithm in Section 5.

We illustrate our framework by using the example in Figure 2. In the first phase, the framework discovers difficulty orderings for song pairs and evaluates the reliability of each ordering. For instance, there are 2 users' singing history supporting $s_1 > s_2$ while only 1 singing history is supporting $s_2 > s_1$. Based on this, we estimate the support and confidence of $s_1 > s_2$ for evaluating the reliability of this ordering. In the second phase, we organize the songs into a graph based on difficulty orderings as shown in the right part of Figure 2. The gray vertices represent the songs in a user's singing history while the white vertices are the candidates to be recommended. Then, our inference algorithm applies an iterative strategy to infer the likelihood that each white vertex is easier than gray vertices and recommends the top songs with the highest likelihood scores.

4. SONG DIFFICULTY ORDERING

This section presents the technique of discovering difficulty ordering of singing-songs. We formalize the notion of song difficulty ordering in Section 4.1 and estimate the reliability of song difficulty orderings in Section 4.2. Finally, we discuss how to discover difficulty orderings from users' singing histories in Section 4.3.

4.1 Song Difficulty Ordering

The knowledge of users' performance on some songs can help us infer their performance on other songs. Intuitively, if a user performs well on a song s_i, then we can conjecture that she is also be capable of singing the songs that are "easier" to perform well than s_i. To formalize this, we introduce the idea of *song difficulty ordering* to capture whether a song is more difficult to perform well than another one. Specifically, given two songs s_i and s_j, we use the notation $s_i > s_j$ to represent one difficulty ordering, which means s_i is more difficult to perform well than s_j.

We introduce a *voting-based* strategy to determine the difficulty ordering of two songs. The basic idea is as follows. Suppose that a group of singers sing and vote which song from s_1 and s_2 is more difficult to get a good performance. Then, we can obtain a set of votes for difficulty comparison of s_1 and s_2. If more singers vote s_i as the difficult one, we can obtain a difficulty ordering $s_i > s_j$ based on these votes. We will discuss how we obtain singers' votes later in Section 4.3. More formally, we first introduce the difficult voting as follows.

DEFINITION 1 (DIFFICULTY VOTING). *Difficulty voting is the process of voting the relative difficulty of two songs s_i and s_j in getting a better performance, where n_{ij} and n_{ji} represent the numbers of votes that support $s_i > s_j$ and $s_j > s_i$ respectively.*

For instance, if there are 7 singers think s_i is more difficult than s_j while 3 singers vote for s_j, then we have $n_{ij} = 7$ and $n_{ji} = 3$ in the difficulty voting of the two songs.

Now we define the song difficulty ordering of two songs.

DEFINITION 2 (SONG DIFFICULTY ORDERING). *The song difficulty ordering of song s_i and s_j is the majority choice in difficulty voting for $s_i > s_j$ and $s_j > s_i$.*

Continuing the above example, because s_i and s_j's difficulty voting results is $n_{ij} > n_{ji}$, we get the song difficulty ordering for the two songs as $s_i > s_j$.

4.2 Reliability of Difficulty Ordering

As singers may not always have agreement on the difficulty ordering, we need to estimate the reliability of difficulty ordering from the corresponding difficulty voting. We consider two constituents of reliability, namely the *support* and the *confidence* of difficulty ordering.

4.2.1 Support

We first consider the factor that how many singers support the ordering $s_i > s_j$. We denote the *Support* of difficulty ordering by $\mathtt{supp}(s_i > s_j)$. Intuitively, a difficulty ordering which is supported by more singers would be more reliable than the one with less support. We define the support of the difficulty ordering

DEFINITION 3 (SUPPORT OF DIFFICULTY ORDERING). *The support of the difficulty ordering $s_i > s_j$, denoted as $\mathtt{supp}(s_i > s_j)$, is the number of votes that $s_i > s_j$ gets.*

Then we need to measure whether a difficulty ordering gets sufficient supports. The difficulty orderings are used for recommendation. s_i will form difficulty orderings with many other songs, for example $s_i > s_t$. It would be more reliable to use the one with more supports to do recommendation. So we estimate the probability that $s_i > s_j$ gets sufficient supports as follow:

$$P_{suff}(s_i > s_j) = \frac{\mathtt{supp}(s_i > s_j)}{\sum_{s_t \in S_\sigma} \mathtt{supp}(s_i > s_t)} \quad (1)$$

where S_σ is a song set and each s_t in S_σ forms a song difficulty ordering $s_i > s_t$.

For example, if we have only two difficulty orderings $s_i > s_j$ and $s_i > s_t$ who have support of 3 and 2 respectively. Then $P_{suff}(s_i > s_j) = 3/(2+3)$.

4.2.2 Confidence

While considering how many singers support an ordering, the *support* does not take into account how many singers oppose that ordering. For example, the vote number of $s_i > s_j$ and $s_j > s_i$ is 10 and 9 respectively, although $s_i > s_j$ has many votes, the reliability of $s_i > s_j$ is doubtful due to the large number of opposing votes. To address this problem, we further consider how confidently can we "trust" a difficulty ordering as the *Confidence* of the difficulty ordering, denoted by $\mathtt{conf}(s_i > s_j)$.

We define the confidence of difficulty ordering

DEFINITION 4 (CONFIDENCE OF DIFFICULTY ORDERING). *The confidence of the difficulty ordering $s_i > s_j$, denoted as $\mathtt{conf}(s_i > s_j)$, is the probability of getting the judgment s_i is more difficult than s_j, given $s_i > s_j$ and $s_j > s_i$'s vote number n_{ij} and n_{ji}.*

As the definition, we represent $\mathtt{conf}(s_i > s_j)$ in the probability form $P(s_i > s_j | n_{ij}, n_{ji})$. To compute $P(s_i > s_j | n_{ij}, n_{ji})$, we first use Bayes's theorem:

$$P(s_i > s_j | n_{ij}, n_{ji}) = \frac{P(n_{ij}, n_{ji} | s_i > s_j) P(s_i > s_j)}{P(n_{ij}, n_{ji})} \quad (2)$$

We assume s_i,s_j have equal probability to be more difficult which makes $P(s_i > s_j)$ and $P(s_j > s_i)$ the same value. Then

$$\frac{P(s_i > s_j | n_{ij}, n_{ji})}{P(s_j > s_i | n_{ji}, n_{ij})} = \frac{P(n_{ij}, n_{ji} | s_i > s_j)}{P(n_{ji}, n_{ij} | s_j > s_i)} \quad (3)$$

If we assume $P(s_i > s_j | n_{ij}, n_{ji}) + P(s_j > s_i | n_{ji}, n_{ij}) = 1$, together with Equation 3, we get

$$P(s_i > s_j | n_{ij}, n_{ji}) = \frac{P(n_{ij}, n_{ji} | s_i > s_j)}{P(n_{ij}, n_{ji} | s_i > s_j) + P(n_{ji}, n_{ij} | s_j > s_i)} \quad (4)$$

Then we need to calculate the probability of the voting result given the difficulty ordering. The subjects can only vote one of s_i and s_j. We consider the process of subject's voting as a Bernoulli trial. We set the human's voting accuracy to be p. The probability of observing n_{ij},n_{ji} is the Bernoulli distribution probability mass function:

$$P(n_{ij}, n_{ji} | s_i > s_j) = C_{n_{ij}+n_{ji}}^{n_{ij}} p^{n_{ij}} (1-p)^{n_{ji}} \quad (5)$$

$$P(n_{ji}, n_{ij} | s_j > s_i) = C_{n_{ij}+n_{ji}}^{n_{ji}} p^{n_{ji}} (1-p)^{n_{ij}} \quad (6)$$

Now we begin to estimate p from user's difficulty voting. We denote τ as our song difficulty ordering set. γ as an opposite difficulty ordering set with τ, their sizes being the same. For example, if $s_i > s_j \in \tau$, then $s_j > s_i \in \gamma$. We estimate p as follows

$$p = \frac{\sum_{(s_i > s_j) \in \tau} V(s_i > s_j)}{\sum_{(s_j > s_i) \in \gamma} V(s_j > s_i) + \sum_{(s_i > s_j) \in \tau} V(s_i > s_j)} \quad (7)$$

Where $V(s_i > s_j)$ is the difficulty votes $s_i > s_j$ gets.

Knowing $P(n_{ij}, n_{ji} | s_i > s_j)$ and $P(n_{ji}, n_{ij} | s_j > s_i)$, using Equation 4 we can obtain $P(s_i > s_j | n_{ij}, n_{ji})$

Similar to the sufficient of the support, we need to measure the probability of the difficulty ordering to be used in recommendation. We estimate whether the probability that $s_i > s_j$ gets a high confidence as follow:

$$P_{conf}(s_i > s_j) = \frac{\mathtt{conf}(s_i > s_j)}{\sum_{s_t \in S_\sigma} \mathtt{conf}(s_i > s_t)} \quad (8)$$

where S_σ is a song set and each s_t in S_σ forms a song difficulty ordering $s_i > s_t$.

4.2.3 Reliability

It is more reliable to make recommendation based on the song difficulty orderings which have both sufficient support and high confidence. We define the reliability of song difficulty ordering as follows.

DEFINITION 5 (RELIABILITY OF DIFFICULTY ORDERING). *The reliability of the difficulty ordering $s_i > s_j$, denotes as $\mathtt{Reli}(s_i > s_j)$, is the probability of the event that $s_i > s_j$ gets sufficient supports and a high confidence.*

We define the event that $s_i > s_j$ gets sufficient supports as $S(s_i > s_j)$, the event $s_i > s_j$ gets a high confidence as $C(s_i > s_j)$. As the definition, $\mathtt{Reli}(s_i > s_j)$ equals to $P(S(s_i > s_j), C(s_i > s_j))$. We can suppose the two events are independent, then

$$P(S(s_i > s_j), C(s_i > s_j)) = P_{supp}(S(s_i > s_j)) * P_{conf}(C(s_i > s_j)) \quad (9)$$

Therefore,

$$\mathtt{Reli}(s_i > s_j) = \frac{\mathtt{supp}(s_i > s_j)}{\sum_{s_t \in S_\sigma} \mathtt{supp}(s_i > s_t)} * \frac{\mathtt{conf}(s_i > s_j)}{\sum_{s_t \in S_\sigma} \mathtt{conf}(s_i > s_t)} \quad (10)$$

where S_σ is a song set and each s_t in S_σ forms a song difficulty orderings $s_i > s_t$.

The reliability of difficulty ordering will be used in the process of song recommendation. See Section 5 for details.

4.3 Discover Song Difficulty Orderings

One essential problem of discovering difficulty orderings is to obtain the difficulty voting introduced in Definition 1. Specifically, we need to obtain the number n_{ij} that support $s_i > s_j$ and n_{ji} that opposes the ordering. To this end, we exploit the users' ratings which implicitly reflect singers' opinions on song difficulty.

Each user of the social singing community is considered a singer. We first deduce the singer's voting for song pair s_i and s_j as follows. Suppose user u_k has sang s_i and s_j, if the listeners' mean ratings for the two songs is $r_i^k < r_j^k$. We know the listeners will give a high rating to the song if the user performs well. So the rating means u_k perform s_j better than s_i. This reflects s_i is more difficult than s_j for u_k. We can deduce u_k's voting preference for songs s_i and s_j is $s_i > s_j$.

We discover song difficulty orderings from user's singing history as follows.

1. Discover the song pairs that are sung by at least θ users.
2. For each song pair s_i,s_j, we deduce each singer's voting from the rating and count the number of votes $s_i > s_j$ and $s_j > s_i$ get as n_{ij} and n_{ji} respectively.
3. Set the one in $s_i > s_j$ and $s_j > s_i$ with more votes as s_i,s_j's song difficulty ordering.

Knowing the difficulty voting results of difficulty orderings, we can also calculate the reliability of the discovered song difficulty orderings.

5. SONG RECOMMENDATION BASED ON DIFFICULTY ORDERINGS

In this section, we propose a song recommendation approach based on the difficulty ordering introduced in the previous section. The basic idea of our approach is to estimate the likelihood that a user can perform the songs well, called *performance degree*. The estimated performance degree is then used for song recommendation. For instance, if we know that the user has larger performance degree on song s_i than s_j, then we would prefer s_i for the recommendation. In this approach, to recommend songs to user u_k, we first estimate user's performance degree on each song outside her singing history (i.e., $S - S_k$), and then rank the songs based on the performance degree as the final recommendation list.

As mentioned in Section 4, we estimate the performance degree based on the song difficulty orderings. Specifically, we first pick the songs in user u_k's singing list S_k that are evaluated by listeners as having been well-performed as *seeds*. Then, we exploit the difficulty orderings to find the songs which have large probabilities to be easier than the seeds, and utilize these probabilities to estimate the performance degree.

We formalize the above-mentioned idea in this section. We formally define performance degree and how we infer the performance degree in Section 5.1, and then develop an iterative algorithm in Section 5.2.

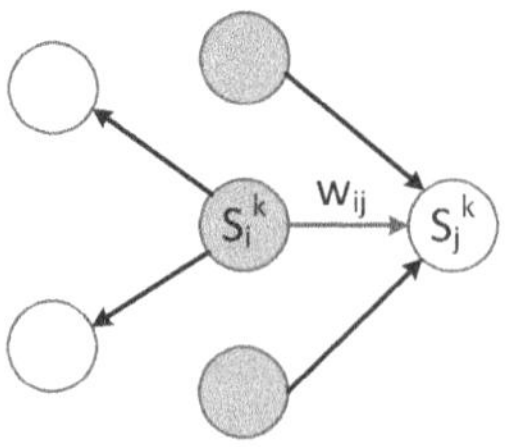

Figure 3: Inference on Difficulty Graph

5.1 Estimating Performance Degree

We formally define the performance degree, denoted by p_j^k, of user u_k on song s_j as the probability that u_k can perform well on s_j, i.e.,

$$p_j^k = Pr\{u_k \texttt{ performs well on } s_j\}$$

To estimate songs' performance degrees based on difficulty orderings. We first organize all difficulty orderings into an ordinary direct graph called *difficulty graph*. We denote the weight of edge from s_i to s_j in the difficulty graph as w_{ij}. We define difficulty graph as follow:

DEFINITION 6 (DIFFICULTY GRAPH). *A difficulty graph G is an ordinary directed weighted graph where the vertex[5] set S are songs, each edge from song s_i to s_j represents a song difficulty ordering with w_{ij} as the weight.*

Next, we present how to estimate performance degree p_j^k for song s_j from the performance degrees of its nearby songs through probabilistic inference. Specifically, suppose that the performance degrees of the songs in s_j's in-degree song set S_{in}^j are all known, shown in the gray vertices in Figure 3. We denote the event that u_k performs well on s_j as $W(s_j^k)$. Now we discusses how to infer p_j^k from the performance degree of the songs in S_{in}^j.

First we use sum and product rules of probability to get

$$Pr(W(s_j^k)) = \sum_{s_i^k \in S_{in}^j} [Pr(W(s_j^k)|W(s_i^k)) * Pr(W(s_i^k))] \quad (11)$$

We let

$$w_{ij} = Pr(W(s_j^k)|W(s_i^k)) \quad (12)$$

which is the edge weight from s_i to s_j. It represents the probability the user can perform s_j well, given that user performs s_i well. It equals to the probability that judgment $s_i^k > s_j^k$ is correct, i.e., the reliability of the song difficulty ordering $\texttt{Reli}(s_i^k > s_j^k)$. Then, we have

$$\begin{aligned} w_{ij} =& \texttt{Reli}(s_i^k > s_j^k) \\ =& \frac{\texttt{supp}(s_i^k > s_j^k)}{\sum_{s_t^k \in S_{out}^i} \texttt{supp}(s_i^k > s_t^k)} * \frac{\texttt{conf}(s_i^k > s_j^k)}{\sum_{s_t^k \in S_{out}^i} \texttt{conf}(s_i^k > s_t^k)} \end{aligned} \quad (13)$$

where S_{out}^i represents the out-degree vertex set of s_i, shown as the white vertices in Figure 3.

Knowing the performance degree of s_j's in-degree vertices and the edge weight, we can infer s_j's performance degree p_j^k. However, user only sings very few songs in the difficulty graph, how to infer s_j's performance degree if the performance degree of its in-degree vertices are unknown. In the next part, we will introduce an iterative algorithm to deal with this problem.

[5]We use vertex and song interchangeably

5.2 Iterative Probabilistic Inference

Based on the estimation method introduced in Section 5.1, we introduce a graph-based inference algorithm called *Iterative Probabilistic Inference (IPI)* to compute unknown performance degree of songs from the known performance degree of songs in the singing history.

We denote the performance degree of each vertex as $\mathbf{d} = [d_1, d_2, ..., d_{|S|}]$, where $|S|$ is the number of vertices in the difficulty graph. We construct the weight matrix $\mathbf{W}$ which is a $|S| \times |S|$ matrix, where W_{ij} equals to the weight from song s_i to s_j, that is $W_{ij} = w_{ij}$. Based on the performance degree estimation described in Section 5.1, we can perform probabilistic inference in the difficulty graph as follows

$$\mathbf{d}(t+1) = \mathbf{W}^T \mathbf{d}(t) \tag{14}$$

Because the initial performance degree $\mathbf{d}$ of each vertex is the same, each user's recommendation result will be the same. We need to give some "advantage" to user's previous singing songs. We construct a bonus vector as $\mathbf{b} = [b_1, b_2, ..., b_{|S|}]$ and assign bonus 1 to the songs that the user has sung in the past, $b_i = 1$, otherwise $b_i = 0$. The bonus vector allows user's previous singing songs to have a probability of getting an additional performance degree in each iteration. Through the iteration, these vertices will also affect other vertices' performance degrees.

Then the probabilistic inference in each iteration can be represented as

$$\mathbf{d}(t+1) = \alpha \mathbf{W}^T \mathbf{d}(t) + (1-\alpha)\mathbf{b} \tag{15}$$

where α represents the probability of inferring from the in-degree vertices, $1-\alpha$ as the probability of getting the bonus.

Then we repeatedly perform the probabilistic inference in the difficulty graph until the vertices' performance degrees converge. Theoretically, the iteration will converge to $(\mathbf{I} - \alpha * \mathbf{W}^T)^{-1} * \mathbf{b}$ according to [18]. Empirically, we observed that the iteration algorithm took three minutes to converge in our experiments. Because the calculation of edge weight in difficulty graph guarantees the sum of s_i's out-degree edge weight $\sum_{s_t \in S^i_{out}} w_{it} \leq 1$, we set $W_{ii} = 1 - \sum_{s_t \in S^i_{out}} w_{it}$ to make sure the iteration on the difficulty graph will converge. The complete algorithm description is given in Algorithm 1

Algorithm 1: *Iterative Probabilistic Inference*

Input: weight matrix $\mathbf{W}$;bonus vector $\mathbf{b}$
Output: final performance degree vector $\mathbf{d}$
$\delta = 0.0001$; $error = \infty$; $t = -1$;$\alpha \in [0, 1)$;
$\mathbf{d}$ where $d_i = 1/sizeof(\mathbf{d})$
while $error > \delta$ **do**
  $t = t + 1$;
  $\mathbf{d}(t+1) = \alpha \mathbf{W}^T \mathbf{d}(t) + (1-\alpha)\mathbf{b}$;
  $error = \mathbf{d}(t+1) - \mathbf{d}(t)$;
$\mathbf{d}^* = \mathbf{d}(t)$

6. EXPERIMENTS

In this section, we report the experimental setup and results. We first introduce the datasets being used in the experiments. After that, we report the baseline methods used to compare with our algorithm. Then we introduce the evaluation metrics used for measuring the performance of the algorithms. Finally, we present and analyse our experimental results.

6.1 Datasets

6.1.1 Song Difficulty Ordering Dataset

Since there is no publicly available dataset for singing-song recommendation, we have collected the data from 5sing which is the largest social singing community in China. In 5sing, users can upload their song recordings, listen and rate other user's recording. We chose this website because it has sufficient performance ratings for most users' singing songs.

For song difficulty orderings discovery, we crawl song pairs which have been sung by at least 10 users. The rating score for these song pairs must satisfy two conditions: the songs' rating scores in each song pair are non-zero and different. We model these song pairs into song difficulty orderings. Note that we will ignore song pairs whose ratings for both songs are the same. Finally we get a song difficulty ordering dataset. It contains total 5877 songs. We get totally 257666 song difficulty orderings.

6.1.2 Singing-song Recommendation Dataset

Now we describe the acquisition of our singing-song recommendation dataset. We download user's singing history from 5sing. Only songs appearing in the song difficulty orderings are kept. Because most of the users sing only a limited number of songs, we crawl the users who have sung at least 60 songs to partly overcome the data sparsity problem. Finally, we obtain a total of 2705 users. The number of songs sung by each user is 96. Despite this selection, the recommendation dataset is still very sparse. Note that the evaluation result of the recommendation for sparse dataset is usually not so high. For example, the best MAP reported by [12] is 0.048 which has 500 songs listened by each user in a 30520 song set. So we focus on comparing the relative increase in performance. We expect that in the future, the social singing community will develop the singing-song recommendation system and provides abundant data for the singing-song recommendation research.

For evaluation purposes, we randomly select 30% songs as the testing set, while the remaining one are used as the training set. We make sure there is no overlapping song between each user's training set and testing set.

6.2 Evaluation Metric

For evaluation, we use precision@n, recall@n and precision recall curve to compare the recommendation accuracy of our method with the baseline methods. We use mean average precision (MAP), Normalized Discount Cumulative Gain@n (NDCG@n) to measure ranking performance.

Precision@n and recall@n shows the precision and recall value at the specific position in the ranking list. Precision@n is defined as the number of correctly recommended songs divided by the total number of songs recommended at position n. While recall@n is defined as the correctly recommended songs divided by the total number of songs should be recommend in the test set.

We also use 11-point interpolated average precision to demonstrate the precision change at all recall levels. We plot the precision at 11 recall levels (0, 0.1, 0.2,..., 1.0) for the average of all users. For each user, the precision at each recall level i is determined by taking the maximum precision at any actual recall levels which are bigger than i. This is the precision recall curve for one user. After calculating the recall levels for each user, we average the precision at the corresponding recall levels over all users to get the final precision recall curve.

We use mean average precision (MAP) [2] to compare the ranking accuracy measured from the whole rank list. For each user, it first calculates the precision at the position of each relevant song in the recommend list. Then these precision values are reduced by their rank positions so that top ranked relevant documents contribute more to the final score. The sum of the precision values is averaged by the total number of correctly recommended items. Now we get the average precision (AP). MAP is calculated by averaging the AP value of each query.

$$MAP = \frac{1}{|Q|}\sum_{q\in Q}\frac{\sum_{n=1}^{N}(Precision@n * rel(n))}{R_q} \tag{16}$$

where Q is the test query set, R_q is q's relevant document, $rel(n)$ is a binary function on the relevance of a given rank, N is the number of retrieved documents.

We use NGCG@n [11] to measure the accuracy of the rank order at specific position of the ranking result. It calculates as follow

$$NDCG(n) = \frac{1}{Z_n}\sum_{j=1}^{n}\frac{2^{r(j)}-1}{log_2(j+1)} \tag{17}$$

where j is the predicted rank position , $r(j)$ is the rating value of j-th document in the ground-truth rank list, Z_n is the normalization factor which is the discounted cumulative gain in the $n-th$ position of the ground-truth rank list. We consider $r(j)$ as 1 if the song is sang by the user, otherwise 0.

6.3 Baseline Methods

We denote our iterative probabilistic inference algorithm as *IPI*. We compare IPI with four baselines.

The first classic baseline is the user-based *Collaborative Filtering (CF)* method. We build the user-song matrix using user's singing history. Songs sang by each user will have a 5-graded rating. Our objective is to predict the rating for other unrated songs. CF utilizes users' current song ratings and the similarity between users to predict the other songs' rating. We recommend songs which have high predicted rating scores. Suppose we want to get the predicted rating value for user u_t and song s_i, we get the rating value r_i^t as

$$r_i^t = \sum_{u_j\in S(u_t,k)\cap N(s_i)}\frac{Sim(u_t,u_j)}{\sum_{u_j\in S(u_t,k)\cap N(s_i)}Sim(u_t,u_j)} * r_i^j \tag{18}$$

Where $S(u_t, k)$ is the top k similar users with the target user u_t, $N(s_i)$ is the user set that has rating for song s_i, r_i^j is user u_j's rating for song s_i and $Sim(u_t, u_j)$ is the similarity between user u_t and u_j. We set the number of the nearest neighbor k to 20 to achieve the best performance. For the user's similarity, we use the cosine distance to calculate the similarity between two users' song rating vectors.

Another popular baseline is graph based song recommendation algorithm. We use the similar baseline as [7]. We build an undirected graph with song and user as vertex, user's singing relation as edge. We use the graph ranking algorithm proposed in [9]. We call this baseline as *Ordinary Graph based Recommendation (OGR)*.

Because measuring the reliability of song difficulty orderings is the key for singing-song recommendation. We compare the result of singing-song recommendation using only support or confidence to estimate the reliability of difficulty orderings. We denote these two baselines as *IPI-supp* and *IPI-conf* respectively.

For IPI-supp, the edge weight of difficulty graph can be calculated as

$$w_{ij} = \frac{\texttt{supp}(s_i > s_j)}{\sum_{s_t\in S_{out}^i}\texttt{supp}(s_i > s_t)} \tag{19}$$

For IPI-conf, the edge weight of difficulty graph can be calculated as

$$w_{ij} = \frac{\texttt{conf}(s_i > s_j)}{\sum_{s_t\in S_{out}^i}\texttt{conf}(s_i > s_t)} \tag{20}$$

6.4 Experimental Results

6.4.1 Baseline Comparison

We use the metrics mentioned in Section 6.2 to compare the performance of different algorithms. We fix the common random walk parameter α shared by OGR, IPI-supp, IPI-conf, IPI as 0.85. We estimate human's voting accuracy using the equation 7, we get $p = 0.71$. Figure 4 demonstrates the song ranking performance of the five algorithms.

Figure 4(a) and Figure 4(b) are the precision and recall results of the five algorithms. We find our method IPI outperform baseline CF, OGR, IPI-supp and IPI-conf by an average of 180%, 36%, 28% 18% in precision and 190%, 32%, 29% 19% in recall. For IPI, IPI-supp, IPI-conf, those methods that make recommendation on difficulty graph perform better than the traditional song recommendation algorithms OGR and CF. This is because CF and OGR ignore the song's difficulty in performance during recommendation. It proves the effectiveness of song difficulty orderings in the singing-song recommendation. Figure 4(c) and Figure 4(d) are the performance results measured by NDCG@n and precision recall curve, it shows the similar results. IPI is always the best and those baselines who do recommendation on difficulty graph are also much better than the traditional song recommendation algorithms.

The above results show that IPI is better than IPI-supp and IPI-conf in all metrics. The difference between IPI and IPI-supp, IPI-conf is that the later only uses single factor support or confidence to estimate the reliability of the song difficulty orderings. This proves that using both factors to measure the reliability is better than the single one. This is reasonable because difficulty orderings with high support only represent the absolute number of people who support the difficulty orderings, it is possible that there are also many people who do not agree with the difficulty orderings. However, confidence considers the agreement of two sides, while ignoring the possible bias caused by the shortage of judgments. Adding both of them in reliability estimation overcomes the shortage of both factors.

Table 1 is the performance result measured from MAP. We find IPI outperform CF and OGR by an average of 160% and 40% respectively. But the absolute values are quite low, this is caused by the sparseness problem of the dataset. We compare the sparseness of our data set with the one reported in [12]. In their dataset, the number of songs listened by each user is 1.6% of the total song set. Their precision recall curve also shows a fast decrease in the precision and the best MAP is 0.048. [17] is another example. In our dataset, the number of songs sang by each user is also about 1.6% of the total song set. The low performance value is reasonable.

Table 1: Ranking accuracy in terms of MAP

Algorithm	IPI	IPI-conf	IPI-supp	OGR	CF
MAP value	0.061	0.051	0.048	0.043	0.024

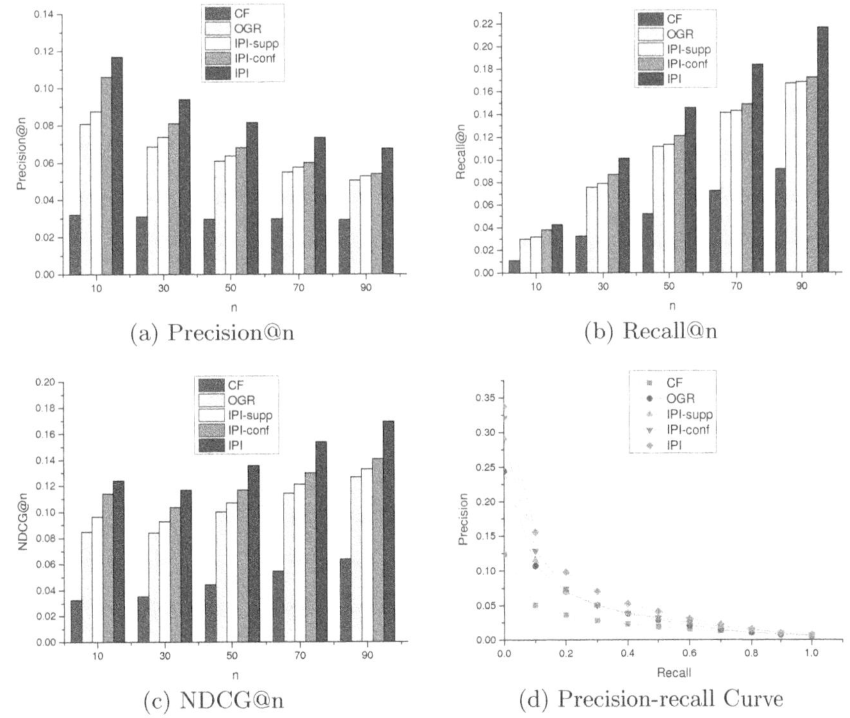

(a) Precision@n (b) Recall@n

(c) NDCG@n (d) Precision-recall Curve

Figure 4: Performance Comparison of the Five Algorithms

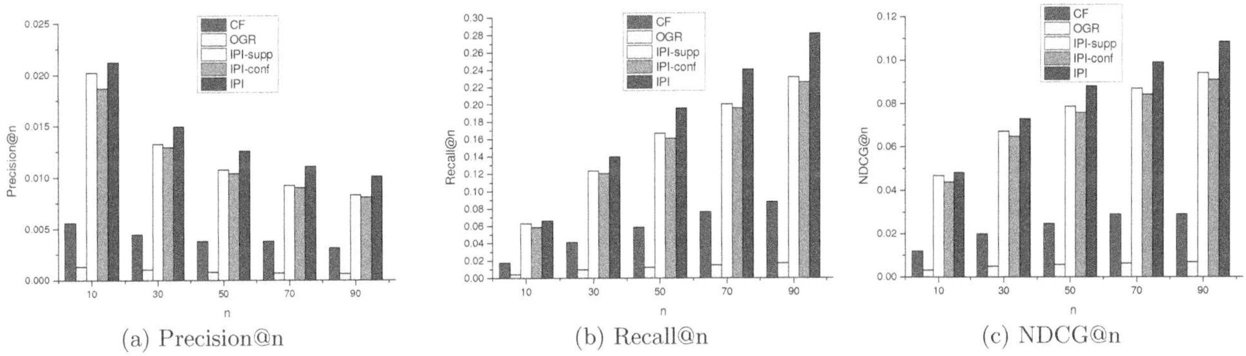

(a) Precision@n (b) Recall@n (c) NDCG@n

Figure 5: Performance Comparison for Cold Start User

6.4.2 *Test for Cold Start User*

We also test the performance of the algorithms for cold start users. We consider those users who sing between 7 to 10 songs in the training set as cold start users. Limiting the number of each user's singing-song is to ensure there will be at least 3 songs in the testing set for the evaluation purpose. The number of users in the sparse dataset is 3000.

Figure 5(a) and Figure 5(b) is the precision and recall results of the five methods on the sparse dataset. We find the performance of IPI-conf is lower than IPI-supp which is opposite to the above results. This is caused by the error in reliability estimation using only support factors. For those conjectures with few supports, even if the confidence is high, it still exhibits errors when estimating the reliability. For cold start users, they do not have enough previous singing songs as query to overcome the error cause by confidence factor. While support can also reflect the popularity of the song difficulty ordering. Large number of support means it is more possible that many people had sung the song pair. For cold start user, recommending popular songs through popular difficulty orderings may perform better. Our IPI again performs better than the two baselines which shows again the measuring the reliability through both the support and confidence is effective. Figure 5(c) is the performance measured from NDCG@n which shows the same results.

Table 2: Statistical significance comparison between IPI and two IPI variants

Precision@n	P@10	P@30	P@50	P@70	P@90
IPI-supp	1.384	5.2259	8.4185	11.0886	13.2275
IPI-conf	3.9934	6.5927	10.3389	12.7425	15.097

Because the precision differences between IPI and two IPI variants are minor in the cold start dataset. We conduct the significance test(t-Test) on the results. For each method, we compute a list of precisions@n, each corresponding to the recommendation for a user. Given IPI and a baseline(IPI-supp or IPI-conf), we compute t-ratio over their precision lists. Table 2 shows the t-ratios between IPI and two baselines. We find most t-ratios are larger than the cutoff of 3.3 (nearest df in t-test table is 1000 under $p<0.001$), which shows IPI's improvement is significant. The only exception is the result of the precision@10 for IPI-supp, which is caused by the data sparse problem.

For the baseline OGR, the performance drops a lot on the sparse dataset. It is caused by the existence of large amounts of isolated vertices in song-user graph. Due to the sparseness of the dataset, many songs in the test set had not been sung by any user in the train set. It is impossible to be recommended based on the song-user graph. By looking into the graph, we find 1391 out of 5877 songs had not been sung by any user in the training set. While our difficulty graph will not be affected by this data sparseness problem. This is because our difficulty graph is pre-built, the iterative algorithm will not largely be affected by the shortage of user's singing relations.

7. CONCLUSIONS

In this paper, we address the singing-song recommendation problem in social singing communities. We propose a method to discover song difficulty orderings from the song performance ratings of each user. We also estimate the reliability of the discovered difficulty orderings based on the support and confidence of the difficulty orderings. For singing-song recommendation, we model the discovered difficulty orderings as a difficulty graph that captures the difficulty relation in performance between different songs. An iterative probabilistic inference algorithm is proposed to estimate the performance degrees of all the other vertices in the graph from each user's past singing history. The experiments have been performed on a dataset collected from an actual social singing community (5sing). The result shows our proposed framework is more effective than the traditional song recommendation methods.

For future work, we will conduct user study to see if the amateur singers are satisfied with the recommendation generated by this system. Secondly, because the discovered song difficulty orderings can also be used in other social singing communities, we will focus on discovering more difficulty orderings from other sources of social singing community to maintain a complete difficulty orderings database. Another direction for singing song recommendation is that we will exploit other factors such as users' singing preference as well as friendship relations to see if they can help make the recommendation better.

8. ACKNOWLEDGEMENT

This research was carried out at the NUS-ZJU SeSaMe Centre. It is supported by the Singapore NRF under its IRC@SG Funding Initiative and administered by the IDM-PO. This research was also supported by the National High Technology Research and Development Program of China (Grant No. 2014AA015205).

9. REFERENCES

[1] S. Agarwal. Ranking on graph data. In W. W. Cohen and A. Moore, editors, *ICML*, volume 148, pages 25–32. ACM, 2006.

[2] R. Baeza-Yates and B. Ribeiro-Neto. *Modern Information Retrieval.* Addison-Wesley, 1999.

[3] S. Baluja, R. Seth, D. Sivakumar, Y. Jing, J. Yagnik, S. Kumar, D. Ravichandran, and M. Aly. Video suggestion and discovery for youtube: Taking random walks through the view graph. WWW '08, pages 895–904, New York, NY, USA, 2008. ACM.

[4] M. Belkin, I. Matveeva, and P. Niyogi. Regularization and semi-supervised learning on large graphs. volume 3120, pages 624–638. Springer, 2004.

[5] M. Belkin and P. Niyogi. Semi-supervised learning on riemannian manifolds. *Machine Learning*, 56(1-3):209–239, 2004.

[6] J. S. Breese, D. Heckerman, and C. M. Kadie. Empirical analysis of predictive algorithms for collaborative filtering. *CoRR*, abs/1301.7363, 2013.

[7] J. Bu, S. Tan, C. Chen, C. Wang, H. Wu, L. Zhang, and X. He. Music recommendation by unified hypergraph: Combining social media information and music content. MM '10, pages 391–400, New York, NY, USA, 2010. ACM.

[8] D. Goldberg, D. A. Nichols, B. M. Oki, and D. B. Terry. Using collaborative filtering to weave an information tapestry. *Commun. ACM*, 35(12):61–70, 1992.

[9] T. H. Haveliwala. Topic-sensitive pagerank. In *Proceedings of the Eleventh International World Wide Web Conference*, 2002.

[10] K. Hoashi, K. Matsumoto, and N. Inoue. Personalization of user profiles for content-based music retrieval based on relevance feedback. In *ACM Multimedia*, pages 110–119, 2003.

[11] K. Järvelin and J. Kekäläinen. Ir evaluation methods for retrieving highly relevant documents. In *SIGIR*, pages 41–48, 2000.

[12] I. Konstas, V. Stathopoulos, and J. M. Jose. On social networks and collaborative recommendation. SIGIR '09, pages 195–202, New York, NY, USA, 2009. ACM.

[13] K. Mao, X. Luo, K. Chen, G. Chen, and L. Shou. myDJ: recommending karaoke songs from one's own voice. In *SIGIR*, page 1009. ACM, 2012.

[14] B. M. Sarwar, G. Karypis, J. A. Konstan, and J. Riedl. Item-based collaborative filtering recommendation algorithms. In *WWW*, pages 285–295. ACM, 2001.

[15] L. Shou, K. Mao, X. Luo, K. Chen, G. Chen, and T. Hu. Competence-based song recommendation. In *SIGIR*, pages 423–432. ACM, 2013.

[16] X. Wu, Q. Liu, E. Chen, L. He, J. Lv, C. Cao, and G. Hu. Personalized next-song recommendation in online karaokes. In *Proceedings of the 7th ACM Conference on Recommender Systems*, RecSys '13, pages 137–140, New York, NY, USA, 2013. ACM.

[17] M. Ye, P. Yin, W.-C. Lee, and D. L. Lee. Exploiting geographical influence for collaborative point-of-interest recommendation. In *SIGIR*, pages 325–334. ACM, 2011.

[18] D. Zhou, J. Huang, and B. Schölkopf. Learning from labeled and unlabeled data on a directed graph. In *ICML*, volume 119, pages 1036–1043. ACM, 2005.

[19] D. Zhou, J. Weston, A. Gretton, O. Bousquet, and B. Schölkopf. Ranking on data manifolds. In *Advances in Neural Information Processing Systems 16*. MIT Press, 2004.

"Sheldon speaking, bonjour !" – Leveraging Multilingual Tracks for (Weakly) Supervised Speaker Identification

Hervé Bredin
Anindya Roy
Nicolas Pécheux
Alexandre Allauzen
–
LIMSI - CNRS
BP 133, Orsay, France
bredin@limsi.fr

ABSTRACT

We address the problem of speaker identification in multimedia data, and TV series in particular. While speaker identification is traditionally a supervised machine-learning task, our first contribution is to significantly reduce the need for costly preliminary manual annotations through the use of automatically aligned (and potentially noisy) fan-generated transcripts and subtitles. We show that both speech activity detection and speech turn identification modules trained in this weakly supervised manner achieve similar performance as their fully supervised counterparts (*i.e.* relying on fine manual speech/non-speech/speaker annotation). Our second contribution relates to the use of multilingual audio tracks usually available with this kind of content to significantly improve the overall speaker identification performance. Reproducible experiments (including dataset, manual annotations and source code) performed on the first six episodes of *The Big Bang Theory* TV series show that combining the French audio track (containing dubbed actor voices) with the English one (with the original actor voices) improves the overall English speaker identification performance by 5% absolute and up to 70% relative on the five main characters.

Categories and Subject Descriptors

H.3 [**Information Storage and Retrieval**]: Content Analysis and Indexing

General Terms

Algorithms

Keywords

speech activity detection; speaker identification; multimedia data; weak supervision; multilingual fusion

MM'14, November 03 – 07 2014, Orlando, FL, USA.

ACM 978-1-4503-3063-3/14/11 ...$15.00.
http://dx.doi.org/10.1145/2647868.2654929.

1. INTRODUCTION

Rich in interactions between characters and enjoying a wide fan base, movies or TV series such as *Harry Potter* or *The Big Bang Theory* are a potential source of data for both natural language processing applications (*e.g.* summarization) and information retrieval tasks (*e.g.* fans may like to retrieve all scenes where *Leonard* invites *Penny* to dinner). Second screen applications could rely on the textual transcription of dialogues between the main characters of a TV series to provide an efficient way to browse a TV series scene by scene [6] or from punchline to punchline (*e.g. Sheldon*'s famous *"Penny, Penny, Penny"* or *"That's my spot!"*) [18].

The main objective of this work is to automatically augment TV series with additional metadata that might eventually lead to those novel multimedia retrieval applications. While automatic speech transcription (or DVD subtitles when they are available) can be used to gain a clear insight of what is being said at any time, the metadata describing which character pronounced a particular line is usually missing, though this information is crucial for content-based video retrieval purposes. We propose to apply speaker identification to automatically obtain this missing information. Figure 1 summarizes our contributions towards this objective.

Thanks to speaker recognition evaluations (SRE) organized by NIST since 1996 [24] and more recent initiatives such as ESTER, ETAPE and REPERE [21], many studies have been devoted to speaker recognition in conversational phone calls or radio and TV broadcast news. However, to the best of our knowledge, it is the first time speaker recognition is also applied to TV series. Section 2 details the different challenges raised by this new task and introduces our baseline approach to solve the problem.

The main limitation of automatic speaker identification is that it relies on a time consuming manual annotation step for the initial training of speaker models. To address this issue in a fully unsupervised manner, a typical approach is to detect speaker names from speech transcripts or subtitles and try to propagate them to speaker clusters [10, 39, 26]. However, reported results show that unsupervised speaker identification performance decreases rapidly (down to less than 30% accuracy) when relying on automatic modules (*i.e.* speech transcription, name detection and speech turns clustering) [16, 20].

Our first major contribution – described in Section 3 – is to show how one can dramatically reduce the cost of

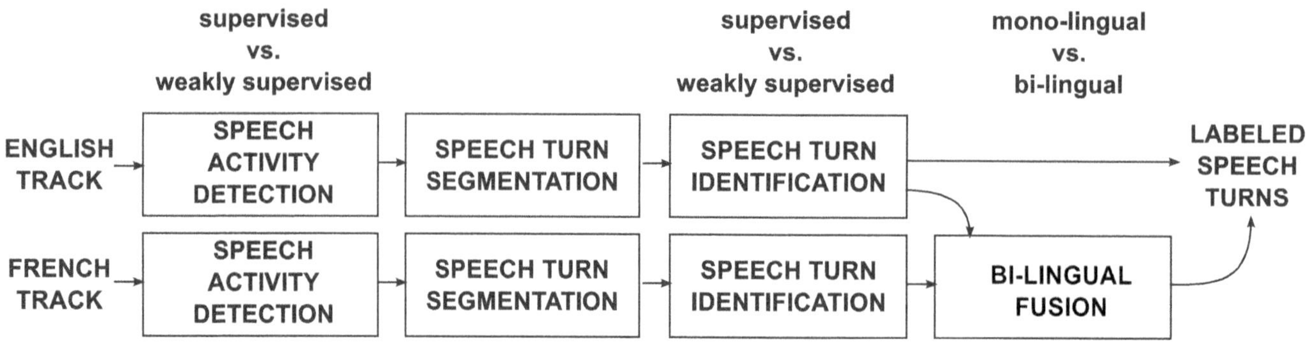

Figure 1: Speaker identification in TV series. Our contributions include weakly supervised speech activity detection, weakly supervised speaker identification, and bi-lingual speaker identification.

this preliminary manual annotation step, with almost no performance loss, via automatic temporal alignment of fan-generated transcripts with corresponding TV series episodes. Alignment of screenplays and transcripts has been used before in the computer vision community for face recognition in movies or TV series in [17, 34, 13, 36, 4]. Though these annotations are often noisy and incomplete, experiments show that the overall speaker identification performance is only slightly degraded, in comparison with the same approach based on precise – but costly – manual annotation of the same training set.

Our second main contribution relates to the use of multilingual audio tracks to further improve speaker identification. While the combination of multiple sources of information (such as voice, face and text) has been used before for multimodal person identification [8, 30], we are not aware of any previous work combining synchronized audio tracks in multiple languages to improve character (or more generally, speaker) identification as done in this work.

As a matter of fact, with the advent of digital broadcasting, most movies and TV series episodes are distributed at least in both the production original language and the viewers' language (with dubbed voices). Section 4 describes how one can take advantage of these multiple audio tracks to reach nearly perfect speaker identification among main characters.

The experimental protocol described in Section 5 follows the reproducible research principle: not only is the used corpus reproducible locally, but the necessary source code to reproduce the experiments is also distributed on the corpus webpage (`tvd.niderb.fr`). Finally, results are reported and discussed in Section 6. Section 7 concludes the paper.

2. SPEAKER IDENTIFICATION

In this section, we describe the speaker identification approach that will serve as a baseline for the rest of the paper. The upper part of Figure 1 summarizes it graphically. As this is the first time speaker identification in TV series is addressed, we first motivate several design choices by a few characterics specific to TV series.

Spontaneous speech While speech is usually prepared in TV broadcast news, dialogues between characters can be considered as spontaneous speech (even though they are acted); thus resulting into short speech turns with lots of fast interactions between characters.

Small set of characters While a large number of speakers are supposed to be recognized in above-mentioned evaluation campaigns, the number of characters in TV series is very limited and mostly main characters are of interest to the end user; the task can therefore be considered as closed-set speaker identification with a small number of targets.

Clean audio The audio track of a TV series is usually the result of a well-controlled production pipeline where the speech signal is carefully recorded on a dedicated channel before being mixed with other audio channels (*e.g.* music, stage noise or recorded laughs). Even though this *clean speech channel* is not available directly, the speech signal resulting from controlled post-production is still much cleaner than if it was recorded in a noisy environment.

2.1 Speech activity detection

Speech activity detection is addressed as a two-classes classification problem. Given the input audio stream, one has to decide for each instant whether a character is currently speaking (*speech* class) or not (*non-speech* class).

While standard speech activity detection usually divides the *speech* class into several sub-classes (*e.g.* clean speech, noisy speech or speech over music) [3], we do not. Indeed, as stated earlier, TV series audio tracks result from a careful post-production process leading to much higher audio quality than phone calls or broadcast news historically addressed by the community.

A two-states hidden Markov model (HMM) is used to tackle this problem: *speech vs. non-speech*. The states emission probability distributions are modeled by Gaussian mixture models. Given annotated (either manually or automatically) audio tracks and acoustic features extracted from them, the HMM parameters are estimated using an iterative Expectation-Maximization (EM) approach: the Baum-Welch algorithm [31].

At test time, given a previously unseen audio track, the Viterbi algorithm [31] is used to estimate the optimal sequence of hidden states (*i.e. speech* or *non-speech*). Finally, a median filter with a sliding window of 250 ms is applied to this sequence to get rid of too short *speech* (or *non-speech*) segments.

2.2 Speech turn segmentation

Due to the rapid interactions between characters in TV series, it is frequent that one continuous speech segment contains speech turns from multiple interacting characters. Therefore, before trying to label speech segments, they are further segmented into smaller homogeneous segments by detecting speaker changes [12]. This is achieved by detecting every maximum of the local Gaussian divergence $G(w_L, w_R)$ between two adjacent sliding windows w_L (left) and w_R (right) of 1 second. The Gaussian divergence is defined as follows:

$$G(w_L, w_R) = (\mu_R - \mu_L)^T \cdot \Sigma_L^{-1/2} \cdot \Sigma_R^{-1/2} \cdot (\mu_R - \mu_L) \quad (1)$$

where the set of acoustic features of each window is modeled as a Gaussian $\mathcal{N}(\mu, \Sigma)$ with diagonal covariance matrix Σ [3].

2.3 Speech turn identification

In this paper, we are only focusing on recognizing main characters as they are usually the ones of interest for the user willing to retrieve a particular moment in a TV series. Moreover, as shown later in Section 6, secondary characters only account for 10% of speech time in a TV series such as *The Big Bang Theory*. Therefore, we address the issue of identifying speech turns as a closed-set speaker identification problem: for each speech turn t, decide which of the N main characters is currently speaking.

We rely on a standard Gaussian mixture model (GMM) system based on adapted universal background model (UBM). It has proved to be very successful for text-independent speaker recognition, since it allows for robust estimation of speaker models λ_i even with a limited amount of enrollment data [32].

Given audio segments annotated as speech turns and acoustic features extracted from them, the UBM parameters are estimated using the iterative Expectation-Maximization (EM) algorithm. Then, for each main character i, a speaker-specific GMM λ_i is trained by MAP adaptation [19] of the means of the UBM.

While standard speaker identification algorithms (for telephone calls or broadcast news) usually rely on a preliminary step of feature normalization to compensate for channel and speaker variability [2], we do not. Indeed, as already stated before in Section 2.1, the audio post-production pipeline in TV series results in a readily normalized audio channel.

At test time, given a speech turn t and a target identity i, the speaker identification score ρ_{ti} is defined as the standard log-likelihood ratio [32]. Finally, the decided identity i^* of speech turn t is obtained as the one with the largest score: $i^* = \text{argmax}_{\ i}\, \rho_{ti}$.

A common practice for speaker identification in broadcast news is to rely on a preliminary speaker diarization step (*i.e.* speech turns clustering) and perform identification at cluster level rather than speech turn level [38]. However, because of the specificity of dialogues in TV series (spontaneous speech, short speech turns and fast interactions between characters), we found that state-of-the-art speaker diarization approaches do not perform well for this kind of content and tend to group speech turns of multiple interacting speakers into a unique cluster: we chose to perform identification at speech turn level, rather than at (likely noisy) cluster level.

3. REDUCING MANUAL SUPERVISION

Both speech activity detection and speech turn identification steps introduced in the previous paragraphs are supervised machine-learning techniques in need of on annotated training data to learn speech, non-speech and speaker models. However, as already stated, this mandatory annotated data is usually very costly (both in terms of time and human resources) to produce manually. Furthermore, while speech/non-speech classification models are quite generic and can be trained once and for all, speaker models are specific to a TV series and need to be updated for every new appearing character.

Named speaker identification techniques [10, 20, 7] could be used to achieve fully unsupervised speaker identification. However, this type of approaches rely on the combination of several error-prone processing stages (including automatic speech transcription, named entity detection, speaker diarization and name propagation), leading to overall bad performance.

Luckily, fan-generated manual transcripts containing speaker identities can be downloaded from the Internet for a limited number of episodes. Once temporally aligned with subtitles, they constitute a reliable source of annotations that can be used to train speaker models, consequently applied to the remaining episodes.

3.1 Aligning transcripts with subtitles

As shown in Figure 2, subtitles (a) typically consist of a sequence of dialogue lines $\mathcal{S} = \{s_i\}_{1 \le i \le N}$ associated with a time span. However, they do not provide information about speaker identity. On the other side, manual transcripts (b) consist of a sequence of dialogue lines $\mathcal{T} = \{t_j\}_{1 \le j \le M}$ each associated with a speaker name, but no temporal information. The objective of automatic alignment is to merge time spans from subtitles with speaker identities from manual transcripts – thus leading to the availability of speaker time spans (e).

3.1.1 Pre-processing

Subtitles may originally cover multiple dialogue lines from several speakers. In such cases, the subtitle time span is divided and allotted to each line proportionally to their number of words. For instance, the first subtitle of Figure 2 (a) is divided into two dialogue lines s_1 (*"...it will not've gone through both slits"*) and s_2 (*"Agreed."*). This simple heuristic is definitely not optimal as it may cut those multi-speaker subtitles at incorrect positions. More advanced techniques could be used instead (*e.g.* forced alignment of text and audio).

3.1.2 Word overlap statistics

In the case of *The Big Bang Theory* TV series, standard word-level alignment [17, 35, 27] in English reveals that around 97% words in manual transcripts have an exact match in subtitles while around 98% words in the subtitles have a match in manual transcripts. The mismatched cases are mostly due to deliberate dropping of uninformative words, simplification of sentences or contractions in the subtitles, *e.g. "it will not have gone"* in manual transcript t_1 is contracted to *"it will not've gone"* in subtitle s_1.

However, in the French language, the situation is less advantageous. While French subtitles can be obtained from DVDs, manual transcripts are not directly available in the

(a) English subtitles

00:11.27 → 00:13.83
s_1 -...it will not've gone through both slits.
s_2 -Agreed.

00:13.99 → 00:15.06
s_3 What's your point?

00:15.23 → 00:18.07
s_4 There's no point. I just think it's a good idea for a T-shirt

(b) Manual transcript

Sheldon:
t_1 it will not have gone through both slits.

Leonard:
t_2 Agreed, what's your point?

Sheldon:
t_3 There's no point, I just think it's a good idea for a tee-shirt.

(c) Translated transcript

Sheldon:
il ne sera pas ont traversé deux fentes.

Leonard:
D'accord, quel est votre point ?

Sheldon:
Il n'y a aucun point, je pense que c'est une bonne idée pour un T-shirt.

(d) French subtitles

00:11.11 → 00:13.84
-il n'aura pas traversé les deux fentes.
-Je sais.

00:13.99 → 00:15.07
Où tu veux en venir ?

00:15.23 → 00:18.07
Nulle part. mais c'est pas une mauvaise idée. pour un t-shirt.

(e) Speaker time spans (English)

00:11.27 → 00:13.37	Sheldon	$s_1 \leftrightarrow t_1$
00:13.37 → 00:13.83	Leonard	$s_2 \leftrightarrow t_2$
00:13.99 → 00:15.06	Leonard	$s_3 \leftrightarrow t_2$
00:15.23 → 00:18.07	Sheldon	$s_4 \leftrightarrow t_3$

(f) Speaker time spans (French)

00:11.11 → 00:13.29	Sheldon
00:13.29 → 00:13.84	Leonard
00:13.99 → 00:15.07	Leonard
00:15.23 → 00:18.07	Sheldon

Figure 2: DVD subtitles (a and d), available English manual transcripts (b), English manual transcripts automatically translated into French (c) and time spans automatically annotated with speaker identity obtained after alignment of subtitles with transcripts (e and f).

French language and an additional step of automatic translation (described later in Section 4.2) is needed to obtain a French version of the English manual transcripts. A similar analysis of word-level alignment in French reveals that only 26% words in the translated manual transcripts are matched with the same word in French subtitles, while 32% words in French subtitles have a match with the same word in translated manual transcripts.

3.1.3 Alignment algorithm

Based on this observation, we chose not to use the standard word-level alignment algorithm as in [17, 35]. Instead, we consider manual transcripts and subtitles as *comparable corpora* and use a dedicated sentence-level alignment algorithm [28]. Let $\mathcal{W}$ be the overall set of words used either in manual transcripts or subtitles. Each subtitle or transcript line $\ell \in \mathcal{S} \cup \mathcal{T}$ is then described by a TF-IDF vector φ_ℓ defined as follows:

$$\forall w \in \mathcal{W}, \;\; \varphi_\ell(w) = \mathrm{TF}_\ell(w) \cdot \log\left(\frac{N+M}{\mathrm{DF}(w)}\right) \tag{2}$$

where $\mathrm{TF}_\ell(w)$ is a binary indicator of whether word w occurs in (subtitle or transcript) line ℓ, N is the number of subtitle lines, M is the number of transcript lines and $\mathrm{DF}(w)$ is the total number of lines in which word w occurs. The local similarity between a subtitle s and a manual transcript t is defined as the cosine similarity between their respective TF-IDF vectors:

$$\sigma(s,t) = \frac{\sum_{w\in\mathcal{W}} \varphi_s(w)\cdot\varphi_t(w)}{\sqrt{\sum_{w\in\mathcal{W}} \varphi_s^2(w) \cdot \sum_{w\in\mathcal{W}} \varphi_t^2(w)}} \tag{3}$$

The standard Dynamic Time Warping (DTW) approach is then applied to obtain the alignment. First, the global alignment score $\kappa(s_i, t_j)$ is computed as follows:

$$\kappa(s_1,t_1) = \sigma(s_1,t_1) \tag{4}$$

$$\kappa(s_i,t_j) = \sigma(s_i,t_j) + \max\begin{cases}\kappa(s_{i-1},t_{j-1})\\ \kappa(s_{i-1},t_j)\\ \kappa(s_i,t_{j-1})\end{cases} \tag{5}$$

Then, we find the best alignment path by backtracking from $\kappa(s_N, t_M)$ to $\kappa(s_1, t_1)$. Pairs of lines (s_i, t_j) on this path are considered as aligned and time spans from the subtitle lines are merged with speaker names from the aligned manual transcript lines. This results in a sequence of time spans annotated with speaker identity as shown in columns (e) and (f) of Figure 2.

3.2 Weak supervision

This automatic alignment process removes the need for costly manual annotations and allow us to achieve weakly supervised speaker identification:

Speech activity detection. Subtitles time spans are marked as *speech* segments, while the rest of the audio track is marked as *non-speech*. Then, the HMM-based approach is trained the usual way as described in Section 2.1.

Speech turn segmentation is left unchanged as it does not rely on any supervision in the first place.

Speech turn identification. Automatically labeled subtitles are used as groundtruth for training of the identification module described in Section 2.3.

However, those automatic annotations do not have the same quality as manual annotations. Figure 3 illustrates this issue for both speech activity detection and speech turn identification. In particular, by comparing time spans of speech turns and DVD subtitles, one notices that DVD subtitles tend to last longer than the corresponding speech turns and therefore overlap non-speech regions (colored as light grey

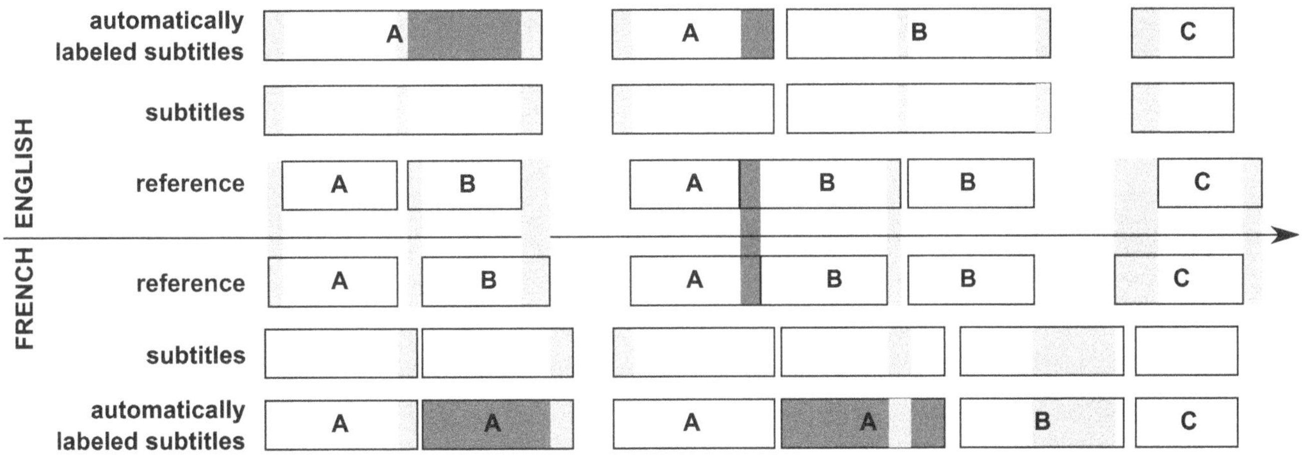

Figure 3: Badly segmented (light grey) regions in subtitles highlight the fact that subtitles time spans only provide coarse annotations for weakly supervised training of speech activity detection. Similarly, incorrectly labeled (dark grey) regions in automatically labeled subtitles highlight that they provide noisy supervision for speaker identification training. Finally, comparing English and French reference speech turns shows that they are approximately synchronized and therefore can be combined for bilingual speaker identification.

regions in Figure 3). This is actually deliberate because subtitles need to be displayed long enough for the viewer to be able to read them entirely. More precisely, statistics reported in column *subtitles* of Table 1 indicate that subtitles do cover most (95.6%) of *speech* regions. However, as anticipated, they also contain 25.4% of *non-speech* regions.

Similarly, errors in the automatic alignment of manual transcripts and subtitles may results in noisy speaker labels (colored as dark grey regions in Figure 3). However, we will show in Section 6 that the performance of both speech activity detection and speech turn identification is not degraded when those noisy annotations are used in place of manual annotations.

4. BILINGUAL IDENTIFICATION

In an increasingly multilingual and multicultural world, many TV programs come as rich multi-lingual content. TV series or movie DVDs, for example, usually contain multilingual audio tracks and/or subtitles. Original characters' voices are dubbed in alternative languages by professional voice actors. In a given language, each character is always dubbed by the same voice actor and no two main characters share the same voice actor.

While a speaker identification system may have trouble distinguishing the voices of two characters in the original language, it is quite unlikely to be also the case with their dubbed voices (and reciprocally). Hence, we show how one can take advantage of these complementary sources of information.

4.1 Bilingual fusion

In this work, we focus on a bilingual (English + French) fusion approach to make the most of the multi-lingual additional audio tracks and improve speaker identification in the original language (English). As illustrated in Figure 3, and for obvious lip-sync reasons, the French speech turns tend to strongly follow the segmentation in the original English language, though they are not perfectly synchronous. Therefore, we propose to train two distinct mono-lingual speaker identification systems (one for English and one for French) and combine them at score level:

$$\rho_{ti} = \alpha \cdot \rho_{ti}^{\mathrm{EN}} + (1-\alpha) \cdot \rho_{ti}^{\mathrm{FR}} \tag{6}$$

where $\alpha \in [0,1]$ is a weighting coefficient.

While we could directly transfer English annotations onto the French track (leading to potentially noisier annotations) in order to train the French speaker identification module, we chose to automatically translate English transcripts into French before aligning them with French subtitles as described in Section 3.1.

4.2 Manual transcripts translation

To translate transcripts, we use NCODE, an open source n-gram Statistical Machine Translation (SMT) system[1]. This system achieved state-of-the-art performance in recent *Workshop on Statistical Machine Translation* (WMT) evaluation campaigns [9, 5]. NCODE implements the bilingual n-gram approach to SMT [11, 23, 14] that is closely related to the standard phrase-based approach [22].

In this approach, to translate a source sentence $\mathbf{s}$ into a target sentence $\mathbf{t}$, the translation process is decomposed into two steps: first the source sentence is reordered according to a set of rewriting rules so as to reproduce the target word order; this generates a word lattice containing the most promising source permutations. Then, this candidate lattice is translated in a monotonic way from left to right. The monotonic translation step involves to consider all the possible segmentation of the candidates in translation units (segments of contiguous words) and to propose several possible translations for these source segments. The best translation is then selected by maximizing the following inference term:

$$\underset{\mathbf{t},\mathbf{a}}{\operatorname{argmax}}\ p(\mathbf{t},\mathbf{a}|\mathbf{s}) = \underset{\mathbf{t},\mathbf{a}}{\operatorname{argmax}}\ \frac{1}{\mathcal{Z}_{\mathbf{s}}} \exp\Big(\sum_{k=1}^{K} \lambda_k f_k(\mathbf{s},\mathbf{t},\mathbf{a})\Big) \tag{7}$$

[1] `http://ncode.limsi.fr`

where K feature functions (f_k) are weighted by a set of coefficients (λ_k), $\mathcal{Z}_{\mathbf{s}}$ is a normalizing factor, and $\mathbf{a}$ denotes the set of hidden variables corresponding to the reordering and segmentation of the source sentence. Since the translation step is monotonic, the peculiarity of this approach relies on the use of a n-gram translation model that estimates the probability of a sequence of bilingual units. Along with the n-gram translation model and a target n-gram language model, 13 conventional features are combined in Equation 7: 4 *lexicon models* similar to the ones used in standard phrase-based systems; 6 *lexicalized reordering models* [37, 15] aimed at predicting the orientation of the next translation unit; a "weak" distance-based *distortion model*; and finally a *word-bonus model* and a *tuple-bonus model* which compensate for the system preference for short translations.

In the following experiments, we use the state-of-the-art system submitted to the WMT 13 campaign [5]. This large-scale system is fully described in [1] and was built using all the available data provided by the workshop organizers.

The French translated transcripts are then aligned with French subtitles as described for English in Section 3.1. Empirical results showed that the automatic translation were of reasonable quality. It is worth noticing that perfect translations are not required, but they must exhibit a sufficient word recall to obtain accurate alignments with subtitles.

5. EXPERIMENTAL SETUP

5.1 Evaluation corpus

Audio tracks, subtitles and manual transcripts are obtained from the publicly available TVD corpus [33] that provides all the necessary tools to generate these resources (either from physical DVDs of the series or from the Internet).

For evaluation purposes, reference annotations of the English audio tracks are obtained from previous work on the very same TV series [36, 4]. These reference annotations contains the speech turns of the five main characters of the series (*Sheldon*, *Leonard*, *Penny*, *Howard* and *Raj*) with all secondary characters grouped into a sixth class (*other*). Though they are not used here, it is worth mentioning that the *non-speech* regions are also segmented into several subclasses such as *music*, *silence* or *laughter*. Note that reference annotations are only available for the English audio tracks. Therefore, although the French track is used to improve the English one, the speaker identification approach cannot be directly evaluated for French alone.

5.2 Evaluation protocol

Experiments are conducted on the first six episodes of the first season of *The Big Bang Theory* TV series because manual speech turns annotations are only available for these very episodes. This amounts to a total duration of approximately two hours (each episode being twenty minutes long).

Due to the relatively limited size of the evaluation corpus, we opted for the leave-one-out cross-validation paradigm. Putting one episode aside, all other episodes are used to train both speech activity detection and speaker identification models. These models are then applied on the previously unseen test episode. This process is repeated for each episode and reported values are averaged over each run.

5.3 Evaluation metrics

Speech activity detection results are reported using three complementary evaluation metrics. We define the *Detection error rate* (DER) as the ratio of the duration incorrectly classified as *speech* or *non-speech* over the total duration of the episode. *Precision* is the ratio of the total duration reported as *speech* that is indeed annotated as *speech* in the reference annotation. *Recall* is the ratio of the total duration of *speech* according to the reference annotation that is is indeed detected as *speech* in the hypothesis.

Speaker identification results are reported using *Identification error rate* (IER), defined as follows:

$$\text{IER} = \frac{\text{miss} + \text{fa} + \text{confusion}}{\text{speech}} \tag{8}$$

where speech is the total duration of *speech* according to the reference annotation, miss (respectively fa) is the total duration of segments incorrectly classified as *non-speech* (resp. *speech*) and confusion is the total duration of *speech* segments whose detected label is incorrect. In other words, it is a compound metric that accounts for both speech turns detection and identification errors.

5.4 Implementation details

All three modules (speech activity detection, speech turn segmentation and speech turn identification) rely on Mel-Frequency Cepstral Coefficients (MFCC) features extracted every 16ms from a 32ms Hamming sliding window, using *Yaafe* open-source toolkit [25]. For speech activity detection, we use 12 MFCCs and energy first derivative, and 16 Gaussians with diagonal covariance matrix for each state (*speech* and *non-speech*). For speech turn segmentation, we use 12 MFCCs and energy, 1s-long left/right windows with a sliding step of 100ms. Speech turn identification relies on 13 MFCCs, their first and second derivatives and the energy first and second derivatives. The UBM is made of 256 Gaussians with diagonal covariance. Both GMM and HMM implementations are based on the *scikit-learn* toolkit [29]. Finally, bilingual fusion parameter α is set to 0.5 in our experiments – thus giving the same weight to both English and French tracks.

5.5 Reproducible research

Alongside the reproducible corpus, the source code necessary to reproduce and evaluate the results of all speaker identification experiments (including feature extraction, speech activity detection, speech turn segmentation and classification) is available as open-source software from the corpus webpage (`tvd.niderb.fr`).

6. RESULTS

6.1 Speech activity detection

The first set of experiments aims at showing that one can rely solely on DVD subtitles to train a speech activity detection module in a weakly supervised fashion. Table 1 compares the performance obtained by the fully supervised (*i.e.* trained using reference annotations) and weakly supervised (*i.e.* trained using readily available subtitles time spans) speech activity detection.

It shows that the latter achieves performance nearly as good as the former (8.1% *vs.* 7.8%), though they differ in

Approach	Subtitles	Supervised	Unsupervised
DER	19.8%	**7.8%**	**8.1%**
Precision	74.6%	94.8%	91.2%
Recall	95.6%	90.4%	94.1%

Table 1: Speech activity detection.

their behavior (better recall for the weakly supervised approach and better precision for the fully supervised one). Column *Subtitles* gives us a first explanation of why this is happening. It shows that subtitles cover most (95.6%) *speech* regions but also contain 25.4% of *non-speech* regions – therefore leading to a weakly supervised approach with an expected tendency to detect *non-speech* segments as *speech*.

6.2 Speaker identification

The second set of experiments focuses on speaker identification. Results are reported in Table 2 depending on whether identification is applied on *reference* speech turns (*i.e.* with perfect speech activity detection and speech turns segmentation) or speech turns obtained *automatically* via the fully/weakly supervised speech activity detection modules.

Speaker identification approach	Segmentation		
	Reference	Fully supervised	Weakly supervised
Oracle	10.0%	24.5%	25.4%
Labeled subtitles	12.8%	27.0%	28.2%
Fully supervised	18.6%	35.9%	37.9%
Weakly supervised	18.5%	35.6%	37.8%

Table 2: Speaker identification error rate (IER) with manual or automatic speech turn segmentation.

For a given speech turn, the *oracle* always projects onto it the correct reference label. If the reference label is a secondary character, then the oracle chooses the most frequent main character (here *Sheldon*). In case of ambiguity (*e.g.* when the speech turn covers more than one reference label), it is solved by choosing the reference label with maximum overlap duration. Therefore, its errors result either from secondary characters (for which no model is trained) or from segmentation errors (*i.e.* detected speech turns that actually cover speech turns of multiple characters). Its performance allows to estimate a lower bound of the impact of segmentation errors on other approaches. In particular, it shows that secondary characters account for only 10% of total speech duration and that incorrect speech activity detection and segmentation adds another 15.4% errors in total.

The *labeled subtitles* approach projects labeled subtitles (obtained in Section 3.1) onto the speech turns in the same way as the *oracle* does with reference labels. Its performance can be used as a measure of how noisy the data used for training the *weakly supervised* approach are. Moreover, its performance close to that of the *oracle* also indicates that, when subtitles and transcripts are available, one should use them directly instead of relying on automatic processing.

Finally, the *fully supervised* (resp. *weakly supervised*) approach rely on reference annotations (resp. automatically labeled subtitles) to train models for the five main characters. We conclude that it is not necessary to go through the costly process of manual annotation to train a speaker identification system. Indeed, relying on automatically obtained coarse annotations lead to the exact same overall error rates (19% for perfect segmentation and 38% for automatic segmentation). The p-value of 78% obtained in a *paired-samples t-test* confirms that the performance of the two approaches are not statistically different from each other.

6.3 Bilingual speaker identification

Finally, the last set of experiments is related to bilingual fusion as described in Section 4.1. Table 3 shows that bilingual (English and French) speaker identification significantly improves monolingual (English) speaker identification performance (down to 32.8% from 37.8%). A detailed analysis of the error rate shows that confusion errors on the five main characters are reduced from 7.1% to 2.1% – corresponding to a relative improvement of 70%. Most of the remaining errors are coming either from speech segmentation (15.4%) or secondary characters (15.3%) with no associated models.

	IER	Confusion	
		all characters	5 main char.
English	37.8%	22.5%	7.1%
Bilingual	32.8%	17.5%	2.1%
Improvement	−13%	−22%	**−70%**

Table 3: Bilingual speaker identification for $\alpha = 0.5$

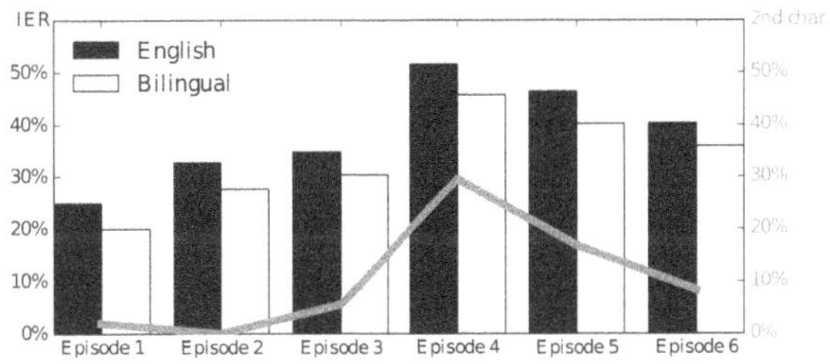

Figure 4: Performance breakdown per episode. Superimposed is the ratio of total speech duration uttered by secondary characters.

As highlighted by Figure 4, absolute improvement is consistent across all 6 episodes, on average 5% with a small standard deviation of 0.7%. Moreover, a *paired-samples t-test* (p-value $< 0.01\%$) confirms that the bilingual approach statistically and significantly outperforms the monolingual one. Additionally, note that the variation of performance between episodes is mostly explained by the ratio of total speech duration uttered by secondary characters for which no biometric models are available.

Though α was arbitrary set to 0.5 in the reported results, Figure 5 allows to better understand its influence on the overall performance. It shows that combining English and French approaches always outperforms the English-only system, whichever value is chosen for α. However, we notice the unexpected property that French speaker identification performs better than its English counterpart, even though the task is evaluated on the English track. This could mean that French actors' voices are easier to distinguish from each other than original actors' voices.

Figure 6 provides additional insight at the complementary information provided by the multilingual audio tracks.

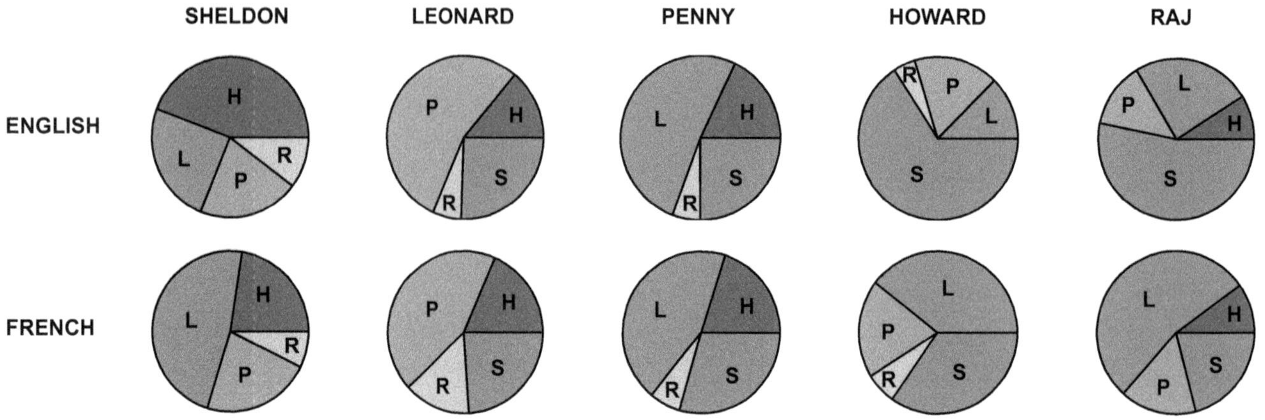

Figure 6: Distribution of confusion errors for each language and each main character (*Sheldon* (S), *Leonard* (L), *Penny* (P), *Howard* (H) and *Raj* (R)). For instance, the top-left pie chart shows that *Sheldon* is mostly mistaken for *Howard* by the English speaker identification module.

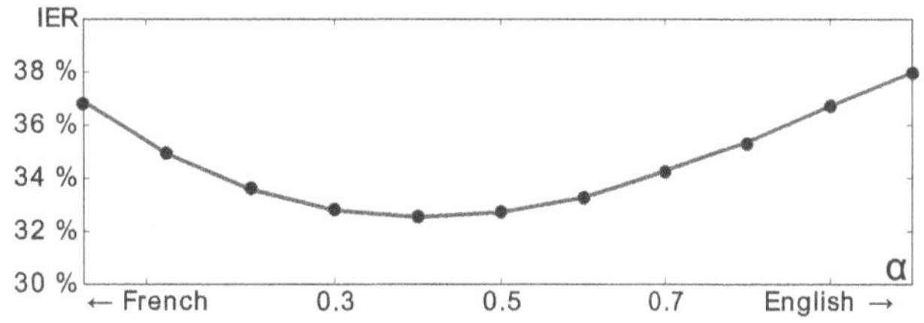

Figure 5: Influence of parameter α on the overall multilingual speaker identification performance.

While *Penny* – the only female character – is mostly confused with *Leonard* by both English and French systems, the English confusion patterns for *Sheldon*, *Howard* and *Raj* strongly differ from the French ones. In English *Sheldon* and *Howard* are mainly mistaken for each other, while in French both are mostly confused with *Leonard*. This confirms our initial motivation for multilingual speaker identification and explains why a simple fusion approach is able to circumvent monolingual confusions by leveraging complementary multilingual behaviors: two characters with similar voices in one language are unlikely to be confusable in the other language.

7. CONCLUSION

In this paper, we described a weakly supervised speaker identification system focusing on main characters of TV series. It relies on the combination of DVD subtitles and fan-made transcripts available on the Internet. It reaches the same overall performance as would a system trained using costly manual annotations (both for speech activity detection and speaker identification). Leveraging bilingual (English and French) audio tracks, we were able to further reduce main characters speaker identification errors from 7% to 2% (a 70% relative improvement).

Once the proposed system is trained, DVD subtitles and fan-made transcripts are no longer necessary to automatically detect and tag main characters speech turns as soon as a new episode airs. However, in case subtitles and/or transcripts are available, experimental results reported in Table 1 show that one should preferably rely on automatically *labeled subtitles* using the proposed alignment technique.

The two remaining main sources of errors of the proposed approaches are imperfect speech turn segmentation and missing speaker models for secondary characters (accounting for a total of 30% error rate). The proposed approach can be directly extended to secondary characters as long as they appear in at least one episode for which both subtitles and transcripts are available. However, we have yet to evaluate the influence of adding extra speaker models on the overall performance of speech turn identification. As far as speech turn segmentation is concerned, the shortness of speech turns and fast interactions between characters is a serious problem that needs to be addressed in the future.

Acknowledgments

This work was done in the context of the QCOMPERE project (funded by ANR) and the CHIST-ERA CAMOMILE project (funded by ANR, FNR and Tübitak).

8. REFERENCES

[1] A. Allauzen, N. Pécheux, Q. K. Do, M. Dinarelli, T. Lavergne, A. Max, H.-S. Le, and F. Yvon. LIMSI @ WMT13. In *Proceedings of the Eighth Workshop on Statistical Machine Translation*, pages 62–69, Sofia, Bulgaria, 2013. Association for Computational Linguistics.

[2] C. Barras and J.-L. Gauvain. Feature and Score Normalization for Speaker Verification of Cellular Data. In *Proceedings of the International Conference on Acoustics, Speech, and Signal Processing*, volume 2, pages 49–52, 2003.

[3] C. Barras, X. Zhu, S. Meignier, and J.-L. Gauvain. Multi-Stage Speaker Diarization of Broadcast News. *IEEE Transactions on Audio, Speech and Language Processing*, 14(5):1505–1512, 2006.

[4] M. Bäuml, M. Tapaswi, and R. Stiefelhagen. Semi-supervised Learning with Constraints for Person Identification in Multimedia Data. In *International Conference on Computer Vision and Pattern Recognition*, 2013.

[5] O. Bojar, C. Buck, C. Callison-Burch, C. Federmann, B. Haddow, P. Koehn, C. Monz, M. Post, R. Soricut, and L. Specia. Findings of the 2013 Workshop on Statistical Machine Translation. In *Proceedings of the Eighth Workshop on Statistical Machine Translation*, pages 1–44, Sofia, Bulgaria, 2013.

[6] H. Bredin. Segmentation of TV Shows into Scenes using Speaker Diarization and Speech Recognition. In *International Conference on Acoustics, Speech, and Signal Processing*, Kyoto, Japan, March 2012.

[7] H. Bredin, A. Laurent, A. Sarkar, V.-B. Le, S. Rosset, and C. Barras. Person Instance Graphs for Named Speaker Identification in TV Broadcast. In *Odyssey 2014, The Speaker and Language Recognition Workshop*, Joensuu, Finland, June 2014.

[8] H. Bredin and J. Poignant. Integer Linear Programming for Speaker Diarization and Cross-Modal Identification in TV Broadcast. In *Proceedings of the 14th Annual Conference of the International Speech Communication Association*, Lyon, France, August 2013.

[9] C. Callison-Burch, P. Koehn, C. Monz, M. Post, R. Soricut, and L. Specia. Findings of the 2012 Workshop on Statistical Machine Translation. In *Proceedings of the Seventh Workshop on Statistical Machine Translation*, pages 10–51, Montréal, Canada, 2012.

[10] L. Canseco, L. Lamel, and J.-L. Gauvain. A Comparative Study Using Manual and Automatic Transcriptions for Diarization. In *Proceedings of the IEEE Automatic Speech Recognition and Understanding Workshop*, pages 415–419, 2005.

[11] F. Casacuberta and E. Vidal. Machine Translation with Inferred Stochastic Finite-State transducers. *Computational Linguistics*, 30(3):205–225, 2004.

[12] S. S. Chen and P. Gopalakrishnan. Speaker, Environment and Channel Change Detection and Clustering via the Bayesian Information Criterion. In *DARPA Broadcast News Transcription and Understanding Workshop*, Virginia, USA, 1998.

[13] T. Cour, B. Sapp, A. Nagle, and B. Taskar. Talking Pictures: Temporal Grouping and Dialog-Supervised Person Recognition. In *International Conference on Computer Vision and Pattern Recognition*, 2010.

[14] J. M. Crego and J. B. Mariño. Improving Statistical MT by Coupling Reordering and Decoding. *Machine Translation*, 20(3):199–215, 2006.

[15] J. M. Crego, F. Yvon, and J. B. Mariño. N-code: an open-source bilingual N-gram SMT toolkit. *Prague Bulletin of Mathematical Linguistics*, 96:49–58, 2011.

[16] Y. Estève, S. Meignier, P. Deléglise, and J. Mauclair. Extracting true speaker identities from transcriptions. In *Proceedings of the International Speech Communication Association*, pages 2601–2604, 2007.

[17] M. Everingham, J. Sivic, and A. Zisserman. “Hello! My name is... Buffy” Automatic Naming of Characters in TV Video. In *British Machine Vision Conference*, 2006.

[18] G. Friedland, L. R. Gottlieb, and A. Janin. Joke-o-mat: browsing sitcoms punchline by punchline. *ACM Multimedia*, pages 1115–1116, 2009.

[19] J.-L. Gauvain and C.-H. Lee. Maximum A Posteriori Estimation for Multivariate Gaussian Mixture Observations of Markov Chains. *IEEE Transactions on Speech and Audio Processing*, 2(2):291–298, April 1994.

[20] V. Jousse, S. Petitrenaud, S. Meignier, Y. Estève, and C. Jacquin. Automatic Named Identification of Speakers using Diarization and ASR Systems. In *Proceedings of the International Conference on Acoustics, Speech, and Signal Processing*, Taïpei, Taïwan, April 2009.

[21] J. Kahn, O. Galibert, L. Quintard, M. Carre, A. Giraudel, and P. Joly. A Presentation of the REPERE Challenge. In *International Workshop on Content-Based Multimedia Indexing*, pages 1–6, 2012.

[22] P. Koehn. *Statistical Machine Translation*. Cambridge University Press, New York, NY, USA, 1st edition, 2010.

[23] J. B. Mariño, R. E. Banchs, J. M. Crego, A. de Gispert, P. Lambert, J. A. Fonollosa, and M. R. Costa-Jussà. N-gram-based Machine Translation. *Computational Linguistics*, 32(4):527–549, 2006.

[24] A. F. Martin and M. A. Przybocki. The NIST 1999 Speaker Recognition Evaluation - An Overview. *Digital Signal Processing*, 10(1–3):1–18, 2000.

[25] B. Mathieu, S. Essid, T. Fillon, J. Prado, and G.Richard. YAAFE, an Easy to Use and Efficient Audio Feature Extraction Software. In *Proceedings of the 11th ISMIR Conference*, Utrecht, Netherlands, 2010.

[26] J. Mauclair, S. Meignier, and Y. Estève. Speaker Diarization : about whom the Speaker is Talking? In *IEEE Odyssey*, 2006.

[27] E. Myers. An O(ND) Difference Algorithm and its Variations. *Algorithmica*, 1(2):251–266, 1986.

[28] R. Nelken and S. Shieber. Towards Robust Context-Sensitive Sentence Alignment for Monolingual Corpora. In *Proceedings of the 11th Conference of the European Chapter of the ACL*, 2006.

[29] F. Pedregosa, G. Varoquaux, A. Gramfort, V. Michel, B. Thirion, O. Grisel, M. Blondel, P. Prettenhofer, R. Weiss, V. Dubourg, J. Vanderplas, A. Passos, D. Cournapeau, M. Brucher, M. Perrot, and E. Duchesnay. Scikit-learn: Machine Learning in Python. *Journal of Machine Learning Research*, 12:2825–2830, 2011.

[30] J. Poignant, L. Besacier, V.-B. Le, S. Rosset, and G. Quénot. Unsupervised Naming of Speakers in Broadcast TV: using Written Names, Pronounced Names or Both? In *Proceedings of the 14th Annual Conference of the International Speech Communication Association*, Lyon, France, August 2013.

[31] L. R. Rabiner. A Tutorial on Hidden Markov Models and Selected Applications in Speech Recognition. *Proceedings of the IEEE*, 77(2):257–286, 1989.

[32] D. A. Reynolds, T. F. Quatieri, and R. B. Dunn. Speaker Verification Using Adapted Gaussian Mixture Models. *Digital Signal Processing*, 10(1-3):19–41, 2000.

[33] A. Roy, C. Guinaudeau, H. Bredin, and C. Barras. TVD: a Reproducible and Multiply Aligned TV Series Dataset. In *LREC 2014, 9th Language Resources and Evaluation Conference*, 2014.

[34] J. Sivic, M. Everingham, and A. Zisserman. "Who are you?" - Learning Person Specific Classifiers from Video. In *Proceedings of the IEEE Conference on Computer Vision and Pattern Recognition*, 2009.

[35] J. Sivic and A. Zisserman. Efficient Visual Search of Videos Cast as Text Retrieval. *IEEE Transactions on Pattern Analysis and Machine Intelligence*, 31(4):591–606, 2009.

[36] M. Tapaswi, M. Bäuml, and R. Stiefelhagen. "Knock! Knock! Who is it?" Probabilistic Person Identification in TV-Series. In *International Conference on Computer Vision and Pattern Recognition*, 2012.

[37] C. Tillmann. A unigram orientation model for statistical machine translation. In *Proceedings of HLT-NAACL*, pages 101–104, 2004.

[38] S. E. Tranter. Who Really Spoke When? Finding Speaker Turns and Identities in Broadcast News Audio. In *Proceedings of the International Conference on Acoustics, Speech, and Signal Processing*, pages 1013–1016, 2006.

[39] S. E. Tranter and D. A. Reynolds. An Overview of Automatic Speaker Diarization Systems. *IEEE Transactions on Audio, Speech, and Language Processing*, 14(5):1557–1565, September.

What's Making that Sound ?

Kai Li
Dept. of Electrical Engineering & Computer Science
University of Central Florida
Orlando, FL 32816, USA
kaili@eecs.ucf.edu

Jun Ye
Dept. of Electrical Engineering & Computer Science
University of Central Florida
Orlando, FL 32816, USA
jye@cs.ucf.edu

Kien A. Hua
Dept. of Electrical Engineering & Computer Science
University of Central Florida
Orlando, FL 32816, USA
kienhua@eecs.ucf.edu

ABSTRACT

In this paper, we investigate techniques to localize the sound source in video made using one microphone. The visual object whose motion generates the sound is located and segmented based on the synchronization analysis of object motion and audio energy. We first apply an effective region tracking algorithm to segment the video into a number of spatial-temporal region tracks, each representing the temporal evolution of an appearance-coherent image structure (i.e., object). We then extract the motion features of each object as its average acceleration in each frame. Meanwhile, Short-term Fourier Transform is applied to the audio signal to extract audio energy feature as the audio descriptor. We further impose a nonlinear transformation on both audio and visual descriptors to obtain the audio and visual codes in a common rank correlation space. Finally, the correlation between an object and the audio signal is simply evaluated by computing the Hamming distance between the audio and visual codes generated in previous steps. We evaluate the proposed method both qualitatively and quantitatively using a number of challenging test videos. In particular, the proposed method is compared with a state-of-the-art audiovisual source localization algorithm. The results demonstrate the superior performance of the proposed algorithm in spatial-temporal localization and segmentation of audio sources in the visual domain.

Categories and Subject Descriptors

I.4.0 [**Computing Methodologies**]: Image Processing and Computer Vision—*General*; G.3 [**Mathematics of Computing**]: Probability and Statistics—*correlation and regression analysis*

Keywords

Audiovisual processing; multimodal analysis; comparative reasoning; winner-take-all hash

1. INTRODUCTION

MM'14, MM '14, November 03 - 07 2014, Orlando, FL, USA

http://dx.doi.org/10.1145/2647868.2654936.

Multimodal information fusion concerns the study of integrating information from multiple sensory modalities that describe the same event. It has been shown for long that combining complementary information from different modalities can improve the performance of a system that uses only a single modality [12][4][14]. An intuitive explanation to this fact is that real-life events are inherently multimodal, while an unimodal system utilizes only a portion of the available information leaving the rest wasted. One particular research area that takes advantage of multimodal information fusion is audiovisual analysis that combines visual information with correlated audio information for improved performance in tasks such as event detection [10], speech recognition [23], video concept classification [15] etc.

Although audio and visual modality provides complementary information to each other, one should be aware that, they may also bring in noise. For example, combining unrelated audio background in the detection of a visual event may undermine rather than boost the performance of an audiovisual event detection system; an irrelevant talking face might distract the audiovisual speech recognition system from focusing on the right person whose speech is being interpreted. The above problems can be effectively alleviated if the system can correctly associate the audio signal with the right sound source in the video. The ability to associate sound with the right visual object is essential for many applications. For example, a pan-tilt camera can automatically follow the active speaker in video conferencing [8];the robot can correctly identify the target that is speaking to her during interaction with a human. Other applications include audio-video stream synchronization [13], audio source separation [24], lip reading [12], object tracking [3][26] etc.

In this paper, we address the audiovisual correlation problem in general videos captured using a single microphone. The sound sources we deal with in this paper is not restricted to any specific type (e.g. a talking person), but rather it could be any object whose motion generates sound. For example, the sound source could be a musical instrument, a talking face, or even a bouncing basketball. Moreover, we aim to accurately segment out the sounding object (i.e. an image structure). Such audiovisual correlation problem is known to be hard for several reasons: there are always multiple distracting motions in the video occasionally synchronous with the soundtrack; signals captured by audio and visual sensors are essentially different in terms of spatial-temporal resolution and semantic meaning.

Most previous research on sound source localization either

rely on multiple microphones in controlled environment [24], or deal with quasi-stationary [6] or specific sound sources such as a talking face [18]. Some recent work [2][22][16] attempt to remove such restrictions and achieve sound source localization in general videos. However, few of them attempt segmentation of the audiovisual object, that is, they merely identify a number of pixels scattered around the object. We believe cross-modal localization of image structures is semantically more meaningful than identifying independent pixels. To achieve such goal, we propose a novel method for simultaneous localization and segmentation of the visual object that is most correlated with the primary audio signals. We use a two-step frame segmentation followed by a label propagation procedure to represent the entire video as a number of spatial-temporal region tracks, each representing the temporal evolution of a semantic object. The motion features of those spatial-temporal tracks are used as the visual descriptors of the objects. The audio energy descriptors are used for audio signals to capture the temporal changing pattern. Finally, a powerful yet efficient comparative reasoning technique, the Winner-Take-All Hash [25], is applied to audio and visual descriptors to generate the audio and visual hash codes. The measure of correlations between visual objects and audio signals are finally computed as the Hamming distance between the audio and visual hash codes.

The remainder of the paper is organized as follows: Section 2 briefly reviews the related work. Section 3 gives an overview of the proposed method. Section 4 explains audio and visual features we used for correlation analysis. Section 5 describes our audiovisual correlation method. In Section 6, we present the experimental results on the test videos. Finally, the paper is concluded in Section 7.

2. RELATED WORK

In controlled environments such as multimedia conferencing rooms [26] and user interfaces [24], one or multiple cameras with microphone arrays have been used for speaker localization. Some other works [8] also use multiple microphones for audiovisual tracking [3][8]. However, such controlled environment and special devices are not typical of general videos, for example, taken by a cellphone or a surveillance camera, thus limiting the applicability of such techniques. A more challenging problem is to locate the visual sound source in videos captured with a single microphone by means of audiovisual correlation analysis.

The existing work that localizes visual objects associated with audio signals using a single microphone approximately fall into two categories: pixel-level localization [16], [22], [2], [6] and object level localization and/or segmentation [13], [5], [19], [7]. In [16], Kdiron et al. propose to use Canonical Correlation Analysis (CCA) to find the image pixels that are most correlated with audio signals. The authors reveal the ill-posedness of CCA due to the high dimensionality of visual features and insufficient samples of stationary signals, and exploit the spatial sparsity of audiovisual events to seek sparse solution with L-1 norm. Sigg [22] further consolidates the problem of CCA in its original form and presents a reformulation that incorporates nonnegativity and sparsity constraints on the coefficients of projection directions. Through this reformulation, the author is able to locate sound sources in a test movie and separate the corresponding audio signals by filtering. Barzelay et al. [2] address the problem of audiovisual source separation in both modalities. They represent the audio and visual signals as audio and visual onsets. The audio and visual onsets measure the drastic change of audio and visual features respectively. The correlation of audio onset with each visual onset is evaluated using a simple coincidence-based measure. A major drawback of pixel-level correlation technqiues is that they are sensitive to visual noises and the localization results (i.e. isolated pixels) do not carry too much high-level semantic meaning. Therefore, those methods are generally not very useful for higher-level reasoning that builds upon the results of audiovisual correlation.

On the other hand, object-level correlation techniques aim at a higher level of abstraction that carries more semantic information about what makes the sound. Casanovas et al. [6] propose to use non-linear diffusion to focus on the audio source in visual domain. The diffusion process is controlled by a diffusion coeffecient based on an estimate of the synchrony between audio energy and motion in the video. The result of the diffusion process is an image region whose motion is most consistent with changes of audio energy. In [18], Liu et al. propose an algorithm to find quasi-stationary speaker faces using audiovisual correlation. The video in a time window is analyzed and the audio source is found by using Quadratic Mutual Information. The analyzed results are incorporated into a Graph-cut based image segmentation to extract the face region of the speaker. The same authors further extend their work to locate general non-stationary sound sources [19]. In this later work, a motion inconsistency measure of small spatial-temporal patches (ST-patch) centered at a pixel is used as the pixel's visual feature. A similar inconsistency measure is defined for audio energy as the audio feature. The audiovisual correlation is analyzed using the incremental Mutual Information, which is able to find each pixel's visual trajectory that best matches the audio energy change. Similar to [18], the results of such audiovisual analysis is fed into a segmentation algorithm to extract the sounding object. In [5], the video signals are first decomposed into a number of video atoms. The sound source is subsequently reconstructed by clustering the visual atoms that have a high audiovisual correlation. This technique tends to extract circular-shaped region irrespective of the original shape of the actual source, because all visual atoms within a radius are used in the reconstruction. The authors address this limitation in [7] by using video diffusion followed by a Graph cut segmentation procedure that keeps together pixels in regions with high audiovisual synchrony.

Those techniques are similar in the sense that they first seek audiovisual correlation at a finer level (i.e. pixels or small atoms) and then apply clustering or segmentation afterwards to group pixels based on the synchrony. The limitation of such methods is that the extracted sounding object boundaries are quite irregular due to the noise in fine-grained synchronization analysis and the shape of the object hardly observes the shape of the actual object.

A different method that reverses the above correlation-before-segmentation process is proposed in [13]. [13] first oversegments each video frame into small segments. K-means clustering is then applied to segments in the entire video such that each resultant spatial-temporal visual cluster represents an object. The velocity and acceleration of visual clusters and the audio Mel-frequency Cepstral Coefficients (MFCCs) are used as the audio and visual features respectively. Canonical Correlation Analysis (CCA) is finally used to identify the objects most correlated with the audio signal. Our work also adopts the correlation-after-segmentation scheme. However, a major difference is that we use region tracking rather than clustering to decompose the video into a number of spatial-temporal region tracks. Our method is able to obtain a consistent labeling of objects that move over a large area. Such spatial-temporal region track representation effectively lends itself to independent motion pattern analysis of each object present in the scene. Another primary distinction is that [13] seeks the maximum correlation of two modalities by means of linear feature transformation (i.e. CCA), while the correlation analysis we utilize is based on a nonlinear transformation of the audio and visual features.

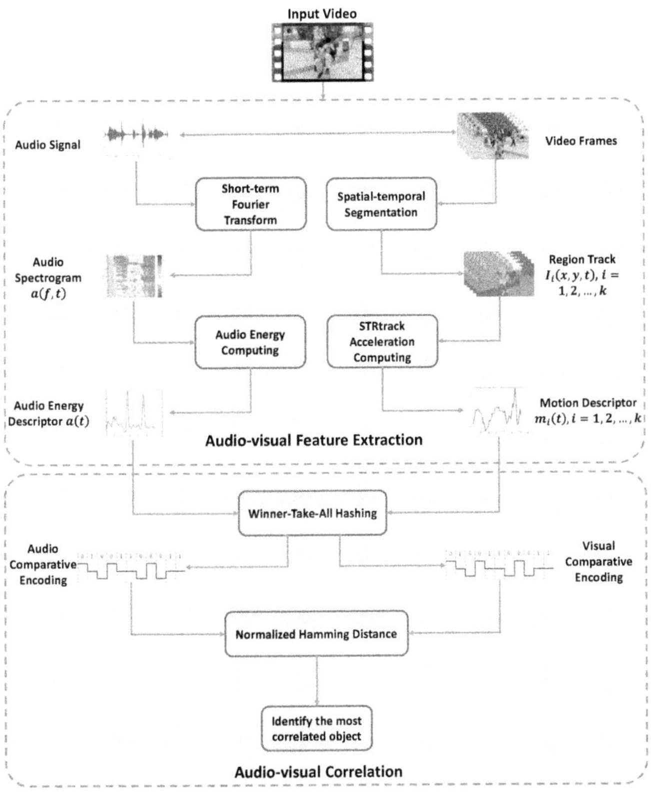

Figure 1: Block diagram of the proposed audiovisual source localization method. In the audiovisual feature extraction step, audio and visual features are extracted independently. The audio spectrogram is computed by applying short-term fourier transform to the audio samples with proper framing. Next, audio power spectrum is integrated over all frequencies to get the audio energy. For the video frames, a two-step segmentation is applied to each frame, and a region tracking algorithm is used to obtain a consistent labeling of all videos. Regions sharing the same label form a spatial-temporal region track. Each region track i is represented by a single vector $[m_i(1), m_i(2), \cdots, m_i(T)]^T$, where $m_i(t)$ is computed as the average acceleration of that region track at frame t. Both audio and visual features go through the same hashing that generates a single audio code for the audio signal and one visual code for each of the spatial temporal region track. The correlation between each region track and the audio signal is simply computed as the Hamming distance between each visual code and audio code. The most correlated objects can be selected by sorting the correlation measure, or selecting those greater than a threshold.

3. AN OVERVIEW OF THE METHOD

This section provides a brief overview of the general steps of the proposed algorithm, leaving the details to be discussed in Section 4 and Section 5.

As illustrated in Fig. 1, the overall process involves two phases: audiovisual feature extraction and audiovisual correlation. In the audiovisual feature extraction phase, audio and visual descriptors are extracted independently. The audio descriptors we use is the smoothed audio energy. Briefly, this is obtained by applying short-term fourier transform to the raw audio signal followed by an integration over all frequencies at each time instant. The resultant audio energy descriptor is further smoothed using a Gaussian filter. The audio energy descriptor represents the change of audio signal strength over time, which we believe is caused by correlated motion in the visual domain. Such audio representation bridges the sampling rate gap between audio and visual signals, thus making it possible to perform audiovisual correlation analysis under the same temporal resolution.

Compared with audio signals, visual signals are characterized by high spatial resolution. We bridge this gap by first using a region tracking algorithm to consistently label the same image structure (i.e. regions in different frames that corresponds to the same semantic object/part) across all video frames. Each label generated in this manner indexes a spatial-temporal region track (STRtrack). In this way, the whole video $I(x, y, t)$ is decomposed into a set of N STRtracks $\{I_1(x, y, t), I_2(x, y, t), \cdots, I_N(x, y, t)\}$, where $t = 1, 2, \cdots, T$ is the frame index, and x, y is pixel's coordinate in a frame. For the ith STRtrack, its motion descriptor in t^{th} frame $m_i(t)$ is computed as the average acceleration of all pixels labeled as i in that frame. In this way, the video is compactly represented as a number of visual descriptors $\{m_1(t), m_2(t), \cdots, m_N(t)\}$.

The audiovisual correlation takes as input the resultant audio and visual descriptors and outputs the correlation scores χ_i for each STRtrack. We believe that the sounding object's motion pattern must be highly correlated to the audio energy in some feature space. We propose to capture this similarity using a nonlinear feature transformation technique, the Winner-Take-All (WTA) hash [25]. The correlation between audio and visual modalities is simply computed as the Hamming distance between the two WTA has codes.

4. AUDIO AND VIDEO REPRESENTATION

The compact representation of audio and video signals are critical for the effectiveness of the proposed method. Our motivation for the proposed audio and video representation is to seek a compact yet informative representation that retains the most relevant information in both modalities and allows for audiovisual comparison in a common feature space.

4.1 Audio Representation

The audio signal $f(t)$ is transformed into the time frequency domain using the Short-term Fourier Transform [1] (STFT) that provides simultaneous time and frequency localization. The capability of STFT for analyzing time-varing, non-stationary signals makes it applicable for general sound sources.

In detail, the signal is first framed according to the frame rate of the video such that each audio frame corresponds to a

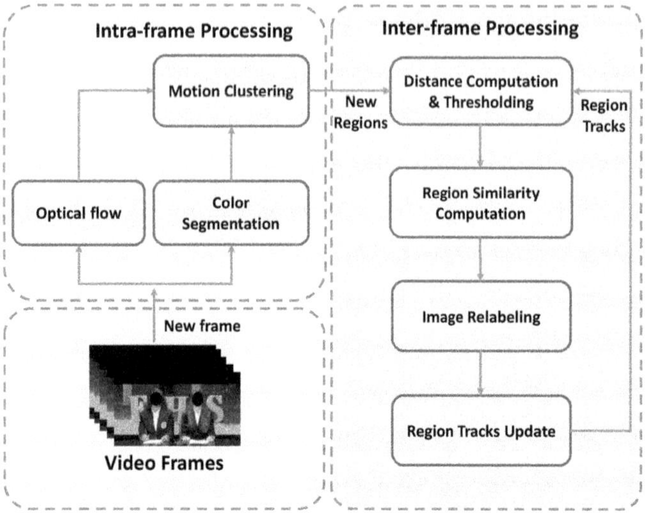

Figure 2: Block diagram of the proposed region tracking algorithm. The algorithm processes video in a streaming manner starting from the first frame. Optical flow and the color segmentation are performed in parallel for each new coming frame. Small regions of color segmentation are then clustered using optical flow information. The initial set of spatial-temporal region tracks are created using clustered regions in the first frame. Regions in later frames are compared with existing region tracks and are added to the right track based on location and appearance. At the same time, regions in the new frame are relabeled in accordance with their instances in previous frames.

video frame. The framing window size h is chosen such that neighboring windows overlap by 50% of the window size. Fourier transform is then applied to the sampling points within each window to get the spectrogram of the audio signal at that frame. Finally, the audio energy feature $a(t)$ is attained by integrating the spectrogram over all frequencies. Formally, the above process can be represented as

$$a(t) = \int_0^\infty \int_0^T f(t').W(t'-t).e^{-j2\pi ft'}dt'df,$$

where T is the length of the audio, and the windowing function $W(t)$ is defined as

$$W(t) = \begin{cases} 1 & \text{if } |t| < h/2 \\ 0 & \text{otherwise.} \end{cases}$$

The resultant audio energy descriptor $a(t)$ is further filtered using a 1-D Gaussian kernel. Intuitively, the audio energy descriptor captures the changing patterns of audio signal strength in the same temporal resolution as the video frames.

4.2 Video Representation

The basic idea of the proposed video representation method is to extract and analyze the motion patterns of all objects present in a scene. We define an object to be an appearance-motion-coherent image structure. We aim to identify image structures corresponding to the same object across all video frames so as to analyze the object's motion patterns.

As shown in Fig. 2, we use a region tracking procedure to propagate first-frame segmentation labeling to all the rest frames. The procedure starts with a two-step segmentation for the first frame. In detail, we first apply Mean shift segmentation of the color image using LUV color features. If the resultant number of small regions is greater than a predefined threshold k, they are further clustered using location and motion features. The reason for such 2-step frame segmentation is to combine color and motion features for segmenting images into regions with highly coherent motion and appearance. To be specific, each region is represented as a 5-dimensional feature vector where the first two dimensions are the spatial centroid coordinates and the last three dimensions are the region's average LUV color values in the color-coded optical flow image. Formally, we compute the forward and backward dense optical flow $\mathbf{F}^+(x, y, t)$ and $\mathbf{F}^-(x, y, t)$ for each frame, where $\mathbf{F}^+(x, y, t)$ is the 2-D flow vector at pixel (x, y) estimated between frame t and $t+1$, and $\mathbf{F}^-(x, y, t)$ is that from t to $t-1$. The average flow is computed as

$$\mathbf{F}(x, y, t) = \frac{1}{2}(\mathbf{F}^+(x, y, t) - \mathbf{F}^-(x, y, t))).$$

Since spatial coordinates and the optical flow values are in different metric spaces, they need to be transformed into a common feature space for direct concatenation and distance computation. We opt to transform the optical flow into the LUV color feature space such that color differences can be measured by the Euclidean distance. In detail, the normalized optical flow (u_x, u_y) is converted to its polar representation (ρ, θ). Then the direction θ is used to access a discretized RGB color wheel adapted from [21]. The accessed RGB values are modulated with ρ to obtain the final RGB colors. The resultant RGB color image are further transformed into the LUV color space.

After the frame segmentation procedure, each region is represented using its color histogram. Specifically, the LUV color space is quantized into $n = 5^3 = 125$ bins and the number of pixels in each bin is counted. The regions in the first frame (i.e. their color histograms) are used as instances to initialize the same number of STRtracks. A new frame first goes through the same segmentation procedure as the first frame. Then for each region in the new frame, it's assigned to one of the track based on spatial proximity and appearance similarity. Specifically, the distance between an STRtrack and a new region is computed as the Euclidean distance between the centroid coordinates of the new region and that of the most recent instance of that STRtrack. The STRtracks whose distance are within a search radius are identified as the candidate matches. The appearance similarity is computed between a new region and it's candidate STRtracks. We define the appearance similarity between a region and an STRtrack as the cosine value of the angle between the color histogram of the region and the average color histogram of all instances of that STRtrack. It's reasonable to use the average color histogram because the same object typically doesn't change too much in appearance. And the average color histogram is more robust to outliers than the color histogram of a single instance (e.g. the most recent instance). Finally, if the similarity value of the most similar STRtrack is greater than a threshold, we simply assign the new region to that STRtrack (i.e. relabel the region using the STRtrack ID). Otherwise, we create a new STRtrack and add to it the new region as the first instance.

The result of the above region tracking algorithm is a number of STRtracks each representing the temporal evolution of an object. We then extract the motion descriptor for an

STRtrack ST_i as its average acceleration. Specifically, the acceleration of a pixel (x, y) at frame t is defined as

$$\mathbf{g}(x,y,t) = \mathbf{F}^+(x,y,t) + \mathbf{F}^-(x,y,t),$$

where $\mathbf{F}^+(x,y,t)$ and $\mathbf{F}^-(x,y,t)$ is the same as defined before. The motion descriptor of ST_i at time t is therefore

$$m_i(t) = \frac{1}{|ST_i^t|} \sum_{(x,y)\in ST_i^t} ||\mathbf{g}(x,y,t)||.$$

where $|ST_i^t|$ is the number of pixels of ST_i in the tth frame. Similar to the audio descriptor, the motion descriptor $m_i(t)$ is smoothed using a Gaussian kernel to reduce the effect of visual noises. In addition, we pick the the top 15 $m_i(t)$s in terms of standard deviation as the candidates in order to filter out objects whose motion is random or minimal.

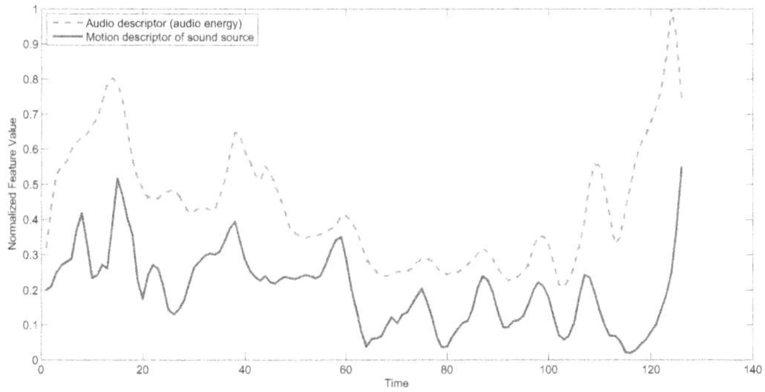

(a) Continuous Sound

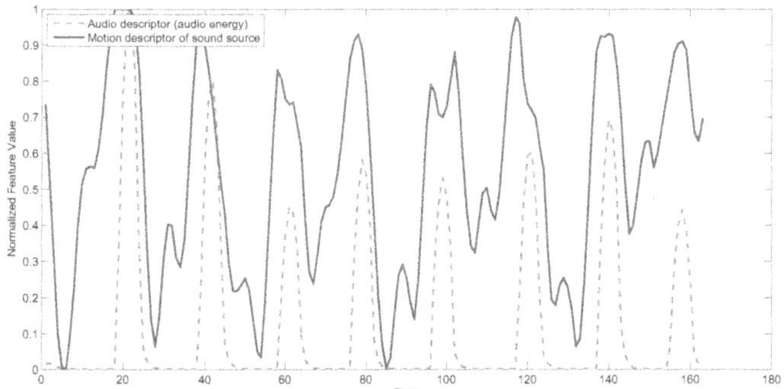

(b) Discrete Sound

Figure 3: Examples of audio descriptors and the motion descriptors of the sound source. (a) is the intermediate results of the video *Violin Yanni*. The visual descriptor represents the motion of the violin player's left hand. (b) is the intermediate result of the video *Basketball*, in which the visual descriptor describes the motion of the basketball.

5. AUDIOVISUAL CORRELATION

Audiovisual correlation is analyzed between audio and visual descriptors obtained in the previous section. We have used the temporal functions $a(t)$ and $m_i(t)s$ to represent the audio and visual descriptors. Another way to look at those functions is to consider them as a vector in the T-Dimensional feature space, where T is the number of frames. Let $\mathbf{a}$ and $\mathbf{m_i}$ represent those feature vectors, they are formally defined as

$$\mathbf{a} = [a(1), a(2), \cdots, a(T)]^T$$

and

$$\mathbf{m_i} = [m_i(1), m_i(2), \cdots, m_i(T)]^T, i = 1, 2, \cdots, k.$$

Now as both modality are in a T-D vector space, an intuitive way to measure the synchrony χ_i between object i with the audio signal is to use Euclidean distance between the two corresponding feature points. However, this does not work because the precise values of variables captured by auditory and visual sensors carry essentially different semantic meanings. In other words, a larger distance doesn't necessarily mean they are less synchronized. Nor does correlation measures such as cosine distance work well, especially for discrete sounds [1] generated by continuous motion (i.e. a bouncing basketball). Fig.3 shows two examples of the audio descriptor of a sound and the motion descriptor of that sound source. As can be observed from the examples, the two descriptors do exhibit similar changing patterns (i.e. similar relative ordering of feature values at different time instant). However, the differences are even more if we look at the precise feature values, which explains why common metrics based on the precise feature values fail to capture the correlation.

We address the above problem by performing a non-linear transformation of the original feature into the ordinal space, using the Winner-Take-All (WTA) technique. Briefly, WTA hash is a ordinal space embedding technique that captures the partial ordering statistics of the original feature dimensions. Such ordinal space embedding techniques have shown success in other tasks such as dimension reduction [20], feature extraction [11] etc. However, they have not been explored in the area of multimodal information analysis. We extract the partial ordering information encoded by ordinal space embedding in an effort to bridge the semantic gap between features in audio and visual modality.

5.1 Winner-Take-All Hash

The WTA hash is a subfamily of hashing functions introduced in [25]. WTA hash is controlled by two parameters: the number of random permutations N and window size S. Fig. 4 illustrates the computation of WTA hash for a 5-dimensional feature vector with parameters $N = 3$ and $S = 3$. The index of the maximum entry among the first S entries of a permutation Θ is chosen as the hash code for that permutation. In our example, the first permutation $[2, 1, 5, 4, 3]$ reorder the feature vector as $[0.2, 0.5, 1.0, 0.30.7]$. The index of the maximum value among the first 2 entries $[0.2, 0.5]$, is taken as the encoding for that permutation. Note that N permutations generate a length-N hash code and each code entry is an integer value between 0 and $S - 1$.

Each WTA hash function encodes a partial ordering statistics of the feature dimensions and defines an ordinal embeding of the features in the rank correlation space. An intuitive way to understand such encoding is to consider the case when $S = 2$. Choosing the first 2 entries from a random permutation is essentially same as randomly choosing 2 entries from the feature vector. If the first entry is larger, the output code is 0, and it's 1 otherwise. When N is sufficiently large, the binary code for the feature vector encodes a com-

[1] Audio signals exhibiting clear intervals of silence is referred to as discrete sounds. An example is the sound produced by a bouncing basketball. While continuous sounds refer to audio signals without clear intervals of silence, such as that generated by violin.

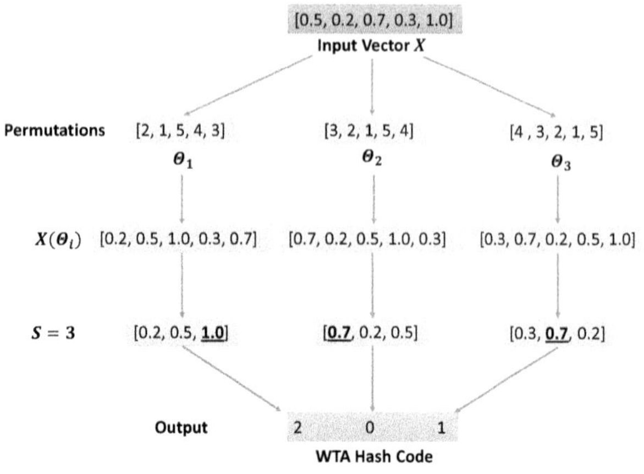

Figure 4: An example of WTA hash with 5-dimensional input vector $X = [0.5, 0.2, 0.7, 0.3, 1.0]$, $N = 3$ and $S = 3$. Θ_i is a permutation of the input vector X, and $X(\Theta_i)$ is the result of the permutation. $X(\Theta_i)$ is further windowed, resulting in a vector containing only its first S entries. Index of the maximum entry in the windowed $X(\Theta_i)$ is output as the WTA hash code for the given permutation.

plete pairwise ordering of different feature dimensions. Note that for a d-dimensional feature vector, the complete pairwise ordering can be encoded with a binary code of length $A_d^2 = d(d-1)$. Larger values of S also encodes the pairwise ordering, however with more emphasis on paring with the head of the S-sized subset of the feature dimensions.

In general, if two vectors are close in their original feature space, they must be close in the rank correlation space. However, the opposite is not true because differences in the numerical values that do not affect the ordering might have bigger effect for other metric spaces (e.g. Euclidean). This characteristic of rank correlation naturally provides certain degree of stability in face of perturbations in numerical values. Another advantage of WTA hash that merits discussion is that compared with a complete ordering, multiple partial orderings offers another degree of resilience to noise and gives considerations to local support (with $S \geq 2$) on feature dimensions. Those advantages of WTA hash makes it perfect for measuring the synchrony between signals in different modalities, such as audio and visual in our case. Synchronized signals in audio and visual modalities demonstrate similar temporal changing patterns, which are precisely the orderings of feature dimensions when we represent the signals as vectors. Therefore, we use the same WTA hash function to encode audio and visual signals for similarity computation.

5.2 Correlation Analysis

Before measuring the synchrony between audio and visual signals, we first use WTA hash to encode the partial ordering statistics of audio descriptor $\mathbf{a}$ and visual descriptors $\mathbf{m}_i$. Note that same set of random permutations are used for both audio and visual descriptors. This encoding transforms features in two different modalities into the common rank correlation space for correlation analysis. Then the synchrony $\chi(\mathbf{a}, \mathbf{m}_i)$ between a visual descriptor $\mathbf{m}_i$ and the audio, denoted as χ_i is simply

$$\chi_i = \frac{H_d(\mathbf{a}, \mathbf{m}_i)}{Dim(\mathbf{x})},$$

where $H_d(\mathbf{a}, \mathbf{m}_i)$ is the Hamming distance between them (i.e. the number of different entries). Finally, the object that corresponds to the sound source can be determined as

$$s = \arg\max_i \chi_i.$$

After identifying the sounding object, we create a confidence map and set the localization confidence for pixels belonging to this object in every frame to 1, while the rest to 0. Similar to [13], instead of dealing with binary localization confidence, the confidence map is convolved with a Gaussian kernel in both spatial and temporal domain to generate a smooth confidence surface. However, rather than fixing the standard deviation of Gaussian kernel for all videos, we make it a function of the average velocity and object size. This is reasonable as objects with large motion has less temporal locality coherency, and the temporal Gaussian kernel should therefore use smaller standard deviation. Formally, let fr be the frame rate of a video, ma be the average acceleration of the sounding object, the standard deviation of the Gaussian kernel is computed as $\sigma_t = \rho_t \cdot fr/ma$, where ρ_t is a coefficient and we set it to 0.5 in the experiments. Similarly, the spatial Gaussian kernel size should be related with the size of an object, and we define it to be $\sigma_s = \rho_s \cdot sqrt(A)$, where A is the average area of the object and ρ_s is an coefficient set to 0.2 in our experiments.

6. EXPERIMENTS

In this section, we show performances of the proposed algorithm on a number of challenging test videos. Specifically, we compared with the state-of-the-art method proposed in [13] both qualitatively and quantitatively.

We gather challenging test videos from previous research

Table 1: Experimental Parameters

Algorithm	Parameter	Value
Mean shift	Spatial bandwidth	13.0
	Range bandwidth	13.0
	Minimum area	400
Optical flow	Regularization weight	0.012
	Downsample ratio	0.75
	Width of the coarsest level	40
Frame segmentation	Maximum no. of segments	25
Region tracking	Searching radius	55
AV correlation	No. of permutations	2000
	Window size	5

and Youtube. In detail, *Violin Yanni* is used in [13]. The audience clapping in *Violin Yanni* adds much noise to the audio; *Wooden Horse* is used in [7], [13] and [16]. The swaying wooden horse in this video is uncorrelated to the audio; *Guitar Lessons*, *Student News* and *Guitar Street* are downloaded from Youtube. In *Guitar Lessons*, the unintentional movement of the player head and body are all somewhat harmonious with the sound; *Guitar Street* contains lots of background noise and moving passengers in the street; In *Student News*, the left reporter's movement occasionally sycrhonizes with the right one's speech. In addition, we also created an additional test video *Basketball* with a distracting moving cushion, which is challenging as the motion of the sounding objects (i.e. basketball) is not constrained within a small range.

The proposed framework takes only a few parameters other than those required by Mean shift [9] and optical flow [17] component algorithms. The primary parameters used in the experiments are summarized in Table 1 unless otherwise specified. We also implemented the algorithm proposed in [13] for comparison. The three parameters for the Quick-Shift algorithm used in [13], namely, the tradeoff between the color and spatial importance, the kernel size for density estimation and the maximum within-cluster distance is set to 0.25, 0.4, and 10 respectively. The number of top visual clusters in terms of velocity and acceleration standard deviation are both set to 5. The spatial-temporal smoothing of localization confidence uses the same settings as our algorithms for a fair comparison.

6.1 Qualitative Performance

We show the sample frames of localization results produced by the proposed method in Fig. 5. The ground truth and results of the algorithm in [13] are also shown for a visual comparison. We produce the ground truth data by manually labeling the most correlated moving object in each video frame using interactive segmentation. As can be observed from the results, our algorithm successfully identified the sound sources in all of the test videos, with close-to-groundtruth localization results. Several factors contribute to the superior performance of our algorithm. First, our region tracking algorithm effectively identify the same object across all video frames, which lays the foundation for motion pattern analysis. Second, smoothing both the audio and visual descriptors in temporal domain before performing correlation analysis greatly reduces the feature noise and well captures the temporal changing pattern in both modalities. Third, the WTA hash technique we use provides further robustness to noise through rank correlation space encoding. The algorithm in [13] is able to roughly identify regions most correlated to the audio in most videos. However, the localization is less accurate than the proposed method. This is largely due to the fact that regions in the visual clusters produced by spatial-temporal clustering of small segments in [13] tend to undersegment the audiovisual object. In [13], small segments within a certain neighborhood around the sounding object are very likely to be grouped into the same cluster, resulting in a very coarse estimation of the most correlated object. We also note that, [13] fails to focus on the right sound source in *Guitar Street* and the first half of *Wooden Horse* as a result of dominance of distracting motion.

6.2 Quantitative Performance

We quantify the performance of the proposed sound source localization method using similar metrics as in [13]. Specifically, *precision* and *recall* are used to assess the spatial localization performance. In detail, if the set of detected pixels is denoted as P, and the set of pixels in ground truth as T, then *precision* and *recall* are defined as

$$precision = \frac{|P \bigcap T|}{|P|}, recall = \frac{|P \bigcap T|}{|T|},$$

where $|\cdot|$ is the cardinality operation. The detected region (i.e. pixel set) P is controlled by a threshold applied to the smoothed localization confidence. The threshold is varied from 0 to 1 to get the precision-threshold and recall-threshold curve for each frame. Then those curves are averaged over all frames. In addition, the precision-recall curve is also plotted to show how *precision* and *recall* change against each other. Those results are shown in Fig. 6. Note that we only showed the quantitative results on videos that both methods have correctly localized the audio source in most of the frames. Therefore, *Guitar Street* and *Wooden Horse* are not included in the quantitative results.

Obviously, the proposed method is able to achieve higher precision consistently across all test videos under different threshold settings. The primary reason for the good precision of our method is that the proposed frame segmentation and region tracking algorithm can accurately segment the objects and reliably track the same object across the entire video. We also note that the recall performance gap between the two methods is much smaller compared to that of precision. In videos such as *Guitar Lessons* and *Basketball*, the recall of [13] is almost on par with our method. This is a natural effect of under-segmentation in [13], which sacrifices precision for recall. Our method, however, is able to achieve good results for both metrics. This is further consolidated by the precision-recall curve shown in Fig. 6c, where larger area under the curves means better performance.

For temporal localization performance, we use the detection rate and hit ratio as the evaluation metric. Detection rate is defined as the ratio of number of frames in which the object is successfully detected to the total number of frames. A successful detection is characterized by a localization containing more than half of pixels of the actual audiovisual object (i.e. recall is greater than 0.5). Hit ratio is defined as the ratio of number of frames in which the localization is accurate to the total number of frames. A localization is said to be accurate if the precision is greater than 0.5. The same threshold as in spatial localization performance evaluation is used to generate a continuous curve. As shown in Fig. 7, the proposed method outperforms [13] in terms of hit ratio. As for detection rate, our method produces steep curves, rapidly increasing to the best performance above a certain threshold. In comparison, [13]'s detection rate increases slowly with changing threshold.

Another view of the above results is shown in Table 2. It's reasonable to look at the above performance metrics given a specific recall value. We set recall to 0.5 to evaluate the other performance metrics, as this represents a successful detection in the test. As shown in the table, our method again outperforms the state-of-the-art method. And interestingly, the performance gap difference between detection rate and hit ratio is similar to that in the precision and recall in the spatial localization performance. This is reasonable as detection rate is more closely related with recall and hit ratio is more related to precision based on the definition. [13] tends to perform worse in metrics related with recall than precision. An example video is *Violin Yanni*. Although the algorithm in [13] successfully detected the left hand of the violin player, which is the ground truth, the hit ratio is essentially zero because more than half of the localized region is false positive. However, for video *Student News* the hit ratio is better than the detection rate. This is because the localization results is a number of small scattering within the speaker's face.

7. CONCLUSIONS AND FUTURE WORK

In this paper, we address the problem of sound source localization and segmentation in general videos captured using

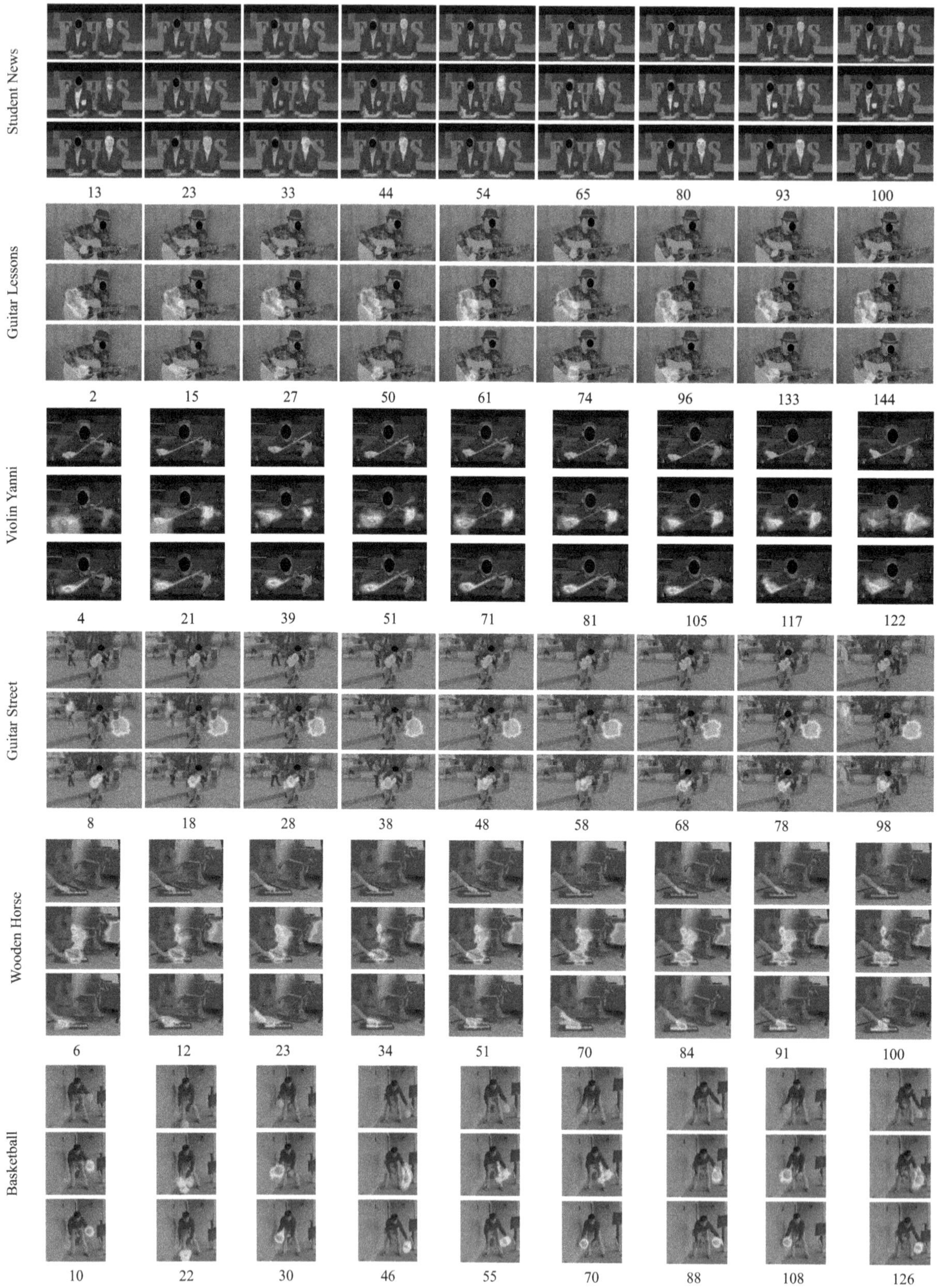

Figure 5: Sample frames of the audiovisual source localization and segmentation results. For each test video, the top row is the manually labeled ground truth.The second row is the results of the method proposed by [13]. The third row the results of our method. The frame number of each column is marked at the bottom of the sample frames.

Algorithm	Our method			Compared method [13]		
Video Name	$prc@rec = 0.5$	$hit@rec = 0.5$	$det@rec = 0.5$	$prc@rec = 0.5$	$hit@rec = 0.5$	$det@rec = 0.5$
Basketball	95.54	98.87	100.0	77.06	92.02	99.39
Violin Yanni	92.42	98.43	92.91	23.01	0.0	39.37
Guitar Lessons	88.40	98.05	100.0	10.03	0.0	100.0
Student News	76.04	100.0	100.0	34.80	6.06	0.0

Table 2: Quantitative results of the proposed algorithm against that of [13]. The numbers are in percentile. "prc", "hit" and "det" denotes precision, hit ratio and detection rate respectively. "prc@rec=0.5" denotes the precision when recall is set to 0.5, and the rest notations are interpreted in a similar way.

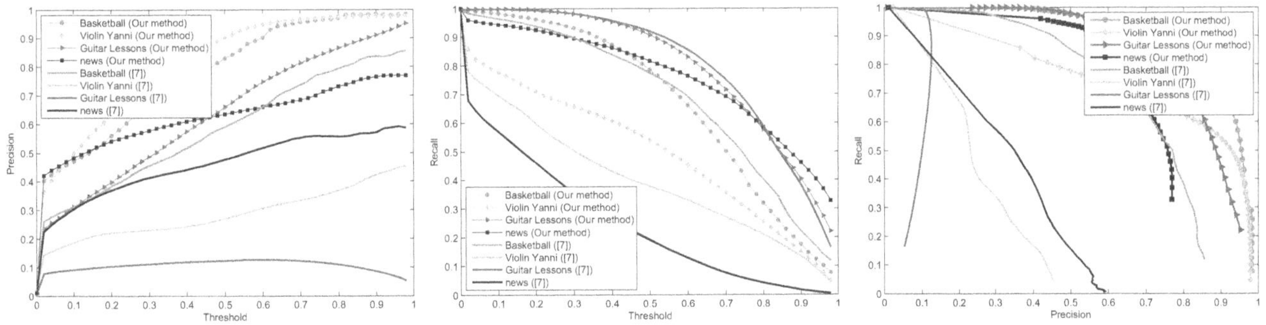

(a) Precision under varying threshold. (b) Recall under varying threshold. (c) Precision-Recall Curve.

Figure 6: Quantitative results of spatial localization performance.

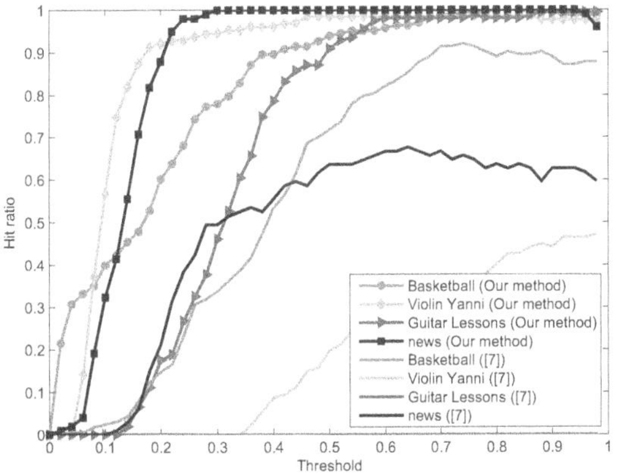

(a) Hit ratio under varying threshold.

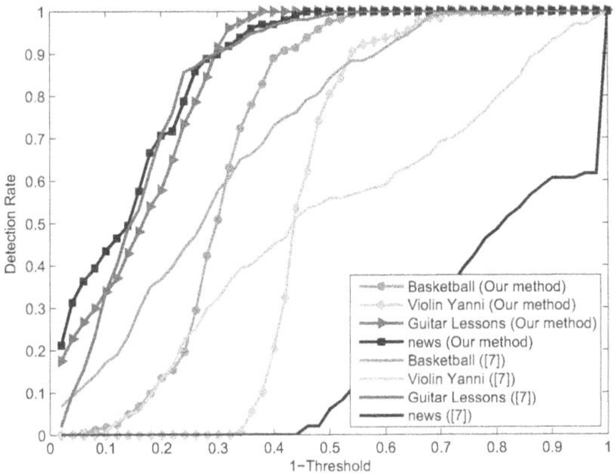

(b) Detection rate under varying threshold.

Figure 7: Quantitative results of temporal localization performance.

Figure 8: Failure case. Top: Audio source detected by the proposed algorithm. Bottom: Manually labeled ground truth. The current algorithm is susceptible to the audio background distraction. The accompany music from the loudspeaker (on the player's left) is mixed with violin sounds, which effectively results in the algorithm's failure to capture the correct moving object.

a single microphone. The proposed approach uses a novel region tracking algorithm to represent the entire video as a number of spatial-temporal region tracks. The synchronization between each region track and the audio energy are analyzed efficiently with the Winner-Take-All hash. We have evaluated our approach with a number of challenging test videos and compared with the state-of-the-art, thus demonstrating its superior performance.

Currently, the performance of our algorithm can be susceptible to the background audio distraction, as illustrated in Fig. 8. The mixed audio signal effectively attenuates the synchronization measure with motion of the correct audio source. In the future, we plan to combine with audio source separation techniques to effectively preprocess the audio signal and improve the algorithm's robustness to background audio distraction.

8. REFERENCES

[1] J. Allen. Short term spectral analysis, synthesis, and modification by discrete fourier transform. *Acoustics, Speech and Signal Processing, IEEE Transactions on*, 25(3):235–238, Jun 1977.

[2] Z. Barzelay and Y. Schechner. Harmony in motion. In *Computer Vision and Pattern Recognition, 2007. CVPR '07. IEEE Conference on*, pages 1–8, June 2007.

[3] M. J. Beal, N. Jojic, and H. Attias. A graphical model for audiovisual object tracking. *Pattern Analysis and Machine Intelligence, IEEE Transactions on*, 25(7):828–836, July 2003.

[4] S. Bengio. Multimodal authentication using asynchronous hmms. In *Proceedings of the 4th International Conference on Audio- and Video-based Biometric Person Authentication*, AVBPA'03, pages 770–777, Berlin, Heidelberg, 2003. Springer-Verlag.

[5] A. Casanovas, G. Monaci, P. Vandergheynst, and R. Gribonval. Blind audiovisual source separation based on sparse redundant representations. *Multimedia, IEEE Transactions on*, 12(5):358–371, Aug 2010.

[6] A. Casanovas and P. Vandergheynst. Audio-based nonlinear video diffusion. In *Acoustics Speech and Signal Processing (ICASSP), 2010 IEEE International Conference on*, pages 2486–2489, March 2010.

[7] A. Casanovas and P. Vandergheynst. Unsupervised extraction of audio-visual objects. In *Acoustics, Speech and Signal Processing (ICASSP), 2011 IEEE International Conference on*, pages 2284–2287, May 2011.

[8] N. Checka and K. Wilson. Person tracking using audio-video sensor fusion. *MIT Artificial Intelligence Laboratory*, 2002, 2001.

[9] D. Comaniciu and P. Meer. Mean shift: A robust approach toward feature space analysis. *Pattern Analysis and Machine Intelligence, IEEE Transactions on*, 24(5):603–619, May 2002.

[10] M. Cristani, M. Bicego, and V. Murino. Audio-visual event recognition in surveillance video sequences. *Multimedia, IEEE Transactions on*, 9(2):257–267, Feb 2007.

[11] T. Dean, M. Ruzon, M. Segal, J. Shlens, S. Vijayanarasimhan, and J. Yagnik. Fast, accurate detection of 100,000 object classes on a single machine. In *Proceedings of IEEE Conference on Computer Vision and Pattern Recognition*, Washington, DC, USA, 2013.

[12] J. Driver. Enhancement of selective listening by illusory mislocation of speech sounds due to lip-reading. *Nature*, 381:66–68, 1996.

[13] H. Izadinia, I. Saleemi, and M. Shah. Multimodal analysis for identification and segmentation of moving-sounding objects. *Multimedia, IEEE Transactions on*, 15(2):378–390, Februray 2013.

[14] W. Jiang, C. Cotton, S.-F. Chang, D. Ellis, and A. Loui. Short-term audio-visual atoms for generic video concept classification. In *Proceedings of the 17th ACM International Conference on Multimedia*, MM '09, pages 5–14, New York, NY, USA, 2009. ACM.

[15] W. Jiang and A. C. Loui. Audio-visual grouplet: Temporal audio-visual interactions for general video concept classification. In *Proceedings of the 19th ACM International Conference on Multimedia*, MM '11, pages 123–132, New York, NY, USA, 2011. ACM.

[16] E. Kidron, Y. Schechner, and M. Elad. Cross-modal localization via sparsity. *Trans. Sig. Proc.*, 55(4):1390–1404, April 2007.

[17] C. Liu. *Beyond Pixels: Exploring New Representations and Applications for Motion Analysis*. PhD thesis, Massachusetts Institute of Technology, May 2009.

[18] Y. Liu and Y. Sato. Finding Speaker Face Region by Audiovisual Correlation. In *Workshop on Multi-camera and Multi-modal Sensor Fusion Algorithms and Applications - M2SFA2 2008*, Marseille, France, 2008. Andrea Cavallaro and Hamid Aghajan.

[19] Y. Liu and Y. Sato. Visual localization of non-stationary sound sources. In *Proceedings of the 17th ACM International Conference on Multimedia*, MM '09, pages 513–516, New York, NY, USA, 2009. ACM.

[20] Y. Pang, Z. Ji, P. Jing, and X. Li. Ranking graph embedding for learning to rerank. *Neural Networks and Learning Systems, IEEE Transactions on*, 24(8):1292–1303, Aug 2013.

[21] J. Savard. http://members.shaw.ca/quadibloc/other/colint.htm.

[22] C. Sigg, B. Fischer, B. Ommer, V. Roth, and J. Buhmann. Nonnegative cca for audiovisual source separation. In *Machine Learning for Signal Processing, 2007 IEEE Workshop on*, pages 253–258, Aug 2007.

[23] M. M. H. Vahid Asadpour and F. Towhidkhah. Audio-visual speaker identification using dynamic facial movements and utterance phonetic content. *Applied Soft Computing*, 11(2):2083–2093, 2011.

[24] K. Wilson, N. Checka, D. Demirdjian, and T. Darrell. Audio-video array source separation for perceptual user interfaces. In *Proceedings of the 2001 Workshop on Perceptive User Interfaces*, PUI '01, pages 1–7, New York, NY, USA, 2001. ACM.

[25] J. Yagnik, D. Strelow, D. A. Ross, and R.-s. Lin. The power of comparative reasoning. In *Proceedings of the 2011 International Conference on Computer Vision*, ICCV '11, pages 2431–2438, Washington, DC, USA, 2011. IEEE Computer Society.

[26] D. N. Zotkin, R. Duraiswami, and L. S. Davis. Joint audio-visual tracking using particle filters. *EURASIP J. Appl. Signal Process.*, 2002(1):1154–1164, January 2002.

Deep Learning for Content-Based Image Retrieval: A Comprehensive Study

Ji Wan[1,2,5], Dayong Wang[3], Steven C.H. Hoi[2], Pengcheng Wu[3], Jianke Zhu[4], Yongdong Zhang[1], Jintao Li[1]
[1]Key Laboratory of Intelligent Information Processing of Chinese Academy of Sciences (CAS), Institute of Computing Technology, CAS, Beijing, China
[2]School of Information Systems, Singapore Management University, Singapore
[3]School of Computer Engineering, Nanyang Technological University, Singapore
[4]College of Computer Science, Zhejiang University, Hangzhou, China
[5]University of Chinese Academy of Sciences, Beijing, China
chhoi@smu.edu.sg; {dywang,wupe0003}@ntu.edu.sg; {wanji,zhyd,jtli}@ict.ac.cn; jkzhu@zju.edu.cn

ABSTRACT

Learning effective feature representations and similarity measures are crucial to the retrieval performance of a content-based image retrieval (CBIR) system. Despite extensive research efforts for decades, it remains one of the most challenging open problems that considerably hinders the successes of real-world CBIR systems. The key challenge has been attributed to the well-known "semantic gap" issue that exists between low-level image pixels captured by machines and high-level semantic concepts perceived by human. Among various techniques, machine learning has been actively investigated as a possible direction to bridge the semantic gap in the long term. Inspired by recent successes of deep learning techniques for computer vision and other applications, in this paper, we attempt to address an open problem: if deep learning is a hope for bridging the semantic gap in CBIR and how much improvements in CBIR tasks can be achieved by exploring the state-of-the-art deep learning techniques for learning feature representations and similarity measures. Specifically, we investigate a framework of deep learning with application to CBIR tasks with an extensive set of empirical studies by examining a state-of-the-art deep learning method (Convolutional Neural Networks) for CBIR tasks under varied settings. From our empirical studies, we find some encouraging results and summarize some important insights for future research.

Categories and Subject Descriptors

H.3.1 [**Information Storage and Retrieval**]: Content Analysis and Indexing; I.2.6 [**Artificial Intelligence**]: Learning; I.4.7 [**Image Processing and Computer Vision**]: Feature Measurement

General Terms

Algorithm; Experimentation

Keywords

Deep Learning; Content-Based Image Retrieval; Convolutional Neural Networks; Feature Representation

MM'14, November 3–7, 2014, Orlando, Florida, USA.

http://dx.doi.org/10.1145/2647868.2654948.

1. INTRODUCTION

The retrieval performance of a content-based image retrieval system crucially depends on the feature representation and similarity measurement, which have been extensively studied by multimedia researchers for decades. Although a variety of techniques have been proposed, it remains one of the most challenging problems in current content-based image retrieval (CBIR) research, which is mainly due to the well-known "semantic gap" issue that exists between low-level image pixels captured by machines and high-level semantic concepts perceived by human. From a high-level perspective, such challenge can be rooted to the fundamental challenge of Artificial Intelligence (AI), that is, how to build and train intelligent machines like human to tackle real-world tasks. Machine learning is one promising technique that attempts to address this grand challenge in the long term.

Recent years have witnessed some important advances of new techniques in machine learning. One important breakthrough technique is known as "deep learning", which includes a family of machine learning algorithms that attempt to model high-level abstractions in data by employing deep architectures composed of multiple non-linear transformations [,]. Unlike conventional machine learning methods that are often using "shallow" architectures, deep learning mimics the human brain that is organized in a deep architecture and processes information through multiple stages of transformation and representation. By exploring deep architectures to learn features at multiple level of abstracts from data automatically, deep learning methods allow a system to learn complex functions that directly map raw sensory input data to the output, without relying on human-crafted features using domain knowledge. Many recent studies have reported encouraging results for applying deep learning techniques to a variety of applications, including speech recognition [,], object recognition [,], and natural language processing [,], among others.

Inspired by the successes of deep learning, in this paper, we attempt to explore deep learning techniques with application to CBIR tasks. Despite much research attention of applying deep learning for image classification and recognition in computer vision, there is still limited amount of attention focusing on the CBIR applications. In this paper, we investigate deep learning methods for learning feature representations from images and their similarity measures towards CBIR tasks. In particular, we aim to address the following open research questions:

(i) Are deep learning methods effective for learning good feature representations from images to tackle CBIR tasks?

(ii) How much improvements can be achieved by deep learning techniques when compared with traditional features crafted by experts in multimedia and computer vision?

(iii) How to apply and adapt an existing deep learning model trained in one domain to a new CBIR task in another domain effectively?

In order to answer the above questions, we investigate a framework of deep learning for content-based image retrieval (CBIR) by applying a state-of-the-art deep learning method, that is, convolutional neural networks (CNNs) for learning feature representations from image data, and conduct an extensive set of empirical studies for a variety of CBIR tasks. From the empirical studies, we obtain some encouraging results and reveal several important insights for addressing the open questions. As a summary, we make the following major contributions in this work:

- We introduce a deep learning framework for CBIR by training large-scale deep convolutional neural networks for learning effective feature representations of images;
- We conduct an extensive set of empirical studies for comprehensive evaluations of deep convolutional neural networks with application to learn feature representations for a variety of CBIR tasks under varied settings.

The rest of this paper is organized as follows. Section 2 reviews related work. Section 3 briefly introduces the framework of deep learning for CBIR. Section 4 introduces all the evaluated datasets and the adopted performance measurement. Section 5 shows the experimental results of our empirical studies. Finally, Section 6 discusses the limitations and concludes this paper.

2. RELATED WORK

Our research lies in the interplay of *content-based image retrieval*, *distance metric learning* and *deep neural network learning*. We briefly review each group of related work below.

2.1 Content-Based Image Retrieval

Content-based image retrieval (CBIR) is one of the fundamental research challenges extensively studied in multimedia community for decades [, ,]. CBIR aims to search for images through analyzing their visual contents, and thus image representation is the crux of CBIR. Over the past decades, a variety of low-level feature descriptors have been proposed for image representation [ ], ranging from global features, such as color features [ ], edge features [ ], texture features [ ], GIST [,], and CENTRIST [ ], and recent local feature representations, such as the bag-of-words (BoW) models [, , ,] using local feature descriptors (e.g. SIFT [ ], and SURF [ ], etc.). Conventional CBIR approaches usually choose rigid distance functions on some extracted low-level features for multimedia similarity search, such as Euclidean distance or cosine similarity. However, the fixed rigid similarity/distance function may not be always optimal to the complex visual image retrieval tasks due to the grand challenge of the semantic gap between low-level visual features extracted by computers and high-level human perceptions.

Hence, recent years have witnessed a surge of active research efforts in the design of various distance/similarity measures on some low-level features by exploring machine learning techniques [, ,]. Among these techniques, some works have focused on learning to hashing or compact codes [, , , ,]. For example, Norouzi et al [ ] proposed a mapping learning scheme for large-scale multimedia applications from high-dimensional data to binary codes that preserve semantic similarity. Jegou et al [ ] adopted the fisher kernel to aggregate local descriptors and adopted a joint dimension reduction in order to reduce an image to a few dozen bytes while preserving high accuracy. Another way to enhance the feature representation is distance metric learning (DML), as discussed in detail as follows.

2.2 Distance metric Learning

Distance metric learning for image retrieval has been extensively studied in both machine learning and multimedia retrieval communities [, , , , , , ,]. In the following, we briefly discuss different groups of existing work for distance metric learning organized by different learning settings and principles.

In terms of training data formats, most existing DML studies often work with two types of data (a.k.a. side information): *pairwise constraints* where must-link constraints and cannot-link constraints are given and *triplet constraints* that contains a similar pair and a dissimilar pair. There are also studies that directly use the class labels for DML by following a typical machine learning scheme, such as the Large Margin Nearest Neighbor (LMNN) algorithm [ ], which however is not essentially different.

In terms of different learning approaches, distance metric learning techniques are typically categorized into two groups: the *global supervised approaches* [,] that learn a metric on a global setting by satisfying all the constraints simultaneously, the *local supervised approaches* [,] that learn a metric on the local sense by only satisfying the given local constraints from neighboring information.

In terms of learning methodology, most existing DML studies generally employ batch learning methods which often assume the whole collection of training data must be given before the learning task and train a model from scratch. Unlike the batch learning methods, in order to handle large-scale data, online DML algorithms have been actively studied recently [,].

The key idea of distance metric learning is to learn an optimal metric which minimizes the distance between similar images and simultaneously maximizes the distance between dissimilar images. In this condition, another technique named similarity learning is closely related to distance metric learning. For example, Chechik et al. proposed an online algorithm for scalable image similarity (OASIS) [ ] for improving image retrieval performance.

2.3 Deep Learning

Deep learning refers to a class of machine learning techniques, where many layers of information processing stages in hierarchical architectures are exploited for pattern classification and for feature or representation learning. It lies in the intersections of several research areas, including neural networks, graphical modeling, optimization, pattern recognition, and signal processing, etc.

Deep learning has a long history, and its basic concept is originated from artificial neural network research. The feed-forward neural networks with many hidden layers are indeed a good example of the models with a deep architecture. Back-propagation, popularized in 1980's, has been a well-known algorithm for learning the weights of these networks. For example, LeCun et al. [ ] successfully adopt the deep supervised back-propagation convolutional network for digit recognition. Recently, it has become a hot research topic in both computer vision and machine learning, where deep learning techniques achieve stat-of-the art performance for various tasks. The deep convolutional neural networks (CNNs) proposed in [ ] came out first in the image classification task of ILSVRC-2012 [1]. The model was trained on more than one million

[1] http://www.image-net.org/challenges/LSVRC/2012/

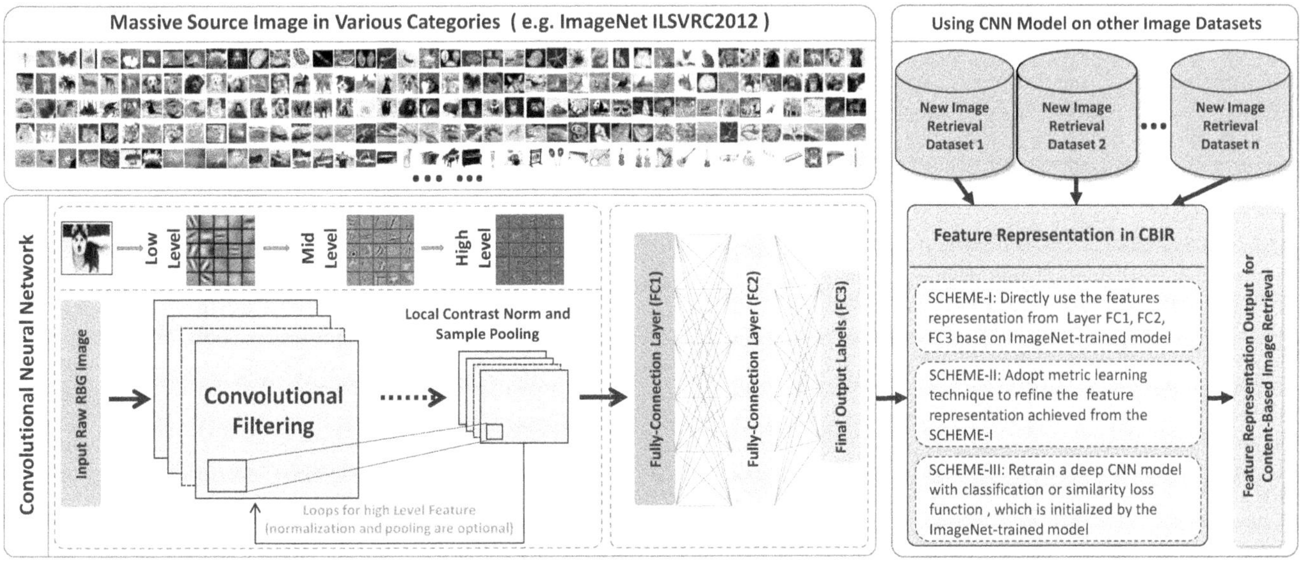

(a) Training deep CNN models in an existing domain (ImageNet) (b) Adopting trained model for CBIR in a new domain

Figure 1: A Framework of Deep Learning with Application to Content-based Image Retrieval.

images, and has achieved a winning top-5 test error rate of 15.3% over 1,000 classes. After that, some recent works got better results by improving CNN models. The top-5 test error rate decreased to 13.24% in [ ] by training the model to simultaneously classify, locate and detect objects. Besides image classification, the object detection task can also benefit from the CNN model, as reported in [ ]. Generally speaking, three important reasons for the popularity of deep learning today are drastically increased chip processing abilities (e.g., GPU units), the significantly lower cost of computing hardware, and recent advances in machine learning and signal/information processing research.

Over the past several years, a rich family of deep learning techniques has been proposed and extensively studied, e.g., Deep Belief Network (DBN) [ ], Boltzmann Machines (BM) [ ], Restricted Boltzmann Machines (RBM) [ ], Deep Boltzmann Machine (DBM) [ ], Deep Neural Networks (DNN) [ ], etc. More detailed survey of latest deep learning studies can be found in [ ]. Among various techniques, the deep convolutional neural networks, which is a discriminative deep architecture and belongs to the DNN category, has found state-of-the-art performance on various tasks and competitions in computer vision and image recognition [, , ,]. Specifically, the CNN model consists of several convolutional layers and pooling layers, which are stacked up with one on top of another. The convolutional layer shares many weights, and the pooling layer sub-samples the output of the convolutional layer and reduces the data rate from the layer below. The weight sharing in the convolutional layer, together with appropriately chosen pooling schemes, endows the CNN with some "invariance" properties (e.g., translation invariance). We will discuss more details of the deep convolutional architecture in Section 3.1.

Our work is also related to some recent works in [,]. Donahue et al. [ ] evaluated whether features extracted from the activation of a deep convolutional network trained in a fully supervised fashion on a large, fixed set of object recognition tasks can be re-purposed to novel generic recognition tasks. For feature representation, they directly use the activation of the layer $DeCAF_5$, $DeCAF_6$ ("FC1" layer in our framework), and $DeCAF_7$ ("FC2" layer in our framework), and adopt LogReg or SVM to train a new classification model over the new dataset. Zeiler and Fergus [ ] introduced a novel visualization technique that gives insight into the function of intermediate feature layers and the operation of the classifier. For feature representation, they keep the top $1-7$ layers of the ImageNet-trained model fixed and retrain a new softmax classifier on top using the training images in the new database. Our work is fundamentally different from these studies in that we focus on evaluating feature representation performance on CBIR tasks, where we aim to learn an effective distance measure for retrieval tasks instead of classifiers in recognition tasks. Finally, we note that our work is also very different from another recent study in [ ] which aims to address multimodal image retrieval using deep learning and their raw input still rely on human-crafted features. By contrast, we aim to learn features directly from images without domain knowledge.

3. DEEP LEARNING FOR CBIR

In this section, we introduce the proposed deep learning framework for CBIR, which consists of two stages: (i) training a deep learning model from a large collection of training data; and (ii) applying the trained deep model for learning feature representations of CBIR tasks in a new domain. Specifically, for the first stage, we adopt the deep architecture of Convolutional Neural Networks (CNNs) as proposed in [ ]. In the following, we first briefly introduce the basics of CNNs, and then focus on discussing how to generalize the trained deep models for feature representations in a new CBIR task.

3.1 Deep Convolutional Neural Networks

Figure 1 gives an overall view of the proposed framework by applying deep learning for CBIR tasks. For the implementation of deep CNNs learning, we follow the similar framework as discussed in [ ] by adapting their publicly released C++ implementation [2]. This model has been successfully trained on the "ILSVRC-2012" dataset from ImageNet and found state-of-the-art performance with 1,000 categories and more than 1 million training images.

[2]https://code.google.com/p/cuda-convnet/

In general, the deep convolutional network, as shown in Figure 1 (a), consists of two parts: 1) the convolution layers and max-pooling layers, and 2) the fully connection layers and the output layers. Specifically, the first layer is the input layer which adopts the mean-centered raw RGB pixels in intensity value. To reduce overfitting, two data augmentation tricks are performed: first, the input images are generated with translation and horizontal reflections by extracting random 224×224 patches from the original 256×256 images and our network is trained on these extracted patches; second, to capture the invariance in illumination and color, they add random multiples of the principle components of the RGB pixel values throughout the dataset. According to the authors [ ], this scheme reduced their models' test set error by over 1%.

Following the input layers, there are five convolutional layers. The first and the second convolution layers are following with a response normalization layers and a max pooling layers, while the third, fourth, and fifth convolution layers are connected to one another without any intervening pooling or normalization. There are several novel or unusual features in Krizhevsky's convolutional neural network, which makes it work better than previous convolutional neural networks. First, the neuron output function f is the nonlinear function: Rectified Linear units (ReLUs), which can reduce the training time of the deep convolutional neural networks several times than the equivalents with "$tanh$"' units. Second, they adopt the "local response normalization", which is helpful for generalization. Last but not least, they adopt the "overlapping pooling" scheme. Max pooling layers are very common in general convolutional neural networks, which summarize the outputs of neighboring groups of neurons in the same kernel map. The max pooling step can enhance the transformation invariance of the feature mapping. Traditionally, the neighborhoods summarized by adjacent pooling units do not overlap. By adopting overlapped neighborhoods, they can reduce the top-1 and top-5 error rates by 0.4% and 0.3%, respectively.

Following the convolutional layers, there are two more fully-connected layers with $4,096$ neurons, denoted as "FC1" and "FC2". The last output layer, which is fed by the "FC2" layer, is a 1000-way softmax layer which produces a distribution over the $1,000$ class labels in ImageNet. In the whole deep convolutional neural network, there are about 60 million parameters in total. We train our deep convolutional neural network based on the ImageNet's ILSVRC-2012 training set, which contains about 1.2 million images. It takes about 200 hours to train a model with an error rate of 0.424 over the validation set ($50,000$ images), which is close to the error rate 0.407 reported in [ ]. All the experiments were conducted on a Linux server with NVIDIA Tesla K20 GPUs. K20 is featuring 13 active SMXes along with 5 memory controllers and 1.25MB of L2 cache, attached to 5GB of GDDR5. In our experiments, the CNN model was trained on only one K20 GPU which has enough memory for our training tasks.

3.2 Feature Representation for CBIR

Although CNNs have been shown with promising results for classification tasks, it remains unknown how it can perform for CBIR tasks. In this paper, our goal is to investigate effective techniques by extending the trained models for learning feature representations in CBIR tasks. In particular, we want to address two open issues: (i) how to apply the trained CNNs from classification to CBIR tasks in ImageNet? and (ii) how to generalize the trained CNNs model in learning feature representation for CBIR tasks in a new domain, which may or may not have enough training data?

Specifically, to apply a trained CNNs model for direct feature representation, we take the activations of the last three fully connected layers (FC1, FC2, and FC3) as the feature representations for CBIR tasks. In our experiments, we denote the feature vector of this direct feature generalization as "DF.FC1", "DF.FC2", and "DF.FC3", respectively. DF.FC3 is the feature taken from the final output layer, DF.FC2 is the features taken from the final hidden layer, and DF.FC1 is the activations of the layer before DF.FC2. We do not evaluate features from lower convolutional layers in the network since the lower layers are unlikely to contain richer semantic representations than the later features which form higher-level hypothesis from the low-level to mid-level local information [ ]. We note that the similar approach was also used for retraining classification models using other techniques (e.g., SVM) in some previous studies [,].

The above direct feature generalization may work on the dataset used for training the CNNs model, but may not work well for CBIR tasks on a new dataset, as shown Figure 1 (b), which may be very different from the original training data set. In the following, we discuss three kinds of feature generalization schemes in detail.

3.2.1 Scheme I: Direct Representation

This is the direct feature representation as discussed above. We assume the retrieval domain is similar to the original dataset for training the CNN model. In this scenario, we will simply adopt one of the activation features DF.FC1, DF.FC2, and DF.FC3, directly. To obtain the feature representation, we directly feed the images in new datasets into the input layer of the pre-trained CNN model, and then take the activation values from the last three layers. Since we only need to compute the feedforward network based on the matrix multiplication for one time, the whole scheme will be very efficient. In our experiment, we also normalize the feature representation with l_2-norm.

3.2.2 Scheme II: Refining by Similarity Learning

Instead of directly using the features extracted by the pre-trained deep model, we attempt to explore similarity learning (SL) algorithms to refine the features in scheme I. Various distance metric learning or similarity learning algorithms can be used, as discussed in Section 2.2, according to the training data available in the new CBIR tasks. In our experiment, we adopt the stat-of-the-art online similarity learning algorithm: Online Algorithm for Scalable Image Similarity Learning ("OASIS") [ ] for SL, which aims to learn a bilinear similarity measure over sparse representation.

Specifically, consider a triplet constraint set $\mathcal{X}$ given as follows:

$$\mathcal{X} = \{(\mathbf{x}_i, \mathbf{x}_i^+, \mathbf{x}_i^-)|(\mathbf{x}_i, \mathbf{x}_i^+) \in \mathcal{S}; (\mathbf{x}_i, \mathbf{x}_i^-) \in \mathcal{D}, i = 1, \ldots, T\}$$

where $\mathcal{S}$ contains relevant pairs and $\mathcal{D}$ includes irrelevant pairs, and T denotes the cardinality of the entire triplet set. We denote the similarity function of two samples as a bilinear form:

$$S_W(\mathbf{x}_i, \mathbf{x}_j) = \mathbf{x}_i^\top W \mathbf{x}_j$$

where $W \in \mathbb{R}^{d \times d}$. We define the hinge loss for a triplet:

$$l_W(\mathbf{x}_i, \mathbf{x}_i^+, \mathbf{x}_i^-) = \max\{0, 1 - S_W(\mathbf{x}_i, \mathbf{x}_i^+) + S_W(\mathbf{x}_i, \mathbf{x}_i^-)\}$$

Hence the global loss L_W over all possible triplets in the training set can be computed as:

$$L_W = \sum_{(\mathbf{x}_i, \mathbf{x}_i^+, \mathbf{x}_i^-) \in \mathcal{X}} l_W(\mathbf{x}_i, \mathbf{x}_i^+, \mathbf{x}_i^-)$$

The OASIS algorithm aims to minimize the overall loss L_W using the same idea of the online Passive-Aggressive (PA) algorithm [ ].

In our framework, we construct the triplets by simply considering relationships of instances in same class as relevant (positive),

(a) ImageNet (b) Caltech256 (c) Oxford (d) Paris (e) Pubfig83LFW

Figure 2: Example images of experimental datasets used in our experiments.

and relationships of instances belonging to different classes as irrelevant (negative). Scheme II is similar to the ones in [ ]. However, they adopt the LogReg or SVM algorithm for classifier training and focus on object recognition. In the following experiments, we denote the feature representation of scheme II as "DF.FC1+SL", "DF.FC2+SL", and "DF.FC3+SL", respectively.

3.2.3 Scheme III: Refining by Model Retraining

Scheme III will retrain the deep convolutional neural networks on the new image dataset for different CBIR tasks by initializing the CNN model with the parameters of the ImageNet-trained models. Depend on the available label information, there are two ways to retrain the CNN model.

1) Refining with class labels. For datasets with class labels, we can retrain the model by optimizing the classification objective function. In this case, all layers of the new model will be initialized based on our ImageNet-trained model except the last output layer, which is adapted to the number of class labels of the new dataset and initialized randomly. Then, we update the whole convolutional neural networks by training on images from the new dataset. In our experiments, we denote the feature vector of this scheme as "ReCLS.FC1", "ReCLS.FC2", and "ReCLS.FC3", respectively.

2) Refining with side information. In some special real-world applications, obtaining the class information directly is expensive, but gathering the side information is easier. We can retrain the CNN model with similarity learning objective function, like what we do in scheme II, and back-propagate the errors to previous layers in order to refine the entire model on the new dataset. In our experiment, we adopt the online distance metric learning algorithm with cosine similarity proposed in [ ]. In particular, denote $\mathbf{y} = \phi(\mathbf{x})$ the output of CNN model on input image $\mathbf{x}$, the cosine similarity of two input images $\mathbf{x}_1, \mathbf{x}_2$ is defined as:

$$S_{cos}(\mathbf{x}_1, \mathbf{x}_2) = \mathbf{y}_1^\top \mathbf{y}_2 / (\|\mathbf{y}_1\| \times \|\mathbf{y}_2\|)$$

Given a training triplet input $(\mathbf{x}, \mathbf{x}^+, \mathbf{x}^-)$, we could define the hinge loss as follow:

$$l((\mathbf{x}, \mathbf{x}^+, \mathbf{x}^-); S_{cos}) = \max\{0, \gamma - S_{cos}(\mathbf{x}, \mathbf{x}^+) + S_{cos}(\mathbf{x}, \mathbf{x}^-)\}$$

where γ is the parameter of margin. Given $(\mathbf{y}, \mathbf{y}^+, \mathbf{y}^-)$ as the output achieved by the CNN network, the derivation of the l with respect to $\mathbf{y}, \mathbf{y}^+, \mathbf{y}^-$ can be computed individually. The entire CNN model can be updated by back-propagation algorithm following the same scheme in [ ]. In our experiments, we denote the feature vector of this scheme as "ReDSL.FC1", "ReDSL.FC2", and "ReDSL.FC3", respectively.

Remark. We set a small learning rate for lower convolutional layers in order to preserve the original CNN model in lower-level feature layers. The original ImageNet-trained model has found a good starting point for the deep CNN model by optimizing a 1000-way classification problem, thus the good initialization will make the new model converge fast. Scheme III is similar to the ones in [ ], which shows that the initialized CNN model could significantly outperform the one with random initializations.

4. IMAGE DATASETS

Our empirical studies aim to evaluate the performance of the three feature generalization schemes based on different image datasets, including the general image database "ImageNet", the object image database "Caltech256", the landmark image datasets "Oxford" and "Paris", and the facial image dataset "Pubfig83LFW". We briefly introduce each of them as follows.

ImageNet: is a large-scale dataset with over 15 million labeled high-resolution images belonging to roughly $22,000$ categories. The images were collected from the web and labeled by human labelers using Amazon's Mechanical Turk crowd-sourcing tool. Starting in 2010, as part of the Pascal Visual Object Challenge, an annual competition called the ImageNet Large-Scale Visual Recognition Challenge (ILSVRC) has been held. ILSVRC uses a subset of ImageNet with roughly $1,000$ images in each of $1,000$ categories. In all, there are roughly 1.2 million training images, $50,000$ validation images, and $150,000$ testing images. The Deep CNN model in our framework is trained based on ILSVRC2012.

Caltech256: contains $30,607$ images of objects, which were obtained from Google image search and from PicSearch.com. Images were assigned to 257 categories and evaluated by humans in order to ensure image quality and relevance.

Oxford: contains $5,063$ high resolution images automatically downloaded from Flickr. It defines 55 queries used for evaluation, which consists of 5 for each of the 11 chosen Oxford landmarks. It is quite challenging due to substantial variations in scale, viewpoint and lighting conditions.

Paris: is analogously to the previous "Oxford" datasets. Its $6,412$ images were obtained from Flickr, and there are also 55 queries for evaluation. As it contains images of Paris it is considered to be an independent dataset from "Oxford".

Pubfig83LFW: is an open-universe web facial image dataset [ ], which combines two widely used face databases: PubFig83 [ ] and LFW [ ]. The 83 individuals from PubFig represent the test images and training gallery, and all the remaining individuals from LFW represent the distractor gallery or background faces. All the faces from each individual in PubFig83 are randomly divided into two-third training faces and one third test faces. All overlapping individuals from LFW are manually removed, and the left LFW dataset is used as distractors to PubFig83. All the facial images are resized to 250×250, and only the facial images that can be detected by a series commercial software are remained. In summary, the PubFig83+LFW dataset has 83 individuals with $8,720$ faces for training and $4,282$ faces for testing and over $5,000$ individuals from LFW with $12,066$ faces for background and distractor faces.

Table 1: Image Retrieval Performance on ImageNet

Feature	mAP	P@K=1	P@K=10	P@K=50	P@K=100	R@K=1	R@K=10	R@K=50	R@K=100
BoW.1200*	0.0007	0.0472	0.0234	0.0144	0.0118	0.0000	0.0002	0.0006	0.0009
BoW.4800*	0.0008	0.0487	0.0243	0.0148	0.0121	0.0000	0.0002	0.0006	0.0009
BoW.1K	0.0012	0.0243	0.0170	0.0124	0.0108	0.0000	0.0001	0.0005	0.0008
BoW.10K	0.0013	0.0212	0.0142	0.0106	0.0094	0.0000	0.0001	0.0004	0.0007
BoW.100K	0.0015	0.0216	0.0140	0.0110	0.0099	0.0000	0.0001	0.0004	0.0008
BoW.1M	0.0016	0.0286	0.0174	0.0132	0.0117	0.0000	0.0001	0.0005	0.0009
GIST	0.0002	0.0137	0.0080	0.0056	0.0049	0.0000	0.0001	0.0002	0.0004
DF.FC1	0.0748	0.4427	0.3650	0.2967	0.2637	0.0003	0.0028	0.0116	0.0205
DF.FC2	0.1218	0.4711	0.4105	0.3547	0.3254	0.0004	0.0032	0.0138	0.0254
DF.FC3	0.1007	0.4282	0.3726	0.3183	0.2898	0.0003	0.0029	0.0124	0.0226

* BoW.1200 and BoW.4800 are extracted by other groups, which are publicly available [3].

Table 2: Image Retrieval Performance on Caltech256

		Euclidean				Various Metric Learning on BoW*				OASIS on Deep Feature		
	Features	BoW*	DF.FC1	DF.FC2	DF.FC3	OASIS	MCML	LEGO	LMNN	DF.FC1	DF.FC2	DF.FC3
10 classes	mAP	0.2300	0.6424	0.7695	0.7109	0.3300	0.2900	0.2700	0.2400	0.8617	0.9153	0.8512
	P@K=1	0.3700	0.8800	0.9200	0.8800	0.4300	0.3900	0.3900	0.3800	0.9360	0.9560	0.9440
	P@K=10	0.2700	0.7748	0.8624	0.7928	0.3800	0.3300	0.3200	0.2900	0.9084	0.9400	0.8944
	P@K=50	0.1800	0.3614	0.4188	0.3930	0.2300	0.2200	0.2000	0.1800	0.4457	0.4614	0.4498
20 classes	mAP	0.1400	0.4984	0.5609	0.5493	0.2100	0.1700	0.1600	0.1400	0.6962	0.7388	0.6399
	P@K=1	0.2500	0.7840	0.7960	0.8020	0.2900	0.2600	0.2600	0.2600	0.8320	0.8780	0.7860
	P@K=10	0.1800	0.6228	0.6772	0.6588	0.2400	0.2100	0.2000	0.1900	0.7768	0.8130	0.7186
	P@K=50	0.1200	0.2998	0.3315	0.3290	0.1500	0.1400	0.1300	0.1100	0.3905	0.4084	0.3764
50 classes	mAP	0.0900	0.4011	0.4624	0.4286	0.1200	-	0.0900	0.0800	0.5186	0.5410	0.4603
	P@K=1	0.1700	0.6792	0.7240	0.6912	0.2100	-	0.1800	0.1800	0.7288	0.7320	0.6840
	P@K=10	0.1300	0.5333	0.5913	0.5519	0.1600	-	0.1300	0.1200	0.6194	0.6394	0.5600
	P@K=50	0.0800	0.2509	0.2836	0.2700	0.1000	-	0.0800	0.0700	0.3155	0.3308	0.2980

The results marked with ⋆ are taken directly from the study in [ ].

5. EXPERIMENTS

In this section, we design an extensive set of experiments to evaluate the performance of deep learning techniques for CBIR tasks. Specifically, the first experiment is to examine how the deep CNN model performs for CBIR tasks on the same dataset that was used to train the model, and the rest experiments aim to test the generalization of the pre-trained deep model to CBIR tasks on other new domains, which may be very different from the training data used for training the original CNN models.

For performance evaluation metrics, we use three standard evaluation measures widely used in CBIR tasks, including the mean average precision (mAP), the precision at particular ranks ("P@K"), and the recall at particular ranks ("R@K").

5.1 Experiment on ImageNet

In this experiment, we aim to evaluate the CBIR performance using scheme I. We evaluate the retrieval performance on the ILSRVC 2012 dataset. We use the $50,000$ validation images as query set, and search on the 1.2-million training image set. We compare scheme I with several bag-of-words (BoW) feature representations, which are widely used for large-scale image retrieval. Among these BoW features, "BoW.1200" and "BoW.4800" are extracted by other groups [3]. The experimental results are shown in Table 1. Several image retrieval results on ImageNet dataset are shown in Figure 3.

[3] http://cloudcv.org/objdetect/

Several observations can be achieved from the results. Firstly, we can observe that this is a very challenging CBIR task. The best BoW feature representation based on a codebook with the vocabulary size $1,000,000$ can only achieve the mAP of 0.0016, and the performance of global GIST feature is even much worse. The results of "BoW.1200" and "BoW.4800" are generated based on the features released in other works, which is similar to the other BoW representations generated by ourselves.

Secondly, the activations based feature vector from the fully-connected layer FC1/FC2/FC3 achieve significantly much better results, among which the "DF.FC2" (the last hidden layer) achieved the best performance with top-1 precision of 47.11%. Although the last output layer DF.FC3 is the classification output of the ImageNet-trained CNN model, which contains the best sematic information, it seems not a good feature representation for CBIR tasks. By examining the standard evaluation measures: *precision* and *recall*, we can find the same observations. When $K = 1$, the P@K=1 of DF.FC2 is about 0.4711. It means the error rate of the nearest neighbor classification with $K = 1$ is 0.529, which is very close to the classification error rate of the ImageNet trained model (0.424). Finally, we note that our current experiments did not add extra post processing step to improve the CBIR performance, although some techniques (such as "geometric constraint based reranking" [ ] or "query expansion" [ ]) often can further boost the image retrieval performance, which however is out of the scope of this study.

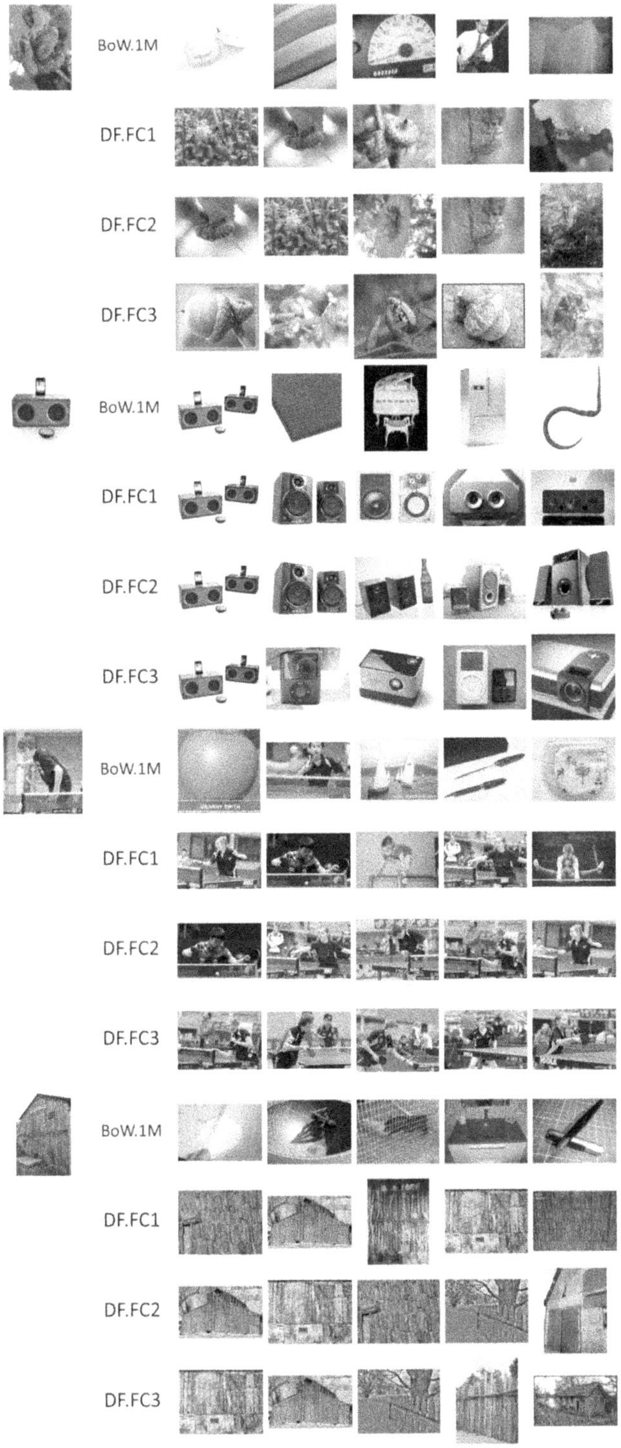

Figure 3: Qualitative evaluation of image retrieval results on ImageNet. For each row, the image on the left-hand side is the query, and the images on the right are the top-5 returned results by each retrieval scheme.

5.2 Experiments on Various CBIR Tasks

In this section, we aim to evaluate the performance of feature representation schemes in Figure 1 (b) on new diverse CBIR tasks. Specifically, we examine the performance of the models for feature representations on three different CBIR tasks: (i) object retrieval tasks using the "Caltech256" dataset, which is an object-based image dataset, and different categories are quite distinct; (ii) landmark retrieval tasks using the "Oxford" and "Paris" datasets, which consist of landmark photos where all the images are captured under various conditions (scale, viewpoint and lighting conditions); and (iii) facial image retrieval tasks using the "Pubfig83LFW" dataset, which is challenging as intra class difference sometimes could be even larger than inter class difference.

5.2.1 Object Image Retrieval

In this experiment, we evaluate the retrieval performance of scheme I and scheme II on the Caltech256 dataset. Following exactly the same experimental setting in [ ], we use subsets of sizes 10, 20, 50 classes, and images from each class were randomly split into a training set of 40 images and a test set of 25 image. Several kinds of distance metric learning algorithms are used to refine the original BoW feature vector (note that these experimental results were taken directly from the study in [ ]). For scheme II, we adopt the OASIS algorithm for similarity learning. All the experimental results are shown in Table 2.

Several observations can be drawn from the results. Firstly, considering scheme I, the performances of DF.FC1/2/3 are consistently better than the general BoW representation. Similar to the previous experiment, the feature vector of the last hidden layer DF.FC2 achieved the best performance.

Second, similar to the previous experiment, based on the Caltech256 dataset, the output layer feature DF.FC3 generally performs better than the feature DF.FC1. Since the Caltech256 dataset is similar to the ImageNet dataset, and the difference between different categories is significant, the last layer feature that represents the final semantics information is also a good representation.

Thirdly, by adopting the similarity learning algorithm, the OASIS algorithm achieves the best performance, which can boost the mAP value from 0.23 to 0.33 for the 10-classes case. However, the performance of the refined BoW feature representation is still much lower than DF.FC2 in scheme I (0.7695). If we consider scheme II by refining the first feature generalization scheme with OASIS algorithm, the performance can be further improved, as shown in the last three columns in Table 2. Last but not least, we observe that after using similarity learning, the performance of DF.FC1 is better than that of the DF.FC3, especially for the harder problems with more categories (e.g. 50 classes). This shows that with DML, one can explore more useful information from the high-dimensional hidden layers than the final class output layers.

The overall encouraging results show that by adapting the pretrained deep model on a new dataset using similarity learning, we can achieve significantly better performance than the original features.

5.2.2 Landmark Image Retrieval

In this experiment, we evaluate the retrieval performance of the three different feature representation schemes for landmark retrieval tasks on the "Oxford" and "Paris" datasets. Following the previous studies [ ], we construct the BoW feature using a codebook with vocabulary size of $100K$ and $1M$, respectively. In additional, we take the experimental results on "Oxford" and "Paris" from [ ] for comparison, which tried to use the features extracted from a CNN model in a different way. The experimental results are shown in Table 3 and Table 4. Since there are no explicit class label available in these datasets, we adopt the SL objective function in scheme III.

Several observations can be drawn from the results. Firstly, we observe that the BoW feature representation works well on both

Table 3: Image Retrieval Performance on "Oxford"

Feature	mAP	P@K=1	P@K=10	R@K=10
BoW-100K	0.5193	0.7636	0.6127	0.2764
BoW-1M	0.6044	0.8000	0.7073	0.3352
CNNaug-ss [ ]	0.6800	-	-	-
DF.FC1	0.4170	0.8364	0.5273	0.2091
DF.FC2	0.3875	0.8364	0.4873	0.1810
DF.FC3	0.3347	0.7091	0.4309	0.1495
DF.FC1+SL	0.4658	0.4909	0.4909	0.1044
DF.FC2+SL	0.4441	0.5273	0.4836	0.1013
DF.FC3+SL	0.3019	0.4364	0.3818	0.0646
ReDSL.FC1	0.7834	0.8727	0.7291	0.2948
ReDSL.FC2	0.6770	0.7455	0.6309	0.2169
ReDSL.FC3	0.7332	0.8727	0.6927	0.2574

Table 4: Image Retrieval Performance on "Paris"

Feature	mAP	P@K=1	P@K=10	R@K=10
BoW-100K	0.5841	0.9455	0.8709	0.0711
BoW-1M	0.6298	1.0000	0.9491	0.0766
CNNaug-ss [ ]	0.7950	-	-	-
DF.FC1	0.5808	0.9818	0.9200	0.0740
DF.FC2	0.6009	0.9636	0.9145	0.0739
DF.FC3	0.5168	0.9455	0.8836	0.0716
DF.FC1+SL	0.8683	0.9455	0.9582	0.0775
DF.FC2+SL	0.8479	0.9818	0.9600	0.0770
DF.FC3+SL	0.7007	0.8545	0.8873	0.0718
ReDSL.FC1	0.9474	0.9818	0.9727	0.0782
ReDSL.FC2	0.9122	1.0000	0.9655	0.0775
ReDSL.FC3	0.9233	1.0000	0.9473	0.0760

datasets, which is consistent with the previous studies. For example, based on a vocabulary with size 1 million, the mAP performances of BoW on the "Oxford" and "Paris" datasets are 0.6044 and 0.6298, respectively. Generally, the landmark images contain lots of useful interesting points, which are corresponding to the corner or edge information of the inside buildings. Hence, the BoW feature representation is a suitable solution for such kinds of datasets. The performances on the Paris dataset are generally better than those on the Oxford dataset.

Secondly, the feature representation of scheme I performs poorly on the two landmark datasets, and the performances of feature representations in different levels are different. In particular, the hidden layer features (DF.FC1 and DF.FC2) are quite comparable, and obviously better than the output layer feature (DF.FC3). By adopting the SL technique in scheme II, the retrieval performance can be improved on both datasets, especially for the Paris dataset.

Thirdly, for scheme III, the model retrained with SL objective achieves the best retrieval performance on both datasets. It indicates that the "deep" retraining step in scheme III is more effective to explore the hidden semantic information than the "shadow" similarity learning step in scheme II. This is reasonable since scheme III has the ability of refining the similarity measurements of the extracted feature and tuning the underlying feature representations simultaneously. However, the extra retraining cost of scheme III is also much higher than that of scheme II using similarity learning.

Finally, we compare our methods to the spatial search method with feature augmentation, named "CNNaug-ss", in [ ]. From Table 3 and Table 4 we can see that "CNNaug-ss" is much better than scheme I, but worse than scheme III with SL objective. Compared with scheme II, "CNNaug-ss" is better on "Oxford" but worse on "Paris". Generally, "CNNaug-ss" has relatively better results on "Oxford" than on "Paris", since it explores sub-patches over multiple scales and the scale variation on Oxford dataset is larger. Exploring a large number of sub-patches over multiple scales makes "CNNaug-ss" computational expensive and limits its scalability.

5.2.3 *Facial Image Annotation*

In this experiment, we evaluate the search-based facial image annotation performance with the first and third feature generalization schemes on the Pubfig83LFW facial dataset. We conduct this experiment because the performance of search-based annotation scheme highly depends on the performance of content-based facial image retrieval. Specifically, we conduct the whole experiment based on the evaluation framework in [ ], in which all the feature are evaluated based on the same settings. For feature representation, we use scheme I and scheme III with classification objective, since the class label information is available on this dataset. We compare them with a state-of-the-art feature representation, Hog-LBP-Gabor, which fuses three kinds of famous facial image representation features [4]. All the experimental results are shown in Table 5 and Fig. 4.

Several observations can be drawn from these results. First, similar to the previous experiments on the landmark datasets, scheme I does not work well on the facial image dataset, by comparing with the well-known facial image representation features. In particular, the best mAP value of scheme I (DF.FC1) is only 0.51.

Second, by using scheme III and retraining a new deep CNN model on the new facial image dataset, the performance of deep features can be significantly boosted. For example, the mAP of ReCLS.FC2 is about 0.81. The improvement over the regular Hog-LBP-Gabor feature is almost 23%, which indicate scheme III can considerably extract a set of suitable feature representation for new image retrieval task. In general, the intra-personal differences might be even larger than the inter-personal differences on facial image datasets, which also indicates that we need a higher level feature generalization scheme for facial image retrieval problem.

Finally, based on the KNN annotation method, we compare the Precision-Recall curves of scheme I and scheme III, as shown in Figure 4. We can see that the retrieval performance can be significantly boosted by adopting scheme III. This encouraging results again validate the good generalization performance of the CNN models for learning effective features in a new domain.

6. CONCLUSIONS

Inspired by recent successes of deep learning techniques, in this paper, we attempt to address the long-standing fundamental feature representation problem in Content-based Image Retrieval (CBIR). We aim to evaluate if deep learning is a hope for bridging the semantic gap in CBIR for the long term, and how much empirical improvements in CBIR tasks can be achieved by exploring the state-of-the-art deep learning techniques for learning feature representations and similarity measures. In particular, we investigate a framework of deep learning with application to CBIR tasks with an extensive set of empirical studies by examining a state-of-the-art deep learning method (convolutional neural networks) for CBIR tasks under varied settings.

Our encouraging results from the extensive empirical studies reveal that (i) deep CNN model pre-trained on large scale dataset

[4] http://goo.gl/QQUvjj

Table 5: The Recall (@Precision=95%) and mean Average Precision on the Pubfig83LFW Dataset.

	Hog-LBP-Gabor		DF.FC1(Best)		ReCLS.FC1		ReCLS.FC2		ReCLS.FC3	
Algorithm	Recall	mAP	Recall	mAP	Recall	mAP	Recall	mAP	Recall	mAP
Nearest Neighbor(NN)	0.249	0.655	0.330	0.514	0.434	0.790	**0.421**	**0.805**	0.259	0.733

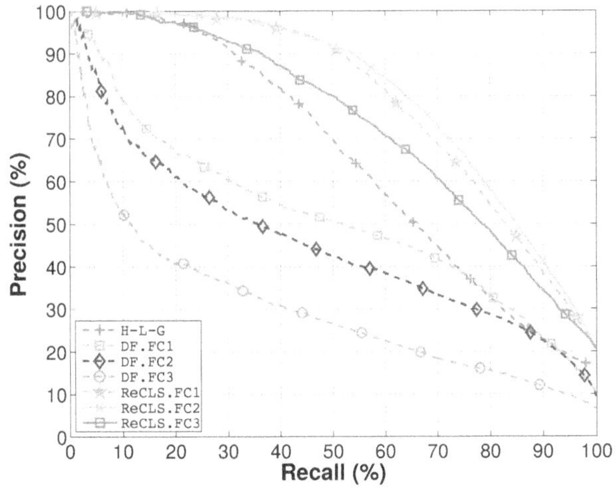

Figure 4: Precision-recall result on the Pubfig83LFW dataset.

can be directly used for features extraction in new CBIR tasks, the promising results on Caltech256 dataset demonstrate that the pre-trained model are able to capture high semantic information in the raw pixels; (ii) The features extracted by pre-trained CNN model may or may not be better than the traditional hand-crafted features, but with proper feature refining schemes, the deep learning feature representations consistently outperform conventional hand-crafted features on all datasets; (iii) When being applied for feature representation in a new domain, we found that similarity learning can further boost the retrieval performance of the direct feature output of pre-trained deep models; and (iv) Finally, by retraining the deep models with classification or similarity learning objective on the new domain, we found that the retrieval performance could be boosted significantly which is much better than the improvements made by "shallow" similarity learning. Despite encouraging results achieved, we believe this is just a beginning for deep learning with application to CBIR tasks, and there are still many open challenges. In future work, we will investigate more advanced deep learning techniques and evaluate more other diverse datasets for more in-depth empirical studies so as to give more insights for bringing the semantic gap of multimedia information retrieval in the long term.

7. ACKNOWLEDGEMENT

This work was supported by the National High Technology Research and Development Program of China (2014AA015202), the National Nature Science Foundation of China (61173054, 61428207), the National Key Technology Research and Development Program of China (2012BAH39B02).

8. REFERENCES

[1] D. H. Ackley, G. E. Hinton, and T. J. Sejnowski. A learning algorithm for boltzmann machines*. *Cognitive science*, 9(1):147–169, 1985.

[2] A. Bar-Hillel, T. Hertz, N. Shental, and D. Weinshall. Learning distance functions using equivalence relations. In *ICML*, pages 11–18, 2003.

[3] H. Bay, T. Tuytelaars, and L. J. V. Gool. Surf: Speeded up robust features. In *ECCV (1)*, pages 404–417, 2006.

[4] B. C. Becker and E. G. Ortiz. Evaluating open-universe face identification on the web. In *CVPR Workshops*, pages 904–911, 2013.

[5] Y. Bengio, A. C. Courville, and P. Vincent. Unsupervised feature learning and deep learning: A review and new perspectives. *CoRR*, abs/1206.5538, 2012.

[6] H. Chang and D.-Y. Yeung. Kernel-based distance metric learning for content-based image retrieval. *Image and Vision Computing*, 25(5):695–703, 2007.

[7] G. Chechik, V. Sharma, U. Shalit, and S. Bengio. Large scale online learning of image similarity through ranking. *Journal of Machine Learning Research*, 11:1109–1135, 2010.

[8] D. C. Ciresan, A. Giusti, L. M. Gambardella, and J. Schmidhuber. Deep neural networks segment neuronal membranes in electron microscopy images. In *NIPS*, pages 2852–2860, 2012.

[9] K. Crammer, O. Dekel, J. Keshet, S. Shalev-Shwartz, and Y. Singer. Online passive-aggressive algorithms. *Journal of Machine Learning Research*, 7:551–585, 2006.

[10] J. Dean, G. Corrado, R. Monga, K. Chen, M. Devin, Q. V. Le, M. Z. Mao, M. Ranzato, A. W. Senior, P. A. Tucker, K. Yang, and A. Y. Ng. Large scale distributed deep networks. In *NIPS*, pages 1232–1240, 2012.

[11] L. Deng. A tutorial survey of architectures, algorithms, and applications for deep learning. *APSIPA Transactions on Signal and Information Processing*, 3:e2, 2014.

[12] C. Domeniconi, J. Peng, and D. Gunopulos. Locally adaptive metric nearest-neighbor classification. *IEEE Trans. Pattern Anal. Mach. Intell.*, 24(9):1281–1285, 2002.

[13] J. Donahue, Y. Jia, O. Vinyals, J. Hoffman, N. Zhang, E. Tzeng, and T. Darrell. Decaf: A deep convolutional activation feature for generic visual recognition. *CoRR*, abs/1310.1531, 2013.

[14] R. B. Girshick, J. Donahue, T. Darrell, and J. Malik. Rich feature hierarchies for accurate object detection and semantic segmentation. *CoRR*, abs/1311.2524, 2013.

[15] M. Guillaumin, J. J. Verbeek, and C. Schmid. Is that you? metric learning approaches for face identification. In *ICCV*, pages 498–505, 2009.

[16] G. Hinton, L. Deng, D. Yu, G. E. Dahl, A.-r. Mohamed, N. Jaitly, A. Senior, V. Vanhoucke, P. Nguyen, T. N. Sainath, et al. Deep neural networks for acoustic modeling in speech recognition: The shared views of four research groups. *Signal Processing Magazine, IEEE*, 29(6):82–97, 2012.

[17] G. E. Hinton, S. Osindero, and Y. W. Teh. A fast learning algorithm for deep belief nets. *Neural Computation*, 18(7):1527–1554, 2006.

[18] S. C. H. Hoi, W. Liu, M. R. Lyu, and W.-Y. Ma. Learning distance metrics with contextual constraints for image retrieval. In *CVPR (2)*, pages 2072–2078, 2006.

[19] E. H. Huang, R. Socher, C. D. Manning, and A. Y. Ng. Improving word representations via global context and multiple word prototypes. In *ACL (1)*, pages 873–882, 2012.

[20] G. B. Huang, M. Ramesh, T. Berg, and E. Learned-Miller. Labeled faces in the wild: A database for studying face recognition in unconstrained environments. Technical Report 07-49, University of Massachusetts, Amherst, October 2007.

[21] A. K. Jain and A. Vailaya. Image retrieval using color and shape. *Pattern Recognition*, 29(8):1233–1244, 1996.

[22] P. Jain, B. Kulis, I. S. Dhillon, and K. Grauman. Online metric learning and fast similarity search. In *NIPS*, pages 761–768, 2008.

[23] H. Jégou, F. Perronnin, M. Douze, J. Sánchez, P. Pérez, and C. Schmid. Aggregating local image descriptors into compact codes. *IEEE Trans. Pattern Anal. Mach. Intell.*, 34(9):1704–1716, 2012.

[24] R. Jin, S. Wang, and Y. Zhou. Regularized distance metric learning: Theory and algorithm. In *NIPS*, pages 862–870, 2009.

[25] Y. Jing and S. Baluja. Visualrank: Applying pagerank to large-scale image search. *IEEE Trans. Pattern Anal. Mach. Intell.*, 30(11):1877–1890, 2008.

[26] A. Krizhevsky, I. Sutskever, and G. E. Hinton. Imagenet classification with deep convolutional neural networks. In *NIPS*, pages 1106–1114, 2012.

[27] N. Kumar, A. C. Berg, P. N. Belhumeur, and S. K. Nayar. Attribute and simile classifiers for face verification. In *ICCV*, pages 365–372, 2009.

[28] Y. LeCun, L. Bottou, Y. Bengio, and P. Haffner. Gradient-based learning applied to document recognition. *Proceedings of the IEEE*, 86(11):2278–2324, 1998.

[29] J.-E. Lee, R. Jin, and A. K. Jain. Rank-based distance metric learning: An application to image retrieval. In *CVPR*, 2008.

[30] M. S. Lew, N. Sebe, C. Djeraba, and R. Jain. Content-based multimedia information retrieval: State of the art and challenges. *TOMCCAP*, 2(1):1–19, 2006.

[31] D. G. Lowe. Object recognition from local scale-invariant features. In *ICCV*, pages 1150–1157, 1999.

[32] B. S. Manjunath and W.-Y. Ma. Texture features for browsing and retrieval of image data. *IEEE Trans. Pattern Anal. Mach. Intell.*, 18(8):837–842, 1996.

[33] A. S. Mian, Y. Hu, R. Hartley, and R. A. Owens. Image set based face recognition using self-regularized non-negative coding and adaptive distance metric learning. *IEEE Transactions on Image Processing*, 22(12):5252–5262, 2013.

[34] T. Mikolov, W. tau Yih, and G. Zweig. Linguistic regularities in continuous space word representations. In *HLT-NAACL*, pages 746–751, 2013.

[35] M. Norouzi, D. J. Fleet, and R. Salakhutdinov. Hamming distance metric learning. In *NIPS*, pages 1070–1078, 2012.

[36] A. Oliva and A. Torralba. Modeling the shape of the scene: A holistic representation of the spatial envelope. *International Journal of Computer Vision*, 42(3):145–175, 2001.

[37] A. Oliva and A. Torralba. Scene-centered description from spatial envelope properties. In *Biologically Motivated Computer Vision*, pages 263–272, 2002.

[38] J. Philbin, O. Chum, M. Isard, J. Sivic, and A. Zisserman. Object retrieval with large vocabularies and fast spatial matching. In *CVPR*, 2007.

[39] A. S. Razavian, H. Azizpour, J. Sullivan, and S. Carlsson. Cnn features off-the-shelf: an astounding baseline for recognition. *CoRR*, abs/1403.6382, 2014.

[40] R. Salakhutdinov and G. E. Hinton. Deep boltzmann machines. In *AISTATS*, pages 448–455, 2009.

[41] R. Salakhutdinov and G. E. Hinton. Semantic hashing. *Int. J. Approx. Reasoning*, 50(7):969–978, 2009.

[42] R. Salakhutdinov, A. Mnih, and G. E. Hinton. Restricted boltzmann machines for collaborative filtering. In *ICML*, pages 791–798, 2007.

[43] P. Sermanet, D. Eigen, X. Zhang, M. Mathieu, R. Fergus, and Y. LeCun. Overfeat: Integrated recognition, localization and detection using convolutional networks. *CoRR*, abs/1312.6229, 2013.

[44] J. Sivic, B. C. Russell, A. A. Efros, A. Zisserman, and W. T. Freeman. Discovering objects and their localization in images. In *ICCV*, pages 370–377, 2005.

[45] A. W. M. Smeulders, M. Worring, S. Santini, A. Gupta, and R. Jain. Content-based image retrieval at the end of the early years. *IEEE Trans. Pattern Anal. Mach. Intell.*, 22(12):1349–1380, 2000.

[46] D. Wang, S. C. H. Hoi, P. Wu, J. Zhu, Y. He, and C. Miao. Learning to name faces: a multimodal learning scheme for search-based face annotation. In *SIGIR*, pages 443–452, 2013.

[47] Z. Wang, Y. Hu, and L.-T. Chia. Learning image-to-class distance metric for image classification. *ACM TIST*, 4(2):34, 2013.

[48] K. Q. Weinberger, J. Blitzer, and L. K. Saul. Distance metric learning for large margin nearest neighbor classification. In *NIPS*, 2005.

[49] J. Wu and J. M. Rehg. Centrist: A visual descriptor for scene categorization. *IEEE Trans. Pattern Anal. Mach. Intell.*, 33(8):1489–1501, 2011.

[50] L. Wu and S. C. H. Hoi. Enhancing bag-of-words models with semantics-preserving metric learning. *IEEE MultiMedia*, 18(1):24–37, 2011.

[51] L. Wu, S. C. H. Hoi, and N. Yu. Semantics-preserving bag-of-words models and applications. *IEEE Transactions on Image Processing*, 19(7):1908–1920, 2010.

[52] P. Wu, S. C. H. Hoi, H. Xia, P. Zhao, D. Wang, and C. Miao. Online multimodal deep similarity learning with application to image retrieval. In *ACM Multimedia*, pages 153–162, 2013.

[53] H. Xie, Y. Zhang, J. Tan, L. Guo, and J. Li. Contextual query expansion for image retrieval. *IEEE Transactions on Multimedia*, 16(4):1104–1114, 2014.

[54] J. Yang, Y.-G. Jiang, A. G. Hauptmann, and C.-W. Ngo. Evaluating bag-of-visual-words representations in scene classification. In *Multimedia Information Retrieval*, pages 197–206, 2007.

[55] D. Yu, M. L. Seltzer, J. Li, J.-T. Huang, and F. Seide. Feature learning in deep neural networks - a study on speech recognition tasks. *CoRR*, abs/1301.3605, 2013.

[56] M. D. Zeiler and R. Fergus. Visualizing and understanding convolutional networks. *CoRR*, abs/1311.2901, 2013.

[57] L. Zhang, Y. Zhang, X. Gu, J. Tang, and Q. Tian. Scalable similarity search with topology preserving hashing. *IEEE Transactions on Image Processing*, 23(7):3025–3039, 2014.

[58] Y. Zhang, L. Zhang, and Q. Tian. A prior-free weighting scheme for binary code ranking. *IEEE Transactions on Multimedia*, 16(4):1127–1139, 2014.

Exploring Inter-feature and Inter-class Relationships with Deep Neural Networks for Video Classification

Zuxuan Wu[1], Yu-Gang Jiang[1], Jun Wang[2], Jian Pu[1], Xiangyang Xue[1]
[1]School of Computer Science, Shanghai Key Laboratory of Intelligent Information Processing, Fudan University, Shanghai, China
[2]Institute of Data Science and Technology, Alibaba Group, Seattle, WA, USA
{zxwu, ygj, jianpu, xyxue}@fudan.edu.cn, wongjun@gmail.com

ABSTRACT

Videos contain very rich semantics and are intrinsically multimodal. In this paper, we study the challenging task of classifying videos according to their high-level semantics such as human actions or complex events. Although extensive efforts have been paid to study this problem, most existing works combined multiple features using simple fusion strategies and neglected the exploration of inter-class semantic relationships. In this paper, we propose a novel unified framework that jointly learns feature relationships and exploits the class relationships for improved video classification performance. Specifically, these two types of relationships are learned and utilized by rigorously imposing regularizations in a deep neural network (DNN). Such a regularized DNN can be efficiently launched using a GPU implementation with an affordable training cost. Through arming the DNN with better capability of exploring both the inter-feature and the inter-class relationships, the proposed regularized DNN is more suitable for identifying video semantics. With extensive experimental evaluations, we demonstrate that the proposed framework exhibits superior performance over several state-of-the-art approaches. On the well-known Hollywood2 and Columbia Consumer Video benchmarks, we obtain to-date the best reported results: 65.7% and 70.6% respectively in terms of mean average precision.

Categories and Subject Descriptors

H.3.1 [**Information Storage and Retrieval**]: Content Analysis and Indexing—*Indexing methods*

Keywords

Multimodal Features; Class Relationships; Deep Neural Networks; Action and Event Recognition

1. INTRODUCTION

Techniques for recognizing high-level semantics in diverse unconstrained videos can be deployed in many applications, such as Web video search and video surveillance systems. However, it is well-known that recognizing or classifying the video semantics is an extremely challenging task due to various factors, such as the semantic gap between low-level video features and the complex semantics. While significant progress has been made in recent years, most state-of-the-art solutions often utilized a large set of features with simple fusion strategies to model high-level video semantics. For instance, two popular ways of combining multiple video features are early fusion and late fusion [41]. Early fusion concatenates all the feature vectors into a long representation for model training and testing, while late fusion trains a model using each feature separately and combines the outputs of all the models. Both methods do not have the capability of explicitly modeling the correlations among the video features, which can be exploited for deriving better representations. In addition, the existing video classification methods often neglected the inter-class relationships among video semantics. Note that such semantic correlations can be exploited to boost the classification performance since knowing the presence of one class may help predict other correlated semantics contained in the same video. Although there exist a few works investigating multi-feature fusion or exploring the inter-class relationships, as will be discussed in the next section, they mostly addressed the two problems separately. Also, many existing methods are computationally expensive; thus, they are less feasible for large scale applications.

Realizing the limitations of the existing works, in this paper, we propose a unified framework based on deep neural network (DNN), which jointly learns feature relationships and class relationships, and simultaneously carries out video classification within the same framework utilizing the learned relationships. Figure 1 gives a conceptual diagram of the proposed approach. First, we extract various video features including local visual descriptors and audio descriptors. The features are then used as the inputs of a DNN, where the first two layers are input layer and feature transformation layer. The third layer of the network is called *fusion layer*, where structural regularization is imposed on the network weights to identify and utilize the feature relationships. Specifically, the regularization terms are designed based on the observation of two natural properties of the inter-feature relationships, *correlation* and *diversity*. The former means that different features may share some common patterns in a middle level representation lying between the original features and the high-level semantics. The latter emphasizes the unique characteristics of different features,

MM'14, November 03 - 07 2014, Orlando, FL, USA

http://dx.doi.org/10.1145/2647868.2654931.

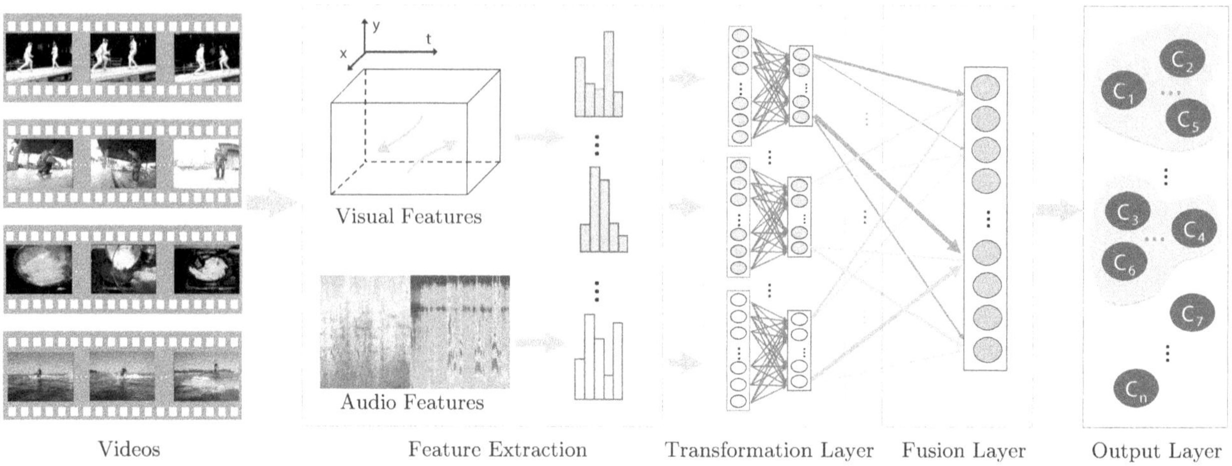

Figure 1: Overview of the proposed DNN-based video classification framework. Various visual/audio features are first extracted and then used as inputs of a DNN. The features are transformed (abstracted) using one layer of neurons before fusion. On the fusion layer, regularization on the network parameters is imposed to ensure that different features can share correlated dimensions while preserving their unique characteristics. As indicated by line width in the figure, some dimensions of different features may be highly correlated (the thick lines pointing to the same neuron). After that, the weights between the fusion and the output layer are also regularized to identify groups of classes. Both the learned inter-feature and inter-class relationships are utilized for improved classification performance.

which serve as complementary information for predicting the video semantics. Through modeling these two properties using a feature correlation matrix, we impose a trace-norm regularization over the fusion weights to reveal the hidden correlation and diversity of the features.

For the inter-class relationships, we impose regularizations on the weights of the final *output layer* to automatically identify the grouping structures of video classes, as well as the outlier classes. Semantic classes within the same group share commonalities or correlations that can be utilized as knowledge sharing for improved classification performance, while the outlier classes should be excluded from negative knowledge sharing. We will show that by imposing a similar trace-norm based regularization on the weights of the output layer, we are able to explore such complex inter-class relationships effectively to produce better video classification results. Therefore, this allows us to develop a unified framework using a regularized DNN, which can be easily implemented using a GPU with affordable training cost.

Notice that it is feasible to use raw video data as inputs instead of the hand-crafted features like the recent works on image classification using deep learning [22]. In this case, the convolutional neural network (CNN) can be adopted for performing feature extraction from the raw data. The reasons of using the hand-crafted features in our proposed framework are two-folds. First, the hand-crafted features are widely used in video classification and remain the central components of some video analytical systems that generated recent state-of-the-art results on tasks like human action recognition [46] and event recognition [1, 23]. By using these features it is easy to make fair comparisons with the traditional semantic classification approaches such as the popular SVM classifiers. Second, extracting features using neural networks needs more layers of neurons that incur a significant number of additional parameters to be tuned, requiring much more training data. Note that in many video classification tasks, the amount of available training data is far less from sufficient for training a neural network with too many layers. Therefore, in this paper, we focus the proposed regularized DNN on the tasks of feature fusion and video semantic classification.

To the best of our knowledge, this work represents the first attempt to capture both the feature and the class relationships in a DNN for video classification. Our major contributions are summarized as follows:

1. We propose to impose structural regularization on the *fusion layer* in a DNN to identify the correlations of multiple features, while still maintaining their diversities. This unique capacity distinguishes the proposed method from most of the existing works that often adopted shallow fusion process without considering the deep exploration of the feature correlations.

2. We also propose to explore inter-class relationships through imposing a similar structure regularization on *output layer* of the DNN. Therefore, both the inter-feature and the inter-class relationships are formulated and explored in a unified framework, which can be easily implemented with a GPU and trained with an affordable time cost.

3. Extensive empirical evaluations are provided to corroborate the effectiveness of the proposed framework in detail, and we attained to-date the highest performance on the widely used real-world benchmarks.

The remaining sections of this paper are organized as follows. Section 2 discusses related works. Section 3 elaborates the proposed framework, including both formulation and optimization. Extensive experimental results and comparisons with alternative methods and the state of the arts are reported and discussed in Section 4. Finally, Section 5 concludes this paper.

2. RELATED WORK

Extensive studies have been conducted in the field of video classification, and typical approaches often combined several multiple features in a standard machine learning pipeline using classifiers like the SVM. Most of the existing work focused on developing effective features [10, 24, 46], novel recognition methods [29, 39], or comprehensive systems that integrate multiple features and classifiers for competitive classification performance [23, 30]. Besides accuracy, efficiency is another important factor that should be considered in the design of a modern video classification system. Several recent studies focused on this issue by using efficient classification methods [27] or parallel computing [49].

In the following we focus our discussion on works investigating multi-feature fusion, and on those exploring inter-class relationships, which are more relevant to this paper.

2.1 Fusing Multiple Features

As aforementioned, there exist two popular fusion strategies, known as early fusion and late fusion. Although both strategies are not able to explore hidden feature relationships such as the correlations between features, they are widely used in many state-of-the-art systems due to the simplicity [1]. In addition, both of them require to design fusion weights that indicate the importance of each individual feature. The weights can be set as equal using heuristics (a.k.a. average fusion), or learned using the cross validation method. Some other works also employed multiple kernel learning (MKL) [5] to estimate the fusion weights [7, 31], which may lead to performance gain that is nevertheless often observed to be insignificant [45].

More recently, several advanced feature fusion approaches have been proposed. In [50], an optimization framework was used for robust late fusion to derive better combination of multiple feature modalities. It seeks a shared low-rank matrix to remove noises of certain modalities, which requires to iteratively compute singular value decomposition with a cubic time complexity, and thus is less scalable for large scale real-world applications. In a following up work by Liu et al. [25], dynamic fusion was adopted to find the best feature combination for each sample. This approach was proved effective but is extremely time-consuming. In [17], Jiang et al. proposed to construct an audio-visual joint codebook based on the discovered correlations between audio and visual features for video concept classification. The approach pointed out a promising direction as this is among the first works performing deep mining of feature correlations. However, the used visual features were computed on each segmented patches from video frames, which is computationally prohibitive for most real-word scenarios. The approach was further enhanced in [18], where the temporal interaction of audio-visual features was investigated. Jhuo et al. [16] improved the speed of training the audio-visual joint codebook by using standard local visual features like the SIFT, instead of the segmentation-based region features.

There are also a few studies on combining multiple features in neural networks, which are closely related to our work. A deep denoised auto-encoder was adopted to learn a shared representation from mutimodal inputs [32], and similarly, a deep Boltzmann machine was utilized to fuse visual and textual features [42]. However, both methods integrated multiple features without elaborately considering the feature correlation and diversity. One important message delivered in this paper is that *regularized fusion* of multiple features is intuitively reasonable and empirically effective, compared with those "free" forms of fusion approaches.

2.2 Exploring Inter-class Relationships

There are many existing works on exploring class relationships, often called context, for improved classification performance. In [44], Torralba et al. highlighted the importance of context in object detection. In [6, 37], co-occurrence context was utilized to enforce object recognition in images. For video classification, Qi et al. [36] proposed to use a multi-label learning method based on ideas from the Gibbs random field. Jiang et al. [19] proposed a semantic diffusion method to utilize class-relationships for video annotation. The algorithm is also capable of adapting the pre-defined class relationships to a new test data domain. Weng et al. [47] proposed a domain-adaptive method that not only explored the class relationships, but also utilized temporal structural information in long broadcast news videos for better annotation performance. Most of these approaches, however, are largely based on the co-occurrence statistics of the video classes, and cannot be used in the cases where the classes share commonalities but do not explicitly co-occur. Our approach can automatically learn such commonalities via a regularized DNN using a rigorous formulation.

The regularization terms used in our approach are partly motivated by recent advances in Multiple Task Learning (MTL) [14, 52]. MTL trains multiple models simultaneously and improves the performance of a task (classifier) with the help of other related tasks. Recent years have witnessed practical successes of MTL in many applications, such as disease prediction [51, 53] and financial stock selection [13]. Sharing commonalities between different tasks is the central idea of MTL and several approaches have been developed with regularizations on shared common patterns across classes [9, 21, 35]. These works considered the class relationships in classification or regression tasks with conventional shallow learning models, but never injected similar regularizations into neural networks.

In fact, multi-layered neural network can be considered as one of the earliest MTL models [8] (see Figure 2 (b)). In such a neural network, each unit in the output layer corresponds to a task and the hidden layer neurons can be regarded as shared common patterns. In this paper, we argue that imposing explicit forms of regularization ensures the deep modeling of complex class relationships for video classification, and thus generates better performance than the traditional neural network with implicit task sharing.

3. METHODOLOGY

This section elaborates our proposed method. We start from introducing the notations and the problem setup. Then a brief introduction of standard DNN is given to support later discussions.

3.1 Notations and Problem Setup

Assume that we are given a training set with N video clips, which are associated with C semantic classes. Here each video clip is represented by M different features, such as various visual and audio descriptors. Therefore, we can denote each training sample as an $(M+1)$-tuple:

$$(\mathbf{x}_n^1, \cdots, \mathbf{x}_n^m, \cdots, \mathbf{x}_n^M, \mathbf{y}_n), n = 1, \cdots, N,$$

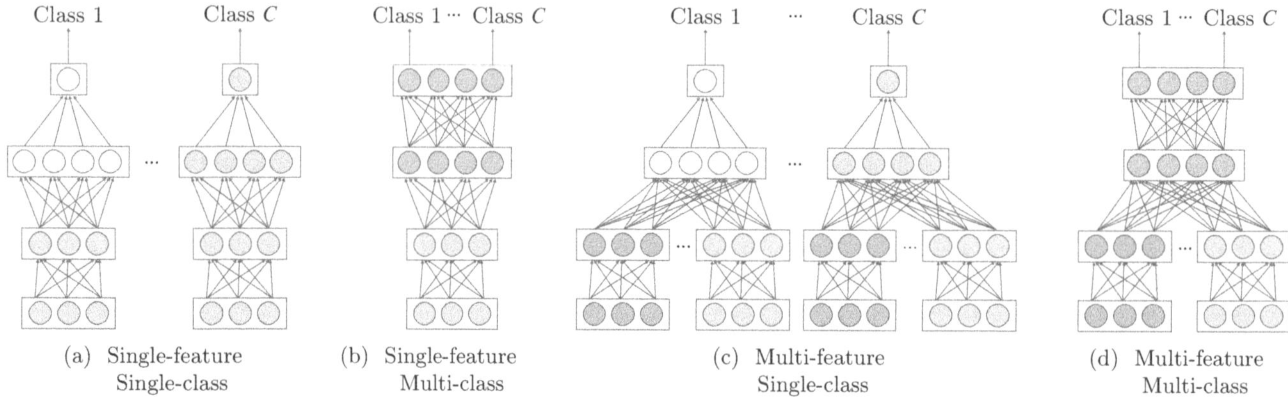

Figure 2: Illustration of different neural network structures. (b) is the most popular structure for multi-class prediction, while (d) was used in works like [42] to combine multiple features, where features are processed separately in the network and then merged through a middle layer. In this paper, we impose regularizations on the same structure as shown in (d) to explore both the inter-feature and the inter-class relationships.

where $\mathbf{x}_n^m$ represents the m-th feature representation of the n-th video sample, and $\mathbf{y}_n = [y_{n1} \cdots y_{nc} \cdots y_{nC}]^\top \in \mathbb{R}^C$ is the corresponding semantic label with the c-th element $y_{nc} = 1$ if the n-th video sample is associated with the c-th semantic class. The goal is to train prediction models that can classify new test videos. A straightforward way is to independently train one classifier for each semantic class, and different features can be combined using either the early fusion or the late fusion scheme. However, such an independent training strategy does not explore the inter-feature as well as the inter-class relationships. Here, we propose a DNN based video classification model that carries out *feature sharing* in the fusion layer through exploring the correlation and diversity of multiple features, as shown in Figure 1. In addition, the prediction layer of our deep neural network is also regularized to enforce *knowledge sharing* across different classes. Hence, both kinds of relationships are explicitly explored in a uniform learning process. Below we first introduce the standard DNN with a single feature and then present the details of our proposed regularized DNN.

3.2 DNN Learning with Single Feature

Inspired by the biological nervous systems, DNN uses a large number of interconnected neurons to construct complex computational models. Through organizing the neurons in multiple layers, this method possesses strong non-linear abstraction capacity and is able to learn arbitrary mapping functions from inputs to outputs as long as being given sufficient training data. Below we briefly review a standard DNN with only one feature as the input, i.e., $M = 1$.

In a DNN with a total of L layers, we denote $\mathbf{a}_{l-1}$ and $\mathbf{a}_l$ as the input and the output of the l-th layer for a single feature, $l = 1, \cdots, L$, while $\mathbf{W}_l$ and $\mathbf{b}_l$ refer to the weight matrix and the bias vector of the l-th layer, respectively. The transition function from the $(l-1)$-th layer to the l-th layer can be formulated as:

$$\mathbf{a}_l = \begin{cases} \sigma(\mathbf{W}_{l-1}\mathbf{a}_{l-1} + \mathbf{b}_{l-1}), & l > 1; \\ \mathbf{x}, & l = 1. \end{cases} \quad (1)$$

Here $\sigma(\cdot)$ is a nonlinear sigmoid function, which is often defined as

$$\sigma(\mathbf{x}) = \frac{1}{1 + e^{-\mathbf{x}}}.$$

Figure 2 (a) and (b) show two types of four-layered neural networks using a single feature as the input.

To derive the optimal weights for each layer, one can formulate the following optimization problem:

$$\min_{\mathbf{W}} \sum_{i=1}^{N} \ell(f(\mathbf{x}_i), \mathbf{y}_i) + \frac{\lambda_1}{2} \sum_{l=1}^{L-1} \|\mathbf{W}_l\|_F^2, \quad (2)$$

where the first part measures the empirical loss on the training data by summing the discrepancy between the outputs of the network $\hat{\mathbf{y}}_i = \mathbf{a}_L = f(\mathbf{x}_i)$ and the ground-truth labels $\mathbf{y}_i$, and the second part is a regularization term preventing overfitting. For simplicity, we can absorb $\mathbf{b}$ into the weights coefficient $\mathbf{W}$ by adding an additional dimension to the feature vectors with a constant value one.

3.3 Regularization on Feature Relationships

A single feature based DNN can be powerful in some cases. However, it can only be used with a single aspect of the data to perform semantic prediction. For complex data like the videos, the semantic information can be carried by different feature representations including both visual and audio clues. Note that simple fusion strategies, such as the early or late fusion, usually result in limited performance gain since the intrinsic relations among multiple feature representations are overlooked [4]. In addition, such simple fusion methods often incur extra efforts for training the classifiers. Therefore, it is desired to obtain a compact yet meaningful fused representation that fully leverages the complementary clues from various features. Below we extend the basic DNN to a regularized variant that is able to accommodate the deep fusion process of multiple features.

We are given a total of M features

$$\{\mathbf{x}_i^1, \cdots, \mathbf{x}_i^m, \cdots, \mathbf{x}_n^M\}, i = 1, \cdots, n$$

for each video sample. Motivated by the multisensory integration process of primary neurons in biological systems [33,

43], we propose to use one additional layer for the fusion of all the features, as shown in Figure 1. Accordingly, the transition equation for this fusion layer can be written as the following:

$$\mathbf{a}_F = \sigma\left(\sum_{m=1}^{M} \mathbf{W}_E^m \mathbf{a}_E^m + \mathbf{b}_E\right), \tag{3}$$

where E and F are the indices of the last layer of feature extraction and the fusion layer respectively (i.e., $F = E+1$). Here $\mathbf{a}_E^m \in \mathbb{R}^P$ denotes the extracted mid-level representation for the m-th feature which is first linearly transformed by the weight $\mathbf{W}_E^m$ and then non-linearly mapped to the new representation $\mathbf{a}_F$ using a sigmoid function.

Since all the feature representations correspond to the same video data, it is easy to understand that various features can be used to reveal the common latent patterns related to the video semantics. In addition, as mentioned earlier, different features could also be complementary because they have distinct characteristics. Therefore, the fusion process should aim to capture the relations among the features, while being able to reserve their unique characteristics at the same time. Instead of simply adding up multiple feature information, we specifically formulate an objective function that can regularize the fusion process to explore such correlations and diversity among the multiple features simultaneously. In particular, the weights, $\mathbf{W}_E^1, \cdots, \mathbf{W}_E^M$, which transform all features into a shared representation, are first vectorized into P dimensional vectors separately, where P is the product of the $\mathbf{a}_E^m$'s $(m = 1, \cdots, M)$ dimension and the $\mathbf{a}_F$'s dimension. Here, we assume the extracted features are of the same dimension. Then we stack these coefficient vectors into a matrix $\mathbf{W}_E \in \mathbb{R}^{P\times M}$, where each column of $\mathbf{W}_E$ corresponds to the weights of a single feature. Hence, the element $\mathbf{W}_E(i,j)$ is given as

$$\mathbf{W}_E(i,j) = \mathbf{W}_E^i(j), \quad i = 1, \cdots, M, \quad j = 1, \cdots, P.$$

Then we can formulate the following objective to design a regularized DNN:

$$\begin{aligned} \min_{\mathbf{W},\mathbf{\Psi}} \quad & \mathcal{L} + \frac{\lambda_1}{2}\left(\sum_{l=1}^{E}\sum_{m=1}^{M} \|\mathbf{W}_l^m\|_F^2 + \sum_{l=F}^{L-1}\|\mathbf{W}_l\|_F^2\right) \\ & + \frac{\lambda_2}{2}\mathrm{tr}(\mathbf{W}_E \mathbf{\Psi}^{-1}\mathbf{W}_E^T) \\ \text{s.t.} \quad & \mathbf{\Psi} \succeq 0, \end{aligned} \tag{4}$$

where $\mathcal{L} = \sum_{i=1}^{N} \ell(\hat{\mathbf{y}}_i, \mathbf{y}_i)$. Compared with the objective function in Equation 2 for the standard single feature neural network, the above cost function includes one additional regularization term. Note that the matrix $\mathbf{W}_E$ represents the coefficients over all the features. Here we use a symmetric and positive semidefinite matrix $\mathbf{\Psi} \in \mathbb{R}^{M\times M}$ to model the inter-feature correlation and introduce the last regularization term with the trace norm that can help learn the inter-feature relationship [12, 52]. Note that the entries with large values in $\mathbf{\Psi}$ indicate strong feature correlations, while small-valued entries denote the diversity among different features since they are less correlated. The coefficients λ_1 and λ_2 control the contributions from different regularization terms. Finally, the objective of learning the regularized DNN is performed as a joint optimization procedure over the weight matrix $\mathbf{W}$ and the feature correlation matrix $\mathbf{\Psi}$.

3.4 Regularization on Class Relationships

To recognize or classify C semantic categories, one can simply adopt the one-vs-all strategy to independently train C classifiers. Figure 2 (a) and (c) illustrate this one-vs-all training scheme with a total of C four-layered neural networks for the single-feature and multi-feature settings, respectively. Clearly, each of these C neural networks is separately learned, where knowledge sharing among different semantic categories is completely neglected. However, it is well recognized that video semantics also share some *commonality*, which indicates that certain semantic categories could be strongly correlated [19, 36]. Therefore, it is critical to explore such a commonality by simultaneously learning multiple video semantics, which can often lead to better learning performance. Note that, the commonality among multiple classes is often represented by the parameter sharing among different prediction models [3, 26]. Compared with the popular SVM method, it is more natural for DNN to perform multi-class training simultaneously. As shown in Figure 2 (b), by adopting a set of C units in the output layer, a single-feature based DNN can be easily extended to multi-class problems, and this structure has been widely adopted. Motivated by the regularization framework used in the standard MTL methods [3, 26], here we present a regularized DNN that aims at training multiple classifiers simultaneously with deeper exploration of the class relationships. To enforce the semantic sharing, we extend the original objective for a standard DNN to the following form:

$$\begin{aligned} \min_{\mathbf{W},\mathbf{\Omega}} \quad & \sum_{i=1}^{N} \ell(f(\mathbf{x}_i), \mathbf{y}_i) + \frac{\lambda_1}{2}\sum_{l=1}^{L-1}\|\mathbf{W}_l\|_F^2 \\ & + \lambda_2 \mathrm{tr}(\mathbf{W}_{L-1}\mathbf{\Omega}^{-1}\mathbf{W}_{L-1}^T). \\ \text{s.t.} \quad & \mathbf{\Omega} \succeq 0. \end{aligned} \tag{5}$$

Note that some previous MTL works assumed that the class relationships are explicitly given and are ready for use as prior knowledge [26], while our method does not require this. Following the convex formulation of MTL [52], here we impose a trace norm regularization term over the coefficients $\mathbf{W}_{L-1}$ of the output layer with the class relationships augmented as a matrix variable $\mathbf{\Omega} \in \mathbb{R}^{C\times C}$. Note that the constraint $\mathbf{\Omega} \succeq 0$ indicates that the class relationship matrix is positive semidefinite since it can be viewed as the similarity measure of the semantic classes. The coefficients λ_1 and λ_2 are regularization parameters. During the learning procedure, the optimal weight matrices $\{\mathbf{W}_l\}_{l=1}^{L}$ and the class relationship matrix $\mathbf{\Omega}$ are simultaneously derived.

3.5 The Unified Objective

To unify the above objectives into a joint framework, we now present a novel DNN formulation that explores both the inter-feature and the inter-class relationships. In our framework, we use one layer of neurons to fuse multiple features, where the objective is to bridge the gap between low-level features and the high-level video semantics. In the final layer of generating the predictions, we impose a trace norm regularization among different semantics to better learn the predictions of multiple classes. Mathematically, we incorporate the feature regularization in Equation 4 and the class regularization in Equation 5 into the following objective function:

$$\begin{aligned}\min_{\mathbf{W},\boldsymbol{\Psi},\boldsymbol{\Omega}} \quad & \mathcal{L} + \frac{\lambda_1}{2}\left(\sum_{l=1}^{E}\sum_{m=1}^{M}\|\mathbf{W}_l^m\|_F^2 + \sum_{l=F}^{L-1}\|\mathbf{W}_l\|_F^2\right) \\ & + \frac{\lambda_2}{2}\mathrm{tr}(\mathbf{W}_E\boldsymbol{\Psi}^{-1}\mathbf{W}_E^T) \\ & + \frac{\lambda_3}{2}\mathrm{tr}(\mathbf{W}_{L-1}\boldsymbol{\Omega}^{-1}\mathbf{W}_{L-1}^T), \\ \text{s.t.} \quad & \boldsymbol{\Psi} \succeq 0 \quad \mathrm{tr}(\boldsymbol{\Psi}) = 1, \\ & \boldsymbol{\Omega} \succeq 0 \quad \mathrm{tr}(\boldsymbol{\Omega}) = 1,\end{aligned} \tag{6}$$

where λ_1, λ_2, and λ_3 are regularization parameters. Compared with the original objective in Equation 2, we have two trace-norm regularization terms that are tailored for the fusion of multiple features and the exploration of the inter-class relationships, respectively. Two additional constraints $\mathrm{tr}(\boldsymbol{\Psi}) = 1$ and $\mathrm{tr}(\boldsymbol{\Omega}) = 1$ are used to restrict the complexity, as suggested in [52]. Finally, the above cost function is minimized with respect to the network weights $\{\mathbf{W}_l\}_{l=1}^{L}$, the inter-feature relationship matrix $\boldsymbol{\Psi}$, and the inter-class correlation matrix $\boldsymbol{\Omega}$.

3.6 Optimization

Among the variables in the minimization problem of Equation 6, two pairs of variables, i.e., $(\mathbf{W}_E, \boldsymbol{\Psi})$ and $(\mathbf{W}_{L-1}, \boldsymbol{\Omega})$, are coupled with each other. Therefore, we adopt the alternative optimization method to iteratively minimize the objective with respect to $\mathbf{W}_l^m$ $(l = 1, \cdots L, m = 1, \cdots, M)$, $\boldsymbol{\Psi}$, and $\boldsymbol{\Omega}$.

By fixing both $\boldsymbol{\Psi}$ and $\boldsymbol{\Omega}$, we first consider the minimization problem over $\mathbf{W}_l^m$, which is degenerated to a set of unconstrained univariate optimization problems:

$$\begin{aligned}\min_{\mathbf{W}_l^m} \quad & \mathcal{L} + \frac{\lambda_1}{2}\left(\sum_{l=1}^{E}\sum_{m=1}^{M}\|\mathbf{W}_l^m\|_F^2 + \sum_{l=F}^{L-1}\|\mathbf{W}_l\|_F^2\right) \\ & + \frac{\lambda_2}{2}\mathrm{tr}(\mathbf{W}_E\boldsymbol{\Psi}^{-1}\mathbf{W}_E^T) + \frac{\lambda_3}{2}\mathrm{tr}(\mathbf{W}_{L-1}\boldsymbol{\Omega}^{-1}\mathbf{W}_{L-1}^T).\end{aligned} \tag{7}$$

As all the terms of the above objective function are smooth, the gradient can be easily evaluated. Denote $\mathbf{G}_l^m$ as the gradient with respect to $\mathbf{W}_l^m$, the weight matrix for the l-th layer and the m-th feature is updated as:

$$\mathbf{W}_l^m = \mathbf{W}_l^m - \eta\mathbf{G}_l^m, \tag{8}$$

where η is the step length of the gradient descent.

We then introduce the solution of minimizing the objective function over $\boldsymbol{\Psi}$ with other variables being fixed. The problem in Equation 6 degenerates to:

$$\begin{aligned}\min_{\boldsymbol{\Psi}} \quad & \mathrm{tr}(\mathbf{W}_E\boldsymbol{\Psi}^{-1}\mathbf{W}_E^T), \\ \text{s.t.} \quad & \boldsymbol{\Psi} \succeq 0 \quad \mathrm{tr}(\boldsymbol{\Psi}) = 1.\end{aligned} \tag{9}$$

Adopting the Cauchy-Schwarz inequality, we obtain the analytical solution for the above minimization problem as:

$$\boldsymbol{\Psi} = \frac{(\mathbf{W}_E^T\mathbf{W}_E)^{\frac{1}{2}}}{\mathrm{tr}((\mathbf{W}_E^T\mathbf{W}_E)^{\frac{1}{2}})}. \tag{10}$$

Similarly, the optimal solution for $\boldsymbol{\Omega}$ is derived as:

$$\boldsymbol{\Omega} = \frac{(\mathbf{W}_{L-1}^T\mathbf{W}_{L-1})^{\frac{1}{2}}}{\mathrm{tr}((\mathbf{W}_{L-1}^T\mathbf{W}_{L-1})^{\frac{1}{2}})}. \tag{11}$$

Algorithm 1 Training Procedure of Regularized DNN

Require: $\mathbf{x}_n^m$: the representation of the m-th feature for the n-th video sample; $\mathbf{y}_n$: the semantic label of the n-th video sample;

1: Initialize $\mathbf{W}_l^m$ randomly, $\boldsymbol{\Psi} = \frac{1}{M}\mathbf{I}_M$ and $\boldsymbol{\Omega} = \frac{1}{C}\mathbf{I}_C$, where $\mathbf{I}_M$ and $\mathbf{I}_C$ are identity matrices;

2: **for** *epoch* = 1 to K **do**

3: Back propagate the prediction error from layer L to layer 1 by evaluating the gradient $\mathbf{G}_l^m$, and update the weight matrix $\mathbf{W}_l^m$ for each layer and each feature as:

$$\mathbf{W}_l^m = \mathbf{W}_l^m - \eta\mathbf{G}_l^m;$$

4: Update the feature relationship matrix $\boldsymbol{\Psi}$ according to Equation 10:

$$\boldsymbol{\Psi} = \frac{(\mathbf{W}_E^T\mathbf{W}_E)^{\frac{1}{2}}}{\mathrm{tr}((\mathbf{W}_E^T\mathbf{W}_E)^{\frac{1}{2}})};$$

5: Update the class relationship matrix $\boldsymbol{\Psi}$ according to Equation 11:

$$\boldsymbol{\Omega} = \frac{(\mathbf{W}_{L-1}^T\mathbf{W}_{L-1})^{\frac{1}{2}}}{\mathrm{tr}((\mathbf{W}_{L-1}^T\mathbf{W}_{L-1})^{\frac{1}{2}})}.$$

6: **end for**

Note that Zhang et al. adopted a similar solution as in Equation 11 to identify task correlations for a linear kernel based regression and classification task [52]. However, our method integrates more complex structural regularizations in a neural network architecture, where both the inter-feature and the inter-class relationships are explored for a completely different application. Hence, the difference of our method is fairly significant.

In our approach, the inter-feature and inter-class relationships are first estimated based on the corresponding weights in the neural networks. The relationships are then used in turn to adjust the network weights for improved classification performance. Using the trace norm allows us to derive the analytical solution in Equation 10 and Equation 11, which satisfies our goal of learning the relationships $\boldsymbol{\Psi}$ and $\boldsymbol{\Omega}$ based on $\mathbf{W}$. More specifically, the training procedure of the proposed method is summarized in Algorithm 1. For each epoch, additional efforts are required to compute the gradient matrix $\mathbf{G}_l^m$ for updating $\mathbf{W}_l^m$, as well as to update the matrices $\boldsymbol{\Omega}$ and $\boldsymbol{\Psi}$. The complexity of calculating the trace norms is the same as that of the $\ell 2$ norm. The update of $\boldsymbol{\Omega}$ and $\boldsymbol{\Psi}$ requires operations with a cubic complexity with respect to the number of features M and the number of video classes C, respectively. Note that these two numbers are often relatively much smaller than the number of data points used for DNN training. Therefore, the training cost of the proposed regularized DNN is very similar to that of a standard DNN. Our empirical study further confirms the efficiency of our method, as will be discussed in the next section.

4. EXPERIMENTS

4.1 Experimental Setup

4.1.1 *Datasets and Evaluation Measure*

We adopt three challenging benchmarks on action and event recognition to evaluate our method, as described in the following.

Hollywood2 [24]. The Hollywood2 dataset is one of the most popular benchmarks on action recognition in videos. Collected from 69 Hollywood movies, it contains 1,707 action video clips covering 12 classes: answering phone, driving car, eating, fighting, getting out of car, hand shaking, hugging, kissing, running, sitting down, sitting up and standing up. Following [24], the dataset is split into a training set with 823 videos and a test set with 884 videos.

Columbia Consumer Videos (CCV) [20]. The CCV dataset is a well-known benchmark on Internet consumer video analysis. It contains 9,317 videos collected from YouTube with annotations of 20 semantic classes, including objects (e.g., "cats"), scenes (e.g., "playground"), and events (e.g., "parade"). Since most of the classes are complex events, it requires a joint use of multiple feature clues like visual and audio representations to perform better classification. The dataset is evenly split into a training set and a test set.

CCV+. Since both the Hollywood2 and the CCV datasets are small in terms of the number of annotated classes, we additionally collected and annotated another 20 classes with in total of 5,159 video clips. These clips are merged with the CCV to form a larger dataset of 40 classes, named CCV+, containing 7,244 videos for training and 7,232 videos for testing. See Figure 3 for the list of class names and a few example frames.

For all the three datasets, the performance is measured by average precision (AP) for each class and mean AP (mAP) for overall results of all the classes.

4.1.2 Feature Representations

Visual Features. For the visual features, we consider the dense trajectory descriptors [46], which have exhibited strong performance on various benchmark datasets. Briefly, densely sampled local frame patches are first tracked over time and four descriptors are then computed for each trajectory: a 30-d trajectory shape descriptor, a 96-d histogram of oriented gradients (HOG) descriptor, a 108-d histogram of optical flow (HOF) descriptor, and a 108-d motion boundary histogram (MBH) descriptor. Finally, each descriptor is quantized into a 4,000-d bag-of-words representation, same as the settings used in [46].

Audio Features. It is well-known that the audio soundtracks contain useful clues for identifying some video semantics. Two types of video features are considered in our study. The first one is the popular MFCCs (Mel-Frequency Cepstral Coefficients), which are computed for every 32ms time-window with 50% overlap and then quantized into a bag-of-words representation. The second one is called Spectrogram SIFT [54]. The 1-d soundtrack of a video is transformed into a 2-D image based on the constant-Q spectrogram, on which standard SIFT descriptors are extracted and quantized into the bag-of-words representation.

Note that all these visual and audio features are adopted because they have demonstrated strong performance on various benchmarks; however, evaluating the performance of each single feature in detail is beyond the scope of this work. All the representations are normalized with RootSift [2], which has been shown to be more suitable for histogram-based features than the conventional L2 normalization.

4.1.3 Compared Approaches

To validate the effectiveness of our method, we compare with the following approaches:

Early Fusion with Neural Networks (NN-EF). All the features are concatenated into a long vector and then used as the input to train a neural network.

Late Fusion with Neural Networks (NN-LF). A separate neural network is trained using each feature independently and then the outputs of all the networks are fused to obtain the final classification results.

Early Fusion with SVM (SVM-EF). The popular χ^2 kernel SVM is adopted and the features are combined on the kernel level before classification.

Late Fusion with SVM (SVM-LF). A separate SVM classifier is trained for each feature and prediction results are then combined.

Multimodal Deep Boltzmann Machines (M-DBM). It is a fusion model proposed in [42], where multiple feature representations are used as the inputs of the Deep Boltzmann Machines.

Discriminative Model Fusion (DMF) [40]. As one of the earliest approaches in multimedia for context-based classification, DMF uses the outputs of an initial classifier, e.g., a standard DNN in our case, as features to train an SVM model as the second level classifier for final prediction.

Domain Adaptive Semantic Diffusion (DASD) [19]. This method uses a graph diffusion formulation for context-based classification. The prediction outputs of a normal DNN (without the regularizations) are used as inputs of the DASD in a post-processing refinement step. The approach also requires input of precomputed class relationships, which are usually estimated based on statistics of label co-occurrences in training data.

The first five approaches can be regarded as alternatives for feature fusion, while the last two approaches focus on the use of the class relationships. All the neural network based experiments are conducted on a single Nvidia Telsa K20 5GB GPU with MATLAB Parallel Computing Toolbox, which speeds up the training procedure by about 5 times than a decent Intel XEON CPU with 16 cores.

4.2 Results and Analysis

In this section, we first report results of our approach by disabling the regularizations on the output layer and the fusion layer respectively, in order to understand the contributions of only exploring the inter-feature or the inter-class relationships. This also ensures fair comparisons with the competing approaches. After that, we report results of using the entire framework, compare with recent state-of-the-art results, and analyze the effect of the number of training samples. Finally, we provide discussions on computational efficiency.

Throughout the experiments, we set the learning rate of the neural networks to 0.7, fix λ_1 to 3×10^{-5} in order to prevent overfitting, and tune λ_2 and λ_3 in the same range as λ_1. Following the conventional settings of DNN, we also adopt the mini batch gradient descent with the batch size being 70.

4.2.1 Effect of Exploring Feature Relationships

We first report results by only using fusion layer regularization on the DNN with the output layer regularization being disabled. Table 1 compares our approach, namely DNN-Fusion Regularization (DNN-FR), with the alternative feature fusion methods. As seen in the table, our approach achieves the best performance with clear gains over

Approaches	Hollywood2	CCV	CCV+
NN-EF	62.0%	66.7%	70.5%
NN-LF	58.5%	61.9%	64.7%
SVM-EF	62.6%	67.5%	70.0%
SVM-LF	62.1%	64.9%	68.5%
M-DBM[42]	61.5%	67.2%	70.1%
DNN-FR	**64.5%**	**69.1%**	**71.8%**

Table 1: Performance comparison (mAP) on the three datasets, using approaches that only explore the inter-feature relationships.

Approaches	Hollywood2	CCV	CCV+
DMF [40]	61.8%	67.6%	68.5%
DASD [19]	60.9%	66.8%	70.2%
DNN-CR	**63.0%**	**69.3%**	**72.1%**

Table 2: Performance comparison (mAP) on the three datasets, using approaches that only explore the inter-class relationships.

all the compared methods. Note that the M-DBM approach also utilizes a neural network for feature fusion, but in a *free* manner without explicitly taking feature relations into the learning process. These results validate the effectiveness of imposing the proposed fusion regularization in neural networks. Notice that, since these adopted datasets are very challenging and have been widely used, an absolute performance gain of 2% is generally considered as a significant improvement.

Comparing across the alternative approaches, early fusion tends to generate better results than late fusion. This observation is consistent with recent works, where the early fusion was more popularly used [1]. The neural network based approaches do not show significant gain over the SVM-based ones because the amount of training data in video classification is limited. With more training samples, the margin is expected to be significantly larger. In addition, for the contribution of the audio clues, we observed that for the classes with strong audio clues, such as "answering phone", adding audio features clearly improves the performance. On the contrary, for classes like "sitting down", using audio features may slightly degrade the result, which is easy to understand.

4.2.2 *Effect of Exploring Class Relationships*

Next we analyze the effect of solely imposing the regularization on the classification/output layer to explore the inter-class relationships, while disabling the regularization on the fusion layer. We compare our method, named as DNN-Classification Regularization (DNN-CR), with DMF and DASD and report the results in Table 2. Clearly, DNN-CR outperforms these two compared approaches, both of which use the outputs of the conventional DNN as inputs for context-based refinement. These results corroborate the effectiveness of the proposed regularization on the output layer. Note that the simple DMF is superior than the DASD because the latter requires pre-computed inter-class relationships, which are normally estimated based on the label co-occurrences in training data. However, some classes that share commonalities may not visually co-occur, resulting in

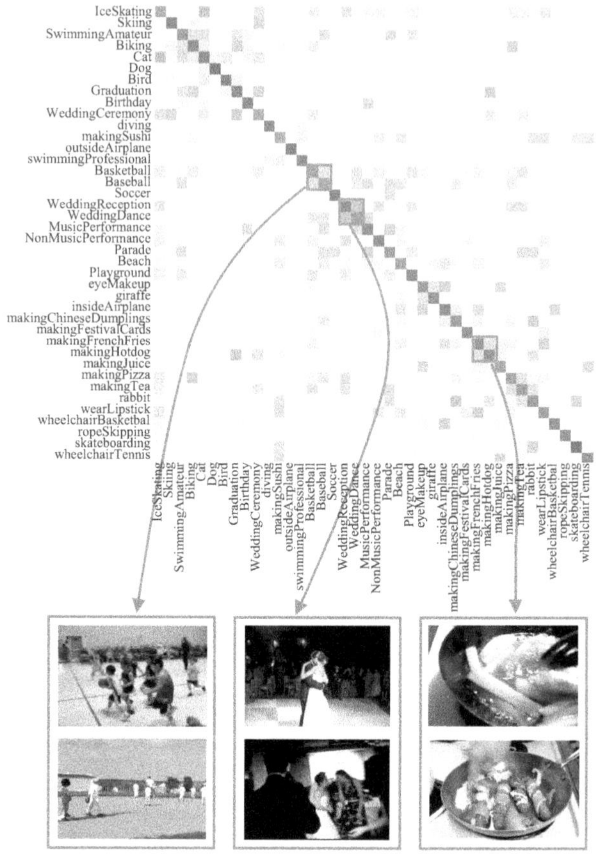

Figure 3: Class relationships in CCV+ indicated by the learned matrix $\boldsymbol{\Omega}$. Example video frames of a few found class groups are shown at the bottom.

a very sparse class relationship matrix that is insufficient for context-based learning. Several other alternative methods such as those based on the conditional random field [37] also rely on the relationship matrix and thus suffer from the same limitation.

To further show the power of our method in learning the class relationships, we visualize some results in Figure 3. As discussed in Section 3, values in the matrix $\boldsymbol{\Omega}$ can reflect the learned correlations among the classes. Hence, we can adopt spectral clustering on the matrix $\boldsymbol{\Omega}$ to group the video semantics, which are then re-ordered for the ease of visualization. We see that many classes sharing commonalities are grouped together, which confirms that our method can reveal the hidden class relationships.

4.2.3 *Results of the Entire Framework*

We now discuss the results of the entire framework, i.e., using regularizations on both the fusion layer and the output layer. In addition, to evaluate the performance using different amounts of training data, we plot the performance w.r.t. the number of training samples in Figure 4. Overall, substantial performance gains are observed from using the regularized DNN framework. Using regularizations on both layers also clearly achieves higher performance than solely imposing regularization on a single layer (i.e., only on $\mathbf{W_E}$) with clear margins. When there are less training samples, the improvement of our method is even more

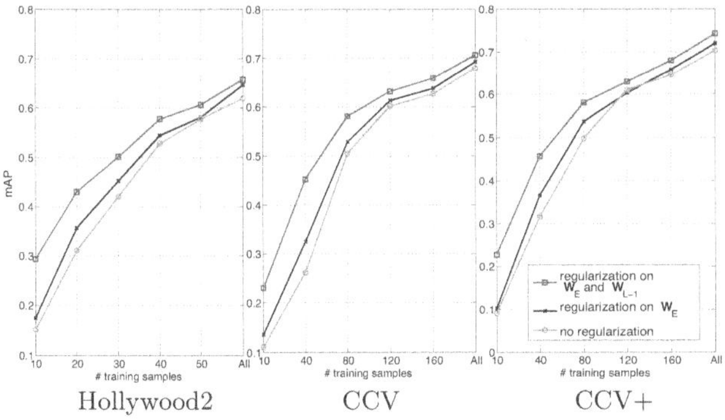

Figure 4: Performance on the three datasets using different number of training samples. We plot the results of DNN without regularization (red), DNN with regularization only on the fusion layer (black), and DNN with regularization on both the fusion and the output layers (blue). Consistent performance gains are obtained from imposing the proposed regularizations.

significant. An improvement of around 100% is obtained on all the three datasets when there are just 10 training samples per class. This demonstrates that the regularized DNN requires much less training data to achieve comparable performance to the non-regularized DNN. In addition, comparing the performance across the three datasets using all the training samples, the gain from exploring the class relationships is more significant on CCV+. This is because CCV+ has more classes and thus contains richer inter-class relationships that are helpful for classification.

Table 3 further compares our best results (from regularization on both layers) with several recently reported results on the Hollywood2 and the CCV datasets. On Hollywood2, our proposed method achieves the best mAP of 65.7%, outperforming all the recent results [15, 28, 46]. All these works are based on the dense trajectory features, and they performed classification using the simple early fusion method. Note that Wang et al. [46] and Oneata et al. [34] used the Fisher vector to encode the features, which has been shown to be more effective than the traditional bag-of-words representation [38]. However, the dimension of the Fisher vectors is too high to be used as inputs of the neural networks, since there is no sufficient training data to tune the numerous parameters. Therefore, we adopt the standard bag-of-words in this work, and it is very appealing to observe higher performance than the approaches using the Fisher vectors.

For the CCV dataset, several recent works have focused on the joint use of multiple audio-visual features. Xu et al. [48] and Ye et al. [50] adopted late fusion with specially designed methods to remove the noise of individually trained classifiers, and Jhuo et al. used a joint audio-visual codebook for classification [16]. Our approach is fundamentally different from these state-of-the-art methods in its design and produces significantly higher performance.

4.2.4 *Computational Efficiency*

Finally, we briefly compare and discuss the computational efficiency, using the Hollywood2 dataset. The average training time of each epoch for NN-EF, NN-LF and M-DBM are presented in Table 4, using a GPU-based implementation as

Hollywood2	mAP	CCV	mAP
Mathe et al. [28]	61.0%	Jiang et al. [20]	59.5%
Jain et al. [15]	62.5%	Jhuo et al. [16]	64.0%
Oneata et al. [34]	63.4%	Xu et al. [48]	60.3%
Wang et al. [46]	64.3%	Ye et al. [50]	64.0%
Regularized DNN	**65.7%**	Regularized DNN	**70.6%**

Table 3: Comparison with state-of-the-art results in the literature. Our method (Regularized DNN) achieves to-date the highest mAP on both the Hollywood2 and the CCV datasets.

Approaches	Training Time (s)
NN-EF	1.068±0.021
NN-LF	0.782±0.007
Regularized DNN	**0.640±0.002**

Table 4: Training time per epoch (seconds) of the neural network based approaches on the Hollywood2 dataset.

mentioned in Section 4.1.3. Our proposed method is more efficient than NN-EF and NN-LF as our regularized DNN contains less parameters to be learned. Specifically, compared with the early fusion, our framework processes the features separately in the first two layers and thus avoids the parameters interacting among them. The late fusion method requires the training of separate networks, which is also more expensive. Note that we exclude the M-DBM approach in this comparison, because it requires significant additional time to pre-train the network for weight initialization. For all the methods, several hundreds of epochs are normally needed to finish the training process (several minutes in total). Once the training is done, all these neural network based methods are extremely fast in terms of performing predictions on testing videos.

5. CONCLUSION

We have introduced a novel DNN framework that explores both inter-feature and inter-class relationships to achieve better classifications on video semantics. By imposing trace-norm based regularizations on a specially designed fusion layer and an output layer in the neural network, our method can learn a fused representation of multiple feature inputs and utilize the commonalities among the semantic classes for improved classification performance. Extensive experiments on popular benchmarks of action and event recognition have shown that our method consistently outperforms the alternative approaches as well as the recent state-of-the-art works. In addition, the proposed method is also similar to even faster than the traditional approaches in terms of the model training, which is very important for large scale applications. One important future work is to add the function of learning feature representations directly from raw video data in the framework, which would require much more training data as discussed earlier but may lead to substantial further performance improvements. Therefore, it would also be interesting and valuable if this extension could be done with an effort of collecting and annotating a larger collection of videos, like the Image-Net effort for image analysis [11], which is urgently needed to stimulate the research on large scale video classification.

Acknowledgement

This work was supported in part by a National 863 Program (#2014AA015101), a National Key Technologies Research and Development Program (#2013BAH09F01), a grant from NSF China (#61201387), and three grants from the Science and Technology Commission of Shanghai Municipality (#13PJ1400400, #13511504503, #12511501602).

6. REFERENCES

[1] R. Aly, R. Arandjelovic, K. Chatfield, and et al. The AXES submissions at TrecVid 2013. In *NIST TRECVID Workshop*, 2013.

[2] R. Arandjelovic and A. Zisserman. Three things everyone should know to improve object retrieval. In *CVPR*, 2012.

[3] A. Argyriou, T. Evgeniou, and M. Pontil. Convex multi-task feature learning. *Machine Learning*, 2008.

[4] P. K. Atrey, M. A. Hossain, A. El Saddik, and M. S. Kankanhalli. Multimodal fusion for multimedia analysis: a survey. *Multimedia systems*, 2010.

[5] F. R. Bach, G. R. Lanckriet, and M. I. Jordan. Multiple kernel learning, conic duality, and the smo algorithm. In *ICML*, 2004.

[6] S. Bengio, J. Dean, D. Erhan, E. Ie, Q. Le, A. Rabinovich, J. Shlens, and Y. Singer. Using web co-occurrence statistics for improving image categorization. *arXiv:1312.5697*, 2013.

[7] L. Cao, J. Luo, F. Liang, and T. S. Huang. Heterogeneous feature machines for visual recognition. In *ICCV*, 2009.

[8] R. Caruana. Multitask learning. *Machine learning*, 1997.

[9] J. Chen, J. Zhou, and J. Ye. Integrating low-rank and group-sparse structures for robust multi-task learning. In *ACM SIGKDD*, 2011.

[10] C. V. Cotton and D. P. Ellis. Subband autocorrelation features for video soundtrack classification. In *ICASSP*, 2013.

[11] J. Deng, W. Dong, R. Socher, L.-J. Li, K. Li, and L. Fei-Fei. ImageNet: A large-scale hierarchical image database. In *CVPR*, 2009.

[12] H. Fei and J. Huan. Structured feature selection and task relationship inference for multi-task learning. *Knowledge and information systems*, 2013.

[13] J. Ghosn and Y. Bengio. Multi-task learning for stock selection. In *NIPS*, 1997.

[14] L. Jacob, F. Bach, J.-P. Vert, et al. Clustered multi-task learning: A convex formulation. In *NIPS*, 2008.

[15] M. Jain, H. Jégou, P. Bouthemy, et al. Better exploiting motion for better action recognition. In *CVPR*, 2013.

[16] I.-H. Jhuo, G. Ye, S. Gao, D. Liu, Y.-G. Jiang, D. T. Lee, and S.-F. Chang. Discovering joint audio-visual codewords for video event detection. *Machine Vision and Applications*, 2014.

[17] W. Jiang, C. Cotton, S.-F. Chang, D. Ellis, and A. Loui. Short-term audio-visual atoms for generic video concept classification. In *ACM Multimedia*, 2009.

[18] W. Jiang and A. C. Loui. Audio-visual grouplet: temporal audio-visual interactions for general video concept classification. In *ACM Multimedia*, 2011.

[19] Y.-G. Jiang, Q. Dai, J. Wang, C.-W. Ngo, X. Xue, and S.-F. Chang. Fast semantic diffusion for large-scale context-based image and video annotation. *IEEE TIP*, 2012.

[20] Y.-G. Jiang, G. Ye, S.-F. Chang, D. Ellis, and A. C. Loui. Consumer video understanding: A benchmark database and an evaluation of human and machine performance. In *ACM ICMR*, 2011.

[21] Z. Kang, K. Grauman, and F. Sha. Learning with whom to share in multi-task feature learning. In *ICML*, 2011.

[22] A. Krizhevsky, I. Sutskever, and G. E. Hinton. Imagenet classification with deep convolutional neural networks. In *NIPS*, 2012.

[23] Z.-Z. Lan, L. Jiang, S.-I. Yu, S. Rawat, Y. Cai, C. Gao, S. Xu, H. Shen, X. Li, Y. Wang, et al. Cmu-informedia@ trecvid 2013 multimedia event detection. In *NIST TRECVID Workshop*, 2013.

[24] I. Laptev, M. Marszalek, C. Schmid, and B. Rozenfeld. Learning realistic human actions from movies. In *CVPR*, 2008.

[25] D. Liu, K.-T. Lai, G. Ye, M.-S. Chen, and S.-F. Chang. Sample-specific late fusion for visual category recognition. In *CVPR*, 2013.

[26] J. Liu, S. Ji, and J. Ye. Multi-task feature learning via efficient l 2, 1-norm minimization. In *UAI*, 2009.

[27] S. Maji, A. C. Berg, and J. Malik. Classification using intersection kernel support vector machines is efficient. In *CVPR*, 2008.

[28] S. Mathe and C. Sminchisescu. Dynamic eye movement datasets and learnt saliency models for visual action recognition. In *ECCV*, 2012.

[29] M. Mazloom, X. Li, and C. G. M. Snoek. Few-example video event retrieval using tag propagation. In *ACM ICMR*, 2014.

[30] P. Natarajan, P. Natarajan, S. Wu, X. Zhuang, A. Vazquez-reina, S. N. Vitaladevuni, C. Andersen, R. Prasad, G. Ye, D. Liu, et al. Bbn viser trecvid 2012 multimedia event detection and multimedia event recounting systems. In *NIST TRECVID Workshop*, 2012.

[31] P. Natarajan, S. Wu, S. Vitaladevuni, X. Zhuang, S. Tsakalidis, U. Park, and R. Prasad. Multimodal feature fusion for robust event detection in web videos. In *CVPR*, 2012.

[32] J. Ngiam, A. Khosla, M. Kim, J. Nam, H. Lee, and A. Ng. Multimodal deep learning. In *ICML*, 2011.

[33] T. Ohshiro, D. Angelaki, and G. DeAngelis. A normalization model of multisensory integration. *Nature Neuroscience*, 2011.

[34] D. Oneata, J. Verbeek, C. Schmid, et al. Action and event recognition with fisher vectors on a compact feature set. In *ICCV*, 2013.

[35] J. Pu, Y.-G. Jiang, J. Wang, and X. Xue. Multiple task learning using iteratively reweighted least square. In *IJCAI*, 2013.

[36] G.-J. Qi, X.-S. Hua, Y. Rui, J. Tang, T. Mei, and H.-J. Zhang. Correlative multi-label video annotation. In *ACM Multimedia*, 2007.

[37] A. Rabinovich, A. Vedaldi, C. Galleguillos, E. Wiewiora, and S. Belongie. Objects in context. In *ICCV*, 2007.

[38] J. Sánchez, F. Perronnin, T. Mensink, and J. Verbeek. Image classification with the fisher vector: Theory and practice. *IJCV*, 2013.

[39] K. Simonyan, A. Vedaldi, and A. Zisserman. Deep Fisher networks for large-scale image classification. In *NIPS*, 2013.

[40] J. R. Smith, M. Naphade, and A. Natsev. Multimedia semantic indexing using model vectors. In *ICME*, 2003.

[41] C. G. Snoek, M. Worring, and A. W. Smeulders. Early versus late fusion in semantic video analysis. In *ACM Multimedia*, 2005.

[42] N. Srivastava and R. Salakhutdinov. Multimodal learning with deep boltzmann machines. In *NIPS*, 2012.

[43] B. E. Stein and T. R. Stanford. Multisensory integration: current issues from the perspective of the single neuron. *Nature Reviews Neuroscience*, 2008.

[44] A. Torralba. Contextual priming for object detection. *IJCV*, 2003.

[45] A. Vedaldi, V. Gulshan, M. Varma, and A. Zisserman. Multiple kernels for object detection. In *ICCV*, 2009.

[46] H. Wang and C. Schmid. Action recognition with improved trajectories. In *ICCV*, 2013.

[47] M.-F. Weng and Y.-Y. Chuang. Cross-domain multicue fusion for concept-based video indexing. *IEEE TPAMI*, 2012.

[48] Z. Xu, Y. Yang, I. Tsang, N. Sebe, and A. Hauptmann. Feature weighting via optimal thresholding for video analysis. In *ICCV*, 2013.

[49] R. Yan, M.-O. Fleury, M. Merler, A. Natsev, and J. R. Smith. Large-scale multimedia semantic concept modeling using robust subspace bagging and mapreduce. In *ACM Workshop on Large-scale Multimedia Retrieval and Mining*, 2009.

[50] G. Ye, D. Liu, I.-H. Jhuo, and S.-F. Chang. Robust late fusion with rank minimization. In *CVPR*, 2012.

[51] D. Zhang and D. Shen. Multi-modal multi-task learning for joint prediction of multiple regression and classification variables in alzheimer's disease. *Neuroimage*, 2012.

[52] Y. Zhang and D.-Y. Yeung. A convex formulation for learning task relationships in multi-task learning. In *UAI*, 2010.

[53] J. Zhou, L. Yuan, J. Liu, and J. Ye. A multi-task learning formulation for predicting disease progression. In *ACM SIGKDD*, 2011.

[54] B. Zhu, W. Li, Z. Wang, and X. Xue. A novel audio fingerprinting method robust to time scale modification and pitch shifting. In *ACM Multimedia*, 2010.

Error-Driven Incremental Learning in Deep Convolutional Neural Network for Large-Scale Image Classification

Tianjun Xiao†, Jiaxing Zhang‡, Kuiyuan Yang‡, Yuxin Peng†*, and Zheng Zhang‡
†Institute of Computer Science and Technology, Peking University, Beijing 100871, China
‡Microsoft Research, Beijing, P.R.China
{xiaotianjun,pengyuxin}@pku.edu.cn; {jiaxz,kuyang,Zheng.Zhang}@microsoft.com

ABSTRACT

Supervised learning using deep convolutional neural network has shown its promise in large-scale image classification task. As a building block, it is now well positioned to be part of a larger system that tackles real-life multimedia tasks. An unresolved issue is that such model is trained on a static snapshot of data. Instead, this paper positions the training as a continuous learning process as new classes of data arrive. A system with such capability is useful in practical scenarios, as it gradually expands its capacity to predict increasing number of new classes. It is also our attempt to address the more fundamental issue: a good learning system must deal with new knowledge that it is exposed to, much as how human do.

We developed a training algorithm that grows a network not only incrementally but also hierarchically. Classes are grouped according to similarities, and self-organized into levels. The newly added capacities are divided into component models that predict coarse-grained superclasses and those return final prediction within a superclass. Importantly, all models are cloned from existing ones and can be trained in parallel. These models inherit features from existing ones and thus further speed up the learning. Our experiment points out advantages of this approach, and also yields a few important open questions.

Categories and Subject Descriptors

I.5.1 [**Pattern Recognition**]: Models—*Neural nets*

General Terms

Algorithms, Experimentation, Performance

Keywords

Incremental Learning; Deep Convolutional Neural Network; Large-scale Image Classification

*Corresponding author.

MM'14, November 3–7, 2014, Orlando, Florida, USA.

http://dx.doi.org/10.1145/2647868.2654926.

1. INTRODUCTION

This paper focuses on incremental learning of deep convolutional neural network (DCNN) [14] in image classification task. By *incremental*, we mean that batches of labeled data of new classes are made available gradually. Our objective is to train a deep neural network that performs well at each of such steps. Figure 1 illustrates incremental learning in a multiclass classification model.

Three aspects motivate this study. The first is from the perspective of end applications. The net trained by image classification task can perform as a critical building block in many multimedia tasks. A DCNN model can map images to text, in tasks such as image tagging and annotation, the tags can be further used in image retrieval tasks [18]. Other tasks applies DCNN indirectly. For example, researchers have used a fine-tuned DCNN trained by image classification using ImageNet data to extract features in the detection task of TRECVID [20]. In all such real-world scenarios, classes and their associated labeled data are always collected in an incremental manner. As such, incremental learning plays a critical role.

The second is a performance one. Applying deep learning to image classification has made rapid progress. In a short span of one year, DCNN has improved the top-5 error rate on the challenge of ImageNet 1K-category classification from 26.2% to 15.3% [14]. Yet, the same network performs poorly on the more general 22K-category classification. One obvious culprit is the relatively limited network capacity. Thus, one option is to substantially increase the network capacity. The difficulties are two-folds. First, large models are inherently difficult to train, probably exponentially so. Second, it is not clear at all how and where new capacities should be allocated. It is more prudent to incrementally evolve the network capacity onwards, which is one principle behind the model proposed in this study.

The third motivation is more fundamental: we believe that this is a more general pattern of learning. As we are exposed to new and more data, we don't start learning from a blank slate. Rather, we leverage what's been learned and absorb new knowledge in a continuous process. Unlike other transfer-learning tasks where the features extracted in one domain is applied to a different but similar one (e.g. applying ImageNet feature sets to PASCAL VOL data [6]), the problem here is to transfer the existing features and learn new one in the *same* task with an ever expanding scope. This process can be emulated with the setting we outlined above, and the goal is to understand what alternatives would work well.

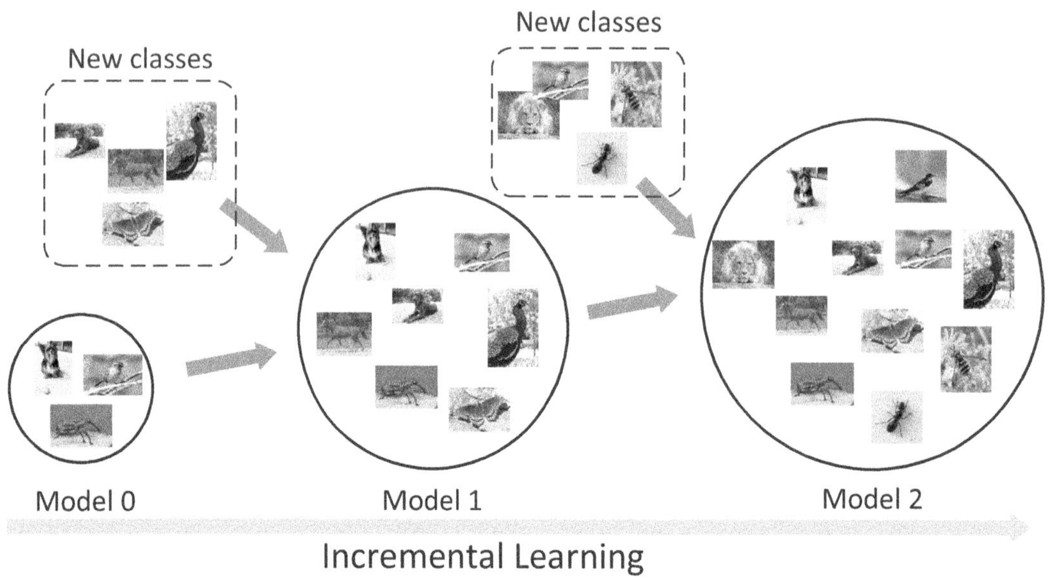

Figure 1: Incremental Learning in Multiclass Classification: the model needs to evolve with arrival of data of new classes.

There have been relatively little study in putting learning in such a dynamic and evolving context. One reason is that large amount of labeled data is only available more recently. Second, doing incremental learning using deep neural network is a new problem and faces inherent technical challenges. Unlike SVM-based approaches, neural networks embed feature extraction and classification in one coherent architecture and within the same model. A consequence is that the modification of parts of the parameter space immediately affects the rest of the model globally. For instance, the so-called "catastrophic forgetting" problem [10] refers to the destruction of existing features learned from earlier data, when the model is exclusively trained with data of new classes. A related difficulty is the allocation of new parameters, as mentioned earlier.

We draw intuition from our everyday experience of learning. For natural objects, there is an inherent ontology hierarchy due to the process of evolution. Artifacts, too, borrow elements from existing ones as one key factor of innovation. As such, it is highly unlikely that there is one flat space where we assign probability to predictions (i.e. with one softmax output layer for the entire 22K ImageNet classes). Rather, we first make a reasonable guess, and zoom into a sub-space where classes are similar. This process is inherently iterative and may involve multiple levels. If that's the case, the model should similarly have a hierarchical structure and the inference should allow iterative refinement.

In this paper, we propose a model that grows organically and hierarchically, as new classes become available. We make the following contributions. First, the model is hierarchical, and the total classes are split gradually towards the leaf of the tree, where similar classes are grouped. Importantly, this process is guided by a pragmatic, error-driven preview process. Second, we carefully control the growth of the network capacity, allocating them according to the responsibility of the components (i.e. coarse-grained routing versus fine-grained prediction). Third, we initialize the new parameters using cloning, thereby maximally retain the learned features. Finally, we perform a detailed study and reveal how learning propagates, with and without cloning.

Our preliminary results show that this approach is promising. Cloning, rather than starting from scratch, can learn faster or better, and often both. Comparing with the existing approaches that always train from scratch, we can reach similar performance by starting from an existing model, but with up to 25% few samples. The results of hierarchical model are mixed, in the sense that the performance gain is limited, due to the errors of superclass prediction. We have gained a few important lessons and insights to guide our future work.

The rest of the paper is organized as follows. We cover related work in Section 2 and then describe our overall architecture in Section 3. We then explain the training algorithm in Section 4, which also depicts how the network grows. Detailed performance study is covered in Section 5. We discuss what we learned, future work and conclude in Section 6.

2. RELATED WORK

Our work attempts to bring the promise of deep learning to the practical and more general paradigm of incremental learning. We organize the discussion of related work according to researches in these areas.

Multi-class image classification and deep learning . The last decade has witnessed a great progress in multi-class image categorization, both in terms of the number of categories and accuracy. For instance, ImageNet has about 22K categories [4], compared to hundreds in the Caltech series [9, 11], and the collection is growing. When the dataset grows bigger, hierarchy pattern in the class set becomes more obvious. Jia *et al.* [3] researched on the classification result in ImageNet_10K dataset and report the phenomenon where misclassification information has some correlation with the semantic hierarchy of ImageNet. Griffin *et al.* [12] utilized the taxonomy hierarchy in the class set to do hierarchical classification to pursue greater speedup. Besides those two works, others mainly focused on the classification accuracy on different dataset. The accuracy has been improving steadily with new developed image features over the years [17, 23, 19], and achieved a great leap with the renewed Deep Convolutional Neural Network [14]. The superiority of DCNN comes from its ability in simultaneously learning the feature extractor and classifier via the network with many layers. Besides image classification task, the DCNN model has been applied to some multimedia tasks directly or indirectly [4, 20].

Incremental learning. A crude definition of incremental learning is that learning is a continuous process with new data. Prior work has addressed two major scenarios, out of which the second one is relevant to this study. The first is concept drift in the training dataflow, and therefore the classifier learns in a non-stationary environment [5, 24]. The second is when there are existing classifiers that are related to the new classes to be learned [1, 7, 8, 9, 15, 16, 21, 22].

Thrun [21] proposed the question as whether leaning the n-th classifier is easier (than learning the first), and since then researchers began to tackle this problem using transfer learning intuition, with techniques using fewer samples to get new models or better generalization. Two of the hot research topics derived from this problem is one-shot learning and zero-shot learning. Fei-Fei *et al.* [8] proposed a Bayesian transfer learning method to avoid learning new categories from scratch and instead using very few training samples. Tommasi *et al.* [22] proposed a multi model knowledge transfer method where source classifiers were weighted by learned coefficient. Lampert *et al.* [16] achieved zero-shot learning by introducing attribute-based classification. Kuzborskij *et al.* [15] pointed out that prior work mostly focused on binary classification problem (object detection), and proposed a discriminative method in the One-Versus-All multi-class classification task by transferring knowledge to a new class while preserving what has already been learned. Those works rely on shallow models instead of DCNN, and the category size is small in comparison.

The particular challenge with DCNN in the context of incremental learning (and in same sense transfer learning as well) is that it mingles feature extractor and classifier in one architecture. Goodfellow *et al.* [10] investigated the catastrophic forgetting problem in gradient-based neural networks. The study is however on the small MNIST dataset with small network, and the proposal of using dropout is already in the default DCNN configuration. Nevertheless it qualitatively re-affirms the difficulty of achieving good performance on old and new tasks simultaneously. Many works have focused on performing domain adaptation, one such example is the one-shot learning by adapting features learned form ImageNet_1K dataset to other datasets [13]. The recent work of zero-shot learning assumes the availability of a semantic embedding space to which outputs of DCNN are projected. Our work differs in the goal, as we want to transfer the learning *within*the same task with larger dataset.

While many incremental learning works paid more attention on efficiency than accuracy, Bengio [2] offered a deeper insight that speed and quality can be obtained simultaneously if increments are made properly, noted as curriculum learning. Its key idea is to start learning on easier aspects of tasks and then gradually increase the difficulty. This setting

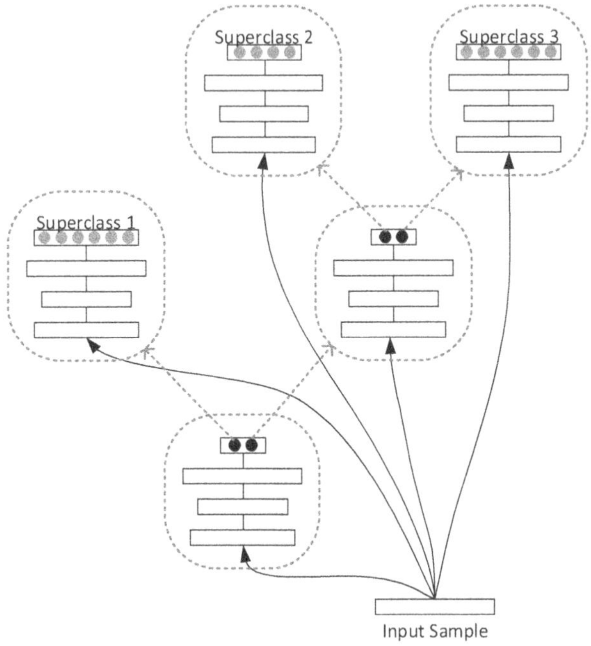

Figure 2: A hierarchy of models: branch models predict superclasses, leaf models return final predictions.

may have positive effect on both the convergence speed and the quality of local minimum obtained. This work can help analyzing our results.

3. INCREMENTAL LEARNING MODEL

In this section, we will introduce our proposal of incremental learning model and its inference process. Without loss of generality, we assume there is a model M_0 that is already trained on N_0 classes. The goal of incremental learning is to evolve from M_{i-1} to M_i, to train N_i classes, in which $N_i - N_{i-1}$ are *new* classes. For example, we might have a DCNN classifier for 500 animal classes out of the 22K categories in ImageNet, we want to grow the network to classify 1000 and then the complete collection of animal classes.

Obviously, the model must increase its capacity to accommodate more classes. The simplest way to grow is widening the top softmax layer to output the extra probabilities on new classes. In other words, M_i share the same structure as M_{i-1} except it has N_i softmax units at the output. One obvious drawback is that the capacity increment is small: if the width of the layer before softmax is H then the additional parameters amounts to $H \times (N_i - N_{i-1})$. To put it more concretely, if we use the default configuration of DCNN [14] for the 500-class model, when we increase it to 1000 classes, the number of parameter increment is merely 1%.

We can make the model bigger by injecting units in the fully-connected layers or having more feature maps in the convolutional layers. However, it is not clear how this should be done. We could end up putting many untrained new parameters into the model everywhere, and their initialization becomes a black magic: too big or too small a random value will either ruin the existing model or making training tediously long.

A better approach must maximize the transfer of learned features, and still conservatively grow the capacity. The architecture we explore in this paper is a hierarchy of models, as shown in Figure 2. In our default setting, all the models (in each blue box) share the same topology and the amount of parameters, except the top output layers. All of them receive the same input sample, and have a softmax output. They logically make up a tree during the inference process. Models at different positions play different roles. Each leaf model performs the final prediction among a non-overlapping subset of the total classes. The branch models, on the other hand, have each of their output unit points to a child model, directing the prediction (eventually) to the correct leaf model. More specifically, the total classes are partitioned into *superclasses*, and each superclass is assigned to a leaf model (the red units in Figure 2). An input sample triggers the root model which outputs the probabilities of which branch the sample belongs to, and then the child model (can be a leaf or branch model) with the highest probability is chosen. This recursion continues until a leaf model is selected, and we take the output in this superclass as the final prediction.

The intuition in this tree-style prediction is that each branch model, being constrained by capacity, is only optimized for predicting a coarse collection of classes. A leaf model, on the other hand, concentrates on a more accurate fine-grained classification on a smaller set of classes. This architecture mirrors the hierarchical and iterative inference process that human brain seems to be adept at, as we do a crude prediction first, and then refine it further by discriminating against close competitors. It also allows the total model capacities to be divided according to responsibilities (coarse vs fine-grained classification). In such a hierarchy of models, the capacity growth is done by cloning new models from the exiting ones and expanding the tree. The cloning reduces the difficulty of initializing the added capacity. We will discuss the details of this incremental learning in the next section.

4. ALGORITHM

For ease of disposition, we will describe the algorithm when there is only one single model, and then generalize the procedure.

4.1 Starting from a Single Superclass

In the starting point of the training, all N_0 classes are in one single superclass and predicted by one model L_0. Thus, L_0 is a leaf model by itself. When new classes come and the superclass size increases to N_1, we have two choices to make the model bigger. One choice is simply extending L_0 to L_0' by inserting more output units, which conservatively increases a small amount of capacity. The second choice that substantially scales up the capacity is partitioning the superclass into K superclasses, and clone L_0 into several new leaf models $L_1, L_2, \ldots, L_K$ to predict within each of these new superclasses. A branch model B with K final output units is also cloned from L_0 to direct the prediction to the correct leaf model on a given input sample. These two choices are illustrated in Figure 3. We call the former *flat increment*, and the latter *clone increment*. There are three problems we need to address: 1) how to partition a superclass; 2) how to re-train these models with changed data and objectives; 3) most importantly, how to decide the best strategy out of the two alternatives.

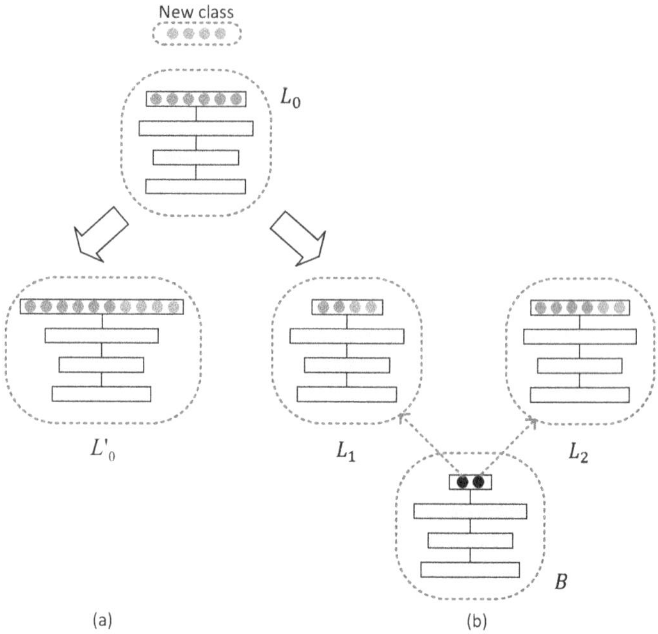

Figure 3: Two choices of capacity increment. (a) Flat increment. The output units is increased to hold more classes. (b) Clone increment. A single leaf model is duplicated to clones for more classes. A branch model is also cloned to direct the correct prediction of superclass.

In clone increment, the network grows by one level, and the total N_1 classes are first clustered to superclasses by similarity. This allows the branch model B and the leaf models to focus on inter- and intra-superclass discriminative features, respectively. This is done using *error-driven preview*, which essentially *error-driven preview* observes the error distribution using current model L_0 on samples drawn from all the data, including both new and old. A validation set of N_0 are tested through L_0, and calculating a confusion matrix $C \in \mathbb{R}^{N_0 \times N_0}$ from the output. The entry C_{ij} denotes the probability that the i-th class is predicted to j-th class, which also measures the similarity between class i and j. We then use spectral clustering partition to split N_0 classes into K clusters based on the confusion matrix. The classes that are easy to confuse with each other are grouped into the same cluster as a superclass, with the desired side effects to minimize the confusion between superclasses. Next, $N_1 - N_0$ new classes are assigned to superclasses based on their confusion rates among the superclasses.

After the superclass partitioning, there are a total of K leaf models to train. Each of them has the same topology as L_0 except the output layer. Compared with L_0 which is only trained to predict N_0 old classes, each new leaf model L_i inherits a portion of old classes plus with some new classes. This change of data and objective requires each leaf model to be retrained. Instead of training from scratch, we train these new leaf models incrementally by copying L_0's parameters as initialization and using random initialization on the remaining new parameters (i.e. the weights connecting the

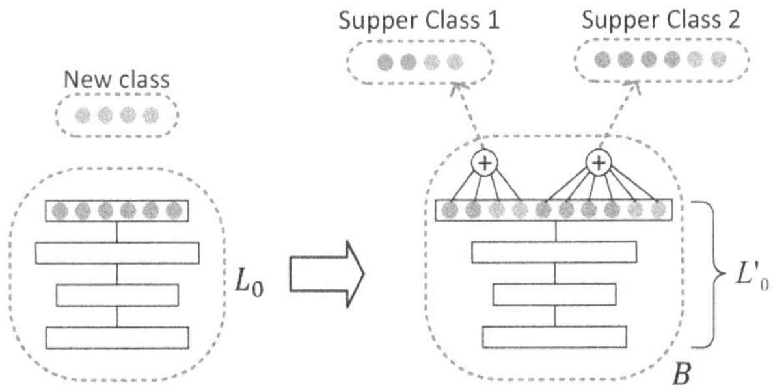

Figure 4: Cloning a branch model. We first do the flat increment and train the new leaf model L'_0. The units in L'_0 for each superclass are summed up for a branch model output unit.

units of the last hidden layer to the newly added output layer units). This training is much more efficient than from scratch.

We also evolve a new leaf model L'_0 to have N_1 output units, trained with flat incremental with data of N_1 classes. Finally, we clone the branch model B by copying parameters from L'_0. As illustrated in Figure 4, and simply sum up the softmax units belonging to each superclass as the predicted probability of that superclass.

At this point, we have built two separate models, the first is L'_0, and the second is the branch model B and its leaf models L_1 to L_K. Strictly speaking, choosing one over the other depends on the estimation of extra model capacity demanded by the new classes. We adopt a simpler strategy to simply let the two compete. This is illustrated in Algorithm 1.

Algorithm 1: ExtendLeafModel

input $(\mathbf{L_0}, \mathbf{S})$: leaf model L_0, superclass S
output $(\mathbf{L'_0}, \mathbf{B}, \mathbf{L_1}, \mathbf{L_2}, \ldots, \mathbf{L_K})$: leaf model L'_0 by flat increment, leaf models $\{L_1, L_2, \ldots, L_K\}$ and branch model B by clone increment
`/* flat increment*/`
incrementally train L_0 to L'_0
`/* clone increment */`
error-driven preview of S
partition S into $\{S_1, S_2, \ldots, S_K\}$
clone L_0 into new leaf models $\{L_1, L_2, \ldots, L_K\}$
for $i = 1$ to K **do**
  incrementally train L_i
end for
clone branch model $B \leftarrow L'_0$
`/* use clones or not */`
if prediction accuracy $\{B, L_1, L_2, \ldots, L_K\} > L'_0$ **then**
  $L'_0 \leftarrow \varnothing$
else
  $B \leftarrow \varnothing$
end if
return $(L'_0, B, L_1, L_2, \ldots, L_K)$

Note that all these models can be trained in parallel. More importantly, the process of cloning and incremental leaf model training automatically transfers features learned from the old model L_0 to the new leaf and branch models. Comparing with training such new models from scratch, the hope is that we can reach better accuracy with the same amount of time budget, or retain the accuracy with shorter training time, or both. Therefore, this is a building block whose performance is critical, and is the subject of much deeper analysis in later part of this paper.

4.2 Incremental Learning

Incremental learning from a single superclass can be generalized to a deeper hierarchy, at each step receiving new batches of classes (Algorithm 2). The first step is to distribute all the new classes into the existing superclasses by error-driven preview in a coarse granularity of superclass (line 1 to 6). Next, for each leaf model l, we grow it using flat increment or clone increment by Algorithm 1, discussed previously. Note that if the clone increment is selected, l is itself expanded to a subtree.

This algorithm can be applied repeatedly with new batches of classes, and naturally support more levels of hierarchy, independent of how many leaf models and how many levels of hierarchy exists in the current model. As the hierarchy deepens, the original trained branch models, especially those near the root, might lose accuracy due to update in their subtrees. We can choose to retrain each branch model by simple flat increment training.

Algorithm 2: IncrementalLearning

input $(\mathcal{S}, \mathcal{L}, \mathcal{B}, \mathcal{S}_{\mathbf{new}})$: superclass set $\mathcal{S}$, leaf model set $\mathcal{L}$ (each $l \in \mathcal{L}$ is corresponding to a $s \in \mathcal{S}$), branch model set $\mathcal{B}$, new class set $\mathcal{S}_{new}$
output $(\mathcal{S}, \mathcal{L}, \mathcal{B})$: updated superclass set $\mathcal{S}$, leaf model set $\mathcal{L}$, branch model set $\mathcal{B}$
`/* ditribute new classes to superclasses* /`
calculate the confusion matrix Φ with entry $\Phi(c, s)$ for probability of predicting $c \in S_{new}$ to $s \in \mathcal{S}$
for all $c \in \mathcal{S}_{new}$ **do**
  select $s \in \mathcal{S}$ with maximum $\Phi(c, s)$
  $s = s \cup \{c\}$
end for
`/* incremental training */`
for all $s \in \mathcal{S}$ and the corresponding $l \in \mathcal{L}$ **do**
  $(l', b, l_1, l_2, \ldots, l_K) =$ **ExtendLeafModel**(s, l)
  if $b \neq \varnothing$ **then**
    insert b to $\mathcal{B}$, replace l by $\{l_1, l_2, \ldots, l_K\}$ in $\mathcal{L}$
  else
    replace l by l' in $\mathcal{L}$
  end if
end for
`/* refine brach models (optional) */`
for all $b \in \mathcal{B}$ **do**
  incrementally train b according to updated subtrees
end for
return $(\mathcal{S}, \mathcal{L}, \mathcal{B})$

---

5. EXPERIMENTS

In this section, we will evaluate our framework on two datasets, using convergence speed and classification accuracy as criterion to show how to learn faster and better incrementally.

Dataset.

We prepare two datasets for our study. The first smaller dataset include all the 398 animal classes in ImageNet_1K, in which 501K and 18K images are used as the training set and validation set, respectively. We call it ImageNet_1K_Animal. It is used primarily to understand the performance of initialization with existing model parameters. We perform a fuller experiment growing a model incrementally with the second larger dataset selected from the 3998 animal synsets in ImageNet_22K. Samples of these synsets have a few problems:

- Not all of them have image samples. For those that do, there are severe unbalance in the number of samples; some of them contain fewer than 10 images.
- The image samples of an inner node in the ImageNet hierarchy can also belong to a leaf node. For such an image, there are multiple labels.

We therefore take all the leaf nodes of animals in the ImageNet_22K hierarchy. We also remove classes with fewer than 100 images, results in 2282 classes. The training, validation and testing set contains 85%, 5%, 10% of the data respectively, with 1.6M, 91K and 183K images each. We call it ImageNet_22K_Animal.

To create an incremental training process, the small dataset is incremented from 195 randomly drawn classes to 398 classes, whereas the big dataset is incremented from 1000 to the full 2282 classes.

Model.

The baseline model is the one 8-layer convolutional network as described in [14], with configuration shown in Table 1. As discussed in Section 4.1, we have two ways to extend the capacity, *flat increment* by increasing the softmax output layer size, and *clone increment* by duplicating more models. In either case, the configurations stay the same except the top output layer, and network parameters are initialized by copying from an existing model, which we call *incremental learning*. We also compare the results against a baseline where the training starts from scratch, which is called *from-scratch learning*.

Training Details.

One of the "black magics" in training a deep network is the scheduling of learning rate adjustment. As we are interested in possible training time savings, we apply an adaptive learning rate tuning strategy to avoid tuning by hand. After training every 30K samples, we test with 1K samples randomly drawn from the whole validation set. We compute and monitor the average validation error for each epoch, and if it doesn't drop by more than 0.1% for three consecutive epochs, we stop the training or cut the learning rate by 10-folds. For one complete training, the learning rate is adjusted twice, starting from 0.01.

5.1 Result Overview

Results on ImageNet_1K_Animal.

With the model well trained on 195 animals, we can train it for 398 animals incrementally or from scratch. Table 2 summarizes the comparison between these two choices, by the error rates trained for different epochs. We hand-tuned the learning rate of the incremental runs for we want them to train for certain epochs. We observe that we can achieve better performance if we incrementally train from the existing 195-animal-model (36.8% versus 38.6%), taking slightly less time than the scratch run. On the other hand, with 25% few data (stopping with 30 epochs), incremental learning already beating the from-scratch one (37.9% versus 38.6%).

Table 2: Incremental/from-scratch learning results in ImageNet_1K_Animal from 195 animals to 398 animals

Training	Epochs	Error Rate
from-scratch	41	38.6%
incremental	10	41.6%
incremental	20	39.2%
incremental	30	37.9%
incremental	40	**36.8%**

The scenario we consider here is one where a model of smaller net has already been trained. From-scratch training simply throws that model away, whereas ours leverages it. The simple flat-incremental method actually creates a curriculum learning [2] scenario. Training a net classifying 195 animals is an easier task compared with a net for 398 animals. We observed positive effects both on convergence speed and the quality of local minimum obtained. More analysis is needed because curriculum learning study is currently empirical.

Results on ImageNet_22K_Animal.

When class number grows from 1000 to 2282, we split the superclass and do a clone increment from the 1000-animal-model. The branch model and the two leaf models are all incrementally trained by copying exiting parameters as initialization. Figure 5 shows the confusion matrices of the existing 1000 and the new 1282 classes before clone increment. All these classes are partitioned into two superclasses with 1350 and 932 classes, respectively (shown in red and blue boxes in Figure 5). One can observe the similar error distribution on the old and new classes.

Table 3: Incremental training result in ImageNet_22K_Animal dataset

Increment	Training	Error Rate	Examples
flat	from-scratch	49.46%	74.74M
flat	incremental	49.15%	**61.45M**
clone	incremental	**48.52%**	117.79M

Table 3 shows advantage of the incremental learning over other training strategies. Column `Increment` shows how the model capacity are extended, flat increment or clone increment. Column `Training` tells how the new models are trained, from-scratch or incremental. Column `Examples` accounts the training examples sweeped to reach that accuracy. Note that if the model has several parts, the examples of each part are summed up to fill the entry. Compared with the baseline (the first row) with flat increment and from-scratch learning, the flat increment combining incremental learning (the second row) performs slightly better, with 0.3% accuracy gain and 18% fewer training examples. Finally, our increment (the last row), with more extra capacity from clone, gains some more (48.52% versus 49.46% of

Table 1: Architecture of the baseline model

Layer	1	2	3	4	5	6	7	8
Type	conv+max+norm	conv+max+norm	conv	conv	conv+max	full	full	full
Channels	96	256	384	384	256	4096	4096	Output Dim
Filter Size	11*11	5*5	3*3	3*3	3*3	-	-	-
Convolution Stride	4*4	1*1	1*1	1*1	1*1	-	-	-
Pooling Size	3*3	3*3	-	-	3*3	-	-	-
Pooling Stride	2*2	2*2	-	-	2*2	-	-	-
Padding Size	2*2	1*1	1*1	1*1	1*1	-	-	-

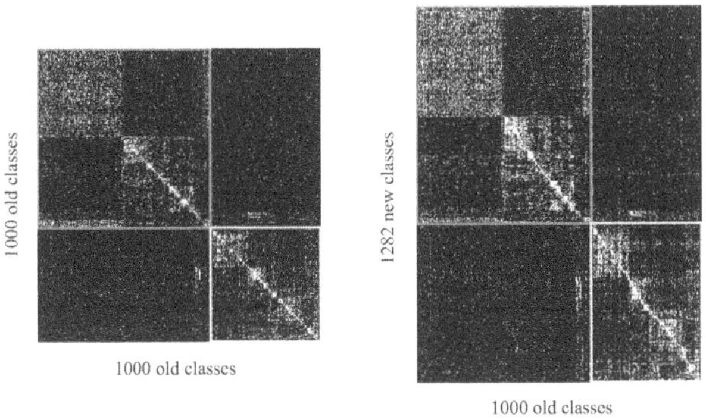

Figure 5: Confusion matrix among 1000 original classes (left), and the confusion matrix between new 1282 classes and original 1000 classes (right). The partitioning has been done (in red and blue boxes, respectively).

baseline) but with substantially more data training the leaf models. The total amount of time needed won't increase if trained in parallel.

To understand the benefit of clone increment, we do a breakdown analysis in Table 4 and Table 5. Flat-incremental model achieved 49.15% overall error rate, in which the superclass 1 and 2 have 45.79% and 56.02% error rates, respectively. If the branch model is perfect, the two leaf models obtain 44.43% and 54.79% error rates, gaining more than 1.2% accuracy each. Accounting the prediction error of the branch model, the 2-level model achieves 45.03% and 55.63%.

Table 4: Breakdown comparison between cloned models and the flat-incremented model

Model	Superclass 1	Superclass 2
cloned leaf$_1$	44.43%	N/A
cloned leaf$_2$	N/A	54.79%
cloned branch	* 2.20%	* 4.11%
cloned leafs+branch	45.03%	55.63%
flat-incremented model	45.79%	56.02%

The end performance on a given superclass can *not* be derived from the average accuracy of a leaf model (i.e. 55.57% superclass 1) and the branch accuracy (i.e. 97.80%). For superclass 1, this will yield the error rate to be $1 - 0.5557 \cdot 0.9780$, which is 45.65%. This is higher than we actually get (45.03%). Why is that?

The reason is that the images misclassified by the branch are also more difficult to be classified correctly by the leaf model. Table 5 shows the error rate if we divide the data according to the branch decision. It is clear that there exists such a strong correlation. This is both subtle and intuitive, and explains the apparent discrepancy described earlier. The correct way to compute the performance on a given superclass is:

Table 5: Conditional Leaf Model Error

SuperClass	Branch Correct	Branch Miss
SuperClass$_1$	43.79%	72.89%
SuperClass$_2$	53.72%	79.76%

$$E_{whole} = 1 - (1 - E_{L|B_{Correct}}) * (1 - E_B) \quad (1)$$

The conditional probability that an image is correctly classified given that it is correctly predicted by the branch $(1 - E_{L|B_{Correct}})$ is not equal to and higher than its average $(1 - E_L)$. Improving the branch model will help, but with a diminishing return.

5.2 Leaf Model Learning Analysis

In our architecture, each leaf model is cloned to deal with one superclass, which includes part of the old classes and some extra new classes. In this section we perform a detailed analysis, showing why initialization with existing parameters is advantageous, and furthermore how new features fight a continuous "tug-of-war" with the old ones. The study is on the 1350 superclass partition, which includes 602 old classes and 748 new ones.

5.2.1 Advantage of Incremental Learning

In Figure 6, we compare the error curves of incremental learning versus one that is trained from scratch. It is obvious that the error rate of incremental learning drops much faster. Such speedup benefits are the results of bigger gradients on weights, which subsequently relate to activations in the forward pass, and derivatives in the backward pass.

Figure 7 shows the ℓ^2 norms of the weight gradients between different layers as a function of training epochs. To save space, only the gradient between layer 7 and 8, and that between layer 1 and 2 are shown, as representatives of classification layers and low feature extraction layers, respectively. The gradient curves between other layers have similar trends. In the first 150 batches, the incremental learning produces much bigger gradient than the from-scratch learning in both high and low layers. This explains why error rate of the incremental learning drops quickly in the same period, as it is able to descend the error surface faster. As training progresses to later epochs, the differences between incremental and from-scratch gradually disappears.

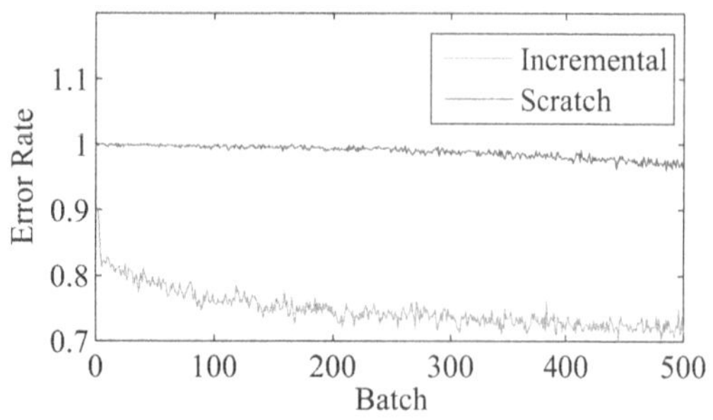

Figure 6: Learning curves of incremental run and scratch run in the first 500 batches

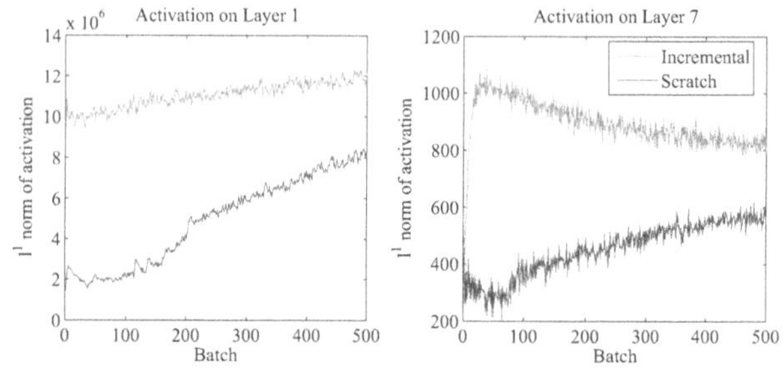

Figure 8: l^1 norm of the activation in layer 1 and layer 7 in the incremental run and the scratch run

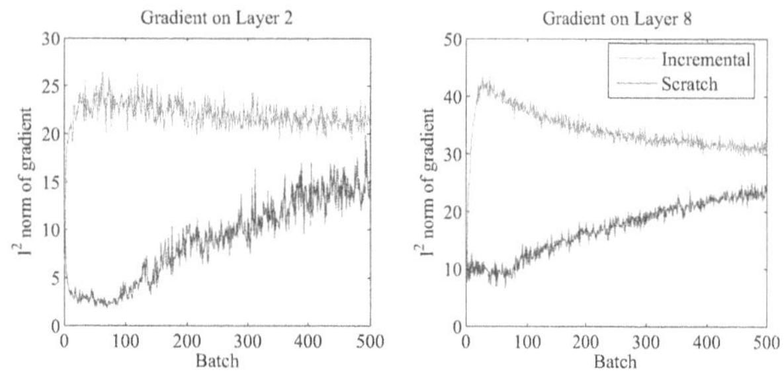

Figure 7: l^2 norm of the gradient in layer 2 and layer 8 in the incremental run and the scratch run

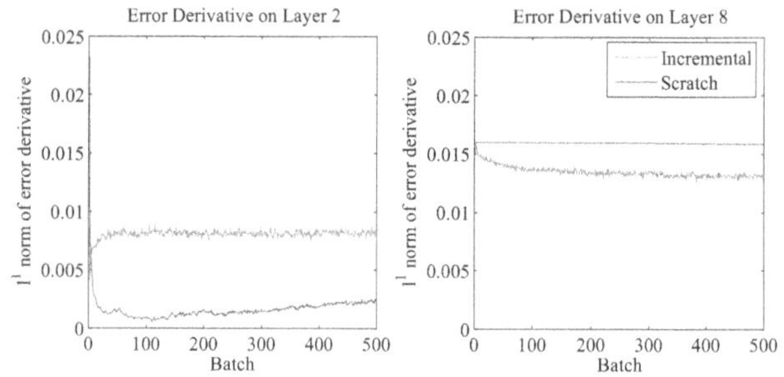

Figure 9: l^1 norm of the error derivative in layer 2 and layer 8 in the incremental run and the scratch run

What leads to the bigger gradients? In back-propagation, the gradient of the weights between layer $i-1$ and i, $\mathbf{g}_{i-1,i} \equiv \frac{\partial E}{\partial W_{i-1,i}}$, is the outer product of $\mathbf{x}_{i-1}$, the activation of layer $i-1$ computed in the forward pass, and $\mathbf{e}_i$, the error derivatives of layer i computed in the back propagation pass. In other words, $\mathbf{g}_{i-1,i} = \mathbf{e}_i \cdot \mathbf{x}_{i-1}^T$. For example, $\mathbf{g}_{7,8} = \mathbf{e}_8 \cdot \mathbf{x}_7^T$.

First, we dive into the activations. In Figure 8, we plot the ℓ^1 norm of the activations in layer 7 and layer 1. We can see that in the feature extraction layers (e.g. layer 1), the activations all rise, signaling the learning and activation of new features. The one with incremental learning starts with bigger values (roughly five times bigger) and increase slowly, the reason is that incremental learning is able to reuse existing features and is therefore less motivated to learn new ones. In the classification layer, activations of incremental learning are also much higher, since from-scratch are gradually moving forward with random (and therefore lower) activations.

Next, we look at error derivatives to check how the error signals are propagated down by the back-propagation algorithm. The last layer's error derivative $\mathbf{e}_8$ is simply the gap between label and output. While from-scratch is essentially making random guesses and suffering from high errors, incremental learning at least are getting most of the predictions of the old classes correct. As such, higher classification layers in from-scratch learning has bigger errors to start the propagation, as shown in Figure 9. Things are different for lower layers. The back-propagation is governed by

$$\mathbf{e}_i = \frac{\partial \mathbf{x}_i}{\partial \mathbf{z}_i} \odot W_{i,i+1}^T \cdot \mathbf{e}_{i+1} \tag{2}$$

and a series of randomly initialized weights of the layers diminishes the error derivatives towards lower layer, as is the case of from-scratch learning. Weights in the incremental learning start with structures that allow the prediction of existing classes, and thus allow easier propagation of error signals. As such, in lower layers (such as layer 2) the error derivatives are larger.

The above observations can be summarized as the followings. Incremental learning has higher activation due to learned features being reused, which also allows errors to propagate more smoothly downwards. Neither is true for from-scratch learning, whose only drive is the bigger error at the output layer. As such, incremental learning has bigger gradients and descent faster.

5.2.2 Interference between new and old classes

By the virtue of the error-driven preview and the subsequent partitioning, classes within a superclass is similar. Since the cloned leaf model was originally trained on old classes (some of them have been moved to another superclass), at the beginning of the training all new classes are misclassified as old ones (see Figure 10). Figure 12 is an illustration of some new classes being classified into similar old classes.

The leaf model slowly learn the new classes. Meanwhile, the prediction accuracy of old classes recovers from some damages. As it turns out, such interference is the driving force for low layers to learn new features that helps separate new classes from old ones. We offer a detailed analysis below.

To make things simple, we will only concentrate on the interference between a pair of similar classes, one old and one new. As illustrated in Figure 11, y_1, t_1 and $\mathbf{w}_1$ are the

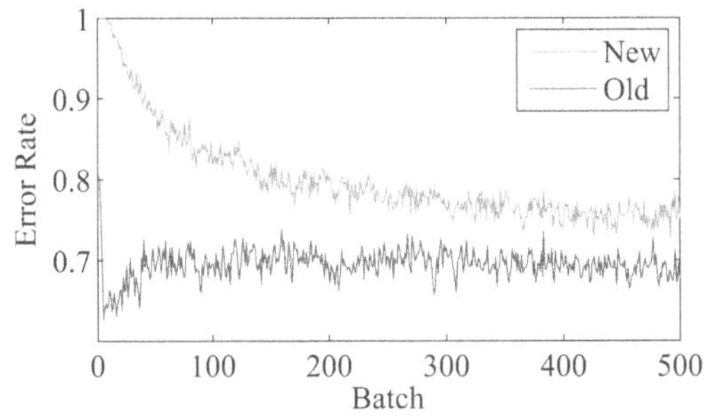

Figure 10: Learning curves of old and new classes.

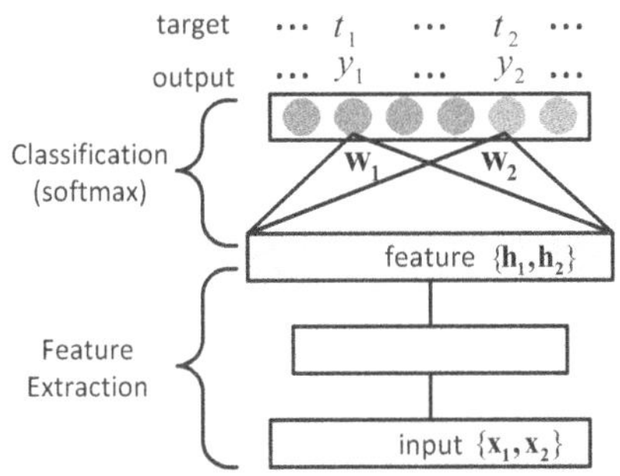

Figure 11: Inference between new and old classes. Input $\mathbf{x}_1$ with feature $\mathbf{h}_1$ belongs to old classes (target $t_1 = 1$); $\mathbf{x}_2$ with $\mathbf{h}_2$ belongs to new classes (target $t_2 = 1$).

output, target, output weight vector for the old class unit respectively, as are y_2, t_2 and $\mathbf{w}_2$ for the new class unit. At the beginning of incremental training, $\mathbf{w}_1$ is copied from the previous training result, and $\mathbf{w}_2$ is just randomly initialized. Given an input sample vector $\mathbf{x}_1$ in old class, the last hidden layer outputs its feature vector $\mathbf{h}_1$. Since the model is well trained on old classes, $y_1 = t_1 = 1$. Because softmax output $y_1 = \frac{e^{\langle \mathbf{w}_1, \mathbf{h}_1 \rangle}}{\sum_k e^{\langle \mathbf{w}_k, \mathbf{h}_1 \rangle}}$, this correct prediction is due to a big inner product $\langle \mathbf{w}_1, \mathbf{h}_1 \rangle$. Without any error on this sample, back-propagation doesn't make any update on weight $\mathbf{w}_1$ and $\mathbf{w}_2$.

Instead, $\mathbf{x}_2$, being similar to x_1, is wrongly predicted as the old class because of the big inner product $\langle \mathbf{w}_1, \mathbf{h}_2 \rangle$. That means that, unsurprisingly, h_1 and h_2 are highly correlated, with a big inner product $\langle \mathbf{h}_1, \mathbf{h}_2 \rangle$. Back-propagation starting from the mismatch between output ($y_1 = 1$, $y_2 = 0$) and the target ($t_1 = 0$, $t_2 = 1$) makes update on both $\mathbf{w}_1$ and $\mathbf{w}_2$,

$$\begin{aligned} \mathbf{w}_1' &= \mathbf{w}_1 - \epsilon \cdot \mathbf{h}_2(y_1 - t_1) = \mathbf{w}_1 - \epsilon \cdot \mathbf{h}_2 \\ \mathbf{w}_2' &= \mathbf{w}_2 - \epsilon \cdot \mathbf{h}_2(y_2 - t_2) = \mathbf{w}_2 + \epsilon \cdot \mathbf{h}_2 \end{aligned} \quad (3)$$

where ϵ is the learning rate. It effectively "shaves" some weights off $\mathbf{w}_1$ and moves them to $\mathbf{w}_2$, and damages $\mathbf{w}_1$ in the sense that if the model sees $\mathbf{x}_1$ again, y_1 is a little less to be turned on. That's formulated by

$$\langle \mathbf{w}_1', \mathbf{h}_1 \rangle = \langle \mathbf{w}_1, \mathbf{h}_1 \rangle - \epsilon \cdot \langle \mathbf{h}_2, \mathbf{h}_1 \rangle \quad (4)$$

So the stronger the correlation between $\mathbf{h}_1$ and $\mathbf{h}_2$, the more damage it is. As the training proceeds by alternating between these two samples, the net result is a compromising accuracy for either one of the class. To see why this is so, consider a state when both classes are correctly predicted. This state cannot be a stable state as the correlation between $\mathbf{h}_1$ and $\mathbf{h}_2$ will cause interferences that will weaken their weights in turn.

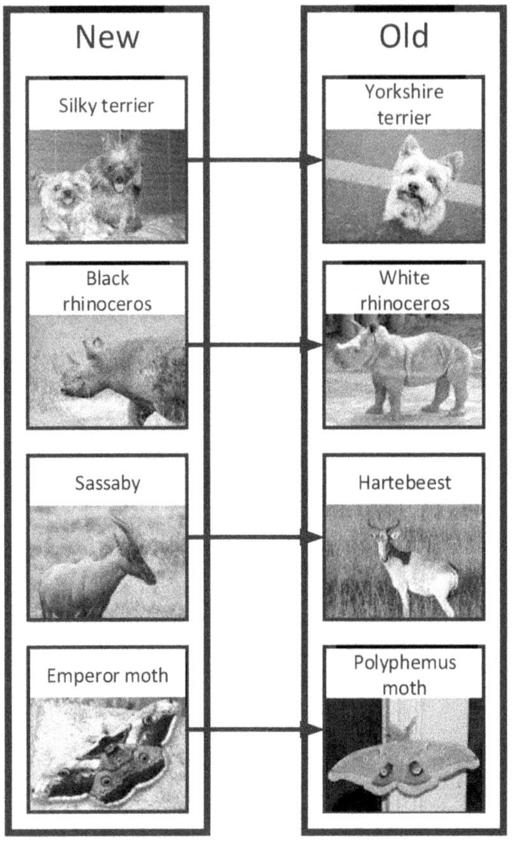

Figure 12: Examples of some new classes being misclassified into similar old classes at the beginning of training.

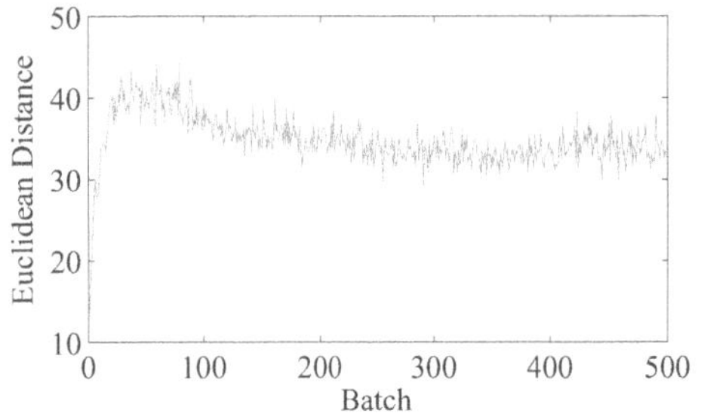

Figure 13: Changing of feature distance between new class *'silky terrier'* and old class *'yorkshire terrior'*.

That means, however, that the back-propagation, being optimum-pursuing, will eventually separate $\mathbf{h}_1$ and $\mathbf{h}_2$ by forcing the error propagates downwards. As shown in Figure 13, old class *'yorkshire terrior'* and new class *'silky terrier'* have very close features at the beginning of training, with the latter misclassfied as the former. Quickly, their feature distance widens, driven by the interference in classification layer to improve the prediction accuracy. The growth of the capacity for this fine-grained feature learning is hopefully s-tolen from classes that are moved away into other superclass (and not seen by the model any more).

6. CONCLUTION

We believe that tackling large-scale image classification task can and should take a divide and conquer approach, and do so incrementally. This study establishes a framework to do so with a training procedure that grows the network capacity hierarchically. The overall performance numbers are positive, but not overwhelmingly so. We take this as a steppingstone and the experiences point out a few lessons and future directions, which we summarize as the followings:

- Cloning naturally inherits leaned features. However, there is a tug-of-war between old and new features, in addition to removing old features that were acquired on removed classes. The current way of training with vanilla back-propagation does not seem to be efficient.
- At the time of performing superclass partition, we have a fair amount of knowledge of errors within each partition. Cloning with the exact same configuration simplifies parameter initialization, at the expense of missing needed capacity increase.
- The branch model should focus on differentiating superclasses, our current training model deprives it from such opportunities.

We are actively pursuing the above directions.

7. ACKNOWLEDGMENTS

This work was supported by National Hi-Tech Research and Development Program (863 Program) of China under Grants 2014AA015102 and 2012AA012503, National Natural Science Foundation of China under Grant 61371128, and Ph.D. Programs Foundation of Ministry of Education of China under Grant 20120001110097.

8. REFERENCES

[1] Y. Aytar and A. Zisserman. Tabula rasa: Model transfer for object category detection. In *Computer Vision (ICCV), 2011 IEEE International Conference on*, pages 2252–2259. IEEE, 2011.

[2] Y. Bengio, J. Louradour, R. Collobert, and J. Weston. Curriculum learning. In *Proceedings of the 26th annual international conference on machine learning*, pages 41–48. ACM, 2009.

[3] J. Deng, A. C. Berg, K. Li, and L. Fei-Fei. What does classifying more than 10,000 image categories tell us? In *Computer Vision–ECCV 2010*, pages 71–84. Springer, 2010.

[4] J. Deng, W. Dong, R. Socher, L.-J. Li, K. Li, and L. Fei-Fei. Imagenet: A large-scale hierarchical image database. In *Computer Vision and Pattern Recognition, 2009. CVPR 2009. IEEE Conference on*, pages 248–255. IEEE, 2009.

[5] R. Elwell and R. Polikar. Incremental learning of concept drift in nonstationary environments. *Neural Networks, IEEE Transactions on*, 22(10):1517–1531, 2011.

[6] M. Everingham, L. Van Gool, C. K. I. Williams, J. Winn, and A. Zisserman. The pascal visual object classes (voc) challenge. *International Journal of Computer Vision*, 88(2):303–338, June 2010.

[7] L. Fe-Fei, R. Fergus, and P. Perona. A bayesian approach to unsupervised one-shot learning of object categories. In *Computer Vision, 2003. Proceedings. Ninth IEEE International Conference on*, pages 1134–1141. IEEE, 2003.

[8] L. Fei-Fei, R. Fergus, and P. Perona. One-shot learning of object categories. *Pattern Analysis and Machine Intelligence, IEEE Transactions on*, 28(4):594–611, 2006.

[9] L. Fei-Fei, R. Fergus, and P. Perona. Learning generative visual models from few training examples: An incremental bayesian approach tested on 101 object categories. *Computer Vision and Image Understanding*, 106(1):59–70, 2007.

[10] I. J. Goodfellow, M. Mirza, X. Da, A. Courville, and Y. Bengio. An empirical investigation of catastrophic forgeting in gradient-based neural networks. *arXiv preprint arXiv:1312.6211*, 2013.

[11] G. Griffin, A. Holub, and P. Perona. Caltech-256 object category dataset. 2007.

[12] G. Griffin and P. Perona. Learning and using taxonomies for fast visual categorization. In *Computer Vision and Pattern Recognition, 2008. CVPR 2008. IEEE Conference on*, pages 1–8. IEEE, 2008.

[13] J. Hoffman, E. Tzeng, J. Donahue, Y. Jia, K. Saenko, and T. Darrell. One-shot adaptation of supervised deep convolutional models. *arXiv preprint arXiv:1312.6204*, 2013.

[14] A. Krizhevsky, I. Sutskever, and G. E. Hinton. Imagenet classification with deep convolutional neural networks. In *NIPS*, volume 1, page 4, 2012.

[15] I. Kuzborskij, F. Orabona, and B. Caputo. From n to n+1: Multiclass transfer incremental learning. In *Computer Vision and Pattern Recognition (CVPR), 2013 IEEE Conference on*, pages 3358–3365. IEEE, 2013.

[16] C. H. Lampert, H. Nickisch, and S. Harmeling. Learning to detect unseen object classes by between-class attribute transfer. In *Computer Vision and Pattern Recognition, 2009. CVPR 2009. IEEE Conference on*, pages 951–958. IEEE, 2009.

[17] S. Lazebnik, C. Schmid, and J. Ponce. Beyond bags of features: Spatial pyramid matching for recognizing natural scene categories. In *Computer Vision and Pattern Recognition, 2006 IEEE Computer Society Conference on*, volume 2, pages 2169–2178. IEEE, 2006.

[18] Z. Lu and Y. Peng. Image annotation by semantic sparse recoding of visual content. In *Proceedings of the 20th ACM international conference on Multimedia*, pages 499–508. ACM, 2012.

[19] F. Perronnin, J. Sánchez, and T. Mensink. Improving the fisher kernel for large-scale image classification. In *ECCV*, pages 143–156. Springer, 2010.

[20] C. Snoek, K. van de Sande, D. Fontijne, A. Habibian, M. Jain, S. Kordumova, Z. Li, M. Mazloom, S. Pintea, R. Tao, et al. Mediamill at trecvid 2013: Searching concepts, objects, instances and events in video. In *NIST TRECVID Workshop*, 2013.

[21] S. Thrun. Is learning the n-th thing any easier than learning the first? *Advances in neural information processing systems*, pages 640–646, 1996.

[22] T. Tommasi, F. Orabona, and B. Caputo. Safety in numbers: Learning categories from few examples with multi model knowledge transfer. In *Computer Vision and Pattern Recognition (CVPR), 2010 IEEE Conference on*, pages 3081–3088. IEEE, 2010.

[23] J. Wang, J. Yang, K. Yu, F. Lv, T. Huang, and Y. Gong. Locality-constrained linear coding for image classification. In *Computer Vision and Pattern Recognition (CVPR), 2010 IEEE Conference on*, pages 3360–3367. IEEE, 2010.

[24] G. Widmer and M. Kubat. Learning in the presence of concept drift and hidden contexts. *Machine learning*, 23(1):69–101, 1996.

Start from Scratch: Towards Automatically Identifying, Modeling, and Naming Visual Attributes

Hanwang Zhang[†], Yang Yang[‡], Huanbo Luan[†§], Shuicheng Yan[†], Tat-Seng Chua[†]
[†]National University of Singapore
[‡]University of Electronic Science and Technology of China
[§]Tsinghua University
{hanwangzhang,dlyyang,luanhuanbo}@gmail.com;{eleyans,dcscts}@nus.edu.sg

ABSTRACT

Higher-level semantics such as visual attributes are crucial for fundamental multimedia applications. We present a novel attribute discovery approach that can automatically identify, model and name attributes from an arbitrary set of image and text pairs that can be easily gathered on the Web. Different from conventional attribute discovery methods, our approach does not rely on any pre-defined vocabularies and human labeling. Therefore, we are able to build a large visual knowledge base without any human efforts. The discovery is based on a novel deep architecture, named Independent Component Multimodal Autoencoder (ICMAE), that can continually learn shared higher-level representations across the visual and textual modalities. With the help of the resultant representations encoding strong visual and semantic evidences, we propose to (a) identify attributes and their corresponding high-quality training images, (b) iteratively model them with maximum compactness and comprehensiveness, and (c) name the attribute models with human understandable words. To date, the proposed system has discovered 1,898 attributes over 1.3 million pairs of image and text. Extensive experiments on various real-world multimedia datasets demonstrate the quality and effectiveness of the discovered attributes, facilitating multimedia applications such as image annotation and retrieval as compared to the state-of-the-art approaches.

Categories and Subject Descriptors

H.3.3 [**Content Analysis and Indexing**]: Abstracting methods

Keywords

attribute discovery; deep learning; multimodal analysis

1. INTRODUCTION

With the evolution of machine understanding of visual attributes (*e.g.*, concepts, objects, and visual patterns) over the years[1], we have witnessed the advances in content-based multimedia applications such as annotation and retrieval, which have been reforming the way we interact with the world [26, 40]. It is believed that the success is mainly derived from the intelligent machinery built on large and diverse databases with high-quality attribute annotation. But constructing such databases is a challenging and expensive task. Recent studies, using crowdsourcing and bootstrapping strategies to collect attributes from the Web data at a vast scale with minimum human intervention, offer a promising route towards this task [8, 24, 28].

However, as we migrate these collected attributes to real-world applications, we may find that they adapt poorly to the ever-evolving visual world [35]. One fundamental issue is that until recently researchers have no idea on how many attributes are enough for multimedia applications. They generally resort to a pre-defined vocabulary constructed by domain experts. Since it is manually built with limited scale, the resultant attributes can hardly keep up with the ever-evolving interests of the general users. For instance, the overlap between the items of ImageNet [8]/LSCOM [24] and user-provided tags crawled from Flickr is only 1.4%/7.6%,

Vocabulary	ImageNet	LSCOM
#item	117,023	483,034
#item∩tag (% of #tag)	79,215 (1.42%)	427,440 (7.66%)

(a) Overlap of Pre-defined Vocabularies with User-Generated Tags

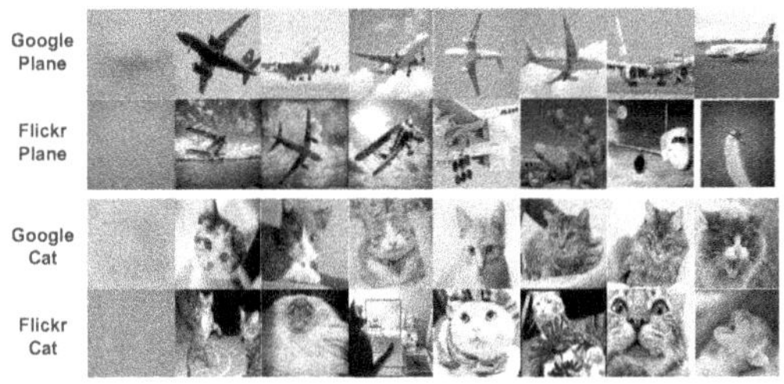

(b) Images Collected by Search Engine and User Tags

Figure 1: Problems with the conventional Web-scale attribute learning paradigm. (a) The pre-defined vocabularies (*i.e.*, items) hardly cover the user-generated tags with 623,464 non-repeated terms from Flickr. (b) Images collected from Google search engine hardly represent user-generated images from Flickr. Images averaged over the most relevant results are shown on the left.

[1]Besides the conventional attribute definition such as object parts, visual properties [12], we refer the term "attribute" to more general semantic meanings such as concepts, objects.

MM'14, November 3–7, 2014, Orlando, Florida, USA.
Copyright 2014 ACM 978-1-4503-3063-3/14/11 ...$15.00.
http://dx.doi.org/10.1145/2647868.2654915.

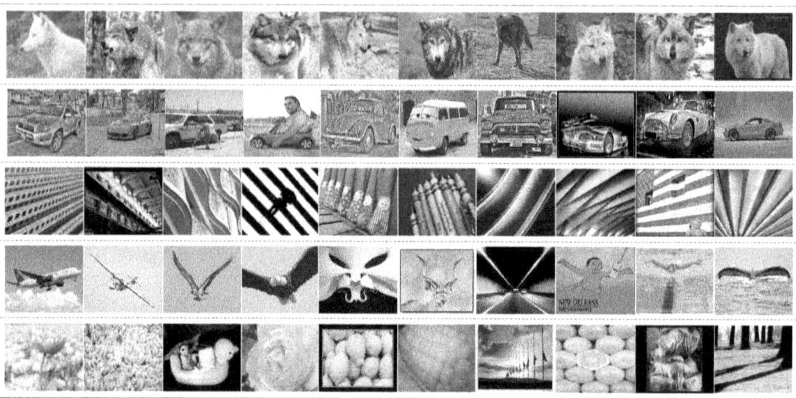

Representative Samples	Names	AP
	Wolf Dog	0.95
	Fourwheeler Car	0.97
	Stripped Rainbow	0.84
	Wing Sky	0.81
	Yellow Russet	0.92

Figure 2: Illustrative examples of 5 discovered attributes. Our approach can automatically identify, model and name attributes without any human efforts. We show 10 representative images with the most model confidence, top 2 names and the performances of attribute models in terms of Average Precision (AP).

as shown in Figure 1(a). On the other hand, due to the noisy tags of the Web images, people exploit search engines to collect much more relevant images given the attributes as queries and invite human labelers to refine the results. However, despite the expensive human labor, the search results may not be informative and comprehensive because of duplicate or near-duplicate visual contents of images, resulting in attribute models heavily biased towards them [16]. For example, as shown in Figure 1(b), given certain attributes as queries, images from a photo sharing community (*e.g.*, Flickr) and a search engine are very different (*e.g.*, Google), causing the models built on the latter can hardly adapt to applications in the former, which nevertheless has begun to dominate the Web content [7].

Intrigued, we raise a question: is it possible to start from scratch to discover and build up the visual attributes directly from the data? In other words, we want to develop an intelligent system that can automatically acquire user-interested attributes solely from images and tags, which can be easily crawled on the Web without any constraints. Here, we refer the "unconstrained crawling" to dataset collection from any sources, rather than need to leverage on search engines to gather data related to a pre-defined set of attributes. In this paper, we describe a novel approach that automatically harvests visual attributes *without any human supervision*. Figure 2 shows some examples of attributes discovered by our system. We want to highlight three key components of our approach that make it effective and distinguishable from state-of-the-art methods [6, 20].

Identification. We do not need any pre-defined vocabulary of semantic attributes or search engines to collect attribute-related images. Instead, our system can automatically identify a set of attributes from a large number of image-text pairs. Motivated by the psychological and cognitive findings [23] that attributes are shared and constructive higher-level abstractions of multi-source sensory perceptions, we develop an unsupervised deep architecture that correlates image and textual data through the shared hidden layer, where the variables are encouraged to be de-correlated from each other. In this way, we are able to fully exploit the rich but noisy visual and semantic information of Web-scale multimodal data to discover useful patterns. Then, the hidden variables are expected to be informative semantic representations for both modalities and are thus ideal surrogates for identifying attributes. For example, a hidden variable may jointly represent the occurrence of the words "furry dog" and the visual properties of a furry dog image.

Modeling. As compared to recent automatic attribute modeling methods that rely on search engines to refine attribute training images [6, 20], our modeling approach incorporates the inherent correlations of visual and textual data encoded in the shared hidden variables, resulting in training images of larger diversity and leading to more generalizable attribute models that are evident in both modalities. Moreover, we propose a model update mechanism for the new data. Hence, besides discovering new attributes, our system can also update old attribute models by merging new but redundant ones. Therefore, the attributes can evolve into a more compact and comprehensive knowledge base from the inexhaustible amount of data.

Naming. Yet, the attributes discovered are not applicable to end-user applications since they have no meaningful utterable names. In order to make the machine-recognized attributes understandable by humans, we propose to name the attributes by using the associated tags of images. For each attribute, we rank the tags as tentative attribute names not only based on their noisy frequencies but also on their relatedness to the corresponding visual properties, namely visualness. This results in more accurate and informative names. It is worth noting that our naming strategy does not rely on any pre-defined vocabularies but directly mines from the user-generated data. The key advantage of this approach is that the attributes are no longer limited in semantic scale and are able to cover general user interest.

The overview of the proposed fully automatic approach is illustrated in Figure 3. We start with nothing but an arbitrary set of image-text pairs as the input data. In order to mine the correlations of the multimodal data, we propose a novel unsupervised deep architecture, called Independent Component Multimodal Autoencoder (ICMAE), which underpins the overall automatic system. ICMAE has two pathways for image and text modalities. The two pathways are then merged into a shared hidden layer. Given the higher-level representations of both pathways (*i.e.*, "Layer 2" as shown in Figure 3), we can learn higher-order correlations across modalities through the shared layer.

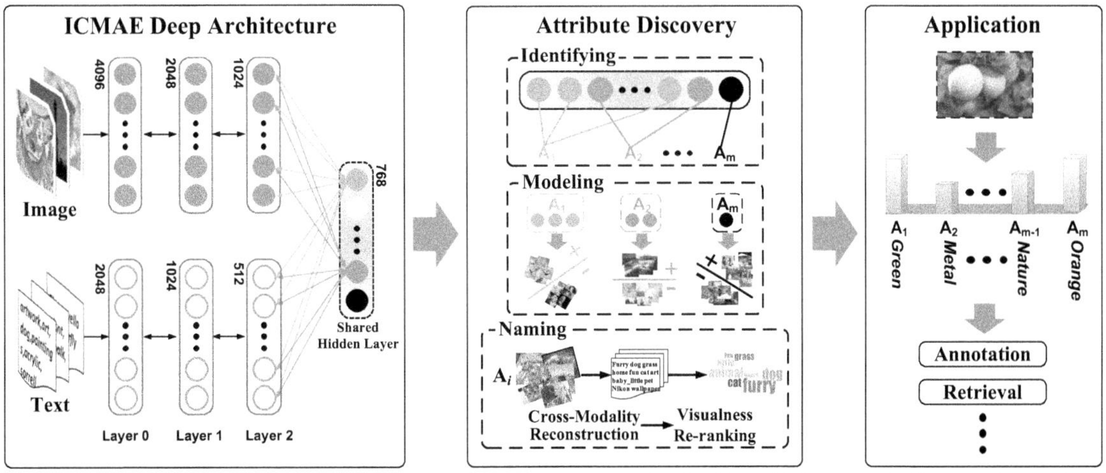

Figure 3: The overview of the proposed system towards automatically identifying, modelling and naming visual attributes. The proposed unsupervised deep architecture, Independent Component Multimodal Autoencoder (ICMAE), underpins the overall system. The number of neurons in each layer is marked.

Based on ICMAE, the attribute discovery works as follows. First, in order to constrain the hidden variables of the shared layer as potential attributes to be **identified**, we propose to impose Independent Component Analysis (ICA) constraints in the architecture to de-correlate the relationships among the variables (colored connections in Figure 3). Then, given a set of images, the response values of the hidden variables of an attribute indicate how strong the attribute is present, guiding us to divide the images into two clusters, namely, positive and negative samples, which are used to **model** the attribute. Finally, for **naming** an attribute, we provide the most confident images of the attribute model as input to the image pathway of ICMAE to reconstruct the textual counterpart. The reconstructed textual data of the images are considered as most visually related to the attribute. Together with their term frequencies, we finally score the text as potential attribute names. So far, the system has discovered 1,898 attributes from 1.3M images and tags pairs. Experimental results on real-world datasets demonstrate that the discovered attributes are effective in supporting fundamental multimedia applications such as image annotation and retrieval.

In the era of big data, we believe that our work has a great potential in relieving human labor for learning visual semantics, due to the following contributions.

- We propose a novel attribute discovery system that can constantly and automatically identify, model and name visual attributes from the exhaustible amount of Web data. To the best of our knowledge, this is the first work to explore the possibility of a fully machine-built visual knowledge base.
- We develop a novel deep architecture named ICMAE that effectively mines the higher-level correlations of noisy multimodal data from the images and the corresponding tags.
- Through fundamental applications such as image annotation and retrieval, we demonstrate that the attributes discovered by our automated system considerably outperform others with human efforts.

The rest of the paper is organized as follows. Section 2 reviews related work. Section 3 describes the machine learning framework of the proposed ICMAE. Section 4 illustrates the proposed automatic attribute discovery approach based on ICMAE, including identifying, modeling, and naming attributes. Experimental results and analysis are reported in Section 5, followed by conclusions in Section 6.

2. RELATED WORK

2.1 Attribute Discovery

The research trend of learning semantic attributes has changed from using small benchmark datasets to large-scale knowledge base, towards real-world applications [35, 38]. However, constructing a desired large dataset is challenging. With the development of crowdsourcing techniques such as Mechanical Turk, large-scale high-quality datasets in terms of size and diversity such as ImageNet [8], LSCOM [24] and Visipedia [28] are constructed at a reasonable cost. Such valuable datasets have successfully spawned many widely-used attribute models such as Classemes [36], Picodes [4], and DeCAF [10]. On the other hand, several studies focus on automatically mining attributes from the Web. For example, Li *et al.* [20] used a multiple instance learning framework to learn sub-image-level features from images returned by querying attribute names from the search engine. Moreover, some bootstrapping strategies are applied to improve the quality of the collected data and their induced attribute models. Li *et al.* [19] developed a system that incrementally updates attribute models, which in turn refines the collected data. Chen *et al.* [6] developed a never-ending image learner that cycles between discovering attribute relationships and then retrain attribute models constrained by the relationships.

However, all the above methods start from a pre-defined vocabulary with poor coverage on general user interests and rely on the less informative images retrieved by search engines. Alternatively, we are able to harvest attributes directly from image-text pairs without the help of any vocabularies and search engines. In this way, our work relates to several recent studies, such as Bergamo *et al.* [4] and Rastegari *et al.* [30] that considered attributes as random split [12] of the visual space enhancing the classification performance. But these discovery methods require class-level image annotations and the discovered attributes have no human understandable names. Instead, our approach does not only discover them but also name them explicitly. Parikh and Grauman [27] invited humans in the discovering process to name attributes by active learning strategy. Similarly, Kankuekul *et al.* [17] incrementally labeled attributes via online interaction with users. As compared to these semi-automatic methods, our naming is fully automatic. There are also automatic attribute discovery and naming methods that fall into specific domains like butterfly [37] and fashion productsbengio2009learning recogntion [3]. However, we tackle the problem in general domain which is more fundamental and challenging.

2.2 Multimodal Deep Learning

Recent advances in machine learning community have examined that deep architecture can be trained to produce useful representations for visual [14], acoustic [9] and textual [21] modalities. However, there are only few studies focusing on multimodal deep learning. Ngiam *et al.* [25] proposed a deep autoencoder that jointly learns shared representations from visual and acoustic modalities. This model correlates the multimodalities by reconstructing one modality given that others missing. Our deep architecture follows this cross-modality reconstruction strategy since it is very similar to the reconstructive and reusable properties of attributes. Andrew *et al.* [1] proposed to use Canonical Correlation Analysis criterion in the overall fine-tuning of independent deep networks of multimodalities. But this model is not reconstructive and hence fails to learn representations optimized for attributes. Srivastava and Salakhutdinov [32] developed a multimodal Deep Boltzmann Machines that jointly model the image and text data. This model learns similar representations as that of Ngiam *et al.* [25] but it may suffer from the early-stopping issue since there is no explicit objective when training Deep Boltzmann Machines. It is worth noting that the learnt representations by the above models are not optimized for identifying informative attributes since the shared representations are highly correlated, resulting in very redundant attributes. Therefore, we propose to incorporate the Independent Correlation Analysis criterion [18] in a deep Multimodal Autoencoder to overcome this issue.

3. INDEPENDENT COMPONENT MULTIMODAL AUTOENCODER

In this section, we introduce the architecture and details of the proposed Independent Component Multimodal Autoencoder (ICMAE), which underpins the subsequent attribute discovery. Technically, learning ICMAE includes layer-wise pre-training and overall fine-tuning. Note that this learning procedure can be applied once again to update the old ICMAE if a new batch of crawled data comes in. Here, we use the parameters of the old model as initializations for the new round of pre-training using the new data. Thus, we can always obtain an updated ICMAE that adapts to the ever-evolving visual world. Without loss of generality, in this section, we only introduce how we train ICMAE based on one batch of training data.

3.1 Architecture Overview

The basic architecture of the network we use is similar to the one used in [25]. As shown in Figure 3, it has two parallel pathways for two input modalities and one shared hidden layer. Each input datum is a feature pair of image $\mathbf{x}^0 \in \mathbb{R}^{4096}$ and its associated text $\mathbf{t}^0 \in \mathbb{R}^{2048}$ (cf. Section 5.1.2 for details of feature extraction from noisy data). Then, $(\mathbf{x}^0, \mathbf{t}^0)$ is *encoded* (*i.e.*, fed forward) to the shared layer along both pathways, namely, $(\mathbf{x}^0, \mathbf{t}^0) \rightarrow (\mathbf{x}^1, \mathbf{t}^1) \rightarrow (\mathbf{x}^2, \mathbf{t}^2) \rightarrow \mathbf{z}$, where the dimensions of the variables $\mathbf{x}^1$ (or $\mathbf{t}^1$) and $\mathbf{x}^2$ (or $\mathbf{t}^2$) are respectively 2048 (or 1024) and 1024 (or 512), and the dimensions of the hidden variable $\mathbf{z}$ is 768. Here, we gradually reduce the dimensionality through each pathway in order to learn higher-level, nonlinear abstractions [14], and merge them into the shared hidden layer to model the relationships between the two modalities. Finally the stimuli of the shared layer is *decoded* (*i.e.*, fed backward) through the two pathways to reconstruct the input data of both modalities, namely, $\mathbf{z} \rightarrow (\widehat{\mathbf{x}}^2, \widehat{\mathbf{t}}^2) \rightarrow (\widehat{\mathbf{x}}^1, \widehat{\mathbf{t}}^1) \rightarrow (\widehat{\mathbf{x}}^0, \widehat{\mathbf{t}}^0)$. Such multimodal deep autoencoder aims to jointly model the distributions of the image and text data, resulting in shared hidden variables that have strong connections to variables from both modalities. Interestingly, this property meets the meanings of semantic attributes [23] and therefore the variables of the shared hidden layer are ideal as attribute candidates. Next, we detail the encoding and decoding functions of ICMAE.

Without loss of generality, we only formulate the image pathway. The encoding functions are computed as

$$\begin{aligned} &\mathbf{x}^1 = \sigma(\mathbf{W}_v^0 \mathbf{x}^0 + \mathbf{c}^1),\ \mathbf{x}^2 = \sigma(\mathbf{W}_v^1 \mathbf{x}^1 + \mathbf{c}^2), \\ &\mathbf{z} = \sigma\left([\mathbf{W}_v^2\ \mathbf{W}_t^2] \begin{bmatrix} \mathbf{x}^2 \\ \mathbf{t}^2 \end{bmatrix} + \mathbf{c}^3 \right), \end{aligned} \tag{1}$$

where $\sigma(\cdot)$ is the element-wise sigmoid function that has been shown to be useful for autoencoders [14]. $\mathbf{W}_v^i$ and $\mathbf{c}^i$, $i = 0, 1$ are trainable weights and encoding biases of the image pathway, respectively. $\mathbf{W}_v^2$ and $\mathbf{W}_t^2$ are the weights of the image and text pathways, respectively. $\mathbf{c}^3$ is the bias of the shared layer. The decoding functions are computed as

$$\widehat{\mathbf{x}}^2 = \sigma(\mathbf{W}_v^{2^T} \mathbf{z} + \mathbf{b}^2),\ \widehat{\mathbf{x}}^1 = \sigma(\mathbf{W}_v^{1^T} \widehat{\mathbf{x}}^2 + \mathbf{b}^1),\ \widehat{\mathbf{x}}^0 = \mathbf{W}_v^{0^T} \widehat{\mathbf{x}}^0 + \mathbf{b}^0, \tag{2}$$

where $\mathbf{b}^i$ is the decoding bias. Note that the decoding function from Layer 1 to the input Layer 0 is not sigmoidal. This is because we need to retain the intrinsic Gaussian distribution for the features of the input data.

3.2 Layer-wise Pre-training

It is well-known that deep architecture only works well if the trainable parameters are properly initialized to a good solution. In this section, we introduce how to use the Restricted Boltzmann Machine (RBM) [2] to pre-train the proposed ICMAE. The RBM is an undirected graphical model that connects two layers of random variables. Without loss of generality, we denote $\mathbf{v}$ as visible variables and $\mathbf{h}$ as hidden variables corresponding to any two connected layers in ICMAE. In particular, for the combined image and text variables at Layer 2, we have $\mathbf{v} \leftarrow [\mathbf{x}^{2^T}, \mathbf{t}^{2^T}]^T$, and for the shared hidden layer, we have $\mathbf{h} \leftarrow \mathbf{z}$. The connections in RBM are parameterized by $\mathbf{W}$ between $\mathbf{v}$ and $\mathbf{h}$. The optimization is to minimize the negative logarithm of the likelihood $p(\mathbf{v}) = \sum_{\mathbf{h}} p(\mathbf{v}, \mathbf{h}) = \sum_{\mathbf{h}} \frac{e^{-E(\mathbf{v},\mathbf{h})}}{Z}$, where Z is a partition function.

One form of RBM is to assume that $\mathbf{v}$ and $\mathbf{h}$ are $\{0, 1\}$-valued binary variables. This RBM type is consistent with the sigmoidal decoding/encoding functions in Eq. (1) and (2).

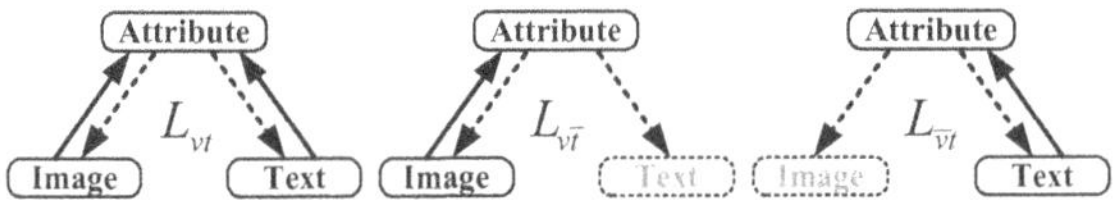

(a) Cross-modality Reconstruction

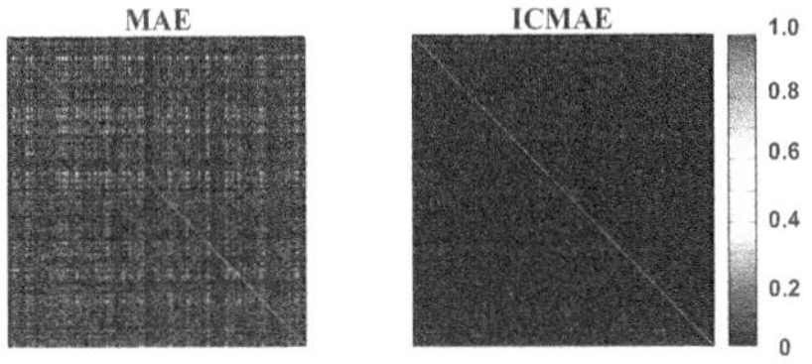

(b) Correlation of Hidden Variables

Figure 4: Illustration of the two objectives of ICMAE. (a) Three types of cross-modality reconstruction error as shown in Eq. (3). The solid and dashed arrows denote encoding and decoding, respectively. The lighter font color denotes missing modalities. (b) Visualizations of the correlation matrices of the resultant hidden variables of MAE (Multimodal AE [25]) and the proposed ICMAE. We can see that most of the hidden variables of ICMAE are de-correlated with each other by the use of independent component constraints as shown in Eq. (4).

Another form of RBM is to assume $\mathbf{h}$ as binary but $\mathbf{v}$ as real-valued Gaussian variables with unit variance and is consistent with the linear encoding/decoding functions in Eq. (2). Therefore, we use the Gaussian-binary RBM to initialize the parameters that connect between Layer 0 and Layer 1 of ICMAE and use the binary-binary RBM to initialize parameters of other layers. In total, we train 5 RBMs (4 along the two pathways, and 1 for the joint layer and the shared hidden layer) for ICMAE pre-training. As it is intractable to compute the gradient of the log-likelihood, we learn the parameters of the RMBs using contrastive divergence as in [34]. Moreover, in order to learn sparse models in an efficient way, we set the initial biases of the RMBs as sufficiently small (*e.g.*, -2).

3.3 Overall Fine-tuning

After pre-training ICMAE by using RBMs as above, we are able to fine-tune the entire ICMAE using stochastic gradient descent to minimize the objective function of ICMAE. If we only define the objective function as the reconstruction error between the mutimodal input $(\mathbf{x}^0, \mathbf{t}^0)$ and output $(\widehat{\mathbf{x}}^0, \widehat{\mathbf{t}}^0)$, the deep autoencoder may easily overfit to each of the modality and fail to learn useful cross-modality correlations. For example, it is possible for shared hidden layer to find representations such that some of the variables are tuned only for images while others are tuned only for tags. So, the shared hidden variables may result in attributes that are only responsive to one single modality, thus losing important information for the subsequent attribute discovery. Inspired by [25], we propose to encourage cross-modality reconstruction. As shown in Figure 4(a), given one modality present and the other one absent, we hope to reconstruct both modalities. According to the encoding/decoding functions in Eq. (1) and (2), we can see that the reconstructed of any modality is a function of both input modality, *i.e.*, $\widehat{\mathbf{x}}^0 = \widehat{\mathbf{x}}^0\left(\mathbf{x}^0, \mathbf{t}^0\right)$. For example, we can define the reconstruction error when the image modality is present while the text modality is absent as

$$L_{v\bar{t}} = \|\mathbf{x}^0 - \widehat{\mathbf{x}}^0\left(\mathbf{x}^0, \mathbf{0}\right)\|_2^2 + \|\mathbf{t}^0 - \widehat{\mathbf{t}}^0\left(\mathbf{x}^0, \mathbf{0}\right)\|_2^2, \quad (3)$$

where the subscript $v\bar{t}$ denote the presence of the image and the absence of text modalities. L_{vt} and $L_{\bar{v}t}$ can be defined in a similar way.

On the other hand, we want to regularize the hidden variables to be statistically independent with each other. Intuitively, attributes in nature are independent semantic meanings that constitute the visual or semantical world [23]. For example, an image of "beach sunset" may be composed by independent attributes such as "round", "water", "sun", "horizontal line". Therefore, we propose to impose the Independent Component Analysis (ICA) criterion on the overall objective function of ICMAE. Different from traditional ICA [15] that optimizes a ℓ_1-norm penalty with "hard" orthonormality constraints, we use a "soft" version with the reconstruction cost [18], which meets our formulation in Eq. (3). In particular, the penalty term is the sum of the activation value of the hidden variables $\mathbf{z}$. For example, when the input modality is image while the text modality is absent, the ICA regularization term is defined as

$$I_{v\bar{t}} = \left\|\mathbf{z}(\mathbf{x}^0, \mathbf{0})\right\|_1, \quad (4)$$

and I_{vt}, $I_{\bar{v}t}$ can be defined in a similar way.

Hence, the overall objective function of ICMAE that we are going to minimize is

$$F\left(\mathbf{x}, \mathbf{t}; \mathcal{W}\right) = L_{vt} + L_{v\bar{t}} + L_{\bar{v}t} + \lambda(I_{vt} + I_{v\bar{t}} + I_{\bar{v}t}) + \gamma R(\mathcal{W}), \quad (5)$$

where $\mathcal{W} = \{\mathcal{W}^i\} = \{(\mathbf{W}_v^i, \mathbf{W}_t^i, \mathbf{b}^i, \mathbf{c}^i)\}$, $i = 0, 1, 2$, is the set of trainable parameters, $R(\mathcal{W})$ is an ℓ_2-norm regularizer, λ and γ are trade-off parameters. We update $\mathcal{W}$ using the stochastic gradient descent method with a dynamic momentum tric [29].

4. ATTRIBUTE DISCOVERY

The deep architecture ICMAE have mined the strong correlations of multimodal data and learnt useful higher-level representations, in which the attributes are encoded. In this section, we will detail how we identify, model and name attributes based on ICMAE.

4.1 Identification

Recall that we identify attributes without any pre-defined vocabularies. Instead, we identify them from the learnt shared hidden variables of ICMAE. Recall that such variables are (a) higher-level features which can reconstruct both modalities; and (b) as independent as possible with each other. On one hand, the hidden variables are high-level abstractions of visual and semantic evidences from a large amount of image-text data and are in turn encouraged to reconstruct these evidences [23]. For example, attribute "furry" is abstracted from visual and semantic cues such as furry animals. Meanwhile, "furry" is indispensable to compose those evidences. On the other hand, we humans in nature hope that attributes are compact and independent semantic meanings which compose the world. Therefore, the hidden variables are expected to be an ideal feature pool to extract attributes.

However, there are still correlated hidden variables relating to the same attribute. Hence, it is possible to identify several clusters, each of which holds the variables with large correlation values. We adopt the Affinity Propagation (AP) [13] that can cluster data given a pair-wise similarity matrix without fixing the number of clusters. In our case, the similarity matrix is the correlation matrix of the

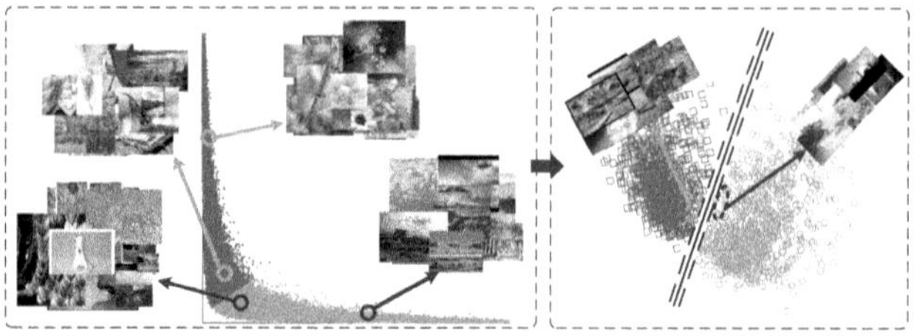

Figure 5: Illustrations of an attribute identified in the hidden space and modeled in the visual space. The attribute corresponds to two hidden variables, which are strongly correlated (left). Images that are sufficiently far from the MMC boundary are chosen. Then, the attribute is modeled by the chosen samples in the visual space using SVM (right, visualized by using PCA to 2-D). The support vectors of images (marked near the hyperplane) are considered as the attribute model representations, which are used to check model redundancy.

hidden variables based on training data. Then, each resultant cluster is considered as an attribute, denoted as a while its hidden variables is denoted as $\mathbf{a}$, where $\mathbf{a} \subseteq \mathbf{z}$. For an identified attribute a, we should further identify its positive and negative samples for the subsequent attribute modeling. To achieve this, we use Maximum Margin Clustering (MMC) [41] to automatically divide samples in the hidden space into two clusters with maximum marginal separation. Denoting $\{\mathbf{a}_i\}$ as the hidden representations of samples with respect to attribute a, MMC iteratively seeks for two clusters by Support Vector Regression (SVR) [31]. It is worth noting that, as shown in Figure 5, images associated with the hidden variables near the decision boundary are ambiguous and not as visually separable as those associated with the hidden variables far from the boundary. Therefore, for better attribute modeling, we identify the high-quality positive and negative images with respect to the attribute as $Pos(a) = \{\mathbf{x}_i | \mathbf{w}^T\mathbf{a}_i > T\}$ and $Neg(a) = \{\mathbf{x}_i | \mathbf{w}^T\mathbf{a}_i < -T\}$, where $\mathbf{w}$ is the model parameter of SVR and $T > 0$ is a positive threshold.

4.2 Modeling

Provided with the training samples $Pos(a)$ and $Neg(a)$ of attribute a, we use a linear Support Vector Machine (SVM) to model the attribute in the visual space. Due to the imperfection of AP clustering of the hidden variables, some attributes may still correlate with each other, resulting in redundant attribute models. In order to obtain a compact set of attribute models, we propose to merge redundant models.

Our merging strategy is based on checking the Mutual Information (MI) shared between model $\mathcal{M}_a$ of attribute a and model $\mathcal{M}_b$ of attribute b. MI measures how much information the knowledge of either $\mathcal{M}_a$ or $\mathcal{M}_b$ provides for the other. For instance, if the MI between $\mathcal{M}_a$ and $\mathcal{M}_b$ is small, it indicates that $\mathcal{M}_a$ provides minimal information for determining whether $\mathcal{M}_b$ is redundant as compared to $\mathcal{M}_a$. Specifically, we represent any model $\mathcal{M}$ by a set of images which are support vectors $\mathcal{S}$ of the model since the support vectors sufficiently characterize the decision boundary of the attribute model (see the right of Figure 5). Therefore, the MI between attribute model $\mathcal{M}_a$ and $\mathcal{M}_b$ is defined as

$$I(\mathcal{M}_a; \mathcal{M}_b) = \sum_{\mathbf{x}' \in \mathcal{S}_b} \sum_{\mathbf{x} \in \mathcal{S}_a} p(\mathbf{x}, \mathbf{x}') \log \left(\frac{p(\mathbf{x}, \mathbf{x}')}{p(\mathbf{x})p(\mathbf{x}')} \right), \quad (6)$$

where we use kernel density estimation [22] to estimate the distribution $p(\mathbf{x})$, $p(\mathbf{x}')$ and $p(\mathbf{x}, \mathbf{x}')$. Note the estimation is efficient since the number of support vectors is relatively small as compared to the number of training samples. We accept to merge two attribute models if the MI between them is larger than a pre-defined threshold. For merging the two models, we first align the direction of their hyperplanes and then combine the samples on either side with response concensus on both models. Finally, we train a merged attribute model with the combined samples.

We can also use this merging strategy to update old attribute models by merging new but redundant ones which are discovered from a new batch of data. Thus, we will acquire more compact and comprehensive attribute models from the inexhaustible amount of Web data.

4.3 Naming

Yet, the discovered attributes are not assigned with any human nameable annotations. In this section, we show how to name attributes directly from the tags associated with representative images (*i.e.*, images with the most confidence of the attribute models). Since the attribute models are binary classifiers, representative images on both sides are considered. That is to say, we will assign *two* names for *one* identified attribute. As compared to standard attribute naming that only express one property (*e.g.*, "green" or "not green"), our naming is more descriptive. Note that this is reasonable since images on the opposite side of "flower" could be endowed various semantics and thus should not be coarsely named as "non-flower" [30].

A straightforward approach to name an attribute is to mine highly frequent tags associated with the representative images of the attribute. However, the user-generated tags are very noisy and thus are usually irrelevant to the visual properties of the attribute. For example, as illustrated in Figure 6, highly frequent words in user tags can be very general concept (*e.g.*, "nature", "sky"), device (*e.g.*, "cannon", "nikon"), or sentiment (*e.g.*, "a-big-fave", "diamond-class photographer"). Moreover, some obvious visual properties are unlikely to ever be mentioned by users. For example, the frequencies of "green", "violet" are low as shown in Figure 6. Therefore, naming attributes only from tag frequency is not a proper approach.

We propose to incorporate the visualness of words to name attributes. Here, visualness refers to how strong the textual words relate to visual properties. Conventional visualness measurement methods [39, 16, 3] still fundamentally rely on word statistics and hence cannot recover missing words with high visualness. Fortunately, thanks to ICMAE that correlates the cross-modality data of images and textual tags, we can directly choose tags which are responsive to the target visual attributes. First, as shown in Figure 6, we feed the representative images of the attribute into ICMAE and reconstruct the text counterpart. In particular, the textual reconstruction is formulated as $\widetilde{\mathbf{t}}^0(\mathbf{x}^0, \mathbf{0})$, which is the cross-modality reconstruction given images but missing text (cf. Section 3.3). Then, since each dimension of the textual data refers to several words (cf. Section 5.1.2), the value of the dimension is considered as the visualness of these words with respect to the attribute. As analogous to word frequencies, we can also visualize the visualness of words in Figure 6. We can see that words like flower names (*e.g.*, "fuchsia", "rosebuds") are strongly related to the images. Moreover,

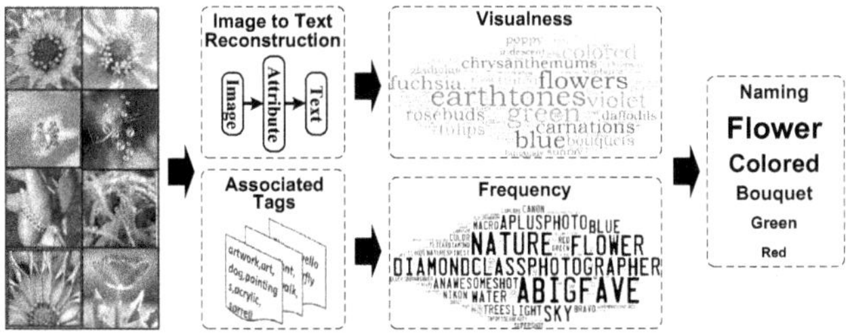

Figure 6: Illustration of attribute naming by jointly considering word visualness and frequency, which are visualized as word clouds. Images shown on the left are representative samples on one side of the attribute model.

some obvious properties like "colored", "green" and "red" have emerged. Finally, we respectively normalize visualness and frequencies, and add the two scores as the final scores for potential attribute names. Figure 2 illustrates the top 2 ranked names for several discovered attributes.

5. EXPERIMENTS

We systematically evaluate the effectiveness of the proposed ICMAE deep architecture and the quality of attribute identification, modeling and naming methods.

5.1 Data and Methodology

5.1.1 Experimental Data Sets

We crawled the image-text multimodal data from a photo-sharing website Flickr. The crawling protocol is as follows. First, we started from 500 seed users who contribute most interesting photos using Flickr API. Next, for each of the seed user, we select at most 100 users from his/her contact. This results in around 50,000 users. Finally, we crawled all their uploaded photos which have tags. In this paper, we used 1,321,496 pairs which are crawled in 10 continuous days of Jan, 2014. In order to examine how our approach can evolve to new data, we split the data into four batches of equal size from earlier to latter periods. We trained ICMAE and discovered attributes from one batch to another. The trained parameters of ICMAE using the former batch were used to initialize the training using the next one.

In order to quantitatively evaluate the quality of the discovered attributes, we conducted two fundamental multimedia tasks, *i.e.*, image annotation and content-based image retrieval, on two benchmark data sets: **MIR-Flickr** that contains 25,000 images across 24 concepts, and **NUS-WIDE** that contains 269,648 images across 81 concepts. For annotation experiments, we followed the "train/test" split protocol in the official documentary, *i.e.*, "15,000/10,000" for MIR-Flickr and "161,789/107,859" for NUS-WIDE. For retrieval experiments on both data sets, we randomly selected 10% images from each concept as query examples.

5.1.2 Visual and Textual Features

For image features, we adopted the 4096-D DeCAF generic visual feature [10], which is the activations of the 6-th layer of a deep CNN trained in a fully supervised fashion on ImageNet [8]. This feature has been demonstrated to be effective on modern benchmark data sets. For each batch of the image data, we normalized the visual features into a zero-mean unit-variance Gaussian distribution. For textual feature, we developed a novel feature towards extreme sparse and noisy tags. The extraction pipeline was conducted as follows.

First, we transformed each word in a tag list into a 300-D vector using Word2Vec [21], which is a model trained on Google News data of 100 billion words. Note that there are about 100,000 words from our data contained in this model. Second, we learnt a 2048-D dictionary from the overlapped 100,000 words using K-means. Third, for each word in a tag list, we obtained a 2048-D sparse codes using any off-the-shelf sparse coding toolbox. Finally, each tag list can be transformed into a 2048-D textual feature by max pooling all the words in it. As compared to traditional word-frequency feature which is extremely sparse (*e.g.*, 1-5 non-zero dimensions using most frequent 2,048 words), our textual features have 30-50 non-zero dimensions. The features have richer semantic meanings, resulting in better representation of textual data. We normalized the textual features into a zero-mean unit-variance Gaussian distribution.

5.1.3 Implementation Details

For training the RBMs (cf. Section 3.2), we initialized the weights uniformly as in the range of $[-0.05, +0.05]$ and the biases as -2. For stochastic gradient of the likelihood, we used Persistent Contrastive Divergence (PCD) [34] with 5-step Gibbs sampling of 100 Markov chains, and the coefficient of the ℓ_2-norm weight decay was set as 0.0001. There were 500 training data in a mini-batch. The initial learning rate was set as 0.1 and we decayed it by dividing 1.000015 at each epoch. We stopped the training of each RBM after 1000 epochs. It took about 5 days to train RBMs on each batch of the multimodal data along each modality pathway.

For training the ICMAE (cf. Section 3.3), we initialized the parameters using the pre-trained RBMs. The hyper-parameters λ and γ in Eq. (5) are set as 1 and 0.0001, respectively. The size of the mini-batch of the stochastic gradient descent is 500 and the initial learning rate was set to 0.001, which will be dynamically adjusted by monitoring the objective function. We stopped the training of ICMAE after 600 epochs. It took about 6 days to train on each batch of the multimodal data. The above deep architectures were built using PyLearn2 and trained on an NVIDIA TITAN 600 GPU.

For attribute identification (cf. Section 4.1), the AP [13] and MMC [41] clustering was implemented by using the codes provided by the authors. Besides using the default parameters, we set the preference in AP algorithm as 0.5 to obtain clusters of hidden variables with sufficient correlations. The threshold T was set as such that the selected samples contribute at least 90% of the sum of the confidence scores. For attribute modeling (cf. Section 4.2) and image annotation experiments (cf. Section 5.2.2), we used the linear SVMs and tuned the trade-off parameter within the set $\log C \in \{-3, -2, ..., 3\}$ on the 10% training data, which were used as the validation set.

5.1.4 Compared Methods

To evaluate the effectiveness of the proposed **ICMAE** in attribute identification, we compared it against the following three state-of-the-art multimodal deep architectures: a) **DCCA**, Deep Canonical Correlation Analysis [1], which exploits Canonical Correlation Analysis to connects the hidden layer of the two pathways of multimodal data in order to fine-tune the overall deep networks, b) **MDBM**, Multimodal Deep Boltzman Machine [32], which connects two Deep Boltzmann Machine of multimodalities by a shared

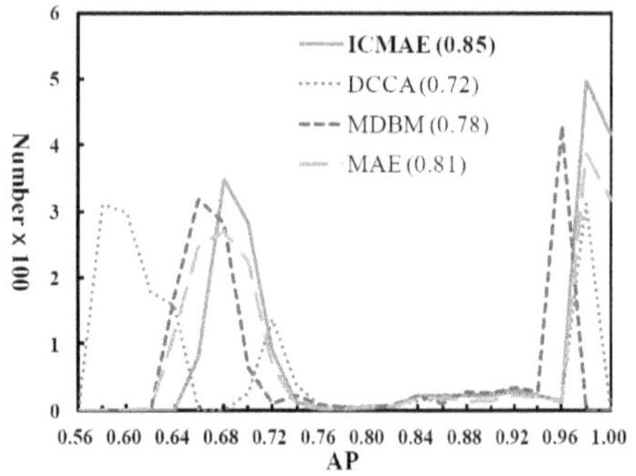

(a) AP Distribution of Attributes

(b) Attributes with Low AP

Figure 7: Evaluations of the attribute identification. (a) Distributions of the number of the discovered attributes by four multimodal deep architectures over a range of AP, with mAP shown in bracket. (b) 10 representative images on both side of the model hypothesis (red dashed line) are shown.

hidden layer, and c) **MAE**, Multimodal Autoencoder, [25] which connects two deep autoencoders of multimodalities by a shared hidden layer. For fair comparisons, all the compared deep architectures have the same number of layers and the same number of neurons in each layer, and we used the same pre-training methods (cf. Section 3.2). We used Average Precision (AP) of the discovered attribute models to evaluate the quality, *i.e.*, the strength of the visual separability of the automatically identified attributes.

To evaluate the effectiveness of attribute modeling, we represented images by the responses of the discovered attribute classifiers. Such representations of images can be considered as semantic features, which are expected to support high performance image annotation and retrieval tasks. We compared our semantic features, named **Auto**, with three state-of-the-art semantic features: a) **Classeme** [36], the 2659-D output of classifiers trained on images collected from Bing Image Search by querying 2,659 concepts from LSCOM [24], b) **DeCAF** [10], the 1000-D output of a deep CNN trained on 1,000 classes of ImageNet [8], and c) **PiCoDes** [4], the 2048-D binary codes obtained by optimizing the classification across 2,659 classes of ImageNet. All the above three compared features were extracted by the software provided by the authors. For annotation, we trained 1-vs-all concept classifiers using the semantic features and used the mean AP (mAP) of the classifiers as the evaluation metric. For retrieval, all the query images and the gallery images are represented using these features and then the retrieval was then performed by similarity search. In particular, we used ℓ_1-norm distance for Classeme, DeCAF and the proposed Auto since they are classifier outputs and used Hamming distance for PiCoDes since it is binary code. We used the mAP at top K, for $K \in \{1, .., 100\}$, and averaged over all the queries as the evaluation metric for retrieval.

To evaluate the quality of attribute naming, we conducted two experiments: quantitative evaluation and human evaluation. For quantitative evaluation, given an image in MIRFlickr or NUS-WIDE, we calculated the average cosine similarities of the predicted attribute names and the ground-truth labels. Specifically, we applied all the discovered attribute classifiers on an image and collected the corresponding top 5 names of each attribute. Recall that each attribute name or the ground-truth label can be represented by a 300-D vector, we then calculated the cosine similarity between any pair of a name and the label. We averaged the similarities over all the pairs as the final similarity between the attribute names and the ground-truth label. For human evaluation, we invited 30 graduate students and showed them 20 representative images and top 5 names of each attribute. We asked them to judge whether the naming is "good", "fair" or "bad". We compared the proposed naming strategy using term frequency and visualness (cf. Section 4.3), named **Freq+Visual** with that using only term frequency (**Freq**) or visualness (**Visual**). Note the Freq naming method is widely adopted in state-of-the-art attribute naming approaches [37, 3].

5.2 Experimental Results

5.2.1 Evaluations of Identification

Figure 7(a) plots the distributions of the number of the discovered attributes by four multimodal deep architectures: the proposed ICMAE, DCCA [1], MDBM [32] and MAE [25]. We can see that all the multimodal deep learning methods can identify a lot of attributes with good AP (*e.g.*, above 0.9). This demonstrates that jointly deep learning representations from visual and textual modality is useful in identifying meaningful visual patterns. In particular, there are 1898, 1691, 1502 and 1778 attributes identified by ICMAE, DCCA, MDBM and MAE, respectively. We can also see that the discovered attributes by ICMAE have stronger visual evidences in terms of the number of good attribute models and the overall mAP. The superiority of ICMAE to other methods arises from the following aspects. a) ICMAE is designed to learn strong cross-modality representations that can reconstruct any of the modality while the other is missing. This guarantees that the identified attributes are good higher-level abstractions from both visual and textual sources, resulting in high-quality labeled images which are strongly related to attributes. b) ICMAE aims to learn hidden representations that are as independent as possible and thus the resultant attributes will have less redundant information. This helps to identify a compact and comprehensive set of attributes.

Figure 2 shows some successful examples of the discovered attributes. However, there are also some attributes with relative low AP (*e.g.*, below 0.7). Figure 7(b) illustrates some examples of attributes with AP around 0.65. We can observe that there is no consistent visual patterns on either side of the attribute model hypothesises. This indicates that the corresponding hidden variables fail to capture any stable semantic meanings. One possible reason is that these variables are isolated from clusters to which they are supposed to belong, due to the imperfection of AP clustering.

Table 1: **Performance (mAP%) of image annotation on MIR-Flickr and NUS-WIDE. Note that our Auto with simple linear SVM considerably outperforms the best published results (43.67% on MIR-Flickr [33] and 27.1% on NUS-WIDE [11]), which were obtained by complicated features and classification models.**

Dataset/Method	Classeme	PiCoDes	DeCAF	Auto
MIR-Flickr	15.90	15.98	52.67	**61.02**
NUS-WIDE	24.09	20.29	27.08	**32.71**

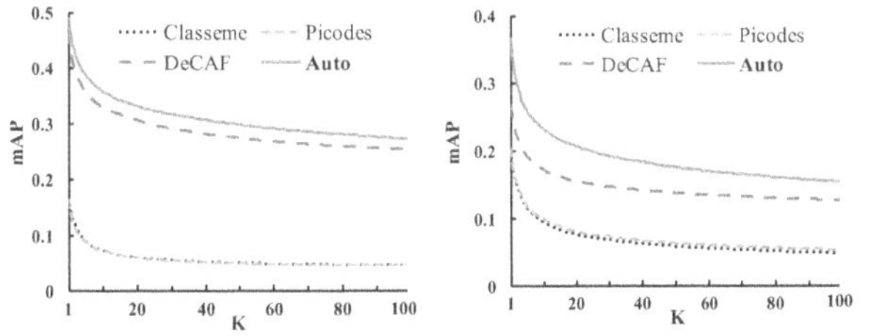

(a) MIR-Flickr (b) NUS-WIDE

Figure 8: Performance (mAP@K) of image retrieval over 10% random queries of MIR-Flickr and NUS-WIDE

5.2.2 *Evaluations of Modeling*

Table 1 and Figure 8 respectively shows the performance of the four semantic features in two fundamental multimedia tasks: image annotation and retrieval. In particular, Figure 10 presents the detailed annotation and retrieval results over all the concepts. Due to page limit, we here only report the 81 concepts of NUS-WIDE. It is worth noting that as compared to the three semantic features which require huge human efforts, *e.g.*, exploiting manually built knowledge base such as ImageNet [8], the proposed feature Auto was extracted from 1,898 attributes discovered in a fully automatic way. From the results, we can observe that Auto considerably outperforms the other three state-of-the-art semantic features. The reasons are two folds. First, our attributes were discovered automatically without the limitations of a pre-defined vocabulary. Hence, the derived feature Auto has a better representation of image semantics. Second, our discovery does not rely on the results of any search engine, which may only provide duplicate and simple images with respect to an attribute. In contrast, we directly mine an arbitrary set of Web images, resulting in attribute models that retain the intricate visual patterns of the visual world.

Table 2: Averaged cosine similarities between the predicted attribute names and the ground-truth labels for images of the combined NUS-WIDE and MIR-Flickr

Method	Freq	Visual	Freq+Visual
Avg. Cos. Similarity	0.10	0.21	**0.28**

5.2.3 *Evaluations of Naming*

Table 2 lists the averaged cosine similarities between the top 5 predicted attribute names and the ground-truth labels for images in NUS-WIDE and MIR-Flickr. From the results, we can see that Freq+Visual improves the naming quality significantly to 0.28. Note that this value suggests that the attribute names are generally relevant to the ground-truth labels. For reference, the cosine similarity between "car" and "fourwheeler" is 0.48 and that between "airplane" and "sky" is 0.23. Interestingly, using solely visualness can obtain 0.21 similarity. This demonstrates that ICMAE can recover missing texts meaningfully using only visual data. Figure 9 shows the average percentage of "Good", "Fair" and "Bad" attribute naming judgement from 30 regular users over the discovered 1,898 attributes. We can clearly see that the users are more satisfied with the Freq+Visual naming strategy. The better performance of jointly considering term frequency and visualness is because the visualness of words obtained by textual reconstruction can effectively eliminate the irrelevant but highly frequent words in the very noisy user-provided tag set.

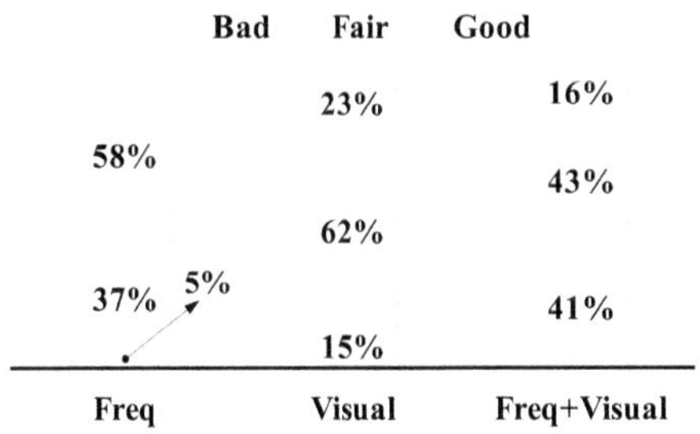

Figure 9: Average percentage of "Good", "Fair", "Bad" attribute naming judgement from the 30 regular users over the discovered 1,898 attributes

6. CONCLUSIONS

We presented a novel automatic attribute discovery approach that can automatically identify, model and name attributes from the inexhaustible image and tag pairs on the Web. We started from scratch without any pre-defined vocabulary or human labelling. Hence, our approach requires no human efforts. In particular, We proposed a novel deep architecture, called Independent Component Multimodal Autoencoder (ICMAE), to mine useful higher-level representations, based on which we developed strategies to identify, model and name attributes. So far, 1,898 attributes have been discovered from 1.3 million crawled data pairs. Extensive experiments on benchmark datasets have demonstrated the feasibility and effectiveness of the proposed approach, which has a great potential in relieving human labor for learning visual semantics from big Web data. In the near future, we will launch a live system based on this work. Peer researchers are welcome to download the attribute models to facilitate their research.

Although this work is an ambitious attempt to build a fully machine-built visual knowledge base, it has left the following two open issues not addressed. First, the system is not a real end-to-end system because we rely on "engineered" but not pixel- or word-level "raw" features. Second, there is still a large gap between human and machine attribute naming qualities (*e.g.*, our result is only 0.28 as compared to 0.50, which is the result we empirically find that human can achieve), especially the names corresponding to attribute models of relatively low reliability. One possible solution for the first issue is to connect CNNs to the inputs of the two pathways [5]. However, it is still unknown on how to design a proper learning strategy to synchronize the behavior of the multimodal heterogeneous network. For the second issue, it is mainly due to the limitation of multimodal correlation. Therefore, we will investigate more effective corre-

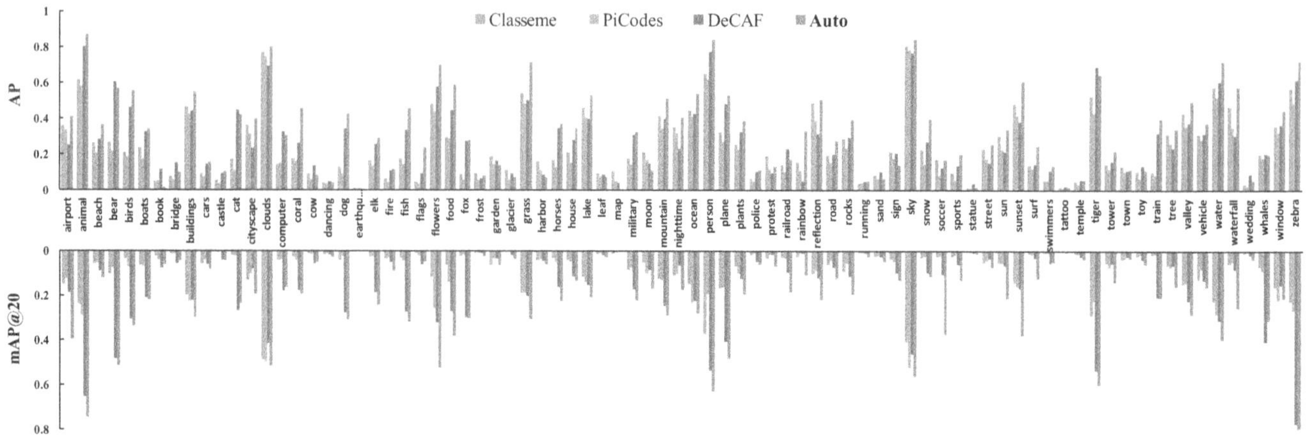

Figure 10: Detailed performance of annotation (AP) and retrieval (mAP@20) over the 81 concepts of NUS-WIDE

lation strategy such as adding new fine-tune objectives [1] and deepening the shared hidden layers.

7. ACKNOWLEDGMENTS

This work was supported by NUS-Tsinghua Extreme Search (NExT) project under the grant No.: R-252-300-001-490 and the National Natural Science Foundation of China, No. 61303075.

8. REFERENCES

[1] G. Andrew, R. Arora, J. Bilmes, and K. Livescu. Deep canonical correlation analysis. In *ICML*, 2013.

[2] Y. Bengio. Learning deep architectures for ai. *Foundations and Trends in Machine Learning*, 2009.

[3] T. L. Berg, A. C. Berg, and J. Shih. Automatic attribute discovery and characterization from noisy web data. In *ECCV*, 2010.

[4] A. Bergamo, L. Torresani, and A. W. Fitzgibbon. Picodes: Learning a compact code for novel-category recognition. In *NIPS*, 2011.

[5] P. Blunsom, E. Grefenstette, N. Kalchbrenner, et al. A convolutional neural network for modelling sentences. In *ACL*, 2014.

[6] X. Chen, A. Shrivastava, and A. Gupta. Neil: Extracting visual knowledge from web data. In *ICCV*, 2013.

[7] T.-S. Chua, H. Luan, M. Sun, and S. Yang. Next: Nus-tsinghua center for extreme search of user-generated content. *MultiMedia*, 2012.

[8] J. Deng, W. Dong, R. Socher, L.-J. Li, K. Li, and L. Fei-Fei. Imagenet: A large-scale hierarchical image database. In *CVPR*, 2009.

[9] L. Deng, J. Li, J.-T. Huang, K. Yao, D. Yu, F. Seide, M. Seltzer, G. Zweig, X. He, J. Williams, et al. Recent advances in deep learning for speech research at microsoft. In *ICASSP*, 2013.

[10] J. Donahue, Y. Jia, O. Vinyals, J. Hoffman, N. Zhang, E. Tzeng, and T. Darrell. Decaf: A deep convolutional activation feature for generic visual recognition. *arXiv preprint arXiv:1310.1531*, 2013.

[11] J. Dong, B. Cheng, X. Chen, T.-S. Chua, S. Yan, and X. Zhou. Robust image annotation via simultaneous feature and sample outlier pursuit. *TOMCCAP*, 2013.

[12] A. Farhadi, I. Endres, D. Hoiem, and D. Forsyth. Describing objects by their attributes. In *CVPR*, 2009.

[13] B. J. Frey and D. Dueck. Clustering by passing messages between data points. *Science*, 2007.

[14] G. E. Hinton and R. R. Salakhutdinov. Reducing the dimensionality of data with neural networks. *Science*, 2006.

[15] A. Hyvärinen, J. Karhunen, and E. Oja. *Independent component analysis*, volume 46. John Wiley & Sons, 2004.

[16] J.-W. Jeong, X.-J. Wang, and D.-H. Lee. Towards measuring the visualness of a concept. In *CIKM*, 2012.

[17] P. Kankuekul, A. Kawewong, S. Tangruamsub, and O. Hasegawa. Online incremental attribute-based zero-shot learning. In *CVPR*, 2012.

[18] Q. V. Le, A. Karpenko, J. Ngiam, and A. Y. Ng. Ica with reconstruction cost for efficient overcomplete feature learning. In *NIPS*, 2011.

[19] L.-J. Li and L. Fei-Fei. Optimol: automatic online picture collection via incremental model learning. *IJCV*, 2010.

[20] Q. Li, J. Wu, and Z. Tu. Harvesting mid-level visual concepts from large-scale internet images. In *CVPR*, 2013.

[21] T. Mikolov, K. Chen, G. Corrado, and J. Dean. Efficient estimation of word representations in vector space. In *ICLR*, 2013.

[22] Y.-I. Moon, B. Rajagopalan, and U. Lall. Estimation of mutual information using kernel density estimators. *Physical Review E*, 1995.

[23] G. L. Murphy. *The big book of concepts*. The MIT Press, 2004.

[24] M. Naphade, J. R. Smith, J. Tesic, S.-F. Chang, W. Hsu, L. Kennedy, A. Hauptmann, and J. Curtis. Large-scale concept ontology for multimedia. *MultiMedia*, 2006.

[25] J. Ngiam, A. Khosla, M. Kim, J. Nam, H. Lee, and A. Y. Ng. Multimodal deep learning. In *ICML*, 2011.

[26] P. Over, G. Awad, M. Michel, J. Fiscus, G. Sanders, B. Shaw, W. Kraaij, A. F. Smeaton, and G. Quéenot. Trecvid 2012 – an overview of the goals, tasks, data, evaluation mechanisms and metrics. In *TRECVID*, 2012.

[27] D. Parikh and K. Grauman. Interactively building a discriminative vocabulary of nameable attributes. In *CVPR*, 2011.

[28] P. Perona. Vision of a visipedia. *Proceedings of the IEEE*, 2010.

[29] N. Qian. On the momentum term in gradient descent learning algorithms. *NN*, 1999.

[30] M. Rastegari, A. Farhadi, and D. Forsyth. Attribute discovery via predictable discriminative binary codes. In *ECCV*, 2012.

[31] B. Scholkopf and A. Smola. Learning with kernels, 2002.

[32] N. Srivastava and R. Salakhutdinov. Multimodal learning with deep boltzmann machines. In *NIPS*, 2012.

[33] B. Thomee and A. Popescu. Overview of the imageclef 2012 flickr photo annotation and retrieval task. In *CLEF*, 2012.

[34] T. Tieleman. Training restricted boltzmann machines using approximations to the likelihood gradient. In *ICML*, 2008.

[35] A. Torralba and A. A. Efros. Unbiased look at dataset bias. In *CVPR*, 2011.

[36] L. Torresani, M. Szummer, and A. Fitzgibbon. Efficient object category recognition using classemes. In *ECCV*. 2010.

[37] J. Wang, K. Markert, and M. Everingham. Learning models for object recognition from natural language descriptions. In *BMVC*, 2009.

[38] M. Wang, R. Hong, X.-T. Yuan, S. Yan, and T.-S. Chua. Movie2comics: Towards a lively video content presentation. *TMM*, 2012.

[39] L. Xie and X. He. Picture tags and world knowledge: Learning tag relations from visual semantic sources. In *MM*, 2013.

[40] H. Zhang, Z.-J. Zha, S. Yan, J. Bian, and T.-S. Chua. Attribute feedback. In *MM*, 2012.

[41] K. Zhang, I. W. Tsang, and J. T. Kwok. Maximum margin clustering made practical. *TNN*, 2009.

What are the Fashion Trends in New York?

Shintami C. Hidayati[1,2], Kai-Lung Hua[1], Wen-Huang Cheng[2], and Shih-Wei Sun[3]
[1]Dept. of CSIE, National Taiwan University of Science and Technology, Taipei, Taiwan (R.O.C)
[2]Research Center for Information Technology Innovation, Academia Sinica, Taipei, Taiwan (R.O.C)
[3]Dept. of New Media Art, Taipei National University of the Arts, Taipei, Taiwan (R.O.C)
{d10115802, hua}@mail.ntust.edu.tw, whcheng@citi.sinica.edu.tw, swsun@newmedia.tnua.edu.tw

ABSTRACT

Fashion is a reflection of the society of a period. Given that New York City is one of the world's fashion capitals, understanding its change in fashion becomes a way to know the society and the times. To keep up with fashion trends, it is important to know what's "in" and what's "out" for a season. Though the fashion trends have been analyzed by fashion designers and fashion analysts for a long time, this issue has been ignored in multimedia science. In this paper, we present a novel algorithm that automatically discovers visual style elements representing fashion trends for a certain season. The visual style elements are discovered based on the stylistic coherent and unique characteristics. The experimental results demonstrate the effectiveness of our proposed method through a large number of catwalk show videos.

Categories and Subject Descriptors

H.3.3 [**Information Search and Retrieval**]: Retrieval Models

Keywords

Clothing image analysis; fashion trend; data mining; visual summarization

1. INTRODUCTION

New York City (NYC) is one of the world's fashion capitals which have major influences on international fashion trends. Understanding the change in fashion becomes an important way to know the society and the times. Therefore, we see there is a need for fashion trends spotting.

Particularly, fashion is a style in clothing, footwear, accessories, or makeup that have been carried by a wide audience during a particular time. Fashion trends reflect to what's "in" and what's "out" for the season. So far, fashion trend analysis is mainly performed by fashion experts who have intensive fashion knowledge. However even for fashion experts, it is time-consuming to collect and analyze fashion trends since there are numerous fashion shows each year. In literature, clothing recognition [1], segmentation [2], and recommendation [3] have received much attention in computer vision and multimedia research. However, to the best of our knowledge, there is no automatic fashion trends analysis framework existed. Hence, this paper is the first work that offers this service.

MM'14, November 3–7, 2014, Orlando, Florida, USA.

http://dx.doi.org/10.1145/2647868.2656405 .

Figure 1: Change of the women's dress fashion on New York Fashion Week, where models present the fashions during a catwalk fashion show.

One major channel to determine fashion trends is fashion show [4], where the latest fashion trends are debuted. In this event, fashion designers showcase their upcoming lines of clothing through models during fashion week, as illustrated in Figure 1. According to [5], color, cut, head decorations, and pattern, as illustrated in Figure 2, are four major elements to investigate fashion style. These fashion elements are considered as fashion trends at a particular fashion week if they satisfy two requirements: 1) coherence, i.e. frequently occurring within a fashion week, and 2) uniqueness, i.e. they occur much more often in a fashion week than in other fashion weeks.

In this work, therefore, we propose a novel framework for automatically discovering visual style elements that well represent fashion trends, with initial focus on New York Fashion Week (NYFW). Given fashion show videos, we first detect

Figure 2: Four major elements for fashion style investigation.

the catwalk model. Then, we seek patterns that are both frequently occurring within the given fashion week event and unique for this fashion week, by integrating unsupervised and supervised learning. As research pioneers in this field, we collected a fashion show image dataset that are extracted from videos [6] of several designers that have presented their collections at ten different seasons of NYFW. Our experiments confirmed that the proposed algorithm offers a satisfactory fashion trends identification through subjective and objective evaluations.

2. SYSTEM FRAMEWORK

In this section, we reveal the details of how the proposed framework exploits NYFW videos available on Fashion TV [6] as the input to discover fashion trends at NYFW.

2.1 Catwalk Model Detection

In order to identify fashion styles during fashion week events, we need to identify catwalk models first, so that we will be able to extract photos with showcased garments. Catwalk models are people who demonstrate clothing and accessories on a long and narrow stage, called catwalk, at fashion shows. Let $\vartheta_v^{\omega,x}$ denotes fashion show video of designer x who has an exhibition at NYFW season ω. Assume there are M frames in $\vartheta_v^{\omega,x}$, that is, $\vartheta_v^{\omega,x} = \{\mu_{v1}^{\omega,x}, \mu_{v2}^{\omega,x}, ..., \mu_{vM}^{\omega,x}\}$, we represent our dataset containing fashion show videos as $\mathcal{D}_v = \{\vartheta_v^{1,1}, \vartheta_v^{1,2}, ..., \vartheta_v^{1,G}, \vartheta_v^{2,1}, \vartheta_v^{2,2}, ..., \vartheta_v^{E,G}\}$, where E is the number of NYFW events and G is the number of designers.

Following [7], we track the presence of faces over all video frames in $\vartheta_v^{\omega,x}$ and then identify if the detected faces belong to the same person. Since catwalk models in general show their frontal faces and the audiences show their side faces, we further employ a constraint for frontal faces when using [7]. Next, we make use of the detected faces to obtain model's full-body by employing [8]. Through [8], which estimates the spatial layout of humans via pictorial structure model, we obtain a full-body image with clean background. We denote $\vartheta_i^{\omega,x}$ be a subset of $\vartheta_v^{\omega,x}$, where $\vartheta_i^{\omega,x}$ contains only one frame for distinct models while $\vartheta_v^{\omega,x}$ contains more than just one frame for a model. A set containing full-body image of catwalk models in our dataset can be represented as $\mathcal{D}_i = \{\vartheta_i^{1,1}, \vartheta_i^{1,2}, ..., \vartheta_i^{1,G}, \vartheta_i^{2,1}, \vartheta_i^{2,2}, ..., \vartheta_i^{E,G}\}$.

2.2 Visual Style Element Initialization

Having the collection of full-body image of catwalk models, $\mathcal{D}_i$, we divide it into two sets: (1) one set containing catwalk models from the selected fashion week event whose visual style elements of the fashion trends are to be discovered, namely positive set $\mathcal{D}_i^+$ (e.g. catwalk models at NYFW S/S 2014), and (2) the other set containing catwalk models from other NYFW events, namely negative set $\mathcal{D}_i^-$ (e.g. all catwalk models at NYFW except from NYFW S/S 2014).

Table 1: Number of fashion styles in our dataset.

Designer \ Season	Spring / Summer 2010	Autumn / Winter 2010	Spring / Summer 2011	Autumn / Winter 2011	Spring / Summer 2012	Autumn / Winter 2012	Spring / Summer 2013	Autumn / Winter 2013	Spring / Summer 2014	Autumn / Winter 2014
BCBG Max Azria	31	29	37	34	30	34	34	30	32	32
Calvin Klein	35	34	34	34	32	33	33	32	35	34
DKNY	46	40	37	34	13	40	48	40	47	42
Nicole Miller	39	37	37	34	39	36	39	44	39	39
Ralph Lauren	50	50	57	53	33	56	52	58	52	38
Rebecca Taylor	44	34	35	39	41	40	33	36	40	41
Richard Chai	26	27	29	28	26	28	27	26	31	27
Ruffian	33	34	36	32	30	31	13	32	31	23
Vera Wang	31	39	44	36	40	39	38	48	40	40
Total	**335**	**324**	**346**	**324**	**284**	**337**	**317**	**346**	**347**	**316**
	3,276									

The representations of visual information at a pixel level generally could not provide enough information to support a useful feature. In addition, using the whole image would require huge amounts of training data to represent spatial configuration of objects. Thus, we consider representing visual elements of fashion styles using image patches. We partition every full-body image of catwalk model from both $\mathcal{D}_i^+$ and $\mathcal{D}_i^-$ into non-overlapping square patches.

As aforementioned, the coherence (to occur frequently) and uniqueness (to be sufficiently different from other fashion shows) of visual style elements are the two key factors for discovering fashion trends. If we somehow knew that a set of patches of the dataset had similar visual style element, we could train a discriminative classifier to build a similarity metric of visual features for these patches. Therefore, we first initialize cluster of patches.

We capture the 4 major elements of fashion trends (Figure 2) by exploiting color and texture information. For color information, the extracted features include HSV color histogram, color correlogram [9], and color moments. For texture information, the extracted features include HOG [10], Haar wavelet transform, and 2D Gabor wavelets [11]. Thus, throughout our algorithm, we represent each patch using 3 different type of focus: (1) color features to discover fashion trends in terms of color information; (2) texture features to discover fashion trends in terms of texture information; and (3) the combination of color and texture features to discover fashion trends in terms of both color and texture information.

To determine candidate patches that might represent visual style element of fashion trends, for each patch in positive set, we search the top 20 nearest neighbor patches in the full dataset of $\mathcal{D}_i$ (both positive set, $\mathcal{D}_i^+$, and negative set, $\mathcal{D}_i^-$) and we use normalized correlation distance as the similarity measure. Since patches portraying stylistic coherence and uniqueness of visual style elements in positive set tend to have higher proportion to match similar patches in positive set, we keep the patches that pass the following rule: for any patch, if there are more than 10 patches, from its top 20 nearest neighbors, belong to $\mathcal{D}^+$. Given there are P number of surviving candidate patches from previous step, we then cluster similar visual style elements by running the standard k-means clustering. In our experiments, we set k with a quite high value of $k = \frac{P}{5}$ since k-means clustering tends not to generalize high-dimensional data well. After that, we further remove candidate patches from clusters that have less than 3 members. Finally, we obtain groups of similar visual style element as the initial cluster.

Table 2: The average accuracy of our fashion trend element detector.

		Extracted Features		
		Color	Texture	Color + Texture
NY Fashion Week	Spring/Summer 2010	80.33 %	90.67 %	88.00 %
	Autumn/Winter 2010	64.67 %	91.00 %	88.67 %
	Spring/Summer 2011	87.00 %	92.00 %	92.33 %
	Autumn/Winter 2011	67.00 %	74.00 %	72.33 %
	Spring/Summer 2012	90.67 %	88.33 %	89.00 %
	Autumn/Winter 2012	50.33 %	67.67 %	60.33%
	Spring/Summer 2013	67.67 %	84.67 %	83.67 %
	Autumn/Winter 2013	66.33 %	65.67 %	68.00 %
	Spring/Summer 2014	94.67 %	90.67 %	92.33 %
	Autumn/Winter 2014	81.00 %	76.00 %	71.67 %

2.3 Iterative Clustering

As discussed in [13], the standard distance metric of unsupervised clustering (e.g. k-NN and k-means clustering) does not work well for capturing the important parts within medium-sized patches because it treats all the pixels equally. If the candidate patch has irrelevant visual representation, the retrieved matches from unsupervised clustering will also have that irrelevant element. Thus, to improve stylistic coherence and uniqueness of patches that serve as visual style elements of fashion trends, we learn the distance metric in an iterative manner to keep improving our initial visual element detector obtained from the previous step.

To be more specific, with an initial set of clusters containing the surviving candidate patches, we train a linear SVM classifier [12] for each cluster, treating patches within the cluster as positive examples and all negative-set patches as negative examples. However, when we iterate the SVM learning directly by utilizing the top t detectors from previous round as positive set, it would just improve the top t detectors a little bit due to the overfitting problem [13].

To prevent overfitting, we further apply cross-validation at each round. We divide both positive and negative sets into two equal, non-overlapping subsets. At each iteration, we run the detectors trained on the previous round to select the top t detection for retraining. We form new clusters from the top t firings of each detectors by considering all SVM scores above -1 to be firings. We repeat this procedure for 4 iterations, in which most of top t patches in a cluster converge. In this work, we set $t = 5$ for all experiments.

After the final iteration, we sort the resulting detectors according to the percentage of top 30 firings that are in the positive set. We return the top ten detectors as the visual style elements that represent fashion trends at a certain season of New York Fashion Week.

3. EXPERIMENTAL RESULTS

3.1 Dataset and Experimental Settings

Dataset: In this work, we constructed a fashion show dataset composed of images with the resolution of 1024×1024, these images are extracted from Fashion TV [6] through the proposed method explained in section 2.1. As shown in Table 1, our dataset collected 3,276 different catwalk models that had been presented by nine fashion design companies for the past 10 seasons of NYFW.

Experimental settings: We represented visual style elements of catwalk models by square patches at the size of 128×128. For color features, we quantized HSV color histogram of each patch into $8 \times 2 \times 2$ color bins and quantized color correlogram of each patch in RGB space into $4 \times 4 \times 4$ bins. For HOG feature, the cell size is set as 8×8 with a stride of 8 pixel/cell. During iterative learning, we employed a linear SVM [12] with C fixed to 0.1.

3.2 Results and Validation

Figure 3 shows the most representative fashion trends of different NYFW identified from the proposed algorithm, in which they are both coherent (frequently occurring within a fashion week) and unique (recognizable from other fashion weeks). For each subfigure of Figure 3, the element inside the dotted line rectangle indicates the identified visual trend at a certain NYFW event. For example, pastel green is identified as the most representative color trend at NYFW based on the investigated nine designers exploited for the season S/S 2014. That is pastel green is widely applied for the season S/S 2014 at NYFW, but it is unlikely to be observed elsewhere. As for the season A/W 2010, the high bun together with a neck scarf is identified as the most representative fashion trend in terms of texture information. Note that though the style (high bun with a neck scarf) occurs more frequently for the season A/W 2010, this element might not be beneficial to help identify color trend in this season since the colors of bun and scarf varied and hence it does not satisfy "stylistic coherence" which is one of the key fashion trend criteria. Besides, based on the discovered fashion patch from our proposed framework, we are capable of telling if the fashion trend of a certain season focuses on a specific location or spreads to several parts of the clothing and/or accessories. A practical prototype of the proposed system is demonstrated in Figure 4.

As a quantitative evaluation, for each top 10 fashion trend elements identified from our proposed algorithm for each season, we computed the percentage of instances corresponding to the positive set out of the top 30 extracted fashion styles. This evaluation is performed on an unseen dataset, containing 50% from positive set and 50% from negative set. Table 2 reports the average accuracy of our fashion trend detector for each season. Based on the high accuracy numbers showed in Table 2, we conclude that our proposed framework is very effective to discover both the stylistic coherence and the uniqueness of visual style elements over a variety of fashion shows. Besides, it can be learned from this table that fashion week with higher average accuracy has more coherent and unique fashion styles comparing to fashion week with lower average accuracy (e.g. the average accuracy of A/W 2012 is low and this implies the fact that the designers of A/W 2012 had less fashion elements in common comparing to the other seasons). Moreover, considering the highest average accuracy among three types of features (color, texture, color+texture) for each fashion week shown in Table 2, it is also interesting to note that from S/S 2010 to S/S 2013, the NYFW designers had put more concern in designing new textures rather than employing new color, while for S/S 2014 and A/W 2014 they had put more efforts in finding new colors and color schemes.

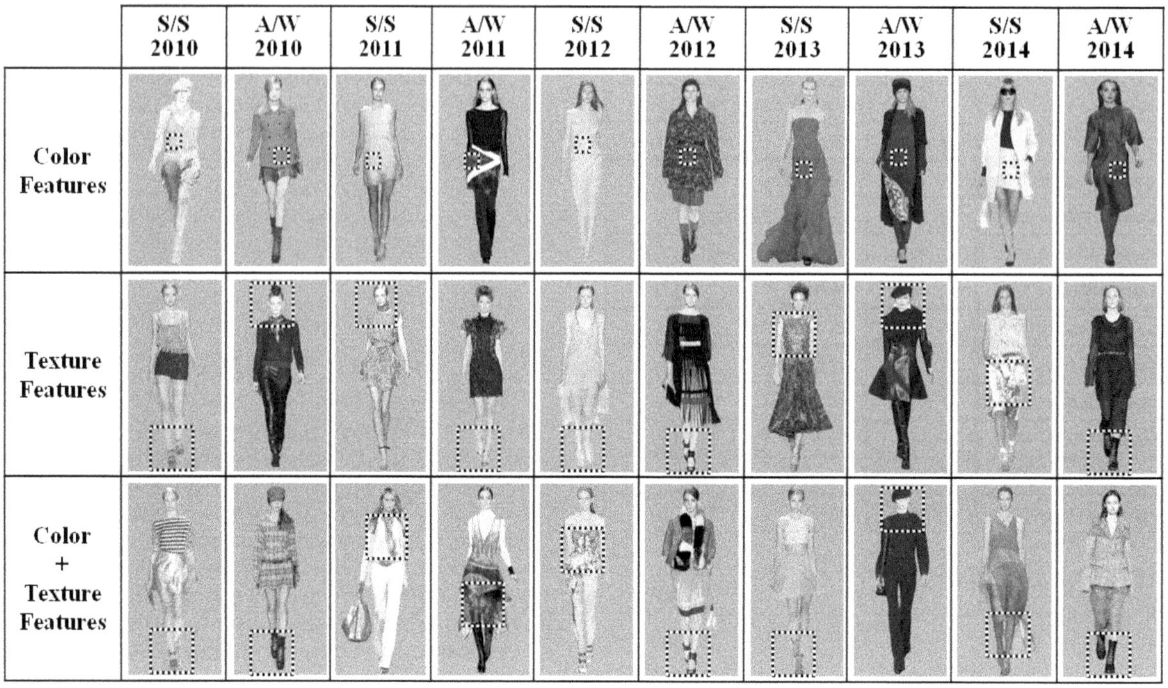

Figure 3: The most representative fashion trend element at NYFW.

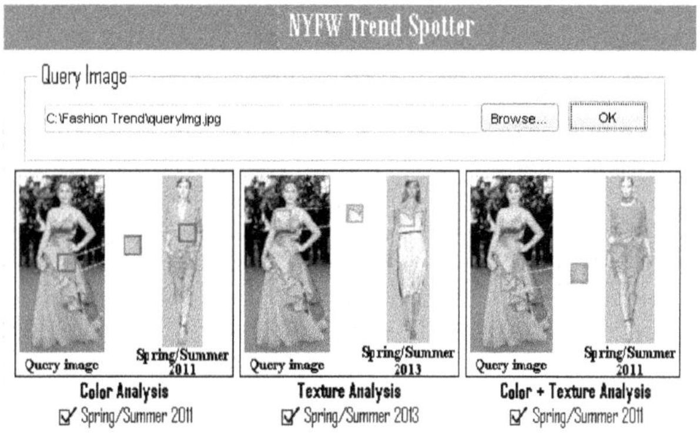

Figure 4: Interface of the proposed system: recognized fashion elements and their corresponding fashion events given a photo query.

4. CONCLUSIONS

In this paper, we presented a novel approach for automatic fashion trends analysis. As research pioneers in this field, we collected a fashion style image dataset that are extracted from fashion show videos of several designers that have presented their collections at ten different seasons of New York Fashion Week (NYFW). By investigating the coherence and uniqueness of four major style elements, i.e. color, cut, head decoration, and pattern, with iterative clustering techniques, we showed what are the fashion trends in New York for the past ten seasons. Our experiments confirmed that the proposed algorithm offers a satisfactory fashion trends identification through subjective and objective evaluations.

5. REFERENCES

[1] S. C. Hidayati *et al.* Clothing Genre Classification by Exploiting the Style Elements. In *ACM MM, 2012.*

[2] Y. Kalantidis *et al.* Getting the look: clothing recognition and segmentation for automatic product suggestions in everyday photos. In *ICMR, 2013.*

[3] S. Liu *et al.* Hi, magic closet, tell me what to wear!. In *ACM MM, 2012.*

[4] Vogue. Fashion show — Vogue, Fashion magazine. 2013. `http://www.vogue.co.uk/fashion/trends`

[5] CNN.com International. 2013. `http://edition.cnn.com/interactive/2013/09/` newblock `living/fashion-week-trends/`

[6] Fashion TV Network's Official Websites. 2013. `http://www.fashiontv.com/videos/fashion-weeks`

[7] J. Sivic *et al.* "Who are you?" – Learning Person Specific Classifiers from Video. In *CVPR*, 2009.

[8] M. Eichner *et al.* 2D articulated human pose estimation and retrieval in (almost) unconstrained still images. *IJCV*, vol. 99, 2012.

[9] J. Huang *et al.* Image indexing using color correlogram. In *CVPR*, 1997.

[10] N. Dalal and B. Triggs. Histograms of oriented gradients for human detection. In *CVPR*, 2005.

[11] T.S. Lee. Image representation using 2D gabor wavelets. *IEEE TPAMI*, 1996.

[12] C.-C. Chang and C.-J. lin LIBSVM: A library for support vector machines. *ACM TIST*, vol. 2, 2011.

[13] S. Singh *et al.* Unsupervised discovery of mid-level discriminative patches. In *ECCV*, 2012.

[14] C. Doersch *et al.* What makes Paris look like Paris. *ACM TOG (SIGGRAPH)*, vol. 31, 2012.

Discovering the City by Mining Diverse and Multimodal Data Streams

Yin-Hsi Kuo*, Yan-Ying Chen, Bor-Chun Chen[1], Wen-Yu Lee, Chun-Che Wu, Chia-Hung Lin, Yu-Lin Hou, Wen-Feng Cheng, Yi-Chih Tsai, Chung-Yen Hung, Liang-Chi Hsieh, Winston Hsu
National Taiwan University and [1]Academia Sinica, Taipei, Taiwan

ABSTRACT

This work attempts to tackle the IBM grand challenge – seeing the daily life of New York City (NYC) in various perspectives by exploring rich and diverse social media content. Most existing works address this problem relying on single media source and covering limited life aspects. Because different social media are usually chosen for specific purposes, multiple social media mining and integration are essential to understand a city comprehensively. In this work, we first discover the similar and unique natures (e.g., attractions, topics) across social media in terms of visual and semantic perceptions. For example, Instagram users share more food and travel photos while Twitter users discuss more about sports and news. Based on these characteristics, we analyze a broad spectrum of life aspects – trends, events, food, wearing and transportation in NYC by mining a huge amount of diverse and freely available media (e.g., 1.6M Instagram photos, 5.3M Twitter posts). Because transportation logs are hardly available in social media, the NYC Open Data (e.g., 6.5B subway station transactions) is leveraged to visualize temporal traffic patterns. Furthermore, the experiments demonstrate that our approaches can effectively overview urban life with considerable technical improvement, e.g., having 16% relative gains in food recognition accuracy by a hierarchy cross-media learning strategy, reducing the feature dimensions of sentiment analysis by 10 times without sacrificing precision.

Categories and Subject Descriptors

H.4.0 [**Information Systems Applications**]: General

Keywords

Multiple media sources; cross-media mining; visualization

1. INTRODUCTION

Due to the explosion of social media, people are used to sharing their daily life on the Internet. Over the decade, there have been many social websites developed for different user groups. Based on the characteristics within, people will choose different media to share their thoughts, photos, personal preferences, etc. For example, people may utilize Foursquare for recording places where they go, Instagram for sharing their visual experiences via photos or videos, and Twitter for updating things that interest them. Therefore, these social media capture different moments in the daily life. The popularity of social media also brings an emerging need of social marketing campaigns for brands [6]; hence, it is essential to discover and mine the user behaviors on diverse social media.

*All authors contributed equally to this work. The work was supported in part by Intel-NTU Connected Context Computing Center.

MM'14, November 3–7, 2014, Orlando, Florida, USA.

http://dx.doi.org/10.1145/2647868.2656406.

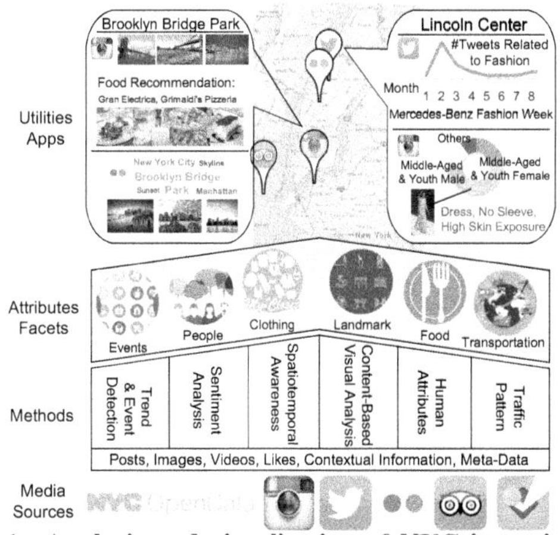

Figure 1: Analysis and visualization of NYC in various perspectives. We collect multiple media sources and adopt different methods for discovering the latent facets. Observing the complementary properties across sources, we enable a systematic framework to leverage the cross-domain and multimodal data for numerous applications for NYC analytics.

Table 1: The percentage of overlapped attractions among Twitter, Instagram, TripAdvisor, and subway traffics (open data).

	Twitter	Instagram	TripAdvisor	subway
Twitter	1	0.35	0.08	0.22
Instagram	0.35	1	0.18	0.43
Tripadvisor	0.08	0.18	1	0.32
subway	0.22	0.43	0.32	1

It is expected that each social website has unique information and features. As a case study, we conducted an experiment for three major social media, including Twitter, Instagram, TripAdvisor, and one NYC open data. The goal is to preliminarily understand the synergies and differences between the data streams, sampled and contributed for human activities. We collected data from the four websites to generate the datasets, and then extracted the top-100 popular places respectively. Table 1 shows the overlaps of each pair of the datasets. We observed that the top-100 places from Twitter and Instagram mainly focus on office buildings, residential places, and chain stores (such as Starbucks and Subway), while those from TripAdvisor focus on the places of famous landmarks, museums, and busy restaurants. The locations of the places obtained from Twitter are denser than those in Instagram. As has been mentioned, using single source is not enough. To obtain richer information, integrating multiple media sources is in dire need. In addition, based on the four datasets, we further observed that many of the popular places are close to subway stations in NYC.

Prior works usually rely on single media source (e.g., Flickr) with different modalities (e.g, image, tag, user) to address traditional applications such as image annotation, travel recommendation, tag ranking, and user preference mining [2][5]. Instead of relying on single source, for this challenge, we aim to leverage multiple data streams including social media and open data for mining

Table 2: **Sentiment analysis results over noisy tweets. The letter trigram is robust to textual noises, compact, yet informative.**

Methods	Error	Feature Dimensions
letter trigram	0.1447	17,030
BoW	0.1611	178,717
letter trigram + BoW (early fusion)	**0.1289**	195,747
letter trigram + BoW (late fusion)	0.1295	195,747

urban activities. We argue a systematic framework (Fig. 1) which detects rich and multi-angle semantics and attributes to facilitate further applications. Moreover, we devise advanced methods to leverage complementary information across sources and deal with the noises in such user-contributed data streams.

Our contributions include, 1) leveraging the complementary information for data analytics, 2) discovering the latent behaviors, synergies and differences among media sources, 3) mining effective factors parameterizing emerging applications from heterogeneous and multi-granularity signals, 4) devising detection and learning methods robust to noisy user-contributed data, and 5) identifying the opportunities and challenges for mining diverse data streams.

2. MEDIA SOURCE COLLECTION

Social media presents rich aspects to overview life in a city. To gain from the diverse and complementary resources, we collect the visual/text content along with metadata in NYC from four social media: 1) *Instagram* – almost ten thousands check-in locations from Instagram which contains 1.6 million photos from October 2010 to May 2014; 2) *Twitter* – 5,337,958 geotag tweets from January 2013 to September 2013; 3) *Flickr* – 261,907 geotag photos from 2012 to 2014; 4) *TripAdvisor* – 842 attractions (e.g., interesting points, landmarks) and 11,566 restaurants in 2014.

Open data is gaining more popularity because it is freely available without copyright concerns. We exploit two sorts of open transportation logs which are hardly available from social media. The first includes 5.5 million trip logs of public bike sharing system (*CitiBike*) from July 2013 to February 2014 and the second comprises 6.5 billion accumulated entries/exits of the turnstiles at NYC subway stations (*MTA*) from January 2012 to May 2014.

3. MINING FROM MULTIPLE MEDIA

3.1 Trend and Event Detection

Detecting what is buzzing on multiple media sources is a good way to understand the urban life, while using Twitter as text-oriented media and Instagram as image-oriented media. When dealing with social media, we use both bottom-up and top-down methods. The bottom-up means detecting trends from social media with multiple granularities. In *spatial aspect*, we detect the trends not only of the whole NYC, but also of some popular regions. As for *temporal aspect*, some big news or large scale events like "World Cup" may lead to monthly trends, but some, such as the news "Suarez Bite Italian Defender" which may survive for a day. On the other hand, the top-down means analyzing a known event. It is easy to show an event's volume change by analyzing its temporal distribution. While considering both spatial and temporal information, we can even see how an event moves.

We brief our trend and event detection method, mainly consisting four parts. 1) *Preprocessing.* We apply stemming and stop word removal on text messages (i.e., Instagram's hash tags, and both Twitter's surrounding text and hash tags). 2) *Trending term detection.* We aim to extract the term which is buzzing at current time, and calculate the buzz score which is similar to the method [3][8]. 3) *Trending topic generation.* After the trending terms are collected, the next step is to group them into topics. To achieve the goal, we aggregate the trending terms with frequent concurrences. 4) *Event analysis.* While we have known an event, we can distinct what is related to the event, and see how it distributes on spatial and temporal domains. A result is illustrated in Fig. 3(b).

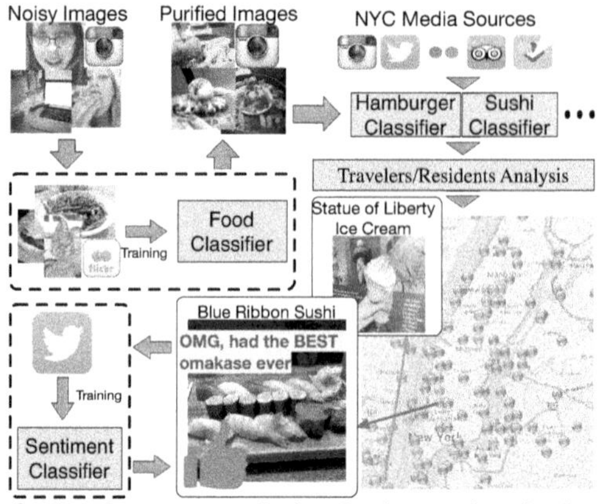

Figure 2: Food recommendation by leveraging food recognition (images), user analysis (logs), and sentiment analysis (comments) over multiple media sources. Red spots on the map are restaurants popular among travelers, while blue spots show the favorites for the (local) residents.

3.2 Sentiment Analysis

Sentiment is another important information contained in social media. For training data, we collect 210,000 (noisy) tweets with emoticons. Half of these tweets with ":)" means containing positive sentiment; others with ":(" means containing negative sentiment. We use word unigram (BoW model) and letter trigram as features. However, there are many typos and variant tags of the same targets. We are the first to adopt letter trigram [4] to represent nosiy textual data in social media. We add starting and ending marks to a word (e.g., #goal# and #gooooal#), break the word into letter trigrams (e.g., **#go**, goa, **oal**, **al#** and **#go**, goo, ooo, ooo, ooa, **oal**, **al#**), and use logistic regression to train data. As shown in Table 2, we can predict sentiment on user comments by only 12.89% error rate.

3.3 Human Attributes

Human attributes such as gender, clothing are important dimensions to understand a city. Because user profiles are very sparse, we detect human attributes in visual content from user contributed photos to observe this city. These photos are like million social sensors which can profile not only social media users but also their communities in real life.

Clothing Attributes Detection. Motivated by [1], we aim to learn semantic attributes to mine fashion trends in urban life. We first use a face detector to trim false positive examples incurred by the pose estimator. We then use Log Gabor, SURF, Skin, and LAB-color to extract low-level features from the five parts (i.e., torso, upper and lower arms). We train classifiers using SVM with totally 26 attributes. We use the dataset in [1] as the training data and test the media sources mentioned in Sec. 2. We focus on those significant attributes across time, e.g., clothing categories for season, patterns for fashion and trend.

Facial Attributes Detection. We construct 11 facial attribute detectors including gender, age, race and glasses by using a generic framework for learning facial attributes adaptively [7]. We collect training data with 10,000 images from Flickr. Given an image, we detect face regions and locate facial parts (eyes, nose and mouth) to extract low-level features (edge, color, texture); mid-level features are then learned by SVM with low-level features from facial parts. Each attribute detector is an ensemble with mid-level features weighted by Adaboost. We apply this framework to each test photo and predict the presence of each attribute.

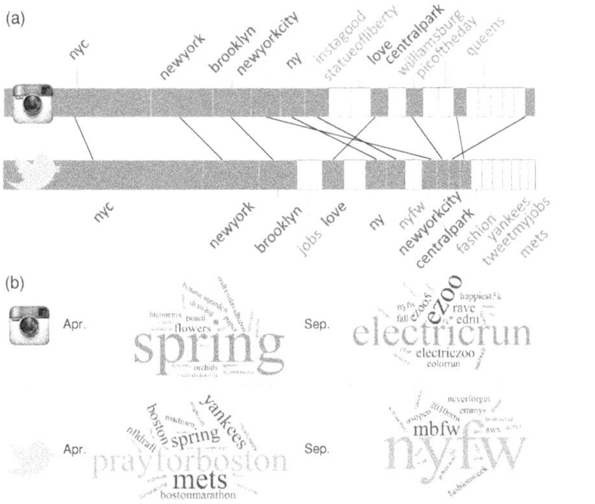

Figure 3: The upper is the top 20 hashtags in Instagram and Twitter. The overlapped tags in grey bricks are linked, and the unique tags are in colors. The bottom shows tag clouds of different trends discovered in April and September. They tend to cover different topics in different contexts so that we argue to integrate emerging and diverse media sources.

3.4 Food Recognition

A large proportion of the images in social media contains food (e.g., more than 100 million images contains hashtag "food" in Instagram). To mine information from these images, it is insufficient to simply use tags to decide what is in the image since tags are really noisy (in our preliminary study, only about 30% of images tagged food on Instagram are correct). Therefore, we adopt state-of-the-art recognition method, convolution neural network (CNN), to recognize food in images. By analyzing different social media sources, we found that Instagram contains more images that can represent users' daily life, but images in Instagram also contain more noises (our experiment shows that about 26% of images tagged food are selfies instead of food images, while the same number is 7.5% in Flickr). Hence, we propose a hierarchy cross-media learning (Fig. 2), where the less noisy Flickr images is used to train a general food classifier and is used to clean the images in Instagram, and purified Instagram images are then further used to train 9 food sub-categories such as hamburger. Using the proposed method, we can achieve 65% accuracy on testing compared to 56% when Instagram data is directly used for training and testing.

3.5 Traffic Patterns

City-scale traffic patterns reveal rich people activities, e.g., commuting, economics and leisure, which are essential for urban computing, advertising and trip planning. To comprehensively analyze NYC traffics, we address the differences between travelers and (local) residents, and the temporal impacts by using Instagram data and open transportation data (CitiBike and subway data in Sec. 2).

Travelers and Residents may care about different matters, and thus have divergent trip patterns. To differentiate their patterns, we calculate the proportion of NYC photos (p_i) in a given user's Instagram album i. If $p_i > 0.5$, the user is classified as a resident and otherwise a traveler. Meanwhile, we treat the CitiBike users registered in "Customer" (one-day/week pass) as travelers and those of "Subscriber" (annual use) as residents. By the trip logs and registrations, we can figure out their visiting patterns for validation.

Daily and Hourly Patterns can roughly depict how residents move for the purpose of working or leisure. Such trends reflect commuting behavior and economic activities that help traffic flow and transportation management. Because subway is a major transportation services in NYC, we use 6.5B entries and exits of each turnstile to discover moving patterns. The accumulated counts of entries and exits indicate how many people leave and enter somewhere near this station, respectively. Since subway logs are not sampled by hour, we leverage the accumulated trips leaving and arriving CitiBike stations, to discover the hourly patterns.

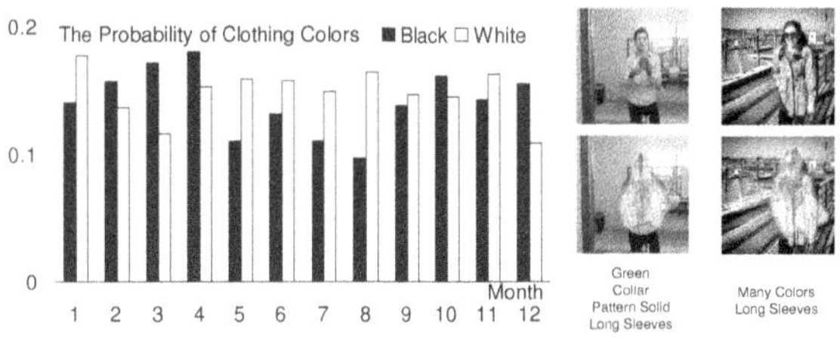

Figure 4: Varying clothing colors across months and two clothing attribute examples. It shows that people tend to wear clothing with dark color in winter whereas light color in summer.

4. VISUALIZATION AND APPLICATIONS

We believe that the data are of the users, by the users, and for the users. In order for the public to easily get across NYC through our rich mining aspects, we design various visualizations and apps to draw those technical data closer to the users. With the interactive interfaces, we can add priceless values in these data and help users to explore by themselves.

4.1 Social Media Association and Comparison

To integrate multiple media sources, we investigate the differences of hashtags between Instagram and Twitter by the proposed method (Sec. 3.1). For overall comparisons, Fig. 3(a) shows the stacked bar charts of the top 20 hashtags. The overlapped hashtags in grey bricks are linked and the unique tags are colored in red/blue. In Fig. 3(b), we show the monthly trends by tag clouds with the top 20 trending hashtags in April and September 2013. Most hot terms (grey bricks) are always popular and ranked higher in (a). Moreover, each media source has their own special tags, e.g., "instagood," "tweetmyjobs." We find that Twitter could provide detailed information of events or institutions, e.g., jobs or the fashion week. In addition, Twitter hashtags are more about the issues which highly concerned by but might not directly happen to users. For example, Boston marathon explosion and MLB season opening in April or New York fashion week in September are public events or news for the New Yorkers. On the other hand, we see fewer sports posts in Instagram (like "yankees," "mets" in Twitter) because it is hard to take photos in person. So, in Instagram, there are more check-in locations and posts regarding to the events which users are directly engaged. For example, many participants of "electricrun" posted relevant photos in April. The different user behaviors suggest that Instagram is a visually-oriented media for users to share their daily life. Conversely, Twitter is a platform for users to publish the opinions of trending events. Due to various purposes, the trending hashtags are quite different and provide complementary information indicating diverse aspects of urban life.

4.2 Human Activities and Fashion Styles

The photos for analyzing in the challenge are much noisier than the training data commonly used in vision community; for example, selfies usually contain only faces without bodies, and people have various poses. For clothing analysis, only about 20% data have the poses detected correctly. These phenomenon lead to more uncertainty in traditional clothing detection methods, but we can still find some significant information. As shown in Fig. 4, we can see that people wear clothing with black color more in winter and

Figure 5: Facial attributes demonstrate that Instagram users have different behaviors when sharing photos. Sports are favored by men, and restaurant visitings or fashion activities are favored by women.

less in summer, while white color has the opposite tendency. Besides, we might observe the fashion and trend as the seasons change and some special fashion styles for each area. As shown in Fig. 1, we can analyze the fashion styles for the New York Fashion Week (NYFW) which is automatically discovered from Twitter.

Facial attributes is one of important information to analyze the user behaviors when sharing photos. We choose top 500 locations based on the number of images to detect 11 facial attributes and classify each location by the proportion of each attribute in the same type which is more than 50%, for example, gender, race, and glasses. As shown in Fig. 5, men prefer sport activities and women commonly share the fun in restaurants or during shopping. The attribute "glasses" dominated locations are always at open spaces like beaches and parks because many people will wear sunglasses in these spaces. Besides, we might combine other applications such as food recommendation or event detection to personalize the results with the detected attributes. For example, the female favourite restaurants in New York or what kind of people will attend the New York Fashion Week (Fig. 1). Such visual information is very different and complementary to traditional methods by text only.

4.3 Food Recommendation

Eating is one of the most important things in our live, therefore we provide a food recommendation system to recommend popular food in New York City. We combine food detection results (Sec. 3.4) with similar geo-locations together to automatically find popular restaurant locations. Comparing with traditional food review websites like Yelp, our system can provide more real-time information since people will upload their images and comments to social media websites (e.g., Instagram) while they are eating, but they might post the restaurant review on Yelp days after they ate when they have free time. We can also provide more user-centered information since all of our data are directly come from users while some of the reviews on Yelp might be paid advertisements. Comparing solely using image tags to find restaurants, our system can provide more informative food images since directly using image tags might found many noisy images like selfies. In order to provide more accurate recommendation, our system further combined two different techniques. First, we combined travelers and residents information (cf. Sec. 3.5) and found restaurants that are preferred by travelers and residents respectively. As shown in Fig. 2, the restaurants around Liberty Island and Central Park mainly serve for travelers. Second, we use sentiment analysis (cf. Sec. 3.2) to find positive and negative sentiments in the image comments and use it to find whether the foods are recommended by the user or not. For example, "Quite possibly my most favourite food..Looks Devine!!" is predicted as a positive comments whereas "Waited an hour for just the 4 bowls of not so great noodle" is negative one.

4.4 Traffic Flow

As Fig. 2 shows, the popular locations for travelers (red spots) and residents (blue spots) mined from Instagram data and CitiBike logs have similar distribution in NYC. For example, both the data show that travelers prefer southern area of Central Park while residents are gathered around financial centres probably near their workplace. The phenomenon matches their moving patterns on weekdays – most heavy traffics appear in transportation centers (e.g., Penn Station, Grand Central Station) and the Financial District in NYC (Fig. 6 (a)). Overall, more traffic flow enters centre of Manhattan but partial flow on weekends (Fig. 6 (b)) turns to enter the suburban in its neighborhood (e.g., Botanical Garden in Brooklyn) or the travel landmarks (e.g., Metropolitan Museum). That suggests people tend to escape from city centers for their leisure outings or cultural activities on weekends. Meanwhile, the traffic flow around commuting time (Fig. 6 (c) and (d)) again confirms that the major commercial transactions are densely located at Manhattan midtown and downtown (green area in (c)) while the traffic flow after business hours spreads to the periphery of Manhattan (green area in (d)).

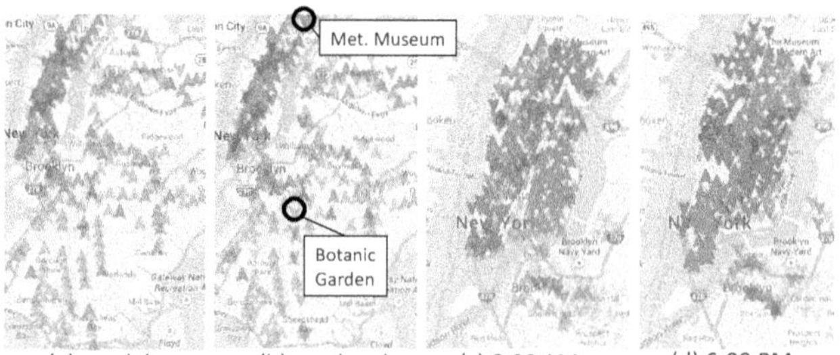

(a) weekday (b) weekend (c) 8:00 AM (d) 6:00 PM

Figure 6: Traffic flow in NYC by open data. Green/red arrows indicate in/out the pointed spots. Higher color saturation means more visitors. Overall, more traffics enter Manhattan on weekdays (a) but partially turn to its neighborhood on weekends (b). The traffics during business hours (c)(d) shows the commercial areas are densely located in midtown/downtown.

5. CONCLUSIONS AND FUTURE WORK

In this work, we show that (1) different social media do behave differently according to our experiments, such that cross-media mining is helpful to overview urban life in comprehensive perspectives, (2) the daily life has been broadly discovered in plentiful aspects by our proposed methods, (3) open data is a complementary resource beyond social media, especially good for transportation. Based on the preliminary results, a comprehensive system can be constructed outstandingly.

6. REFERENCES

[1] H. Chen et al. Describing clothing by semantic attributes. In *ECCV*, 2012.

[2] T.-S. Chua et al. Next: Nus-tsinghua center for extreme search of user-generated content. *IEEE MultiMedia*, 2012.

[3] A. Dong et al. Towards recency ranking in web search. In *WSDM*, 2010.

[4] P.-S. Huang et al. Learning deep structured semantic models for web search using clickthrough data. In *CIKM*, 2013.

[5] L. Kennedy et al. How flickr helps us make sense of the world: Context and content in community-contributed media collections. In *ACM MM*, 2007.

[6] G. Kim and E. P. Xing. Visualizing Brand Associations from Web Community Photos. In *ACM WSDM*, 2014.

[7] N. Kumar et al. FaceTracer: A Search Engine for Large Collections of Images with Faces. In *ECCV*, 2008.

[8] C.-C. Wu et al. Learning to personalize trending image search suggestion. In *ACM SIGIR*, pages 727–736, 2014.

New Yorker Melange: Interactive Brew of Personalized Venue Recommendations

Jan Zahálka
ISLA, Informatics Institute
University of Amsterdam
Amsterdam, The Netherlands
j.zahalka@uva.nl

Stevan Rudinac
ISLA, Informatics Institute
University of Amsterdam
Amsterdam, The Netherlands
s.rudinac@uva.nl

Marcel Worring
ISLA, Informatics Institute
University of Amsterdam
Amsterdam, The Netherlands
m.worring@uva.nl

ABSTRACT

In this paper we propose *New Yorker Melange*, an interactive city explorer, which navigates New York venues through the eyes of New Yorkers having a similar taste to the interacting user. To gain insight into New Yorkers' preferences and properties of the venues, a dataset of more than a million venue images and associated annotations has been collected from Foursquare, Picasa, and Flickr. As visual and text features, we use semantic concepts extracted by a convolutional deep net and latent Dirichlet allocation topics. To identify different aspects of the venues and topics of interest to the users, we further cluster images associated with them. New Yorker Melange uses an interactive map interface and learns the interacting user's taste using linear SVM. The SVM model is used to navigate the interacting user's exploration further towards similar users. Experimental evaluation demonstrates that our proposed approach is effective in producing relevant results and that both visual and text modalities contribute to the overall system performance.

Categories and Subject Descriptors

H.3.3 [**Information Storage and Retrieval**]: Information Search and Retrieval; H.3.5 [**Information Storage and Retrieval**]: Online Information Services

General Terms

Algorithms; Human Factors; Experimentation

Keywords

Interactive city exploration; social media; user-centered design; deep nets; semantic concept detectors; topic models

1. INTRODUCTION

New York's reputation of being a melting pot of cultures is well-earned. Millions of people with diverse ethnicities, nationalities, and tastes live in the city, contributing to its vibrant, cosmopolitan atmosphere. Tens of millions of visitors come to the Big Apple yearly to enjoy the city, pondering what places in New York to visit. There are numerous resources that help with the choice, such as Foursquare, Yelp, or TripAdvisor. These are excellent when searching venues enjoying general popularity. Does *vox populi*, however, sufficiently reflect the individuality of New Yorkers?

Personal prism can reveal interesting places off the beaten track. Indeed, virtually everyone has "this little place" they like to frequent in their hometown. These places often do not show up in conventional travel guides and recommender systems. However, if the patrons of these venues exhibit a taste similar to our own in their online multimedia trail, we might want to visit them. Hence, we propose the *New Yorker Melange*, an interactive venue exploration system which allows the interacting users (hereafter referred to as *actors*) to brew their own melange of venues frequented by New Yorkers (hereafter referred to as *users*) similar to them.

Understanding user's preference towards a particular venue and the aspects that make two venues similar is a non-trivial task. Although venue categories (e.g., art museum, bar, park, and restaurant) assigned by some social media platforms make the analysis easier, in practice the variety of aspects of interest to the users may be considered too wide to be captured by such categories. We conjecture that those aspects may be naturally encoded in venue-related images and the metadata associated with them. While some location-based social networking platforms, such as Foursquare, offer a detailed venue description together with the images of the venues contributed by the users, with regard to content quantities and topical richness of community-contributed metadata, they can hardly match content-sharing platforms (e.g., Flickr and Picasa). Therefore, in our approach we choose to utilize a large amount of information automatically collected from multiple platforms, which we effectively integrate by performing topical analysis in visual and text domain.

In Section 2 we reflect on the related work. In sections 3 and 4 we describe our data collection procedure and our proposed interactive venue exploration system. The proposed approach is evaluated in Section 5, while Section 6 provides concluding remarks.

2. RELATED WORK

In recent years, a number of location recommendation and exploring applications using community-contributed content have been proposed. For example, Pang et al. mine user-generated travelogues to select representative Flickr images for a particular tourist destination [7]. Kofler et al. con-

MM'14, November 3–7, 2014, Orlando, Florida, USA.
Copyright 2014 ACM 978-1-4503-3063-3/14/11 ...$15.00.
http://dx.doi.org/10.1145/2647868.2656403.

ceived a system analyzing users' previously-captured Flickr images to provide personalized recommendations of off-the-beaten-track locations at a destination city of interest [5]. Popescu et al. analyzed a collection of Flickr images to discover existing tourist routes within a city and recommend new ones [8]. Another personalized travel recommendation system, proposed by Cheng et al., recommends optimal routes for a particular user demographic based on user attributes extracted from community-contributed images [2]. Rudinac et al. proposed a visual summarization approach, using community-contributed images and associated metadata to discover various aspects of a geographic area [9]. Finally, Zhao et al. devised a multimodal approach to detecting overlapping communities in Foursquare [12].

What sets us apart from related work is an interactive approach to venue recommendation and city exploring in which the user preferences are learned on-line. Additionally, in our approach the venues are recommended indirectly, as a part of the like-minded users' profiles, which puts a strong accent on user-centricity. Finally, to gain a better insight into user preferences and venue properties, we integrate multimedia data from content-sharing and location-based social networking platforms.

3. DATA COLLECTION

The first step of the data obtaining process involved getting the list of venues of interest. To this end, we queried the Foursquare API using geo coordinates corresponding to New York City. This resulted in a JSON database containing the respective venue listings. Each listing comprises information about the venue, such as *name*, *venue category*, and *geo coordinates*. In total, we obtained information about 7,246 verified venues. For each venue, we downloaded up to 200 images associated with it, resulting in a collection of 429,921 Foursquare images.

To diversify, enrich, and enlarge our dataset, we have systematically crawled Picasa and Flickr, two popular image sharing social sites. Each query targeted a particular venue, using the venue name and geo coordinates as parameters. To alleviate incorrect geo coordinate assignments by camera GPS systems and users, we set the geo radius, i.e., the tolerated deviation from the venue's geo coordinates, to 1 kilometer. Each query retrieved up to 500 images along with associated annotations. This process yielded 243,292 images from Flickr, and 398,968 images from Picasa.

In total, our collection contains 1,072,181 images of New York and associated annotations. We believe we have significantly increased the signal-to-noise ratio in our dataset by including both the venue name and the geo coordinates in the query. The quality of the dataset can be further improved at the expense of the size by reducing the geo radius and/or reducing the number of images retrieved per venue. Furthermore, grouping images by categories of interest opens up exciting possibilities for further research. Moreover, the same type of data can be obtained for any location in the world. Our dataset thus presents an interesting data resource for multimedia research in general.

4. APPROACH

This section discusses our approach to providing content-driven topical recommendations of venues frequented by New Yorkers. The data preprocessing pipeline, conceptually depicted in Figure 1, consists of three key steps: extraction of visual features from the images (Section 4.1), extraction of text features from the image annotations (Section 4.2), and representing individual venues and users as topical clusters (Section 4.3). Finally, Section 4.4 describes the interactive exploration system as used by the actor.

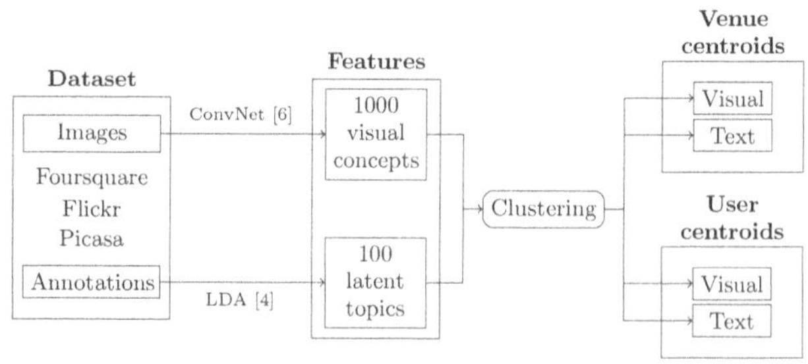

Figure 1: Data collection and preprocessing.

4.1 Visual Features

Guided by an assumption that the venues of interest to the actor may share visual attributes, we extract visual features from the images associated with them. To this end, we use a deep convolutional neural network as conceived by Krizhevsky et al. [6]. The deep net was trained on the ImageNet Large Scale Visual Recognition Challenge (ILSVRC) 2012 dataset of 1000 semantic concepts [3]. We choose to represent each Foursquare, Flickr, and Picasa image by the respective output of the deep net, i.e., the distribution over the 1000 semantic concepts.

4.2 Text Features

For all Flickr images we index the text from *title*, *description*, and *tags*. In case of Picasa images, we utilize the *title*, *summary*, *description*, *keywords*, *albumtitle*, *albumdesc*, and *snippet* fields. We further tokenize the text using the Natural Language Toolkit (NLTK) [1] and remove all HTML elements. Finally, we remove common stopwords and words appearing only once. To index the text in a persistent manner, we use the Gensim framework [11] designed for topic modeling of large corpora. After computing the bag of words representation for each document, we perform online Latent Dirichlet Allocation (LDA) [4] to identify a small number of topics associated with the images. To ensure a reasonable granularity, we set the number of topics to 100.

4.3 Clustering

Processing million images places a non-trivial computational load on the machine, thus prohibiting interactivity. Hence, a compact representation of individual venues and users is needed. We conjecture that each venue and user has a number of topics of interest within the respective set of images. For example, images of a restaurant might depict the food, the interior, or groups of people enjoying their drink. A user's images, while potentially diverse and numerous, will typically share topics corresponding to the user's main interests. Determining a reasonable number of topics to represent users and venues provides not only a more compact representation, but also a basis for matching them.

To obtain the topics of interest, we cluster all images associated with a venue using the k-means clustering algorithm. The cluster centroids represent the individual topics. Simi-

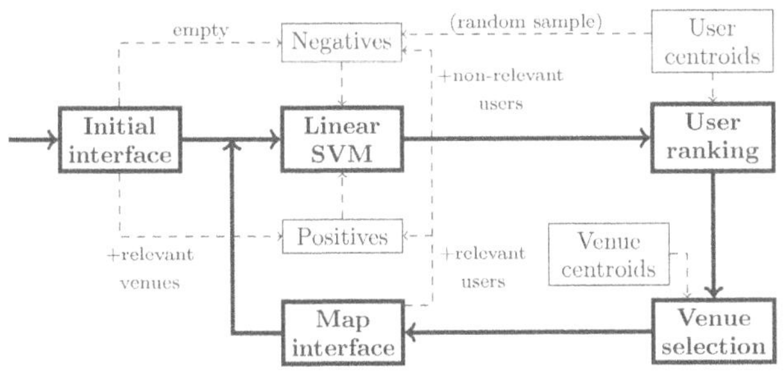

Figure 2: Interactive exploration; thick components represent the system flow, non-thick nodes and dashed arrows depict the data flow.

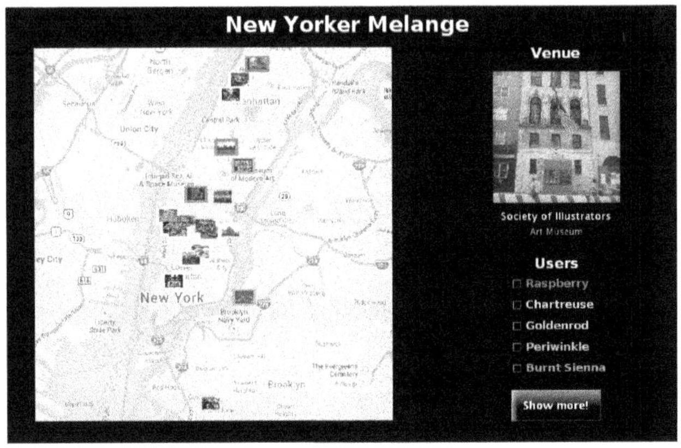

Figure 3: A screenshot with user recommendations generated by our New Yorker Melange system.

larly, we apply the k-means clustering algorithm to cluster all images uploaded by a particular user and select cluster centroids to represent user interests. To ensure a reasonable topical granularity, we choose to use $k = 5$ clusters. The clustering is performed independently for the visual and the text domain.

4.4 Interactive Exploration

The interactive exploration pipeline within the New Yorker Melange, conceptually depicted in Figure 2, can be decomposed into five steps described in this section. Steps 2–4 take around a second on a standard PC, which makes New Yorker Melange a responsive, truly interactive system.

Step 1: Initial interface: The actor is first presented with a set of images arranged in a grid interface. These images illustrate individual venues, and each is the top-ranked Foursquare image for the respective venue. The actor selects the venues of interest by clicking on the images. Then, two sets of positive examples are initialized to contain the cluster centroids of the clicked-on venues for each respective modality (cf. Section 4.3). The sets of negative examples (again, one for each modality) are initially empty.

Step 2: Linear SVM: To identify users similar to the actor, we train a linear SVM separately for visual and text modalities using the respective sets of positive and negative examples as training data. If the size of the set of negatives for any modality is smaller than two times the size of positives, the system supplements the set of negatives with random samples from the collection of user centroids to ensure good positives-negatives balance.

Step 3: User ranking: Each user's relevance score per modality is the maximum of SVM scores assigned to the user's cluster centroids, i.e., each user is as relevant as their most relevant topic. The overall user relevance ranking is determined by aggregating the score rankings across modalities using Borda count. The top-5 ranked users are selected to be displayed to the actor.

Step 4: Venue selection: For each displayed user, up to 5 relevant visited venues are selected. The venue representativeness score per modality is the maximum of cosine similarities between the venue's cluster centroids and the user's cluster centroids. These scores are again aggregated using Borda count.

Step 5: Map interface: The users and their venues are displayed within the map interface depicted in Figure 3. Each venue is represented by a thumbnail of the same image as in step 1. Each thumbnail is placed on the map of New York at the venue's coordinates and color-coded by the visiting user(s). The users themselves are anonymized. The anonymization does not prohibit the manifestation of individual New Yorker stories, but ensures the users' privacy. Clicking on an image thumbnail enables the actor to inspect the image and basic information about the venue. The actor can indicate which user(s) are relevant using the checkboxes. Upon pressing the "Show more!" button, the cluster centroids of users indicated as relevant are added to the positive data and the cluster centroids of users not indicated as relevant are added to the negative data. The cluster centroids of all five displayed users are removed from the collection of user centroids, and these users will not show up in subsequent iterations. After these adjustments to the data, the system proceeds with step 2.

5. EXPERIMENTAL RESULTS

To evaluate the effectiveness of our system in recommending the users and venues of interest to the actor, we apply a protocol inspired by the common practices in evaluation of recommender systems [10]. First, we select 100 users with the largest number of visited venues to be used as artificial actors. For each, we use 4-fold cross-validation as follows. In each step, 25% of the venues visited by the user are withheld as test data. The remaining venues are indicated as relevant (cf. Section 4.4, step 1). The artificial actor then goes through 10 interaction rounds (cf. Section 4.4, steps 2–4). Whenever it encounters a venue from the test set, it marks the corresponding user(s) as relevant. The system's performance at each interaction round is measured by recall, i.e., the ratio of the number of encountered test venues to the total number of test venues, averaged across four folds.

As the *baseline* for comparison we use an interactive recommender system architecture, utilizing the *user-venue matrix*, which encodes users' preference towards venues. The values in the matrix are 1 when the user visited a particular venue, and 0 otherwise. Initially, the actor is represented with a binary vector of relevant venues. To identify users similar to the actor (cf. Section 4.4, step 2), we compute the Jaccard similarity coefficient between the actor's vector and the vectors of all users in the collection. The five users most similar to the actor are then selected and displayed on the screen. The displayed users are represented by their visited venues, selected and sorted again by Jaccard similarity to

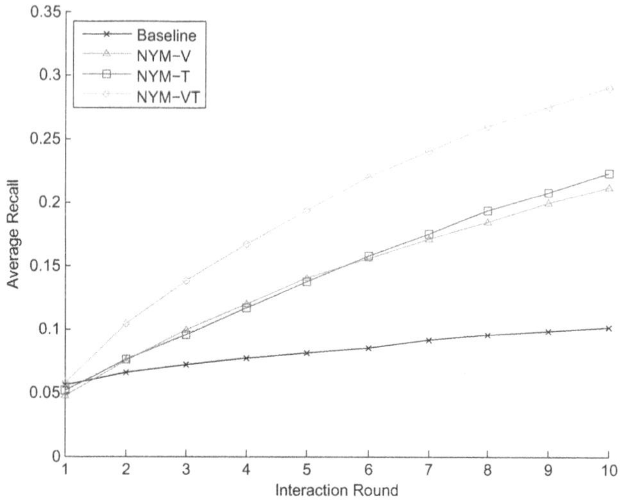

Figure 4: Performance comparison of several variants of our New Yorker Melange system; the performance is expressed in terms of average recall at interaction round.

the actor's profile. When the actor selects one of the displayed users, all venues visited by that user are added to the actor's venue vector.

The results presented in Figure 4 show that the New Yorker Melange (NYM-VT) clearly outperforms baseline at each interaction round. This proves the added benefit of topical modeling of venues and users. While the recall of 0.29 yielded by our approach at round 10 may not seem particularly high at a first glance, one should not forget that the evaluation protocol is rather challenging. Note that the artificial actors will not mark displayed users that prefer different venues of the same type as relevant. A closer analysis of the experimental results reveals that when the set of the actor's categories of interest is reasonably sized ($\sim$ 5 categories), the system yields a performance well above average. Conversely, the cases where the performance is lacking are those when the system tries to learn too many categories at once. This is an expected result because, intuitively, the taste of users having preference towards many different categories is difficult to model. This apparent weakness can be easily overcome by splitting the exploration of many different topics into several smaller sessions, each focusing on a small number of topics at once.

We further investigate contribution of each modality to the overall performance of our proposed approach. Therefore, in Figure 4 we compare the performance of the New Yorker Melange system (NYM-VT) with its variants utilizing only visual (NYM-V) and text (NYM-T) information. The results show that both visual and text modalities contribute equally to the overall system performance and that combining them leads to a clear performance improvement.

6. CONCLUSION

We have presented the New Yorker Melange, a system that gives the users an opportunity to interactively explore the city through the eyes of New Yorkers sharing their taste. Our experiments have shown that the proposed user-centric approach, which treats venues as part of the like-minded user profiles and iteratively learns topical preferences of the interacting user, is effective in producing relevant recommendations. The experiments further suggest that even though useful information about venue properties and user preferences may be extracted from both visual and text content, the performance of our multi-modal approach cannot be matched by its uni-modal variants. Additionally, our work led to a good-quality, large-scale and cross-platform dataset whose value extends beyond the use case addressed in this paper. By performing topical modeling in visual and text domain on the dataset, our approach succeeds in integrating communities and content originating from very different social media platforms.

7. ACKNOWLEDGMENTS

This research is partly supported by the Dutch Technology Foundation STW, which is part of the Netherlands Organisation for Scientific Research (NWO), and which is partly funded by the Ministry of Economic Affairs.

8. REFERENCES

[1] S. Bird, E. Klein, and E. Loper. *Natural language processing with Python.* " O'Reilly Media, Inc.", 2009.

[2] A.-J. Cheng, Y.-Y. Chen, Y.-T. Huang, W. H. Hsu, and H.-Y. M. Liao. Personalized travel recommendation by mining people attributes from community-contributed photos. In *ACM MM*, pages 83–92, 2011.

[3] J. Deng, A. Berg, S. Satheesh, H. Su, A. Khosla, and F.-F. Li. Large scale visual recognition challenge 2012. `www.image-net.org/challenges/LSVRC/2012`.

[4] M. Hoffman, F. R. Bach, and D. M. Blei. Online learning for latent dirichlet allocation. In *NIPS*, pages 856–864, 2010.

[5] C. Kofler, L. Caballero, M. Menendez, V. Occhialini, and M. Larson. Near2me: An authentic and personalized social media-based recommender for travel destinations. In *ACM WSM*, pages 47–52, 2011.

[6] A. Krizhevsky, I. Sutskever, and G. E. Hinton. ImageNet classification with deep convolutional neural networks. In *NIPS*, pages 1097–1105. 2012.

[7] Y. Pang, Q. Hao, Y. Yuan, T. Hu, R. Cai, and L. Zhang. Summarizing tourist destinations by mining user-generated travelogues and photos. *Comput. Vis. Image Und.*, 115(3):352 – 363, 2011.

[8] A. Popescu, G. Grefenstette, and P.-A. Moëllic. Mining tourist information from user-supplied collections. In *ACM CIKM*, pages 1713–1716, 2009.

[9] S. Rudinac, A. Hanjalic, and M. Larson. Generating visual summaries of geographic areas using community-contributed images. *IEEE TMM*, 15(4):921–932, 2013.

[10] G. Shani and A. Gunawardana. Evaluating recommendation systems. In *Recommender Systems Handbook*, pages 257–297. Springer US, 2011.

[11] R. Řehůřek and P. Sojka. Software framework for topic modelling with large corpora. In *LREC*, pages 45–50, 2010.

[12] Y.-L. Zhao, Q. Chen, S. Yan, T.-S. Chua, and D. Zhang. Detecting profilable and overlapping communities with user-generated multimedia contents in LBSNs. *ACM TOMCCAP*, 10(1):3:1–3:22, 2013.

ATLAS: Automatic Temporal Segmentation and Annotation of Lecture Videos Based on Modelling Transition Time

Rajiv Ratn Shah
School of Computing, National University of Singapore, Singapore
rajiv@comp.nus.edu.sg

Yi Yu
School of Computing, National University of Singapore, Singapore
yuy@comp.nus.edu.sg

Anwar Dilawar Shaikh
Department of Computer Engineering, Delhi Technological University, India
anwardshaikh@gmail.com

Suhua Tang
Graduate School of Informatics and Engineering, UEC, Japan
shtang@uec.ac.jp

Roger Zimmermann
School of Computing, National University of Singapore, Singapore
rogerz@comp.nus.edu.sg

ABSTRACT

The number of lecture videos available is increasing rapidly, though there is still insufficient accessibility and traceability of lecture video contents. Specifically, it is very desirable to enable people to navigate and access specific slides or topics within lecture videos. To this end, this paper presents the ATLAS system for the VideoLectures.NET challenge (MediaMixer, transLectures) to automatically perform the temporal segmentation and annotation of lecture videos. ATLAS has two main novelties: (i) a SVM^{hmm} model is proposed to learn temporal transition cues and (ii) a fusion scheme is suggested to combine transition cues extracted from heterogeneous information of lecture videos. According to our initial experiments on videos provided by VideoLectures.NET, the proposed algorithm is able to segment and annotate knowledge structures based on fusing temporal transition cues and the evaluation results are very encouraging, which confirms the effectiveness of our ATLAS system.

Categories and Subject Descriptors

H.3.1 [**Information Storage and Retrieval**]: Content Analysis and Indexing; K.3.1 [**Computers and Education**]: Computer Uses in Education—*Distance learning*

Keywords

Lecture video segmentation; lecture video annotation; lecture video recommendation

1. MOTIVATION AND BACKGROUND

The ATLAS system presented in this paper is our solution to the ACM Multimedia 2014 Grand Challenge on automatic temporal segmentation and annotation. ATLAS stands for *automatic temporal segmentation and annotation of lecture videos based on modelling transition time.* The number of lecture video recordings on the web has increased rapidly due to the ubiquitous availability of cameras and the affordable network infrastructure. However, the accessibility and traceability of lecture video content is still a challenging task. To solve this problem, ATLAS first predicts temporal transitions (TT_1) using supervised learning on video content and temporal transitions (TT_2) by text (transcripts and/or slides) analysis using an N-gram based language model. In the next step, TT_1 and TT_2 are fused by our algorithm to obtain a list of transition times for lecture videos. Moreover, text annotations corresponding to these temporal segments are determined by assigning the most frequent N-gram token of the subtitle resource tracks (SRT) block under consideration (and similar to the N-gram token of slide titles, if available). In this way, the proposed ATLAS system improves the automatic temporal segmentation and annotation of lecture videos so that online learning becomes much easier and users can search sections within a lecture video.

ATLAS introduces new algorithms to automatically segment lecture videos based on video and text analysis. Furthermore, it automatically annotates the segments using an N-gram based language model. A color histogram of a keyframe at each shot-boundary is used as a visual feature to represent the slide transition in the video content. The relationship between the visual features and the transition time of a slide is established with a training dataset of lecture videos provided by the grand challenge organizers, using a machine-learning SVM^{hmm} technique. The SVM^{hmm} model predicts temporal transitions for a lecture video. Furthermore, our solution can help in recommending similar content to the users using text annotations as keywords for searching. The ATLAS system can determine temporal segments and annotations of lecture videos offline rather than at search time, therefore, our system is time-efficient and scales well to large repositories of lecture videos. Our initial experiments have confirmed that our system recommends reasonable temporal segmentations and annotations for lecture videos.

MM '14, November 3–7, 2014, Orlando, Florida, USA.

http://dx.doi.org/10.1145/2647868.2656407.

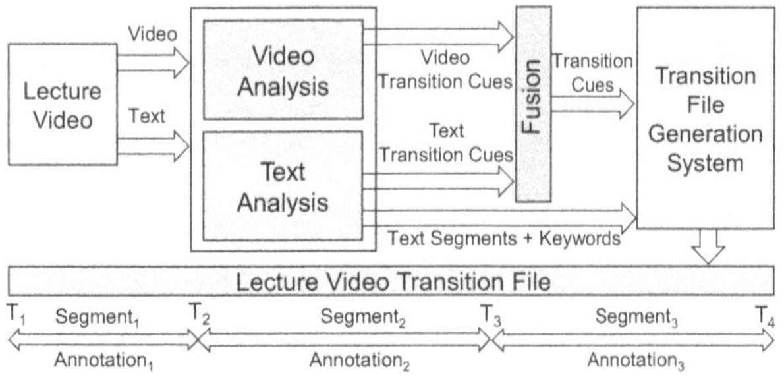

Figure 1: System Framework of ATLAS.

The paper is organized as follows. In Section 2, we review related work and Section 3 describes the ATLAS system. The evaluation results are presented in Section 4. Finally, we conclude the paper with a summary in Section 5.

2. RELATED WORK

Automatic temporal segmentation and annotation of lecture videos is a challenging task, since it depends on many factors such as speaker presentation style, characteristic of camera (*i.e.*, video quality, static or dynamic position/view, *etc*), and others. Moreover, it is a cross-disciplinary area which requires knowledge of text analysis, visual analysis, speech analysis, machine learning and others. In the last a few years, several researchers attempted to solve the problem of automatic segmentation and annotation of lecture videos. Earlier work [5, 7–9] attempted to segment videos automatically by exploiting visual, audio and linguistic features. Fan *et al.* [4] tried to match slides with presentation videos by exploiting visual content features. Chen *et al.* [3] attempted to automatically synchronize presentation slides with the speaker video. Repp *et al.* [10] proposed the segmentation and annotation of audiovisual recordings based on automated speech recognition. Recently, Bhatt *et al.* [1] and Che *et al.* [2] attempted to automatically determine the temporal segmentation and annotation for lecture videos.

3. SYSTEM OVERVIEW

Our system has several novel components which together form its innovative contributions (see Figure 1 for the system framework). The ATLAS system performs the temporal segmentation and annotation of a lecture video in three steps. First, transition cues are predicted from the visual content, using supervised learning described in Section 3.1. Second, transition cues are computed from the available texts using an N-gram based language model described in Section 3.2. Finally, transition cues derived from the previous steps are fused to compute the final temporal transitions and annotations with text, as described in Section 3.3.

3.1 Prediction of Video Transition Cues

A lecture video is composed of several shots combined with cuts and gradual transitions. Kucuktunc *et al.* [7] proposed a video segmentation approach based on fuzzy color histograms which detects shot-boundaries. Therefore, we train two machine learning models using a SVM^{hmm} [6] technique by exploiting the color histograms (64-D) of keyframes to detect the slide transitions automatically in a lecture video. As described in the later Section 4.1, we use lecture videos (V_T) with known transition times as the test set and the remaining in the dataset as the training set. We employ human annotators to annotate ground truths for lecture videos in the training set (see Figure 2 for an illustration of the annotation with both models).

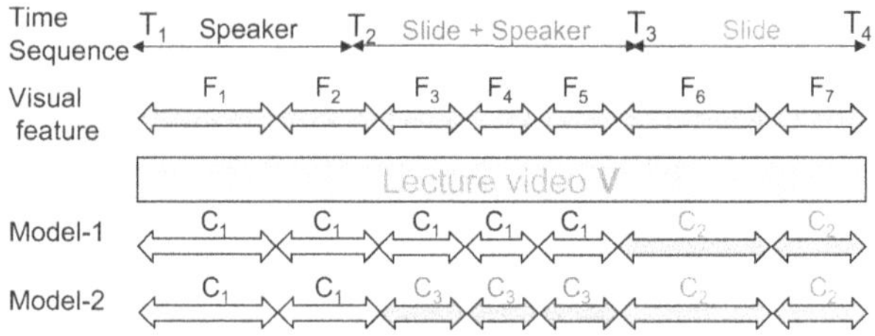

Figure 2: Slide transition models.

First, a SVM^{hmm} model M_1 is trained with two classes C_1 and C_2. Class C_2 represents the segment of a lecture video when only a slideshow is visible (or the slideshow covers a major fraction of a frame) and class C_1 represents the remaining part of the video (see Model-1 in Figure 2). Therefore, whenever a transition occurs from a sequence of classes C_1 (*i.e.*, from speaker only or, both speaker and slide) to C_2 (*i.e.*, slideshow only), it indicates a temporal transition with high probability in the majority of cases. However, we find that for some videos this model detects very few transitions (less than five transitions only). We notice that there are mainly three reasons for this issue, first, when lecture videos are recorded with a single shot, second, when the transition occurs from a speaker to a slideshow but the speaker is still visible in the frame most of the time, and third, when the transition occurs between two slides only.

To resolve the above issues, we train another SVM^{hmm} model M_2 by adding another class C_3, which represents the part of a video when a slideshow and a speaker are both visible. We use this model to predict transitions from only those videos for which M_1 predicted very few transitions. We do not use this model for all videos due to two reasons. First, the classification accuracy of M_1 is better than that of M_2 when there is a clear transition from C_1 to C_2. Second, we want to focus on only those videos which exhibit most of their transitions from C_1 to C_3 throughout the video (this is the reason M_1 was predicting very few transitions), hence, a transition from a sequence of classes C_1 to C_3 is considered a slide transition for such kind of videos.

3.2 Computation of Text Transition Cues

3.2.1 Preparation

In the preparation step, we convert slides (a PDF file) of a lecture video to a HTML file using Adobe Acrobat software. However this can be done with any other proprietary or open source software as well. The benefit of converting the PDF to an HTML file is that we obtain the text from slides along with their positions and font sizes, which are very important cues to determine the title of slides.

3.2.2 Title/Sub-Title Text Extraction

Algorithm 1 extracts titles/sub-titles from the HTML file derived from slides, which represent most of the slide titles of lecture videos accurately. A small variation of this algorithm produces the text content of a slide by extracting the text between two consecutive title texts.

3.2.3 Transition Time Recommendation from SRT File

We employ an N-gram based language model to calculate the relevance score R for every block of thirty tokens from

Algorithm 1 Title/sub-title text extraction from slides

procedure TITLEOFSLIDES(S)
INPUT: A HTML file for slides (H)
OUTPUT: A list of title text T
extractFontFreq(H, $fontList$, $freq$) ▷ this function finds all font and their frequency counts in slides.
$titleFontSize$ = findTitleFontSize($fontList$, $freq$) ▷ this function determines the font size of the title of slides.
$numSlides$ = findNumSlides($titleFontSize$) ▷ this function calculates the approx number of slides.
T = findTitleText($titleFontSize$, $position$) ▷ this function determines the text for titles of all slides which located in top 1/3 of vertically or 2/3 of horizontally in slides.
end procedure

a SRT file. We use a hash map to keep track of all N-gram tokens and their respective term frequencies (TF). The relevance score is defined by the following equation,

$$R(B_i) = \sum_{j=1}^{N}\sum_{k=1}^{n} W_j * w(t_k),$$

$$\text{and } w(t_k) = \frac{TF(t_k|B_i) * log(TF(t_k|SRT) + 1)}{log\frac{TF(t_k|SRT)+1}{TF(t_k|B_i)}},$$

where, $TF(t_k|B_i)$ is the TF of an N-gram token t_k in a block B_i and $TF(t_k|SRT)$ is the TF of the token t_k in the SRT file. N is the N-gram count (we consider up to $N = 3$, *i.e.*, trigram), W_j is the weight for different N-gram counts such that the sum of all W_j is equal to one, and n is the number of unique tokens in the block B_i. We place more importance to a higher order N-gram count by assigning high values to W_j in the relevance score equation.

If slides of a lecture video are available then we calculate the approximate number of slides (*numSlides*) using the Algorithm 1. We consider the *numSlides* number of SRT blocks with the highest relevance scores to determine transitions using text analysis. We infer the start time of these blocks from the hash-map and designate them as the temporal transitions derived from the available texts.

3.3 Transition File Generation

We fuse the temporal transitions derived from the visual contents and the speech transcript file by replacing two transitions less than ten seconds apart by their average transitions time and keeping the remaining transitions as the final temporal transitions for the lecture video. Next, we compare N-gram tokens of blocks corresponding to the final temporal transitions and calculate their similarity with N-gram tokens derived from the title of slides. We assign the most similar N-gram token of a block B_i as a text annotation A for a temporal segment which consists of B_i. If slides of lecture videos are not available then an N-gram token with high TF is assigned as a text annotation for the lecture segment.

4. EVALUATION

4.1 Dataset and Experimental Settings

A total of 65 videos (V) were provided with several metadata annotations such as speech transcriptions, slides, transitions, *etc.*, for the VideoLectures.NET Challenge. A transition file contains details of all transitions and corresponding title texts for a lecture video. Therefore, details in the transition file are treated as ground truth for the lecture video segmentation and annotation task. V_T is the test set for the evaluation of our approach, consisting of videos with transition files.

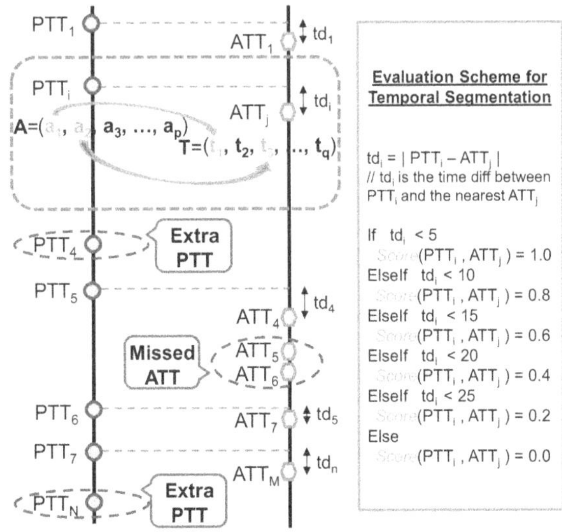

Figure 3: Mapping of PTT, ATT and their respective text to calculate precision, recall and F-1 scores.

4.2 Results

The ATLAS system determines the temporal transitions and the corresponding annotations of lecture videos, with details described earlier in Sections 3.1, 3.2 and 3.3. To evaluate the effectiveness of our approach, we compute precision, recall and F-1 scores for each video in V_T. For a few videos in V_T, precision, recall and F-measure values are very low because our SVM^{hmm} models are not able to detect transitions in lecture videos if lectures are recorded with a single shot, or without zoom-in, zoom-out, or when the slide transitions occur between two slides without any other change in the background. For example, precision and recall for the lecture video *cd07_eco_thu* are *zero*, since only a speaker is visible in the whole video except for a few seconds at the end when both the speaker and a slide consisting of an image with similar color as the background are visible. Therefore, for videos in which our machine learning techniques are not able to detect transitions, we determine transitions from analyzing the speech transcripts (and the text from slides if available) using an N-gram based language model as described in the earlier Section 3.2.

For an evaluation of the temporal segmentation, we connect one predicted transition time (PTT) with only one nearest actual transition time (ATT) from the provided transition files. It is possible that some PTTs are not connected with any ATT and vice versa, as shown in Figure 3. For example, PTT_4 and PTT_N are not connected with any ATT. Similarly, ATT_5 and ATT_6 are not connected with any PTT. We refer to these PTTs and ATTs as *ExtraPTT* and *MissedATT*, respectively. We compute the score for each (PTT_i, ATT_j) pair based on the time difference between them, by employing a relaxed approach as depicted in Figure 3 because it is very difficult to predict exactly the same transition time at the granularity of seconds. Therefore, to evaluate the accuracy of the temporal segmentation,

Table 1: Evaluation of temporal segmentation for the lecture videos in test set V_T.

	Segmentation Accuracy with Visual Transition Cues (I)			Segmentation Accuracy with Text Transition Cues (II)			Segmentation Accuracy with Fused Transition Cues (III)		
Video Name	Precision	Recall	F-1	Precision	Recall	F-1	Precision	Recall	F-1
sparsemethods_01	0.536	0.728	0.618	0.245	0.185	0.211	0.393	0.638	0.486
scholkopf_kernel_01	0.434	0.451	0.442	0.186	0.255	0.219	0.258	0.506	0.341
denberghe_convex_01	0.573	0.487	0.526	0.397	0.296	0.339	0.452	0.496	0.473
bartok_games	0.356	0.246	0.291	0.156	0.938	0.268	0.169	0.831	0.281
abernethy_learning	0.511	0.192	0.279	0.340	0.625	0.441	0.379	0.600	0.465
agarwal_fgc	0.478	0.287	0.358	0.440	0.367	0.400	0.358	0.393	0.375
abernethy_strategy	0.600	0.235	0.338	0.518	0.496	0.507	0.500	0.435	0.465
cd07_eco_thu	0	0	-	0.166	0.154	0.160	0.183	0.154	0.167
szathmary_eol	0.545	0.988	0.702	0.109	0.225	0.147	0.307	0.825	0.447
2011_agarwal_model	0.350	0.088	0.140	0.366	0.331	0.348	0.366	0.331	0.348
2010_agarwal_itl	0.571	0.174	0.267	0.371	0.339	0.354	0.320	0.348	0.333
leskovec_mlg_01	0.492	0.451	0.471	0.356	0.251	0.294	0.397	0.419	0.408
taylor_kmsvm_01	0.650	0.325	0.433	0.260	0.232	0.245	0.391	0.489	0.435
green_bayesian_01	0.473	0.492	0.483	0.362	0.353	0.357	0.339	0.539	0.416
icml08_agarwal_mpg	0.200	0.012	0.023	0.363	0.352	0.357	0.500	0.121	0.190
nonparametrics_01	0.384	0.571	0.459	0.231	0.331	0.272	0.301	0.584	0.397
bubeck_games	0.655	0.465	0.543	0.280	0.452	0.347	0.379	0.574	0.456
Overall_score	**0.459**	**0.364**	**0.375**	**0.303**	**0.363**	**0.310**	**0.352**	**0.487**	**0.381**

we use the following equations to compute precision and recall, and then compute F-measure (F-1 score) using the standard formula $(2 \times \text{precision} \times \text{recall})/(\text{precision} + \text{recall})$.

$$Precision\_segmentation = \frac{\sum_{k=1}^{r} Score(PTT_i, ATT_j)}{N}$$

$$Recall\_segmentation = \frac{\sum_{k=1}^{r} Score(PTT_i, ATT_j)}{M}$$

where N is the number of ATTs, M is the number of PTTs and r is the number of (PTT_i, ATT_j) pairs.

Table 1 shows the precision, recall and F-1 scores for the temporal segmentation of the lecture videos, (I) when visual transition cues are predicted by our SVM^{hmm} models, (II) when text transition cues are predicted by our N-gram based approach, and (III) when the visual transition cues are fused with text transition cues. Furthermore, it shows that the proposed scheme (III), improves the average *recall* much and the average *F-1* slightly, compared with the other two schemes. Therefore, the transition cues determined from the text analysis are also very helpful, especially when the supervised learning fails to detect temporal transitions.

5. CONCLUSIONS

The proposed ATLAS system provides a novel and time-efficient way to automatically determine the temporal segmentation and annotation of lecture videos. First, it determines the temporal segmentation by fusing the transitions cues computed from the visual contents and the text analysis. Second, it annotates the texts corresponding to the determined temporal transitions. ATLAS can effectively segment and annotate lecture videos to facilitate the accessibility and traceability within their content. In our future work, we plan to extend the approach to apply supervised learning on all available texts using features derived from a confusion matrix based on an N-gram language model.

ACKNOWLEDGMENTS

This research has been supported by the Singapore National Research Foundation under its International Research Centre @ Singapore Funding Initiative and administered by the IDM Programme Office through the *Centre of Social Media Innovations for Communities* (COSMIC).

6. REFERENCES

[1] C. A. Bhatt, A. Popescu-Belis, M. Habibi, S. Ingram, S. Masneri, F. McInnes, N. Pappas, and O. Schreer. Multi-factor Segmentation for Topic Visualization and Recommendation: the MUST-VIS System. In *ACM Multimedia*, pages 365–368, 2013.

[2] X. Che, H. Yang, and C. Meinel. Lecture Video Segmentation by Automatically Analyzing the Synchronized Slides. In *ACM Multimedia*, pages 345–348, 2013.

[3] Y. Chen and W. J. Heng. Automatic Synchronization of Speech Transcript and Slides in Presentation. In *IEEE ISCS*, volume 2, pages 568–571, 2003.

[4] Q. Fan, K. Barnard, A. Amir, A. Efrat, and M. Lin. Matching Slides to Presentation Videos using SIFT and Scene Background Matching. In *ACM Multimedia*, pages 239–248, 2006.

[5] A. Haubold and J. R. Kender. Augmented Segmentation and Visualization for Presentation Videos. In *ACM Multimedia*, pages 51–60, 2005.

[6] T. Joachims, T. Finley, and C.-N. Yu. Cutting-plane Training of Structural SVMs. *In Machine Learning Journal*, 77(1):27–59, 2009.

[7] O. Kucuktunc, U. Gudukbay, and O. Ulusoy. Fuzzy Color Histogram-based Video Segmentation. *In Computer Vision and Image Understanding*, 114(1):125–134, 2010.

[8] M. Lin, J. F. Nunamaker Jr, M. Chau, and H. Chen. Segmentation of Lecture Videos based on Text: A Method Combining Multiple Linguistic Features. In *IEEE Hawaii ICSS*, pages 9–17, 2004.

[9] C.-W. Ngo, T.-C. Pong, and T. S. Huang. Detection of Slide Transition for Topic Indexing. In *IEEE ICME*, volume 2, pages 533–536, 2002.

[10] S. Repp, J. Waitelonis, H. Sack, and C. Meinel. Segmentation and Annotation of Audiovisual Recordings based on Automated Speech Recognition. In *Springer IDEAL*, pages 620–629. 2007.

Predicting Viewer Perceived Emotions in Animated GIFs

Brendan Jou
Electrical Engineering
Columbia University
New York, NY 10027

Subhabrata Bhattacharya
Imaging and Computer Vision
Siemens Research
Princeton, NJ 08540

Shih-Fu Chang
Electrical Engineering
Columbia University
New York, NY 10027

{bjou,sfchang}@ee.columbia.edu, subhabrata.bhattacharya@siemens.com

ABSTRACT

Animated GIFs are everywhere on the Web. Our work focuses on the computational prediction of emotions perceived by viewers after they are shown animated GIF images. We evaluate our results on a dataset of over 3,800 animated GIFs gathered from MIT's GIFGIF platform, each with scores for 17 discrete emotions aggregated from over 2.5M user annotations – the first computational evaluation of its kind for content-based prediction on animated GIFs to our knowledge. In addition, we advocate a conceptual paradigm in emotion prediction that shows delineating distinct types of emotion is important and is useful to be concrete about the emotion target. One of our objectives is to systematically compare different types of content features for emotion prediction, including low-level, aesthetics, semantic and face features. We also formulate a multi-task regression problem to evaluate whether viewer perceived emotion prediction can benefit from jointly learning across emotion classes compared to disjoint, independent learning.

Categories and Subject Descriptors

H.1.2 [**Models and Principles**]: User/Machine Systems; I.2.10 [**Artificial Intelligence**]: Vision and Scene Understanding

Keywords

affective computing; emotion prediction; animated gifs; perceived emotion; multi-task learning

1. INTRODUCTION

Our work focuses on the computational prediction, or recognition, of emotions perceived by viewers in animated Graphical Interchange Format (GIF) images. First, we explain why GIFs are an important media type for studying human emotion. Animated GIF images, or just GIFs for short, are a largely unexplored media in Multimedia and Computer Vision research. Their use for conveying emotions has become widely prevalent on the Web, and are now massively found on digital forums, message boards, social media, and websites of every genre. Videos, on one hand, are as popularly used for education and documentation as they are for car chases and explosions in a movie. The challenge with both general consumer videos [10] and professional video content [2, 11, 15, 14] is that this range of emotional expressiveness is too broad and a proper sampling scheme is difficult to determine. On the other hand, still images lack the temporal context necessary for observing concrete emotions. Meanwhile, animated GIFs have quickly become a channel for visually expressing emotion in our modern society. Their role in popular culture has even contributed to the rise of widely, rapidly spread cultural references called *memes*. This social function of GIFs today provides confidence that GIFs gathered from the Web for research are emotionally expressive.

Next, we make an explicit distinction among different types of emotions and justify the importance of perceived emotion in affective study. Affective Computing today is largely rooted in the task of recognizing human emotion (or synonymously, human affect) [13] – and more specifically, "induced" human emotion [9]. Much research in this direction follows a canonical process of presenting stimuli to human subjects, measuring their physiological signals (as well as facial, voice, and body expression), and then manually or computationally analyzing the outcome [7, 15]. Subjects are often asked to complete a survey to qualitatively or quantitatively describe their emotions to the stimuli post hoc [11, 14, 15]. A key issue with this paradigm is it assumes there is only one type of emotion to study; when in fact, *not all affect is induced.* While traditional Affective Computing has assumed a single emotion or-

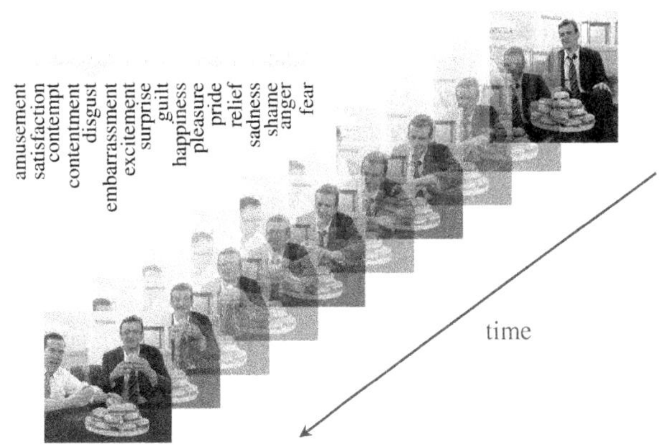

Figure 1: Example Animated GIF with Emotion Scores. Ten frames of an animated GIF sequence are shown with its respective emotion scores from user annotation on the upper-left. Scores that reflect positive presence of emotions are shown in green and negative are shown in red. The diversity of emotions illustrates the various types of emotions involved in multimedia interactions, e.g. intended, perceived, and induced.

MM'14, November 3–7, 2014, Orlando, Florida, USA.

http://dx.doi.org/10.1145/2647868.2656408.

acle as the target, we propose that there are in fact, many different types of emotion.

In Figure 1, we show an example of how there may be different categories of emotion, or affect. The example animated GIF shows two characters, one in white, one in black, are seated in front of a large pile of hamburgers. As they dig into this pile of burgers, the one in black makes a wide-eyed expression, while the character in white makes a wide-mouthed expression. Perhaps the author of this image sequence designed it for a setting where they *intended* to make their audience feel "disgusted" at gluttony of these two characters. What we show at the top-left of Figure 1 though is that viewers can *perceive* that the GIF expresses "pleasure," "happiness," "excitement," and "satisfaction" – that is, they cognitively understand that the image sequence portrays those emotions. Ultimately though, despite what they perceive, they may actually feel (or, be *induced* with) something different – "guilt" or "shame" for having done something similar before or, for others, a sense of "amusement" because they find the GIF to be funny.

Perceived emotion is an important phenomena to study because it is more concrete and objective than induced emotion, where labels are less reliable due to their subjectivity. In addition, computationally recognizing (or, predicting) what an author truly intended is challenging because such labels often do not exist. In this work, we aim to evaluate features and computational models for predicting perceived emotions of GIFs. Specifically, we compare features of different types, including low level features like color histogram, aesthetics, mid-level semantic features inspired by emotion modeling, and face features. Also, in view of the relatedness of multiple emotions, we apply and evaluate multi-task learning, which has been designed to perform multiple machine learning tasks jointly.

The key contributions of our work include: (1) the first work to computationally predict emotion in animated GIFs to the best of our knowledge, (2) the introduction of different types of emotion, while explicitly focusing on perceived emotion, one of the first works for this emotion type, and (3) the prediction of 17 discrete emotion perceived by viewers using multi-task learning.

2. RELATED WORK

In [4], the authors propose a bank of visual classifiers that form a mid-level representation for modeling affect in images called SentiBank. Briefly, the representation is a set of 1,200 Linear SVM outputs where the SVMs are trained using a taxonomy of "adjective-noun pairs" (ANPs). The ANPs combine a "noun" for visual detectability and an "adjective" for affective modulation of the noun, resulting in pairs like "cute dog," "beautiful sunset," "disgusting food," and "terrible accident." These ANPs were mined from Flickr, where authors uploaded images along with tag metadata to describe their content. Although not acknowledged by the authors in [4], because of this way that SentiBank is trained, the representation actually describes an uploader's or originator's intended emotion, not emotion in general. Recent work in [6] studied the metadata of images and used a text-based model to extract "publisher affect concepts" and "viewer affect concepts", but tries to divide emotion along the axis of human roles, e.g. publishers and viewers, but does not acknowledge that emotion can also be divided along how they arise in those humans, e.g. intended, perceived, and induced. We also set a more ambitious goal of predicting viewer perceived emotion using content-based methods where such metadata and comments are not available, as is often the case.

In Affective Computing for visual data, [12] develops a set of color, texture, and composition features inspired by concepts in art theory and psychology and uses Naïve Bayes classifiers for emotion recognition in still images. In [18], a global color-based feature

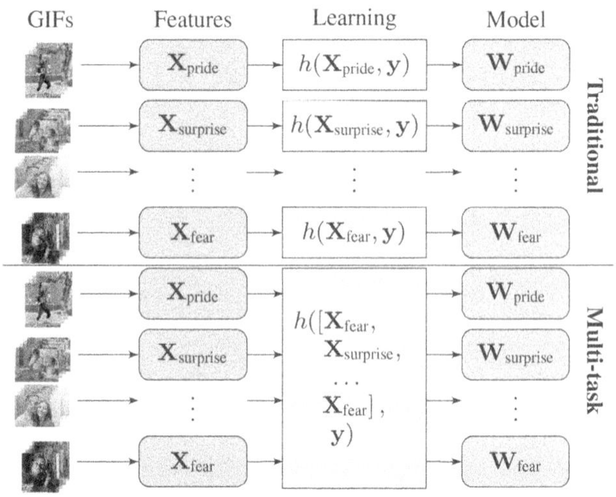

Figure 2: Traditional and Multi-task Learning. Top: Traditional pipeline for discrete emotion recognition where classifier or regressor h is learned independently for each emotion with training labels y. Bottom: Multi-task learning jointly learns over all emotion classes yielding multiple regressors.

is designed for a semi-supervised factor graph formulation to predict emotion in images and modify the "feel" of an image. Both of these representations model visual emotion using early fusion and independently trained classifiers for each emotion. We use multi-task regression to learn multiple regressors jointly across emotions, resulting in a fast, low-cost linear projection at test time.

There are several existing public datasets available to the community for recognizing emotion in visual media, but all focused on induced emotion to best of our knowledge. The International Affective Picture System (IAPS) was an early dataset that does deviate slightly from induced emotion, but only provides a small set of ~1,000 still images. The DEAP dataset [11] consists of 40 one-minute excerpts from music videos and spontaneous physiological signals from 32 subjects. The MAHNOB-HCI Tagging dataset [15] has 20 short film clips with ~27 subjects with physiological signals like EEG and audio recordings of the subjects. FilmStim [14] and LIRIS-ACCEDE [2] are two other datasets consisting also of short film clips, 64 and 9,800 clips respectively, but use scores and rankings by participant ratings instead of strict classifications. These datasets use an emotion model called the "valence-arousal(-dominance) space" that represents emotion along a "valence" axis measuring sentiment positivity and an "arousal" axis capturing reactiveness to a stimuli. An issue with the valence-arousal model is its difficulty to immediately apply in real-world applications, where applications benefit most when there is a describable entity that can be tied to the output of some computational machinery. On the other hand, discrete emotions like sadness, happiness, and anger, provide us exactly this descriptive power. We note also that recent work in [10] studied discrete emotions for 1,101 user-generated videos, but labels data using 10 annotators following an unspecified "detailed definition of each emotion." Meanwhile, we present baselines on a dataset of animated GIFs annotated by over 2.5M users with soft labels on 17 discrete emotions.

3. GIFGIF DATASET

We gathered data from a website created by Human-Computer Interaction researchers at the MIT Media Lab called GIFGIF[1]. We

[1] http://gifgif.media.mit.edu

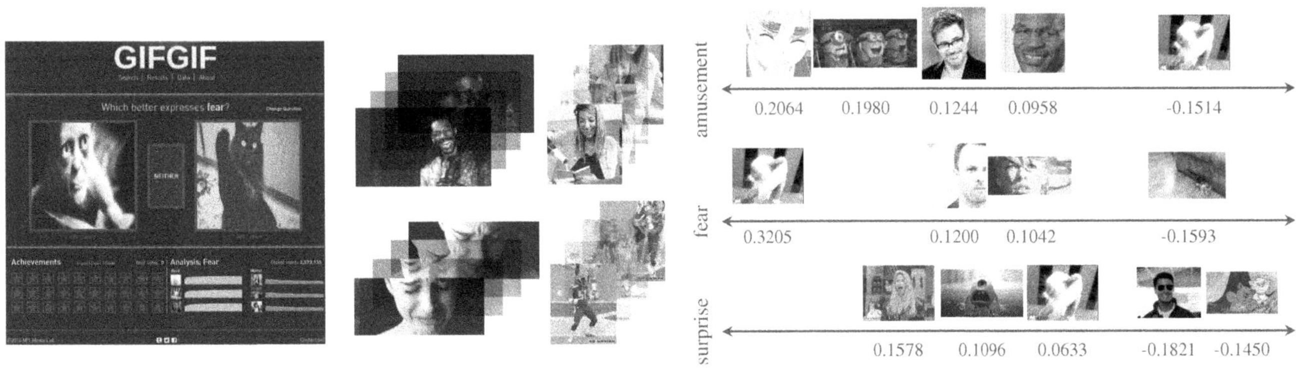

GIF-to-GIF Comparison | Animated GIFs | Emotion Scores

Figure 3: GIFGIF Dataset. Left: Screenshot of the GIFGIF interface designed at the MIT Media Lab. Users are asked to vote which GIF best expresses an emotion. Center: Several example animated GIFs from the dataset collected from GIFGIF. Right: Last frame of example GIFs for three emotions along with their emotion scores, shown sorted by their score on a [-1,1] scale where 0 is neutral.

collected 3,858 GIFs on April 29, 2014 from GIFGIF along with their crowdsourced annotations. The GIFs, which have at most 303 frames each, are sourced from a large variety of domains from films, television shows, cartoons/anime, sports, video games, advertisements, user generated content, and user-edited content. The GIFs span a wide range of camera angles, illumination, special effects, humans & non-humans, B/W & color, zooming, resolution, and some original content from as early as the 1930's.

As shown in Figure 3, the website that the MIT researchers designed presents users with a pair of GIFs and asks "Which better expresses X?" where X is one of 17 emotions: amusement, anger, contempt, contentment, disgust, embarrassment, excitement, fear, guilt, happiness, pleasure, pride, relief, sadness, satisfaction, shame and surprise. Users answer with the GIF they perceive expresses the emotion best or select neither.8 This particular question of "expression" is precisely an effort to capture emotions users perceive in the content rather than what users feel after seeing the GIF.

At the time of our data collection, GIFGIF aggregated over 2.5M user annotations to produce a 17-dimensional vector for each GIF containing a score between 0 and 50 for each emotion where 25 is neutral. The creators of GIFGIF chose to calculate these scores using the TrueSkill algorithm [8], a method originally designed for ranking video game players given the outcome of a game. Here, GIFs replace players and GIFGIF users provide outcomes of GIF pair match-ups. The range $[0, 50]$ comes from heuristic parameters in the TrueSkill algorithm that define a mean performance $\mu = 25$ and uncertainty $\sigma = 25/3$ per player or GIF. In all our experiments and analysis, we normalize this range to [-1,1] for convenience. GIFGIF labels are unique in that each GIF has a soft labels for each emotion whereas other datasets [2, 10, 11, 14, 15] have traditionally only had one categorical emotion assignment per image or video.

4. PERCEIVED EMOTION PREDICTION

Given animated GIFs and emotional scores along 17 discrete perceived emotions, we seek to computationally predict these scores in a regression framework and evaluate performance.

4.1 Feature Representations

To better understand what features aid the prediction of viewer perceived emotion, we use four image feature representations, each chosen for their previous use or connection to emotion recognition in visual content. The interested reader is encouraged to see the individual references relevant to each feature for details.

Color histograms. We compute frame-level color histograms in HSV color space for its classical use in vision and affect computing.

Face expression: Facial expressions in GIFs intuitively impact how viewers perceive conveyed emotions. We use a convolutional neural network with top-level one-vs-all SVMs with squared hinge losses which achieved the best validation performance of 69.4% in a public evaluation [16] and represents the current state-of-the art. The training set of [16] consisted of 28,708 48×48 face images over seven emotions: angry, disgust, fear, happy, sad, surprise and neutral. We perform face detection using OpenCV's Haar-like cascade and apply facial expression recognition on the largest face for a 6-D vector of SVM score outputs as a feature.

Image-based aesthetics: Earlier works have shown that emotion has some intrinsic correlation with visual aesthetics [3, 10, 12]. We compute a subset of well-known image-based aesthetic features as described in [3]. GIF frames are divided into 3×3 cells from which cell-level statistics are computed including the dark channel, luminosity, sharpness, symmetry, white balance, colorfulness, color harmony, and eye sensitivity. The normalized area of dominant object and distances from the dominant object's centroid to grid-line intersections are also computed at the frame-level. Together these form a 149-D feature vector for each frame.

SentiBank: We use a recent mid-level visual representation composed of visual sentiment detectors called SentiBank [4] discussed earlier. The feature consists of a 1,200-D vector of Linear SVMs outputs estimating the originator's intended emotion via "adjective-noun pairs" (ANPs). SentiBank has been shown to work well other emotion recognition tasks [3, 4, 6, 10] and achieved a F-score for recognizing ANPs of over 0.6 on a controlled test set [4].

4.2 Multi-task Emotion Regression

Traditional independent regression like logistic regression or support vector regression ignores the fact that emotion classes can often be related – for example, the sensation of "surprise" is not necessarily orthogonal to the feeling of "fear." We present a novel application of multi-tasking learning (MTL), also known as multi-task regression (MTR), to solve this problem. In multi-task learning, our goal is to learn the weight matrix $\mathbf{W}$ comprised of t tasks via the optimization $\min_{\mathbf{W}} \mathcal{L}(\mathbf{W}) + \Omega(\mathbf{W})$, where $\mathcal{L}(\mathbf{W})$ is the empirical training loss and $\Omega(\mathbf{W})$ is a regularization encoding task-relatedness. Our "tasks" are the 17 discrete emotion classes.

To model the relationship between emotions, one approach is to constrain regressors of different emotions to share a low dimen-

Table 1: Perceived Emotion Prediction on GIFGIF. The normalized mean square error (nMSE) is reported across 17 emotions over five random repetitions of a 20/80% train/test split for color histogram (CH), face expression (FE), Aesthetics (AS) and SB features with ordinary least squares linear regression (OLS), logistic regression (Logit), and low rank multi-task regression (MTR). Lower nMSE indicates better performance.

	OLS	Logit	MTR
CH	1.7398 ± 0.1868	1.6618 ± 0.2991	1.4641 ± 0.1935
FE	0.8925 ± 0.0036	0.9130 ± 0.0030	0.8955 ± 0.0024
AS	1.0440 ± 0.0133	1.0571 ± 0.0116	1.0361 ± 0.0093
SB	1.5694 ± 0.0614	1.4944 ± 0.0593	2.2901 ± 0.1981

sional subspace. Formally, this means we want a low rank weight matrix $\mathbf{W}$ and need to solve the rank minimization $\min_{\mathbf{W}} \mathcal{L}(\mathbf{W}) + \lambda \cdot \text{rank}(\mathbf{W})$. This problem is NP-hard in general [17], and a popular solution is to minimize the trace (or nuclear) norm $\|\cdot\|_*$ instead of the rank function. Trace norm regularization in multi-task learning [19] for a data matrix $\mathbf{X}$ takes the form

$$\min_{\mathbf{W}} \sum_{i=1}^{t} \left\| \mathbf{W}_i^T \mathbf{X}_i - \mathbf{y}_i \right\|_F^2 + \rho_1 \|\mathbf{W}\|_* ,$$

where a least squares loss is used for $\mathcal{L}(\mathbf{W})$. We sample ten equally spaced frames for each GIF, or less for shorter GIFs, and apply the emotion labels from GIFGIF's TrueSkill algorithm as weakly supervised labels $\mathbf{y}$ over each of the frames. We ran our experiments over five random repetitions of a 20/80% train/test ratio, find regularization parameters using cross-validation, and report results on the test set where regression outputs are computed by the averaging frame-level scores for GIFs in each emotion category. We adopt the normalized mean squared error (nMSE) used in previous studies [1, 5] for our experiments. The nMSE is defined as the mean squared error (MSE) divided by the variance of the target vector and assures that the error is not biased toward models that over or under predict.

We compare our approach to classical linear regression with ordinary least squares (OLS), i.e. no weighting, and logistic (logit) regression. We note that methods like support vector regression could have been used in place of LR, but would still learn emotion models independently; and despite the pairwise comparison in GIFGIF, methods like RankSVM could not be used because GIFGIF only exposes TrueSkill score outputs, not pair comparison outcomes.

From Table 1, we see that color histograms expectedly performs poorly since emotion is more complex than can be captured by color. The aesthetics feature, though not designed specifically for emotion recognition, still does encode some information related to the perceptual emotion and achieved the second best nMSE. Surprisingly, the SentiBank feature which is tailored as a mid-level semantic feature for aspects of emotion does not perform well. This may be explained by the facts that there is a cross-domain issue from the training set that SentiBank used to our current dataset, and that SentiBank has a fairly conservative F-score of 0.6 for its detectors [4]. Of all features, the face expression feature performs the best. The simple intuition is that humans express and perceive much of their emotions through their faces. We predict the training label average when no faces are detected.

Overall, we consistently observed that the best performing emotion was "happiness" followed by "amusement" for all regressors using face expression features, and the worst performing emotion was also consistently "embarrassment." Inspecting the GIFs in the "embarrassment" category, we found that this emotion was heavily dominated by sequences where a person or cartoon would hide their faces with their hands or another object, or would look down hiding their faces via their pose. In these cases, as one would expect, face detection fails because of occlusions. We believe that the "embarrassment" emotion would benefit most from gesture recognition as many of the occlusions are due to hand movement. The good performance on the "happiness" and "amusement" emotions are unsurprising as both emotions are visually expressed with smiles and laughter. However, due the subtle differences between these two emotions, we also believe that this is also one of the reasons why multi-task learning sometimes performs marginally worse due to ambiguities like this in the model. We believe it maybe important for future multi-task emotion models to also regularize on the similarity and not just the dissimilarity of emotion tasks.

5. CONCLUSIONS

We showed there are be different delineations of emotions and presented a computational approach to predicting viewer perceived emotions on a dataset of animated GIFs. Additionally, we showed that emotions need not be decoupled from each other by presenting a multi-task regression approach for jointly learning over 17 discrete emotions. In the future, we will study the gap between intended, perceived and induced emotion as well as study the temporal patterns of emotion.

Acknowledgments

The first author was supported by the U.S. Department of Defense (DoD) through the National Defense Science & Engineering Graduate Fellowship (NDSEG) Program.

6. REFERENCES

[1] A. Argyriou, T. Evgeniou, and M. Pontil. Convex multi-task feature learning. In *Machine Learning*, 2008.

[2] Y. Baveye, J.-N. Bettinelli, E. Dellandrea, L. Chen, and C. Chamaret. A large video data base for computational models of induced emotion. In *ACII*, 2013.

[3] S. Bhattacharya, B. Nojavanasghari, T. Chen, D. Liu, S.-F. Chang, and M. Shah. Towards a comprehensive computational model for aesthetic assessment of videos. In *ACM Multimedia*, 2013.

[4] D. Borth, R. Ji, T. Chen, T. Breuel, and S.-F. Chang. Large-scale visual sentiment ontology and detectors using adjective-noun pairs. In *ACM Multimedia*, 2013.

[5] J. Chen, J. Zhou, and J. Ye. Integrating low-rank and group-sparse structures for robust multi-task learning. In *KDD*, 2011.

[6] Y.-Y. Chen, T. Chen, W. H. Hsu, H.-Y. M. Liao, and S.-F. Chang. Predicting viewer affective comments based on image content in social media. In *ACM ICMR*, 2014.

[7] J. Fleureau, P. Guillotel, and I. Orlac. Affective benchmarking of movies based on the physiological responses of a real audience. In *ACII*, 2013.

[8] R. Herbrich, T. Minka, and T. Graepel. TrueSkill™: A Bayesian skill rating system. In *NIPS*, 2006.

[9] W. James. What is an Emotion? *Mind Association*, 1883.

[10] Y.-G. Jiang, B. Xu, and X. Xue. Predicting emotions in user-generated videos. In *AAAI*, 2014.

[11] S. Koelstra, C. Mühl, M. Soleymani, J.-S. Lee, A. Yazdani, T. Ebrahimi, T. Pun, A. Nijholt, and I. Patras. DEAP: A database for emotion analysis using physiological signals. *IEEE TAffC*, 2011.

[12] J. Machajdik and A. Hanbury. Affective image classification using features inspired by psychology and art theory. In *ACM Multimedia*, 2010.

[13] R. W. Picard. *Affective Computing*. MIT Press, 1997.

[14] A. Schaefer, F. Nils, X. Sanchez, and P. Philippot. Assessing the effectiveness of a large database of emotion-eliciting films: A new tool for emotion researchers. *Cognition and Emotion*, 2010.

[15] M. Soleymani, J. Lichtenauer, T. Pun, and M. Pantic. A multimedia database for affect recognition and implicit tagging. *IEEE TAffC*, 2012.

[16] Y. Tang. Deep learning using linear support vector machines. In *ICML*, 2013.

[17] L. Vandenberghe and S. Boyd. Semidefinite programming. *SIAM Review*, 1996.

[18] X. Wang, J. Jia, P. Hu, S. Wu, J. Tang, and L. Cai. Understanding the emotional impact of images. In *ACM Multimedia*, 2012.

[19] J. Zhou, J. Chen, and J. Ye. MALSAR: Multi-tAsk Learning via StructurAl Regularization. Technical report, ASU, 2012.

Context-Based Photography Learning using Crowdsourced Images and Social Media

Yogesh Singh Rawat
School of Computing
National University of Singapore
yogesh@comp.nus.edu.sg

Mohan S Kankanhalli
School of Computing
National University of Singapore
mohan@comp.nus.edu.sg

ABSTRACT

This paper presents a photography model based on machine learning which utilizes crowd-sourced images along with social media cues. As scene composition and camera parameters play a vital role in aesthetics of a captured image, the proposed system addresses the problem of learning photographic composition and camera parameters. Further, we observe that context is an important factor from a photography perspective, we therefore augment the learning with associated contextual information. We define context features based on factors such as time, geo-location, environmental conditions and type of image, which have an impact on photography. The meta information available with crowd-sourced images is utilized for context identification and social media cues are used for photo quality evaluation. We also propose the idea of computing the photographic composition basis, *eigenrules* and *baserules*, to support our composition learning method. The trained photography model can provide assistance to the user in determining image composition and camera parameters.

Categories and Subject Descriptors

H.4 [**Information Systems Applications**]: Miscellaneous

Keywords

Composition Learning; Social Media; Camera Parameters

1. INTRODUCTION

The method proposed in this paper is our solution to the ACM Multimedia 2014 Grand Challenge on Machine Learning for Computational Photography proposed by Huawei. The main focus of this work is to provide a system for learning photographic composition and camera parameters (exposure, aperture, ISO and shutter speed) based on the environmental characteristics and objects of the scene. Figure 1 presents the overview of our proposed method.

MM'14, November 03 - 07, 2014, Orlando, Florida, USA
Copyright 2014 ACM 978-1-4503-3063-3/14/11 ...$15.00.
http://dx.doi.org/10.1145/2647868.2656409.

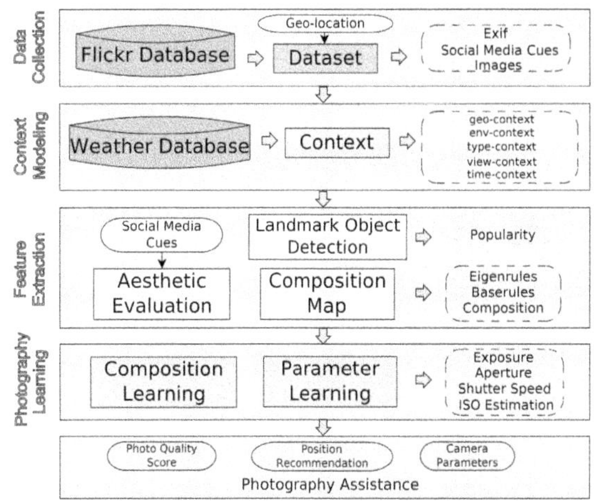

Figure 1: **System Overview**

Scene composition and camera parameter settings are two most important factors in the art of photography [11]. Photographers follow some widely accepted principles such as *rule of thirds, leading lines, repeating patterns, layering, horizon lines, relative scale, etc.* as they compose the scene [9]. Based on this fact the authors of [3, 4, 14, 15, 20] proposed photography assistance based on image composition and make use of some well known photography rules along with some heuristics (clear theme, position of main object, region of interest, etc.) to assist users in capturing photographs. However, these methods are limited to some well known heuristic rules and also lack contextual knowledge which plays a vital role in photography.

In contrast to rule based approaches, the authors of [13, 16–18] proposed the data driven approach and make use of crowd-sourced images to build aesthetic evaluation models which can provide feedback regarding image quality. However, the proposed methods do not make use of any context information. Yin et al. [22] proposed a more comprehensive photography learning model which make use of context information and also make suggestions regarding camera parameters. However, the proposed method does not consider presence of people in images and the composition recommendation is based on one iconic image selected for a given view. Also, the parameter learning model is independent of objects in a scene. Recently, Xu et al. [21] proposed a human position recommendation system for selected landmark locations. However, their method considers only a single person and does not provide any feedback regarding scene composition.

Professional photographers use their experience and knowledge to capture high quality images based on the context. Motivated by this fact, we propose a comprehensive system for photography assistance using crowd-sourced images which takes into account available contextual information for composition and camera parameter learning. Our main contributions are: 1) We propose a context based composition learning system which accounts for human objects in the scene and is not limited by the number of main objects in the scene, 2) We introduce the concepts of *eigenrules* and *baserules* to support composition learning, 3) We propose context based camera parameter learning which takes into account the presence of human objects in the scene, and finally, 4) We present human position recommendation in a scene for landmark locations which is not limited by number of people.

2. PROPOSED METHODOLOGY

The crowd-sourced image database is augmented with *Exif* information and social media cues corresponding to each image. The *Exif* meta data is utilized for context modeling and social media cues are used for image aesthetic quality evaluation. Based on the context features and aesthetic score, independent models are trained for image composition, exposure, aperture and shutter speed.

2.1 Context

We define five context features, *time-context, geo-context, env-context, view-context* and *type-context*. Time is an important factor for learning camera parameters as it has direct impact on lighting conditions. Time of image capture is used along with sunrise, sunset and sunpeak time to define *time-context*. Image composition reflects how the visual elements are organized in the photograph. Different geo-locations may have different visual elements therefore geo-location is important from composition perspective. Geo-location also affects camera parameters as lighting conditions may also vary from location to location. To define the *geo-context* we use the latitude and longitude of the location. Lighting condition of a location also depends on the weather and therefore weather will have an impact on camera parameters. Factors such as temperature, visibility, humidity, haze, rain conditions, month of capture, dew, mist and cloud details are utilized to define *env-context*.

For a given geo-location we can have multiple views based on the direction we are facing. Different views for a geo-location will mostly have different color composition. Based on this assumption we make use of localized color(HSV) histogram to define *view-context*. A photograph with and without human objects will have different image composition as well as camera parameters. To differentiate between images with and without people, we define *type-context*. Feature descriptor for *type-context* is formed using face recognition on the image.

2.2 Aesthetic Score Evaluation

Number of user-favorites and user-views of any photo on social media indicates its popularity in social media. Apart from social media cues '*interestingness*' score [6] of an image can also be used for inferring its quality. We employ the logistic function (to well separate bad and good images, instead of exponential [22]) to assign aesthetic score(A) between 0 and 1 to each image based on number of user-views(v), number of user-favorites(f) and *'interestingness'* score(i) using equation 1. $\alpha, \beta, \gamma, \delta$ and κ are constants which are empirically calculated.

$$A(v, f, i) = \frac{1}{1 + e^{-(\alpha log(v) + \beta f + \frac{\gamma f}{v+1} + \delta i - \kappa)}} \tag{1}$$

2.3 Composition Learning

Photographic composition is defined as organization of important objects in the image [9]. For composition representation popular landmark objects are identified for a geo-location. We make use of image segmentation [1] and saliency detection [2] to identify salient objects in an image. A pool of salient objects (visual words) is generated for a geo-location and clustering (K-means) is performed to identify popular landmark objects. Each visual word is represented using a set of features (HOG [8], SURF [5] and RGB histogram). For each detected landmark object a popularity score is generated using equation 2.

$$popularity(V_i) = average(\frac{N_i}{N_{max}}, \frac{\sum_{j=1}^{N_i} s_j}{N_i}) \tag{2}$$

where, V_i is the ith landmark object, N_i is the size of cluster i, N_{max} is size of the largest cluster for a given geo-location and s_j is the saliency value for visual word j for a given cluster i.

Visual words extracted after segmentation [1] for each image are classified into popular landmark objects from similar geo-context employing the Nearest Neighbor approach. Composition map for each image is formed using detected popular landmark objects and their corresponding popularity value. There can be faces present in the image which may change the composition of a view. To take this into account we make use of face detection and all the detected faces are assigned popularity score of 1. The composition map is divided into $n \times n$ grids of rectangular cells. Spatially connected cells ($m \times m$) are merged to form blocks. A histogram of popularity is extracted for each block using b bins. Blocks can have overlapping cells and composition descriptor is formed by combining histogram of saliency for all the blocks. Viewpoint and type of view are two factors which can bring variation in scene composition. Therefore, we use composition descriptor along with *view-context* and *geo-context* to train a classifier for composition learning.

2.3.1 *Eigenrules and Baserules*

Depending on the scene composition different photography rules may apply for different geo-locations. To find out popular photographic compositions for any geo-location we employ matrix decomposition on the composition feature of images. Composition map is divided into m × m grids of rectangular cells and average popularity score is calculated for each cell. Feature vector is formed by combining the average popularity score of all the cells in the grid. We employ Principal Component Analysis (PCA) to find the basis for the composition rules. The idea is inspired by [19] where *eigenfaces* are used as basis for human faces. Here we are using similar technique for finding out the basis for photographic composition rules. The components which contributes most towards the variance in composition are chosen as basis vectors and are called *eigenrules*.

To explore photographic composition further we employ Non-Negative Matrix Factorization (NMF) [12] to find popular position in image where objects are placed by the photographers. NMF has been used for learning parts of faces and semantic features of text by researchers [12]. Here we aim to factorize the image composition into basic components. The top basic components are extracted from NMF decomposition to learn the basis rules and are called *baserules*. The motivation behind *eigenrules* and *baserules* is to visualize and support the proposed composition learning. Since NMF [12] decomposition gives only positive basis, complex compositions can be formed by adding different combinations of *baserules*. On the other hand *eigenrules* can have negative components as well, therefore inferring complex compositions involve addition as well as subtraction of *eigenrules*. Therefore, from users perspective, *baserules* are more important and easy to visualize as they indicate positions where salient objects should be placed.

2.4 Parameter Learning

Exposure value (EV) represents a combination of camera's shutter speed, ISO and f-number (aperture), such that all combinations that yield the same exposure have the same EV value. For a given *geo-context*, *env-context* and *time-context* different combination of aperture, ISO and shutter speed can lead to same exposure value, therefore we propose to learn these parameters independently based on relevant context information. Exposure value is a base-2 logarithmic scale defined as [10],

$$EV_{100} = log_2 \frac{A^2}{T} - log_2 \frac{S}{100} \tag{3}$$

where, A is the relative aperture (f-number), T is the exposure time ('shutter speed') in seconds, S is the ISO value, EV_S is the exposure value at ISO S and EV_{100} is the exposure value at ISO 100. Time, geo-location, weather conditions and direction of camera lens are the main factors affecting exposure value, therefore we use *time-context, geo-context, env-context* and *view-context* for exposure learning.

Although aperture has a direct impact on exposure value it also controls the *depth of field* [11]. Photographs with human objects will have greater depth of field as compare to images without human objects. Also, the size of human objects will affect depth of field as bigger human objects will be closer to the camera leading to a larger depth of field as compared to smaller human objects. We use *time-context, geo-context, view-context, env-context* and *type-context* for aperture learning.

Apart from controlling the exposure value, shutter speed is also utilized to capture dynamic scene content. For a given geo-location *view-context* can be used to differentiate between various views based on the assumption that scene dynamics will not vary much for landmark locations. Therefore *view-context* is used along with *time-context, env context* and *geo-context* to learn shutter speed. Exposure, aperture, ISO and shutter speed are related [11] and therefore we directly employ equation (3) to estimate the ISO parameter.

3. EXPERIMENTS

We utilize crowd-sourced landmark photos to train and test our proposed method. We used Flickr API's to download crowd-sourced images along with social media data.

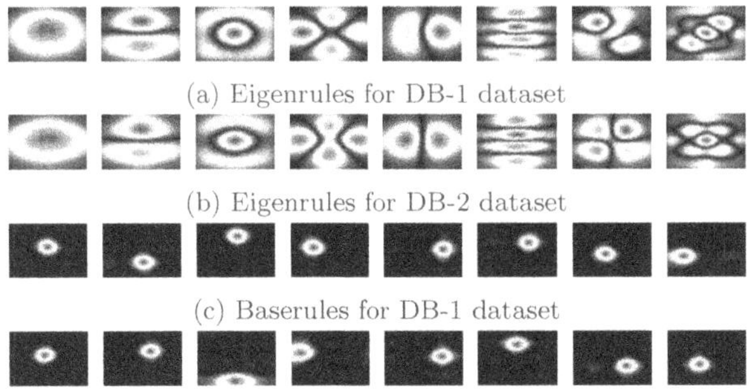

(a) Eigenrules for DB-1 dataset

(b) Eigenrules for DB-2 dataset

(c) Baserules for DB-1 dataset

(d) Baserules for DB-2 dataset

Figure 2: **Visualization of Eigenrules and Baserules**

We collected around 62K images for 12 different tourist locations. Apart from images of tourist locations we also collected popular photographs from Flickr for learning composition bases. We constructed two independent datasets using '*interestingness*' API with 21K (DB-1) and 51K (DB-2) images respectively. High ranked images (aesthetic score >0.80) for a given geo-location are used for landmark object detection. Images with low aesthetic score are left out to filter out noise in the process. We employ K-means algorithms with 200 centers on pool of visual words to identify popular landmark objects.

In composition learning we aim to train a classification model which can differentiate between good and bad compositions. We consider images with aesthetic score >0.6 as good and <0.4 as bad. We use binary SVM [7] with RBF kernel to train separate classification model for each location. We employ 10 fold cross validation to determine the accuracy rate and precision of the classifier. Composition feature is extracted as described in section 2.3 with n=9, m=3 and b=10. Table 1 presents the classification accuracy and precision score for some of the locations. The probabilistic score from classification is used to evaluate the aesthetic score of the image. For position recommendation, composition grid is searched to find locations for detected faces to obtain maximum aesthetic score. Figure 3 shows sample images from '*Merlion Park*' location with predicted aesthetic scores along with position recommendations(red blocks).

Eigenrules and Baserules.

Figure 2 shows top *eigenrules* and *baserules* extracted for the two datasets (DB-1, DB-2) with high quality images. Some of the *eigenrules* reflect popular heuristic rules of photography which are used by photographers. For example, the first *eigenrule* corresponds to 'rule of center', the second *eigenrule* corresponds to 'rule of symmetry' and the third *eigenrule* corresponds to 'rule of framing' [9]. Similarly, some of the *baserules* shown in figure 2 correspond to popular photography rules used by the photographers. For example, 'rule of thirds' is a popular and mostly utilized composition rule which recommend four positions (power points) in the frame to place the salient objects. All these four power points are found in top *baserules* for both the datasets. Also, we observed that both the set with high quality images share most of the *eigenrules* and *baserules*. Moreover, similar *eigenrules* and *baserules* are observed for all the locations in our dataset. Based on this observation we can infer that various photographic compositions can be expressed as combinations of some basic rules.

Location	Dataset Size	Composition		Exposure		Aperture		Shutter Speed	
		Accuracy	Precision	R2 Score	MSE	R2 Score	MSE	R2 Score	MSE
Merlion Park	3385	0.74	0.71	0.76	0.062	0.42	0.036	0.45	0.194
Esplanade	1837	0.71	0.80	0.70	0.171	0.20	0.021	0.53	0.085
Float at Marina Bay	3862	0.71	0.87	0.65	0.047	0.33	0.038	0.59	0.004
Eiffel Tower	17093	0.72	0.73	0.70	0.049	0.47	0.047	0.32	0.037
Statue of Liberty	5667	0.72	0.74	0.51	0.028	0.31	0.050	0.66	0.014
India Gate	1498	0.76	0.71	0.64	0.065	0.51	0.039	0.47	0.017
Gateway of India	1536	0.68	0.64	0.45	0.090	0.43	0.033	0.59	0.016
Leaning Tower of Pisa	5133	0.67	0.63	0.70	0.048	0.48	0.011	0.56	0.025
Arc de Triomphe	5500	0.70	0.71	0.63	0.065	0.34	0.036	0.39	0.041
Cologne Cathedral	6056	0.69	0.63	0.58	0.092	0.41	0.018	0.41	0.018
St. Peter's Basilica	4964	0.72	0.76	0.54	0.105	0.36	0.030	0.32	0.044

Table 1: **Results for Composition and Camera Parameter Learning**

Parameter Learning.

We employ ϵ-Support Vector Regression (ϵ-SVR) with RBF kernel for training separate models for the three camera parameters. Images with aesthetic score >0.6 are used for learning. Table 1 shows mean squared error and R^2 score (coefficient of determination) for the trained model for various locations with ten fold cross validation. It can be observed that the results for exposure learning is better as compared to aperture and shutter speed learning. This is because various combination of aperture, ISO and shutter speed can produce similar exposure and thus can lead to similar image quality. However, getting exposure correct is more important than other parameters as the right amount of light entering the camera lens is the major factor affecting image quality.

Image	Actual Values/Predicted Values			
	Exposure	Aperture	Shutter Speed	ISO
a	11.96/12.37	4.0/5.05	0.0050/0.0026	80/180
b	12.26/11.75	2.8/5.70	0.0020/0.0063	80/147
c	12.26/12.43	2.8/4.06	0.0020/0.0016	80/176
d	12.26/13.0	2.8/5.18	0.0020/0.0016	80/196
e	9.61/13.44	2.8/5.99	0.0125/0.0023	80/134

(a) 0.64 (b) 0.76 (c) 0.80 (d) 0.84 (e) 0.81

Figure 3: **Sample images from 'Merlion Park' location along with predicted aesthetic scores and camera parameters**

Sample images from '*Merlion Park*' location are shown in figure 3 with position recommendation (red region) and corresponding actual/predicted camera parameters. Figure 3b and 3c shows similar views with and without a person standing in the foreground. As we can see from the predicted value of aperture the image with face requires larger aperture value as compared to the image without face.

4. CONCLUSION AND FUTURE WORK

We have presented a context based photography learning method which utilizes crowd-sourced images and associated social media cues. The proposed method for learning photographic composition and camera parameters (exposure, aperture and shutter speed) takes into account the relevant context information. We also presented the idea of photographic composition basis, *eigenrules* and *baserules* to substantiate the proposed composition learning. The preliminary experiments support the effectiveness of our approach. The proposed method can be extended to provide camera motion suggestions (pan/tilt/zoom) to the user and will be focus of our future work. Also, the idea of *eigenrules* and *baserules* can be further exploited to better understand the photographic composition. In future we also plan to pursue a user study to evaluate the performance of our system.

Acknowledgment

This research was carried out at the SeSaMe Centre. It is supported by the Singapore NRF under its IRC@SG Funding Initiative and administered by the IDMPO.

References

[1] R. Achanta, A. Shaji, K. Smith, A. Lucchi, P. Fua, and S. Susstrunk. SLIC Superpixels Compared to State-of-the-art Superpixel Methods. *TPAMI*, 34(11):2274 – 2282, 2012.
[2] R. Achanta and S. Susstrunk. Saliency Detection using Maximum Symmetric Surround. (ICIP), Hong Kong., 2010.
[3] S. Banerjee and B. Evans. In-camera automation of photographic composition rules. *IEEE TIP*, 16(7):1807–1820, 2007.
[4] W. Bares. A photographic composition assistant for intelligent virtual 3d camera systems. In *Smart Graphics*, pages 172–183. Springer Berlin Heidelberg, 2006.
[5] H. Bay, A. Ess, T. Tuytelaars, and L. V. Gool. Speeded-up robust features (surf). *J CVIU*, 110(3):346 – 359, 2008.
[6] D. Butterfield, C. Fake, C. Henderson-Begg, and S. Mourachov. Interestingness ranking of media objects, Oct. 26 2006. US Patent App. 11/350,981.
[7] C.-C. Chang and C.-J. Lin. LIBSVM: A library for support vector machines. *ACM TIST*, 2:27:1–27:27, 2011.
[8] N. Dalal and B. Triggs. Histograms of oriented gradients for human detection. In *CVPR 2005*, pages 886–893 vol. 1, 2005.
[9] M. Freeman. *The Photographer's Eye: Composition and Design for Better Digital Photos.* Focal Press, May 2007.
[10] R. E. Jacobson. *The Manual of Photography: Photographic and Digital Imaging.* Focal Press, 2000.
[11] S. Kelby. *The digital photography book.* Peachpit Press, [Berkeley, CA], 2006.
[12] D. D. Lee and H. S. Seung. Learning the parts of objects by non-negative matrix factorization. *Nature*, 401:788–791, 1999.
[13] K.-Y. Lo, K.-H. Liu, and C.-S. Chen. Intelligent photographing interface with on-device aesthetic quality assessment. In *ACCV 2012*, volume 7729, pages 533–544. Springer Berlin Heidelberg.
[14] C. Lujun, Y. Hongxun, S. Xiaoshuai, and Z. Hongming. Real-time viewfinder composition assessment and recommendation to mobile photographing. In *PCM 2012*, pages 707–714. Springer Berlin Heidelberg, 2012.
[15] H. Mitarai, Y. Itamiya, and A. Yoshitaka. Interactive photographic shooting assistance based on composition and saliency. In *ICCSA 2013*, volume 7975, pages 348–363. Springer Berlin Heidelberg.
[16] B. Ni, M. Xu, B. Cheng, M. Wang, S. Yan, and Q. Tian. Learning to photograph: A compositional perspective. *IEEE Transactions on Multimedia*, 15(5):1138–1151, Aug. 2013.
[17] J. Park, J.-Y. Lee, Y.-W. Tai, and I. S. Kweon. Modeling photo composition and its application to photo re-arrangement. In *ICIP*, pages 2741–2744, 2012.
[18] H.-H. Su, T.-W. Chen, C.-C. Kao, W. Hsu, and S.-Y. Chien. Preference-aware view recommendation system for scenic photos based on bag-of-aesthetics-preserving features. *IEEE Transactions on Multimedia*, 14(3):833–843, 2012.
[19] M. Turk and A. Pentland. Face recognition using eigenfaces. In *CVPR '91*, pages 586–591, 1991.
[20] P. Wang, W. Zhang, J. Li, and Y. Zhang. Online photography assistance by exploring geo-referenced photos on MID / UMPC. In *IEEE 10th Workshop on MSP*, pages 6–10, 2008.
[21] P. Xu, H. Yao, R. Ji, X.-M. Liu, and X. Sun. Where should i stand? learning based human position recommendation for mobile photographing. *Multimedia Tools and Applications*, 69(1):3–29, 2014.
[22] W. Yin, T. Mei, C. W. Chen, and S. Li. Socialized mobile photography: Learning to photograph with social context via mobile devices. *IEEE Transactions on Multimedia*, (1):184–200, 2014.

Virtual Portraitist: Aesthetic Evaluation of Selfies Based on Angle

Mei-Chen Yeh and Hsiao-Wei Lin
Department of Computer Science and Information Engineering
National Taiwan Normal University, Taipei, Taiwan
myeh@csie.ntnu.edu.tw, allison1125@hotmail.com

ABSTRACT
This work addresses the Huawei Grand Challenge that seeks solutions of quality improvement and functionality extension in computational photography. We propose *virtual portraitist*—a new method that helps users take good selfies in angle. Dissimilar to current solutions that mostly use a post-processing step to fix a photograph, the proposed method enables a novel function of recommending a good look *before* the photo is captured. This is achieved by using an automatic approach for estimating the aesthetic quality score of a selfie based on angle. In particular, a set of distinctive patterns discovered from a collection of online profile pictures are combined with head pose and camera orientation to rate the quality of a selfie. Experiments validate the effectiveness of the approach.

Categories and Subject Descriptors
I.4.9 [**Image Processing and Computer Vision**]: Applications.

General Terms
Algorithms, Experimentation.

Keywords
Computational photography, self-portrait, image quality, data mining.

1. INTRODUCTION
With developments in handsets equipped with enhanced computational power and expanded communication capabilities, current mobile devices are capable of taking photographs and transferring images/videos to the Internet. Alternatively, research progress on machine learning has enabled new technologies in processing multimedia data. The ACM Multimedia 2014 Huawei Grand Challenge calls for solutions that can be used to improve the capturing quality of a photograph (or a video) and extend the range of functionalities supported by current consumer cameras and mobile phones.

This paper addresses the aesthetic quality assessment problem of photographs. Among many themes/subjects of interest, we particularly focus on self-portrait photographs, also referred to as selfies. Selfies have been becoming popular because social media websites have helped popularize the phenomenon whereby people can easily use a smartphone to take and share their self-portrait photographs. In November 2013, the Oxford Dictionaries announced the word "selfie" as their international word of the year 2013 [8]. However, taking good selfies is not always a trivial task for general users. For example, it remains unclear how does one take a good selfie and what qualities may make for an unsuccessful one?

Figure 1. The concept of "virtual portraitist." A camera is not limited to displaying frames on screen when it is activated. It guides users to take an attractive self-portrait photograph. Image source.

Figure 2. An example outcome of the proposed approach. The red bar below each face indicates the aesthetic score based on angle, estimated by detecting the distinctive patterns (i.e. triangles) discovered from a collection of online profile pictures. Image source.

MM'14, November 3–7, 2014, Orlando, Florida, USA.

http://dx.doi.org/10.1145/2647868.2656401

Numerous mobile apps such as CreamCam [9] and YouCam Perfect [10] have been launched to enhance the aesthetic quality of selfies; however, those tools use a post-processing procedure to fix a photograph (e.g. complexion enhancement and blemish removal). Certain flaws are unfortunately not easy to adjust by using a post-processing step. For example, angle is one of the important factors in taking a selfie. Adjusting the subject's pose after taking the photograph would be difficult.

We present a fully automatic approach for estimating the aesthetic quality of a selfie based on angle. The approach is readily implemented in a smartphone, providing a novel function of recommending a good look *before* the photo is captured. An example outcome of the approach is shown in Fig. 2. Good selfie photographs may have common patterns because several guidelines can be used to take good one. Therefore, we collected images from "The Beauty of Facebook" [11], named the Beauty dataset, from which we discovered frequent and distinct patterns (see Fig. 6). Each colored triangle represents a good pattern detected on the image. The red bar below each face indicates the estimated aesthetic score ranging from 0 to 10.

In the remainder of this paper, we describe in detail the proposed solution, including the discovery of distinctive patterns from online profile pictures, head pose and camera orientation estimation, and score computation for evaluating the aesthetic quality of a selfie based on angle. We finally present experiments and conclude the paper with a short discussion.

2. THE PROPOSED SOLUTION

Given a selfie, the proposed approach aims to estimate an aesthetic score of the selfie from device orientation and image content. Among many factors such as facial expression and lighting condition that may affect the quality of a selfie, we focus on angle, in which the variations may be caused by the way a smartphone is positioned and orientation a subject turns his (or her) face to the camera. The aesthetic evaluation is performed on a selfie image by considering the following factors: 1) the occurrence of good patterns mined from a collection of profile pictures; 2) head pose estimation, and 3) camera orientation.

2.1 Distinctive Pattern Discovery

2.1.1 Pattern Formation

This work describes a pattern by using a triangle that connects three facial landmarks on a face. A simplified version of the method [7] is used to detect eleven facial fiducial points, as shown in Fig. 3. A triangle is formed by connecting three facial points, creating a set of 165 triangles. Each angle in a triangle is quantized into seven bins. The quantization associated with a particular triangle and angle is performed by using a uniform scalar quantizer [6], in which the decision boundaries are determined by analyzing the angle distribution of face images in the Labeled Faces in the Wild (LFW) dataset [4]. We observe that the angles follow a normal distribution. Therefore, we use the mean and standard deviation of the distribution to determine the decision boundaries. An example is shown in Fig. 4. As a result, a triangle is indexed by one of the 343 (7^3) possible combinations.

2.1.2 Pattern Mining

Next, frequent and distinctive patterns are discovered as follows. First, we collect a set of profile pictures from the Beauty dataset, from which a transaction database D is built. Each triangle is considered as an item; therefore, a transaction (i.e. a profile picture) is a set of 165 items (i.e. triangles). An itemset A is called *frequent* in D if the support of A is larger than or equal to a threshold. Since frequent itemsets are subject to the monotonicity property, the APriori algorithm [1] can be used to efficiently find the frequent itemsets.

In order to obtain frequent patterns with a sufficiently large support value, we estimate the head pose of each face image (detailed in the next subsection) upon which the affinity propagation clustering algorithm (AP) [2] is applied on images of the Beauty dataset to form face clusters. Figure 5 illustrates the clustering results based on head pose. Next, the frequent itemsets are discovered from each cluster, and the union of all discovered frequent itemsets creates a collection of triangles, frequently occurring on face images of the Beauty dataset.

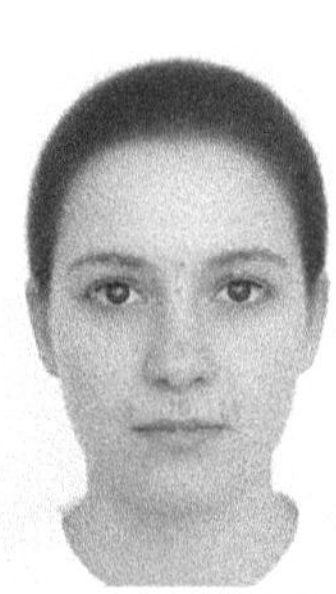

Figure 3. Patterns are computed from 11 facial fiducial points, which are subsequently used to rate a selfie.

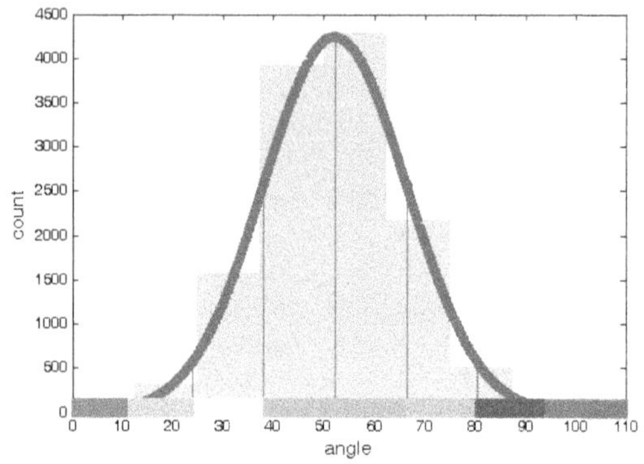

Figure 4. Quantization of an angle based on its distribution computed from the LFW dataset [4].

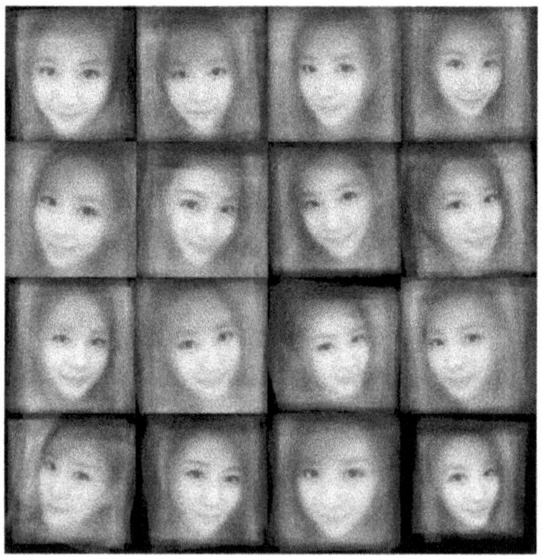

Figure 5. Clustering results of the Beauty of Facebook based on head pose. Each face is an average face of the images in the same cluster.

Figure 6. Discriminant patterns discovered from the "Beauty of Facebook" [11] and "Faces in the Wild" [4] datasets.

The discovered frequent patterns may not necessarily be distinctive, because we observe that a few discovered patterns also occur frequently in the LFW dataset. However, those patterns are not useful for distinguishing good selfies from the others. Therefore, we also discover the frequent itemsets in the LFW images. Let P_B and P_R be the frequent pattern sets mined from the Beauty and LFW datasets, respectively. The final pattern set is P_B–P_R. Each pattern is weighted by its occurrence ratio in the Beauty dataset. Figure 6 shows the patterns with the top 16 weight values.

To understand the discriminative capability of the triangle patterns, we build a beauty detector by thresholding the number of detected patterns on a face. Figure 7 shows the ROC curve for the detector on the Beauty+LFW test set. Using the triangle patterns alone, we obtain a good detection accuracy rate (over 80%) with a low false positive rate (less than 20%).

2.2 Head Pose Estimation

Head pose estimation is the process of inferring the orientation of a person's head relative to the view of a camera [5]. Under the assumption that a human head can be modeled as a disembodied rigid object, it is limited to three degrees of freedom in pose, characterized by *pitch*, *roll*, and *yaw* angles. In this work, we apply a geometric method [3] to estimate head pose orientations from the relative configuration of facial landmarks. The reason of using a geometric method is threefold. First, the geometric method is fast and simple. Second, the approach operates on just a few facial fiducial points, which are also used for computing the pattern described in the previous subsection. Third, the approach directly exploits properties that are known to influence human head pose estimation, delivering a decent estimate of head pose in most cases.

The approach uses five facial fiducial points, including the inner and outer corners of each eye, and the tip of the nose. By assuming that the four eye points are on the same plane, yaw can be determined from the observable difference in size between the left and right eye. Roll can be computed simply from the angle of this line from the horizon. Finally, pitch is determined by comparing the distance between the nose tip and the eye-line to an anthropometric model. In summary, a selfie photograph is described by a three-dimensional angle vector, indicating the head pose of the person being captured.

2.3 Aesthetic Evaluation

The aesthetic evaluation of a selfie image I is performed by combining the following criteria—the occurrence of discovered patterns $f_b(I)$, estimate of head pose $f_p(I)$, and orientation of camera f_c:

$$f(I) = f_b(I) \times f_p(I) \times f_c. \quad (1)$$

The score function $f_b(I)$ returns the weighted sum of discovered patterns detected on I. Consequently, we infer the orientation of a person's head relative to the view of camera and derive an angle vector (i.e. pitch, roll, and yaw). The angle vector is then compared to those extracted from the Beauty dataset. The score function $f_p(I)$ computed as:

$$f_p(I) = \exp\left(-\frac{1}{A} d(I, \mathcal{B})\right), \quad (2)$$

where $d(I, \mathcal{B})$ is the average Mahalanobis distance of the angle vector to its top 10 neighbors in the Beauty dataset, and A is a scaling parameter. Finally, we access the gyroscope and retrieve the pitch, roll and yaw angles of smartphone (if available). Because the roll angle is mostly stable in selfie photographs, we use only the pitch and yaw angles to compute f_c. Observing that selfies are usually captured with a pitch angle ranging from -130 to -50 and a yaw angle ranging from -180 to -90, -20 to 70, or 120-180, the f_c value is set 1 if the angle falls into those specified areas, and is set less than 1 (to reduce the overall score) otherwise.

3. EXPERIMENTS

3.1 Setup

Because rating a selfie is subjective, we conducted a user study to evaluate the performance of the proposed approach. We used FaceGen [12] to create ten simulated selfies, as shown in Fig. 8. Real selfie photographs were not used because collecting a set of selfie photographs that only differ in angle would be rather difficult. Since we attempt to understand the relationship between angle and perceived quality of a selfie photograph, other factors that may change how a selfie is rated should be eliminated as much as possible.

Twenty-five college students (both male and female) were invited to participate in the experiment. The simulated selfie images were shown to the participants and they were requested to rank the images from their most (1) to less (10) desirable images. The

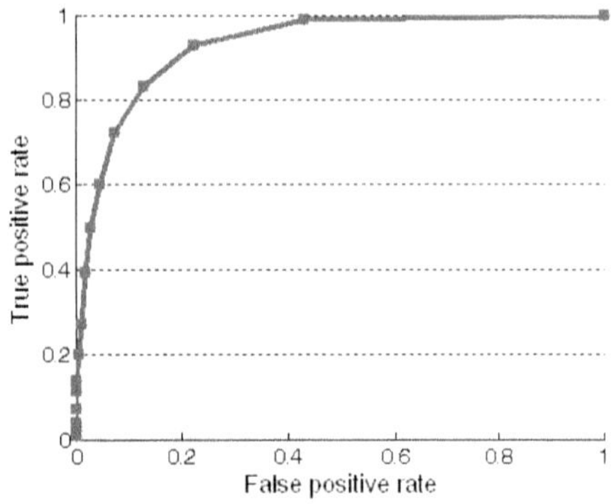

Figure 7. ROC curve for the beauty detector on the Beauty+LFW test set.

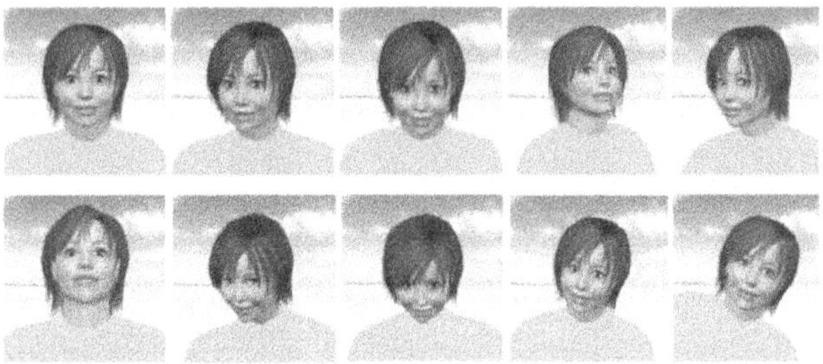

Figure 8. Ten simulated selfies were used for evaluating the performance of the proposed approach.

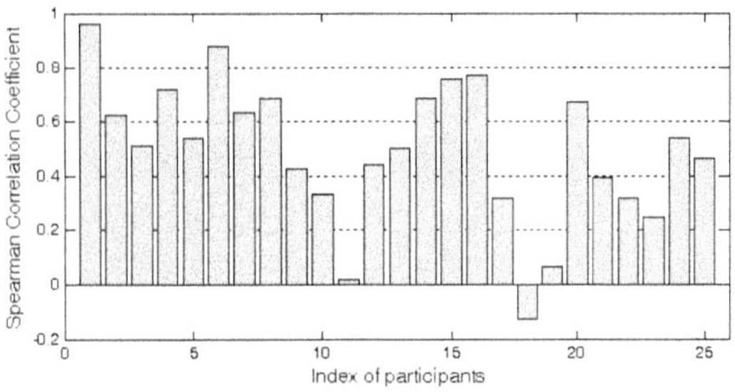

Figure 9. Spearman correlation coefficients of the ranked results between the automatic approach and 25 participants.

Spearman's rho correlation coefficient was used to quantify the similarity between two ranked lists.

Since the camera orientation f_c is not available in creating the simulated selfie images, the aesthetic score described in Equation (1) was computed by using only the occurrence of discovered patterns $f_b(I)$ and estimate of head pose $f_p(I)$.

3.2 Results

We observed that the participants' opinions may vary regarding how the selfies should be ranked. We computed the correlation of the paired user rankings, and the correlation coefficient values ranged from -0.6 to 1, indicating that most of the rankings are moderately correlated, but a few participants held very different opinions. The result of automatic ranking is shown in Fig. 9. Each bar represents the correlation coefficient of two ranked lists returned by the automatic approach and a particular participant. The ranked list derived by the automatic approach is moderately or highly correlated to a majority of the rankings (17 among 25) collected from the participants.

A problem with the correlation analysis is that the rank position of an item has no effect on the final similarity score. In the case of ranking selfies, the top ranked images are more important than those with a lower rank. Another usage of the proposed approach is to select a few good selfies from a range of photos. Therefore, we computed the percent of the participants of choosing top k ranked images if two selections (i.e. user and automatic selection) overlap. The selfies of great interest (i.e. among the top 3 of the ranked list) in 96% of the participants were successfully identified by using the proposed approach.

4. CONCLUSION

This paper presents a new approach for evaluating the aesthetic quality of a selfie based on angle. In particular, a set of frequent and distinct patterns are automatically discovered from profile pictures and a benchmark face dataset based upon which a new selfie photograph is rated. The proposed approach can be used to develop "virtual portraitist," which is readily implemented in current smartphones, enabling novel functionalities for guiding users to take appealing selfie photographs.

5. ACKNOWLEDGMENTS

This work was supported in part by Ministry of Science and Technology, Taiwan, under Grant No. NSC 102-2221-E-003-026.

6. REFERENCES

[1] R. Agrawal, T. Imielinski, and A. N. Swami, "Mining association rules between sets of items in large databases," *Proc. of ACM Int'l Conf. SIGMOD*, 1993.

[2] B. J. Frey and D. Dueck, "Clustering by passing messages between data points," *Science*, pp. 972–976, 2007.

[3] T. Horprasert, Y. Yacoob and L. Davis, "Computing 3-D head orientation from a monocular image sequence," *Proc. of IEEE Int'l Conf. Automatic Face and Gesture Recognition*, 1996.

[4] G. B. Huang, M. Ramesh, T. Berg and E. Learned-Miller, "Labeled faces in the wild: a database for studying face recognition in unconstrained environments," University of Massachusetts, Amherst, Technical Report, 2007.

[5] E. Murphy-Chutorian and M. M. Trivedi, "Head pose estimation in computer vision: a survey," *IEEE Trans. Pattern Analysis and Machine Intelligence*, 31(4): 607-626, 2009.

[6] K. Sayood, *Introduction to Data Compression, 4th Edition*. Morgan Kaufmann, 2012.

[7] X. Xiong and F. De la Torre, "Supervised descent method and its application to face alignment," *Proc. of IEEE Int'l Conf. Computer Vision and Pattern Recognition*, 2013.

[8] Oxford Dictionaries Word of the Year 2013. http://blog.oxforddictionaries.com/press-releases/oxford-dictionaries-word-of-the-year-2013

[9] CreamCam. http://creamcamapp.com/

[10] YouCam Perfect. http://www.cyberlink.com/stat/product/CyberLink_app/YouCam_Perfect/enu/YouCam_Perfect.jsp

[11] The Beauty of Facebook. http://beauty.zones.gamebase.com.tw/wall

[12] FaceGen. http://www.facegen.com/

Cross Modal Deep Model and Gaussian Process Based Model for MSR-Bing Challenge*

Jian Wang, Cuicui Kang, Yonghao He, Shiming Xiang, Chunhong Pan
Institute of Automation, Chinese Academy of Sciences, Beijing 100190, China
{jian.wang, cckang, yhhe, smxiang, chpan}@nlpr.ia.ac.cn

ABSTRACT

In the MSR-Bing Image Retrieval Challenge, the contestants are required to design a system that can score the query-image pairs based on the relevance between queries and images. To address this problem, we propose a regression based cross modal deep learning model and a Gaussian Process scoring model. The regression based cross modal deep learning model takes the image features and query features as inputs respectively and outputs the relevance scores directly. The Gaussian Process scoring model regards the challenge as a ranking problem and utilizes the click (or pseudo click) information from both the training set and the development set to predict the relevance scores. The proposed models are used in different situations: matched and miss-matched queries. Experiments on the development set show the effectiveness of the proposed models.

Categories and Subject Descriptors

H.3.3 [**Information Storage and Retrieval**]: Information Search and Retrieval—*Retrieval models*

Keywords

Image Retrieval; Deep Network; Gaussian Process; Convolutional Neural Network; Clickthrough Data

1. INTRODUCTION

The arrival of the big data era encourages the researchers to develop more creative methods so as to facilitate the real-word applications. Image retrieval is one of the hot topics in the field of multimedia. This challenge focuses on the task of image retrieval. The traditional image retrieval [12] is roughly divided into two categories: keyword based and content based. The keyword based image retrieval takes advantages of extra data such as captions, tags and descriptions to the images. Differently, the content based image retrieval takes the images as the input queries and performs the retrieval via measuring the visual similarities between the images. However, the challenge puts forward a new scenario: directly scoring the query-image pairs without any extra information but the clickthrough data [6]. In the challenge, we are given a training set and a development set. The training set consists of triads: ⟨query, image, click count⟩, and the development set is used to validate the performance of the system.

In the previous challenge, some methods [16, 15, 3, 13, 11] are proposed. In general, these methods concentrate on several points: image content based model, text based model and some other models. In the image content based model [16, 3, 11], the basic idea is that the visually similar images will have similar queries. The model first retrieves images and their associated queries by computing the visual similarities between the images, and then computes the textual similarities between the queries. The final relevance scores are based on the textual similarities. However, the model is difficult to retrieve reliable visually similar images in the big image collection with a crowd of noisy samples. The text based model [16, 15, 3, 13] can be said as an inverse process of the image content based model: 1) retrieve semantically similar queries and their related images; 2) compute the visual similarities between the images. Then the scores are given by the visual similarities.

Beyond these algorithms, in [16] a modified PageRank model is proposed, which achieved the first place in the last challenge. The model follows the assumption that the majority images under the same query are relevant to the query. We found that this assumption holds in the development set. The higher similarities to the other images, the higher relevance score the image will get. However, this method abandons the semantics of queries. The name and face correspondences are also studied in [16]. For those names appearing in the training set, the authors train identity models using corresponding faces. Additionally, some names are missing in the training set, so another strategy is used in [16]: the final score is decided by the number of names and faces detected in the query and the image. When the numbers are identical, the score will be higher than those in other cases.

In this paper, we propose two models to deal with the challenge: the regression based cross modal deep learning model and the Gaussian Process scoring model. The image features and the query features are fed into the regression based cross modal deep learning model separately, and then

*This work was supported in part by the National Basic Research Program of China under Grant 2012CB316304, and the National Natural Science Foundation of China under Grants 61272331, 61203277, 61331018, and 91338202.

MM'14, November 3–7, 2014, Orlando, Florida, USA.
Copyright 2014 ACM 978-1-4503-3063-3/14/11 ...$15.00.
http://dx.doi.org/10.1145/2647868.2656400.

the deep network outputs the relevance scores directly, providing an end-to-end scoring fashion. Although the previous works [14, 10] focus on the multi-modal deep learning, their deep networks are learned in the form of generative models and are not adaptive in this case. The details of the deep network will be described in Section 2. We use this model only when the incoming query exists (or has highly semantical one) in the training set. In [7], the Gaussian Process has been used to rank the images of the same query by requiring that all the images must have click counts. The proposed Gaussian Process scoring model makes a modification based on the original one in [7]. If the incoming query has identical or highly semantical query in the training set, the images of the incoming query as well as the images of the identical query in the training set are all used in Gaussian Process scoring model. Since those images of the incoming query have no click counts (they are what we want to predict), their click counts are set to the same value. As for the queries that are not matched in the training set, only the images of the incoming query are used, and the pseudo click counts of these images are generated based on an assumption: the images highly related to the query are in the same cluster, whereas the other images scatter in the feature space. Accordingly, we use meanshift [1] to find the center of the cluster and assign higher click counts to those images near the center and lower click counts to those far away from the center. Notice that the Gaussian Process scoring model can handle all the incoming queries (matched and miss-matched), but the semantics of miss-matched queries are neglected. The experiments are conducted on the development set, and the results show the effectiveness of our models.

2. THE PROPOSED MODELS

In this section, the proposed models are introduced in detail. In subsection 2.1, there is a brief description of image feature extraction. Then, subsection 2.2 depicts the query match strategy. The regression based cross modal deep learning model and the Gaussian Process scoring model are described in subsection 2.3 and subsection 2.4, respectively.

2.1 CNN Feature for Images

The deep neural network has received popular attentions because it shows the remarkable capacity of feature learning in recent years. The convolutional neural network (CNN) [8] is one of the widely used architectures for image feature extraction. In this challenge, we only use deep CNN features for all images. The source code is available at the authors' website [2]. The network contains five convolution layers and three fully-connected layers, which has been trained on the ILSVRC-2012 database of 1000 categories. The outputs of the *6th* layer are used as the image features, which is 4096-dimensional.

2.2 Query Matching Strategy

As mentioned in [5], the original queries suffer some problems: meaningless words, such as "picture" and "image"; misspelling, such as "girl" vs "gril"; near-duplicate queries, such as "cat", "cats" and "cat pictures". To deal with these problems, we first remove meaningless words, then get the stems of each query by using the OpenNLP tool[1]. In this way,

[1]https://opennlp.apache.org/index.html

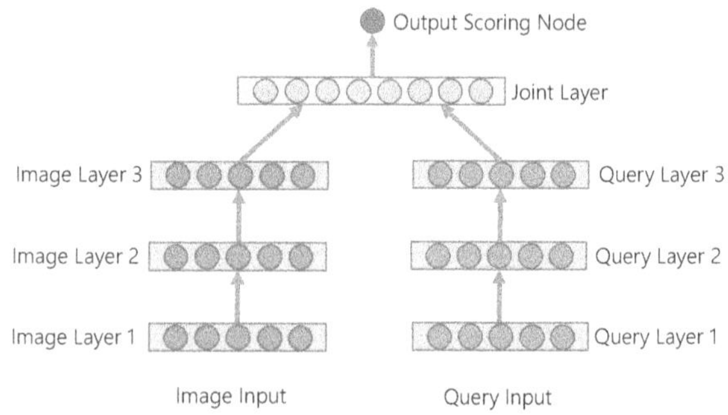

Figure 1: Structure of the proposed regression based cross modal deep learning model.

some triads are merged to a single triad, reducing 23094592 triads to 9195452 triads in the training set.

For each unigram in the training set, we collect all the queries that contain the unigram. In this way, it is easy to get a query list and the frequency of unigram. The importance of each unigram is measured by its frequency reciprocal. The amount of information contained in a query is defined as the sum of the importance of its unigrams. For an incoming query, first its amount of information is calculated. Then we start to search the similar queries in the query list of unigrams. In order to speed up this process, the search is from the list of unigram with the highest importance to the lowest. The ratio of the amount of information is used to measure the similarity between queries. We set a large threshold, say 0.9, to determine whether the two queries are matched or not. By using the strategy, in the development set, there are 438 queries that are matched and the rest are not matched.

2.3 Regression based Cross Modal Deep Learning Model

The architecture of the proposed deep model is presented in Fig. 1. For each modal, there is an input layer, followed by two hidden layers. The joint layer merges the information from two modals and connects to the scoring node. Since the features of queries are difficult to extract, we represent query features in the image feature space by using linear weighting via clickthrough data. In the training set, assume that the image set is $\mathcal{I} = \{\mathbf{x}_i\}_{i=1}^N$, N is the number of images, and the query set is $\mathcal{Q} = \{q_i\}_{i=1}^M$, M is the number of queries. For each query q_i, its associated image set is $\mathcal{I}_i = \{\mathbf{x}_{i,j}\}_{j=1}^{n_i}$ and the click count set is $\mathcal{C}_i = \{c_{i,j}\}_{j=1}^{n_i}$, where n_i is the number of images of query q_i. Thus, the feature of query q_i can be formulated as:

$$\mathbf{f}_i = \sum\nolimits_{j=1}^{n_i} \hat{c}_{i,j}\mathbf{x}_{i,j}, \tag{1}$$

where $\hat{c}_{i,j} = c_{i,j} / \sum_{j=1}^{n_i} c_{i,j}$ is the normalized count. In this way, each query in the training set is allocated to a feature point in the image feature space. In our view, such kind of representations of the queries can obtain a good property that image features around a query point are semantically related to the query.

All the image and query features are mean-centered and normalized to unit length. The input layers are real-valued and the other layers are binary. The output scoring node rates the relevance via the sigmoid activation. The click

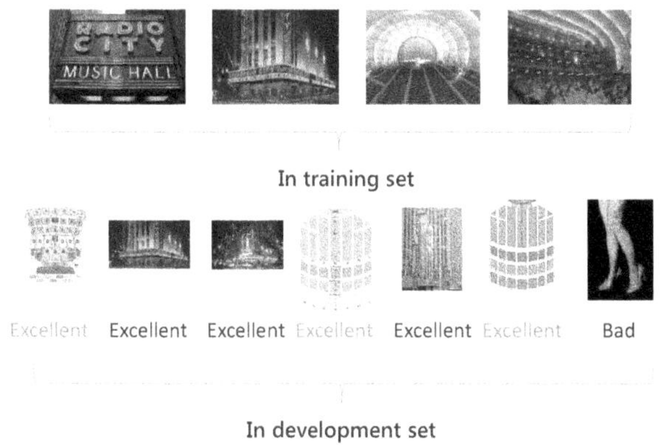

Figure 2: Images of query "radio city music hall" in both training set and development set. We can see that the images in the training set depict the building itself, but there are three images (labeled with red "Excellent") describing the inside layout of the building.

counts c are scaled into the float points by:

$$\tilde{c} = \frac{2}{1 + exp(-c)} - 1, \quad (2)$$

which are used as the true similarity scores in the deep learning. Evidently, $\tilde{c} \in [0, 1)$. In the training process, the squared error is used for the output scoring node. All the parameters are pre-trained using Contrastive Divergence [4] based on the Restricted Boltzmann Machine (RBM) (Gaussian RBM for the input layers and Binary RBM for the other layers). The backpropagation algorithm is used to fine-tune the parameters. The numbers of nodes in each layers are set as follows: image input layer and query input layer are 4096, 1000 nodes are for the image layers 2-3 and query layers 2-3, and the joint layer contains 2000 nodes.

It should be pointed out that the queries in the training set are self matched, hence the learned deep model is only suitable for the matched queries. As a result, there are only 438 queries in the development set that can be processed by the deep model. If all the queries can be semantically represented by feature vectors through an image-independent method[2], the deep learning model may be better learned and can tackle all the queries.

2.4 Gaussian Process Scoring Model

The key assumption in Gaussian Process scoring model is that the more click counts an image received, the more relevant it will be to its query. The basic form of Gaussian Process based ranking is formulated as follows [7]:

$$y(\mathbf{x}) = \mathbf{K}(\mathbf{x}, \mathbf{X}_c)[\mathbf{K}(\mathbf{X}_c, \mathbf{X}_c) + \sigma^2\mathbf{I}]^{-1}\mathbf{y}_c, \quad (3)$$

where $y(\mathbf{x})$ is the relevance prediction of image $\mathbf{x}$, $\mathbf{K}$ is a kernel function (here Gaussian kernel is adopted), $\mathbf{X}_c$ is a matrix collecting all clicked image feature vectors, and $\mathbf{y}_c$ is the normalized click counts of all images. In Gaussian Process, the clicked images of the queries are preconditions. For those matched queries, they have clicked images in the training set. However, we found that the clicked images are very limited for these queries and cannot fully represent the semantics of the queries, such as the example in Fig. 2. Thus, Gaussian Process with the training images dose not perform well. Considering this, we regard the challenge as a ranking problem. Therefore, the images in the development set under the test query can be also involved into Gaussian Process by assigning them the same pseudo click count ($\frac{1}{5}$ of the max count in those of training images). The formulation in (3) is rewritten as:

$$y(\mathbf{x}) = \mathbf{K}\left(\mathbf{x}, [\mathbf{X}_c^{tr}; \mathbf{X}^{dev}]\right) \cdot \left[\mathbf{K}\left([\mathbf{X}_c^{tr}; \mathbf{X}^{dev}], [\mathbf{X}_c^{tr}; \mathbf{X}^{dev}]\right) + \sigma^2\mathbf{I}\right]^{-1} [\mathbf{y}_c^{tr}; \mathbf{y}^{dev}],$$

where $\mathbf{X}_c^{tr}$ are feature vectors from training set, $\mathbf{X}^{dev}$ are feature vectors from development set, $\mathbf{y}_c^{tr}$ and $\mathbf{y}^{dev}$ are normalized click counts of images from training set and development set, respectively. Each feature vector in $\mathbf{X}^{dev}$ is assigned to $\mathbf{x}$ to obtain a refined relevance score. We apply this Gaussian Process scoring model to those matched queries (438 queries) in the development set.

As for the queries that are not matched, a pseudo click count generation strategy is employed. In our opinion, the majority of images that are related to the query are in the same cluster with relatively small distances with each other, whereas those unrelated images scatter in feature space. Based on this assumption, we use meanshift [1] to find the center of the cluster and set higher click counts to the images that are near the center. Specifically, a radius threshold is set, when the distances are smaller than the radius, the pseudo click counts are set to 2, otherwise 1. After completing this, we can get the relevance scores using Eqn. (3).

3. EXPERIMENT

The Challenge provides two datasets, a training set for model learning and a development set for evaluation. The training set consists of 1M images with 23M click logs, and the development set contains more than 70K query-image pairs of 1000 unique queries and around 80K images.

As for the evaluation, the Discounted Cumulated Gain at 25 (DCG_{25}) for the same query is used. Then the average of all queries is computed as the result. The DCG_{25} for each query is computed as

$$DCG_{25} = 0.01757 \sum_{i=1}^{25} \frac{2^{rel_i} - 1}{\log_2(i+1)}$$

where the rel_i={Excellent=3,Good=2,Bad=0} is the manually judged relevance for each image with respect to the query, and 0.01757 is a normalizer to make the score for 25 Excellent results 1.

The experimental results on the development set are reported in Table 1. We also compared our method with those methods proposed in the previous challenges, and the results are shown in Table 2. From Table 1, we can observe that the ideal NDCG of matched queries is much higher than that of miss-matched queries, indicating that there are many miss-matched queries having less than 25 images which are "excellent" or "good" related to the queries. The Gaussian Process scoring model achieves the highest NDCG among three models with matched queries, particularly better than the original Gaussian Process model, and it is the only model that can be applied to all queries. Although the regression

[2]As far as we know, there exist some methods for extracting semantic feature vectors for a single word, such as word2vect [9]. However, the queries with short text are difficult to extract semantic features. We have tried some methods, but got unsatisfactory results.

Table 1: Performances of three models, namely regression based cross modal deep learning model, original Gaussian Process and Gaussian Process scoring model. The original and ideal NDCG scores are also presented for each part of development set. "-" means that it is not available.

	Matched Queries (438)	Miss-mathced Queries (562)	All Queries (1000)
Original NDCG	0.603	0.362	0.469
Ideal NDCG	0.800	0.580	0.684
Deep Network	0.660	-	-
Original GP	0.656	-	-
Our GP	0.678	0.433	0.540

Table 2: Comparisons between our method and other proposed methods on the entire development set. We take Gaussian Process scoring model as the final model.

	Our method	MPM [16]	CQRA [15]	EDM [3]	GLP [11]	BA [13]
NDCG	0.540	0.537	0.529	0.503	0.505	0.487

based cross modal deep learning model shows a lower performance than that of Gaussian Process scoring model, it directly bridges two different modalities and promotes the original NDCG from 0.603 to 0.660, making it worthy to be explored further. In Table 2, Gaussian Process scoring model outperforms the other methods.

The final test set of the challenge contains 147346 images and 9449 queries. The feature extraction of CNN costs about 2 hours and 40 minutes on our PC with one intel i7-4770 CPU and one Intel GTX780 GPU. As for the scoring stage, the proposed algorithm just need 43ms to process an image-query pair on average. The performance of the proposed models are listed below:

- Random: 0.3906
- Ideal: 0.5266
- Deep learning model (matched queries) + GP scoring model (miss-matched queries): 0.4877
- GP scoring model: 0.4965

4. CONCLUSIONS

In this work, we propose two models: regression based cross modal deep learning model and Gaussian Process scoring model, to assign relevance scores to the query-image pairs. The regression based cross modal deep learning model takes separated image features and query features as inputs and outputs the relevance scores directly. We represent the query features in the image feature space by using linear weighting via the clickthrough data. This model can only tackle the queries that have highly semantical or identical queries in the training set. The Gaussian Process scoring model regards the challenge as a ranking problem. It generates the relevance scores by using images with click counts in the training set and images with pseudo click counts in the development set, and we adapt it to those miss-matched queries. The experimental results on development set demonstrate the effectiveness of the proposed models.

5. REFERENCES

[1] Y. Cheng. Mean shift, mode seeking, and clustering. *IEEE Transactions on PAMI*, 17(8):790–799, 1995.

[2] J. Donahue, Y. Jia, O. Vinyals, J. Hoffman, N. Zhang, E. Tzeng, and T. Darrell. DeCAF: A deep convolutional activation feature for generic visual recognition. *arXiv preprint arXiv:1310.1531*, 2013. Software available at https://github.com/UCB-ICSI-Vision-Group/decaf-release/wiki.

[3] Q. Fang, H. Xu, R. Wang, S. Qian, T. Wang, J. Sang, and C. Xu. Towards MSR-Bing Challenge: Ensemble of diverse models for image retrieval. In *MSR-Bing IRC 2013 Workshop*, 2013.

[4] G. Hinton. Training products of experts by minimizing contrastive divergence. *Neural Computation*, 14(8):1771–1800, 2002.

[5] X. Hua. Looking into "MSR-Bing Challenge on Image Retrieval". 2013.

[6] X. Hua, L. Yang, J. Wang, J. Wang, M. Ye, K. Wang, Y. Rui, and J. Li. Clickage: Towards bridging semantic and intent gaps via mining click logs of search engines. In *Proceedings of ACM International Conference on Multimedia*, pages 243–252, 2013.

[7] V. Jain and M. Varma. Learning to re-rank: query-dependent image re-ranking using click data. In *Proceedings of International Conference on World Wide Web*, pages 277–286, 2011.

[8] A. Krizhevsky, I. Sutskever, and G. Hinton. Imagenet classification with deep convolutional neural networks. In *Advances in NIPS*, pages 1106–1114, 2012.

[9] T. Mikolov, K. Chen, G. Corrado, and J. Dean. Efficient estimation of word representations in vector space. *arXiv preprint arXiv:1301.3781*, 2013.

[10] J. Ngiam, A. Khosla, M. Kim, J. Nam, H. Lee, and A. Ng. Multimodal deep learning. In *Proceedings of International Conference on Machine Learning*, pages 689–696, 2011.

[11] Y. Pan, T. Yao, H. Li, and C. Ngo. USTC-CityU at MSR-Bing IRC: Image search by graph-based label propagation. In *MSR-Bing IRC 2013 Workshop*, 2013.

[12] Y. Rui, T. Huang, and S. Chang. Image retrieval: Current techniques, promising directions, and open issues. *Journal of Visual Communication and Image Representation*, 10(1):39–62, 1999.

[13] A. Sayko and A. Slesarev. Report on a baseline approach to the 2nd MSR-Bing challenge on image retrieval. In *MSR-Bing IRC 2013 Workshop*, 2013.

[14] N. Srivastava and R. Salakhutdinov. Multimodal learning with deep boltzmann machines. In *Advances in Neural Information Processing Systems*, pages 2222–2230, 2012.

[15] L. Wang, S. Cen, H. Bai, C. Huang, N. Zhao, B. Liu, and Y. Feng. France telecom orange labs a MSR-Bing challenge on image retrieval 2013. In *MSR-Bing IRC 2013 Workshop*, 2013.

[16] C. Wu, K. Chu, Y. Kuo, Y. Chen, W. Lee, and W. Hsu. Search-based relevance association with auxiliary contextual cues. In *MSR-Bing IRC 2013 Workshop*, 2013.

Bag-of-Words Based Deep Neural Network for Image Retrieval

Yalong Bai[1]
ylbai@mtlab.hit.edu.cn

Wei Yu[1]
w.yu@hit.edu.cn

Tianjun Xiao[2]
xiaotianjun@pku.edu.cn

Chang Xu[3]
changxu@nkjl.nankai.edu.cn

Kuiyuan Yang, Wei-Ying Ma[4]
{kuyang, wyma}@microsoft.com

Tiejun Zhao[1]
tjzhao@hit.edu.cn

[1]Harbin Institute of Technology, Harbin, China [2] Peking University, Beijing, China
[3]Nankai University, Tianjin, China [4]Microsoft Research Asia, Beijing, China

ABSTRACT

This work targets image retrieval task hold by MSR-Bing Grand Challenge. Image retrieval is considered as a challenge task because of the gap between low-level image representation and high-level textual query representation. Recently further developed deep neural network sheds light on narrowing the gap by learning high-level image representation from raw pixels. In this paper, we proposed a bag-of-words based deep neural network for image retrieval task, which learns high-level image representation and maps images into bag-of-words space. The DNN model is trained on the large scale clickthrough data, and the relevance between query and image is measured by the cosine similarity of query's bag-of-words representation and image's bag-of-words representation predicted by DNN, the visual similarity of images is computed by high-level image representation extracted via the DNN model too. Finally, PageRank algorithm is used to further improve the ranking list by considering visual similarity of images for each query. The experimental results achieved state-of-the-art performance and verified the effectiveness of our proposed method.

Categories and Subject Descriptors

I.4 [**IMAGE PROCESSING AND COMPUTER VISION**]: Miscellaneous

General Terms

Algorithms; Experimentation

Keywords

Image Retrieval; Deep Neural Network; Click Data

MM'14, November 3–7, 2014, Orlando, Florida, USA.

ACM 978-1-4503-3063-3/14/11 ...$15.00.
http://dx.doi.org/10.1145/2647868.2656402 .

1. INTRODUCTION

According to settings of MSR-Bing Grand Challenge, in this work, we developed a system to assess the relevance between image and query pair for image retrieval. That is, given a pair of query and image, the system could produce a floating-point score that reflects how relevant the images could describe the query. The database of MSR-Bing Grand Challenge contains 11.7 million of queries and 1 million of images which were collected from the user click log of Bing image Search in the EN-US market [4].

Bridging the semantic gap between visual representation and textual representation is the core issue of getting better image retrieval. The traditional solutions compute the relevance between images and textual descriptions based on features extracted from the surrounding text of images or some low-level image representation features (such as SIFT, HOG, and LBP), where the information from the image itself is still far from fully used. With large number of training data, deep neural network has demonstrated its great success in learning high-level image representation from raw pixels. In this task, large scale clickthrough is available as training data, thus we can learn high-level image representations by deep neural networks.

Deep neural network has been used for image retrieval task in [1], which trained a set of classifiers for different queries based on high-level image features learned by a transfer learning DNN architecture. But this kind of solution is hard to scale up when dealing with a huge number of queries considering that training classifier for each query is impractical. In this work, we proposed a new deep neural network architecture which can handle large scale of queries and be directly used for computing the relevance between image and query. Our model aims two main objectives: 1) query-image relevance assessment; 2) high-level visual features based image-image similarity assessment.

For query-image relevance assessment, our DNN maps the image from raw pixels into a bag of words space, the relevance of a query-image pair is computed via their cosine similarity in the bag-of-words space. The high-level visual features of each image can also be extracted by our DNN model, the image-image similarity is computed based on these high-level visual features. Finally, the scores of query-image

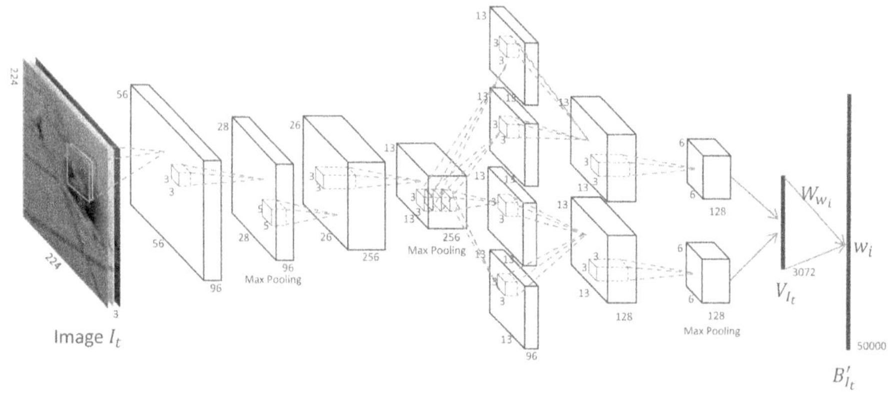

Figure 1: The architecture of bag-of-words based deep neural network.

relevance and image-image similarity are both considered to get final ranking score.

The rest of the paper is structured as follows. In Section 2, we introduce the architecture of Bag-of-Words based DNN and do some analysis on our proposed model. Three different ranking methods are presented on section 3. Section 4 introduces the real experimental verification of our proposed method, Finally, we conclude the paper in section 5.

2. BAG-OF-WORDS BASED DEEP NEURAL NETWORK

Bag-of-words is a simplifying representation widely used in natural language processing and information retrieval task. In this work, we regard each query as a short document built up by several individual words. Consider a query set with m queries $\{q_1, q_2, ..., q_m\}$, there are totally $|W|$ split single words $\{w_1, w_2, ..., w_{|W|}\}$, we firstly compute idf score for each single word as following

$$idf_{w_i} = log\frac{m}{|j : w_i \in q_j|} \tag{1}$$

where $|j : w_i \in q_j|$ is the number of queries that contains w_i. To decrease the computational complexity of our system, only top 50000 words with high frequency are kept as the vocabulary of bag-of-words representation. Given an image I, all of its related queries are merged as one document D_I. D_I can be regarded as the textual description for I. To represents D_I as bag-of-words B_{D_I}, the value of each word is set as the accumulation of corresponding idf value. For example, there is a puppy image clicked under query "small dog", "white dog" and "dog chihuahua", while $idf_{dog} = 0.3$, $idf_{small} = 0.1$, $idf_{white} = 0.05$, $idf_{chihuahua} = 0.9$, the bag-of-words representation of this image should be "dog:0.9; white:0.05; small:0.1; Chihuahua:0.9". The image and related bag-of-words representation vector pairs $<I, B_{D_I}>$ are used as supervised data to train our deep neural network.

2.1 Overall Architecture

As depicted in Fig. 1, the proposed bag-of-words based deep neural network (BoWDNN) contains four convolutional layers and two fully-connected layers, drop out with rate 0.5 is added to the first fully-connected layer for avoiding overfitting [3]. The output of last fully-connected layer is fed to cosine similar loss function to represent the relevance degree between image and query. The first, second and fourth convolutional layers are followed by max-pooling layers. Response-normalization layers follow the first and second convolutional layers. To accelerate the learning process, ReLU[2] non-linearity is applied as activation function in every convolutional layers and first full-connected layer.

As the input size of deep neural network is fixed, we resize each image with small dimension to 256 and crop out the central 256×256 patch. During training, 224×224 patches will be randomly extracted (four corner patches and one center patch for each image) from the 256×256 images. The first convolutional layer filters the $224 \times 224 \times 3$ input RGB image with 96 kernels of size $11 \times 11 \times 3$ with a stride of 4 pixels. The second convolution layer is with 256 kernels of size $5 \times 5 \times 96$. The third convolutional layer has 384 kernels of size $3 \times 3 \times 64$ which are split into four groups, and the fourth convolutional layer has 256 kernels of size $3 \times 3 \times 192$ which are split into two groups. The first full-connected layer has 3072 neurons, and the number of neurons in the last full-connected layer is determined by the vocabulary size of bag-of-words representation. The loss function of BoWDNN based on the cosine similarity between a predicted image's bag-of-words representation and the corresponding queries' bag-of-words representation.

2.2 Training Objective

The intent of our Bag-of-Words based deep neural network is to map images into their corresponding bag-of-words representation vectors. The objective function is to maximize the following average cosine similarly

$$J = \frac{1}{T}\sum_{t=1}^{T} Rel(B'_{I_t}, B_{D_{I_t}}) \tag{2}$$

where T is the amount of images in training data, the bag-of-words relevance of image-query pair $Rel(B'_{I_t}, B_{D_{I_t}})$ is defined as the cosine similarity in the bag-of-words space

$$Rel(B'_{I_t}, B_{D_{I_t}}) = \frac{B'_{I_t} \cdot B_{D_{I_t}}}{\|B'_{I_t}\| \, \|B_{D_{I_t}}\|} \tag{3}$$

where $B_{D_{I_t}}$ is the bag-of-words representation for queries of image I_t, B'_{I_t} is the bag-of-words vector predicted by

BoWDNN as following

$$B'_{I_t} = < r_{I_t,w_1}, r_{I_t,w_2}, ..., r_{I_t,w_n} > \quad (4)$$

where r_{I_t,w_i} indicates the relevance between image I_t and word w_i, given by

$$r_{I_t,w_i} = V_{I_t} \cdot W_{w_i} \quad (5)$$

where V_{I_t} is the high-level image representation features learned by BoWDNN, W_{w_i} is the weights to compute the relevance between V_{I_t} and word w_i as shown in Fig. 1.

For an image I and query q, their relevance is measured via Eq. 3.

2.3 Visual Similarity Measurement

Figure 2: Visual similarity images measured by the learned high-level image feature. The first row shows some query images, the left rows are their visual similarity images ordered by the similarity degree.

The high-level image features learned by BoWDNN are employed to measure the visual similarity. Given an image pair I_a and I_b, feed them into the BoWDNN architecture as Fig. 1 shown, the outputs of first full-connected layer V_{I_a} and V_{I_b} are used as visual features of I_a and I_b respectively. The visual similarity between I_a and I_b is define as:

$$Rel(V_{I_a}, V_{I_b}) = \frac{V_{I_a} \cdot V_{I_b}}{||V_{I_a}|| \, ||V_{I_b}||} \quad (6)$$

Fig 2 shows the images which are similar to the query image, all of these images were retrieval from whole training dataset by using the above visual similarity measurement.

3. RANKING METHODS

Our proposed ranking method as illustrated in Fig. 3 which contains two main parts: bag-of-words based query-image relevance assessment and extracting high-level image features for computing image-image visual similarity. The outputs of these two parts will be used as the inputs of our ranking methods.

In this section, we introduce three different approaches for compute the score $s(I, q)$ an image-query pairs (I, q).

1) BoWDNN-R (Bag-of-Words similarity based ranking method). The idea of this method is to measure the image-query relevance based on the similarity between the query bag-of-words representation and image bag-of-words representation learned by BoWDNN. The relevance scores could be formulated as $s(I, q) = Rel(B'_I, B_q)$, where B'_I is the bag-of-words vector computed by BoWDNN, and B_q is the bag-of-words representation of query q.

2) BoWDNN-S (Visual similarity based ranking method). Considering that the given image-query pairs in this MSR-Bing Grand Challenge comes from users' click through, the images relevant to a query are tend to be similar. That is, an image's relevance to a query can be measured by how other candidate images similar to this image. In the other words, the visual similarity (connections) among images deserve the relevance scores. Similar to the modified PageRank model(MPM) in [6] , the relevance scores can be formulated as $s(I, q) = 1/N \sum_{j=1}^{N} sim(I_j, I) = 1/N \sum_{j=1}^{N} Rel(V_{I_j}, V_I)$, where I_j is one of the top-N most similarity images. To avoid the influence of noisy images, only the top-5 most similar images are considered.

3) BoWDNN-J (Joint ranking method). Inspired by the website ranking based on hyperlinks, we use the PageRank[5] to fuse the both bag-of-words similarity scores and visual similarity scores. Firstly, we build a visual similarity matrix P for each query q, let $P(i, j) = sim(I_i, I_j)$, where I_i and I_j is two images related to query q. Then normalize the scale of $P(i, j)$ from [-1,1] to [0,1], and iterate $s(I_i, q) = \alpha \cdot s(I_i, q) + (1-\alpha) \sum_{n=1}^{N} s(I_n, q) \cdot s(I_i, I_m)$ for several times, where α is a parameter in [0,1), I_m is one of the N images which are most similar to I_i, $s(I_i, q)$ is initialized to the image-query relevance score of BoWDNN-R. Finally, rank each image I_i according its ranking score $s(I_i, q)$.

4. EXPERIMENT SETUP AND RESULTS

We used the entire development set including 1000 queries and the final test set to evaluate our proposed Bag-of-words based deep neural network on the image retrieval task. The evaluation metric is Discounted Cumulated Gain (DCG). To compute DCG, for each query, we sort the images based on the floating point scores produced by BoWDNN-R, BoWDNN-S and BoWDNN-J. DCG for each query is calculated as

$$DCG_{25} = 0.01757 \sum_{i=1}^{25} \frac{2^{rel_i - 1}}{log_2(i+1)} \quad (7)$$

where $rel_i = Excellent = 3, Good = 2, Bad = 0$ is the human judged relevance for each image with respect to the query, and 0.01757 is a normalizer so that the perfect ranking has a NDCG value of 1. The final result is averaged over all queries in the test set.

Our BoWDNN was trained on single NVIDIA Tesla K20Xm 6GB GPU, limited by GPU memory size, we only used top-50000 words with high frequency as the vocabulary of bag-of-words representation.

Table 4 summarizes the DCG@25 of different approaches conducted on the DEV and TEST dataset. Both MPM (the winner of last year in MSR-Bing Grand Challenge) in [6] and BoWDNN-S are considering only top-5 similar images and compute relevance scores by the modified PageRank model, but the MPM in [6] measures image similarity based on state-of-the-art bag-of-visual-words features, while BoWDNN-S uses high-level visual features learned by BoWDNN, the DCG@25 was improved from 0.537 to 0.544 after using the learned features. It may be due to the learned high-level visual features are more suitable to describe the content of images. Meanwhile, BoWDNN-S also achieves

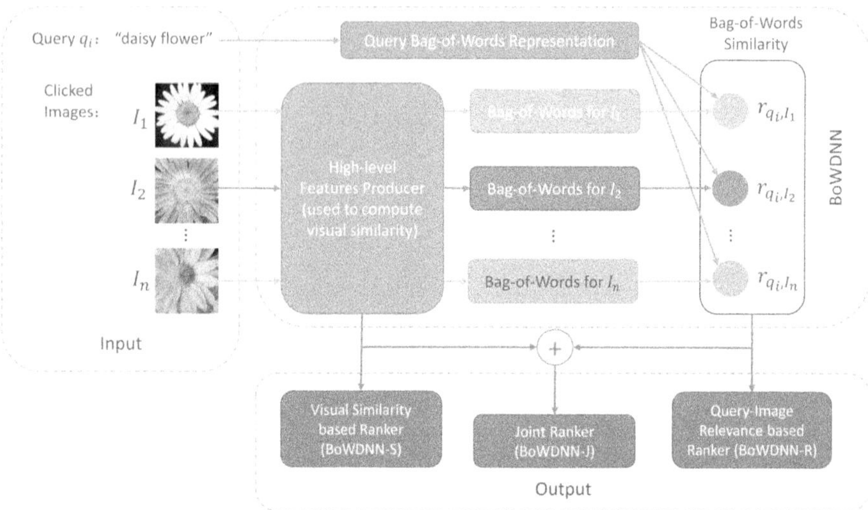

Figure 3: The system diagram of our proposed method: given query and its clicked images, the query-image relevance score will be computed according to the bag-of-words representations of image and the high-level visual features.

Table 1: Performance of three different ranking methods powered by Bag-of-words based deep neural network.

Methods	Dataset	
	Dev set	Test set
Random	0.4683	0.3906
Upper Bound	0.6840	0.5266
Ring Training	0.5021	-
BoWDNN-R	0.5089	0.4677
MPM in [6]	0.5370	-
BoWDNN-S	0.5436	0.4969
BoWDNN-J	0.5441	0.4968

better performance than BoWDNN-R, there are three possible limitations in current BoWDNN-R. 1) the size of bag-of-words vocabulary is not large enough to cover the all user intensions. There are many rare word in query log, and lots of words in queries are missed in current vocabulary. 2) the unigram representation is limited in some situations like query about people's name, each single word in a name can not represent any visual information about the related people, all of the words in people's name will be projected to human visual feature in BoWDNN, it's hard to learn some special and exact features for each person. 3) there is large numbers of queries which is hard to mining the relevance with images, like "if you really knew me" which is a title of video having no word to describe the visual content. On the other hand, the performance of visual similarity propagation methods like BoWDNN-S to a large extent depends on the quality of the initial search results, different with BoWDNN-R, this kind of method can only be used to rerank the search results. Finally, we joint these two different ranking methods and get further improvement.

5. CONCLUSIONS

In this paper, we proposed a bag-of-words based deep neural network for image retrieval task and trained on large scale clickthrough dataset from MSR-Bing Grand Challenge. By utilizing the predicted bag-of-words image representations and high-level visual features learned by BoWDNN, we propose three different methods, bag-of-words similarity based, visual similarity based, and their joint. The experiments evaluated on dev and test dataset demonstrate the effectiveness of our proposed approach for image retrieval.

6. REFERENCES

[1] Y. Bai, K. Yang, W. Yu, W.-Y. Ma, and T. Zhao. Learning high-level image representation for image retrieval via multi-task dnn using clickthrough data. *ICLR*, 2014.

[2] X. Glorot, A. Bordes, and Y. Bengio. Deep sparse rectifier networks. In *Proceedings of the 14th International Conference on Artificial Intelligence and Statistics. JMLR W&CP Volume*, volume 15, pages 315–323, 2011.

[3] G. E. Hinton, N. Srivastava, A. Krizhevsky, I. Sutskever, and R. R. Salakhutdinov. Improving neural networks by preventing co-adaptation of feature detectors. *arXiv preprint arXiv:1207.0580*, 2012.

[4] X.-S. Hua, L. Yang, J. Wang, J. Wang, M. Ye, K. Wang, Y. Rui, and J. Li. Clickage: Towards bridging semantic and intent gaps via mining click logs of search engines. In *Proceedings of the 21st ACM international conference on Multimedia*, pages 243–252. ACM, 2013.

[5] L. Page, S. Brin, R. Motwani, and T. Winograd. The pagerank citation ranking: Bringing order to the web. 1999.

[6] C.-C. Wu, K.-Y. Chu, Y.-H. Kuo, Y.-Y. Chen, W.-Y. Lee, and W. H. Hsu. Search-based relevance association with auxiliary contextual cues. In *Proceedings of the 21st ACM international conference on Multimedia*, pages 393–396. ACM, 2013.

Click-through-based Subspace Learning for Image Search

Yingwei Pan †, Ting Yao ‡, Xinmei Tian †, Houqiang Li †, Chong-Wah Ngo ‡
† University of Science and Technology of China, Hefei, China
‡ City University of Hong Kong, Kowloon, Hong Kong
{panyw, tingyao}.ustc@gmail.com; {xinmei, lihq}@ustc.edu.cn; cscwngo@cityu.edu.hk

ABSTRACT

One of the fundamental problems in image search is to rank image documents according to a given textual query. We address two limitations of the existing image search engines in this paper. First, there is no straightforward way of comparing textual keywords with visual image content. Image search engines therefore highly depend on the surrounding texts, which are often noisy or too few to accurately describe the image content. Second, ranking functions are trained on query-image pairs labeled by human labelers, making the annotation intellectually expensive and thus cannot be scaled up.

We demonstrate that the above two fundamental challenges can be mitigated by jointly exploring the subspace learning and the use of click-through data. The former aims to create a latent subspace with the ability in comparing information from the original incomparable views (i.e., textual and visual views), while the latter explores the largely available and freely accessible click-through data (i.e., "crowdsourced" human intelligence) for understanding query. Specifically, we investigate a series of click-through-based subspace learning techniques (CSL) for image search. We conduct experiments on MSR-Bing Grand Challenge and the final evaluation performance achieves $DCG@25 = 0.47225$. Moreover, the feature dimension is significantly reduced by several orders of magnitude (e.g., from thousands to tens).

Categories and Subject Descriptors

H.3.3 [**Information Storage and Retrieval**]: Information Search and Retrieval—*Retrieval models*

General Terms

Algorithm, Experimentation.

Keywords

Image search; subspace learning; click-through data; DNN image representation.

MM'14, November 3–7, 2014, Orlando, Florida, USA.

http://dx.doi.org/10.1145/2647868.2656404.

1. INTRODUCTION

Keyword-based image search has received intensive research attention since the early of 1990s [8]. The significance of the topic can be partly reflected from the huge volume of published papers, particularly for addressing the problems of learning the rank or similarity functions. Despite these efforts, the fact that the queries (texts) and search targets (images) are of two different modalities (or views) has resulted in the open problem of "semantic gap." Specifically, a query in the form of textual keywords is not directly comparable with the visual content of images. The commercial search engines to date primarily reply on textual features extracted from the surrounding texts of images. This kind of visual search approach may not always achieve satisfying results as textual information is sometimes noisy and even unavailable. Moreover, image rankers trained on query-image pairs labeled by human experts may lead to poor generalization performance due to the label noise problem and difficulty associated with understanding the user's intent.

Inspired by the success of subspace learning [9], this paper studies the cross-view (i.e., text to image views) search problem by learning a common latent subspace that allows direct comparison of text queries and images. Specifically, by mapping to the latent subspace, the similarity between a textual query and a visual image can be directly measured between their projections, making the information from original incomparable cross-view space comparable in the shared latent subspace.

Moreover, we consider exploring user click-through data, aiming to understand the user's intent for image search. In general, image rankers obtain training data by having human experts label the relevance of query-image pairs. However, it is difficult to fathom the user's intent based on the query keywords alone, especially for those ambiguous queries. For example, given the query "gorilla hummer," experts tend to label images of animals "gorilla" and "hummer" as highly relevant. However, empirical evidence suggests that most users wish to retrieve images of a car of "gorilla hummer" type. The experts' labels might therefore be erroneous resulting in training sets with label noise and the ranker is learnt to be sub-optimal. In this work, our click-through-based learning provides an alternative to address this problem. Most image search engines display results as thumbnails. The user can browse the entire image search results before clicking on a specific image. As such, users predominantly tend to click on images that are relevant to their query. Therefore, the click data can serve as a reliable and implicit feedback for image search.

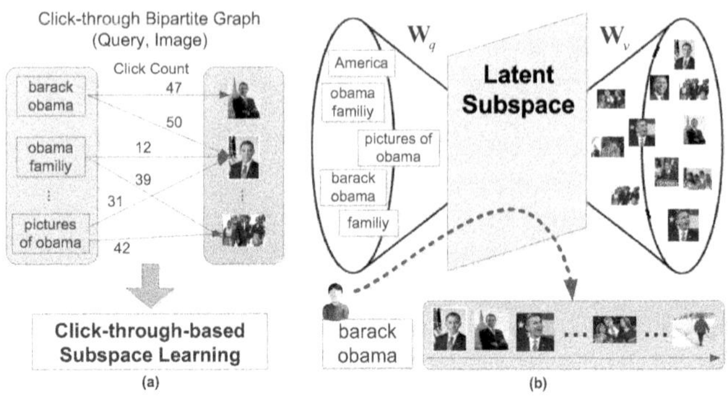

Figure 1: Click-through-based image search framework (better viewed in color). (a) Latent subspace learning between textual query and visual image based on click-through bipartite graph. (b) With the learnt mapping matrices $\mathbf{W}_q$ and $\mathbf{W}_v$, queries and images are projected into this latent subspace and then the distance in the latent subspace is directly taken as the measurement of query-image relevance. Then for each query, the images are ordered based on the relevance scores to the query.

By jointly integrating subspace learning and click-through data, this paper investigates click-through-based subspace learning approaches (CSL) for image search, as shown in Figure 1. Specifically, a bipartite graph between the user queries and images is constructed on the search logs from a commercial image search engine. An edge between a query and an image is established, if the users who issue the query clicked the image. Subspace learning aims to learn a latent subspace in the way of minimizing the distance between the mappings of query and image, or maximizing the correlation between the two views. After the optimization of subspace learning, the relevance score between a query and an image in the original space can be directly computed based on their mappings. For any query, the image search list will be returned by sorting their relevance scores to the query.

In summary, this paper makes the following contributions:

- We study the problem of keyword-based image search by jointly exploring subspace learning and the use of click-through data.
- We investigate click-through-based subspace learning methods, which aim to learn a latent subspace. By mapping to the subspace, textual queries and visual images can be directly compared.

The remaining sections are organized as follows. Section 2 presents click-through-based subspace learning methods. Section 3 provides empirical evaluations, followed by the discussions and conclusions in Section 4.

2. CLICK-THROUGH-BASED SUBSPACE LEARNING

The main goal of click-through-based subspace learning (CSL) method is to create a latent common subspace with the ability of directly comparing semantic textual query and image visual content. Four subspace learning techniques are investigated, i.e., Canonical Correlation Analysis (CCA) [2], Click-through-based Cross-view Learning (CCL) [6], Polynomial Semantic Indexing (PSI) [10], and Passive-Aggressive Model (PA) [3]. After we obtain the latent subspace, the relevance between query and image is directly measured by their mappings. The approach overview is shown in Figure 1.

In the following, we will first define the bipartite graph that naturally encodes user actions in the query log, followed by briefly presenting the four subspace learning approaches. Finally, the CSL algorithm for image search is presented.

2.1 Notation

Let $\mathscr{G} = (\mathcal{V}, \mathcal{E})$ denote a click-through bipartite. $\mathcal{V} = Q \cup V$ is the set of vertices, which consists of a query set Q and an image set V. $\mathcal{E}$ is the set of edges between query vertices and image vertices. The number associated with the edge represents the clicked times in the image search results of the query. Suppose there are n triads $\{q_i, v_i, c_i\}_{i=1}^n$ generated from the click-through bipartite in total, where c_i is the click counts of image v_i in response to query q_i. Let $\mathbf{Q} = \{\mathbf{q}_1, \mathbf{q}_2, \ldots, \mathbf{q}_n\}^\top \in \mathbb{R}^{n \times d_q}$ and $\mathbf{V} = \{\mathbf{v}_1, \mathbf{v}_2, \ldots, \mathbf{v}_n\}^\top \in \mathbb{R}^{n \times d_v}$ denote the query and image feature matrix, where $\mathbf{q}_i$ and $\mathbf{v}_i$ are the textual and visual feature of query q_i and image v_i, and d_q and d_v are the feature dimensionality, respectively. The click matrix $\mathbf{C}$ is a diagonal $n \times n$ matrix with its diagonal elements as c_i.

2.2 Canonical Correlation Analysis

Canonical Correlation Analysis (CCA) is a classical technique, which explores the mapping matrices by maximizing the correlation between the projections in the subspace. We assume that a low-dimensional common subspace exists for the representation of the query and image. The linear mapping function can be derived from the common subspace by

$$f(\mathbf{q}_i) = \mathbf{q}_i \mathbf{W}_q, \quad \text{and} \quad f(\mathbf{v}_i) = \mathbf{v}_i \mathbf{W}_v, \tag{1}$$

where d is the dimensionality of the common subspace, and $\mathbf{W}_q \in \mathbb{R}^{d_q \times d}$ and $\mathbf{W}_v \in \mathbb{R}^{d_v \times d}$ are the transformation matrices that project the query textual semantics and image content into the common subspace, respectively. CCA aims to find the two linear projections making $(\mathbf{Q}\mathbf{W}_q, \mathbf{V}\mathbf{W}_v)$ maximally correlated as

$$(\mathbf{W}_q, \mathbf{W}_v) = \underset{\mathbf{W}_q, \mathbf{W}_v}{\operatorname{argmax}} \ \operatorname{corr}(\mathbf{Q}\mathbf{W}_q, \mathbf{V}\mathbf{W}_v). \tag{2}$$

Specifically, we view the click number of a query and an image as an indicator of their relevance. All the query-image pairs generated from click-through bipartite graph are used for learning the linear mapping projections.

2.3 Click-through-based Cross-view Learning

The training of Click-through-based Cross-view Learning (CCL) is performed simultaneously by minimizing the distance between query and image mappings in the latent subspace weighted by their clicks, and preserving the structure relationships between the training examples in the original feature space. In particular, the objective function of CCL is composed of two components, i.e., distance between views in the latent subspace, and the structure preservation in the original space. The overall objective function of CCL is as

$$\begin{aligned} \min_{\mathbf{W}_q, \mathbf{W}_v} \ & tr((\mathbf{Q}\mathbf{W}_q - \mathbf{V}\mathbf{W}_v)^\top \mathbf{C}(\mathbf{Q}\mathbf{W}_q - \mathbf{V}\mathbf{W}_v)) \\ & + \lambda (\sum_{i,j=1}^{n} \mathbf{S}_{ij}^q \|\mathbf{q}_i \mathbf{W}_q - \mathbf{q}_j \mathbf{W}_q\|^2 + \sum_{i,j=1}^{n} \mathbf{S}_{ij}^v \|\mathbf{v}_i \mathbf{W}_v - \mathbf{v}_j \mathbf{W}_v\|^2) \end{aligned}, \tag{3}$$

Table 1: The DCG@25 (%) of different approaches on Dev dataset.

Appr.	NGS	GLP	CCA	CCL	PSI	PA	FUS
	48.99	50.25	50.55	50.59	49.91	50.17	51.12

where λ is the tradeoff parameter, $\mathbf{S}^q \in \mathbb{R}^{n\times n}$ and $\mathbf{S}^v \in \mathbb{R}^{n\times n}$ denote the affinity matrices defined on the queries and images, respectively. The first term is the cross-view distance, while the second term represents structure preservation.

The underlying assumption of CCL is that the higher the click number, the smaller the distance between the query and the image in the latent subspace. Furthermore, the similarity between examples in the original space can be preserved in the learned latent subspace.

2.4 Polynomial Semantic Indexing

Given a query q_i and an image v_j, a polynomial ranking model with 2-degree is given by

$$f(q_i, v_j) = (\mathbf{q}_i\mathbf{W}_q)(\mathbf{v}_j\mathbf{W}_v)^T. \quad (4)$$

The training of $\mathbf{W}_q$ and $\mathbf{W}_v$ could be many forms. From our click-through data, we can easily get a set of triplets $\mathcal{T}$, where each tuple (q, v^+, v^-) consists of the query q, an image v^+ with higher click and a lower clicked image v^-. Deriving from the idea of "learning to rank" [5], it aims to optimize $\mathbf{W}_q$ and $\mathbf{W}_v$ which makes $f(q, v^+) > f(q, v^-)$, i.e., image v^+ should be ranked higher than image v^-. The margin ranking loss is employed and the optimization problem is defined as

$$minimize: \sum_{(q,v^+,v^-)\in\mathcal{T}} \max(0, 1 - f(q, v^+) + f(q, v^-)). \quad (5)$$

2.5 Passive-Aggressive Model

Similar in spirit, Passive-Aggressive model measures the match between a query q_i and an image v_j by first projecting the query into the image space. Accordingly, the ranking function is defined as

$$f(q_i, v_j) = \mathbf{q}_i\mathbf{W}_q\mathbf{v}_j^T. \quad (6)$$

For a tuple (q, v^+, v^-), the change of $\mathbf{W}_q$ is determined by whether the constrains of $f(q, v^+) > f(q, v^-)$ is verified. The optimization of $\mathbf{W}_q$ is performed by adapting the Passive-Aggressive algorithm [3]. It is worth noticing that here the subspace is set to image space and hence $\mathbf{W}_v$ is the identity matrix.

2.6 CSL Algorithm

After the optimization of $\mathbf{W}_q$ and $\mathbf{W}_v$, we can obtain the linear mapping functions defined in Eq.(1). With this, original incomparable textual query and visual image become comparable. Specifically, given a test query-image pair, we can compute the similarity or distance value between the pair as reflecting how relevant the query could be used to describe the given image. For any query, sorting by its corresponding values for all its associated images gives the retrieval ranking for these images.

3. EXPERIMENTS

We conducted experiments on the MSR-Bing Image Retrieval Challenge dataset, i.e. Clickture [4], which contains a

Figure 2: Examples in Clickture dataset (upper row: clicked images; lower row: search query with click times on the upper image).

training and a development (Dev) sets. It was collected from one year click-through data of one commercial image search engine. There are more than 11.7 millions distinct queries and 1.0 million unique images of the training set. Figure 2 shows a few exemplary images with their clicked queries and click counts in the Clickture. For example, users clicked the first image 12 times in the search results when submitting query "red wine" in total. Note that there is no surrounding text or description of images provided in the dataset.

In the Dev set, there are 79,926 $\langle query, image \rangle$ pairs generated from 1,000 queries, where each image to the corresponding query was manually annotated on a three point ordinal scale: Excellent, Good, and Bad. In the experiments, the training set is used for learning the latent subspace, while the Dev set is used for performance evaluation. In addition, there is an official test set for the final evaluation.

3.1 Experimental Settings

Textual and Visual Features. We take the word in queries as "word features." Words are stemmed and stop words are removed. With word features, each query is represented by a tf vector in the query space. In our experiments, we use the top 50,000 most frequent words as the word vocabulary. Visual feature derived from Convolutional Neural Networks (CNN) by using DeCAF [1] is extracted as image representation.

Compared Approaches. We compare the following approaches for performance evaluation:

- N-Gram SVM Modeling (NGS). We use all the clicked images of a given query as positive samples and randomly select negative samples from the rest of the training dataset to build a support vector machine (SVM) model for each query, and then use this model to predict the relevance of the query to a new image. When a query is not in the training set, but its n-grams appear in some queries of the training set, we generate the model by linearly fusing the SVM models of these queries. We name this run as *NGS*.
- Graph-based Label Propagation (GLP) [7]. GLP employs neighborhood graph search to find the nearest neighbors on an image similarity graph built up with visual representations and further aggregates their clicked queries/click counts to get the labels of the new image. This run is named as *GLP*.
- Click-through-based Subspace Learning. We design five runs for CSL approaches: *CCA*, *CCL*, *PSI*, *PA*, and their linear fusion *FUS*.

Table 2: The DCG@25 (%) of our three submitted runs on test dataset.

Run	FUS	FUG	FUA
	47.225	46.404	47.441

Table 3: Run time (ms) of six different approaches. The experiments are conducted on a regular PC (Intel dual-core 2.0GHz CPU and 100 GB RAM).

Appr.	NGS	GLP	CCA	CCL	PSI	PA
	7500	14.8	4.5	1.0	1.0	1.5

Evaluation Metrics. Following the challenge's measurement, for each query, we use Discounted Cumulated Gain (DCG) to evaluate the performance of top 25 images.

3.2 Performance Comparison

Table 1 shows the DCG performance of seven runs averaged over 1,000 queries in Dev dataset. Overall, all the CSL approaches consistently lead to a performance boost against *NGS*. Particularly, the DCG@25 performance of *CCL* can achieve 0.5059, which improves *NGS* by 3.5%. As a result of linear fusion, *FUS* improves the performance up to 0.5112. Furthermore, *CCA*, *CCL* and *FUS* all exhibit better performance than *GLP*, while the performance of *PA* is slightly less than *GLP*. More importantly, by learning a low-dimensional latent subspace, the dimension of the mappings of textual query and visual image is reduced by several orders of magnitude. In our experiments, the dimensionality of latent subspace is empirically set to 50 for *CCA*, *CCL*, and *PSI*. Figure 3 shows the top ten images for query "college station texas" by using five CSL approaches, respectively.

Table 2 details the performances of our three submitted runs on test dataset. In addition to *FUS*, *FUG* is late fusion by performing GLP on several visual features including color moments, wavelet texture, histograms of oriented gradients, and CNN feature. *FUA* is average fusion of *FUS* and *FUG*. As indicated by our results, *FUS* significantly outperforms *FUG* and *FUA* achieves the best performance.

3.3 Run Time

Table 3 lists the detailed run time for each compared methods. The CSL approaches are extremely efficient, completing relevance prediction of each image-query pair within five milliseconds on average. They are much faster than *NGS* which needs beyond five seconds and *GLP* which requires about 15 milliseconds, respectively.

4. CONCLUSION

In this paper, we tackled two major limitations of existing image search rankers - highly depends on surrounding texts and learning from training data with label noise. We have investigated the issues of directly learning the cross-view distance between a textual query and an image by leveraging both click data and subspace learning techniques. The click data represent the click relations between queries and images, while the subspace learning aims to learn a latent common subspace between multiple views. The extensive experiments evaluated on 1,000 queries show that CSL approaches gave better results than SVM-based and graph-based methods. Moreover, CSL approaches have good properties on both feature dimension reduction and speed, making them good candidates for online image search applications.

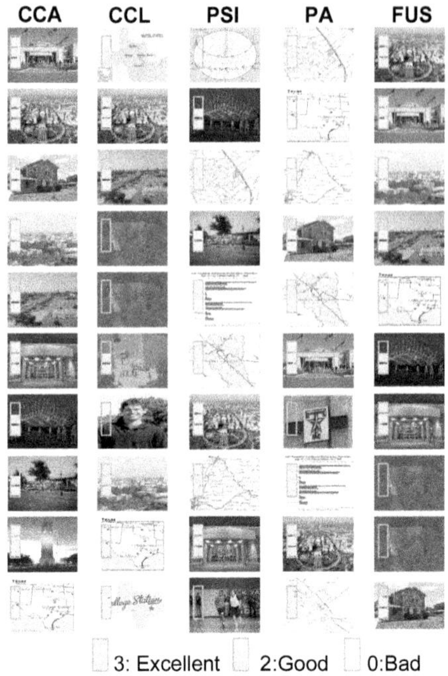

Figure 3: The exemplary list of top ten images for query "college station texas" ranked by CSL approaches.

Acknowledgments

This work was partially supported by the National Natural Science Foundation of China (No. 61272290), the Fundamental Research Funds for the Central Universities (No. WK2100060011), and the Shenzhen Research Institute, City University of Hong Kong.

5. REFERENCES

[1] J. Donahue, Y. Jia, O. Vinyals, J. Hoffman, N. Zhang, E. Tzeng, and T. Darrell. Decaf: A deep convolutional activation feature for generic visual recognition. *arXiv preprint arXiv:1310.1531*, 2013.

[2] Y. Gong, Q. Ke, M. Isard, and S. Lazebnik. A multi-view embedding space for modeling internet images, tags, and their semantics. *IJCV*, pages 210–233, 2014.

[3] D. Grangier and S. Bengio. A discriminative kernel-based model to rank images from text queries. *IEEE Trans. on PAMI*, 30(8):1371–1384, 2008.

[4] X.-S. Hua, L. Yang, J. Wang, J. Wang, M. Ye, K. Wang, Y. Rui, and J. Li. Clickage: Towards bridging semantic and intent gaps via mining click logs of search engines. *In ACM MM*, 2013.

[5] T. Joachims. Optimizing search engines using clickthrough data. In *KDD*, 2002.

[6] Y. Pan, T. Yao, T. Mei, H. Li, C.-W. Ngo, and Y. Rui. Click-through-based cross-view learning for image search. In *SIGIR*, 2014.

[7] Y. Pan, T. Yao, K. Yang, H. Li, C.-W. Ngo, J. Wang, and T. Mei. Image search by graph-based label propagation with image representation from dnn. In *ACM MM*, 2013.

[8] Y. Rui, T. Huang, and S. Chang. Image retrieval: current techniques, promising directions, and open issues. *VCIR*, 10(1):39–62, 1999.

[9] C. Xu, D. Tao, and C. Xu. A survey on multi-view learning. *CoRR abs/1304.5634*, 2013.

[10] T. Yao, T. Mei, C.-W. Ngo, and S. Li. Annotation for free: Video tagging by mining user search behavior. *In ACM MM*, 2013.

Perception-Guided Multimodal Feature Fusion for Photo Aesthetics Assessment

Luming Zhang[†], Yue Gao[†], Chao Zhang[‡], Hanwang Zhang[†], Qi Tian[◇], Roger Zimmermann[†]
[†]School of Computing, National University of Singapore, Singapore
[‡]Department of Computer Science, University of Illinois at Urbana-Champaign, USA
[◇]Department of Computer Science, University of Texas at San Antonio, USA
{zhanglm,gaoyue,hanwang,rogerz}@comp.nus.edu.sg, czhang82@illinois.edu, qitian@cs.utsa.edu

ABSTRACT

Photo aesthetic quality evaluation is a challenging task in multimedia and computer vision fields. Conventional approaches suffer from the following three drawbacks: 1) the deemphasized role of semantic content that is many times more important than low-level visual features in photo aesthetics; 2) the difficulty to optimally fuse low-level and high-level visual cues in photo aesthetics evaluation; and 3) the absence of a sequential viewing path in the existing models, as humans perceive visually salient regions sequentially when viewing a photo.

To address and solve these challenges, we propose a new aesthetic descriptor that mimics the way humans sequentially perceive visually/semantically salient regions in a photo. In particular, a weakly supervised learning paradigm is developed to project the local aesthetic descriptors (graphlets in this work) into a low-dimensional semantic space. Thereafter, each graphlet can be described by multiple types of visual features, both at low-level and in high-level. Since humans usually perceive only a few salient regions in a photo, a sparsity-constrained graphlet ranking algorithm is proposed that seamlessly integrates both the low-level and the high-level visual cues. The top-ranked graphlets are the discerned visually/semantically prominent graphlets in a photo. They are sequentially linked into a path that simulates the process of humans actively viewing. Finally, we learn a probabilistic aesthetic measure based on such actively viewing paths (AVPs) from the training photos that are marked as aesthetically pleasing by multiple users. Experimental results show that: 1) the AVPs are 87.65% consistent with real human gaze shifting paths, as verified by the eye-tracking data; and 2) our photo aesthetic measure outperforms many of its competitors.

Categories and Subject Descriptors

I.2.10 [**Artificial Intelligence**]: Vision and Scene Understanding; H.3.3 [**Information Storage and Retrieval**]: Information Search and Retrieval

MM '14, November 3–7, 2014, Orlando, Florida, USA.
Copyright 2014 ACM 978-1-4503-3063-3/14/11 ...$15.00.
http://dx.doi.org/10.1145/2647868.2654903.

Keywords

Weakly supervised; multimodal; sparsity; actively viewing; gaze shifting; path

1. INTRODUCTION

Photo aesthetic quality evaluation is a useful technique in multimedia applications. For example, a successful photo management system should rank photos based on the human perception of photo aesthetics, so that users can conveniently select their favorite pictures into albums. Moreover, an effective photo aesthetics prediction algorithm can help photographers to crop an aesthetically pleasing sub-region from an original poorly framed photo. However, photo aesthetics evaluation is still a challenging task due to the following three reasons.

- Semantics is an important cue to describe photo aesthetics, but the state-of-the-art models cannot exploit semantics effectively. Typically, a photo aesthetic model [12] only employs a few heuristically defined semantics according to a specific data set. They are determined by whether photos in a data set are covered by objects like sky, water, and *etc*. In addition, the semantics are typically detected using a set of external object detectors, *e.g.*, a human face detector. There is no guarantee that all the pre-specified semantic objects can be accurately discovered.

- Eye tracking experiments [6] have shown that humans allocate gazes to important regions in a sequential manner. As shown in Fig. 4, most people start with viewing the player, and then shift gazes to the grass, and finally to the audiences and the red track. Existing photo aesthetic models, however, fail to encode such a gaze shifting sequence.

- Psychophysics studies [7] have shown that both the bottom-up and the top-down visual features draw the attention of human eye. It is generally accepted that an aesthetic model should integrate both the low-level and the high-level visual cues. However, current models typically fuse multiple types of features in a linear or nonlinear way, where the cross-feature information is not well utilized. Even worse, these integration schemes cannot emphasize the visually/semantically salient regions within a photo.

To solve these problems, a sparsity-constrained ranking algorithm jointly discovers visually/semantically important graphlets along the human gaze shifting path, based on which a photo aesthetic model is learned. An overview of our proposed aesthetic model is presented in Fig. 1. By transferring semantics of image labels into

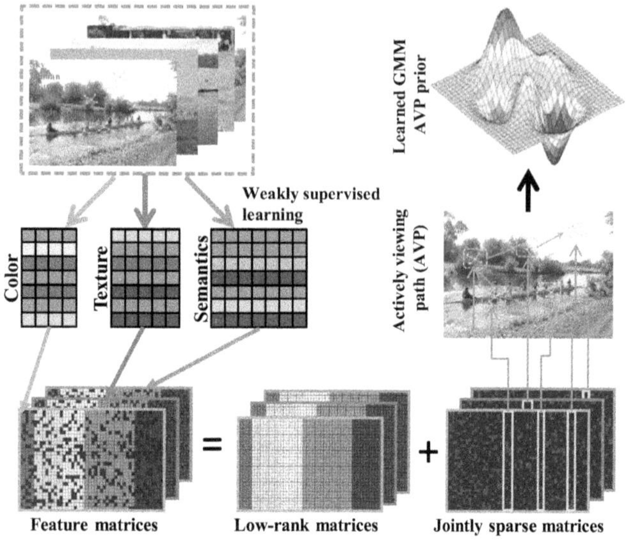

Figure 1: The pipeline of the proposed photo aesthetic model.

different graphlets of a photo, we represent each graphlet by a couple of low-level and high-level visual features. Then, a sparsity-constrained framework is proposed to integrate multiple types of features for calculating the saliency of each graphlet. Particularly, by constructing the matrices containing the visual/semantic features of graphlets in a photo, the proposed framework seeks the consistently sparse elements from the joint decompositions of the multiple-feature matrices into pairs of low-rank and sparse matrices. Compared with previous methods that linearly/non-linearly combine multiple global aesthetic features, our framework can seamlessly integrate multiple visual/semantic features for salient graphlets discovery. These discovered graphlets are linked into a path, termed actively viewing path (AVP), to simulate a human gaze shifting path. Finally, we employ a Gaussian mixture model (GMM) to learn the distribution of AVPs from the aesthetically pleasing training photos. The learned GMM can be used as the aesthetic measure, since it quantifies the amount of AVPs that are shared between the aesthetically pleasing training photos and the test image.

The main contributions of this paper are two-fold:

- A sparsity-constrained ranking framework that discovers visually/semantically important graphlets that draw the attention of the human eye, by seamlessly combining a few low-level and high-level visual features;
- Actively viewing path (AVP), a new aesthetic descriptor that mimics the way humans actively allocate gazes to visually/semantically important regions in a photo.

2. RELATED WORK

In recent years, many photo aesthetic quality evaluation methods have been proposed. Roughly, these methods can be divided into two categories: global feature-based approaches and local patch integration-based approaches.

Global feature-based approaches design global low-level and high-level visual features that represent photo aesthetics in an implicit manner. Ke *et al.* [10] developed a group of high-level visual features, such as an image simplicity based on the spatial distribution of edges, to imitate human perception of photo aesthetics. Datta *et al.* [3] proposed 58 low-level visual features, *e.g.*, shape convexity, to capture photo aesthetics. Dhar *et al.* [5] proposed a set of high-level attribute-based predictors to evaluate photo aesthetics. In [12], Luo *et al.* adopted a GMM-based hue distribution and a prominent lines-based texture distribution to represent the photo global composition. To capture the photo local composition, regional features describing human faces, region clarity, and region complexity were developed. In [15], Marchesotti *et al.* proposed using generic descriptors, *i.e.*, the bag of visual words and the Fisher vector, to access photo aesthetics. Experiments shown that the two generic descriptors outperform many specifically designed photo aesthetic descriptors. It is worth noting the limitations of the above approaches: 1) Luo *et al.* [12]'s approach relies on category-dependent regional feature extraction, requiring that photos can be 100% accurately classified into one of the seven categories. This prerequisite is infeasible in practice; 2) the attributes proposed by Dhar *et al.* [5] are designed manually and are data set dependent. Thus, it is difficult to generalize them to different data sets; and 3) all these global low-level and high-level visual features are designed heuristically. There is no strong indication that they can capture the complicated spatial configurations of different photos.

Local patch integration-based approaches extract patches within a photo and then integrate them to measure photo aesthetic quality. In [2], Cheng *et al.* proposed the omni-range context, *i.e.*, the spatial distribution of arbitrary pairwise image patches, to model photo composition. The learned omni-range context priors are combined with the other cues, such as the patch number, to form a posterior probability to measure the aesthetics of a photo. One limitation of Cheng *et al.*'s model is that only the binary correlation between image patches is considered. To describe high-order spatial interactions of image patches, Nishiyama [17] *et al.* first detected multiple subject regions in a photo, where each subject region is a bounding rectangle containing the salient parts of an object. Then, an SVM classifier is trained for each subject region. Finally, the aesthetics of a test photo is computed by combining the scores of the SVM classifier corresponding to a photo's internal subject regions. One limitation of Nishiyama *et al.*'s approach is that it cannot model the spatial interaction of multiple image regions explicitly. In [18], Nishiyama *et al.* proposed a color harmony-based photo aesthetic evaluation method. A color harmony model is first applied to the patches within a photo to describe their color distribution. The patch-level color distribution is then integrated into a bag-of-patches histogram. The histogram is further classified by an SVM to identify whether a photo is high or low aesthetics. It is noticeable that Nishiyama *et al.* [18] evaluates photo aesthetics by utilizing visual features in the color channel only. Features describing photo aesthetics in other channels, such as texture, are neglected. Bhattacharya *et al.* [1] proposed a spatial recomposition that allows users to interactively select a foreground object. The system presents recommendations to indicate an optimal location of the foreground object, which is detected by combining multiple aesthetic features, *e.g.*, the relative position of the foreground objects. The major shortcoming of Bhattacharya *et al.*'s method is the necessity of human interaction, limiting its application for large-scale photo aesthetics evaluation.

3. LOW-LEVEL AND HIGH-LEVEL LOCAL AESTHETICS DESCRIPTION

3.1 The Concept of Graphlets

There are usually a number of of components (*e.g.*, the human and the red track in Fig. 2) in a photo. Among these components, a few spatially neighboring ones and their spatial interactions capture the local aesthetics of a photo. Since graph is a powerful tool to describe the relationships among objects, we use it to model the spatial interactions of components in a photo. Our technique is to segment a photo into a set of atomic regions[1], and then construct graphlets to characterize the local aesthetics of this photo. In particular, a graphlet is a small-sized graph defined as:

$$\mathcal{G} = (\mathcal{V}, \mathcal{E}), \quad (1)$$

where $\mathcal{V}$ is a set of vertices representing those spatially neighboring atomic regions; and $\mathcal{E}$ is a set of edges, each of which connects pairwise spatially adjacent atomic regions. We call a graphlet with t vertices a t-sized graphlet. It is worth emphasizing that the number of graphlets within a photo is exponentially increasing with the graphlet size. Therefore, only small graphlets (*i.e.*, vertex number less than 10) are employed.

In this work, we characterize each graphlet in both color and

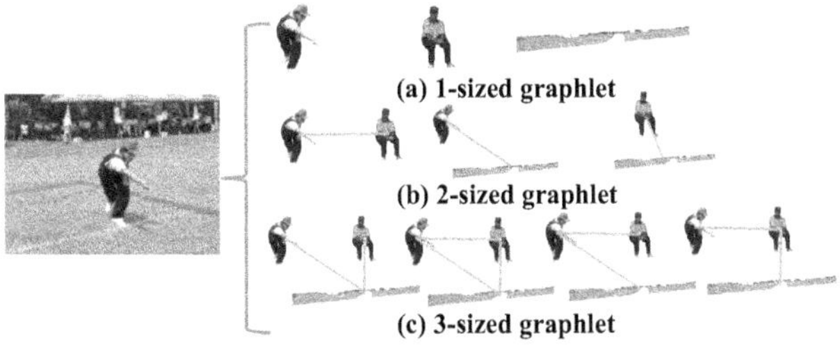

Figure 2: An example of differently sized graphlets extracted from a photo.

texture channels. Given a t-sized graphlet, each row of matrix $\mathbf{M}_r^c$ represents the 9-dimensional color moment [19] and each row of matrix $\mathbf{M}_r^t$ denotes the 128-dimensional HOG [8] of an atomic region. To describe the spatial interactions of atomic regions, we employ a $t \times t$ adjacency matrix as:

$$\mathbf{M}_s(i,j) = \begin{cases} \theta(R_i, R_j) & \text{if } R_i \text{ and } R_j \text{ are spatially adjacent} \\ 0 & \text{otherwise} \end{cases}, \quad (2)$$

where $\theta(R_i, R_j)$ is the horizontal angle of the vector from the center of atomic region R_i to the center of atomic region R_j. Based on the three matrices $\mathbf{M}_r^c$, $\mathbf{M}_r^t$, and $\mathbf{M}_s$, the color and texture channel of a graphlet is described by $\mathbf{M}^c = [\mathbf{M}_r^c, \mathbf{M}_s]$ and $\mathbf{M}^t = [\mathbf{M}_r^t, \mathbf{M}_s]$, respectively. Moreover, similar to many feature fusion algorithms [22, 23] that allow only vector representation of a sample, the color channel matrix $\mathbf{M}^c$ and the texture channel matrix $\mathbf{M}^t$ of a graphlet are further converted into vectors by staking each of them in row-wise.

3.2 Semantically Local Aesthetics Pursuit

In addition to color and texture channels description, high-level semantic cues should also be exploited for photo aesthetics evaluations. In this paper, the semantic cues are integrated based on a weakly supervised paradigm. Particularly, we transfer the semantics of image labels[2] into different graphlets in a photo. This is implemented based on a manifold embedding algorithm described as follows:

$$\arg\min_{\mathbf{Y}} [\sum_{i,j} ||y_i - y_j||^2 l_s(i,j) - \sum_{i,j} ||y_i - y_j||^2 l_d(i,j)]$$
$$= \arg\min_{\mathbf{Y}} \text{tr}(\mathbf{YRY}^T), \quad (3)$$

where $\mathbf{Y} = [y_1, y_2, \cdots, y_N]$ denotes a collection of d-dimensional post-embedding graphlets; $l_s(\cdot,\cdot)$ and $l_b(\cdot,\cdot)$ are functions measuring the similarity and discrepancy between graphlets; $\mathbf{R} = [\vec{\mathbf{e}}_{N-1}^T, -\mathbf{I}_{N-1}]W_1[\vec{\mathbf{e}}_{N-1}^T, -\mathbf{I}_{N-1}] + \cdots + [-\mathbf{I}_{N-1}, \vec{\mathbf{e}}_{N-1}^T]\mathbf{W}_N[-\mathbf{I}_{N-1}, \vec{\mathbf{e}}_{N-1}^T]$; $\mathbf{W}_i$ is an $N \times N$ diagonal matrix whose h-th diagonal element is $[l_s(h,i) - l_d(h,i)]$.

More specifically, $l_s(\cdot,\cdot)$ and $l_d(\cdot,\cdot)$ are functions measuring

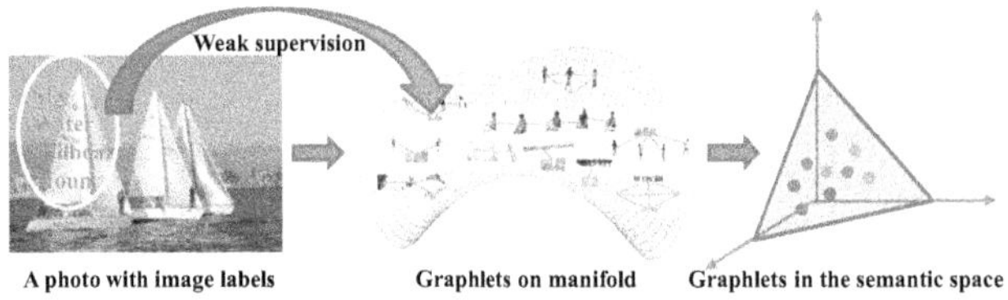

Figure 3: An illustration of embedding graphlets into the semantic space on manifold.

the semantic similarity and difference between graphlets, respectively. Denote $\mathbf{b}_i$ as the C-dimensional row vector containing the multiple labels of the photo from which graphlet $\mathcal{G}_i$ is extracted; and $\vec{\mathbf{N}} = [N^1, \cdots, N^C]^T$ where N^c is the number of photos for category c, then l_s and l_d are defined as:

$$l_s(i,j) = \frac{[\mathbf{b}_i \cap \mathbf{b}_j]\vec{\mathbf{N}}}{\sum_c N^c} \cdot d_{GW}(\mathcal{G}_i, \mathcal{G}_j), \quad (4)$$

$$l_d(i,j) = \frac{[\mathbf{b}_i \oplus \mathbf{b}_j]\vec{\mathbf{N}}}{\sum_c N^c} \cdot d_{GW}(\mathcal{G}_i, \mathcal{G}_j), \quad (5)$$

where $d_{GW}(\mathcal{G}_i, \mathcal{G}_j) = ||\mathbf{M}_i^o - \mathbf{M}_j^o||_2$; $\mathbf{M}_i^o$ and $\mathbf{M}_j^o$ are the orthonormal basis to the matrices of graphlets $\mathcal{G}_i$ and $\mathcal{G}_j$, respectively.

Inspired by many manifold algorithms [22], we assume a linear approximation of the graphlet embedding process. Therefore, we suppose $\mathbf{Y} = \mathbf{U}^T\mathbf{X}$ and thus (3) can be reorganized into:

$$\arg\min_{\mathbf{U}} \text{tr}(\mathbf{U}^T\mathbf{XRX}^T\mathbf{U})$$
$$= \arg\min_{\mathbf{U}} \text{tr}(\mathbf{U}^T\mathbf{LU}) \;\; s.t. \;\; \mathbf{U}^T\mathbf{U} = \mathbf{I}_d, \quad (6)$$

where $\mathbf{X}$ is obtained by row-wise stacking matrix $[\mathbf{M}_r^c, \mathbf{M}_r^t, \mathbf{M}_s]$ into a vector, $\mathbf{U}$ is the linear projection matrix, and $\mathbf{L} = \mathbf{XRX}^T$. The above objective function (6) is a basic optimization problem that can be solved using the Lagrangian multiplier. The optimal solution is the d eigenvectors associated with the d smallest eigenvalues of matrix $\mathbf{L}$.

4. SPARSITY-CONSTRAINED SALIENT GRAPHLETS DISCOVERY

In a human vision system, usually only the distinctive sensory information is selected for further processing. From this perspective, only a few visually/semantically salient graphlets within a photo are usually perceived by humans. These salient graphlets are significantly different from those non-salient ones, either in their appearances or in their semantics. Inspired by this, a sparsity-constrained ranking scheme is developed to discover salient graphlets, by exploring color, texture, and semantic channels collaboratively. More specifically, the ranking algorithm can be formulated as follows:

[1]The atomic regions are superpixels segmented using SLIC [4]. The codes are publicly available. Experiments show SLIC is efficient and the generated superpixels are neatly adherent to object boundaries.

[2]With the advances of supervised image retrieval, nowadays image labels are cheaply available. They can be efficiently and accurately acquired by many existing models, *e.g.*, SPM [24] and its variants.

Formulation: Let $\mathbf{X}_1, \mathbf{X}_2$, and $\mathbf{X}_3$ be the three feature matrices in color, texture, and semantic channels respectively, where the columns in different matrices with the same index correspond to the same graphlet. The size of each $\mathbf{X}_i$ is $d_i \times N$, where d_i is the feature dimension and N is the number of graphlets. Then, the task is to find a weighting function to each graphlet $S(\mathcal{G}_i) \in [0, 1]$ by integrating the three feature matrices $\mathbf{X}_1, \mathbf{X}_2$, and $\mathbf{X}_3$.

Based on the theory of visual perception [27], there are usually strong correlation among the non-salient regions in a photo. That is to say, the non-salient graphlets can be self-represented. This analysis suggests that feature matrix $\mathbf{X}$ ($\mathbf{X}$ can be any one of matrices $\mathbf{X}_1, \mathbf{X}_2$, and $\mathbf{X}_3$) can be decomposed into a salient part and a non-salient part, *i.e.*,

$$\mathbf{X} = \mathbf{X}\mathbf{Z}_0 + \mathbf{E}_0, \tag{7}$$

where $\mathbf{X}\mathbf{Z}_0$ denotes the non-salient part that can be reconstructed by itself, $\mathbf{Z}_0$ denotes the reconstruction coefficients, and $\mathbf{E}_0$ denotes the remaining part corresponding to the salient targets.

Without a constraint, there are an infinite number of possible decompositions with respect to $\mathbf{Z}_0$ and $\mathbf{E}_0$. Toward a unique solution that indicates those salient graphlets, we need some criteria for characterizing matrices $\mathbf{Z}_0$ and $\mathbf{E}_0$. Aiming at this, two observations are made. On one hand, motivated by many approaches in computer vision, we assume that only a small fraction of graphlets are salient, *i.e.*, matrix $\mathbf{E}_0$ is sparse. The connection between sparsity and saliency is also consistent with the fact that only a small subset of sensory information is selected for further processing in a human vision system. On the other hand, the strong correlation among the background graphlets suggests that matrix $\mathbf{Z}_0$ is with low rankness. Based on the above analysis, we can infer the salient graphlets by adding a sparsity and low-rankness constraint to (7), thereby the graphlet saliency detection can be formulated as a low-rank representation (LRR) [25] problem:

$$\min_{\mathbf{Z}_0, \mathbf{E}_0} ||\mathbf{Z}_0||_* + \lambda||\mathbf{E}_0||_{2,1}, \quad s.t. \ \mathbf{X} = \mathbf{X}\mathbf{Z}_0 + \mathbf{E}_0, \tag{8}$$

where $||\cdot||_*$ denotes the matrix nuclear norm that is a convex relaxation of the rank function, parameter $\lambda > 0$ is used to balance the effects of the two parts, and $||\cdot||_{2,1}$ is the $l_{2,1}$ norm defined as the sum of the $l_{2,1}$ norms of the columns of a matrix:

$$||\mathbf{E}_0||_{2,1} = \sum_i \sqrt{\sum_j (\mathbf{E}_0(j,i))^2}. \tag{9}$$

It is noticeable that the minimization of the $l_{2,1}$ norm encourages the columns of $\mathbf{E}_0$ to be zero, and hence it fits well with our saliency detection problem. For a column corresponding to the i-th graphlet $\mathcal{G}_i$, a larger magnitude implies that the corresponding graphlet is more salient in drawing the attention of the human eye.

Let $\mathbf{E}_0^*$ be the optimal solution (with respect to $\mathbf{E}_0$) to problem (7). To obtain the saliency value of graphlet $\mathcal{G}_i$, we quantify the response of the sparse matrix as follows:

$$S(\mathcal{G}_i) = ||\mathbf{E}_0^*(:,i)||_2 = \sqrt{\sum_i (\mathbf{E}_0^*(j,i))^2}. \tag{10}$$

where $||\mathbf{E}_0^*(:,i)||_2$ denotes the l_2 norm of the i-th column of $\mathbf{E}_0^*(:,i)$. A larger score of $S(\mathcal{G}_i)$ means that graphlet $\mathcal{G}_i$ has a higher probability to be salient.

The objective function (7) calculates the saliency of a graphlet based on one type of visual feature, which is suboptimal since multiple visual features determine graphlet saliency collaboratively. To combine together visual features in color, texture, and semantic channels, we generalize the objective function (7) into a multimodal version:

$$\min_{\substack{\mathbf{Z}_1,\mathbf{Z}_2,\mathbf{Z}_3 \\ \mathbf{E}_1,\mathbf{E}_2,\mathbf{E}_3}} \sum_{i=1}^{3} ||\mathbf{Z}_i||_* + \lambda||\mathbf{E}||_{2,1}, \quad s.t. \ \mathbf{X}_i = \mathbf{X}_i\mathbf{Z}_i + \mathbf{E}_i, \tag{11}$$

where $\mathbf{E} = [\mathbf{E}_1; \mathbf{E}_2; \mathbf{E}_3]$ is formed by vertically concatenating $\mathbf{E}_1$, $\mathbf{E}_2$, and $\mathbf{E}_3$ together along a column. The integration of multiple features is seamlessly performed by minimizing the $l_{2,1}$ norm of $\mathbf{E}$. That is, we enforce the columns of $\mathbf{E}_1$, $\mathbf{E}_2$, and $\mathbf{E}_3$ to have jointly consistent magnitude values.

Let $\{\mathbf{E}_1^*, \mathbf{E}_2^*, \mathbf{E}_3^*\}$ be the optimal solution to (11), to obtain a saliency score for graphlet $\mathcal{G}_i$, we quantify the response of the sparse matrices as follows:

$$S(\mathcal{G}_i) = \sum\nolimits_{j=1}^{3} ||\mathbf{E}_j^*(:,i)||_2, \tag{12}$$

where $||\mathbf{E}_j^*(:,i)||_2$ denotes the l_2 norm of the i-th column of $\mathbf{E}_j^*$. A larger score of $S(\mathcal{G}_i)$ means that graphlet $\mathcal{G}_i$ has a higher probability to be salient. Algorithm 1 summarizes the procedure of our proposed multimodal graphlet saliency detection. The details of solving (11) are illustrated in the Appendix.

Algorithm 1 Multimodal Salient Graphlets Discovery

input: Graphlets from a labeled photo, the projection matrix $\mathbf{U}$;
output: A number of graphlets ranked by their saliency values;

1) Compute the feature matrices $\{\mathbf{X}_1, \mathbf{X}_2, \mathbf{X}_3\}$ in color, texture, and semantic channels to describe each graphlet;
2) Obtain the sparsity matrices $\{\mathbf{E}_1, \mathbf{E}_2, \mathbf{E}_3\}$ in color, texture, and semantic channels respectively, by solving the objective function (11);
3) Compute the graphlet saliency based on (12), and a few top-ranked graphlets are deemed as the salient ones.

5. PERCEPTION-GUIDED PROBABILISTIC AESTHETIC MEASURE

Based on the above discussion, the top-ranked graphlets are the salient ones that can draw the attention of the human eye. That is, humans first fixate on the most salient graphlet in a photo, and then shift their gazes to the second salient one, and so on. Inspired by the scan path used in human eye-tracking experiments, we propose an actively viewing path (AVP) to mimic the sequential manner biological species perceive a visual scene. The procedure of generating an AVP from a photo is described in Fig. 4. It is noticeable that all the AVPs from a data set are with the same number of graphlets K. Typically, we set K to 4 and its influence on photo aesthetics prediction is evaluated in our experiments.

Given a set of aesthetically pleasing training photos $\{I^1, \cdots, I^H\}$

Figure 4: An illustration of AVP generation based on the top-ranked graphlets.

and a test image I^*, they are highly correlated through their respective AVPs $\mathcal{P}$ and $\mathcal{P}^*$. Thus, a probabilistic graphical model is utilized to describe this correlation. As shown in Fig. 5, the graphical model contains two types of nodes: observable nodes (blue color) and hidden nodes (gray color). More specifically, it can be divided into four layers. The first layer represents all the training photos, the second layer denotes the AVPs extracted from the training photos, the third layer represents the AVP of the test photo, and the last layer denotes the test photo. The correlation between the first and the second layers is $p(\mathcal{P}|I^1, \cdots, I^H)$, the correlation between the second and the third layers is $p(\mathcal{P}^*|\mathcal{P})$, and the correlation between the third and the fourth layers is $p(I^*|\mathcal{P}^*)$.

According to the formulation above, photo aesthetics can be

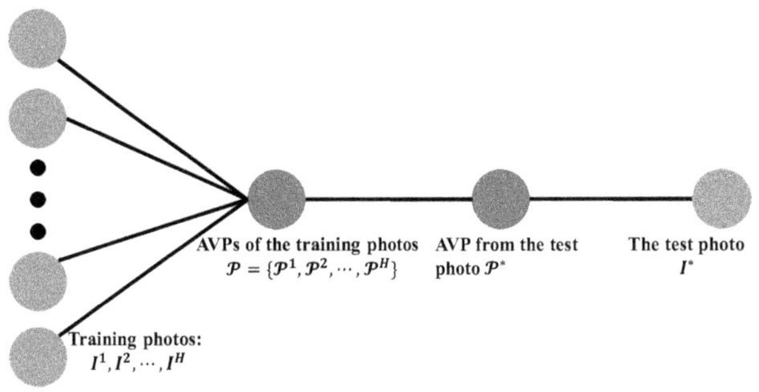

Figure 5: An illustration of the probabilistic graphical model.

quantified as the similarity between the AVPs from the test photo and those from the training aesthetically pleasing photos. The similarity is interpreted as the amount of AVPs that can be transferred from the training photos into the test image. That is, the aesthetic quality of the test photo I^* can be formulated as:

$$\begin{aligned}\gamma(I^*) &= p(I^*|I^1, \cdots, I^H) \\ &= p(I^*|\mathcal{P}^*) \cdot p(\mathcal{P}^*|\mathcal{P}) \cdot p(\mathcal{P}|I^1, \cdots, I^H). \quad (13)\end{aligned}$$

The probabilities $p(I^*|\mathcal{P}^*)$, $p(\mathcal{P}^*|\mathcal{P})$, and $p(\mathcal{P}|I^1, I^2, \cdots, I^H)$ in (13) are computed respectively as:

$$\begin{aligned}p(I^*|\mathcal{P}^*) &= \prod_{\mathcal{G}^* \in \mathcal{P}^*} p(I^*|\mathcal{G}^*) \\ &= \prod_{\mathcal{G}^* \in \mathcal{P}^*} \frac{p(\mathcal{G}_1^*, \cdots, \mathcal{G}_T^*|I^*)p(I^*)}{p(\mathcal{G}_1^*, \cdots, \mathcal{G}_T^*)} \\ &\propto \prod_{\mathcal{G}^* \in \mathcal{P}^*} p(\mathcal{G}_1^*, \cdots, \mathcal{G}_T^*|I^*)p(I^*) \\ &= \prod_{\mathcal{G}^* \in \mathcal{P}^*} \prod_{i=1}^{T} \prod_{j=1}^{Y_t} p(\mathcal{G}_t^*(j)|I^*), \quad (14)\end{aligned}$$

where T is the maximum graphlet size, Y_i is the number of i-sized graphlets in the test photo I^*, and $\mathcal{G}_t^*(j)$ is the j-th t-sized graphlet of AVP from the test photo. $p(\mathcal{G}_t^*(j)|I^*)$ denotes the probability of extracting graphlets $\mathcal{G}_t^*(j)$ from the test photo I^*, which is calculated as described next.

As shown in Fig. 6, the graphlet extraction is based on random walk. We first index all atomic regions in a photo and choose a starting one with probability $\frac{p(Y)}{Y}$, where Y means there are Y atomic regions in photo I and $p(Y)$ is the corresponding probability. We then visit a spatially adjacent larger-indexed vertex[3] with probability $\frac{1}{2\sum_d p_d(R_l)d(R_l)}$, where $d(R_l)$ is the degree of the current atomic region R_l and $p_d(R_l)$ denotes the probability of atomic region R_l with degree $d(R_l)$. In our implementation, $p_d(R_l) \propto$

[3]It is with the same probability of visiting a larger-indexed vertex or visiting a smaller-indexed one.

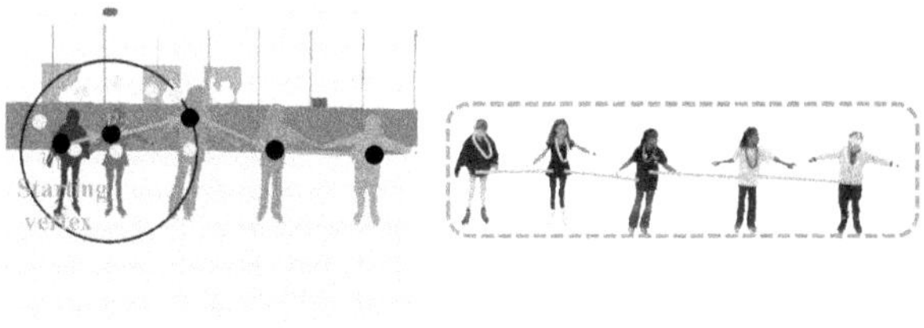

Figure 6: Graphlet extraction based on a random walk model.

$\exp\left(-\frac{1}{||d(R_l)-\bar{d}p(R_l)d(R_l)||}\right)$ and $p(Y) \propto \exp\left(-\frac{||Y-\bar{Y}||^2}{\sigma_Y^2}\right)$. The random walk process stops when the maximum graphlet size is reached. Therefore, we obtain

$$p(\mathcal{G}|I) \propto \frac{p(Y)}{Y} \prod_{l=1}^{T-1} \frac{1}{2\sum_d p_d(R_l)d(R_l)}, \quad (15)$$

The probability $p(\mathcal{P}^*|\mathcal{P})$ measures the similarity between AVPs from the training photos and that from the test photo:

$$p(\mathcal{P}^*|\mathcal{P}) = \prod_{i=1}^{H} \prod_{\substack{\mathcal{G}^* \in \mathcal{P}^* \\ \mathcal{G} \in \mathcal{P}^i}} p(\mathcal{G}^*|\mathcal{G}), \quad (16)$$

where $p(\mathcal{G}^*|\mathcal{G})$ measures the similarity between the same-indexed graphlets from the test and the training photos, respectively. In our implementation, $p(\mathcal{G}^*|\mathcal{G})$ is implemented as a Gaussian kernel.

The probability $p(\mathcal{P}|I^1, \cdots, I^H)$ measures the probabilities of AVPs generated from the training photos, which is calculated as:

$$\begin{aligned}p(\mathcal{P}|I^1, \cdots, I^H) &= \prod_{i=1}^{H} p(\mathcal{P}^i|I^i) \\ &= \prod_{i=1}^{H} \prod_{\mathcal{G} \in \mathcal{P}^i} p(\mathcal{G}|I^i), \quad (17)\end{aligned}$$

In summary, the procedure of our proposed photo aesthetics evaluation algorithm is presented in Algorithm 2.

Algorithm 2 Perception-Guided Photo Aesthetic Model

input: A set of training aesthetically pleasing $\{I^1, \cdots, I^H\}$, the number of graphlets in an AVP: K, and the test photo I^*;
output: The aesthetic score of the test photo I^*;

1) Extract graphlets from each training photo; represent them in both color and texture channels; learn the embedding model and represent each graphlet in semantic channel;
2) Construct the AVPs of each photo by selecting K salient graphlets, based on the sparsity-constrained ranking algorithm described in Sec. 4;
3) Compute the aesthetic score of the test photo I^* using (13).

6. EXPERIMENTS AND ANALYSIS

This section evaluates the effectiveness of the proposed method, which can be divided into four parts. The first part compares our approach with well-known photo aesthetic models. The second part step-by-step evaluates each component of the proposed approach. Third, based on an eye-tracking experiment, we make a quantitative comparison between the proposed AVP and a real human gaze shifting path. Lastly, we analyze the influence of different parameter settings on our aesthetic model.

6.1 Data Sets and Implementation Details

To the best of our knowledge, there exist three off-the-shelf data sets for evaluating photo aesthetics: the CUHK [10], the Photo.net,

Table 1: **Comparison of aesthetics prediction accuracies.**

	CUHK	PNE	AVA
Dhar *et al.*	0.7386	0.6754	0.6435
Luo *et al.*	0.8004	0.7213	0.6879
Marchesotti *et al.* (FV-Color-SP)	0.8767	0.8114	0.7891
Cheng *et al.*	0.8432	0.7754	0.8121
Nishiyama *et al.*	0.7745	0.7341	0.7659
The proposed method	**0.9059**	**0.8552**	**0.8413**

and the AVA [16]. A rough description of the three data sets is as follows: 1) The CUHK [10] contains 12,000 photos collected from DPChallenge.com. These photos have been labeled by ten independent viewers. Each photo is classified as highly aesthetic if more than eight viewers agree on the assessment. We use a standard split of training/test sets on this data set. 2) The Photo.net [3] consists of 3581 images. Only URLs of the original photos are provided. Approximately half of the images have since been removed from the websites, leaving only nearly 1,700 images available. Thus, we extend this data set by online crawling 4,000 photos and name the extended Photo.net data set PNE. The aesthetics of these additionally crawled photos are manually labeled. They are randomly split into equal partitions, one for training and the rest for testing. 3) The AVA [16] data set contains 25,000 highly- and low-aesthetic photos, each of which is associated with two semantic tags. The selection criteria is based on the aesthetic quality of each photo, which is scored by 78 to 549 amateur/professional photographers. The training and test photos of the AVA data set are pre-specified.

For the classifier-based photo aesthetic models, such as those proposed by Marchesotti *et al.* [15] and Nishiyamma *et al.* [18], both the highly- and low-aesthetic photos are adopted to learn the model. More specifically, the highly aesthetic photos are used as positive samples and the low aesthetic ones are used negative samples. For those models that are based on transferring aesthetic features (*e.g.*, Cheng *et al.* [2]'s model), they employ only the "good" aesthetic features to score a test photo. Thus, it is necessary to assign a weight for each training AVP indicating its "goodness", *i.e.*, a larger weight reflects a higher aesthetic level. The weight is determined by the aesthetics of the photo from which the graphlet is extracted. For the three data sets, different settings are used to assign the weight of each photo. For the CUHK, we use the probabilistic output described in Yan *et al.*'s work [10] to rank the aesthetics of each photo. For the PNE, we manually select 674 highly aesthetic photos and leave the rest as the low-aesthetic ones. Then, we extract the aesthetic features based on [10], and further use a probabilistic SVM output to score the aesthetics of each photo. For the AVA, each training photo is rated by multiple users. We average the rating scores of a photo as its overall aesthetic score.

All the experiments were carried out on a personal computer with an Intel X5482 processor and 8GB RAM. The algorithm is implemented on the Matlab 2011 platform.

6.2 A Comparative Study

The first experiment compares our approach with five photo aesthetics evaluation methods. The compared algorithms include three global feature-based approaches proposed by Dhar *et al.* [5], Luo *et al.* [12], and Marchesotti *et al.* [15], respectively; and two local patch integration-based methods proposed by Cheng *et al.* [2] and Nishiyama *et al.* [18], respectively.

In the comparative study, we notice that the source codes of the above five compared methods are not provided and some experimental details are not mentioned, therefore it is difficult to strictly

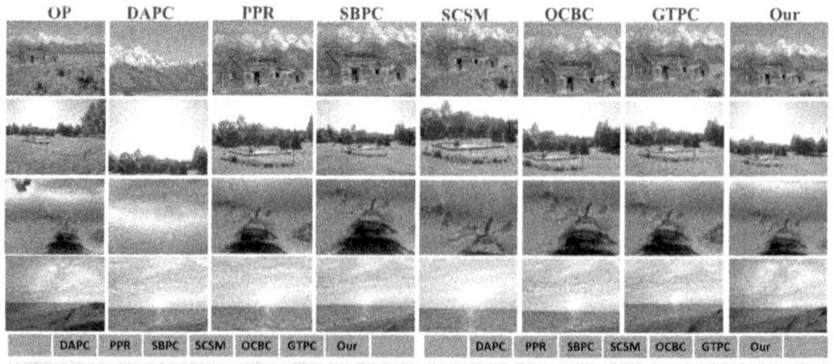

	DAPC	PPR	SBPC	SCSM	OCBC	GTPC	Our	
DAPC	--	5	8	7	8	6	2	36
PPR	25	--	8	12	11	14	9	79
SBPC	22	22	--	12	15	14	10	95
SCSM	23	18	18	--	12	9	7	87
OCBC	22	19	15	18	--	12	9	95
GTPC	24	16	16	21	18	--	8	103
Our	28	21	20	23	21	22	--	135

	DAPC	PPR	SBPC	SCSM	OCBC	GTPC	Our	
DAPC	--	16	15	18	19	11	6	85
PPR	14	--	13	12	13	9	7	68
SBPC	15	17	--	17	18	12	9	88
SCSM	12	18	13	--	16	8	4	71
OCBC	11	17	12	14	--	6	3	63
GTPC	19	21	18	22	24	--	9	113
Our	24	23	21	26	27	21	--	142

	DAPC	PPR	SBPC	SCSM	OCBC	GTPC	Our	
DAPC	--	21	19	17	16	12	11	96
PPR	9	--	15	17	18	21	10	90
SBPC	11	15	--	14	12	19	12	83
SCSM	13	13	16	--	13	14	8	77
OCBC	14	12	18	17	--	15	9	85
GTPC	18	9	11	16	15	--	6	75
Our	19	20	18	22	21	24	--	124

	DAPC	PPR	SBPC	SCSM	OCBC	GTPC	Our	
DAPC	--	3	6	5	7	5	8	34
PPR	27	--	14	17	18	15	11	102
SBPC	24	16	--	21	22	19	8	110
SCSM	25	13	9	--	14	13	8	82
OCBC	23	12	8	16	--	16	7	82
GTPC	25	15	11	17	14	--	6	88
Our	22	19	22	22	23	24	--	132

Figure 7: Cropped photos produced by the compared methods and the preference matrices (OP: the original photo; the red numbers denote the scores of the algorithms).

implement them. Toward a convincing comparative study, we try to strengthen some components of the compared methods. Based on this, we adopt the following implementation settings. For Dhar's approach, we use the public codes from Li *et al.* [14] to extract the attributes from each photo. These attributes are combined with the low-level features proposed by Yeh *et al.* [21] to train the aesthetic classifier. For Luo *et al.*'s approach, not only are the low-level and high-level features in their publication implemented, but also the six global features from Getlter *et al.* [29]'s work are used to strengthen the aesthetic prediction ability. For Marchesotti *et al.*'s approach, similar to the implementation of Luo *et al.*'s method, the six additional features are also adopted. For Cheng *et al.*'s approach, we implement it as a simplified version of our approach, *i.e.*, only 2-sized graphlets are employed for aesthetics measure. Notably, for the three probabilistic model-based aesthetics evaluation methods (*i.e.*, Cheng *et al.*'s method, Nishiyama *et al.*'s method, and our model), if the aesthetic score is larger than 0.5, then this photo is deemed as highly aesthetic, and vice versa. We choose 0.5 as the threshold because for each of the three data sets, about half of the photos are highly aesthetic.

We present the aesthetics prediction accuracy on the CUHK, the PNE, and the AVA in Table 1. On the three data sets, our approach outperforms Marchesotti *et al.*'s approach by nearly 3%, and exceeds the rest of the compared methods by more than 6%, which demonstrates the effectiveness our approach.

Last but not least, we evaluate the proposed aesthetic model in comparison with several well-known cropping methods. For our approach, the sub-region with the highest aesthetic score in each photo is cropped. The compared cropping methods are sparse coding of saliency maps (SCSM [30]), sensation based photo cropping (SBPC [18]), omni-range context-based cropping (OCBC [2]), personalized photo ranking (PPR [21]), describable attribute for photo cropping (DAPC [5]), and the graphlet transferring-based photo cropping(GTPC) [20], respectively. We conduct a paired comparison-based user study [20] and present the preference matrix obtained from the above methods. Each preference matrix is

Table 2: Aesthetics prediction accuracy decrement.

	CUHK	PNE	AVA
Graphlet→single atomic region	-4.31%	-3.55%	-4.76%
Remove adj. mat from graphlet	-3.38%	-3.65%	-2.77%
Mani. Grap. emb.→Single-ch. emb.	-3.16%	-2.81%	-2.89%
Mani. Grap. emb.→kernel PCA	-6.21%	-5.12%	-4.33%
Prob. mea. → clasf. mea.	-3.31%	-2.81%	-2.91%

filled by 25∼40 volunteers. As shown in Fig. 7, the result again demonstrates the advantage of the proposed method.

6.3 Step-by-Step Model Justification

The proposed photo aesthetic model includes three main components: the multimodal graphlet representation, the sparsity-constrained graphlet ranking, and the probabilistic aesthetics measure, which are theoretically indispensable and inseparable. To demonstrate the effectiveness of each step, we replace each component by a functionally reduced counterpart and report the corresponding aesthetics prediction accuracy.

- To illustrate the effectiveness of the first component, two experimental settings are applied: 1) reducing the multimodal graphlet representation to a single channel one (Mani.Grap→ Sing-ch), where only the color channel is used. The color channel is preserved here because as shown by several photo aesthetics methods [18], it is the most important channel for representing photo aesthetics; and 2) replacing the manifold graphlet embedding by kernel PCA (Mani.Grap.emb→ kernel PCA), where the kernel is calculated as:

$$k(\mathcal{G}, \mathcal{G}') \propto \exp(-d_{GW}(\mathbf{M}, \mathbf{M}')), \qquad (18)$$

  where $\mathbf{M} = [\mathbf{M}_r^c, \mathbf{M}_r^t, \mathbf{M}_r^s, \mathbf{M}_s]$ and $d_{GW}(\cdot, \cdot)$ is the Golub-Werman distance between identically sized matrices.

- To justify the usefulness of the sparsity-constrained graphlet ranking, we replace this component by the locality preserving active learning paradigm proposed by Zhang *et al.* [31]. In Zhang *et al.*'s model, the weighting matrix (W in Eqn. (12) of Zhang *et al.* [31]) is calculated by considering a graphlet and its spatially neighboring graphlets in a photo. As the comparative aesthetic features shown in Fig. 8, our approach prefers to select small graphlets due to the sparsity constraint in our model. More importantly, our approach can explicitly model the gaze shifting sequence of each photo, while the other methods fail.

- To demonstrate the effectiveness of the third component, we replace the probabilistic aesthetics measure by a kernel SVM-based one (Prob.mea.→Clas.mea.), wherein the kernel is computed the same as that in the above kernel PCA.

As shown in Table 2, when replacing one component of the proposed approach by an existing one, the aesthetics prediction accuracy reduces dramatically. This demonstrates that each component of the proposed approach is indispensable and inseparable.

6.4 Visualization of the Active Viewing Paths and the Photos Ranked by Aesthetics

This subsection quantitatively and qualitatively compares the proposed actively viewing path (AVP) with real human gaze shifting path. In particular, we record the eye fixations of five viewers by making use of the eye-tracker EyeLink II, and then link the fixations into a path in a sequential manner. As can be seen from Fig. 9, in most photos, the proposed AVPs are consistent with human gaze shifting paths. In addition, we calculate the proportion of the human gaze shifting path that overlaps with an AVP. The overlapping between our proposed AVP and a real human gaze shifting path is computed as shown in Fig. 10. Given the five real gaze shifting paths, we connect all the segmented regions on the gaze shifting path and then obtain the human gaze shifting path with segmented regions. Based on this, the similarity between an AVP and a gaze shifting path with segmented regions is calculated by:

$$s(P_1, P_2) = \frac{nPixel(P_1 \cap P_2)}{nPixel(P_1) + nPixel(P_2)}, \qquad (19)$$

where P_1 and P_2 denote an AVP and the gaze shifting path with segmented regions, respectively, $nPixel$ counts the pixels within an image region, and $P_1 \cap P_2$ denotes the shared region between P_1 and P_2. Based on (19), we observe that the overlapping percentage between an AVP and a real human gaze shifting path is 87.65% on average. This observation shows that the AVP can accurately predict the human gaze shifting process.

Next, we visualize the top-ranked graphlets from images in

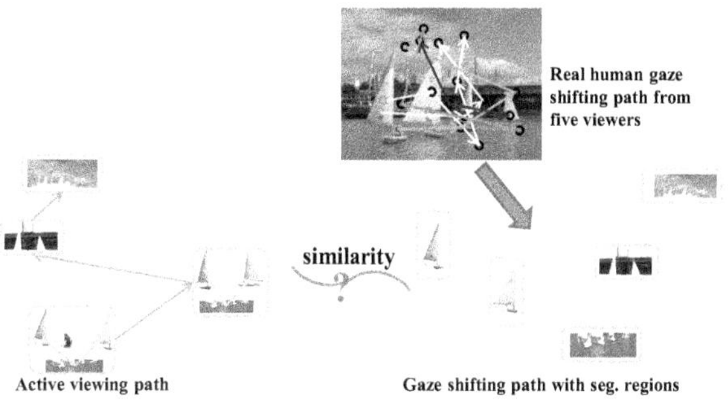

Figure 9: An illustration of the overlapping between an AVP and a human gaze shifting path.

the LHI [32] data set. As shown in Fig. 12, for each image, the first four most visually/semantically salient graphlets are presented. The results again demonstrate the importance of mining the spatial interaction of image regions for describing photo aesthetics.

Further, we visualize photos of the AVA data set that are ranked by our probabilistic photo aesthetics measure. As can be seen from Fig. 11, we made the following three observations.

- As shown in the photos whose aesthetics are ranked between 0.8 and 1, highly aesthetic photos with multiple interacting objects are assigned with very high scores, which shows that our proposed AVPs well predict how humans perceive local/global aesthetics in these beautiful photos.

- As seen from the photos whose aesthetics are ranked between 0.5 and 0.8, highly aesthetic photos with a single object are also appreciated by the proposed aesthetics model. This is because graphlets are naturally local composition descriptors, and they influence photo aesthetics by making use of the proposed probabilistic model.

- Objects from the photos whose aesthetics are ranked between 0 and 0.5 are either spatially disharmoniously distributed or blurred. Thus, these photos are considered as aesthetically low by our model.

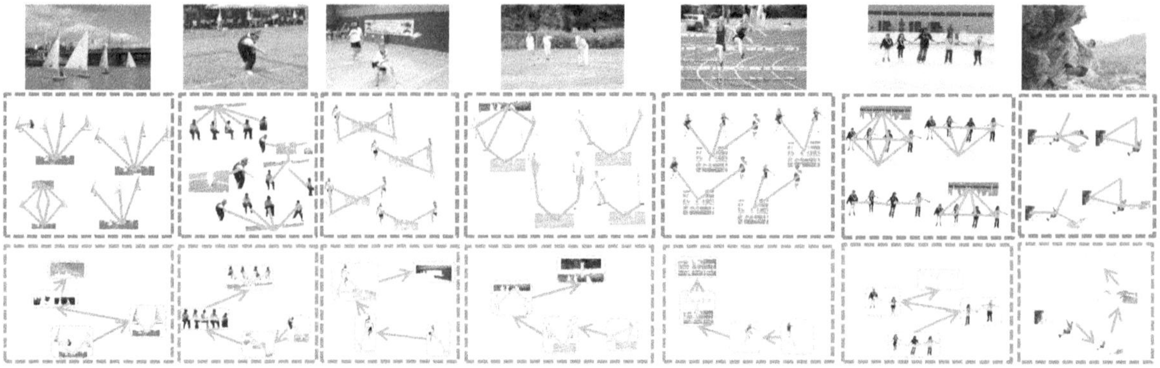

Figure 8: A comparison of representative graphlets (blue rectangles) and the AVPs (red rectangles).

Figure 10: Comparison of gaze shifting paths from five observers (differently colored) and the proposed AVPs.

Figure 11: Ranking results on the AVA data set. The yellow paths denote the AVPs predicted by our model, where each circle indicates the location of a graphlet. The three pie charts show statistics of photos from the three data sets based on our model.

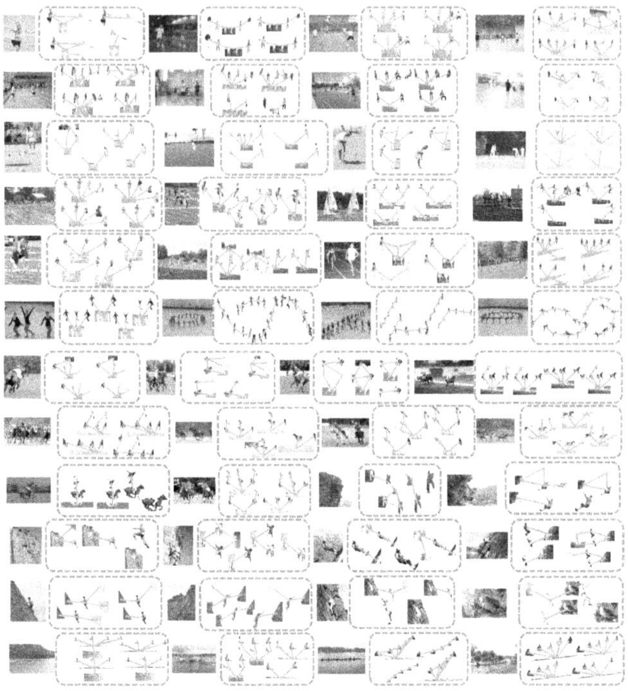

Figure 12: Visualized highly ranked graphlets of the LHI data set.

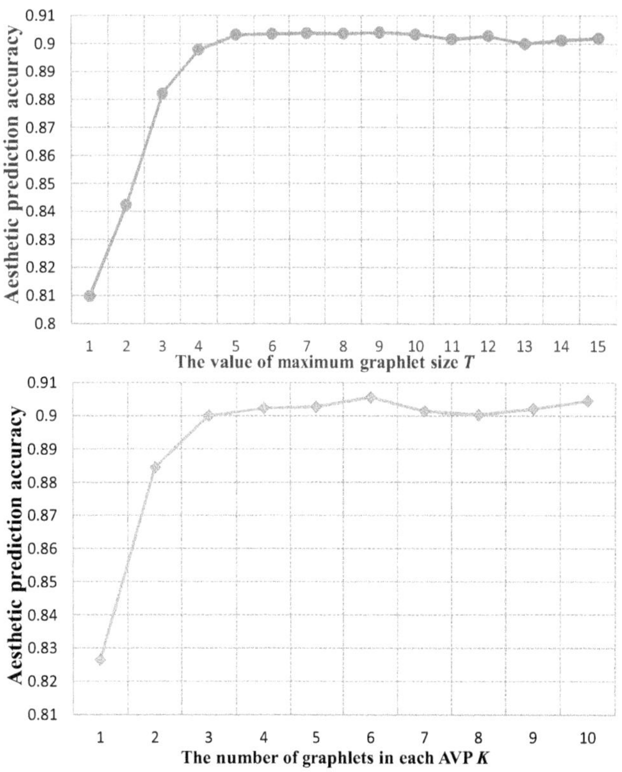

Figure 13: Photo aesthetics evaluation performance under different parameters.

We compare the AVPs predicted by our approach, under both low aesthetic and high aesthetic photos. As shown in Fig. 11, neither low nor high aesthetic photo have particular path geometry, such as the angle between pairwise shifting vectors (yellow arrows). However, for high aesthetic photos, the fixation points (yellow circles) are aesthetically pleasing and the objects along the path are harmoniously distributed.

6.5 Parameter Analysis

The experiment evaluates the influence of the graphlet size T and the number of graphlets of each AVP K on the performance of the proposed photo aesthetics model.

To analyze the effects of the maximum graphlet size T on predicting photo aesthetics, we set up an experiment by varying T continuously. In the top graph of Fig. 13, we present the aesthetics prediction accuracy (on the CUHK data set) when the maximum size of the graphlet is tuned from 1 to 10. As can be seen, prediction accuracy increases moderately when $T \in [1, 5]$ but remains almost unchanged when $T \in [6, 10]$. This observation implies that 5-sized graphlets are sufficient for capturing the local composition of photos in the CUHK data set. In the bottom graph of Fig. 13, we present the performance when the number of graphlet in an AVP (K) is tuned from 1 to 10. As can be seen, the prediction accuracy increases quickly when $K \in [1, 4]$ but remains stable when $K \in [5, 10]$.

7. CONCLUSIONS

Image/video aesthetics quality assessment is a useful technique in multimedia field [28, 11, 13]. In this paper, a new model is proposed to evaluate the aesthetics of a photo by simulating the process of humans sequentially perceiving semantics of a photo. By discovering visually/semantically salient graphlets using a sparsity-constrained ranking paradigm, an active viewing path is constructed to mimic the process where humans actively look at important components in a photo. Thereafter, we develop a probabilistic model that quantifies photo aesthetics as the amount of AVPs that can be transferred from a set of aesthetically pleasing training photos into the test image. Extensive experiments demonstrate the effectiveness of our model.

In the future, we will apply our model to video aesthetics evaluation. The aesthetics of a video clip is determined by accumulating the aesthetic scores of all its constituent frames, using a probabilistic model.

8. APPENDIX

Problem (11) is convex and can be optimized efficiently. We first convert it into the following equivalent problem:

$$\min_{\mathbf{J}_i,\mathbf{Z}_i,\mathbf{E}_i} \sum_{i=1}^{3} ||\mathbf{J}_i||_* + \lambda||\mathbf{E}||_{2,1}, \quad s.t.\ \mathbf{X}_i = \mathbf{X}_i\mathbf{Z}_i + \mathbf{E}_i, \mathbf{Z}_i = \mathbf{J}_i, \tag{20}$$

This problem can be solved with the ALM method which minimizes the following augmented Lagrange function:

$$\mathcal{L} = \lambda||\mathbf{E}||_{2,1} + \sum_{i=1}^{3}(||\mathbf{J}_i||_* + \langle \mathbf{Y}_i, \mathbf{X}_i - \mathbf{X}_i\mathbf{Z}_i - \mathbf{E}_i\rangle + \langle \mathbf{W}_i, \mathbf{Z}_i - \mathbf{J}_i\rangle + \frac{\mu}{2}||\mathbf{X}_i - \mathbf{X}_i\mathbf{Z}_i - \mathbf{E}_i||_F^2 + \frac{\mu}{2}||\mathbf{Z}_i - \mathbf{J}_i||_F^2) \tag{21}$$

where $\mathbf{Y}_1, \mathbf{Y}_2, \mathbf{Y}_3$ and $\mathbf{W}_1, \mathbf{W}_2, \mathbf{W}_3$ are Lagrange multipliers and $\mu > 0$ is a penalty parameter. The inexact ALM method, which is also called the alternating direction method, is illustrated in Algorithm 3. Note that the subproblems of the algorithm are convex

Algorithm 3 Inextact ALM-based solution of (11)

input: Data matrices $\{\mathbf{X}_i\}$, parameter λ;
output: The optimal solution $\mathbf{E}^*$;

while not converged **do**

1) Fix the others and update $\mathbf{J}_1, \mathbf{J}_2, \mathbf{J}_3$ by:
$\mathbf{J}_i = \arg\min_{\mathbf{J}} \frac{1}{\mu}||\mathbf{J}||_* + \frac{1}{2}||\mathbf{J}_i - (\mathbf{Z}_i + \frac{\mathbf{W}_i}{\mu})||_F^2$.

2) Fix the others and update $\mathbf{Z}_1, \mathbf{Z}_2, \mathbf{Z}_3$ by:
$\mathbf{Z}_i = \mathbf{M}(\mathbf{X}_i^T(\mathbf{X}_i - \mathbf{E}_i) + \mathbf{J}_i + \frac{\mathbf{X}_i^T\mathbf{Y}_i - \mathbf{W}_i}{\mu})$
where $\mathbf{M} = (\mathbf{I} + \sum_{i=1}^{3} \mathbf{X}_i^T\mathbf{X}_i)^{-1}$.

3) Fix the others and update $\mathbf{E} = [\mathbf{E}_1; \mathbf{E}_2; \mathbf{E}_3]$ by
$\mathbf{E} = \arg\min_{\mathbf{E}} \frac{\lambda}{\mu}||\mathbf{E}||_{2,1} + \frac{1}{2}||\mathbf{E} - \mathbf{G}||_F^2$,
where $\mathbf{G}$ is formed by vertically concatenating the matrices $\mathbf{X}_i - \mathbf{X}_i\mathbf{Z}_i + (\mathbf{Y}_i/\mu)$, $i = 1, 2, 3$ together along column.

4) Update the multipliers
$\mathbf{Y}_i = \mathbf{Y}_i + \mu(\mathbf{X}_i - \mathbf{X}_i\mathbf{Z}_i - \mathbf{E}_i)$; $\mathbf{W}_i = \mathbf{W}_i + \mu(\mathbf{Z}_i - \mathbf{J}_i)$;

5) Update the parameter μ by
$\mu = \min(\rho\mu, 10^{10})$
where the parameter ρ controls the convergence speed. It is set as $\rho = 1.1$ in all experiments.

6) Check the convergence condition: $\mathbf{X}_i - \mathbf{X}_i\mathbf{Z}_i - \mathbf{E}_i \to 0$ and $\mathbf{Z} - \mathbf{J}_i \to 0, i = 1, 2, 3$;

end while

and they have closed-form solution. Step 1 is solved via the singular value thresholding operator [26], whereas Step 3 is solved via [25].

Acknowledgements

This research has been supported by the Singapore National Research Foundation under its International Research Centre @ Singapore Funding Initiative and administered by the IDM Programme Office through the Centre of Social Media Innovations for Communities (COSMIC). Dr. Tian was also supported for this work in part by ARO grant W911NF-12-1-0057, Faculty Research Award by NEC Laboratories of America, and in part by the National Science Foundation of China (NSFC) under contract No. 61128007, respectively.

9. REFERENCES

[1] Subhabrata Bhattacharya, Rahul Sukthankar, Mubarak Shah, A Framework for Photo-Quality Assessment and Enhancement based on Visual Aesthetics, *in Proceedings of ACM Multimedia*, pages: 271–280, 2010.

[2] Bin Cheng, Bingbing Ni, Shuicheng Yan, Qi Tian, Learning to Photograph, *in Proceedings of ACM Multimedia*, pages: 291–300. 2010.

[3] Ritendra Datta, Dhiraj Joshi, Jia Li, James Z. Wang, Studying Aesthetics in Photographic Images using a Computational Approach, *in Proceedings of ECCV*, pages: 288–301, 2006.

[4] Radhakrishna Achanta, Appu Shaji, Kevin Smith, Aurelien Lucchi, Pascal Fua, and Sabine Sĺźsstrunk, SLIC Superpixels compared to State-of-the-Art Superpixel Methods, *T-PAMI*, 34(11): 2274–2282, 2012.

[5] Sagnik Dhar, Vicente Ordonez, Tamara L. Berg, High Level Describable Attributes for Predicting Aesthetics and Interestingness, *in Proceedings of CVPR*, pages: 1657–1664. 2011.

[6] Neil D. B. Bruce, John K. Tsotsos, Saliency, Attention, and Visual Search: An Information Theoretic Approach, *Journal of Vision*, 9(3), article 5, 2009.

[7] Ali Borji, Boosting Bottom-up and Top-down Visual Features for Saliency Estimation, *in Proceedings of CVPR*, pages: 438–445, 2012.

[8] N. Dalal, B.Triggs, Histograms of Oriented Gradients for Human Detection, *in Proceedings of CVPR*, pages: 886–893. 2005.

[9] Jonathan Harel, Christof Koch, Pietro Perona, Graph-based Visual Saliency, *in Proceedings of NIPS*, pages: 545–552. 2007.

[10] Yan Ke, Xiaoou Tang, Feng Jing, The Design of High-level Features for Photo Quality Assessment, *in Proceedings of CVPR*, pages: 419–426, 2006.

[11] Luming Zhang, Yue Gao, Rongrong Ji, Qionghai Dai, Xuelong Li, Actively Learning Human Gaze Shifting Paths for Photo Cropping, *IEEE T-IP*, 21(5), pages: 2235–2245, 2014.

[12] Wei Luo, Xiaogang Wang, Xiaoou Tang, Content-based Photo Quality Assessment, *in Proceedings of ICCV*, pages: 2206–2213. 2011.

[13] Xiao Liu, Mingli Song, Dacheng Tao, Zicheng Liu, Luming Zhang, Jiajun Bu, Chun Chen, Semisupervised Node Splitting for Random Forest Construction, *in Proceedings of CVPR*, pages: 492–499, 2013.

[14] Fei-Fei Li, Pietro Perona, A Bayesian Hierarchical Model for Learning Natural Scene Categories, *in Proceedings of CVPR*, pages: 524–531, 2005.

[15] Luca Marchesotti, Florent Perronnin, Diane Larlus, Gabriela Csurka, Assessing the Aesthetic Quality of Photographs using Generic Image Descriptors, *in Proceedings of ICCV*, pages: 1784–1791, 2011.

[16] Naila Murray, Luca Marchesotti, Florent Perronnin, AVA: A Large-Scale Database for Aesthetic Visual Analysis, *in Proceedings of CVPR*, pages: 2408–2415, 2012.

[17] Masashi Nishiyama, Takahiro Okabe, Yoichi Sato, Imari Sato, Sensation-based Photo Cropping, *in Proceedings of ACM Multimedia*, pages: 669–672, 2009.

[18] Masashi Nishiyama, Takahiro Okabel, Imari Sato, Yoichi Sato, Aesthetic Quality Classification of Photographs based on Color Harmony, *in Proceedings of CVPR*, pages: 33–40, 2011.

[19] Markus Stricker, Markus Orengo, Similarity of Color Images, *Storage and Retrieval of Image and Video Databases*, pages: 381–392, 1995.

[20] Luming Zhang, Mingli Song, Qi Zhao, Xiao Liu, Jiajun Bu, Chun Chen, Probabilistic Graphlet Transfer for Photo Cropping, *IEEE T-IP*, 21(5), pages: 2887–2897, 2013.

[21] Che-Hua Yeh, Yuan-Chen Ho, Brian A. Barsky, Ming Ouhyoung, Personalized Photograph Ranking and Selection System, *in Proceedings of ACM Multimedia*, pages: 211–220, 2010.

[22] Xinchao Wang, Zhu Li, Dacheng Tao, Subspaces Indexing Model on Grassmann Manifold for Image Search, *IEEE T-IP*, 20(9), pages: 2627–2635, 2011.

[23] Tian Xia, Dacheng Tao, Tao Mei, Yongdong Zhang, Multiview Spectral Embedding, *IEEE T-SMC-B*, 40(6), pages: 1438–1446, 2010.

[24] Svetlana Lazebnik, Cordelia Schmid, Jean Ponce, Beyond Bags of Features: Spatial Pyramid Matching for Recognizing Natural Scene Categories, *in Proceedings of CVPR*, pages: 2169–2178, 2006.

[25] Guangcan Liu, Zhouchen Lin, Yong Yu, Robust Subspace Segmentation by Low-Rank Representation, *in Proceedings of ICML*, pages: 663–670, 2010.

[26] Jianfeng Cai, Emmanuel J. Candès, Zuowei Shen, A Singular Value Thresholding Algorithm for Matrix Completion, *SIAM Journal on Optimization*, 20(4), pages: 1956–1982, 2010.

[27] Xiaodi Hou, Jonathan Harel, Christof Koch, Image Signature: Highlighting Sparse Salient Regions, *IEEE T-PAMI*, 34(1), pages: 194–201, 2012.

[28] Luming Zhang, Yue Gao, Rongrong Ji, Yingjie Xia, Qionghai Dai, Xuelong Li, Actively Learning Human Gaze Shifting Paths for Semantics-Aware Photo Cropping, *IEEE T-IP*, 23(5), pages: 2235–2245, 2014.

[29] Peter Gehler, Sebastian Nowozin, On Feature Combination for Multiclass Object Classification, *in Proceedings of ICCV*, pages: 221–228, 2009.

[30] Jieying She, Duo Wang, Mingli Song, Automatic Image Cropping Using Sparse Coding, *in Proceedings of ACPR*, pages: 490–494, 2007.

[31] Lijun Zhang, Chun Chen, Jiajun Bu, Deng Cai, Xiaofei He, Thomas S. Huang, Active Learning Based on Locally Linear Reconstruction, *IEEE T-PAMI*, 33(10), pages: 2026–2038, 2011.

[32] Benjamin Yao, Xiong Yang, Song-Chun Zhu. Introduction to a Large Scale General Purpose Ground Truth Dataset: Methodology, Annotation Tool, and Benchmarks. *EMMCVPR*, pages:169–183, 2007.

Impact of Ultra High Definition on Visual Attention

Hiromi Nemoto
MMSPG, EPFL
hiromi.nemoto@epfl.ch

Philippe Hanhart
MMSPG, EPFL
philippe.hanhart@epfl.ch

Pavel Korshunov
MMSPG, EPFL
pavel.korshunov@epfl.ch

Touradj Ebrahimi
MMSPG, EPFL
touradj.ebrahimi@epfl.ch

ABSTRACT

Ultra high definition (UHD) TV is rapidly replacing high definition (HD) TV but little is known of its effects on human visual attention. However, a clear understanding of this effect is important, since accurate models, evaluation methodologies, and metrics for visual attention are essential in many areas, including image and video compression, camera and displays manufacturing, artistic content creation, and advertisement. In this paper, we address this problem by creating a dataset of UHD resolution images with corresponding eye-tracking data, and we show that there is a statistically significant difference between viewing strategies when watching UHD and HD contents. Furthermore, by evaluating five representative computational models of visual saliency, we demonstrate the decrease in models' accuracies on UHD contents when compared to HD contents. Therefore, to improve the accuracy of computational models for higher resolutions, we propose a segmentation-based resolution-adaptive weighting scheme. Our approach demonstrates that taking into account information about resolution of the images improves the performance of computational models.

Categories and Subject Descriptors

I.2.10 [**Artificial Intelligence**]: Vision and Scene Understanding—*perceptual reasoning, representations, data structures, and transforms*; H.5.1 [**Information Interfaces and Presentation**]: Multimedia Information Systems—*evaluation/methodology, video*

Keywords

Visual attention; ultra high definition; saliency map; subjective evaluations; eye-tracking

1. INTRODUCTION

Ultra high definition (UHD), a rapidly emerging immersive video technology, is expected to replace high definition (HD) as the next standard video format of digital TV. Most of the TV displays and video cameras manufacturers, as well as broadcasting companies, strongly promote UHD video content, since this technology enhances sensation of presence and provides better viewing experience [15, 24]. The increased resolution of UHD TV typically leads to larger display sizes and, hence, for the full enjoyment of UHD content, ITU standardization body recommends certain viewing conditions [18], as illustrated in Figure 1. The figure demonstrates the difference in viewing conditions between HD and UHD, suggesting that there might be also large differences in viewing strategies and in visual attention patterns of people watching HD and UHD TVs.

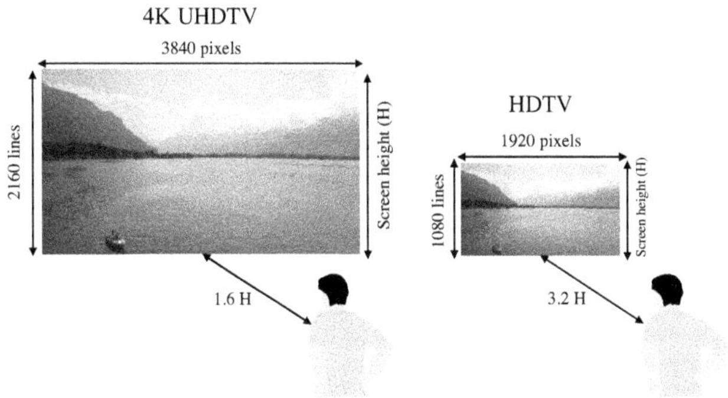

Figure 1: Recommended viewing conditions for 4K UHD and HD.

Visual attention is a widely studied topic and its practical applications include gaze-adaptive image and video compression [16, 6], objective image quality metrics [26], image retargeting [30], and image retrieval [29]. It even reaches beyond computing, proving useful in areas such as attention-based advertising, art, and cinema. To take advantage of visual attention information in practical applications, *salient regions* in images, i.e., regions that attract most of the attention, are either detected using an eye-tracking device or predicted using computational models of visual attention. One of the first computational model was proposed by Itti and Koch [17] in 1998, which uses image features such as luminance intensity, color, and orientation to construct a *saliency map*, i.e., a map predicting visual attention of a corresponding visual scene. The practical usefulness of computational models fueled the research for many years, resulting in many visual attention models, creation of different evaluation datasets with ground truth eye-tracking data, and various evaluation methodologies and metrics.

Although a significant number of public image and video datasets for visual attention exist [31], no dataset with eye-tracking data is available for UHD content. However, without this subjective data, it is hard to understand what is the impact of UHD on visual attention and whether it is significant for practical applications. In addition, computational models of visual attention are also evaluated using existing public databases, featuring images with resolution of HD or less, which means that little is known about the accuracy of these models when used for UHD content.

MM'14, November 3–7, 2014, Orlando, Florida, USA.
Copyright 2014 ACM 978-1-4503-3063-3/14/11 ...$15.00.
http://dx.doi.org/10.1145/2647868.2654917.

Since UHD has the ability to provide more details and requires higher data rate when compared to HD, understanding human attention patterns and viewing strategies for UHD content is important for developing efficient data compression algorithms and accurate objective quality metrics. The knowledge of visual attention for UHD can also help electronics manufactures to create better acquisition and display devices and content creators, such as photographers, movie and TV makers, to create images and video sequences with higher appeal value.

Therefore, this paper investigates the impact of UHD content on visual attention and on existing computational models of visual attention. To answer this question, a dataset is created first, which consists of 45 UHD 4K images with high variety of content (see examples in Figure 3 and refer to [25] for more details). Then, a subjective experiment involving 20 naïve subjects is conducted to collect eye-tracking data for these images using a professional eye-tracking system (Smart Eye Pro 5.8) and a professional reference monitor (Sony Trimaster SRM-L560). A similar experiment is also conducted with images resized to HD resolution for comparison with UHD. Fixation density maps (FDM) computed from the eye-tracking data for UHD and HD resolutions are compared using three metrics: attentional focus [20], similarity score [22], and Kullback-Leibler divergence (KLD) [10, 2]. Five representative models of visual attention were selected: 'Judd' by Judd *et al.* [23], 'GBVS' by Harel *et al.* [14], 'Itti' by Itti *et al.* [17], 'AIM' by Bruce [4], and 'Context-Aware' by Goferman *et al.* [12]. Their saliency maps were computed for UHD and HD contents and compared with corresponding subjective eye-tracking data using three metrics: similarity score, KLD, and area under the curve (AUC) [13].

The aim of this work is not only to evaluate the behavior of visual attention on UHD content, but also to investigate the impact on current computational models of visual attention and, if possible, to improve these models by making them adaptive to the content resolution. In summary, the main contributions of the paper are:

1. Dataset of UHD and HD images with corresponding subjective eye-tracking data;
2. Similarity analysis of FDMs for HD and UHD contents to understand if there is a difference in visual attention between UHD and HD resolutions;
3. Evaluation of five existing computational models of visual attention computed for UHD images to see if their performance is degraded when compared to HD;
4. Proposed resolution-adaptive weighting scheme to improve the accuracy of computational models of visual attention for UHD contents.

The rest of this paper is organized as follows. Section 2 presents related works including computation of FDM and several metrics for comparison of FDMs or FDM and saliency map. Section 3 describes eye tracking experiments, while Section 4 presents the results of subjective experiments. Sections 5 compares the performances of computational models of visual attention and Section 6 proposes the improvement of their performance for UHD content. Section 7 concludes the paper.

2. BACKGROUND AND RELATED WORK

A lot of work have been done over the years on fixation density map and computational visual attention modeling. In this section, we first give a brief overview of state of the art in visual attention, then describe how fixation density map (FDM) is computed and follow up with different approaches to measure the similarity of two FDMs or a FDM and a saliency map.

2.1 Related Work

A number of eye tracking experiments have been conducted for the purpose of investigating human visual attention mechanism. Previous research has suggested that a variety of factors influence human fixation patterns. The Delft Image Quality Lab carried out two eye tracking experiments in free-viewing task and in quality assessments task conditions [1] and found that there are significant differences on eye fixation patterns between these two different task conditions. In [27], the authors also reported that image distortion affects visual attention, especially for low quality images. The authors of [5] demonstrated that human faces are significant attentive regions in both free-viewing and searching conditions.

MIT CSAIL Saliency Database [21] provides a saliency database of low resolution images and tests the effect of resolution on fixation patterns. The results of the study showed that lower image resolutions contribute to the consistency of eye fixations and also noted that humans have a tendency to look at the image center for all resolutions. Image appeal is another feature that affects human fixation pattens. According to [11], more appealing images grab more attention than less appealing images. It also has been reported that current visual attention models are not able to capture this difference. The work by Engelke *et al.* [7] is the first comparative study to investigate the similarity between FDMs from independent experimental laboratory. Three eye tracking experiments were conducted independently using the same contents, though, they used somewhat different experimental conditions, e.g., viewing distance and image presentation time. It was shown that FDMs are very similar with each other and the impact of the dissimilarity of FDMs is not significant on practical applications such as visual attention modeling and image quality metrics.

Despite the large body of work on eye tracking and visual attention, to the best of our knowledge, no study have been reported on the influence of higher resolution images such as UHD resolution on human fixations or visual attention. Therefore, in this paper, we conduct subjective experiments with an eye tracking system under UHD viewing condition and perform rigorous analysis of visual attention using FDMs obtained in the subjective experiments.

2.2 Computation of fixation density maps

Fixation density maps (FDMs) are computed by convolving the recorded gaze points with a Gaussian filter, and then normalizing the result to values between 0 and 1. Only gaze points corresponding to fixation points are used to compute an FDM. Gaze points associated with saccades are not used in the computation. The eye tracking system used in our experiments (see Section 3.3) automatically discriminates between saccades and fixations based on the gaze velocity information. More specifically, during a time frame, all gaze points associated with gaze velocity below a fixation threshold are classified as fixation points, while saccades are detected when the gaze velocity lies above the fixation threshold. Blinks are also detected automatically by the eye tracking system based on the distance between the two eyelids of each eye. All detected saccades and blinks are excluded from the experimental data by the eye tracker and only the gaze points classified as fixation points are used further. These points are then filtered with a Gaussian kernel to compensate the eye tracker inaccuracies and to simulate the foveal point spread function of the human eye. As suggested in the state of the art [8, 22], the standard deviation of the Gaussian filter used for computing the FDMs is set to 1 degree of visual angle, which corresponds to $\sigma = 60$ pixels in our experiments for both HD and UHD. This standard deviation value is based on the assumption that the fovea of the human eye covers approximately 2 degrees of visual angle.

2.3 Assessment measures

Although several metrics have been proposed to measure the similarity between two FDMs or between a FDM and a saliency map computed by visual attention models, there is no standardized procedure. In [28], 12 similarity metrics have been compared using Kendall's W coefficient with a conclusion that a lot of these metrics are redundant. To avoid redundancies, the authors suggested to use three metrics, area under the curve (AUC) [3], Kullback-Leibler divergence (KLD) [10, 2], and one other optional metric (we selected the similarity score [22]) to capture different aspects of saliency maps. Since AUC is mostly used for comparison between computational saliency maps and the distributions of humans' fixation points, we used only KLD and similarity score metrics to analyze the similarities between two FDMs computed from our HD and UHD experiments (see Section 3 for more details). Additionally, the attentional focus measure [20] was used to characterize the visual focus of the subjects.

2.3.1 *Attentional focus*

Attentional focus [20] is defined as the number of objects that are viewed by the subjects during image observation. The rationale is to distinguish between cases where subjects look at few objects versus cases where they look more or less uniformly at several objects. To compute attentional focus, the FDM was first partitioned into blocks of $N \times N$ pixels. Then, the average intensity was computed for each block. Finally, the attentional focus was computed as the entropy of the normalized intensity across different blocks. Low entropy indicates high attentional focus while high entropy indicates low attentional focus. Figure 2 shows a schematic representation of this concept. The size of the blocks was determined so as to match the size of fovea, corresponding to 2 degrees of visual angle, which corresponds to 120×120 pixels in our experiments.

2.3.2 *Similarity score*

The similarity score is a distribution-based metric of how similar two saliency maps are. The similarity score S between two normalized maps P and Q is

$$S = \sum_{i,j} min(P_{i,j}, Q_{i,j}),\ where \sum_{i,j} P_{i,j} = \sum_{i,j} Q_{i,j} = 1 \quad (1)$$

If a similarity score is one, the two saliency maps are the same, if it is zero, the maps do not overlap at all.

2.3.3 *Kullback-Leibler divergence*

The Kullback-Leibler divergence (KLD) is usually used to estimate the dissimilarity between two probability distributions. In context of saliency maps or fixation density maps, this is a measure of dissimilarity between two histograms. If, in the corresponding histograms, $p(x)$ and $h(x)$ represent the probabilities of a pixel to have value x, the symmetric KLD is

$$KLD = \frac{1}{2} \sum_{x} \left[p(x) log \frac{p(x)}{h(x)} + h(x) log \frac{h(x)}{p(x)} \right] \quad (2)$$

When two probability distributions are strictly equal, KLD value is zero, and when histograms do not overlap at all, it tends to infinity.

2.3.4 *Area under the curve*

Area under the curve (AUC) metric is the area under the receiver operating characteristics (ROC) curve [13]. In this metric, the human fixation points are treated as the positive set and the same number of points are randomly extracted from the image to form a negative set. Then, the saliency map is used as a classifier to separate

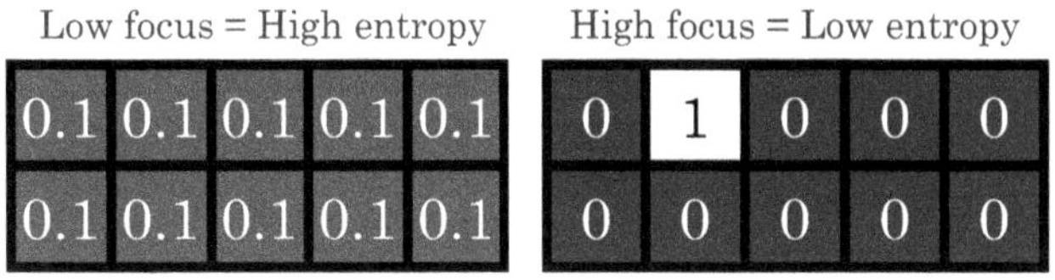

*The values in the windows indicate normalized average intensity of FDM.

Figure 2: Illustration of attentional focus metric.

the positive points from the negatives points. For a given threshold, all points in the saliency map having a value above this threshold are considered as fixation points. The fixation points in the positive and negative sets are labeled as true positive and false positive, respectively. By varying the threshold, the ROC curve is constructed from the corresponding false positive and true positive rates. The area under this curve indicates how well the saliency map estimates human fixations. An AUC value of 1 corresponds to perfect prediction and a value of 0.5 corresponds to random prediction.

The classical AUC method is often criticized, because its value can be artificially increased if a computational model considers the center bias technic, i.e., considering that human eye fixations are rarely located near the borders of typical test images. To overcome this drawback, the shuffled AUC has been proposed for better saliency maps validation [32]. In the shuffled AUC metric, to moderate center-bias effects, human fixations of other images from the same dataset are used to create the negative set instead of uniformly random points. To fairly compare computational models, the shuffled AUC was used in this paper.

3. EYE TRACKING EXPERIMENTS

To investigate how different are visual attention and viewing strategies for HD and UHD resolutions, we conducted extensive experiments to acquire eye movements while a set of still images was shown in both HD and UHD resolutions to the subjects.

3.1 Test images

Since there is no publicly available standard dataset, at least to our knowledge, of UHD resolution images suitable for visual attention modeling, we constructed such dataset. For the dataset, we used still images with native resolution higher than UHD acquired by some of the latest digital cameras, including Sony DSC-RX100 II, Sony NEX-5N, FUJIFILM XF1, Olympus E-PL2, and RED SCARLET-X. Additionally, some high resolution painting images were obtained from the Europeana internet portal[1]. A total of 45 images were selected to cover a wide variety of content, e.g., natural scenes (both indoor and outdoor), humans, ships, animals, music gigs, historical scenes, etc. For the dataset, all images were cropped to 3840×2160 pixels for UHD resolution and then downsampled to 1920×1080 pixels for HD resolution using Lanczos resampling. Figure 3 shows some examples of the images and more details about the dataset can be found in [25].

3.2 Participants

A total of 20 naïve subjects (7 females and 13 males) took part in the experiments. Subjects were between 18 and 28 years old with an average of 23.8 years of age. Before the experiment, a consent form was handed to subjects for signature. All subjects were screened for correct visual acuity and color vision using Snellen and Ishiara charts respectively.

[1] Europeana: think culture, http://www.europeana.eu

Figure 3: Examples of images from our UHD dataset. The dataset is publicly accessible.[2]

3.3 Test environment

The experiments were conducted at the MMSPG quality test laboratory, which fulfills the recommendations for the subjective evaluation of visual data issued by ITU-R [19]. The test room was equipped with a controlled lighting system with a 6500 K color temperature and an ambient luminance at 15% of the maximum screen luminance, whereas the color of all the background walls and curtains present in the test area were in mid grey. The test room was separated in two by a curtain to isolate the subject and equipment from the test operators, which were present during the test session to supervise the recording of the eye tracking data. The laboratory setup was intended to ensure the reproducibility of the results and to avoid unintended influence of external factors.

Test stimuli were displayed on a professional high-performance 4K/QFHD 56" LCD reference monitor Sony Trimaster SRM-L560. A Smart Eye Pro 5.8 remote eye tracking system was employed to determine the gaze position on the screen of the left and right eyes independently. The system was equipped with three Sony HR-50 cameras at a frame rate of 60 fps and two infrared flashes, which enabled us to measure the gaze position with under 0.5 visual degrees error, while an accurate gaze output was available for at least ± 45 degrees of head rotation. All measurements from the eye tracker were recorded on a separate computer.

The experiment involved one subject per test session. The subject was seated in line with the center of the monitor at the distance of 3.2 and 1.6 times the image height for HD and UHD contents, respectively, as suggested in [18] as optimal viewing distance, which corresponds to roughly 1.1 meters from the monitor in both cases. The eye tracking system was placed at 0.7 meters from the monitor such that the face was well captured by the cameras. Figure 4 depicts the conditions of the experiments.

At the beginning of the test, the aperture and focus settings of the eye tracker cameras were adjusted for optimal conditions and a full camera calibration was performed to maximize the accuracy of the measurements. For each subject, a personal profile was created by recording several head poses and gaze calibrations using four calibration points close to the screen corners and one at the center of the screen. To ensure the accuracy of the eye tracking data, subjects were instructed to hold their head still while watching the images, and test operators made sure that all features were correctly detected by at least two out of three cameras during the experiment.

3.4 Experimental protocol

The experiment was separated into two different sessions to avoid inter-resolution comparison: one sessions was dedicated to UHD resolution only and another session to HD resolution only. To reduce the influence of potential memory effects on visual attention from viewing the same contents twice, the participants were divided into two groups of ten subjects each: the first group watched the images in UHD resolution first and then in HD resolution, while the reverse order was considered for the second group. Table 1 depicts the arrangement of the test sessions. To reduce contextual effects, the stimuli orders of display were randomized by applying different permutation for each subject. To reduce fatigue effects, each subject took a 15 minutes break between the two sessions.

[2]Ultra-Eye dataset, http://mmspg.epfl.ch/ultra-eye

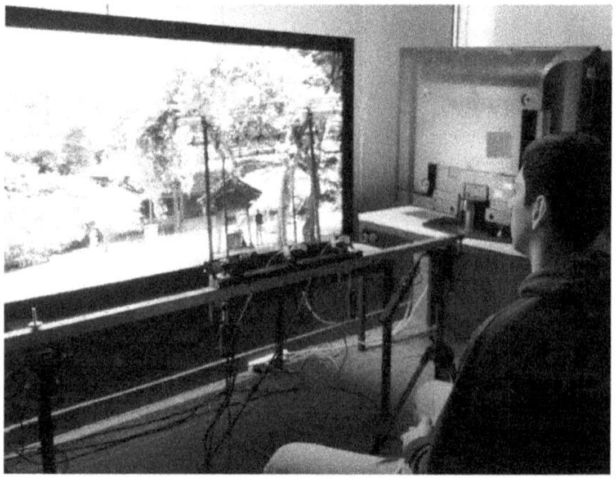

Figure 4: Experimental setup.

Table 1: Arrangement of test sessions for HD and UHD resolutions.

	Group #1	Group #2
First session	UHD resolution	HD resolution
Second session	HD resolution	UHD resolution

According to [7], the FDM is almost saturated at about four seconds presentation time. However, since the images used in our experiments were about four times larger than the ones used in [7], it is possible that the subjects are not able to watch all salient regions in the image if the presentation time is too short. Therefore, each image was shown for 15 seconds in our experiments. Additionally, a two seconds mid-grey background was displayed prior to the presentation of each test stimuli to reset subject's attention. With this timing, each session was approximately 15 minutes long.

Since the purpose of these experiments was to investigate the difference in visual attention and viewing strategies for HD and UHD resolutions, subjects were instructed to watch the images in a free-viewing scenario. Additionally, a training session was organized to allow subjects to familiarize with the procedure. The training materials were presented to subjects exactly as for the test materials.

To understand the influence of the memory effect on the subjective data, the following categories of FDMs were analyzed separately:

1. **UHD-First:** Group #1, first session (10 subjects).
2. **HD-First:** Group #2, first session (10 subjects).
3. **UHD-Second:** Group #2, second session (10 subjects). They watched UHD contents after watching the same images with HD resolution, followed by a 15 minutes resting phase.
4. **HD-Second:** Group #1, second session (10 subjects). They watched HD contents after watching the same images with UHD resolution, followed by a 15 minutes resting phase.
5. **UHD-All:** All 20 subjects.
6. **HD-All:** All 20 subjects.

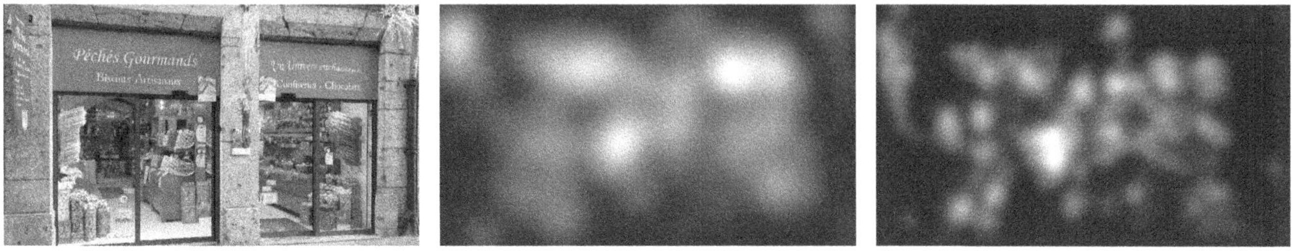

(a) Presented image (b) FDM of HD resolution (HD-all) (c) FDM of UHD resolution (UHD-all)

Figure 5: Examples of FDMs for a presentation time of 15 s.

4. IMPACT ON VISUAL ATTENTION

Figure 5 shows examples of FDMs for HD and UHD resolutions computed from the eye-tracking data (across all subject groups). It can be noted from the figure that FDM of UHD resolution is more scattered and more 'focused' compared to FDM of HD resolution. In both cases, subjects look at various objects in the images. However, subjects watched specific objects in UHD images with higher intensity but browsed HD images in a more 'relaxed' way.

In this section, we compare FDMs for UHD and HD contents using the similarity metrics discussed in Section 2.3: attentional focus, similarity score, and KLD.

4.1 Attentional focus

Figure 6 shows the attentional focus computed separately for categories of FDMs described in Section 3.4 vs. varying presentation time. From the figure, it can be noted that, at each presentation time, the attentional focus of UHD resolution has lower value, which means that UHD has lower entropy or higher focus when compared to HD resolution, regardless of the presentation order. A possible explanation is that the higher level of details in UHD images make subjects' attention more focused and concentrated compared to HD images.

Also, attentional focus saturates faster for HD resolution than for UHD resolution, since UHD resolution images are four times bigger. To estimate the presentation time at which the FDMs are saturated, the attentional focus values were fitted using the response curve of a first order lag system according to the equation:

$$f(t) = a\left[1 - \exp\left(-\frac{t}{\tau}\right)\right] + b, \tag{3}$$

where t is the presentation time (how long the image was viewed by the subjects), a and b are the amplitude and the offset of the resulted attentional focus curve, and τ is a constant representing the time at which the attentional focus reaches 63.2% of its maximum value.

Considering that the saturation (95% of the maximum value) is achieved at 3τ, the FDMs are saturated after about 10.67 s for HD and after about 13.02 s for UHD. It means that 10 s is not enough to get a stable FDM for UHD resolution and that a longer presentation time is required.

Figure 6 shows that there is no influence of presentation order on the attentional focus and there is a difference between UHD and HD resolutions, but it does not show if these findings are statistically significant. To answer this question, we performed an analysis of variance (ANOVA) on attentional focus results at the presentation time equal to 15 seconds. ANOVA analysis was done for different pairs of FDMs with results shown in Table 2. The table shows that attentional focus is statistically significantly different for HD and UHD resolutions, while the presentation order of HD or UHD content, i.e., the order in which a subject viewed content, does not affect attentional focus in a statistically significant way. It means that even though each image was presented twice to the subjects, the influence of potential memory effects does not significantly impact attentional focus, indicating that the results from both groups of subjects can be combined.

Table 2: p-value computed for attentional focus ($t = 15$ s).

	HD-Second	UHD-First	UHD-Second
HD-First	0.074	< 0.001	< 0.001
HD-Second		< 0.001	< 0.001
UHD-First			0.11

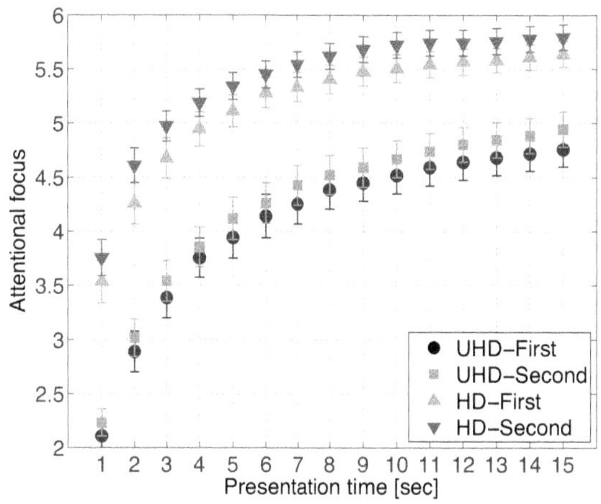

Figure 6: Attentional focus of FDMs with confidence intervals.

4.2 Similarity score

While attentional focus only measures one FDM, similarity score compares two different FDMs. We computed similarity scores for all meaningful pairs of FDMs (see Section 3.4 for explanation of different FDMs): HD-First vs. UHD-First, HD-Second vs. UHD-Second, HD-First vs. HD-Second, and UHD-First vs. UHD-Second; and the corresponding scores are shown in Figure 7 for all presentation times varying from 1 to 15 seconds. The figure demonstrates that HD-First (HD images were viewed before UHD) is more similar to HD-Second (UHD images were viewed before HD) than UHD-First and UHD-Second FDMs. This high similarity between FDMs for HD can also be noticed visually, for instance by comparing FMD of HD-First in Figure 8 (b) of a sample image in Figure 8 (a) with FDM of HD-Second in Figure 8 (c). In turn, the FDMs of UHD-First, shown in Figure 8 (d), and UHD-Second, shown in Figure 8 (e), are quite different visually too.

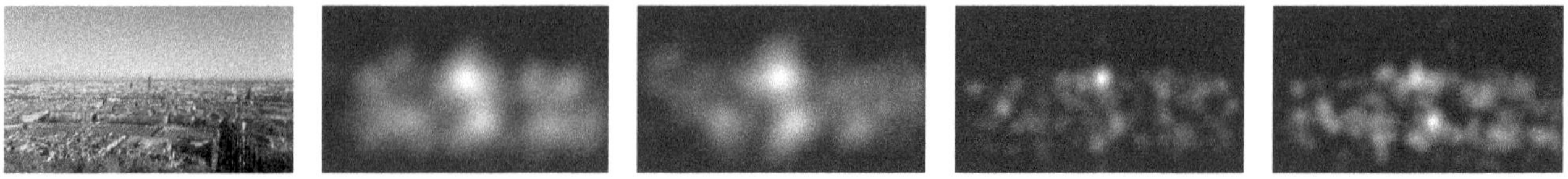

(a) Presented image (b) FDM of HD-First (c) FDM of HD-Second (d) FDM of UHD-First (e) FDM of UHD-Second

Figure 8: Examples of FDMs for different resolutions and viewing orders.

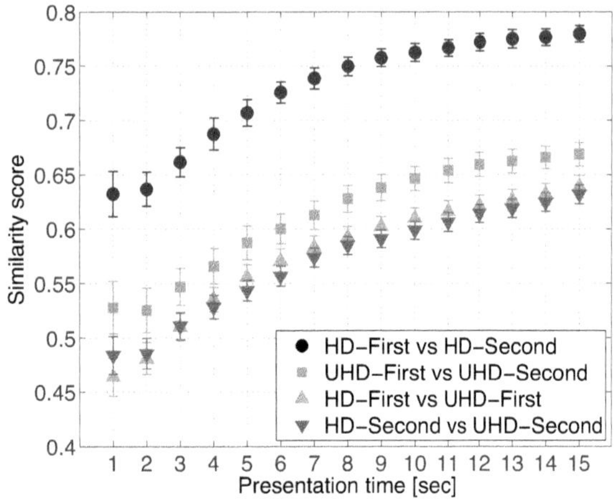

Figure 7: Similarity score of FDM pairs with confidence intervals.

This observation with the fact that other two pairs, HD-First vs. UHD-First and HD-Second vs. UHD-Second have almost the same similarity as UHD-First vs. UHD-Second, indicate that the fixation patterns for UHD resolution have higher diversity compared to HD resolution, i.e., different subjects look at UHD images in many different ways compared to a more unified way of viewing HD images. It also means that the presentation order does not influence the similarity score.

To analyze the statistical significance of the similarity score results, we performed an ANOVA analysis and computed p-values, comparing similarity scores between different pairs of FDMs as shown in Table 3. The table demonstrates that all results show statistically significant difference, except when comparing HD-First vs. UHD-First with HD-Second vs. UHD-Second. This analysis confirms the observation that there is a significant difference between FDMs of HD and UHD resolutions but the presentation order, in other words, memory effect, has no influence on the results, confirming the conclusions given in Section 4.1.

To better understand the dissimilarity between HD and UHD resolutions, scatter-like plot of the conjoint intensity values between two FDMs can be used [7]. Figure 9 shows such plot for the FDMs given in Figure 5 (b) and (c). In this plot, highly correlated FDM values lie closer to the main diagonal (dashed line). As it can be observed, there are several structural dissimilarities, especially for highly fixated points, which are due to the difference in the number of peaks and their respective positions in the actual FDMs.

Table 3: p-value computed for similarity score ($t = 15$ s).

	UHD-1st vs. UHD-2nd	HD-1st vs. UHD-1st	HD-2nd vs. UHD-2nd
HD-1st vs. HD-2nd	< 0.001	< 0.001	< 0.001
UHD-1st vs. UHD-2nd		< 0.001	< 0.001
HD-1st vs. UHD-1st			0.30

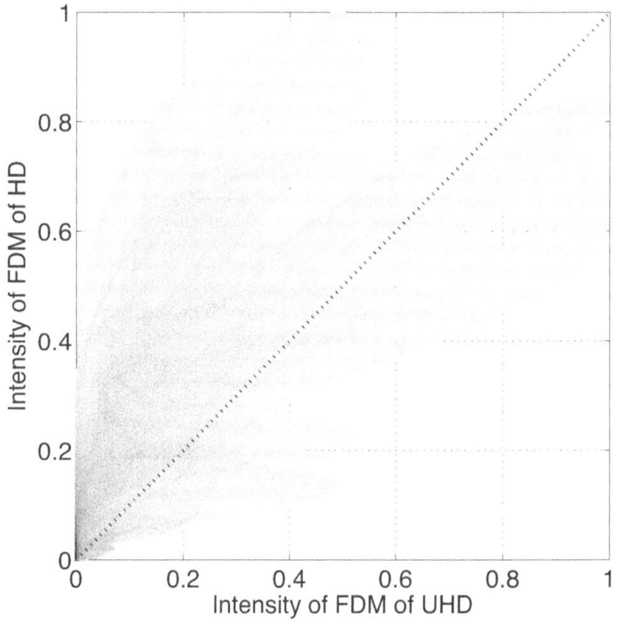

Figure 9: Scatter-like plot of the conjoint intensity values between the two FDMs of Figure 5.

Also, similarly to attentional focus, estimated τ time constant of similarity scores for HD ($\tau = 4.2$ s) is lower than for UHD resolution ($\tau = 5.1$ s).

4.3 Kullback-Leibler divergence

KLD metric was computed in the same way as similarity scores metric and results are shown in Figure 10. As it can be observed, KLD values are clearly saturated after 3 s for both HD and UHD. Since KLD measures the dissimilarity of the two histograms, this metric does not consider the spacial distribution but only evaluates the difference in the number of points of attention and their intensities. Therefore, this metric shows the difference between the viewing strategy of the subjects. Results in Figure 10 show very small KLD values when comparing FDMs of the same resolution, which suggests that the strategy to browse the images does not change much across subjects for a specific resolution. The fact that KLD values for UHD resolution (UHD-First vs. UHD-Second pair) are the lowest suggests that subjects are focusing on a fewer attentive regions in UHD compared to HD, probably, due to the higher resolution and higher level of details in UHD images. It can also be noted from the figure that KLD values for HD vs. UHD FDM pairs are much higher than for the same resolution pairs, which means that viewing strategies for HD and UHD resolutions are different.

Table 4: p-value computed for KLD ($t = 15$ s).

	UHD-1st vs. UHD-2nd	HD-1st vs. UHD-1st	HD-2nd vs. UHD-2nd
HD-1st vs. HD-2nd	< 0.001	< 0.001	< 0.001
UHD-1st vs. UHD-2nd		< 0.001	< 0.001
HD-1st vs. UHD-1st			0.53

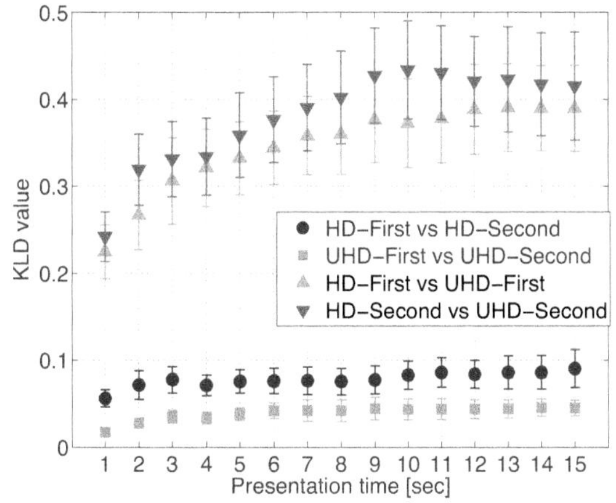

Figure 10: KLD of FDM pairs with confidence intervals.

To investigate the statistical significance of KLD results, we performed an ANOVA analysis in the same way as for similarity score metric. Table 4 shows p-values of the ANOVA analysis for KLD metric computed on different pairs of FDMs. From the table, it is clear that only HD-First vs. UHD-First is not significantly different compared to HD-Second vs. UHD-Second, which, similarly to the earlier observations, means that influence of memory effects is insignificant, but HD is significantly different from UHD.

5. IMPACT ON SALIENCY MAPS

In this section, we investigate the impact of UHD viewing on the performance of computational models of visual attention using three metrics: similarity score, KLD, and AUC.

5.1 Selection of computational models

In [22], Judd *et al.* benchmarked 10 computational models of visual attention using human fixations recorded with an eye tracker as ground truth. The authors have reported that Judd *et al.* [23] and graph-based visual saliency (GBVS) [14] models have the best and second best performance respectively. Other computational models of visual attention in the top five of their benchmarking are the Itti's [17], AIM [4], and Context-Aware [12] models. Following this benchmark, we use these five computational models of visual attention to estimate human fixations and to investigate whether using UHD content affect their performances. The selected models cover the whole spectrum of approaches. Context-Aware is top-down, Judd is hybrid, and the rest are bottom-up models. All models take image size into account when computing saliency map, therefore, we used UHD and HD images in their original sizes as inputs in the models.

5.2 Benchmarking of computational models

The performance of the computational models of visual attention is evaluated by comparing saliency maps generated by the models to the ground truth FDMs from our eye tracking experiments (see Section 3 for details). The similarity score, KLD, and AUC metrics are used as performance indexes. The FDMs of HD-All and UHD-All (see Section 3.4 for the explanation of the terms), obtained after 15 seconds presentation time, are used for the performance comparison, as our analysis showed that these FDMs are stable enough (see Section 4).

Table 5 reports the similarity scores, KLD, and AUC computed between saliency maps and FDMs. In case of UHD resolution, the performance of the models is very close to random (values are near 0.5) according to the similarity score metric. In particular, the Judd and GBVS models, which are reported to be the best models according to [22], show a drastic drop in performance between HD and UHD. ANOVA analysis was performed to determine whether the difference between the results of HD and UHD was statistically significant. The p-values are reported in Table 5. As it can be observed, the performances of all computational models of visual attention significantly decrease under UHD viewing condition when compared to HD viewing condition, with $p < 0.001$ in most cases, except for the AUC metric. Unlike the other metrics, according to the AUC metric, there is no significant difference between HD and UHD resolutions with regards to the performance of computational models of visual attention. This is most likely because AUC metric considers only the location of the fixation points, which are similar for HD and UHD, but it does not capture their intensity [33].

For KLD metric, the performance of computational models of visual attention was significantly lower in case of UHD resolution when compared to HD resolution, except for the AIM model. As the AIM model generates saliency maps having narrower probability distribution when compared to the other models, its performance is barely affected by the difference of the saliency map's statistical distribution between HD and UHD when benchmarked using the KLD metric. According to the KLD metric, the performance of Judd's model drops drastically. Looking at the saliency maps of this model (see Figure 11 (a) and (b)) show that the visual attention predicted by this model is quite spread, which is somewhat comparable to the FDM of HD resolution (see Figure 11 (c)), whereas this property does not match well with the structure of the FDM of UHD resolution (see Figure 11 (d)).

Overall, the results of the similarity and KLD metrics show that the current computational models of visual attention are not reliable to predict visual attention of the UHD content.

Table 5: Performance assessment of computational saliency maps compared to the FDMs of both HD and UHD.

	Judd [23]		GBVS [14]		Itti [17]		AIM [4]		Context-Aware [12]	
	HD	UHD	HD	UHD	HD	UHD	HD	UHD	HD	UHD
Similarity score	0.64	0.51	0.69	0.54	0.63	0.52	0.58	0.47	0.62	0.52
p-value	< 0.001		< 0.001		< 0.001		< 0.001		< 0.001	
KLD	4.48	8.12	0.69	2.40	1.99	5.73	0.93	1.03	0.99	2.59
p-value	< 0.001		< 0.001		< 0.001		0.29		< 0.001	
AUC	0.61	0.61	0.61	0.61	0.63	0.65	0.62	0.62	0.64	0.65
p-value	0.87		0.97		0.16		0.51		0.58	

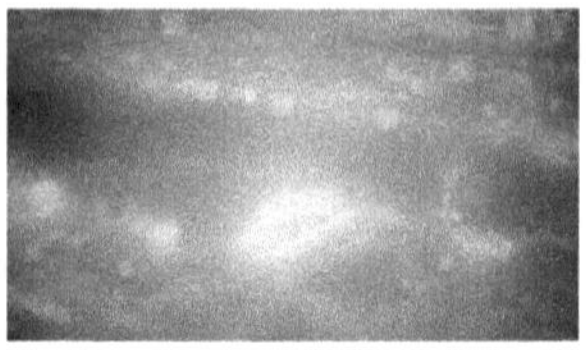

(a) HD saliency map

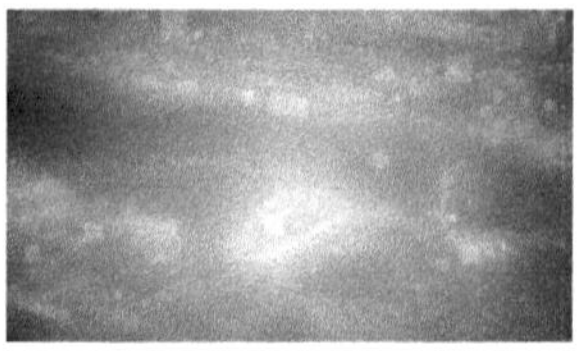

(b) UHD saliency map

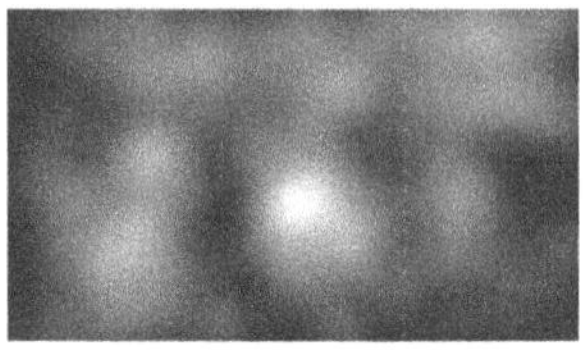

(c) FDM of HD-All

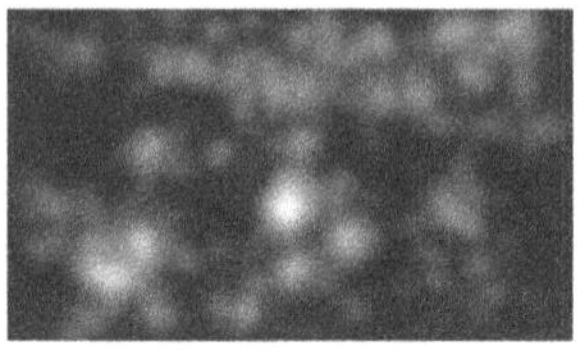

(d) FDM of UHD-All

Figure 11: Performance of Judd model's saliency map vs. FDMs.

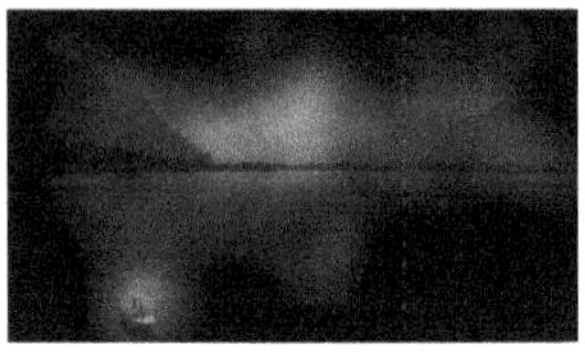

(a) HD

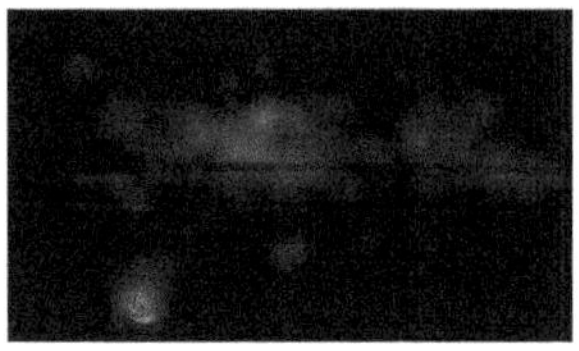

(b) UHD

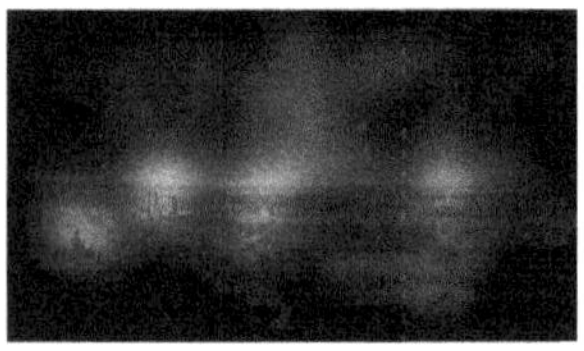

(c) HD

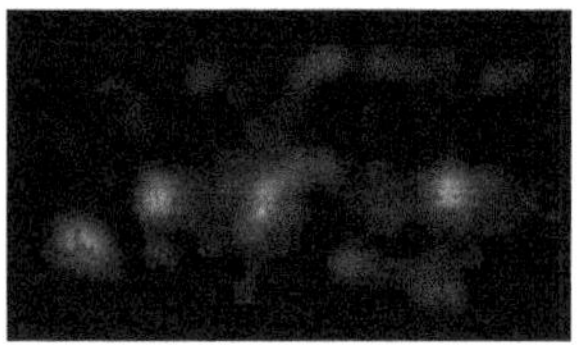

(d) UHD

Figure 12: FDMs of HD-All and UHD-All overlaid on the images.

6. RESOLUTION-BASED WEIGHTING

The decrease in the performance of computational visual attention models for UHD resolution demonstrated in Section 5.2 indicates that these models should take viewing condition associated with image resolution into account. To verify this hypothesis, we propose a simple resolution-weighting scheme and show that it can be used to improve the performance of computational models when the higher resolution content is used.

6.1 Proposed method

By studying FDMs of UHD content, we noticed that subjects seem to look at smaller objects more when watching UHD images than when watching HD images. For example, in Figure 12 (b), subjects looked at the small boat in a focused way in UHD version (see the original image in Figure 3), while they browse other areas equally in HD (see Figure 12 (b)). Also, in Figure 12 (d) the subjects focused at the small house, the stone architecture, and humans (refer to Figure 3 for the original image) in a more concentrated manner when viewing UHD than when viewing HD (see Figure 12 (c)). Following this observation, we propose to tune saliency maps according to the sizes of objects in images. To automatically estimate these sizes, we use a graph-based image segmentation [9]. This particular segmentation technique was chosen because it ignores details in high-variability regions, which matches our purpose of estimating the sizes of main objects only. An example of

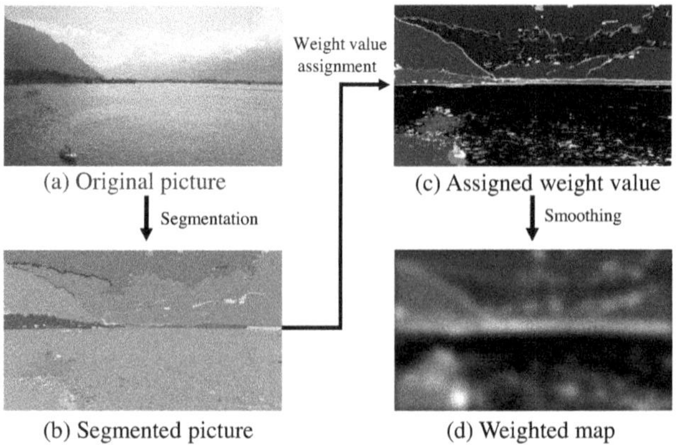

Figure 13: Computation of weighted map.

the segmentation is shown in Figure 13 (b). The authors of the segmentation use certain parameters to adjust the behaviors of the algorithm, which we set according to values in Table 6. These values may not work for other resolutions than UHD but, in this paper, we only want to demonstrate the possibility of improving saliency maps for UHD resolutions. The development of computational model of visual attention that is automatically adaptive to changing resolution is out of the scope of this paper.

Table 6: Parameters for the segmentation.

Parameter	Value	Explanation
$sigma$	1	Smoothing coefficient
k	100	Value for the threshold function
min	20	Minimum component size

Computation of the proposed resolution-adaptive weighting map is illustrated by Figure 13. For each segmentation component in the segmented image, a weight value is assigned depending on its size in the range between 0 and 1. Since subjects tend to look at smaller objects in UHD images, the weight value should be high when the area of the segmentation component is small. However, with such approach many small segmentation fragments, which mainly come from trivial textures in larger objects, will receive a high weight value, leading to an incorrect weighting. To avoid this, for each segmentation component C_n, we compute its weight value W_n using the following equation:

$$W_n = \begin{cases} n(1-A)/B + A & \text{if } n \leq B \\ (B-n)/(N-1-B) + 1 & \text{if } n > B \end{cases} \tag{4}$$

where A and B are tuning parameters that depend on resolution of the images and $n \in \{0, ..., N-1\}$ is the index of the list of N segmentation components sorted by size. For a fixed resolution (in our case UHD), one can fine-tune these parameters, so that the small fragments and large components receive small weights, while medium-sized components of interest receive large weights.

An example of the map with assigned weight values using this approach is shown in Figure 13 (c). This map is smoothed with a Gaussian filter (see Figure 13 (d)) to avoid sharp transitions. The standard deviation of the filter kernel is the same $\sigma = 60$ as it was used for computation of FDMs (see Section 2.2 for details). The saliency map of a given computational model of visual attention is then multiplied by this weighted map resulting in a new saliency map weighted according to the object sizes in the image.

Table 7: Comparison of saliency maps of original computational models (Original) with weighted models (Proposed) for UHD.

	Judd [23]		GBVS [14]		Itti [17]		AIM [4]		Context-Aware [12]	
	Original	Proposed	Original	Proposed	Original	Proposed	Original	Proposed	Original	Proposed
Similarity score	0.51	0.55	0.54	0.56	0.52	0.52	0.47	0.51	0.52	0.51
p-value	< 0.001		0.36		0.82		0.02		0.58	
KLD	8.12	1.66	2.40	0.53	5.73	0.96	1.03	2.0	2.59	0.76
p-value	< 0.001		< 0.001		< 0.001		< 0.001		< 0.001	
AUC	0.61	0.68	0.61	0.66	0.65	0.68	0.62	0.68	0.65	0.67
p-value	< 0.001		< 0.001		0.1		< 0.001		0.2	

This simple approach allows to indirectly embed a resolution information into the saliency map computation. The examples of the new saliency maps are shown in Figure 14 side-by-side with saliency maps obtained using the original computational models as presented in Section 5.1.

6.2 Assessment of the proposed method

To test the effectiveness of these new weighted maps, we compared them with the original saliency maps by computing similarity score, KLD, and AUC metrics, similar to how we evaluated the performance of the original saliency maps for HD and UHD resolutions in Section 5.2. The results shown in Table 7 demonstrate that the new weighted saliency maps improve the performance of the most of the computational models. Only in case of AIM model and KLD metric, the new weighted saliency map shows decrease in the performance. It means that by using a rather simple approach, taking into account resolution of the images and their content structure, we could improve the performance of the existing models on higher resolution images.

7. CONCLUSION

In this paper, we studied the influence of UHD resolution on human visual attention and attention models. We conducted subjective eye tracking experiments with both HD and UHD resolution images covering wide variety of scenes. We then created the fixation density maps for HD and UHD images and evaluated them using three different objective metrics: attentional focus, similarity score, and KLD, effectively creating a visual attention dataset for HD and UHD contents.

The assessment results demonstrated that (i) UHD resolution images can grab the focus of attention more than HD images; (ii) humans tend to look at a few attentive regions in the images with more intent when viewing UHD; and (iii) viewing strategy is different for HD and UHD.

We also compared five different computational models of visual attention when applying to HD and UHD images, showing that models' performance degrade with the increase in resolution. The evaluation suggests that an image resolution and the structural content information of an image should be taken into account when developing a resolution-independent computational model. Adding such information into several existing computational models via a simple segmentation-based weighting scheme increased the performance of these models.

Acknowledgments

This work has been conducted in the framework of the Swiss National Foundation for Scientific Research (FN 200021-143696-1), EC funded Network of Excellence VideoSense, and COST IC1003 European Network on Quality of Experience in Multimedia Systems and Services QUALINET.

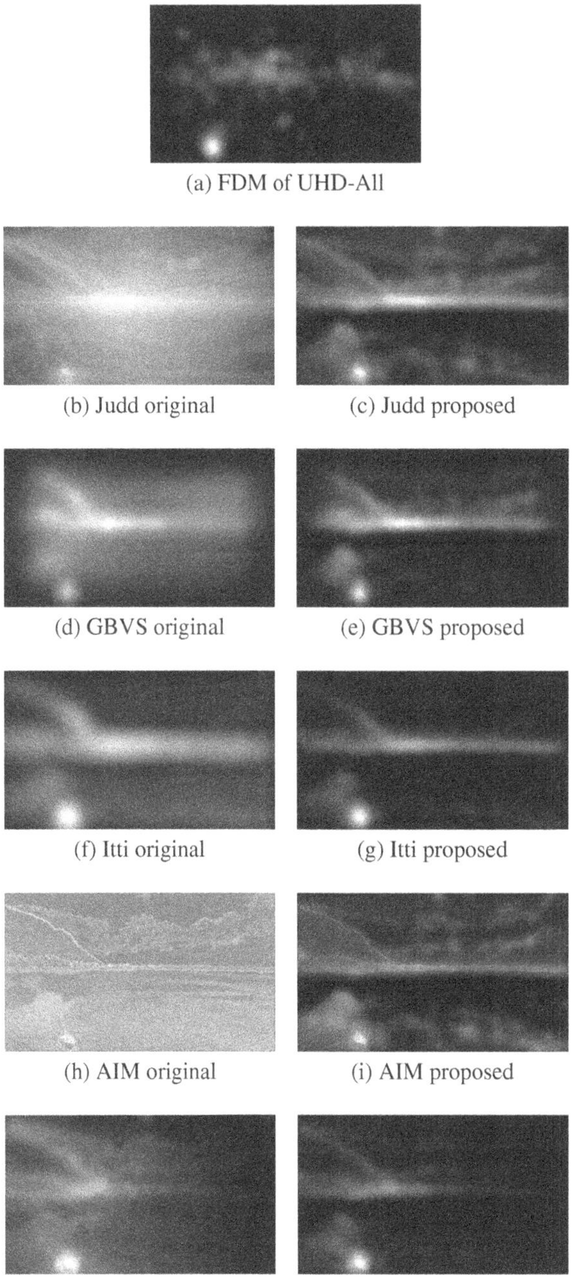

(a) FDM of UHD-All

(b) Judd original (c) Judd proposed

(d) GBVS original (e) GBVS proposed

(f) Itti original (g) Itti proposed

(h) AIM original (i) AIM proposed

(j) Context-Aware original (k) Context-Aware proposed

Figure 14: Left column: original saliency maps. Right column: improved saliency maps with resolution adaptive weighting.

8. REFERENCES

[1] H. Alers, L. Bos, and I. Heynderickx. How the task of evaluating image quality influences viewing behavior. In *International Workshop on Quality of Multimedia Experience (QoMEX)*, pages 167–172, Sept. 2011.

[2] A. Borji and L. Itti. State-of-the-art in visual attention modeling. *IEEE Transactions on Pattern Analysis and Machine Intelligence*, 35(1):185–207, Jan. 2013.

[3] A. Borji, D. N. Sihite, and L. Itti. Quantitative Analysis of Human-Model Agreement in Visual Saliency Modeling: A Comparative Study. *IEEE Transactions on Image Processing*, 22(1):55–69, 2013.

[4] N. D. B. Bruce. *Saliency, Attention and Visual Search: An Information Theoretic Approach*. PhD thesis, York University, Canada, 2008. AAINR45988.

[5] M. Cerf, J. Harel, W. Einhaeuser, and C. Koch. Predicting human gaze using low-level saliency combined with face detection. In J. Platt, D. Koller, Y. Singer, and S. Roweis, editors, *Advances in Neural Information Processing Systems 20*, pages 241–248. Curran Associates, Inc., 2008.

[6] Z. Chen, W. Lin, and K. N. Ngan. Perceptual video coding: Challenges and approaches. In *IEEE International Conference on Multimedia and Expo (ICME)*, pages 784–789, July 2010.

[7] U. Engelke, H. Liu, J. Wang, P. L. Callet, I. Heynderickx, H.-J. Zepernick, and A. J. Maeder. Comparative Study of Fixation Density Maps. *IEEE Transactions on Image Processing*, 22(3):1121–1133, 2013.

[8] U. Engelke, A. Maeder, and H. Zepernick. Visual attention modelling for subjective image quality databases. In *IEEE International Workshop on Multimedia Signal Processing (MMSP)*, pages 1–6, Oct. 2009.

[9] P. F. Felzenszwalb and D. P. Huttenlocher. Efficient Graph-Based Image Segmentation. *International Journal of Computer Vision*, 59(2):167–181, Sept. 2004.

[10] M. S. Gide and L. J. Karam. Comparative evaluation of visual saliency models for quality assessment task. In *International Workshop on Video Processing and Quality Metrics for Consumer Electronics (VPQM)*, pages 37–40, Jan. 2012.

[11] S. Gilani, R. Subramanian, H. Hua, S. Winkler, and S.-C. Yen. Impact of image appeal on visual attention during photo triaging. In *IEEE International Conference on Image Processing (ICIP)*, pages 231–235, Sept. 2013.

[12] S. Goferman, L. Zelnik-Manor, and A. Tal. Context-aware saliency detection. In *IEEE Conference on Computer Vision and Pattern Recognition (CVPR)*, pages 2376–2383, June 2010.

[13] D. M. Green and J. A. Swets. *Signal Detection Theory and Psychophysics*. Wiley, New York, 1966.

[14] J. Harel, C. Koch, and P. Perona. Graph-based visual saliency. In *Advances in neural information processing systems*, volume 19, pages 545–552. MIT Press, 2007.

[15] T. Ito. Future television — Super Hi-Vision and beyond. In *IEEE Asian Solid State Circuits Conference (A-SSCC)*, pages 1–4, Nov. 2010.

[16] L. Itti. Automatic foveation for video compression using a neurobiological model of visual attention. *IEEE Transactions on Image Processing*, 13(10):1304–1318, Oct. 2004.

[17] L. Itti, C. Koch, and E. Niebur. A model of saliency-based visual attention for rapid scene analysis. *IEEE Transactions on Pattern Analysis and Machine Intelligence*, 20(11):1254–1259, Nov. 1998.

[18] ITU-R BT.2022. General viewing conditions for subjective assessment of quality of SDTV and HDTV television pictures on flat panel displays. International Telecommunication Union, Aug. 2012.

[19] ITU-R BT.500-13. Methodology for the subjective assessment of the quality of television pictures. International Telecommunication Union, Jan. 2012.

[20] P. Jermann, M.-A. Nuessli, and K. Sharma. Attentional Episodes and Focus. In *Dual Eye-Tracking workshop in ACM Conference on Computer Supported Cooperative Work*, Seattle, Washington, USA, Feb. 2012.

[21] T. Judd, F. Durand, and A. Torralba. A model of saliency-based visual attention for rapid scene analysis. *Journal of Vision 2011*, 11(4):1254–1259, Apr. 2011.

[22] T. Judd, F. Durand, and A. Torralba. A Benchmark of Computational Models of Saliency to Predict Human Fixations. Technical Report MIT-CSAIL-TR-2012-001, CSAIL, MIT, Jan. 2012.

[23] T. Judd, K. Ehinger, F. Durand, and A. Torralba. Learning to predict where humans look. In *IEEE International Conference on Computer Vision (ICCV)*, pages 2106–2113, Sept. 2009.

[24] K. Masaoka, M. Emoto, M. Sugawara, and Y. Nojiri. Contrast effect in evaluating the sense of presence for wide displays. *Journal of the Society for Information Display*, 14(9):785–791, 2006.

[25] H. Nemoto, P. Hanhart, P. Korshunov, and T. Ebrahimi. Ultra-Eye: UHD and HD images eye tracking dataset. In *International Workshop on Quality of Multimedia Experience (QoMEX)*, Sept. 2014.

[26] J. Redi, H. Liu, P. Gastaldo, R. Zunino, and I. Heynderickx. How to apply spatial saliency into objective metrics for JPEG compressed images? In *IEEE International Conference on Image Processing (ICIP)*, pages 961–964, Nov. 2009.

[27] J. Redi, H. Liu, R. Zunino, and I. Heynderickx. Interactions of visual attention and quality perception. In *Proc. SPIE*, volume 7865, pages 78650S–78650S–11, Feb. 2011.

[28] N. Riche, M. Duvinage, M. Mancas, B. Gosselin, and T. Dutoit. Saliency and Human Fixations: State-of-the-Art and Study of Comparison Metrics. In *IEEE International Conference on Computer Vision (ICCV)*, pages 1153–1160, Dec. 2013.

[29] K. Vu, K. A. Hua, S. Member, and W. Tavanapong. Image Retrieval Based on Regions of Interest. *IEEE Transactions on Knowledge and Data Engineering*, 15:1045–1049, 2003.

[30] D. Wang, G. Li, W. Jia, and X. Luo. Saliency-driven Scaling Optimization for Image Retargeting. *Visual Computing*, 27(9):853–860, Sept. 2011.

[31] S. Winkler and R. Subramanian. Overview of Eye tracking Datasets. In *International Workshop on Quality of Multimedia Experience (QoMEX)*, pages 212–217, July 2013.

[32] L. Zhang, M. H. Tong, T. K. Marks, H. Shan, and G. W. Cottrell. SUN: A Bayesian framework for saliency using natural statistics. *Journal of vision*, 8(7):32.1–20, 2008.

[33] Q. Zhao and C. Koch. Learning a saliency map using fixated locations in natural scenes. *Journal of vision*, 11(3):1–15, Mar. 2011.

An Objective Quality of Experience (QoE) Assessment Index for Retargeted Images

Jiangyang Zhang, C.-C. Jay Kuo
Ming Hsieh Department of Electrical Engineering
University of Southern California
Los Angeles, CA, USA
jiangyaz@usc.edu, cckuo@sipi.usc.edu

ABSTRACT

Content-aware image resizing (or image retargeting) is a technique that resizes images for optimum display on devices with different resolutions and aspect ratios. Traditional objective quality of experience (QoE) assessment methods are not applicable to retargeted images because the size of a retargeted image is different from its source. In this work, three determining factors for humans visual QoE on retargeted images are analyzed. They are global structural distortion (G), local region distortion (L) and loss of salient information (S). Different features are selected to quantify their respective distortion degrees. Then, an objective quality assessment index, called GLS, is proposed to predict viewers' QoE by fusing selected features into one single quality score. Several regression models used for feature fusion are discussed and compared. Experimental results demonstrate that the proposed GLS quality index has stronger correlation with human QoE than other existing objective metrics in retargeted image quality assessment.

Categories and Subject Descriptors

I.4.7 [**Computation Methodologies**]: Image Processing and Computer Vision—*Feature Measurement*

Keywords

Image retargeting; Quality assessment; QoE assessment; Content-aware image resizing

1. INTRODUCTION

Content-aware image resizing (or image retargeting) is a technique that addresses the increasing demand to display image contents on devices of different resolutions and aspect ratios. Traditional resizing techniques do not meet this requirement since they either discard important information (e.g. cropping) or introduce visual artifacts by oversqueezing the content (e.g. homogenous scaling). The goal of image retargeting is to change the aspect ratio and the resolution of images while preserving its visually important content and avoiding noticeable artifacts.

Several content-aware image retargeting solutions have been proposed in the last 7-8 years. They can be classified into two types: discrete and continuous approaches [19]. A discrete approach resizes an image by removing unimportant pixel regions iteratively [1, 15, 18] while a continuous approach conducts resizing through non-uniform image warping [7, 21, 25]. Most previous work has demonstrated novelty in problem formulation and algorithmic design. However, evaluation on the performance of different retargeting methods remains to be ad hoc as most of them rely on simple visual comparison or small-scale user studies. Clearly, there is a need to develop a better methodology for evaluating all retargeting results in a systematic and quantitative way.

Recently, Rubinstein *et al.* [17] conducted a systematic study on eight state-of-the-art retargeting algorithms through a large scale user study. Besides collecting and analyzing subjective evaluation results, they evaluated the performance of six distances as possible objective measures for retargeted images. However, there exists significant disagreement between their chosen measures and subjective evaluation results. Thus, a better objective QoE assessment index for retargeted images is still in need.

Objective image QoE assessment indices have been extensively studied in the last decade [8, 22]. They can be divided into three categories: full-reference (FR), reduced-reference (RR) and no-reference (NR). However, traditional image QoE assessment indices are not applicable in the context of image retargeting for the following reasons. For FR and RR methods, one underlying assumption is that the size of the original image should be matched with that of the distorted image. Since the original and retargeted images differ significantly in sizes and aspect ratios, this assumption does not hold. Furthermore, a retargeted image should preserve as much important information in its original image as possible. Thus, referring to the original image is an indispensable part in evaluating a retargeted result which rules out NR methods.

In this paper, we attempt to address the QoE assessment issue and propose a novel objective index that accounts for three major determining factors for humans visual perception on retargeted images. These factors include: the global structural distortion (G), the local region distortion (L) and the loss of salient information (S). Various features are chosen to quantify their respective distortion degrees. Then, an objective quality assessment index, called GLS, is developed to predict viewers' QoE by fusing these features into one

MM'14, November 3–7, 2014, Orlando, Florida, USA.

http://dx.doi.org/10.1145/2647868.2654922.

quality score. In developing the GLS quality index, we compare several regression models in fusing multiple features. It is shown by experimental results that the proposed GLS index has stronger correlation with human QoE than other existing objective indices in retargeted image quality assessment. The effectiveness of new extracted features is the basis for the impressive performance gain of the proposed GLS index as compared with other existing QoE indices.

The rest of this work is organized as follows. Related previous work on image retargeting, distorted image quality assessment, and retargeting image QoE assessment is reviewed in Section 2. Three major distortion types for image retargeting are analyzed in Section 3. Then, the GLS assessment index for retargeted images is proposed in Section 4. Experimental results and related discussion are presented in Section 5. Finally, concluding remarks are given and future research directions are pointed out in Section 6.

2. REVIEW OF RELATED WORK

2.1 Image Retargeting

Content-aware image resizing methods can be classified into discrete and continuous approaches [19]. For the discrete approach, image resizing is achieved by identifying and discarding unimportant image contents. The cropping-based method [2] identifies the most prominent components in an image with saliency-based measures and cuts out a rectangular region as the desired retargeting result. This method clearly fails when there are two salient objects located at the two ends of an image. The seam carving method [1] resizes an image by iteratively removing paths of pixels with the least amount of saliency. This method may lead to local distortion of a salient object such as a human fact and yield an unpleasant result. Realizing that no single retargeting operator could perform well on all images, Rubinstein, Shamir and Avidan proposed the multi-operator method [18] that combines three different operators; namely, scaling, cropping and seam carving, to achieve a more robust result across a wide range of images. For the continuous approach, image retargeting is formulated as a global optimization problem [25, 21] where the salient image regions ought to be well preserved while non-salient regions are allowed to be squeezed or stretched.

2.2 Distorted Image QoE Assessment

Objective image QoE assessment, which studies the degree of quality degradation due to distortions such as additive noise, blurring and compression, is a hot research topic in recent years [8]. Early work evaluates degraded image quality using the pixelwise distortion measure such as the mean squared errors (MSE) and the peak signal-to-noise ratio (PSNR). Although the MSE and PSNR values are simple to calculate, they do not correlate with human subjective visual experience well. To overcome this problem, other quality indices have been proposed to account for characteristics of the human visual system (HVS). Examples include contrast sensitivity function (CSF) masking [3], just noticeable difference (JND) threshold [24], structure similarity (SSIM) [23], feature similarity (FSIM) [27], etc. One common assumption of the aforementioned full-reference image quality indices is that the size and the aspect ratio of the source image and its distorted one are the same. Since the size of a retargeted image is different from its source, these indices are not applicable to the QoE assessment of retargeted images.

2.3 Retargeted Image QoE Assessment

The first comparison study on retargeted image quality was presented in [17]. In this work, the authors conducted a large scale user study to compare the performance of eight representative state-of-the-art image retargeting methods. In addition to performance evaluations based on user responses, six objective image distance measures were evaluated and compared with actual human perception. Since none of these six measures was in well alignment with human ranking, there is a need to search for other retargeted image quality indices that can offer better agreement. A similar study was conducted by Ma *et al.* [12], in which a different image retargeting database was built and evaluated by human viewers. Several existing objective QoE measures were evaluated. It was concluded that a better quality index could be obtained by combining the shape distortion measure and the content information loss. Although in-depth performance analysis on QoE index design was conducted in [12] and [17], none of them offers a satisfactory retargeted image QoE index. Recently, Liu *et al.* [10] proposed an objective QoE assessment method for image retargeting using a top-down approach. Although the method is capable of measuring both local and geometric distortions using the SSIM index, it does not account for information completeness which will be shown to play an important role in the quality assessment of retargeted images.

In this work, we will start with identifying three dominant distortion types for image retargeting; namely, the global structural distortion (G), the local region distortion (L) and the loss of salient information (S). Then, features are extracted to characterize the severity of these distortions. Finally, we propose a GLS quality index that adopts a machine learning methodology to fuse all distortion features.

3. IMAGE RETARGETING DISTORTION ANALYSIS

In this section, we identify three main distortion types of image retargeting – global structural distortion, local region distortion and loss of salient information. The first two distortion types introduce visual unpleasing artifacts to retargeted results such as over-squeezing the object shapes (global) or breaking the prominent lines (local). The third type does not necessarily introduce visually noticeable artifacts, yet the retargeted result fails to preserve all salient information in the original image. Understanding the characteristics of these major distortion types would lay out a basis for the GLS quality index design, which will be elaborated in Section 4.

3.1 Global Structural Distortion

Global structural distortion occurs when an image is over-squeezed or over-stretched after retargeting, leading to unpleasing shape deformation of prominent objects. This distortion is especially noticeable when the salient object is improperly deformed and/or different parts of a salient object are deformed unproportionally, leading to inconsistency as compared with the original image. This type of distortion produces artifacts at the global scale.

Both discrete and continuous image retargeting methods could potentially produce global structural distortion. For

Figure 1: Two examples of global structural distortion. Upper row: the original image of *face* (left) and the retargeted result by [1] (right). Lower row: the original image of *lotus* (left) and the retargeted result by scaling (right).

example, as shown in Fig. 1, the global structure of the prominent object in the *face* image is heavily distorted because the relative positions of eyes, nose and mouth are misaligned after retargeting. However, the shape of each individual face component (eyes, nose, mouth, etc.) are kept intact. In other words, there is no distortion in local regions. For image *lotus*, there is also heavy global structural distortion as the prominent object (flower) is over-squeezed after retargeting.

3.2 Local Region Distortion

After retargeting, some local regions in the image may be heavily distorted, especially near those regions with prominent edges. Discrete retargeting methods, such as seam carving [1], may introduce broken lines when the removed region overlaps with a prominent edge region. On the other hand, continuous retargeting methods may result in heavy edge bending when the underlying mesh behind the edge region undergoes significant warping. The local region distortions become less noticeable at regions with homogeneous textures, (e.g. sky, surface, wall, etc.) and irregular textures (e.g. trees, grass, sand, etc.) [26]. We show an example of heavy local region distortion using the seam carving method in Fig. 2. Prominent edges are heavily bended after retargeting since many of the removed seams passed through the edge of pencils.

3.3 Loss of Salient Information

Besides reducing visual artifacts, a good retargeted image should be able to include all important content in its original image as much as possible. Loss of salient information is a distortion type commonly introduced by discrete operators such as cropping. When the salient object is too large and/or spans across the whole image, cropping will inevitably discard some important information. For example, as shown in Fig. 3(a), there are four different buildings in the original image, each of them with similar visual importance. To retarget this image to half of its original width, a simple cropping method will inevitably discard some salient information, leaving only two of the buildings in the retargeted result. A better retargeting method for this image should be able to remove redundant information from each

Figure 2: Illustration of local region distortion. Left: the original image of *pencil*. Right: the retargeted result using the seam carving method in [1] with three zoomed-in local regions.

building but preserve all four buildings as shown in Fig. 3(b) (b). This type of distortion is less observable for continuous retargeting methods, since different regions of an image are scaled disproportionately without discarding pixels in them.

(a) (b)

Figure 3: Illustration of loss of salient information: (a) the original image of *Marble* and its cropping result, where the yellow box shows the optimum cropping result. (b) a better retargeted result obtained by [18].

The objective quality indices examined in [10, 17] primarily focus on measuring distortions (global or/and local). However, they do not pay much attention to the importance of information completeness. In contrast, we attempt to find good features to characterize all three distortion types and combine them into one single score for quantitative evaluation of retargeted results in this work.

4. GLS QUALITY INDEX FOR RETARGETED IMAGES

In this section, we will introduce the proposed GLS quality index for retargeted images. Given the original image, I, and its retargeted results $\hat{I}_i$ (i=1,2,3,...), we would like to compute an objective quality score S_i for each result to achieve the following two objectives:

1. the relative rank of retargeted results is consistent with the subjective ranking;
2. the predicted quality score matches with subjective quality scores.

We will first introduce the overall framework in Section 4.1 and, then, describe each stage in detail in Sections 4.2-4.5.

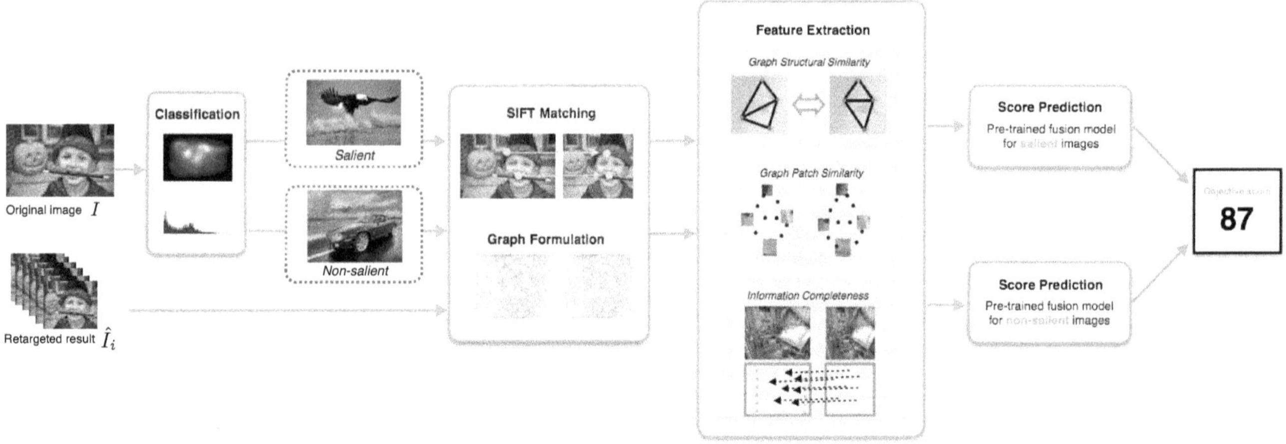

Figure 4: The system framework in computing the proposed GLS quality index for retargeted images.

4.1 Overview of System Framework

The challenge of objective image QoE assessment lies in formulating effective features and fusing them into a single number to predict the quality score. In the proposed GLS scheme, we first conduct saliency analysis and SIFT feature mapping to determine whether I is a *salient* or *non-salient* image and build the mapping correspondence between I and $\hat{I}_i$. For each retargeted result $\hat{I}_i$, we extract features to quantify the three types of distortions as mentioned in Section 3. A pre-trained machine learning model is used to fuse all features into one single quality score as the final result. The machine learning model is trained using subjective evaluation results of existing image retargeting databases [12, 17]. Fig. 4 shows the overall system framework in computing the proposed GLS quality index.

4.2 Saliency-based Classification

The first step is to determine whether the source image, I, is a *salient* or *non-salient* image. If an image contains one salient object which does not cover the entire image, it is considered as salient. Otherwise, if all contents in I have equal visual importance or its salient object is too large and fills up the entire image, I is viewed as non-salient. This classification step is commonly known as data grouping in handling large-scale databases. The main purpose of image grouping is to separate images of different characteristics into multiple disjoint groups so that we can train different prediction models for them separately. This grouping process allows us to design a more accurate prediction model since there is a stronger correlation between the training and test images.

There are many algorithms proposed for saliency computation and, without loss of generality, we simply choose one and adopt the GBVS method [5] here. The salient image classification problem is conducted based on analyzing the histogram of the obtained saliency map, which takes a value ranging from 0 to 255. The saliency value "0" means the lowest saliency level (i.e., no saliency) and "255" means the highest saliency level (i.e. strongest saliency). As shown in Fig. 5, the saliency histogram of a typical salient image usually consisting of a steep peak followed by a quickly descending tail as shown in Fig. 5(a). On the other hand, for a typical non-salient image, the histogram usually has a low-rising peak and a slowly decaying tail as shown in Fig. 5(b). The canal boat image in Fig. 5(b) is classified to a non-salient one since its salient region is too large.

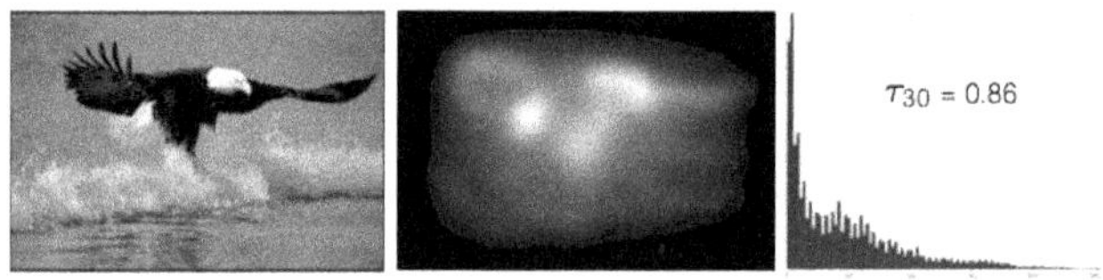

(a) *salient* image (*eagle*)

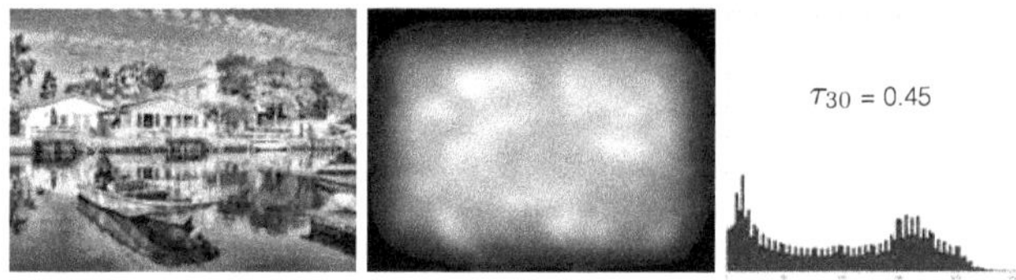

(b) *non-salient* image (*canal boat*)

Figure 5: Classification based on the saliency map histogram analysis for two representative images: the original image I (left), the saliency map (middle) and its histogram (right).

We define the percentage of pixels below brightness level x as

$$\tau_x = \frac{\sum_x h(x)}{N}, \quad x = 1, 2, \cdots, 256,$$

where $h(x)$ is the number of pixels at bin x in the histogram and N is the total number of pixels in image I. In our experiments, we adopt the following simple rule to decide whether an image is a salient one or not. If $\tau_{30} > \delta$ with threshold $\delta = 0.70$, it is a salient image. Otherwise, it is a non-salient one.

4.3 SIFT Mapping and Mesh Formulation

The next step is compute the mapping correspondence between SIFT features [11] of the original image, I, and its retargeted results, $\hat{I}_i$. This correspondence will help serve as the basis for feature extraction as elaborated in Section 4.4.

We first extract the SIFT features from I and match them with those of each retargeted image $\hat{I}_i$. We discard all SIFT features that are not successfully matched so that we have an equal number of SIFT features for each image pair, I and $\hat{I}_i$, at the end of the matching process. Then, we formulate two graphs for each image pair $(I, \hat{I}_i)$. Each vertex in the graph represents one matched feature in the original image. The graph formulation is completed by connecting all neighboring vertices using delaunay triangulation as shown in Fig. 6.

As a result, we associate each image pair, I and $\hat{I}_i$, with two graphs denoted by $\mathbf{G} = (\mathbf{V}, \mathbf{E})$ and $\hat{\mathbf{G}}_\mathbf{i} = (\hat{\mathbf{V}}_\mathbf{i}, \hat{\mathbf{E}}_\mathbf{i})$, where $|\mathbf{V}| = |\hat{\mathbf{V}}_\mathbf{i}|$ and, for each vertex $\mathbf{v} \in \mathbf{V}$, there is a unique mapping $m(\mathbf{v}) = \hat{\mathbf{v}}_\mathbf{i}$, where $\hat{\mathbf{v}}_\mathbf{i} \in \hat{\mathbf{V}}_\mathbf{i}$. With such a mapping in place, we have converted the problem of measuring the distance between I and $\hat{I}_i$ to the problem of computing the graph similarity between $\mathbf{G}$ and $\hat{\mathbf{G}}_\mathbf{i}$.

(a) (b)

Figure 6: SIFT feature mapping and graph formulation between the original image and its retargeted result: (a) original image I (top), matched SIFT features (middle) and its formulated graph $\mathbf{G} = (\mathbf{V}, \mathbf{E})$ (bottom), (b): retargeted result $\hat{I}_i$ (top), matched SIFT features (middle) and its formulated graph $\hat{\mathbf{G}}_\mathbf{i} = (\hat{\mathbf{V}}_\mathbf{i}, \hat{\mathbf{E}}_\mathbf{i})$ (bottom).

4.4 Extraction of Features

There are two key issues in objective image QoE assessment: 1) extraction and representation of appropriate features, and 2) pooling of features into one single number to represent quality score. We will address the first issue in this section and focus on the issue of feature fusion in Section 4.5.

4.4.1 Graph Structure Similarity

The graph structure similarity feature measures the amount of global structural distortion in the retargeted image. To compute this feature, we make use of the results in Section 4.3, where the problem of comparing image pair, I and $\hat{I}_i$, is reformulated as comparing the graph similarity between $\mathbf{G} = (\mathbf{V}, \mathbf{E})$ and $\hat{\mathbf{G}}_\mathbf{i} = (\hat{\mathbf{V}}_\mathbf{i}, \hat{\mathbf{E}}_\mathbf{i})$.

If there is little global structural distortion during the retargeting process, the relative positions of $\hat{\mathbf{V}}_\mathbf{i}$ should be close to those of $\mathbf{V}$ and the shape of each triangle in $\mathbf{G}$ should be similar to the corresponding matched triangle in $\hat{\mathbf{G}}_\mathbf{i}$. As a result, the global structural distortion in $\hat{I}_i$ can be measured using shape deformation of each mesh triangle.

To measure the shape deformation of each triangle, we make use of the log-polar spatial representation scheme [16], which is computationally more efficient than methods such as RANSAC. It encodes the relative positions and orientations between each pair of nodes in the graph. Fig. 7 shows an example of 5-bit (32 regions) log-polar representations and its corresponding spatial and orientation codes. In our case, we use a spatial code with 8 bits, where the first 3 bits represent the relative orientation angle (quantized into 8 sectors) and the remaining 5 bits represents the relative distance (quantized into 32 levels).

The shape deformation between two triangles is measured using the modified inconsistency sum method [16]. That is, to compare the log-polar codes of nodes in the triangle, we compute the distance between two triangles T_k and $\hat{T}_k$ as

$$d_k = \sum_{i=1}^{3} C_{i,k} \otimes \hat{C}_{i,k},$$

where k and i are indices for triangles and its three nodes, respectively, and $C_{i,k}$ (i=1,2,3) are the codes for node i in triangle T_k, and $\otimes$ denotes the XOR operator. For the test images used in our experiments, the typical range for k is between 200 and 1000. If a triangle in $\mathbf{G}$ is perfectly matched with the corresponding triangle in $\hat{\mathbf{G}}_\mathbf{i}$, then $d_k = 0$. Then, we add up the distances for all triangle pairs and obtain the distance between two graphs, $\mathbf{G}$ and $\hat{\mathbf{G}}_\mathbf{i}$, as

$$f_1 = \sum_k d_k.$$

4.4.2 Graph Patch Similarity

To measure the degree of local region distortion in the retargeted result, we consider a feature called the graph patch similarity. If there is prominent local region distortion such as broken edges or edge bending, the patch difference should be significant.

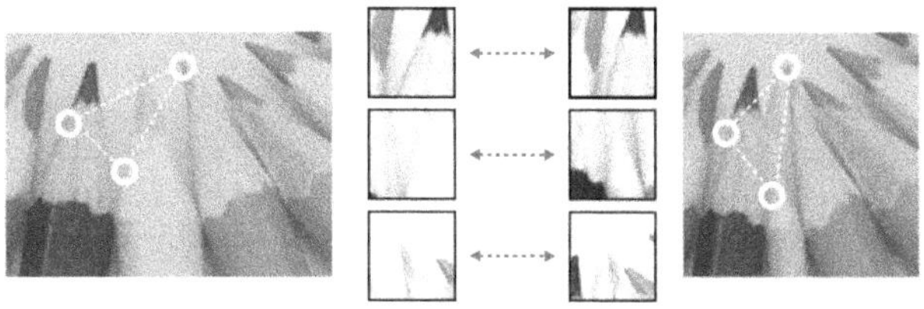

Figure 8: The degree of local region distortion is measured by using the graph patch similarity, where the Euclidean distance of local patches of matched graph nodes are computed and summed up over the entire graph.

For each image pair I and $\hat{I}_i$, we compare the similarity of local patches of size $N \times N$ centered around each node in graphs $\mathbf{G}$ and $\hat{\mathbf{G}}_\mathbf{i}$, where N is chosen to be 15 in our

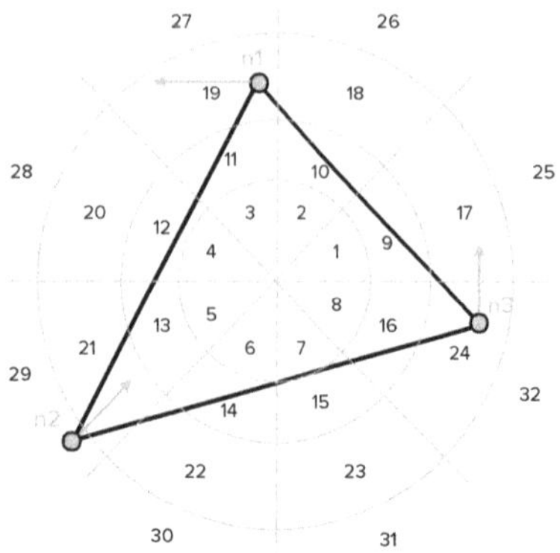

Node	Position	Orientation
n1	19	π
n2	29	π/4
n3	24	π/2

Figure 7: Log-polar spatial representation scheme [16]. This example shows the 5-bit (32 regions) log-polar representation of a triangle: the position and orientation codes of each triangle node.

experiment. We use $p_{i,k}$ and $\hat{p}_{i,k}$ to denote patches centered at the node with index i of the triangle with index k in these two graphs, respectively. Then, the graph patch similarity feature can be computed as

$$f_2 = \sum_k \sum_{i=1}^{3} d(p_{i,k}, \hat{p}_{i,k}),$$

where $d(p_{i,k}, \hat{p}_{i,k})$ represents the Euclidean distance between patches $p_{i,k}$ and $\hat{p}_{i,k}$. We show an example of three matched features and the corresponding local patches for comparison in Fig. 8.

4.4.3 Information Completeness

The features of information completeness characterizes how well the retargeted image, $\hat{I}_i$, preserves the important content of the original image, I. When I is a salient image and contains a prominent object, preserving this salient object and its surrounding region is important at the expense of regions of lower saliency. However, all contents that possess similar importance for non-salient images, they should be preserved in a more uniform manner.

First, we need to determine a region in I that should be present in the retargeted image $\hat{I}_i$. This region, denoted by $\hat{P}_i$, is called the impact area of $\hat{I}_i$. To determine the impact region $\hat{P}_i$, we reverse-map all matched SIFT nodes in $\hat{I}_i$ back to I as shown in Fig. 9, and find a tight rectangular bounding box, which is denoted as $\hat{P}_i$. Based on the saliency map, we classify pixels in I into three regions: critical, important and ordinary as shown in Fig. 10. For a good retargeted result, its impact area $\hat{P}_i$ should contain as much critical and important regions as possible.

Then, to quantify the information completeness, we can define a feature that measures the amount of saliency value covered by the impact region. It is written as

$$f_3 = \alpha \cdot \frac{P_c}{N_c} + (1-\alpha) \cdot \frac{P_i}{N_i},$$

where N_i and N_c are the total numbers of pixels of important and critical regions and P_i and P_c are the total numbers of important and critical region pixels inside the impact area $\hat{P}_i$, respectively. The weighting parameter α is empirically chosen to be 0.70. The value of f_3 ranges from 0 to 1. If all the important and critical regions are encircled by the impact area, we have $f_3 = 1.0$.

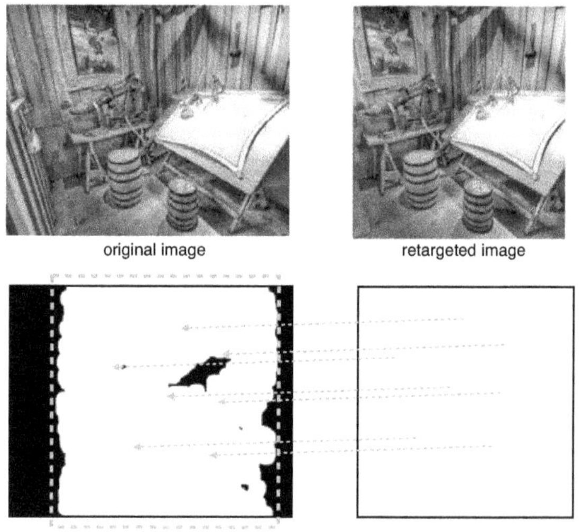

Figure 9: Illustration of the reverse mapping of the matched SIFT nodes in the retargeted image to the source image to compute the impact area $\hat{P}_i$ in the source image. The white region in the bottom left indicates a region where the underlying information can be found in the retargeted image while the black region means this part of information is lost after retargeting.

4.5 Feature Fusion and Model Selection

For effective image quality prediction, not only is the feature selection important but also the mechanism to fuse all features into one single quality score. There is no straightforward solution to feature fusion since the contribution of each feature to the final quality score may be different and is difficult to determine. A few basic pooling methods can be employed, including simple summation, multiplication and linear combinations of features. However, all these methods implicitly make assumptions on the relative importance of each feature, and there is lack of convincing ground for the assumptions.

In the proposed GLS quality index, we take advantage of the subjective human evaluation results and employ the machine learning technique to find a mapping function between the features discussed in Section 4.4 and the final quality score.

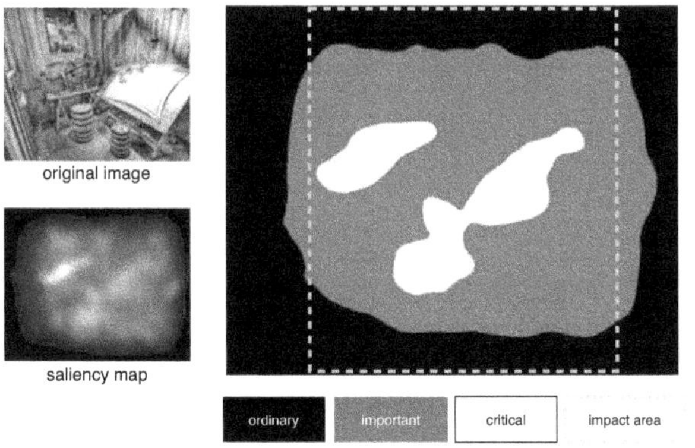

Figure 10: Illustration of the information completeness feature computation: the original image (left top), the saliency map (left bottom) and the segmentation of the saliency map into the critical region (white), the important region (gray) and the ordinary region (black), and the impact area $\hat{P}_i$ encircled by the green dash line.

In addition to features f_1, f_2 and f_3, we consider three more auxiliary features. They are:

- f_4: the total number of matched SIFT node pairs between I and $\hat{I}_i$;
- f_5: the average matching strength of all matching SIFT node pairs;
- f_6: the average matching strength of top 50 matched SIFT node pairs.

These three features measure how good the matching is between I and $\hat{I}_i$. The matching strength represents the distance between each matching feature pair. For each retargeted result, we extract the six features $\{f_1, f_2, ..., f_6\}$ from the given image and normalize them to the range of $[0, 1]$.

To determine the optimal fusion rule, we conduct experiments with the following eight fusion methods and compare their performance in our current application context:

1. Direct feature addition (*add*)
2. Direct feature multiplication (*multi*)
3. Linear regression (*lin*)
4. Logistic regression (*log*)
5. Logistic regression with L_1 penalty (*log-L1*)
6. Support vector regression with linear kernel (*svr-lin*)
7. Support vector regression with polynomial kernel (*svr-pol*)
8. Support vector regression with RBF kernel (*svr-rbf*)

Note that the last six of the above eight fusion methods are based on machine learning.

In the training phase, each candidate model is presented with a training set $\{f_p, y_p\}$ and the model parameters are estimated. The training sets are obtained from subjective evaluation results from existing public datasets, where f_p are the feature descriptors and y_p corresponds to the subjective score. We utilize the cross-validation scheme for each candidate model and choose the optimal model whose objective scores have the highest correlation with human subjective evaluation results. During the test phase, the trained optimal model is presented with the feature descriptors of the test image, and it predicts the estimated objective quality score.

5. EXPERIMENTAL RESULTS

5.1 Datasets

For the experiments, we make use of two public databases for image retargeting: the RetargetMe database [17] and the CUHK database [12].

The RetargetMe database contains 80 images, each with eight retargeted results obtained by eight methods: Nonhomogeneous Warping (WARP) [25], Seam-Carving (SC) [1], Scale-and-Stretch (SNS) [21], Multi-Operator (MULTI) [18], Shift-Map (SM) [15], Streaming Video (SV) [7], Cropping (CR) and Homogeneous Scaling (SCL). The subjective evaluation results on 37 images for all eight retargeting methods are provided in this database ($37 \times 8 = 296$ results). The evaluation was conducted with 210 human participants and scores were computed using pairwise comparison method, in which participants were shown two retargeted images side-by-side and were asked to choose their preferred ones.

The CUHK database contains 171 retargeted results from 57 image sources. In addition to the eight retargeting methods studied by [17], this database includes results from two more targeting methods; namely, the optimized seam carving and scale method [4] and the energy-based deformation method [6]. Unlike the pair-wise comparison scheme used in [17], the subjective evaluation in this study employed the 5-category discrete scale ("Bad", "Poor", "Fair", "Good" and "Excellent") to obtain the mean opinion scores (MOS) of viewers for each retargeted result.

5.2 Test Methodology

For both databases, we employ the 10-fold cross-validation method to evaluate the performance of the proposed GLS quality index. That is, the data is equally divided into ten parts: one chunk is used for testing and the remaining nine parts are used for training. The experiment is repeated with each of the ten chunk used for testing. The averaged accuracy of the test based on all ten chunks is taken as the final performance measure.

5.3 Comparison of Feature Fusion Methods

For performance evaluation, we consider the following five metrics: 1) the Kendall rank coefficient τ, 2) the Pearson linear correlation coefficient r, 3) the Spearman rank order correlation coefficient ρ, 4) the root mean square error ($RMSE$) between subjective and objective quality scores, and 5) the outliers ratio (OR).

For a perfect match between the objective and subjective scores (or rank), we have

- $\tau = 1.0$
- $r = 1.0$
- $\rho = 1.0$
- $RMSE = 0$
- $OR = 0$

Table 1 shows the Kendall rank coefficient of the eight different fusion methods as discussed in Section 4.5 for the RetargetMe database. Since the subjective evaluation for

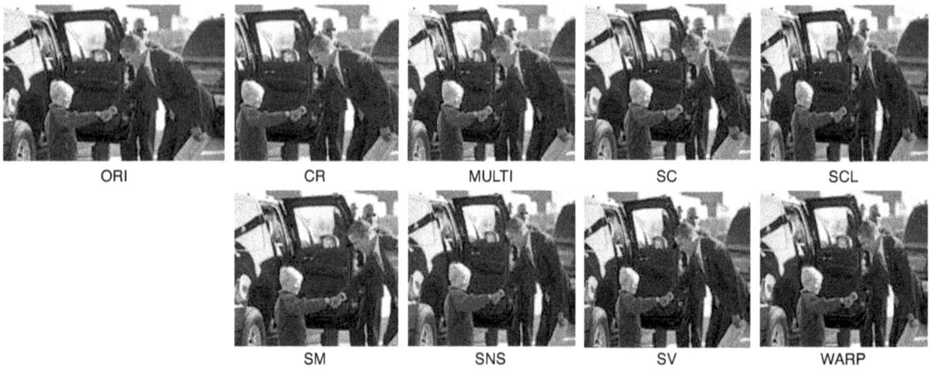

$\tau = 0.857$

Rank	1	2	3	4	5	6	7	8
Subjective	CR	MULTI	SV	SCL	SM	SNS	WARP	SC
Objective	CR	SV	SCL	MULTI	SM	SNS	WARP	SC

Figure 11: An example where the proposed GLS index is strongly correlated with the subjective rank (with Kendall rank coefficient $\tau = 0.857$). The original and eight retargeted images of the *Obama* image and the corresponding subjective rank [17] and the objective rank computed using the GLS index are shown.

this database is based on the pairwise comparison, it is difficult to determine the mean opinion score (MOS) and we evaluate the performance of these fusion methods with the Kendall rank coefficient only. We see from Table 1 that the machine-learning-based fusion methods perform significantly better than simple feature addition or multiplication. In particular, the logistic regression fusion method outperforms all others. Furthermore, adding the L_1 penalty further improves the Kendall rank coefficient from 0.355 to 0.382.

Table 1: Kendall rank coefficient τ of different fusion models for RetargetMe database [17]

	add	*multi*	*lin*	*log*	*log-L1*	*svr-lin*	*svr-pol*	*svr-rbf*
τ	0.058	0.095	0.301	0.355	**0.382**	0.307	0.308	0.306

Table 2 compares the performance of different fusion methods for the CUHK database. Since the mean opinion scores (MOS) are provided in this database, we can conduct performance comparison using multiple metrics. As shown in Table 2, the logistic regression (yet without L_1 penalty) outperforms all other fusion methods under almost all performance metrics except for SROCC, where the linear regression is slightly better than the logistic regression.

5.4 Comparison of Objective Quality Indices

Table 3: Performance comparison of five objective image QoE indices for RetargetMe database [17]

	BDS[20]	EH[13]	SIFT-Flow[9]	EMD[14]	GLS
τ	0.083	0.004	0.145	0.251	**0.382**

In this section, we compare the proposed GLS quality index with four other objective QoE indices for retargeted images. They are:

- Bidirectional Similarity (BDS) [20]
- Edge Histogram (EH) [13]
- SIFT-Flow [9]
- Earth Mover Distance (EMD) [14]

Table 3 and Table 4 compare the performance among all five QoE indices for the RetargetMe and the CUHK databases, respectively. We see from the experimental results that the proposed GLS index performs better than all existing QoE indices by a significant margin in all four performance metrics.

5.5 Discussion

The proposed GLS index outperforms all other existing QoE indices for two main reasons. First, the GLS index design is based upon three dorminant distortion types for image retargeting as discussed in Section 3. The other quality indices consider only one or two of these distortion types but none of them consider all three together. For example, EH [13], SIFT-Flow [9] and EMD [14] do capture the global structural distortion and the local region distortion of retargeted images, but fail to consider the information completeness factor. The BDS index [20] measures information completeness in a bidirectional way, but it fails to consider either global or local distortions that occurred in the retargeting result fully.

The second reason that explains the good performance of the proposed GLS index is that the machine-learning technique is adopted to fuse features effectively to yield one final quality score. Although our feature design takes into consideration all three distortion types, determining relative weights of multiple features still remains a challenge. In the GLS index, we address this challenge by training a machine learning model that learns from existing subjective evaluation results and intelligently determines the optimal feature weights for each specific image. The more subjective evaluation results we have for the fusion model training, the better the predicted objective score for each retargeted result.

We offer further insights into the performance of the GLS quality index by examining two examples. We show the evaluation of eight retargeted results for image *Obama* in Fig. 11. This image contains two salient objects: President Obama and the boy. As shown in the subjective result,

Table 2: LCC, SROCC, RMSE and OR of different fusion models for CUHK database [12]

	lin	*log*	*log-L1*	*svr-lin*	*svr-pol*	*svr-rbf*
r	0.4402	**0.4622**	0.3961	0.3656	0.3711	0.3658
ρ	**0.4939**	0.4760	0.4002	0.4038	0.3821	0.3961
$RMSE$	12.204	**10.932**	14.026	12.894	13.259	13.212
OR	0.2046	**0.1345**	0.2163	0.2339	0.2022	0.2267

Table 4: Comparison with other objective image QoE metrics for CUHK database [12]

	BDS[20]	EH[13]	SIFT-Flow[9]	EMD[14]	GLS
r	0.2896	0.3422	0.3141	0.2760	**0.4622**
ρ	0.2887	0.3288	0.2899	0.2904	**0.4760**
$RMSE$	12.922	12.686	12.817	12.977	**10.932**
OR	0.2164	0.2047	0.1462	0.1696	**0.1345**

cropping performs the best since the two salient objects can perfectly fit into one cropping window and very little salient information is lost. On the other hand, seam carving [1] and warping [25] perform the worst as they introduce heavy global structural distortion (on President Obama) and local region distortion (the document in President's hand).

As shown in the rank order table of Fig. 11, the objective rank computed with the proposed GLS index correlates well with the subjective rank in [17]. The Kendall rank coefficient is equal to $\tau = 0.857$. The best one and the poorest four image retargeting methods identified by the GLS index are identical with subjective evaluation results. The only slight difference lies in the methods that are ranked from 2 to 4. The GLS index favored the result of the streaming video method [7] while the subjective evaluation ranks the multi-operator method [18] as the second.

However, there are individual cases where the proposed GLS index does not agree well with the subjective evaluation results. We show the evaluation results of the *Buddha* image in Fig. 12. For this case, there is a large discrepancy between the subjective and objective evaluation results with Kendall rank coefficient $\tau = -0.357$. The GLS index gives the highest preference to cropping, seam-carving [1] and warping [25]. However, these three are among the worst performing methods according to subjective evaluation results, thereby leading to a negative Kendall rank coefficient value. The mismatch between the objective and subjective ranks may be explained by the shortage of training data. In the training data set, there is no image similar to the Buddha image which contains the face of a human statue as opposed to an authentic human face. If similar cases are available in the training data or face-detection is added to the saliency detection module, we may expect the proposed machine-learning-based GLS index to learn from these cases and provide more accurate prediction.

6. CONCLUSION AND FUTURE WORK

In this paper, we proposed a novel objective quality of experience (QoE) index, called the GLS index, to evaluate image retargeting results. We first identified three key factors related to human perception on the quality of retargeted images. They are global structural distortion, local region distortion and loss of salient information. Using this knowledge as guidance, we found effective features that capture these distortion types and utilized machine learning to fuse all features into one single quality score. One major advantage of applying the machine learning tool is that the feature weights can be determined automatically. It was shown by experimental results that the proposed GLS index outperforms four other existing objective indices by a significant margin in all performance metrics of consideration.

Since the performance of the machine learning method will be improved with more training data, a larger database with more subjective evaluation results for image retargeting is desired. The prediction of objective scores will be greatly improved with a model trained with more complete data set that contains all distortion types. In addition, this work is mainly focused on evaluating retargeting results of images. Objective QoE assessment for retargeted video will be an important extension of the current work.

7. REFERENCES

[1] S. Avidan and A. Shamir. Seam carving for content-aware image resizing. In *ACM Transactions on graphics (TOG)*, volume 26, page 10. ACM, 2007.

[2] L.-Q. Chen, X. Xie, X. Fan, W.-Y. Ma, H.-J. Zhang, and H.-Q. Zhou. A visual attention model for adapting images on small displays. *Multimedia systems*, 9(4):353–364, 2003.

[3] B. Chitprasert and K. Rao. Human visual weighted progressive image transmission. *Communications, IEEE Transactions on*, 38(7):1040–1044, 1990.

[4] W. Dong, N. Zhou, J.-C. Paul, and X. Zhang. Optimized image resizing using seam carving and scaling. *ACM Transactions on Graphics (TOG)*, 28(5):125, 2009.

[5] J. Harel, C. Koch, P. Perona, et al. Graph-based visual saliency. *Advances in neural information processing systems*, 19:545, 2007.

[6] Z. Karni, D. Freedman, and C. Gotsman. Energy-based image deformation. In *Computer Graphics Forum*, volume 28, pages 1257–1268. Wiley Online Library, 2009.

[7] P. Krähenbühl, M. Lang, A. Hornung, and M. Gross. A system for retargeting of streaming video. In *ACM Transactions on Graphics (TOG)*, volume 28, page 126. ACM, 2009.

[8] W. Lin and C.-C. Jay Kuo. Perceptual visual quality metrics: A survey. *Journal of Visual Communication and Image Representation*, 22(4):297–312, 2011.

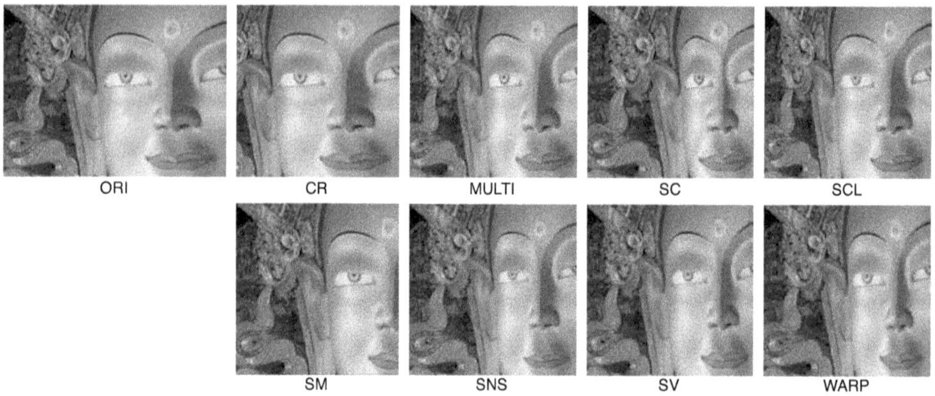

τ = -0.357

Rank	1	2	3	4	5	6	7	8
Subjective	MULTI	SCL	SV	SM	CR	SNS	WARP	SC
Objective	CR	SC	WARP	SV	MULTI	SM	SNS	SCL

Figure 12: An example where the proposed GLS index is poorly correlated with the subjective rank (with Kendall rank coefficient $\tau = -0.357$). The original and eight retargeted images of the *Buddha* image and the corresponding subjective rank [17] and the objective rank computed using the GLS index are shown.

[9] C. Liu, J. Yuen, A. Torralba, J. Sivic, and W. T. Freeman. Sift flow: Dense correspondence across different scenes. In *Computer Vision–ECCV 2008*, pages 28–42. Springer, 2008.

[10] Y.-J. Liu, X. Luo, Y.-M. Xuan, W.-F. Chen, and X.-L. Fu. Image retargeting quality assessment. In *Computer Graphics Forum*, volume 30, pages 583–592. Wiley Online Library, 2011.

[11] D. G. Lowe. Object recognition from local scale-invariant features. In *Computer vision, 1999. The proceedings of the seventh IEEE international conference on*, volume 2, pages 1150–1157. IEEE, 1999.

[12] L. Ma, W. Lin, C. Deng, and K. N. Ngan. Image retargeting quality assessment: a study of subjective scores and objective metrics. *Selected Topics in Signal Processing, IEEE Journal of*, 6(6):626–639, 2012.

[13] B. S. Manjunath, J.-R. Ohm, V. V. Vasudevan, and A. Yamada. Color and texture descriptors. *Circuits and Systems for Video Technology, IEEE Transactions on*, 11(6):703–715, 2001.

[14] O. Pele and M. Werman. Fast and robust earth mover's distances. In *Computer vision, 2009 IEEE 12th international conference on*, pages 460–467. IEEE, 2009.

[15] Y. Pritch, E. Kav-Venaki, and S. Peleg. Shift-map image editing. In *Computer Vision, 2009 IEEE 12th International Conference on*, pages 151–158. IEEE, 2009.

[16] S. Purushotham, Q. Tian, and C.-C. J. Kuo. Picture-in-picture copy detection using spatial coding techniques. In *Proceedings of the 2011 ACM international workshop on Automated media analysis and production for novel TV services*, pages 25–30. ACM, 2011.

[17] M. Rubinstein, D. Gutierrez, O. Sorkine, and A. Shamir. A comparative study of image retargeting. In *ACM transactions on graphics (TOG)*, volume 29, page 160. ACM, 2010.

[18] M. Rubinstein, A. Shamir, and S. Avidan. Multi-operator media retargeting. In *ACM Transactions on Graphics (TOG)*, volume 28, page 23. ACM, 2009.

[19] A. Shamir and O. Sorkine. Visual media retargeting. In *ACM SIGGRAPH ASIA 2009 Courses*, page 11. ACM, 2009.

[20] D. Simakov, Y. Caspi, E. Shechtman, and M. Irani. Summarizing visual data using bidirectional similarity. In *Computer Vision and Pattern Recognition, 2008. CVPR 2008. IEEE Conference on*, pages 1–8. IEEE, 2008.

[21] Y.-S. Wang, C.-L. Tai, O. Sorkine, and T.-Y. Lee. Optimized scale-and-stretch for image resizing. In *ACM Transactions on Graphics (TOG)*, volume 27, page 118. ACM, 2008.

[22] Z. Wang and A. C. Bovik. Modern image quality assessment. *Synthesis Lectures on Image, Video, and Multimedia Processing*, 2(1):1–156, 2006.

[23] Z. Wang, A. C. Bovik, H. R. Sheikh, and E. P. Simoncelli. Image quality assessment: from error visibility to structural similarity. *Image Processing, IEEE Transactions on*, 13(4):600–612, 2004.

[24] A. B. Watson and J. A. Solomon. Model of visual contrast gain control and pattern masking. *JOSA A*, 14(9):2379–2391, 1997.

[25] L. Wolf, M. Guttmann, and D. Cohen-Or. Non-homogeneous content-driven video-retargeting. In *Computer Vision, 2007. ICCV 2007. IEEE 11th International Conference on*, pages 1–6. IEEE, 2007.

[26] J. Zhang and C.-C. Kuo. Region-adaptive texture-aware image resizing. In *Acoustics, Speech and Signal Processing (ICASSP), 2012 IEEE International Conference on*, pages 837–840. IEEE, 2012.

[27] L. Zhang, D. Zhang, and X. Mou. Fsim: a feature similarity index for image quality assessment. *Image Processing, IEEE Transactions on*, 20(8):2378–2386, 2011.

Acceptability-based QoE Management for User-centric Mobile Video Delivery: A Field Study Evaluation

Wei Song, Dian Tjondronegoro, Ivan Himawan
Science and Engineering Faculty, Queensland University of Technology, Brisbane, QLD, Australia
{w1.song, dian, i.himawan} @qut.edu.au

ABSTRACT

Effective Quality of Experience (QoE) management for mobile video delivery – to optimize overall user experience while adapting to heterogeneous use contexts – is still a big challenge to date. This paper proposes a mobile video delivery system to emphasize the use of acceptability as the main indicator of QoE to manage the end-to-end factors in delivering mobile video services. The first contribution is a novel framework for user-centric mobile video system that is based on acceptability-based QoE (A-QoE) prediction models, which were derived from comprehensive subjective studies. The second contribution is results from a field study that evaluates the user experience of the proposed system during realistic usage circumstances, addressing the impacts of perceived video quality, loading speed, interest in content, viewing locations, network bandwidth, display devices, and different video coding approaches, including region-of-interest (ROI) enhancement and center zooming.

Categories and Subject Descriptors

H.5.1 [**Multimedia Information Services**]: Evaluation/methodology; H.5.m [**Miscellaneous**]

General Terms

Performance; Design; Experimentation.

Keywords

Acceptability; evaluation; field study; QoE; mobile video delivery

1. INTRODUCTION

It is increasingly common for people to watch videos on mobile devices. Over half-a-billion increase in global mobile devices and connections in 2013, 53% accounts for mobile video traffic [2]. The huge amount of mobile video consumption exerts pressure on delivering the services in a resource- or cost-efficient manner, while still ensuring user experience. Quality of experience (QoE) has been widely accepted to measure the success of mobile video services as it measures the overall acceptability of a service, based on end-users' subjective perceptions [10].

MM '14, November 3-7, 2014, Orlando, FL, USA.

ACM 978-1-4503-3063-3/14/11 $15.00
http://dx.doi.org/10.1145/2647868.2654923

The core of a QoE-based video delivery system is the QoE prediction model, which are usually established based on the results of subjective video quality assessments. As most of the subjective assessment studies follow the methods recommended by ITU [8], the existing QoE models [19, 21, 28, 29], are often indicated by *mean opinion score* (MOS) (1-5 scales). However, *acceptability* has been suggested as a better measure to indicate user's acceptance to the quality of mobile video [12, 15]. To date, only a few QoE models have been developed to predict acceptability [1, 26]. Since these models were based on user studies conducted in a lab or under a simulated delivery scenario, the collected user data may not truly reflect user perception and satisfaction in real usage contexts. Thus, some researchers proposed the use of mobile "living lab" setting to closely represent realistic situations by gathering user feedback from an online (i.e. live) system [4]. Such approach would improve the accuracy of the resulting QoE prediction models, as mobile users are more likely to watch videos anywhere rather than in a laboratory-simulated situation.

To the best of our knowledge, acceptability based QoE (A-QoE) has not been used in current mobile video systems. Agboma et al. [1] demonstrated significant resource savings while using acceptability threshold for managing the network resources for various types of videos and terminals, in contrast to conventional solutions. However, the conceptual framework was not fully implemented in real application, and subjective evaluation was not explored. Moreover, research in real mobile video delivery environment has rarely considered: region-of-interest (ROI) enhancements which was found to improve user perceived quality at low bitrate such as 300kbps, particularly for videos with large objects and faces [7, 23]; and center zooming which can benefit to user experience for sports videos [23].

This paper aims to address the aforementioned challenges by presenting an A-QoE based video management system for end-to-end mobile video delivery, which manages acceptability from multiple dimensions: video quality, delivery network, and viewing device. It also presents results from a comprehensive field study to evaluate the performance of the system and the potential impacts of parameters from end-to-end video delivery system.

The rest of this paper is organized as follows. Section 2 introduces the related work. Section 3 describes the detail of the A-QoE based mobile video delivery system. Section 4 describes the field study design and hypotheses. Section 5 presents the data analysis results. Section 6 discusses the findings, and Section 7 is conclusion and future work.

2. RELATED WORK

QoE-based video delivery system needs to consider all aspects in the whole process of mobile video provision that may influence users' (perceptual) acceptability, including transcoding existing videos to suit mobile platforms [17], adaptive transmission under wireless network constraints [13], and supporting individual requirements, such as user's willingness to pay [16] and preference for video content [24]. Many works were devoted in exploring these key factors however, most QoE-based video systems only focus on network-level adaptation (e.g., packet loss, jitter, delay, and congestion) [6, 28]. Only few studies have incorporated more factors for QoE management across the whole (end-to-end) process of video delivery – from video coding, transmission, to display. For example, some frameworks involve video content features [13, 27], viewing devices, and multimedia content types [1] for network bandwidth adaptation.

Acceptability as the index of QoE has not been practically used in mobile video delivery, as majority of quality measurement methods is based on MOS. It is interesting to examine whether the acceptability-based quality management can achieve good experience as the MOS does. Effective A-QoE based mobile video delivery systems (A-QoE based MVS) should consider the end-to-end influencing factors that may affect end-user's overall acceptability [10]. Studies found that user acceptability is influenced by different encoding settings [1], mobile device's characteristics (particularly the screen resolution) [25], user profile (e.g. content type preference and prior experience) [24], usage contexts (e.g. on bus or stay at a place) [11], and user's wiliness to pay [16].

The key requirement for A-QoE based MVS is A-QoE prediction models which objectively measure subjective acceptability or perception to dynamic usage contexts of mobile videos. These prediction models usually apply no-reference (NR) and reduced-reference (RR) metrics, which are generally more applicable for practical applications. NR metrics rely on the computed distortions (e.g., noise, blur, and blockiness) of the delivered video or the causes of degradations (e.g., network bandwidth, packet loss, jitter, delay) [18] to predict the user's perception of quality. RR metrics are usually based on the impacts of network parameters and application parameters (e.g., video resolution, frame rate, codec type, and bitrate) on user's perception [1, 13].

To design the proposed MVS, we adopted the most up-to-date A-QoE models [26], which were developed based on a comprehensive study of subjective acceptability assessment with 80 participants, and considered a wide range of influencing factors. The models took into account: a) *application-level parameters* such as video resolution, frame rate and video content motion features; b) *network-level parameters* such as bitrate or network throughout; and c) *end-user parameters* such as mobile device's display features. Moreover, the quality assessments have combined the use of standard video sequences provided by ITU-T Study Groups and some additional videos from the World Wide Web. The importance of using "mainstream" materials for user-centric study had been argued in [20].

3. A-QoE BASED MOBILE VIDEO SYSTEM

The specific A-QoE models [26] used in our system are described in equation (1) and (2), to tackle the application scenarios of having original source videos in compressed domain and either when the mobile device's display capability is known or not.

$$QoE = \frac{1}{\left(1+\left(\frac{LBR}{a+b\cdot SSR+c\cdot FR+d\cdot MAP+e\cdot MAD}\right)^{h\cdot FR\cdot SDPPI+i}\right)^{g+f\cdot SDPPI}} \quad (1)$$

$$QoE = \frac{1}{\left(1+\left(\frac{LBR}{a+b\cdot SSR+c\cdot FR+d\cdot MAP+e\cdot MAD}\right)^{h\cdot FR+i}\right)^{g}} \quad (2)$$

where $LBR = \log_{10}(BR)$, $SDPPI$ is scaled device screen PPI (pixel per inch), SSR is Scaled Spatial Resolution - calculated as the ratio of video resolution over the maximum in-screen pixels, and FR is the frame rate. The *MAP* and *MAD* are motion features of a video (see the definitions in Section 3.2.1). Coefficients of the parameters are indicated as $a-g$.

3.1 Overall Framework

The overall framework (Figure 1) of the user-centric mobile video system is designed based on a typical structure of video delivery systems, which consists of: server, proxy (optional), network, and client. The *server module* uses a database to store outputs from *video codec* that encodes the video sources from their original format into a set of different formats for supporting adaptations to various viewing context (such as network conditions and device-specific requirements). The *video delivery module* selects a suitable video quality (from the video database) that best matches the user and application conditions and maximizes A-QoE. The *video application module* captures the viewing conditions and plays back the delivery video.

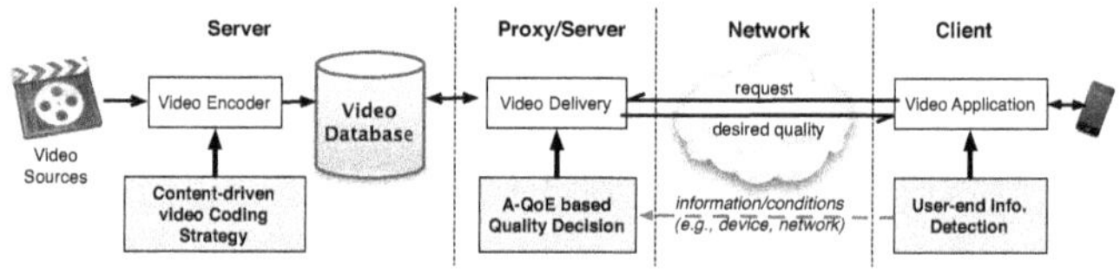

Figure 1. Framework of A-QoE based Mobile Video Delivery System.

As the main purpose of our study is evaluating the A-QoE management strategy for mobile video delivery, we adopted simple progressive download technique to establish the system and enabled the QoE-based adaptation by using multiple quality streams of video sequences. Since short-duration videos were used for the evaluation, adaptive video streaming strategy (such as [22]) is not necessary. Moreover, the progressive download can avoid the packet loss and jitter by means of packet retransmissions and buffer. Therefore, only delay (re-buffering interruption) needs to be handled by network-bandwidth adaptation. The novelty of this framework lies on the underpinning user-centered strategies for QoE management, including content-driven video coding, acceptability based quality decision, and user-end (client) information detection and response.

3.2 Content-driven Video Coding

The video coding takes into account the impacts of encoding parameters and video content features on users acceptability. In order to support various viewing conditions (e.g., screen sizes of mobile devices and network bandwidths), five quality levels for each video are generated with the criteria of consistent expected acceptability. The whole encoding process consists of three steps: 1) classify a source video into a particular content group based on its content features; 2) determine the optimal encoding parameters of the five quality levels, corresponding to its content group; 3) encode the source video into five degraded videos using the defined encoding parameters.

3.2.1 *Classification of Video Content Group*

Studies have found that videos with high motion intensity (e.g., sports videos) require higher encoding bitrate than those with small or slow motion (e.g., news videos), in order to achieve similar use-perceived quality or acceptability [1, 25, 26]. Hence, when encoding videos, it is necessary to distinguish video contents and encode them using proper parameters.

Video content classification is usually based on a video's spatial and temporal complexity. A conventional measure of video content characteristics is to extract SI and TI from pixel level, suggested in ITU-T Recommendation P.910 [9]. In this study, however, we used three motion characteristics that can be easily extracted from a compressed video in order to speed up the video classification and to re-use them for A-QoE prediction [26]. They are: *motion activity intensity* (MAI) defined as the mean magnitude of motion vector (MV); *motion activity proportion* (MAP) defined as the proportion of the number of non-zero MVs in the total number of MVs; and *motion activity direction* (MAD) defined as the deviation of MV directions from the dominant movement direction. Their values for one video were computed at every 50 P-frames by (3) and averaged in order to ensure the overall system efficiency.

$$MAI = \frac{1}{N_t}\sum_i \sqrt{x_i^2 + y_i^2};\quad MAP = \frac{N_{nz}}{N_t};\quad MAD = \sqrt{\frac{1}{N_t}\sum_i D_i^2} \quad (3)$$

where, x and y are the coordinate of a MV; N_t is the total number of MVs, and N_{nz} is the number of non-zero MVs; D_i is the variation of the ith direction from the dominant direction.

Pearson Correlation Analysis for controlling video resolution and frame rate suggests that the encoding bitrate is significantly correlated to MAI and MAP with R>0.7 (p<.01). Three groups were distinguished through Hierarchical Cluster Analysis based on video bitrate and acceptability. Thus, we only need to use MAI and MAP to classify content groups as shown in (4). Most videos with fast movement fall into CG1 and stable videos fall into CG2.

$$\begin{aligned} &CG1: if\ MAP > 0.4\ OR\ MAI > 15; \\ &CG2: if\ MAP < 0.2\ AND\ MAI < 10; \\ &CG3: other \end{aligned} \quad (4)$$

3.2.2 *Video Encoding Settings*

Based on A-QoE study results, we have determined the typical encoding settings for each CG, so that source videos can be degraded into five quality levels Q1 – Q5. Taking account of the characteristics of recent smart phones in the market, we have set the special resolution (SR) at the lowest quality level Q1 as 480×270 pixels for 16:9 aspect ratios. The SR at the highest level Q5 is set as 1280×720 pixels to support HD quality.

The encoding bitrate (BR) for Q1 is defined as <=200kbps for supporting wireless EDGE (Exchanged Data rates for GSM Evolution) network access, which often leads to a very low download speed based on our local testing. Since CG2 and CG3 represent relatively slow motion videos, we give them a relative lower frame rate (FR) 15fps than 25fps for CG3. Similarly, the bitrate for CG2 and CG3 can be even lower due to the frame rate reduction.

The rest of the BR and FR is determined using equation (2) with the threshold as 80%±3% acceptability. The MAI and MAP were chosen as the average values for each content group. Table 1 summarizes the encoding parameters.

Table 1. Encoding parameter settings for 5 quality levels for 3 video content groups

		Q1	Q2	Q3	Q4	Q5
CG1	SR	480×270	480×270	640×360	960×540	1280×720
	FR	25	25	25	25	25
	BR	200	500	800	1000	1500
CG2	SR	480×270	480×270	640×360	960×540	1280×720
	FR	15	15	25	25	25
	BR	100	250	300	500	700
CG3	SR	480×270	480×270	640×360	960×540	1280×720
	FR	15	15	25	25	25
	BR	150	300	500	700	1000

3.2.3 *ROI and Zooming Approaches*

The quality of mobile video can be further enhanced using specialized coding strategies, such as region-of-interest (ROI) based enhancements and center-region zooming [14, 23], we have implemented the algorithms in the proposed video delivery system (so that its benefits can be confirmed in our field study). The ROI detection is based on the knowledge that human eyes can only observe a particular region that is visually interesting, thus, capturing our attention when watching a video segment. In this paper, we adopted the algorithms in [7] for ROI detection and ROI-based video coding. The principle of ROI-based video coding is to enhance the quality of ROI regions by allocating more encoding bits at the cost of reducing encoding bits for the non-ROI region(s). The center-region zooming coding is realized by cutting off a part of video frame from the edges so that the rest of the frame appears "zoomed-in" when displaying on a screen. In this study, we simply zoomed the video from the center of frame and determined the size by the following calculations.

Let's first define:

- The width and height of the input video as W_1 and H_1; its aspect ratio as $In_{ar} = W_1/H_1$;
- The width and height of the output video after cropping as W_2 and H_2; its aspect ratio as $Out_{ar} = W_2/H_2$;
- The zooming factor ZF as 1.1. Although Knoche et al.'s research [14] suggested that a ZF between 1.14-1.33 was preferred by participants for small resolution videos on a mobile phone (e.g., 320×240 pixels), we did not use a bigger zooming factor than 1.1, as we were concerned about the loss of content information.

Then, the output video's resolution can be measured by the following equation (5).

$$\frac{W_1 \cdot H_1}{W_2 \cdot H_2} \le ZF \quad (5)$$

$if\ In_{ar} > Out_{ar}, compute\ H_2\ first:$

$$H_2 \ge H_1 \cdot \sqrt{\frac{In_{ar}}{Out_{ar} \cdot ZF}};\quad W_2 = H_2 \cdot Out_{ar}$$

$if\ In_{ar} \le Out_{ar}, comput\ W_2\ first:$

$$W_2 \ge W_1 \cdot \sqrt{\frac{Out_{ar}}{In_{ar} \cdot ZF}};\quad H_2 = \frac{W_2}{Out_{ar}}$$

Due to the algorithmic limitation and specific evaluation purposes, the encoding parameters for the ROI and zooming approaches were different from those presented in Table 1 and will be specified in Section 5.1.1.

3.3 A-QoE based Video Quality Adaptation

When the server or proxy module receives a user's request for a particular video, the delivery module will decide the optimal video quality for the current viewing circumstances, based on QoE estimation. Together with the user request, the server will also receive context information including network bandwidth, device resolution, and screen pixel density.

The adaption process has three steps: 1) filter out quality levels (from the five quality levels Q1-Q5) that are higher than the device resolution and the current bandwidth, in order to avoid overprovisioning; 2) compute the QoE values for the remaining quality levels using the A-QoE prediction model, which formula is shown in (1); 3) return the quality that achieves the highest QoE. If the first step cannot obtain any suitable quality level, the Q1 (<=200kbps) will be selected. To speed-up processing time, variables used in (1) can be determined in advance, while QoE lookup-tables (codebook) for popular mobile devices can be used.

3.4 Collection of User-end Information

The user-end information is collected using a custom client application, namely *iPlayer*, developed for iOS devices – both iPhone and iPad. Screenshots are shown in Figure 2. The collected data includes two parts: detected context information automatically and recorded user evaluations. The automatic detected information consists of network bandwidth, device screen resolution, viewing location and time, viewed video name and its quality level. The bandwidth is calculated by measuring the data bits downloaded in the first 2 seconds after a user clicks a video to watch. Strictly, it is the instant connection speed between the client app and the video server.

Figure 2. iPlayer user interface for iPhone and iPad, and user feedback screenshot on iPhone

User feedback is collected at the completion of viewing a video, through a series of questions on: overall user experience, perceived clarity and fluency (/smoothness) of a video, perceived loading speed, level of interest in video content, and semantic viewing location. The design of the questions listed in Table 2 has referred to relative research on mobile video quality assessment under semi-living lab context [5]. These questions (except location) are answered using a 1-5 scale to match the Absolute Category Rating [9]: 1-bad, 2-poor, 3-fair, 4-good, 5-excellent. As not all the scales' descriptions are explicitly displayed on the mobile app, more detailed instructions have been given to the participants when conducting a user study. On submission, the user feedback data linking with the detected context information, is sent to and stored in a data server.

Table 2: Questions of User Evaluation

No.	Question (1-bad, 2-poor, 3-neutral/fair, 4-good, 5-excellent)
1	How do you evaluate the overall experience of viewing the video?
2	How do you feel the clarity of the viewed video?
3	How do you feel the smoothness of the viewed video?
4	How do you feel the loading speed?
5	How do you like the video content? (1-dislike, 3-neutral, 5-like)
6	Where did you watch the video? (bus, home, school, or other)

3.5 System Implementation

The proposed mobile video delivery system has been fully implemented for experimental testing and evaluations. The video encoding process was implemented for both Linux and Windows OS. It can automatically fetch the recently added/updated video sources from a real media company's server, then perform video content analysis and video coding in a Linux server and a Windows Server in parallel. It stores the transcoded videos into the video database (with the key metadata). In client, when the iPlayer (i.e., mobile video client) is launched, it downloads the .xml file to show the video list; it organizes user feedback on video quality in text and sends to the Server to be stores into a feedback.csv file. The communication between the client and the video server is achieved through *sockets* for estimating bandwidth/transmission speed, sending user-end viewing conditions, and receiving the determined optimal quality URL.

4. EVALUATION

4.1 Hypotheses

Before the field user study, we listed a range of hypotheses to examine. We assume that the user-centric video delivery system will perform well in terms of providing the mobile users with good viewing experience.

H1: The video delivery system with optimal quality decision strategy can achieve good user experience.

We also assume that the overall user experience is related to how users feel the video quality and data loading speed, as well as how much people like the video content. Although video content features have been considered in this delivery system (i.e., motion features for content-driven video coding and A-QoE prediction), we wonder whether semantic difference between video content types (e.g., news, movie, etc.) is still influencing user experience.

H2: Overall user experience has correlations with user-perceived video clarity, fluency, loading speed, and interest to video content

H2a: Overall user experience is different between video content types

With the view of the context influence, we consider that:

H3: Overall user experience varies with viewing locations

To examine whether different coding approaches – normal H.264/AVC, ROI-enhancement, and Zooming – have a significant impact on user experience, the fourth hypothesis is defined as:

H4: Overall user experience is different when the videos are encoded with different coding approaches

It is also interesting to see how devices affect user experience.

H5a: Overall user experience is better when viewing videos on a bigger screen than a smaller one at a given point of pixel (PPI).

H5b: Overall user experience is better when viewing videos on a device with higher display resolution than lower display resolution at a given screen size

4.2 Field Study Design

Aiming at obtaining more realistic user experience of viewing mobile videos, this user study was designed to allow users using their own iOS devices to watch videos anywhere and anytime. The following introduces the details of the user study.

4.2.1 Preparation of Test videos

We used 50 video clips (around 1-3 min each) as the video resources, of which 30 news videos were from Fairfax Media in 2012 and 20 movie trailers were downloaded from online. Both types of resources are in H.264 video format with AAC audio format. The movie trailers are at a resolution of 1920×1080 pixels and encoding bitrate 4Mbps, while the news videos are at only 1024×576 pixels and 800kbps. The deficiency in news video quality potentially affects our user study results.

To evaluate whether or not the coding strategies of ROI-enhancement and zooming can increase overall user experience in nature setting of video delivery, we divided the 50 video clips into three groups, termed 'Normal, 'ROI', and 'Zoom' hereafter. The assignment was as: Normal – a total of 26 videos with 18 news and 8 movie trailers; ROI – a total of 12 videos with 6 news and 6 trailers; Zoom – a total of 12 videos with 6 news and 6 trailers.

The encoding settings of audio for all the videos are identical: AAC 44.1kHz and 96kbps. The video encoding settings are different for the three groups. The *Normal* group was encoded as normal H.264/AVC format using open source codec x264 r2310; the encoding parameters for five quality levels are shown in Table 1 in Section 3.2.2.

For the *ROI* group, automatic ROI detection [7] was firstly run to gain the ROI regions of a video with a fixed size ratio to a frame - 25%. Then, the video was encoded with a self-developed algorithm upon the same x264 codec with 2-pass option. In the first pass, the video is encoded at a slightly (about 25%) higher bitrate than that for Normal; in the second pass, the ROIs are maintained the same quality as the first pass, and the encoding bits for non-ROIs are reduced by increasing the QP value. The QP delta was set to 6 in this study, determined by experimental observation to maintain an effective balance, so that improved quality of the important region is perceivable without increasing bandwidth, while the rest of the frame is not degraded to the point where users see it as a distraction. The frame rates were as the same as the source video, due to the limitation of ROI detection in handling frame drops when we conducted this study.

For the *Zoom* group, the same x264 codec was used to crop and encode the cropped frames. With the mobile device's screen resolution as the targeted output video resolution, the output aspect ratio for most iOS devices (e.g., iPhone 4 and iPad) will be smaller than the input video's aspect ratio (16:9). Using (5), we can calculate the crop size as: 1720×1080 pixels for 1920×1080 pixels movie trailers, and 920×576 pixels for 1024×576 pixels news. Then, the cropped source videos were encoded into 480×300 pixels for quality level Q1 and Q2; 640×400, 960×600, and 1280×800 pixels for Q3, Q4 and Q5 respectively. Frame rate was also not restricted. Using the default setting of x264, the cropped videos were encoded with the enable of constant rate factor CRF and QP=23. As a result, the bitrate for each quality is not fixed and is generally higher than that in Normal. The CRF setting is commonly regarded as the best quality settings objectively. Whether Zoom with the CRF setting can achieve better subjective quality will be examined by our user study.

4.2.2 Participants recruitment

We recruited 20 people from a university through emails and Facebook advertisement. Due to 3 drop-outs, in the end we had 17 completed participants – 9 females and 8 males, at the age of 21-40 (1 over 50). They were all iOS device users and mobile video viewers, most of whom (11 out of 17) were frequent viewers – watching videos on mobile at least once a week and the rest were about once a week.

The participants were asked to watch at least 30 videos on their own iOS devices (e.g., iPhone, iPod touch, and iPad 2) using the *iPlayer* app within two weeks, and answer the evaluation questions that will pop-up on screen each time when finish watching a video. One-week extension was applied to a few people who could not complete on time.

Prior to the participation, we instructed each subject about how to install and use the iPlayer app, and made sure they understood the evaluation questions and knew how to rate. The participants were also informed that their watching session (such as video's type, start and end times, network condition and location) would be recorded on the devices automatically, but their personal information would be confidential. Where and when to watch videos was not limited, but they were strongly suggested to watch videos according to their daily-life routine (e.g., watch videos when taking a bus, relaxing at home, and eating at a café) and under different networks. Free movie vouchers were provided for the participants' time.

By the end of our study (i.e. November 2013), we have collected 663 valid data from the 17 participants.

4.2.3 Data collection

The 17 participants brought a total of 18 iOS devices into the field study because one participant used two devices: iPhone 3GS and iPad 2. These devices covered five different models. Table 3 lists these models and their screen properties in terms of screen size (inch), resolution (pixels), and pixel per inch. Evaluation records gathered from each device show that most of the data (84.5%) were collected from retina display devices, which are iPhone 4/4S 33.6%, iPhone 5 33.5% and iPad retina 17.4%, respectively.

Geographically, where the testing videos have been watched are across the city and suburbs nearby, and many data were submitted in the university which the participants were recruited from. This is consistent with the participants' self-reported locations. The time distribution of viewing videos indicated that the peak viewing times were between 16:00-22:00 and 9:00-14:00, which may explains why most of videos were viewed at home and university.

Table 3. iOS devices involved in the user study

	iPhone 3GS	iPhone 4/4S	iPhone 5	iPad 2	iPad Retina
Screen (inch)	3.5	3.5	4	9.7	9.7
Resolution (pixel)	480×320	960×640	1136×640	1024×768	2048×1536
Pixel per inch	163	326	326	132	264
Number of device	1	6	6	2	3

5. RESULTS

With the data collected, statistical data analysis was conducted to examine our hypotheses. We firstly defined a number of variables in Table 4 to represent different aspects of the collected data. In the following content, we will use these variables to simplify the description of data analysis results.

Table 4: Variables of the collected data

Variable	Data Type	Description
OverallExp	Scale	Scores of user's overall experience (1-5)
Clarity	Scale	Scores of user-perceived clarity of video quality (1-5)
Fluency	Scale	Scores of user-perceived smoothness of video quality (1-5)
LoadingSpeed	Scale	Scores of user-perceived loading speed of a video (1-5)
ContentInterest	Scale	User's interest (or like) level to a video content (1-5)
LocationType	Nominal	Location types of viewing videos: bus, home, school/work, and other
DevType	Nominal	iOS device types: iPhone3GS, iPhone 4/S, iPhone 5, iPad2, and iPad retina
DevPPI	Ratio	iOS device display screen pixels per point (PPI)
VideoCT	Nominal	Semantic types of video contents: movie and news
CodingType	Nominal	Video coding approaches: N-normal, R-ROI enhancement, Z-zooming
NetworkBW	Ratio	Detected network bandwidth of video transmission (kbps)
BR	Ratio	Video encoding bit rate (kbps)

To choose proper statistic tests, we had verified whether the data followed normal distribution or not. Since the values of OverallExp, Clarity, Fluency, LoadingSpeed, and ContentInterest are highly skewed and traditional data transformation techniques (e.g., logarithm and exponent) may break the data interpretative, we used non-parametric tests such as the Mann-Whitney U test and the Kruskal-Wallis test for these variables. We did not filter out the outliers from the data because in a field study the outliers may be caused by specific viewing conditions.

5.1 Mobile Video Delivery Performance (H1)

In alignment with the system design objectives, we can define a "good" experience as over 80% of delivered videos are acceptable (that is, the overall experience scale >= 3) and 70% of them can be rated to "good" and better (that is, the scale of overall experience is equal and greater than 4). Translating the description into a more measurable way, we expected the system performance would be: 15%, 15%, and 70% of the user ratings for overall experience will go for scale 1-2, 3, and 4-5, respectively.

A chi-square test for goodness of fit (with alpha = 0.05) was used to access whether the real overall user experience fit in our expectation in a sample of 663 ratings. Table 5 lists the numbers and percentages of the sample nominating each rating scale, as well as the expected numbers.

Table 5: Summary of overall experience score

Scale	Observed N	Percentage (%)	Expected N	Expected percentage (%)
1	26	3.9	100	15
2	22	3.3		
3	118	17.8	100	15
4	241	36.3	464	70
5	256	38.6		
Total	**663**	**100**	**663**	**100**

The chi-square test was statistically significant, $\chi^2(4, N = 663) = 37.42, p < .001$, indicating that some scales were with significantly different frequency than the expected. However, the effect size is considered small as Cohen's $w = 0.24$, which is smaller than 0.3 [28]. From Table 5, it can be observed that the actual rating percentages of lower scales (1 and 2) are much lower than the corresponding expectations; those of higher scales (4 and 5) are slightly higher than the expectations. This shows that our system performed even better than what we expected.

Evaluating the other aspects of the system performance, Clarity, Fluency and LoadingSpeed, we could obtain similar results: less than 10% of ratings went into the scales 1 and 2, and over 70% of ratings into the scales 4 and 5.

A boxplot graph Figure 3 was generated to summarize the values of OverallExp and other testing variables. Figure 3 indicates that except a few outliers (the circles), the majority of assessments (the box) are greater than or equal to 3 – fair; the median (the heavy black line) is at about 4; and about 75 percent of the data is between 4-5.

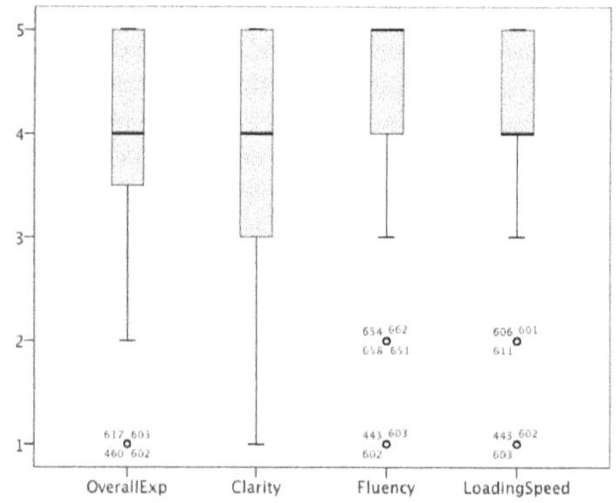

Figure 3. Boxplot of OverallExp, Clarity, Fluency and LoadingSpeed

5.2 Factors Affecting Overall Experience (H2)

Pearson and Spearman Correlation Analysis show that the overall experience is strongly associated with clarity, fluency, loading speed, and content interest (r>0.6, p<0.01) (Table 6). Figure 4 shows that the overall experience is generally increasing with the increase of the user-perceived image clarity, fluency, loading speed and user's interest in video content, but it is dragged down by a low interest (e.g., ContentInteret = 2) even if when the user-perceived video quality is rather high (e.g., Fluency = 3).

Table 6. Pearson and Spearman correlations between OverallExp and other system performance measurements

		Overall Exp	Clarity	Fluency	Loading Speed	Content Interest
Pearson	Correlation	1	.694**	.712**	.606**	.681**
	Sig. (2-tailed)		.000	.000	.000	.000
Spear-man	Correlation	1.000	.680**	.662**	.560**	.723**
	Sig. (2-tailed)	.	.000	.000	.000	.000

** Correlation is significant at 0.01 level (2-tailed).

Overall experience is also significantly affected by video content type (*H5a*) based on the Mann-Whitney U test. The "movie" trailers (mean rank=382.59, n=300) received a higher rating than the "news" (mean rank=290.19, n=363) (z=-6.558, p<.001). This is probably due to the fact that people more like movie content than news, evidenced by that ContentInterest of movie is significantly higher than that of news (z=-8.698, p<.001, medium effect size Cohen's w = 0.34). However, it does not rule out another possibility: the resource quality of "news" is lower than the movie's in terms of bitrate and resolution (refer to section 4.2.1 for more details).

To further reveal the impact of content type, we conducted a range of Mann-Whitney U tests under the control of the ContentInterest level. As only 10 records of movie at ContentInterest level 1 and 2 were received, the tests were run at only the levels 3, 4 and 5. It turned out that at the same interest level, Clarity was significant higher for movie than news (p<=0.03), seen in Figure 5; however, this does not seem to affect much on OverallExp (p>=0.499). It may be because no significant difference between the two types of videos for Fluency (p>=0.55) and LoadingSpeed (p>0.55).

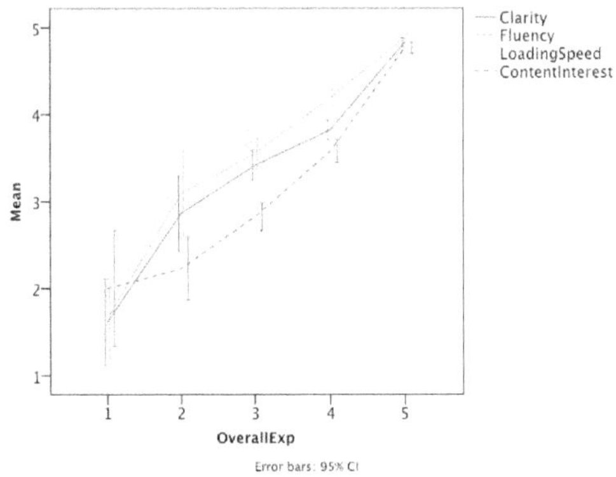

Figure 4. Relations between OverallExp and Clarity, Fluency, LoadingSpeed and ContentInterest

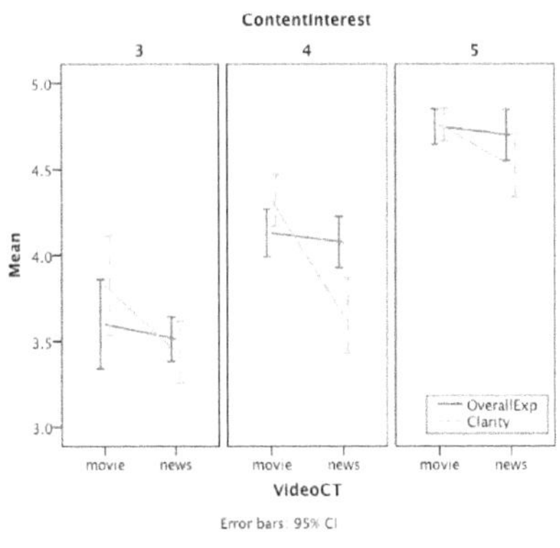

Figure 5. Barchart of content type influence on OverallExp and Clarity at ContentInterest level 3, 4 and 5

5.3 Impacts of Viewing Locations (H3)

Among the 663 user data, 92 were recorded on a moving vehicle (bus, ferry or train), 358 at home, 176 at school (e.g., university or working place), and 37 at other places such as café shop, bus/train station, barber, and some places with public WiFi networks. Figure 6 shows the means of OverallExp at different locations. Based on the Kruskal-Wallis test, the overall experience was significantly different at different viewing locations (vehicle: mean rank=290.02, home: mean rank=358; school: mean rank=352.02; other: mean rank=259.15; chi-square (3)=15.463, p<.001). Follow-up Mann-Whitney U tests between each pair of location categories evidenced that the OverallExp between "home" and "school" was not significantly different (p>.05), but OverallExp was significantly higher at "home" and "school" than "vehicle" or "other" (p<.05). We wondered whether this might be caused by poor network connection while travelling, and therefore further examined network bandwidth of these location types.

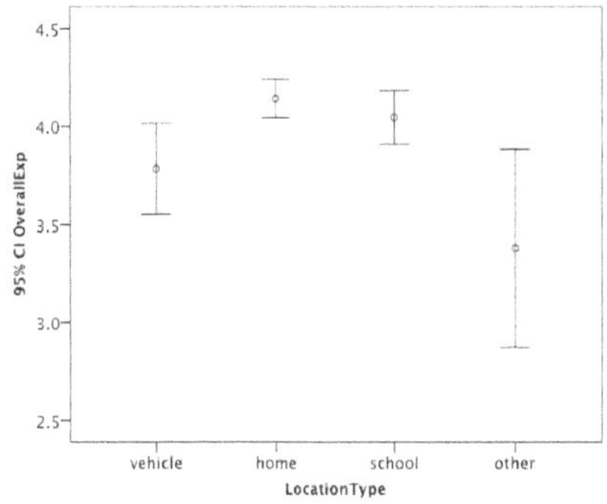

Figure 6. Mean scores of overall experience at four viewing locations

Figure 7 displays the distribution of the detected network bandwidths for four location types. It is not supervised that network connection at "school" is the best (median=3161kbps) because the university where the user study conducted has excellent Wi-Fi networks. Interestingly, the "home" network connections with normally ADSL+ or ADSL 2+ are not better than "vehicle" networks with cellular networks (we assume that when people are on the move, they mainly use cellular networks to access our video database, but we were not able to distinguish whether the cellular network was 3G, 4G, or GSM). 'vehicle' network bandwidth (median=946kbps) is even slightly higher than 'home' networks (median = 778kbps). Even though 'home' had a relative lower bandwidth than other locations, it actually achieved the best overall experience (see Figure 6). Furthermore, the participants felt the loading speed was faster at 'home' than at other places even 'school', albeit not significant. Two reasons may explain the phenomena. First, due to the bitrate adaptation by the A-QoE based delivery strategy, the difference of network bandwidth will not importantly affect the video delivery speed. Second, in a comfortable viewing environment, such as home, user's viewing experience can be enhanced.

Considering the important influence of people's like to video content on their viewing experience (*H2a*), we compared the viewing locations' effect under the control of interest level. Because there were inadequate data at low interest levels when distributing them to different locations, we only observed the ContentInterest level 3, 4 and 5. Due to the same reason, "other" category was also excluded from the analysis. Kruskal-Wallis tests indicated that the differences of OverallExp among the three location categories "vehicle", "home" and "school" were not significant anymore (p>=.66). In spite of this, the participants did notice the variation of loading speeds at different viewing locations: the Kruskal-Wallis tests indicated a significant LoadingSpeed difference at ContentInterest level 3 and 4 (p<.05). At the highest interest level 5, the LoadingSpeed was reported high at all types of viewing locations. This can be explained by that network bandwidths in those cases when ContentInterest = 5 are wide enough to support smooth video downloading.

To conclude, when video delivery has adapted to network bandwidth condition, overall experience becomes more affected by user interest and where to watch.

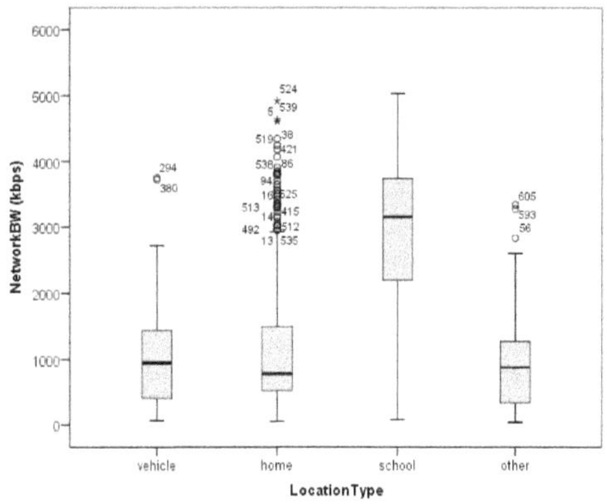

Figure 7. Boxplot of network bandwidth in different viewing locations

5.4 Impacts of Video Coding Approaches (H4)

A Kruskal-Wallis ANOVA indicated that the overall user experience has no statistically significant differences between the coding approaches "Normal" (mean rank = 326.08), "ROI" (mean rank=343.90) and "Zoom" (mean rank = 331.79), where $\chi^2(2)$ = 1.087, n=663, p=0.581. Given eta-squared $\eta^2 = \chi^2/(N-1)$), which is interpreted as the proportion of variance in the DV that can be attributed to the IV, is far less than 0.01, the effect size is considered very small, according to Cohen's guideline [3]. Similarly, the coding approaches did not have a statistically significant impact on the variables: Clarity (p=0.414), Fluency (p=0.220), and LoadingSpeed (p=0.259).

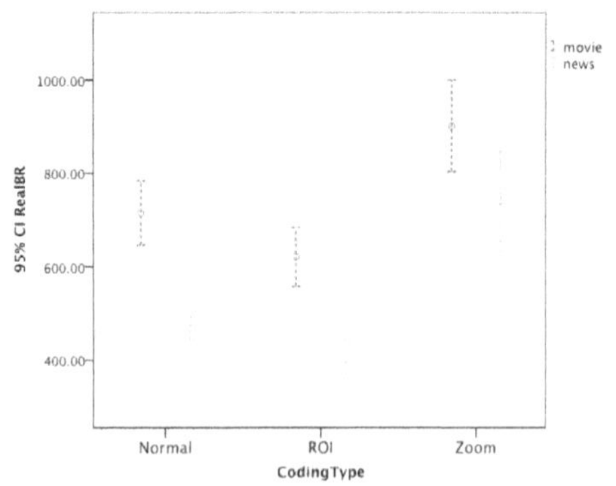

Figure 8. Average encoding bitrates of Normal, ROI and Zoom for movie and news videos.

Follow-up Mann-Whitney U tests on each pair of the coding approaches were conducted under the control of devices, video content types, and viewing locations. The results showed that there was no significant difference between each pair of the three approaches for all the four dependent variables (p>0.05). In other words, we have to reject the hypothesis H4.

Although there was no significant influence of the coding approaches on user's viewing experience, the encoding bitrate of ROI is significantly lower than Normal (Figure 8). Mann-Whitney U tests showed: for movies, Normal (n=105) mean rank=114.79 and ROI (n=100) mean rank = 90.63 with $\chi^2(1)$ = -2.934, p =.003; for news videos, Normal (n=227) mean rank =155.59 and ROI (n=68) mean rank=122.68 with $\chi^2(1)$ = -2.911, p=.004. This indicates that, to achieve a similar level of overall experience, ROI coding approach will use less encoding bitrate than Normal H.264 coding.

For Zoom, given similar conditions – video width 960 pixels and on iPhone5, the bitrate of delivered videos is significantly higher than Normal (p<.001) due to the CRF encoding settings (see Section 4.2.1), but it could not perform better. It only reached a slightly higher rank of Clarity but not significant based on Mann-Whitney U Test (n=76, mean rank=46.05 for Normal; n=22, mean rank=56.83 for Zoom; p=.08).

Based on the comparisons, we may conclude that a high video bitrate is not necessary for a high QoE; resource saving can be achieved by proper QoE management which guarantees the overall user experience with the minimization of network bandwidth occupancy.

5.5 Impacts of Viewing Devices (H5)

Comparisons were carried out between between iPhone 4/4S and iPhone 5. Despite the similar display capability (both are 326ppi), the OverallExp on iPhone 5 achieved a significant higher rank than that on iPhone 4/4S (iPhone 4/4S: mean rank=185.07, n=223; iPhone 5: mean rank = 261.11, n=222; z=-6.6, p<.001). We attribute this to the larger iPhone 5 screen,, and might be also the faster processing speed, because the other system performance indexes – Fluency and LoadingSpeed – are also significantly higher on iPhone 5 (p<.001).

With the same screen size of 9.7 inches but higher display PPI (264 vs. 132), iPad retina was significantly superior to iPad 2 in terms of overall experience (z=-5.991, p<.001) (see Figure 9), but not in Clarity, Fluency and LoadingSpeed (p>.025).

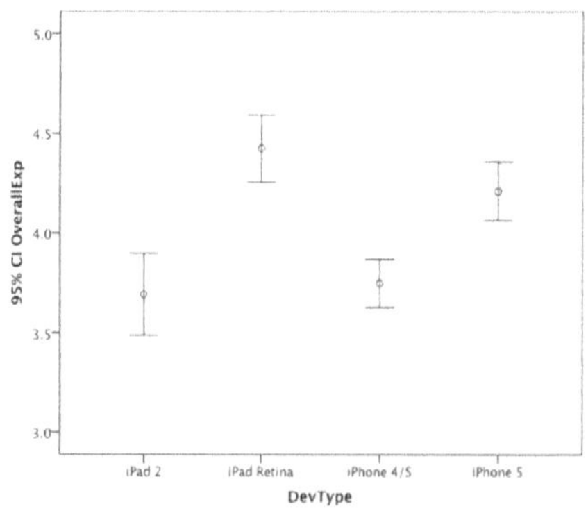

Figure 9. Comparison of overall experience when viewing videos on different iOS devices

In order to examine if the influence of devices on overall experience is independent on viewing locations and video content types, we conducted further Mann-Whitney U tests between the two types of iPhones and iPads while controlling the types of location (vehicle, home, or school) and content (news or movie). It was confirmed that the significance between iPhone 4/4S and iPhone 5 existed at any location and video content ($p<.001$); between iPad 2 and iPad retina, it existed with all video content types and "home" location ($p<.001$) (Other locations were not studied because there were no videos viewed on iPad retina at "vehicle" and only 20 records at "school"). We conclude that the influence of the device on overall experience is independent.

6. DISCUSSIONS

Based on the statistical data analysis of the five hypotheses groups, we draw the following conclusions.

First, the video delivery system worked well in providing good overall viewing experience. This reaches the desired goal of establishing the video system. It is confirmed that by adapting to user viewing conditions and maximizing the QoE, overall user experience can be maintained at a certain good level (e.g., OverallExp >= 4).

Second, the overall experience is strongly associated with not only the user-perceived video quality such as clarity and smoothness, and video loading speed through networks, but also to what extent the user likes the video content. This is consistent with pervious research [25]. At the same interest level, the overall experience will not be significantly different between different content types (e.g., movie and news). The accuracy of acceptability-QoE models can be further improved by considering individual interest, which may be measured by individual viewing history.

Third, "home" is the best location to watch videos compared with public transport (e.g., bus and train), workplace (e.g., school), and other places such as a café or bus station. It is not just because 'home' has a stable network connection (as a workplace usually has much better network connections), but more because of the comfort or ease of viewing circumstance. Despite the fact that the network connection speed at home was three times slower than that at school, participants felt the loading speed at home was the same as, if not higher, at school. This means the network variation is well managed by the delivery strategy.

Fourth, the assumption of coding approaches effect on overall experience was not supported by the statistical analysis. Neither ROI nor Zoom could provide a better viewing experience than the Normal H.264 coding. This result is completely opposite to the lab experiment of subjective video quality assessment on ROI video coding [7], and the study of comparing zooming effectiveness on user experience for mobile sports videos [23]. Several implicit factors may have led to these results: 1) Video delivery strategy: the video system was designed to ensure good experience. As a result, when all the three coding approaches could achieve a high score of overall experience, their differences would not be distinct anymore. 2) Environment: unlike a lab experiment in controlled conditions, the real-life experiment of this study was in a natural and uncontrolled environment. These results are probably more ecologically valid. 3) Codec: compared to the older version of x264 used in previous studies [7, 23] , the relatively new version (i.e., in the year of 2010 vs. 2013) used in this study may have improved in retaining high video quality. 4) Coding strategy: the zooming coding was zoomed in from the center of a video with a zooming factor of 1.1, which might be not an appropriate setting because the effective zooming factor is related to the video resolution [14], and cropping from the center might also cut off some important information from the frame.

From the bitrate perspective, the ROI did show a small benefit in network resource saving. Whereas, the Zoom case indicated the video encoding settings that target a good objective quality at the cost of a high encoding bitrate, do not explicitly benefit the overall user experience in real mobile video applications, although the user-perceived video clarity is slightly good. It should be noted that this conclusion may be influenced by the Zoom cropping strategy itself, thus independent studies may be required to further address this issue.

Fifth, as for the mobile devices, the screen size and its display resolution have a combined impact on overall user experience. At the same PPI, the device with a bigger screen will achieve better overall experience than that of a smaller screen. Meanwhile, at the same screen size, a device with higher PPI will outperform a counterpart. Given the fact that the A-QoE models were developed based on the evaluation data collected from only the same screen size of mobile phones (i.e., iPhone 3GS and iPhone 4) [26], it is understandable why the effect of screen size was not captured and properly handled by the A-QoE based system. Further subjective evaluation on bigger screens will help improve the A-QoE models.

7. CONCLUSION

This paper proposes an adaptive mobile video delivery system to achieve optimum QoE. The end-to-end QoE based video delivery framework incorporates a holistic view on the impacts of: video content and encoding, bandwidth limitation, features of mobile devices, and viewing context. The experimental user-driven video delivery system highlights the importance of each key component: 1) content-driven video coding techniques; 2) acceptability-based QoE to determine the optimal video quality suits for the current bandwidth and mobile device resolution; and 3) a video client that can collect real-time (online) user-end information, such as device features, usage context, and perceived experience feedback. The user evaluation in field was conducted with 17 subjects within 2-3 weeks to cover natural mobile viewing contexts. The results demonstrated promising evidence that the proposed A-QoE based management in mobile video delivery system can help to maximize overall user experience and minimize the cost of resource for diverse mobile devices. The results also revealed that the adopted A-QoE models have prediction limitations in handling user interest, semantic viewing location, and relatively larger screen of a mobile device. Furthermore, it was found that in contrast to the previous research findings [7, 14, 23], the ROI and zooming video coding strategies could not significantly improve overall user experience in this field study.

The field user study has been limited by the number of participants, video content, and video delivery system implementation. Future work on a large-scale user study is needed to collect more real-time (online) feedback, and enable a more comprehensive analysis about A-QoE based video adaptation affected by various factors. Also proposed is a comparison study between A-QoE based video delivery and conventional video delivery, on the performance of improving QoE. Machine Learning techniques may be applied for automatic and continuous A-QoE model refinement, based on real-time user feedback under diverse viewing contexts.

8. ACKNOWLEDGMENTS

This research was carried out as part of the activities of, and funded by, the Smart Services Cooperative Research Centre (CRC) through the Australian Government's CRC Programme.

9. REFERENCES

[1] Agboma, F. and Liotta, A. 2012. Quality of experience management in mobile content delivery systems. *Telecommun Syst*, 49, 1, 85-98.

[2] Cisco. 2014 *Cisco Visual Networking Index: Global Mobile Data Traffic Forecast Update, 2013–2018.*

[3] Cohen, J. 1988 *Statistical Power Analysis for the Behavioral Sciences*. Lawrence Erlbaum Associates.

[4] De Moor, K., Ketyko, I., Joseph, W., Deryckere, T., De Marez, L., Martens, L. and Verleye, G. 2010. Proposed framework for evaluating quality of experience in a mobile, testbed-oriented living lab setting. *Mobile Networks and Applications*, 15, 3, 378-391.

[5] De Pessemier, T., De Moor, K., Joseph, W., De Marez, L. and Martens, L. 2012. Quantifying subjective quality evaluations for mobile video watching in a semi-living lab context. *IEEE T Broadcast*, 58, 4, 580-589.

[6] Fu, B., Kunzmann, G., Wetterwald, M., Corujo, D. and Costa, R. 2013. QoE-aware traffic management for mobile video delivery. In *Proceedings of the IEEE International Conference on Communications Workshops* (Budapest, Hungary, June 9-13, 2013). IEEE.

[7] Himawan, I., Song, W. and Tjondronegoro, D. 2012. Impact of Region-of-Interest video coding on perceived quality in mobile video. In *Proceedings of IEEE International Conference on Multimedia & Expo (ICME 2012)* (Melbourn, Australia, 2012). IEEE.

[8] ITU-R. 2004 *Methodology for the Subjective Assessment of Quality for Television Pictures*. Recommendation BT. 500-11.

[9] ITU-T. 1999 *Subjective Video Quality Assessment Methods for Multimedia Applications*. P.910 Recommendation.

[10] ITU-T SG 12. *Definition of Quality of Experience*. 2007.

[11] Jumisko-Pyykkö, S. and Hannuksela, M. M. 2008. Does context matter in quality evaluation of mobile television? In *Proceedings of MobileHCI'08* (Amsterdam, The Netherlands, Sept 2–5, 2008). ACM, NY, 63-72.

[12] Jumisko-Pyykkö, S., Vadakital, V. K. M. and Hannuksela, M. M. 2008. Acceptance threshold: A bidimensional research method for user-oriented quality evaluation studies. *Int J Digital Multimedia Broadcasting*, 2008.

[13] Khan, A., Sun, L., Jammeh, E. and Ifeachor, E. 2010. Quality of experience-driven adaptation scheme for video applications over wireless networks. *Iet Commun*, 4, 11 (Jul. 2010), 1337-1347.

[14] Knoche, H., Papaleo, M., Sasse, M. A. and Vanelli-Coralli, A. 2007. The kindest cut: enhancing the user experience of mobile TV through adequate zooming. In *Proceedings of MM'07* (Augsburg, Germany, Sept 23–28, 2007). ACM, 87-96.

[15] McCarthy, J. D., Sasse, M. A. and Miras, D. 2004. Sharp or smooth?: comparing the effects of quantization vs. frame rate for streamed video. In *Proceedings of CHI'04* (Vienna, Austria, April 24-29, 2004). ACM, NY, 535-542.

[16] Molnar, A. and Muntean, C. H. 2013. Cost-oriented adaptive multimedia delivery. *IEEE T Broadcast*, 59, 3, 484-499.

[17] Muller, C., Renzi, D., Lederer, S., Battista, S. and Timmerer, C. 2012. Using Scalable Video Coding for dynamic adaptive streaming over HTTP in mobile environments. In *Proceedings of the 20th European Signal Processing Conference (EUSIPCO)* (Aug 27-31, 2012), 2208-2212.

[18] Piamrat, K., Viho, C. e., Ksentini, A. and Bonnin, J.-M. 2009. Quality of experience measurements for video streaming over wireless networks. In *Proceedings of the 6th Internnational Conference on Information Technology: New Generation* (2009). IEEE Computer Society, 1184-1189.

[19] Pinson, M. H. and Wolf, S. 2004. A new standardized method for objectively measuring video quality. *IEEE T Broadcas*, 50, 3 (Sep. 2004), 312-322.

[20] Sasse, M. A. and Knoche, H. 2006. Quality in context-an ecological approach to assessing QoS for mobile TV. In *Proceedings of the 2nd ISCA/DEGA Tutorial & Research Workshop on Perceptual Quality of System* (Berlin, Germany, Sep 3-5, 2006).

[21] Seshadrinathan, K. and Bovik, A. C. 2010. Motion tuned spatio-temporal quality assessment of natural videos. *IEEE T Image Process*, 19, 2 (Feb 2010), 335-350.

[22] Sodagar, I. 2011. The MPEG-DASH standard for Multimedia streaming over the Internet. *MultiMedia, IEEE*, 18, 4, 62-67.

[23] Song, W., Tjondronegoro, D., Wang, S.-H. and Docherty, M. 2010. Impact of zooming and enhancing Region of Interests for optimizing user experience on mobile sports video. In *Proceedings of MM'10* (Firenze, Italy, Oct 25-29, 2010). ACM, NY, 321-330.

[24] Song, W., Tjondronegoro, D. and Docherty, M. 2011. Quality delivery of mobile video: In-depth understanding of user requirements. In *Proceedings of the OZCHI'11* (Canberra, Australia, Nov 28 – Dec 2 , 2011). ACM.

[25] Song, W., Tjondronegoro, D. and Docherty, M. 2011. Saving bitrate vs. pleasing users: Where is the break-even point in mobile video quality? In *Proceedings of MM'11* (Scottscale, Arizona, USA). ACM, 403-412.

[26] Song, W. and Tjondronegoro, D. 2014. Acceptability-based QoE models for mobile video., *IEEE T. Multimedia*, 16, 3, 738 - 750.

[27] Ukommi, U., Arachchi, H. K., Dogan, S. and Kondoz, A. M. 2013. Content-aware bitrate adaptation for robust mobile video services, In *Proceedings of 2013 IEEE International Symposium on Broadband Multimedia Systems and Broadcasting (BMSB)*. IEEE, 1-4.

[28] Venkataraman, M. and Chatterjee, M. 2011. Inferring video QoE in real time. *Network, IEEE*, 25, 1, 4-13.

[29] Wang, Z., Bovik, A. C., Sheikh, H. R. and Simoncelli, E. P. 2004. Image quality assessment: From error visibility to structural similarity. *IEEE T Image Process*, 13, 4, 600-612.

Weakly-Supervised Image Parsing via Constructing Semantic Graphs and Hypergraphs

Wenxuan Xie, Yuxin Peng*, Jianguo Xiao
Institute of Computer Science and Technology, Peking University, Beijing 100871, China
{xiewenxuan, pengyuxin, xiaojianguo}@pku.edu.cn

ABSTRACT

In this paper, we address the problem of weakly-supervised image parsing, whose aim is to automatically determine the class labels of image regions given image-level labels only. In the literature, existing studies pay main attention to the formulation of the weakly-supervised learning problem, i.e., how to propagate class labels from images to regions given an affinity graph of regions. Notably, however, the affinity graph of regions, which is generally constructed in relatively simpler settings in existing methods, is of crucial importance to the parsing performance due to the fact that the weakly-supervised image parsing problem cannot be handled within a single image, and that the affinity graph facilitates label propagation among multiple images. Therefore, in contrast to existing methods, we focus on how to make the affinity graph more descriptive through embedding more semantics into it. We develop two novel graphs by leveraging the weak supervision information carefully: 1) Semantic graph, which is established upon a conventional graph by utilizing the proposed weakly-supervised criteria; 2) Semantic hypergraph, which explores both intra-image and inter-image high-order semantic relevance. Experimental results on two standard datasets demonstrate that the proposed semantic graphs and hypergraphs not only capture more semantic relevance, but also perform significantly better than conventional graphs in image parsing. More remarkably, due to the complementariness among the proposed semantic graphs and hypergraphs, the combination of them shows even more promising results.

Categories and Subject Descriptors

I.4.6 [**Image Processing and Computer Vision**]: Segmentation—*pixel classification*

General Terms

Algorithms, Experimentation, Performance

*Corresponding author.

MM'14, November 3–7, 2014, Orlando, Florida, USA.

http://dx.doi.org/10.1145/2647868.2654910.

Keywords

Weakly-supervised image parsing; Semantic graph construction; Semantic hypergraph construction

1. INTRODUCTION

Image parsing, whose aim is to assign semantic labels to image regions [28], is a fundamentally challenging problem [17, 16, 36, 12]. Being a sort of fine-grained image analysis, an effective image parsing system facilitates many higher-level image understanding tasks, e.g., image editing [26] and region-based image retrieval [39]. However, although the goal of image parsing is to classify pixels, directly modeling pixels may lead to unreliable predictions due to the fact that a single pixel contains little information. In order to yield semantically consistent results, existing image parsing approaches are generally based on image regions (aka, superpixels).

In the literature, most image parsing methods suppose that a training dataset with superpixel-level labels is given and then either establish an appearance-based model which propagates labels from training superpixels to test superpixels [35] or resort to non-parametric methods to transfer labels from training images to query images [14]. However, it is generally too laborious and time-consuming to annotate superpixel-level labels manually. Fortunately, thanks to the rapid spread of online photo sharing websites (e.g., Flickr), a large amount of images with user-provided image-level labels become available. These labels can be further refined by modeling visual consistency and error sparsity [43]. In contrast to superpixel-level labels, it is more challenging to develop an image parsing algorithm based on image-level labels only. In this paper, such a problem is called weakly-supervised image parsing.

In traditional image parsing, labels are propagated from training superpixels to test superpixels; however, in weakly-supervised image parsing, the propagation is from images to superpixels. To handle such a weakly-supervised learning problem, several approaches have been proposed in the literature. For example, [17] has first proposed a bi-layer sparse coding model for uncovering how an image or superpixel could be reconstructed from superpixels of the entire image repository, and then used the learned relevance to facilitate label inference. What is more, [16] has developed a weakly-supervised graph propagation model, where the final results can be directly inferred by simultaneously considering superpixel consistency, superpixel incongruity and the weak supervision information. It can be observed that, superpixel

Figure 1: Illustrations of our motivation in constructing semantic graphs by reducing the number of *candidate superpixels*. An image is in a green box if its corresponding superpixel (which is bounded by a magenta closed curve) is semantically relevant to (i.e., has the same ground-truth label with) the original superpixel, otherwise it is in a red box.

graphs are necessary and important to the aforementioned image parsing methods.

However, despite the effectiveness of the aforementioned approaches, the superpixel graphs are constructed in relatively simpler settings. These approaches are mainly based on the assumption that a given superpixel from an image can be sparsely reconstructed via the superpixels belonging to the images with common labels, and that the sparsely selected superpixels are relevant to the given superpixel. In order to state conveniently, we define *candidate superpixels* to be the set of superpixels which are possibly adjacent to a given superpixel, where the adjacency denotes a non-zero similarity in a superpixel graph. Under this definition, the candidate superpixels of the above approaches are those belonging to the images which have common labels with the image containing the given superpixel. Due to the large number of candidate superpixels in these approaches, the graph construction process tends to incur more semantically irrelevant superpixels and thus the parsing performance is degraded.

Therefore, it is crucial to construct a superpixel graph with more semantic relevance. In order to handle this task, we start from the following three observations:

- *An ideal graph yields nearly perfect results.* Suppose there is an ideal graph, in which all pairs of semantically relevant superpixels are adjacent, and all pairs of semantically irrelevant superpixels are non-adjacent. The parsing accuracy with such a graph is 99% (where the 1% loss lies in the error of over-segmentation).
- *Reducing the number of candidate superpixels is beneficial.* As shown by the illustrative examples in Fig. 1, by reducing the number of candidate superpixels, the graph can be made more descriptive. If all the candidate superpixels are selected correctly, the parsing accuracy on MSRC-21 dataset is 89%.
- *It is important to explore high-order semantic relevance.* For example, superpixels (usually more than two) that are both visually similar and spatially adjacent within an image tend to be semantically relevant.

It can be concluded from the *first* observation that, although the ideal graph is unavailable due to the fact that the ground-truth labels of superpixels are unknown in advance, it is worthwhile to construct a superpixel graph with more semantic relevance. Based on the *second* observation, we can construct a descriptive graph by reducing the number of candidate superpixels. Concretely, we impose novel criteria on conventional graphs by exploiting the weak supervision information carefully, and develop semantic graphs. Moreover, as shown by the *third* observation, we may further enrich the superpixel graph by resorting to hypergraphs [42]. In this paper, semantic hypergraphs are constructed to model both intra-image and inter-image high-order relevance by leveraging the weak supervision information.

The rest of the paper is organized as follows. A brief overview of related studies is presented in Section 2. In Section 3, the graph propagation approach to weakly-supervised image parsing is introduced as a preliminary. Then, we present the proposed semantic graph construction approach and semantic hypergraph construction approach in Section 4 and Section 5, respectively. In Section 6, we show how the aforementioned graphs and hypergraphs are combined by using random walk. The proposed methods are evaluated on two standard datasets in image parsing in Section 7. Finally, Section 8 draws the conclusions.

2. RELATED WORK

In this section, we review some studies related to the proposed approach in the following aspects: image parsing, weakly-supervised image segmentation, graph construction and hypergraph construction.

2.1 Image Parsing

The image parsing problem has received wide interests in the vision community, and numerous methods have been proposed. Earlier studies mainly focus on modeling shapes [33, 5]. These methods, however, can only handle images either with a singe object or without occlusions between objects. Some other approaches are mostly based on discriminative learning techniques, e.g., conditional random field [37], dense scene alignment [14] and deep learning [8]. All of these algorithms require pixel-level labels for training, however, which are very expensive to obtain in practice.

Besides the aforementioned approaches, there have been a few studies on weakly-supervised image parsing, where superpixel labels are propagated along a predefined graph. As a first attempt, [17] has proposed a bi-layer sparse coding model for mining the relation between images and superpixels. The model has also been extended to a continuity-biased bi-layer sparsity formulation [18]. In [16], a weakly-supervised graph propagation model is developed to directly infer the superpixel labels. Moreover, in [15], a multi-edge graph is established to simultaneously consider both images and superpixels, and is then used to obtain superpixel labels through a majority voting strategy. Different from the above approaches which pay main attention to the formulation of the weakly-supervised learning problem, our focus is to construct a superpixel graph with more semantic relevance by using the weak supervision information carefully.

2.2 Weakly-Supervised Image Segmentation

The weakly-supervised image segmentation task is similar to weakly-supervised image parsing, where the only difference lies in that, images are split into a training set and a test set, and the aim is to infer the labels of test image pixels by exploiting only the image-level labels in the training set. In the literature, [29] has proposed to handle this task by using the Markov field aspect model. In [30], multiple instance learning and multi-task learning strategies are adopted. Multi-image model [31] and criteria on multiple feature fusion [32] have also been studied.

What is more, recent approaches contain criteria on probabilistic graphlet cut [41], weakly-supervised dual clustering [20] and classifier evaluation [40]. However, in practice, due to the easy access of image-level labels on photo sharing websites such as Flickr, we assume all image-level labels are available in this paper, which is different from the aforementioned weakly-supervised image segmentation task.

2.3 Graph Construction

A number of methods have been proposed for graph construction, among which the most popular ones include sparse linear reconstruction (L_1) graph [34], ϵ-ball graph and k-nearest neighbor (k-NN) graph. Recent studies are mostly based on the combinations and extensions of these graphs. As an example, [44] has proposed to handle semi-supervised learning with a non-negative low rank and sparse graph. In [13], a two-stage non-negative sparse representation has been proposed for face recognition. Furthermore, a k-NN sparse graph is applied to handle image annotation in [27].

However, different from conventional graph construction in either supervised or unsupervised setting, constructing a descriptive graph under weak supervision in this paper is a novel and interesting task to handle.

2.4 Hypergraph Construction

A hypergraph is a graph in which an edge can connect more than two vertices [4]. Similar to simple graphs, hypergraphs can also be used in learning tasks [42]. For example, [22] has proposed to handle latent semantic learning in action recognition through sparse coding and hypergraph regularization. Moreover, hypergraphs enable visual-textual joint relevance learning for tag-based social image search [11]. In [10], hypergraphs are exploited in codebook learning for image classification.

Besides the aforementioned approaches and applications, we propose to model high-order relevance among superpixels in weakly-supervised image parsing by resorting to hypergraphs in this paper.

3. WEAKLY-SUPERVISED IMAGE PARSING BY GRAPH PROPAGATION

In order to handle weakly-supervised image parsing, the proposed semantic graph and hypergraph construction approaches are based on the weakly-supervised graph propagation model in [16]. As a preliminary, we begin by formally defining the problem, and then present the formulation and solution. In this paper, we only show the key steps here. Please refer to [16] for detailed derivations.

3.1 Problem Definition

Given an image collection $\{X_1, \dots, X_m, \dots, X_M\}$, where X_m denotes the m-th image, and its label information is denoted by an indicator vector $y_m = [y_m^1, \dots, y_m^c, \dots, y_m^C]^\top$, where $y_m^c = 1$ if X_m has the c-th label, and $y_m^c = 0$ otherwise. C denotes the number of classes, and the image-level label collection is denoted as $Y = [y_1, \dots, y_m, \dots, y_M]^\top$. After image over-segmentation with a certain approach, e.g., SLIC [1], X_m is represented by a set of superpixels $X_m = \{x_{m1}, \dots, x_{mi}, \dots, x_{mn_m}\}$, where n_m is the number of superpixels in X_m. x_{mi} stands for the i-th superpixel of X_m, and its corresponding label information is also denoted by an indicator vector $f_{mi} = [f_{mi}^1, \dots, f_{mi}^c, \dots, f_{mi}^C]^\top$, where $f_{mi}^c = 1$ if superpixel x_{mi} has the c-th label, and $f_{mi}^c = 0$ otherwise. Moreover, $N = \sum_{m=1}^M n_m$ denotes the total number of superpixels in the image collection, and $F \in \mathbb{R}^{N \times C}$ denotes all the superpixel labels. In the weakly-supervised setting, all the image labels Y are given, and the superpixel labels F are to be inferred.

3.2 Formulation

In a traditional label propagation formulation, both the graph and the labeled information are considered; however, in a weakly-supervised label propagation formulation, both the graph and the weak supervision information are taken into account. First of all, given an $N \times N$ matrix W denoting the affinity graph of superpixels, we can obtain the smoothness regularizer [3] as follows

$$T_1 = \mathrm{tr}(F^\top LF) \tag{1}$$

where L is a Laplacian matrix defined as $L = D - W$, and D is the degree matrix of W. The smoothness regularizer enforces similar superpixels in feature space to share similar labels, which also resembles the idea of spectral clustering [23]. Furthermore, the image-level supervision information can be formulated in the following form

$$T_2 = \sum_m \sum_c |\max_{x_{mi} \in X_m} f_{mi}^c - y_m^c| \tag{2}$$

According to Eq. 2, if $y_m^c = 1$, at least one superpixel should interpret the label. Moreover, if $y_m^c = 0$, no superpixels will be assigned to that label, which is equivalent to require $\max f_{mi}^c = 0$. According to such equivalence, and due to the fact that the image-level label y_m^c can only be either 1 or 0, Eq. 2 can be rewritten in the following form

$$T_3 = \sum_m \sum_c (1 - y_m^c) h_c F^\top q_m + \sum_m \sum_c y_m^c (1 - \max_{x_{mi} \in X_m} g_{mi} F h_c^\top) \tag{3}$$

where h_c is a $1 \times C$ indicator vector whose all elements, except for the c-th element, are zeros, and q_m is an $N \times 1$ indicator vector whose all elements, except for those elements corresponding to the m-th image, are zeros. Moreover, g_{mi} is a $1 \times N$ vector whose elements corresponding to the i-th superpixel in X_m are ones and others are zeros. Through simultaneously considering Eq. 1 and Eq. 3, the final formulation is shown as follows

$$\begin{aligned} \min_F \;& \lambda \operatorname{tr}(F^\top L F) + \sum_m \sum_c (1 - y_m^c) h_c F^\top q_m \\ &+ \sum_m \sum_c y_m^c (1 - \max_{x_{mi} \in X_m} g_{mi} F h_c^\top) \\ s.t. \;& F \geq 0, \;\; F\mathbf{e}_1 = \mathbf{e}_2 \end{aligned} \tag{4}$$

where λ is a positive parameter. It should be noted that, the equality $\sum_{c=1}^{C} f_{mi}^c = 1$ always holds due to $F\mathbf{e}_1 = \mathbf{e}_2$, where $\mathbf{e}_1 = \mathbf{1}_{C \times 1}$, and $\mathbf{e}_2 = \mathbf{1}_{N \times 1}$.

3.3 Solution

Eq. 4 can be efficiently solved via concave-convex programming [38] iteratively. Let η be the subgradient of $l = [f_{m1}^c, \ldots, f_{mi}^c, \ldots, f_{mn_m}^c]^\top$, which is an $n_m \times 1$ vector and its i-th element is shown as follows

$$\eta_i = \begin{cases} \frac{1}{n_\alpha}, & f_{mi}^c = \max_j f_{mj}^c \;\text{ where } x_{mj} \in X_m \\ 0, & \text{otherwise} \end{cases} \tag{5}$$

where n_α is the number of superpixels with the largest label value. According to [38], Eq. 4 can be derived and further relaxed as the following quadratic programming problem

$$\begin{aligned} \min_F \;& \lambda \operatorname{tr}(F^\top L F) + \sum_m \sum_c (1 - y_m^c) h_c F^\top q_m \\ &+ \sum_m \sum_c y_m^c (1 - h_c \beta U_m F h_c^\top) + \gamma \|F\mathbf{e}_1 - \mathbf{e}_2\|^2 \\ s.t. \;& F \geq 0 \end{aligned} \tag{6}$$

where U_m is an $N \times N$ diagonal block matrix , whose diagonal elements are equal to q_m. β is a $C \times n_m$ matrix corresponding to X_m and $\beta_{mc} = \eta^\top$. Moreover, γ is a weighting parameter. To efficiently solve Eq. 6, the non-negative multiplicative updating procedure in [19] is adopted, which facilitates the following element-wise updating rule

$$F_{ij} = F_{ij} \times \frac{[2\lambda W F + 2\gamma \mathbf{e}_2 \mathbf{e}_1^\top + \sum_m \sum_c y_m^c U_m^\top \beta^\top h_c^\top h_c]_{ij}}{[2\lambda D F + 2\gamma \mathbf{e}_1 \mathbf{e}_1^\top + \sum_m \sum_c (1 - y_m^c) q_m h_c]_{ij}} \tag{7}$$

Therefore, Eq. 4 can be solved by alternatively updating β and F according to Eq. 5 and Eq. 7, respectively. After convergence, the superpixel labels F are obtained as the final results of image parsing.

4. SEMANTIC GRAPH CONSTRUCTION

Although the graph propagation method shown in the previous section is capable of inferring superpixel labels, the superpixel graph W is constructed by adopting relatively simpler settings. For example, the L_1 graph used in [16] is built up by reconstructing each given superpixel via the superpixels belonging to the images with common labels. However, as a key factor to the final performance of weakly-supervised image parsing (as shown by the *first* observation in Section 1), the superpixel graph W can be made more descriptive by leveraging the weak supervision information carefully. In this section, we focus on the construction process of a novel superpixel graph, i.e., k-NN semantic graph.

4.1 Preliminaries

Based on the *second* observation in Section 1, we propose to construct graphs with more semantic relevance by reducing the number of candidate superpixels. To begin with, we denote all the feature vectors of the superpixels as $Z \in \mathbb{R}^{d \times N}$, where d is the dimensionality of a feature vector. Furthermore, based on the image-level labels, all the superpixels belonging to images with the c-th label is denoted as $Z_c \in \mathbb{R}^{d \times N_c}$. According to the illustrative examples in Fig. 1, given a superpixel x_{mi} (belonging to image X_m) whose ground-truth label is c and whose corresponding feature vector is denoted as p_{mi}, using Z_c as candidate superpixels can provide better results than using Z or other Z_j, where $j \neq c$.

The aforementioned fact can be easily verified due to the following reasons: 1) Since all the superpixels which belong to Z but not Z_c are semantically irrelevant to p_{mi}, it is beneficial to represent p_{mi} by excluding these superpixels, and thus using Z_c may yield better results than Z; 2) Z_c contains more semantically relevant superpixels and fewer irrelevant superpixels to p_{mi} than other Z_j, where $j \neq c$. Therefore, our aim is to find the most appropriate candidate superpixels for each superpixel.

Notably, this is a paradox, since we can precisely obtain Z_c according to the ground-truth label of x_{mi} (i.e., c) and thus provide a descriptive graph. However, the superpixel label c is to be inferred and unknown in advance. In order to handle this problem, we develop k-NN semantic graphs, which is based on the proposed criteria in selecting Z_c in conventional k-NN graphs.

4.2 k-NN Semantic Graph

In this subsection, we present the construction process of k-NN semantic graphs. Since using Z as candidate superpixels is always a suboptimal choice, we focus on selecting candidate superpixels from Z_j where $j \in \{1, \ldots, C\}$. Given a superpixel x_{mi} (belonging to image X_m) whose feature vector is p_{mi}, we begin by denoting S_j as the set of k-NN superpixels of p_{mi} in Z_j, and S_j^{cp} as the set of k-NN superpixels in Z_j^{cp}, where Z_j^{cp} is the complementary set of Z_j, i.e., $Z_j^{cp} = Z \backslash Z_j$. Based on these notations, we select the k-NN superpixels of p_{mi} according to the following criterion.

$$\begin{aligned} \min_{j, S_j} \;& \sum_{a=1}^{k} \sum_{b=1}^{k} \operatorname{sim}(S_{ja}, S_{jb}^{cp}) \\ s.t. \;& S_{ja} \in S_j, \; S_{jb}^{cp} \in S_j^{cp}, \; y_m^j = 1, \; j \in \{1, \ldots, C\} \end{aligned} \tag{8}$$

where S_{ja} and S_{jb}^{cp} are superpixels belonging to sets S_j and S_j^{cp}, respectively. Moreover, $\operatorname{sim}(\cdot, \cdot)$ denotes a similarity measure of two feature vectors of superpixels. According to Eq. 8, we select S_j as the k-NN superpixels of p_{mi}, where the sum of pairwise similarity between superpixels in S_j and S_j^{cp} is minimized.

Eq. 8 is optimized in two steps: 1) Enumerate S_j for all possible values of j which satisfy $y_m^j = 1$ (i.e., all labels of the image containing the given superpixel p_{mi}); 2) Select the specific S_j which minimizes Eq. 8 (i.e., the sum of pairwise similarity) as the final result. Solving Eq. 8 requires $O(CN + Ck^2)$ for a single superpixel. Since C and k are much smaller than N, the complexity is linear with respect to N (i.e., the total number of superpixels).

As a consequence, after selecting neighbors for each superpixel in the entire image repository by reducing the number of candidate superpixels based on Eq. 8, the affinity graph W is constructed. We further assign $W = \frac{1}{2}(W + W^\top)$ to ensure its symmetry, and use it as the k-NN semantic graph in this paper.

4.3 Interpretation

Eq. 8 makes sense due to the following reasons. Generally, superpixels with the same labels tend to be visually similar, whereas the similarity between superpixels belonging to different classes tends to be small. Through minimizing the pairwise similarity between superpixels in S_j and S_j^{cp}, the superpixels in the selected S_j are likely to have the same label with p_{mi}.

For example, given an image X_m with labels 'grass' and 'bird', we denote a 'grass' superpixel and a 'bird' superpixel in X_m as p_{grs} and p_{brd}, respectively. Moreover, candidate superpixels Z_{grs}, Z_{grs}^{cp}, Z_{brd} and Z_{brd}^{cp} are defined accordingly. Given p_{grs}, since 'grass' superpixels may appear as neighbors in both Z_{brd} (superpixels in 'bird' images) and Z_{brd}^{cp} (superpixels in 'non-bird' images), the pairwise similarity between superpixels in S_{brd} and S_{brd}^{cp} is relatively large. In contrast, the pairwise similarity between superpixels in S_{grs} and S_{grs}^{cp} is small since 'grass' superpixels are absent in S_{grs}^{cp}. Therefore, the selected set of neighbors for p_{grs} is S_{grs} but not S_{brd}. Moreover, the same applies to p_{brd}, where S_{brd} is chosen as its k-NN superpixels.

It should be noted that, although we focus only on constructing k-NN semantic graphs in this paper, the idea of constructing a superpixel graph with more semantic relevance by reducing the number of candidate superpixels is also applicable to other types of graphs, e.g., L_1 graphs. What is more, Eq. 8 is not the only choice for constructing k-NN semantic graphs, and can be readily substituted by other feasible criteria.

More notably, our aim is to show that reducing the number of candidate superpixels is beneficial. We have conducted experiments and observed that L_1 semantic graph (with some criteria) performs better than original L_1 graph. However, constructing L_1 graph is time-consuming. Therefore, our experiments are mainly based on k-NN (semantic) graphs, which are more efficient to construct.

5. SEMANTIC HYPERGRAPH CONSTRUCTION

Besides constructing semantic graphs which only contain second-order relevance, we also model high-order semantic relevance by resorting to hypergraphs (as shown by the *third* observation in Section 1). We begin by presenting some notations along with our motivation in exploiting hypergraphs. After that, we introduce the proposed approaches to establishing intra-image hyperedges and inter-image hyperedges, respectively. Finally, we discuss the complementariness among the semantic graphs and hypergraphs.

5.1 Notation and Motivation

A hypergraph $G(A, \mathcal{E})$ consists of a vertex set A and a hyperedge set $\mathcal{E}$ [42]. Each hyperedge e is a subset of the vertex set A, where the weight corresponding to the hyperedge e is denoted as $w(e)$. The degree of a vertex a is defined as $d(a) = \sum_{\{e \in \mathcal{E} | a \in e\}} w(e)$. Moreover, the incidence matrix H is an $|A| \times |\mathcal{E}|$ matrix, whose entry $H(a, e) = 1$ if $a \in e$, and $H(a, e) = 0$ otherwise. The degree of a hyperedge e is defined as $\delta(e) = |e|$. Therefore, we have $d(a) = \sum_{e \in \mathcal{E}} w(e)H(a, e)$ and $\delta(e) = \sum_{a \in A} H(a, e)$. Note that, the hyperedge weight $w(e)$ in this paper is defined as

$$w(e) = \frac{1}{|e|} \sum_{a_1 \in e, a_2 \in e} \text{sim}(a_1, a_2) \tag{9}$$

where $\text{sim}(\cdot, \cdot)$ denotes a predefined similarity measure of two vertices. Based on these definitions, we define the Laplacian matrix of the aforementioned hypergraph as follows

$$L^h = D_a - HW_eD_e^{-1}H^\top \tag{10}$$

where D_a, D_e, and W_e denote the diagonal matrices of the vertex degrees, the hyperedge degrees, and the hyperedge weights of the hypergraph, respectively.

According to Eq. 10, the affinity graph can be defined as $W^h = HW_eD_e^{-1}H^\top$, and thus a hypergraph can be viewed as a graph with pairwise similarities. It can be observed after some derivation that, for any two vertices $a_1 \in e$ and $a_2 \in e$, the affinity between them in W^h is $\frac{w(e)}{\delta(e)}$. Consequently, the high-order relevance among vertices in a hypergraph can be decomposed into a set of second-order relevance (as shown in W^h). With this in mind, the hypergraph can be viewed to have a cluster-based structure partitioned by hyperedges (if these hyperedges do not overlap), and we present two types of cluster-based structures in weakly-supervised image parsing in the next two subsections.

5.2 Intra-Image Hyperedges

We begin by analyzing the cluster-based structure within a single image. Intuitively, superpixels that are both visually similar and spatially adjacent tend to be semantically relevant. In order to achieve this goal, we establish a graph W_m for the image X_m whose vertices correspond to superpixels of X_m, and only retain the pairwise visual similarities of spatially adjacent superpixels on W_m. Then, the cluster-based structure is learned on W_m by spectral clustering [23], which can be viewed as a graph partitioning task [24]. The spectral clustering algorithm is summarized as follows:

1. Find K smallest nontrivial eigenvectors $v_1, \ldots, v_K$ of the Laplacian matrix $L_m = D_m - W_m$, where D_m is the degree matrix of W_m.
2. Form $E = [v_1, \ldots, v_K]$, and normalize each row of E to have unit length.
3. Perform K-means clustering on the vectors $E_{i.}$ (where $i = 1, \ldots, n_m$) to partition the n_m superpixels into K clusters.

After performing spectral clustering for each image, superpixels belonging to the same cluster form an intra-image hyperedge. By stacking all the hyperedges into a single incidence matrix H, we can obtain the Laplacian matrix according to Eq. 10. In order to state conveniently, we denote

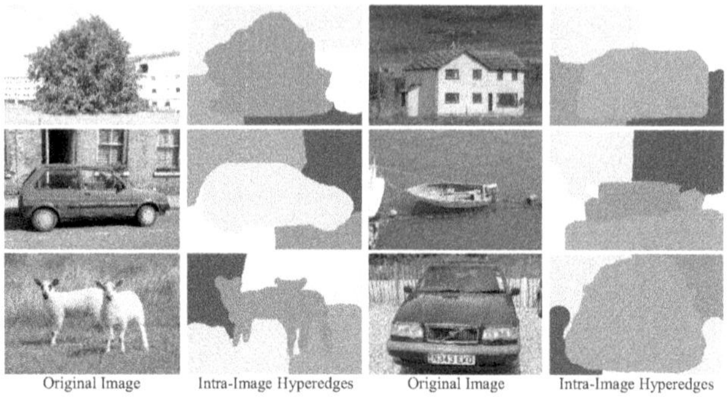

Figure 2: Illustration of some intra-image hyperedges. Superpixels in the area of the same color share an intra-image hyperedge. Please note that an area generally contains more than one superpixel, and that the number of clusters here is set to 5.

the resultant hypergraph as HG_{intra}. Some example results are shown in Fig. 2.

It should be noted that, spatial adjacency has already been utilized in image segmentation in the literature. For example, all pairwise similarities between spatially adjacent superpixels are retained in [20]. However, such a setting may cause all the superpixel labels to be similar, which may not be a good choice.

5.3 Inter-Image Hyperedges

Besides intra-image hyperedges, there is a second type of cluster-based structures, i.e., inter-image hyperedges. Recall that in Subsection 4.1, we define $Z_j \in \mathbb{R}^{d \times N_j}$ to be all the superpixels belonging to images with the j-th label. Moreover, the necessary condition of two superpixels being semantically relevant is that, the two images to which they belong have at least one label in common. Therefore, instead of discovering the cluster-based structure in Z (i.e., all the superpixels), we focus on the subsets Z_j, where $j \in \{1, \dots, C\}$.

The approach to learning inter-image hyperedges consists of two steps: 1) Establish an $N_j \times N_j$ visual similarity graph W_j for all superpixels in Z_j; 2) Patition W_j by spectral clustering [23].

Similarly with Subsection 5.2, after performing spectral clustering for each category, superpixels belonging to the same cluster form an inter-image hyperedge. By stacking all the hyperedges into a single incidence matrix H, we can obtain the Laplacian matrix according to Eq. 10. We denote the resultant hypergraph as HG_{inter}.

Please note that, rather than using the full graph W_j, we observe in the experiments that the k-NN version of W_j results in better performance.

5.4 Discussion

We discuss the complementariness between HG_{intra} and HG_{inter} here. Moreover, the k-NN semantic graph proposed in Section 4 is also taken into account.

- HG_{intra} vs HG_{inter}. HG_{inter} is based on visual appearance only, while HG_{intra} leverages the spatial adjacency information in a single image.
- k-NN semantic graph vs HG_{intra}. Similarly with the above, k-NN semantic graph and HG_{intra} exploit visual appearance and spatial adjacency, respectively.
- k-NN semantic graph vs HG_{inter}. There may be errors in predicting candidate superpixels in k-NN semantic graph, and thus the neighbors of a given superpixel are not really semantic relevant ones. Fortunately, the cluster-based structure learned in HG_{inter} may help reduce the errors caused by k-NN semantic graph.

Therefore, the aforementioned three graphs (hypergraphs) are complementary with each other, and thus the combination of them can yield better parsing performance.

6. GRAPH COMBINATION BY RANDOM WALK

Currently, we have proposed three semantic graphs (hypergraphs) in total, i.e., k-NN semantic graph, HG_{intra} and HG_{inter}. As discussed in the previous section, these graphs are complementary with each other, and thus it is beneficial to combine them for image parsing. Hence, in this section, we present an approach to combine these graphs based on random walk. Recall that according to Eq. 10, the affinity graph is defined as $W^h = HW_eD_e^{-1}H^\top$, and thus a hypergraph can be viewed as a graph with pairwise similarities.

In order to state clearly, assume that we have S undirected and symmetric graphs $G_s = (A, W_s)$, where $s = 1, \dots, S$. Each element $W_s(a,b)$ in the $N \times N$ similarity matrix W_s measures the similarity between superpixels x_a and x_b on the s-th graph. It should be noted that, these graphs share the same set of vertices while having different similarity matrices. With respect to each graph G_s, as in [6], for the vertex $a \in A$,we denote its degree on G_s as $d_s(a) = \sum_b W_s(a,b)$. Furthermore, the volume of graph G_s is defined as $\mathrm{vol}_s A = \sum_{a \in A} d_s(a) = \sum_{a \in A, b \in A} W_s(a,b)$. The natural random walk on G_s can be defined as follows. That is, for any two vertices a and b on G_s, their transition probability on G_s is

$$p(a \to b|G_s) = W_s(a,b)/d_s(a) \qquad (11)$$

and the stationary probability of a on G_s is

$$p(a|G_s) = d_s(a)/\mathrm{vol}_s A \qquad (12)$$

Denote $p(G_s)$ (where $s = 1, \dots, S$) as the prior probabilities of the random walker choosing the graph G_s, and we have $p(G_s) \geq 0$ and $\sum_s p(G_s) = 1$. Therefore, the posterior probability in selecting the graph G_s at vertex a is

$$p(G_s|a) = \frac{p(G_s,a)}{\sum_s p(G_s,a)} = \frac{p(a|G_s)p(G_s)}{\sum_s p(a|G_s)p(G_s)} \qquad (13)$$

For any two vertices a and b, their transition probability on multiple graphs can be computed as

$$p(a \to b) = \sum_s p(a \to b|G_s)p(G_s|a) \qquad (14)$$

In addition, the stationary probability of vertex a on multiple graphs is computed as

$$p(a) = \sum_s p(a|G_s)p(G_s) \qquad (15)$$

Finally, according to [9], the combined Laplacian matrix $\hat{L}$ of multiple graphs is defined as follows

$$\hat{L} = \Pi - \frac{\Pi P + P^\top \Pi}{2} \qquad (16)$$

where P denotes the transition probability matrix with its elements being $p(a \to b)$, and Π is the diagonal stationary probability matrix with its diagonal elements being $p(a)$.

7. EXPERIMENTS

In this section, we evaluate the proposed semantic graphs and hypergraphs in weakly-supervised image parsing. We begin by describing the experimental setup and then compare our method with other closely related methods. Moreover, the parameter setting details are presented.

7.1 Experimental Setup

We conduct experiments on two standard datasets: PASCAL VOC'07 (PASCAL for short) [7] and MSRC-21 [26]. Both datasets contain 21 different classes and are provided with pixel-level labels, which are used to evaluate the performance measured by classification accuracy. In weakly-supervised image parsing, we assume all the image-level labels are known for both training and test set, i.e., 632 images in PASCAL dataset and 532 images in MSRC-21 dataset [25]. Moreover, we adopt SLIC [1] to obtain superpixels for each image, and represent each superpixel by the bag-of-words model while using SIFT [21] as the local descriptor. Histogram intersection kernel [2] is adopted to measure the similarity between two feature vectors of superpixels. To present fair comparisons, we adopt the same parameters for the graph propagation model shown in Eq. 4. Furthermore, the setting of parameters in constructing semantic graphs and hypergraphs will be investigated in Subsection 7.3.

Notably, besides computing the parsing accuracy on the entire image repository, we also measure the semantic relevance captured by a graph with a percentage value

$$\text{percentage} = \frac{\#(\text{adjacent superpixels with the same label})}{\#(\text{adjacent superpixels})} \tag{17}$$

where the term *adjacent superpixels* denotes a pair of superpixels whose similarity in a graph is non-zero.

Apart from comparing with the state-of-the-arts [17, 16], we mainly focus on the comparisons with some closely related baselines. For example, to demonstrate the effectiveness of the proposed k-NN semantic graph (k-NN SG for short), we compare with the following two baselines: 1) k-NN original graph (k-NN OG), where all superpixels are candidates for a given superpixel; 2) k-NN label intersection graph (k-NN LIG), where all the candidate superpixels belong to images which have at least one common label with the image containing the given superpixel. Our aim is to show that it is beneficial to reduce the number of candidate superpixels in establishing superpixel graphs.

In addition, since HG_{intra} exploits the spatial adjacency information, we compare it with an adjacency graph G_{adj}, where all pairwise similarities between spatially adjacent superpixels are retained [20]. We also compare HG_{inter} with baseline k-NN graphs, since HG_{inter} is based on a partition of k-NN visual similarity graphs as shown at the end of Subsection 5.3. Finally, we enumerate all the possible graph combination strategies to demonstrate the complementariness among the proposed semantic graphs and hypergraphs.

7.2 Empirical Results

The per-class accuracies on PASCAL dataset and MSRC-21 dataset are listed in Table 1 and Table 2, respectively.

Table 3: Percentages (%) of semantically relevant superpixels in different graphs along with the corresponding mean parsing accuracies (%) on PASCAL dataset.

Graphs	Percentage	Accuracy
k-NN OG	11	19
k-NN LIG	34	37
k-NN SG	38	42
HG_{inter}	32	41
G_{adj}	43	n/a
HG_{intra}	49	n/a

Table 4: Percentages (%) of semantically relevant superpixels in different graphs along with the corresponding mean parsing accuracies (%) on MSRC-21 dataset.

Graphs	Percentage	Accuracy
k-NN OG	33	65
k-NN LIG	52	65
k-NN SG	59	73
HG_{inter}	51	70
G_{adj}	50	n/a
HG_{intra}	66	n/a

Note that we have numbered the compared methods in these two tables for convenience.

It can be observed that trends on both datasets are similar, and that the results achieved by (11) are significantly better than the state-of-the-arts [17, 16]. In addition, we have the following findings based on the results in Table 1 and Table 2:

- (3) vs {(1), (2)}: k-NN SG outperforms the other two baselines, and thus it is beneficial to reduce the number of candidate superpixels in graph construction.
- (5) vs (1), (8) vs (6), (10) vs (3): HG_{intra} takes into account the spatial adjacency information of superpixels, which is complementary to the visual appearance. Therefore, combining HG_{intra} with graphs considering only visual appearance can improve the performance.
- (5) vs (4), (8) vs (7): G_{adj} retains the similarity of all spatially adjacent superpixels, which may cause all the superpixel labels to be similar after label propagation. In contrast to such an undesirable setting, HG_{intra} only impose regularization on superpixels which are *both spatially adjacent and visually similar.*
- (6) vs (1): Although HG_{inter} is based on a partition of k-NN visual similarity graphs, the high-order semantic relevance is a key factor to the parsing performance.
- (8) vs (6), (9) vs {(3), (6)}, (10) vs (3), (11) vs {(8), (9), (10)}: It can be observed that the proposed k-NN SG, HG_{intra} and HG_{inter} are complementary with each other, which is in correspondence with the discussion in Subsection 5.4.

Furthermore, we report the semantic relevance captured by different graphs along with the corresponding mean parsing accuracy on PASCAL dataset and MSRC-21 dataset in Table 3 and Table 4, respectively. By comparing among k-NN OG, k-NN LIG and k-NN SG, we observe that, generally, the more semantic relevance captured by the graph, the better the parsing accuracy is. However, although the

Table 1: Accuracies (%) of the proposed semantic graphs and hypergraphs for individual classes on PASCAL dataset, in comparison with other methods. The last column shows the mean accuracy over all classes.

Methods	plane	bike	bird	boat	bottle	bus	car	cat	chair	cow	table	dog	horse	motor	person	plant	sheep	sofa	train	tv	bkgd	mean
bi-layer sparse coding [17]	24	25	40	25	32	35	27	45	16	49	24	32	13	25	56	28	17	16	33	18	**82**	32
L_1 graph+χ^2 distance graph [16]	28	20	52	28	46	41	39	60	25	68	25	35	17	**35**	56	36	46	17	31	20	65	38
(1) k-NN OG	20	16	16	16	12	16	14	15	15	22	11	13	14	13	25	17	24	16	11	20	76	19
(2) k-NN LIG	41	20	58	41	48	30	38	44	**31**	42	**31**	36	**28**	26	37	30	50	25	42	40	47	37
(3) k-NN SG	**85**	55	87	45	42	31	34	57	21	**81**	23	16	6	11	42	31	72	24	49	40	41	42
(4) k-NN OG+G_{adj}	28	24	9	14	13	19	22	12	18	14	8	12	9	12	**59**	14	17	15	12	27	76	21
(5) k-NN OG+HG_{intra}	30	35	11	16	15	21	26	11	17	20	13	16	9	12	57	22	18	16	16	26	74	23
(6) HG_{inter}	56	21	71	**57**	44	40	43	**62**	16	76	19	**45**	17	23	46	30	48	10	49	38	53	41
(7) HG_{inter}+G_{adj}	57	17	72	49	53	42	**55**	54	18	64	23	38	23	30	45	24	48	17	41	27	54	41
(8) HG_{inter}+HG_{intra}	62	18	77	56	**58**	44	54	51	15	65	26	41	**28**	**35**	46	29	46	22	48	34	50	43
(9) k-NN SG+HG_{inter}	76	34	**89**	55	36	41	41	**62**	21	80	20	25	17	21	48	19	**77**	20	**58**	34	46	44
(10) k-NN SG+HG_{intra}	76	**62**	79	49	49	39	49	53	26	73	23	23	12	15	48	**40**	55	**32**	47	**42**	38	44
(11) k-NN SG+HG_{inter}+HG_{intra}	77	48	87	50	56	**48**	44	60	27	76	18	38	25	31	52	38	59	31	51	34	41	**47**

Table 2: Accuracies (%) of the proposed semantic graphs and hypergraphs for individual classes on MSRC-21 dataset, in comparison with other methods. The last column shows the mean accuracy over all classes.

Methods	bldg	grass	tree	cow	sheep	sky	plane	water	face	car	bike	flower	sign	bird	book	chair	road	cat	dog	body	boat	mean
L_1 graph+χ^2 distance graph [16]	70	92	49	10	10	83	36	**82**	62	20	52	98	88	48	98	70	75	95	76	43	23	61
(1) k-NN OG	74	**94**	64	29	12	**94**	36	75	65	40	81	96	83	56	**99**	77	**78**	93	73	34	17	65
(2) k-NN LIG	71	92	61	25	9	92	33	75	67	39	82	98	90	54	98	85	73	**99**	87	32	10	65
(3) k-NN SG	49	82	45	59	51	90	78	68	66	68	**98**	**99**	94	84	**99**	**99**	48	**99**	98	30	20	72
(4) k-NN OG+G_{adj}	74	92	67	36	18	92	47	74	71	50	84	96	88	57	**99**	81	77	96	78	32	**25**	68
(5) k-NN OG+HG_{intra}	**75**	**94**	63	55	28	93	45	74	72	59	80	96	86	63	98	86	77	97	84	37	18	70
(6) HG_{inter}	70	87	72	25	13	91	81	79	54	70	80	97	86	61	98	92	68	**99**	92	**50**	9	70
(7) HG_{inter}+G_{adj}	70	88	74	20	14	91	82	78	77	69	82	97	88	58	98	93	65	98	93	44	15	71
(8) HG_{inter}+HG_{intra}	72	88	**76**	30	18	93	84	80	80	75	81	97	90	61	98	92	67	98	94	49	19	73
(9) k-NN SG+HG_{inter}	67	88	59	45	38	93	82	75	81	78	95	98	**95**	**85**	**99**	98	62	**99**	98	34	16	75
(10) k-NN SG+HG_{intra}	53	84	46	63	**62**	89	72	67	78	69	96	**99**	90	84	98	97	53	**99**	98	27	20	74
(11) k-NN SG+HG_{inter}+HG_{intra}	71	89	60	**64**	57	93	**90**	76	**90**	**85**	95	**99**	**95**	83	**99**	**99**	66	**99**	**99**	34	**25**	**80**

semantic relevance captured by k-NN LIG is much more than k-NN OG, there is nearly no improvement in parsing accuracy on MSRC-21 dataset. It may be due to the fact that k-NN LIG only discards the adjacencies of superpixels whose corresponding images have no common labels. These adjacencies do not affect the parsing accuracy much, since the inferred label of a superpixel is constrained to be one of the labels of its corresponding image. In contrast, k-NN SG further improves the percentage of semantically adjacent superpixels, which is beneficial for the final performance.

Moreover, although HG_{inter} is based on a partition of k-NN visual similarity graphs, it contains more semantic relevance than k-NN OG and thus performs better. Besides, by learning the cluster-based structure within each image, HG_{intra} obtains more semantic relevance than G_{adj}, where some semantically irrelevant adjacencies are discarded. It should be noted that, since neither HG_{intra} nor G_{adj} models the relevance among images, they cannot be directly used in image parsing.

Notably, the criterion shown in Eq. 8 is to select candidate superpixels belonging to images containing a specific label, which can be viewed as initial predictions for all superpixel labels, although these predictions are not used to evaluate the parsing accuracy directly. However, we can still calculate an accuracy for these predictions. We empirically discover that these predictions achieve relatively lower results. For example, on MSRC-21 dataset, the accuracy achieved by initial predictions in constructing k-NN SG is 64%, whereas the accuracy of label propagation with k-NN SG is 73%. The result shows the effectiveness of the whole framework. Moreover, some example results for image parsing by graph propagation using (11) in comparison with the ground-truth on MSRC-21 dataset are shown in Fig. 3.

However, the proposed method may fail in several cases. For example, the 'boat' category in MSRC-21 dataset performs relatively poor, since the number of 'boat' superpixels is small, and the intra-class variance of the 'boat' category is large. For another example, it is difficult to distinguish between the 'face' category and the 'body' category in MSRC-21 dataset, since images containing label 'face' generally contains label 'body'. As we only know the image-level label, the difference between these two labels is small. Moreover, the visual appearance of these two categories is similar (since both of them contain human skins), and thus the selection of candidate superpixels may fail sometimes.

Besides, we also conduct qualitative experiments on NUS-WIDE dataset. It should be noted that, NUS-WIDE dataset does not contain pixel-level labels for quantitative evaluation. [16] only evaluates the parsing results qualitatively. We have conducted experiments on a subset of NUS-WIDE dataset and qualitatively observed that our methods generally perform well. In order to allow for quantitative evaluation, we plan to manually annotate some pixel-level labels and conduct thorough experiments in the future.

7.3 Parameter Setting

There are four parameters in constructing the proposed semantic graphs and hypergraphs: 1) the number of neighbors k_1 in k-NN SG; 2) the number of clusters K_2 in HG_{intra}; 3) the number of neighbors k_3 in visual similarity graph W_j for constructing HG_{inter}; 4) the number of clusters K_4 in HG_{inter}. Note that subscripts are added to distinguish among these parameters. Moreover, since the sizes of visual similarity graphs $W_j \in \mathbb{R}^{|Z_j|\times|Z_j|}$ (where $j \in \{1,\ldots,C\}$) vary a lot among different classes in constructing HG_{inter}, we empirically set $K_4 = |Z_j|/k_3$ to allow for a flexible choice

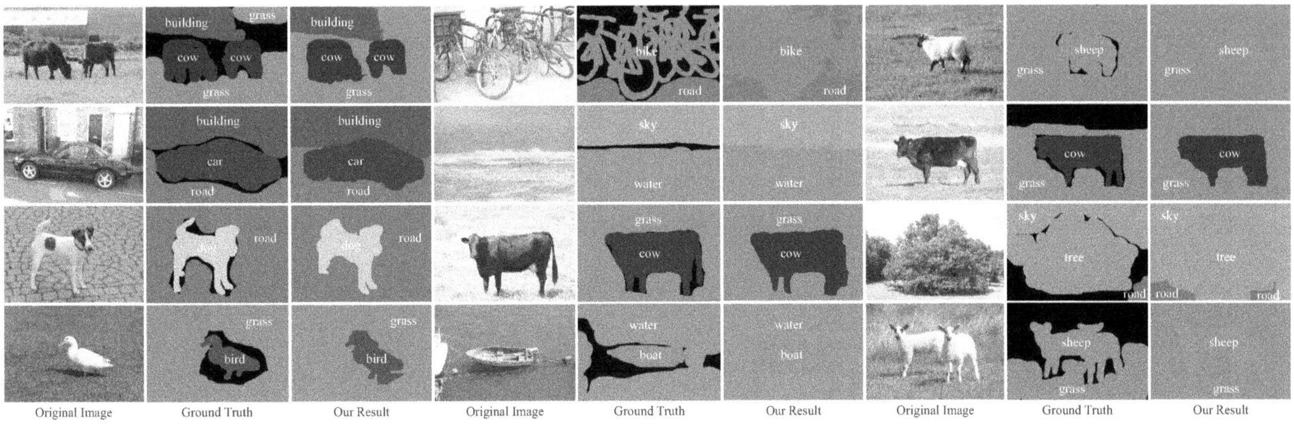

Figure 3: Some example results for image parsing by graph propagation using (11) k-NN SG+HG_{inter}+HG_{intra} (i.e., our result) in comparison with the ground-truth on MSRC-21 dataset.

of K_4 for different classes. Hence, we focus on the setting of k_1, K_2 and k_3, where the parsing accuracies by varying these parameters on MSRC-21 dataset are shown in Fig. 4.

We have the following observations according to Fig. 4:

- As k_1 increases, the performance generally decreases, which may be due to the fact that taking into account more neighbors also incurs more semantically irrelevant superpixels. Hence, we set k_1 to a relatively small value in the experiments, i.e., $k_1 = 20$.
- K_2 is the number of partitions in an image, as shown in Fig. 2. A small K_2 enforces the labels of most superpixels to be similar, whereas a large K_2 makes superpixels within an image disjoint with each other, neither of which are good ideas. Consequently, we set $K_2 = 5$ to exploit the spatial adjacency information effectively.
- Due to similar reasons with k_1, k_3 should not be too large, either. Although there are better results when k_3 is set to some large value (e.g., $k_3 = 80$), the results are unstable as k_3 goes large. In the experiments, we adopt $k_3 = 20$ in order to obtain reliable results.

Please note that we use the same parameters as discussed above on PASCAL dataset.

8. CONCLUSIONS

Based on the observations listed in Section 1, it is important to construct superpixel graphs with more semantic relevance in order to achieve better results in weakly-supervised image parsing. Since it is difficult to directly train a classifier (i.e., modeling the relationship between visual features and labels of superpixels) in weakly-supervised learning problems, it is an interesting and important issue to establish descriptive graphs in weakly-supervised setting by exploiting the weak supervision information carefully.

Moveover, we empirically observe that it is beneficial to reduce the number of candidate superpixels and to explore high-order semantic relevance. Therefore, we investigate in this paper the semantic graph and hypergraph construction. As shown in the experiments, the proposed semantic graphs and hypergraphs perform significantly better than conventional graphs. What is more, due to the complementariness among these graphs, the combination of them yields even more promising results. More notably, as a general framework, the proposed approach is suitable for other weakly-supervised learning tasks besides image parsing.

9. ACKNOWLEDGMENTS

This work was supported by National Hi-Tech Research and Development Program (863 Program) of China under Grants 2014AA015102 and 2012AA012503, National Natural Science Foundation of China under Grant 61371128, and Ph.D. Programs Foundation of Ministry of Education of China under Grant 20120001110097.

10. REFERENCES

[1] R. Achanta, A. Shaji, K. Smith, A. Lucchi, P. Fua, and S. Süsstrunk. Slic superpixels compared to state-of-the-art superpixel methods. *TPAMI*, 34(11):2274–2281, 2012.

[2] A. Barla, F. Odone, and A. Verri. Histogram intersection kernel for image classification. In *ICIP*, pages 513–516, 2003.

[3] M. Belkin and P. Niyogi. Laplacian eigenmaps and spectral techniques for embedding and clustering. *NIPS*, 14:585–591, 2001.

[4] C. Berge. *Hypergraphs*. North-Holland, Amsterdam, 1989.

[5] Y. Chen, L. Zhu, A. Yuille, and H. Zhang. Unsupervised learning of probabilistic object models (POMs) for object classification, segmentation, and recognition using knowledge propagation. *TPAMI*, 31(10):1747–1761, 2009.

[6] F. R. Chung. *Spectral graph theory*. American Mathematical Society, 1997.

[7] M. Everingham, L. Van Gool, C. Williams, J. Winn, and A. Zisserman. The PASCAL visual object classes (VOC) challenge. *IJCV*, 88(2):303–338, 2010.

[8] C. Farabet, C. Couprie, L. Najman, and Y. LeCun. Learning hierarchical features for scene labeling. *TPAMI*, 35(8):1915–1929, 2013.

[9] Z. Fu, H. H. Ip, H. Lu, and Z. Lu. Multi-modal constraint propagation for heterogeneous image clustering. In *ACM MM*, pages 143–152, 2011.

[10] S. Gao, I.-H. Tsang, and L.-T. Chia. Laplacian sparse coding, hypergraph laplacian sparse coding, and applications. *TPAMI*, 35(1):92–104, 2013.

[11] Y. Gao, M. Wang, Z.-J. Zha, J. Shen, X. Li, and X. Wu. Visual-textual joint relevance learning for tag-based social image search. *TIP*, 22(1):363–376, 2013.

[12] Y. Han, F. Wu, J. Shao, Q. Tian, and Y. Zhuang. Graph-guided sparse reconstruction for region tagging. In *CVPR*, pages 2981–2988, 2012.

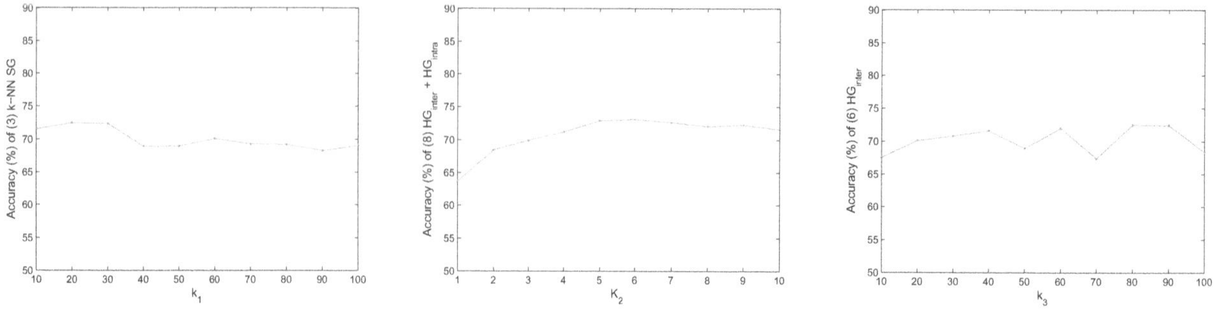

(a) (b) (c)

Figure 4: Mean accuracies (%) by varying parameters in graph construction on MSRC-21 dataset: (a) the number of neighbors k_1 in k-NN SG; (b) the number of clusters K_2 in HG_{intra}; (c) the number of neighbors k_3 in visual similarity graph W_j for constructing HG_{inter}.

[13] R. He, W.-S. Zheng, B.-G. Hu, and X.-W. Kong. Two-stage nonnegative sparse representation for large-scale face recognition. *TNNLS*, 24(1):35–46, 2013.

[14] C. Liu, J. Yuen, and A. Torralba. Nonparametric scene parsing: Label transfer via dense scene alignment. In *CVPR*, pages 1972–1979, 2009.

[15] D. Liu, S. Yan, Y. Rui, and H.-J. Zhang. Unified tag analysis with multi-edge graph. In *ACM MM*, pages 25–34, 2010.

[16] S. Liu, S. Yan, T. Zhang, C. Xu, J. Liu, and H. Lu. Weakly supervised graph propagation towards collective image parsing. *TMM*, 14(2):361–373, 2012.

[17] X. Liu, B. Cheng, S. Yan, J. Tang, T. S. Chua, and H. Jin. Label to region by bi-layer sparsity priors. In *ACM MM*, pages 115–124, 2009.

[18] X. Liu, S. Yan, B. Cheng, J. Tang, T.-S. Chua, and H. Jin. Label-to-region with continuity-biased bi-layer sparsity priors. *ACM TOMCCAP*, 8(4):50, 2012.

[19] X. Liu, S. Yan, J. Yan, and H. Jin. Unified solution to nonnegative data factorization problems. In *ICDM*, pages 307–316, 2009.

[20] Y. Liu, J. Liu, Z. Li, J. Tang, and H. Lu. Weakly-supervised dual clustering for image semantic segmentation. In *CVPR*, pages 2075–2082, 2013.

[21] D. G. Lowe. Distinctive image features from scale-invariant keypoints. *IJCV*, 60(2):91–110, 2004.

[22] Z. Lu and Y. Peng. Latent semantic learning by efficient sparse coding with hypergraph regularization. In *AAAI*, pages 411–416, 2011.

[23] A. Y. Ng, M. I. Jordan, and Y. Weiss. On spectral clustering: Analysis and an algorithm. *NIPS*, 14:849–856, 2001.

[24] J. Shi and J. Malik. Normalized cuts and image segmentation. *TPAMI*, 22(8):888–905, 2000.

[25] J. Shotton, M. Johnson, and R. Cipolla. Semantic texton forests for image categorization and segmentation. In *CVPR*, pages 1–8, 2008.

[26] J. Shotton, J. Winn, C. Rother, and A. Criminisi. Textonboost for image understanding: Multi-class object recognition and segmentation by jointly modeling texture, layout, and context. *IJCV*, 81(1):2–23, 2009.

[27] J. Tang, R. Hong, S. Yan, T.-S. Chua, G.-J. Qi, and R. Jain. Image annotation by knn-sparse graph-based label propagation over noisily tagged web images. *ACM TIST*, 2(2):14, 2011.

[28] J. Tighe and S. Lazebnik. Superparsing: scalable nonparametric image parsing with superpixels. *IJCV*, 101(2):329–349, 2013.

[29] J. Verbeek and B. Triggs. Region classification with markov field aspect models. In *CVPR*, pages 1–8, 2007.

[30] A. Vezhnevets and J. M. Buhmann. Towards weakly supervised semantic segmentation by means of multiple instance and multitask learning. In *CVPR*, pages 3249–3256, 2010.

[31] A. Vezhnevets, V. Ferrari, and J. M. Buhmann. Weakly supervised semantic segmentation with a multi-image model. In *ICCV*, pages 643–650, 2011.

[32] A. Vezhnevets, V. Ferrari, and J. M. Buhmann. Weakly supervised structured output learning for semantic segmentation. In *CVPR*, pages 845–852, 2012.

[33] J. Winn and N. Jojic. Locus: Learning object classes with unsupervised segmentation. In *ICCV*, pages 756–763, 2005.

[34] S. Yan and H. Wang. Semi-supervised learning by sparse representation. In *SDM*, pages 792–801, 2009.

[35] Y. Yang, Z. Huang, Y. Yang, J. Liu, H. T. Shen, and J. Luo. Local image tagging via graph regularized joint group sparsity. *PR*, 46(5):1358–1368, 2013.

[36] Y. Yang, Y. Yang, Z. Huang, H. T. Shen, and F. Nie. Tag localization with spatial correlations and joint group sparsity. In *CVPR*, pages 881–888, 2011.

[37] J. Yuan, J. Li, and B. Zhang. Scene understanding with discriminative structured prediction. In *CVPR*, pages 1–8, 2008.

[38] A. L. Yuille and A. Rangarajan. The concave-convex procedure. *Neural Computation*, 15(4):915–936, 2003.

[39] D. Zhang, M. M. Islam, G. Lu, and I. J. Sumana. Rotation invariant curvelet features for region based image retrieval. *IJCV*, 98(2):187–201, 2012.

[40] K. Zhang, W. Zhang, Y. Zheng, and X. Xue. Sparse reconstruction for weakly supervised semantic segmentation. In *IJCAI*, pages 1889–1895, 2013.

[41] L. Zhang, M. Song, Z. Liu, X. Liu, J. Bu, and C. Chen. Probabilistic graphlet cut: Exploiting spatial structure cue for weakly supervised image segmentation. In *CVPR*, pages 1908–1915, 2013.

[42] D. Zhou, J. Huang, and B. Schölkopf. Learning with hypergraphs: Clustering, classification, and embedding. *NIPS*, 19:1601–1608, 2007.

[43] G. Zhu, S. Yan, and Y. Ma. Image tag refinement towards low-rank, content-tag prior and error sparsity. In *ACM MM*, pages 461–470, 2010.

[44] L. Zhuang, H. Gao, Z. Lin, Y. Ma, X. Zhang, and N. Yu. Non-negative low rank and sparse graph for semi-supervised learning. In *CVPR*, pages 2328–2335, 2012.

Fused One-vs-All Mid-Level Features for Fine-Grained Visual Categorization

Xiaopeng Zhang[1], Hongkai Xiong[1], Wengang Zhou[2], Qi Tian[3]

[1] Dept. of Electronic Engineering, Shanghai Jiao Tong University, Shanghai, 200240, China

[2] Dept. of EEIS, University of Science and Technology of China, Hefei, 230027, China

[3] Dept. of Computer Science, University of Texas at San Antonio, Texas, TX 78249

{zxphistory, xionghongkai}@sjtu.edu.cn[1], zhwg@ustc.edu.cn[2], qitian@cs.utsa.edu[3]

ABSTRACT

As an emerging research topic, fine-grained visual categorization has been attracting growing attentions in recent years. Due to the large inter-class similarity and intra-class variance, recognizing objects in fine-grained domains is extremely challenging, and sometimes even humans can not recognize them accurately. Traditional bag-of-words model could obtain desirable results for basic-level category classification by weak alignment using spatial pyramid matching model, but may easily fail in fine-grained domains since the discriminative features are not only subtle but also extremely localized. The fine differences often get swamped by those irrelevant features, and it is virtually impossible to distinguish them.

To address the problems above, we propose a new framework for fine-grained visual categorization. We strengthen the spatial correspondence among parts by including foreground segmentation and part localization. Based on the part representations of the images, we learn a large set of mid-level features which are more suitable for fine-grained tasks. Comparing with the low level features directly extracted from the images, the learned one-vs-all mid-level features enjoy the following advantages. First, the dimension of the mid-level features is relatively small. In order to obtain high classification accuracy, the dimension of the low level features usually reaches several thousand to tens of thousand, and becomes even larger when introducing spatial pyramid model. However, the dimension of our mid-level features is related to the number of classes, which is far less. Second, each entry of the proposed mid-level features is meaningful, which forms a more compact representation of the image. Third, the mid-level features are more robust than the low level ones, which is helpful for classification. Fourth, the learning process of the mid-level features is independent and can be easily combined with other techniques to boost the performance. We evaluate the proposed approach on the extensive fine-grained dataset CUB 200-2011 and Stanford Dogs, by learning the mid-level features based on the popular Fisher vectors and convolutional neural network, we boost the classification accuracy by a considerable margin and advance the state-of-the-art performance in fine-grained visual categorization.

Categories and Subject Descriptors

H.4 [**Information Systems Applications**]: Miscellaneous

General Terms

Algorithms, Experimentation

Keywords

Mid-level Features; Fine-Grained Visual Categorization; Convolutional Neural Networks; Image Similarity

1. INTRODUCTION

As an emerging research topic, fine-grained visual categorization discriminates typically hundreds of sub-categories belonging to the same basic-level category. It lies between the basic-level category classification (*e.g.* The PASCAL VOC dataset including bikes, boats, cars and so on) and the identification of individual instances (*e.g.* face recognition). The major challenge lies in great intra class variation and sometimes small inter-class variation. Taking the widely used fine-grained dataset CUB 200-2011 as an example, as shown in Fig. 1, it is even difficult for the humans to recognize them accurately. The basic-level categorization such as distinguishing a car from a dog is easy because there are plenty of helpful visual cues to tell them apart, while for fine-grained visual categorization, there are much fewer discriminative features compared with that at the basic-level. The differences between fine-grained classes are very subtle and extremely localized, *e.g.* only the shape of the beak or the color of the crown matter when recognizing similar birds species.

Traditional Bag-of-Features [7] framework has been widely used in various image classification applications due to its simpleness and effectiveness. However, with the ignorance of spatial layout information of the features, it suffers severely limited descriptive capability. A standard way to introduce weak geometry in Bag-of-Features representation is the use of spatial histogram [17], which defines pooling regions based on a uniform grid at predefined scales (typically the whole image, then quadrants, sixteenths, *etc.*). The spatial pyramid matching method is effective for basic-level category classification, but suffers in fine-grained domains

MM'14, November 3–7, 2014, Orlando, Florida, USA.

http://dx.doi.org/10.1145/2647868.2654937.

Figure 1: Sample images from the CUB-200-2011 dataset, which shows (a) great intra class variance and (b) small inter-class variance. It's hard even for humans to recognize them accurately.

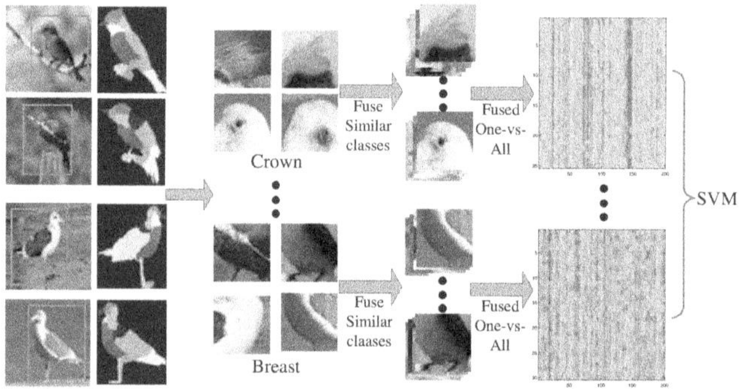

Figure 2: An overview framework of our proposed algorithm. Foreground segmentation and part localization are performed before feature extraction. The fused one-vs-all mid-level features are defined by specifying any part, fusing classes with similar parts into one super-class, and supervised learning one-vs-all mid-level features with SVM, then another SVM classifier is learned based on the mid-level features to get the final classification results.

due to the highly localized nature of distinguished features. The fact implies that a stronger correspondence should be considered to achieve higher classification accuracy. Hence, all of current works on fine-grained visual categorization use part-based features in one way or another. As a matter of fact, fine-grained visual categorization conveniently enables part-based models, as all the sub-categories share the same type of parts and attributes. For example, all birds should have beaks, wings and legs. Once the discriminative parts are determined, they are encoded into different parts of visual words, enabling the classifier to pick up the differences based on parts. On the other hand, it is well known that the background information often offers useful clues in basic-level categorization. For example, the background road is helpful for classifying cars from other categories. However, backgrounds are seldom discriminative for fine-grained visual categorization because all of them are in the similar scene. For example, all birds are usually either on trees or flying in the sky. Hence, ignoring the background information is a reasonable operation. In the light of these observations, it is necessary to incorporate foreground segmentation and part localization into fine-grained categorization to improve the classification accuracy.

Most of current classification tasks follow the pipeline of extracting basic descriptors like SIFT and HOG, quantizing the descriptors into compact visual words and pooling the visual word histograms for image representation. However, these low level features may not be optimal for specific classification tasks due to the well-known semantic gap [18] between low level features and high-level image semantics. Furthermore, extremely large dimension of the low level features, especially for Fish vectors, leads to overfitting in a discriminative hyperplane spanned by the linear classifiers, which degrades the classification accuracy and increases the computational complexity. Various methods are proposed to address these problems. Since single descriptor might fail to capture the rich information within local pathes, it is reasonable to extract multiple descriptors for compensation. They are more discriminative for classification as they describe the image from multiple aspects. By simply concatenating different descriptors together, [3] has outperformed the state-of-the-art result using single descriptor. The others [25], [4], [29] learn semantic representations of the images by aggregating neighboring descriptors to form micro-features or visual phrases. In comparison to the low level features, they are more meaningful. However, they are de facto low level features suffering from the dimension dilemma.

This paper proposes a new framework for fine-grained visual categorization based on the above observations. As shown in Fig. 2, first, we infer the foreground objects and localize the parts to enable part-based feature extractions. Coarse-to-fine part localization is obtained according to the accessibility of the ground truth part annotations. Second, we learn one-vs-all mid-level features part by part based on the extracted low level features. Compared with the high-dimensional low level features directly extracted from the images, the proposed mid-level features are dimension friendly, entry meaningful and robust for classification. The dimension of the mid-level features is related to the number of classes, which is far less than that of the low level ones and each entry of the mid-level features has specific meaning. Furthermore, our proposed learning algorithm can be easily combined with other techniques to boost the performance. Integrating all these techniques produces a more powerful framework for fine-grained visual categorization, and outperforms the state-of-the-art classification accuracy by a noticeable margin.

The rest of this paper is organized as follows. In Section 2, we review related works on fine-grained visual categorization. In Section 3, foreground segmentation and part localization are performed before feature extraction. Depending on the accessibility of the ground truth part annotations, alternative methods are selected to obtain fine or coarse segmentation and localization results. Section 4 presents the detailed algorithm of learning one-vs-all mid-level features with elaborated analysis of their principles. Furthermore, the fused one-vs-all mid-level features are proposed to enhance the performance. Experimental results are shown in Section 5. Finally, we draw our conclusion in Section 6.

2. RELATED WORK

Fine-grained categorization has been studied only recently and quickly becomes a popular topic in recognition. Previous works have aimed at various aspects of fine-grained categorization, such as the localization of parts, the description of the part objects and the human in the loop techniques to boost recognition accuracy.

2.1 Fine-Grained Part Localization

Part-based methods have recently experienced renewed interest and success [12]. Fine-grained visual categorization also conveniently enables the part-based approaches because objects belong to the same basic level often share the same parts. The detection of fine-grained categories includes segmenting the objects of interest from the background and localizing the individual parts of the objects. In [6] Chai *et al.* introduce techniques that can improve both segmentation and part localization accuracy by co-segmentation. Considering the varied poses and appearances of bird species, Zhang *et al.* [27] propose pose pooling kernel to define semantic pooling regions and aggregate features from each part regions. In [19] Parkhi *et al.* propose to use deformable part models to detect the head of the cats and the dogs. Berg *et al.* [2] propose to automatically detect part locations using the face localization methods. The work in [26] accomplishes unsupervised learning of a deformable part model to find discriminative parts for fine-grained categorization. These methods attempt to find parts of the images that are discriminative in different ways without the explicit part labels, but can't achieve the accuracy performance of a supervised part-based approach. In [24], Xie *et al.* use the Ultrametric Contour Map as an unsupervised algorithms to calculate the closed boundaries with the guidance of the part annotations. Although its accuracy performance is promising, it suffers the debate of using too many human annotations, which is unrealistic in real-word applications.

2.2 Fine-Grained Descriptors

For the description of fine-grained objects, different proposals have been made in the literature. The most widely used descriptors are color SIFT, gray SIFT descriptors plus color histogram [6], [13]. Zhang *et al.* [28] use gradient, local binary pattern, RGB color and normalized RGB color based kernel descriptors. A common characteristic of these descriptors is that they are largely handcrafted. They are all comprising dense sampling of local image patches, describing them by means of low level visual descriptors, encoding them into a high-dimensional representation, and pooling over the images. There are also works trying to learn features from the dataset. Berg *et al.* [2] build part-based one-vs-one features library which are discriminative mid-level features, and use these features for classification.

Recently, these handcrafted descriptors have been substantially outperformed by the introduction of convolutional neural networks [15], which have a more complicated structure than traditional representations. They contain several layers of non-linear feature extractors, and are said to be deep representation of images (in contrast, traditional descriptors such as SIFT would be referred as shallow representation). These networks have achieved competition-winning numbers on large benchmark dataset. It has been demonstrated that training a convolutional network to simultaneously classify, locate and detect objects in images can boost both the classification accuracy and localization accuracy [20]. The advantage of convolutional neural networks is that the system is end-to-end, and alleviates the requirement to manually design a suitable feature extractor. Though not specifically designed to model subcategory level differences, it has been demonstrated that [10] the convolutional neural network features capture such information well and obtain the state-of-the-art results for fine-grained visual categorization so far.

2.3 Human Interaction

Since fine-grained visual categorization is difficult for both humans and computers, an interactive method that assists a human in discovering the true class is useful and preferable. Human interaction methods have recently experienced a strong resurgence in popularity. Deng *et al.* [9] propose a "human-in-the-loop" approach to find accurate distinctive regions for recognition. It resorts to an online game Bubble to help find which part/parts are more helpful for categorization, then SIFT descriptors are extracted from these labeled regions for training classifiers. Duan *et al.* [11] propose to use a latent conditional random field to generate localized attributes that are both machine and human friendly, and employ a recommender system that selects attributes likely to be semantically meaningful, then human interaction is used to provide semantic names for the discovered attributes.

3. SEGMENTATION AND PART LOCALIZATION

For the fine-grained visual categorization, almost all the categories share similar background clutters. Ignoring the background information is a reasonable preprocessing step since background seldom offers useful clues for recognition of sub-categories. On the other hand, the regular spatial pyramid model often fails to align the corresponding parts in the fine-grained tasks, we need a more accurate part alignment method to capture the semantic parts of the objects. We chose two different kinds of foreground segmentation and part localization methods, namely fine part localization and coarse part localization, according to the accessibility of the ground truth part annotations.

3.1 Segmentation and Part Localization with Ground Truth Part Annotations

The ground truth part annotations provided in the CUB 200-2011 [22] dataset include the locations of fifteen parts, *e.g* back, beak, belly and so on. With the help of the provided bounding boxes and part annotations, we could obtain accurate foreground masks and fine part localization results. We use the Grab-Cut algorithms [5] for foreground segmentation as in [24]. The initial mask is constructed using ground truth part annotations, the pixels outside the bounding boxes are regarded as definite background, the annotations are regarded as definite foreground and the others are regarded as possible foreground. In the vast majority of cases the algorithms are able to return a rather precise contour of the object.

With the guidance of part annotations, we calculate the Ultrametric Contour Map [1] of the foreground object, which generates closed contours with decreasing boundary intensities to cut the image into smaller and smaller regions. De-

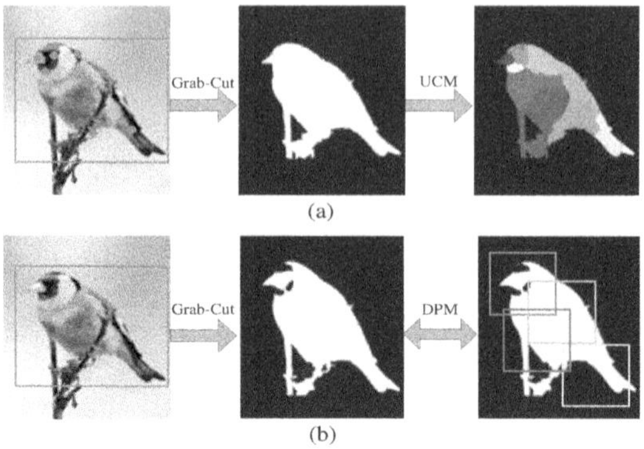

Figure 3: The foreground segmentation and part localization in different situations. (a) With ground truth part annotations, fine part localization can be obtained via Grab-Cut and Ultrametric Contour Map segmentation. (b) Using the Grab-Cut and Deformable Part Model interactively to obtain coarse part localization with only provided bounding boxes, the color boxes frame the detected part regions.

note the image as $U = (u_{i,j})_{W \times H}$, where $u_{i,j}$ is the pixel values at position (i, j), we construct a directed graph $G = (V, \varepsilon)$, where $V = \{v_{ij}\}$ consists of all pixels, and ε represents edges connecting adjacent pixels:

$$\varepsilon = \{(v_{ij} \to v_{i'j'}) | \mid i - i' \mid + \mid j - j' \mid = 1\} \quad (1)$$

The weight of an edge is related to the boundary intensity at the tail node, which is denoted as:

$$\omega = (v_{ij} \to v_{i'j'}) = u_{i'j'} + \lambda \quad (2)$$

here, λ is called step penalty, which takes the geometric distance into consideration. After the graph is complete, we take the part annotation points as seed nodes, and calculate their shortest paths to the other nodes. The segmentation process is to assign each node to its nearest part annotation nodes, taking both the intensity values and coordinate distance into consideration. The segmentation and part localization process is illustrated in Fig. 3(a), the foreground in different colors represents different part regions.

3.2 Segmentation and Part Localization without Ground Truth Part Annotations

The ground truth part annotations need trivial manual calibration and do not give automatically classification performance. To accomplish automatical classification, without loss of generality, we also include segmentation and part localization results without the ground truth part annotations. The deformable part model [12] is the most widely used part-based object detection model for automatic part localization. Chai *et al.* [6] have demonstrated that the foreground segmentation and part localization can boost each other if they are performed interactively, better segmentation results can be obtained by taking part localization into account when performing segmentation and likewise, more accurate parts can be detected if the foreground masks are considered when performing part localization. Based on the deformable part model W and saliency model S trained using a set of training images, the model is fitted to an image I via jointly optimizing the Grab-Cut and deformable part model objective functions:

$$E(p, f, c|W, S, I) = \alpha E^{dpm}(p|W, I) + \beta E^{gc}(f, c|I) + E^{c}(p, f|S) \quad (3)$$

Here, p, f, c represent the part localization, the foreground mask and the color distributions of the foreground and background, respectively. α and β are weights controlling the balance between the energy terms. E^{dpm} and E^{gc} are the deformable part model and grab cut energy function, E^{c} is a penalty function which penalizes the case where the foreground segmentation f and part localization p do not agree. By imposing the consistency between foreground segmentation and part localization, better segmentation and part localization results can be obtained comparing to simply concatenation of the two operations. Sample segmentation and part localization results are shown in Fig. 3(b).

4. LEARNING MID-LEVEL FEATURES

Based on the foreground segmentation and part localizations, different features can be extracted from each part. The image I can be represented as a set of local features:

$$D = \{(f_1, R_1), (f_2, R_2), ..., (f_M, R_M)\} \quad (4)$$

where f_i, R_i, $i \in \{1, 2, ..., M\}$ denote the ith feature vector and the occupied region respectively, and M is the total number of regions. The features can be obtained via traditional methods such as Fisher vector aggregating SIFT-like low level descriptors or convolutional neural networks.

We could get the representation of the image by simply concatenating different part features into a long feature vector, then traditional SVM classifier is learned and evaluated based on the long feature vectors. It's the pipeline that most of the classification tasks follow. However, this kind of image representation is not only high dimensional (to achieve high classification accuracy, the dimension of the low level features could be as large as tens of thousand, and even larger when concatenating different parts into a long one) but also entry meaningless, from which we could not interpret what does each entry of the features mean. Furthermore, with these high-dimensional feature vectors, a discriminative hyperplane can be easily obtained even using linear classifier, but it may also introduce overfitting and perform badly on the test features. Based on these observations, we try to learn mid-level features which are dimensional friendly and semantic meaningful, and robust to some extent when performing classification.

4.1 One-vs-All Mid-Level Features

Our method requires as input part-based features extracted from the same part of different objects, and annotated with class labels. Attempting to learn mid-level features is intuitive since they share more semantic meanings than low level ones. Given the reference dataset, let the training set consists of images belong to N classes $\{1, ..., N\}$ and includes P parts $\{1, ...P\}$. The one-vs-all mid-level features are learned as follows:

1. Select any part $p \in \{1, ..., P\}$ from the objects.

2. Learning one-vs-all mid-level features based on the part p features. Choosing the part features from all the classes $\{1, ..., N\}$ which describe the part p, except those zero vectors, we denote these features as f^p . Based on the part features f^p, we learn a one-vs-all SVM classifier, and project

the part features f^p to get one-vs-all scores based on the learned SVM weights. The dimension of the projected scores is equal to the number of classes, which is N dimension in our definitions.

3. According to the projection transformation, all the low level training features are mapped into the new mid-level feature space. After an L_2 normalization, we simply concatenate the mid-level features part by part, by this way we can obtain our mid-level feature representation for any training image.

4. For any image in the test set, we extract low level features based on part p, and project corresponding part features to N dimensional vector according to the learned SVM weights. Concatenating the mid-level features the same as the training ones, from which we can get our one-vs-all mid-level features for test images.

After a simple one-vs-all transformation, all the low level features are projected to the mid-level feature space. The advantages of the learned mid-level features over the low level ones are obvious. Firstly, the dimension of the mid-level features is far less than that of the low level ones, since the transformation projects the low level features to N dimensional feature vectors regardless of the dimension of the low level features, where N is the number of classes, so the total dimension of the mid-level features is NP, which are only several thousand in most situations. We would demonstrate the super-performance of the learned mid-level features in the following sections. Secondly, comparing with the low level features which are entry meaningless, every entry of the mid-level features has specific semantic meaning. For example, given a reference image x, denote the mid-level features for part p as $X^p = \{X_1^p, X_2^p, ...X_N^p\}$, The score $X_i^p(i \in \{1, ...N\})$ represents the signed distance between current image to category i for part p. The larger the value X_i^p is, the more similar of image x with category i for part p. This kind of formulation is very helpful and understandable for classification, if X_i^p is larger than any other scores in X_p, we can say that part p of image x is most similar with that of class i.

4.2 Deep Insights for One-vs-All Mid-Level Features

Now we have a deep insight into the one-vs-all mid-level features. The learned method is easy to understand, however, the intuition behind the simple algorithm is not that straightforward. Here, we clarify the advantages of our proposed one-vs-all mid-level features to give a better understanding of it. For a given part $p \in \{1, ..., P\}$, given a set of part-level features together with their corresponding labels (x_i^p, y_i^p), $i = 1, ..., l$, $x_i^p \in R^n$ and $y_i^p \in \{1, ..., N\}$, where l, n, N denote the number of training instances, the dimension of low level features and the number of classes, respectively. The one-vs-all SVM classifier based on this part tries to solve the following optimization problem:

$$\min_{w_m, \xi_i^p} \quad \frac{1}{2}\sum_{m=1}^{N} w_m^T w_m + C\sum_{i=1}^{l} \xi_i^p \qquad (5)$$
$$s.t. \quad w_{y_i^p}^T x_i^p - w_m^T x_i^p \geq e_i^{pm} - \xi_i^p, i = 1, ..., l$$

where

$$e_i^{pm} = \begin{cases} 0, & \text{if } y_i^p = m \\ 1, & \text{if } y_i^p \neq m \end{cases}$$

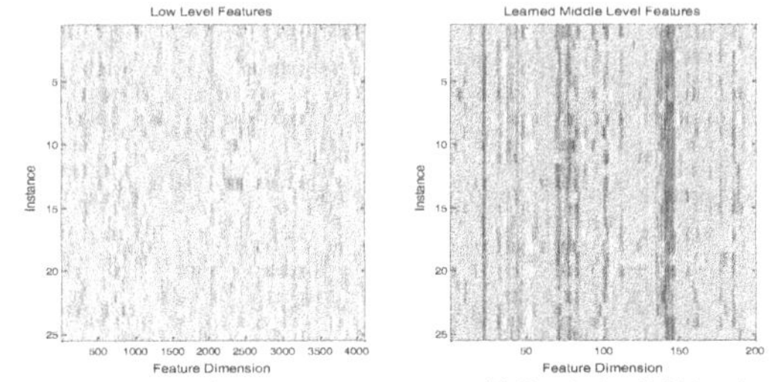

(a) Magnitude of Low-Level Features (b) Magnitude of Mid-Level Features (c) Weight Coefficient Distribution of Low-Level Features (d) Weight Coefficient Distribution of Mid-Level Features

Figure 4: The upper row shows the magnitude distribution of (a) the low level features and (b) the learned mid-level features for a given part, both from the same class. The lower row shows the corresponding SVM weights learned from the two kinds of features. Different colors represent different magnitudes, which are sorted in descending order and correspond to colors of red, yellow and blue. Note that in (a), the magnitude distribution is irregular while in (b) it exhibits regular stripes, especially the red line around dimension 25. The weights lie on the diagonal from upper left to lower right are dominant in (d), while the weights are irregular in (c).

The decision function is

$$\arg\max_{m=1,\dots,N} \quad w_m^T x_i^p \qquad (6)$$

The mid-level features are the projection of the low level ones based on the learned weights, which are the signed distance to the decision hyperplane. Denote the mid-level features of x_i^p as $X_i^p = \{X_{i1}^p, X_{i2}^p, ..., X_{iN}^p\}$, each entry of X_i^p are obtained according to the following equation:

$$X_{im}^p = \frac{w_m^T x_i^p}{\|w\|_2}, \quad m = 1, 2, ..., N \qquad (7)$$

From the constrained conditions in Eq. (5), we can see that SVM classifier tends to fit the positive samples and makes the positive sample scores larger than that of the negative ones during every one-vs-all comparison in Eq. (6). Hence, for the mid-level feature X_i^p (instance i and part p) learned from the SVM classifier, $X_{iy_i^p}^p$ is usually larger than all the other entries in $X_i^p = \{X_{i1}^p, X_{i2}^p, ..., X_{iN}^p\}$. As shown in Fig. 4, the upper row of this figure shows an example of the magnitude distribution of the low level features and learned mid-level features for a given part, all belongs to the same sub-category. The magnitude of the low level features are orderless, while the learned mid-level features exhibit regular stripes, especially the one around feature dimension 25, the dark red line indicates that the magnitudes are large,

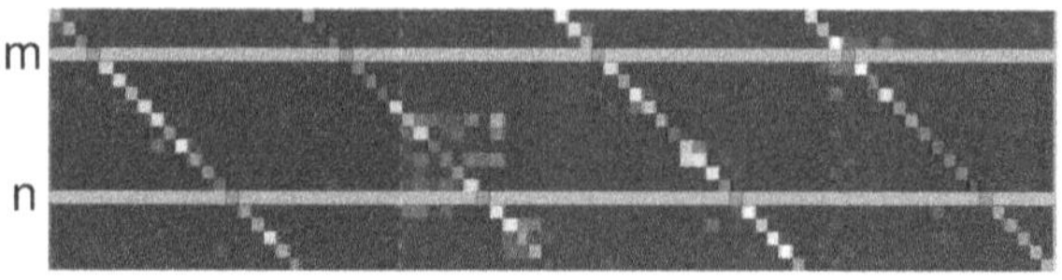

Figure 5: Illustration of robustness of the one-vs-all mid-level features. The dominant weight coefficients lie in the diagonal locations for each part. The response is robust to the disturbance in the non-dominant locations.

which means that this part is more likely belonging to the corresponding category. We simply concatenate the mid-level features part by part to obtain the representation of an image.

Next, another one-vs-all SVM classifier is trained based on these mid-level features. As Fig. 4(b) shows, for a given part p the magnitudes at the specific positions are large and stable , which makes these mid-level features robust, so the model coefficients trained on the mid-level features are large at these positions. More specifically, for a given part p, the largest coefficients in the learned model $W^p_{(N\times N)}$ are focused on $\{w_{(1,1)}, w_{(2,2)}, ..., w_{(N,N)}\}$ if the training mid-level features are ordered. As shown in Fig. 4(d), The weight coefficients lie on the diagonal from upper left to lower right are large and we call these dominate weight coefficients. As a comparison, we also show the weight coefficients learned directly based on the low level features, which are shown in Fig. 4 (c), the coefficients are irregular and we can't find any dominant weight coefficients.

Finally, based on the learned mid-level features and the weight coefficients, the ultimate classifier assigns result which has the max response in decision function just like (6). Now we elaborate the robust advantage of this kind of representation and analyze in what situations misclassification would happen. We denote the weight coefficients learned from the mid-level features as $W_{N\times NP}$. Suppose a test instance belong to class m with mid-level features $X \in R^{NP}$. Considering the following objective function:

$$\min\,(W_m^T - W_n^T)X \quad n \in \{1, 2, ..., N\}, n \neq m \tag{8}$$

If the objective value of Eq. (8) is positive, then we success this classification. Note that for weight vector W_m, $m \in \{1, 2, ..., N\}$, the most largest weight coefficients are focused on $\{W_{m,m}, W_{m,m+N}, ..., W_{m,m+(P-1)N}\}$, we call these dominant weight coefficients which contribute most to the final decision scores, as shown in Fig. 5. So the disturbance in the non-dominant entries would not influence the score $W_m^T X$ too much, hence manifest the robustness of this representation. On the other hand, the dominant weight coefficients for class n lie in $\{W_{n,n}, W_{n,n+N}, ..., W_{n,n+(P-1)N}\}$, the equation would become negative when and only when disturbance happened in both of these two locations. At this situation, classes m and n are very similar, and most of their corresponding parts are similar and couldn't tell them apart.

4.3 Fused One-vs-All Mid-Level Features

The analysis above has demonstrated the fact that in some situations the discriminative features are subtle and extremely localized. These subtle features may be easily swamped by plenty of irrelevant features. The misclassification would happen when the misclassified results are very similar with the correct ones. In the one-vs-all comparisons, we divide each part into N different classes, where N is the total number of classes. This kind of partition is not optimal since different classes may also share similar parts. It might bring into overfitting if we try to separate these very similar parts (actually they can't be distinguished only by the similar parts) and swamp discriminative features when recognizing classes sharing these similar parts. These observations suggest us to down weight the features which are not informative to discriminate similar classes. In this section, we propose a method which fuses the similar parts into a super-one to avoid dividing them into different classes, and learn one-vs-all mid-level features based on these fused classes. In order to fuse the similar classes into a bigger one, we first need to find the most similar classes for a given part. A standard L_1 or L_2 distance-based measurement is appealing for its simplicity, but considers all features to be equally important, which is unlikely to be a good idea. The low level features are high dimensional, some of them are not helpful to discriminate the classes. We wish to down weight the features that are not discriminative, and emphasize those that are. We apply a linear discriminate analysis to project the features into a low dimensional subspace and then measure the similarity between them. For consistency, we use the same notations as the last section. For a specified part p, given a set of part-level pairs (x_i^p, y_i^p), $i = 1, ..., l$, $x_i^p \in R^n$ and $y_i^p \in \{1, ..., N\}$, denote the number of samples belonging to each class as $\{n_1, n_2, ..., n_N\}$. Linear discriminant analysis projects the n dimensional features x_i^p to $K(K < n)$ dimensional subspace via finding the optimal projection matrix $W = [w_1|w_2|...|w_K]$, $w_i \in R^n, i = 1, 2, ..., K$ that minimize the ratio of within-class variance to between-class variance.

Figure 6: The similar parts found by linear discriminant analysis. The upper row shares similar back while the lower shares similar breast. Note that the classes in the same row are all different. During the one-vs-all mid-level features learning, it is better to treat the classes with similar parts as one.

After projecting the features into K dimensional subspace, for any given two classes, we measure the similarity of part features as

$$s_f = \frac{(\mu_1 - \mu_2)^2}{\sigma_1^2 + \sigma_2^2} \tag{9}$$

where μ_1 and μ_2 are the mean feature values for the two classes, and σ_1 and σ_2 are the corresponding standard de-

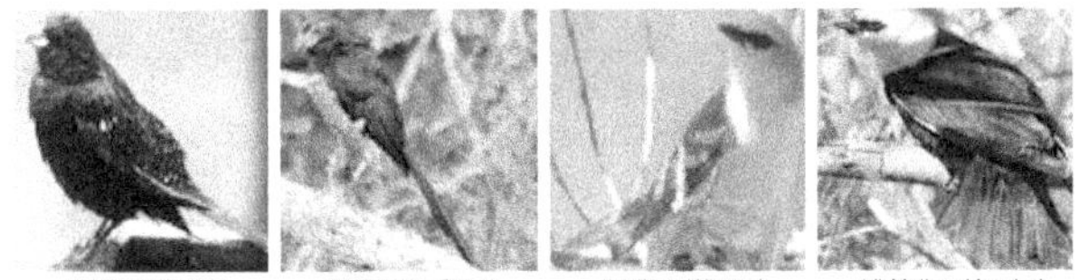

Figure 7: Classification result comparisons between the one-vs-all and the fused one-vs-all mid-level features. The one-vs-all mid-level features correctly recognize (c) Blue Winged Warbler but misclassify (a) Red Winged Blackbird as (b) Groove Billed Ani. While the fused ones correctly recognize (a) Red Winged Blackbird but misclassify (c) Blue Winged Warbler as (d) Yellow Headed Blackbird.

viations. We could get the similarity measure for any class pairs, and rank the similar classes for a given part. Fig. 6 shows an example of applying LDA similarity measurement to find the most similar classes for a given part. The upper are for part back and the lower are for part breast. All the classes in the same row are different, from which we can see that these parts are not discriminative to recognize the similar classes. As an alternative, we first fuse these similar classes into a bigger one, and learn the one-vs-all mid-level features based the fused classes.

5. EXPERIMENTAL RESULTS

5.1 Dataset

We test our method on CUB-200-2011 dataset, which is one of the most extensive datasets in fine-grained literature. It contains 11788 images spanning 200 sub-species, several of which share so tremendous similarities that even humans can't recognize them easily. Each image is labeled with its sub-species, a bounding box which encloses the object and at most 15 ground truth part annotations which indicate the locations of different parts of the images, *e.g.* beak, wings, throat and so on. Without loss of generality, we test our method in both situations: with and without part annotations. We make use of the provided bounding boxes as do most of the approaches we compared to. During Preprocessing, each image is resized to the same size, *i.e.* width and height do not exceed 500 pixels. We use the fixed train/test split provided in the dataset for all experiments. There are roughly 30 images per category to train and the rest for test. We mirror the train images to double the size of the training set, since it has been demonstrated an effective way to improve the classification accuracy to some extent. We also include results for Stanford Dogs [8], using similar experimental settings as for CUB-200-2011 Birds. For accuracy evaluation, we use the standard evaluation metric which is the average classification accuracy by category.

5.2 Implementation Details

We extract convolutional neural network features for its powerful classification capacity. The implementation [20] is used to extract CNN features. For a given part region (ground truth part or detected part), we crop the image to the minimal rectangle which enclose the given part. The output features of layer 21 are used for final representation of the given input part for its efficiency, which is a 4096 dimensional vector. In order to compute features for a part region, we must convert the image data in that region into a form that is compatible with the CNN (the structure requires inputs of a fixed 221×221 pixel size). Among the many possible transformations of arbitrary-shaped regions, we choose to resize the image to make the short side 221 and feed it to the CNN input. The output at this situation is no longer a 4096 dimensional vector, but $4096 \times n$ dimension. We chose max pooling on the multidimensional vector to get the feature vector with length 4096. Experiments show that this kind of resizing method gives higher performance than directly resizing it to 221×221 because it does not bring into aspect ratio deformation.

When it comes to encoding the images using Fisher vectors, we extract grayscale SIFT descriptors (the implementation [21] is adopted) at each part with a spatial stride of 5 and at four scales, defined by setting the width of the SIFT spatial bins to $12, 16, 20, 24$ pixels respectively. After extracting SIFT descriptors, we apply a PCA transformation to reduce the dimension to 80 and use a Gaussian mixture model with 128 components. In order to code the color information, we choose LLC [23] coded discriminative color descriptors [14] with a vocabulary of size 500. Both Fisher vectors and color features are l_2 normalized after encoding and then concatenated. For ease of expression, we denote Fisher vectors plus LLC coded color descriptors as Fisher vectors in the following experiments.

In situations with ground truth part annotations, since there are very few images in the dataset with 15 parts visible, according to the symmetry, we combine the left eye and right eye into one part, and apply the same operations on wings and legs. Thus we have 12 parts in total used for part-based recognition. In situations with detected parts, considering detecting more parts are inaccurate, we choose the same number of parts as in [6] to fix it at 4. For classification, we use a linear SVM classifier and the regularization strength is set by cross-validation.

5.3 One-vs-All vs Fused One-vs-All

We first compare the performance of our proposed two kinds of features, the one-vs-all and the fused one-vs-all mid-level features. The comparison is based on the ground truth part annotations and features extracted from convolutional neural network. By simply learning the one-vs-all mid-level features and performing another SVM classification, we could get an accuracy of 78.1%, which outperforms the state-of-the-art result [2]. One step further, we fuse the classes which share similar parts, and the number of classes decreases after fusing. We iteratively fuse the classes to a specified number according to their similarity rankings in Eq. (9) and learn the one-vs-all features based on the fused classes. For simplicity, each part has the same number of classes after fusing. The results are shown in Table 1. It is surprising that classification accuracy improves by 0.8% after the dimension for each part is reduced to 175 (which means the total dimension is 2275 after concatenation). It demonstrates that even the one-vs-all mid-level features (2600 dimension vector) are redundant to some extent, and the improvement lies in that some classes share similar parts and the fused method combines them into one to reduce the disturbance. The accuracy decreases when the fused number becomes smaller since the dimension is too small to classify correctly.

Number	200	175	150	[200;175]	All
Accuracy	78.1%	78.9%	77.0%	79.6%	78.3%

Table 1: Classification accuracies using the one-vs-all and the fused one-vs-all mid-level features.

Method	Accuracy
CNN (low level features)	75.9%
CNN (mid-level features)	79.6%
FV (low level features)	72.3%
FV (mid-level features)	75.8%
FV+CNN (low level features)	77.1%
FV+CNN (mid-level features)	81.2%

Table 2: Classification accuracies on Birds with ground truth annotations using different methods.

At the last two columns in Table 1, we concatenate the mid-level features with the fused ones and get an accuracy of 79.6%, better than any single mid-level features. It implies us to use both features to complement each other. As shown in Fig. 7, the one-vs-all mid-level features could correctly recognize (c) *Blue Winged Warbler* but misclassify (a) *Red Winged Blackbird* as (b) *Groove Billed Ani*, mainly because the subtle discriminative features (red wings) are swamped by other irrelevant features. While the fused one-vs-all mid-level features (fused number 175) could correctly recognize (a) *Red Winged Blackbird* but misclassify (c) *Blue Winged Warbler* as (d) *Yellow Headed Blackbird* . By combining these two features, both classes can be recognized correctly. In the following experiments, we combine the one-vs-all and the fused one-vs-all mid-level features for classification. We only set the fused number as 175 , and concatenate them with the one-vs-all mid-level features.

5.4 Ground Truth Part Annotations Results

In this section, we first show the experimental results with ground truth part annotations. The concatenated mid-level features have dimension of 375 per part, so the total number of dimension is 4875. The classification results are shown in Table 2 for both CNN features and Fisher vectors. As a comparison, we also list the results directly based on the low level features, because the Fisher vector for one part is already high dimensional (tens of thousand), computing similarity based on Fisher vectors is time consuming, so we directly use the similarity measurement results based on the CNN features to compute the fused classes. From results in Table 2 we can see that the learned mid-level features can boost the classification accuracy by a large margin, achieving 3.7% and 3.5% improvements comparing with the results on the low level features respectively. The last line shows the result of combing Fisher vectors and CNN features, which gives another improvement and achieves an accuracy of 81.2%, which demonstrates that these two mid-level features are complementary with each other, as far as we know, it is the highest accuracy achieved so far.

5.5 Detected Part Locations Results

To enable automatic classification without the ground truth part annotations, we also perform experiments with detected parts. We segment the object into 4 parts, together with the whole image as an extra part, extracting features within each part, and learn the one-vs-all and fused one-vs-all

Method	Birds	Dogs
CNN (low level features)	61.8%	50.1%
CNN (mid-level features)	65.3%	52.6%
FV (low level features)	58.7%	44.8%
FV (mid-level features)	61.2%	47.1%
FV+CNN (low level features)	62.9%	50.9%
FV+CNN (mid-level features)	67.6%	53.5%

Table 3: Classification accuracies with detected parts using different methods.

mid-level features for classification. The results are listed in Table 3. We obtain an accuracy of 67.6% using both Fisher vectors and CNN features, which further demonstrates that the two features complement with each other. We also include the results on Sanford Dogs dataset in the last column of Table 3, and our mid-level features achieve 2.5% and 2.3% improvements comparing with the low level ones using CNN and Fisher vectors respectively, and get an accuracy of 53.5% when combining the two kinds of features.

5.6 Time Complexity

Now we analyze time complexity of our proposed method. The training and testing based on the mid-level features is faster comparing with that on the low level ones. Taking the classification on the detected parts as an example, on our computer (Inter Core i7, CPU 3.2GHz), classification based on the mid-level features (dimension 4875) takes about 90s, mainly due to its low dimensionality, while direct classification based on the low level features costs about 190min for Fisher vectors (dimension around 100K) and 450s for C-NN features (dimension around 20K). We need extra time to learn the mid-level features. For Fisher vectors, it spends about 8min in average for each part (dimension around 20K) and 40min in total, while the time on CNN features is 80s in average (dimension 4096) and 400s in total respectively. Note that the learning process is part by part, so the time consuming is far less than that based on the whole features.

5.7 Comparisons to Previous Works

Finally, we compare our method with existing works. Many researchers have reported classification results on Birds and Dogs dataset. The comparison results on Birds using ground truth part annotations are listed in Table 4, our method outperforms the state-of-the-art result (73.3%) by a large margin. To make fare comparisons, we use our mid-level features learning algorithm directly on the extracted features in [24], and obtain an improvement about 3% with an accuracy of 69.1%, which demonstrates the effectiveness of our method. Fig. 8 shows some easiest (accuracy 100%) and hardest (accuracy below 40%) classes of our method. Even with the help of ground truth part annotations, some subcategories are still challenging due to the existence of confusing counterpart, such as *American Crow* and *Fish Crow*, *California Gull* and *Herring Gull*. Exploiting methods overcoming these problems would be a challenging future work.

More works try to perform classification without the ground truth part annotations. We compare our method with these works under the same conditions, the results are listed in Table 5. It can be seen from the results that our method outperforms all the other results, partially benefit from convolutional neural network. The result in [10] could directly demonstrate our superior performance of using mid-level

Method	Accuracy
Xie (hierarchical part matching)[24]	66.35%
Xie (mid-level features)	69.1%
Berg (POOF)[2]	73.3%
Ours (FV+CNN mid-level features)	81.2%

Table 4: Classification accuracies comparisons on Birds with ground truth part annotations.

Method	Birds	Dogs
Berg (POOF)[2]	56.78%	-
Chai (symbiotic segmentation)[6]	59.4%	45.6%
E.Gavves (alignments)[13]	62.7%	50.1%
Zhang (deformable descriptors)[28]	50.98%	-
Jia (DeCAF)[10]	64.96%	-
Ours (FV+CNN mid-level features)	67.6%	53.5%

Table 5: Classification accuracies comparisons with detected part regions.

features, which also extracts features from the convolutional neural network. By using the mid-level features, our method outperforms 2.7% comparing with their result. The improvement on Dogs is also obvious, our method exceeds the state-of-the-art result [13] by around 3.5%, to the best of our knowledge, this is the best accuracy reported so far in the literature.

At last, we compare our method with Berg's POOF [2] method, which also tries to learn some mid-level features for classification. Their features are also learned based on SVM classifier, but aim to learn one-vs-one mid-level features between any two classes for a given part. Though discriminative these features are, the shortcomings are that some entries are not informative. For example, if the binary classifier is trained based on class i and j, the meaning of the scores for other classes are not so clear, and in most situations can't be used as discriminative features for other classes. On the other hand, since the one-vs-one part pairs are so large, in order to ensure effectiveness, it randomly samples some pairs and learns mid-level features based on these pairs, which may also decrease the accuracy. Different from the POOF method, we try to learn one-vs-all mid-level features at one time, which is more effective, and the fuse algorithm further boosts the discriminative power of our mid-level features. As a comparison, we learn POOF based on CNN features, the pairs are randomly sampled and the dimension is set as 5000, which is the same as [2]. The classification accuracy is 74.2%, which is comparable with Berg's but much lower than that of our method even without combing with Fisher vectors. Besides, our learning algorithm is independent of the feature extraction steps, and can be easily combined with other methods.

6. CONCLUSIONS

In this paper, we propose a novel method to learn one-vs-all mid-level features, which is more suitable for fine-grained visual categorization. It is dimension friendly since the dimension of the learned mid-level features is only related with the number of the classes and far less than that of the low level ones. The learned mid-level features are more compact representations of images since each entry of the features represents the signed distance to the corresponding class. The novel mid-level features are more robust than the low level ones. Considering different classes may share similar parts, we fuse classes with similar parts to super one and learn fused one-vs-all mid-level features based on the fused classes. We combine the two kinds of mid-level features into a powerful discriminative features for fine-grained visual categorization. Furthermore, we demonstrate the complementary characteristics of Fisher vectors and convolutional neural network features. Combining all the techniques we outperform the state-of-the-art results by a large margin on both Birds and Dogs dataset.

Our one-vs-all mid-level features are somewhat attribute features, which are similar with [16]. They are both mid-level semantic representations of the images. The fused one-vs-all mid-level features coincide with the characteristic of attributes that several classes share the same attributes. If we treat each class of a given part as an attribute, each entry of the mid-level features can be regarded as a continuous attribute value corresponding to that class. Different from the binary attributes extracted from [16] which need human annotations and have the form like black, water, eat fish, our features are relative attributes and don't need human interactions. Though overlapping to some extent (different classes may share similar attributes), they are applicable to detect unseen object classes, which needs to be verified in the future works.

7. ACKNOWLEDGMENTS

This work was supported in part by National Science Foundation of China (NSFC) under contact No. U1201255, 61271218, 61228101 and 61128007, in part to Dr. Zhou by the Fundamental Research Funds for the Central Universities under contract No. WK2100060014, the start-up funding from the University of Science and Technology of China under contract No. KY2100000036, and in part to Dr. Tian by ARO grant W911NF-12-1-0057, and Faculty Research Award by NEC Laboratories of America, respectively.

8. REFERENCES

[1] P. Arbelaez, M. Maire, C. Fowlkes, and J. Malik. From contours to regions: An empirical evaluation. *Computer Vision and Pattern Recognition*, pages 2294–2301, 2009.

[2] T. Berg and P. N. Belhumeur. POOF: Part-based one-vs-one features for fine-grained categorization, face verification, and attribute estimation. *Computer Vision and Pattern Recognition*, pages 955–962, 2013.

[3] A. Bosch, A. Zisserman, and X. Munoz. Image classification using random forests and ferns. *International Conference on Computer Vision*, pages 1–8, 2007.

[4] Y.-L. Boureau, F. Bach, Y. LeCun, and J. Ponce. Learning mid-level features for recognition. *Computer Vision and Pattern Recognition*, pages 2559–2566, 2010.

[5] Y. Boykov, O. Veksler, and R. Zabih. Fast approximate energy minimization via graph cuts. *IEEE Transactions on Pattern Analysis and Machine Intelligence*, 23(11):1222–1239, 2001.

[6] Y. Chai, V. Lempitsky, and A. Zisserman. Symbiotic segmentation and part localization for fine-grained

Figure 8: Example classification results on Birds with ground truth part annotations. Top: some classes our method achieves 100% accuracy. Bottom: some classes our method performs poorly.

categorization. *International Conference on Computer Vision*, pages 321–328, 2013.

[7] G. Csurka, C. Dance, L. Fan, J. Willamowski, and C. Bray. Visual categorization with bags of keypoints. *Workshop on Statistical Learning in Computer Vision, ECCV*, 1(1-22):1–2, 2004.

[8] E. I. D. Dataset. Novel datasets for fine-grained image categorization. *First Workshop on Fine Grained Visual Categorization, CVPR*, 2011.

[9] J. Deng, J. Krause, and L. Fei-Fei. Fine-grained crowdsourcing for fine-grained recognition. *Computer Vision and Pattern Recognition*, pages 580–587, 2013.

[10] J. Donahue, Y. Jia, O. Vinyals, J. Hoffman, N. Zhang, E. Tzeng, and T. Darrell. Decaf: A deep convolutional activation feature for generic visual recognition. *arXiv preprint arXiv:1310.1531*, 2013.

[11] K. Duan, D. Parikh, D. Crandall, and K. Grauman. Discovering localized attributes for fine-grained recognition. *Computer Vision and Pattern Recognition*, pages 3474–3481, 2012.

[12] P. Felzenszwalb, D. McAllester, and D. Ramanan. A discriminatively trained, multiscale, deformable part model. *Computer Vision and Pattern Recognition*, pages 1–8, 2008.

[13] E. Gavves, B. Fernando, C. G. Snoek, A. W. Smeulders, and T. Tuytelaars. Fine-grained categorization by alignments. *International Conference on Computer Vision*, pages 1713–1720, 2013.

[14] R. Khan, J. Van de Weijer, F. S. Khan, D. Muselet, C. Ducottet, and C. Barat. Discriminative color descriptors. *Computer Vision and Pattern Recognition*, pages 2866–2873, 2013.

[15] A. Krizhevsky, I. Sutskever, and G. E. Hinton. Imagenet classification with deep convolutional neural networks. *Advances in Neural Information Processing Systems*, pages 1097–1105, 2012.

[16] C. H. Lampert, H. Nickisch, and S. Harmeling. Learning to detect unseen object classes by between-class attribute transfer. *Computer Vision and Pattern Recognition*, pages 951–958, 2009.

[17] S. Lazebnik, C. Schmid, and J. Ponce. Beyond bags of features: Spatial pyramid matching for recognizing natural scene categories. *Computer Vision and Pattern Recognition*, pages 2169–2178, 2006.

[18] Y. Lu, L. Zhang, J. Liu, and Q. Tian. Constructing concept lexica with small semantic gaps. *IEEE Transactions on Multimedia*, 12(4):288–299, 2010.

[19] O. M. Parkhi, A. Vedaldi, A. Zisserman, and C. Jawahar. Cats and dogs. *Computer Vision and Pattern Recognition*, pages 3498–3505, 2012.

[20] P. Sermanet, D. Eigen, X. Zhang, M. Mathieu, R. Fergus, and Y. LeCun. Overfeat: Integrated recognition, localization and detection using convolutional networks. *arXiv preprint arXiv:1312.6229*, 2013.

[21] A. Vedaldi and B. Fulkerson. Vlfeat: An open and portable library of computer vision algorithms. *ACM Multimedia*, pages 1469–1472, 2010.

[22] C. Wah, S. Branson, P. Welinder, P. Perona, and S. Belongie. The Caltech-UCSD Birds-200-2011 dataset. *Technical Report*, CNS-TR-2011-001.

[23] J. Wang, J. Yang, K. Yu, F. Lv, T. Huang, and Y. Gong. Locality-constrained linear coding for image classification. *Computer Vision and Pattern Recognition*, pages 3360–3367, 2010.

[24] L. Xie, Q. Tian, R. Hong, S. Yan, and B. Zhang. Hierarchical part matching for fine-grained visual categorization. *International Conference on Computer Vision*, pages 1641–1648, 2013.

[25] L. Xie, Q. Tian, and B. Zhang. Spatial pooling of heterogeneous features for image applications. *ACM Multimedia*, pages 539–548, 2012.

[26] S. Yang, L. Bo, J. Wang, and L. G. Shapiro. Unsupervised template learning for fine-grained object recognition. *Advances in Neural Information Processing Systems*, pages 3122–3130, 2012.

[27] N. Zhang, R. Farrell, and T. Darrell. Pose pooling kernels for sub-category recognition. *Computer Vision and Pattern Recognition*, pages 3665–3672, 2012.

[28] N. Zhang, R. Farrell, F. Iandola, and T. Darrell. Deformable part descriptors for fine-grained recognition and attribute prediction. *International Conference on Computer Vision*, pages 729–736, 2013.

[29] L. Zheng and S. Wang. Visual phraselet: Refining spatial constraints for large scale image search. *IEEE Transactions on Signal Processing Letters*, 20(4):391–394, 2013.

Scalable Visual Instance Mining with Threads of Features *

Wei Zhang†, Hongzhi Li‡, Chong-Wah Ngo†, Shih-Fu Chang‡
† Dept. of Computer Science, City University of Hong Kong
‡ Dept. of Computer Science, Columbia University
wzhang34-c@my.cityu.edu.hk, hongzhili@cs.columbia.edu
cscwngo@cityu.edu.hk, sfchang@cs.columbia.edu

ABSTRACT

We address the problem of visual instance mining, which is to extract frequently appearing visual instances automatically from a multimedia collection. We propose a scalable mining method by exploiting Thread of Features (ToF). Specifically, ToF, a compact representation that links consistent features across images, is extracted to reduce noises, discover patterns, and speed up processing. Various instances, especially small ones, can be discovered by exploiting correlated ToFs. Our approach is significantly more effective than other methods in mining small instances. At the same time, it is also more efficient by requiring much fewer hash tables. We compared with several state-of-the-art methods on two fully annotated datasets: MQA and Oxford, showing large performance gain in mining (especially small) visual instances. We also run our method on another Flickr dataset with one million images for scalability test. Two applications, instance search and multimedia summarization, are developed from the novel perspective of instance mining, showing great potential of our method in multimedia analysis.

Categories and Subject Descriptors

H.3.3 [**Information Storage and Retrieval**]: Information Search and Retrieval

Keywords

Instance Mining; Thread of Features; min-Hash; Clustering; Summarization

1. INTRODUCTION

In the past decade, multimedia researchers mainly focused on visual search (given a query, retrieve similar images), while visual mining has not yet been fully studied. This paper addresses the problem of *visual instance mining*, which is to automatically discover and extract frequent visual instances out of a data collection. The term "*instance*" in this paper is referred as a specific "visual entity" (e.g., an object/location/logo/person). We highlight this problem by comparing with its relatives: (1) different from visual search, instance mining does not have any query as entry point; (2) compared to general "object class" discovery (e.g., car, dog) [2, 8, 18, 23], specific instances (e.g., this car, this dog) are expected as output; (3) compared to image-level clustering [15], instance mining also extracts objects covering small image areas.

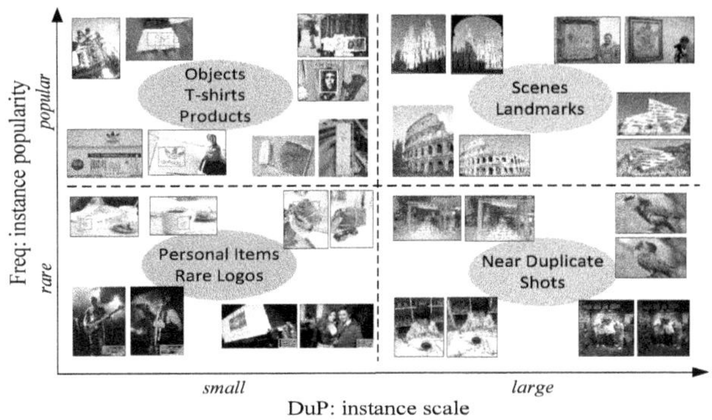

Figure 1: A wide range of visual instances, plotted on a 2D plane of "Freq-DuP". Note *Freq* is the number of images sharing an instance, and *DuP* indicates the instance scale. We propose a robust instance mining method, particularly effective for small scale instances.

As shown in Fig. 1, there are various instances in a real-world data collection. Roughly, they can be characterized by two dimensions: "Frequency" (Freq) and "Duplicate Proportion" (DuP). "Freq" of an instance is the number of images sharing that instance, and "DuP" denotes the duplicate proportion among images with the instance. Roughly speaking, "Freq" depicts the popularity (rare or popular) of an instance, and "DuP" indicates the instance scale (small or large). Small and rare instances (Fig. 1 bottom-left) correspond to personal belongings (e.g., a personal mug) or rare logos. Large and popular instances (top-right) are mostly famous landmarks or scenes, while large and rare ones (bottom-right) are often near duplicates shots (probably taken by the same user within a short time of period). Small and popular instances (top-left) are usually consistent patterns featuring popular objects (e.g., famous prod-

*Area chair: Xian-Sheng Hua

MM'14, November 3–7, 2014, Orlando, Florida, USA.
Copyright 2014 ACM 978-1-4503-3063-3/14/11 ...$15.00.
http://dx.doi.org/10.1145/2647868.2654942.

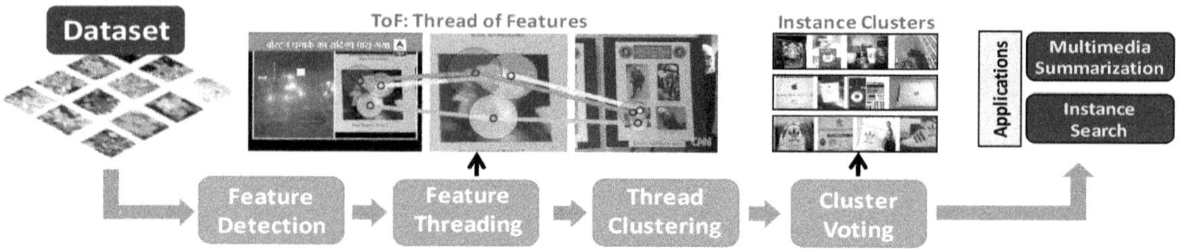

Figure 2: The framework of our proposed instance mining approach.

ucts, visual memes). For a real application, Freq is usually positively correlated with the popularity/significance of an instance, and DuP is negatively correlated with the mining difficulty.

Mining frequent instances from large multimedia collection is essential for many tasks in multimedia analysis, such as multimedia summarization, trend predication, product recommendation and instance search. For example, given the photos uploaded in a certain time and location (e.g., Flickr photos uploaded during last year in New York City), instance mining could be applied to (1) organize the collection for browsing; (2) discover popular items (e.g., restaurant, tee) or events (e.g., Macy's parade); (3) analyze trends for fashion/product/tourism. As shown in Fig. 8, 9 and 10, popular instances mined from a dataset could be treated as a "high-level" feature for understanding the dataset. People can grasp the key ideas of the data collection with a quick glance at the mining results, saving a lot of time and effort. Another interesting aspect to note is the serendipity in mining results. Some instances in the dataset could be very difficult to be noticed by a human. However, automatic mining could reveal some of these underlying features.

Instance mining is still challenging in terms of efficiency and effectiveness. Most existing methods suffer from either scalability or quality issue. Methods designed for small instances [11, 22, 24, 20] can only handle few thousands of images. On the other hand, scalable methods [14, 4, 5] are mostly less compatible with small instances. Scalable instance-level mining remains to be a problem. In this work, we address both problems at the same time, targeting for mining all frequent instances, especially small ones, at million scale dataset. Specifically, a two-step framework is adopted. As shown in Fig. 2, we first thread features that potentially share an instance via efficient pruning, and then cluster these threads to vote for instance clusters. The first step is motivated by the fact that only a very small fraction of local features, which are likely to repeat among images, are helpful in instance mining. We highlight these features by threading them together. The second step is featured by threads clustering rather than image clustering, which significantly boosts the chance of mining small instances.

The main contribution of this paper is the proposal of a visual mining approach that addresses the scalability and small issues at the same time. Compared to other methods, our approach is more effective in mining small instances, while being scalable for million scale dataset. Furthermore, through two applications, we show novel solutions to the problem of instance search and multimedia summarization. Both of our applications are the first attempts to solve the original problems (search/summarization) from a new perspective of data mining.

2. RELATED WORKS

In this section, we review related works based on their targeting instance types.

Small Instances Mining. Methods designed for *small* instances usually work on small scale dataset.

Early studies on Common Pattern Discovery [11, 22, 24] model this as an optimization problem. These methods are computational expensive, thus can only operate on small scale dataset (up to few hundreds images). It is reported in [11] that two hours of running time is required for a dataset with 600 images.

Another approach is Frequent Itemset Mining, which are initially used to find sets of products bought together by customers (e.g., beer and diaper). Sophisticated algorithms, i.e., APriori [1], Eclat [25], and FP-growth [7], have been developed for this purpose. Quack introduces FIM to visual mining in [17], by treating local image patches as transactions and visual words as items. This method is effective object discovery, but slow in support-counting. In practice, it can only deal with thousands of images.

Sivic [20] extracts key objects and characters from a featured movie by directly clustering grouped local features. Each feature is first grouped with its neighbours. Then frequent objects are extracted as clusters of the grouped features. This is a direct and effective approach for instance mining. However, the scalability remains a big issue, since pairwise similarity evaluation is essentially quadratic. Moreover, only instances with fixed size can be mined, since features must be grouped before clustering.

Large Instances Mining. Methods designed for *large* instances are much scalable.

Philbin [15] constructs a matching graph by searching each image in turn, and then partitions dense sub-graph as clusters. They managed to discover large instances (mostly landmarks). However, small instances could be extremely difficult to mine, since the graph is constructed by full-image search. As for speed, it takes two hours for clustering a 37k dataset, since searching every image against the whole dataset is costly.

Chum [4] mines similar images efficiently by min-Hash [3] with the representation of BoW. Correspondingly, key collisions are extracted as clusters. This method is capable of finding landmarks in large dataset. However, it does not apply to small instance discovery, since Jaccard similarity between images sharing an small instance can be extremely low, and the probability of collision for such images decays quickly as the similarity drops.

Mining Both Small and Large Instances. There only exist a few methods that are both efficient for large dataset and compatible for small instances.

Letessier [10] use Random Maximum Margin Hashing to generate a prior distribution and then adaptively sample and verify frequent objects. A fundamental difference from our method is that [10] mines small instances by clustering local points (versus ToFs in our approach). Our method is potentially more effective and robust, since we uniquely consider the co-occurrence of multiple local points in instances through clustering feature threads.

Pineda [16] extracts instances by clustering visual words, where each visual word is represented as a set of images that have features quantized to it. This method is effective in mining both small and large instances, but can only work on small scale dataset. The performance decays quickly as more images are involved, since more noises are introduced to the representation of visual words.

Geometric min-Hash (GmH) [5] extends min-Hash by considering the dependency among visual words. For a sketch, it computes the first hash key as standard min-Hash does. Secondary hash values are then chosen within a local proximity of the first key. This method improves the collision probability for small instances. However, this performance boosting only exists when the first key repeats, which is still difficult for small instances.

This paper targets for instance-level mining in large dataset (up to million scale). We build our method upon min-Hash for efficient processing, and address the small problem by threading features.

3. INSTANCE MINING

As in Fig. 2, our method consists of two major steps: Feature Threading and Thread Clustering. We start by introducing how to thread features efficiently (Section 3.1), and then show how to mine both small and large instances effectively with these threads (Section 3.2).

3.1 Feature Threading

Our mining algorithm adopts a bottom-up approach, building up visual instances with the elementary components: Thread of Features (ToF). As illustrated in Fig. 2, a ToF corresponds to a set of consistent local features across multiple images. It keeps potential features that link instances, and discards noisy features that are unlikely located on frequent instances. This is motivated by the fact that only a small fraction of features are helpful in instance mining. This phenomena is different from image search, where every feature must be indexed since the query stays unknown.

For mining, ToF serves as an important cue for identifying frequent instances. Whenever there is an instance among a set of images, there must exist several ToFs connecting these images. On the other hand, we can hardly extract any ToFs among random images sharing no common instance. In principle, ToFs should be (1) compact to only link potential features from instances; (2) complete to cover as many instances as possible; (3) efficient to extract and thus be scalable on large dataset. Next, we will discuss our solution to these challenges.

In our work, local SIFT features are quantized to visual words before processing, since comparing raw features is too costly. In image search [19], features quantized to the same visual word are considered to be matched. However, such matching is too noisy. In other words, most of the features quantized to the same visual word are not necessarily consistent enough for threading. Therefore, we also consider the neighbouring points around each feature F for robust matching. In particular, l nearest features are considered to augment the central feature F as a small local patch. These neighbouring features are selected within a small region centered at F, and with the similar scale[1] as F. In our implementation, a local patch is created around each local point by concatenating its $l = 10$ neighboring visual words. The term "central feature" indicates the SIFT feature of the local point.

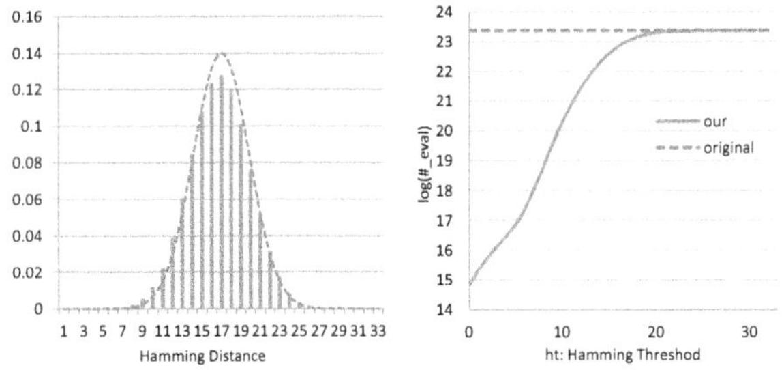

Figure 3: Left: The distribution of Hamming distances among features extracted from a 10k subset of Flickr images. The curve $Bin(32, 0.5)$ is overlaid as red dashed line. Right: the number of evaluations with respect to different Hamming signature threshold, ht. The red dashed line indicates the case without using Hamming code.

Threading among these augmented features involves lots of similarity evaluations, i.e., intersection of two sets: counting the number of common visual words between a pair of patches. Two features are threaded if their local patches share at least $t = 2$ common visual words. For a dataset with N images and each with n local features on average, the direct way requires $(Nn)^2$ evaluations. By restricting the threading among features quantized to the visual word [20], the evaluation is reduced to $(\frac{Nn}{w})^2 \times w = (Nn)^2/w$, where w is the size of the visual vocabulary. However, this number is still too large for large dataset.

We noticed that, even for features quantized to the same visual word, most of the similarity evaluations are still unnecessary and lead to no intersection. In this paper, we further reduce the computation by using a short binary Hamming signature [9] for early pruning. A short binary code, extracted from the central feature, is embedded to each central feature as its "signature". This signature is computed by randomly projecting the feature vector to lower dimensional space and thresholding to binary codes. Hamming distance is checked prior to the actual similarity evaluation. Only patches with low Hamming distance are subject to actual similarity evaluation. Note that Hamming distance is much efficient ("XOR") to compute compared to full similarity evaluation. In this way, the set intersection is evaluated only if two patches are with the same central visual word, and their signatures are with a distance less than the Hamming Threshold (ht). Consequently, the total number of evaluations is further reduced to:

$$(\frac{Nn}{w} \times \mathrm{CDF}(ht))^2 \times w = \frac{(Nn)^2}{w} \times \mathrm{CDF}^2(ht), \qquad (1)$$

[1]The scale of local SIFT feature.

where CDF(ht) is the Cumulative Distribution Function of Hamming distance, which could be approximated as a Binomial distribution $Bin(K, 0.5)$ for K-bits Hamming signature [9]. We use $K = 32$-bits Hamming codes throughout this paper. Fig. 3 (left) plots the distribution of Hamming distances for a 10k image subset of Flickr dataset (see Section 4.1 for details). As shown, the probability mass function of $Bin(32, 0.5)$ roughly fits the actual distribution. According to Eq. 1, our method only involves a fraction of $\text{CDF}^2(ht)$ evaluations compared with [20]. For commonly used Hamming threshold $ht = 10 \sim 12$, this fraction is around $(\sum_{i=0}^{10\sim 12} \text{PMF}(i))^2 = 0.06\% \sim 1.16\%$. Fig. 3 (right) plots the actual number of evaluations when mining on this 10k dataset. Compared with [20], the computation is significantly reduced. With the help of Hamming signature, we efficiently extract several ToFs from each visual word, by traversing the inverted file structure.

In summary, one ToF corresponds to a set of reliably matched local patches with (1) same central visual word; (2) small Hamming distances for their signatures; and (3) roughly consistent neighbourhood. Thus, ToF serves as a reliable link connecting images sharing consistent features. In practice, only a small fraction of features are linked as threads, while large portion features are discarded as noises. Compared to traditional BoW, ToFs are much smaller in size and cleaner in quality, which enables efficient and reliable instance mining in large dataset.

3.2 Instances Mining with ToF

After feature threading, each ToF is represented as a set of image IDs. In this section, we show that this neat representation is efficient for processing, while being effective in mining both small and large instances. Since our method is also based on min-Hash for efficient clustering, we first analyze the main problems of min-Hash in instance mining, then show how our strategy avoids these problems.

3.2.1 Min-Hash Revisited

Here we only briefly summarize min-Hash, and more details can be found in [3, 6]. Min-Hash (mH) is a randomized algorithm for efficient sets-similarity estimation. It hashes a set to the minimal index according to a random permutation, where the collision probability of two sets equals to their Jaccard similarity. Thus a large number k of min-Hash functions approximates the actual similarity. In practice, multiple (s) hashing keys are grouped together as a s-tuple called sketch. In the scenario of mining, images with at least one sketch collision are treated as similar images. With images represented as BoW vector, the probability [6] that two images I_1 and I_2 having at least one sketch collision is given by:

$$P_C(\text{I}_1, \text{I}_2) = 1 - (1 - sim(\text{I}_1, \text{I}_2)^s)^k. \quad (2)$$

Small Instances: The first problem is on small instances. The probability of collision decays rapidly as the similarity drops, especially when a large sketch s is used. In our experiments, $sim(\text{I}_1, \text{I}_2)$ is around 0.02 (see Section 4.1 for details), thus $P_C \approx 0.3\%$ even with $k = 500$ hash tables. To have a decent probability of observing at least one collision, usually we have to use very large number of hash tables, which requires more computation. As a result, most of the mining results [4, 15] in previous works are about large landmarks.

Random Collisions: Next, we analyze the other problem: random collisions (false positives), which is an important aspect but often ignored by previous methods. That is, besides true patterns, how many random image pairs are extracted. Let us consider a dataset with N random images, each of which has n local features on average, and a visual vocabulary $\mathcal{V} = \{v_1, v_2, ..., v_w\}$ of size w for quantization. Assume local features in this dataset are quantized to each visual word with equal chance. For a pair of random images I_A and I_B, let $X_1, X_2, ..., X_w$ be a list of indicator random variables with

$$X_i = \begin{cases} 1, & \text{if } v_i \in \text{I}_A \;\&\; v_i \in \text{I}_B, \\ 0, & \text{otherwise.} \end{cases} \quad (3)$$

That is, $X_i = 1$ only if both images have the i-th visual word. Since each X_i is identical and independent to each other, the expected number of common visual words m is given by:

$$m = \mathbf{E}[\sum_{i=1}^{w} X_i] = w \times \mathbf{E}[X_1] = w(1 - (\frac{w-1}{w})^n)^2. \quad (4)$$

Let $x = 1/w$, the term $(\frac{w-1}{w})^n = (1-x)^n$ can be expanded with Taylor expansion near $x = 0$ as $1 - nx + \mathcal{O}(x)$. This linear approximation for $m = n^2/w$ is already accurate enough, since x is approaching 0 for a large vocabulary. Then the Jaccard similarity between a random pair of images can be written as:

$$\epsilon = \frac{|\text{I}_A \cap \text{I}_B|}{|\text{I}_A \cup \text{I}_B|} = \frac{m}{2n - m} \approx \frac{n}{2w - n}. \quad (5)$$

This ϵ is important as it estimates the average similarity for random image pairs, which can be used to threshold large number of false positives. For each $\binom{N}{2}$ pairs of images, the number of image pairs found in k hash tables follows the binomial $Bin(k, \epsilon^s)$. As a result, the expected number of random image pairs mined from the whole dataset is:

$$RC = \binom{N}{2} \times k \times \epsilon^s. \quad (6)$$

Take Oxford105k used in [4] for example, where $N = 104,844$, $n = 2,805$, $w = 2^{17}$, $k = 512$, and $s = 3$. According to Eq. 6, $RC = 3.34 \times 10^6$, which roughly matches the number reported in [4]: $38.4 \times N = 4.02 \times 10^6$, where both *random* and *true* collisions are counted. That is to say, besides true image pairs, more than 3 million random pairs are expected to be extracted from a 100k dataset. Note RC grows quadratically in N, which becomes a big problem for large scale mining. These random pairs need to be verified with expensive post-operations, such as spatial verification and image retrieval.

3.2.2 ToF Mining

After Feature Threading, the rest part of our method can be briefly summarized as follows. ToFs are first clustered using min-Hash, where clusters are extracted as key collisions in hash tables. Then instance clusters are discovered with a simple voting.

Thread Clustering. Our method solves the Small-Instance problem by clustering ToFs instead of images. A ToF may only give a single "link" over a set of images Ω, while multiple ToFs would indicate a strong evidence of an instance over Ω. Although min-Hash is not good for mining images sharing a small instance, we show that it is quite suitable for mining correlated ToFs.

Suppose a set of images that share a small instance, where $m \ll n$ and ϵ goes to 0. Thus hashing images can hardly find the instance. In this work, we turn to exploit correlated ToFs (Co-ToF), instead of clustering images. Correlated ToFs are the set of threads that consistently show up (or disappear) together on images. Clusters of correlated ToFs lead to instance hypotheses. Intuitively, it suggests that these images are sharing several consistent local regions. This strategy is especially good for mining small instances. Luckily, ToFs consisting the pattern can still show high similarities, though the images are with low ϵ between each other. Note that the probability of ToFs collision is totally independent on the instance scale, which makes it suitable for instance mining. The only factor that matters is the similarity among ToFs composing an instance, which is usually high after feature threading.

Note that our strategy also addresses the Random Collision problem. With compact and clean ToF, similarities among ToFs composing an instance are much higher than similarities among images sharing the instance. The reason is that Feature Threading has discarded large portion of noisy features. According to Eq. 2, to ensure a high probability of collision $P_C > \alpha$, we need at least $k > \log_{1-sim^s}(1-\alpha)$ hash tables. That is, much fewer k hash tables are needed with a slightly higher sim, since $\log_{1-sim^s}(1-\alpha)$ is steep when $sim \approx 0.02$ and $\alpha \approx 0.8$. This property is very useful, since large computation can be saved with fewer hash tables.

Cluster Voting. After Threads Clustering, we adopt a voting step to get instance clusters from threads clusters. For each cluster of ToFs, all images that are linked by these threads are considered as potential instance holders. To further reduce noises, only the candidate images linked by most (80%) ToFs are voted as instance clusters.

Our method helps small instances mining. There may only a few threads extracted for small instances. But the probability of collision (these threads are hashed to the same key) only depends on the similarity of these threads. It has nothing to do with the number of threads. Small objects would just lead to a small cluster with only a few threads. In summary, the main advantages of our mining strategy can be summarized as follows: (1) fewer hashing tables (k) are needed, since the noises are significantly reduced with ToFs; (2) we have better probability to extract small instances.

4. QUANTITATIVE EVALUATION

We compare our method (Co-ToF) with three baselines: (1) mH: image discovery via min-Hash [4]; (2) Co-VW: object mining via co-occurring visual words [16]; (3) GmH: Geometric min-Hash for objects discovery [5]. The first one (mH) is included in our evaluation as a baseline using standard min-Hash. The other two methods are selected as representatives for scalable instance-level mining methods, as discussed in Section 2.

4.1 Datasets

MQA: A total number of 438 images are crawled from Flickr and Google Image, by querying 52 instances names (e.g., Wall Street Bull). This dataset[2] is originally used for visual instance naming [27], such that a wide range of real-life instances are covered, including fashion, vehicle, flower, pet, food, product, logo, landmark and art. Each visual

[2]http://vireo.cs.cityu.edu.hk/mqa/

Table 1: Summary for the dataset used in our experiment.

Dataset	# image	# cluster	cluster size	ϵ for GT
MQA	438	52	8.5 ± 2.2	0.0185
Oxford5k	5,062	364	6.5 ± 21.6	0.0251
Oxford100k	99,782	-	-	-
Flickr	1,000,000	-	-	-

instance has 5~15 (8.5 on average) image examples with different background (i.e., small duplicate proportion). We use this dataset to test the performance on small instances.

Oxford5k: This dataset[3] has 5,062 Flickr images by crawling landmarks in Oxford. As for the ground-truth, the 11 landmark buildings are labeled manually. Different with image search, our evaluation takes all images with labels {"Good", "OK", "Junk"} as true results, since we are evaluating instance level mining. However, we still found this dataset heavily under-annotated: besides 11 labeled landmarks, there still exist large number of unlabeled instance clusters. Such annotation is reasonable for image-search evaluation, but is inadequate for instance mining. In this case, we re-annotate this dataset by (1) searching each image in turn with traditional image search system, and (2) pooling the top results for manual annotation. With our fine annotation[4], it ended up with 364 clusters (including the original 11 landmarks) involving 2,369 images in total.

Oxford100k: This dataset [13] has 99,782 Flickr images by crawling popular tags. Note images in this dataset are not annotated, and are treated as negative images in our quantitative evaluation, although there might be some frequent instances inevitably.

Flickr: This dataset has one million images downloaded from Flickr by crawling "recent uploaded photos". No restrictions on tags, users, or locations are enforced at the time of dataset construction. Though we expect this dataset to be random, it still has several patterns inside, since there might be some popular objects/landmarks shared by different users and consistent images uploaded in same location. Note that we do not have the ground-truth for this dataset, and it serves as a "blind" dataset for scalability test.

General Settings. A hierarchical vocabulary with one million leaf nodes is constructed [12]. With this vocabulary, each image is representated as a set of visual words. As shown in Table 1, the average Jaccard similarity (ϵ) of ground-truth (GT) images for MQA (Oxford5k) is 0.0185 (0.0251), while ϵ for random image pairs is around 0.0013. For hashing, k sketches of size 3 ($s = 3$) are used for all methods.

4.2 Evaluation Metric

In this paper, we adopt F-measure as the evaluation metric, which is frequently used in clustering. Instance mining is essentially a clustering problem, where both false positive and false negative decisions should be penalized. Specifically, *recall* is computed as the number of detected true image pairs divided by total number of true pairs, and *precision* is calculated as the percentage of true image pairs among all

[3]http://www.robots.ox.ac.uk/~vgg/data/oxbuildings/

[4]This annotation has already been made available at: http://vireo.cs.cityu.edu.hk/gt_clusters.oxford5k

Figure 5: Example instances mined from MQA dataset. Each row corresponds to a sample instance cluster.

the detected pairs. Then F-measure is the harmonic mean of precision and recall.

4.3 Mining MQA dataset

Fig. 4 compares different methods on MQA, which is a small dataset with small instances. In terms of F-measure, all methods, except mH, perform strongly on this small scale dataset. As discussed in Section 3.2, mH is not suitable for mining small instances, where similarities between true image pairs are low. In such case, mH can hardly distinguish true images out of random pairs, resulting in poor precision and recall. On the other hand, other methods are much compatible to small instances. Our method Co-ToF converges quickly and leads the performance at different k. It only needs very few tables to produce a decent result. Co-VW also performs well on this dataset, and reaches its peak around $k = 20$. For this small dataset (438 images) indexed with a large vocabulary (1M), the sets of visual words for different instance patterns are unlikely to overlap. Thus there are not too much noises in the posting list of each visual words. This situation is ideal for Co-VW, but does not hold, as more and more images (e.g., 100k$\sim$1M) are added to the dataset, e.g., Oxford dataset in Section 4.4. GmH also performs well on this dataset by choosing secondary hashing keys from the proximity of the first key. This strategy prevents random collisions effectively, which significantly improves precision over mH. However, it is still difficult for the first key to collide for small instances, since the first key is generated randomly as mH does. The chance for these randomly selected features to collide is low, and it is even lower when the images share a small instance (as in MQA). Therefore, low recall is still a problem for GmH.

Fig. 5 shows several example instances mined from MQA dataset. Based on our observation, (1) instances with high-Freq and large-DuP are easy to mine, e.g., buildings, scenes; (2) our method is effective in mining small instances, e.g., Coca-Cola, Wii-mote; (3) some instances, e.g., animals, flowers, are still difficult to mine, since features extracted on these smooth, non-rigid instances are not stable, which corrupts feature threading.

4.4 Mining Oxford Dataset

Fig. 6 compares different methods on Oxford dataset. We first evaluate the performance on the fully annotated Oxford5k (top), and then report the performance on the complete Oxford105k (bottom). Note that this 105k dataset

Figure 7: Example instances mined from Oxford105k dataset, using our method. Top 3 rows: example instances in ground-truth set. Images with green-solid border are in the "junk" set of Oxford dataset, while red-dashed border indicates false positives. Bottom 3 rows: example instances outside ground-truth set. The last row is a false cluster.

is a combination of Oxford5k and Oxford100k, where Oxford100k is added as distracting images.

The performance on Oxford dataset is roughly consistent as MQA. The main differences between Oxford and MQA are two folds: larger instances and more distracting images.

First, the average Jaccard similarity between true image pairs is higher on Oxford dataset[5]. In this case, mH suits better for this dataset by effectively discovering large instances. However, it is still not comparable with GmH and Co-ToF, which work for both small and large instances. Second, more and more distracting images, which do not belong to any cluster, are included in our evaluation. Generally, more distracting images bring more irrelevant/noisy features, which makes instance mining even harder. For Co-VW, more noisy features are attached to the posting list of each visual word, which brings down the similarity of visual words composing an instance. As a result, the performance of Co-VW degenerates quickly as dataset grows. For mH, the number of random collisions grows quadratically in the dataset size (Eq. 6). Thus it gives lower precision on larger dataset. For GmH, more random collisions are observed as more distracting images are added, but it is less sensitive due to the way of choosing secondary hash keys. As expected, our method performs consistently better than other methods, and the performance gap is even larger as the dataset grows. We noticed in our experiments that the size[6] of threads does not grow as fast as dataset size, since our method only threads potential features for mining.

Performance on Small Instances. As shown, Oxford dataset is with both small and large instances. Since our method is tailored for small instances, we are also interested in the performance on particular small instances. To separate small instances from large ones, we first calculate the average Jaccard similarity for pairwise images in each ground-truth cluster, and then cut the whole ground-truth

[5]From 0.0185 to 0.0251 is adding 35% more common local features.

[6]Number of threaded features.

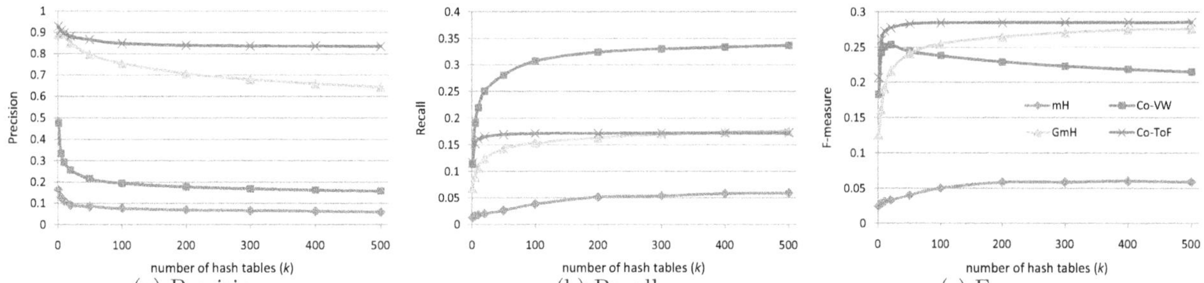

(a) Precision (b) Recall (c) F-measure

Figure 4: Performance comparison on MQA dataset.

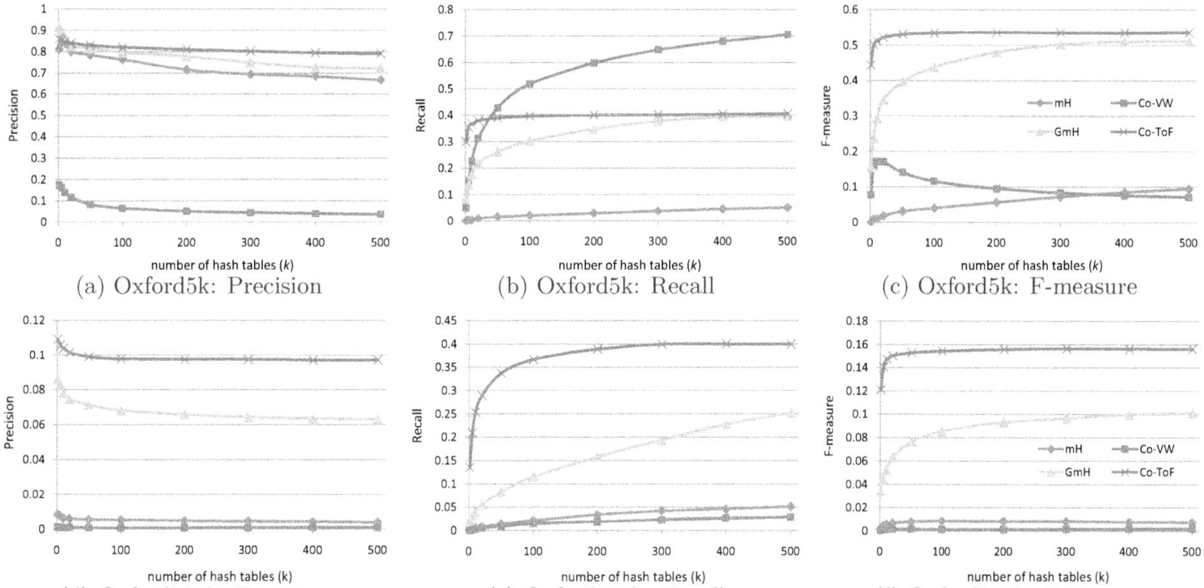

(a) Oxford5k: Precision (b) Oxford5k: Recall (c) Oxford5k: F-measure

(d) Oxford105k: Precision (e) Oxford105k: Recall (f) Oxford105k: F-measure

Figure 6: Performance comparison on Oxford dataset. Top: Oxford5k, Bottom: Oxford105k.

Table 2: The performance (F-measure) on the *small* subset of instances in Oxford dataset. A mid-level value of $k = 300$ ($1 \sim 500$ evaluated in Fig. 6) is adopted for all methods.

	mH	Co-VW	GmH	Co-ToF
Oxford5k	0.0006	0.1370	0.1670	0.1836
Oxford105k	0.0006	0.0005	0.0347	0.0994

instances into halves according to this similarity. Instance clusters with lower half similarities are regarded as *small*. Table 2 presents the detailed performance on this *small* subset. On Oxford5k, Co-ToF, GmH, and Co-VW show significant advantage over mH, which does not work on small instances. Co-VW works on Oxford5k, but the performance decays badly with more distracting images added. Both GmH and Co-ToF work for small instances, and give decent performance on this subset. GmH extracts small instances effectively by improving the collision probability when the first hash key repeats. Co-ToF outperforms GmH by removing noisy background features, such that both first and secondary hash keys are with high chance to collide.

Table 3: Precision of the mining results for Flickr dataset, estimated on 1000 random image pairs.

	mH	Co-VW	GmH	Co-ToF
Precision	0.233	0.011	0.363	0.423

Fig. 7 shows several examples mined from Oxford105k. In addition to the patterns included in the ground-truth set (top 3 rows), we also show some patterns mined on Oxford100k (bottom 3 rows), what are not labeled. As observed, some of the patterns labeled as "junk" (less than 25% region is visible) in the original paper [13] are also discovered by our method, which demonstrates the ability of small instance discovery.

Failure cases. Some instances, mostly with non-rigid motion and non-planar surfaces, are missed by our method, since the local features are not always repeatable across different images and the ToFs cannot be established through feature matching. Some false-alarm instances (e.g., last row of Fig. 7) are mined, because some locally consistent local patches could appear frequently in irrelevant images. However, this problem can be alleviated by post-operations as spatial verification.

Figure 8: Example instances mined from Flickr dataset. Due to space limitation, this figure only shows example instances with 5∼10 ToFs. Instances from top to bottom: the dart board, Starbucks, logo in the corner, Apple logo, Adidas logo, a border style.

4.5 Mining Flickr Dataset

Since it is impossible for us to annotate such a large dataset, Flickr dataset is mainly used for scalability test in this paper. We do not evaluate recall on this dataset, and the precision is roughly estimated by sampling 1000 random image pairs from the mining results. As shown in Table. 3, Co-VW gives most noisy result, due to the large scale of this dataset. Min-Hash is good at finding highly similar images, but it also returns large number of false positives. GmH gives better precision by carefully selecting secondary hash keys. Co-ToF achieves the best precision by removing noises through feature threading. Note that the precision alone may not be able to tell the full story on performance, but it gives a gist on noise levels of different method.

The mined instances on this dataset are dominated by near duplicates probably uploaded by the same user, which are less-interesting. Thus in Fig. 8, we only show example instances with small-DuP and high-Freq. As shown, some of the small patterns corresponds to popular objects (the dart board) or product logos (Apple, and Adidas), since they are heavily shared by a wide range of users. The mining results could indicate the instance popularity. Since these objects only occupy a small area on the images with different background, most of them are missed in other mining methods. There is also a small logo found as in the 3rd row of Fig. 8, which is small and embedded in a corner of the images. Perhaps these photos are uploaded by a TV station or an organization. The last row gives a serendipity. These set of photos seem to be irrelevant, if judged by human. In fact, by careful investigation, we notice that the instance is the common style along the borders. A possible explanation is probably a photo editing tool (e.g., Instagram), with this special border-style, is getting popular among Flickr users.

4.6 Discussion

Performance on small instances. In our evaluation, we have separated and focused on the *small* instances in the Oxford dataset in Table 2. For MQA, the majority of the dataset is of small sizes (confirmed by the small ϵ in Table 1). Hence, results in Fig 4 have been meant to evaluate the performance focusing on small instances. The Flickr dataset is diverse and too large to manually set aside only small instances for performance comparison. However, Fig 8 only shows instances with small DuP and high Freq.

Parameter sensitivity. The parameter settings $(K; s)$ follow the recommendation of previous works [4, 6, 9, 20] with similar scenarios. Figures 4 and 6 show the performances with different values of k. The choice of parameters $(l; t)$ are selected based on a separate validation experiment ($l = 5\sim20, t = 1\sim5$), considering the tradeoff between efficiency and accuracy.

Open Issues. Since our method relies on extraction of local feature and their threading, its performance may degrade when dealing with large media quality variations introduced by significant viewpoint change, domain changes and high noises.

Table 4: The running time for each method on different datasets. For Co-ToF, the total time (C) is decomposed to Feature Threading (A) and Hashing (B) as: A + B = C.

	MQA	Oxford5k	Oxford105k	Flickr
mH	2.1 s	27.0 s	9.5 m	1.7 h
Co-VW	8.7 s	68.2 s	8.0 m	1.7 h
GmH	2.2 s	27.3 s	9.6 m	1.8 h
Co-ToF	1.0+2.8 =3.8 s	13.5+4.6 =18.1 s	6.3+1.3 =7.6 m	1.4+0.4 =1.8 h

s: second, m: minute, h: hour

4.7 Speed Efficiency

Table 4 gives a summary for the running time of different methods. These experiments were all conducted on a 8-core machine with 2.67GHz CPU, 16GB memory. The processing time excludes feature extraction and quantization, which are the same for all methods. As shown in the last row of Table 4, the total running time of our method (Co-ToF) consists of two parts: Feature Threading (Section 3.1) and Threads Hashing (Section 3.2), while other methods only have a hashing step. In general, all methods take roughly similar time on large dataset. Although Co-ToF needs an extra step for Feature Threading, the Hashing step is much efficient compared to other methods. Essentially, the hashing time is mainly affected by two factors: the total time is linear in the number of sets; computing the hash key for a set is linear in the size of the set. After feature threading, both factors are reduced significantly due to the compactness of ToF. Other methods, mH, Co-VW and GmH, need much longer time for hashing, since they take the full set of features during hashing. Note in this table, all methods adopt the same number ($k = 100$) of hash tables for the purpose of comparison. However, our method usually requires much fewer hash tables in practice, which reduces the running time significantly in real applications. As observed, the running time for our method is mainly dominated by Feature Threading. However, the extra time spent is compensated by efficient hashing step and much better results.

5. APPLICATIONS

In this section, we demonstrate two applications from the new perspective of visual instance mining. To suppress similar consective frames within a video shot, local points from the same video are not linked at the time of feature threading, which can be done conveniently and efficiently by incorporating video ID to each feature. Therefore, only inter-video threads are kept.

5.1 Multimedia Summarization

We first present a multimedia summarization application with two recent events "E1: Boston Bombing" and "E2: Malaysia Airlines Flight 370". To demonstrate, the datasets are constructed by crawling Youtube videos with keyword search "Boston Bomb" and "Malaysia Airlines Flight 370". Returned videos are then filtered with specific upload-time constraint[7]. We construct the dataset this way such that (1) there exist some repeated instances for mining; and (2) people roughly know what kind of instances should be expected, since we do not have ground-truth for these videos. Finally, we ended up with 355 videos for E1 ($\sim$92k frames) and 406 videos for E2 ($\sim$103k frames), which include official TV news as well as amateur reviews.

We apply our instance mining to summarize the video collection as shown in Fig. 9 (Left: Boston Bombing, Right: Malaysia Airlines Flight 370). The tag-cloud (top) is generated by extracting frequent terms (verbs and nouns) by parsing video metadata (title, description). Visual patterns (bottom) are extracted with the proposed method. We further select several "small (first two rows in Fig. 9 bottom), medium (3rd row), and large (last row)" size instances for visualization. As observed, most visual instances are meaningful: small instances are mostly faces of key characters, logos of TV stations; medium-size ones correspond to iconic sub-images cited in multiple videos; large instances are mostly cover photos for each event.

Compared with traditional summarization by image-level clustering, whose results are very similar as the last row in Fig. 9, our instance level summarization is much precise and complete in identifying salient items and scenes. Compared to texts summarization, which only conveys general ideas, our result gives much concrete and intuitive visual entities on what (and probably who/where) is about the data collection. One drawback of visual instance summarization would be the lack of semantic meaning for visual entities. Thus in this application, we adopt both results to give complementary summarization.

5.2 Instance Search

Instance Search (INS) [21] is a realistic problem proposed by TRECVID, which is to retrieve all occurrences of the query instance from a video collection. Compared to traditional image search, the query instance is usually specified with a small Region Of Interest on the query image, and the target instances on reference images could also be small and with different background. Apparently, this phenomenon poses small-DuP problem. However, most state-of-the-art methods [28, 26] ignore this problem and still rank images based on traditional similarity as: $sim(Q, R_i) = \frac{Q \cdot R_i}{\|Q\| \|R_i\|}$, where Q is the BoW vector extracted within the query ROI, while R_i covers full reference image. Apparently, $\|R_i\|$ *over-norms* the score for small-DuP reference images by including dense features on background, which gives lower ranking accordingly.

We apply instance mining to solve this "over-norm" problem. Our solution is straight-forward: (1) we first apply instance mining on the reference dataset to get frequent instance set $\mathcal{P}$; (2) query instance Q is then matched against $\mathcal{P}$, which is indexed with an inverted file; (3) images sharing matched instances are boosted in the initial retrieval rank-list. Though simple, this strategy solves the "over-norm" problem by leveraging small instances extracted through instance mining, which does not suffer from the small-DuP problem. We test this strategy on TRECVID'13 Instance Search task, which includes 30 query instances defined by TRECVID, and 470k reference video clips cut from 464 hours of TV series.

After mining, it ended up with 22k instance clusters ($\mathcal{P}$) that are verified with spatial consistency. Some of these instances are presented in Fig. 10 (top). As shown, there are both large instances ("the curtain") and small ones ("the Parking sign", "this pendent"). These inter-links across clips, especially on small instances, could be helpful to address the "over-norm" problem.

By matching each Q to $\mathcal{P}$, we can get a list of relevant instances. However, we found in our experiments that not every Q can be matched against $\mathcal{P}$. In other words, our mining results only partially overlap with the 30 queries defined by TRECVID. Therefore, we only re-rank the queries which are closely matched with $\mathcal{P}$ by thresholding the matching score. After this, 10 out of 30 queries are considered as "overlap" and are further re-ranked with the mining results. As shown in Fig. 10 (bottom), most of these queries are improved by our re-ranking. The Average Precision is boosted in the range of 3.3% to 11.0%. Such examples of queries include "no smoking logo", "bust of queens" and "Parking sign". These queries originally suffer from the "over-norm" issue badly because of their small area on the reference images. To the best of our knowledge, this is the first attempt to address the search problem with data mining. This application may shed some light on new directions for instance search.

6. CONCLUSIONS

We have presented a technique and two applications on visual instance mining for multimedia collections. Our method is effective for both small and large instances, while being efficient on million scale dataset. For efficiency, ToF is proposed as a clean and robust representation, and min-Hash is adopted for fast clustering. For effectiveness, correlated ToFs are exploited for generating instance hypotheses. The quantitative evaluation shows that our method is more effective than other methods in mining instances (especially small ones) while being scalable. Two applications on instance search and multimedia summarization demonstrate the potential of our method in solving multimedia problems.

7. ACKNOWLEDGMENTS

The work described in this paper was supported by a grant from the Research Grants Council of the Hong Kong Special Administrative Region, China (CityU 118812).

8. REFERENCES

[1] R. Agrawal and R. Srikant. Fast algorithms for mining association rules in large databases. In *Proc. VLDB*, pages 487–499, 1994.

[2] D. M. Blei, A. Y. Ng, and M. I. Jordan. Latent dirichlet allocation. *Journal of Machine Learning Research*, pages 993–1022, 2003.

[7] E1: 04/15/2013$\sim$06/15/2013; E2: 03/08/2014$\sim$03/25/2014.

Figure 9: Youtube videos summarization for the events "Boston Bomb" (left) and "Malaysia Airlines MH370" (right), through text mining (top) and visual instance mining (bottom).

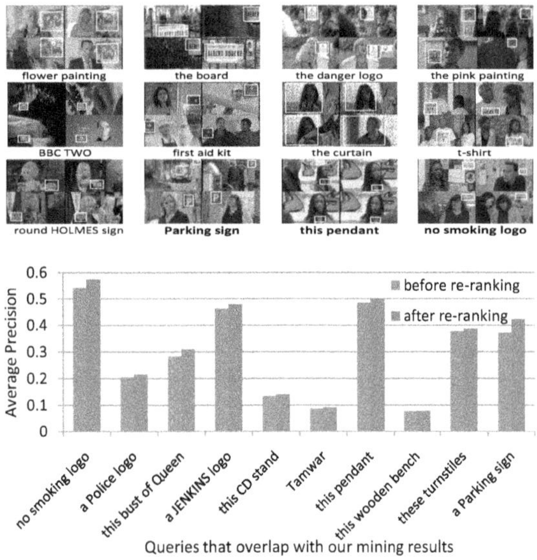

Figure 10: Top: example instances mined from TRECVID'13 Instance Search dataset. Texts below each instance cluster are labeled manually. Instances that overlap with TRECVID's 30 queries are bolded. Bottom: the performances before and after re-ranking with instance mining, for queries that are also our mined instances.

[3] A. Broder. On the resemblance and containment of documents. In *SEQUENCES*, 1997.

[4] O. Chum and J. Matas. Large-scale discovery of spatially related images. *IEEE Trans. PAMI*, 32:371–377, 2010.

[5] O. Chum, M. Perdoch, and J. Matas. Geometric min-hashing: Finding a (thick) needle in a haystack. *Proc. CVPR*, pages 17–24, 2009.

[6] O. Chum, J. Philbin, M. Isard, and A. Zisserman. Scalable near identical image and shot detection. In *Proc. CIVR*, 2007.

[7] J. Han, J. Pei, and Y. Yin. Mining frequent patterns without candidate generation. In *Proc. SIGMOD*, pages 1–12, 2000.

[8] T. Hofmann. Probabilistic latent semantic indexing. *Proc. SIGIR*, pages 50–57, 1999.

[9] H. Jégou, M. Douze, and C. Schmid. Improving bag-of-features for large scale image search. *IJCV*, 87(3):192–212, May 2010.

[10] P. Letessier, O. Buisson, and A. Joly. Scalable mining of small visual objects. In *ACM Multimedia*, 2012.

[11] H. Liu and S. Yan. Common visual pattern discovery via spatially coherent correspondences. In *Proc. CVPR*, pages 1609–1616, 2010.

[12] D. Nister and H. Stewenius. Scalable recognition with a vocabulary tree. In *Proc. CVPR*, pages 2161–2168, 2006.

[13] J. Philbin, O. Chum, M. Isard, J. Sivic, and A. Zisserman. Object retrieval with large vocabularies and fast spatial matching. In *Proc. CVPR*, 2007.

[14] J. Philbin, J. Sivic, and A. Zisserman. Geometric LDA: A generative model for particular object discovery. In *Proc. BMVC*, 2008.

[15] J. Philbin and A. Zisserman. Object mining using a matching graph on very large image collections. In *Proc. ICVGIP*, pages 738–745, 2008.

[16] G. F. Pineda, H. Koga, and T. Watanabe. Scalable object discovery: A hash-based approach to clustering co-occurring visual words. *IEICE Trans. on Information and Systems*, pages 2024–2035, 2011.

[17] T. Quack, V. Ferrari, and L. V. Gool. Video mining with frequent itemset configurations. In *Proc. CIVR*, pages 360–369, 2006.

[18] B. C. Russell, W. T. Freeman, A. A. Efros, J. Sivic, and A. Zisserman. Using multiple segmentations to discover objects and their extent in image collections. In *Proc. CVPR*, pages 1605–1614, 2006.

[19] J. Sivic and A. Zisserman. Video Google: A text retrieval approach to object matching in videos. In *Proc. ICCV*, 2003.

[20] J. Sivic and A. Zisserman. Video data mining using configurations of viewpoint invariant regions. In *Proc. CVPR*, 2004.

[21] A. F. Smeaton, P. Over, and W. Kraaij. Evaluation campaigns and trecvid. In *Proc. MIR*, 2006.

[22] H.-K. Tan and C.-W. Ngo. Localized matching using earth mover's distance towards discovery of common patterns from small image samples. *Image Vision Computing*, 27(10):1470–1483, 2009.

[23] G. Xin, L. Dong, J. Brendan, Z. Mojun, C. Anni, and S.-F. Chang. Robust object co-detection. In *Proc. CVPR*, 2013.

[24] J. Yuan and Y. Wu. Spatial random partition for common visual pattern discovery. In *Proc. ICCV*, 2007.

[25] M. J. Zaki. Scalable algorithms for association mining. *IEEE Trans. on KDE*, pages 372–390, 2000.

[26] W. Zhang and C.-W. Ngo. Searching visual instances with topology checking and context modeling. In *Proc. ICMR*, 2012.

[27] W. Zhang, L. Pang, and C. W. Ngo. Snap-and-ask: Answering multimodal question by naming visual instance. In *ACM Multimedia*, 2012.

[28] C. Zhu and S. Satoh. Large vocabulary quantization for searching instances from videos. In *Proc. ICMR*, 2012.

Multi-modal Mutual Topic Reinforce Modeling for Cross-media Retrieval

Yanfei Wang, Fei Wu, Jun Song, Xi Li, and Yueting Zhuang
College of Computer Science, Zhejiang University
Hangzhou, Zhejiang, China
{yanfeiwang07, wufei, songjun54cm, xilizju, yzhuang}@zju.edu.cn

ABSTRACT

As an important and challenging problem in the multimedia area, multi-modal data understanding aims to explore the intrinsic semantic information across different modalities in a collaborative manner. To address this problem, a possible solution is to effectively and adaptively capture the common cross-modal semantic information by modeling the inherent correlations between the latent topics from different modalities. Motivated by this task, we propose a supervised multi-modal mutual topic reinforce modeling (M^3R) approach, which seeks to build a joint cross-modal probabilistic graphical model for discovering the mutually consistent semantic topics via appropriate interactions between model factors (e.g., categories, latent topics and observed multi-modal data). In principle, M^3R is capable of simultaneously accomplishing the following two learning tasks: 1) modality-specific (e.g., image-specific or text-specific) latent topic learning; and 2) cross-modal mutual topic consistency learning. By investigating the cross-modal topic-related distribution information, M^3R encourages to disentangle the semantically consistent cross-modal topics (containing some common semantic information across different modalities). In other words, the semantically co-occurring cross-modal topics are reinforced by M^3R through adaptively passing the mutually reinforced messages to each other in the model-learning process. To further enhance the discriminative power of the learned latent topic representations, M^3R incorporates the auxiliary information (i.e., categories or labels) into the process of Bayesian modeling, which boosts the modeling capability of capturing the inter-class discriminative information. Experimental results over two benchmark datasets demonstrate the effectiveness of the proposed M^3R in cross-modal retrieval.

Categories and Subject Descriptors

H.3.3 [**Information Search and Retrieval**]: Retrieval models

ACM Multimedia 2014, Nov. 3-7, 2014, Orlando, Florida, USA

http://dx.doi.org/10.1145/2647868.2654901.

Keywords

Multi-modal Analysis; Mutual Topic; Topic Reinforcement; Cross-media Retrieval

1. INTRODUCTION

Nowadays, many real-world applications involve multimodal documents, where information inherently consists of data with different modalities, such as a web image with loosely related narrative text descriptions, or a news article with paired text and images. Since multi-modal documents exploit the symbiosis of multiple-modality data to deliver high-level semantics, it is desirable to disentangle the underlying latent correlations between data objects with different modalities in multi-modal documents and support similarity search across different modalities. However, the so-called *heterogeneity-gap* has been widely understood as a fundamental barrier of multi-modal document modeling. Therefore, effectively understanding the multi-modal data as well as their underlying semantic properties plays a crucial role in cross-media analysis.

To achieve the goal of multi-modal data understanding, a number of approaches have been proposed for multi-modal document modeling in the recent literature. According to the model-constructing mechanisms, these approaches can be typically categorized into two classes: statistical dependency modeling and probabilistic graphical modeling. Specifically, the first class of approaches mainly focuses on maximizing the statistical dependency (e.g., measured by the mutual information) of different modalities in the common latent space [12, 24, 23, 7]. In contrast, the second class of approaches is derived from the joint modeling of data objects with different modalities in a probabilistic manner[2, 22, 26]. These approaches tend to maximize the likelihood of observed multi-modal data in terms of their latent topics. They are usually based on some assumptions about how multi-modal data is correlated such as all modalities share same topic proportions, or have one-to-one topic correspondences, or have commonly sharing topics.

In order to learn discriminative correlated latent representations, a group of approaches integrate the side information (e.g., class labels) into the process of multi-modal document modeling, to enhance representation performance for within-class multi-modal data. For instance, canonical correlation analysis (CCA) and support vector machine (SVM)are combined in [8] to multi-view classification. A generic multi-view latent space Markov network was proposed in [5] to jointly maximize the likelihood of multi-view data and their supervising labels. By introducing the class label information, the

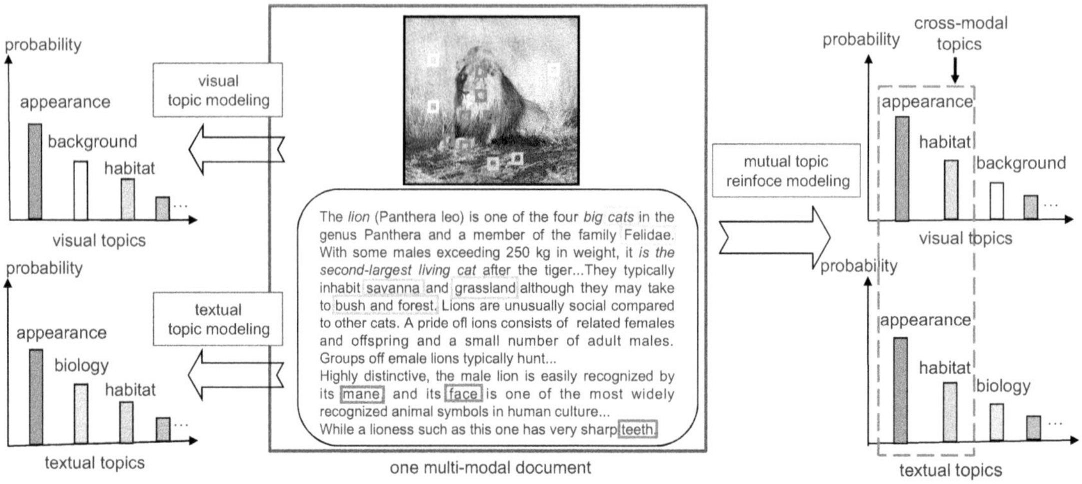

Figure 1: The intuitive illustration of multi-modal mutual topic reinforce modeling. Given one multi-modal document, its textual units or the visual units respectively describe individual text-specific topics (i.e., appearance,biology and habitat) or image-specific topics (i.e., appearance, background and habitat) with different probabilities. The proposed M^{3}R attempts to assign a high priority to the sharing cross-modal topics (i.e., appearance and habitat). The areas in the image and the words in the text highlighted by the same color share a same latent topic. (Figure best viewed in color)

generalized multi-view analysis (GMA) [24] extended original unsupervised two-view CCA to supervised multi-view counterpart. In [31], coupled dictionary learning (DL) was introduced to discover the correlations of multi-modal data. It is worth noting that various forms of side-information can potentially offer "free" supervision in many scenarios for multi-modal data modeling such as category belonging, user tagging, ratings and so on.

However, the aforementioned approaches to multi-modal modeling are generally incapable of explicitly and effectively modeling the intrinsic interactions between modalities and usually suffer from the modeling weakness in the following two aspects: 1) distinguishing the relative importance information on the latent topics for multi-modal data understanding; and 2) discovering the cross-modal topic consistency information. To alleviate the limitations, we propose a multi-modal mutual topic reinforce modeling (M^{3}R) approach that can adaptively encode the cross-modal topic consistency information by multi-modal reinforcement modeling. Here, "*cross-modal topic*" means the topics simultaneously remarked by multi-modal data (i.e., images and texts) within the same multi-modal documents. Using such cross-modal topic consistency information, M^{3}R is able to adaptively learn a set of more semantically meaningful latent topics via the interactions between multi-modal topics. As a result, the mutually consistent cross-modal topics (reflecting the same semantic information) are encouraged with a relatively high priority, while the remaining modality-specific topics are discouraged but still preserved. Therefore, the process of discovering the mutually consistent cross-modal topics is associated with the concept of mutual topic reinforcement.

Figure 1 gives out an intuitive illustration of M^{3}R. Given one multi-modal document about a "lion" with an image and corresponding text, the textual units (e.g., words or sentences) or the visual units (e.g., patches or regions) respectively describe individual modality-specific textual topics (i.e., appearance,biology and habitat) or visual topics (i.e., appearance, background and habitat) with different probabilities. However, some of textual units and visual units all remark several cross-modal topics (i.e., appearance and habitat). In principle, M^{3}R tends to assign a high priority to cross-modal topics by mutual topic reinforcement and at the same time preserves other modality-specific topics.

To obtain discriminative multi-modal data representations, we further incorporate the class label information into the process of probabilistic graphical modeling, and then formulate M^{3}R as a generative probabilistic model driven by a supervised learning manner. Therefore, the main contributions of our work are two-fold. First, we introduce the concept of multi-modal mutual topic reinforcement into multi-modal data understanding. Second, we establish a hybrid generative-discriminative probabilistic graphical model that adaptively learns a set of semantically meaningful latent topics via cross-modal mutual topic reinforcement in a supervised learning manner.

2. RELATED WORKS

As aforementioned, the modeling of multi-modal documents can be typically categorized into two classes: statistical dependency modeling and probabilistic graphical modeling. Representative works of the first class are Canonical Correlation Analysis (CCA) [12] and its extensions [24, 23] which project multi-modal data into a common (or shared) subspace so that the correlations between multi-modal data is preserved or maximized. For examples, after the maximally correlated subspace of text and image features is obtained by CCA, logistic regression is employed to cross-media retrieval in [23]. As a supervised kernelizable extension of CCA, Generalized Multiview Analysis [24] is conducted to map data in different modality spaces to a single (non)linear subspace. Although the aforementioned methods are able to effectively discover the desired latent representations, they generally lack intuitive explanations since the obtained representations are projections of the multi-modal data in a common space without apparently interpretable meanings.

Representative works of probabilistic graphical modeling include multi-modal latent Dirichlet allocation (mmLDA)[2], Correspondence LDA (Corr-LDA) [2], Topic-regression Multimodal LDA (tr-mmLDA) [22] and Factorized Multi-Modal Topic Model [26]. These approaches introduce shared latent variables which either indicate the topic proportions as in mmLDA or the indexes of topics as in CorrLDA [2]. Therefore, they either assume that all modalities share same topic proportions, or have one-to-one topic correspondences, or have commonly shared topics. Nevertheless, those predefined assumptions inherently restrain a more flexible application of cross-media retrieval in the setting involved uncontrolled multi-modal data. Thus, other topic model based methods such as Multi-modal Document Random Field (M-DRF) [14] are proposed to deal with more realistic scenarios. All the above models learn the latent representations of the multi-modal data in an unsupervised manner though they are able to offer intuitive probabilistic interpretations. The most similar work with us is the so-called nonparametric Bayesian supervised multi-modal topic modal [16], which present a nonparametric Bayesian approach to learning upstream supervised topic models for analyzing multi-modal data. However, our proposed method is a downstream supervised topic model and encourages the learning of cross-modal topics through topic distribution interactions.

Other methods based on dictionary learning for multi-view/multi-modal retrieval such as factorized/coupled dictionary learning were proposed in [13][31]. There are also methods for cross-modal similarity metric learning based on learning to rank such as [18] and [28], where the authors proposed uni-directional and bi-directional cross-modal ranking methods via structural SVM. Hashing based methods for multi-modal similarity search were initiated by Bronstein et al. in CMSSH [4]. After that, CVH [15], MLBE [30] and sparse multi-modal hashing [29] were proposed respectively. These methods bear some resemblance with CCA and its extensions that they directly utilize intra-modality and inter-modality similarities to map multi-modal data into a comparable subspace and thus lack the interpretability for the latent representations.

Motivated by the recent remarkable advance of deep learning, several deep architectures have been conducted to learn the joint multi-modal representation. A multi-modal Deep Boltzmann Machine for learning a generative model for data with multiple modalities is proposed in [25]. Methods like stacked autoencoders [21] and deep CCA [1] have similar incentive. However, these methods all build their models on an unsupervised manner. In [10], a deep visual-semantic embedding model was presented to identify visual objects using both labeled image data as well as semantic information gleaned from unannotated text. However, this supervised deep learning method is for image labeling and can not be extended to multi-modal analysis in a straightforward manner.

3. THE MODEL OF M^{3}R

In this section, we illustrate the detailed information of our model. Notations and formulations are first presented followed by the generative process and model inference. Finally, we derive the prediction algorithm using our model for multi-modal retrieval.

3.1 Problem Formulation

With some training data of multi-modal documents and their corresponding labels, we aim to learn the latent representations in terms of mutually reinforced cross-modal topics as well as maintaining discriminative information of multi-modal documents. Terminologies from text modeling such as "words", "documents", and "vocabulary" are generalized in modeling data of other modalities and are used throughout the paper.

Suppose that we have a labeled training set of D multi-modal documents with M modalities from C categories: $\Omega = \{\boldsymbol{x}_d = (\mathbf{x}_{d1}, \cdots, \mathbf{x}_{dm}, \cdots, \mathbf{x}_{dM}, c_d)\}_{d=1}^{D}$, where $\mathbf{x}_{dm}$, which has N_{dm} words (e.g., textual words for texts or visual words for images) $\{x_{dmn}\}$, represents the unimodal document of m-th modality inside d-th multi-modal document while $c_d \in \{1, \cdots, C\}$ is the category of d-th multi-modal document. We assume that each word x_{dmn} from $\mathbf{x}_{dm}$ takes a discrete value from its modality-specific vocabulary $\{V_m\}_{m=1}^{M}$. There is no constraint that all the multi-modal document must have all M modalities, we just assume full correspondence for presentation convenience. This will be apparent in the section of generative process.

As aforementioned, the modality correlations in multi-modal documents are adaptively learned by the interactions of latent topic distributions while discriminations are acquired by integration of label information into the probabilistic graphic model. Figure 2 illustrates our model as a graphic model. The shaded nodes indicate observations, while the others represent latent variables. The dashed edges indicate that the topic proportion of each unimodal document is determined not only by the prior, but also by the topic proportions of other unimodal documents with the same multi-modal documents as it. Note that M^{3}R systematically models the observed multi-modal data, the class labels and the interactions between cross-modal latent topics.

Following the notations in Figure 2, our model follows the tradition of latent Dirichlet allocation (LDA) that the topic proportions $\boldsymbol{\pi}_{d1}, \cdots, \boldsymbol{\pi}_{dM}$ are generated from Dirichlet distribution with hyper-parameter α while the topic z_{dmn} of the word in a document with certain modality is drawn from a multinomial distribution. Each word x_{dmn} is drawn from the corresponding topic-word multinomial distribution ϕ_{mk} while ϕ_{mk} is drawn from a Dirichlet distribution with prior $\beta_{1:M}$. In addition to that, we introduce the correlation (interaction) among topic proportions inside a multi-modal document as well as the supervision (label) information.

3.2 Correlation and Supervision Modeling

Given the d-th multi-modal document $\boldsymbol{x}_d$, there must be some correlations between different modality data $\{\boldsymbol{x}_{dm}\}_{m=1}^{M}$ to synthetically express the whole semantic delivered by $\boldsymbol{x}_d$. For example, given one multi-modal document with an image and corresponding text, the image and corresponding text are complementary to each other for describing the same semantics embedded in the multi-modal document. Here we assume that if two data objects in one multi-modal document are similar or correlated, the same should be with their topic proportions. Therefore, we learn the correlations and further reinforce the cross-modal topics of different modalities inside the multi-modal document through topic proportion similarities. If π_i and π_j are topic proportions of two data objects in one multi-modal document respectively, the similarity between topic proportions π_i and π_j can be calculated by the potential function as follows [14]:

$$\Psi(\pi_i, \pi_j) = \exp(-\lambda f(\pi_i, \pi_j)) \tag{1}$$

where λ is a positive scaling factor for the potential function, and $f(\pi_i, \pi_j)$ is the symmetric KL-divergence which can be defined as follows:

$$\begin{aligned} f(\pi_i, \pi_j) &= \frac{1}{2}(D_{KL}(\pi_i||\pi_j) + D_{KL}(\pi_j||\pi_i)) \\ &= \frac{1}{2}\sum_{k=1}^{K}(\pi_{ik}\log\frac{\pi_{ik}}{\pi_{jk}} + \pi_{jk}\log\frac{\pi_{jk}}{\pi_{ik}}) \end{aligned} \tag{2}$$

where K is the dimension of topic proportions π_i and π_j, i.e., the number of topics.

To model the discriminative (label) information, we referred to downstream supervised models such as supervised latent Dirichlet allocation (LDA) and its variants [3] [27], which have gained much success in many applications such as document or image classification in uni-modal scenarios. Inspired by these works, the label information of the multi-modal documents is modeled through the softmax function. We generate the labels using the softmax regression based on the empirical topic frequencies of the multi-modal documents which are the concatenations of the empirical topic frequencies for unimodal documents within the multi-modal documents.

Thus, referred to Figure 2, the parameters of our model include the hyper-parameter α for topic proportions, a set of M hyper-parameter $\beta_{1:M}$ for topic-words distributions in different modalities, a parameter λ for the correlation (interaction) term, and a set of C class coefficients $\eta_{1:C}$. Each coefficient η_c is a $M \times K$-vector of real values.

3.3 The Generative Process

For generating a unimodal document within a multi-modal document, we start with choosing the category label of the multi-modal document, then we generate the topic proportion of this unimodal document, next the topic of each word of this unimodal document is assigned, finally we generate the word according to the topic. This process is repeated until we draw the whole multi-modal document. Denoting Dirichlet and Multinomial distributions as "Dir" and "Multi", the whole generative process can be described as follows:

1. For each topic k in each modality m, sample the V_m dimensional topic-word distribution $\phi_{mk} \sim \mathrm{Dir}(\phi|\beta_m)$

2. For each multi-modal document x_d:

   a) Draw the M topic proportions $\pi_{d1}, \cdots, \pi_{dM}$ of x_d from the distribution

$$p(\pi_{d1}, \cdots, \pi_{dM}) = \frac{1}{Z}\exp(-\lambda\sum_{m_i=1}^{M}\sum_{m_j \neq m_i} f(\pi_{dm_i}, \pi_{dm_j})) \times \prod_{m=1}^{M}\mathrm{Dir}(\pi_{dm}|\alpha)$$

where Z is a normalization constant. If some modalities are missing in a multi-modal document, we just adjust M to the accurate number of modalities in the

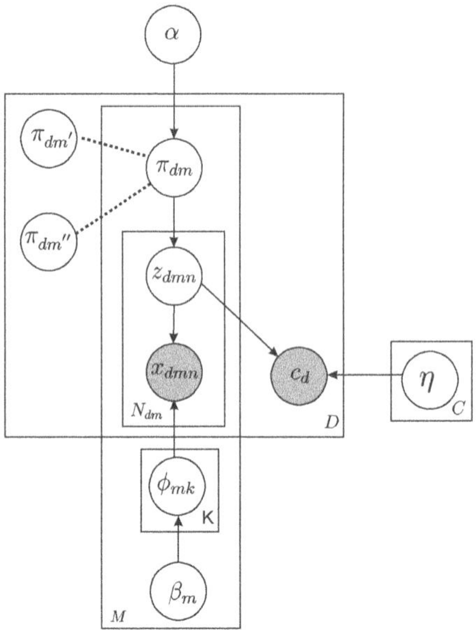

Figure 2: The graphical structure of our model. Given one multi-modal document x_d, the dashed edges denote the topic proportion of each uni-modal document (π_{dm} here) is determined not only by the prior, but also by the topic proportions of other uni-modal documents (such as $\pi_{dm'}$ and $\pi_{dm''}$) in the same multi-modal document.

multi-modal document. For example, in the retrieval stage, $M = 1$ and the first term (similarity term) is disregarded.

b) For each word x_{dmn} in $\mathbf{x}_{dm}$ of the multi-modal document x_d :

Draw a topic $z_{dmn} \sim \mathrm{Multi}(z|\pi_{dm})$;

Draw a word $x_{dmn} \sim \mathrm{Multi}(x|\phi_{mz_{dmn}})$.

c) Draw class label $c_d|z_{(1\ldots M)1:N_{dm}} \sim$ softmax $(\bar{z}_d, \eta)$, where $\bar{z}_d = [\bar{z}_{d1} \cdots \bar{z}_{dm} \cdots \bar{z}_{dM}]$ and $\bar{z}_{dm} = \frac{1}{N_{dm}}\sum_{n=1}^{N_{dm}} z_{dmn}$ denotes the empirical topic frequencies. The softmax function provides the following distribution,

$$p(c|\bar{z}_d, \eta) = \exp(\eta_c^T \bar{z}_d) / \sum_{l=1}^{C}\exp(\eta_l^T \bar{z}_d)$$

Given the parameters α, η , β and λ, following the generative process above, we can now write the joint probability of a corpus with D multi-modal documents as follows:

$$\begin{aligned} & p(x, z, \pi, c, \phi) \\ =& \frac{1}{Z}\prod_{d=1}^{D} p(c_d|\bar{z}, \eta)\exp(-\lambda\sum_{m_i=1}^{M}\sum_{m_j \neq m_i} f(\pi_{dm_i}, \pi_{dm_j})) \\ & \prod_{m=1}^{M}\Big(\prod_{k=1}^{K}\mathrm{Dir}(\phi_{mk}|\beta_m)\Big)\mathrm{Dir}(\pi_{dm}|\alpha) \\ & \Big(\prod_{n=1}^{N_{dm}}\mathrm{Multi}(z_{dmn}|\pi_{dm})\mathrm{Multi}(x|\phi_{mz_{dmn}})\Big) \end{aligned} \tag{3}$$

3.4 Inference

In this section, we come to the learning strategy of our model. The hidden variables of the model are the topic-words distribution parameters $\boldsymbol{\phi}$, topic proportions $\boldsymbol{\pi}$, and the topic assignments $\boldsymbol{z}$ for the whole corpus. As with other topic models, the exact inference of the model is in general intractable. Some commonly used approximate methods are usually conducted in parameter inference as substitutes, such as variational inference[2], expectation propagation[20], or Gibbs sampling[11]. In this paper, we utilize the collapsed Gibbs sampling method for its simplicity and effectiveness.

With the joint probability of Eq.(3) for a corpus, we then conduct collapsed Gibbs sampling for inference. Gibbs sampling samples the topic assignment for one word based on its conditional probability with the observations and the topic assignments for the other words given, while the latent variables $\boldsymbol{\pi}$ and $\boldsymbol{\phi}$ are integrated out. We only perform Gibbs sampling on the $\boldsymbol{z}$ in this case. The probability of observations and sampling variable conditioned on the hyper-parameters can be calculated by integrating out the latent variables:

$$\begin{aligned}&\int p(\boldsymbol{x},\boldsymbol{z},\boldsymbol{\pi},\boldsymbol{c},\boldsymbol{\phi})d\boldsymbol{\pi}d\boldsymbol{\phi}\\ =&\frac{1}{Z}\prod_{d=1}^{D}\exp(\eta_{c_d}^T\bar{\boldsymbol{z}}_d)/\sum_{l=1}^{C}\exp(\eta_l^T\bar{\boldsymbol{z}}_d)\times\\ &\prod_{m=1}^{M}\frac{\Gamma(\sum_{k=1}^K\alpha)}{\prod_{k=1}^K\Gamma(\alpha)}\frac{\prod_{k=1}^K\Gamma(n_{dmk}+\alpha)}{\Gamma(\sum_{k=1}^K(n_{dmk}+\alpha))}\\ &\prod_{k=1}^{K}\frac{\Gamma(\sum_{v=1}^V\beta_m)}{\prod_{v=1}^V\Gamma(\beta_m)}\frac{\prod_{v=1}^V\Gamma(n_{mkv}+\beta_m)}{\Gamma(\sum_{v=1}^V(n_{mkv}+\beta_m))}\\ &\int\exp(-\lambda\sum_{m_i=1}^{M}\sum_{m_j\neq m_i}f(\boldsymbol{\pi}_{dm_i},\boldsymbol{\pi}_{dm_j}))d\boldsymbol{\pi}\end{aligned} \tag{4}$$

where n_{mkv} is the occurrence number of word v in topic k for modality m while n_{dmk} is the occurrence number of words assigned to topic k of $\mathbf{x}_{dm}$ in multi-modal document $\boldsymbol{x}_d$, respectively.

Noticing that the topic proportions for different modality data inside the multi-modal document are coupled, which makes the integration difficult. Inspired by [2], we introduce an empirical topic proportion instead of the original one to relax the coupled topic proportions of our model. We use the empirical model for the rest of our paper. We define the empirical topic proportion distribution given the topic assignments as follows:

$$\hat{\pi}_{dmk}=\frac{n_{dmk}+\alpha}{\sum_{k=1}^K(n_{dmk}+\alpha)} \tag{5}$$

where n_{dmk} is the occurrence number of topic k of $\mathbf{x}_{dm}$ in multi-modal document $\boldsymbol{x}_d$.

At this point, the markov chain updates of the topic assignment for one word based on the observations and the topic assignments for the other words can be derived as follows:

$$\begin{aligned}&p(z_{dmn}=k|\mathcal{D},\mathbf{z}_{-x_{dmn}},\alpha,\boldsymbol{\beta},\boldsymbol{\eta},\lambda)\propto\\ &\frac{n_{dmk}+\alpha}{\sum_{k=1}^K(n_{dmk}+\alpha)}\times\frac{n_{mkx}+\beta_m}{\sum_{x=1}^V(n_{mkx}+\beta_m)}\\ &\times\frac{\exp(\eta_{c_d}^T\bar{\boldsymbol{z}}_{d,z=k})/\sum_{l=1}^C\exp(\eta_l^T\bar{\boldsymbol{z}}_{d,z=k})}{\exp(\eta_{c_d}^T\bar{\boldsymbol{z}}_{d,-z})/\sum_{l=1}^C\exp(\eta_l^T\bar{\boldsymbol{z}}_{d,-z})}\\ &\prod_{m_j\neq m}\exp\left(\lambda f(\hat{\boldsymbol{\pi}}_{dm,-z},\hat{\boldsymbol{\pi}}_{dm_j})-\lambda f(\hat{\boldsymbol{\pi}}_{dm,z=k},\hat{\boldsymbol{\pi}}_{dm_j})\right)\end{aligned} \tag{6}$$

where n_{mkx} is the occurrence number of word x_{dmn} in topic k for modality m while n_{dmk} is the occurrence number of words assigned to topic k of $\mathbf{x}_{dm}$ in multi-modal document $\boldsymbol{x}_d$ respectively, both exclude the current word. $\hat{\boldsymbol{\pi}}_{dm,-z}$ is the empirical topic distribution for $\mathbf{x}_{dm}$ in multi-modal document $\boldsymbol{x}_d$ excluding the current word, and $\hat{\boldsymbol{\pi}}_{dm,z=k}$ is the empirical topic distribution for modality m of multi-modal document d when the topic for the current word is k.

After getting $\boldsymbol{z}$, we can estimate $\boldsymbol{\pi}$ according to Eq.(5) and $\boldsymbol{\phi}$ as follows:

$$\hat{\phi}_{mkv}=\frac{n_{mkv}+\beta_m}{\sum_{x=1}^V(n_{mkv}+\beta_m)} \tag{7}$$

For determining the hyper-parameters, we choose to automatically update the hyper-parameters. We initialize α to be identical for all the dimensions and $\boldsymbol{\beta}$ to be identical for all the modalities, then we update them according to the training data as follows [19]:

$$\alpha\leftarrow\frac{\alpha\Big[\sum_{d=1}^D\sum_{m=1}^M\sum_{k=1}^K\Big(\Psi(n_{dmk}+\alpha)-\Psi(\alpha)\Big)\Big]}{K\Big[\sum_{d=1}^D\sum_{m=1}^M\Big(\Psi(\sum_{k=1}^K(n_{dmk}+\alpha))-\Psi(\sum_{k=1}^K\alpha)\Big)\Big]} \tag{8}$$

$$\beta_m\leftarrow\frac{\beta_m\Big[\sum_{k=1}^K\sum_{v=1}^V\Big(\Psi(n_{mkv}+\beta_m)-\Psi(\beta_m)\Big)\Big]}{V_m\Big[\sum_{k=1}^K\Big(\Psi(\sum_{v=1}^V(n_{mkv}+\beta_m))-\Psi(V_m\beta_m)\Big)\Big]} \tag{9}$$

where $\Psi(\cdot)$ is the digamma function $\Psi(x)=\frac{d}{dx}\ln\Gamma(x)$. For the updating of η, we resort to the general gradient descent method of softmax regression parameter update. We summarize the learning process in Algorithm 1.

3.5 Multi-modal Retrieval

After the training stage, we aim to verify whether the proposed M^{3}R can find the corresponding modality data given the query of certain modality and rank the corresponding modality data with the same category as the query forward than those with other categories, when it is applied to cross-media retrieval. Suppose we are given a query $\boldsymbol{x}$ which consists of N words, i.e. $\boldsymbol{x}=\{x_1,x_2,\cdots,x_N\}$ from p-th modality and aim to find its similar data from the q-th modality by cross-media retrieval. First we compute the topic proportion of all the q-th modality data, then we rank the q-th modality data using scores of the likelihood for the

Algorithm 1 The Learning Process of M^{3}R

Input: $\Omega = \{\boldsymbol{x}_d = (\mathbf{x}_{d1}, \cdots, \mathbf{x}_{dm}, \cdots, \mathbf{x}_{dM}, c_d)\}_{d=1}^{D}$
Randomly initialize topics $\boldsymbol{z}$, set values of document-topic occurrence number vector $\boldsymbol{ndmk} = \{\cdots, n_{dmk}, \cdots\}$ and topic-word occurrence number vector $\boldsymbol{nmkv} = \{\cdots, n_{mkv}, \cdots\}$ to 0
Initialize $\alpha, \beta_{1:M}$ and $\eta_{1:C}$
Calculate $\boldsymbol{nmkv}$ and $\boldsymbol{ndmk}$ according to Ω and $\boldsymbol{z}$
repeat
  for $d \leftarrow 1$ to D **do**
    for $m \leftarrow 1$ to M **do**
      for $n \leftarrow 1$ to N_{dm} **do**
        $k \leftarrow z_{dmn}$
        $n_{dmk} \leftarrow n_{dmn} - 1$
        $n_{mkv} \leftarrow n_{mkv} - 1$
        calculate $\bar{\boldsymbol{z}}_{d,-z}$ and $\hat{\boldsymbol{\pi}}_{dm,-z}$
        for $k \leftarrow 1$ to K **do**
          calculate $\bar{\boldsymbol{z}}_{d,z=k}$ and $\hat{\boldsymbol{\pi}}_{dm,z=k}$
          calculate $p(z_{dmn} = k)$ according to Eq.(6)
        end for
        sample a topic k of current word according to $\boldsymbol{p} = \{\cdots, p(k), \cdots\}$
        $n_{dmk} \leftarrow n_{dmn} + 1$
        $n_{mkv} \leftarrow n_{mkv} + 1$
        $z_{dmn} \leftarrow k$
      end for
    end for
  end for
  update $\alpha, \beta_{1:M}$ and $\eta_{1:C}$
until convergence or maximum iteration
calculate $\hat{\boldsymbol{\pi}}$ and $\hat{\boldsymbol{\phi}}$ according to Eq.(5) and Eq.(7).
return $\hat{\boldsymbol{\pi}}$, $\hat{\boldsymbol{\phi}}$;

Output:
Latent representations for multi-modal documents $\hat{\boldsymbol{\pi}}$, the topic-words distributions $\hat{\boldsymbol{\phi}}$

query document which can be calculated as follows:

$$s_i = p(\boldsymbol{x}|\boldsymbol{\pi}_i) = \prod_{n=1}^{N} p(x_n|\boldsymbol{\pi}_i) = \prod_{n=1}^{N}\sum_{k=1}^{K} p(x_n|z=k)p(z=k|\boldsymbol{\pi}_i), \quad (10)$$

where $\boldsymbol{\pi}_i$ is the latent topic proportion for the i-th document of the q-th modality data, while $p(x_n|z=k)$ looks into the topic-word distribution $\hat{\boldsymbol{\phi}}_{pk}$ of p-th modality learned in the training stage. Note that the marginal probabilities $p(x_n|\boldsymbol{\pi}_i)$ can be pre-computed during learning time, so we use this method rather than the KL-divergence between the topic proportions of the two modalities to avoid time-consuming inference step for each query.

4. EXPERIMENTS

In this section, we evaluate the performance of our proposed method when applied to cross-media retrieval (specified to *image-query-texts* and *text-query-images*). We first introduce the data sets and evaluation criteria we adopted, and then elaborate parameter setting and tuning in our experiments. At last, we compare our method with other state-of-the-art algorithms and demonstrate the results.

4.1 Data Sets

One of our experimental data sets is the Wiki Text-Image data from Wikipedia feature articles [23]. Wiki Text-Image contains 2866 text-image pairs from ten different categories with each image associated with a text snippet describing the image. After SIFT features [17] are extracted, k-means clustering is conducted to obtain the representation of bag-of-visual-words (abbreviated as *BoVW*) [9] for each image. Each text is represented as a 5000-dimensional bag-of-textual-words (abbreviated as *BoTW*) vector by term frequency. In this dataset, there are on average 117.5 surrounding textual words for each image. We randomly choose 1/5 pairs of the dataset for test with the remaining pairs for training.

The other data set we used is the NUS-WIDE data set [6], which contains 133,208 images with 1000-dimensional tags and 81-dimensional concepts. Each image with its annotated tags in NUS-WIDE can be treated as a pair of image-text data while the concepts are regarded as the labels. We only select those pairs that belong to the 10 largest categories (concepts) with each pair has a unique category (concept). As a result, we get 26813 paired data samples and then we randomly choose 1/5 of them for test with the remaining pairs for training. We use the 500-dimension BoVW based on SIFT features for the representation of each image and 1000-dimensional tags for the representation of each text as the authors supplied. There are on average 7.7 surrounding textual words per image for this data set.

4.2 Evaluation Metrics

In the experiments, we aim to evaluate the quantitative performance of different methods in the following two aspects:(1) evaluation of the category relevance between query data and the retrieved results. A retrieved result is considered relevant if it belongs to the same category as the query data [24]. (2) investigation of cross-modal relevance for image-text pairs. The relevant retrieved result refers to the corresponding unique data object paired with the query [14]. The former aspect reveals the capability of learning discriminative cross-modal latent representations while the latter one can indicate the ability of learning correlated latent concepts. In this paper, we use three metrics regarding the two aspects as follows:

MAP : MAP is defined here to measure whether the retrieved data belong to the same category as the query (*relevant*) or does not belong to the same category (*irrelevant*). Given a query (one image or one text) and a set of its corresponding R retrieved results, the Average Precision is defined as

$$AP = \frac{1}{L}\sum_{r=1}^{R} prec(r)\delta(r), \quad (11)$$

where L is the number of relevant data in the retrieved set, $prec(r)$ represents the precision of the top r retrieved data (i.e., the ratio of the relevant results in the top r retrieved results). $\delta(r) = 1$ if the r-th retrieved data object is relevant to the query and $\delta(r) = 0$ otherwise. MAP is defined as the average AP of all the queries. Same as [30], we set $R = 50$ in the experiments.

Percentage: Since there is only one ground-truth match for each image/text regarding the above mentioned aspect (2), to evaluate the multi-modal performance we can resort to the position of the ground-truth textt/image in the ranked list obtained. In general, one query image (or text) is considered correctly retrieved if its corresponding ground-truth text (or image) appears in the first t percent of the ranked list obtained by submitting the query according to [14]. Percentage is ratio of correctly retrieved query samples among all the query samples. t is set to equal to 0.2 in our experiments.

MRR: We also use Mean Reciprocal Rank (MRR) to evaluate the performances of different methods in our experiments regarding the position of the corresponding unique ground-truth paired with the query. The definition of Mean Reciprocal Rank (MRR) is as follows:

$$MRR = \frac{1}{|Q|}\sum_{i=1}^{|Q|}\frac{1}{rank_i}, \qquad (12)$$

where $|Q|$ is the number of query samples, $rank_i$ represents the position of the corresponding unique ground-truth paired with the ith query in the retrieved list.

4.3 Compared Methods

We make a comparison with three state-of-the-art supervised cross-modal methods as follows:

- **SLDA-KL**: sLDA [3] is first individually employed to obtain the latent representations (i.e.,topic proportions) of each image or text. When one image (text) is submitted, we get its nearest neighboring image (text), take the corresponding paired text (image), then obtain the ranked list of retrieved texts (images) via the symmetric KL-divergence between the paired text (image) and the retrieved texts (images) in term of their topic proportions.
- **Generalized Multiview Analysis (GMA)**[24]: GMA is a supervised method in cross-modal retrieval which utilizes both pair-wised and label information of multi-modal data. As stated by authors , GMA is a supervised kernelizable extension of CCA and maps data in different modality spaces to a single subspace.
- **Supervised coupled dictionary learning with group structures for Multi-Modal retrieval (SliM^2)** [31]: SliM^2 is a supervised dictionary learning approach with group structures utilizing the class information to jointly learn discriminative multi-modal dictionaries as well as mapping functions between different modalities for multi-modal retrieval.

4.4 Parameter Tuning

As indicated before, the parameters of our model are the hyper-parameter α for topic proportions, a set of M hyper-parameter $\beta_{1:M}$ for topic-words distributions in different modalities, the parameter of potential function λ , and a set of C class coefficients $\eta_{1:C}$. The hyper-parameters α and $\beta_{1:M}$ can be learned directly from the training data using Eq.(8) and Eq.(9). The initial values of α and $\beta_{1:M}$ are set to the value commonly used in text modeling[11]. The class coefficients $\eta_{1:C}$ can also be learned in the training process but their initial values may influence the results. We set the initial values of $\eta_{1:C}$ same for all categories and all dimensions making it a variable base on a single value η. Then we perform grid-search for λ and η. The setting of λ and η is 500 and 0.6 on Wiki data set while 40 and 6 on NUS-WIDE data set, respectively.

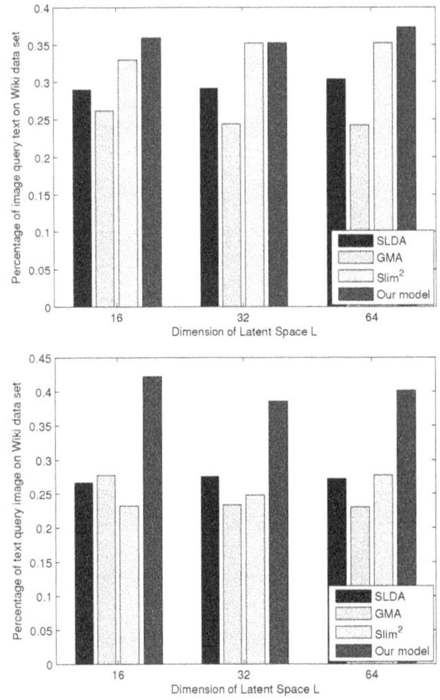

Figure 3: The Performance comparison of different methods according to Percentage metric with varied dimension of latent space on Wiki data set. Top is for image query text while bottom is for text query image.

4.5 Results

4.5.1 Performance Comparison

The performances of each algorithm are shown in Table 1 and Table 2 in terms of MAP, Percentage and MRR.

Here, two kinds of cross-media retrieval tasks are evaluated: (1) submitting one image to retrieve texts (image-query-texts), (2) submitting one text to retrieve images (text-query-images). From Table 1 and Table 2, we can see our proposed method achieves the best average performance in almost all of metrics for two data sets. Compared to the second best methods, we gain relatively 7.8%, 7.8% and 0.84% average performance improvement in terms of MAP, Percentage and MRR respectively on wiki data set while gain relatively 7.8% and 33% average performance improvement in terms of Percentage and MRR respectively on NUS-WIDE data set.

For NUS-WIDE data set, GMA and SliM^2 performs better than M^{3}R in the average performance of MAP metric. The reason is probably that one image in NUS-WIDE is associated with about only seven words in average, which restricts the power of our proposed algorithm. Moreover, for cross-media retrieval, the Percentage and MRR metrics are considered as more accurate indicators of true performance than the MAP metric. Since the underlying motivation of cross-media retrieval is to learn the correlations of data objects with different modalities and perform similarity search across different modalities, the Percentage and MRR metrics which evaluate the performance according to the position of the corresponding unique ground-truth paired with the query is more close to the goal of cross-modal retrieval than

Table 1: The performance comparison on the Wiki data set. The results shown in boldface are best results.

Wiki	Image query Texts			Text query Images			Average Performance		
	MAP	Percentage	MRR	MAP	Percentage	MRR	MAP	Percentage	MRR
SLDA	0.2116	0.3037	0.0369	0.2146	0.2723	0.0241	0.2131	0.2880	0.0305
GMA	0.2074	0.2792	0.0153	0.2542	0.2827	0.0208	0.2308	0.2810	0.0181
SliM^2	**0.2548**	**0.4084**	**0.0454**	0.2021	0.3106	0.0261	0.2285	0.3595	0.0358
M^3R	0.2298	0.3735	0.0321	**0.2677**	**0.4014**	**0.0400**	**0.2488**	**0.3875**	**0.0361**

Table 2: The performance comparison on the NUS-WIDE data set. The results shown in boldface are best results.

Wiki	Image query Texts			Text query Images			Average Performance		
	MAP	Percentage	MRR	MAP	Percentage	MRR	MAP	Percentage	MRR
SLDA	0.1976	0.2396	0.0022	0.2078	0.2640	0.0035	0.2027	0.2518	0.0029
GMA	0.2202	0.3765	0.0043	**0.4199**	0.3752	0.0045	**0.3201**	0.3759	0.0044
SliM^2	**0.3154**	**0.4639**	0.0057	0.2924	0.3877	0.0045	0.3039	0.4258	0.0051
M^3R	0.2445	0.3896	**0.0065**	0.3044	**0.4853**	**0.0071**	0.2742	**0.4375**	**0.0068**

the MAP metric evaluating the performance according to the labels.

For text-query-images task,our proposed method also achieves the best performance in almost all of metrics for two data sets except for NUS data set measured by MAP, which can be explained by the aforementioned same reason.

For image-query-texts, SliM^2 is superior except for NUS-WIDE data set measured by MRR. SliM^2 performs cross-media retrieval by the minimization of reconstruction error through coupled multi-modal dictionary learning. The performance by SliM^2 is noticeably unbalanced. The reason is that SliM^2 is prone to be over-fitting over one modality data and at the same time be under-fitting over another modality. Mathematically speaking, the minimization of reconstruction error in image-query-text retrieval direction will unavoidably increase the reconstruction error in text-query-image direction. However, our approach achieves an attractive balance performance of cross-media retrieval due to its intrinsic power of learning a unified space (e.g., topic space) via multi-modal mutual topic reinforce modeling, in which the pair-correspondence of images and text documents ensure an equal contribution to the learned metric, which is essential in practical interest.

We also do performance comparison of different methods in best parameter setting according to Percentage metric with varied dimension of latent space on Wiki data set as illustrate on Figure 3. The results on top row is for image query text while results on bottom row is for text query image. From Figure 3, we can see our method outperform all the other methods and are relatively stable to the dimension of latent space.

4.5.2 Results Demonstration

As one of topic model based method, our model has the advantage to mine the interpretable latent topics. Since textual topics bear more explicit semantics and visual topics can be hardly illustrated, we only demonstrate the latent topics in text modality. We select some topics (indicated by their corresponding topical words) that apparently have some meanings related to the categories and illustrate them in Table 3 with each topic assigned to its most relevant category. The table indicates that our method is able to discover the latent topics. For example, the topic related to music consists of words like "Punk","video" and "bands" which all reveals the semantics of music from different aspects.

Figure 4 illustrates one example of image query text and one example of text query image over Wiki image-text data set. The retrieved results by different methods are compared.

The query image and the query text come from a paired document from the "geography" category. The underlined semantics are mainly about "Fanno creek", "park" and "trail". For the example of image-query-texts, we use the corresponding images together with keywords of the retrieved texts to demonstrate the results. Though all of retrieved texts (and their corresponding images) come from the "geography" category same as the query image but the third retrieved text of GMA is irrelevant to the query image in semantics. For the example of text-query-images, The retrieved images by SliM^2 and our method (M^3R) all come from "geography" category, while there are images coming from other categories rather than "geography" by the other two methods. Retrieved results irrelevant to the query in semantics are marked with red color. From the results, we can observe that our proposed method are more semantically correlated with the query both for images and texts.

5. CONCLUSION

M^3R is proposed in this paper for multi-modal data understanding. M^3R is a supervised multi-modal mutual topic reinforce modeling (M^3R) approach which can learn correlated yet discriminative latent representations for multi-modal data by introducing of topic interaction and label information. We have demonstrated the superior performance of M^3R in terms of several metrics on two data sets for cross-modal retrieval. M^3R gains interpretable latent representations for multi-modal retrieval and is effective for cross-modal retrieval in terms of MAP, Percentage and MRR.

6. ACKNOWLEDGEMENTS

This work is supported in part by National Basic Research Program of China (2012CB316400), NSFC (NO. 61103099, 61105074), 863 program (2012AA012505), the Fundamental Research Funds for the Central Universities and Chinese Knowledge Center of Engineering Science and Technology

Table 3: Exemplar topics from the Wiki dataset. We assign each learned topic to its most probable category. Topic words are sorted by their importance values in the descending order.

Category	Topic Words
Literature	Literature Poets Capture Inspired Tradition God Admiral Volume Duke Piece
Media	Episode Davis Filming Cast Murray Hollywood Drama Actors Angeles Round
Music	Punk Video Studio Bands Award Albums Tracks Billboard POP Guitar
Sport	Football Cup Ball Marshall Conference Players Wales Professional Competition Africa
Warfare	Infantry Battalion Regiment Corps Units Artillery Marine Lieutenant Brigade Ridge

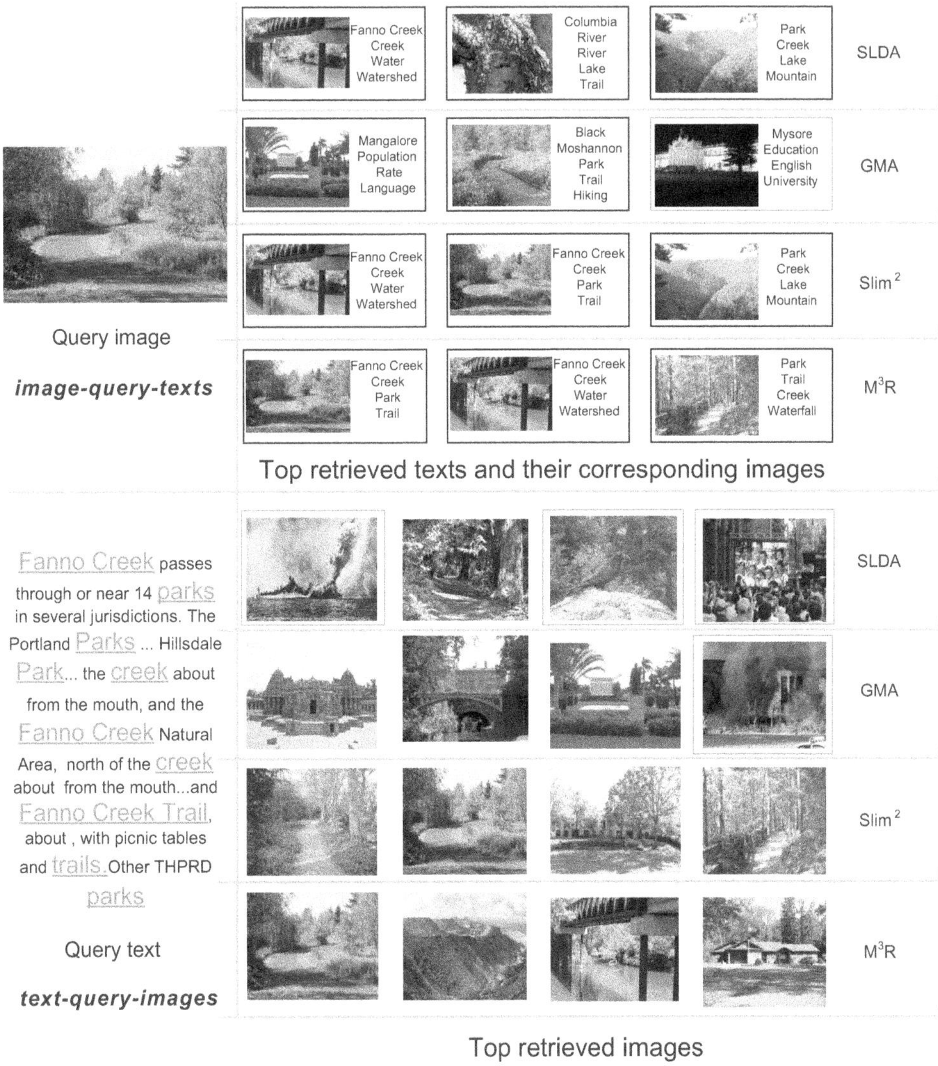

Figure 4: Two examples of image-query-texts and text-query-images over Wiki data set by four algorithms. For image-query-texts, we use the corresponding images of retrieved texts and key words of the texts to demonstrate the results. The query image and text are paired data from the "geography" category. Retrieved results irrelevant to the query in semantics are marked with red color.

(CKCEST) and Program for New Century Excellent Talents in University.

7. REFERENCES

[1] G. Andrew, R. Arora, J. Bilmes, and K. Livescu. Deep canonical correlation analysis. In *Proceedings of International Conference on Machine Learning*, pages 1247–1255, 2013.

[2] D. Blei and M. Jordan. Modeling annotated data. In *Proceedings of the international ACM SIGIR conference on Research and development in informaion retrieval*, pages 127–134, 2003.

[3] D. M. Blei and J. D. McAuliffe. Supervised topic models. *arXiv preprint arXiv:1003.0783*, 2010.

[4] M. M. Bronstein, A. M. Bronstein, F. Michel, and N. Paragios. Data fusion through cross-modality

metric learning using similarity-sensitive hashing. In *Computer Vision and Pattern Recognition, IEEE Conference on*, pages 3594–3601, 2010.

[5] N. Chen, J. Zhu, F. Sun, and E. P. Xing. Large-margin predictive latent subspace learning for multiview data analysis. *Pattern Analysis and Machine Intelligence, IEEE Transactions on*, 34(12):2365–2378, 2012.

[6] T.-S. Chua, J. Tang, R. Hong, H. Li, Z. Luo, and Y.-T. Zheng. Nus-wide: A real-world web image database from national university of singapore. In *Proceedings of ACM Conference on Image and Video Retrieval*, July 2009.

[7] J. Costa Pereira, E. Coviello, G. Doyle, N. Rasiwasia, G. Lanckriet, R. Levy, and N. Vasconcelos. On the role of correlation and abstraction in cross-modal multimedia retrieval. *Transactions of Pattern Analysis and Machine Intelligence*, 36(3):521–535, March 2014.

[8] J. Farquhar, D. Hardoon, H. Meng, J. S. Shawe-taylor, and S. Szedmak. Two view learning: Svm-2k, theory and practice. In *Advances in neural information processing systems*, pages 355–362, 2005.

[9] L. Fei-Fei, R. Fergus, and P. Perona. Learning generative visual models from few training examples: an incremental bayesian approach tested on 101 object categories. In *Computer Vision and Pattern Recognition Workshop, IEEE Conference on*, pages 178–178, 2004.

[10] A. Frome, G. S. Corrado, J. Shlens, S. Bengio, J. Dean, T. Mikolov, et al. Devise: A deep visual-semantic embedding model. In *Advances in Neural Information Processing Systems*, pages 2121–2129, 2013.

[11] T. L. Griffiths and M. Steyvers. Finding scientific topics. *Proceedings of the National academy of Sciences of the United States of America*, 101(Suppl 1):5228–5235, 2004.

[12] H. Hotelling. Relations between two sets of variates. *Biometrika*, 28(3/4):321–377, 1936.

[13] Y. Jia, M. Salzmann, and T. Darrell. Factorized latent spaces with structured sparsity. *Advances in Neural Information Processing Systems*, 23:982–990, 2010.

[14] Y. Jia, M. Salzmann, and T. Darrell. Learning cross-modality similarity for multinomial data. In *Computer Vision and Pattern Recognition, IEEE Conference on*, pages 2407–2414, 2011.

[15] S. Kumar and R. Udupa. Learning hash functions for cross-view similarity search. In *Proceedings of international joint conference on Artificial Intelligence*, pages 1360–1365, 2011.

[16] R. Liao, J. Zhu, and Z. Qin. Nonparametric bayesian upstream supervised multi-modal topic models. In *Proceedings of the ACM international conference on Web search and data mining*, pages 493–502, 2014.

[17] D. G. Lowe. Object recognition from local scale-invariant features. In *Proceedings of the IEEE international conference on Computer vision*, volume 2, pages 1150–1157, 1999.

[18] X. Lu, F. Wu, S. Tang, Z. Zhang, X. He, and Y. Zhuang. A low rank structural large margin method for cross-modal ranking. In *Proceedings of the 36th international ACM SIGIR conference on Research and development in information retrieval*, pages 433–442, 2013.

[19] T. Minka. Estimating a dirichlet distribution. *Technical report, MIT*, 2000.

[20] T. P. Minka. Expectation propagation for approximate bayesian inference. In *Proceedings of the conference on Uncertainty in artificial intelligence*, pages 362–369. Morgan Kaufmann Publishers Inc., 2001.

[21] J. Ngiam, A. Khosla, M. Kim, J. Nam, H. Lee, and A. Y. Ng. Multimodal deep learning. In *Proceedings of the International Conference on Machine Learning*, pages 689–696, 2011.

[22] D. Putthividhy, H. Attias, and S. Nagarajan. Topic regression multi-modal latent dirichlet allocation for image annotation. In *Computer Vision and Pattern Recognition, IEEE Conference on*, pages 3408–3415, 2010.

[23] N. Rasiwasia, J. Costa Pereira, E. Coviello, G. Doyle, G. Lanckriet, R. Levy, and N. Vasconcelos. A new approach to cross-modal multimedia retrieval. In *Proceedings of the international conference on Multimedia*, pages 251–260, 2010.

[24] A. Sharma, A. Kumar, H. Daume, and D. Jacobs. Generalized multiview analysis: A discriminative latent space. In *Computer Vision and Pattern Recognition, IEEE Conference on*, pages 2160–2167, 2012.

[25] N. Srivastava and R. Salakhutdinov. Multimodal learning with deep boltzmann machines. In *NIPS*, pages 2231–2239, 2012.

[26] S. Virtanen, Y. Jia, A. Klami, and T. Darrell. Factorized multi-modal topic model. *arXiv preprint arXiv:1210.4920*, 2012.

[27] C. Wang, D. Blei, and F.-F. Li. Simultaneous image classification and annotation. In *Computer Vision and Pattern Recognition, IEEE Conference on*, pages 1903–1910, 2009.

[28] F. Wu, X. Lu, Z. Zhang, S. Yan, Y. Rui, and Y. Zhuang. Cross-media semantic representation via bi-directional learning to rank. In *Proceedings of ACM international conference on Multimedia*, pages 877–886, 2013.

[29] F. Wu, Z. Yu, Y. Yang, S. Tang, Y. Zhang, and Y. Zhuang. Sparse multi modal hashing. *IEEE Trans. Multimedia*, 2013. doi: 10.1109/TMM.2013.2291214.

[30] Y. Zhen and D.-Y. Yeung. A probabilistic model for multimodal hash function learning. In *Proceedings of ACM SIGKDD international conference on Knowledge discovery and data mining*, pages 940–948, 2012.

[31] Y. Zhuang, Y. Wang, F. Wu, Y. Zhang, and W. Lu. Supervised coupled dictionary learning with group structures for multi-modal retrieval. In *Proceedings of Conference on Artificial Intelligence*, pages 1070–1076, 2013.

Quality-adaptive Prefetching for Interactive Branched Video using HTTP-based Adaptive Streaming

Vengatanathan Krishnamoorthi[†] Niklas Carlsson[†] Derek Eager[‡]
Anirban Mahanti[§] Nahid Shahmehri[†]
[†] Linköping University, Sweden, firstname.lastname@liu.se
[‡] University of Saskatchewan, Canada, eager@cs.usask.ca
[§] NICTA, Australia, anirban.mahanti@nicta.com.au

ABSTRACT

Interactive branched video that allows users to select their own paths through the video, provides creative content designers with great personalization opportunities; however, such video also introduces significant new challenges for the system developer. For example, without careful prefetching and buffer management, the use of multiple alternative playback paths can easily result in playback interruptions. In this paper, we present a full implementation of an interactive branched video player using HTTP-based Adaptive Streaming (HAS) that provides seamless playback even when the users defer their branch path choices to the last possible moment. Our design includes optimized prefetching policies that we derive under a simple optimization framework, effective buffer management of prefetched data, and the use of parallel TCP connections to achieve efficient buffer workahead. Through performance evaluation under a wide range of scenarios, we show that our optimized policies can effectively prefetch data of carefully selected qualities along multiple alternative paths such as to ensure seamless playback, offering users a pleasant viewing experience without playback interruptions.

Categories and Subject Descriptors

C.4 [**Information Systems Organization**]: Performance of Systems; C.2.2 [**Network Protocols**]: Applications; H.5.1 [**Multimedia Information Systems**]: Video

Keywords

HTTP-based adaptive streaming (HAS); Branched video; Multipath/nonlinear streaming; Seamless playback

1. INTRODUCTION

On-demand video streaming has gained tremendous popularity and currently accounts for a large fraction of Internet traffic [24]. In contrast to the original UDP-based services, most of today's on-demand video streaming services are using HTTP over TCP. The use of HTTP-based streaming simplifies caching and facilitates simple traversal of NATs and firewalls. With the introduction of HTTP-based adaptive streaming (HAS) protocols, the player can now also easily adapt the streaming quality based on the user's current bandwidth conditions [3, 5].

Another important development has been the increased level of personalization on the Web. As companies and users become increasingly used to personalized services, we expect increasing personalization of video. For example, a viewer may find a movie too sad, too violent, or too scary. What if the content provider could customize the video playback sequence based on the taste of each user?

Interactive branched video (previously also called "nonlinear" and "multipath" video) that allow users to traverse different plot sequences, depending on their interactions with the video (e.g., by pushing a button on a keyboard, TV remote, or with the help of a mouse click) have been proposed in the research literature [11, 12, 17, 27], and explored through clever (but non-trivial) use of navigation captions in YouTube videos. Recently, Interlude[1] even launched a Web-based service that offers content creators an easy way to create interactive videos hosted by the company.

While these types of media provide many advantages and opportunities, they also present new challenges. For example, with the user playback experience (at least of linear video) being dominated by the number and durations of any potential playback interruptions [9], branched video presents a unique challenge as the player may not know in advance which of the potential paths a user will take. Therefore, video must be prefetched along multiple paths to ensure that playback is seamless, without playback interruptions, even when users defer their choices to the last possible moment.

We argue that HTTP-based Adaptive Streaming (HAS) provides an excellent framework for implementing interactive branched video streaming (Section 2). Using HAS together with a simple media description and path tracking mechanism (i) provides the creator with full flexibility when designing personalized content, (ii) does not add any additional overhead on the content servers storing the media files compared to delivery of regular linear non-interactive media, and (iii) ensures that the solution is TCP friendly, easily traverses firewalls/NATs, and can leverage all of the benefits of content replication and proxy caches.

In this paper, we describe a design and full implementation of such a HAS-based interactive branched video stream-

[1] Interlude, `http://www.interlude.fm`, Mar. 2014.

MM'14, November 03 - 07, 2014, Orlando, FL, USA
Copyright 2014 ACM 978-1-4503-3063-3/14/11 ...$15.00.
http://dx.doi.org/10.1145/2647868.2654951.

ing system. Using a relatively simple model and this implementation, we explore the key question of what policy a branched video player should use when deciding which video chunks to download when. Such a policy is analogous to the rate adaptation policy in HAS, but is made greatly more complex by uncertainty regarding future user path selections. The contributions of this paper are as follows.

We first develop a simple analytic model that allows definition of the basic prefetch problem as an optimization problem in which the expected playback quality is maximized, while avoiding playback interruptions. Within this framework we argue that it is optimal to download back-to-back video chunks in a round-robin manner, and that there exists a natural tradeoff between playback quality and the use of additional parallel TCP connections to build up buffer workahead and ensure seamless playback.

Second, based on these findings, we design optimized policies that determine (i) when different chunks of the video should be downloaded, (ii) at what quality level each such chunk should be encoded with, and (iii) how to manage playback buffers and TCP connections such as to ensure a smooth playback experience without excessive workahead. By extending the existing buffer management policies used for HAS our policies carefully balance the buffer workahead needed to ensure seamless playback against potential wasted bandwidth from prefetching data along non-used paths or for an early terminated session.

Finally, we present the design, implementation (Section 4) and experimental evaluation (Section 5) of our framework. In addition to providing concrete evidence that the optimized policies perform well under a wide range of scenarios, our experiments provide insights into the importance of careful adaptive policies. For example, it is shown that the use of parallel connections can be particularly valuable when building workahead in environments with much competing traffic, and our optimized prefetching policies together with a capped workahead policy is shown to provide a good tradeoff between ensuring a smooth playback experience and avoiding excessive workahead.

The remainder of the paper is organized as follows. Section 2 presents our general HAS-based branched video framework. Section 3 defines our system model, problem formulation, and optimized prefetching policies. Section 4 describes our system design implementation. Our experimental evaluation is presented in Section 5. Section 6 discusses related work, and Section 7 concludes the paper.

2. PERSONALIZED CONTENT DELIVERY

2.1 Chunks, Segments, and Branch Points

HAS players typically either use byte-range requests or split the video file into *chunks*, each addressable with a unique URL. While the general design in this paper is applicable to both types, we will present a chunk-based solution. A manifest file providing URLs for individual chunks is used to bootstrap the player. Each chunk is typically 2-5 seconds long, and chunk boundaries coincide for the different encodings, allowing the client to switch to any available encoding at chunk boundaries.

Branched video, as we define it here, generalizes traditional linear HAS video in that it allows (i) the video designer to define arbitrary playback sequences through the underlying linear video, and (ii) the users to select among multiple alternative playback sequences. In order to allow for such customization and interactivity, the designer can define both linear and nonlinear *segments*. These are linked together using *branch points* at which the user can chose among multiple path options [17].

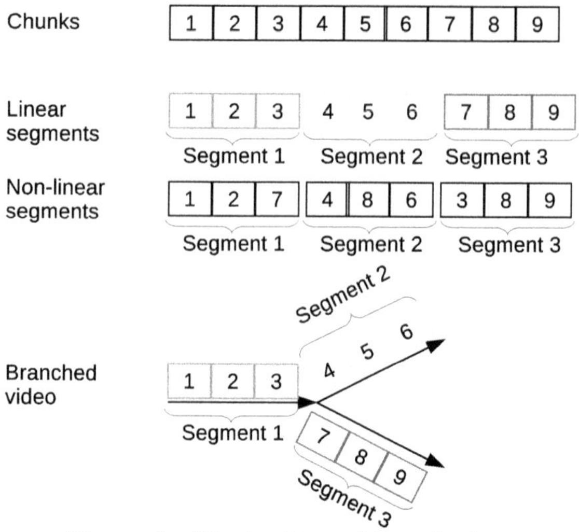

Figure 1: Illustration of terminology

Figure 1 illustrates our terminology. Here, as with regular HAS video, a chunk contains a small fixed duration of the video and is defined within the video manifest file. Each segment (linear or nonlinear) consists of a sequence of chunks that are played in the specified order without the need for any user interaction. Branch points are used to give users the option of alternative video playback paths. While playing the segment leading up to an applicable branch point, the user is given the option of which of several possible next segments the player should play next.

2.2 Branched Video Structure

Our client-driven design does not add any client tracking or additional processing overhead to the HAS servers. The designer simply specifies segments and branch point rules in a potentially-personalizable, text-based metafile, separate from the manifest file that comes with the underlying HAS media. The player is responsible for determining which branch points to consider and chunks to download.

Segments can be specified as any arbitrary sequence of chunks and the applicable branch points can be defined using rich branch point rules that specify (i) the playback path that the client must have taken for the branch point rule to be applied, (ii) the options for what path to follow after the branch point, (iii) the weight associated with each path choice, and (iv) the message to be displayed to the user whenever that branch point is in play. When playing the video, our player keeps track of the playback sequence of the user and checks the applicability of each of the branch point rules associated with the next upcoming branch point. Among all matching branch point rules, the player picks the one with the longest match. In the remainder of this paper we will focus on how the player performs prefetching, given the outcome from applying this rule.

Consider a branched video that consists of $E = |\mathcal{E}|$ segments and $B = |\mathcal{B}|$ branch points. Here, each segment $e \in \mathcal{E}$ is of playback length L_e and consists of n_e chunks each with playback duration $l_{e,i}$, where $1 \leq i \leq n_e$. Each chunk can

Table 1: Notation for branched video

Symbol	Definition
$\mathcal{E}$	Set of all segments e (linear or nonlinear)
L_e	Media playback duration in segment e
n_e	Total number of chunks in segment e
$l_{e,i}$	Total media playback length of chunk i in segment e
$\mathcal{Q}$	Set of quality encodings
$q_{e,i}$	The quality encoding of chunk i in segment e
$\mathcal{B}$	Set of all branch points b
$\mathcal{E}^b$	Set of branch edges e associated with branch point b
w_e^b	Relative weight for branch-point edge e of branch point b
Δ^u	Protocol threshold time used by client u
t_i^s	Start of download of chunk i
t_i^c	Download completion of chunk i
t_i^d	Playback deadline of chunk i
l_i	Total media playback duration of the ith chunk among those in segment e and those immediately following branch point b
q_i	The quality encoding of the ith chunk among those in segment e and those immediately following branch point b
r_i	Estimated per-connection download rate between download initiation times t_i^s and t_{i+1}^s
c_i	Number of parallel connections between download initiation times t_{i-1}^s and t_i^s
$R_i(c)$	Estimated total download rate between the initiations of the ith and $(i+1)^{\text{st}}$ chunk downloads, when using c connections

be downloaded in one of $Q = |\mathcal{Q}|$ qualities, where $\mathcal{Q}$ is the set of qualities, each corresponding to a particular video bitrate. We use $q_{e,i}$ to denote the quality (bitrate) of chunk i of segment e, and hence the size of this chunk is $q_{e,i}l_{e,i}$.

We denote by $\mathcal{E}^b$ the set of branch options (in particular, possible choices for the next segment to play) available to a particular client reaching branch point $b \in \mathcal{B}$. Each is given a weight w_e^b. In the following, we will assume that all weights are normalized, such that $\sum_{e\in\mathcal{E}^b} w_e^b = 1$, and the weights reflect relative priorities (e.g., the probability that a path is selected). Table 1 summarizes our notation.

3. PLAYER MANAGEMENT

3.1 Problem Description

We design optimized prefetching policies and buffer management schemes that (i) provide uninterrupted playback with seamless switches from one segment to another, and (ii) given such uninterrupted playback, maximize the playback quality. Our HAS-based solution takes advantage of parallel TCP connections to build up a workahead buffer to keep unnecessary stalls at a minimum, but must also make careful tradeoffs among workahead, playback quality, and the potentially wasted bandwidth associated with downloading chunks the client later does not use.

As an illustration of these design choices, consider first Figure 1. Assume that the player is currently playing segment 1. To ensure seamless playback when reaching the branch point, the first chunk of each path choice (i.e., chunks 4 and 7) must have been retrieved before reaching the branch point. To make good prefetch decisions, the client must keep track of how much time there is until the branch point, and

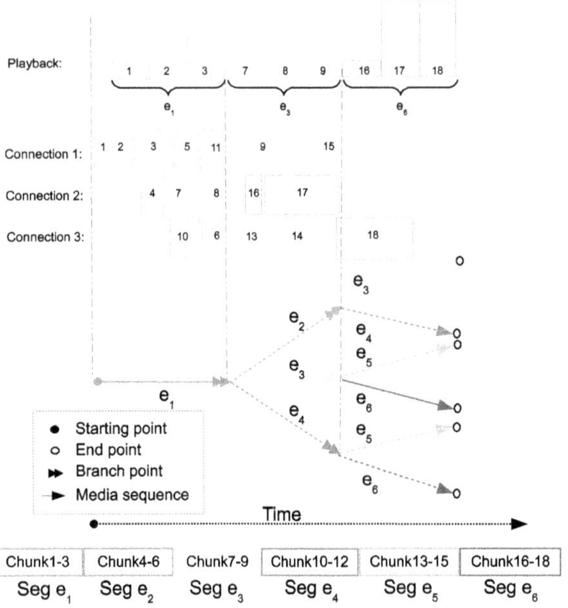

Figure 2: Round-robin parallel downloading

how much bandwidth is available, so as to determine when and at what quality each chunk should be downloaded.

Figure 2 illustrates a more complex branched video structure in which the client must make multiple path decisions (bottom half of the figure), the download schedule (middle) and the playback schedule (top) for an example player implementing a basic policy. Note how all chunks along the selected (solid lines) playback path are obtained in time of their playback deadlines (i.e., the time by which the player needs that chunk for it to be played without a stall), how up to three parallel connections are used to build up workahead and prefetch the first chunk of each potential path choice (chunks 4, 7, and 10 for the first branch point, and then chunks 13 and 16 for the second branch point) before reaching the branch points, as well as how different qualities are selected for the different chunks depending on how much workahead is available before each (potential) playback deadline. In this scenario a simple round-robin schedule is used for determining which chunk to download next.

This example illustrates the importance of careful prefetching. More generally, important design considerations in determining a good download schedule include:

- **Download ordering and playback quality.** With different chunks being associated with paths of different likelihood and with different delay constraints, both the order of downloads and the chosen quality for each chunk play an important role in ensuring seamless playback at the highest possible playback quality.

- **Concurrent downloads.** To allow improved download speeds and prefetching we allow multiple parallel connections. However, when doing so, we must consider the tradeoff between improving the overall download rate and meeting individual playback deadlines.

- **Capped workahead.** To avoid excessive workahead and wasted bandwidth usage when a user terminates a session early, most HAS players use on-off control and do not allow the buffer to fill up beyond a certain threshold. In the context of branched video this concept must be extended to take into account the number of path options at each encountered branch point. Depending on the underlying structure, our player sets the target buffer size dynamically.

The player must determine when chunks should be downloaded, at what qualities, and how much parallelism should be utilized, such as to maximize the playback quality and meet playback deadlines. Given a network constraint on how much data can be downloaded over a given time period, there is a tradeoff between quality (higher quality implies larger chunks) and the number of chunks that can be downloaded. The stall probability depends on network conditions and the prefetching policy (such as concerning prefetching of chunks from after a branch point).

3.2 Objectives and Constraints

In this section we formulate the prefetching problem as an optimization problem. Without loss of generality, we consider a client downloading a single segment e that has been determined to have an upcoming branch point b. We want to maximize the playback quality of the chunks of the current segment e and the first chunk of each of the $|\mathcal{E}^b|$ different path choices, conditioned on each chunk, including the first chunk of each potential segment following the branch point, being downloaded prior to its (potential) playback deadline.

Objective function: Assuming that a client picks path $e' \in \mathcal{E}^b$ at branch point b with a probability $w^b_{e'}$, we can formulate our objective function as:

$$\text{maximize} \sum_{i=1}^{n_e} q_{e,i} l_{e,i} + \sum_{e' \in \mathcal{E}^b} w^b_{e'} q_{e',1} l_{e',1}. \tag{1}$$

Round-robin ordering: Without loss of generality, we enumerate the chunks associated with a segment e and the first chunk in all potential following segments as follows: (i) the chunks of segment e are enumerated from 1 to n_e, and (ii) the first chunk from all of the segments following the branch point b are enumerated from n_e+1 to $n_e+|\mathcal{E}^b|$ with chunk n_e+1 having the highest weight $w^b_{e'}$ and $n_e+|\mathcal{E}^b|$ the lowest. With this numbering, let q_i and l_i be the quality and chunk length, respectively, of the ith chunk of the combined segment-branch-point pair $\{e, b\}$.

Clearly, the downloads of the chunks in segment e should be initiated before those for chunks following the branch point. Furthermore, to avoid stalls, in the case where all of the probabilities $w^b_{e'}$ are significant, it is optimal to use a round-robin ordering for workahead from after the branch point; i.e., the downloads for the first chunk from all of the possible following segments should be initiated, prior to initiating downloads of any subsequent chunks. These "first chunk" downloads should be initiated in order of the respective weights $w^b_{e'}$. Therefore, workahead downloads should be initiated in the same order as in our enumeration. Finally, for similar reasons, it may be desirable to choose non-increasing quality levels for successive workahead downloads.

Motivated by the above observations, in the following we only consider round-robin schedules following the above order. In fact, in the case that additional workahead is possible after downloading all the $|\mathcal{E}^b|$ chunks and our workahead rule (Section 3.4) allows for greater workahead beyond the branch point, we again use round-robin among the second chunk of the candidate segments.

With our chunk order and notation, we can rewrite the objective function as:

$$\text{maximize} \sum_{i=1}^{n_e} q_i l_i + \sum_{i=n_e+1}^{n_e+|\mathcal{E}^b|} q_i l_i. \tag{2}$$

Playback deadlines: Let t^c_i and t^d_i represent the time at which the client completes download of chunk i and the playback deadline of chunk i, respectively.

Our optimization problem has the constraint that the download completion time t^c_i of each chunk ($1 \le i \le n_e + |\mathcal{E}^b|$) must be before the playback deadline of that chunk:

$$t^c_i \le t^d_i = \begin{cases} \tau + \sum_{j=1}^{i-1} l_j, & \text{if } 1 \le i \le n_e \\ \tau + \sum_{j=1}^{n_e} l_j, & \text{if } n_e < i \le n_e + |\mathcal{E}^b| \end{cases} \tag{3}$$

Here, τ is used to denote the time at which the first chunk of segment e begins playback. If time is measured relative to the time at which video download is initiated, then for the first segment on a client's playback path, τ corresponds to the startup delay. For subsequent segments, τ is given by the value of τ for the preceding segment on the client's playback path, plus the total playback duration of that segment.

Startup delays: For simplicity, we calculate the startup delay considering only the first segment e on a client's playback path, and the subsequent branch point b. Further, we use the minimum possible startup delay when all downloaded chunks are downloaded sequentially at some minimum desired quality q^*. The startup delay τ can then be calculated as the maximum of $\max_{1 \le i \le n_e} [\sum_{j=1}^{i} \frac{q^* l_j}{R(1)} - \sum_{j=1}^{i-1} l_j]$ and $\sum_{j=1}^{n_e+|\mathcal{E}^b|} \frac{q^* l_j}{R(1)} - \sum_{j=1}^{n_e} l_j$, where $R(1)$ is the download rate when using a single TCP connection. Here, the first expression uses the tightest download completion time constraint over all of the chunks of segment e (typically yielding a startup delay equal to the download time of the first chunk, t^c_1) and the second expression uses the constraint of obtaining the first chunk of each branch choice in time for playback. The same method is used again anytime that there is a playback interruption and τ must be re-calculated.

Download times: Constraint (3) is on download completion times. Here we relate these completion times to total download rate and the policy variables (number of parallel connections, prefetching policy decisions). We restrict attention to policies that only initiate new chunk downloads and open new TCP connections at the time of a download completion. Such policies simplify connection management.

With a measured total download rate of $R_i(c_i)$ between the initiations of the ith and $(i+1)^{\text{st}}$ chunk downloads, the average download rate per connection is equal to $r_i = R_i(c_i)/c_i$, where c_i is the number of active parallel connections during this time period. Letting t^s_i denote the time at which the download of chunk i is initiated, and assuming that the per-connection rates r_i are known, we can formulate the following conservation equation:

$$\sum_{j=i}^{i+k} r_j (t^s_{j+1} - t^s_j) = q_i l_i, \tag{4}$$

where we have assumed that k new chunk downloads are initiated over the download time of the ith chunk; i.e., $t^c_i = t^s_{i+k}$. Here, the left-hand side gives the total amount of data downloaded on a single connection during the download time of chunk i, recognizing that the download rate on that connection will change with the number of active parallel connections. The right-hand side gives the chunk size.

Download rates: In practice, neither the rates r_j nor any of the future download completion times are known at the time of a download completion, when the player must determine (i) how many parallel connections to use until the next completion, and (ii) at what quality any new chunk should be downloaded. At one extreme the client has no competition on the network bottleneck link. In this case $R_i(c_i)$ is independent of c_i and $r_{i+1} = \frac{c_i}{c_{i+1}} r_i$. At the other extreme, the client has very many competing flows, $R_i(c_i)$ is approximately proportional to c_i, and r_i can be assumed to be independent of c_i.

To help ensure that delay constraints are satisfied even under uncertainty, our policies use the conservative assumption that there will be no additional bandwidth gains from using additional TCP connections, but prioritize parallelism when possible without violating these delay constraints.

3.3 Prefetching Policies

The player initially opens one connection to the server, and subsequently opens additional connections at download completion time instants, depending on the policy. Idle connections are reused, and, as shown in Figure 2, HTTP GETs for different paths can share a single connection.

To determine the number of new chunks to request next, and the quality at which each of these chunks should be downloaded, we use our optimization problem formulation. At the completion of a chunk download, we pick the quality and number of parallel new downloads that maximizes the expected weighted playback quality, as defined by the objective function (2), and that satisfies all constraints.

We consider two policies that both restrict the number of candidate schedules to consider, but differ in their complexity and how aggressive they are. The first policy, called *Optimized non-increasing quality*, considers all possible candidate schedules that (i) do not exceed the maximum number of parallel connections allowed C, (ii) do not count on opening additional connections in future steps, and (iii) in which the qualities of consecutive chunks are non-increasing. This policy reduces the number of possible schedules per number of parallel connections from M^Q, where $M = n_e + |\mathcal{E}^b| - m$ is the number of remaining chunks, m is the number of already requested chunks, and Q is the number of possible quality levels for each remaining chunk, down to $\binom{M+Q-1}{Q-1}$.

As condition (iii) can still allow for a large number of candidate schedules, we also consider a more conservative policy that modifies condition (iii) so as to require the quality of the requested chunks to be sustainable for the remaining chunks. This policy, called *Optimized maintainable quality*, requires only Q candidate schedules to be considered per number of parallel connections. Both policies pick the highest feasible quality for the next chunk, and open up additional parallel connections only if this quality can still be sustained.

To explore the tradeoff between aggressively picking high quality segments and prioritizing opening up additional parallel connections, we also consider two additional policies. Both these policies use the same three schedule constraints used with *Optimized maintainable quality*. In the first policy, called *Single connection*, we only allow a single connection to be open at each point in time. The second policy, called *Greedy bandwidth*, is much more bandwidth aggressive, and chooses chunk quality and the number of parallel new downloads so as to maximize the number of requested bytes $\sum_{i=j}^{j+m} q_i l_i$, when chunks j through $j+m$ are requested at this time instance. Table 2 summarizes our policies.

3.4 Capped Workahead

A common on-off control strategy used by HAS players is to stop requesting chunks whenever the buffer occupancy exceeds a threshold T_{max}, until the buffer occupancy drops below another threshold T_{min} [1,3].

We generalize this idea to the context of branched video. Consider a player that is currently playing a segment $e \in \mathcal{E}$ and is approaching branch point b with $|\mathcal{E}^b|$ path choices. We define a minimum buffer threshold $T_{min} = T_{single}|\mathcal{E}^b|$, where T_{single} is the amount of data that should be buffered for each path choice to be confident that a stall will not occur, but such as to avoid excessive buffering along that path, in the case that path was not selected. Using the minimum buffer threshold, we then simply set the maximum buffer threshold $T_{max} = (T_{min} + \Delta)$, where Δ is an additional buffer margin.

4. IMPLEMENTATION DESCRIPTION

Our client is implemented using the Open Source Media Framework (OSMF v2.0) libraries and the front-end player is built from Strobe Media Playback (SMP). While most modifications are focused on the classes under the `http-streaming` directory, responsible for HAS, some modifications to the files under the `StrobeMediaPlayback` directory were needed to implement user interaction[2].

4.1 High-level System Overview

After having downloaded the HAS manifest file (that describes the HAS media file and the different encodings at which the chunks are available) and the metafile for the branched video (that describes the branched video structure), the client bootstraps the player using the information from the two files.

Our modified HAS player can open parallel TCP connections, and request and download multiple chunks in parallel. The chunks belonging to the segment currently being played back are delivered in-order to the playback buffer, whereas prefetched chunks from past an upcoming branch point are downloaded into the browser cache, from which they can be very quickly retrieved when the client makes a path decision. This design has been tested and compared against in-player memory solutions such as those presented by Krishnamoorthi et al. [17], showing significant reductions in in-player memory requirements and most importantly in the time that it takes to load a new path. This is important when masking the load times from cache to player, so as to ensure that users do not observe any playback interruptions.

Finally, to minimize fetch times from the cache, our current implementation uses the browser RAM cache (of our Mozilla Firefox version 25.0.1 browser), and requests from the player are checked against the index of cache content before placing a request to the server. While we have found benefits to using a RAM cache, relative to the use of a disk cache, these differences are negligible compared to the overall benefits of prefetching to cache in general.

---

[2]Our data files and source code for our software framework are available at `http://www.ida.liu.se/~nikca/papers/mm14.html`

Table 2: Summary of prefetching policies.

Policy	Connections	Schedules considered	Objective
Optimized non-increasing quality	$1 \leq c_i \leq C^{max}$	M^Q, where $M = n_e + \lvert\mathcal{E}^b\rvert - m$	Equation (2)
Optimized maintainable quality	$1 \leq c_i \leq C^{max}$	$\binom{M+Q-1}{Q-1}$	Equation (2)
Single connection	1	$\binom{M+Q-1}{Q-1}$	Equation (2)
Greedy bandwidth	$1 \leq c_i \leq C^{max}$	$\binom{M+Q-1}{Q-1}$	$\sum_{i=j}^{j+m} q_i l_i$

4.2 Interactive Playback

Once playback is close to a branch point, a message is displayed to the user requesting selection of the desired path option. The player reads the user input and this information is communicated to the class that handles branch-point transitions. The player also maintains a record of chunks and segments it has played previously. This information is used whenever the player has to use the longest matching rule (Section 2.2).

Once playback reaches a branch point, a branch-point event is triggered. Using the time associated with the branch point, the player calculates the chunk that should be played first following the branch point. Using this chunk number, our modified player checks if the chunk has been requested (at any quality level), and if so, determines its URL. Having determined the cached URL, the player can now quickly retrieve the content and move it into the playback buffer.

The likelihood of a stall event at a branch point is strongly impacted by the `BufferTime` parameter. This gives the minimum amount of data (in seconds) the player needs to have in the playback buffer before resuming playback after a stall or avoid a stall event at a branch-point event. Whenever our download manager triggers a branch-point event, we therefore set `BufferTime` to a small value so that there is no interruption in playback. As soon as playback is resumed after a branch point event, `BufferTime` is reset to the player's default value and additional requests are placed so as to fetch all the prefetched content for the new segment from the cache. The request module then resumes its normal operation and continues prefetching of the remaining chunks in the new segment and the first chunks following the next branch point.

4.3 Parallel Connections

An important aspect of allowing seamless playback is effective workahead prefetching. Researchers have found that HAS players often experience a large degradation in performance when exposed to competing flows [1, 13, 14]. Based on initial experiments and related literature (e.g., [4]) we conjecture that multiple parallel TCP connections will help ensure stable throughput in such scenarios.

We schedule new chunk downloads and open new TCP connections based on our workahead prefetching policies, as described in Section 3, which take into account playback deadlines, current download rate estimates, and the priority order of the chunks. Our policies are conservative, in that when calculating expected download completion times it is assumed that an additional TCP connection will not increase the total achieved download rate (and so would correspondingly reduce the rate achieved by each of the existing connections). At the end of each chunk download, new parallel connections are initiated only if this is not expected to lead to violations of the playback deadlines of chunks currently being downloaded or chunks yet to be downloaded.

4.4 Rate Estimation

Rate estimation is a critical component of any HAS player. Typically, rate estimates of the available bandwidth are generated based on the download rates observed during previous downloads. To avoid placing too much weight on the most recent chunk download, most HAS players make use of a weighted average of past download times/rates.

With our branched video player, we must also account for the fact that a chunk may have been downloaded in parallel with other chunks. For this reason, each new rate measurement is scaled up accordingly, using the conservative approximation that the number of such parallel connections was constant and equal to the minimum number of parallel connections during the chunk download. As with the default player, these measurements are then used to update an exponentially weighted moving average with weight 0.4.

5. EXPERIMENTAL RESULTS

5.1 Experimental Setup

To validate our general system design and evaluate the performance of different prefetching policies, we use a basic experimental testbed, in which a client and the server are connected over a high-speed LAN. To emulate a wide range of network conditions the client machine runs `dummynet` [23], allowing us to control the available bandwidth and round-trip-times (RTTs) observed between the two machines.

The server runs Flash Media Server (FMS) version 4.5, and hosts a HAS video encoded at four bit rates (250Kb/s, 500Kb/s, 850Kb/s, and 1300Kb/s), which we refer to as quality levels 0, 1, 2, and 3, respectively. The chunk size is 4 seconds. This HAS video was generated from the Big Buck Bunny video using Adobe's encoding and HAS packaging suite. Different numbers of segments and branch points were defined from the base video for different experiments.

The player is instrumented to continually write its internal state and actions to a log file, which we later process to evaluate the performance experienced by the client. Of particular interest is the buffer occupancy, the frequency and duration of stall events, as well as the general playback rate and quality experienced by the client.

The performance of our system design, is evaluated under each of the four prefetching policies *Optimized non-increasing quality*, *Optimized maintainable quality*, *Single connection*, and *Greedy bandwidth*, all defined in Section 3.3, as well as a *Naïve* player that is capable of handling interactive branched video, but that does not perform prefetching along the different alternative paths, but simply downloads chunks only along the current default path. Naturally, this policy stalls at each branch point that the default path is not selected and simply serves as a baseline for comparison.

By comparing the two optimized policies, *Optimized non-increasing quality* and *Optimized maintainable quality*, we can evaluate the value of being conservative, as the second policy should be considerably more conservative in its quality selection for the next segment. By comparing the performance of this policy with the *Single connection* policy, we can assess the value of using parallel connections. Finally, *Greedy bandwidth* helps further capture the tradeoffs associated with aggressively opening up parallel connections.

In the following subsections we present experiments in which we vary one parameter at a time. Starting from a default scenario, we give initial insights into the impact that factors such as the available bandwidth, end-to-end RTTs, number of chunks per segment, number of branches, and amount of competing traffic have on the playback performance. Results are presented both for the first branch point and for later branch points. For Sections 5.2-5.4 we use $T_{single} = 8$, but do not place any workahead (buffer size) limitations (Section 4.4). This limitation is instead separately validated in Section 5.5. The focus of the evaluation is on client playback performance (as measured by stall probability and playback rate[3]) and we only consider a single player (possibly competing against other TCP flows, but not other similar players). Interesting directions for future work include multi-factor experiments, experiments with competing players, and experiments with more dynamic bandwidth conditions (e.g., as seen by mobile users).

5.2 Single-branch Experiments

Consider first a scenario in which the client views a basic branched video (e.g., as shown in Figure 1) with a single initial segment e with n_e chunks, and a single branch point b, with $|\mathcal{E}^b|$ branch options. In our default scenario we let $n_e = 5$ and $|\mathcal{E}^b| = 4$. Furthermore, we use a default end-to-end bandwidth of 2,500Kb/s, RTT of 150ms, and no competing traffic. The use of an RTT of 150ms is motivated by typical values observed on our networks. For example, trace route measurements to the top million websites on the Web, according to `www.alexa.com` on June 12, 2012, suggests that a client within our campus would see an average RTT of 177.4ms to these sites.

To evaluate the impact that each of the above experiment parameters has on performance, we use a "one-factor-at-a-time" approach in which we run multiple series of experiments. In each series we vary one parameter at a time, and for each configuration in that series, we perform 30 experiments per policy, and report averages and standard deviations for the average video quality and stall probabilities.

In our experiments, we consider a worst-case scenario in which the client always picks the least likely branch, which is the last branch that our prefetching policies prefetch.

Figure 3 shows the video quality distribution for our default scenario, based on which we perform our one-factor experiments. Figure 4 shows the impact of the available bandwidth on the average video playback rate and stall probability. Here, the data points for 2500 Kb/s corresponds to our default scenario, and the average quality simply corresponds to the weighted sum of the quality distributions in Figure 3. As expected, the Naïve policy, which does not perform prefetching, always results in the most stall events. Clearly, the high playback rate of this policy is misleading when evaluating the playback quality. All of the prefetching policies successfully employ some of the bandwidth that the Naïve policy uses for downloading the current segment, for prefetching instead, so as to avoid stalls. The most successful tradeoff is achieved by the *Optimized maintainable quality* policy, which adapts its quality entirely based on our optimization formulation. In contrast to the *Optimized non-increasing quality* policy, this policy is conservative in that it does not schedule high quality downloads unless it expects this quality to be sustainable. The success of a more conservative policy is particularly evident when comparing against the *Greedy bandwidth* policy, which sees both higher stall probability and lower playback rate than the *Optimized maintainable quality* policy.

We next take a closer look at the impact of the end-to-end RTTs, number of chunks n_e in the initial segment, and the number of branch options $|\mathcal{E}^b|$. Figures 5 and 6 show the playback rate and stall probability as a function of these variables. As expected, the average quality observed by the quality-aware policies increase with (i) decreasing RTTs, (ii) increasing number of chunks n_e in the initial segment, and (iii) decreasing number of branch options $|\mathcal{E}^b|$. In the case of decreasing RTTs, the TCP throughput quickly ramps up. In the case of increasing number of chunks n_e, the policies have more time to build a workahead before reaching the branch point, and finally, in the case of decreasing number of branch options, less data must be downloaded ahead of the branch point, leaving bandwidth which instead can be used to download higher quality chunks.

As when comparing across different bandwidth conditions, the quality-aware policies consistently outperform the *Greedy bandwidth* policy. Under challenging conditions, the *Optimized maintainable quality* policy is the clear winner, and consistently sees the lowest stall probabilities.

5.3 Multiple Branch Point Scenarios

In general, we assume that the distance between successive branch points is long enough that it is never worthwhile to prefetch beyond more than a single branch point. We have also performed experiments in which the branched video structure has multiple branch points, to assess how the performance differs at the later branch points. In these experiments we have used symmetric structures in which all segments have the same number of chunks n_e and all branch points have the same number of branch options $|\mathcal{E}^b|$.

Figures 7 and 8 show the average playback rate and stall probabilities for the later segments and branch points for experiments with a symmetric tree structure with depth three. While these results are consistent with those observed for the first branch point, we observe slightly higher overall playback rate for these later segments, especially for the prefetching policies with multiple parallel connections. This can be explained by the fact that these policies can continue to utilize any initiated parallel connections after passing the first branch point. However, in a few cases we also observe higher stall probabilities than for the first branch point. This is particularly apparent where there are only two chunks per segment. In this case, segments are too short to allow sufficient time for prefetching chunks from beyond the next branch point, before it is reached.

5.4 Competing Flows

We compare performance in scenarios with different numbers of competing TCP flows, and a total available bandwidth of 5Mb/s. Each competing flow was generated by downloading a large file from the same server.

[3]Startup delay is another important metric, but this is small in our experiments and does not differ among the policies.

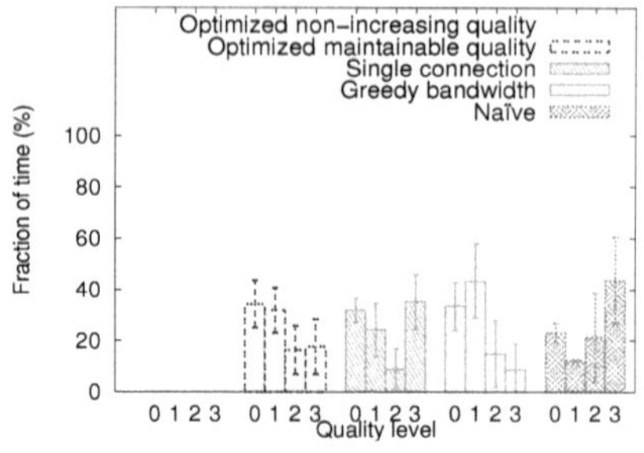

Figure 3: Playback qualities in default scenario.

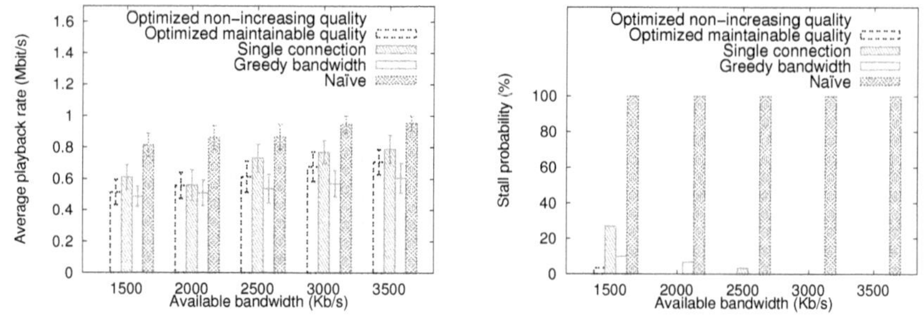

(a) Playback rate (b) Stall probability

Figure 4: Impact of the available bandwidth.

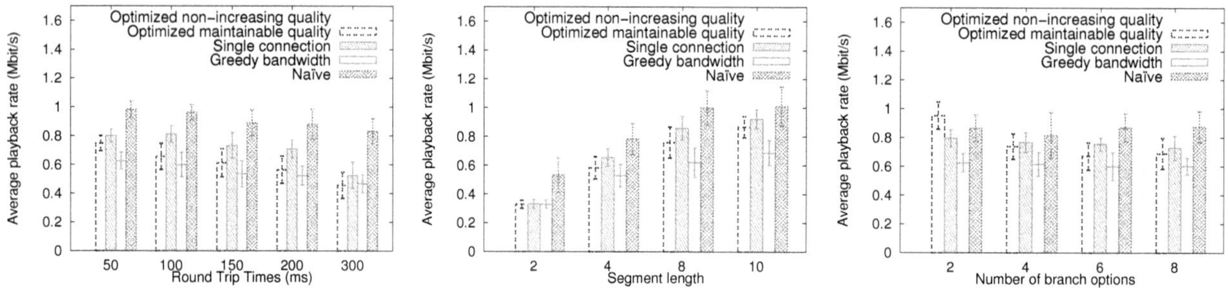

(a) End-to-end RTTs (b) Chunks n_e (c) Branch options $|\mathcal{E}^b|$

Figure 5: The average playback rate under different end-to-end RTTs, number of chunks n_e in the initial segment, and the number of branch options $|\mathcal{E}^b|$.

As seen from the results shown in Figure 9, there is a clear overall performance degradation as the number of competing flows increases. This is to be expected, as in these cases, the fair share of bandwidth available to the player quickly decreases, and the player must adapt the playback quality accordingly. However, in these cases, we can also see significant advantages to our prefetching policies that open multiple parallel connections, compared to the baseline *Single connection* policy.

5.5 Capped Workahead

The policies used in Sections 5.2-5.4 do not consider workahead (buffer size) limitations. While much of our analysis and that evaluation is focused on seamless playback, we have found that our capped workahead policy (Section 3.4) can save substantial bandwidth. To illustrate its operation, we include example results for a high-bandwidth scenario in which a client with 6Mb/s connection is playing a branched video with maximum rate encoding at 1.3Mb/s.

Figure 10 shows the variation in the buffer occupancy over time. In this scenario, we use the *Optimized maintainable quality* policy and the next upcoming branch point has 4 branch alternatives. With our default settings of $T_{single} = 8$ and $\Delta = 4$, this gives us $T_{min} = 32$ and $T_{max} = 36$.

It may appear unintuitive that we reach a buffer occupancy much higher than T_{max}. However, this can be explained by the use of many parallel connections. With a high available bandwidth, the player can be fairly aggressive in opening new parallel connections, especially initially when building up the initial buffer to T_{max}. With the buffer only accounting for completed in-order chunk downloads, the buffer occupancy can therefore easily overshoot. However, when reaching (and exceeding) T_{max} some connections are terminated. With less parallel connections being able to accumulate during the later on periods, as we can see in the figure, the later peaks in buffer occupancy are significantly smaller than the original peak.

6. RELATED WORK

Much research on on-demand streaming of branched video, sometimes referred to as nonlinear media, has focused on server-side optimizations for popular content [7, 11, 27], including the development of multicast-based solutions [7, 27]. Other works have designed authoring and media representation tools for the development of interactive media [21, 25, 26], or tag-based systems that allow tagged parts of different videos to be automatically stitched together into a single playback sequence [16].

Recently, Krishnamoorthi et al. [17] proposed the idea of using HTTP-based Adaptive Streaming (HAS) together with branched video. HAS provides an excellent framework for delivering interactive branched video. While they provide a basic proof-of-concept implementation, the focus is on the general flexibility the framework enables, both for the content designer (of the interactive branched video) and the player (which can select to prefetch chunks of different qualities). This paper substantially extends this prior work by addressing the key policy question of how the player should decide what chunks to download when. This includes optimized policies, improved connection/data management, and a detailed evaluation. Meixner et al. [20] have also considered download and caching strategies for playback of branched video, but do not consider HAS.

Motivated by their widespread usage [10, 24], linear HAS players have been widely studied. For example, Akhskabi et al. [3] present an experimental evaluation of HAS players, and the impact their different quality adaption algorithms,

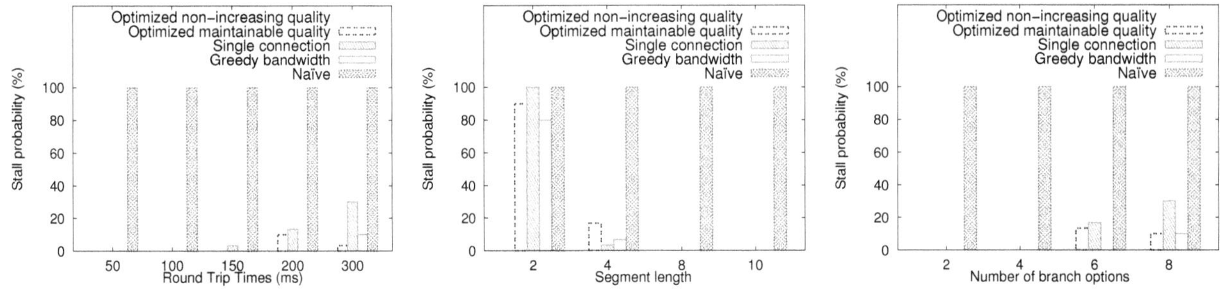

(a) End-to-end RTTs (b) Chunks n_e (c) Branch options $|\mathcal{E}^b|$

Figure 6: The stall probability under different end-to-end RTTs, number of chunks n_e in the initial segment, and the number of branch options $|\mathcal{E}^b|$.

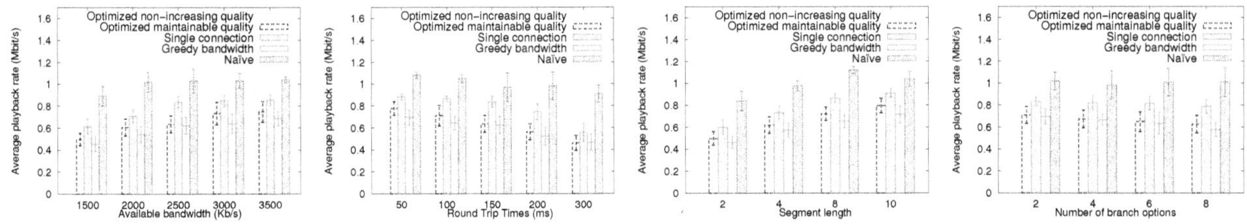

(a) Available bandwidth (b) End-to-end RTT (c) Chunks n_e (d) Branch options $|\mathcal{E}^b|$

Figure 7: Average playback rate in scenario with multiple branch points, under different conditions.

buffer management policies, and other design choices have on the users' playback quality. Huang et al. present a detailed analysis on rate estimation at the HTTP layer and different factors that contribute to instability and unfairness in HAS players [13], and propose a buffer occupancy based solution for rate adaptation [14]. De Cicco et al. [8] propose an alternative buffer occupancy based solution, which generates a long-lived TCP flow instead of an on-off flow.

For the purpose of addressing oscillations and instability in quality choices made by the player, Akhshabi et al. [2] propose using a server-based traffic shaper, while Jiang et al. [15] develop an algorithm for chunk scheduling, quality selection and bit-rate estimation that improves fairness, efficiency and stability in HAS players. HAS performance is also influenced by player interaction with caches and other middle boxes [6, 18]. Both competing HAS traffic and regular TCP flows have an effect on the rate estimation and quality adaptation of the player [1, 13].

Other works have considered the impact of quality switching on the Quality of Experience (QoE) [19, 22], typically suggesting that QoE is improved with less quality switching. While our policies by design select rates such as to avoid future down switches in playback quality, we note that the least weighted branches (which are more likely to be obtained at a lower quality) are more likely to see a temporal quality degradation. Future work could investigate potential quality oscillations in the context of branched video.

7. CONCLUSIONS

Playback interruptions and stall times can greatly impact the users' playback experience. In this paper we present the implementation of a branched video streaming player that achieves seamless transition between segments in a branched video structure without playback interruptions. Using a simple optimization framework, we design optimized prefetching policies that maximize the playback quality while ensuring sufficient workahead to avoid stall events. To achieve these goals, our policies (i) adjust the quality levels of the prefetched chunks based on the bandwidth conditions that the client experiences, and (ii) determine the appropriate number of parallel connections to ensure good download speeds and improved workahead buffering. Our results show that our solution is able to achieve rate adaptive streaming and buffer management, such as to ensure seamless playback. We also show that the proposed solution effectively adapts the quality selection and number of parallel connections so as to provide the user with the best possible video quality under scenarios with different bandwidths, RTTs, segment lengths leading to a branch point, number of branch options after a branch point, and number of competing TCP flows. While our current system is entirely client-driven, future work includes server-side optimizations.

8. ACKNOWLEDGEMENTS

The authors are thankful to our shepherd Carsten Griwodz and the anonymous reviewers for their feedback, which helped improve the clarity of the paper. This work was supported by funding from Center for Industrial Information Technology (CENIIT) and the Swedish National Graduate School in Computer Science (CUGS) at Linköping University, the Natural Sciences and Engineering Research Council (NSERC) of Canada, and National ICT Australia (NICTA).

9. REFERENCES

[1] S. Akhshabi, L. Anantakrishnan, A. C. Begen, and C. Dovrolis. What happens when HTTP adaptive streaming players compete for bandwidth? In *Proc. ACM NOSSDAV*, Feb. 2012.

[2] S. Akhshabi, L. Anantakrishnan, C. Dovrolis, and A. C. Begen. Server-based traffic shaping for stabilizing oscillating adaptive streaming players. In *Proc. ACM NOSSDAV*, Feb. 2013.

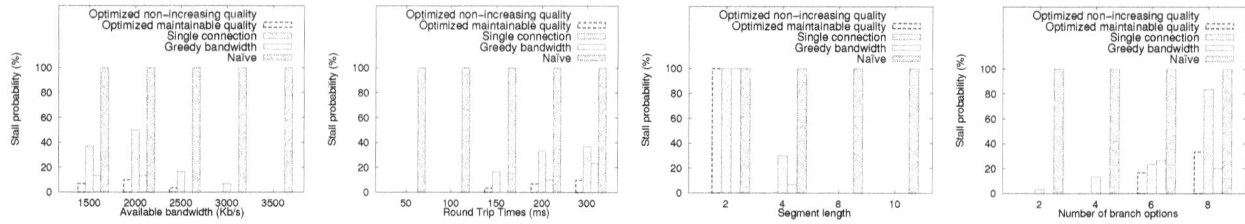

(a) Available bandwidth (b) End-to-end RTT (c) Chunks n_e (d) Branch options $|\mathcal{E}^b|$

Figure 8: Stall probability at the second branch point under different conditions.

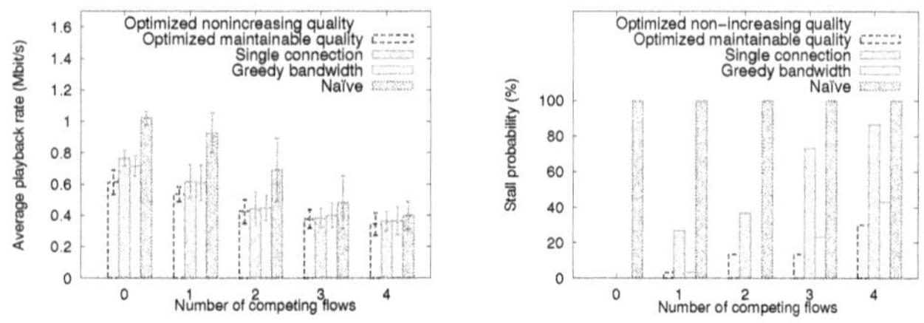

(a) Playback rate (b) Stall probability

Figure 9: The average video playback rate and stall events for different numbers of competing flows.

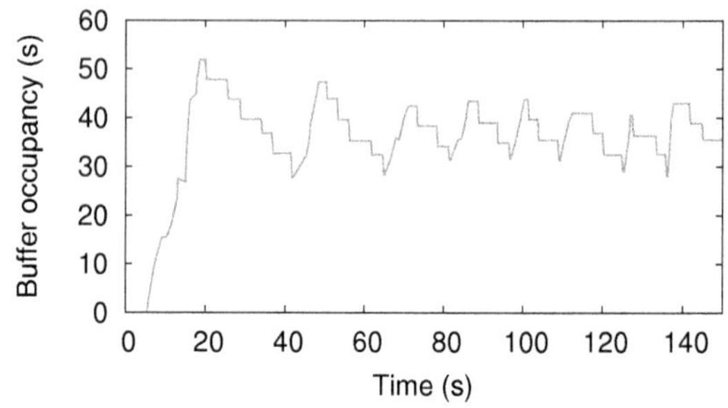

Figure 10: Buffer occupancy over time

[3] S. Akhshabi, A. C. Begen, and C. Dovrolis. An experimental evaluation of rate-adaptation algorithms in adaptive streaming over HTTP. In *Proc. ACM MMSys*, Feb. 2011.

[4] E. Altman, D. Barman, B. Tuffin, and M. Vojnovic. Parallel TCP sockets: Simple model, throughput and validation. In *Proc. IEEE INFOCOM*, Apr. 2006.

[5] A. C. Begen, T. Akgul, and M. Baugher. Watching video over the web: Part 1: Streaming protocols. *IEEE Internet Computing*, (15):54–63, 2011.

[6] S. Benno, J. O. Esteban, and I. Rimac. Adaptive streaming: The network HAS to help. *Bell Lab. Tech. Journal*, 16(2):101–114, Sep. 2011.

[7] N. Carlsson, A. Mahanti, Z. Li, and D. L. Eager. Optimized periodic broadcast of nonlinear media. *IEEE Trans. on Multimedia*, 10(5):871–884, 2008.

[8] L. De Cicco, V. Caldaralo, V. Palmisano, and S. Mascolo. ELASTIC: A client-side controller for dynamic adaptive streaming over HTTP (DASH). In *Proc. IEEE Packet Video Workshop*, Dec. 2013.

[9] F. Dobrian, V. Sekar, A. Awan, I. Stoica, D. Joseph, A. Ganjam, J. Zhan, and H. Zhang. Understanding the impact of video quality on user engagement. In *Proc. ACM SIGCOMM*, Aug. 2011.

[10] J. Erman, A. Gerber, K. K. Ramadrishnan, S. Sen, and O. Spatscheck. Over the top video: The gorilla in cellular networks. In *Proc. ACM IMC*, Nov. 2011.

[11] D. Gotz. Scalable and adaptive streaming for non-linear media. In *Proc. ACM MM*, Oct. 2006.

[12] C. Griwodz, F. T. Johnsen, S. Rekkedal, and P. Halvorsen. Caching of interactive multiple choice MPEG-4 presentations. In *Proc. IEEE IPCCC*, Apr. 2006.

[13] T. Huang, N. Handigol, B. Heller, N. McKeown, and R. Johari. Confused, timid, and unstable: Picking a video streaming rate is hard. In *Proc. ACM IMC*, Nov. 2012.

[14] T. Huang, R. Johari, and N. McKeown. Downton abbey without the hiccups: Buffer-based rate adaptation for HTTP video streaming. In *Proc. ACM SIGCOMM FhMN Workshop*, Aug. 2013.

[15] J. Jiang, V. Sekar, and H. Zhang. Improving fairness, efficiency, and stability in HTTP-based adaptive video streaming with FESTIVE. In *Proc. ACM CoNEXT*, Dec. 2012.

[16] D. Johansen, P. Halvorsen, H. D. Johansen, H. Riiser, C. Gurrin, B. Olstad, C. Griwodz, Å. Kvalnes, J. Hurley, and T. Kupka. Search-based composition, streaming and playback of video archive content. *Multimedia Tools and Applications*, 61:419–445, 2012.

[17] V. Krishnamoorthi, P. Bergström, N. Carlsson, D. Eager, A. Mahanti, and N. Shahmehri. Empowering the creative user: Personalized HTTP-based adaptive streaming of multi-path nonlinear video. In *Proc. ACM SIGCOMM FhMN Workshop*, Aug. 2013 (Also ACM SIGCOMM CCR, 43(4):591-596, Oct. 2013.).

[18] V. Krishnamoorthi, N. Carlsson, D. Eager, A. Mahanti, and N. Shahmehri. Helping hand or hidden hurdle: Proxy-assisted HTTP-based adaptive streaming performance. In *Proc. IEEE MASCOTS*, Aug. 2013.

[19] Z. Li, X. Zhu, J. Gahm, R. Pan, H. Hu, A. C. Begen, and D. Oran. Probe and adapt: Rate adaptation for http video streaming at scale. *IEEE Journal on Selected Areas in Communications*, 2014.

[20] B. Meixner and J. Hoffmann. Intelligent download and cache management for interactive non-linear video. *Multimedia Tools and Applications*, pages 1–44, June. 2012.

[21] B. Meixner and H. Kosch. Interactive non-linear video: Definition and XML structure. In *Proc. ACM DocEng*, Sep. 2012.

[22] R. K. P. Mok, X. Luo, E. W. W. Chan, and R. K. C. Chang. Qdash: A QoE-aware DASH system. In *Proc. MMSys*, Feb. 2012.

[23] L. Rizzo. Dummynet: A simple approach to the evaluation of network protocols. *ACM CCR*, 27:31–41, 1997.

[24] Sandvine. Global Internet phenomena report- 2H 2013, Technical report, Nov. 2013.

[25] A. Sobe, L. Böszörmenyi, and M. Taschwer. Video Notation (ViNo): A Formalism for Describing and Evaluating Non-sequential Multimedia Access. *International Journal on Advances in Software*, 3(1 and 2):19–30, Sep 2010.

[26] U. Spierling, S. A. Weiß, and W. Müller. Towards accessible authoring tools for interactive storytelling. In *Proc. ACM TIDSE*, Dec. 2006.

[27] Y. Zhao, D. L. Eager, and M. K. Vernon. Scalable on-demand streaming of nonlinear media. *IEEE/ACM Trans. on Networking*, 15(5):1149–1162, Oct 2007.

Self-Organized Inter-Destination Multimedia Synchronization for Adaptive Media Streaming

Benjamin Rainer
Institute of Information Technology
Alpen-Adria-Universität Klagenfurt
9020 Klagenfurt, Austria
benjamin.rainer@itec.aau.at

Christian Timmerer
Institute of Information Technology
Alpen-Adria-Universität Klagenfurt
9020 Klagenfurt, Austria
christian.timmerer@itec.aau.at

ABSTRACT

As social networks have become more pervasive, they have changed how we interact socially. The traditional TV experience has drifted from an event at a fixed location with family or friends to a location-independent and distributed social experience. In addition, more and more Video On-Demand services have adopted pull-based streaming. In order to provide a synchronized and immersive distributed TV experience we introduce self-organized Inter-Destination Multimedia Synchronization (IDMS) for adaptive media streaming. In particular, we adapt the principles of IDMS to MPEG-DASH to synchronize multimedia playback among geographically distributed peers. We introduce session management to MPEG-DASH and propose a Distributed Control Scheme (DCS) to negotiate a reference playback timestamp among the peers participating in an IDMS session. We evaluate our DCS with respect to scalability and the time required to negotiate the reference playback timestamp. Furthermore, we investigate how to compensate for asynchronism using Adaptive Media Playout (AMP) and define a temporal distortion metric for audio and video which allows the impact of playback rate variations to be modeled with respect to QoE. This metric is evaluated based on a subjective quality assessment using crowdsourcing.

Categories and Subject Descriptors: C.2.4 Computer-Communication Networks: Distributed Systems; H.5.1 Information Interfaces and Presentation:Multimedia Information Systems

General Terms: Algorithms, Design, Measurement, Experimentation

Keywords: Inter-Destination Multimedia Synchronization; Adaptive Media Streaming; Self-Organization; Quality of Experience; Dynamic Adaptive Streaming over HTTP

MM'14, November 03 - 07 2014, Orlando, FL, USA.

http://dx.doi.org/10.1145/2647868.2654938.

1. INTRODUCTION

Over the past decade social communication has evolved extensively through the introduction of platforms such as Facebook, Twitter, and Google+. These cutting-edge forms of social interaction place new requirements on the underlying technologies that help us create, distribute and view multimedia content. The traditional TV scenario as we know it, watching TV with friends and family, is becoming increasingly location independent with people wanting to experience multimedia together even if they are geographically distributed. This new form of togetherness utilizes real-time communication channels such as text, voice, or even video telephony in order to share the experience.

The presence of a real-time communication channel requires a synchronized playback of the multimedia among the participating users. Asynchronism may lead to an unpleasant viewing experience and may diminish the feeling of togetherness of the users as reported in [8]. Consider for example, if, out of a group of friends watching a soccer game together using multiple devices, some experience playback that is a few seconds ahead of the others. This kind of asynchronism between individual users may lead to a low system acceptance. Thus, playback synchronization is a key feature of such a system. In general, the synchronization of the playback among geographically distributed users is termed Inter-Destination Multimedia Synchronization (IDMS) [19]. The technical challenges of IDMS can be summarized based on the type of streaming technology employed (e.g., pull- or push-based), the selection of an appropriate synchronization point, and in cases where asynchronism does occur, an appropriate mechanism should be used to smoothly and imperceptibly synchronize the multimedia playback at the peers.

Our approach differs from existing push-based IDMS approaches that utilize RTP/RTCP receiver reports to signal timing and control information and instead extends IDMS to pull-based over-the-top streaming by adopting MPEG Dynamic Adaptive Streaming over HTTP (MPEG-DASH) [23]. Specifically, it relies on the following mechanisms: *i)* **Session management** which is responsible for managing the session to which peers belong; *ii)* **Signalling of timing and control information** allows the exchange of timing information and, if necessary, control information between peers; *iii)* **Negotiation on a reference playback timestamp** deals with the selection of a playback timestamp within a session to which the peers have to synchronize their playback; *iv)* **Carrying out the synchronization** overcome the identified asynchronism by modifying the multimedia playback of each peer.

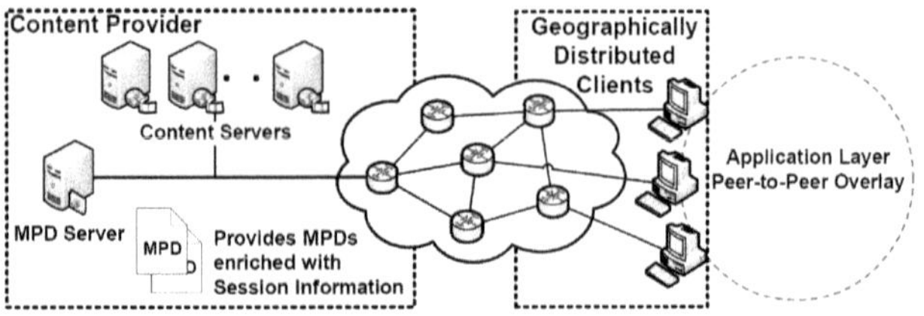

Figure 1: Architecture of IDMS for DASH.

In an RTP/RTCP-based environment these mechanisms are typically implemented at the server level whereas MPEG-DASH adopts a client-centric approach and, hence, migrates these mechanisms to the client. This facilitates simple HTTP servers that provide content in an MPEG-DASH compliant format (e.g., segmented ISO Base Media File Format or MPEG-2 Transport Stream). Furthermore, MPEG-DASH provides a Media Presentation Description (MPD) which describes the various spatial, temporal and quality dimensions of the content as well as different encodings. The MPD also contains information on the location of the content with support for multiple content servers [23].

Figure 1 illustrates our IDMS approach for pull-based streaming and, in particular, for MPEG-DASH. Rather than modifying the server side for IDMS, we introduce **session management** by defining IDMS Session Objects (ISOs). These ISOs are referenced from within the MPD and are stored at the server providing the MPD (i.e., *MPD Server*). We assume that there is a dedicated *MPD Server* that handles MPD requests from peers.

The contribution of this paper is as follows: *1)* Section 3.1 discusses our MPD extensions by including ISOs. Our actual IDMS approach adopts a Distributed Control Scheme (DCS) where peers within a session build a peer-to-peer (P2P) overlay for **signalling timing information** and **negotiating on a reference playback timestamp**. *2)* Section 3.2 describes the creation of the P2P overlay and how the playback timestamp is negotiated among the peers within a session. Furthermore, we address the scalability and reachability of peers in the P2P overlay. When peers in a session have agreed on a reference playback timestamp, the question arises how to overcome the identified asynchronism at each peer (i.e., **carrying out the synchronization**). *3)* Section 3.3 proposes a new approach that adopts Adaptive Media Playout (AMP) and aims on minimizing the impact on the Quality of Experience (QoE) when synchronizing the playback. In Section 4 we provide an evaluation of our IDMS approach and Section 5 concludes the paper.

2. RELATED WORK

2.1 Inter-Destination Multimedia Synchronization

The common assumption of most IDMS solutions is that clocks are already synchronized using existing time protocols (e.g., the Network Time Protocol (NTP) or the Precision Time Protocol (PTP)). Thus, most schemes only deal with the signalling of timing and control information to achieve IDMS among the participating clients [2, 19]. Current IDMS solutions tend to be tailored to very specific use cases, for example, the synchronization of multiplayer online games [12] or synchronization in collaborative work [11]. In general, the existing solutions can be grouped into three different schemes [2, 19]:

Master-/Slave (MS) scheme uses a dedicated master for signalling timing information which is elected from the participating peers or determined by the media source and thus implies a single point of failure. If the selected master leaves the sessions a new master must be selected or elected from the peers. Furthermore, the peers have to *trust* that the control and timing information received from the master is correct. The advantage of this scheme is that the content provider is not required to provide a central instance for signalling control and timing information. This allows the re-election of a master if the previously elected master leaves the IDMS session.

Synchronization Master Scheme (SMS) is a centralized approach where the synchronization is controlled by a synchronization master which is either the media source or a separate node (not a peer). The synchronization master collects timing information and sends timing instruction to which the peers have to adhere. This approach suffers from scalability issues because a central instance can only handle a certain number of peers. Furthermore, if more than one synchronization instance is used, dedicated communication must be implemented between them. However, the approach has the advantage that the peers can trust the synchronization instance because it is in control of the content provider.

Distributed Control Scheme (DCS) uses distributed protocols to determine a common playback timestamp to which the peers may synchronize. Here, timing information is exchanged in a P2P manner among the peers. This scheme has the highest robustness in terms of overall failure probability as the content provider is only required to host the multimedia content. Nevertheless, the peers have to trust each other. Furthermore, Network Address Translators (NATs) may cause problems, especially if the peers are behind symmetric NATs.

In [24] the authors present a *Master-/Slave scheme* to achieve IDMS, which adopts the local lag and time warp algorithm to compensate for media playback inconsistencies [14]. Therefore, a peer or the source is selected as the master to which the media playback of all clients is synchronized. In [4] and [16] a SMS approach using RTP and RTCP for achieving IDMS is presented. Therefore, the receiver report message and the application-specific message of RTCP were extended. In a *Distributed Control Scheme* all the clients signal timing information by either unicasting or multicasting messages to each other. [9] presents the *iNEM4U* approach where a DCS is used to achieve IDMS among heterogeneous network infrastructures, thus, providing IDMS as a service using the synchronized multimedia integration language. Furthermore, it introduces *iSession* for the session management, which provides an XML description of each session including the users or clients, content source, and other service-specific data.

A very recent DCS for achieving IDMS which uses an extended version of RTCP messages is presented by [18]. The proposed DCS is designed on top of RTP/RTCP and assigns peers to a specific cluster. Within a cluster the peers regularly exchange RTCP RR packets including playback timestamps in order to achieve intra-cluster synchronization. This solution uses multicast for exchanging the RTCP RR packets between the peers. Another DCS which uses multicast for intra-stream synchronization is presented in [12]. It appears that in contrast to our approach, most existing DCSs use multicast. We believe that it is risky to presume that multicast is supported by the open Internet. Furthermore, our DCS approach does not require a fully connected network where all peers can communicate with each other and our DCS approach is not directly coupled with the streaming technology employed. Pull-based streaming, typically MPEG-DASH, is used as an enabler and to store the session information that is needed to build the application layer P2P overlay (cf. Figure 1). As a result, our DCS approach may also be used in conjunction with other streaming technologies.

A crucial aspect of IDMS systems, specifically in distributed systems, is the selection of a reference or master to which other peers synchronize their media playback. In [3] three different reference selection policies are discussed: *i*) synchronization to the slowest peer, i.e., the client that is displaying the lowest frame number among the group of clients; *ii*) synchronization to the fastest peer, i.e., the client that is displaying the highest frame number; and *iii*) synchronization to the average frame number among a group of clients.

These policies assume that the playback is paused or audio/video frames are skipped to compensate for asynchronism which is in contrast to our approach where the playback rate is dynamically increased or decreased.

2.2 Adaptive Media Playout

Adaptive media playout (AMP) deals with overcoming the asynchronism and a common approach is adopting the skipping or pausing of media units. In [10] the effect of stalls during media playback was subjectively assessed. The results indicate that the Mean Opinion Score (MOS) degrades with an increase in stalls during media playback. Thus, using stalls to overcome asynchronism may lead to a low QoE for the users. AMP was introduced to overcome these shortcomings, and the approach described in [17] deals with increasing or decreasing the playback rate of media units without considering the influence on the QoE of the user. Furthermore, we assume that the playback rate of both audio and the video domain are altered simultaneously and preserving the inter-stream synchronization between audio and video.

Initially, AMP was thought to be used to compensate for buffer under-flows or over-flows by decreasing or increasing the media playback rate to allow the stabilization of the playback buffer. The authors of [25] modelled the adaptation of the media playback rate depending on the buffer variance. In [13] the buffer fill state was used to decide whether the playback rate should be increased/decreased. All these schemes try to avoid buffer under-flows or buffer over-flows in an error prone environment. In [6] the authors attempt to combine the decision with content features and use the spatial resolution of the video frames to influence the adaptive playback in wireless video streaming. We apply AMP to overcome identified asynchronisms and try to find time windows in the content where a playback rate increase or decrease has the least impact on the QoE.

The synchronization thresholds for IDMS using different communication methods were investigated by [8]. The authors found that the upper bound on acceptable asynchronism varies depending on the communication tool. For example, when users are provided with a voice communication tool, asynchronism is only subjectively perceived for delays greater than two seconds.

3. SELF-ORGANIZED IDMS FOR ADAPTIVE MEDIA STREAMING

3.1 Session Management

We adopt MPEG-DASH [23] as an enabler for our IDMS approach to pull-based streaming, extending the MPD with so-called IDMS Session Objects (ISOs) that are matched against a session key provided by users. Nevertheless, our solution remains compliant to the MPEG-DASH standard because non-IDMS peers will ignore the additional session description when parsing the MPD. Pull-based streaming such as MPEG-DASH represents multimedia content as equally sized, self-contained time units (e.g, 2s, 4s, 10s, etc.) which are referred to as segments. These segments may be stored as separate files or are indexed by byte ranges in a contiguous file. Additionally, the multimedia content may be provided in different representations – described with the MPD – offering various scalability (e.g., spatial, temporal, quality) of the multimedia content. The adaptation between representations takes place at segment boundaries.

Definition: In the context of IDMS we define an ISO as a time bounded entity to which a set of peers is assigned to. Each ISO shall have an unique identifier for a certain multimedia content.

We assume that an ISO is identified by an unique session key which is provided by the user or the application. The session key is signalled by adding it to the HTTP GET message that requests a MPD from the *MPD Server*. As peers may use Network Address Translation (NAT), Session Traversal Utilities for NAT (STUN, RFC 5389) is applied to determine the public IP address and port number to be used during the synchronization. We use the same ports for STUN negotiation and our synchronization protocols. Each peer communicates with a STUN server (in our case the *MPD Server*) in order to determine whether the peer is behind a NAT and, if available, the type of NAT. Appendix A outlines how the type of the NAT is identified and how it can be traversed.

The resulting public IP (IPv4 or IPv6) address, port number, and NAT type is added along with the session key to the initial HTTP GET message that requests the MPD from the *MPD Server* as URL parameters. The initiation of an IDMS session and the provision of the session key is out of the scope of this paper. With the initiation of an IDMS session an ISO with a specific session key is created. The *MPD Server* adds the peers that request a certain MPD with a specific session key to the corresponding ISO. When a peer requests a MPD, the *MPD Server* adds the peer to the ISO associated with the session key and returns both. As peers may join the session at different points in time, each peer may only have partial information about the actual number of peers in an IDMS session.

```
<xs:schema xmlns:xs="http://www.w3.org/2001/XMLSchema" xmlns="
    http://www.aau.at/DASH/Session" targetNamespace="http://www
    .aau.at/DASH/Session" xmlns:xlink="http://www.w3.org/1999/
    xlink">
  <xs:import namespace="http://www.w3.org/1999/xlink"
      schemaLocation="xlink.xsd"/>
  <xs:element name="IDMSSessionObject">
    <xs:complexType>
      <xs:sequence>
```

```
                <xs:element name="PeerList" type="PeerListType"
                    minOccurs="0" maxOccurs="unbounded"/>
                <xs:element name="TTL" type="xs:dateTime"
                    minOccurs="1" maxOccurs="1"/>
            </xs:sequence>
            <xs:attribute ref="xlink:href"/>
            <xs:attribute ref="xlink:actuate" default="onLoad"/>
        </xs:complexType>
    </xs:element>
    <xs:complexType name="PeerListType">
        <xs:sequence>
            <xs:element name="Peer" type="PeerType" minOccurs="0"
                maxOccurs="unbounded"/>
        </xs:sequence>
    </xs:complexType>
    <xs:complexType name="PeerType">
        <xs:sequence>
            <xs:element name="Identifier" type="
                PeerIdentifierType" minOccurs="1"
                maxOccurs="unbounded"/>
        </xs:sequence>
    </xs:complexType>
    <xs:complexType name="PeerIdentifierType">
        <xs:sequence>
            <xs:element name="IP" type="xs:string"/>
            <xs:element name="Port" type="xs:integer"/>
        </xs:sequence>
        <xs:attribute name="nat" type="xs:string"/>
    </xs:complexType>
</xs:schema>
```

Listing 1: IDMS Session Object for MPEG-DASH.

Listing 1 depicts the XML Schema for an ISO. The ISO includes a list of peers (represented by *@PeerListType*) in the IDMS session and a Time-To-Live (TTL). The maximum TTL for an IDMS session is the duration of the requested multimedia content. The *@PeerIdentifierType* contains the public IP address, port number, and the NAT type of a specific peer. Note that a peer may have more than one identifier if it has several network interfaces that are connected to different networks.

```
<MPD xmlns="urn:mpeg:dash:schema:mpd:2011" xmlns:iso="http://www
    .aau.at/DASH/Session" type="static"
    mediaPresentationDuration="PT3256S" minBufferTime="PT1.2S"
    profiles="urn:mpeg:dash:profile:isoff-on-demand:2011">
<BaseURL>http://www.example.com/</BaseURL>
<Period>
    <AdaptationSet>
        <Representation id="0" mimeType="video/mp4" codecs="avc1,
            mp4a" startWithSAP="1" bandwidth="1713804">
            <!-- ... representation info -->
        </Representation> <!-- ... more representations -->
    </AdaptationSet>
</Period>
<iso:IDMSSessionObject>
    <iso:PeerList>
        <iso:Peer>
            <iso:Identifier nat="NoNAT">
                <iso:IP>143.205.122.242</iso:IP>
                <iso:Port>8029</iso:Port>
            </iso:Identifier>
            <iso:Identifier nat="FullCone">
                <iso:IP>143.205.199.149</iso:IP>
                <iso:Port>8030</iso:Port>
            </iso:Identifier>
        </iso:Peer> <iso:Peer>
            <iso:Identifier nat="PortRestricted">
                <iso:IP>10.0.0.5</iso:IP>
                <iso:Port>8029</iso:Port>
            </iso:Identifier>
        </iso:Peer> <!-- ... more peers -->
      </iso:PeerList> <iso:TTL>2014-07-26T21:32:52</iso:TTL>
</iso:IDMSSessionObject>
</MPD>
```

Listing 2: Excerpt of an example MPD with an ISO.

Byte 0	1	17	21	25	29
Type	IP	Port	PTS	NTP TS	

Figure 2: Message structure for the *coarse synchronization.*

Listing 2 shows an excerpt of an MPD comprising an ISO. Peers requesting the MPD will be added to the ISO. The process of adding peers to the ISO induces an implicit ordering of the peers which is used by the subsequent P2P synchronization algorithms. Every peer numbers the peers in the ISO strict monotonically increasing beginning with one.

3.2 Signalling of Timing Information and Negotiation of the Playback Timestamp

For creating the P2P overlay in order to signal timing information and negotiating a reference playback timestamp among the peers, we propose to determine the playback timestamp to which the peers shall synchronize their playback in two steps. In the first step, referred to as *coarse synchronization*, new peers request the segments which are currently played by other peers within the IDMS session, thus reducing the synchronization effort and building the P2P overlay. In a second step, *fine synchronization*, peers agree on a reference playback timestamp in a self-organized manner by using the constructed P2P overlay. In general, we assume that the clocks of the peers are synchronized (e.g. using NTP or PTP).

3.2.1 Peer-To-Peer Overlay Construction and Coarse Synchronization

The P2P overlay is created using the information contained in the ISO. Prior to any communication among the peers, each peer uses STUN to detect the NAT type and, in the case of a restricted NAT or port restricted NAT, it follows the procedure described in Appendix A. UDP is used as the transport protocol between the peers because reliable communication is not essential. Each peer that receives the ISO requests the current playback timestamp from all peers it lists. Figure 2 depicts the message structure for the *coarse synchronization* which is used for both response and request as specified by the *Type* field. For requests, the fields *IP* and *Port* are set to the public IP address and port number of the requesting peer – other fields are empty – which indicates that the receiving peer shall respond with its current playback timestamp. The responding peer sets its own IP address (field *IP*) and port number (field *Port*) allowing peers to track which peers responded to which requests. The field *PTS* is set to the current playback timestamp and the field *NTP TS* is the corresponding NTP timestamp. The NTP timestamp is used to align all received timestamps to the same point in time. As the list of peers in the ISO grows over time, peers joining the session early will only have a subset of available peers. Therefore, if a peer is asked for its playback timestamp by an unknown peer it adds the associated IP address and port to the list of known peers.

Algorithm 1 implements *coarse synchronization*. The peer requesting the playback timestamps waits until either all requests have been satisfied or a given time period T_C has elapsed. If no timestamp arrives during T_C the peer starts over by requesting playback timestamps from the known peers (i.e., *request_timestamps*). Each peer that receives a request (i.e., *receive_request*) responds with its IP address, port number, playback timestamp, and the corresponding

Algorithm 1 Coarse Synchronization.

```
function request_timestamps
    for all p ∈ peers do
        sendPacket(Type.Request, p.IP, p.Port, myIP,
            myPort, null, null)
    end for
    wait(T_C) ∨ receivedTS.size() = peers.size()
    if receivedTS.size() = 0 then
        request_timestamps()
    else
        calculateSegment()
    end if
end function
function receive_request(pt : packet)
    if isPeerKnown(pt.srcIP, pt.srcPort) ≠ true then
        addPeer(pt.srcIP, pt.srcPort)
    end if
    sendPacket(Type.Response, pt.srcIP, pt.srcPort,
        myIP, myPort, PTS, NTPTS)
end function
function receive_timestamp(pt : packet)
    receivedTS.add(pt.PTS, pt.NTP)
end function
```

NTP timestamp. The timestamps from the responses may be combined to calculate the start segment using one of four strategies, namely the *i)* maximum, *ii)* minimum, *iii)* average, and *iv)* weighted average of the received timestamps. Which strategy should be selected depends on the application and may be influenced by Quality of Service (QoS) parameters like bandwidth, delay, and maximum selectable bit-rate of the multimedia content. In our application, we determine the start segment using the average of the playback timestamps.

Let T_{ref} be the timestamp resulting from such a strategy. We calculate the segment to start with by $\lceil \frac{T_{ref}}{T_s} \rceil$, where T_s is the segment size in seconds. Suppose that M is the theoretical reference timestamp to which all peers will adjust their playback. Therefore, without loss of generality the asynchronism ξ after asking the other peers for their playback timestamp and downloading N segments until the playback starts is given by:

$$0 \leq |\xi| \leq |M - \lceil \frac{T_{ref}}{T_s} \rceil \cdot T_s + \sum_{i=1}^{N} \frac{b_c(t_i)}{b_r(t_i)}| \qquad (1)$$

where $b_c(t)$ is the bit-rate of the transmission channel in bit/s at time instant t and $b_r(t)$ is the bit-rate of the current representation of the multimedia content. The *coarse synchronization* ensures that if a peer joins an IDMS session it starts with a segment that is as closest as possible to the segment the other peers are currently playing.

3.2.2 Self-organized Fine Synchronization

The second synchronization phase starts once playback commences at the segment determined by *coarse synchronization* with the goal of agreeing on a reference timestamp to which all the peers in an IDMS session should synchronize. We propose *Merge and Forward*, a flooding-based algorithm that calculates the average playback timestamp among the peers in a distributed and self-organized manner. Here, the average playback timestamp is utilized because it favors neither the peers already within the IDMS session or those that have just joined. Selecting the minimum would privilege

Algorithm 2 Merge and Forward.

```
B_i, L_i, P_i, NTP_i, I_i^M, I_i^m, S_i, C_i ← 1
function broadcastToNeighbors
    update(P_i, NTP_i)
    for all p ∈ peers do
        sendPacket(P_i, NTP_i, I_i^M, I_i^m, S_i, C_i, B_i)
    end for
end function
function receiveBloomFilter(P_j, NTP_j, I_j, S_j, C_j, B_j)
    if S_j > S_i then
        B_i ← H(i), L_i ← ∅, S_i ← S_j, C_i ← 1
    end if
    update(P_i, NTP_i), update(P_j, NTP_j)
    if B_i ⊕ B_j ≠ 0 ∧ B_i ∩ B_j = ∅ then
        B_i ← B_i + B_j, P_i ← (P_i·C_i + P_j·C_j) / (C_i + C_j)
        I_i^M = max{I_i^M, I_j^M}, I_i^m = min{I_i^m, I_j^m}
        C_i = C_i + C_j
    end if
    if B_i ⊕ B_j ≠ 0 ∧ B_i ∩ B_j ≠ 0 ∧ B_j ∉ L_i then
        if C_j ≥ C_i ∧ i ∈ B_i ∩ B_j then
            B_i ← B_j, P_i ← P_j, C_i ← C_j
        else if C_j ≥ C_i then
            B_i ← B_j + H(i), P_i ← (P_j·C_j + P_i) / (C_j + 1)
            C_i ← C_j + 1
        end if
        I_i^M = max{I_i^M, I_j^M}, I_i^m = min{I_i^m, I_j^m}
    end if
    L_i ← {B_j} ∪ L_i
end function
```

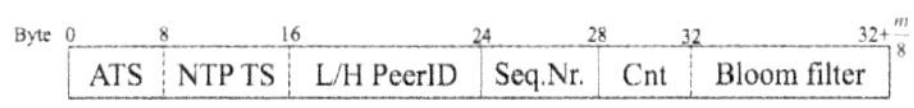

Figure 3: Message structure for the *fine synchronization.*

peers that recently joined an IDMS session and it will force all other peers to synchronize to this playback timestamp. The maximum will have the opposite effect. *Merge and Forward* focuses on reducing the overhead introduced when exchanging playback timestamps using unicast between all peers in contrast to other algorithms which use multicast [18]. Furthermore, by avoiding *pure flooding* it maintains media throughput and thus the QoE.

For tracking which and how many peers have contributed to the average playback timestamp we use a Bloom filter. Therefore, each peer uses the same set of hash functions $h_1(x)$, ..., $h_k(x)$ for computing the bits to set when inserting itself into the Bloom filter [5]. This allows us to exchange a fixed length packet and contributes to the scalability of our P2P approach. Figure 3 depicts the message structure for the P2P communication once the overlay has been constructed by the *coarse synchronization* with the following semantics: *a)* ***ATS***: average playback timestamp. *b)* ***NTP TS***: NTP timestamp for aligning the playback timestamp. *c)* ***L/H PeerID***: the lowest and highest peer identification number seen by the sending peer according to the ISO (i.e., number of *Peer* elements within the ISO). *d)* ***Seq.Nr.***: indicates the current synchronization round. *e)* ***Cnt.***: the number of peers contributed to current average playback timestamp. *f)* ***Bloom filter***: fixed length Bloom filter with a length of m bits. The *PeerID* is used later for determining how many peers are in a certain Bloom filter. The overall size of such a message is $24 + \frac{m}{8}$ bytes. The *Seq.Nr.* allows the peers to trigger a re-synchronization by increasing the sequence number (e.g., due to asynchronism or MPD update). Other peers receiving a message with a higher sequence number will reset to the initial condition and start over. The P2P algorithm making use of this message structure is shown in Algorithm 2 and referred to as *Merge and Forward (M&F)*.

Each peer i maintains a Bloom filter B_i and inserts itself with its own peer id according to the indices obtained by the use of a common set of k hash functions $h_1(x), ..., h_k(x)$, a list of already seen Bloom filters L_i, a playback timestamp P_i and its corresponding NTP timestamp depicted by NTP_i, a sequence number S_i which is initially set to zero, and the highest peer id seen I_i. $H(x)$ depicts the function that generates the bit-sequence for peer x by applying $h_1(x), ..., h_k(x)$. Each peer **forwards** B_i, P_i, C_i, I_i^M and I_i^m periodically to its neighbors depicted by the function $broadcastToNeighbors$, with period τ. If peer i receives a Bloom filter from one of its neighbors j, it checks whether it can **merge** the Bloom filters. The Bloom filters can only be merged if they are disjoint to avoid introducing a bias to the weighted average. If the Bloom filters are merged by using the bit-wise OR depicted by $+$, then we calculate the weighted average between P_i and P_j. C_i depicts the number of peers that contributed to the average playback timestamp. If the Bloom filters are not disjoint and if we have not seen the received Bloom filter yet, we store the received Bloom filter and add it to the list of already seen Bloom filters. Finally, the peer id I_i^M is set to the maximum of I_i^M and I_j^M and I_i^m is set to the minimum of I_i^m and I_j^m. After a synchronization round has finished (all peers hold the same reference playback timestamp), a peer may trigger a new synchronization round by increasing S_i. If a peer receives an sequence number that is higher than its own, it resets B_i such that it only includes itself, empties the list L_i and sets $S_i \leftarrow S_j$. The re-synchronization may be triggered if a peer has paused the playback of the multimedia content or if it is unable to synchronize its playback to the negotiated reference. In the latter case, the peer may increase the importance of its timestamp by introducing a weight (e.g., $PTS = w_i \cdot PTS$, $w_i \geq 1$).

In order to calculate the overlap or the intersection of two Bloom filters ($B_i \cap B_j$), the algorithm must know which peers have already been inserted. Due to the nature of Bloom filters testing if peers are in a filter may identify peers that were not inserted (false positives). Consider a test function $test(B, x)$ that returns true if peer x was inserted into the Bloom Filter. Let's assume we know that peer x is not in Bloom filter B and that when we receive the Bloom filter of size m, s bits are set by the use of k hash functions. If we test whether peer x was inserted into the Bloom filter and this test returns true we have encountered a false positive. The probability of encountering a false positive for the received Bloom filter is given by $(\frac{s}{m})^k$, s the number of bits set [5]. Therefore, if we try to determine which and how many peers $(p_1, p_2, ..., p_n)$ have contributed to the timestamp represented by the Bloom filter, assuming that we test for n peers and h peers are really in the Bloom Filter ($h \leq n$) the false positive rate is given by: $P_{false}(p_1 \vee p_2 \vee ... \vee p_n) = \sum_{i=1}^{n-h}(\frac{s}{m})^k = (n-h) \cdot (\frac{s}{m})^k$ (due to independence). *Merge and Forward* uses the *L/H PeerID* as the upper limit and lower limit to test for peers in a Bloom filter. Nevertheless, this has no impact on the calculated average playback timestamp because the false positives have only an impact on which Bloom filters are merged and, thus, only increase the required time. Therefore, we assume that the size of Bloom filter is chosen sufficiently large. It can be proven that the resulting average playback timestamp equals to real average playback timestamp of the peers [*Sketch of proof*: solving the recursive construction of the weighted average playback timestamp (binary tree) leads to the real average playback timestamp. Furthermore, through contradiction it is shown that the calculated average playback timestamp is unique for the same number of peers and playback timestamps among different network graphs].

3.3 Dynamic AMP for IDMS

In this section we describe our dynamic AMP approach for IDMS which dynamically increases/decreases the playback rate to overcome the asynchronism without impacting the QoE. Other approaches neither consider the impact on the QoE nor vary the playback rate dynamically every time a peer synchronizes its playback (cf. Section 2). We propose using the current buffer contents of a peer for determining when and for which duration we should change the playback rate and formulate the following general constrained optimization problem:

$$\arg\min_X f(X) \tag{2a}$$

$$x_2 \cdot (x_3^{sign(\xi)} - 1) \cdot sign(\xi) = |\xi| \tag{2b}$$

$$L \leq B - x_2 \cdot x_3 + x_2 \cdot \frac{b_c}{b_r} \tag{2c}$$

$$x_1 \leq T \tag{2d}$$

$$x_2 \leq t_{max} \tag{2e}$$

where $X \in \mathbb{R}^3$ is our vector with $(x_1, x_2, x_3)^T$, x_1 denotes the starting time of the playback rate change relative to the current buffer, x_2 denotes the duration of the playback rate change, and x_3 denotes the target playback rate. Our aim is to find values for X such that X^* is a minimizer for $f(X)$ $(\forall X \in \mathbb{R}^3 : f(X^*) \leq f(X))$. $f(X)$ can be any function that models the impact of changing the playback rate for the given duration on the QoE. Furthermore, we define constraints that reduce the set of feasible points. First, we introduce the constraint as depicted by Equation 2b which states that the given asynchronism should be compensated for by selecting appropriate values for x_2 and x_3, respectively. ξ denotes the asynchronism identified by comparing the current playback timestamp to the reference timestamp. If $\xi < 0$ the playback rate is reduced and if $\xi > 0$ the playback rate is increased in order to compensate for the asynchronism. Equation 2c avoids buffer underflows and, thus, stalls in the multimedia playback. This constraint only applies if the playback rate is increased. In particular, L denotes the lower buffer threshold in seconds, B the current buffer fill state in seconds, b_c the client's bandwidth, and b_r the bit-rate of the selected representation. Furthermore, we constrain the starting time (T) of the playback rate variation by bounding x_1 (cf. Equation 2d). Equation 2e limits the duration (t_{max}) of the playback variation.

By measuring distortion in the audio and video domain we attempt to approximate the impact of playback rate changes on the QoE. Therefore, we define a metric that allows measuring the playback rate variations with respect to the (visual) motion intensity and the (audio) spectral energy. We derive the visual feature (motion intensity) from the average length of the motion vectors between two consecutive frames whereas the audio featrue is extracted from the spectral energy of the audio frames (for each channel). We compare these audio-visual (AV) features from a given content section with a given duration (e.g., 2s) for the increased/decreased playback rate and the nominal playback rate. As the length of the asynchronism is known, both the target playback rate and the duration of the playback rate change can be calculated. Importantly, introducing an increase/decrease in the playback rate will alter the duration of the respective content section which may or may not be perceived by the user.

The video metric is defined in Equation 3.

$$d_v(X) = \sum_{j=s_v}^{\widetilde{e_v}} f_v(j) - \sum_{j=s_v}^{e_v} f_v(j) \tag{3}$$

where s_v denotes the number of the first frame of the content section for which the playback rate should be changed. $\widetilde{e_v} = s_v + \lfloor (t_e - t_b) \cdot fps_{\Delta\mu} \rfloor$ is the index of the last frame when using the increased/decreased playback rate, t_e the end timestamp of the content section, t_a the start timestamp of the content section, $fps_{\Delta\mu}$ the frame rate of the changed playback rate $\Delta\mu$, and e_v is the number of the last frame using the nominal playback rate for a given duration. f_v denotes the average motion intensity.

The audio metric is defined in Equation 4.

$$d_a(X) = \sum_{c=1}^{C} \Big(\big(\sum_{u=s_a}^{\widetilde{e_a}} \sum_{k=0}^{S_f} |\widehat{a}_{c_u}(k)| - \sum_{u=s_a}^{e_a} \sum_{k=0}^{S_f} |\widehat{a}_{c_u}(k)| \big) \Big) \tag{4}$$

where C denotes the number of available audio channels and S_f denotes the highest frequency. s_a, $\widetilde{e_a}$, and e_a are defined in the same way as for video. The Fourier transformed audio frames are denoted by $\widehat{a}_c$ (we use a half overlapping Hamming window) for a given audio channel c.

The combined AV metric is defined in Equation 5.

$$g(X) = \sqrt{d_v(X)^2 + d_a(X)^2} \tag{5}$$

$g(X)$ is neither convex nor continuous because it depends on the features which are derived from the actual content.

The highest asynchronism in our IDMS system is given by Equation 1. The initial asynchronism of a newly joined peer depends on the time the peer requires for downloading sufficient segments such that it can start the playback. If the asynchronism is greater than the current buffer fill state the peer will not be able to compensate the asynchronism. In such cases, the synchronization process must be partitioned into a number of smaller synchronization processes. Therefore, we define the asynchronism for each synchronization process as $\delta_{k+1} = \min(\xi - \delta_k, B - L)$, starting with $\delta_0 = \min(\xi, B - L)$. This has no effect if ξ is lower than zero because reducing the playback rate does not affect the buffer fill state.

Using the sequential unrestricted minimization technique, we transform the general optimization problem given in Equation 2 into the following optimization problem:

$$\arg\min_X f(X) = \begin{cases} g(X) + \gamma \cdot \sum_{i=1}^{3} p_i(X) & \text{if } \xi \geq 0 \\ g(X) + \gamma \cdot \sum_{i=2}^{3} p_i(X) & \text{if } \xi < 0 \end{cases} \tag{6a}$$

$$p_1(X) = \min\{0, B - x_2 \cdot x_3 + x_2 \cdot \frac{b_c}{b_r} - L\}^2 \tag{6b}$$

$$p_2(X) = \min\{0, T - x_1\}^2 \tag{6c}$$

$$p_3(X) = \min\{0, t_{max} - x_2\}^2 \tag{6d}$$

Equation 6a shows the transformed cost function. To reduce the set of feasible points we use the constraint given in Equation 2b and apply the implicit function theorem, reducing x_2 to a function of x_3 by $u(x_3) = sign(\delta_k) \cdot \frac{|\delta_k|}{x_3^{sign(\delta_k)} - 1}$ for $x_3 \neq 1$ [*Proof*: by application of the implicit function theorem on $f(x_3, x_2) = x_2 \cdot (x_3^{sign(\delta_k)} - 1) \cdot sign(\delta_k) - |\delta_k|$]. Thus, we try to find values x_1 and x_3 that minimize $f(X)$. The penalty function $p_1(X)$ (cf. Equation 6b) states that the buffer fill state shall not be drained below the threshold L when increasing the playback rate. $p_2(X)$ (cf. Equation 6c) depicts the costs that depend on the starting point of the playback rate variation. $p_3(X)$ (cf. Equation 6d) states that a peer should be synchronized within t_{max} seconds. γ sets the penalty factor for the transformed constraints ($\gamma > 0$). For solving the optimization problem during the multimedia playback we use multiple instances of the Nelder-Mead algorithm with different starting points [20].

To conclude, our dynamic AMP approach overcomes asynchronism by searching for content sections where the playback rate may be increased/decreased having the least impacting on the QoE.

4. EXPERIMENTAL RESULTS

The evaluation of our self-organized IDMS for DASH approach comprises two aspects. First, we investigate the proposed DCS by simulation with respect to the traffic generated during the negotiation on the reference playback timestamp and the time needed until all peers have the necessary information for calculating the average playback timestamp. Second, we conduct a subjective quality assessment for evaluating the introduced A/V metric and the dynamic AMP approach.

4.1 Evaluation of Merge and Forward

To evaluate the performance of the *Merge and Forward* algorithm, we compare our algorithm to an approach that is similar to the one described in [18]. As this approach uses multicast, we modify it such that each peer aggregates all received playback timestamps into a single message and sends them periodically to its neighbors using unicast because we do not assume that multicast is in place. We call this approach *Aggregate*. We compare the two algorithms based on the overhead produced by peers agreeing on the average playback timestamp and the duration of the process. The evaluation scenario foresees that a certain number of peers will join the P2P overlay over the lifetime of the session. If the peers join one by one after the existing peers have already synchronized, the time required by *Merge and Forward* to synchronize is the same as *Aggregate*. Furthermore, peers may leave the P2P overlay during the negotiation process as any reference timestamp they have contributed persists until a re-synchronization is triggered.

We simulated the algorithms on Erdös-Renyi random networks [7] implemented using OMNeT++ [21]. A period τ of 250 milliseconds was used for both algorithms, with the round trip time set to 300 milliseconds and a maximum clock skew of 30 milliseconds randomly (uniformly) chosen from an interval of $[-15, 15]$. For *Merge and Forward* we set the size of the Bloom filter to 512 bit. We generate random net-

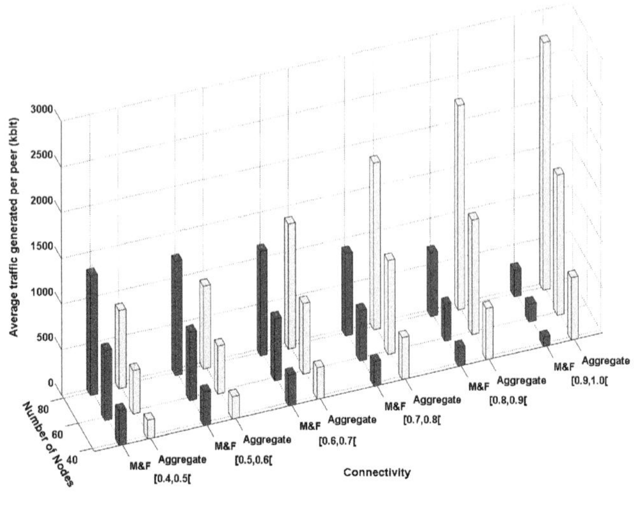

Figure 4: Traffic overhead per peer until all peers have the same reference playback timestamp using *Merge and Forward* (M&F) and *Aggregate* (95% CI).

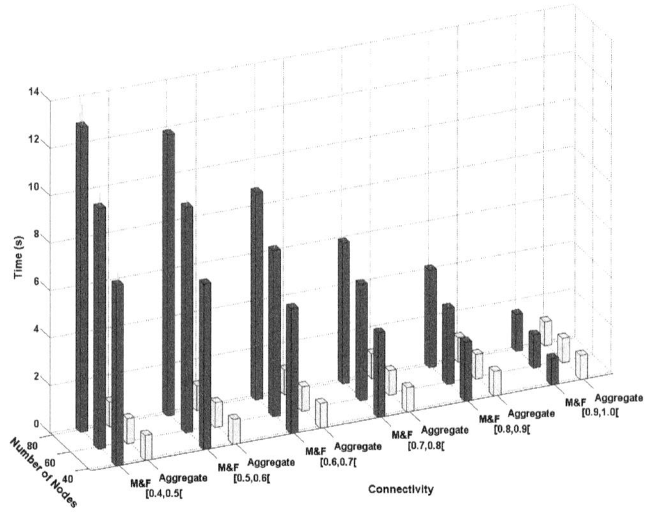

Figure 5: Time for the distributed calculation of the average playback timestamp using *Merge and Forward* (M&F) and *Aggregate* (95% CI).

works for the following number of peers: 40, 60, and 80 with following probabilities for creating a connection between two peers: 0.1 to 0.9 increased in 0.1 steps. We use these numbers of peers and connectivities in order to show how the algorithms scale when increasing the number of peers and their connectivity. For each of the parameter settings we conducted 30 simulation runs and taking the average of the results.

Figure 4 illustrates the average network traffic (in kbit) generated at each peer by both algorithms during the agreement phase with respect to the overall connectivity of the network. The connectivity is given by the ratio of the average node degree and the number of peers in the network ($c = \frac{\frac{1}{|V|}\sum_{i=1}^{|V|} d_G(v)}{|V|-1}$, V is the set of vertices and $d_G(v)$ is the degree of node $v \in V$). The x-axis represents connectivity in intervals which increase in 0.1 steps. With low connectivity, *Merge and Forward* generates more traffic than *Aggregate* but this is due to the time required to compute the average playback timestamp among all peers. If the connectivity increases the fixed length messages of *Merge and Forward* start to pay off and it subsequently outperforms the *Aggregate* algorithm.

Figure 5 depicts the time for the distributed calculation of the average playback timestamp. Here, *Aggregate* represents the optimum case because lists of timestamps can be merged even if they overlap because the contribution of each peer can be clearly identified. Using Bloom filters and only a single field for the average playback timestamp, the contribution of a single peer cannot be uniquely identified anymore. If a peer receives a Bloom filters where a subset of the peers contributed to the received one and to one that the peer holds, calculating the weighted average would yield a skewed weighted averaged compared to the real weighted average without the overlap. However, with an increase in the connectivity, the time needed by *Merge and Forward* converges to the time needed by *Aggregate*. This shows that the negotiation time required by *Merge and Forward* does not solely depend on the number of peers in the overlay.

Combining Figure 4 and Figure 5 yields the average traffic in kbit/s generated at each peer by both algorithms during the agreement phase, *Merge and Forward* always outperforms *Aggregate*. If a peer does join an IDMS session, the whole process of calculating the reference playback timestamp is restarted. Compared to *Merge and Forward*, using *Aggregate* or any other pure flooding algorithm will generate more overhead as the number of peers or connectivity increases. The assumption that *Merge and Forward* has to calculate the average among all playback timestamps and the low overhead result in an increase in the time until all peers hold the same timestamp.

4.2 Evaluation of the dynamic AMP

We evaluated our dynamic AMP approach by conducting a subjective quality assessment using crowdsourcing [22]. The aim is to determine how the AV metrics introduced in Equation 3, Equation 4, and Equation 5 reflect the actual impact on the QoE when increasing or decreasing the playback rate.

To carry out our user study we used the Microworkers [15] crowdsourcing platform which hosts so-called campaigns to which users (microworkers) can subscribe. These campaigns include a detailed description of the task and ask subjects to submit proof that they participated in the campaign. Our user study was designed with a duration of 15 minutes and offered \$0.25 as a reward, slightly more that the typical \$0.20 paid for such a campaign. The design of our study is as follows: *1.)* We present an introduction where we explain the task and the test procedure in detail. *2.)* A pre-questionnaire is presented to the subject which asks for demographic data. *3.)* A short training phase is conducted in order to mitigate the surprise effect. *4.)* The main evaluation takes place using a Single Stimulus method as defined in [1]. *5.)* At the end a post-questionnaire is presented which allows for comments. *6.)* A unique token is provided as proof for a successful participation.

For the training phase we selected a short video sequence from Babylon A. D. The training sequence is presented with three different media playback rates $\mu \in \{1, 0.5, 2\}$ in order to introduce AMP to the subject and and the corresponding effect on the playback. A playback rate of one depicts the

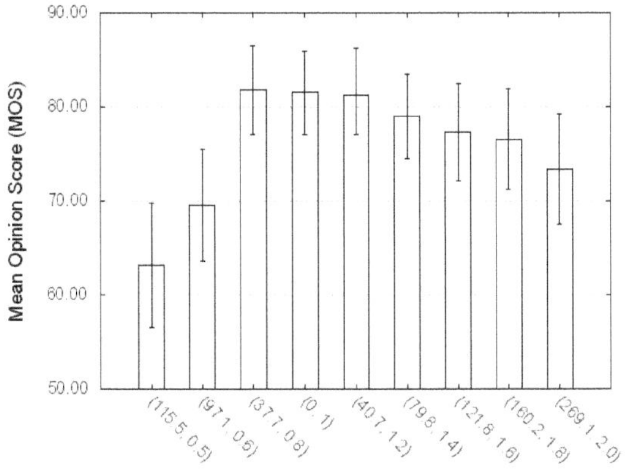

Figure 6: MOS and 95% CI for $(\overline{g(X)}, \mu)$.

nominal playback rate of the video sequence (e.g., 25 frames per second). A playback rate of 2 is twice as fast as the nominal playback rate and 0.5 is half the nominal playback rate. The stimulus for the main evaluation is the first 51 seconds of Big Buck Bunny (http://www.bigbuckbunny.org). This content provides high and low motion scenes as well as scenes with high and low audio volume. We introduce four content sections for which the playback rates are increase and decreased. The playback timestamps for the selected content sections in seconds are as follows (start-end): 6.4–7.2, 9–10, 16–18, 35–38, and 46–49. These content sections are presented with following playback rates: 0.5, 0.6, 0.8, 1, 1.2, 1.4, 1.6, 1.8, 2. The multimedia player that is employed uses the Waveform Similarity based Overlap-Add algorithm [26] that tries to preserve pitch for the audio domain while increasing or decreasing the playback rate. For rating the QoE we use a continuous rating scale [0, 100] displayed as a slider. Furthermore, we randomly insert a control question after a stimulus presentation which asks the participants what they have seen in the previous video sequence.

For the statistical analysis of the results, we screened the subjects according to [1] and specifically removed participants who failed to correctly answer to the control question. This yielded 55 (48 male and 7 female) subjects for the statistical analysis out of a total of 80 participants.

The QoE ratings for each stimulus presentation were subject to a Shapiro-Wilk-test to assess whether the ratings were normally distributed. The null hypothesis ($H0$), stating that no normal distribution is present, was rejected for each configuration of playback rates. Furthermore, we calculate the average distortion $\overline{g(X)}$ for each stimulus presentation.

Figure 6 depicts the assessed Mean Opinion Score (MOS) for each tuple $(\overline{g(X)}, \mu)$. The hidden reference condition is given by $\mu = 1$. The results state that playback rates below (i.e, $\mu = 0.8$) and above (i.e., $\mu \in \{1.2, 1.4, 1.6, 1.8\}$) the nominal playback rate have no significant impact on the QoE. This confirmed a Student's t-test for equal sample variances which showed no significant difference in MOS between the reference condition and the playback rates as follows: $\mu = 0.8 : p = 0.93, t = -0.083; \mu = 1.2 : p = 0.92, t = 0.096; \mu = 1.4 : p = 0.81, t = 0.42; \mu = 1.6 : p = 0.22, t = 1.23; \mu = 1.8 : p = 0.16, t = 1.41$ for $\alpha = 5\%$. These results indicate that the subjects could not notice a significant difference for playback rates within the range of [0.8, 1.8]. For the other playback rates, the QoE significantly degrades. A Student's t-test revealed that there is a statistical significant difference between the MOS of the reference condition and the playback rates $\mu = 0.5 : p = 0.00, t = 4.5217; \mu = 0.6 : p = 0.002, t = 3.2; \mu = 2 : p = 0.03, t = 2.19$ for $\alpha = 5\%$.

Finally we investigated how well our distortion metric defined in Equation 5 correlates with the assessed MOS. For playback rates greater than the nominal playback rate the Pearson correlation coefficient is $\rho = 0.975$ with the probability of encountering a false positive being $p = 0.0009$. Playback rates lower than the nominal playback rate exhibit a high negative correlation with $\rho = -0.995$ and $p = 0.0047$. This indicates a strong linear correlation between our distortion metric and the MOS assessed by the subjective quality assessment, supporting our approach to the optimization problem as stated in Section 3.3. Furthermore, such an optimizer will always perform equal or better than skipping or pausing the multimedia playback in terms of QoE.

5. CONCLUSION AND FUTURE WORK

In this paper we develop IDMS for pull-based streaming by using a DCS to negotiate a reference playback timestamp among the peers participating in a session. Specifically, we introduce the notion of an IDMS session for pull-based streaming and showed how MPEG-DASH can be adopted to incorporate these IDMS sessions in the MPD. Following this, we describe a DCS for negotiating a reference playback timestamp among the peers in an IDMS Session. The proposed DCS was evaluated with respect to scalability and the time required to synchronize a certain number of peers. The results show that *Merge and Forward* scales very well with the number of peers. Furthermore, the overhead saved may allow the peers to request higher quality streams which can improve the overall QoE of the IDMS system.

The selection of the average playback timestamp as the reference has the potential drawback that certain peers may be unable to synchronize to it due to a shortage of bandwidth. Therefore, we introduce a re-synchronization method that allows a peer to influence the calculation of the reference playback timestamp such that all peers are guaranteedly able to synchronize their multimedia playback. We leave the problem of determining an appropriate weight for a given peer's playback timestamp as subject to future work.

The synchronization of an IDMS system is crucial because it directly impacts the QoE, with skipping and pausing leading to an undesirable degradation. As a result, we adopt AMP and formulate an optimization problem which selects appropriate parameters such that the impact of the resulting playback rate adjustment on the QoE is minimized while avoiding asynchronism. We use a distortion metric as the objective function whose validity for modeling the impact of playback rate adjustments on the QoE is supported by the results of a subjective quality assessment. The evaluation of our IDMS approach in a real world environment and the QoE provided by the system remain as future work.

6. ACKNOWLEDGMENTS

This work was supported in part by the EC in the context of the SocialSensor (FP7-ICT-287975) and QUALINET (COST IC 1003) projects and partly performed in the Lakeside Labs research cluster at Alpen-Adria-Universität. The authors thank the anonymous reviewers for their helpful and insightful comments that have greatly improved this paper.

7. REFERENCES

[1] Rec. ITU-R BT.500-11. Technical report.

[2] F. Boronat, J. Lloret, and M. García. Multimedia group and inter-stream synchronization techniques: A comparative study. *Inf. Syst.*, 34(1):108–131, 2009.

[3] F. Boronat, M. Montagud, and V. Vidal. Master Selection Policies for Inter-destination Multimedia Synchronization in Distributed Applications. In *IEEE 19th Int. Symp. on MASCOTS*, pages 269–277, 2011.

[4] F. Boronat Seguí, J. Guerri Cebollada, and J. Lloret Mauri. An RTP/RTCP based approach for multimedia group and inter-stream synchronization. *MTAP*, 40:285–319, 2008.

[5] K. Christensen, A. Roginsky, and M. Jimeno. A New Analysis of the False Positive Rate of a Bloom Filter. *Inf. Process. Lett.*, 110(21):944–949, Oct. 2010.

[6] H.-C. Chuang, C. Huang, and T. Chiang. Content-Aware Adaptive Media Playout Controls for Wireless Video Streaming. *IEEE Trans. on Multimedia*, 9(6):1273–1283, 2007.

[7] P. Erdös and A. Rényi. On random graphs. *Publicationes Mathematicae*, 6:290–297, 1959.

[8] D. Geerts, I. Vaishnavi, R. Mekuria, O. van Deventer, and P. Cesar. Are we in sync?: synchronization requirements for watching online video together. In *Proc. of the SIGCHI*, CHI '11, pages 311–314, New York, NY, USA, 2011. ACM.

[9] C. Hesselman, D. Abbadessa, W. Van Der Beek, D. Gorgen, K. Shepherd, S. Smit, M. Gulbahar, I. Vaishnavi, J. Zoric, D. Lowet, R. De Groote, J. O'Connell, and O. Friedrich. Sharing enriched multimedia experiences across heterogeneous network infrastructures. *IEEE Comm. Mag.*, 48(6):54–65, 2010.

[10] T. Hossfeld, M. Seufert, M. Hirth, T. Zinner, P. Tran-Gia, and R. Schatz. Quantification of YouTube QoE via Crowdsourcing. In *IEEE ISM*, pages 494–499, 2011.

[11] Y. Ishibashi, T. Hasegawa, and S. Tasaka. Group synchronization control for haptic media in networked virtual environments. In *12th Int. Symp. on HAPTICS.*, pages 106 – 113, 2004.

[12] Y. Ishibashi and S. Tasaka. A distributed control scheme for causality and media synchrnoization in networked multimedia games. In *IEEE Proc. of the 11th ICCN*, pages 144–149, 2002.

[13] M. Kalman, E. Steinbach, and B. Girod. Adaptive media playout for low-delay video streaming over error-prone channels. *IEEE Trans. on Circuits and Systems for Video Technology*, 14(6):841–851, 2004.

[14] M. Mauve, J. Vogel, V. Hilt, and W. Effelsberg. Local-lag and Timewarp: Providing Consistency for Replicated Continuous Applications, 2002.

[15] Microworkers. http://www.microworkers.com.

[16] M. Montagud. Design, development and evaluation of an adaptive and standardized rtp/rtcp-based idms solution. In *Proc. of the 21st ACM MM*, pages 1071–1074, New York, NY, USA, 2013. ACM.

[17] M. Montagud and F. Boronat. On the Use of Adaptive Media Playout for Inter-Destination Synchronization. *IEEE Communications Letters*, 15(8):863–865, 2011.

[18] M. Montagud, F. Boronat, and H. Stokking. Design and Simulation of a Distributed Control Scheme for Inter-destination Media Synchronization. In *IEEE 27th AINA*, pages 937–944, March 2013.

[19] M. Montagud, F. Boronat, H. Stokking, and R. Brandenburg. Inter-destination multimedia synchronization: schemes, use cases and standardization. *Multimedia Sys.*, 18:459–482, 2012.

[20] J. A. Nelder and R. Mead. A Simplex Method for Function Minimization. *The Computer Journal*, 7(4):308–313, 1965.

[21] OMNET++ 4.3.1. http://www.omnetpp.org/.

[22] B. Rainer and C. Timmerer. A quality of experience model for adaptive media playout. In *6th QoMEX*. IEEE, September 2014.

[23] I. Sodagar. The MPEG-DASH Standard for Multimedia Streaming Over the Internet. *IEEE MultiMedia*, 18(4):62–67, 2011.

[24] H. Stokking, M. Van Deventer, O. Niamut, F. Walraven, and R. Mekuria. IPTV inter-destination synchronization: A network-based approach. In *14th ICIN*, pages 1–6, 2010.

[25] Y.-F. Su, Y.-H. Yang, M.-T. Lu, and H. H. Chen. Smooth control of adaptive media playout for video streaming. *Trans. Multi.*, 11(7):1331–1339, Nov. 2009.

[26] W. Verhelst and M. Roelands. An overlap-add technique based on waveform similarity (WSOLA) for high quality time-scale modification of speech. In *IEEE ICASSP*, volume 2, pages 554–557, April 1993.

APPENDIX

A. NETWORK ADDRESS TRANSLATION

We differentiate between the following types of NAT: no NAT, symmetric firewall, full cone NAT, restricted cone NAT, port restricted NAT, and symmetric NAT. In the case of a full cone NAT, where the mapping is done statically by the NAT such that any address is allowed to send packets by using the public IP address and port number to a peer, the communication with the STUN instance has already registered the necessary ports at the peer's NAT. If the peer detects that its NAT is a restricted cone NAT or port restricted NAT, the peer's NAT allows only incoming packets from an address if the peer has already send a packet to this address. Therefore, we add a relaying function to the STUN instance which is used by peers with a restricted cone NAT or port restricted NAT. The procedure for a peer with a restricted cone NAT or port restricted NAT is as follows: first, it sends a UDP packet to the address with which it wants to communicate using the IP and port signalled by the ISO, this tells the NAT that incoming packets from the destination address are allowed; second, if the other peer has one of the mentioned NATs it uses the relaying function of the STUN instance to signal the other peer that it shall send a packet to the given public IP and port; third, the other peer uses the signalled information to open its NAT. After this *handshake* the P2P synchronization protocol can be carried out as described in Section 3.2. This allows to have more than one peer behind the same NAT. If there is no NAT but a symmetric firewall or a symmetric NAT there is no peer to peer communication possible. If the router supports Universal Plug and Play it is possible to add forwarding rules for the ports used by our synchronization protocols but this is out of scope of this paper.

Anahita: A System for 3D Video Streaming with Depth Customization

Kiana Calagari[1,3] Krzysztof Templin[2] Tarek Elgamal[1] Khaled Diab[3] Piotr Didyk[2]
Wojciech Matusik[2] Mohamed Hefeeda[1]

[1]Qatar Computing Research Institute, Doha, Qatar
[2]Computer Science and Artificial Intelligence Laboratory, MIT, Cambridge, MA
[3]School of Computing Science, Simon Fraser University, Burnaby, BC, Canada

ABSTRACT

Producing high-quality stereoscopic 3D content requires significantly more effort than preparing regular video footage. In order to assure good depth perception and visual comfort, 3D videos need to be carefully adjusted to specific viewing conditions before they are shown to viewers. While most stereoscopic 3D content is designed for viewing in movie theaters, where viewing conditions do not vary significantly, adapting the same content for viewing on home TV-sets, desktop displays, laptops, and mobile devices requires additional adjustments. To address this challenge, we propose a new system for 3D video streaming that provides automatic depth adjustments as one of its key features. Our system takes into account both the content and the display type in order to customize 3D videos and maximize their perceived quality. We propose a novel method for depth adjustment that is well-suited for videos of field sports such as soccer, football, and tennis. Our method is computationally efficient and it does not introduce any visual artifacts. We have implemented our 3D streaming system and conducted two user studies, which show: (i) adapting stereoscopic 3D videos for different displays is beneficial, and (ii) our proposed system can achieve up to 35% improvement in the perceived quality of the stereoscopic 3D content.

Categories and Subject Descriptors

H.5.1 [**Information Interfaces and Presentation**]: Multimedia Information Systems—*video*; I.3.3 [**Computer Graphics**]: Picture/Image Generation—*display algorithms, viewing algorithms*

Keywords

Video streaming; 3D video; stereoscopic retargeting; depth optimization

MM '14, November 03 - 07 2014, Orlando, FL, USA.

http://dx.doi.org/10.1145/2647868.2654899.

1. INTRODUCTION

Stereoscopic 3D (S3D) has already become main stream in movie theaters. Many productions are released in stereoscopic format and there is a significant audience that enjoys this more immersive experience [17, 14]. Moreover, S3D is becoming increasingly popular at home. This trend is largely facilitated by widely available stereoscopic 3D content and displays—most of new TV-sets are 3D-ready. Furthermore, enabling stereoscopic viewing on mobile devices is viable and useful for a wide range of applications.

Although S3D is already well established in the movie industry, popularizing it among home and mobile users is still a challenging and unsolved problem. The most challenging problem is content adaptation. This is because both 3D perception and visual comfort highly depend on viewing conditions (e. g., display size, viewing distance) [33, 9, 30, 31, 27]. In the case of movie theaters, the same version of the content can be shown on different screens, as viewing conditions do not vary significantly among them. However, due to the wide range of TV-sets or mobile displays, such an assumption does not hold anymore. In addition, stereoscopic content should be manipulated to account for differences in user preferences. A content that provides a good experience for one user does not necessarily provide a good experience for others. As a result, providing the same content for all displays and users results in sub-optimal quality, both in terms of depth perception and visual comfort. Finally, there is a large variety of different 3D display types. Each of them needs a different video input, e. g., side-by-side, temporal interleaving (shutter glasses), spatial interleaving (e. g., polarized glasses, autostereoscopic) etc. They also have different capabilities and limitations [6]. This requires further content customization based on the display type.

To address these issues, we propose *Anahita* – a system for 3D video streaming. In contrast to previous systems, it utilizes an additional information about viewing conditions and display technology, and uses it to improve viewing experience by adjusting depth. To the best of our knowledge, this is the first 3D streaming system with such capabilities. Furthermore, the additional information enables a smart bandwidth management, i. e., sending the information that is not ultimately displayed can be avoided. In particular, the contributions of this paper are as follows:

- A new system design for adaptive 3D video streaming: The goal of this system is to optimize stereoscopic 3D videos for a wide range of display sizes, video representations, viewers' preferences, and network conditions. The system efficiently organizes the creation of various versions of 3D videos using a structure that we refer to as the 3D version tree. The system uses the Dynamic Adaptive Streaming over HTTP (DASH) to dynamically switch among different versions and optimize the quality and depth perception for different viewers.

- A novel method for depth expansion and compression for stereoscopic 3D videos: Our method performs simple image processing operations, it does not require creating accurate depth maps, and it does not introduce visual artifacts. The main target application for our method is sport videos e.g., soccer, football, tennis, and cricket. In such applications, preserving the scene structure, e.g., the straightness of the lines, is extremely important. Our method guarantees to preserve the scene structure.
- A complete end-to-end implementation and two user studies to evaluate its benefits: We implement the server side of our system and deploy it on the Amazon cloud. The server implements our depth customization method as well as several off-the-shelf video processing operations to adapt 3D videos. In addition, we provide multiple clients on 3D-enabled mobile phones, tablets, desktop displays, and large TV displays. We conduct two user studies. The first study shows the need for our system in general. The second study shows the achieved gain in depth enhancements by the proposed system, which was up to 35%.

The rest of this paper is organized as follows. In Sec. 2, we summarize previous efforts in academia and industry in designing 3D video streaming systems. We also describe different 3D content customization methods and how our method is different from them. Then, we present the design of our system (Sec. 3), and the depth customization method (Sec. 4). Sec. 5 discusses details of the implementation. In Sec. 6, we present our user studies which evaluate our system. Sec. 7 concludes the paper.

2. RELATED WORK

There has been a significant interest both in the academia and in the industry in 3D video processing. However, as discussed below, the problem of depth optimization for different displays sizes and types has not received much attention. In addition, in contrast to previous methods, our depth manipulation method does not rely on accurate depth maps, it does not introduce any significant distortions to the videos, and it is computationally inexpensive.

2.1 3D Streaming Systems

Multiple systems for 3D content streaming have been proposed in the literature. For example, Baicheng et al. [35] describe a 3D video streaming system, but their main focus is on the 3D media encoder and decoder. Whereas Diab et al. [11] focus on optimizing the storage in 3D streaming systems. Pehlivan et al. [26] propose a video streaming system that switches between 2D and 3D videos depending on the available bandwidth and display equipment. The work by Wu et al. [34] adapts 3D video quality and balances/trades off the temporal and spatial (color plus depth) quality in real-time, but it does not enhance or customize the depth signal for different display types/sizes/technologies. Our work could potentially leverage their method to provide smarter rate adaptation in our 3D streaming system. 3D teleconferencing has been also proposed. For example, early work [19] focused on extending the transport protocol to associate left and right views. Whereas the more recent ViewCast [37] enables multi-party 3D tele-immersion and prioritizes stream transmissions based on the client's viewing angle. Similarly, Telecast [5] prioritizes streams based on viewing angles, but supports a large number of non-interactive viewers, using a hybrid P2P+CDN architecture. Depth customization is not addressed in these works. In addition, multiview client-server systems, where a scene can be displayed from different viewpoints has been considered, for example in [22], [20] and [15].

In addition to the academic works mentioned above, there has been significant interest from the industry, including YouTube, 3DVisionLive, Trivido, and 3DeeCentral. YouTube [4] supports multiple 3D formats including anaglyph (red-cyan, blue-yellow or green-magenta), side by side, row and column interleaved. In addition, it supports HTML5 stereo view, which is the format for active-shutter displays that utilizes NVIDIA 3D Vision. Unlike our system, YouTube does not change or customize the depth of videos for different displays. 3DVisionLive [2] is a web channel for 3D video streaming and 3D photo sharing. It uses the Microsoft Silverlight and IIS smooth streaming technologies. It is, however, limited to one display technology. Trivido [3] is a 3D Internet video platform. It supports anaglyph, side by side, row interleaved 3D formats, and the 3D NVIDIA Vision format. However, it does not address the problem of customizing the content for different displays. 3DeeCentral [1] supports 3D content on multiple 3D-enabled devices, but it does not provide adjusted depth for different displays.

In summary, previous works on 3D streaming have addressed various problems including content acquisition, content representation, encoding, storage, and transmission of both stereoscopic and multiview content. However, we are not aware of any 3D streaming system that adaptively customizes the depth based on the display size, display technology, and viewer's preferences.

2.2 Depth Customization

There are two basic requirements stereoscopic content has to meet in order to be comfortable to watch. First, every object in the scene needs to fit within the "comfort zone", i. e., it cannot be too far from the screen plane [27]. A rule of thumb used by stereographers (*percentage rule*) is that the pixel disparity should not be greater than 2–3 percent of the screen width [27]. Second, the relative distance (in z-direction) between nearby objects (in xy-plane) cannot be too large, i. e., the disparity needs to be within the limit known as Panum's fusional area [8]; otherwise, one of the objects will not be fused by the observer. Meeting those constraints is dependent on two stereoscopic parameters that influence the depth distribution of a stereo shot – the camera separation and the convergence. The former influences the *range* of depth (and thus distances between the objects), whereas the latter influences the *placement* of that range relative to the screen plane. Oscam et al. [23] developed a method for real-time optimization of these parameters, however, it is limited to synthetic content, and cannot be applied as a post-process.

The convergence is relatively easy to modify in post-production by simply shifting either one or both views. Fixing the camera separation, however, is more difficult, since it requires synthesizing new camera views. Lang et al. [21] show how this, and even more sophisticated operations, can be accomplished via nonlinear disparity mapping. Unfortunately, their method relies to a large extent on stereo correspondences, and it requires recovering pixel values for points that have not been registered by the camera. Therefore, it is difficult to reliably generate clean, artifact-free output without manual intervention, not to mention real-time performance. Furthermore, nonlinear disparity mapping can severely degrade the quality of videos of field sports such as soccer, due to objectionable curving of the lines.

Depth can also be manipulated as a consequence of depth compression performed to limit the bandwidth of 3D content. Although some of these techniques can adapt to different viewing conditions [34, 24], their primary goal is to maintain the original depth. In contrast, our technique intentionally modifies the depth to enhance viewer experience.

Our depth customization method is a simple, yet efficient post-production technique that can expand or compress the depth in stereo content. It targets depth customization in field sports such as soccer, football, tennis, and cricket. Our method preserves lines and planes, and thus it maintains the structure of the scene, which is important in sports videos.

3. SYSTEM ARCHITECTURE

The main goal of the proposed 3D streaming system, called Anahita[1], is to provide depth-optimized videos to different 3D display types and sizes. As shown in Fig. 1, the proposed system consists of: (i) server that processes the content and creates a customized version for each display based on its size and technology, and (ii) multiple clients from which 3D devices connect to the server and receive the suitable versions. The following subsections provide more details.

3.1 Server Side

The server adjusts the depth of 3D videos and adaptively streams them to clients. It also manages the creation and storage of different versions of the 3D videos. Specifically, the server has four main components: (i) Depth Enhancer, (ii) 3D Version Manager, (iii) Storage Manager, and (iv) Adaptive Streamer.

The Depth Enhancer customizes the depth of 3D videos based on the target clients. It can either increase or decrease the amount of depth to be perceived in the video. This is done using simple image processing operations that can be performed in real time as a post-processing step (Sec. 4).

The 3D Version Manager component handles the creation of different versions of the same 3D video. This is done through what we call 3D Version Tree, which is shown in Fig. 2. We note that current 2D streaming systems, e. g., YouTube, typically store a *few* (2–4) versions of the same 2D video, but at different qualities (bitrates) to accommodate the variability in network bandwidth of different clients. The number of versions in the proposed 3D streaming system needs to be much larger than traditional 2D streaming systems. The classification of 3D displays presented in [11] suggests that more than 35 versions may be needed to accommodate current 3D displays. This is because, in addition to the variability of network bandwidth, clients requesting 3D videos use different displays in terms of size, depth rendering method, and the amount of depth that can be perceived.

The 3D version tree in Fig. 2 manages the creation of all different 3D versions. Specifically, the input video is assumed to be in the side-by-side format, which is currently the most commonly used 3D representation. Our depth enhancement method creates up to D versions with different depth values, where D is the number of different display sizes supported by the system. These D versions represent the first level of the version tree. In this level, all versions are still in the side-by-side format. In the second level of the tree, we apply various video conversion methods to support displays with different depth rendering technologies, which include anaglyph, frame interleaved, row interleaved, column interleaved, and video plus depth. In our system, we implement conversion methods known from the literature. For each display size in level 1 of the tree, up to R versions can be created in level 2, where R

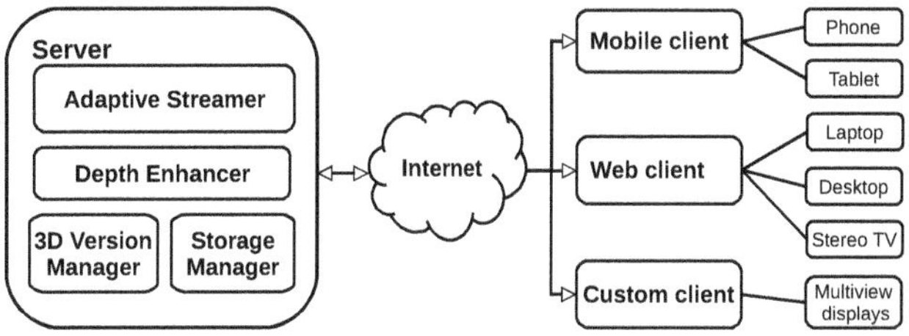

Figure 1: Design of the proposed 3D streaming system. The Depth Enhancer customizes the depth based on display sizes and viewing conditions. The creation of multiple versions of each 3D video is managed by the 3D Version Manager, and the storage of these versions is handled by the Storage Manager. The Adaptive Streamer uses DASH to serve segments of different versions to various clients.

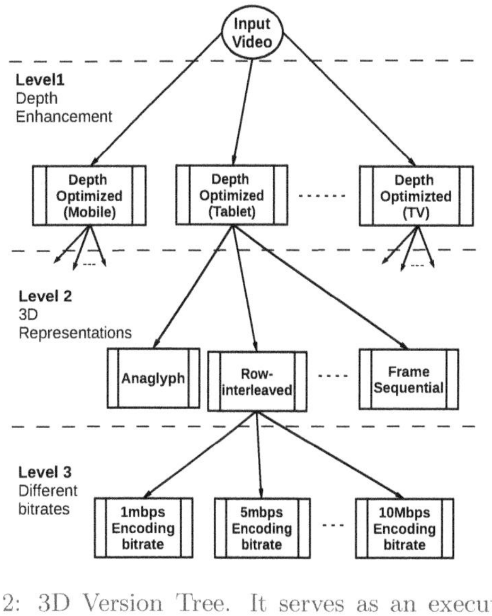

Figure 2: 3D Version Tree. It serves as an execution or master plan to create different versions of each 3D video.

[1]In ancient times, Anahita was the source of all clean water streams that flowed through golden channels to all lands and oceans on Earth. In the Internet age, Anahita is the source of all high-quality 3D video streams that flow through network channels to all types of displays.

is the number of different 3D video representations supported by the system. In the third level of the 3D version tree, we create up to B versions for each 3D representation in level 2 to accommodate clients with heterogeneous and varying network bandwidth, where B is the number of different bitrates (qualities) offered by the system. We note that the depth enhancement method is applied in the first level of the tree because it is more expensive than other operations. Since the first level handles only a few number of display sizes, the number of times that the depth enhancement method is invoked is minimized. In addition, the depth enhancement method should be applied on the original, side-by-side, video in order to create consistent and optimized depth perception regardless of the different 3D video representations.

The third component of our system is the Storage Manager, which organizes the storage of different versions. Notice, that the 3D version tree can have up to $D \times R \times B$ different versions for each video to support optimized 3D video quality on displays with different sizes, 3D video representations, and dynamic network conditions. With current display technologies and sizes, the parameters D, R, and B are roughly in the ranges $[4-6]$, $[5-7]$, and $[2-4]$. That is, more than 100 versions of the same 3D video could be needed to support the large diversity of clients. Creating and storing all versions for all videos may waste storage and processing resources of the system, especially for videos with low popularity. A recent work [11] studied this problem and proposed an algorithm to store some versions while creating others on demand, based on video popularity, video size, and processing requirements to create each version. This algorithm, or similar ones, can be used in our system.

The final component of our system is the Adaptive Streamer, which adopts the Dynamic and Adaptive Streaming over HTTP (DASH) protocol [18, 29, 28]. DASH enables the server to scale to many concurrent sessions, uses off-the-shelf HTTP servers, facilitates switching among different versions, and provides wide client accessibility because it uses the standard HTTP protocol which is allowed in most networks. The server side of the DASH protocol divides a video into a sequence of small segments. Current 2D streaming systems that use DASH create few versions of each segment at different bitrates. In our 3D streaming system, however, we create different versions of each segment using the 3D version tree to adapt not only to the network bandwidth, but also to different display sizes and technologies.

In addition to the depth customization feature that supports different 3D displays, our 3D streaming system offers another feature: *depth personalization*, which is adjusting the depth of a video based on the preferences of individual viewers. This is a desirable feature, as it improves the engagement of viewers and allows them to choose the most visually comfortable depth perception. This feature is realized as follows. The user interface at the client side displays multiple depth options. The default selection is our depth-optimized version, created for the viewer's display. The viewer is allowed to choose other versions with more or less depth. After selection, the client side translates this request to the corresponding segment ID and submits it to the DASH server.

3.2 Client Side

As shown in Fig. 1, the client side of our streaming system supports various platforms, including: (i) mobile, (ii) web-based, and (iii) custom. All three platforms implement the client side of the DASH protocol to adaptively request segments of the different versions of 3D videos stored at the streaming server. Specifically, the client starts by requesting the manifest file from the server, which contains meta data about the requested 3D video and its available versions. Then, it decides on the most suitable 3D version based on the display characteristics and the current network conditions. The client then starts requesting videos segments from the server and the media player is notified to start playing these segments.

For the mobile client, we developed an application to work on various mobile devices such as smartphones and tablets. Most 3D-enabled mobile devices use autostereoscopic displays, which do not require glasses. Rendering of 3D content on these displays depend on five main parameters including: pitch (spatial frequency or the period of the parallax barrier), duty cycle (parallax barrier ratio of opacity to transparency), optical thickness (distance between the parallax barrier and the display), angle (barrier degree of rotation from vertical), and shift (horizontal offset of the parallax barrier relative to the display). Since different manufacturers can choose different values for these parameters, we built a mobile client to adjust the content according to the display characteristics provided by the manufacturer. We designed the mobile client application to have two parts. The first (lower) part calls specific APIs supplied by the manufacturer of the mobile device. The second part is independent of the manufacturer and implements all high-level functions such as the adaptive streaming.

The web-based client uses standard web interfaces to render the encoded 3D video (e.g., side-by-side or frame interleaved) and the 3D display as well as its associated glasses (if any) create the 3D perception to the viewer. Finally, there are displays that require special handling of 3D videos, such as the multi-view displays. Such displays usually require the 3D video in the form of video-plus-depth (2D images and the associated depth map). From the video-plus-depth input, view synthesis methods are used to create multiple virtual views. In our system, we implemented a custom client for such displays, which includes a component to generate depth maps that are needed for the view synthesis method.

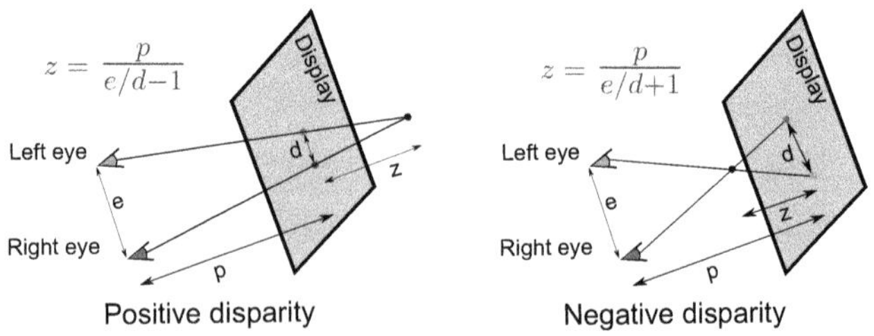

Figure 3: Disparity (d) vs. perceived depth (z). p is the viewing distance, and e is the inter-ocular distance.

4. DEPTH CUSTOMIZATION

In order to perceive binocular stereopsis, we need to display a different view to each eye. The two views show the same scene but from two slightly different viewing points. For each pixel in the left view, its corresponding pixel in the right view is located a few pixels away. Given a pair of corresponding pixels, the signed distance $d = x_r - x_l$ between their x-positions is called *disparity*. The disparities are detected by the human visual system and interpreted as depth. As shown in Fig. 3, an object is perceived behind the screen plane if the disparity is positive, and in front of the screen plane if the disparity is negative. In the special case of zero disparity, the object appears on the screen plane. The amount of perceived depth (z) is a function of disparity (d), viewing distance (p), and inter-ocular distance (e). Perceived virtual depth, both for positive and negative disparities, is commonly approximated as in Fig. 3, with larger disparities resulting in perception of larger distances [16].

In addition to viewing conditions, the perception of depth varies from person to person [10, 12], and is a matter of preference. Thus, using the same content in all situations is sub-optimal, and clearly there is a need for techniques enabling customization of the depth distribution in 3D videos. In the context of streaming sports videos, such techniques need to meet three requirements: (i) they need to work as a post-process, since we do not have influence on the recording process, (ii) they need to be fast, and (iii) they need to automatically produce high quality results, without objectionable artifacts. We propose a new method of depth expansion/compression that meets these requirements. It targets videos of various field sports such as soccer, football, and tennis.

4.1 Structure Preserving Scene Shifting

Adjusting depth is not a straightforward task. As discussed in Sec. 2, it can be achieved using a disparity remapping. This is, however, a viable option only in off-line applications with some form of supervision. The only safe automatic adjustment for general scenes is convergence manipulation, which can be easily performed using a horizontal shift of the two views. We observed, however, that for some scenes, especially in sports videos, the geometry has approximately planar structure. In such cases, disparity maps can be well described by a single disparity gradient $g = (g_x, g_y)$.

This observation led us to devise a Structure Preserving Scene Shifting (SPSS) method for depth expansion/compression, which adjusts the depth range of the scene by means of 2D geometric transformations. The basic idea behind the SPSS method is to estimate the disparity gradient g and adjust its magnitude. The gradient is estimated by fitting a plane to the scene's disparity map which is obtained using a stereo-correspondence algorithm. In contrast to the depth remapping approach, we use stereo correspondences only to estimate the single depth gradient, hence the accuracy of the correspondences is not critical.

Modification of the gradient is achieved via a remapping operation, in which a parallelogram-shaped region of the input image is selected and mapped back onto the whole image area. Such a mapping can be applied to one of the views or both, and in the latter case, the depth modifications caused by each transformation will add up. To minimize visibility of the distortion, we split the desired depth adjustment between the two views, so that each mapping of one view is accompanied by a complementary mapping of the other. The top and bottom edges of the mapping parallelogram are always kept horizontal, and its shape is described by a combination of two parameters: the *slant* and the *stretch*.

The *slant* operation regulates the skewness of the mapping region by horizontally moving its top and bottom edges in opposite directions. This operation modifies g_y. An example is given in Fig. 4. The *stretch* operation re-scales the mapping region horizontally. The stretch is done linearly to assure that any plane structure remains planar. This transformation modifies g_x. An example is given in Fig. 5.

Following the convention of the percentage rule, we express the amount of slant and stretch as a fraction of the image width, and denote it as σ_{sl} and σ_{st}, respectively. Additionally, a *shift* operation, that moves the mapping region to the left or right can be used, to adjust the convergence. Depending on the direction of the shift, the scene disparities are uniformly increased or decreased, and as a result, the scene appears closer or farther from the user. As previously, we express the size of the shift as a fraction of the image width, and denote it as σ_{sh}.

Assuming, that image x- and y-coordinates are in the range $[-\frac{1}{2}, \frac{1}{2}]$, the three operations are combined into one operator, mapping a pair of old coordinates (x, y) to a pair of new coordinates $(\hat{x}, \hat{y})$ as shown in Eq. 1. To accommodate slanting, stretching, and shifting, the mapping region has to be slightly smaller than the input image, therefore the factor r (typically 0.95) is used to re-scale the coordinates. Recall, that the depth transformation is split equally between the two views of the stereo image, hence the factor ± 0.5.

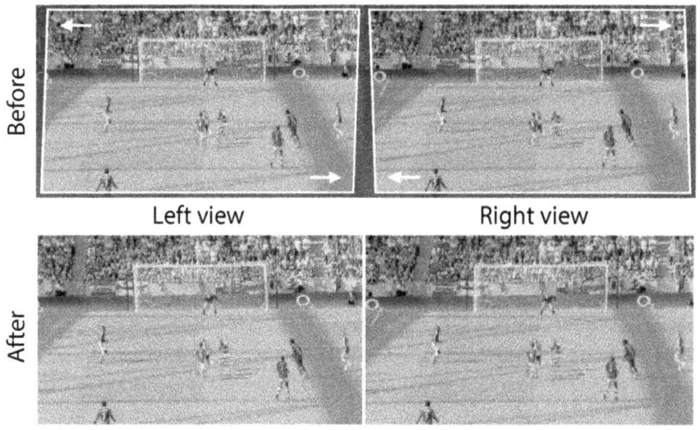

Figure 4: Example of the slant operation. A parallelogram-shaped region is mapped back onto the whole image area, modifying the vertical component g_y of the disparity gradient g. Note, how the opposing slants in the left and right view complement each other to minimize the distortion.

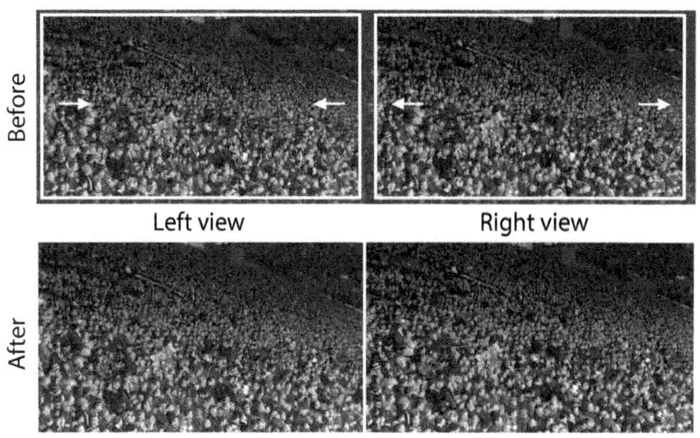

Figure 5: Example of the stretch operation. The left and right views are horizontally scaled. In effect, the horizontal component g_x of the disparity gradient g is changed.

$$(\hat{x}, \hat{y}) = (x \pm 0.5 \cdot (\sigma_{\mathrm{sl}} \cdot y + \sigma_{\mathrm{st}} \cdot x + \sigma_{\mathrm{sh}}),\ y) \cdot \frac{1}{r}. \quad (1)$$

Formally, for any scene classified as suitable for the SPSS method, the following steps are taken:

1. The gradient $g = (g_x, g_y)$ of the scene's disparity map is calculated.

2. The slant and stretch are calculated as follows, where e is the *expansion value*, dependent on the viewing conditions and the content.

$$\sigma_{\mathrm{sl}} = e \cdot \frac{g_y}{|g_x| + |g_y|} - g_y, \quad \sigma_{\mathrm{st}} = e \cdot \frac{g_x}{|g_x| + |g_y|} - g_x,$$

3. The shift σ_{sh} is set in such a way that there are no negative disparities on the edges of the image.

4. In order to maintain temporal coherency, $\sigma_{\mathrm{sl}}, \sigma_{\mathrm{st}}$, and σ_{sh} are temporally smoothed, using the history of their values in the n previous frames.

5. The views are remapped according to Eq. (1) using linear interpolation.

(a) (b)

Figure 6: Examples of shots in a soccer video that have planar depth structure. The depth maps were determined using optical flow estimation methods [32, 7], and were further enhanced by cross bilateral filtering [25]. Vectors in the maps visualize depth gradients. Note, that they are provided for visualization purposes, and our method does not require computationally expensive estimation of accurate, dense stereo correspondences.

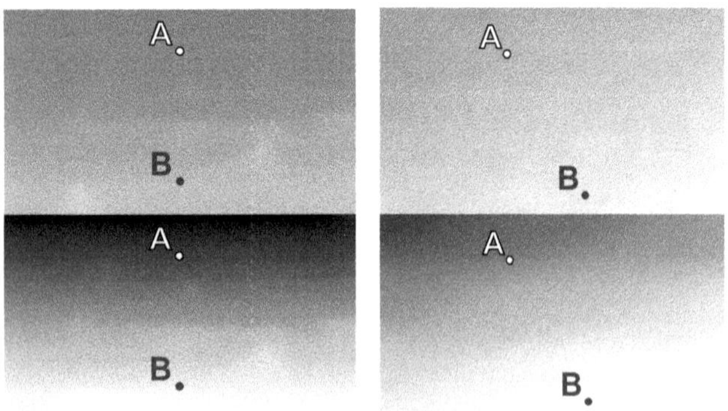

(a) (b)

Figure 7: Our method has increased the disparity range while preserving the depth structure and orientation (the top images are the original disparity maps, while the bottom ones show depth after our optimization.)

Ekin et al. distinguish four types of camera shots in soccer games: long shots, medium shots, close-ups, and out-of-field shots [13]. Long shots provide a global view, in which the field takes most of the screen-space, and multiple small player silhouettes are visible. Medium shots show a smaller portion of the field, usually with couple larger silhouettes, while close-ups show the above-waist portion of one player. Finally, out-of-field shots show the audience, coaches, etc.

Close-ups, out-of-field, and medium shots usually have quite complicated geometry. Long shots, however, are different, because their geometry can be very well approximated by a plane, therefore, they are perfect candidates for the SPSS (see Fig. 6a for an example of a long shot). Occasionally, some medium or out-of-field shots, such as the one shown in Fig. 6b, are also well fitted by a plane, and thus can benefit from the proposed depth adjustment. In the evaluation section, we analyze the shot types in different sports videos and show that the proposed SPSS method can cover a significant portion (60–70%) of the shots in field sports.

Fig. 7 shows the depth maps of the two samples from Fig. 6, before and after SPSS. It can be seen that SPSS enhances the depth contrast, while preserving the original scene structure. In both samples, the depth difference between points A and B has increased, while, the direction of the depth gradient has remained unchanged. In the following, we focus exclusively on long shots, which are the most important use case of SPSS. In Sec. 6, we describe a perceptual study, in which optimal expansion values are found.

4.2 Shot Classifier

Our depth adjustment technique assumes that the scene can be well approximated by a plane. This makes the technique suitable for long shots. Therefore, in order to decide which frame can be manipulated, the type of a shot needs to be determined.[2] Although some techniques performing this exist [13], our scenario is specific. First, we need to detect long shots only. Second, if the classification reports false positives our method should provide acceptable quality. Moreover, previous techniques considered only a single image as an input, whereas our classification can take an advantage of having stereoscopic version of the content.

To detect shots suitable for our technique, we estimate how well a scene can be approximated by a single plane. To this end, we first recover depth using [36]. Next, we fit a plane to it using least squares method and compute the coefficient of determination (R^2) to measure its goodness. To detect scenes suitable for our depth manipulation we construct a binary classifier, which classifies a scene based on the R^2 value, i.e., if the goodness is above a certain threshold q, the scene is considered suitable for our manipulations. Otherwise, it remains unchanged. In order to determine a good threshold q, we processed 1,015 randomly chosen frames from one soccer game and classified them manually into two groups: long shots and the rest. Then, we analyzed how our binary

[2] A shot in our definition is just a pair of images, and we do not need any shot boundary detection algorithms.

classifier performs for different threshold values using the relation between true positive and false positive ratios. Fig. 8 presents the ROC curve. Based on the analysis we chose $q = 0.693$, which gives true positive ratio = 0.8981, and false positive ratio = 0.1925.

5. SYSTEM IMPLEMENTATION

The server-side operations of our system have been developed using C++ and OpenCV. The system is implemented in an extensible and modular manner. Specifically, all video processing operations, e.g., depth expansion, frame interleaving, etc., are implemented as independent components with standard interfaces. This enables us to chain any sequence of these video operations to create different 3D versions. The sequence of operations to create any 3D version is pre-defined using our 3D version tree as illustrated in Fig. 2. Only one 3D version tree is maintained in the system, which is consulted upon the creation of any 3D version. For example, to serve a viewer using a stereoscopic 3D TV with polarized glasses, the system creates the corresponding version by performing three operations: depth optimization, row-interleaving, and scaling. We note that to create a version in Level 3 in the version tree (Fig. 2), the ancestor versions at Levels 1 and 2 have to be created first. The system is designed to have the most time-consuming operations in Level 1. Therefore, these time-consuming operations are executed once instead of being executed in every branch of the tree.

In our prototype, we implemented the anaglyph, row-interleaving, column-interleaving, frame-sequential, depth optimization, and depth estimation operations. Additionally, we implemented some auxiliary operations, such as scale, which resizes the images uniformly, and split, which splits a side-by-side image into separate left and right images.

During initialization, the system decides which versions to create from each 3D video in the system. This decision depends on the storage requirements and available processing capacity to create any missing version on demand. The chosen versions are not necessarily leaf nodes, but they can be at any level of the 3D version tree. To create a version, the system recursively traverses up the 3D version tree starting from the node corresponding to that version until it reaches an already-created version or it hits the root node (the original 3D video). The system pushes the non-created versions to a stack. Then, it creates these versions using the order in the stack. We note that this version creation process is highly parallelizable, and a separate thread can be spawned for each version. However, multiple versions may share an ancestor that should be created. To avoid multiple creations of the same version, we chose to parallelize Level-1 branches. With this setup, one thread is spawned for each branch, and versions inside each branch are generated in series.

At the client side, we have implemented three applications. First, a web application using HTTP and DASH-JS, which is a JavaScript DASH library for the Google Chrome browser. Second, a mobile application for the autostereoscopic mobile devices using Java and the Android SDK. We tested the application on HTC and LG 3D smartphones, and on a Gadmei 3D tablet. Third, we implemented a MS Windows application for a multiview display (Dimenco 55" TV). We implemented the DASH client using Java. The application has been developed to perform view-synthesis before presenting the content to the multiview display.

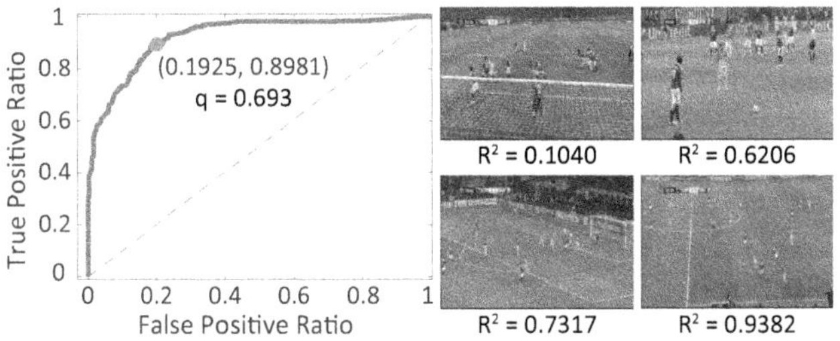

Figure 8: Left: ROC curve for our binary shot classifier. Right: Four examples of shots with corresponding R^2 values. Top two have low R^2 value, therefore, their depth will be unchanged. On the other hand, bottom two are long shots and due to the high R^2 value (above the threshold) their depth will be modified.

6. EVALUATION

We start our evaluation by showing the need for depth customization through a subjective study. Next, we briefly describe our implementation of a complete, end-to-end, prototype of the proposed 3D streaming system. Then, we use this prototype to conduct another subjective study to show that the proposed system significantly improves the perceived depth in 3D videos. Finally, we analyze the percentage of video shots in field sports that can benefit from the proposed depth customization method.

6.1 The Need for Depth Customization

In this subjective study, we displayed 3D videos to multiple subjects using different displays. We manipulated depth with different degrees to study its impact on the subjects.

Subjects: Ten subjects took part in this study. They were all members of a computer graphics group. They had normal/corrected-to-normal vision, and could perceive stereoscopic 3D effect.

Experimental Setup: We tested two trial conditions: smartphone and TV. In the smartphone condition, the content was presented using an LG Optimus 3D MAX P725 phone (the stereo effect is achieved by means of a parallax barrier). The observation distance was about 30 cm. In the TV condition, the content was shown using a 55-inch Sony Bravia XBR-55HX929 TV-set, and a pair of active shutter glasses. The observation distance was about 2 m.

Content: We used a series of short clips taken from the Manchester United vs. Wigan Athletic FA Community Shield game (2–0, 12 August, 2013) as the test sequence. Each clip was a few seconds long, and the entire sequence was 54 seconds long. The initial depth range of the test sequence was small, and the whole image appeared flat.

Protocol: The subjects were shown six versions of the test sequence, with increasing expansion values, in the two above-mentioned conditions. The values used were: −0.5 % (depth compression), 0 % (original sequence, no slant), 1 %, 2 %, 3 %, and 4 % (depth expansion). Half of the subjects saw the TV condition first, and the other half saw the smartphone condition first. In each condition, the subjects were asked to choose the preferred version, assuming that they were to watch the entire 90-minute soccer game.

Results and Discussion: The average preferred values for expansion were: 1.4 % in the TV condition and 2.3 % in the smartphone condition. The results together with

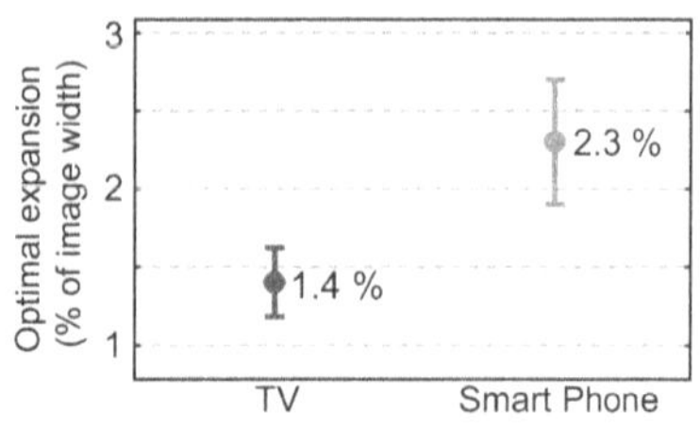

Figure 9: Mean expansion value and standard error of the mean for both conditions.

the standard error of the mean are shown in Fig. 9. The experiment shows that the original 3D videos were not the best choice for subjects. Instead, the depth-manipulated 3D videos scored higher than the original ones. In addition, the level of depth manipulation depended on the used display. Therefore, we can conclude that for optimized viewing of 3D videos on different displays, the depth of the videos needs to be adjusted.

In addition, we use the results of this experiment to set the expansion values in the rest of our evaluation. That is, the expansion values for the TV and smartphone are set to 1.4 % and 2.3 %, respectively. Our experiment in this section tested only two viewing conditions – a smartphone and a TV. We used linear interpolation of the expansion value for the other display sizes used in the experiments in Sec. 6.2.

We assumed that displays are always viewed from a particular, standard distance which depends on the display size. Therefore, the size is the only parameter that our depth adjustment technique accounts for. For non-standard viewing distances, the amount of depth expansion/compression our method needs to perform could be derived in a similar experiment, and the server could adjust the content accordingly also in such cases. The viewing distance could be indicated manually by the user or inferred using an embedded camera.

Existing studies demonstrate that there is a significant variation in depth perception among observers [10, 12]. We did not explicitly analyze how much the ideal depth varies across subjects, however, it is unclear how the system could take such variability into account without some prior knowledge about the user. Therefore, we decided to use by default the mean expansion value, and to provide the user with the possibility of overriding that setting.

6.2 Depth Improvement

We conduct a subjective study to measure the perceptual depth enhancements achieved by our system, for different videos and viewing conditions. The system was deployed on Amazon cloud and fully tested over the Internet. For our subjective studies, however, the experiments were done over a LAN to assess the effectiveness of the proposed depth adjustment method. For handling network dynamics, our system supports encoding the video in different bitrates and it can switch among them in real time using the standard DASH protocol. Our depth adjustment method does not increase the bitrate and it is independent of the rate adaptation method.

Subjects: Fifteen new subjects took part in this experiment. They were all computer science students and researchers, had normal/corrected-to-normal vision, and could perceive stereoscopic 3D effect.

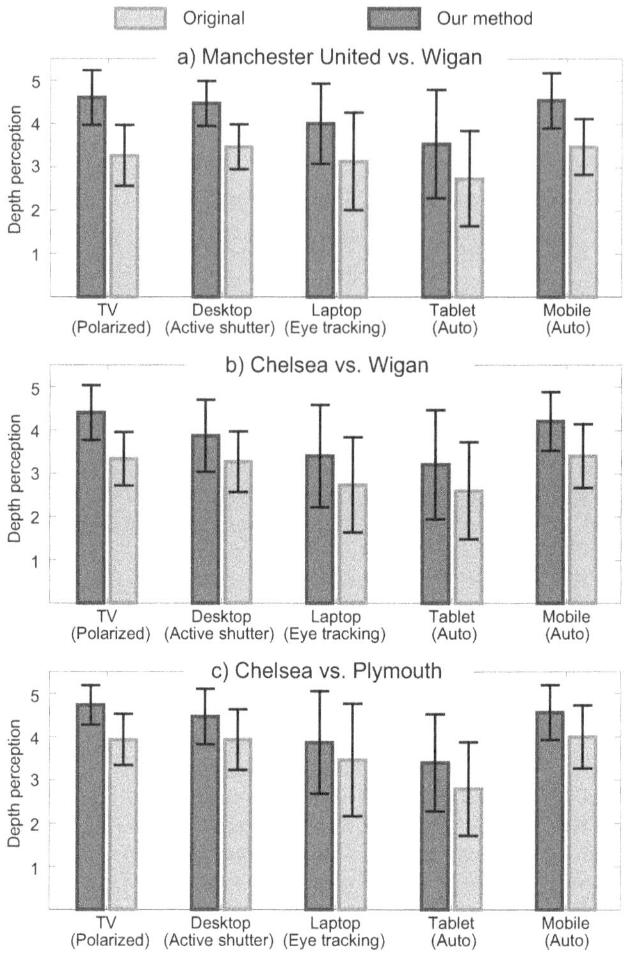

Figure 10: Our method improves depth perception for all tested videos on all displays. Error bars represent the standard deviation of the user ranking.

Experimental Setup: We tested 5 conditions: (i) Smartphone: LG Optimus 3D MAX P725 phone (autostereoscopic), with observation distance about 30 cm. (ii) Tablet: GADMEI tablet (autostereoscopic), with observation distance about 40 cm. (iii) Laptop: 15.6" Toshiba Qosmio F755-3D350 laptop (autostereoscopic with eye tracking), with observation distance about 60 cm. (iv) Desktop: 27" Samsung desktop (active shutter glasses), with observation distance about 1 m. (v) Big TV: 55" Philips TV-set (passive polarized glasses), with observation distance about 3 m.

Content: We used three soccer 3D video clips downloaded from YouTube. From each video, we extracted a series of shots with the following total lengths. (i) Manchester United vs. Wigan: 60 sec. (ii) Chelsea vs. Wigan: 24 sec. (iii) Chelsea vs. Plymouth: 20 sec. All shots were of long-view nature, thus suitable for our method. In our system, these shots are automatically identified by the classifier in Sec. 4.2. Other shots are not subjected to our depth customization.

Protocol: All subjects viewed the five 3D displays. For each display, the subjects were shown the original sequence and the optimized version. Both the order in which participants saw the displays and the video sequences were randomized. The subjects were asked to rank the depth perception of each version between 1 and 5 as follows: 5–Excellent, 4–Very Good, 3–Good, 2–Fair, and 1–Poor.

Results and Discussion: We plot the ranking results for each 3D video in Fig. 10. The figure shows the mean ranking values for the depth-optimized 3D videos created by our method as well as the original 3D videos. The error bars visualize the standard deviation of the rankings. In order to analyze the obtained data we computed a series of t-tests. All differences reported in the figure are statistically significant (p-value < 0.05) except the tablet version of the second game (Fig. 10b). Regardless of the original depth perception which depends on filming style, depth range of the scene, artistic choice, and shooting angles, the study demonstrates that our method always improves the depth perception. The improvement can be as high as 35% in the case of the TV Fig. 10a.

6.3 Coverage

To demonstrate how many shots can benefit from our depth customization method, we analyze two full 3D soccer games (each is more than 90 minutes), and a 10-min segment of 3D tennis game. The two soccer games were from different broadcasters and different competitions. We watched each video and manually classified shots. In Table 1, we summarize our analysis of the first full 3D soccer game, Milan vs. Barcelona, showing the percentage of long, medium, close-ups, and out-of-field shots. Similar to any usual soccer game, the game included goals, injuries, player changes, offsides, etc. It can be seen that the percentage of shots are similar throughout the two halves of the game. During the second half, two injuries, two player changes, and two goals happened, which decreased the percentage of long shots. This is because these events typically have more close-up shots. However, it can be seen that, on average, over 70 % of full 3D soccer games are long shots. Table 2 shows the

Time/Shot Type	Long	Medium	Close-up	Out-of-field
00:00:00 - 00:02:10	*Introduction*			
00:02:10 - 00:48:17	73.1 %	24.4 %	1.3 %	1.2 %
00:48:17 - 1:03:20	*Half-time*			
1:03:20 - 1:53:52	67.1 %	28.4 %	1.4 %	3.1 %

Table 1: Shot analysis of the Milan vs. Barcelona full 3D soccer game on 20/2/2013 in the UEFA Champions League.

Time/Shot Type	Long	Medium	Close-up	Out-of-field
00:00:00 - 00:04:30	*Introduction*			
00:04:30 - 00:55:10	68.25 %	26.25 %	4.1 %	1.4 %
00:55:10 - 1:06:56	*Half-time*			
1:06:56 - 1:58:10	61.3 %	29.4 %	6.6 %	2.7 %

Table 2: Shot analysis of the Manchester United vs. Liverpool full 3D soccer game on 16/3/2014 in the English Premiere League.

Time/Shot Type	Long	Medium	Close-up	Out-of-field
00:00:00 - 00:00:28	*Introduction*			
00:00:28 - 00:09:41	64.4 %	16.8 %	2 %	16.8 %

Table 3: Shot analysis of the R. Nadal vs. N. Djokovic 3D tennis clip on 3/7/2011 in the Wimbledon competition.

analysis of another full 3D soccer game (Manchester United vs. Liverpool). The main difference between the two games is the percentage of close-up shots. Nevertheless, the shot percentage is still dominated by long shots in both games.

Our analysis of the 3D segment from the tennis game between Rafael Nadal and Novak Djokovic is summarized in Table 3. The table shows that more than 64 % of the game can be enhanced by our method.

In summary, our analysis of various 3D games shows that our method can enhance between 60 % to 70 % of the shots in 3D videos in field sports, such as soccer and tennis.

7. CONCLUSIONS

It is challenging to stream and render 3D stereoscopic videos for different displays. This is not only because of the different technologies used to render depth, but also because the perceived depth depends on the size of the display, viewing distance, and the viewer's preferences. This is further complicated by the dynamic nature of the Internet used to stream 3D videos from a server to clients. Through a user study, we have shown that there is indeed a need to customize 3D videos for different displays. In our study, subjects ranked our depth-manipulated versions of the videos higher than the original ones. We have also shown that the amount of manipulation is dependent on the display size. We have presented a novel system that allows for an adaptive streaming of 3D videos to heterogeneous receivers in terms of display sizes, 3D video representations, viewers' preferences, and network conditions. Our system employs the DASH protocol for adaptive streaming and switching among different versions of 3D videos in order to improve the user viewing experience. In addition, we have proposed a new method for depth customization of 3D sport videos such as soccer, football, and tennis. Our method is computationally inexpensive and it maintains the scene structure of 3D videos. We have implemented a complete prototype of the proposed system and assessed its performance through another user study with 15 subjects viewing several 3D videos on five different 3D displays, ranging from a mobile phone to a large 55" TV set. Our results have shown that the proposed system significantly improves the depth perception in all scenarios.

8. REFERENCES

[1] 3DeeCentral. `http://www.3deecentral.com/`.

[2] 3DVisionLive. `https://www.3dvisionlive.com/`.

[3] Trivido. `http://www.trivido.com/`.

[4] Youtube. `http://www.youtube.com/`.

[5] A. Arefin, Z. Huang, K. Nahrstedt, and P. Agarwal. 4D TeleCast: Towards large scale multi-site and multi-view dissemination of 3DTI contents. In *Proc. of IEEE Conference on Distributed Computing Systems (ICDCS'12)*, pages 82–91, Macau, China, June 2012.

[6] P. Benzie, J. Watson, P. Surman, I. Rakkolainen, K. Hopf, H. Urey, V. Sainov, and C. von Kopylow. A survey of 3DTV displays: Techniques and technologies. *IEEE Transactions on Circuits and Systems for Video Technology*, 17(11):1647–1658, 2007.

[7] T. Brox, A. Bruhn, N. Papenberg, and J. Weickert. High accuracy optical flow estimation based on a theory for warping. In *Proc. of European Conference on Computer Vision (ECCV'04)*, pages 25–36, Prague, Czech Republic, May 2004.

[8] P. Burt and B. Julesz. Modifications of the classical notion of Panum's fusional area. *Perception*, 9(6):671–682, 1980.

[9] L. Chauvier, K. Murray, S. Parnall, R. Taylor, and J. Walker. Does size matter? The impact of screen size on stereoscopic 3DTV. In *IBC conference*, 2010.

[10] B. E. Coutant and G. Westheimer. Population distribution of stereoscopic ability. *Ophthalmic and Physiological Optics*, 13(1):3–7, 1993.

[11] K. Diab, T. Elgamal, K. Calagari, and M. Hefeeda. Storage optimization for 3D streaming systems. In *Proc. of ACM Conference on Multimedia Systems (MMSys'14)*, pages 59–69, Singapore, March 2014.

[12] P. Didyk, T. Ritschel, E. Eisemann, K. Myszkowski, and H.-P. Seidel. A perceptual model for disparity. *ACM Transactions on Graphics*, 30(4), 2011.

[13] A. Ekin, A. M. Tekalp, and R. Mehrotra. Automatic soccer video analysis and summarization. *IEEE Transactions on Image Processing*, 12(7):796–807, 2003.

[14] J. Freeman and S. E. Avons. Focus group exploration of presence through advanced broadcast services. In *Proc. of SPIE Human Vision and Electronic Imaging Conference*, pages 530–539, San Jose, CA, June 2000.

[15] A. Hamza and M. Hefeeda. A DASH-based Free-Viewpoint Video Streaming System. In *Proc. of ACM NOSSDAV'14 workshop, in conjunction with ACM Multimedia Systems (MMSys'14) Conference*, pages 55–60, Singapore, March 2014.

[16] N. S. Holliman. Mapping perceived depth to regions of interest in stereoscopic images. In *Proc. of SPIE Stereoscopic Displays and Virtual Reality Systems Conference*, pages 117–128, San Jose, CA, May 2004.

[17] W. IJsselsteijn, H. de Ridder, R. Hamberg, D. Bouwhuis, and J. Freeman. Perceived depth and the feeling of presence in 3DTV. *Displays*, 18(4):207–214, 1998.

[18] ISO/IEC 23009-1:2012. Information technology – Dynamic adaptive streaming over HTTP (DASH) – Part 1: Media presentation description and segment formats.

[19] M. Johanson. Stereoscopic video transmission over the internet. In *Proc. of IEEE Workshop on Internet Applications (WIAPP'01)*, pages 12–19, Washington, DC, USA, July 2001.

[20] H. Kimata, K. Fukazawa, A. Kameda, Y. Yamaguchi, and N. Matsuura. Interactive 3D multi-angle live streaming system. In *Proc. of IEEE International Symposium on Consumer Electronics (ISCE'01)*, pages 576–579, Singapore, June 2011.

[21] M. Lang, A. Hornung, O. Wang, S. Poulakos, A. Smolic, and M. Gross. Nonlinear disparity mapping for stereoscopic 3D. *ACM Transactions on Graphics*, 29(3):10, 2010.

[22] J.-G. Lou, H. Cai, and J. Li. A real-time interactive multi-view video system. In *Proc. of ACM Multimedia Conference (ACM MM'05)*, pages 161–170, Singapore, November 2005.

[23] T. Oskam, A. Hornung, H. Bowles, K. Mitchell, and M. Gross. OSCAM - Optimized stereoscopic camera control for interactive 3D. *ACM Transactions on Graphics*, 30(6):189:1–189:8, 2011.

[24] D. Pająk, R. Herzog, R. Mantiuk, P. Didyk, E. Eisemann, K. Myszkowski, and K. Pulli. Perceptual depth compression for stereo applications. *Computer Graphics Forum*, 33(2):195–204, 2014.

[25] S. Paris and F. Durand. A fast approximation of the bilateral filter using a signal processing approach. *International Journal of Computer Vision*, 81(1):24–52, 2009.

[26] S. Pehlivan, A. Aksay, C. Bilen, G. B. Akar, and M. R. Civanlar. End-to-end stereoscopic video streaming system. In *Proc. of IEEE International Conference on Multimedia and Expo (ICME'06)*, pages 2169–2172, Toronto, Canada, July 2006.

[27] T. Shibata, J. Kim, D. M. Hoffman, and M. S. Banks. The zone of comfort: Predicting visual discomfort with stereo displays. *Journal of Vision*, 11(8):11, 2011.

[28] I. Sodagar. The mpeg-dash standard for multimedia streaming over the internet. *IEEE Multimedia Magazine*, 18(4):62–67, 2011.

[29] T. Stockhammer. Dynamic adaptive streaming over HTTP: Standards and design principles. In *Proc. of ACM Conference on Multimedia Systems (MMSys'11)*, pages 133–144, San Jose, CA, USA, February 2011.

[30] W. J. Tam, F. Speranza, S. Yano, K. Shimono, and H. Ono. Stereoscopic 3D-TV: Visual comfort. *IEEE Transactions on Broadcasting*, 57(2):335–346, 2011.

[31] J. R. Thorpe and M. J. Russell. Perceptual effects when scaling screen size of stereo 3D presentations. In *Proc. of Society of Motion Picture and Television Engineers Conferences(SMPTE'11)*, pages 1–10, Hollywood, CA, USA, October 2011.

[32] Ugo Capeto. Depth Map Automatic Generator. `http://3dstereophoto.blogspot.com/2013/04/depth-map-automatic-generator-dmag.html`.

[33] A. J. Woods, T. Docherty, and R. Koch. Image distortions in stereoscopic video systems. In *Proc. of SPIE Stereoscopic Displays and Applications Conference*, pages 36–48, San Jose, CA, September 1993.

[34] W. Wu, A. Arefin, G. Kurillo, P. Agarwal, K. Nahrstedt, and R. Bajcsy. Color-plus-depth level-of-detail in 3D tele-immersive video: A psychophysical approach. In *Proc. of ACM Multimedia Conference (ACM MM'11)*, pages 13–22, Scottsdale, Arizona, USA, November 2011.

[35] B. Xin, R. Wang, Z. Wang, W. Wang, C. Gu, Q. Zheng, and W. Gao. Avs 3D video streaming system over internet. In *Proc. of IEEE International Conference on Signal Processing, Communication and Computing (ICSPCC'12)*, pages 286–289, Hong Kong, August 2012.

[36] Q. Yang, L. Wang, and N. Ahuja. A constant-space belief propagation algorithm for stereo matching. In *Proc. of IEEE Conference on Computer Vision and Pattern Recognition (CVPR'10)*, pages 1458–1465, San Francisco, CA, USA, June 2010.

[37] Z. Yang, W. Wu, K. Nahrstedt, G. Kurillo, and R. Bajcsy. Viewcast: View dissemination and management for multi-party 3D tele-immersive environments. In *Proc. of the ACM Multimedia Conference (ACM MM'07)*, pages 882–891, Augsburg, Bavaria, Germany, September 2007.

LiveRender: A Cloud Gaming System Based on Compressed Graphics Streaming

Li Lin[†] Xiaofei Liao[†*] Guang Tan[‡] Hai Jin[†] Xiaobin Yang[†] Wei Zhang[†] Bo Li[§]
[†] Service Computing Technology and System Lab, Cluster and Grid Computing Lab
School of Computer Science and Technology, Huazhong University of Science and Technology, China
[‡]Shenzhen Institutes of Advanced Technology, Chinese Academy of Sciences, China
[§]Department of Computer Science and Engineering, Hong Kong University of Science and Technology, China
{llin, xfliao, hjin, xbyang, alanzw}@hust.edu.cn guang.tan@siat.ac.cn bli@cse.ust.hk

ABSTRACT

In cloud gaming systems, the game program runs at servers in the cloud, while clients access game services by sending input events to the servers and receiving game scenes via video streaming. In this paradigm, servers are responsible for all performance-intensive operations, and thus suffer from poor scalability. An alternative paradigm is called *graphics streaming*, in which graphics commands and data are offloaded to the clients for local rendering, thereby mitigating the server's burden and allowing more concurrent game sessions. Unfortunately, this approach is bandwidth consuming, due to large amounts of graphic commands and geometry data. In this paper, we present LiveRender, an open source gaming system that remedies the problem by implementing a suite of bandwidth optimization techniques including intra-frame compression, inter-frame compression, and caching, establishing what we call *compressed graphics streaming*. Experiments results show that the new approach is able to reduce bandwidth consumption by 52-73% compared to raw graphics streaming, with no perceptible difference in video quality and reduced response delay. Compared with the video streaming approach, LiveRender achieves a traffic reduction of 40-90% with even improved video quality and substantially smaller response delay, while enabling higher concurrency at the server.

Categories and Subject Descriptors

H.4 [**Information Systems Applications**]: Multimedia information systems—*Massively multiplayer online games*; I.3.2 [**Computer Graphics**]: Graphics Systems—*Distributed /network graphics*

General Terms

Algorithms, Design, Experimentation, Performance

*Corresponding Author

MM'14, November 03 - 07 2014, Orlando, FL, USA.

http://dx.doi.org/10.1145/2647868.2654943.

Keywords

cloud gaming; video streaming; graphics streaming; model compression

1. INTRODUCTION

Recently, cloud gaming has become a promising approach to providing online gaming services [25]. A typical way of implementing cloud gaming is via video game streaming, in which the servers are responsible for interpreting user input, executing game code, rendering graphics contents, and transmitting game scenes to clients by video streaming. This paradigm frees players from downloading and upgrading the game content while allowing service providers to publish new games easily. A thin client such as a mobile device can readily access the gaming service provided it is connected to a medium to high speed network. Over the past few years there has been an increasing number of companies providing such a service, including OnLive [9], Gaikai [7], CiiNow [4] and Ubitus [14].

While offering the clients maximum convenience, the video streaming approach imposes great pressures on the servers. Game computing involves extensive use of both CPU and GPU, which requires an expensive CPU/GPU fusion architecture to support smooth game execution. Our experiments show that a powerful machine with an Intel Xeon E5620 processor, 12GB memory and Radeon HD 6990 graphics card allows merely *two* moderate-quality (20 frames per second) concurrent sessions of the popular game Trine [13]. This means that a large number of powerful servers need to be used to support massive numbers of players, which present a daunting challenge to cloud gaming as a business. It is reported, for example, that OnLive spends 5 million dollars per month on its operation in 2012, a large portion of which goes to the maintenance of its tens of thousands of servers, each supporting but a *single* game session [1].

To address the scalability problem, an alternative approach, *graphics streaming* [22], is proposed that attempts to ease the server's burden by moving part of the computation back to the client side. In this approach, 3D graphics data and commands are intercepted and transmitted to clients for local rendering. As graphic process units (GPUs) are becoming standard modules on today's portable devices such as smartphones and tablets, the clients can continue to enjoy the benefit of download-free gaming services. The increased capacity of the servers potentially translates to less cost on the client side, which likely stimulates a wider adoption of cloud gaming. This paradigm, however, still faces a technical challenge. Our measurement shows that raw graphics streaming[1] is highly bandwidth consuming, due to large numbers of graphic commands and models to be transmitted. For example, the game Trine consumes an average bandwidth of 15 Mbps with raw graphics streaming, which is higher than the maximum access speed of some major U.S. Internet service providers, and far exceeds the average broadband speed 9.8 Mbps in the U.S. as of the 3rd quarter 2013 [2]. This will cause network congestion and unacceptable delay in the interaction between the client and server, which is a crucial aspect of quality of gaming experience.

In this paper we present LiveRender, a graphics streaming based cloud gaming system that addresses the above bandwidth problem. The highlight of LiveRender is a new approach of game streaming, which we call *compressed graphics streaming* (CGS). CGS features a suite of graphics-specific compression techniques, including intra-frame compression, inter-frame compression, and caching, that help to reduce data traffic by exploiting the inherent redundancy of geometry models and the locality property of graphics commands. We show that CGS can save data transmission by 52-73%, with practically unnoticeable difference in video quality and smaller response delay compared with raw graphic streaming. Compared with the video streaming approach, LiveRender achieves a bitrate reduction of 40-90% with even improved video quality and much smaller response delay, while enabling higher concurrency at the server.

To the best of our knowledge, LiveRender is the first open source implementation[2] of graphics streaming based cloud gaming system. It is also the first of its kind demonstrated to support complex interactive games. We view its improvement on bandwidth efficiency a necessary step toward truly scalable and high quality of experience (QoE) cloud gaming services, and hope that its openness and practicality will be of interest to the Internet gaming community.

2. RELATED WORK

Cloud gaming technology [26] is closely related to remote rendering, which separates rendering tasks from the client to remote servers. In this section we provide a brief review of related work.

2.1 Streaming-based Remote Rendering

Remote rendering is motivated by the need to allow thin clients to display graphics efficiently by migrating rendering tasks to remote servers. WireGL [19] presents a system for scalable interactive rendering on a cluster of workstations. In a WireGL system, clients can simultaneously submit graphics commands to graphics servers, which jointly render a single output image. Following a similar goal and to better exploit the aggregate power of clusters for general algorithms, Humphreys et al. build a system named Chromium [20] based on WireGL. Chromium provides a flexible module – the stream processors – to manipulate graphics API commands on clusters. The stream processors are well extensible to combine with commodity graphics accelerators.

[1]Here 'raw' means no graphics-aware operations being performed on the data. For the obvious benefit, the data will still undergo a generic lossless compression algorithm (e.g., LZO [8]) before network transmission.

[2]https://github.com/llfjfz/LiveRender.git

A mobile devices oriented solution for remote 3D graphics rendering is designed by Lamberti and Sanna [23]. The solution proposes a three-tier architecture in which a server renders complex 3D models and encodes them into a video stream to the clients. A client equipped with a 3D viewer can view the rendering results and interact with the server. Chromium's stream processors are used in the server to manage components of 3D models and distribute graphics commands. Pazzi et al. [24] introduce an image-based virtual environment streaming scheme. In the scheme the server streams rendering output to a client, where an image-based rendering strategy assists in displaying the output. Streaming and rate control protocols with buffering and scheduling mechanisms are devised to sustain stable frame rates in wireless network. Baratto et al. [15] implement THINC, a virtual display architecture which transparently intercepts the application's drawing commands and translates them to low-level commands compatible with the client's hardware. THINC provides a multilevel remote display protocol that achieves improved interactive performance in both local and wide area networks.

2.2 Cloud Gaming Systems

There are two basic approaches to implementing a cloud gaming service: video streaming and graphics streaming.

Video streaming approach. Commercial cloud gaming service providers under this category include OnLive [9], Gaikai [7], CiiNow [4] and Ubitus [14]. GamingAnywhere [18] is an open source cloud gaming system that integrates a number of components to enable extensible, portable, and reconfigurable gaming services. The H.264 standard is adopted for video encoding and decoding, and the SDL library [11] is used to handle inputs as LiveRender does. Shi et al. [27,28] introduce a 3D image warping assisted real-time video coding method that can use graphics rendering contexts to improve the performance of video encoding in cloud gaming services. It is a post-rendering video streaming technique; in one way it encodes the game screens as video steaming, and in another it uses graphics command semantics to assist the encoding.

In this approach, the servers are responsible for all computation intensive tasks including game code execution, graphics rendering, and video coding. To guarantee high quality of experience at the client, an expensive CPU/GPU fusion architecture needs to be used, whose power hungry nature further adds to the operation cost.

Graphics streaming approach. Games@Large [16, 21, 22] is the earliest project that realizes graphics streaming for cloud gaming. In Games@Large, game execution occurs at the servers, and graphics commands are captured and transmitted to clients for screen renderings. Its main limitation is that it is very bandwidth consuming. For complex games, the rendering of a game frame has to deal with a large number of graphics commands and a large amount of geometry data, which can easily go beyond 10 Mbps. For an average broadband connection, this will likely cause network congestion and result in playback jitters. The design of LiveRender specifically aims to solve this problem by reducing the redundancy of graphics data. The compression considers redundancies within a frame, across adjacent frames, and among graphic commands, and can be adjusted to provide tradeoffs between degrees of compression and video quality.

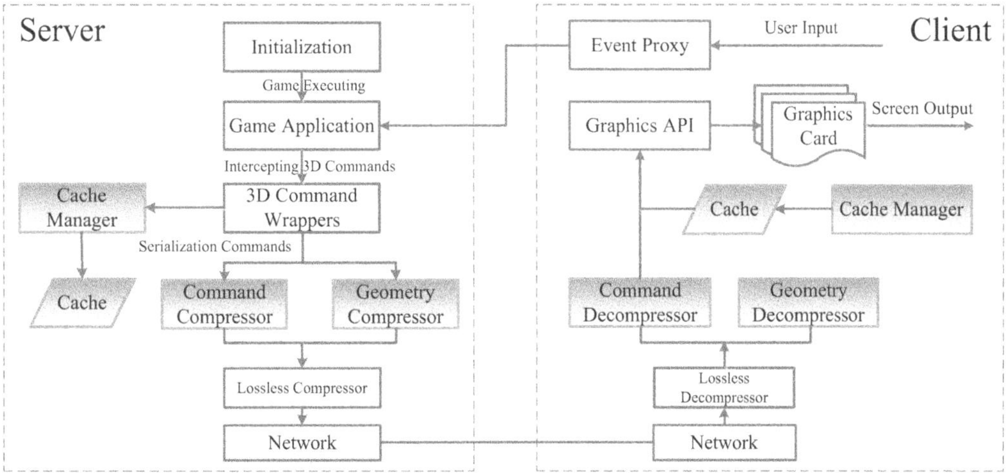

Figure 1: LiveRender architecture. The gray boxes represent compression specific modules provided by LiveRender and that work underneath the game engine. The Lossless Compressor module right above the Network module is implemented by both raw graphics streaming and LiveRender.

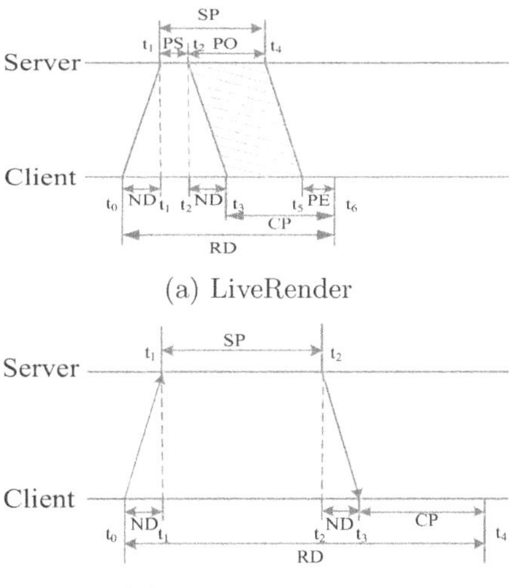

Figure 2: Client-Server interaction and response delay. The shaded area represents the period of pipelined processing. RD: response delay, SP: server processing time, CP: client processing time, ND: network delay, PS: pipeline start, PO: pipeline overlap, PE: pipeline end.

3. SYSTEM OVERVIEW

In LiveRender, the server executes game programs, intercepts graphics commands and geometry data, and transmits them to the client. The client performs graphics rendering for local display, and handles user input. Figure 1 depicts the architecture of LiveRender. In this section, we describe the main modules of LiveRender, shown in gray boxes, and the interactive procedure between the client and server as compared with GamingAnywhere.

LiveRender deals with three types of graphics data: (1) graphics commands, which manipulate geometric objects to generate game scenes; (2) geometry data, which is further divided into vertex data and index data. Vertices define the geometric objects, and indices are used as references or pointers to vertices, and (3) texture data, which mainly comprises static pictures.

3.1 Server Side

At the server side, LiveRender implements a proxy library to intercept graphics commands and associated data, and migrate them to the client. The proxy library is able to encapsulate 3D graphics calls and route them by messages. The library also contains a set of wrapper classes that inherit from 3D graphics APIs (e.g., Direct3D [5] and OpenGL [10], which are employed to perform compression and caching. When game rendering starts, a hook mechanism is used to route graphics calls to the proxy library, which then takes over the execution of graphics commands.

In Figure 1, the Cache Manager module is in charge of storing reusable graphics commands, geometry data, and texture data. The Command Compressor module implements the logic of commands compression by exploiting the cache. The Geometry Compressor module performs lossy compression on vertices and indices with intra- and inter-frame model compression.

3.2 Client Side

There are two tasks for the client: input handling and graphics rendering. LiveRender handles input events using the SDL (Simple DirectMedia Layer) library, which provides low-level access to keyboard, mouse, joystick, and graphics hardware via Direct3D and OpenGL. For graphics rendering, the client receives compressed graphics data from the network, and recovers the original commands and geometry data through local cache and graphics interpolation. The local graphics APIs are then called to render the graphics content for display.

3.3 Client-Server Interaction

Figure 2 shows the interaction and response delay between server and client in LiveRender in comparison with GamingAnywhere. Response delay is defined as the differ-

(a) Intra-frame compression.

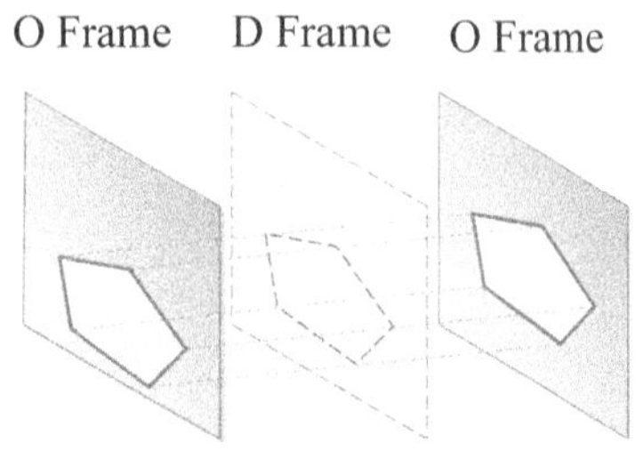

(b) Inter-frame compression.

Figure 3: Illustration of model compression.

ence between the time when a client's input is generated and the time when the client sees the resulting game scene. In GamingAnywhere, a user's input is generated and then transmitted over the network and arrives at the server's network interface after ND (network delay) time units. The server spends SP (server processing) time on processing the input, rendering the graphics, and generating H.264 video, which is finally sent to the client. The client spends CP (client processing) time units on decoding and displaying the scene on the screen. The processing flow in LiveRender is more complex. After the user's input arrives at the server, the server processes the game logic and starts generating graphic commands. After a short period of preparation time PS (pipeline start), the graphics commands and associated data are packetized and start being sent to the client, which starts rendering immediately after receiving the first batch of graphics commands. The transmission process is parallel to the server's processing, lasting a period of PO (pipeline overlap). The client keeps rendering until PE (pipeline end) time units after receiving all the graphics commands. Note that the illustrations in Figure 2 are only schematic and the lengths of line segments do not necessarily reflect the true time spans.

4. GRAPHICS COMPRESSION AND CACHING

LiveRender reduces transmission bandwidth by compressing graphics data and using caches. Graphics compression mainly involves geometric model data, including intra-frame compression for static models and inter-frame compression for dynamic time-dependent models. Caching is aimed to reduce redundant transmission by replacing reusable data structures with short references. The specific strategies are designed with a proper balance between compression ratio, computation load, and ultimate rendering quality.

4.1 Intra-Frame Compression

LiveRender compresses graphic models using an existing surface simplification algorithm, QSlim [17]. In complex video games, a scene can easily contain tens of thousands of model vertices structured in a way opaque to the LiveRender module. The ignorance of game semantics and geometrical structures makes it challenging to approximate geometry objects effectively. LiveRender provides a solution based on a new concept, *abstract model*, which allows partial reconstruction of graphic models. The following details the design.

Algorithm 1 Model simplification algorithm

Input:
The original vertex set $\{v_1, v_2, ..., v_n\}$,
The target vertex number: **m**,
The original edge set $\{e_1, e_2, ..., e_r\}$,
Output:
The simplified vertex set $\{v'_1, v'_2, ..., v'_m\}$,
The simplified edge set $\{e'_1, e'_2, ..., e'_p\}$

// Initialization state
for i ← 1 to n **do**
  compute the quadric error of $\mathbf{v}_i$: $\mathbf{Q}_i$;
end for
// Cost computation
for i ← 1 to r **do**
  extract vertex pair ($\mathbf{v}_1$, $\mathbf{v}_2$) of $\mathbf{e}_i$;
  compute the position of $\bar{v}$ in ($\mathbf{v}_1$,$\mathbf{v}_2$) → $\bar{v}$;
  compute the contraction cost of (v_1, v_2): c_i;
  put c_i in priority queue;
end for
// Vertex pair contraction
while n>m **do**
  take the vertex pair (v_1, v_2) at head of queue;
  contract this vertex pair;
  n ← n - 1;
  update cost of all vertex pairs connecting to v_1 or v_2;
end while
return $\{v'_1, v'_2, ..., v'_m\}$, $\{e'_1, e'_2, ..., e'_p\}$;

4.1.1 *Model Surface Simplification*

LiveRender adopts a fast and high-quality surface simplification algorithm, QSlim [17]. QSlim is a vertex pair contraction algorithm based on the quadric error metric (QEM). The quadric error of every vertex $\mathbf{v} = [x\ y\ z\ 1]^T$ is defined as $Q(\mathbf{v}) = \mathbf{v}^T\mathbf{Q}\mathbf{v}$, where matrix $\mathbf{Q}$ represent vector product $\mathbf{p}\mathbf{p}^T$, and $\mathbf{p}$ stands for the plane equation $ax + by + cz + d = 0$ with a unit normal (i.e.,$a^2 + b^2 + c^2 = 1$). The cost of contraction $(\mathbf{v}_1,\mathbf{v}_2) \to \bar{v}$ can be computed as $\bar{Q} = \mathbf{Q}_1 + \mathbf{Q}_2$. Every iterative contraction of a vertex pair will choose the minimum pair cost, then reconnect all vertex pairs related to $\mathbf{v}_1$ or $\mathbf{v}_2$ to the new position $\bar{v}$ and update the cost.

An example of the QSlim algorithm is given in Figure 3(a). The algorithm details in LiveRender are described in Algorithm 1, where the bolded text are modifications made to fit in practical game execution. During initialization, when computing the QEM, we add a boundary constraint: that every vertex of a boundary edge is initialized with a large weight which promises a better quality for simplification. For cost computation, we only select vertex pair $(\mathbf{v}_1,\mathbf{v}_2)$ which is an edge without considering the options $\|\mathbf{v}_1,\mathbf{v}_2\| < \varepsilon$. The second optimization is that we simply choose $\mathbf{v}_1$ as the position of $\bar{v}$. These optimizations help LiveRender preform fast model simplification with good quality.

Algorithm 2 Cache Updating Algorithm

Input:
    The command parameters: *cmd_params*
Output:
    If cache hit happens, then return *hit_id*.
    Otherwise, return *rep_id* representing a new cache id.

```
hit_id ← -1;
rep_id ← -1;
key ← hash(cmd_params);
hashnode ← search(key);
if hashcode ≠ NULL then
    return hit_id ← getCacheIndex(&hashcode);
else if cache is not full then
    hashnode ← createNode();
else
    hashnode ← getReplaceNode();
end if
return rep_id ← getCacheIndex(&hashnode);
```

4.1.2 Model Reconstruction and Selection

Working beneath the game engine, the LiveRender module cannot really see complete models; what it receives from the upper layer is only a set of vertices and static graphics data (e.g., texture) in addition to graphics commands. The lack of geometrical information prevents LiveRenders from fully recovering the original models. However, our investigation of the rendering behavior of mainstream games indicates that a complete model is often divided into multiple fixed, and possibly inconsecutive, *rendering sequences*. For example, suppose a model in the current frame is divided into three independent rendering sequences, then the subsequent processing of the model will continue to be done on these sequences. Such a property allows us to encapsulate the rendering sequences into abstract models, which serve as basic units for later geometric approximation.

A game scene often contains thousands of models with great variety of complexity and update frequency, thus compressing all of the models is not cost-effective. LiveRender implements two strategies to improve the efficiency. First, it performs simplification to a model only once, even if the model is updated later. We build new indices that map model vertices to simplified ones, to which follow-up model operations are performed. The simplification process is transparent to the game engine. Second, the model simplification is done only to frequently updated models, which account for only a small percentage of all models. The updating frequency can be inferred from graphics API lock and unlock operations. We using a static profiling mechanism to pre-run the games to obtain an empirical threshold for this strategy.

4.2 Inter-Frame Compression

Inter-frame compression aims to reduce redundancy of geometry data between consecutive frames. For most games, the geometry data undergo only minor changes across two adjacent frames. It is thus possible to save transmission of some frames and recover them using interpolation at the client, with negligible sacrifice of video quality. To that end, we divide frames into original frames (O frames) and derived frames (D frames), and the transmitted frame sequence will be repeated in the form $O, D_1, D_2, \ldots, D_k, O\ldots$, where k is a parameter. A D frame from the server is a simplified version of its original frame with geometry data removed, but keeping the graphic commands and texture data. In particular, render settings such as lighting, space transformation matrix, and texture are transmitted without omission, which provides a basis for high quality rendering at the client. The missing part of a D frame will be approximately recovered from the two O frames before and after itself using linear interpolation. An illustration of the compression principle is given in Figure 3(b). The larger the k, the more saving in data transmission, but more increase in response delay and more loss of video quality. We have found that $k = 1$ strikes a good balance between the benefit and cost. This brings bandwidth savings of 20-34% than without inter-frame compression in our experiments. In LiveRender, the transmission of frames are pipelined, so the increase of response delay is equal to the time for the server to process and transmit an extra frame of data, which is small compared to the whole loop of distributed game execution.

Commands	Hit rate	#Calls	L	$\widehat{L}$
SetStreamSource	99.9%	526822	23.0	3.0
SetRenderState	99.9%	204896	15.0	3.0
SetVertexShader	99.9%	102972	1496.6	3.0
SetPixelShader	99.9%	101787	11.0	3.0
SetTexture	99.9%	174300	15.0	3.0
DrawIndexedPrimitive	97.8%	526814	28.0	3.5
DrawPrimitiveUP	97.5%	30858	137.7	10.7
VertexBufferUnlock	98.9%	526814	471.7	75.6
SetPixelShaderConstantF	97.8%	511038	63.0	15.5
SetVertexShaderConstantF	95.4%	555046	291.1	54.2

Table 1: Cache hit rate and transmission savings of some major graphics commands in Trine. L and $\widehat{L}$, both in bytes, mean the average length of original and transmitted commands, respectively.

4.3 Caching

LiveRender's caching mechanism deals with three types of graphics data: graphics commands, geometry data, and texture. Caching not only helps reduce network traffic, but also results in smaller response delay due to faster local access of data structures.

4.3.1 Graphics Commands

We define the set of graphics commands involved in a graphics frame as a *command frame*. A command frame normally contains thousands of commands, some of which can be hundreds of bytes long. These graphics commands are closely related during game rendering, and some special graphics commands are frequently called in a short period of time. As such, buffering the parameters of the graphics commands will be very helpful for reducing network traffic.

We buffer parameters on both the server and client. The caching operations are driven by the server, which synchronizes with the client on buffered data. The server uses a LRU (Least Recently Used) cache with double linked lists, and the client uses arrays for buffer maintenance. A hash table is used by the server to assist inserting, searching, deleting the cache items wrapped by hashnodes. A hashnode is a structure that stores a command's parameters. When a new command is intercepted, the server first calculates a hash code of the parameters, then it searches the hash ta-

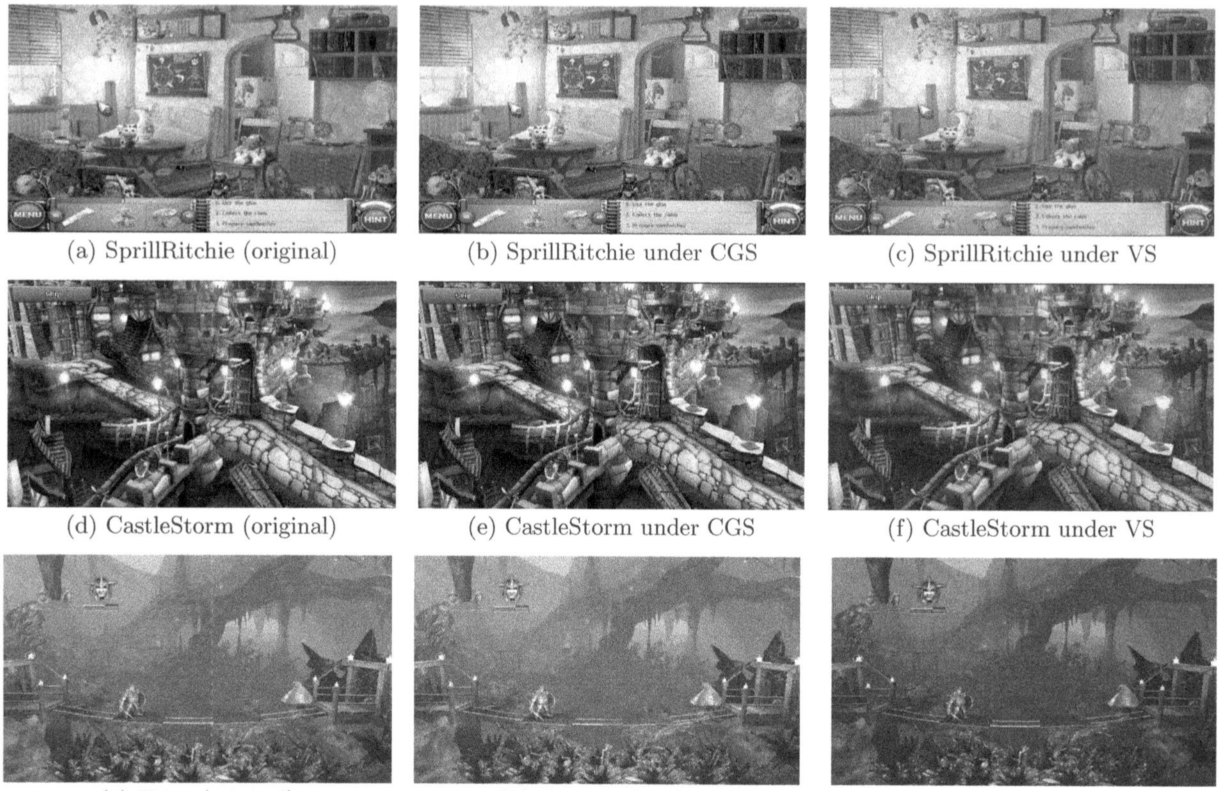

(a) SprillRitchie (original) (b) SprillRitchie under CGS (c) SprillRitchie under VS

(d) CastleStorm (original) (e) CastleStorm under CGS (f) CastleStorm under VS

(g) Trine (original) (h) Trine under CGS (i) Trine under VS

Figure 4: Game screenshots under CGS (LiveRender) and VS (GamingAnywhere).

ble with the hash code. If a hit event happens, the server sends an index to the client, which can retrieve the command from its local buffer. If instead a miss event happens, the server sends the complete command with its parameters to the client, while inserting or replacing an item in the cache. Algorithm 2 presents the pseudocode of the cache maintenance process.

The client's cache operations are triggered by messages from the server. Every received command contains a flag to indicate whether the parameters are stored in the server's cache. If the flag is true, the client obtains the parameters locally; otherwise, it receives the parameters from network and updates its cache to ensure data consistency with the server. A simple processing logic is run at the client without using hash tables in order to make the computation efficient.

Table 1 provides the cache hit rate of some major graphics commands in Trine, as well as the average command length transmitted with and without using the cache during a play of 1470 consecutive frames (about one minute). Those commands are invoked frequently with a strong locality property, as a result great savings of transmission can be attained with caching.

4.3.2 Geometry Data and Texture

Geometry data comprise vertices and indices, which we cache for model reconstruction, model simplification, and generation. Considering that only a small proportion of geometry data change in the majority of static models during game execution, we implement an incremental updating mechanism by which only the updated data blocks are retransmitted with their address offsets. Texture data are transmitted only once, and we provide texture pre-loading when the the game starts up, then new textures will be transmitted progressively as the game execution goes on.

5. EVALUATION

LiveRender has been implemented based on Direct3D on Windows. The software package contains 20,000+ lines of C/C++ code and is made available online at GitHub. In this section, we evaluate the performance of three schemes of game streaming: (1) Compressed graphics streaming (CGS) as used by LiveRender; (2) Raw graphics streaming (RGS), implemented by having CGS disable all graphics-aware compression operations; (3) Video streaming, as used by GamingAnywhere, whose open source allows us to insert testing code for performance measurement. Note that both CGS and RGS use a content-ignorant lossless compression algorithm before network transmission. The comparative study is mainly focused on four aspects of gaming performance: network bandwidth usage, video quality and response delay at the client side, and concurrency at the server side.

Game	CPU%	GPU%	FPS	#Cmds/Frame
SprillRitchie	18.01	71.26	421.24	479
CastleStorm	16.89	20.31	59.84	4363
Trine	17.82	38.72	66.43	4708

Table 2: Performance characteristics of games running on a virtual machine.

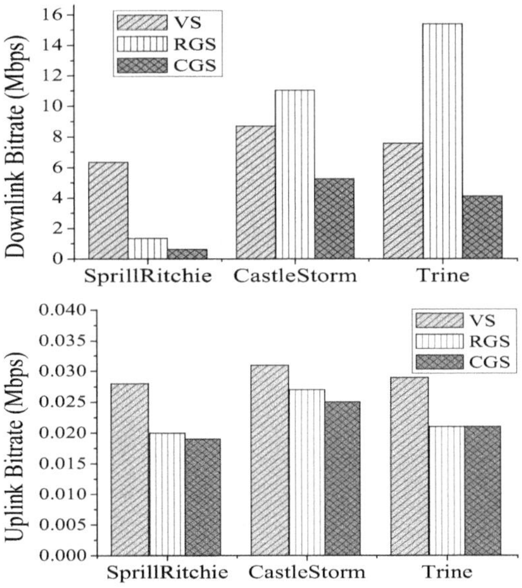

Figure 5: Bitrates of the games for the three game streaming schemes.

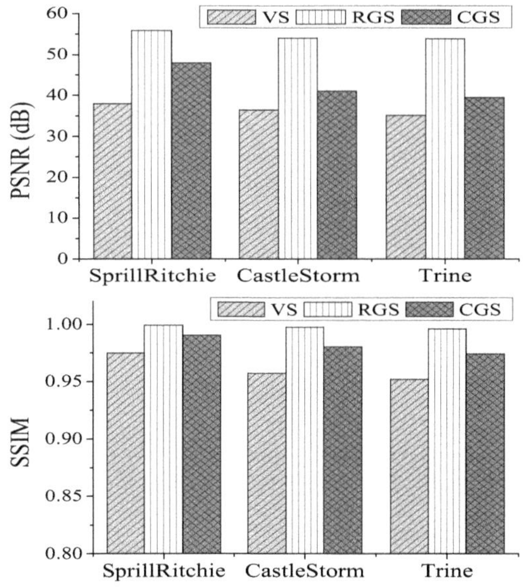

Figure 6: Video quality of games for the three game streaming schemes.

5.1 Experimental Setup

We run games on a server with an Intel Xeon E5620 2.4GHZ processor, 12GB DDR3 memory containing three 4GB chips, an AMD Radeon HD 6990 GPU with 4GB GDDR5 dedicated memory. Several laptop clients serve as clients, each configured with an Intel core i7 processor, an Intel HD graphics card and 4GB DDR3 memory. We launch virtual machines (VMs) on the server, each supporting a game session. We use VMWare Workstation version 9 as the virtualization solution, in which the host operation system (OS) is Windows7 ultimate 64 bit version and every guest OS is assigned one core processor, 1GB memory with Windows7 ultimate 32 bit. The server and the clients are connected with 100Mbps Ethernet.

We choose three games from different categories for evaluation: a casual game, SprillRitchie [12], a strategy game, CastleStorm [3], a physics-based action game, Trine [13]. These games are highly popular and represent various levels of complexity. Table 2 summarizes their characteristics when run on a virtual machine separately, in terms of CPU utilization, GPU utilization, average frames per second (FPS) and average graphics rendering commands per frame. FPS is an important parameter that reflects a game's comprehensive performance.

We implement a game replay function in the client program to facilitate repeated testing or concurrency experiments. For each game, we have a player play the game for ten minutes and record the user's inputs (e.g., key presses and mouse clicks) with respect to the indices of frames. In future tests, the user's inputs are injected to the system following the same sequence of frames.

5.2 Bandwidth and Video Quality

In this section we study the bandwidth consumption of the different schemes and the video quality as perceived by the client. For each run of a game, we select 20 frames of typical scenes (see Figure 4 for example) at the server side as the ground truth of video quality. At the client we capture frames of the same locations and evaluate their quality using two standard metrics: peak signal-to-noise ratio (PSNR) and structural similarity (SSIM). PSNR (in dB) is defined as the noise error between the original and compressed images. SSIM is defined as the structural similarity between lossless and distorted images, which reflects user-perceived quality of image fidelity. The PSNR and SSIM of the twenty frames are averaged to give the final results of video quality.

The GamingAnywhere system uses an H.264 codec for video streaming. We set the encoding bitrate to 10 Mbps, corresponding to a frame rate of 25 FPS. This is only an upper limit for the bitrate; in our experiments the GamingAnywhere system normally achieves 18-22 FPS, generating bitrate around 8 Mbps on average. By default, the network bandwidth is 100Mbps, and CGS uses intra-frame compression, inter-frame compression, and caching.

Figure 5 shows the downlink and uplink bitrates of the three schemes for the games. The downlink carries all the graphics data and is thus vital to video quality, while the uplink deals with only user input which is minimal compared with today's network access bandwidth. The data shows that CGS achieves a 52-73% reduction of bitrate compared with RGS, and a 40-90% reduction compared with VS. As a result of the aggressive compression, CGS causes a 27% reduction of PSNR and a 2% reduction of SSIM index compared to the lossless RGS scheme. Nevertheless the resulting PSNR remains above 35 and generates almost unnoticeable degradation of image quality. In all cases, the video quality of CGS is higher than VS despite the much lower bitrate. A close inspection of the screenshots in Figure 4 shows that CGS produces (slightly) more vivid and sharp images, especially for texture data which is losslessly recovered by CGS. For a small number of objects, CGS may generate a distorted version because of the lossy graphics compression, while the images of VS appear a little more blurry in a uniform way, which results in missing of tiny objects such as light spots. In practical gaming, the loss of fidelity is imperceptible for both schemes.

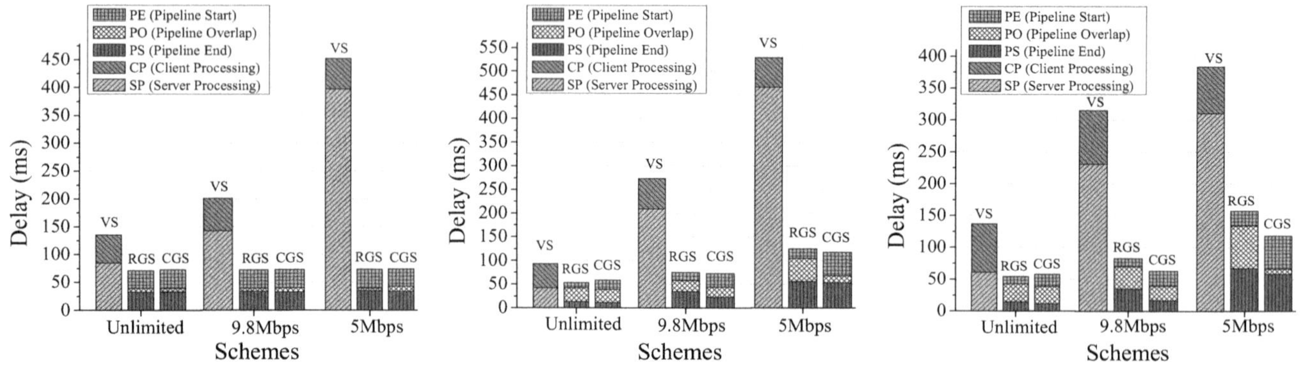

(a) SprillRitchie (b) CastleStorm (c) Trine

Figure 7: Breakdown of response delay for the games under different bandwidth settings. In all the figures the network delay $ND = 0$, so is not shown.

5.3 Response Delay

Response delay (RD) is a critical aspect of gaming experience, especially for highly interactive games. Recall that response delay is defined as the difference between the time when a client's input is generated and the time when the client sees the resulting game scene. Response delay covers a number of complex processes, as detailed in Section 3. In particular, the RD of graphics streaming is $RD = PS + PO + PE$, and for video streaming, $RD = SP + CP$.

To examine the impact of network bandwidth on gaming performance, we use the dummynet tool [6] to simulate a bandwidth-constrained access network. Dummynet simulates typical network behavior such as queuing and packet losses to limit network throughput according to the user's specification. We use dummynet on the client's machine and limit the outbound bandwidth to three possible levels: unlimited (actually 100 Mbps), 9.8 Mbps, which is the average broadband access bandwidth in the U.S. as of Q3, 2013 [2], and 5 Mbps, which is the minimum recommended bandwidth by OnLive for the VS scheme.

To obtain the delays of different sub-processes, we insert testing code into LiveRender and GamingAnywhere. In particular, we collect delay statistics related to system and network queuing under bandwidth restricted scenarios, which make up a significant portion of RD but are left out in the original evaluation of GamingAnywhere. We manually injected 100 user inputs in each game, measure the different components of delay, and then take the average as our final evaluation results. The experiments are all carried out in a local area network where the physical network delay is negligible, so it should be understood that the true response delay in a realistic environment is the measured result plus a network delay in a broad area network. Since the latter is a shared factor of all the schemes and varies across environments, the ideal setting of $ND = 0$ does not invalidate the comparative analysis.

Figure 7 shows the breakdown of the different schemes' response delays under three levels of bandwidth limitation. Take the game Trine in Figure 7(c) for example. With unlimited access bandwidth, $RD_{VS} = 60.65+75.97 = 136.62$ms, while $RD_{RGS} = 54$ms and $RD_{CGS} = 57.55$ms. The great difference between video and graphics streaming schemes is attributed to two reasons. First, the VS approach involves two additional computation tasks compared to the graphics streaming approach: video encoding and decoding. At the server side, the extra process incurs not only additional computation time, but also more coordination overhead between the GPU memory and main memory. Second, the multiple processing phases in the VS scheme are serialized, while they are pipelined in graphics streaming, as suggested by the absence of separate rendering processes in Figure 2. The overlap of processing at both the server and client greatly reduces the total delay in the interaction loop.

In Figure 7, one can also notice that CGS produces a slightly larger RD than RGS, due to the extra compression and decompression operations involved at the server and client. Though the traffic is much lower with CGS, the unlimited bandwidth setting makes the difference in bitrate largely irrelevant. If we consider a more restrictive bandwidth setting, for example the 5Mbps case in Figure 7(c), the results are quite different. Recall that the RGS scheme generates a bitrate of 15.4 Mbps, far exceeding the capacity of the access bandwidth. In this case, $RD_{RGS} = 157$ms while $RD_{CGS} = 117.5$ms, indicating that the reduced traffic successfully reduces the network queuing time (reflected by PO) and makes the totally delay smaller.

The comparative results of delay also hold for the games SprillRitchie and CastleStorm. In summary, we make two observations: (1) CGS and RGS produce less than half of the delay incurred by VS, and (2) CGS and RGS have comparable delay in large bandwidth networks, while the former is obviously superior to the latter in bandwidth restricted environments.

5.4 Concurrency

In this section we study the server's scalability in terms of number of concurrent game sessions supported. Since the games assume an exclusive use of a system's resources, we run multiple virtual machines (VMs) to support concurrent game sessions. Perhaps because of the internal limitations of the VM, only a single GamingAnywhere session is supported by a VM. For LiveRender, it is possible to start multiple LiveRender sessions on a VM, but the performance is very poor. As such, we run a single game session for each game on each VM. We measure FPS, CPU and GPU utilization at the server, and take the average FPS of all the VMs as the final FPS.

Figures 8, 9, and 10 show the system's performance for varying numbers of VMs. As can be seen, the average FPS steadily declines with more VMs because of the increasing

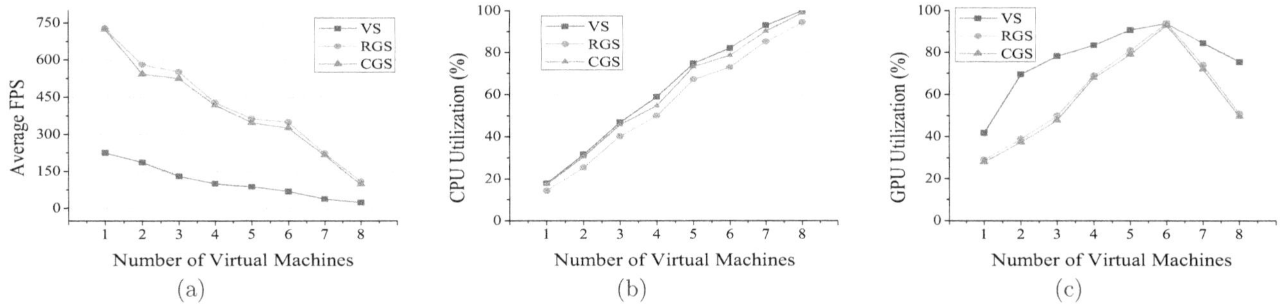

Figure 8: Concurrency performance for SprillRitchie.

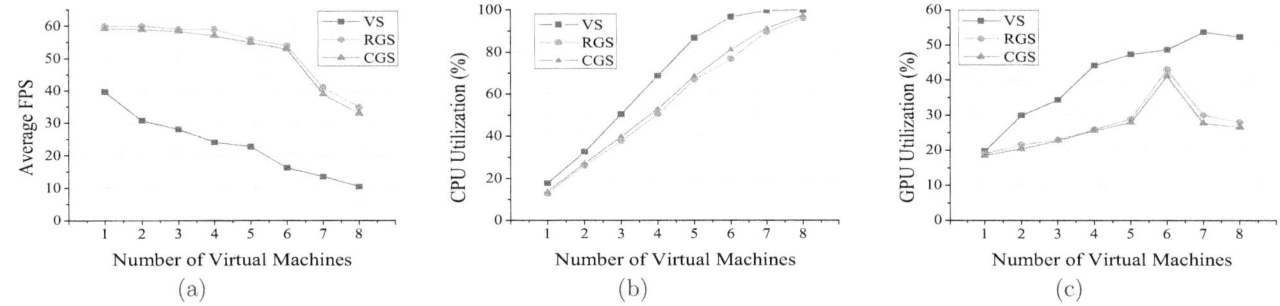

Figure 9: Concurrency performance for CastleStorm.

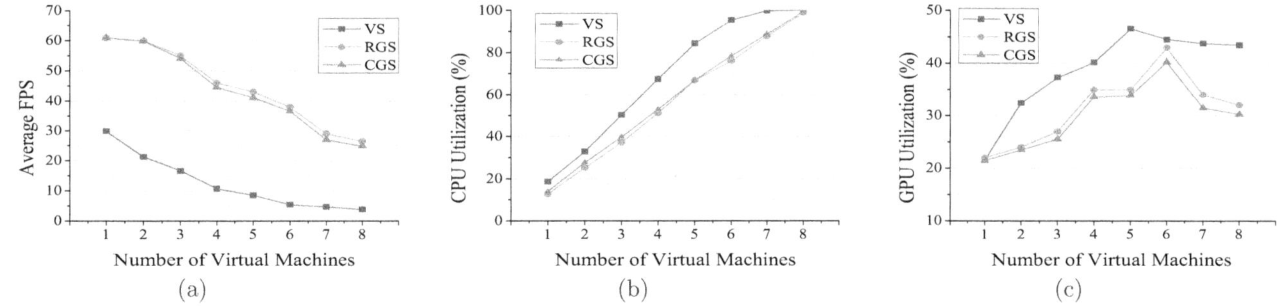

Figure 10: Concurrency performance for Trine.

workload. In all cases, CGS's average FPS remains above 25, a threshold for good gaming experience. In contrast, the GA's FPS quickly drops below this threshold for the games except the simple one SprillRitchie. For example, the Trine fails to maintain such a level of FPS beyond one session. Using the threshold of 25 FPS, CGS supports eight times as many concurrent sessions as GA does for Trine, and the improvement is 2.67× for CastleStorm. Due to the extra compression overhead, CGS delivers equal or slightly lower FPS as RGS does, and consumes a little more CPU than RGS in all cases.

One can also see that the GPU utilization increases with more VMs for both RGS and CGS within six VMs. Though graphics rendering does not take place at the server, graphic tasks such as commands generation, model loading, and texture handling still involve GPU and thus the overhead will rise with more game sessions. GPU utilization does not always increase – it reaches highest at six VMs and starts to decline afterwards. This is because that the VM manager is saturated with six VMs; further workload only causes excessive overhead on the VM manager and more system I/O operations, which brings down the GPU's performance. This trend is in agreement with the FPS results in Figures 8, 9 and 10, which see a steep drop of FPS after six VMs.

5.5 Impact of Compression Strategies

In this section, we provide insight into the impact of compression strategies. Figure 11 shows the impact of k, the number of D frames in inter-frame compression, on bandwidth optimization. We can see that a larger k does bring more savings in bitrate, but the improvement becomes quite marginal for $k > 2$. Considering the extra delay and loss of graphics quality, we find $k = 1$ to offer a proper tradeoff between the different aspects of performance.

We also measure the bitrate of the games under different combinations of compression strategies. Take Trine for example, the original bitrate is 15.4Mbps; with only the caching strategy the bitrate is reduced to 7.03Mbps. On top of this, applying intra-frame compression further reduces the bitrate to 6.24Mbps, and finally the additional inter-frame compression strategy with $k = 1$ brings the bitrate down to 4.12Mbps.

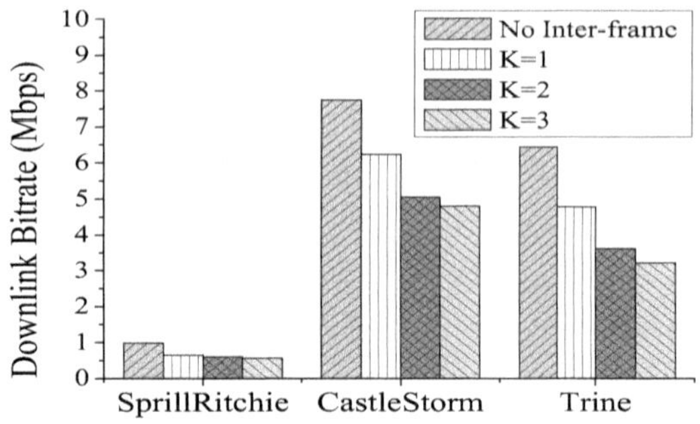

Figure 11: Impact of k, the number of D frames, on downlink bitrate.

We have used the LRU cache replacement policy in our design, which is the most widely used algorithm. We compared it with two additional policies, FIFO (First In First Out) and LFU (Least Frequently Used). We test the three policies with increasing cache size for the three games, and the results show that LRU requires a much smaller cache size to reach the same hit rate (about 95%) as indicated in Table 1. Specifically, LRU's cache usage is only 40% and 5% of those of FIFO and LFU, respectively. Moreover, LRU has computation complexity of only $O(1)$, which is lower than that of LFU.

6. CONCLUSIONS

In this paper, we have presented the design and implementation of a cloud gaming system, LiveRender, using a new technique called compressed graphics streaming. Compared with the raw graphics streaming approach, LiveRender considerably reduces network transmission by compressing graphics data and caching data on the server and the client. Experiments show LiveRender's significant advantages over the raw graphics streaming approach and the video streaming approach in terms of bandwidth consumption, response delay, as well as server concurrency.

So far we have only considered basic compression techniques in LiveRender, ignoring the possibility of further optimizations within a frame and across different frames. For example, a more discriminative treatment of the models could improve compression ratio while retaining the video quality. This is a subject for our future study. Moreover, we will investigate how graphics compression can be performed automatically in accordance with network conditions, which will provide better gaming experience than allowed by static settings.

7. ACKNOWLEDGMENTS

This paper is supported by China National Natural Science Foundation under grant No. 61272408, 61322210, National High-tech Research and Development Program of China (863 Program) under grant No. 2012AA010905, CCCPC Youngth Talent Plan, Doctoral Fund of Ministry of Education of China under grant No. 20130142110048. Guang Tan's work was partly supported by NSFC under grants 61103243 and 61379135. The research was also supported in part by grants from RGC 615613, NSFC U1301253, NSFC/RGC N_HKUST610/11, and ChinaCache Int. Corp. CCNT12EG01.

8. REFERENCES

[1] OnLive lost. http://www.theverge.com/2012/8/28/3274739/onlive-report, 2012.

[2] The state of the internet. http://www.akamai.com/dl/akamai/akamai-soti-q313.pdf?WT.mc_id=soti_Q313, 2013.

[3] CastleStorm. http://www.castlestormgame.com/, 2014.

[4] Ciinow. http://www.ciinow.com/, 2014.

[5] Direct3D. http://en.wikipedia.org/wiki/Direct3D, 2014.

[6] Dummynet. http://info.iet.unipi.it/~luigi/dummynet/, 2014.

[7] Gaikai. http://www.gaikai.com, 2014.

[8] LZO. http://www.oberhumer.com/opensource/lzo/, 2014.

[9] OnLive. http://game.onlive.com, 2014.

[10] OpenGL. http://en.wikipedia.org/wiki/Opengl, 2014.

[11] SDL. http://www.libsdl.org/, 2014.

[12] Sprill and Ritchie. http://www.bigfishgames.com/, 2014.

[13] Trine. http://trine-thegame.com/site/, 2014.

[14] Ubitus. http://www.ubitus.net/en/index.html, 2014.

[15] R. A. Baratto, L. N. Kim, and J. Nieh. Thinc: A virtual display architecture for thin-client computing. In *SOSP'05*, pages 277–290. ACM, 2005.

[16] P. Eisert and P. Fechteler. Low delay streaming of computer graphics. In *ICIP'08*, pages 2704–2707. IEEE, 2008.

[17] M. Garland and P. S. Heckbert. Surface simplification using quadric error metrics. In *SIGGRAPH'97*, pages 209–216. ACM, 1997.

[18] C.-Y. Huang, C.-H. Hsu, Y.-C. Chang, and K.-T. Chen. GamingAnywhere: An open cloud gaming system. In *MMSys'13*, pages 36–47. ACM, 2013.

[19] G. Humphreys, M. Eldridge, I. Buck, G. Stoll, M. Everett, and P. Hanrahan. WireGL: A scalable graphics system for clusters. In *SIGGRAPH'01*, pages 129–140. ACM, 2001.

[20] G. Humphreys, M. Houston, R. Ng, R. Frank, S. Ahern, P. D. Kirchner, and J. T. Klosowski. Chromium: A stream-processing framework for interactive rendering on clusters. In *SIGGRAPH'02*, pages 693–702. ACM, 2002.

[21] A. Jurgelionis, F. Bellotti, A. De Gloria, P. Eisert, J. Laulajainen, and A. Shani. Distributed video game streaming system for pervasive gaming. *STreaming Day*, 9, 2009.

[22] A. Jurgelionis, P. Fechteler, P. Eisert, F. Bellotti, H. David, J. P. Laulajainen, R. Carmichael, V. Poulopoulos, A. Laikari, P. Perälä, A. De Gloria, and C. Bouras. Platform for distributed 3D gaming. *International J. of Computer Games Technology*, 2009:1:1–1:15, Jan. 2009.

[23] F. Lamberti and A. Sanna. A streaming-based solution for remote visualization of 3D graphics on mobile devices. *IEEE Trans. on Visualization and Computer Graphics*, 13(2):247–260, 2007.

[24] R. Pazzi, A. Boukerche, and T. Huang. Implementation, measurement, and analysis of an image-based virtual environment streaming protocol for wireless mobile devices. *IEEE Trans. on Instrumentation and Measurement*, 57(9):1894–1907, 2008.

[25] P. Ross. Cloud computing's killer app: Gaming. *IEEE Spectrum*, 46(3):14–14, 2009.

[26] R. Shea, J. Liu, E.-H. Ngai, and Y. Cui. Cloud gaming: architecture and performance. *IEEE Network*, 27(4):16–21, July 2013.

[27] S. Shi, K. Nahrstedt, and R. Campbell. A real-time remote rendering system for interactive mobile graphics. *ACM Trans. on Multimedia Computing, Communications and Applications*, 8(3s):46:1–46:20, Oct. 2012.

[28] W. Yoo, S. Shi, W. Jeon, K. Nahrstedt, and R. Campbell. Real-time parallel remote rendering for mobile devices using graphics processing units. In *ICME'10*, pages 902–907. IEEE, 2010.

We are not All Equal: Personalizing Models for Facial Expression Analysis with Transductive Parameter Transfer

Enver Sangineto*, Gloria Zen*
University of Trento
Trento, Italy

Elisa Ricci
FBK University of Perugia
Trento, Italy Perugia, Italy

Nicu Sebe
University of Trento
Trento, Italy

ABSTRACT

Previous works on facial expression analysis have shown that person-specific models are advantageous with respect to generic ones for recognizing facial expressions of new users added to the gallery set. This finding is not surprising, due to the often significant inter-individual variability: different persons have different morphological aspects and express their emotions in different ways. However, acquiring person-specific labeled data for learning models is a very time consuming process. In this work we propose a new transfer learning method to compute personalized models without labeled target data. Our approach is based on learning multiple person-specific classifiers for a set of *source* subjects and then directly transfer knowledge about the parameters of these classifiers to the *target* individual. The transfer process is obtained by learning a regression function which maps the data distribution associated to each source subject to the corresponding classifier's parameters. We tested our approach on two different application domains, Action Units (AUs) detection and spontaneous pain recognition, using publicly available datasets and showing its advantages with respect to the state-of-the-art both in term of accuracy and computational cost.

Categories and Subject Descriptors

I.2.10 [**Vision and Scene Understanding**]: [Video Analysis]; H.1.2 [**User/Machine Systems**]: [Human factors; Human information processing]

General Terms

Human factors

Keywords

Facial Expression Recognition; Action Unit Detection; Transductive Transfer Learning; Learning from Distributions

*These two authors contributed equally to this work

MM'14, November 3–7, 2014, Orlando, Florida, USA.

http://dx.doi.org/10.1145/2647868.2654916 .

1. INTRODUCTION

Social interaction among individuals is regulated by a complex communication code. Everyday people naturally sense and convey social signals (*e.g.* interest, approval, disagreement). Automatic understanding this communication code is one of the priorities for the interpretation of human social activities. Aiming to face the challenges of creating socially aware computers, in the last few years the research in the area of social signal processing [34] has made considerable progresses. Social signals are conveyed (also) through a great variety of non-verbal behavioral cues such as facial expressions, gaze, gestures, body postures and vocal outbursts. Automatic detection of non-verbal behavioral cues and specifically of facial expressions [19, 37] is of crucial importance in many areas, including ambient assisted living, human-computer interfaces, entertainment, education, and multimedia content analysis. For instance, in [36] facial expressions are employed to estimate the level of interest of a user watching a video, in [15] they are used for group meeting analysis and in [30] for affective labeling of multimedia contents. However, human beings express their emotions in different ways. Cultural factors, age, gender and personality strongly influence the intensity and the way in which emotions are exhibited [37]. Other important variability factors are the person-specific morphological appearance as well as the illumination conditions or the camera viewpoint.

State-of-the-art facial expression analysis systems achieve excellent performance in controlled laboratory conditions, with limited illumination variations, frontal head pose and posed expressions. However, the accuracy of these systems often drastically drops in real world situations with spontaneous expressions. This drop is largely due to the fact that the datasets used for training models do not sufficiently well represent the variability of real-world scenarios. Technically, this issue can be seen as a special case of the well known *dataset bias* effect [14]: the assumption that training and test data are drawn from the same distribution often does not hold in realistic conditions and the performance of a classifier typically degrades when tested in a different setting from the training one. On the other hand, learning person-specific or scenario-specific classifiers is often practically infeasible, due to the need of collecting large number of task-specific labeled samples. This problem has recently motivated a large series of efforts in the computer vision and multimedia communities in developing transfer learning and domain adaptation approaches [25, 35]. These methods are specifically designed to exploit the informations acquired in different but related *source* domains/tasks when training a classifier for a novel *target* task or domain.

However, few attempts have been done so far for using these techniques in the context of facial expression analysis and in particular to learn *person-specific* models [4, 5]. In [4] Chen *et al.* proposed a transfer learning approach for spontaneous pain recognition. Their method can be used both in an *inductive* and in a *transductive* setting. In both cases labeled data are provided for a set of individuals (source). In the inductive setting, few labeled samples are also available for the subject of interest, while in the more challenging transductive scenario no annotated data for the target individual are collected. In [5] a transductive transfer learning approach named Selective Transfer Machine is introduced for AU detection. These methods provide significant advantages over generic classifiers in term of recognition accuracy. However, their computational cost is usually not negligible when large datasets are considered as they rely on re-weighting all source samples according to their similarity with target data.

In this paper we present a radically different knowledge transfer strategy to learn personalized models for facial expression analysis in a transductive setting (Fig. 1). Transfer learning is formulated as the problem of learning from a set of data distributions. Specifically, we assume to have at disposal N source datasets. Every source domain corresponds to a specific individual. Source data are labeled (*e.g.* indicating an emotion type or a specific AU). Our goal is to learn a *person-specific* classifier for a new subject (target) improving the accuracy over the *generic* classifier, *i.e.* the classifier trained only on source samples. Data in the target domain are not annotated. In our approach, first a set of N classifiers, parameterized by the vectors $\boldsymbol{\theta}_1, ..., \boldsymbol{\theta}_N$, is obtained from source data. In a second phase, we propose to use a vector-valued regression framework to learn a mapping $f(\cdot)$ between each source data distribution and the parameters of the associated classifier $\boldsymbol{\theta}_i$. Once $f(\cdot)$ is obtained, it is used to predict the optimal classifier $\boldsymbol{\theta}_t$ for the target distribution.

Our method has been applied to two different problems, facial AUs detection and pain expression recognition, and evaluated using two publicly available datasets: the Extended Cohn-Kanade dataset [17] and the UNBC-McMaster Shoulder Pain Expression Archive Database [18]. Our experiments demonstrate the advantages of the proposed approach over state-of-the-art generic classifiers, confirming the findings of previous works proposing personalized models. When comparing with methods based on transfer learning [4, 5], our approach achieves similar or better recognition accuracy but radically outperforms them in term of computational cost.

Contributions. To summarize, the main contributions of this paper are the following: (i) We propose a novel transfer learning approach to obtain personalized models for facial expression analysis. To the best of our knowledge, this is the first approach for *Transductive Parameter Transfer (TPT)*, where the parameters of the source classifiers are "transferred" to the target domain using a regression framework without the need of labeled target data. Previous methods either rely on *instance transfer* (source sample selection or re-weighting) or look for a *shared feature space* between sources and target data [21]. (ii) Our approach is computationally very efficient both at training and at testing time, a crucial aspect in many applications (*e.g.* HCI). (iii) In this work, we assume that the different domains correspond to different users expressing the same emotions but our approach can be applied to cope with many other variability sources such as, for instance, viewpoint changes.

2. RELATED WORK

Facial Expression Analysis. In the last few years research on facial expression analysis have made significant progresses. Many approaches have proved to be effective for recognizing the seven basic facial expressions (*i.e.* happiness, sadness, fear, anger, disgust, and surprise plus the neutral state) or for detecting AUs on which the facial emotions are based [19, 37]. The common approach adopted in the state-of-the-art face analysis systems for still images consists of three main steps: face registration, feature extraction (possibly followed by dimensionality reduction) and classification. Face registration is commonly achieved by the localization of anatomically salient facial points [27, 28]. Once the face has been registered, different features can be extracted either from the whole face image (*e.g.* Local Binary Pattern Histograms [1]) or from patches centered around (a subset of) the facial landmarks (*e.g.* SIFT features). Concerning the classification step, SVM, Boosting, Random Forests and many other approaches have been proposed [19, 37]. However, most state-of-the-art systems have been trained and tested in laboratory conditions, with datasets mainly composed of frontal face images and posed emotions [19, 32, 37]. Much little attention has been payed to personalized systems and realistic scenarios. Many authors have recently focused on recognizing spontaneous facial emotions [7, 16, 33], while others have focused on the recognition of non-basic emotions such as pain or frustration [13, 29]. However, all these works are based on generic detectors, *i.e.* detectors trained using a dataset as much as possible realistic and which is supposed to generalize to different individuals and acquisition conditions. Unfortunately, having at disposal only datasets of few hundreds/thousands of images, generalization is hard to achieve.

To cope with this issue few recent works have proposed solutions to integrate weakly labeled or unlabeled data. In [29] Sikka *et al.* adopted a Multiple Instance Learning approach for training a pain expression classifier using video-level labels assuming that frame-level labels are not available. Pain/no-pain expression classification in a partially labeled and unlabeled setting is also considered in [4] where an extension of AdaBoost is proposed. However, their method did not achieve significant improvement in terms of accuracy with respect to the generic classifier in the transductive scenario. In [5] Chu *et al.* presented Selective Transfer Machine for person-specific AU detection. Their approach is based on the Kernel Mean Matching technique [9], which is modified using an iterative minimization procedure where labeled source data drive a progressive movement of the generic SVM hyperplane toward the target space. Even if effective, this approach is very slow at training time, being the proposed minimization strategy very time consuming. On the other hand, user-specific adaptation algorithms are required to be computationally efficient to be used in real world applications. Our method is mainly motivated based on this need and our experiments confirm that it is particularly advantageous with respect to [5].

Transfer learning. Transfer learning approaches have recently become popular as a means to solve or alleviate the scarceness of (labeled) training samples [35, 25]. Since a complete survey of transfer learning techniques is beyond the scope of this article, we refer the reader to [21] where a taxonomy of the existing approaches is presented showing how most of them can be classified in instance-transfer, features-transfer and parameter-transfer approaches.

When the target domain is completely unlabeled, usually instance-transfer approaches are commonly adopted. For instance, in *covariate shift* problems, the basic assumption is that the source and the target feature spaces are the same but the marginal probability distributions of the input data are different [21]. In [9] Gretton *et al.* compare the centroids of the source and the target distributions and estimate the source sample weights which reduce this discrepancy. These weights are then used to assign importance to the source samples when training a model on target data.

There are two main drawbacks with instance-transfer approaches. The first is the computational burden. All the source samples need to be stored as they will be selected or re-weighted when training a model on target data. This is not very efficient both in terms of memory requirements and computational cost. The second issue is that computing the distance between the means of the source and the target data distributions in the Reproducing Kernel Hilbert Space as in many previous works [5, 9] may poorly approximate the real difference between distributions. We propose to solve both problems by learning the relation between the "shape" of each task-specific data distribution and the corresponding classifiers' parameters. Once this mapping has been learned using source data, source samples can be completely discarded. In Sec. 3 we show that we only need to store a kernel matrix representing the distribution similarity. Moreover, we show that our method is flexible as it permits to define several measures to compare source and target data distributions, each corresponding to a specific kernel function.

Learning from Distributions. There is a long track of works on learning from data distributions, showing successful results in several fields, such as text analysis [11], bioinformatics [2], and computer vision [8]. The common approach is to map a distribution into a Reproducing Kernel Hilbert Space, introduce a suitable kernel function, and then use a traditional kernel machine. In this context, the large majority of methods [10, 11] operates by fitting a parametric density function (*e.g.* a Gaussian distribution) to the training data, and using the density parameters to compute the inner products between distributions. Another class of methods does not make any assumption on the distribution form and defines kernels among sets of objects [8]. To our knowledge, no previous works have considered kernel among distributions to perform domain adaptation. An interesting exception is [2], where Blanchard *et al.* proposed a learning framework based on kernel machines and the kernel matrix is the product between two terms: a "standard" kernel defined on feature vectors is multiplied by a kernel defined on the corresponding pairs of distributions. However in [2] there is no regression framework or explicit transfer of the source classifier's parameters to the target domain. Finally, the solution proposed by Blanchard and colleagues involves storing and comparing all the source and target samples which gives no computational advantages with respect to other techniques like instance-reweighting.

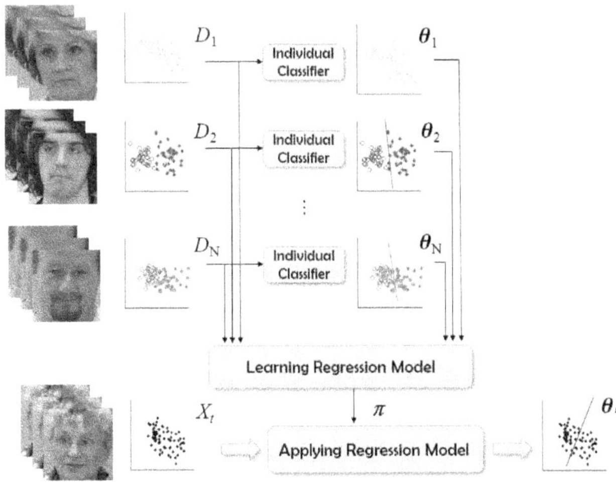

Figure 1: Overview of the proposed *Transductive Parameter Transfer (TPT)* learning approach for facial expression analysis.

3. A REGRESSION FRAMEWORK FOR PARAMETER TRANSFER

In this section we present our method for Transductive Parameter Transfer. Let $\mathcal{X}, \mathcal{Y}$ be, respectively, a feature space and a label space. In this paper we consider $\mathcal{Y} = \{-1, 1\}$ but generalizing our approach to a multiclass setting is straightforward. We assume that N *labeled source* datasets $D_1^s, ..., D_N^s$, $D_i^s = \{\mathbf{x}_j^s, y_j^s\}_{j=1}^{n_i^s}$, and an *unlabeled target* dataset $X^t = \{\mathbf{x}_j^t\}_{j=1}^{n_t}$, $\mathbf{x}_j^s, \mathbf{x}_j^t \in \mathcal{X}$, $y_j^s \in \mathcal{Y}$, are available. Moreover, let denote $X_i^s = \{\mathbf{x}_j^s\}_{j=1}^{n_i^s}$ the set of points in D_i^s obtained by discarding the labels. We assume that the elements in X_i^s are generated by a marginal distribution P_i^s defined on $\mathcal{X}$ and similarly the vectors X^t are generated by P_t. We generally assume that $P_t \neq P_i^s$ and $P_i^s \neq P_j^s$ ($1 \leq i, j \leq N$, $i \neq j$). Finally, we call $\mathcal{P}$ the space of all the possible distributions on $\mathcal{X}$ and we assume that P_t, P_i^s are drawn from $\mathcal{P}$ according to the meta-distribution Π, *i.e.* $P_t, P_i^s \sim \Pi$.

Our goal is to learn a classifier on the target data X^t without acquiring label information. The approach we propose is based on three main steps (Fig. 1). First, a set of source-specific classifiers is learned on each training set D_i^s. In the second step a regression algorithm is adopted in order to learn the relation between the marginal distributions P_i^s and the source classifiers' parameter vectors $\boldsymbol{\theta}_i$. Finally, the desired target classifier is obtained applying the learned distribution-to-classifier mapping and using as input the distribution P_t. In the following, the three steps are described in details.

In the first phase, each source dataset D_i^s is used to train a classifier solving an optimization problem as:

$$\boldsymbol{\theta}_i = \min_{\boldsymbol{\theta} \in \Theta} \mathcal{R}(\boldsymbol{\theta}) + \lambda_L L(\boldsymbol{\theta}, D_i^s) \tag{1}$$

where $\boldsymbol{\theta}_i$ is the parameter vector associated to the learned classifier, Θ is the parameter space, $\mathcal{R}(\cdot)$ a regularizer and $L(\cdot)$ is the empirical risk weighted with λ_L. Specifically, in this paper we use a set of linear SVM classifiers, thus $\boldsymbol{\theta}_i = [\mathbf{w}_i', b_i]$, $\mathbf{w}_i \in I\!R^M, b_i \in I\!R$, defines a hyperplane in the feature space $\mathcal{X} \equiv I\!R^M$ (see Fig. 1) and it can be estimated solving:

$$\min_{\mathbf{w},b} \frac{1}{2}||\mathbf{w}||^2 + \lambda_L \sum_{j=1}^{n_i^s} l(\mathbf{w}'\mathbf{x}_j^s + b, y_j^s) \tag{2}$$

where $l(\cdot)$ is the hinge loss.

In the second phase, we propose to use a regression approach to learn a mapping $f : \mathcal{P} \to \Theta$. The intuition here is that each hyperplane, defined by $\boldsymbol{\theta}_i$, depends on the distribution P_i^s generating the datapoints X_i^s. Thus, if using the source data we are able to learn the relationship between the "shape" of the underlying distribution and its corresponding hyperplane, then, for computing the optimal hyperplane on target data, we do not need label information anymore and we can simply apply the learned mapping $f(\cdot)$, *i.e.* $f(P_t) = [\mathbf{w}_t', b_t]$.

Of course, we do not know P_i^s $(1 \leq i \leq N)$ neither P_t, but we assume they can be approximated with the associated sample sets X_i^s and X^t, respectively. Thus, given a training set $\mathcal{T} = \{X_i^s, \boldsymbol{\theta}_i\}_{i=1}^N$ we propose to learn a mapping:

$$\widehat{f} : 2^{\mathcal{X}} \to \Theta \tag{3}$$

which approximates $f(\cdot)$. The function $\widehat{f}(\cdot)$ is a vector-valued set function, *i.e.* a function which takes as input a set of datapoints X and outputs a vector $\boldsymbol{\theta} = [\mathbf{w}', b]$. If $\mathcal{X} \equiv I\!R^M$, *i.e.* $\boldsymbol{\theta}$ is a $M+1$ dimensional vector, $\widehat{f}(\cdot)$ can be learned using $M+1$ independent scalar regressors. However, as it is reasonable to assume that the elements in $\boldsymbol{\theta}$ are correlated, we use a vector-valued regression approach where the output dimensions are jointly estimated. In our implementation, we adopt the Multioutput Support Vector Regression (M-SVR) framework proposed in [31]. In preliminary experiments we also tested a k-nearest neighbour approach, averaging the $\boldsymbol{\theta}$ values corresponding to the k-closest sources, based on the kernels presented in the next sections, but we obtained much worse results with respect to the proposed Multioutput SVR. We believe that this is due to the fact that SVR is a better tool for regression.

The M-SVR is a generalization of the ϵ-insensitive Support Vector Regression to a multi-dimensional case. In the M-SVR framework, $\widehat{f}(\cdot)$ can be defined by a set of parameters $\boldsymbol{\pi} = (\mathbf{B}, \mathbf{c})$:

$$\widehat{f}(X) = \phi(X)'\mathbf{B} + \mathbf{c}' \tag{4}$$

where $\mathbf{B} = [\boldsymbol{\beta}_1, \ldots, \boldsymbol{\beta}_{M+1}]$ and $\mathbf{c} = [c_1, \ldots, c_{M+1}]'$ are the weight matrix and the bias vector, respectively, and $\phi(X)$ is a nonlinear mapping of the set of data X to a higher-dimensional space. In turn $\boldsymbol{\pi}$ can be found by minimizing:

$$\min_{\boldsymbol{\pi}} \frac{1}{2} \sum_{i=1}^{M+1} ||\boldsymbol{\beta}_i||^2 + \lambda_E \sum_{i=1}^{N} E(\|\boldsymbol{\theta}_i' - \widehat{f}_{\boldsymbol{\pi}}(X_i)\|) \tag{5}$$

where $E(\cdot)$ is a loss function which extends to the multi-dimensional case the ϵ-insensitive loss proposed by Vapnik for scalar-valued Support Vector Regression, *i.e.*:

$$E(u) = \begin{cases} 0 & u < \epsilon \\ u^2 - 2u\epsilon + \epsilon^2 & u \geq \epsilon \end{cases} \tag{6}$$

As for scalar-valued SVR, the problem (5) can be solved in its dual form introducing the kernel matrix $\mathbf{K} \in I\!R^{N \times N}$,

Algorithm 1 Optimization algorithm to solve (5)

Input: The set $\mathcal{T} = \{X_i^s, \boldsymbol{\theta}_i\}_{i=1}^N$, the parameters λ_E, ϵ.

Initialize $k = 0$, $\mathbf{V}^k = \mathbf{0}$, $\mathbf{c}^k = \mathbf{0}$.
Inner Loop:
- Compute a_i using (9), $i = 1, \ldots, N$.
- Compute $\hat{\mathbf{V}}$, $\hat{\mathbf{c}}$ solving (8) $\forall\, j = 1, \ldots, M+1$.
- Compute η_k using a backtracking algorithm.
- Compute $\mathbf{V}^{k+1} = \mathbf{V}^k + \eta_k(\hat{\mathbf{V}} - \mathbf{V}^k)$.
- Compute $\mathbf{c}^{k+1} = \mathbf{c}^k + \eta_k(\hat{\mathbf{c}} - \mathbf{c}^k)$.
- Set $k = k + 1$.

Until Convergence

Output: $\mathbf{V}, \mathbf{c}$

Algorithm 2 The proposed TPT approach

Input: The sets $D_1^s, ..., D_N^s$, X^t, the regularization parameters λ_L, λ_E, ϵ.

Compute $\{\boldsymbol{\theta}_i = (\mathbf{w}_i, b_i)\}_{i=1}^N$ using (2).
Create a training set $\mathcal{T} = \{X_i^s, \boldsymbol{\theta}_i\}_{i=1}^N$.
Compute the kernel matrix $\mathbf{K}$, $\mathbf{K}_{ij} = \kappa(X_i^s, X_j^s)$ using (10), (13) or (14)
Given $\mathbf{K}$, $\mathcal{T}$, compute $\widehat{f}(\cdot)$ solving (5).
Compute $(\mathbf{w}_t, b_t) = \widehat{f}(X^t)$ using (7).

Output: $\mathbf{w}_t, b_t$

$\mathbf{K}_{ij} = \kappa(X_i, X_j) = \phi(X_i)'\phi(X_j)$ [31] and the decision function (4) can be rewritten as:

$$\widehat{f}(X) = \sum_{i=1}^{N} \mathbf{V}_{i.}\kappa(X_i, X) + \mathbf{c}' \tag{7}$$

where $\mathbf{V} \in I\!R^{N \times M+1}$ is the matrix of the optimal parameters computed solving the dual optimization problem associated to (5) and $\mathbf{V}_{i.}$ denotes the i-th row. To compute $\mathbf{V}$ and $\mathbf{c}$ in this paper we follow [31] and adopt an iterative reweighted least-squares procedure. This procedure is summarized in Algorithm 1. We define the matrix $\boldsymbol{\Theta} \in I\!R^{N \times M+1}$ $\boldsymbol{\Theta} = [\boldsymbol{\theta}_1, \ldots, \boldsymbol{\theta}_N]'$. At each iteration k, the values of $\mathbf{V}$ and $\mathbf{c}$ are updated solving a series of $M+1$ independent weighted least-squares problems, one for each column of $\mathbf{V}$ (here denoted as $\mathbf{V}_{.j}$) and for each c_j:

$$\begin{bmatrix} \mathbf{K} + \mathbf{A} & \mathbf{1} \\ \mathbf{a}'\mathbf{K} & \mathbf{1}'\mathbf{a} \end{bmatrix} \begin{bmatrix} \mathbf{V}_{.j} \\ c_j \end{bmatrix} = \begin{bmatrix} \boldsymbol{\Theta}_{.j} \\ \mathbf{a}\boldsymbol{\Theta}_{.j} \end{bmatrix} \tag{8}$$

where $\boldsymbol{\Theta}_{j.}$ is the j-th row of the matrix $\boldsymbol{\Theta}$ and $\mathbf{1}$ is an all-one column vector. The vector $\mathbf{a} = [a_1, \ldots, a_N]$ and the matrix $\mathbf{A} \in I\!R^{N \times N}$, $\mathbf{A}_{ij} = a_i\delta(i-j)$ are computed at each step using:

$$a_i = \begin{cases} 0 & u_i^k < \epsilon \\ \frac{2\lambda_E(u_i^k - \epsilon)}{u_i^k} & u_i^k \geq \epsilon \end{cases} \tag{9}$$

and $u_i^k = \|\boldsymbol{\theta}_i' - \sum_{i=1}^N \mathbf{V}_{i.}^k \kappa(X_i, X) - (\mathbf{c}^k)'\|$. Due to lack of space, for more details on the M-SVR framework we refer the reader to the original paper [31].

Finally, once (5) is solved, in the last phase of our method, (7) is used to compute the parameter vector of the target classifier, *i.e.* $\boldsymbol{\theta}_t = \widehat{f}(X^t)$.

From Algorithm 1 and from (7) it is clear that, both for computing $\widehat{f}(\cdot)$ and to apply $\widehat{f}(\cdot)$ to X^t, we only need a kernel $\kappa(X_i, X_j)$ which represents the similarity between pairs of datasets X_i, X_j. In Sec. 3.1-3.3 we propose different choices for such a kernel, but it is worth noting that other kernels can be used as well.

In Algorithm 2 we summarize the whole *training* procedure. The *test* phase is standard as in classification with SVM. Given a new target feature vector $\mathbf{x}$, the corresponding label y is predicted using: $y = sign(\mathbf{w}_t'\mathbf{x} + b_t)$.

3.1 Fisher Kernel

Fisher kernels [10], originally proposed in machine learning and statistics to measure the similarity between distributions, have recently become common tools in the computer vision and multimedia fields [20, 22].

Suppose that the set of points $X = \{\mathbf{x}_t\}_{t=1}^n$ is generated by the marginal distributions P on $\mathcal{X}$. Let p_γ be a probability density function which models the generative process of elements in X where γ is the parameter vector governing p_γ. In statistics, the score function is defined as $G_\gamma = \nabla_\gamma \log p_\gamma(X)$, *i.e.* it is the gradient of the log-likelihood of the data with respect to the model parameters and describes how the parameters of the generative model p_γ should be modified to better fit the data [10]. Typically p_γ is chosen as a Gaussian Mixture Model and $\gamma = \{\alpha_h, \mu_h, \Sigma_h, h = 1, ..., H\}$, being H the number of components and $\alpha_h, \mu_h, \Sigma_h$ the component weight, its mean and its covariance matrix, respectively. In our experiments we set $H = 20$. As it is common, we also assume that every matrix Σ_h is diagonal, *i.e.* $\Sigma_h = \text{diag}(\sigma_h)$.

Given two sets of points X_i and X_j generated by the two distributions P_i and P_j, their similarity can be measured using the Fisher Kernel [10]:

$$\kappa_{FK}(X_i, X_j) = (G_\gamma^{X_i} Z_\gamma)' Z_\gamma G_\gamma^{X_j} = (\mathcal{G}_\gamma^{X_i})' \mathcal{G}_\gamma^{X_j} \tag{10}$$

where $F_\gamma = Z_\gamma' Z_\gamma$ is the Cholesky decomposition of the Fisher Information Matrix [10] and $\mathcal{G}_\gamma^X$ is the so called Fisher vector. The Fisher vector [22] is obtained computing $\mathcal{G}_\gamma^X = [\mathcal{G}_{\alpha_1}^X, \dots, \mathcal{G}_{\alpha_H}^X, \mathcal{G}_{\mu_1}^X, \dots, \mathcal{G}_{\mu_H}^X, \mathcal{G}_{\sigma_1}^X, \dots, \mathcal{G}_{\sigma_H}^X]$, *i.e.* calculating and concatenating the following terms ($\forall h = 1, \dots, H$):

$$\begin{aligned} \mathcal{G}_{\alpha_h}^X &= \frac{1}{\sqrt{\omega_h}} \sum_t (\psi_t(h) - \omega_h) \qquad (11) \\ \mathcal{G}_{\mu_h}^X &= \frac{1}{\sqrt{\omega_h}} \sum_t \psi_t(h) \frac{\mathbf{x}_t - \mu_h}{\sigma_h} \\ \mathcal{G}_{\sigma_h}^X &= \frac{1}{\sqrt{2\omega_h}} \sum_t \psi_t(h) \left[\frac{(\mathbf{x}_t - \mu_h)^2}{\sigma_h^2} - 1 \right] \end{aligned}$$

where $\omega_h = \frac{\exp(\alpha_h)}{\sum_j \exp(\alpha_j)}$ and $\psi_t(h)$ represents the soft assignment of $\mathbf{x}_t$ to the h-th Gaussian. We refer to [22] for further details.

3.2 EMD-based kernel

The Earth Mover's Distance [26, 24] has been widely used in computer vision as it represents a simple and practical approach to measure the distance between distributions. To compute the EMD between X_i and X_j, first a clustering algorithm is applied separately to the two datasets (we use a simple k-means algorithm in our experiments). In this way the signatures of each set $\mathcal{I} = \{(\boldsymbol{\nu}_1^i, w_1^i), \dots (\boldsymbol{\nu}_Q^i, w_Q^i)\}$ and $\mathcal{J} = \{(\boldsymbol{\nu}_1^j, w_1^j), \dots (\boldsymbol{\nu}_Q^j, w_Q^j)\}$ are computed, where $\boldsymbol{\nu}_q^i$, $\boldsymbol{\nu}_q^j$ are the cluster centroids respectively obtained on the X_i and X_j datasets and w_q^i, w_q^j denote the weights associated to each cluster. In this paper, for sake of simplicity, we consider the same number of clusters $Q = 20$ for both datasets and the cardinality of each cluster is used as cluster weight.

Given two signatures $\mathcal{I}$ and $\mathcal{J}$, the EMD between the associated datasets X_i and X_j is defined as the solution of the following transportation problem:

$$D_{EMD}(X_i, X_j) = \min_{f_{pq} \geq 0} \sum_{p,q=1}^{Q} d_{pq} f_{pq} \tag{12}$$

$$\text{s.t.} \qquad \sum_{p=1}^{Q} f_{pq} = w_q^i \qquad \sum_{q=1}^{Q} f_{pq} = w_p^j$$

where f_{pq} are flow variables and d_{pq} is the ground distance defined as $d_{pq} = \|\boldsymbol{\nu}_p^i - \boldsymbol{\nu}_q^j\|$. In a nutshell, the EMD represents the minimum cost needed to transform one distribution into another. Using EMD we define a kernel:

$$\kappa_{EMD}(X_i, X_j) = e^{-\rho D_{EMD}(X_i, X_j)} \tag{13}$$

where ρ is a user defined parameter. Despite this is not a valid kernel as it is not semi-definite positive we observe excellent performance in our experimental evaluation. This is in line with the findings of previous works [6].

3.3 Density Estimate-based Kernel

The last choice for a kernel measuring the similarity of two distributions we present here is taken from [2]. It is based on a Density Estimate (DE) kernel and it is defined as follows:

$$\kappa_{DE}(X_i, X_j) = \frac{1}{nm} \sum_{p=1}^{n} \sum_{q=1}^{m} \kappa_{\mathcal{X}}(\mathbf{x}_p, \mathbf{x}_q), \tag{14}$$

where n, m are the cardinality of X_i, X_j, respectively, and $\kappa_{\mathcal{X}}(\cdot)$ is a normalized gaussian kernel defined on $\mathcal{X}$.

4. EXPERIMENTS

In this section we present two series of experiments to demonstrate the effectiveness of the proposed TPT approach in two different application domains: AU detection (Sec. 4.1) and pain recognition (Sec. 4.2). We deliberately choose these in order to compare our approach with the only other transductive domain adaptation methods for facial expression analysis we are aware of: the Transductive AdaBoost (TA) algorithm proposed in [4] and the Selective Transfer Machine (STM) in [5]. For this reason, we adopt the same experimental protocols presented in [4, 5], *i.e.* we use the same benchmarks, the same image registration and features extraction pipelines and the same evaluation scheme (on a frame basis) and metrics (Area Under ROC and/or F_1 Score). In the following subsections we present the results of our experimental evaluation in details. Note that in [5] the authors also use the RU-FACS dataset which is no more publicly available. Therefore, we could not test our system on that benchmark. We conclude this section analyzing the

Table 1: Performance on Cohn-Kanade+ dataset, F_1 Score

AU	SVM	KMM [9]	TSVM [12]	DASVM [3]	STM [5]	TPT EMD	TPT Fisher	TPT DE
1	61.1	44.9	56.8	57.7	62.2	72.2	74.0	74.4
2	73.5	50.8	59.8	64.3	76.2	81.8	75.5	84.2
4	62.7	52.3	51.9	57.7	69.1	71.5	71.8	66.3
6	75.7	70.1	47.8	68.2	79.6	75.1	74.9	74.8
12	76.7	74.5	59.6	59.0	77.2	85.5	83.5	85.1
17	76.0	53.2	61.7	81.4	84.3	82.8	83.5	76.1
Avg	70.9	57.6	56.3	64.7	74.8	**78.2**	77.2	76.8

Table 2: Performance on Cohn-Kanade+ dataset, AUC.

AU	SVM	KMM [9]	TSVM [12]	DASVM [3]	STM [5]	TPT EMD	TPT Fisher	TPT DE
1	79.8	68.9	69.9	72.6	88.9	88.0	89.0	88.2
2	90.8	73.5	69.3	71.0	87.5	93.5	92.9	92.6
4	74.8	62.2	63.4	79.9	81.1	88.1	85.0	84.3
6	89.7	87.7	60.5	94.7	94.0	92.2	91.3	91.1
12	88.1	89.5	76.0	95.5	92.8	97.5	97.2	97.1
17	90.3	66.6	73.1	94.7	96.0	95.9	94.3	94.3
Avg	85.6	74.7	68.7	83.1	90.1	**92.5**	91.6	91.3

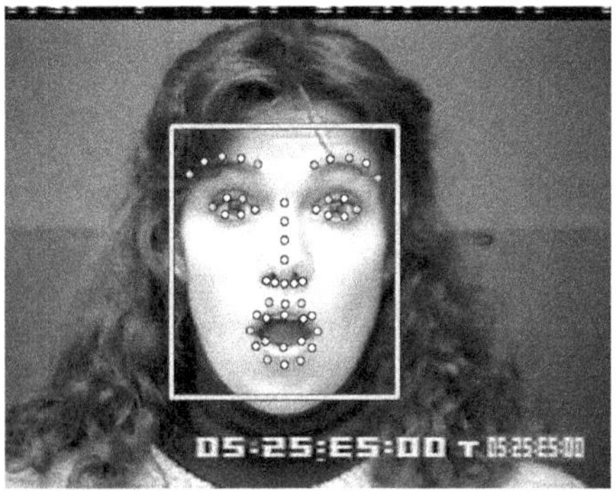

Figure 2: CK+ dataset: sample frame. The green rectangle shows the cropped part of the image and the dots are the detected facial landmarks (the 16 selected landmarks are in green).

influence of the cardinality of the source datasets (N) and the number of target samples (n_t) on the accuracy of the proposed method (Sec. 4.3).

4.1 Facial Action Unit Detection

4.1.1 Dataset

The **Extended Cohn-Kanade**[1] (CK+) dataset [17] contains a set of spontaneous and posed expressions with only frontal faces. The dataset includes 593 videos from 123 users. The number of videos per user ranges from 1 to 11. The video length varies from 4 to 71 frames. A sample frame extracted from this dataset is shown in Fig. 2.

4.1.2 Feature Extraction

In order to compare our results with [5], we followed the same experimental protocol and we implemented the same feature extraction pipeline. First, the subject's face and facial landmarks are detected, the face is aligned, cropped and resized to a 200×200 pixel window. We use the code available at the author's website[2]. Then, as in [5] we select 16 landmarks (Fig. 2) from which we extract SIFT descriptors using OpenCV from 36 × 36 pixel regions around them. In [5] the authors do not specify what landmarks to select, so we chose the external corners of the mouth, of the eyes and of the eyebrows plus other 10 equally spaced landmarks in the mouth, the eyes and the eyebrows. Finally, all these descriptors are concatenated and dimensionality is reduced using Principal Component Analysis. We retain 90% of the energy, obtaining a final feature vector of size 51. Similarly to [5], we select the most frequent AUs in the dataset and the detection of each AU is considered as an independent binary classification problem. However, differently from [5], we could not test our system on AU7 and AU15 because the number of samples for these two AUs is too small. This fact, in combination with the low number of persons (N) in the CK+ dataset, makes it difficult for our system to learn the relation between the data point distributions and the hyperplane parameters. Thus, the average performance values showed in Tables 1-2 are computed using 6 AUs.

Figure 3: UNBC-MSPEAD dataset: sample frames. Spontaneous facial expressions of patients under shoulder mobility tests are shown.

4.1.3 Results

Following [5], our experiments are conducted using a leave-one-subject-out evaluation scheme. The performance are computed using the F_1 score, defined as $F_1 = \frac{2 \cdot recall \cdot precision}{recall + precision}$, and the Area Under ROC (AUC).

We compare our approach with a generic classifier learned on the entire source data (SVM), a semi-supervised Trans-

[1] http://www.pitt.edu/~emotion/ck-spread.htm

[2] http://humansensing.cs.cmu.edu/intraface/

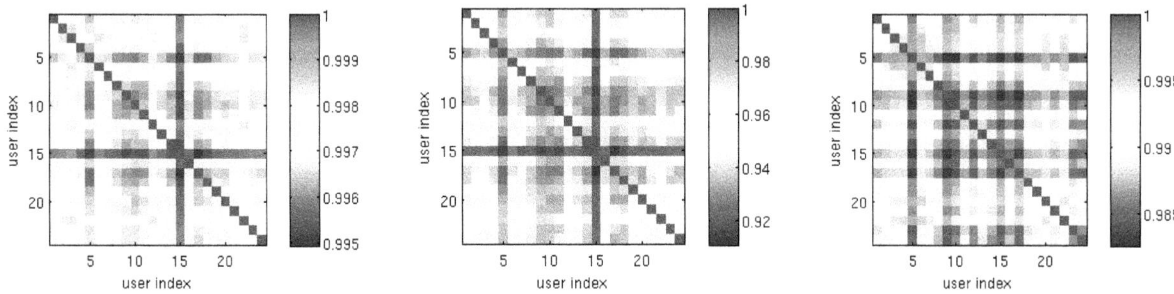

Figure 4: UNBC-MSPEAD dataset: similarity matrices of the learnt θ_i for each subtask, obtained with (a) our method, (b) individual "ideal" classifiers and (c) generic classifiers.

ductive SVM (TSVM) [12] and transfer learning-based methods: STM [5], Kernel Mean Matching (KMM) [9] and Domain Adaptation SVM (DASVM) [3]. The results are shown in Tables 1 and 2. The values concerning the performance of STM, SVM, KMM, TSVM and DA-SVM are reported from [5]. The parameters of our system (λ_E, ρ and ϵ) are computed using an inner cross-validation loop on the source subjects.

Our method outperforms all the other approaches considering both the AUC and the F_1 Score. Specifically, the best performances are obtained using the EMD kernel, while with the DE kernel and the Fisher kernel they are slightly inferior. Among competing methods, TSVM performs poorly. We argue that this is due to the fact that all the source samples are retained in the training process. This may bias the classifier because training samples from irrelevant subjects can be included. KMM, DASVM and STM, instead, re-weight and possibly retain only significant samples, according to different criteria. In particular, only STM outperforms a generic classifier, underlying the importance of an appropriate re-weighting scheme. However, our approach achieves even better performance than STM. We believe this is due to the fact that STM represents the discrepancy between source and target distributions by the distance of the associated centroids. Conversely, the kernel functions of TPT better capture the similarity between data distributions.

4.2 Pain Expression Recognition

4.2.1 Dataset

The **UNBC-McMaster Shoulder Pain Expression Archive Database**[3] (UNBC-MSPEAD) [18] is composed of 200 video sequences of patients with shoulder injuries. It depicts 25 patients performing a series of active and passive range-of-motion tests with either their affected limb or the unaffected one. The dataset is annotated on a frame basis (48398 frames are labeled by experts using the Prkachin and Solomon Pain Intensity, PSPI, metric system [23]). Some frames are shown in Fig. 3.

4.2.2 Feature Extraction

To extract features from video sequences we follow the approach proposed in [4]. For each frame we use the eye locations provided in the UNBC-MSPEAD database to crop and warp the face region into a 128×128 pixel image. Then the resulting face image is divided into 8×8 blocks and Local Binary Pattern Histograms features [1] are extracted on each block. Following the pipeline reported in [4] we adopt *uniform* $LBP^{u2}_{8,1}$, where *u2* means "uniform" and $(8, 1)$ represents 8 sampling points on a circle of radius 1. The resulting 59-dimensional feature vectors for each block are concatenated resulting into a descriptor of $8 \times 8 \times 59 = 3776$ dimensions. Finally, Principal Component Analysis is applied to reduce feature dimensions retaining 90% of the variance. The dimension of the final feature vectors is 334.

4.2.3 Results

Following [4], our experiments are conducted using a leave-one-subject-out evaluation scheme. However, since there is no pain exhibited in the videos of one subject (*i.e.* PSPI score is equal to 0 for all the frames), we exclude them from the experiments. Hence, the final number of subjects considered, both at training and at testing time, is 24. As in [4], every fame is tested independently of the others (no temporal information is used) and with a binary output (pain/no pain).

In order to allow a comparison of our results with [4], we evaluate the performance using AUC and we compare against: a generic classifier (SVM) trained using only the source samples (no domain adaptation), Transductive Transfer Adaboost (TTA) [4], Transductive SVM (TSVM) [12] and Selective Transfer Machine (STM) [5]. For TTA, we report the performances published by Chen *et al.* in [4], while for the last two algorithms, we use the codes publicly available[4,5]. The parameters of our system (λ_E, ρ and ϵ) are computed using an inner cross-validation loop on the source subjects. The results are shown in Fig. 5 and Fig. 6. Figure 5 compares different kernel choices in our approach. As in the case of the CK+ dataset, the best performances are obtained using the EMD kernel. In the rest of the experiments, we refer as TPT our method with the EMD kernel.

Figure 6 shows the accuracy of our approach with respect to the baseline methods. TPT outperforms all the other algorithms. However, the improvement is modest with respect to what observed on the CK+ dataset (see Sec. 4.1.3). In general, for this dataset, personalization does not provide much benefits with respect to a generic classifier (SVM). We attribute this finding to the following two main reasons. Firstly, this dataset is much more difficult than the CK+: while in the latter all the faces have a frontal pose, in UNBC-MSPEAD there are large pan and pitch rotations, expressions are spontaneous and inter-individual differences are pronounced. Moreover, in the CK+, only the emotion peaks are annotated (*i.e.* the last frame of each video), while in UNBC-MSPEAD all the frames are labeled, and the dif-

[3]http://www.pitt.edu/~emotion/um-spread.htm

[4]http://svmlight.joachims.org/

[5]http://humansensing.cs.cmu.edu/software.html

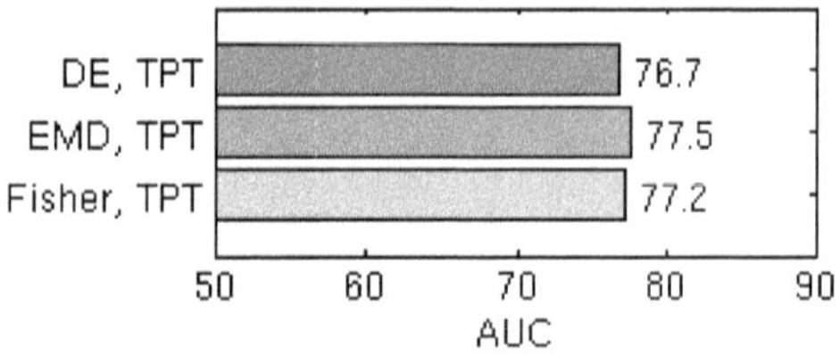

Figure 5: UNBC-MSPEAD dataset. Performances obtained with our method with different kernels.

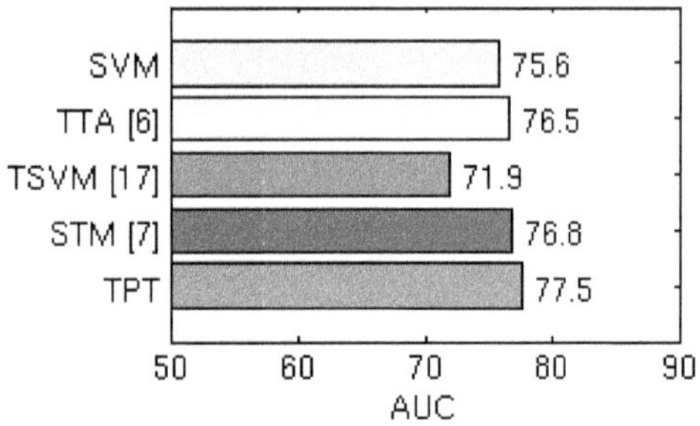

Figure 6: UNBC-MSPEAD dataset. Performances obtained with our method and baselines.

ference between pain and non pain expressions is more subtle. In fact, the pain intensity of positive samples varies from 1 to 16 and these samples are considered all equally positive. Sample frames of pain expressions at varying intensity levels are shown in Fig. 8. The second reason may be found in the fact that in the UNBC-MSPEAD dataset the number of subjects (and thus the number of individual classifiers $\boldsymbol{\theta}_i$) is lower than those in CK+ (24 vs. about 80-90, depending on the AU). In Sec. 4.3 we show how the accuracy of our approach varies as a function of N. Finally, comparing TPT with SVM on a subject basis (i.e., counting the number of persons for which there is an improvement of TPT over SVM), we observe that TPT achieves a higher AUC than SVM on 18 out of 24 subjects.

In order to further validate our approach, in Fig. 4 we show the similarity matrix $\mathbf{S}$ of the classifiers computed for each of the 24 subjects of the UNBC-MSPEAD dataset, defined as: $\mathbf{S}_{ij} = e^{-||\boldsymbol{\theta}_i - \boldsymbol{\theta}_j||_2}$, with $i, j = 1, ..., N$. In the leftmost matrix, each $\boldsymbol{\theta}_i$ is the classifier vector obtained with our method. In the center matrix, $\boldsymbol{\theta}_i$ is the "ideal" classifier for the i-th subject, *i.e.*, an SVM classifier computed using only the samples of the i-th individual, in the "ideal" hypothesis of having labeled samples for this target user. For sake of comparison, we also report the classifiers computed with a generic SVM using a leave-one-user-out protocol, in other words, using all the training samples excluding the ones of the i-th subject. The similarity matrix of the $\boldsymbol{\theta}_i$ learned with generic SVM are shown in the rightmost matrix. It is interesting to notice that the structure of the similarity matrix obtained with our method is very similar to the structure of the ideal classifier matrix, which visually confirms that our regression framework is effective in building personalized models.

Figure 8 shows the results obtained with our method on a sample video sequence. In details, it compares the values of the decision function obtained with TPT (*i.e.* $z = \mathbf{w}_t'\mathbf{x} + b_t$) and the original PSPI values (GT). GT and z have been normalized between 0 and 1 for ease of visual comparison. It is interesting to notice that the values of z are significantly aligned with the pain intensity values.

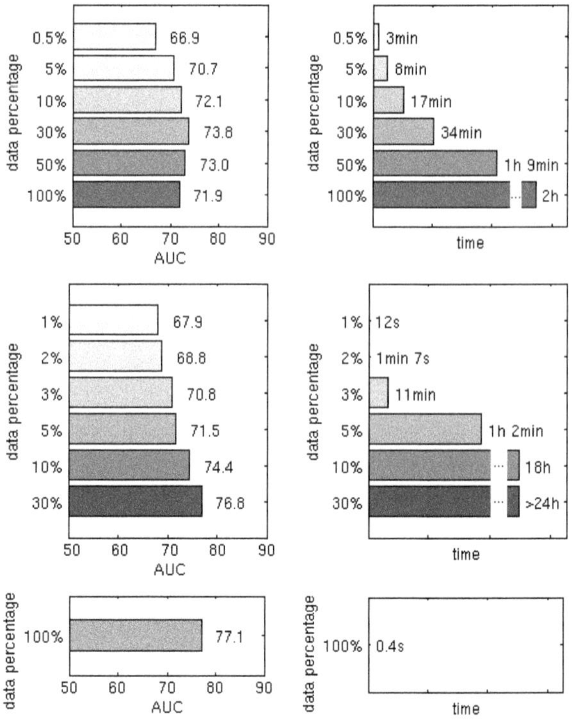

Figure 7: UNBC-MSPEAD dataset: (left) AUC and (right) average time for training a target classifier with different transfer learning methods: (top) TSVM [12], (center) STM [5] and (bottom) TPT. Results for [5, 12] are reported considering different percentage of source data samples.

The last part of this section is dedicated to compare TPT and state-of-the-art approaches with respect to the computational times. In Fig. 7 we report the performance and the training time of the methods for which code is available online, *i.e.* TSVM and STM. In [4] Chen *et al.* report the training time for TTA on UNBC-MSPEAD (17.6 minutes) but they do not mention the workstation they used, thus the results are not directly comparable. Our experiments were run on a 4 Cores 2.40GHz CPU machine.

The training times reported in Fig. 7 indicate the average times for training a single target classifier. All the methods but ours use all the source samples (suitably re-weighted) for training a target classifier, thus they require a much higher computational load. Conversely, in TPT training is split in three phases (Sec. 3), whose average time are the following: (i) computing domain-specific classifiers, ~40 seconds, (ii) computing the kernel matrix, ~4 seconds, (iii) computing the target-specific classifier using a pre-calculated kernel matrices, 0.4 seconds. It is worth noting that steps (i) and (ii) involve only source samples and are executed a single time. Only step (iii) is target-specific and it is the phase that realizes adaptation on a new subject. Thus in Fig. 7 we only report the computational times of step (iii). It is clear from these plots that both TSVM and STM do not scale well as the number of training samples increases. For instance, using only 10% of the source samples, TSVM needs 17 minutes on average for training an individual classifier, STM 18 hours and TPT only 0.4 seconds. Even if the accuracy of all the methods are comparable in this difficult dataset, our pro-

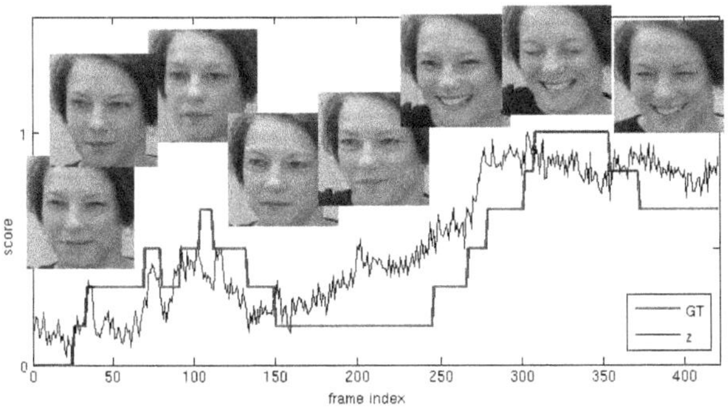

Figure 8: UNBC-MSPEAD dataset: ground truth labels (GT) compared to the value $z = \mathbf{w}_t'\mathbf{x}+b_t$ of the decision function obtained with TPT for one sample video sequence.

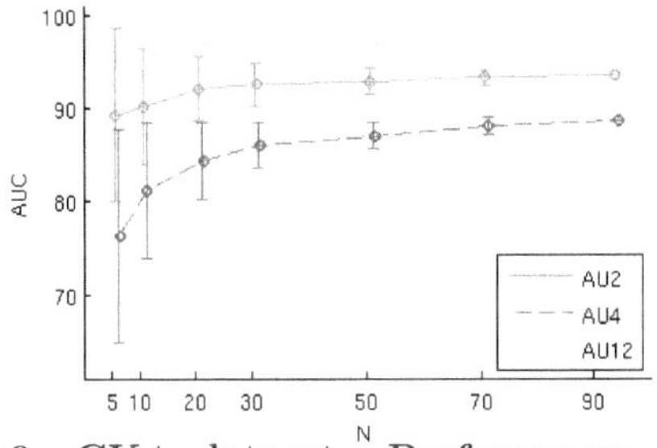

Figure 9: CK+ dataset. Performance of TPT at varying number of source users.

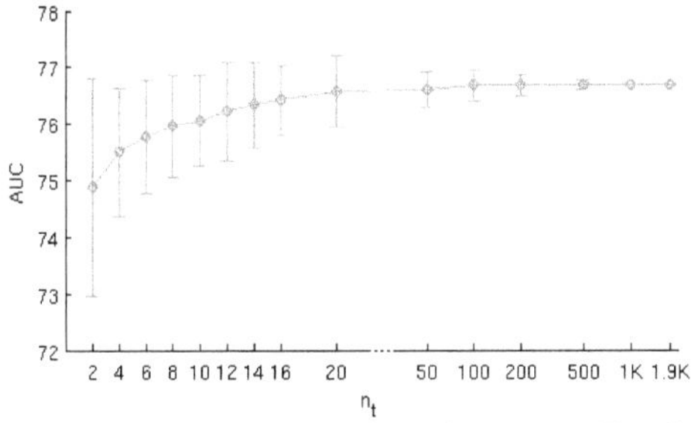

Figure 10: UNBC-MSPEAD dataset. Performance of TPT at varying number of target samples n_t.

posed approach largely outperforms all the other algorithms with respect to the computational cost. Moreover, independently from the kernel choice, we do not need to store the source samples. Indeed, the regression function value for a new target task is computed considering only on the kernel matrix. We believe that both memory storage and time efficiency are crucial in real world multimedia applications, where the construction of a personalized classifier needs to be fast and memory resources are usually limited (*e.g.*, with personal devices).

4.3 Relation between performance and number of source users and samples

In this section we analyse how the performance of our method depends on the number of source datasets N and target samples n_t. These experiments have been conducted respectively on the CK+, which contains the highest number of subjects - up to $\sim$90 (depending on the specific AU), while UNBC-MSPEAD dataset has only 25 subjects - and on the UNBC-MSPEAD, which contains a higher number of samples per subjects - around 1900 samples per user, while for CK+ it is around 150.

In the CK+ experiments, we randomly select a subset of $N + 1$ users over all the subjects, varying N from 5 to $\sim$90. Then we test our method using a leave-one-user-out approach, in which in turn one user is chosen as the target subject and the remaining N are used as sources. For a given value of N, we repeat the experiments 100 times and the average values are reported in Fig. 9. The performances are measured computing the AUC. Error bars show the standard deviation from the mean. As expected, with a low number of source datasets the performance of TPT are rather modest, expecially for the AU which are more difficult to detect (*e.g.* AU4). In fact, the regression function $\widehat{f}(\cdot)$ (Sec. 3) is learned using N training samples (*i.e.* data distributions) and, if N is too small, it generalizes poorly.

We also analyse the impact of the number of target data points n_t on the recognition accuracy for the UNBC-MSPEAD dataset. Fig. 10 reports the average AUC obtained on 100 runs. On each run, a random subset of n_t points is selected for each target user. A leave-one-user-out protocol is used. When n_t increases the performance improves, as data distributions are better approximated when a large number of data points is employed.

5. CONCLUSIONS

In this paper we proposed a method for building person-specific facial expression classifiers as a way to deal with the inter-individual variability of the emotions. A personalized classifier for a new target subject is inferred without the need of acquiring labeled data. The proposed method is based on a regression framework which directly maps the unlabeled data distribution of a given person to the parameters of her/his personalized classifier. As far as we know, this is the first transductive parameter transfer approach in literature. Oppositely to previous transfer learning approaches operating in a transductive setting and based on instance reweighting the main advantage of our method is that we do not need to store and compare all the source and target samples. This leads to a significantly reduced computational cost. We empirically showed that our system achieves state-of-the-art accuracy on public benchmarks while being different orders of magnitude faster.

6. ACKNOWLEDGMENTS

This work was partially supported by the European 7th Framework Program, under grant VENTURI (FP7-288238) and xLiMe (FP7-611346) and by the cluster project Ageing at Home.

7. REFERENCES

[1] T. Ahonen, A. Hadid, and M. Pietikäinen. Face description with local binary patterns: Application to face recognition. *IEEE Trans. on PAMI*, 28(12):2037–2041, 2006.

[2] G. Blanchard, G. Lee, and C. Scott. Generalizing from several related classification tasks to a new unlabeled sample. In *NIPS*, 2011.

[3] L. Bruzzone and M. Marconcini. Domain adaptation problems: A DASVM classification technique and a circular validation strategy. *IEEE Trans. on PAMI*, 32(5):770–787, 2010.

[4] J. Chen, X. Liu, P. Tu, and A. Aragones. Learning person-specific models for facial expression and action unit recognition. *Pattern Recognition Letters*, 34(15):1964–1970, 2013.

[5] W.-S. Chu, F. D. L. Torre, and J. F. Cohn. Selective transfer machine for personalized facial action unit detection. In *CVPR*, 2013.

[6] M. R. Daliri. Kernel earth mover's distance for eeg classification. *Clinical EEG and Neuroscience*, 44(3):182–187, 2013.

[7] H. Dibeklioğlu, T. Gevers, A. A. Salah, and R. Valenti. A smile can reveal your age: Enabling facial dynamics in age estimation. In *ACM Multimedia*, 2012.

[8] K. Grauman and T. Darrell. The pyramid match kernel: Discriminative classification with sets of image features. In *CVPR*, 2005.

[9] A. Gretton, A. Smola, J. Huang, M. Schmittfull, K. Borgwardt, and B. Schölkopf. Covariate shift by kernel mean matching. *Dataset shift in machine learning*, 3(4):5, 2009.

[10] T. Jaakkola, D. Haussler, et al. Exploiting generative models in discriminative classifiers. *NIPS*, 1999.

[11] T. Jebara, R. Kondor, and A. Howard. Probability product kernels. *The Journal of Machine Learning Research*, 5:819–844, 2004.

[12] T. Joachims. Transductive inference for text classification using support vector machines. In *ICML*, 1999.

[13] A. Kapoor, W. Burleson, and R. W. Picard. Automatic prediction of frustration. *International Journal of Man-Machine Studies*, 65(8):724–736, 2007.

[14] A. Khosla, T. Zhou, T. Malisiewicz, A. A. Efros, and A. Torralba. Undoing the damage of dataset bias. In *ECCV*, 2012.

[15] S. Kumano, K. Otsuka, D. Mikami, and J. Yamato. Recognizing communicative facial expressions for discovering interpersonal emotions in group meetings. In *Proceedings of the 2009 International Conference on Multimodal Interfaces*, ICMI-MLMI '09, 2009.

[16] G. Littlewort, M. S. Bartlett, and K. Lee. Faces of pain: automated measurement of spontaneousallfacial expressions of genuine and posed pain. In *ICMI*, 2007.

[17] P. Lucey, J. F. Cohn, T. Kanade, J. Saragih, Z. Ambadar, and I. Matthews. The extended cohn-kanade dataset (ck+): A complete dataset for action unit and emotion-specified expression. In *CVPR Workshops*, 2010.

[18] P. Lucey, J. F. Cohn, K. M. Prkachin, P. E. Solomon, S. W. Chew, and I. Matthews. Painful monitoring: Automatic pain monitoring using the unbc-mcmaster shoulder pain expression archive database. *Image Vision Comput.*, 30(3):197–205, 2012.

[19] A. Martinez and S. Du. A model of the perception of facial expressions of emotion by humans: Research overview and perspectives. *Journal of Machine Learning Research*, 13:1589–1608, 2012.

[20] I. Mironica, J. Uijlings, N. Rostamzadeh, B. Ionescu, and N. Sebe. Time matters!: capturing variation in time in video using fisher kernels. In *ACM Multimedia*, 2013.

[21] S. J. Pan and Q. Yang. A survey on transfer learning. *IEEE Trans. on Knowledge and Data Engineering*, 22(10):1345–1359, 2010.

[22] F. Perronnin and C. Dance. Fisher kernels on visual vocabularies for image categorization. In *CVPR*, 2007.

[23] K. M. Prkachin and P. E. Solomon. The structure, reliability and validity of pain expression: Evidence from patients with shoulder pain. *Pain*, 139(2):267–274, 2008.

[24] E. Ricci, G. Zen, N. Sebe, and S. Messelodi. A prototype learning framework using emd: Application to complex scenes analysis. *IEEE Trans. on PAMI*, 35(3):513–526, 2013.

[25] S. D. Roy, T. Mei, W. Zeng, and S. Li. Socialtransfer: cross-domain transfer learning from social streams for media applications. In *ACM Multimedia*, 2012.

[26] Y. Rubner, C. Tomasi, and L. J. Guibas. The earth mover's distance as a metric for image retrieval. *International Journal of Computer Vision*, 40(2):99–121, 2000.

[27] E. Sangineto. Pose and expression independent facial landmark localization using dense-surf and the hausdorff distance. *IEEE Trans. on PAMI*, 35(3):624–638, 2013.

[28] J. M. Saragih, S. Lucey, and J. F. Cohn. Deformable model fitting by regularized landmark mean-shift. *International Journal of Computer Vision*, 91(2):200–215, 2011.

[29] K. Sikka, A. Dhall, and M. Bartlett. Weakly supervised pain localization using multiple instance learning. *IEEE FG*, 2013.

[30] M. Tkalcic, A. Odic, A. Kosir, and J. Tasic. Affective labeling in a content-based recommender system for images. *IEEE Trans. on Multimedia*, 15(2):391–400, Feb 2013.

[31] D. Tuia, J. Verrelst, L. Alonso, F. Perez-Cruz, and G. Camps-Valls. Multioutput support vector regression for remote sensing biophysical parameter estimation. *IEEE Geoscience and Remote Sensing Letters*, 8(4):804–808, July 2011.

[32] M. F. Valstar, B. Jiang, M. Mehu, M. Pantic, and K. Scherer. The first facial expression recognition and analysis challenge. In *IEEE FG*, 2011.

[33] M. F. Valstar, M. Pantic, Z. Ambadar, and J. F. Cohn. Spontaneous vs. posed facial behavior: automatic analysis of brow actions. In *ICMI*, 2006.

[34] A. Vinciarelli, M. Pantic, and H. Bourlard. Social signal processing: Survey of an emerging domain. *Image and Vision Computing*, 27(12):1743–1759, 2009.

[35] Y. Yang, Y. Yang, Z. Huang, J. Liu, and Z. Ma. Robust cross-media transfer for visual event detection. In *ACM Multimedia*, 2012.

[36] M. Yeasin, B. Bullot, and R. Sharma. Recognition of facial expressions and measurement of levels of interest from video. *IEEE Trans. on Multimedia*, 8(3):500–508, 2006.

[37] Z. Zeng, M. Pantic, G. I. Roisman, and T. S. Huang. A survey of affect recognition methods: Audio, visual, and spontaneous expressions. *IEEE Trans. on PAMI*, 31(1):39–58, 2009.

Object-Based Visual Sentiment Concept Analysis and Application

Tao Chen, Felix X. Yu, Jiawei Chen, Yin Cui, Yan-Ying Chen, Shih-Fu Chang

Columbia University, USA

{tc2650,xy2154,jc3960,yc2776,sc250}@columbia.edu yanying@gmail.com

ABSTRACT

This paper studies the problem of modeling object-based visual concepts such as "crazy car" and "shy dog" with a goal to extract emotion related information from social multimedia content. We focus on detecting such adjective-noun pairs because of their strong co-occurrence relation with image tags about emotions. This problem is very challenging due to the highly subjective nature of the adjectives like "crazy" and "shy" and the ambiguity associated with the annotations. However, associating adjectives with concrete physical nouns makes the combined visual concepts more detectable and tractable. We propose a hierarchical system to handle the concept classification in an object specific manner and decompose the hard problem into object localization and sentiment related concept modeling. In order to resolve the ambiguity of concepts we propose a novel classification approach by modeling the concept similarity, leveraging on online commonsense knowledgebase. The proposed framework also allows us to interpret the classifiers by discovering discriminative features. The comparisons between our method and several baselines show great improvement in classification performance. We further demonstrate the power of the proposed system with a few novel applications such as sentiment-aware music slide shows of personal albums.

Categories and Subject Descriptors

H.3.3 [**Information Storage and Retrieval**]: Information Retrieval and Indexing

Keywords

social multimedia; visual sentiment; affective computing

1. INTRODUCTION

The explosive growth of social media and the ever-growing volume of online visual content have greatly motivated the research on large-scale social multimedia analysis. Among

MM'14, November 3–7, 2014, Orlando, Florida, USA.

Copyright 2014 ACM 978-1-4503-3063-3/14/11 ...$15.00.

http://dx.doi.org/10.1145/2647868.2654935.

Figure 1: We propose a novel framework to detect visual concepts corresponding to adjective-noun pairs that statistically correlate with sentiments or emotions expressed in images. The proposed framework focuses on detection of objects and associated attributes. Photo on the left, ©Gordon (Monkey Mash Button) of Flickr. Photo on the right, ©allen watkin (allenthepostman) of Flickr. Bounding boxes are added to highlight difference between objects and background.

these research efforts, understanding the emotion and sentiment in visual media content shows its emerging importance. Images and videos embedding strong sentiments can strengthen the opinion conveyed in the content and influence the public viewer with viral effects. Understanding sentiment expressed in visual content will greatly benefit social media communication and enable broad applications in education, advertisement and entertainment.

While the modeling of generic visual concepts (nouns) such as "sky" and "dog" has been studied extensively in computer vision, modeling adjectives correlated with visual sentiments like "amazing" and "shy" directly is very difficult, if not impossible, due to the big "affective gap" between the low-level visual features and the high-level sentiment. Therefore, we follow a more tractable approach proposed by Borth et al. [3] which models sentiment related visual concepts as a mid-level representation to fill the gap. Those concepts are Adjective Noun Pairs (ANPs), such as "happy dog" and "beautiful sky", which combine the sentimental strength of adjectives and detectability of nouns. Though these ANP concepts do not directly express emotions or sentiments, they were discovered based on strong co-occurrence relationships with emotion tags of web photos, and thus are useful as effective statistical cues for detecting emotions depicted in the images. In this work, we systemically study the modeling of these sentiment related visual concepts (termed visual sentiment concepts in this paper) by addressing two important challenges:

Many concepts are object based and need to be localized. These include popular content in social media such as "face", "dog" and "car". Modeling concepts using the features extracted from the whole image as in [3] will lose the specific characteristics of the objects and unavoidably encompass noise from the background. However, it is very difficult and time consuming to localize each concept because of the lack of bounding box annotation of the ANPs, and the prohibitive computational complexity required in training the local concept detectors.

The ambiguity of the visual sentiment annotation. The existing annotation of visual sentiment concepts are highly ambiguous and they are often hard to distinguish since semantically related adjectives often have similar visual reflexes in images. For example, "cute dog" and "adorable dog". Traditional multiclass classification using hard labels will not work. In contrast, the nouns representing objects are much less ambiguous.

Therefore a natural and efficient approach is to model the object (noun) first, and then model the object based sentiment attributes (adjective) with a specific aim to tackle the ambiguity. The requirement of the hierarchical scheme can be further justified by several observations. First, visual sentiment concepts are inconsistent across objects. For example, the visual characteristics that indicate a girl is beautiful could be very different from those indicate a beautiful sunset scene. Second, the features that effectively detect sentiment concepts is usually different from those effective for object detection. For example, Machajdik et al. [21] proposed to use features inspired by psychology and art to model affect in images. Third, to extract the features such as the composition of the image and the color distribution inside the object, we also need to first localize the object. Moreover, instead of modeling visual sentiment concepts directly with an object detection method such as Deformable Part Model (DPM) [11], the hierarchical method allows us to apply special approaches like soft weight SVM to address the concept overlap among multiple adjectives of the same noun. Traditional object detection methods do not allow this.

In this work we first build object detection models to recognize six frequent objects in social media including "car", "dog", "dress", "face", "flower" and "food" to model the 135 ANP concepts associated with those nouns. We then build object-based sentiment concept models, based on the detected objects, with location and composition information. In order to resolve the visual ambiguity among the adjectives, we propose a novel method exploiting rich semantic similarity information computed from an online commonsense knowledgebase, conceptNet [20]. The method models the ambiguity by two kinds of visual similarity, namely attributive and proportional similarity. The implementation is based on a fusion of weighted SVM and a recently proposed machine learning model, called proportion-SVM or pSVM. Several visual sentiment concepts detected by our system are shown in Figure 1. The very significant performance improvement (up to 50% relatively) compared to the previous work proves the success of our model. To understand how these high-level models work, we interpret the classifiers by discovering the discriminative features for each visual sentiment concept classifier.

Additionally, we demonstrate an innovative application that benefit from our model. The application is to automatically generate sentiment-aware personalized music slide show. We also show our model can improve the existing affective application such as an image commenting assistant. The user studies and comparisons show that our hierarchical classification greatly improves the quality of these applications.

To the best of our knowledge, this is the first work systematically studying the modeling of sentiment concepts related to objects. Our technical contributions include a complete hierarchical system for object based visual sentiment modeling in which we i) exploit an online commonsense knowledgebase to model the visual sentiment relations from ambiguous and incomplete Internet labels, ii) propose a unique classification model to handle attributive and proportional similarity between visual sentiment concepts. We prove the sentiment modeling technique is a highly useful tool for solving various real-world problems by demonstrating novel applications and improving existing ones.

The rest of the paper is organized as follows. Section 2 summarizes the related work. Section 3 includes an overview of the problem and our solution. In Section 4 and Section 5, we present the proposed object-based visual sentiment models in detail. Section 6 evaluates our results by various comparisons and further explains and justifies our hierarchical classification framework. Section 7 shows applications that greatly benefit from our new visual sentiment concept detection.

2. RELATED WORK

2.1 Modeling Sentiment

Most work on sentiment analysis so far has been based on textual information [32, 9, 29]. Sentiment models have been demonstrated to be useful in various applications including human behavior prediction [9], business [24], and political science [30].

Compared to text-based sentiment analysis, modeling sentiment based on images is much less studied. Perhaps the most relevant work is [3], which proposed to *design* a large-scale visual sentiment ontology based on Adjective-Noun Pairs (the sentiment modeling is then based on one-vs-all SVMs). Our work is clearly distinct from [3], as we focus on the fundamental understanding of visual sentiment concepts, rather than ontology construction and basic detector training. Such understanding is important for identifying successful components and open issues in designing features and detection models. This work is also necessary as the performance of the modeling has been shown to be critical for various applications of visual sentiment analysis [3, 4].

2.2 Modeling Visual Concepts

Concept modeling has been widely studied in multimedia [23, 28], and computer vision (often referred as "attributes") [12]. The concepts being modeled are mostly objects [28], scenes [25], or activities [13]. There is work trying to solve the "fine grained recognition" task, where the categories are usually organized in a hierarchical structure. [7, 8, 6]. There is also work trying to model "non-conventional" concepts or properties of the images, such as image aesthetic and quality [18, 22], memorability [16], interestingness [16], and affection/emotions [21, 31, 17, 21, 31, 33]. Our work

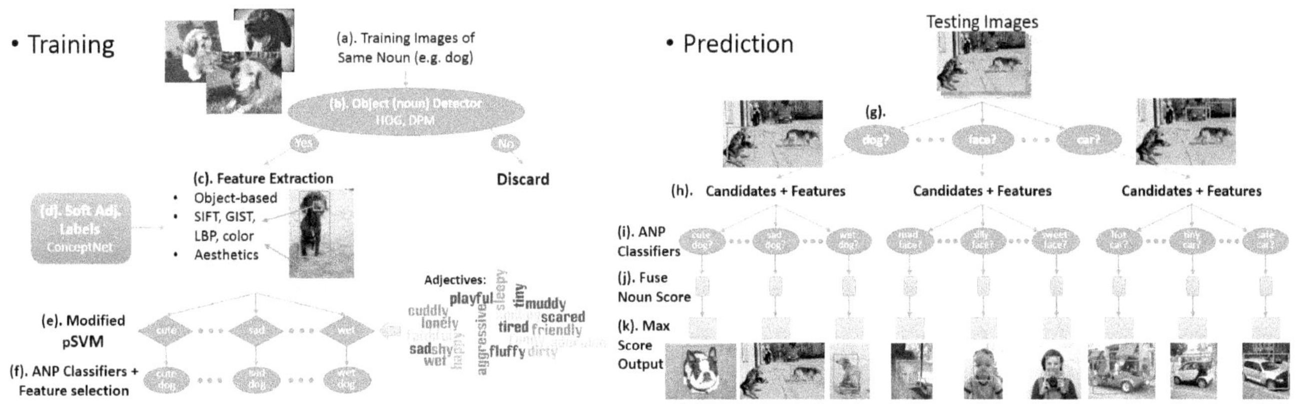

Figure 2: The pipeline of our hierarchical system (details in Section 3).

is different from the above as our objective is to model mid-level sentiment concepts, e.g., "beautiful flower", and "happy dog", which have been shown promising in supporting several exciting applications [3, 4], but have not been analyzed with sufficient rigors and robustness.

We propose to use a hierarchical approach to model object-based sentiment concepts by firstly localizing the objects, and then modeling the object-specific adjectives. An alternative approach is to train a detection model for each object-based sentiment concept separately. One piece of related work is [26], where a DPM model is trained for each "visual phrase" such as "person riding a horse", and "dog laying on sofa". Different from the a visual phrase, which is a combination of two objects, an object-based sentiment concept is an adjective noun pair. As mentioned in the introduction, the hierarchical approach is necessary due to the ambiguity of the ANP labels and efficiency considerations.

3. OVERVIEW

Our goal is to detect visual sentiment concepts from images. Following [3], visual sentiment concepts are defined as Adjective Noun Pairs (ANPs), such as "beautiful girl" and "happy dog". In [3], more than 3,000 ANPs were discovered by a data-driven method and form the Visual Sentiment Ontology (VSO). Image based classifiers were trained for these ANPs with standard SVM. 1,200 ANPs among VSO were considered detectable based on the classifier performance and their classifiers are known as SentiBank. The 1,200 dimensional detector response of SentiBank has been proven effective as mid-level features in tasks such as predicting the sentiments of photo tweets.

However we find the individual concept detector of SentiBank less reliable and interpretable, especially for object-based concepts such as "adorable dress" and "abandoned car". The ANPs containing the same noun are often confused with each other. This drawback limits the application and reliability of SentiBank as mentioned in [4]. This is due to the fact that the difference of the sentiment concepts of these objects are usually reflected in the subtle difference *within* the image region of the object in addition to the context in the surrounding background. Because the classifiers trained in SentiBank use features extracted from the whole image without considering object localization, the inability to separate foreground and background features as expected limits the detection accuracy and interpretability of ANP concept classifiers. To address this problem, we propose a hierarchical classification system that detects and localizes the object first, and then classify the sentiment concepts.

3.1 Data Collection

Our data is from the VSO image dataset mentioned in [3]. For each ANP, it contains URLs of about 500 Flickr images, which are tagged with the ANP by the image uploader. Note that as the tags may not be fully reliable, such labels are considered as pseudo labels, rather than the ground truth. Figure 3 shows example images of several ANPs. Without losing generality, we focus on the aforementioned "detectable" ANPs and our experiment in this paper is limited to the six most popular nouns, namely "car", "dog", "dress", "face", "flower" and "food". These nouns are not only frequently tagged in the social multimedia, but also associated with diverse adjectives to form a large set of ANPs. In addition, if we can successfully model such ANPs, we can easily extend the proposed approach to cover more nouns. The total number of ANPs associated with the 6 nouns is 135, as shown in Table 1. We download the images of these ANPs as our training and test data. The data partition will be discussed in Section 6.1.

3.2 Pipeline

Figure 2 shows the pipeline of our hierarchical classification. The left part of the figure shows the training pipeline. Given the training images of the same noun Figure 2(a), we first train an object (noun) detector and apply it to those images (b). Only the images with relatively high detection response will be kept on into the next level of the hierarchy. Each training image passed contains at least one object bounding box. Next, for each bounding box a group of comprehensive features including low-level visual features and aesthetic features are extracted (c) for the sentiment concept classification. The details of the features will be described in Section 5. To train each classifier, the ANP pseudo labels of each object passed from the image is treated as soft labels to take into account the semantic overlap of multiple ANPs. We use semantic similarities between concepts to compute the weights (d). Fusion of weighted

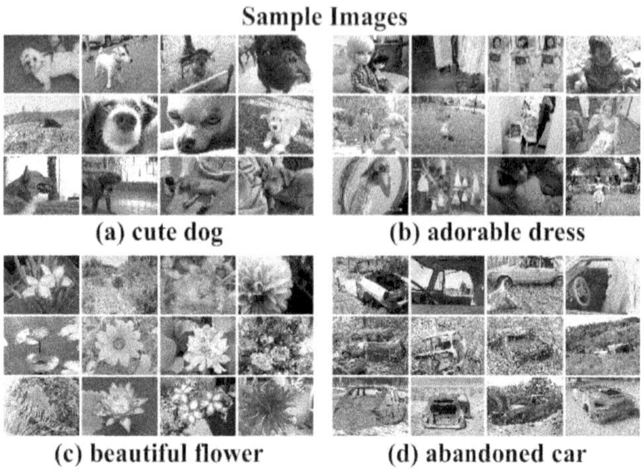

Figure 3: Example images with ANP pseudo label.

Table 1: ANPs used in our experiment (categorized by nouns).

Adjective	Noun
abandoned, amazing, awesome, bad, broken, classic, clean, crazy, damaged, derelict, dirty, expensive, famous, fancy, fantastic, filthy, hot, lonely, powerful, safe, shiny, super, tiny, ugly	car
adorable, aggressive, cuddly, cute, dirty, faithful, fluffy, friendly, funny, happy, lonely, muddy, playful, sad, scared, shy, silly, sleepy, smiling, tiny, tired, wet	dog
adorable, colorful, cute, elegant, fancy, favorite, gorgeous, pretty, sexy, stunning, traditional	dress
adorable, angry, attractive, bright, chubby, clean, crazy, crying, cute, dirty, dumb, excited, funny, grumpy, handsome, hilarious, innocent, mad, pensive, pretty, scared, scary, sick, silly, sleepy, stupid, sweet, tired, tough, ugly, weird, worried	face
amazing, attractive, awesome, beautiful, cheerful, colorful, delightful, dry, dying, fantastic, fascinating, favorite, fragile, fresh, gentle, golden, little, magical, magnificent, pretty, prickly, smelly, strange, stunning, sunny, tiny, wild	flower
amazing, awesome, colorful, delicious, dry, excellent, fancy, favorite, greasy, great, gross, healthy, hot, natural, super, tasty, traditional, weird, yummy	food

SVM and proportional SVM [35] (e) is specifically used to learn from the overlapped class labels. The fusion employs a rank minimization technique, which also provides us the ability to select the most discriminative features (f).

The predicting pipeline is illustrated on the right part of Figure 2. In the first level of the hierarchy, we apply all the noun detectors to the test image (g). All the detected bounding box candidates will be considered in the second level. For each candidate, we extract the aforementioned comprehensive features (h) and apply the ANP classifiers corresponding to (e.g., "shy dog" after "dog" detector) detected nouns (i). The ANP predicted probability score is fused with the corresponding noun detection score so that the confidence of noun detection is taken into consideration (j). The maximum score among all the candidates is then chosen as the ANP score (k).

4. NOUN DETECTION

Our object dependent visual sentiment classifiers are designed as hierarchical classifiers. The goal of the first level of the hierarchy is to detect the object. There are several reasons for such a design. First, the objects or nouns are much easier to detect than the visual sentiment attributes described in the adjectives. Second, the features suitable for object detection and sentiment attribute detection are usually different. For example, Histogram of Oriented Gradients (HOG) is known to be efficient for object detection, but sentiment attributes may be more sensitive to aesthetic based features [21]. Third, object detectors can localize an object and enable the extraction of object-based features for training the sentiment attributes. Removal of the interference from the background improves the possibility of success for the difficult task of sentiment attribute classification.

For objects that have clear parts (car, dog, and dress), we adopt the 5th release [14] of Deformable Part Model (DPM) [11], one of state-of-the-art object detection methods. The method models the object as several movable parts attached to a root and uses latent SVM to train the model. Specifically, for car and dog, we use the pre-trained models in the release. For dress, we train our own models using manually labeled bounding boxes on 500 randomly selected images from all the training images associated with the noun "dress". For the objects which has no clear parts (flower and food), we train SVM models for them (with the same features used for DPM). For "face", instead of using a general object detector, we apply a rotation invariant multiview face detection method [15] for face images.

In the prediction step, we apply the noun detector on test images with a loose threshold, so that more object candidates can be detected to improve the recall. The detection scores are also fused with the subsequent ANP classifier step.

5. MODELING VISUAL ADJECTIVES

The second step in the hierarchy is the ANP classification. The goal is to train classifiers for different ANPs that contain the same noun, e.g., "happy dog" vs. "sad dog" vs. "lonely dog". In this subsection, when we mention ANPs, we are referring to ANPs of the same noun by default.

Training set and pseudo labels.

For each noun, every instance in the training set corresponds to a detected object bounding box passed from the noun detection step. This implies multiple instances may come from same training image and some training images are discarded. Each instance inherits the pseudo ANP labels from its original training image.

Feature extraction.

Intuitively, the best set of features is different for different adjectives. Instead of manually designing features for each adjective, we target extracting a comprehensive set of features for all images, and we then rely on automatic feature selection to choose the most discriminative features. The features we used can be classified as low-level features and aesthetic features.

The *low-level features* include BoW features of SIFT, Gist, LBP and Color. The dictionary size of BoW is 500. These features are extracted in an "object-based" manner based on three different settings: whole image, inside the object bounding box, and background only. For the features of the whole image, we further apply two-level Spatial Pyramid Matching. Thus each BoW feature has 3,500 dimensions and the overall low-level feature has 14,000 dimensions. We further extract *aesthetic features* including dark channel, luminosity feature, sharpness, symmetry, low depth of field, white balance, colorfulness, color harmony, eye sensitivity as well as the relative position and size of the bounding box. Details of such features can be found in [2]. These features are also computed for both the whole image and inside the bounding box if applicable. Overall the aesthetic features have 301 dimensions. By extracting object-based features we are able to utilize the object localization in the ANP classification.

Leveraging ConceptNet.

With the extracted features and pseudo labels, one naive way of modeling the ANPs is to train a one-vs-all classifier for each ANP. However, this is not a good approach as different adjectives with related meanings can be applied to the same images. For example, an image of "cute dog" can also be an image of "lovely dog". Therefore, the adjective modeling process is a multi-label learning problem rather than a multi-class learning problem. Unfortunately, although there might be multiple labels for each image, due to the image collection process, one image is usually associated with a single adjective label. The incomplete labels create difficulties in training the ANP classifiers.

Labeling training images manually is infeasible due to the large number of categories and instances. While there exist abundant accurately labeled image datasets for various objects and even fine grained categories, there are no annotated datasets for ANPs.

We propose to learn ANP from incomplete labels by incorporating an additional similarity measure between ANPs. We observed two types of similarity between adjectives related to visual sentiment, which we call "attributive similarity" and "proportional similarity". The former refers to cases in which every instance of one ANP shares certain visual similarity with another. For example, every "cute dog" is usually considered as "adorable dog" too. The later refers to cases in which a certain proportion of the instances of one ANP can be labeled as another. For example, some "dirty dogs" are also "wet dogs", but not all. Modeling these similarities are very challenging. Our hypothesis is that both types are correlated with the *semantic similarity* between adjectives in the domain of language. Thus we build a $n \times n$ matrix of semantic similarities S for n ANPs. Each entry $S_{i,j}$ indicates the semantic similarity between the adjectives of the ith and the jth ANPs. Note we also normalize each row of S so that $S_{i,i} = 1$ and the entry of the least similar ANP in each row equals to -1.

We compute the semantic similarities between adjectives by ConceptNet [20]. The ConceptNet is a hypergraph that links a large amount of concepts (words) by the knowledge discovered from Wikipedia and WordNet, or provided by community contributors. The concept similarity can be computed by searching for the shortest path in this graph. We apply the association function of the Web API of ConceptNet 5 [1] to get the semantic similarity of two adjectives. If an adjective does not exist as a concept in ConceptNet, we manually select one of its synonyms or derivatives instead. The similarity value generated by ConceptNet is between -1 and 1, where 1 corresponds to the similarity to itself. We will explain how we approximate the attributive and proportional similarity by semantic similarity in the next paragraph.

Training the Classifiers.

By considering the two types of similarity between visual sentiment attributes, we design our classification methods as follows.

For "attributive similarity" it is natural to use weighted SVM (wSVM), where each instance in the training data has a weight between 0 and 1 to regulate its contribution to the classifier. Given training samples of multiple ANPs of the same noun, when training a classifier for an ANP_i, an image of the ANP_j will be treated as a training sample with a label equaling the sign of $S_{i,j}$ and a sample weight equaling the absolute value of $S_{i,j}$. We subsample from the training instances so that the ratio of positive to negative is 1:1. We employ weighted linear SVM to train the classifiers for each ANP.

To deal with "proportional similarity", our solution is pSVM ($\propto$SVM) [35]. The input of pSVM is a "bag" of the training instances. Each bag is assigned a proportion value indicating the proportion of positive instances in the bag. In our case each bag consists of the instances with the same ANP pseudo labels, and while training the classifier for the ith ANP the proportion value of the jth bag is set as follows:

$$p_{i,j} = \begin{cases} 0 & \text{if } S_{i,j} \leq 0 \\ S_{i,j} & \text{if } S_{i,j} > 0 \end{cases}$$

We use the alter-$\propto$SVM algorithm [35]. It iteratively trains the linear SVM model and updates the inferred labels until convergence.

Model fusion and feature selection.

To combine multiple features and select the most discriminative features for each ANP model, we employ the low-rank fusion proposed by Ye et al. in [34], which has been shown to work much better than naive late fusion. Multiple models trained from wSVM and pSVM with different low-level features and aesthetic features, different regions of the image (whole, object, background) are used for prediction and their confidence scores are fused by rank minimization as mentioned above. The process also provides us individual feature weights that can be used to find the most discriminative features for each ANP classifier.

Following the approach used in detecting noun phrase [26], we further combine the noun detection score with the ANP detection score of each candidate bounding box. If a test image has multiple candidates for an ANP, the maximal score is chosen as the final ANP score.

6. EXPERIMENTS AND DISCUSSIONS

6.1 Test Set and Ground Truth

To evaluate the performance of hierarchical classification, we prepare two test sets from the dataset. Test set A

[1]http://conceptnet5.media.mit.edu/

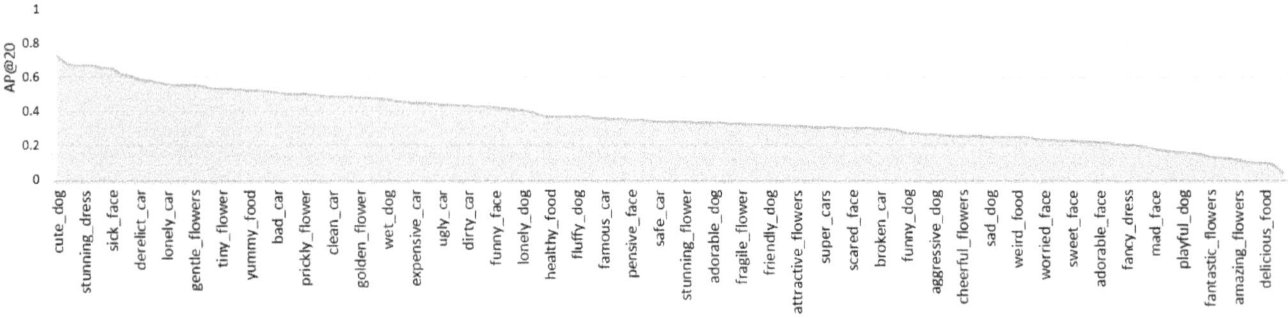

Figure 4: The curves show AP@20 (avg. over 5 runs) for test set A. Only a subset of ANP names are shown due to space limit.

evaluates the performance of distinguishing multiple related ANPs of the same noun. For each ANP, we choose 240 images from the dataset; 40 of them are randomly sampled from pseudo-labeled images of each ANP class. The other 200 are randomly sampled from the pseudo-labeled images of other ANPs containing the same noun. Since we cannot rely on the pseudo labels from testing, each image is manually labeled by three individuals (graduate students without detailed knowledge of our work). Each individual answers yes or no to the question "Does the image contain the ANP". The ANP ground truth label of the image is decided by the majority vote of the individual labels. All 240 images are excluded from the training set of the ANP; 20 positives and 40 negatives are randomly sampled from the 240 images to form the test set A of the ANP.

Test set B evaluates the overall visual sentiment classification performance on the real world data. For each ANP (whose noun is denoted by N), 20 positives are sampled in the same way as test set A. To get the negatives, we first randomly select one image from each of the 1,200 SentiBank ANPs by using the pseudo labels from the web except those containing the same noun N. Then we sample additional negatives from the manually labeled ground truth set of the ANPs sharing the same noun. The total number of negative examples in the test set B for each ANP is 1,200.

Our test sets and the trained ANP detectors will be made available to the community at http://visual-sentiment-ontology.appspot.com/.

6.2 Performance and Comparisons

We conduct our experiments on a eight-core CPU workstation. In the training step, training each noun detector takes about six hours including feature extraction, which is the most time consuming step. Fortunately we only need to train once for each noun. In the second level of the hierarchy, feature extraction takes two seconds for each image. Training each ANP classifier in the second level of the hierarchy only takes ten seconds on average using LibLinear library [10]. In the prediction step, it takes about three seconds to compute all 135 ANP scores for each image including feature extraction.

In our experiments all the parameters are chosen by 5-fold cross validation on the training set with pseudo labels. For both test sets, we evaluate the classification performance in terms of AP@20 averaged over five runs, and in each run we randomly sample the test images as mentioned above. The result for test set A is shown in Figure 4. It shows

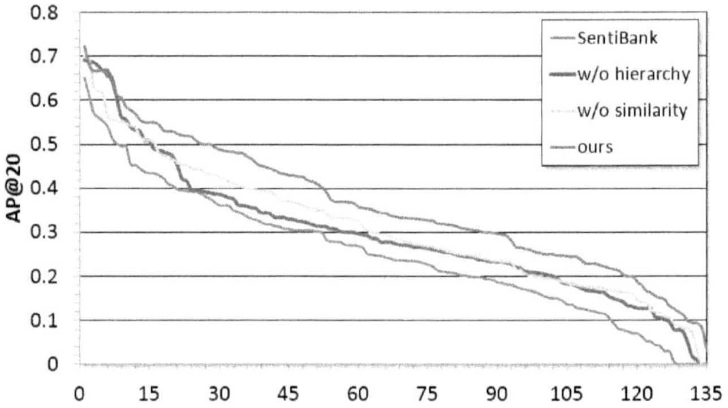

Figure 5: Comparison of ANP detectors with different baselines. ANPs are sorted on the horizontal axis based on the detection performance. Performance is computed by averaging over 5 runs on test set A.

two thirds of ANPs have a AP@20 score above 0.3. The hierarchical classification results are also compared with following baseline and variations:

- SentiBank. A straightforward linear SVM classification in a one-against-all setting using pseudo labels and features extracted from the whole images.
- Without hierarchy. Noun detection is skipped. Features are extracted only from the whole image. Weighted SVM and pSVM are used to handle similarity over multiple related ANPs
- Without similarity among concepts. One-vs-all classification is directly trained based on pseudo labels in the second level of the hierarchy.

The comparison results on test set A are shown in Figure 5. The mean AP on test set A and B for each noun and all nouns along with comparison are also shown in Figure 6.

Figure 7 further shows the top results detected by ANP classifiers using our method. The corresponding object bounding box is shown as blue rectangle. Misclassified images are surrounded by red frames.

For both test set A and test set B, our proposed approach improves over the SentiBank classifiers reported in [3] by a very large margin. The improvement can be as high as

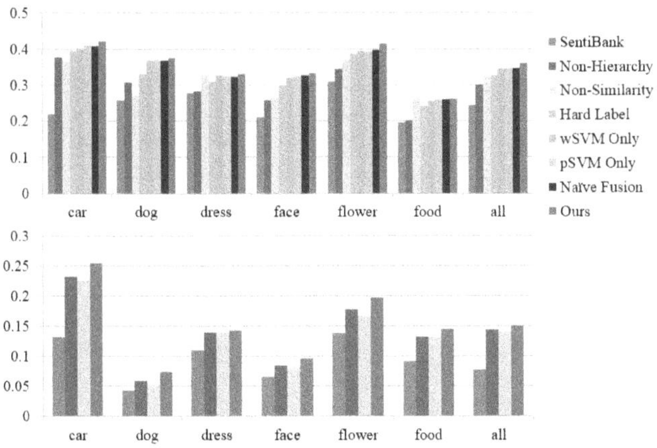

Figure 6: The mean AP on test set A (top) and B (bottom) for each noun and all nouns.

Figure 7: Top detection results of ANP classifiers trained by our hierarchical model. Detected concept regions are shown as blue bounding boxes. Photo on the first row, from left to right, ©Andrey Belenko, ©Cavin (CavinB), ©Clayton Parker (claytron), ©vxla, ©artfulblogger of Flickr. Photo on the second row, from left to right, ©Laurie Avocado (lavocado@sbcglobal.net), ©BLDUMMY, ©SurFeRGiRL30, ©Andrew Hitchcock (adpowers), ©Enric Martinez of Flickr. More top detection results can be found on supplemental webpage [1].

50% as shown in Fig 6: the AP for all nouns for test set A increases from 0.24 to 0.36. The results also provide justification for both the hierarchical framework in Section 3 and the similarity modeling technique in Section 5 proposed in this paper.

6.3 Evaluation of Components

We further justify each component of our system. These experiments are conducted on test set A and measured by the mean AP@20 of all nouns averaged over 5 runs. We first evaluate the multi-concept similarity model. In the second level of the hierarchy, if we only use semantic similarity to generate hard labels for each instance and use standard SVM for classification, the AP@20 will be reduced from 0.36 to 0.33. The result for each noun and all nouns are shown as the "Hard Label" in Figure 6. It indicates that leveraging ConceptNet similarity as soft labels is more effective. Next we evaluate the classification model. If we only use weighted SVM or pSVM, the mean AP will both decline to around 0.35. The two groups of results are shown as "wSVM Only" and "pSVM Only" in Figure 6 respectively, and thus confirm the benefit of fusing the two models. At last, we test the classification model with naive late fusion instead of the low-rank fusion, the mean AP is also reduced to 0.35. The result is shown as "Naive Fusion" in Figure 6. It verifies our assumption that it is useful to fuse models of different visual features. Although the improvement due to low-rank fusion is not significant, the more important benefit of this fusion method is generating a sparse error matrix for each feature so that we can achieve feature selection, as well as classifier interpretation, which will be discussed in Section 6.4.

6.4 Discussion

Further justification of the hierarchical framework.

Previous research suggests that phrase detection or a combination of phrase and object detection performs better than general object detection [26]. For example, "jumping dog" can be better detected using a combination of "jumping dog" detector and "dog" detector. Therefore, one may argue against our choice of general object detector and suggest using specific object detector for each ANP. Several observations lead to our decision. First, most ANPs are different from the visual phrases mentioned in [26]. The additional visual cues involving many global and aesthetic related features extracted from localized regions usually do not contribute much to the typical object detection features such as HoG. However, there are exceptions such as "sleepy dog", which has a very different pose from normal dogs. Second, it is very difficult and inefficient to integrate our comprehensive features into the object detection method such as DPM. Third, it is too time consuming and impracticable to label object bounding boxes for each ANP. Therefore, our hierarchical classification offers the best trade-off between accuracy and efficiency.

Extension to scenes or settings.

According to Figure 6, even without object localization our method still outperforms the baseline, thanks to the soft labels that exploit the concept similarity and the deliberately designed model. This means that we can apply our method to "global nouns" such as "sunset" and "sky". These concepts do not need localization.

The factors for classification accuracy.

Some of our ANP classifiers cannot achieve good classification accuracy. An important reason is that some ANP categories may still be ambiguous. Some adjectives, such as "favourite", are subjective because the interpretations may vary significantly among individuals. This causes greater diversity in the image labels and also the visual features. Other reasons include the lack of visual cues of the adjective such as "smelly", low performance of noun detection such as "food" and the lack of more efficient features such as the lack of facial marker features for "face".

Discriminative features.

Other than improving the classification accuracy, it is also interesting to understand how the classification works by studying the contributions of different features. Specifically we try to interpret the classifiers by discovering discriminative features.

Table 2: The examples of the discriminative features of ANP.

ANP	Discriminative features
abandoned car	object SIFT, white balance, background color histogram, background Gist
crazy car	object LBP, object colorfulness, color harmony, object color histogram
lonely dog	background Gist, composition, depth of field, colorfulness
shy dog	object luminosity, dark channel, object symmetry, object white balance
ugly face	object color harmony, object symmetry, object Gist, color histogram

Low-rank fusion [34] provides us with statistics on the discrimination ability of each feature during ANP classification. For each ANP we rank the features according to the average over the fusion weights of all the test examples. Table 2 shows the top features for some ANPs. The result shows the features extracted from the object are more discriminative than those extracted from the whole image, and the background features are also useful. For example, images of "abandoned car" are usually shot in the wild and with a dim tone, thus the white balance and background features are important. Many crazy cars modeled by our method are with exaggerated color combinations. Images of "lonely dog" contain more uniform background, and are mostly black and white with relatively small object (dog). "Shy dogs" images usually show half face, thus object symmetry is important. The similar reasons can be found for "ugly face".

Limitations and future work.
Our work has several limitations. First, object detection may not be always reliable, especially when applied to ANPs associated with unique postures of the corresponding noun such as "sleepy dog". Training specific object detectors for such ANPs may be a solution. Second, the semantic similarity derived from ConceptNet might be incorrect. For such cases manually provided similarity can be helpful. Third, our feature set can be more comprehensive, for example including the shape based and "Wang histogram" features that are proved efficient for aesthetics and emotion classification [5, 21], or even the recently proposed "OverFeat" feature based on deep learning [27]. And finally, our discriminative features are limited to our feature set, further work can be done to discover new features for better interpretation of sentiment concept model.

7. APPLICATIONS

We demonstrate two applications that benefit from our visual sentiment concept detection. Note since our experiments are limited to six nouns, the following applications also focus on the images associated with these nouns. More nouns can be easily incorporated by training more ANP detectors using our system.

7.1 Mood-Aware Personalized Music Slide Show

Music slide shows are popular for personal entertainment and photo sharing. Modern music playing software is capable of showing visual effects, album covers or photo albums when playing music. Recently, GettyImages presents Moodstream[2], a web-based application that is able to show photos according to the mood of the music. However the photos are from a pre-selected set where the mood labels are already available. Given the ability of our system to detect visual sentiment concepts, we can generate such mood-aware music slide shows directly from users' personal photo albums.

To generate a slide show, we first compute the real-time mood of the music. We adopt Mood Cloud [19] to detect the mood of the music. This method predicts a five dimensional mood vector for any given time stamp of the music in real-time using SVM model trained from manually labeled data. The five dimensions correspond to aggressive, happy, relaxed, sad and party. Next we classify every candidate photo to one of these five moods. We build a 135×5 matrix to map each of the 135 ANPs to the mood vector, where each entry of the matrix is the mean of the semantic similarity and co-occurrence rate between corresponding ANP and name of the mood. The semantic similarity is computed from ConceptNet. The co-occurrence rate is a normalized value of the returned image count while searching the ANP and mood together on Flickr. The mood vector of the photo can be estimated by the mean mood vector of its top three detected ANPs, and we classify the photo to the mood class with the highest score.

Given a music track, we repeatedly decide the slide show photo of each segment from the beginning of the track. Each time we take three seconds of music to compute a dominant mood. A photo of same mood is randomly selected for this segment. If the mood is sad or relaxed, the segment is extended to three seconds. The next segment starts right after the previous one. This process repeats until the end of the track. We also apply several rules for photo transition. The length of each transition is 0.5 seconds. The type includes fade, zoom in and out, and flying in from eight surrounding directions. If the detected mood is "aggressive" and "party", the transition type is restricted to zoom in and flying in, randomly selected otherwise. Since our system also provides ANP bounding boxes, we generate the zooming path according to the center of the top ANP bounding box.

We conduct the experiment on five music tracks and three Creative Common licensed personal photo albums with a total of 100 images downloaded from Flickr. The music tracks are within the length of 15 to 20 seconds. Generating all the slide shows on the machine mentioned in Section 6 takes 4.5 minutes, where 99% of the time is spent on ANP detection of the photos. This indicates that our method can generate a slide show of a real-time music stream with pre-processed photo albums. Figure 8 shows several screenshots from the music slide shows. Please refer to the video on supplemental webpage [1] for better illustration of the sidle show results.

We evaluated our result by a preliminary user study. We generate another five slide shows by randomly selecting photos, and ask evaluators to choose the preferred one. Each pair of the five music slide shows is shown to ten evaluators. These evaluators are graduate students majoring in computer science, engineering, art and physics without detailed knowledge of our project. In 42 of 50 evaluations, the evaluator preferred the mood-aware music slide show.

[2]http://moodstream.gettyimages.com/

sad happy aggressive

Figure 8: Screenshots of the music slide show with detected moods. Please refer to the supplemental webpage [1] for the video. All photos ©Jennifer Morton (jennratonmort) of Flickr.

7.2 Image Commenting Assistant

A novel application of visual sentiment concept detection presented in [4] is the automatic image commenting assistant. In their work, the authors first compute the ANP response of the image by SentiBank, then select proper elements from a comment database as the comment on the image. The selection is based on the correlation between the top three detected visual sentiment concepts and affective concepts extracted from large-scale user comments. While showing promising results, this method suffers from low detection accuracy of the object-based ANPs. We follow this pipeline and replace the sentiment concept predictors with our hierarchical predictors to generate comments. The quality of the comments generated by the two methods is compared. For fair comparison, we only consider the response of the 135 object based ANPs for both SentiBank and our method. We randomly select 20 images from test set A to test the commenting assistants.

Figure 2 of supplemental webpage [1] shows the comments of five images generated by the two commenting assistants. The top three detected concepts are listed for both methods. The concepts detected by our method are constantly better than [4]. The comparison of top three detected concepts clearly shows two advantages of our method. Our approach can more reliably detect the objects (nouns), especially when they are relatively small in the image, as shown in the first example. Second, our method provides better classifiers for the sentiment attributes (adjective) since ambiguity is considered. We further evaluate the comment quality with a user study. The two comments generated from each of the 20 images are shown to five evaluators. These evaluators are graduate students majoring in engineering and art without detailed knowledge of our project. For each comparison, they are asked "which comment is from the real user". In 78 of the 100 evaluations, the evaluator prefers the comment generated by our approach.

8. CONCLUSIONS

This paper presents a novel hierarchical system to model object-based visual sentiment concepts. The system is designed to handle sentiment concept classification in an object specific manner and tackle the challenge of concept localization and resolving sentiment attribute ambiguity. By leveraging an online commonsense knowledgebase and proposing novel classification to model concept similarity, our system has greatly improved the classification performance over previous work (by up to 50%). The proposed framework also allows us to interpret the classifiers by discovering discriminative features. We demonstrate the power of the proposed system with a few novel applications such as sentiment-aware music slide show of personal albums. Although our experiments currently focus on a visual sentiment dataset, the proposed framework of discovering visual concepts as mid-level representation may be extended to handle other important yet challenging topics such as in aesthetics, style, credibility and intent.

9. ACKNOWLEDGEMENT

The authors would like to thank the anonymous reviewers and Dr. Martha Larson for their invaluable input. Research was sponsored in part by the U.S. Defense Advanced Research Projects Agency (DARPA) under the Social Media in Strategic Communication (SMISC) program, Agreement Number W911NF-12-C-0028. The views and conclusions contained in this document are those of the author(s) and should not be interpreted as representing the official policies, either expressed or implied, of the U.S. Defense Advanced Research Projects Agency or the U.S. Government. The U.S. Government is authorized to reproduce and distribute reprints for Government purposes notwithstanding any copyright notation hereon.

10. REFERENCES

[1] Supplemental Webpage. http://www.ee.columbia.edu/dvmm/vso/supplemental.html.

[2] Subhabrata Bhattacharya, Behnaz Nojavanasghari, Tao Chen, Dong Liu, Shih-Fu Chang, and Mubarak Shah. Towards a comprehensive computational model for aesthetic assessment of videos. In *Proceedings of the 21st ACM International Conference on Multimedia*. ACM, 2013.

[3] Damian Borth, Rongrong Ji, Tao Chen, Thomas Breuel, and Shih-Fu Chang. Large-scale visual sentiment ontology and detectors using adjective noun pairs. In *Proceedings of the 21st ACM International Conference on Multimedia*. ACM, 2013.

[4] Yan-Ying Chen, Tao Chen, Winston H. Hsu, Hong-Yuan Mark Liao, and Shih-Fu Chang. Predicting viewer affective comments based on image content in social media. In *Proceedings of the International Conference on Multimedia Retrieval*. ACM, 2014.

[5] Ritendra Datta, Dhiraj Joshi, Jia Li, and James Z Wang. Studying aesthetics in photographic images using a computational approach. In *European Conference on Computer Vision*. Springer, 2006.

[6] J. Deng, W. Dong, R. Socher, L.J. Li, K. Li, and L. Fei-Fei. ImageNet: A Large-Scale Hierarchical Image Database. In *Computer Vision and Pattern Recognition*, 2009.

[7] Jia Deng, Jonathan Krause, and Li Fei-Fei. Fine-grained crowdsourcing for fine-grained recognition. In *Computer Vision and Pattern Recognition (CVPR), 2013 IEEE Conference on*, pages 580–587. IEEE, 2013.

[8] Kun Duan, Devi Parikh, David Crandall, and Kristen Grauman. Discovering localized attributes for fine-grained recognition. In *Computer Vision and Pattern Recognition*. IEEE, 2012.

[9] Andrea Esuli and Fabrizio Sebastiani. SentiWordNet: A publicly available lexical resource for opinion

mining. In *Proceedings of the Conference on Language Resources and Evaluation*, volume 6, 2006.

[10] Rong-En Fan, Kai-Wei Chang, Cho-Jui Hsieh, Xiang-Rui Wang, and Chih-Jen Lin. Liblinear: A library for large linear classification. *The Journal of Machine Learning Research*, 9:1871–1874, 2008.

[11] P. F. Felzenszwalb, R. B. Girshick, D. McAllester, and D. Ramanan. Object detection with discriminatively trained part based models. *IEEE Transactions on Pattern Analysis and Machine Intelligence*, 32(9):1627–1645, 2010.

[12] V. Ferrari and A. Zisserman. Learning visual attributes. In *Neural Information Processing Systems*, 2007.

[13] Yanwei Fu, Timothy M Hospedales, Tao Xiang, and Shaogang Gong. Attribute learning for understanding unstructured social activity. In *European Conference on Computer Vision*. Springer, 2012.

[14] R. B. Girshick, P. F. Felzenszwalb, and D. McAllester. Discriminatively trained deformable part models, release 5. http://people.cs.uchicago.edu/~rbg/latent-release5/.

[15] Chang Huang, Haizhou Ai, Yuan Li, and Shihong Lao. High-performance rotation invariant multiview face detection. *Pattern Analysis and Machine Intelligence, IEEE Transactions on*, 29(4):671–686, 2007.

[16] P. Isola, J. Xiao, A. Torralba, and A. Oliva. What makes an image memorable? In *Computer Vision and Pattern Recognition*, 2011.

[17] Jia Jia, Sen Wu, Xiaohui Wang, Peiyun Hu, Lianhong Cai, and Jie Tang. Can we understand van Gogh's mood?: Learning to infer affects from images in social networks. In *Proceedings of the 20th ACM international conference on Multimedia*, pages 857–860. ACM, 2012.

[18] Dhiraj Joshi, Ritendra Datta, Elena Fedorovskaya, Quang-Tuan Luong, James Z Wang, Jia Li, and Jiebo Luo. Aesthetics and emotions in images. *Signal Processing Magazine, IEEE*, 28(5):94–115, 2011.

[19] Cyril Laurier and Perfecto Herrera. Mood Cloud: A real-time music mood visualization tool. In *Proceedings of the 2008 Computers in Music Modeling and Retrieval Conference*, 2008.

[20] Hugo Liu and Push Singh. ConceptNet - a practical commonsense reasoning tool-kit. *BT technology journal*, 22(4):211–226, 2004.

[21] J. Machajdik and A. Hanbury. Affective image classification using features inspired by psychology and art theory. In *Proceedings of ACM Multimedia*, pages 83–92, 2010.

[22] L. Marchesotti, F. Perronnin, D. Larlus, and G. Csurka. Assessing the aesthetic quality of photographs using generic image descriptors. In *Proceedings of the International Conference on Computer Vision*, 2011.

[23] M. Naphade, J. Smith, J. Tesic, S.-F. Chang, W. Hsu, L. Kennedy, A. Hauptmann, and Curtis J. Large-scale concept ontology for multimedia. In *IEEE Multimedia*, 2006.

[24] Bo Pang and Lillian Lee. Opinion mining and sentiment analysis. *Information Retrieval*, 2(1-2):1–135, 2008.

[25] Genevieve Patterson and James Hays. Sun attribute database: Discovering, annotating, and recognizing scene attributes. In *Computer Vision and Pattern Recognition*. IEEE, 2012.

[26] Mohammad Amin Sadeghi and Ali Farhadi. Recognition using visual phrases. In *Computer Vision and Pattern Recognition*. IEEE, 2011.

[27] Pierre Sermanet, David Eigen, Xiang Zhang, Michael Mathieu, Rob Fergus, and Yann LeCun. Overfeat: Integrated recognition, localization and detection using convolutional networks. *arXiv:1312.6229*, 2013.

[28] J.R. Smith, M. Naphade, and A. Natsev. Multimedia semantic indexing using model vectors. In *International Conference on Multimedia and Expo*, 2003.

[29] Mike Thelwall, Kevan Buckley, Georgios Paltoglou, Di Cai, and Arvid Kappas. Sentiment strength detection in short informal text. *Journal of the American Society for Information Science and Technology*, 61(12):2544–2558, 2010.

[30] Andranik Tumasjan, Timm O Sprenger, Philipp G Sandner, and Isabell M Welpe. Predicting elections with Twitter: What 140 characters reveal about political sentiment. In *Proceedings of the 4th International AAAI Conference on Weblogs and Social Media*, 2010.

[31] Weining Wang and Qianhua He. A survey on emotional semantic image retrieval. In *Image Processing, 2008. ICIP 2008. 15th IEEE International Conference on*, pages 117–120. IEEE, 2008.

[32] Theresa Wilson, Janyce Wiebe, and Paul Hoffmann. Recognizing contextual polarity in phrase-level sentiment analysis. In *Proceedings of the Conference on Human Language Technology and Empirical Methods in Natural Language Processing*, 2005.

[33] V. Yanulevskaya, J. van Gemert, K. Roth, A. Herbold, N. Sebe, and J.M. Geusebroek. Emotional valence categorization using holistic image features. In *Proceedings of the IEEE International Conference on Image Processing*, pages 101–104, 2008.

[34] Guangnan Ye, Dong Liu, I-Hong Jhuo, and Shih-Fu Chang. Robust late fusion with rank minimization. In *Computer Vision and Pattern Recognition*. IEEE, 2012.

[35] Felix X. Yu, Dong Liu, Sanjiv Kumar, Tony Jebara, and Shih-Fu Chang. $\propto$SVM for learning with label proportions. In *International Conference on Machine Learning*, 2013.

An Event Driven Fusion Approach for Enjoyment Recognition in Real-time

Florian Lingenfelser
Human Centered Multimedia
University of Augsburg
lingenfelser@hcm-lab.de

Johannes Wagner
Human Centered Multimedia
University of Augsburg
wagner@hcm-lab.de

Elisabeth André
Human Centered Multimedia
University of Augsburg
andre@hcm-lab.de

Gary McKeown
School of Psychology
Queen's University Belfast
g.mckeown@qub.ac.uk

Will Curran
School of Psychology
Queen's University Belfast
w.curran@qub.ac.uk

ABSTRACT

Social signals and interpretation of carried information is of high importance in Human Computer Interaction. Often used for affect recognition, the cues within these signals are displayed in various modalities. Fusion of multi-modal signals is a natural and interesting way to improve automatic classification of emotions transported in social signals. Throughout most present studies, uni-modal affect recognition as well as multi-modal fusion, decisions are forced for fixed annotation segments across all modalities. In this paper, we investigate the less prevalent approach of event driven fusion, which indirectly accumulates asynchronous events in all modalities for final predictions. We present a fusion approach, handling short-timed events in a vector space, which is of special interest for real-time applications. We compare results of segmentation based uni-modal classification and fusion schemes to the event driven fusion approach. The evaluation is carried out via detection of enjoyment-episodes within the audiovisual Belfast Story-Telling Corpus.

Categories and Subject Descriptors

I.5 [**PATTERN RECOGNITION**]: Applications—*Computer vision; Waveform analysis; Signal processing*

Keywords

affect recognition; social signal processing; multi–modal fusion; event–driven fusion

1. INTRODUCTION

Affective states of human beings refer to the experience of feelings or emotions. These conditions are expressed by the experiencing person through various channels and can be naturally understood by other humans. One of the goals of human computer interaction (HCI) is to automate this perception process and give machines the capability to assess affective states of users [18, 24]. Through the appliance of appropriate sensor technologies and recognition techniques, multi-modal cues that point to certain affective states can be measured and recognized. These sources of evidence lead to the automatic classification of human emotions.

Since emotions are generally observable in multiple channels, the obvious approach is to incorporate as much multi-modal information as possible in the classification process [30]. Meaningful features and hints of monitored signals are then to be combined through fusion strategies in order to generate a final prediction. For example, if confronted with a classical audio-visual emotion recognition problem, one would probably first have a look at single spoken sentences, calculate prosodic features from the audio signal and classify the whole sentence with a statistical feature set. In order to enrich descriptive information about the observed signal segment and assumably enhance recognition performance, additional descriptors can be extracted from the video images that are recorded during the spoken sentence in the audio signal. At this point fusion of information from both modalities has to be applied. In the simplest case the two feature sets are merged to be used by a single classifier [26]. More elaborate ways of fusing multiple modalities are in use throughout many affect recognition studies [22, 31, 29, 28, 16, 17]. These fusion strategies and their effects on recognition accuracies will be discussed in the following sections. Some facts can however be anticipated here: Present studies have shown varying degrees of success or even failure of classical fusion approaches [2]. Assuming decent data content in all considered modalities, one would generally expect a steady classification gain from adding additional information.

A possible reason for the unsteady performance of presented fusion schemes could lie in the initiation of consideration of multiple signals and appliance of the above mentioned fusion algorithms. In off-line studies, the triggering of fusion processes is simply given by the annotation boundaries; in a real-time scenario this is typically done by detecting the on and offset of a relevant time-interval in one modality. Afterwards fusion techniques are called for classification throughout all available modalities. Consequently, the seg-

MM'14, November 3–7, 2014, Orlando, FL, USA
Copyright 2014 ACM 978-1-4503-3063-3/14/11$15.00.
http://dx.doi.org/10.1145/2647868.2654924.

mentation of a cue in one modality is forced upon other available channels. What if nothing is happening in the face at this point in time, as emotional reactions are time-shifted between modalities or not present at all? Meaningful information in additional modalities is assumed - but it is not guaranteed. Cutting fixed segments through multi-layered signals does seem to be undesirable. One could think of adding deltas to additionally concerned modalities, but this approach would most likely lead to a hard-wired construct, that is hard to define and not generalizable. So how do we solve the problem of non-aligned cues in multiple signals?

A first step is to reject the assumption that all relevant cues happen at the same time in all modalities. Practical observations demonstrate the need to detect events for each modality separately. But if all signal–events are treated individually, we have to find ways to relate them for proper fusion of identified information. Therefore, we introduce an event driven fusion model that incorporates the temporal relation between the events. It is specially suited for real-time applications. An early prototype has been already successfully applied at the eNTERFACE 13 workshop in Lisbon[13]. For evaluation we will analyse a suitable corpus for recognition of enjoyable emotions.We compare single modality accuracy to segmentation based fusion approaches and event driven fusion - concerning framewise classification of enjoyment. We define enjoyment as an episode of positive emotion, indicated by visual and auditory cues of enjoyment, such as smiles and voiced laughters. This enables us to compare overarching enjoyment–annotations to accumulated indication-events. Based on this evaluation we can finally discuss advantages and disadvantages of event driven fusion for affect recognition.

2. MULTI-MODAL FUSION

In a standard classification task, recognizers are trained with samples of pre-segmented data. This segmentation is achieved by annotation of the recorded data. Experts review the data, marking time-segments of interest and providing them with a pre-defined label that describes the nature of the respective time period. Resulting data samples are then subject to feature extraction techniques. When dealing with one modality, this procedure is carried out on one specific kind of signal and one classification model can be trained with the resulting samples. In multi-modal classification, every single signal needs an adapted feature extraction step, resulting in feature sets for every observed signal. Reasonable combination of available information is the challenge of multi-modal fusion approaches.

2.1 Segmentation–Based Fusion Approach

When confronted with fusion of multiple signals, a vast amount of eligible strategies come into consideration [20]. Possible methods can be differentiated by the levels at which they are executed. Authors in [30] cite 18 studies dealing with audio-visual fusion. Here, they distinguish between feature-, decision- and model-level fusion.

A very straightforward way to fuse all observed modalities is to merge all calculated features into a single and high dimensional feature set for one single classification model (feature level fusion). The accumulated features contain a greater amount of information than a single modality. Prediction based fusion, as proposed in [19], tries to discriminate classes by modelling spatial and temporal relationships between multi-modal features. Decision level fusion sums up combination rules for the probabilistic outputs of several classification models. Instead of using all available features for a single classifier, the available feature set is divided into subgroups (e. g. one classifier per modality). Standard decision techniques include class-label combination (e. g. voting, look-up tables and algebraic combination rules such as sum rule or product rule). Feature and decision level fusion include the most standard approaches used in most studies concerning multi-modal fusion experiments. In model level fusion (e. g. stacked generalisation [23] the outputs of several classifiers are not fused by predefined combination rules. Instead their results are used as input for one or more meta classification models that generate the final decision.

A fair amount of studies incorporate these segmentation based fusion techniques for combination of observed signals and final classification. Meta studies like [2] compare gathered results and give an overview: Some report remarkable accuracy gains over uni-modal classification, others do not notice statistically relevant benefits. Even substantial drops in classification quality are sometimes registered. In numbers, the effect of multi-modal fusion in comparison to uni-modal classification range from a +27.4% gain in recognition performance to a -9.0% drop in overall accuracy for a total of 30 compared studies. The study also points out, that classification improvements are far more likely to be achieved on acted data than on natural or semi-natural recordings. Such meta comparisons do not go into detail about the applied fusion schemes. Studies like [3, 11, 10, 6] examine rather basic fusion strategies and sometimes advise on which scheme dominates others. Results are not consistent throughout mentioned experiments. Furthermore, the success of fusion is obviously not primarily dependent on the chosen algorithm (though of course there are differences in performance between the single fusion strategies).

2.2 Asynchronous Fusion Approach

In segmentation based fusion approaches, analysis of all modalities is initiated and margined by a comprehensive annotation for the given classification problem [12]. For example, when doing audiovisual emotion recognition it is a common strategy to trigger analysis of further modalities by voice activity detection in the vocal modality. Whenever there is activity in the voice, classification of facial expressions is done during this time segment. Fusion algorithms are then applied to the cues of the extracted time-slice. This approach of triggering multi-modal fusion from a single annotation or modality has at least one severe drawback: Additional cues in further modalities can be expected but are not guaranteed to coexist at the time frames or in the worst case, are not present at all. Imagine the audio-visual affect recognition scenario: The vocal component of an emotional expression may be signalled before the facial component. This way, the observed segment of modalities does indeed fit to relevant data in the audio signal, but boundaries of facial activity are shifted. Such component asynchronicity fully contributes to the multi-modal fusion and negatively influences final classification.

An elegant way of fusing modalities without forcing decisions from all channels in every time slot is offered by dynamic classification. Since dynamic classifiers work on continuous streams of short-term features, it is not necessary to force a fusion decision "from above". Instead, they (principally) have the ability to model temporal relations between the streams and learn when and how multimodal information should be combined. Dupont *et. al* [4] were among the first to tackle the asynchronous nature of audio and video streams by modelling temporal topologies with multi-stream HMMs for continuous speech recognition. Song *et. al* [22] proposed a tripled Hidden Markov Model (THMM), which is able to integrate three or more streams of data and allows the state asynchrony of the sequences while preserving their natural correlation over time. Zeng *et. al* [31] applied Multi-stream Fused Hidden Markov Model (MFHMM), where state transitions of different component HMMs do not necessarily occur at the same time across different streams so that the synchrony constraint among different streams is also relaxed. Coupled Hidden Markov Models (CHMM), where the probability of the next state of a sequence depends on the current state of all HMMs and therefore enables an improved modelling of intrinsic temporal correlations between multiple modalities, have also been proposed [15].

To overcome the computational complexity of asynchronous Hidden Markov model (AHMM), Wöllmer *et. al* [29] suggested a multidimensional dynamic time warping (DTW) algorithm for hybrid fusion of asynchronous data, requiring significantly less decoding time while providing the same data fusion flexibility as the AHMM. Finally, Artificial Neural Networks (ANN) offer a third alternative for asynchronous fusion; in particular in the form of Long Short-Term Memory Neural Networks (LSTM-NNs), which replace the traditional neural network nodes with memory cells, essentially allowing the network to learn when to store or relate to bimodal information over long periods of time. In fact, LSTM-NNs have been successfully applied to combine acoustic and linguistic features to continuously predict the current quadrant in a two-dimensional emotional space spanned by the dimensions valence and activation [28]. Likewise, in a similar emotion recognition task, this approach successfully fuses facial expressions, shoulder gestures and audio cues [17].

2.3 Event Driven Fusion Approach

While the aforementioned asynchronous fusion approaches theoretically outperform segmentation based schemes, they also have some drawbacks. One severe disadvantage comes from their complexity in terms of training and decision taking. Since it is difficult to understand how the network reaches a decision, applying it in a real-time system bears the risk that the learned model parameters may poorly translate if applied in a possibly less controllable environment. Furthermore, once trained, they function as a black box whose hard-wired parameters leave little opportunity for adjustments to the new conditions. Another issue, which is gladly overlooked in pure offline studies, is the problem of *missing data*. Missing data can occur when either no useful information *can* be detected (e.g. the user is not looking into the camera), or because there *is* nothing useful to detect (e.g. the user is not talking), or last but not least, due to a failure of one of the sensors.

A possible way to make the fusion process more transparent is by shifting from a frame-by-frame based processing towards an event driven approach. Introducing events as an abstract intermediate layer effectively decouples uni-modal processing from the final decision making. Each modality serves as a client which individually decides when to add information. Signal processing components can be added or replaced without having to touch the actual fusion system and missing input from one of the modalities does not cause the collapse of the whole fusion process. In some sense this kind of event-driven fusion is similar to semantic fusion used to analyse the semantics of multi-modal commands, and typically investigates the combination of gestures and speech in new-generation multi-modal user interfaces [14]. However, only few attempts have been made to apply event-driven concepts for automated emotion detection.

In an artistic Augmented Reality installation, the Callas Emotional Tree [7], Gilroy *et. al* uses event-based fusion to derive the affective state of a user in real-time. The basic idea of their approach was to derive emotional information from different modality-specific sensors and map it onto a continuous affective space spanned by the three dimensions Pleasure, Arousal and Dominance (PAD model). Since the application depended on a continuous assessment of the affective user state, the current state of the fusion system was constantly represented by a vector in the PAD space. And the direction into which the vector would move was set by a bunch of vectors representing the single modality-specific contributions. The values of those guiding vectors was updated whenever a new affective cue was detected or otherwise decayed over time. A different approach for predicting user affect in a continuous dimensional space based on verbal and non-verbal behavioural events (e.g. smiles, head shakes, or laughter), has been published by Eyben *et. al* [5]. In their system events are seen as "words", which are joined for each time segment and converted to a feature vector representation through a binary bag-of-words (BOW) approach. Tests on an audiovisual database proved the proposed string-based fusion to be superior over conventional feature-level modelling.

3. EVENT BASED VECTOR FUSION

As implied by first attempts for event driven fusion, a possible way to avoid the problem of restricting segmentations is to have customized annotations for every single modality, from which the recognition of single events – that indicate the sought classification – can be learned. The task of the event driven fusion algorithm then has to be to accumulate these indicating events, take their temporal flow into account and, finally, to classify each single time frame and give boundaries for the recognition on the timescale.

3.1 General Requirements

A real-time event driven fusion scheme, meant to reduce negative effects of the segmentation problem, must meet certain requirements. It should be based on separated event detection in observed signals and its inherent fusion rules must consider the temporal flow of all detected events.

Temporal Component

Once recognized, an event enters the fusion process and influences the continuous result with potency given by the strength of the recognized cue. An event's influence then has to decrease over time - as the moment of occurrence shifts further back in time – until the influential potency reaches a value of zero and the event is discarded. This way, current events are given a stronger impact on the fusion process than the ones that lie further down the time-axis.

Combining Modality Based Events
The additional effort of detecting events in every single modality leads to a fusion model that should link independent signal-events. If complementary events are detected in multiple signals during overlapping time-segments, the cues reinforce each other by amplifying the prediction probability of the continuous fusion output. On the other hand, the detection of contradictory cues leads to events that neutralise each other and therefore have a lesser negative effect on the fusion result. This way, additional information from multiple modalities is more likely to enhance the overall classification performance.

Real–Time Fusion Result
The result of the fusion scheme is calculated by temporal influences (expressed through momentary weights) of registered events. This result will consist of n continuous confidence values (typically valued and normalized between zero and one) for an n-dimensional classification problem. The continuous fusion result is accessible at any point in time. This circumstance is especially valuable in real–time scenarios, where reactions to changing conditions have to be carried out as fast as possible.

Handling Missing Data
The last demand on the real–time system, is an implementation that resists the temporal absence of cues from one or more modalities. This can result for example from missing activity in a modality, tracking problems, or even the breakdown of attached devices. If recognizers involved in decision making each represent the observations of an associated modality, the absence of a single contribution to the final decision is unlikely to result in a drastic quality fall–off for overall classification accuracy – especially if the malfunction is recognized and the corresponding classifier's (most likely counter–productive) contribution is accordingly rated or completely left out of the fusion process.

3.2 Algorithm

The proposed fusion algorithm is based on preceding work done by [8] (section 2.3). We generalize this approach by designing a fusion scheme that operates in a user-defined vector space.

3.2.1 Vector Space and Event Vectors

In the simplest scenario, the vector space is a one-dimensional axis, typically describing a likelihood between zero and one. Events, generated from observed signals, are mapped into this space as vectors. The vectors are provided with the following parameters:

- Confidence Value
  One for each defined axis in the event space. This defines the position of the vector within the dimensional model. For instance, it can be dynamically calculated from the probabilities of a detected cue.

- Vector Weight
  The vector weight is a quantifier for the initial weighting the event has in the calculation of the fusion result. It is defined by the modality the event is detected in and serves as a regulation instrument for emphasizing more reliable information sources. If, for example, one modality is generally better suited for the given classification problem, it can be assigned a higher overall weight. The weight can also be defined by the context. For example, in case of a high noise level, audio might be given less weight.

- Decay Speed
  This is also defined for each modality and describes the average lifespan of cues extracted from the respective signal. If determines the time it takes for the event's influence to decrease to zero and get discarded. Events that strongly indicate the fusion's target class can be given longer decay times, in order to prolong their influence on the result.

In our case, these parameters are empirically determined by systematically testing a large number of combinations for the enjoyment recognition task (see 5.4 for detailed analysis). Figure 1 shows a series of events and their confidence values in the event space. The weight (and therefore influence on the fusion result) of an event vector decrease over time (see dotted line) until the vector is completely removed.

For real-time enjoyment recognition, each frame of audiovisual data undergoes checking for correct face tracking and voice activity. If consequently possible, a SVM classifier for smile recognition (trained with 36 statistical features over action units and smile annotation) and a SVM classifier for laughter recognition (trained with 1451 statistical prosodic features and laughter annotation) each give a normalized probability for the respective event. These confidence values directly map the probabilities given by the SVM models and are used to create uni-modal event-vectors in the multimodal vector space (with resulting event-values in the range of zero to one). Influences (weights) of these events hyperbolically decrease over time, precisely calculated by the initial weight-parameter and speed-parameter of the corresponding modality.

t [s]	Description	e(E)
5.4	vocal event indicating enjoyment	0.9
6.2	facial expression indicating enjoyment	1.0
8.0	vocal event indicating enjoyment	0.8

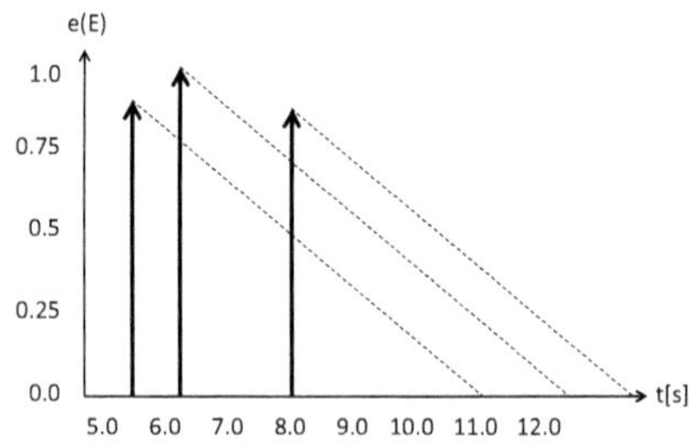

Figure 1: Multi-modal events mapped into the event space.

3.2.2 Fusion Vector

A mass centre is calculated at each frame for all active (weight greater zero) events, by summing up all event-values modified by their current influence (decreased weight) and averaging over the number of active events. The fusion result itself is a vector, which approaches the calculated mass centre with a predefined speed-parameter (figure 2). If this vector rises above a specified classification threshold, we classify the frame to contain enjoyment. This way, we logically fuse smile and laughter events for enjoyment recognition and can evaluate the fusion result against enjoyment annotations frame by frame.

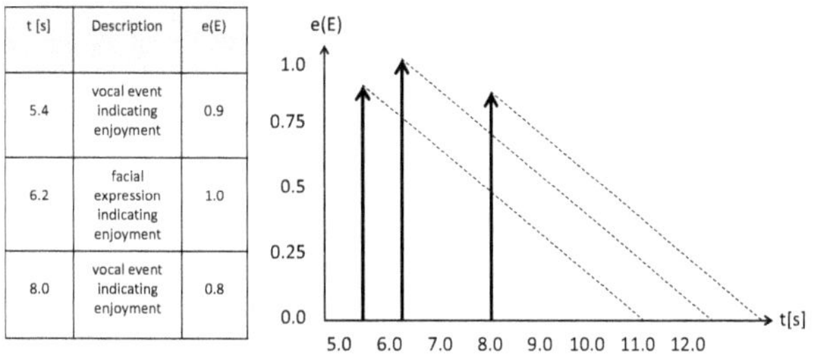

Figure 2: The fusion vector (solid line) approaching the temporary mass centre (bars) and then decreasing to a neutral state.

3.2.3 Characteristics

The fact that the fusion vector does not instantly assume the value of the mass centre, but instead approaches it in a predefined speed, gives the continuous result of event driven vector fusion a special characteristic: The fusion result reacts inertially to new events. Some misclassifications that happen during a row of correct interpretations do not directly shift the overall result in a wrong direction. On the other hand, this slow reaction time can have negative effects, for example if quick classification switches between classes is desired. A possible countermeasure is to raise the speed of the fusion vector towards the mass centre or lower the lifespan of active events – of course this goes along with lowering the mentioned robustness to single misinterpretations. As a consequence, the decay speed and weights of vectors have to be adapted to the observed classification problem.

Realizing the premise of separated events turns out to be a labour–intensive task. In practice, it takes considerably more effort to independently identify events in different signals than triggering interpretation in all modalities by a single signal–event. A deeper understanding of every single modality is needed and the signal processing tasks rise proportionally, as meaningful segments now have to be found in each modality. These unrelated segments need to be interpreted and forwarded to the fusion algorithm as events. A strong technical framework for multi–modal event detection in real–time is needed as a foundation for the realisation of an event driven fusion scheme.

4. A FRAMEWORK FOR EVENT DRIVEN FUSION

The Social Signal Processing framework (SSI)[1] [27] offers special support for the development of online recognition systems from multiple sensors. A list of special traits make the SSI framework a good choice for implementing the event driven fusion approach: An architecture is established to handle diverse signals in a coherent way, no matter if it is a waveform, a heart beat signal, or a video image. Live sensor input is available for a long list of hardware devices and new ones can be implemented via offered interfaces. Thereby, implementation details related to real–time processing such as buffering, synchronization, and threading are hidden from the developer of additional content. Components to process captured signals and assemble machine learning pipelines are included in the framework. Possibilities range from real–time signal processing to high-level feature extraction and online classification.

[1] http://www.openssi.net/

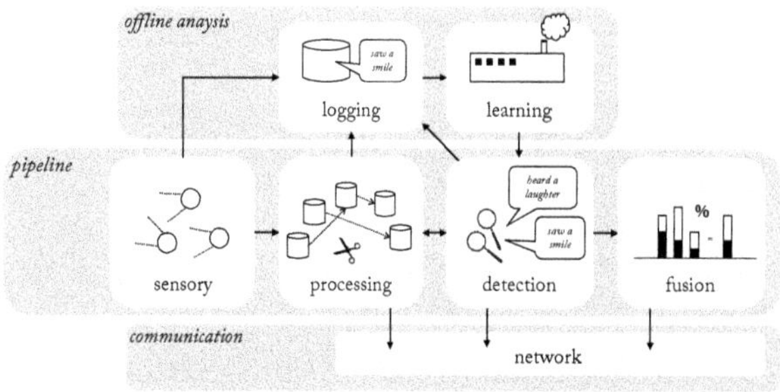

Figure 3: SSI framework: Offline trained recognizers applied in a pipeline for event fusion in real–time.

SSI breaks data handling down to two basic data structures, that perfectly fit the idea of event driven fusion: Streams and events. Data read from a sensor is transformed into a stream, i.e. a continuous flow of samples with fixed sample rate and size. Various transformation algorithms (e. g. filtering, feature calculation, etc.) can be applied to manipulate and further process a raw data stream.

In addition to streams, SSI features the concept of events. Events are meant to describe relevant parts of streams. Single events are usually generated from continuous streams by applying some kind of activity detection. Their length is variable and they may contain additional data, such as a feature set or textual descriptions. Whenever on and offsets are detected, events are sent to the event board. Recognition components that have subscribed to the event are now informed. According to the segment they can request stream chunks or corresponding feature sets and feed them, for example to a single classifier. Classification probabilities are again published as events and can be further processed by event driven fusion schemes.

5. ENJOYMENT RECOGNITION

For evaluation of the event driven fusion approach, we picked the task of enjoyment recognition. We define enjoyment as an episode of enjoyable emotion. These episodes are typically accompanied by visual and auditory cues: We summarize voiced laughters and unvoiced laughters in the audio modality as laughters. The visual component of a laugh as well as visual smiles are in the following denoted as smiles. An annotation of an enjoyment segment will most likely contain one or more of these indicators of enjoyment (figure 4).

5.1 Belfast Story–Telling Corpus

The training corpus for evaluation was taken from the first session of the Belfast Storytelling corpus. The corpus was comprised of six sessions of groups of three or four people telling stories to one another in either English or Spanish. The storytelling task was based on the 16 Enjoyable Emotions Induction Task [9]. Participants were recruited at least a week ahead of the recording session, and were instructed to prepare or think of stories that relate to each of 16 listed positive emotions or sensory experiences. During the storytelling session the participants were seated in com-

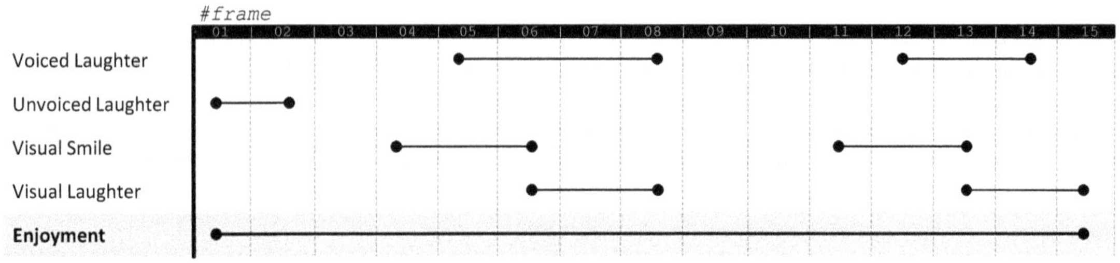

Figure 4: Exemplary annotation of a full enjoyment episode aligned with various voiced and visual cues emitted by the user. For each frame (bordered by dotted lines) a decision has to be made by the fusion system. In a conventional segmentation–based approach each frame is seen in isolation, i.e. a decision is derived from the multi–modal information within the frame. However, we can see that the single cues only partly overlap with the enjoyment episode: While other frames align with cues from a single modality (see e.g. frame 2 and 4), some of the frames, which are spanned by the enjoyment episode do actually not overlap with any observable cues (see e.g. frame 9 and 10). Those frames are likely to be misclassified by a segmentation–based approach. The event–driven fusion approach proposed in this paper, which takes in account the temporal asynchronicity of the events, is able to overcome frames with sparse cues of enjoyment based on information of preceding frames.

fortable chairs around a central table, and each participant wore a head-mounted microphone to capture high quality audio recordings. Video signals were recorded using Logitech Pro HD webcams. Kinect motion capture technology was used to capture facial features, gaze direction and depth information. Participants took turns at recalling a story associated with each enjoyable emotion. The list of enjoyable emotions was randomised for each story telling session, and all of the participants told stories associated with the same emotion in each round of stories. The amount of laughter varied depending on which emotion was being recalled and the nature of the story that was being recounted. The story-telling events occasionally evolved into an open discussion, which further facilitated episodes of laughter. First session involved three male native English speakers recounting stories to one another. Manual annotations of enjoyment episodes and laughter / smile events have been created for this session with the ELAN annotation tool [21] (see figure 4 for an exemplary excerpt).

To capture synchronised data we required the use of 9 computers and a Network Attached Storage (NAS) system. Streaming the visual data from a single participant required a dedicated computer for each HD webcam and Kinect, making a total of 8 computers to capture the data. The audio signals were captured using a ninth computer. The HD Webcams streamed video data to the computers at 25fps, with a resolution of 1024x576 for three of the cameras and 960x720 for the fourth camera. We also used standard video recording equipment as a backup recording system. Webcam streams were compressed with the Huffyuv lossless codec and later compressed using the lossy H264 to make more usable file sizes. The audio from each head mounted microphone was fed into a MOTU 8pre FireWire audio interface preamp, and from there into another computer with Firewire 800 recording hard drives. Audio was recorded using wav format files (mono, 48000Hz, 24-bit PCM). Each session lasted about 120 minutes, resulting in approximately 75 minutes recording time. Synchronized recording of data streams was achieved using the SSI software (section 4).

5.2 Enjoyment Recognition Systems

Figure 4 depicts multiple annotation tracks for the Belfast Story–Telling Corpus. The overarching enjoyment episode includes several segments of smiles and laughters. Training of the following recognition systems is based on these annotations. All classification systems perform recognition on a framewise basis: A decision, if enjoyment is present within the evaluated person or not, is made every 400 milliseconds within a window of one second. Each recognition system is subject independent – two of the persons of session one (section 5.1) are used for training the recognizers needed for compared approaches, one person is used for testing. Given a recording length of approximately one hour per person, this leads to a rough total of 18.000 samples for training and 9.000 samples for testing. Considering class imbalances within testing samples, we use the unweighted average as evaluation criterion.

Uni–Modal Classification

Based on the segmentation given by the annotations, we recognize enjoyment directly from the single modalities audio and video. As feature–sets for characterizing the raw audio streams, we use 1451 statistical prosodic EmoVoice features [25]. Recognizers for video classification are trained with 36 features, gained from statistics over action units provided by the Microsoft Kinect^{TM}. Both feature extraction steps are calculated within the SSI framework (section 4). As computational model for classification, we use LibSVM's support vector machines [1] with a linear kernel.

Segmentation Based Fusion

Segmentation based fusion approaches on the feature, decision and model level (section 2.1) are applied to combine both modalities for direct enjoyment classification (using the same enjoyment annotation track as the uni–modal classification systems). From these experiments we can draw first conclusions if the multi–modal information can deliver classification improvements, if the same annotated time segments are sliced through modalities.

	Uni–Modal Classification		Segmentation–Based Fusion		
	Audio	Video	Feature	Decision	Model
Enjoyment	50.26%	66.85%	73.75%	76.41%	76.08%
¬ Enjoyment	60.47%	76.90%	66.17%	61.53%	56.04%
UA	**57.14%**	**73.62%**	**68.64%**	**66.39%**	**62.58%**
WA	**55.37%**	**71.88%**	**69.96%**	**68.97%**	**66.06%**

Table 1: Results for uni–modal classification and segmentation based fusion on feature, decision and model level. Trained on overall enjoyment annotations.

Modality-Tailored Fusion
Afterwards we try to recognize the annotated enjoyment segments indirectly from tailored annotations: Instead of using the annotations for whole enjoyment episodes for both modalities, we annotate audible occurrences of laughters within the audio channel and visible laughters and smiles in the video separately. These tailored annotations are then used to train classification models for detecting these enjoyment indicating cues, rather than recognizing enjoyment directly (same feature sets as for enjoyment classification are applied).

Modality-tailored fusion is meant as an intermediate and experimental step, in which these modality tailored cue-recognizers are used directly in decision and model level fusion schemes. The models trained on enjoyment segmentations are therefore replaced, probabilities given to each frame by classifiers meant for detecting audible and visual laughters are mapped to the corresponding enjoyment classes.

Event Driven Vector Fusion
Finally we apply event–based vector fusion to compare this indirect, event–based way of fusing multi–modal information to single channel classification and segmentation based fusion performance. The events have to be detected and generated by the framework. Before classification, activity recognition is performed for each modality, for example testing if there is more than noise in the audio channel. Such pre–processing can introduce additional prediction errors (as the activity recognition is also not always correct), but a very crucial point in robust real–time systems. For this reason we simulate the process also for evaluation. Recognizers consider every frame that pass activity recognition and generate events for smiles and laughters respectively. Confidence values of these events correspond to the recognition probabilities of smile and laughter detectors. All currently active events are finally considered for mass–centre calculation and therefore influence the course of the fusion vector (section 3). For every frame, we calculate the current position of the fusion vector and based on its current position we decide if enjoyment is present or not within the observed time frame.

In order to simulate a true real–time system it should be noted that evaluation has been carried out for the full recordings, i.e. no frames were excluded at any time. Consequently, in case of segmentation-based fusion a decision had to be forced even for frames where no signal was detected (i.e. no face tracked and silence detected in the audio channel). We decided to map those frames onto the class with the highest a priori probability (i.e. no enjoyment).

5.3 Results

Result tables report unweighted (average accuracy across frames) and weighted (average accuracy across classes) recognition results (UA / WA). During the discussion, we will focus on the weighted recognition performance, as classified frames contain less samples of occurring enjoyment as well as audible and visible laughter. Table 1 shows recognition results for single channel classification and segmentation based fusion algorithms that use classification models trained directly on enjoyment annotations. Recognition of enjoyment via the audio modality is close to random (55.37%). Expressive cues for enjoyment are located within the boundaries of an amused episode, but do not fit them very well, which leads to noisy features and poor classification rates (figure 4). With a weighted 71.88%, the video modality yields far better capabilities of determining enjoyment frames. Facial expressions, which express enjoyable emotions, correspond much better to the overarching annotation, as hints of smiles are mostly present during enjoyment. These discrepancies pass on to segmentation based fusion approaches: Feature, decision and model level fusion perform on an intermediate level between the merged modalities (69.96%, 68.97% and 66.06%)[2]. This is to be expected, as the problematic classification models trained on the vocal modality fully contribute to the fusion result.

	Event Detection		
	Audio	Video	
Laughter	76.51%	78.15%	**Smile**
¬ Laughter	91.66%	79.61%	**¬ Smile**
UA	**90.99**	**79.31**	**UA**
WA	**84.09**	**78.88**	**WA**

Table 2: Result for uni–modal event recognizers for laughters and smiles. Trained on modality tailored annotations.

Table 2 gives insight into the capability of event detection recognizers for the audio and video modality. These are not trained with the bi–modal annotations of enjoyment, but with tailored, more narrow uni–modal annotations for actual laughter occurrences and smiles respectively. When looking at laughter classification within the audio channel, it becomes clear that detection of these short indication–

[2]Several representative fusion schemes for decision and model level have been tested with very close average recognition rates. Presented results are generated with the product rule (decision level) and stacking (model level) – as described in section 2.1.

	Modality–Tailored Fusion		Event–Driven Fusion
	Decision	Model	Vector Based
Enjoyment	55.16%	66.75%	76.18%
¬ Enjoyment	90.32%	80.54%	81.37%
UA	**78.84%**	**76.04%**	**79.68%**
WA	**72.74%**	**73.65%**	**78.78%**

Table 3: Results for modality tailored fusion on decision and model level and event driven vector fusion.

events is by far more reliable than recognition of whole enjoyment episodes (84.09% to 55.37%). Differences between smile– and enjoyment recognition on basis of the video channel is not as massive: The low recognition difference of 7.00% (compared to auditory enjoyment and laughters) depicts the high correlation of experienced enjoyment and positive facial expressions.

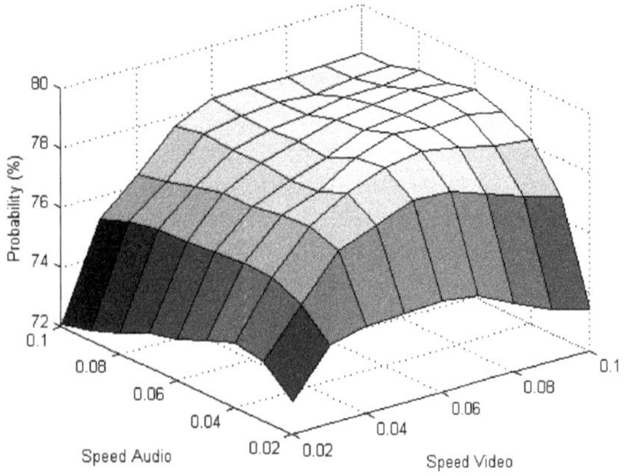

Figure 5: Influence of audio and video decay speed on vector fusion performance.

However, we can not directly use these event recognition models for enjoyment detection. They are meant to be further processed by an event–driven fusion algorithm, such as vector fusion. But first we experiment with an intermediate step: Event recognition models are used in segmentation based fusion algorithms on decision and model level. Laughter and smile detections are simply mapped to the enjoyment class and fed into the fusion process. Results of this procedure are described in the first entries of Table 3 (modality–tailored fusion). Both fusion approaches deliver good results. With a weighted average of 72.74% on decision– and 73.65% on model–level they exceed uni–modal classification of enjoyment on the more qualified video channel (71.88%). By combining laughter and smile detections, these approaches are able to partially capture the course of enjoyment episodes, but they do not take temporal relations of recognized events into account. Table 3 shows clearly, that the main improvements in recognition performance is based on the detection of ¬Enjoyment. This means they mostly predict the absence of indicating events during the periods of enjoyment, there are still many misclassifications. At this point, event–driven fusion schemes can gain further improvements over previous approaches.

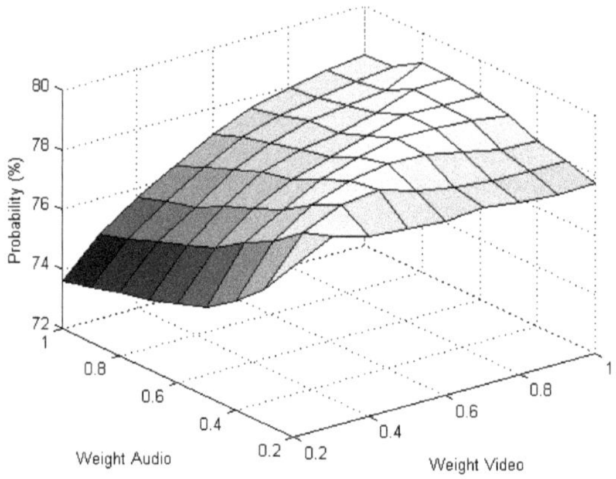

Figure 6: Influence of audio and video weights on vector fusion performance. Stable performance is observed if audio and video events are weighted in a ratio of 8 to 10.

5.4 Parameter Analysis

As described earlier (section 3), the performance of event driven fusion depends on the three parameters confidence, weight and speed of the events. To achieve optimal results, a reasonable configuration of the three parameters has to be found. Confidence is directly derived from probabilities given by the event detectors. This derivation only makes sense if confidence values of given classifiers are comparable. To prove this assumption, Figure 7 plots the confidence values of event detectors against the correctness of the estimation. Prediction behaviours of modalities resemble each other clearly.

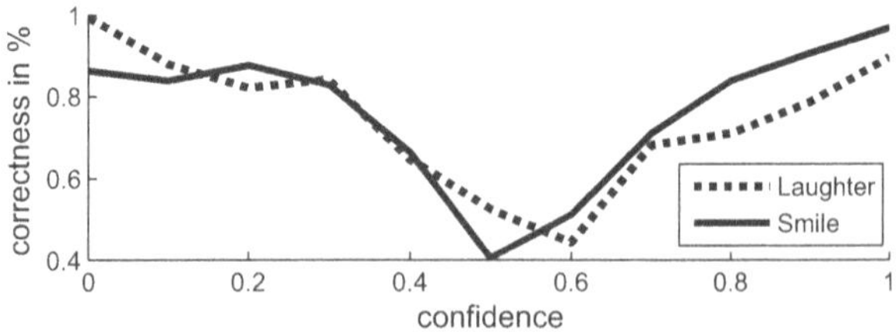

Figure 7: Frequency of correctly classified frames according to laughter / smile confidence. Similar prediction behaviour allows to directly combine confidence values during the fusion process.

Optimal configuration of weight and speed parameters have been empirically determined by systematically testing a large number of combinations (figures 5 and 6): Smile events are weighted with full influence, as the occurrence of smiles correlate well with the boundaries of enjoyment episodes. Their decay speed is regulated high, as the beginning and ending of enjoyment are often similar to presence and absence of smiles in the face and the fusion vector should rise and fall fast whenever smiles are detected or not. The decay speed of laughter events is regulated low. Laughters are considered a strong indicator of enjoyment and whenever they occur we expect the enjoyment episode to last for several frames afterwards. Best performance is achieved if laughters are weighted less than smile events – again due to the fact that smiles better describe the limits of enjoyment segments. The optimal ratio lies around 8 to 10 (figure 6).

Taking these findings and the possibility to temporarily relate the detected events into account, event–driven vector fusion achieves an average recognition rate of 78.78%. This is the best result we were able to achieve for enjoyment recognition during our experiments with examined approaches. According to McNemar's Chi-Squared Test ($p < 0.05$), improvements in comparison to the second best approach (modality tailored fusion on model and decision level) are significant. Table 3 also shows a well balanced distribution of accuracies among classes (76.18% for Enjoyment and 81.37% for ¬Enjoyment), which shows that event driven fusion is accurate in detecting whole episodes of enjoyment and models their boundaries well.

6. CONCLUSION

Affect recognition systems apply multi–modal fusion under the reasonable assumption that combination of information from several modalities does improve classification accuracy. However, studies over the last years have shown that the concrete enhancements of fusion systems compared to uni–modal classification are – to say the least – unstable. A possible problem causing this varying performance is that overarching segmentations for given classification problems are used throughout observed modalities, resulting in segmentation based fusion approaches. In this study we have specified and implemented an event driven real–time fusion system for affect recognition. This kind of approach does not directly fuse identical timeframes throughout modalities, but calculates probabilities indirectly by accumulating shorter, detection–indicating and possibly time–shifted events. This approach demands additional annotation, segmentation and training steps, but our evaluation shows a promising potential of the event driven approach:

Given the affect recognition task of enjoyment classification on the Belfast Story–Telling Corpus, we exemplary compare uni–modal and segmentation based, multi–modal fusion systems to event driven vector vector fusion. While the segmentation for enjoyment episodes indeed fits well for classification via the video modality, it is not very suitable for the audio channel. This fact results in acceptable recognition accuracy when using only the video modality and very bad results for audio classification. Segmentation based fusion aligns between these accuracies and performs on an intermediate level. It then, recognizes the enjoyment–indicating events of laughters and smiles and processes them further with event driven vector fusion. We empirically determined parameters for speed and weight distributions among modalities. Best performance was yielded when smile events were given a higher weight and speed than laughters. Laughters are a strong indicator of enjoyment and should therefore have a long–term influence on fusion; smiles on the other hand need quick reaction time as they describe well the margins of enjoyment. They also profit from higher weightings as this allow smiles to hold steady during longer enjoyment–periods with no vocal activity. Based on this configuration (78.78%), we were able to enhance enjoyment recognition accuracy by 6.09% compared to uni–modal classification (video channel), 8.82% compared to segmentation based fusion (feature level) and 5.13% compared to modality-tailored fusion (model level).

7. FUTURE WORK

Having identified potential problems of segmentation based fusion and the capabilities of an event driven approach, many interesting investigations open up: By now, we have trained few event recognizers for a valence related affect classification problem. The amount of event detectors can be raised by a great amount and expanded to further modalities. Arousal related classification, e.g. on the basis of physiological signals and events, potentially enables recognition coverage of the 2–dimensional valence–arousal emotion space. The presented vector fusion implementation is just one way of relating event detections for multi–modal fusion. Because of its accessible and understandable logic and structure, vector fusion is a very good starting point for analysis of the event driven fusion approach. However, more complicated network structures seem very promising and are to be examined and compared in future studies.

8. ACKNOWLEDGMENTS

The work described in this paper is funded by the European Union under research grant ILHAIRE, a Seventh Framework Programme (FP7/2007-2013) under grant agreement n°270780 and CEEDs (FP7-ICT-2009-5).

9. REFERENCES

[1] C.-C. Chang and C.-J. Lin. LIBSVM: A library for support vector machines. *ACM Transactions on Intelligent Systems and Technology*, 2:27:1–27:27, 2011.

[2] S. K. D'Mello and J. Kory. Consistent but modest: a meta-analysis on unimodal and multimodal affect detection accuracies from 30 studies. In L.-P. Morency, D. Bohus, H. K. Aghajan, J. Cassell, A. Nijholt, and J. Epps, editors, *ICMI*, pages 31–38. ACM, 2012.

[3] R. Duin and D. Tax. Experiments with classifier combining rules. In *Lecture Notes in Computer Science*, volume 1857, pages 16–29. Springer, 2000.

[4] S. Dupont and J. Luettin. Audio-visual speech modeling for continuous speech recognition. *IEEE Transactions on Multimedia*, 2(3):141 – 151, 2000.

[5] F. Eyben, M. Wöllmer, M. F. Valstar, H. Gunes, B. Schuller, and M. Pantic. String-based audiovisual fusion of behavioural events for the assessment of dimensional affect. In *IEEE International Conference on Automatic Face & Gesture Recognition and Workshops, FG 2011*, pages 322–329, USA, March 2011. IEEE Computer Society.

[6] G. Fumera and F. Roli. A theoretical and experimental analysis of linear combiners for multiple classifier systems. *IEEE Transactions on Pattern Analysis and Machine Intelligence*, 27(6):942–956, 2005.

[7] S. W. Gilroy, M. Cavazza, R. Chaignon, S.-M. Mäkelä, M. Niranen, E. André, T. Vogt, J. Urbain, M. Billinghurst, H. Seichter, and M. Benayoun. E-tree: Emotionally driven augmented reality art. In *Proceedings of the 16th ACM International Conference on Multimedia*, MM '08, pages 945–948, New York, NY, USA, 2008. ACM.

[8] S. W. Gilroy, M. Cavazza, M. Niranen, E. Andre, T. Vogt, J. Urbain, M. Benayoun, H. Seichter, and M. Billinghurst. Pad-based multimodal affective fusion. In *Affective Computing and Intelligent Interaction and Workshops, 2009. ACII 2009. 3rd International Conference on*, 2009.

[9] J. Hofmann, F. Stoffel, A. Weber, and T. Platt. The 16 enjoyable emotions induction task (16-eeit). 2012.

[10] L. I. Kuncheva. Switching between selection and fusion in combining classifiers: An experiment. *IEEE Transactions on Systems, Man, and Cybernetics, Part B: Cybernetics*, 32(2):146–156, 2002.

[11] L. I. Kuncheva. A theoretical study on six classifier fusion strategies. *IEEE Transactions on Pattern Analysis and Machine Intelligence*, 24(2):281–286, 2002.

[12] F. Lingenfelser, J. Wagner, and E. André. A systematic discussion of fusion techniques for multi-modal affect recognition tasks. In *Proceedings of the 13th International Conference on Multimodal Interfaces*, ICMI '11, pages 19–26, New York, NY, USA, 2011. ACM.

[13] M. Mancini, L. Ach, E. Bantegnie, T. Baur, N. Berthouze, D. Datta, Y. Ding, S. Dupont, H. Griffin, F. Lingenfelser, R. Niewiadomski, C. Pelachaud, O. Pietquin, B. Piot, J. Urbain, G. Volpe, and J. Wagner. Laugh when you're winning. In C. T. R. J. C.-M. Rybarczyk, Y., editor, *Innovative and Creative Developments in Multimodal Interaction Systems, Proceedings of 9th IFIP WG 5.5 International Summer Workshop on Multimodal Interfaces, eNTERFACE 2013*, volume 425, Lisbon, Portugal, 2014. Springer.

[14] G. U. Mehlmann and E. André. Modeling multimodal integration with event logic charts. In L.-P. Morency, D. Bohus, H. K. Aghajan, J. Cassell, A. Nijholt, and J. Epps, editors, *ICMI*, pages 125–132. ACM, 2012.

[15] A. V. Nefian, L. Liang, X. Pi, L. Xiaoxiang, C. Mao, and K. Murphy. A coupled hmm for audio-visual speech recognition. In *in International Conference on Acoustics, Speech and Signal Processing (CASSP'02)*, pages 2013–2016, 2002.

[16] M. A. Nicolaou, H. Gunes, and M. Pantic. Audio-visual classification and fusion of spontaneous affective data in likelihood space. In *ICPR*, pages 3695–3699. IEEE, 2010.

[17] M. A. Nicolaou, H. Gunes, and M. Pantic. Continuous prediction of spontaneous affect from multiple cues and modalities in valence-arousal space. *T. Affective Computing*, 2(2):92–105, 2011.

[18] M. Pantic, A. Pentland, A. Nijholt, and T. Huang. *Human Computing and Machine Understanding of Human Behavior: A Survey*, volume 4451, pages 47–71. 2007.

[19] S. Petridis, M. Pantic, and J. F. Cohn. Prediction-based classification for audiovisual discrimination between laughter and speech. In *Automatic Face and Gesture Recognition and Workshops (FG 2011), 2011 IEEE International Conference*, pages 619–626, 2011.

[20] R. Polikar. Ensemble based systems in decision making. *IEEE Circuits and Systems Magazine*, (3):21 – 45, 2006.

[21] H. Sloetjes, A. Russel, and A. Klassmann. Elan: a free and open-source multimedia annotation tool. In *INTERSPEECH*, pages 4015–4016. ISCA, 2007.

[22] M. Song, J. Bu, C. Chen, and N. Li. Audio-visual based emotion recognition - a new approach. In *CVPR (2)*, pages 1020–1025, 2004.

[23] K. M. Ting and I. H. Witten. Issues in stacked generalization. *Journal of Artificial Intelligence Research*, 10:115–124, 1999.

[24] A. Vinciarelli, M. Pantic, D. Heylen, C. Pelachaud, I. Poggi, F. D'ericco, and M. Schroeder. Bridging the gap between social animal and unsocial machine: A survey of social signal processing. *IEEE Transactions on Affective Computing*, 3:69–87, April 2012. Issue 1.

[25] T. Vogt, E. André, and N. Bee. Emovoice - a framework for online recognition of emotions from voice. In *Perception in Multimodal Dialogue Systems, 4th IEEE Tutorial and Research Workshop on Perception and Interactive Technologies for Speech-Based Systems, Kloster Irsee, Germany*, LNCS, pages 188–199. Springer, 2008.

[26] J. Wagner, F. Lingenfelser, E. Andre, J. Kim, and T. Vogt. Exploring fusion methods for multimodal emotion recognition with missing data. *IEEE Transactions on Affective Computing*, 2(4):206–218, 2011.

[27] J. Wagner, F. Lingenfelser, T. Baur, I. Damian, F. Kistler, and E. André. The social signal interpretation (ssi) framework: multimodal signal processing and recognition in real-time. In A. Jaimes, N. Sebe, N. Boujemaa, D. Gatica-Perez, D. A. Shamma, M. Worring, and R. Zimmermann, editors, *ACM Multimedia*, pages 831–834. ACM, 2013.

[28] M. Wöllmer, B. Schuller, F. Eyben, and G. Rigoll. Combining long short-term memory and dynamic bayesian networks for incremental emotion-sensitive artificial listening. *J. Sel. Topics Signal Processing*, 4(5):867–881, 2010.

[29] M. Wöllmer, M.llmer, M. Al-Hames, F. Eyben, B. Schuller, and G. Rigoll. A multidimensional dynamic time warping algorithm for efficient multimodal fusion of asynchronous data streams. *Neurocomput.*, 73(1-3):366–380, Dec. 2009.

[30] Z. Zeng, M. Pantic, G. I. Roisman, and T. S. Huang. A survey of affect recognition methods: Audio, visual, and spontaneous expressions. *IEEE transactions on pattern analysis and machine intelligence*, 31(1):39–58, January 2009.

[31] Z. Zeng, J. Tu, B. M. Pianfetti, and T. S. Huang. Audio-visual affective expression recognition through multistream fused hmm. *Trans. Multi.*, 10(4):570–577, June 2008.

Correlating Speaker Gestures in Political Debates with Audience Engagement Measured via EEG

John R. Zhang
Dept. Computer Science
Columbia University
New York NY, USA
jrzhang@cs.columbia.edu

Jason Sherwin
Dept. Biomedical Engineering
Columbia University
New York NY, USA
jss2212@columbia.edu

Jacek Dmochowski
Dept. Psychology
Stanford University
Stanford CA, USA
jdmochow@stanford.edu

Paul Sajda
Dept. Biomedical Engineering
Columbia University
New York NY, USA
psajda@columbia.edu

John R. Kender
Dept. Computer Science
Columbia University
New York NY, USA
jrk@cs.columbia.edu

ABSTRACT

We hypothesize that certain speaker gestures can convey significant information that are correlated to audience engagement. We propose *gesture attributes*, derived from speakers' tracked hand motions to automatically quantify these gestures from video. Then, we demonstrate a correlation between gesture attributes and an objective method of measuring audience engagement: electroencephalography (EEG) in the domain of political debates. We collect 47 minutes of EEG recordings from each of 20 subjects watching clips of the 2012 U.S. Presidential debates. The subjects are examined in aggregate and in subgroups according to gender and political affiliation. We find statistically significant correlations between gesture attributes (particularly extremal pose) and our feature of engagement derived from EEG both with and without audio. For some stratifications, the Spearman rank correlation reaches as high as $\rho = 0.283$ with $p < 0.05$, Bonferroni corrected. From these results, we identify those gestures that can be used to measure engagement, principally those that break habitual gestural patterns.

Categories and Subject Descriptors

H.1.2 [**User/Machine Systems**]: Human information processing; H.3.3 [**Information Storage and Retrieval**]: Information Search and Retrieval

General Terms

Experimentation

Keywords

Gestures; video; electroencephalography (EEG); neuroscience; engagement; political debates; attributes

MM'14, November 3–7, 2014, Orlando, Florida, USA.

ACM 978-1-4503-3063-3/14/11 ...$15.00.
http://dx.doi.org/10.1145/2647868.2654909.

1. INTRODUCTION

The increasing availability of video online provides countless benefits to the public, but leads to the problem of information overload to viewers. The automatic identification of engaging segments through visual signals presents one possible solution. We explore one possible source of visual signals: speaker gestures. Because how a speaker gesticulates gives insight on the their emotions toward the subject at hand, we hypothesize that human gestures can convey significant information which can be correlated to audience engagement. The analysis of how media engages audiences is itself an interesting and difficult problem. In this paper, we study how speaker gestures engage audiences in the socially relevant domain of political debates. Future work can apply these results toward video retrieval applications and affective interfaces.

Our contributions are as follows. First, we propose a number of *gesture attributes*, which seek to capture the properties of human gesture. These include: velocity, direction change, and extremal pose. We also present methods on automatically deriving these attributes from tracked hand motions in digital video. Second, we examine how these gesture attributes correlate with audience engagement. We asked 20 subjects to watch clips of the 2012 U.S. Presidential Debates while simultaneously measuring their electroencephalography (EEG), resulting in a total of 47 minutes of EEG data per subject. The method of [10] is applied to identify temporal moments of audience engagement, which are then correlated against our gesture attributes. We compute Spearman rank correlations between gesture attributes and our measure of engagement and statistically significant correlations across various stratifications of video, subjects and presence of audio. For some stratifications, correlations reach as high as $\rho = 0.283$ ($p < 0.05$, Bonferroni corrected).

This paper is organized as follows. In Section 2, we review related work. In Section 3 we describe our domain of interest and the video dataset we experiment with. In Section 4 we propose a number of computer vision techniques for automatically extracting gesture attributes from video. In Section 5 we describe the measurement of audience engagement while watching debate videos. In Section 6, we show statistically significant correlations between gesture attributes and viewers' neural activity. We discuss other observations in Section 7. Finally, we conclude with a discussion of future work in Section 8.

2. RELATED WORK

Here we briefly review related work across linguistics, computer science and neuroscience as our work lies at the intersection of these fields.

2.1 Psychological Impact of Speaker Gestures

There is substantial psychological research which has demonstrated the importance of body language in conveying emotion, particularly in asserting dominance (with regard to the PAD model of Mehrabian *et al.* [24]). The body gestures of speakers are known to have an emotional impact on the audience [13]. As such, research in the field of affective interfaces frequently studies gestures to infer emotion. Glowinski *et al.* proposed a framework and a set of features for upper body gestures which characterize emotional behavior of the person gesticulating [14]. Kapur *et al.* proposed a full-body motion-capture system for inferring emotion [20]. Related to this, our work proposes gesture attributes and explicitly studies the relationship between them and audience engagement.

A number of studies have been done on gestures in the context of political speeches and debates. In the 2012 U.S. Presidential Debates, psychologists and linguists were hired in an attempt to infer personality traits of the candidates through their gesticulations [32]. Bull examined the relationship between the style and content of political speeches with the gesticulations of the speaker [3]. Three British political speeches made by three different speakers with varying levels of oratory reputation were videotaped and analyzed. The author annotated gestures using his own system [4] and annotated speech content according to purpose (e.g., an attack on another speaker, advocacy, naming, addressing, etc.) After analysis, the author noted that gestures were correlated to vocal intonation and often used to elicit and control applause, although this result varied heavily based on speaker. The deliberate use of gestures to control the audience is another reason we believe that gestures are valid as semantic cues.

More recently, Casasanto *et al.* examined the co-occurrence of certain hand gestures and the sentiment (i.e., positivity or negativity) of the accompanying speech [7]. The authors demonstrate their hypothesis that the sentiment of a person's spoken clauses and the handedness of their gestures are highly correlated. That is, right-handed speakers tend to say more positive things while gesticulating with their right hand, and similarly for left-handed speakers. This analysis was done by manually examining the 2004 and 2008 U.S. Presidential Debates: two linguists separated the transcripts into clauses, assigning each a sentiment, and then watched the corresponding video, identifying the handedness of each gesture.

These studies support the significance of gesture in engaging audiences, and their significance in political discourse.

2.2 Pose and Gesture Recognition

To automatically capture the properties of human gesture from video, we can begin by identifying individual body parts. While the proliferation of infrared-based cameras allowing for depth information to be captured along with imagery has led to an explosion of gesture-based applications and research, we restrict our literature review to those methods using only single-camera video information. This is because for our purpose of video analysis, this is usually the only information available.

Work on pictorial structures have been applied to improve pose estimation. In pictorial structures, objects (in our case, upper bodies) are represented as a collection of parts arranged in a configuration with pairs connected by "springs" that pull each other to be in a relative location with respect to the other. Ferrari *et al.* applies this approach to the task of estimating upper- and full-body poses in humans [12]. The human (upper) body is modeled with 6 parts: upper and lower left and right arms, the torso and the head, where each part is parameterized by location, scale and orientation. A method is introduced for estimating these parameters. Yang *et al.* uses a similar parts-based model but does not parameterize parts with orientation, resulting in significantly faster performance [33] . In one interesting application of gesture analysis using pictorial structures-based posed estimation, Buehler *et al.* demonstrates a system whereby British Sign Language is automatically learned from captioned video [2].

In our work, we derive attributes through tracked hands alone. Buehler *et al.* shows how this can be done accurately if upper body pose information is also available [1]. They propose a method of hand detection and tracking via a part-based model which infers the position of the hands based largely on the position of the other body parts, starting with the head. However, in our domain, this is not always the case, as the arms may be out of view or occluded by a podium.

Hand detection can be done using a number of features, often combined: skin color, Haar-like features, and HOGs. Mittal *et al.* combine skin color and shape features (as determined by HOGs) to produce hand detectors robust to different poses and backgrounds [26]. However, the method is trained on images of entire hands. Similarly, Kadir *et al.* trained a boosted classifier using Haar-like features to detect entire hands [19]. Such detection techniques would, in general, be unable to detect when one hand is occluded by another hand. Furthermore, our own attempts to train models using these features to recognize partial hands (e.g., just a thumb sticking out) resulted in poor performance. This capability is desirable for the purpose of propagating bounding boxes across frames, when hands may appear in and out of view. However, color and shape features are still useful for hand blob detection. Zhang *et al.* uses skin color in their method to track and distinguish clasping and occluded hands [34]. We apply this method as a first step toward deriving gesture attributes.

2.3 Measuring Engagement

As our ultimate goal is to demonstrate a correlation between points of interest in videos and the speaker's gestures, then in order to build a ground-truth, we must be able to examine when the audience's attention is piqued. To this end, we briefly review the literature for different methods of measuring audience engagement—itself an unsolved and difficult problem.

A number of different methods exist for capturing a person's engagement. The most straight-forward method is perhaps a direct user study. For instance, in their study of video summarization, Ma *et al.* propose a fully automatic multi-modal video summarization scheme and perform user studies to evaluate its efficacy [23]. The authors recruit 20 subjects to first watch summarized video clips, followed by the original video before assigning scores for "enjoyment" and "informativeness". While this approach may be effective for determining which segments of video may be more relevant *after* their extraction, it would be difficult to apply this to gathering a ground-truth of relevant segments of video without prior candidates. Furthermore, the task we face is even more subjective, as what catches a viewer's attention can be highly idiosyncratic.

Another approach, eye tracking—the process by which the gaze is tracked—has found numerous applications in determining web usability [5], assessing the efficacy of advertising media [6] and in the automotive industry to identify when drivers may be distracted [29]. Nakano *et al.* use eye tracking to estimate a person's engagement in a conversation [27]. In their approach, the subject's gaze is classified as looking at the speaker's face, the speaker's body, or some object. They conclude that the subject is least likely to be engaged when their gaze is not on the speaker (face or body) and propose a system for automatically recognizing these moments.

A third approach uses signals from social networks, particularly Twitter. Diakopoulos *et al.* use Twitter to gauge audience sentiment during the 2008 U.S. Presidential Debates [9]. Tweets are aggregated by searching for related hashtags (e.g., #current, #debate08, etc.) and then assigned a sentiment label manually using Amazon Mechanical Turk. As the Tweets can be time-synced to the debate, the authors are able to derive conclusions regarding audience sentiment with regard to the candidates and to the debate topics. Naturally, there is a lag between a moment in the debate and the corresponding Tweet.

The methods discussed so far all require conscious actions by the subject. That is, we assume a person is paying attention if they indicate it in a questionnaire, or if their eyes follow a target, or if they Tweet about it. Functional magnetic resonance imaging (fMRI) [16, 17], and EEG allow us to measure neural correlates of engagement from a subject without interfering or interrupting their viewing of the video. EEG has long demonstrated that it can capture neurological information related to attention. For instance, EEG devices have been approved for use as tests for attention deficit hyperactivity disorder (ADHD) in children [30]. Dmochowski *et al.* propose a method for interpreting EEG data to identify moments of engagement in subjects [10]. Intuitively, the method works under the hypothesis that neural activity would be most similar across subjects at moments when something piques their interest. Therefore, the method identifies these moments by computing the points of maximum correlation of EEG measurements across subjects and comparing it against a significance derived from a permutation test. This is the approach we ultimately apply to gather a corroborating signal of when subjects are engaged when watching video. Unlike the other methods reviewed here, it is direct, less sensitive to lag (i.e., the subject does not need to interrupt their viewing to give feedback) and less intrusive for the subject.

3. DOMAIN

In this paper, we focus on the domain of political debates, particularly the 2012 U.S. presidential debates. This simplifies the parameters of our experiment as the American political landscape is dominated by two parties: the Democratic Party and the Republican Party. Although voters who identify as Independent have seen a resurgence in popularity in recent times according to Gallup's [18] from 33% in 1988 to 40% in 2011, the vast majority of voters voted for one of these two parties while only 1.6% voted for others in the 2012 election. Each party was also represented by a single leader: U.S. President Barack Obama for the Democratic Party and former Massachusetts Governor Mitt Romney for the Republican Party.

Despite restricting the experiment to such a narrow domain, the results of the study could nonetheless have significant impact due to the importance of the domain. Political consulting is big business in America, where even the slightest edge in capturing audiences' attention could command lucrative fees, and ultimately change the outcome of an election.

We use recorded video of the first (original air date October 3, 2012) and third (original air date October 22, 2012) debates between Obama and Romney, which are publicly available. These videos are rigidly structured and of high quality. The videos have a resolution of 640×360 pixels and are recorded at 24.58 frames per second using a stationary camera, and tend to focus on the upper bodies of the speakers, who are largely stationary but gesticulate frequently while they speak. The number of speakers are limited to the presidential candidates and the debate moderators, and this study will only focus on the candidates. The speakers are dressed formally in a suit and tie, and the background and foreground are clearly distinguishable. In the first debate, speakers are standing behind a podium. In the second, speakers are sitting at a table. We focus here on the gestural habits of the two U.S. presidential candidates. Examples of the videos are shown in Figure 1.

Figure 1: Examples of the 2012 U.S. Presidential Debates. Speakers' hands appear in and out of view, and speakers may gesticulate with one or both hands.

We restrict our analysis to these two debates (out of the total four debates that year). We discard the vice-presidential debate in order to reduce the number of speakers. We also discard the second presidential debate as the speakers are walking while carrying a microphone, therefore biasing any gesture information that can be derived.

From these videos we construct a collection of clips, which we will use to train our gesture models and use as stimulus for human subjects. Each clip shows a continuous frontal shot of a single speaker. Given the high quality and structured nature of the recording, most clips satisfy this constraint. To extract these clips from the full videos, we first automatically segment the videos using HSV color histogram comparison with 3D histograms with 16 bins for each dimension, and we compare them using the L2 distance and a threshold of 0.1 similar to [28], resulting in 322 shots, totaling 142.8 minutes. Next, we manually discard the shots which do not contain a frontal view of a single candidate, leaving us with 291 shots of interest, totaling 136.4 minutes.

4. GESTURE ATTRIBUTES

We propose methods for extracting the following gesture attributes from video, which seek to capture the minute properties of human gesture.

We begin by applying the hand detection and tracking algorithm described in [34] to distinguish and track left and right hands. From this we can derive our attributes, anchored at each frame, computed solely from the positions of the bounding boxes of detected hands and faces.

The attributes we initially explored include: distance from hands to each other (in cases where there are two hands), distance from each hand to the face, velocity of motion for each hand, and direction change for each hand. Preliminary analysis using PCA on the set of all attributes suggested that velocity and direction change were responsible for a significant part of the variation in the features, therefore, we focus on these two attributes here.

4.1 Velocity

For each frame f, we can compute the velocity of a hand's motion simply by summing up the distances that a point on the hand (e.g., the upper left corner of the bounding box) moves within a neighborhood of the anchor frame, and dividing by the number of frames elapsed. The neighborhood of a frame is defined as its immediately preceding and following sampled frames. In our case, the velocity can also be normalized to the range of $[0, 1]$ by dividing by the maximum velocity across all videos. This is acceptable since the speakers are centered in the shots in roughly the same way. We denote the normalized velocity at frame f by $\mathbf{v}_f$. This

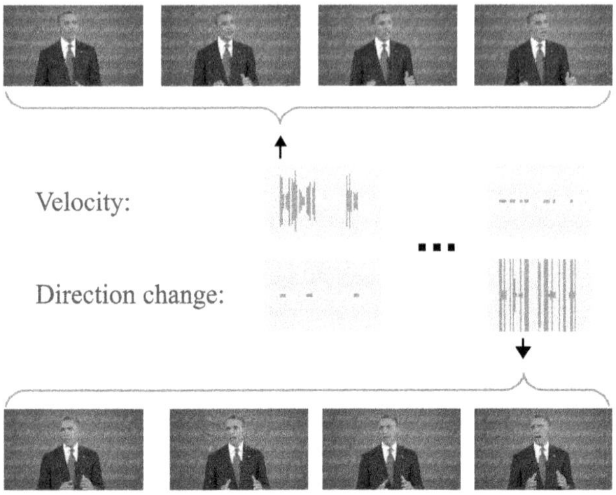

Figure 2: Examples of gestures with high velocity and a low amount of direction change (e.g., a "swipe" motion) and low velocity and high amount of direction change (e.g., a "jittery" beat motion). The graphs of the velocity and direction change are center-aligned.

is computed for each hand, and can be combined simply by taking the maximum across hands for each frame.

4.2 Direction Change

For each frame f, we can also compute the degree of change of direction in the gestures. First, for each hand, we record as a row vector the (x, y) positions of the centroids of each hand bounding box within the neighborhood of each frame g within a row matrix M_g. We subtract the mean of these centroids from each row of the matrix and apply PCA to recover the principal components and the amount of variance associated with each. If a principal component is responsible for a majority of the variance (in our work, at least 75%) then that component is retained as a measure of the direction of the hand movement within the window of frames. We denote this vector at frame g by $\vec{\mathbf{p}}_g$

Next, to compute the degree of direction change in the neighborhood of frame f, we find the maximum angle between principal components in the set of frames. Since the angle is between $[0, \pi]$, it can also be normalized to the range $[0, 1]$. We can compute the normalized angle by:

$$\mathbf{d}_f = \max_{i,j} \left\{ \arccos\left(\frac{\vec{\mathbf{p}}_i \cdot \vec{\mathbf{p}}_j}{||\vec{\mathbf{p}}_i|| \cdot ||\vec{\mathbf{p}}_j||} \right) \right\} / \pi \quad (1)$$

for all i, j in the neighborhood of f.

Like velocity, this is computed for each hand and can be combined by taking the maximum across hands for each frame. Based on both the velocity and direction change attributes, it is possible to identify certain types of motions, such as long "swipe" motions or short and quick "jittery" motions, as shown in Figure 2.

4.3 Extremal Poses

One frequent observation across the related literature and our own research is that gestures vary greatly from person to person. Even so, each individual often forms their own habits. This means that given sufficient information about a person's gestural habits during speech across time, we can therefore identify the moments when they use unusual or extremal poses. We hypothesize that

	First	Third
# Frames w/ Obama's hand(s)		
Only right	1949	907
Only left	6532	12343
Both	11023	4377
# Frames w/ Romney's hand(s)		
Only right	2662	3517
Only left	4774	786
Both	6228	1023

Table 1: Summary of video data used to learn extremal pose models for Obama and Romney. It is interesting to note that Obama's left-handedness is very apparent.

these moments when their body language deviates from their regular patterns may correlate to significant events in the corresponding speech.

We apply [34] to the entire set of 291 shots from Section 3 at 12 Hz to identify the bounding boxes of left and right hands, stratified by speaker and video. This allows us to build a gesture "profile" for each speaker. A summary of the number of frames for each speaker-video-hand grouping is shown in Table 1.

We model the likelihood of a pose as defined by the position of centroids of the bounding boxes of the visible hand(s) in a frame. To do this, we first stratify the video data according to speaker and video. The poses cannot be combined across different debates as their poses vary. That is, in the first debate they stand in front of a podium while in the third, they sit a table.

The model will also depend on how many hands are present—whether it is a left-handed gesture, a right-handed gesture, or a gesture using both hands. The hands in our videos may be partially occluded or simply out of view, but since we are focusing on how gestures affect the audience who sees it, this is nevertheless valid.

We examine the position of the hands for each speaker, across each video, as seen for each speaker in the first debate in the heatmaps in Figure 3. We model the position of each hand as a 2D gaussian distribution. Estimating the gaussians in the cases where only one hand is visible is straightforward. In the case where both hands are visible, we model the positions as a mixture of 2 gaussians, estimated using the expectation-maximization (EM) algorithm.

Finally, as a measure of the likelihood of a given pose, we use a function of the Mahalanobis distance between the position of a hand and its distribution for a given speaker. Since the distance is bounded in our case (i.e., the size of the image is finite), this also provides us a way to normalize the measure to the range $[0, 1]$ consistent with the velocity and direction change attributes described above. In the case where there are two hands, we simply take the maximum Mahalanobis distance of the two (i.e., the most unlikely position).

Formally, for each frame of video, we can compute the likelihood that a pose is unusual as follows. Let $H = \{\text{left}, \text{right}, \text{both}\}$ be the set of hand(s) which may be detected in the frame. Suppose we have trained gaussian mixture models G_i for each $i \in H$ representing the likelihood of the hand position. Let $X = \{(x_i, y_i), \ldots | i \in H\}$ be the set of hand positions in the frame and $h \in H$ be the hand(s) detected in the frame, then the likelihood measure M is simply:

$$M(X|h) = \max_{x \in X} \left\{ \frac{D_{G_i}(x)}{D_{\max}} \right\} \quad (2)$$

where D is the Mahalanobis distance and $D_{\max}$ is the maximum Mahalanobis distance given the size of the image, which we use as a normalization factor.

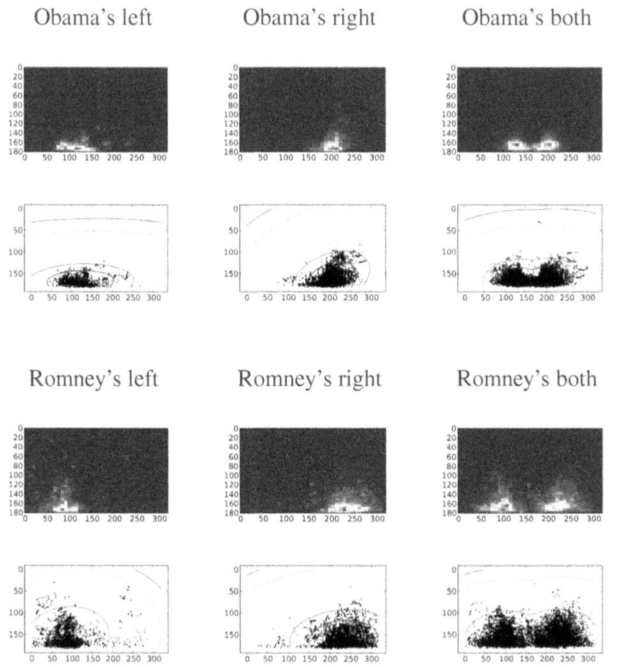

Figure 3: Hand positions and estimated mixtures of Gaussians for the first debate. Contours represent Mahalanobis distances.

5. AUDIENCE ENGAGEMENT

To collect audience engagement data, we showed 6 videos totaling 61 minutes to each of 20 human subjects in an electrostatically shielded room[1]. After discarding noisy data, 47 minutes worth of EEG data (per subject) were retained for analysis. Subjects were instructed to sit comfortably and view the debates attentively, refraining from overt movements. This experiment was approved by the Institutional Review Board of Columbia University and all subjects gave written informed consent prior to the experiment. The order of the video clips were kept the same across subjects. In between each of the 6 videos, subjects were given a break and the experiment did not resume until the subject indicated they were comfortable.

Subjects were fitted with a standard 64-electrode cap following the international 10/10 system, as shown in Figure 4. EEG data was recorded using a BioSemi Active Two AD Box ADC-12[2] system at 2048 Hz which was downsampled to 512 Hz for processing.

5.1 Video Stimuli

We selected 28 of the 291 clips in Section 3: 8 from the first debate and 6 from the third debate featuring Obama, and 8 from the first debate and 6 from the third debate featuring Romney. The total duration of the clips is approximately 30.5 minutes, so each clip is 65 seconds on average.

Next, we manually selected clips in a way that equalizes video time featuring each candidate. The debates also covered a range of topics, as defined by the moderators of the respective debates

[1]ETS-Lindgren, Glendale Heights, IL, USA.

[2]BioSemi, The Netherlands.

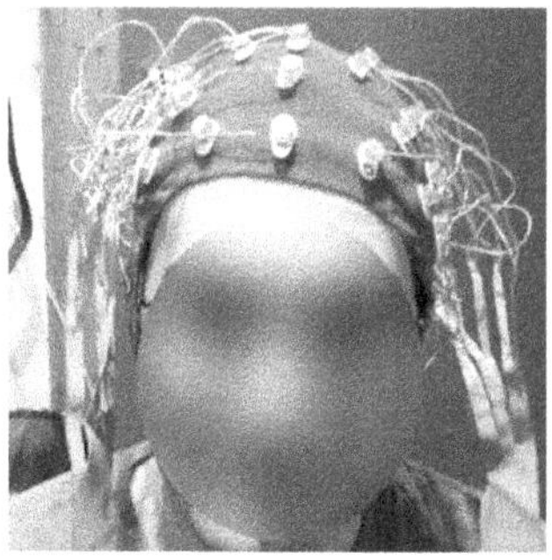

Figure 4: Subject wearing 64-electrode wet-gel EEG cap.

and listed in Figure 5. We also attempted to balance the time each speaker spends discussing each of these topics, i.e., each speaker spends approximately the same amount of time discussing each topic, but the time discussing each topic may differ.

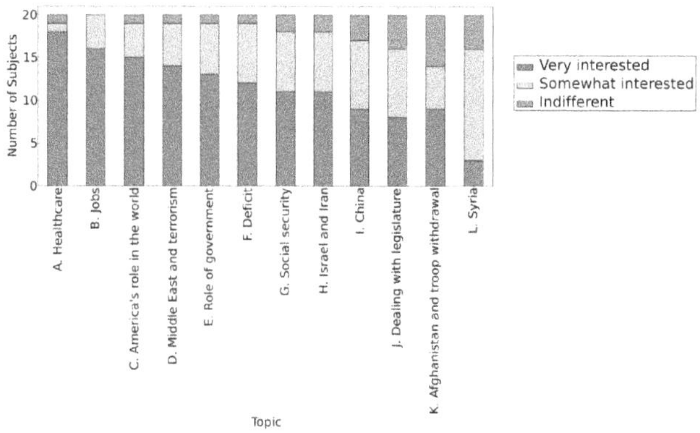

Figure 5: List of topics covered in the video stimuli as defined by the debate moderators, along with subjects' level of interest. Topics are listed in order of increasing weighted subject interest.

Finally, to produce the video stimuli to present to subjects, we randomly shuffled the 28 clips, and then made silent versions of each by removing the audio track. The silent versions were meant to serve as control. In total, we showed 61 minutes of video to each subject. In order to allow for a break approximately every 10 minutes, we separated this into 6 videos. We create each of these 6 "long videos" by concatenating the smaller clips (both audible and silent versions) together, as shown in Figure 6. In each case, the audible clip was always played after its silent version, so that subjects do not associate visual scenes with the spoken content on a second viewing of each clip. Each of the long videos began with a 5-second video of a countdown, followed by the clips, each separated with a 3-second blank (i.e., black screen). The silent and audible versions of each clip were always placed in the same long video, and often shown in pairs (i.e., Silent 1, Silent 2, Audible 1, Audible 2) to reduce the likelihood of subjects associating the audible clip with its silent version (much less likely than the reverse). Randomness in the order (i.e., sometimes the ordering may be Silent 1, Silent 2, Audible 2, Audible 1) as well as the blank video in between clips serve to further mitigate carryover effects. The final durations of the 6 videos were 9.32 minutes, 10.39 minutes, 10.72 minutes, 11.93 minutes, 9.82 minutes and 8.94 minutes.

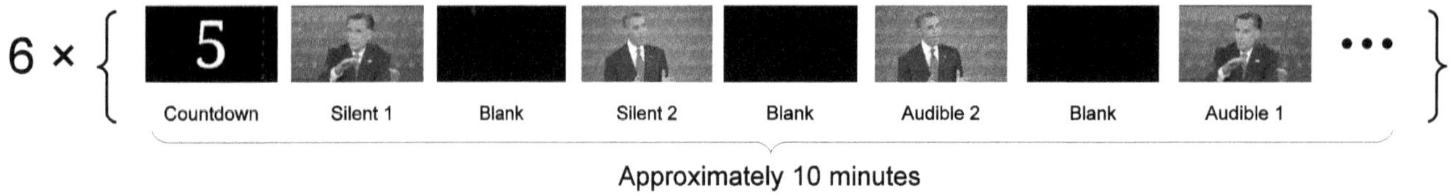

Figure 6: Each of the 6 videos shown to each subject began with a 5-second countdown, followed by silent then audible versions of clips of the debates, each separated with a 3-second blank screen.

Group	No. Subjects	Age		
		Min	Med	Max
All	20	18	21	31
Democrats	10	18	21	29
Republicans	10	18	22	31
Females	10	18	21	29
Males	10	18	21.5	31

Table 2: Range and medians of ages of subjects divided by group.

However, as previously mentioned, noise and artifacts which occurred during the EEG data collection process led us to discard data recorded during both the audible and silent versions of 7 video clips for all subjects. Due to the sensitive nature of the data collection process, noise appears to have been introduced for a number of reasons, including loose electrodes. The audible and silent versions of these 7 clips totaled 14 minutes in duration, therefore leaving us with 47 minutes of EEG data for each subject for analysis.

5.2 Subjects

For this study, we recruited 20 college students and young professionals of various ethnic backgrounds and nationalities. In addition to their age and gender, they were also asked to identify their political leanings on a scale from 1 to 5, where 1 is Strongly Democrat and 5 is Strongly Republican. Only those who were not neutral (i.e., 3) were considered for this experiment. Those who were not American and therefore did not vote but nonetheless followed American politics and thus identified with a political party were included in this experiment.

We stratify subjects according to their political affiliation (Democrat or Republican) and their gender (male or female). The 20 subjects are divided by political affiliation and gender, with ages ranging from 18 to 31 with a median age of 21, as summarized in Table 2.

To account for possible topic bias (i.e., what if one group was overwhelmingly interested in candidates' opinions on healthcare while another was only interested in their thoughts on the Middle East), subjects were also asked to indicate their level of interest in each of the topics from Figure 5 as one of: *indifferent*, *somewhat interested*, or *very interested*. Subjects were selected randomly restricted only by age, gender and political affiliation independent of their interests in the topics. Their responses are aggregated by group and shown in Figure 7. It can be seen that Democrats and Republicans have roughly equal numbers of subjects that are at least somewhat interested in each of the topics. However, more males expressed indifference in each topic than females, therefore we do not believe personal interest in topics is a confounding factor in our correlation analysis of Democrats versus Republicans, but may be one when comparing females versus males. One possible confounding factor when comparing Democrats versus Republicans is the fact that this experiment took place beginning roughly 6 months *after* the 2012 U.S. presidential election, so the outcome was already known. Nevertheless, we believe this should not significantly affect our main hypothesis, that is, how audiences react to speakers' gestures, but it is something to keep in mind when making observations across party lines.

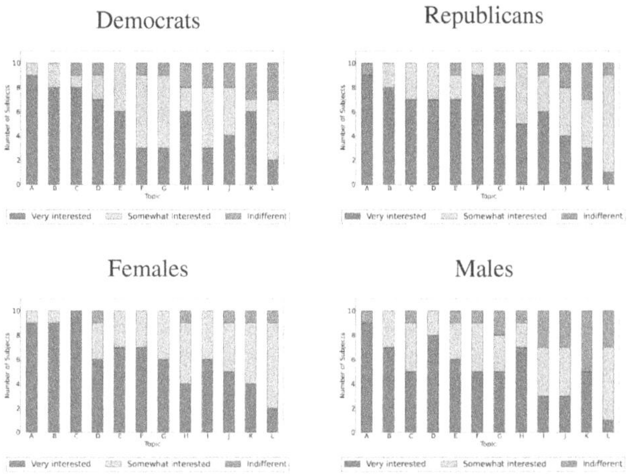

Figure 7: Subjects' interests in each topic, separated by group. Topics correspond to Figure 5. Democrats and Republicans have roughly equal numbers of subjects that are at least somewhat interested in each of the topics. However, more males expressed indifference in each topic than females.

5.3 Deriving Engagement from EEG

Once EEG data was collected from all subjects for each clip, we apply standard post-processing. A software-based 0.5 Hz high pass filter was used to remove DC drifts, and 60 Hz and 120 Hz notch filters were used to minimize line noise. Eye blink artifacts were removed by independent component analysis (ICA) through EEGLAB [8]. EEG samples whose squared magnitude falls above four standard deviations of the mean power of their respective channels were replaced with zero.

To identify moments of engagement, we apply the method of Dmochowski *et al.* [10] on EEG data across all subjects for each clip. Intuitively, this method works on the hypothesis that only moments of stimulus which engage audiences will elicit a common neural response from most audience members, and therefore seeks to find maximal inter-subject correlations between subjects' EEG responses. Lack of engagement, i.e., boredom, would not result in a common neural response as subjects would each focus on different stimuli or at best be randomly time-locked across the subjects so that inter-subject correlation would be minimized.

In this method, for a given clip, let $\mathbf{X}^{(i)} \in \mathbb{R}^{D \times T}$ be the EEG data of subject i where D is the number of channels (electrodes, so $D = 64$) and T is the number of time samples (on average for each clip, $T = 33280$). To estimate engagement from a group of N subjects, we form aggregated matrices $\mathbf{X}_1, \mathbf{X}_2$ as follows:

$$\mathbf{X}_1 = \left[\mathbf{X}^{(1)} \cdots \mathbf{X}^{(1)} \cdots \mathbf{X}^{(N-2)} \; \mathbf{X}^{(N-1)} \right] \quad (3)$$

$$\mathbf{X}_2 = \left[\mathbf{X}^{(2)} \cdots \mathbf{X}^{(N)} \cdots \mathbf{X}^{(N)} \; \mathbf{X}^{(N)} \right] \quad (4)$$

That is, columns of $\mathbf{X}_1, \mathbf{X}_2$ correspond to $\binom{N}{2}$ combinations of pairs of subjects. Therefore, $\mathbf{X}_1, \mathbf{X}_2 \in \mathbb{R}^{D \times \binom{N}{2} T}$. We wish to find a weight vector $\mathbf{w} \in \mathbb{R}^D$ such that the Pearson product-moment correlation coefficient between $\mathbf{y}_1 = \mathbf{X}_1^T \mathbf{w}$ and $\mathbf{y}_2 = \mathbf{X}_2^T \mathbf{w}$ is highest, that is:

$$\mathbf{w} = \arg\max_{\mathbf{w}} \frac{\mathbf{y}_1^T \mathbf{y}_2}{\|\mathbf{y}_1\| \|\mathbf{y}_2\|} \quad (5)$$

After differentiating, $\mathbf{w}$ can be found by solving a generalized eigenvalue problem, following the full derivation in [10]. As such, there are multiple solutions. The weight vector $\mathbf{w}$ that maximizes the correlation coefficient between $\mathbf{y}_1$ and $\mathbf{y}_2$ corresponds to the largest eigenvalue, and similarly for the second, third, etc. Based on prior work and our own examination that most of the variation is carried by the first three components, we take the three weight vectors corresponding to the three largest eigenvalues (i.e., the three strongest correlations) and compute correlations between EEG data after applying these weight vectors. We refer to the results (i.e., correlations) computed from the weight vectors as components 1, 2, 3 (corresponding to the largest eigenvalues and descending).

We can compute correlation at a finer time granularity and determine significance by computing Pearson correlation between corresponding 5-second EEG segments (across subjects for a given clip) at 1-second intervals. To determine significance, a permutation test is applied by splitting the EEG data into 5-second non-overlapping windows, randomly shuffling and taking the correlation at $p = 0.05$ (Bonferroni corrected). An example of inter-subject correlations for a video clip for 3 components and its significance threshold is shown in Figure 8. Distributions of inter-subject correlations for the first component during both audible and silent playback are shown in Figure 9.

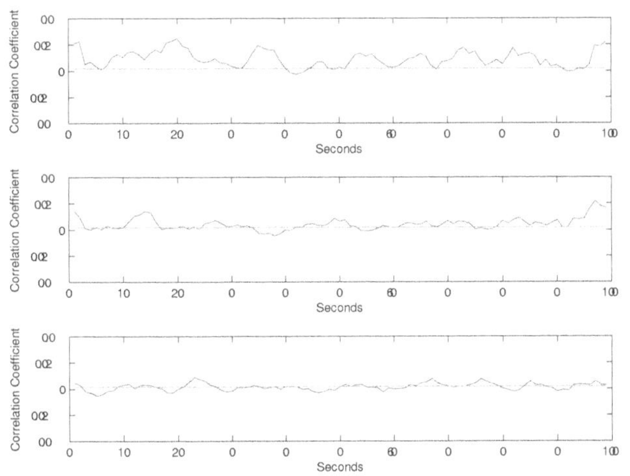

Figure 8: Inter-subject correlation for a video clip for three components (blue line), as computed according to [10]. The red line is the significance threshold. The first component is on top. Note the granularity of the horizontal axis (time).

To summarize, for each clip, the method of [10] gives us a correlation coefficient $r_{t,c} \in [-1, 1]$ at time sample t and the corresponding correlation coefficient $R_{t,c}$ from a permutation test at $p = 0.05$ (a threshold of significance) for each of the top three components c.

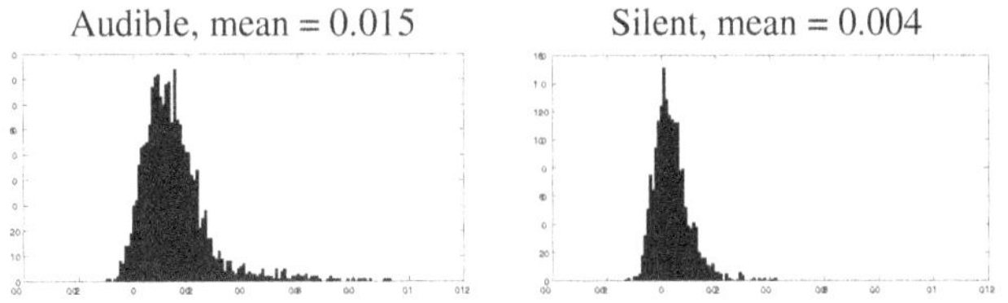

Figure 9: Distributions of the inter-subject correlations during silent and audible playback and their means.

From the weight vector $\mathbf{w}$, we can also compute the scalp projections of the synchronized activity since each weight corresponds to an electrode. This is computed on a per-clip basis across all subjects. We show representative scalp projections for EEG data collected during both audible and silent playbacks of three clips in Figure 10.

In the audible group, electrodes near the visual cortex are given more weight in the first component, potentially implying that subjects are attentively watching the videos. In the second component, more weight is given in regions near the prefrontal cortex—the region of the brain associated with executive function and decision making [25]. One possible implication is that subjects are judging the speakers. The scalp projections for the corresponding clips during silent playback are more difficult to interpret as they are more varied. One possible explanation is that subjects were not paying attention. This is consistent with feedback from subjects after the experiment, who stated that they were "confused" about what to do during the silent videos clips. This is also corroborated by the higher inter-subject correlations during audible playback, as seen in Figure 9. Interpretations for the third component are unclear at this time and we leave that for future work.

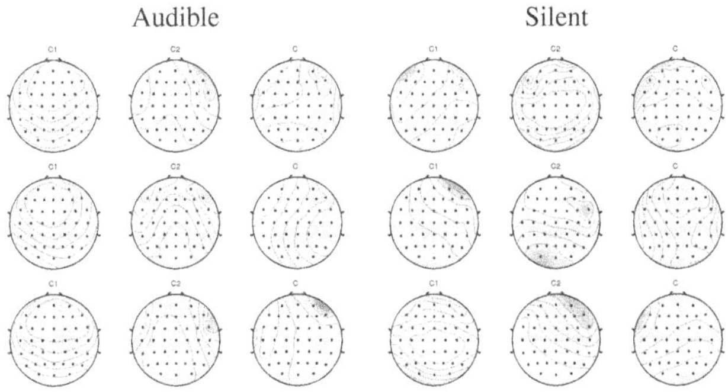

Figure 10: Scalp projections (as seen from above with subject facing 12 o'clock) showing weights given to EEG channels (electrodes) in order to produce the maximally correlated components. The scalp projections are for all subjects for each of three video clips—one on each row—for each audio mode.

6. CORRELATIONS

For both of the silent and audible versions of each clip and each one of the five subject groups, we now have three components of engagement features derived from EEG data. We can also compute three types of gesture attributes for the clip: velocity, direction change, extremal pose, each computed according to Section 4. All of these features are time-synced. The visual features are computed at 12 Hz, so the engagement features (EEG) which were originally computed at 1 Hz must also be upsampled to 12 Hz by linear interpolation. To summarize, for each of the 28 video clips originally selected, we have the following feature vectors:

- **3 gesture attributes**: velocity, direction change, extremal pose.
- **30 engagement features**: 5 subject groups (all, Democrats, Republicans, females, males) $\times$ 2 audio modes (silent, audible) $\times$ 3 components of inter-subject correlations of EEG data with accompanying significance thresholds.

We now wish to find the correlations between the gesture attributes and the engagement features. These are usually computed on a per-clip basis, but to compute the correlations, we concatenate the vectors for all clips. As we are only interested in scenes involving gestures, we discard time samples where no hands were visible. Furthermore, we only wish to consider time samples where our measure of engagement was statistically significant. Therefore, all time samples where inter-subject correlation fell below the significance threshold were also discarded.

Because we do not hypothesize that there is a direct correlation between the exact magnitude of the gesture attributes and the "level" of engagement (i.e., magnitude of the engagement feature)—that is, there is no reason a slightly more emphatic gesture should result in slightly more engagement—we choose a correlation measure that is less dependent on magnitude. Therefore, instead of Pearson product-moment correlation, we use Spearman rank correlation.

In addition to stratifying subjects according to political and gender groups, and audio mode (i.e., whether or not the video clip was audible or silent), we can also stratify the videos according to speaker (Obama or Romney), and debate (first or third).

Tables 3, 4 and 5 show all cases where a statistically significant correlation was found between a visual feature and an EEG component for the various stratifications by speaker, debate and subject group. For conciseness, some stratifications are not shown. The corresponding correlation coefficient at $p = 0.05$ (Bonferroni corrected, assuming 30 hypotheses) is also shown in each table. We discuss observations in Section 7.

To show that the correlation values are significant and meaningful, standard statistical measures are not sufficient. Instead, to determine statistical significance, we take an approach similar to [10]. We perform a permutation test whereby random samples are created by shuffling non-overlapping 5-second windows of the EEG data and correlating against the visual features to form the null distribution.

Subj.	Audio?	ρ	Gesture	EEG	Thres.
Dem	N	0.139	Extremal	1	0.129

Table 3: Statistically significant Spearman rank correlations ρ between gesture attributes and components of engagement features with significance threshold $p < 0.05$ (Bonferroni corrected) for all videos showing Romney or Obama from both the first and third debate. As this is aggregated across both speakers and both debates, statistical significance is less likely.

7. DISCUSSION

From these results, we can make several observations. As we could not account for many of the nuances in political science or the inherent biases in the population from which we selected our subjects, we refrain from making observations regarding differences between groups of subjects.

Subj.	Audio?	ρ	Gesture	EEG	Thres.
Obama					
None					
Romney					
All	N	0.079	Velocity	1	0.069
		0.167	Dir Change	1	0.090
		0.178	Extremal	2	0.133
Rep	Y	0.129	Dir Change	2	0.092
		0.163	Extremal	1	0.132
	N	0.083	Velocity	1	0.069
		0.190	Dir Change	1	0.090
Dem	Y	0.144	Extremal	1	0.132
	N	0.135	Dir Change	1	0.090
		0.254	Extremal	1	0.129
Fem	N	0.141	Extremal	2	0.133
		0.164	Extremal	3	0.131
Male	Y	0.105	Dir Change	1	0.092
		0.249	Extremal	2	0.132
	N	0.098	Velocity	2	0.072
		0.165	Dir Change	2	0.089
		0.167	Extremal	1	0.129

Table 4: Statistically significant Spearman rank correlations ρ between gesture attributes and components of engagement features with significance threshold $p < 0.05$ (Bonferroni corrected) for only the first debate. The implication that Obama did not engage the audience via gesture compared to Romney in the first debate is consistent with bipartisan reports that Obama "lacked energy" in the first debate [22].

Gestures are significant and may augment speech. Statistically significant correlations between gesture attributes and audience engagement exist during both silent and audible playback, suggesting that gestures may help engage audiences even in the presence of sound, although they have a bigger effect in the absence of sound.

Extremal poses and direction change are the most significant gesture attributes. In the majority of the stratifications we examined, the extremal pose gesture attribute resulted in the highest correlations with engagement followed by direction change. This suggests that audience engagement is driven by moments of gesture atypical of the candidate.

The first and second components of the engagement features drives correlation. As these components should correspond to highest and second-highest amounts of variance in the EEG data respectively, this result is consistent. This is also consistent with the results of Dmochowski *et al.* [10].

While audible videos are more engaging in general, silent videos are more likely to engage via gesture. The original goal of having subjects watch clips without sound was to use those results as a control. However, it appears that without sound, subjects paid less attention. As previously mentioned in Section 5.3 and Figure 10, the first component of the scalp projections for subjects watching audible clips shows higher weights around the visual cortex, while the scalp projections for the silent clips appear to be less focused. This is further corroborated by the higher average inter-subject correlation during audible versus silent playback, as seen in Figure 9. However, higher correlations were more likely to occur between gestures and engagement during silent playback, sug-

Subj.	Audio?	ρ	Gesture	EEG	Thres.
Obama					
All	N	0.113	Velocity	2	0.072
		0.243	Extremal	3	0.131
Dem	N	0.182	Dir Change	1	0.090
		0.256	Extremal	1	0.129
Fem	Y	0.179	Extremal	3	0.133
Male	Y	0.107	Dir Change	1	0.092
	N	0.176	Extremal	2	0.133
Romney					
All	Y	0.080	Velocity	1	0.073
		0.149	Velocity	3	0.073
		0.261	Dir Change	3	0.096
		0.198	Extremal	1	0.132
	N	0.106	Dir Change	1	0.090
		0.130	Extremal	1	0.129
		0.156	Extremal	2	0.133
Rep	Y	0.142	Extremal	3	0.133
	N	0.227	Extremal	2	0.133
Dem	Y	0.114	Dir Change	3	0.096
		0.189	Extremal	2	0.132
	N	0.106	Dir Change	1	0.090
		0.221	Extremal	3	0.131
Fem	Y	0.097	Dir Change	2	0.092
	N	0.117	Velocity	3	0.068
		0.194	Dir Change	2	0.089
		0.123	Dir Change	3	0.087
Male	Y	0.190	Velocity	2	0.072
		0.223	Extremal	1	0.132
	N	0.283	Extremal	2	0.133

Table 5: Statistically significant Spearman rank correlations ρ between gesture attributes and components of engagement features with significance threshold $p < 0.05$ (Bonferroni corrected) for only the third debate.

gested that in the absence of sound, gestures were more effective at engaging the audience. It is certainly encouraging to see that, for the most part, people watch debates to listen to what the candidates have to say.

Obama did not engage the audience through gesture in the first debate, whereas Romney did so in both debates. This is consistent with bipartisan reports that Obama "lost" the first debate and lacked energy [22]. As can be seen in Table 4, there were no statistically significant correlations between gesture and engagement during playback of Obama's videos. However, Obama recovered in his third debate, with many significant correlations, as seen in Table 5. Romney, on the other hand, showed many significant correlations in both the first and third debates.

8. CONCLUSION

We have built an argument for using speaker gestures as visual cues for video indexing by demonstrating their correlation with an EEG-derived signal believed to encode group-level engagement. By indexing based on speaker gestures, video search and browsing applications could potentially highlight video segments that are more likely to engage viewers.

Psychologists and linguists have long observed the importance of gestures in communication. We studied this relationship by taking a more quantitative approach and sought to find an application by building tools for automatically extracting gesture attributes.

8.1 Future Work

More gesture attributes. In this paper, we have closely examined three automatically extracted gesture attributes against audience engagement. While we found interesting results, we do not claim that these span the breadth of human gesture. Indeed our attributes were limited to those which could be derived solely from hand positions. Other possible attributes include: hand poses (e.g., the shape of the hand—is it pointing, in a fist, an open palm, etc.), body orientation, and head movements (e.g., head shaking, nodding, etc.).

Study the co-occurrence of words, gesture and engagement. Some words may naturally co-occur with gesture and catch audiences' attention. We attempted a preliminary study of this by examining temporally-aligned stemmed words in the presidential debates and their corresponding segments (within a 5-second window) of Spearman correlations between extremal pose and engagement, and we plotted these values in histograms for words with at least 15 occurrences, as shown in Figure 11. Clearly the amount of data is insufficient for any conclusions, but do suggest potentially interesting results, e.g., the words *business* and *(interest) rate*, which are very politically charged, appear to have a skewed distribution of correlation coefficients. An interpretation remains for future work.

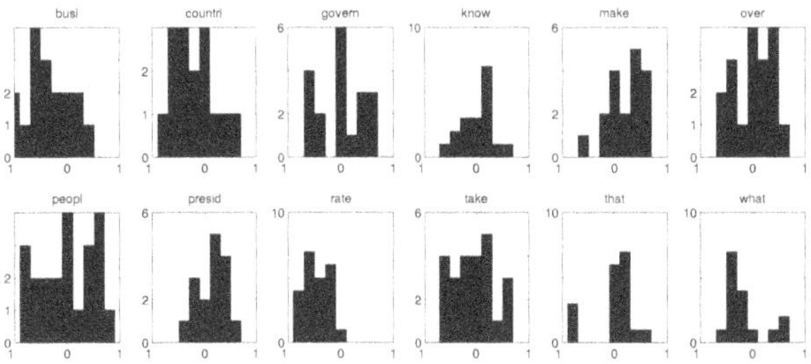

Figure 11: Co-occurrences of specific word stems and speaker gestures and audience engagement. The histograms show the correlation coefficients between extremal pose and engagement features which co-occurred within a 5-second window of a specific word (the word stem is shown).

How other modalities correlate with engagement. We have collected an interesting dataset of audience engagement as measured through neural activity. Naturally, it would be interesting to see what other features beyond gesture may elicit audiences' attention. Some existing works have demonstrated the multimodal nature of gestures and how speech may affect engagement (e.g., [11, 15, 21, 31]). Our dataset offers an opportunity to study other features against engagement in a quantitative way. Examining how low-level audio features may correlate with engagement is one obvious direction for future work.

9. ACKNOWLEDGMENTS

This research was partially supported by the Army Research Laboratory (under Cooperative Agreement Number W911NF-10-2-0022 and W911NF-12-2-0019), the Army Research Office (W911NF-11-1-0219) and a fellowship funded by the David and Helen Gurley Brown Institute for Media Innovation at the Columbia University Graduate School of Journalism. The views and conclusions contained in this document are those of the authors and should not be interpreted as representing the official policies, either expressed or implied, of the Army Research Laboratory or the U.S. Government.

10. REFERENCES

[1] P. Buehler, M. Everingham, D. P. Huttenlocher, and A. Zisserman. Long term arm and hand tracking for continuous sign language TV broadcasts. In *Proc. British Machine Vision Conference*, 2008.

[2] P. Buehler, M. Everingham, and A. Zisserman. Learning sign language by watching TV (using weakly aligned subtitles). In *Proc. Computer Vision and Pattern Recognition*, 2009.

[3] P. Bull. The use of hand gesture in political speeches: Some case studies. *J. Language and Social Psychology*, 5(2):103–118, 1986.

[4] P. E. Bull and G. Connelly. Body movement and emphasis in speech. *J. Nonverbal Behavior*, pages 169–187, 1985.

[5] G. Buscher, E. Cutrell, and M. R. Morris. What do you see when you're surfing?: using eye tracking to predict salient regions of web pages. In *Proc. SIGCHI Conf. Human Factors in Computing Systems*, pages 21–30, 2009.

[6] G. Buscher, S. T. Dumais, and E. Cutrell. The good, the bad, and the random: an eye-tracking study of ad quality in web search. In *Proc. SIGIR Conf. Research and Development in Information Retrieval*, pages 42–49, 2010.

[7] D. Casasanto and K. Jasmin. Good and bad in the hands of politicians: Spontaneous gestures during positive and negative speech. *PLoS One*, 5(7):e11805, 2010.

[8] A. Delorme and S. Makeig. EEGLAB: an open source toolbox for analysis of single-trial EEG dynamics including independent component analysis. *J. Neuroscience Methods*, 134(1):9–21, 2004.

[9] N. A. Diakopoulos and D. A. Shamma. Characterizing debate performance via aggregated twitter sentiment. In *Proc. SIGCHI Conf. Human Factors in Computing Systems*, pages 1195–1198, 2010.

[10] J. P. Dmochowski, P. Sajda, J. Dias, and L. C. Parra. Correlated components of ongoing EEG point to emotionally laden attention–a possible marker of engagement? *Frontiers in Human Neuroscience*, 6, 2012.

[11] J. Eisenstein and R. Davis. Visual and linguistic information in gesture classification. In *SIGGRAPH 2006 Courses*, page 30, New York, NY, USA, 2006.

[12] V. Ferrari, M. Marin-Jimenez, and A. Zisserman. Progressive search space reduction for human pose estimation. In *Proc. Computer Vision and Pattern Recognition*, June 2008.

[13] N. Freedman. Hands, words, and mind: On the structuralization of body movements during discourse and the capacity for verbal representation. In *Communicative Structures and Psychic Structures*, pages 109–132. 1977.

[14] D. Glowinski, N. Dael, A. Camurri, G. Volpe, M. Mortillaro, and K. R. Scherer. Multi-scale entropy analysis of dominance in social creative activities. *T. Affective Computing*, 2(2):106–118, 2011.

[15] B. J. Grosz and C. L. Sidner. Attention, intentions, and the structure of discourse. *Computational Linguistics*, 12(3):175–204, 1986.

[16] S. J. Hanson, A. D. Gagliardi, and C. Hanson. Solving the brain synchrony eigenvalue problem: conservation of temporal dynamics (fmri) over subjects doing the same task. *J. Computational Neuroscience*, 27(1):103–114, 2009.

[17] U. Hasson, Y. Nir, I. Levy, G. Fuhrmann, and R. Malach. Intersubject synchronization of cortical activity during natural vision. *Science*, 303(5664):1634–1640, 2004.

[18] J. M. Jones. Record-high 40% of americans identify as independents in '11. http://www.gallup.com/poll/151943/record-high-americans-identify-independents.aspx, 2012.

[19] T. Kadir, R. Bowden, E. Ong, and A. Zisserman. Minimal training, large lexicon, unconstrained sign language recognition. In *Proc. British Machine Vision Conference*, volume 1, 2004.

[20] A. Kapur, A. Kapur, N. Virji-Babul, G. Tzanetakis, and P. F. Driessen. Gesture-based affective computing on motion capture data. In *Affective Computing and Intelligent Interaction*, pages 1–7. Springer, 2005.

[21] S. Kettebekov, M. Yeasin, and R. Sharma. Improving continuous gesture recognition with spoken prosody. In *Proc. Computer Vision and Pattern Recognition*, 2003.

[22] M. Landler and P. Baker. After debate, Obama team tries to regain its footing. http://www.nytimes.com/2012/10/05/us/politics/obama-team-tries-to-change-course-after-debate-disappoints.html, 2012.

[23] Y.-F. Ma, L. Lu, H.-J. Zhang, and M. Li. A user attention model for video summarization. In *Proc. ACM Multimedia*, 2002.

[24] A. Mehrabian. Pleasure-arousal-dominance: A general framework for describing and measuring individual differences in temperament. *Current Psychology*, 14(4):261–292, 1996.

[25] E. K. Miller, D. J. Freedman, and J. D. Wallis. The prefrontal cortex: categories, concepts and cognition. *Philosophical Transactions of the Royal Society of London. Series B: Biological Sciences*, 357(1424):1123–1136, 2002.

[26] A. Mittal, A. Zisserman, and P. Torr. Hand detection using multiple proposals. In *Proc. British Machine Vision Conference*, 2011.

[27] Y. I. Nakano and R. Ishii. Estimating user's engagement from eye-gaze behaviors in human-agent conversations. In *Proc. Int. Conf. Intelligent User Interfaces*, 2010.

[28] A. Smeaton, P. Over, and A. Doherty. Video shot boundary detection: Seven years of trecvid activity. *Computer Vision and Image Understanding*, 114(4):411–418, 2010.

[29] D. L. Strayer, J. M. Watson, and F. A. Drews. Cognitive distraction while multitasking in the automobile. *Psychology of Learning and Motivation-Advances in Research and Theory*, 54:29, 2011.

[30] S. Tavernise. Brain test to diagnose A.D.H.D. is approved. http://www.nytimes.com/2013/07/16/health/brain-test-to-diagnose-adhd-is-approved.html, 2013.

[31] M. Watanabe, Y. Den, K. Hirose, S. Miwa, and N. Minematsu. Features of pauses and conjunctions at syntactic and discourse boundaries in japanese monologues. In *INTERSPEECH*, 2007.

[32] G. V. Xaquin, A. McLean, A. Tse, and S. Peçanha. What Romney and Obama's body language says to voters. http://www.nytimes.com/interactive/2012/10/02/us/politics/what-romney-and-obamas-body-language-says-to-voters.html, 2012.

[33] Y. Yang and D. Ramanan. Articulated pose estimation with flexible mixtures-of-parts. In *Proc. Computer Vision and Pattern Recognition*, 2011.

[34] J. R. Zhang and J. R. Kender. Recognizing and tracking clasping and occluded hands. In *Proc. Int. Conf. Image Processing*, Sept 2013.

How 'How' Reflects What's What: Content-based Exploitation of How Users Frame Social Images

Michael Riegler[2], Martha Larson[3], Mathias Lux[1], Christoph Kofler[3]
[1]Institute for Information Technology, University of Klagenfurt, Austria
[2]Media Performance Group, Simula Research Laboratory AS, Norway
[3]Multimedia Computing Group, Delft University of Technology, Netherlands
michael@simula.no, {m.a.larson, c.kofler}@tudelft.nl, mlux@itec.aau.at

ABSTRACT

In this paper, we introduce the concept of *intentional framing*, defined as the sum of the choices that a photographer makes on *how* to portray the subject matter of an image. We carry out analysis experiments that demonstrate the existence of a correspondence between image similarity that is calculated automatically on the basis of global feature representations, and image similarity that is perceived by humans at the level of intentional frames. Intentional framing has profound implications: The existence of a fundamental image-interpretation principle that explains the importance of global representations in capturing human-perceived image semantics reaches beyond currently dominant assumptions in multimedia research. The ability of fast global-feature approaches to compete with more 'sophisticated' approaches, which are computationally more complex, is demonstrated using a simple search method (SimSea) to classify a large (2M) collection of social images by tag class. In short, intentional framing provides a principled connection between human interpretations of images and lightweight, fast image processing methods. Moving forward, it is critical that the community explicitly exploits such approaches, as the social image collections that we tackle, continue to grow larger.

Categories and Subject Descriptors

H.3.3 [**Information Storage and Retrieval**]: Information Search and Retrieval

Keywords

Intentional framing; human interpretation of images; user intention; image classification

1. INTRODUCTION

Conventionally, multimedia researchers assume that what an image is about is primarily related to its literal subject matter, i.e., the visually depicted entities, events or scenes.

MM'14, November 3–7, 2014, Orlando, Florida, USA.
Copyright 2014 ACM 978-1-4503-3063-3/14/11 ...$15.00.
http://dx.doi.org/10.1145/2647868.2654894.

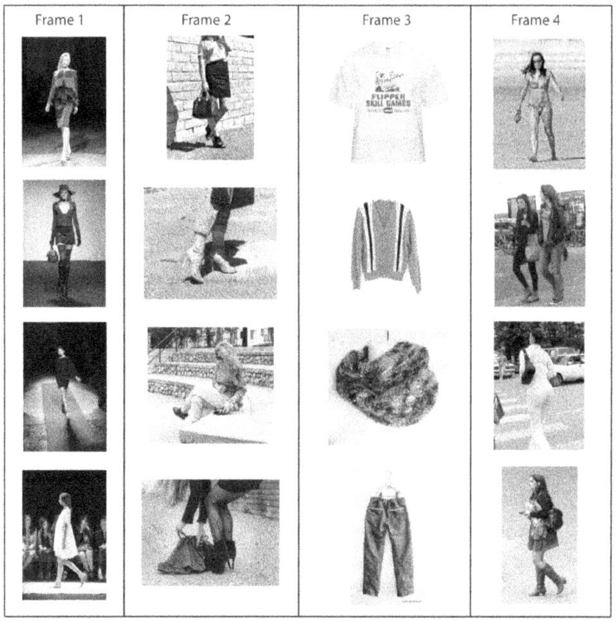

Figure 1: Four intentional frames reflect four different photographer intents (i.e., *how* users took the images). They are all indicative of the overall topic 'fashion' (i.e., *what* the images depict). Global-feature similarity suffices to capture intentional frames. Computationally intensive approaches are not necessarily required.

In this paper, we go beyond this conventional viewpoint and demonstrate that *what* an image is about is also reflected in *how* that image was taken. This new perspective benefits content-based approaches to large-scale social image collections, since it can be exploited in a simple, computationally lightweight fashion.

The core of the new perspective is the principle that we refer to as the *intentional framing*. We define intentional framing as, 'the sum of the choices made by photographers on exactly *how* to portray the subject matter that they have decided to photograph.' Note that intentional framing is a photographic act carried out by a photographer. Automatically captured images, such as security camera images, are not expected to exhibit framing effects. Fig. 1 provides an illustration of four ways in which 'fashion' is depicted in user photos on Flickr, a large online social photo-sharing community. These four different cases of *how* the subject matter of a photo is portrayed, correspond to four visually distinctive *intentional frames.* In Sections 2 and 4, we will return to discuss this figure in more detail, including the relationship between these intentional frames and image similarly calculated automatically on the basis of global image features. Here, we first focus on introducing intentional framing, and describing its importance for multimedia research.

Our definition of intentional framing arises from the following considerations. When taking a photograph, the photographer does not click the shutter randomly, but first decides on a message and a subject. The decision process involves applying, either consciously or unconsciously, a set of conventions. These conventions can be thought as a recipe for a certain kind of image. This recipe is the intentional frame. The fact that the photographer applies a specific intentional frame leads to the generation of an image with distinguishable characteristics. These characteristics are visible in the image, and are used, again, either consciously or unconsciously, by humans in order to interpret the image.

When human viewers interpret an image at the level of its intentional frame, they are making a very high-level semantic judgement. The important role that intentional frame judgements play in human interpretations of images can be illustrated using a short thought experiment. Imagine a home with portraits of family members hanging on the wall. The subject matter (i.e., the *what*) of a portrait image is a person. In taking the image (i.e., the *how*), the photographer had the intent of creating a portrait. What would happen if the portraits of the family members were replaced with mugshots of the family members? This would be a strange situation. A visitor to this home would not easily be able to interpret the wall. A mugshot, like a portrait, portrays a person (i.e., the subject matter has remained the same). However, it is a very different image. The photographer who captures a mugshot has the intention of taking a picture that will be used by the police for identification purposes. This thought experiment demonstrates that two photos with the same literal subject matter (n.B. both a portrait and a mugshot are a photo of a person) are interpreted by the human mind in radically different ways.

The distinction between 'portrait' and 'mugshot' is a simple example used for the purposes of illustration. In this paper, we will investigate neither portraits nor mugshots specifically, but rather use a data-driven approach to explore intentional framing effects in large social image collections. However, by conducting this thought experiment, it is already possible to appreciate the profound implications of the concept of intentional framing for the multimedia field.

First, in order to arrive at image analysis algorithms that are truly capable of mimicking human image interpretation, image analysis algorithms should be 'aware' of the photographer's intention. In other words, they should be able to capture the visual differences that characterize images that were taken with different intents. For example, if humans find the difference between the intentional frames 'mugshot' and 'portrait' to be important, multimedia analysis algorithms need to make this distinction, too.

Second, sensitivity to very high-level semantic judgements, such as those related to intentional frames, will become critical as social image collections continue to grow larger. As pointed out by [13], an image retrieval system that indexes images by detecting basic concepts such as 'dog' cannot effectively support users to search huge social image collections. Even if the relative number of images depicting a 'dog' in the collection is small, if the collection is large enough, a 'dog' detector will detect thousands of dog images, i.e., many more than a user can use in a results' list. Instead, image analysis algorithms are needed which focus on specific aspects of images that are important to users and go beyond the basic concepts they depict. We do not claim that intentional framing is the only way in which human interpretations transcend the literal subject matter of an image. However, it is clear that it is an important contributing factor, and should for this reason be taken into account.

Finally, because of the fact that intentional framing impacts the overall 'look and feel' of images, differences in intentional framing can be captured by simple, lightweight approaches that exploit global representations. Such approaches are critical for allowing image analysis algorithms to scale and handle more and more images, as techniques for image indexing and retrieval are needed for larger and larger collections.

In short, intentional framing is important to the multimedia research community because it provides a principled motivation for applying lightweight approaches, exploiting global-feature representations to large-scale social image collections. The purpose of this paper is to establish the existence of intentional framing as a fundamental principle of human image interpretation, and to demonstrate its importance for content-based approaches to large-scale collections of social images. This paper makes three major contributions: (i) introduce intentional framing as a fundamental principle important for human interpretation of images at a high level of semantic abstraction, (ii) demonstrate that human-perceived similarity with respect to intentional frame corresponds to automatic similarity computed using global-feature representations of images and (iii) show that adopting the intentional framing perspective leads to a back-to-the-basics approach that relies exclusively on global-features to capture image semantics. Our approach delivers image classification rates that compete with the state of the art, while saving significantly in computational complexity.

We finish this section with an overview of the line of argumentation followed in the remainder of the paper. In Section 2, we discuss the related work, and demonstrate that although intentional framing is related to other phenomena studied in the literature, it cannot be reduced to any of them. In Section 3, we explain the concept of intentional framing in greater detail and provide illustrative examples.

Next, Section 4 presents two analysis experiments on human interpretations of images with respect to intentional framing. The experiments involve a user study and explore the judgments that humans make about images at the level of intentional frames. They establish the existence of a correspondence between automatic image similarity calculated on the basis of global features and human perceptions of images with respect to intentional frame.

This correspondence motivates us, in Section 5, to propose a back-to-the-basics simple search approach (SimSea) that leverages global feature representations to classify social images. We report results on standard image-classification task, 2013 Yahoo! Large-scale Flickr-tag Image Classification ACM Multimedia Grand Challenge. The results are surprising: a simple global-feature approach such as SimSea is able to compete with more 'sophisticated' content-based algorithms. Intentional framing, however, constitutes a principled reason why we should actually expect such results. Our conclusion, presented Section 6, opens up a future perspective.

2. RELATED WORK

Our coverage of related work first positions intentional framing with respect to other phenomena related to image semantics. We point to previous work that, plausibly, has taken advantage of the principle of intentional framing, without being aware of its existence. Finally, we cover the lightweight, search-based image classification approaches.

2.1 Intentional Frames and Image Semantics

Intentional framing is distinct from other aspects of image semantics because it focuses on 'how' the photographer has realized an image rather than 'what' is depicted in the image. There are three major research areas that seek to analyze images in terms of 'what' they portray: concepts, scenes, and events, which all focus on the literally depicted subject material of an image. Here, we cover each in turn.

Concepts: In context of image retrieval and analysis, concepts are objects and other entities that are literally depicted in images. The larger notion of a 'concept' derives from psychology and cognitive science, which has put forth various theories on human concept representations, e.g., concepts as definitions vs. concepts as mental images [33]. Independently of the exact mechanism involved, it is clear that concepts play a role in how humans store, organize and manipulate information about the world around them. For this reason, image analysis research has invested a great deal of effort into developing algorithms capable of detecting visual concepts [10].

An example of the variety covered by concepts is provided by the *ImageCLEF* concept detection task. Here, both categories of high-level semantic abstraction, such as 'fauna', 'age' or 'weather', are used alongside categories of lower abstraction levels, such as 'cat' and 'plant' [1]. Essentially, anything that is nameable by human observer can be considered a concept. Under this perspective, a scene or an event is considered a concept—scenes emphasize the positioning of elements and events include temporal sequence [23]. We turn to discuss both scenes and events in more detail.

Scenes: Scene interpretation has its roots in perception psychology. Scene perception describes the visual perception of an environment as seen by an observer at a given time. Rensink [27] describes perception of a scene as high, mid and low level processing steps. Long-term human learning results in a *scene schema* that interlinks the types of objects that occur together.

In the area of machine learning and content-based image retrieval, the notion of *gist* has been used to address the analysis of scenes. Gist originated in language analysis, and was introduced into image analysis by Friedman [7]. In the context of images, the gist is a description of a scene's overall meaning, such as 'farmyard', 'shopping center', or 'city' [27]. Olivia et al. [24] used global features to detect the gist of a scene. Global features capture global attributes of an image related to edges, colors or texture. Hays et al. [8, 9] used the idea of gist to address tasks related to geo-coordinates, such as geo-location detection and geo-scene completion.

The gist of a scene and the intentional framing of an image are related in the way that they both aim to capture global image characteristics. For this reason, global feature representations are suitable for both. However, intentional framing is a much broader notion that gist, since gist is restricted to 'what' is depicted in *scenes*, and intentional framing encompasses 'how' the subject material is presented in a *general social image*. The difference between scenes and intentional frames can be appreciated by considering Fig. 1. The notion of scenes is not adequate to account for the difference between the four frames. Instead we introduce intentional framing to go beyond the gist of scenes and to capture these differences.

Events: An event is a specific incident taking place at or over a given time span, involving one or more actors or objects and a specific place. Events often provide subject material for social images: weddings, parties, concerts, and sports events are favorite subjects of photos that users take and share online. Specific to the area of image analysis, an image may depict an event, but it is usually just a snapshot of the event and cannot cover every single aspect of it [12].

Work that has been done on Multimedia Event Detection, exemplified by the work in [22], is devoted to the detection of specific types of human activities, corresponding to types of events. This work focuses on detecting instances of particular event types, e.g., identify multimedia content that depicts a 'kiss' as a human activity. In contrast, a newer breed of work done on Social Event Detection is devoted to detect multimedia content that depicts a specific social event. This work focuses on identifying, for example, whether a photo was captured at a particular wedding. Examples of work on social events include [28], which uses candidate-retrieval methods and machine learning functions to automatically detect events in a stream and [26], which tackles social event detection by using multi-modal clustering and the integration of supervisory signals. Image analysis aiming to identify events, does not cover the same range of phenomena addressed by intentional framing. Note that although human activities and events are depicted in the images in Fig. 1, they do not provide a complete characterization of the differences between the four intentional frames.

To sum up, intentional framing, which focuses on 'how' images are taken, plays a significant role in human image interpretation. This role goes beyond aspects of image semantics that focus on 'what' is depicted in images, including concepts, scenes, and events. We close by mentioning a additional difference between 'the how' and 'the what' of images. Users/viewers recognize that two pictures are similar with respect to an intentional frame—referring again to Fig. 1, note the similarities among the images in each column. This recognition does not imply that it is easy, or even possible, to give an intentional frame a specific name. In contrast, concepts, scenes and events are often readily nameable (e.g., 'cat', 'farmyard' and 'kiss' above). We find that the fact that intentional frames are so difficult to be named, helps to explain why this important principle has been overlooked by the multimedia community thus far. This paper aims to compensate for past inattention.

2.2 Covert Exploitation of Framing

Although our basic position is that intentional framing has been overlooked by the multimedia community, we do *not* claim that it has never before been exploited. In this paper, we make the case that intentional framing is an integral part of the act of creating a photo and that, for this reason, we should expect the visual reflexes of intentional framing to act as a social signal that gives rise to exploitable patterns in large collections of social images. If we consider intentional framing to be a fundamental principle underlying human image interpretation, then it is odd to assume that the multimedia community has entirely missed its existence up until this moment. Instead, we consider it to be highly likely that past work in the area of image analysis and retrieval has made use intentional framing effects without being aware of it. Specifically, we make the point that any approach that exploits content based comparison, e.g., pairwise similarity, of images may also be capturing regularities in 'how' the images were photographed alongside of regularities in 'what' the images depict.

Here we mention a two specific social image analysis approaches that we suspect might already exploiting 'how' alongside of 'what'. In Li et al. [15], social tag relevance is learned with a visual neighbor voting algorithm. The approach searches for similar images based on a query image. It cannot be excluded that such similarity is indirectly picking up on 'how' images are taken, in addition to 'what' they literally depict. Another example is Liu et al.'s [16] work on tag propagation. This work makes use of a tag-specific visual sub-vocabulary. Such a sub-vocabulary could easily be exploiting 'how' images are photographed alongside of 'what' they depict. We believe that there are a large number of examples of research that may be unwittingly exploiting intentional framing. An key contribution of this paper is to point out the existence of intentional framing, with the goal of stimulating research on its explicit exploitation. If an algorithm already benefits implicitly from intentional framing, we believe it can only be improved by understanding the extent of this benefit, and by actively seeking to enhance it. In this paper, we do not directly quantify the benefits of intentional framing, but rather focus on laying a solid groundwork for future work in that direction.

2.3 Search-based Image Classification

Finally, we turn to discussing work related to our search-based image classification approach, SimSea. We would like to explicitly point out that SimSea itself does not constitute a major contribution of this paper. Rather, we introduce SimSea as a back-to-the-basics algorithm that exploits global-feature representations. Its effectiveness is rather mysterious, until we take the perspective that global features are capable of capturing the semantics of large-scale social image collections because they are sensitive to the semantics associated with intentional frames.

SimSea is a search-based approach representing a variant of the well-known k-NN algorithm. The multimedia item to be classified is used as a query, and a similarity metric is applied to retrieve a ranked list of the most similar items in a collection of multimedia items that has been labeled with category labels. The category labels of the top-ranked items are then propagated to the query image. The work most closely related to ours is the geo-visual ranking approach to content-based prediction of image location [14]. Here, the location of a photo is predicted by using the photo as a query to retrieve a list of geo-visual neighbors from a social image collection, and propagating the most visual likely location to the photo.

Additionally, Wang et al. [34] and Yang and Hanjalic [35] use similar approaches in their work. However, these use both image features and text features, and focus on re-ranking search results. In contrast, our approach relies exclusively on the visual channel, is not deployed for concept detection, and is tested at a much larger scale.

3. INTENTIONAL FRAMING

In this section, we present the concept of framing in more detail. Specifically, we discuss photographers' choices that lead to intentional framing, and we provide examples of intentional framing in social image collections, illustrating its link to human interpretations and its generality.

In the most general sense, frames are organizational structures in which information is communicated or understood. They have been extensively studied in the field of communication, which investigates a wide and disparate range of framing phenomena [6, 29]. Across phenomena, however, it is agreed that frames regulate *how* information is communicated, rather than directly determining *what* is communicated. In describing how frames work, Entman [6] states, 'Frames highlight some bits of information about an item that is the subject of a communication, thereby elevating them in salience' (p. 53). Similarly, the decisions that a photographer makes when taking a photograph determine which information in the photographs gets noticed or interpreted as important by the viewer.

3.1 Photographers' Choices

Recall that we have defined intentional framing as, 'the sum of the choices made by photographers on exactly *how* to portray the subject matter that they have decided to photograph.' We use the term 'intentional framing', rather than simply 'framing' to emphasize that the 'frame' is the visible reflexes of the *intent* of the photographer to create a certain type of image. The term 'intentional framing' also disambiguates our use of the word 'framing' from another use common in photography. Specifically, photographers use 'framing' to refer to positioning the subject of a photo within a door or other opening that acts like a window frame in a photograph. This sense of 'framing' is not the one that we are addressing here.

Choices a photographer makes to achieve certain types of framing include color distribution, lighting, positions of objects and people, camera angle, depth of field, and focus. They also include the choice of the precise moment during ongoing action at which the image is shot. In this way, the photographer also influences exactly what is depicted in the image, for example, facial expressions of the people appearing in the image. In general, the influence of the photographer reflects not so much personal choices, but rather shared expectations between photographers and viewers about how photos portray the world. These expectations constitute a set of conventions that allow viewers to interpret photos. Radically creative photography may make breaks with conventions, but photos that stray too far from familiar recipes are difficult to interpret.

The importance of intentional framing for photographers is witnessed by the way how it is described on websites that teach photography. For example, Fodors provides a web tutorial for travel photography [31]. Several different methods for framing photos are described, each related to different subject matter: 'classic vacation shots', 'the man-made world', 'the natural world', 'the elements' and 'people'. Each is broken down into finer-grained topic related categories.

Clearly, the decisions that photographers make that determine intentional framing are closely related to composi-

Figure 2: Example Flickr images that depict the same visual contents (a woman and a man), but correspond to two different intentional frames (left: holiday memories and right: fashion)

Table 1: The metadata for the images in Fig. 2 reflecting the different underlying intents of the user/photographer

	Left image	**Right image**
Title	Thingvellir	DCU Fashion Show 2009
Tags	trip, iceland, reykjavik, ...	fashion, Cirque Du Couture dcu, Couture, ...
Description	Iceland 2009.	DCU Style Society presents DCU FASHION SHOW 2009 ...

tion. The composition of a photograph includes the arrangement of objects, the angle, the focus or the distribution of colors in a photograph. Although composition choices contribute to intentional framing, intentional framing cannot be reduced to composition. We explicitly point out that intentional framing also includes choices beyond composition, such as whether human subjects are visibly expressing emotion, and the choice of the exact setting. The fact that photographers consider intentional framing as a way to extend beyond composition is illustrated by the organization of the tutorial [31]. Here, methods for framing photos are *not* treated under the heading 'Photography composition rules'. There are rather separate sections dedicated to composition and to framing. We are interested in the broader concept of framing rather than the narrower concept of composition as it is more tightly related to the topic of the image, which makes it a better indicator of image semantics.

3.2 Intentional Frames in Practice

In Fig. 2, we present two social images from Flickr that both depict the same basic content, a woman and a man, but differ in respect to their intentional framing. We can gain insight into the intent of the users that took these images by inspecting their titles, tags and descriptions, shown in Tab. 1. This metadata leads to the conclusion that the intent behind the image on the left is to capture a memory of a trip and the intent behind the image on the right is to depict fashion.

This difference in intent can also be seen in how the users who took the photos have chose to frame them. Although both images show a man and a woman, in the image on the left, the user has chose to make a 'selfie' in an outdoor setting that focuses on faces and smiles, and in the image on the right, the setting is an illuminated stage and the focus is on the clothing. An inspection of Fig. 2 reveals that these choices have visual reflexes in the photos. The visual manifestations of intentional framing signal to the viewer that one photo should be interpreted as representing holiday memories and the other as depicting fashion.

With this example we would also like to stress the point that textual metadata could possibly help in the differentiation of photos on the basis of their intentional frame. Our focus here, however, is on visually observable intentional framing effects and on content-based approaches. For this reason, we do not consider textual features any further.

3.3 Viewers' Interpretations

The study of framing has its roots in the field of social psychology, where a frame describes a general, mainly subliminal, basic idea at play during perception or interpretation. The notion of 'frame' is thus tightly related to *Gestalt*, the perception of the essence or shape of an entity's complete form [11]. Specific to image perception is the notion of 'gist' [7], i.e., what is perceived from an image at a glance. We have already noted that gist-based methods have been applied by multimedia researchers to the problem of analyzing images that depict scenes.

Viewer interpretations of images are tightly synchronized with the intentional framing that is chosen by a photographer. In fact, the intentional framing of the image constitutes a signal from the photographer to the viewer about how the image should be interpreted. For some subject material, photographers often use highly conventionalized intentional frames. For example, nearly everyone can bring a standard picture in mind of how a traditional bridal pair appears in a wedding photo, or a how a public figure is represented in a certain role, e.g., a politician delivering an inspiring speech.

For other subject material, the intentional framing is less tightly linked to the subject matter, but rather more closely related to the underlying goal or purpose. For example, [18] establishes a typology of photographer intentions. This work demonstrates the reasons for which people take social images range from sharing emotions to recalling a feeling or collecting and storing information.

Our work does not depend on explicitly identifying or cataloguing intentional frames corresponding to all possible image topics, or photographer goals and purposes. We are rather interested in the fact that photographers use intentional frames to create photos, and that users/viewers differentiate photos on the basis of intentional frames. In other words, our work is focused on establishing that, alongside of *what* photos depict, *how* photos are taken is important for human interpretation of image semantics.

We point out that intentional framing is closely linked to the notion of *connotation*. In the area of images, connotation refers to those aspects of image interpretation that go beyond the literally depicted subject material of the image. In his seminal essay in [2], *The Photographic Message*, Roland Barthes characterizes connotation as 'the imposition of second meaning on the photographic proper' (p. 20). Intentional framing can also be considered a 'second meaning'. However, understanding connotation involves interpreting 'what' is depicted in an image. For example, red roses are commonly considered to have connotations of love. In contrast, intentional framing keeps the focus specifically on 'how' image content is depicted, and the way that photog-

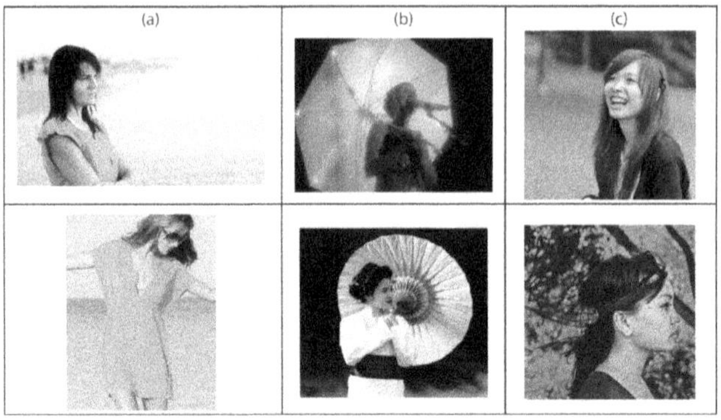

Figure 3: Pairs of photos that contrast with respect to intentional frame. The pairs differ with respect to the interpretations of human viewers, impressionistically described as: (a) feeling vs. fashion, (b) performance vs. history (c) personality vs. art

rapher choices related to 'how' are reflected in visual characteristics of an image. We remark that ultimately intentional framing may lead the multimedia research community to more effective exploitation of overall image connotations.

3.4 Generality of Intentional Framing

Intentional framing is a general phenomenon underlying social images. The visual reflexes of photographers' intent constitute a social signal that influences the global patterns that exist in a large collection of social images. Some photographers might take images unthinkingly, but most conceptualize their images to at least a minimum extent. Photographer choices, in turn, impact exactly *how* the subject material is depicted in the image. We do not claim that intentional framing constitutes a strong signal within a social image collection. Rather, our position is that this signal exists, and that it is strong enough to be effectively exploited. Here, we present additional examples to demonstrate that intentional framing takes different forms, and that a large range of images can be differentiated on the basis of intentional framing.

The Flickr images in Fig. 3 are arranged in pairs that differ with respect to intentional framing. The contrast between the two photos in each pair demonstrates that if two photos depicting the same concept or entity use different intentional frames, the result is two images with different interpretations. Consider the two photos in column (a). The top photo is about what the woman in the blue dress is feeling, and the bottom photo is about the blue dress. The contrast is due to the framing choices made by the photographers who took these photos. These choices include not only the ratio of the frame filled by the dress vs. the ratio filled by the background water, but also with the depth of field, the overall color palette, and the emotion projected by the human subject, and the subject's posture. In other words, it is intentional framing and not the depicted visual concepts that serve to distinguish these images from the point of view of a human interpreter.

Similar observations can be made about the photo pairs in (b) and (c). In (b), one set of photographer choices leads to an image depicting an ongoing performance (top), and the other to an image that documents history (bottom). Note that these two photos are very similar with respect to their basic composition, but different in their interpretation. This pair illustrates how intentional framing includes, but goes beyond, photographers' composition choices. In (c), one set of photographer choices leads to an image that conveys the happy personality of the subject (top) and another set of choices lead to a photo with a somber mood (bottom) that could be considered a work of art, more than a testimony to the personality of the person displayed.

It is important to note that the descriptions we use to refer to viewer interpretations of framing are impressionistic. We do *not* claim that these are the only possible descriptions, or that algorithms should predict these interpretations directly. Our point is that intentional framing is important for human image interpretations, and content-based algorithms should not be 'blind' to its existence. The larger message is that multimedia researchers should not indiscriminately assume that content-based image methods must 'compensate' for the visual variability of depicted objects, scenes, and images. Such approaches will lead to image analysis and retrieval systems that cannot possibly be sensitive to the difference in human interpretation between the pair of images in (a). Instead we advocate systems that admit the possibility that differences important for human semantic interpretation of images are related to intentional frames.

4. HUMAN VIEWS ON FRAMING

In this section, we empirically investigate the phenomenon of intentional framing. On the basis of the discussion in Section 3, we expect intentional framing to manifest itself in a collection of social images in the form of clusters of images that are homogenous in terms of their overall 'look and feel'. For this reason, we study clusters of images that are created automatically using global feature representations. We are interested in two aspects of these clusters, which we investigate in two analysis experiments involving human judgments collected via user studies.

The first experiment explores the correspondence of global-feature clusters with human judgements of photographer intent. The second experiment explores the correspondence of global-feature clusters with image semantics in the form of a higher level topic, in this case, 'fashion'. Each experiment consists of two steps, first, the *clustering step*, in which we create clusters in a social image collection, and, second, the *correlation step* in which we analyze the relationship between the clusters and human judgements related to intentional framing.

4.1 Global Features and Photographer Intent

According to the principle of intentional framing, the intent of the photographer guides the decisions made by the photographer while conceptualizing an image, resulting in an image with a particular intentional frame. However, since intentional framing results from a general recipe for a photograph, rather than specific rules, and, since photographers apply this recipe only to varying degrees, we, yet, know nothing about the visual variability that characterizes intentional frames. For this reason, the goal of our first experiment, is to demonstrate that it is indeed conceivable that global features can capture the regularities of frames.

For this experiment, we use the *Photo Intentions* data set that has been created by Lux et al. [20], and consists of 1,310 Flickr photos annotated with *photographer intent categories*. The categories correspond to general photographer goals in taking a picture: (i) *preserve a good feeling*, (ii) *preserve a bad feeling*, (iii) *show it to family and friends*, (iv) *publish it on-line*, (v) *support a task of mine* and (vi) *recall a specific situation*, and were chosen on the basis of a previous user study carried out by [18]. The images in the data set were annotated by the users who took them, who were contacted by Lux et al. [20] via Flickr. The category labels provided by the photographers were verified using a crowdsourcing experiment carried out on Mechanical Turk. As explained in detail in [20], five crowdworkers judged each image, and rated it with respect to each of the six intent categories. These ratings, used in our experiment, reflected the association of the image with each of the six categories using a 5-point Likert scale.

It is important to note that in this experiment, we do not assume that the photographer's intent category corresponds just to one single intentional frame. Instead, we take these categories to involve multiple closely related intentional frames that photographers use to accomplish a particular goal or purpose. We assume that if visual clusters correspond to intentional frames, then they will also be correlated with intent categories that encompass multiple frames. To our knowledge, our data set is the largest publicly available collection of social images that includes information about the intent of the photographer.

The *clustering step* in our experiment was carried out as follows. A selection of common global features was made, and the features were extracted from the images using *LIRE* (latest version[1]) [19]. For each type of global feature, clustering is performed using *Weka* (version 3[2]). We chose X-means clustering [25], since it determines the number of the clusters automatically, which is important for the experiment.

The *correlation step* was carried out for each different global-featuring clustering of the images. The purpose of the correlation step was to compare the visual closeness of the images in a cluster, with the human perception of whether the images were 'close' with respect to the intent of the photographer. We analyze each global feature clustering with respect to each intent category separately. Specifically, we calculate the Pearson correlation between the mean square distance of the images in a cluster from their cluster centroid and the mean of the Likert-scale ratings reflecting the degree to which the images in the cluster are associated with the intent category.

Tab. 2 summarizes the results, and demonstrates that the experiment uncovered the existence of a number of cases in which the tightness of visual clusters correlates (> 0.3) with human agreement on the photographer's intent.

These cases (n.B. they are negative correlations) are indicated with black. It can be seen that certain features seem to be particularly well suited for certain categories. For example, FCTH is the best feature for detecting photos for which the photographer's intent was *publish on-line* (i.e., in a blog). It is important to note that the results of this experiment must be seen as a *suggestion* that global features can capture photographer intent. There are also cases of positive correlation, which are marked in white, where it is clear that other effects are at play. However, if there was no relationship between global features and photographer intent, we would have expected a table that was entirely grey,

[1]https://code.google.com/p/lire/source/checkout

[2]http://www.cs.waikato.ac.nz/ml/weka/downloading.html

Table 2: Correlation of global-feature-based clusters (MSE) and human agreement on photographer intent on the *Photo Intentions* data set.

Feature	recall situation	preserve good feeling	publish online	show to family and friends	support task	preserve bad feeling
CEDD						
FCTH						
Gabor						
Tamura						
Luminance Layout						
Scaleable Color						
Opponent Histogram						
AutoColor Correlogram						
JPEG Coefficent						
Edge Histogram						
PHOG						
JCD						
JointHistogram						

which is not the case. Encouraged by this initial experiment, we turned to a second, larger-scale experiment, that investigates the connection between image clusters and topical semantics.

4.2 Intentional Framing and Topic

Our second analysis experiment is closely related to the title of this paper. It investigates the connection between 'how' an image is taken and 'what' that image depicts. Recall that the intentional frame that a photographer chooses is related to the particular subject material that is portrayed in the image (i.e., the topic). The importance of the relationship between intentional framing and topic is the following: if visual patterns of intentional framing in social data sets are indicative of topic, then they can be exploited for content-based tasks such as analysis of image semantics, and image retrieval.

For this experiment we use the *Fashion 10000* data set for Flickr images, which was created by Loni et al. [17] for the purpose of developing classifiers to detect fashion images in social image collections. The data set consists of 30,000 images and was collected to contain a significant portion of images (>10,000 of them) that are related to fashion and clothing. Further details on how the +fashion/-fashion labels were generated can be found in [17].

On the basis of the results of the previous experiment, we expect that clustering using global feature representations are indeed capable of picking up visual regularities in the data related to intentional framing. This experiment had the goal of uncovering a relationship between the visual tightness of clusters and human judgements that these clusters were related to the overall topic of fashion.

Because the *Fashion 10000* data set is an order of magnitude larger than the intention data set, we first carried out clustering, and then submitted the clusters to a group of human judges. The *clustering step* in this experiment was carried out by first determining an optimal global feature representation for the data using average information gain. Under this assumption, the following features were identified as useful for the data set: CEDD, FCTH, JCD, PHOG, ColorLayout, JPEG coefficient histogram and ScalableColor [19]. As before, X-means clustering was applied, resulting in 62 clusters.

In the *correlation step*, a set of human subjects were presented with 62 screens of images, each screen containing images sampled from one of the 62 clusters (n.B. the clusters were too large to judge in their entirety). In total, there were 10 participants who judged the images. The participants were selected by convenience sampling from the immediate environment of the authors, and briefed to ensure that they had an adequate understanding of social fashion. The participants then judged the consistency of the clusters with respect to fashion.

As in the previous experiment, we calculate the Pearson correlation between the mean square distance of the images in a cluster from the cluster's centroid (reflecting visual tightness of the cluster) and the average human agreement about the fact that the cluster reflects fashion. The result was a negative correlation, -0.56 (i.e., small, tight clusters are associated with clear human judgements of topic focus). This result provides evidence that global features are indeed able to build clusters that partition fashion from non-fashion images in the data set. This experiment supports the conclusion that 'how' images are taken, as reflected in global-feature-based clustering, is indicative of the topical subject matter that they contain.

We conclude this section by mentioning that qualitatively the outcomes of the second experiment were striking. Specifically, the four groups of intentional frames in Fig. 1 in Section 1 were *not* hand selected from the data. Rather, these four intentional frames represent clusters that were formed using global-feature-based clustering in the second analysis experiment. These clusters serve as a compelling illustration of the link between global features and semantic image content. Our position is that this link exists, because of the photographer's tendency to take pictures of specific content which follows a set of intentional frames. This effect is stable enough to be a useful visual signal within large-scale social image collections.

5. CONTENT-BASED CLASSIFICATION

The evidence in Section 4 suggest that there is a link between global feature representations and image topic that is mediated by intentional framing. Motivated by this evidence, we carry out an experiment designed to exploit that link. The experiment involves large-scale classification of social images into tag-classes. Intentional framing gives us reason to believe that images belonging to a certain tag-class, and therefore containing certain topical subject material, will be characterized by patterns of intentional framing. These patterns reflect typical sets of choices made by users on 'how' to make a photograph that are related to the subject material that they are photographing. We do not expect the effects to be strong. Instead, our goal is to present plausible proof that the effects of intentional framing are exploitable for a task related to image semantics.

5.1 Data Set and Experimental Setup

We carry out our content-based classification experiment on the *Yahoo! Flickr Creative Common Images tagged with ten concepts, version 1.0 data set*[3] that was used for the 2013 Yahoo! Large-scale Flickr-tag Image Classification ACM Multimedia Grand Challenge. The data set consists of 1.5 million training images associated with ten equally-sized tag-classes and 500,000 test images. The tag-classes are: *2012*, *beach*, *food*, *london*, *music*, *nature*, *people*, *sky*, *travel*, and *wedding*. This data set is considered challenging not only due to its scale, but also because each topical tag-class is characterized by a very high degree of visual variability. Our choice of a standard data set allows us to compare our approach to the performance achieved by current state-of-the-art methods.

In order to make clear how the theory of intentional framing is expected to contribute to the performance of a classifier on such a classification task, we consider the class 'London' in more detail. Images taken all over London will be tagged 'London', giving rise to a high level of visual diversity. However, because we are looking specifically at social images, we expect that people are taking pictures of London mainly with the intention of documenting the city, for example, as tourists, as residents or as journalists. For this reason, we expect photos to be generally associated with key intentional frames, examples might be, cityscape photos, photos that emphasize a sense of place, and photos taken to preserve memories. These intentional frames are indicative of the topic 'London' the way that the four frames in Fig. 1 are indicative of the topic 'fashion'.

The intentional frames are not expected to be mutually exclusive among tag-classes. However, they are expected to support discrimination well enough to act as indicators of tag-classes. For example, it is reasonable to expect that more cityscape photos would be anticipated in the tag-class 'London' than in the tag-class 'Food'. In this way, intentional framing can be anticipated to deliver performance on this task—sensitivity to the specific literally depicted content of the images (i.e., detecting specific food items or specific city landmarks) is not necessary.

Our simple search classification approach, SimSea, is a variant of the k-NN algorithm. We choose a back-to-the-basics approach because of its computational simplicity and the speed that it delivers on large scale image classification problems. As previously mentioned, SimSea is not itself novel. Our novel contribution is that intentional framing provides a principled explanation as to why an algorithm such as SimSea should work well on a large collection of social images.

SimSea is implemented by extending the LIRE framework [19] with an implementation of a search based classifier. The following global features were used: JCD [5], CL [4], OH [32] and PHOG [3]. These features were selected using information gain calculated on the development set (a subset of the training set).

For retrieval we employ the inverted index strategy to index the hash values, like terms describing the actual image. To query the system, we create a term-based query from the hashes of the query image.

Classification proceeds as follows. Each search result of a given tag-class is counted as one vote in favor of assigning the query image to that tag-class. The class with the most votes wins, and is returned as the classified class for the query image. In case of a draw, the occurrences of the class is weighted by the rank of each image with the same class. The weight function is defined as:

$$c = \arg\max_{c \in C}\{ClassScore(c)\}$$

$$ClassScore(c) = |c|. \sum_{I_i \in \{I_i | Class(I_i) = c\}} rank(I_i)^{-1}$$

The class with the highest $ClassScore$ of all classes $c \in C$ is chosen as class c of the image. The $ClassScore$ is calculated

[3]see http://webscope.sandbox.yahoo.com

Table 3: *iAP* per class on the development set.

	JCD	CL	OH	PHOG
2012	0.198	0.128	0.13	0.104
beach	0.448	0.487	0.342	0.534
food	0.531	0.492	0.389	0.352
london	0.244	0.201	0.146	0.347
music	0.526	0.457	0.495	0.164
nature	0.502	0.41	0.435	0.503
people	0.264	0.227	0.244	0.105
sky	0.628	0.601	0.544	0.473
travel	0.139	0.101	0.128	0.112
wedding	0.463	0.272	0.262	0.235

by counting the occurrences of each class c and multiply it with the summed $WeightedRankScore$. $rank(I_i) : \{I_i\} \rightarrow \mathbb{N}$ gives the rank of an image. The $WeightedRankScore$ is the sum of $rank(I_i)^{-1}$ scores for each class. The search time of this approach is well below 300 ms for the 1,500,000 indexed images. Due to the nature of the global feature search, the search time will scale sub-linearly with the number of images in the index.

5.2 Experimental Results

For evaluation metric, we adopt mean interpolated averaged precision ($MiAP$), which was also used to evaluate the results of the Grand Challenge.

Our first step is to use the development set to determine optimal settings. Our development set is based on a sub-set of the training data that includes 1,000 randomly selected images per class. A setting of $k = 50$, was determined to be optimal. Tab. 3 reports results for $k = 50$ using a variety of global features. It can be seen that average precision is very similar for all choices of features. However, JCD achieves the highest overall mean interpolated average precision (0.417), and is therefore chosen for the experiment on the test set.

Our second step is to carry out classification on whole test data set (500k images; 50k images per tag-class). Applying the optimal settings determined on the development set, i.e., $k = 50$ and JCD features, we performed our second experiment with the test data set featuring 50k images per class which leads to a $MiAP$ over all classes of 0.391.

Tab. 4 shows the $MiAP$ over all classes for the 500k test set and all 1.5 million training images to train the model, compared with the best results of the ACMMM Grand Challenge 2013 from Mantziou et al. [21]. The best performing reported result from the second approach from Su et al. [30] is not compared because the reported $MiAP$ excludes the tag-class *2012*. However, they also use a concept detection approach, Hessian affine (Concept 1 (HA)), which is more comparable. The comparison shows that our *SimSea* approach which uses *only one* global feature, nearly can reach the performance of the other approaches and in one case, Concept 1 (HA) [30], can reach better performance.

As baseline we use the results of SMaL [21] (Local 1 (SMaL)) and SVM [21] (Local 2 (SVM)), which both rely on local features and complex learning algorithms, because they report the $MiAP$ for each class which makes it better comparable with our results. Based on the $MiAP$ We calculated the statistical significance (Wilcoxon Signed-Rank Test) with a significance level of 0.01. This leads to p-value of 0.5754 for SimSea versus Local 1 (SMaL) and a p-value of 0.3320 for SimSea versus Local 2 (SVM). This test shows that the difference is not statistically significant and

Table 4: SimSea vs. best results from the ACMMM Grand Challenge 2013. The difference with Local 1 and Local 2 is not statistically significant

	SimSea	Local 1 (SMaL) [21]	Local 2 (SVM) [21]	Concept 1 (HA) [30]
$MiAP$	0.391	0.422	0.413	0.37

therefore our methods performance cannot be interpreted as worse (or better) than the Local 1 and Local 2 approach. For the sake of completeness we mention that all approaches outperform the dominant class baseline, which is 0.1.

It is important to point out that the run-time performance of our approach is very good. Classification of a single image takes roughly 300 ms on a current Windows 7, Intel Core i7, 16GB PC. This is faster than 10 minutes for Local 1 (SMaL) and 2.5 seconds for Local 2 (SVM) on a 24-core Intel Xeon Q6600 2.0Ghz with 128GB RAM reported in [21].

6. CONCLUSION AND OUTLOOK

This paper has presented a proof for the importance of visual patterns in large collections of social images that exist due to underlying consistencies in how photographers choose to make images. Conceptually, we have turned from considering an image as something that is viewed by a user ('what' is shown in the image) to considering an image to be something that was created by a photographer ('how' the image was captured by the photographer). This shift of perspective allows us open up a new set of commonalities between images. These commonalities are useful for image analysis and retrieval because they both connect images at the level of pixels, and also correspond to connections perceived by humans interpreting images.

Specifically, this paper has introduced intentional framing, a principle that accounts for the connection between the decisions made by photographers that are related to the subject material they photograph, and visual characteristics of social images. We show that global feature representations of images are connected to human perceptions of photographer intent, and also that intentional frames chosen by photographers are connected to the semantics of images at the level of topic

We report the results of a large-scale image classification experiment that makes use of a back-to-the-basics simple search approach exploiting global feature representations of images. If we consider that the perspective image topic is exclusively related to 'what' images predict, the good performance of this simple approach is mysterious. Global features are known to be related to the overall 'look and feel' of images and not necessarily to specific semantic content. However, once we understand that intentional framing has the ability to act as a bridge between global characteristics of an image, and interpretations of image semantics, these results are expected.

The principled account that intentional framing provides for the results of our content-based classification experiment opens a new vista for multimedia research. We consider the results of this experiment to reflect the force of intentional framing at work in a large-scale social image collection. However, it measures that force, at best, only indirectly. Additional work is required to understand the exact nature of that force, the factors that influence it, and how it can best be harnessed in the service of image analysis and retrieval. For example, we would not expect an intentional-framing-sensitive approach to work well on a collection of images not taken by human photographers, e.g., Google street view images. Such a collection would have only a single robotically created frame, and image semantics would not be differentiated at this level. Further experimentation is necessary to test this hypothesis and to discover how to exploit the intentional framing principle to its full potential.

Taken as a whole, the evidence presented in this paper serves to demonstrate the high promise of the 'how' perspective for social images. We conclude that intentional framing opens the possibility of the exploitation of lightweight approaches that contribute to the development of a new breed of fast image analysis and content-based retrieval algorithms for large-scale social image collections.

7. ACKNOWLEDGMENTS

We would like to thank Xinchao Li, Yue Shi and Oge Marques for fruitful discussion of framing. M. Riegler is a recipient of the Excellence Scholarship of the Industrialists' association Carinthia. which provided partial support for this research. Support was also received from Lakeside Labs GmbH, Klagenfurt, Austria, the European Regional Development Fund, the Carinthian Economic Promotion Fund (KWF-20214/25557/37319), EC FP7 project CUbRIK (287704), the iAD center for Research-based Innovation (174867) funded by the Norwegian Research Council, and the Dutch national program COMMIT. C. Kofler is a recipient of the Google Europe Doctoral Fellowship in Video Search, which also provided partial support.

8. REFERENCES

[1] ImageCLEF Task. http://imageclef.org/2012. [lv., 08, 13].

[2] R. Barthes. *Image Music Text.* Hill and Wang, 1977.

[3] A. Bosch, A. Zisserman, and X. Munoz. Representing Shape with a Spatial Pyramid Kernel. In *Proceedings of the CIVR '07*, pages 401–408, New York, NY, USA, 2007.

[4] S.-F. Chang, T. Sikora, and A. Puri. Overview of the MPEG-7 Standard. *IEEE Transactions on Circuits and Systems for Video Technology*, 11(6):688–695, June 2001.

[5] S. A. Chatzichristofis, Y. S. Boutalis, and M. Lux. Selection of the Proper Compact Composite Descriptor for Improving Content Based Image Retrieval. In *Proceedings of the SPPRA 09'*, 2009.

[6] R. M. Entman. Framing: Toward Clarification of a Fractured Paradigm. *Journal of communication*, 43(4):51–58, 1993.

[7] A. Friedman. Framing Pictures: The Role of Knowledge in Automatized Encoding and Memory for Gist. *Journal of experimental psychology: General*, 108(3):316, 1979.

[8] J. Hays and A. A. Efros. IM2GPS: Estimating Geographic Information from a Single Image. In *Proceedings of the CVPR 08'*, pages 1–8.

[9] J. Hays and A. A. Efros. Scene Completion Using Millions of Photographs. In *Proceedings of the ACM TOG 07'*, volume 26, page 4, 2007.

[10] M. J. Huiskes, B. Thomee, and M. S. Lew. New Trends and Ideas in Visual Concept Detection: The MIR Flickr Retrieval Evaluation Initiative. In *Proceedings of the ACM ICMR 10'*, pages 527–536, 2010.

[11] G. Humphrey. The Psychology of the Gestalt. *Journal of Educational Psychology*, 15(7):401, 1924.

[12] J. Kim. Events as Property Exemplifications. In *Action theory*, pages 159–177. Springer, 1976.

[13] M. Larson, M. Melenhorst, M. Menéndez, and P. Xu. Using Crowdsourcing to Capture Complexity in Human Interpretations of Multimedia Content. In *Fusion in Computer Vision*, pages 229–269. Springer, 2014.

[14] X. Li, M. Larson, and A. Hanjalic. Geo-visual Ranking for Location Prediction of Social Images. In *Proceedings of ACM ICMR 13'*, pages 81–88. ACM, 2013.

[15] X. Li, C. G. Snoek, and M. Worring. Learning Social Tag Relevance by Neighbor Voting. *Multimedia, IEEE Transactions on*, 11(7):1310–1322, 2009.

[16] D. Liu, S. Yan, X.-S. Hua, and H.-J. Zhang. Image Retagging Using Collaborative Tag Propagation. *Multimedia, IEEE Transactions on*, 13(4):702–712, 2011.

[17] B. Loni, L. Y. Cheung, M. Riegler, A. Bozzon, L. Gottlieb, and M. Larson. Fashion 10000: An Enriched Social Image Dataset for Fashion and Clothing. In *Proceedings of ACM MMSys 14'*, pages 41–46, New York, NY, USA, 2014. ACM.

[18] M. Lux, M. Kogler, and M. del Fabro. Why Did You Take This Photo: A Study on User Intentions in Digital Photo Productions. In *Proceedings of SAPMIA 10'*, SAPMIA '10, pages 41–44, New York, NY, USA, 2010. ACM.

[19] M. Lux and O. Marques. Visual Information Retrieval Using Java and LIRE. *Synthesis Lectures on Information Concepts, Retrieval, and Services*, 5(1):1–112, 2013.

[20] M. Lux, M. Taschwer, and O. Marques. A Closer Look at Photographers' Intentions: A Test Dataset. In *Proceedings of the ACM CrowdMM 12'*, pages 17–18. ACM, 2012.

[21] E. Mantziou, S. Papadopoulos, and Y. Kompatsiaris. Scalable Training with Approximate Incremental Laplacian Eigenmaps and PCA. In *Proceedings of the ACM MM 13'*, pages 381–384, 2013.

[22] T. B. Moeslund, O. Javed, Y.-G. Jiang, and R. Manmatha. Special Issue on Multimedia Event Detection. *Mach. Vision Appl.*, 25(1):1–4, Jan. 2014.

[23] M. Naphade, J. R. Smith, J. Tesic, S. Chang, W. Hsu, L. Kennedy, A. Hauptmann, and J. Curtis. Large-scale Concept Ontology for Multimedia. *MM IEEE*, pages 86–91, 2006.

[24] A. Oliva and A. Torralba. Building the Gist of a Scene: The Role of Global Image Features in Recognition. *Progress in brain research*, 155:23–36, 2006.

[25] D. Pelleg, A. W. Moore, et al. X-means: Extending K-means with Efficient Estimation of the Number of Clusters. In *Proceedings of ICML 00'*, pages 727–734, 2000.

[26] G. Petkos, S. Papadopoulos, and Y. Kompatsiaris. Social Event Detection Using Multimodal Clustering and Integrating Supervisory Signals. In *Proceedings of ACM ICMR 12'*, page 23, 2012.

[27] R. A. Rensink. Scene Perception. 7:151–155, 2000.

[28] T. Reuter and P. Cimiano. Event-based Classification of Social Media Streams. In *Proceedings of ACM ICMR 12'*, page 22, 2012.

[29] D. A. Scheufele. Framing as a Theory of Media Effects. *Journal of communication*, 49(1):103–122, 1999.

[30] Y.-C. Su, T.-H. Chiu, G.-L. Wu, C.-Y. Yeh, F. Wu, and W. Hsu. Flickr-tag Prediction Using Multi-modal Fusion and Meta Information. In *Proceedings of ACM MM 13'*, pages 353–356, 2013.

[31] F. Travel. Framing of Images from Photographers View. http://www.fodors.com/travel-photography/. [lv., 11, 13].

[32] K. E. van de Sande, T. Gevers, and C. G. Snoek. Evaluating Color Descriptors for Object and Scene Recognition. *Pattern Analysis and Machine Intelligence, IEEE Transactions on*, 32(9):1582–1596, 2010.

[33] S. Vinner. Concept Definition, Concept Image and the Notion of Function. *International Journal of Mathematical Education in Science and Technology*, 14(3):293–305, 1983.

[34] L. Wang, L. Yang, and X. Tian. Query Aware Visual Similarity Propagation for Image Search Reranking. In *Proceedings of ACM MM 09'*, pages 725–728. ACM, 2009.

[35] L. Yang and A. Hanjalic. Supervised Reranking for Web Image Search. In *Proceedings of ACM MM 10'*, pages 183–192. ACM, 2010.

A Group Testing Framework for Similarity Search in High-dimensional Spaces

Miaojing Shi*
Peking University

Teddy Furon
Inria

Hervé Jégou
Inria

ABSTRACT

This paper introduces a group testing framework for detecting large similarities between high-dimensional vectors, such as descriptors used in state-of-the-art description of multimedia documents. At the crossroad of multimedia information retrieval and signal processing, we produce a set of group representations that jointly encode several vectors into a single one, in the spirit of group testing approaches. By comparing a query vector to several of these intermediate representations, we screen the large values taken by the similarities between the query and all the vectors, at a fraction of the cost of exhaustive similarity calculation.

Unlike concurrent indexing methods that suffer from the curse of dimensionality, our method exploits the properties of high-dimensional spaces. It therefore complements other strategies for approximate nearest neighbor search.

Our preliminary experiments demonstrate the potential of group testing for searching large databases of multimedia objects represented by vectors. We obtain a large improvement in terms of the theoretical complexity, at the cost of a small or negligible decrease of accuracy. We hope that this preliminary work will pave the way to subsequent works for multimedia retrieval with limited resources.

1. INTRODUCTION

With the apparition and massive growth of social networks, and simultaneously the massive proliferation of personal capture devices such as smartphones, research in multimedia has entered the age of "big data". In this context, the scale to be considered by search engines is in the order of billions of heterogeneous documents: mixtures of image, sound, video, text, or even more complex data such as links of various nature in social networks.

This raises the issue of resources required to search and organize such large collections. Both efficiency and memory

*Miaojing Shi has worked on this paper while he was a visiting student at Inria Rennes.

MM'14, November 3–7, 2014, Orlando, Florida, USA.

http://dx.doi.org/10.1145/2647868.2654895.

Group testing was born during World War II [6]. Facing an increasing number of injuries, the US army decided to make blood donation mandatory for soldier recruits. However, a fraction of them were infected by syphilis. Unfortunately, syphilis testing back then was expensive. Realizing that there is no point running an exhaustive testing procedure over a large population if a small fraction of individuals are infected, some blood samples were pooled into one mixture and tested against syphilis. If the test was positive, the blood samples were individually tested.

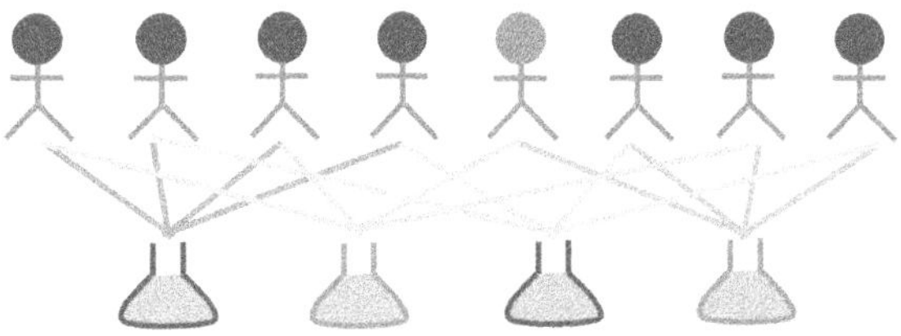

This very promising idea was not actually put to use. The seminal paper on it dates back to 1943 due to Robert Dorfman [5]. Nowadays, group testing finds application in pharmacology, bioinformatics, genome screening, etc. This paper considers the potential of this approach for similarity search, a key ingredient of multimedia systems.

Figure 1: Group testing: An historical motivation.

are critical issues. The need for efficient search has maintained a sustained effort of research in various communities, leading to some major improvements in the last decades. One of the most noticeable advances is arguably the introduction of Locality-sensitive hashing [7] (LSH). This indexing strategy and its derivatives, such as E2LSH [4], were the first to exhibit provable sub-linear search in arbitrary spaces. However, this method trades memory for efficiency, and the practical complexity grows dramatically with the dimensionality. For descriptors of intermediate dimensionality such as SIFT descriptors [15], many hash functions are required and the indexing structure has a prohibitive memory cost. Data-aware methods like FLANN [20] or LSH variants employing the multiple-probe mechanisms [18] are preferred in practice. The situation is even worse when considering the high-dimensional vectors used for image retrieval, such as Fisher vectors [22] or bag-of-words [24]. To our knowledge, all sub-linear indexing strategies are ineffective for such vectors, and not used in state-of-the-art image search engines.

Sketching is another class of approximate search commonly used for high-dimensional vectors. Sketches in Hamming space, also derived from LSH, are popular [3, 17, 25]. In this case, each vector is mapped to a compact code, typically a binary vector, in order to reduce the complexity by a constant factor. The search is exhaustive, meaning that the code associated with the query is compared to all the database codes. The speed-up comes from the fact that it is faster to compare short binary vectors than long floating-point vectors, typically saving one to two orders of magnitude in terms of search efficiency. This approach is supported by theoretical results [3, 2] showing that the Hamming distance between binary vectors provides an approximation of the cosine similarity between the original Euclidean vectors. Note that this approach is also termed LSH in the recent literature. However, we stress that this approach does not offer the sub-linear complexity underlying the first LSH algorithms [7]. Recent developments in this line of research include compressed-domain distance estimation based on more general codes, such as product quantization [11].

In this paper, in a complementary manner, we are interested in reducing the number of measurements by avoiding the exhaustive comparison of the query with all the documents. The motivation is therefore in the spirit of the recent super-image approach [16]. Yet our approach is not specific to a particular image search setup and only requires that the indexed vectors satisfy some properties: being truly high-dimensional, with zero mean and unit norm, and compared with cosine similarity[1]. These assumptions are satisfied by state-of-the-art descriptors such as the Fisher vector [22], VLAD [12] or more recently the T-embedding [13].

In other terms, the framework proposed in this paper is an attempt to explicitly exploit the properties underlying high-dimensional spaces in a search mechanism. More precisely, we consider a group testing approach as illustrated in Figure 1. In our similarity search scenario, for a given query we aim at detecting the largest similarities from a limited number of measurements, typically one order of magnitude smaller than what is formally required with an exhaustive comparison.

Our framework is formally introduced in Section 2, where we detail how we form overlapping groups of images, with each group being represented by a simple vector. Section 3 considers several score estimation strategies relying on pseudo-inverse reconstruction, sparse decoding and group testing methods. Section 4 presents a simple mathematical model to stress an important phenomenon known as dilution in group testing. The potential of our approach is evaluated in the experimental Section 5. Section 6 concludes the paper.

2. THE GROUP TESTING FRAMEWORK

Let us consider a collection of images described by vectors $\mathcal{X} = \{x_1, \ldots, x_j, \ldots, x_N\}$, $x_j \in \mathbb{R}^D$, and a D-dimensional query vector $q \in \mathbb{R}^D$ representing the query image. The images are compared with cosine similarity. We denote by $u_j = \langle q|x_j\rangle = q^\top x_j$ the similarity between the query and the jth database image.

[1]The three last assumptions can be obtained by performing PCA and re-normalizing the resulting vector. This modifies the comparison metric but often has little impact of the performance for the application.

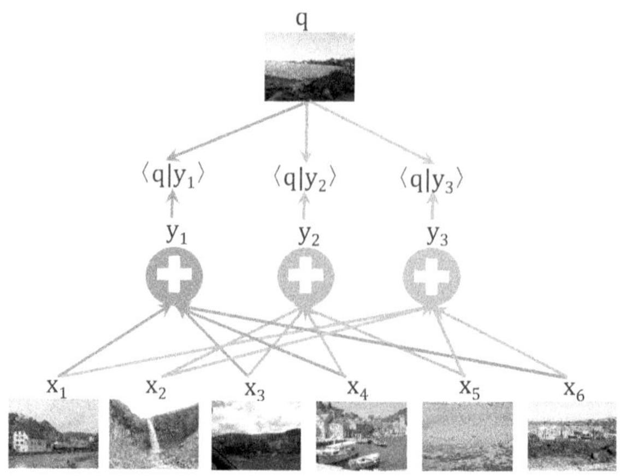

(a) Group representation

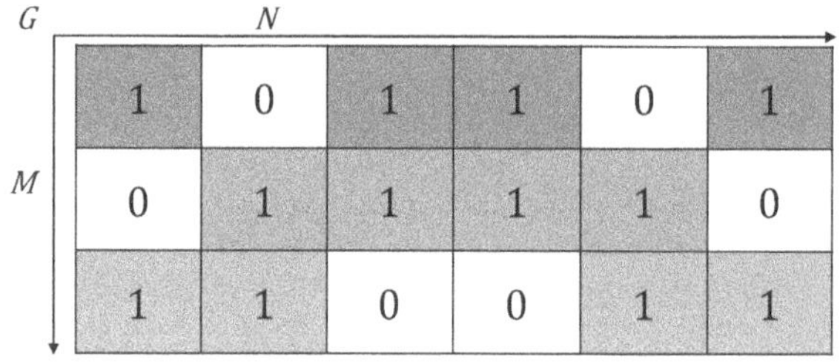

(b) Group matrix

Figure 2: Top: an illustration of the proposed group testing framework for image search. y_i denotes the ith group vector, which is the sum of the image vectors of current group, e.g., $y_1 = x_1 + x_3 + x_4 + x_6$; $\langle q|y_i\rangle$ corresponds to the cosine similarity between group vector y_i and query vector q. Bottom: Group matrix G with its element g_{ij} being one if the jth image belongs to the ith group, otherwise $g_{ij} = 0$.

The similarities between a given query and the entire collection are therefore obtained by

$$\mathbf{u} = [u_1, \ldots, u_N]^\top = X^\top q, \tag{1}$$

where X is a $D \times N$ matrix with each column being the corresponding image vector x_j in database.

To avoid this costly matrix-vector operation, we consider the group testing framework illustrated in Figure 2. The image database vectors $x_1, ..., x_N$ are gathered into M overlapping groups $\mathcal{H}_1, \ldots, \mathcal{H}_M$. Each group $\mathcal{H}_i$ is described by a D-dimensional vector y_i, which is the sum of its image vectors:

$$y_i = \sum_{j \in \mathcal{H}_i} x_j. \tag{2}$$

Formally, the membership of an image to a group is given by a sparse $M \times N$ matrix $G = [g_{ij}]$, such that $g_{ij} = 1$ if image x_j belongs to group $\mathcal{H}_i$, otherwise $g_{ij} = 0$. Therefore, the group representation is obtained as

$$Y = X \cdot G^\top. \tag{3}$$

For a given query image q, our objective is to avoid the exhaustive comparison (1) of the query with the N images in the database. Instead, we calculate its similarities with the M group vectors Y as

$$\mathbf{v} = [v_1, ..., v_M]^\top = Y^\top q, \tag{4}$$

The group similarity vector $\mathbf{v}$ is M-dimensional, and is related to the image similarity vector by

$$\mathbf{v} = GX^{\top}q = G\mathbf{u}. \quad (5)$$

The objective is to infer the similarity values $\mathbf{u}$ from the measurements $\mathbf{v}$. Equation (5) is underdetermined because $M < N$, meaning that it has infinite number of solutions. In other terms, without any further assumptions, it is not possible to recover $\mathbf{u}$ from $\mathbf{v}$.

However, there are many ways to single out a solution. For instance, the standard approach described in Section 3.1 relies on the pseudo-inverse.

Sparse recovery [14] is another approach, where the typical assumption is that $\mathbf{u}$ is sparse: over N components, only a few of them are not null. Under some assumptions on matrix G and the sparsity of $\mathbf{u}$, perfect recovery is possible even in situations where $M \ll N$. For our particular problem of similarity search, we want to exploit the following **key assumption**: Most images are *not* related to the query, whence most components of $\mathbf{u}$ are nearly 0 especially for high-dimensional spaces. On the contrary, the few images matching with the query produce positive similarities. Section 3.2 is devoted to this particular problem of similarity estimation with a sparsity assumption.

Notice that in very large scale database, storing the whole matrix G is not desirable, or not even possible. In practice, we simply store the group IDs each image belongs to, and the image IDs each group consists of. Section 5.1 gives a random construction of matrix G where each group has the same size $N_{\mathcal{H}}$, and each image belongs to the same number of groups $N_{\mathcal{L}}$. Specifically, when M is pre-fixed such that N divides $N_{\mathcal{H}}M$, $N_{\mathcal{L}}$ is guaranteed to be an integer such that

$$N_{\mathcal{L}} = N_{\mathcal{H}} \times \frac{M}{N}. \quad (6)$$

3. SCORE ESTIMATION STRATEGY

This section presents three score estimation strategies, namely based on pseudo-inverse, sparse decoding and group testing. They are introduced in a progressive manner, from the more standard ones to our group testing recovery method.

3.1 Pseudo-inverse PI

A standard method to solve (5) is to employ the pseudo-inverse of the grouping matrix G:

$$\tilde{\mathbf{u}} = (G^{\top}G)^{-1}G^{\top}\mathbf{v}. \quad (7)$$

This estimation provides the solution satisfying (5) minimizing the ℓ_2 norm $\|\tilde{\mathbf{u}}\|$ of the estimated similarity vector.

Albeit standard, this strategy has several drawbacks, both in terms of efficiency and accuracy. First, computing equation[2] (7) is time consuming: although the pseudo-inverse is fixed and computed offline, it is not sparse and multiplying it by a vector requires $N \times M$ elementary computations. Since M may be larger than D, especially for large databases, there is no computational advantage of using this strategy compared to the exhaustive search, whose complexity is $N \times D$. The lack of sparsity of the pseudo-inverse has another consequence: the variance of the similarity estimator for both the relevant and irrelevant images is large. This remark is related to the theoretical discussion provided in Section 4. Finally, this estimation does not exploit any particular assumption on $\mathbf{u}$, that is, the similarities associated with relevant images are expected to be significantly larger than the other measurements, *i.e.*, the distribution of the scores is closely distributed around 0, but has a heavy tail.

For these reasons, this method must be understood as a baseline, with respect to estimation quality, for the strategies that we propose in the rest of this section.

[2]We denote by $\mathbf{u}$ the true similarity vector, which, in our case, is the cosine similarity. We use $\tilde{\mathbf{u}}$ to denote the estimated image score vector.

3.2 Sparse decoding SD

As long as $\mathbf{u}$ is sparse enough, sparse decoding is capable of recovering $\mathbf{u}$ by solving the equation

$$\tilde{\mathbf{u}} = \min_{\mathbf{u}} \|\mathbf{v} - G\mathbf{u}\| + \lambda\|\mathbf{u}\|_1, \quad (8)$$

where $\|\mathbf{u}\|_1$ is the l_1-norm penalty added to regularize $\|\mathbf{v} - G\mathbf{u}\|$ [19]. The penalty ensures that most components of $\mathbf{u}$ are stuck around 0, hence providing a sparse solution.

In practice, irrelevant images have small similarity values and we do not really care about an exact recovery of these values. We are only interested in spotting large positive similarity values, while large negative similarities are assumed unlikely to occur. Therefore, we add positivity constraints on the solution $\mathbf{u}$,

$$\tilde{\mathbf{u}} = \min_{\mathbf{u}} \|\mathbf{v} - G\mathbf{u}\| + \lambda \textstyle\sum u_j. \quad s.t. \quad u_j \geq 0 \quad (9)$$

Nevertheless, we are facing the following difficulties: the sparsity of vector $\mathbf{u}$, defined as the number of large components and presumably also equal to the number of relevant database images, depends a lot on the query. Moreover, as the similarities of the irrelevant images are not strictly 0, we are in the context of noisy sparse signals recovery. Therefore, we can not perfectly reconstruct $\mathbf{u}$ but only aim at producing an estimation $\tilde{\mathbf{u}}$.

The design of matrix G also has its importance, because accurate recovery is guaranteed only if G satisfies the Restricted isometry property (RIP). Verifying this property for a given matrix G is NP-hard in general.

There are probabilistic constructions giving birth to RIP compliant matrices almost surely: for instance, generating its entries according to an i.i.d. sub-Gaussian distribution providing that $M = \mathcal{O}(W \log N)$, where W is an upper bound of the sparsity of $\mathbf{u}$. However, these sensing matrices are not sparse at all and difficult to handle for our large scale application. Note that algorithms solving (9) are iterative; each iteration requires a vector multiplication by matrix G.

To achieve a better trade-off between efficiency and effectiveness, we keep the matrix G sparse, while getting away from the compressed sensing framework: we have no guarantee on the reconstruction quality since our setup a priori does not necessarily fulfill the RIP and sparsity conditions. Yet, we find experimentally that, despite the inaccuracy of sparse decoding, nearly all the relevant images are assigned with large values in the estimation $\tilde{\mathbf{u}}$. Therefore, the sparse decoding algorithm is useful to indicate likely relevant images. We no longer see $\tilde{u}_j$ as the estimation of the similarity u_j but as a quantity indicating the likelihood that the jth image matches the query, *i.e.* u_j is somehow 'big'.

Re-ranking. We calculate the true similarities between query and R images with largest likelihood scores $\tilde{u}_j$. By

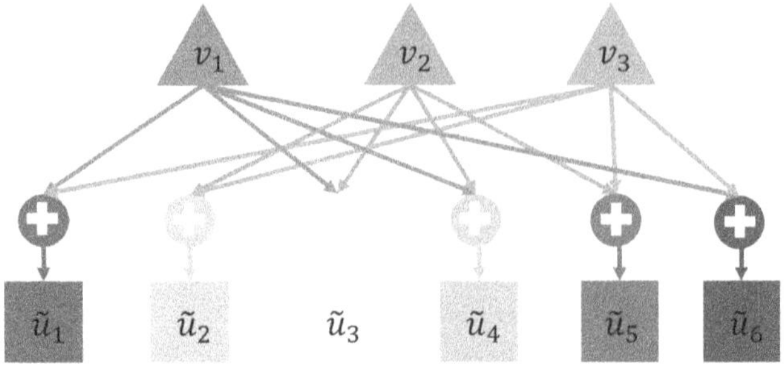

Figure 3: The basic score estimation strategy proposed in the group testing framework. v_1, v_2 and v_3 denote the corresponding group similarities in Figure 2. The image likelihood score $\tilde{u}_j$ is initially estimated by the sum the similarities of those groups that image j is connected with, *e.g.*, $\tilde{u}_1 = v_1 + v_3$.

revisiting only a fraction of image vectors ($R \ll N$), we are able to remove those irrelevant images and retain close to state-of-the-art retrieval accuracy. From this point view, the idea is closer to the adaptive group testing described in Figure 1 than to compressed sensing. The quantity $v_i = q^\top y_i$ is regarded as a test over the group of images $\mathcal{H}_i$ indicating whether some images in this group match the query.

3.3 Group testing GT

Revisiting the image vectors adds complexity and slows down the search. To relieve this concern, we further simplify the first stage discarding any iterative sparse decoding algorithm but employing the group testing approach. As illustrated in Figure 3, the 'likelihood' score for each image is estimated by summing the corresponding group similarities it belongs to:

$$\tilde{u}_j = \sum_{i \in \mathcal{L}_j} v_i, \tag{10}$$

where $\mathcal{L}_j$ denotes the set of groups image j belongs to. Vector-wise:

$$\tilde{\mathbf{u}} = G^\top \mathbf{v}. \tag{11}$$

Thanks to the sparsity of matrix G, the computational complexity is $M \times N_\mathcal{H}$, which is significantly smaller than $M \times N$.

Once again, $\tilde{\mathbf{u}}/N_\mathcal{L}$ is an estimation of $\mathbf{u}$ whose variance is relatively large. Despite its inaccuracy, the relevant images are usually assigned with large values in the estimation $\tilde{\mathbf{u}}$. To confirm the relevance of an image j with a large score $\tilde{u}_j$, we directly calculate its true similarity with the query vector.

This is the key: in order to improve the overall estimator, we consider an *adaptive* group testing strategy, which takes advantage of the direct measurement between the query and a few database images. This is done by an online back propagation update. More precisely, we take out the highest score from $\tilde{\mathbf{u}}$:

$$n = \arg\max_j \tilde{u}_j, \tag{12}$$

and in turn we calculate the exact similarity value

$$u_n = q^\top x_n \tag{13}$$

between query q and image n. Now that we have the true knowledge of nth image's similarity to query, in order to eliminate its influence on those groups it is attached to, we subtract u_n from the initial group similarity $v_m^0 = v_m$ to yield an updated similarity v_m^1:

$$v_m^1 = v_m^0 - u_n = q^\top \left(\sum_{j \in \mathcal{H}_m^0} x_j - x_n \right) \tag{14}$$

$$= q^\top \sum_{j \in \mathcal{H}_m^0 \setminus \{n\}} x_j, \tag{15}$$

where m denotes the mth group connected with image n. The new estimator v_m^1 is more accurate than v_m^0 to infer a possible match amongst the remaining images inside the group. We update the $N_\mathcal{L}$ group similarities connected with image n following (14). Subsequently, we back propagate the updated group similarities to their images as in Figure 3. The initial estimated image score vector $\tilde{\mathbf{u}}^0 = \tilde{\mathbf{u}}$ (11) is updated to $\tilde{\mathbf{u}}^1$. We repeat this update R times:

$$v_m^R = v_m^{R-1} - u_n = q^\top \sum_{j \in \mathcal{H}_m^{R-1} \setminus \{n\}} x_j. \tag{16}$$

At each iteration, the selected image of highest score is excluded as well as its connections with groups. Thereby, n is not the same in each update, the corresponding groups (m, $\mathcal{H}_m^{R-1}$) it connects with might also be different. The updated group similarities are back propagated to their images at each iteration. After $\tilde{\mathbf{u}}^{R-1}$ is updated to $\tilde{\mathbf{u}}^R$, we already calculate the cosine similarities of R images in total to the query, and they are ranked by their true similarity values during the back propagation stage.

Batch processing. In practice, when R is large, calculating and back-propagating the true similarity one vector by one affects the efficiency. To overcome this problem, we do not select only one image with the largest score, but instead the $\frac{R}{t}$ largest scores and propagate these messages at once, where t is a parameter setting the desired number of back propagations steps (instead of R). With t being small enough, the propagation phase is significantly accelerated and the bottleneck becomes the vector-level operations, *i.e.*, the query-group measurements and the direct measurements between the query and the selected images.

Computational cost. The overall computational cost in the proposed method is summarized as

$$\begin{aligned} T &= \mathcal{O}(M \times D) + \mathcal{O}(M \times N_\mathcal{H}) + \mathcal{O}(R \times D) \\ &\simeq \mathcal{O}((M + R) \times D) = \mathcal{O}(2M \times D). \end{aligned} \tag{17}$$

T can be approximated to $\mathcal{O}(2M \times D)$ as $D \gg N_\mathcal{H}$ and $R = M$. Compared to the baseline time complexity,

$$T_\text{B} = \mathcal{O}(N \times D), \tag{18}$$

the retrieval efficiency is guaranteed ($T \ll T_\text{B}$), *i.e.* as long as $2M \ll N$. We ignore the complexity of back propagation. $\frac{R}{t}$ images' true similarities are calculated each time, supposing all the M groups' similarities are correspondingly updated, then the additional operations will amount to $t \times M \times N_\mathcal{H}$ at most for t updates. As long as t is small, it is still negligible in high-dimensional spaces (large D) and large scale database (large N).

Variant (GT-V). In the Appendix, we present a simplified version of our GT-based estimator, denoted by GT-V (GT Variant). It works in the particular case that there exists highly relevant database images to a query, such as near duplicate images. When we take out the largest score from $\tilde{\mathbf{u}}$ (11), we will find that $\tilde{u}_n$ is clearly larger than the other $\tilde{u}_j$. We could directly subtract $\tilde{u}_n/N_{\mathcal{L}}$ from the group similarities without calculating the true similarity, since we have a high confidence that the nth image is highly relevant to the query. The corresponding image scores are updated following the same protocol with GT. In the end, we do t times back propagation with each time only one estimated image similarity being subtracted from the group similarities. We select the top-R ranked images with the largest scores from $\tilde{\mathbf{u}}^t$ and re-rank them according to their cosine similarities with query. The performance can reach the same level with GT, however, the additional computation during back propagation is further reduced to $t \times N_{\mathcal{H}} \times N_{\mathcal{L}}$.

Notice that GT-V is only effective for the databases that have highly relevant images with the query (perhaps the query's duplicate matched images). Notwithstanding GT-V is not a general method, it is almost as effective as GT for all the databases used in our experimental investigation.

4. DISCUSSION

We introduce a very simple probabilistic model to get some hints on how to tune our setup. By no means, we pretend that this model closely reflects reality. It is only a toy example illustrating a given phenomena, known as dilution in the group testing literature.

4.1 Model of the image similarity

Let x_j and q be two uniformly distributed random unit vectors of D dimension. We assume that two irrelevant images produce two statistically independent vectors. Denote by U_j the random variable modeling their cosine similarity u_j. It is asymptotically (for large D) distributed as a Gaussian law with null expectation and variance $1/D$: $U_j \sim \mathcal{N}\left(0, \frac{1}{D}\right)$. It indicates that, the larger D is, the sparser $\mathbf{u}$ will be, the easier it will be reconstructed.

When the images are relevant, we model the distribution of U_j by another Gaussian distribution: $U_j \sim \mathcal{N}(\mu, \sigma^2)$ with a positive expectation $\mu > 0$. We define $\mathcal{G}(x; \mu, \sigma^2) = \exp(-(x-\mu)^2/2\sigma^2)/\sqrt{2\pi}\sigma$ the probability density function (pdf) of $\mathcal{N}(\mu, \sigma^2)$.

4.2 Model of the group similarity

The distribution of the group similarity is a mixture of the above Gaussian distributions depending on how many relevant images there are in the group.

Suppose that there are c images matching with the query in the database of size N. Denote by K the random variable modeling the number of matching images in a given group of size $N_{\mathcal{H}}$. Since the group has been created at random, K follows a hypergeometric distribution:

$$\mathbb{P}[K = k] = \begin{cases} \frac{\binom{c}{k}\binom{N-c}{N_{\mathcal{H}}-k}}{\binom{N}{N_{\mathcal{H}}}} & \text{if } 0 \leq k \leq \min(c, N_{\mathcal{H}}), \\ 0 & \text{otherwise.} \end{cases} \quad (19)$$

We denote this probability by $P_N^c(k, N_{\mathcal{H}})$.

We assume now that the similarities of the images composing the group are mutually independent, which is reasonable since the group has been composed randomly. When there are k matches in the group, the random variable V related to the group similarity v is then distributed as $\mathcal{N}(k\mu, (N_{\mathcal{H}} - k)/D + k\sigma^2)$. In other words, its pdf is

$$f(v|K = k) = \mathcal{G}(x; k\mu, (N_{\mathcal{H}} - k)/D + k\sigma^2). \quad (20)$$

When we do not know how many matches there are in a group, the pdf of V is as follows:

$$\begin{aligned} f(v) &= \sum_{k=0}^{N_{\mathcal{H}}} \mathbb{P}[K = k] \cdot f(v|K = k) \\ &= \sum_{k=0}^{N_{\mathcal{H}}} P_N^c(k, N_{\mathcal{H}}).\mathcal{G}\left(x; k\mu, \frac{N_{\mathcal{H}} - k}{D} + k\sigma^2\right). \end{aligned}$$

4.3 Hypothesis test

The philosophy of group testing is to infer about the relevance of image j from the group similarities. We need to test the two following hypotheses:

Image j matches the query. When $g_{ij} = 1$, we know that image j belongs to group $\mathcal{H}_i$, therefore this group has at least one match. This knowledge transforms the pdf of the group similarity V_i into:

$$f_1^+(v) = \sum_{k=1}^{N_{\mathcal{H}}} P_{N-1}^{c-1}(k-1, N_{\mathcal{H}} - 1).\mathcal{G}\left(x; k\mu, \frac{N_{\mathcal{H}} - k}{D} + k\sigma^2\right)$$

In the same way, when $g_{ij} = 0$, this knowledge transforms the pdf of the group similarity V_i into:

$$f_0^+(v) = \sum_{k=0}^{N_{\mathcal{H}}} P_{N-1}^{c-1}(k, N_{\mathcal{H}}).\mathcal{G}\left(x; k\mu, \frac{N_{\mathcal{H}} - k}{D} + k\sigma^2\right).$$

Image j does not match the query. When $g_{ij} = 1$, we know that this group cannot be composed of matching images only:

$$f_1^-(v) = \sum_{k=0}^{N_{\mathcal{H}}-1} P_{N-1}^{c}(k, N_{\mathcal{H}} - 1).\mathcal{G}\left(x; k\mu, \frac{N_{\mathcal{H}} - k}{D} + k\sigma^2\right).$$

When $g_{ij} = 0$, this knowledge transforms the pdf of the group similarity V_i into:

$$f_0^-(v) = \sum_{k=0}^{N_{\mathcal{H}}} P_{N-1}^{c}(k, N_{\mathcal{H}}).\mathcal{G}\left(x; k\mu, \frac{N_{\mathcal{H}} - k}{D} + k\sigma^2\right).$$

Which groups bring information. In reality, we do not know wether image j is a match. If it is, $N_{\mathcal{L}}$ group similarities are distributed according to f_1^+ and $M - N_{\mathcal{L}}$ according to f_0^+. If it is not, then $N_{\mathcal{L}}$ group similarities are distributed according to f_1^- and $M - N_{\mathcal{L}}$ according to f_0^-. Since $c \ll N$, we have indeed that

$$f_0^+(v) \approx f_0^-(v), \quad \forall v \in \mathbb{R}. \quad (21)$$

This means that knowing whether image j matches the query or not has no impact on the similarities of the groups which image j doesn't belong to. It is only the similarities of the $N_{\mathcal{L}}$ groups where image j is, that bring some information about the match with the query.

4.4 Amount of information

The group similarities provide an amount of information about the match of image j which can be measured by the Kullback Leibler distance between their distributions under

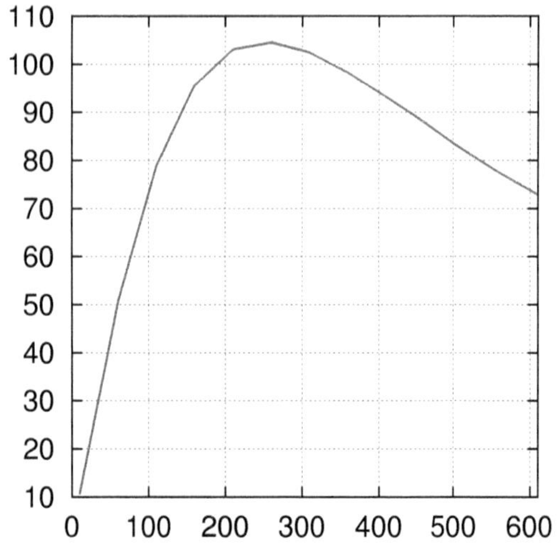

Figure 4: Total Kullback Leibler distance in nats, as a function of $N_{\mathcal{H}}$. Setup: $D = 1920$, $\mu = 0.47$, $\sigma^2 = 0.16$, $c = 3$, $n = 10^6$.

both hypothesis. We assume that the group similarities are statistically independent (which is not exactly true). The total Kullback Leibler distance between the distribution of the M group similarities under both hypothesis is simply (thanks to approximation (21)):

$$D_{KL} = N_{\mathcal{L}} \cdot D(f_1^+ || f_1^-) = M \frac{N_{\mathcal{H}}}{N} \cdot D(f_1^+ || f_1^-), \quad (22)$$

where $D(f_1^+||f_1^-)$ is the Kullback-Leibler distance between pdf f_1^+ and f_1^-.

This last quantity heavily depends on $N_{\mathcal{H}}$: The bigger $N_{\mathcal{H}}$, the bigger the variances of the involved Gaussian distributions (20), the smoother and more similar f_1^+ and f_1^-, and the lower $D(f_1^+||f_1^-)$. This means that the quantity of information brought by one group similarity about the matching of a given image in the database is getting lower. This phenomenon is known in group testing as the dilution: composing groups with too many items dilute the detectability of the match of one particular item.

However, this phenomenon is partly compensated by the fact that, for a fixed ratio M/N, larger groups (*i.e.* big $N_{\mathcal{H}}$) implies that a given image is present in more groups (*i.e.* big $N_{\mathcal{L}}$ thanks to (6)). Each group brings less information, but we have more groups to detect whether a particular image is a match. In the end, it is not possible to theoretically derive the best value of $N_{\mathcal{H}}$ maximizing the total Kullback Leibler distance D_{KL}. Figure 4 plots this quantity for this toy example showing that there is an optimal value for $N_{\mathcal{H}}$. In the experimental session, we will show the optimal value of $N_{\mathcal{H}}$ in the enumerable test of $N_{\mathcal{L}}$ as appearing in (6).

5. EXPERIMENTS

This section evaluates and compares the algorithms proposed in our framework. We consider an image retrieval scenario. We, first, present the evaluation protocol and give some implementation details. Then we discuss the parameters and analyze the results.

5.1 Dataset and evaluation protocol

We use public benchmarks commonly used by papers on image retrieval for the evaluation.

INRIA Holidays is a set of images which mainly contains holidays photos [9]. It includes a large variety of scene types (natural, man-made, water and fire effects, etc.) and has 500 queries and 1,491 images in total. The evaluation is carried out in a leave-one-out manner, meaning the query image is retrieved from the set prior to retrieval.

UKB. The University of Kentucky Benchmark dataset [21] consists of 10,200 images grouped into 2,550 subsets of corresponding images. Each subset contains four images. For a given query, the system is expected to return the four relevant images in the first four positions.

Flickr1M. The Flickr1M dataset consists of 1 million images downloaded from Flickr [23]. The images have been downloaded by searching Flickr and are used as distractors in our experiment.

Evaluations are first conducted on a small and medium-sized datasets (Holidays and UKB). To evaluate the performance on larger scale, we gradually add images from the Flickr1M dataset as distractors. In this case, the evaluation is performed on the 500 Holidays queries, since the images from Flickr1M are not relevant to the queries. Note that some methods, like pseudo-inverse and sparse decoding, are not evaluated on the larger sets because they are not tractable: although they use less group-to-query operations, deducing the image similarities is their bottleneck.

Evaluation protocol. The performance for the Holidays and Flickr1M datasets is measured in terms of the average precision (AP), which is defined as the area under the precision-recall curve [23] for each query. The AP score is computed for each query and averaged to obtain a mean average precision (mAP). For the UKB dataset, the score is standardly computed as the average number of correct images in the top-4 positions (4-recall@4), the best score is 4. In the same test, there is always a small variance of the performance due to the randomness of the group matrix. We report here the median value (maximum and minimal values for the variances) out of 5 repetitions. The baseline is obtained from a recent paper [13].

5.2 Implementation notes

Design of Matrix G. Referring to the model discussion session, $N_{\mathcal{H}}$ and $N_{\mathcal{L}}$ have a strong impact on the variances of the group similarities. These parameters should not be very large, so that the detectability of the match of one particular relevant image in a group is not diluted too much, as discussed in Section 4.

The parameter $N_{\mathcal{H}}$ is chosen to be a small value, Figure 6 shows a simple example on how to construct the matrix: starting from a $M \times N$ zero matrix $\widetilde{G}$, we set some values to 1s: $N_{\mathcal{H}}$ elements (red) in the first row as one, and $N_{\mathcal{H}}+1$: $2N_{\mathcal{H}}$ elements (green) in the second row as one, *etc.* When it comes to the end, we restart from the beginning (brown) until M rows are initialized. This construction guarantees that each group has approximately the same number of images $N_{\mathcal{H}}$, and each image belongs to approximately the same number of groups $N_{\mathcal{L}}$. To make it

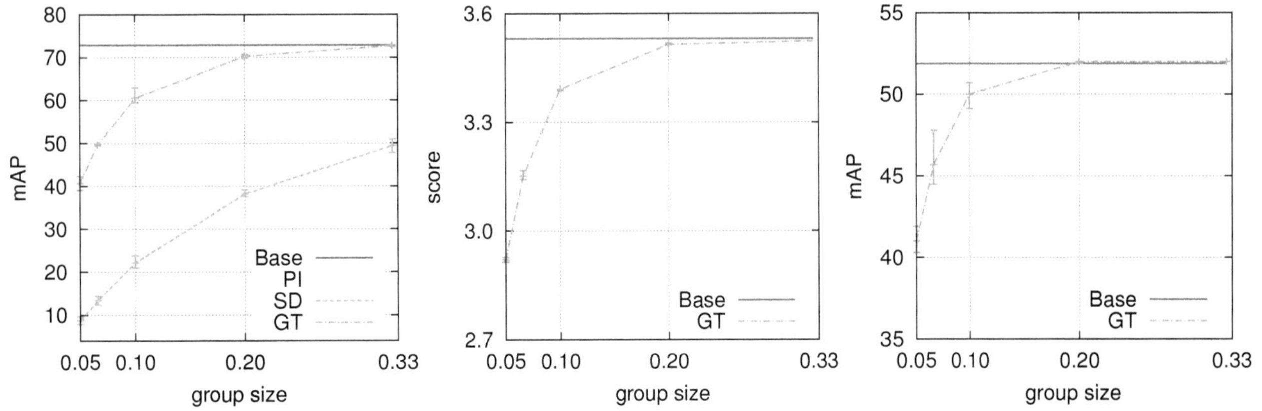

(a) Holidays (b) UKB (c) Holidays+Flickr1M

Figure 5: Group size varied in the range of $\{\frac{1}{20}, \frac{1}{15}, \frac{1}{10}, \frac{1}{5}, \frac{1}{3}\}$ of the database size. $N_{\mathcal{L}}$ is chosen as 2 according to Table 1. Vocabulary size is 16.

Table 1: Performance as a function of the number of groups per image $N_{\mathcal{L}}$ on Holidays (+ Flickr1M) and UKB datasets. $N_{\mathcal{L}}$ varies from 1 to 20, while M is 1/10 of database size. The results are given for *(top)* 8064- and *(bottom)* 1920-dimensional image descriptors.

$N_{\mathcal{L}}(k_c = 64)$	Holidays	UKB
	GT	GT
1	68.3	3.56
2	**69.6**	**3.57**
5	68.3	3.56
10	63.8	3.56
20	60.3	3.56
baseline	77.2	3.63

$N_{\mathcal{L}}(k_c = 16)$	UKB	Holidays+Flickr1M
	GT	GT
1	3.37	49.4
2	**3.39**	**50.0**
5	3.37	49.2
10	3.36	49.2
20	3.37	48.3
baseline	3.53	51.9

random, we apply some random permutations on the matrix columns, and consequently, we could produce a random matrix satisfying (6). Note that this construction is similar to the one considered in a paper for projecting sparse vectors [10].

Experimental setup. The local descriptors are extracted with the Hessian-affine detector and described by SIFT [15]. We use the RootSIFT variant [1, 8] in all our experiments. Overall, the descriptor extraction follows the procedure in our baseline [13]. The triangulation embedding and democratic aggregation [13] are used to aggregate the features with a vocabulary size k_c being set to either 16 or 64. We obtain the vocabulary independently from the dataset Flickr60k. Given the SIFT descriptor's length of 128, the dimension

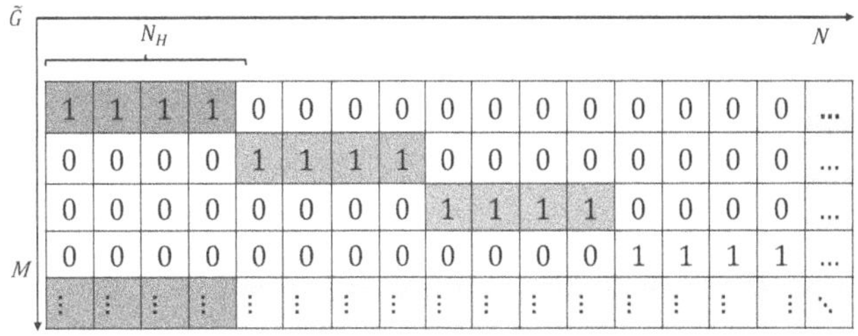

Figure 6: An illustration of how to construct the group matrix.

of our representation is thus $128 \times 16(64) = 2,048(8,192)$. In real implementation, the first 128 components associated with the largest eigenvalues are discarded to reduce the interferences between the coded descriptors. The final dimensionality D of the representation is therefore $1,920(8,064)$. The number of groups M is by default $\frac{1}{10}$ of the database size, and we calculate the cosine similarities of the same number of images in back propagation stage ($R = M$). Considering both the efficiency and effectiveness, t is set to 10 in GT. $N_{\mathcal{L}}$ varies in different datasets and score estimation strategies, as discussed in the following subsection evaluating the impact of the parameter. The quantity $N_{\mathcal{H}}$ is obtained by (6).

5.3 Impact of the parameters

Number of groups per image $N_{\mathcal{L}}$. Table 1 shows the performance of varying number of groups per image in Holidays, UKB and Flickr1M datasets. The best $N_{\mathcal{L}}$ is 2 for both vocabulary size and dataset. The performance is not very sensitive to $N_{\mathcal{L}}$, we can generally take it as small as 2 for better efficiency.

Total number of groups M. For a fixed value of $N_{\mathcal{L}}$, we evaluate the impact of the total number of groups in Holidays, UKB, and Holidays + Flickr1M datasets. We vary M from 1/20 to 1/3 of the database size, and obtain similarity scores reported in Figure 5 and Table 2 for vocabulary sizes $k_c = 16$ and 64. Increasing the group size appear to help. Indeed, with M simply being 1/10 of database size and

Table 2: The number of groups M varies in the range of $\{\frac{1}{20}, \frac{1}{15}, \frac{1}{10}, \frac{1}{5}, \frac{1}{3}\}$ of the database size N. $N_{\mathcal{L}}$ is chosen as 2 according to Table 1. The vocabulary size is $k_c = 64$.

$\frac{M}{N}$	Holidays	UKB
	GT	GT
1/20	52.5	3.32
1/15	59.7	3.46
1/10	69.5	3.57
1/5	75.5	3.63
1/3	77.2	3.63
baseline	77.2	3.63

$k_c = 16$, the mAP using back propagation reaches around 96% of the baseline benchmark in Holidays+Flickr1M. This means that we only need 2/10 (another 1/10 is for the back propagation) of the original computational cost to recover 96% of the baseline precision.

Pseudo-inverse and sparse decoding results on Holidays dataset are also presented. They are more time consuming: it is not feasible to carry out them for a large dataset. For pseudo-inverse, it only works when the matrix G is very dense ($N_{\mathcal{L}}$ is very large), which makes the reconstruction very inefficient. For sparse decoding, we add positive constrains in the coefficients of $\mathbf{u}$ (9), otherwise, the mAP is a bit higher.

As previously reported [13], the performance improves by increasing the vocabulary size k_c from 16 to 64. In our framework, it is important to use a large dimensionality: the dimensionality D ($k_c \times 128 - 128$) significantly impacts the level of noisy variance in group testing. Increasing D has a beneficial on this variance (see Section 4.1), and the overall performance is therefore improved.

Back propagation times. Table 3 shows the results, for UKB and Holidays+Flickr1M datasets, with different numbers of back-propagation stages t . GT is improved with a larger number of back propagation iterations. Setting $t = 10$ appears a good compromise both in terms of efficiency and effectiveness. Take Holidays+Flickr1M as an example, we apply $t = 10$ back propagations steps, each involving direct measurements for $10k$ images (those with the highest ranks). Assuming that all group similarities are updated by one back propagation, the additional computation is thus approximated to $t \times (10k \times N_{\mathcal{H}}) = 20 \times N$, where $N_{\mathcal{H}}$ is 20 when $N_{\mathcal{L}}$ is chosen as 2 for the best. Compared to the $N \times D$ computations of the baseline, the overall increase in efficiency is still guaranteed because $D = 1,920 \gg 20$.

We also present the result for GT-V. The performance drop for large values of t. In our opinion, this is because, for UKB and Holidays+Flickr1M, there is only one duplicate image per query (the query itself). Refer to the Appendix for more details about this variant.

Group *vs* back propagation. Assuming that $M + R = 100k$ is fixed in Holidays + Flickr1M, Figure 7 analyzes the trade-off between M and R. We achieve the best performance for $M = R = 50k$. The default setting follows this observation. It is also interesting that, 1) the performance is obviously better with a larger ratio M/R; 2) when $M = 100k$ and $R = 0$ (no back propagation), the mAP is only 3.3.

Table 3: Performance as a function of the number of back propagation stages t (Holidays + Flickr1M and UKB datasets). The number of groups is set by default to $\frac{N}{10}$ and $N_{\mathcal{L}}$ is the optimal value. $k_c = 16$.

t	UKB		Holidays+Flick1M	
	GT	GT-V	GT	GT-V
0	3.28		48.9	
1	3.34	**3.34**	49.5	**49.4**
4	3.38	2.04	48.9	19.6
8	3.37	2.05	49.5	16.3
10	**3.39**	2.04	**50.0**	16.4

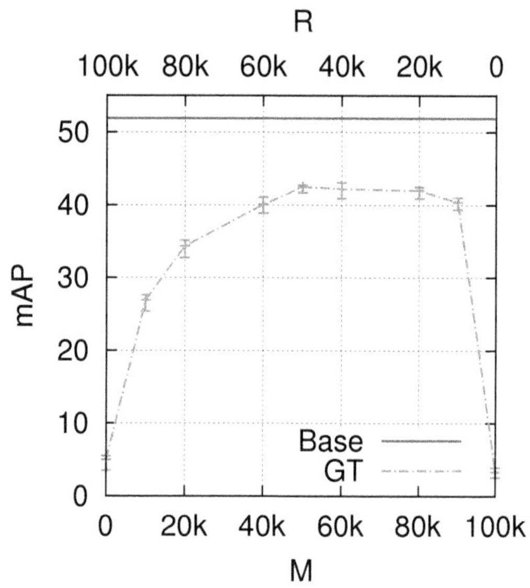

Figure 7: Performance (mAP) on Holidays + Flickr1M dataset corresponding to different combinations of M and R when $M + R$ is fixed to $100k$ and vocabulary size $k_c = 16$.

5.4 Overall performance

Database size. Figure 8 reports the mAP values obtained when we gradually add images from Flickr1M as distractors to Holidays dataset. For larger databases, the mAP of our methods approaches the baseline. This behavior is expected because group testing is more effective when the number of positive tests is small compared to the total number of tests: there is comparatively less interferences in the score estimation. This advocates the practical interest of our group testing framework for very large scale image retrieval.

The results of GT-V are also given in this figure as an alternative choice. Although GT-V is not provably good in general, it is competitive in all the databases we use, for there are always images that are highly relevant to the query. Nevertheless, we generally observe some loss compared to our main GT approach.

PCA dimensionality reduction. Another way to reduce the computational cost is to use dimensionality reduction. We demonstrate that our approach is complementary with PCA dimensionality reduction. To evaluate this, we keep the first D' components of the representation (as evaluated

Table 4: Performance after dimensionality reduction to short vectors. This evaluation follows our default settings. There are two set of descriptors used in rows 3–6 and 7–9, corresponding to vectors of dimensionality 1920 and 8064, respectively. We compare the methods PCA, GT, and P+G (PCA + GT) for two different operating points, aiming at reducing the complexity of the baseline by a factor 8 (columns 3 to 5) and 32 (columns 6 to 8). The number of operations is reflected by $N_s \times D'$, where N_s denotes the number of vector comparisons. The combination of PCA with group testing always achieves the best result for a fixed complexity.

Method	Base	PCA	GT	P+G	PCA	GT	P+G
N_s	N	N	$\frac{N}{8}$	$\frac{N}{2}$	N	$\frac{N}{32}$	$\frac{N}{2}$
D'	1920	$\frac{1920}{8}$	1920	$\frac{1920}{4}$	$\frac{1920}{32}$	1920	$\frac{1920}{16}$
Holidays	72.8	65.6	49.1	**67.2**	56.2	7.3	**60.3**
UKB	3.53	3.45	3.08	**3.48**	3.26	1.55	**3.33**
Flickr1M	51.9	42.9	44.6	**46.6**	32.0	15.9	**39.8**
D'	8064	$\frac{8064}{8}$	8064	$\frac{8064}{4}$	$\frac{8064}{32}$	8064	$\frac{8064}{16}$
Holidays	77.2	71.7	60.7	**73.8**	65.6	20.3	**68.5**
UKB	3.63	3.59	3.41	**3.62**	3.52	2.31	**3.56**

in our image retrieval baseline [13]): Table 4 reports the performance with different D', k_c and N_s. Our goal is to measure the performance for a fixed overall complexity. N_s denotes the total number of vector comparisons, *e.g.*, in GT, $N_s = R + M$, it is $\frac{N}{8}$ meaning that $\frac{N}{16}$ for the M group similarities and another $\frac{N}{16}$ for the R image similarities in the back propagation. The overall computations in different methods is approximately summarized by the cost $N_s \times D'$.

Compared to the baseline, there is a drop in performance in GT due to the smaller number of measurements (and therefore small number of computations). The same remark holds for the PCA: if we divide the dimensionality by 8 and 32 in PCA, so that the computation of PCA is the same with that of GT, the performance decreases. Yet, our method is better than PCA on the large Holidays+Flickr1M dataset. For the smaller datasets, *i.e.* UKB and Holidays, it is inferior but could be close to PCA as long as N_s is not too small and k_c is large. In essence, these experiments show that the proposed group testing framework are comparatively more effective for large scale database and high-dimensional spaces.

We also conduct the experiment by combining PCA with GT (P + G). First, we divide the original dimensionality by 4, and 16; second, we embed GT by setting M as $\frac{N}{4}$ ($R = M$), which means that N_s is $\frac{N}{2}$. Considering the results that achieves the same overall complexity, it appears that the combination of PCA with GT outperforms both PCA and GT. Again, the performance is comparatively better on the large scale databases and high-dimensional spaces.

6. CONCLUSION

Our framework for similarity search in high-dimensional spaces amounts to replacing the individual query-database similarity computations by group measurements, in a way strongly inspired by adaptive group testing algorithms. In this context, the key algorithmic component is to estimate the individual image similarities from the group measurements. The first conclusion of our paper is that sparse recovery algorithms with positivity constraints, such as those used in compressed sensing, already give better results than the regular pseudo-inverse method. Yet this strategy has a limited practical interest due to its high computational cost.

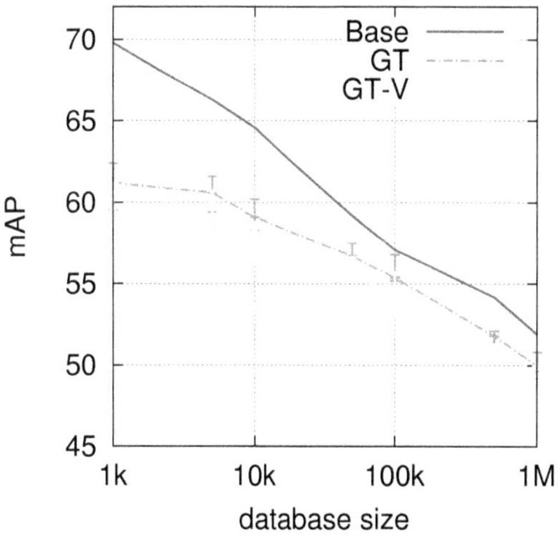

Figure 8: mAP values corresponding to different sizes of Holidays + Flickr (1k, 5k, 10k, 50k, 100k, 500k, 1M). Group size is $\frac{1}{10}$ of the database size while vocabulary size is 16.

Moreover, sparse recovery makes the (invalid) assumption that most similarities are zeros. For this reason, our main strategy based on adaptive group testing demonstrates a better performance, especially for large datasets and for the higher-dimensional spaces. As a result, our strategy offers competitive performance with respect to the compromise between retrieval efficiency and accuracy, and is shown complementary to PCA dimensionality reduction.

As a final note, we mention that this exploratory strategy is certainly not optimum with respect to the achievable trade-offs. From a group testing perspective, our algorithm is very simple and does not formally optimize the accuracy under a constraint on the number of measurements. Similarly, the group design is not directly optimized. For these reasons, we believe that further possible improvement is possible in this promising framework.

7. ACKNOWLEDGEMENTS

This work was supported by ERC grant VIAMASS no. 336054 and ANR project FIRE-ID. Miaojing Shi was supported by NBRPC 2011CB302400, NSFC 61121002, 61375026 and JCYJ 20120614152136201, he thanks his supervisor Prof. Chao Xu for encouraging him to work on this paper.

8. REFERENCES

[1] R. Arandjelovic and A. Zisserman. Three things everyone should know to improve object retrieval. In *CVPR*, June 2012.

[2] R. Balu, T. Furon, and H. Jégou. Beyond "project and sign" for cosine estimation with binary codes. In *ICASSP*, 2014.

[3] M. S. Charikar. Similarity estimation techniques from rounding algorithms. In *STOC*, pages 380–388, May 2002.
[4] M. Datar, N. Immorlica, P. Indyk, and V. Mirrokni. Locality-sensitive hashing scheme based on p-stable distributions. In *Proceedings of the Symposium on Computational Geometry*, pages 253–262, 2004.
[5] R. Dorfman. The detection of defective members of large populations. *The Annals of Mathematical Statistics*, 14(4):436–440, December 1943.
[6] D.-Z. Du and F. K. Hwang. *Combinatorial group testing and its applications*. World Scientific, 1993.
[7] P. Indyk and R. Motwani. Approximate nearest neighbors: towards removing the curse of dimensionality. In *STOC*, pages 604–613, 1998.
[8] M. Jain, R. Benmokhtar, P. Gros, and H. Jégou. Hamming embedding similarity-based image classification. In *ICMR*, June 2012.
[9] H. Jégou, M. Douze, and C. Schmid. Hamming embedding and weak geometric consistency for large scale image search. In *ECCV*, October 2008.
[10] H. Jégou, M. Douze, and C. Schmid. Packing bag-of-features. In *ICCV*, September 2009.
[11] H. Jégou, M. Douze, and C. Schmid. Product quantization for nearest neighbor search. *IEEE Trans. PAMI*, 33(1):117–128, January 2011.
[12] H. Jégou, F. Perronnin, M. Douze, J. Sánchez, P. Pérez, and C. Schmid. Aggregating local descriptors into compact codes. In *IEEE Trans. PAMI*, September 2012.
[13] H. Jégou and A. Zisserman. Triangulation embedding and democratic kernels for image search. In *CVPR*, June 2014.
[14] F. Krzakala, M. Mézard, F. Sausset, Y. Sun, and L. Zdeborová. Statistical-physics-based reconstruction in compressed sensing. *Physical Review X*, 2(2), 2012.
[15] D. Lowe. Distinctive image features from scale-invariant keypoints. *IJCV*, 60(2):91–110, 2004.
[16] Q. Luo, S. Zhang, T. Huang, W. Gao, and Q. Tian. Superimage: Packing semantic-relevant images for indexing and retrieval. In *ICMR*, April 2014.
[17] Q. Lv, M. Charikar, and K. Li. Image similarity search with compact data structures. In *CIKM*, pages 208–217, November 2004.
[18] Q. Lv, W. Josephson, Z. Wang, M. Charikar, and K. Li. Multi-probe LSH: Efficient indexing for high-dimensional similarity search. In *Proceedings of the International Conference on Very Large DataBases*, pages 950–961, 2007.
[19] J. Mairal, F. Bach, J. Ponce, and G. Sapiro. Online dictionary learning for sparse coding. In *ICML*, 2009.
[20] M. Muja and D. G. Lowe. Fast approximate nearest neighbors with automatic algorithm configuration. In *VISAPP*, February 2009.
[21] D. Nistér and H. Stewénius. Scalable recognition with a vocabulary tree. In *CVPR*, pages 2161–2168, June 2006.
[22] F. Perronnin and C. R. Dance. Fisher kernels on visual vocabularies for image categorization. In *CVPR*, June 2007.
[23] J. Philbin, O. Chum, M. Isard, J. Sivic, and A. Zisserman. Object retrieval with large vocabularies and fast spatial matching. In *CVPR*, June 2007.
[24] J. Sivic and A. Zisserman. Video Google: A text retrieval approach to object matching in videos. In *ICCV*, pages 1470–1477, October 2003.
[25] A. Torralba, R. Fergus, and Y. Weiss. Small codes and large databases for recognition. In *CVPR*, June 2008.

APPENDIX: Group testing variant GT-V

This appendix details the variant mentioned at the end of Section 3. It specifically assumes that some searched images (for instance duplicate images) in the database are very similar to the query. The groups connected with these highly relevant images have thus strong similarities, but the presence of other relevant images in these groups might be consequently hidden. To cancel this shadowing in these groups, we propose an alternative method: group testing variance.

Likewise (11) and (12), we obtain the initial scores $\tilde{\mathbf{u}}$ and spot the image with the highest score. Empirically, we observe that $\tilde{u}_n$ is significantly larger than the other $\tilde{u}_j$. This gives us a high confidence that the nth image is highly relevant to the query, and all the groups in which it occurs have relatively larger similarities.

This n^{th} image may hide the presence of other relevant images in the groups of $\mathcal{L}_n$. We subtract $\tilde{u}_n^0 = \tilde{u}_n$ from initial group similarities $v_m^0 = v_m$, $m \in \mathcal{L}_n$, to yield an update similarity v_m^1:

$$v_m^1 = v_m^0 - \tilde{u}_n^0 . \frac{1}{|\mathcal{L}_n|} = q^\top \left(\sum_{j \in \mathcal{H}_m^0} x_j - \frac{1}{|\mathcal{L}_n|} \sum_{i \in \mathcal{L}_n} v_i^0 \right). \quad (23)$$

Update v_m^1 more precisely depicts the likelihood scores of the group composed of the remainging images.

Following the same protocol as in the main GT method, all the $N_{\mathcal{L}}$ group similarities connected with image n are updated and back propagated to the images (the nth image being excluded) connected with these groups. The image scores in $\tilde{\mathbf{u}}$ is updated, and we repeat the update t times:

$$v_m^t = v_m^{t-1} - \tilde{u}_n^{t-1} . \frac{1}{|\mathcal{L}_n|}. \quad (24)$$

Afterwards, we rank the image list according to their values in $\tilde{\mathbf{u}}^t$ and re-rank the top-R ones by calculating their true cosine similarities.

The computational cost is comparable to GT, as discussed below for the two main steps of these algorithms.

1. largest score removal: once $N_{\mathcal{L}}$ connected group similarities are changed, the scores of the $N_{\mathcal{H}} \times N_{\mathcal{L}}$ images connected with these groups are updated. The additional computation thus amounts to $t \times N_{\mathcal{H}} \times N_{\mathcal{L}}$ operations for a number of t updates;
2. image list re-ranking: the computation is $\mathcal{O}(N \log R)$ for selecting the top-R ranked images, plus $\mathcal{O}(R \log R)$ for re-ranking them by their true similarities. With R equalling M and small enough, it is comparable to the time complexity of ranking the entire list $\mathcal{O}(N \log N)$.

If there is no highly relevant images in the database, the image with the largest estimated score might not truly matching the query. In this case, we suggest adopting the more reliable GT estimation.

Object Segmentation in Images using EEG Signals

Eva Mohedano[1]
eva.mohedano@insight-centre.org

Graham Healy[1]
ghealy@computing.dcu.ie

Kevin McGuinness[1]
kevin.mcguinness@dcu.ie

Xavier Giró-i-Nieto[2]
xavier.giro@upc.edu

Noel E. O'Connor[1]
noel.oconnor@dcu.ie

Alan F. Smeaton[1]
alan.smeaton@dcu.ie

[1]Insight Centre for Data Analytics
Dublin City University
Glasnevin, Dublin 9, Ireland

[2]Image Processing Group
Universitat Politècnica de Catalunya
C. Jordi Girona, 1-3. 08034 Barcelona

ABSTRACT

This paper explores the potential of brain-computer interfaces in segmenting objects from images. Our approach is centered around designing an effective method for displaying the image parts to the users such that they generate measurable brain reactions. When an image region, specifically a block of pixels, is displayed we estimate the probability of the block containing the object of interest using a score based on EEG activity. After several such blocks are displayed, the resulting probability map is binarized and combined with the GrabCut algorithm to segment the image into object and background regions. This study shows that BCI and simple EEG analysis are useful in locating object boundaries in images.

Categories and Subject Descriptors

H.1.2 [**User/Machine System**]: Human information processing; I.4.6 [**S**]: egmentation; C.3 [**Special-Purpose and Application-Based Systems**]: Signal processing systems

General Terms

Experimentation, Design, Algorithms

Keywords

Brain-computer interfaces, Electroencephalography, rapid serial visual presentation, Object segmentation, Interactive segmentation, GrabCut algorithm

1. INTRODUCTION

The human brain is capable of processing audiovisual information in a fashion that, nowadays, clearly outperforms machines in several applications. The multimedia research community is constantly trying to simulate the brain's behaviour to later leverage its innate computational possibilities through machinery. However, a deep understanding of the human brain remains one of the greatest scientific challenges. Recent initiatives, such us the Human Brain Project in Europe or the the BRAIN Initiative in the United States, have identified its exploration as one of the Grand Challenges of our time.

Although humans consistently outperform computers in the semantic interpretation of multimedia signals [12], the computational and storage power of machines can be scaled and networked dramatically beyond individual human capacities. These two observations are the foundation of the human computational technologies, which exploit the best of both by defining collaborative strategies. The steady decrease in the cost of EEG (Electroencephalography) systems in recent years has made these non-invasive Brain-Computer Interfaces (BCIs) accessible beyond the traditional disciplines that typically availed of this technology [18, 23]. Visual analysis is one such field, with recent publications exploring the potential of EEG signals for image retrieval [10, 26, 25] and object detection [5, 14].

The use of brain-computer interfaces is, however, still limited, primarily because the motor (or speech) capabilities of most humans provide richer interaction methods than BCIs. For this reason, many current applications use BCIs as a secondary interaction source to complement another primary one, or as a tool for scientists to study human behaviour [11]. Brain-computer interfaces, however, have the potential to be enormously beneficial for seriously impaired people, such as those affected by *Locked In Syndrome* (LIS). These individuals are paralysed of nearly all voluntary muscles, so are disabled from motion and speech. Vision is always intact, although in extreme cases even eye movement is restricted [1], in which cases BCIs represent the only opportunity to interact with the world.

Although a controversial discussion topic between neuroscientists, some authors claim to have observed consciousness with EEG devices on patients with persistent vegetative state [7], which may open a door to a certain interaction with them. For these reasons, and as explained in [9], *BCI systems hold great promise for effective basic communication capabilities through machines, e.g. by controlling a spelling program or operating a neuroprosthesis.* The use of EEGs for these type of assistive technologies has been previously explored in applications like letter-by-letter spelling [21] or the control of robots [2, 19].

The objective of this work is to demonstrate that BCI interfaces are useful in tasks beyond spelling out words. We

MM'14, November 3–7, 2014, Orlando, Florida, USA.

http://dx.doi.org/10.1145/2647868.2654896 .

focus here on interaction with multimedia: specifically, object selection and segmentation in images. The capacity to perform such segmentation using a BCI interface potentially has both practical and creative applications, such as selection of specific objects for similarity search, and mixing objects from different sources to create a new composition. We propose a system capable of accurately selecting an object in an image in a manner that is completely hands-free, using only measured signals from an EEG interface. In this way, previous work exploring image retrieval (global image scale) [10, 26, 25] and object detection (coarse local scale) [5, 14] are extended to a pixel-level object segmentation. This task is addressed by applying the human computation paradigm, using noisy EEG signals to seed the well-known GrabCut [22] segmentation algorithm.

This remainder of the paper is structured as follows. Section 2 reviews previous work exploring the use of EEG signals for multimedia analysis. Section 3 provides an overview of the entire system architecture, which is described in detail in Sections 4, 5, and 6. Section 7 presents the results from out experiments. Section 8 gives conclusions and outlines future research directions.

2. RELATED WORK

Previous work combining BCI and computer vision [10, 25, 13] have been focused primarily on image retrieval and object detection. In such work images are presented to participants according to the *oddball paradigm*. This approach consists of presenting a "target" image among many "distractor" images via Rapid Serial Visual Presentation (RSVP) [24]. The presentation rate of the images is high, around 10Hz, so that a specific signature in the corresponding EEG signals is produced when the user observes the target images (or rare stimulus). This signature is known as a P300 wave and it is a kind of Event-Related Potential (ERP) associated to the process of recognising a relevant visual stimulus [15]. The wave's primary characteristic is a positive peak in the EEG signal 300ms after the visual stimulus was observed.

Two previous works describing a BCI system applied to image retrieval and detection were presented by Wang [25] and Healy [10]. In both cases the authors perform RSVP of images from known datasets at 10Hz to detect those images in which a specific object appears. The main difference between them is that in Wang's paper the user is not asked to press any additional button when a target image is seen. Our work differs from these because it focuses on target windows (or regions) instead of target image detection. The most similar work to ours is Bigdely-Shamlo's paper [5], in which satellite images are explored using local windows to detect those containing airplanes. Bigdely-Shamlo's work, however, assumes that the object fits in a single window, while in our contribution objects are partially represented in an unknown number of windows.

3. SYSTEM ARCHITECTURE

We propose a system that aims to both detect and segment an object from an image using the measured brain signals of the user at the moment of observing a specific region. The idea is to transform the measured EEG responses into a map that gives an estimate of how probable it is that a particular region seen by the user contains the target object, and then use this map to seed a segmentation algorithm. The construction of this map is based on EEG signal classification, as the electrical responses of the brain are known to differ when the user detects a target or rare stimulus in a RSVP scenario.

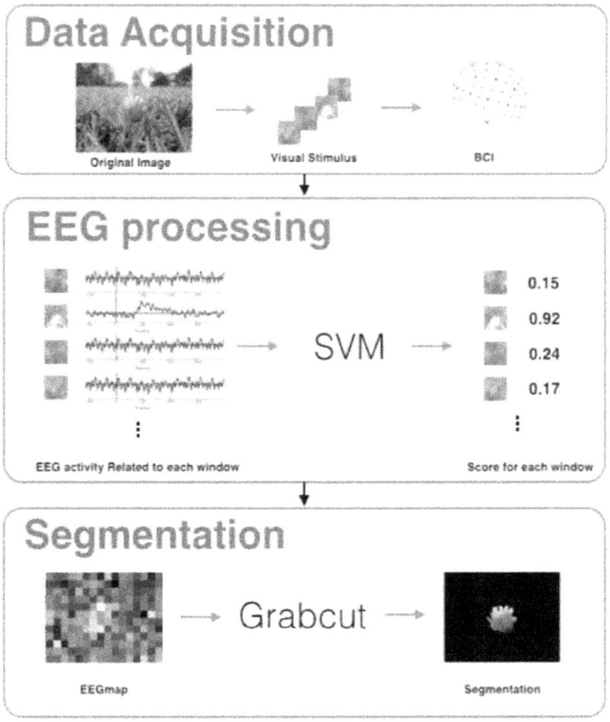

Figure 1: Block diagram of the system.

Figure 1 illustrates the three primary stages of the proposed system:

1. **Data acquisition** (Section 4): in this stage we capture the brain signals related to the visual stimulus.

2. **EEG processing** (Section 5): pre-processing and classification are used to generate the probability maps for the object location. As these maps are built by using EEG analysis, they will be referred to as *EEG maps*.

3. **Segmentation** (Section 6): EEG maps are used to seed the GrabCut object segmentation algorithm [22].

The following sections of the paper describe each stage in more detail.

4. DATA ACQUISITION

This section describes the experimental set-up used to capture the data. First, a new image dataset was created and each image partitioned in blocks of equal size. Each of these blocks are presented at a high rate, in order to generate a measurable response on EEG signals. This stage was validated with a preliminary test with a single user, an important step before starting a larger campaign of data acquisition. After the positive output from the preliminary test, the final experiments reported in the remainder of the paper were based on a population of five people between 21 and 32 years old.

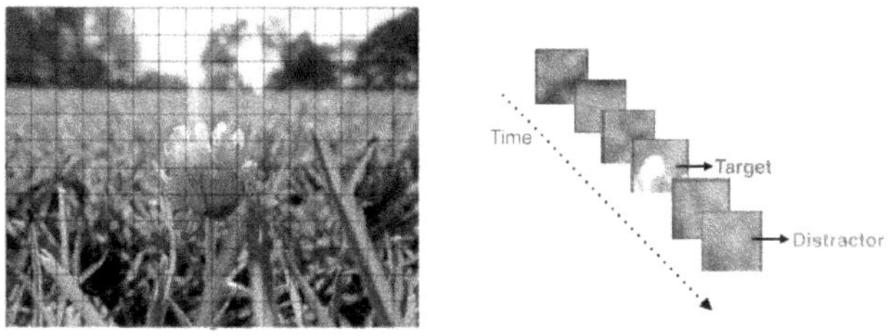

Figure 2: Illustration of RSVP to randomly display different regions of an image.

4.1 Image dataset

A novel dataset of 22 images was created to run the experimentation described in this paper. Given the exploratory nature of this work, the images were chosen to include a single object in a background of limited complexity. The dataset includes different configurations regarding the color, shape, and texture of the objects, as well as their relative similarity with the foreground.

The collection consists of 20 new images captured for the purpose of this work and images 38082 and 123074 from the *Berkeley Segmentation Dataset and Benchmark (BSDB)* [16]. The later allow the comparison of the obtained results with other object segmentation approaches. Each of the images has an associated ground truth in the form of a binary mask. In the case of the two BSDS images, the ground truth masks were obtained from a previous work where 100 binary masks from objects where generated from a subset of 96 images [17].

4.2 Windows presentation

The goal of this stage is the generation of the visual stimulus in such a way that they generate a different and measurable cognitive reaction depending on whether they are associated to object or background pixels. The approach adopted is based on the Rapid Serial Visual Presentation (RSVP) [24] of the different windows that compose an image containing an object of interest. The approach follows the same idea described in the papers for image retrieval by using BCI [10, 25, 13] but applied at local scale. This involves partitioning an image into 192 windows and displaying each of them in a fast and random succession (Figure 2). Given the homogeneous scale of the objects in the dataset and the amount of windows, these windows will usually only contain part of the object. In particular, the adopted ratio generated an average of 15% of windows containing parts of the object.

A non-invasive 31 channel BCI with a sample rate of 1kHz was used to capture the brain reaction of the users during the image presentation. The electrodes were located according to the 10-20 system distribution and the experiment was run in a Faraday Cage. This room isolates the participant and equipment to minimize the interference from any other unrelated acoustic or visual events.

Image presentation in the experiments was carried out as follows. First, the entire image was displayed to the participant for five seconds. This allows the user to memorise the visual features of both object and background. Afterwards, the 192 windows of each image were presented at a rate of 5Hz. Each region is shown zoomed and centered on the screen. Preliminary experiments showed participants attention decreased with time. To minimise this effect, we asked participants to count the number of windows containing a part of the object.

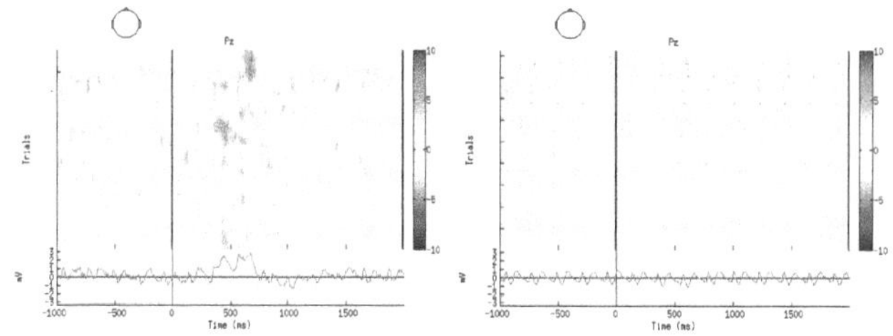

Figure 3: One second before and two seconds after the visual stimulus recorded in the Pz channel for all participants (grand average). Shown are: the amplitudes of the brain waves (top), and the averaged values over all the waves for the target window (bottom-left), and distractor window epochs (bottom-right).

4.3 Preliminary experiments

Acquiring EEG data on real users is both laborious and time consuming: in addition to the time required to actually perform the experiments (approximately one hour), it requires scheduling time with volunteers, equipment setup, and precise positioning of the various BCI sensors in a controlled environment. To ensure maximum benefit from each experiment trial, we decided to carry out a set of preliminary small-scale and simulated experiments. The objective of these experiments were: first, to establish whether classification of EEG signals with some reasonable degree of accuracy using our equipment and experiment setup is indeed feasible; second, to determine whether, given a imprecise classification of an EEG signal for a window, it is possible to use this to locate and segment the corresponding object from an image; and third, to guide us in making reasonable choices for the parameters such as the number and size of windows and their presentation rate. We include some details on these experiments here for reproducibility and to justify our design decisions. Positive results at this stage indicated that the system could indeed be effective and helped underpin the full-scale experiments.

4.3.1 Averaging of targets and distractors

The first study focused on the temporal evolution of the EEG signal in those cases where this was captured at the presentation of a target or a distractor window. Given the noisy nature of EEG signals, the observation of any difference between two individual plots from the two classes is challenging. Nevertheless, this noise can be reduced by averaging several signals from the same class and, in this way, distinguish a clear ERP waveform.

Figure 3 compares the same number of target (left) and distractor (right) signals captured in one electrode. The time span goes from one second before the visual stimulus and two seconds after it. The behaviour on the target reactions is different to the distractors, evidencing a peak around 500ms after the stimulus visualization, which is clearly noticed in the averaged waveform across all the erptarget$_{d}istractortrials$.

This first result provided the evidence that the adopted RSVP strategy was capable of generating different and measurable brain responses for the two classes of windows. It must be made clear that the future sections in the remainder

Figure 4: Left: original image; centre: simulation of the window labels (white: windows with object, black: window with background); right: probability map from simulating the SVM scores.

of this paper do not apply any averaging strategy on the EEG signals associated to an image window. All future results presented in late sections (Section 7) are based on the classification the EEG signal obtained with a single trial.

4.3.2 Binary classification and simulated EEG maps

A second test was performed to establish the feasibility of distinguishing between target and distractor windows using EEG signals. We posed this as a binary classification problem and trained a binary SVM with RBF kernel classifier with target and distractor EEG signals. 459 EEG signals were used to train the classifier (229 targets and 230 distractors), and 153 EEG signals for testing (76 targets and 77 distractors). The zero-one accuracy obtained was 0.68, which shows sufficient signal is present to achieve better than random classification.

This final preliminary experiment was intended to determine if, given a noisy classification signal from an SVM trained on EEG signals, this could be used to seed a segmentation. We simulated the output of a binary classifier on ground truth images using draws from a Bernoulli distribution with $P(X = 1) = 0.68$ for windows containing a target. Figure 4 (center) illustrates the resulting binary classification maps. The results are, clearly, quite noisy; significant information is lost when the SVM scores are binarized. We therefore chose to use the normalized SVM scores, rather than thresholded decisions, to estimate a soft probability. To simulate SVM scores, we model the distribution of scores given the classification decision as Gaussian, fitting parameters from the data used in the first preliminary experiment, and draw from these Gaussians conditioned on the binary classification decision. Figure 4 (right) shows the resulting generated probability maps, which clearly highlight the object of interest. We chose conditioned Gaussians based on histogram observations; note, however, that this assumption has no bearing on the remainder of the experiments. The simulation results indicate that SVM scores are a useful estimator of the probability that a particular region contains a target.

Table 1: Area Under the Curve (AUC) and Averaged Precision (AP) obtained per user

User	1	2	3	4	5	avg	std
AUC	.63	.75	.73	.78	.65	.71	.06
AP	.22	.33	.30	.45	.23	.31	.08

5. EEG PROCESSING

In this section we describe the actual procedure (i.e. based on what was learnt from the preliminary experiments reported in the previous section) followed to clean and classify the brain signals related to the windows presented to the users. The output generated in this stage are the EEG maps that will be used to produce the final object segmentation for the images.

5.1 Data cleaning and feature vectors

The data was referenced to the Tp9 channel and subsampled from the original 1000Hz rate to 250Hz. For 3 of the users the Tp10 channel was used instead due it was cleaner and, therefore, introduced less noise to the raw signals of the rest of the channels. Then, a band-pass filter from 0.1Hz to 70Hz was applied. By visual inspection, we rejected manually the noisy segments. With the data filtered, we extracted the brain reaction related to the stimulus by selecting one and two seconds pre and post-window presentation (epochs).

For the feature selection, we selected the time region within the epoch that best characterizedd the difference between targets and distractors. As shown in Figure 3, this region is contained between 200ms and 900ms after the visual presentation. The feature vectors are built by concatenating the 31 channels for this time region. The final feature vector is obtained by applying a second subsample to the vectors to reduce the sample rate to 20Hz.

5.2 Binary classification of windows

We worked with the scikit-learn Python library [20] to train the SVM with RBF kernel classifier. The feature vectors were normalized with zero mean and unit standard deviation across each feature component. From the total amount of 22 images, 17 were selected to train the classifier. The EEG vectors related to these images formed an imbalanced set of 435 examples of targets and 2829 examples of distractors, respectively labeled with 1 and 0. An SVM with RBF kernel was trained, and grid search with 5-fold cross validation was used for hyperparameter selection. The parameters selected were the ones that obtained the maximum averaged Area Under the Curve value (AUC) across all the folds.

The final model was tested on 5 images, which contained a set of 130 targets and 830 distractors. Table 1 gives the measured performance.

5.3 EEG maps

The confidence scores provided by the classifier can be graphically represented as an image in the form of *EEG maps*. This score represents the distance that separates the classified sample from the hyperplane [20]. Depending on the sign of this distance, the binary classifier assigns a target or distractor label. The maps are built by normalizing the values assigned to each window between 0 and 1 according

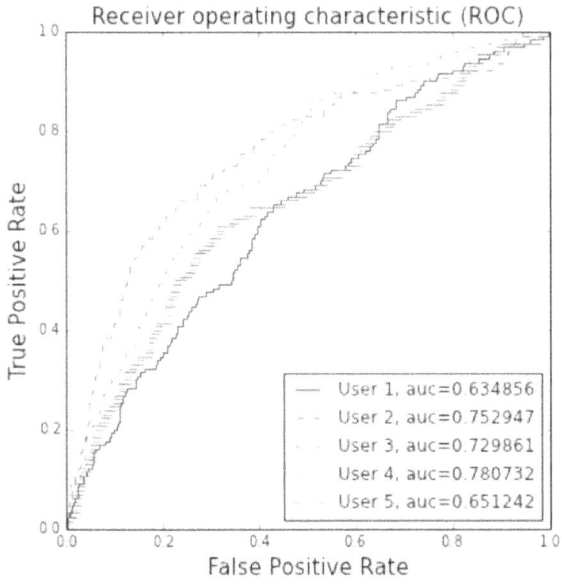

Figure 5: Classification performance per each user in the Reciever Operating Characteristic (ROC) space.

to:

$$X' = \frac{X - min(X)}{max(X) - min(X)}, \quad (1)$$

where X' represents the EEG map normalized and X the original EEG map.

6. OBJECT SEGMENTATION

The EEG maps constructed in the previous section provide local information about how likely is to find an object part in each window. The final segmentation requires a post-processing of the EEG maps to obtain a pixel-wise binary mask of the object location. Three configurations have been assessed for this task, and for each it was required learn a different set of parameters:

1. Binarization of the EEG maps
2. Filtering and binarization of the EEG maps
3. Filtering and binarization of the EEG maps to seed a segmentation algorithm.

EEG maps are generated after training the SVM model on 17 images. The different values for the segmentation parameters were learned on these training images based on the average performance of the 17 processed EEG maps.

The quality of the segmentation was evaluated with the Jaccard Similarity Index, a popular metric for object segmentation used, for example, in Pascal Visual Object Classes (VOC) Challenge [8]. This measure is made to evaluate the similarity between the final segmentation and ground truth masks. The Jaccard Index has values between 0 an 1, with 1 the maximum similarity between the masks. The measure is defined as the intersection of the two final binary masks divided by the union of both masks:

$$J(A, B) = \frac{A \cap B}{A \cup B}, \quad (2)$$

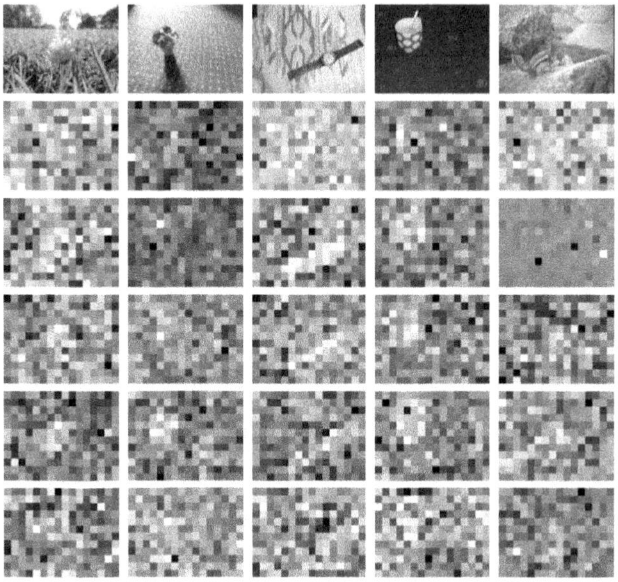

Figure 6: EEG maps for a test set of images. The top row is the original images and the remaining rows are the generated EEG maps for five different participants. Brighter pixels represent higher probabilities.

where A is the segmentation mask and B is the ground truth mask.

6.1 Binarizing the EEG maps

The simplest strategy to quantitatively assess the EEG maps in terms of object localization is to directly convert them into a binary mask. Such binarization is achieved by setting a threshold α, which will consider as targets all those pixels in the EEG map which are higher than α, and label as distractors all the rest. An optimal binarization threshold α_i was estimated for each individual user i by averaging the $\alpha_{i,j}$ values that provided the highest Jaccard index for each training image I_j.

$$\alpha_{i,j} = \underset{\alpha}{\operatorname{argmin}}\, J(M_{i,j}(\alpha), GT_j) \quad (3)$$

where $M_{i,j}$ is the EEG map thresholded by α for user i and image I_j, and GT_j is the ground truth mask for image I_j.

Quantitative results for this approach are presented in Figure 7 have a high density set of windows labelled as target around the object location, especially for user 4.

Table 2 contains the thresholds learned for each of the six users in the test by using 17 images for training. The table also includes the Jaccard index for each user when these thresholds are applying on the 5 test images. The averaged Jaccard index through all the users corresponds to a low 0.14, which points at the poor performance of a direct binarization on the EEG map.

6.2 Filtering and binarization of EEG maps

The binarization approach presented in the previous section presents a first limitation because of the block artefacts introduced by the window boundaries. The window contours do not need to match with the object ones, so in general this

Table 2: Final threshold per user obtained from the EEG maps for training and the final average value obtained applying the threshold on the test set.

User	1	2	3	4	5	avg	std
α	.59	.74	.65	.61	.67	.65	.06
J	.10	.15	.18	.21	.11	.23	.17

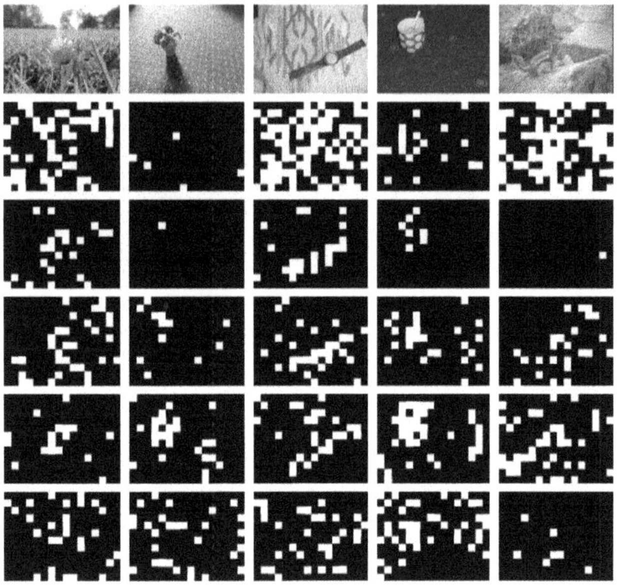

Figure 7: Binary masks after thresholding the EEG maps. The top row is the original images and the remaining rows are the binary masks for five different participants.

lack of resolution is partially responsible of the bad performance of the solution. In addition, the spatial relationship between the windows is completely ignored, without any contextual analysis that may provide coherence to the overall composition.

In this section, a low-pass filter is added before thresholding the maps to reduce block artefacts. With this filter, the isolated false positive windows of the background can be reduced and the high compact windows around the object will mutually reinforce. Equation (4) describes the filter mask (kernel) that is convoluted with the image. The (x, y) values are the horizontal and vertical distances from the origin to a certain point of the kernel. The kernel takes standard deviation σ as a parameter defining the spatial extension of the filter:

$$G(x,y) = \frac{1}{\sqrt{2\pi\sigma^2}} \exp - \frac{x^2+y^2}{2\sigma^2} \quad (4)$$

The Gaussian filtering and posterior binarization of the resulting EEG map requires defining the two parameters α and σ. As in the previous section, these were selected via minimizing error the training dataset. In this case, though, the Gaussian filtering changes the dynamic range of the EEG maps the threshold, which is no longer between 0 and 1. For this reason, the binarization threshold is not learnt as an absolute value but as a normalised coefficient $p \in [0, 1]$

Table 3: Averaged percentage (normalized to one) and σ per user obtained from the train set and final Jaccard index obtained on the test set by using these parameters.

User	1	2	3	4	5	avg	std
p	.61	.70	.63	.65	.69	.66	.04
σ	39.24	33.29	26.35	29.18	33.53	32.32	4.89
J	.16	.30	.27	.41	.24	.27	.09

referred to the dynamic range of the EEG map:

$$\alpha_{i,j}(p) = min(F_{i,j}) + p \cdot (max(F_{i,j}) - min(F_{i,j})), \quad (5)$$

where $F_{i,j}$ the filtered EEG map of user i for image I_j.

The procedure used for optimisation was to select the parameters (σ, α) that generated the maximum averaged Jaccard Index over all the images of the train set. 70 values for sigma ($\sigma \in [0, 70]$) were tested to filter the EEG map. For each filtered map, 100 different values were tried by varying p from 0 to 1, and the binarization threshold $\alpha_{i,j}$ that maximized the Jaccard was selected, as previously presented in Equation (3). Then, for each image a optimal combination (σ, α) that maximized the Jaccard was obtained. Finally, the parameters used in the test set were set by averaging the 17 pairs of optimal parameters computed for the training set.

The new binary masks shown in Figure 8 present in many cases a single patch located near the actual position of the object, with a shape which is much more natural than the sparse blocks generated in Figure 7. A quantitative analysis of the results is presented in Table 3 and results in an important gain of 79% when comparing the averaged Jaccard indices of thresholding with our without the Gaussian filtering. The results combining a low-pass filter with thresholding the EEG maps produce a cleaner binary masks which contain a better estimation for the object location (Figure 8). However, these values are still too poor to consider these results an accurate segmentation of the object.

6.3 Seeding the segmentation algorithm

The results obtained in the previous section, based only on EEG data, already provide in many cases a rough estimation of the object location. The configuration explored in this section explores the synergy between BCI data and computer vision algorithms. The EEG maps filtered with a Gaussian kernel are used to seed an object segmentation algorithm that can exploit the spatial dependencies between neighbouring pixels. This way the computer vision algorithm is guided by the user in a noisy and approximate fashion.

The segmentation algorithm used is GrabCut [22]. This technique performs a segmentation of an image based on a rough initial segmentation defined by the user, typically by drawing a box around the target object. The pixels outside the box are initially considered as background and the pixels inside as unknown. The technique models separately the pixels labeled as background and the ones labeled as unknown by using a Gaussian Mixture Model (GMM). The unknown pixels are considered foreground pixels in the first iteration. Then, the two GMMs obtained are used to solve a minimization problem via min-cut and produce a first segmentation of the object. After the initial iteration, with the new labels for background and foreground, GMM are

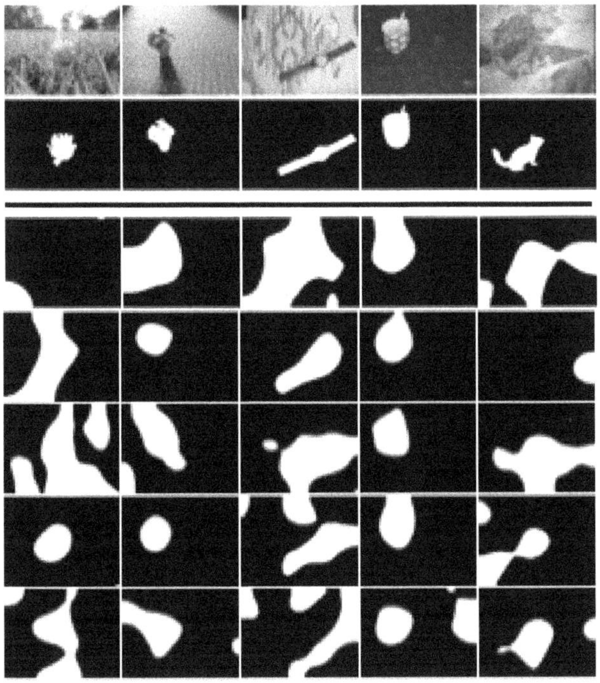

Figure 8: Binary mask after filtering and thresholding the EEG maps. Each row represent the final masks per user.

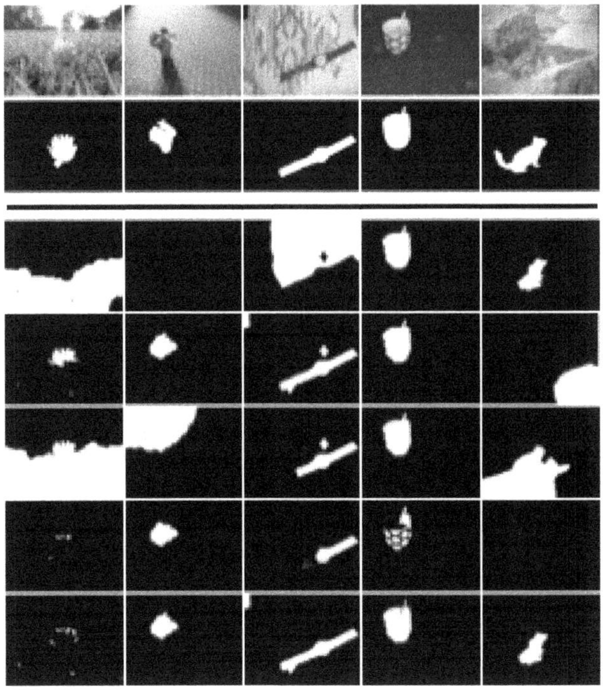

Figure 9: Final binary segmentations. The images and the ground truth masks are displayed (first an second row). Below, each row represents a different user.

updated and the process is repeated until converge on the final segmentation. Our proposal here is to replace the drawn rectangle by using the EEG maps.

The popular OpenCV [6] implementation of GrabCut was selected for this purpose. The algorithm requires an input a map with pixels marked as: *a*) definitely background; *b*) possible background; *c*) possible foreground; and *d*) definitely foreground. The algorithm requires labels *a* and *b* or *c*. Label *d* is optional, and we have not considered to assign this value due to the noisy nature of the signals.

The initialization of GrabCut with EEG maps requires thresholding the Gaussian filtered map by applying two thresholds: α_1 to separate pixels (a) from the rest, and α_2 to separate the pixels labeled as (b) from pixels of (c). Both thresholds are defined as relative percentages (p_1, p_2), as in the Section 6.2 eq. (5) for the same reason: after applying the low pass filter, the EEG map is unnormalized.

The optimization is realized by randomized search [3], trying combinations of (p_1, p_2, σ) and computing the final Jaccard Index. We used the hyperopt python package [4] for the optimization problem.

The function to optimize (eq. (6)) is the one that computes the average of all the Jaccard Index for the training set given a parameters combination. The optimization is to find the parameters that minimize the error on the averaged Jaccard index:

$$E(p_1, p_2, \sigma) = 1 - \frac{\sum_{j=1}^{N} J(M_{i,j}(p_1, p_2, \sigma), GT_j)}{N}, \quad (6)$$

where $N = 17$ is the number of training images. First, the EEG maps are filtered by applying a Gaussian filter with the sigma parameter $\sigma \in [0, 70]$, then the filtered map is thresholded at two levels by applying two thresholds: $p_1 \in [0, 0.5)$ and $p_2 \in [0.5, 1.0]$. We randomly pick 1,000 combinations.

Table 4: Optimal parameters (p_1, p_2, σ) per user. p_1, p_2 are the percentages normalized to 1. Accuracy is the final Jaccard index on the test set.

User	1	2	3	4	5	avg	std
t_1	.04	.15	0.02	.27	.17	.17	.18
t_2	.77	.76	.64	.81	.69	.73	.07
σ	35.65	29.56	37.53	3.18	19.10	25.00	14.16
Jacc.	.28	.62	.31	.36	.69	.45	.19

7. RESULTS

As the number of images for testing the system is limited, a cross-validation is performed by switching the images on the test and training set 5 times and producing that way the segmentation of all the dataset. That means that 5 different systems are generated following the pipeline described (Figure 10), where the 5 testing images are always independent from the training.

The results obtained are plotted in Figure 11 for the three strategies to produce the final binary mask introduced in Section 6. Averaged Jaccard accuracies indicate that the configuration of using GrabCut with the filtered and thresholded EEG maps performs better than the other configurations, producing a good binary mask in many of the images. However, in other images, the Jaccard Index is not high enough and the segmentation is noisy.

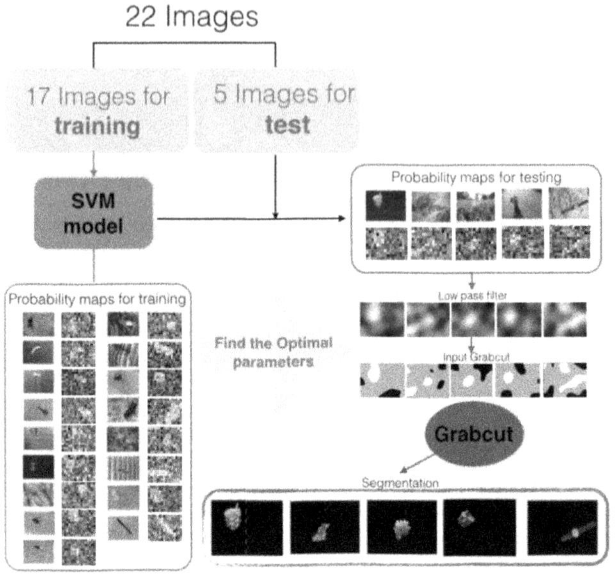

Figure 10: Diagram of the segmentation procedure. The training set is used to generate the SVM model to produce the EEG maps. The same SVM is used on the training images to produce a EEG maps for training, from where the system parameters are estimated. The separated test images ares classified by the SVM and the final segmentation is performed by using the learned parameters.

Table 5: Final Jaccard for each of the five iterations of the cross-validation of the system

	Jaccard A	Jaccard B	Jaccard C
avg	.13	.21	.47
std	.03	.04	.12

Figure 12 presents the visual segmentation for five examples, as well as the intermediate stages. The first three results offer a good qualitative segmentation, while the two last do not succeed in the task. These two failing examples share the characteristic of a very similar distribution between the object and the background. While the EEG map offers a reasonable quality, the GrabCut algorithm fails in the segmentation. This effect is possibly due to the color-driven approach adopted by GrabCut, which basically models foreground and background with color GMM.

It is possible to see that the filtered EEG maps produce a good estimation of the object location that in three of the five examples produce a good segmentation. The segmentation is less accurate in two images, although the location in the processed EEG map is reasonable.

These results show that it is possible to successfully classify the brain reaction produced to detect different parts of a target object, and to produce useful information based on the EEG waves to locate the target object on the images.

7.1 Combining EEG maps of different users

To reduce the noise of the EEG maps, we compute an unique map per image by averaging the EEG maps of the

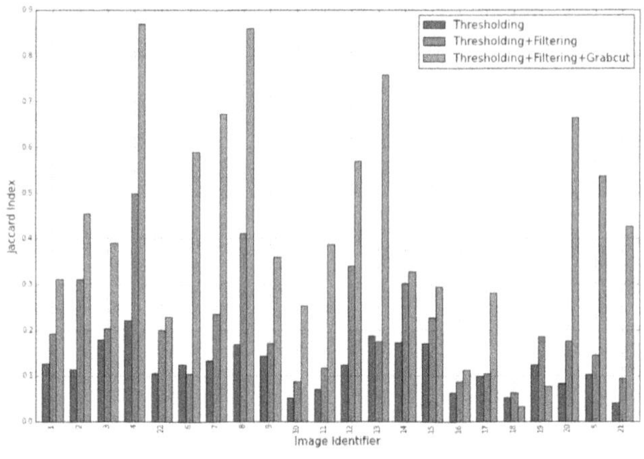

Figure 11: Average Jaccard index across users per image.

different users. The final segmentation is performed following the approach described in the section 6.3. The parameters are picked by averaging across iterations and users ($p_1 = 0.23$, $p_2 = 0.74$, $\sigma = 24.10$).

Qualitative results of the averaged EEG maps provide evidence that combining the individual maps of different users it is possible to generate cleaner EEG maps (Figure 13). The final Jaccard combining the EEG maps of the users outperform in 18 of the 22 images, getting an averaged Jaccard of 0.72, 1.6 times superior to the global result obtained before (Table 13).

7.2 EEG vs. mouse-based interfaces

The analysis of the proposed BCI-based solution is compared with a state-of-the-art solution using a mouse instead of the human-computer interface. The study is based on the two images from the Berkeley Segmentation DataSet (BSDS) [16] we used, which were also considered in a previous study on mouse-based segmentation tools [17]. In that work, four different segmentation techniques were compared in an interactive set up where users draw scribbles to seed the algorithm. That experimentation measured the evolution of Jaccard index with respect to the amount of time that a user was engaged in the operation of the tool.

For the sake of a fair comparison, only the image processing algorithm referred as Interactive Graph Cuts (IGC) has been considered because it is the most similar to the GrabCut solution adopted in our paper. In terms of time evolution, we selected the Jaccard index obtained 45 seconds after the start of the interactive segmentation because this is the closest time stamp to the total display time of an image in our EEG-based system: 43.4 seconds distributed in an initial display of the full image during 5 seconds and 38.4 seconds for the RSVP of 192 windows at a rate of 5 Hz.

The average Jaccard indexes for the EEG- and mouse-based segmentations are presented in the Table 6. The obtained figures clearly show that mouse-based interaction outperforms the proposed EEG-based method which, in addition, requires the costly task of installing the BCI on the user. Note that the high variability on the standard deviation associated to the averaged Jaccard evidence a high variability in the users performance for the EEG results, different to the mouse-based interface, where all the users perform similar.

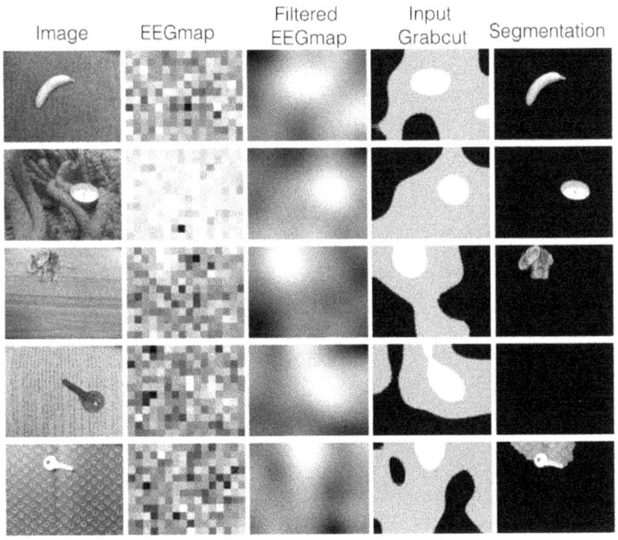

Figure 12: All steps to produce the segmentation combining the EEG maps with GrabCut. Results are from the user 2; segmented images are the set used on the second iteration of the cross-validation.

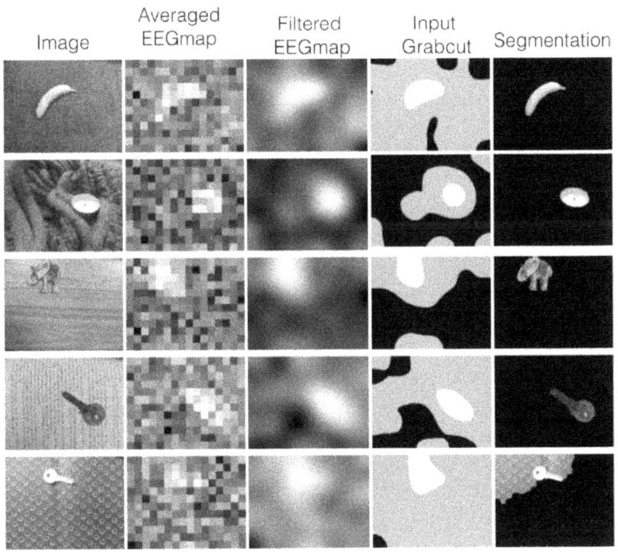

Figure 13: All steps to produce the segmentation combining the EEG maps with GrabCut. The EEG maps are the average of the all the user's maps generated.

8. CONCLUSIONS AND FUTURE WORK

We proposed a system for object segmentation using brain signals. The system is posed as a proof of concept, with the objective being to determine if such a system is feasible.

We designed a specific method of presenting images to associate each image region with its visual brain reaction. Our use of non-overlapping blocks limits the resolution of the generated EEG maps; future work will consider overlapping windows increase the spatial resolution.

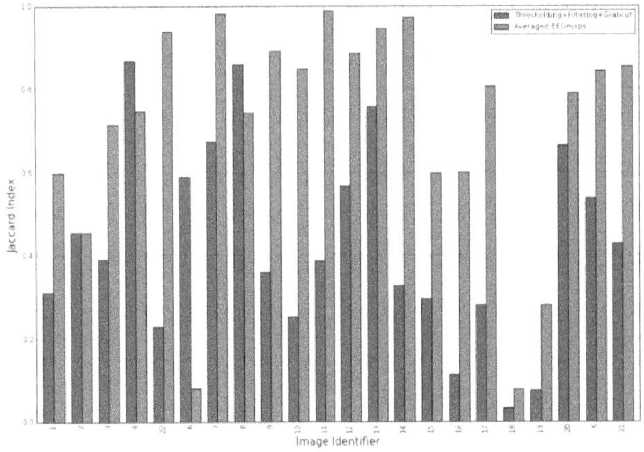

Figure 14: Final Jaccard per image. In blue, EEG maps combined with GrabCut. In green, averaged EEG maps across users combined with GrabCut.

Table 6: Jaccard Index for EEG and mouse-based interaction methods.

	BSDS 38082	BSDS 123074
EEG	$.36 \pm .33$	$.23 \pm .23$
Mouse	$.74 \pm .06$	$.89 \pm .02$

The EEG processing performed in the paper (Section 5) is based on low-pass filtering the EEGdata, epoching the data to identify each window with its brain reaction, training an SVM with the the down-sampled signal, and concatenating EEG channels to form a feature vector. This simple processing gives an AUC of .71; more sophisticated analysis, e.g. Independent Component Analysis (ICA) for channel selection and artifact removal, may improve classifier performance. Better EEG features, such as wavelet features, may also improve classification and, consequently, the quality of the EEG maps.

In Section 6 we investigated three different configurations to produce binary masks. The EEG maps obtained are noisy and require post-processing; a Gaussian low-pass filter was effective in reducing the effect of noise and improves Jaccard accuracy (6.2). Using other filters or morphological operators on the binarized EEG map may improve results. Subsection 6.3 discusses our preprocessing of the EEG maps to set the initial inputs to GrabCut. Future work will consider using the values of the EEG maps directly to set initial terminal capacities of the min-cut graph.

We have shown that the fusion of different user's EEG maps helps to reduce the noise on the probability masks and perform a segmentation that, once combined with GrabCut, notably outperforms the segmentation performance acquired.

Our system shows that it is possible to roughly locate and delineate an object in an image using EEG data, but is far from get the quality on the segmentation of other state-of the art interactive segmentation tools. Nonetheless, this proof of concept opens the door to new interaction modes which may become specially valuable for those people affected by Locked in Syndrome. For them, this work may represent a promising direction in improving their communication for applications such as object selection. If the accuracy of BCI keeps increasing, and their cost decreasing, it is expected that new applications will appear for this novel human computer interface that has raised the interest in different fields of the multimedia community.

9. ACKNOWLEDGMENTS

This publication has emanated from research conducted with the financial support of Science Foundation Ireland (SFI) under grant number SFI/12/RC/2289 and partially funded by the Project TEC2013-43935-R BigGraph of the Spanish Government.

10. REFERENCES

[1] G. Bauer, F. Gerstenbrand, and E. Rumpl. Varieties of the locked-in syndrome. *Journal of Neurology*, 221(2):77–91, 1979.

[2] C. J. Bell, P. Shenoy, R. Chalodhorn, and R. Rao. Control of a humanoid robot by a noninvasive brain computer interface in humans. *Journal of Neural Engineering*, 16(5):432–441, 2008.

[3] J. Bergstra and Y. Bengio. Random search for hyper-parameter optimization. *J. Mach. Learn. Res.*, 13:281–305, Feb. 2012.

[4] J. Bergstra, D. Yamins, and D. D. Cox. Making a science of model search: Hyperparameter optimization in hundreds of dimensions for vision architectures. In *ICML (1)*, volume 28 of *JMLR Proceedings*, pages 115–123. JMLR.org, 2013.

[5] N. Bigdely-Shamlo, A. Vankov, R. Ramirez, and S. Makeig. Brain activity-based image classification from rapid serial visual presentation. *IEEE Transactions on Neural Systems and Rehabilitation Engineering*, 16(5):432–441, 2008.

[6] G. Bradski. *Dr. Dobb's Journal of Software Tools*, 2000.

[7] D. Cruse, S. Chennu, C. Chatelle, T. A. Bekinschtein, D. Fernández-Espejo, J. D. Pickard, S. Laureys, and A. M. Owen. Bedside detection of awareness in the vegetative state: a cohort study. *The Lancet*, 378(9809):2088–2094, 2012.

[8] M. Everingham, L. Van Gool, C. K. I. Williams, J. Winn, and A. Zisserman. The Pascal visual object classes (VOC) challenge. *International Journal of Computer Vision*, 88(2):303–338, June 2010.

[9] D. Fernandez-Canellas. Modeling the temporal dependency of brain responses to rapidly presented stimuli in erp based bci. Master's thesis, Northeastern University, 2013.

[10] G. Healy and A. F. Smeaton. Optimising the number of channels in eeg-augmented image search. In *Proceedings of the 25th BCS Conference on Human-Computer Interaction*, BCS-HCI, pages 157–162, 2011.

[11] R. Hebbalaguppe, K. McGuinness, J. Kuklyte, G. Healy, N. O. Connor, and A. Smeaton. How Interaction Methods Affect Image Segmentation : User Experience in the Task. In *Proc. The 1st IEEE Workshop on User-Centred Computer Vision (UCCV)*, 2013.

[12] X. Hu, K. Li, J. Han, X. Hua, L. Guo, and T. Liu. Bridging the semantic gap via functional brain imaging. *Multimedia, IEEE Transactions on*, 14(2):314–325, 2012.

[13] Y. Huang, D. Erdogmus, M. Pavel, S. Mathan, and K. E. Hild, II. A framework for rapid visual image search using single-trial brain evoked responses. *Neurocomputing*, 74(12-13):2041–2051, June 2011.

[14] A. Kapoor, P. Shenoy, and D. Tan. Combining brain computer interfaces with vision for object categorization. In *Computer Vision and Pattern Recognition (CVPR)*, pages 1–8, 2008.

[15] S. J. Luck. *An introduction to the event-related potential technique.* MIT Press, 2005.

[16] D. Martin, C. Fowlkes, D. Tal, and J. Malik. A database of human segmented natural images and its application to evaluating segmentation algorithms and measuring ecological statistics. In *ICCV*, volume 2, pages 416–423, July 2001.

[17] K. McGuinness and N. E. O'Connor. A comparative evaluation of interactive segmentation algorithms. *Pattern Recogn.*, 43(2):434–444, Feb. 2010.

[18] S. Motomura, Y. Ojima, and N. Zhong. Eeg/erp meets act-r: A case study for investigating human computation mechanism. In N. Zhong, K. Li, S. Lu, and L. Chen, editors, *Brain Informatics*, volume 5819 of *Lecture Notes in Computer Science*, pages 63–73. 2009.

[19] I. Pathirage, K. Khokar, E. Klay, R. Alqasemi, and R. Dubey. A vision based p300 brain computer interface for grasping using a wheelchair-mounted robotic arm. In *2013 IEEE/ASME International Conference on Advanced Intelligent Mechatronics (AIM)*, pages 188–193, July 2013.

[20] F. Pedregosa, G. Varoquaux, A. Gramfort, V. Michel, B. Thirion, O. Grisel, M. Blondel, P. Prettenhofer, R. Weiss, V. Dubourg, J. Vanderplas, A. Passos, D. Cournapeau, M. Brucher, M. Perrot, and E. Duchesnay. Scikit-learn: Machine learning in Python. *Journal of Machine Learning Research*, 12:2825–2830, 2011.

[21] B. Roark, B. Oken, F.-O. M., U. Orhan, and D. Erdogmus. Offline analysis of context contribution to erp-based typing bci performance. *Journal of Neural Engineering*, 10(6):432–441, 2013.

[22] C. Rother, V. Kolmogorov, and A. Blake. "GrabCut": Interactive foreground extraction using iterated graph cuts. *ACM Transactions on Graphics*, 23(3):309–314, August 2004.

[23] P. Sajda, E. Pohlmeyer, J. Wang, L. C. Parra, C. Christoforou, J. Dmochowski, B. Hanna, C. Bahlmann, M. K. Singh, and S.-F. Chang. In a blink of an eye and a switch of a transistor: cortically coupled computer vision. *Proceedings of the IEEE*, 98(3):462–478, 2010.

[24] R. Spence. Rapid, Serial and Visual: a presentation technique with potential. *Information Visualization*, 1(1):13–19, 2002.

[25] J. Wang, E. Pohlmeyer, B. Hanna, Y.-G. Jiang, P. Sajda, and S.-F. Chang. Brain state decoding for rapid image retrieval. In *Proceedings of the 17th ACM International Conference on Multimedia*, MM '09, pages 945–954, 2009.

[26] A. Yazdani, J.-M. Vesin, D. Izzo, C. Ampatzis, and T. Ebrahimi. Implicit retrieval of salient images using brain computer interface. In *ICIP*, pages 3169–3172, 2010.

Help Save The Planet: Please Do Adjust Your Picture

Oche Ejembi
School of Computer Science
University of St Andrews, UK
ooe@st-andrews.ac.uk

Saleem N. Bhatti
School of Computer Science
University of St Andrews, UK
saleem@st-andrews.ac.uk

ABSTRACT

Allowing digital video users to make choices of picture size and codec would significantly reduce energy usage, electricity costs and the carbon footprint of Internet users. Our empirical investigation shows a difference of up to a factor of 3 in energy usage for video decoding using different codecs at the same picture size and bitrate, on a desktop client system. With video traffic already responsible for the largest and fastest growing proportion of traffic on the Internet, a significant amount of energy, money and carbon output is due to video. We present a simple methodology and metrics that can be used to give an intuitive, quantitative and comparable assessment of the energy usage of video decoding. Providing energy usage information to users would empower them to make sensible choices. We demonstrate how small energy savings for individual client systems could give significant energy savings when considered at a global scale.

1. INTRODUCTION

Video has become a popular use-case for many of today's Internet users. With 65% of all Internet traffic being some form of video [1], it is already the largest and fastest growing class of traffic today. This percentage is expected to rise to as much as ~80% – ~90% by 2017, as new technology makes it easier, cheaper and more accessible to send and receive video. While it is still most popularly used for entertainment / leisure purposes (e.g YouTube, Netflix, Vine etc.) and communication purposes (e.g Skype, Facetime, etc.), Internet video is also used in several other crucial, important applications such as education [2], surveillance [3], healthcare [4], and agriculture [5].

With this growth in its usage, there must be a commensurate growth in its energy consumption and carbon footprint. Considering that the developing regions of the world e.g. parts of Asia, Africa and South America, have very large populations and already contribute significantly to the global number of Internet users, but still have relatively low Internet penetration (typically well below 50%), the energy load of video could be extremely significant. Indeed, video is a great enabler for countries where functional literacy is low: video communication has greater utility for users than text-based communication. It has been conservatively estimated that in 2014, ICT would contribute 3.2% of all carbon emissions globally, greater than that produced by the aviation sector [6], and so video will be responsible for a significant proportion of this.

MM'14, November 3–7, 2014, Orlando, Florida, USA.

ACM 978-1-4503-3063-3/14/11 ...$15.00.
http://dx.doi.org/10.1145/2647868.2654897.

1.1 Video diversity

Today, there are many video codecs that are widely used. The diversity of video codecs also provides an opportunity for users to exercise choice in their usage. There are several trade-offs involved in such a decision. Some codecs might offer a wider range of options and configurability than others, while some perform best for particular use-cases and scenarios. Consequently, there are several metrics for Quality of Service (QoS) and Quality of Experience (QoE) involved in benchmarking and selection of codecs. While energy usage is of some concern to users, especially for mobile devices which have a constrained energy supply in the form of battery, there are currently no well-defined metrics which specifically take energy usage of codecs into consideration in a way that can be (i) integrated into applications, and (ii) be understood by users so that they can be empowered to make appropriate choices.

1.2 Contribution

We have investigated client-side energy usage of a number of popular and important video codecs: Flash video (Sorenson Spark/FLV1); MPEG-4 Part 2 (two variants); MPEG-4 Part 10 / H.264; H.265 / High Efficiency Video Codec (HEVC); and Google's VP8 & VP9. We have used a simple testbed to examine the energy and compute-resource usage of these codecs. Our contributions are:

1. We define a simple methodology and metrics to provide intuitive, quantitative and comparable energy usage and quality assessment for video codecs.

2. Applying our methodology in an inexpensive desktop testbed, we present empirical measurements and assessment of significant differences in energy usage across the codecs.

3. We propose ways in which the energy metrics can be integrated into video applications and how users can be empowered to make choices about codec usage based on measured energy usage information.

We focus here on decoding (playback) of pre-existing video content, as video decoding events today far outnumber video encoding (creation) events, e.g. consider video downloads from YouTube. However, YouTube is also a prime example of how video creation is becoming widespread, so we also include a discussion of how our methodology and findings would apply to encoding of video. We also consider some hardware issues for video decoding, but as most of the video codecs available to users are software only, the energy savings we present are complimentary to energy-efficient hardware, can be applied to legacy systems that are not 'green', and so have the potential to offer huge energy savings *globally*, from relatively small *individual* client-side and server-side savings, especially as use of ICT grows.

2. RELATED WORK

In recent years, studies in energy awareness for ICT systems (or 'Green IT') have gained increasing interest, both in research and industry. While most of these studies have focused either on hardware or data-centre optimisations, some have investigated how software behaviour can have significant impacts on energy usage. For example, Sabharwal et. al. [7] discuss several aspects of software architecture which can affect energy use. Based on testbed measurements, they show how relatively simple optimisations in source code can lead to considerable energy savings (e.g. improved laptop battery life).

The human users of these software applications also have an important role to play in energy-efficiency. In our previous work [8], we show through a 2-year study, how providing feedback and incentives to IT-system users encouraged behavioural changes towards saving energy. We recorded savings of up to 56% in individual energy consumption. Similarly, Amsel et. al. [9] present a tool which provides measurement-based feedback on application energy usage to users, who may then modify their behaviour accordingly.

With the widespread use of video in ICT, previous work has looked into making video 'greener'. Again, while the bulk of the work has looked at improving hardware, some have looked at software based optimisations at various levels. Li et.al. [10] examine improving energy efficiency at the application layer using mechanisms such as dynamic cache management. Nencioni et. al. [11] present a predictive pre-fetching algorithm to save energy used by the BBC iPlayer TV-catchup service. Song et. al. [12] examine optimising the energy use of video transcoding CPUs using a modified DVFS algorithm.

Video diversity, as discussed in Section 1.1 above, has also generated considerable research interest. Several works, e.g. [13–15], have compared various video codecs for typical quality of experience (QoE) metrics, such as peak signal to noise ratio (PSNR), structural similarity index metric (SSIM) and mean opinion scores (MOS). Also quality of service (QoS) metrics, such as network bit-rate variability and bit-error or delay tolerance, have been considered. Other works have investigated the characteristics, performance and resource usage of various popular video *applications* such as YouTube, Netflix and Vine e.g. [16–18]

Surprisingly, very little work has explicitly examined the energy use of different codecs as used in these popular applications. However, Lin et.al [19] present a (now dated) investigation on the energy use of some codecs on a mobile platform. Sharrab et. al. [20] present an analytical model of the power consumption of capturing and *encoding* using H.264 and MPEG4 codecs.

We have investigated how choice of codec and picture size for video playback impact client-side energy usage. This is the first work to investigate the energy consumption of the newest codecs, VP9 and H.265, which might increase in popularity, and compare them with popular codecs including H.264, VP8, Flash Video (FLV) and MPEG-4 Part 2. This is also the first work to propose providing information to users of video energy usage.

3. EXPERIMENT METHODOLOGY

The aim of our experiment was to perform an empirical investigation of the energy and resource consumption of various popular codecs during encoding and decoding (playback). Based on that energy usage, we have defined how energy usage information can be presented to users to enable choice of codec to be made.

3.1 Overview

We chose two opensource, high-definition (HD) video files, as summarised in Table 1. These were then re-encoded at different picture sizes, and with several different codecs, using the opensource FFmpeg[1] software. The picture sizes we chose cover a range of common use-cases, as described in Table 2. The video codecs are a mix of some that are commonly used and some that might become popular, and are listed in Table 3. Only default settings were used for encoding the test video files, whilst varying only the picture size of the output video and target bit-rate to obtain similar file attributes.

Table 1: Opensource video files used in experiments.

Big Buck Bunny: A popular *animation* video, featured in a number of published experiments, e.g [21]. We used the first 2 minutes of this video.
Tears of Steel: A science-fiction, *CGI-enhanced, live-action movie*. We used 2 minutes starting from the 6:00 mark, containing fast-paced action scenes.

Both files, from Blender (http://www.blender.org – an opensource movie project) were retrieved from an open, public repository (http://www.media.xiph.org) in YUV format.

Table 2: Video picture sizes and example use cases.

Label	Picture size	Target bit rate (Kbps)
QCIF[a]	176x144	128 (Older handheld devices)
CIF[b]	352x288	256 (Handheld mobile devices)
360p	480x360	640 (Smartphones)
480p	720x480	728 (Smartphones, tablets)
720p	1080x720	1456 (HD, desktops, TV)
1080p	1920x1080	2912 ('full' HD, desktops, TV)

[a]Also known as 144p. [b]Also known as 288p.

3.2 Testbed

The testbed is shown Figure 1. A single host was used to decode and playback the encoded video files – two of these units are shown in the left of the figure. Each system is a Shuttle XPC Glamor SG31G2[2], with Intel® Core™ 2 Quad

[1]http://ffmpeg.org

[2]http://global.shuttle.com/unique/productsSpec?productId=646

Table 3: Video codecs: libraries and software.

Label	Library & software version
FLV	from fmpeg-libavcodec v55.52
H264	libx264 v0.125
H265	libx265 v0.8
MPEG4	from fmpeg-libavcodec v55.52
MSMPEG4	from fmpeg-libavcodec v55.52
VP8	libvpx VP8 v1.3.0-1780-g1f08824[a]
VP9	libvpx VP9 v1.3.0-1780-g1f08824[a]

[a]From the WebM Project http://www.webmproject.org/

Q6600, 2.40GHz CPU with a Intel 82G33/G31 chipset and an Express Integrated Graphics Controller core, 4GB RAM (128MB used for graphics, set in BIOS). To examine the effects of hardware-assisted video decoding, we performed experiments with a PCI-express Nvidia® G86 GeForce™ 8400GS with 256MB GDRAM. This is considered a mid-range desktop configuration. The machine ran a minimal installation of Ubuntu Linux 13.10 64-bit (x86-64) Server installation, with no desktop environment, and with a minimal set of background processes running. This was to avoid any unnecessary load on the machines when measuring energy usage. However, to enable video playback on the client machine, we used the lightweight *Openbox*[3] window manager. We played-back the video files using the opensource VLC media player application, version 2.2.git Weatherwax (revision 2.1.0-git-2995-dgf36375)[4].

The machine used for encoding the video files from the YUV source was a mini-tower workstation (on the right in Figure 1) with an Intel Core i5 4440, 3.1GHz, Quad-Core (Haswell) processor, 4GB (2x2GB) Corsair DDR3 (1333MHz) memory, and a C220 Series Chipset. This ran the Ubuntu Linux 13.10 64-bit (x86-64) Desktop installation. This is considered a mid-range workstation configuration, which is affordable for home use. No hardware assist was available for encoding video and so this was not assessed. This is fairly typical at the time of writing, though hardware assisted encoding is becoming available, and we would expect this to be more common in the future.

Figure 1: Desktop testbed. The black Shuttle systems on the left were used for the decoding experiments, and are connected to the Kill-A-Watt/MoteWatt power meters in the centre. The mini-tower on the right is the workstation used for encoding the videos form the YUV HD source.

We obtained power readings for the experiments using our modified Prodigit 'Kill-a-Watt' 2000MU power meter[5], dubbed the 'WattMote' (the two units in the centre). The unmodified meter is a cheap but sensitive and accurate real-time home power meter. Using instructions available online [22], the meter was modified with an RFM12B radio to enable captured readings to be sent to a receiver (one of the other Shuttle units, on the left).

[3]http://openbox.org
[4]http://www.videolan.org
[5]http://www.p3international.com/products/p4400.html

3.3 Measurement regime and observables

We took power measurements for decoding and encoding for each combination of the 7 codecs (*vvv*) and 6 picture sizes (*ppp*), a total of 42 combinations. The measurement was for the system as a whole, as this is the power usage seen by the user when undertaking the {de,en}encoding tasks. Each power measurement was repeated 20 times for decoding, and 5 times for encoding, which we found to give acceptable variations for either experiment. As each video sample was 2 minutes long, for the 2 films this is a total of 3360 minutes of measurements for decoding. Encoding times varied greatly, depending on codec and picture size, from 0.5 seconds to 360 minutes.

Each *vvv* – *ppp* combination used only the software codecs and the main system CPU. The NVIDIA graphics card supports hardware assist for H.264 decoding using libVDPAU v304.88, so a separate set of measurements were conducted for H.264 with hardware assist – 6 picture sizes, 20 runs, 2 minutes per run for each film, for an additional 480 minutes of tests. We also measured the system power usage when idle to assess the additional power usage of the systems as a whole due to the {de,en}coding tasks.

The observables we capture for this experiment are summarized in Table 4. The derived metrics we used are explained in Section 4. Our results are detailed in Section 5.

Table 4: Summary of observables for experiments

Observable	Units	Measured using
Power	Watts	MoteWatt power meter
{De,En}coding Time	Seconds (s)	*time(1)*[a]
Energy	K Joules (KJ)	Power × time for {de,en}coding
CPU usage	Percentage	*time(1)*[a]
RAM usage	MiB	*time(1)*[a]
PSNR	dB	*tiny_ssim*[b]
SSIM	–	*tiny_ssim*[b]

[a]Note that this is /usr/bin/time and not the *time* command that is built into the default *bash* shell on linux.
[b]http://ffmpeg.org/doxygen/trunk/tiny_ssim_8c_source.html

4. ENERGY AND QUALITY METRICS

We describe the metrics we have used to (i) evaluate our measurement-based study; and (ii) demonstrate how energy information could be used within video applications.

4.1 Energy usage for video

For video, we are concerned with energy usage with respect to the video stream, so we choose to define a metric which measures *energy used per second of video stream content*. Such a definition is independent of the way the video is encoded, and so can be used to make comparisons across different codecs. It is also a simple metric for users and developers to understand. Note that the units of our metric, which we will call P_{xv} (where $x = d$ for video *decoding* and $x = e$ for video *encoding*) , are then *Joules per second (of video content), i.e.* J/s_v . These are the same units as electrical power (Watts, W = J/s), but we choose to write the units as J/s_v to make clear the different assessment we are making. However, this does mean that we can also translate directly from measured power usage for a system to our video energy metric P_{xv}, which is very convenient.

$$\begin{aligned} P_{xv} &= \frac{\text{energy usage for video \{en,de\}coding}}{t_v} \\ &= P_a - P_{idle} \end{aligned} \quad (1)$$

where P_{xv} is the mean energy usage per second of video (J/s_v) by video encoding (P_{ev}) or decoding (P_{dv}), and t_v is the duration of the video stream in seconds. P_a is the mean measured power of the system during encoding or decoding of the video. P_{idle} is the mean measured power when the system lies idle. This is summarised in Table 5.

Table 5: Definitions for P_{xv} (Eqn. (1)).

P_{xv}	mean energy usage per second during video encoding*(x=e)* or decoding*(x=d)* $[J/s_v]$
P_a	measured mean *system* power usage during video encoding or decoding [W]
P_{idle}	mean system power usage when idle [W]

4.2 Energy metric

We wish to assess the amount of energy used for a system (workstation or server) as a whole in either encoding or decoding video. It would also be possible to assess the energy usage for individual components of a system, including hardware components (e.g. CPU memory, graphics card) and software (e.g. operating system, graphics driver, etc). For now, our concern is with energy usage as a whole, but more detailed analyses of energy usage of individual components may yield benefits for targeting or optimising energy efficient operations – we leave this for future work.

4.3 Decoding video

We wish to create a normalised decoding metric, E_{dv}. We define ${}_{vvv}E_{dv-ppp}$ as the energy metric for decoding video using codec *vvv* (from Table 3) at picture size *ppp* (from Table 2). We define ${}_{vvv}E_{dv-ppp}$ for decoding video:

$$\begin{aligned} {}_{vvv}E_{dv-ppp} &= \frac{P_{idle}}{P_a} && (2) \\ &= \frac{P_{idle}}{{}_{vvv}P_{dv-ppp} + P_{idle}} && (3) \end{aligned}$$

with P_a, P_{dv} and P_{idle} as defined in Section 4.1. Note that the denominator is simply the mean power measured during the decoding process. For example, for decoding using H.264 to 720p, we would define:

$${}_{h264}E_{dv-720p} = \frac{P_{idle}}{{}_{h.264}P_{dv-720p} + P_{idle}} \quad (4)$$

4.4 Encoding video

For our experiments here, we chose to use the measured energy required to convert the full-quality source, which is a YUV encoding of picture size 1920x1080 and 30fps, to the encoding scheme supported by the video codec while maintaining picture size and frame rate. So, using similar notation to that for decoding, we define E_{ev}:

$${}_{vvv}E_{ev-ppp} = \frac{P_{idle}}{{}_{vvv}P_{ev-ppp} + P_{idle}} \quad (5)$$

where *vvv*, *ppp* and P_{idle} are as defined for the complementary decoding expression given in Eqn. 3. For example, for encoding using H.264 at 720p, we would define:

$${}_{h264}E_{ev-720p} = \frac{P_{idle}}{{}_{h.264}P_{ev-720p} + P_{idle}} \quad (6)$$

4.5 Limitations of E_{xv}

From the discussion above, the metric, E_{xv} is defined in terms of real energy measurements. This has the advantage that, being defined in terms of P_{xv} from Eqn. (1), values are comparable across the system for different codecs. Creating a purely analytic model for evaluating an energy metric might be more convenient from a methodical viewpoint, but it is not practical: it would need to encompass the complexities of the different video encoding/decoding algorithms, the specific implementations of those algorithms, and the range of hardware and software components that are involved. Our measurement-based approach removes that complexity by treating the system as a black box.

However, one drawback of a measurement-based approach is that all measurements are system-specific: the same methods used to conduct the same measurements on a different system would yield different results. Differences in implementation of the same video encoding and decoding algorithms, as well as differences in hardware and software components and configuration mean that the actual values of ${}_{vvv}P_{dv-ppp}$ and ${}_{vvv}P_{ev-ppp}$ could be very different for the same coding scheme (*vvv*) when measured on different systems (or even on the same system but with different configurations of codecs, drivers, etc). Additionally, some systems might have hardware assist for specific algorithms, reducing their values of ${}_{vvv}P_{dv-ppp}$ and ${}_{vvv}P_{ev-ppp}$, where as other systems might use only software. For example, many modern smartphones will have hardware assist for H.264, but many low-end desktop machines may not. However, where a set of measurements are made relative to the same system, the values of ${}_{vvv}P_{dv-ppp}$ and ${}_{vvv}P_{ev-ppp}$ do provide indicative energy performance comparisons, and additional measurements can be made to cater for hardware assist for direct comparison also. Indeed, this is what we have done in our measurements.

4.6 Combined quality-energy metric

To demonstrate how the energy values could be incorporated into an application, we take a simple approach, using a compound metric as in Eqn. (7) and Table 6.

$$Q_M = \sum_{m=1}^{M} \alpha_m Q_m \quad (7)$$

$$0 \le Q_m \le 1 \quad (8)$$

$$\sum_{m=1}^{M} \alpha_m = 1 \ , \ 0 \le \alpha_m \le 1 \quad (9)$$

Table 6: Definitions for Q_M (Eqn. 7).

Q_m	an application quality metric, e.g. for a video codec or some other relevant quality metric
α_m	a weight

With respect to Eqn. (7), E_{xv} (from Eqn. 3 or 5) would be treated as a quality measure. This is very convenient to incorporate into applications, allowing application control and decision policies to use energy along with traditional quality measures. Additionally, if more than one video quality metric was required for assessment of quality, then those multiple metrics could also be integrated as different Q_m, using appropriate weights α_m.

However, if such a method of composing the energy metric into an applications is not suitable, then a more appropriate algorithm could be used, as required. The intention of our presentation here is to demonstrate that from a measurement-based approach, it is possible to derive an energy metric that could be incorporated into applications.

4.7 Examples of codec quality metric Q_m

There has been much debate within the community about which objective video metrics are appropriate for measuring video quality, e.g. [23]. Rather than take a position in that discussion, our quality assessment leaves the choice of metric to the user and only requires that it conform to the normalised range and semantic as given in expression (8). Existing quality metrics should be transformed in order to be used as we have expressed in Eqn. (7).

For example with SSIM [24], the value is already normalised to the range [0,1]. However, PSNR must be converted in a way that makes sense to the applications. One method for converting PSNR is to note that some studies have observed a near-linear correspondence between PSNR and MOS [25], allowing normalisation and mapping to the appropriate range for Q_m as given in expression (8).

5. RESULTS

Our focus is on our decoding results, but we also consider briefly some of our encoding experiments.

5.1 Decoding measurements

Figure 2 shows the results from the decoding experiments entirely by software using the CPU without the hardware card installed. The H.265 codec, overall, consumes the greatest energy, followed by VP9. H.264 and VP8 consume an equal amount of energy and system resources during playback, while FLV consumes the least amount of resources during playback. It is important to note that these differences in energy and resource usage are at roughly the same target bit-rates. There are differences in the perceived quality of the decoded file, which we capture using SSIM and PSNR values in Figures 4. While the use of such metrics (especially PSNR) remain in debate, they do give indications of the level of perceived video quality (especially the SSIM metric), and help us to explain how video quality and energy usage can be used together (Section 6). More suitable metrics could be substituted as requirements dictate.

5.2 Limitations of QoE measurements

The results of the PSNR and SSIM assessments are shown in Figure 4. We observed that the popular opensource x264 codec (considered to be the best implementation of the H.264 codec standard [14]), produces poor results when analysed by the tiny_ssim tool [26]. However, a quick visual examination of the resultant videos shows that the quality is good, comparable to VP8, VP9 and H.265, and visibly better than MPEG4 and FLV. A possible explanation is that x264's default psycho-visual optimisations provide improved visual quality to human viewers, but negatively impact calculated PSNR and SSIM scores. Another limitation is in how tiny_ssim is implemented. It requires that the comparison it makes is on two YUV files, so we need to transcode our encoded video files to YUV, e.g. the H.264 video file is converted to YUV format before being used by tiny_ssim, and some of x264's optimisations may not be visible in the YUV format.

We used tiny_ssim as it allowed us to assess all the codecs. Other tools (e.g. the widely-used MSU Video Quality Measurement tool [14]), do not support H.265, VP8 and VP9.

6. TRADE-OFFS AND SAVINGS

We focus on discussing decoding, for the sake of brevity, but similar analysis is possible for encoding also.

6.1 Software only decoding

Values for metrics for P_{dv}, E_{dv}, and Q_{dSSIM} are shown in Fig. 6. P_{dv} is as from Eqn. 1, and the graph shows the energy consumption of video playback. We observe very small differences among the various codecs for picture sizes up to 360p. For example, at 360p (which is YouTube's default size) all but one of the codecs consume approximately 4-5J/s_v. H.265 consumes the most energy at this picture size, $\sim 7J/s_v$. From 480p, we begin to notice significant differences among the codecs. At 1080p we see a difference of factor of 3 between FLV (lowest P_{dv}) at $15J/s_v$ (3 times more than at 360p), and H.265 (highest P_{dv}) at $53J/s_v$ for 'Tears of Steel' (~8 times more than at 360p).

The E_{dv} graphs show the normalized values of P_{dv} as calculated using Eqn. (5). These values for E_{dv} are used to create Q_{dSSIM} as in Eqn. 7, along with measured SSIM values to represent quality, each with equal weight. For Q_{dSSIM}, we find that at QCIF picture size, the VP9 codec provides the best energy-quality tradeoff for the 'Big Buck Bunny' movie, whereas for 'Tears of Steel', it is the HEVC codec. MPEG4 and H.264 rank lowest at this picture size, because for approximately the same amount of energy, they provide a relatively poor quality. At 360p, the MSPEG4 codec provides the best energy-quality trade-off, while at 1080p it is FLV (for 'Tears of Steel'). However, please note our comments in Section 5.2 on our use of tiny_ssim.

We have observed that at different picture sizes, different codecs may provide the best trade-off between energy use and picture quality. Based on this, an energy-aware application could dynamically adapt its picture-size and/or video

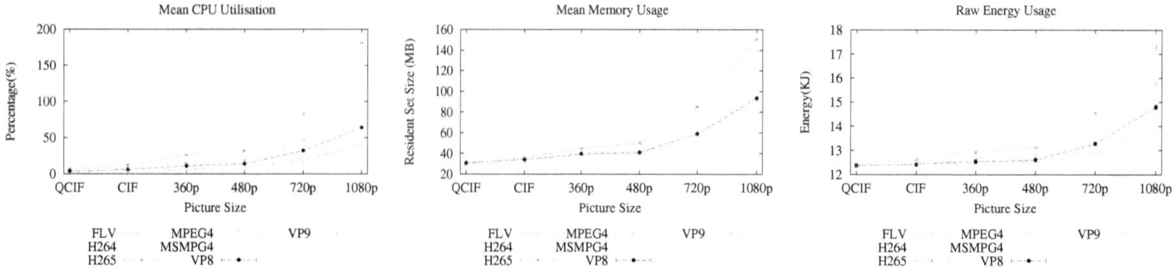

(a) 'Big Buck Bunny'

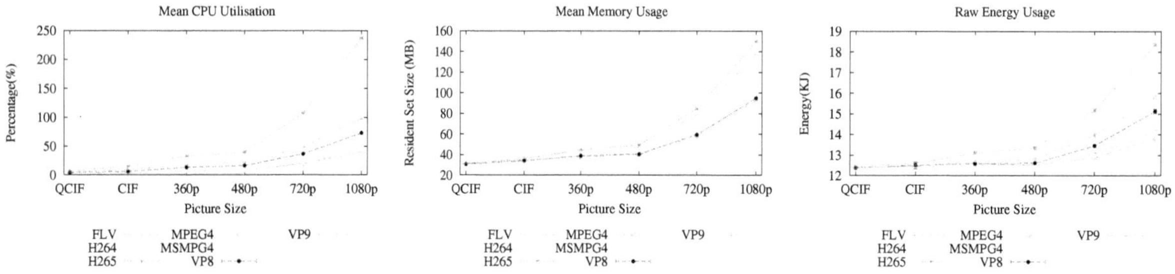

(b) 'Tears of Steel'

Figure 2: Resource usage for decoding of video files. 20 runs were used to plot each point, with 95% confidence (error bars not always visible as they are very small in some cases). The lines joining the points are visual aids only and do not imply interpolation to intermediate picture sizes.

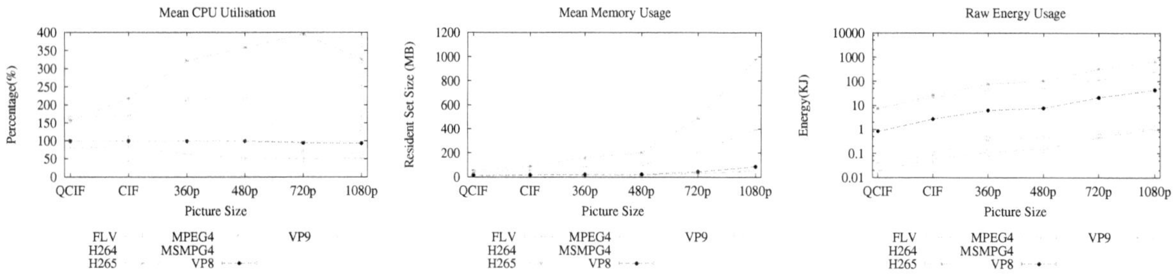

(a) 'Big Buck Bunny'

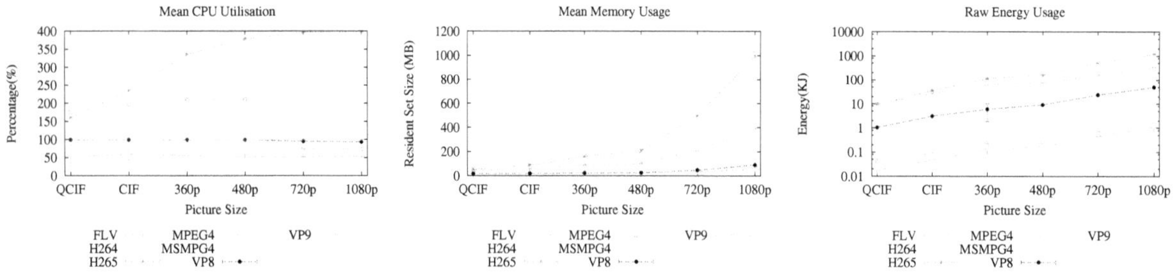

(b) 'Tears of Steel'

Figure 3: Resource usage during encoding video files. 5 runs were used to plot each point, with 95% confidence (error bars not always visible as they are very small in some cases). The lines joining the points are visual aids only and do not imply interpolation to intermediate picture sizes.

codec with the aim of conserving energy while maintaining the best possible quality [27, 28]. (A similar analysis is possible for the encoding results.)

6.2 Hardware assisted decoding

Our NVIDIA G86 (Geforce 8400) graphics card supports only decode for H.264 from our chosen codecs. However, we can still draw some general conclusions. We compared the energy use of the system using hardware and software and present results in Fig. 5. Using hardware can make the playback process more energy efficient. At 360p, while software decoding consumes $\sim 5J/s_v$, hardware-assisted decoding consumes just $\sim 3J/s_v$. The difference is greater at 1080p, with software decoding consuming $\sim 25J/s_v$ compared

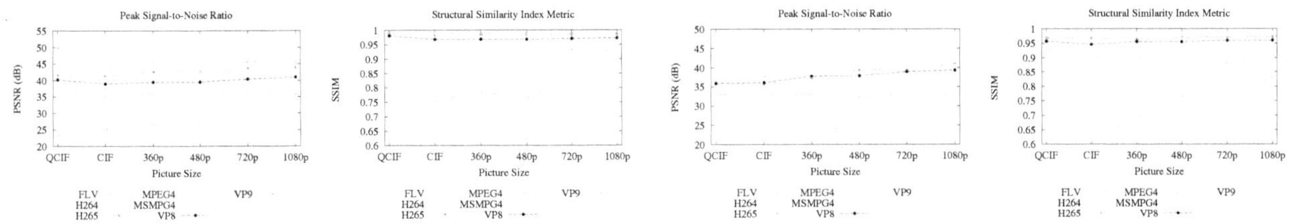

(a) 'Big Buck Bunny' (b) 'Tears of Steel'

Figure 4: QoE measurements for both video sources at various picture sizes. The lines joining the points are visual aids only and do not imply interpolation to intermediate picture sizes.

to $\sim 10J/s_v$ using hardware assist. System resource usage (i.e. CPU and RAM) is also much reduced using hardware assist, leaving the system available to perform other tasks. However, the video card adds ~25W to the system's idle power. So, it is only when there is an energy saving of at least $25J/s_v$ that we gain from hardware assist.

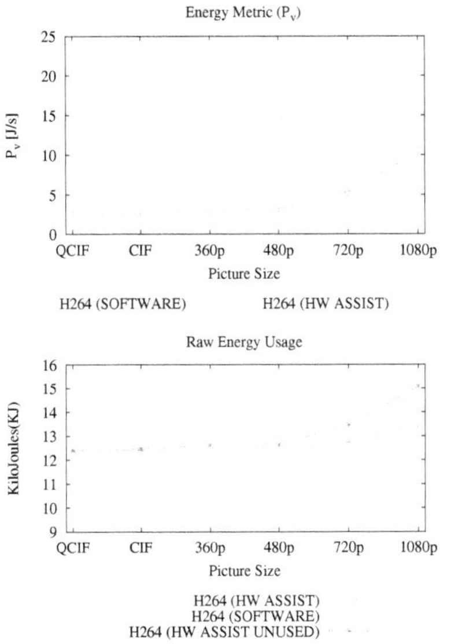

Figure 5: Energy for video decoding of H.264 with and without hardware assistance. 20 runs were used to plot each point, with 95% confidence (error bars not always visible as they are very small in some cases). The lines joining the points are visual aids only and do not imply interpolation to intermediate picture sizes.

In future systems, energy savings could be gained by turning on hardware assist only when it would yield an energy benefit. This would require changes to hardware and software (e.g. drivers), and would also require new interfaces for the user to control this behaviour. A system profiling tool would need to execute in order to determine when the hardware control should be applied, the result being stored as part of a configuration file on the system, which is updated when system configuration changes (hardware or software).

6.3 Impact of energy savings

From Figures 2 and 6, we see how the differences in energy consumption of the codecs and picture sizes can be significant. For the same picture size, by using different codecs, we see that there are small and large differences in in energy usage, e.g. $1J/s_v$ between FLV and H.264 at 360p for 'Big Buck Bunny', and $40J/s_v$ between FLV and H.265 at 1080p for 'Tears of Steel'. Also, even with the same codec, we can see large differences with energy usage depending on picture size, e.g. $40J/s_v$ difference between 1080p and 480p for 'Tears of Steel' with H.265. This allows us to gain some measure of upper and lower bounds of savings that could be made by users exercising choice in the video stream they select. Our evaluation of the related impact is in the spirit of a Fermi estimate.

It is estimated that there are 6 billion hours of video streamed from YouTube every month[6], a total of 72 billion hours per year, and we use this with UK energy consumption data in Table 7 to give an estimate of impact.

Table 7: Estimate of potential annual impact of energy savings based on 72 billion YouTube hours per year and UK energy consumption data.

J/s_v	KWh	Cost[a]	$KgCO_2$[b]
1	72M	GB£10.8M (US$17.8M)	12.2M
40	2880M	GB£432.0M (US$712.8M)	189.6M

[a]From [29], mean cost of GB£577 / year per household.
[b]UK government data, 10 May 2014, 0.17 $KgCO_2$/KWh[7].

At energy savings of just $1J/s_v$ (the difference between FLV and H264 software decoding at 360p) for example, and assuming similar savings could be made on all client systems (in reality, it would vary), this would be enough to power 18947 homes in the UK for a year (mean annual home usage is 3800KWh [29]). In monetary terms, this represents ~£10.8M (~US$17.8M) per year, and in terms of carbon emissions, 12.2M $KgCO_2$ emissions. The second row in Table 7 shows equivalent numbers for a reduction of $40J/s_v$ (the difference between using 480p instead of 1080p with H.265). Real savings will depend on the choices users make and the specific software, hardware and video sources, and will be subject to regional variations (e.g. the US emits 0.69$KgCO_2$ / KWh[8], over 3 times as much as the UK). It is clear that the potential benefits economically and environmentally are significant at a global scale.

However, we believe our numbers in Table 7 are likely to be an underestimate by at least an order of magnitude because (i) we do not include other substantial video sources similar to YouTube (e.g. TED and news agencies such as the BBC), or movie services (e.g. Netflix, Amazon, etc.), or

[6]http://www.youtube.com/press/statistics.html
[7]http://www.rensmart.com/Information/KWHToCO2Conversion
[8]http://www.epa.gov/cleanenergy/energy-resources/refs.html

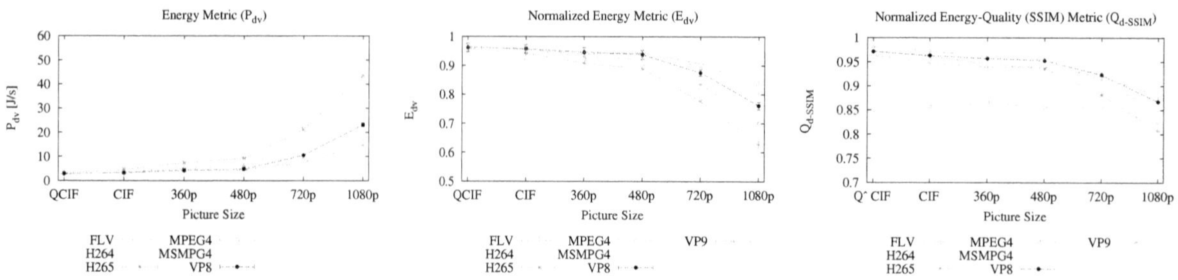

(a) 'Big Buck Bunny'

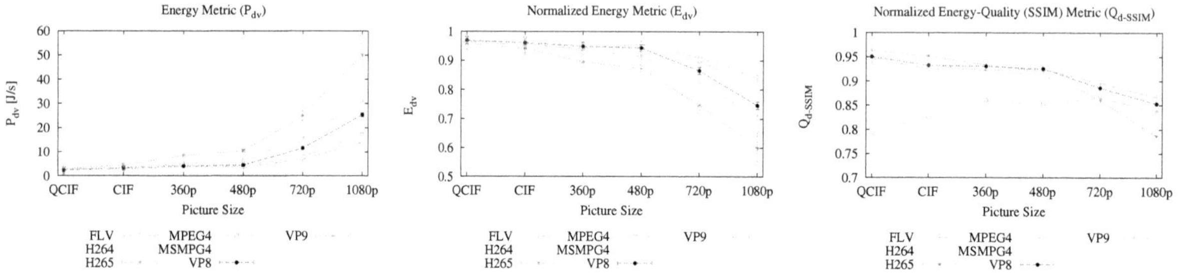

(b) 'Tears of Steel'

Figure 6: Derived energy metrics for decoding. 20 runs were used to plot each point, with 95% confidence (error bars not always visible as they are very small in some cases). The lines joining the points are visual aids only and do not imply interpolation to intermediate picture sizes.

real-time video (e.g. Skype, Facetime, etc.); and (ii) we do not assess the impact of transmitting fewer video bits across network infrastructure to the client and possible savings in network systems and devices [30]. There are also likely to be secondary impact factors, e.g. the energy use of content caches and proxies. Both of these will be significant when considered at a global scale. Also, different platforms will behave differently, e.g. on smartphones and tablets with hardware support for H.264, the situation is likely to be different, with other codecs decoded in software having much higher energy-consumption than H.264.

7. EMPOWERING USERS

Users must be given enough information to be empowered to make choices about video streams. We make two suggestions in this section, each with different levels of detail for client systems. Each scheme would allows users to make assessments based only on codec and picture size. So, for example, if a video stream provider only gives a choice of picture size and not of video codec, the user is still empowered with suitable knowledge to make a choice with respect to energy usage. As our methodology is measurement-based, we discuss first the use of a benchmark tool to provide data on the client system. Providing appropriate information in the correct format would require further analyses, additional experimentation, software development, testing and human factors work for real use.

7.1 System benchmark tool

Users are familiar with the use of benchmarks in order to assess the performance of equipment. For example, the Standard Performance Evaluation Corporation (SPEC)[9] is a non-profit organisation that produces many benchmarks[10] that are widely used for IT equipment and components, e.g. SPEC CPU2006 for CPU, SPECvirt_sc2013 for virtualisation, etc. SPEC also produces SPECpower_ssj2008[11], which assesses power usage using a suite of Java code that can be downloaded and executed on systems.

Consider a similar benchmark tool for video, which we shall call *vEQ-benchmark*. This would be downloaded by client systems, executed, and result in the creation of a system file containing information about energy usage of the system when decoding (and encoding) video. That is, it would be a suite that would produce a machine-readable summary, which we shall call *vEQ-summary*, based on the methodology presented in this paper, along with other data (e.g. video hardware information). The vEQ-summary file would contain information on codec types, estimates on energy usage for those codec types, QoE information, and other relevant information for users. It would be executed on system initialisation and when the system configuration changes. Especially at the larger picture sizes, there is a difference in energy usage between the two different types of content we have used in our experiments, both for encoding and decoding. So a benchmark would need to allow for such variation, e.g. by using a suite of reference video files.

SPECpower_ssj2008 relies on power analyser hardware to provide power information. However, future hardware would have power usage information available through an API much like the Advanced Configuration & Power Interface (ACPI)[12] already provides today for a range of systems.

Based on the contents of the vEQ-summary file, a video codec, video component (such as a browser plugin) could, along with information about the video, provide an interface to the user, to inform them about the energy usage and other information for a specific video file. A future applica-

[9]http://www.spec.org/

[10]http://www.spec.org/benchmarks.html

[11]http://www.spec.org/power_ssj2008/

[12]http://acpi.info

tion adaptation mechanism could use that information along with user preferences to automatically adapt video quality to trade-off energy usage and QoE as required.

7.2 Simple user information

A simple way of presenting feedback to the user would be to indicate how 'green' a video file is, with a simple visual symbol, indicating the relative 'greenness' of a video file with respect to another. Figure 7 shows a mock-up for such an indicator from the YouTube video playback control bar in a web browser. The video plugin for the browser would, based on the contents of the vEQ- summary file, place green markers (a 'leaf' logo in this case) next to the different video formats that are already offered for playback. More green leaf markers indicate a 'greener' file.

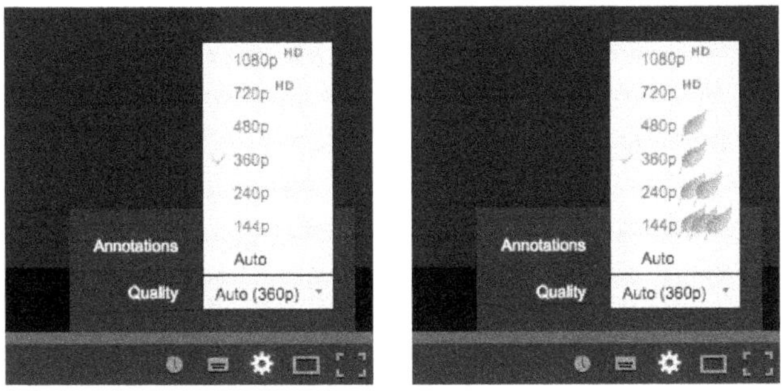

Figure 7: A YouTube control panel (left), modified to show 'green' choices for video playback for the different picture size options (right). More green 'leaf' markers indicate a more energy efficient stream.

7.3 Detailed energy labelling

For many appliances, standard energy labelling is being used to indicate energy usage. For example, the "Directive 2010/30/EU of the European Parliament and of the Council of 19 May 2010"[13] defines the indication by labelling and standard product information of the consumption of energy and other resources by energy-related products[14]. Many regions of the world have similar schemes and labelling. Such labels are now required on many appliances in the EU.

We propose that such a labelling scheme also be devised for video. However, rather than a printed label, a dynamic, adaptive label would be displayed on screen, using the vEQ-summary information to generate detailed energy and performance information. For example, in place of the YouTube display above in Figure 7, when a video file is selected the video file meta-data, along with the information from the vEQ-summary could be used to generate a label as shown in the mock-up of Figure 8. Qualitative indicators (top) as well as detailed quantitative information (bottom, for more technically aware users) allow users to make their selection. The qualitative indicators would be evaluated from using a combined quality/energy measure such as in Eqn. 7, using appropriate weights. Like other labels, e.g. for domestic appliances, our label contains other relevant information, such as QoE, file size, detailed video coding information, and availability of hardware assist.

[13] http://ec.europa.eu/energy/efficiency/eed/eed_en.htm

[14] http://www.newenergylabel.com/

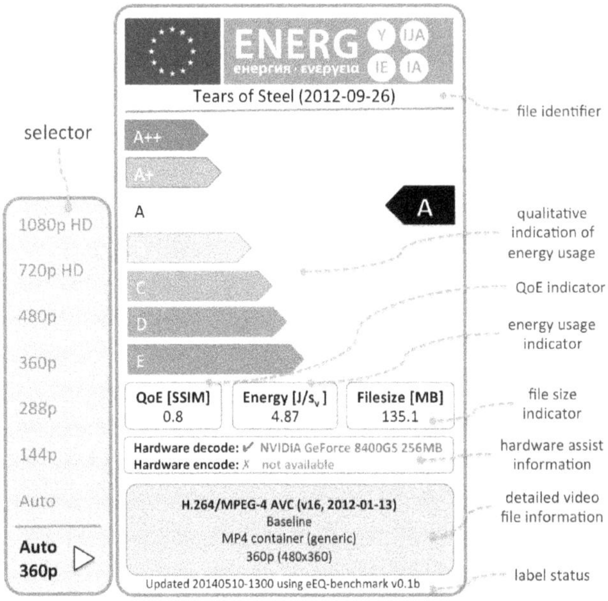

Figure 8: A future interactive, video energy and performance label. A qualitative indicator allows quick and easy evaluation by the user. Detailed information at the bottom of the label could include: a QoE measure; energy usage; file size (downloading more bits uses more energy); and the availability of hardware assist for video encode and decode.

(Such a scheme could be applied to software components and systems more generally, not just video codecs, to complement labelling on hardware components and systems. This is an item for future study.)

8. CONCLUSION

Suitably informed users could provide economic and environmental benefits when using video. We have presented empirical results from our test-bed evaluations of the system energy usage of decoding and encoding of video streams. We examined seven popular codecs: FLV, H.264, H.265 (HEVC), MPEG4-II, Microsoft MPEG4-II (MSMPEG4), VP8 and VP9. Using a simple, measurement-based methodology, we have shown that the differences in energy usage between these codecs can be significant, e.g. a factor of 3 between decoding FLV and H.265 at a large picture size (1080p), and up to a factor of 10 for encoding. Both picture size and video codec choice impact energy usage. We presented simple energy metrics and demonstrated how these could be used with QoE to make an energy performance trade-off. We have also proposed two schemes to present energy usage information to users, to empower them to make choices on video usage. When considered across a global population of video users, individual client-side savings sum to show a potential for significant energy and cost savings, as well as environmental impact.

Acknowledgements

This work was partly supported by the IU-ATC project, funded by grant EP/J016756/1 from the Engineering and Physical Sciences Research Council (EPSRC). Oche Ejembi is funded by the Scottish Informatics and Computer Science Alliance (SICSA). Special thanks to Jim Park (School of

Computer Science, University of St Andrews) for modifying the Kill-A-Watt power meter.

9. REFERENCES

[1] Cisco Systems, "Cisco visual networking index: Global mobile data traffic forecast update, 2012–2017," Feb 2013. [Online]. Available: http://goo.gl/OL6mYY

[2] W.-J. Hsin and J. Cigas, "Short Videos Improve Student Learning in Online Education," *J. Comput. Sci. Coll.*, vol. 28, no. 5, pp. 253–259, May 2013.

[3] M. Chen, S. GonzÃąlez, H. Cao, Y. Zhang, and S. Vuong, "Enabling low bit-rate and reliable video surveillance over practical wireless sensor network," *The Jrnl of Supercomputing*, vol. 65, no. 1, pp. 287–300, 2013.

[4] C. T. E. R. Hewage, M. G. Martini, and N. Khan, "3D Medical Video Transmission over 4G Networks," in *Proc. 4th Intl. Symp. on Applied Sciences in Biomedical and Communication Technologies*, 2011, pp. 180:1–180:5.

[5] T. Cai, E. Abbott, and N. Bwambale, "The Ability of Video Training to Reduce Agricultural Knowledge Gaps Between Men and Women in Rural Uganda," in *6th Intl. Conf. on Information and Communications Technologies and Development: Notes - Vol. 2*, 2013, pp. 13–16.

[6] M. Webb, "SMART 2020: Enabling the low carbon economy in the information age, a report by The Climate Group on behalf of the Global eSustainability Initiative (GeSI)," Global eSustainability Initiative (GeSI), Tech. Rep., 2008. [Online]. Available: http://goo.gl/EOqSB4

[7] M. Sabharwal, A. Agrawal, and G. Metri, "Enabling Green IT through Energy-Aware Software," *IT Professional*, vol. 15, no. 1, pp. 19–27, Jan 2013.

[8] Y. Yu and S. N. Bhatti, "The Cost of Virtue: Reward As Well As Feedback Are Required to Reduce User ICT Power Consumption," in *e-energy 2014 - 5th ACM Intl. Conf. on Future Energy Systems*, Jun 2014.

[9] N. Amsel and B. Tomlinson, "Green Tracker: A Tool for Estimating the Energy Consumption of Software," in *ACMCHI 2010 Extended Abstracts on Human Factors in Computing Systems*, 2010, pp. 3337–3342.

[10] X. Li, M. Dong, Z. Ma, and F. C. Fernandes, "GreenTube: power optimization for mobile videostreaming via dynamic cache management," in *Proc. ACM SIGMM 2012*, Oct 2012, pp. 279–288.

[11] G. Nencioni, N. Sastry, J. Chandaria, and J. Crowcroft, "Understanding and Decreasing the Network Footprint of Catch-up Tv," in *Proc. 22nd Intl. Conf. on World Wide Web*, 2013, pp. 965–976.

[12] M. Song, Y. Lee, and J. Park, "CPU Power Management in Video Transcoding Servers," in *Proc. NOSSDAV 2014*, Nov 2014, pp. 91:91–91:96.

[13] Y. Sharrab and N. Sarhan, "Detailed Comparative Analysis of VP8 and H.264," in *IEEE Intl. Symp. Multimedia (ISM 2012)*, 2012, pp. 133–140.

[14] D. Vatolin, D. Kulikov, and M. Arsaev. (2012, November) 8th MPEG-4 AVC/H.264 Video Codecs Comparison - Standard Version. [Online]. Available: http://www.compression.ru/video/codec_comparison/h264_2012/

[15] A. Ravi and K. Rao, "Performance analysis and comparison of the Dirac video codec with H. 264/MPEG-4 Part 10 AVC," *Intl. Jrnl. Wavelets, Multiresolution and Information Processing*, vol. 9, no. 04, pp. 635–654, 2011.

[16] A. Rao, A. Legout, Y.-s. Lim, D. Towsley, C. Barakat, and W. Dabbous, "Network characteristics of video streaming traffic," in *ACM CoNEXT 2011*, 2011, pp. 25:1–25:12.

[17] Y. Liu, L. Guo, F. Li, and S. Chen, "An empirical evaluation of battery power consumption for streaming data transmission to mobile devices," in *ACM SIGMM 2011*, 2011, pp. 473–482.

[18] L. Zhang, F. Wang, and J. Liu, "Understand instant video clip sharing on mobile platforms: Twitter's vine as a case study," in *NOSSDAV 2014 - Network and Operating System Support on Digital Audio and Video Workshop*, 2013, pp. 85:85–85:90.

[19] C.-H. Lin, J.-C. Liu, and C.-W. Liao, "Energy analysis of multimedia video decoding on mobile handheld devices," *Computer Standards & Interfaces*, vol. 32, no. 1 - 2, pp. 10 – 17, 2010.

[20] Y. O. Sharrab and N. J. Sarhan, "Aggregate power consumption modeling of live video streaming systems," in *MMSys 2013*, 2013, pp. 60–71.

[21] R. Trestian, A.-N. Moldovan, O. Ormond, and G. Muntean, "Energy consumption analysis of video streaming to Android mobile devices," in *IEEE NOMS 2012*, Apr 2012, pp. 444–452.

[22] M. Tranchemontagne, "Moteino kill-a-watt: Hardware," http://goo.gl/TdoF5M, 2013.

[23] R. Serral-Gracià, E. Cerqueira, M. Curado, M. Yannuzzi, E. Monteiro, and X. Masip-Bruin, "An Overview of Quality of Experience Measurement Challenges for Video Applications in IP Networks," in *WWIC2010 - 8th Intl. Conf. on Wired/Wireless Internet Communications*, 2010, pp. 252–263.

[24] Z. Wang, A. Bovik, H. Sheikh, and E. Simoncelli, "Image quality assessment: from error visibility to structural similarity," *IEEE Trans. Image Processing*, vol. 13, no. 4, pp. 600–612, April 2004.

[25] D. Vatolin, D. Kulikov, A. Parshin, and O. Petrov. (2006, January) MSU Subjective Comparison of Modern Video Codecs. [Online]. Available: goo.gl/3CpNWJ

[26] L. Merritt, R. S. Bultje, and M. Niedermayer, "tiny_ssim.c, codec-independent objective quality measurement," http://git.videolan.org/?p=ffmpeg.git;a=blob;f=tests/tiny_ssim.c, 2013.

[27] S. N. Bhatti and G. Knight, "Enabling QoS adaptation decisions for Internet applications," *Computer Networks*, vol. 31, no. 7, pp. 669–692, Apr 1999.

[28] M. Tauber, S. N. Bhatti, and Y. Yu, "Towards Energy-Awareness In Managing Wireless LAN Applications," in *NOMS2012 - IEEE Network Operations and Management Symp.*, Apr 2012.

[29] "UK Energy Statistics, Statistical Press Release," UK Dept. of Energy and Climate Change, Tech. Rep., Mar 2014. [Online]. Available: http://goo.gl/gqxSWl

[30] M. Gupta and S. Singh, "Greening of the Internet," in *ACM SIGCOMM 2003*, 2003, pp. 19–26.

Media Experience of Complementary Information and Tweets on a Second Screen

Kenta Kusumoto, Teemu Kinnunen, Jari Kätsyri, Heikki Lindroos, Pirkko Oittinen
Aalto University School of Science, Department of Media Technology
P.O. Box 15500, Espoo, FI-00076 AALTO, Finland
[kenta.kusumoto, teemu.kinnunen, jari.katsyri, heikki.lindroos, pirkko.oittinen]@aalto.fi

ABSTRACT

Television (TV) programs are increasingly augmented with second-screen applications that can provide complementary information and social media interaction related to the program. However, there is a lack of understanding about the optimal design of such applications. In this paper, we study the effects of complementary information and tweets on the media experience indexed by a comprehensive self-report questionnaire. We built a custom second-screen tablet application and conducted an experiment to investigate the effects of complementary information and tweets on the media experience of TV programs. Apart from reducing concentration and immersion, neither the presence of complementary information nor the presence of tweets affected the media experience of the TV programs, whereas the media experience of second-screen content depended on which program it accompanied. Our results demonstrate that the media experience of complementary information and tweets presented on second screens differs between TV programs.

Categories and Subject Descriptors

H.5.2 [**Information interfaces and presentation**]: User interfaces; J.4 [**Computer applications**]: Social and behavioral sciences

Keywords

Second screen; complementary information; tweets; TV; media experience; tablet; media multitasking

1. INTRODUCTION

The use multiple media simultaneously (media multitasking) is becoming increasingly more common [13]. In particular, the consumption of content from a combination of television (TV) and a second screen (e.g., a laptop, smartphone, or tablet) has gained interest in recent years. Second-screen usage can be related to TV content (e.g., chatting online about a TV program) or unrelated to this content (e.g., checking email). Although the TV industry is concerned that unrelated second-screen usage may reduce audience engagement with TV programs, the industry also views related usage as an opportunity that may lead to increased engagement.

Many existing commercial second-screen applications augment TV content with related complementary information and social media conversations (e.g., zeebox[1], Shazam[2]). Recently, second screens have appeared in gaming environments as well (e.g., Xbox SmartGlass[3], Battlefield 4 Battlescreen[4]). However, these applications have evolved mainly as a result of trial and error, and empirical research to understand the usage of these applications, particularly the media experience associated with them, has been negligible.

Most of the research on media multitasking, especially in second-screen environments, has focused on performance [1]. Additionally, several descriptive studies [13] and uses and gratifications studies [16, 17] have provided insight on how much, in what ways, and why people engage in media multitasking. From an application standpoint, it is also important to understand how second-screen use affects the media experience. Therefore, in this work, we focus on the way that complementary information and tweets affect the media experience in a second-screen environment. For this purpose, we built a custom second-screen tablet application for presenting TV program-related complementary information and tweets, and we conducted an experiment to measure the media experience of second-screen use (Figure 1).

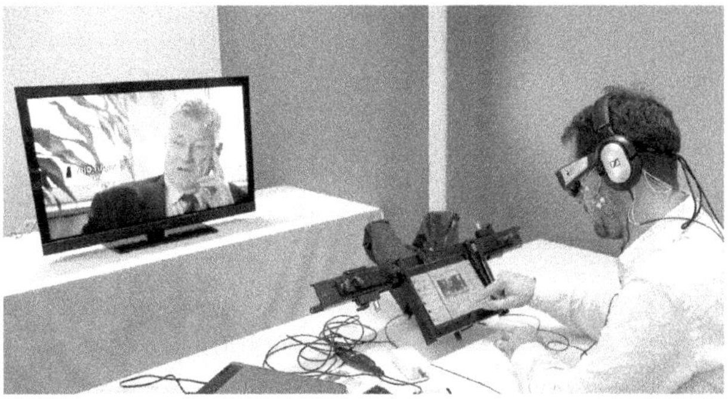

Figure 1: The second-screen environment of the experiment.

MM'14, November 3–7, 2014, Orlando, Florida, USA.

ACM 978-1-4503-3063-3/14/11 ...$15.00.
http://dx.doi.org/10.1145/2647868.2654925.

[1] http://zeebox.com/
[2] http://www.shazam.com/music/web/productfeatures.html?id=1266
[3] http://www.xbox.com/smartglass
[4] http://bf4central.com/battlefield-4-battlescreen/

2. MEASURING THE MEDIA EXPERIENCE

The concept of media is multifaceted and vague. It may refer to content, device, or channel. In the present study, we define media as content such as text, images, or video. Different media have different properties that all contribute to how the media are experienced. Several instruments have been developed to measure various aspects of the media experience, including (but not limited to) engagement [10], flow [9], spatial presence [15], social presence [3], emotion [12], and user experience [14]. Each of these captures unique perspectives on the media experience, but they also share overlapping aspects. In recent years, the concept of multimedia experience has emerged and developed into the research field of Quality of Experience (QoE) [7]. This field has received substantial attention because traditional performance-based methods (i.e., Quality of Service) lack the ability to measure subjective aspects of the multimedia experience.

In this study, we present the measurements of media experience with a questionnaire based on the Model of Media Experience [4], which is able to capture multifaceted dimensions of media-related experiences. As far as we know, the present experimental study is the first attempt to operationalize the model. The model defines three levels, namely, the meta, macro, and micro levels. The meta level considers the effects of societal, economic, and technological changes on media usage. The macro level addresses the social aspect of media use. Finally, the micro level represents media experience at the individual level. The micro level comprises 16 dimensions with regard to which media experience of an individual is assessed (similar to the features of QoE [7]). The present study employs questions from each appropriate dimension. The Model of Media Experience emphasizes the experience of media content rather than the system; thus, it is considered suitable for the present study.

Because the study involved three different types of media content (TV programs, complementary information, and tweets), the media experience was measured separately for each type of content with self-report questions (see Tables 6, 7, 8 in the Appendix). Some questions were common to all media content regarding involvement (e.g., interestingness), hedonic liking, and spatial presence (e.g., immersion). Questions related to informativeness (trustworthiness, novelty, and understandability) were exclusive to TV programs and complementary information, and social presence-related questions (social presence and connectedness) were exclusive to tweets. Additionally, some questions were administered regardless of the presence of tablet content but were specific to either complementary information (search willingness) or tweets (follow willingness) and a question was asked regarding which screen was perceived to be the main screen. Furthermore, eye tracking was used to measure how much the participants looked at the TV and the tablet screens. Eye tracking provides information about visual attention and thus provides insight into what a person finds interesting. In the present study, eye tracking was also used to check whether the participants actually used the second screen.

3. EXPERIMENT

3.1 Design

In the present experiment, the participants interacted freely with a second-screen tablet application while watching TV programs presented on a TV screen (Figure 1). The implemented application offered complementary information and tweets that were related to and synchronized with the TV programs.

The experiment had an $8 \times 2 \times 2$ mixed design with the following independent variables: different TV programs (see Table 1), the presence (or absence) of complementary information, and the presence (or absence) of tweets.

Table 1: TV program labels that are used throughout this paper with short descriptions and genres.

Label	Description	Genre
MAGA1	The program reports in a critical tone how an orphanage foundation defrauded an orphanage of 25 million euros.	Magazine
MAGA2	The program criticizes the accidental leak in a gypsum pond caused by a mining company and presents tweets on the topic.	
DOCU1	The program talks about the barnacle goose that has inhabited urban areas and whose feces cause aesthetic damage to the scenery.	Documentary
DOCU2	The program interviews celebrities and discusses the realities of partners moving in and living together in a humorous tone.	
REAL1	The program documents somewhat humorously the competition of two teams that have to build a car within a month with 3000 euros.	Reality
REAL2	A dance competition program that conforms to the British Got to Dance program format.	
SPOR1	A European boxing heavyweight title match between a national and a foreign boxer.	Sports
SPOR2	A floorball match between a national and a foreign team in the European Floorball Tour 2013.	

As shown in Table 1, the TV programs were selected from four different TV genres: magazine, documentary, reality, and sports (two programs per genre). However, because our preliminary analyses demonstrated that there were considerable differences between individual TV programs, we chose to consider each TV program separately. Common genres such as drama and movies were not included because their intense plot structure would have required continuous following [2] and they would have been less suitable for concurrent second-screen use.

The combinations of complementary information and tweets presented on the tablet formed the experimental conditions

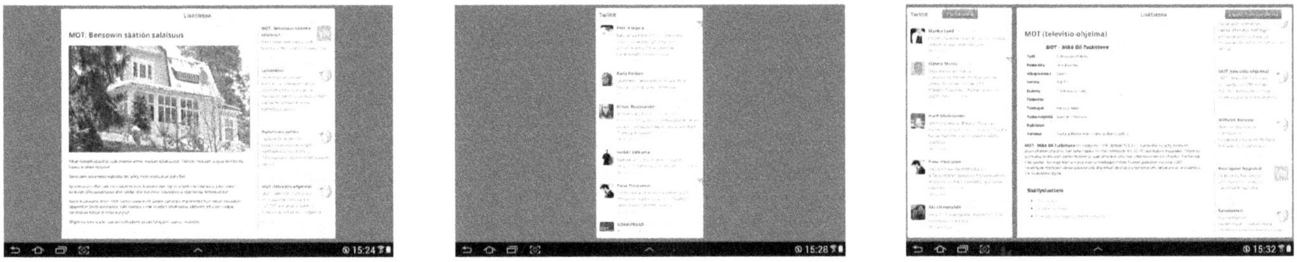

(a) Complementary information only (condition 2).

(b) Tweets only (condition 3).

(c) Both (condition 4).

Figure 2: The graphical user interface of the second-screen application for the different conditions. In the TV-only condition when no tablet content was presented (condition 1), the tablet screen remained blank.

(Table 2). Figure 2 shows the user interface of the second-screen tablet application in the various conditions.

Furthermore, the TV programs were presented with different condition combinations arranged in four different condition sets, as demonstrated in Table 3. The participants were assigned different condition sets in the order of participation. The combination of complementary information and tweets presented with a particular TV program was the same in a given condition set. The same complementary information and tweets were presented with a particular TV program, and their presentation order and time during the program were always the same (due to synchronization with the progress of the program). Every participant saw each TV program only once and in a random order.

Table 2: The experimental conditions.

Condition	Content combination
1	TV program only
2	TV program + complementary information
3	TV program + tweets
4	TV program + complementary information + tweets

Table 3: The condition sets and conditions they comprise (for conditions, see Table 2).

Condition set	TV program condition			
	Magazine	Documentary	Reality	Sports
1	1	2	3	4
2	4	1	2	3
3	3	4	1	2
4	2	3	4	1

For example, if a participant was assigned to condition set 1, then he/she was presented with the programs MAGA1 and MAGA2 without any tablet content, DOCU1 and DOCU2 with complementary information only, REAL1 and REAL2 with tweets only, and SPOR1 and SPOR2 with both complementary information and tweets. The TV programs were within-subject variables, and the presence of complementary information and the presence of tweets were partially between-subject variables.

3.2 Dependent variables

The dependent variables were composed of the answers to the self-report media experience questions for each content including TV programs, complementary information, and tweets listed in Tables 6, 8, and 7, respectively, and eye-tracking variables (see Section 4.6). The TV program-related questions were administered in all conditions, whereas the complementary information and tweet-related questions were administered only when the tablet content was presented.

Additionally, regardless of the condition, the participants were asked to evaluate their willingness to search for complementary information about the TV programs and their willingness to follow tweets related to the TV program.

When either or both of the tablet contents were presented, the participants were asked to evaluate whether they considered the TV or the tablet to be the main screen. It should be noted that the main screen question regarded the tablet as a whole and did not discriminate between complementary information and tweets.

The self-report questions were answered using the tablet after each TV program. All items were evaluated on a 7-point Likert scale in which 1 = "strongly disagree" and 7 = "strongly agree," except for the main screen question, which had a binary scale with 1 = "TV" or 2 = "tablet."

3.3 Stimuli

The TV programs were video clips of approximately five minutes in length that were edited from full-length videos. Based on convention, the duration of five minutes was expected to be sufficient for the participant to concentrate on the TV program and still have time to read complementary information articles.

The complementary information articles consisted of online news and Wikipedia articles. These two complementary information types were selected because they were not tied to any specific TV genre (as opposed to sports statistics, for example). The articles were collected manually based on terms in the TV programs. The selected articles were stripped of all annotations, external links, and information that was unavailable at the time of airing of the TV program. Each TV program was accompanied by 10 articles.

The tweets were collected by querying them with the name of the TV program and with the terms associated with the program. Tweets that contained images or web links or in which the message was unrelated to the TV program were excluded manually. The number of tweets presented during each of the TV programs ranged from 29 to 57.

3.4 Apparatus

The TV used to show the TV program stimuli was a Sony Bravia KDL-40HX800 with a screen size of 40 inches and an aspect ratio of 1920 × 1080 pixels. The luminance of the screen was measured to be approximately 160 cd/m^2.

A Samsung Galaxy Tab 10.1 tablet was used as the second screen. The tablet had a screen size of 10.1 inches and an aspect ratio of 1280 × 800 pixels with 149 ppi resolution. The luminance of the tablet was measured to be approximately 130 cd/m^2.

SMI Eye-Tracking Glasses (ETG), a head-mounted eye-tracking system, was used to track the gaze of the participants. As opposed to fixed eye trackers that have a limited tracking range and headbox, the ETG allowed the participants to move their heads freely, making the TV viewing more comfortable. More importantly, the ETG tracked the gaze on multiple screens at various distances. In the present experiment, the ETG was calibrated to the TV screen. The ETG tracked binocular eye movement at 30 Hz and captured scene video at 24 fps. Because the ETG lacked exposure adjustment, the TV and the tablet screens became overexposed in the scene video if the room was too dark compared to the screens. The overexposure was avoided by adjusting the room lighting and the brightness of the screens.

Sennheiser HD201 corded closed circumaural headphones were used to mitigate any distracting external noise and to improve the participants' concentration. The headphones had a frequency response of 21–18000 Hz and a sound pressure level of 108 dB at 1 kHz according to the product specifications.

3.5 Environment

To avoid the overexposure of TV and tablet screens in the ETG scene videos (see previous section) caused by dim ambient lighting, the room was illuminated brightly. Three fluorescent lights, two pointing up and one down, were used. Room illuminance was approximately 340 lux, corresponding to normal office lighting.

The distance between the participant and the TV screen was approximately 225 cm, conforming to the International Telecommunication Union (ITU) recommendation [11]. The distance between the participant and the tablet was maintained at approximately 50 cm because the ETG required the target to be at least 40 cm from the wearer for the tracking to be accurate.

As described above, any environmental noises were blocked effectively by the closed headphones. In addition, a partitioning screen was placed between the participant and the experimenter to increase the participant's concentration on the experimental task.

3.6 Second-screen application

The second-screen application developed for the experiment in this study was implemented with HTML5. In particular, the CSS animation and WebSocket communication features were utilized.

Complementary information and tweets were presented on the tablet in three distinct graphical user interface components (Figure 2c). A feed component on the left presented tweets, and another feed component on the right presented short descriptions of the complementary information articles. The area in the middle between the two feeds was used to present the full complementary information articles. When only complementary information or only tweets were presented, the component was centered, as shown in Figures 2a and 2b. When neither of the tablet contents was presented, the tablet screen remained blank.

The tweet-feed items were composed of a profile image, Twitter name, full name, time elapsed since the creation of the tweet, and the message. The complementary information-feed items had a title, the first sentence of the full article as a short description of the article, and an icon of the information source type. The full article was positioned to the left of the complementary information feed and could contain text, tables, images, and internal links.

The complementary information and tweet feeds were updated automatically, and new items were presented at the top of the feed. For the updates to be noticeable with peripheral vision, they were emphasized with the following animations: the new item flashed once, and the old items slid downwards to make space for a new item.

Older items could be revealed by scrolling down the feed. When the feed was not in the top position, the updates were not animated. Instead, the number of new items was indicated by a button in the header of the feed. By tapping the button, the feed scrolled automatically back to the top position, which also restarted the update animation. The participants could open and read the full articles by tapping the items in the complementary information feed. The full articles could be navigated by scrolling and with internal links. This setting was intended to replicate a plausible real-world application as closely as possible.

3.7 Procedure

Prior to taking part in the experiment, the participants were asked to complete an online questionnaire consisting of sociodemographic questions. Upon their arrival at the experiment room, the participants were given a brief description of the experimental procedure, after which they signed an informed consent form. The participants were instructed to watch the TV programs and simultaneously read complementary information articles and/or tweets on the tablet and interact with the tablet application freely. The participants wore the ETG and headphones, after which the ETG was calibrated and the sound level of the headphones was adjusted.

After the initial preparations, the participants completed a practice session in which they watched a TV program accompanied by both complementary information and tweets on the tablet. The TV program presented in the practice session was not one of the actual stimuli presented during the experiment.

In the experiment, the participants watched all of the TV program stimuli and, upon finishing each program, fixated on a fixation cross presented on the TV screen and answered the media experience questions presented on the tablet. The fixation cross was used to estimate the drift in eye tracking.

3.8 Participants

In total, 43 people (32 male, 11 female), mostly undergraduate students at a Finnish university, participated in the experiment. The average age of the participants was 27.4 years (SD = 7.2 years). Most of the participants had a degree in higher education and an engineering background. Remarkably, nearly half of the participants (42.9%) reported owning a tablet. This proportion is substantially larger than the percentage of Finnish households that have a tablet, which, according to Statistics Finland, was 20% in 2013 [6]. Clearly, this sample represented typical technology-oriented second-screen users and hence was suitable for the present experiment. The participants received two movie tickets for their participation.

4. RESULTS

4.1 Data analysis

The data were analyzed using a Linear Mixed Model procedure in the IBM SPSS statistical analysis software[5] version 22.0. This procedure was equivalent to conventional ANOVA analysis but allowed the inclusion of TV programs and different experimental conditions as independent variables.

The TV programs, the presence of complementary information, the presence of tweets, and the order of the trials were selected as fixed effects. The order of the trials was included as a covariate to take into account the effect of the order of the presentation of each stimulus.

A participant identifier was used as a contextual variable (level-two variable), and the order of the trials was used as a repeated-effects variable. Compound symmetry was used as the repeated residual error covariance type. Significance was tested with a 5% significance threshold, and restricted maximum likelihood was used as the fitting method.

As a post-hoc test, pairwise comparisons were performed for the TV programs, the presence of complementary information, and the presence of tweets.

Eye-tracking events (e.g., saccades and fixations) were detected using the SMI BeGaze 3.3 analysis software.[6] An annotation of the detected fixations into areas of interest, namely, the TV and the tablet screens, was performed semi-automatically. The annotation process was assisted by clustering the fixation points spatially with K-means clustering. Clustering proved to be a feasible method for annotation because most of the fixation points that fell on the TV screen were at the top, whereas most of the fixation points that fell on the tablet were at the bottom, creating two distinct clusters. The automatically annotated clusters were confirmed manually. Eye-tracking variables were calculated only for the conditions in which either or both of the tablet contents were presented (conditions 2, 3, and 4).

4.2 Differences in media experience between TV programs

Cronbach's alpha was $\alpha = .87$ (8 items) for the TV program-related questions, $\alpha = .91$ (11 items) for the complementary information-related questions, and $\alpha = .91$ (8 items) for the tweet-related questions, all indicating good reliability.

4.2.1 TV programs

The media experience characteristics of the TV programs were examined first because these characteristics may affect the media experience of complementary information and tweets. All TV program-related variables differed significantly ($p < .01$) between individual programs (detailed statistics are not shown). Figure 3 shows the differences in TV program-related variables. Although there were differences between the variables, in general, most variables were evaluated significantly higher for MAGA1, and variables excluding the informativeness variables (trustworthiness, novelty, and understandability) scored lower for DOCU1 and REAL1. The trustworthiness and novelty of DOCU2, REAL1, and REAL2 were evaluated significantly lower than those of the other programs. REAL1 differed from the other programs by being significantly less understandable.

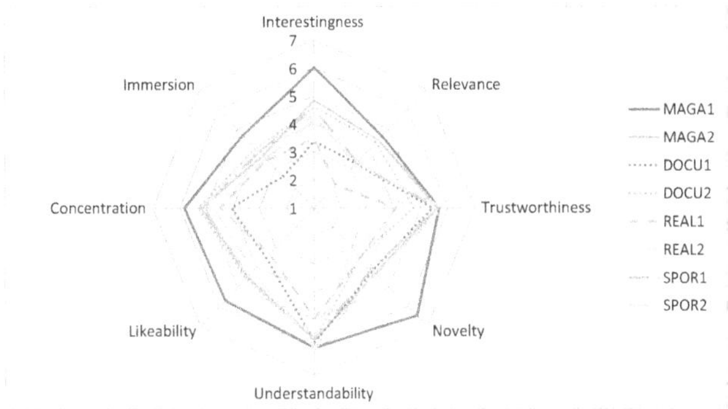

Figure 3: Media experience characteristics of TV programs.

4.2.2 Complementary information

As Table 4 shows, the interestingness, trustworthiness, likability, and relatedness of complementary information varied significantly, and relevance and novelty varied almost significantly between the programs.

Table 4: Differences in complementary information-related variables between the programs. Degrees of freedom (df) are rounded values. $^{**}p < .01$, $^{*}p < .05$, $^{\dagger}p < .10$.

Variable	df	F	p
Interestingness	(7, 112)	2.60	.02*
Relevance	(7, 110)	1.95	.07†
Trustworthiness	(7, 112)	2.71	.01*
Novelty	(7, 111)	1.86	.08†
Understandability	(7, 105)	.99	.44
Likability	(7, 107)	3.78	.00**
Concentration	(7, 104)	1.51	.17
Immersion	(7, 107)	1.16	.33
Valuableness	(7, 107)	1.22	.30
Experience enhancement	(7, 110)	.54	.80
Relatedness	(7, 110)	3.29	.00**

Figure 4 shows the differences in complementary information-related variables. In general, most variables were evaluated significantly higher for MAGA1, MAGA2, and SPOR1. However, with respect to novelty, likability, and concentration, the evaluations for REAL1 were on par with those for the aforementioned programs.

Figure 5 shows TV program likability for the programs plotted against complementary information likability for the programs. The figure illustrates that complementary information likability is relatively high for REAL1 even though the TV program likability of REAL1 is low. The relatively

[5]http://www.ibm.com/software/analytics/spss/

[6]http://www.smivision.com/en/gaze-and-eye-tracking-systems/products/begaze-analysis-software.html

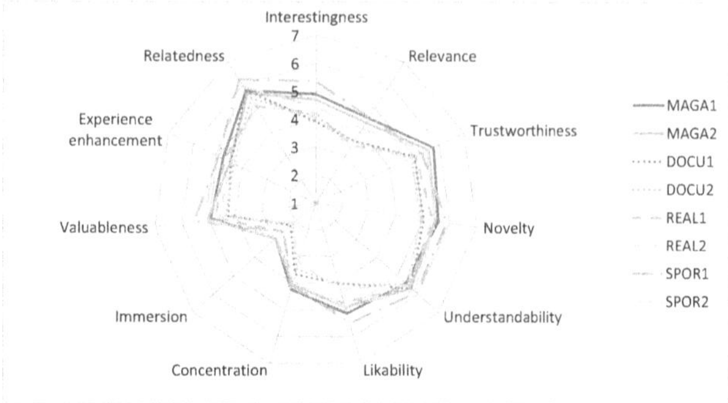

Figure 4: Media experience characteristics of complementary information.

high score for REAL1 in complementary information likability (and novelty and concentration) may result from the fact that the REAL1 program was disengaging due to its poor media experience (see Section 4.2.1), and the participants found the complementary information to be more appealing. This can be contrasted with DOCU1, for which likability was low for both the TV program and complementary information. A possible reason for this incongruity is that REAL1 was significantly less understandable compared to the other programs and thus resulted in the increased usefulness and appeal of the complementary information.

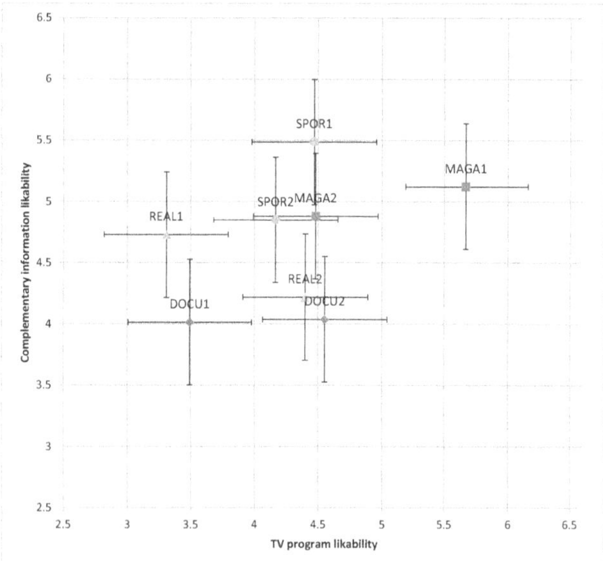

Figure 5: Complementary information likability against TV program likability (means with 95% CIs).

4.2.3 Tweets

All tweet-related variables differed significantly ($p < .01$) between the programs (detailed statistics are not shown). Figure 6 shows the differences in tweet-related variables. In general, most evaluated items were significantly higher for SPOR1 and SPOR2. Notably, in many cases, the scores for MAGA1 and MAGA2 were also relatively high; hence, they did not differ significantly from the scores for SPOR1 and SPOR2. However, with respect to novelty, likability, and concentration, the evaluations for REAL1 were on par with the aforementioned programs. Tweets for DOCU1 and DOCU2 were evaluated as significantly less related to the TV program than tweets for the other programs.

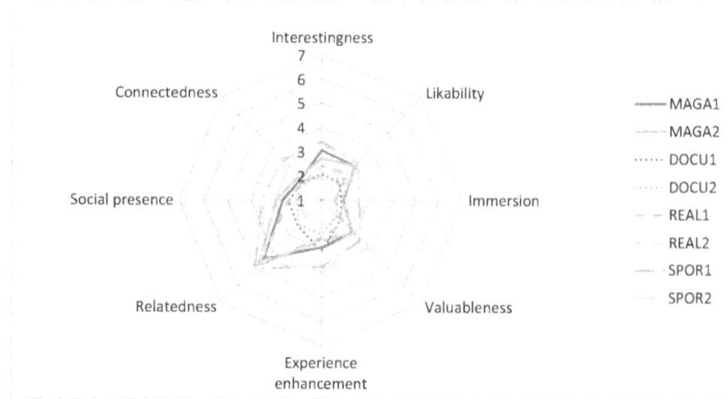

Figure 6: Media experience characteristics of tweets.

Figure 7 shows TV program likability for the programs plotted against tweet likability for the programs. At first glance, the figure resembles Figure 5, but in Figure 7, tweet likability for DOCU1, DOCU2, REAL1, and REAL2 is consistently at a lower level compared to MAGA1, MAGA2, SPOR1, and SPOR2 and has no incongruity as in Figure 5.

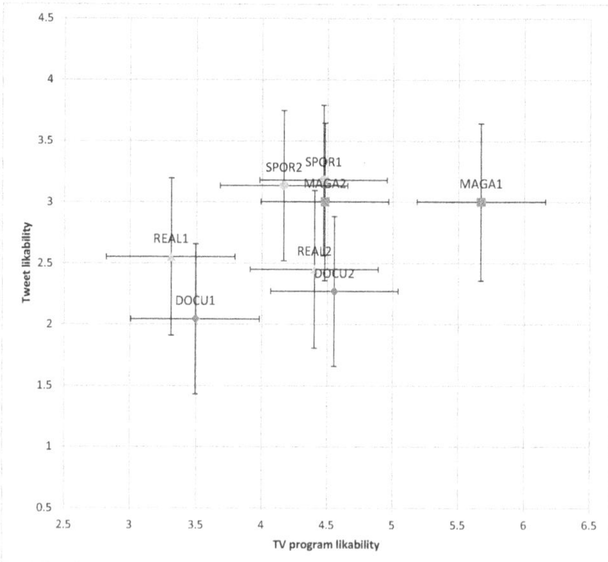

Figure 7: Tweet likability against TV program likability (means with 95% CIs).

4.3 Cross-content effects

Neither the presence of complementary information nor that of tweets had an effect on the TV program-related variables, except that both significantly decreased TV program concentration ($p < .01$) and immersion ($p < .01$).

Although the presence of complementary information did not have an effect on any of the tweet-related variables, the presence of tweets had a deteriorating effect on several complementary information-related variables, including complementary information novelty, understandability, concentration, valuableness, and relatedness, as shown in Table 5. The presence of tweets also had a marginally negative effect on complementary information immersion and experience enhancement.

Table 5: The effect of tweet presence on complementary information-related variables. Degrees of freedom (df) are rounded values. $^{**}p < .01$, $^{*}p < .05$, $^{\dagger}p < .10$.

Variable	df	F	p
Interestingness	(1, 113)	1.56	.21
Relevance	(1, 113)	1.62	.21
Trustworthiness	(1, 112)	.28	.60
Novelty	(1, 113)	9.59	.00**
Understandability	(1, 113)	6.00	.02*
Likability	(1, 113)	.89	.35
Concentration	(1, 113)	10.69	.00**
Immersion	(1, 113)	2.94	.09†
Valuableness	(1, 113)	5.12	.01*
Experience enhancement	(1, 113)	3.90	.05†
Relatedness	(1, 113)	12.07	.00**

4.4 Willingness to search for complementary information and to follow tweets

Figure 8 shows that the willingness to search for complementary information related to the TV program was significantly higher for MAGA1, MAGA2, and SPOR1. While search willingness for SPOR2 did not differ significantly from DOCU1 and REAL2, it was significantly larger than search willingness for DOCU2 and REAL1. The presence of complementary information did not affect search willingness (F(1, 271) = 1.58, p = .21), confirming that the presented complementary information did not bias the responses.

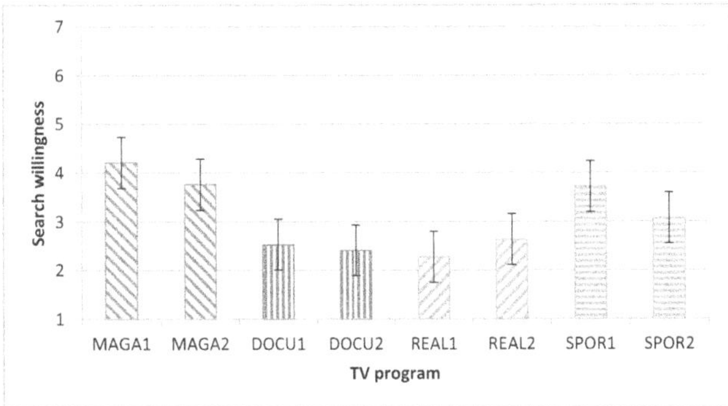

Figure 8: Willingness to search for complementary information for the programs (means with 95% CIs).

Figure 9 shows that the willingness to follow TV program-related tweets was significantly higher for SPOR1 and SPOR2, with the exceptions of MAGA1 and MAGA2, for which the score did not differ significantly from any of the programs. As with search willingness, the presence of tweets did not affect the willingness to follow (F(1, 270) = .97, p = .32).

4.5 Perceived main screen

The participants were asked whether they considered the TV or the tablet to be the main screen when either or both tablet contents were presented (conditions 2, 3, and 4). There were close to significant differences in the main

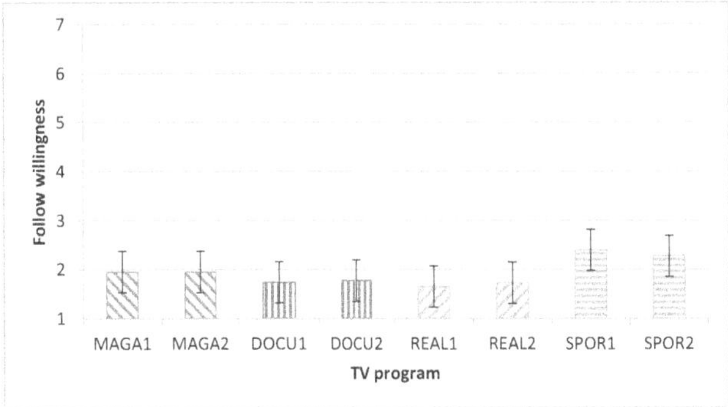

Figure 9: Willingness to follow tweets for the programs (means with 95% CIs).

screen variable between the programs (F(7, 193) = 2.04, p = .05). Post-hoc tests showed that DOCU1 scored significantly higher than the other programs (Figure 10). REAL1 also scored significantly higher than MAGA2, REAL2, and SPOR1.

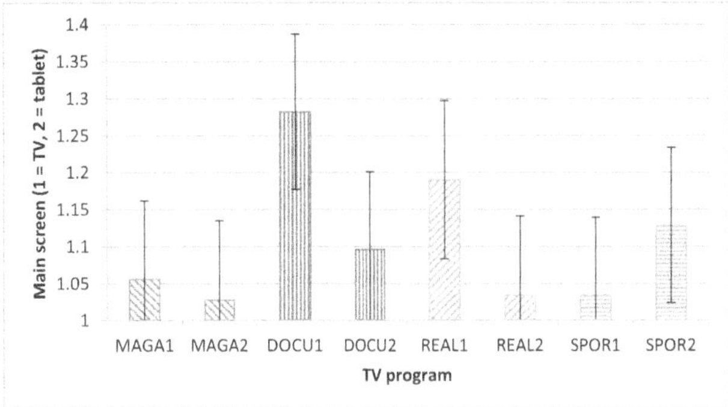

Figure 10: Perceived main screen for the TV programs (means with 95% CIs). 1 = TV, 2 = tablet.

The pattern bears a close inverse resemblance to the pattern in the TV program-related variables, which indicated that the media experience was poor for DOCU1 and REAL1. The Pearson correlation between the TV program interestingness and the main screen variable was r = -.57 (p < .001), indicating a large effect size with a negative correlation.

However, because the mean scores in Figure 10 are close to 1 for most of the TV programs, it is clear that the TV had a firm position as the main screen, and the tablet became the main screen on rare occasions.

Although the presence of complementary information predicted whether the tablet was perceived to be the main screen (F(1, 189) = 4.66, p <.05), the presence of tweets did not (F(1, 189) = .04, p = .84).

4.6 Eye tracking

The proportional dwell time on the tablet, that is, the proportion of total fixation duration on the tablet, was extracted from the eye-tracking data. In practice, the proportional dwell time on the TV was the opposite of that on the tablet because the number of fixations that fell outside the two screens was very small.

The mean proportional dwell time on the tablet was 37.8% (SD = 18.7%). There were no significant differences in the proportional dwell time on the tablet between the TV programs ($F(7, 131) = 1.42$, $p = .20$). These results resemble those of Holmes et al. [5], who did not find significant differences in the proportional dwell times between genres in a second-screen environment. Naturally, both the presence of complementary information ($F(1, 187) = 9.45$, $p < .01$) and the presence of tweets ($F(1, 187) = 6.11$, $p < .05$) predicted the proportional dwell time on the tablet. As Figure 11 shows, the proportional dwell time on the tablet was higher when only complementary information was presented on the tablet than when only tweets were presented and was highest when both tablet contents were presented.

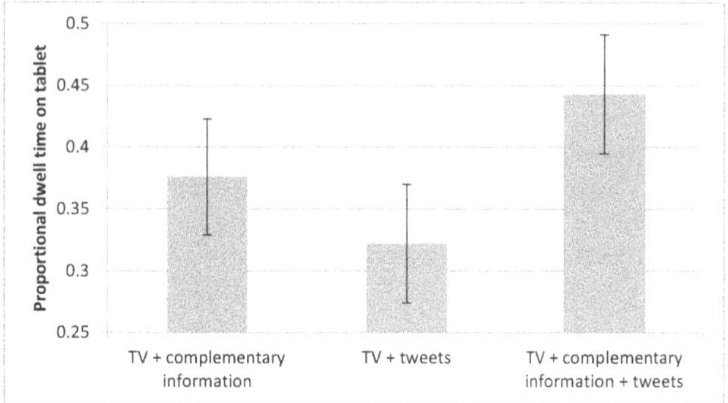

Figure 11: Proportional dwell time on the tablet for different conditions (means with 95% CIs).

Moreover, the mean number of gaze transitions per minute between the TV and the tablet screens was 8.8 ($SD = 4.0$), which translates to a mean dwell time of 6.8 seconds. This number aligns with the findings of the study by Brasel and Gips [1], in which the authors conclude that the dwell time for media multitasking is considerably lower than that found in previous studies.

5. DISCUSSION

The presence of complementary information and tweets reduced TV program concentration and immersion, which may be a sign of reduced engagement with TV programs. However, the presence of complementary information and tweets did not affect any other TV program-related variables. Although the reduction in concentration and immersion can be explained by divided attention (see Section 4.6), it is not trivial that the media experience of the TV programs was otherwise unaffected. Complementary information and tweets neither improved nor deteriorated the media experience of the TV programs. Although the results imply reduced engagement with TV programs, they may also imply that second screens could be used to enrich TV programs without sacrificing the media experience of these programs.

Nevertheless, there were clear differences in the way that complementary information and tweets were experienced with different TV programs. Apparently, complementary information and tweets are meaningful companions for some, but not all, TV programs.

In general, both complementary information- and tweet-related variables scored higher for MAGA1, MAGA2, SPOR1, and SPOR2, suggesting that the tablet contents suited these programs better than the other programs.

Differences in the willingness to search for complementary information and in the willingness to follow tweets between the programs resembled the pattern of complementary information and tweet-related variables. In general, the willingness to search for complementary information and the willingness to follow tweets were evaluated higher for MAGA1, MAGA2, SPOR1, and SPOR2, which supports the idea that the tablet contents suited these programs better than the other programs.

The tablet was more likely to be considered the main screen for DOCU1 and REAL1, which were the TV programs that were the least pleasing to viewers. This finding suggests that participants attempted to counter the boredom of watching a disengaging TV program by reading more appealing tablet content and thus were more likely to recognize the tablet as the main screen. Hence, the second screen has some potential to become the main screen if the TV program fails to satisfy the viewer. It is also possible that this potential may manifest in temporarily disengaging parts of otherwise satisfactory TV programs, thereby keeping the viewer more engaged in TV viewing.

Interestingly, there was an imbalance between the effects of complementary information and the presence of tweets as well as differences in complementary information and tweet-related variables between the programs. Although the presence of complementary information did not affect tweet-related variables, the presence of tweets negatively affected several complementary information-related variables. Furthermore, all tweet-related variables varied significantly between the programs, whereas only some of the complementary information-related variables were significantly different between the programs. This finding indicates that complementary information was less affected by individual programs and may imply that complementary information was regarded as independent main content that coexisted with the TV program, whereas tweets were regarded as side content. Tweets acted as a distraction for complementary information; thus, the presence of tweets deteriorated the media experience of complementary information. The finding that the presence of complementary information predicted that the tablet would become the main screen, whereas the presence of tweets did not predict this result, further supports the above formulation.

6. LIMITATIONS

The present study involved a number of limitations that should be addressed in future studies. A generalization of the results for the TV genres was not feasible due to the differences in TV programs within the genres and the small number of genres. Additionally, presenting previously broadcast TV programs about temporary events, such as magazine and sports programs, may affect the results depending on the participant's familiarity with the program or topic. The quantification and more rigorous control of the structure of the TV programs and tablet contents is necessary for a more detailed examination of the effects. The number of female participants was clearly smaller than the number of male participants in the present study, which could have biased our results. However, it should be noted that the higher number of male participants reflected the demographics of the participant sample (i.e., technologically oriented students). Finally, the study considered only the concurrent use of the second screen while watching TV. There is evidence that complementary information may work better with particular genres before and after broadcasting

[8]. Measuring the media experience of second-screen use before and after broadcasting is necessary to investigate long-term effects. Although we have striven for a realistic multimedia setting, some possibly artificial compromises were made to ensure sufficient experimental rigor (the laboratory environment, a wearable eye tracker, and identical research stimuli).

7. CONCLUSION

In this study, we investigated the media experience of TV viewing and the simultaneous consumption of complementary information and tweets on a second-screen tablet application. An experiment was conducted in which the participants watched TV programs and simultaneously interacted freely with a second-screen tablet application. The participants evaluated the media experience associated with the TV programs, complementary information, and tweets using comprehensive self-report questionnaires. Furthermore, we used a head-mounted eye-tracking device to determine how much visual attention was paid to the tablet when complementary information and/or tweets were presented.

We found that apart from reducing concentration and immersion, neither the presence of complementary information nor the presence of tweets exerted an effect on TV program-related variables, indicating that the participants were able to distinguish between the media experiences of different media content. Complementary information and tweets emerged as suitable companions for magazine and sports programs. The findings also indicate that a second screen may become the main screen when the TV program is not appealing.

The results suggest that the selection of second-screen content types is an important design principle to consider when developing second-screen applications. Furthermore, the media experience could be used to index media content to realize, for example, experience-based video enrichment and content recommendation systems.

8. ACKNOWLEDGMENTS

This study was part of the Digile Next Media Programme and was funded by Tekes (Finnish Funding Agency for Technology and Innovation). We would like to thank Yle (the Finnish national public broadcasting company) for providing the TV programs.

9. REFERENCES

[1] S. A. Brasel and J. Gips. Media multitasking behavior: Concurrent television and computer usage. *Cyberpsychology, Behavior, and Social Networking*, 14(9):527–534, 2011.

[2] D. Geerts, P. Cesar, and D. Bulterman. The implications of program genres for the design of social television systems. In *Proceedings of the 1st International Conference on Designing Interactive User Experiences for TV and Video*, UXTV '08, pages 71–80, New York, NY, USA, 2008. ACM.

[3] C. Harms and F. Biocca. Internal consistency and reliability of the networked minds measure of social presence. 2004.

[4] M. Helle, N. Ravaja, H. Heikkilä, J. Kallenbach, A. Kankainen, J. Kätsyri, J. Laine, and D. Marghescu. A theoretical model of media experience and research methods for studying it. Technical report, Next Media, 2011.

[5] M. E. Holmes, S. Josephson, and R. E. Carney. Visual attention to television programs with a second-screen application. In *Proceedings of the Symposium on Eye Tracking Research and Applications*, ETRA '12, pages 397–400, New York, NY, USA, 2012. ACM.

[6] R. Kohvakka, P. Melkas, and R. Harala. Suomen virallinen tilasto (svt): Väestön tieto- ja viestintätekniikan käyttö -tutkimus 2013. Technical report, Statistics Finland, 2013.

[7] P. Le Callet, S. Möller, and A. Perkis. Qualinet white paper on definitions of quality of experience. *European Network on Quality of Experience in Multimedia Systems and Services (COST Action IC 1003)*, 2013.

[8] Miso. The miso sync experiment: Delivering real-time, relevant information on the second screen. Technical report, Miso, 2011.

[9] T. P. Novak and D. L. Hoffman. Measuring the flow experience among web users. *Interval Research Corporation*, 31, 1997.

[10] H. L. O'Brien and E. G. Toms. The development and evaluation of a survey to measure user engagement. *Journal of the American Society for Information Science and Technology*, 61(1):50–69, 2010.

[11] Radiocommunication Sector of ITU. Recommendation itu-r bt.2022: General viewing conditions for subjective assessment of quality of sdtv and hdtv television pictures on flat panel displays. Technical report, International Telecommunication Union, 2012.

[12] N. Ravaja. Effects of a small talking facial image on autonomic activity: The moderating influence of dispositional bis and bas sensitivities and emotions. *Biological Psychology*, 65(2):163–183, 2004.

[13] V. J. Rideout, U. G. Foehr, and D. F. Roberts. Generation m2: Media in the lives of 8-to 18-year-olds. *Henry J. Kaiser Family Foundation*, 2010.

[14] T. Tullis and W. Albert. *Measuring the user experience: collecting, analyzing, and presenting usability metrics.* Morgan Kaufmann, 2010.

[15] P. Vorderer, W. Wirth, F. R. Gouveia, F. Biocca, T. Saari, L. Jäncke, S. Böcking, H. Schramm, A. Gysbers, T. Hartmann, C. Klimmt, J. Laarni, N. Ravaja, A. Sacau, T. Baumgartner, and P. Jäncke. Mec spatial presence questionnaire (meq-spq): Short documentation and instructions for application. 2004.

[16] Z. Wang and J. M. Tchernev. The "myth" of media multitasking: Reciprocal dynamics of media multitasking, personal needs, and gratifications. *Journal of Communication*, 62(3):493–513, 2012.

[17] W. Zhang and L. Zhang. Explicating multitasking with computers: Gratifications and situations. *Computers in Human Behavior*, 28(5):1883–1891, 2012.

APPENDIX

A. MEDIA EXPERIENCE VARIABLES

Table 6: TV program-related variables, their associated self-report questions, and conditions in which the questions were administered (for conditions, see Table 2).

Variable	Questions	Conditions
Interestingness	The TV program was interesting.	1, 2, 3, 4
Relevance	The TV program was relevant to me.	1, 2, 3, 4
Trustworthiness	The TV program was trustworthy.	1, 2, 3, 4
Novelty	The TV program provided novel information.	1, 2, 3, 4
Understandability	The TV program was understandable.	1, 2, 3, 4
Likability	I liked the TV program.	1, 2, 3, 4
Concentration	I concentrated on the TV program.	1, 2, 3, 4
Immersion	I immersed myself completely into the TV program.	1, 2, 3, 4

Table 7: Tweet-related variables, their associated self-report questions, and conditions in which the questions were administered (for conditions, see Table 2).

Variable	Questions	Conditions
Interestingness	The tweets were interesting.	3, 4
Likability	I liked the tweets.	3, 4
Immersion	I immersed myself completely into the tweets.	3, 4
Valuableness	The tweets added value to the TV program.	3, 4
Experience enhancement	TV watching experience was enhanced by the tweets.	3, 4
Relatedness	The tweets were related to the TV program.	3, 4
Social presence	The tweets made me feel socially present.	3, 4
Connectedness	I felt connected to other Twitter users.	3, 4

Table 8: Complementary information-related variables, their associated self-report questions, and conditions in which the questions were administered (for conditions, see Table 2).

Variable	Questions	Conditions
Interestingness	The complementary information articles were interesting.	2, 4
Relevance	The complementary information articles were relevant to me.	2, 4
Trustworthiness	The complementary information articles were trustworthy.	2, 4
Novelty	The complementary information articles provided novel information.	2, 4
Understandability	The complementary information articles were understandable.	2, 4
Likability	I liked the complementary information articles.	2, 4
Concentration	I concentrated on the complementary information articles.	2, 4
Immersion	I immersed myself completely into the complementary information articles.	2, 4
Valuableness	The complementary information articles added value to the TV program.	2, 4
Experience enhancement	TV watching experience was enhanced by the complementary information articles.	2, 4
Relatedness	The complementary information articles were related to the TV program.	2, 4

Interactive Line Drawing Recognition and Vectorization with Commodity Camera

Pradeep Kumar Jayaraman
School of Computer Engineering
Nanyang Technological University, Singapore
pradeepk001@e.ntu.edu.sg

Chi-Wing Fu
School of Computer Engineering
Nanyang Technological University, Singapore
cwfu@ntu.edu.sg

ABSTRACT

This paper presents a novel method that interactively recognizes and vectorizes hand-drawn strokes in front of a commodity webcam. Compared to existing methods, which recognize strokes on a completed drawing, our method captures both spatial and temporal information of the strokes, and faithfully vectorizes them with timestamps. By this, we can avoid various stroke recognition ambiguities, enhance the vectorization quality, and recover the stroke drawing order. This is a challenging problem, requiring robust tracking of pencil tip, accurate modeling of pen-paper contact, handling pen-paper and hand-paper occlusion, while achieving interactive performance. To address these issues, we develop the following novel techniques. First, we perform robust spatio-temporal tracking of pencil tip by extracting discriminable features, which can be classified with a fast cascade of classifiers. Second, we model the pen-paper contact by analyzing the edge-profile of the acquired trajectory and extracting the portions related to individual strokes. Lastly, we propose a spatio-temporal method to reconstruct meaningful strokes, which are coherent to the stroke drawing continuity and drawing order. By integrating these techniques, our method can support interactive recognition and vectorization of drawn strokes that are faithful to the actual strokes drawn by the user, and facilitate the development of various multimedia applications such as video scribing, cartoon production, and pen input interface.

Categories and Subject Descriptors

I.4 [**Image Processing and Computer Vision**]: Applications

Keywords

line drawing; vectorization; online computation; pen interface; webcam

1. INTRODUCTION

The acquisition and vectorization of hand-drawn strokes on paper is beneficial to a wide range of multimedia applications: from handwriting recognition to cartoon production, video scribing and sketch-based modeling. This bridges the gap between paper and digital representations, and facilitates the development of computational methods for editing and interaction.

In general, there are four major approaches for recognizing and vectorizing paper-based line drawings according to the kind of inputs being processed:

- *Manual approach* involves manual effort of tracing individual strokes in a scanned input image. While being accurate and flexible, this approach can be extremely tedious subject to the complexity of the drawing.
- *Image-based approach* [2, 20] takes a scanned image of a completed drawing as an input, and attempts to automatically analyze the drawing contours to infer the stroke geometry and produce the vector representation. Major challenges of this approach are the image noise and the ambiguities in reconstructing the strokes due to image resolution and line junctions.
- *Sensor-based approach* [25, 30] employs hardware devices to track the pen trajectory on paper to detect the pen strokes. This approach, however, requires specially-designed devices that are not common, e.g., sensors in the ballpoint tip of a pen, etc.
- *Camera-based approach* [19, 23] captures the video of the drawing process, and recognizes strokes on paper by tracking and analyzing the pen-tip trajectory by computer-vision methods. The two main advantages of this approach are 1) the use of original writing instruments, i.e., pens/pencils, so involving no learning overhead in practice, and 2) the availability of temporal information from the captured video.

Our goal in this work is to develop an interactive camera-based method to capture and vectorize hand-drawn strokes on paper through a commodity low-cost webcam that captures at 480p/720p resolution and 30 frames/second. By this, we can faithfully vectorize drawn strokes with improved stroke continuity, and also recover the temporal information and drawing order of the strokes. With the emergence of recent ubiquitous devices like the Google Glass [9], camera-based approach could be particularly useful to help recognize hand-drawn inputs in front of the embedded camera, and to facilitate the development of pen input interface.

Previous methods for vectorizing hand-drawn strokes either exist as online/offline approaches, which are constrained by the stroke length, size, and direction, or strictly offline methods, which process the scanned images of the final drawings. To the best of our knowledge, this is the first attempt of developing an online camera-based method to acquire and

MM'14, November 3–7, 2014, Orlando, Florida, USA.
Copyright 2014 ACM 978-1-4503-3063-3/14/11 ...$15.00.
http://dx.doi.org/10.1145/2647868.2654939.

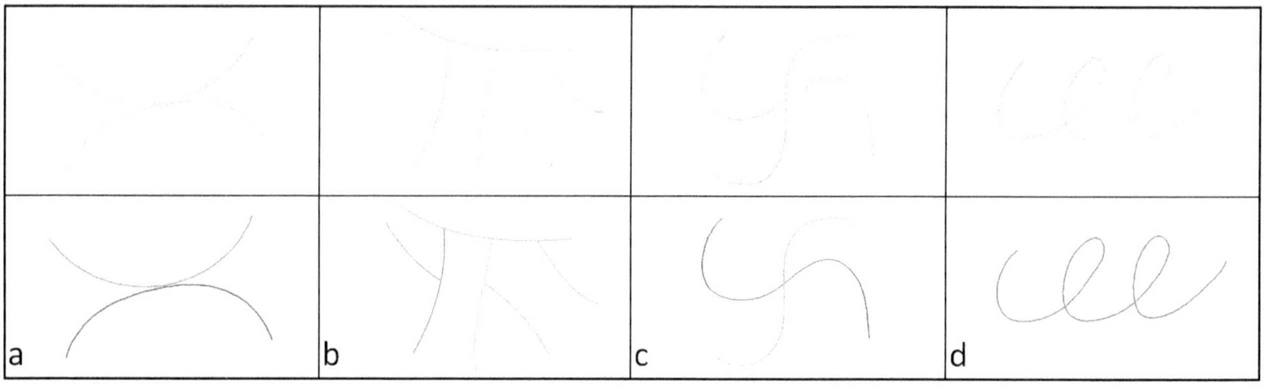

Figure 1: *Top row: four line drawings on paper, revealing four common stroke recognition ambiguities: (a) spatial adjacency, (b) junction ambiguities, (c) multiple-stroke intersection, and (d) self-intersection. Existing vectorization methods may mis-recognize the original strokes as strokes of some other drawing continuity or break the original strokes into several shorter strokes at the junctions and intersections. Bottom row: our method can faithfully recognize and vectorize these strokes even in the presence of the ambiguities; color-coding is used to indicate individual recognized strokes.*

vectorize freehand line drawings.

However, such problem is very challenging since we need to robustly track the tip of the pen in the video, accurately model the pen-paper contacts, handle the pen-paper as well as hand-paper occlusion, and complete the entire computation with interactive performance. To address these issues, we propose the following novel techniques, which are the major technical contributions of this work:

- First, we identify three distinctive features, i.e., variance, color, and shape, and integrate them to robustly locate the tip of pen/pencil while quickly rejecting negative samples. We also exploit a domain-specific idea to generalize our shape feature to be invariant to rotation and partial perspective distortion.
- Second, we model the pen-paper contact implicitly by analyzing the zero-crossings of the Laplacian of Gaussian filter response along the pen-tip trajectory, and extracting an appropriate subset of it to estimate the potential region of the drawing strokes.
- Lastly, we combine the spatio-temporal information to define a cost function to reconstruct a stroke while preserving the stroke continuity and drawing order even in the presence of recognition ambiguities.

Our method has several advantages over existing offline vectorization methods, which work only with completed drawings. First, it is *online*, so it can capture and produce vectorized strokes with real-time feedback. Second, it involves only everyday pens/pencils and a simple camera rather than specialized pen/paper hardware. Third, our online method enables the capture of strokes with temporal information and drawing order, thus facilitating the development of various multimedia applications, and could potentially be integrated with camera-based interaction device such as the Google Glass. Lastly, by using temporal information, we can effectively avoid various stroke recognition ambiguities that are common in existing vectorization methods, see Figure 1: spatial adjacency, junction ambiguities, multiple-stroke intersection, and self-intersection, see also [20]. From the results shown in Figure 1, we can see our method can avoid these recognition ambiguities and faithfully recover each stroke natural to the actual stroke drawn by the user while preserving the stroke continuity in the vectorization.

2. RELATED WORK

Line Drawing Vectorization. Line drawing is a common form of raster images for vectorization. For example, manga artists traditionally create their cartoon drawings on paper with pencils, and then scan and vectorize their drawings for further digital processing and editing.

Early methods for line drawing vectorization can only deal with rather simple drawings such as technical layout plans and maps, where the methods could approximate the drawings with straight line segments [11] or employ morphological operations such as thinning [14] and skeletonization [31, 34] to extract the pixel-wide contours. Hilaire and Tombre [10] also attempted to fit line segments and arcs in a least-squares sense to images of technical drawings. As such, these methods are generally incapable of handling freehand drawings.

Several research works have been proposed to handle the vectorization of higher-order primitives. Among them, Chang et al. [5] studied piecewise fitting of Bezier curves for vectorizing cartoon images. Bao et al. [2] proposed to trace near-constant-width lines in line drawings by estimating a dense orientation field that guides the tracing direction. Noris et al. [20] reconstructed robust centerlines in topologically-complex line drawings in the presence of certain junction ambiguities. Some works that estimate temporal information and tracing directions of strokes [8, 13] and extract curves to trace contours with connectivity and orientation [26, 6] may also be used in vectorizing line-drawings.

While recent methods mentioned above and commercial software like Adobe Illustrator [28] and WinTopo [24] could produce reasonable vectorized lines given in line drawing images, they often cause fragmentation and/or stroke distortion problems especially near line junctions due to various stroke recognition issues, see Figure 1. Moreover, none of them could faithfully reconstruct strokes with spatio-temporal coherence following how the artist creates a drawing.

Pen Interface. Another relevant research area is the development of pen interfaces to capture and reconstruct pen strokes in an environment that mimics how people use pens, see [27] for a related survey. Generally, there are two major approaches for pen interface:

i) Sensor-based approach develops pen interfaces [25, 7] by using a combination of specially-designed hardware, e.g.,

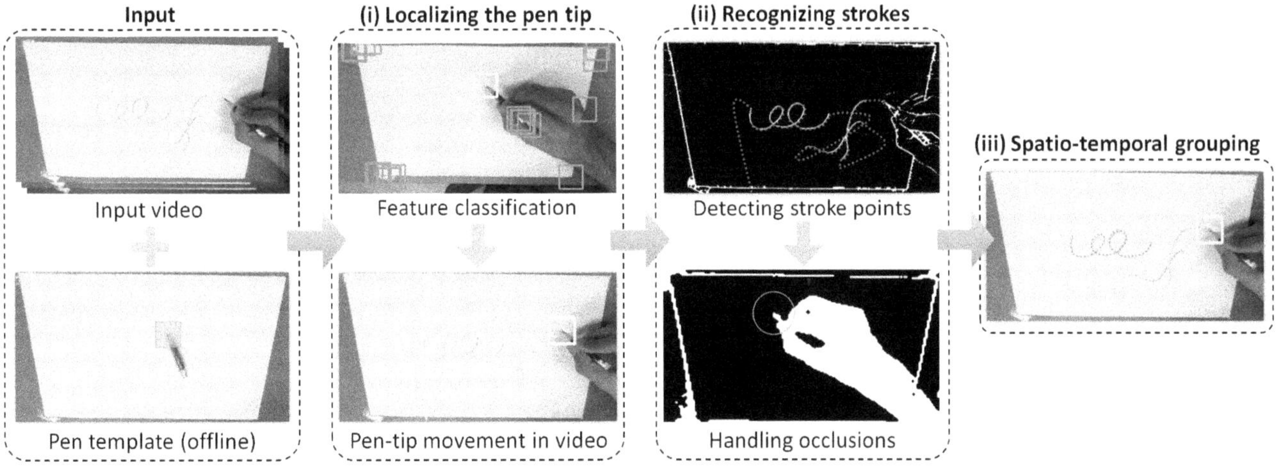

Figure 2: *Overview of our stroke recognition and vectorization method. From left to right: our input is a video stream and a simple pen-tip template; (i) potential patches are searched in video frames to localize the pen tip and track its trajectory; (ii) Laplacian of Gaussian filter response helps extract stroke points to estimate the actual drawn stroke; hand and pen occlusions are also tracked; and (iii) lastly, spatio-temporal clustering is performed to identify individual strokes (color coded).*

special paper with invisible dot pattern, camera-augmented pen, capacitive touch sensor, infrared camera, etc. Though there are some related commercial products, e.g., Anoto Digital pens [1] and the Wacom Inkling [30], this approach requires special hardware devices that are not as common as everyday pens and paper.

ii) Camera-based approach captures video frames of the pen writing/drawing process through a camera, and attempts to either localize or track the pen tip in each frame to obtain the pen-tip trajectory and stroke. Lin et al. [15] and Tang et al. [29] proposed various video-analysis schemes to recover the spatio-temporal grouping of strokes in Chinese characters. They first extract strokes by thinning/skeletonizing the final video frame of the completed drawing, and then infer the stroke continuity by analyzing the evolution of strokes over time. However, their method does not track the pen tip and attempts to infer stroke connectivity by analyzing the relevant pixels in the stroke skeleton throughout the video. Hence, the method is highly sensitive to shadow and noise, and requires tedious fine-tuning before the operation. Since the occlusion problem is not handled, the analysis is performed offline, and there is no interactive feedback.

Munich and Perona [18, 19] captured handwriting strokes by analyzing visual input from a conventional camera. The method was later extended to support handwriting recognition by Wienecke et al. [32]. In detail, they used a correlation-based template matching method to detect the pen tip. Hence, the method cannot handle planar rotations and perspective distortions. Pen-paper contact is estimated based on a simple local analysis of intensity, which can be easily affected by shadow or neighboring strokes. Since it assumes a small image region that confines the handwriting strokes, occlusions are handled with a fixed-size mask. More recently, Seok et al. [23] assumed a specific conical-shaped colored pen, and tracked the pen tip by simple color detection and geometric cues. While robust to orientation and illumination changes, this method restricts the color and shape of the pen tip. Though the method is online, it cannot handle the occlusion problem because it assumes that the handwriting strokes are unidirectional, and the hand and pen body would move away from the video view constantly. This assumption does not hold in our case for freehand drawing since user's hand may move around and occlude previous strokes. Moreover, [23] does not consider temporal information to disambiguate strokes (see again Figure 1) to support meaningful stroke-based editing, and assumes specific color and shape constraints to detect the pen tip.

In sharp contrast, our proposed method is more general and can overcome a number of problems and assumptions taken by existing state-of-the-art methods: it considers hand and pen occlusions over the paper; it can retain stroke continuity and drawing order; it is stable for local cluttering caused by neighboring strokes; it is an online method capable of delivering interactive feedback; and it has the potential for meaningful stroke-based editing.

3. OVERVIEW

Figure 2 overviews our method with a running example. Our system setup includes a drawing space with a sheet of paper fixed on a desk, an everyday pen/pencil for drawing, a commodity webcam that oversees the drawing space from the top, and a desktop computer that processes the webcam's video stream and performs our method to recognize and vectorize the drawing strokes. In summary, our method consists of the following three major steps:

i) **Localizing the pen tip.**
Extracting discriminable features around the pen tip for efficient, rotation-invariant, and illumination-invariant per-frame detection of pen tip (Section 4.2); *Pruning* the search space by corner detection to accelerate the performance (Section 4.3.1); and *Classifying* the extracted feature vectors using a cascaded approach to quickly identify and track the pen tip over time to obtain a meaningful pen-tip trajectory (Section 4.3.2).

ii) **Reconstructing Strokes.**
Extracting a subset of points along the pen-tip trajectory to estimate the footprint of the drawn strokes by analyzing the edge profile along the trajectory (Section 5.1); and *Resolving* occlusion problem caused by user's hand and pen over the paper (Section 5.2).

iii) **Spatio-temporal Grouping.**
Grouping the extracted points into a stroke by formulat-

ing a cost function that considers the stroke connectivity, and spatial and temporal distance information (Section 6); and *Vectorizing* the clustered stroke by fitting a cubic spline over the grouped points, and outputting the final result in SVG vector format.

In our implementation, the above computation takes only ~0.072 sec. per video frame, showing that our method can support online stroke recognition and vectorization at interactive speed. However, since some drawn strokes may be occluded fully or partially by user's hand or pen, we can only reconstruct their unoccluded parts during the online computation. Our method keeps tracking the hand and pen locations (see Section 5.2) to determine if the occlusion has been removed, and then reconstructs and renders the previously-occluded strokes once they become visible and can be detected by our method. Hence, in a single video frame, our method may recover more than one stroke at a time.

4. LOCALIZING THE PEN TIP

4.1 Initialization

Our input consists of a video stream of the pen drawing process and a pen-tip template. To prepare a new pen-tip template, which is just an offline one-time step, it only takes a few seconds to mark a 60×60 image region on a frame of the video stream to enclose the pen tip. Here we only assume the pen is placed over the paper, on which the drawing would be done, and place no restrictions on the pen orientation as our method can later automatically normalize the template input to a canonical form that is rotation-invariant.

In detail, when extracting the pen-tip template, we also need a foreground-background segmentation [33] on the video frame to obtain a background-subtracted binary image, assuming that the pen is not part of the initial scene. Here we set a high adaptation time period in the background model to avoid too-early merging of foreground into the background.

4.2 Feature Extraction

Given a patch, which could be a pen-tip template or a 60×60 region in a video frame, we next need to extract distinctive features in the patch for supporting the pen-tip localization. The set of features we carefully selected in this work are *background confidence*, *intensity variance*, *color*, and *shape*. These features are simple-to-compute and yet discriminative to help identify the pen tip under rotation, illumination variation, and mild perspective distortions.

i) *Background Confidence* ($\mathcal{B}_i$). By applying foreground-background segmentation [33] on every video frame (including the one for the pen-tip template and also the video frames of the drawing process), we can obtain a background-subtracted binary image M whose background pixels take zero values. Hence, given a patch in M, we can count the number of background pixels in it, and compute the patch's background confidence ($\mathcal{B}_i$), i.e., the ratio of the number of background pixels to the total number of pixels in the patch.

ii) *Intensity Variance* (σ^2). The second feature we employed is the statistical variance of pixel grayscale values. This feature helps to measure the uniformity of pixel intensities in a patch. Moreover, after we obtain the pen-tip template, we pre-compute its intensity variance, say σ^2, and define low and high intensity variance thresholds $0.5\sigma^2$ and $1.5\sigma^2$, respectively, to support the fast cascaded classifier later on.

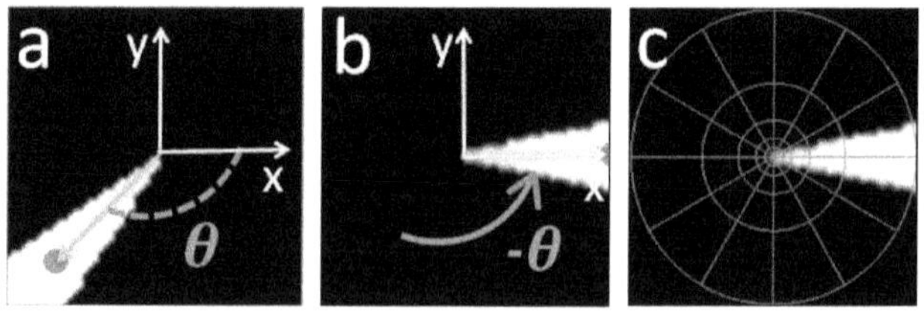

Figure 3: *Rotation-invariant shape feature. Given a binary patch extracted around a detected corner point in a video frame, we compute (a) the center of mass (red) of the largest foreground blob, rotate and normalize the patch into (b) a canonical shape representation, and then use (c) a log-polar histogram to extract the shape feature vector.*

iii) *Color* ($\mathcal{C}_i$). Third, we use the CIELab color-space to compute the color feature of a patch. Since the L channel represents the color luminance, we discard it for the sake of illumination invariance. Then, we quantize the chrominance by computing a 2D histogram of a and b channels with 16 bins in each dimension, and flattening the histogram as a 256-dimensional color feature vector. By this, we can compute the color feature vector of the pen tip template, say $v_t^{(c)}$, as well as the color feature vector of any patch in a video frame, say $v_i^{(c)}$. Hence, we can further compute the color similarity measure between them by Euclidean distance: $\mathcal{C}_i = \|v_t^{(c)} - v_i^{(c)}\|$.

iv) *Shape* ($\mathcal{S}_i$). Lastly, we compute the shape feature of a patch by devising an efficient rotation-invariant method based on the shape context [3]. Note that from the video frames, since we create candidate patches to be centered at detected corner points (Section 4.3.1), we can be certain that the pen tip (if any) would always appear at the center of a patch. Hence, for each patch, we can compute the shape feature as follows:

(a) Find the largest connected foreground blob in the given patch, and compute its center of mass, see the red dot in Figure 3(a);

(b) Compute its offset angle, say θ, from the positive x-axis in the image space, see again Figure 3(a);

(c) Rotate the patch image about its center (pen tip, if any) by $-\theta$ in order to normalize the patch to a canonical representation, see Figure 3(b);

(d) Calculate a 60-dimensional shape feature vector by centering a log-polar histogram (5 radial bins and 12 angular bins) at the patch center and computing its shape context, see Figure 3(c); and

(e) Lastly, compute shape similarity measure $\mathcal{S}_i$ for a given patch against the pen-tip template similar to the mechanism for the color similarity measure.

Note that the advantages of using the log-polar histogram here are: 1) it is simple and efficient to compute; 2) its coarse binning can sufficiently describe the pen-tip shape; and 3) its uneven binning relates and helps alleviate the effect of mild perspective distortion.

4.3 Feature Classification

4.3.1 Pruning the search space

In typical object localization, a sliding window is often used to go over a given video frame and extract all possible patches (potentially hundreds of thousands) for feature matching.

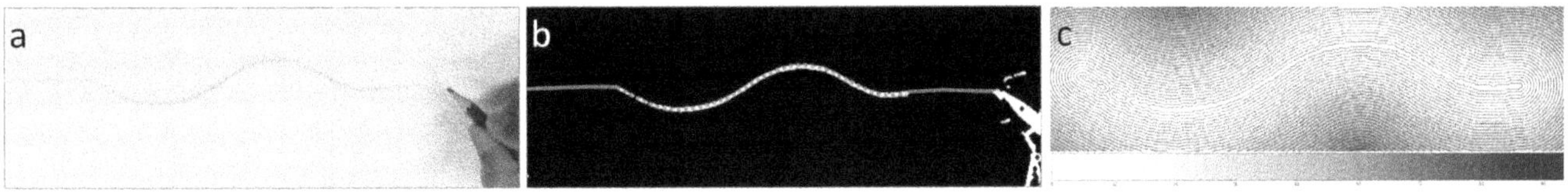

Figure 4: *Detecting drawn strokes: (a) captured pen-tip trajectory in green; (b) thresholded* $\mathbf{L} \circ \mathbf{G}$ *filter response reveals the drawn stroke; stroke points (red) are further extracted by using (c) level-sets defined around the detected stroke.*

Clearly, this approach is infeasible to deal with a large search space for interactive applications, so we prune the search space by two key observations in our problem:

- First, we assume fixed camera and paper. This is a reasonable assumption in most camera-based methods. Given that, we assume that the pen-tip relatively retains it's scale while drawing, so we only consider patches of the same size as the pen-tip template.
- Second, since the pen tip is always a *sharp corner*, we perform corner detection [22], which is a very fast process, to extract fixed-size patches around detected corners to accelerate the search for the pen tip.

By these, we can reduce the cardinality of the search space to the number of corners detected in each video frame and greatly accelerate the pen-tip localization.

4.3.2 Cascaded Classifier

Given the set of patches $\{s_i\}$ extracted from the pruning method above, we exploit the four features described in the previous subsection, and devise a fast cascaded approach to further classify patches in $\{s_i\}$. Note that this is a lazy approach in applying the features, so that we do not need to compute all the four features for every patch in $\{s_i\}$.

- In the first step, we compute the background confidence score $\mathcal{B}_i$ of each candidate patch in $\{s_i\}$, and retain only those with $\mathcal{B}_i$ less than a threshold T_b, where T_b is empirically set to be 0.95. This feature is highly discriminative, and it helps to quickly filter out most of the patches that belong to the background.
- In the second step, we compute the intensity variance of the remaining patches, and filter out those with intensity variance outside the prescribed threshold range $[0.5\sigma^2, 1.5\sigma^2]$. This step enables us to quickly reject almost all irrelevant patches that are not similar to the pen-tip template.
- In the third step, we compute the color similarity measure $\mathcal{C}_i$ of each remaining patch using the color feature vectors of the patch and the pen-tip template. By this, we can filter and retain only the patches whose $\mathcal{C}_i$ is less than a threshold T_c, which is set to be 0.15 in all our experiments.
- The last step is similar to the third step, but now we compute the shape feature vector of the remaining patches, and employ the shape similarity measure $\mathcal{S}_i$ to retain only the patches with $\mathcal{S}_i$ less than a threshold T_s, which is set to be 0.3 in all our experiments.

Since the fast cascaded filtering process above may still retain more than one patch in the end, we may need to further compute the average value of color and shape similarity measures for each remaining patch, and select the one with the largest average to locate the pen-tip patch.

4.4 Tracking

There may also be scenarios where the pen tip is not detected, i.e., no pen-tip patches are identified by the cascaded classifier above, e.g., missing the pen tip in the corner detection, and severe visual interference such as noise, shadow, and clutter. Hence, in addition to per-frame detection, we also employ the detected pen-tip location in the previous video frame to perform short-term tracking of the pen tip using the Lucas-Kanade optical flow method [16]. By this, we can improve the pen-tip localization, and avoid breaking the pen-tip trajectory due to the above mentioned reasons. In detail, we initialize the tracker by each detected pen-tip location from the cascade classifier, and continue the short-term tracking until the cascade classifier finds a subsequent detection, at which time the tracker is reinitialized. By combining detection and tracking, we can obtain a highly smooth pen-tip's trajectory, say $\mathbf{T}$, over the drawing space as a function of time (e.g., see Figure 4(a)):

$$\mathbf{T} = \left\{(p_1, t_1), (p_2, t_2), \ldots, (p_n, t_n) \mid p_i \in \mathbb{R}^2, t \in \mathbb{R}\right\},$$

where $p_i = (x_i, y_i)$ denotes a spatial coordinate, and t_i a monotonically-increasing timestamp (frame index).

5. RECONSTRUCTING STROKES

5.1 Detecting Stroke Points

Once we capture the pen-tip trajectory across the video frames, our next step is to determine the set of stroke points on the paper, say $\mathbf{S}$ (see Figure 4(a)). In detail, we determine $\mathbf{S}$ by analyzing the response of the Laplacian of Gaussian ($\mathbf{L} \circ \mathbf{G}$) filter over the video frames. The $\mathbf{L} \circ \mathbf{G}$ filter corresponds to how the human visual system observes sudden changes in contrast and downplays subtle differences [17]. Mathematically, it is represented by the curvature, or the second derivative of the image intensity, see Figure 4(c).

The intensity profile of strokes in clean line drawings are generally in the form of a parabolic profile (see Figure 5(top)), and the maxima of the filter response corresponds to the cen-

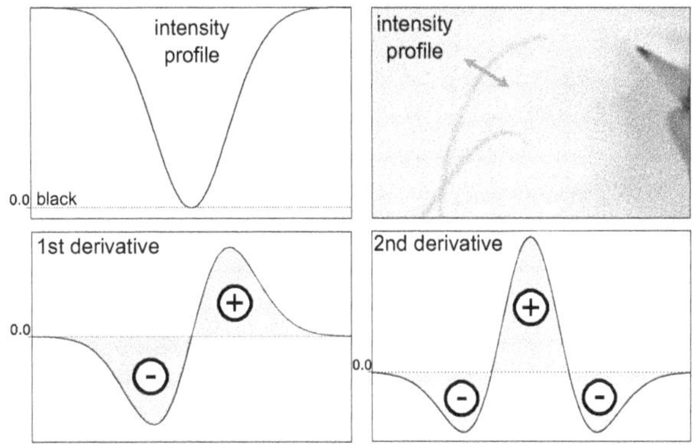

Figure 5: *Stroke intensity profile. Top: intensity profile across a stroke (perpendicular to stroke direction). Bottom: first and second derivatives of the intensity profile, respectively. The maxima of the second derivative corresponds to the centerline of the stroke.*

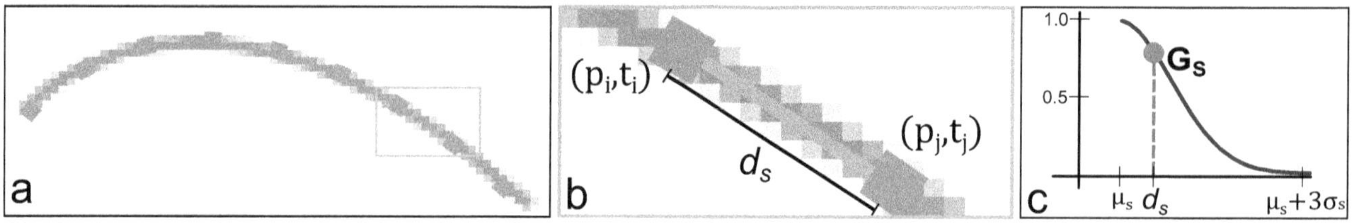

Figure 7: *Spatio-temporal grouping of stroke points: (a) a subset of stroke points in red; (b) edge connectivity estimated between two temporally-consecutive stroke points; and (c) the Gaussian function f for computing the spatio-temporal grouping criterion* $\mathbf{G_S}$ *(and similarly also for* $\mathbf{G_T}$*).*

terline of edges, or in our case, the centerline of the drawn strokes (see Figure 5(bottom)). From each frame, say F, we derive a new image $\mathcal{L} = \max(0, \mathbf{L} \circ \mathbf{G}(F))$ by applying the $\mathbf{L}\circ\mathbf{G}$ filter on F and clamping negative filter response to zero. After that, we further threshold $\mathcal{L}$ at a value of 15 to remove noise and weak responses, and obtain a set of edge pixels over the video frame, say $\{\mathbf{q}\}$. Next, we can define a level-sets around the edge pixels in $\mathcal{L}$ using a distance transform with the Euclidean distance metric: $D(\mathbf{x}) = \min_q \|\mathbf{x} - \mathbf{q}\|$, where $\mathbf{x}$ is each pixel in the video frame. By this, we can extract a set of stroke points $\mathbf{S}$ as a subset of the trajectory $\mathbf{T}$ lying close to the drawn strokes within a threshold:

$$\mathbf{S} = \{(p_i, t_i) \; | D(p_i) \leq \tau; \forall (p_i, t_i) \in \mathbf{T}\} \ ,$$

where τ defines the maximum level set below which points are on the drawn strokes; in practice, it is set to be 2.0.

5.2 Handling Occlusions

In the previous subsection, we presented an analysis method to obtain stroke points on the paper based on the $\mathbf{L}\circ\mathbf{G}$ filter response. However, it is important to note that not all edges in the filtered image $\mathcal{L}$ actually correspond to the drawn strokes. Typically, the user's hand and pen inside the video frames may occlude some of the drawn strokes, and affect the edge profile and the stroke point analysis. Hence, to obtain meaningful strokes points, we continuously track the positions of pen and hand in the video stream, and perform the stroke point analysis (Section 5.1) only on the non-occluded image region. In other words, we postpone the stroke point analysis until the occlusion is clear. In detail, we estimate the pen and hand occluding regions as follows:

- By the pen-tip localization method in Section 4, we can always locate the pen tip over the video frames. Hence, we can approximate the pen occluding region by a small circular region around the pen tip (radius equal to the size of the pen-tip template), see the gray circle in Figure 6(c).
- To estimate the hand occluding regions, we first convert the colors in each frame to the HSV color space. Then, we perform a pixel-level classification based on [21] to determine the skin color, and generate an initial mask of the hand. Note that the V channel is ignored in the computation to account for illumination invariance. By further applying morphological post-processing operations such as erosion and closing, we can obtain a clean mask of the user's hand as shown in Figure 6(c). Note also that we experimented our method with three users of different skin colors, and obtained the following threshold ranges in the classification model for hand tracking: $0 \leq hue \leq 10°$ and $0.08 \leq saturation \leq 0.59$, see Figure 6(a).

Figure 6: *Occlusion detection: (a) thresholding skin color in the hue-saturation space; (b) a sample frame from the video; and (c) masks obtained for the pen (gray circle) and for the hand (white).*

6. SPATIO-TEMPORAL GROUPING

Given a set of strokes points $\mathbf{S}$ obtained from the previous stage, our next task is to group them and form meaningful drawing strokes that are spatio-temporally coherent. To do so, we first need to remove redundant points with exactly the same spatial coordinates. Note that redundant points could be produced if the pen tip stays on the same image location for more than one video frame.
After that, we define a cost function to measure whether two temporally-consecutive stroke points, say (p_i, t_i) and (p_j, t_j), should be grouped together in forming a drawing stroke. The cost function has the following three components:

i) **Edge Connectivity ($\mathbf{G_E}$).** This criterion explores the presence/absence of a stroke between (p_i, t_i) and (p_j, t_j). In detail, we sum the $\mathbf{L}\circ\mathbf{G}$ response along the line from (p_i, t_i) to (p_j, t_j) (e.g., the green line in Figure 7(b)), and normalize the sum by the length of the line; if the sum is above a threshold value of 0.4, we put $\mathbf{G_E}$ as 1, and 0 otherwise.

ii) **Spatial Cost ($\mathbf{G_S}$).** The second criterion explores the spatial proximity between (p_i, t_i) and (p_j, t_j) since we should not group stroke points that are too far away from each other. To compute this criterion, we measure the spatial distance, say d_s, between the two stroke points using the L^2 norm, i.e., $d_s = \|p_i - p_j\|$, and compute $\mathbf{G_S}$ by mapping the distance value to range $[0, 1]$ (see Figure 7(b&c)): $\mathbf{G_S} = f(\ d_s,\ \mu_s,\ \sigma_s\ )$, where μ_s and σ_s are set to be 1.0 and 3.0, respectively, and f is a Gaussian function:

$$f(x, \mu, \sigma) = \exp\left(\frac{-(x-\mu)^2}{2\sigma^2}\right) .$$

iii) **Temporal Cost ($\mathbf{G_T}$).** The third criterion is similar to the second one, but it explores the temporal proximity between (p_i, t_i) and (p_j, t_j). Here it computes the temporal distance, say d_t, between the two points using the L^1 norm, and again use f to map the distance value to range $[0, 1]$: $\mathbf{G_T} = f(\ d_t,\ \mu_t,\ \sigma_t\ )$, where μ_t and σ_t are set to be 1.0 and 5.0, respectively.

Figure 8: *Vectorization results of six different line drawings generated by our method. In each box, we show the vectorization result with randomly-colored strokes on the right and a contrast-enhanced scanned image of the original drawing on the left. From left to right: the drawings are* OLD MAN, CAT, DUCK, GIRL, CHEETAH, *and* HELLO-WORLD; *our method recognizes 42, 44, 17, 24, 25, and 6 strokes from them, respectively.*

The combined cost $\mathbf{G}$ of grouping points (p_i, t_i) and (p_j, t_j) to a continuous stroke is then defined as:

$$\mathbf{G}(i,j) = \mathbf{G_E} \left[(1-w) \cdot \mathbf{G_S}(i,j) + w \cdot \mathbf{G_T}(i,j) \right],$$

where w is set to be 0.6 for putting more emphasis on the temporal information. If $\mathbf{G}$ is greater than 0.5, we consider the two points to go along a common continuous stroke. Once we examine and group each pair of temporally-consecutive points, we can form longer strokes, and then vectorize each of them by cubic spline fitting.

7. RESULTS AND EVALUATION

7.1 Implementation

We implement and run our method on a desktop computer with a 3.20 GHz Intel i7 CPU, 12 GB memory, and 64-bit Windows 7. We employ the Logitech C615 webcam to capture video streams at 480p/720p and 30 frames/sec. See Figure 9: the webcam is fixed at $\sim$1.5ft above the drawing space opposite to the user at an evaluation angle of $\sim$60 degree and a field-of-view of 74 degree.
Estimating the homography transformation between the webcam view and paper is a one-time process: During the system initialization, we first identify the largest white blob in the image, and then use Hough line transform to extract straight lines around the blob's boundary edges. After that, we compute line intersections to obtain the paper corners, show them to the user for confirmation, and then estimate the homography matrix by assuming the paper dimension. We implement our software in Python 2.7, and use the following library APIs: OpenCV [4], NumPy, and SciPy [12] for vision-based methods and numerical computation.

7.2 Evaluation: Performance

First, we perform an experiment to evaluate the performance of our method in delivering interactive online computation. To do so, we measure the time taken (in sec.) to process each video frame (resolution 720p) for each stage in the pipeline (see again Figure 2). Two drawing cases, CHEETAH and HELLO-WORLD (see Figure 8), with totally 7680 and 3150 frames, respectively, are used here. The average processing time taken by each stage is reported in Table 1.

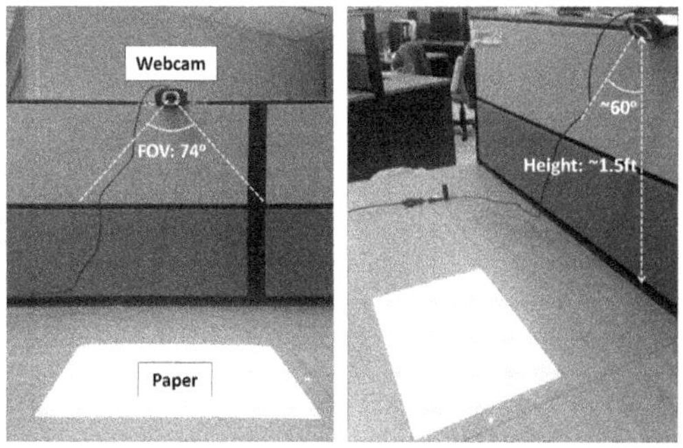

Figure 9: *System setup from two different views.*

From the performance results, we see that the entire computation consistently takes around 0.07-0.08 sec. per frame, showing that it can attain interactive performance.

stage	**method**	**avg. time (sec)**	
		CHEETAH	HELLO-WORLD
1	pen-tip localization	0.035	0.035
2a	detecting stroke points	0.012	0.012
2b	handling occlusions	0.009	0.008
3	spatio-temporal grouping	0.012	0.021

Table 1: *Performance evaluation result: average time taken to complete the various stages in our method.*

7.3 Evaluation: Accuracy

Second, we evaluate the accuracy of our results by comparing them with the actual strokes drawn on paper, as well as with the vectorization results produced from the commercial tool WinTopo Professional [24] (with the default option *One-Touch Vectorization* in our experiments). The six line drawings shown in Figure 8 are used in our evaluation and the following four criteria are used:

i) Number of Strokes. First, we compare the total number of actual strokes drawn on paper against the total number of strokes vectorized by our method, and also by WinTopo, see Table 2. From the results, we can see that our online method is able to accurately recognize all the user-drawn strokes without missing any stroke. In sharp contrast, WinTopo produces a lot more strokes than the actual num-

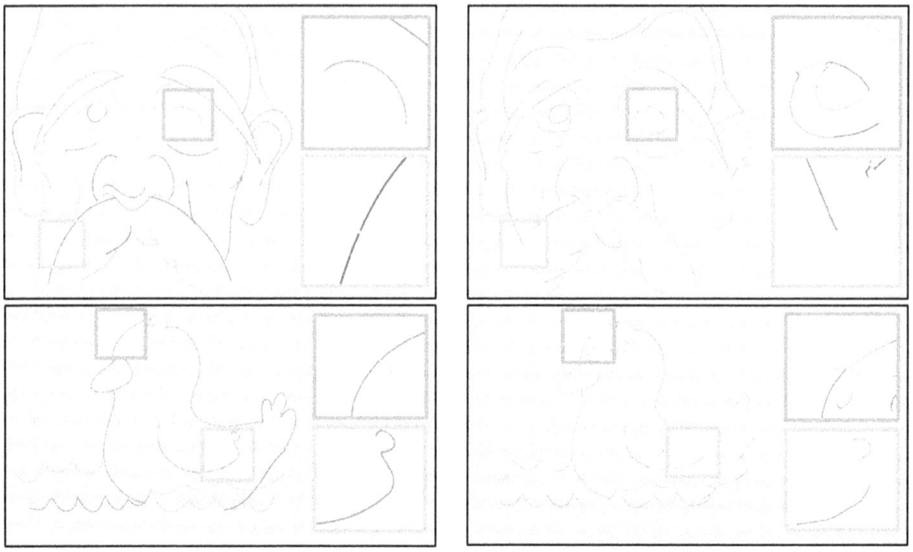

Figure 10: *Visual comparison of stroke reconstruction results: our method (left) and WinTopo (right).*

drawing	# actual strokes	# reconstructed		overlap %	avg. deviation
		ours	WinTopo		
CAT	44	44	74	88.77	1.568
GIRL	24	24	43	88.50	1.520
HELLO-WORLD	6	6	30	94.89	1.215
OLD-MAN	42	42	50	86.29	2.957
DUCK	17	17	35	87.34	2.135
CHEETAH	25	25	42	83.66	1.994

Table 2: *Evaluation of accuracy: the number of reconstructed strokes, overlap percentage, and average deviation.*

ber of strokes drawn by user due to its deficiency in resolving various stroke recognition ambiguities, see again Figure 1.

ii) Overlap Percentage. Second, we evaluate how close our vectorization results are to the actual drawing. Here we first scan the paper drawing and use a simple binary segmentation to extract the actual strokes. Then, we transform and overlay our vectorized strokes onto the scanned image (through the recovered homography) and compute the overlap percentage: $|A \cap B|/|B|$, where A and B are sets of pixels covered by the scanned strokes and the vectorized strokes, respectively. Note that this measure aims to see how the vectorized strokes (actually one-pixel-wide lines) are contained within the actual strokes in the scanned image space.

From Table 2, we can see that our method can attain very high overlap percentage, but not yet perfect, because: 1) the homography recovered for computing the overlap percentage is not perfect, and 2) we use a discrete set of stroke points (captured in each frame) to reconstruct a stroke by spline-fitting. Since WinTopo vectorizes strokes by binary-thinning the scanned images, its vectorized results can always perfectly overlap with the original strokes. However, from Figure 8, we can still see how similar our vectorization results are with respect to the scanned drawings.

iii) Average Deviation. Third, we quantitatively measure the deviation of our reconstructed strokes from the scanned drawings in pixel units. Like overlap measure, this is done in the image space of the scanned drawings.

Let P and Q be the set of pixels belonging to the scanned strokes and our reconstructed strokes (1-pixel wide), respectively. We compute the average deviation between them as $dev(P, Q) = \sum_{q_i \in Q} \min \|q_i - p_j\|/|Q|$, where p_j is the pixel in P that is the nearest to q_i in the image space. From the results shown on the rightmost column of Table 2, we can see that the average deviation is consistently around 1 to 2 pixels, indicating that our results are sufficiently close to the original strokes. Note that the resolution of the scanned images used in this experiment is 877×637 pixels.

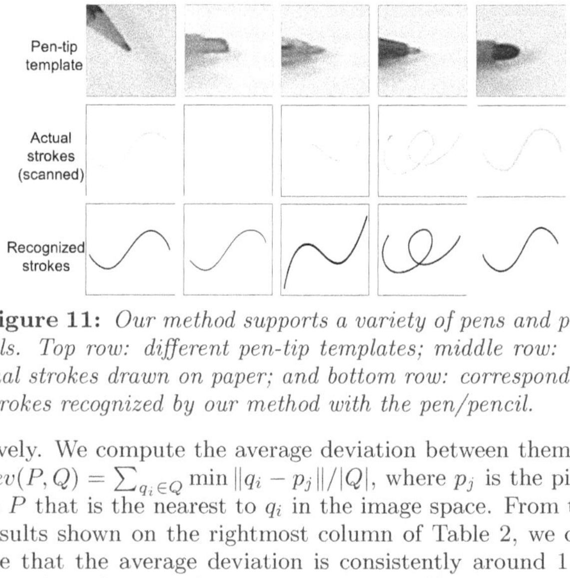

Figure 11: *Our method supports a variety of pens and pencils. Top row: different pen-tip templates; middle row: actual strokes drawn on paper; and bottom row: corresponding strokes recognized by our method with the pen/pencil.*

iv) Visual Comparison. Lastly, we randomly colorize the recognized strokes for both our results and WinTopo, and perform a visual comparison. Two comparison examples are shown in Figure 10. From the zoomed views shown in the figure, we can clearly see that WinTopo suffers from stroke recognition ambiguities, and tends to break strokes at junctions, thereby producing excessive strokes. On the contrary, our method, which employs temporal information, can accurately reconstruct the long strokes while retaining the original stroke continuity and avoiding various stroke recognition ambiguities.

7.4 Evaluation: Variety of Pens and Pencils

Our method supports a variety of pens and pencils, see Figure 11 (first row). To include a new pen/pencil to stroke recognition, we only need a few seconds' time to take a picture of the pen tip in front of the camera, and then apply our

Figure 13: *Video scribing. Our method enables us to easily re-render the vectorized strokes, which have temporal information, and produce a video scribing effect. The drawing video is spatio-temporal coherent with the original drawing by the user but goes without the pen and the user's hand.*

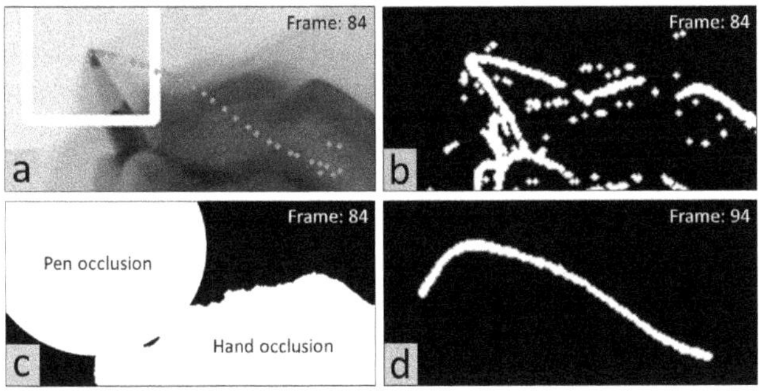

Figure 12: *Example of how occlusion could interfere the analysis of stroke points: (a) notice a number of stroke are points occluded by the hand and the pen-tip at the moment; (b)* $\mathbf{L} \circ \mathbf{G}$ *response affected by the occlusion; attempting to recognize stroke points in the presence of occlusion is error-prone; (c) occlusion mask computed by our method; and (d) valid* $\mathbf{L} \circ \mathbf{G}$ *response of the stroke after the occlusion is clear.*

interface to crop the picture and create a pen-tip template. After that, our method can employ the pen-tip template to automatically locate the pen-tip trajectory.

Figure 11 presents the related results with five different kinds of pens and pencils. The top, middle and bottom rows in the figure show the pen-tip templates, scanned image of a drawn stroke, the recognition results respectively.

7.5 Evaluation: Occlusion Detection

Next, we explore and illustrate how occlusion detection helps to improve the stroke recognition. A typical case is presented in Figure 12. During the drawing process, hand and pen occlusions could seriously interfere the stroke point analysis process described in Section 5.1. See the drawing in Figure 12(a) and the resulting $\mathbf{L} \circ \mathbf{G}$ response in Figure 12(b). If we analyze this response and extract the stroke points around the pen-tip trajectory at this moment (video frame #84), the analysis result would be error-prone.

Hence, we detect and track the hand and pen occlusion regions over the video frames, see Figure 12(c), and postpone the stroke point analysis and extraction till the occlusion is clear, see Figure 12(d). By this mechanism, we can improve the extraction quality while attaining full automation.

7.6 Evaluation: Vectorization Results

Figure 8 presents the vectorization results generated by our method and compares them side by side with scanned images of the original drawings. Notice the individual reconstructed strokes (each randomly-colored). They are free of the various stroke recognition ambiguities we mentioned in Section 1 (see also Figure 1); in addition, they can correspond nicely to the actual strokes drawn by the user. This demonstrates one key advantage of our online method in improving the stroke recognition quality.

Furthermore, we develop a video-scribing application, which renders the vectorized strokes on a virtual paper according to their spatio-temporal orders but without the pen and user's hand, see Figure 13 for image snapshots. By this, we can simulate and visualize the actual drawing process, and create visually-pleasing animation effects.

8. CONCLUSION

This paper presents a novel interactive camera-based method to capture and vectorize freehand line drawings on paper. There are three key contributions in this work. First, we propose a robust spatio-temporal tracking technique that can efficiently localize and track the pen tip in video frames. This technique combines the strength of a fast-cascade classifier with discriminable features and optical-flow tracking (which is less accurate) to achieve high performance and accuracy. Second, we extract stroke points in the video frames by considering not only the edge profiles around the estimated pen-tip trajectory but also the hand and pen occlusion to improve the stroke recognition accuracy. Lastly, we develop an efficient spatio-temporal clustering method to produce meaningful strokes that are coherent with the actual strokes drawn by the users. As for the evaluation, we perform a number of experiments to examine different aspects of our method: computation performance, accuracy against actual drawings and an offline commercial tool for vectorization, as well as pen and hand occlusion. In the end, we use the method to produce assorted vectorization results, as well as apply it to produce the video-scribing animation effect with some of our results.

Future Work. First, we would look for ways to enable a moving camera, so that we could extend our interface for smart-glasses. Second, we would also like to improve the system performance, e.g., by multi-core processing on commodity CPUs. Third, we would explore the use of a parameter calibration module for better adaptation to varying lighting conditions. Lastly, we also plan to explore the use of crowdsourcing to study and evaluate our interface.

Acknowledgments. We thank reviewers for various constructive comments that helped to improve this paper. This work is funded in part by MOE Tier-2 grant (MOE2011-T2-2-041 (ARC 5/12)) and MOE Tier-1 grant (RG 29/11).

9. REFERENCES

[1] Anoto. Anoto Digital Pens. http://www.anoto.com.

[2] B. Bao and H. Fu. Vectorizing line drawings with near-constant line width. In *IEEE International Conference on Image Processing*, pages 805–808, 2012.

[3] S. Belongie and J. Malik. Matching with shape contexts. In *IEEE Workshop on Content-based Access of Image and Video Libraries*, pages 20–26, 2000.

[4] G. Bradski. OpenCV. *Dr. Dobb's Journal of Software Tools*, 2000.

[5] H.-H. Chang and H. Yan. Vectorization of hand-drawn image using piecewise cubic bézier curves fitting. *Pattern Recognition*, 31(11):1747 – 1755, 1998.

[6] M.-M. Cheng. Curve structure extraction for cartoon images. In *Harmonious Human Machine Env.*, pages 13–25, 2009.

[7] M. Chikano, K. Kise, M. Iwamura, S. Uchida, and S. Omachi. Recovery and localization of handwritings by a camera-pen based on tracking and document image retrieval. *Pattern Recognition Letters*, 35:214–224, 2014.

[8] D. Doermann and A. Rosenfeld. Recovery of temporal information from static images of handwriting. *International Journal of Computer Vision*, 15(1-2):143–164, 1995.

[9] Google. Google Glass. http://www.google.com/glass/start/, 2013.

[10] X. Hilaire and K. Tombre. Robust and Accurate Vectorization of Line Drawings. *IEEE Trans. on Pattern Analysis Machine Intell.*, 28(6):890–904, 2006.

[11] R. D. Janssen and A. M. Vossepoel. Adaptive vectorization of line drawing images. *Computer Vision and Image Understanding*, 65(1):38 – 56, 1997.

[12] E. Jones, T. Oliphant, P. Peterson, et al. SciPy: Open source scientific tools for Python, 2001.

[13] Y. Kato and M. Yasuhara. Recovery of drawing order from scanned images of multi-stroke handwriting. In *Proceedings of International Conference on Document Analysis and Recognition.*, pages 261–264, 1999.

[14] L. Lam, S.-W. Lee, and C. Suen. Thinning methodologies - A comprehensive survey. *IEEE Transactions on Pattern Analysis Machine Intelligence*, 14(9):869–885, 1992.

[15] F. Lin and X. Tang. Dynamic stroke information analysis for video-based handwritten chinese character recognition. In *IEEE International Conference on Computer Vision*, volume 1, pages 695–700, 2003.

[16] B. D. Lucas and T. Kanade. An iterative image registration technique with an application to stereo vision. In *Proc. of International Joint Conference on Artificial Intelligence*, volume 2, pages 674–679, 1981.

[17] D. Marr and E. Hildreth. Theory of edge detection. *Proceedings of the Royal Society of London Series B*, 207(1167):187–217, 1980.

[18] M. Munich and P. Perona. Visual input for pen-based computers. In *Proceedings of the 13th International Conference on Pattern Recognition, 1996.*, volume 3, pages 33–37, 1996.

[19] M. Munich and P. Perona. Visual Input for Pen-based Computers. *IEEE Transactions on Pattern Analysis Machine Intelligence*, 24(3):313–328, 2002.

[20] G. Noris, A. Hornung, R. W. Sumner, M. Simmons, and M. Gross. Topology-driven Vectorization of Clean Line Drawings. *ACM Transactions on Graphics*, 32(1):4:1–4:11, 2013.

[21] S. Phung, A. Bouzerdoum, and S. Chai, D. Skin segmentation using color pixel classification: analysis and comparison. *IEEE Transactions on Pattern Analysis Machine Intelligence*, 27(1):148–154, 2005.

[22] E. Rosten and T. Drummond. Machine learning for high-speed corner detection. In *European Conference on Computer Vision*, volume 1, pages 430–443, 2006.

[23] J.-H. Seok, S. Levasseur, K.-E. Kim, and J. H. Kim. Tracing handwriting on paper document under video camera. In *Proceedings of the International Conference on Frontiers in Handwriting Recognition*, pages 109–110, 2008.

[24] SoftSoft. WinTopo. http://wintopo.com/, 2012.

[25] M. Sperber, M. Klinkigt, K. Kise, M. Iwamura, B. Adrian, and A. Dengel. Handwriting reconstruction for a camera pen using random dot patterns. In *International Conference on Frontiers in Handwriting Recognition*, pages 160–165, 2010.

[26] C. Steger. Extracting curvilinear structures: A differential geometric approach. In *Computer Vision - ECCV '96*, volume 1064 of *Lecture Notes in Computer Science*, pages 630–641. 1996.

[27] J. Steimle. Survey of pen-and-paper computing. In *Pen-and-Paper User Interfaces*, Human-Computer Interaction Series, pages 19–65. 2012.

[28] A. Systems. Adobe Illustrator. http://www.adobe.com/products/illustrator.html.

[29] X. Tang, F. Lin, and J. Liu. Video-based handwritten Chinese character recognition. *IEEE Trans. on Circuits and Sys. for Video Tech.*, 15(1):167–174, 2005.

[30] Wacom. Inkling. http://inkling.wacom.com/.

[31] L. Wenyin and D. Dori. A survey of non-thinning based vectorization methods. In *Advances in Pattern Recognition*, volume 1451 of *Lecture Notes in Computer Science*, pages 230–241. 1998.

[32] M. Wienecke, G. A. Fink, and G. Sagerer. A handwriting recognition system based on visual input. 2nd International Workshop on Computer Vision Systems, pages 63–72, 2001.

[33] Z. Zivkovic and F. van der Heijden. Efficient adaptive density estimation per image pixel for the task of background subtraction. *Pattern Recognition Letters*, 27(7):773 – 780, 2006.

[34] J. J. Zou and H. Yan. Cartoon Image Vectorization Based on Shape Subdivision. In *Proceedings of the International Conference on Computer Graphics*, CGI '01, pages 225–231, 2001.

RAPID: Rating Pictorial Aesthetics using Deep Learning*

Xin Lu[1] Zhe Lin[2] Hailin Jin[2] Jianchao Yang[2] James Z. Wang[1]
[1]The Pennsylvania State University
[2]Adobe Research
{xinlu, jwang}@psu.edu, {zlin, hljin, jiayang}@adobe.com

ABSTRACT

Effective visual features are essential for computational aesthetic quality rating systems. Existing methods used machine learning and statistical modeling techniques on handcrafted features or generic image descriptors. A recently-published large-scale dataset, the AVA dataset, has further empowered machine learning based approaches. We present the RAPID (RAting PIctorial aesthetics using Deep learning) system, which adopts a novel deep neural network approach to enable automatic feature learning. The central idea is to incorporate heterogeneous inputs generated from the image, which include a global view and a local view, and to unify the feature learning and classifier training using a double-column deep convolutional neural network. In addition, we utilize the style attributes of images to help improve the aesthetic quality categorization accuracy. Experimental results show that our approach significantly outperforms the state of the art on the AVA dataset.

Categories and Subject Descriptors

I.4.7 [**Image Processing and Computer Vision**]: Feature measurement; I.4.10 [**Image Processing and Computer Vision**]: Image Representation; I.5 [**Pattern Recognition**]: Classifier design and evaluation

General Terms

Algorithms, Experimentation

Keywords

Deep Learning; Image Aesthetics; Multi-Column Deep Neural Networks

*The research has been primarily supported by Penn State's College of Information Sciences and Technology and Adobe Research. The authors would like to thank the anonymous reviewers.

MM'14, November 03-07, 2014, Orlando, FL, USA.

http://dx.doi.org/10.1145/2647868.2654927.

1. INTRODUCTION

Automated assessment or rating of pictorial aesthetics has many applications. In an image retrieval system, the ranking algorithm can incorporate aesthetic quality as one of the factors. In picture editing software, aesthetics can be used in producing appealing polished photographs. Datta *et al.* [6] and Ke *et al.* [13] formulated the problem as a classification or regression problem where a given image is mapped to an aesthetic rating, which is normally quantized with discrete values. Under this framework, the effectiveness of the image representation, or the extracted features, can often be the accuracy bottleneck. Various handcrafted aesthetics-relevant features have been proposed [6, 13, 21, 3, 20, 7, 26, 27], including low-level image statistics such as distributions of edges and color histograms, and high-level photographic rules such as the rule of thirds.

While these handcrafted aesthetics features are often inspired from the photography or psychology literature, they share some known limitations. First, the aesthetics-sensitive attributes are manually designed, hence have limited scope. It is possible that some effective attributes have not yet been discovered through this process. Second, because of the vagueness of certain photographic or psychologic rules and the difficulty in implementing them computationally, these handcrafted features are often merely approximations of such rules. There is often a lack of principled approach to improve the effectiveness of such features.

Generic image features [23, 24, 22] are proposed to address the limitations of the handcrafted aesthetics features. They used well-designed common image features such as SIFT and Fisher Vector [18, 23], which have been successfully used for object classification tasks. The generic image features have been shown to outperform the handcrafted aesthetics features [23]. However, because these features are meant to be generic, they may be unable to attain the upper performance limits in aesthetics-related problems.

In this work, we intend to explore beyond generic image features by learning effective aesthetics features from images directly. We are motivated by the recent work in large scale image classification using deep convolutional neural networks [15] where the features are automatically learned from RGB images. The deep convolutional neural network takes pixels as inputs and learns a suitable representation through multiple convolutional and fully connected layers. However, the originally proposed architecture cannot be directly applied to our task. Image aesthetics relies on a combination of local and global visual cues. For example, the rule of thirds is a global image cue while sharpness and noise

Figure 1: Global views and local views of an image. Global views are represented by normalized inputs: center-crop, warp, and padding (shown in the top row). Local views are represented by randomly-cropped inputs from the original high-resolution image (examples shown).

levels are local visual characteristics. Given an image, we generate two heterogeneous inputs to represent its global cues and local cues respectively. Figure 1 illustrates global vs. local views. To support network training on heterogeneous inputs, we extend the method in [15] by developing a double-column neural network structure which takes parallel inputs from the two columns. One column takes a global view of the image and the other column takes a local view of the image. We integrate the two columns after some layers of transformations to form the final classifier. We further improve the aesthetic quality categorization by exploring style attributes associated with images. We named our system RAPID, which stands for RAting PIctorial aesthetics using Deep learning. We used a recently-released large dataset to show the advantages of our approach.

1.1 Related Work

Earlier visual aesthetics assessment research focused on examining handcrafted visual features based on common cues such as color [6, 26, 27], texture [6, 13], composition [21, 20, 7], and content [20, 7], as well as generic image descriptors [23, 31, 24]. Commonly investigated color features include lightness, colorfulness, color harmony, and color distribution [6, 26, 27]. Texture descriptors vary from wavelet-based texture features [6], distribution of edges, to blur descriptors and shallow depth-of-field descriptors [13]. Composition features typically include the rule of thirds, size and aspect ratio [20], and foreground and background composition [21, 20, 7]. There have been attempts to represent the content of images using people and portrait descriptors [20, 7], scene descriptors [7], and generic image features such as SIFT [18], GIST [28], and Fisher Vector [23, 24, 22].

Despite the success of handcrafted and generic visual features, the usefulness of automatically learned features have been demonstrated in many vision applications [15, 4, 32, 30]. Recently, trained deep neural networks are used to build and associate mid-level features with class labels. Convolutional neural network (CNN) [16] is one of the most powerful learning architectures among the various types of neural networks (e.g., Deep Belief Net [10] and Restricted Boltzmann Machine [9]). Krizhevsky *et al.* [15] significantly advanced the 1000-class classification task in ImageNet challenge with a deep architecture of CNN in conjunction with dropout and normalization techniques, Sermanet *et al.* [30] achieved the-state-of-the-art performance on all major pedestrian detection datasets, and Ciresan *et al.* [4] reached a near-human performance on the MNIST[1] dataset.

The effectiveness of CNN features has also been demonstrated in image style classification [12]. Without training deep neural network, Karayev *et al.* extracted existing Decaf features [8] and used those features as input for style classification. There are key differences between that work [12] and ours. First, they mainly targeted style classification whereas we focus on aesthetic categorization, which is a different problem. Second, they used existing features as input to classification and did not train specific neural networks for style or aesthetics categorization. In contrast, we train deep neural networks directly from RGB inputs, which are optimized for the given task. Third, they relied on features from global views, while we leverage heterogeneous input sources, i.e., global and local views, and propose double-column neural networks to learn features jointly from both sources. Finally, we propose a regularized neural network based on related attributes to further boost aesthetics categorization.

As designing handcrafted features has been widely considered an appropriate approach in assessing image aesthetics, insufficient effort has been devoted to automatic feature learning on a large collection of labeled ground-truth data. The recently-developed AVA dataset [24] contains 250,000 images with aesthetic ratings and a 14,000 subset with style labels (e.g., rule of thirds, motion blur, and complementary colors), making automatic feature learning using deep learning approaches possible.

[1] http://yann.lecun.com/exdb/mnist/

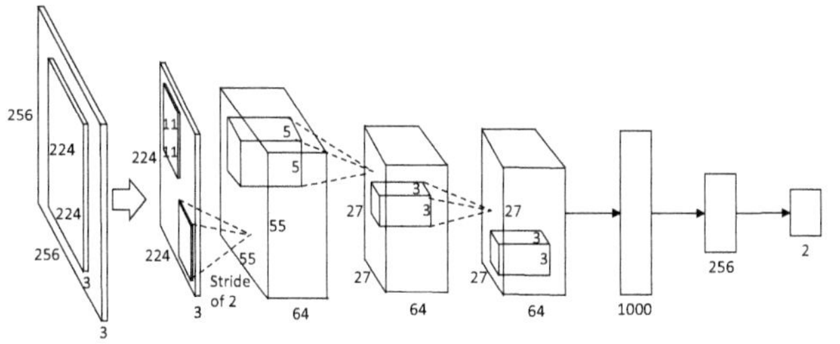

Figure 2: Single-column convolutional neural network for aesthetic quality rating and categorization. We have four convolutional layers and two fully-connected layers. The first and second convolutional layers are followed by max-pooling layers and normalization layers. The input patch of the size $224 \times 224 \times 3$ is randomly cropped from the normalized input of the size $256 \times 256 \times 3$ as done in [15].

In this work, we train deep neural networks on the AVA dataset to categorize image aesthetic quality. Specifically, we propose a double-column CNN architecture to automatically discover effective features that capture image aesthetics from two heterogeneous input sources. The proposed architecture is different from the recent work in multi-column neural networks [4, 1]. Agostinelli *et al.* [1] extended stacked sparse autoencoder to a multi-column version by computing the optimal column weights and applied the model to image denoising. Ciresan *et al.* [4] averaged the output of several columns trained on inputs with different standard preprocessing methods. Our architecture is different from that work because the two columns in our architecture are jointly trained using two different inputs: The first column of the network takes global image representation as the input, while the second column takes local image representations as the input. This allows us to leverage both compositional and local visual information.

The problem of assessing image aesthetics is also relevant to recent work of image popularity estimation [14]. Aesthetic value is connected with the notion of popularity, while there is a fundamental difference between the two concepts. Aesthetics concerns primarily with the nature and appreciation of beauty, while in the measurement of popularity both aesthetics and how interesting the visual stimulus is to the viewer population are important. For instance, a photograph of some thought-provoking subject may not be considered of high aesthetic value, but can be appreciated by many people based on the subject alone. On the other hand, a beautiful picture of flowers may not be able to reach the state of popularity if the viewers don't consider the subject of sufficient interestingness.

1.2 Contributions

Our main contributions are as follows.

- We conducted systematic evaluation of the single-column deep convolutional neural network approach with different types of input modalities for aesthetic quality categorization;
- We developed a double-column deep convolutional neural network architecture to jointly learn features from heterogeneous inputs;
- We developed a regularized double-column deep convolutional neural network to further improve aesthetic categorization using style attributes.

2. THE ALGORITHM

Patterns in aesthetically-pleasing photographs often indicate photographers' visual preferences. Among those patterns, composition [17] and visual balance [25] are important factors [2]. They are reflected in the global view (e.g., top row in Figure 1) and the local view (e.g., bottom row in the Figure). Popular composition principles include the rule of thirds, diagonal lines, and golden ratio [11], while visual balance is affected by position, form, size, tone, color, brightness, contrast, and proximity to the fulcrum [25]. Some of these patterns are not well-defined or even abstract, making it difficult to calculate those features for assessing image aesthetic quality. Motivated by this, we aim to leverage the power of CNN to automatically identify useful patterns and employ learned visual features to rate or to categorize the aesthetic quality of images.

However, applying CNN to the aesthetic quality categorization task is not straightforward. The different aspect ratios and resolutions in photographs and the importance of image details in aesthetics make it difficult to directly train CNN where inputs are typically normalized to the same size and aspect ratio. A challenging question, therefore, is to perform automatic feature learning with regard to both the global and the local views of the input images. To address this challenge, we take several different representations of an image, i.e., the global and the local views of the image, which can be encoded by jointly considering those heterogeneous representations. We first use each of the representations to train a single-column CNN (SCNN) to assess image aesthetics. We further developed a double-column CNN (DCNN) to allow our model to use the heterogeneous inputs from one image, aiming at identifying visual features in terms of both global and local views. Finally, we investigate how the style of images can be leveraged to boost aesthetic classification accuracy [29]. We present an aesthetic quality categorization approach with style attributes by learning a regularized double-column network (RDCNN), a three-column network.

2.1 Single-column Convolutional Neural Network

Deep convolutional neural network [15] takes inputs of fixed aspect ratio and size. However, an input image can be of arbitrary size and aspect ratio. To normalize image sizes, we propose three different transformations: center-crop (g_c), warp (g_w), and padding (g_p), which reflect the global view (I_g) of an image I. g_c isotropically resizes original images by normalizing their shorter sides to a fixed length s. Center-crop normalizes the input to generate a $s \times s \times 3$ input. g_c was adopted in a recent image classification work [15]. g_w anisotropically resizes (or warps) the original image into a normalized input with a fixed size $s \times s \times 3$. g_p resizes the original image by normalizing the longer side of the image to a fixed length s and padding border pixels with zeros to generate a normalized input of a fixed size $s \times s \times 3$. For each image I and each type of transformation, we generate an $s \times s \times 3$ input I_g^j with the transformation g_j, where $j \in \{c, w, p\}$. As resizing inputs can cause harmful information loss (i.e., the high-resolution local views) for aesthetic assessment, we also use randomly sampled fixed size

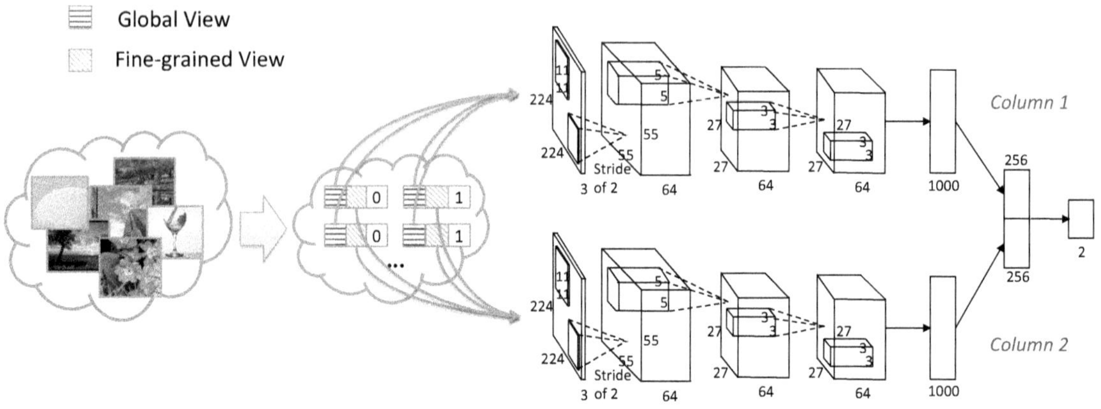

Figure 3: Double-column convolutional neural network. Each training image is represented by its global and local views, and is associated with its aesthetic quality label: 0 refers to a low quality image and 1 refers to a high quality image. Networks in different columns are independent in convolutional layers and the first two fully-connected layers. The final fully-connected layer are jointly trained.

(at $s \times s \times 3$) crops with the transformation l_r. Here we use g to denote global transformations and l to denote local transformations. This results in normalized inputs $\{I_l^r\}$ (r is an index of normalized inputs for each random cropping), which preserve the local views of an image with details from the original high-resolution image. We used these normalized inputs $I_t \in \{I_g^c, I_g^w, I_g^p, I_l^r\}$ for CNN training. In this work, we set s to 256, thus the size of I_t is $256 \times 256 \times 3$. To alleviate overfitting in network training, for each normalized input I_t, we extracted a random $224 \times 224 \times 3$ patch I_p or its horizontal reflection to be the input patch to our network.

We present an example for the four transformations, g_w, g_c, g_p, and l_r, in Figure 1. As shown, the global view of an image is maintained via the transformations of g_c, g_w, and g_p. Among the three global views, I_g^w and I_g^p maintain the relative spatial layout among elements in the original image. I_g^w and I_g^p follow rule of thirds whereas the I_g^c does not. In the bottom row of the figure, the local views of an original image are represented by randomly-cropped patches $\{I_l^r\}$. These patches depict the local details in the original resolution of the image.

The architecture of the SCNN used for aesthetic quality assessment is shown in Figure 2. It has a total of four convolutional layers. The first and the second convolutional layers are followed by max-pooling layers and normalization layers. The first convolutional layer filters the $224 \times 224 \times 3$ patch with 64 kernels of the size $11 \times 11 \times 3$ with a stride of 2 pixels. The second convolutional layer filters the output of the first convolutional layer with 64 kernels of the size $5 \times 5 \times 64$. Each of the third and forth convolutional layers has 64 kernels of the size $3 \times 3 \times 64$, and the two fully-connected layers have 1000 and 256 neurons respectively.

Suppose for the input patch I_p of the i-th image, we have the feature representation $\mathbf{x}_i$ extracted from layer fc256 (the outcome of the convolutional layers and the fc1000 layers), and the label $y_i \in \mathcal{C}$. The training of the last layer is done by maximizing the following log likelihood function:

$$l(\mathbf{W}) = \sum_{i=1}^{N} \sum_{c \in \mathcal{C}} \mathbb{I}(y_i = c) \log p(y_i = c \mid \mathbf{x}_i, \mathbf{w}_c) \ , \quad (1)$$

where N is the number of images, $\mathbf{W} = \{\mathbf{w}_c\}_{c \in \mathcal{C}}$ is the set of model parameters, and $\mathbb{I}(x) = 1$ iff x is true and vice versa. The probability $p(y_i = c \mid \mathbf{x}_i, \mathbf{w}_c)$ is expressed as

$$p(y_i = c \mid \mathbf{x}_i, \mathbf{w}_c) = \frac{\exp(\mathbf{w}_c^T \mathbf{x}_i)}{\sum_{c' \in \mathcal{C}} \exp(\mathbf{w}_{c'}^T \mathbf{x}_i)} \ . \quad (2)$$

The aesthetic quality categorization task can be defined as a binary classification problem where each input patch is associated with an aesthetic label $c \in \mathcal{C} = \{0, 1\}$. In Section 2.3, we explain a SCNN for image style categorization, which can be considered a multi-class classification task.

As indicated by the previous study [15], the architecture of the deep neural network may critically affect the performance. Our experiments suggest that the general guideline for training a good-performing network is to first allow sufficient learning power of the network by using sufficient number of neurons. Meanwhile, we adjust the number of convolutional layers and the fully-connected layers to support the feature learning and classifier training. In particular, we extensively evaluate the network trained with different numbers of convolutional layers and fully-connected layers, and with or without normalization layers. Candidate architectures are shown in Table 1. To determine the optimal architecture for our task, we conduct experiments on candidate architectures and pick the one with the highest performance, as shown in Figure 2.

With the selected architecture, we train SCNN with four different types of inputs (I_g^c, I_g^w, I_g^p, I_l^r) using the AVA dataset [24]. During training, we handle the overfitting problem by adopting dropout and shuffling the training data in each epoch. Specifically, we found that l_r serves as an effective data augmentation approach which alleviates overfitting. Because I_l^r is generated by random cropping, an image contributes to the network training with different inputs when a different patch is used.

We experimentally evaluate the performance of these inputs with SCNN. Results will be presented in Section 3. I_g^w performs the best among the three global input variations (I_g^c, I_g^w, I_g^p). I_l^r yields an even better results compared with I_g^w. Hence, we use I_l^r and I_g^w as the two inputs to train the proposed double-column network. In our experiments, we fix the dropout rate as 0.5 and initiate the learning rate with 0.001. Given a test image, we compute its normalized input and followed by generating the input patch, with which we calculate the probability of the input patch being assigned to each aesthetic category. We repeat this process for 50 times, average those results, and pick the class with the highest probability.

2.2 Double-column Convolutional Neural Network

For each image, its global or local information may be lost when transformed to a normalized input using g_c, g_w, g_p, or l_r. Representing an image through multiple inputs can somewhat alleviate the problem. As a first attempt, we generate one input to depict the global view of an image and another to represent its local view.

We propose a novel double-column convolutional neural network (DCNN) to support automatic feature learning with heterogeneous inputs, i.e., a global-view input and a local-view input. We present the architecture of the DCNN in Figure 3. As shown in the figure, networks in different columns are independent in convolutional layers and the first two fully-connected layers. The inputs of the two columns are I_g^w and I_l^r. We take the two 256×1 vectors from each of the fc256 layer and jointly train the weights of the final fully-connected layer. We avoid the interaction between two columns in convolutional layers because they are in different spatial scales. During training, the error is back propagated to the networks in each column respectively with stochastic gradient descent. With the proposed architecture, we can also automatically discover both the global and the local features of an image from the fc1000 layers and fc256 layers.

The proposed network architecture could easily be expanded to multi-column convolutional networks by incorporating more types of normalized inputs. DCNN allows different architectures in individual networks, which may facilitate the parameter learning for networks in different columns.

In our work, network architectures are the same for both columns. Given a test image, we perform a similar procedure as we do with SCNN to evaluate the aesthetic quality of an image.

2.3 Learning and Categorization with Style Attributes

The discrete aesthetic labels, i.e., high quality and low quality, provided weak supervision to make the network converge properly due to the large intra-class variation. This motivates us to exploit extra labels from the training images to help identify their aesthetic characteristics. We propose to leverage style attributes, such as complementary colors, macro, motion blur, rule of thirds, shallow depth-of-field (DOF), to help determine the aesthetic quality of images because they are regarded as highly relevant attributes [24].

There are two natural ways to formulate the problem. The first is to leverage the idea of multi-task learning [5], which jointly construct feature representation and minimize the classification error for both labels. Assuming we have aesthetic quality labels $\{y_{ai}\}$ and style labels $\{y_{si}\}$ for all training images, the problem becomes an optimization prblem:

$$\max_{\mathbf{X},\mathbf{W}_a,\mathbf{W}_s} \sum_{i=1}^{N} \Big(\sum_{c \in \mathcal{C}_A} \mathbb{I}(y_{ai} = c) \log p(y_{ai} \mid \mathbf{x}_i, \mathbf{w}_{ac}) + \sum_{c \in \mathcal{C}_S} \mathbb{I}(y_{si} = c) \log p(y_{si} \mid \mathbf{x}_i, \mathbf{w}_{sc}) \Big) \;, \quad (3)$$

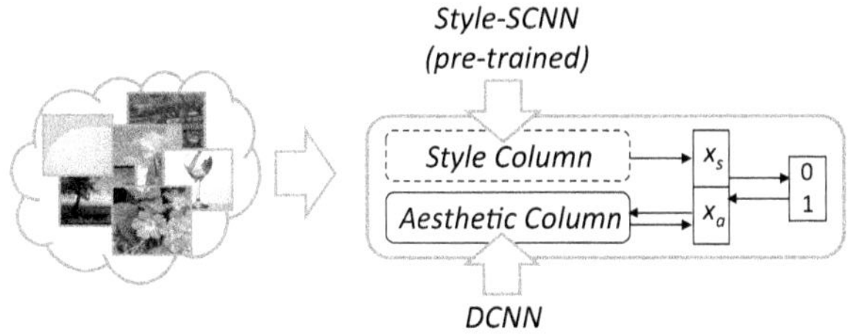

Figure 4: Regularized double-column convolutional neural network (RDCNN). The style attributes $\mathbf{x}_s$ are generated through pre-trained Style-SCNN and we leveraged the style attributes to regularize the training process of RDCNN. The dashed line indicates that the parameters of the style column is fixed during RDCNN training. While training the RDCNN, we only fine-tuned the parameters in the aesthetic column and the learning process is supervised by the aesthetic label.

where $\mathbf{X}$ is the features of all training images, $\mathcal{C}_A$ is the label set for aesthetic quality, $\mathcal{C}_S$ is the label set for style, and $\mathbf{W}_a = \{\mathbf{w}_{ac}\}_{c \in \mathcal{C}_A}$ and $\mathbf{W}_s = \{\mathbf{w}_{sc}\}_{c \in \mathcal{C}_S}$ are the model parameters. It is more difficult to obtain images with style attributes. In the AVA benchmark, among 230,000 image with aesthetic labels only 14,000 of them have style labels. As a result, we cannot jointly perform aesthetics categorization and style classification with a single neural network due to many missing labels.

Alternatively, we can use ideas from inductive transfer learning [29], where we target minimizing the classification error with one label, whereas we construct feature representations with both labels. As we only have a subset of images with style labels, we first train a style classifier with them. We then extract style attributes for all training images, and applied those attributes to regularize the feature learning and classifier training for aesthetic quality categorization.

To learn style attributes for 230,000 training images, we first train a style classifier by performing the training procedure discussed in Section 2.1 on 11,000 labeled training images (Style-SCNN). We adopted the same architecture as shown in Figure 2. The only difference is that we reduced the number of filters in the the first and fourth convolutional layers to a half due to the reduced number of training images. With Style-SCNN, we are maximizing the log likelihood function in Equation 1 where $\mathcal{C}$ is the set of style labels in the AVA dataset. We experimentally select the best architectures (to be shown in Table 4) and inputs (I_g^c, I_g^w, I_g^p, I_l^r). The details are described in Section 3. Given an image, we apply the learned weights and extract the features from the fc256 layer as its style attribute.

To facilitate the network training with style attributes of images, we propose a regularized double-column convolutional neural network (RDCNN) with the architecture shown in Figure 4. Two normalized inputs of the aesthetic column are I_g^w and I_l^r, same as in DCNN (Section 2.2). The input of the style column is I_l^r. The training of RDCNN is done by solving the following optimization problem:

$$\max_{\mathbf{X}_a,\mathbf{W}_a} \sum_{i=1}^{N} \sum_{c=1 \in \mathcal{C}_a} \mathbb{I}(y_{ai} = c) \log p(y_{ai} \mid \mathbf{x}_{ai}, \mathbf{x}_{si}, \mathbf{w}_{ac}) \;, \quad (4)$$

where $\mathbf{x}_{si}$ are the style attributes of the i-th training image, $\mathbf{x}_{ai}$ are the features to be learned. Note that the maximiza-

Table 1: **Accuracy for Different SCNN Architectures**

	conv1 (64)	pool1	rnorm1	conv2 (64)	pool2	rnorm2	conv3 (64)	conv4 (64)	conv5 (64)	conv6 (64)	fc1K	fc256	fc2	Accuracy
Arch 1	√	√	√	√	√	√	√	√			√	√	√	**71.20%**
Arch 2	√	√	√	√	√	√					√	√	√	60.25%
Arch 3	√	√	√	√	√	√	√				√	√	√	62.68%
Arch 4	√	√		√	√		√	√	√	√	√	√	√	65.14%
Arch 5	√	√	√	√	√	√	√	√				√	√	70.52%
Arch 6	√	√	√	√	√	√	√	√	√		√	√	√	62.49%
Arch 7	√	√	√	√	√	√	√	√	√	√	√	√	√	70.93%

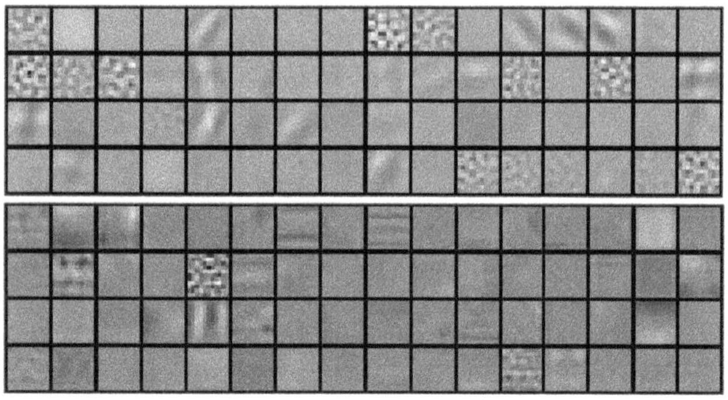

Figure 5: 128 convolutional kernels of the size $11 \times 11 \times 3$ learned by the first convolutional layer of DCNN for aesthetic quality categorization. The first 64 are from the local view column (with the input I_l^r) and the last 64 are from the global view column (with the input I_g^w).

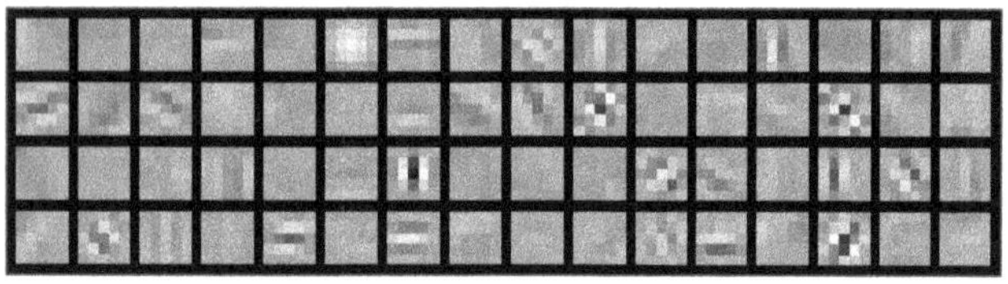

Figure 6: 64 convolutional kernels of the size $5 \times 5 \times 3$ learned by the first convolutional layer of CNN for object classification on the CIFAR dataset.

tion does not involve style attributes $\mathbf{x}_s$. In each learning iteration, we only fine-tuned the parameters in the aesthetic column and the learning process is supervised by the aesthetic label. The parameters of the style column are fixed and the style attributes $\mathbf{x}_{ls}$ essentially serve as a regularizer for training the aesthetic column.

3. EXPERIMENTAL RESULTS

We evaluated the proposed method for aesthetics quality categorization on the AVA dataset [24]. We first introduce the dataset. Then we report the performance of SCNN with different network architectures and normalized inputs. Next, we present aesthetic quality categorization results with DCNN and qualitatively analyze the benefits of the double-column architecture over a single-column one. We also demonstrate the performance of RDCNN with the accuracy of trained style classifier and aesthetic categorization results with style attributes incorporated. Finally, we summarize the computational efficiency of SCNN, DCNN, and RDCNN in training and testing.

Table 2: Accuracy of Aesthetic Quality Categorization with Different Inputs

δ	I_l^r	I_g^w	I_g^c	I_g^p
0	71.20%	67.79%	65.48%	60.43%
1	68.63%	68.11%	69.67%	70.50%

Table 3: Accuracy of Aesthetic Quality Categorization for Different Methods

δ	[24]	SCNN	AVG_SCNN	DCNN	RDCNN
0	66.7%	71.20%	69.91%	73.25%	74.46%
1	67%	68.63%	71.26%	73.05%	73.70%

3.1 The Dataset

The AVA dataset contains a total of 250,000 images, each of which has about 200 aesthetic ratings ranging from one to ten. We followed the experimental settings in [24], and used the same collection of training data and testing data: 230,000 images for training and 20,000 images for testing. Training images are divided into two categories, i.e., low-quality images and high-quality images, based on the same criteria as [24]. Images with mean ratings smaller than $5-\delta$ are referred to as low-quality images, those with mean ratings larger than or equal to $5+\delta$ are high-quality images. We set δ to 0 and 1 respectively to generate the binary ground truth labels for the training images. Images with ratings between $5-\delta$ and $5+\delta$ are discarded. With $\delta = 0$, there are 68,000 low-quality images and 167,000 high-quality images. With $\delta = 1$, there are 7,500 low-quality images and 45,000 high-quality images. For the testing images, we fix δ to 0, regardless what δ is used for training. This results in 5,700 low-quality images and 14,000 high-quality images for testing.

To learn style attributes, we use the subset of images with style labels from the AVA dataset as the training set. The 14 style classes include complementary colors, duotones, HDR, image grain, light on white, long exposure, macro, motion blur, negative images, rule of thirds, shallow DOF, silhouettes, soft focus, and vanishing point. The subset contains 11,000 images for training and 2,500 images for testing.

3.2 SCNN Results

We compare the performance of SCNN with different layer combinations and normalized inputs on aesthetic quality categorization task. Table 1 presents seven different architectures and their overall accuracy. As shown, the selected layer for each architecture is labeled with a check mark. In all seven architectures, we use I_l^r as the input with $\delta = 0$. The results show that the architecture Arch 1 performs the best, which partially indicates the importance of choosing a proper number of convolutional layers and fully connected layers, and having normalization layers.

(a) Images ranked the highest in aesthetics by DCNN

(b) Images ranked the lowest in aesthetics by DCNN

Figure 7: Images ranked the highest and the lowest in aesthetics generated by DCNN. Differences between low-aesthetic images and high-aesthetic images heavily lie in the amount of textures and complexity of the whole image.

With the network architecture fixed to Arch 1, we compare the performance of SCNN with different inputs, i.e., I_g^c, I_g^w, I_g^p, I_l^r. We train classifiers with both $\delta = 0$ and $\delta = 1$ for each input type. The overall accuracy is presented in Table 2. The results show that I_l^r yields the highest accuracy among four types of inputs, which indicates that l_r serves as an effective data augmentation approach to capture the local aesthetic details of images. I_g^w performs much better than I_g^c and I_g^p, which is the best among the three inputs for capturing the global view of images.

Based on the above observation, we choose Arch 1 as the architecture of our model, with I_l^r as input. As shown in

Figure 8: Test images correctly classified by DCNN but misclassified by SCNN. The first row shows the images that are misclassified by SCNN with the input I_l^r. The second row shows the images that are misclassified by SCNN with the input I_g^w. The label on each image indicates the ground-truth aesthetic quality.

Table 4: Accuracy for Different Network Architectures for Style Classification

	conv1 (32)	pool1	rnorm1	conv2 (64)	pool2	rnorm2	conv3 (64)	conv4 (32)	conv5 (32)	conv6 (32)	fc1K	fc256	fc14	MAP	Accuracy
Arch 1	√	√	√	√	√	√	√	√			√	√	√	**56.81%**	**59.89%**
Arch 2	√	√	√	√	√	√					√	√	√	52.39%	54.33%
Arch 3	√	√	√	√	√	√	√				√	√	√	53.19%	55.19%
Arch 4	√	√		√	√		√	√	√	√	√	√	√	54.13%	55.77%
Arch 5	√	√	√	√	√	√	√	√				√	√	53.94%	56.00%
Arch 6	√	√	√	√	√	√	√	√	√		√	√	√	53.22%	57.25%
Arch 7	√	√	√	√	√	√	√	√	√	√	√	√	√	47.44%	52.16%

Table 3, the performance of this setting is better than the state of the art on the AVA dataset for both $\delta = 0$ and $\delta = 1$.

3.3 DCNN Results

We adopt the SCNN architecture Arch 1 for both columns in DCNN. Figure 5 illustrates the filters of the first convolutional layer for trained DCNN. The first 64 are from the local column (with the input I_l^r), while the last 64 are from the global column (with the input I_g^w). Compared with the filters trained in the object recognition task on CIFAR dataset[2] (shown in Figure 6), the filters learned with image aesthetic labels are smoother and cleaner without radical intensity changes. This indicates that differences between low-aesthetic and high-aesthetic image cues mainly lie in the amount of texture and the complexity of the whole image. The difference can be observed from typical test images presented in Figure 7. The images ranked the highest in aesthetics are generally smoother than those ranked the lowest. This finding substantiates the importance of simplicity and complexity features recently proposed for analyzing visual emotions [19].

To quantitatively demonstrate the effectiveness of trained DCNN, we compare its performance with that of the SCNN as well as [24]. As shown in Table 3, DCNN outperforms SCNN for both $\delta = 0$ and $\delta = 1$, and significantly outperforms the earlier work. To further demonstrate the effectiveness of joint training of DCNN, we compare DCNN with AVG_SCNN, which averaged the two SCNN results with I_g^w and I_l^r as inputs. As shown in Table 3, DCNN outperforms the AVG_SCNN for both δ values.

[2]http://www.cs.toronto.edu/~kriz/cifar.html

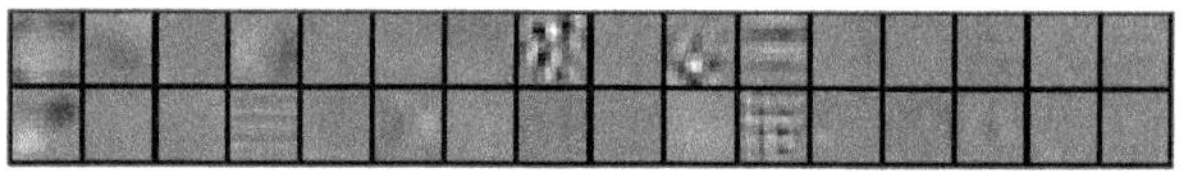

Figure 9: 32 convolutional kernels of the size $11 \times 11 \times 3$ learned by the first convolutional layer of Style-SCNN for style classification.

To qualitatively analyze the benefits of the double-column architecture, we visualize ten test images correctly classified by DCNN but incorrectly by SCNN. We present the examples in Figure 8. Images in the first row are misclassified by SCNN with the input I_l^r. Images in the second row are misclassified with the input I_g^w. The label on each image indicates the ground-truth aesthetic quality. As shown, images misclassified by SCNN with the input I_l^r usually contain a dominant object, which is because I_l^r does not consider the global information in an image. Images misclassified by SCNN with the input I_g^w often have detailed information in their local views that can improve the classifier if can be properly leveraged.

3.4 Categorization with Style Attributes

To demonstrate the effectiveness of the style attributes for aesthetic quality categorization, we first evaluate the style classification accuracy with SCNN. We then compare the performance of RDCNN with DCNN.

3.4.1 *Style Classification*

We train the style classifier with SCNN, and visualize the filters learned by the first convolutional layer of SCNN in Figure 9. We test the trained model on 2,573 images.

Figure 10: Test images correctly classified by RDCNN and misclassified by DCNN. The label on each image indicates the ground truth aesthetic quality of images.

Table 5: Accuracy of Style Classification with Different Inputs

	I_l^r	I_g^w	I_g^c	I_g^p
AP	56.93%	44.52%	45.74%	41.78%
MAP	56.81%	47.01%	48.14%	44.07%
Accuracy	59.89%	48.08%	48.85%	46.79%

For each image, we randomly sample 50 patches of the size $224 \times 224 \times 3$, and average the prediction results. To compare our results with the results reported in [24], we use the same experimental setting. We perform similar experiments as discussed in Section 3.2 by comparing different architectures and normalized inputs. The comparison results for different architectures are shown in Table 4. The selected layer for each architecture is labeled with a check mark. We achieve the best accuracy for style classification with Arch 1 and I_l^r as input (Table 5). It indicates the importance of local view in determining the style of an image. It shows the effectiveness of l_r as a data augmentation strategy in case of limited training data. We did not compare our style classification results with Karayev *et al.* [12] as their evaluations were done on a randomly selected subset of test images.

The Average Precision(AP) and Mean Average Precision (MAP) are also calculated. The best MAP we achieved is 56.81% which outperforms the accuracy of 53.85% reported in [24].

3.4.2 Aesthetic Quality Categorization with Style Attributes

We demonstrate the effectiveness of style attributes by comparing the best aesthetic quality categorization accuracy we have achieved with and without style attributes. As shown in Table 3, RDCNN outperforms DCNN for both δ values.

To qualitatively analyze the benefits brought with the regularized double-column architecture, we show typical test images that have been correctly classified by RDCNN but misclassified by DCNN in Figure 10. Those examples correctly classified by RDCNN are mostly with the following styles: rule-of-thirds, HDR, black and white, long exposure, complementary colors, vanishing point, and soft focus. This indicates that styles attributes help aesthetic quality categorization.

3.5 Computational Efficiency

Training SCNN for a specific input type takes about two days. Training DCNN takes about three days. For RDCNN, style attribute training takes roughly a day, and RDCNN training three to four days. Classifying 2,000 images (each with 50 views) takes about 50 minutes, 80 minutes, and 100 minutes for SCNN, DCNN, and RDCNN, respectively, with Nvidia Tesla M2070/M2090 GPU.

4. CONCLUSIONS

We present a double-column deep convolutional neural network approach for aesthetic quality rating and categorization. Rather than designing handcrafted features or adopting generic image descriptors, aesthetic-related features are learned automatically. Feature learning and classifier training are unified with the proposed deep neural network approach. The double-column architecture takes into account both the global view and local view of an image for judging its aesthetic quality. Besides, image style attributes are leveraged to improve the accuracy. Evaluating with the AVA dataset, which is the largest benchmark with rich aesthetic ratings, our approach shows significant better results than earlier-reported results on the same dataset.

5. REFERENCES

[1] F. Agostinelli, M. Anderson, and H. Lee. Adaptive multi-column deep neural networks with application to robust image denoising. In *Advances in Neural*

Information Processing Systems (NIPS), pages 1493–1501. 2013.

[2] R. Arnheim. In *Art and visual Perception: A psychology of the creative eye*. Los Angeles. CA: University of California Press., 1974.

[3] S. Bhattacharya, R. Sukthankar, and M. Shah. A framework for photo-quality assessment and enhancement based on visual aesthetics. In *ACM International Conference on Multimedia (MM)*, pages 271–280, 2010.

[4] D. Ciresan, U. Meier, and J. Schmidhuber. Multi-column deep neural networks for image classification. In *IEEE Conference on Computer Vision and Pattern Recognition (CVPR)*, pages 3642–3649, 2012.

[5] R. Collobert and J. Weston. A unified architecture for natural language processing: Deep neural networks with multitask learning. In *International Conference on Machine Learning (ICML)*, pages 160–167, 2008.

[6] R. Datta, D. Joshi, J. Li, and J. Wang. Studying aesthetics in photographic images using a computational approach. In *European Conference on Computer Vision (ECCV)*, pages 288–301, 2006.

[7] S. Dhar, V. Ordonez, and T. Berg. High level describable attributes for predicting aesthetics and interestingness. In *IEEE Conference on Computer Vision and Pattern Recognition (CVPR)*, pages 1657–1664, June 2011.

[8] J. Donahue, Y. Jia, O. Vinyals, J. Hoffman, N. Zhang, E. Tzeng, and T. Darrell. DeCAF: A deep convolutional activation feature for generic visual recognition. In *Technical report, 2013. arXiv:1310.1531v1*, 2013.

[9] G. Hinton. Training products of experts by minimizing contrastive divergence. *Neural Computation*, 14(8):1771–1800, 2002.

[10] G. E. Hinton, S. Osindero, and Y.-W. Teh. A fast learning algorithm for deep belief nets. *Neural Computation*, 18(7):1527–1554, 2006.

[11] D. Joshi, R. Datta, E. Fedorovskaya, Q. T. Luong, J. Z. Wang, J. Li, and J. B. Luo. Aesthetics and emotions in images. In *IEEE Signal Processing Magazine*, 2011.

[12] S. Karayev, A. Hertzmann, H. Winnermoller, A. Agarwala, and T. Darrel. Recognizing image style. In *British Machine Vision Conference (BMVC)*, 2014.

[13] Y. Ke, X. Tang, and F. Jing. The design of high-level features for photo quality assessment. In *IEEE Conference on Computer Vision and Pattern Recognition (CVPR)*, volume 1, pages 419–426, 2006.

[14] A. Khosla, A. Das Sarma, and R. Hamid. What makes an image popular? In *International World Wide Web Conference (WWW)*, pages 867–876, 2014.

[15] A. Krizhevsky, I. Sutskever, and G. E. Hinton. Imagenet classification with deep convolutional neural networks. In *Advances in Neural Information Processing Systems (NIPS)*, pages 1106–1114, 2012.

[16] Y. LeCun, L. Bottou, Y. Bengio, and P. Haffner. Gradient-based learning applied to document recognition. In *Proceedings of the IEEE*, pages 2278–2324, 1998.

[17] O. Litzel. In *On Photographic Composition*. New York: Amphoto Books, 1974.

[18] D. Lowe. Distinctive image features from scale-invariant keypoints. *International Journal of Computer Vision (IJCV)*, 60(2):91–110, 2004.

[19] X. Lu, P. Suryanarayan, R. B. Adams Jr, J. Li, M. G. Newman, and J. Z. Wang. On shape and the computability of emotions. In *ACM International Conference on Multimedia (MM)*, pages 229–238. ACM, 2012.

[20] W. Luo, X. Wang, and X. Tang. Content-based photo quality assessment. In *IEEE International Conference on Computer Vision (ICCV)*, pages 2206–2213, 2011.

[21] Y. Luo and X. Tang. Photo and video quality evaluation: Focusing on the subject. In *European Conference on Computer Vision (ECCV)*, pages 386–399, 2008.

[22] L. Marchesotti and F. Perronnin. Learning beautiful (and ugly) attributes. In *British Machine Vision Conference (BMVC)*, 2013.

[23] L. Marchesotti, F. Perronnin, D. Larlus, and G. Csurka. Assessing the aesthetic quality of photographs using generic image descriptors. In *IEEE International Conference on Computer Vision (ICCV)*, pages 1784–1791, 2011.

[24] N. Murray, L. Marchesotti, and F. Perronnin. AVA: A large-scale database for aesthetic visual analysis. In *IEEE Conference on Computer Vision and Pattern Recognition (CVPR)*, pages 2408–2415, 2012.

[25] W. Niekamp. An exploratory investigation into factors affecting visual balance. In *Educational Communication and Technology: A Journal of Theory, Research, and Development*, volume 29, pages 37–48, 1981.

[26] M. Nishiyama, T. Okabe, I. Sato, and Y. Sato. Aesthetic quality classification of photographs based on color harmony. In *IEEE Conference on Computer Vision and Pattern Recognition (CVPR)*, pages 33–40, 2011.

[27] P. O'Donovan, A. Agarwala, and A. Hertzmann. Color compatibility from large datasets. *ACM Transactions on Graphics (TOG)*, 30(4):63:1–12, 2011.

[28] A. Oliva and A. Torralba. Modeling the shape of the scene: A holistic representation of the spatial envelope. *International Journal of Computer Vision (IJCV)*, 42(3):145–175, 2001.

[29] J. Pan and Q. Yang. A survey on transfer learning. *IEEE Transactions on Knowledge and Data Engineering (TKDE)*, 22(10):1345–1359, 2010.

[30] P. Sermanet, K. Kavukcuoglu, S. Chintala, and Y. LeCun. Pedestrian detection with unsupervised multi-stage features learning. In *IEEE Conference on Computer Vision and Pattern Recognition (CVPR)*, pages 3626–3633, 2013.

[31] H.-H. Su, T.-W. Chen, C.-C. Kao, W. Hsu, and S.-Y. Chien. Scenic photo quality assessment with bag of aesthetics-preserving features. In *ACM International Conference on Multimedia (MM)*, pages 1213–1216, 2011.

[32] Y. Sun, X. Wang, and X. Tang. Hybrid deep learning for face verification. In *The IEEE International Conference on Computer Vision (ICCV)*, 2013.

Fashion Parsing with Video Context

Si Liu*[1], Xiaodan Liang*[2,1], Luoqi Liu[1], Ke Lu[3], Liang Lin[2], Shuicheng Yan[1]
[1]National University of Singapore
[2]Sun Yat-Sen University
[3]University of Chinese Academy of Sciences
{dcslius, eleyans}@nus.edu.sg,
{xdliang328, llq667}@gmail.com, {linliang}@ieee.org, {luk}@ucas.ac.cn,

ABSTRACT

In this paper, we explore how to utilize the video context to facilitate fashion parsing. Instead of annotating a large amount of fashion images, we present a general, affordable and scalable solution, which harnesses the rich contexts in easily available fashion videos to boost any existing fashion parser. First, we crawl a large unlabelled fashion video corpus with fashion frames. Then for each fashion video, the cross-frame contexts are utilized for human pose co-estimation, and then video co-parsing to obtain satisfactory fashion parsing results for all frames. More specifically, Sift Flow and super-pixel matching are used to build correspondences across frames, and these correspondences then contextualize the pose estimations and fashion parsing in individual frames. Finally, these parsed video frames are used as the reference corpus for the non-parametric fashion parsing component of the whole solution. Extensive experiments on two benchmark fashion datasets as well as a newly collected challenging Fashion Icon (FI) dataset demonstrate the encouraging performance gain from our general pipeline for fashion parsing.

Categories and Subject Descriptors

H.3.3 [**Information Search and Retrieval**]: Retrieval models; I.2.6 [**Learning**]: Knowledge acquisition

General Terms

Algorithms, Experimentation, Performance

Keywords

Fashion parsing, video segmentation, video context, human pose estimation

*indicates equal contribution

Figure 1: Illustration of images for fashion parsing and their parsing results obtained by our proposed system. Note that the girls are photographed with quite diverse poses, with some girl in side-view or back-view even, which are very challenging circumstances for fashion parsing. For better viewing of all figures in this paper, please see the original zoomed-in color pdf file.

1. INTRODUCTION

Fashion parsing aims to predict the label (e.g. skin, t-shirt, etc.) for each pixel in a fashion image. The performance of traditional fashion parsers are constrained by the limited training data, and thus cannot well parse the fashion images which contain human bodies in arbitrary, even exaggerated poses and various views. In this paper, we propose a fashion parsing algorithm which can potentially make use of unlimited fashion videos on the web, and thus can parse the challenging fashion images well. Some exemplar parsing results are shown in Fig. 1.

Fashion parsing has the potential to benefit a wide range of applications [2, 12, 11]in the multimedia area. For example, it can be used to analyse the numerous photos shared by users on social networks, so that the information about the users' personalities and preferences can be obtained and exploited for friend recommendation, advertisement, etc. Besides, fashion parsing can also be used in intelligent surveillance, e.g., person re-identification. A good understanding of one's apparel may provide useful cues to identify a person. Despite its various potential applications, current fashion parsing systems [17, 3, 16, 10] still have many limitations,

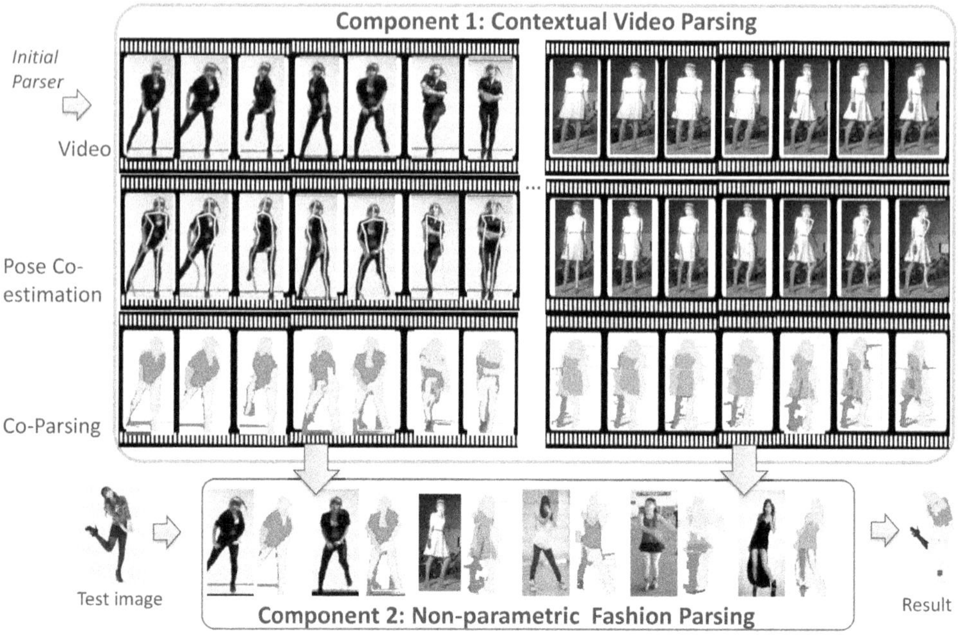

Figure 2: Framework overview of our system. It contains two components, i.e., contextual video parsing and non-parametric fashion parsing. Any off-the-shelf constrained pose estimator and fashion parser can initialize the human pose estimation and parsing results. To leverage the video contexts represented by Sift Flow and super-pixel matching, the videos have much better human pose estimation and fashion parsing results by the proposed video human pose co-estimation and fashion co-parsing algorithms. Since no supervision is required for the video data, a large number of video frames and their video parsing results can be obtained and used as a gallery set to facilitate the non-parametric label transfer to the test image.

since they cannot handle fashion parsing well, which is the common case in real life.

To solve fashion parsing in the wild, there are mainly two challenges. Firstly, there is a great diversity in human poses, which results in the unsatisfactory performance of even the state-of-the-art human pose estimator [18]. As an important embedded component of all fashion parsers, the poor performance of a human pose estimator may greatly degrade the fashion parsing results. Secondly, there has been no dataset specially designed for the fashion parsing task. All existing publicly available fashion parsing datasets [16, 10, 16] contain only constrained images. Lack of training data makes training an unconstrained fashion parser impossible.

In this paper, we propose a novel framework which leverages video contexts to tackle the fashion parsing task without extra annotation. Here, the videos are not required to be labelled, thus can be easily obtained from the web (e.g., youtube.com). The framework is illustrated in Fig 2. It contains two components: 1) contextual video parsing, and 2) non-parametric fashion parsing. As for the contextual video parsing component, the goal is to parse the unlabelled unconstrained videos which are also assumed to be in the wild, yet with valuable cross-frame contexts. Since human pose estimation is the prerequisite for fashion parsing, a human pose co-estimation step (Sec. 4.1.1) is implemented first in the contextual video parsing component. In this step, we first apply the off-the-shelf constrained human pose estimator to the videos, and then refine the estimated results by incorporating the pixel-level correspondences between sequential frames, which are described by Sift Flow [9]. After the human pose co-estimation, we first apply a constrained fashion parser (pre-trained on a small amount of constrained labeled data). It can provide a rough initialization for unconstrained video parsing. Then we use the super-pixel-level correspondences between two sequential frames, which are described by a super-pixel matching technique to refine the parsing results. That is, we co-parse all the frames in one video simultaneously (Sec. 4.1.2). In the fashion parsing in the wild component, these parsed video frames are used as the gallery set which transfers labels to testing images by the proposed non-parametric method (Sec. 4.2). To verify the effectiveness of the proposed framework, we conduct extensive experiments. The results proof that our framework better parses fashion images in the wild than state-of-the-art parsers.

Our whole framework is inspired by physiology. More specifically, our whole system simulates how a baby gradually gains more knowledge. Initially, a little baby has a simple and original understanding of the world (corresponding to the initial fashion parser in our paper). Then the baby gradually learns more knowledge by linking what he/she already knows with the world (corresponding to label propagation from initial fashion parser to the whole video). After gaining much more knowledge about the world (finish the video parsing), the baby can apply his/her enriched knowledge to handle the problem (using enlarged video corpus to transfer labels to testing image). The first component of our system, i.e., contextual video parsing, simulates the process that a baby gradually learns more knowledge. The second component, i.e., the non-parametric label transfer, simulates the process that determines how the baby uses the knowledge he/she learns to better solve a problem.

The contributions of this work can be summarized as:

- Our work differs from other existing fashion parsing works in that we parse fashion images with the help of the large scale of web videos without extra annotation. Extensive experiments on three datasets prove the effectiveness of the proposed framework.

- In order to robustly parse the web videos, we leverage the rich temporal and semantic video contexts. It contains two components, i.e., the contextual video parsing and the non-parametric fashion parsing.
- We construct two new datasets, one large video dataset and one Fashion Icon (FI) dataset, which can serve as the benchmark datasets for the fashion parsing task.

2. RELATED WORK

In this section we review the recent research development in the fields of fashion parsing and video parsing sequentially.

2.1 Fashion Parsing

The first clothing parsing work was conducted by Yamaguchi *et al.* [17]. Their fashion parsing performance was not quite high due to the large human pose variation and background clutter. Later, Yamaguchi *et al.* [16] dramatically improved the fashion parsing performance by using a retrieval based approach. Their approach combines parsing from pre-trained global clothing models, local clothing models learned on the fly from retrieved examples, and transferred parse masks (paper doll item transfer) from retrieved examples. Dong *et al.* [3] used Parselets as the building blocks of the parsing model. Parselets are a group of parsable segments which can generally be obtained by low-level over-segmentation algorithms. They built a Deformable Mixture Parsing Model (DMPM) for human parsing to simultaneously handle the deformation and multi-modalities of Parselets. Liu *et al.* [10] addressed the problem of automatically parsing the fashion images with weak supervision from the user-generated color-category tags. They proposed to combine the human pose estimation module, the MRF-based inference module and the category classifier learning module. However, all the existing algorithms can only parse the constrained fashion images, which are still far from practical use. To our best knowledge, we are the first to explore the fashion parsing task.

2.2 Video Parsing

The main difficulty of video parsing lies in the great burden of labelling training samples. According to the amount of required labelling, video parsing algorithms can be classified into four categories. The first category is supervised video parsing [14], which requires a large amount of labelled video data and thus is extremely tedious for human labelling. To reduce the burden of labelling, semi-supervised video segmentation [1, 15] is proposed, which reduces the labellers' burden to some extent. Later, weakly supervised video segmentation was explored [13] where semantic labels are associated with training videos but not spatially or temporally localized. Our video parsing technique belongs to the last category, i.e., unsupervised video parsing. No pixel-level labels are required when we parse the video data, thus ideally an infinite number of videos can be parsed, which partially alleviates the lack of unconstrained training data.

3. DATASET COLLECTION

We collect two datasets, including a video dataset and a Fashion Icon (FI) image dataset for our ultimate purpose of fashion parsing. The first video dataset contains $1,500$ videos. The second FI image dataset contains $1,082$ images.

Video Dataset: Three requirements are considered during the data collection. First, all the videos are HD videos so that the clothes can be seen clearly to facilitate the later fashion parsing. Second, at least one girl in the video is unoccluded from head to toe during the entire video sequence. Third, to balance the informativeness of the videos and the processing efficiency, the lengths of all video clips retained range from 2 seconds to 10 seconds. We mainly collect five categories of videos, including: 1) MVs of the singers; 2) dance teaching videos; 3) fashion shows of some clothing brands; 4) fashion TV dramas or movies; and 5) big evening parties or talent shows.

To balance the efficiency of video processing and the informativeness of videos, we sample from each video and keep the frame number in each video less than 50. In order to filter the background of each frame, all the crawled videos are automatically preprocessed to be human-centric and with less background clutter before fed to our video parsing system. The automatic preprocessing process contains two steps. We first use Grammar Models [6] to automatically detect the human body. Then, the detected human-centric bounding box is used as the seed for the tracking algorithm [7, 19]. Thus all the video frames are roughly aligned and mostly occupied by the human body, which greatly facilitates the later video parsing. Alternatively, we can detect the human body in each frame, but this solution suffers from the relatively low detection speed. We believe that using detection as the initialization for the later tracking algorithm is a balance between accuracy and efficiency. Due to the fully unsupervised processing of the videos, our video dataset is easily scalable by continuously downloading more data.

Fashion Icon (FI) Image Dataset: We collect $1,082$ images from the web to construct the Fashion Icon dataset (FI). The FI dataset is quite different from existing fashion parsing datasets [16, 3] in two aspects. Firstly, some images in FI each contain multiple humans. Secondly, the humans in the images of the FI dataset are in very diverse poses, which is more consistent with reality. In order to compare the performances of different parsing systems, the FI dataset is thoroughly labelled based on the label set defined by Dong *et al.* [3], which includes 18 categories: face, sunglass, hat, scarf, hair, upper clothes, coat, left-arm, right-arm, belt, pants, left-leg, right-leg, skirt, left-shoe, right-shoe, bag, dress and background.

4. FRAMEWORK

In this section we introduce the proposed framework. We detail the contextual video parsing component and the non-parametric fashion parsing component sequentially in the following.

4.1 Contextual Video Parsing

The goal of our contextual video parsing is to parse all the frames in each video simultaneously. The main challenge comes from the large variations in human poses and views within the video frames. The performance of existing fashion parsers often relies on a perfect human pose estimator to localize the human as well as the body parts. However, most of the previous pose estimators, limited by the small amount of training data, tend to fail in predicting arbitrary poses in images from the web. In this paper, we propose a novel generic graphical model to better infer the poses

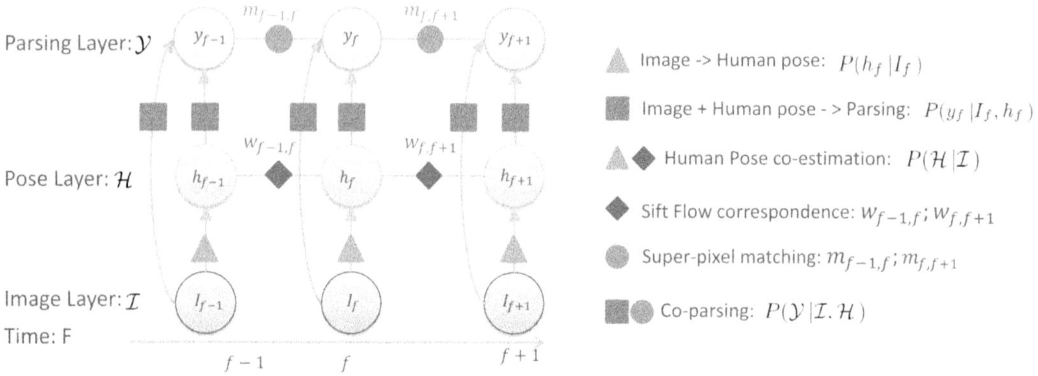

Figure 3: The whole video parsing framework. The graphical model has three layers: image layer, pose layer and parsing layer. Green triangles and blue squares respectively represent the traditional human pose estimation and fashion parsing. By incorporating Sift Flow correspondences indicated by purple diamonds, video pose co-estimation is conducted. The refined human pose results, along with the mined super-pixel matching indicated by red circles, are fed into the video co-parsing step.

and the parsing results of any frames. Intuitively, we utilize the temporal coherence and appearance consistency characteristics within video frames to refine the estimated poses and parsing results obtained from the existing constrained models. By regarding these informative contexts as the regularization constraints, the pose co-estimation and fashion co-parsing can be largely improved.

We denote the parsing results of all frames $\mathcal{I}$ as $\mathcal{Y}$ and human pose estimation results as $\mathcal{H}$. We estimate the pixel-wise semantic labelling, where the whole label set is denoted as $\mathcal{C} = \{1, \cdots, N_C\}$ and N_C is the number of labels. The three factors $(\mathcal{I}, \mathcal{Y}, \mathcal{H})$ are dependent upon each other for the fashion parsing task. Video co-parsing can be viewed as maximizing the conditional probability over parsing results $\mathcal{Y}$, human poses $\mathcal{H}$ and video frames $\mathcal{I}$, formulated as

$$P(\mathcal{H}, \mathcal{Y}|\mathcal{I}) = P(\mathcal{H}|\mathcal{I})P(\mathcal{Y}|\mathcal{I}, \mathcal{H}). \quad (1)$$

As illustrated in Fig. 3, our graphical model can be viewed as the composition of three layers. The bottom layer I contains all the input frames $\mathcal{I} = \{I_f\}_1^F$. The middle layer represents the estimated poses for each frame $\mathcal{H} = \{h_f\}_1^F$. Finally in the top layer, the fashion parsing results for all frames are denoted as $\mathcal{Y} = \{y_f\}_1^F$. For simplicity, only three temporal adjacent frames I_{f-1}, I_f and I_{f+1} are shown. Note that the nodes in the middle layer h_f are conditioned on the input observations I_f and the temporal constraints $w_{f,f+1}$ and $w_{f-1,f}$ from the adjacent human poses. The inference of all nodes is denoted as the video pose co-estimation. Furthermore, the video co-parsing task can be converted to inferring the states of nodes y_f in the top layer. The probability of each node y_f relies on the prediction of the corresponding pose h_f, the appearance constraints $m_{f,f+1}$ and $m_{f-1,f}$ as well as the inputs I_f. Because there are numerous hypotheses of locations of poses and all the frames are required to be parsed simultaneously, the joint inference of $P(\mathcal{H}|\mathcal{I})P(\mathcal{Y}|\mathcal{I}, \mathcal{H})$ can be NP-hard and impossible to solve efficiently. We approximate the inference task in Eq. (1) by separately optimizing the two sequential tasks: pose co-estimation $P(\mathcal{H}|\mathcal{I})$ and video co-parsing $P(\mathcal{Y}|\mathcal{I}, \mathcal{H})$. Note that the results of video pose co-estimation are the inputs of video co-parsing.

4.1.1 Video Human Pose Co-estimation $P(\mathcal{H}|\mathcal{I})$

Our pose co-estimation stage has two steps. First, we estimate the initial pose for each frame, illustrated as green triangles in Fig. 3. Second, all poses of all the frames are refined together by considering the confidence ranking of poses and the Sift-Flow correspondences between the successive frames, represented by purple diamonds in Fig. 3.

Image Human Pose Estimation $P(h_f|I_f)$ **:** Human pose estimation in the image has been extensively studied. We adopt the articulated pose estimation technique with flexible mixtures-of-parts method [18]. The human pose model can be represented by a K-node skeleton graph $G_s = (V_s; E_s)$, where the K nodes V_s correspond to different human parts, such as left shoulder, right shoulder, etc., and the edges E_s represent the relationships of human parts.

Given a frame I_f, we estimate the locations $\{l_f^i\}_{i=1}^K$ for all K key-points and the associated part types $\{t_f^i\}_{i=1}^K$ for each point within the hunan skeleton. The human pose can be calculated as $h_f = \{l_f, t_f\}$, where $l_f = \{l_f^i\}_{i=1}^K$ and $t_f = \{t_f^i\}_{i=1}^K$. We denote the hypotheses set of l_f^i as $\{1, \cdots, L\}$ and that of t_f^i as $\{1, \cdots, T\}$, where L is the image lattice and T is the number of types for each part.

Given a pose configuration h_f (including part types t_f and positions l_f), the confidence $P(h_f|I_f)$ is computed by combining 3 factors: the corresponding confidence for the part type assignments t_f, the unary score for each key point and the pairwise scores for the skeleton relations by [18]. It is worth noting that the probability $P(h_f|I_f)$ can be used to roughly predict the accuracy of the human pose estimator. That is, the high probability means the estimator has strong confidence for the estimated pose. We rank the probabilities of all the poses for all frames in each video, and then we can select the most confident poses, used as the "seeds" for the following pose co-estimation.

Video Human Pose Co-Estimation $P(\mathcal{H}|\mathcal{I})$**:** As aforementioned, even the state-of-the-art pose estimators may fail when parsing the fashion images. To process the numerous frames, we consider the video frames as a chain structure and the contextual relationships between adjacent frames are used to regularize the poses of all the frames. In this chain model, each node is the pose h_f of the frame $\mathcal{I}$, and the edges E_W are the chains. As shown in Fig. 3, the frame

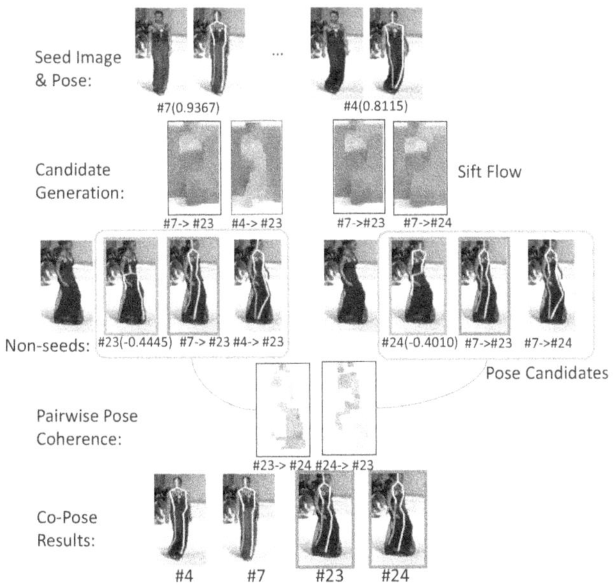

Figure 4: Illustration of human pose co-estimation. The frames ♯4, ♯7, ♯23, ♯24 of the video are shown. The constrained human pose estimator is applied and the confidences are shown in parentheses. Then the frames with high confidences (e.g., ♯7 with confidence 0.9367) are regarded as seeds. Each frame has 3 candidate poses. The first candidate is generated by the frame itself, while the other two are transferred from seeds by Sift-Flow correspondences (in second row). For each possible candidate pair, we calculate the pairwise term according to the Sift Flow field. Based on the context between successive frames, the optimal poses among all pose candidates are selected, which are highlighted by red bounding boxes. The final pose co-estimation results are shown in the last row, which are much better than the original estimated poses, such as the initial pose estimation results for frames ♯23 and ♯24, highlighted by green bounding boxes.

h_f connects only with h_{f-1} and h_{f+1}. By using the temporal constraints, more accurate human pose estimations for all frames can be obtained simultaneously.

We use the Sift Flow [9] method to capture the temporal displacements between successive frames. For the frame pair (i, j), we denote the corresponding flow field as $w_{i,j}$, which is a 2D flow vector indexed by pixel positions. Given the flow field $w_{i,j}$, the position of each pixel p in the frame i can be mapped to $p + w_{i,j}(p)$ in the frame j. Note that w is not symmetric, i.e., $w_{i,j} \neq w_{j,i}$, according to the Sift Flow computational framework.

As for human pose co-estimation, we consider two items for jointly refining the poses of all the frames: single pose confidence for each frame and the pairwise pose coherence. First, the single pose confidence is obtained by $P(h_f|I_f)$, which evaluates the quality of the estimated pose of each frame. Second, the pairwise term assesses the coherence of poses in two adjacent frames. We map the estimated pose of one frame by the flow vector to its adjacent frame, and hope the mapped pose to be close to the estimated pose of the adjacent frame. This means that pose estimation results should be consistent with the temporal flow field. We thus formulate the human pose co-estimation as maximizing the probability $P(\mathcal{H}|\mathcal{I})$,

$$P(\mathcal{H}|\mathcal{I}) \propto \prod_{f \in I} \mathcal{P}(l_f, t_f|I_f) \cdot \exp(-\eta \sum_{\{f_1, f_2\} \in E_W} (\sum_{i \in V_s} \left| l^i_{f_2} - \{l^i_{f_1} + w_{f_1,f_2}(l^i_{f_1})\} \right|_2^2 + \sum_{i \in V_s} \left| l^i_{f_1} - \{l^i_{f_2} + w_{f_2,f_1}(l^i_{f_2})\} \right|_2^2)) \quad (2)$$

where η is used to balance the single pose confidence and the pairwise pose coherence, which is empirically set in our experiments. Given the pose l_{f_1} of the frame I_{f_1}, we map it into the frame I_{f_2} by using the Sift Flow vector w_{f_1,f_2} for all locations of l_{f_1}, denoted as $l^i_{f_1} + w_{f_1,f_2}(l^i_{f_1})$. The temporal displacement between the estimated pose l_{f_1} and the transfered pose $l^i_{f_1} + w_{f_1,f_2}(l^i_{f_1})$ is calculated using the Euclidean distance. The pairwise term is computed by the summation of the displacements of all key points.

The difficulty of optimizing Eq. (2) lies in two aspects. 1) We estimate the pose locations $\{l_f\}_{i=1}^{K}$ of all frames simultaneously, which leads to a very huge hypotheses set of the size FK^L. 2) The whole graph for the pose co-estimation can be viewed as a hierarchical model. The bottom is a common skeleton graph, of which the nodes are human key points and the edges are skeleton relations within each frame. Then the top is a chain structure, where the nodes are the single pose confidences obtained from the bottom and the edges E_W are the cross-frame pose coherences. This hierarchical graph makes inferring pose locations intractable for each video, not to mention our large-scale video set.

For efficiency, we consider all within-frame nodes (i.e. key points) for each frame as a super node (i.e. an integrated pose candidate). In this way, our graph can be simplified into a chain structure from a hierarchical model, which can be effectively solved by the well-known belief propagation method [1]. To generate a set of reasonable pose candidates for each frame, we use the pose propagation strategy with the selected pose seeds. Specifically, we rank all confidences $\{P(h_f|I_f)\}_{f=1}^{F}$ of initialized poses for all frames and select the top 5 candidates with the highest confidences as the pose seeds. We then propagate these seeds to all other frames via Sift Flow [9]. Except the frames with pose seeds, each frame I_f has 6 candidate poses, including 5 propagated pose candidates and the estimated pose from I_f itself. We consider these pose candidates as the possible hypotheses of each frame, which largely reduces the searching space for each node. During the inference procedure, the unary term for each super node I_f is $P(h_f|I_f)$ and the probabilities of propagated pose candidates are directly transferred from the original pose confidence of seeds. In addition, given a specific pair of frames, we obtain different pairwise terms if we select different pose candidate pairs. The pairwise term for each pose candidate pair is calculated by the summation of two temporal displacements using the Sift Flow vector, as described in Eq. (2). The whole procedure of our pose co-estimation is illustrated in Fig. 4. Two pose seeds with highest confidences are selected and then used to generate the candidate poses for the non-seeds frames.

4.1.2 Video Co-Parsing $P(\mathcal{Y}|\mathcal{I}, \mathcal{H})$

Given the refined human poses for all frames, we can perform the video co-parsing, conditioned on the image and

[1] http://www.di.ens.fr/~mschmidt/Software/UGM.html

Figure 5: **Non-parametric fashion parsing. For each testing image, 25 similar images in the video corpus are retrieved. Parsing results are then transferred from the retrieved video frames to the testing image at the super-pixel level. We show the transfer process of 5 fashion items, i.e., leg/right leg, left/right shoes and upper-clothing.**

pose layer as displayed in Fig. 3. Our co-parsing algorithm includes two steps: computing pixel-level confidences w.r.t. the fashion items $P(y_{f,i'}|I_f, h_f)$ for all pixel $i' \in I_f$ (denoted as blue rectangles), and then co-parsing all frames by considering the super-pixel correspondences (denoted as red circles) to obtain $P(\mathcal{Y}|\mathcal{I}, \mathcal{H})$.

Image Parsing $P(y_f|I_f, h_f)$**:** Given one frame I_f and the refined human pose h_f, we compute the confidence score of assigning the possible clothing item label to each pixel. Let us denote $y_{f,i'}$ as the clothing item label at pixel i'. The confidence score $P(y_{f,i'}|I_f, h_f)$ of assigning clothing item labels to $y_{f,i'}$ can be computed by the existing fashion parser, e.g. [16]. And $P(y_f|I_f, h_f)$ can be denoted as the set of $P(y_{f,i'}|I_f, h_f)$.

Note that our algorithm can easily adapt to any other fashion parser, such as [3], by properly redesigning video co-parsing solution.

Video Co-parsing $P(\mathcal{Y}|\mathcal{I}, \mathcal{H})$**:** Based on the pixel-level confidences, we refine the parsing results of all frames together by considering the within-frame and cross-frame super-pixel consistencies. Intuitively, the super-pixels in the spatial neighbours within each frame are encouraged to take the same fashion labels; and similarly, the matched super-pixels across the adjacent frames also favor the same labels. We can thus rectify and smooth the label map of super-pixels of all frames together.

Following the previous parsing works, we build dense appearance correspondences for super-pixels instead of pixels. We first compute over-segmentations of all frames using a fast segmentation method [4]. Then the confidence score of assigning the clothing item label to each super-pixel s is computed as the average of the pixel-wise confidences $P(y_{f,i'}|I_f, h_f)$ of $i' \in s$ which represents all pixels within this super-pixel. We denote the confidence score of each super-pixel by $\phi_s(y_f(s))$. To smooth the label maps of all frames, we utilize two kinds of relationships to consider the appearance consistency. First, the within-image relationship N_{int} is computed for the spatial neighbors of super-pixels. Second, we consider the cross-image relationship N_{ext} for each super-pixel with its most similar counterpart in the previous/subsequent frame.

Mathematically, our co-parsing task aims to maximize the probability $P(\mathcal{Y}|\mathcal{I}, \mathcal{H})$, formulated as

$$P(\mathcal{Y}|\mathcal{I}, \mathcal{H}) \propto \exp(-(\sum_{f \in I} \sum_{s \in \wedge_f} \phi_s(y_f(s)) + \sum_{(s,q) \in N_{\text{int}}} \varphi_{\text{int}}(y_f(s), y_f(q)|I_f) + \sum_{(s,q) \in N_{ext}} \varphi_{ext}(y_f(s), y_{f'}(q)|I_f, I_{f'}))) \tag{3}$$

where $\wedge_f$ denotes all super-pixels within each image I_f. (s, q) represents each pair of neighboured super-pixels within images and across images. The within-image smoothness term φ_{int} and the cross-image smoothness term φ_{ext} are defined as

$$\begin{aligned} &\varphi_{\text{ext}}(y_f(s), y_f(q)|I_f) \\ &= \delta(y_f(s) \neq y_f(q)) \exp(-\lambda_{ext} |\mathcal{F}(s) - \mathcal{F}(q)|) \\ &\varphi_{\text{int}}(y_f(s), y_f(q)|I_f, I_{f'}) \\ &= \delta(y_f(s) \neq y_{f'}(q)) \exp(-\lambda_{int} |\mathcal{F}(s) - \mathcal{F}(q)|) \end{aligned} \tag{4}$$

where $\delta(\cdot)$ is the indicator function and $\mathcal{F}(s)$ is the feature of the super-pixel, which is computed by a concatenation of bag-of-words from RGB, Lab and Gradient for each super-pixel. We also pick the closest super-pixel pairs (s, q) across the sequent frames using L2-distance on these bag-of-words features. λ_{ext} and λ_{int} are the weights of two kinds of pairwise terms. Because our pairwise term Eq. (4) is a submodular function, the optimization of maximizing Eq. (3) becomes a tractable graphical model. We solve this optimization problem by the well-studied α-expansion method [5]. Thus the optimal parsing results of all frames can be calculated as $\mathcal{Y}$.

4.2 Non-parametric Fashion Parsing

Based on our contextual video parsing algorithm, we can efficiently process the large scale video data to generate the gallery set of images. In the following, we propose a non-parametric method for transferring the parsing results of our parsed gallery to the test image.

Given a testing image I, we first use the human detection technique [6] to roughly locate the human body. The caffe feature [8] for each human is computed, which can intrinsically capture the style, pose and appearance characteristics of the whole image. We use L2-distance over the DeCAF feature to find 25 nearest neighbors in our gallery. After that, the testing images are over-segmented and each super-pixel of the testing image finds the closest super-pixel from each retrieved image using L2-distance of the caffe features.

More specifically, we denote the retrieved images for the image I as D. For each super-pixel s, the selected corresponding super-pixel from the reference image r in D is denoted as s_r, and the caffe feature of the super-pixel s is denoted as $h(s)$. Then, our transfered label y_s for each super-pixel s is computed by

$$P(y_s|s, D) = \frac{1}{Z} \sum_{r \in D} \frac{M(y_s, s_r)}{1 + \|h(s) - h(s_r)\|} \tag{5}$$

where we define:

$$M(y_s, s_r) = \frac{1}{|s_r|} \sum_{i' \in s_r} \delta(y_{r,i'} = y_s), \tag{6}$$

where $|s_r|$ is the number of pixels within the super-pixel s_r and i' denotes each pixel. Z is a normalization constant. Our parsing results are computed as the weighted average of the parsing results of closest super-pixels for all retrieved images in D. The obtained transferred parsing results $P(y_s|s, D)$ for all super-pixels are further refined by

Figure 6: The top row shows images from FS and CFPD while the bottom row shows images from FI.

Markov Random Filed to respect boundaries of actual clothing items.

5. EXPERIMENTS

We first introduce our experimental setting, including the datasets and the baselines we compare with. Then we report the step-by-step results of the whole framework, including the quantitative and qualitative results of video pose co-estimation, video co-parsing and test image parsing.

5.1 Experimental Setting

We conduct the experiments on three datasets. The first is the Fashionista (FS) dataset [17] containing 685 photos with good visibility of the full body and covering a variety of clothing items. 456 out of the 685 images are used for training and the rest 229 images are used for testing. The second dataset is the Colorful Fashion Parsing Data (CFPD) [10] dataset which consists of 2,682 images. The training set and the testing set are split into half-half. The third dataset is our newly collected Fashion Icon (FI) dataset which contains 1,028 images. The images in this dataset contain one or multiple humans with quite diverse human poses. Some exemplar images of the three datasets are shown in Fig. 6. It can be seen that humans in constrained fashion images are in (near)-frontal view and well-posed. However, in unconstrained fashion images, the girls cross or stretch their arms or legs freely, and may be in arbitrary view. In our experiments, the label sets of FS and CFPD contain 18 and 13 kinds of fashion items, respectively. FI has two sets of label sets, one containing 18 kinds of fashion items as FS, and the other containing 13 kinds as CFPD, where the later is obtained by merging from the former. Our experiments are conducted on a PC with Core I7 3.4GHz GPU and 6GB memory, and the average processing time for testing an image with resolution $600 * 400$ is 2 seconds. The parameter η, λ_{ext} and λ_{int} are set as 0.1, 0.5 and 0.5 empirically in this work.

5.2 Experimental Results

In this subsection, we first evaluate the effectiveness of human pose co-estimation and video co-parsing sequentially. Then, we compare the results of our system and the baselines on the three datasets.

5.2.1 Video Pose Co-estimation Evaluation

We evaluate our human pose co-estimation method in predicting the poses of frames. We randomly select 100 videos from our collected video dataset and manually label 14 key points of the human skeleton for each selected video frame. We compare our results with the state-of-the-art image-based pose estimator, mixtures-of-parts model [18], which is trained on FS and predicts the pose of each frame separately. The standard PCK (Probability of Correct Key point) metric [18] is used to evaluate the performance of pose estimation. Table 1 displays the results of the frame based pose estimator (denoted as "Pose") and the video pose co-estimator (denoted as "Co-Pose"). The results demonstrate that our video pose co-estimator can generally improve the key points localization accuracies for 9 out of all 14 key points. In particular, the accuracy for the left knee point has been increased by 9.6%. Moreover, Our average PCK of all 14 key points reaches high accuracy of 78.17% and improves the "Pose" by 1.73%.

In addition, we also visualize the pose estimation results of the two comparison methods in Fig. 7. For the dancing video frames with large variations in pose and view, our method shows superior performance in predicting the key points of human poses, especially for the left and right knees. As shown in Fig. 7(a), only the left knee point of the first frame is predicted correctly for "Pose" while our method can rectify the left knee key points of all frames by benefiting from the Sift-Flow and temporal coherence constraints.

Table 3: Comparison between frame based parsing and video co-parsing

Method	Accuracy	F.g. accuracy	Avg. precision	Avg. recall	Avg. F-1
Parsing	80.48	44.79	31.98	40.64	33.18
Co-Parsing	**82.38**	**48.47**	**33.02**	**42.54**	**34.69**

5.2.2 Video Co-Parsing Evaluation

We compare the performances of our video co-parsing method with the existing image-based fashion parser [16], whose code is publicly available [2]. The 100 videos are randomly selected and all frames are manually labeled. Similar to [16], we evaluate the parsing results of all frames with 5 metrics, including accuracy, foreground accuracy, average precision, average recall and average F-1 score. The comparison results are shown in Table 3. Significant improvements of our co-parsing method for all 5 metrics can be observed.

More exemplar results are shown in Fig. 8. Video co-parsing predicts more consistent fashion labels for all video frames than the image-based fashion parser. For example, in the left panel, "Parsing" predicts that the girl wears upper clothing in three frames yet dress in two frames. Through the contextual inference of "Co-Parsing", all five frames are correctly predicted. Another example is shown in the right panel of Fig. 8. The left/right arms and left/right legs are more accurately estimated benefiting from the temporal regularizations during the co-parsing procedure.

5.2.3 Evaluation of Fashion Parsing in FS and CFPD

We report the fashion parsing performance of Paper Doll and our method on testing images in the FS and CFPD datasets. In addition, we evaluate the superiority of our pose co-estimator and video co-parsing components. The "Co-Pose+Co-Parsing" utilizes the pose co-estimator and the video co-parser sequentially. The "Co-Parsing" solution does not implement pose co-estimation and directly uses the image-based pose estimator.

The results are listed in the first two rows of Table 2. It is obvious that both of our two solutions achieve higher perfor-

[2]http://www.cs.sunysb.edu/~kyamagu/research/paperdoll/

Table 1: The PCK comparison between frame based pose estimation and video based pose co-estimation.

key point	lank	lkne	lhip	rhip	rkne	rank	lwr	lelb	lsho	rsho	relb	rwr	hbot	htop
Pose	68.88	74.13	83.39	83.92	79.37	**71.50**	43.88	**73.43**	**93.01**	90.04	**71.50**	**47.38**	94.93	94.76
Co-Pose	**74.48**	**83.73**	**87.94**	**91.78**	**80.94**	70.80	**44.58**	72.55	92.65	**91.78**	69.06	38.63	**98.08**	**97.38**

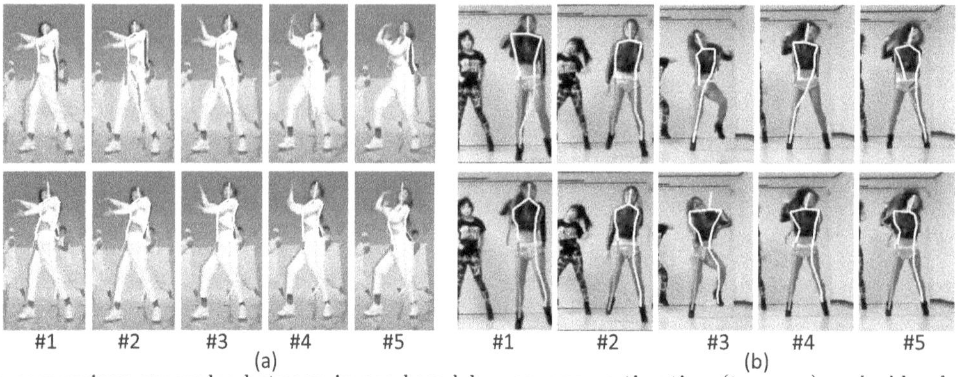

Figure 7: Two comparison examples between image based human pose estimation (top row) and video based human pose co-estimation (bottom row).

Figure 8: Comparison examples between image based fashion parsing (middle row) and video based co-parsing (bottom row).

Table 2: Comparison among Paper Doll [16] and two solutions of our method in FS, CFPD and FI.

Data set	Method	Accuracy	F.g. accuracy	Avg. precision	Avg. recall	Avg. F-1
FS-FS	Paper Doll	85.69	52.09	41.74	**45.15**	37.43
	Co-Parsing	87.21	54.03	54.73	39.36	39.15
	Co-Pose + Co-Parsing	**88.34**	**57.08**	**56.97**	42.25	**43.69**
CFPD-CFPD	Paper Doll	82.79	44.08	**49.20**	32.00	32.66
	Co-Parsing	83.73	49.03	43.56	40.36	39.96
	Co-Pose + Co-Parsing	**84.70**	**52.49**	42.31	**42.31**	**41.42**
FS-FI	Paper Doll	84.63	47.43	36.12	**39.65**	35.20
	Co-Parsing	86.26	42.09	35.96	29.30	28.31
	Co-Pose + Co-Parsing	**87.33**	**51.09**	**41.63**	39.33	**37.07**
CFPD-FI	Paper Doll	81.81	37.11	34.20	28.04	25.20
	Co-Parsing	83.84	45.77	35.14	36.04	34.00
	Co-Pose + Co-Parsing	**85.65**	**50.29**	**37.13**	**38.05**	**36.05**

mances than the Paper Doll in general, which demonstrates the capability of our contextual video co-parser. In addition, the necessity of human pose co-estimation is proven, where the avg. F1-score of "Co-Pose+Co-Parsing" outperform "Co-Parsing" by 4.54%.

We also present the F1-scores for each fashion item label in Fig. 9(a) and Fig. 9(b). Generally, the "Co-Pose+Co-Parsing" shows the highest performance, especially in predicting the human part labels, such as "LeftLeg", "LeftArm", "RightLeg" and "RightArm". We can also observe this superior performance from the visualization of parsing results in Fig. 11(a) and Fig. 12(a). The first row shows the parsing results of Paper Doll and the second row shows ours. Our parser performs better on predicting the fashion items, such as skirt, pants, and upper-clothes. In addition, our results can be less disturbed by the background clutter and show relatively clear boundary and appearance consistency, e.g. the leg regions of the second and third images in the first

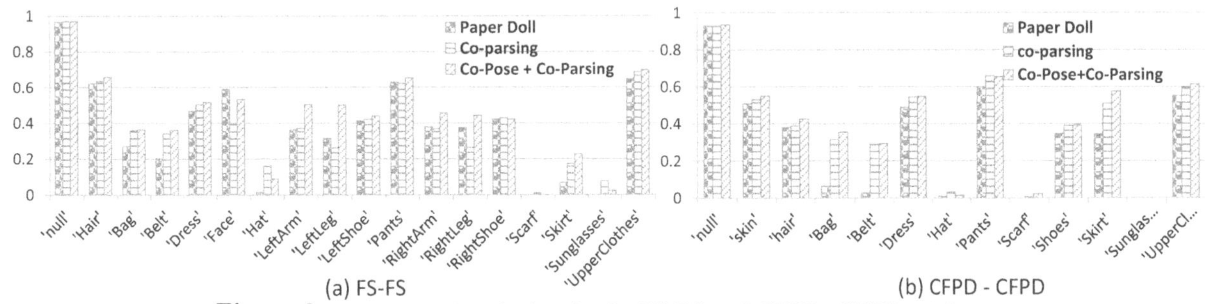

Figure 9: F-1 score of each class in the FS-FS and CFPD -CFPD settings.

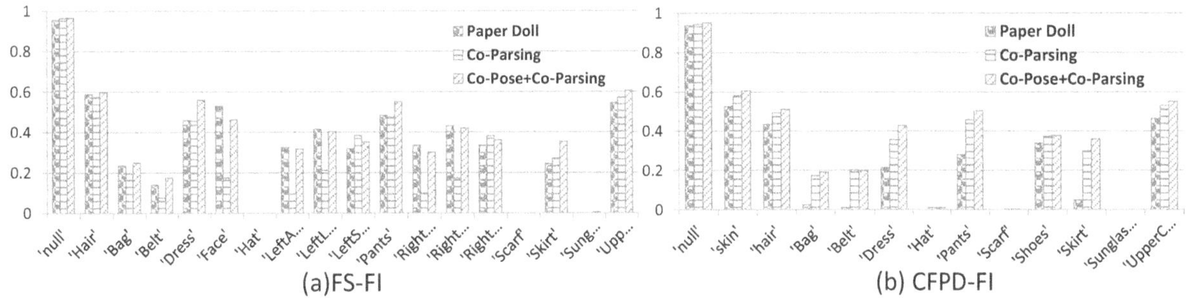

Figure 10: F-1 scores of each class in the FS-FI and CFPD-FI settings.

Figure 11: Comparison of two settings: (a) FS-FS, (b) FS-FI. In each triple, the original image, the parsing result by Paper Doll and our result are shown sequentially.

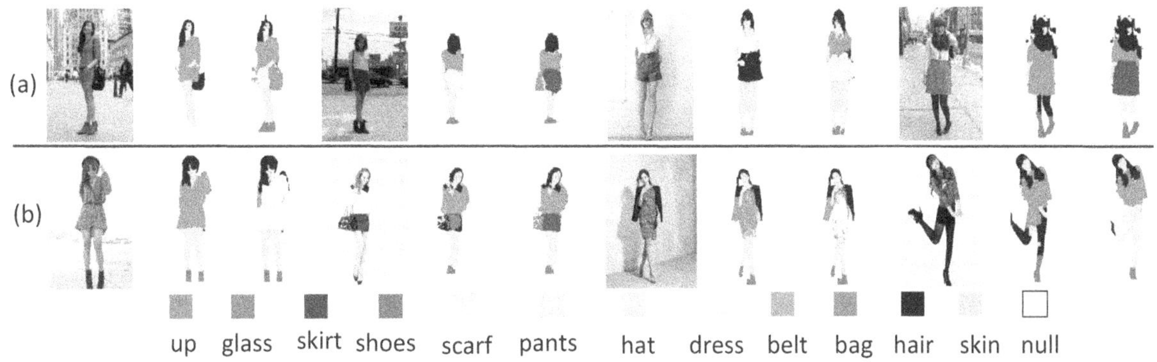

Figure 12: Comparison of two settings: (a) CFPD-CFPD, (b)CFPD-FI. In each triple, the original image, the parsing result by Paper Doll and our result are shown sequentially.

row of Fig. 11(a). Moreover, our parser can also correctly localize small fashion items, such as the bags in the second and third images in the second row of Fig. 11(a) and the third image in the first row of Fig. 11(b).

5.2.4 *Evaluation of Fashion Parsing in FI*

Our collected FI dataset contains more images with diverse poses and arbitrary views. We parse images in the FI dataset with the trained model from two training image sets, FS and CFPD, separately. The main difference between $FS-FI$ and $CFPD-FI$ is that we train two super-

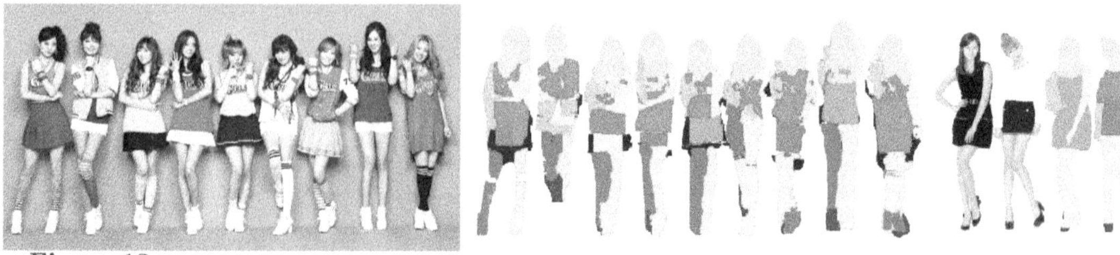
Figure 13: The results of our system in parsing images with multiple humans in the FS-FI setting.

vised parsing models with different training data and label sets. Similarly, we compare two solutions of our method, i.e., "Co-Pose+Co-Parsing" and "Co-Parsing" with the baseline Paper Doll. The quantitative comparison results show that our method largely improves the performance of Paper Doll in both settings, shown in the last two rows of Table 2. It is worth noting that our method shows larger improvements on the FI dataset than on FS and CFPD datasets. Specifically, with the same training dataset CFPD, the performance of FI is increased by 3.82% compared with 1.91% of CFPD in terms of accuracy. This well proves the advantages of our method on parsing fashion images.

The detailed comparison of each fashion item label among "Paper Doll", "Co-Parsing" and "Co-Pose+ Co-Parsing" in both FS-FI and CFPD-FI settings is illustrated in Fig. 10. In general, "Co-Pose+ Co-Parsing" outperforms "Co-Parsing" and performs much better than Paper Doll.

Moreover, the visual parsing comparisons are shown in Fig. 11(b) and Fig. 12(b) for the FS and CFPD datasets, respectively. Our system can correctly predict the fashion items for images with very diverse human poses, e.g., the second image of the first row of Fig. 11(a).

Additionally, we also conduct experiments of parsing the multi-human images under the FS-FI setting, as shown in Figure. 13. We use the detection method [6] to cut the images into several smaller images with single human only. The single human image is then fed into our system and the parsing results are generated. Then the final parsing result for each multi-human image is merged by combining the parsing of each single image. We show several results of parsing images with multiple humans and prove that our method can predict reliable parsing results when the humans are not heavily occluded.

6. CONCLUSION AND FUTURE WORK

In this paper we propose a novel framework for fashion parsing in the wild which leverages video contexts without extra annotation. It contains two components, i.e., the contextual video parsing and the non-parametric fashion parsing. Extensive experiments on two benchmark fashion datasets as well as a newly collected FI dataset demonstrate the effectiveness of our proposed framework well. We can optionally label more unconstrained images and train an unconstrained fashion parser. However, the great burden of human labelling may considerably limit the scalability of the fashion parser. Since our method only needs the unsupervised videos which can be easily crawled from the web, our solution can easily scale up to new videos with even more challenging poses and views, e.g. lying on the floor or sitting in the chair.

Two possible research directions can be considered in the future. First, we plan to develop a mobile App, which can parse images uploaded by users in an online way. Second, we can select images with uncertain results through active learning, and then annotate more frame poses and fashion parsing ground truths, which may lead to better video parsing results with a small amount of user interaction.

Acknowledgement

This work was supported by the Singapore National Research Foundation under its International Research Centre@Singapore Funding Initiative and administered by the IDM Programme Office. The work is also supported by the Hi-Tech Research and Development (863) Program of China (no. 2013AA013801) and Guangdong Science and Technology Program (no. 2012B031500006).

7. REFERENCES

[1] Vijay Badrinarayanan, Fabio Galasso, and Roberto Cipolla. Label propagation in video sequences. In *CVPR*, 2010.

[2] Huizhong Chen, Andrew Gallagher, and Bernd Girod. Describing clothing by semantic attributes. In *ECCV*. 2012.

[3] Jian Dong, Qiang Chen, Wei Xia, Zhongyang Huang, and Shuicheng Yan. A deformable mixture parsing model with parselets. In *ICCV*, 2013.

[4] Pedro F Felzenszwalb and Daniel P Huttenlocher. Efficient graph-based image segmentation. *IJCV*, 2004.

[5] Brian Fulkerson, Andrea Vedaldi, and Stefano Soatto. Class segmentation and object localization with superpixel neighborhoods. In *CVPR*, 2009.

[6] Ross B Girshick, Pedro F Felzenszwalb, and David A McAllester. Object detection with grammar models. In *NIPS*, 2011.

[7] Sam Hare, Amir Saffari, and Philip HS Torr. Struck: Structured output tracking with kernels. In *ICCV*, 2011.

[8] Yangqing Jia, Evan Shelhamer, Jeff Donahue, Sergey Karayev, Jonathan Long, Ross Girshick, Sergio Guadarrama, and Trevor Darrell. Caffe: Convolutional architecture for fast feature embedding. 2014.

[9] Ce Liu, Jenny Yuen, and Antonio Torralba. Sift flow: Dense correspondence across scenes and its applications. *TPAMI*, 2011.

[10] Si Liu, Jiashi Feng, Csaba Domokos, Hui Xu, Junshi Huang, Zhenzhen Hu, and Shuicheng Yan. Fashion parsing with weak color-category labels. *TMM*, 2014.

[11] Si Liu, Jiashi Feng, Zheng Song, Tianzhu Zhang, Hanqing Lu, Changsheng Xu, and Shuicheng Yan. Hi, magic closet, tell me what to wear! In *MM*, pages 619–628, 2012.

[12] Si Liu, Zheng Song, Guangcan Liu, Changsheng Xu, Hanqing Lu, and Shuicheng Yan. Street-to-shop: Cross-scenario clothing retrieval via parts alignment and auxiliary set. In *CVPR*, 2012.

[13] X Liu, D Tao, M Song, J Bu, and C Chen. Discriminative segment annotation in weakly labeled video. In *CVPR*, 2014.

[14] Jamie Shotton, Matthew Johnson, and Roberto Cipolla. Semantic texton forests for image categorization and segmentation. In *CVPR*, 2008.

[15] Meng Wang, Richang Hong, Xiao-Tong Yuan, Shuicheng Yan, and T-S Chua. Movie2comics: Towards a lively video content presentation. *TMM*, 2012.

[16] Kota Yamaguchi, M Hadi Kiapour, and Tamara L Berg. Paper doll parsing: Retrieving similar styles to parse clothing items. In *ICCV*, 2013.

[17] Kota Yamaguchi, M Hadi Kiapour, Luis E Ortiz, and Tamara L Berg. Parsing clothing in fashion photographs. In *CVPR*, 2012.

[18] Yi Yang and Deva Ramanan. Articulated pose estimation with flexible mixtures-of-parts. In *CVPR*, 2011.

[19] T Zhang, B Ghanem, S Liu, and N Ahuja. Robust visual tracking via multi-task sparse learning. 2012.

Daily Stress Recognition from Mobile Phone Data, Weather Conditions and Individual Traits

Andrey Bogomolov
University of Trento,
SKIL Telecom Italia Lab
Via Sommarive, 5
I-38123 Povo - Trento, Italy
andrey.bogomolov@unitn.it

Bruno Lepri
Fondazione Bruno Kessler
Via Sommarive, 18
I-38123 Povo - Trento, Italy
lepri@fbk.eu

Michela Ferron
Fondazione Bruno Kessler
via Sommarive, 18
I-38123 Povo - Trento, Italy
ferron@fbk.eu

Fabio Pianesi
Fondazione Bruno Kessler
Via Sommarive, 18
I-38123 Povo - Trento, Italy
pianesi@fbk.eu

Alex (Sandy) Pentland
MIT Media Lab
20 Ames Street
Cambridge, MA, USA
pentland@mit.edu

ABSTRACT

Research has proven that stress reduces quality of life and causes many diseases. For this reason, several researchers devised stress detection systems based on physiological parameters. However, these systems require that obtrusive sensors are continuously carried by the user. In our paper, we propose an alternative approach providing evidence that daily stress can be reliably recognized based on behavioral metrics, derived from the user's mobile phone activity and from additional indicators, such as the weather conditions (data pertaining to transitory properties of the environment) and the personality traits (data concerning permanent dispositions of individuals). Our multifactorial statistical model, which is person-independent, obtains the accuracy score of 72.28% for a 2-class daily stress recognition problem. The model is efficient to implement for most of multimedia applications due to highly reduced low-dimensional feature space (32d). Moreover, we identify and discuss the indicators which have strong predictive power.

Categories and Subject Descriptors

I.5 [**Computing Methodologies**]: PATTERN RECOGNITION—*Models, Design Methodology, Implementation*; J.4 [**Computer Applications**]: SOCIAL AND BEHAVIORAL SCIENCES—*Sociology, Psychology*

General Terms

Algorithms; Experimentation; Measurement; Theory

MM'14, November 3–7, 2014, Orlando, Florida, USA.

http://dx.doi.org/10.1145/2647868.2654933.

Keywords

stress recognition; mobile sensing; pervasive computing

1. INTRODUCTION

Nowadays, the number of mobile phones in use worldwide is about 5 billion, with millions of new subscribers everyday [1]. Mobile phones allow for unobtrusive and cost-efficient access to huge streams of previously inaccessible data related to daily social behavior [29]. These devices are able to sense a wealth of behavioral data such as (i) location, (ii) other devices in physical proximity through Bluetooth scanning, (iii) communication data, including both metadata (logs of who, when, and duration) of phone calls and text messages (sms), etc. Correspondingly, the availability is continuously growing of huge streams of *personal data* related to activities, routines and social interactions [11, 29] which represent a novel opportunity to address fundamental problems of our societies in different fields, such as mobility and urban planning [19], finance [46], healthy living and subjective well-being [31, 33].

In this work, we focus on one of the most widespread and debilitating problem of our subjective well-being and our society: stress. Stress is a well-known condition in modern life and research has shown that the amount of cumulative stress plays a role in a broad range of physical, psychological and behavioural conditions, such as anxiety, low self-esteem, depression, social isolation, cognitive impairments, sleep and immunological disorders, neurodegenerative diseases and other medical conditions [8], while also significantly contributing to healthcare costs. Hence, measuring stress in daily life situations has become an important challenge [39]. Today, the availability of huge and diverse streams of pervasive data produced by and about people allows for automatic, unobtrusive, and fast recognition of daily stress levels. An early prediction of stress symptoms can indeed help to prevent situations that are risky for human life [23].

Several studies have produced interesting results that support the feasibility of detecting stress levels through phys-

[1]http://www.ericsson.com/ericsson-mobility-report

iological sensors (see [23], [26]). However, the use of physiological sensors is limited by several shortcomings. Stress detection systems based on physiological measurement such as heart-rate variability or skin conductance are intrusive and need to be easily wearable to be exploited in natural settings; the data they produce can be confounded by daily life activities such as speaking or drinking; they exhibit important between-person differences [39].

Recently, social psychologist Miller wrote "The Smartphone Psychology Manifesto" in which he argued that the smartphones should be seriously considered as new research tools for psychology. In his opinion, these tools could revolutionize all fields of psychology and other behavioral sciences making these disciplines more powerful, sophisticated, and grounded in real-world behavior [36] and [30]. Indeed, several works have started to use smartphone activity data in order to detect and predict personality traits [6, 9, 37, 48], mood states [31], and daily happiness [38]. Stopczynski et al. [49] described the Copenhagen Networks Study, a large-scale study designed to measure human interactions spanning multiple years.

Smartphones data can be used to detect stress levels as well. Indeed, stress levels are associated with the type of activities people engage in, including those executed at/through their smartphone (for instance, a high number of phone calls and/or e-mails from many different people could be associated with higher stress levels). Weather conditions – an environmental transitory property – in turn, have been argued [24], [41] to be often associated with stress, acting either directly (as stressors) or indirectly (by affecting individual sensitivity to stressors). Finally, the impact of all these transitory factors – (smartphone) activities and weather conditions – on stress induction can be expected to be modulated by personal characteristics and differences [50], [52]. For example, a neurotic person could react with higher levels of stress to a high number of interactions (call, sms or proximity interactions) than an emotionally stable person; an extrovert or agreeable person, in turn, might well find him/herself at ease with a high number of interactions.

In this paper, we approach the automatic recognition of daily stress as a 2-class classification problem (non-stressed vs stressed) based on information concerning different types of data: a) people activities, as detected through their smartphones; b) weather conditions; c) personality traits. The information about people activities is represented by features extracted from call and sms logs and from Bluetooth hits, able to capture (i) the amount of calls, of sms and of proximity interactions; (ii) the diversity of calls, of sms, and of proximity interactions; and (iii) regularity in user behaviors. In addition, we use weather conditions (environmental and transitory factors) along with personality traits (internal and stable factors); the latter are mediating factors that can modulate people responses to stressors (e.g., weather, daily activity). This multifactorial approach will be compared to approaches based only on a family of features (personality, weather conditions, mobile phone features) or simpler combinations of families of features (personality and weather conditions; personality and mobile phone features; weather conditions and mobile phone features).

Classification experiments are performed using a variety of approaches and the best solution for our classification problem was found using an ensemble of tree classifiers based on a Random Forest algorithm. Our multifactorial approach obtains an accuracy score of 72.28% for a 2-class daily stress recognition problem, providing evidence that individual daily stress can be reliably predicted from the combination of smartphone usage data, weather conditions and individual dispositions (personality traits). Interestingly, if one of these information sources is dropped, the recognition performances decrease drastically.

In sum, the main contributions of this paper are as follows:

1. We propose a multi-factorial data-driven approach to the prediction of individual daily stress;
2. We validate our approach with a seven-months dataset collected from 111 subjects;
3. We provide a comprehensive analysis of the predictive power of the proposed approach and a comparison with approaches based only on single families of features (personality, weather conditions, mobile phone features) or pairwise combinations thereof (personality and weather conditions, personality and mobile phone features, weather conditions and mobile phone features).

2. RELATED WORK

A large body of research on stress detection focused on physiological measurements to infer stress levels (see [23], [34], [39]). Heart-rate variability, galvanic skin response, respiration, muscle activity and temperature are among the most relevant features. However, despite providing reliable insights on stress levels, this approach has major limitations because it comprises wearable sensors that need to be carried at all times to allow for continuous monitoring.

Among the different changes in physiological parameters that happen during stressful situations, variation in speech production has inspired a number of studies using acoustic sensing on smartphones. Research on stress detection based on voice analysis considered different speech characteristics such as pitch, glottal pulse, spectral slope and phonetic variations. For example, Lu and colleagues [32] proposed StressSense, an Android application for stress detection from human voice in real-life conversation, and they achieved 81% and 76% accuracy for indoor and outdoor environments.

However, these methods depend on sound quality, which is not granted in natural settings (e.g., crowded public places, noisy outdoor), and the correlation between speech and emotion is subjected to large individual differences [43]. Hence, our performance of 72.28% is a good and reliable alternative to stress detection. Other studies focused on the video analysis of behavioural correlates of psychological stress [18]. These systems, despite providing an unobtrusive method for stress monitoring, cannot be employed in a large variety of real world and mobile environments and pose privacy concerns related to the recording of people's behaviour.

A promising approach that can overcome the major shortcomings of stress detection based on physiological measures and on audio/video analysis is activity recognition from smartphone usage patterns. Studies in this field have been mainly focused on the understanding of relational dynamics of individuals [14]. Recently studies have started to investigate how smartphone usage habits can provide insights into users' affective state [31] and stress levels [1]. LiKamWa and colleagues [31] proposed MoodScope, a mobile software system that recognizes the users' mood, but not stress states, from smartphone usage analysis. They collected usage data and self-reported mood in a two months longitudinal study and used them to train mood models. Smartphone usage data consisted in phone calls, SMSes, e-mail messages, application use, web browsing histories and location changes, while self-reported mood was collected from users' input at least four times a day. MoodScope reached a 66% accuracy of participants' daily-average mood, with phone calls and categorized applications as the most useful features for mood discrimination.

Bauer and Lukowicz [1] focused on mid-term stress detection, monitoring 7 students during a two week exam session followed by two weeks of non-stressful period. The recorded data were related to participants' mobility patterns and social interactions, and included users' location, Bluetooth proximity, phone calls and SMSes. These features allowed to detect an average behaviour modification of 53% for each user during the exam session. A limitation of this study is the small number of subjects. Our multifactorial approach outperforms the approach proposed by [1] although a direct comparison may be not adequate given the different focus: our approach tend to daily classify people as "not stressed" or "stressed", while Bauer and Lukowicz try to detect stressful situations.

In 2013, Sano and Picard [42] reported an accuracy performance in stress recognition of 75% using a combination of features obtained from mobile phones and wearable sensors. However, the limited number of subjects used in their experiments (18) and the limited number of days (5) make preliminary the results of this study.

3. DATA COLLECTION

From November 12, 2010 to May 21, 2011, we collected a dataset capturing the lives of 117 subjects living in a married graduate student residency of a major US university. Our sample of subjects has a large variety in terms of provenance and cultural background: we have subjects from 16 countries such as USA, China, Israel, India, Iran, Russia, etc. During this period, each participant was equipped with an Android-based cellular phone incorporating a sensing software explicitly designed for collecting mobile data. Such software runs in a passive manner and does not interfere with the every day usage of the phone. The data collected consisted of: (a) call logs, (b) sms logs, (c) proximity data, obtained by scanning near-by phones and other Bluetooth devices every five minutes, and (d) data from surveys administered to participants, which provided self-reported information about personality traits ("Big Five") and self reported information about daily stress.

Proximity interaction data were derived from Bluetooth hits in a similar way as in previous reality mining studies [13]. Bluetooth scans were performed every 5 minutes in order to keep the battery from draining while achieving a high enough temporal resolution. The Bluetooth log of a given smartphone were then used to extract the list of the other participants' phones which were in proximity.

In total, the dataset consisted of 33497 phone calls, 22587 SMS, and 1460939 Bluetooth hits.

3.1 Stress data

At the evening, the participants were also asked to fill daily surveys about their daily self-perceived stress level. The stress information was reported by the participants filling a seven items scale with 1 = "not stressed", 4 = "neutral" and 7 = "extremely stressed". In our experiments we used the data only for the subjects (111 subjects) who had provided at least 2 weeks of consecutive data.

The distribution of daily stress is visualized in Fig. 1. We see that it has a small negative skew – the density is moved to the higher region of stress score. The distribution has negative excess kurtosis, which in our case means that the sample reported a specific daily stress score more often than the neutral. Fig. 2 shows that within-person daily stress variance is more spread than between-person, but the density of between-person variance is higher.

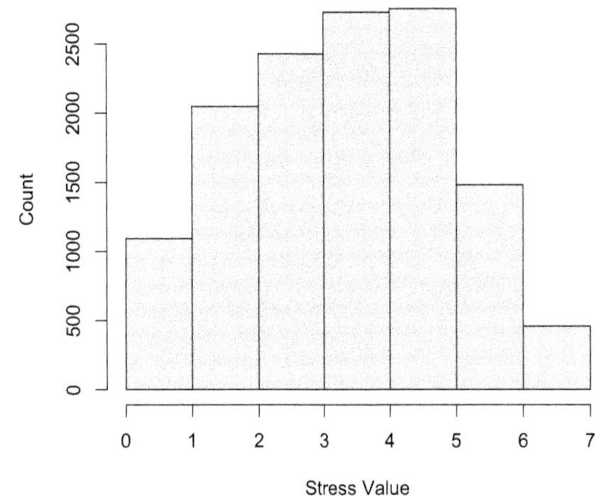

Figure 1: Recorded Stress Scores Density

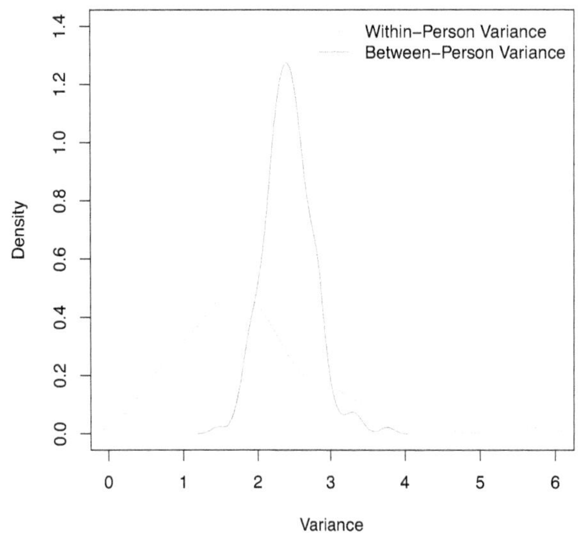

Figure 2: Within- and between-subject variance

3.2 Personality Data

Several studies in social psychology investigated the relationships between personality traits and psychological stress. Personalities that tend to be more negative are usually associated with greater distress, while outgoing and positive

Table 1: Selected Features Ranked by Mean Decrease in Accuracy

Rank	Feature	0	1	Mean Decrease in Accuracy	Mean Decrease in Gini Index
1	personality.Conscientiousness	13.65	18.04	23.35	159.96
2	personality.Agreeableness	14.22	19.73	22.92	167.30
3	personality.Neuroticism	15.96	21.04	22.56	183.87
4	personality.Openness	14.20	14.18	21.38	139.23
5	personality.Extraversion	15.75	15.02	21.07	158.51
6	weather.MeanTemperature	14.50	6.34	17.44	322.27
7	sms.RepliedEvents.Latency.Median	8.83	13.85	15.63	48.74
8	weather.Humidity	15.33	2.10	15.45	298.13
9	sms.AllEventsPerDay	8.61	0.56	10.50	42.91
10	bluetooth.Q95TimeForWhichIdSeen	4.99	6.05	9.94	32.47
11	bluetooth.MaxTimeForWhichIdSeen	6.24	7.23	9.47	32.12
12	sms.IncomingAndOutgoingPerDay	7.45	1.26	9.38	41.59
13	weather.Visibility	9.94	1.26	9.22	251.27
14	weather.WindSpeed	8.77	1.30	8.67	282.10
15	bluetooth.Q90TimeForWhichIdSeen	4.24	6.75	8.64	28.41
16	bluetooth.TotalEntropyShannon	5.04	3.51	8.56	31.37
17	call.EntropyMillerMadowOutgoingTotal	4.25	4.10	8.54	27.49
18	call.EntropyShannonOutgoingAndIncomingTotal	4.23	4.86	8.53	26.28
19	bluetooth.TotalEntropyMillerMadow	5.06	4.22	8.50	32.09
20	bluetooth.IdsMoreThan09TimeSlotsSeen	6.11	5.85	8.43	27.88
21	bluetooth.IdsMoreThan04TimeSlotsSeen	6.34	4.59	8.04	24.64
22	call.EntropyShannonMissedOutgoingTotal	3.13	4.92	7.85	24.34
23	bluetooth.IdsMoreThan19TimeSlotsSeen	2.97	5.16	7.78	20.87
24	call.EntropyShannonOutgoingTotal	3.10	6.45	7.78	24.79
25	bluetooth.Q75TimeForWhichIdSeen	5.16	4.70	7.76	22.07
26	call.EntropyMillerMadowMissedOutgoingTotal	4.09	5.45	7.55	24.64
27	call.EntropyMillerMadowOutgoingAndIncomingTotal	3.87	6.29	7.51	28.63
28	sms.OutgoingAndIncomingTotalEntropyMillerMadow	4.68	3.84	7.19	17.63
29	sms.OutgoingTotalEntropyMillerMadow	5.22	1.49	7.19	18.88
30	bluetooth.Q50TimeForWhichIdSeen	1.53	7.29	7.08	18.91
31	bluetooth.Q68TimeForWhichIdSeen	2.36	5.96	6.68	19.05
32	sms.OutgoingTotalEntropyShannon	2.53	2.77	5.13	17.59

personalities generally experience less distress [50], [52]. The majority of the studies that have examined the relationship between personality and distress focused on the Big Five traits [25], a personality model owing its name to the five traits it takes as a constitutive of people's personality: Extraversion, Neuroticism, Agreeableness, Conscientiousness, and Openness to experience. Researchers showed significant associations between psychological stress, on the one hand, and Neuroticism, Extraversion and Conscientiousness, on the other. Duggan et al. [12] found that individuals high in Neuroticism may be more vulnerable to experiencing distress as they respond more negatively to daily stressors and report more daily stressful events and higher levels of daily stress. When people with high scores in Neuroticism encounter stressful events, they tend to experience them as more aversive than those low in this trait [3], [21]. Finally, in a study with university students, Volrath and Torgensen [52] showed that students with more adaptive personalities such as Extraversion and Conscientiousness are more positive and sociable and hence less affected by daily stress.

In our study, Big Five personality traits were measured by asking subjects to answer the online version of the 44 questions Big Five questionnaire developed by John et al. [25], by means of 5-point likert scales. The scores on the five traits were the average over the raw scores (inverted when needed) of the items pertaining to each trait.

3.3 Weather data

The question about the relationship between mood, health and weather has been extensively debated [22], [41]. Studies in environmental psychology investigated the role of weather as a stressor and showed significant effects of temperature, hours of sunshine and humidity on mood [24], [41]. A large-scale study by Faust and colleagues [15] on 16,000 students in Switzerland showed an association between weather and sleep disorders, depressed mood and irritability. More recently, Denissen et al. [10] investigated the effects of six daily weather variables (temperature, wind power, sunlight, precipitation, air pressure, photoperiod) on three mood variables (positive affect, negative affect, and tiredness). Their results revealed main effects of temperature, wind power, and sunlight on negative affect, while sunlight had also a main effect on tiredness and mediated the effects of precipitation and air pressure on tiredness.

In our experiments, we used the following weather variables: (i) mean temperature, (ii) pressure, (iii) total precipitation, (iv) humidity, (v) visibility and (vi) wind speed (measured in m/s) metrics. The source weather data were collected from Wolfram Alpha [2]. All weather metrics are computed on a daily scale for the same day that is under investigation and the source data are extracted from the Boston area weather stations (e.g. KBOS) located on the same relative elevation as the campus where the data collection was performed.

4. FEATURE EXTRACTION

Based on previous works that characterize social interactions by means of mobile phone data and use social interactions data to predict people's behaviors, states [2,31], and traits [6,9,37], we derived the 25 call and sms basic features reported in Table 2 and the 9 proximity basic features reported in Table 3.

For each basic feature, we calculated second order features, such as mean, median, min, max, 99%, 95% quan-

[2]http://www.wolframalpha.com

tiles, quantiles corresponding to 0.5, 1, 1.5 and 2 standard deviations (applying Chebyshev's inequality), variance and standard deviation functions. Moreover, for each basic feature we calculated the same functions as above for 2 and 3 days backward-moving window to account for the possibility that past events influenced the current stress state.

In the following subsections we will describe more in detail the 25 call and sms basic features and the 9 proximity basic features.

4.1 Call and Sms Features

The features reported in Table 2 fall under four broad categories: (i) general phone usage, (ii) active behaviors, (iii) regularity, and (iv) diversity.

Table 2: List of Basic Features

General Phone Usage
1. Total Number of Calls (Outgoing+Incoming)
2. Total Number of Incoming Calls
3. Total Number of Outgoing Calls
4. Total Number of Missed Calls
5. Number of SMS received
6. Number of SMS sent
Diversity
7. Number of Unique Contacts Called
8. Number of Unique Contacts who Called
9. Number of Unique Contacts Communicated with (Incoming+Outgoing)
10. Number of Unique Contacts Associated with Missed Calls
11. Entropy of Call Contacts
12. Call Contacts to Interactions Ratio
13. Number of Unique Contacts SMS received from
14. Number of Unique Contacts SMS sent to
15. Entropy of SMS Contacts
16. Sms Contacts to Interactions Ratio
Active Behaviors
17. Percent Call During the Night
18. Percent Call Initiated
19. Sms response rate
20. Sms response latency
21. Percent SMS Initiated
Regularity
22. Average Inter-event Time for Calls (time elapsed between two events)
23. Average Inter-event Time for SMS (time elapsed between two events)
24. Variance Inter-event Time for Calls (time elapsed between two events)
25. Variance Inter-event Time for SMS (time elapsed between two events)

Features for *general phone usage* consist of: the total number of outgoing, incoming and missed calls and the total number of sent/received sms. Moreover, we also computed the following ratios: outgoing to incoming calls, missed to (outgoing + incoming) calls, sent to received sms.

Then, we captured the *active behaviors* of an individual computing the following features: (i) percentage of calls done during the night, (ii) percentage of initiated calls during the night, (iii) the sms response rate, (iv) the sms response latency, and (v) the percentage of initiated sms. In particular, we consider a text from a user (A) to be a response to a text received from another user (B) if it is sent within an hour after user A received the last text from user B. The response rate is the percentage of texts people respond to. The latency is the median time it takes people to answer a text. Note that by definition, latency will be less or equal to one hour.

Diversity and *regularity* have been shown to be important for the characterization of different facets of human behavior. In particular, entropy, used as a measure of diversity, has been successfully applied to predict mobility [47], spending patterns [28, 46], online behavior [44] and personality traits [37]. Concerning *regularity* features, we measured the time elapsed between calls, the time elapsed between sms exchanges and the time elapsed between call and sms. More precisely, we consider both the average and the variance of the inter-event time of one's call, sms and sum thereof (call+sms). Noticeably, in fact, even when two users have the same inter-event time for both call and sms, that quantity can be different for their sum.

Diversity measures how evenly an individual's time is distributed among others. In our case, the diversity of user behavior is addressed by means of three kinds of features: (i) entropy of contacts, (ii) unique contacts to interactions ratio, (iii) number of unique contacts, all computed both on calls and on sms. In particular, the entropy of an individual is the ratio between his/her total number of contacts and the relative frequency at which he/she interacts with them. The more one interacts equally often with a large number of contacts, the higher the entropy will be. For entropy calculation, we applied *Miller-Madow correction* [35], which is explained in Equation 1.

$$\hat{H}_{MM}(\theta) \equiv -\sum_{i=1}^{p} \theta_{ML,i} \log \theta_{ML,i} + \frac{\hat{m}-1}{2N}, \qquad (1)$$

where $\hat{m}$ is a number of bins with nonzero θ-probability. The likelihood function is given as the product of probability density functions $P(\theta) = f(x_1;\theta)f(x_2;\theta)\cdots f(x_n;\theta)$ for a random sample $X_1, \cdots, X_n$. θ_{ML} is the maximum likelihood estimate of θ, which maximizes $P(\theta)$. Miller-Madow correction was applied, dealing with the data quality problems, to get bias-corrected empirical entropy estimate.

4.2 Proximity Features

Starting from the Bluetooth hits collected, we filtered out all the cases with $RSSI < 0$. From the filtered Bluetooth proximity data we extracted the following basic Bluetooth proximity features (Table 3). In this case, the extracted features fall under three broad categories: (i) general proximity information, (ii) diversity, and (iii) regularity. As for call and sms, we applied Miller-Madow correction for entropy calculation.

Table 3: List of Basic Bluetooth Proximity Features

General Bluetooth Proximity
1. Number of Bluetooth IDs
2. Times most common Bluetooth ID is seen
3. Bluetooth IDs accounting for n% of IDs seen
4. Bluetooth IDs seen for more than k time slots
5. Time interval for which a Bluetooth ID is seen
6. Entropy of Bluetooth contacts
Diversity
7. Contacts to interactions ratio
Regularity
8. Average Bluetooth interactions inter-event time (time elapsed between two events)
9. Variance of the Bluetooth interactions inter-event time (time elapsed between two events)

5. METHODOLOGY

We formulated the automatic recognition of daily stress as a binary classification problem ("not stressed" vs "stressed"), with labels 0 for "not stressed" and label 1 for "stressed". The two classes included all the cases with scores <= 4 and scores > 4, respectively. The sizes of the resulting two classes are

36.16% for "stressed" and 63.84% for "not stressed". The inclusion of the cases with stress=4 in the 0 class meant to provide a more clearcut distinction between the "stressed" and the "non-stressed" cases.

The data set was then randomly split into a training (80% of data) and a testing (20% of data) dataset, carefully avoiding that data for the same subjects appeared in both the training- and in the test-set. In order to accelerate the convergence of the models, we *normalized* each dimension of the feature vector [4]. Additionaly, we also used a leave-one-subject-out cross-validation strategy. Hence, 111 models for each personality trait were trained on 110-subject subsets, evaluating them against the remaining ones and finally averaging the results. The results obtained are not significantly different from the ones obtained using the random split 80% vs 20%. In the rest of the paper, we will discuss only the results obtained with the random split 80% vs 20%.

5.1 Feature Selection

As an initial step, we carried out a *Pearson correlation analysis* to visualize and better understand the relations between variables in the feature space. We found quite a large subset of features with strong mutual correlations and another subset of uncorrelated features. Hence, there was room for feature space reduction. We excluded using *principal component analysis* (PCA) because the transformation it is based on produces new variables that are difficult to interpret in terms of the original ones making the interpretation of the results more complex.

Therefore, we turned to a pipelined *variable selection* approach, based on *feature ranking* and *feature subset selection*, which was perfomed using only data from the training set. The metric used for feature ranking was the mean decrease in the *Gini coefficient of inequality*. This choice was motivated because it outperformed other metrics, such as mutual information, information gain and chi-square statistic with an average improvement of approximately 28.5%, 19% and 9.2% respectively [45]. The Gini coefficient ranges between 0, expressing perfect equality in predictive power and 1, expressing maximal inequality in predictive power. The feature with maximum mean decrease in Gini coefficient is expected to have the maximum influence in minimizing the out-of-the-bag error. It is known in the literature that minimizing the out-of-the-bag error results in maximizing common performance metrics used to evaluate models (*e.g.* accuracy, F1, AUC, etc.) [51].

The feature selection procedure produced a reduced subset of 32 features from an initial pool of about 500 features. Hence, we obtained a low-dimensional feature space that makes our approach efficient to implement into mobile and multimedia applications.

5.2 Model Building

We trained a variety of classifiers: (i) an ensemble of tree classifiers based on a Random Forest algorithm [5], (ii) a Generalized Boosted Model (GBM) [16], (iii) Support Vector Machines with linear and Gaussian radial basis kernels, and (iv) Neural Networks. The best solution of the classification problem was found using an ensemble of tree classifiers based on *Random Forest* algorithm. In the rest of the paper, we report the performance results only for Random Forest.

Random forest algorithm produces a combination of simple decision tree predictors, such that each tree is dependent on the values of a random vector sampled independently with the same distribution for all the classification trees in the forest [5]. The decision boundary is formed according to the margin function. Given an ensemble of tree classifiers $h_1(\mathbf{x}), h_2(\mathbf{x}), ..., h_K(\mathbf{x})$ and if the training set is drawn at random from the empirical distribution of the random vector $Y, \mathbf{X}$ the margin function is defined as:

$$mg(\mathbf{X}, Y) = avg_k I(h_k(\mathbf{X}) = Y) - \max_{j!=Y} avg_k I(h_k(\mathbf{X}) = j), \tag{2}$$

where $I(\cdot)$ is the characteristic function. The margin function measures the distance between the average votes at $(\mathbf{X}, Y)$ for the right class and the average vote for any other class. For this model the generalization error function is:

$$PE^* = P_{\mathbf{X},Y}(mg(\mathbf{X}, Y) < 0), \tag{3}$$

where $P_{\mathbf{X},Y}$ is the probability over $\langle \mathbf{X}, Y \rangle$ space. For any event $A \subset \Omega$ of the feature space the characteristic function $I(\cdot)$ of A is:

$$I_A(x) = \begin{Bmatrix} 1 & \iff (x \subset A) \\ 0 & otherwise \end{Bmatrix} \begin{Bmatrix} 1 & \iff \exists x \\ 0 & otherwise \end{Bmatrix} \tag{4}$$

Random Forests classifiers were trained with a stepwise increase of the number of trees equal to the upper limit of 2^{11}. Optimal number of trees for model generalization as measured by mean misclassification rate for 10-fold cross-validation strategy is estimated to be 112 trees.

In order to find the final model, we trained a number of models and selected the best one based on κ metrics for the 10-fold validation strategy. The Cohen's κ measures pairwise agreement among a set of functions which are making classification decisions with correction for an expected chance agreement [7]:

$$\kappa = \frac{P(A) - P(E)}{1 - P(E)} \tag{5}$$

$\kappa = 0$ if there is no agreement more than expected by chance following the empirical distribution; while $\kappa = 1$ when there is a *max* agreement. κ is a state-of-the-art statistics about how significantly the classification model is different from chance. Importantly, κ is a more robust measure than the simple percent agreement, given that it takes into account chance agreement occurring without being too conservative.

During the learning and model selection process we used a random sampling with replacement to generate a new set of data for each fold from the basic training set, and followed leave-one-out 10-fold cross validation scheme. We adopted this strategy in order to prevent data overfitting and to deal with potential data loss in cases where calls, sms and Bluetooth proximities existed in the real world but were not registered by the smartphone logger software. Our *structural risk minimization*, as opposed to empirical risk minimization solution to prevent data overfitting, was incorporated by working with a regularization penalty into the learning process, balancing the model's complexity against training data fitting and by sampling the model training sets in such a way that they mimic the empirical distributions without most probable erroneous outliers.

Model parameter estimation selection was done iteratively on the basis of our exploratory analysis, inferred knowledge of the relationships between variables and model performance metrics (κ and Accuracy). Confounding variables are identified but not removed from the dataset during training and test phases.

6. EXPERIMENTAL RESULTS

The performance metrics used to evaluate our approach are: accuracy, κ, sensitivity, and specificity. The recognition model based on random forest algorithm shows 90.68% accuracy on the training set and 72.28% accuracy on the test set. In Table 4 we provide the final stress recognition model performances on the test set along with their statistical significance [17].

Metric	Value
Accuracy	0.7228
95% CI	(0.7051, 0.7399)
No Information Rate	0.6384
P-Value [Acc > NIR]	< 2.2e-16
Kappa	0.3752
Sensitivity	0.5272
Specificity	0.8335
'Positive' Class	"stressed"

Table 4: Recognition Model Performance Metrics

Information about accuracy and κ metrics distribution using 10-fold cross validation strategy is provided in Table 5. As we can see, the distribution of the estimated performance metrics does not vary substantially among folds, signaling a good generalization despite the possible existence of heterogeneous data in each fold and the "noise" coming from the resampling procedure.

	Accuracy	Kappa
Min.	0.6959	0.2995
1st Qu.	0.7156	0.3535
Median	0.7282	0.3817
Mean	0.7232	0.3684
3rd Qu.	0.7312	0.3869
Max.	0.7404	0.4010

Table 5: 10-fold Cross-Validation Metrics

We also compared our approach based on combining multiple indicators with simpler approaches using as predictors (i) only personality traits, (ii) only weather conditions, (iii) only activities inferred from mobile phone data, (iv) a combination of personality traits and weather conditions, (v) a combination of personality traits and activities inferred from mobile phone data, (vi) a combination of weather conditions and activities inferred from mobile phone data. Table 6 reports accuracy, κ, sensitivity, specificity and F1 for each approach. In this table we also report the performance of (vii) a simple majority classifier, which always returns the majority class as prediction (accuracy = 63.84%). Finally, we also ran experiments with three classes ("not stressed", "neutral", "stressed"), with labels -1 for "not stressed", label 0 for "neutral", and label 1 for "stressed". The class "not stressed" included all the cases with scores < 4, the class "neutral" included all the cases with scores $= 4$, and the class "stressed" included all the scores > 4. The sizes of the resulting three classes are 42.83% for "not stressed", 20.98% for "neutral", and 36.15% for "stressed". The global accuracy obtained by our multifactorial model, 59.57%, significantly outperformed the performance of simple majority classifier, which always returns the class "not stressed" as prediction.

7. DISCUSSION

The comparison among the performance of the various models in Table 6 provides convincing evidence that none of the features sets (personality, weather, smartphone activity) considered alone is endowed with a good enough predictive power. This conclusion applies also to pairwise combinations of the same features sets to the extent that neither personality+smartphone activity, nor personality+weather, nor weather+smartphone activity do any better than the majority classifier (accuracy=63.84%). Interestingly, significant improvements over the latter can only be obtained by the simultaneous usage of the three features sets: our final model based on a Random Forest classifier using 32-dimensional feature vectors obtained a 72.28% accuracy for our 2-class classification problem.

As pointed out in Section 2, some recent works have used mobile phones data for stress recognition [1,42]. Bauer and Lukowicz [1] reported a 53% of accuracy in detecting the transition from stressful periods (a two week exam session) to non-stressful periods (two weeks after the exam session). Our multifactorial approach outperforms the approach proposed by [1] altough a direct comparison may be not adequate given the different task. More recently, Sano and Picard reported an accuracy performance of 75% using a combination of features from mobile phones and more obtrusive wearable sensors. However, the limited number of subjects (only 18) and the limited number of days (only 5) make the results preliminary. Other approaches used video and audio features for stress recognition [18,32]. For instance, StressSense, an application for stress detection from human voice, achieved a 76% of accuracy in outdoor environments. However, this method depends on sound quality and it may pose privacy concerns for people perceiving voice recording and analysis as a threat to their privacy. Hence, our performance of 72.28 shows that the proposed multifactorial approach is a reliable and less obtrusive alternative.

An investigation of the most important predictors of daily stress reveales interesting associations. Table 1 reports the 32 features selected and used in our model ranked by their mean reduction in accuracy. All the personality traits contributes significantly in predicting the daily stress variable. These results are interesting because the previous studies in social psychology focused their analyses mainly on the associations between stress and Neuroticism, Extraversion and Conscientiousness. Instead, our work shows the important contribution played also by Agreeableness and Openness to Experience to the automatic classification of daily stress. Moreover, these results open us the possibility of creating a multi-step stochastic model in which we first estimate the personality and then we use those estimates as independent variables for the daily stress recognition problem. Our current approach uses self-reported information on personality and this strategy could be a limitation for scaling to larger sample of users. However, recent studies showed that personality traits may be reliable recognized from mobile phone data [6,9,37,48].

With regard to weather, we found confirmation for the association between temperature and stress. Moreover, sig-

Table 6: Model Metrics Comparison for Feature Subsets

Model	Accuracy	Kappa	Sensitivity	Specificity	F1
Our Multifactorial Model	72.28	37.52	52.72	83.35	57.89
Baseline Majority Classifier	63.84	0.00	100.00	0.00	0.00
Weather Only	36.16	0.00	100.00	0.00	0.00
Personality Only	36.16	0.00	100.00	0.00	0.00
Bluetooth+Call+Sms	48.59	6.80	73.80	34.32	50.94
Personality+Weather	43.55	2.96	81.90	21.83	51.20
Personality+Bluetooth+Call+Sms	46.40	7.01	83.17	25.57	52.88
Weather+Bluetooth+Call+Sms	49.60	-5.45	38.45	55.91	35.55

nificant effects of other meteorological variables – humidity, visibility, and wind speed – for predicting daily stress were also found.

Regarding the mobile phone data, it is interesting to note the contribution of proximity features. Out of the selected 32 features, 11 features are proximity ones, 6 comes from call data and 6 from sms data. In particular, an interesting predictive role is played by the number of time intervals for which an id is seen. The results obtained using proximity features seem to confirm previous findings in social psychology: in particular, the relevant role played by face-to-face interactions and by interactions with strong ties in determining the stress level of a subject [27]. For sure, this result requires further investigation. In addition, two features capturing the entropy in proximity interactions are among the selected ones. This finding seems to confirm results available in the social psychological literature about the associations between stress and the richness/diversity of social interactions [20]. Further confirmation to this conclusion comes from the similalry important role played by entropy-based call and sms features.

The remaining selected features related to sms interactions are (i) the latency in replying to a text message, defined as the median time to answer a text message and (ii) the amount of sms communications (outgoing+incoming).

8. IMPLICATIONS AND LIMITATIONS

Stress has become a major problem in our society. Ubiquitous connectivity, information overload, increased mental workload and time pressure are all elements contributing to increase general stress levels. While in some cases people may realize that they are undergoing stressful situations, severe and chronic stress may be more difficult to detect. Moreover, stress may be considered the norm in a modern and demanding society. Nonetheless, while slightly increased stress levels may be functional for productivity, prolonged and severe stress can be at the source of several physical dysfunctions like headache, sleep or immunological disorders, unhealthy behaviours such as smoking and bad eating habits, as well as of psychological and relational problems. Beside manifest social costs, stress also entails considerable financial costs for our economies, which are estimated by the World Health Organization in 300 billion dollars a year for American enterprises, and 20 billion euro for Europe ones, in terms of absenteeism and low productivity.

Our technology provides a cost-effective, unobtrusive, widely available and reliable tool for stress recognition. It detects daily stress levels with a 72.28% accuracy combining real life data from different sources, such as personality traits, social relationships (in terms of calls, sms and proximity interactions), and weather data. The development of a reliable stress recognition system is a first but essential step toward wellbeing and sustainable living, and its scope can be extended to different areas of applicability. Providing people with a tool capable of gathering rich data about real life, and transforming them into meaningful insights about stress levels, paves the way to a new generation of context-aware technologies that can target therapists, enterpises and common citizens.

This technology can inform the design of automatic systems for the assessment and treatment of psychological stress. With such a tool, therapists could monitor and record patients' daily stress levels, access longitudinal data, identify recurrent or significant stressors and modulate treatment accordingly.

In work environments, where stress has become a serious problem affecting productivity, leading to occupational issues and causing health diseases, our system could be extended and employed for early detection of stress-related conflicts and stress contagion, and for supporting balanced workloads. Awareness is a first but crucial step to motivate people to change their behaviour and take informed and concrete steps toward a healthy lifestyle and appropriate stress coping strategies. Mobile applications developed on the basis of our technology could provide feedback to increase people's awareness of their stress levels, alerts when they reach a warning threshold, and suggest stress management and relaxation techniques when appropriate.

However, our study has also some limitations. We can list the following ones: (i) our sample comes from a population living in the same environment. Our subjects were all married graduate students living in a campus facility of a major US university; and (ii) the non-availability of proximity data concerning the interaction with people not participating in the data collection, a fact that is common to many other relevant studies and that has been also pointed out by [40]. The first problem is at least partially attenuated by the large variability of the sample in terms of provenance and cultural background (in our sample we have subjects from 16 countries and from all the continents), which can be expected to correspond to a wide palette of interaction behaviors that efficaciously counterbalance the effects of living-place homogeneity.

9. CONCLUSION

The goal of this paper was to investigate the automatic recognition of people's daily stress from three different sets of data: a) people activity, as detected through their smartphones (data pertaining to transitory properties of individuals); b) weather conditions (data pertaining to transitory properties of the environment); and c) personality traits (data concerning permanent dispositions of individuals). The problem was modeled as a 2-way classification one. The results convincingly suggest that all the three types of data are necessary for attaining a reasonable predictive power. As long as one of those information sources is dropped, performances drop below those of the baselines. Moreover, the distributional data for accuracy and κ show the robustness and generalization power of our multifactorial approach.

Taken together, and despite the limitations discussed above, our results not only provide evidence that individual daily stress can be reliably predicted, but they also point to the necessity of considering at the same time people's transitory properties (smartphone activity), transitory properties of the environment and information about stable individual characteristics. For the sake of transitory individual properties, mobile phone usage patterns have important advantage over alternative methods: they are less unobtrusive and raise limited privacy problems as compared to, e.g., voice analysis or the exploitation of data from physiological sensors. Moreover, and importantly, automatic stress detection based on mobile phone data can take advantage of the extensive usage and diffusion of these devices, it can be applied in several real world situations and it can be exploited for a variety of applications that are delivered by means of the same device. For example, applications used to inform the design of clinical decision support systems or self-monitoring applications of stress levels in work settings and in other daily life situations, which allows people to identify personal stressors and enforces their proactive role in stress prevention and management.

Acknowledgment

This work was partially supported by Telecom Italia Semantics and Knowledge Innovation Laboratory (SKIL) with research grant T.

10. REFERENCES

[1] G. Bauer and P. Lukowicz. Can smartphones detect stress-related changes in the behaviour of individuals? In *Pervasive Computing and Communications Workshops (PERCOM Workshops), 2012 IEEE International Conference on*, pages 423–426. IEEE, 2012.

[2] A. Bogomolov, B. Lepri, and F. Pianesi. Happiness recognition from mobile phone data. *Proceedings of the 2013 International Conference on Social Computing (SocialCom 2013)*, pages 790–795, 2013.

[3] N. Bolger and E. A. Schilling. Personality and the problems of everyday life: The role of neuroticism in exposure and reactivity to daily stressors. *Journal of Personality*, 59(3):355–386, 1991.

[4] G. E. P. Box and D. R. Cox. An Analysis of Transformations. *Journal of the Royal Statistical Society. Series B (Methodological)*, 26(2):211–252, 1964.

[5] L. Breiman. Random forests. *Mach. Learn.*, 45(1):5–32, Oct. 2001.

[6] G. Chittaranjan, J. Blom, and D. Gatica-Perez. Mining large-scale smartphone data for personality studies. *Personal Ubiquitous Comput.*, 17(3):433–450, Mar. 2013.

[7] J. Cohen. A Coefficient of Agreement for Nominal Scales. *Educational and Psychological Measurement*, 20(1):37–46, Apr. 1960.

[8] S. Cohen, K. R. C., and L. U. Gordon. *Measuring stress: A guide for health and social scientists.* Oxford University Press, USA, 1997.

[9] R. de Oliveira, A. Karatzoglou, P. Concejero Cerezo, A. Armenta Lopez de Vicuña, and N. Oliver. Towards a psychographic user model from mobile phone usage. In *CHI'11 Extended Abstracts on Human Factors in Computing Systems*, pages 2191–2196. ACM, 2011.

[10] J. Denissen, L. Butalid, L. Penke, and M. Van Aken. The effects of weather on daily mood: A multilevel approach. *Emotion Researcher*, 8(5):662–667, 2008.

[11] W. Dong, B. Lepri, and A. Pentland. Modeling the co-evolution of behaviors and social relationships using mobile phone data. In *MUM*, pages 134–143, 2011.

[12] C. Duggan, P. Sham, A. Lee, C. Minne, and R. Murray. Neuroticism: a vulnerability marker for depression evidence from a family study. *Journal of Affective Disorders*, 35(3):139 – 143, 1995.

[13] N. Eagle and A. Pentland. Reality mining: sensing complex social systems. *Personal and Ubiquitous Computing*, 10(4):255–268, 2006.

[14] N. Eagle, A. S. Pentland, and D. Lazer. Inferring friendship network structure by using mobile phone data. *Proceedings of the National Academy of Sciences*, 106(36):15274–15278, 2009.

[15] V. Faust, M. Weidmann, and W. Wehner. The influence of meteorological factors on children and youths: A 10% random selection of 16,000 pupils and apprentices of basle city (switzerland). *Acta Paedopsychiatrica: International Journal of Child & Adolescent Psychiatry*, 1974.

[16] Y. Freund and R. E. Schapire. A decision-theoretic generalization of on-line learning and an application to boosting. *Journal of Computer and System Sciences*, 55(1):119 – 139, 1997.

[17] S. Garcia and F. Herrera. An Extension on "Statistical Comparisons of Classifiers over Multiple Data Sets" for all Pairwise Comparisons. *Journal of Machine Learning Research*, 9:2677–2694, Dec. 2008.

[18] D. Giakoumis, A. Drosou, P. Cipresso, D. Tzovaras, G. Hassapis, A. Gaggioli, and G. Riva. Real-time monitoring of behavioural parameters related to psychological stress. *Studies in health technology and informatics*, 181:287, 2012.

[19] M. Gonzalez, C. Hidalgo, and L. Barabasi. Understanding individual mobility patterns. *Nature*, 453(7196):779–782, 2008.

[20] W. J. Goode. A theory of role strain. *American Sociological Review*, 25(4):pp. 483–496, 1960.

[21] L. H. A. S. Gunthert, Kathleen Cimbolic; Cohen. The role of neuroticism in daily stress and coping. *Journal of Personality and Social Psychology*, 77:1087–1100, 1999.

[22] J. Hardt and H. Gerbershagen. No changes in mood with the seasons: observations in 3000 chronic pain patients. *Acta Psychiatrica Scandinavica*, 100(4):288–294, 1999.

[23] J. Healey and R. Picard. Detecting stress during real-world driving tasks using physiological sensors. *Intelligent Transportation Systems, IEEE Transactions on*, 6(2):156–166, 2005.

[24] E. Howarth and M. S. Hoffman. A multidimensional approach to the relationship between mood and weather. *British Journal of Psychology*, 75(1):15–23, 1984.

[25] O. P. John and S. Srivastava. The Big Five trait taxonomy: History, measurement, and theoretical perspectives. In L. A. Pervin and O. P. John, editors, *Handbook of Personality: Theory and Research*, pages 102–138. Guilford Press, New York, second edition, 1999.

[26] E. Jovanov, A. O'Donnell Lords, D. Raskovic, P. Cox, R. Adhami, and F. Andrasik. Stress monitoring using a distributed wireless intelligent sensor system. *Engineering in Medicine and Biology Magazine, IEEE*, 22(3):49–55, 2003.

[27] D. Krackhardt. The strength of strong ties: The importance of philos in organizations. pages 216–239, 1992.

[28] C. Krumme, A. Llorente, M. Cebrian, A. Pentland, and E. Moro. The predictability of consumer visitation patterns. *Scientific Reports*, (1645), 2013.

[29] N. D. Lane, E. Miluzzo, H. Lu, D. Peebles, T. Choudhury, and A. T. Campbell. A survey of mobile phone sensing. *IEEE Communications Magazine*, 48(9):140–150, 2010.

[30] N. Lathia, K. K. Rachuri, C. Mascolo, and P. J. Rentfrow. Contextual dissonance: Design bias in sensor-based experience sampling methods. *Proceedings of Ubicomp 2013*, pages 183–192, 2013.

[31] R. LiKamWa, Y. Liu, N. D. Lane, and L. Zhong. Moodscope: building a mood sensor from smartphone usage patterns. In *Proceeding of the 11th annual international conference on Mobile systems, applications, and services*, MobiSys '13, pages 389–402, New York, NY, USA, 2013. ACM.

[32] H. Lu, D. Frauendorfer, M. Rabbi, M. S. Mast, G. T. Chittaranjan, A. T. Campbell, D. Gatica-Perez, and T. Choudhury. Stresssense: detecting stress in unconstrained acoustic environments using smartphones. In *Proceedings of the 2012 ACM Conference on Ubiquitous Computing*, UbiComp '12, pages 351–360, New York, NY, USA, 2012. ACM.

[33] A. Madan, M. Cebrián, S. T. Moturu, K. Farrahi, and A. Pentland. Sensing the "health state" of a community. *IEEE Pervasive Computing*, 11(4):36–45, 2012.

[34] D. Majoe, P. Bonhof, T. Kaegi-Trachsel, J. Gutknecht, and L. Widmer. Stress and sleep quality estimation from a smart wearable sensor. In *Pervasive Computing and Applications (ICPCA), 2010 5th International Conference on*, pages 14–19, 2010.

[35] G. Miller. Note on the bias of information estimates. *Information theory in psychology: Problems and methods*, 2(95):100, 1955.

[36] G. Miller. The smartphone psychology manifesto. *Perspectives on Psychological Science*, 7(3):221–237, 2012.

[37] Y.-A. Montjoye, J. Quoidbach, F. Robic, and A. Pentland. Predicting personality using novel mobile phone-based metrics. In A. Greenberg, W. Kennedy, and N. Bos, editors, *Social Computing, Behavioral-Cultural Modeling and Prediction*, volume 7812 of *Lecture Notes in Computer Science*, pages 48–55. Springer Berlin Heidelberg, 2013.

[38] A. Muaremi, B. Arnrich, and G. Tröster. A survey on measuring happiness with smart phones. In *6th International Workshop on Ubiquitous Health and Wellness (UbiHealth 2012)*, 2012.

[39] K. Plarre, A. Raij, S. Hossain, A. Ali, M. Nakajima, M. Al'absi, E. Ertin, T. Kamarck, S. Kumar, M. Scott, D. Siewiorek, A. Smailagic, and L. Wittmers. Continuous inference of psychological stress from sensory measurements collected in the natural environment. In *Information Processing in Sensor Networks (IPSN), 2011 10th International Conference on*, pages 97–108, 2011.

[40] D. Quercia, J. Ellis, L. Capra, and J. Crowcroft. Tracking "gross community happiness" from tweets. In *CSCW*, pages 965–968, 2012.

[41] J. L. Sanders and M. S. Brizzolara. Relationships between weather and mood. *The Journal of General Psychology*, 107(1):155–156, 1982.

[42] A. Sano and R. W. Picard. Stress recognition using wearable sensors and mobile phones. *Proceedings of the 2013 Humaine Association Conference on Affective Computing and Intelligent Interaction*, pages 671–676, 2013.

[43] K. R. Scherer, D. Grandjean, T. Johnstone, G. Klasmeyer, and T. Bänziger. Acoustic correlates of task load and stress. In *INTERSPEECH*, 2002.

[44] R. Sinatra and M. Szell. Entropy and the predictability of online life. *Entropy*, (16):543–556, 2014.

[45] S. R. Singh, H. A. Murthy, and T. A. Gonsalves. Feature selection for text classification based on gini coefficient of inequality. *Journal of Machine Learning Research-Proceedings Track*, 10:76–85, 2010.

[46] V. K. Singh, L. Freeman, B. Lepri, and A. S. Pentland. Predicting spending behavior using socio-mobile features. In *Social Computing (SocialCom), 2013 International Conference on*, pages 174–179. IEEE, 2013.

[47] C. Song, Z. Qu, N. Blumm, and A. Barabasi. Limits of predictability in human mobility. *Science*, (327):1018–1021, 2010.

[48] J. Staiano, B. Lepri, N. Aharony, F. Pianesi, N. Sebe, and A. Pentland. Friends don't lie: inferring personality traits from social network structure. In *Proceedings of the 2012 ACM Conference on Ubiquitous Computing*, pages 321–330. ACM, 2012.

[49] A. Stopczynski, V. Sekara, P. Sapiezynski, A. Cuttone, M. M. Madsen, J. E. Larsen, and S. Lehmann. Measuring large-scale social networks with high resolution. *PLoS ONE*, (9), 2014.

[50] J. Suls, P. Green, and S. Hillis. Emotional reactivity to everyday problems, affective inertia, and neuroticism. *Personality and Social Psychology Bulletin*, 24(2):127–136, 1998.

[51] E. Tuv, A. Borisov, G. Runger, and K. Torkkola. Feature selection with ensembles, artificial variables, and redundancy elimination. *The Journal of Machine Learning Research*, 10:1341–1366, 2009.

[52] M. Vollrath and S. Torgersen. Personality types and coping. *Personal. Individ. Differ.*, 29:367–378, 2000.

Validating an iOS-based Rhythmic Auditory Cueing Evaluation (iRACE) for Parkinson's Disease

Shenggao Zhu[1], Robert J Ellis[2], Gottfried Schlaug[3], Yee Sien Ng[4], and Ye Wang[1,2]
[1]NUS Graduate School for Integrative Sciences and Engineering, National University of Singapore, Singapore
[2]School of Computing, National University of Singapore, Singapore
[3]Department of Neurology, Beth Israel Deaconess Medical Center and Harvard Medical School, USA
[4]Department of Rehabilitation Medicine, Singapore General Hospital, Singapore
shenggaozhu@nus.edu.sg; {ellis, wangye}@comp.nus.edu.sg;
gschlaug@bidmc.harvard.edu; ng.yee.sien@sgh.com.sg

ABSTRACT

Movement disorders such as Parkinson's disease (PD) will affect a rapidly growing segment of the population as society continues to age. Rhythmic Auditory Cueing (RAC) is a well-supported evidence-based intervention for the treatment of gait impairments in PD. RAC interventions have not been widely adopted, however, due to limitations in access to personnel, technological, and financial resources. To help "scale up" RAC for wider distribution, we have developed an iOS-based Rhythmic Auditory Cueing Evaluation (iRACE) mobile application to deliver RAC and assess motor performance in PD patients. The touchscreen of the mobile device is used to assess motor timing during index finger tapping, and the device's built-in tri-axial accelerometer and gyroscope to assess step time and step length during walking. Novel machine learning-based gait analysis algorithms have been developed for iRACE, including heel strike detection, step length quantification, and left-versus-right foot identification. The concurrent validity of iRACE was assessed using a clinic-standard instrumented walking mat and a pair of force-sensing resistor sensors. Results from 10 PD patients reveal that iRACE has low error rates ($<\pm 1.0\%$) across a set of four clinically relevant outcome measures, indicating a potentially useful clinical tool.

Categories and Subject Descriptors

K.4.2 [**Computing Milieux**]: Computers and Society—*Social Issues*; H.1.2 [**Information Systems**]: Models and Principles—*User/Machine Systems*; J.3 [**Computer Applications**]: Life and Medical Sciences

General Terms

Design, Experimentation, Measurement

Keywords

Rhythmic Auditory Cueing (RAC); Mobile app; Motor performance; Gait analysis; Tapping; Concurrent validity

MM'14, November 3–7, 2014, Orlando, Florida, USA.

http://dx.doi.org/10.1145/2647868.2654952.

1. INTRODUCTION

A 2007 review of published prevalence studies projects that the number of individuals over the age of 50 with Parkinson's disease (PD) living in 15 of the world's most populous nations will double between 2005 (roughly 4.4 million) and 2030 (roughly 9.0 million) [11]. Although administration of carbidopa/levodopa remains the "gold-standard" treatment for motor impairments in PD [32], gait parameters such as cadence, stride length, and velocity remain significantly reduced in PD patients relative to age-matched healthy controls, even when patients are tested during the "peak" effect of medication [25]. Together, these concerns motivate the search for additional strategies or therapies to help maintain motor functions in PD patients.

1.1 Rhythmic Auditory Cueing for PD

The use of physical therapy for the treatment of gait impairments in PD (e.g., bradykinesia, freezing, falling) has been the subject of systematic reviews and "best practice" treatment recommendations for therapy delivery [20]. A specific, evidence-based treatment recommendation was the use of *rhythmic sensory cueing* (RSC)—in particular, rhythmic auditory cueing (RAC) (for reviews, see [22, 36]). RAC is the use of an auditory pacing stimulus (either a simple metronome, or music with a steady beat) to which patients attempt to synchronize while walking.

The beneficial effects of RAC on gait in PD have been noted for several decades. Single-session RAC leads to improvements along multiple gait parameters (e.g., velocity, stride length, and stepping rate [22]), and a handful of multiweek interventions have found sustained improvements in gait parameters during a post-intervention follow-up (e.g., [7, 33]). Perhaps most importantly, RAC leads to a reduction in *motor timing variability* (MTV), quantified as stride-to-stride timing fluctuations during walking (for a detailed discussion, see [15]). PD patients have significantly higher MTV during gait than healthy controls, even under normal medication regimens [23]. Furthermore, MTV is both prospectively and retrospectively associated with fall risk [14]. The incidence of falls in PD is high: an estimated two-thirds of patients fall at least once a year, and half experience multiple falls per year [13]. Therefore, reduced MTV by RAC means less falls (and thus less cost of falls) in PD.

1.2 Assessment of PD Motor Performance

Although the efficacy of RAC for PD (i.e., statistically significant improvements in gait parameters) is well supported (e.g., [8, 22, 36]), RAC has not been widely adopted due to the lack of affordable and convenient *clinimetric tools* that would enable a medical professional (e.g., neurologist, physical therapist) to accurately assess a patient's motor performance in the short term, which could provide insight into whether that patient would respond to RAC in the longer term [7, 33].

With the rapid growth of mobile devices (e.g., smartphones) and the emergence of mobile cloud computing technology [10], mobile devices are becoming a ubiquitous computing platform in our daily life and healthcare. Compared to traditional devices in human gait assessment, such as foot-mounted force sensors [16], sensor-embedded walkways [27] and motion-capture cameras [30], mobile devices have clear advantages in portability, convenience, cost efficiency, and comprehensiveness of platform features (e.g., on-device data collection, analysis and visualization).

Here, we describe such a tool to facilitate and "scale up" RAC interventions: an iOS-based Rhythmic Auditory Cueing Evaluation (iRACE) mobile application ("app"). iRACE operates on an iPhone or iPod touch, and connects to a cloud-based website. iRACE records activities during walking (via the on-board accelerometer and gyroscope) and index finger tapping (via the touchscreen). Motor production is assessed both with and without RAC, and the auditory cues can be highly customized by each user. The recorded walking and tapping data is analyzed to obtain the basic motor parameters (step time/length, tapping intervals, etc.), as well as a set of four clinically relevant outcome measures. These results may then be visualized on the iRACE app as well as the website.

We have developed novel machine learning-based algorithms for iRACE gait analysis, including heel strike detection, step length quantification, and left-vs.-right foot identification. These algorithms were validated against ground truth measures obtained from a clinic-standard instrumented walking mat and force-sensing resistor sensors. Results from 10 PD patients revealed that iRACE had less than $\pm 1.0\%$ error rates (averaged across subjects) across four outcome measures, indicating a potentially useful clinical tool.

Using iRACE, medical professionals can easily assess whether RAC is effective to an individual patient, and if so, use iRACE to deliver long-term RAC-based therapy and monitor the patient's performance over time, benefiting the patient physically, mentally, and financially.

The rest of the paper is structured as follows. Section 2 reviews related literature on smartphone-based gait analysis. Section 3 describes the iRACE system. The clinical validity study design of iRACE is outlined in Section 4. iRACE-based gait analysis, clinical outcome measures, and tapping analysis are detailed in Sections 5, 6 and 7, respectively. Experiment results are presented in Section 8. Section 9 concludes our work and explores future directions.

2. RELATED WORK

A number of recent studies have investigated the viability of smartphone's built-in inertial measurement unit (IMU; accelerometer and/or gyroscope) to measure and quantify human gait [6, 18, 21, 26, 31, 34, 42, 43], with key details summarized in Table 1. A careful reading of this group of studies, however, reveals several concerns.

First, in some cases [6, 18, 21], only a single healthy subject's data was examined, precluding the ability to infer whether the specific algorithms or analyses that were used would generalize across individuals.

Table 1: Smartphone-based gait investigations

Ref.	Subject	N	Device	Location	Fs
[6]	HC	1	iOS	Left pocket	100
[18]	HC	1	Android	Front waist	60
[21]	HC	1	iOS	Left ankle	100
[26]	HC	49	Android	L3	50
[31]	HC	30	Android	L3	33
[34]	HC	49	Android	L3	50
[42]	HC/RA	20/39	Android	L3	33
[43]	HC	13	Android	L3	100

Notes: N is the number of healthy controls (HC) or patients with rheumatoid arthritis (RA) tested. "L3" indicates device placed in the vicinity of the third lumbar vertebrae on the lower back. Fs is the sampling frequency of the device's IMU in Hz.

Second, in some cases [21, 42], no concurrent ground-truth gait analysis was utilized, precluding any assessment of the sensitivity, specificity, and temporal precision of smartphone-derived calculations. In other cases [26, 31, 43], larger samples of healthy adults were studied, and a conventional waist-mounted tri-axial accelerometer was employed as ground truth. Such a design, however, is suboptimal, in that it would reveal only whether the smartphone's accelerometer functions as well as a conventional accelerometer, rather than whether the smartphone *actually* (and accurately) captures the spatio-temporal dynamics of human gait, as measured by "gold standard" devices: foot-mounted force-sensing resistors [16], sensor-embedded walkways [27], ground reaction force plates [39], or motion-capture cameras [30].

Third, some studies [21, 31, 42, 43] did not utilize traditional step-level spatio-temporal analysis (i.e., heel strike detection and step time/length quantification), which is standard in classic IMU-based gait analysis [46, 47]. Instead, these studies used statistics which quantify properties of the raw accelerometer waveform, such as its peak frequency after a fast Fourier transform, or the period at which successive peaks appear in the waveform's autocorrelation. Although such statistics are mathematically *valid*, they lack clinical *utility*, as there are no large-scale studies which provide normative or relative (e.g., PD patients versus age-matched controls) values for these statistics, unlike traditional outcome measures (for reviews, see [17, 24]; cf. Section 6 below).

Finally—and most relevant to the current project—no previous study has evaluated the validity of smartphone-based gait analysis in PD patients.

3. SYSTEM DESCRIPTION

iRACE consists of three main components: an iOS-based mobile device such as an iPhone or iPod touch (the "iRACE device"), a mobile application (the "iRACE app"), and a back-end cloud computing service (the "iRACE website"). An iPhone or iPod touch is equipped with an inertial measurement unit (IMU) comprising a microelectromechanical tri-axial linear accelerometer and Coriolis vibratory gyroscope, each with a maximum nominal sampling frequency of 100 Hz. The device's capacitive touchscreen has a maximum refresh rate of 60 Hz. The IMU data and touchscreen tap events are recorded during walking and tapping, respectively, which are then uploaded to the iRACE website.

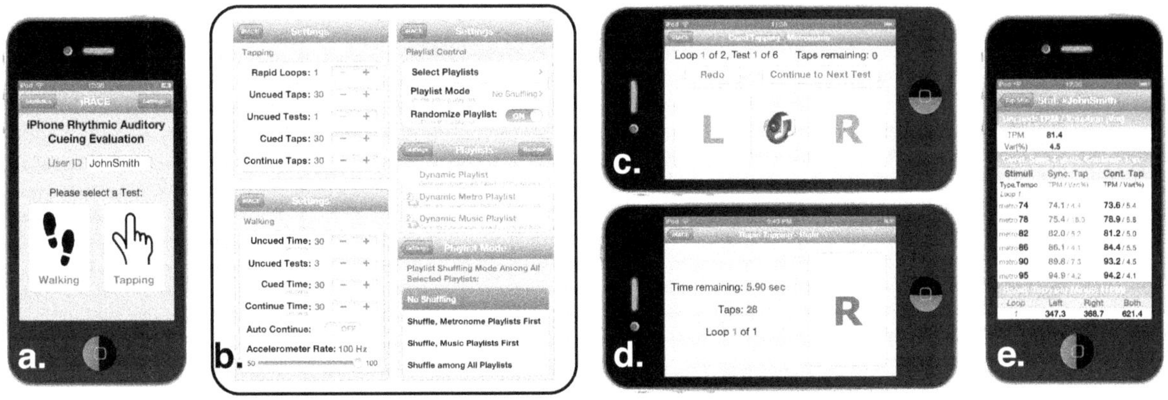

Figure 1: iRACE app screenshots. (a.) Home screen. (b.) Settings for evaluation parameters and playlists. (c.) RAC bimanual tapping. (d.) Rapid tapping. (e.) Tapping analysis and visualization.

3.1 iRACE App

3.1.1 Overview

iRACE administers three widely used tests of motor performance of both walking and finger tapping movements: (1) self-paced bilateral performance, (2) synchronization–continuation bilateral performance, and (3) rapid unilateral and bilateral performance. Launching iRACE (Figure 1a) provides the option to conduct a Walking Evaluation (using tests 1–2) or a Tapping Evaluation (using tests 1–3).

iRACE has a number of flexible settings (Figure 1b), including the number of iterations of each test and the desired playlist of RAC stimuli. The playlist can be pre-defined and fixed across subjects, or *dynamically* generated such that its range of tempos can automatically "bracket" each subject's self-paced walking/tapping tempo.

iRACE guides the user through all tests in succession. In a self-paced test, no RAC is provided; the subject will walk or tap at a rate deemed most comfortable. In a synchronization–continuation test, the RAC stimulus is delivered during the first part of the test (synchronization), during which the subject attempts to walk or tap with the stimulus beat. After a pre-specified number of events (steps or taps), the stimulus fades to silence over a few seconds, whereupon the subject attempts to continue the same pattern of movement at the same rate (continuation).

3.1.2 Walking and Tapping Evaluations

Quantitative evaluations of self-paced [23] and RAC-based synchronization (for reviews, see [22, 36]) walking are widely reported in the PD literature. During an iRACE Walking Evaluation, the iRACE device is secured to the ventral surface of the lower trunk (at the navel) using an elastic sleeve and waist band (Figure 2a). Although several previous studies have positioned the accelerometer on the dorsal surface of the body (e.g., over the third lumbar vertebrae; cf. Table 1), securing the device at the navel enables the user to more easily interact with the iRACE device (with an eye towards eventual home-based use). Both self-paced walking and synchronization–continuation walking tests are performed in this manner.

Index finger tapping is a widely used motor timing assessment in PD, both as a "fast-as-possible" test [12] and as a synchronization–continuation test [40]. To our knowledge, there exist no smartphone-implemented evaluations of finger tapping in either healthy controls or patients with movement disorders. During all tapping tests (self-paced, synchronization-continuation, and rapid; cf. Figure 1c–d), the iRACE device is positioned on a desk or table such that the subject's arms and wrists are comfortably supported, permitting smooth index finger movements. iRACE can process and visualize the tapping data in-app immediately after a test (Figure 1e). (In-app gait analysis will be implemented in a future version of iRACE.)

3.2 iRACE Website

A cloud-based service has been established to facilitate iRACE data management and visualization. Each iRACE user can create an account to login the iRACE app and website. The website has the following main features: (1) To build user profiles and manage user roles and relationships (patients, therapists, etc.); (2) To receive and analyze data files uploaded from iRACE app; (3) To visualize walking and tapping analysis results in tables and graphs; (4) To review evaluation history and track user progress over time.

4. CLINICAL STUDY DESIGN

This section describes the novel fusing of clinic-standard ground truth measures with iRACE, and the testing protocol into which they were incorporated.

4.1 Ground Truth Gait Measures

As noted in Section 2, no previous investigation has validated smartphone-based gait analysis using ground truth data that directly samples heel strikes in the temporal and/or spatial dimensions. In our study, we utilized both: a GAITRite electronic walkway[1], and a force-sensing resistor assembly[2] and telemetry unit (DataLOG[3]).

GAITRite is a 61 cm × 610 cm roll-up mat embedded with pressure sensors arranged with 1.27-cm spacing, with a maximum sampling frequency of 240 Hz. GAITRite computes various spatio-temporal gait parameters for each walk across the mat, such as cadence, step time and step length. Its accuracy has been validated by concurrent analyses using insole footswitch sensors [2] and motion-capture cameras [41]. GAITRite has been the primary data collection

[1] http://www.gaitrite.com
[2] http://www.biometricsltd.com/forcesensors.htm
[3] http://www.biometricsltd.com/datalog.htm

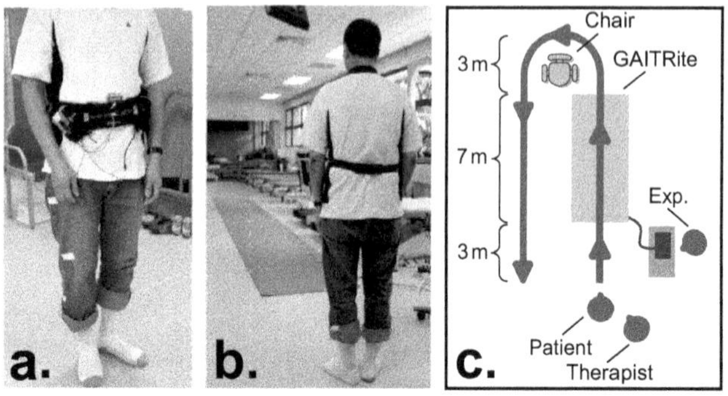

Figure 2: Clinical study settings. (a.) iRACE device and DataLOG secured to a belt on patient's lower trunk. (b.) Straight line walking segment on GAITRite. (c.) Illustration of the walking path.

device in numerous gait investigations in the elderly, including PD patients (e.g., [8, 24]).

In the present study, a force-sensing resistor (FSR) sensor was attached to the heel pad of each foot to record the moment of each heel strike. Both FSR sensors were wired to a telemetry unit (DataLOG) and sampled at 1000 Hz as binary values (0 if the pressure on FSR exceeds a certain threshold, and 1 otherwise). FSR sensors are widely used in gait analysis, including gait analysis in PD (for reviews, see [14, 15]). When a heel strikes the ground, the pressure placed on the FSR toggles its reading from 1 to 0; that toggling timestamp was used as the "ground truth" heel strike time. DataLOG also received an analog audio signal directly from the iRACE app, which was used to synchronize iRACE and DataLOG clocks (detailed in Section 5.2).

As DataLOG has a higher sampling frequency (i.e., with millisecond-level temporal resolution) than GAITRite, FSR and DataLOG recorded heel strike timestamps were used as the ground truth to validate the temporal precision of iRACE (cf. Section 5.3), and GAITRite was used to evaluate the step length algorithm of iRACE (cf. Section 5.5).

4.2 Subjects and Testing Protocol

Ten patients (4 female) diagnosed with idiopathic Parkinson's disease were recruited from Singapore General Hospital. The average age of the patients was 66.3 (range: 58 to 81), and average duration of PD was 5.7 years (range: 2 to 14). The patients had a Hoehn and Yahr stage of 2.0 ($N = 1$), 2.5 ($N = 5$), 3.0 ($N = 3$) and 4.0 ($N = 1$), where N is the number of patients. None of the patients had a coexisting dementia (Mini-Mental State Examination score > 24 points) or other diagnosed neurological impairments. All patients were under stable medication regimens for the preceding four weeks, and were tested at least 30 minutes after taking morning medications.

All testing procedures were approved by the institutional review board (IRB) at Singapore General Hospital. The iRACE "belt" and FSR sensors (Figure 2a) were attached as described above (cf. Section 3.1.2 and 4.1). The experimenter then demonstrated the target walking path (Figure 2c), including a 3-meter acceleration/deceleration phase to allow for steady-state walking while on the GAITRite mat.

Each subject then completed four or more walking trials (i.e., enough to record at least 40 steps on GAITRite) in each of three sequential RAC conditions: (1) self-paced (no RAC), (2) RAC with metronome tempo set to 100% of mean self-paced cadence, (3) RAC with metronome tempo set to 110% of mean self-paced cadence; these two tempos are common in RAC [36]. (The mean self-paced cadence was computed using GAITRite, as the data was collected *before* the algorithms detailed in Section 5 were developed.)

The iRACE Tapping Evaluation (cf. Section 3.1.2) was conducted after the completion of the Walking Evaluation.

5. WALKING ANALYSIS

This section describes the processing pipeline used to transform the raw IMU data recorded by iRACE into temporal and spatial gait parameters (step time, step length, etc.).

5.1 Preprocessing

During a Walking Evaluation, the iRACE device was oriented with its screen facing forward and its "home" button facing up. iRACE simultaneously records 6 channels of IMU data in the iOS device xyz coordinate system: tri-axial acceleration (a_x, a_y and a_z) and tri-axial rotation rate (ω_x, ω_y and ω_z). For simplicity, from the subject's perspective, we define anterior–posterior (A–P) acceleration as $a_{AP} = -a_x$ (positive values for anterior acceleration), up–down (U–D) acceleration as $a_{UD} = -a_y$ (positive values for upward acceleration), and left–right (L–R) acceleration as $a_{LR} = a_z$ (positive values for leftward acceleration). Similarly, we define the rotation rate around the A–P axis (i.e., roll) as $\omega_{AP} = -\omega_x$, around the U–D axis (i.e., yaw) as $\omega_{UD} = -\omega_y$, and around the L–R axis (i.e., pitch) as $\omega_{LR} = -\omega_z$.

Four preprocessing steps were applied: (1) IMU waveform interpolation; (2) straight-line walking identification; (3) device tilt compensation; and (4) low-pass filtering.

First, since the time interval between successive IMU samples varies stochastically, raw IMU data is usually interpolated and resampled at a fixed frequency [18, 26, 31]. In the present study, all IMU data was cubic-spline interpolated and resampled at 1000 Hz, which as a result could refine the peak and trough locations (i.e., improve temporal resolution) in the IMU waveforms (e.g., Figure 3a).

Second, an algorithm was implemented to isolate straight-line walking segments from turn segments (cf. Figure 2c), stationary segments, or other non-walking segments (e.g., freezing). This was achieved by analyzing the acceleration amplitude of a_{AP} (to identify actual walking) and rotation rate ω_{UD} (to identify turning). For simplicity, only straight-line segments will be analyzed further.

Third, because the iRACE device usually pitches (around the L–R axis) as the subject walks (thus affecting IMU waveforms and the accuracy of subsequent heel strike detection), the A–P and U–D waveforms were adjusted (using a trigonometric algorithm) according to the estimated device tilt angle (based on rotation rate ω_{LR} and average gravity in A–P and U–D axes; derived from [29]).

Fourth, all IMU data was low-pass filtered with a 4th-order zero-lag Butterworth filter with a cut-off frequency of 20 Hz, as suggested by [46, 47].

5.2 iRACE & Ground Truth Synchronization

Since the internal clocks in the iOS device and DataLOG are independent and not synchronized, a novel synchronization method was developed via an acoustic signal. Specifically, iRACE generated a 2-second square-wave audio (using the iOS Audio Units API). iRACE toggled the volume

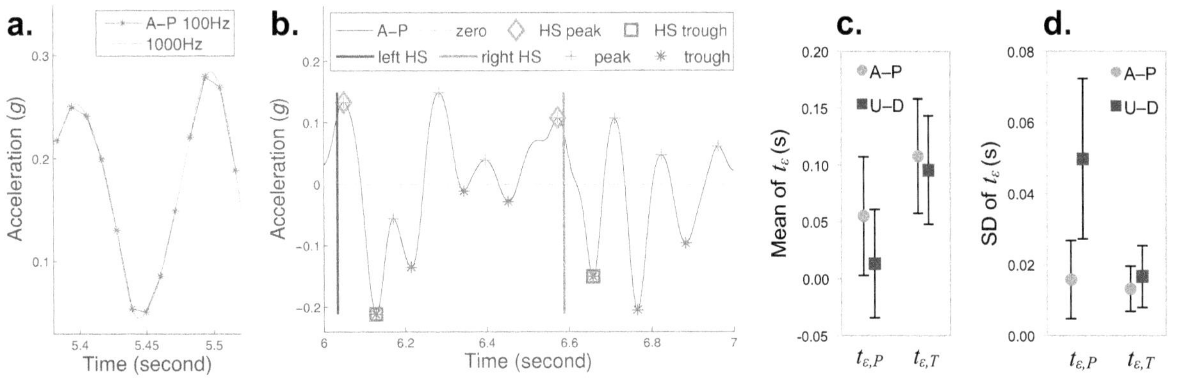

Figure 3: (a.) Interpolation and resampling of iRACE acceleration data. (b.) Annotation of heel strike points (HS peak and HS trough) in the A–P waveform. (c.) and (d.) Group mean and standard deviation (SD) of the temporal error (t_ε) between HS timestamps and annotated waveform peaks ($t_{\varepsilon,P}$) and troughs ($t_{\varepsilon,T}$).

of this audio repeatedly (approximately every 30 ms) between silence and normal volume, and saved the toggling timestamps (in iRACE's clock). DataLOG recorded this audio (at 2 kHz), which was then analyzed to locate these volume toggling timestamps (in DataLOG's clock), i.e., the rising and falling edges of the audio volume contour. The temporal offset between the two clocks was found by linearly regressing the DataLOG timestamps onto the iRACE timestamps; the y-axis intercept was the "best fitting" offset in the least-squares sense, with sub-millisecond level accuracy.

GAITRite records the session start time to the millisecond level, so that the steps measured by GAITRite can be correctly matched to those measured by DataLOG and iRACE.

5.3 Waveform Annotation & Timing Analysis

Previous accelerometry-based gait analysis methods have used waveform peaks (i.e., local maxima) in the A–P channel [26, 47] and/or U–D channel [28] as analogues of physical heel strike (HS) events (for a review, see [19]). As noted in Section 2 (cf. Table 1), however, the above papers were primarily focused on gait analysis in healthy individuals, and have not been extended to gait analysis in PD patients. Even a brief glance at the waveform excerpt from a PD patient in Figure 3b reveals that the widely used convention of "an A–P peak preceding a zero-crossing" as a HS analogue [44, 46, 47] is problematic, as *multiple* zero-crossings may be present between successive ground truth HS events (i.e., as recorded by DataLOG and FSR sensors).

To find out which accelerometry waveform event was the most temporally stable analogue of a true HS event, a more systematic approach was taken in the present study. For each ground truth HS timestamp (t_{HS}), the timestamps of a peak (t_P) and its subsequent trough (t_T, i.e., local minimum) that were most likely to correspond to t_{HS} were manually annotated on the A–P and U–D accelerometry waveforms. In general, t_P (or t_T) was closest to t_{HS} among all peaks (or troughs), but exceptions existed due to irregular waveform fluctuations (i.e., irregular gait). For convenience, manually annotated peaks and troughs will be referred to as "HS peaks" and "HS troughs", respectively (cf. Figure 3b).

After annotation, the signed temporal errors (t_ε) of four waveform event timestamps (i.e., $t_{P,AP}$, $t_{P,UD}$, $t_{T,AP}$, $t_{T,UD}$) relative to the corresponding t_{HS} were calculated for each t_{HS}, and the mean (M_{t_ε}) and standard deviation (SD_{t_ε}) of t_ε were computed for each subject. Figure 3c–d present the group-level mean and standard deviation (as error bars) of M_{t_ε} and SD_{t_ε} across all subjects, respectively. Logically, temporal *variability* (i.e., SD_{t_ε}) rather than temporal *delay* (i.e., M_{t_ε}) is the more critical statistic, as a physical delay is inherent between a HS event and the corresponding waveform peak/trough recorded in a waist-mounted accelerometer. A 2 (*Channel*: A–P or U–D) × 2 (*Event*: SD of $t_{\varepsilon,P}$ or $t_{\varepsilon,T}$) repeated-measures analysis of variance (ANOVA) was performed, revealing a significant effect for *Channel* ($F_{1,9} = 26.86$, $p = .0006$; i.e., A–P had lower SDs than U–D), *Event* ($F_{1,9} = 32.16$, $p = .0003$; i.e., HS troughs had lower SDs than HS peaks), and their interaction ($F_{1,9} = 15.96$, $p = .003$). Because A–P troughs ($t_{T,AP}$) had the smallest group-level mean and variance of SD_{t_ε} (cf. Figure 3d), they may be considered the most temporally stable analogue of HS events.

5.4 Heel Strike Detection

As highlighted in Figure 3b, conventional rule-based algorithms using hand-crafted rules or hard-coded thresholds (e.g., a simple zero-crossing rule to identify HS analogues) may be imprecise in PD patients, due to individual differences in disease staging, bradykinesia, freezing, and so forth.

To address this limitation, a machine learning-based HS detection algorithm was proposed, which formulates HS detection as a binary classification problem: whether a given accelerometry A–P trough was a HS analogue (i.e., a HS trough) or not. (A–P troughs are the most temporally stable waveform events relative to true HS events; cf. Section 5.3.)

Firstly, two sets of features were extracted for each A–P trough: (1) Features from the A–P trough (including the trough amplitude, the difference in time or amplitude between a trough and its adjacent peaks, etc.); and (2) Features from all accelerometer and gyroscope waveforms. The average step time (T_s; i.e., the duration of a step) was previously derived from the A–P waveform autocorrelation [43]. A segment (about $0.2 \times T_s$) centered on the trough timepoint was selected in each waveform, and features (mean, standard deviation, etc.) from these segments were extracted and concatenated. These two sets of features together formed a feature vector, denoted as $\mathbf{f}_i$ for the i-th trough.

Next, a set of features based on a trough sequence (i.e., combinations of adjacent troughs) was constructed for the i-th trough, including $\mathbf{f}_i - \mathbf{f}_{i-1}$, $\mathbf{f}_i - \mathbf{f}_{i+1}$, $\mathbf{f}_i + 0.5\mathbf{f}_{i-1} - 0.5\mathbf{f}_{i+1}$, etc. After that, a set of the most statistically significant features are selected among all the extracted features using the `rankfeatures`[4] function in MATLAB (with a two-sample t-test used as the class separability criteria).

A two-layer neural network classifier [3] then took the selected features as input. The ground truth of whether each trough was a HS trough was derived from the waveform annotation. Different numbers of selected features and units in the hidden layer of the classifier were iterated and tested; the optimal parameter combination was obtained, which yielded the highest classification accuracy based on 10-fold cross-validation (for more details about parameter selection, see [3]). In the present study, 100 selected features and 20 units in the hidden layer were used.

For each trough, a number (continuously valued from 0 to 1) was output by the classifier, indicating the probability of that trough being a HS trough. This number was then thresholded at 0.5, giving an initial prediction of the identify of a HS trough or a non-HS trough. Next, this initial prediction was refined, as follows. Based on the previously derived average step time (T_s), a pair of rules was applied: (1) If any two adjacent HS troughs were separated by less than $0.7 \times T_s$, the one with the lower probability was adjusted to a non-HS trough; (2) If no HS trough existed in the window $[0.7 \times T_s, 1.3 \times T_s]$ before or after the timestamp of a given HS trough, the trough with highest probability in that window was selected as a HS trough.

5.5 Step Length Calculation

After HS detection, the spatial displacement (i.e., step length) between successive HS troughs was calculated. Algorithms for IMU-based step length calculation can be generally grouped into two categories: double integration of acceleration [5, 45], and machine learning-based regression methods [37]. For trunk-mounted smartphones, the main difficulties of the double integration method lie in the integration drift over time and the estimation of initial velocity at the beginning of a step (i.e., the HS trough time), since the trunk velocity at that time is typically non-zero. For example, in the present PD patients' data, if the initial velocity were set to zero (as assumed in [5]), the resultant step length based on double integration usually drifted to a negative value.

To overcome these difficulties, a hybrid machine learning algorithm was proposed, which took the double integration results together with other low-level waveform features as the input, and uses neural network regression [3] to calculate step length. Specifically, for each step, features were extracted from segments of tri-axial acceleration and the "energy waveform" (i.e., $\sqrt{a_{AP}^2 + a_{LR}^2 + (a_{UD}+1)^2}$; e.g., [6]) including single and double integration, time duration, standard deviation, and so on. These segments include the exact step segment (between successive HS troughs) and its shifted versions (by half a step duration before or after it). Similar features were also extracted from tri-axial gyroscope waveforms. Next, Principal Component Analysis [3] was used to select the most significant features, which were then input to a two-layer neural network regression model [3]. Model parameters were trained using 10-fold cross-validation.

5.6 Left-versus-Right Foot Identification

Left versus right foot identification is important for clinical gait measures, but presents some challenges when the measurement device is attached centrally at the trunk. Some studies use L–R acceleration to distinguish left and right foot, based on the sign of L–R acceleration, or the sign of its single or double integration [5, 46, 47]. These methods assume that the direction of trunk displacement is different for different feet. However, the validity of these assumptions has not been tested using smartphones, or in PD patients. We tested these methods in our PD patient data, and confirmed that they worked for a majority of patients, but some failure cases still existed due to weak and irregular L–R acceleration. At the same time, we observed that the gyroscope data (especially rotation rate around U–D axis) usually also showed different patterns for different feet, which relates to the different rotation directions of the trunk.

To fully utilize all accelerometer and gyroscope data, a machine learning-based method was proposed for left-versus-right foot classification. For each step between successive HS troughs, two sets of features were extracted. First, step-based features (single/double integration, maximum, minimum, etc.) from segments of all accelerometer and gyroscope waveforms. The durations of these segments include the exact step duration (between successive HS troughs) and its shifted versions (by half a step duration before or after it). These features are denoted as a vector $\mathbf{f}_i$ for the i-th step. Second, features from a step sequence, including $\mathbf{f}_i - \mathbf{f}_{i-1}$, $\mathbf{f}_i - \mathbf{f}_{i+1}$, $\mathbf{f}_i - 0.5\mathbf{f}_{i-1} - 0.5\mathbf{f}_{i+1}$, etc. The ground truth of left-vs.-right foot was obtained from DataLOG left and right foot sensors. As in the HS detection method (cf. Section 5.4), feature selection was performed, and the neural network classifier was evaluated using 10-fold cross-validation.

6. CLINICAL OUTCOME MEASURES

iRACE calculates four clinically relevant outcome measures that quantify specific statistical properties of an event series (ES) $\{e_1, e_2, \ldots, e_N\}$ of N successive finger tap or heel strike timestamps (in elapsed seconds, relative to an arbitrary "0" timepoint) or N successive heel strike displacements (in meters, relative to an arbitrary starting position). An inter-event series (IES) refers to the first-order difference (i.e., intervals) of an event series, with $N-1$ elements.

6.1 Outlier Flagging

Outliers in an ES come in two forms: false positives (i.e., a "double tap" of the same button during bimanual tapping, or a "double trough" in an A–P acceleration waveform; cf. Figure 3b), or false negatives (i.e., "missing" events due to inadequate heel strike pressure or touchscreen contact, or by *a priori* exclusion of turns during a walk; cf. Section 5.1).

For all walking and tapping trials other than Rapid Tapping, a simple "successive percentage change" (S_{SPC}) transformation was used to flag outliers in the original ES. For all adjacent elements of an IES, $S_{SPC,i}$ is defined as:

$$S_{SPC,i} = 100\frac{|IES_{i+1} - IES_i|}{IES_i}. \qquad (1)$$

S_{SPC} will have $N-2$ elements relative to the original ES.

A single threshold percentage value (P) was then set; here, $P = 75$. For any $S_{SPC,i} \geq P$, the associated ES element e_{i+2} was flagged as an outlier. Additionally, any repeated event on the same side of the body (i.e., the second of two successive left or successive right taps or heel strikes) was flagged as an outlier. The first-order difference of a series of ≥ 6 consecutive ES elements without an outlier flag will be

[4]http://www.mathworks.com/help/bioinfo/ref/rankfeatures.html

labeled a "ΔES". (For rapid tapping trials, a simpler logic was applied: an outlier was identified as any IES_{i+1} which followed IES_i by less than 50 ms. This threshold was established to eliminate moments of near-synchronous tapping that are more likely to occur during alternate bimanual tapping, particularly at fast rates.)

6.2 Outcome Measures

Two statistics were calculated from a ΔES. First, the mean of a ΔES (Δ_M) is straightforward, and can be taken for either a timestamp ΔES ($\Delta_{M,T}$) or a displacement ΔES ($\Delta_{M,D}$). Two transformations yield the commonly reported statistics of *cadence* (= $60/\Delta_{M,T}$, in steps-per-minute) and *velocity* (= $\Delta_{M,D}/\Delta_{M,T}$, in meters-per-second). Second, the coefficient of variation of a ΔES (Δ_{CV}) is widely used in analyses of motor timing in PD [15]:

$$\Delta_{CV} = 100\frac{\text{std}(\Delta ES)}{\text{mean}(\Delta ES)}, \quad (2)$$

where std(·) is the sample standard deviation.

Two other statistics were derived from a transformation of an outlier-free ES proposed by [35] to quantify motor timing during walking. For each string of N ($N \geq 3$) right (e_R) and N left (e_L) events without an outlier flag, $\{e_{R,1}, e_{L,1}, e_{R,2}, e_{L,2}, \ldots, e_{R,N}, e_{L,N}\}$, two relative phase series were defined using the right (Φ_R) or left (Φ_L) foot as the "reference" foot (the following formulas assume the first R event precedes the first L event):

$$\Phi_{R,i} = 360\frac{e_{L,i} - e_{R,i}}{e_{R,i+1} - e_{R,i}}, \quad \Phi_{L,i} = 360\frac{e_{R,i+1} - e_{L,i}}{e_{L,i+1} - e_{L,i}}. \quad (3)$$

For example, a $\Phi_{R,i} = 180$ indicates that the left event $e_{L,i}$ precisely bisects the time (or displacement) between successive right events $e_{R,i}$ and $e_{R,i+1}$.

The mean absolute percentage deviation from 180 (Φ_M) indicates the presence of an overall phase asymmetry (e.g., right steps do not evenly divide left strides, or vice versa):

$$\Phi_{M,R} = 100\frac{\text{mean}(|\Phi_R - 180|)}{180}, \quad (4)$$

$$\Phi_{M,L} = 100\frac{\text{mean}(|\Phi_L - 180|)}{180}. \quad (5)$$

The coefficient of variation of Φ (Φ_{CV}) was calculated in an analogous fashion to Δ_{CV}:

$$\Phi_{CV,R} = 100\frac{\text{std}(\Phi_R)}{\text{mean}(\Phi_R)}, \quad \Phi_{CV,L} = 100\frac{\text{std}(\Phi_L)}{\text{mean}(\Phi_L)}. \quad (6)$$

The nature of the Φ transform means that Φ_{CV} reflects *local* (i.e., event-to-event) variability relative to the mean, while Δ_{CV} reflects *global* variability relative to the mean.

For parsimony, the maximum of $\Phi_{M,R}$ and $\Phi_{M,L}$ (referred to simply as Φ_M), and the maximum of $\Phi_{CV,R}$ and $\Phi_{CV,L}$ (referred to as Φ_{CV}) will be retained for a given test. Thus, any reduction in the magnitude of Δ_{CV}, Φ_M, or Φ_{CV} would reflect an improvement on that particular aspect of gait stability, which may be caused by the positive facilitation of RAC (relative to without RAC).

7. TAPPING ANALYSIS

Two limitations that occur when recording iOS touchscreen events have the potential to affect the outcome measures of iRACE tapping. First, this touchscreen has a relatively slow maximum sampling frequency (60 Hz) compared to the iOS IMU (100 Hz). Second, the touchscreen datastream is effectively binary (0 = no contact; 1 = contact) rather than continuously valued like the IMU, precluding it from interpolation (and the resulting refinement of temporal resolution; cf. Figure 3a). Together, these limitations suggest that iRACE estimates of inter-tap interval variability (i.e., Δ_{CV} and Φ_{CV}) may be inflated.

For example, as an IES becomes faster (i.e., with a smaller Δ_M) or more temporally stable (i.e., a smaller Δ_{CV}, Φ_M, or Φ_{CV}), the impact of 60-Hz sampling error becomes more prominent; the potential error in each timestamp is a larger proportion of the underlying period. This is highlighted in Figure 4a, which visualizes an inter-tap interval series with a true $\Delta_M = 0.25$ s and $\Delta_{CV} = 2.0\%$ (blue trace). However, after downsampling this series at 60 Hz (by advancing each timestamp in the original series forward to the next possible 60-Hz sample point, yielding the red trace), the observed Δ_M is accurate (= 0.25 s) but the observed Δ_{CV} is inflated (= 3.8%). By contrast, in Figure 4b, a series with a true Δ_M = 1.0 s and $\Delta_{CV} = 8.0\%$ has both an accurate observed Δ_M (= 1.0 s) and Δ_{CV} (= 8.1%) after downsampling.

To systematically quantify the error induced by 60-Hz sampling on the four temporal outcome measures (Δ_M, Δ_{CV}, Φ_M, and Φ_{CV}), the following simulation was conducted. A random "pull" of 30 values (which forms an IES) was drawn from the normal distribution ($\mu = 0$, $\sigma = 1$), and shifted to have a mean of M (where $M = 0.125$ to 1.0 in ten geometric steps). The corresponding ES series was generated by taking the cumulative sum of the IES. Next, the value of Δ_{CV}, Φ_M, or Φ_{CV} was rescaled (over separate manipulations) to have a value of exactly P% (where $P = 2.0$, 4.0, or 8.0). The rescaled ES was then downsampled to 60 Hz. Finally, the four outcome measures were calculated from the downsampled timestamps. In total 10 (M) × 3 (P) × 2000 iterations were performed.

The simulation results are presented in Figure 4c–f, plotting the error induced by 60-Hz sampling (y-axis) at different values of M (x-axis) and P (different colors) for each outcome measure (separate panels). The median (heavy line) and central 95% (lighter lines) of all iterations are shown for each P value. Several conclusions can be made. First, Δ_M is accurately captured at all levels of P; this finding is perhaps expected, as even with a fast M (e.g., Figure 4a), the numerous underestimated and overestimated elements (relative to the simulated ground truth) tend to cancel each other out. Second, as predicted, the accuracy of all outcome measures increases (i.e., the y-axis width between each pair of 95% lines decreases) as M increases. Most importantly, for the range of "plausible" walking and tapping rates (i.e., $\Delta_M \geq 0.5$ s, or 120 events-per-minute or slower), outcome measures differ from ground truth by less than ±1.0%.

8. RESULTS

This section presents the concurrent validation results, including the accuracy of iRACE-quantified gait parameters, outcome measures, and measures of RAC facilitation.

8.1 Gait Measurement Accuracy

A heel strike dataset of 3898 HS events was combined across all Walking Evaluations of all ten subjects. Each HS event has both a ground truth HS timestamp from the DataLOG FSR sensor, and an annotated HS trough in iRACE A–P waveform. A total of 16295 A–P troughs (including

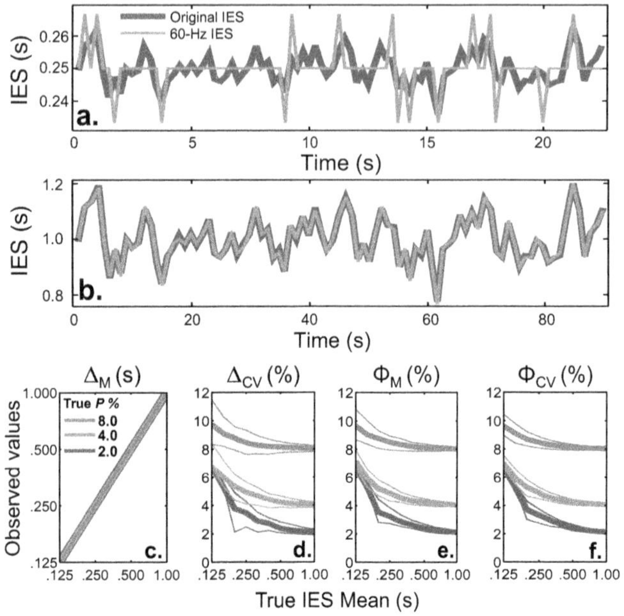

Figure 4: Tapping simulation. (a.) and (b.) 60-Hz downsampled inter-event interval (IES) series with a mean of 0.25 s and 1.0 s. (c.–f.) Outcome measures.

HS troughs and non-HS troughs) were identified. Based on 10-fold cross-validation, our HS detection algorithm (cf. Section 5.4) achieved 100% precision and recall. If the binary output was directly obtained from the classifier using a decision boundary of 0.5 (i.e., no further rule-based refinement was applied), the precision and recall were 99.98% and 99.87%, respectively (F_1 score = 99.93%).

On the same HS dataset, our left-vs.-right foot identification algorithm (cf. Section 5.6) also achieved 100% accuracy.

A step length dataset of 1668 steps was combined across all walks of all subjects with ground truth step lengths collected from GAITRite. The root mean square error (RMSE) of our step length calculation algorithm was 3.22 cm based on 10-fold cross-validation, or 6.95% when expressed as a CV value (i.e., RMSE divided by mean step length).

8.2 Outcome Measure Accuracy

A repeated-measures Bland–Altman (B–A) analysis [4] is presented for Step Time (Figure 5) and Step Length (Figure 6). As used here, a B–A analysis summarizes the accuracy of an experimental device (iRACE) against a control device (ground truth device; DataLOG or GAITRite). Outcome measures from individual trials (blue points) are averaged to create a single value per subject (red points). The key statistics in a B–A plot are the y-axis mean (dashed red line) and 2×SD error bars (solid red lines), which indicate the expected mismatch between the two devices at the population level (with the error term adjusted for multiple trials per subject, per [4]). Similar to the tapping simulation (cf. Figure 4c), Δ_M was very accurately estimated for both Step Time (Figure 5a) and Step Length (Figure 6a). Although the amount of y-axis error in iRACE-quantified variability measures (Δ_{CV}, Φ_M, Φ_{CV}) was greater than that of Δ_M, this error was less than ±1.0% in most subjects (i.e., averaged across individual walks). This indicates that iRACE

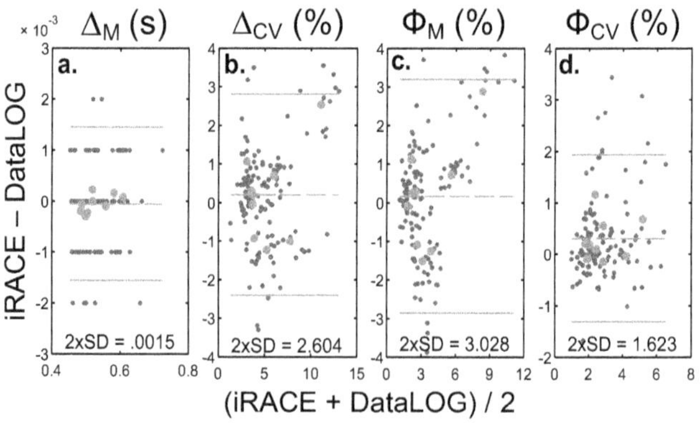

Figure 5: Bland–Altman step time analysis.

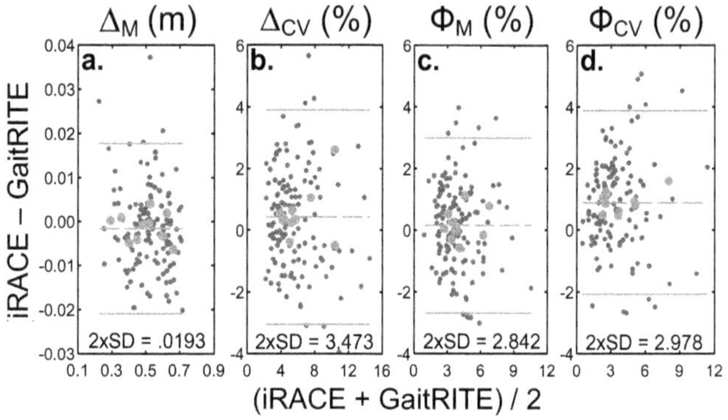

Figure 6: Bland–Altman step length analysis.

would be able to distinguish parkinsonian gait from normal gait based on their percentage-based variability measures, which can differ by as much as 5% for stride time variability [9] and 2.5% for stride length variability [1].

8.3 Accuracy of RAC Facilitation

Finally, to quantify whether any effect of RAC facilitation was significantly different between iRACE and the relevant ground truth, a 2 (*Device*: iRACE vs. ground truth) × 3 (*RAC* conditions: Self-paced, 100%, 110%; cf. Figure 7) repeated-measures ANOVA was performed separately on each outcome measure. A significant effect for *RAC* was found for Step Time Δ_M ($F_{2,16} = 7.17$, $p = .006$), Step Time Δ_{CV} ($F_{2,16} = 4.05$, $p = .038$), and Step Length Δ_M ($F_{2,16} = 8.43$, $p = .003$), indicating the expected influence of RAC: decreasing inter-step durations and increasing inter-step lengths as tempo increased. Importantly, no significant *Device* × *RAC* interactions were present in any of the ANOVAs (each $p > .10$, as shown in Figure 7), indicating no systematic difference between iRACE and ground truth outcome measures in the ability to detect RAC facilitation when it actually occurred.

9. DISCUSSION AND CONCLUSION

The current paper presents the first-ever systematic ground truth validation of the accuracy of smartphone-based gait analysis in PD, and describes an iOS-based Rhythmic Auditory Cueing Evaluation (iRACE) mobile application to facilitate RAC efficacy diagnosis, via an assessment of upper motor (finger tapping) and lower motor (walking) perfor-

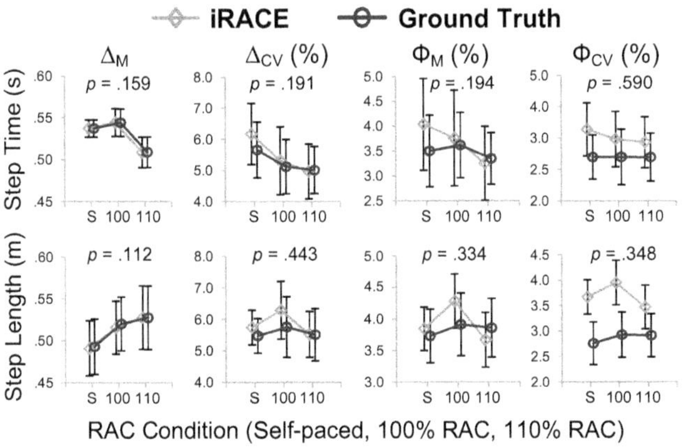

Figure 7: Outcome measures of step time and step length under 3 RAC conditions: self-paced ("S"), and cued with metronomes set to 100% ("100") and 110% ("110") of self-paced walking cadence.

mance. Novel machine learning-based gait analysis algorithms have been developed for iRACE, and the present pilot study reveals that iRACE has low error rates relative to clinic-standard ground truth measures, indicating a potentially useful clinical tool.

It is important to note that the present paper is concerned with evaluating the *accuracy* of smartphone-based gait measurement, not the *efficacy* of RAC (which has been the focus of prior studies [22, 23, 36, 38]). RAC has been widely noted for its facilitative effects on gait [12, 40]. iRACE enables medical professionals to quickly and accurately quantify the *degree* of RAC facilitation (cf. Section 8.3), enabling a decision of whether RAC might be useful as a "neurophysiological adjuvant" for individual PD patients.

The flexibility, portability, and validity of iRACE suggest both prognostic and analytic applications. First, because it is smartphone implemented, an entire world of RAC stimuli can be made available, ranging from the user's own music collection to commercially available streaming music (e.g., Deezer[5], Google Play[6], Spotify[7]), matched to the user's music preference and the requirements of RAC therapy (e.g., steady tempo and strong beats). Second, iRACE could be used to track the improvement of motor performance over time (e.g., in a longitudinal clinical trial) or in conjunction with a behavioral, pharmacological, or neurostimulatory intervention. Third, iRACE would enable clinicians to evaluate correlations between (1) upper motor and lower motor timing variability, and (2) step time and step length variability during gait, both of which remain largely unexplored in the clinical literature. Fourth, the portability of iRACE would enable it to be used by neurologists and physical therapists around the globe. The resultant surge in collected data (archived and managed on the iRACE website; cf. Section 3.2) could then be used to explore large-sample correlations with other disease-relevant variables, revealing potentially novel insights into how PD affects the motor system. Together, this future work may lead to an improved ability to characterize—and, ultimately, treat—motor dysfunction in Parkinson's disease.

[5]http://www.deezer.com
[6]https://play.google.com/music
[7]https://www.spotify.com

ACKNOWLEDGEMENTS

We thank Haotian "Sam" Fang, Hang Guo, Dr. Dawn Tan, Dr. Patsy Tan, Jacqueline Chen, Christal Chiang, and Lee Meng Ho for their help with clinical data collection, and Boyd Anderson for helpful comments. This project was partially funded by the National Research Foundation (NRF) and managed through the multi-agency Interactive & Digital Media Programme Office (IDMPO) hosted by the Media Development Authority of Singapore (MDA) under Centre of Social Media Innovations for Communities (COSMIC), and partially funded by the Agency for Science, Technology and Research (A*STAR) under grant R-252-000-510-305.

10. REFERENCES

[1] P. Arias and J. Cudeiro. Effects of rhythmic sensory stimulation (auditory, visual) on gait in Parkinson's disease patients. *Exp. Brain Res.*, 186(4):589–601, 2008.

[2] B. Bilney, M. Morris, and K. Webster. Concurrent related validity of the GAITRite walkway system for quantification of the spatial and temporal parameters of gait. *Gait & Posture*, 17(1):68–74, 2003.

[3] C. M. Bishop. *Pattern recognition and machine learning.* Springer, 2006.

[4] J. M. Bland and D. G. Altman. Measuring agreement in method comparison studies. *Statistical Methods in Medical Research*, 8(2):135–160, 1999.

[5] F. Bugané, M. Benedetti, et al. Estimation of spatial-temporal gait parameters in level walking based on a single accelerometer. *Comp Meth and Prog in Biomed*, 108(1):129–137, 2012.

[6] H. K. Chan, H. Zheng, et al. Feasibility study on iPhone accelerometer for gait detection. In *Proc. PervasiveHealth*, pages 184–187. IEEE, 2011.

[7] N. de Bruin, J. B. Doan, et al. Walking with music is a safe and viable tool for gait training in Parkinson's disease: the effect of a 13-week feasibility study on single and dual task walking. *Parkinson's Disease*, 2010, 2010.

[8] N. de Bruin, J. B. Doan, G. Turnbull, et al. Walking with music is a safe and viable tool for gait training in Parkinson's disease. *Parkinson's Disease*, 2010, 2010.

[9] M. F. del Olmo and J. Cudeiro. Temporal variability of gait in Parkinson disease: Effectsof a rehabilitation programme based on rhythmic sound cues. *Parkinsonism & Related Disorders*, 11(1):25–33, 2005.

[10] H. T. Dinh, C. Lee, D. Niyato, and P. Wang. A survey of mobile cloud computing: architecture, applications, and approaches. *Wireless Communications and Mobile Computing*, 13(18):1587–1611, 2013.

[11] E. Dorsey, R. Constantinescu, J. Thompson, et al. Projected number of people with Parkinson disease in the most populous nations, 2005 through 2030. *Neurology*, 68(5):384–386, 2007.

[12] C. G. Goetz, S. Fahn, et al. Movement Disorder Society-sponsored revision of the Unified Parkinson's Disease Rating Scale (MDS-UPDRS): Process, format, and clinimetric testing plan. *Movement Disorders*, 22(1):41–47, 2007.

[13] Y. A. Grimbergen, M. Munneke, and B. R. Bloem. Falls in Parkinson's disease. *Current Opinion in Neurology*, 17(4):405–415, 2004.

[14] J. M. Hausdorff. Gait dynamics, fractals and falls: finding meaning in the stride-to-stride fluctuations of human walking. *Human Movement Science*, 26(4):555–589, 2007.

[15] J. M. Hausdorff. Gait dynamics in Parkinson's disease: common and distinct behavior among stride length, gait variability, and fractal-like scaling. *Chaos: Interdiscipl J Nonlinear Sci*, 19(2):026113, 2009.

[16] J. M. Hausdorff, Z. Ladin, and J. Y. Wei. Footswitch system for measurement of the temporal parameters of gait. *J Biomechanics*, 28(3):347–351, 1995.

[17] J. H. Hollman, E. M. McDade, and R. C. Petersen. Normative spatiotemporal gait parameters in older adults. *Gait & Posture*, 34(1):111–118, 2011.

[18] T.-V. How, J. Chee, E. Wan, and A. Mihailidis. Mywalk: a mobile app for gait asymmetry rehabilitation in the community. In *Proc. PervasiveHealth*, pages 73–76. ICST, 2013.

[19] J. J. Kavanagh and H. B. Menz. Accelerometry: a technique for quantifying movement patterns during walking. *Gait & Posture*, 28(1):1–15, 2008.

[20] S. H. Keus, M. Munneke, et al. Physical therapy in Parkinson's disease: evolution and future challenges. *Movement Disorders*, 24(1):1–14, 2009.

[21] R. LeMoyne, T. Mastroianni, and W. Grundfest. Wireless accelerometer iPod application for quantifying gait characteristics. In *Proc. EMBC*, pages 7904–7907. IEEE, 2011.

[22] I. v. Lim, E. Van Wegen, et al. Effects of external rhythmical cueing on gait in patients with Parkinson's disease: a systematic review. *Clin Rehab*, 19(7):695–713, 2005.

[23] S. Lord, K. Baker, et al. Gait variability in Parkinson's disease: an indicator of non-dopaminergic contributors to gait dysfunction? *J Neurol*, 258(4):566–572, 2011.

[24] S. Lord, T. Howe, et al. Gait variability in older adults: a structured review of testing protocol and clinimetric properties. *Gait & Posture*, 34(4):443–450, 2011.

[25] M. E. McNeely, R. P. Duncan, and G. M. Earhart. Medication improves balance and complex gait performance in Parkinson disease. *Gait & Posture*, 36(1):144–148, 2012.

[26] S. Mellone, C. Tacconi, and L. Chiari. Validity of a smartphone-based instrumented Timed Up and Go. *Gait & Posture*, 36(1):163–165, 2012.

[27] H. B. Menz, M. D. Latt, et al. Reliability of the GAITRite walkway system for the quantification of temporo-spatial parameters of gait in young and older people. *Gait & Posture*, 20(1):20–25, 2004.

[28] H. B. Menz, S. R. Lord, and R. C. Fitzpatrick. Acceleration patterns of the head and pelvis when walking are associated with risk of falling in community-dwelling older people. *J Gerontology Series A: Bio Sci and Med Sci*, 58(5):M446–M452, 2003.

[29] R. Moe-Nilssen. A new method for evaluating motor control in gait under real-life environmental conditions. part 1: The instrument. *Clin Biomech*, 13(4):320–327, 1998.

[30] T. B. Moeslund, A. Hilton, and V. Krüger. A survey of advances in vision-based human motion capture and analysis. *Computer Vision and Image Understanding*, 104(2):90–126, 2006.

[31] S. Nishiguchi, M. Yamada, et al. Reliability and validity of gait analysis by Android-based smartphone. *Telemedicine and e-Health*, 18(4):292–296, 2012.

[32] C. W. Olanow, Y. Agid, et al. Levodopa in the treatment of Parkinson's disease: current controversies. *Movement Disorders*, 19(9):997–1005, 2004.

[33] C. Pacchetti, F. Mancini, et al. Active music therapy in Parkinson's disease: an integrative method for motor and emotional rehabilitation. *Psychosomatic Medicine*, 62(3):386–393, 2000.

[34] L. Palmerini, S. Mellone, L. Rocchi, and L. Chiari. Dimensionality reduction for the quantitative evaluation of a smartphone-based Timed Up and Go test. In *Proc. EMBC*, pages 7179–7182. IEEE, 2011.

[35] M. Plotnik, N. Giladi, and J. M. Hausdorff. A new measure for quantifying the bilateral coordination of human gait. *Exp. Brain Res*, 181(4):561–570, 2007.

[36] T. C. Rubinstein, N. Giladi, and J. M. Hausdorff. The power of cueing to circumvent dopamine deficits: a review of physical therapy treatment of gait disturbances in Parkinson's disease. *Movement Disorders*, 17(6):1148–1160, 2002.

[37] Y. Song, S. Shin, S. Kim, D. Lee, and K. Lee. Speed estimation from a tri-axial accelerometer using neural networks. In *Proc. EMBC*, pages 3224–3227, Aug 2007.

[38] S. J. Spaulding, B. Barber, et al. Cueing and gait improvement among people with Parkinson's disease: A meta-analysis. *Archives Phys Med and Rehab*, 94(3):562–570, 2013.

[39] D. H. Sutherland. The evolution of clinical gait analysis part III–kinetics and energy assessment. *Gait & Posture*, 21(4):447–461, 2005.

[40] A. L. Taylor Tavares, G. S. Jefferis, et al. Quantitative measurements of alternating finger tapping in Parkinson's disease correlate with UPDRS motor disability and reveal the improvement in fine motor control from medication and deep brain stimulation. *Movement Disorders*, 20(10):1286–1298, 2005.

[41] K. E. Webster, J. E. Wittwer, and J. A. Feller. Validity of the GAITRite walkway system for the measurement of averaged and individual step parameters of gait. *Gait & Posture*, 22(4):317–321, 2005.

[42] M. Yamada, T. Aoyama, et al. Using a smartphone while walking: a measure of dual-tasking ability as a falls risk assessment tool. *Age and Ageing*, 40(4):516–519, 2011.

[43] M. Yang, H. Zheng, et al. Assessing the utility of smart mobile phones in gait pattern analysis. *Health and Technology*, 2(1):81–88, 2012.

[44] M. Yang, H. Zheng, et al. igait: An interactive accelerometer based gait analysis system. *Comp Meth and Prog in Biomed*, 108(2):715–723, 2012.

[45] S. Zhu, H. Anderson, and Y. Wang. A real-time on-chip algorithm for IMU-based gait measurement. In *Advances in Multimedia Information Processing–PCM 2012*, pages 93–104. Springer, 2012.

[46] W. Zijlstra. Assessment of spatio-temporal parameters during unconstrained walking. *European J Applied Physiology*, 92(1-2):39–44, 2004.

[47] W. Zijlstra and A. L. Hof. Assessment of spatio-temporal gait parameters from trunk accelerations during human walking. *Gait & Posture*, 18(2):1–10, 2003.

Towards Efficient Privacy-preserving Image Feature Extraction in Cloud Computing

Zhan Qin[1] Jingbo Yan[1] Kui Ren[1] Chang Wen Chen[1] Cong Wang[2]
[1]Department of Computer Science and Engineering, SUNY at Buffalo, Buffalo, NY 14214 USA
[2]Department of Computer Science, City University of Hong Kong, Hong Kong
zhanqin@buffalo.edu, jbyan@xidian.edu.cn, kuiren@buffalo.edu, chencw@buffalo.edu, congwang@cityu.edu.hk

ABSTRACT

As the image data produced by individuals and enterprises is rapidly increasing, Scalar Invariant Feature Transform (SIFT), as a local feature detection algorithm, has been heavily employed in various areas, including object recognition, robotic mapping, etc. In this context, there is a growing need to outsource such image computation with high complexity to cloud for its economic computing resources and on-demand ubiquitous access. However, how to protect the private image data while enabling image computation becomes a major concern. To address this fundamental challenge, we study the privacy requirements in outsourcing SIFT computation and propose SecSIFT, a high performance privacy-preserving SIFT feature detection system. In previous private image computation works, one common approach is to encrypt the private image in a public key based homomorphic scheme that enables the original processing algorithms designed for plaintext domain to be performed over ciphertext domain. In contrast to these works, our system is not restricted by the efficiency limitations of homomorphic encryption scheme. The proposed system distributes the computation procedures of SIFT to a set of independent, co-operative cloud servers, and keeps the outsourced computation procedures as simple as possible to avoid utilizing homomorphic encryption scheme. Thus, it enables implementation with practical computation and communication complexity. Extensive experimental results demonstrate that SecSIFT performs comparably to original SIFT on image benchmarks while capable of preserving the privacy in an efficient way.

Categories and Subject Descriptors

H.3.3 [**Information Systems Applications**]: Information Search and Retrieval

General Terms

Security, Algorithm

MM'14, November 3–7, 2014, Orlando, Florida, USA.

http://dx.doi.org/10.1145/2647868.2654941.

Keywords

Image Feature Detection; SIFT; Privacy-preserving; Cloud Computing

1. INTRODUCTION

Nowadays, it is getting more and more popular for owners to outsource image data from local devices to cloud for its great flexibility and cost saving [2]. Popular social network providers commonly utilize image data to realize behavioral advertising, preference analytics, etc., [16]. For example, Facebook and Flickr are extracting qualified features from users' images and constructing corresponding data mining models to improve their user experiences in social discovery [20]. To manage the massive computation workload in image feature extraction and utilization on the "Big Data", more and more image owners choose to outsource the computation of image feature extractions to cloud [32]. However, this trend creates the privacy concerns. The outsourced image data reveals private information of the owner, like personal identity, location, or even financial profiles. Moreover, even features extracted from the image may leak important private information. The attacker can deduce the content of image via feature comparisons in a benchmark image database, or even recover part of the image based on these features. Thus, exploring privacy-preserving image feature detection over encrypted cloud data becomes of paramount importance.

There is an emerging research field on discovering solutions to enable image processing over encrypted data [15]. In secure multimedia data search [26, 19], the authors propose designs to protect the privacy of the query image when searching over a public database by utilizing oblivious retrieval techniques. Some existing works are interested in the manipulation of encrypted image data in different forms, e.g., face recognition system [10, 25, 23], ECG signals [4], and fingercode authentication system [3]. Others focus on extracting/detecting image features from the ciphertext domain, e.g., Scalar Invariant Feature Transform (SIFT) [14], and shape-based image features [29].

However, all previous works on private image feature detection impose either heavy workload for image owners or unacceptable computational complexity at the cloud side, if not both. Thus, none of them is suitable for practical usages. In [10, 5], image owners have to perform very expensive operations of homomorphic encryption before outsourcing. In [12, 14], existing solutions require the cloud to perform massive homomorphic evaluations in the ciphertext domain (Details refer to Sec. 6). Another common weakness is that no previous work can protect the location information of the feature points, which may subsequently lead to significant information leakage to the cloud server depending the nature of the images [29].

Hence, in this paper, we focus on enabling practical and privacy-preserving SIFT computation over outsourced image. We present SecSIFT, a system for performing privacy-preserving image feature detection over private user image data, which scales substantially better than the previous systems. SecSIFT operates under the similar trust model as used in several recent private proposals, i.e., honest-but-curious and independent servers. There are two key points that differentiate our proposal from other homomorphic encryption based solutions [19, 29, 12]: How the privacy of local feature's locations is defined, and How the computation procedures are distributed among cloud servers. Prior works only protect the image data by encrypting them through a homomorphic encryption scheme. They either leak the locations of feature points to the cloud [13] or require impractical computational resources [19]. In our security model, the privacy of image content is defined in two aspects: the *confidentiality of values* and the *delocalization of keypoints*. Both of them are protected. The proposed design also divides the SIFT algorithm into several computation procedures and distributing them to different cloud entities. The efficiency of the proposed system is promised by utilizing splitting based encryption, Order Preserving Encryption (OPE), random permutation, and dummy point perturbation as its crypto primitives in different components of the system.

Altogether, this paper makes the following contributions:

- It presents the design of SecSIFT, a private system for performing SIFT computation without leaking the private information of the processed image. SecSIFT is typically one to two orders of magnitude more efficient in bandwidth and computation complexity than previous comparable systems (i.e., the systems with similar features and trust model).
- It gives formal security proofs to justify the correctness and privacy-preserving guarantee of the proposed mechanism. A detailed evaluation on the utility, privacy, and efficiency of SecSIFT is provided.
- It describes a complete implementation of SecSIFT. Extensive experiments on Microsoft Azure cloud instance with real dataset across thousands of images (Caltech256) demonstrate the effectiveness and efficiency of the proposed system.

The rest of this paper is organized as follows: The next section gives a brief introduction to SIFT algorithm. Section 3 gives the problem formulation of SecSIFT, and states the design goals of the proposed system. Section 4 presents the system design. We describe analysis and evaluation of the correctness, privacy, and efficiency of the proposed system in Section 5.1, 5.2, and 5.3. Finally, we present related work and conclude in Section 6 and 7, respectively.

2. PRELIMINARY ON SIFT

Scale Invariant Feature Transform (SIFT) is one of the most popular algorithms in computer vision to extract and describe local features in images. We separate it into mainly two stages to describe the algorithm briefly below. Detailed elaboration can be found in [17]:

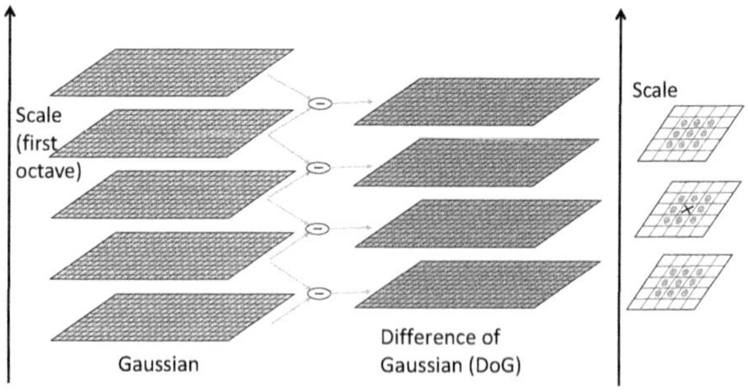

Figure 1: *Scale-space Extrema Detection*: The image forms a series of octave via convolutions and subtractions [17].

- *Scale-space Extrema Detection*: This is the stage where the keypoints are detected (located). In this stage, the image is convolved with Gaussian filters at multiple scales, and then successive Gaussian-blurred images are taken. The keypoints are taken as extreme points of the Difference of Gaussians (DoG) that occur at multiple scales. Specifically, a DoG image $D(x, y, \sigma)$ is given by

  $$D(x, y, \sigma) = L(x, y, k_i\sigma) - L(x, y, k_j\sigma) \quad (1)$$

  where $L(x, y, k\sigma)$ is the convolution of the original image $I(x, y)$ with the Gaussian-blur $G(x, y, k\sigma)$ at scale $k\sigma$, i.e., $L(x, y, k\sigma) = G(x, y, k\sigma) * I(x, y)$. Hence a DoG image between scales $k_i\sigma$ and $k_j\sigma$ is just the difference of the Gaussian-blurred images at scales $k_i\sigma$ and $k_j\sigma$. As shown in Fig. 1, for *Scale-space Extrema Detection*, the convolved images are grouped by octave (an octave corresponds to doubling the value of σ). The DoG images are taken from adjacent Gaussian-blurred images per octave.

  Once DoG images are obtained, keypoints are identified as local extrema of the DoG images across scales. This is done by comparing each pixel in the DoG images to its eight neighbors at the same scale and nine corresponding neighboring pixels in each of the neighboring scales. If a pixel value is an extrema among all neighboring pixels, it is selected as a keypoint.

- *Feature Descriptor Generation*: In this step, the keypoints are assigned orientations based on local image gradient directions. The keypoint descriptor can be represented relative to this orientation, which explaines the invariance to image rotation.

  First, the Gaussian-blurred image $L(x, y, \sigma)$ at the keypoint's scale σ is taken so that all computations are performed in a scale-invariant manner. For an image sample $L(x, y, \sigma)$, the gradient vector consists of magnitude $m(x, y)$ and orientation $\theta(x, y)$, which are calculated using pixel differences: Let the gradient magnitudes be, respectively, denoted as $\mathsf{Diff_X} = L(x+1, y, \sigma) - L(x-1, y, \sigma)$, and $\mathsf{Diff_Y} = L(x, y+1, \sigma) - L(x, y-1, \sigma)$ along different directions. For each 4×4 block, the gradient magnitude and orientation are, respectively, computed for each position (x, y) within the block as:

  $$m(x, y) = \sqrt{(\mathsf{Diff_X})^2 + (\mathsf{Diff_Y})^2} \quad (2)$$

  $$\theta(x, y) = tan^{-1}\frac{\mathsf{Diff_X}}{\mathsf{Diff_Y}} \quad (3)$$

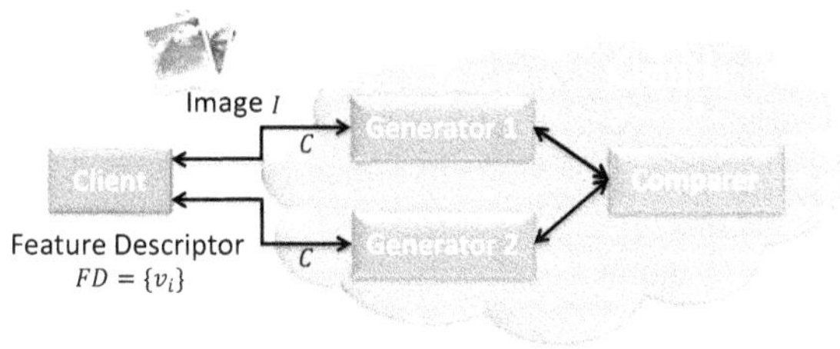

Figure 2: System Architecture: Three independent entities (cloud servers) ensure the privacy of image is preserved in SecSIFT.

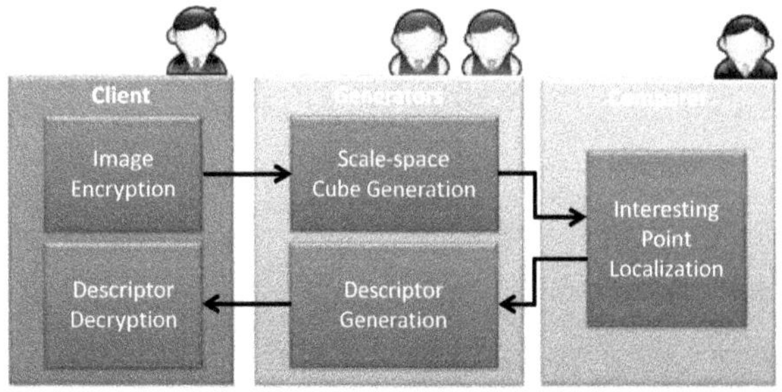

Figure 3: Architecture and Workflow of SecSIFT.

The magnitude and direction computations for the gradient are done for every pixel in a neighboring region around the keypoint in the Gaussian-blurred image. Note that this gradient vector can also be represented in other forms, besides magnitude and direction, while the accuracy of the SIFT algorithm can still remain largely unchanged. However, different representation forms may lead to different computational complexity in the ciphertext domain, which will be discussed in Sec 4.4. After the computations of the magnitude and direction, an orientation histogram with 36 bins is formed, with each bin covering 10 degrees. Each sample in the neighboring window added to a histogram bin is weighted by its gradient magnitude and a Gaussian-weighted circular window with a σ that is 1.5 times that of the keypoint's scale. The peaks in this histogram correspond to dominant orientations. Once the histogram is filled, the orientations corresponding to the highest peak and local peaks that are larger than 80% of the highest peaks are assigned to the keypoint.

3. PROBLEM FORMULATION

3.1 System Architecture

As illustrated in Fig. 2, we consider a high-level architecture of SecSIFT. At the core, the system consists of two parties: Client and Cloud. Client may represent either an individual or an enterprise customer, who owns private image data and aims to outsource the computation task on SIFT Feature Descriptors (*FDs*) over these images to cloud. Specifically, to keep sensitive image data confidential against unauthorized access, cryptographic techniques need to be applied to the image data before outsourcing. In our system, Client encrypts the image, denoted by plaintext matrix I, into a ciphertext matrix, denoted by C, and then uploads it to Cloud. The expected image processing results from Cloud are a set of SIFT descriptors, which are FD vectors of keypoints in the image obtained by the SIFT algorithm. Cloud consists of three entities: two Generators and a Comparer, which are independent cloud server providers. These entities are named according to the functionality they perform in SecSIFT:

- Generators: Generators are composed of two cloud entities (servers) that perform mirrored procedures over encrypted image. Thus, for simplicity, we consider them as one entity: It receives encrypted image from Client. And then it generates the scale-space and corresponding scale-space cubes (27 neighboring pixels from 3 scales). After that, it sends permuted scale-space cubes to Comparer, and receives the locations of keypoints from Comparer. Finally it outputs FD vectors as the results of SIFT algorithm to Client.
- Comparer: Comparer performs the comparison procedures, which is designed for performing the discovery of keypoints in SIFT algorithm. More specifically, this procedure is performed through a series of comparisons of neighboring pixels in the scale-space to find local extrema in the image. In our design, the output of Comparer is the cube identifier of the corresponding the keypoint, which is conducted to protect the privacy of the image against both Generator and Comparer at the same time (formally defined in Sec. 4.2.2).

3.2 Security Model

We consider the image I owned by Client to be private. The clients' goal is to protect the privacy of the image content, while enabling Cloud to execute SIFT algorithm over it. Specifically, we consider the information of image content: pixel values, keypoint locations, and descriptive features extracted from the image, to be clients' private information.

In our security model, we consider the Cloud to be "honest-but-curious" and "independent". We assume that Cloud acts in an "honest but curious" fashion, which means it correctly follows the designated protocol specification, but is interested in inferring from or analyzes the data flow to learn additional information. In our design, Client uploads his/her image in a split form to multiple cloud entities, which carry out the computations regarding SIFT. Similar to the secure multiparty computation schemes, we assume the cloud entities to be "independent" to each other. This assumption is promised by the independent reputation and financial interests of the cloud server provider. Here, Generators and Comparer would explicitly state non-collusion in their legally binding documents. Thus, the independence among cloud entities can be assured in practice [8].

3.3 Design Goals

Our ultimate goal is to design a privacy-preserving SIFT feature detection system that supports the outsourced image feature detection service, while providing the strongest possible protection on the image content privacy and simultaneously maintaining the efficiency. In particular, we have the following design goals:

Image Content Privacy: As claimed in our security model, the cloud entities should get no access to the image content like pixel values and detected features. According to the accepted security standard in image encryption [28], the *confidentiality* of the image is protected when each pixel of the image is encrypted. Consider an image as a matrix, if ev-

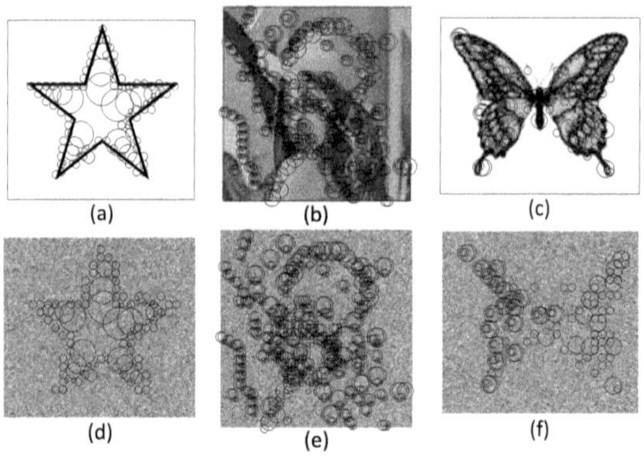

Figure 4: SIFT features (intermediate) in plaintext domain (a), (b), (c) and ciphertext domain (d), (e), (f).

ery element is protected (depending on different encryption scheme), the whole matrix, i.e., the image is protected. Following this methodology, we define the privacy of image data values to be the *confidentiality* of values. Moreover, in outsourced image local feature extraction like SIFT algorithm, the location of keypoints may also leak image content, e.g., the shape of objects in the image. As shown in Fig. 4, though not considered in general image retrieval applications, intermediate result such as feature points along strong edges and their locations form crude object shapes, which reveal sensitive information of images. To solve this problem, we define the *delocalization* of keypoints: For each cloud entities, it is computationally hard to get the location of keypoints in the image, which means the keypoint's location of the image is protected against Cloud. The delocalization property can prevent the cloud entities deducing private content shapes from the images.

Computational Savings: Client's workload in SecSIFT should be substantially less than the workload of completing a local SIFT program.

Cloud Efficiency: It is further desirable to reduce the computational complexity on Cloud process as much as possible and finally make it acceptable when compared with a local SIFT program.

4. SecSIFT SYSTEM DESIGN

As shown in Fig. 3, SecSIFT algorithm consists of five sequential components: *Image Encryption, Scale-space Cube Generation, Keypoint Discovering, Descriptor Generation,* and *Descriptor Decryption*. The detailed construction of each component will be shown in Sec. 4.1-4.5. Here, we first give a high-level description on the system workflow of SecSIFT.

At the beginning, Client takes an image and security parameters as the system inputs and passes the encrypted (split) image C and $seed_c$ to Generators and $seed_d$ to Comparer (Sec. 4.1). After receiving the ciphertext from Client, Generator generates the corresponding scale-space and cubes. Then it shuffles surrounding pixels and encrypts the cube through an OPE scheme and passes the encrypted cubes attached with corresponding identifiers to Comparer (Sec. 4.2). Comparer decrypts the received cubes from both Generators and locates the keypoints by discovering the cubes that include extrema. The corresponding identifiers attached to the keypoints are then sent back to two Generators, inserted with some dummy identifiers (Sec. 4.3). Generators locate the

Algorithm 1 Splitting based Image Encryption

Input:
The matrix of the image, I, security parameter κ;

Output:
The ciphertext pair: C_1 and C_2; Control parameters s_{id}, s_p, and s_d;

Generate prime modulus $t := Gen_{prime}(1^\kappa)$, and matrix $R \leftarrow PRG(1^\kappa)$;
for each pixel at position (x, y) in I **do**
  Encrypt $I(x, y)$ by splitting the value: $C_1(x, y) = R(x, y)$, $C_2(x, y) = (I - R(x, y)) \ mod \ q$;
end for
Generate control parameters $s_{id} \leftarrow PRG_{id}(1^\kappa)$, $s_p \leftarrow PRG_p(1^\kappa)$, and $s_d \leftarrow PRG_d(1^\kappa)$;
return C_1, C_2, s_{id}, s_p, and s_d.

corresponding pixel points in the image after receiving those identifiers from Comparer, and then generate feature descriptors of keypoints over ciphertext domain and sends them back to Client (Sec. 4.4). Finally, Client discards the feature descriptors corresponding to the dummy identifiers, and then decrypts the rest of feature descriptors as the system output (Sec. 4.5).

4.1 Client: Image Encryption

Before outsourcing an image to Cloud, Client needs to encrypt the image and generate a set of control parameters to control the privacy-preserving mechanisms on different cloud entities. Instead of encrypting each pixel of the image through a public key based homomorphic encryption scheme as in the existing works [25, 14], Client additively splits the image matrix I into two ciphertext matrices: It first generates a prime modulus q, which defines the message space of the encryption scheme, and a random matrix R, whose elements are chosen from $[0, q-1]$. Then, it encrypts the image by splitting the matrix I into two matrices: $C_1 = R$ and $C_2 = (I - R) \ mod \ q$ and sends them to Generators, respectively: Client $\rightarrow$ Generator1 : C_1; Client $\rightarrow$ Generator2 : C_2. The details are illustrated in Alg. 1. After that, Client generates and sends control parameters s_{id}, s_p, and s_d to Generators and Comparer: Client $\rightarrow$ Generators : (s_{id}, s_p); Client $\rightarrow$ Comparer : s_d. Specifically, s_{id} and s_p synchronize the generation of scale-space cubes' identifiers and permutations on Generators (Sec. 4.2.2). And s_d controls the generation of dummy identifiers on Comparer (Sec. 4.3).

4.2 Generator: Scale-space Cube Generation

4.2.1 Scale-space Generation

After receiving ciphertexts C_1 and C_2 from Client, both Generators perform convolutions and subtractions, as in the original SIFT algorithm, to generate scale-space. Specifically, for each pixel in the ciphertext matrix C_i, Generator performs the following computations to generate the DoG images at scale σ:

$$D(x, y, \sigma) = (G(x, y, k_i\sigma) - G(x, y, k_j\sigma)) * C_i(x, y) \qquad (4)$$

where $G(x, y, \sigma) = \frac{1}{2\pi\sigma^2} e^{-(x^2+y^2)/2\sigma^2}$. The results of Gaussian function at different scales are a set of constant matrices, which are considered to be public information to all participants. Thus, the generation of these matrices can be performed by Generator over plaintext domain. Note that Generators work over encrypted images, which are split into two homologous ciphertexts. Therefore, both Generators must compute in the same operation order for each encrypted pixel to generate a homologous scale-space.

4.2.2 Cube Encryption

After generating the scale-space, Cloud needs to discover keypoints as local extrema from the scale-space through comparisons. However, these comparisons cannot be performed by a cloud entity. It could leak the pixel values in the image, though the image is encrypted. If only one cloud entity performs all the tasks, it will lead to pixel value leakage to the cloud. Note that even if the cloud performs the comparisons in the ciphertext domain, it can still learn the values of encrypted pixels: The comparable ciphertexts enables Cloud to deduce the content of the image through comparing all encrypted pixel values in the image. To solve this problem, we assume the existence of three non-colluding cloud entities. Our scheme is designed in such a way that none of them alone can deduce any pixel value information by itself. Comparer is introduced as a cloud server to discover keypoints through comparing neighboring pixels in scale-space. To better illustrate the balance between privacy and effectiveness of the proposed solution, we first analyze two naive solutions and their shortcomings:

- *Cube Permutation:* A naive solution is dividing the scale-space into multiple cubes, which contain 27 pixels acrossing 3 scales, and permutating these cubes randomly before sending them to Comparer. However, only permutation alone cannot break the space correlations of neighboring cubes completely. It is still computationally possible for Comparer to discover the space order of cubes through traversing all cubes and finding the overlapping pixels (18 pixels at maximum) among neighboring cubes.

- *Noise Perturbation:* Another naive solution is perturbing noises into pixels to hide the overlapping pixels in neighboring cubes. The perturbed noises make it computational impossible for Comparer to find overlapping pixels in neighboring cubes. However, the noise perturbation based solution may badly weaken the effectiveness of the system. Specifically, the precision of comparisons is compromised by noise perturbation. The reason is that the effectiveness on comparisons and the protection on ciphertexts inherently contradict to each other in noise perturbation mechanisms.

Based on the previous analysis on the possible solutions, we propose a novel solution to discover the keypoints in the scale-space without compromising the privacy of the image. In this solution, the OPE scheme proposed in [1] is adopted to enable the ciphertext comparisons to be performed by Comparer. However, since the image data uploaded by Client is over ciphertext domain, we cannot directly use the scheme in [1]. Thus, we need to carefully modify a piece-wise linear spline to enable Comparer to recover the split image from OPE ciphertexts. The complete construction is explained in the following:

Cube Encryption: As illustrated in the *Cube Permutation*, Generator first divides the scale-space into cubes, as shown in Fig. 1. At the beginning, Generator encrypts all pixels in the processed image cubes through an OPE scheme, as shown in Alg. 2. The modeling of target distribution yields a set of buckets $\{B_1^t, ..., B_k^t\}$. For every bucket of length

Algorithm 2 OPE based Cube Encryption

Require:
The split image cube $Cube_i$;
Ensure:
The encrypted split image cube $\widehat{Cube_i}$;
for each pixel in $Cube_i$ **do**
  for predefined bucket $j = 1...\|m\|$ **do**
    Generating a set of bucket $[p_l, p_h)$, with $h - l - 1$ points;
  end for
  if a distribution over $[0, p_h)$ has the density function $pq + r$ for constant q and r; **then**
    For any constant $z > 0$;
    $\mathcal{M}(p) = z(\frac{q}{2r}p^2 + p)$;
  end if
  At bucket width w, flat value f is $f = f_{min} + \sum_{j=1}^{i-1} w_j^f + \mathcal{M}_i(p - p_{min} - \sum_{j=1}^{i-1} w_j)$;
  Encrypted the pixel in split image $\widehat{Cube_i} := c_{min} + \sum_{j=1}^{i-1} w_j^c + (\mathcal{M}_i^c)^{-1}(f - f_{min} - \sum_{j=1}^{i-1} w_j^f)$,
end for
return $\widehat{Cube_i}$;

w^t, we also get the mapping function $\mathcal{M}^t$ and associated parameters s^t and z^t. Assume the maximum width for each bucket is $K = max[w_i]$. Note that f denotes flatten space, t denotes target stage, and c denotes cipher space:

$$\mathcal{M}^c(w^c) = z^c(s^c(w^c)^2 + w^c), \quad z = \frac{K^t n^t}{s^t(w^t)^2 + w^t}; \tag{5}$$

where $s = q/2r$. After that, we save the bucket boundaries in the cipher space in the data structure $\mathcal{K}^c$. For every bucket, we also save the quadratic coefficients s^c and the scale factor z^c.

The scheme enables the split image recovery as follows: First, when computing the scale factors for each bucket by using the constraint. In this step, the bucket should map to a space proportional to the number of points in the bucket, in which the duplicate points are excluded. Thus, adjacent plaintext values in the regions will be mapped to flattened values that are relatively close. Suppose that using our modified scheme, a plaintext value p maps into a value f in the flat space, and $p + 1$ maps into f'. When encrypting p, we choose the random value close to the interval's center $[\frac{f'-f}{2})$. Thus, the encrypted value of p will be uniformly spread in the interval $[f, f')$. Combining the intra-bucket uniformity generated by the linear splines, and the inter-bucket uniformity from the scale factors together results in the flattened distribution to be uniform. In addition, to identify the extent, the OPE scheme maintains distance between plaintexts, and we start from analyzing the distance of any two random plaintexts. The size of the ciphertext depends on the skew in the plaintext and target distributions. Assume g_{min}^p to be the smallest gap between sorted values in the plaintext. Similarly, we can define g_{max}^p, g_{min}^t, and g_{max}^t. Then, the additional number of bits needed by the ciphertext in the worst case is approximated as:

$$l_{add} = \log(\frac{g_{max}^p}{g_{min}^p}) + \log(\frac{g_{max}^t}{g_{min}^t}) \tag{6}$$

Algorithm 3 Cube ID Perturbation

Input:
The random number s_{id}, the ID set of keypiont $\{ID\}$;
Output:
The perturbed cube ID: $\{\bar{ID}\}$;
Generating a binomial pseudorandom matrix $M = PRG_M(|I|, s_{id})$;
for All $(x, y) \in I$ **do**
  if $M(x, y) > 0$ **then**
    Computing $DID := H(s_{id}, x, y)$;
    for each $DID \notin \{ID\}$
    $\{\bar{ID}\} = \{ID\} \cup \{DID\}$;
  end if
end for
return $\{\bar{ID}\}$;.

Note that we can explicitly control g^t, i.e., the length introduced by the target stage, while g^p depends on the different format of the image data.

Permutation: After the encryption of OPE scheme, both Generators generate cube identifiers and permutate the cubes under a same set of control parameters. First, each Generator generates an identifier for each cube, denoted as *CID*. It generates it with the control parameter and corresponding position in the image matrix as the inputs: $CID = H(s_{id}, x, y)$. Recall that (x, y) is the position in the image matrix, and H is a predefined random hash function. Since both Generators use the same control parameter s_id in identifier generation, the identifiers of the cubes at same positions can be synchronized. After that, Generators performs the permutation of cubes with the s_p from Client, pixel position and scales as the inputs: $Seq = H_p(s_p, x, y, \sigma)$. For this procedure, s_id from *CID* generation and s_p from cube permutation guarantee the synchronization of operations in Generators.

4.3 Comparer: Keypoint Discovering

After receiving split image cubes $\widehat{Cube_1}$ and $\widehat{Cube_2}$ from Generators, Comparer recovers the encrypted cubes through additions: $\widehat{Cube} = \widehat{Cube_1} + \widehat{Cube_2}$. Then, it identifies cubes that include extremum through comparing 26 pixels with the centre pixel in the cube. After that, to protect the location of keypoints against Generators, Comparer generates a set of dummy identifiers, i.e., *DID*s, with the s_d from Client. Then, it mixes them with *CID*s connected with extrema, before sending them back to Generators, as shown in Alg. 3. The detailed privacy analysis of inserting *DID*s will be shown in Sec. 5.2.

4.4 Generator: Descriptor Generation

Generators perform the adjusted feature descriptor generation procedures, after receiving the perturbed cube ID set $\{\bar{ID}\}$ from Comparer. As described in Sec. 2, SIFT derives the feature descriptor of keypoint from computing the magnitude and direction of its neighboring pixels in the plaintext domain. The orientation assignment is executed for each detected feature point. The histogram of weighted magnitudes, which are defined on a number of restrictive directions, is derived based on the Eq. (3). A normalized region of size 16×16, which is expanded from the region covering the derived orientation, is built. A 128-dimensional SIFT feature descriptor is established for the 16×16 region, which is further divided into sixteen 4×4 blocks, around a feature point.

Algorithm 4 Descriptor Generation

Input:
The perturbed cube ID set $\{\bar{ID}\}$;
Output:
The descriptor of keypoint V_{di};
for Each $\bar{ID} \in \{\bar{ID}\}$ **do**
  Compute the position of keypoint from the ID set: $(x, y) = H^{-1}(\bar{ID})$;
  for each surrounding block of keypoint **do**
    $V(0) = V(0) + (L(x+1, y, \sigma) - (L(x-1, y, \sigma)$;
    $V(1) = V(1) + (L(x, y+1, \sigma) - (L(x, y-1, \sigma)$;
    $V(2) = V(2) + (L(x-1, y-1, \sigma) - (L(x+1, y+1, \sigma)$;
    $V(3) = V(3) + (L(x+1, y-1, \sigma) - (L(x-1, y+1, \sigma)$;
    Concatenate region features together: $V_d = (V_d || V(0) || V(1) || V(2) || V(3))$;
  end for
end for
return V_{di};.

For feature descriptor extraction conducted over ciphertext domain, the histogram and vector computations require high computational complexity and are too complicated to be implemented over ciphertext domain. Thus, we modify the original descriptor to generate the weighted magnitudes located at four directions (i.e., $0°, 45°, 90°$, and $135°$) in the proposed system, which constitutes a 4-dimensional vector, as shown in Fig. 5. Since a 16×16 region contains sixteen 4×4 blocks, a 64-dimensional feature descriptor for a keypoint is established. Due to the security constraint on comparisons, no additional information of encrypted feature descriptor can be extracted from the ciphertext domain by Generators. Our experimental results reveal that modified SecSIFT descriptors successfully maintain the robustness of the proposed system, as illustrated in Fig. 6(b).

In our design, the feature descriptor calculated in the ciphertext domain for each 4×4 block is conducted as follows: Let $V(k), k = \{0, 1, 2, 3, \}$ denote the feature vector of a 16×16 block:

$$\begin{aligned} \text{Diff}_{0°} &= (L(x+1, y, \sigma) - (L(x-1, y, \sigma) \\ \text{Diff}_{90°} &= (L(x, y+1, \sigma) - (L(x, y-1, \sigma) \\ \text{Diff}_{45°} &= (L(x-1, y-1, \sigma) - (L(x+1, y+1, \sigma) \\ \text{Diff}_{135°} &= (L(x+1, y-1, \sigma) - (L(x-1, y+1, \sigma) \end{aligned} \quad (7)$$

As shown in Alg. 4, each Generator generates a descriptor as split 64-dimensional vector V_d. Then, it sends V_d attached with the *CID* to Client. Note that the descriptors of keypoints include vectors of dummy points. To protect the privacy of location of the keypoints, Generator is designed to perform the descriptor generation of these dummy points. The corresponding computation complexity depends on the number of inserted dummy points from the security parameter settings. However, these dummy points do not affect the decryption workload on Client end. Client can distinguish the dummy descriptors from the real descriptors by simulating Comparer to generate $\{DID\}$.

4.5 Descriptor Decryption

Before recovering the encrypted descriptor (feature vector) by subtracting the split feature descriptors: $V_d = V_{d2} - V_{d1}$, Client needs to identify and discard the dummy feature descriptors. Recall that *DID*s are computed from the pseudorandom matrix M, which only depends on the size of the image and the control parameter s_{id}. Thus, Client can ef-

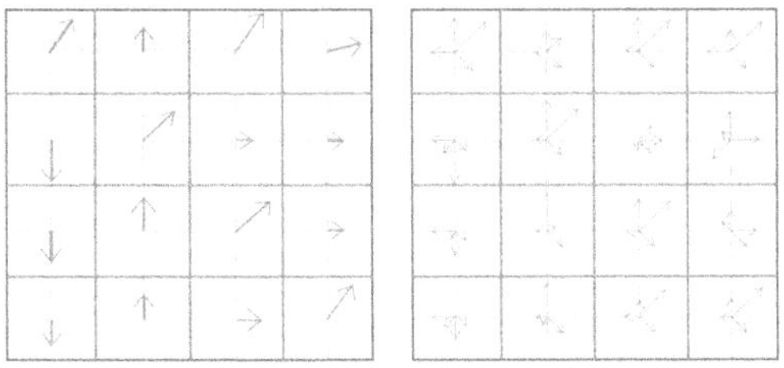

(a) (b)

Figure 5: Original SIFT feature gradient vector (a) and modified feature descriptor (b).

ficiently regenerate the dummy matrix M and discard the descriptors with the corresponding DIDs.

After recovering the feature vectors, Client can perform the orientation calculation to get the assigned orientations and convert the feature vectors of each block to the main orientation as the original SIFT. The effectiveness of adjusted descriptors will be discussed in Sec. 5.1. From the client's perspective, the encryption and decryption computational complexity are both linear to the size of the image. The communication complexity between Cloud and Client contains the upload bandwidth ($2|I|$) and the download bandwidth ($|FD|$), which depend on the size and content of the image.

5. SYSTEM EVALUATION

We conduct a thorough experimental evaluation of the proposed system on real image database: Caltech256, which contains 30,607 images with total size 1.2GB. Our experiment is implemented using C programming language on both local workstation and Microsoft Azure cloud instance. The local workstation runs with an Intel Core2 Duo CPU (E6550) running at 2.33GHz, 4GB of RAM and a 7200RPM disk drive. The cloud side process is conducted on Azure with large standard instance type. We analyze and present our evaluation result in three aspects: correctness, privacy, and efficiency.

5.1 Correctness Analysis and Evaluation

5.1.1 Correctness of Feature Descriptors

Since neighboring input value must have similar output ciphertext under order preserving encryption, the proposed algorithm may not return the exact answers. In the scenario of SIFT algorithm, SecSIFT algorithm should output a noisy list of keypoint at Comparer. Recall that given a plaintext space of size M, i.e., the domain size $|D| = M$, and ciphertext space N, assuming $m_1 < m_2 \in [M]$. The following theorem provides the utility guarantee of SecSIFT:

THEOREM 1. *Let $t = (N-1)/(M-1)$, and assume $t > 7$. Let $m_1 \leftarrow [M], m_2 \leftarrow [M]\{m_1\}$, $(c_1, c_2) = Enc_{r,k}(m_1, m_2), w = c_2 - c_1 \bmod M$, and $d = m_2 - m_1 \bmod M$. Then*

$$Pr_{m_1,m_2}[2d > w] < \frac{3}{t}\frac{1}{\sqrt{(M-1)/lnM}} \tag{8}$$

PROOF. Let $t = (N-1)(M-1)$. Let b be a fixed value (less than $\sqrt{M-1}$) to be determined later. Define $\beta = \frac{2tb\sqrt{M-1}}{t-2}$. Assume w is uniformly random in $[N-1]$, so

$$Pr_{m_1,m_2}[w < \beta + 1] < \frac{\beta+1}{N-1} \tag{9}$$

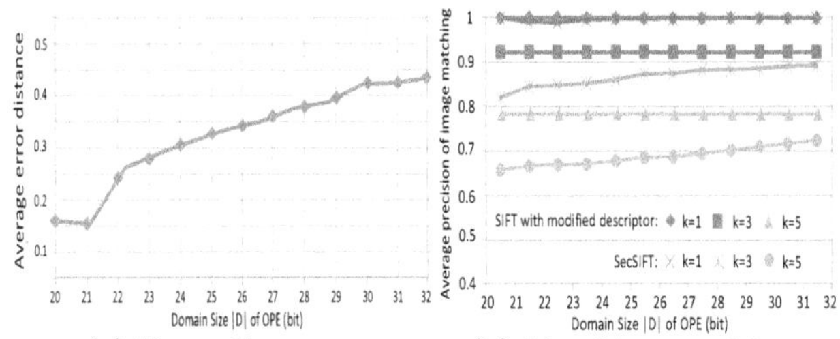

(a) Error distance. (b) Matching precision.

Figure 6: Correctness Evaluation.

Define $d_R = min\{(M-1)w/N + b(M-1)/\sqrt{M-1}, M-1\}$. Note that $(M-1)w/N$ is the most likely plaintext distance of w. Then we can deduce that $d_R < w/2$, whenever $w > \beta+1$. Hence

$$\begin{aligned} Pr_{m_1,m_2}[2d > w] &< Pr_{m_1,m_2}[2d > w | w > \beta + 1] \\ &\quad + Pr_{m_1,m_2}[|w < \beta + 1] \\ &< 2/M + \frac{2b}{(t-2)\sqrt{M-1}} + \frac{1}{N-1} \\ &< 2/M + \frac{2}{t-2}\frac{1}{\sqrt{(M-1)/lnM}} \end{aligned} \tag{10}$$

assuming $t > 7$. This bound gives us the idea of good values for $t = N/M$. In particular, we can find that choosing a constant for $t > 7$, which means choosing N to be a constant multiple of M, is sufficient in order to make the above probability negligible. Whether the constant should be large or small depends on the tolerance for random intervals to be shallow. The upper bound of noise introduced by the OPE scheme to the image value is $\frac{3}{t}\ln(1/M)$. □

5.1.2 Experimental Results

We first analyze the correctness of the proposed system from the view of keypoint localizations. We conduct the experiments regarding comparison between keypoints detected from the plaintext domain and the ones from the ciphertext domain in SecSIFT. The Euclidean distances between the closest keypoints from different domains are computed: The keypoints from SecSIFT and original SIFT are obtained respectively. After that, the corresponding keypoints in SecSIFT based on the ones from original SIFT are discovered. The standard Euclidean Distance is utilized to quantify these distances. Fig. 6(a) illustrates the average error distance between corresponding keypoints. The error is introduced by the randomness from the OPE scheme. In fact the maximum distance between corresponding keypoints from different domains is smaller than 3.56, which means they still have more than 63% overlapping neighboring pixels.

Given the descriptor generated by SecSIFT, we next focus on the precision of the matching results. Basically, the experiments are analogous to the application of image matching. We randomly select 1,000 images from 10 categories, and perform original SIFT, SIFT with modified descriptors and SecSIFT to extract their feature descriptors. Then these descriptors are utilized to compute their Euclidean distance to find the corresponding matching image in the image set. The results regarding the top-k matching images are examined here. As shown in Fig. 7, the left column images are the query (target) image, and the right column images are the top-k (k=4) matching images in the database. Fig. 6(b) illustrates the result of image matching performed over SIFT

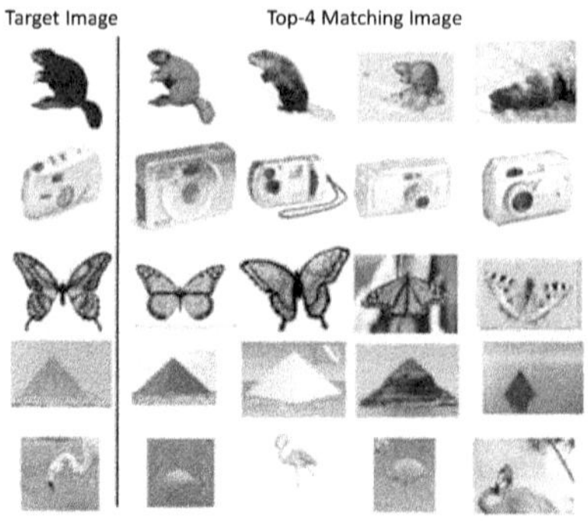

Figure 7: An example of image matching using SecSIFT.

with modified descriptors and SecSIFT, compared with the original SIFT as the ground truth. When $k = 1$, the precision is above 99%. The matching results are almost the same. When $k > 2$, the precision of the proposed system reduces, but still remains above 80% on average.

5.2 Privacy Analysis and Evaluation

5.2.1 Confidentiality of Pixel Values & Descriptive Feature Vectors

To analyze the confidentiality of the image content, we start with the observed data by each cloud entity. For Generator, it can only observe the encrypted (split) image and the cube identifier *CID* returned by Comparer. The image splitting mechanism provides the security guarantee of image content against Generator, as long as the client generate a new key every time to encrypt the image. The security strength of the ciphertext depends on the security of the utilized pseudorandom generator function. The information leakage from *CID* like the location of the keypoints to Generator will be analyzed in Sec. 5.2.2.

For Comparer, though the OPE scheme leaks the order of the ciphertext, the information disclosed to Comparer contains only the statistical information [31] (e.g., the counts of different pixel values) over ciphertexts in the scale-space domain. The confidentiality of the image values relies on the security strength of the OPE scheme. Recall that the security of the image content against Comparer is quantified by the domain size $|D| = M$. Assume for any challenge set size z, there exists an efficient adversary A as a curious Comparer, and we have the following theorem:

THEOREM 2. *For any z and A, if $N > 2M$, $M > 16 + z$, such that:*

$$Adv^{z}_{[M],[N]}(A) < \frac{4z}{\sqrt{M - z + 1}} \tag{11}$$

PROOF. Let $N > M, 0 < y < N, 0 < x < M$. Recall hypergeometric and negative hypergeometric probabilities:

$$P_{hgd}(N, M, y, x) < \frac{(\binom{y}{x})(\binom{N-y}{M-x})}{(\binom{N}{M})}$$

$$P_{nhgd}(N, M, y, x) < \frac{(\binom{y-1}{x-1})(\binom{N-y}{M-x})}{(\binom{N}{M})} \tag{12}$$

As shown in [6], random OPE are naturally linked to negative hypergeometric probabilities. This allows us to construct an efficient adversary against OPE scheme, which yields the result that:

$$Adv^{z}_{[M],[N]}(A) < Pr[Exp^{z}_{[M],[N]}(A) = 1] \tag{13}$$

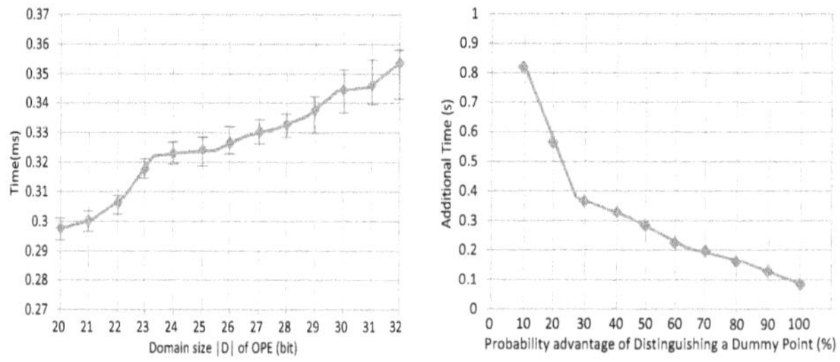

(a) OPE encryption time. (b) Descriptor generation time.

Figure 8: Privacy Evaluation.

where the security experiment is as follows: The experiment $Exp^{z}_{[M],[N]}(A)$ is performed by the adversary. It returns 1, if $(m_R - m_L + 1 \ mod \ M) < r$, while $m_0 \in [m_L, m_R]$, and returns 0 otherwise. Note that the experiment demands that the adversary returns the specified ciphertext that $c_0 \in c$, rather than any ciphertext from ciphertext set c. Thus we can use the simple bound deduced from Eq. 12 and 13:

$$Pr[Exp^{z}_{[M],[N]}(A) = 1] = \frac{4z}{\sqrt{M - z + 1}} \tag{14}$$

□

5.2.2 Delocalization of Keypoint Locations

Since Comparer is enabled to read the encrypted pixels in scale cubes for comparisons, Comparer can only attack the system through reconstructing the image from cubes, which means reconstructing the relative location relations among pixels. The permutation algorithm is utilized in our design to protect the locations of keypoints against Comparer. In this case, the permutation of surrounding pixels in a scale cube can effectively sabotage the reconstruction algorithm. For neighboring cubes, the maximum number of overlapping pixels is 18. Assume each cube has 6 directions to discover its neighboring cube. The maximum number of overlapping pixels for two neighboring directions is 12. Through probability deduction, we can discover that the permutation algorithm can decrease the probability of discovering the correct neighboring cubes to be one out of six, which is 16.6%. Assume the size of the image is n, then the possibility of reconstruct the half of the image is approximately 2^{3n}.

For Generators, the dummy points are inserted into the returned cube identifiers to hide the keypoints locations in the image. Due to the functionality requirements in SIFT, the locations of real keypoints must be revealed to Generators for generating descriptors. However, the dummy keypoints observed by Generators can effectively prevent it distinguishing the location of real keypoints. The experiment $Exp_{|r|,|d|}(A)$ for adversary A, which has $|r|$ real keypoints and $|d|$ dummy points, is described as follows: It returns 1, if A choose a real keypoint from the mixed keypoints group, and returns 0 otherwise. Thus we can get a simple bound:

$$Pr[Exp^{z}_{|r|,|d|}(A) = 1] = \frac{|r|}{|r| + |d|} \tag{15}$$

5.2.3 Experimental Results

We conduct the experiments regarding computation time of OPE procedure and additional descriptor generation time for dummy points to test the additional computation complexity introduced by privacy-preserving mechanisms. Fig. 8

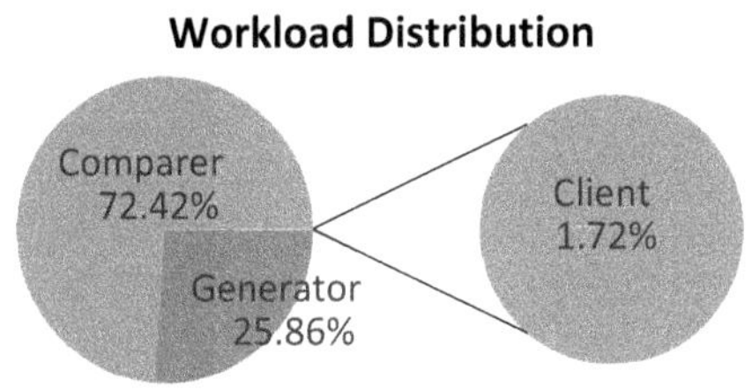

Figure 9: The workload distribution of SecSIFT.

(a), (b) show the results. As the strength of the strength of the confidentiality and delocalization property grows, the additional time complexity increases: The time complexity of one OPE encryption procedure grows, as the domain size $|D|$ of OPE increases (from 20 to 30 bits). In Fig. 8(b), we conduct the experiments of the additional computational time of descriptor generation procedures for different scales of dummy point insertion. Regarding the growth additional time complexity of descriptor generation, the probability of distinguishing the dummy points from the mixed descriptors decreases.

5.3 Efficiency Evaluation

In order to evaluate the efficiency of the proposed system, the experiments are conducted regarding the time cost of data preprocessing phase and image feature detection phase. Fig. 9 shows the computational complexity on the different entities in SecSIFT for an image with size of 300×300. The result shows that the Client takes a minimum computational complexity, since most of the workloads, like scale-space generation and extreme discovering, are taken by Generators and Comparer. As shown in Fig. 10, the time complexity of the proposed system remains to be fully practical, i.e., about the order of seconds. Meanwhile, the homomorphic encryption based scheme requires time complexity at the order of minutes [12] under the same security parameters. The reason is that the public key based homomorphic encryption schemes require massive multiplications and exponentials over ciphertext domain as the homomorphic additions and multiplications.

6. RELATED WORK

This outsourced privacy-preserving SIFT is proposed to explore the prospects of private image computation outsourcing, inspired by works [19], [14], [18], [21]. In secure multimedia data search [26], the authors propose a design to protect the privacy of the query image when searching over a public non-encrypted database. In [19], features extracted from images are encrypted in a distance-preserving scheme to enable the direct comparisons for similarity evaluation. Secure image retrieval allows content-based search over encrypted multimedia databases, and therefore offers flexible approaches to manage private multimedia collections online [15]. In [18], the state-of-the-art search indexes for multimedia data are encrypted while the efficient search capabilities are preserved. In [9], authors analyze the security flaws of the typical technology blocks used in state-of-the-art content-based image retrieval system. Most of existing works are interested in the manipulation of encrypted image data: A privacy-preserving face recognition system, based on Paillier cryptosystem, is proposed by Erkin [10]. Bianchi [5] generalizes the packing encryption technique proposed by Troncoso-Pastoriza [27]. By utilizing the garbled circuit and homomorphic encryption scheme, [25] and [23] propose privacy-preserving face recognition systems. The

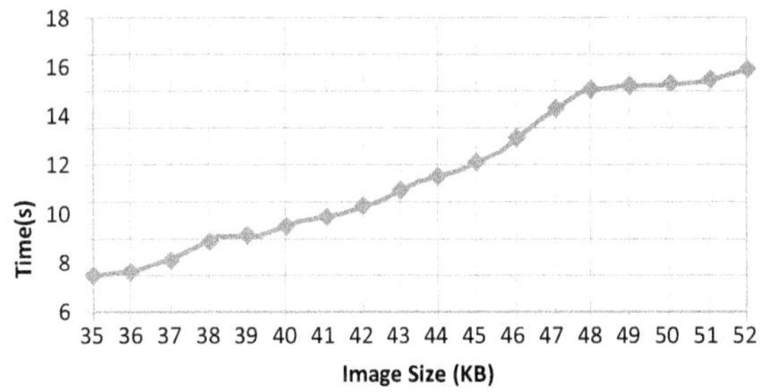

Figure 10: The computation time of SecSIFT on different size of images.

privacy-preserving classification of ECG signal and privacy-preserving fingercode authentication system are presented in [4] and [3] by Barni. Another orthogonal work [22] proposes a privacy-preserving identical image copies searching system based on the signs of DCT image coefficient. In [7], the utilization of secure multiparty computation techniques is proposed in a biometric identification system. The most similar work to this paper is Hsu's work [12], which utilizes homomorphic encryption scheme (Paillier) to enable a secure SIFT computation over the ciphertext. However, the proposed scheme has two drawbacks: 1) It introduces unrealistic computational complexity on encrypted data comparison. The proposed algorithm requires the cloud to traverse half of the ciphertext space for each comparison. Assuming a 512-bit modulus of the Paillier cryptosystem, the cloud needs to perform 2^{256} multiplications (homomorphic additions) for each ciphertext comparison. 2) The data owner needs to encrypt and decrypt each pixel in the image under Paillier scheme. It is an unpractical workload to the data owner, especially compared with the splitting based encryption scheme in our system (0.02-0.5s/pixel vs. 0.04-0.08μs/pixel). Another work [29] demonstrates that shape-based image feature extraction can be carried out within ciphertext domain in a multiple cloud server structure.

Based on Yao's garbled circuits [30] and Gentry's work on fully homomorphic encryption (FHE) [11], a general solution has been shown to allow homomorphic evaluations over ciphertext domain. However, applying these general mechanisms to our image computation application would be far from practical, due to its extremely large size of the circuit that cannot be handled in practice and the huge computation complexity of FHE operations. Another existing list of work that loosely relates to (but is also significantly different from) our research proposal is secure multiparty computation (SMC) [30]. However, schemes in the context of SMC are in general ill-suited when applied to practical system models, as they usually assume no single party knows all the problem input and impose comparable computation burden on each involved parties [24]. In short, practically efficient mechanisms with immediate practices for private image computation outsourcing in cloud are still missing.

7. CONCLUSION

In this paper, we proposed a privacy-preserving SIFT system over encrypted image data. The proposed system explores the techniques of splitting based encryption, order-preserving encryption, random permutation, and dummy points perturbation to enable secure image computation outsourcing with practical performance. The correctness, privacy, and efficiency of the proposed system were analyzed and evaluated. We further constructed a prototype system

SecSIFT and conducted extensive experiments. The experimental results show that the proposed system is correct and effective for different image categories in Caltech256 image database. As our ongoing work, we will continue to research on privacy-preserving image detection algorithms for the effective utilization over encrypted data.

8. ACKNOWLEDGEMENT

We thank the helpful comments from the anonymous reviewers and Mohan S. Kankanhalli for shepherding our paper. This work was supported in part by US National Science Foundation under grants CNS-1262277 and CNS-1262275, and by RGC of Hong Kong under the ECS grant 9041983.

9. REFERENCES

[1] R. Agrawal, J. Kiernan, R. Srikant, and Y. Xu. Order preserving encryption for numeric data. In *Proc. of ACM SIGMOD*, 2004.

[2] M. J. Atallah, K. N. Pantazopoulos, J. R. Rice, and E. E. Spafford. Secure outsourcing of scientific computations. *Advances in Computers*, Vol. 54, pp. 215-272, 2002.

[3] M. Barni, T. Bianchi, D. Catalano, M. Di Raimondo, et al. Privacy-preserving fingercode authentication. In *Proc. of ACM MMSec*, 2010.

[4] M. Barni, P. Failla, R. Lazzeretti, A. Sadeghi, and T. Schneider. Privacy-preserving ecg classification with branching programs and neural networks. *IEEE TIFS*, Vol.6, No. 2, pp. 452-468, 2011.

[5] T. Bianchi, A. Piva, and M. Barni. Composite signal representation for fast and storage-efficient processing of encrypted signals. *IEEE TIFS*, Vol. 5, No. 1, pp. 180-187, 2010.

[6] A. Boldyreva, N. Chenette, Y. Lee, and A. Oneill. Order-preserving symmetric encryption. In *Proc. of EUROCRYPT*, 2009.

[7] J. Bringer, H. Chabanne, and A. Patey. Privacy-preserving biometric identification using secure multiparty computation: An overview and recent trends. *Signal Processing Magazine*, 2013.

[8] R. Chen, I. E. Akkus, and P. Francis. Splitx: high-performance private analytics. In *Proc. of ACM SIGCOMM*, 2013.

[9] T.-T. Do, E. Kijak, T. Furon, and L. Amsaleg. Challenging the security of content-based image retrieval systems. In *Proc. of IEEE MMSP*, 2010.

[10] Z. Erkin, M. Franz, J. Guajardo, S. Katzenbeisser, I. Lagendijk, and T. Toft. Privacy-preserving face recognition. In *Proc. of PET*, 2009.

[11] C. Gentry. *A fully homomorphic encryption scheme.* PhD thesis, Stanford University, 2009.

[12] C.-Y. Hsu, C.-S. Lu, and S.-C. Pei. Image feature extraction in encrypted domain with privacy-preserving sift. *IEEE Trans. Image Processing*, Vol. 21, No. 11, pp. 4593-4607, 2012.

[13] C.-Y. Hsu, C.-S. Lu, and S.-C. Pei. Secure and robust sift. In *Proc. of ACM MM*, 2009.

[14] C.-Y. Hsu, C.-S. Lu, and S.-C. Pei. Homomorphic encryption-based secure sift for privacy-preserving feature extraction. In *Proc of IEEE SPIE*, 2011.

[15] Y. Ke and R. Sukthankar. Pca-sift: A more distinctive representation for local image descriptors. In *Proc. of IEEE CVPR*, 2004.

[16] P. Leon, B. Ur, R. Shay, Y. Wang, R. Balebako, and L. Cranor. Why johnny can't opt out: A usability evaluation of tools to limit online behavioral advertising. In *Proc. of ACM SIGCHI*, 2012.

[17] D. G. Lowe. Distinctive image features from scale-invariant keypoints. *International journal of computer vision*, Vol. 60, No. 2, pp. 31-110, 2004.

[18] W. Lu, A. Swaminathan, A. L. Varna, and M. Wu. Enabling search over encrypted multimedia databases. In *Proc. of IEEE SPIE*, 2009.

[19] W. Lu, A. L. Varna, A. Swaminathan, and M. Wu. Secure image retrieval through feature protection. In *Proc. of IEEE ICASSP*, 2009.

[20] M. Malheiros, C. Jennett, S. Patel, S. Brostoff, and M. A. Sasse. Too close for comfort: A study of the effectiveness and acceptability of rich-media personalized advertising. In *Proc. of ACM SIGCHI*, 2012.

[21] B. Moskovich and M. Osadchy. Illumination invariant representation for privacy preserving face identification. In *Proc. of IEEE CVPRW*, 2010.

[22] F. Movahedi Naini, P. Thiran, M. Vetterli, and J. Unnikrishnan. Privacy-preserving function computation by exploitation of friendships in social networks. In *Proc. of IEEE ICASSP*, 2014.

[23] M. Osadchy, B. Pinkas, A. Jarrous, and B. Moskovich. Scifi-a system for secure face identification. In *Proc. of IEEE S&P*, 2010.

[24] S. J. Patel, A. Chouhan, and D. C. Jinwala. Comparative evaluation of elliptic curve cryptography based homomorphic encryption schemes for a novel secure multiparty computation. *Journal of Information Security*, Vol. 5, No.1, pp. 12-18, 2014.

[25] A.-R. Sadeghi, T. Schneider, and I. Wehrenberg. Efficient privacy-preserving face recognition. In *Proc. of ICISC*, 2009.

[26] J. Shashank, P. Kowshik, K. Srinathan, and C. Jawahar. Private content based image retrieval. In *Proc. of IEEE CVPR*, 2008.

[27] J. R. Troncoso-Pastoriza, S. Katzenbeisser, M. Celik, and A. Lemma. A secure multidimensional point inclusion protocol. In *Proc. of ACM MMSec*, 2007.

[28] Y. Wang, K.-W. Wong, X. Liao, and G. Chen. A new chaos-based fast image encryption algorithm. *Applied soft computing*, Vol. 11, No. 1, pp. 514-522 2011.

[29] S. Wang, M. Nassar, M. Atallah, and Q. Malluhi. Secure and private outsourcing of shape-based feature extraction. In *Proc. of ICISC*, 2013.

[30] A. C.-C. Yao. Protocols for secure computations. In *Proc. of IEEE FOCS*, 1982.

[31] Z. Qin, J. Yan, C. Wang, K. Ren, C. W. Chen, and X. Fu. Privacy-preserving Outsourcing of Image Global Feature Detection. In *Proc. of IEEE Globecom*, 2014.

[32] X. Yuan, X. Wang, C. Wang, A. Squicciarini, and K. Ren. Enabling Privacy-preserving Image-centric Social Discovery. In *Proc. of IEEE ICDCS*, 2014.

User-Level Psychological Stress Detection from Social Media Using Deep Neural Network

Huijie Lin[1,2], Jia Jia[1,2], Quan Guo[3], Yuanyuan Xue[1], Qi Li[1], Jie Huang[1], Lianhong Cai[1,2], Ling Feng[1]

1 Department of Computer Science and Technology, Tsinghua University, Beijing, China
2 TNList and Key Laboratory of Pervasive Computing, Ministry of Education
3 Machine Intelligence Laboratory, College of Computer Science, Sichuan University, Chengdu, China
linhuijie@gmail.com, jjia@tsinghua.edu.cn, guoquanscu@gmail.com, xue-yy12@mails.tsinghua.edu.cn, liqi0422@gmail.com, qazwsxed_3372@qq.com, clh-dcs@tsinghua.edu.cn, fengling@tsinghua.edu.cn

ABSTRACT

It is of significant importance to detect and manage stress before it turns into severe problems. However, existing stress detection methods usually rely on psychological scales or physiological devices, making the detection complicated and costly. In this paper, we explore to automatically detect individuals' psychological stress via social media. Employing real online micro-blog data, we first investigate the correlations between users' stress and their tweeting content, social engagement and behavior patterns. Then we define two types of stress-related attributes: 1) low-level content attributes from a single tweet, including text, images and social interactions; 2) user-scope statistical attributes through their weekly micro-blog postings, leveraging information of tweeting time, tweeting types and linguistic styles. To combine content attributes with statistical attributes, we further design a convolutional neural network (CNN) with cross autoencoders to generate user-scope content attributes from low-level content attributes. Finally, we propose a deep neural network (DNN) model to incorporate the two types of user-scope attributes to detect users' psychological stress. We test the trained model on four different datasets from major micro-blog platforms including Sina Weibo, Tencent Weibo and Twitter. Experimental results show that the proposed model is effective and efficient on detecting psychological stress from micro-blog data. We believe our model would be useful in developing stress detection tools for mental health agencies and individuals.

Categories and Subject Descriptors

H.3.3 [**Information Retrieval**]: Information Retrieval and Indexing

General Terms

Algorithms, Human Factors.

Keywords

Stress detection; convolutional neural network; cross auto encoders; deep learning; micro-blog; social media

MM'14, November 3–7, 2014, Orlando, Florida, USA.
Copyright © 2014 ACM 978-1-4503-3063-3/14/11…$15.00.

1. INTRODUCTION

1.1 Motivation

Psychological stress is the root cause to many health problems and mental diseases. Chronic stress increases the risk of developing health problems such as insomnia, obesity, heart diseases, cancer etc. [1]. Many studies have revealed a link between stress and mental diseases like anxiety disorders, depression etc. [2]. Stress has been a threat to human health for a long time. Time magazine's June 6, 1983 cover story called stress "The Epidemic of the Eighties" and referred to it as our leading health problem (http://www.stress.org/americas-1-health-problem/). Meanwhile, stress has been progressively worsened and spread recent years. With the rapid development of modern society, many people feel increasingly stressed under the rapid pace of life. Numerous surveys have confirmed that adult Americans are feeling under much more stress than a decade or two ago. A 1996 Prevention magazine survey found that almost 75% feel they have "great stress" one day a week and with more than 30% indicating they feel this way more than twice a week, which is 55% compared to the same survey conducted in 1983 (http://www.anxietycentre.com/stress.shtml). In a word, the rapid increase of stress has become a great challenge to human health and life quality.

Psychological stress detection remains a large problem at the present stage. Detecting and managing stress before it turns into severe problems is of significant importance. Recent decades, many efforts have been devoted to stress detection by researchers from diverse areas. They have developed many methods to measure psychological stress, including psychological questionnaire based interviews [3, 4] and physiological signal based measures [5, 6]. However, these methods have their limitations in many aspects. Psychological questionnaires often contain a range of questions designed by psychologists. People are usually unwilling to do these questionnaires unless they have to. Physiological methods usually require professional devices to measure users' physiological and biochemical properties and need specialists to analyze the acquired data. Thus, it is very important and useful to find a way to detect user's stress state reliably, automatically and non-invasively.

With the fast development of social networks, people are widely using social media platforms to share their thoughts and feelings. A statistic report from statisticbrain.com (http://www.statisticbrain.com/twitter-statistics/) shows that by 2014.1.1, the total number of active registered users on Twitter has reached more than 645 million, with an average 58 million tweets posted per day. As for Sina weibo (the largest micro-blog platform in China), the number of weibo users has reached more than 600 million (http://www.comsoc.org/blog?page=3). People post tweets containing text and images on micro-blog platforms to share opinions, express emotions, record daily routines and communicate with friends. We can obtain linguistic and visual content that may indicate stress related symptoms. This makes the detection of users' psychological stress through their tweets and posting patterns from micro-blog feasible.

1.2 Related Work

Existing methods for stress detection. Many efforts have been devoted to developing convenient tools for individual stress detection recent years. Researchers are trying to leverage pervasive devices like personal computers and mobile phones for routine stress detection. Hong L. etc. [7] proposed StressSense to unobtrusively recognize stress from human voice using smartphones. Paredes, P. etc. [8] investigated the initial lab evidence of the use of a computer mouse in the detection of stress. However, such applications rely on collecting one's real-life data, which is easy to trigger antipathy. It makes stress detection invasive to normal life, and can't be used widely in more people.

Researches on using social media for healthcare. With the rapid spread of social networks, researches on using social media data for physical and mental healthcare are also increasingly growing. Sadilek et al. [9] leverage Tweeter postings to identify the spread of flu symptoms. Paul M.J. etc. [10] apply the Ailment Topic Aspect Model to over 1.5 million health related tweets and discover correlations between behavioral risk factors and aliments. Munmun etc. [11] leverage behavioral cues indicated from Twitter postings to predict depression before it is reported. These studies show the feasibility of harnessing social media data for developing healthcare tools. However, they mainly leverage the textual content in the social media data, while other equally important content, like images and social behavior are ignored.

Deep learning approaches for cross-media data modeling. Micro-blog data is typical cross-media data. Items may come from diverse sources and modalities. It is difficult to handle the heterogeneous cross-media data. Recent years, extensive researches on deep learning show superior ability of deep neural networks (DNN) in learning features from large scale unlabeled data [12-14]. [15, 16] further extend the deep models for multimodal learning. [17] design a cross-media learning method based on DNN, and leverage the model for detecting psychological states and corresponding categories from a single tweet. However, stress is a continuous state compared to instant emotions, indicating that the stressed stated can last for several days in psychology [3]. It remains a challenge to make use of aggregated cross-media data for user-level modeling.

1.3 Our Work

In this paper, we explore the potential to use social media to detect psychological stress for individuals. Micro-blog is one of the most popular social media that can be publicly accessed. People can post text with no more than 140 words, upload images or have social interactions with others. Employing real online micro-blog data, we first investigate the correlations between users' stress and their tweeting content, behavior patterns and social engagement. Then we define two types of stress-related attributes: 1) low-level content attributes from a single tweet, including text, images and social interactions like comments, retweets and favorites; 2) user-scope statistical attributes through their weekly micro-blog

Table 1. The details of the observation dataset (DB1).

Tweets' label	Number of tweets	Number of users	Number of weeks	Number of tweets per week
Non-Stressed	253638	12230	17861	14.2
Stressed	239038	11074	19136	12.5
Summation	492676	23304	36997	13.3

postings, leveraging information of tweeting time, tweeting types, linguistic styles, and social engagement with friends indicated from the @-mentions and @-replies, etc. To combine low-level content attributes with user-scope statistical attributes, we further design a convolutional neural network (CNN) with cross autoencoders to learn the latent high-level attributes on cross-modal units [17][18]. Finally, we propose a deep neural network (DNN) model to incorporate the two types of user-scope attributes to detect users' psychological stress. The experimental results on four datasets from different Micro-blog platforms indicate the effectiveness and efficiency of the proposed method.

We have to face several challenges in this work. And the corresponding contributions are:

1) **Challenge 1**: Micro-blog platforms contain massive data. It is infeasible to manually label the data. How to find effective methods to automatically label the ground truth remains a challenge.
Our solution: Inspired by previous research [19], we have built a stressed-twitter-posting database using the "I feel stressed" sentence pattern as the ground-truth label for detecting stress from micro-blog data. With a small set of psychological stress scale score labeled dataset as test, it is proved that our ground truth labeling method is reliable;

2) **Challenge 2**: Attributes in a tweet come with multiple modalities and the components are often incomplete, which is a typical problem in cross-media. Numbers of tweets in a certain period of time also differ from person to person and from week to week. Traditional models have limited abilities to extract modality-invariant attributes from such data.
Our solution: We design a convolutional neural network with cross autoencoders to aggregate low-level content attributes and generate modality-invariant user-scope attributes which support user-level stress detection;

3) **Challenge 3**: Modeling stress in user-level is more difficult than in discrete tweet-level, since both the overview and detailed attributes should be concerned about.
Our solution: We propose a stress detection model based on DNN to incorporate content attributes and statistical attributes together. The DNN model along with CNN forms a unified integral deep network which can extract attributes from single tweets and detect user-level continuous psychological stress.

2. DATA OBSERVATION

2.1 Observation dataset

We first crawl 350 million tweets data via Sina Weibo's streaming APIs from 2009.10 to 2012.10. Then we collect tweets containing sentence patterns like "I feel stressed this week" and "I feel stressed so much this week" as the weekly stressed state label, and tweets containing "I feel relaxed" and "I feel non-stressed" as the non-stressed state label. The "I feel" pattern has been proved to be

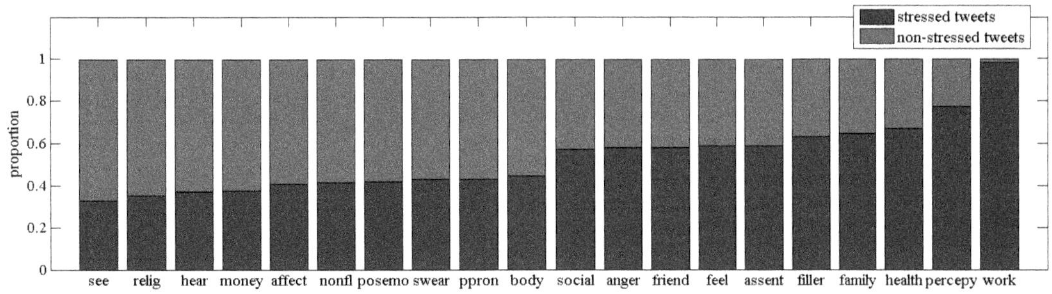

Figure 1. The proportion of top 12 most frequently occurred word categories from non-stressed and stressed weeks of tweets

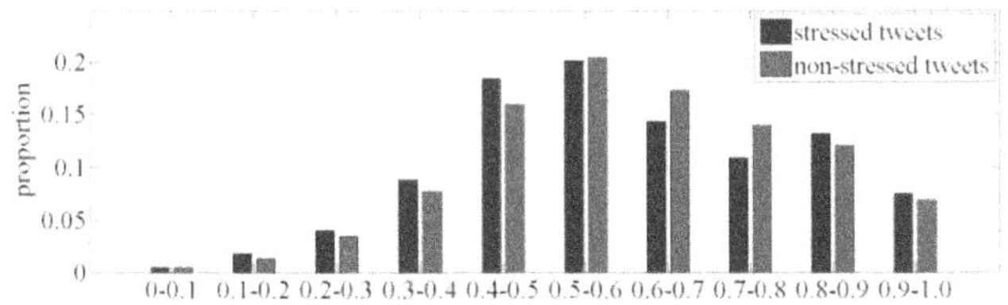

Figure 2(a). Brightness distribution from tweets' image

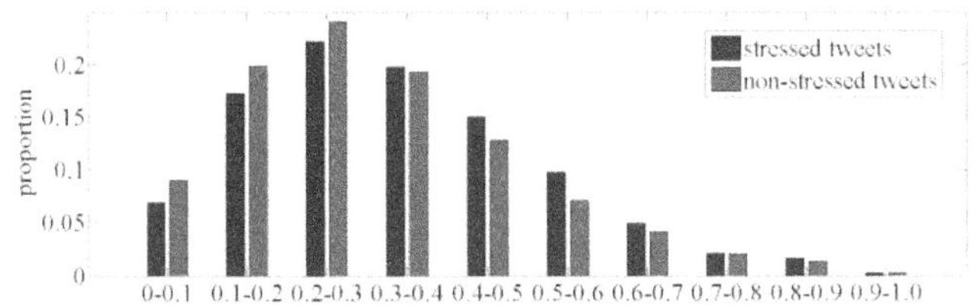

Figure 2(b). Saturation distribution from tweets' image

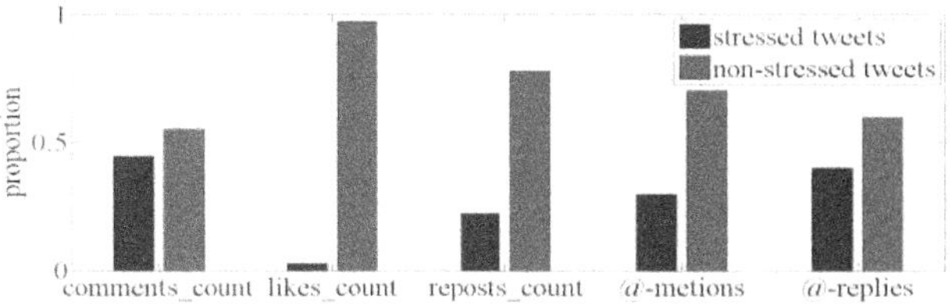

Figure 3. Social engagement observation

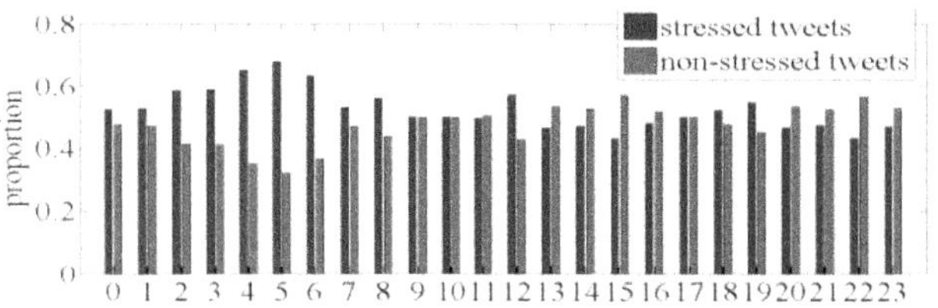

Figure 4. Tweeting time observatio

effective as ground truth data labels in emotion analysis in [19]. In this way, we collect over 19000 weeks of users' tweets that are labeled as stressed, and over 17000 weeks of non-stressed users' tweets. There are 492,676 tweets from 23304 users in total. We take this dataset for observation and further experiments, which is represented by DB1 in this paper. The details of the dataset are shown in Table 1.

2.2 Observation and analysis

We first conduct a series of analyses on the DB1 and present some patterns related to individuals' psychological stress reflected by tweets. In the analysis, we randomly pick 1000 weeks of stressed and non-stressed tweets from the DB1 and focus on the following aspects:

- *Content correlation*: the difference of stressed and non-stressed tweets in tweets' content, including text and images;
- *Social engagement correlation*: the difference between stressed and non-stressed weekly tweets on users' social interactions with friends via @-mentions, @-replies and tweets' comments, retweets and likes;
- *Behavioral correlation*: the difference of stressed and non-stressed tweeting behavior in tweeting frequency, tweeting types and tweeting time.

2.2.1 Observations on content correlation

Tweets on micro-blog mainly consist of text and images. We leverage a widely used psychological dictionary LIWC [20] to measure the most frequently occurred words in stressed and non-stressed tweets text content. The results are shown in Figure 1. From the figure, we observe that there is evident difference in text content between the stressed and non-stressed tweets. For the stressed tweets, there are more words categories from negative emotions, social, friends and family etc. While for the non-stressed tweets, there exist more word categories from positive emotions, work, health and anxiety etc.

As for the image content of tweets, we consider brightness and saturation as observed visual features. The results are shown in Figure 2(a) and Figure 2(b). From Figure 2(a), we can observe that the presence of images with low brightness (<0.3) from stressed class is obviously higher than that from non-stressed class, indicating that stressed users are more likely to post images with lower brightness.

As for the saturation distribution in Figure 2(b), we observe that the saturation of non-stressed users' images are more likely to be lower (<0.5), while the stressed class is more likely to be in the higher range (>0.5).

2.2.2 Observations on social engagement correlation

Micro-blog is an important platform for users to share information and interact with friends. The social interactions on micro-blog usually consist of @-mentions, @-replies, retweets, comments and likes etc. We analyze the correlation between social interactions and users' stress states.

Figure 3 shows the social interaction patterns from tweets of users in stressed and non-stressed states. The patterns are measured as the proportion of the numbers of comments, likes, retweets, @-mentions and @-replies in users' weekly tweets.

From the figure, we observe that for the non-stressed class, users' tweets get more comments, likes and retweets from friends, indicating that people are generally more likely to interact with the followed users when they are at a non-stressed state. Meanwhile, compared to non-stressed weeks, the stressed weeks have less @-mentions and @-replies of friends. This also proves that stressed users are less social active than non-stressed users.

2.2.3 *Observations on Behavioral Correlation*

As revealed by psychology theories [1], there are many common symptoms may be related to stress, including insomnia, social withdrawal .etc. These symptoms can also be reflected by tweeting behavior changes on micro-blog. We observe tweeting time distributions to measure users' tweeting behavior.

Figure 4 shows the results of tweeting time distribution of users from the two classes. Tweeting time distribution is measured in tweet postings in hours of a day. From the result, we observe that there are more stressed postings during 0 to 6 in the morning, revealing that stressed users are more likely to be insomnia.

Summary To very briefly summarize, we have the following intuitions which will be further leveraged and incorporated in our method design:

- The different content of a single tweet including text, image and social interactions are all related to different one's stress state at some point.
- One's stress state can be related to the social engagement with friends in weekly unit.
- One's stress state can also be related to the tweeting behavior on micro-blog.

3. ATTRIBUTES DEFINITION

The micro-blog data is a typical type of cross-media data, containing text, emoticons, images and social interactions. Besides, the patterns of micro-blog usage behavior in a period such as one week unit also contain useful information for stress detection. To leverage both content information contained in single cross-media micro-blog tweet and the micro-blog usage behavior in weekly tweets, guided by psychological theories, we define two sets of attributes to measure the differences of the stressed and non-stressed users on micro-blog: 1) *content attributes* from the content of a single tweet; 2) *statistical attributes* from the users' behavior of weekly tweet postings.

3.1 Content Attributes

The content of a tweet from micro-blog usually consists of text, image and social interaction. We define linguistic, visual and social attributes from each part of a tweet respectively as follows:

1) Linguistic Attributes:

As users usually express their emotions using tweets, we measure the emotions in a single tweet using linguistic attributes. To describe the linguistic attributes, we leverage a psychological dictionary named "Language Inquiry and Word Count Dictionary" [20]. The simplified Chinese LIWC dictionary [21] is developed by Chinese psychologists and linguists, based on the psycholinguistic dictionary LIWC (http://www.liwc.net), which has been proved to be effective on determining affect in Twitter. It is composed of almost 4500 words and categorized into over 60 categories [20].

Based on the dictionary, we define the text content related features as the tweet's linguistic attributes:

- **Positive and Negative Emotion Words** (2 dimension). Measured by the number of positive and negative emotion words in the tweet's text, indicating how positive or negative emotions are expressed in the tweet.
- **Positive and Negative Emoticons** (2 dimensions). Measured by the number of positive and negative emotions. Emoticons are widely used in micro-blog platforms to express users' emotional states. We manually categorize the 129 emoticons provided by Sina Weibo platform into positive and negative categories.
- **Punctuation Marks and Associated Emotion Words** (4 dimensions). We use this attribute to signify the intensity of emotion in a tweet, either positive or negative according to the associated emotional words. Four typical punctuation marks (exclamation mark, question mark, dot mark and the Chinese full stop mark "。") are considered.
- **Degree Adverbs and Associated Emotion Words** (2 dimensions). Degree adverbs are also used to express the degree of emotions. For example, "I feel a little bit sad" and "I feel terribly sad" express different level of negative feelings. We use a number range of 1-3 to represent neural, moderate and severe degrees of positive expression and the minus to represent the negative ones.

Thus, we get 10-dimensional vector to denote the linguistic attributes from a tweet's text content.

2) Visual Attributes:

Based on previous work on affective image classification [22] and color psychology theories [23], we combine the following features as the visual middle-level representation:

- Five-color theme (15 dimensions): a combination of five dominant in the HSV color space, representing the main color distribution of an image. It has been revealed to have important impact on human emotions according to psychology and art theories [22].
- Saturation (2 dimensions): the mean value of saturation and its contrast.
- Brightness (2 dimensions): the mean value of brightness and its contrast.
- Warm or cool color (1 dimension): ratio of cool colors with hue ([0-360]) in the HSV space between 30 and 110.
- Clear or dull color (1 dimension): ratio of colors with brightness ([0-1]) and saturation less than 0.6.

Thus, based on the psychological studies and color theories, we finally get a 21 dimensional attributes from the tweet's image content.

3) Social Attributes:

Besides the text content and image content of a tweet, some additional features like comments, retweets and likes indicate the tweet's social attention from one's friends. They can also imply one's stress state to some degree. We use the number of comments, retweets and likes of a tweet to measure the tweet's social attention degree into social attributes. Thus, we get a 3-dimensional vector to represent the social attributes of a tweet.

3.2 Statistical Attributes

Statistical attributes are summarized from users' tweets in a specific sampling period. We use one week as the sampling period in this paper. On one hand, psychological stress often results from cumulative events or mental states; on the other hand, users may express their chronic stress in a series of tweets rather than one. Appropriately designed statistical attributes can provide a macro-scope of a user's stress states, and avoid noise or missing data. We define statistical attributes from three aspects to measure the differences between stressed and non-stressed states based on users' weekly tweet postings. The details of the statistical attributes are described as follows:

1) Social Engagement:

We consider 3 measures to characterize the social engagement from users' weekly tweet postings: the @-mentions, @-replies and the retweets from a user's friend. These three behaviors are the most commonly used ways to interact with friends on micro-blog platforms. Unlike the social attributes in a single tweet, the social engagement attributes are measured in numbers of @-mentions and @-replies in weekly tweet postings, indicating one's social interaction activeness with friends.

2) Behavioral Attributes:

We define a set of behavioral measures for users, including tweeting time and tweeting types, based on the weekly tweet postings. These measures are described as follows:

- **Tweeting time:**

Tweeting time can indicate users' daily routines at some point. We consider two measures that derive from the tweeting time information of tweets: tweeting frequency and tweeting time distribution. Tweeting frequency is measured in the average number of tweets posted in a day, while tweeting time distribution is measured in numbers of tweets posted in hours with a 24 dimensional vector.

- **Tweeting Type:**

Users usually post tweets on micro-blog with diverse motivations, making the tweets to be presented in different types. We categorize users' tweets into mainly four types: 1) image tweets (tweets containing images) 2) original tweets (tweets that are originally posted by tweets' users) 3) information query tweets 4) information sharing tweets (tweets that contain outside hyperlinks). We use a 4-dimensional vector of the numbers of tweets in the above 4 types respectively to represent the tweeting type attribute.

3) Linguistic Style:

We introduce measures to characterize linguistic styles in users' weekly tweet postings using the psychological dictionary LIWC [20]. LIWC categorizes frequently-used words into more than 60 categories. We adapt 10 categories from LIWC that are related to daily life, social events, e.g.: personal pronouns, home, work, money, religion, death, health, ingestion, friends and family. We extract words from users' weekly tweet postings and use a 10 dimensional vector of numbers of words in the 10 categories to represent the linguistic style attribute. Different from the linguistic attributes of a single tweet which mainly measures the emotions, the linguistic style can measure one's linguistic behavior in aggregated tweets.

Table 2. List of notations used in the following sections.

.x	An input pattern to the network
y	Hidden activation of units in an AE
x	Reconstruction of input pattern x from an AE
W^{l}	Connection weight matrix of layer l in a network
b^{l}	Activation bias of units of layer l in a network
g^{l}	Activation function of units of layer l in a network
S, S	Sigmoid function and its derivate
θ	The set of parameters in a network
J	Performance function of a network
λ	Weight decay penalty
Ω	Set of all modalities in the problem domain
K	Number of modalities in the problem domain
M	Subset of modalities, whose elements are actually presented to the network
x_i	An input pattern with modality i
x_s	An input pattern with modalities in set s
f_i	Modality specified mapping of modality i
w_i	Weight matrix of modality i
x_i	Reconstruction of input pattern with modality i from CAE
x_s	Reconstruction of input pattern with modalities in set s from CAE
P	Subset of modalities, whose elements are available in dataset

4. MODEL AND LEARNING

4.1 Architecture

As described in section 3, we define low-level content attributes from each single tweet in tweet-scope, and statistical attributes from aggregated tweets in user-scope. In tweet-scope, we concern about the low-level content attributes of a single tweet as defined in Section 3.1, while in user-scope, we concern about one's states reflected by several tweets in a period. These two sets of attributes cannot be combined directly since their mathematical descriptions are not in the same domain. So we need to generate latent user-scope content attributes from low-level content attributes at first. After that, both of the two user-scope attribute sets, including the content attributes and statistical attributes, can be finally fed into a classifier for user-level stress detection.

In the following sections, we will address our solution through the following two key components: 1) First we design a convolutional neural network with cross autoencoders to generate user-scope content attributes from low-level content attributes, thus the tweet-scope content attributes can be combined with the user-scope statistical attributes; 2) We propose a deep neural network model to incorporate the two types of user-scope attributes for user-level psychological stress detection.

4.2 Cross auto encoders

Rather than summarizing the user's state alone, we further incorporate the detail attributes with multiple modalities of every tweets by utilizing a recently proposed cross-media model, namely the Cross Autoencoders (CAE) [17].

An auto encoder is a basic unit in deep neural networks for learning distinctive attributes from data [12-14]. It is a shallow network containing one hidden layer and paired input/output layers. The network is trained to reconstruct input pattern from activation of the hidden layer, which is actually stimulated by the input itself. The reconstruction can be formulated by

$$\begin{aligned} y &= g^{1}\ \ W^{1} x + b^{1} \\ x &= g^{2}\ \ W^{2} y + b^{2} \end{aligned} \quad (1)$$

where x is the input pattern and y is the activation of hidden units. x denotes the reconstruction result from the hidden units. W^{1} and W^{2} are the connection weights while b^{1} and b^{2} are bias to the postsynaptic units. g^{1} and g^{2} are activation functions of the units, where sigmoid functions are rational choice in many scenario. In this work, we use the following sigmoid function as activation function of all neurons:

$$S(x) = \frac{1}{1+e^{-x}}, \quad (2)$$

and its derivative is then given by $S'(x) = S(x)(1-S(x))$.

To train the autoencoder to reconstruct input pattern and learn distinctive attributes on the hidden layer, we minimize the following performance function by updating the parameter set $\theta = \{W^{(1)}, W^{(2)}, b^{(1)}, b^{(2)}\}$ with gradient descent

$$J(\theta; x) = \frac{1}{2}\|x - \hat{x}\|^2 + \frac{\lambda}{2}\sum_{i,j,l}\left(W_{ij}^{(l)}\right)^2, \quad (3)$$

where the second term is a regularization to prevent model over fitting which is known as weight decay.

In order to learn attributes robust to partial corruption of the input pattern, Vincent et al. proposed a noticeable extension to the autoencoders, namely the denoising Autoencoder (dA) [24]. The autoencoders are trained to reconstruct a repaired input from corrupted ones, what is done by first corrupting original input pattern to get the corrupted version with stochastic sampling. Part of the components is randomly chosen and set to 0 while others remain unchanged. The trained model is robust to small irrelevant changes in input.

Researchers further extended the model for multimodal learning [15, 16] and cross-modal learning [17]. Lin et al. proposed an autoencoder structure to leverage data with different modalities from different sources for utilizing superior attribute learning power of deep networks on cross-media data [17], namely the CAE. Similar to dA, CAE holds back part of components of training data and require the model to reconstruct the held back part. Rather than select randomly like dA do, CAE orderly hold back each combination of modalities. The feedforward pass of CAE can be formulated by

$$\begin{aligned} f_i(s) &= w_i s, \ i \in M \\ y &= g^{(1)}\left(\sum_{i\in M} f_i(x_i) + b^{(1)}\right) \\ \hat{x}_\Omega &= g^{(2)}\left(W^{(2)} y + b^{(2)}\right) \end{aligned} \quad (4)$$

where f_i is the modality specified mapping and x_i is data of modality $i \in M$. Denoting $\Omega = \{1,2,\dots,K\}$ as the set of all modalities, $M \subseteq \Omega$ is the set of modalities that data are available with. $W^{(1)} = [w_1, w_2, \dots, w_K]$ is the encoder layer weight matrix while $b^{(1)}$ is the bias. $g^{(1)}$ is the activation function of hidden neurons and y is activities of them. The last equation represents the decoder part. $W^{(2)}$ is the weight matrix and $b^{(2)}$ is the bias. $g^{(2)}$ is the activation function of reconstruction neurons. $\hat{x}_\Omega = [\hat{x}_1; \hat{x}_2; \dots; \hat{x}_K]$ is the reconstruction for all modalities in the problem domain.

CAE can be trained with standard gradient descent algorithms, but with a special designed data set. Data available with all modalities are used for training. The network is fed with data which contain combination of modalities. Error feedback is calculated on all modalities and updates the network by back-propagation. The new performance function can be formulated by

$$J(\theta; x) = \frac{1}{2}\sum_{i\in\Omega}\|\hat{x}_i(x_M) - x_i\|^2 + \frac{\lambda}{2}\sum_{i,j,l}\left(W_{ij}^{(l)}\right)^2, \quad (5)$$

where we explicitly denote $\hat{x}_i$ as a deterministic function of x_M.

Figure 5 demonstrates a comparison on structure of standard autoencoder and CAE. The key idea here is, as data with M is presented, data with all modalities Ω are required to reconstruct.

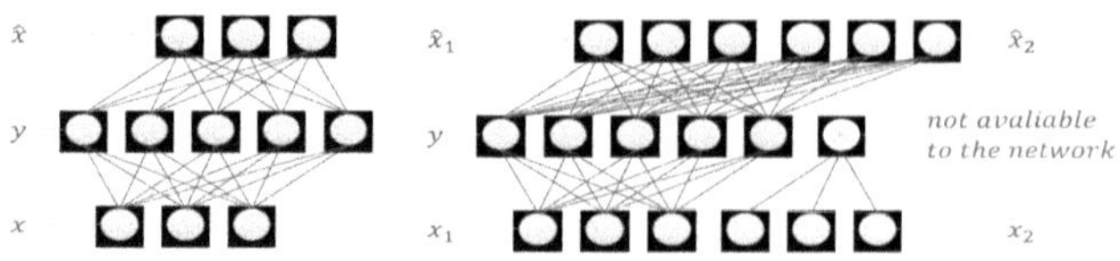

Figure 5. Comparison of standard autoencoder and CAE.

One limitation of this training method is that, in a real world problem, data with all modalities are rare. To make use of more data available with a couple of (not all) modalities, we further employ the Extended Feature Learning (EFL) phase. In this phase, error feedback is calculated for available modalities. Thus the performance function is given by

$$J(\theta; x) = \frac{1}{2}\sum_{i\in P}\|\hat{x}_i(x_P) - x_i\|^2 + \frac{\lambda}{2}\sum_{i,j,l}\left(W_{ij}^{(l)}\right)^2, \quad (6)$$

where $P \subset \Omega$ is the set of available modalities.

It has to be noticed that EFL should be carried out after initial training of CAE that general correlation between modalities are learned. Otherwise the network may tend to learn trivial attributes for each modality as mentioned in [15].

Micro-blog data is typical cross-media data. It consists of text body, emoticons, attached images, replies and retweets from other users etc. Meanwhile, these parts do not necessarily exist for any tweet item. Using CAE, we can model tweets to capture relationship of information with different modalities and learn modality-invariant attributes.

4.3 Convolutional neural networks with CAE

The attributes of tweets from a user's weekly tweet postings in timeline form a time-series. To further model a user as a subject of series of tweets, we apply Convolutional Neural Networks (CNN) [18, 25]. CNNs have large learning capacity while having much fewer connections and parameters to learn comparing to similar size standard network layer. They focus on learning stationary local attributes for series like images (pixel series), speeches and other time-series. We can learn user-scope content attributes from a series of single tweet in time-series to describe one's stress state in a week.

After this step, all attributes of tweets in time-series are formed to a 1-Dimensional series. Figure 6 demonstrates a 2-D unit (left) which is often used in image processing and a 1-D unit (right) which is used in our model.

We propose to use CAE rather than standard units in CNN for tweet-series. 1) On one hand, CAE units works directly on multi-modality attributes of tweets because CAE can learn modality-invariant attributes of tweets directly. Consequently the generated attribute maps are also modality-invariant and the rest of the network can work in modality-invariant domain. 2) On the other hand, individuals may have fewer tweets than the patch size of convolutional units. We call it "missing tweet" phenomenon. In such case, we cannot apply attribute extraction with standard units, while we can handle such users with CAE by treating their tweet-series as incomplete patches.

Figure 7 presents a detailed view of CNN with CAE units. Each cylinder is a tweet instance with multiple modalities. Red circles with cross are attributes with missing modalities. The cylinders form a 1-D sequence along the time-line in a week. The leftmost red crosses are 'missing tweet' instances when the patch is applied to the first instance of the week. In our case, three continuous instances make a patch. CAE units are listed in the attribute maps. They connect to a patch of instance. CAE units take patches with missing modalities as well as 'missing' instance, and generate the modality-invariant attribute maps. The CAE units are used as filters in the 1D CNN (Fig.7) and convolute over the sequence of tweets to form one feature map. Thus the latent user-scope attributes can be generated from the low-level attributes from the single tweets.

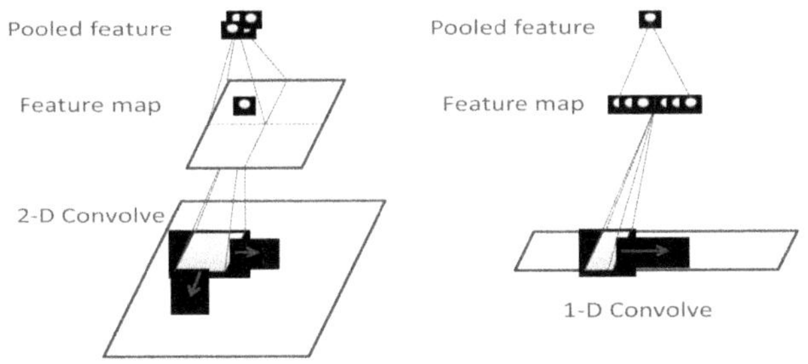

Figure 6. CNN units for 2-D convolution and 1-D convolution.

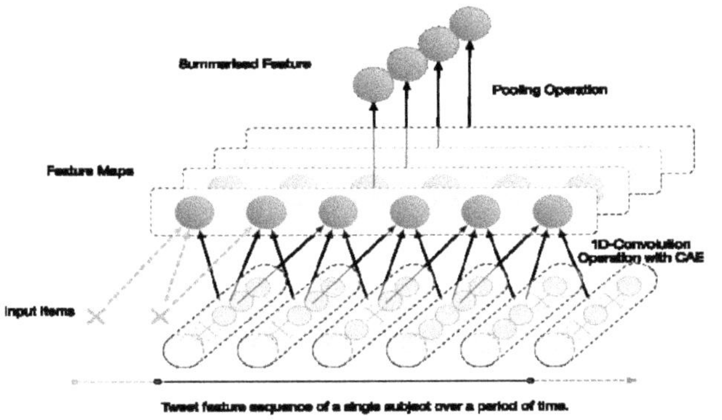

Figure 7. CNN with CAE units.

Pooling is another important step to summarize attribute maps into fewer attribute instances. Though different users have different number of tweets in different weeks, the period of time that the tweets are sampled are the same. We simply pool each attribute map into one pooled attribute. There are two commonly used pooling operations: max-pooling and mean-pooling. When max pooling is used, the pooled attribute unit is assigned with the maximally activation among all units in the attribute map. When mean-pooling is applied, the mean of activations of all units in the attribute map is assigned to the pooled attribute unit. Since we pool over the period of time rather than a certain number of tweets, we consider using mean-over-instances (MOI) and mean-over-time (MOT). Mean-over-instances is simply the average value of activations of the units while mean-over-time can be calculated by summing up the activations since they are sampled in same length of time. We test all the three pooling methods in our experiments in Section 5.

4.4 Classifiers

Through the key steps in the above section, we get two types of user-scope attributes: content attributes learnt by CNN with CAE units, and the manually defined statistical attributes (Section 3.2). We can measure one's stress using these user-scope attributes now. Determining the stress states of a user can be formulated as a typical binary classification problem. In general, any state-of-the-art classifier can be utilized to predict one's stress states with the extracted attributes. In our work, we focus on using a deep neural network (DNN) over the extracted attributes for classification [14]. Deep neural networks have shown superior ability in a variety of classification tasks. The deep architecture of the network can further learn higher-level semantically related attributes from the user-scope attributes. Since both the content attributes learnt by CNN with CAE units and the manually defined statistical attributes are modality-invariant, we use standard fully-connected layers of stacked autoencoders and classify with a final logistic regression unit. A 4-layer architecture is used in this paper. Figure 8 demonstrates an overall architecture of our proposed model with DNN classifier.

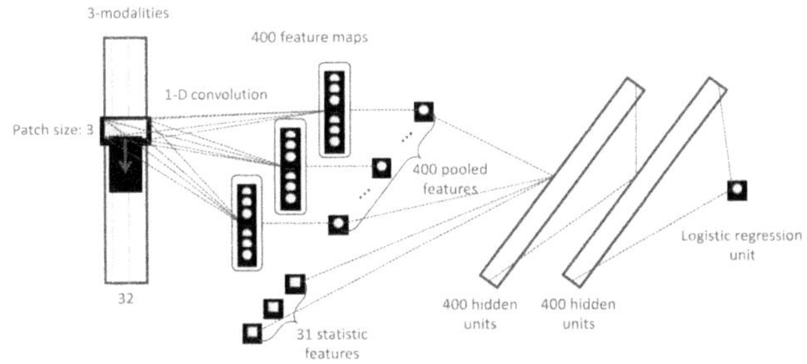

Figure 8. Overall architecture of the proposed model with DNN classifier.

Table 3. The details of the collected tweet dataset DB2-DB4 from different micro-blog platforms.

Platform	Stress label	Number of tweets	Number of users	Number of weeks	Tweets per week
DB2:Sina Weibo (2010.2-2011.9)	stressed	1459	98	98	14.9
	non-stressed	1845	112	112	16.5
	summation	3304	210	210	15.7
DB3:Tencent Weibo (2011.11-2013.3)	stressed	138570	7845	8974	15.4
	non-stressed	172585	8239	9976	17.3
	summation	311155	16084	18950	16.4
DB4:Twitter (2009.6-2009.12)	stressed	54748	4905	6081	9.0
	non-stressed	75357	4018	6545	11.5
	summation	130105	8923	12626	10.3

5. EXPERIMENTS

5.1 Experimental setup

Dataset. We perform our experiments on four datasets DB1-DB4 collected from three different micro-blog platforms: Sina Weibo, Tencent Weibo[1], and Twitter. DB1 from Sina Weibo has the most number of tweets and users which has been described in Section 2, Table 1. The details of the other 3 datasets are shown in Table 3. The Tencent Weibo (DB3) and Twitter (DB4) are labeled using the sentence pattern method described in Section 2. Especially, to avoid the noise in data ground truth, we establish a small scale dataset DB2 from Sina Weibo. DB2 is collected from the users that have shared the score of a psychological stress scale[2] with 50 items via Sina Weibo. If the resulted score is over 80, then the test subject is claimed to be stressed. We crawl the shared scores and the corresponding users' information and weeks' tweets. In this way, for DB2 we finally get 98 weeks of stressed tweets (scale

[5] http://t.qq.com another popular micro-blog platform in China.

[6] http://types.yuzeli.com/survey/pstr50

Table 4. Comparison of results using different classification models.

Pooling Method	Classifier	SVM			RF			NB			DNN		
	Feature	statistic	content	both	statistic	content	both	statistic	content	both	statistic	content	both
Max	Accuracy		0.7117	**0.7562**		0.7340	**0.7675**		0.6714	0.6727		0.7186	0.7635
	F1-score		0.7921	**0.8312**		0.8109	**0.8341**		0.7493	0.7504		0.8049	0.8284
MOI	Accuracy	0.6987	0.6569	0.7433	0.7329	0.7327	0.7630	0.6432	**0.7099**	0.6813	0.7146	0.7201	0.7640
	F1-score	0.7999	0.7929	0.8224	0.8124	0.8071	0.8292	0.7496	**0.7896**	0.7567	0.7965	0.8040	0.8285
MOT	Accuracy		0.7165	0.7457		0.7186	0.7556		0.6480	0.6484		0.7227	**0.7857**
	F1-score		0.8062	0.8261		0.7970	0.8255		0.7701	0.7700		0.8072	**0.8443**

score > 80) and 112 weeks of non-stressed tweets (scale score < 80) as a small but reliable ground truth data to further validate the reliability of the sentence pattern based ground truth labeling method.

In the following experiments, we first train and test our model on the large-scale Sina Weibo dataset DB1. Then we further test our model on the other 3 datasets to show effectiveness of the proposed model on different data sources or different ground truth labeling methods. For all of our analyses, we use 5-fold cross validation, over 10 randomized experimental runs.

Comparison Methods. We compare the following classification methods for user-level psychological stress detection:

- **Naive Bayes (NB)** is a simple probabilistic classifier based on Bayes' theorem that calculates the posterior probability by calculating prior probability of attributes. The classifier assigns sample with the largest calculated posterior [26].
- **Support Vector Machine (SVM)** is a popular and binary classifier that is proved to be effective on a huge category of classification problems. It tries to find a hyperplane that divides training samples into their classes with maximum margin [27]. In our problem we use SVM with RBF kernel which can handle most nonlinear binary classifications better.
- **Random Forest (RF)** is an ensemble learning method for decision trees by building a set of decision trees with random subsets of attributes and bagging them for classification results [28].
- **Deep Neural Network (DNN)**. The proposed model in this paper. We use a 4-layer DNN with a softmax classifier for the detection task. We also evaluate the influence of using different size of networks.

Measures. For a fully investigation of proposed methods, we consider the following aspects:

- **Performance**. To evaluate the detection performance of our method, we evaluate the results with Accuracy and F1-score. By dividing user samples as stressed (positive) and non-stressed (negative) ones, detection results of testing data can be categorized into the following classes:
  - **True Positive (TP)**: stressed user sample correctly detected (true) as stressed (positive).
  - **False Negative (FN)**: stressed user sample incorrectly determined (false) as non-stressed (negative).
  - **False Positive (FP)**: non-stressed user sample incorrectly detected (false) as stressed (positive).
  - **True Negative (TN)**: non-stressed user sample correctly determined (true) as non-stressed (negative).

  Accuracy is the proportion of correct prediction or true results among testing samples. More formally it is given by

$$Accuracy = \frac{TP+TN}{TP+FN+FP+TN}. \quad (7)$$

5.2 Detection Performance

To evaluate the effectiveness of the proposed model, we first perform a fully test against large-scale DB1 from Sina Weibo. We consider working with statistical attributes and content attributes extracted by proposed CNN with CAE from cross-modal tweets data of a week respectively, and then using both of them together. For the pooling method, we also test the all three methods: max pooling, mean-over-instance (MOI) pooling and mean-over-time (MOT) pooling. For comprehensive comparisons, we test SVM, RF, NB as well as the proposed DNN as classifiers in this experiment. For this experiment, a 4-layer DNN is used.

Table 4 demonstrates the results of extensive experiments. Regarding different classifiers, SVM gets an accuracy of 75.62% and F1-score 0.8341 using both attributes together and max pooling. RF gets similar results where the accuracy is 76.75% and F1-score is 0.8341. NB does not work well with statistical attributes. It gets its best result working with content based attribute alone using MOI pooling. The proposed DNN classifier reaches the overall best performance with an accuracy of 78.57% and F1-score of 0.8443. Classification using two types of attributes together with MOT pooling outperforms all the baselines. It achieves a ~3% improvement over SVM and ~2% improvement over RF. When it works with the single type of attribute or other pooling methods it also get competitive results.

5.3 Detection Performance

To evaluate the effectiveness of the proposed model, we first perform a fully test against large-scale DB1 from Sina Weibo. We consider working with statistical attributes and content attributes extracted by proposed CNN with CAE from cross-modal tweets data of a week respectively, and then using both of them together. For the pooling method, we also test the all three methods: max pooling, mean-over-instance (MOI) pooling and mean-over-time (MOT) pooling. For comprehensive comparisons, we test SVM, RF, NB as well as the proposed DNN as classifiers in this experiment. For this experiment, a 4-layer DNN is used.

Table 4 demonstrates the results of extensive experiments. Regarding different classifiers, SVM gets an accuracy of 75.62% and F1-score 0.8341 using both attributes together and max pooling. RF gets similar results where the accuracy is 76.75% and F1-score is 0.8341. NB does not work well with statistical attributes. It gets its best result working with content based attribute alone using MOI pooling. The proposed DNN classifier reaches the overall best performance with an accuracy of 78.57% and F1-score of 0.8443. Classification using two types of attributes together with MOT pooling outperforms all the baselines. It achieves a ~3% improvement over SVM and ~2% improvement over RF. When it works with the single type of attribute or other pooling methods it also get competitive results.

As for comparison with previous work, due to the different goal, our results are not comparable with [17]. Actually, the most related user-level prediction work is [11], with the best result of 74% for a binary choice. Our model can achieve a more compelling result of 84%.

5.4 Factor Contribution Analysis

Impact of content and statistical attributes: Table 4 also reveals the impact of two types of attributes. With solely statistical or content attribute, all classifiers get fair results around accuracy of 70%. While both types of attributes are used, there is a growth of about 5%. Trend of F1-score is similar that using both types of attributes provides a better result. These results show the effectiveness of combining both classes of attributes, which also prove that the proposed model is reliable for user-level stress detection.

Impact of pooling methods: Comparison results using max pooling, MOI pooling and MOT pooling are also shown in Table 4. We can see that MOT pooling gets an obvious better result working with DNN. When SVM or RF is considered, all three methods get similar results and max pooling is fractionally ahead in all three pooling methods. In summary, MOT is a better choice for high performance detection.

Impact of different modalities in content attributes: Tweets content come with multiple modalities. To evaluate the contribution of each data modality, we conduct experiments with different combination of attributes. Since text is the necessary part of a tweet, we test using solely text attributes, using combination of text and visual attributes, using combination of text and social attributes, as well as using all attributes.

Table 5. Comparison of results using different attributes.

		Text	Text + visual	Text + Social	All
content	Accuracy	0.7147	0.7187	0.7090	**0.7227**
	F1-score	0.8031	0.8054	0.7993	**0.8072**
both*	Accuracy	0.7613	0.7610	0.7228	**0.7849**
	F1-score	0.8294	0.8265	0.8011	**0.8443**

*both content and statistical attributes

As shown in Table 5, we report predict performance of using content attributes (composed with only the named attributes in Table 5) alone as well as combining with statistical attributes. Using just text attribute gains rather high performance. Simply combining visual or social attributes even reduces the result, especially the social attributes. This trend is even more obvious when both types of attributes (content and statistical) are used. Nevertheless, using all attributes together outperforms using only text attributes. Highest detection performance is observed when using all attribute and working with both types of attributes.

Impact of scale of data. Model learning of the proposed CNN attributes extraction model with CAE is a key link of the whole framework. The model is trained in unsupervised scheme and takes advantage of large-scale unlabeled data. DNN classifier model also utilizes large-scale training data. We investigate the impact of data scale on training the network.

We measure the overall quality by final detection performance. In order to focus the discussion on neural network model, we evaluate with all attributes and only use content attributes. Figure 9 shows the trend of detection performance with different proportion of training data. In our case, the size of time series sets is the number of weeks. We pretrain with all data in DB1 (Table 1) and each filter is trained with roughly 1M patches when 100% data is used. We can see the advantage of using larger training set from the result.

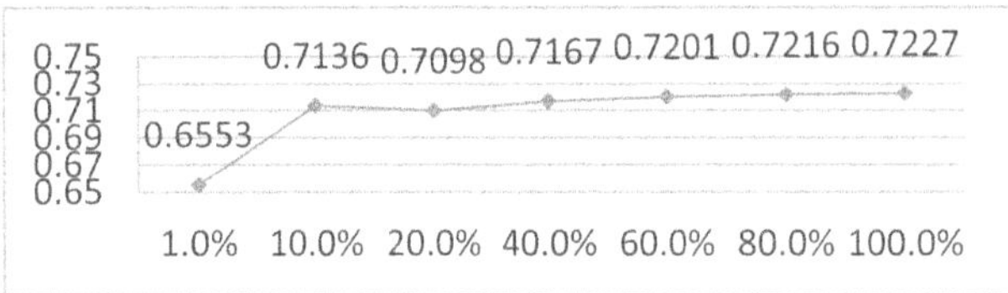

Figure 9. Influence of data scale in training, measured in accuracy. We use DB1(Table 1) in this experiment.

Impact of size of network. Size of network is a critical issue in setting up DNN model. Shallow networks result in trivial model that cannot catch any underlying correlation in data, whereas too deep networks lead to over-complex model which is difficult to tune and may suffer from problems like over-fitting. To choose an appropriate DNN model for classification, we test DNN with different number of layers.

Table 6 summarizes the experiment results. It is clear that 2-layer is not enough for the model to get a satisfactory result. 3-layer model improve significantly while 4-layer model reaches the peak. 5-layer model does not get better result. This is mainly due to the network is too large that it cannot be tuned to a good local minimum with available data and within a feasible training time.

Table 6. Comparison of results using different number of layers in DNN.

	Accuracy	F1-score
DNN-2	0.6843	0.7926
DNN-3	0.7816	0.8423
DNN-4	**0.7857**	**0.8443**
DNN-5	0.7762	0.8386

5.5 Model Efficiency

Table 7. Comparison of results using more classifiers.

	SVM	RF	NB	DNN
CPU time (s)	3.59×10^4	4.59×10^3	3.10	1.93×10^4

For the classification models aforementioned, we also consider their efficiency performance. Though the training of model can be done offline, efficiency is still a considerable factor for evaluating an algorithm. For DNN model, we sum up both pre-training phase and finetuning phase. Table 7 lists the CPU time of each model to train with all labeled data. The results show that training DNN takes around 5 hours which is still reasonable while it get the best detection performance results.

5.6 Results on Other Datasets

We further evaluate our model on other datasets DB2-DB4 to show that our model is a universal model. For this part of experiments, we use statistical attributes together with content attributes using MOT pooling, and with 4-layer DNN model.

DB2 from Sina Weibo with PSTR label. We use a matured model trained with large scale Sina Weibo dataset, and then test it against another set of subject independently sampled from Sina Weibo. For the test set, we collect weekly tweets from the users that have shared the score of a psychological stress scale with 50 items via Sina Weibo. Detection result shows that the test accuracy is 74.13% and f1-score is 0.7778, which approves that the overall model is consistent and the sentence pattern based ground truth labeling method is reliable.

DB3 from Tencent Weibo. We test on data collected from another major Chinese Micro-blog platform. For this test, we use the attribute extractor trained with large scale Sina Weibo dataset and only finetune the network with Twitter dataset in 5-fold. The accuracy is 76.78% and f1-score is 0.7915 which demonstrate the capability of the proposed model.

DB4 from Twitter. We also test against the twitter dataset. We still use the attribute extractor trained with large scale Sina Weibo dataset and only finetune the network with Twitter dataset in 5-fold. The accuracy is 67.43% and f1-score is 0.7224. One reason for this modest result is that users in Twitter dataset and Sina Weibo dataset come from different language and culture background. Another factor could be that the scale of this dataset is rather small. Subjects in the Twitter dataset are on the order of 10% of large scale Sina Weibo dataset. We look into the collected data and find that, by coincidence, all tweets in this dataset have no social activity. We suggest this is also a cause of the unsatisfactory result.

6. CONCLUSION

In this paper, we present a user-level psychological stress detection from users' weekly micro-blog data. First we use the sentence patterns like "I feel stressed" to collect the ground truth labeled micro-blog data in week unit. Then we define a set of low-level content attributes from single tweet's text, images and social interactions. We also present a variety of statistical attributes like behavioral attributes, social engagement and linguistic style attributes from users' weekly tweet postings. A convolutional neural network with cross autoencoders is designed to aggregate weekly low-level content attributes and generate user-scope attributes. Finally we propose a deep neural network model to further learn higher-level attributes in user-scope and predict users' stress. In our proposed method, the user-scope attribute extractor and classification model forms a uniform deep architecture which bridges the gap between each single tweet and user's psychological stress state. We test the model on four different datasets from major micro-blog platforms with different scales and ground truth labeling methods, and deeply discuss the influence of model parameters on experimental results. The results show that the proposed model is effective and efficient on detecting psychological stress from micro-blog data.

7. ACKNOWLEDGMENTS

This work is supported by the National Basic Research Program of China（2011CB302201）, and also partially supported by (2012CB316401) and the National Natural, and Science Foundation of China (61370023, 61373022). We also thank Microsoft Research Asia-Tsinghua Univertity Joint Laboratory project：FY14-RES-SPONSOR-111 for its funding.

8. REFERENCES

[1] Kasl, S. V. (1984). Stress and health. Annual review of public health, 5(1), 319-341.

[2] Hammen, C. (2005). Stress and depression. Annu. Rev. Clin. Psychol., 1, 293-319.

[3] Cohen, S., Kamarck, T., & Mermelstein, R. (1983). A global measure of perceived stress. Journal of health and social behavior, 385-396.

[4] Kanner, A. D., Coyne, J. C., Schaefer, C., & Lazarus, R. S. (1981). Comparison of two modes of stress measurement: Daily hassles and uplifts versus major life events. Journal of behavioral medicine, 4(1), 1-39.

[5] Hetz, C., Martinon, F., Rodriguez, D., & Glimcher, L. H. (2011). The unfolded protein response: integrating stress signals through the stress sensor IRE1α. Physiological Reviews, 91(4), 1219-1243.

[6] Healey, J. A., & Picard, R. W. (2005). Detecting stress during real-world driving tasks using physiological sensors. Intelligent Transportation Systems, IEEE Transactions on, 6(2), 156-166.

[7] Lu, H., Frauendorfer, D., Rabbi, M., Mast, M. S., Chittaranjan, G. T., Campbell, A. T., ... & Choudhury, T. (2012, September). StressSense: Detecting stress in unconstrained acoustic environments using smartphones. In Proceedings of the 2012 ACM Conference on Ubiquitous Computing (pp. 351-360). ACM.

[8] Paredes, P., Sun, D., & Canny, J. (2013, May). Sensor-less sensing for affective computing and stress management technology. In Pervasive Computing Technologies for Healthcare (PervasiveHealth), 2013 7th International Conference on (pp. 459-463). IEEE.

[9] Sadilek, A., Kautz, H. A., & Silenzio, V. (2012, June). Modeling Spread of Disease from Social Interactions. In ICWSM.

[10] Paul, M. J., & Dredze, M. (2011, July). You are what you Tweet: Analyzing Twitter for public health. In ICWSM.

[11] De Choudhury, M., Gamon, M., Counts, S., & Horvitz, E. (2013, July). Predicting depression via social media. In AAAI Conference on Weblogs and Social Media.

[12] Hinton, G. E., & Salakhutdinov, R. R. (2006). Reducing the dimensionality of data with neural networks. *Science*, *313*(5786), 504-507..

[13] Hinton, G. E. (2007). Learning multiple layers of representation. *Trends in cognitive sciences*, *11*(10), 428-434.

[14] Bengio, Y. (2009). Learning deep architectures for AI. *Foundations and trends® in Machine Learning*, 2(1), 1-127.

[15] Ngiam, J., Khosla, A., Kim, M., Nam, J., Lee, H., & Ng, A. Y. (2011). Multimodal deep learning. In *Proceedings of the 28th International Conference on Machine Learning (ICML-11)* (pp. 689-696) .

[16] Srivastava, N., & Salakhutdinov, R. (2012). Multimodal Learning with Deep Boltzmann Machines. In *NIPS* (pp. 2231-2239).

[17] H. Lin, J. Jia, Q. Guo, Y. Xue, J. Huang, L. Cai, L. Feng. Psychological Stress Detection from Cross-media Microblog Data Using Deep Sparse Neural Network. In proceedings of IEEE International Conference on Multimedia & Expo, 2014.

[18] Krizhevsky, A., Sutskever, I., & Hinton, G. E. (2012). ImageNet Classification with Deep Convolutional Neural Networks. In *NIPS* (Vol. 1, No. 2, p. 4).

[19] Kamvar, S. D., & Harris, J. (2011, February). We feel fine and searching the emotional web. In Proceedings of the fourth ACM international conference on Web search and data mining (pp. 117-126). ACM.

[20] Tausczik, Y. R., & Pennebaker, J. W. (2010). The psychological meaning of words: LIWC and computerized text analysis methods. Journal of Language and Social Psychology, 29(1), 24-54.

[21] Rui Gao, Bibo Hao, He Li, Yusong Gao, Tingshao Zhu. Developing Simplified Chinese Psychological Linguistic Analysis Dictionary for Microblog. 2013 International Conference on Brain & Health Informatics (BHI'13). Oct. 2013. Maebashi, Japan.

[22] X. Wang, J. Jia, J. Yin, and L. Cai. Interpretable aesthetic features for a_ective image classi_cation. In ICIP, pages 3230-3234, Melbourne, Australia, 2013.

[23] Wang, X. H., Jia, J., Liao, H. Y., & Cai, L. H. (2012). Affective image colorization. Journal of Computer Science and Technology, 27(6), 1119-1128.

[24] Vincent, P., Larochelle, H., Bengio, Y., & Manzagol, P. A. (2008, July). Extracting and composing robust features with denoising autoencoders. In *Proceedings of the 25th international conference on Machine learning* (pp. 1096-1103). ACM.

[25] LeCun, Y., & Bengio, Y. (1995). Convolutional networks for images, speech, and time series. *The handbook of brain theory and neural networks, 3361*.

[26] Ng, A. Y., & Jordan, M. I. (2002). On discriminative vs. generative classifiers: A comparison of logistic regression and naive bayes. *Advances in neural information processing systems*, 2, 841-848.

[27] Chang, C. C., & Lin, C. J. (2011). LIBSVM: a library for support vector machines. *ACM Transactions on Intelligent Systems and Technology (TIST)*, *2*(3), 27.

[28] Svetnik, V., Liaw, A., Tong, C., Culberson, J. C., Sheridan, R. P., & Feuston, B. P. (2003). Random forest: a classification and regression tool for compound classification and QSAR modeling. *Journal of chemical information and computer sciences*, *43*(6), 1947-1958

Optimized Distances for Binary Code Ranking

Jianfeng Wang[1] Heng Tao Shen[2] Shuicheng Yan[3]
Nenghai Yu[1] Shipeng Li[4] Jingdong Wang[4]
[1] University of Science and Technology of China, Hefei, P. R. China
[2] The University of Queensland, Australia
[3] National University of Singapore, Singapore
[4] Microsoft Research, Beijing, P. R. China
wjf2006@mail.ustc.edu.cn; shenht@itee.uq.edu.au;eleyans@nus.edu.sg;
ynh@ustc.edu.cn; {spli;jingdw}@microsoft.com

ABSTRACT

Binary encoding on high-dimensional data points has attracted much attention due to its computational and storage efficiency. While numerous efforts have been made to encode data points into binary codes, how to calculate the effective distance on binary codes to approximate the original distance is rarely addressed. In this paper, we propose an effective distance measurement for binary code ranking. In our approach, the binary code is firstly decomposed into multiple sub codes, each of which generates a query-dependent distance lookup table. Then the distance between the query and the binary code is constructed as the aggregation of the distances from all sub codes by looking up their respective tables. The entries of the lookup tables are optimized by minimizing the misalignment between the approximate distance and the original distance. Such a scheme is applied to both the symmetric distance and the asymmetric distance. Extensive experimental results show superior performance of the proposed approach over state-of-the-art methods on three real-world high-dimensional datasets for binary code ranking.

Categories and Subject Descriptors

H.3.3 [**Information Search and Retrieval**]: Search Process

General Terms

Algorithms, Measurement, Experimentation

Keywords

Binary Code Ranking; Lookup Table; Approximate Nearest Neighbor Search

MM'14, November 3–7, 2014, Orlando, Florida, USA.
Copyright 2014 ACM 978-1-4503-3063-3/14/11 ...$15.00.
http://dx.doi.org/10.1145/2647868.2654898.

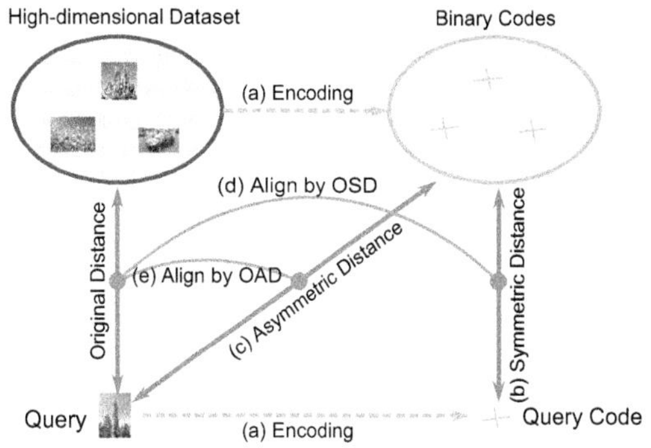

Figure 1: Hashing-based ANN search. (a) encoding of the high-dimensional data to binary codes; (b) distance between binary codes; (c) distance between unbinarized query and the binary code; (d) alignment of the symmetric distance towards the original distance by our OSD; (e) alignment of the asymmetric distance towards the original distance by our OSD.

1. INTRODUCTION

Nearest neighbor (NN) search is a fundamental problem in many multimedia and computer vision applications. Due to the scalability issue and "curse of dimensionality", exact NN search is often intractable for large-scale high-dimensional datasets in practice. Instead, approximate nearest neighbor (ANN) search can provide orders of magnitude faster speed with near-optimal accuracy and is thus more widely applied in real applications than exact NN search [21].

Recently, hashing for ANN search has attracted lots of attention because of its storage and computational efficiency. High-dimensional data points are represented as compact binary codes, and the distance on binary codes is adopted as the approximate measure towards the original distance[1]. Numerous efforts have been devoted to encode the points into binary codes. One representative approach is locality-sensitive hashing (LSH) [6] which employs random projections to compute the binary codes. It is guaranteed that similar data points are mapped into the same binary codes with a high probability. Instead of random projection-based ap-

[1]Here we assume that the original distance is computed by the Euclidean distance in the high-dimensional data space.

proaches, one can learn the hash functions from the databases by preserving the similarities evaluated from the original space in the binary code space [8, 15, 16, 18, 22, 27, 28, 29, 30, 34, 35]. The semantic information can be incorporated to construct the hash functions, which is not our focus. In this paper, we mainly target on the search based on the Euclidean distance. Fig. 1 (a) shows the role of hashing functions in the search pipeline.

After obtaining binary codes, the distance between the query and the code is then used to rank all the database points. The Hamming distance, which counts the number of bits that differ between two binary codes, is mostly employed in existing works [3, 16, 27, 29]. It can be quickly calculated with several hardware instructions. However, its effectiveness is limited, and only $Q + 1$ different values are provided, where Q is the number of bits (i.e., code length). As a consequence, for a query point, many database points may share the same Hamming distance value.

Besides encoding the query into the binary code, another way is to directly define some appropriate distance between the unencoded query and the database binary code, which is usually referred to as *asymmetric distance* (AD) [4]. Comparatively, the distance using the encoded query is referred to as *symmetric distance* (SD). Fig. 1 (b) and (c) illustrate the relations of SD and AD, respectively. Since the unencoded query carries more information than the encoded query, AD generally achieves better accuracy than SD. In [4, 31, 33], query-dependent weights are computed for each bit under some assumptions, such as the uniform distribution assumption [33], and the distance is defined as the summation of a portion of the weights according to the binary codes. For product quantization [8], and composite quantization [32] the space is grouped into multiple clusters. Each database point is encoded by the index of the nearest cluster center and AD is defined as the distance between the query and the cluster center.

Given a query point and binary codes, in this paper we study the problem of *how to effectively measure the distance between the query and the database binary codes for the ANN search*. Here the effectiveness refers to the alignment between the search results based on the approximate distance and those based on the original distance. Suppose the code length is Q, there are in total of 2^Q different possible codes. A simple but effective way is to build up a lookup table with 2^Q entries, each of which represents the distance between the query and the corresponding binary code. Obviously, such a table can contain complete distance information. By carefully setting the values in the lookup table, we expect a much better approximate distance as well as ranking result.

However, when the code length Q increases, storing 2^Q values in the table becomes infeasible. To address this issue, we propose to partition the Q bits into multiple sub codes, each of which generates a much smaller lookup table. Then, the overall approximate distance is defined as the aggregation from these lookup tables of all sub codes. We optimize the entry values in the lookup tables by minimizing the misalignment between the approximate distance and the original distance. We term the proposed idea applied to SD as *Optimized Symmetric Distance* (OSD) while to AD as *Optimized Asymmetric Distance* (OAD). Fig. 1 (d) and (e) depict the alignment of our OSD and OAD, respectively. Extensive experimental results demonstrate the superior effectiveness of our approach over state-of-the-art methods for binary code ranking.

Our approach has the following advantages. 1) It generalizes the existing approaches and achieves better ranking results. 2) It can be applied to a wide range of binary codes, including the codes generated by product quantization [8]. 3) The algorithm makes no specific assumption on the data distribution (e.g. uniform distribution). 4) It is efficient and consumes linear training time to the data size. The extra testing time is minor and is consistent with the data size.

2. RELATED WORK

In this section, we review hashing-based ANN search algorithms that are closely related to our approach. The hashing-based search algorithms consist of two main phases. The first phase is binary code encoding, in which each data point is encoded as a binary code. The second phase is binary code ranking, in which all data points are ranked based on their distances computed on binary codes to the query.

2.1 Binary code encoding

There are generally two types of approaches towards encoding high-dimensional data points into binary codes. One is based on random projections and the other is to learn from the data.

Locality sensitive hashing (LSH) [6] is one of the typical random-based approaches. The key idea is to hash high-dimensional data points using several random hash functions to ensure that the probability of collision is high for close points and vice versa. There are various algorithms extending LSH, e.g. Kernelized LSH [13], Shift-invariant kernel hashing [20], Super-bit LSH [9]. These approaches are blind with the data distribution and usually need longer binary codes or more hash tables to achieve a satisfactory performance.

In contrast, learning-based algorithms compute the hash function explicitly from the training data. Binary reconstructive embedding [12] aims to align the Hamming distance to the original Euclidean distance. Iterative quantization hashing [3] and isotropic hashing [10] are based on PCA and rotate the axis by minimization of the distortion errors and by the equality of variances, respectively. Spectral hashing (SH) [29] learns the hash codes by minimizing the summation of the Hamming distances weighted by the similarities computed in the input space, which is extended from different perspectives in [17, 28]. The sequential projection learning scheme [25] and LDAHash [23] learn hash functions to minimize (maximize) the Hamming distance of similar (dissimilar) pairs. Ranking-based hashing approaches are developed in [15, 27] to expect the ranking order is well aligned from the binary space to the original space.

Product quantization (PQ) [8] encodes the points by the index of the nearest cluster center with the quantization errors minimized. The training time cost for a large number of clusters is reduced through partitioning the original space into multiple disjoint subspaces and clustering each subspace. The quantization errors are further reduced in [2, 18, 26, 32].

2.2 Binary code ranking

Given a query point, its distance to the binary code of each database point is typically used as the approximation of the true distance in the original high-dimensional space. Due to the fast speed of the approximate distance computation, even the exhaustive search over the whole dataset is fast enough in practice. Sophisticated techniques based on the inverted index can further improve the speed, e.g., [1, 8, 19]. In this phase, the approximate distance plays a crucial role on the overall ranking performance.

The distance approximation scheme consists of two groups: symmetric distance (SD) and asymmetric distance (AD). SD is referred to as the distance between the data from the same space while AD is referred to as the distance between the data from different spaces.

Symmetric Distance: The Hamming distance is most widely used and can be computed efficiently by bit operations. However, the Hamming distance is often not sufficiently effective and many retrieved candidates may share the same distance value. The Spherical Hamming distance [5] is based on the hypersphere hashing scheme and is defined as the Hamming distance divided by the number of bits where the points falls into the same hypersphere. Manhattan hashing [11] uses the Manhattan distance with each projected dimension encoded by natural binary codes. The weighted Hamming distance, where each bit is assigned to a real-valued weight, is used in [15, 28] to rank the database points. For product quantization [8] and cartesian K-means [18], the space is split into multiple clusters, and the distance between the cluster centers is used to approximate the original distance.

Asymmetric Distance: AD does not encode the query point as the binary code and thus is able to exploit more accurate query representation. The distance in [31] assigns a bit-level weight, which depends on the *unbinarized hash values* [31] of the query and the database points. Two kinds of ADs are proposed in [4], based on the assumption that the Euclidean distance between the unbinarized hash values is closely related with the original distance. QsRank [33] defines the query-sensitive distance for the PCA-based binary codes. The asymmetric Hamming distance [7] is incorporated within the inverted file structure. In [8, 18, 32], the distance between the original query point and the cluster centers is used to approximate the original distance with each database point encoded as the index of the nearest cluster.

In this paper, we focus on the second phase, and aim to define the optimized distances on binary codes to achieve effective binary code ranking. The first phase to encode the high-dimensional data is not our contribution.

3. OVERVIEW

Given a dataset $\mathcal{X} = \{\mathbf{x}_1, \cdots, \mathbf{x}_N\}$ with $\mathbf{x}_i \in \mathbb{R}^P$ where N is the dataset size and P is the dimensionality of data space, the encoding scheme encodes each data point into a binary code, and can be written as $\mathbf{h} : \mathbb{R}^P \mapsto \{0,1\}^Q$, where Q is the code length. Let $\mathbf{b}_i \in \{0,1\}^Q$ be the binary code of $\mathbf{x}_i$. Provided the high-dimensional dataset and the derived binary codes, we aim to optimize the distance on binary codes to improve the search accuracy.

Given a query point $\mathbf{q} \in \mathbb{R}^P$, the distance comparison is mainly determined by the binary codes of the database points. Since Q bits lead to 2^Q different codes, we can build up a lookup table with 2^Q entries, each of which represents the distance between the query and the corresponding binary code. Fig. 2 (a) illustrates the lookup table with 2^{16} entries when $Q = 16$.

Table 1: Sizes of lookup tables with different numbers of partitions when $Q = 32$.

T	1	2	4	8	16
$T \times 2^{Q/T}$	2^{32}	2^{17}	2^{10}	2^7	2^6

However, with the code length Q increased, storing 2^Q entries becomes infeasible in practice. To address the scalability problem, we propose to partition the Q bits into multiple sub codes, and each sub code generates a much smaller lookup table. Let T be the number of partitions. For the sake of simplicity, we assume Q is divisible by T and the length of each sub code is equal to $S \triangleq Q/T$, where the symbol '$\triangleq$' means 'defined as'. Our approach can be easily applied to partitions with an unequal length. Since the length of the sub code is S, there are $M \triangleq 2^S$ possible binary codes or *buckets* on each partition. Denote the smaller lookup table as $\mathbf{d}^t(\mathbf{q}) \in \mathbb{R}^M, t \in \{1, \cdots, T\}$ for the query $\mathbf{q}$. In certain cases, we eliminate $\mathbf{q}$ and use $\mathbf{d}^t$ to denote the lookup table without confusion. Fig. 2 (b) shows 2 smaller lookup tables when $T = 2$ and $Q = 16$.

Before describing how to aggregate the distance from the lookup tables $\{\mathbf{d}^t\}$, we introduce some notations. Let $\mathbf{b}_i^t \in \{0,1\}^S$ be the t-th sub code of the binary code $\mathbf{b}_i$. Given $\mathbf{b}_i^t$, we further introduce an indicator matrix $\mathbf{R}^t \in \{0,1\}^{N \times M}$, in which the entry $r_{j,m}^t$ on the j-th row and m-th column is defined as

$$r_{j,m}^t \triangleq \begin{cases} 1, & m = \mathcal{P}(\mathbf{b}_j^t) \\ 0, & \text{otherwise,} \end{cases} \tag{1}$$

where $\mathcal{P}(\mathbf{b}_j^t)$ maps the binary representation $\mathbf{b}_j^t$ into the natural decimal representation. For example, $\mathcal{P}(0100) = 4$ and $\mathcal{P}(1001) = 9$. In other words, the condition $m = \mathcal{P}(\mathbf{b}_j^t)$ means that on the t-th partition, the j-th point falls into the m-th bucket. The two representations, $\mathbf{b}_j^t$ and $r_{j,m}^t$ are equivalent, and we can easily derive one from the other.

Then, we arrive at the proposed distance between the query $\mathbf{q}$ and the binary code $\mathbf{b}_j$ with T partitions,

$$\mathcal{D}(\mathbf{q}, \mathbf{b}_j) \triangleq \sum_{t,n} r_{j,n}^t d_n^t(\mathbf{q}), \tag{2}$$

where $d_n^t(\mathbf{q})$ is the n-th entry of $\mathbf{d}^t(\mathbf{q})$. The intuition of the distance definition is to select one entry from each $\mathbf{d}^t$ and aggregate these selected entries. With fixed t, the summation through all n equivalently extracts the entry $d_{n_t}^t$, where on the t-th partition the j-th point falls into the n_t-th bucket. Then over all the possible t values, we sum up $d_{n_t}^t$ to obtain the overall distance.

If no partitioning is performed, i.e. $T = 1$, the lookup table $\{d_n^1\}$ contains 2^Q entries and each entry denotes the distance to the corresponding binary code. When $T > 1$, the distance is constructed as the summation of T entries. By partitioning, the size of lookup tables reduces to $T \times 2^{Q/T}$ from 2^Q. It can be easily proved that with $T \leq Q/2$, the size is strictly decreased with a larger T. Table 1 illustrates the sizes with different numbers of partitions when $Q = 32$.

Then, all the database points can be ranked by the distance defined in Eqn. 2. In Sec. 4 and Sec. 5, we will present the proposed approaches to learn $\{\mathbf{d}^t(\mathbf{q})\}$ for SD and AD.

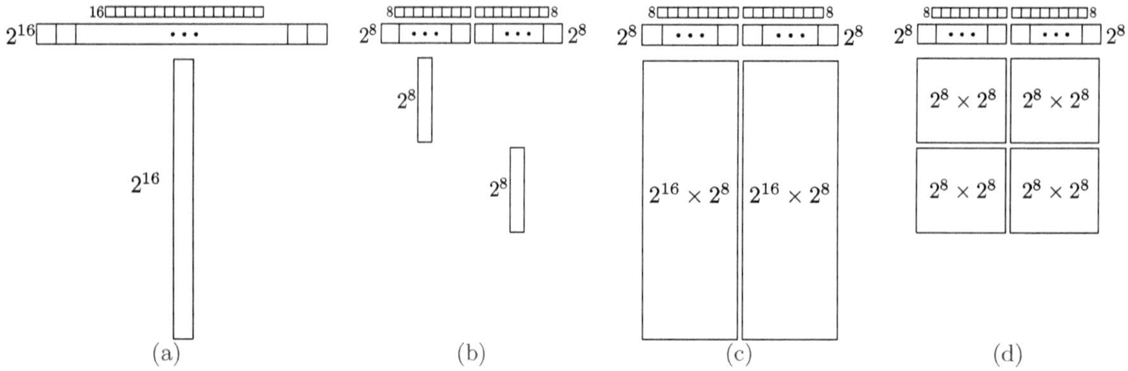

Figure 2: Proposed lookup tables for binary code ranking with 16 bits. (a) a query-dependent lookup table to indicate the distance to any binary code of the database. (b) 2 smaller lookup tables by 2 partitions on the database code. (c) 2 lookup matrices to store all the distance information between the query code and the database code. (d) 4 smaller lookup matrices by further splitting the query code into 2 groups.

4. OPTIMIZED SYMMETRIC DISTANCE

For symmetric distance, the query point is encoded as a binary code, denoted by $\mathbf{b}_q$. Accordingly, the lookup table $\{\mathbf{d}^t(\mathbf{q})\}$ is written as $\{\mathbf{d}^t(\mathbf{b}_q)\}$. Since there are 2^Q different possible query codes and 2^S different codes for each of the T partitions of the database codes, we can imagine to pre-build T lookup matrices with the size $2^Q \times 2^S$. Fig. 2 (c) illustrates the lookup matrix with the size $2^{16} \times 2^8$ when $T = 2$ and $Q = 16$. During the search stage, we can extract the corresponding row as the lookup table $\mathbf{d}^t(\mathbf{b}_q)$.

However, storing the matrix with the size $2^Q \times 2^S$ is infeasible. To address the problem, we propose to partition the query code in the same way as done for the database code $\mathbf{b}_j$. Let $\mathbf{D}^{s,t} \in \mathbb{R}^{M\times M}$ be the lookup matrix between the s-th partition of the query code and the t-th partition of the database code, and $d^{s,t}_{m,n}$ be the entry on the m-th row and the n-th column of $\mathbf{D}^{s,t}$. Fig. 2 (d) shows the example when $T = 2$ and $Q = 16$. Then, the element of the lookup tables is defined as

$$d^t_n(\mathbf{q}) \triangleq \sum_{s,m} r^s_{q,m} d^{s,t}_{m,n}, \tag{3}$$

where $r^s_{q,m}$ is the indicator notation of the query code, similar as in Eqn. 1 for the database code. If r^s_{q,m_s} is non-zero, Eqn. 3 is equivalent to $d^t_n = \sum_s r^s_{q,m_s} d^{s,t}_{m_s,n}$. That is, every partition of the query code contributes one entry to construct d^t_n.

The lookup matrix $\{\mathbf{D}^{s,t}\}$ contains all the distances between any query code to any database codes. We offline learn $\{\mathbf{D}^{s,t}\}$ from the training data, and compute the lookup table $\{\mathbf{d}^t(\mathbf{b}_q)\}$ for the query code $\mathbf{b}_q$ by Eqn. 3.

4.1 Formulation

The original distance between the query point $\mathbf{q}$ and the database point $\mathbf{x}_j$ is

$$\|\mathbf{q} - \mathbf{x}_j\|_2, \tag{4}$$

while the approximate symmetric distance between their binary codes is constructed by Eqn. 2 and Eqn. 3. Obviously, there may exist a distance approximation error, and it is beneficial to minimize it for accurate ANN search. Substituting Eqn. 3 into Eqn. 2, we propose to learn the values $\{d^{s,t}_{m,n}\}$ by minimizing

$$\mathrm{E}_{\mathbf{q}}\left(\sum_j (\|\mathbf{q} - \mathbf{x}_j\|_2^2 - \sum_{t,n} r^t_{j,n} \sum_{s,m} r^s_{q,m} d^{s,t}_{m,n})^2\right), \tag{5}$$

where $\mathrm{E}_{\mathbf{q}}(\cdot)$ represents the expectation over the distribution of the query $\mathbf{q}$.

Assuming that the query and the database points follow the same data distribution, the problem of minimizing Eqn. 5 is transformed to

$$\min_{\{d^{s,t}_{m,n}\}} \mathcal{F}_S \triangleq \frac{1}{2}\sum_{i,j}(\|\mathbf{x}_i - \mathbf{x}_j\|_2^2 - \sum_{s,t,m,n} r^s_{i,m} r^t_{j,n} d^{s,t}_{m,n})^2. \tag{6}$$

In this formulation, $d^{s,t}_{m,n}$ is not required to be non-negative. The only requirement is the overall approximate distance $\sum_{s,t,m,n} r^s_{i,m} r^t_{j,n} d^{s,t}_{m,n}$ should align as well as possible to the squared original distance $\|\mathbf{x}_i - \mathbf{x}_j\|_2^2$. Here we use the squared Euclidean distance rather than the Euclidean distance because of the fact that the squared distance can be exactly written as the summation of multiple values.

4.2 Optimization

The matrix form of Eqn. 6 is

$$\mathcal{F}_S = \frac{1}{2}\|\mathbf{A} - \sum_{s,t} \mathbf{R}^s \mathbf{D}^{s,t} \mathbf{R}^{t\prime}\|_F^2 \tag{7}$$

$$= \frac{1}{2}\|\mathbf{A} - \mathbf{R}\mathbf{D}\mathbf{R}'\|_F^2, \tag{8}$$

where $\mathbf{R}^t$ is the indicator matrix whose entries are defined in Eqn. 1, $\mathbf{D}^{s,t}$ is the lookup matrix, the entries of the distance matrix $\mathbf{A} \in \mathbf{R}^{N\times N}$ are defined as

$$A_{i,j} \triangleq \|\mathbf{x}_i - \mathbf{x}_j\|_2^2, \tag{9}$$

$\mathbf{R}^{t\prime}$ is the transpose matrix of $\mathbf{R}^t$, $\|\cdot\|_F$ represents the Frobenius norm, and $\mathbf{R}$, $\mathbf{D}$ are defined as

$$\mathbf{R} \triangleq \begin{bmatrix}\mathbf{R}^1 & \cdots & \mathbf{R}^T\end{bmatrix}, \tag{10}$$

$$\mathbf{D} \triangleq \begin{bmatrix}\mathbf{D}^{1,1} & \cdots & \mathbf{D}^{1,T} \\ \vdots & \ddots & \vdots \\ \mathbf{D}^{T,1} & \cdots & \mathbf{D}^{T,T}\end{bmatrix}. \tag{11}$$

This is an unconstrained quadratic program. Setting $\partial \mathcal{F}_S / \partial \mathbf{D}$ as 0, we have

$$\mathbf{EDE} = \mathbf{G}, \tag{12}$$

where

$$\mathbf{E} \triangleq \mathbf{R}'\mathbf{R} = \begin{bmatrix} \mathbf{R}^{1'}\mathbf{R}^1 & \cdots & \mathbf{R}^{1'}\mathbf{R}^T \\ \vdots & \ddots & \vdots \\ \mathbf{R}^{T'}\mathbf{R}^1 & \cdots & \mathbf{R}^{T'}\mathbf{R}^T \end{bmatrix}, \tag{13}$$

$$\mathbf{G} \triangleq \mathbf{R}'\mathbf{A}\mathbf{R} = \begin{bmatrix} \mathbf{R}^{1'}\mathbf{A}\mathbf{R}^1 & \cdots & \mathbf{R}^{1'}\mathbf{A}\mathbf{R}^T \\ \vdots & \ddots & \vdots \\ \mathbf{R}^{T'}\mathbf{A}\mathbf{R}^1 & \cdots & \mathbf{R}^{T'}\mathbf{A}\mathbf{R}^T \end{bmatrix}. \tag{14}$$

Both $\mathbf{E}$ and $\mathbf{G}$ are computed from the database points and their binary codes. Then, we can solve $\mathbf{D}$ in a closed form by matrix (pseudo-)inversion: $\mathbf{D} = \mathbf{E}^\dagger \mathbf{G} \mathbf{E}^\dagger$. The *Optimized Symmetric Distance* (OSD) algorithm is decipted in Alg. 1. Below are the details of computing $\mathbf{E}$ and $\mathbf{G}$.

Compute E. Let $\mathbf{E}^{s,t} \triangleq \mathbf{R}^{s'}\mathbf{R}^t$. We compute the entry on the m-th row and n-th column of $\mathbf{E}^{s,t}$ as

$$E^{s,t}_{m,n} = \sum_i r^s_{i,m} r^t_{i,n}. \tag{15}$$

Recalling that $r^s_{i,m}$ in Eqn. 1 indicates whether the i-th point falls into the m-th bucket on the s-th partition, we have the observation that $E^{s,t}_{m,n}$ is equal to the number of points which fall into both the m-th bucket on the s-th partition and the n-th bucket on the t-th partition.

Computing all the entries $\{E^{s,t}_{m,n}\}$ only need to scan all the binary codes one time. Each $E^{s,t}_{m,n}$ is initialized by 0. For the i-th point, $E^{s,t}_{m,n}$ increases by 1 if both $r^s_{i,m}$ and $r^t_{i,n}$ are non-zero. The overall complexity of computing $\{E^{s,t}_{m,n}\}$ is $O(T^2N)$ and the storage complexity is $O(M^2T^2)$.

Compute G. According to the definition of the distance matrix $\mathbf{A}$ in Eqn. 9, we compute the element of $\mathbf{G}^{s,t} \triangleq \mathbf{R}^{s'}\mathbf{A}\mathbf{R}^t$ in Eqn. 14 as

$$G^{s,t}_{m,n} = \sum_{i,j} r^s_{i,m} A_{i,j} r^t_{j,n} \tag{16}$$

$$= \sum_{i,j} r^s_{i,m} \|\mathbf{x}_i - \mathbf{x}_j\|_2^2 r^t_{j,n} \tag{17}$$

$$= E^{s,s}_{m,m} E^{t,t}_{n,n} (\|\mathbf{c}^s_m - \mathbf{c}^t_n\|_2^2 + \epsilon^s_m + \epsilon^t_n), \tag{18}$$

where

$$\mathbf{c}^s_m \triangleq \begin{cases} \frac{1}{E^{s,s}_{m,m}} \sum_i r^s_{i,m} \mathbf{x}_i, & E^{s,s}_{m,m} > 0 \\ \mathbf{0}, & E^{s,s}_{m,m} = 0, \end{cases} \tag{19}$$

$$\epsilon^s_m \triangleq \begin{cases} \frac{1}{E^{s,s}_{m,m}} \sum_i r^s_{i,m} \|\mathbf{x}_i - \mathbf{c}^s_m\|_2^2, & E^{s,s}_{m,m} > 0 \\ 0, & E^{s,s}_{m,m} = 0, \end{cases} \tag{20}$$

and $\mathbf{c}^t_n$ and ϵ^t_n are similarly defined. The transformation from Eqn. 17 to Eqn. 18 can be justfied by simply replacing $\|\mathbf{x}_i - \mathbf{x}_j\|_2^2$ with $\|(\mathbf{x}_i - \mathbf{c}^s_m) + (\mathbf{c}^s_m - \mathbf{c}^t_n) + (\mathbf{c}^t_n - \mathbf{x}_j)\|_2^2$.

From Eqn. 19, one can observe that $\mathbf{c}^s_m$ is the center of all the points which fall into the m-th bucket on the s-th partition, while ϵ^s_m from Eqn. 20 is the average distortion error between the points and the center.

The computation of $\{G^{s,t}_{m,n}\}$ consists of three steps: 1) scanning all the points to obtain the centers $\{\mathbf{c}^s_m\}$ by Eqn. 19, whose complexity is $O(NPT)$; 2) scanning all the points to obtain the distortion errors $\{\epsilon^s_m\}$ in Eqn. 20 whose complexity is $O(NPT)$; 3) and then computing $\{G^{s,t}_{m,n}\}$ by Eqn. 18 whose complexity is $O(M^2PT^2)$.

Algorithm 1 Optimized Symmetric Distance.

Input: Dataset $\{\mathbf{x}_i\}$; Binary codes $\{\mathbf{b}_i\}$; T; $\mathbf{b}_q$
Output: The lookup table $\{d^t_n\}$
1: Compute $\mathbf{E}$ by Eqn. 13 and 15
2: Compute $\{\mathbf{c}^t_m\}$ by Eqn. 19
3: Compute $\{\epsilon^t_m\}$ by Eqn. 20
4: Compute $\mathbf{G}$ by Eqn. 14 and 18
5: Solve $\mathbf{D}$ by Eqn. 12

5. OPTIMIZED ASYMMETRIC DISTANCE

The goal of optimized asymmetric distance (OAD) is to learn distance functions $\{d^t_n(\mathbf{q})\}$, which map the real-valued query $\mathbf{q}$ to the lookup tables storing the distances between the query and the binary codes for all the T partitions. We choose to learn distance functions instead of generating a complete look matrix offline as done optimized symmetric distance, because the query in OAD is any real-valued point and the number of possible queries is infinite while the query in OSD is encoded to binary codes and hence the number is finite.

5.1 Formulation

The objective function for OAD is formulated as follows,

$$\min_{\{d^t_n(\cdot)\}} \mathcal{F}_A \triangleq \frac{1}{2} \mathrm{E}_q \left(\sum_i (\|\mathbf{q} - \mathbf{x}_i\|_2^2 - \sum_{t,n} r^t_{i,n} d^t_n(\mathbf{q}))^2 \right), \tag{21}$$

which minimizes the expectation of the misalignment between the original distance and the approximate distance.

It seems that the optimization is not feasible as there is an expectation with respect to the query $\mathbf{q}$ and there is no prior information for the distribution of the query. We will show that the parameters of the distance functions $\{d^t_n(\mathbf{q})\}$ are independent to the query $\mathbf{q}$. On the other hand, the original distance between the query and each database point is needed in the objective function of Eqn. 21. We will show that the functions $\{d^t_n(\cdot)\}$ are learnt only using $\{\mathbf{c}^t_n\}$ (as defined in Eqn. 19), $\{\epsilon^t_n\}$ (as defined in Eqn. 20), and $\mathbf{E}$ (as defined in Eqn. 13). Consequently, the dataset $\{\mathbf{x}_i\}$ can be discarded and is not required in the online computation.

5.2 Optimization

The matrix form of Eqn. 21 is written as

$$\mathcal{F}_A = \frac{1}{2} \mathrm{E}_q (\|\mathbf{a}(\mathbf{q}) - \sum_t \mathbf{R}^t \mathbf{d}^t(\mathbf{q})\|_2^2) \tag{22}$$

$$= \frac{1}{2} \mathrm{E}_q (\|\mathbf{a}(\mathbf{q}) - \mathbf{R}\mathbf{d}(\mathbf{q})\|_2^2), \tag{23}$$

where

$$\mathbf{d}(\mathbf{q}) \triangleq \left[\mathbf{d}^1(\mathbf{q})' \quad \cdots \quad \mathbf{d}^T(\mathbf{q})' \right]', \tag{24}$$

$$\mathbf{d}^t(\mathbf{q}) \triangleq \left[d^t_1(\mathbf{q}) \quad \cdots \quad d^t_M(\mathbf{q}) \right]', \tag{25}$$

$$\mathbf{a}(\mathbf{q}) \triangleq \left[\|\mathbf{q} - \mathbf{x}_1\|_2^2 \quad \cdots \quad \|\mathbf{q} - \mathbf{x}_N\|_2^2 \right]', \tag{26}$$

and $\mathbf{R}^t$ and $\mathbf{R}$ are defined in Eqn. 1 and Eqn. 10, respectively.

Algorithm 2 Optimized Asymmetric Distance.

Input: Dataset $\{\mathbf{x}_i\}$; Binary codes $\{\mathbf{b}_i\}$; T; $\mathbf{q}$
Output: The lookup table $\{d_n^t\}$
1: Compute $\mathbf{E}$ by Eqn. 13 and 15
2: Compute $\{\mathbf{c}_n^t\}$ by Eqn. 19
3: Compute $\{\epsilon_n^t\}$ by Eqn. 20
4: Compute inv($\mathbf{E}$)

Let the derivative of $\mathcal{F}_{\mathrm{A}}$ w.r.t. $\mathbf{d}(\mathbf{q})$ as 0. We have

$$\mathbf{d}(\mathbf{q}) = \mathrm{inv}(\mathbf{E})\mathbf{g}(\mathbf{q}), \tag{27}$$

where

$$\mathbf{g}(\mathbf{q}) \triangleq \mathbf{R}'\mathbf{a}(\mathbf{q}) = \left[\mathbf{a}(\mathbf{q})'\mathbf{R}^1 \quad \cdots \quad \mathbf{a}(\mathbf{q})'\mathbf{R}^T\right]', \tag{28}$$

and $\mathbf{E}$ is defined in Eqn. 13, and inv($\mathbf{E}$) represents the (pseudo-) inversion of $\mathbf{E}$.

Let $\mathbf{g}^t(\mathbf{q}) \triangleq \mathbf{R}^{t\prime}\mathbf{a}(\mathbf{q})$. According to the definition of the indicator notation $\mathbf{R}^t$ in Eqn. 1, we compute the n-th entry of $\mathbf{g}^t(\mathbf{q})$ as

$$g_n^t(\mathbf{q}) = \sum_i r_{i,n}^t \|\mathbf{q} - \mathbf{x}_i\|_2^2 \tag{29}$$

$$= E_{n,n}^{t,t}(\|\mathbf{q} - \mathbf{c}_n^t\|_2^2 + \epsilon_n^t). \tag{30}$$

where $\mathbf{c}_n^t$, ϵ_n^t and $E_{n,n}^{t,t}$ are defined in Eqn. 19, Eqn. 20, and Eqn. 15, respectively. The above equation means that only a small number of distances rather than the distances between the query $\mathbf{q}$ and all the database points, are required, and thus the computation cost is reduced. To reduce the online computations, we precompute inv($\mathbf{E}$), $\mathbf{c}_n^t$ and ϵ_n^t. Thus, the online process only computes $\{g_n^t\}$ by Eqn. 30 with $O(PT2^{Q/T})$ time and $\mathbf{d}$ by Eqn. 27 with $O(T^2 2^{2Q/T})$ time, both of which are independent to N.

The algorithm of *Optimized Asymmetric Distance* is summarized in Alg. 2.

6. DISCUSSIONS

6.1 Number of Partitions T

6.1.1 Effectiveness vs T

The ranking result is often better if the misalignment of the approximate distance towards the original distance is smaller. Thus, we use the mean squared differences between the true distance and the approximate distance to describe the effectiveness, i.e., the objective function under optimal solutions in Eqn. 6 and Eqn. 21 for OSD and OAD, respectively.

The numbers of the optimization variables in Eqn. 6 and Eqn. 21 are $T^2 \times 2^{2Q/T}$ and $T \times 2^{Q/T}$, respectively, both of which are monotonically decreasing with T when $T \leq Q/2$. The following theorem shows how the number of partitions T influences the effectiveness.

THEOREM 1. *Given a positive integer c, and the numbers of partitions T_1 and T_2 satisfying that $T_1 = cT_2$ and the code length Q is divisible by T_1, under the optimal solutions, we have*

$$\mathcal{F}_{S,T_1}^* \geq \mathcal{F}_{S,T_2}^* \tag{31}$$

$$\mathcal{F}_{A,T_1}^* \geq \mathcal{F}_{A,T_2}^* \tag{32}$$

where $\mathcal{F}_{S,T_i}^*, i = \{1, 2\}$ denotes the optimal objective function value in Eqn. 6 with T_i partitions, and $\mathcal{F}_{A,T_i}^*$ is for Eqn. 21.

The theorem can be easily proved based on the basic fact that the optimal solution for the case with T_1 partitions is a feasible solution for the case with T_2 partitions. We omit the detailed proof. Intuitively, this theorem shows that a smaller T_2 can lead to a potentially smaller distance approximate error than T_1.

6.1.2 Complexity vs T

Storage: To compute the lookup tables, OSD requires the lookup matrix $\{d_{m,n}^{s,t}\}$ with $O(T^2 2^{2Q/T})$ storage. OAD requires the auxiliary matrix inv($\mathbf{E}$) with $O(T^2 2^{2Q/T})$ storage, $\{\mathbf{c}_m^t\}$ with $O(P2^{Q/T}T)$ storage, and $\{\epsilon_m^t\}$ with $O(T2^{Q/T})$ storage. The storage cost is consistent with the data size, and is generally decreasing with a larger T.
Training time: For OSD in Alg. 1, it requires $O(T^2N)$ to compute $\mathbf{E}$, $O(PNT)$ to compute $\{\mathbf{c}_m^s\}$ and $\{\epsilon_m^s\}$, $O(2^{2Q/T}P T^2)$ to compute $\{G_{m,n}^{s,t}\}$, and $O(2^{2Q/T}T^2)$ to solve the linear equation of Eqn. 12 to get $\mathbf{D}$. For OAD in Alg. 2, it requires $O(T^2N)$ to compute $\mathbf{E}$, $O(PNT)$ to compute $\{\mathbf{c}_m^s\}$ and $\{\epsilon_m^s\}$, and $O(2^{3Q/T}T^3)$ to compute the matrix (pseudo-)inversion of $\mathbf{E}$. Practically, to compute $\mathbf{E}$, $\{\mathbf{c}_m^s\}$, $\{\epsilon_m^s\}$, and $\{G_{m,n}^{s,t}\}$ is quite fast. The main time cost is to solve Eqn. 12 for OSD and the matrix (pseudo-)inversion of $\mathbf{E}$ for OAD. Thus, the training time generally decreases with a larger T.
Online query time: For the online search process, each distance computation of both OSD and OAD requires $O(T)$ time by Eqn. 2. To obtain the lookup tables, OSD requires $O(2^{Q/T}T(T-1))$ preprocessing time by Eqn. 3, while OAD requires $O(PT2^{Q/T})$ and $O(T^2 2^{2Q/T})$ for Eqn. 30 and Eqn. 27, respectively.

6.2 Connections with Related Work

In OSD, we first compute the lookup matrix $\{d_{m,n}^{s,t}\}$ and then the lookup table $\{d_n^t\}$ for the query code. In OAD, we compute the functions $\{d_n^t(\cdot)\}$ from the training data and compute the lookup tables for the real-valued query. In this subsection, we show that several existing approaches are special cases of our proposed distances.

The Hamming distance and the symmetric weighted Hamming distance used in [28, 15] is a special case of our proposed symmetric distance under the conditions that $T = Q$ and

$$d_{m,n}^{s,t} = \begin{cases} w_s(m \oplus n), & s = t \\ 0, & s \neq t, \end{cases} \tag{33}$$

where $m \in \{0, 1\}$, $n \in \{0, 1\}$, and $\oplus$ denotes the XOR operation. The coefficient w_s is 1 for Hamming distance or a learnt variable in [28, 15].

In [31], the weights of the weighted Hamming distance are dependent on the un-encoded query as well as the database points. Let w_s be the weight of the sth bit. The distance presented in [31] is the special case of our proposed asymmetric distance under the conditions that $T = Q$ and $d_m^s = w_s(b_{q,s} \oplus m)$, where $b_{q,s}$ represents the s-th bit of the query code $\mathbf{b}_q$, and $m \in \{0, 1\}$. Similarly, it can be shown that QsRank [33], expectation-based and lower-bound based approaches in [4] are also special cases of our proposed asymmetric distance with different settings for $\{d_m^t(\mathbf{q})\}$.

For product quantization [8], the original P-dimensional space is partitioned into multiple disjoint subspaces. Let T

be the number of partitions. In each subspace with P/T dimensions, $2^{Q/T}$ clusters are generated and each point is encoded as the concatenation of the index of the nearest cluster center within each subspace. Denote $\hat{\mathbf{c}}_m^s \in \mathbb{R}^{P/T}$ as the m-th cluster center in the s-th subspace. The symmetric distance introduced in [8] is a special case of our proposed symmetric distance under the conditions that there are T partitions and

$$d_{m,n}^{s,t} = \begin{cases} \|\hat{\mathbf{c}}_m^s - \hat{\mathbf{c}}_n^s\|_2^2 & s = t \\ 0 & s \neq t. \end{cases} \quad (34)$$

We have a similar conclusion for the asymmetric distance introduced in [8] and the proposed optimized asymmetric distance.

7. EXPERIMENTS

7.1 Experiment Settings

7.1.1 High-dimensional datasets

Three widely-used high-dimensional datasets are used, including SIFT1M [8], GIST1M [8], and MNIST [14]. SIFT1M contains 1 million 128-dimensional SIFT descriptors of local image structures, with $10,000$ queries. GIST1M contains 1 million 960-dimensional GIST feature vectors which capture the global image structures, with $1,000$ queries. MNIST has $60,000$ database images, with $10,000$ query images. Each image contains 28×28 pixels, and we vectorize each image as a 784-dimensional feature vector.

7.1.2 Binary code encoding

We adopt several representative binary encoding approaches to encode the high-dimensional data into binary codes.

- Locality sensitive hashing (LSH) [6]: a typical data-independent linear hashing method.
- Iterative quantization (ITQ) hashing [3]: one of the state-of-the-art data-dependent linear hashing methods.
- Kernel-based supervised hashing (KSH) [16]: a typical data-dependent kernel hashing method. Following [16], we use the Gaussian RBF kernel and randomly sample 300 points to construct the hash functions. The supervised information is obtained on $10,000$ randomly sampled points by the Euclidean distance as [16].
- Product quantization (PQ) [8]: a typical non-parametric method, in which the original space is partitioned into multiple disjoint subspaces. Each subspace is clustered into 256 groups.

We generate the binary codes using the above four encoding schemes. For each encoding scheme on each dataset, we generate the codes with different code lengths ranging from 16 to 128.

7.1.3 Binary code ranking

After obtaining the binary codes, we rank all the data points based on the distances between their binary codes and the query. Our optimized distances are compared with the following distances.

Table 2: The methods used in our experiments. ✓(✗) means the corresponding encoding algorithm and the distance are (not) compatible.

	Symmetric			Asymmetric			
	OSD	HM	SD[8]	OAD	QsRank[33]	WhRank[31]	AD[8]
LSH	✓	✓	✗	✓	✗	✓	✗
ITQ	✓	✓	✗	✓	✓	✓	✗
KSH	✓	✓	✗	✓	✗	✓	✗
PQ	✓	✗	✓	✓	✗	✗	✓

- Hamming distance: The distance is applied on LSH, ITQ and KSH. PQ is unsuitable because the code is the index of the nearest cluster center and the Hamming distance cannot represent the dissimilarity.
- Weighted Hamming distance (WhRank) [31]: WhRank computes the data-adaptive and query-sensitive weight for each bit. The distance between the query and each point is the addition of the weights where the corresponding bit differs.
- Query-sensitive ranking (QsRank) [33]: It assigns float-precision weights for each bit, and the distance is computed as the summation of at most Q weights (Q is the code length). Due to the limitation of QsRank, it is only applied to ITQ, which is based on PCA.
- PQ distances [8]: Both the symmetric distance (SD) and the asymmetric distance (AD) are introduced in [8] for the codes generated by PQ. SD is the distance between the cluster centers, while AD is the distance between the original query point and the cluster center.

To distinguish different distances, we append a suffix to the name of the binary encoding scheme. Our proposed approaches are denoted as '-OSD' and '-OAD' for optimized symmetric distance and optimized asymmetric distance, respectively. '-HM' is used to denote the Hamming distance. '-SD' and '-AD' are referred particularly to as the symmetric and asymmetric distancess in [8] for the codes generated by PQ. For instance, LSH-OAD is interpreted as the LSH encoding scheme with our proposed optimized asymmetric distance. Table 2 summarizes the names.

7.1.4 Evaluation criteria

For each query point, we use linear scan to perform the search, i.e., compare it with every database binary code by different distance measures and evaluate the quality of the ranking results. The overall performances are evaluated using two criteria: mean average precision (mAP) and mean average ratio.

The precision at C is defined as the proportion of the number of the true neighbors within the top-ranked C points. The true neighbors of a query are set as the top-2% nearest neighbors in terms of the Euclidean distance as in the work [30]. Average precision (AP) is collected for each query. By averaging over all the queries, we can arrive at the final mAP.

The mean overall ratio [24] reflects the general quality of all top-ranked neighbors. Let $\mathbf{x}_{\hat{q}_c}$ and $\mathbf{x}_{q_c}$ be the c-th nearest point of the query $\mathbf{q}$ measured by the Euclidean distance and the approximate distance, respectively. The overall ratio regarding the top-ranked C points is $\text{Ratio}_C(\mathbf{q}) = \frac{1}{C}\sum_{c=1}^{C} \|\mathbf{q} - \mathbf{x}_{q_c}\|_2 / \|\mathbf{q} - \mathbf{x}_{\hat{q}_c}\|_2$. The mean overall ratio is the mean over all the queries. A lower mean overall ratio means a better performance.

7.2 Comparison Results

Our proposed approaches (OSD and OAD) have only one parameter, i.e., the number of partitions T. As discussed in Sec. 6.1, T controls the trade-off among effectiveness, storage, and speed. In this experiment, we set T in LSH, ITQ and KSH as 2, 3, 6 and 14 for code length 16, 32, 64 and 128, respectively. The length of each partition could be different and we make them as even as possible. For PQ, we follow the number of partitions in the code generation. This parameter will also be studied experimentally in Sec. 7.3.

Fig. 3 shows the experimental results w.r.t. the mAP on the three datasets. From these results, the following observations can be observed.

- Our proposed asymmetric distance achieves the highest mAP in all the settings. This is because the asymmetric distance uses more accurate representation of the query point and generally can achieve better results than the symmetric distance which uses the query binary code directly. Our OAD minimizes the approximation errors, which is beneficial for the ANN search.
- Among the symmetric distances, our OSD performs best, by learning the distance from the original dataset and minimizing the approximation errors.
- For the binary codes generated by KSH and PQ on GIST1M, our OSD is even better than the asymmetric distance WhRank and that of PQ, respectively. This emphasizes that the optimization of minimizing the approximation errors is very promising to improve the ranking accuracy.
- For the PQ code, proposed approaches improve the second best by around 7 percent on the 960-dimensional GIST1M with 1 million points, and gain a small improvement on the other two datasets. This means that our approach achieves significant improvement over the challenging dataset. The reason of different improvements comes from the various data distributions.
- The asymmetric distances QsRank and WhRank generally perform better than the symmetric Hamming distances, which is also demonstrated in [33] and [31].

The experiment results w.r.t. the mean average ratio are shown in Fig. 4 for code length 32. In terms of this criterion, it can be observed that our proposed OAD mostly achieves the lowest mean average ratio. Meanwhile, our proposed OSD is the best among all the symmetric distances.

7.3 Effect of T

In this experiment, we study the effect of T. The experiments run on a server with the Intel(R) Xeon(R) CPU E5-2690 @2.90GHz. The program is in C++ with a single thread to evaluate the time cost of the online query, while in the offline training process, multiple threads are enabled. The results on SIFT1M with the code length 64 generated by ITQ are reported. Similar results can be found on the other datasets with other code lengths.

The results are shown in Fig. 5. Except the similar observations with those in Sec. 7.2, we can also find that the mAP improves for our OSD and OAD as the number of partitions T decreases, because the accuracy of the distance approximation gains in this case. With a small T, the query time of OSD reduces. The reason is that only small numbers of additions are required for each distance computation, and the preprocessing time in Eqn. 3 is quite small. For OAD, the query time decreases first and then increases as T increases. The reason is that a smaller T leads to higher preprocessing cost, while a larger T also causes higher distance computational cost. In general, OAD has higher query cost than OSD since more preprocessing computations are involved in OAD. With a larger T, the difference between OAD and OSD becomes minor, because the preprocessing cost is small, and the distance computational cost is identical.

For the compared distances, the query time of WhRank and QsRank is longest. This is because for each distance computation in WhRank and QsRank, at most Q additions are required. For our OSD and OAD, the number of additions is T, which is much smaller than Q.

As illustrated in Fig. 5(c), the training time for both OSD and OAD decreases as T increases. We find the main training cost is to solve Eqn. 12 for OSD and the matrix (psuedo-)inversion of $\mathbf{E}$ for OAD. Time complexities of both routines are smaller for a larger T. These results also verify the analysis in Sec. 6.1.

8. CONCLUSION

In this paper, we study how to effectively measure the distances for binary code ranking and propose two optimized distance measures: optimized symmetric distance and optimized asymmetric distance. The key novelty lies in the distance table between the (encoded) query and the database codes are explicitly optimized rather than implicitly optimized or heuristically computed as done in the traditional algorithms. Extensive experimental results demonstrate the superiority of our proposed solutions over existing distances.

Acknowledgements

This work was partially supported by the National Basic Research Program of China (973 Program) under Grant 2014CB347600, ARC Discovery Project DP130103252, National Natural Science Foundation of China (No. 61371192), and Singapore National Research Foundation under its International Research Centre@Singapore Funding Initiative and administered by the IDM Programme Office.

9. REFERENCES

[1] A. Babenko and V. S. Lempitsky. The inverted multi-index. In *CVPR*, 2012.

[2] C. Du and J. Wang. Inner product similarity search using compositional codes. *CoRR*, abs/1406.4966, 2014.

[3] Y. Gong and S. Lazebnik. Iterative quantization: A procrustean approach to learning binary codes. In *CVPR*, 2011.

[4] A. Gordo, F. Perronnin, Y. Gong, and S. Lazebnik. Asymmetric distances for binary embeddings. *IEEE Trans. Pattern Anal. Mach. Intell.*, 2014.

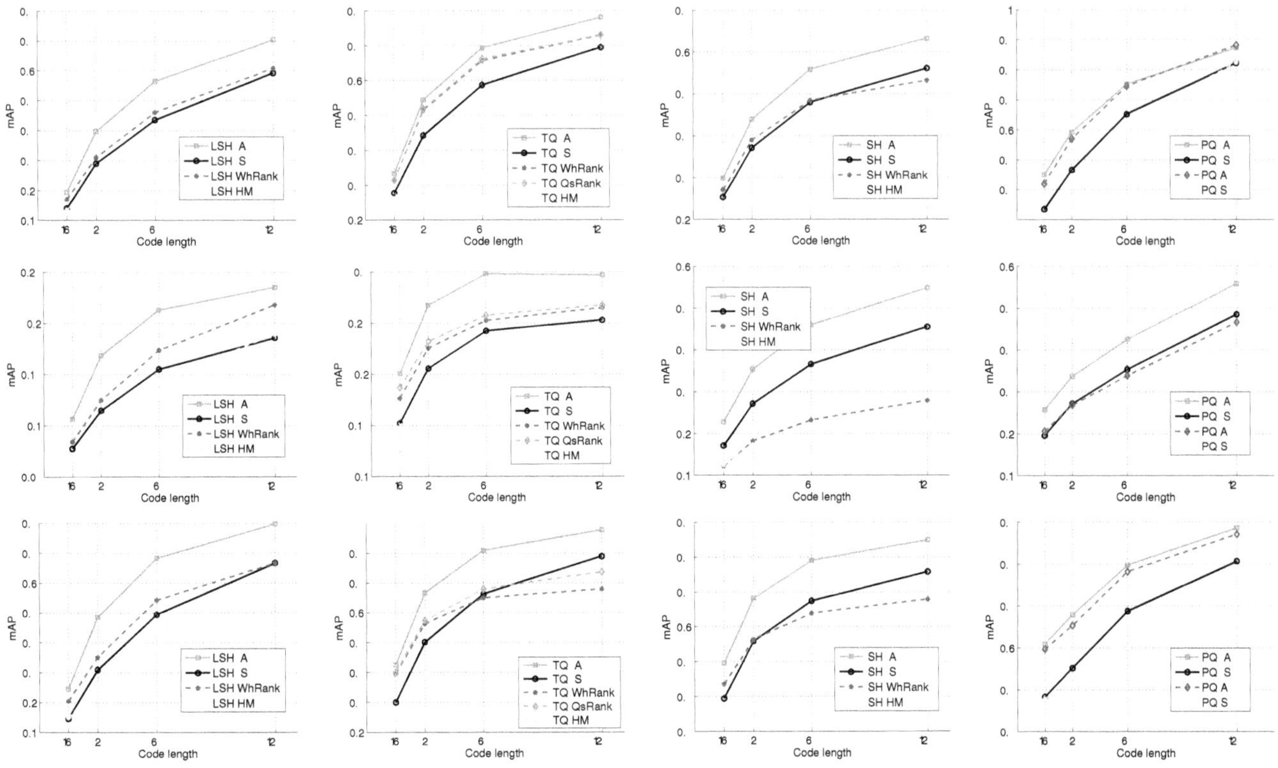

Figure 3: Results on mAP with with different code lengths. The first, second and third row correspond to SIFT1M, GIST1M, and MNIST respectively. The higher the mAP is, the better the approach is.

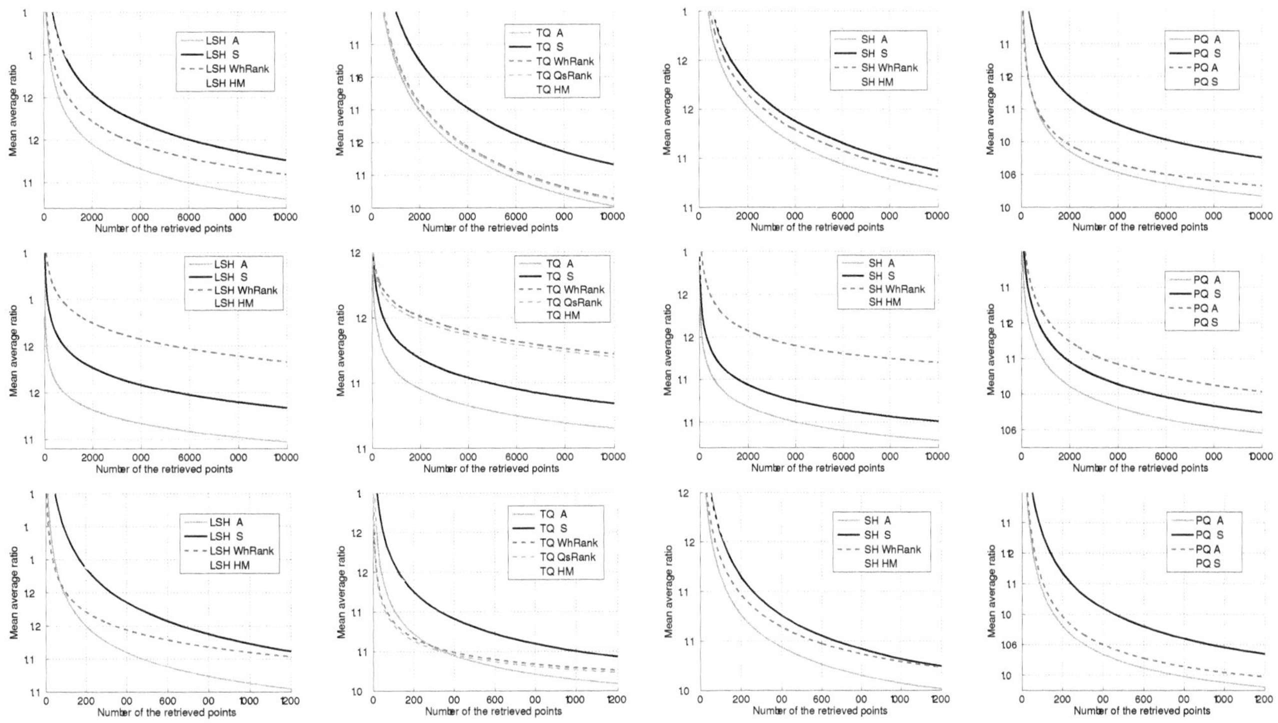

Figure 4: Results on mean overall ratio with 32 bits. The first, second and third row corresponds to SIFT1M, GIST1M, and MNIST respectively. The lower the mean average ratio is, the better the approach is.

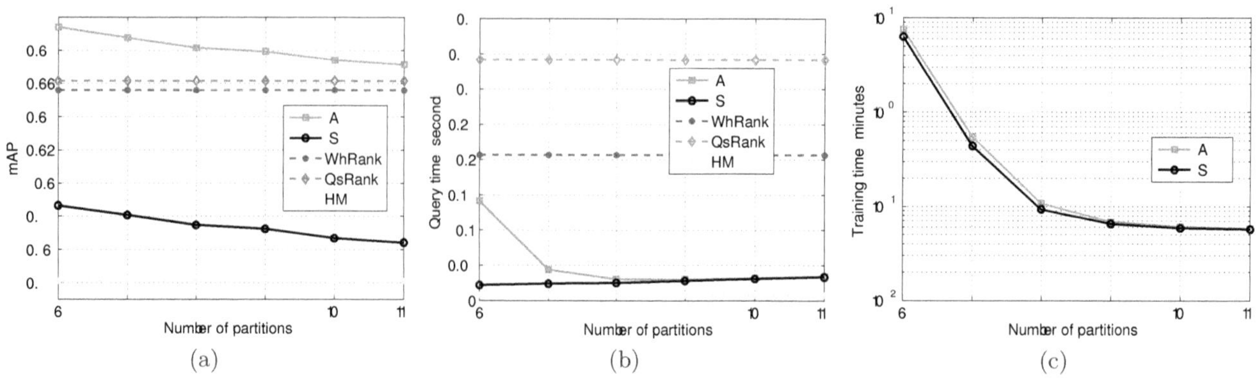

Figure 5: Performance with different numbers of partitions on SIFT1M with 64 bits from ITQ.

[5] J. Heo, Y. Lee, J. He, S. Chang, and S. Yoon. Spherical hashing. In *CVPR*, 2012.

[6] P. Indyk and R. Motwani. Approximate nearest neighbors: Towards removing the curse of dimensionality. In *STOC*, 1998.

[7] M. Jain, H. Jégou, and P. Gros. Asymmetric hamming embedding: taking the best of our bits for large scale image search. In *ACM Multimedia*, 2011.

[8] H. Jégou, M. Douze, and C. Schmid. Product quantization for nearest neighbor search. *IEEE Trans. Pattern Anal. Mach. Intell.*, 33(1), 2011.

[9] J. Ji, J. Li, S. Yan, B. Zhang, and Q. Tian. Super-bit locality-sensitive hashing. In *NIPS*, 2012.

[10] W. Kong and W.-J. Li. Isotropic hashing. In *NIPS*, 2012.

[11] W. Kong, W.-J. Li, and M. Guo. Manhattan hashing for large-scale image retrieval. In *SIGIR*, 2012.

[12] B. Kulis and T. Darrell. Learning to hash with binary reconstructive embeddings. In *NIPS*, 2009.

[13] B. Kulis and K. Grauman. Kernelized locality-sensitive hashing. *IEEE Trans. Pattern Anal. Mach. Intell.*, 34(6), 2012.

[14] Y. LeCun, L. Bottou, Y. Bengio, and P. Haffner. Gradient-based learning applied to document recognition. *Proceedings of the IEEE*, 86(11), 1998.

[15] X. Li, G. Lin, C. Shen, A. van den Hengel, and A. R. Dick. Learning hash functions using column generation. In *ICML*, 2013.

[16] W. Liu, J. Wang, R. Ji, Y.-G. Jiang, and S.-F. Chang. Supervised hashing with kernels. In *CVPR*, 2012.

[17] W. Liu, J. Wang, S. Kumar, and S. Chang. Hashing with graphs. In *ICML*, 2011.

[18] M. Norouzi and D. J. Fleet. Cartesian k-means. In *CVPR*, 2013.

[19] M. Norouzi, A. Punjani, and D. J. Fleet. Fast search in hamming space with multi-index hashing. In *CVPR*, 2012.

[20] M. Raginsky and S. Lazebnik. Locality-sensitive binary codes from shift-invariant kernels. In *NIPS*, 2009.

[21] G. Shakhnarovich, T. Darrell, and P. Indyk. *Nearest-Neighbor Methods in Learning and Vision: Theory and Practice*. The MIT press, 2006.

[22] J. Song, Y. Yang, Z. Huang, H. Shen, and R. Hong. Multiple feature hashing for real-time large scale near-duplicate video retrieval. In *ACM Multimedia*, 2011.

[23] C. Strecha, A. Bronstein, M. Bronstein, and P. Fua. Ldahash: Improved matching with smaller descriptors. *IEEE Trans. Pattern Anal. Mach. Intell.*, 34(1), 2012.

[24] Y. Tao, K. Yi, C. Sheng, and P. Kalnis. Efficient and accurate nearest neighbor and closest pair search in high-dimensional space. *ACM Trans. Database Syst.*, 35(3), 2010.

[25] J. Wang, S. Kumar, and S. Chang. Sequential projection learning for hashing with compact codes. In *ICML*, 2010.

[26] J. Wang, J. Wang, J. Song, X.-S. Xu, H. T. Shen, and S. Li. Optimized cartesian k-means. *CoRR*, abs/1405.4054, 2014.

[27] J. Wang, J. Wang, N. Yu, and S. Li. Order preserving hashing for approximate nearest neighbor search. In *ACM Multimedia*, 2013.

[28] Y. Weiss, R. Fergus, and A. Torralba. Multidimensional spectral hashing. In *ECCV (5)*, 2012.

[29] Y. Weiss, A. Torralba, and R. Fergus. Spectral hashing. In *NIPS*, 2008.

[30] H. Xu, J. Wang, Z. Li, G. Zeng, S. Li, and N. Yu. Complementary hashing for approximate nearest neighbor search. In *ICCV*, 2011.

[31] L. Zhang, Y. Zhang, J. Tang, K. Lu, and Q. Tian. Binary code ranking with weighted hamming distance. In *CVPR*, 2013.

[32] T. Zhang, C. Du, and J. Wang. Composite quantization for approximate nearest neighbor search. In *ICML (2)*, 2014.

[33] X. Zhang, L. Zhang, and H.-Y. Shum. Qsrank: Query-sensitive hash code ranking for efficient ϵ-neighbor search. In *CVPR*, 2012.

[34] X. Zhu, Z. Huang, H. Cheng, J. Cui, and H. T. Shen. Sparse hashing for fast multimedia search. *ACM Trans. Inf. Syst.*, 31(2), 2013.

[35] X. Zhu, Z. Huang, H. T. Shen, and X. Zhao. Linear cross-modal hashing for efficient multimedia search. In *ACM Multimedia*, 2013.

Iterative Multi-View Hashing for Cross Media Indexing

Yao Hu* Zhongming Jin* Hongyi Ren Deng Cai Xiaofei He
State Key Lab of CAD&CG, Zhejiang University, Hangzhou, China
{yaoohu, jinzhongming888, erichongyi, dengcai, xiaofeihe}@gmail.com

ABSTRACT

Cross media retrieval engines have gained massive popularity with rapid development of the Internet. Users may perform queries in a corpus consisting of audio, video, and textual information. To make such systems practically possible for large mount of multimedia data, two critical issues must be carefully considered: (a) reduce the storage as much as possible; (b) model the relationship of the heterogeneous media data. Recently academic community have proved that encoding the data into compact binary codes can drastically reduce the storage and computational cost. However, it is still unclear how to integrate multiple information sources properly into the binary code encoding scheme.

In this paper, we study the cross media indexing problem by learning the discriminative hashing functions to map the multi-view datum into a shared hamming space. Not only meaningful within-view similarity is required to be preserved, we also incorporate the between-view correlations into the encoding scheme, where we map the similar points close together and push apart the dissimilar ones. To this end, we propose a novel hashing algorithm called *Iterative Multi-View Hashing* (IMVH) by taking these information into account simultaneously. To solve this joint optimization problem efficiently, we further develop an iterative scheme to deal with it by using a more flexible quantization model. In particular, an optimal alignment is learned to maintain the between-view similarity in the encoding scheme. And the binary codes are obtained by directly solving a series of binary label assignment problems without continuous relaxation to avoid the unnecessary quantization loss. In this way, the proposed algorithm not only greatly improves the retrieval accuracy but also performs strong robustness. An extensive set of experiments clearly demonstrates the superior performance of the proposed method against the state-of-the-art techniques on both multimodal and unimodal retrieval tasks.

Categories and Subject Descriptors

H.3.1 [**Information Storage and Retrieval**]: Content Analysis and Indexing

*Equal contribution.

MM'14, November 03 - 07 2014, Orlando, FL, USA

http://dx.doi.org/10.1145/2647868.2654906 .

General Terms

Algorithms

Keywords

Multi-View Hashing; Within-View Similarity; Between-View Correlations.

1. INTRODUCTION

In recent years, with the explosive growth of the available media data, hashing method has attracted many researchers' attention due to its great advantages in reducing both the computational cost and storage. A lot of hashing algorithms have been proposed for various applications, such as image and video retrieval [28, 27, 31, 12], duplicate image detection [3], key point detection [29] and so on.

However, most of the existing hashing methods are mainly designed for single type of data, such as sift or gist feature for image [13] and Tf-idf feature for text [8]. In these methods, the hashing functions are designed to learn similarity preserving binary codes for data representation. However, it is well known that multimedia data with same semantics can exist in more than one view [21, 5, 19]. For example, we can describe one topic by text document, image or audio. In each view, the corresponding type of feature only reveals the partial information. The joint consideration of multiple features in the multi-view space can assist us to better understand the underlying data distribution. To model the mutual correlation across different views, traditional cross media retrieval algorithms firstly project all the original features into a shared semantic correlation space [23, 30] and then perform alignments for pair matching between views [18]. However, it is still a puzzle how to construct an effective indexing based on these algorithms.

To build an efficient indexing for cross media retrieval, a series of multi-view hashing algorithms have been proposed to encode the multimodal data sources from different perspectives [24, 33, 15]. Not only the respective information from each individual view but also the mutual information across different views are required to be simultaneously preserved for designing discriminative multi-view hashing functions. Specifically, just as pointed out in [24, 32], we expect to ensure the consistency between the learned hashing codes and the corresponding hashing functions designed for different information sources, which means that small variations of the data should not result in prominent difference for the final binary codes. Furthermore, it is also necessary to push apart the data points with different concepts, no matter in which view they are available, to make the encoding scheme more discriminative [22]. Such properties are understood as between-view similarity and between-view distinctiveness preservation respectively when multi-view data representations are mapped into the

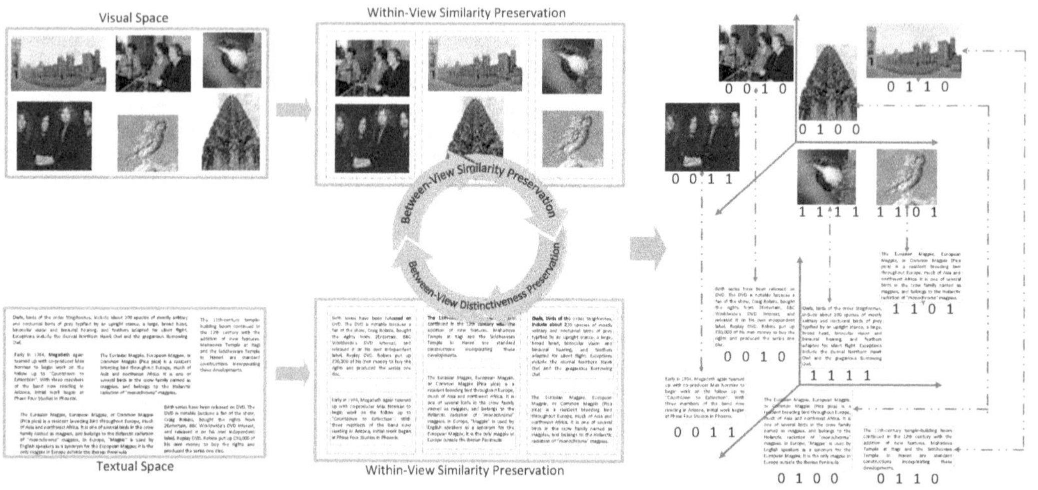

Figure 1: The illustration of our proposed Iterative Multi-View Hashing (IMVH).

produced common Hamming space. In [33], the authors attempt to preserve these two types of information simultaneously in the Euclidean space. However, since the rough incorporation with a weak representative ability for the between-view correlations, it does not take full advantage of the mutual information across different views, which leads a limited performance. Therefore, how to incorporate these two types of information into the multi-view hashing function learning effectively still remains challenging.

To address this problem, in this paper we propose a novel multi-view hashing method called *Iterative Multi-View Hashing* (IMVH) to preserve the within-view similarity and between-view correlations, including between-view similarity and between-view distinctiveness of the original data distribution, into the Hamming space in an iterative scheme. An illustration of the whole flowchart is shown in Figure 1. We begin with learning hashing functions in each view involving the within-view similarity and between-view distinctiveness preservation term, while the between-view similarity is incorporated globally during the optimization process. Specifically, in each iteration, an optimal rotation is learned to align the data points belonging to the same concept in different views to globally preserve the between-view similarity. Furthermore, inspired by the recent proposed idea regarding the binary codes as auxiliary variables for a more flexible model, we update the binary codes by solving a series of binary label assignment problems to reduce the unnecessary cost caused by the rough quantization with the sign function $\text{sgn}(\cdot)$. In this way, the obtained multi-view hashing functions can be guaranteed with enough consistency and discriminative power. Experimental results on several benchmarks confirm that our proposed IMVH greatly improves accuracy with strong robustness on cross-modal retrieval tasks and unimodal retrieval tasks compared with the state-of-the-art multimodal and unimodal hashing approaches respectively.

For the purpose of explaining our basic idea clearly, in the following we firstly focus on the dual-view case, e.g., image feature space $\mathcal{I}$ and textual feature space $\mathcal{T}$.

Notations: We assume $*$ is a placeholder for space $\mathcal{I}$ or $\mathcal{T}$ and denote $\mathbf{X}_* \in \mathbb{R}^{D_* \times N}$ to be the centralized data matrix whose column $\mathbf{X}_*^i$ represents to the i-th sample from either space. D_* is the dimension of the corresponding space. We further define K bits hashing code of sample x as $h_*(x) = [h_*^1(x), \cdots, h_*^K(x)] \in \{1, -1\}^K$ and $h_*^k(x) = \text{sgn}((w_*^k)^T x)$. For simplicity, we denote the projection matrix $\mathbf{W}_* = [w_*^1, w_*^2, \ldots, w_*^K] \in \mathbb{R}^{D_* \times K}$ and the binary code matrix $\mathbf{B}_*$ can be computed as $\mathbf{B}_* = \text{sgn}(\mathbf{X}_*^T \mathbf{W}_*) \in \mathbb{R}^{N \times K}$ [1]. Similarly the vector $\mathbf{B}_*^k$ represents the k-th column of $\mathbf{B}_*$ (the k-th bits of all samples). To obtain the semantic information, we also assume that each pair $(\mathbf{X}_\mathcal{I}^i, \mathbf{X}_\mathcal{T}^j)$ has a label $s_{ij} = 1$ if they have the same concept and $s_{ij} = 0$ otherwise. For clear description, we also assume each pair $(\mathbf{X}_\mathcal{I}^i, \mathbf{X}_\mathcal{T}^i)$ exists in the same concept, *i.e.*, $s_{ii} = 1$.

2. BACKGROUND

Most of the previously proposed hashing methods for single-view data can be decomposed into two steps: (1) Firstly, project all the original data points into a low dimensional space; (2) obtain the binary codes by quantizing the new data representations in the embedding space. In unsupervised case, a series of methods have been proposed based on the different embedding methods, such as random projection [7], spectral decomposition [28] and other learning schemes [25, 14, 20, 11, 10]. Furthermore, when the semantic information is available, the projection directions are constructed to make the binary codes fit the supervision as much as possible [17].

Recently several hashing algorithms for multi-view data have also been studied. Along the lines of single-view hashing, these hashing algorithms also can be decomposed into the similar two steps imposing a couple of constraints. In [9], Canonical Correlation Analysis (CCA) is adopted to extract a common latent space from two views by solving

$$\begin{aligned} \min_{w_\mathcal{I}, w_\mathcal{T}} \quad & w_\mathcal{I}^T \mathbf{X}_\mathcal{I} \mathbf{X}_\mathcal{T}^T w_\mathcal{T} \\ s.t. \quad & w_*^T \mathbf{X}_* \mathbf{X}_*^T w_* = 1, * = \mathcal{I} \text{ or } \mathcal{T}. \end{aligned} \tag{1}$$

Similar latent semantic space such as Multimedia Correlation Space [30], Correlation Semantic Space [23] based on CCA and Parallel Field Embedding Space [18] based on manifold alignment are also introduced from different perspective. Then a joint model can be constructed here after all the data in different views are projected into such intermediate space. An intuitive way to construct a cross media indexing is to directly quantize the results from these

[1]The corresponding hash bit can be computed as $(1 + h_*(x))/2$ simply .

methods. However, it would leads an unbalance encoding scheme. Furthermore, such methods only extract partial information of the correlations and most of the critical information of the data distribution is ignored, which limits the performance of the learned hashing functions. On the other hand, Rastegari *et al.*[24] propose to find the most discriminative hashing functions by enforcing the maximum margin constraints and a block coordinate descent based iterative scheme is applied for the optimization. To preserve the with-in view and between-view similarity, Kumar *et al.*[15] formulate the multi-view hashing problem as an extension of traditional spectral hashing, while Bronstein *et al.*[2] learn the projection directions from the perspective of boosting. Except for the similarity preservation, the between-view distinctiveness has also been pointed out to be critical for the discriminative power of the learned hashing functions [22]. This insight enables the joint preservation of the between-view similarity and distinctiveness in [33], where the authors simultaneously consider these two regularization terms in the optimization procedure. However, this method suffers from the unsatisfactory performance which may be caused by its improper incorporation of between-view correlations.

3. OUR APPROACH

For multi-view hashing problem, the main challenge is how to incorporate the within-view information and between-view correlations into an unified framework properly. To obtain powerful discriminative hashing functions, we expect to force the dissimilar pairs to be far away in the produced Hamming space. Meanwhile, the global similarity across all the views should also be preserved for consistent encoding scheme. In our approach, we explore to incorporate these different aspects of the original data distribution in a global framework. For better description, in this section, we firstly show how to formulate the within-view similarity and between-view correlations. Then an iterative optimization strategy will be provided for optimization later.

3.1 Within-View Similarity Preservation

Within-view similarity preservation is designed to maintain the neighborhood relationships among the data points in each individual view after being mapped into the produced Hamming space. In traditional single view hashing methods, Spectral Hashing [28] preserves the within-view similarity by minimizing the weighted Hamming distance between codewords correlates with the similarity. While for multi-view hashing methods [32], to deal with the multiple information sources, the similarity quantity for each individual view is measured with the same way as in Spectral Hashing. And the total cost is the summation across all the data modalities.

Motivated by the recent progress in Supervised Hashing methods [27, 17], by defining an N-by-N affinity matrix $\mathbf{S}_*$, we expect the similarity between training data points represented by each bit can approximate $\mathbf{S}_*$ as much as possible. And the within-view similarity for each individual view can be measured as the summation of the costs for all the bits. Then the total within-view similarity for all the views can be preserved by minimizing the following term:

$$\frac{1}{2}\sum_{*}\sum_{k=1}^{K}\|\mathbf{B}_*^k(\mathbf{B}_*^k)^T-\mathbf{S}_*\|_F^2=-\sum_{*}Tr(\mathbf{B}_*^T\mathbf{S}_*\mathbf{B}_*)+const.$$

Notice that there are many choices for the affinity matrix $\mathbf{S}_*$. Intuitively, we adopt the same way as in [27]. We define $\mathbf{S}_*^{ij}=1$ if the pair $(\mathbf{X}_*^i,\mathbf{X}_*^j)$ are denoted as similar, $\mathbf{S}_*^{ij}=-1$ if dissimilar and $\mathbf{S}_*^{ij}=0$ if unknown. By minimizing (2), it incurs a heavy penalty if two similar examples are mapped far away in the Hamming space and then the similarity between different examples can be preserved in the learned hashing codes.

3.2 Between-View Correlations Preservation

For multi-view hashing problems, only preserving the within-view similarity in each view is far from enough. It is critical to incorporate the relationships between different views when learning the hashing functions. Specifically, it is natural to assume that the points with the same concept should be binarized consistently wherever they are available. Therefore, we formulate this between-view similarity preservation term as

$$\Phi(\mathcal{I},\mathcal{T}) \quad = \quad \|\mathbf{B}_\mathcal{I}-\mathbf{B}_\mathcal{T}\|_F^2.$$

Meanwhile it is also important to note that the points with different concepts should not be mapped closely together, which may seriously lower the discriminative power of the learned hashing function. To meet this requirement, in the following, we propose to penalize the distinctiveness for data points with different concepts across all the views.

Following the similar way in [22], we need to severely punish the dissimilar pairs if they have similar binary codes, *i.e.*, small hamming distance after encoding, which can be realized by minimizing the between-view distinctiveness term. Taking the distinctiveness term $\Omega_\mathcal{I}(\mathcal{I},\mathcal{T})$ from $\mathcal{I}\to\mathcal{T}$ as example, it can be defined as follows:

$$\Omega_\mathcal{I}(\mathcal{I},\mathcal{T})=\sum_{i=1}^{N}\ell_i,\quad \ell_i=\frac{\sum_{j=1}^{N}(1-s_{ij})\tau(d_{ij})}{\sum_{j=1}^{N}(1-s_{ij})},\tag{2}$$

where $d_{ij}=hamm(h_\mathcal{I}(\mathbf{X}_\mathcal{I}^i),h_\mathcal{T}(\mathbf{X}_\mathcal{T}^j))=\frac{1}{2}\sum_{t=1}^{K}|\mathbf{B}_\mathcal{I}^{it}-\mathbf{B}_\mathcal{T}^{jt}|$ and the distinctiveness term $\Omega_\mathcal{T}(\mathcal{I},\mathcal{T})$ from $\mathcal{T}\to\mathcal{I}$ can also be defined in a similar way. $\tau(d)$ is called the smoothly clipped inverted squared deviation (SCISD) function [22], which is defined as

$$\tau(d)=\begin{cases}\frac{-d^2+ab^2}{2} & \text{if } |d|\le b,\\ \frac{d^2-2ab|d|+a^2b^2}{2(a-1)} & \text{if } b\le|d|\le ab,\\ 0 & \text{if } ab\le|d|,\end{cases}\tag{3}$$

where a and b are two user-specified parameters.

It is important to note the fact that the between-view distinctiveness preservation term $\Omega_*(\mathcal{I},\mathcal{T})$ in (2) is quite different from the regularization term used in [33], where the distinctiveness is preserved for learning the hashing function based on the Euclidean distance between the projected pairs. While in (2), we utilize Hamming distance instead of the Euclidean distance to precisely measure the difference of the projected pairs. In this way, we measure the distinctiveness penalization of $\mathbf{X}_\mathcal{I}^i$ as the average distinctiveness of between all the dissimilar pairs involving $\mathbf{X}_\mathcal{I}^i$ across all the views. Therefore, minimizing the regularization term $\Omega_*(\mathcal{I},\mathcal{T})$ can better assist us to find the hash functions which enjoy the large-margin property.

3.3 The Objective Function

Furthermore, a lot of research works [28, 17] have revealed that the independence between hash functions assists the balance of the learned hashing codes in each feature space. Therefore, we also add a regularization $\sum_*\|\mathbf{B}_*^T\mathbf{B}_*-N\mathbf{I}_K\|_F^2$, where $\mathbf{I}_K\in\mathbb{R}^K$ is an identity matrix. After some simple algebraic operations, it is easy to observe that $\sum_*\|\mathbf{B}_*^T\mathbf{B}_*-N\mathbf{I}_K\|_F^2=\sum_*\Big(\|\mathbf{B}_*^T\mathbf{B}_*\|_F^2-2N\|\mathbf{B}_*\|_F^2+N^2\|\mathbf{I}_K\|_F^2\Big)=\sum_*\|\mathbf{B}_*^T\mathbf{B}_*\|_F^2+const.$ Therefore, we can minimize $\sum_*\|\mathbf{B}_*^T\mathbf{B}_*\|_F^2$ instead to force the independence between the learned hashing functions.

Recall that a discriminative hashing functions should ensure the dissimilar data across different views are forced to be pushed apart and similar pairs are binarized consistently. Therefore, the corresponding regularization terms can be incorporated into the objective function as constraints. Furthermore, to obtain better generalization ability, it is also suggested by the recent research advances [16, 24] to maximize margin between positive and negative samples for each hashing function. Overall, we can formulate the objective function of IMVH as

$$\mathcal{O} = \Phi(\mathcal{I},\mathcal{T}) + \sum_{*} \Big(\mathcal{L}(\mathbf{B}_*, h_*(\mathbf{X}_*)) + \lambda_* \|\mathbf{W}_*\|_F^2 + \alpha_*\Omega_*(\mathcal{I},\mathcal{T}) - \beta_* Tr(\mathbf{B}_*^T \mathbf{S}_* \mathbf{B}_*) + \gamma_* \|\mathbf{B}_*^T \mathbf{B}_*\|_F^2 \Big), \tag{4}$$

where the loss term $\mathcal{L}(\mathbf{B}_*, h_*(\mathbf{X}_*))$ can be defined as the summation of the hinge loss of all the K hash bits as $\mathcal{L}(\mathbf{B}_*, h_*(\mathbf{X}_*)) = \sum_{k=1}^{K} \mathcal{L}(\mathbf{B}_*^k, h_*^k(\mathbf{X}_*)) = \sum_{k=1}^{K}\sum_{i=1}^{N} \max(0, 1 - \mathbf{B}_*^{ik} h_*^k(\mathbf{X}_*^i))$. And the regularization term $\|W\|_F^2$ is proposed to ensure the max-margin constraint for the learned hyperplanes.

To solve problem (4) efficiently, we propose to solve it by using a simple iterative scheme. Firstly we can fix $\mathbf{W}_\mathcal{T}$ and $\mathbf{B}_\mathcal{T}$ and solve the following subproblem in the image feature space:

$$\min_{\mathbf{W}_\mathcal{I},\mathbf{B}_\mathcal{I}} \mathcal{O}_\mathcal{I} = \mathcal{L}(\mathbf{B}_\mathcal{I}, h(\mathbf{X}_\mathcal{I})) + \lambda_\mathcal{I}\|\mathbf{W}_\mathcal{I}\|_F^2 + \Phi(\mathcal{I},\mathcal{T}) + \alpha_\mathcal{I}\Omega_\mathcal{I}(\mathcal{I},\mathcal{T}) - \beta_\mathcal{I} Tr(\mathbf{B}_\mathcal{I}^T \mathbf{S}_\mathcal{I} \mathbf{B}_\mathcal{I}) + \gamma_\mathcal{I}\|\mathbf{B}_\mathcal{I}^T\mathbf{B}_\mathcal{I}\|_F^2. \tag{5}$$

And then we fix $\mathbf{W}_\mathcal{I}$ and $\mathbf{B}_\mathcal{I}$ and minimize the corresponding subproblem in the textual feature space:

$$\min_{\mathbf{W}_\mathcal{T},\mathbf{B}_\mathcal{T}} \mathcal{O}_\mathcal{T} = \mathcal{L}(\mathbf{B}_\mathcal{T}, h(\mathbf{X}_\mathcal{T})) + \lambda_\mathcal{T}\|\mathbf{W}_\mathcal{T}\|_F^2 + \Phi(\mathcal{I},\mathcal{T}) + \alpha_\mathcal{T}\Omega_\mathcal{T}(\mathcal{I},\mathcal{T}) - \beta_\mathcal{T} Tr(\mathbf{B}_\mathcal{T}^T \mathbf{S}_\mathcal{T} \mathbf{B}_\mathcal{T}) + \gamma_\mathcal{T}\|\mathbf{B}_\mathcal{T}^T\mathbf{B}_\mathcal{T}\|_F^2. \tag{6}$$

By solving the above two subproblems alternatively, we can obtain the satisfactory hashing functions with outperforming discriminative power meanwhile preserving relationships between different views. In spite of the seemingly complex appearance of (5) and (6), they can be solved by a quite efficient way. In the next section, we take the subproblem (5) as an example to show the detailed optimization procedure. And the subproblem (6) also can be solved in the same way.

4. OPTIMIZATION METHOD

Note that the between-view correlations preservation terms $\Phi(\mathcal{I},\mathcal{T})$ and $\Omega_\mathcal{I}(\mathcal{I},\mathcal{T})$ in $\mathcal{O}_\mathcal{I}$ are both non-convex and non-smooth since their respective special configuration. Therefore, the main challenge is how to deal with the joint optimization problem in an unified scheme. Following the similar framework proposed by Lin *et al.* [16], we view the binary code matrix $\mathbf{B}_\mathcal{I}$ as an auxiliary variable for hash function learning and can be deviated from $\text{sgn}(\mathbf{X}_\mathcal{I}^T\mathbf{W}_\mathcal{I})$, which makes the optimization process more flexible. In this section, we propose an iterative scheme to solve the subproblem (5) efficiently , where an optimal rotation matrix is learned to preserve the global between-view similarity for a more discriminative projection matrix $\mathbf{W}_\mathcal{I}$ and then we update $\mathbf{B}_\mathcal{I}$ by solving a series of binary assignment problems.

4.1 Update $\mathbf{W}_\mathcal{I}$ by Optimal Rotation

After we fix $\mathbf{B}_\mathcal{I}$, $\mathbf{B}_\mathcal{T}$ and $\mathbf{W}_\mathcal{T}$, we firstly update $\mathbf{W}_\mathcal{I}$ by solving

$$\min_{\mathbf{W}_\mathcal{I}} \mathcal{L}(\mathbf{B}_\mathcal{I}, h(\mathbf{X}_\mathcal{I})) + \lambda_\mathcal{I}\|\mathbf{W}_\mathcal{I}\|_F^2. \tag{7}$$

In this way, we actually learn K independent binary SVM classifiers, one for each bit. The learned projection matrix $\mathbf{W}_\mathcal{I}$ can force the the mapped values far away from 0 and then the corresponding hashing functions have a better generalization ability [20]. However, the lack of the critical between-view similarity information makes $\mathbf{W}_\mathcal{I}$ not powerful enough for a consistent encoding scheme.

Motivated by the recent work [9] which proposes to preserve the global similarity by learning an orthogonal rotation matrix to minimize the quantization loss between the hashing codes and original datum, we refine the previously obtained projection matrix $\mathbf{W}_\mathcal{I}$ in a similar way. We expect such rotation can minimize the distortion between different views as much as possible to globally preserve the between-view similarity. Therefore, we relax the between-view similarity preservation term $\Phi(\mathcal{I},\mathcal{T})$ by minimizing $\|\mathbf{X}_\mathcal{I}^T\mathbf{W}_\mathcal{I} - \mathbf{B}_\mathcal{T}\|_F^2$. Then an orthogonal rotation matrix $\mathbf{R}_\mathcal{I}$ is learned for the coarse projected data $\mathbf{V}_\mathcal{I} = \mathbf{X}_\mathcal{I}^T\mathbf{W}_\mathcal{I}$ by minimizing the following optimization problem:

$$\min_{\mathbf{R}_\mathcal{I}} \|\mathbf{V}_\mathcal{I}\mathbf{R}_\mathcal{I} - \mathbf{B}_\mathcal{T}\|_F^2 \quad s.t. \quad \mathbf{R}_\mathcal{I}^T\mathbf{R}_\mathcal{I} = \mathbf{I}_K, \mathbf{R}_\mathcal{I}\mathbf{R}_\mathcal{I}^T = \mathbf{I}_K. \tag{8}$$

Note that the binary matrix $\mathbf{B}_\mathcal{T}$ in another feature space is fixed and obtained by the previous iteration. Therefore, minimizing (8) actually is equivalent to finding a rotation to align the data in the current feature space with another, which is a classic Orthogonal Procrustes problem [26]. We firstly compute the SVD of the $K \times K$ matrix $\mathbf{B}_\mathcal{T}^T\mathbf{V}_\mathcal{I}$ and then obtain the optimal solution of (8) as

$$\mathbf{B}_\mathcal{T}^T\mathbf{V}_\mathcal{I} = U\Sigma V^T \quad and \quad \mathbf{R}_\mathcal{I} = VU^T. \tag{9}$$

After learning the optimal rotation matrix, we refine the the projection matrix as

$$\mathbf{W}_\mathcal{I} \longleftarrow \mathbf{W}_\mathcal{I}\mathbf{R}_\mathcal{I}. \tag{10}$$

Obviously the problem (8) actually forces the global consistency between the hash codes of different views. Different from [24] adopting a similar regularization for initialization and preserving consistency during learning SVM classifiers, in our approach the between-view consistency information is considered by learning the optimal rotation. In this way, the between-view similarity can be preserved.

4.2 Update $\mathbf{B}_\mathcal{I}$ by Graph Cut

Different from the traditional hashing techniques [28, 24] binarizing the projected data with sign function $\text{sgn}(\cdot)$ to obtain $\mathbf{B}_\mathcal{I}$, some researchers propose to update this binary matrix by solving binary assignment problems indirectly [16] or directly [6], which reduces the unnecessary loss caused by directly binarization and greatly improves the performance . In our approach, we also take the similar way to deal with this binary assignment procedure to update $\mathbf{B}_\mathcal{I}$. With the fixed $\mathbf{W}_\mathcal{I}$, the subproblem (5) degrades to be

$$\min_{\mathbf{B}_\mathcal{I}} \mathcal{L}(\mathbf{B}_\mathcal{I}, h(\mathbf{X}_\mathcal{I})) + \alpha_\mathcal{I}\Omega_\mathcal{I}(\mathcal{I},\mathcal{T}) - \beta_\mathcal{I} Tr(\mathbf{B}_\mathcal{I}^T \mathbf{S}_\mathcal{I} \mathbf{B}_\mathcal{I}) + \gamma_\mathcal{I}\|\mathbf{B}_\mathcal{I}^T\mathbf{B}_\mathcal{I}\|_F^2. \tag{11}$$

It is obvious that the objective function in (11) is separable. Therefore it can be solved by updating each bit while holding all the others fixed, then cycling through this process. For ease of presentation, we denote $\mathbf{z} \triangleq \mathbf{B}_\mathcal{I}^k$ to represent the k-th bit of $\mathbf{B}_\mathcal{I}$ and $\bar{\mathbf{B}}_\mathcal{I}^k$ as the concatenation of all the other fixed bits $\{\mathbf{B}_\mathcal{I}^{k'} : k' \neq k\}$. Then the problem (11) turns into minimizing the following energy

Algorithm 1 Iterative Multi-View Hashing

Input: $\mathbf{X}_* \in \mathbb{R}^{d_* \times N}$, bits number K, maximum iterations $t_{\max}$, parameters α_*, β_* and γ_*.

1: *// Initialization by Canonical Correlation Analysis as in* (1)
2: $\mathbf{W}_\mathcal{I}, \mathbf{W}_\mathcal{T} \leftarrow CCA(\mathbf{X}_\mathcal{I}, \mathbf{X}_\mathcal{T}, K)$
3: $\mathbf{B}_\mathcal{I} \leftarrow \text{sgn}(\mathbf{X}_\mathcal{I}^T \mathbf{W}_\mathcal{I})$, $\mathbf{B}_\mathcal{T} \leftarrow \text{sgn}(\mathbf{X}_\mathcal{T}^T \mathbf{W}_\mathcal{T})$
4: **repeat**
5:   *// Stage 1 : Training in the feature space* $\mathcal{I}$
6:   **for** $t = 1, \ldots, t_{\max}$ **do**
7:     Compute $\mathbf{W}_\mathcal{I}$ by solving K independent SVM classifiers and learn rotation matrix $\mathbf{R}_\mathcal{I}$ according to (9).
8:     $\mathbf{W}_\mathcal{I} \leftarrow \mathbf{W}_\mathcal{I}\mathbf{R}_\mathcal{I}$.
9:     Update $\mathbf{B}_\mathcal{I}$ by solving (12) with graph cut method on each bit.
10:   **end for**
11:   *// Stage 2 : Training in the feature space* $\mathcal{T}$
12:   Solve subproblem (6) in an similar way according to step 6-10.
13: **until** convergence or max iterations reached

Output: $\mathbf{B}_\mathcal{I} \leftarrow \text{sgn}(\mathbf{X}_\mathcal{I}^T \mathbf{W}_\mathcal{I})$, $\mathbf{B}_\mathcal{T} \leftarrow \text{sgn}(\mathbf{X}_\mathcal{T}^T \mathbf{W}_\mathcal{T})$.

function

$$\begin{aligned} \min_z \sum_{i=1}^{N} \mathcal{E}_u(z_i) + \sum_{(i,j)} \mathcal{E}_p(z_i, z_j) \\ s.t. \quad z_i = \{1, -1\}, i = 1, \ldots, N, \end{aligned} \tag{12}$$

where $\sum_{(i,j)}$ sums all the possible pairs of (i, j) and $i \neq j$. Obviously the problem (12) is a typical graph cut problem, which aims to find a cut to minimize the energy of a graph $\mathcal{E}$ including the energy of unary term $\mathcal{E}_u$ and the energy of pairwise term $\mathcal{E}_p$.

Specifically, from the objective function (5), it is easy to see that the unary term $\mathcal{E}_u$ involves the loss term $\mathcal{L}(\mathbf{B}_\mathcal{I}, h(\mathbf{X}_\mathcal{I}))$ and $\Phi_\mathcal{I}(\mathcal{I}, \mathcal{T})$ and can be written as $\mathcal{E}_u(z_i) = \max(0, 1 - z_i h_\mathcal{I}^k(\mathbf{X}_\mathcal{I}^i)) + \alpha_\mathcal{I}\ell_i$, where $\ell_i = \frac{\sum_{j=1}^{N}(1-s_{ij})\tau(|z_i - \mathbf{B}_\mathcal{T}^{jk}| + \sum_{t \neq k}^{K} |\mathbf{B}_\mathcal{I}^{it} - \mathbf{B}_\mathcal{T}^{jt}|)}{\sum_{j=1}^{N}(1-s_{ij})}$ according to the definition of $\Omega_\mathcal{I}(\mathcal{I}, \mathcal{T})$ in (2). From $\mathcal{O}_\mathcal{I}$, we can also see that the pairwise term $\mathcal{E}_p$ only involves the within-view similarity preservation term and the independence term. Therefore with some algebraic operations, we can see that

$$\begin{aligned} & -\beta_\mathcal{I} Tr(\mathbf{B}_\mathcal{I}^T \mathbf{S}_\mathcal{I} \mathbf{B}_\mathcal{I}) + \gamma_\mathcal{I} \|\mathbf{B}_\mathcal{I}^T \mathbf{B}_\mathcal{I}\|_F^2 \\ = \; & \mathbf{z}^T (2\gamma_\mathcal{I} \bar{\mathbf{B}}_\mathcal{I}^k (\bar{\mathbf{B}}_\mathcal{I}^k)^T - \beta_\mathcal{I} \mathbf{S}_\mathcal{I}) \mathbf{z} + const \\ = \; & \mathbf{z}^T Q_\mathcal{I} \mathbf{z} + const, \end{aligned} \tag{13}$$

where $Q_\mathcal{I} = 2\gamma_\mathcal{I} \bar{\mathbf{B}}_\mathcal{I}^k (\bar{\mathbf{B}}_\mathcal{I}^k)^T - \beta_\mathcal{I} \mathbf{S}_\mathcal{I}$. Then pairwise term can be represented as $\mathcal{E}_p(z_i, z_j) = 2Q_\mathcal{I}^{ij} z_i z_j$. To better fit $S_\mathcal{I}$ with $\bar{\mathbf{B}}_\mathcal{I}^k$, we empirically set $\gamma_\mathcal{I} = \frac{1}{2(K-1)}\beta_\mathcal{I}$ to ensure that $Q_\mathcal{I}^{ii} = 0$. Based on the above observations, the traditional graph cut algorithm [1] can be adopted to solve the problem (12) efficiently.

After we update $\mathbf{W}_\mathcal{I}$ and $\mathbf{B}_\mathcal{I}$ as a solution of (5), we take the similar way to deal with subproblem (6). By alternately solving these two subproblems, the global optimization problem (4) converges soon. Overall we summarize the main procedure in Algorithm 1, which is called *Iterative Multi-View Hashing* (IMVH). Following the same setting in [24], we also take the K eigenvectors corresponding to the largest eigenvalues by CCA as in (1) to initialize $\mathbf{W}_\mathcal{I}$ and $\mathbf{W}_\mathcal{T}$. Meanwhile, we also try random initialization for IMVH. From the comparison, we find that the different initialization is not sensitive to the final results and only affects the convergence speed.

Although Algorithm 1 consists of both inner and outer iterations, empirical experimental results show that only 3 inner iterations are enough to solve the subproblem (5) or (6) in each outer iteration, where only one cycling for the sequential bit update (12) is enough to get a satisfactory solution. What's more, usually 3 outer iterations are also sufficient to obtain hashing functions with satisfactory performance. The detailed results can be found in Figure 4 (more details will be discussed in the Section 5). Overall, IMVH successfully utilizes all the useful within-view similarity and between-view correlations across all the data modalities and unifies their respective advantages in a global frame work, which leads a superior performance compared with the existing multimodal hashing methods.

5. EXPERIMENTS

In this section, we validate our proposed method IMVH on two popular publicly available multimodal benchmarks that are fully paired and labeled including:

- **Wiki**: It contains 2,866 image-text pairs, which are selected from the Wikipedia's featured articles. Each image is represented by a 128-dim SIFT feature vector. The text article is represented by the probability distribution over 10 topics , which learned by a latent Dirichlet allocation (LDA) model. Specifically, each pair is labeled with one of 10 semantic classes. This data set is publicly available [2] and has been used in [34, 33].
- **Flickr**: It consists of 186,577 image-tag pairs, which are generated by choosing 10 largest classes from the NUS data set [3]. Each image is represented by a 500-dimensional bag-of-words feature vector based on SIFT descriptors, while each tag is represented by a 1000-dimensional feature vector. This data set is publicly available and has been used in [33].

All the data points in the above data sets are centralized in each view respectively before the subsequent process.

Since IMVH is designed as a binary encoding scheme for multi-view data, we first evaluate its effectiveness on two **Cross Modal Retrieval Tasks**: (1) use an image query in the visual modal to search the relevant texts from the text database, which can be concluded as *Image Query vs. Text Database*; (2) use a text query in the textual modal to search the relevant images from the image database, which can be concluded as *Text Query vs. Image Database*. Furthermore, it is also necessary to explore how much the incorporation of multiple information source can benefit the retrieval. Therefore, we also conduct evaluations on two **Unimodal Retrieval Tasks**: use a query to search the relevant items in the same modal, which can be concluded as (1) *Image Query vs. Image Database* and (2) *Text Query vs. Text Database*.

5.1 Experimental Setting

Following the similar setting in [33], we randomly select 20% and 1% data points as queries in Wiki and Flickr data sets respectively. The remaining is used to form the database. The retrieved points with the same semantic concept of the query are regarded as true neighbors. For the faster training procedure, we randomly select 2000 data pairs (image vs. text) in each database to construct the training set.

It is a great surprise to find that our method IMVH is not sensitive to the parameters. Therefore we unify the parameters for different

[2] http://www.svcl.ucsd.edu/projects/crossmodal/

[3] http://lms.comp.nus.edu.sg/research/NUS-WIDE.htm

tasks in the different data sets. We simply set the parameters $\alpha_* = 1$, $\beta_* = 2$ and $\gamma_* = \frac{1}{2(K-1)}\beta_*$ in the objection function (4). The user-specified parameters a and b in SCISD function (3) are set to be $a = 2$ and $b = 0.2K$. Furthermore, we use the widely used LIBLINEAR package [4] to learn the SVM classifiers in the step 7 in the Algorithm 1. We adopt the GCO package [4] as the graph cut solver to solve the problem (12). For simplicity, we just run 3 outer iterations in Algorithm 1. In each outer iteration, we also only use 3 inner iterations to solve the subproblem (5) or (6). Experimental results show that the above setting works very well.

During all the evaluations, we measure the performance by using Recall curve, Precision-Recall curve (PR curve) and mean Average Precision (mAP) together. Recall curve reflects the effectiveness versus time cost, while Precision-Recall curve is a overall measure considering both precision and recall. mAP score is the average precision at the ranks where recall changes. In our experiments, each point in recall curve or precision-recall curve corresponds to a hamming radius ranging from 0 to K. All of these three evaluation metrics are widely used in the image retrieval literature [28, 9].

5.2 Comparison methods

For cross-modal retrieval tasks, we evaluate and compare the following five multimodal algorithms:

- **IMVH** algorithm, which is proposed in this paper.
- **CRH** algorithm [33], which considers the joint preservation of between-view correlations based on a co-regularized boosting framework.
- **CVH** algorithm [15], which extends traditional spectral hashing in single view to the multi-view case, aiming at preserving the between-view similarity.
- **CMSSH** algorithm [2], which learns linear hash functions based on eigendecomposition and boosting.
- **PDH** algorithm [24], which aims to find the most discriminative hashing functions by enforcing the maximum margin constraints with a block coordinate descent iterative scheme.

For unimodal retrieval tasks, we also compare IMVH with four state-of-the-art hashing methods for single-view data including

- **LSH**: Locality Sensitive Hashing [7], which generates the projection directions fundamentally based on the random projection.
- **SH**: Spectral Hashing [28], which learns the hashing functions based on spectral graph partitioning.
- **ITQ**: Iterative quantization [9], which tries to learn an optimal orthogonal rotation to minimize the quantization error of mapping this data to the vertices of binary hypercube after the PCA projection.
- **ITQ+CCA**: A variation of ITQ, which incorporates the multiview information by using Canonical Correlation Analysis (CCA) to produce the projection matrix instead of PCA.

The implementation of all the algorithms except CVH are generously provided by the authors, where CRH is implemented using C++ and CMSSH, PDH and IMVH are implemented using MATLAB. Since the code of CVH is not publicly available, we implement CVH using MATLAB by ourselves. All the experiments are conducted on a workstation with Intel Xeon(R) E7450 CPU and 256GB memory.

[4]http://vision.csd.uwo.ca/code/

Table 1: mAP comparison results on Wiki for cross-modal retrieval tasks.

Task	Method	Code Length		
		K=24	K=48	K=64
Image Query vs. Text Database	CRH	0.2020	0.2076	0.1858
	CVH	0.1753	0.1515	0.1512
	CMSSH	0.1371	0.1655	0.1637
	PDH	0.1838	0.1581	0.1581
	IMVH	**0.2504**	**0.2715**	**0.2719**
Text Query vs. Image Database	CRH	0.1161	0.1261	0.1195
	CVH	0.1310	0.1222	0.1215
	CMSSH	0.1177	0.1195	0.1156
	PDH	0.1370	0.1287	0.1287
	IMVH	**0.1948**	**0.2084**	**0.2168**

5.3 Experimental Results on Wiki

Figure 2 shows the comparison results of the cross modal retrieval tasks on the Wiki data set with different bits, which includes the recall curves and precision-recall curves for all the algorithms. The first and second columns show the performance of all the methods on recall curves for cross modal retrieval tasks *Image Query vs. Text Database* and *Text Query vs. Image Database* respectively. Given a fixed recall, the smaller of the number of the retrieved samples, the better of the algorithm, which means that the algorithm can obtain higher speed than others for the same recall. Therefore, from Figure 2, we can see that IMVH has the highest recall among all the compared methods. The third and forth columns display the comparison results on precision recall curves of all the method. Obviously, IMVH achieves significant advantage on the precision. From the above comparison results, we can see that IMVH greatly outperforms the state-of-the-art multimodal hashing methods on both cross-modal retrieval tasks. Meanwhile, we find that PDH has a second-best performance over CRH, CVH and CMSSH. However, it is important to note that the starting point of PDH's recall curve is far from zero. This is because PDH suffers from the unbalance encoding in the Wiki data set, i.e., most of the retrieved points fall into only a few hashing buckets. IMVH successfully avoids this situation by incorporating the between-view distinctiveness information, which makes a more balanced encoding scheme.

Table 1 shows the mean Average Precision (mAP) results on the Wiki data set using 24, 48, 64 bits. Obviously, the proposed method IMVH achieves higher mAP than other algorithms across all the cases. Specifically, IMVH outperforms other methods by 4.8%-8.6% in different bits for the task *Image Query vs. Text Database* and 5.7%-8.8% for the task *Text Query vs. Image Database*.

5.4 Experimental Results on Flickr

Similar to the results on the Wiki data set, IMVH also has the best performance on the Flickr data set. The recall curves and precision-recall curves are shown in the Figure 3, where IMVH still always outperforms the other multimodal methods on recall curves with a smaller gap. Similarly, IMVH consistently has the best performance of all the cases. In Table 2, we show the mAP comparison results on the Flickr where IMVH outperforms the other methods in different bits for both tasks.

To verify the claim that the incorporation of multiple information source can assist IMVH to obtain an encoding scheme with better discriminative power. We conduct a group of comparison between our method IMVH, PDH with some traditional hashing methods such as LSH, SH, ITQ and ITQ+CCA on the two uni-

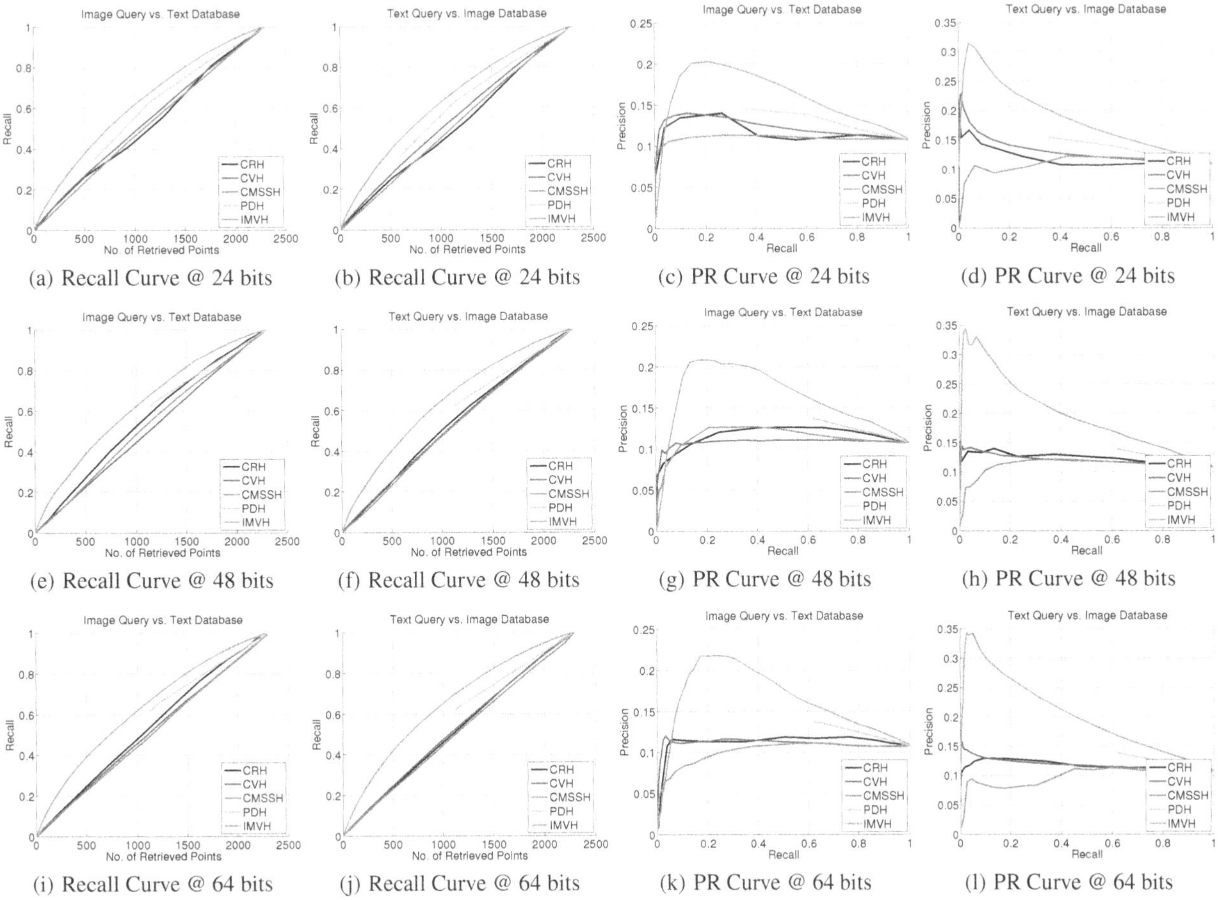

(a) Recall Curve @ 24 bits (b) Recall Curve @ 24 bits (c) PR Curve @ 24 bits (d) PR Curve @ 24 bits

(e) Recall Curve @ 48 bits (f) Recall Curve @ 48 bits (g) PR Curve @ 48 bits (h) PR Curve @ 48 bits

(i) Recall Curve @ 64 bits (j) Recall Curve @ 64 bits (k) PR Curve @ 64 bits (l) PR Curve @ 64 bits

Figure 2: Cross modal retrieval results on Wiki using different bits. The first and second columns show the recall curves of all the algorithms on two cross modal retrieval tasks respectively, while the third and fourth columns show the precision-recall curves of all the algorithms on these tasks. From above results, it is obvious to see that IMVH has the best performance compared with the state-of-the-art multimodal hashing methods.

modal retrieval tasks. Note the fact that the textual feature space in Wiki data set has only 10 dimension, which is not proper for the comparison of hashing methods with more than 10 bits. Therefore we only conduct the evaluation on the Flickr data set. Among these six methods, IMVH, PDH and ITQ+CCA are trained in the multi-modal data space, while LSH, SH and ITQ are trained in the each data modal. We compare the mAP results of all the six methods in each data modality. From Figure 5, we can see that multimodal methods IMVH and PDH significantly outperform the unimodal hashing methods in both data modalities, which implies that the proper incorporation of multiple information sources would be much helpful to learn a better hashing encoding scheme. Furthermore, we can also see that IMVH always obtains a much higher mAP score than PDH with different hashing bits for the unimodal retrieval tasks in the corresponding feature spaces. Overall, from the above results, we demonstrate the effectiveness of IMVH on both unimodal and cross-modal retrieval tasks.

5.5 Convergence Rate

In this subsection, we test the convergence rate of our proposed IMVH. We conduct a series of evaluations to test the convergence rate of IMVH for both cross modal retrieval tasks on Wiki and Flickr data sets. The detailed results are shown in Figure 4. Although IMVH has both outer and inner iterations (see details in Algorithm 1), empirical experimental results show that our proposed IMVH is quite efficient. In Figure 4 (a) (b) (e) (f), we firstly fix the number of outer iterations to be 3 and evaluate the mAP score versus the number of inner iterations. We can see that only 3 inner iterations are needed to get a good enough result in a outer iteration. While in (c) (d) (g) (h), we fix the number of outer iterations to be 3 and evaluate the IMVH's performance versus the number of outer iterations, where show usually 3 outer iterations are sufficient for IMVH to obtain a satisfactory performance.

From Figure 2 and Figure 3, we can see that IMVH and PDH have the best performance during all the tasks. To be fair, we test the training time of CVH, CMSSH, PDH and IMVH since they are implemented using MATLAB while CRH is implemented using C++. From Table 3 we can see that the training time of IMVH and PDH are also far more than others. This phenomenon can be seen as as a trade off between accuracy and efficiency. For IMVH, most of the computation consumption is on solving graph cut problems (12). However, we also find that only a small training data set can guarantee the superior performance for IMVH, which can greatly reduce the computation cost caused by solving graph cut

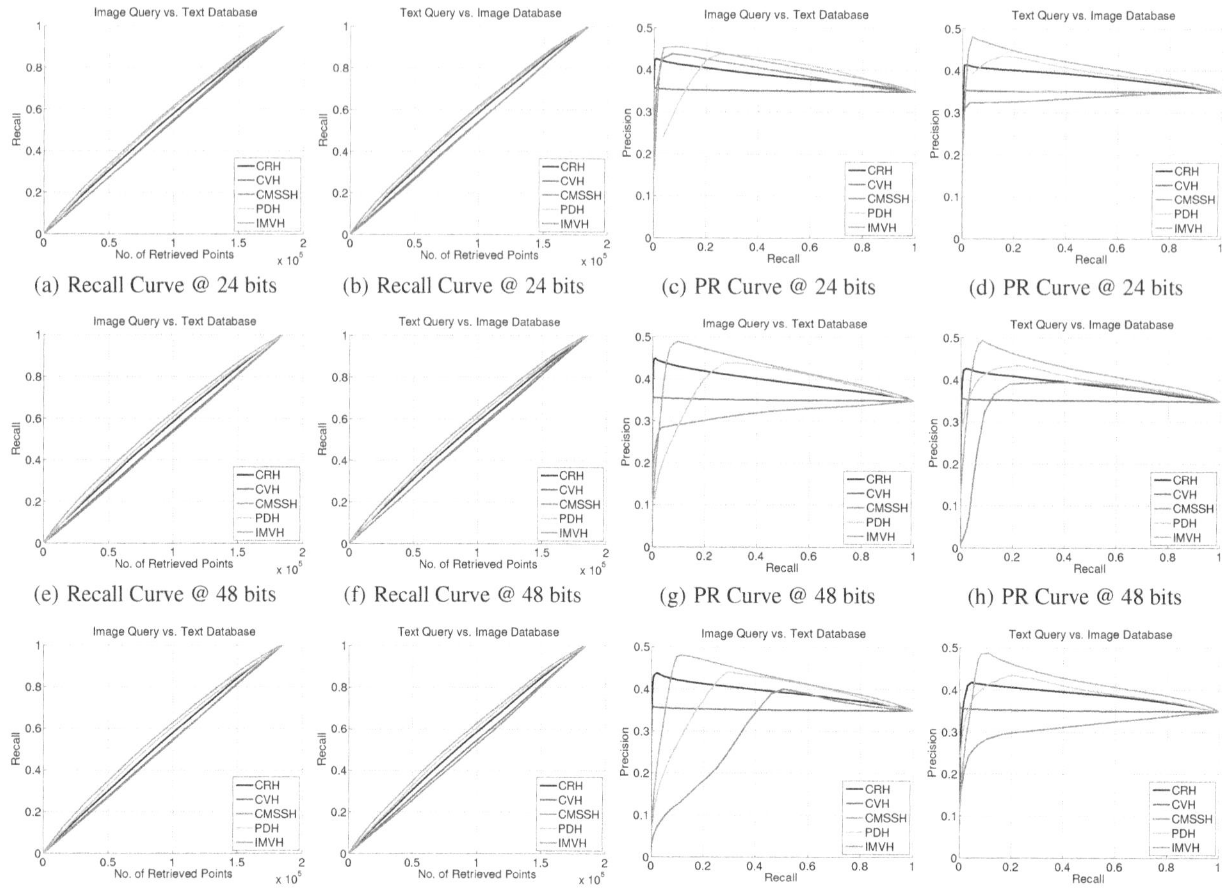

(a) Recall Curve @ 24 bits (b) Recall Curve @ 24 bits (c) PR Curve @ 24 bits (d) PR Curve @ 24 bits

(e) Recall Curve @ 48 bits (f) Recall Curve @ 48 bits (g) PR Curve @ 48 bits (h) PR Curve @ 48 bits

(i) Recall Curve @ 64 bits (j) Recall Curve @ 64 bits (k) PR Curve @ 64 bits (l) PR Curve @ 64 bits

Figure 3: Cross modal retrieval results on Flickr using different bits. The first and second columns show the recall curves of all the algorithms on two cross modal retrieval tasks respectively, while the third and fourth columns show the precision-recall curves of all the algorithms on these tasks. From above results, we can see that IMVH consistently outperforms all the compared methods.

Table 2: mAP comparison results on Flickr for cross modal retrieval tasks.

Task	Method	Code Length		
		K=24	K=48	K=64
Image Query vs. Text Database	CRH	0.3934	0.4016	0.4015
	CVH	0.3505	0.3508	0.3510
	CMSSH	0.3838	0.3546	0.3700
	PDH	0.4250	0.4289	0.4300
	IMVH	**0.4416**	**0.4633**	**0.4658**
Text Query vs. Image Database	CRH	0.3846	0.3854	0.3859
	CVH	0.3500	0.3504	0.3506
	CMSSH	0.3432	0.3624	0.3289
	PDH	0.4063	0.4107	0.4118
	IMVH	**0.4297**	**0.4430**	**0.4444**

problem. Therefore, we can learn the discriminative hashing function by IMVH with acceptable training time even on a large data set.

5.6 Parameters' Sensitivity

Note that solving subproblem (5) or (6) involves essential parameters α_* and β_*, where α_* is used to penalize the dissimilar pairs with similar binary codes and β_* is used to control the independence of the learned hashing functions. In the previous experiments, we simply set $\alpha_* = 1$ and $\beta_* = 2$. In this subsection we conduct a series of evaluations to examine how the performance of IMVH varies with α_* and β_* separately for both cross modal retrieval tasks. The detailed results are displayed in Figure 6, where the first and second row show the respective mAP score @ 64 bits of all the algorithms on Wiki and Flickr data sets. When β_* is fixed to be 2, the impact of α_* for the final mAP score is shown in Figure 6 (a) (b) (e) (f), where we can see that IMVH can obtain consistent good performance with α_* varying from 0.2 to 20. And Figure 6 (c) (d) (g) (h) show the experimental results with different β_* when α_* is fixed to be 1, where IMVH also always has a satisfactory performance with β_* varying from 0.1 to 10. Overall, from these results it is obvious to see that our proposed IMVH is robust enough against the parameters selection.

Table 3: Training time @ 24 bits on Flickr for cross modal retrieval tasks.

Method	CVH	CMSSH	PDH	IMVH
Training time	2.5s	6.3s	297s	1917s

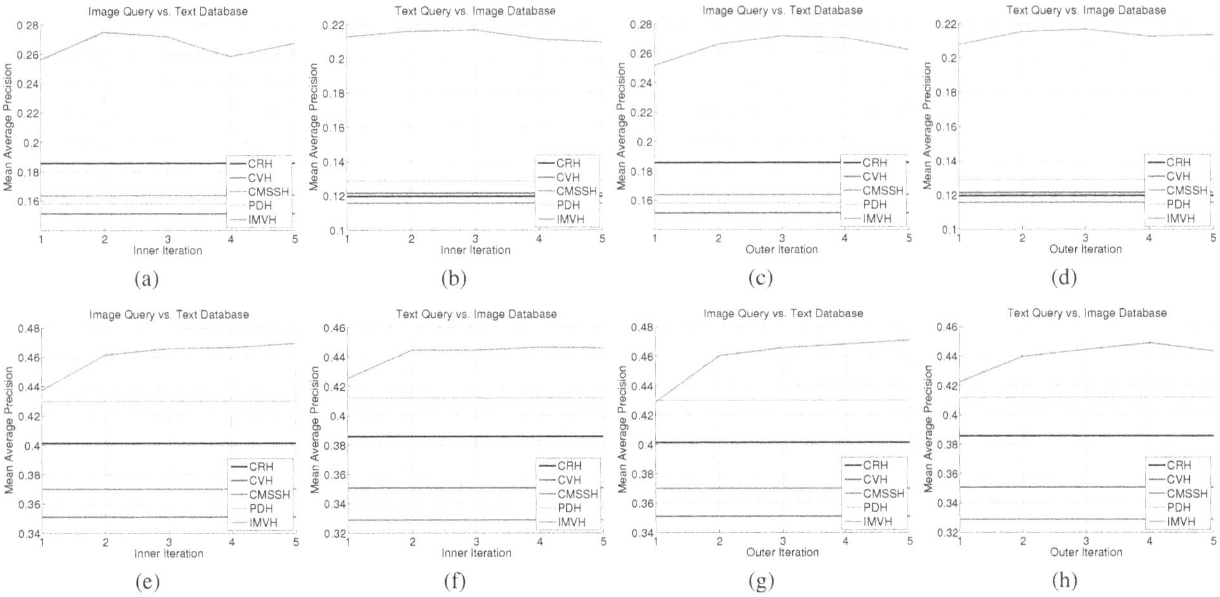

Figure 4: Iterations needed for IMVH to obtain a satisfactory performance for cross modal retrieval tasks. The first and second rows show the respective performance of IMVH on Wiki and Flickr data sets. In (a) (b) (e) (f), we fix the number of outer iterations to be 3 with varying inner iterations and in (c) (d) (g) (h) we fix the number of inner iterations to be 3 with varying outer iterations.

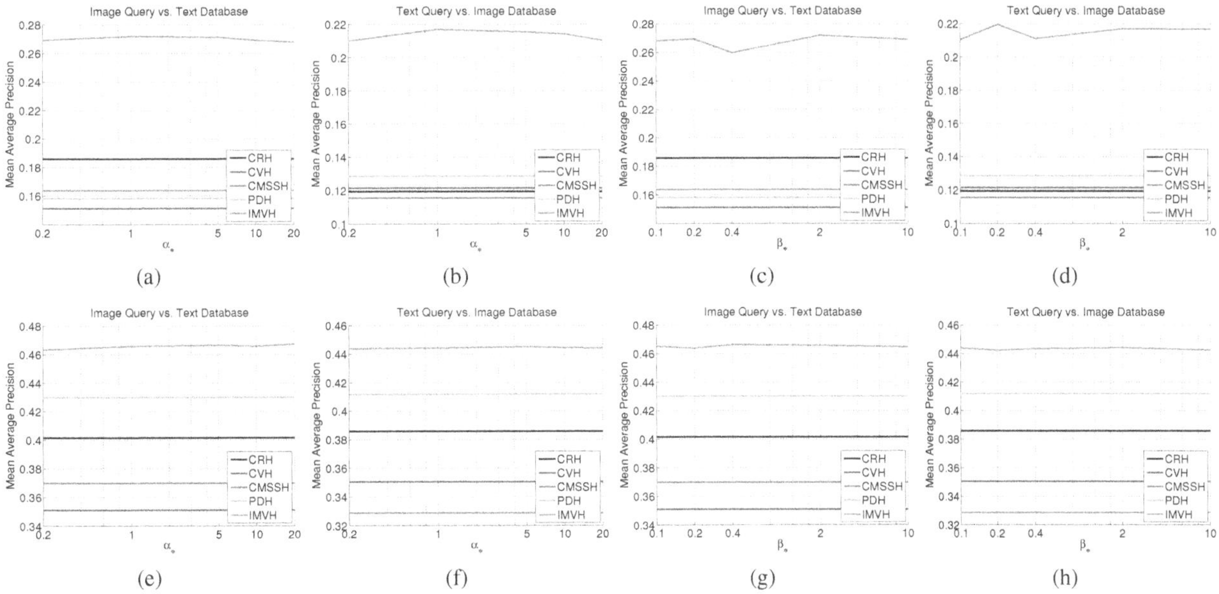

Figure 6: mAP score @ 64 bits versus the parameters β_* and α_* for both cross modal retrieval tasks. The first and second rows show the mAP score of all the algorithms on Wiki and Flickr data sets respectively. In (a) (b) (e) (f), we fix β_* to be 2 and vary α_* from 0.2 to 20. And in (c) (d) (g) (h), we fix α_* to be 1 and vary β_* from 0.1 to 10.

6. CONCLUSIONS

In this paper, we present a novel hashing algorithm for multi-view data called *Iterative Multi-View Hashing* (IMVH) for cross-modal retrieval. By incorporating the critical between-view correlations such as similarity and distinctiveness across all the views in an iterative scheme, the learned hash functions by IMVH have a greater consistent and discriminative power. To further improve the accuracy, we view the hash function learning and code generation processes separately, where the latter can be done by solving a series of binary assignment problems instead of the crucial quantization by $\text{sgn}(\cdot)$. Experimental results on two benchmarks have validated this approach, and show that this new approach outper-

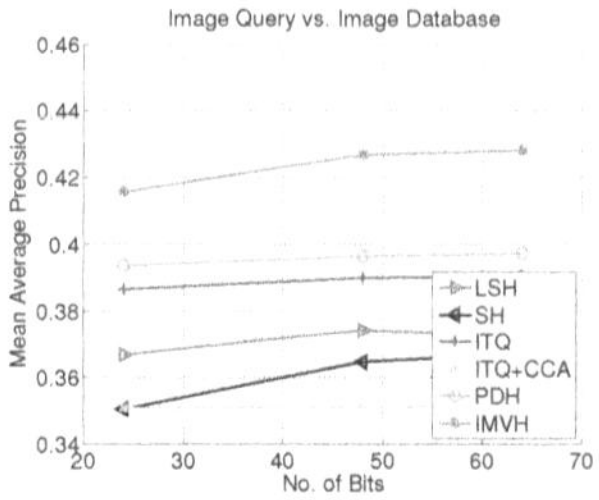

(a)

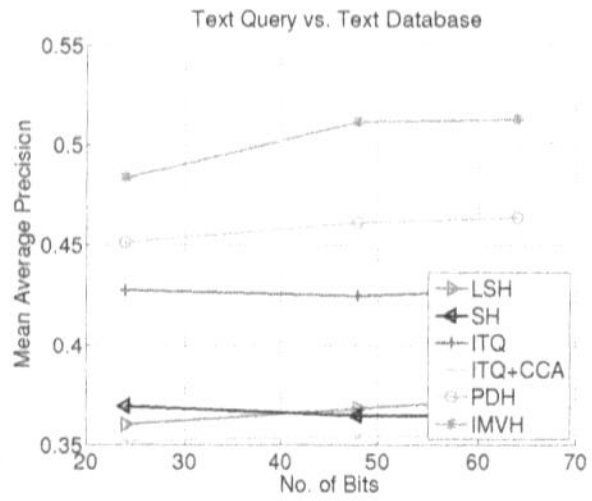

(b)

Figure 5: mAP results on Flickr for unimodal retrieval task.

forms the state-of-the-art multimodal hashing methods. In our future work, we will consider how to further improve the scalability of IMVH by exploring more efficient algorithm to solve the binary assignment problem.

7. ACKNOWLEDGEMENTS

This work was supported in part by the National Basic Research Program of China (973 Program) under Grant 2012CB316400, in part by the National Natural Science Foundation of China under Grant 61233011, Grant 61125203, Grant 91120302, and Grant 61222207, and in part by the National Program for Special Support of Top-Notch Young Professionals. We also appreciate the constructive criticism for this work from Prof. Kaiming He in MSRA.

8. REFERENCES

[1] Y. Boykov, O. Veksler, and R. Zabih. Fast approximate energy minimization via graph cuts. *IEEE Transactions Pattern Analysis Machine Intelligence*, 23(11), 2001.

[2] M. M. Bronstein, A. M. Bronstein, F. Michel, and N. Paragios. Data fusion through cross-modality metric learning using similarity-sensitive hashing. In *Computer Vision and Pattern Recognition*, 2010.

[3] O. Chum, J. Philbin, and A. Zisserman. Near duplicate image detection: min-hash and tf-idf weighting. In *British Machine Vision Conference*, 2008.

[4] R.-E. Fan, K.-W. Chang, C.-J. Hsieh, X.-R. Wang, and C.-J. Lin. Liblinear: A library for large linear classification. *Journal of Machine Learning Research*, 9, 2008.

[5] S. Feng, R. Manmatha, and V. Lavrenko. Multiple bernoulli relevance models for image and video annotation. In *Computer Vision and Pattern Recognition*, 2004.

[6] T. Ge, K. He, and J. Sun. Graph cuts for supervised hashing. In *European Conference on Computer Vision (ECCV)*, 2014.

[7] A. Gionis, P. Indyk, and R. Motwani. Similarity search in high dimensions via hashing. In *International Conference on Very Large Data Bases*, 1999.

[8] Y. Gong, S. Kumar, V. Verma, and S. Lazebnik. Angular quantization-based binary codes for fast similarity search. In *Advances in Neural Information Processing Systems*, 2012.

[9] Y. Gong, S. Lazebnik, A. Gordo, and F. Perronnin. Iterative quantization: A procrustean approach to learning binary codes for large-scale image retrieval. *IEEE Transactions Pattern Analysis Machine Intelligence*, 35(12):2916–2929, 2012.

[10] J. Ji, J. Li, S. Yan, B. Zhang, and Q. Tian. Super-bit locality-sensitive hashing. In *Advances in Neural Information Processing Systems*. 2012.

[11] Z. Jin, Y. Hu, Y. Lin, D. Zhang, S. Lin, D. Cai, and X. Li. Complementary projection hashing. In *International Conference on Computer Vision*. 2013.

[12] Z. Jin, D. Zhang, Y. Hu, S. Lin, D. Cai, and X. He. Fast and accurate hashing via iterative nearest neighbors expansion. In *IEEE Transactions on Cybernetics*. 2014.

[13] W. Kong and W.-J. Li. Isotropic hashing. In *Advances in Neural Information Processing Systems*, 2012.

[14] B. Kulis and T. Darrell. Learning to hash with binary reconstructive embeddings. In *Advances in Neural Information Processing Systems*, 2009.

[15] S. Kumar and R. Udupa. Learning hash functions for cross-view similarity search. In *International Joint Conference on Artificial Intelligence*, 2011.

[16] G. Lin, C. Shen, D. Suter, and A. van den Hengel. A general two-step approach to learning-based hashing. In *International Conference on Computer Vision*, 2013.

[17] W. Liu, J. Wang, R. Ji, Y.-G. Jiang, and S.-F. Chang. Supervised hashing with kernels. In *Computer Vision and Pattern Recognition*, 2012.

[18] X. Mao, B. Lin, D. Cai, X. He, and J. Pei. Parallel field alignment for cross media retrieval. In *Proceedings of the ACM International Conference on Multimedia*, pages 897–906, 2013.

[19] F. Monay and D. Gatica-Perez. Modeling semantic aspects for cross-media image indexing. *IEEE Transactions Pattern Analysis Machine Intelligence*, 29(10):1802–1817, 2007.

[20] Y. Mu, J. Shen, and S. Yan. Weakly-supervised hashing in kernel space. In *Computer Vision and Pattern Recognition*, 2010.

[21] G.-J. Qi, C. Aggarwal, Y. Rui, Q. Tian, S. Chang, and T. Huang. Towards cross-category knowledge propagation for learning visual concepts. In *Computer Vision and Pattern Recognition*, 2011.

[22] N. Quadrianto and C. H. Lampert. Learning multi-view neighborhood preserving projections. In *International Conference on Machine Learning*, 2011.

[23] N. Rasiwasia, J. C. Pereira, E. Coviello, G. Doyle, G. R. G. Lanckriet, R. Levy, and N. Vasconcelos. A new approach to cross-modal multimedia retrieval. In *Proceedings of the ACM International Conference on Multimedia*, pages 251–260, 2010.

[24] M. Rastegari, J. Choi, S. Fakhraei, H. D. III, and L. S. Davis. Predictable dual-view hashing. In *International Conference on Machine Learning*, 2013.

[25] M. Rastegari, A. Farhadi, and D. Forsyth. Attribute discovery via predictable discriminative binary codes. In *European Conference on Computer Vision*, 2012.

[26] P. Schonemann. A generalized solution of the orthogonal procrustes problem. *Psychometrika*, 31, 1966.

[27] J. Wang, S. Kumar, and S.-F. Chang. Sequential projection learning for hashing with compact codes. In *International Conference on Machine Learning*, 2010.

[28] Y. Weiss, A. Torralba, and R. Fergus. Spectral hashing. In *Advances in Neural Information Processing Systems*, 2005.

[29] C. Wu, J. Zhu, J. Zhang, C. Chen, and D. Cai. A convolutional treelets binary feature approach to fast keypoint recognition. In *European Conference on Computer Vision*, 2012.

[30] Y. Yang, D. Xu, F. Nie, J. Luo, and Y. Zhuang. Ranking with local regression and global alignment for cross media retrieval. In *Proceedings of the ACM International Conference on Multimedia*, pages 175–184, 2009.

[31] G. Ye, D. Liu, J. Wang, and S.-F. Chang. Large-scale video hashing via structure learning. In *International Conference on Computer Vision*, 2013.

[32] D. Zhang, F. Wang, and L. Si. Composite hashing with multiple information sources. In *International ACM SIGIR Conference on Research and Development in Information Retrieval*, 2011.

[33] Y. Zhen and D.-Y. Yeung. Co-regularized hashing for multimodal data. In *Advances in Neural Information Processing Systems*, 2012.

[34] X. Zhu, Z. Huang, H. T. Shen, and X. Zhao. Linear cross-modal hashing for efficient multimedia search. In *Proceedings of the ACM International Conference on Multimedia*, pages 143–152, 2013.

Rescue Tail Queries: Learning to Image Search Re-rank via Click-wise Multimodal Fusion

Xiaopeng Yang †, Tao Mei ‡, Yongdong Zhang †

† Key Lab of Intelligent Information Processing of Chinese Academy of Sciences (CAS)
Institute of Computing Technology, CAS, Beijing 100190, P. R. China
‡ Microsoft Research, Beijing 100080, P. R. China
yangxiaopeng@ict.ac.cn; tmei@microsoft.com; zhyd@ict.ac.cn

ABSTRACT

Image search engines have achieved good performance for head (popular) queries by leveraging text information and user click data. However, there still remain a large number of tail (rare) queries with relatively unsatisfying search results, which are often overlooked in existing research. Image search for these tail queries therefore provides a grand challenge for research communities. Most existing re-ranking approaches, though effective for head queries, cannot be extended to tail. The assumption of these approaches that *the re-ranked list should not go far away from the initial ranked list* is not applicable to the tail queries. The challenge, thus, relies on how to leverage the possibly unsatisfying initial ranked results and the very limited click data to solve the search intent gap of tail queries.

To deal with this challenge, we propose to mine relevant information from the very few click data by leveraging click-wise-based image pairs and query-dependent multimodal fusion. Specifically, we hypothesize that *images with more clicks are more relevant to the given query than the ones with no or relatively less clicks* and *the effects of different visual modalities to re-rank images are query-dependent*. We therefore propose a novel query-dependent learning to re-rank approach for tail queries, called "click-wise multimodal fusion." The approach can not only effectively expand training data by learning relevant information from the constructed click-wise-based image pairs, but also fully explore the effects of multiple visual modalities by adaptively predicting the query-dependent fusion weights. The experiments conducted on a real-world dataset with 100 tail queries show that our proposed approach can significantly improve initial search results by 10.88% and 9.12% in terms of NDCG@5 and NDCG@10, respectively, and outperform several existing re-ranking approaches.

Categories and Subject Descriptors

H.3.3 [**Information Search and Retrieval**]: Retrieval models

General Terms

Algorithms, Experimentation, Performance

MM'14, November 3–7, 2014, Orlando, Florida, USA.

http://dx.doi.org/10.1145/2647868.2654900.

(a) "kim kardashian" (b) "kim and kanye's baby"

Figure 1: Examples of the initial image search results of a head query ("kim kardashian") and a tail query ("kim and kanye's baby"). The red rectangles mark irrelevant images [best viewed in color]. Existing commercial search engines achieve very limited image search performance for tail queries.

Keywords

Image search; search re-ranking; tail queries; click-through data; multimodal fusion.

1. INTRODUCTION

As Web 2.0 and social networks developed, billions of images have been contributed and shared in the media-centered communities. The increasing number of images has posed a grand challenge to image search. Most existing commercial search engines adopt keyword-based technique for image search. However, the textual information of web images is often noisy and even unavailable. In order to boost the performance of web image search and overcome the "semantic gap" (the gap between the low-level features and high-level semantics) and "intent gap" (the gap between the representation of users' query/demand and the real intent of the users), many image search re-ranking approaches have been proposed in recent years [17].

However, most re-ranking methods target at improving search performance of head (popular) queries, while the tail (rare) queries have often been overlooked. In this paper, we focus on image search re-ranking for tail queries for the following reasons. First, head queries are frequently issued, which are mostly about celebrities, movies and so on. The corresponding image source material, textual information, and user clicks are generally substantial. By applying existing effective re-ranking methods, consequently, the search performance of head queries is usually satisfying. In contrast, the search performance of tail queries is poor due to the lack of enough source information and user clicks. As a result, most existing re-ranking approaches, with the assumption that *the re-ranked list should be close to the initial ranked list* or *the top ranked images from the initial ranked list suppose relevant to the given query*, cannot be extended to solve the problems of tail queries. Second, since query frequencies follow such a power-law distribution that there are large numbers of tail queries in query logs

[1], search performance of those queries would potentially affect the popularity and relevance of search engines significantly in fierce market competition. For example, Fig. 1 shows the initial search results of head query "kim kardashian" and tail query "kim and kanye's baby," respectively. We can see that the top 10 search results of head query "kim kardashian" are absolutely satisfying, while, for tail query "kim and kanye's baby," there are only two relevant images that satisfy user search intent. To summarize, we believe that appropriately handling tail queries is a newly emerging direction in image search.

To address these challenges for tail queries, we seek to leverage multiple visual features and pair-wise click-through data simultaneously. In general, most image search re-ranking approaches treat different modalities (features), such as shape, color and texture, independently. However, for different queries, discriminative modalities may have distinct effects. For instance, for the queries like "heart" and "sun," color feature may be more useful, while for the queries such as "buildings," texture feature will be more effective. The same situation happens to tail queries, for example, shape feature may be more helpful for "kim and kanye's baby" shown in Fig. 1(b) to detect the "baby." Although several approaches, which learn and predict fusion weights in a linear or non-linear way to combine multiple modalities, have proved effective [22][27], the problem of how to fuse multiple modalities adaptively and in a query-dependent way still remains. Conversely, since users browse image thumbnails before selecting the images to click, we believe that the click data can reflect users' search intent as "implicit" relevance feedback [9][26]. Intuitively, images with more clicks are more relevant to the given query than the ones with no or less clicks. However, clicked images always hold a low percentage in the search results to a given tail query, even less than 10%. It is difficult to learn the similarity among them to facilitate re-ranking for all the images. How to mine useful information from such limited click-through data is a problem that most existing re-ranking work does not take into consideration.

To address the above issues, we propose a novel query-dependent learning to re-rank approach, called "click-wise multimodal fusion," to improve the search performance for tail queries. In our paper, we define "click-wise" as the difference value of clicks for pair-wise images. Our key assumptions are based on two aspects: 1) the effects of different visual modalities to re-rank images are query-dependent, and 2) images with more clicks are more relevant than the ones with no or relatively less clicks in response to a given query. In click-wise multimodal fusion, we extract multiple visual features from all the images, and select image pairs containing click-wise information, no matter clicked-clicked image pairs or clicked-unclicked ones. On the one hand, click-wise multimodal fusion can learn and predict the fusion weights of multiple modalities adaptively and query-dependently. On the other hand, it can make full use of click-wise-based image pairs to correctly re-rank the clicked images with larger clicks higher through penalizing the misclassified pairs with different click-wise information.

Note that our re-ranking approach is general, yet, it is applicable to tail queries owing to the use of click-wise information. Specifically, as click-through data can be viewed as the footprints of user search behavior, we mine click-wise information adequately to guide image search re-ranking regardless of the initial ranked list. For a given tail query, even the number of clicked images is relatively small, such as 10 or less, we can still get enough training data by detecting the click-wise-based pairs. Moreover, the clicked images of tail queries are usually uncertain and diverse resulting in the difficulty to learn from the "similarity" among them, while using our approach, we can learn from the "dissimilarity" via click-wise information to re-rank images.

The contributions of this paper can be summarized as follows.

- We have investigated the image search re-ranking for tail queries which is often overlooked by most previous research. To the best of our knowledge, this represents one of the first attempts for formally studying the problem of image search re-ranking for tail queries.
- We propose a novel learning to re-rank approach, called "click-wise multimodal fusion," which can not only adaptively learn the fusion weights of multiple modalities in a query-dependent way, but also leverage image pairs with click-wise information to facilitate image search re-ranking.
- We conduct experiments on a one-week real-world dataset consisting of 2,682,666 queries and 20,165,208 image URLs collected from a commercial search engine. The evaluation validates that our approach is able to significantly improve search performance for tail queries, while maintaining slightly better performance for head queries.

The rest of this paper is organized as follows. Section 2 presents related work. Section 3 analyzes a one-week query log and details the definition of tail queries. Section 4 introduces our proposed query-dependent re-ranking approach, called "click-wise multimodal fusion." Section 5 reports the experimental results on the performance of our re-ranking approach. Section 6 draws the conclusion.

2. RELATED WORK

Our work is mainly related to image search re-ranking and search with click-through data. In this section, we first present image search re-ranking along two directions, i.e., recurrent pattern mining and multimodal visual feature fusion. Then, we introduce the work on search with click-through data, especially for image search.

2.1 Image Search Re-ranking

According to how many visual features are leveraged and explored, we categorize visual search re-ranking into two major directions, i.e., recurrent pattern mining and multimodal visual feature fusion. Most of them are developed based on the hypotheses that 1) the re-ranked results should not change too much from the initial ranked results or the top ranked images from the initial ranked list suppose relevant to the given query, and 2) visually similar images should be close in the re-ranked list.

Recurrent pattern mining seeks to mine recurrent patterns from relevant images to improve the re-ranking performance. For instance, Hsu *et al.* formulate re-ranking as a random walk problem along the context graph, where video stories are represented as nodes and the edges between them are weighted by contextual similarities [7]. Yan *et al.* propose to re-rank using a binary classifier where the top-ranked (bottom-ranked) documents from the initial ranked results are chosen as pseudo-positive (pseudo-negative) samples, which is the so-called pseudo-relevance feedback (PRF) [23]. Compared with exploiting the initial search results without any external knowledge, Yang and Hanjalic leverage query examples and formulate learning to re-rank as an optimization function by minimizing the distance between the re-ranked list and the initial one, while maximizing the coherence of similar ranked images in terms of the visual features [24]. Similarly, crowd-sourced knowledge, e.g., multiple initial ranked results from various search engines [15] and the suggested queries augmented from the image collection on the Web [28], is mined to find relevant visual patterns. In order to further satisfy users' search intent, many researchers

Table 1: Query frequency distribution for one-week query log.

query frequency	number of queries	region in Fig. 2
(100, 3251]	767	HEAD
(1, 100]	310,274	TAIL-A
1	2,371,625	TAIL-B

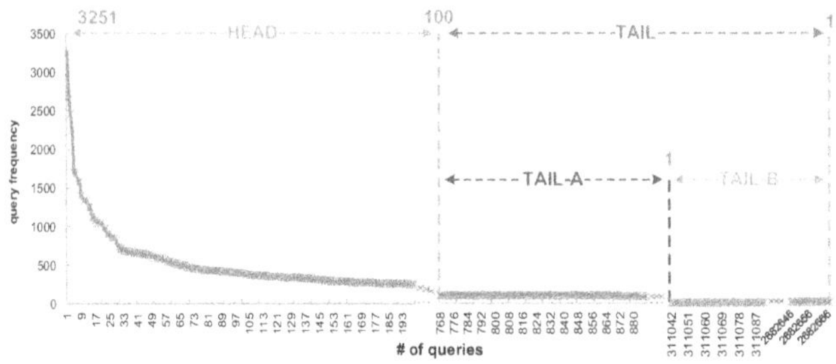

Figure 2: The power-law distribution for the query frequencies of 2,682,666 queries. Note that regions are divided by *dotted* lines [best viewed in color].

involve user interaction, such as human labeling and feedback, to guide the re-ranking process. Hauptmann *et al.* propose to employ active learning technique to exploit both the human bandwidth and machine capability for video search re-ranking [6]. For reducing the efforts of users' labeling, Tian *et al.* propose a sample selection strategy based on images' structural information, and then use a discriminative dimension reduction algorithm to capture user intent in the visual feature space [21].

Multimodal visual feature fusion aims to fuse different modalities in a unified way and make them function well accordingly. To deal with this problem, one natural way is to concentrate multiple features into a long feature vector and then use this joint modality to perform specific task. Alternatively, we can fuse the re-ranking results produced by applying modalities separately in a re-ranking algorithm. These two methods are the so-called "early fusion" and "late fusion" separately [20]. Even though the early and late fusion approaches are advantageous compared with ones using an individual modality, yet, they still suffer from "curse of dimensionality" and incapability of determining proper fusion weights for different modalities, respectively. Thus, in order to learn appropriate fusion weights of multiple modalities, Snoek *et al.* propose to assign weights heuristically and manually based on the type of query, such as text-, concept- and visual-oriented queries [19]. This "rule-based fusion," though easy to implement, may degrade the retrieval performance due to the wrong weights assigned by users. To address this issue, Kennedy *et al.* recommend to use "query-class-dependent fusion" [13]. They first classify each user query into categories learnt by cluster algorithms, and then aggregate retrieval results with the help of query-class associated weights. Nevertheless, it is difficult to categorize a user query into a specific class accurately due to its complicated semantic meanings. Therefore, "adaptive fusion" is introduced to learn query-dependent fusion weights for multiple modalities [22][25].

Overall, though proved effective for head queries, the above mentioned approaches cannot be extended to tail queries, mainly because the initial ranked results of tail queries are always so unsatisfying that they cannot support the assumptions. Moreover, click-through data, which can be viewed as an indicator of image relevance, are mostly not taken into consideration in those methods.

2.2 Search with Click-through Data

Click-through data have been studied in web search for a few years [3][4][5][12]. Compared with web document search, where users can only browse a two-line snippet in response to a given query, in image search, users browse image thumbnails before selecting the images to click. Thus, it is much more convincing that the decision to click is likely dependent on the relevance of an image. In recent years, mining click-through data from query logs to facilitate image search has attracted some researchers' attention [8][9][26]. For instance, Jain *et al.* employ Gaussian Process regression to predict the normalized click count for each image, and combine it with the original ranking score for re-ranking [9]. In [26], Yang *et al.* leverage click-through data and detect recurrent visual patterns of images simultaneously to boost the performance of image retrieval. Based on the assumption that clicked images are highly correlated with relevant ones to the given query, it is inspiring to use click-through data, which are readily available and freely accessible from query logs, to guide image search instead of human intervention. As the above work presents, the click counts of images have been fully explored, yet, for tail queries, there are not enough clicked images, let alone the images' click counts. In order to increase data volume containing click information, we attempt to use click-wise-based image pairs, i.e., image pairs with the difference value of clicks. Then, our concerns are: 1) what is the influence of *the difference value of clicks*? 2) can *the difference value of clicks* be leveraged to improve search performance of images, especially for tail queries?

3. QUERY LOGS AND TAIL QUERIES

Since we focus on improving search performance of tail queries, we first analyze query logs, and then give the general definition of tail queries. We have collected query logs from a commercial image search engine for one week in Oct. 2013. The query logs are represented as plain text files that contain a line for each HTTP request satisfied by the Web server. For each record, the following fields are used in our data collection:

<*Query, ClickedURL, ClickCount, Thumbnail*>

where the *ClickedURL* and *ClickCount* represent the URL and the number of clicks on this URL when users submit the *Query*, respectively. *Thumbnail* denotes the corresponding image information on the *ClickedURL*.

In order to study the effect of click-through data, we use all the queries in the log with at least one click. There are 2,682,666 queries and 20,165,208 image URLs in total. Generally, a tail query is identified based on its query frequency. As Table 1 shows, there are over 88% queries with one query frequency, indicating they are issued only once by users during one week. In contrast, the number of queries with frequency larger than 100 is 767, accounting for less than 0.03% of all queries. We sort all the queries according to their frequencies in a descending order and draw Fig. 2 which shows that the query frequency distribution follows the power laws. Empirically, we believe that queries issued more than 100 times during a week can be viewed as popular (head) queries. Thus, based on the query frequency of 100, we divide the entire query frequency distribution into "HEAD" region and "TAIL" region shown in Fig. 2. Moreover, since the number of queries issued only once is extremely large, we further divide "TAIL" region into "TAIL-A" (including queries issued between 1 and 100 times) and "TAIL-B" (including queries issued only once). In our work, we mainly focus on region "TAIL-A" and "TAIL-B" consisting of tail queries.

Following the general concept based on query frequencies, we give the definition of tail queries below.

DEFINITION 1. A $Query$ is represented as a record:

<*QueryText, QueryFrequency*>

where $QueryText$ stands for the textual information of $Query$, $QueryFrequency$ indicates the query frequency during a certain time period. A tail query is a query with $QueryFrequency$ no more than T_q, where T_q is the threshold which equals to a certain query frequency for identifying tail queries.

Since the time period of query logs varies, the threshold T_q can be defined accordingly. In our work, we set T_q to 100 for a one-week query log. Taking query "kim and kanye's baby" shown in Fig. 1(b) as an example, its query frequency equals to 29 which is less than $T_q = 100$, then we can define it as a typical tail query. Concerning queries with clicks, i.e. the queries in the log with at least one click, the definition of tail queries is different from the general one as follows.

DEFINITION 2. A $Query$ with clicks is represented as a record:

<*QueryText, QueryFrequency, ClickedImages*>

where $ClickedImages$ indicates the number of clicked images in response to $Query$. A tail query with clicks is a query with *QueryFrequency* no more than T_q, and *ClickedImages* no more than T_c, where T_q and T_c are the thresholds of *QueryFrequency* and *ClickedImages*, respectively.

Similarly, the thresholds of T_q and T_c can be set depending on the time period of query logs and the requirement of click information. Compared with general definition of tail queries given in Def. 1, we add $ClickedImages$ for tail queries with clicks mainly for the following reason. A dispersive distribution of clicked images equals with diverse search intent of users. By narrowing down the range of the number of clicked images, we can get more centralized user intent via a certain number of clicked images. In our work, we set T_q and T_c all to 100 for a one-week query log. For example, as the query frequency and the number of clicked images of query "kim and kanye's baby" is 29 and 22 respectively, we can use it as a representative tail query with clicks.

4. LEARNING TO RE-RANK: CLICK-WISE MULTIMODAL FUSION

In this section, we introduce our proposed novel re-ranking approach, called click-wise multimodal fusion (CWMF). First, we present traditional ranking SVM (Supported Vector Machine), which is a commonly used "pair-wise" learning to rank algorithm. We do not introduce other learning to rank algorithms, such as "point-wise" and "list-wise," because in our work we try to use click-wise information between two images, which more matches the form of "pair-wise." Then, we extend ranking SVM to a learning to re-rank paradigm and detail our re-ranking approach.

In the following sections, we use q to denote the issued query, x to denote an image returned by a search engine, y to denote the relevance of image x, and c to denote the click count of image x.

4.1 Ranking SVM

Ranking SVM, in which the preference relations between instances are used, can be viewed as a special case of SVM [11]. Suppose we are given a set of training query-image-label triples (q_i, x_i, y_i), where $q_i \in \mathcal{Q}$ ($\mathcal{Q}$ is the set of queries), $x_i \in \mathcal{R}^n$ (n is the dimension of image's feature), $y_i \in \mathcal{R}$, $i = 1, 2, ..., N$ (N is the number of triples). Label y_i annotates the relevance of x_i in response to q_i, then we can define the set of image preference pairs as

$$\bar{\mathcal{P}} \triangleq \{(i,j)|q_i = q_j, y_i > y_j\}, \tag{1}$$

where $i, j = 1, 2, ..., N$. We use $\bar{P}$ to denote the size of set $\bar{\mathcal{P}}$, i.e., $\bar{P} \triangleq |\bar{\mathcal{P}}|$.

Then, ranking SVM can be formulated as learning for classification on the preference pairs shown as Eqn. (2).

$$\begin{aligned} \min_{\omega,\xi} \quad & F(\omega, \xi) = \tfrac{1}{2}\omega^T\omega + C\textstyle\sum_{(i,j)\in\bar{\mathcal{P}}} \xi_{ij} \\ \text{s.t.} \quad & \omega^T\left(\Phi(x_i) - \Phi(x_j)\right) \geq 1 - \xi_{ij} \\ & \xi_{ij} \geq 0, \quad \forall (i,j) \in \bar{\mathcal{P}}, \end{aligned} \tag{2}$$

where ω is a weight vector that is adjusted by learning, C is the regularization parameter and $C > 0$, Φ is a mapping onto instance feature that describes the match between q_i and x_i, ξ_{ij} is a L1 loss term. Overall, the first term of Eqn. (2) is called regularization term, and the second one is the Hinge Loss term.

Note that the optimization is equivalent to that of SVM as a quadratic optimization problem. Assume that ω^* is the optimal solution of Eqn. (2) and $f(x)$ is a ranking function, then we can leverage ω^* to calculate the ranking score of image x as follows

$$f(x) = {\omega^*}^T \Phi(x). \tag{3}$$

4.2 Click-wise Multimodal Fusion

4.2.1 Overview

Since the initial search results of tail queries are usually unsatisfying and the corresponding click data are very limited, most existing re-ranking approaches cannot be extended to tail queries. The reason lies on the basic assumption of re-ranking, i.e., *the re-ranked list should not go far away from the initial ranked list.* To address these issues, we propose to mine relevant information from the very few click data by leveraging click-wise-based image pairs (image pairs with click-wise information) and query-dependent multimodal fusion. Note that in our paper we define "click-wise information" as the difference value of clicks. Then, we develop our re-ranking approach based on the following two assumptions:

- images with more clicks are more relevant to the given query than the ones with no or relatively less clicks, and
- the effects of different visual modalities to re-rank images are query-dependent.

In order to leverage the click-wise information from click-through data, we formulate image search re-ranking as a "pair-wise" learning to re-rank problem based on ranking SVM. However, on one hand, traditional ranking SVM cannot deal with the problem of multimodal fusion resulting in the impossibility to leverage query-dependent effects of different modalities. On the other hand, without considering the difference value of clicks, ranking SVM treats the image pairs with different click-wise information equally [2]. Nevertheless, it is not desirable that the ranking model tends to be close to the clicked-clicked instance pairs, especially of which the click-wise information is relatively small. On the opposite, the ranking model should be in proximity to the clicked-unclicked instance pairs containing large click-wise information. To summarize, in order to adequately learn the multi-modality influence and adjust the ranking SVM training bias, we extend ranking SVM to make it capable of learning query-dependent multi-modality fusion weights and penalizing the misclassified click-wise-based instance pairs.

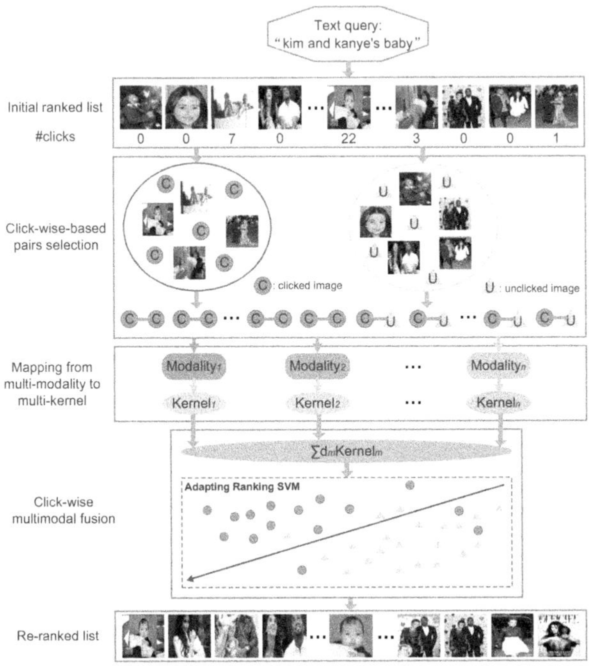

Figure 3: The overview of the proposed click-wise multimodal fusion re-ranking [best viewed in color]. Note that "♯clicks" denote the corresponding click count of each image. "Click-wise-based pairs selection" chooses image pairs with click-wise information. "Mapping from multi-modality to multi-kernel" projects different modalities into their corresponding kernel space. "Click-wise multimodal fusion" integrates multiple kernel learning with a click-based adapting ranking SVM.

The overview of the proposed query-dependent image search re-ranking approach, called "click-wise multimodal fusion," is shown in Fig. 3. Given a tail query, such as "kim and kanye's baby," to mine relevant information from click data, we first identify the set of clicked images and the set of unclicked ones from the initial ranked list based on the click counts of images (♯clicks). Since clicked images of tail queries are very limited, we select two images with different click counts as a pair to expend training data. In other words, we choose click-wise-based image pairs not only between the set of clicked images and the set of unclicked ones, but also from the interior of the set of clicked images. Then, in order to facilitate re-ranking by exploring the query-dependent effects of multiple visual features, we transform multiple visual modalities into the same dimension by mapping them to their corresponding kernel space. Finally, in our proposed query-dependent learning to re-rank approach, click-wise multimodal fusion can not only adaptively learn the linear fusion weight d_m for each modality by leveraging multiple kernel learning algorithm, but also directly output the re-ranks of images based on a click-based adapting ranking SVM.

Compared with ranking SVM, the advantages of click-wise multimodal fusion are twofold. First, we revise the Hinge Loss function by setting various losses for misclassification of image pairs between different click-wise-based pairs (pairs with discriminative difference value of clicks). To reduce errors on determining ranks of images with more clicks, the loss function heavily penalizes errors with regard to click-wise-based pairs with large difference value of clicks. This modification can be viewed as a click-based adapting ranking SVM. Second, we integrate a multiple kernel learning algorithm with the click-based adapting ranking SVM into a uniform framework. By automatically learning and predicting the query-dependent fusion weights for multiple features, we can explore how consistent (contradictory) modalities could incorporate (compromise) with each other.

4.2.2 Formulation

For a given query q, we represent the image instances as a set of query-instance-clicks triples (q, x_i, c_i), where $q \in \mathcal{Q}$, $x_i \in \mathcal{R}^n$, $c_i \in \mathcal{R}$, $i = 1, 2, ..., l$ (l is the number of images to be re-ranked). Suppose there are M modalities of images in total. Based on modality m, image x_i can be expressed as $x_{m,i}$ ($m = 1, 2, ..., M$). For lightening notations, we specify $\sum_m$ to represent the summation from the 1st modality to the Mth one, and use $\phi_m(x_i)$ to represent the mapping onto feature m that describes the match between query q_i and image $x_{m,i}$. Based on the click-wise information, we define the set of click-wise-based instance pairs as

$$\mathcal{P} \triangleq \{(i,j) | (c_i - c_j) \geq \delta\}, \tag{4}$$

where δ is the threshold controlling the selection of click-wise-based pairs and $\delta > 0$. Accordingly, the difference value of clicks between x_i and x_j is expressed as c_{ij}, which equals to $|c_i - c_j|$. We also use P to denote the size of set $\mathcal{P}$, i.e., $P \triangleq |\mathcal{P}|$.

We define a new loss function which integrates multiple kernel learning with a click-based adapting ranking SVM as follows.

$$\begin{aligned} \min_{d,\omega,\xi} \ & L(d,\omega,\xi) = \tfrac{1}{2}\textstyle\sum_m \tfrac{1}{d_m}\omega_m^{\mathrm{T}}\omega_m + C\sum_{(i,j)\in\mathcal{P}} \xi_{ij}\lambda_{ij} \\ \text{s.t.} \ & \textstyle\sum_m \omega_m^{\mathrm{T}}\big(\phi_m(x_i) - \phi_m(x_j)\big) \geq 1 - \xi_{ij} \\ & \xi_{ij} \geq 0, \ \ \forall (i,j) \in \mathcal{P} \\ & \lambda_{ij} = \exp\left\{\tfrac{c_{ij}}{2\gamma^2}\right\} \\ & \textstyle\sum_m d_m = 1, \ \ d_m \geq 0, \ \ \forall m, \end{aligned} \tag{5}$$

where d denotes the fusion weight vector for M modalities, λ denotes the adapting penalty parameter, γ denotes the average difference value of clicks among all click-wise-based pairs for query q, i.e., $\gamma = \frac{\sum_{(i,j)\in\mathcal{P}} c_{ij}}{P}$, where $i \neq j$ and $i, j = 1, 2, ..., l$. Note that in Eqn. (5) we define that when $d_m = 0$, ω_m has to be a zero vector so as to yield a finite objective value [18].

4.2.3 Optimization

Due to the introduction of the last constraint, it is difficult to directly solve Eqn. (5) by its corresponding dual problem. Thus, we deform Eqn. (5) as a constrained optimization problem with regard to d as follows.

$$\min_d J(d), \quad \text{such that} \sum\nolimits_m d_m = 1, \ d_m \geq 0, \tag{6}$$

where

$$J(d) = \left\{ \begin{aligned} & \min_{\omega,\xi} \left\{ \tfrac{1}{2}\textstyle\sum_m \tfrac{1}{d_m}\omega_m^{\mathrm{T}}\omega_m + C\sum_{(i,j)\in\mathcal{P}} \xi_{ij}\lambda_{ij} \right\} \\ & \text{s.t.} \ \textstyle\sum_m \omega_m^{\mathrm{T}}\big(\phi_m(x_i) - \phi_m(x_j)\big) \geq 1 - \xi_{ij} \\ & \quad \xi_{ij} \geq 0, \ \ \forall (i,j) \in \mathcal{P} \\ & \quad \lambda_{ij} = \exp\left\{\tfrac{c_{ij}}{2\gamma^2}\right\}. \end{aligned} \right. \tag{7}$$

To solve the above problem, we first write the Lagrange function of $J(d)$ as

$$L_p = \frac{1}{2}\sum\nolimits_m \frac{1}{d_m}\omega_m^{\mathrm{T}}\omega_m + C\sum\nolimits_P \xi_{ij}\lambda_{ij} - \sum\nolimits_P \alpha_{ij}W - \sum\nolimits_P u_{ij}\xi_{ij}, \tag{8}$$

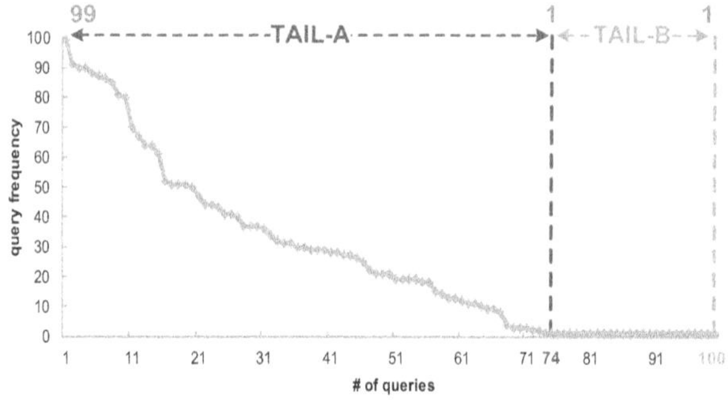

Figure 4: Query frequency distribution for the 100 tail queries dataset.

where α_{ij} and u_{ij} are the Lagrange multipliers, $\sum_{\mathcal{P}}$ is the abbreviation for $\sum_{(i,j)\in\mathcal{P}}$ and

$$W = \sum_m \omega_m^{\mathrm{T}}(\phi_m(x_i) - \phi_m(x_j)) - (1 - \xi_{ij}). \quad (9)$$

After setting the respective derivatives with respect to ω_m and ξ_{ij} to zero, we can obtain the Lagrange dual function below.

$$\begin{array}{ll} \max\limits_{\alpha} & L_D(\alpha) = -\frac{1}{2}\alpha^{\mathrm{T}}G\alpha + e^{\mathrm{T}}\alpha \\ \text{s.t.} & 0 \le \alpha_{ij} \le C\lambda_{ij}, \ \forall (i,j) \in \mathcal{P}, \end{array} \quad (10)$$

where $\alpha \in \mathcal{R}^P$ is indexed by click-wise-based pairs in set $\mathcal{P}$, $e \in \mathcal{R}^P$ is a vector of ones, and G is a P by P symmetric matrix. Specifically,

$$G_{(i,j),(u,v)} = \sum_m d_m \Phi_{m,ij}^T \Phi_{m,uv}, \ \forall (i,j),(u,v) \in \mathcal{P}, \quad (11)$$

where $\Phi_{m,ij} \triangleq \Phi_m(x_i) - \Phi_m(x_j)$.

Clearly, the dual problem of (7) is similar to that of ranking SVM. There are two differences lying on: 1) G in (10) is a weighted mapping from M modality, while G in ranking SVM is based on a single modality; 2) the upper bounds of α vary according to various click-wise information from pairs, i.e., pairs with larger difference value of clicks get a larger upper bounds, in contrast, the upper bounds of α in ranking SVM are the same.

In order to facilitate the calculation of fusion weight vector d and also avoid the situation that mapping Φ is infinite dimensional, we assign a kernel function $K(\cdot,\cdot)$, such as linear kernel, RBF kernel, etc., to each modality accordingly. Then, G can be indicated as

$$G = \sum_m d_m A\tilde{G}_m A^{\mathrm{T}} \quad (12)$$

where $\tilde{G}_m \in \mathcal{R}^{l\times l}$, with $\tilde{G}_m(i,j) = K_m(x_i,x_j) = \Phi_m(x_i)^{\mathrm{T}}\Phi_m(x_j)$ and $A \in \mathcal{R}^{P\times l}$ is a particular matrix with the following format

$$A = \begin{array}{c} \\ \vdots \\ (i,j) \\ \vdots \end{array} \begin{array}{c} \cdots \quad i \quad \cdots \quad j \quad \cdots \\ \begin{bmatrix} 0...0 & +1 & 0...0 & -1 & 0...0 \end{bmatrix} \end{array} \quad (13)$$

meaning that if $(i,j) \in \mathcal{P}$, the ith entry of the corresponding row in A is 1, the jth entry is -1, and other entries are all zeros. The reason of introducing matrix A is to save the computation cost of G from $O(l^4)$ to $O(l^2)$.

Then, by treating the weighted mapping G as a unified single one, the standard ranking SVM algorithms [11][14] can be leveraged to directly solve this problem. Once the $J(d)$ is solved, we compute the gradient of $J(d)$ with respect to d_m, and then use a reduced gradient algorithm proposed in [18] to update the fusion weight vector d for M modalities. The updating scheme is $d \leftarrow d + \theta D$, where θ is the step size which can be determined by line search and D is the descent direction

Table 2: Statistic property values of 100 tail queries.

	QueryFrequency	*ClickedImages*	*MaxClicks*
Max. value	99	69	31
Min. value	1	1	1
Avg. value	27	23.21	9.98

$$D_m = \begin{cases} 0 & \text{if } d_m = 0 \text{ and } \frac{\partial J}{\partial d_m} - \frac{\partial J}{\partial d_\mu} > 0 \\ \frac{\partial J}{\partial d_\mu} - \frac{\partial J}{\partial d_m} & \text{if } d_m > 0 \text{ and } m \neq \mu \\ \sum\limits_{v\neq\mu, d_v>0} (\frac{\partial J}{\partial d_v} - \frac{\partial J}{\partial d_\mu}) & \text{for } m = \mu, \end{cases} \quad (14)$$

where μ is the index of the largest component of vector d.

Finally, when the terminated criterion is met, such as the duality gap, the KKT condition, the variation of d between two consecutive steps or simply a maximal number of iterations, the re-ranking score of image x can be represented as

$$\begin{aligned} f(x) &= \sum_m \omega_m^{*\,\mathrm{T}} \Phi_m(x) \\ &= \sum_m d_m^* \sum_{(i,j)\in\mathcal{P}} \alpha_{ij}^* K_m(x_i - x_j, x), \end{aligned} \quad (15)$$

where ω_m^*, d_m^* and α_{ij}^* are the optimal values.

5. EXPERIMENTS

In this section, we describe our experimental settings and present the experimental results. To adequately validate the effectiveness of our approach, we first compare our approach with those methods lacking of multimodal fusion and several existing re-ranking methods, respectively. Then, we analyze the sensitivity of parameters used in our approach and the complexity of our approach. Finally, we give some detailed re-ranking examples of tail queries.

5.1 Experimental Settings

To facilitate evaluation and compare our proposed approach with other ones, we randomly select 100 tail queries from the one-week query log mentioned in Sect. 3 according to the settings $T_q = 100$ and $T_c = 100$, in other words, these queries belong to region "TAIL" defined in Fig. 2. Figure 4 shows the query frequency distribution of these 100 tail queries with clicks. We can find that query frequencies of these 100 tail queries follow a nearly power-law distribution as Fig. 2, indicating that these queries have certain representativeness. Among the 100 tail queries, there are 73 and 27 queries belonging to region "TAIL-A" and "TAIL-B" as shown in Fig. 2, respectively. Note that there are almost triple queries in "TAIL-A" than the ones in "TAIL-B," since we assign a larger selection weight for queries in "TAIL-A." The reason originates from the fact that the click data of queries in "TAIL-B" are provided by an individual user, which are possibly biased compared with click data aggregated by users. Moreover, there are various types of queries, such as people ("pewdiepie," and "josh freeman girlfriend"), object ("first computer," and "corner wall waterfall"), concept ("internet safety," and "small caribbean house plans"), scenery ("sea sparkle," and "east coast of the united states from space") and event ("jodie foster dating," and "elizabeth smart wedding"). Note that some typical tail queries belonging to these semantic categories are shown in the bracket next to their name severally.

Since source materials of tail queries are usually limited and the images after the top 100 results are typically irrelevant, we

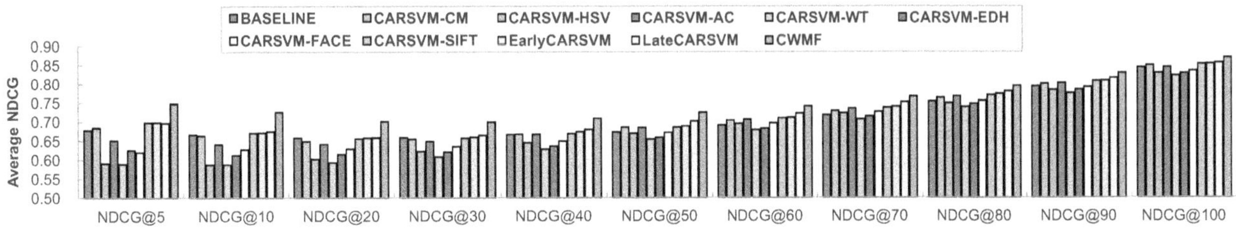

Figure 5: Comparison of re-ranking approaches using different modalities in terms of NDCG

use the top 100 images from the initial search results to perform re-ranking, which means that the number of images $l = 100$. Among the 10,000 query-image-clicks triples, the property values defined in Def. 2 are demonstrated in Table 2. The last column $MaxClicks$ recorded in Table 2 denotes the maximum click count among all the $ClickCount$ for a given query.

For these images, we extract seven features, i.e., $M = 7$, including: 225-dimensional block-wise color moments, 64-dimensional HSV color histogram, 144-dimensional color autocorrelogram, 128-dimensional wavelet texture, 75-dimensional edge distribution histogram, 7-dimensional face features, and 2000-dimensional scale-invariant feature transform (SIFT) descriptor. It is noteworthy that in our experiments SIFT descriptor [16] with a Difference of Gaussian (DoG) interest point detector is employed to extract visual patterns of images. Then, K-means is further used to cluster the similar patches into "visual words," and Bag-of-Word (BoW) is used to represent each image. Empirically, the number of visual words is set to 2,000.

In the following parts, we use CARSVM-CM, CARSVM-HSV, CARSVM-AC, CARSVM-WT, CARSVM-EDH, CARSVM-FACE, and CARSVM-SIFT to denote the methods that only use the seven modalities based on the click-based adapting ranking SVM (CARSVM), respectively. Note that CARSVM is also proposed in this paper.

In our experiments, each query-image pair is labeled carefully by annotators on a scale of 0 to 2: 0–"irrelevant," 1–"fair," and 2–"relevant." Before labeling, we first let annotators figure out the meaning of the issued tail query and check some related web documents to determine user search intent. By understanding user intent as much as possible, the relevance scores of images are more convincing relatively. We adopt the Normalized Discounted Cumulative Gain (NDCG) [10] to measure performance, which is widely used in information retrieval when there are more than two relevance levels. Given a ranked list, the NDCG at the depth p is defined as

$$\text{NDCG}@p = Z_p \sum_{i=1}^{p} \frac{2^{r^i} - 1}{\log(1+i)}, \qquad (16)$$

where r^i is relevance score of the ith image, and Z_p is a normalization constant to guarantee that a perfect ranking's $\text{NDCG}@p$ is equal to 1.

5.2 Evaluations of Re-ranking

We first compare our proposed approach, called click-wise multimodal fusion (CWMF), with methods that use only an individual modality, method "early fusion" and method "late fusion" to verify the effectiveness of multimodal fusion in our approach. Methods that use only an individual modality are all based on the click-based adapting ranking SVM (CARSVM), which means the click-wise-based pairs selection parameter δ and the Hinge Loss adapting parameter λ are all concerned. The "early fusion" refers to the method that concentrates all the seven modalities into a long vector and leverages it to perform click-wise learning to re-rank. In the "late fusion," we leverage seven click-based adapting ranking SVM classifiers, each of which uses the data of one of the seven features respectively, and we linearly fuse the re-ranking results of these classifiers, in which the fusion weights are tuned for maximum performance. For simplifying notations, we represent "early fusion" and "late fusion" based on the click-based adapting ranking SVM as EarlyCARSVM and LateCARSVM severally.

For our proposed method CWMF, we first assign a kernel function to each modality accordingly. In our experiments, linear kernel is designated to each modality for its efficiency, i.e., $K_m(x_i, x_j) = x_{m,i}^{\mathrm{T}} x_{m,j}$, where $m = 1, 2, ..., M$. Then, after tuning the parameters C and δ to obtain the optimal performance, we set $C = 0.5$ and $\delta = 5$ for our dataset. Detailed analysis about parameter C and δ will be introduced in Sect. 5.3. Moreover, we take the duality gap, which is equal to 0.01, as the stopping criterion.

Figure 5 illustrates the average measurements from NDCG@5 to NDCG@100 using the above methods. Here we also illustrate the NDCG measurements of the initial ranked lists and regard them as BASELINE results. From Fig. 5, we can find that using only an individual modality can hardly obtain the maximum improvement compared with the baseline. The performance of different single modalities, some of which even degrades to a certain extent, varies at different depths of NDCG. This phenomenon is understandable, because the effect of an individual modality depends on different queries and it is hard to determine its usefulness to a given query. But the "uncertain" single modality is still useful by integrating it with other features to work together. Combining multiple modalities, the NDCG values of EarlyCARSVM and LateCARSVM are relatively larger than those of methods using an individual modality, which demonstrate the effectiveness of the introduction of multiple modalities. Nevertheless, our proposed approach click-wise multimodal fusion achieves the maximum improvements and obviously outperforms other methods at different depths of NDCG. Thus, we can draw a conclusion that the multimodal fusion scheme of our approach can help determine the modality importance and fuse multiple modalities adaptively to obtain ideal performance.

Then, we compare our proposed re-ranking approach with several existing ones, where the parameters are optimized to achieve the best possible performance, including:

- Random walk (RW) [7]. A representative self-re-ranking method which conducts random walk on an image graph where nodes are images and edges are weighted by image visual similarities.
- Pseudo-relevance feedback (PRF) [23]. PRF performs re-ranking as a classification problem assuming that top-ranked results are more relevant than the bottom-ranked results.
- Multimodal graph-based re-ranking (MGR) [22]. An effective re-ranking method which leverages the initial ranked list and explores the effects of multiple modalities in a multi-graph-based learning scheme.

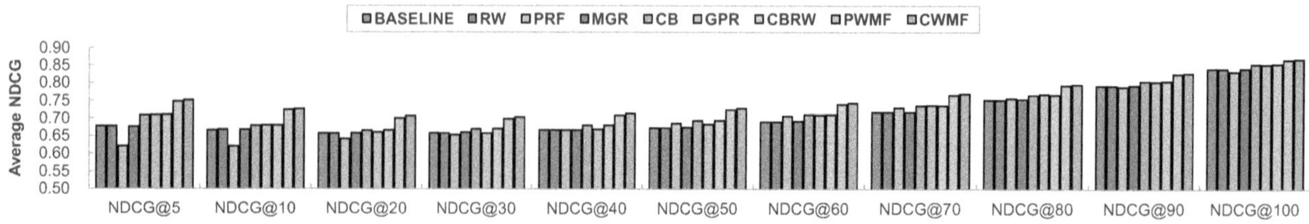

Figure 6: Comparison of re-ranking approaches in terms of NDCG.

- Click-boosting (CB). CB performs re-ranking by leveraging click-through data only, namely, CB re-ranks images according to their click counts in a descending order.
- Gaussian process regression (GPR) [9]. GPR first detects clicked images and performs dimensionality reduction on all the visual features. Then, a Gaussian process regressor is trained on the clicked images to predict the click counts of all images. The final re-ranking scores are calculated based on the predicted click counts and the initial ranking scores.
- Click-boosting random walk (CBRW) [26]. A two-step re-ranking method which is a combination of using click-through data and detecting visual recurrent patterns for image search re-ranking.
- Pair-wise multimodal fusion (PWMF). PWMF is the same as CWMF in dealing with multiple modalities and the selection of click-wise-based image pairs. The only difference is that the Hinge Loss adapting parameter λ is not concerned in PWMF, indicating that PWMF is based on the original ranking SVM with multimodal fusion. Note that PWMF is a deformation of CWMF and also proposed in this paper.

Figure 6 shows the overall performance of different re-ranking approaches in our tail queries dataset. On the whole, our proposed click-wise multimodal fusion (CWMF) outperforms other methods, and the improvements are consistent and stable at different depths of NDCG. Using our re-ranking approach the NDCG values are improved significantly. For example, the NDCG@5 is improved by 10.88% from the baseline of 0.6775 to 0.7512, and NDCG@10 is boosted by 9.12% from 0.6658 to 0.7265 on the entire dataset.

It is noted that the performance of PRF has a serious degradation from NDCG@5 and NDCG@10, respectively. This is mainly because the assumption behind PRF, i.e., top ranked images are typically relevant in response to a given query, is not suitable for tail queries whose baseline results are often much lower than head queries'. Similarly, the re-ranking scores of images by RW and MGR are partially related to the initial ranked lists. Even by tuning the tradeoff parameters, they still obtain weak improvements over the baseline results, which demonstrates the difficulty for tail queries to detect recurrent patterns via "similarity" mining. Compared with RW, PRF and MGR, we can see that CB performs better than BASELINE at all NDCG levels, indicating that the click-through data of tail queries can provide helpful information on user feedback for image re-ranking. Leveraging click counts of images, GPR and CBRW obtain better performance than CB's, however, the improvements are inconspicuous. The reasons, for GPR, possibly originate from the lack of training clicked images for Gaussian process regression and the reliance on the initial ranking scores. CBRW is due to the same reason as RW's. The fact that PWMF and CWMF achieve significant improvements proves the highly usefulness of click-wise information from image pairs. Compared with CWMF, PWMF does not take the problem of punishing the misclassified image pairs into consideration, i.e., there is no Hinge loss adapting parameter λ in PWMF. As we can see from Fig. 6, PWMF gets a comparatively poor performance, which exactly demonstrates the availability and superiority of the click-based adapting ranking SVM used in CWMF.

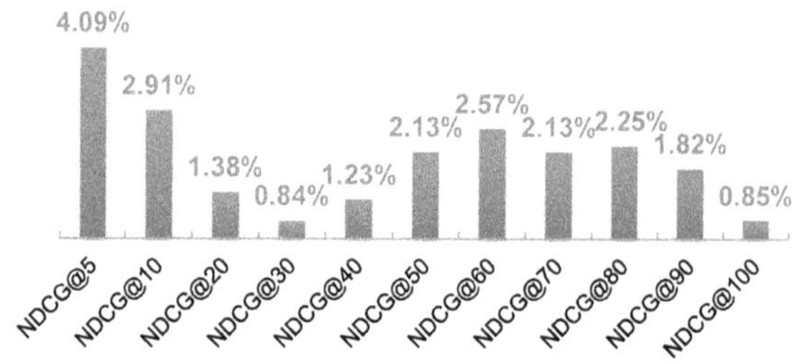

Figure 7: Improvements using click-wise multimodal fusion compared with the baseline in terms of NDCG for 50 head queries.

Overall, by simultaneously leveraging multimodal fusion and click-based adaption, our proposed approach CWMF can significantly improve the performance of image search for tail queries. To the best of our knowledge, this is the first attempt to use the difference values of clicks (click-wise information) and multiple modalities at the same time for image search re-ranking of tail queries.

As click-wise multimodal fusion re-ranking proved significantly effective for tail queries, it is worth noting that CWMF is general and can be applied to head queries. We randomly select 50 queries with more than 100 query frequency in the one-week query log, which means that these queries belong to the "HEAD" region in Fig. 2. Due to the space limitation, for the 50 head queries, we only demonstrate the improvements using our proposed approach compared with the baseline results from NDCG@5 to NDCG@100 in Fig. 7. The improvements can be observed at all levels of NDCG, though the improvements are comparatively small because of the good initial search performance of head queries already obtained by search engines.

5.3 Parameter Analysis

We adopt five-fold cross validation to test the sensitivity of parameters δ and C in our proposed approach. We first set C to 0.5 and vary δ from 1 to 30 with an interval of 5. Figure 8(a) demonstrates the performance curve with various δ. We can find that though higher than the baseline's, the NDCG degrades when $\delta = 1$ or as δ gets larger compared with $\delta = 5$. It is understandable that when $\delta = 1$ our approach cannot obtain the best performance, because it is hard to tell the relevance relation between two images from a pair with only one click difference. For the larger δ, since the click counts of images are comparatively small for tail queries, δ should not go too far to select the possible click-wise-based pairs. If there is no pair matching the filter criterion, in our experiments, we relax the filter criterion and define the set of click-wise-based pairs as $\mathcal{P} \triangleq \{(i,j)|(c_i - c_j) > 0\}$. However, the Hinge Loss adapting parameter λ is not concerned for pairs in this $\mathcal{P}$. Thus,

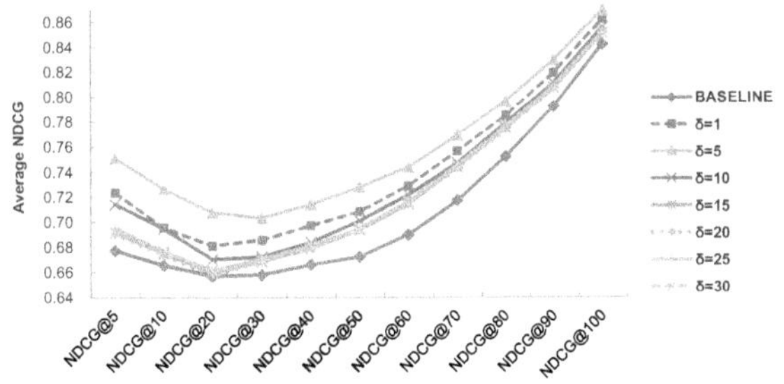

(a) Re-ranking performance variation with various δ.

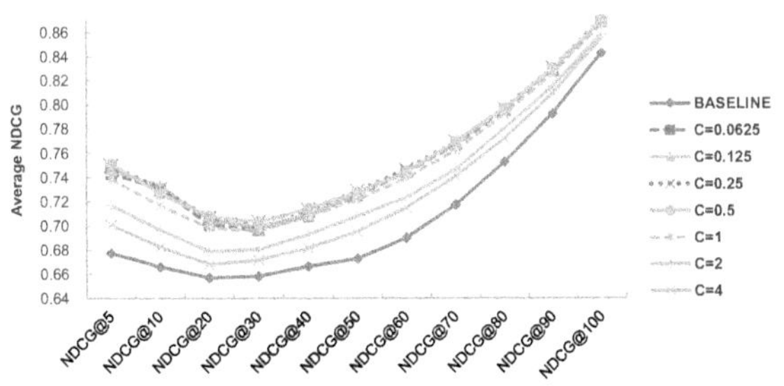

(b) Re-ranking performance variation with various C.

Figure 8: The sensitivity of re-ranking parameters.

the NDCG drops relatively due to the lack of click-wise-based pairs or the influence of λ. We then set δ to 5 and vary C from 0.0625 (2^{-3}) to 32 (2^5). Figure 8(b) demonstrates the performance curve with various C. We can see that the performance of our approach will not significantly degrade when C varies in a certain range.

5.4 Complexity Analysis

Since our proposed CWMF is query-dependent and computed by an approximate optimal solution through an iterative strategy, its complexity is mainly determined by the number of click-wise-based pairs, the ranking SVM solver, the reduced gradient algorithm and the iterations controlled by the terminated criterion. Take the 100 tail queries used in our experiments for example, i.e., each query corresponds to 100 images to be re-ranked by seven modalities, our approach takes 1.20 seconds on average for a given query on a regular PC (Intel quad-core 3.30GHz CPU and 8GB RAM) to complete the entire re-ranking process. To obtain satisfying results for tail queries, there is a tradeoff between the performance and the computation time using our approach. We will seek to reduce the time complexity in our consequent work.

5.5 Examples of Tail Query Re-ranking

To further verify the effectiveness of our proposed approach, in this section, we show some specific examples of tail queries. As mentioned in Sect. 5.2, most existing re-ranking approaches cannot be scaled well to tail queries, thus, in Fig. 9 we show the initial ranked list and the re-ranked list using our proposed click-wise multimodal fusion re-ranking of three typical tail queries severally.

For instance, "pewdiepie" is an online alias of a Swedish video game commentator on YouTube. Game fans may issue this query for checking on what "pewdiepie" looks like, however, we can find that there are only three "real" faces from the top 10 images returned by a search engine. Through mining the click-wise information and multiple modalities, our re-ranking approach achieves excellently satisfying results. It is worth mentioning that all the top 10 images in the re-ranked list of "pewdiepie" are portraits of himself and comply with user search intent.

6. CONCLUSIONS

In the paper, we have studied the problem of image search re-ranking for tail queries, which is often overlooked in the research communities. We have proposed a novel re-ranking approach based on the assumptions that *images with more clicks are more relevant to the given query than the ones with no or relatively less clicks* and *the effects of different visual modalities to re-rank images are query-dependent*. Our proposed approach can not only fully explore the effects of multiple visual modalities by adaptively predicting the query-dependent fusion weights, but also effectively expand training data by learning relevant information from click-wise-based image pairs. The experiments conducted on a real-world dataset demonstrate that different modalities, though the local feature SIFT is always assigned a high fusion weight, can incorporate with each other to improve search performance in a query-dependent way. For instance, a proper linear fusion of face feature and SIFT learnt by our approach is proved effective for improving the search performance of queries about characters, such as "pewdiepie" ($d_{FACE} = 0.1849, d_{SIFT} = 0.8151$). As mentioned in Sect. 5.1, there are two types of tail queries: one is from region "TAIL-A" in Fig. 2 and the other is from "TAIL-B." Using our proposed approach, the NDCG@5 of queries from "TAIL-A" is improved by 10.96% compared with the initial search results, and the corresponding improvement of queries from "TAIL-B" is 10.64%. This further shows the superiority of relevant information mined from click-wise-based image pairs used in our approach.

Intuitively, the click data provided by an individual user are believed to be possibly biased, yet from the experimental results of queries in "TAIL-B," they can be used as a useful indicator of relevance feedback. Thus, we believe that using click-through data for personal search is an interesting research topic in the future.

7. ACKNOWLEDGMENTS

This work was performed when the first author Xiaopeng Yang was visiting Microsoft Research as a research intern. In addition, this work was partially supported by National High Technology Research and Development Program of China (2014AA015202), the National Key Technology Research and Development Program of China (2012BAH39B02), the National Natural Science Foundation of China (61173054, 61172153), the Beijing New Star Project on Science & Technology (2007B071).

8. REFERENCES

[1] R. Baeza-Yates and A. Tiberi. Extracting semantic relations from query logs. *ACM SIGKDD*, pages 76–85, 2007.

[2] Y. Cao, J. Xu, T.-Y. Liu, H. Li, Y. Huang, and H.-W. Hon. Adapting ranking SVM to document retrieval. *ACM SIGIR*, pages 186–193, 2006.

[3] B. Carterette and R. Jones. Evaluating search engines by modeling the relationship between relevance and clicks. *Advances in Neural Information Processing Systems*, 2007.

[4] O. Chapelle and Y. Zhang. A dynamic bayesian network click model for web search ranking. *WWW*, pages 1–10, 2009.

[5] G. Dupret and C. Liao. A model to estimate intrinsic document relevance from the clickthrough logs of a web search engine. *ACM WSDM*, pages 181–190, 2010.

[6] A. G. Hauptmann, W.-H. Lin, R. Yan, J. Yang, and M.-Y. Chen. Extreme video retrieval: Joint maximization of human and computer performance. *ACM Multimedia*, pages 385–393, 2006.

(a) "pewdiepie" (81, 57)

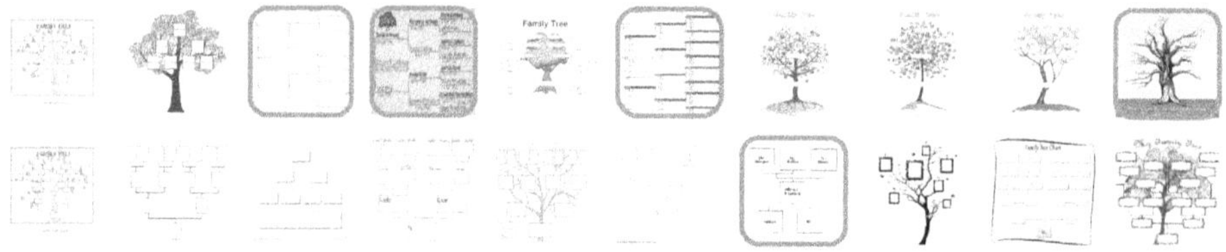

(b) "blank family tree" (8, 20)

(c) "old engine" (1, 28)

Figure 9: The initial ranked list and the re-ranked list using our proposed approach for specific tail queries. First row of each tail query corresponds to the initial ranked list, and the second row corresponds to the re-ranked list using click-wise multimodal fusion. The red rectangles mark irrelevant images. The brackets next to the query show the corresponding query frequency and the number of clicked images during one week, respectively [best viewed in color].

[7] W. H. Hsu, L. S. Kennedy, and S.-F. Chang. Video search reranking through random walk over document-level context graph. *ACM Multimedia*, pages 971–980, 2007.

[8] X.-S. Hua, L. Yang, J. Wang, J. Wang, M. Ye, K. Wang, Y. Rui, and J. Li. Clickage: Towards bridging semantic and intent gaps via mining click logs of search engines. *ACM Multimedia*, pages 243–252, 2013.

[9] V. Jain and M. Varma. Learning to rerank: Query-dependent image reranking using click data. *WWW*, pages 277–286, 2011.

[10] K. Järvelin and J. Kekäläinen. IR evaluation methods for retrieving highly relevant documents. *ACM SIGIR*, pages 41–48, 2000.

[11] T. Joachims. Optimizing search engines using clickthrough data. *ACM SIGKDD*, pages 133–142, 2002.

[12] T. Joachims, L. Granka, and B. Pan. Accurately interpreting clickthrough data as implicit feedback. *ACM SIGIR*, pages 154–161, 2005.

[13] L. S. Kennedy, A. P. Natsev, and S. Chang. Automatic discovery of query-class-dependent models for multimodal search. *ACM Multimedia*, pages 882–891, 2005.

[14] T.-M. Kuo, C.-P. Lee, and C.-J. Lin. Large-scale kernel rankSVM. *SIAM International Conference on Data Mining*, pages 812–820, 2014.

[15] Y. Liu, T. Mei, and X.-S. Hua. CrowdReranking: Exploring multiple search engines for visual search reranking. *ACM SIGIR*, pages 500–507, 2009.

[16] D. G. Lowe. Object recognition from local scale-invariant features. *IEEE ICCV*, pages 1150–1157, 1999.

[17] T. Mei, Y. Rui, S. Li, and Q. Tian. Multimedia search reranking: A literature survey. *ACM Computing Surveys*, 46(38), 2014.

[18] A. Rakotomamonjy, F. R. Bach, S. Canu, and Y. Grandvalet. SimpleMKL. *Journal of Machine Learning Research*, 9:2491–2521, 2008.

[19] C. G. M. Snoek, K. van de Sande, O. de Rooij, and *et al.* The mediamill TRECVID 2008 semantic video search engine. *NIST TRECVID Workshop*, 2008.

[20] C. G. M. Snoek, M. Worring, and A. W. M. Smeulders. Early versus late fusion in semantic video analysis. *ACM Multimedia*, pages 399–402, 2005.

[21] X. Tian, D. Tao, X.-S. Hua, and X. Wu. Active reranking for web image search. *IEEE Trans. on Image Processing*, 19(3):805–820, 2010.

[22] M. Wang, H. Li, D. Tao, K. Lu, and X. Wu. Multimodal graph-based reranking for web image search. *IEEE Trans. on Image Processing*, 21(11):4649–4661, 2012.

[23] R. Yan and A. Hauptmann. Query expansion using probabilistic local feedback with application to multimedia retrieval. *ACM CIKM*, pages 361–370, 2007.

[24] L. Yang and A. Hanjalic. Supervised reranking for web image search. *ACM Multimedia*, pages 183–192, 2010.

[25] X. Yang, Y. Zhang, T. Yao, C.-W. Ngo, and T. Mei. Click-boosting multi-modality graph-based reranking for image search. *Multimedia Systems*, May 2014.

[26] X. Yang, Y. Zhang, T. Yao, Z.-J. Zha, and C.-W. Ngo. Click-boosting random walk for image search reranking. *ACM ICIMCS*, pages 1–6, 2013.

[27] T. Yao, C.-W. Ngo, and T. Mei. Circular reranking for visual search. *IEEE Trans. on Image Processing*, 22(4):1644–1655, 2013.

[28] Z.-J. Zha, L. Yang, T. Mei, M. Wang, and Z. Wang. Visual query suggestion. *ACM Multimedia*, pages 15–24, 2009.

Easy Samples First: Self-paced Reranking for Zero-Example Multimedia Search

Lu Jiang[1], Deyu Meng[2], Teruko Mitamura[1], Alexander G. Hauptmann[1]
[1] School of Computer Science, Carnegie Mellon University
[2] School of Mathematics and Statistics, Xi'an Jiaotong University
{lujiang, teruko, alex}@cs.cmu.edu, dymeng@mail.xjtu.edu.cn

ABSTRACT

Reranking has been a focal technique in multimedia retrieval due to its efficacy in improving initial retrieval results. Current reranking methods, however, mainly rely on the heuristic weighting. In this paper, we propose a novel reranking approach called Self-Paced Reranking (SPaR) for multimodal data. As its name suggests, SPaR utilizes samples from easy to more complex ones in a self-paced fashion. SPaR is special in that it has a concise mathematical objective to optimize and useful properties that can be theoretically verified. It on one hand offers a unified framework providing theoretical justifications for current reranking methods, and on the other hand generates a spectrum of new reranking schemes. This paper also advances the state-of-the-art self-paced learning research which potentially benefits applications in other fields. Experimental results validate the efficacy and the efficiency of the proposed method on both image and video search tasks. Notably, SPaR achieves by far the best result on the challenging TRECVID multimedia event search task.

Categories and Subject Descriptors

H.3.3 [**Information Search and Retrieval**]: Retrieval Models; I.2.6 [**Artificial Intelligence**]: Learning

General Terms

Algorithms, Measurement, Experimentation

Keywords

Multimodal Reranking; Multimedia Event Detection; Self-paced Learning; Zero-Example Search; Content-based Search

1. INTRODUCTION

In the era where multimedia contents are being produced and shared in an unprecedented pace, multimedia search has become increasingly crucial in providing quality service for users to issue semantic queries, e.g. searching for visual objects or events. Reranking is a focal technique to improve the quality of search results [3]. The intuition is that the initial ranked result brought by the query is noisy [33], and can be refined by the multimodal information residing in the retrieved videos/images. For example, in image search the reranking is performed based on the results of text-based search, in which the initial results are retrieved by matching images' surrounding texts [17, 39]. Studies show that reranking methods can improve the Mean Average Precision (MAP) of the initial result by a relative 17% on a representative dataset [32, 26].

This observation is confirmed by a recent study on multimodal content-based search [13], in which the reranking is performed on multimodal content features extracted from the video content, and no textual metadata, such as the title, is available. Reranking by multimodal content-based search is still an understudied problem. To advance the new technologies in this direction, NIST initiated a task called Multimedia Event Detection (MED) 0Ex (Zero-Example) [7, 13, 4] in TRECVID 2013. The task is to detect the occurrence of a main event occurring in a video clip, e.g. "Birthday party", in the absence of example videos, which resembles a real-world search scenario where example videos are often unavailable. It is more challenging than reranking by text-based search in image search, since the content features not only come from multiple modalities but also much more noisy. Nevertheless, the method in [13] still manages to yield a 158% relative MAP improvement over the plain retrieval result. Due to the significant improvement, NIST includes reranking as an official condition in TRECVID 2014[1].

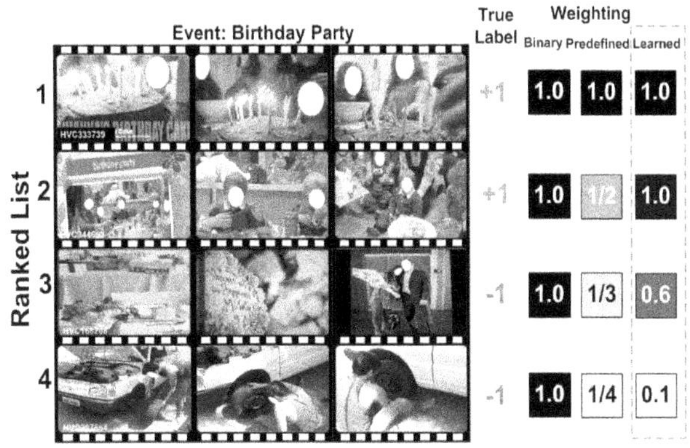

Figure 1: Comparison of binary, predefined and learned weights on the event "Birthday Party". All videos are used as positive in reranking. Learned weights are learned by the proposed method.

[1] See FullSysPRF www-nlpir.nist.gov/projects/tv2014/tv2014.html

MM'14, November 3–7, 2014, Orlando, Florida, USA.

http://dx.doi.org/10.1145/2647868.2654918.

An important step in reranking is to assign weights to videos, based on which the reranking is carried out. The main strategy in current reranking methods is to assign binary (or predefined) weights to videos at different rank positions. These weighting schemes are simple to implement, yet may lead to suboptimal solutions, as demonstrated in our experiments. For example, the reranking methods in [38, 13, 8] assume that top-ranked videos are of equal importance (binary weights). The fact is that, however, videos ranked higher are generally more accurate, and thus more "important", than those ranked lower. On the other hand, the predefined weights [9] are derived independently of reranking models, and thus may not faithfully reflect the latent importance. Fig. 1 illustrates a ranked list of "Birthday Party" videos, where all videos are used as positive in reranking; the top two are true positive; the third video is a negative but closely related video on wedding shower as they share key concepts such as "gift", "cake" and "cheering"; the fourth video is completely unrelated. As illustrated, neither binary nor predefined weights reflect the latent importance residing in the videos. Furthermore, since the binary and predefined weights are designed based on empirical experience lacking of theoretical justifications, it is unclear where, or even whether reranking with these weights converges.

An ideal reranking method would assign appropriate weights to videos in a theoretically sound manner. To this end, we propose a method called Self-Paced Reranking (SPaR) which assigns weights adaptively in a self-paced fashion. The method is established on the self-paced learning theory [1, 19]. The theory is inspired by the learning process of humans and animals, where samples are not presented randomly but organized in a meaningful order which illustrates from easy to gradually more complex ones [1]. In the context of the reranking problem, the easy samples are the top-ranked videos that have smaller loss. As opposed to utilizing all samples to learn a model simultaneously, the proposed model is learned gradually from easy to more complex samples. As the name "self-paced" suggests, in every iteration, SPaR examines the "easiness" of each sample based on what it has already learned, and adaptively determines their weights to be used in the subsequent iterations.

SPaR represents a general method of addressing multimodal pseudo relevance feedback for 0Ex video search. Compared with existing reranking methods, SPaR has the following three benefits. First, it is established on a solid theory, and of useful properties that can be theoretically verified. For example, SPaR has a concise mathematical objective to optimize, and its convergence property can be theoretically proved in Theorem 1. Besides, since the self-paced learning is expected to effectively converge to minima of quality [1, 19], SPaR inherently tends to find reasonably good solutions for reranking problems. The experimental results in Section 5 substantiate this hypothesis. Second, SPaR represents a general framework for reranking on multimodal data, which includes other methods, such as [38, 23, 13], as special cases (See Section 4.2). The connection is significant because once an existing method is modeled as a special case of SPaR, the optimization methods discussed in this paper become immediately applicable to analyze, and even solve the problem. Third, SPaR offers a compelling insight into reranking by multimodal content-based search [7, 13, 4], where the initial ranked lists are retrieved by content-based search. Although reranking may not be a novel idea, reranking by multimodal content-based search is clearly understudied and worthy of exploration, since existing studies mainly concentrate on reranking only by text-based search.

On the other hand, this paper also advances the state-of-the-art self-paced learning frontier. Existing self-paced learning algorithms adopt a simple binary weighting [1, 19] in order to obtain the global optimum for subproblems. We generalize it to real-valued weighting by introducing a spectrum of self-paced functions that preserve the global optimum (See Lemma 1 in Section 4.1). The proposed functions not only augment the choices of weighting schemes in reranking, but also may benefit applications in other fields that need to discriminate samples' importance.

The experimental results show promising results on two challenging datasets. On the TRECVID content-based search task MED 0Ex, SPaR improves the plain retrieval baseline by a relative 230% in terms of the MAP. To the best of our knowledge, the reported MAP is by far the best result on this TRECVID task. In addition, SPaR also outperforms the state-of-the-art reranking methods on an image reranking dataset called Web Query. In summary, the contribution of this paper is fourfold:

- We propose a novel reranking method that has a solid theoretical background and theoretically verifiable properties.
- The proposed method provides a general reranking framework by multimodal content-based search, which includes existing methods as special cases.
- We discuss a spectrum of self-paced functions that substantially augment the choices of self-paced learning. Our work is potentially beneficial to self-paced learning applications that need to discriminate samples.
- The proposed method achieves by far the best result on the TRECVID multimedia event search.

2. RELATED WORK

Existing reranking methods are mainly performed by text-based search, in which the initial ranked list is retrieved by text/keyword matching [39, 33]. In terms of the types of the reranking model, these methods can be categorized into Classification, Clustering, Graph and LETOR (LEarning-TO-Rank) based reranking. In Classification-based reranking [38], a classifier is trained upon the pseudo label set, and then tested on retrieved videos to obtain a reranked list. Similarly, in LETOR-based reranking [6] instead of a binary classifier, a ranking function is learned by the pairwise [23] or list-wise [33, 32] RankSVM. In Clustering-based reranking [9], the retrieved videos are aggregated into clusters, and the clusters' conditional probabilities of the pseudo samples are used to obtain a reranked list. The role of clustering is to reduce the noise in the initial reranking. In Graph-based reranking [10, 27], the graph of retrieved samples needs to be first constructed, on which the initial ranking scores are propagated by collective classification methods such as Random Walk [12], under the assumption that visually similar videos usually have similar ranks. Generally, reranking methods, including the above methods, are unsupervised methods, but there also exist some studies on supervised reranking [17, 39].

Reranking by multimodal content-based search is still an understudied problem. To advance the new technologies in this direction, NIST initiated a content-based search task

1: $t = 0$; //Iteration zero
2: Choose starting values for $\mathbf{y}, \mathbf{v}$;
3: **while** $t \leq$ max iteration **do**
4: $\Theta_1^{(t+1)}, ..., \Theta_m^{(t+1)} = \arg\max \mathbb{E}_{\mathbf{y},\mathbf{v}}(\Theta_1^{(t)}, ..., \Theta_m^{(t)}; C)$;
5: $\mathbf{y}^{(t+1)}, \mathbf{v}^{(t+1)} = \arg\max \mathbb{E}_{\Theta}(\mathbf{y}^{(t)}, \mathbf{v}^{(t)}; k)$;
6: **if** t is small **then** increase $1/k$;
7: **end while**
8: **return** $[v_1 y_1, \cdots, v_n y_n]^T$;

Algorithm 1: Reranking in Optimization Perspective.

1: $t = 0$; //Iteration zero
2: Choose the initial pseudo labels and weights;
3: **while** $t \leq$ max iteration **do**
4: Train a reranking model on the fixed labels and weights;
5: Update the pseudo labels and weights;
6: **if** t is small **then** add more pseudo positives;
7: **end while**
8: **return** The list of samples after reranking;

Algorithm 2: Reranking in Conventional Perspective.

called MED 0Ex (Zero-Example) in TRECVID 2013. Previously, research is mainly concentrated on the event search with 10 or 100 exemplar videos [24, 40, 12, 25]. Only a few methods have been proposed to tackle the 0Ex search problem [7, 13, 4]. A closely related work is [13], in which the authors discussed a reranking method named MMPRF, which yields significant improvements over the plain retrieval result. As we see in Section 4.2, MMPRF is a special case of the proposed method that only uses the binary weighting.

Self-paced (or curriculum) learning [19, 1] is a recently proposed theory, inspired by the teaching of students, where easy concepts are taught before complex ones. The idea is to learn the model gradually from easy to complex examples iteratively in a self-paced fashion. This theory has been successfully applied to various applications, including domain adaptation [30], dictionary learning [31], segmentation [20], tracking [29], etc. Existing methods all adopt a simple binary weighting to obtain the global optimum for subproblems. We generalize it to real-valued weighting that still preserves the global optimum, which is potentially conducive for self-paced learning applications in other fields.

3. SELF-PACED RERANKING

3.1 Objective Function

The proposed Self-paced Reranking is a general reranking framework for multimedia search, which is inherently performed using features from multiple modalities. Given a dataset of n videos with features extracted from m modalities, let $\mathbf{x}_{ij}$ denote the feature of the ith sample from the jth modalities, e.g., $\mathbf{x}_{i1}, \mathbf{x}_{i2}, \mathbf{x}_{i3}$ can be the visual, acoustic and optical character feature vectors extracted from different channels of the ith video. $y_i \in \{-1, 1\}$ is the *pseudo label* for the ith video whose values are assumed since the true labels are unknown to reranking methods. The kernel SVM is used to illustrate the algorithm due to its robustness and decent performance in reranking [21, 8]. We will discuss how to generalize it to other models in Section 4.2. Let $\Theta_j = \{\mathbf{w}_j, b_j\}$ denote the classifier parameters for the jth modality, which includes a coefficient vector $\mathbf{w}_j$ and a bias term b_j. Let $\mathbf{v} = [v_1, ..., v_n]^T$ denote the weighting parameters for all samples. Inspired by the self-paced learning [19], supposed n is the total number of samples and m is the total number of modalities, the objective function $\mathbb{E}$ can be formulated as:

$$\begin{aligned} &\min_{\Theta_1,...,\Theta_m,\mathbf{y},\mathbf{v}} \mathbb{E}(\Theta_1, ..., \Theta_m, \mathbf{v}, \mathbf{y}; C, k) = \\ &\min_{\substack{\mathbf{y},\mathbf{v},\mathbf{w}_1,...,\mathbf{w}_m, \\ b_1,...,b_m,\{\ell_{ij}\}}} \sum_{j=1}^{m} \frac{1}{2}\|\mathbf{w}_j\|_2^2 + C\sum_{i=1}^{n}\sum_{j=1}^{m} v_i \ell_{ij} + mf(\mathbf{v}; k) \\ &\text{s.t. } \forall i, \forall j, y_i(\mathbf{w}_j^T \phi(\mathbf{x}_{ij}) + b_j) \geq 1 - \ell_{ij}, \ell_{ij} \geq 0 \\ &\qquad \mathbf{y} \in \{-1, +1\}^n, \mathbf{v} \in [0, 1]^n, \end{aligned} \tag{1}$$

where ℓ_{ij} is the standard hinge loss, calculated from:

$$\ell_{ij} = \max\{0, 1 - y_i \cdot (\mathbf{w}_j^T \phi(\mathbf{x}_{ij}) + b_j)\}. \tag{2}$$

$\phi(\cdot)$ is a feature mapping function to obtain non-linear decision boundaries. C ($C > 0$) is the standard regularization parameter trading off the hinge loss and the margin. $\sum_{j=1}^{m} v_i \ell_{ij}$ represents the weighted loss of the ith sample. The weight v_i reflects the sample's importance, and when $v_i = 0$, the loss incurred by the ith sample is always zero, i.e. it will be unselected in the training. In the conventional SVM, all samples share the equal weight 1.

$f(\mathbf{v}; k)$ is a regularization term that specifies how the samples are selected and how their weights are calculated. It is called the self-paced function as it determines the learning pace, controlled by the parameter k ($k > 0$), at which the model learns new samples. There is an m in front of $f(\mathbf{v}; k)$ as $\sum_{j=1}^{m} f(\mathbf{v}; k) = mf(\mathbf{v}; k)$. $f(\mathbf{v}; k)$ can be defined in various forms in terms of the learning pace, which will be discussed in Section 3.3. The objective is subjected to two sets of constraints: the first set of constraints in Eq. (1) is the soft margin constraint inherited from the conventional SVM. The second constraints in Eq. (1) define the domains of pseudo labels and their weights, respectively.

Eq. (1) turns out to be difficult to optimize directly due to its non-convexity and complicated constraints. However, it can be effectively optimized by Cyclic Coordinate Method (CCM) [5]. CCM is an iterative method for non-convex optimization, in which the variables are divided into a set of disjoint blocks, in this case two blocks, i.e. classifier parameters $\Theta_1, ..., \Theta_m$, and pseudo labels $\mathbf{y}$ and weights $\mathbf{v}$. In each iteration, a block of variables can be optimized while keeping the other block fixed. Suppose $\mathbb{E}_{\Theta}$ represents the objective with the fixed block $\Theta_1, ..., \Theta_m$, and $\mathbb{E}_{\mathbf{y},\mathbf{v}}$ represents the objective with the fixed block $\mathbf{y}$ and $\mathbf{v}$. Eq. (1) can be solved by Alg. 1, which takes the input of the initial ranked list, and outputs the reranked list. In Step 2, it initializes the starting values for the pseudo labels and weights. Then it optimizes Eq. (1) iteratively via Step 4 and 5, until the convergence is reached.

Alg. 1 provides a theoretical justification for reranking from the perspective of optimization. Alg. 2 lists general steps for reranking that have one-to-one correspondence with the steps in Alg. 1. The two algorithms present the same methodology from two perspectives. For example, optimizing $\Theta_1, ..., \Theta_m$ can be interpreted as training a reranking model. In the first few iterations, Alg. 1 gradually increases the $1/k$ to control the learning pace, which, correspondingly, translates to adding more pseudo positives, e.g. top 10 [13] in training reranking models.

Alg. 1 and 2 offer complementary insights. Alg. 1 theoretically justifies Alg. 2 on the convergence and the decrease of objective. On the other hand, the empirical experience from studying Alg. 2 offers valuable advices on how to set starting values from the initial ranked lists, which is less concerned in the optimization perspective. According to Alg. 2, to use SPaR one needs to alternate between two steps: training reranking models and determining the pseudo samples and their weights for the subsequent iteration. We will discuss how to optimize $\mathbb{E}_{\mathbf{y},\mathbf{v}}$ (training reranking models on pseudo samples) in Section 3.2, and how to optimize $\mathbb{E}_{\Theta}$ (selecting pseudo samples and their weights based on the current reranking model) in Section 3.2.

3.2 Learning with the Fixed Pseudo Labels and Weights

With the fixed $\mathbf{y}, \mathbf{v}$, Eq. (1) represents the sum of weighted hinge loss across all modalities, i.e,

$$\begin{aligned}&\min_{\Theta_1,...,\Theta_m} \mathbb{E}_{\mathbf{y},\mathbf{v}}(\Theta_1, ..., \Theta_m; C)\\ =& \min_{\mathbf{w}_1,...,\mathbf{w}_m,b_1,...,b_m,\{\ell_{ij}\}} \sum_{j=1}^{m} \frac{1}{2}\|\mathbf{w}_j\|_2^2 + C\sum_{i=1}^{n}\sum_{j=1}^{m} v_i\ell_{ij} \\ &\text{s.t. } \forall i, \forall j, y_i(\mathbf{w}_j^T\phi(\mathbf{x}_{ij}) + b_j) \geq 1 - \ell_{ij}, \ell_{ij} \geq 0.\end{aligned} \quad (3)$$

As mentioned, $v_i\ell_{ij}$ is the discounted hinge loss of the ith sample from the jth modality. Eq. (3) represents a non-conventional SVM as each sample is associated with a weight reflecting its importance. Eq. (3) is non-trivial to optimize directly due to its complex constraints. As a result, we introduce a method that finds the global optimum for Eq. (3). The objective of Eq. (3) can be decoupled, and each modality can be optimized independently. Now consider the jth modality ($j = 1, ..., m$). We introduce Lagrange multipliers λ and α, and define the Lagrangian of the problem as:

$$\begin{aligned}\Lambda(\mathbf{w}_j, b_j, \alpha, \lambda) =& \frac{1}{2}\|\mathbf{w}_j\|_2^2 + C\sum_{i=1}^{n} v_i\ell_{ij}\\ &+\sum_{i=1}^{n}\alpha_{ij}(1 - \ell_{ij} - y_i\mathbf{w}_j^T\phi(\mathbf{x}_{ij}) - y_ib_j) + \sum_{i=1}^{n} -\lambda_{ij}\ell_{ij}\\ &\text{s.t. } \forall i, \alpha_{ij} \geq 0, \lambda_{ij} \geq 0.\end{aligned} \quad (4)$$

Since only the jth modality is considered, j is a fixed constant. The Slater's condition trivially holds for the Lagrangian, and thus the duality gap vanishes at the optimal solution. According to the KKT conditions [2], the following conditions must hold for its optimal solution:

$$\begin{aligned}&\frac{\nabla\Lambda}{\mathbf{w}_j} = \mathbf{w}_j - \sum_{i=1}^{n}\alpha_{ij}y_i\phi(\mathbf{x}_{ij}) = \mathbf{0}, \frac{\nabla\Lambda}{b_j} = \sum_{i=1}^{n}\alpha_{ij}y_i = 0,\\ &\forall i, \frac{\partial\Lambda}{\partial\ell_{ij}} = Cv_i - \alpha_{ij} - \lambda_{ij} = 0.\end{aligned} \quad (5)$$

According to Eq. (5), $\forall i, \lambda_{ij} = Cv_i - \alpha_{ij}$, and since Lagrange multipliers are nonnegative, we have $0 \leq \alpha_{ij} \leq Cv_i$. Substitute these inequations and Eq. (5) back into Eq. (4), the problem's dual form can be obtained by:

$$\begin{aligned}&\max_{\alpha}\sum_{i=1}^{n}\alpha_{ij} - \frac{1}{2}\sum_{i=1}^{n}\sum_{k=1}^{n}\alpha_{ij}\alpha_{kj}y_iy_k\kappa(\mathbf{x}_{ij}, \mathbf{x}_{kj}),\\ &\text{s.t. } \sum_{i=1}^{n} y_i\alpha_{ij} = 0, 0 \leq \alpha_{ij} \leq Cv_i,\end{aligned} \quad (6)$$

where $\kappa(\mathbf{x}_{ij}, \mathbf{x}_{kj}) = \phi(\mathbf{x}_{ij})^T\phi(\mathbf{x}_{kj})$ is the kernel function. Compared with the dual form of conventional SVMs, Eq. (6) imposes a sample-specific upper-bound on the support vector coefficient, which is the key in computing decision boundary. A sample's upper-bound is proportional to its weight, and therefore a sample with a smaller weight v_i is less influential as its support vector coefficient is bounded by a small value of Cv_i. Eq. (6) degenerates to the dual form of conventional SVMs when $\mathbf{v} = \mathbf{1}$. According to the Slater's condition, strong duality holds, and therefore Eq. (4) and Eq. (6) are equivalent problems. Since Eq. (6) is a quadratic programming problem in its dual form, there exists a plethora of algorithms/toolkits to solve it [2].

3.3 Learning with the Fixed Classification Parameters

With the fixed classification parameters $\Theta_1, ..., \Theta_m$, the objective function of Eq. (1) becomes:

$$\begin{aligned}&\min_{\mathbf{y},\mathbf{v}} \mathbb{E}_{\Theta}(\mathbf{y}, \mathbf{v}; k) = \min_{\mathbf{y},\mathbf{v}} C\sum_{i=1}^{n}\sum_{j=1}^{m} v_i\ell_{ij} + mf(\mathbf{v}; k)\\ &\text{s.t. } \mathbf{y} \in \{-1, +1\}^n, \mathbf{v} \in [0, 1]^n.\end{aligned} \quad (7)$$

The goal of Eq. (7) is to learn not only the pseudo labels $\mathbf{y}$ but also their weights $\mathbf{v}$. Learning $\mathbf{y}$ is easier as its optimal values are independent of $\mathbf{v}$. Therefore, we first optimize each pseudo label by:

$$y_i^* = \underset{y_i=\{+1,-1\}}{\arg\min}\ \mathbb{E}_{\Theta}(\mathbf{y}, \mathbf{v}) = \underset{y_i=\{+1,-1\}}{\arg\min}\ C\sum_{j=1}^{m}\ell_{ij}, \quad (8)$$

where y_i^* denotes the optimum for the ith pseudo label. Solving Eq. (8) is simple as all labels are independent with each others in the sum, and each label can only take binary values. Its global optimum can be efficiently obtained by enumerating each y_i. For n samples, we only need to enumerate $2n$ times.

Having found the optimal $\mathbf{y}$, the task switches to optimizing $\mathbf{v}$. $f(\mathbf{v}; k)$ is the self-paced function, and in [19], it is defined based on the l_1 norm of $\mathbf{v} \in [0, 1]^n$:

$$f(\mathbf{v}; k) = -\frac{1}{k}\|\mathbf{v}\|_1 = -\frac{1}{k}\sum_{i=1}^{n} v_i. \quad (9)$$

Substituting Eq. (9) back into Eq. (7), the optimal $\mathbf{v}^* = [v_1^*, ..., v_n^*]^T$ is then calculated from

$$v_i^* = \begin{cases} 1 & \frac{1}{m}\sum_{j=1}^{m} C\ell_{ij} < \frac{1}{k} \\ 0 & \frac{1}{m}\sum_{j=1}^{m} C\ell_{ij} \geq \frac{1}{k}. \end{cases} \quad (10)$$

The underlying intuition of the self-paced learning can be justified by the closed-form solution in Eq. (10). If a sample's average loss is less than a certain threshold, $1/k$ in this case, it will be selected, or otherwise unselected, as a training example. The parameter k controls the number of samples to be included in training. Physically, $1/k$ corresponds to the "age" of the model. When $1/k$ is small, only easy samples with small loss will be considered. As $1/k$ grows, more samples with larger loss will be gradually appended to train a "mature" reranking model.

According to Eq. (10), the variable $\mathbf{v}$ takes only binary values. This scheme is called Hard Weighting as a sample can be either selected ($v_i = 1$) or unselected ($v_i = 0$). Hard Weighting is less appropriate in our problem as it cannot discriminate the importance of samples (see Fig. 2). Correspondingly, Soft Weighting, which assigns real-valued weights, reflects the latent importance of samples in training more faithfully. The comparison is analogous to the hard/soft assignment in Bag-of-Words quantization, where an interest point can be assigned either to its closest cluster

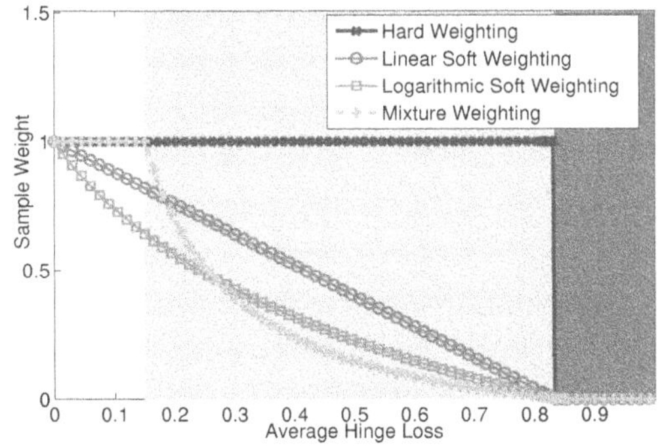

Figure 2: Comparison of different weighting schemes ($k = 1.2$, $k' = 6.7$). Hard Weighting assigns binary weights. The figure is divided into 3 colored regions, i.e. "white", "gray" and "black" in terms of the loss.

(hard), or to a number of clusters in its vicinity (soft). Generally, the soft assignment outperforms the hard assignment [15]. Before introducing specific soft weighting schemes, we first examine the general property of the self-paced function.

DEFINITION 1 (SELF-PACED FUNCTION). *Suppose that v denotes a weight variable, l is the loss, and k is the learning pace parameter. $f(v;k)$ is called a self-paced function, if*

1. *$f(v;k)$ is convex with respect to $v \in [0,1]$.*
2. *$v^*(k,l)$ is monotonically decreasing with respect to l, and it holds that $\lim_{l\to 0} v^*(k,l) = 1, \lim_{l\to\infty} v^*(k,l) = 0$.*
3. *$v^*(k,l)$ is monotonically increasing with respect to $1/k$, and it holds that $\lim_{k\to 0} v^*(k,l) = 1, \lim_{k\to\infty} v^*(k,l) = 0$.*

where $v^*(k,l) = \arg\min_{v\in[0,1]} vl + f(v;k)$.

According to [19], the self-paced function can be decomposed into $f(\mathbf{v};k) = \sum_{i=1}^{n} f(v_i;k)$. The three conditions in Definition 1 provide an axiom for self-paced learning. Condition 2 indicates that the model inclines to select easy samples (with smaller errors) in favor of complex samples (with larger errors). Condition 3 states that when the model "age" $1/k$ gets larger, it embarks on incorporating more, probably complex, samples to train a "mature" model. The limits in these constraints impose the upper bound and lower bound for v. The convexity in Condition 1 further ensures the model can find good solutions.

It is easy to verify that existing functions in self-paced learning [19, 30] follow Definition 1. Lemma 1 in Section 4.1 indicates the global optimum of Eq. (7) can be obtained for all functions following Definition 1. Attributed to this concise definition, a spectrum of rational self-paced learning functions can be formulated, and we discuss three of them, namely, linear, logarithmic and mixture weighting[2]. Note that the proposed functions may not be optimal as there is no single weighting scheme that can always work the best for all datasets. However, they evidently augment the choices of the soft weighting in the literature.

Linear soft weighting: Probably the most common approach is to linearly weight samples with respect to their loss. This weighting can be realized by the following self-paced function:

$$f(\mathbf{v};k) = \frac{1}{k}(\frac{1}{2}\|\mathbf{v}\|_2^2 - \sum_{i=1}^{n} v_i). \tag{11}$$

[2]Exponential weighting is missing in our discussion as it violates the convexity condition in Definition 1.

Eq. (11) is a convex function of $\mathbf{v}$, and thus the global minimum can be obtained at $\nabla_{\mathbf{v}}\mathbb{E}_{\Theta}(\mathbf{v}) = \mathbf{0}$. We have

$$\frac{\partial \mathbb{E}_{\Theta}}{\partial v_i} = \sum_{j=1}^{m} C\ell_{ij} + m(\frac{1}{k}v_i - \frac{1}{k}) = 0. \tag{12}$$

Considering $v_i \in [0,1]$, the close-formed optimal solution for v_i $(i = 1, 2, ..., n)$ can be written as:

$$v_i^* = \begin{cases} -k(\frac{1}{m}\sum_{j=1}^{m} C\ell_{ij}) + 1 & \frac{1}{m}\sum_{i=1}^{m} C\ell_{ij} < \frac{1}{k} \\ 0 & \frac{1}{m}\sum_{i=1}^{m} C\ell_{ij} \geq \frac{1}{k}. \end{cases} \tag{13}$$

Similar as the hard weighting in Eq. (10), the weight is 0 for the samples whose average loss is larger than $1/k$; Otherwise, the weight is linear to the loss (see Fig. 2).

Logarithmic soft weighting: The linear soft weighting penalizes the weight linearly in terms of the loss. A more conservative approach is to penalize the weight logarithmically, which can be achieved by the following function:

$$f(\mathbf{v};k) = \sum_{i=1}^{n}(\zeta v_i - \frac{\zeta^{v_i}}{\log\zeta}), \tag{14}$$

where $\zeta = (k-1)/k$ and $k > 1$. Its partial gradient equals:

$$\frac{\partial \mathbb{E}_{\Theta}}{\partial v_i} = \sum_{j=1}^{m} C\ell_{ij} + m(\zeta - \zeta^{v_i}) = 0. \tag{15}$$

We then can easily deduce:

$$\log(\frac{1}{m}\sum_{j=1}^{m} C\ell_{ij} + \zeta) = v_i \log\zeta. \tag{16}$$

The closed-form optimal solution for the Logarithmic soft weighting is then given by:

$$v_i^* = \begin{cases} \frac{1}{\log\zeta}\log(\frac{1}{m}\sum_{j=1}^{m} C\ell_{ij} + \zeta) & \frac{1}{m}\sum_{i=1}^{m} C\ell_{ij} < \frac{1}{k} \\ 0 & \frac{1}{m}\sum_{i=1}^{m} C\ell_{ij} \geq \frac{1}{k}. \end{cases} \tag{17}$$

Mixture weighting: Mixture weighting is a hybrid of the soft and the hard weighting. One can imagine that the loss range is divided into three colored areas, as illustrated in Fig. 2. If the loss is either too small ("white" area) or too large ("black" area), the hard weighting is applied. Otherwise, for the loss in the "gray" area, the soft weighting is applied. Compared with the soft weighting scheme, the mixture weighting tolerates small errors up to a certain point. To define the start of the "gray" area, an additional parameter k' is introduced. Formally,

$$f(\mathbf{v};k,k') = -\zeta\sum_{i=1}^{n}\log(v_i + \zeta k), \tag{18}$$

where $\zeta = \frac{1}{k'-k}$ and $k' > k > 0$. The partial gradient is:

$$\frac{\partial \mathbb{E}_{\Theta}}{\partial v_i} = \sum_{j=1}^{m} C\ell_{ij} - \frac{m\zeta}{v_i + k\zeta} = 0. \tag{19}$$

The closed-form optimal solution is given by:

$$v_i^* = \begin{cases} 1 & \frac{1}{m}\sum_{i=1}^{m} C\ell_{ij} \leq \frac{1}{k'} \\ 0 & \frac{1}{m}\sum_{i=1}^{m} C\ell_{ij} \geq \frac{1}{k} \\ \frac{m\zeta}{\sum_{i=1}^{m} C\ell_{ij}} - k\zeta & \text{otherwise.} \end{cases} \tag{20}$$

Eq. (20) tolerates any loss lower than $1/k'$ by assigning the full weight. It penalizes the weight by the inverse of the loss for samples in the "gray" area which starts from $1/k'$ and ends at $1/k$ (see Fig. 2). The mixture weighting has the properties of both hard and soft weighting schemes. The comparison of these weighting schemes is listed in the toy example below.

EXAMPLE 1. *Suppose we are given six samples from two modalities. The hinge loss of each sample calculated by Eq. (2) is listed in the following table, where $Loss_1$ and $Loss_2$ column list the losses w.r.t. the first and the second modality, whereas "Avg Loss" column lists the average loss. The last four columns present the weights calculated by Eq. (10), Eq. (13), Eq. (17) and Eq. (20) where $k = 1.2$ and $k' = 6.7$.*

ID	*Loss₁*	*Loss₂*	*Avg Loss*	*Hard*	*Linear*	*Log*	*Mixture*
1	0.08	0.02	0.05	1	0.940	0.853	1.000
2	0.15	0.09	0.12	1	0.856	0.697	1.000
3	0.50	0.50	0.50	1	0.400	0.226	0.146
4	0.96	0.70	0.83	1	0.004	0.002	0.001
5	0.66	1.02	0.84	0	0.000	0.000	0.000
6	1.30	1.10	1.20	0	0.000	0.000	0.000

As we see, Hard Weighting produces less reasonable solutions, e.g. the difference between the first (ID=1) and the fourth sample (ID=4) is 0.78 and they share the same weight 1; on the contrary, the difference between the fourth and the fifth sample is only 0.01, but suddenly they have totally different weights. This abrupt change is absent in other weighting schemes. Log is a more prudent scheme than Linear as it diminishes the weight more rapidly. Among all weighting schemes, Mixture is the only one that tolerates small errors.

3.4 Modality Weighting

The accuracies of different modalities usually vary considerably, and modality weighting may be beneficial for reranking, as suggested in [13, 11]. To incorporate modality weighting, following [13], we rewrite the objective function as:

$$\min_{\mathbf{y},\mathbf{v}} \mathbb{E}_{\Theta}(\mathbf{y},\mathbf{v};k) = \min_{\mathbf{y},\mathbf{v}} C\sum_{i=1}^{n}\sum_{j=1}^{m} v_i\ell_{ij} + mf(\mathbf{v};k) \quad \text{s.t. } \mathbf{y} \in \{-1,+1\}^n, \mathbf{v} \in [0,1]^n \quad \mathbf{A}^T\mathbf{v} \le \mathbf{g}. \tag{21}$$

Eq. (21) degenerates to Eq. (7) when $\mathbf{g} = [n, n, .., n]^T$. The added constraint limits the total weight that each modality can have. For n samples from m modalities, according to [13], $\mathbf{A}_{n\times m}$ is a matrix calculated from:

$$\mathbf{A}_{ij} = \frac{I(\mathbf{w}_j^T\phi(\mathbf{x}_{ij}) + b_j > 0)}{\sum_{j=1}^{m} I(\mathbf{w}_j^T\phi(\mathbf{x}_{ij}) + b_j > 0)}, \tag{22}$$

where $I(\cdot)$ is the indicator function which equals 1 when $\mathbf{w}_j^T\phi(\mathbf{x}_{ij}) + b_j > 0$, and 0 otherwise. For convenience of notation, let $0/0 = 0$. For each sample, Eq. (22) first counts the number of modalities that classify it as positive. Then each row of $\mathbf{A}$ is normalized so that it adds up to 1. According to [13], $\mathbf{A}$ needs to be calculated only once. $\mathbf{A}^T\mathbf{v}$ sums up the total weight for each modality. $\mathbf{g}$ ($\mathbf{g} > \mathbf{0}$) is a prior vector imposing the upper-bound on the total weight, and higher weight should be assigned to accurate modalities [13][3]. Due to the introduced constraint, the analytical solutions in Section 3.3 cannot be directly applied to optimize Eq. (21). To solve it, we first calculate $\mathbf{y}$ using Eq. (8) and then apply gradient descent to find $\mathbf{v}$. Lemma 1 guarantees that this method finds the global optimal solution for Eq. (21).

[3]Estimating $\mathbf{g}$ is beyond the topic of our paper. More information on this topic can be found in [13].

4. THEORETICAL DISCUSSIONS

4.1 Convergence

The proposed SPaR has some useful properties. The following lemma proves that the global optimum can be obtained for any self-paced function following Definition 1.

LEMMA 1. *For any self-paced function that follows Definition 1, the gradient descent method in Section 3.4 finds the global optimal solution for Eq. (7) and Eq. (21).*

PROOF. Consider the objective of Eq. (21). Suppose $\mathbf{y}^* = [y_1^*, ..., y_n^*]^T$ is a solution found by the gradient descent method in Section 3.4. According to Eq. (8), $\forall y_i \in \{-1,+1\}$ and $\forall v_i \in [0,1]$, we have:

$$\mathbb{E}_{\Theta}(y_i^*, v_i; k) \le \mathbb{E}_{\Theta}(y_i, v_i; k). \tag{23}$$

Therefore $\forall \mathbf{y}$, $\forall \mathbf{v}$, the following inequations hold:

$$\mathbb{E}_{\Theta}(\mathbf{y}^*, \mathbf{v}; k) = \sum_{i=1}^{n} \mathbb{E}_{\Theta}(y_i^*, v_i; k) \le \sum_{i=1}^{n} \mathbb{E}_{\Theta}(y_i, v_i; k) = \mathbb{E}_{\Theta}(\mathbf{y}, \mathbf{v}; k). \tag{24}$$

In other words, $\mathbf{y}^*$ found by Eq. (8) is the global optimum for Eq. (21). Now consider the objective with the fixed $\mathbf{y}^*$. According to Definition 1, $f(\mathbf{v})$ is a convex function of $\mathbf{v}$, and because $\mathbf{A}^T\mathbf{v} \le \mathbf{g}$ is a linear constraint, Eq. (21) is a convex function of $\mathbf{v}$. Suppose that $\mathbf{v}^*$ is a solution found by gradient descent, due to the convexity, $\mathbf{v}^*$ is the global optimum for Eq. (21). Therefore, $\mathbf{y}^*, \mathbf{v}^*$ is the global optimal solution for Eq. (21). The proof trivially holds for Eq. (7) when $\mathbf{g} = [n, n, .., n]^T$. □

The following theorem proves the algorithmic convergence.

THEOREM 1. *Alg. 1 converges to a stationary solution for any fixed C and k.*

PROOF. Let the superscript index the variable value in that iteration, e.g. $\mathbf{v}^{(t)}$ represents the value of $\mathbf{v}$ in the tth iteration. Denote $\Theta^{(t)} = \Theta_1^{(t)}, ..., \Theta_m^{(t)}$. $\mathbf{y}^{(0)}$ and $\mathbf{v}^{(0)}$ are arbitrary initial values in their feasible regions. As Eq. (6) is a quadratic programming problem, the solution $\Theta^{(t)}$ is the global optimum for $\mathbb{E}_{\mathbf{y},\mathbf{v}}$, i.e.

$$\mathbb{E}(\Theta^{(t)}, \mathbf{y}^{(t-1)}, \mathbf{v}^{(t-1)}) \le \mathbb{E}(\Theta^{(t-1)}, \mathbf{y}^{(t-1)}, \mathbf{v}^{(t-1)}). \tag{25}$$

According to Lemma 1, $\mathbf{v}, \mathbf{y}$ are also global optimum for $\mathbb{E}_{\Theta}$, i.e.

$$\mathbb{E}(\Theta^{(t)}, \mathbf{y}^{(t)}, \mathbf{v}^{(t)}) \le \mathbb{E}(\Theta^{(t)}, \mathbf{y}^{(t-1)}, \mathbf{v}^{(t-1)}). \tag{26}$$

Substitute Eq. (26) back into Eq. (25), we have that $\forall t \ge 1$,

$$\mathbb{E}(\Theta^{(t)}, \mathbf{y}^{(t)}, \mathbf{v}^{(t)}) \le \mathbb{E}(\Theta^{(t-1)}, \mathbf{y}^{(t-1)}, \mathbf{v}^{(t-1)}). \tag{27}$$

Eq. (27) indicates that the objective decreases in every iteration. Since $\mathbb{E}$ is the sum of finite elements, it is bounded from below. Consequently, according to [34], it is guaranteed that Alg. 1 (an instance of CCM algorithm) converges to a stationary solution of the problem. □

Theorem 1 guarantees the convergence of Alg. 1. Note that the convergence means a stationary solution whose values are finally stable, which may not necessarily mean a global optimal solution. Actually, since the objective function of Eq. (1) is non-convex, the quality of the solution may rely on its the initial ranked lists. If initial lists brought by queries are off-topic, reranking can degrade the initial result. This is a common problem in all reranking methods that has been observed in several studies [32, 39, 13]. There exist some works to alleviate the influence of bad initial values. One is to estimate the quality of a ranked list, and only conduct reranking on "good" ranked lists [32]. Another is to provide some supervision by annotating a few positive videos, also known as supervised reranking [17, 39]. More details can be referred to these papers.

4.2 Relation to Existing Reranking Models

A general form of Eq. (1) is written as

$$\min_{\Theta_1,...,\Theta_m,\mathbf{y},\mathbf{v}} \mathbb{E}(\Theta_1,...,\Theta_m,\mathbf{v},\mathbf{y};k) = \min_{\Theta_1,...,\Theta_m,\mathbf{y},\mathbf{v}} \sum_{i=1}^{n}\sum_{j=1}^{m} v_i Loss(\mathbf{x}_{ij};\Theta_j) + mf(\mathbf{v};k) \quad (28)$$
$$\text{s.t. Constraints on } \Theta_1,...,\Theta_m$$
$$\mathbf{y} \in \{-1,+1\}^n, \mathbf{v} \in [0,1]^n,$$

where $Loss(\mathbf{x}_{ij};\Theta_j)$ is a general function of the loss incurred by the ith sample against the jth modality, e.g., in Eq. (1) it is defined as the sum of the hinge loss and the margin. The constraints on $\Theta_1,...,\Theta_m$ are the constants in the specific reranking model. Alg. 1 is still applicable to solve Eq. (28).

Eq. (28) represents a general reranking framework for 0Ex video search, which includes existing Classification-based and LETOR-based reranking methods as special cases. For example, generally, when $Loss$ takes the negative likelihood of Logistic Regression, and $f(\mathbf{v};k)$ takes Eq. (9) (hard weighting), SPaR corresponds to MMPRF in [13]. When $Loss$ is the hinge loss, $f(\mathbf{v};k)$ is Eq. (9), the pseudo labels are assumed to be $+1$, and there is only one modality, SPaR corresponds to Classification-based PRF [38, 8]. Given $Loss$ and constraints on Θ are from pair-wise RankSVM, SPaR can degenerate to LETOR-based reranking methods [23].

4.3 Time Complexity

The proposed SPaR is efficient. Suppose n and m is the total number of samples and modalities, respectively. u is the average feature dimension. l is the number of pseudo samples selected by the self-paced function. In an iteration, the complexity mainly comes from Step 4 and Step 5 in Alg. 1. In Step 4, the complexity lies in solving the quadratic programming (order $mu \cdot l^2$). In Step 5, it lies in searching the optimal $\mathbf{y}$ (order $mu \cdot n$) and the optimal $\mathbf{v}$ (order $mu \cdot n + l^2$), based on an efficient algorithms which first solves an unconstrained problem on n variables, and then solve a constrained problem on l variables. Therefore, the time complexity for each iteration is order $mu \cdot (l^2 + n)$. As in other reranking methods, the number of pseudo samples is far less than that of total samples, i.e. $l \ll n$. The proposed method is expected to be efficient, and the empirical runtime comparison substantiates this claim.

5. EMPIRICAL EXPERIMENTS

In this section, we empirically verify the efficacy and efficiency of the proposed method on two datasets. The TRECVID MED represents the task of video reranking by multimodal content-based search, and the Web Query represents the task of image reranking by text-based search.

5.1 TRECVID Multimedia Event Detection

Dataset and evaluation: We conduct experiments on the TRECVID Multimedia Event Detection (MED) 2013 development and MEDTest set including around 34,000 videos on 20 Pre-Specified events. The task is to detect the occurrence of a main event in a video clip, where all features have to be extracted from the video content. The performance is evaluated on the MEDTest set consisting of about 25,000 videos, by the official metric Mean Average Precision (MAP). The official test split released by NIST is used, and the reported MAP is comparable with other teams' MAPs on the same split. The experiments are all conducted in the 0Ex setting, in which no ground-truth positive videos are available. In the baseline comparison, we evaluate each experiment 10 times on randomly generated splits to reduce the bias brought by the partition. The mean and 90% confidence interval are reported.

Features: Four types of high-level features are used, namely Automatic Speech Recognition (ASR), Optical Character Recognition (OCR), Semantic INdexing (SIN) and DCNN (Deep Convolutional Neural Network). SIN and DCNN [18] is 346 visual concepts and 1,000 visual objects trained on TRECVID and ImageNet set, respectively. Two types of low-level features are used: dense trajectories [36] and MFCC. The detailed information about these features is in [21].

Baselines: The proposed method is compared against the following baselines: 1) *Without Reranking* is a plain retrieval method without Reranking, and the language model with Jelinek-Mercer smoothing is used [41]. 2)*Rocchio* is a classical reranking model for vector space model under tf-idf representation [16]. 3) *Relevance Model* is a famous reranking method for text, and the variant with the i.i.d. assumption in [22] is used. 4)*CPRF*(Classification-based PRF) is a seminal PRF-based reranking method. Following [38, 8], SVM classifiers with χ^2 are trained using the top-ranked and bottom-ranked videos [38]. 5)*Learning to Rank* is a LETOR-based method. Following [23], it is trained using the pairwise constraints derived from the pseudo-positives and pseudo-negatives. A LambdaMART [37] in the RankLib toolkit is used to train the RankSVM model; 6) *MMPRF* is a multimodal reranking method [13], and the variant with modality weighting is used [13]. The parameters of all methods, including the proposed SPaR, are tuned on MED Research Set that shares no overlap with our development set. The tuned parameters are then applied to the MEDTest set.

The baseline methods are selected based on two considerations: first, the methods cover the reranking methods in the fields of both information retrieval and multimedia retrieval. Second, the comparison between them helps to isolate the contribution of different components.

Predefined weighting schemes: Section 3.3 discusses four weighting schemes including the conventional hard weighting and the proposed three soft weighting schemes. The following two predefined schemes are also included for comparison: 1) Interpolation is a commonly used weighting scheme which assigns weights linearly to a sample' rank order [9, 33]:

$$v_i = \frac{1}{m}\sum_{j=1}^{m}\left(1 - \frac{rank(\mathbf{x}_{ij})}{N}\right), \quad (29)$$

where N is the number of total pseudo samples. The weight for the first sample is 1.0, and 0.0 for the last. $rank(\cdot)$ returns the sample's rank order in its list. 2) Inverse Rank assigns a sample's weight based on its inverse rank order. The weight v_i equals the average inverse rank across m modalities:

$$v_i = \frac{1}{m}\sum_{j=1}^{m}\frac{1}{rank(\mathbf{x}_{ij})}. \quad (30)$$

Our model: Alg. 1 is used. Eq. (6) is solved by the quadratic programming package "quadprog" [28], in which the parameter C is fixed to 1 and the ϕ is set as the χ^2 explicit feature map [35]. By default, Eq. (18) is used. The modality weighting is used. $\mathbf{g}$ vector is calculated using

Table 1: MAP (× 100) comparison with the baseline methods across 20 Pre-Specified events.

Method	NIST's split	10 splits
Without Reranking	3.9	4.9 ± 1.6
Rocchio	5.7	7.4 ± 2.2
Relevance Model	2.6	3.4 ± 1.0
CPRF	6.4	8.3 ± 1.8
Learning to Rank	3.4	4.2 ± 1.4
MMPRF	10.1	13.6 ± 2.4
SPaR	**12.9**	**15.3 ± 2.6**

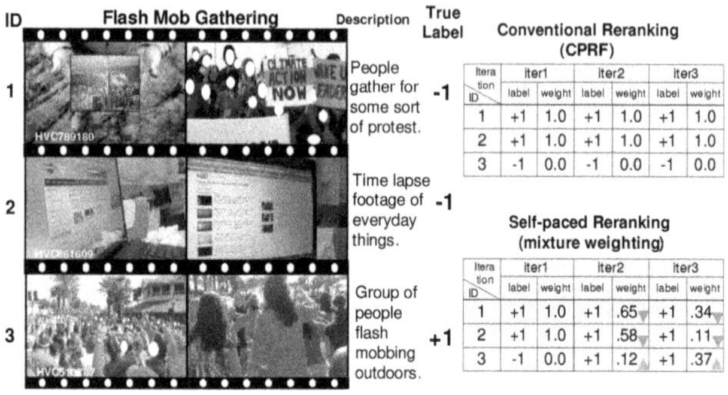

Figure 4: Weights changed by CPRF and SPaR on representative videos in different iterations.

the query likelihood method in [13]. The initial values of the pseudo labels and weights are derived using the method in [13]. Since, according to [13], pseudo negatives has little impact on the MAP, the learning is applied on pseudo positives. Eq. (21) is solved by LM-BFGS [42] in "stats" package. As in the baseline methods, the parameters are tuned on MED Research Set.

5.1.1 *Comparison with Baseline methods*

We first examine the overall MAP in Table 1, in which the best result is highlighted. The MAP of the proposed SPaR is by far the best MAP of the 0Ex task reported on this dataset, according to [13, 7, 4]. As we see, SPaR outperforms all baseline methods by statistically significant differences, on both the official NIST's split and the 10 splits. For example, on the NIST's split, it increases the MAP of the baseline without reranking by a relative 230% (absolute 9%), and the second best method MMPRF by a relative 28% (absolute 2.8%). Fig. 3 plots the AP comparison on each event, where the x-axis represents the event ID and the y-axis denotes the average precision. As we see, SPaR outperforms the baseline without reranking on 18 out of 20 events, and the second best MMPRF on 15 out of 20 events. The improvement is statistically significant at the p-level of 0.05, according to the paired t-test. Fig. 6 illustrates the top retrieved results on two events that have the highest improvement. As we see, the videos retrieved by SPaR are more accurate and visually coherent.

We observed two reasons for the improvements over the conventional reranking methods. First, SPaR can adjust the weights in a more reasonable way. For example, Fig. 4 illustrates the weights assigned by CPRF and SPaR on the event "E008 Flash Mob Gathering". Three representative videos are plotted where the third (ID=3) is true positive, and the others (ID=1,2) are negative. The tables on the right of Fig. 4 list their pseudo labels and weights in each iteration. Since the true labels are unknown to the methods, in the first iteration, both methods made mistakes. In Conventional Reranking, the initial pseudo labels and learned weights stay unchanged thereafter. However, SPaR adaptively assigns the weights as the iteration grows, e.g. it reduces the overestimated weights of videos (ID=1,2) in iteration 2 and 3 probably because of their dissimilarity from other pseudo positive videos. Second, modality weighting seems to be conducive in further improving the MAP. Table 2 lists the MAP with and without modality weighting [13], where the MAPs of MMPRF come from [13]. As we see, in both methods, the variant with modality weighting outperforms the variant without it.

Table 2: MAP (×100) comparison of methods with(w) and without(w/o) modality weighting on the NIST's split.

Method	w/o Weighting	w/ Weighting
MMPRF [13]	9.0	10.1
SPaR	10.8	12.9

Table 3: MAP and MAP@100 comparison with baseline methods on the Web Query dataset.

Method	MAP	MAP@100
Without Reranking [17]	0.569	0.431
CPRF [38]	0.658	-
Random Walk [10]	0.616	-
Bayesian Reranking [33, 32]	0.658	0.529
Preference Learning Model [32]	-	0.534
BVLS [26]	0.670	-
Query-Relative(visual) [17]	0.649	-
Supervised Reranking [39]	0.665	-
SPaR	**0.672**	**0.557**

We found two scenarios where SPaR fails. First, when the initial top-ranked videos retrieved by queries are completely off-topic. SPaR may not recover from the inferior starting values, e.g. the query brought by "E022 Cleaning an appliance" are off-topic (on cooking in kitchen). Second, SPaR may not help when the features used in reranking are not discriminative to the queries, e.g. for "E025 Marriage Proposal", our system lacks of meaningful detectors such as "stand on knees". Therefore even if 10 true positives are used, the AP is still bad (0.003).

5.1.2 *Comparison of Weighting Schemes*

We conduct experiments with different weighting schemes, and plot their MAPs in Fig. 5, where the x-axis denotes the iteration, and the y-axis is the MAP. The same step size is used in all methods. As we see, SPaR with the proposed soft weighting schemes, including linear, log and mixture weighting, consistently outperforms the binary and the predefined weighting across iterations. Among them, the mixture weighting is slightly better than others, suggesting the rationale for tolerating small errors on this dataset. The MAPs of the proposed soft weighting schemes seem to be robust and less sensitive to the iteration change, which is valuable in ranking since the number of true positives is usually unknown to the algorithms. The MAP drop seems to be related to the nature of the MED dataset. Evidence is that the similar pattern can be observed in other methods [13]. Nevertheless, SPaR still outperforms the binary, predefined weights and the baseline methods in Table 1.

5.2 Web Query Dataset

To verify SPaR's performance on image search, we conduct experiments on a web image query dataset consisting of 71,478 images from 353 queries, retrieved by a search engine named Exalead (`http://www.exalead.com/search/`). For each query, the top ranked images generated by Exalead

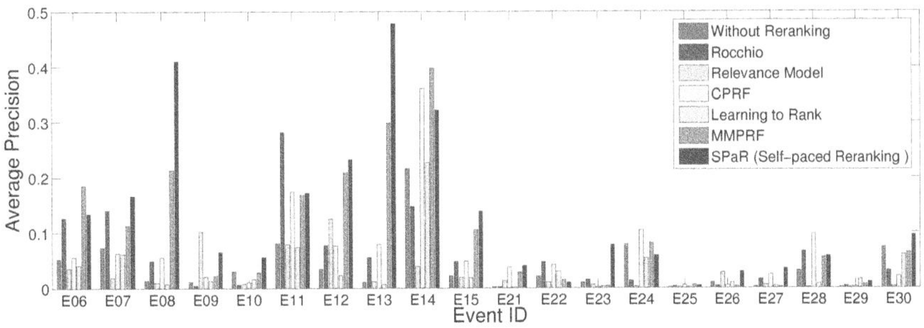

Figure 3: The AP comparison with the baseline methods. The MAP across all events is available in Table 1.

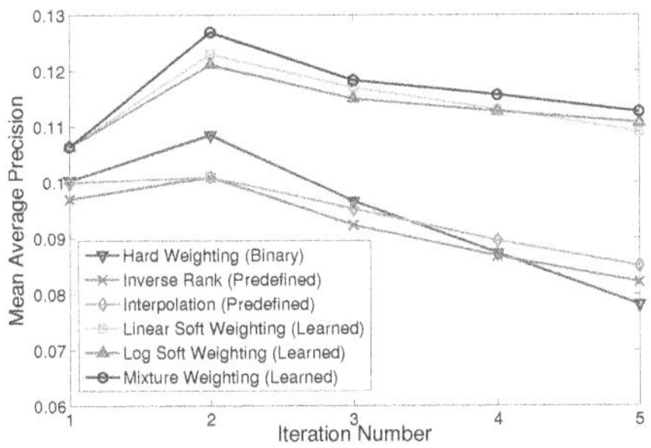

Figure 5: Comparison of binary, predefined, and learned weighting schemes in different iterations.

are provided, along with the true label for every image. The dataset is representative as the 353 queries cover a broad range of topics. The performance is evaluated by the non-interpolated MAP, as used in [17]. MAP@100 is also included for comparison. Note that as the initial result contains a single modality, no modality weighting is applied.

Following [32, 26], densely sampled SIFT are extracted. A codebook of 1,024 centroids is constructed. Spatial Tiling [14] is used to further improve the performance. We compare SPaR with the state-of-the-art reranking methods. SPaR is configured in a similar way as discussed in Section 5.1, and provided initial text-based search results are used. Following [26, 32], the parameters are tuned on a validation set consisting of a subset of queries.

We examine the overall MAP in Table 3. "-" denotes that the number is unavailable in the cited paper. As we see, SPaR achieves the promising MAP among state-of-the-art reranking methods, including Graph-based [10], LETOR-based [33, 32], Classification-based [38] and even supervised reranking methods [17, 39], in terms of both MAP and MAP@100. A similar pattern as in TRECVID MED can be observed that SPaR significantly boosts the MAP of plain retrieval without reranking, and obtain comparable or even better performance than the baseline methods. Generally, SPaR improves about 84% queries over the method without reranking. Since the initial ranked lists are retrieved by text matching, this result substantiates the claim that SPaR is general and applicable to reranking by text-based search.

5.3 Runtime Comparison

To empirically verify the efficiency of SPaR, we compare the runtime (second/query) in a single iteration. The experiments are conducted on Intel Xeon E5649 @ 2.53GHz with 16GB memory and the results are listed in Table 4. To test the speed of Rocchio and Relevance Model, we built our own inverted index on the Web Query dataset, and issue the query against the index. The reranking in MED, which is

Table 4: Runtime Comparison in a single iteration.

Method	MED	Web Query
Rocchio	5.3 (s)	2.0 (s)
Relevance Model	7.2 (s)	2.5 (s)
Learning to Rank	178 (s)	22.3 (s)
CPRF	145 (s)	10.1 (s)
MMPRF	149 (s)	10.1 (s)
SPaR	158 (s)	12.2 (s)

conducted only on semantic features, is slower because it involves multiple features and modalities. As we see, SPaR's overhead over CPRF is marginal on the both sets. This result suggests SPaR is inexpensive, and agrees with the time complexity analysis in Section 4.3. The current implementations for all methods are far from optimal, which involve a number of programming languages. We will accelerate the pipeline in future.

6. CONCLUSIONS AND FUTURE WORK

In this paper, we proposed a novel approach called Self-Paced Reranking (SPaR) for multimodal reranking. SPaR reveals the missing link between reranking and an optimization problem that can be effectively solved by the self-paced learning. The proposed framework is general, and can be used to theoretically explain other reranking methods. This paper also advances the state-of-the-art self-paced learning research by generalizing binary to real-valued self-paced functions that preserve global optimum. Experimental results validate the efficacy and the efficiency of the proposed method on image and video search. SPaR consistently outperforms the plain retrieval without reranking, and obtains decent improvements over the existing reranking methods. Notably, SPaR achieves by far the best result on the challenging TRECVID MED 0Ex task.

Possible directions for future work may include automatically selecting appropriate self-paced functions for different types of reranking problems. Currently, parameters are tuned on a validation set. The tuning may heavily rely on the quality of the validation set. Another direction is to study the parameter tuning based on prior knowledge or heuristics.

7. ACKNOWLEDGMENTS

This work was partially supported by Intelligence Advanced Research Projects Activity (IARPA) via Department of Interior National Business Center contract number D11PC20068. Deyu Meng was partially supported by 973 Program of China (3202013CB329404) and the NSFC project (61373114). The U.S. Government is authorized to reproduce and distribute reprints for Governmental purposes notwithstanding any copyright annotation thereon. Disclaimer: The views and conclusions contained herein are those of the authors and should not be interpreted as necessarily representing the official policies or

Figure 6: Top ranked videos/images ordered left-to-right using (a) plain retrieval without reranking and (b) self-paced reranking. True/false labels are marked in the lower-right of every frame.

endorsements, either expressed or implied, of IARPA, DoI/NBC, or the U.S. Government.

8. REFERENCES

[1] Y. Bengio, J. Louradour, R. Collobert, and J. Weston. Curriculum learning. In *ICML*, pages 41–48, 2009.

[2] S. P. Boyd and L. Vandenberghe. *Convex Optimization*. Cambridge university press, 2004.

[3] S.-F. Chang. How far we've come: Impact of 20 years of multimedia information retrieval. *TOMCCAP*, 9(1):42, 2013.

[4] J. Chen, Y. Cui, G. Ye, D. Liu, and S.-F. Chang. Event-driven semantic concept discovery by exploiting weakly tagged internet images. In *ICMR*, page 1, 2014.

[5] J. Gorski, F. Pfeuffer, and K. Klamroth. Biconvex sets and optimization with biconvex functions: a survey and extensions. *Mathematical Methods of Operations Research*, 66(3):373–407, 2007.

[6] D. Grangier and S. Bengio. A discriminative kernel-based approach to rank images from text queries. *PAMI*, 30(8):1371–1384, 2008.

[7] A. Habibian, T. Mensink, and C. G. Snoek. Composite concept discovery for zero-shot video event detection. In *ICMR*, page 17, 2014.

[8] A. G. Hauptmann, M. G. Christel, and R. Yan. Video retrieval based on semantic concepts. *Proceedings of the IEEE*, 96(4):602–622, 2008.

[9] W. H. Hsu, L. S. Kennedy, and S.-F. Chang. Video search reranking via information bottleneck principle. In *Multimedia*, pages 35–44, 2006.

[10] W. H. Hsu, L. S. Kennedy, and S.-F. Chang. Video search reranking through random walk over document-level context graph. In *Multimedia*, pages 971–980, 2007.

[11] B. Huurnink, C. G. Snoek, M. de Rijke, and A. W. Smeulders. Content-based analysis improves audiovisual archive retrieval. *Multimedia, IEEE Transactions on*, 14(4):1166–1178, 2012.

[12] L. Jiang, A. G. Hauptmann, and G. Xiang. Leveraging high-level and low-level features for multimedia event detection. In *Multimedia*, pages 449–458, 2012.

[13] L. Jiang, T. Mitamura, S.-I. Yu, and A. G. Hauptmann. Zero-example event search using multimodal pseudo relevance feedback. In *ICMR*, page 297, 2014.

[14] L. Jiang, W. Tong, D. Meng, and A. G. Hauptmann. Towards efficient learning of optimal spatial bag-of-words representations. In *ICMR*, page 121, 2014.

[15] Y.-G. Jiang, C.-W. Ngo, and J. Yang. Towards optimal bag-of-features for object categorization and semantic video retrieval. In *CIVR*, pages 494–501, 2007.

[16] T. Joachims. A probabilistic analysis of the rocchio algorithm with tfidf for text categorization. Technical report, DTIC Document, 1996.

[17] J. Krapac, M. Allan, J. Verbeek, and F. Jurie. Improving web image search results using query-relative classifiers. In *CVPR*, pages 1094–1101, 2010.

[18] A. Krizhevsky, I. Sutskever, and G. Hinton. Imagenet classification with deep convolutional neural networks. In *NIPS*, pages 1106–1114, 2012.

[19] M. P. Kumar, B. Packer, and D. Koller. Self-paced learning for latent variable models. In *NIPS*, pages 1189–1197, 2010.

[20] M. P. Kumar, H. Turki, D. Preston, and D. Koller. Learning specific-class segmentation from diverse data. In *ICCV*, pages 1800–1807, 2011.

[21] Z.-Z. Lan, L. Jiang, S.-I. Yu, et al. Cmu-informedia at trecvid 2013 multimedia event detection. In *TRECVID*, 2013.

[22] V. Lavrenko and W. B. Croft. Relevance based language models. In *SIGIR*, pages 120–127, 2001.

[23] Y. Liu, T. Mei, X.-S. Hua, J. Tang, X. Wu, and S. Li. Learning to video search rerank via pseudo preference feedback. In *ICME*, pages 297–300, 2008.

[24] Z. Ma, Y. Yang, Z. Xu, N. Sebe, and A. G. Hauptmann. We are not equally negative: fine-grained labeling for multimedia event detection. In *Multimedia*, pages 293–302, 2013.

[25] M. Mazloom, A. Habibian, and C. G. Snoek. Querying for video events by semantic signatures from few examples. In *Multimedia*, pages 609–612, 2013.

[26] N. Morioka and J. Wang. Robust visual reranking via sparsity and ranking constraints. In *Multimedia*, pages 533–542, 2011.

[27] L. Nie, S. Yan, M. Wang, R. Hong, and T.-S. Chua. Harvesting visual concepts for image search with complex queries. In *Multimedia*, pages 59–68, 2012.

[28] R Core Team. *R: A Language and Environment for Statistical Computing*. R Foundation for Statistical Computing, Vienna, Austria, 2013.

[29] J. S. Supančič III and D. Ramanan. Self-paced learning for long-term tracking. In *CVPR*, pages 2379–2386, 2013.

[30] K. Tang, V. Ramanathan, L. Fei-Fei, and D. Koller. Shifting weights: Adapting object detectors from image to video. In *NIPS*, volume 1, page 2, 2012.

[31] Y. Tang, Y.-B. Yang, and Y. Gao. Self-paced dictionary learning for image classification. In *Multimedia*, pages 833–836, 2012.

[32] X. Tian, Y. Lu, L. Yang, and Q. Tian. Learning to judge image search results. In *Multimedia*, pages 363–372, 2011.

[33] X. Tian, L. Yang, J. Wang, Y. Yang, X. Wu, and X.-S. Hua. Bayesian video search reranking. In *Multimedia*, pages 131–140, 2008.

[34] P. Tseng. Convergence of a block coordinate descent method for nondifferentiable minimization. *Journal of optimization theory and applications*, 109(3):475–494, 2001.

[35] A. Vedaldi and A. Zisserman. Efficient additive kernels via explicit feature maps. *PAMI*, 34(3):480–492, 2012.

[36] H. Wang, A. Klaser, C. Schmid, and C. L. Liu. Action recognition by dense trajectories. In *CVPR*, pages 3169–3176, 2011.

[37] Q. Wu, C. J. Burges, K. M. Svore, and J. Gao. Adapting boosting for information retrieval measures. *Information Retrieval*, 13(3):254–270, 2010.

[38] R. Yan, A. G. Hauptmann, and R. Jin. Multimedia search with pseudo-relevance feedback. In *CVIR*, pages 238–247, 2003.

[39] L. Yang and A. Hanjalic. Supervised reranking for web image search. In *Multimedia*, pages 183–192, 2010.

[40] Q. Yu, J. Liu, H. Cheng, A. Divakaran, and H. Sawhney. Semantic pooling for complex event detection. In *Multimedia*, pages 733–736, 2013.

[41] C. Zhai and J. Lafferty. A study of smoothing methods for language models applied to ad hoc information retrieval. In *SIGIR*, pages 334–342, 2001.

[42] C. Zhu, R. H. Byrd, P. Lu, and J. Nocedal. Algorithm 778: L-bfgs-b: Fortran subroutines for large-scale bound-constrained optimization. *ACM Transactions on Mathematical Software*, 23(4):550–560, 1997.

Mining Cross-network Association for YouTube Video Promotion

Ming Yan[1,2], Jitao Sang[1,2], Changsheng Xu[1,2]
[1]National Lab of Pattern Recognition, Institute of Automation, CAS, Beijing 100190, China
[2]China-Singapore Institute of Digital Media, Singapore, 139951, Singapore
{ming.yan, jtsang, csxu}@nlpr.ia.ac.cn

ABSTRACT

We introduce a novel cross-network collaborative problem in this work: given YouTube videos, to find optimal Twitter followees that can maximize the video promotion on Twitter. Since YouTube videos and Twitter followees distribute on heterogeneous spaces, we present a cross-network association-based solution framework. Three stages are addressed: (1) heterogeneous topic modeling, where YouTube videos and Twitter followees are modeled in topic level; (2) cross-network topic association, where the overlapped users are exploited to conduct cross-network topic distribution transfer; and (3) referrer identification, where the query YouTube video and candidate Twitter followees are matched in the same topic space. Different methods in each stage are designed and compared by qualitative as well as quantitative experiments. Based on the proposed framework, we also discuss the potential applications, extensions, and suggest some principles for future heterogeneous social media utilization and cross-network collaborative applications.

Categories and Subject Descriptors

H.3.5 [**Online Information Services**]: Web-based services

General Terms

Theory

Keywords

video promotion; cross-network analysis; social media

1. INTRODUCTION

Since the launch in 2005, YouTube has established itself as the world's largest video sharing platform. Latest statistics show that within every minute, 100 hours of video are uploaded to YouTube [1], resulting in an estimate of more than 2 billion videos totally. People act on purpose. It has been recognized that YouTube users share videos with an obvious extrinsic motivation of receiving attentions (e.g., video view) [1, 2], especially for the profit-seeking video content providers [2]. In spite of the fact that billions of videos are consumed in YouTube each day, the massive volume makes the exploration of individual videos very difficult. According to research, YouTube video view count distribution exhibits a power-law pattern with truncated tails [3]. Most videos have a short active life span, receiving half of the total views in the first 6 days after being published, and with fewer and fewer access thereafter [4]. Therefore, the mismatch between high attention expectation and rare access opportunity calls for YouTube video promotion to broaden the viewership.

Generally speaking, within YouTube, video can be accessed from internal search, related video recommendation, channel subscription or front page highlight. Some work has been devoted to utilizing these sources to promote internal video views. Zhou et al. studied the impact of related video recommendation on video views, with goal to design a strategy to drive YouTube video popularity [5]. In [6], YouTube search bias phenomenon is investigated to optimize video discovery in YouTube's internal search results. However, essentially as a content repository, YouTube exhibits limited promotion efficiency with the internal mechanisms. Very recent research shows that external referrers, such as external search engines and other social media websites, arise to be important sources to lead users to YouTube videos [7]. Among the social media websites, Twitter has been quickly growing as the top referrer source for web video discovery [3].

Twitter allows users to embed videos in their tweets by posting video links. Followers to these users then receive the tweet feed and become the potential viewers of these videos. The followee-follower architecture has established Twitter as a great platform to promote and engage with the audiences and distinguished itself with the significant information propagation efficiency. Twitter followees, especially those with a lot of followers (which we refer to as *popular followee*), play important roles under social media circumstances by: (1) acting as "we media", via the control of information dissemination channels to millions of audiences, and (2) acting as influential leaders, via their potential impact on the followers' decisions and activities. YouTube video "Gangnam Style" went viral to become the first web video

[1] http://www.youtube.com/yt/press/statistics.html.

[2] YouTube has started to let video content providers be partners to cash in on the videos posted by sharing ad revenue and charging rental fees to viewers.

[3] http://mashable.com/2010/05/25/twitter-online-video/.

MM'14, November 03 - 07, 2014, Orlando, FL, USA.
Copyright 2014 ACM 978-1-4503-3063-3/14/11 ...$15.00.
http://dx.doi.org/10.1145/2647868.2654920.

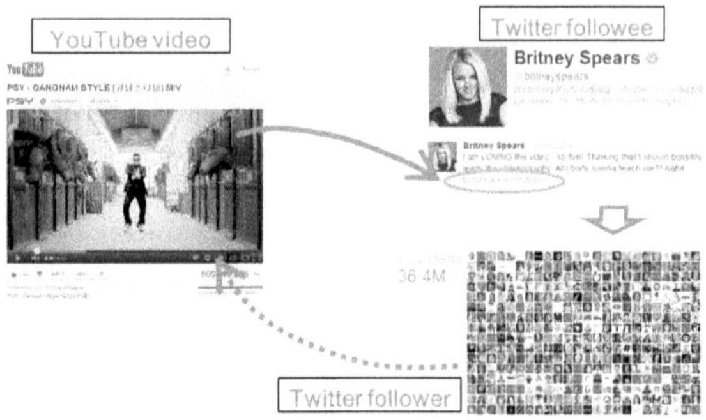

Figure 1: Problem illustration.

that reaches one billion views in 5 months, resulting mainly from its successful strategy of roping in some popularly followed musicians on Twitter, such as Britney Spears, Justin Bieber and Katy Perry. In this context, if we can identify "proper" followees to help disseminate videos, their significant audience accessibility and behavioral impact will guarantee the promotion efficiency. Therefore, the problem of this work is: *For specific ouTube video, to identify proper Twitter followees with goal to maximize video dissemination to the followers* (as shown in Fig. 1).

It is not trivial to measure the "properness" of Twitter followees for specific YouTube videos. The challenge lies in two-fold: (1) The level of "properness" is not necessarily proportional to the number of followers (#follower). While a popular followee with a large #follower will guarantee a huge audiences, what video promotion cares is the number of "effective" audiences, who are likely to show interest to the video and with higher probability to take subsequent consuming actions like watch, reshare, etc. A close analogy to advertising can be made, where the followee is viewed as advertising media, whose bid price is decided by #follower. Twitter followee identification is analogous to advertising media selection [4], with goal to achieve the maximum coverage and exposures in a target audience with the minimum cost. (2) Based on the above discussion, whether a Twitter followee is proper for the promotion task is actually decided by the interest his/her followers show to the YouTube videos. However, we only know the followers' activities on Twitter, based on what only the demographics or interests on the general level can be inferred [8, 9]. While, the YouTube videos are known to distribute more on specific semantic level [10]. The discrepancy in topic granularity and affiliated platform makes it impractical to directly evaluate Twitter followers' interest to YouTube videos, let alone the costly computation in evaluating each follower and the subsequent aggregation.

Our solution to address the above challenges is inspired by the fact that the same individual usually involves with different social media networks, including media sharing - *ouTube* and *Flickr*, microblogging *Twitter* and *Tumblr*, private/professional social networks *LinkedIn* and *Facebook*. Anderson Analytics shows that the different social media networks share remarkable percentage of overlapped users [5]. In this context, if we know the corresponding Twitter accounts of YouTube users who show interest to a given video (e.g., upload, favorite, add to playlist), it is confident to identify the Twitter followee that these Twitter accounts jointly followed as the optimal promotion referrer. In practice, it is impossible to obtain all the overlapped accounts between different networks. Moreover, a practical solution should be not limited to the specific video and followee, but generalizable on the alike sets. Therefore, in this work, we propose to investigate the problem in YouTube video and Twitter followee topic level, and exploit the observed overlapped users to mine the cross-network topic association for solution. Specifically, based on users' interactions with YouTube videos and Twitter followees, we first build heterogeneous video topic and followee topic, respectively. After that, the topic association is mined from the overlapped users' distributions on the two topics. Finally, the optimal Twitter promotion referrers are identified by matching with the transferred video distribution on the Twitter followee topic space.

Our contributions in this work can be summarized in the following three-fold:

1. We introduce a new problem of YouTube video promotion on Twitter platform by identifying proper Twitter followees. There exist both trends and demands in exploring external referrers towards promoting social media content.
2. A cross-network association-based solution framework is presented, under which alternative methods have been examined. The solution is validated to discover heterogeneous topic association and facilitate effective video-followee matching in the same topic space.
3. The discussion in Section 5 on the idea of exploiting overlapped users' activities in different networks towards cross-network knowledge mining opens up possibilities to the utilization of heterogeneous social media sources. This will be the key takeaway for future cross-network analysis and applications.

2. RELATED WORK

2.1 Cross-network Collaboration

With various social media networks growing in prominence, netizens are using a multitude of social media services for social connection and information sharing. Cross-network collaborative applications have recently attracted attentions. One line is on cross-network user modeling, which focuses on integrating various social media activities. In [11], the authors introduced a cold-start recommendation problem by aggregating user profiles in Flickr, Twitter and Delicious. Deng et al. has proposed a personalized YouTube video recommendation solution by incorporating user information from Twitter [12]. Another line is devoted to taking advantage of different social networks' characteristics towards collaborative applications. For example, Suman et al. exploited the real-time and socialized characteristics of the Twitter tweets to facilitate video applications in YouTube [13]. Our work belongs to the second line, where a collaborative application is designed to exploit the propagation efficiency of Twitter to meet the YouTube video promotion demand.

2.2 Social Media Influencer Mining

Previous analysis on Twitter has found that popular users with high in-degree are not necessarily influencers for propagation [14], which calls for research onto the problem of

[4] http://en.wikipedia.org/wiki/Advertising media selection.

[5] See "Anderson Analytics 2009 report: what your favorite social network says about you?".

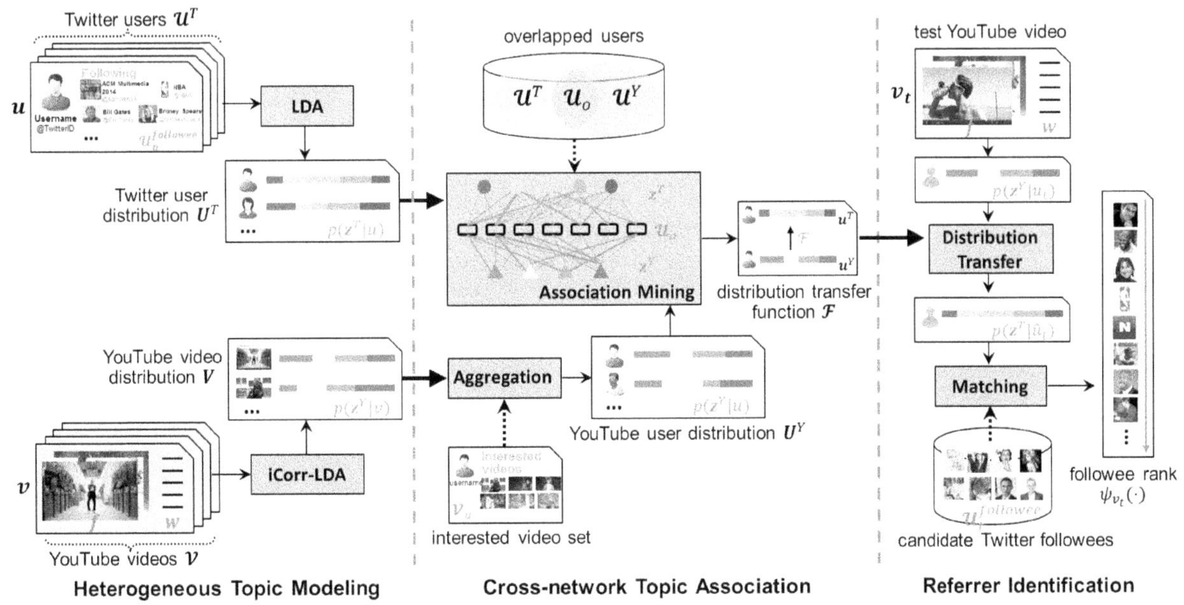

Figure 2: Solution framework.

influencer mining. One line is to identify the domain or topic experts. Representative solutions include the extensions to PageRank by considering topical similarity, e.g, Twitter-Rank [15], and incorporating auxiliary sources like Twitter lists [16]. Another line is concerned with maximizing influence spread by initializing some seed users. David et al. first defined this problem [17], which is then applied to viral marketing [18].

Our introduced problem of Twitter followee identification can be viewed as a special case of influencer mining. The existing influencer mining methods mainly focus on single network and need an explicit relevance metric, e.g. the topical relevance between follower and followee, and the accept rate between the propagation item and follower. In our problem, the relevance of influencer is designed by items distributed on another network. It is difficult to explicitly define the relevance metric between cross-network knowledge. Moreover, to focus on addressing cross-network association, we pay no attention to the complicated social network structure as in the standard maximizing influence problems. What we care is actually about the propagation efficiency in the first level of followee-follower network.

2.3 Heterogeneous Topic Association

The core of our solution lies in the heterogeneous topic association between Twitter followee and YouTube video. Typical applications of existing heterogeneous topic association work include cross-media retrieval and heterogeneous face recognition, where invariant feature extraction and subspace learning based solutions are extensively investigated. Invariant feature extraction methods are devoted to reducing the heterogeneous gap by exploring the most insensitive feature patterns. Klare et al. proposed to extract the SIFT and Multiscale LBP for forensic sketch and mug shot photo matching [19]. In [20], the intra-difference and inter-difference are jointly considered into a discriminant local feature learning framework. The basic idea of subspace learning is to learn a new space where the observed heterogeneous data can be well represented. [21] provides good surveys of CCA and its extensions to learn a semantic representation from multimodal data.

Subspace learning methods focus on maintaining the smoothness for retrieval, i.e., the projected coefficients of two items should be similar if they constitute a training pair. This is different from our goal for heterogeneous topic association and transfer. Invariant feature extraction aims to extract and learn low-level discriminative features, which will largely fail in case of complicated association like heterogeneous social media topics. In this work, we propose a solution framework based on user's collaborative involvement in heterogeneous topics. This avoids low-level analysis and can be viewed as a high-level crowdsourcing strategy.

3. CROSS-NETWORK YOUTUBE VIDEO PROMOTION

This section introduces the cross-network YouTube video promotion problem and the proposed solution. We first formally define the problem:

DEFINITION 1 (CROSS-NETWORK YOUTUBE VIDEO PROMOTION). *Imagine we have a collection of ouTube videos* $\mathcal{V}$ *where each* $v \in \mathcal{V}$ *is represented by its contained textual words and visual keyframes* $[\mathbf{w}_v, \mathbf{f}_v]$, *and a collection of Twitter users* $\mathcal{U}^T$ *whose followees construct the Twitter followee user collection* $\mathcal{U}^{followee} \subset \mathcal{U}^T$. *The goal of outube video promotion is for a given ouTube video* $v \in \mathcal{V}$, *to identify Twitter followee* $u \in \mathcal{U}^{followee}$ *whose followers are most likely to be interested in* v.

3.1 Framework

Our solution consists of three stages: *Heterogeneous Topic Modeling*, *Cross-network Topic Association* and *Referrer Identification*(as illustrated in Fig. 2). The goal of Stage 1 is to discover the latent structure within YouTube video and Twitter user spaces, and facilitate the subsequent analysis and applications in topic level. We conduct this by employing generative topic models, with video as *document*, textual word and visual feature of keyframes as the multi-

Table 1: Input (*In*) & output (*Out*) of each stage.

Stage 1	*In*:	YouTube video $v \in \mathcal{V} : [\mathbf{w}_v, \mathbf{f}_v]$; Twitter user $u \in \mathcal{U}^T : \mathcal{U}_u^{followee}$.
	Out:	YouTube video distri. $V : p(\mathbf{z}^Y \vert v)$; Twitter user distri. $U^T : p(\mathbf{z}^T \vert u)$.
Stage 2	*In*:	V, U^T; YouTube, Twitter and overlapped user set $\mathcal{U}^Y, \mathcal{U}^T, \mathcal{U}_o$; YouTube user interested videos $\mathcal{V}_u \subset \mathcal{V}$.
	Out:	Distri. transfer func. $\mathcal{F} : \mathbf{u}^Y \rightarrow \mathbf{u}^T$. ($\mathbf{u}^Y$: the aggregated YouTube user distri.)
Stage 3	*In*:	$\mathcal{F}$; Test video set $\mathcal{V}_t$; Twitter followee set $\mathcal{U}^{followee}$.
	Out:	Twitter followee rank for $v \in \mathcal{V}_t : \psi_v(\cdot)$.

modal *word* in YouTube, and user as *document*, followee as *word* in Twitter. Through this stage, each YouTube video and Twitter user can be represented as distributions in the derived corresponding topic spaces.

As discussed in the introduction, the discrepancy between the cross-network topic spaces prevents from direct analysis. Stage 2 is designed to address this issue by mining the cross-network topic association. Note that traditional semantic-based criteria tend to fail in capturing the association between heterogeneous entities of video and user. We propose a solution that first aggregates YouTube video distribution to user level, and then exploit the overlapped users among different networks as bridge for association mining. The basic premise is that: if the same group of users heavily involve with topic A in network X and topic B in network Y, it is very likely that topic A and B are closely associated. With the derived topic association, topical distribution transfer between different networks is enabled, i.e., given users' topical interest in YouTube videos, we can infer their most probably followed Twitter followee topics.

Since the ultimate goal is to match video to followee. After the offline Stage 1 and Stage 2, in the online Stage 3, we view each test video as a virtual YouTube user who holds identical topical distribution. It is easy to understand that the virtual user actually represents the typical users in YouTube showing significant interest to the test video, who are exactly potential fans and thus the targeted users. Therefore, after topical distribution transfer, it is promising to identify the Twitter followee that best matches the followee topical distribution of the targeted users as the optimal promotion referrer for the video. In Table 1 we summarize the inputs and outputs for each stage.

3.2 Heterogeneous Topic Modeling

3.2.1 YouTube Video Topic Modeling

In YouTube, the video topics are expected to span over both textual and visual spaces. We introduce a modification to the multi-modal topic model, Corr-LDA [22]. Corr-LDA is proposed for the problem of image annotation, by modeling the correspondence between image segments and caption words. It assumes a generative process that first generates the segment descriptions and subsequently the caption words. In our problem, each YouTube video is represented as a pair $(\mathbf{f}; \mathbf{w})$, where $\mathbf{f} = \{f_1, \cdots, f_N\}$ is a collection of N visual feature vectors associated with the extracted keyframes, $\mathbf{w} = \{w_1, \cdots, w_M\}$ is the collection of M caption and tag words. Different from image where each word corresponds to one segment, video caption and tag word usually distribute in several keyframes.

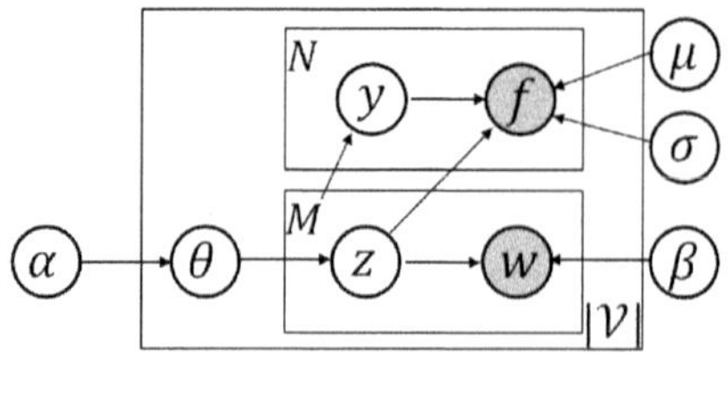

Figure 3: The graphical representation of iCorr-LDA. Note that $\mathbf{y} = \{y_1, \cdots, y_N\}$ are discrete indexing variables that take values from 1 to M with equal probability.

Therefore, we modified the standard CorrLDA and introduce inverse Corr-LDA (iCorr-LDA) to discover the YouTube video multimodal topics. In particular, we first generate M textual words from the standard LDA model. Then, for each of the N keyframes, one of the words is selected and a corresponding keyframe is drawn, conditioned on the same topic generating the word. The graphical model of iCorr-LDA is depicted in Fig. 3. After topic modeling, each video $v \in \mathcal{V}$ can be represented as $\mathbf{v} = \{v_1, \cdots, v_{K^Y}\}$, where K^Y is the number of topics in the derived YouTube video space, $v_k = p(z_k^Y \vert v)$ is video v's topic distribution on the kth topic.

3.2.2 Twitter Followee Topic Modeling

Since the properness of Twitter followee is decided by the followers, we are interested in investigating into the followee-follower architecture in Twitter. Therefore, we represent each Twitter user (*document*) with all his/her followees (*words*) and apply the standard LDA for topic modeling. Since topic modeling exploits co-occurrence relationships, like the YouTube video topics capturing the frequently co-occurred visual features and textual words in videos, the derived Twitter topics actually capture the shared followees by a subset of Twitter users. Particularly, high topic-word distribution indicates the popularity of followees in a group of Twitter followers, and high document-topic distribution indicates user's significant interest in a class of Twitter followees.

After topic modeling, we can obtain Twitter user topic distribution matrix $U^T = \{\mathbf{u}_1^T, \cdots, \mathbf{u}_{\vert\mathcal{U}^T\vert}^T\}$. Each user $u \in \mathcal{U}^T$ is represented as $\mathbf{u}^T = \{u_1^T, \cdots, u_{K^T}^T\}$, where K^T is the number of topics in the derived Twitter followee space, $u_k^T = p(z_k^T \vert u)$ is user u's topic distribution on the kth topic.

3.3 Cross-network Topic Association

3.3.1 YouTube User-Topic Distribution Aggregation

YouTube user's topic distribution can be obtained by aggregating his/her interested videos' distributions. Specifically, for YouTube user u, we construct the interested video set $\mathcal{V}_u \subset \mathcal{V}$ from his/her uploaded videos, favorite videos and videos in the playlists. Given YouTube video $v \in \mathcal{V}_u$ and its topical distribution $p(\mathbf{z}^Y \vert v)$, through simple derivation, we can calculate user u's topical distribution by:

$$p(z_k^Y \vert u_i) = \sum_{v \in \mathcal{V}_u} \frac{N_v(f) + N_v(w)}{N(f) + N(w)} \cdot p(z_k^Y \vert v) \qquad (1)$$

where $N_v(f)$, $N_v(w)$ denote the total number of keyframes and words in video v, $N(f) = \sum_{v \in \mathcal{V}_u} N_v(f)$, $N(w) = \sum_{v \in \mathcal{V}_u} N_v(w)$

denote the total number of keyframes and words in video set $\mathcal{V}_u$. After aggregation, we can obtain the YouTube user topic distribution matrix $U^Y = \{\mathbf{u}_1^Y, \cdots, \mathbf{u}_{|\mathcal{U}^Y|}^Y\}$.

3.3.2 Transition Probability-based Association (TP)

With the derived YouTube and Twitter user topic distributions, we present the solutions for topic association mining. Recall that the basic idea is: if many overlapped users who take interests in the ith YouTube topic also follow the jth Twitter topic, the association between the two topics a_{ij} tends to be strong. One direct way is to examine the joint involvement of cross-network topics in the overlapped users.

We assume YouTube and Twitter user set share the overlapped users $\mathcal{U}_o = \mathcal{U}^Y \cap \mathcal{U}^T$. Viewing as a probabilistic transition problem, the topic association can be calculated by aggregating over all the overlapped users [6]:

$$a_{ij} = p(z_j^T|z_i^Y) = \sum_{u\in\mathcal{U}_o} p(z_j^T|u)\cdot p(u|z_i^Y) = \sum_{u\in\mathcal{U}_o} u_j^T \cdot u_i^Y \cdot \frac{p(u)}{p(z_i^Y)}$$

where $p(u)$ is the user prior which we assume having the uniform distribution, the topic prior $p(z_i^Y) = \sum_{u\in\mathcal{U}_o} p(z_i^Y|u)\cdot p(u)$ indicates the popularity of the ith YouTube topic among the overlapped users. By calculating all cross-network topic pairs and subsequent normalization, we can obtain the topic association matrix $A = \{a_{ij}\}_{K^Y \times K^T}$. The distribution transfer from U^Y to U^T can then be fulfilled. Given a new user u_t and the YouTube video topic distribution $p(\mathbf{z}^Y|u_t)$, his/her Twitter followee topic distribution is estimated as:

$$p(z_j^T|u_t) = \sum_{i=1}^{K^Y} a_{ij}\cdot p(z_i^Y|u_t) \tag{2}$$

3.3.3 Regression-based Association

The above probability-based method directly calculates over all overlapped users, where noisy user topic distributions will deteriorate the derived association matrix. An alternative way to obtain the association matrix is to solve an optimization problem. Rewriting the user topic distribution matrices as $U^Y = [U_o^Y, U_{non}^Y]$ and $U^T = [U_o^T, U_{non}^T]$, where U_o^Y, U_o^T denote the overlapped users' distributions on the corresponding topic spaces, we propose to view the association matrix A as the linear regression from the overlapped users' YouTube distribution U_o^Y to their Twitter distribution U_o^T.

Formally, the regression objective function is:

$$\min_A ||U_o^T - AU_o^Y||^2 + \lambda_1||A||_q \tag{3}$$

where the first term represents the regression error, the second term is the regularization penalty used to avoid overfitting, and $\lambda_1 \in [0,1]$ is the weighting parameter. When $q = 1$, Eqn. (3) is a lasso problem and can be effectively solved by the feature-sign search algorithm [23]. When $q = 2$, Eqn. (3) is a ridge regression problem with analytical solution as:

$$A = U_o^T U_o^{Y\mathrm{T}}(U_o^Y U_o^{Y\mathrm{T}} + \lambda_1 I)^{-1} \tag{4}$$

where $\cdot^{\mathrm{T}}$ is the matrix transpose, and $I \in \mathbb{R}^{K^Y\times K^Y}$ is the identity matrix.

[6] The derivation is based on Bayesian rule, which is omited due to space limitation.

3.3.4 Latent Attribute-based Association (LA)

The aforementioned two association methods are devoted to finding the cross-network association matrix A. Actually, to conduct the topical distribution transfer, the association matrix is not necessarily needed. Moreover, such a matrix exists under the assumption of linear association, which does not hold in complicated cases.

Latent attribute discovery on overlapped users $\mathcal{U}_o^Y$, $\mathcal{U}_o^T$. (LA_overlap) Instead of pursuing an explicit A for "hard" transfer, we also introduce a third association method, by discovering the shared latent structure behind the two topic spaces. For the overlapped users, the different topic distributions can be viewed as their observed activities on different networks. It is reasonable to assume the latent structure behind these observations is actually user attribute. It is the same user's unique attribute values (e.g., age, gender, occupation, home location, etc.) that give birth to his/her different activities and thus the cross-network topic distributions. In each network, a set of representative topic distribution vectors are extracted as network-specific user factors to represent the latent attributes. Specifically, we assume a YouTube factor $\mathbf{d}^Y = \{d_1^Y, \cdots, d_{K^Y}^Y\}$ and a Twitter factor $\mathbf{d}^T = \{d_1^T, \cdots, d_{K^T}^T\}$ are coupled to the same user attribute $d \in \mathcal{D}$. This can be better understood by analogous to coupled dictionary learning [24]. It is reasonable to assume that the same user should have identical attribute representation, and thus identical coefficients when projected to the coupled user factors.

Formally, let $D^Y = \{\mathbf{d}_1^Y, \cdots, \mathbf{d}_{|\mathcal{D}|}^Y\}$, $D^T = \{\mathbf{d}_1^T, \cdots, \mathbf{d}_{|\mathcal{D}|}^T\}$ denote the coupled user factors in YouTube and Twitter, where $|\mathcal{D}|$ is the number of the latent user attributes. By forcing overlapped user's YouTube and Twitter distributions share the same coefficients after projected to the coupled factors, we have the following optimization objective function:

$$\begin{aligned}\min_{D^Y, D^T, S} & ||U_o^Y - D^Y S||_2^2 + ||U_o^T - D^T S||_2^2 + \lambda_2||S||_1 \\ s.t.\ & ||\mathbf{d}^Y||_2^2 \le 1, ||\mathbf{d}^T||_2^2 \le 1, \forall d \in \mathcal{D}\end{aligned} \tag{5}$$

where $S = \{\mathbf{s}_1, ..., \mathbf{s}_{|\mathcal{U}_o|}\}$ with $\mathbf{s}_i$ be the attribute representation for user $u_i \in \mathcal{U}_o$, the constrain $||\mathbf{d}||_2^2 \le 1$ is to prevent D from being arbitrarily large. The reason of using *l1*-norm penalty is to encourage a compact attribute space that users sparsely distribute on. Eqn. (5) can be rewritten as

$$\begin{aligned}\min_{\hat{D}, S} & ||\hat{U}_o - \hat{D}S||_2^2 + \lambda_2||S||_1 \\ & s.t.||\hat{\mathbf{d}}_i||_2^2 \le 1, \forall i\end{aligned} \tag{6}$$

where

$$\hat{U}_o = \begin{bmatrix} U_o^Y \\ U_o^T \end{bmatrix}, \hat{D} = \begin{bmatrix} D^Y \\ D^T \end{bmatrix}$$

The optimization problem (6) can be efficiently solved by the sparse coding algorithm proposed in [23].

Latent attribute discovery on all users $\mathcal{U}^Y$, $\mathcal{U}^T$. (LA_all) The non-overlapped users have been ignored in the proposed association methods. In practical implementation, plenty of non-overlapped users exist. The optimal user factors should both be coupled to unique latent attributes and well represent the latent structure in each network.

Inspired by this, we reformulate Eqn. (5) that the non-overlapped users $\mathcal{U}_{non}^Y$, $\mathcal{U}_{non}^T$ also contribute to the user factor discovery in each network, but with no requirement on identical coefficients. Formally, the optimization objective function is:

$$\min_{D^Y,D^T,S^Y,S^T} ||U^Y - D^Y S^Y||_2^2 + ||U^T - D^T S^T||_2^2 + \lambda_3||S_o||_1 + \lambda_4||S_{non}^Y||_1 + \lambda_5||S_{non}^T||_1$$
$$s.t.\ ||\mathbf{d}^Y||_2^2 \le 1, ||\mathbf{d}^T||_2^2 \le 1, \forall d \in \mathcal{D} \quad (7)$$

where S_{non}^Y,S_{non}^T are user factor coefficients for the non-overlapped users in YouTube and Twitter, $S^Y = [S_o, S_{non}^Y]$, $S^T = [S_o, S_{non}^T]$, $\lambda_3, \lambda_4, \lambda_5$ are tuning parameters controlling the factor distribution sparsity. It can be seen that the above formulation learns user factors not only coupled to unique user attributes over the overlapped users, but minimizing the reconstruction error in each network over all the non-overlapped users.

Since Eqn. (7) is convex to $D^Y, D^T, S_o, S_{non}^Y, S_{non}^T$ respectively, we design an iterative algorithm by alternatively optimizing the following three sub-problems till convergence or maximum iteration:

A. Coupled factor distribution learning

$$\min_{S_o} ||U_o^Y - D^Y S_o||_2^2 + ||U_o^T - D^T S_o||_2^2 + \lambda_3||S_o||_1 \quad (8)$$

This is exactly the same problem in Eqn. (5) with fixed user factors D^Y, D^T.

B. Divided factor distribution learning

$$\min_{S_{non}^Y} ||U_{non}^Y - D^Y S_{non}^Y||_2^2 + \lambda_4||S_{non}^Y||_1$$
$$\min_{S_{non}^T} ||U_{non}^T - D^T S_{non}^T||_2^2 + \lambda_5||S_{non}^T||_1 \quad (9)$$

This is a multi-task lasso problem and can be solved by the feature-sign search algorithm [23].

C. Coupled user factor update

$$\min_{D^Y,D^T} ||U^Y - D^Y S^Y||_2^2 + ||U^T - D^T S^T||_2^2$$
$$s.t.\ ||\mathbf{d}^Y||_2^2 \le 1, ||\mathbf{d}^T||_2^2 \le 1, \forall d \in \mathcal{D} \quad (10)$$

This is a quadratically constrained quadratic program problem (QCQP). We utilize an alternative update strategy for solution [25].

With the derived user factors D^Y and D^T, given a new YouTube user topic distribution $\mathbf{u}^Y \in \mathbb{R}^{K^Y \times 1}$, we can estimate the YouTube user factor distribution as:

$$\mathbf{s}^* = \min_s ||\mathbf{u}^Y - D^Y \mathbf{s}||_2^2 + \lambda||\mathbf{s}||_1 \quad (11)$$

Since unique user shares the same factor coefficients, we can reconstruct his/her Twitter topic distribution as:

$$\mathbf{u}^T = D^T \mathbf{s}^*.$$

3.4 Referrer Identification

With the cross-network distribution transfer function $\mathcal{F}$, we can estimate arbitrary user's Twitter followee topic distribution by inputing his/her YouTube video topic distribution. In our video promotion problem, given a test YouTube video v_t, we simulate a virtual user with identical topic distribution $\mathbf{v}_t^Y = p(\mathbf{z}^Y|v_t)$ to represent the typical YouTube users liking the video [7]. After distribution transfer, the virtual user's Twitter followee topic distribution $\mathbf{v}_t^T = p(\mathbf{z}^T|v_t)$ actually reflects the most probable Twitter following patterns for the video fans.

On the Twitter side, we construct a popular Twitter followee set $\mathcal{U}_t^{followee} \subset \mathcal{U}^{followee}$ serving as the candidate YouTube video promotion referrers. For each popular followee $u \in \mathcal{U}_t^{followee}$, his/her Twitter topic distribution $\mathbf{u}^T$ can be calculated as:

$$p(z_k^T|u) \propto p(u|z_k^T) \cdot p(z_k^T)$$

where $p(z_k^T)$ is the topic prior and can be calculated by aggregating over users. Here $p(z_k^T|u)$ actually reflects followee u's popularity in the kth topic.

Direct product-based matching Given the test YouTube video and candidate Twitter followees represented on the same topic space, one way is to directly use dot product as the properness measure. The properness score of Twitter followee $u \in \mathcal{U}_t^{followee}$ to promote YouTube video v_t is calculated as:

$$properness(u, v_t) = <\mathbf{v}_t^T, \mathbf{u}^T> = \sum_{k=1}^{K^T} v_{t,k}^T \cdot u_k^T \quad (12)$$

A rank $\psi_{v_t}(\cdot)$ defined on the followees can be obtained accordingly to identify the optimal Twitter referrer.

Weighted product-based matching We also investigate a matching strategy by optimizing the weights for each topic. Viewing test video as the query and candidate Twitter followee set as the collection, the referrer identification can be treated as a retrieval problem. In light of this, we design a training scheme and adopt ranking SVM [26] for topic selection.

Ranking SVM model is with the form as:

$$g(\cdot,\cdot) = \mathbf{h} \cdot \phi(\cdot,\cdot) \quad (13)$$

where $\mathbf{h}$ is the model parameter, i.e., the learnt weights for the corresponding topics. The goal of ranking SVM is to learn an optimal $\mathbf{h}$ that best maintains the rank order in the training query-document pairs.

In our problem, we define the feature mapping function as the vector product between video and followee distributions:

$$\phi(\mathbf{v}_t^T, \mathbf{u}^T) = \mathbf{v}_t^T \odot \mathbf{u}^T = \{v_{t,1}^T \cdot u_1^T, ..., v_{t,K^T}^T \cdot u_{K^T}^T\}$$

where $\odot$ indicates the element-wise multiplication. To obtain the ranks in the training set, for each query-document pair v, u, we need to calculate their ground-truth properness score. According to the discussion in introduction, the properness of Twitter followee is decided by how many of his/her followers like the test video. Therefore, we combine two information retrieval metrics of *precision* and *recall* to define the Ground-Truth (GT) properness:

$$\text{precision}(v, u) = \frac{|\mathcal{U}_v \cap \mathcal{U}_u^{followee}|}{|\mathcal{U}_u^{followee}|}$$

$$\text{recall}(v, u) = \frac{|\mathcal{U}_v \cap \mathcal{U}_u^{followee}|}{|\mathcal{U}_v|}$$

$$\text{GT-properness}(v, u) = \frac{2}{\text{precision}(v, u)^{-1} + \text{recall}(v, u)^{-1}}$$

[7] Due to the flexibility of iCorr-LDA, we can also estimate the topic distribution for videos with only visual keyframes or textual words. This extends the applicability of our framework.

Table 2: Statistics of our dataset.

$\lvert\mathcal{U}^Y\rvert$	$\lvert\mathcal{U}^T\rvert$	$\lvert\mathcal{U}_o\rvert$	$\lvert\mathcal{V}\rvert$	Avg.$\lvert\mathcal{U}_u^{followee}\rvert$
38,540	39,400	11,850	2,280,129	891.1

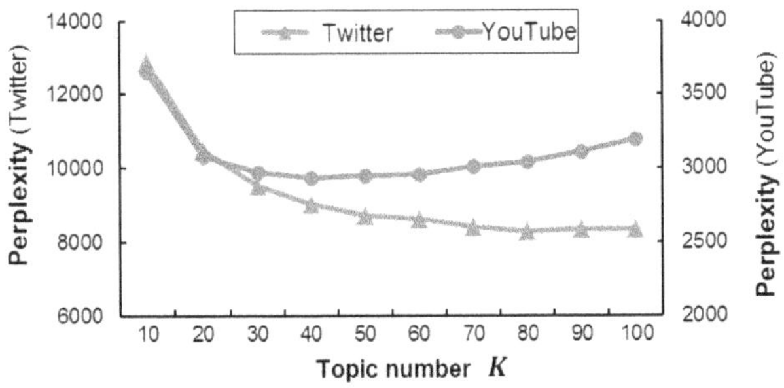

Figure 4: The perplexities for different topic numbers on YouTube and Twitter.

where $\mathcal{U}_v$ is the set of users showing interest in v, $\mathcal{U}_u^{followee}$ is the follower set of u [8]. We can see that *recall* actually concerns with coverage of the interested YouTube audiences, while *precision* is in charge of the virtual cost. With the learnt $\mathbf{h}^*$, the properness of Twitter followee $u \in \mathcal{U}_t^{followee}$ for test video v_t is calculated as:

$$properness(u, v_t) = \mathbf{h}^* \cdot \phi(\mathbf{v}_t^T, \mathbf{u}^T). \quad (14)$$

4. EXPERIMENTS

4.1 Dataset

Since no ready cross-network dataset is available, we construct a new dataset with user account linkage between YouTube and Twitter. Google+ encourages users to provide the external links to their other social media network accounts. We first collected 143,259 Google+ users, among which 38,540 provide YouTube account, 39,400 provide Twitter account, 11,850 provide both accounts [9]. For each YouTube user, we further downloaded his/her uploaded videos, favorite videos, playlists and the involved video information via YouTube API. For each Twitter user, we downloaded his/her followee set and user profiles via Twitter API. Table 2 summarizes the key statistics [10].

4.2 Heterogeneous Topic Modeling

4.2.1 Topic Number Selection

In topic modeling, the selection of topic number is very important. We resort to the perplexity in this paper, which is a standard measure for estimating how well one generative model fits the data [28]. The lower the perplexity score is, the better the performance. We test the perplexity with

Table 3: Visualization of discovered YouTube topics.

Topic #1	Word	gameplay xbox playstation gaming minecraft
	Video	"Epic Mods - MW2 MOD IN CoD4" 
		"HEXXIT COOP ep7 w/ Double" 
		"Halo 4 Adrift Multiplayer Map" 
Topic #17	Word	history german berlin germany poetry
	Video	"GEH STERBEN, DU OPFER!!!" 
		"Syrien - Wahrheit lźber das Massaker" 
		"Volker Pispers - Einzeltater" 

different topic number K^Y and K^T on 490,000 held-out YouTube videos and 9,400 held-out Twitter users, respectively [11]. The perplexity scores on different topic numbers are shown in Fig. 4. We can see that on both YouTube and Twitter, the perplexities decrease dramatically first before reaching a relatively stable level and then have a tendency to increase when the models are overfit. Since larger topic number requires more computational cost and has overfitting risk, we prefer the smallest topic number that leads to perplexity on the stable level. Therefore, we choose the topic number $K^Y = 40$ for YouTube and $K^T = 80$ for Twitter.

4.2.2 Visualization of Discovered Topics

In order to interpret the derived topic spaces, we visualize some of the discovered topics in YouTube and Twitter, respectively. Table 3 shows two sampled YouTube video topics. For each topic, we provide the top-5 probable words and 3 most representative videos. Representative videos are ranked based on the video-topic distribution $p(z_k^Y|v)$ and represented by the keyframes and video titles in Table 3. By visualizing both the semantic and visual information, it is very easy to interpret the domain knowledge associated with each topic. Moreover, the discovered video topics show high consistency between textual semantics and visual patterns.

Table 4 shows three sampled Twitter followee topics, with each visualized by the top-3 probable followees and the followees' profile information. It is conceived that the discovered Twitter topics have a quite wide coverage: the general topic #43 addressing the game-related popular followees, the specific topic #10 consisting of Forbes influencers, and even the geographic topic #38 with the top followees all coming from Berlin. Twitter users' joint following patterns are well captured in modeling the follower-followee relationship, which is very important to the subsequent promotion application.

[8] For a given YouTube video, we can only know whether a specific Twitter followee's followers will like the video if we know these Twitter followers' YouTube accounts, so both the sets $\mathcal{U}_v$ and $\mathcal{U}_u^{followee}$ are counted based on the known overlapped user set $\mathcal{U}_o$.

[9] User linkage mining is a separate topic in cross-network analysis [27]. In our work, to guarantee a promising overlapped user resource, we leverage user self-provided account links on Google+.

[10] Avg.$\lvert\mathcal{U}_u^{followee}\rvert$ is the average number of followees over all the examined Twitter users.

[11] Hyperparameters are fixed as $\alpha = 0.8$ and $\beta = 0.1$ according to the empirical expectation for the output distribution [29].

Table 4: Visualization of discovered Twitter topics.

Topic	User ID	Username	Location	#followers	Self-description
#43	63485337	Markus Persson	Stockholm, Sweden	1,436,534	Hey, you! Play more games! Now!
	36803580	Steam	–	932,044	Steam, The Ultimate Online Game Platform. Follow us...
	11167502	Humble Bundle	San Francisco,CA	192,764	News from the Humble Bundle. For support, please...
#10	21279340	Pam Moore	Orlando, FL	178,101	50% mktg 50% geek CEO, Forbes TOP Social Influencer.
	33057154	Jeff Sheehan	Atlanta, GA	254,984	Social Media Pro | Speaker | Author | 30+ years Mktg.
	15081182	Warren Whitlock	Las Vegas, NV	178,759	Forbes Power Influencer. Radio Host, Author, Speaker...
#38	5876652	Sascha Lobo	Berlin, Germany	161,099	Author, Internet.
	9655032	netzpolitik	Berlin, Germany	120,014	Entrepreneur, activist, organizer of @republica.
	9334352	Mario Sixtus	Berlin, Germany	60,542	Journalist, Photographer. Hier mehr oder weniger

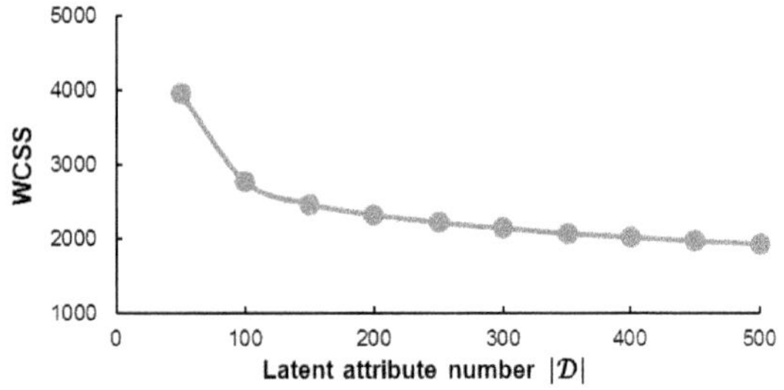

Figure 5: Sum of WCSS over different $|\mathcal{D}|$.

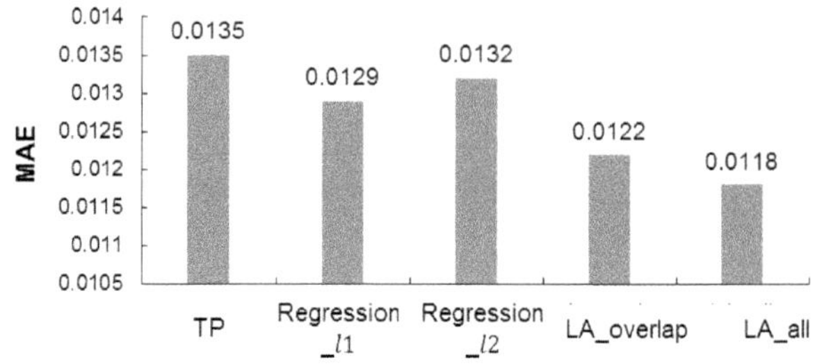

Figure 6: MAE for distribution transfer in Stage 2.

4.3 Cross Network Topic Association

4.3.1 *Experimental Setting*

Given a user with his/her YouTube topic distribution $\mathbf{u}^Y$, the goal of Stage 2 is to estimate his/her Twitter followee topic distribution $\mathbf{u}^T$. Therefore, we utilize Mean Abosolute Error (MAE) as the evaluation metric. We randomly select half of the overlapped users to construct the test set $\mathcal{U}_{test}$, and the rest overlapped users and non-overlapped users as the training set. MAE is calculated over all topics of each test user as:

$$\text{MAE} = \frac{\sum\limits_{u \in \mathcal{U}_{test}} \sum\limits_{k=1}^{K^T} |\hat{u}_k^T - u_k^T|}{|\mathcal{U}_{test}| K^T} \tag{15}$$

where u_k^T and $\hat{u}_k^T$ are the actual and estimated user u's topic distribution on the kth Twitter topic.

For model parameters, we select the regularization coefficient λ_1 in Eqn. (3) by grid search and 5-fold cross validation. Tuning parameters λ_2 in Eqn. (5) and $\lambda_3, \lambda_4, \lambda_5$ in Eqn. (7) are selected by a combined line-search strategy according to the minimal objective energy after converge. As a result, the parameters are set as $\lambda_1 = 0.1, \lambda_2 = 0.2, \lambda_3 = 0.1, \lambda_4 = 0.01, \lambda_5 = 0.01$. It is particularly non-trivial to decide the number of attributes $|\mathcal{D}|$ in the latent attribute-based association methods: small $|\mathcal{D}|$ may fail to capture the intrinsic structures, while big $|\mathcal{D}|$ will lead to overfitting. As discussed in the solution section, the coupled user factors can be understood as a pair of dictionaries in the discovered Twitter and YouTube topic spaces. Classical clustering metrics, e.g., Within-Cluster Sum of Squares (WCSS) [30], are widely used to evaluate how well the observed data can be reconstructed from the learnt dictionary. Therefore, we conduct K-means on YouTube and Twitter user distributions U^Y, U^T with the identical cluster number $|\mathcal{D}|$. In Fig. 5 we draw the curve of WCSS sum on the two networks w.r.t. the change of $|\mathcal{D}|$. We choose $|\mathcal{D}| = 300$ when the aggregated reconstruction error decreases to a steadily low level.

4.3.2 *Experimental Results and Analysis*

The transition probability (TP) and regression based methods all yield explicit topic association matrix. To better understand the association between heterogeneous topics, we first examine the derived association matrix $A \subset \mathbb{R}^{K^Y \times K^T}$ from TP. Among the $K^Y \times K^T = 3,200$ topic association pairs, the most significant are $\{z_1^Y, z_{43}^T\}$ and $\{z_{17}^Y, z_{38}^T\}$, which have been visualized in Table 3 and 4. We can see that the derived association involves with multiple aspects: game-related YouTube topic #1 significantly associates with Twitter topic #43 whose top-ranked followees are official game platforms or developers, and the association between YouTube topic #17 and Twitter topic #38 results from their shared location in Germany. A single association metric, e.g., semantics, tends to fail in this case. Actually, one advantage of exploiting the overlapped users for association mining is its flexibility: there is no need to explicitly design an association metric, and users' collaborative activities on different social networks define the metric.

Performance comparison among the proposed methods is shown in Fig. 6. Several observations are made. (1) With MAE lower than 0.015, all the proposed association solutions achieve satisfied performance. This shows the reasonability by exploiting the overlapped users towards cross-network topic association. (2) The latent attribute-based methods (*LA_overlap*, *LA_all*) outperform the explicit association matrix-oriented methods (*TP*, *Regression*). In addition to the freedom to non-linear association, *LA*-based solutions address the hidden structure behind the observed heterogeneous user activities and enjoy better interpretation. (3) By considering the non-overlapped users, *LA_all* is slightly superior to *LA_overlap*. This validates our assumption that better capturing the latent structure in each network contributes to improved coupled factor discovery.

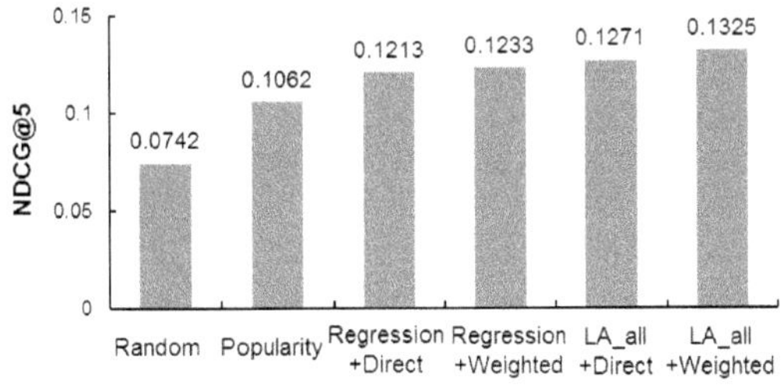

Figure 7: NDCG@5 for different settings in Stage 3.

4.4 Twitter Referrer Identification

4.4.1 Experimental Setting

2,061 videos that more than 15 overlapped users have shown interest to are selected to construct the YouTube test video set $\mathcal{V}_t$. Meanwhile, 21,276 Twitter followees who are followed by more than 50 users construct the candidate Twitter followee set $\mathcal{U}_t^{followee}$.

We use Normalized Discounted Cumulative Gain (NDCG) as the evaluation metric, which is widely used in retrieval problems. NDCG is defined as:

$$NDCG@k = \frac{1}{Z}\sum_{j=1}^{k}\frac{2^{rel(j)}-1}{\log(1+j)} \tag{16}$$

where $rel(\cdot)$ is a relevance function between the test video and the ranked followee candidate. With the goal to identify Twitter followees with optimal coverage-cost balance, we use *GT-properness* as in Eqn. (14) to calculate $rel(\cdot)$. Moreover, the groundtruth for the Twitter referrer ranking is also constructed by sorting the *GT-properness* between the test video and the followee candidate based on the known overlapped user set $\mathcal{U}_o$.

We consider the following settings for comparison:

- *Random*: randomly select k followees from $\mathcal{U}_t^{followee}$;
- *Popularity*: select k popular Twitter followees with the most #followers;
- *Regression+Direct*: distribution transfer by *Regression_l1*, matching by *Direct product*;
- *Regression+Weighted*: distribution transfer by *Regression_l1*, matching by *Weighted product*;
- *LA_all+Direct*: distribution transfer by *LA_all*, matching by *Direct product*;
- *LA_all+Weighted*: distribution transfer by *LA_all*, matching by *Weighted product*.

4.4.2 Experimental Results and Analysis

We show NDCG@5 for different settings in Fig. 7 [12]. It is observed that: (1) *Popularity* fails to identify the optimal Twitter referrer. This is easy to understand. While high #follower guarantees the coverage of potential viewers (*precision*), the retrieved follower set is expected to also include many uninterested users (*recall*), which deviates our goal towards target promotion. (2) Conducting distribution transfer by *LA_all+Direct* and *LA_all+Weighted* obtain better performance than *Regression+Direct* and *Regression+Weighted*. This coincides with our motivation that more accurate distribution transfer contributes to improved referrer identification. (3) The settings with weighted product-based matching consistently outperform those with direct product. This demonstrates the advantage of topic weight optimization. One possible interpretation is that different topics contribute differently in view of referrer identification.

[12]Since the view history of Youtube users is unavailable via public API, the NDCG results are relatively low due to a lack of abundant user behaviors.

5. DISCUSSION

5.1 Application and Extension

Application. The proposed framework also enables solutions to other applications. From Stage 2, we actually obtain the association between YouTube video interests and Twitter following patterns. Based on this association, cross-network personalized recommendation problems on two directions can be enabled: recommending Twitter followee topic or Twitter lists given YouTube video interest [16], and recommending YouTube videos given Twitter followee list.

Another promising application is on examining the value of Twitter followees. Current methods value Twitter followees by directly analyzing their followers' demographics information, e.g., the followee has a lot of young female followers. The proposed framework in this work facilitates application-oriented Twitter followee value analysis, by associating Twitter followee topic space with the needed topic spaces. For example, our work can be viewed as valuing Twitter followee w.r.t. promotion efficiency to YouTube videos. This significantly expands understanding into the value of Twitter followees.

Extension. Our current solution only employs the content feature of YouTube test videos, i.e., title, tags and keyframes. One extension is to combine with social features, e.g., who uploads or favorites the video. The consideration of user social network is also expected to contribute to improved cross-network association.

Moreover, the current referrer identification is on the individual level, i.e., no interaction between followees is considered. In practice, when choosing a group of followees as the promotion referrers, follower intersection of the candidate followees need to be modeled. Analogous to advertising, as discussed in the introduction, this work actually addresses the problem of advertising media selection. Other problems in advertising include advertising anchor text generation (i.e., optimizing video description for promotion), and advertising slot bid (i.e., followee reshare time selection).

Other than crawling user activities from public API, another way for evaluation is to run a real-world system and ask the users for participation. However, the examined users are popular Twitter followees, who are costly or completely unwilling to participate into the study. Therefore in the future, we are expecting to conduct a real-world evaluation by examining some less popular followees instead.

5.2 A Promising Direction

The idea of exploiting overlapped users towards cross-network association actually opens up possibilities to a very interesting direction. People involve with social media by interacting with heterogeneous social media knowledge, e.g., multimedia semantics, geographic patterns, people consuming patterns, social interactions, etc. The association among different social media activities will lead to insightful observations, contribute to collective utilization, and facilitate advanced social media analysis and applications. For example, the association between user watching activity in *ouTube* and transaction activity in *Amazon* leads to understanding between user interest and consuming models, and facilitates cross-network product target advertising. "Multimedia" research under social media circumstances may understand not only text, image, video, but the association among heterogeneous social media knowledge.

The user-generated nature of social media inspires us to understand the heterogeneous knowledge by "how we experience the world". Instead of conducting analysis from scratches, the different activities that overlapped users contribute in different social media networks can be employed as human supervision. This actually borrows the essence of crowdsourcing where the collective human intelligence is aggregated.

The guideline to instantiate the idea is: (1) Determine the heterogeneous knowledge involved in different social media networks, and crawl a dataset of overlapped users and their heterogeneous activities. (2) Extract the latent topic spaces on each network to construct heterogeneous knowledge bases. (3) Conduct cross-network topic association by exploiting the observed overlapped users as supervision. (4) Design cross-network collaborative applications (one-way or two-way) based on the derived knowledge association.

6. CONCLUSION

We have proposed an overlapped user-based association solution framework, to address the novel cross-network YouTube video promotion problem. Alternative methods have been developed and evaluated, to demonstrate the effectiveness of exploiting user collaboration towards heterogeneous knowledge association. The proposed framework is quite flexible, and can be generalized to other cross-network collaborative problems. We hope that this paper could serve as a good chance to emphasize the collective utilization of social media sources and further the agenda of cross-network analysis and application in social multimedia research.

7. ACKNOWLEDGMENT

This work is supported in part by National Basic Research Program of China (No. 2012CB316304), National Natural Science Foundation of China (No. 61225009, 61332016, 61303176), and Beijing Natural Science Foundation (No. 4131004).

8. REFERENCES

[1] Bernardo A Huberman, Daniel M Romero, and Fang Wu. Crowdsourcing, attention and productivity. *Journal of Information Science*, 35(6):758–765, 2009.

[2] Jean Burgess and Joshua Green. *YouTube: Online video and participatory culture*. John Wiley & Sons, 2013.

[3] Meeyoung Cha, Haewoon Kwak, Pablo Rodriguez, Yong-Yeol Ahn, and Sue Moon. I tube, you tube, everybody tubes: analyzing the world's largest user generated content video system. In *IMC 2007*, pages 1–14.

[4] Xu Cheng, Cameron Dale, and Jiangchuan Liu. Statistics and social network of youtube videos. In *IWQoS 2008*, pages 229–238.

[5] Renjie Zhou, Samamon Khemmarat, and Lixin Gao. The impact of youtube recommendation system on video views. In *IMC 2010*, pages 404–410.

[6] Youmna Borghol, Sebastien Ardon, Niklas Carlsson, Derek Eager, and Anirban Mahanti. The untold story of the clones: Content-agnostic factors that impact youtube video popularity. In *KDD 2012*, pages 1186–1194.

[7] Flavio Figueiredo, Jussara M Almeida, Marcos André Gonçalves, and Fabrício Benevenuto. On the dynamics of social media popularity: A youtube case study. *arXiv preprint arXiv:1402.1777*, 2014.

[8] Delip Rao, David Yarowsky, Abhishek Shreevats, and Manaswi Gupta. Classifying latent user attributes in twitter. In *SMUC 2010*, pages 37–44.

[9] Zhiheng Xu, Rong Lu, Liang Xiang, and Qing Yang. Discovering user interest on twitter with a modified author-topic model. In *WI-IAT 2011*, pages 422–429.

[10] John R. Kender, Matthew L. Hill, Apostol (Paul) Natsev, John R. Smith, and Lexing Xie. Video genetics: A case study from youtube. In *ACM Multimedia 2010*, pages 1253–1258.

[11] Fabian Abel, Samur Araújo, Qi Gao, and Geert-Jan Houben. Analyzing cross-system user modeling on the social web. In *Web Engineering*, pages 28–43. Springer, 2011.

[12] Zhengyu Deng, Jitao Sang, and Changsheng Xu. Personalized video recommendation based on cross-platform user modeling. In *ICME 2013*, pages 1–6. IEEE.

[13] Suman Deb Roy, Tao Mei, Wenjun Zeng, and Shipeng Li. Socialtransfer: cross-domain transfer learning from social streams for media applications. In *ACM Multimedia 2012*, pages 649–658. ACM.

[14] Meeyoung Cha, Hamed Haddadi, Fabricio Benevenuto, and P Krishna Gummadi. Measuring user influence in twitter: The million follower fallacy. *ICWSM*, 10:10–17, 2010.

[15] Jianshu Weng, Ee-Peng Lim, Jing Jiang, and Qi He. Twitterrank: finding topic-sensitive influential twitterers. In *WSDM 2010*, pages 261–270. ACM.

[16] Saptarshi Ghosh, Naveen Sharma, Fabricio Benevenuto, Niloy Ganguly, and Krishna Gummadi. Cognos: crowdsourcing search for topic experts in microblogs. In *SIGIR 2012*, pages 575–590. ACM.

[17] David Kempe, Jon Kleinberg, and Éva Tardos. Maximizing the spread of influence through a social network. In *KDD 2003*, pages 137–146. ACM.

[18] Wei Chen, Chi Wang, and Yajun Wang. Scalable influence maximization for prevalent viral marketing in large-scale social networks. In *KDD 2010*, pages 1029–1038. ACM.

[19] Brendan F Klare, Zhifeng Li, and Anil K Jain. Matching forensic sketches to mug shot photos. *Pattern Analysis and Machine Intelligence, IEEE Transactions on*, 33(3):639–646, 2011.

[20] Zhen Lei, Matti Pietikainen, and S Li. Learning discriminant face descriptor. 2013.

[21] David R Hardoon, Sandor Szedmak, and John Shawe-Taylor. Canonical correlation analysis: An overview with application to learning methods. *Neural computation*, 16(12):2639–2664, 2004.

[22] David M Blei and Michael I Jordan. Modeling annotated data. In *SIGIR 2003*, pages 127–134.

[23] Honglak Lee, Alexis Battle, Rajat Raina, and Andrew Y Ng. Efficient sparse coding algorithms. *Advances in neural information processing systems*, 19:801, 2007.

[24] Jianchao Yang, Zhaowen Wang, Zhe Lin, Scott Cohen, and Thomas Huang. Coupled dictionary training for image super-resolution. *Image Processing, IEEE Transactions on*, 21(8):3467–3478, 2012.

[25] Meng Yang, Lei Zhang, Jian Yang, and David Zhang. Metaface learning for sparse representation based face recognition. In *ICIP 2010*, pages 1601–1604.

[26] Thorsten Joachims. Optimizing search engines using clickthrough data. In *KDD 2002*, pages 133–142. ACM.

[27] Jing Liu, Fan Zhang, Xinying Song, Young-In Song, Chin-Yew Lin, and Hsiao-Wuen Hon. What's in a name?: an unsupervised approach to link users across communities. In *WWW*, pages 495–504, 2013.

[28] David M Blei, Andrew Y Ng, and Michael I Jordan. Latent dirichlet allocation. *the Journal of machine Learning research*, 3:993–1022, 2003.

[29] Thomas L Griffiths and Mark Steyvers. Finding scientific topics. *Proceedings of the National academy of Sciences of the United States of America*, 101(Suppl 1):5228–5235, 2004.

[30] John A Hartigan and Manchek A Wong. Algorithm as 136: A k-means clustering algorithm. *Applied statistics*, pages 100–108, 1979.

One of a Kind: User Profiling by Social Curation

Xue Geng[†], Hanwang Zhang[‡], Zheng Song[‡], Yang Yang[‡], Huanbo Luan [‡] and Tat-Seng Chua[‡]
[‡]School of Computing, National University of Singapore
[‡]University of Electronic Science and Technology of China
[§]Tsinghua University
[§]Visenze Pte. Ltd.
{snownus, hanwangzhang, sirius.szh, dlyyang}@gmail.com
{luanhb, chuats}@comp.nus.edu.sg

ABSTRACT

Social Curation Service (SCS) is a new type of emerging social media platform, where users can select, organize and keep track of multimedia contents they like. In this paper, we take advantage of this great opportunity and target at the very starting point in social media: user profiling, which supports fundamental applications such as personalized search and recommendation. As compared to other profiling methods in conventional Social Network Services (SNS), our work benefits from the two distinguishable characteristics of SCS: a) organized multimedia user-generated contents, and b) content-centric social network. Based on these two characteristics, we are able to deploy the state-of-the-art multimedia analysis techniques to establish content-based user profiles by extracting user preferences and their social relations. First, we automatically construct a content-based user preference ontology and learn the ontological models to generate comprehensive user profiles. In particular, we propose a new deep learning strategy called multi-task convolutional neural network (mtCNN) to learn profile models and profile-related visual features simultaneously. Second, we propose to model the multi-level social relations offered by SCS to refine the user profiles in a low-rank recovery framework. To the best of our knowledge, our work is the first that explores how social curation can help in content-based social media technologies, taking user profiling as an example. Extensive experiments on 1,293 users and 1.5 million images collected from Pinterest in fashion domain demonstrate that recommendation methods based on the proposed user profiles are considerably more effective than other state-of-the-art recommendation strategies.

Categories and Subject Descriptors

J.4 [**Computer Applications**]: Social and Behavioral Sciences—*Sociology*

Keywords

Social Curation; User Profiling; Recommendation; Pinterest

MM'14, November 3–7, 2014, Orlando, Florida, USA.
Copyright 2014 ACM 978-1-4503-3063-3/14/11 ...$15.00.
http://dx.doi.org/10.1145/2647868.2654950 .

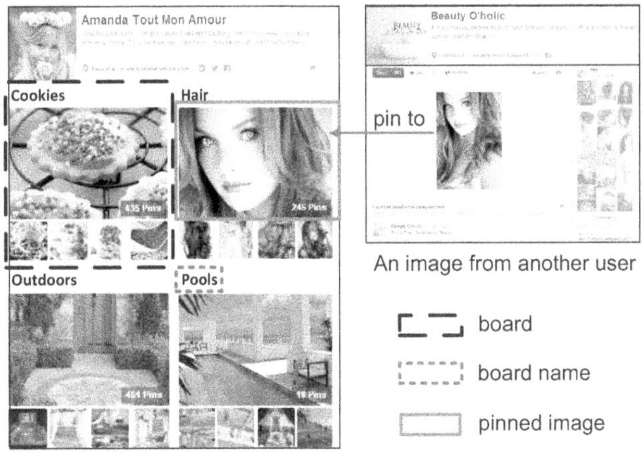

Figure 1: An example of "pin" in Pinterest. A user can curate image bundles called "boards". The curation is done by "pinning" images from other users. Here, the user pins a hairstyle image from another user into her own board named "hair".

1. INTRODUCTION

Social Network Service (SNS), through which people can create, disseminate, and consume information, has evolved themselves while revolutionized our lives over the past 15 years[1]. To date, a large variety of SNSs have thrived on the Internet, focusing on retail market (*e.g.*, Amazon), friendship (*e.g.*, Facebook), movie review (*e.g.*,IMDb), photo sharing (*e.g.*, Flickr), and so on. It is widely acknowledged that social media offers us valuable opportunities in both academia and industry [6].

In this paper, we are interested in user profiling, which is the starting yet fundamental point of SNS [3] in helping to customize large scale web contents to specific users. Here, profiling is the process of establishing users' profiles of interest from the spontaneous data associated with users on SNS, with the aim of capturing the online behavior of the users, including their interest and preferences. Without doubt, user profiling is an indispensable direction in social media, especially for the recommendation-based applications such as viral marketing and e-commerce [14]. User profile can be extracted from explicit or implicit sources. The *explicit* user

[1]The first online social network, FriendsReunited was launched in 1999, founded in Great Britain to reunite past school pals.

profile is provided by users during the registration to some services, and it is often incomplete and inaccurate. *Implicit* profiling is generally content-based, which has been shown to be a useful enhancement based on user relations (*e.g.*, followers or friends) and user-generated contents (*e.g.*, reviews and uploaded/shared photos, videos), which are often multimedia in nature [1]. In fact, the major interest of SNS is rapidly shifting from text-based contents to multimedia[2].

However, content-based user profiling by analyzing the multimedia data in conventional SNSs (*e.g.*, Facebook, Flickr) is a challenging task since the philosophy behind them is rooted in the social connections between the contents creators, *i.e.*, the users, but not the contents themselves. On one hand, the user-user and user-content connections in these conventional networks are *abundant but less informative* to derive personalized user profiles. For example, the friendship of two users does not necessarily suggest that they share the same preference, and the intricate "like" or "dislike" user-content links over the network are extremely diverse in topics, giving rise to difficulties in analyzing the exact user preference. On the other hand, the diverse and noisy user-generated contents prevent us from learning content-based models of user preference, leaving them as the "dark matters" of the "social universe" [5]. Therefore, conventional SNSs are unable to handle the increasingly multimedia nature of users' interactions and experiences.

Recently, Social Curation Service (SCS) has emerged as a new type of social network scheme, attracting many social network users [12]. As compared to the conventional SNSs, SCSs involve human process of remixing social media for the purpose of further consumption. In particular, Pinterest[3], which is the most popular SCS registered by over 70 million users, is a new emerging photo sharing social networking site that allows users to select, organize and keep track of images they like. Pinterest is a "pinboard-style" image sharing social network. Its main innovation is to encourage users to collect and share interesting things in a categorized way. As illustrated in Figure 1, Pinterest innovates a notion called "*Pin to Board*", where users can '*pin*' or '*repin*' items they like into their own "*boards*". The key operation "pin" is to select a photo or video from external websites or another users' pin boards. The boards are bundles of pinned multimedia contents of various interest such as "Animals", "Arts", "Education" and "Fashion". For example, a user can have many bundles named "Cookies", "Outdoors", and "Pools" shown in Figure 1. In this way, social connections are encoded by pins, *e.g.*, users cannot directly send private or public messages to each other and the only social activity is to *like* a pin, *comment* on a pin or *repin* someone's pin into her own boards. Today, many conventional SNSs are inspired by this interesting feature of social curation, such as Flickr's "*add-to-gallery*".

Motivated by the promising outlook of social curation, we attempt to establish high-quality user profiles based on such new social media platforms, *i.e.*, SCSs, with the aim of advancing fundamental social applications such as recommendation. Specifically, our user profiling approach is superior to traditional ones for two key reasons:

Organized vs. Unorganized Contents. Unorganized multimedia contents in conventional SNSs are visually and semantically noisy and diverse, and are thus hard to analyze and exploit even with the state-of-the-art multimedia annotation techniques [11]. In contrast, SCSs contain a considerable amount of manually organized and maintained contents. For example, images in a curated bundle (*e.g.*, the board in Pinterest or the gallery in Flickr) are very focused on the same semantics as shown in Figure 1. Such organized multimedia contents offer us high-quality human labeled training data for multimedia modeling. Moreover, we are able to mine a large amount of curated bundles of user interest to build an content-based ontology to further structuralize the data, resulting in more personalized and accurate user profiles.

[2]http://www.kpcb.com/insights/2013-internet-trends
[3]http://www.pinterest.com

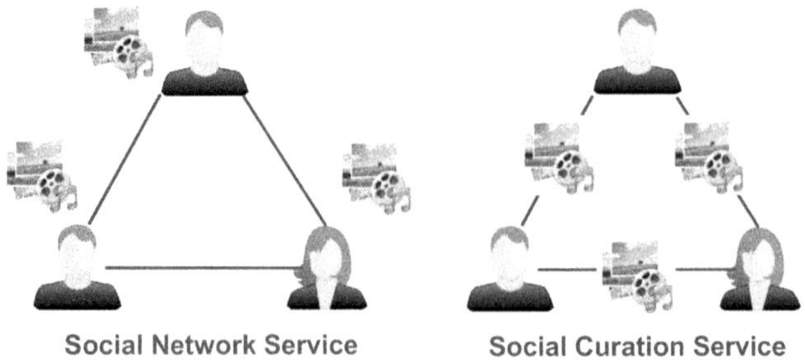

Figure 2: The illustration of the user-centric SNS and the content-centric SCS. Although SNS contains user-generated content, the philosophy behind it is limited to user-user interactions. Alternatively, SCS encourages user interactions at the content level.

Content-centric vs. User-centric Network. As aforementioned, conventional user-centric SNSs are not optimized to create comprehensive user profiles based on user-generated contents. Alternatively, as illustrated in Figure 2, content-centric SCSs are advantageous in reliable social cues on user preference. In particular, user curation through multimedia contents helps to encode multi-level content-content connections, which are expected to pinpoint the user preference in terms of the contents generated by the user. Such connections between two images include: a) *user-level* connection, where the strength indicates how many users have pinned the two images; b) *bundle-level* connection, where the strength indicates how many bundles share the two images; and c) *content-level* connection, where the strength suggests the similarities between the two images. In particular, the first two connections are expected to unravel the diverse user interest hidden in the contents. For example, if two images are only shared by few users (or bundles), the connection between them rarely suggests similar user interest. However, if they are shared by many users (or bundles), they tend to be very likely referring to the same interest. Our user profiling method can leverage rich information to refine the imperfect content-based profile models.

The overview of the proposed user profiling approach based on an example of SCSs, Pinterest, is illustrated in Figure 3. First, we collect multimedia contents curated by users, *i.e.*, the images in bundles as well as the associated user interest description like bundle names and tags. Due to user curation, the collected data are of high-quality and focused according to the user interest. Second, we propose an automatic ontology construction method to structuralize the curated images onto an ontology. The construction is done

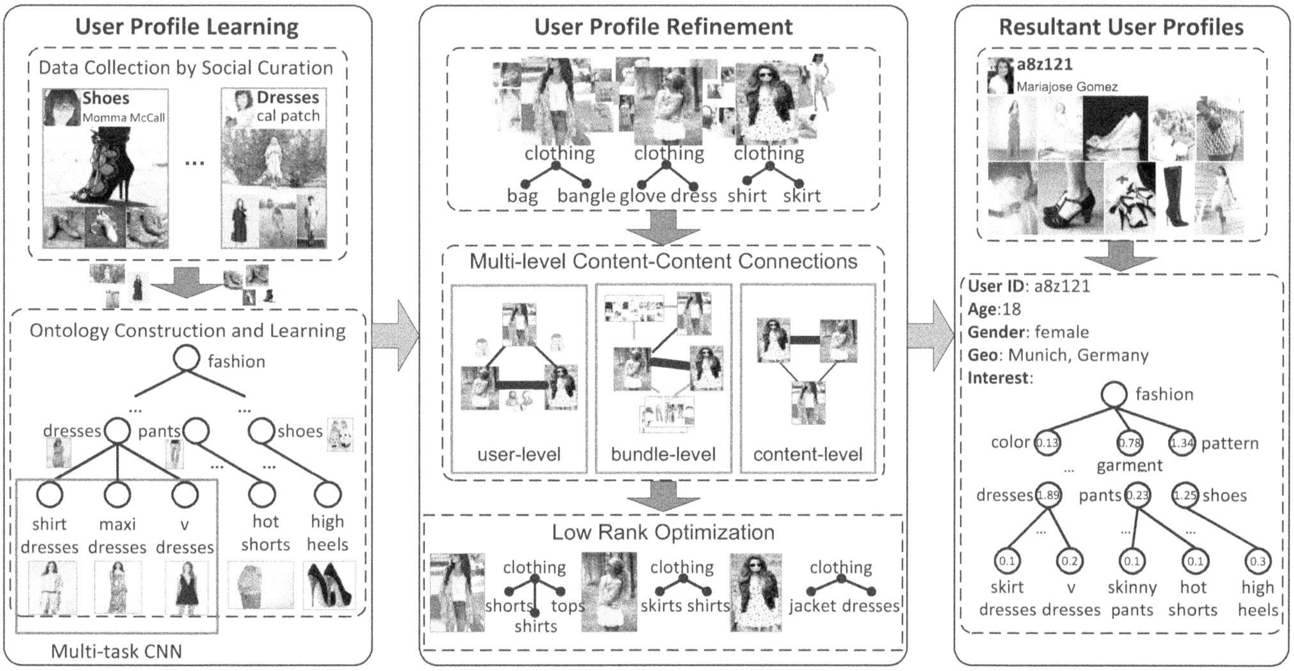

Figure 3: The overview of the proposed user profiling by social curation.

by pruning an expert ontology, *i.e.*, Wikipedia Category, to the desired user interest in a specific domain, such as fashion. Third, based on the constructed ontology, we are able to learn content-based models to generate ontological user profiles, which are more comprehensive and personalized than the traditional text-based profiles. In particular, we propose a novel multi-task convolutional neural network (mtCNN) in order to leverage both the relatedness of sibling items of user interest and the cutting-edge advances in high-performance visual modeling. Fourth, we further propose a low-rank recovery framework to further refine the generated user profiles by the ontological profile models, exploiting the rich user-level, bundle-level and content-level social relations offered by social curations. Therefore, the resultant user profiles are expected to retain: a) the interest of user; b) the interest of user-curated bundles; and c) the semantic affinities with respect to the ontology, supporting effective fundamental social media applications such as recommendation. Experimental results on 1,239 users and 1.5 million images collected from Pinterest in fashion domain demonstrate the effectiveness of the proposed user profiling method as compared to other state-of-the-art methods in terms of recommendation.

With the rapid growing popularity of social curation services, we believe that our research is a pioneering work on content-based social curation analysis, with the following contributions:

- We propose a novel content-based user profiling method based on social curation. Our work concentrates on exploring how social curation can help in content-based social multimedia analysis
- We present a user profiling framework on how to exploit the rich social information in SCS. This framework is fully automated and can be extended to general visual-oriented domain. In this paper, we use the fashion domain in Pinterest as an example.
- Through extensive experiments on fashion recommendation in social media, we demonstrate that our user profiling approach considerably outperforms other state-of-the-art methods.

The rest of the paper is organized as follows. Section 2 reviews related work. Section 3 describes the user profile learning process. Section 4 illustrates the process of user profile refinement. Experimental results and analysis are reported in Section 5, followed by conclusions in Section 6.

2. RELATED WORK

User profiling aims to establish user profiles by obtaining, extracting and representing the characteristics and preferences of users [34]. Current studies on user profiling often analyze either user behaviors (*e.g.*, click streams [32] and posts [28]) or user generated data to model users. From the content-based user profiling point of view, traditional user profiling methods applied either hand-crafted meta-descriptors or a set of latent features by factorizing a user's registered profile data, without considering homophily [29]. Even some researchers considered exploiting collaborative filtering techniques to profile user interest, the social connections are often sparse and noisy, leading to imperfect user profiles. On the other hand, some researchers attempted to exploit user generated contents to profile users. For example, Abel *et al.* [1] enriched user-generated text, *i.e.*, twitter tweets to construct semantic user profiles. Cai *et al.* [4] proposed to build a tag-based user profile for personalized search. Some researchers also attempted to exploit cross-SNS contents to extract comprehensive user profiles [2]. However, traditional content-based user profiles rarely build upon multimedia contents. Even if they do, they are generally unsatisfactory due to the sparse and noisy user-generated data. Alternatively, we propose to use the emerging social network platforms, the social curation services (SCS), to generate content-based user profiles.

SCSs encourage users to curate bundles of multimedia contents from diverse sources, and then re-organize them to show own interest[4] [20, 21]. As introduced by Kimura [12], the key advantage of social curation is the valuable human effort involved in organizing web contents, leading to well-organized contents and content-centric network, which is different from traditional user-centric network. For example, some researchers have worked on exploiting the Flickr groups for image annotation [25, 18] , but the work only focused on the characteristics of the well organized contents without content-centric network; while Kimura's work is just a preliminary study on the potential of social curation in image annotation. Besides, Katsuhiko *et al.* [11] showed that social curation is a promising data source for automatic image understanding and mining in SNSs compared to other state-of-art computer vision methods. Morever, Katsuhiko *et al.* used only the textual meta-data of images, but not utilizing the full power of multimedia and content-centric network. Research on social curation is still in its infancy and thus requires a lot of explorations, especially on some fundamental issues. In this work, we proposed to deploy the power of social curation and state-of-the-art visual model to establish comprehensive content-based user profiles, to support social media applications such as recommendation [22, 15, 7].

3. USER PROFILES LEARNING

Social curation service (SCS), by nature, contains high-quality images in bundles curated by users. Here, "high-quality" means the semantics of images are highly constrained and relevant by the user-provided tags. This gives us a great opportunity to develop well-generalized content-based models to predict the semantics of images, in our cases, the items of user interest.

3.1 Profile Ontology Construction

We use an ontology to organize the items of user interest and their relationships in fashion domain from general to specific, as it has been widely shown to be effective in integrating human knowledge of the domain and data distributions to improve the modeling of visual semantics [31].

After harvesting the user-curated interest concepts for pinned images such as comments and bundle names, we want to automatically generate a profile ontology $\mathcal{O} = (\mathcal{V}, \mathcal{E})$, where $\mathcal{V} = \{v\}$ is a set of concepts such as "leopard", "dresses" and an edge in $\mathcal{E}$ is an ordered pair of concepts in $\mathcal{V} \times \mathcal{V}$. Now, we introduce how to automatically construct the ontology $\mathcal{O}$ by mining the contents in Pinterest. First, we exploit Wikipedia Categories to build a preliminary ontology based on pre-defined general user interest. This ontology is rooted from three general concepts: "color", "garment" and "pattern", voted by the most general WordNet concepts which are hypernyms of the user provided fashion words. However, it is hard to adapt to the real user interest distribution of the user-curated data, since a) some concepts are outdated such as "polonaise", which are missing from the user-curated data; and b) high-frequency concepts such

[4]http://scobleizer.com/2010/03/27/the-seven-needs-of-real-time-curators/

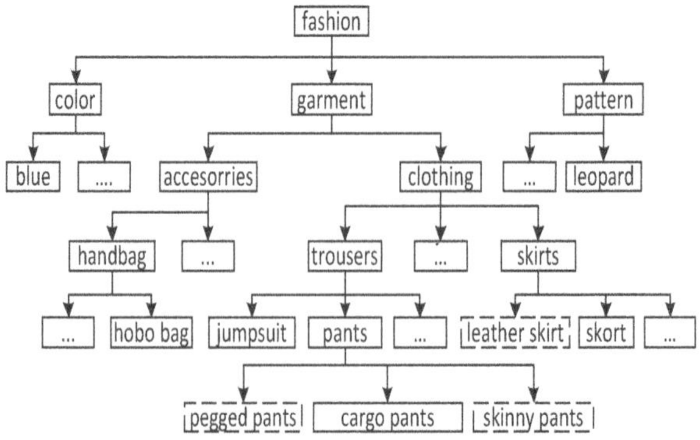

(a) Profile Ontology

#	Statistics
leaf nodes	427
total nodes	464
average samples of leaf nodes	546
least/largest leaf samples	177/11,442
least/largest depth	3/6

(b) Ontology Statistics

Figure 4: (a) The automatic constructed profile ontology in the fashion domain. The dashed boxes denote the automatically augmented concepts. (b) The ontology statistics based on user-generated contents collected from Pinterest.

as "V-dresses", "sleeveless dresses", on the other hand, are missing from this ontology. Therefore, we should prune the Wikipedia ontology to the user interest on demand.

Specifically, to remove the outdated concept, we consider the concepts with low term frequency (*e.g.*, less than 100 times) derived from around 800,000 user-generated items as the outdated ones. Also, we need to add high-frequency concepts into this ontology. This is not a trivial task since it is challenging to find which concept in the ontology is most semantically related to a given high-frequency concept. Here, we propose a novel method for augmenting the ontology with out-of-vocabulary concepts. Suppose we want to add a high-frequency concept h onto the existing ontology $\mathcal{O}$, the key is to find the most probable semantic path from top to bottom and then add h as a sibling of a concept v if v is most semantically similar to h among others along the path. In order to numerically calculate the most probable semantic path, we need to transform concept words into numeric vectors. Here, we use Word2Vec [19] to transform a concept into a 300-D vector, retaining its semantic meanings. Then, we use all the concepts in $\mathcal{V}$ to sparsely represent h as

$$\arg\min_{\mathbf{a}} \|\mathbf{h} - \mathbf{V}\mathbf{a}\|_2^2 + \lambda\|\mathbf{a}\|_1, \quad (1)$$

where $\mathbf{h}$ is the 300-D vector of item h, $\mathbf{V}$ is a dictionary matrix which is arranged by putting vectors of $\mathcal{V}$ column-wisely, $\mathbf{a}$ is a sparse coefficient vector and λ is a trade-off parameter. By doing this, each concept of the ontology $\mathcal{O}$ is assigned a value according to the sparse codes of h [30]. Therefore, we can find the most probable semantic path with the largest sum of sparse codes to achieve the target concept.

As a result, we obtain a comprehensive user profile ontology as shown in Figure 4.

3.2 Profile Ontology Learning

Content-centric SCSs offer well-organized contents which closely relate to user interest. In other words, we are able to collect high-quality training images for every concept in the constructed profile ontology. For learning the model of each concept in the profile ontology, we want to map the images curated by users onto this profile. For example, given an image of "cargo pants", we expect to *visually* reason like: $garment \rightarrow trousers \rightarrow pants \rightarrow cargopants$. As compared to the flat "bag-of-bundles" image organizations in Pinterest, this hierarchical reasoning gives richer semantic interpretations of user interest. In order to achieve this, for each concept v in the profile ontology $\mathcal{O}$, we need to learn a classification model that predicts whether an image belongs to v. Let us start with looking for the training samples of v. Trivially, the images of the concept itself will be the positive samples. Moreover, we consider positive samples of v's siblings as negative samples of v. This myopia way of training is shown to be effective in hierarchical visual task [17]. However, this training strategy suffers from the "error propagation" problem, *i.e.*, the models of v and its siblings are incapable of rejecting the classification errors propagated from higher-level unseen concepts.

In order to alleviate such propagated errors, we expect the model of every concept in the ontology to be as accurate in prediction as possible. To achieve this, we propose to adopt the Multi-task Learning (MTL) framework [9] for jointly learning the models of a concept and its siblings. It has been shown that MTL improves the prediction performance on multiple, different but related, learning problems through shared parameters or representations. In our case, the tasks of learning a concept and its siblings are related since sibling samples are visually similar. For example, "V-dresses" and "strapless dresses" under "dresses" share similar visual cues. Formally, without loss of generality, we only consider a set of sibling concepts $\{v_1, ..., v_M\}$, which share the same parent. Given training images $\{(\mathbf{x}_i, y_i)\}$, where $\mathbf{x}_i$ and y_i are the feature and label of the i-th image in any v_m, respectively. The objective of the MTL is

$$\min_{\mathbf{w}_0,...,\mathbf{w}_M} F(\mathbf{w}_0, ..., \mathbf{w}_M) = -\sum_{m=1}^{M} \sum_{i \in \mathcal{I}_m} \log P(y_i = m | \mathbf{x}_i; \mathbf{w}_0, \mathbf{w}_m) + \lambda \sum_{m=0}^{M} R(\mathbf{w}_m) \tag{2}$$

where $\mathbf{w}_0, ..., \mathbf{w}_M$ are the trainable parameters for M tasks, $\mathcal{I}_m$ is the set of training image indices of v_m, $P(y_i = m|\mathbf{x}_i)$ is a softmax function against other labels $y_i \neq m$ and λ is the trade-off parameter of the regularizer $R(\cdot)$, *e.g.*, ℓ_2-norm regularizer. Particularly, $\mathbf{w}_0$ is the shared parameters of the M tasks, namely, in the last two-layer connection, $\mathbf{w}_0$ is added to $\mathbf{w}_m$ for each task m.

Recent advances in computer vision have shown that deep Convolutional Neural Network (CNN) can learn useful features that outperform the hand-crafted ones [13]. Therefore, we propose a novel multi-task CNN (mtCNN) deep architecture that jointly learns the features and parameters for the tasks. As illustrated in Figure 5, we have M CNNs for each task to learn the feature $\mathbf{x}_i \leftarrow \phi(\mathbf{x}_i; \widetilde{\mathbf{w}}_m)$, where $\phi(\mathbf{x}_i; \widetilde{\mathbf{w}}_m)$ is the output of the m-th CNN (cf. Section 5.1.2 for the details of the mtCNN architecture) and $\widetilde{\mathbf{w}}_m$ is the trainable parameters. Denoting the the overall parameters of mtCNN as $\mathcal{W} = \{\mathbf{w}_0, \mathbf{w}_m, \widetilde{\mathbf{w}}_m\}_{m=1}^{M}$, then the stochastic gradient

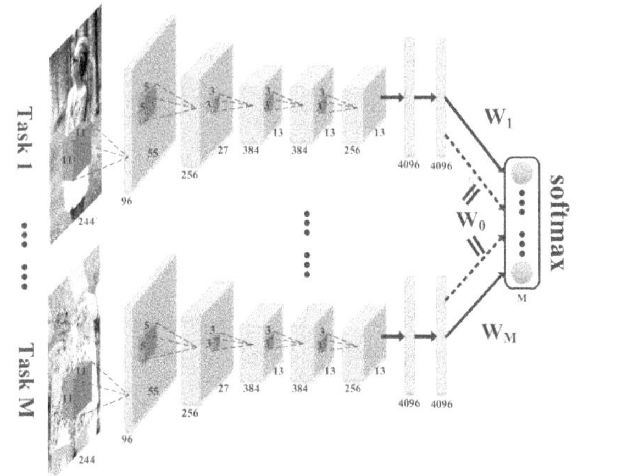

Figure 5: The illustration of the proposed mtCNN. There are M independent CNN pathways for the M tasks. These CNNs share a common parameter $\mathbf{w}_0$ when they eventually feed-forward into the softmax classification layer.

descent update rule of $\mathcal{W}$ in the k-th iteration for solving mtCNN is

$$\begin{cases} \Delta_{k+1} = 0.9 \cdot \Delta_k - 1.5e^{-4} \cdot \eta \cdot \mathcal{W}_k - \eta \cdot \frac{\partial F}{\partial \mathcal{W}_k}, \\ \mathcal{W}_{k+1} = \Delta_{k+1} + \mathcal{W}_k, \end{cases} \tag{3}$$

where Δ is the momentum variable [23], η is the learning rate which is adaptive to the objective function value.

Now we can represent any image in the user-curated bundles as $\mathbf{p}$, where the i-th value p_i is the model output of concept v_i in ontology $\mathcal{O}$. By averaging the $\mathbf{p}$ of all the images, we can eventually obtain the user profiles in a personal hierarchical representation in which the value of each concept node shows the user's interest.

4. REFINEMENT OF USER PROFILES BY SOCIAL CURATION

So far, the above user profiles are only based on visual models, which are insufficient to accurately predict user interest in terms of concepts in the ontology. In this section, we propose to refine the image representations via the multi-level social cues. Since our user profile comes from the integration of all the image representations; through refining the image representation, we can thus refine the user profiles.

4.1 Formulation

We use graph links to model the various types of relations evident from rich social information of curated images. We observe that there are three levels of key relations in the content-centric social curation network. As we will detail soon, these levels of connections play an important role in regularizing the user interest depicted in images.

User-level. This level's connection origins from the fact that "Great minds think alike". For example, if users A, B and C share images i and j simulataneously, then images i and j might be similar. Therefore, images are connected if two or more users have curated them. Formally, we have

$$S_{ij}^{u} = \begin{cases} n, & \text{if } n \text{ users share images } i \text{ and } j, \\ 0, & \text{no users share them.} \end{cases} \tag{4}$$

The strength of user-level link S^u_{ij} indicates how many users consider images i and j belong to the same interest.

Bundle-level. This level's connection is similar to the user-level connection since each bundle often represents one kind of a user's interest. Therefore, at this level, images are connected if two or more bundles include them,

$$S^b_{ij} = \begin{cases} n, & \text{if } n \text{ bundles include images } i \text{ and } j, \\ 0, & \text{no bundles share them.} \end{cases} \tag{5}$$

The strength of bundle-level link S^b_{ij} suggests how many bundles would be curated by users to pin images i and j to the same interest.

Content-level. This level includes two types of image content links: visual link and semantic link. The visual link is based on the visual similarities while the semantic link is based on the hierarchical semantic similarities between two images. Formally, we have

$$S^v_{ij} = \exp\left(-\frac{\|\mathbf{x}_i - \mathbf{x}_j\|_2^2}{\rho^2}\right), \quad S^h_{ij} = \mathbf{p}_i^T \mathbf{H} \mathbf{p}_j = \sum_{k,l} \mathbf{p}_i^k H_{kl} \mathbf{p}_j^l, \tag{6}$$

where ρ is a predefined radius set to the standard variance of the feature norms, $\mathbf{x}$ and $\mathbf{p}$ are the visual and hierarchical semantic representations of images, respectively. The matrix $\mathbf{H}$ can be derived by measuring the closeness of concept relations in the ontology. For instance, let $H_{kl} = \xi(\pi(k,l))$, where $\pi(k,l)$ is the lowest common ancestor of concepts k and l, and $\xi(\cdot)$ is some real function that is non-decreasing going down the hierarchy, *i.e.*, the lower the shared ancestor, the more similar concepts k and l are.

Now, we can combine the above links in order to refine the existing hierarchical representations of images, which are the basis to establish user profiles. Denote the hierarchical representations of all the training images before refinement as $\mathbf{P}$ and those after refinement as $\mathbf{R}$, which is the goal we are pursuing. In particular, we assume that the original $\mathbf{P}$ is noisy and the desired $\mathbf{R}$ is a low-rank recovered noise-free matrix. Intuitively, each column vector of the low-rank matrix $\mathbf{R}$ denotes the hierarchical item representation of an image. Intuitively, due to the relations between concepts in the ontology, the concept "cargo pants" should imply that concepts "pants" and "trousers" are along the semantic path. This indicates, from the viewpoint of linear algebra, that "cargo pants" could be located in a subspace spanned by those concepts along the path, imposing a low-rank nature of the matrix $\mathbf{P}$.

Therefore, by jointly considering the aforementioned multi-level social relations and the low-rank prior, the formulation of the proposed profile refinement objective is

$$\begin{aligned} \min_{\mathbf{R}} J(\mathbf{R}) &= \|\mathbf{P} - \mathbf{R}\|_F^2 + \alpha\|\mathbf{R}\|_* \\ &+ \beta \text{trace}\left\{\mathbf{R}^T\left(\mathbf{L}^u + \mathbf{L}^b + \mathbf{L}^v + \mathbf{L}^h\right)\mathbf{R}\right\}, \end{aligned} \tag{7}$$

where α and β are trade-off parameters, $\mathbf{L}^u$, $\mathbf{L}^b$, $\mathbf{L}^v$, and $\mathbf{L}^h$ are the graph Laplacians of the corresponding graphs in Eq. (4) to (6). For example, $\mathbf{L}^u = \mathbf{D}^u - \mathbf{S}^u$, where $\mathbf{D}^u$ is a diagonal matrix with the i-th entry as $\sum_j S^u_{ij}$. Such graph regularized terms impose the low-rank pursuit of $\mathbf{R}$ to be consistent with the multi-level social connections. The nuclear norm $\|\mathbf{R}\|_*$ is a convex surrogate for matrix rank [27], whose convexity allows an effective optimization for its solution. Next, we show how to solve the formulation in Eq (7).

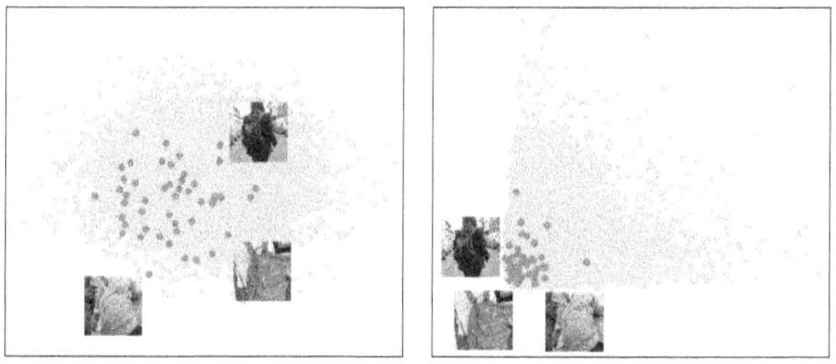

(a) Original User Profiles (b) Refined User Profiles

Figure 6: Illustration of the effectiveness of the proposed profile refinement method. The gray blue points are images represented by user profiles, and the red ones correspond to "bag" images. All these points are visualized by using PCA mapped into a 2-D space. (a) Before refinement, images of the same interest are scattered. (b) After refinement, images of the same interest are clustered.

4.2 Solution

When we investigate the formulation in Eq (7), we find that the profile refinement problem is a convex optimization problem. Therefore, there is a guarantee to obtain a global minimum. However, it does not have a closed-form solution. Fortunately, this problem can be solved by the Proximal Gradient method [24], which uses a sequence of quadratic approximations of the objective function $J(\mathbf{R})$ in order to derive the optimal solution.

We define $H(\mathbf{R}) = \|\mathbf{P} - \mathbf{R}\|_F^2 + \beta\text{trace}(\mathbf{R}^T\mathbf{L}\mathbf{R})$, where $\mathbf{L} = \mathbf{L}^u + \mathbf{L}^b + \mathbf{L}^v + \mathbf{L}^h$, and then the objective function can be re-written as $J(\mathbf{R}) = H(\mathbf{R}) + \alpha\|\mathbf{R}\|_*$. Suppose $\mathbf{R}_{k-1}$ is the solution at the $(k-1)$-th step, we can update to $\mathbf{R}_k$ by solving the following optimization problem which quadratically approximates $J(\mathbf{R})$ by the second-order Taylor expansion of $H(\mathbf{R})$ at $\mathbf{R}_{k-1}$:

$$\begin{aligned} \mathbf{R}_k &= \arg\min_{\mathbf{R}} H(\mathbf{R}_{k-1}) + < \nabla H(\mathbf{R}_{k-1}), \mathbf{R} - \mathbf{R}_{k-1} > \\ &+ \frac{\delta}{2}\|\mathbf{R} - \mathbf{R}_{k-1}\|_F^2 + \alpha\|\mathbf{R}\|_* \\ &= \arg\min_{\mathbf{R}} \frac{\delta}{2}\|\mathbf{R} - \mathbf{G}_k\|_F^2 + \alpha\|\mathbf{R}\|_*, \end{aligned} \tag{8}$$

where the values of $\mathbf{G}_k$ and δ are defined as

$$\begin{aligned} \mathbf{G}_k &= \mathbf{R}_{k-1} - \frac{2}{\delta}\left(\mathbf{R}_{k-1} - \mathbf{P} + \alpha\mathbf{L}\mathbf{R}_{k-1}\right), \\ \delta &= 2\sigma_{max}\left(\mathbf{I} + \alpha\mathbf{L}\right), \end{aligned} \tag{9}$$

where δ satisfies the Lipschitz condition and $\sigma_{max}(\cdot)$ denotes the largest singular value. Note that the solution of Eq. (8) is $\mathbf{R}_k = \mathbf{U}\text{diag}\lfloor\sigma - \frac{\alpha}{\delta}\rfloor_+\mathbf{V}^T$, where $\mathbf{U}\text{diag}(\sigma - \frac{\alpha}{\delta})\mathbf{V}^T$ is the singular value of $\mathbf{G}_k$ [27]. Also, note that even with a large amount of images, the above optimization for profile refinement is tractable. To see this, for solving the singular values of $\mathbf{G}_k$, we can apply the trick to solve it by obtaining the singular values of $\mathbf{G}_k^T$, which can be much smaller. Meanwhile, for solving the largest singular values of $\mathbf{I} + \alpha\mathbf{L}$, we can adopt the efficient power method in matrix analysis.

After the above low-rank approximation, the average value of hierarchical representations of all the images after refinement $\mathbf{R}$ is seen as the user profile. The effectiveness of this profile refinement algorithm is shown in Figure 6. It shows that the proposed methods can refine the user profiles with the same user interest (*i.e.*, "bag" in this example) close to each other so that they have consistent user profile representations. It gives an intuitive interpretation of the expected better recommendation performance of the proposed profile refinement since it is often more accurate to calculate the user-user similarities in collaborative filtering approaches, and user-image similarities in content-based approaches.

5. EXPERIMENT

In this section, we systematically evaluate the effectiveness of our proposed profile learning, profile refinement algorithm and image recommendation using the profiles.

5.1 Data and Methodology

5.1.1 Experimental Data Set

We crawled the Pinterest data based on HTTP requests as there is no open API of Pinterest. The crawling protocol was as follows. First, we started from 50 popular pins from seed data in the fashion domain. Next, for each pinned image, we used a breadth-first search (BFS) strategy to crawl the boards which have pined or re-pined the image. The overall crawling process took a month. As a result, the data set consists of 1,239 users and 1,538,658 images.

In order to populate images into the constructed ontology in Section 3, we matched the items of user interest (*e.g.*, bundle names, tags) with entries in our constructed ontology to annotate the images of the corresponding concepts. Besides, the time when the user pinned the images can be obtained, therefore, we divided the images based on the pinning time for image recommendation. In order to train the profile ontology model, we split the data set equally into training/testing sets. Note that the testing set was used for testing ontology profile models, profile refinement algorithms and image recommendation. For profile refinement, the groundtruths were the same as the profile models. For recommendation, the average number of images per user were 433. In order to simulate real-world recommender system which has data from multiple domains, we added half the number of noisy data (*i.e.*, around 200) that are not in fashion domain.

5.1.2 Implementation Details

The underlying deep architecture we adopted in Section 3.2 is the deep convolutional neural network architecture proposed by Krizhevsky *et al.* [13]. Its inputs were the raw RGB pixel intensity values of a 224×224 image. Those values were forwarded through 5 convolutional neural layers (with pooling and ReLU non-linearities activation function along the way) and 3 fully-connected layers to determine its final neuron activities, namely, a distribution over the sibling concepts of user interest. As a result, neurons of the network in each layer were respectively 150,528-D, 290,400-D, 186,624-D, 64,896-D, 64,896-D, 43,264-D, 4,096-D, 4,096-D, and M-D, where M is the number of sibling concepts. We used the ImageNet pre-trained model, namely DeCAF [8], as the pre-trained network to initialize CNN and mtCNN. For visual features of the images used in Eq. (6) and other content-based baseline methods, we also adopted the 6-th layer output of DeCAF, which is a 4096-D feature vector.

For the sparse coding in section 3.1, we empirically initialized λ as 0.1. For multi-task convolutional neural network, we empirically set λ as 0.0001. For the profile refinement algorithm, we set $\alpha \in \{0.0001, 0.01, 0.1..., 10\}$, $\beta \in \{0.00001, 0.01, 0.1, ..., 10\}$, various pairs of (α, β) values were tried and the one with the best performance was chosen.

For all the experiments, we used an NVIDIA 780X GPU with 2304 cores, 3GB memory, and i7-2600 CPU with 3.40 GHz and 16G memory.

5.1.3 Compared Methods and Evaluation Metric

To evaluate the effectiveness of the proposed multi-task CNN (**mtCNN**), we compared it with state-of-art convolutional neural network [13]. For the model of each concept node in the ontology, we used the average precision (AP) as the evaluation metric.

To study the performance of our proposed profile refinement algorithm (**Ours**), two algorithms were employed as the baselines: a) **LR_ES_CC_TC** [33]: tag refinement algorithm low-rank, error sparsity, content consistency and tag correlation; and b) **TRVSC** [16]: tag refinement algorithm based on visual and semantic consistency. For evaluation metric, we used the widely used F_1-score.

To evaluate the effectiveness of user profiling methods, we proposed to use image recommendation based on user profiling. As mentioned in [3], current recommender systems generally fall into the following two categories: a) content-based recommendations, where users are recommended items similar to those they preferred in the past; and b) collaborative recommendations where users are recommended items that people with similar tastes and preferences liked in the past. Here, we extend the traditional recommendation methods using our proposed visual-based ontology profile. We used the content-based ontology profile vector to represent a user to calculate the user-item and user-user similarity. To evaluate the performance of visual-based profile in image recommendation, we compared it with the state-of-art methods: a) **CB**: this is the traditional content-based recommendation method [22], where users are recommended items similar to those they preferred in the past; b) **CF_WNMF** [10]: this method makes the use of non-negative matrix factorization on user and item graphs for collaborating Filtering; c) **CF_LDA** [26]: this method combines traditional collaborating methods with probabilistic topic modeling to provide an interpretable latent structure for users and items; d) **CB_UP**: this method extends the traditional content-based methods through representing the users with our profile ontology; and e) **CF_UP**: this method extends the traditional collaborating method by computing users' similarities using our proposed profile ontology. We used mean AP (mAP) of the recommendation results as the evaluation metric.

5.2 Experimental Results

5.2.1 Evaluations of Profile Ontology Learning

Figure 7 illustrates the average precision values of different concept classifiers in the hierarchy. From this result, we can see that the multi-task convolutional neural network (**mtCNN**) at most levels achieves a mean average precision about 0.50, which is superior to traditional neural networks. These results demonstrate the effectiveness of **mtCNN** that makes use of hierarchical visual tasks. However, it can be seen that our proposed method has comparatively low performance on some concepts such as "zipper front dresses" and "skinny pants". The reason for the low performance could be: (a) the distinctive attribute of those concepts is too fine-

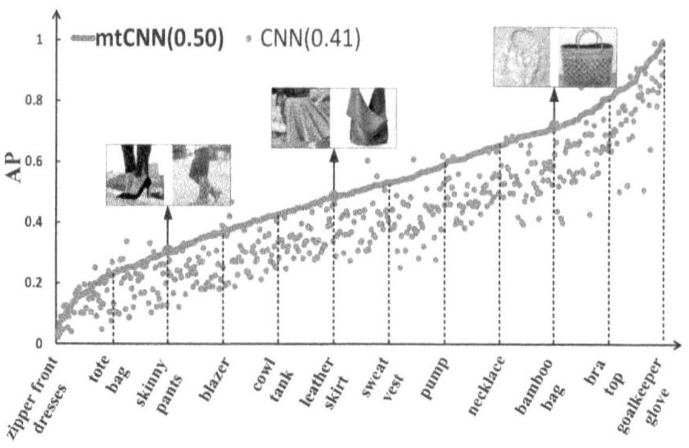

Figure 7: Performance of the 464 user profile models trained by CNN and the proposed mtCNN. mAPs are shown in brackets. Representative user interest and its two most confident images are shown.

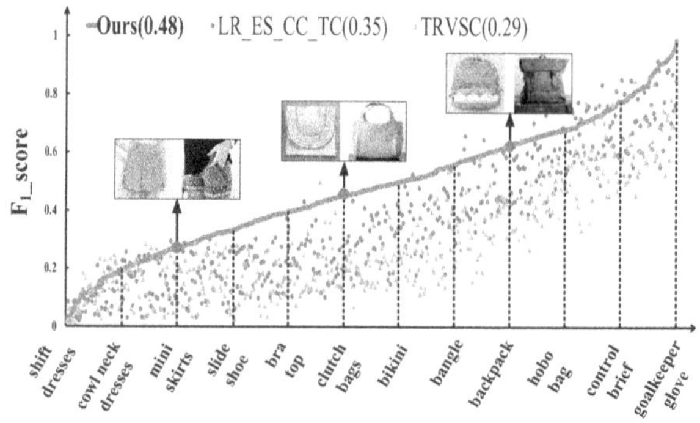

Figure 8: Performance of the three profile refinement methods. Mean F_1-scores are shown in brackets. The profile contains 464 user interests. Representative user interest in the profile and its two most confident images are shown.

grained, e.g. "zipper front", to differentiate those items correctly; and (b) these concepts tend to co-occur frequently with common items in an image. For example, the item "skinny pants" often co-occur with the item "high heels" in an image, then our method would recognize the "high heels" with "skinny pants" as "skinny pants". On the other hand, our method has quite good performance on other items such as "bamboo bag" and "goalkeeper glove". The reason for this is that those items have comparatively clean image samples.

5.2.2 *Evaluations Of Profile Refinement*

Figure 8 shows the detailed performance of image refinement for individual tags between our proposed approach and the baselines. From these results, we can see that the proposed method deploying social curation achieves an average F_1-score of 0.48, much higher than the other two methods. The superiority of our proposed profile refinement algorithms arises from two aspects: a) low rank; and b) multi-level social connections. Thanks to the content-centric network, multi-level connections are encoded to refine the user profiles. The experiment results explicitly illustrate that social curation services provide more structured and accurate information to infer user's preferences.

From Figure 8, we can observe that some classes may have comparatively lower F_1-score. For example, the F-score of the item "mini skirts" is about 0.25. It may be due to the noisy content-level connection since "mini skirts" and "mini dress" are often pinned into the same boards. Moreover, some cases fail because some images may not be that popular and therefore there exist only sparse and noisy content-level connections. In contrast, we observe that popular items tend to have higher F_1-scores;

Figure 9 shows some tag refinement results for some sample images produced by our approach. In the figure, the original user profiles come from tag annotation while the refined profiles comes from low-rank approximation. We can see that our approach can effectively correct and enrich the imprecise and incomplete image tags. For example, in Figure 9(c), our approach removes the irrelevant tags "dresses" and adds the more detailed tags "tote bag" and some other related tags such as "pink skirt" through social curation. Moreover, the enrichment capability of our proposed approaches can be seen in Figure 9(e) and (f), where there is only one irrelevant tag that shows people's intentions such as "comfy" and "outfit" and after refining the incomplete tags by our approaches, the images are associated with reasonable tags. However, some cases fail because of lack of sibling samples. For example, the concepts "bow tie" and "ascot tie" under "tie" have fewer samples than others on the ontology.

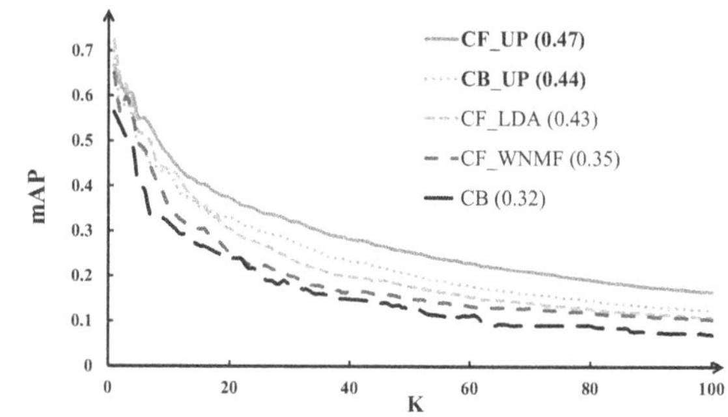

Figure 10: Performance (mAP@K) of the five recommendation methods. mAP@10 are shown in brackets.

5.2.3 *Evaluations of Image Recommendation*

Figure 10 shows the performance comparison between the proposed image recommendation methods and the other four state-of-the-art recommendation methods. We can observe that our proposed recommendation methods based on the visual-based ontology profile achieve the best performance in terms of MAP at all the top K results compared to the other methods. For example, our method improves the performance by 13.3%, 22.6%, 48.0%, 54.2% in terms of MAP at the top 20 results compared to the CB, CF_WNMF, CF_LDA and CB_UP respectively. This verifies the effectiveness of our proposed ontology profile in recommendation systems. However, if the user's interest is too general, the framework doesn't work well since our recommender system will recommend all the images. Some illustrative examples are shown in Figure 11.

The superiority of the proposed ontology profile arises from the following points: a) this profile models the user with a semantic hierarchy consisting of past users' interest; such hierarchy profile provide a more comprehensive interpretation of images of interest of users; and b) through

Figure 9: Illustrative profile refinement results by the proposed method.

computing the users' similarities based on this hierarchy profile, implicitly similar users are obtained which alleviates the sharing sparsity problem in traditional collaborative filtering recommendation methods. For example, there may exist many images that are rarely shared and would not be recommended. Besides, since our ontology construction does not totally rely on Wikipedia, but also the user comments which cover the real interest even if it falls into the long tail. Once a general domain is selected, our ontology can adapt to the true distribution of user interest.

6. CONCLUSIONS

In this paper, we targeted at content-based user profiling on the emerging social curation service (SCS). As compared to the conventional social network service (SNS), which focuses on user-user connections, SCS is based on the content-content connections curated by users. This is a unique characteristic of SCS, which inspires the idea of our profiling method. In particular, we investigated the fashion domain in the most popular SCS, namely Pinterest, on how social curation can help us tackle the existing difficulties in social media analysis. Specifically, we proposed to automatically construct a content-based user preference ontology and learn the ontological models to generate comprehensive user profiles. Then, we proposed to model the multi-level social relations offered by SCS to refine the user profiles in a low-rank recovery framework. Extensive experiments on 1,239 users and 1.5 million images are collected from Pinterest in fashion domain demonstrated the effectiveness of the proposed user profiling method, which outperforms the other state-of-the-art methods.

SCS is still in its infancy and thus requires a lot of explorations. For our initial exploration, we only focused on the fashion domain. However, in order to set up a real application running on a variety of SCSs, we should further investigate how to automatically determine the domains of users' interest. This is not a trivial task due to the extremely large diversity of user interests. Nevertheless, we believe that the proposed user profiling based on multimedia analysis with the help of social curation has a great potential to stimulate future research in social network.

7. ACKNOWLEDGEMENTS

This work was supported by the NUS-Tsinghua Extreme Search (NExT) project under the grant NO.: R-252-300-001-490 and the National Natural Science Foundation of China under the grant No.: 61303075.

8. REFERENCES

[1] F. Abel, Q. Gao, G.-J. Houben, and K. Tao. Analyzing user modeling on twitter for personalized news recommendations. In *UMAP*. 2011.

[2] F. Abel, E. Herder, G.-J. Houben, N. Henze, and D. Krause. Cross-system user modeling and personalization on the social web. *UMUAI*, 2013.

[3] G. Adomavicius and A. Tuzhilin. Toward the next generation of recommender systems: A survey of the state-of-the-art and possible extensions. *TKDE*, 2005.

[4] Y. Cai and Q. Li. Personalized search by tag-based user profile and resource profile in collaborative tagging systems. In *ACM KDD*, 2010.

[5] M. Campbell. Online friendships light up shadow social networks. *NewScientist Magazine*, 2012.

[6] T.-S. Chua, H. Luan, M. Sun, and S. Yang. Next: Nus-tsinghua center for extreme search of user-generated content. *MultiMedia, IEEE*, 2012.

[7] M. Deshpande and G. Karypis. Item-based top-n recommendation algorithms. *ACM TOIS*, 2004.

[8] J. Donahue, Y. Jia, O. Vinyals, J. Hoffman, N. Zhang, E. Tzeng, and T. Darrell. Decaf: A deep convolutional activation feature for generic visual recognition. *arXiv preprint arXiv:1310.1531*, 2013.

[9] T. Evgeniou and M. Pontil. Regularized multi–task learning. In *ACM KDD*, 2004.

[10] Q. Gu, J. Zhou, and C. H. Ding. Collaborative filtering: Weighted nonnegative matrix factorization incorporating user and item graphs. In *SDM*, 2010.

[11] K. Ishiguro, A. Kimura, and K. Takeuchi. Towards automatic image understanding and mining via social curation. In *ICDM*, 2012.

[12] A. Kimura, K. Ishiguro, M. Yamada, A. Marcos Alvarez, K. Kataoka, and K. Murasaki.

Figure 11: Illustrative recommendation results from the proposed collaborative filtering based on our user profiles (CF_UP). Top nine recommended images for six users are shown.

Image context discovery from socially curated contents. In *ACM MM*, 2013.

[13] A. Krizhevsky, I. Sutskever, and G. E. Hinton. Imagenet classification with deep convolutional neural networks. In *NIPS*, 2012.

[14] J. Leskovec, L. A. Adamic, and B. A. Huberman. The dynamics of viral marketing. *TWEB*, 2007.

[15] J. Lin, K. Sugiyama, M.-Y. Kan, and T.-S. Chua. Addressing cold-start in app recommendation: latent user models constructed from twitter followers. In *SIGIR*, 2013.

[16] D. Liu, X.-S. Hua, M. Wang, and H.-J. Zhang. Image retagging. In *ACM MM*, 2010.

[17] M. Marszalek and C. Schmid. Semantic hierarchies for visual object recognition. In *CVPR*, 2007.

[18] J. McAuley and J. Leskovec. Image labeling on a network: using social-network metadata for image classification. In *ECCV*. 2012.

[19] T. Mikolov, K. Chen, G. Corrado, and J. Dean. Efficient estimation of word representations in vector space. *arXiv preprint arXiv:1301.3781*, 2013.

[20] S. Mittal, N. Gupta, P. Dewan, and P. Kumaraguru. The pin-bang theory: Discovering the pinterest world. *arXiv preprint arXiv:1307.4952*, 2013.

[21] R. Ottoni, J. P. Pesce, D. Las Casas, G. Franciscani Jr, W. Meira Jr, P. Kumaraguru, and V. Almeida. Ladies first: Analyzing gender roles and behaviors in pinterest. *ICWSM*, 2013.

[22] M. J. Pazzani and D. Billsus. Content-based recommendation systems. In *The adaptive web*. 2007.

[23] N. Qian. On the momentum term in gradient descent learning algorithms. *NN*, 1999.

[24] K.-C. Toh and S. Yun. An accelerated proximal gradient algorithm for nuclear norm regularized linear least squares problems. *PJO*, 2010.

[25] A. Ulges, M. Worring, and T. Breuel. Learning visual contexts for image annotation from flickr groups. *TMM*, 2011.

[26] C. Wang and D. M. Blei. Collaborative topic modeling for recommending scientific articles. In *ACM KDD*, 2011.

[27] J. Wright, A. Ganesh, S. Rao, Y. Peng, and Y. Ma. Robust principal component analysis: Exact recovery of corrupted low-rank matrices by convex optimization. In *NIPS*, 2009.

[28] Z. Xu, Y. Zhang, Y. Wu, and Q. Yang. Modeling user posting behavior on social media. In *SIGIR*, 2012.

[29] S.-H. Yang, B. Long, A. Smola, N. Sadagopan, Z. Zheng, and H. Zha. Like like alike: Joint friendship and interest propagation in social networks. In *WWW*, 2011.

[30] H. Zhang, Y. Yang, H. Luan, S. Yan, and T.-S. Chua. Start from scratch: Towards automatically identifying, modeling, and naming visual attributes. In *ACM MM*, 2014.

[31] H. Zhang, Z.-J. Zha, Y. Yang, S. Yan, Y. Gao, and T.-S. Chua. Attribute-augmented semantic hierarchy: Towards bridging semantic gap and intention gap in image retrieval. In *ACM MM*, 2013.

[32] Y. Zhang, W. Chen, D. Wang, and Q. Yang. User-click modeling for understanding and predicting search-behavior. In *ACM KDD*, 2011.

[33] G. Zhu, S. Yan, and Y. Ma. Image tag refinement towards low-rank, content-tag prior and error sparsity. In *ACM MM*, 2010.

[34] I. Zukerman and D. W. Albrecht. Predictive statistical models for user modeling. *UMUAI*, 2001.

3D Interest Maps From Simultaneous Video Recordings

Axel Carlier
Université de Toulouse
axel.carlier@irit.fr

Lilian Calvet
Simula Research Laboratory
lcalvet@simula.no

Duong T. D. Nguyen and Wei Tsang Ooi
National University of Singapore
{nguyend1, ooiwt}@comp.nus.edu.sg

Pierre Gurdjos and Vincent Charvillat
Université de Toulouse
{gurdjos,vcharvillat}@irit.fr

ABSTRACT

We consider an emerging situation where multiple cameras are filming the same event simultaneously from a diverse set of angles. The captured videos provide us with the multiple view geometry and an understanding of the 3D structure of the scene. We further extend this understanding by introducing the concept of *3D interest map* in this paper. As most users naturally film what they find interesting from their respective viewpoints, the 3D structure can be annotated with the level of interest, naturally crowdsourced from the users. A 3D interest map can be understood as an extension of saliency maps in the 3D space that captures the semantics of the scene. We evaluate the idea of 3D interest maps on two real datasets, taken from the environment or the cameras that are equipped enough to have an estimation of the poses of cameras and a reasonable synchronization between them. We study two aspects of the 3D interest maps in our evaluation. First, by projecting them into 2D, we compare them to state-of-the-art saliency maps. Second, to demonstrate the usefulness of the 3D interest maps, we apply them to a video mashup system that automatically produces an edited video from one of the datasets.

Categories and Subject Descriptors

H.5.1 [**Multimedia Information Systems**]: Video

General Terms

Algorithms, Human Factors, Experimentation

Keywords

Video Interaction Techniques, 3D interest maps, Crowdsourcing

1. INTRODUCTION

The proliferation of video capturing devices has lead to an explosion of user-generated video content. In this paper, we consider the case of public performances (music, dance, sport, magic, theater etc.) with a spectating crowd that film the performance with either their mobile devices or a static camera. This behavior is particularly interesting as multiple videos of the same scene are captured from multiple diverse viewpoints.

MM'14, November 03–07, 2014, Orlando, Florida, USA.

ACM 978-1-4503-3063-3/14/11 ...$15.00.
http://dx.doi.org/10.1145/2647868.2654947 .

Figure 1: A dance performance from RagAndFlag dataset. Cameras 1 to 6 are located around the stage at ground level. Camera 7 shoots this picture (zoom position 8) and occasionally zoom into the red rectangle (zoom position 7). A 3D interest map is drawn in white in the 3D space and also in the 2D image space after re-projection of the 3D map (with black background).

Figure 1 shows an example of the scenario we consider, where an open air performance has six cameras surrounding the stage at ground level (labeled 1 to 6) and one camera filming the performance from above with two zoom levels (labeled 7 and 8). We can treat the scene being filmed as a type of 3D visual content, with the videos of this scene filmed from different viewpoints containing, collectively, a large part of this 3D content. If we know the parameters of the cameras filming the scene, the 3D structure can be partially reconstructed. But what is more interesting is that what users choose to film in a scene signals the interestingness of the region in 3D space that is being filmed. When a videographer selects his zoom level or his preferred framing, he implicitly reveals the interestingness of the scene he films. For example in Figure 1, the user who is shooting with the top camera (at zoom level 7 represented by the red rectangle) is obviously interested in the stage, because he zoomed in towards it. By generalization, several videographers collectively reveal the most interesting 3D parts of the scene where many view frustums intersect. Thus, it is feasible to label the reconstructed 3D structure with a level of interest. This idea led us to introduce a new concept called *3D interest map* in this paper.

Intuitively, a *3D interest map* represents some hot spots as illustrated in white in Figure 1 and explained by a distribution of interest with several modes or peaks (adjusted to the locations of human performers in this example). Note that the 3D interest maps can also been re-projected into 2D frames and become a standard (2D) saliency maps (as shown on the black and white region of Figure 1), but with the additional advantage that salient regions are consistent between videos filmed from different angles. Estimating such a multi-modal distribution from several synchronized videos is the main contribution of this work.

The constructed 3D interest maps are useful in many applications. We focus on the application of automated video authoring in this paper. In particular, we use 3D interest maps as additional input to a video mashup system that automatically switches between input video streams to produce a single temporally coherent video. The use of 3D interest maps allows the algorithm to exploit interestingness information for close up shots and to generate virtual camera movements. Furthermore, the availability of information *across* videos allows using the system to maintain coherence when it cuts from one camera to another. We show that 3D interest maps lead to better mashup videos. Our improvement of video mashups using 3D interest maps is the second contribution of this paper.

The paper is organized into seven sections. We first review the related work in Section 2. We then formally define the concept of 3D interest maps in Section 3, before explaining our algorithm to compute 3D interest maps in Section 4. Section 5 demonstrate the usefulness of 3D interest maps by applying them to a video mashup system. The experiments and evaluation results are presented in Section 6. Finally, the paper concludes in Section 7.

2. RELATED WORK

Our literature review is organized into three subsections. We first position our 3D interest maps in relation to other attention models. Then, we explain how the proposed approach relates to crowdsourcing, before reviewing several systems similar to ours.

Salient Region Detection. Salient regions or objects from any given image or video direct human attention by definition. In their recent survey [3], Borji and Itti discuss the most important visual attention models that compute saliency maps. In his pioneer work, Itti [15] devised the first bottom-up visual saliency model using differences across multi-scale image features. More recently, Goferman et al. [12] combine local low-level information, higher level features, and a more global spatial context to detect salient objects. This bottom-up detector, along with a few others, have been shown to be effective [4]. We use this detector in our work as a reference for some of our experiments. Top-down models for saliency detection can be even more effective in specific environments, but they usually require a costly learning stage [2].

The temporal dimension is a key factor when detecting dynamic salient regions in video sequences. For a given frame, the most salient regions should be selected from both the current image saliency map and the previous detections [17]. Further, it is natural to predict salient regions from motion maps in a video.

In the context of 3D visual content, Dittrich et al. [9] propose an approach for saliency detection in stereoscopic videos based on color, motion, and disparity. The last factor is used as regions that pops up in the scene tend to catch users' attention.

This existing work aims to determine the salient regions from low-level features of visual content. A salient region, however, does not necessary imply that it is interesting or important, two attributes that require an understanding of the semantics of the content and the users' intentions and are difficult to infer from features alone. Our approach, however, accounts for user intention which are implicitly indicated by the scene they are filming.

Crowdsourcing users' interest. To address the semantic gap, several crowdsourcing-based methods have been proposed to identify interesting regions in images and videos. The idea is that, by polling (either implicitly or explicitly) from multiple users what they find interesting, we can discover the interestingness of a region without needing to explicitly infer the semantic of the content.

In the context of games with a purpose (GWAPs) and human computation, Huang et al. [14] developed a collaborative game, called Photoshoot, for extracting image ROIs from shoot points that serve in the role of gaze points. Crowdsourcing users' interest can be also done more implicitly. As an example, Xie et al. [31] considered a mobile use-case with image browsers, where users tend to zoom and scroll to view interesting regions in detail on a small screen. By crowdsourcing these actions, a ROI extraction model can produce user interest maps. This approach, using implicit feedback while users are browsing still images, has been extended to infer moving ROIs based on video browsing behaviors [5, 6]. In this work, the users naturally zoom into the video and reveal ROIs. In our work, we consider that users around the scene are also implicitly interacting with it by filming the scene; a user filming a 3D region is implicitly designating this region as interesting.

Applications based on simultaneous video capture. Multiple videos captured simultaneously can be automatically edited to produce a new *mashup* video similarly to how a human director would switch between different cameras to produce a show. Shrestha et al. [26] address this problem, and select the cameras by maximizing video quality. They also explain in [25] how to synchronize multiple cameras from the available multimedia content. Saini et al. [23] expand this effort on video mashups with live applications in mind. The system decides which camera to switch to without any reference to future information. Their improved model jointly maximizes the video signal quality, but also the diversity and quality of the view angles, as well as some aesthetic criteria that include shot lengths and distances from the stage. We explain in Section 5 how 3D interest maps make it possible to improve these mashups by introducing automatic zooming and panning on the frame, as well as smoothing the transitions between shots, thanks to 3D information that relates the content of one video with another.

3. WHAT IS A 3D INTEREST MAP?

Understanding and predicting user interest is a key issue in many multimedia applications. In order to efficiently compress, store, retrieve, transmit, recommend, display any media item, it is helpful to estimate users' level of interest in it.

Beyond saliency. In some situations, user interest and attention are guided by a task to be performed; in other free-viewing situations, a user may subjectively gaze at most interesting items. In the latter case, a saliency map associated with an image often serves as a gaze predictor and can be interpreted as a 2D map with a type of "interest level" (preferably normalized, between 0 and 1) assigned to each pixel. Unfortunately 2D saliency models still fall short of predicting semantically interesting objects perfectly. With 3D content in mind, one can formally define a 3D saliency map by generalization, and determine saliency at a given 3D voxel by considering how different a given voxel is from its surroundings in color, orientation, depth etc. Similar to many 2D saliency models, this generalized 3D saliency estimation does not integrate any semantics and is a poor interest predictor for a 3D scene like the one depicted in Figure 2. In this example, a semantic definition of the interest (in 3D) would probably assign the highest interest level to the voxels located on the soloist in front of the band, an intermediate interest value to voxels located on others musicians, and low interest to voxels located on the background buildings. We devised our 3D interest maps with this objective in mind.

Our 3D interest maps are innovative for several reasons. First, we infer 3D interest information from the multiple view geometry of simultaneous video recordings: it is an original 3D generalization of 2D saliency maps. Indeed, a 3D interest map is richer than several saliency maps computed from the original video recordings: as shown later, the correspondences between salient areas seen in range views are naturally established when re-projecting the components of the 3D interest maps. Another important difference with traditional saliency models is that we do not need to predict where the spectators would gaze – we can simply observe it. We can see a user's camera as a third eye that he focuses towards the parts of the scene that he is most interested in. Our 3D interest levels are somehow "crowdsourced" from many videographers and we assume that the semantically important portions of the scene can be statistically revealed by analyzing the selected view frustums (originated by zoom, pan and framing decisions). If many videographers focus towards "the most interesting" musician (e.g., the soloist) shown in Figure 2, a bit of semantically motivated interest is revealed.

A formal approach to 3D interest maps. We define a 3D interest map with respect to a given time instant, and hence we consider a set of J images corresponding to synchronized video frames[1] taken from J cameras capturing the same scene from different angles at this instant. We assume that the camera projection matrices $\mathtt{P}^j$, $j = 1..J$, with respect to some Euclidean projective representation, are given.

We also assume that we have the 2D regions of interest (ROI) in the J range views at our disposal. Note that the simplest user's ROI in a view can be drawn from the central fixation assumption [30], in which it corresponds to an elliptic region centered at the principal point (*i.e.*, at the point where the optical axis meets the image plane). Such elliptic regions are shown in blue in Figure 2 for two cameras. Although this assumption will be relaxed later, it makes sense as it seems natural that the user tends to shoot by steering the camera optical axis towards the scene hot spots.

Figure 2: Central focus assumption on the BrassBand dataset.

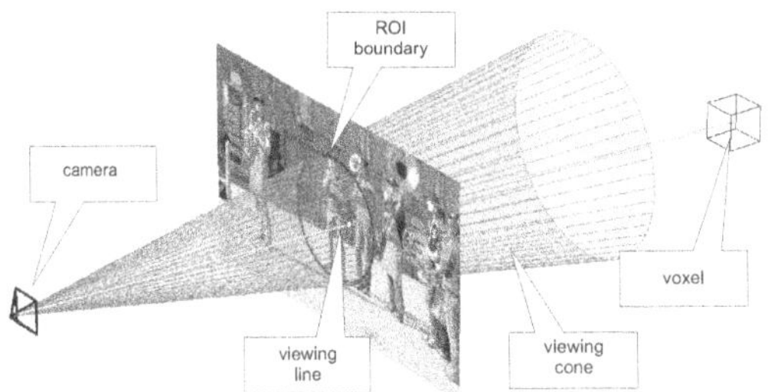

Figure 3: Viewing cone back-projecting a 2D ROI (in blue) and viewing line back-projecting a 2D point (in yellow); see text.

The key ingredient for defining a 3D interest map is the notion of viewing cones. A *viewing cone* is the back-projection of a 2D ROI, *i.e.*, the generalized cone in 3D space that is the assemblage of 3D lines passing through the camera center and every pixel on the 2D ROI boundary (see Figure 3). For the k-th elliptic ROI ($k = 1..K$) in view j, referred to as E_k^j, the corresponding viewing cone can be defined in the projective 3D space by its order-4 symmetric homogeneous matrix [13, p199]

$$\Lambda(E_k^j) = (\mathtt{P}^j)^T \mathtt{E}_{jk} \mathtt{P}^j \quad (1)$$

where $\mathtt{E}_k^j$ is the order-3 symmetric homogeneous matrix of the ellipse [13, p30] describing the boundary of E_k^j, and $\mathtt{P}^j$ is the projection matrix of camera j. In the situation illustrated by Figure 2, we have one elliptic ROI centered in each view with $J = K$. In the more general situation, multiple ROIs in a view are allowed (as explained in the next section).

We now partition the 3D scene into a set of voxels $\mathcal{S} = \{v_i\}_{i \in I}$. The intersection of viewing cones in 3D (as suggested by Figure 5) reveals a region where the voxels are seen by many cameras and can be considered as interesting for that reason. Hence, we can introduce a *measure of interest* of a voxel v_i by looking at how often it is seen. If we let $\mathcal{E}$ be the set of all 2D ROIs and $\mathcal{E}(v_i) \subset \mathcal{E}$ be a subset that depends on v_i, this 3D interest level is related to the 2D ROIs through the following definition:

$$Int(v_i) = \frac{1}{|\mathcal{E}|} \sum_{E \in \mathcal{E}(v_i)} \frac{\mathrm{Vol}(\Lambda(E) \cap v_i)}{\mathrm{Vol}(v_i)} \quad (2)$$

where $\mathrm{Vol}(a)$ stands for the 3D volume of the considered 3D regions in argument a. As the quantity $\mathrm{Vol}(\Lambda(E) \cap v_i)$ computes the volume of intersection of v_i with the viewing cone through E, the measure (2) is maximum when $\mathcal{E}(v_i) = \mathcal{E}$ and v_i is *entirely* included in all ROIs of $\mathcal{E}$, giving $Int(v_i) = 1$. It is minimum when v_i is not included in any ROI, giving $Int(v_i) = 0$. The intermediate values measure how often a given voxel is partially or completely seen.

We will say that the measure of interest (2) is (only) *geometrically consistent* when $\mathcal{E}(v_i) = \mathcal{E}$ and is (both geometrically and) *photometrically consistent* when $\mathcal{E}(v_i) \subset \mathcal{E}$ is the subset in which v_i is (at least partially) visible. In our context, a voxel v_i is said to be *visible with respect to a set of ROIs* $\mathcal{E}' \subset \mathcal{E}$ if there are pixels in each ROI of $\mathcal{E}'$ such that (*i*) all their back-projections as 3D *viewing lines* cut v_i (see Figure 3) and (*ii*) the neighborhoods of all these pixels are photometrically consistent in the views. It is straightforward to compute a geometrically consistent measure of interest, by intersecting all the cones associated with $\mathcal{E}$; it is the information brought by the users that contributed and no sophisticated computer vision algorithm is required. Nevertheless, due to many inter-voxels occlusions, only a subset of viewing cones associated with $\mathcal{E}$ are really seeing a visible voxel, which motivates the notion of photometrically consistent measure of interest. In Figure 6, the red voxel that is located at the intersection of the frustums of the three cameras is only visible (i.e., not occluded) in one frustum. Even if seen by all cameras, this red voxel is clearly not the most interesting since in fact only one user is seeing it. The method to determine $\mathcal{E}(v_i)$, the subset of 2D ROIs in which v_i is visible, will be tackled in the next section.

At this step, it is natural to consider the distribution of interest among the voxels through a histogram and subsequently introduce a normalized interest measure derived from (2) as

$$\widetilde{Int}(v_i) = Int(v_i) / \sum_{i \in I} Int(v_i). \quad (3)$$

Definition 1 *A **3D interest map** is the limit form of the 3D histogram with voxels as bins (diagonal length $\Delta l \to 0$) with respect to the normalized measure of interest (3).*

[1]Both the synchronization and the calibration are assumed to be, at least approximately, available for the J cameras.

In other words, if the voxels decrease in size and become infinitesimally small, the normalized measure of interest (3) behaves like a continuous probability density function.

Finally, we will model our 3D interest map (in our implementation and due to its generality) as a 3D Gaussian Mixture Model (3D GMM) with a satisfying number G of mixed components:

$$\widetilde{Int}(v) = \sum_{g=1}^{G} w_g \mathcal{N}(v; \boldsymbol{\mu}_g, \Sigma_g) \tag{4}$$

where v is now a 3D point (seen as an infinitesimally small voxel), $\mathcal{N}$ is the 3D Gaussian density, and w_g, $\boldsymbol{\mu}_g$, Σ_g are the weights and parameters of the 3D mixture. We detail the estimation of these parameters in the next section.

A GMM is flexible enough to approximate closely any multimodal density of 3D interest. Using GMM, the estimated 3D interest map can also be re-projected in the image spaces to play the role of J dependent 2D interest maps associated with the J cameras (see also the right part of the red rectangle in Figure 1).

Figure 4: 2D elliptic ROIs, as computed in Step (1) of our algorithm, on the RagAndFlag dataset.

4. 3D INTEREST MAP COMPUTATION

In this section, we present a method to build a 3D interest map using several synchronized videos shooting the same scene. The proposed algorithm (see Algorithm 1) is broken down in two successive estimations: a Gaussian mixture is first computed to produce a geometrically consistent 3D interest map (Steps (1)-(3)). The intuition behind this first step is to triangulate interesting 3D regions (Figure 5) from automatically detected 2D regions of interest (Figure 3). At this step, the 3D interest map (i.e., the Gaussian mixture) is coarse. The map is then refined into a final photometrically consistent one (Steps (4)-(6)). These last steps are made possible thanks to the constraints brought the coarse intermediate 3D interest map.

Algorithm 1 Computation of a GMM-based 3D interest map.

(1) Compute K_j ellipses of interest E_k^j for each view j
(2) Compute the intersection of visual cones
(3) Estimate a geometrically consistent 3D GMM
(4) Re-project it to get 2D GMM in image spaces
(5) Compute 2D Masks serving as PMVS input
(6) Estimate the final photometrically consistent 3D GMM from PMVS output

Detection of Ellipses (1). In this step, we look for 2D regions that are likely to contain interesting objects. These regions will then be used, as an implementation of Equation 2, to produce the cones as explained in the previous section. Many algorithms exist for such a task, from saliency maps to object detectors (face or body detectors would fit our use case).

At this stage, we do not need a high precision on these ellipses of interest, since they are primarily a way of reducing the complexity of the following steps. We therefore choose to use off-the-shelf OpenCV blob tracker, which uses standard algorithms for foreground detection (we use a temporal window of 15 frames) followed by blobs detection and tracking, considering the connected components of the foreground mask. In other words, we rely mostly on the apparent motion to detect the ellipses of interest, which is coherent with our use case of live performances. An example of the output of this algorithm can be seen on Figure 4. Note that the detected ellipses are not matched between views.

It is possible that the apparent motion is too low to detect ellipses based on the previously explained algorithm. In that case, we build on our assumption that users naturally tend to focus their camera towards objects of interest. We therefore consider an ellipse of area A_c centered on the camera frame, as shown on Figure 2. If the cumulated area of the ellipses of interest detected during Step (1) of our algorithm is less than $A_c/2$, then we empirically consider that there is insufficient apparent motion on the scene and switch to the central focus assumption.

Intersection of Visual Cones (2). At this stage, only a geometrically consistent 3D interest map can be computed. Indeed, we have no information about the visibility of a detected 2D ellipse number k in view j ($\mathtt{E}_k^j$ in Section 3's formalism) in other views $j' \neq j$. We use Equation (2) with $\mathcal{E}(v_i) = \mathcal{E}$ for defining a first coarse 3D interest map. In other words, the basic idea is to intersect cone-pairs $\Lambda(\mathtt{E}_{k_1}^j)$ and $\Lambda(\mathtt{E}_{k_2}^{j'})$ for all pairs of views (j, j') and for all pairs of 2D ROIs $(\mathtt{E}_{k_1}^j, \mathtt{E}_{k_2}^{j'})$ in these views.

The algorithm for intersecting two visual cones, related to cameras j and j' and 2D ROIs $\mathtt{E}_{k_1}^j$ and $\mathtt{E}_{k_2}^{j'}$, is as follows:

1. In image j, generate M random points inside the ellipse $\mathtt{E}_{k_1}^j$ and back-project each of these points p as a 3D line $\mathtt{L}_p^j$, through p and the camera center.
2. Compute the two intersection points where line $\mathtt{L}_p^j$ meets the viewing cone $\Lambda(\mathtt{E}_{k_2}^{j'})$ associated with image j'. This step can be achieved very efficiently when formulated with projective geometry[2].
3. If such intersection points exist, discretize the line segment, whose endpoints are these two points, into T points so that image j yields MT 3D points.
4. Repeat 1-3 by switching the roles of cameras j and j'.

Now, given a sequence of J views, we can apply the above algorithm for each of the $\frac{1}{2}J(J-1)$ distinct image-pairs and each pair of detected ellipses that can be formed in the image-pairs. Indeed, Figure 4 shows a pair of images for which 5 (left image) and 4 ellipses were detected, which means that, in this particular example, 20 cones intersections are computed. Note that all cones do not necessarily intersect, so 20 cones intersections is an upper bound. The result of this step is a cloud of 3D points with denser regions where the interest is locally high.

Figure 5 illustrates this step on our BrassBand dataset, for which there is little movement in the scene. As a consequence, cones are generated based on the central focus assumption. Thus, there is one cone per camera. We can see on the figure the 3D points (in blue) that are generated in the cones intersection.

[2]Let $\mathbf{x} \in \mathbb{R}^3$ be the homogeneous vector of an image point x. The 3D line, back-projection of x, can be given by a 3D point function $\mathbf{X} : \mathbb{R} \to \mathbb{R}^4$ defined by $\mathbf{X}(\mu) = ((\mu\mathbf{x} - \mathbf{p}_4)^T \mathtt{M}^{-T}, 1)^T$, using the projection matrix decomposition $\mathtt{P} = [\mathtt{M} \mid \mathbf{p}_4]$ ([13, p162]). The line cuts a cone Λ at two points $\mathbf{X}(\mu_1)$ and $\mathbf{X}(\mu_2)$ where μ_1 and μ_2 are the two real roots of the quadratic polynomial $\mathbf{X}(\mu)^T \Lambda \mathbf{X}(\mu)$.

Figure 5: Intersection of visual cones (BrassBand dataset).

3D GMM Estimation (3). Based on the obtained 3D data points, we now estimate the first interest density (a 3D GMM) given by Equation (4). Since we do not know the number G of Gaussian modes and we have no initial parameter estimates, we can not rely on the standard Expectation-Maximization technique for this step. We use Mean-Shift density estimator [7] that is devised to iteratively detect the unknown distribution modes along with the data points that belong to the cluster associated with each mode. The hard assignment between data points and modes given by Mean-Shift then allows us to trivially estimate each weight w_g (ratio of points assigned to the jth cluster vs. total number of data points) and each parameter: both $\boldsymbol{\mu}_g$ and Σ_g are estimated with maximum likelihood formulas.

Mean-Shift clustering is only controlled by one scale parameter: the bandwidth. Theoretically, the bandwidth compromises between the bias and variance of the estimator. In practice, it can be understood as the distance allowed between peaks of the distribution. At the current level (Step (3) in algorithm 1), however, the data points located at the intersection of the visual cones (see also Figure 5) do not fit with any recognizable shape (e.g., human performers). It is discriminative enough to select a relatively large bandwidth to detect the modes of our first 3D interest map: we typically choose $h = 2m$ in our experiments.

Re-projection to 2D GMM (4). Using a GMM in 3D allows the 3D interest maps to be re-projected in the J views. Such re-projection helps with the visualization and the evaluation of the 3D interest maps in the experimental section. Figure 9, second row, shows an example. Note that the 3D multi-modal distribution also appears as a multi-modal density in 2D. Flandin and Chaumette [10] define a model providing, for every 3D point of the scene, the probability that it belongs to an object of interest. They introduce several propagating rules for Gaussian uncertainties, such as subspace projection and back-projection of a distribution from 2D to 3D. Their fourth rule can be reused in our case to characterize the 2D GMM in image spaces resulting from the perspective projection of our 3D interest maps. Modeling the interest with Gaussians allows us to switch back and forth between 3D and 2D.

PMVS Masks Computation (5). We now aim at making the 3D interest map more discriminative. As said before, we used Equation (2) with $\mathcal{E}(v_i) = \mathcal{E}$, leading to a first coarse estimate. To refine it, we must determine whether a voxel is visible or not in a view. In Figure 6, we already noticed (cf. Section 3) that the red voxel that is located at the intersection of the viewing cones is the most interesting according to a *geometrically consistent measure of interest* but it should not be considered as the most interesting with a *photometrically consistent measure*: its red color is not occluded in only one view. The blue voxel is more interesting (seen from several views with photometrically consistent blue projections). In our implementation, this consistency is imposed by a constrained 3D reconstruction, achieved efficiently with multi-view stereo software such as PMVS [11] that is devised to propagate photometric consistency.

Given the extreme difficulty of wide-baseline multiple-view correspondences in our set-up, we use the re-projected GMM to produce 2D masks that will constrain and guide the 3D reconstruction algorithm. For each image, we binarize the 2D GMM (i.e., the 3D interest maps re-projection) in order for the mask to contain 95% of the information from the GMM. Results of this step can be visualized on the third row in Figure 9. As shown in the experiments, PMVS outputs denser 3D reconstructed points in the most interesting regions (e.g., around the human performers) thanks to the 2D masks guidance. The role of the "crowdsourced" masks is quantitatively evaluated in Section 6.

Final Estimation from PMVS Output (6). The PMVS software takes as input the camera projection matrices along with the masks computed during the previous step, and outputs a set of reconstructed 3D points. These points respect the photometric consistency. Note that we need to provide a parameter to PMVS, called the level, which specifies the resolution at which the input images will be processed. We set the level to 4, which means the image resolution considered is 120×68. This choice significantly speeds-up the computation as well as limits the influence of a bad synchronization on the quality of our results. Similarly to Step (4) of the algorithm, we then estimate the parameters of a 3D GMM to model the final 3D interest map. In our public event use case, if we ideally aim at estimating a separate mode for each dancer or singer, the bandwidth for the Mean-Shift clustering should be selected as $h = 60cm$ to typically separate two humans standing next to each other. This bandwidth parameter controls the granularity of the 3D interest map. The re-projection of our refined 3D interest map is shown on the fourth row in Figure 9.

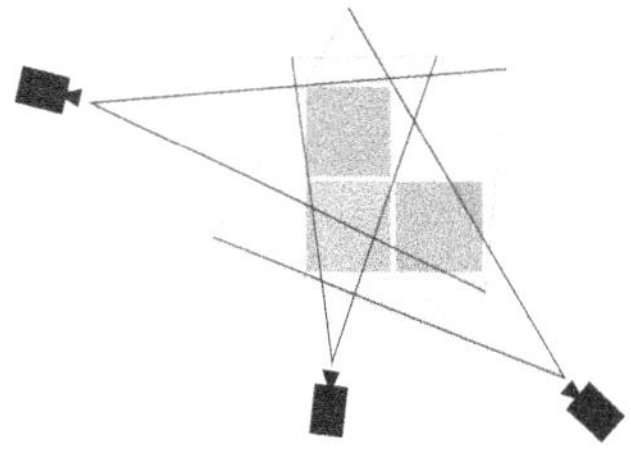

Figure 6: The red voxel has the highest geometrically consistent measure of interest (included in the three viewing cones) but a low photometrically consistent measure (only visible in one).

5. APPLICATION TO VIDEO MASHUP

We now demonstrate the power of 3D interest map, by applying the information we obtained to video mashups.

5.1 Video Mashup

The goal of video mashup is to automatically create a temporally continuous video of an event by splicing together different clips from simultaneously recorded videos of the event, usually shot from a diverse set of angles. A video mashup system aims to replace a human director, and therefore a successful video mashup system should produce videos that are interesting to watch, logically coherent, and cover the important scene that happens during the event.

One of the state-of-the-art systems for video mashup is Jiku Director [21], which focuses on mashing up videos captured with handheld mobile devices. Jiku Director uses an online algorithm [23] to produce the mashup, following a shot-change pattern learnt from professional, human-edited, video. The system also filters out bad quality videos through simple feature analysis and tries to increase the diversity of shots in the mashup by not selecting clips from the same devices when possible.

Jiku Director, however, is limited in two ways. First, it always uses the video clips recorded by users "as-is" without any cropping and scaling, nor introducing any camera movement. As a result, the camera shots in the resulting video are limited to the movement made by the user while recording the video. Furthermore, since the videos are recorded by audiences of an event, the shots are most of type of long/medium shots. The resulting mashup is lacking in diversity of shot types. Second, when Jiku Director introduces a cut, its only consideration is the shot angle (viewing direction of the camera) and shot length (distance of the camera from the stage), without considering the subjects or narrative.

One way to overcome the first limitation is to analyze salient features from each video independently and model the importance of the content. Jiku Director could then introduce virtual camera movement (zooming effects and dolly shots) by cropping out the region-of-interests (ROIs) from the videos. This approach is similar to that adopted by Carlier et al. [5]. This approach, however, could not overcome the second limitation, as there is no way to associate an object of interest that appears in one video clip with another object of interest that appears in another clips.

The proposed 3D interest map allows us to identify such association for objects that appears in the same time instant across two video clips. Furthermore, using the objects' bounding boxes and interest levels, we can add camera movements to pan from one object to another, and to zoom in for close-up shots of the objects, producing better mashups. The rest of this section describes how we apply 3D interest map to a new video mashup algorithm.

5.2 Computing Bounding Boxes

The first step of our mashup algorithm is to compute bounding boxes that contains the most interesting regions of the videos. Since our 3D interest maps are modeled by GMM, one bounding box for each Gaussian in the mixture can be produced easily.

The mashup application, however, needs stable bounding boxes that are tracked over time. The algorithm described in Section 4, however, applies at every time instant without considering temporal consistency. Therefore, to produce bounding boxes for the mashup applications, we change the last step of our algorithm (clustering a 3D point cloud) and compute the bounding boxes in the 4D space (3D and time). We augment the 3D points with a fourth coordinate that corresponds to their frame index, and apply the Mean-Shift algorithm to this 4D point cloud. We compute a bounding box for each cluster that contains all points of the cluster for its entire duration. The bounding boxes are stable over time by construction and can be mapped in all videos. An example of this output can be seen on Figure 7. Note that all bounding boxes are constrained to be of the same aspect ratio as the original video.

Figure 7: Bounding boxes computed from our 3D interest maps. Bounding boxes of the same color are corresponding to the same object of interest.

5.3 Mashup Heuristics

With the set of bounding boxes, we now present a simple algorithm for video mashups to illustrate the power of 3D interest map.

Note that 3D interest map cannot be computed online, but as we will later compare our results with Jiku Director's, which is an online algorithm, we choose to design our mashup algorithm to be online as well, with no knowledge of future frames beyond the current selected shots.

Our algorithm takes, as input, the set of object of interests computed from 3D interest map. For each object appearing in each frame, we have its bounding box, x-y coordinate and depth of its centroid in each frame. The output of our algorithm will be a sequence of *shots* (t, j, B, m), where t is the beginning time of the shot, j is the camera to choose the shot from, B is the set of regions of interest to use in this shot, and m is the virtual camera movement in this shot.

We use the same decision matrix used by Jiku Director to decide Camera j in each shot. Once j is fixed, we determine t, B, and m as follows. We first define a *scene* as a sequence of shots with logical coherence. For instance, a scene can start with a wide angle shot, followed by a zoom in shot to an object x, followed by a close up shot of x. We limit the length of the scene to containing no more than N_s shots (we use $N_s = 3$).

To determine the current shot starting at time t, the algorithm first needs to decide if the current shot belongs to the same scene as previous shot, or starts a new scene. If current scene has reached its limit in number of shots, we simply start a new scene. Otherwise, we try to see if the current shot fits.

Let L_{max} be the maximum possible shot length (we use $L_{max} = 7s$). To determine the current shot, we look at the bounding boxes and objects for the next L_{max} time in the video shot by camera j.

We prioritize the bounding box of each object by their importance in the scene. Each object i has a *camera independent importance*, $I(i, t)$, which is computed from $\sum_j v_i^j(t)/d_i^j(t)$, where $v_i^j(t)$ is 1 if object i appears in Camera j at time t; 0 otherwise, and $d_i^j(t)$ is the depth of the object i from the camera plane of camera j at time t, normalized to 0 and 1. The intuition here is that an object that appears frequently in the collective video clips and closer to the camera is the more important than those that appears fewer number of times/far away from cameras.

In each video clip, we compute the *camera dependent importance* of an object, $I_j(i, t)$ as $I(i, t)/d_i^j(t)$. The importance of the bounding box is then the sum of the camera dependent importance of all objects in the bounding box. Note that even though each bounding box is associated with an object, other objects may appear in the bounding box. Naturally, a bounding box that includes multiple important objects becomes important.

Now, we look at the most important bounding boxes in j at each time instance for the next L_{max} seconds. If at the start of the L_{max} seconds, the same bounding boxes is used as the previous shot, we fit the current shot into the same scene, and set B to these bounding boxes. We may stop the current shot at the time when these bounding boxes disappear. If a bounding box different from that of previous shot become the most important, we introduce a new scene, setting B to the new most important bounding box.

It remains to determine m for the current shot. The choice of m can be either: wide angle shot, close up, move the camera (zoom in, zoom out, or pan). The algorithm follows the following principles: (i) there should not be frequent camera movement, and (ii) the choice of m should lead to "fluid" shots: two consecutive close up shots should have the same object; zooming into an object should be followed by either a close up shot that include that object or a pan shot moving from that object to something else; a zoom out shot should be followed by a wide-angle shot; and a pan shot moving from an source object to a target object should be followed by a zoom out shot from the target, or a close up shot of the target. In Figure 8, a video transition from our heuristics illustrates how the 3D informations can be used for continuity editing.

Figure 8: A video transition keeping the same object(s) of interest in focus between two successive shots from two different cameras.

6. EXPERIMENTS

To evaluate our proposed 3D interest maps and its application to video mashup system, we first introduce two useful datasets and briefly explain our experimental set-up. The interest maps obtained from our experiments are then compared against saliency maps in the 2D image space (a comparison in 3D is difficult to visualize). Finally, we report the major results from our study to evaluate our improvements to video mashups.

6.1 Dataset

We present, in this subsection, the data we have worked on and that we use to evaluate our approach.

RagAndFlag. This dataset consists of videos filmed with seven cameras simultaneously (see Figure 1). This dataset presents a challenging scenario where the cameras have very diverse viewing angles and the videos depict a highly dynamic outdoor scene with variable lightning and about 50 moving objects (dancers, see also [22]). We use this dataset to test our mashup application.

BrassBand. This dataset depicts a more static scene with eight musicians close to each other, moving occasionally. Seven cameras are spread around the scene: three are fixed on a tripod and four are handheld (shot with smartphones) with little movement.

6.2 3D Interest Map

In this section, we evaluate the accuracy of the reconstructed 3D interest maps.

Our experiments use a radius of one fifth of the focal length to produce the cones-based 3D interest map. The parameters M and T are set to 10. We calibrate the cameras for each dataset using specific patterns (orange squares in **RagAndFlag**, concentric circles in **BrassBand**) on the planar stages. Knowing the plane-to-image homography associated with a given plane in the scene, we can (under standard assumptions of square pixels and centered principal point) compute the focal length [13] and then the camera pose [27]. The average re-projection error of our calibration is 2.2 pixels on 1920×1080 images, which is acceptable for our application. We synchronize the videos using an algorithm from Shrestha et. al [16] and observe an average error of 7.25 frames (0.25 sec).

Figure 9 shows examples of our results on the **RagAndFlag** dataset. In this figure, original images are introduced in the top row; the output of Steps (1)-(3) from our algorithm (i.e., a geometrically consistent version of the 3D interest maps computed from the cones intersection) is shown in the second row. This version will be referred as *cones maps* in the following paragraphs. The third row shows the masks that are inferred from the cones maps,

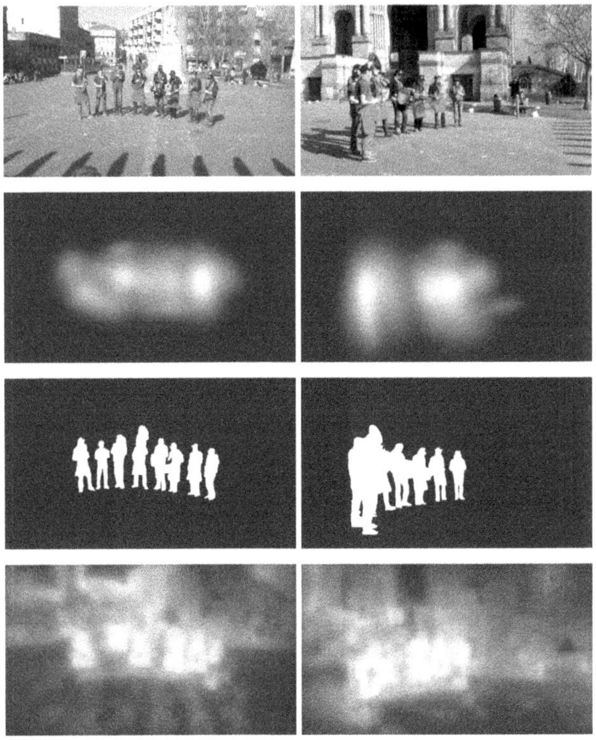

Figure 10: Results on the BrassBand dataset. For each row, from top to bottom: (i) original images; (ii) our 3D interest maps; (iii) manually generated ground truth binary masks; and (iv) state-of-the-art saliency map, as computed by Goferman [12].

as described in Step (4) of our algorithm. The forth row shows the final output of our algorithm, the 3D interest maps. We manually created ground truth masks to evaluate the 3D interest maps, and these ground truth masks are exposed on the fifth row. Finally results from a state-of-the-art saliency algorithm by Goferman et. al [12] are shown on the sixth row.

Similar results are presented for **BrassBand** in Figure 10. Due to space limitations, we only present original images, our final 3D interest maps, Goferman saliency, and the ground truth masks in these figures.

We can observe on all these figures that our 3D interest maps are very precise: almost all regions that are highlighted as salient are recognized as part of some objects of interest.

We can see also on Figure 9 that cones maps (2nd row) are more precise than Goferman's saliency maps (last row). This is the reason why we do not simply binarize state-of-the-art saliency maps to produce the 2D masks. Though the recall from saliency maps is quite high, the precision is insufficient to efficiently serve as a mask for PMVS.

In order to quantitatively evaluate our results, we follow the methodology from [4] and estimate a precision-recall (PR) curve by varying a threshold on the interest values and generating a binary saliency map for each value of the threshold. These experiments have been conducted on four types of interest maps: our final 3D interest maps, Goferman saliency, cones maps (see above) and a version of our interest maps we call *No Masks*. *No Masks* is computed by applying the PMVS algorithm to our data without inputting the masks based on the cones intersection, and estimating 3D interest maps from the set of points obtained from PMVS. We evaluate this version to prove the importance of Steps (1) to (5) in our algorithm.

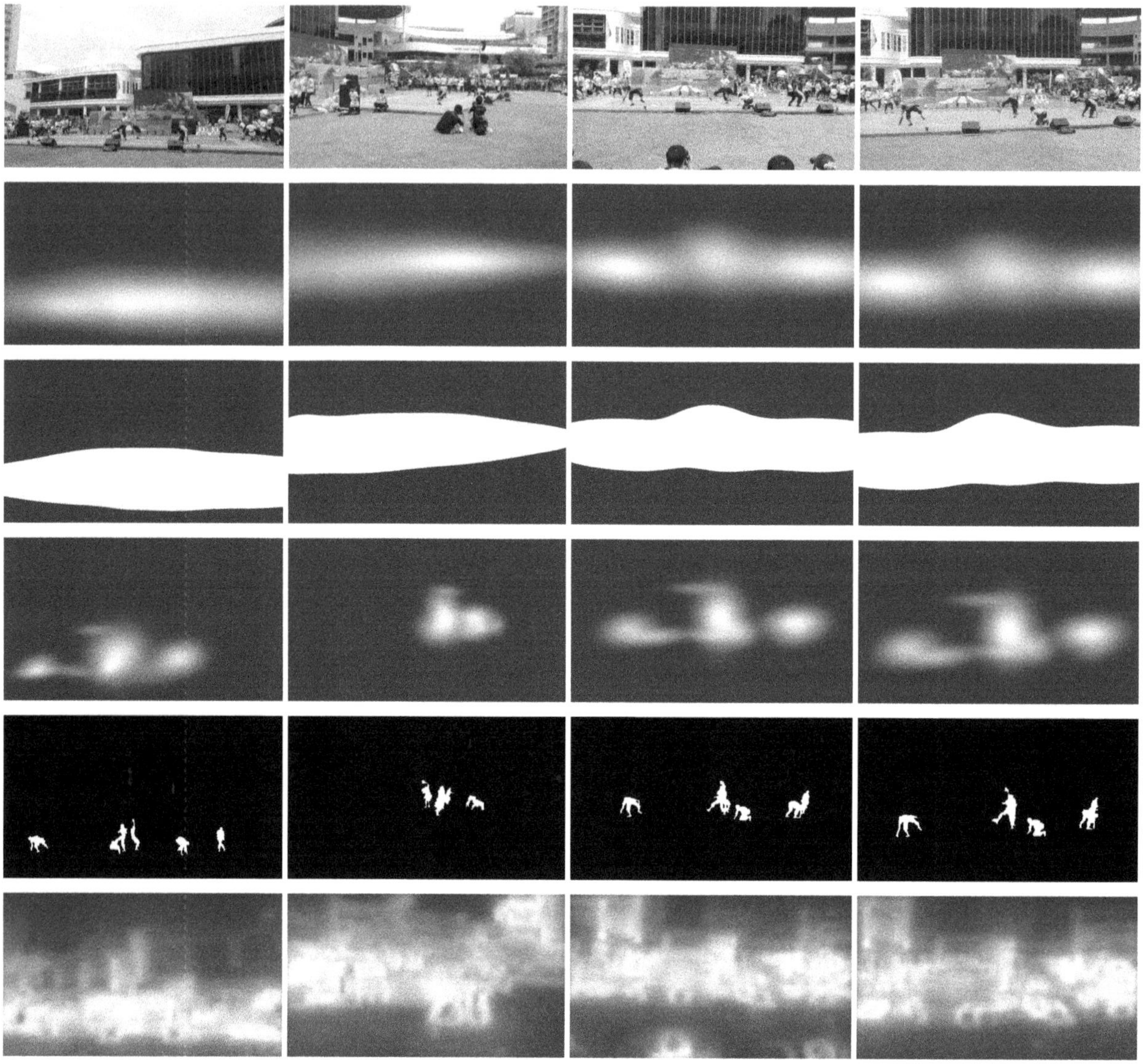

Figure 9: Results on the RagAndFlag dataset. For each row, from top to bottom: (i) original images; (ii) re-projected 3D interest maps computed by intersecting viewpoint frustums (*cones maps*); (iii) masks used as an input to PMVS; (iv) our final results; (v) manually generated ground truth binary masks; and (vi) state-of-the-art saliency map, computed using Goferman's method [12]

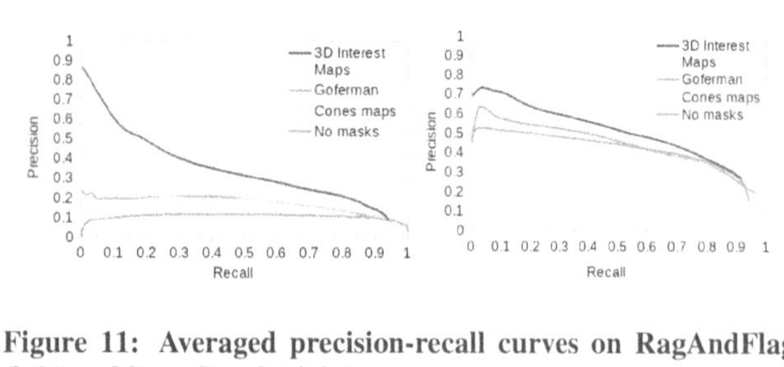

Figure 11: Averaged precision-recall curves on RagAndFlag (left) and BrassBand (right)

We created ground truth masks for 12 instants in our datasets, and resulting PR curves are displayed in Figure 11. Our 3D interest maps spectacularly outperforms Goferman's algorithm on the **RagAndFlag** dataset, which can be explained by the small size of the regions of interest (see Figure 1: the crowd is far from the scene) and the high variety in contrast of many background elements (the mat, the buildings, etc.). Our 3D interest maps is also better than Goferman in the **BrassBand** dataset, but the saliency detection is more performant in this case. Indeed the objects of interest are very salient in the images from **BrassBand**, since most of the musicians are wearing red colors.

Results on *cones* and *no masks* are also not as good as our 3D interest maps, which validates the importance of both steps in our approach. It is interesting, however, to note that cones maps is more precise than Goferman on the curves. This validates our choice to use cones maps to compute the PMVS masks (Step (5) in our algorithm) instead of just using a saliency map, because the more precise the masks are, the less noisy the reconstructed points are, and therefore the more precise our 3D interest maps are. In addition, it takes less than a second to compute cones maps whereas Goferman's saliency takes 5 seconds per image on GPU.

6.3 Evaluation of Mashup Algorithm

We now present the methodology and results of our user study to evaluate the video mashups produced from our algorithm.

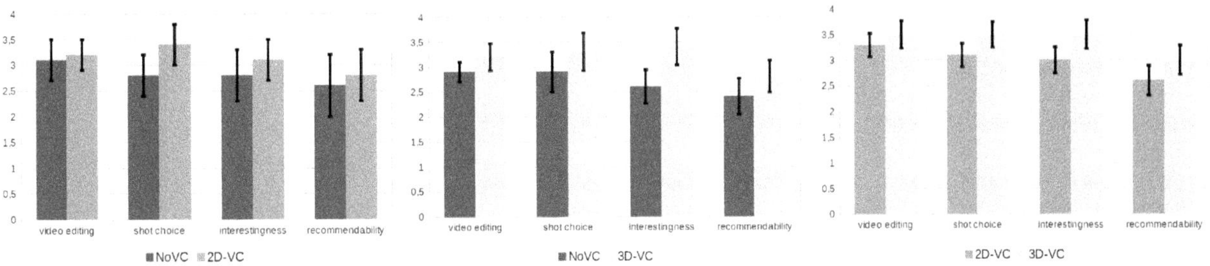

Figure 12: Average responses of the users for the three scenarios: NoVC vs. 2D-VC, NoVC vs. 3D-VC and 2D-VC vs. 3D-VC

Dataset. We pick the Rag&Flag dataset as the input to our algorithm, as it has the most dynamic content. We use a 1-minute sequence from the 7-minute video, to limit the length of the user study, and let users be able to watch the videos several times.

Benchmark. We choose to compare our output with two other methods. The first is the output from the MoviMash algorithm [23]. As MoviMash does not generate virtual camera movements, we denoted the output from this video as NoVC. We also included the output from a version of our algorithm that makes use of 2D saliency maps to generate zoom and pan shots [20]. We use the same saliency detector than the one from step (1) in algorithm 1, by consistency. We track the obtained ROIs with the same technique than the one from paragraph 5.2 except that it is applied in reduced (2D and time) dimension. The difference between this 2D version and ours is that: (i) the saliency information is computed for each video individually (without considering 3D scene information from other videos), and (ii) no interest information across different videos is available. We denoted the output from this video as 2D-VC. The output from our algorithm using 3D interest map is denoted as 3D-VC. Note that the three versions NoVC, 2D-VC, 3D-VC can be downloaded as supplemental material.

Users. We recruited 30 users (10 female, 20 male, age between 21-43) to participate in the user studies. All users have limited experience with video editing and production except for one.

Methodology. The user study is conducted online. Users are presented with the instructions and are told that "the main purpose of the user study is to rate the videos according to the quality of video editing". We created two Web pages for our purpose, each of them displaying two videos. On one of the page, NoVC is displayed along with either 2D-VC or 3D-VC (the choice is random). On the other page, 2D-VC, and 3D-VC are displayed. The order of display of the videos is random on both Web pages, to eliminate bias. The users are allowed to replay the video as many times as they want. A list of rating criteria are presented to the user below the video, where they are asked to rate the videos with a rating from 1 (worst) to 5 (best) according to the criteria of (i) the quality of video editing, (ii) the choice of camera shot, (iii) the interestingness of the video, and (iv) the likelihood that the user would recommend the video to a friend.

Results. The average responses of the users, along with their 95% confidence interval, are plotted in Figure 12.

The first result that is very clear is that users prefer the versions with virtual camera movements (2D-VC, 3D-VC) rather than the output from MoviMash (NoVC). The choice of camera shot (ii) is the criteria where the difference is the most obvious, which is understandable as variety in the choice of shots makes the video more enjoyable to watch.

The interestingness of the video (iii), meaning the capacity of a video to display the interesting subjects in a scene, is also significantly higher in 3D-VC than in NoVC. This proves that the 3D interest maps indeed help the mashup algorithm displaying the interesting regions in the videos. Note that 2D-VC also outperforms NoVC with respect to this criterion but that the difference is less significant. Indeed since the 2D interest maps used to compute this version are mostly based on apparent motion, the 2D-VC mashup has often multiple choices of moving regions to display and does not necessarily focus on the prominent region of interest. The right diagram of figure 12 seems to indicate that 3D-VC performs better than 2D-VC, however the results can not be proven statistically significant. Indeed, to non-expert users, the two videos can look similar because the shots dynamics are the same (zoom in, zoom out, pan).

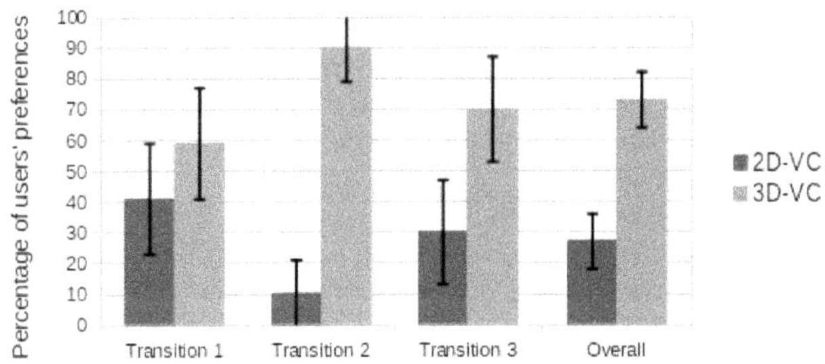

Figure 13: Second user study (99% confidence intervals)

Therefore we conducted another, much shorter, user study. We asked a different pool of 45 users to look at three pairs of very short videos, each depicting a transition between 2 shots (e.g. figure 8). Each pair consisted in the transition computed by 3D-VC and by 2D-VC. We displayed the three pairs in random order, and asked users which transition they preferred. Unlike the results presented in figure 12, this study allows us to clearly (statistically significantly) state that the transitions based on the 3D interest maps are better than the ones based on the 2D interest maps (see figure 13).

7. DISCUSSION AND CONCLUSION

This paper introduces *3D interest maps*, a new concept that associates each 3D point in a scene with its level of interest and can be viewed as extension of saliency maps to 3D. We formally define a 3D interest map and explain how we compute it. We show that our 3D interest maps are more precise in locating interesting objects than state-of-the-art saliency algorithms. A key aspect of our 3D interest maps is that they allow mapping of interesting regions across different videos that depict the same scene at the same time instance. This property is useful for many applications, such as video mashup systems.

The main challenges and limitations of our work are obviously the strong assumptions about estimation of the camera poses and synchronization between them. In our experiments, cameras were calibrated from a single view in order to avoid matching features between views, as we benefited from the existence of geometric patterns lying on the stage ground. In many man-made environments, it might be worthwhile to calibrate the camera by automatically detecting vanishing points corresponding to orthogonal directions [8, 29]. Multiple tags and projected patterns (e.g., multiple tags or projections on the walls behind the stage) [19] also have clear potentials for solving this problem. Alternatively, we may also rethink our work following uncalibrated approaches. The authors of [1] exploit sparse feature flows in-between neighbouring images/cameras and structure these visual data using distances and angles. In our case, the idea would be to replace the 3D space where interest levels are estimated with descriptor spaces where relationships between videos crowd-sourced from different cameras could also be established.

Regarding future work, we are convinced, among other authors, that calibration might become a real-time commodity using both the smartphone cameras and inertial measurement units (IMU) as well as, in the very near future, depth sensors (e.g., as in Google's Project Tango). In any of the above-mentioned approaches, some information from the IMU (namely the gravity vector) and Exif data (namely the focal length) can be very helpful, as it can basically provide the vanishing point of the vertical direction or, equivalently, the vanishing line of the ground plane [18]. In some recent work [28], an inertial tracker provides camera poses which are subsequently refined by visual tracking. And last but not least, pose estimation by relocalization [24] form another promising, yet still challenging, paradigm.

3D interest maps is built from video clips filmed by users, where the interest levels of the scene emerges naturally from the users' shot framing. The quality of the interest map can only be improved with more videos.

Acknowledgments. This research is supported by the Singapore National Research Foundation under its International Research Centre @ Singapore Funding Initiative and administered by the IDM Programme Office.

8. REFERENCES

[1] A. Arpa, L. Ballan, R. Sukthankar, G. Taubin, M. Pollefeys, and R. Raskar. Crowdcam: Instantaneous navigation of crowd images using angled graph. In *3DTV-Conference*, pages 422–429, 2013.

[2] A. Borji, M. N. Ahmadabadi, and B. N. Araabi. Cost-sensitive learning of top-down modulation for attentional control. *MVA*, 22(1):61–76, Jan. 2011.

[3] A. Borji and L. Itti. State-of-the-art in visual attention modeling. *IEEE Tr. PAMI*, 35(1):185–207, 2013.

[4] A. Borji, D. N. Sihite, and L. Itti. Salient object detection: A benchmark. In *ECCV*, pages 414–429, 2012.

[5] A. Carlier, V. Charvillat, W. T. Ooi, R. Grigoras, and G. Morin. Crowdsourced automatic zoom and scroll for video retargeting. In *ACM Multimedia*, pages 201–210, 2010.

[6] A. Carlier, G. Ravindra, V. Charvillat, and W. T. Ooi. Combining content-based analysis and crowdsourcing to improve user interaction with zoomable video. In *ACM Multimedia*, pages 43–52, 2011.

[7] D. Comaniciu and P. Meer. Mean shift: A robust approach toward feature space analysis. *IEEE Tr. PAMI*, 24(5):603–619, 2002.

[8] A. Criminisi, I. D. Reid, and A. Zisserman. Single view metrology. In *IJCV*, pages 123–148, 2000.

[9] T. Dittrich, S. Kopf, P. Schaber, B. Guthier, and W. Effelsberg. Saliency detection for stereoscopic video. In *MMSys*, 2013.

[10] G. Flandin and F. Chaumette. Visual data fusion for objects localization by active vision. In *ECCV*, pages 312–326, 2002.

[11] Y. Furukawa and J. Ponce. Accurate, dense, and robust multiview stereopsis. *IEEE Tr. PAMI*, 32(8):1362–1376, 2010.

[12] S. Goferman, L. Zelnik-Manor, and A. Tal. Context-aware saliency detection. In *CVPR*, pages 2376–2383, 2010.

[13] R. I. Hartley and A. Zisserman. *Multiple View Geometry in Computer Vision*. Cambridge University Press, 2004.

[14] T.-H. Huang, K.-Y. Cheng, and Y.-Y. Chuang. A collaborative benchmark for region of interest detection algorithms. In *CVPR*, pages 296–303, 2009.

[15] L. Itti, C. Koch, and E. Niebur. A model of saliency-based visual attention for rapid scene analysis. *IEEE Tr. PAMI*, 20(11):1254–1259, 1998.

[16] Y. Ke, D. Hoiem, and R. Sukthankar. Computer vision for music identification. In *CVPR*, pages 597–604, 2005.

[17] F. Liu and M. Gleicher. Video retargeting: automating pan and scan. In *ACM Multimedia*, pages 241–250, 2006.

[18] J. Lobo and J. Dias. Vision and inertial sensor cooperation using gravity as a vertical reference. In *IEEE Tr. PAMI*, pages 1597–1608, 2003.

[19] I. Martynov, J.-K. Kamarainen, and L. Lensu. Projector calibration by "inverse camera calibration". In *SCIA*, pages 536–544. 2011.

[20] D.-T.-D. Nguyen, A. Carlier, W. T. Ooi, and V. Charvillat. Jiku director 2.0: A mobile video mashup system with zoom and pan using motion maps. In *ACM Multimedia*, 2014.

[21] D.-T.-D. Nguyen, M. Saini, V.-T. Nguyen, and W. T. Ooi. Jiku director: a mobile video mashup system. In *ACM Multimedia*, pages 477–478, 2013.

[22] M. Saini, S. P. Venkatagiri, W. T. Ooi, and M. C. Chan. The jiku mobile video dataset. In *MMSys*, pages 108–113, 2013.

[23] M. K. Saini, R. Gadde, S. Yan, and W. T. Ooi. Movimash: online mobile video mashup. In *ACM Multimedia*, pages 139–148, 2012.

[24] T. Sattler, B. Leibe, and L. Kobbelt. Improving image-based localization by active correspondence search. In *ECCV*, pages 752–765. 2012.

[25] P. Shrestha, M. Barbieri, H. Weda, and D. Sekulovski. Synchronization of multiple camera videos using audio visual features. *IEEE Tr. Multimedia*, 12(1):79–92, 2010.

[26] P. Shrestha, P. H. N. de With, H. Weda, M. Barbieri, and E. H. L. Aarts. Automatic mashup generation from multiple-camera concert recordings. In *ACM Multimedia*, pages 541–550, 2010.

[27] P. F. Sturm. Algorithms for plane-based pose estimation. In *CVPR*, pages 1706–1711, 2000.

[28] P. Tanskanen, K. Kolev, L. Meier, F. Camposeco, O. Saurer, and M. Pollefeys. Live metric 3d reconstruction on mobile phones. In *ICCV*, pages 65–72, 2013.

[29] J.-P. Tardif. Non-iterative approach for fast and accurate vanishing point detection. In *ICCV*, pages 1250–1257, 2009.

[30] B. W. Tatler. The central fixation bias in scene viewing: selecting an optimal viewing position independently of motor biases and image feature distributions. *J. of Vision*, 7(14):1–17, 2007.

[31] X. Xie, H. Liu, S. Goumaz, and W.-Y. Ma. Learning user interest for image browsing on small-form-factor devices. In *CHI*, pages 671–680, 2005.

Crowdsourcing a Reverberation Descriptor Map

Prem Seetharaman
Northwestern University
EECS Department
prem@u.northwestern.edu

Bryan Pardo
Northwestern University
EECS Department
pardo@northwestern.edu

ABSTRACT

Audio production is central to every kind of media that involves sound, such as film, television, and music and involves transforming audio into a state ready for consumption by the public. One of the most commonly-used audio production tools is the reverberator. Current interfaces are often complex and hard-to-understand. We seek to simplify these interfaces by letting users communicate their audio production objective with descriptive language (e.g. "Make the drums sound bigger."). To achieve this goal, a system must be able to tell whether the stated goal is appropriate for the selected tool (e.g. making the violin warmer using a panning tool does not make sense). If the goal is appropriate for the tool, it must know what actions lead to the goal. Further, the tool should not impose a vocabulary on users, but rather understand the vocabulary users prefer. In this work, we describe SocialReverb, a project to crowdsource a vocabulary of audio descriptors that can be mapped onto concrete actions using a parametric reverberator. We deployed SocialReverb, on Mechanical Turk, where 513 unique users described 256 instances of reverberation using 2861 unique words. We used this data to build a concept map showing which words are popular descriptors, which ones map consistently to specific reverberation types, and which ones are synonyms. This promises to enable future interfaces that let the user communicate their production needs using natural language.

Categories and Subject Descriptors

H.1.2 [**User/Machine Systems**]: Human factors; H.5.1 [**Multimedia Information Systems**]: Audio input/output; H.5.2 [**User Interfaces**]: User-centered design; H.5.5 [**Sound and Music Computing**]: Signal analysis, synthesis, and processing

MM'14, November 3–7, 2014, Orlando, Florida, USA.

ACM 978-1-4503-3063-3/14/11 ...$15.00.
http://dx.doi.org/10.1145/2647868.2654908.

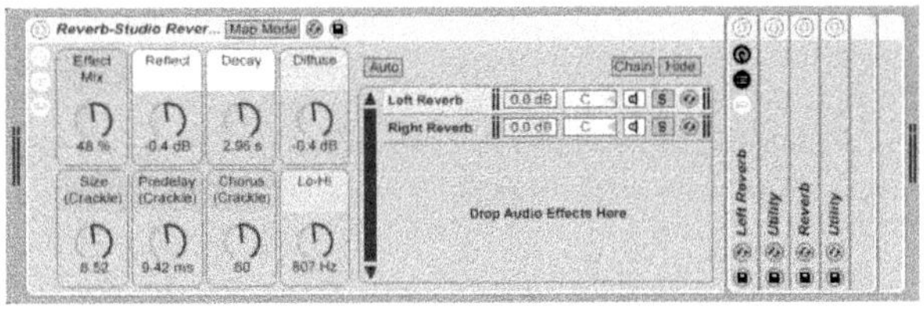

Figure 1: A parametric reverberator from Ableton Live, a digital audio workstation.

General Terms

Human factors; crowd-sourced vocabulary; reverberation; audio

Keywords

Human computation; audio descriptors; audio synonyms; audio engineering; interfaces

1. INTRODUCTION

Audio production is central to every kind of media that involves sound, such as film, television, and music. It involves using tools such as parametric reverberators, equalizers, compressors, and limiters, to transform audio into a state ready for consumption by the public.

One of the most commonly-used audio production tools is the reverberator. In the physical world, reverberation is created by the reflections of a sound off of the solid surfaces (e.g. walls) of an enclosed space. These reflections result in a decaying series of echoes that modify the sound's loudness, timbre, and perceived spatial characteristics. In the digital realm, reverberation (reverb) can be simulated using networks of delays and gains to create a decaying series of echoes.

Reverberators allow the creation of echo effects. They can make the audio sound as if it were recorded in a different acoustic environment (e.g. change a recording made in a sound booth to sound like one recorded in a cathedral), and are used to increase the pleasantness of the sound. Nearly all commercially-recorded singing has reverberation added. People often describe reverb as making a sound "deep", "spacious" and "warm", although the exact relationships between these words and the changes in the control parameters for reverberators are not widely known.

Figure 1 shows the interface of a professional quality parametric reverberator. While the "effect mix" and the "decay" dials may make intuitive sense, the other dials like "predelay" and "Lo-Hi" have no intuitively obvious meaning to the average person or to many musicians (e.g. acoustic and orchestral musicians). This is because the controls are conceptualized in terms of the underlying processes used to create the reverberation effect, as opposed to perceptually relevant terms that people may commonly use to describe reverberation, like "boomy." The result is that musicians without technical expertise can spend a great deal of time stumbling through numerous parameter settings, disrupting the creative process. Musicians should not have to reconceptualize their ideas in terms of a fixed interface with esoteric parameters.

Musicians, both amateur and professional, often conceptualize creative goals for production in terms of natural language that may not have obvious, clear mappings onto the controls available on the audio production tools. Much of the work of audio production involves bridging the gap between artistic goals that are expressed in natural language ("Make the guitar sound 'bigger'") and the tools available to manipulate the sound (e.g. the controls of a parametric reverberator).

We seek a vocabulary that makes audio production interfaces accessible to laypeople, rather than experts. We do this by finding mappings between commonly used descriptive words ("boomy") and the hard-to-understand controls of production tools ("predelay"). The point of this is to develop interfaces that give novices an easy point of entry into audio production. This will support the creativity of acoustic musicians without forcing them to learn interfaces with opaque and esoteric controls. What is more, mappings between the vocabulary of non-technical people and the parameters of production tools may give expert audio engineers an easier way to communicate with their clients. The following quote from Jon Burton, a respected audio engineer, illustrates the communication problem many audio engineers face.

"The idea had sprung from a problem that has arisen in studios ever since the beginning of the recording age: how can you best describe a sound when you have no technical vocabulary to do so? It's a situation all engineers have been in, where a musician is frustratedly trying to explain to you the sound he or she is after, but lacking your ability to describe it in terms that relate to technology, can only abstract. I have been asked to make things more 'pinky blue', 'Castrol GTX'y' and... 'buttery'." [5]

In this work, we describe SocialReverb, a project to crowdsource a vocabulary of audio descriptors that can be mapped onto concrete actions using a parametric reverberator. Using the data collected by SocialReverb, we can create a map that places audio descriptors in relation to one another. This allows us to answer questions about the relationships between descriptors in terms of how they map onto reverberation. We can find descriptive terms whose definitions vary across users, and words that have high agreement between users.

A crowdsourced concept map of terms relating to reverberation would also allow the creation of a reverberator that responds to simple commands in plain English ("make the sound boomy"). To achieve this goal, the tool must be able to determine whether or not the stated goal can be achieved using the selected tool (e.g. making a violin sound "warmer" using a panning tool does not make sense). It should also know what actions must be taken, given the correct tool ("Use a parametric reverberator with an RT60 of 4 seconds and a cutoff frequency of 100 Hz to make the drums rumble warmly"). Further, it should be aware of possible variations in the mapping between word and audio among users (Bob's "warm" $\neq$ Alice's "warm". The concept map learned by SocialReverb is key to learning these mappings and building a plain English interface for reverberation tools.

2. BACKGROUND AND RELATED WORK

There has been much prior work on learning descriptive terms for audio. One common approach to creating a dictionary of descriptors is that of using using text co-occurrence, lexical similarity and dictionary definitions (e.g. WordNet [12]). Approaches based strictly on text are not applicable to our task, because they do not provide mappings between words and measurable sound features or control settings for audio manipulation tools.

Psychologists have explored the mappings between descriptive terms and measurable signal characteristics for sound. Some terms, specifically terms that relate to pitch (high, low) and loudness (soft, loud) have relatively well understood [8, 19] mappings onto measurable sound features. Many other terms, however (e.g. "muffled" sound) do not have simple correlations that have been identified by psychologists.

There have been numerous studies performed in the past half century that hope to find universal sound descriptors that relate to a set of canonical perceptual dimensions [7, 11, 21, 23]. In the past decade, researchers from many different backgrounds, such as recording engineering [9], music composition [20], and computer science [17], have sought a universal set of English terms that describe sound. [22] extracted features from onomatopoeia recordings and computed distances between words, similar to this work. They embedded these distances into a 2D space, similar to the one in Figure 7. This work, however, addresses the distances between onomatopoeia, rather than reverberation. It also has no crowdsourcing element, as the words and sounds were generated by 4 lab members. Our work involves hundreds of users across thousands of sessions, contributing thousands of words.

These studies have varied from finding a vocabulary of descriptors for sound in general to finding a specific set of descriptors for particular instruments. The typical approach is to start by determining a set of natural descriptors by performing a survey. The descriptors provided by participants of the survey are then mapped onto sound measures such as spectral tilt, sound pressure level, or spectral centroid. The research community, however, has not focused on learning vocabularies of words that map to actionable sound manipulations using audio production tools. They have also focused on words to describe timbre, rather than the effect of reverberation. Our work is distinct in both these regards.

Recording engineers [9] use a few specific terms that are used to describe effects produced by recording and production equipment which are straightforward to map onto measurable sound properties. In the case of reverberation, "wet" is, perhaps, the best-known term and refers to the "wet/dry" mix control found on many reverberators. This gives the amplitude ratio between the direct audio signal and the reverberated signal. The "wetter" the sound is, the more reverberation there is. Unfortunately, many descriptive terms applied to reverberation (e.g. "boomy" and "warm") do not map clearly onto single reverberation parameters and the general population of acoustic musicians do not share the vocabulary of recording engineers. Our goal is to discover the vocabulary of this more general population.

The SocialEQ project is the most similar work to the current project. SocialEQ was a project to crowdsource sound adjectives relevant to parametric equalization [6]. It creates a dictionary of words defined both in terms of subjective experiential qualities and measurable properties of a sound. The current work is distinct in that it crowdsources a vocabulary of audio descriptors relevant to reverberation, rather than equalization. Further, the collection technique described in [6] is a time-consuming task that involves rating 40 equalization settings to learn a single word. Their task takes around 15 minutes per word. This limited the size of the resulting vocabulary learned. The simple task in the current work takes just 2 to 3 minutes for multiple words, letting us learn many more word associations.

[14] describes a reverberator that can be controlled through measures of reverberation (RT60, echo density, clarity, central time, spectral centroid). This reverberator is the one used in this work. We also map audio descriptors to these same 5 measures of reverberation. [15] expands on this reverberator to develop a system for learning the settings of a parametric reverberator by users teaching words to the system and rating examples, like in [6]. However, [15] is limited to only a few words that were given to the users to teach to the system (bright, clear, boomy, church-like, bathroom-like). Our system expands and greatly extends this approach by collecting far more audio descriptors (thousands, instead of five) from far more people (hundreds, instead of dozens), priming the pump for a future system where relevant words can be taught to the system using fewer audio examples.

3. SOCIALREVERB

Simplifying interfaces, such as the controller shown in Figure 1, to a simple dial that makes the sound more "church-like" or less "church-like," or more "rumbly" or less "rumbly" requires the collection of a vocabulary that we can map onto actionable changes made by a parametric reverberator. However, it is not immediately obvious what words actually describe reverb and how those descriptions map on to changes in signal statistics or the parameters controlling a reverberator.

We address this problem by asking a large number of users to describe the difference between pairs of audio recordings: an original recording, and that same recording after reverberation is applied. This creates a folksonomy of words that relate to reverberation. It also gives us the data needed to map these words into both a feature space describing the audio and the space of parameter settings for a reverberator.

3.1 The Software

To deploy the software to a large audience for data collection, we have implemented it as a web application using Web Audio API, an experimental low-level audio processing API implemented in Chrome, Opera, and Safari. We implement the reverberation unit with Web Audio API using the built in Gain nodes, Delay nodes, and Lowpass filter, so all of the audio processing required for the reverberation is done within the user's browser. The software is deployed on Google App Engine.

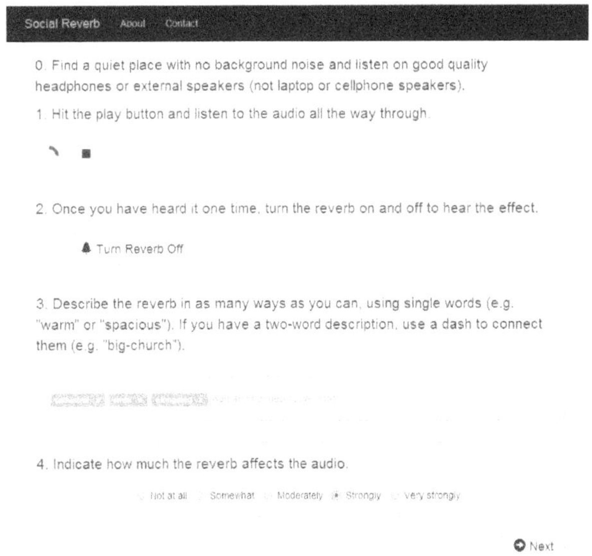

Figure 2: First part of survey for participants. Here they contribute words freely, and rate how much the reverb affects the audio.

3.2 The Interaction

Participants are recruited through Amazon's Mechanical Turk [2]. Once someone agrees to participate, they are presented with a brief (30 second) listening test to ensure they have a listening environment conducive to hearing reverberation (see Section 4.2 for details).

If they pass the listening test, they begin the task and are presented with a looped 10-15 second audio recording of a musical instrument (drums, guitar, or piano) recorded without reverberation. When the audio example has played through once, the 'Turn Reverb On' button is enabled, letting the user turn the reverb on and off to hear the effect of the reverberator. The user can only add or remove reverb. No manipulation of the reverberator parameters is allowed. Once they have toggled the reverb on and off and listened for at least another iteration of the audio example, they are asked to provide a list of words that describe the effect of the reverberator. We encourage the user to use single words, like "warm" and "spacious", but also allow them to use multi-word descriptions by connecting them with a dash.

We ask each participant to contribute words before being presented words other participants contributed to avoid any premature convergence of user vocabularies. This avoids a narrowly focused resulting vocabulary. Since we collected 2861 unique words, we achieved this goal. The prompt in the task mentions three words (warm, spacious, and big-church). While one might expect these words would end up over represented in the final data set, these are just three words out of 2861 provided by participants and none of these three words ended up in the top ten words, ranked by consistency. We then ask them to rate how much the reverb affects the audio, using a Likert scale with values 'not at all', 'somewhat', 'moderately', 'strongly', 'very strongly'.

If there are prior user responses for the current reverberation settings, we then present 15 random words from the set of words previously used to describe the reverb. We ask

Figure 3: Second part of survey for participants. Here they are presented with a list of words and asked whether or not they agree that they describe the reverberation effect. They are asked two questions about their listening environment for inclusion criteria purposes.

them to select words from this list that are good descriptors of the reverberation, or indicate that none are good descriptors. An important note is that this set of words is selected randomly to avoid any bias in the resultant data. If a participant contributes a new word to the data in the first part of the survey, it now has a chance of being presented to other users.

Finally, we ask two questions about the listening environment. We ask what sort of speakers the user has (headphones, stand-alone speakers, laptop/tablet/phone speakers, other) and whether the listening environment is quiet. These are used as inclusion criteria (see Section 4.2). One session consists of repeating this process 5 times, labeling 5 reverberation settings. Each reverberation setting in a single session has a random audio file associated with it. The audio changes between the piano, drums, and guitar sample. In the Amazon Mechanical Turk task used to collect the data, we restrict users to at most 3 sessions.

3.3 The Reverberator

To implement the data collection, we needed a reverberator able to generate a wide variety of impulse response functions on the fly. Rather than use a convolution reverberator, which selects from a fixed library of precomputed impulse responses, we used a digital stereo reverberation unit inspired by Moorer's work ([13]), described in [15] and [14] and seen in Figure 4. The developed reverberator is a version of a well known state-of-the-art algorithm, comparable to reverberators found in professional digital audio work stations such as Ableton, Cubase, etc.

The reverberator is controlled with 5 parameters: the delay and gain of the first comb filter, the delay between the channels of the all-pass filter, the cutoff frequency of the low pass filter and the gain of the overall reverberation. The

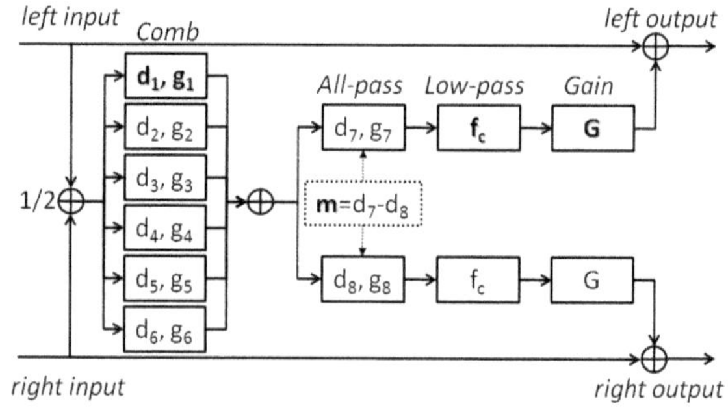

Figure 4: The digital stereo reverberation unit.

reverberation is added back to the dry signal to produce the modified signal. The reverberator uses six comb filters in parallel to simulate the complex modal response of a room by adding the echoes together. The delays and gains of the other five comb filters are derived from the delay (d_1) and gain (g_1) of the first comb filter. After this is computed, the signal is doubled into a left and right channel. The left channel is delayed by $d_a + m$ seconds, while the right channel is delayed by $d_a - m$ seconds, where d_a is .01 sec, and m ranges between 0 and 12 msec. This creates a slight stereo effect. The signal is then put through a low-pass filter with a cutoff frequency f_c to simulate air and walls absorption. Finally, a gain parameter G, controls the wet/dry effect.

These five parameters (d_1, g_1, m, f_c, G) provide us direct control over the sound of the reverberator. To make data collected using this reverberator useful for other reverberatiors with different control parameters, we use the methods described in [14] to map these five control parameters to five signal measures of the resulting impulse response function. The signal measures are:

1. *Reverberation time (RT60)*, the time it takes for the reflections of a direct sound to decay by 60 dB below the level of the direct sound [1].
2. *Echo density*, the number of echoes per second at a time t.
3. *Clarity*, the ratio in dB of the energies of the impulse response before and after a given time t, indicating how "clear" the sound is.
4. *Central time*, the time of the center of the energy in the impulse response.
5. *Spectral centroid*, the frequency of the center of energy in the magnitude spectrum of the impulse response.

By characterizing the reverberation in this way, results from this study can be used for any reverberation unit where a mapping has been made between the control parameters and the resulting impulse response characteristics, regardless of the construction of the reverberator. This makes the learned data highly generalizable.

In selecting reverberation settings to present, we chose a set of 1024 impulse response functions that evenly cover a wide range of reverberations. The reverberation time ranged from .5 to 8 seconds, the echo density from 500 to 10000 echoes/sec, the clarity from -20 to 10 dB, the central time from .01 to .5 sec, and the spectral centroid from 200 to 11025 Hz.

From this set S of 1024 settings, we estimate a maximally varying subset P of 256 settings as described in [16]. First, we select a random setting $s \in S$ and initialize P to include s. Then we search through S to find the next setting that maximizes the variance of P, if included. That is,

$$s_{next} = \arg\max_{s \in S} v(s)$$

, where $v(s) = \frac{1}{D}\sum_d std_d(P \cup f)$. Here, d is a dimension (one of the five signal measures) and D is the number of dimensions (5). We normalize each dimension so one does not dominate the sum. This process walks through the space of reverberation settings, finding ones that are maximally different from ones that we have already chosen. This set of 256 widely-varying reverberation settings was used for all sessions in the study.

For each session with a participant we select a setting from P as described in 4.3, and present it to the user. Our selection method ensures even coverage across P, and the nature of P is such that a single user is unlikely to get two similar reverberation settings in a single session.

3.4 The Audio

We selected three monophonic (as opposed to stereo) dry (no reverberation) signals for source audio that are representative of sounds that would be used in real musical projects. The first is a dry electric guitar sound with no effects processing, playing a 10 second chord progression. The second is a 16 second passage from Bach's Chaconne in D minor recorded with a dry piano sound, created using a dry sampled piano from the East West Quantum Leap Pianos Gold library. The last is a 14 second recording of a drum kit performing in a rock style, taken from a studio recording used in a commercially released album. Each of these signals is representative of real-world music. We chose three very different signals that each broadly cover the frequency range. In the "agreement" part of the survey, we present words from other sessions with the same reverberation, but applied to all 3 sounds. High-agreement words are likely in the intersection of descriptions of three audio signal/reverberation combinations. As the three audio signals are very different, we see the words in the intersection as descriptions of the effect, rather than the audio signal.

The audio was recorded with a sample rate of 48000 Hz. We then compressed each audio file as a high-quality .mp3 file using the LAME [10] .mp3 encoder at a bitrate of 320kbps. This bitrate has been shown to produce audio that listeners over the internet find indistinguishable from uncompressed compact disc quality audio [3]. Compression was done to limit the bandwidth cost of sending the audio to the client's computer. Once the audio is transferred to the client, the audio is expanded again to a 16-bit pulse-code-modulated (PCM) audio buffer. Reverberation is then applied locally to the audio in the buffer.

4. DATA COLLECTION

4.1 Participant Recruiting

We recruited participants through Amazon's Mechanical Turk. We paid participants \$.50 (USD) for every 5 audio examples described, if they pass certain inclusion criteria. Participants could elect to perform the task from 1 to a maximum of 3 times. A single Amazon Mechanical Turk user thus describes 5, 10, or 15 reverberation settings.

4.2 Inclusion Criteria

We ensure cooperative and attentive participants in a variety of ways. Amazon Mechanical Turk provides measures of worker reliability that may be used to pre-screen participants. For this study, we only allowed workers wtih a 97% positive review rating and who have performed at least 1000 tasks on Mechanical Turk.

Much of the effect of reverberation occurs in low frequencies (below 100 Hz). Many laptop speakers are not able to reproduce sounds below 100 Hz. To ensure quality contributions, participants were asked to take a listening test prior to performing the task. The test randomly selects 2 audio files from a set of 8. These audio files consists of high, mid-range, and low tones in some random sequence. The high tones were selected to be audible on any speaker. The mid-range tones were selected to be slightly audible on laptop, phone, or tablet speakers, but clear on any quality speakers or headphones. The low tones were selected to be completely inaudible on laptop, phone, or tablet speakers. The user is asked how many tones they heard clearly in each audio file. The correct answers vary between 1 and 8 depending on the audio file selected. The user is given three chances to pass the speaker test. If they fail, they cannot participate.

Remaining participants are filtered further. We measure the total amount of time spent listening to the audio example, with the effect on and off. If the user listens to the clean audio for less than the length of the audio file, we exclude them from the data. If the user listens to the audio with the effect on for less than the length of the audio file, we exclude them from the data. We also removed sessions where the participant answered no to the question: "Was the listening environment quiet?" Finally, we only include participants who self-report listening on "headphones (including earbuds") and "stand-alone speakers", excluding those listening on "laptop/tablet/phone speakers" or "other."

4.3 Experimental Design

There are 3 possible audio recordings and 256 possible reverberation settings, making for a total of 768 combinations. The audio examples are selected randomly for each session. The reverberation settings are selected carefully for each session to ensure even coverage of the 256 settings. Each time the system selects a reverberation setting to present, a count for that reverberation is incremented by one. When we select a reverberation setting, we select randomly amongst the settings with the minimum count in the database. This is equivalent to random selection without replacement until all reverberation settings have been used an equal number of times.

Each time a participant performs the task, they are asked to describe 5 reverberation settings (see Section 3.2 for a description of the interaction). A single user may perform the task at most 3 times, describing at most 15 reverberation settings. Recall there are 768 combinations of reverberation and audio file to be labeled. This requires a minimum of 52 (if each describes 15 reverberations) and a maximum of 154 (if each describes only 5 reverberations) participants to ensure each combination was labeled at least once.

5. RESULTS

As of this writing, 513 unique users have described 256 instances of reverberation using 2861 unique words. We have made the data available for use by the research community at `interactiveaudiolab.org/data/socialreverb`. We have also included audio examples, where a descriptor is applied to one of the dry sounds described in 3.4.

5.1 Definitions

1. **example**: A reverberation applied to an audio file for a participant to describe.
2. **descriptor**: An adjective used to describe the effect of reverberation on one or more examples.
3. **session**: A participant takes the SocialReverb survey, providing descriptors for 5 examples. Participants may perform up to 3 sessions.
4. **descriptor instance**: Each time a descriptor is entered in the free-response question (Question 3 in Figure 3.2) or a user agreed that it described a reverberation from the list of words (Question 5, Figure 3.2).
5. **reverberation measure vector**: a vector of measures of reverberation described in Section 3.3. Each descriptor instance is associated with a corresponding reverberation measure vector.
6. **reverberation parameter vector**: a vector of control parameter settings for the reverberator described in Section 3.3. Each descriptor instance is associated with a corresponding reverberation parameter vector.
7. **descriptor definition**: The set of reverberation measure vectors that share a common descriptor, and built as described in 5.3. The preciseness of the definition depends on the normalized variance in the set of measure vectors.

5.2 The descriptors

There were a total of 1074 sessions, in which we collected 14628 descriptor instances from 513 users. These 14628 descriptor instances represented 2861 unique descriptors. Of the 2861 descriptors, 1791 had at least 2 instances. The most popular descriptor by far was *echo*. Other popular terms include *warm* and *spacious*. While these words were expected, we now have correlations between specific reverberation effects and the words used to describe them. This is a unique contribution as no prior study has done this for a vocabulary of more than 5 descriptors. The top ten most common descriptors are shown in Table 1. These words are those one would expect to crop up in a discussion of reverberation. Interestingly, they are not those with the most specific definitions, in terms of the measured qualities of the reverberation, as we shall see in Section 5.4.

5.3 Representing reverberation concepts

Recall that these words were elicited from users in a format that asks them to describe the change to a sound when the reverb is applied, as opposed to an absolute measure of what is a "warm" sound. This lets us correlate the actual signal changes caused by the reverberator to the descriptive term elicited by that reverberator.

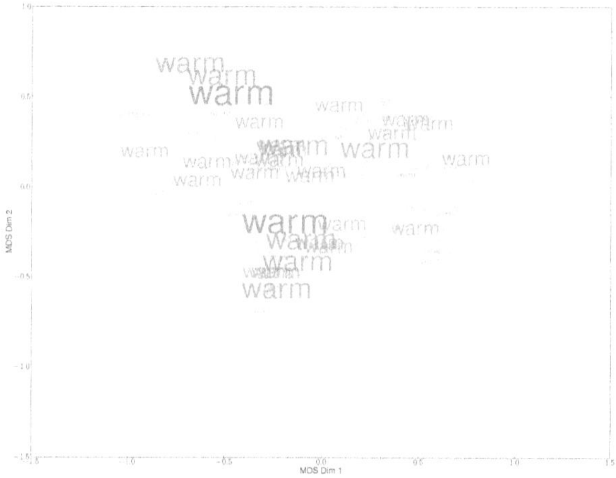

Figure 5: A map of reverb measure vectors for "warm". Font size encodes how much agreement there was on the word for that specific reverb measure vector. "Warm" is a less consistent descriptor, than "underwater," as can be seen by its spread across the map above.

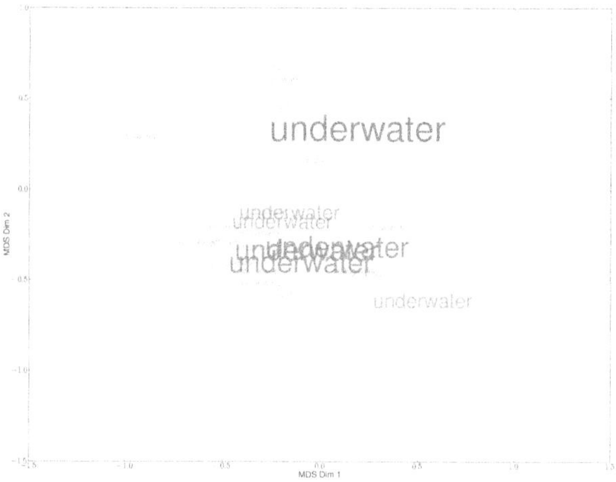

Figure 6: The same visualization technique as in Figure 5 for "underwater", rather than "warm". This map is more consistent than Figure 5, as it has much less spread across the map.

Rank	Word	Instances
1	echo	1220
2	distant	662
3	warm	596
4	spacious	596
5	loud	538
6	muffled	451
7	deep	423
8	church	327
9	echoing	312
10	big	255

Table 1: Top ten words in database by number of descriptor instances.

Using the parameters and measures associated with each descriptor (see Section 3.3), we can calculate an actionable definition for the descriptor. Each instance of a descriptor is associated with an example that had a particular reverberation applied. To define the actionable meaning of a descriptor, we add the associated reverberation measurement vector (consisting of reverberation time, echo density, clarity, central time, and spectral centroid) to the set of associated measurement values.

Once we find all reverberation measures associated with a word (e.g. "warm"), we take the average of each measure and use the resultant vector as a first approximation of the descriptor definition. Here, by definition, we mean the changes in the measurable signal qualities that a typical listener would label as making the sound "warm." This gives us a definition that can be used to change a sound to make it more "boomy" (or "warm", or some other word). This can be done using the same technique applied in [14].

5.4 Consistent reverberation descriptors

Some words are more specific than others. For example, "echo" or "echoing" is a very broad term that we know from the data is applied to many varied examples of reverberation. While it is true that taking the average, as described in the previous section will result in something many would call "echoing," we seek words that would let a user have more nuance than merely having or not having echo effect. Therefore, we would like to establish how specific reverberation descriptors are. For example, does the word "boomy" describe a specific range of reverberation settings, or is it used more generally? To answer this, we calculate the normalized variance within each descriptor's definition.

A descriptor definition is the set of reverberation measure vectors (one five-element vector per instance) associated with the descriptor. Each of the measures is normalized to the range from 0 to 1, so that one measurement (e.g. RT60) does not dominate the calculations. For each descriptor, we then calculate the within-measurement variance (e.g. variance of normalized RT60 for all instances of "boomy"). The variances for all five measures (e.g. the variance of RT60, echo density, clarity, central time and spectral centroid) are then averaged for each descriptor. The top 10 descriptors that had at least 15 instances in the database each are shown in Table 2 , ranked by variance of descriptor definition. Note that none of the top 10 highly-specific terms is in the top 10 most-used descriptors. This indicates that the most widely-used words may contain less specifically applicable information than many less-used words.

Figures 5 and 6 are a visual representation of consistency. They were generated by gathering every unique reverberation measure vector associated with the descriptor, and performing multidimensional scaling [4] on the resultant data. Here, the size of a word indicates the number of instances where that descriptor shared the same specific reverberation measure vector. The larger the text, the more times that specific reverberation setting was given this label. Less consistent maps have the descriptor spread across the map. This means many different reverberation settings elicited the same description. More consistent maps have descriptors more focused in specific areas of the map. This indicates the word has a specific meaning, particular to a certain kind of reverb.

Rank	Word	Normalized Variance	# of Instances
1	chaotic	.17452	26
2	underwater	.19031	70
3	watery	.20074	29
4	boomy	.2014	31
5	distorted	.20172	235
6	messy	.20595	35
7	haunting	.21077	157
8	broad	.21518	26
9	overdone	.21743	18
10	ominous	.21839	84

Table 2: Top ten descriptors with at least 15 instances, sorted by variance of the definition. Lower variance means higher cross-participant agreement in the definition of the word.

Figure 5 shows that some words have multimodal definitions not captured by the averaging scheme we use for the descriptor definition. We can see that "warm" appears to group into 3 clusters. This would indicate that there are 3 different "warm" reverberations in the data. This is in contrast to Figure 6, which has a single definition, since the distribution of reverberation settings is clearly centered on one location.

5.5 Mapping the reverb word space

A reverberation setting is described by the five-parameter signal descriptor of the reverberation described in Section 3.3. We can thus place any word-label applied by a participant to a reverberation setting in a five dimensional-space, defined by the signal descriptor values.

We can visualize the reverberation measure space by using descriptor definitions. For each descriptor with 15 or more instances, we calculate a definition and measure the variance of the definition as described in Section 5.4. From the resultant descriptor definitions, we calculate pairwise Euclidean distances. We use these distances to project the original five dimensional space onto two dimensions, using multidimensional scaling [4]. Each descriptor is scaled using its variance. The resultant reverberation descriptor map is shown in Figure 7. To rephrase, word position is the center of the distribution of reverberation settings associated with the word. Word size is associated with the variance of the distribution. Larger words indicate greater consistency (less variance) among participants.

5.6 Audio descriptor synonyms

Distance between descriptor definitions is measured using Euclidean distance in the space of reverberation measures. We consider two descriptors synonyms if the pairwise distance between their descriptor definitions is within the first percentile of all pairwise distances between descriptor definitions. We restrict the set of possible words to those whose descriptor definition variance score falls in the lower 50th percentile of all descriptor definition variance scores. We only create a descriptor definition for a word if it was mentioned in the database (either agreed with or contributed freely) at least 15 times.

Table 3 shows synonyms of some high consistency descriptors found through comparing descriptor definitions.

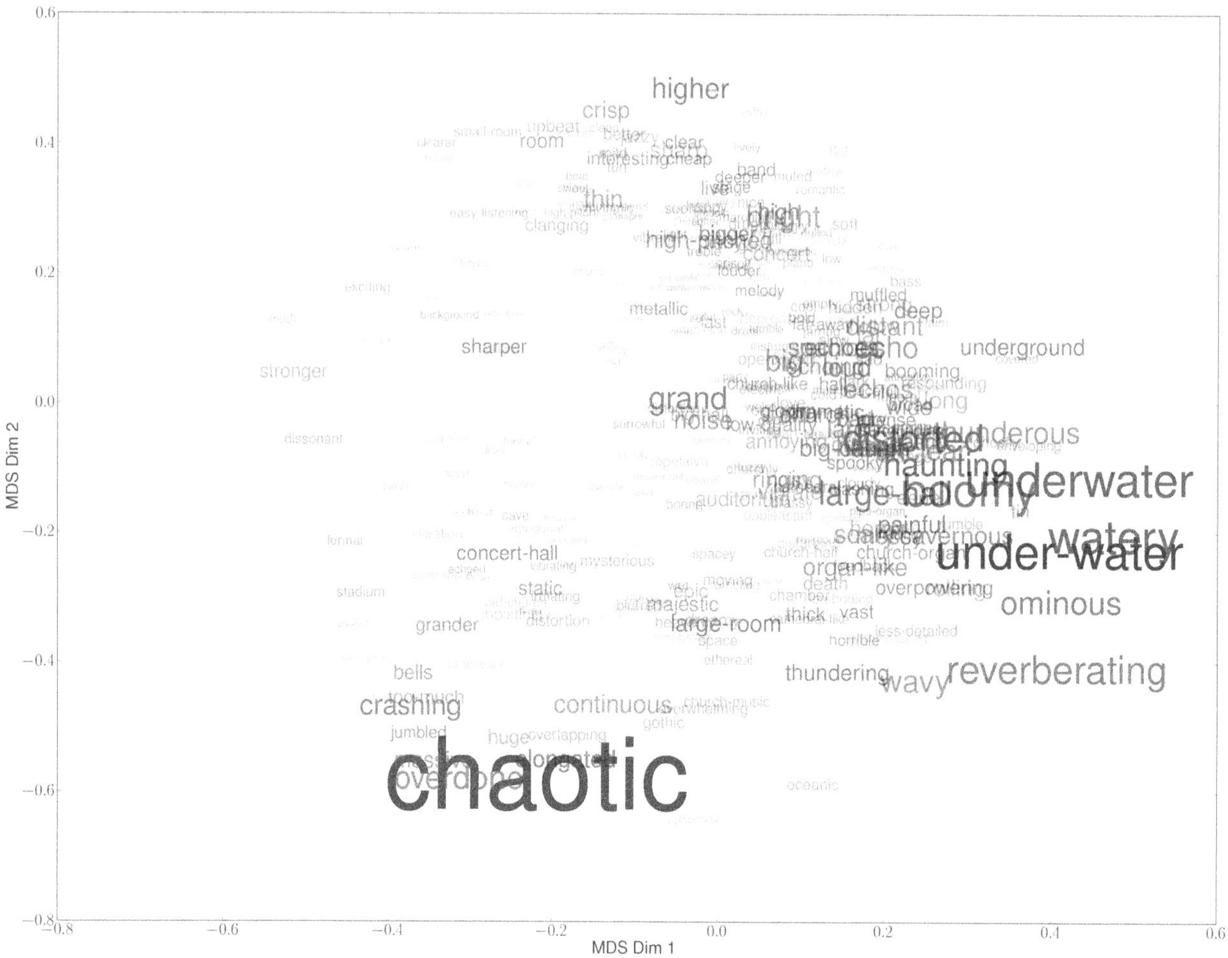

Figure 7: A visualization of the reverberation descriptor space. The map was created using multidimensional scaling to project the data onto the two dimensions shown. The font size of a word inversely correlates to the variance in its definition among participants. Big words that are close together can be interpreted as reliable audio synonyms for reverberation.

Descriptor	Synonyms
distorted	big-church, strange
harsh	big-church, bad, strange
echo	loud, spacious, echos
spacious	echo, distant, echoing, far, slow, cool, jumbled
deep	distant, hollow, bass
church	dramatic, dark
far	distant, spacious
wide	airy, peaceful
ringing	annoying, spooky, intense
hollow	distant, deep, far-away, muffled, bass, thick
big-church	distorted, harsh, surrounding, strange

Table 3: Some descriptors with low normalized variance and their synonyms.

5.7 Parameter space versus measure space

To this point, all figures and tables have shown words in the space of measured signal statistics for reverberated sounds. We did this so that the data would be usable across multiple kinds of reverberators that do not share the same set of control parameters. A question may arise, however, about whether new insight can be gained by building a map of descriptors using the distance in parameter space rather than measure space. The resultant map is shown in Figure 8.

The parameters control the reverberation directly, manipulating the coefficients and delay times of the reverberator shown in Figure 4. The measures of the impulse response generated by the parameters are what we use to measure distance between reverberation effects. In Figure 7, the words are more evenly spaced around the environment, and the space can be divided cleanly into a few different types of reverberation by looking at it. Around "chaotic" falls reverberations in large halls, to the point of distortion, like in a parking garage. Around "underwater" falls calmer reverberations in slightly smaller halls. Above "underwater" are stranger reverberations ("clashing", "distorted") in small

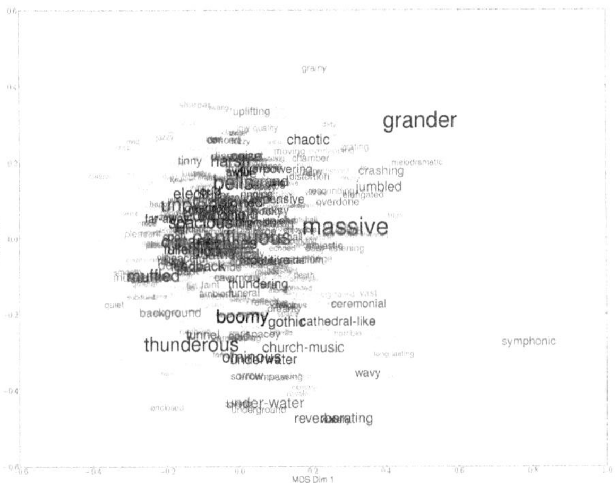

Figure 8: The same visualization technique as in Figure 7, except now done in parameter space rather than measure space

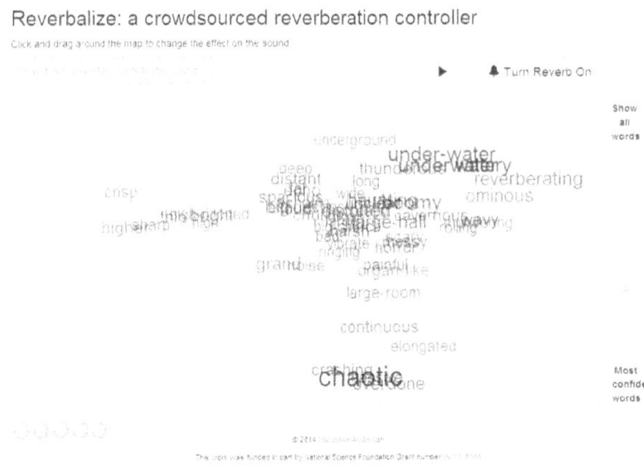

Figure 9: Reverbalize: a novel reverberation controller implemented using the data collected via SocialReverb.

halls (bathrooms, stairwells, perhaps) and above that are the more realistic reverberations, that sound like churches and auditoriums. Around "upbeat" exist reverberations that sound like studio recordings, or very small rooms.

In parameter space, shown in Figure 8, we cannot draw these divisions so easily. The words are clustered together much more closely and evenly. While some of the relationships in measure space are somewhat preserved ("massive", "jumbled", "crashing" are still near each other), many are not. "Upbeat", for example, is now close to "low quality" and much closer to "chaotic" than it was before. This suggests that there are larger perceptual discontinuities in parameter space than in measure space. From this map, we see that operating a parametric reverberator using the measures of the reverberation, rather than direct control of the system that produces the reverberation is more predictable, making it easier to use. Indeed, many parametric reverberators behave this way, such as the one in Figure 1. This is, in fact, what makes them difficult to use and is, in part, a motivation for this work.

6. FUTURE WORK

We have used the data collected to implement a novel reverberation controller [18], shown in Figure 6. Words are projected onto a map, using a mapping from their 5 dimensional descriptor definitions to the 2 dimensional space of the map. Users traverse the map to explore effects, using the words as a guide. They can also search for a word, and if it's in the map, it's applied to the audio.

This interface lays the groundwork for a future validation study on the effectiveness of an interface built using the data from the current work. In this validation study, we will focus on a population of acoustic musicians who have musical ideas and goals, but are not the typical population of tech-savvy production engineers and electronic musicians that are the typical user base of existing audio production tools. We will compare our vocabulary-map interface to a traditional parametric interface, where both interfaces control the same underlying reverberation tool.

Participants will be given two kinds of production tasks. In the first task, an audio file with reverberation already applied to it will be presented. Then the participant will be given the original, un-reverberated audio and asked to match the reverberation effect using either the new interface or a traditional parametric reverberation interface. We will measure two parameters: how quickly does the participant complete the task and how closely does the participant-applied reverberation match the original reverberation. Participants will also be asked to complete a survey about their satisfaction with the interface along various dimensions (e.g. ease of use, clarity of affordances, etc.).

In the second task, users will be given a production goal (e.g. "make the music sound as if it is being played underwater.") and asked to achieve that goal using either the traditional or the new interface. We will measure how quickly the user reports having achieved the goal, as well as the users' level of satisfaction with how well the goal was achieved. Further, the outcome will be presented to a second set of users who will be asked to measure how well the stated goal was achieved. As with the first task, participants will be asked to complete a survey about their satisfaction with the interface along various dimensions (e.g. ease of use, clarity of affordances, etc.).

Other future work includes a tool to automatically apply appropriate descriptive labels to the output of any existing reverberator. This can be done by measuring the impulse response, placing it on the descriptor map, and using the words nearby as a description of the reverberation effect. This will allow the creation of two-way language-based control of reverberation tools. The user can ask the question "What is the effect of changing knob A?" and the tool could predict "It will make the sound 'boomy'." Similarly, one could ask "How do I make the sound 'boomy'?" and be told by the tool. This opens up the possibility of a new kind of interactive instruction for such tools, informed by a real understanding of the mappings between words and audio effects.

7. CONCLUSIONS

In this work, we described an approach to learning actionable words to describe reverberation that could be used to produce a crowd-sourced folksonomy of descriptive terms for reveberation. This was embodied in a web-based data collection tool, SocialReverb.

We also developed methods to determine which descriptors are commonly used to describe reverberation, which are specific to a range of reverberation settings, and which are synonymous. We also created a map of words visualizing their relationship to each other and examined the map in both measure space (abstract control of the reverberator) and parameter space (direct control of reverberator). The data underlying this map has been made available to the broader community.

This map of descriptors, allows the creation of reverberation tools whose controls are conceptualized in terms of perceptually relevant terms ("make the drums sound chaotic") rather than in terms of the underlying processes used to create the reverberation (reverberation time, echo density, and so on). The data we gathered also tells us which words are actionable by a reverberator, like "echo", "distant", or "underwater". By collecting this vocabulary, we can create audio production tools that are accessible to novices, as well as understand the way people interact with reverberation tools and audio effects in general.

8. ACKNOWLEDGEMENTS

This work was supported by the National Science Foundation, Grant No. IIS-1116384. Additional thanks to Zach Puller for providing source audio for the study.

References

[1] Fons Adriaensen. "Acoustical Impulse Response Measurement with ALIKI". In: *4th International Linux Audio Conference.* 2006.

[2] Amazon. *Amazon Mechanical Turk.* 2005-2014. URL: `http://mturk.com`.

[3] Jeff Atwood. *Concluding the Great MP3 Bitrate Experiment.* 2012. URL: `http://blog.codinghorror.com/concluding-the-great-mp3-bitrate-experiment/`.

[4] Ingwer Borg and Patrick JF Groenen. *Modern multidimensional scaling: Theory and applications.* Springer, 2005.

[5] Jon Burton. *Ear Machine iQ: Intelligent Equaliser Plug-in.* June 2011. URL: `http://www.soundonsound.com/sos/jun11/articles/em-iq.htm`.

[6] Mark Cartwright and Bryan Pardo. "Social-eq: Crowdsourcing an equalization descriptor map". In: *14th International Society for Music Information Retrieval.* 2013.

[7] J. Grey. *Multidimensional perceptual scaling of musical timbres.* The Journal of the ASA, 61(5):1270-1277, 1977.

[8] H. Helmholtz and A. Ellis. *On the sensations of tone as a physiological basis for the theory of music.* Dover, New York, 2nd english edition, 1954.

[9] D. Huber and R. Runstein. *Modern recording techniques.* Focal Press/Elsevier, Amsterdam ; Boston, 7th edition, 2010.

[10] LAME. *LAME MP3 Encoder.* 1998-2014. URL: `http://lame.sourceforge.net/`.

[11] S. McAdams et al. *Perceptual scaling of synthesized musical timbres: Common dimensions, specificities, and latent subject classes.* Psychological Research, 58(3):177-192, 1995.

[12] George A. Miller. *WordNet: a lexical database for English.* 1995. DOI: `10.1145/219717.219748`.

[13] James A. Moorer. "About this Reverberation Business". In: *Computer Music Journal* (1979).

[14] Zafar Rafii and Bryan Pardo. "A Digital Reverberator Controlled through Measures of the Reverberation". In: *Northwestern Electrical Engineering and Computer Science Department* (2009).

[15] Zafar Rafii and Bryan Pardo. "Learning to Control a Reverberator using Subjective Perceptual Descriptors". In: *10th International Society on Music Information Retrieval* (2009).

[16] AT Sabin, Zafar Rafii, and Bryan Pardo. "Weighted-Function-Based Rapid Mapping of Descriptors to Audio Processing Parameters". In: *Journal of the Audio Engineering Society* (2011), pp. 419–430.

[17] M. Sarkar, B. Vercoe, and Y. Yang. "Words that describe timbre: a study of auditory perception through lan- guage". In: *Proc. of Language and Music as Cognitive Systems Conference.* 2007.

[18] Prem Seetharaman and Bryan Pardo. "Reverbalize: a crowdsourced reverberation controller". In: *ACM Multimedia, Technical Demo* (2014).

[19] R. Shepard. *Geometrical approximations to the structure of musical pitch.* Psychological Review, 89(4):305-333, 1982.

[20] D. Smalley. *Spectromorphology: explaining sound-shapes.* Organised Sound, 2(02):107-126, 1997.

[21] L. Solomon. *Search for physical correlates to psychological dimensions of sounds.* The Journal of the ASA, 31(4):492-497, 1959.

[22] S Sundaram and S Narayanan. "Analysis of audio clustering using word descriptions". In: *ICASSP: Acoustics, Speech and Signal Processing* (2007).

[23] A Zacharakis, K Pastiadis, and G Papadelis. "An Investigation Of Musical Timbre: Uncovering Salient Semantic Descriptors And Perceptual Dimensions". In: *12th International Society for Music Information Retrieval Conference.* 2011.

What Videos Are Similar with You? Learning a Common Attributed Representation for Video Recommendation

Peng Cui, Zhiyu Wang and Zhou Su
Department of Computer Science and Technology, Tsinghua University, Beijing, China
cuip@tsinghua.edu.cn, zy-wang08@mails.tsinghua.edu.cn, suhmily@gmail.com

ABSTRACT

Although video recommender systems have become the predominant way for people to obtain video information, their performances are far from satisfactory in that (1) the recommended videos are often mismatched with the users' interests and (2) the recommendation results are, in most cases, hardly understandable for users and therefore cannot persuade them to engage. In this paper, we attempt to address the above problems in data representation level, and aim to learn a common attributed representation for users and videos in social media with good interpretability, stability and an appropriate level of granularity. The basic idea is to represent videos with users' social attributes, and represent users with content attributes of videos, such that both users and videos can be represented in a common space concatenated by social attributes and content attributes. The video recommendation problem can then be converted into a similarity matching problem in the common space. However, it is still challenging to balance the roles of social attributes and content attributes, learn such a common representation in sparse user-video interactions and deal with the cold-start problem. In this paper, we propose a REgularized Dual-fActor Regression (REDAR) method based on matrix factorization. In this method, social attributes and content attributes are flexibly combined, and social and content information are effectively exploited to alleviate the sparsity problem. An incremental version of REDAR is designed to solve the cold-start problem. We extensively evaluate the proposed method for video recommendation application in real social network dataset, and the results show that, in most cases, the proposed method can achieve a relative improvement of more than 20% compared to state-of-the-art baseline methods.

Categories and Subject Descriptors

H.3.3 [**Information Search and Retrieval**]: Retrieval models

Keywords

video recommendation, attributed representation, social attributes

MM'14, November 3–7, 2014, Orlando, Florida, USA.

http://dx.doi.org/10.1145/2647868.2654946.

1. INTRODUCTION

Recommender systems are becoming increasingly important because of the overload of information brought about by today's Internet. Video recommender systems are required, in particular, because of the high timing costs of watching videos. Netflix reported that 75% of the content that people watch follows a recommendation. These video recommender systems therefore play the role of a bridge between users and videos, where a common representation of videos and users is required to measure the matching degree of user-video pairs. Developing an interpretable and stationary common representation method for both videos and users is of paramount significance for effective and efficient video recommendation.

In the literature, collaborative filtering (CF) has achieved great success in recommender systems. User-based CF methods represent users with videos as features, such that user-video matching can be conducted in the item space. In contrast, item-based CF methods represent videos with users as features and calculate the matching degree of user-video pairs in user space. However, the performances of these methods are seriously affected by the sparsity of the user-video collaborative matrix; they are unable to infer meaningful information about videos (or users) that lack interactions with different users (or videos). More recently, matrix factorization based CF has become more popular. It assumes a common low-dimensional latent factor representation for both users and items such that the user-item matching degree is measurable in the latent space. However, the latent factors are hardly interpretable, which makes it difficult to generalize the learned representations to new data. In addition, all CF methods suffer from the cold start problem, i.e., making recommendations for new users or new videos difficult, owing to a lack of information in the collaborative matrix. To address this, content-based video recommendation methods are currently being investigated, where users' interests and preferences are represented in detail by either content features or metadata (for example, title, or tags) of videos. However, the low-level representation is often too specific to capture users' broad interests [6]. Representing videos and users in a common space with good interpretability, stability, and appropriate levels of granularity is still an open problem.

Fortunately, the emergence of social media brought us with vast amount of users, videos and the observable interaction behaviors between users and videos. With the *Homophily* hypothesis[1], it is possible and reasonable to extract a middle-level representation

[1]Homophily is the tendency of individuals to associate and bond with others who are similar. It is often used to account for the similar behaviors of similar people towards new ideas or innovations, which implies that user-item interactions can be predicted by similarity matching of users and items in a common space.

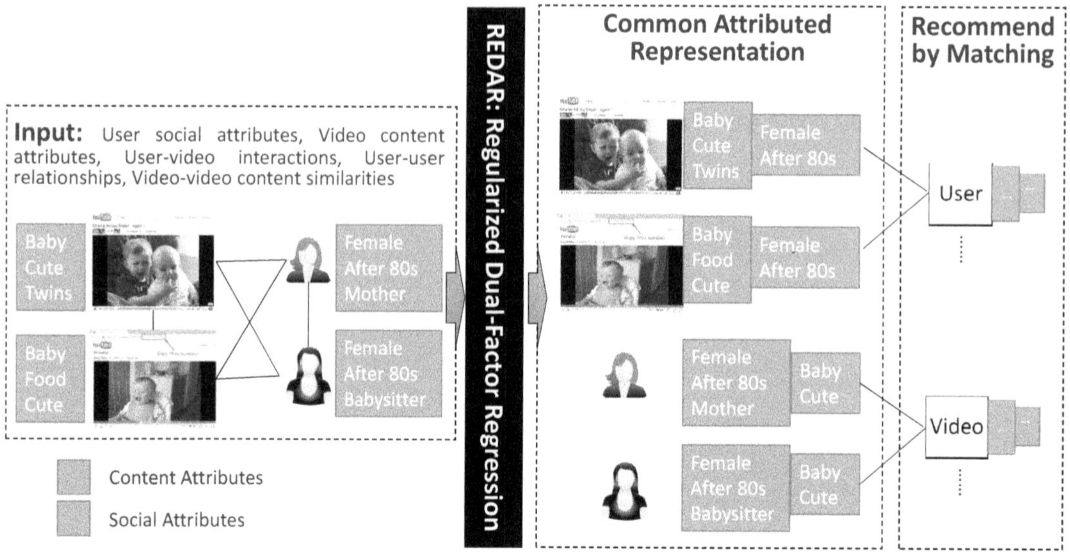

Figure 1: The framework of attributed representation based video recommendation.

layer from the social-enriched environment a middle-level representation layer to represent both videos and users. Attributes, which lie in the middle of low low-level features and high-level semantics, have been intensively investigated in recent years to characterize the visual contents. And Furthermore, it has been demonstrated that such a middle middle-level representation is in a properan appropriate level of granularity for various application scenarios . It is natural and straightforward to extract content attributes from videos to depict their contents. Also In addition, we can extract social attributes from user profiles to capture users' characteristics in social aspects. Through the interactions between users and videos, the video content attributes and user social attributes are no longer isolated. For If a video being is watched by a number of users, the social attributes of the users who watched the video can be aggregated into the social attributes of the video. For example, in Figure 1, a video can be represented by social attributes such as "after 80s " and "female,", which means that the video is more probably liked by after 80s female users. Similarly, for a user having watched a number of videos, the content attributes of the videos that are watched by the user can be aggregated into the content attributes of the user. It is shown in Figure 1 shows that the user can be represented by content attributes such as "baby" and "cute", which means that the user is more likely to watch the videos with such contents. In this way, both social attributes and content attributes can be used as the common representation for user-video matching, and such representations are interpretable (compared with latent space models), stable (compared with CF models), and in a properhave an appropriate level of granularity.

However, it is still challenging to make video recommendations in the social and content attribute space.

(1) **The balance of social attributes and content attributes.** User-video interactions are often triggered by both long-term preference and instantaneous interest, alongside the general topic or style of the video, or detailed elements of the video content that attracted the user. Comparatively, social attribute-based representation is more stable and general. Users' social attributes are often abstract (e.g., after 80s) and remain unchanged for quite a long time. Although videos dynamically propagate among users with different social attributes, their aggregated social attributes are unlikely to dramatically vary over time. In contrast, users' content attributes can capture user preferences in detail and are therefore more dynamic with users watching videos with different content attributes. A method which integrates a user's content attributes incorporating different aspects of a user-video interaction mechanism requires a subtle design.

(2) **The sparsity of user-video interactions.** Extracting both a user's social attributes from user profiles and content attributes for videos from their surrounding texts is straightforward. However, in order to learn social attributes for videos and vice versa, user-video interactions play an important bridging role. Nevertheless, the high volumes of users and videos intrinsically determine the sparsity of user-video interactions. Therefore, effective priors are required to alleviate the sparsity problem. Embedding rich information, in addition to user-video interactions in social media, into the recommendation framework is a critical problem.

(3) **The cold-start problem.** Making recommendations for cold users (who have not watched any videos) and cold videos (that have not been watched by any users), the so-called cold-start problem, always proves difficult to overcome in video recommender systems. As mentioned above, we rely on user-video interactions to bridge users and content attributes, as well as videos and social attributes. For new users and videos, we need an effective method to link them with other active users and popular videos, whose attribute-based representations have been learned from rich information.

In this paper, we analyze the significance of social attributes for videos and content attributes for users. We find that most videos can obtain a number of representative social attributes by aggregating the social profiles of the users who watched them. This is also the case for users and content attributes. Furthermore, we find that videos having similar content are prone to have similar social attributes, and users having social relationships are prone to have similar content attributes. These interesting discoveries imply the possibility of video recommendation in social and content attribute space. Thus we further propose a REgularized Dual fActor Regression (REDAR) method based on matrix factorization. In particular, with the aim of predicting user-video interactions, we factorize the observed user-video interactions into two factors, which respectively correspond to the matching degree of user-video pairs in both social attribute space and content attribute space. These two factors are flexibly combined to optimize the approximation of the user-video interactions. In order to alleviate the sparsity problem of user-video interactions, we use video content similarities to regularize the similarities between the social attributes of videos, and we also use social relationships to regularize the similarities between the users' content attributes. For new users and videos, we propose a cold-start strategy, where new videos (or users) are efficiently linked with other videos (or users) by content similarity (or social relationship). We evaluate our proposed method on real online social media data collected from a Twitter-style website. The experiments on the real data validate our hypotheses and demonstrate the superiority of REDAR for video recommendation.

It is worthwhile to highlight the key contributions of this paper:

(1) In contrast with the representation methods in traditional recommender systems, we attempt to represent (a) videos with social attributes and (b) users with content attributes by harvesting video propagation traces among users and users' interactive behavior with videos. The resulting common attribute-based representation is interpretable with an appropriate level of granularity, in which videos can be effectively and efficiently recommended to users by directly measuring the user-video similarities (see Sections 1 and 2).

(2) We validate the rationality for representing videos (or users) with social (or content) attributes using data statistics in a real social network dataset, and find the patterns of these representations among videos with similar visual contents and users with social relationships. These discoveries pave the way for recommending videos to users in the representation space with common attributes (see Section 3).

(3) We propose our REDAR method based on matrix factorization to predict user-video interaction behavior and present video recommendations accordingly. The model can attain a superior trade-off between social attribute-based representation and content attribute-based representation, and incorporate flexible regularizers from social and visual information to alleviate the sparsity problem. In addition, a cold-start strategy for REDAR is proposed, which can also be used to efficiently deal with online and incremental data (see Section 4).

(4) We extensively evaluate the proposed methods using a reasonable scale real dataset. The experimental results show that our proposed REDAR method can significantly and consistently outperform other state-of-the-art baseline methods. Several variants of REDAR are compared and analyzed to demonstrate the rationality of the design (see Section 5).

2. RELATED WORK

In this section, we will briefly survey the related work, introduce the corresponding taxonomies, and position the uniqueness of this paper.

(1) **Traditional Recommendation Methods**

Content-based filtering and CF have been widely used to help users discover the most valuable information to them. Content-based filtering introduces the basic idea of studying the item content for the ranking problem. With the emergence of topic modeling techniques such as LDA [3], recent content-based approaches [21] rank candidate items by how well they match the topic interest of the user as their preference. These methods represent detailed users and items, enabling them to recommend similar items to what the user has previously adopted. CF methods, consisting of memory-based and model-based methods, are widely used. The memory-based approaches [20] calculate the similarity between all users based on their ratings of items. They represent users (or items) by the item-sets (or user-sets), which are often unstable and can only obtain good performance for active users or popular items. The model-based methods learn a model based on patterns recognized in the ratings of users. Several matrix factorization methods [13] have recently been proposed. The matrix approximation models all focus on representing the user-item rating matrix with low-dimensional latent vectors. These learned latent representations are hardly interpretable and are therefore difficult to generalize to new data. Although these methods have achieved success in real applications, the representation methods they adopt limit space for improvement.

(2) **Social Recommendation**

Recognizing that influence is a subtle force that governs the dynamics of social networks, influence-based recommendation [14] involves interpersonal influence into social recommendation cases. Trust-based approaches[8] exploit the trust network among users and make recommendations based on the ratings of users who are directly or indirectly trusted. [9][11] proposed a probabilistic factor analysis framework, which fuses users' preference and social influence together. Furthermore, [10] investigated the social recommendation problem in a multiple domain setting. Most of these works are based on traditional content-based filtering or CF-based filtering methods, and their common goal is to embed social information into traditional methods to improve the recommendation accuracy. However, few authors have targeted the problem of how to learn a new common representation for users and items in social networks, which is indeed feasible and important for boosting social recommendation performance.

(3) **Video Recommendation**

Video recommendation plays an important role in delivering videos to users. The most well-known real video recommendation system is running on YouTube, where personalized sets of videos are recommended to users based on their activities on the site [5]. The recommendation system is one of the most important techniques to find videos [29], preceded by video searching. Compared with YouTube's recommendation system, which only considers user ratings and user-video interaction information, the following research on video recommendation attempted to incorporate more aspects of user and content information[23]. Park et al. [19] proposed to construct user profiles as an aggregation of tag clouds and generate recommendations according to similar viewing patterns. Bertini et al. [2] built a demo to show how to create user profiles containing the users' interests and apply them to a friend's suggestion and video recommendation. Ma et al. [16] assumed that social friends have higher common interests and their sharing behaviors are an important clue to enhance video recommendation. These methods pay more attention to user representation by discovering user profiles and behavior patterns [24]. Further, Zhu et al. [30] decomposed the recommendation process into video representation and recommendation generation, and represented videos with topics to match user interests. Fu et al. [7] tackled the problem of attribute learning for videos with sparse labels. These methods focus on video representation, yet the representations of videos and users are still isolated [18, 26]. Previous works focused on either user representation or video representation, and only a few works investigated integration strategies [25, 15] by first separately processing and then aggregating for recommendation. Our work is the first to uniformly learn a common representation for both users and videos in an interpretable way and with proper granularity.

(4) **Attribute based Methods**

Recently, attributes have aroused much interest in the research community because attribute-based representations are in a proper granularity to bridge low-level information and high-level seman-

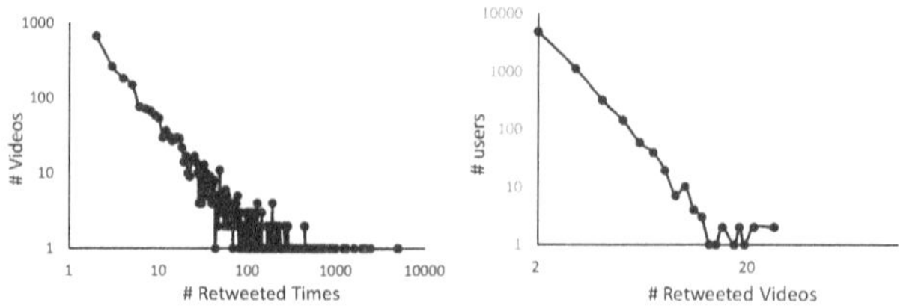

Figure 2: Distribution of users (or videos) with respect to the number of videos they retweeted (or the number of times they are retweeted).

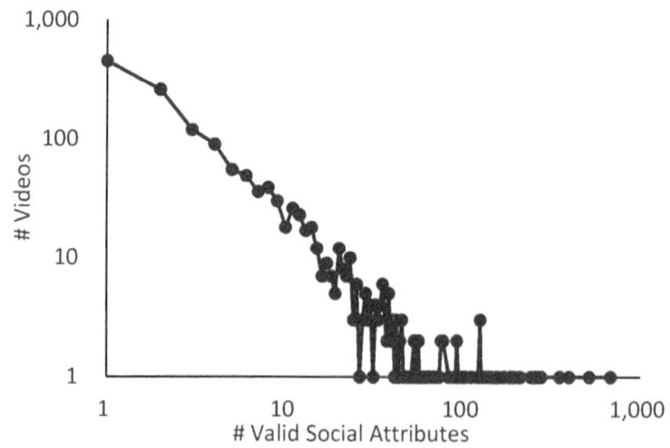

Figure 3: Distribution of videos with respect to the number of valid social attributes.

tics. Khalid et al. [6] represented documents by attributes of users who read these documents. Zhang et al. [28] used an attribute-augmented semantic hierarchy to bridge the semantic gap and intention gap. Ma et al. [17] extracted visual, audio, and linguistic attributes for video summarization, which outperforms traditional visual-only methods, while Cha et al. [4] conducted statistical analysis on video attributes to analyze user behavior on Youtube, giving an intuitive observation of the video sharing platform. Yu et al. [27] regarded user behaviors as their attributes to explore large-scale video-on-demand systems. These methods investigated attribute representations either for videos or for users. However, only a limited number of them explored the possibility of a common attribute-based representation for both users and videos, which is the focus of this paper.

3. PRELIMINARY STUDY

In this section, we will introduce the characteristics of the dataset and validate the rationality of representing videos (or users) by social attributes (or content attributes).

3.1 Data Description

The dataset is collected from Tencent Weibo, a Twitter-style social network platform in China with more than 300 million users. Video sharing is an important and popular feature of this platform. Users proactively forward the videos from external Youtube-style video sharing websites onto this microblog platform; the video then propagates over the social graph. We collected these kinds of videos with their text descriptions between June 20, 2012 and June 26, 2012. We then selected the videos that had been retweeted at least two times, collected the profiles (including demographic information and self-labeled tags such as "after 90s," "soccer fans," etc.) of the users that were involved in the propagation processes of these videos at least two times, and the social relations among the collected users. Therefore, we have 2357 videos, 6572 users, and 1271 social relations among the users. We show the distribution of videos with respect to the times they are retweeted, and the distribution of users with respect to the number of videos that they retweeted in Figure 2. It can be seen that both distributions obey the power law, which indicates that the user-video interactions are sparse. Thus, the dataset is adequate for simulating real application scenarios and evaluating the performances of the proposed method and other baselines.

3.2 Social Attributes of Videos

Here, we use a simple method to intuitively approximate the social attribute-based representations for videos, while a formal method will be proposed in Section 4 under the motivation of this preliminary study. We first extract social attributes for users. The demographic information is easily transformed into labels. For the self-labeled tags, we filter the tags with very low or very high frequency, while retaining the mid-frequency tags as labels. All these labels are used as the social attribute candidate set of users. For each video, we aggregate the social attributes of the users who retweeted the video. If the frequency of a social attribute exceeds 20% of the total number of users who retweeted the video, this attribute is regarded as a valid social attribute for the video. The distribution of videos with respect to the number of valid social attributes is shown in Figure 3. It can be seen that the agglomeration phenomenon of social attributes universally exists among videos, which validates the hypothesis of videos being watched by users with similar social attributes. However, the figure also shows that most videos only have a small number of valid social attributes, which pose a significant challenge to video recommendation based on such a sparse representation.

There is a well-accepted belief that a user is more likely to like videos that are similar to those videos they have watched previously. This is the fundamental hypothesis of content-based video recommendation methods. Motivated by this, we presume that videos with similar visual contents should have similar valid social attributes. To validate this, we calculate the visual content similarity of each pair of videos (the detail method for calculating the visual content similarity is referred to in Section 4.1) and the social attribute similarity of each pair of videos, and plot the relationship between the visual content similarity and the social attribute similarity, as shown in Figure 4. It can be seen that, on average, social attribute similarities of videos positively correlates with their visual content similarities. That is, videos that have similar visual contents are more likely to have similar social attributes.

3.3 Content Attributes of Users

We deal with the content attributes of users in a similar approach. We first extract content attributes for videos. Almost all videos have text descriptions to indicate the high-level semantics of the video contents. These text descriptions are segmented into words, and after filtering the words with very low or very high frequency, we retain the mid-frequency words as labels. All these labels are used as the content attribute candidate set of videos. For each user, we aggregate the content attributes of the videos that the user watched. If the frequency of a content attribute exceeds 20% of the total number of videos that the user watched, this attribute is regarded as a valid content attribute for the user. The distribution of videos with respect to the number of valid social attributes is shown in Figure 5. Similarly, the agglomeration phenomenon of content attributes

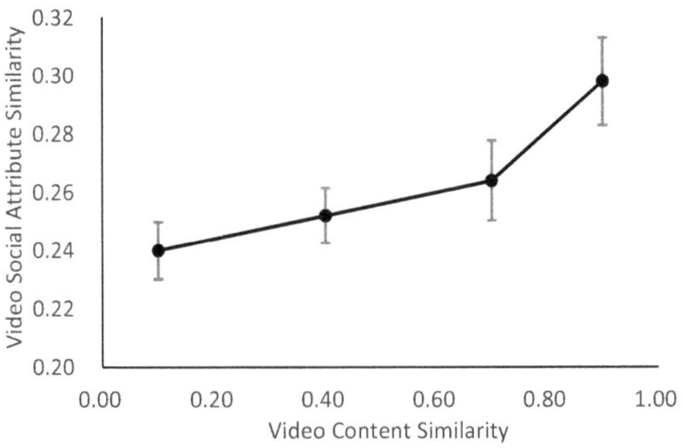

Figure 4: The correlation between videos' social attribute similarity and their content similarity.

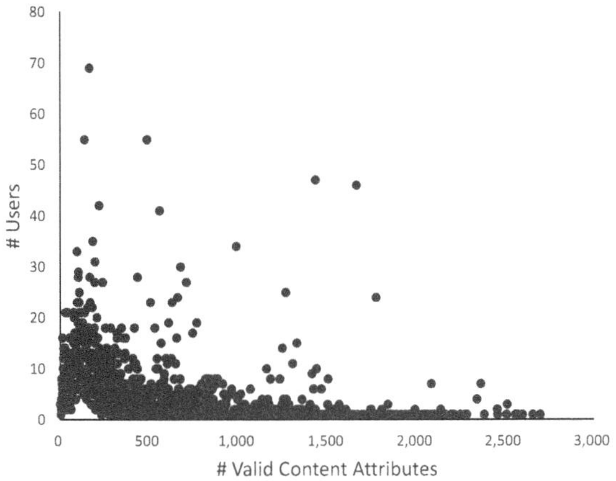

Figure 5: Distribution of users with respect to the number of valid content attributes.

universally exists among users, yet the valid content attributes for each user are very sparse.

The homophily hypothesis is a commonly accepted hypothesis in sociology to interpret the interpersonal relations within social networks. It presumes that users with similar demographic information or attributes are more prone to establish social relations. In our case, we use the hypothesis conversely and presume that users with social relations are more likely to have similar content attributes. To validate this, we measure the content attribute similarities of all pairs of users, and calculate the average and standard deviation of content attribute similarity for the pairs of users with and without social relations, respectively. We show the results in Figure 6, and it can be seen that, on average, the content attribute similarities of users who are socially linked are much higher than those of users without social relations.

We have now validated the important hypotheses in this work, including (1) the agglomeration phenomenon exists in social attributes among videos and content attributes among users; (2) videos with similar visual contents are more likely to have similar social attributes; and (3) users with social relations are more likely to have similar content attributes. The first one is fundamental for representing videos (or users) with social attributes (or content attributes), while the latter two provide important clues for alleviating the sparsity and cold-start problem in attribute-based representation video recommendation.

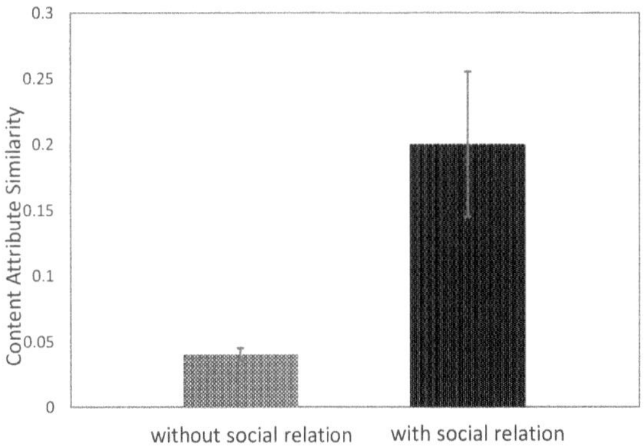

Figure 6: The correlation between users' content attribute similarity and their social relationship.

4. THE REDAR MODEL

4.1 Problem Formulation

Suppose that we have collected abundant information from a social media platform, with large sets of users $\mathcal{U}$ and videos $\mathcal{V}$ with $M = |\mathcal{U}|$ and $N = |\mathcal{V}|$. We denote the watching relationship matrix as $\mathbf{W} \in \{0,1\}^{M \times N}$, with its (u,v)-th entry

$$W_{uv} = \begin{cases} 1, & \text{if user } u \text{ watched video } v; \\ 0, & \text{otherwise.} \end{cases} \tag{1}$$

However, in real cases, most of the elements in $\mathbf{W}$ are zero because of the sparse interactions between users and videos. Thus, in order to focus more on the valid elements, we propose to only measure the approximation loss on observed elements on $\mathbf{W}$. To formulate this, we introduce the *masking matrix* $\mathbf{Y} \in \{0,1\}^{M \times N}$, with its (u,v)-th entry

$$Y_{uv} = \begin{cases} 1, & \text{if user } u\text{'s behavior on video } v \text{ is observed;} \\ 0, & \text{otherwise.} \end{cases} \tag{2}$$

where observed behaviors could be either positive or negative. Please refer to Section 5.1 for details on how to determine whether an entry is observed.

We denote the the friendship relationship matrix as $\mathbf{R} \in \{0,1\}^{M \times M}$, with its (u_1,u_2)-th entry

$$R_{u_1 u_2} = \begin{cases} 1, & \text{if user } u_1 \text{ is a friend of user } u_2; \\ 0, & \text{otherwise.} \end{cases} \tag{3}$$

We denote the content similarity matrix as $\mathbf{C} \in [0,1]^{N \times N}$, with its (v_1,v_2)-th entry

$$C_{v_1 v_2} = e^{-distance(v_1,v_2)} \tag{4}$$

where $distance(v_1, v_2)$ is measured by visual features. Given two videos, keyframes are extracted respectively, with SIFT descriptors pre-extracted on these keyframes, so that it won't consume a lot of online calculations. Keyframes from the two videos are matched to count the matched number of descriptors, and the total ratio of matched descriptors is used as the video distance [12].

Besides visual features, tags are also considered in social media to describe videos and users. Tags of a video come from accompanying text of the video. The video tag set is denoted as $\mathcal{T}^{\mathcal{V}}$ with $P = |\mathcal{T}^{\mathcal{V}}|$, and the relationships of videos and video tags are denoted by a matrix $\mathbf{V} \in [0,1]^{N \times P}$, with

$$V_{v,t} = TF_v(v,t) \cdot IDF_v(t) \tag{5}$$

where TF_v is calculated on video v's accompanying text, and IDF_v is calculated on all video accompanying texts. Tags of a user can be extracted from the user's profile and his/her self-labeling tags. The user tag set is denoted as $\mathcal{T}^{\mathcal{U}}$ with $Q = |\mathcal{T}^{\mathcal{U}}|$, and the relationship of users and user tags is denoted by a matrix $\mathbf{U} \in [0,1]^{M \times Q}$, with

$$U_{u,t} = TF_u(u,t) \cdot IDF_u(t) \quad (6)$$

where TF_u is calculated on user u's profile, and IDF_u is calculated on all user profiles.

With all these matrices as input, according to the observations in Section 3, we can define our targeting matrices. The first targeting matrix is $\mathbf{E} \in [0,1]^{M \times P}$, which links users with videos' attributes. The second targeting matrix is $\mathbf{F} \in [0,1]^{N \times Q}$, which links videos with users' social attributes. In order to learn the targeting matrices from the input information, we use the following principles to define our objective function:

- User-video matching with both social attributes and content attributes should be consistent with the real user-video interactions.
- User-user similarity with content attributes should be consistent with user friendship.
- Video-video similarity with social attributes should be consistent with videos' visual similarity.
- Both social attributes and content attributes should be sparse.

Therefore, the objective function is defined as

$$\begin{aligned}(\mathbf{E},\mathbf{F}) = \arg\min_{\mathbf{E},\mathbf{F}} (&||\mathbf{Y} \odot (\alpha \mathbf{E}\mathbf{V}^T + (1-\alpha)\mathbf{U}\mathbf{F}^T - \mathbf{W})||_F^2 \\ &+ \lambda_1 ||\mathbf{E}\mathbf{E}^T - \mathbf{R}||_F^2 + \lambda_2 ||\mathbf{F}\mathbf{F}^T - \mathbf{C}||_F^2 \\ &+ \lambda_3 ||\mathbf{E}||_1 + \lambda_4 ||\mathbf{F}||_1)\end{aligned} \quad (7)$$

where $\alpha \in [0,1]$ is a weighting factor between video tags and user tags, and λ_1, λ_2, λ_3, λ_4 are non-negative parameters less than 1, with λ_1 weighting for user relationships and λ_2 weighting for visual similarities. $\odot$ stands for an element by element multiply operation. Although there are five parameters to tune in this model, $alpha$, λ_1 and λ_2 are more important, and the result is not sensitive with λ_3 and λ_4. In this objective function, both social attribute based representation and content attribute based representation are flexibly integrated, and rich side information are embedded into regularizers to alleviate the sparsity problem. Thus we denote the proposed method as *REgularized Dual-fActor Regression* (REDAR).

4.2 The Model Solution

To solve the problem, we apply Iterative Shrinkage Thresholding Algorithm [1]. To simplify the description, we define

$$\begin{aligned}f(\mathbf{E},\mathbf{F}) =&||\mathbf{Y} \odot (\alpha \mathbf{E}\mathbf{V}^T + (1-\alpha)\mathbf{U}\mathbf{F}^T - \mathbf{W})||_F^2 \\ &+ \lambda_1 ||\mathbf{E}\mathbf{E}^T - \mathbf{R}||_F^2 + \lambda_2 ||\mathbf{F}\mathbf{F}^T - \mathbf{C}||_F^2\end{aligned} \quad (8)$$

$$g(\mathbf{E},\mathbf{F}) = \lambda_3 ||\mathbf{E}||_1 + \lambda_4 ||\mathbf{F}||_1 \quad (9)$$

So that the iterative formulas to solve the model are

$$\mathbf{E}^{(k)} = T_{\lambda_3 t_k^E}(\mathbf{E}^{(k-1)} - t_k^E \nabla_{\mathbf{E}} f(\mathbf{E}^{(k-1)}, \mathbf{F}^{(k-1)})) \quad (10)$$

$$\mathbf{F}^{(k)} = T_{\lambda_4 t_k^F}(\mathbf{F}^{(k-1)} - t_k^F \nabla_{\mathbf{F}} f(\mathbf{E}^{(k-1)}, \mathbf{F}^{(k-1)})) \quad (11)$$

where $\mathbf{E}^{(k)}$, $\mathbf{F}^{(k)}$ are the k-th round of results of our targeting matrices $\mathbf{E}$ and $\mathbf{F}$. t_k^F and t_k^E are step sizes. The function T_λ is defined as

$$T_\lambda(x) = (|x| - \lambda)_+ sgn(x) \quad (12)$$

In order to solve $\nabla_{\mathbf{E}} f$ and $\nabla_{\mathbf{F}} f$, we have

$$f(\mathbf{E},\mathbf{F}) = f_1(\mathbf{E},\mathbf{F}) + \lambda_1 f_2(\mathbf{E}) + \lambda_2 f_3(\mathbf{F}) \quad (13)$$

where

$$f_1(\mathbf{E},\mathbf{F}) = ||\mathbf{Y} \odot (\alpha \mathbf{E}\mathbf{V}^T + (1-\alpha)\mathbf{U}\mathbf{F}^T - \mathbf{W})||_F^2 \quad (14)$$

$$f_2(\mathbf{E}) = ||\mathbf{E}\mathbf{E}^T - \mathbf{R}||_F^2 \quad (15)$$

and

$$f_3(\mathbf{F}) = ||\mathbf{F}\mathbf{F}^T - \mathbf{C}||_F^2 \quad (16)$$

By solving their derivations, we get

$$\frac{\partial f_1}{\partial \mathbf{E}} = 2\alpha(\mathbf{Y} \odot (\alpha \mathbf{E}\mathbf{V}^T + (1-\alpha)\mathbf{U}\mathbf{F}^T - \mathbf{W}))\mathbf{V} \quad (17)$$

$$\frac{\partial f_1}{\partial \mathbf{F}} = 2(1-\alpha)(\mathbf{Y}^T \odot (\alpha \mathbf{E}\mathbf{V}^T + (1-\alpha)\mathbf{U}\mathbf{F}^T - \mathbf{W})^T)\mathbf{U} \quad (18)$$

$$\frac{\partial f_2}{\partial \mathbf{E}} = 4(\mathbf{E}\mathbf{E}^T - \mathbf{R})\mathbf{E} \quad (19)$$

$$\frac{\partial f_3}{\partial \mathbf{F}} = 4(\mathbf{F}\mathbf{F}^T - \mathbf{C})\mathbf{F} \quad (20)$$

Therefore, we get

$$\nabla_{\mathbf{E}} f(\mathbf{E},\mathbf{F}) = \frac{\partial f_1}{\partial \mathbf{E}} + \lambda_1 \frac{\partial f_2}{\partial \mathbf{E}} \quad (21)$$

$$\nabla_{\mathbf{F}} f(\mathbf{E},\mathbf{F}) = \frac{\partial f_1}{\partial \mathbf{F}} + \lambda_2 \frac{\partial f_3}{\partial \mathbf{F}} \quad (22)$$

More details about the flow of the algorithm is presented in Algorithm 1.

Algorithm 1 Iterative Solution of REDAR Model.

Input: $\mathbf{W}, \mathbf{R}, \mathbf{C}, \mathbf{U}, \mathbf{V}$
$t_k^E, t_k^F, \lambda_1, \lambda_2, \lambda_3, \lambda_4$
Output: $\mathbf{E}, \mathbf{F}$
1: Initialize: $\mathbf{E}^{(0)} = \mathbf{W}\mathbf{V}$, $\mathbf{F}^{(0)} = \mathbf{W}^T\mathbf{U}$
2: **for** $k = 1, 2, \ldots$ **do**
3: Calculate $\frac{\partial f_1^{(k-1)}}{\partial \mathbf{E}}, \frac{\partial f_1^{(k-1)}}{\partial \mathbf{F}}, \frac{\partial f_2^{(k-1)}}{\partial \mathbf{E}}, \frac{\partial f_3^{(k-1)}}{\partial \mathbf{F}}$
4: $\nabla_{\mathbf{E}} f(\mathbf{E}^{(k-1)}, \mathbf{F}^{(k-1)}) = \frac{\partial f_1^{(k-1)}}{\partial \mathbf{E}} + \lambda_1 \frac{\partial f_2^{(k-1)}}{\partial \mathbf{E}}$
5: $\nabla_{\mathbf{F}} f(\mathbf{E}^{(k-1)}, \mathbf{F}^{(k-1)}) = \frac{\partial f_1^{(k-1)}}{\partial \mathbf{F}} + \lambda_2 \frac{\partial f_3^{(k-1)}}{\partial \mathbf{F}}$
6: $\mathbf{E}^{(k)} = T_{\lambda_3 t_k^E}(\mathbf{E}^{(k-1)} - t_k^E \nabla_{\mathbf{E}} f(\mathbf{E}^{(k-1)}, \mathbf{F}^{(k-1)}))$
7: $\mathbf{F}^{(k)} = T_{\lambda_4 t_k^F}(\mathbf{F}^{(k-1)} - t_k^F \nabla_{\mathbf{F}} f(\mathbf{E}^{(k-1)}, \mathbf{F}^{(k-1)}))$
8: **end for**
9: **return** $\mathbf{E}^{(k)}, \mathbf{F}^{(k)}$

With the optimized results of $\mathbf{E}$ and $\mathbf{F}$, which are denoted as $\hat{\mathbf{E}}$ and $\hat{\mathbf{F}}$, respectively, we can estimate the user-video interactions by

$$\hat{\mathbf{W}} = \alpha \hat{\mathbf{E}}\mathbf{V}^T + (1-\alpha)\mathbf{U}\hat{\mathbf{F}}^T \quad (23)$$

Time complexity analysis. The time complexity of the algorithm depends on the matrix calculations and number of iterations. Since both matrix linear combinations and lasso take linear time, we only need to consider matrix calculation of the gradients. More specifically, the running time is

$$\begin{aligned}&T(k,M,N,P,Q) \quad (24)\\ =&O(k)(O(\frac{\partial f_1}{\partial \mathbf{E}}) + O(\frac{\partial f_1}{\partial \mathbf{F}}) + O(\frac{\partial f_2}{\partial \mathbf{E}}) + O(\frac{\partial f_3}{\partial \mathbf{F}}))\\ =&O(k(M(P+Q)N + MNP + MNQ + MPM + NQN))\\ =&O(k((M+N)(M+N)(P+Q) - MMQ - NNP))\\ \leq&O(k(M+N)(||\mathbf{E}||_0 + ||\mathbf{F}||_0 + ||\mathbf{U}||_0 + ||\mathbf{V}||_0))\end{aligned}$$

We use MP, NQ, MQ, and NP to denote the 0-norm of $\mathbf{E}$, $\mathbf{F}$, $\mathbf{U}$, and $\mathbf{V}$, respectively, which stands for the number of non-zero elements in the matrix. That is to say, our algorithm can compute $||\mathbf{E}||_0 + ||\mathbf{F}||_0$ and scan $||\mathbf{U}||_0 + ||\mathbf{V}||_0$ elements with each in time of $O(k(M+N))$ on average. Further, with the scope matrix $\mathbf{Y}$, the matrix calculation can avoid the calculation of most elements, which results in a small const factor of the time complexity.

4.3 Incremental REDAR Model

Our model can also handle the cold-start problem with an incremental algorithm. To deal with new users and new videos, we do not learn the entire $\mathbf{E}$ and $\mathbf{F}$, but only focus on the incremental part of the data. More specifically, suppose we have a set of new users $\Delta\mathcal{U}$ with $\Delta M = |\Delta\mathcal{U}|$ and a set of new videos $\Delta\mathcal{V}$ with $\Delta N = |\Delta\mathcal{V}|$. We do not know their watching histories, i.e., the relationships between the new users and the new videos. We represent the friendship of the new users and all users by a matrix $\Delta\mathbf{R} \in \{1,0\}^{(M+\Delta M)\times\Delta M}$, with the same entity meaning to $\mathbf{R}$. We represent the visual feature similarity of new videos and all videos as a matrix $\Delta\mathbf{C} \in [0,1]^{(N+\Delta N)\times\Delta N}$, with the same entity meaning to $\mathbf{C}$. We denote new video tag set by $\Delta\mathbf{V} \in [0,1]^{\Delta N\times P}$, with the same entity meaning to $\mathbf{V}$. We denote new user tag set by $\Delta\mathbf{U} \in [0,1]^{\Delta M\times Q}$, with the same entity meaning to $\mathbf{U}$. Also, we denote our targeting matrices by $\Delta\mathbf{E} \in [0,1]^{\Delta M\times P}$ and $\Delta\mathbf{F} \in [0,1]^{\Delta N\times Q}$, with the same entity meaning to $\mathbf{E}$ and $\mathbf{F}$, respectively.

Since the missing of new user-video watching relationship, we only need to focus on the friendship and visual feature similarity terms. Thus we get the following objective function

$$(\Delta\mathbf{E},\Delta\mathbf{F}) = \arg\min_{\Delta\mathbf{E},\Delta\mathbf{F}} \lambda_1 || \begin{bmatrix} \mathbf{E} \\ \Delta\mathbf{E} \end{bmatrix} \times \Delta\mathbf{E}^T - \Delta\mathbf{R}||_F^2 \quad (25)$$
$$+\lambda_2 || \begin{bmatrix} \mathbf{F} \\ \Delta\mathbf{F} \end{bmatrix} \times \Delta\mathbf{F}^T - \Delta\mathbf{C}||_F^2$$
$$+\lambda_3||\Delta\mathbf{E}||_1 + \lambda_4||\Delta\mathbf{F}||_1$$

which can be solved in a similar way with Equation 7 as follows. We define

$$\Delta f(\Delta\mathbf{E},\Delta\mathbf{F}) = \lambda_1 || \begin{bmatrix} \mathbf{E} \\ \Delta\mathbf{E} \end{bmatrix} \times \Delta\mathbf{E}^T - \Delta\mathbf{R}||_F^2 \quad (26)$$
$$+ \lambda_2 || \begin{bmatrix} \mathbf{F} \\ \Delta\mathbf{F} \end{bmatrix} \times \Delta\mathbf{F}^T - \Delta\mathbf{C}||_F^2$$

$$\Delta g(\Delta\mathbf{E},\Delta\mathbf{F}) = \lambda_3||\Delta\mathbf{E}||_1 + \lambda_4||\Delta\mathbf{F}||_1 \quad (27)$$

So that the iterative solution is:

$$\Delta\mathbf{E}^{(k)} = T_{\lambda_3 t_k^{\Delta E}}(\Delta\mathbf{E}^{(k-1)} - t_k^{\Delta E}\nabla_{\Delta\mathbf{E}} f(\Delta\mathbf{E}^{(k-1)},\Delta\mathbf{F}^{(k-1)})) \quad (28)$$

$$\Delta\mathbf{F}^{(k)} = T_{\lambda_4 t_k^{\Delta F}}(\Delta\mathbf{F}^{(k-1)} - t_k^{\Delta F}\nabla_{\Delta\mathbf{F}} f(\Delta\mathbf{E}^{(k-1)},\Delta\mathbf{F}^{(k-1)})) \quad (29)$$

To solve $\nabla_{\Delta\mathbf{E}} f$ and $\nabla_{\Delta\mathbf{F}} f$, we have

$$\Delta f(\Delta\mathbf{E},\Delta\mathbf{F}) = \lambda_1 \Delta f_1(\Delta\mathbf{E}) + \lambda_2 \Delta f_2(\Delta\mathbf{F}) \quad (30)$$

where

$$\Delta f_1(\Delta\mathbf{E}) = || \begin{bmatrix} \mathbf{E} \\ \Delta\mathbf{E} \end{bmatrix} \times \Delta\mathbf{E}^T - \Delta\mathbf{R}||_F^2 \quad (31)$$

$$\Delta f_2(\Delta\mathbf{F}) = || \begin{bmatrix} \mathbf{F} \\ \Delta\mathbf{F} \end{bmatrix} \times \Delta\mathbf{F}^T - \Delta\mathbf{C}||_F^2 \quad (32)$$

By solving their derivations, we get

$$\frac{\partial \Delta f_1}{\partial \Delta\mathbf{E}} = 2(\begin{bmatrix} \mathbf{E} \\ \Delta\mathbf{E} \end{bmatrix} \times \Delta\mathbf{E}^T - \Delta\mathbf{R})^T \begin{bmatrix} \mathbf{E} \\ 2\Delta\mathbf{E} \end{bmatrix} \quad (33)$$

$$\frac{\partial \Delta f_2}{\partial \Delta\mathbf{F}} = 2(\begin{bmatrix} \mathbf{F} \\ \Delta\mathbf{F} \end{bmatrix} \times \Delta\mathbf{F}^T - \Delta\mathbf{C})^T \begin{bmatrix} \mathbf{F} \\ 2\Delta\mathbf{F} \end{bmatrix} \quad (34)$$

Therefore, we get

$$\nabla_{\Delta\mathbf{E}} f = \lambda_1 \frac{\partial \Delta f_1}{\partial \Delta\mathbf{E}} \quad (35)$$

$$\nabla_{\Delta\mathbf{F}} f = \lambda_2 \frac{\partial \Delta f_2}{\partial \Delta\mathbf{F}} \quad (36)$$

With the optimized $\Delta\mathbf{E}$ and $\Delta\mathbf{F}$, which are denoted by $\Delta\hat{\mathbf{E}}$ and $\Delta\hat{\mathbf{F}}$, respectively, we can estimate the user-video watching relationship as $\Delta\hat{\mathbf{W}}^{\Delta\mathcal{U}} \in [0,1]^{\Delta M\times(N+\Delta N)}$ and $\Delta\hat{\mathbf{W}}^{\Delta\mathcal{V}} \in [0,1]^{(M+\Delta M)\times\Delta N}$ for new users and new videos, respectively, where

$$\Delta\hat{\mathbf{W}}^{\Delta\mathcal{U}} = \alpha\Delta\hat{\mathbf{E}} \begin{bmatrix} \mathbf{V} \\ \Delta\mathbf{V} \end{bmatrix}^T + (1-\alpha)\Delta\mathbf{U} \begin{bmatrix} \hat{\mathbf{F}} \\ \Delta\hat{\mathbf{F}} \end{bmatrix}^T \quad (37)$$

$$\Delta\hat{\mathbf{W}}^{\Delta\mathcal{V}} = \alpha \begin{bmatrix} \hat{\mathbf{E}} \\ \Delta\hat{\mathbf{E}} \end{bmatrix} \Delta\mathbf{V}^T + (1-\alpha) \begin{bmatrix} \mathbf{U} \\ \Delta\mathbf{U} \end{bmatrix} \Delta\hat{\mathbf{F}}^T \quad (38)$$

Note that $\Delta\hat{\mathbf{W}}^{\Delta\mathcal{U}}$ and $\Delta\hat{\mathbf{W}}^{\Delta\mathcal{V}}$ are consistent in their common elements.

Time complexity analysis. With the entire data, we have to process matrices with sizes MN, MQ, MP, NQ, and NP. With the incremental data, we only need to process matrices with sizes $\Delta M \times Q$, $\Delta M \times P$, $\Delta N \times Q$, and $\Delta N \times P$. When $\Delta M \ll M$ and $\Delta N \ll N$, the incremental algorithm is much faster than a re-calculation approach. More detailedly, the time complexity of the incremental algorithm can be solved in a similar way with Algorithm 1.

$$\begin{aligned} &T(k,M,N,\Delta M,\Delta N,P,Q) \quad (39) \\ =&O(k)(O(\frac{\partial \Delta f_1}{\partial \Delta\mathbf{E}}) + O(\frac{\partial \Delta f_2}{\partial \Delta\mathbf{F}})) = O(k(MP\Delta M + NQ\Delta N)) \\ =&O(k(M \times ||\Delta\mathbf{E}||_0 + N \times ||\Delta\mathbf{F}||_0)) \end{aligned}$$

which keeps the low average computation time for each output element.

5. EXPERIMENTS

In this section, we will present the empirical study results on the REDAR method for video recommendation.

5.1 Experimental Settings

Training and Testing. For all recommendation methods in a social network environment, there is an inevitable problem of unobservable negative samples. In $\mathbf{W}$, $\mathbf{W}_{ij} = 1$ is used to indicate that the user i was interested in video j. However, $\mathbf{W}_{ij} = 0$ does not necessarily indicate that user i was not interested in video j, but rather user i never received and saw video j. To guarantee that all the 0-entries are correct signals that reflect the users decision to reject retweeting the videos after seeing them, we estimate the online sessions of users according to their behaviors reflected by the 1-entries of $\mathbf{W}$ as in [9]. We suppose that the users should be able to see all the videos that they received during online sessions. For example, if a user retweets a video at time t, then we suppose that the user can see all the videos they received from their friends during $[t-\Delta t, t+\Delta t]$. In our case, Δt is set to five minutes. Thus,

$\mathbf{W}_{ij} = 0$ is valid only if video j is received by user i during their online session, which is controlled by $\mathbf{Y}$. We randomly select 80% of the observed entries in $\mathbf{W}$ as training data, and use the remaining entries as testing data. The random selection is conducted 10 times, and the average results are reported.

Groundtruth. According to the above training and testing strategy, the testing entries are in actual known. Therefore, we use the actual value of these entries as the ground truth to evaluate the testing performance.

Evaluation Criteria.In the following experiments, we use the RMSE (Root Mean Square Error) and MAE (Mean Average Error) to calculate the reconstruction loss of $\mathbf{W}$ on testing entries, which evaluates the prediction performance in the value aspect. We also evaluate the ranking performance using Kendall's and Spearman's ranking coefficients. Finally, we calculate the Precision@K to evaluate the prediction accuracy of the top recommended videos, which is important in real recommendation applications.

5.2 Baselines

In order to demonstrate the advantages and characteristics of the proposed method, we implemented the following four state-of-the-art methods and five variants of REDAR.

- *UserCF*. Implemented according to [22], where only user-video interaction information is used.
- *ItemCF*. Implemented according to [20], where only user-video interaction information is used.
- *SVD-based CF*. Implemented according to [13], where only user-video interaction information is used.
- *User-Label-Item*. Implemented according to [6]. A video is represented by aggregating the labels of the users who watched the video, and the video recommendation is conducted by matching video label representation and user labels.
- *REDAR-SocialAttribute*[2]. Implemented by setting $\alpha = 1$ in Equation 7.
- *REDAR-ContentAttribute*. Implemented by setting $\alpha = 0$ in Equation 7.
- *REDAR-SocialRegularizer*. Implemented by setting $\lambda_1 = 0$ in Equation 7.
- *REDAR-ContentRegularizer*. Implemented by setting $\lambda_2 = 0$ in Equation 7.
- *REDAR-LassoRegularizer*. Implemented by setting $\lambda_3 = \lambda_4 = 0$ in Equation 7.

5.3 Parameters Setting

We have five parameters in REDAR in total. α is the trade-off parameter for balancing social attribute-based representation and content attribute-based representation. $\lambda_1 - \lambda_4$ respectively control the weight of the social relation prior, the visual content prior, and the sparse prior on the social attributes of the videos and the content attributes of the users. For the parameter setting, we use grid search to obtain the optimal parameters. To demonstrate the importance of both social attributes and content attributes, we show how α affects the performance of REDAR in Figure 7. It can be seen that the RMSE of testing data significantly varies with different α values,

[2]In all variants of REDAR, "-" means "minus".

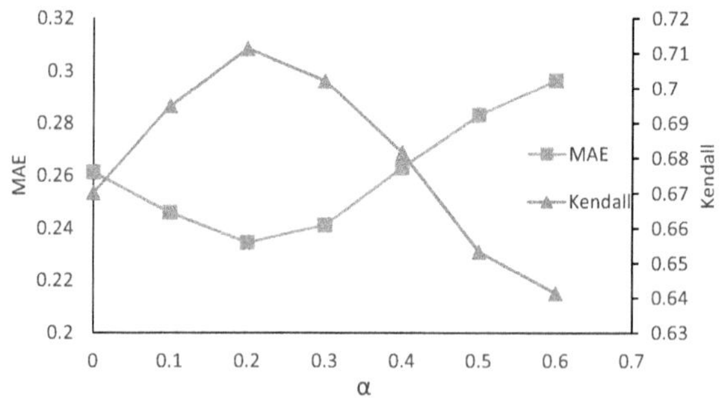

Figure 7: The parameter tuning of α to balance social attributes and content attributes.

which indicates the importance of subtly balancing social attributes and content attributes. The proposed method attains the best performance when $\alpha = 0.3$, which also indicates that, comparatively, the social attribute-based representation is more effective for video recommendation, while the role of content attributes cannot be ignored.

5.4 Video Recommendation Performances

Firstly, we evaluate the prediction accuracy of the proposed method with the measures including prediction errors (MAE and RMSE) and ranking coefficients (Kendall and Spearman). As shown in Table 1, the proposed REDAR method achieves the best performance across all measures. In addition, the relative improvement of REDAR from other baseline methods is significant. For example, in RMSE, REDAR achieves 25% relative improvement compared to the best baseline method *User-based Representation*. By comparing the results of baseline methods and REDAR, we arrive at the following observations.

	MAE	RMSE	Kendall	Spearman
UserCF	0.3664	0.5744	0.5430	0.5961
ItemCF	0.3958	0.6067	0.5082	0.5578
SVD-CF	0.3204	0.5412	0.5858	0.6360
User-Label-Item	0.3104	0.5366	0.6189	0.6910
REDAR	**0.2345**	**0.4299**	**0.7113**	**0.8539**

Table 1: Video recommendation performances.

(1) *UserCF*, *ItemCF* and *SVD-based CF* depend only on the collaborative matrix information, yet *SVD-based CF* performs much better than *UserCF* and *ItemCF*. The significant improvement should be attributed to the learned latent representation for users and videos, which is more optimal than item-based or user-based representation in approximating user-video interactions.

(2) The *User-Label-Item* method performs better than *SVD-based CF*. The main reason is that the common representation of items and users learned in the *User-Label-Item* method is interpretable and stationary. Another possible explanation is that User-Label-Item method incorporates richer information than *SVD-based CF*, such as the user profiles.

(3) Although the ultimate goal of both REDAR and *User-Label-Item* is to learn a common representation of videos and users with good interpretability, stability, and appropriate granularity, the results show that REDAR performs better than *User-Label-Item*. After translating *User-Label-Item* into our scenario, *User-Label-Item* only considers the social attributes of the videos, but ignores the importance of the users' content attributes. This makes the learned

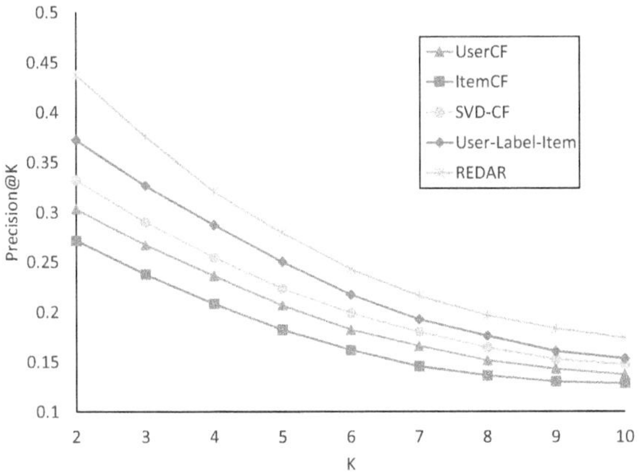

Figure 8: Performance evaluation in Precision@K.

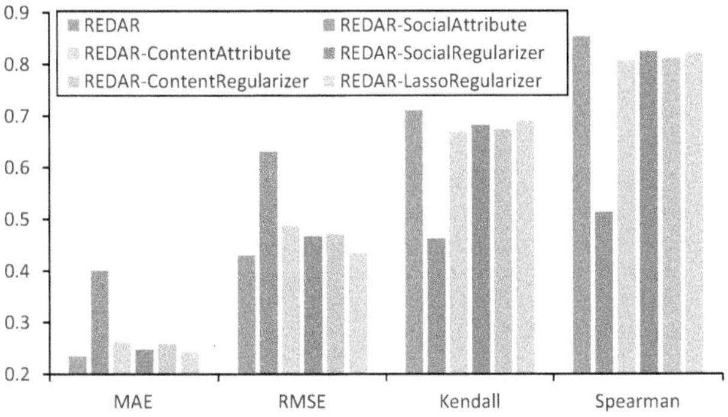

Figure 9: Performance evaluation on the variants of REDAR method.

representation difficult to capture the dynamic characteristics of users' preferences. Moreover, the REDAR method is more flexible at incorporating effective priors, such as the social relationship information.

We also evaluate the methods in Precision@K, and show the results in Figure 8. We observe that REDAR performs the best in all testing cases, and the improvement is more obvious when K is reduced. This is important in real recommendation applications, where users often only browse the top recommended videos.

5.5 Effects of Regularizers

In order to understand the characteristics and demonstrate the rationality of REDAR, we evaluate the performances of several variants of the REDAR model with a leave-one-out strategy. That is, we remove the factors and regularizers one by one and observe the change of model performances. The degree of performance degradation indicates the importance and effectiveness of the removed factor or regularizer. The results are shown in Figure 9. From the results, we can reach several observations.

(1) The largest degree of performance degradation occurs when changing REDAR into REDAR-SocialAttribute by removing the social attribute factor, which means that representing videos with social attributes is effective in video recommendation scenarios. In comparison to visual feature-based video representation and surrounding text-based video representation methods, social attribute-based video representation is at an appropriate granularity. In addition, it can avoid the semantic gap problem of low-level features and the problems brought by the absence of surrounding texts. More importantly, social attribute-based video representation can directly account for users' interaction behaviors on videos.

(2) Although content attribute-based representation produces the worst results, it complements the social attribute-based representation method, meaning they can achieve better results together than they can individually.

(3) All the regularizers imposed to the main regression term play important roles in addressing the sparsity problem. Comparatively, the social regularizer is more important than the content regularizer, which is reasonable because the social influence factor embedded in social relations is important for predicting user behaviors in a social network environment [9]. Nevertheless, the non-trivial improvement from REDAR-ContentRegularizer to REDAR justifies the contribution of visual content, which is also demonstrated in our preliminary study.

5.6 Cold-Start Recommendation Performances

In this subsection, we analyze the capability of REDAR to deal with new users and videos. We first randomly select 10% of the users in our dataset as new users, and then hide the historical video retweeting behaviors from $\mathbf{W}$ and use the data of the remaining users to learn $\mathbf{E}$ and $\mathbf{F}$. After that, we apply our incremental version ΔREDAR to learn representations for the new users, recommend videos to these new users accordingly, and evaluate the performances of these recommendations. To demonstrate the performance of ΔREDAR, we also evaluate the performance of REDAR on these new users. We deal with new videos in a similar way to new users.

	MAE	RMSE	Kendall	Spearman	Time
REDAR	0.2362	0.4338	0.7094	0.8522	4.16h
ΔREDAR-V	0.2761	0.4719	0.6892	0.7914	13.30m
ΔREDAR-U	0.2913	0.5025	0.6775	0.7745	16.86m

Table 2: Performances of video recommendation for cold-start users and videos. ΔREDAR-V stands for recommendation of new videos, and ΔREDAR-U stands for recommendation for new users.

The results are shown in Table 2. The ΔREDAR can deal with new users and new videos effectively. Although, undoubtedly, REDAR performs better than ΔREDAR, the degree of degradation of ΔREDAR from REDAR is acceptable. Further, by comparing Table 2 and Table 1, we can see that the performances of ΔREDAR, which does not use any user-video interaction, information of these new users and new videos is still better than other baselines that use this information. Moreover, the ΔREDAR can also be used for online processing of new data in an efficient way. In Table 2, the running time of the incremental processing method ΔREDAR is much less than that of the offline recommendation REDAR for the same number of new users and new videos. The running time is reduced from hours to minutes.

6. CONCLUSION

In this paper, we significantly improved the performance and interpretability of video recommendation systems by learning a common attribute-based representation for users and videos in social media with good interpretability, stability, and appropriate granularity. In order to address the critical challenges including the balance of social attributes and content attributes, the sparsity problem of user-video interactions, and the cold-start problem, we propose our REDAR method based on matrix factorization, in which social attributes and content attributes are flexibly combined, while social and content information is effectively exploited to alleviate the sparsity problem. An incremental version of REDAR is also designed to solve the cold-start problem. The experimental results show that, in most cases, the proposed method can achieve more than 20% relative improvement than state-of-the-art baseline methods.

7. ACKNOWLEDGEMENT

This work was supported by National Natural Science Foundation of China, No. 61370022, No. 61303075 and No. 61210008; International Science and Technology Cooperation Program of China, No. 2013DFG12870; National Program on Key Basic Research Project, No. 2011CB302206. Thanks for the support of NExT Research Center funded by MDA, Singapore, under the research grant, WBS:R-252-300-001-490.

8. REFERENCES

[1] A. Beck and M. Teboulle. A fast iterative shrinkage-thresholding algorithm for linear inverse problems. *SIAM Journal on Imaging Sciences*, 2(1):183–202, 2009.

[2] M. Bertini, A. Del Bimbo, A. Ferracani, F. Gelli, D. Maddaluno, and D. Pezzatini. A novel framework for collaborative video recommendation, interest discovery and friendship suggestion based on semantic profiling. In *Proceedings of the 21st ACM international conference on Multimedia*, pages 451–452. ACM, 2013.

[3] D. M. Blei, A. Y. Ng, and M. I. Jordan. Latent dirichlet allocation. *the Journal of machine Learning research*, 3:993–1022, 2003.

[4] M. Cha, H. Kwak, P. Rodriguez, Y.-Y. Ahn, and S. Moon. I tube, you tube, everybody tubes: analyzing the world's largest user generated content video system. In *Proceedings of the 7th ACM SIGCOMM conference on Internet measurement*, pages 1–14. ACM, 2007.

[5] J. Davidson, B. Liebald, J. Liu, P. Nandy, T. Van Vleet, U. Gargi, S. Gupta, Y. He, M. Lambert, B. Livingston, et al. The youtube video recommendation system. In *Proceedings of the fourth ACM conference on Recommender systems*, pages 293–296. ACM, 2010.

[6] K. El-Arini, M. Xu, E. B. Fox, and C. Guestrin. Representing documents through their readers. In *Proceedings of the 19th ACM SIGKDD international conference on Knowledge discovery and data mining*, pages 14–22. ACM, 2013.

[7] Y. Fu, T. M. Hospedales, T. Xiang, and S. Gong. Attribute learning for understanding unstructured social activity. In *Computer Vision–ECCV 2012*, pages 530–543. Springer, 2012.

[8] M. Jamali and M. Ester. Trustwalker: a random walk model for combining trust-based and item-based recommendation. In *Proceedings of the 15th ACM SIGKDD international conference on Knowledge discovery and data mining*, pages 397–406. ACM, 2009.

[9] M. Jiang, P. Cui, R. Liu, Q. Yang, F. Wang, W. Zhu, and S. Yang. Social contextual recommendation. In *Proceedings of the 21st ACM international conference on Information and knowledge management*, pages 45–54. ACM, 2012.

[10] M. Jiang, P. Cui, F. Wang, Q. Yang, W. Zhu, and S. Yang. Social recommendation across multiple relational domains. In *ACM CIKM*. ACM, 2012.

[11] M. Jiang, P. Cui, F. Wang, W. Zhu, and S. Yang. Scalable recommendation with social contextual information. *IEEE Transactions on Knowledge Discovery and Engineering*, 2014.

[12] S. Jiang, Y. Zhao, S. Wei, R. Ni, and Z. Zhu. Frame filtering and path verification for improving video copy detection. In *Proceedings of the Fifth International Conference on Internet Multimedia Computing and Service*, pages 34–37. ACM, 2013.

[13] Y. Koren, R. Bell, and C. Volinsky. Matrix factorization techniques for recommender systems. *Computer*, 42(8):30–37, 2009.

[14] J. Leskovec, A. Singh, and J. Kleinberg. Patterns of influence in a recommendation network. In *Advances in Knowledge Discovery and Data Mining*, pages 380–389. Springer, 2006.

[15] H. Luo, J. Fan, D. A. Keim, and S. Satoh. Personalized news video recommendation. In *Advances in Multimedia Modeling*, pages 459–471. Springer, 2009.

[16] X. Ma, H. Wang, H. Li, J. Liu, and H. Jiang. Exploring sharing patterns for video recommendation on youtube-like social media. *Multimedia Systems*, pages 1–17, 2013.

[17] Y.-F. Ma, L. Lu, H.-J. Zhang, and M. Li. A user attention model for video summarization. In *Proceedings of the tenth ACM international conference on Multimedia*, pages 533–542. ACM, 2002.

[18] T. Mei, B. Yang, X.-S. Hua, L. Yang, S.-Q. Yang, and S. Li. Videoreach: an online video recommendation system. In *Proceedings of the 30th annual international ACM SIGIR conference on Research and development in information retrieval*, pages 767–768. ACM, 2007.

[19] J. Park, S.-J. Lee, S.-J. Lee, K. Kim, B.-S. Chung, and Y.-K. Lee. Online video recommendation through tag-cloud aggregation. *IEEE Multimedia*, 18(1):78–87, 2011.

[20] B. Sarwar, G. Karypis, J. Konstan, and J. Riedl. Item-based collaborative filtering recommendation algorithms. In *Proceedings of the 10th international conference on World Wide Web*, pages 285–295. ACM, 2001.

[21] K. Stefanidis, E. Pitoura, and P. Vassiliadis. Managing contextual preferences. *Information Systems*, 36(8):1158–1180, 2011.

[22] J. Wang, A. P. De Vries, and M. J. Reinders. Unifying user-based and item-based collaborative filtering approaches by similarity fusion. In *Proceedings of the 29th annual international ACM SIGIR conference on Research and development in information retrieval*, pages 501–508. ACM, 2006.

[23] Z. Wang, L. Sun, W. Zhu, S. Yang, H. Li, and D. Wu. Joint social and content recommendation for user-generated videos in online social network. *IEEE Transactions on Multimedia*, 15(3):698–709, 2013.

[24] S. Xu, H. Jiang, and F. Lau. Personalized online document, image and video recommendation via commodity eye-tracking. In *Proceedings of the 2008 ACM conference on Recommender systems*, pages 83–90. ACM, 2008.

[25] B. Yang, T. Mei, X.-S. Hua, L. Yang, S.-Q. Yang, and M. Li. Online video recommendation based on multimodal fusion and relevance feedback. In *Proceedings of the 6th ACM international conference on Image and video retrieval*, pages 73–80. ACM, 2007.

[26] J. C. Yang, Y. T. Huang, C. C. Tsai, C. I. Chung, and Y. C. Wu. An automatic multimedia content summarization system for video recommendation. *Journal of Educational Technology & Society*, 12(1), 2009.

[27] H. Yu, D. Zheng, B. Y. Zhao, and W. Zheng. Understanding user behavior in large-scale video-on-demand systems. In *ACM SIGOPS Operating Systems Review*, volume 40, pages 333–344. ACM, 2006.

[28] H. Zhang, Z.-J. Zha, Y. Yang, S. Yan, Y. Gao, and T.-S. Chua. Attribute-augmented semantic hierarchy: towards bridging semantic gap and intention gap in image retrieval. In *Proceedings of the 21st ACM international conference on Multimedia*, pages 33–42. ACM, 2013.

[29] R. Zhou, S. Khemmarat, and L. Gao. The impact of youtube recommendation system on video views. In *Proceedings of the 10th ACM SIGCOMM conference on Internet measurement*, pages 404–410. ACM, 2010.

[30] Q. Zhu, M.-L. Shyu, and H. Wang. Videotopic: Content-based video recommendation using a topic model. In *Multimedia (ISM), 2013 IEEE International Symposium on*, pages 219–222. IEEE, 2013.

ADVISOR – Personalized Video Soundtrack Recommendation by Late Fusion with Heuristic Rankings

Rajiv Ratn Shah, Yi Yu, Roger Zimmermann
School of Computing, National University of Singapore
Singapore 117417
{rajiv,yuy,rogerz}@comp.nus.edu.sg

ABSTRACT

Capturing videos anytime and anywhere, and then instantly sharing them online, has become a very popular activity. However, many outdoor user-generated videos (UGVs) lack a certain appeal because their soundtracks consist mostly of ambient background noise. Aimed at making UGVs more attractive, we introduce *ADVISOR*, a personalized video soundtrack recommendation system. We propose a fast and effective heuristic ranking approach based on heterogeneous late fusion by jointly considering three aspects: venue categories, visual scene, and user listening history. Specifically, we combine confidence scores, produced by SVM^{hmm} models constructed from geographic, visual, and audio features, to obtain different types of video characteristics. Our contributions are threefold. First, we predict scene moods from a real-world video dataset that was collected from users' daily outdoor activities. Second, we perform heuristic rankings to fuse the predicted confidence scores of multiple models, and third we customize the video soundtrack recommendation functionality to make it compatible with mobile devices. A series of extensive experiments confirm that our approach performs well and recommends appealing soundtracks for UGVs to enhance the viewing experience.

Categories and Subject Descriptors

H.3.3 [**Information Storage and Retrieval**]: Information Search and Retrieval; I.4.8 [**Image Processing and Computer Vision**]: Scene Analysis—*Sensor fusion*

Keywords

Video soundtrack generation; geographic category; user preference; scene mood prediction; music retrieval

1. INTRODUCTION

In the era of ubiquitous availability of mobile devices with wireless connectivity, user-generated videos (UGV) have become popular since they can be easily acquired using most modern smartphones or tablets and are instantly available for sharing on social media web sites (*e.g.*, YouTube, Vimeo, Dailymotion). In addition, people enjoy listening to music online. Thus, various user-generated data of online activities (*e.g.*, sharing videos, listening to music) can be rich sources containing users' preferences. It is very interesting to extract activity-related data with a user-centric point of view. Exploiting such data may be very beneficial to individual users, especially for preference-aware multimedia recommendations [35]. We consider location (*e.g.*, GPS information) and online listening histories as user-centric preference-aware activities. We categorize user activity logs from different data sources, correlate them with user preferences by using semantic concepts, *i.e.*, moods, and leverage them to complement recommendations for personal multimedia events. To enhance the appeal of a UGV for viewing and sharing, we have designed ADVISOR, which replaces the ambient background noise of a UGV with a soundtrack that matches both the video scenes and a user's preferences. A generated music video (the UGV with the recommended soundtrack) enhances the video viewing experience because it not only provides the visual experience but simultaneously renders music that matches the captured scenes and locations. ADVISOR can be used in many applications such as to recommend music for a slideshow of sensor-rich Flickr images or for outdoor UGV live streaming, *etc.*

In terms of the target environment, this work mainly studies soundtrack recommendations for outdoor UGVs in places where different geo-categories such as beach, temple, *etc*, would be relevant. Thus, ADVISOR may not work well for indoor scenes (*e.g.*, parties). The reader may imagine the following scenario: a mom brings her son outdoors where she records a video of the little boy playing on a beach and swimming in the sea. Subsequently they would like to add music of their own style to this video to make it more appealing. Since video and audio have quite different low level features they are linked via a high level semantic concept – moods – in this work. As shown in Figure 1, the ADVISOR system consists of two parts: an offline training and an online processing component. Offline a training dataset with geo-tagged videos is used to train SVM^{hmm} models that map videos to mood tags. The online processing is further divided into two modules: a smartphone application and a server backend system. The smartphone application allows users to capture sensor-annotated videos[1]. Geographic contextual information (*i.e.*, geo-categories such as *Theme*

MM '14, November 3–7, 2014, Orlando, Florida, USA.

http://dx.doi.org/10.1145/2647868.2654919.

[1] We use the terms sensor-annotated videos and UGVs interchangeably in this study to refer to the same outdoor videos acquired by our custom Android application.

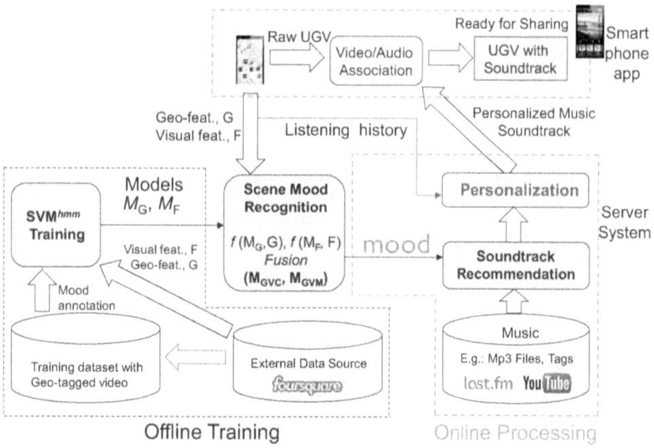

Figure 1: System overview of soundtrack recommendations for UGVs with ADVISOR.

Park, *Lake*, *Plaza* and others derived from Foursquare[2]) captured by geo-sensors (GPS and compass), can serve as an important dimension to represent valuable semantic information of multimedia data while video frame content is often used in scene understanding. Hence, scene moods are embodied in both the geographic context and the video content. The sensor data streams are mapped to a geo feature G, and a visual feature F is calculated from the video content. With the trained models, G and F are mapped to mood tags. Then, songs matching these mood tags are recommended. Among them, the songs matching a user's listening history are considered as user preference-aware.

In the ADVISOR system, first, we classify the 20 most frequent mood tags of Last.fm[3] into four mood clusters (see Table 1) and then use these mood tags and mood clusters to generate ground truths for the collected music and video datasets. Next, in order to effectively exploit multi-modal (geo, visual and audio) features, we propose late fusion methods to predict moods for a UGV. We construct two offline learning models (see M_{GVM} and M_{GVC} in Figure 1) which predict moods for the UGV based on the late fusion of geo and visual features. Furthermore, we also construct an offline learning model (Figure 2, M_{Eval}) based on the late fusion of visual and concatenated audio features (MFCC, mel-spectrum and pitch [33]) to learn from the experience of experts who create professional *soundtracks* in Hollywood movies. We leverage this experience in the automatic selection of a matching soundtrack for the UGV using M_{Eval} (see Figure 2). We deploy these models (M_{GVM}, M_{GVC} and M_{Eval}) in the backend system. To generate the music soundtrack for the UGV, the Android application first uploads its recorded sensor data and selected key-frames to the backend system. Next, the backend system computes geo and visual features for the UGV and forwards these features to M_{GVM} and M_{GVC} to predict scene *mood tags* and *mood clusters*, respectively, for the UGV. Moreover, we also construct a novel heuristic method to retrieve a list of songs from an offline music database based on the predicted scene moods of the UGV. The soundtrack recommendation component of the backend system re-ranks a list of songs retrieved by the heuristic method based on user preferences and recommends them for the UGV (see Figure 5). Next, the

[2]www.foursquare.com

[3]Last.fm is a popular music website.

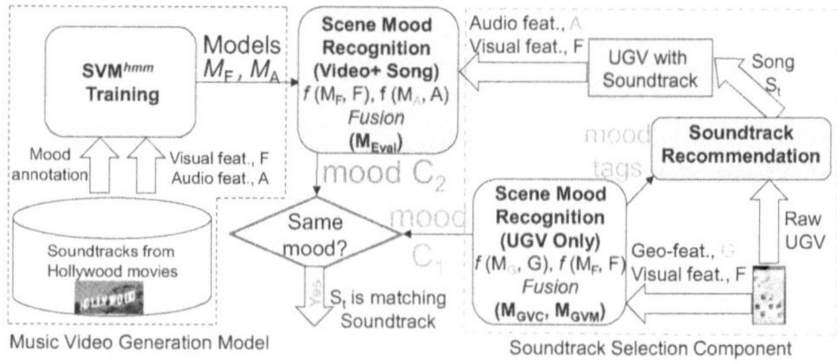

Figure 2: Soundtrack selection process for UGVs in ADVISOR.

Table 1: Four mood clusters.

Mood Cluster	Cluster Type	Mood Tags
$Cluster_1$	High Stress, High Energy	Angry, Quirky, Aggressive
$Cluster_2$	Low Stress, High Energy	Fun, Playful, Happy, Intense, Gay, Sweet
$Cluster_3$	Low Stress, Low Energy	Calm, Sentimental, Quiet, Dreamy, Sleepy, Soothing
$Cluster_4$	High Stress, Low Energy	Bittersweet, Depressing, Heavy, Melancholy, Sad

backend system determines the most appropriate song from the recommended list by comparing the characteristics of a composition of a selected song and the UGV with a *soundtrack* dataset of Hollywood movies of all movie genres using the learning model M_{Eval}. Finally, the Android application generates a music video using that song as a soundtrack for the UGV. The remaining parts of this paper are organized as follows. In Section 2, we review the related literature, and we describe the ADVISOR system in Section 3. The experiments and results are presented in Section 4. Finally, we conclude the paper with a summary in Section 5.

2. RELATED WORK

Our purpose is to support real-time user preference-aware video soundtrack recommendations via mobile devices. The steps of such a process can be described as follows. (1) A user captures a video on a smartphone. (2) An emotion cognition model predicts video scene moods based on a heterogeneous late fusion of geo and visual features. (3) A list of songs are automatically recommended for the video matching with the user's listening history. (4) The system sets the most appropriate song from the recommended list as the soundtrack for the video by leveraging the experience of professional mood-based associations between music and movie contents. In this section, we briefly provide some recent progress on emotion recognition and music recommendation systems and techniques.

Despite significant efforts that have focused on music recommendation techniques [9, 14, 18, 22] in recent years, little attention has been paid to music recommendation for sets of images or UGVs. Kuo *et al.* [14] investigated the association discovery between emotions and music features of film music and proposed an emotion-based music recommendation system. As of now, the music recommendation area for a set of images has been largely unexplored and consists of only a few state-of-the-art approaches such as an emotion-based impressionism slideshow system from images of paintings by Li *et al.* [16]. This method extracts features such as the dominant color, the color coherence vector, and the color moment for color and light. It also extracts some statistical measures from the gray level co-occurrence matrix for textures, and computes the primitive length of textures. Furthermore, Wei *et al.* [30] tried to establish an association between color and mood by exploiting the color-related features using an SVM classifier.

There exist a few approaches [6,27,29] to recognize emotions from videos but the field of video soundtrack recommendation for UGVs [24,34] is largely unexplored. Hanjalic *et al.* [6] proposed a computational framework for affective video content representation and modeling based on the dimensional approach to affect. They developed models for arousal and valance time curves using low-level features extracted from video content, which map the affective video content onto a 2D emotion space characterized by arousal and valence. Soleymani *et al.* [27] introduced a Bayesian classification framework for affective video tagging which takes contextual information into account since emotions that are elicited in response to a video scene contain valuable information for multimedia indexing and tagging. Based on this, they proposed an affective indexing and retrieval system which extracts features from different modalities of a movie, such as video, audio, *etc.* To understand the affective content of general Hollywood movies, Wang *et al.* [29] formulated a few effective audiovisual cues to help bridge the affective gap between emotions and low-level features. They introduced a method to extract affective information from multifaceted audio streams and classified every scene of Hollywood domain movies probabilistically into affective categories. They further processed the visual and audio signals separately for each scene to find the audio-visual cues and then concatenated them to form scene vectors which were sent to a SVM to obtain probabilistic membership vectors. Audio cues at the scene level were obtained using the SVM and the visual cues were computed for each scene by using the segmented shots and key-frames.

Cristani *et al.* [4] introduced a music recommendation policy for a video sequence taken by a camera mounted on board a car. They established the association between audio and video features from low-level cross-modal correlations. Yu *et al.* [34] presented a system to automatically generate soundtracks for UGVs based on their concurrently captured contextual sensor information. The proposed system correlates viewable scene information from sensors with geographic contextual tags from OpenStreetMap[4] to investigate the relationship between geo-categories and mood tags. Since the video soundtrack generation system by Yu *et al.* does not consider the visual content of the video or the contextual information other than geo-categories, soundtracks recommended by this system are very subjective. Furthermore, the system used a pre-defined mapping between geo-categories and mood tags, and hence the system is not adaptive in nature. In our recent work [24], we recommend soundtracks for a UGV based on modeling scene moods using a SVM^{hmm} model. In particular, first, the SVM^{hmm} model predicts scene moods based on the sequence of concatenated geo and visual features. Next, a list of matching songs corresponding to the predicted scene moods are retrieved.

Currently, sensor rich media content is receiving increasing attention because sensors provide additional external information such as location from GPS, viewing direction from a compass unit, and so on. Sensor-based media can be useful in applications such as life log recording, location-based queries and recommendations [1]. Kim *et al.* [11] discussed the use of textual information such as web documents, social tags and lyrics to derive an emotion of a music sample. Rahmani *et al.* [19] proposed context-aware movie recommendation techniques based on background information such as users' preferences, movie reviews, actors and directors of movie, *etc.* Chen *et al.* [2] proposed an approach by leveraging a tripartite graph (user, video, query) to recommend personalized videos. Kaminskas *et al.* [9] proposed a location-aware music recommendation system using tags, which recommends songs that suit a place of interest. Park *et al.* [18] proposed a location-based recommendation system based on location, time, the mood of a user and other contextual information in mobile environments. Recently, Schedl *et al.* [22] proposed a few hybrid music recommendation algorithms that integrate information of the music content, the music context, and the user context, to build a music retrieval system. For the ADVISOR system, these earlier works inspired us to mainly focus on sensor-annotated videos that contain additional information provided by sensors and other contextual information such as a user's listening history, music genre information, *etc.*

Multi-feature late fusion techniques have been advocated in various applications such as video event detection and object recognition [32]. Snoek *et al.* [25, 26] performed early and late fusion schemes for semantic video analysis and found that a late fusion scheme performs better. Ghias *et al.* [5] and Lu *et al.* [17] used heuristic approaches for querying desired songs from a music database by humming a tune. These earlier works inspired us to build the ADVISOR system by performing heterogeneous late fusion to recognize moods from videos and retrieve a ranked list of songs using a heuristic approach. To the best of our knowledge, this is the first work that correlates preference-aware activities from different behavioral signals of individual users, *e.g.*, online listening activities and physical activities.

3. SYSTEM DESCRIPTION

To generate a music video for a UGV, ADVISOR first predicts scene moods from the UGV using learning models described next in Section 3.1. The scene moods used in this study are the 20 most frequent mood tags of Last.fm, described in detail in Section 4.1.1. Next, the *soundtrack recommendation component* in the backend system recommends a list of songs, using a heuristic music retrieval method, described in Section 3.2. Finally, the *soundtrack selection component* selects the most appropriate song from the recommended list to generate the music video of the UGV, using a novel method, described in Section 3.3.

3.1 Scene Moods Prediction Models

In our custom Android recording app, a continuous stream of geo-sensor information is captured together with each video using GPS sensors. This sensor information is mapped to geo-categories such as *Concert Hall*, *Racetrack*, and others using the Foursquare API. Then the geo-categories are mapped to a geo-feature G using the bag-of-word model. With the trained SVM^{hmm} model (M_G), mood tags C_G with geo-aware likelihood are generated. Furthermore, a vi-

[4]www.openstreetmap.org

Table 2: SVM^{hmm} models used in this study.

Model	Input-1	Input-2	Output
M_F	F	-	T
M_G	G	-	T
M_A	A	-	C
M_{GVC}	M_G	M_F	$C = f_1(M_G, M_F)$
M_{GVM}	M_G	M_F	$T = f_2(M_G, M_F)$
M_{Eval}	M_A	M_F	$C = f_3(M_A, M_F)$
M_{Cat}	G	F	$T = f_4(G, F)$
G, F, and A represent the geo, visual and audio features, respectively. T and C denote the set of predicted mood tags and mood clusters, respectively. M_{GVC} and M_{GVM} are models constructed by the late fusion of M_G and M_F. M_{Eval} is constructed by the late fusion of M_A and M_F.			

sual feature such as a color histogram is calculated from the video content. With the trained SVM^{hmm} model (M_F), mood tags C_F associated with visual-aware likelihood are generated. In the next step, the mood tags associated with location information and video content are combined by late fusion. Finally, mood tags with high likelihoods are regarded as scene moods of this video.

3.1.1 Geo and Visual Features

Based on the geo-information, a UGV is split into multiple segments with timestamps, with each segment representing a video scene. The geo-information (GPS location) for each video segment is mapped to geo-categories using APIs provided by Foursquare. The Foursquare API also provides distances of geo-categories with respect to the queried GPS location, which describe the typical objects near the video scene in the video segments. We treat each geo-tag as a word and exploit the bag-of-words model [12] on a set of 317 different geo-tags in this study. Next, for each video segment, a geo-feature with 317 dimensions is computed from geo-tags with their score used as weights.

A color histogram [13,24] with 64 dimensions is computed from each UGV video frame by dividing each component of RGB into four bins. Next, the UGV is divided into multiple continuously correlated parts (CCP), within each of which color histograms have high correlations. Specifically, starting with an initial frame, each subsequent frame is regarded as part of the same CCP if its correlation with the initial frame is above a pre-selected threshold. Next, a frame with its timestamp, which is most correlated with all the other frames in the same CCP, is regarded as a key-frame. Color histograms of key-frames are treated as visual features.

3.1.2 Scene Moods Classification Model

Wang *et al.* [29] classified emotions for a video using an SVM-based probabilistic inference machine. To arrange scenes depicting *fear*, *happiness* or *sadness*, Kang [10] used visual characteristics and camera motion with hidden Markov models (HMMs) at both the shot and scene levels. In order to effectively exploit multi-modal features, late fusion techniques have been advocated in various applications and semantic video analysis [25,26,32]. These approaches inspired us to use SVM^{hmm} models [8] based on the late fusion of various features of UGVs to learn the relationships between UGVs and scene moods. Table 2 shows the summary of all the SVM^{hmm} learning models used in this study.

To establish the relation between UGVs and their associated scene moods, we train several offline learning models with the *GeoVid dataset* as described later in Section 4.1.2.

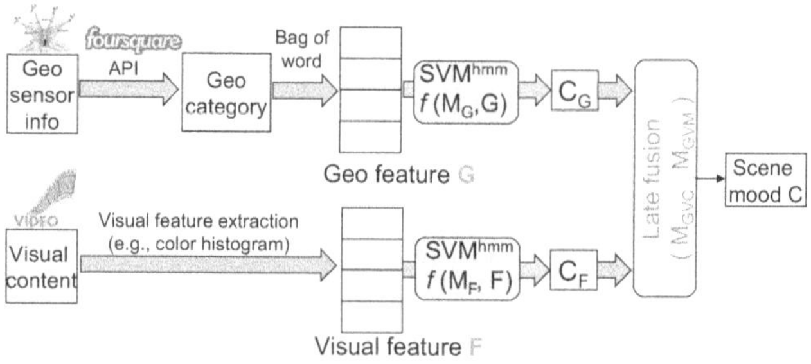

Figure 3: Mood recognition from UGVs using M_{GVC} and M_{GVM} SVM^{hmm} models.

Experimental results in Section 4.2.1 confirm that a model based on late fusion outperforms other models in scene mood prediction. Therefore, we construct two learning models based on the late fusion of geo and visual features and refer to them as *emotion prediction models* in this study. A geo feature computed from geo-categories reflects the environmental atmosphere associated with moods and a color histogram computed from key-frames represents moods in the video content. Next, the sequence of geo-features and the sequence of visual features are synchronized based on their respective timestamps to train *emotion prediction models* using SVM^{hmm} method. Figure 3 shows the process of mood recognition from UGVs based on heterogeneous late fusion of SVM^{hmm} models constructed from geo and visual features. M_{GVC} and M_{GVM} are *emotion prediction models* trained with mood clusters and mood tags, respectively, as ground truths for the training dataset. Hence, M_{GVC} and M_{GVM} predict mood clusters and mood tags, respectively, for a UGV based on heterogeneous late fusion of SVM^{hmm} models constructed from geographic and visual features.

3.1.3 Scene Moods Recognition

UGVs acquired by our Android application are enhanced with geo-information by using sensors such as GPS and compass. When a user requests soundtracks for a UGV then the Android application determines timestamps for multiple video segments of the UGV with each segment representing a video scene based on geo-information of the UGV. Furthermore, the Android application extracts key-frames of the UGV based on timestamps of video segments and uploads them to the backend system along with the geo-information of video segments. The backend system computes geo and visual features of the UGV from the uploaded sensor information and key-frames. The SVM^{hmm} models, M_{GVC}, M_{GVM} and M_{Cat} read the sequence of geo and visual features and recognize moods for the UGV. For example, M_{Cat} is trained with the concatenation of geo and visual features as described in the following sequence (see Figure 4).

$$\langle V, G_1, F_1, m_1\rangle,\ \langle V, G_1, F_1, m_2\rangle,\ \langle V, G_2, F_1, m_2\rangle,\ \ldots$$

In this specific example, in the emotion recognition step, when M_{Cat} is fed with geo features G and visual features F using $f_4(G, F)$, then it automatically predicts a set of scene mood tags $m = \{m_1, m_2, m_2, m_2, m_3\}$ for the UGV.

3.2 Music Retrieval Techniques

We prepared an offline music dataset of candidate songs in all main music genres, with details described later in Section 4.1.3. We refer to this dataset as the *soundtrack dataset*.

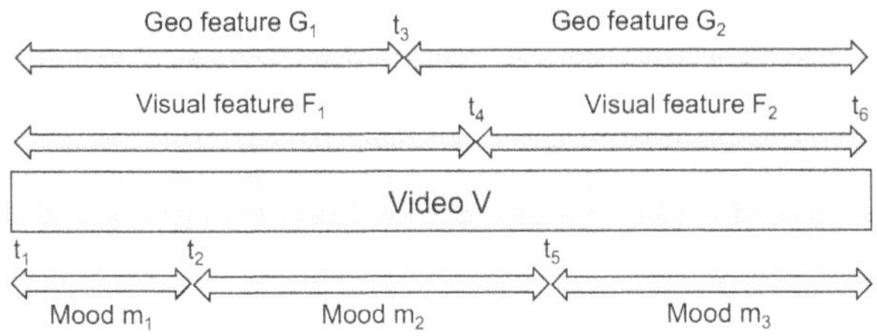

Figure 4: The concatenation model M_{Cat} from [24].

The next step in the ADVISOR system is to find music from the *soundtrack dataset* that matches with both the predicted mood tags and the user preferences. With the given mood tags, the soundtrack retrieval stage returns an initial song list L_1. For this task we propose a novel music retrieval method. Many state-of-the-art methods for music retrieval use heuristic approaches [5,17]. This inspired us to propose a heuristic method which retrieves a list of songs based on the predicted scene moods by M_{GVM} and M_{GVC}. We take the user's listening history as user preferences, and calculate the correlation between audio features of songs in the initial list L_1 and in the listening history. From the initial list, songs with high correlations are regarded as user specific songs L_2, and recommended to users as video soundtracks.

3.2.1 Heuristic Method for Soundtrack Retrieval

An improvement in mood tag prediction accuracy for a UGV is also an improvement in matching music retrieval because songs in the *soundtrack dataset* are organized in a hash table with mood tags as keys. However, retrieving songs based on only one mood tag suffers from subjectivity because the *mood clusters* prediction accuracy of M_{GVC} is much better than the *mood tags* prediction accuracy of M_{GVM} for an UGV (see Table 5). Since a song may have multiple mood tags, when the *emotion prediction models* predict multiple mood tags, a song may be matched with several tags. Therefore, we calculate the total score of each song to reduce this subjectivity issue and propose a heuristics based on a music retrieval method to rank all the predicted mood tags for the UGV and then normalize them as the likelihood to retrieve the final ranked list L_1 of N songs. Algorithm 1 describes this retrieval process and its *composition operation* $*$ is defined such that it outputs only those most frequent *mood tags* T from the list of mood tags predicted by $f_2(M_G, M_F)$ which belong to the most frequent *mood clusters* predicted by $f_1(M_G, M_F)$. Thus, the *composition operation* $*$ is defined by the following equation:

$$T = f_1(M_G, M_F) * f_2(M_G, M_F)$$

where T, G, F, f_1 and f_2 have the usual meaning, with details described in Table 2.

3.2.2 Post-filtering with User Preferences

A new paradigm shift in music information retrieval (MIR) is currently creating a move from a system-centric perspective towards user-centric approaches. Therefore, addressing user-specific demands in music recommendation is receiving increased attention. User preference-aware music recommendations based on users' preferences observed from their listening history is very common. Music genres of the user's frequently listened to songs are treated as his/her listening preference and later used for the re-ranking of a list of songs

Algorithm 1 Heuristic based song retrieval procedure

```
procedure HEURISTICSONGSRETRIEVAL(H)
    INPUT: geo and visual features (G, F) of the UGV
    OUTPUT: A ranked list of songs L1 for the UGV
    T = f1(M_G, M_F) * f2(M_G, M_F)
    L = []                                  ▷ Initialize with empty list.
    for each mood tag i in T do
        p(i) = likelihood(i)                ▷ Likelihood of mood tag i.
        Lt(i) = songList(i)                 ▷ Song list for mood tag i.
        L = L ∪ Lt(i)                       ▷ L has all unique songs.
    end for
            ▷ isPrsnt returns 1 if s is present in Lt(i) else 0.
            ▷ scr(s, i) is the score of song s with mood tag i.
    for each song s in L do
        Score(s) = 0                        ▷ Initialize song score.
        for each mood tag i in T do
            Score(s)+ = p(i) * scr(s, i) * isPrsnt(s, Lt(i))
        end for
    end for
    L1 = sortSongScore(L)                   ▷ Sort songs.
    Return L1                               ▷ A ranked list of N songs.
end procedure
```

L_1 recommended by the heuristics method. Our system extracts audio features including MFCC [21] and pitch from audio tracks of the user's frequently listened to songs. These features help in re-ranking the list of recommended songs L_1 by comparing the correlation coefficients of songs matching the genres preferred by the user, and then recommending a list of user preference-aware songs L_2 (see Figure 5). Next, the *soundtrack selection component* automatically chooses the most appropriately matching song from L_2 and attaches it as the soundtrack to the UGV.

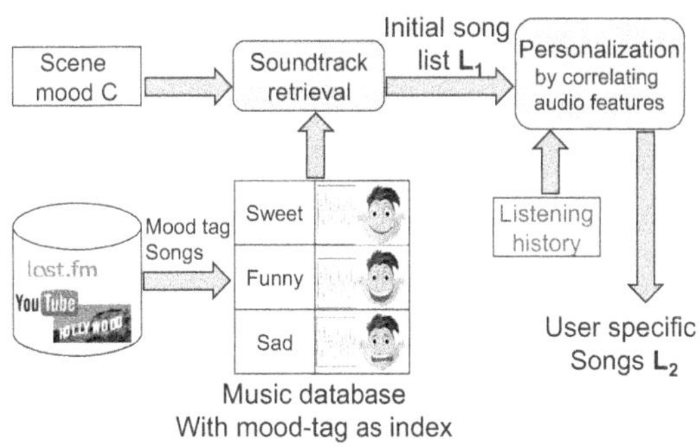

Figure 5: Matching songs with a user's preferences.

3.3 Automatic Music Video Generation Model

Wang *et al.* [29] concatenated audio and visual cues to form scene vectors which were sent to a SVM method to obtain high-level audio cues at the scene level. We propose a novel method to automatically select the most appropriate soundtrack from the list of songs L_2 recommended by our music retrieval system as described in the previous Section 3.2, to generate a *music video* from the UGV.

We use soundtracks of Hollywood movies in our system to select appropriate UGV soundtracks since music in Hollywood movies is designed to be emotional and hence is easier to associate with mood tags. Moreover, music used by Hollywood movies is generated by professionals, which ensures a good harmony with the movie contents. Therefore, we learn from the experience of such experts using their professional *soundtracks* of Hollywood movies through a SVM^{hmm} learning model. We refer to the collection of such soundtracks as the *evaluation dataset*, with details described later in Section 4.1.4. We construct a *music video generation model* (M_{Eval}) using the training dataset of the *evaluation dataset*, which can predict mood clusters for any music video. We leverage this model to select the most appropriate soundtrack for the UGV. We construct M_{Eval} based on heterogeneous late fusion of SVM^{hmm} models constructed from visual features such as a color histogram and audio features such as MFCC, mel-spectrum and pitch. Similar to our findings with the learning model to predict *scene moods* based on the late fusion of geo and visual features of UGVs, we find that the learning model M_{Eval} based on the late fusion of visual features and concatenated ⟨MFCC, mel-spectrum and pitch⟩ audio features also performs well.

Figure 2 shows the process of soundtrack selection for a UGV. It consists of two components, first, music video generation model (M_{Eval}), and second, a soundtrack selection component. M_{Eval} maps visual features F and audio features A of the UGV with a soundtrack to mood clusters C_2, *i.e.*, $f_3(F, A)$ corresponds to mood clusters C_2 based on the late fusion of F and A. The soundtrack selection component compares moods (C_2 and C_1) of the UGV predicted by M_{Eval} and, M_{GVC} and M_{GVM}.

Algorithm 2 describes the process of the most appropriate soundtrack selection from the list of songs recommended by the heuristic method to generate the music video of the UGV. To automatically select the most appropriate soundtrack, we compute audio features of a selected song and visual features of the UGV and refer to this combination as the *prospective music video*. We compare the characteristics of the *prospective music video* with video songs of the *evaluation dataset* of many famous Hollywood movies. Next we predict mood clusters (C) for the *prospective music video* using M_{Eval}. We treat the predicted mood clusters (C_1) of the UGV by M_{GVC} as ground truth for the UGV, since the mood clusters prediction accuracy of M_{GVC} is very good (see Section 4.2.1). Finally, if the most frequent mood cluster C_2 from C for the *prospective music video* is similar to the ground truth (C_1) of the UGV, then the selected song (S_t) is treated as the soundtrack and the music video of the UGV is generated. If both mood clusters are different then we repeat the same process with the next song in the recommended list L_2. In the worst case, if none of the songs in the recommended list L_2 satisfies the above criteria then we repeat the same process with the second most frequent mood cluster from C, and so on.

Algorithm 2 Music video generation for a UGV

```
procedure MusicVideoGeneration(MV)
    INPUT: A UGV V by the Android application
    OUTPUT: A music video MV for V
    m = moodTags(V)                  ▷ M_GVM predicts mood tags.
    C_1 = moodClusters(V)            ▷ M_GVC predicts clusters.
    L_2 = HeuristicSongsRetrieval(m, C_1)
    F = visualFeatures(V)            ▷ Compute visual features.
    for rank = 1 to numMoodCluster do
        for each song S_t in L_2 do
            a_1 = calcMFCC(S_t)                  ▷ MFCC feat.
            a_2 = calcMelSpec(S_t)               ▷ Mel-spec feat.
            a_3 = calcPitch(S_t)                 ▷ Pitch feat.
                                ▷ Concatenate all audio features.
            A = concatenate(a_1, a_2, a_3)
            C = findMoodCluster(F, A)            ▷ using M_Eval.
            C_2 = mostFreqMoodCluster(rank, C)
                                ▷ Check for similar mood clusters
                                ▷ predicted by M_GVC and M_Eval.
            if C_2 == C_1 then
                                ▷ Android app generates music video.
                MV = generateMusicVideo(S_t, V)
                Return MV                        ▷ Music video for V.
            end if
        end for
    end for
end procedure
```

4. EXPERIMENTS AND RESULTS

4.1 Dataset and Experimental Settings

The input dataset in our study consists of sensor-annotated videos acquired from a custom Android (or iOS) application running on smartphones. As described in Section 3, we train several learning models to generate a music video from a UGV. To train effective models for the ADVISOR system, it is important to have good ground truths for the training and the testing dataset. However, due to the difference in age, occupation, gender, environment, cultural background and personality, music perception is highly subjective among users. Hence generating ground truths for the evaluation of various music mood classification algorithms are very challenging [11]. Furthermore, there is no standard music dataset with associated mood tags (ground truths) available due to the lack of an authoritative taxonomy of music moods and an associated audio dataset. Therefore, we prepare our own datasets in Sections 4.1.1, 4.1.2, 4.1.3 and 4.1.4 to address the above issues.

4.1.1 Emotion Tag Space

Mood tags are important keywords in digital audio libraries and online music repositories for effective music retrieval. Furthermore, oftentimes, music experts refer to music as the finest *language of emotion*. Therefore it is very important to learn the relationship between music and emotions (mood tags) to build a robust ADVISOR. A number of prior methods [11,15] have described state-of-the-art classifications of mood tags into different emotion classes. The first type of approach is the *categorical approach* which classifies mood tags into emotion clusters such as *happy*, *sad*, *fear*, *anger* and *tender*. Hevner [7] categorized 67 mood tags into eight mood clusters with similar emotions based on musical characteristics such as *pitch*, *mode*, *rhythm*, *tempo*, *melody* and *harmony*. Thayer [28] proposed an energy-stress model, where the mood space is divided into four clusters such as *low energy / low stress*, *high energy / low stress*, *high energy / high stress*, and *low energy / high stress* (see Figure 6). The second type of method is based on the *dimensional approach* to affect, which represents music samples along a two-dimensional emotion space (characterized by arousal and valence) as a set of points.

We consider the *categorical approach* of music mood classification to classify the mood tags used in this work. We extracted the 20 most frequent mood tags of Last.fm from the crawled dataset of 575,149 tracks with 6,814,068 tag annotations in all main music genres by Laurier *et al.* [15]. Last.fm is a music website with more than 30 million users, who have created a site-wide folksonomy of music through end-user tagging. We classified these 20 mood tags into four mood clusters based on mood tag clustering introduced in earlier work [7,20,24]. Four mood clusters represent four

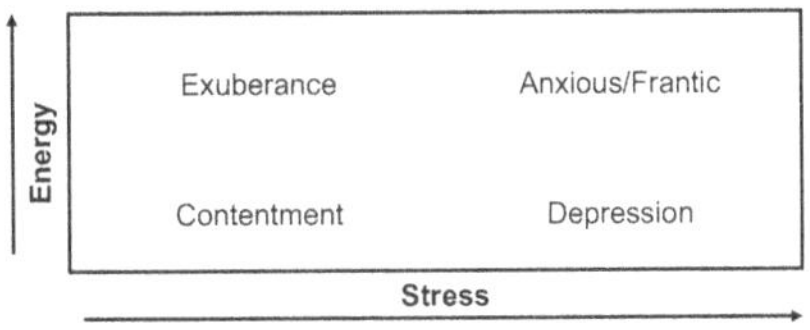

Figure 6: Thayer's [28] model of moods.

quadrants of a 2-dimensional emotion plane with energy and stress characterized as its two dimensions (see Table 1).

However, emotion recognition is a very challenging task due to its cross-disciplinary nature and high subjectivity. Therefore experts have suggested the need for the use of multi-label emotion classification. Since the recommendation of music based on low-level mood tags can be very subjective, many earlier approaches [11, 31] on emotion classification and music recommendation are based on high-level mood clusters. Therefore, in order to calculate the annotator consistency, accuracy and inter-annotator agreement, we compare annotations at four high-level *mood clusters* instead of the 20 low-level *mood tags* in this study. Moreover, we leverage the mood tags and mood clusters together to improve the scene mood prediction accuracy of ADVISOR.

4.1.2 GeoVid Dataset

To create an offline training model for the proposed framework of scene mood prediction of a UGV we utilized 1,213 UGVs which were captured during eight months (4 March 2013 to 8 November 2013) using the GeoVid[5] application. These videos were captured with iPhone 4S and iPad 3 devices. The video resolution of all videos was 720×480 pixels, and their frame rate 24 frames per second. The minimum sampling rate for the location and orientation information was 5 samples per second (*i.e.*, a 200 millisecond sampling rate). In our case, we mainly focus on videos that contain additional information provided by sensors and we refer to these videos as *sensor-annotated videos*. The captured videos cover a diverse range of rich scenes across Singapore and we refer to this video collection as the *GeoVid dataset*.

Since emotion classification is highly subjective and can vary from person to person [11], generating ground truths for the evaluation of the various emotion classifications from video techniques are difficult. It is necessary to use some filtering mechanism to discard bad annotations. In the E6K music dataset for MIREX[6], IMIRSEL assigns each music sample to three different evaluators for mood annotations. They then evaluate the quality of ground truths by the degree of agreement on the music samples. Only those annotations are considered as ground truths where the majority of evaluators selected the same mood cluster. The ground truth of music samples for which all annotators select different mood clusters are resolved by music experts.

For the *GeoVid dataset* we recruited 30 volunteers to annotate emotions (the mood tags listed in Table 1). First, we identified annotators who are consistent with their annotations by introducing redundancy. We repeated one of the videos in the initial sets of the annotation task with

[5]The GeoVid app and portal at http://www.geovid.org provide recorded videos annotated with location meta-data.

[6]The MIR Evaluation eXchange is an annual evaluation campaign for various MIR algorithms hosted by IMIRSEL (International MIR System Evaluation Lab) at the University of Illinois at Urbana-Champaign.

Table 3: Ground truth annotation statistics with three annotators per video segment.

All Different	Two The Same	All The Same
298	1293	710

ten videos given to each of the evaluators. If any annotated mood tag belonged to a different mood cluster for a repeated video then this annotator's tags were discarded. Annotators passing this criteria were selected for mood annotation of the *GeoVid dataset*. Furthermore, all videos of the *GeoVid dataset* were split into multiple segments with each segment representing a video scene, based on its geo-information and timestamps. For each video segment, we asked three randomly chosen evaluators to annotate one mood tag each after watching the UGV carefully. In order to reduce subjectivity and check the inter-annotator agreement of the three human evaluators for any video, we inspected whether the majority (at least two) of the evaluators chose mood tags that belonged to the same mood cluster. If the majority of evaluators annotated mood tags from the same mood cluster then that particular cluster and its associated mood tags were considered as ground truth for the UGV. Otherwise the decision was resolved by music experts. Due to the subjectivity of music moods, we found that all three evaluators annotated different mood clusters for 298 segments during annotation for the *GeoVid dataset*, hence their ground truths were resolved by music experts (see Table 3).

4.1.3 Soundtrack Dataset

We prepared an offline music dataset of candidate songs (729 songs altogether) in all main music genres such as *classical*, *electronic*, *jazz*, *metal*, *pop*, *punk*, *rock* and *world* from the ISMIR'04 genre classification dataset[7]. We refer to this dataset as the *soundtrack dataset* and we divided it into 15 *emotion annotation tasks* (EAT). We recruited 30 annotators and assigned each EAT (with 48–50 songs) to two randomly chosen annotators and asked them to annotate one mood tag for each song. Each EAT had two randomly selected repetitive songs to check the annotation consistency of each human evaluator, *i.e.*, if the evaluator-chosen mood tags belonged to the same mood cluster for redundant songs then the evaluator was consistent, otherwise the evaluator's annotations were discarded. Since the same set of EATs was assigned to two different annotators, their inter-annotator agreement is calculated by *Cohen's kappa coefficient* (κ) [3]. This coefficient is considered to be a robust statistical measure of inter-annotator agreement and defined as follows:

$$\kappa = \frac{Pr(a) - Pr(e)}{1 - Pr(e)}$$

where $Pr(a)$ is the relative observed agreement among evaluators, and $Pr(e)$ is the hypothetical probability of chance agreement, using the observed data to calculate the probabilities of each annotator randomly indicating each category. If $\kappa = 1$ then both annotators for an EAT are in complete agreement while there is no agreement when $\kappa = 0$. According to Schuller *et al.* [23], an agreement level with a κ value of 0.40 and 0.44, respectively, for the music mood assessment with regard to valence and arousal, are considered to be *moderate to good*. Table 4 shows the summary of the mood annotation tasks for the *soundtrack dataset* with a

[7]ismir2004.ismir.net/genre contest/index.htm

Table 4: Summary of the emotion annotation tasks.

Total number of songs	729
Pairs of annotators	15
Common songs per pair	48–50
κ : Maximum	0.67
κ : Minimum	0.29
κ : Mean	0.47
κ : Standard deviation	0.12

mean κ value of 0.47, which is considered to be *moderate to good* in music judgment. For four EATs, annotations were carried out again since evaluators for these EATs failed to fulfill the *annotation consistency* criteria.

For a fair comparison of music excerpts, samples were converted to a uniform format (22,050 Hz, 16 bits, and a mono channel PCM WAV) and normalized to the same volume level. Yang *et al.* [31] suggested to use 25-second music excerpts from around the segment middle to reduce the burden on evaluators. Therefore, we manually selected 25-second music excerpts from near the middle such that the mood was likely to be constant within the excerpt by avoiding drastic changes in musical characteristics. Furthermore, songs were organized in a hash structure with their mood tags as hash keys, so that ADVISOR was able to retrieve the relevant songs from the hash table with the predicted mood tags as keys. We then considered a sequence of the most frequent mood tags T predicted by the *emotion prediction model*, with details described in Section 3.1, for song retrievals.

The *soundtrack dataset* was stored in a database, indexed and used for soundtrack recommendation for UGVs. A song with ID s and k tags is described by a list of tag attributes and scores from $\langle s, tag_1, scr_1\rangle$ to $\langle s, tag_k, scr_k\rangle$, where tag_1 to tag_k are mood tags and scr_1 to scr_k are their corresponding scores. Tag attributes describe the relationship between mood tags and songs, and are organized in a hash table where each bucket is associated with a mood tag. With the aforementioned song s as an example, its k tag attributes are separately stored in k buckets. Since a tag is common to all songs in the same bucket, it is sufficient to only store tuples consisting of song ID and tag score.

4.1.4 Evaluation Dataset

We collected 402 soundtracks from Hollywood movies of all main movie genres such as *action, comedy, romance, war, horror* and others. We refer to this video collection as the *evaluation dataset.* We manually selected 1-minute video segments from around the middle for each clip in the *evaluation dataset* such that the emotion was likely to be constant within that segment by avoiding drastic changes in scene and musical characteristics. We ignored segments having dialogues in a scene while selecting 1-minute excerpts. Since the segments in the *evaluation dataset* are professionally produced and their genres, lyrics and context are known, emotions elicited by these segments are easy to determine. Mood clusters (listed in Table 1) were manually annotated for each segment based on its movie genre, lyrics and context and treated as ground truth for the *evaluation dataset.*

4.2 Experimental Results

4.2.1 Scene Moods Prediction Accuracy

To investigate the relationship between *geo* and *visual features* to predict video scene moods for a UGV, we trained four SVM^{hmm} models and compared their accuracy. First, the *Geo model* (M_G) was trained with geo features only, second, the *Visual model* (M_F) was trained with visual features only and third, the *Concatenation model* (M_{Cat}) was trained with the concatenation of both geo and visual features (see Figure 4). Finally, fourth, the *Late fusion models* (M_{GVM}, M_{GVC}) were trained by the late fusion of the first (M_G) and second (M_F) models.

Table 5: Accuracy of emotion prediction models.

SVM^{hmm} Learning Model Accuracy (Performed 10-fold cross validation.)					
Ratio	Model Type	Exp-1 (in %)	Exp-2 (in %)	Exp-3 (in %)	Feature Dimens.
70:30	M_F	18.87	52.62	64.63	64
	M_G	25.56	60.12	74.22	317
	M_{Cat}	24.47	60.79	73.52	381
	M_{GVM}	**37.18**	**76.42**	-	317
	M_{GVC}	-	-	**84.56**	317
80:20	M_F	17.76	51.65	63.93	64
	M_G	24.68	60.83	73.06	317
	M_{Cat}	25.97	61.96	71.97	381
	M_{GVM}	**34.86**	**75.95**	-	317
	M_{GVC}	-	-	**84.08**	317

Exp-1: Model trained at mood *tags* level and predicted moods accuracy checked at mood *tags* level.
Exp-2: Model trained at mood *tags* level and predicted moods accuracy checked at mood *cluster* level.
Exp-3: Model trained at mood *cluster* level and predicted moods accuracy checked at mood *cluster* level.

We randomly divided the *GeoVid dataset* into training and testing datasets with 80:20 and 70:30 ratios. We performed 10-fold cross validation experiments on various learning models as described above to compare their scene mood prediction accuracy for UGVs in the test dataset. We used three experimental settings. First, we trained all models from the training dataset with *mood tags* as ground truth and compared their scene mood prediction accuracy at the *mood tags level* (*i.e.*, whether the predicted *mood tags* and ground truth *mood tags* were the same). Second, we trained all models from the training dataset with *mood tags* as ground truth and compared their scene mood prediction accuracy at the *mood clusters level* (*i.e.*, whether the most frequent mood cluster of predicted *mood tags* and ground truth *mood tags* were the same).

Lastly, we trained all models from the training dataset with *mood clusters* as ground truth and compared their scene mood prediction accuracy at the *mood clusters level* (*i.e.*, whether the predicted *mood clusters* and ground truth *mood clusters* were the same). Our experiments confirm that the model based on late fusion of geo and visual features outperforms the other three models. We noted that the scene mood prediction accuracy at the *mood tag level* does not perform well because the accuracy of the SVM classifier degrades as the number of classes increases. A comparison of the scene mood prediction accuracies for all four models is listed in Table 5.

4.2.2 Soundtrack Selection Accuracy

We randomly divided the *evaluation dataset* into a training and a testing dataset with a 80:20 ratio, and performed 5-fold cross validation experiments to calculate the scene

Table 6: M_{Eval} emotion classification accuracy.

Training M_{Eval}	# Training Videos *Evaluation dataset*	322	Accuracy (in %)
Prediction (Exp-1)	**# Test Videos** *Evaluation dataset*	80	68.75
Prediction (Exp-2)	**# UGVs with soundtrack** *GeoVid dataset*	80	70.00
(Performed 5-fold cross validation.)			

mood prediction accuracy of M_{Eval} for UGVs in the test dataset. We performed two experiments. First, we trained M_{Eval} from the training set with *mood clusters* as ground truth and compared their scene mood prediction accuracy at the *mood clusters level* for UGVs in the test dataset of the *evaluation dataset* (*i.e.*, whether the predicted *mood clusters* and ground truth *mood clusters* matched). In the second experiment, we replaced the test dataset of the *evaluation dataset* with the same number of *music videos* generated by our system for randomly selected UGVs from the *GeoVid dataset*. The M_{Eval} maps visual features F and audio features A of a video V to mood clusters C, *i.e.*, $f_3(F, A)$ corresponds to mood clusters C based on the late fusion of F and A (see Figure 2). An input vector (in time order) for M_{Eval} can be represented by the following sequence (see Figure 7): $\langle F_1, A_1\rangle$, $\langle F_1, A_2\rangle$, $\langle F_2, A_2\rangle$, $\langle F_2, A_3\rangle$, ...

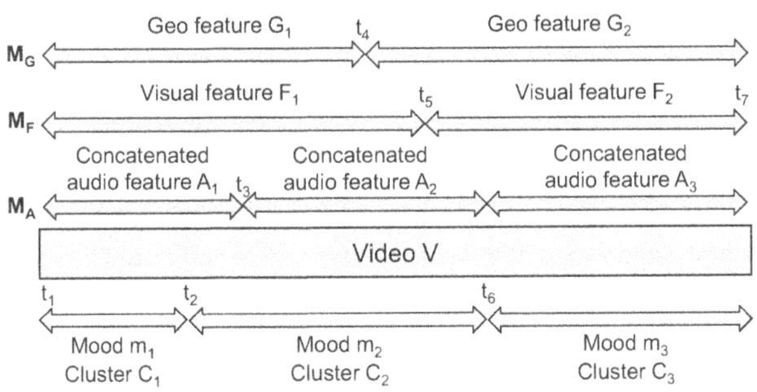

Figure 7: Features to mood tags/clusters mapping.

M_{Eval} reads the above input vector and predicts mood clusters for it. Table 6 shows that the emotions (mood clusters) prediction accuracy (68.75%) of M_{Eval} for *music videos* is comparable to the emotion prediction accuracy at the scene level in movies by state-of-the-art approaches such as introduced by Soleymani *et al.* [27] (63.40%) and Wang *et al.* [29] (74.69%). To check the effectiveness of the ADVISOR system, we generated *music videos* for 80 randomly selected UGVs from the *GeoVid dataset* and predicted their mood clusters by M_{Eval} with 70.0% accuracy, which is again comparable to state-of-the-art algorithms for emotion prediction at the scene level in movies. The experimental results in Table 6 confirm that ADVISOR effectively combines objective scene moods and music to recommend appealing soundtracks for UGVs.

4.3 User Study

Based on the techniques introduced earlier, we implemented the ADVISOR system to generate music videos for UGVs. All UGVs were single-shot clips with sensor metadata, acquired by our Android application designed specifically for recording sensor-annotated videos. We randomly selected five UGVs each for six different sites of Singapore as listed in Table 7, from a set of acquired videos. To judge whether the recommended songs capture the scene moods of videos, we recruited fifteen volunteers to assess the appropriateness and entertainment value of the music videos (UGVs with recommended songs). We asked every user to select one video for each site by choosing the most likely candidate that they themselves would have captured at that site. The predicted scene moods listed in Table 7 are the first three mood tags belonging to the most frequent mood cluster predicted by M_{GVC} for five videos at different sites. A soundtrack for all selected videos was generated using ADVISOR and users were asked to assign a score 1 (worst) to 5 (best) to the generated music videos. Finally, we calculated the average score of music videos for all sites. Table 7 summarizes the ratings and the most appropriate scene moods from a list of predicted mood tags for videos from the aforementioned six sites. The feedback from these volunteers was encouraging, indicating that our technique achieves its goal of automatic music video generation to enhance the video viewing experience.

Table 7: User study feedback from 15 volunteers.

Video Location	Predicted Scene Moods	1	2	3	4	5	Avg. Rating
Cemetery	melancholy, sad, sentimental	0	0	3	4	8	4.3
Clarke Quay	fun, sweet, calm	0	2	5	7	1	3.5
Gardens by the Bay	soothing, fun, calm	0	3	3	9	0	3.4
Marina Bay Sands	fun, playful	0	0	2	6	7	4.3
Siloso Beach	happy, fun, quiet	0	0	1	6	8	4.5
Universal Studios	fun, intense, happy, playful	0	2	5	5	3	3.6
Ratings on a scale from 1 (worst) to 5 (best).							

5. CONCLUSIONS

Our work represents one of the first attempts for user preference-aware video soundtrack generation. We categorize user activity logs from different data sources by using semantic concepts. This way, the correlation of preference-aware activities based on categorization of user-generated heterogeneous data complements video soundtrack recommendations for individual users. The ADVISOR system automatically generates a matching soundtrack for a UGV in four steps. More specifically, first, a learning model based on the late fusion of geo and visual features recognizes scene moods in the UGV. Second, a novel heuristic method recommends a list of songs based on the predicted scene moods. Third, the soundtrack recommendation component re-ranks songs recommended by the heuristics method based on the user's listening history. Finally, our Android application generates a music video from the UGV by automatically selecting the most appropriate song using a learning model based on the late fusion of visual and concatenated audio features. In the future, each one of these steps could be further enhanced. The experimental results and our user study confirm that ADVISOR can effectively combine objective scene moods and individual music tastes to recommend appealing soundtracks for UGVs.

Acknowledgments

The authors are very grateful to Dr. Suhua Tang and the anonymous reviewers for their insightful and constructive suggestions to improve the quality of this work. The research has been supported by the Singapore National Research Foundation under its International Research Centre @ Singapore Funding Initiative and administered by the IDM Programme Office through the Centre of Social Media Innovations for Communities (COSMIC).

6. REFERENCES

[1] K. Aizawa, D. Tancharoen, S. Kawasaki, and T. Yamasaki. Efficient Retrieval of Life Log based on Context and Content. In *ACM Workshop on Continuous Archival and Retrieval of Personal Experiences*, pages 22–31, 2004.

[2] B. Chen, J. Wang, Q. Huang, and T. Mei. Personalized Video Recommendation through Tripartite Graph Propagation. In *ACM International Conference on Multimedia*, pages 1133–1136, 2012.

[3] J. Cohen. A Coefficient of Agreement for Nominal Scales. *Educational and Psychological Measurement*, 20(1):37–46, 1960.

[4] M. Cristani, A. Pesarin, C. Drioli, V. Murino, A. Rodà, M. Grapulin, and N. Sebe. Toward an Automatically Generated Soundtrack from Low-level Cross-modal Correlations for Automotive Scenarios. In *ACM Int'l Conference on Multimedia*, pages 551–560, 2010.

[5] A. Ghias, J. Logan, D. Chamberlin, and B. C. Smith. Query by Humming: Musical Information Retrieval in an Audio Database. In *ACM International Conference on Multimedia*, pages 231–236, 1995.

[6] A. Hanjalic and L.-Q. Xu. Affective Video Content Representation and Modeling. *In IEEE Transactions on Multimedia*, 7(1):143–154, 2005.

[7] K. Hevner. Experimental Studies of the Elements of Expression in Music. *The American Journal of Psychology*, pages 246–268, 1936.

[8] T. Joachims, T. Finley, and C.-N. Yu. Cutting-plane Training of Structural SVMs. *Machine Learning Journal*, 77(1):27–59, 2009.

[9] M. Kaminskas and F. Ricci. Location-adapted Music Recommendation using Tags. In *User Modeling, Adaption and Personalization*, pages 183–194. Springer, 2011.

[10] H. B. Kang. Affective Content Detection using HMMs. In *ACM International Conference on Multimedia*, pages 259–262, 2003.

[11] Y. E. Kim, E. M. Schmidt, R. Migneco, B. G. Morton, P. Richardson, J. Scott, J. A. Speck, and D. Turnbull. Music Emotion Recognition: A State of the Art Review. In *International Society for Music Information Retrieval (ISMIR)*, pages 255–266, 2010.

[12] Y. Ko. A Study of Term Weighting Schemes using Class Information for Text Classification. In *ACM Special Interest Group on Information Retrieval (SIGIR)*, pages 1029–1030, 2012.

[13] O. Kucuktunc, U. Gudukbay, and O. Ulusoy. Fuzzy Color Histogram-based Video Segmentation. *In Computer Vision and Image Understanding*, 114(1):125–134, 2010.

[14] F.-F. Kuo, M.-F. Chiang, M.-K. Shan, and S.-Y. Lee. Emotion-based Music Recommendation by Association Discovery from Film Music. In *ACM International Conference on Multimedia*, pages 507–510, 2005.

[15] C. Laurier, M. Sordo, J. Serrà, and P. Herrera. Music Mood Representations from Social Tags. In *Int'l Society for Music Information Retrieval (ISMIR)*, pages 381–386, 2009.

[16] C. T. Li and M. K. Shan. Emotion-based Impressionism Slideshow with Automatic Music Accompaniment. In *ACM Int'l Conference on Multimedia*, pages 839–842, 2007.

[17] L. Lu, H. You, and H. Zhang. A New Approach to Query by Humming in Music Retrieval. In *IEEE Int'l Conference on Multimedia and Expo (ICME)*, pages 22–25, 2001.

[18] M. H. Park, J. H. Hong, and S. B. Cho. Location-based Recommendation System using Bayesian User's Preference Model in Mobile Devices. In *Ubiquitous Intelligence and Computing*, pages 1130–1139. Springer, 2007.

[19] H. Rahmani, B. Piccart, D. Fierens, and H. Blockeel. Three Complementary Approaches to Context Aware Movie Recommendation. In *ACM Workshop on Context-Aware Movie Recommendation*, pages 57–60, 2010.

[20] J. A. Russell. A Circumplex Model of Affect. *Journal of Personality and Social Psychology*, 39:1161–1178, 1980.

[21] M. Sahidullah and G. Saha. Design, Analysis and Experimental Evaluation of Block based Transformation in MFCC Computation for Speaker Recognition. In *Speech Communication*, volume 54, pages 543–565, 2012.

[22] M. Schedl and D. Schnitzer. Location-Aware Music Artist Recommendation. In *MultiMedia Modeling*, pages 205–213. Springer, 2014.

[23] B. Schuller, C. Hage, D. Schuller, and G. Rigoll. Mister DJ, Cheer Me Up!: Musical and Textual Features for Automatic Mood Classification. *In Journal of New Music Research*, 39(1):13–34, 2010.

[24] R. R. Shah, Y. Yu, and R. Zimmermann. User Preference-Aware Music Video Generation Based on Modeling Scene Moods. In *ACM Int'l Conference on Multimedia Systems (MMSys)*, pages 156–159, 2014.

[25] C. G. Snoek, M. Worring, and A. W. Smeulders. Early versus Late Fusion in Semantic Video Analysis. In *ACM Int'l Conference on Multimedia*, pages 399–402, 2005.

[26] C. G. Snoek, M. Worring, J. C. Van Gemert, J.-M. Geusebroek, and A. W. Smeulders. The Challenge Problem for Automated Detection of 101 Semantic Concepts in Multimedia. In *ACM International Conference on Multimedia*, pages 421–430, 2006.

[27] M. Soleymani, J. J. M. Kierkels, G. Chanel, and T. Pun. A Bayesian Framework for Video Affective Representation. In *IEEE Int'l Conference on Affective Computing and Intelligent Interaction and Workshops*, pages 1–7, 2009.

[28] R. E. Thayer. *The Biopsychology of Mood and Arousal.* Oxford University Press, 1989.

[29] H. L. Wang and L. F. Cheong. Affective Understanding in Film. *In IEEE Transactions on Circuits and Systems for Video Technology*, 16(6):689–704, 2006.

[30] C. Y. Wei, N. Dimitrova, and S.-F. Chang. Color-mood Analysis of Films based on Syntactic and Psychological Models. In *IEEE International Conference on Multimedia and Expo (ICME)*, pages 831–834, 2004.

[31] Y. H. Yang, Y. C. Lin, Y. F. Su, and H. H. Chen. A Regression Approach to Music Emotion Recognition. *In IEEE Transactions on Audio, Speech, and Language Processing*, 16(2):448–457, 2008.

[32] G. Ye, D. Liu, I.-H. Jhuo, and S.-F. Chang. Robust Late Fusion with Rank Minimization. In *IEEE Conference on Computer Vision and Pattern Recognition (CVPR)*, pages 3021–3028, 2012.

[33] Y. Yu, K. Joe, V. Oria, F. Moerchen, J. S. Downie, and L. Chen. Multi-version Music Search using Acoustic Feature Union and Exact Soft Mapping. *In International Journal of Semantic Computing*, 3(02):209–234, 2009.

[34] Y. Yu, Z. Shen, and R. Zimmermann. Automatic Music Soundtrack Generation for Outdoor Videos from Contextual Sensor Information. In *ACM International Conference on Multimedia*, pages 1377–1378, 2012.

[35] R. Zimmermann and Y. Yu. Social Interactions over Geographic-aware Multimedia Systems. In *ACM Int'l Conference on Multimedia*, pages 1115–1116, 2013.

Social Embedding Image Distance Learning

Shaowei Liu[1], Peng Cui[1], Wenwu Zhu[1], Shiqiang Yang[1] and Qi Tian[2]
[1]Computer Science Department, Tsinghua University, China
[2]Department of Computer Science, University of Texas at San Antonio
liu-sw11@mails.tsinghua.edu.cn, cuip/wwzhu/yangshq@tsinghua.edu.cn,
qitian@cs.utsa.edu

ABSTRACT

Image distance (similarity) is a fundamental and important problem in image processing. However, traditional visual features based image distance metrics usually fail to capture human cognition. This paper presents a novel Social embedding Image Distance Learning (*SIDL*) approach to embed the similarity of collective social and behavioral information into visual space. The social similarity is estimated according to multiple social factors. Then a metric learning method is especially designed to learn the distance of visual features from the estimated social similarity. In this manner, we can evaluate the cognitive image distance based on the visual content of images. Comprehensive experiments are designed to investigate the effectiveness of *SIDL*, as well as the performance in the image recommendation and reranking tasks. The experimental results show that the proposed approach makes a marked improvement compared to the state-of-the-art image distance metrics. An interesting observation is given to show that the learned image distance can better reflect human cognition.

Categories and Subject Descriptors

H.3.3 [**Information Search and Retrieval**]: Retrieval models

Keywords

image search and recommendation; social similarity; user behavior; metric learning

1. INTRODUCTION

With the fast development of Internet, image search and recommendation play an important role in delivering information in our daily life. In these applications, measuring the distance (or similarity) of pair-wise images is a fundamental and important issue. *If an effective image distance metric is obtained, we can easily employ existing technologies to achieve satisfactory performance in image search [12] and recommendation [21].*

MM'14, November 03 - 07 2014, Orlando, FL, USA.

http://dx.doi.org/10.1145/2647868.2654905.

However, to date, existing image distance metrics do not perform well to achieve this goal, due to the fact that they usually focus on measuring similarity of visual features but are not mature to capture human cognition, which is one of the most important factors in image search and recommendation. Here human cognition includes many aspects, such as semantics, attributes, user intention, image emotion, etc. Although the problem of capturing human cognition has received increasing attention in recent years, how to identify users' cognition is still a great challenge because we can hardly obtain the knowledge.

With the development of social network, a huge amount of users share their beautiful pictures and view others' in the social media platforms, such as Flickr and Twitter. Within these platforms, we can obtain not only vast amounts of images but also a series of collective social and behavioral information, such as annotated tags, favorite images and interest groups of users. In social psychology, it has been proved that human cognition and user behavior influence each other [2]. Therefore, social behavioral information in social media platform can be regarded as the reflection of their cognition to images. Given user behavior information in the social media platforms, we can use to better evaluate image distance. However, this idea faces the following challenges:

(1) **The lack of social information in Web image.** Although behavioral information does help to estimate user cognition, most of the Web images do not have user behavior information due to the fact that they are not produced by social media platforms. If the image distance relies on social behavioral data, our method will be extremely circumscribed in social images. Therefore, how to make our distance metric universal in common Web images is a great challenge in our problem.

(2) **The unreliability of social media data.** In social network, collective social and behavioral information is usually uncertain and unreliable. If the amount of user behavior information is not enough, the social similarity may have contingency. For example, although two images are both favored by a user, they may be still dissimilar because the user might have more than one interest. Thus, we also need to consider the reliability of social similarity.

(3) **The sparsity of user behavior.** In traditional image distance learning task, the knowledge of similarity graph is very dense: in most cases, the similarity of any two images is fixed. However, in social network, most of pair-wise images are not related socially. Thus, we cannot determine

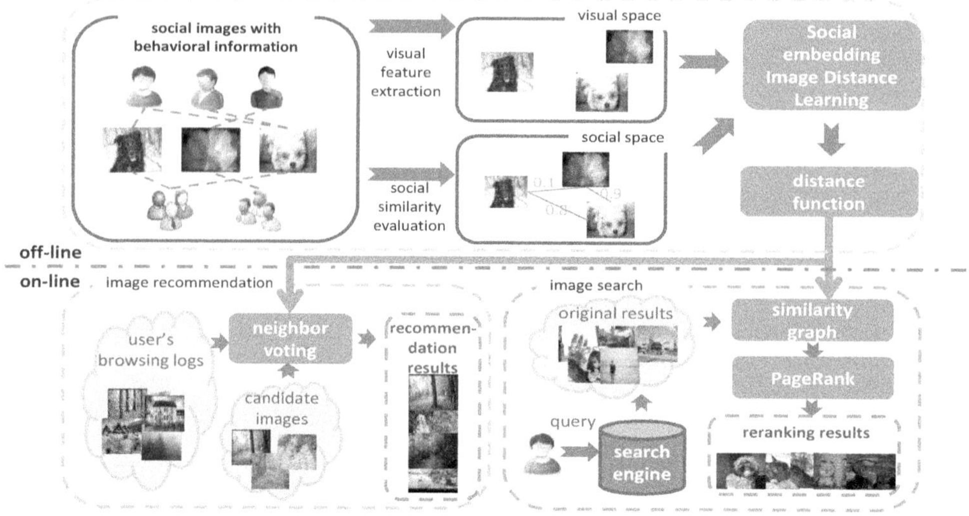

Figure 1: Illustration of the proposed Social embedding Image Distance Learning (*SIDL*) approach and the image search and recommendation system developed on *SIDL*.

whether these two images are socially similar or not. In this case, the visual similarity should be maintained.

To address the above problems, we propose a Social embedding Image Distance Learning (*SIDL*) approach to learn image distance from user behavior information in social media platforms, which is shown in Figure 1. In the approach, we use metric learning technique to learn an image distance function of visual features. Different from traditional metric learning work, our distance function aims at making image distance consistent to their social distance in user behavior. Thus, although the distance function is learned from social images (i.e., the images in social media platforms), it can measure the distance of ordinary Web images because it learns the weight and correlation of visual features. We call this idea "learn from social image, work beyond social image". In our method, we first estimate the social similarity among social images, where the reliability of social entities is evaluated. Next, we conduct our metric learning method to reduce the distance of socially similar images and enlarge the distance of socially dissimilar images. Finally, the learned image distance function is used to evaluate the distance of Web images based on their visual features. The image distance can be applied to a lot of applications, such as image recommendation and reranking. We not only conduct comprehensive experiments to show the effectiveness of our approach, but also give an interesting observation about the relationship between the learned distance and our intuitive cognition.

The contributions of our proposed approach are summarized as follows:

(1) We propose a novel image distance learning approach, which aims at using user behavior information in social media to capture human cognition in Web image distance measuring. To the best of our knowledge, we are the first who use the idea of "learn from social media, work beyond social media" to solve this problem.

(2) In this paper, we propose a Social Embedding Image Distance Learning approach, where an image distance metric function based on visual features is learned to make image distance consistent to social distance defined from user behavior. In our approach, social distance is well estimated in multimodal social factors. The metric learning method is especially designed to learn the similarity of visual features from social distance. Furthermore, we design two basic application scenarios based on the proposed *SIDL* method, including image recommendation and image reranking.

(3) To evaluate the performance of our approach, comprehensive experiments are conducted based on real social media and image reranking datasets. The experimental results have shown the effectiveness of the learning method. In addition, compared to the state-of-the-art image distance metrics the superiority of our image distance metric in the applications of image recommendation and reranking is also demonstrated.

(4) More than quantitative evaluation, an interesting observation of the relationship between the learned distance and our intuitive cognition is also given to show our results subjectively. We can observe that the key points of images, such as eyes, salient objects, are more important in measuring image similarity.

The rest of the paper is organized as follows: Section 2 gives a brief overview and comparison of related work. Section 3 introduces the evaluation of image social similarity. In Section 4, we introduce optimization of the proposed *SIDL* method and present two applications including image reranking and recommendation based on our distance learning method. Then, we introduce our experiments and report the results in Section 5. Finally, Section 6 summarizes the paper.

2. RELATED WORK

Aiming at improving the performance of image search, a series of methods have been proposed to capture human cognition , including query log based methods [11, 10], query analysis based methods [18, 19], relevance feedback based methods [22, 28], etc. In query log based methods, user click data in image search engines are used to estimate user intention. However, if a query contains less training images, the performance will not be very good. Besides, the image with low rank will not be easily seen by others. Query analysis based methods usually use the techniques in IR, such as query suggestion to capture different aspects of user intention. Zha *et al.* proposed a visual query suggestion approach [27] to suggest more detailed queries for ambiguous queries. In these methods, an important assumption is that visually similar images should have similar user intentions, which is not always tenable. Relevance feedback is another effective way to collect the cognition information by collecting users' feedback. However, the complex operation of feedback may sometimes reduce the user experience.

With the development of social media, a series of social-sensed image search and recommendation approaches have been proposed[5]. The social factors, such as image tags, users, interest groups are considered to replace the original manually labeled data. Image tagging methods [14] by user annotation show their significant improvements in bridging the semantic gap. Liu *et al.* proposed an image reranking method [15] that considers both visual factor[30, 24] and social factor. In this work, interest group in Flickr is utilized to evaluate the image similarity in user intention level. The research indicates that the interest groups can help understanding user intention in image reranking. However, this work is based on the images in Flickr, which cannot be well generalized to the ordinary Web images without social information such as interest groups.

Image distance metric plays an important role in many machine learning problems. Traditional metric learning researches usually aim at learning metric from labeled examples. The methods can be categorized into supervised ones [26] and semi-supervised ones [9]. In supervised metric learning, labels of images are complete, such as the categories of the images. Kilian *et al.* proposed a method named LMNN [25], which aims at reducing the margin of nearest neighbors. In semi-supervised metric learning, we do not have all the labels but only know some pairs of images are similar and some pairs are dissimilar. Thus, these methods aim at reducing the distance among the similar set and enlarging the distance among the dissimilar set. In our work, we do not have any labeled images but the images with social behavioral information. Although the social similarity can be evaluated by the social information, its reliability is not guaranteed because the social data are very noisy and uncertain. In addition, social similarity is a wholly new dimension to evaluate image similarity and it is very sparse. Thus visual distance needs to be maintained when an image does not have a socially similar neighbor.

3. SOCIAL SIMILARITY

Given the training social images with both visual features and social factors, our aim is to learn a distance function of visual features, which is consistent to the social similarity. Therefore, we first need to explore how to evaluate social similarity of images according to their social behavioral information.

3.1 Image Presentation

In this paper, we aim at embedding social behavioral information into visual space. Thus it is very important to present the complex and unstructured social behavioral information in a structured feature space. Here we call each dimension of social behavioral information as a social factor. Similar to the "Bag of Visual Words" model in visual descriptor presentation, each social factor is presented in a "Bag of social entity" way. For example, in Flickr, the typical social factors we can obtain include user favoring, group sharing, and user tagging, etc. Thus an image can be presented by a set of users who favor it, groups that share it and tags that belong to it, which are defined as social entities. Therefore, a social image can be presented in visual and social dimensions, i.e., $\mathcal{I}_i = \{x_i, \mathcal{S}_i\}$, where x_i is the vector of visual features ,and $\mathcal{S}_i = \cup_{k=1}^{m} \mathcal{V}_i^k$ is a set that includes m social factors. $\mathcal{V}_i^k$ is the kth social factor of image $\mathcal{I}_i$. Each social factor $\mathcal{V}_i^k$ can be represented as a bag of social entities. To make our formulation more general, we use the symbol V_i to represent a social factor, and v_i to denote a social entity. For example, we can use $\mathcal{V}^1$ to denote the social factor of user favoring. Therefore, $\mathcal{V}_i^1 = \{v_{t_1}, \cdots, v_{t_n}\}$ denotes that there are n users $v_{t_1}, \cdots, v_{t_n}$ that favor the image $\mathcal{I}_i$.

Given the training social images with both visual features and social factors, our aim is to learn a distance function $d(x_i, x_j)$ of visual features, which is consistent to the social similarity $sim_{social}(\mathcal{I}_i, \mathcal{I}_j)$. In this section, we will show some analysis of social factors and introduce how to evaluate the social similarity in our approach.

3.2 Preliminary Study of Social Factors

In our problem, the first question is whether the social similarity, i.e., the similarity of social factors is helpful in understanding image similarity in user behavioral aspect. To demonstrate this, we collect a social image dataset from Flickr, which includes 19,888 images, 6,843 users, 1,490 groups and 17,922 tags. For each user, we hope that all images that he/she favors should have low variance in feature space because they confirm to his/her interests. Therefore, for the images that are favored by a given user, we extract visual features and social features and calculate the variance. Here the visual features are presented in a "Bag of Visual Word" model. For each social factor, social feature is presented as the distribution vector of social entities. For example, if user j favors image i, the jth element of the image i's user feature is 1, otherwise it is 0. So are the group feature and tag feature. Each feature vector is normalized to make the 2-norm to be 1 for scale unification. For each user and group, the variances of the images in different feature spaces are illustrated in Figure 2. From Figure 2, we can observe that variance of visual feature is the largest among four features. Thus if we want to recommend images to a user or a group, social similarity is more reliable than visual similarity. Among three social factors, we can find that the user favoring factor obtains the smallest variance. In other words, using others' favoring information to recommend images will obtain a good performance. This result is consistent with the idea of Collaborative Filtering (CF). In addition, we can see that most of the variance values are relatively large. It indicates that the images favored by a user or a group are usually very diverse in feature space.

3.3 Reliability of Social Entities

In social media, the user behavior information is usually noisy and uncertain. Thus not all social entities are equally reliable in evaluating social similarity. For example, images in the group named "iphone club" should be similar but images in the groups named "beautiful world" may be very diverse. In this case, the former group is more reliable than the latter one in similarity evaluation. Therefore, it is important to evaluate the reliability of social entities.

Take users as an example, if an image is favored by two users, we can assume that the interests of these two users are partially similar. Based on this assumption, we can build a

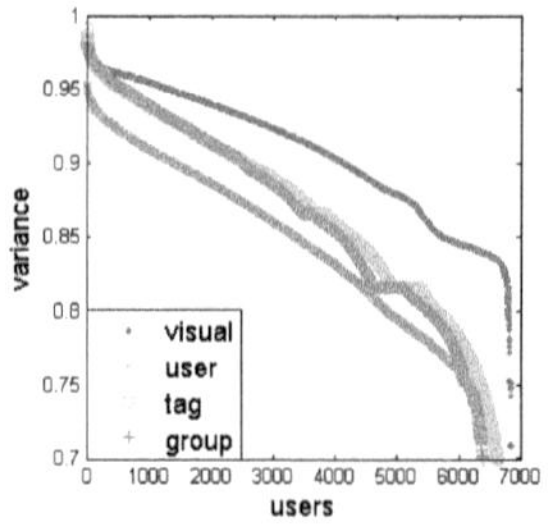

(a)

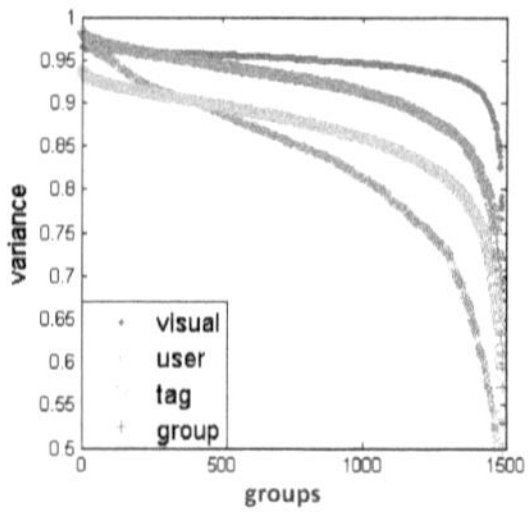

(b)

Figure 2: The variance of the visual features and social factors of the images that are favored by each (a) user (b) group. The results are sorted in a descending order.

similarity graph based on user interests. The nodes are users and the weight of an edge denotes the similarity of the users. We use $Im(v_i)$ to denote the images that are favored by user v_i, i.e.,

$$Im(v_i) = \{\mathcal{I}_t | v_i \in \mathcal{V}_t\}. \quad (1)$$

In this equation, $\mathcal{V}_t$ denotes the all entities that belongs to image $\mathcal{I}_t$. Then, the similarity of the social entities can be defined as the Jaccard distance of the images:

$$sim(v_i, v_j) = \frac{|Im(v_i) \cap Im(v_j)|}{|Im(v_i) \cup Im(v_j)|}. \quad (2)$$

Based on the similarity graph, we utilize spectral clustering method to divide users into c clusters. For a given entity v_i, if all of its neighbors belong to the same cluster with v_i, we can think v_i is a reliable social entity. The images belongs to user v_i should have high probability to be similar. Thus, the reliability score of v_i is defined as follows,

$$r(v_i) = \frac{1}{|c(v_i) \cup_{v_j \in N(v_i)} c(v_j)|}, \quad (3)$$

where $N(v_i)$ is the set of neighbor nodes of v_i; $c(v_i)$ is the label of v_i's cluster. If all of v_i's neighbors belong to the same cluster with it, the reliability score $r(v_i)$ is defined as 1. On the contrary, if his neighbors cover all of c clusters, $r(v_i)$ is defined as $1/c$.

This method is also suitable for the cases of using group or tag as social entity. For any entity v_i, the pair-wise similarity can be similarly calculated by Equation 2 and the reliability score can be calculated by Equation 3.

3.4 Evaluation of Social Similarity

We explore evaluating the social similarity of pair-wise images based on the reliability scores of the corresponding social entities. For two images $\mathcal{I}_i$ and $\mathcal{I}_j$, we analyze their similarity by their social factors $\mathcal{V}_i$ and $\mathcal{V}_j$. If $\mathcal{V}_i \cap \mathcal{V}_j$ is empty, i.e.,they share no common entities, we define the social similarity as 0. Otherwise, the social similarity is determined by the overlap of the entities and their reliability. Taking users as an example, intuitively, when the users have the same reliability, the images that are jointly favored by more users should be more similar. If the images are both favored by a fixed number of users, the images that are favored by more reliable users should have higher similarity. Based on the above two considerations, the social similarity of image in the social factor $\mathcal{V}_i$ and $\mathcal{V}_j$ is defined as follows,

$$sim(\mathcal{V}_i, \mathcal{V}_j) = \begin{cases} 0, & \mathcal{V}_i \cap \mathcal{V}_j = \phi \\ \frac{\sum_{v_t \in \mathcal{V}_i \cap \mathcal{V}_j} r(v_t)}{\sum_{v_t \in \mathcal{V}_i \cup \mathcal{V}_j} r(v_t)}, & \text{otherwise} \end{cases} \quad (4)$$

where $r(v_t)$ is the reliability score defined in Equation 3. In Equation 4, the similarity is defined as the weighted Jaccard similarity of $\mathcal{V}_i$ and $\mathcal{V}_j$. Obviously, this definition of similarity satisfies the previous heuristics. For a social image has multiple social factors, the final similarity of images $\mathcal{I}_i$ and $\mathcal{I}_j$ is defined as the average of all the social factors' similarity:

$$sim_{social}(\mathcal{I}_i, \mathcal{I}_j) = \frac{1}{m} \sum_{k=1}^{m} sim(\mathcal{V}_i^k, \mathcal{V}_j^k). \quad (5)$$

In this equation, we use average because different social factors reflect different aspects of image similarity. The final social similarity values range from 0 to 1. When the similarity is close to 1, the images are judged very similar in social dimension. On the other hand, when the similarity is near to 0, we are not very certain that the images are very dissimilar because similar images may also have no social relation. This problem can be solved by multiple sampling. Because of the diversity of the images, for a given image, if we randomly select many socially dissimilar images, the vast majority of them will be truly dissimilar to it.

4. SOCIAL EMBEDDING IMAGE DISTANCE LEARNING

When social similarity of images is estimated, our target is to learn an image distance function to reduce the distance of socially similar image and enlarge the distance of socially dissimilar images. In this section, we first introduce our proposed image distance learning method. Next, we give the algorithm of our approach and analyze the complexity. Finally, we design two applications based on the proposed image distance metric, including image recommendation and text-based image reranking.

4.1 Mahanalobis Distance Function

In traditional metric learning researches, *Mahalanobis* Distance is a widely used metric function because it is very efficient in optimization and calculation, as well as effective enough in most problems. Although some kernel functions are proposed to improve the performance. We do not consider them because the metric function is not the main contribution of this work and it may make our method not scalable. Therefore, we use *Mahalanobis* Distance to evaluate the image distance, which is defined as follows,

$$d_M(x_i, x_j) = \sqrt{(x_i - x_j)^T M (x_i - x_j)}, \quad (6)$$

where M is the *Mahalanobis* matrix, which needs to be learned in our problem; x_i is the visual feature vector of image $\mathcal{I}_i$. To guarantee d to be a distance function, M must be positive semidefinite, which is noted as $M \succeq 0$.

4.2 Distance Learning with Social Constraints

In our metric learning approach, our goal is to learn the *Mahanalobis* matrix M from the social images, which makes the image distance $d_M(x_i, x_j)$ consistent to social similarity. i.e., the distance between socially similar images is close and the distance between socially dissimilar images is far.

In metric learning, "triple" is a widely used concept for optimization. In our approach, a "triple" $< i, j, k >$ is defined as three images I_i, I_j and I_k, where I_i and I_j are socially similar and I_i and I_k are socially dissimilar. Thus, we can train our metric function by reducing $d_M(x_i, x_j)$ and enlarging $d_M(x_i, x_k)$. In our method, the training set of triples $\mathcal{T}$ based on social similarities is defined as:

$$\mathcal{T} = \{< i, j, k > | sim_{social}(\mathcal{I}_i, \mathcal{I}_j) > \delta, sim_{social}(\mathcal{I}_i, \mathcal{I}_k) < \epsilon\}, \quad (7)$$

where δ and ϵ are the thresholds to specify socially similar images and socially dissimilar images. In social media, there are a lot of socially dissimilar images and a few socially similar images. For a given $< x_i, x_j >$, there are a lot of x_k that satisfies the equation 7. In our approach we just randomly select some of them to avoid explosion of scale and reduce the redundancy. After the set of of triples $\mathcal{T}$ is selected, we need to find the optimal *Mahanalobis* matrix M that satisfies the following constraints:

$$d_M^2(x_i, x_k) - d_M^2(x_i, x_j) > 1, \forall < i, j, k > \in \mathcal{T} \quad (8)$$

Following the traditional margin-based metric learning methods[25, 23], the margin between two distances is defined as the squared error because it is very easy to optimize and have a good performance. In Equation 8, the matrix M that satisfies all the constraints is typically not unique. In this case, we aim to select M that is close to the original unweighted Euclidean Distance, which represents the original visual similarity in our problem. This leads to the following optimization problem:

$$\begin{aligned} &\min_M ||M - I||_F^2 \\ s.t.\quad & d_M^2(x_i, x_k) - d_M^2(x_i, x_j) > 1, \forall < i, j, k > \in \mathcal{T} \\ & M \succeq 0 \end{aligned} \quad (9)$$

where I is the identity matrix with the same dimensions with M and $|| \cdot ||_F$ donotes *Frobenius* norm. As in other margin-based methods, we add slack variables [4] to account for the constraints that cannot be satisfied. Thus our problem can be written as follows,

$$\begin{aligned} &\min_M ||M - I||_F^2 + C \sum_{i,j,k} sim_{social}(\mathcal{I}_i, \mathcal{I}_j)\epsilon_{ijk} \\ s.t.\quad & d_M^2(x_i, x_k) - d_M^2(x_i, x_j) > 1 - \epsilon_{ijk}, \forall < i, j, k > \in \mathcal{T} \\ & M \succeq 0, \quad \epsilon_{ijk} \geq 0 \end{aligned} \quad (10)$$

where ϵ_{ijk} is the slack variable and $sim_{social}(\mathcal{I}_i, \mathcal{I}_j)$ is the social similarity defined in Equation 5. C is a parameter that denotes the stringency of the slack variables. Different from traditional methods, we use social similarity as the coefficient of the slack variables because we have different confidence for different training triples. When the images $\mathcal{I}_i$ and $\mathcal{I}_j$ are very socially similar, i.e. $sim_social(\mathcal{I}_i, \mathcal{I}_j)$ is close to 1, we hope the corresponding constraint to be satisfied as far as possible. On the contrary, when $sim_{social}(\mathcal{I}_i, \mathcal{I}_j)$ is very small, the value of slack variable can be relatively greater. This problem is a Semi-Definite Programming (SDP) problem. It can be solved by the existing solvers [7].

4.3 Algorithm and Complexity

We summarize the procedure of the whole Social Embedding Image Distance Learning approach as described in Algorithm 1.

There are four main steps in our approach: entity reliability evaluation step, social similarity computation step, triple selection step, and optimization step. In entity reliability evaluation step, the time complexity is $\mathcal{O}(\sum_{i=1}^{m} f_i^2)$, m is the number of social factors and f_i is the size of the ith social factor. In social similarity computation step, the complexity is $\mathcal{O}(n^2 m)$. In the triple selection step, the time complexity is $\mathcal{O}(r \cdot \sum_{i=1}^{n} |S_i|)$, where n is the total number of the training images, $|S_i|$ is the number of the images that are socially similar to the ith image and r is a constant that denotes the number of socially dissimilar images sampled. Usually, we have $|S_i| << n$, thus the complexity of this step is usually much less than $\mathcal{O}(n^2 r)$. In the last optimization step, the complexity of SDP is $\mathcal{O}(c|T|)$, where c is a constant that is determined by the number of iteration and the length of visual features, as well as $|T|$ denotes the number of selected triples. At the same time, we have $|T| \leq n^2 r$. Based on the above analysis, the total complexity of our algorithm is no more than $\mathcal{O}(crn^2)$. Therefore, the time complexity of our algorithm is square with respect to the number of training images.

Algorithm 1: Social embedding Image Distance Learning

Input: the number of the social factors m;
the number of social entities in the ith social factor f_i;
the number of the training images n;
the visual features x_i and social factors $\mathcal{S}_i = \cup_{k=1}^{m} \mathcal{V}_i^k$ for each training image $\mathcal{I}_i$
Output: the *Mahanalobis* matrix M for the distance metric in Equation 6.

```
for (i = 1 : m) do
    for j = 1 : f_i − 1 do
        for k = k + 1 : f_i do
            Compute the pair-wise similarity of social entity
            sim(v_i^j, v_i^k) using Equation 2;
        end
    end
    Conduct spectral clustering on the similarity graph;
    Compute the reliability score of the social entity v_i^k
    using Equation 3;
end
for (i = 1 : n − 1) do
    for j = i + 1 : n do
        Compute the social similarity of the training images
        sim(I_i, I_j) using Equation 5;
    end
end
T = Φ;
for i = 1 : n do
    for j ∈ {j|sim(I_i, I_j) > δ} do
        for t=1:r do
            Randomly generate k ∈ {1, 2, · · · , n},
            sim(I_i, I_k) < ε;
            Add < i, j, k > to T;
        end
    end
end
Formulate the Problem in Equation 10;
Optimize the SDP problem by standard solvers;
```

4.4 Applications

In image search and recommendation tasks, human cognition plays an important role. Thus, our approach is very useful in these tasks. In this section, we introduce how and why our image distance metric can be used in the corresponding application scenarios.

4.4.1 Image recommendation

In the image recommendation task, our target is to recommend new images based on his/her historical browsing logs.

In our approach, we learn the image distance function from users in social platforms. Then, for general Web images, we can judge whether two images will have similar favored users according to their visual contents. Given a set of images $Train = \{I_1, I_2, \cdots, I_m\}$ that have been viewed by the current user, we need to recommend the top k images in the candidate set $Test = \{J_1, J_2, \cdots, J_n\}$. Intuitively, the image that are similar to the images in $Train$ should be recommended. In our distance learning method, when the optimal *Mahanalobis* matrix M is obtained, the pair-wise image distance $d_M(I_i, I_j)$ can be calculated accordingly. Thus, the next question is how to select the images that are similar to the training set based on the distance function. Here we provide the Borda Fusion model to solve the problem.

Borda Count has been widely used in meta-search and recommendation [3]. It simulates a democratic voting process: each voter gives a preference rank to d candidates; the top ranked candidate gets d points, the second ranked one gets $d-1$ points and so on so forth. Then, for each candidate, the total points from all voters are used for ranking. The top k results are returned for recommendation. In this model, each image in the training data is regarded as a voter. For each training image, we calculate the distance from it to the testing images J_q in $Test$. Then, the distance $d_M(I_p, J_q)$ are ranked in ascending order. The top d test images obtain their points. Finally, after all the training images in $Train$ are traversed, we rank the testing images in $Test$ with respect to their total points. We return the top k images as the recommendation results.

To notice, our recommendation process is purely content-based. Thus, in this paper, we do not compare our method to other user-centric recommendation methods such as *Collaborative Filtering (CF)* because we do not need any user information. In addition, as CF suffers from cold-start problem, hybrid recommendation (e.g. CF+content-based) becomes more popular, where image distance metric is also a fundamental problem.

4.4.2 Image reranking

When people search a query in the image search website, the search engine will return a lot of images that are judged as relevant to the query. Reranking the images to better meet the demands of users is an important problem. Jing *et al.* [12] proposed a VisualRank method for image reranking. In this method, the similarity of two images are evaluated by their visual features. Then, a PageRank [20] based iterative calculation is conducted to give the images rank scores. This method selects the images that are visually similar to most of the other images. It has been proven that VisualRank performs well in product search. However, in general image search task, the performance is not very desirable because it ignores human cognition factor. Our approach learns the social similarity, which can better estimate human cognition. In our approach, the pair-wise image similarity is evaluated by the learned distance function $d_M(\mathcal{I}_i, \mathcal{I}_j)$. The PageRank model is used to select the images that are interesting to most of the users.

In this method, we first generate the image similarity matrix P, whose elements are calculated as:

$$P_{ij} = \frac{e^{-d_M(x_i, x_j)}}{\sum_{k=1}^{n} e^{-d_M(x_k, x_j)}} \tag{11}$$

where $d_M(x_i, x_j)$ is the learned *Mahanalobis* distance in Equation 6, n is the number of candidate images. Here we use negative exponent function to convert distance to similarity and chose $\sigma^2 = 0.5$. The denominator aims at normalizing the sum of each column to 1. Then, the PageRank process is conducted:

$$pr = d \cdot P \cdot pr + (1-d)e \tag{12}$$

where pr denotes the rank score vector, d is the damping factor to guarantee the connectivity of the similarity graph, and e is a normalized n-dimension vector whose elements are all $1/n$. In PageRank, the empirical value of d is about 0.8. After the PageRank process, each image has a rank score in pr. Finally we can rerank images by their rank scores.

5. EXPERIMENTS

In this section, we first introduce our experimental settings. Then we evaluate the proposed approach in three aspects: the effectiveness of our learning method, as well as the performance of the learned distance function in recommendation task and image reranking task. Finally, we show some learning results and give some interesting insights of our distance learning method.

5.1 Experimental Setup

5.1.1 Datasets

In our experiments, we have prepared three datasets, including:

Training dataset and test dataset. To train the distance function and test the effectiveness of our distance learning method, we crawl the images and their social contextual information in Flickr through Flickr API. This dataset includes 101,496 images, 54,173 users, 6,439 groups and 35,844 tags in total. We crawl the data by the following criteria: first, we search for 500 hot queries[1], such as sunset, portrait, etc. to obtain the seed images. Then the images that belong to the same user or group with the seed images are expanded. We crawl the social information of the images, including: the users who favor them, the groups that the images belong to, as well as the tags annotated to the images. Some images may have no favored users or interest groups. We divide this dataset into two parts: 80% for training and 20% for test.The social entities in the training and test datasets may have overlap. It will not impact the fairness of our experiments because we do not evaluate the similarity between training and test data in our method.

Recommendation dataset. We also prepare a recommendation dataset for the application scenario of image recommendation. We select 1,793 users' favorite images in Flickr. The users selected must have at least 40 favorite images. For each user, we randomly select 20 images for training and 20 as ground truth for testing. Then we sample other 80 images from the whole image dataset as candidates. Each candidate image must have at least one tag that is the same as one of the ground truth images.

MSR dataset. We utilize Bing Image Retrieval Grand Challenge (MSR) dataset [10] to prove that our distance learning method can improve the performance of image reranking. Different from traditional image retrieval datesets, MSR dataset is based on user click data, which can capture not only semantic relevance but also human cognition.

The first two datasets are crawled from Flickr because our methods rely on social behavioral infomation. However, to the best of our knowledge, there is no public benchmark including such information. In our image reranking method,

[1]https://www.flickr.com/photos/tags/.

we do not need any personalized information. Thus a public dataset is utilized to make our approach comparable to others.

5.1.2 Visual Features

Visual feature is an important setting in our method because it determines the performance of transfer learning. If there is no relationship between the used visual feature and the social similarity of the images, our method will not work. Although using multiple features may improve the performance, it will bring much higher complexity at the same time. The key point of this paper is distance learning but not feature selection. Therefore, we only use a simple and effective visual feature in our experiments. In our approach, local features are better than global features because local features represent images in object level, which can better reflect user interests. Among the various local features, we utilize a Bag-of-Words (BoW) histogram based on SIFT descriptors [29, 16] in our experiments, which is one of the most widely used presentation of images. The SIFT descriptors are extracted by a VLFeat implementation [1]. Then a hierarchical k-means visual vocabulary tree is constructed with 4 layers and 10 branches for each layer. After clustering, each leaf node in the vocabulary tree is defined as a visual word. An image is presented as the histogram of the visual words occurred. In our datasets, all images are rescaled to the normal size in Flickr for uniformity: the length of the longest edge is rescaled to 400 pixels.

5.1.3 Baselines

To demonstrate the advantages of our proposed distance learning approach *SIDL*, we implement the following baseline methods for comparison.

(1) **Euclidean distance.** When the BoW features are extracted, the Euclidean distance is commonly used to evaluate the image distance, i.e.:

$$d(x_i, x_j) = \sqrt{(x_i - x_j)^T(x_i - x_j)}. \quad (13)$$

(2) **Jaccard similarity.** If we regard an image as a document, when it is presented as a bag of words, the Jaccard distance [17], which is a set similarity function for documents can also be utilized:

$$sim(I_i, I_j) = \frac{|I_i \cap I_j|}{|I_i \cup I_j|}, \quad (14)$$

where I_i denotes the ith image that is presented as a set of visual words. For it is a similarity function, we convert it to distance by negative exponent function if needed.

(3) **TagProp [8].** Guillaumin *et al.* proposed a method named *TagProp* for image annotation. This method use metric learning technology to learn the image distance with respect to their tags. Although the final output of this method is the tag relevance, it evaluates the pair-wise image similarity in the optimization process. In our experiments, we only use the results of image distance.

(4) **LMNN [25].** Weinberger *et al.* proposed a metric learning method named Large Margin Nearest Neighbor (LMNN). *LMNN* uses metric learning to reduce the margins of the nearest neighbors. It is designed for image classification, which relies on the pre-labeled data. For our training data do not contain the label of classification, we use the image classification benchmark Caltech101 [6] as the training dataset, which includes 102 categories, and 40 to 800 images per category. We select 30 images per category for training. Then, the trained *Mahanalobis* distance function is compared to our method.

(5) **social+LMNN.** In this baseline, we use the social similarity estimation in Equation 5 to select the nearest neighbor of an image, and then use *LMNN* for optimization. Here we use this as a baseline to compare the metric learning optimization step in the same condition of social similarity estimation.

In the area of image processing, there are a variety of methods for image search and recommendation. However, in this paper, we only want to prove that our cognition-based image distance performs better than the traditional image distance metrics. Thus we fix the Borda Fusion model in recommendation and PageRank model in reranking and use the above distance metrics as baselines.

The code of our algorithm is realized in MATLAB 2010b. The toolbox of VLFeat [1] is used for SIFT feature extraction and hierarchical k-means clustering of visual words. We use SeDuMi [7] toolbox as the solver of the proposed optimization problem. All the experiments were conducted on a server with Intel(R) Xeon(R) CPU X5645 at 2.40 GHz on 24 cores, 192GB RAM and 64-bit Windows Server 2008 operating system.

5.2 Effectiveness of SIDL

The goal of our approach is to learn the social similarity in visual space. Thus, we first need to prove the feasibility of this idea. When we have learned a distance function from the training set, can this function reflect the social similarity in the test data? Here we evaluate the effectiveness in ranking because ranking order is much more important than absolute value in our problem. For a given image in the test dataset, we calculate the social similarity to the other images by Equation 5 and then can obtain a rank order as ground truth. On the other hand, we can calculate the image distance based on the learned distance function by Equation 6 and get another rank order of similar images. The consistency of these two orders can reflect the effectiveness of our method. We use $Kendall - \tau$ rank correlation [13] as the evaluation measure. Give two ranking sequence X and Y. The $Kendall - \tau$ is defined as:

$$\tau = \frac{n_c - n_d}{\frac{1}{2}n(n-1)}, \quad (15)$$

where n is the total number of images, n_c is the number of concordant pairs and n_d is the number of discordant pairs. A concordant is defined as the pair (i, j) that satisfies $x_i \geq x_j$ when $y_i \geq y_j$ or $x_i \leq x_j$ when $y_i \leq y_j$. Otherwise, (i, j) is a discordant pair. The scale of $Kendall - \tau$'s value is $[-1, 1]$. If X and Y are the same, $\tau = 1$. If X and Y are completely inverted, $\tau = -1$.

In training process, we fix the value of δ and ϵ in Equation 7 as $\delta = 0.7, \epsilon = 0.1$. In this setting, an image in the training dataset has 179 socially similar images and about 70,000 socially dissimilar images in average. To reduce the complexity of our optimization process, for each image, we randomly select 200 socially dissimilar images in the triple selection step in Equation 7. We use a 5-folds cross validation to tune the parameter C in the Equation 10. The best performance of τ is obtained when $C = 0.15$.

In social similarity evaluation step, we need to discover what social factors are helpful in evaluating social similarity. Therefore, before comparing our methods to the baselines, we first use different social factors to demonstrate their

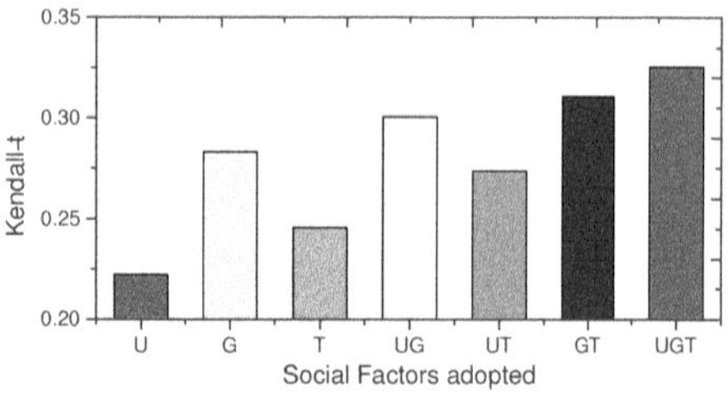

Figure 3: The Performance on the test dataset in $Kendall-\tau$ **using different social factors. "U" denotes users, "G" denotes groups and "T" denotes tags.**

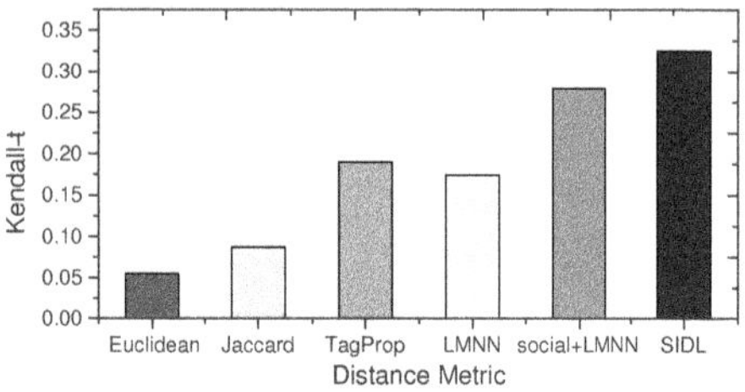

Figure 4: The performance on the test dataset in $Kendall-\tau$ **of different image distance metrics.**

effects on the final performance. Figure 3 illustrates the results.

Figure 3 is generated by using different social factors to calculate the social similarity in Equation 5. In Figure 3, "U" denotes users, "G" denotes groups, "T" denotes tags and multiple symbols denotes using multiple social factors. When we use different factors, the value of δ and ϵ are adjusted at the same time to guarantee that the number of socially similar images is about 200 and the number of socially dissimilar images is about 70,000. In Figure 3, we can observe that our algorithm obtains the best performance when using "UGT". It shows that all these factors are helpful to improve the performance. If we only use one factor, group is the best and user is the worst. This is because images in the same group are relatively concentrated in user interests but the images belong to the same user sometimes may be very diverse. If we use two social factors, the best performance is obtained when using groups and tags. It is interesting that using group and user also has a not bad performance. It reflects that the knowledge of group and user has less overlap than group and tag.

We compare our method to the baselines to demonstrate the effectiveness. The results are illustrated in Figure 4.

From Figure 4, it can be observed that the proposed *SIDL* method achieves the best performance. In baseline methods, Euclidean distance and Jaccard similarity are unsupervised. The τ values of these metrics are less than 0.1, which means the rank orders are likely to be random. *LMNN* performs the worst among the four supervised methods. It is mainly due to the difference in the training datasets. In Flickr, most of the images are usually informal and noisy. However, images in Caltech101 dataset is well structured and have obvious objects. Besides, the amount of images in Caltech101 is only about 1/10 scale of our Flickr training dataset. The fact that *social+LMNN* performs better than *TagProp* shows that tag similarity in the training data cannot represent social similarity in the test data well.

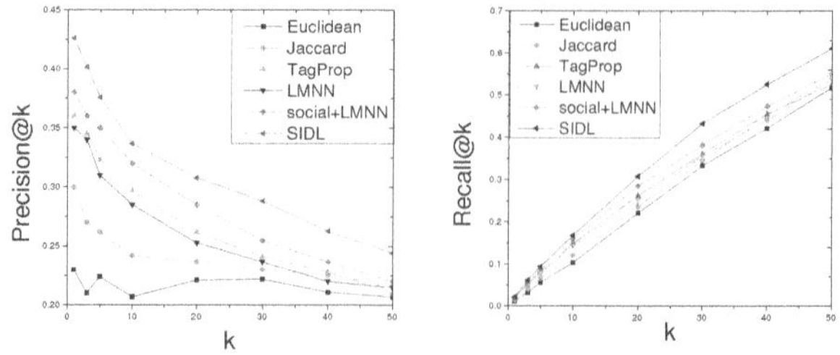

(a) Precision (b) Recall

Figure 5: The performance on recommendation dataset in (a) Precision@k and (b) Recall@k with different number of top k **images using different image distance metrics in our Borda-fushion based image recommendation model.**

Both *social+LMNN* and *SIDL* use social and visual information. The difference between these two methods exists in the optimization step. In the training dataset, an image usually only has less than 200 socially similar images. Compared to the total 80,000 images, socially similarity is very sparse. Thus if two visual words A and B do not occur in any pair of socially similar images, we can learn nothing in metric learning process. In *SIDL*, we initialize the distance function as the Euclidean distance, for the images whose distance cannot be learned, their visual similarity is maintained. Besides, in Equation 10, we add reliability scores as coefficients to the relax variables, which can make the constraints of highly similar pairs more accurate.

In this experiment, all the testing ground truth are based on the social similarity defined in Equation 5 because we only want to prove that it is effective to learn image distance of visual features from social similarity. Thus we will demonstrate the effectiveness of our approach in real applications in the next section.

5.3 Performance in Image Recommendation and Image Reranking

Here we first show the performance of our method in the image recommendation task. In the image recommendation dataset, each user has 20 images for training and 100 for testing. In the 100 testing images, 20 should be recommended. For each image distance metric, we use the Borda Fusion model in Section 4 to calculate the voting points of the testing images according to their distance to the training images. Top k images are returned as the recommendation results. Here we use *Precision@k* and *Recall@k* as the measures. The results are illustrated in Figure 5. In the figure, it can be seen that *SIDL* performs the best in both Precision and Recall for all k values. If we recommend images randomly, the precision will be 0.2. Similar to the last experiment, the result of Euclidean is near to random, which indicates the Euclidean distance of BoW features can hardly reflect the image similarity in recommendation task. The relative performance of the baselines is similar to the previous experiment except for *LMNN* and *TagProp*. In recommendation dataset, *LMNN* performs better than *TagProp*, which indicates the general category information might be effective than the specific tag information in recommendation task. Compared to *social+LMNN*, *SIDL* performs 10% higher in

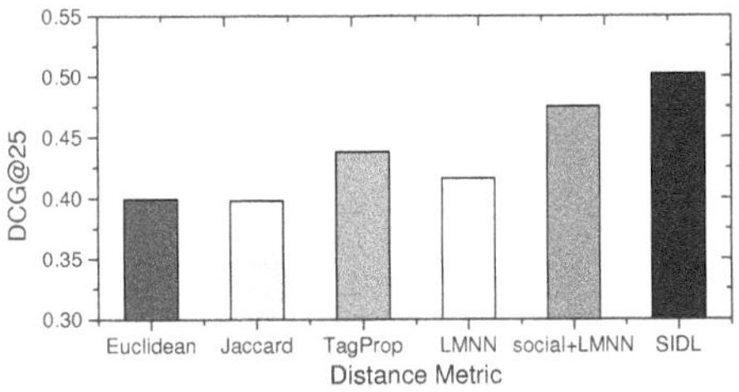

Figure 6: The performance on the MSR dataset in terms of DCG@25 with using different image distance metrics in the PageRank model.

Precision. It indicates the proposed metric learning optimization method has superiority to traditional *LMNN* in embedding social information.

To show the performance in the image reranking task, we use different distance metrics in the PageRank model in Section 4. For each query in MSR dataset, a similarity graph is constructed for each metric. Then the PageRank score can be calculated by Equation 12. Following the measurements in the grand challenge, we use Discounted Cumulated Gain of the top 25 images ($DCG@25$) to evaluate the performance. When the rank order is given, the $DCG@25$ for each query is calculated as:

$$DCG@25 = 0.01757 \sum_{i=1}^{25} \frac{2^{rel_i - 1}}{\log_2^{i+1}}, \quad (16)$$

where rel_i is the relevance score of the ith ranked image (Excellent=3, Good=1, Bad=0), 0.1757 is to normalize the value of $DCG@25$ up to 1. Note that for the queries with less than 25 images, we simply supply some "Bad" images after the original ranking list. Figure 6 shows the results. From Figure 6, we can observe that the Euclidean distance performs well in $DCG@25$, which is different with the previous results. It is mainly because for a given query, most of the images are visually similar. The visual words occurred are relatively concentrated. In this case, the Euclidean distance can measure the image similarity more accurate than the general images. Similar to the first experiment, *TagProp* performs worse than *LMNN*, which may be also caused by imbalanced training data. Based on the unsupervised PageRank model, our approach achieves 0.5017 of $DCG@25$, which is comparable to the supervised methods reported in Multimedia Grand Challenge. It verifies the effectiveness of our approach in image reranking.

5.4 Show Case and Insights

In our approach, it is very interesting to observe the learned similarity from the user behavioral information. In the *Mahanalobis* matrix M, the meaning of the ith diagonal element denotes the difference brought when we only add/delete the ith visual word in an image. Therefore, the value of the diagonal elements can be regarded as the weight of the corresponding visual words. Figure 7 illustrates four typical visual words with high weights in matrix M. Some representative images are presented at the same time. Among a huge amount of the images that include the visual word, we select the images where the visual word have similar meaning in semantic as the representative images. From Figure 7, we can observe that the visual words that can represent characteristics of objects will obtain high weights in our distance learning approach, such as fruits of plants, petals, eyes of animals, branches of trees.

Figure 8: The observations of the weight of visual words learned in our approach. In each row, The first image and the second image are socially similar, and the first and the third are socially dissimilar. Visual features with high weights are labeled with red rectangles and the ones with low weight are labeled with green rectangles.

Figure 8 reflects another interesting phenomenon. For the three images in the first row, the first one and the second one have a common visual word on the butterfly with high weight; the first one and the third one have a common visual word on the flower with low weight. In human cognition, it is natural that the first and the second are similar because the butterfly is the focus and the flower is not very important. Here the weight of visual word can reflect this well. In the second row, three images are all about dogs. The first and the second have both eyes; the first and the third have similar furs. In emotion level, the first two images give us a feeling of "lovely" but the third image make us fell "lonely". Eyes of the dogs indeed play an important role in the emotion of these images, which is consistent to the weights of visual words, too. Of course, the final image distance is not determined by these several visual words. Besides, due to the semantic gap, most of visual words do not correspond to an object. Here we just try to catch a glance of the relationship between the learning results and human cognition.

6. CONCLUSION

In this paper, we tackled evaluating image distance in the angle of human cognition for image search and recommendation. An Social embedding Image Distance Learning (*SIDL*) approach was proposed to embed collective social behavioral information into visual space. *SIDL* first evaluated the social similarity, where the reliability of social entities were estimated to reduce the noise and unreliability of the social data. Then a margin based metric learning algorithm was designed to learn the social similarity in visual space. In addition, we designed two application scenarios including image recommendation and image reranking where our cognitive distance can be used to reduce the cognition gap. The experiment results demonstrated that the cognitive image distance learning method was effective to learn the social similarity from BoW features. As well as the superiority of the learned image distance in image recommendation and reranking tasks had been proved.

This work is a trial to bridge the visual features and social factors to learn a "different" cognitive image distance. Thus we only use relatively simple methods to combine the multi-

Figure 7: The illustration of the visual words with high weights in our approach. The location of the visual word is marked in a red rectangle in each image.

dimensions of information. In the future, the power of the method can be further increased if we employ more complex features and models, for example, using deep learning on multimodal visual features.

7. ACKNOWLEDGEMENT

This work was supported by National Natural Science Foundation of China, No. 61370022, No. 61303075 and No. 61210008; International Science and Technology Cooperation Program of China, No. 2013DFG12870; National Program on Key Basic Research Project, No. 2011CB302206. This work was also supported in part to Dr. Qi Tian by ARO grant W911NF-12-1-0057, Faculty Research Award by NEC Laboratories of America, respectively. This work was supported in part by NSFC 61128007.Thanks for the support of NExT Research Center funded by MDA, Singapore, under the research grant, WBS:R-252-300-001-490.

8. REFERENCES

[1] http://www.vlfeat.org.

[2] D. Albarracin and R. S. Wyer Jr. The cognitive impact of past behavior: influences on beliefs, attitudes, and future behavioral decisions. *Journal of personality and social psychology*, 79(1):5, 2000.

[3] J. A. Aslam and M. Montague. Models for metasearch. In *ACM SIGIR*, pages 276–284. ACM, 2001.

[4] C. Cortes and V. Vapnik. Support-vector networks. *Machine learning*, 20(3):273–297, 1995.

[5] P. Cui, S.-W. Liu, W.-W. Zhu, H.-B. Luan, T.-S. Chua, and S.-Q. Yang. Social-sensed image search. *ACM TOIS*, 32(2):8, 2014.

[6] L. Fei-Fei, R. Fergus, and P. Perona. Learning generative visual models from few training examples: An incremental bayesian approach tested on 101 object categories. *CVIU*, 106(1):59–70, 2007.

[7] M. Grant and S. Boyd. CVX: Matlab software for disciplined convex programming, version 2.0 beta. http://cvxr.com/cvx, 2013.

[8] M. Guillaumin, T. Mensink, J. Verbeek, and C. Schmid. Tagprop: Discriminative metric learning in nearest neighbor models for image auto-annotation. In *ICCV*, pages 309–316. IEEE, 2009.

[9] S. C. Hoi, W. Liu, and S.-F. Chang. Semi-supervised distance metric learning for collaborative image retrieval. In *CVPR*, pages 1–7. IEEE, 2008.

[10] X.-S. Hua, L. Yang, J. Wang, J. Wang, M. Ye, K. Wang, Y. Rui, and J. Li. Clickage: towards bridging semantic and intent gaps via mining click logs of search engines. In *ACM Multimedia*, pages 243–252, 2013.

[11] B. J. Jansen. Search log analysis: What it is, what's been done, how to do it. *Library & information science research*, 28(3):407–432, 2006.

[12] Y. Jing and S. Baluja. Visualrank: Applying pagerank to large-scale image search. *PAMI*, 30(11):1877–1890, 2008.

[13] M. G. Kendall. A new measure of rank correlation. *Biometrika*, 1938.

[14] X. Li, C. G. Snoek, and M. Worring. Learning social tag relevance by neighbor voting. *TMM*, 11(7):1310–1322, 2009.

[15] S. Liu, P. Cui, H. Luan, W. Zhu, S. Yang, and Q. Tian. Social visual image ranking for web image search. In *MMM*, pages 239–249. Springer, 2013.

[16] D. G. Lowe. Object recognition from local scale-invariant features. In *ICCV*, volume 2, pages 1150–1157. Ieee, 1999.

[17] M. Nei. Genetic distance between populations. *American naturalist*, pages 283–292, 1972.

[18] L. Nie, S. Yan, M. Wang, R. Hong, and T.-S. Chua. Harvesting visual concepts for image search with complex queries. In *ACM Multimedia*, pages 59–68, 2012.

[19] M. Ou, P. Cui, F. Wang, J. Wang, W. Zhu, and S. Yang. Comparing apples to oranges: a scalable solution with heterogeneous hashing. In *ACM SIGKDD*, pages 230–238. ACM, 2013.

[20] L. Page, S. Brin, R. Motwani, and T. Winograd. The pagerank citation ranking: Bringing order to the web. 1999.

[21] M. J. Pazzani. A framework for collaborative, content-based and demographic filtering. *Artificial Intelligence Review*, 13(5-6):393–408, 1999.

[22] Y. Rui, T. S. Huang, M. Ortega, and S. Mehrotra. Relevance feedback: a power tool for interactive content-based image retrieval. *CSVT*, 8(5):644–655, 1998.

[23] M. Schultz and T. Joachims. Learning a distance metric from relative comparisons. In *NIPS*, 2003.

[24] Z. Wang, P. Cui, L. Xie, W. Zhu, Y. Rui, and S. Yang. Bilateral correspondence model for words-and-pictures association in multimedia-rich microblogs. *ACM TOMM*, 10(4):34, 2014.

[25] K. Q. Weinberger and L. K. Saul. Distance metric learning for large margin nearest neighbor classification. *The Journal of Machine Learning Research*, 10:207–244, 2009.

[26] L. Yang and R. Jin. Distance metric learning: A comprehensive survey. *Michigan State Universiy*, 2, 2006.

[27] Z.-J. Zha, L. Yang, T. Mei, M. Wang, and Z. Wang. Visual query suggestion. In *ACM Multimedia*, pages 15–24, 2009.

[28] H. Zhang, Z.-J. Zha, S. Yan, J. Bian, and T.-S. Chua. Attribute feedback. In *ACM Multimedia*, pages 79–88. ACM, 2012.

[29] S. Zhang, Q. Tian, G. Hua, Q. Huang, and S. Li. Descriptive visual words and visual phrases for image applications. In *ACM Multimedia*, pages 75–84. ACM, 2009.

[30] L. Zheng and S. Wang. Visual phraselet: Refining spatial constraints for large scale image search. *Signal Processing Letters, IEEE*, 20(4):391–394, 2013.

Improving Content-based and Hybrid Music Recommendation using Deep Learning

Xinxi Wang and Ye Wang
School of Computing, National University of Singapore
{wangxinxi, wangye}@comp.nus.edu.sg

ABSTRACT

Existing content-based music recommendation systems typically employ a *two-stage* approach. They first extract traditional audio content features such as Mel-frequency cepstral coefficients and then predict user preferences. However, these traditional features, originally not created for music recommendation, cannot capture all relevant information in the audio and thus put a cap on recommendation performance. Using a novel model based on deep belief network and probabilistic graphical model, we unify the two stages into an automated process that simultaneously learns features from audio content and makes personalized recommendations. Compared with existing deep learning based models, our model outperforms them in both the warm-start and cold-start stages without relying on collaborative filtering (CF). We then present an efficient hybrid method to seamlessly integrate the automatically learnt features and CF. Our hybrid method not only significantly improves the performance of CF but also outperforms the traditional feature based hybrid method.

Categories and Subject Descriptors

H.3.3 [**Information Search and Retrieval**]: Retrieval models; H.5.5 [**Sound and Music Computing**]: [Modeling, Signal analysis, synthesis and processing]

General Terms

Model, Algorithm, Experimentation

Keywords

music recommendation; deep learning; feature learning; probabilistic graphical model

1. INTRODUCTION

A music recommendation system automatically recommends songs that match a user's music preference from a large database. The quality of a match is influenced by many factors concerning the user (e.g., personality, emotional states, activities, social environment) and the song (e.g., music audio content, novelty, diversity).

Among song-related factors, *music audio content* is of great importance. In most cases, we like/dislike a song as a result of characteristics from its audio content, such as vocal, melody, rhythm, timbre, genre, instrument, or lyrics. Without listening to the content, we know almost nothing about the song's quality, let alone whether we would like it. Because music content largely determines our preferences, it should be able to provide good predictive power for recommendation.

However, existing music recommenders relying on music audio content usually produce unsatisfactory recommendation performance. They all follow a *two-stage* approach: extracting traditional audio content features such as Mel-frequency cepstral coefficients (MFCC), then using these features to predict user preferences [1, 2, 3]. Traditional audio content features, however, were not created for music recommendation or music related tasks (For example, MFCC was originally used for speech recognition [4]). They only became attached to music recommendation after the discovery that they can also describe high-level music concepts like genre, timbre, and melody. Using such features can result in poor recommendation performance in two ways. First, the high-level concepts cannot be described accurately due to the so-called *semantic gap* [5]. Second, even if the feature descriptions are accurate, the high-level concepts may not be essential to the user's music preferences. Therefore, traditional features could fail to take into account information relevant to music recommendation.

We believe that the key to an effective content-based music recommendation method is a set of good content features. *Manually* crafting such features is possible but time consuming and painstaking. A better approach is to combine the existing two-stage approach into a unified and automated process: features are *learnt* automatically and directly from audio content to maximize recommendation performance. Recent development in *deep learning* techniques [6] has made such a unified approach possible. In fact, people have already started using deep learning to learn features for other music tasks such as music genre classification [7] and music emotion prediction [8] with promising results.

Content-based methods also frequently combines *collaborative filtering* (CF), which recommends songs based on the interests of like-minded users. Most existing recommenders are based on CF because of its superior accuracy [9]. How-

MM'14, November 3–7, 2014, Orlando, Florida, USA.

http://dx.doi.org/10.1145/2647868.2654940 .

ever, as it depends solely on usage data, CF is powerless when confronted with the new-song problem — it cannot recommend songs without prior usage history. Content-based methods do not suffer from this problem because they can predict based on a song's audio content, which is usually available for online merchants. Therefore, content-based methods can rescue CF in the new-song scenario. Because CF and content-based methods take advantage of different dimensions of information, it is possible to combine them into a *hybrid method* for better predictions.

Thus motivated, we first develop a content-based model that automatically and simultaneously extracts features from audio content and makes personalized recommendations. We then develop a hybrid method to combine both CF and content features. Specifically, this paper seeks to make the following contributions:

- *Content-based method*: We develop a novel content-based recommendation model based on probabilistic graphical model and the *deep belief network* (DBN) proposed by the deep learning community [10]. It unifies feature learning and recommendation. While it does not rely on collaborative filtering, it outperforms baseline content-based models, which rely on CF, in both the *cold-start* stage and *warm-start* stage.

- *Hybrid method:* To combine CF and music content, we apply the automatically learnt audio features to an efficient hybrid model. Experimental results show that the learnt features complement CF and also outperform traditional features in hybrid methods.

The remainder of this paper is organized as follows. Section 2 briefly reviews the prevailing method in music recommendation and briefly introduces deep belief network as well as its applications in music tasks. Section 3 describes our content-based and hybrid recommendation model and discusses the baseline content-based model used in our experiments. Section 4 describes our extensive experimental evaluations. Section 5 concludes this work and discusses future research directions.

2. RELATED WORK

We will enumerate the current music recommendation techniques before introducing deep belief network and other deep learning techniques. We will then review applications of deep learning techniques in music tasks including music recommendation.

2.1 Music recommendation

Currently music recommender systems can be classified into four categories: collaborative filtering (CF), content-based methods, context-based methods and hybrid methods.

Collaborative filtering recommends songs by considering the preferences of other like-minded users. For instance, if user A and B have similar music preferences, then songs liked by A but not yet considered by B will be recommended to B. The state-of-the-art methods for performing CF are based on matrix factorization (MF), which is well summarized by [11]. In Section 3.1, we will elaborate on one of the MF method, probabilistic matrix factorization.

Content-based methods recommend songs that have similar audio content to the user's preferred songs. Most existing content-based methods first extract traditional audio features such as MFCC and then recommend based on the similarities between the feature vectors of songs. However, the similarity metrics used are often ad hoc, because they are not optimized with respect to the recommendation objective and are usually chosen from a very restrictive set of distance functions such as Euclidean distance [12, 13], Earth Mover's distance [14], or Pearson correlation distance [15, 16]. While two recent works tried to employ machine learning techniques to automatically learn a similarity metric [17, 18], they still relied on traditional features. Attempts have been made to perform feature selection or transformation on traditional features [13, 15], but they remain suboptimal as the traditional features may fail to take into account essential information.

Context-based methods recommend songs to match various aspects of the user context (e.g., activities, environment, or physiological states [3, 19]). They have become increasingly popular in recent years with the advent of sensor-rich and computationally powerful smartphones.

Hybrid methods combine two or more of the above methods. Hybrid CF and content-based methods[1] have been explored extensively in recommenders for other products such as movies [20, 21, 22, 23]. Although such approaches can potentially generalize to music recommendation, we do not use them due to efficiency issues: (1) they use full Bayesian inference [20, 22, 23] or Monte Carlo simulation [24] and are thus much slower than our algorithm; (2) they have been applied to a dataset with thousands of users and items and 1 million ratings, while our dataset has hundreds of thousands of users and items and 28 million ratings. Directly applying these algorithms on our dataset is thus not trivial.

To our knowledge, Yoshii *et al.* [2] are the first to combine CF and content-based methods in music recommendation. In this work, MFCC features were quantized into codewords and used together with rating data in the three-way aspect model, a probabilistic model, originally proposed in [25] for bibliographic recommendation. Almost concurrently, Li *et al.* [26] built a probabilistic hybrid approach to unify CF and traditional features.

While Yoshii and Li's works were promising starting points for *model-based* hybrid methods, subsequent studies all focused on content similarity based methods. Castillo [27] proposed a hybrid recommender by linearly combining the results of a content similarity based recommender and a collaborative filtering based one. Tiemann *et al.* [28] and Shruthi *et al.* [29] developed approaches that successfully fused CF and content similarities but revealed little information about the fusion process. Bu *et al.* [30] and Shao *et al.* [31] used hyper-graphs to combine usage data and content similarity information. Domingues *et al.* [32] first obtained song similarities based on CF and content features separately before integrating the two kinds of similarities into a hybrid similarity metric. Similarly, Bogdanov *et al.* [16] also combined content similarity and Last.fm's similarity, which is likely based on CF. Combining the similarities of different modalities is relatively easy and may work to some extent in practice, but the similarity metrics are usually selected in an ad hoc way.

[1]In subsequent part of this paper, we will use "hybrid method" to refer to "hybrid collaborative filtering and content-based method".

To summarize, most existing content-based methods and all hybrid methods use traditional features. This could change with the advent of deep learning, which we will introduce in the following section.

2.2 Deep learning

Deep learning methods mimic the architecture of mammalian brains. They can automatically learn features at multiple levels directly from low-level data without resorting to manually crafted features. We give a very brief introduction to *deep belief networks* (DBN), which will be used in this work, and refer the readers to Bengio *et al.* [33] for a more comprehensive review of deep learning techniques.

A deep belief network is a generative probabilistic graphical model with many layers of hidden nodes at the top and one layer of observations at the bottom. Connections are allowed between two adjacent layers but not between the same layer. Connections of the top two layers are undirected while the rest are directed. Jointly training all layers is computationally intractable, so Hinton *et al.* [10] developed an efficient algorithm to train the model layer by layer from bottom to top in a greedy manner. This unsupervised training process is usually called *pre-training*. Afterward, the DBN can be converted to a *multi-layer perceptron* (MLP) for supervised learning. This stage is called *finetune* and is usually implemented as *back-propagation*. It is also possible to directly train a MLP using back-propagation without the pre-training step, but this is prone to overfitting, especially when the MLP is deep (has more than two hidden layers). Pre-training may help by implicitly effecting a form of regularization [34].

2.3 Deep learning in music related tasks

The field of music information retrieval (MIR) has only recently begun to embrace the power of deep learning. Lee *et al.* [35] used a convolutional deep belief network to extract features in an unsupervised fashion for tasks such as music genre classification. Results show that the automatically learnt features significantly outperforms MFCC. In Hamel *et al.* [7], deep belief network was used for music genre classification and autotagging, with performance surpassing that based on MFCC and MIM feature sets. In [36, 37], Humphrey *et al.* proposed that the traditional two-stage machine learning process — feature extraction and classification/regression — should be conducted simultaneously. To classify the rhythm style of a piece of music, Pikrakis applied DBN to engineered features representing rhythmic signatures [38]. Schmidt *et al.* [39] found that DBN easily outperforms traditional features in understanding rhythm and melody based on music audio content. Other feature learning techniques like sparse coding also started to be used in music tasks. In [40], a sparse coding based approach was used to learn interpretable audio features in an unsupervised way, and good performance was achieved in music genre classification.

To the best of our knowledge, the first deep learning based approach for music recommendation was almost concurrently proposed by Oord *et al.* [41] within the last year. They first conducted matrix factorization to obtain latent features for all songs, and then used deep learning to map audio content to those latent features. Comparisons between their methods and ours will be detailed later.

Symbol	Description
u	User u
v	Song v
r_{uv}	The rating that user u gives to song v
γ_u	The latent features for u estimated by MF
y_v	The latent features for v estimated by MF
β_u	User u's preference of content features
μ	All users' common preference
x_v	The learnt content features for song v
Ω	The parameters of DBN
$\mathcal{U}, \mathcal{V}$	User and song sets, respectively
U, V	The number of users and songs, respectively
I	All user, song pairs in the training dataset

Table 1: Frequently used symbols

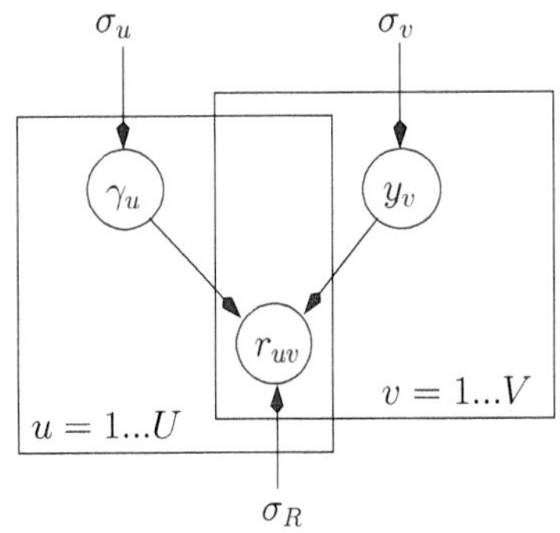

Figure 1: Probabilistic matrix factorization

To summarize, all content-based music recommendation methods except [41] and all hybrid methods are based on traditional features, which are not created for music recommendation. To enable simultaneous feature extraction and recommendation, we will build a unified model for pure content-based recommendation. We will also show that the automatically learnt features can be applied to our efficient hybrid method.

3. RECOMMENDATION MODELS

In this section, we will introduce our content-based model and hybrid model, as well as the two baseline content-based models with which to compare our models.

3.1 Collaborative filtering via probabilistic matrix factorization

Collaborative filtering is a popular recommendation method. The state-of-the-art CF methods are based on matrix factorization (MF). A MF method named probabilistic matrix factorization (PMF) [42] is used in this paper for its simplicity, accuracy, and efficiency. In addition, PMF's principled probabilistic interpretation enables it to be extended to incorporate content information more easily.

PMF assumes that each user $u \in \mathcal{U}$ and song $v \in \mathcal{V}$ can be represented as latent feature vectors γ_u and y_v, respectively. The rating that user u gives to song v is the inner product of γ_u and y_v. The training data is usually very sparse, and without regularization the model is crippled by severe overfitting. Therefore, Gaussian priors are used for both γ_u and y_v as regularization. Formally, the model is specified as the

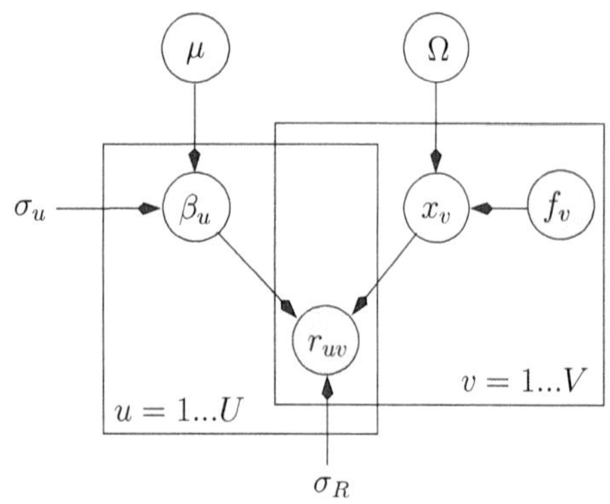

Figure 2: Hierarchical linear model with deep belief network

following[2] (see graphical representation in Figure 1):

$$r_{uv}|\gamma_u, y_v, \sigma_R \sim \mathcal{N}\left(\gamma_u' y_v, \sigma_R^2\right)$$
$$\gamma_u|\sigma_u \sim \mathcal{N}\left(\mathbf{0}, \sigma_u^2 \mathbf{I}\right)$$
$$y_v|\sigma_v \sim \mathcal{N}\left(\mathbf{0}, \sigma_v^2 \mathbf{I}\right)$$

The negative log-likelihood of the model can be simplified as Equation (1), where I is the user-song pairs in the training set. λ_u and λ_v are usually tuned using a validation data set [42].

$$L_{\text{MF}} = \sum_{u,v \in I} \left(r_{uv} - \gamma_u' y_v\right)^2 + \lambda_u \sum_u \|\gamma_u\|^2 + \lambda_v \sum_v \|y_v\|^2 \tag{1}$$

Since a new user/song without rating data has no vector representation in the model, their ratings cannot be predicted. This cold-start problem is endemic to all CF methods. In the following sections, we will introduce our solution to the new-song problem.

3.2 Content-based Music Recommendation

3.2.1 *Hierarchical linear model with deep belief network (HLDBN)*

We assume that the audio content of song v is f_v, and its automatically learnt feature vector is x_v. User u's music preference is represented as a vector β_u. The rating that u gives to song v, denoted as r_{uv}, is the inner product of x_v and β_u. We use μ to represent all users' common music preference, which is the mean of all users' β_u-s. The model (Figure 2) is formulated as:

$$r_{uv} \sim \mathcal{N}\left(\beta_u' x_v, \sigma_R^2\right)$$
$$\beta_u \sim \mathcal{N}\left(\mu, \sigma_u^2 \mathbf{I}\right)$$
$$x_v = \text{DBN}\left(f_v; \Omega\right)$$

σ_u indicates the variance of user preferences. The smaller the σ_u, the more similar the user preferences are to the common preference μ and the more strongly β_u is regularized. The Gaussian prior for β_u models user common interests as *one* cluster. However, users of different genders, ages and different culture backgrounds could form different groups. To capture this grouping effect, we could change the single Gaussian prior to a mixture of Gaussians. We tried such a prior and used Monte Carlo Expectation Maximization to estimate the parameters, but it resulted in overfitting. Therefore, we chose single Gaussian as the prior.

Automatic learning of features x_v from music content f_v is achieved by deep belief network (DBN), which is briefly introduced in Section 2.2 and 2.3. DBN can be treated as a very flexible deterministic function that maps f_v to x_v. It has hundreds of thousands, perhaps even millions, of parameters (denoted as Ω) to be learnt from training data. We assume that r_{uv} follows a normal distribution to account for the noise in user ratings.[3]

Learning - Maximum Likelihood Estimation (MLE) is used to train the model. The negative log-likelihood of the model is shown in Equation (2), where irrelevant constants are omitted. The hyperparameter λ is the ratio σ_u^2/σ_R^2, with a larger λ indicating stronger regularization.

$$L_{\text{HLDBN}} = \sum_{u,v \in I} \left(r_{uv} - \beta_u' \text{DBN}\left(f_v, \Omega\right)\right)^2 + \lambda \sum_u \|\beta_u - \mu\|^2 \tag{2}$$

Since Ω consists of a large amount of parameters, directly optimizing L_{HLDBN} using gradient descent could easily overfit. Following the DBN training procedure established in [10], we first pre-train the DBN as stacked layers of Restricted Boltzmann Machines in an unsupervised fashion and then optimize L_{HLDBN} using mini-batch stochastic gradient descent, where the gradient descent part of DBN is implemented as back-propagation.[4]

Unlike traditional two-stage methods, our model automatically and simultaneously optimizes audio features (x_v) and user preference parameters (β_u-s). This provides a unified and more principled method to content-based recommendation.

Prediction - After the learning phase, the rating that user u gives to song v can be estimated as $\hat{r}_{uv} = \gamma_u' \text{DBN}(f_v, \Omega)$. As the predictions are based on audio content, new songs can be recommended accurately as well.

3.2.2 *Baseline models*

We now turn our attention to the two content-based approaches proposed in Oord *et al.* and hereby used as our baseline methods [41]. The models are based on convolutional neural network (CNN), another popular deep learning method. To make their approach directly comparable with ours, we replace CNN with DBN while keeping the other parts unchanged.

Content-based baseline model 1 (CB1) - This model first uses PMF to learn latent features γ_u and y_v for all users and songs and then trains a DBN to map from audio content to the latent features y_v. Formally, the objective can be formulated as:

$$\min_{\Omega} \sum_v \left(y_v - \text{DBN}\left(f_v, \Omega\right)\right)^2 \tag{3}$$

[2] $\mathcal{N}(a, b)$ is the normal distribution with mean a and variance b. $x \sim p$ indicates that x satisfies the distribution p or x is drawn/generated from p.

[3] The normal distribution may be replaced with a softmax or probit model. In this paper, we follow PMF and use the normal distribution to keep the model clean.

[4] For the following DBN-based models, the same training approach is used.

Let $x_v = \text{DBN}(f_v, \Omega)$; the rating that user u gives to song v can be predicted as $\hat{r}_{uv} = \gamma_u' x_v$. This model, however, fails because of a fundamental flaw shown in Theorem 1.

THEOREM 1. *Model CB1 does not minimize the sum of squared errors of predicted ratings.*

PROOF. Let $\epsilon_v = y_v - x_v$. The optimization objective Equation (3) is equivalent to

$$\min_{\Omega} \sum_{v} \|\epsilon_v\|^2 \tag{4}$$

Instead of predicting the latent features, our *true objective* is to predict ratings, so we actually need to minimize the sum of squared errors of predicted ratings:

$$\min_{\Omega} \sum_{u,v \in I} \left(r_{uv} - \gamma_u' x_v\right)^2 \tag{5}$$

which can be transformed as:

$$\begin{aligned} &\min_{\Omega} \sum_{u,v \in I} \left(r_{uv} - \gamma_u' x_v\right)^2 \\ =&\min_{\Omega} \sum_{u,v \in I} \left(r_{uv} - \gamma_u' \left(y_v - \epsilon_v\right)\right)^2 \\ =&\min_{\Omega} \sum_{v} \epsilon_v \left(\sum_{u:u,v \in I} \gamma_u \gamma_u' \right) \epsilon_v' + 2 \sum_{u:u,v \in I} \gamma_u' \left(r_{uv} - \gamma_u' y_v\right) \epsilon_v \end{aligned} \tag{6}$$

Since ϵ_v is not constrained because MLPs are universal approximators [43], we can see that Equation (6) and (4) have different optimal solutions. □

The original model in Oord et al. [41] uses weighted sum of squared errors. Following the same approach, we can prove that CB1 does not minimize the weighted version, either.

Content-based baseline model 2 (CB2) - This is the other model proposed by Oord et al. [41]. It is presented as the following,

$$\min_{\Omega} \sum_{u,v \in I} \left(r_{uv} - \gamma_u' \text{DBN}(f_v, \Omega)\right)^2 \tag{7}$$

where γ_u is obtained from MF beforehand. Rating r_{uv} is predicted as $\gamma_u' x_v$, where $x_v = \text{DBN}(f_v, \Omega)$.

This model uses the correct objective and thus does not have the issue of CB1 discussed in Theorem 1. However, it lacks regularization on the parameters, which may cause overfitting. We will show this empirically in Section 4.5.

Another issue of both CB1 and CB2 is that they are directly based on the results of MF and thus their prediction results are strongly correlated with the collaborative filtering (CF) results. As we will show in Section 4.5 and 4.6, this hinders us from combining CB1 or CB2 with CF to form an effective hybrid approach.

3.3 Hybrid CF and content-based music recommendation

Collaborative filtering and content-based methods use different information. To fuse all the information available for more accurate predictions, we can combine the two in a hybrid method.

Information fusion has been studied extensively in other domains such as sensor fusion and multimedia information fusion. There are mainly two approaches for our problem. Decision fusion combines the prediction results from existing CF and content-based methods. On the other hand, data fusion develops a new unified model to incorporate both CF and audio content. Our hybrid method is based on the latter, but it also uses the features learnt by HLDBN.

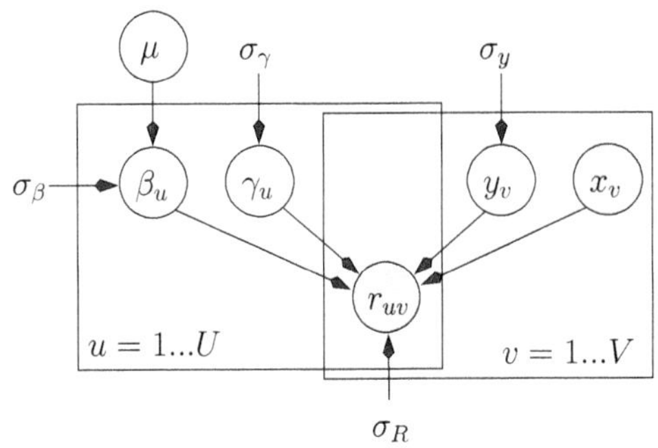

Figure 3: Hybrid recommendation

In our hybrid model (Figure 3), we assume that the audio features x_v for every song is already known. γ_u, y_v and β_u are not directly adopted from the results of PMF and HLDBN but need to be jointly learnt from data. Rating r_{uv} is predicted by the sum of the CF part $\gamma_u' y_v$ and the content part $\beta_u' x_v$. The priors for γ_u and y_v are set following the PMF model, and β_u the HLDBN model.

$$\begin{aligned} r_{uv}|\beta_u, x_v, \gamma_u, y_v, \sigma_R &\sim \mathcal{N}\left(\beta_u' x_v + \gamma_u' y_v, \sigma_R^2\right) \\ \beta_u|\sigma_\beta &\sim \mathcal{N}\left(\mu, \sigma_\beta^2 \mathbf{I}\right) \\ \gamma_u|\sigma_u &\sim \mathcal{N}\left(\mathbf{0}, \sigma_\gamma^2\right) \\ y_v|\sigma_v &\sim \mathcal{N}\left(\mathbf{0}, \sigma_y^2\right) \end{aligned} \tag{8}$$

The negative log-likelihood can be simplified as the following, where $\lambda_\beta = \sigma_R^2/\sigma_\beta^2$, $\lambda_\gamma = \sigma_R^2/\sigma_\gamma^2$, and $\lambda_y = \sigma_R^2/\sigma_y^2$.

$$\begin{aligned} L_{\text{Hybrid}} = &\sum_{u,v \in I} \left(r_{uv} - \beta_u' x_v - \gamma_u' y_v\right)^2 + \lambda_\beta \|\beta - \mu\|_F^2 \\ &+ \lambda_\gamma \|\gamma\|_F^2 + \lambda_y \|y\|_F^2 \end{aligned}$$

L_{Hybrid} is not a convex function, but if we fix any three of β_u, μ, γ_u, and y_v, it is convex and the optimal solution can be obtained in closed form. We thus optimize L_{Hybrid} using the alternative least square (ALS) algorithm: we first set the derivatives of L_{Hybrid} with respect to each of the four parameters to zero and solve the equations, which results in the following four updating formulas. We then iterate them until L_{Hybrid} converges or until the prediction performance on a validation set reaches the highest point.

$$\begin{aligned} \beta_u &\leftarrow \left(\sum_{v:u,v \in I} x_v x_v' + \lambda_\beta \mathbf{I} \right)^{-1} \left(\lambda_\beta \mu + \sum_{v:u,v \in I} \left(r_{uv} - \gamma_u' y_v\right) x_v \right) \\ \gamma_u &\leftarrow \left(\sum_{v:u,v \in I} y_v y_v' + \lambda_\gamma \mathbf{I} \right)^{-1} \left(\sum_{v:u,v \in I} \left(r_{uv} - \beta_u' x_v\right) y_v \right) \\ y_v &\leftarrow \left(\sum_{u:u,v \in I} \gamma_u \gamma_u' + \lambda_y \mathbf{I} \right)^{-1} \left(\sum_{u:u,v \in I} \left(r_{uv} - \beta_u' x_v\right) \gamma_u \right) \\ \mu &\leftarrow \frac{1}{U} \sum_{u \in \mathcal{U}} \beta_u \end{aligned}$$

To achieve faster convergence, γ_u, y_v are first initialized using PMF.

We could create a pure data fusion model by adding $x_v = \text{DBN}(f_v, \Omega)$ after Equation 8, and optimizing Ω jointly with other parameters. However, we found its performance inferior to the one above.

4. EXPERIMENTS

4.1 Dataset

Deep belief network has a large number of parameters, and a large amount of data is required to adequately train such a model. We chose The Echo Nest Taste Profile Subset [9] because it is the largest publicly available music recommendation dataset as far as we know. The original dataset has 1,019,318 users, 384,546 songs, and 48,373,586 listening histories. We were able to crawl preview audio clips with length of about half a minute from 7digital[5] for 282,508 of the songs. We selected the top 100,000 users mainly to reduce the training time.

Implicit feedback - From the Taste Profile Subset, we know the songs that a user has listened to, so the dataset can be presented as a set of (user, song) pairs. We assign a rating of 1 to each pair and use them as the positive samples. To generate negative samples, we use the well-established User-Oriented Sampling method built in [44]: for user u who listened to songs $\mathcal{V}_u$, we randomly sampled $|\mathcal{V}_u|$ songs from $\mathcal{V}\backslash\mathcal{V}_u$ and assign a rating 0 to each generated (user, song) pair. We now have equal number of positive and negative samples for every user.

Instead of using the sampling method described above, HLDBN could theoretically use the weighted matrix factorization method proposed in Hu *et al.* [45] to directly handle the implicit feedback. While the method may be more accurate, the computational overhead is prohibitive: there will be about 2.83×10^{10} rating data points, which can make all algorithms about 1000 times slower and take years to finish.

Table 2 gives the statistics of the final dataset. The density of the rating matrix is only 0.1%.

Splitting the dataset - The dataset was then split into 5 disjoint sets: the training set, warm-start validation/test sets, and cold-start validation/test sets. All users and songs in the warm-start sets need to be in the training set. To simulate the new-song problem, songs in the cold-start validation/test sets cannot exist in the training set, while all users in the cold-start sets still need to be in the training set because the new user problem is not our focus. The statistics of the five datasets are shown in Table 2, where WS and CS stand for warm-start and cold-start, respectively.

Audio content preprocessing - We first converted all audio clips to WAV files with mono channel, 8kHz sampling rate, and 16 bit depth. We then randomly sampled a 5-second continuous segment from each audio clip, because directly using the half-minute clips requires too much memory and computation while segments shorter than 5 seconds may lose too much information. We next converted each 5-second segment into a 166×120 spectrogram (30ms window, no overlap). PCA was then used to transform the spectrograms into vectors whose dimensions were ranked according to their significance. The top-K dimensions were finally normalized to have zero mean and unit variance and fed into

[5]http://7digital.com

	# of users	# of songs	# of ratings
Total	100,000	282,508	28,258,926
Train	100,000	262,508	18,382,954
WS Valid	100,000	262,454	3,939,204
WS Test	100,000	262,457	3,939,206
CS Valid	99,963	10,000	1,025,654
CS Test	99,933	10,000	971,908

Table 2: Dataset statistics

DBN. The normalization step is required because we use Gaussian-Bernoulli RBM for the DBN's input layer [46]. K, the dimensionality of f_v and the number of nodes of the DBN's input layer, is determined by a validation step.

4.2 Implementation and Training of deep belief network

We implemented our DBN using Theano[6], because it supports convenient GPU programming and automatic symbolic differentiation. Since our input for DBN is continuous, we used the Gaussian-Bernoulli RBM for the input layer and binary RBMs for the rest [46].

Training DBN on CPUs is extremely slow. GPUs with large memory are thus indispensable in the deep learning experiments. Training and testing of every model takes three to four days using a single GPU with 6GB GPU memory. Since DBN has many hyperparameters that could have great impact on the prediction performance, tuning seems unavoidable at this stage. Sequentially trying each configuration of the hyperparameters on a single GPU is too time consuming. We thus utilized a GPU cluster with 15 computing nodes, each of which containing two Tesla M2090 GPU cards.

Mini-batch stochastic gradient descent was used as the training algorithm. We cannot transfer all data into one GPU because of its memory limit. Sequentially transferring one batch after computing the previous batch is slow because of the low bandwidth of the bus between the GPU memory and main memory. Our solution is to use multithreading to enable computing and transferring next batch at the same time.

4.3 Evaluation Metrics

The Root Mean Square Error (RMSE) metric was used to evaluate most models in this paper. It is defined as:

$$\text{RMSE} = \sqrt{\frac{\sum_{i=1}^{N}(\hat{r}_i - r_i)^2}{N}}$$

where r_i, $\hat{r}_i$ are the true and predicted ratings, respectively. We prefer RMSE to the truncated mAP used in the million song dataset challenge [9] because our models are regression models, for which RMSE is a more accurate and sensible metric [9]. Moreover, RMSE is feasible in our case because the sampling step in the preprocessing of the dataset described in Section 4.1 have converted all implicit feedback into explicit ratings.

For models which rank songs instead of predicting ratings, we still resort to truncated mAP. mAP was originally widely used in information retrieval to measure the ranking quality of search results. Suppose the system recommends user u a

[6]http://deeplearning.net/software/theano/

list of songs $l_{u,1}, l_{u,2} \ldots l_{u,M}$, we first define the precision-at-k (P_k) metric as:

$$P_k(u, l_u) = \frac{1}{k} \sum_{i=1}^{k} r_{u,l_{u,i}}$$

Then we define the average precision as the following,

$$\text{AP}(u, l_u) = \frac{1}{n_u} \sum_{k=1}^{M} r_{u,l_{u,k}} P_k(u, l_u)$$

where n_u is the number of songs preferred by user u, i.e. $n_u = \sum_{v=1}^{V} r_{u,v}$. Finally, mAP is defined as:

$$\text{mAP} = \frac{1}{U} \sum_{u=1}^{U} \text{AP}(u, l_u)$$

4.4 Probabilistic Matrix Factorization

Because CB1, CB2 and the hybrid method all depend on the results of PMF, we trained several PMF models with different configurations using the Alternative Least Square algorithm. The training procedure was stopped when the performance on the warm-start validation set converged. We found that the best performance on the validation set was achieved when the dimensionality of the latent features was 100 and $\lambda_u = \lambda_v = 4$. Further increasing the dimensionality of the latent features brought little improvement.

The results for CF are shown in Table 4. We should note that a rating predictor which randomly generates 0s or 1s have RMSE = 0.707, and a mean predictor which constantly gives 0.5s has RMSE = 0.5.

There is no result for PMF on the cold-start validation/test sets, as PMF cannot recommend during the cold-start stage (see Section 3.1).

4.5 Content-based music recommendation

Comparisons between deep learning based methods and traditional features (e.g. MFCC) based methods have been conducted in [41]. We avoid repeating those comparisons and only compare HLDBN with CB1 and CB2.

Because the objectives for the warm-start and cold-start scenarios are different, we discuss them separately in the following two sections.

4.5.1 *Warm-start*

Evaluating the performance of a content-based model in the warm-start stage is important for two reasons. First, the warm-start stage is a crucial stage to a recommender. Second, a content-based model performing well in the warm-start stage would serve as a better building block for a good hybrid model, whose performance in the warm-start stage is determined by both the collaborative filtering part and the content part. In the warm-start stage, all songs in the validation/test sets are in the training set. Therefore, whether the content-based model generalizes to new songs or not is not of our focus.

To determine the structure of DBN, we tried different number of layers as well as different number of nodes for each layer. For HLDBN, we finally used DBN with four layers (the input layer included), each containing 500 nodes. Increasing the number of nodes of each layer does not produce better results. Unsupervised pre-training was conducted for 200 iterations. The mini-batch size for both pre-training and finetune is 5000. The learning rate for the Gaussian-Bernoulli RBM is 5×10^{-5} and binary RBM 10^{-2}. The finetune learning rate of the supervised training stage is 0.5, and the regularization parameter $\lambda = 0.1$. The finetune process was stopped when the model's predictive performance on the warm-start validation set started to drop.

	Warm start		Cold start	
	Valid	Test	Valid	Test
PMF	0.270	0.270	-	-
HLDBN	**0.323**	**0.323**	**0.477**	**0.478**
CB1	0.679	0.679	0.688	0.669
CB2	0.325	0.325	0.495	0.495
Mean	0.500	0.500	0.500	0.500

Table 3: Predictive performance of CF and content-based methods using DBN (Root Mean Squared Error).

For CB1 and CB2, the number of nodes of their output layer is determined by the dimensionality of the PMF's latent features, i.e. 100 (see Section 4.4). Other layers use the same configuration as HLDBN.

The results of HLDBN, CB1, and CB2 are shown in Table 3. Although HLDBN only slightly outperforms CB2, we should notice that while CB2 is trained based on the results of PMF, HLDBN is a unified model and does not rely on PMF, which makes it easier to train and more principled.

The results also show that CB1 has RMSE larger than 0.5, which is worse than the trivial mean predictor. In fact, the RMSE of CB1 on the training set is also as large as 0.7, and increasing the size of DBN does not lead to improvement. These observations support our assertion in Section 3.2.2 that CB1 used the incorrect objective.

4.5.2 *Cold-start*

The major practical advantage of content-based methods over CF is that content-based methods work even in the new-song scenario. Thus an effective content-based model should generalize well to new songs.

Most experimental settings are the same as those in the warm-start evaluation except the configuration of DBN. Even with pre-training, large DBN is prone to overfitting. We tried many configurations and decided on using four layers, each of which contains 300 nodes. Increasing the number of input nodes makes the model overfit.

The results are shown in Table 3. We can see that HLDBN outperforms CB1 and CB2 significantly. CB1 has very poor results due to its incorrect objective function. CB2 performs only slightly better than the mean predictor. We tried to reduce the size of its DBN and also applied the deep convolutional neural network directly on the spectrogram following the same settings as [41] (the RMSEs of CB2+CNN on WS Valid, WS Test, CS Valid, and CS Test are 0.325, 0.326, 0.492, and 0.492, respectively), but there were no significant changes, which suggests that CB2 does not generalize well. This could be due to the lack of proper regularization. Therefore, among the three models, only HLDBN generalizes to new songs.

4.6 Hybrid music recommendation

The focus of our hybrid method is to boost the recommendation performance in the warm-start stage instead of solving the new-song problem, for which we can simply fall

	WS Valid	WS Test
Hybrid w/ HLDBN	**0.255**	**0.255**
Hybrid w/ CB2	0.270	0.270

Table 4: Predictive performance of our hybrid method with the features learnt by our HLDBN model and the baseline CB2 model (Root Mean Squared Error). WS stands for warm-start.

	WS Valid	WS Test
PMF	0.0109	0.0110
Hybrid w/ HLDBN	**0.0132**	**0.0131**
AM w/ traditional features	0.0108	0.0108
AM w/ features from HLDBN	0.0123	0.0120

Table 5: Comparison between hybrid methods using features learnt from HLDBN and traditional features (mean Average Precision).

back to HLDBN. It is also possible to build a model to handle both scenarios seamlessly, and we leave it as future work.

As CB1 performs worse than the trivial mean predictor, it makes little sense to train a hybrid model based on its learnt features. We thus only consider the hybrid methods based on the features learnt by HLDBN and CB2. Table 4 shows that the hybrid approach based on CB2's features does not bring any improvement over PMF's results shown in Table 3. This is because the content features learnt by CB2 are highly correlated with the latent features from PMF and do not provide much new information. On the other hand, HLDBN does not rely on PMF, and its learnt features have incorporated audio content information that PMF fails to take into account. The results show that HLDBN performs significantly better than PMF.

To show that the learnt features are better than traditional features in hybrid music recommendation, the aspect model (AM, introduced in Section 2.1), one of the two existing model-based hybrid music recommenders (Section 2.1), was chosen as the baseline. Because AM ranks songs instead of predicting ratings, we switched our evaluation metric from RMSE to truncated mAP, for which the top-500 recommended songs were considered.

For AM, we first extracted a rich set of traditional features. Marsyas [47] was used on the 30-second WAV files described in Section 4.1. A window size of 512 was used without overlapping. Descriptions about the features are shown in Table 6. Because AM cannot handle continuous features directly, we built a codebook using k-means based on 8 million feature vectors from 10,000 randomly sampled songs. K-means was used instead of GMM in [2] mainly for better efficiency. Hadoop[7] was used to handle the large amount of data and computation. Finally, feature vectors of each song were quantized as codewords, which were further aggregated into a vector with each element representing occurrences of the corresponding codeword. Other parts remain the same as [2]. To use HLDBN's learnt features in AM, we also quantized the learnt features and aggregated each song's codewords into one vector.

The results of our hybrid method and AM are shown in Table 5. We can see that AM with traditional features performs slightly worse than PMF. However, AM performs significantly better with the features learnt by HLDBN. This may suggest that the automatically learnt features are more effective than the traditional features in hybrid music recommendation.

[7]http://hadoop.apache.org/

Feature name	Description
MFCC	Mel-Frequency Cepstral Coefficients. It models the auditory perception system and is widely used in speech and music domain.
Zero Crossings	The rate of sign-changes along a signal.
Spectral Centroid	The "center of mass" of the spectrum. Measures the brightness of the sound.
Spectral Flux	The squared change in normalized amplitude between two consecutive time frames. It measures how much the sound changes between frames.
Spectral Rolloff	Measures the amount of the right-skewness of the power spectrum.
Spectral Flatness Measure	Measures how much the audio signal sounds like a tone instead of noise.
Spectral Crest Factor	Another measure of noisiness. Similar to Spectral Flatness Measure.
Chroma	Pitch based feature. It projects the spectrum into 12 bins, representing the 12 distinct pitches of the chromatic musical scale.
Tempo	Beats per minute

Table 6: Traditional audio features used

In addition, our hybrid method performs significantly better than AM. The possible reasons could be: (1) our model has regularization terms but AM does not; (2) our method can directly use the features, but AM has to quantize feature vectors, which results in information loss.

5. CONCLUSION

In this paper, we have described a novel model for content-based music recommendation leveraging on deep belief network and probabilistic graphical model. Instead of splitting feature extraction and recommendation into separate steps, our model unifies them in an automated process. Compared with existing deep learning based models, our model outperforms them in both the warm-start and cold-start stages without relying on collaborative filtering. Based on the automatically learnt features, we created a hybrid collaborative filtering and content-based recommendation method, which not only significantly improves the performance of CF but also outperforms the traditional feature based hybrid method.

As deep learning strives to provide a model for human cognition, it has the potential to reveal many secrets behind our preferences for music. Our study on HLDBN serves as a mere starting point to tap into that potential. One practical future direction could be to further improve the recommendation performance by explicitly modeling the temporal structure of music content using deep recurrent neural network [48]. Another interesting direction could be to interpret the automatically learnt features to discover interesting characteristics of music. Also, it may be interesting to take advantage of recent advances in matrix factorization (e.g. Lee *et al* [49]) by combining them with the deep learning methods.

6. ACKNOWLEDGMENT

This project is funded by the National Research Foundation (NRF) and managed through the multi-agency Interactive & Digital Media Programme Office (IDMPO) hosted by the Media Development Authority of Singapore (MDA) under Centre of Social Media Innovations for Communities (COSMIC). We are also grateful to Haotian Fang for proofreading the manuscript.

7. REFERENCES

[1] P. Cano, M. Koppenberger, and N. Wack, "Content-based music audio recommendation," in *Proceedings of the 13th annual ACM international conference on Multimedia*, MULTIMEDIA '05, (New York, NY, USA), pp. 211–212, ACM, 2005.

[2] K. Yoshii, M. Goto, K. Komatani, T. Ogata, and H. G. Okuno, "Hybrid Collaborative and Content-based Music Recommendation Using Probabilistic Model with Latent User Preferences," in *ISMIR*, pp. 296–301, 2006.

[3] X. Wang, D. Rosenblum, and Y. Wang, "Context-Aware Mobile Music Recommendation for Daily Activities," in *ACM Multimedia 2012*, Oct. 2012.

[4] P. Mermelstein, "Distance measures for speech Recognition–Psychological and instrumental," in *Joint Workshop on Pattern Recognition and Artificial Intelligence*, 1976.

[5] M. A. Casey, R. Veltkamp, M. Goto, M. Leman, C. Rhodes, and M. Slaney, "Content-Based Music Information Retrieval: Current Directions and Future Challenges," *Proceedings of the IEEE*, vol. 96, pp. 668–696, Mar. 2008.

[6] Y. Bengio, A. Courville, and P. Vincent, "Representation Learning: A Review and New Perspectives," Oct. 2012.

[7] P. Hamel and D. Eck, "Learning features from music audio with deep belief networks," in *11th International Society for Music Information Retrieval Conference*, 2010.

[8] E. M. Schmidt and Y. E. Kim, "Learning emotion-based acoustic features with deep belief networks," in *ISMIR*, 2011.

[9] B. McFee, T. Bertin-Mahieux, D. P. W. Ellis, and G. R. G. Lanckriet, "The million song dataset challenge," in *21st International Conference Companion on World Wide Web*, pp. 909–916, 2012.

[10] G. E. Hinton, S. Osindero, and Y. W. Teh, "A fast learning algorithm for deep belief nets," *Neural Comput.*, vol. 18, pp. 1527–1554, July 2006.

[11] Y. Koren, R. Bell, and C. Volinsky, "Matrix Factorization Techniques for Recommender Systems," *Computer*, vol. 42, pp. 30–37, Aug. 2009.

[12] H. C. Chen and A. L. P. Chen, "A Music Recommendation System Based on Music Data Grouping and User Interests," in *Proceedings of the Tenth International Conference on Information and Knowledge Management*, CIKM '01, (New York, NY, USA), pp. 231–238, ACM, 2001.

[13] B. Zhang, J. Shen, Q. Xiang, and Y. Wang, "CompositeMap: a Novel Framework for Music Similarity Measure," *SIGIR*, 2009.

[14] B. Logan and A. Salomon, "A Content-Based music similarity function," tech. rep., Cambridge Research Laboratory, 2001.

[15] D. Bogdanov, M. Haro, F. Fuhrmann, E. Gómez, and P. Herrera, "Content-based music recommendation based on user preference examples," in *The 4th ACM Conference on Recommender Systems. Workshop on Music Recommendation and Discovery (Womrad 2010)*, 2010.

[16] D. Bogdanov, M. Haro, F. Fuhrmann, A. Xambó, E. GóMez, and P. Herrera, "Semantic audio content-based music recommendation and visualization based on user preference examples," *Inf. Process. Manage.*, vol. 49, pp. 13–33, Jan. 2013.

[17] B. McFee, L. Barrington, and G. Lanckriet, "Learning content similarity for music recommendation," *Audio, Speech, and Language Processing, IEEE Transactions on*, vol. 20, pp. 2207–2218, Oct. 2012.

[18] N.-H. Liu, "Comparison of content-based music recommendation using different distance estimation methods," *Applied Intelligence*, vol. 38, pp. 160–174, June 2013.

[19] M. Schedl and D. Schnitzer, "Location-Aware Music Artist Recommendation," in *MultiMedia Modeling* (C. Gurrin, F. Hopfgartner, W. Hurst, H. Johansen, H. Lee, and N. O'Connor, eds.), vol. 8326 of *Lecture Notes in Computer Science*, pp. 205–213, Springer International Publishing, 2014.

[20] I. Porteous, A. Asuncion, and M. Welling, "Bayesian Matrix Factorization with Side Information and Dirichlet Process Mixtures," in *Proceedings of the Twenty-Fourth AAAI Conference on Artificial Intelligence (AAAI-10)*.

[21] L. M. de Campos, J. M. Fernández-Luna, J. F. Huete, and M. A. Rueda-Morales, "Combining content-based and collaborative recommendations: A hybrid approach based on Bayesian networks," *International Journal of Approximate Reasoning*, vol. 51, pp. 785–799, Sept. 2010.

[22] H. Shan and A. Banerjee, "Generalized Probabilistic Matrix Factorizations for Collaborative Filtering," in *Data Mining (ICDM), 2010 IEEE 10th International Conference on*, pp. 1025–1030, IEEE, Dec. 2010.

[23] S. Park, Y. D. Kim, and S. Choi, "Hierarchical Bayesian Matrix Factorization with Side Information," in *Proceedings of the Twenty-Third International Joint Conference on Artificial Intelligence*, IJCAI'13, pp. 1593–1599, AAAI Press, 2013.

[24] D. Agarwal and B. C. Chen, "Regression-based latent factor models," in *Proceedings of the 15th ACM SIGKDD international conference on Knowledge discovery and data mining*, KDD '09, (New York, NY, USA), pp. 19–28, ACM, 2009.

[25] R. Popescul and L. H. Ungar, "Probabilistic models for unified collaborative and content-based recommendation in sparsedata environments," in *UAI 2011*, 2001.

[26] Q. Li, S. H. Myaeng, and B. M. Kim, "A probabilistic music recommender considering user opinions and audio features," *Information Processing and Management*, vol. 43, pp. 473–487, Mar. 2007.

[27] H. S. Del Castillo, "Hybrid Content-Based Collaborative-Filtering music recommendations,"

Master's thesis, University of Twente, The Netherlands, 2007.

[28] M. Tiemann and S. Pauws, "Towards ensemble learning for hybrid music recommendation," in *Proceedings of the 2007 ACM conference on Recommender systems*, RecSys '07, (New York, NY, USA), pp. 177–178, ACM, 2007.

[29] J. Shruthi, S. Sneha, U. R. Shetty, and D. Jayalakshmi, "A hybrid music recommender system.".

[30] J. Bu, S. Tan, C. Chen, C. Wang, H. Wu, L. Zhang, and X. He, "Music recommendation by unified hypergraph: Combining social media information and music content," in *Proceedings of the International Conference on Multimedia*, MM '10, (New York, NY, USA), pp. 391–400, ACM, 2010.

[31] B. Shao, D. Wang, T. Li, and M. Ogihara, "Music Recommendation Based on Acoustic Features and User Access Patterns," *Audio, Speech, and Language Processing, IEEE Transactions on*, vol. 17, pp. 1602–1611, Nov. 2009.

[32] M. A. Domingues, F. Gouyon, A. M. Jorge, J. P. Leal, J. . Vinagre, L. Lemos, and M. Sordo, "Combining usage and content in an online music recommendation system for music in the long-tail," in *Proceedings of the 21st International Conference Companion on World Wide Web*, WWW '12 Companion, (New York, NY, USA), pp. 925–930, ACM, 2012.

[33] Y. Bengio, "Learning Deep Architectures for AI," *Foundations and Trends in Machine Learning*, vol. 2, pp. 1–127, Jan. 2009.

[34] D. Erhan, Y. Bengio, A. Courville, P. A. Manzagol, P. Vincent, and S. Bengio, "Why Does Unsupervised Pre-training Help Deep Learning?," *J. Mach. Learn. Res.*, vol. 11, pp. 625–660, Mar. 2010.

[35] H. Lee, Y. Largman, P. Pham, and A. Y. Ng, "Unsupervised feature learning for audio classification using convolutional deep belief networks," in *Advances in Neural Information Processing Systems*, 2009.

[36] E. J. Humphrey, J. P. Bello, and Y. LeCun, "Moving Beyond Feature Design: Deep Architectures and Automatic Feature Learning in Music Informatics," in *13th International Society for Music Information Retrieval Conference*, 2012.

[37] E. Humphrey, J. Bello, and Y. LeCun, "Feature learning and deep architectures: new directions for music informatics," *Journal of Intelligent Information Systems*, vol. 41, no. 3, pp. 461–481, 2013.

[38] A. Pikrakis, "A deep learning approach to rhythm modelling with applications," in *6th International Workshop on Machine Learning and Music (MML13)*, 2013.

[39] E. M. Schmidt and Y. E. Kim, "Learning rhythm and melody features with deep belief networks," in *ISMIR*, 2013.

[40] M. Henaff, K. Jarrett, K. Kavukcuoglu, and Y. LeCun, "Unsupervised Learning of Sparse Features for Scalable Audio Classification," in *International Society for Music Information Retrieval Conference*, 2011.

[41] A. van den Oord, S. Dieleman, and B. Schrauwen, "Deep content-based music recommendation," in *NIPS*, 2013.

[42] R. Salakhutdinov and A. Mnih, "Probabilistic Matrix Factorization," in *Advances in Neural Information Processing Systems*, 2008.

[43] K. Hornik, M. Stinchcombe, and H. White, "Multilayer feedforward networks are universal approximators," *Neural Networks*, vol. 2, pp. 359–366, Jan. 1989.

[44] R. Pan, Y. Zhou, B. Cao, N. N. Liu, R. Lukose, M. Scholz, and Q. Yang, "One-Class Collaborative Filtering," in *Data Mining, 2008. ICDM. Eighth IEEE International Conference on*, vol. 0, (Los Alamitos, CA, USA), pp. 502–511, IEEE, Dec. 2008.

[45] Y. Hu, Y. Koren, and C. Volinsky, "Collaborative Filtering for Implicit Feedback Datasets," in *Proceedings of the 2008 Eighth IEEE International Conference on Data Mining*, vol. 0 of *ICDM '08*, (Washington, DC, USA), pp. 263–272, IEEE Computer Society, Dec. 2008.

[46] G. Hinton, "A Practical Guide to Training Restricted Boltzmann Machines," in *Neural Networks: Tricks of the Trade* (G. Montavon, G. Orr, and K.-R. Müller, eds.), vol. 7700 of *Lecture Notes in Computer Science*, pp. 599–619, Springer Berlin Heidelberg, 2012.

[47] G. Tzanetakis and P. Cook, "MARSYAS: a framework for audio analysis," *Org. Sound*, vol. 4, pp. 169–175, Dec. 1999.

[48] M. Hermans and B. Schrauwen, "Training and analyzing deep recurrent neural networks," in *Advances in Neural Information Processing Systems*, 2013.

[49] J. Lee, S. Kim, G. Lebanon, and Y. Singer, "Local Low-Rank matrix approximation," in *Proceedings of the 30th Annual International Conference on Machine Learning*, 2013.

Author Index

www.ingramcontent.com/pod-product-compliance
Ingram Content Group UK Ltd.
Pitfield, Milton Keynes, MK11 3LW, UK
UKHW051419290926
15471UKWH00009B/1675

9 781450 334259